July 28–August 1, 2013
Dublin, Ireland

Association for
Computing Machinery

Advancing Computing as a Science & Profession

SIGIR'13 VOL 1 of 2

The Proceedings of the 36th International ACM SIGIR Conference on

Research & Development in Information Retrieval

Sponsored by:

ACM SIGIR

Supported by:

Baidu, Google, Microsoft, SFI, Yahoo!, Aol., IBM, Yandex, Facebook, CNGL, DCU, Failte Ireland, and Trinity College Dublin

Association for
Computing Machinery

Advancing Computing as a Science & Profession

The Association for Computing Machinery
2 Penn Plaza, Suite 701
New York, New York 10121-0701

Notice to Past Authors of ACM-Published Articles
ACM intends to create a complete electronic archive of all articles and/or other material previously published by ACM. If you have written a work that has been previously published by ACM in any journal or conference proceedings prior to 1978, or any SIG Newsletter at any time, and you do NOT want this work to appear in the ACM Digital Library, please inform permissions@acm.org, stating the title of the work, the author(s), and where and when published.

ISBN: 978-1-4503-2034-4 (Digital)

ISBN: 978-1-4503-2702-2 (Print)

Additional copies may be ordered prepaid from:

ACM Order Department
PO Box 30777
New York, NY 10087-0777, USA

Phone: 1-800-342-6626 (USA and Canada)
+1-212-626-0500 (Global)
Fax: +1-212-944-1318
E-mail: acmhelp@acm.org
Hours of Operation: 8:30 am – 4:30 pm ET

Printed in the USA

Welcome from the General Chairs

Céad míle fáilte - Welcome - to Dublin, Ireland for the 36th Annual ACM SIGIR conference on research and development in information retrieval.

SIGIR has long been the premier international forum for the presentation of new research results and the demonstration of new systems and techniques in the field of information retrieval. Since it was last hosted in Dublin in 1994, the SIGIR conference has grown enormously in participation and technical diversity, and search and information retrieval has become a ubiquitous part of the lives of many millions of people across the world. Returning to Dublin after almost 20 years gives the information retrieval research community the chance to reflect on how the field has developed, and to celebrate the continuing innovation of leading researchers in information retrieval.

We would like to take this opportunity to recognize that a conference of the scale of SIGIR would not be possible without the dedicated work of a great many people. Principal among these are the Program Committee Chairs, Maarten de Rijke, Diane Kelly and Tetsuya Sakai who worked with 50 area chairs and many reviewers to select the papers for the Full Paper program. A special thanks to Cathal Gurrin and Udo Kruschwitz who took on the new and demanding role of Short Paper and Demonstration Chairs, and their reviewers who assisted them in selecting the excellent short paper and demonstration programs from record numbers of submissions. We thank also Noriko Kando and Séamus Lawless, Tutorial Chairs; Arjen de Vries and Vincent Wade, Workshop Chairs, Alan Smeaton, Best Paper Awards Chair; Jaime Arguello, Mounia Lalmas and Grace Hui Yang, Doctoral Consortium Chairs; Susan Feldman and Jimi Shanahan, Industry Track Chairs; and Liadh Kelly and Lorraine Goeuriot, Proceedings Chairs. We are indebted to Séamus Lawless, Local Organisation Chair and his team in Dublin. Special thanks also to Laura Grehan, Publicity Chair and Fiona Maguire, Treasurer, for their involvement throughout the planning and preparation for the conference.

While SIGIR 2013 is sponsored by ACM, we acknowledge the generous financial support of a large number of companies and organizations that has enabled us to provide for a great conference experience. Baidu, Google, Microsoft and Science Foundation Ireland (SFI) generously supported the conference at the Gold level, Yahoo! at the Silver level and AOL, IBM and Yandex provided support at the Bronze level. Facebook, itself a newcomer SIGIR supporter, underwrote the Newcomers Breakfast on the first day of the conference. In addition, Morgan & Claypool, Springer, Now Publishers and the Qatar Computing Research Institute have all made arrangements to support and exhibit at the conference. Local financial support was also provided by CNGL, Dublin City University, and Fáilte Ireland. Finally, we are extremely grateful to Sarah Collins and her colleagues at Conference Partners Ltd. in Dublin for their support and management of the conference website, registration, venues, catering, and all local logistics.

We hope that you enjoy the conference and take the opportunity to catch up with old friends and make new ones in our beautiful and historic surroundings here in Dublin and Ireland.

Gareth J. F. Jones
Dublin City University

Páraic Sheridan
Dublin City University

Program Chairs' Welcome

Welcome to SIGIR, the 36th annual international ACM conference on research and development in Information Retrieval. SIGIR is the premier, international venue for research and development in information retrieval. We believe the breadth and diversity of research that comprises the program reflects the health of the organization and major future directions of the field. We are grateful to all those who submitted papers to the conference and gave the Committee an opportunity to evaluate their work for potential inclusion in the program. We are also grateful to the 50 Area Chairs and 204 general program committee members, who represent 30 countries and over 120 institutions, for all the hard work they put into evaluating submissions.

The conference received 366 full paper submissions this year. Of these, 73 (20%) were accepted, essentially the same as last year's acceptance rate and the year before. The top five countries in terms of accepted papers (according to contact author affiliation) were the U.S.A. (28), China (9), the Netherlands, Singapore, and U.K. (5 each). The top five technical areas covered by the accepted papers (as indicated by the primary keyword assigned by paper authors) were users and interactive IR (16%), search engine architecture and scalability (15%), queries and query analysis (15%), evaluation (11%), and retrieval models and ranking (11%). This represents only a slight re-ordering of topics from last year. Two hundred fifty papers were submitted to the short papers track, which represents a 20% increase in the number of submissions made to last year's poster track. Eighty-five (34%) short papers were accepted. In addition, 46 demonstrations were proposed, of which 23 (50%) were accepted. The program also consisted of 7 workshops and 10 tutorials. Finally, the Doctoral Consortium hosted 11 students this year from 10 countries and 11 institutions.

As has been customary for many years, SIGIR 2013 used a two-tier double-blind review process. In the first stage, at least three reviewers read every paper and provided ratings and comments. Papers were evaluated according to seven main criteria: relevance, originality, soundness, quality of the presentation, impact, coverage of the literature, and, for the first time, reproducibility of the results. In the second stage, the primary and secondary Area Chairs ensured the quality of the reviewing process by studying, validating, and summarizing these reviews, and adding their own feedback and ratings. Area Chairs initiated discussions among reviewers to resolve any controversial issues or significant differences of opinion. Once the discussion stage was completed, the two Area Chairs made a recommendation regarding the paper for nearly all submissions. This year we allowed Area Chairs to indicate that a paper should be accepted if room. At the program committee meeting held in Amsterdam, The Netherlands, the Program Chairs and the attending Area Chairs went over the reviews, verified the process, gathered additional input, and discussed and decided on papers that were balloted as accept if room, papers from which the primary Area Chair abstained and papers that had unusual score distributions. For papers that were balloted as accept if room, we especially considered the potential for the paper to provoke interesting and fruitful discussion at the conference. Ultimately 73 papers were selected for inclusion in the program.

One important change to this year's program was renaming the poster paper submission type to short papers and increasing the length of the paper from two to four pages. Short papers were presented at the conference in poster format and two separate short paper sessions were included as part of the main conference program, rather than a single event collocated with an evening reception. We believe that increasing the length of the accompanying paper allows researchers to better communicate their experiments and results, which in turn, will allow this submission type to function as a more comprehensive and substantial container for small, but significant findings. We further believe this change better allows research presented in this format to get the attention it deserves. We would like to thank the Short Paper Co-Chairs for all the extra work they did this year managing this new format and the Short Paper reviewers for the great job they did handling both the larger volume of submissions and their increased size. We believe the large increase in number of submissions to this track indicates the community's receptiveness to this change.

We hope you find this program interesting, provocative and inspiring, and that the conference provides you with a valuable opportunity to share ideas with other researchers, practitioners and students from institutions around the world. The deadline for SIGIR 2014 is, after all, only six months away!

Diane Kelly
Program Chair
University of North Carolina

Maarten de Rijke
Program Chair
University of Amsterdam

Tetsuya Sakai
Program Chair
Microsoft Research Asia

Table of Contents

Session 2A: Users and Interactive IR I

Session 2B: Efficiency I

Session 2C: Topic Modeling

Session 3A: Users and Interactive IR II

Session 3B: Recommender Systems

Session 3C: Retrieval Models and Ranking I

Session 4A: Time

Session 4B: Evaluation I

Session 4C: Multimedia

Session 5A: Search Sessions

Session 5B: Click Models

Session 6A: Social Media and Network Analysis II

Session 6B: Queries II

Session 7A: Diversity

Session 7B: Evaluation II

Session 8A: Retrieval Models and Ranking II

Session 8B: Efficiency II

Author Index for Volume 1 of SIGIR'13 Proceedings 733

Short Papers 1 -- Evaluation

Short Papers 1 — Filtering and Recommending

Short Papers 1 -- Multimedia IR

Short Papers 1 — Queries and Query Analysis

Short Papers 1 — Retrieval Models and Ranking

Short Papers 1 — Social Media IR

Short Papers 1 — Topic Models

Short Papers 1 — Users and Interactive IR

Short Papers 2 — Evaluation

Short Papers 2 — Filtering and Recommending

Short Papers 2 — Multimedia IR

Short Papers 2 — Queries and Query Analysis

Short Papers 2 — Retrieval Models and Ranking

Short Papers 2 — Social Media IR

Short Papers 2 — Topic Models

Short Papers 2 -- Users and Interactive IR

Demonstrations 1 — Users and Interactive IR

Demonstrations 1 — IR and Structured Data

Demonstrations 1 — Information Extraction

Demonstrations 1 — Filtering and Recommending

Demonstrations 1 — Classification and Clustering

Demonstrations 2 — Users and Interactive IR

Demonstrations 2 — IR and Structured Data

Demonstrations 2 — Information Extraction

Demonstrations 2 — Filtering and Recommending

Demonstrations 2 — Classification and Clustering

Tutorials

Workshops

Doctoral Consortium

SIGIR 2013 Organization

General Co-Chairs:	Gareth J. F. Jones *(Dublin City University, Ireland)* Páraic Sheridan *(Dublin City University, Ireland)*
Program Co-Chairs:	Diane Kelly *(University of North Carolina, Chapel Hill, USA)* Maarten de Rijke *(University of Amsterdam, The Netherlands)* Tetsuya Sakai *(Microsoft Research Asia, China)*
Short Papers & Demos Co-Chairs:	Cathal Gurrin *(Dublin City University, Ireland)* Udo Kruschwitz *(University of Essex, UK)*
Tutorial Co-Chairs:	Noriko Kando *(National Institute of Informatics, Japan)* Séamus Lawless *(Trinity College Dublin, Ireland)*
Workshop Co-Chairs:	Arjen de Vries *(Centrum Wiskunde and Informatica & Delft University of Technology, The Netherlands)* Vincent Wade *(Trinity College Dublin, Ireland)*
Best Paper Awards Chair:	Alan Smeaton *(Dublin City University, Ireland)*
Doctoral Consortium Co-Chairs:	Jaime Arguello *(University of North Carolina, Chapel Hill, USA)* Mounia Lalmas *(Yahoo! Labs, Spain)* Grace Hui Yang *(Georgetown University, USA)*
Industrial Track Co-Chairs:	Susan Feldman *(Synthexis, LLC, USA)* Jimi Shanahan *(Consultant, USA)*
Sponsorship Chair:	Páraic Sheridan *(Dublin City University, Ireland)*
Publicity Chair:	Laura Grehan *(Dublin City University, Ireland)*
Local Organization Chair:	Séamus Lawless *(Trinity College Dublin, Ireland)*
Treasurer:	Fiona Maguire *(Dublin City University, Ireland)*
Publications Co-Chairs:	Lorraine Goeuriot (*Dublin City University, Ireland)* Liadh Kelly *(Dublin City University, Ireland)*
Webmaster:	Conference Partners *(Dublin, Ireland)*

SIGIR 2013 Area Chairs

Diane Kelly *(University of North Carolina, Chapel Hill, USA)* – Chair

Maarten de Rijke *(University of Amsterdam, The Netherlands)* – Chair

Tetsuya Sakai *(Microsoft Research Asia, China)* – Chair

Document Representation and Content Analysis

James Allan *(University of Massachusetts Amherst, USA)*

Paul Bennett *(Microsoft Research, USA)*

Kevyn Collins-Thompson *(Microsoft Research, USA)*

Shlomo Geva *(Queensland University of Technology, Australia)*

Wessel Kraaij *(Radboud University Nijmegen & TNO, The Netherlands)*

Oren Kurland *(Technion, Israel)*

Edleno S. de Moura *(Federal University of Amazonas, Brazil)*

Arjen de Vries *(Centrum Wiskunde and Informatica & Delft University of Technology, The Netherlands)*

Ming Zhou *(Microsoft Research Asia, China)*

Queries and Query Analysis

Carlos Castillo *(Qatar Computing Research Institute, Qatar)*

Nick Craswell *(Microsoft, USA)*

Fernando Diaz *(Microsoft Research, USA)*

Evgeniy Gabrilovich *(Google, USA)*

Fabrizio Silvestri *(Information Science and Technology Institute CNR, Italy)*

Ryen White *(Microsoft Research, USA)*

Web IR and Social Media Search

Eugene Agichtein *(Emory University, USA)*

Charles L. A. Clarke *(University of Waterloo, Canada)*

Aristides Gionis *(Aalto University, Finland)*

Matthew Lease *(University of Texas at Austin, USA)*

Mounia Llamas *(Yahoo! Labs, Spain)*

Yoelle Maarek *(Yahoo! Labs, Israel)*

Marc Najork *(Microsoft Research, USA)*

Elad Yom-Tov *(Microsoft Research, Israel)*

Search Engine Architectures and Scalability

B. Barla Cambazoglu *(Yahoo! Labs, Spain)*

Vanja Josifovski *(Google, USA)*

Retrieval Models and Ranking

Leif Azzopardi *(University of Glasgow, UK)*

Peter Bruza *(Queensland University of Technology, Australia)*

David Carmel *(Yahoo! Labs, Israel)*

Bruce Croft *(University of Massachusetts Amherst, USA)*

Eric Gaussier *(Université Joseph Fourier, France)*

Donald Metzler *(Google, USA)*

Tao Qin *(Microsoft Research Asia, China)*

Filtering and Recommendation

Jamie Callan *(Carnegie Mellon University, USA)*

Brian Davison *(Lehigh University, USA)*

Yi Zhang *(University of California, USA)*

Evaluation

Ben Carterette *(University of Delaware, USA)*

Mark Sanderson *(RMIT University, Australia)*

Ellen Voorhees *(NIST, USA)*

William Webber *(University of Maryland, USA)*

Users and Interactive IR

Susan Dumais *(Microsoft Research, USA)*

Kalervo Järvelin *(University of Tampere, Finland)*

Ian Ruthven *(University of Strathclyde, UK)*

Jaime Teevan *(Microsoft Research, USA)*

IR and Structured Data

Krisztian Balog *(University of Stavanger, Norway)*

Andrew Trotman *(University of Otago, New Zealand)*

Multimedia IR

Franciska de Jong *(University of Twente, The Netherlands)*

Stephane Marchand-Maillet *(University of Geneva, Switzerland)*

Other Applications

Tat-Seng Chua *(National University of Singapore, Singapore)*

Vanessa Murdock *(Microsoft, USA)*

Douglas W. Oard *(University of Maryland, USA)*

SIGIR 2013 Program Committee

Virgil Pavlu *(Northeastern University, USA)*
Jan Pedersen *(Microsoft Corporation, USA)*
Jian Pei *(Simon Fraser University, Canada)*
Raffaele Perego *(ISTI-CNR, Italy)*
Benjamin Piwowarski *(University Pierre et Marie Curie and CNRS, France)*
Barbara Poblete *(University of Chile and Yahoo! Labs Santiago, Chile)*
John Prager *(IBM Research, USA)*
Kunal Punera *(RelateIQ, USA)*
Kira Radinsky *(SalesPredict, Israel)*
Filip Radlinski *(Microsoft, UK)*
Hema Raghavan *(IBM Research, USA)*
Edie Rasmussen *(University of British Columbia, Canada)*
Berthier Ribeiro-Neto *(Federal University of Minas Gerais, Google Engineering, Brazil)*
Dmitri Roussinov *(University of Strathclyde, UK)*
Rodrygo Santos *(University of Glasgow, UK)*
Ralf Schenkel *(Max Planck Institut for Informatics, Germany)*
Falk Scholer *(RMIT University, Australia)*
Pavel Serdyukov *(Yandex, Russia)*
Chirag Shah *(Rutgers University, USA)*
Milad Shokouhi *(Microsoft, UK)*
Anna Shtok *(Technion, Israel)*
Luo Si *(Purdue University, USA)*
Altigran S. da Silva *(Universidade Federal do Amazonas, Brazil)*
Catherine L. Smith *(Kent State University, USA)*
Mark D. Smucker *(University of Waterloo, Canada)*
Cees Snoek *(University of Amsterdam, The Netherlands)*
Ian Soboroff *(NIST, USA)*
Aya Soffer *(IBM Research, Israel)*
Oren Somekh *(Yahoo! Labs, Israel)*
Ruihua Song *(Microsoft Research Asia, China)*
Young-In Song *(NHN Corp., Korea)*
Julia Stoyanovich *(Drexel University, USA)*
Jian-Tao Sun *(Microsoft Research Asia, China)*
Idan Szpektor *(Yahoo! Research, Israel)*
Jie Tang *(Tsinghua University, China)*
Paul Thomas *(CSIRO and Australian National University, Australia)*
Qi Tian *(University of Texas, San Antonio, USA)*
Anastasios Tombros *(Queen Mary University of London, UK)*
Dolf Trieschnigg *(University of Twente, The Netherlands)*
Manos Tsagkias *(University of Amsterdam, The Netherlands)*
Theodora Tsikrika *(Royal School of Library & Information Science, Denmark)*
Andrew Turpin *(University of Melbourne, Australia)*
Olga Vechtomova *(University of Waterloo, Canada)*
Emre Velipasaoglu *(Magnet Systems, USA)*
Robert Villa *(University of Sheffield, UK)*
Meng Wang *(Hefei University of Technology, China)*
Xin-Jing Wang *(Microsoft Research Asia, China)*
Wouter Weerkamp *(University of Amsterdam, The Netherlands)*
Gerhard Weikum *(Max Planck Institute for Informatics, Germany)*
Ji-Rong Wen *(Microsoft Research Asia, China)*
Thijs Westerveld *(Teezir Search Solutions, The Netherlands)*
Max L. Wilson *(University of Nottingham, UK)*
Xiaobing Xue *(Twitter, USA)*
Yiming Yang *(Carnegie Mellon University, USA)*
Grace Hui Yang *(Georgetown University, USA)*
Emine Yilmaz *(Microsoft Research Cambridge, UK)*
Minoru Yoshida *(University of Tokyo, Japan)*
Yisong Yue *(Carnegie Mellon University, USA)*
Zhengjun Zha *(National University of Singapore, Singapore)*
ChengXiang Zhai *(University of Illinois, Urbana-Champaign, USA)*
Lei Zhang *(Microsoft Research Asia, China)*
Lanbo Zhang *(University of California, Santa Cruz, USA)*
Min Zhang *(Tsinghua University, China)*
Le Zhao *(Google Inc., USA)*
Nivio Ziviani *(Federal University of Minas Gerais, Brazil, Brazil)*
Justin Zobel *(University of Melbourne, Australia)*
Guido Zuccon *(CSIRO, Australia)*

Short Papers Committee

Cathal Gurrin *(Dublin City University, Ireland)* – Chair
Udo Kruschwitz *(University of Essex, UK)* – Chair

Eytan Adar *(University of Michigan, USA)*
Mikhail Ageev *(Moscow State University, Russian Federation)*
Ahmet Aker *(University of Sheffield, UK)*
Elif Aktolga *(University of Massachusetts Amherst, USA)*
M-Dyaa Albakour *(University of Glasgow, UK)*
Rami Albatal *(Dublin City University, Ireland)*
Omar Alonso *(Microsoft, USA)*
Peter Anick *(Brandeis University, USA)*
Javed A. Aslam *(Northeastern University, USA)*
Niranjan Balasubramanian *(University of Massachusetts Amherst, USA)*
Timothy Baldwin *(University of Melbourne, Australia)*
Krisztian Balog *(University of Stavanger, Norway)*
Alberto Barron-Cedeo *(Universitat Politecnica de Catalunya, Spain)*
Gerald Benoit *(Simmons College, Harvard University, USA)*
Roi Blanco *(Yahoo! Research, Spain)*
Marco Bonzanini *(Queen Mary University of London, UK)*
Emanuele Di Buccio *(University of Padova, Italy)*
Rui Cai *(Microsoft Research Asia, China)*
Silvia Calegari *(University of Milan-Bicocca, Italy)*
Rodrigo Tripodi Calumby *(State University of Feira de Santana, Brazil)*
Fazli Can *(Bilkent University, Turkey)*
Annalina Caputo *(University of Bari Aldo Moro, Italy)*
Mark J. Carman *(Monash University, Australia)*
Ben Carterette *(University of Delaware, USA)*
Marc-Allen Cartright *(University of Massachusetts, Amherst, USA)*
Khe Chai Sim *(National University of Singapore, Singapore)*
Yi Chang *(Yahoo! Labs, USA)*
Francine Chen *(FX Palo Alto Laboratory, USA)*
Yi Chen *(Dublin City University, Ireland)*
Yun Chi *(NEC Laboratories America, USA)*
Paul Clough *(University of Sheffield, UK)*
Kevyn Collins-Thompson *(Microsoft Research, USA)*
Eli Cortez *(Neemu Technologies, Brazil)*
Bin Cui *(Peking University, China)*
Ronan Cummins *(University of Greenwich, UK)*
Sally Jo Cunningham *(Waikato University, New Zealand)*
Na Dai *(Yahoo!, USA)*
Jeff Dalton *(University of Massachusetts Amherst, USA)*
Mariam Daoud *(York University, Toronto, Canada)*
Kareem Darwish *(Qatar Computing Research Institute, Qatar)*
Debora Donato *(StumbleUpon, USA)*
Koji Eguchi *(Kobe University, Japan)*
David Eichmann *(University of Iowa, USA)*
Carsten Eickhoff *(Delft University of Technology, The Netherlands)*
Yi Fang *(Santa Clara University, USA)*
Fabio Faria *(University of Campinas, Brazil)*
Nicola Ferro *(University of Padua, Italy)*
Luanne Freund *(University of British Columbia, Canada)*
Ingo Frommholz *(University of Bedfordshire, UK)*
Norbert Fuhr *(University Duisburg-Essen, Germany)*
Debasis Ganguly *(Dublin City University, Ireland)*
Bin Gao *(Microsoft Research Asia, China)*
Wei Gao *(Qatar Computing Research Institute, Qatar)*
Susan Gauch *(University of Arkansas, USA)*
Shima Gerani *(University of Lugano, Switzerland)*
Shlomo Geva *(Queensland University of Technology, Australia)*
M. Rami Ghorab *(Trinity College Dublin, Ireland)*
C. Lee Giles *(Pennsylvania State University, USA)*
Brigitte Grau *(LIMSI-CNRS & ENSIIE, France)*
Mark A. Greenwood *(University of Sheffield, UK)*
Daniel Gruhl *(IBM, USA)*
Preben Hansen *(Stockholm University, Sweden)*
Claudia Hauff *(TU Delft, The Netherlands)*
Ben He *(Chinese Academy of Sciences, China)*
Daqing He *(University of Pittsburgh, USA)*
Jiyin He *(Centrum Wiskunde & Informatica, The Netherlands)*
Zhouzhou He *(Zhejiang University, China)*
Andreas Henrich *(University of Bamberg, Germany)*
Katja Hofmann *(University of Amsterdam, The Netherlands)*
Frank Hopfgartner *(TU Berlin, Germany)*

Vivian (Qinmin) Hu *(York University, Canada)*
Jimmy Huang *(York University, Canada)*
Yoshiyuki Inagaki *(Yahoo! Labs, USA)*
Giacomo Inches *(University of Lugano, Switzerland)*
Diana Inkpen *(University of Ottawa, Canada)*
Jagadeesh Jagarlamudi *(IBM T.J Watson Research Center, USA)*
Adam Jatowt *(Kyoto University, Japan)*
Jiwoon Jeon *(Google Inc., USA)*
Daxin Jiang *(Microsoft Research Asia, China)*
Hideo Joho *(University of Tsukuba, Japan)*
Joemon M. Jose *(University of Glasgow, UK)*
Leszek Kaliciak *(Robert Gordon University, UK)*
Jaap Kamps *(University of Amsterdam, The Netherlands)*
Noriko Kando *(National Institute of Informatics, Japan)*
Nattiya Kanhabua *(Norwegian University of Science and Technology, Norway)*
Evangelos Kanoulas *(Google, Switzerland)*
David Karger *(MIT, USA)*
Sarvnaz Karimi *(CSIRO, Australia)*
Maryam Karimzadehgan *(University of Illinois, Urbana-Champaign, USA)*
Mostafa Keikha *(University of Massachusetts Amherst, USA)*
Diane Kelly *(University of North Carolina, Chapel Hill, USA)*
Liadh Kelly *(Dublin City University, Ireland)*
Jin-Dong Kim *(Database Center for Life Science, Japan)*
Jinyoung Kim *(Microsoft Corp., Bing, USA)*
Seokhwan Kim *(Institute for Infocomm Research, Singapore)*
Donald H. Kraft *(Department of Computer Science, U.S. Air Force Academy, USA)*
Abhimanyu Lad *(LinkedIn, USA)*
Dmitry Lagun *(Emory University, USA)*
Ni Lao *(Carnegie Mellon University, USA)*
Neal Lathia *(University of Cambridge, UK)*
Victor Lavrenko *(University of Edinburgh, UK)*
Jung-Tae Lee *(NHN Corp., South Korea)*
Teerapong Leelanupab *(King Mongkut's Institute of Technology, Thailand)*
Miro Lehtonen *(Kasetsart University, Finland)*
Na Li *(Dublin City University, Ireland)*
Wei Li *(Dublin City University, Ireland)*
Yingming Li *(Zhejiang University, China)*
Xia Lin *(Drexel University, USA)*
Christina Lioma *(University of Copenhagen, Denmark)*
Suzanne Little *(Dublin City University, Ireland)*
Ting Liu *(Harbin Institute of Technology, China)*
Deirdre Lungley *(University of Essex, UK)*
Mihai Lupu *(Vienna University of Technology, Austria)*
Yuanhua Lv *(Microsoft Research, USA)*
Hao Ma *(Microsoft Research, USA)*
Andrew MacFarlane *(City University London, UK)*
Takuya Maekawa *(Osaka University, Japan)*
Walid Magdy *(Qatar Computing Research Institute, Qatar)*
Prasenjit Majumder *(Dhirubhai Ambani Institute of Information and Communication Technology, India)*
Yi Mao *(Microsoft, USA)*
Stephane Marchand-Maillet *(University of Geneva, Switzerland)*
Ilya Markov *(University of Lugano, Switzerland)*
Paul McNamee *(Johns Hopkins University, USA)*
Edgar Meij *(Yahoo! Research, Spain)*
David Milne *(CSIRO ICT Centre, Australia)*
Stefano Mizzaro *(University of Udine, Italy)*
Marie-Francine Moens *(Katholieke Universiteit Leuven, Belgium)*
Alistair Moffat *(University of Melbourne, Australia)*
Vanessa Murdock *(Microsoft, USA)*
Preslav I. Nakov *(Qatar Computing Research Institute, Qatar)*
Michael L. Nelson *(Old Dominion University, USA)*
Charles Nicholas *(University of Maryland, USA)*
Jian-Yun Nie *(University of Montreal, Canada)*
Tae-Gil Noh *(Heidelberg University, Germany)*
Giorgio Maria Di Nunzio *(University of Padua, Italy, Italy)*
Neil O'Hare *(Yahoo! Research, Spain)*
Iadh Ounis *(University of Glasgow, UK)*
Gabriella Pasi *(University of Milano-Bicocca, Italy)*
Virgil Pavlu *(Northeastern University, USA)*
Karen Pinel-Sauvagnat *(IRIT, France)*
Tamara Polajnar *(University of Cambridge, UK)*
Luca Pretto *(University of Padua, Italy)*
Filip Radlinski *(Microsoft, UK)*
Hema Raghavan *(IBM Research, USA)*
Fiana Raiber *(Technion, Israel)*
Edie Rasmussen *(University of British Columbia, Canada)*

Maarten de Rijke *(University of Amsterdam, The Netherlands)*

Adam Roegiest *(University of Waterloo, Canada)*

Haggai Roitman *(IBM Research Lab, Haifa, Israel)*

Stefan Rueger *(Knowledge Media Institute, The Open University, UK)*

Ian Ruthven *(University of Strathclyde, UK)*

Jun Sakuma *(University of Tsukuba, Japan)*

Kazuhiro Seki *(Kobe University, Japan)*

Jangwon Seo *(Google Inc., USA)*

Jialie Shen *(Singapore Management University, Singapore)*

Fabrizio Silvestri *(Information Science and Technology Institute, Italy)*

Mark D. Smucker *(University of Waterloo, Canada)*

Dawei Song *(The Open University, UK)*

Vassilios Stathopoulos *(University College London, UK)*

Juliane Stiller *(Humboldt University, Berlin, Germany)*

Aixin Sun *(Nanyang Technological University, Singapore)*

Mingxuan Sun *(Georgia Institute of Technology, USA)*

S.M.M. Tahaghoghi (Microsoft, USA)

Bin Tan *(Amazon, USA)*

Michael J. Taylor *(Microsoft Research Cambridge, UK)*

Carla Teixeira Lopes *(University of Porto, Portugal)*

Martin Theobald *(Max-Planck Institute for Informatics, Germany)*

Ulrich Thiel *(Fraunhofer Gesellschaft, Germany)*

James A. Thom *(RMIT University, Australia)*

Paul Thomas *(CSIRO, Australia)*

Paul Thompson *(Dartmouth College, USA)*

Qi Tian *(University of Texas at San Antonio, USA)*

Anastasios Tombros *(Queen Mary University of London, UK)*

Ricardo Torres *(University of Campinas, Brazil)*

Dolf Trieschnigg *(University of Twente, The Netherlands)*

Andrew Trotman *(University of Otago, New Zealand)*

Manos Tsagkias *(University of Amsterdam, The Netherlands)*

Andrew Turpin *(University of Melbourne, Australia)*

Howard Turtle *(Syracuse University, USA)*

Sarah Tyler *(University of California, Santa Cruz, USA)*

Sumithra Velupillai *(Stockholm University, Sweden)*

Stephen Wan *(CSIRO, Australia)*

Changhu Wang *(Microsoft Research Asia, China)*

Lidan Wang *(University of Maryland, College Park, USA)*

Mengqiu Wang *(Stanford University, USA)*

Taifeng Wang *(Microsoft Research Asia, China)*

Xin-Jing Wang *(Microsoft Research Asia, China)*

Wouter Weerkamp *(University of Amsterdam, The Netherlands)*

Xing Wei *(Google Inc., USA)*

John Whissell *(University of Waterloo, Canada)*

Stewart Whiting *(University of Glasgow, UK)*

Tak-Lam Wong *(The Hong Kong Institute of Education, Hong Kong)*

Justin Wu *(York University, Toronto, Canada)*

Mingfang Wu *(RMIT University, Australia)*

Xiaobing Xue *(University of Massachusetts, Amherst, USA)*

Grace Hui Yang *(Georgetown University, USA)*

Ming Yang *(Zhejiang University, China)*

Yang Yang *(Dublin City University, Ireland)*

Zheng Ye *(York University, Toronto, Canada)*

Emine Yilmaz *(Microsoft Research Cambridge, UK)*

Minoru Yoshida *(University of Tokyo, Japan)*

Xiaojun (Jenny) Yuan *(University at Albany, The State University of New York, USA)*

Dell Zhang *(Birkbeck, University of London, UK)*

Jiayue Zhang *(York University, Toronto, Canada)*

Lanbo Zhang *(University of California, Santa Cruz, USA)*

Peng Zhang *(Robert Gordon University, UK)*

Zhenxing Zhang *(Dublin City University, Ireland)*

Zhongfei Zhang *(State University of New York, Binghamton, USA)*

Jessie Zhao *(York University, Toronto, Canada)*

Dong Zhou *(Hunan University of Science and Technology, China)*

Lijuan Zhou *(Dublin City University, Ireland)*

Guido Zuccon *(CSIRO, Australia)*

Demonstrations Committee

Cathal Gurrin *(Dublin City University, Ireland)* – Chair
Udo Kruschwitz *(University of Essex, UK)* – Chair

Rami Abatal *(Dublin City University, Ireland)*
Mikhail Ageev *(Moscow State University, Russia)*
Omar Alonso *(Microsoft, USA)*
Steve Beitzel *(Applied Communication Sciences, USA)*
Kevyn Collins-Thompson *(Microsoft Research, USA)*
Silviu Cucerzan *(Microsoft Research, USA)*
Sally Jo Cunningham *(Waikato University, New Zealand)*
Debora Donato *(StumbleUpon, USA)*
Gregory Grefenstette *(Exalead, France)*
Jer Hayes *(IBM, Ireland)*
Ben He *(Graduate Univ. of Chinese Academy of Sciences, China)*
Frank Hopfgartner *(TU Berlin, Germany)*
Mark Hughes *(Dublin City University, Ireland)*
Jiwoon Jeon *(Google, USA)*
Daxin Jiang *(Microsoft Research Asia, China)*
Håvard D Johansen *(University of Tromsø, Norway)*
Joemon M. Jose *(University of Glasgow, Scotland)*
Hyowon Lee *(Singapore University of Technology and Design, Singapore)*
Jochen L. Leidner *(Thomson Reuters, Switzerland)*
Johannes Leveling *(Dublin City University, Ireland)*
Christina Lioma *(University of Copenhagen, Denmark)*
Suzanne Little *(Dublin City University, Ireland)*
Rao Shen *(Yahoo!, USA)*
Bin Tan *(Amazon, USA)*
Tyler R. Tate *(Twigkit, UK)*
Mitul Tiwari *(LinkedIn, USA)*
Su-Lin Wu *(Google, USA)*
Lijuan Zhou *(Dublin City University, Ireland)*

Tutorials Committee

Noriko Kando *(National Institute of Informatics, Japan)* – Chair
Séamus Lawless *(Trinity College Dublin, Ireland)* – Chair

Maristella Agosti *(University of Padua, Italy)*
Leif Azzopardi *(University of Glasgow, UK)*
Hideo Joho *(University of Tsukuba, Japan)*
Jaap Kamps *(University of Amsterdam, The Netherlands)*
Liadh Kelly *(Dublin City University, Ireland)*
Don Metzler *(Google, USA)*
Douglas W. Oard *(University of Maryland, USA)*
Jaime Teevan *(Microsoft Research, USA)*
Andrew Trotman *(University of Otago, New Zealand)*
Yi Zhang *(University of California, Santa Cruz, USA)*
Dong Zhou *(Hunan University of Science and Technology, China)*

Workshops Committee

Arjen de Vries *(Centrum Wiskunde and Informatica & Delft University of Technology, The Netherlands)* – Chair
Vincent Wade *(Trinity College Dublin, Ireland)* – Chair

Giambattista Gianni Amati *(Fondazione Ugo Bordoni, Italy)*
Alejandro Bellogín *(Centrum Wiskunde and Informatica, The Netherlands)*
Bruce Croft *(University of Massachusetts Amherst, USA)*
J. Shane Culpepper *(Royal Melbourne Institute of Technology, Australia)*
Norbert Fuhr *(University of Duisburg-Essen, Germany)*
Gabriella Kazai *(Microsoft Research, Cambridge, UK)*
Barbara Prolete *(University of Chile & Yahoo! Labs Santiago, Chile)*
Dong Zhou *(Hunan University of Science and Technology, China)*

Best Paper Awards Committee

Alan Smeaton *(Dublin City University, Ireland)* – Chair

Peter Bruza *(Queensland University of Technology, Australia)*

David Elsweiler *(University of Regensburg, Germany)*

Alan Hanjalic *(Delft University of Technology, The Netherlands)*

Winston Hsu *(National Taiwan University, Taiwan)*

Birger Larsen *(Royal School of Library and Information Science, Denmark)*

Dik Lee *(The Hong Kong University of Science and Technology, Hong Kong)*

Isabelle Moulinier *(Thomson Reuters, USA)*

Padmini Srinivasan *(University of Iowa, USA)*

Doctoral Consortium Mentors

Jaime Arguello *(University of North Carolina, Chapel Hill, USA)* – Chair

Mounia Lalmas *(Yahoo!, Spain)* – Chair

Grace Hui Yang *(Georgetown University, USA)* – Chair

David Carmel *(Yahoo! Labs, Israel)*

Tat-Seng Chua *(National University of Singapore, Singapore)*

Kevyn Collins-Thompson *(Microsoft Research, USA)*

Hui Fang *(University of Delaware, USA)*

Julio Gonzalo *(UNED, Spain)*

Djoerd Hiemstra *(University of Twente, The Netherlands)*

Joemon Jose *(University of Glasgow, UK)*

Oren Kurland *(Technion, Israel Institute of Technology, Israel)*

Donald Metzler *(Google, USA)*

Vanessa Murdock *(Bing, USA)*

Jian-Yun Nie *(Université de Montréal, Canada)*

Yanjun Qi *(NEC Labs America, USA)*

Ian Ruthven *(University of Strathclyde, UK)*

Fabrizio Silvestri *(ISTI - CNR, Italy)*

John Tait *(johntait.net Ltd)*

Jun Wang *(University College London, UK)*

Local Organization Committee

Séamus Lawless *(Trinity College Dublin, Ireland)* – Chair

M. Rami Ghorab *(Trinity College Dublin, Ireland)*

Johannes Leveling *(Dublin City University, Ireland)*

SIGIR 2013 Sponsors & Supporters

Sponsors

Corporate Supporters

Gold Level

Silver Level

Bronze Level

Aol.

IBM

Yandex

Newcomers' Breakfast Supporter

facebook

Local Supporters

Riding the Multimedia Big Data Wave

John R. Smith
IBM T. J. Watson Research Center
Kitchawan Road
Yorktown Heights, NY 10532 USA
jsmith@us.ibm.com

ABSTRACT

Across multiple generations of information technology that have dealt with structured and unstructured data, the explosion of multimedia data is creating the biggest wave of all. Huge volumes of multimedia – images, video and audio are being generated and consumed daily. Currently, multimedia makes up 60% of internet traffic, 70% of mobile phone traffic and 70% of all available unstructured data. To give specific examples, Web users are uploading 72 video-hours to YouTube per minute, and on an average day, social media users post 300 hundred million photos to Facebook. Consumers using mobile phones and digital cameras are taking 500 billion photos per year, or 78 per person on the planet [1]. Specialized domains are participating too. Medical institutions are acquiring one billion radiological images per year, and cities are installing hundreds of millions of video cameras worldwide for safety, security and law enforcement. Industries across life sciences, petroleum exploration, astronomy, insurance, retail and many others are faced with huge and growing volumes of multimedia data.

Multimedia clearly is "big data". But, it it big data not just because there is a lot of it. Multimedia is big data because increasingly it is becoming a valuable source for insights and information. Multimedia data can tell us about things happening in the world, point out places, events or topics of interest (memes), give clues about a person's preferences and even capture a rolling log of human history [1, 2]. However, the challenge with multimedia big data is that images, video and audio require much more sophisticated algorithms for content analysis than previous waves of structured and unstructured data. This is spurring on a tremendous amount of research on efficient and effective techniques for "bridging the semantic gap" to enable large-scale multimedia information extraction and retrieval [3, 4].

In this talk we present a perspective across multiple industry problems, including safety and security, medical, Web, social and mobile media, and motivate the need for large-scale analysis and retrieval of multimedia data. We describe a multi-layer architecture that incorporates capabilities for audio-visual feature extraction, machine learning and semantic modeling and provides a powerful framework for learning and classifying contents of multimedia data. We discuss the role semantic ontologies for representing audio-visual concepts and relationships, which are essential for training semantic classifiers [5]. We discuss the importance of using faceted classification schemes in particular for organizing multimedia semantic concepts in order to achieve effective learning and retrieval [6]. We also show how training and scoring of multimedia semantics can be implemented on big data distributed computing platforms to address both massive-scale analysis and low-latency processing [7]. We describe multiple efforts at IBM on image and video analysis and retrieval, including IBM Multimedia Analysis and Retrieval System (IMARS), and show recent results for semantic-based classification and retrieval. We conclude with future directions for improving analysis of multimedia through interactive and curriculum-based techniques for multimedia semantics-based learning and retrieval.

SIGIR'13, July 28–August 1, 2013, Dublin, Ireland.
ACM 978-1-4503-2034-4/13/07.

Categories and Subject Descriptors

H.2.4 [**Systems**]: Multimedia databases; I.2.10 [**Artificial Intelligence**]: Vision and Scene Understanding—*Video analysis*; I.2.4 [**Artificial Intelligence**]: Knowledge Representation Formalisms and Methods—*Semantic networks*; I.2.6 [**Artificial Intelligence**]: Learning—*Concept learning*

Keywords

Multimedia information retrieval, video analysis, content-based search, machine learning, semantic modeling

Biography

Dr. John R. Smith is Senior Manager, Intelligent Information Management Dept, IBM T. J. Watson Research Center. He received his Ph.D., Electrical Engineering from Columbia University in 1997. He currently leads IBM's research in multimedia information retrieval including image and video content extraction, multimedia content-based search, video event detection and retrieval and social media analysis. Dr. Smith is currently principal investigator for IBM Multimedia Analysis and Retrieval

System (IMARS), which has been recognized by multiple awards including a Wall St. Journal innovation award. Dr. Smith is a long-time participant in the NIST TRECVID video retrieval evaluation and co-led the development of the Large Scale Concept Ontology for Multimedia (LSCOM), which has been incorporated into the TRECVID evaluation. From 2000-2004, Dr. Smith served as Chair, ISO/IEC MPEG Multimedia Description Schemes Group and led the development of multiple parts of the MPEG-7 Multimedia Metadata Standard and MPEG-21 Digital Framework Standard. While a student with Prof. Shih-Fu Chang at Columbia University, Dr. Smith conducted some of the earliest work on content-based image retrieval (VisualSEEk) and Web image/video search (WebSEEk), which has been highly influential for researchers and practitioners. Dr. Smith has published more than two hundred papers (>14K citations, h-index of 55, i-index of 166). Dr. Smith is currently a member of ACM SIGMM, Fellow of IEEE and Editor-in-Chief of *IEEE MultiMedia*.

1. REFERENCES

[1] John R. Smith. History made everyday. *IEEE MultiMedia*, 18(2), July-Sept 2011.

[2] L. Xie, A. Natsev, J. R. Kender, M. Hill, and J. R. Smith. Visual memes in social media: Tracking real-world news in youtube videos. In *Proc. of the 19th ACM Intl. Conf. on Multimedia*, pages 53–62. ACM, November 2011.

[3] John R. Smith. Minding the gap. *IEEE MultiMedia*, 19(2), January-March 2012.

[4] A. Hanjalic, R. Lienhart, W.-Y. Ma, and J. R. Smith. The holy grail of multimedia information retrieval: So close or yet so far away? *Proc. IEEE*, 96(4):541–547, 2008.

[5] M. Naphade, J. R. Smith, J. Tesic, S.-F. Chang, W. Hsu, L. Kenendy, A. Hauptmann, and J. Curtis. Large-scale concept ontology for multimedia. *IEEE MultiMedia*, 13(3), July-Sept 2006.

[6] John R. Smith. Just the facets. *IEEE MultiMedia*, 20(1), January-March 2013.

[7] R. Yan, M. O. Fleury, M. Merler, A. Natsev, and J. R. Smith. Large-scale multimedia semantic concept modeling using robust subspace bagging and map-reduce. In *Proc. of the 1st ACM Workshop on Large-Scale Multimedia Retrieval.* ACM, October 2009.

Beliefs and Biases in Web Search

Ryen W. White
Microsoft Research
One Microsoft Way
Redmond, WA 98052 USA
ryenw@microsoft.com

ABSTRACT

People's beliefs, and unconscious biases that arise from those beliefs, influence their judgment, decision making, and actions, as is commonly accepted among psychologists. Biases can be observed in information retrieval in situations where searchers seek or are presented with information that significantly deviates from the truth. There is little understanding of the impact of such biases in search. In this paper we study search-related biases via multiple probes: an exploratory retrospective survey, human labeling of the captions and results returned by a Web search engine, and a large-scale log analysis of search behavior on that engine. Targeting yes-no questions in the critical domain of health search, we show that Web searchers exhibit their own biases and are also subject to bias from the search engine. We clearly observe searchers favoring positive information over negative and more than expected given base rates based on consensus answers from physicians. We also show that search engines strongly favor a particular, usually positive, perspective, irrespective of the truth. Importantly, we show that these biases can be counterproductive and affect search outcomes; in our study, around half of the answers that searchers settled on were actually incorrect. Our findings have implications for search engine design, including the development of ranking algorithms that consider the desire to satisfy searchers (by validating their beliefs) and providing accurate answers and properly considering base rates. Incorporating likelihood information into search is particularly important for consequential tasks, such as those with a medical focus.

Categories and Subject Descriptors

H.3.3 [**Information Storage and Retrieval**]: Information Search and Retrieval – *Search process, Selection process.*

Keywords

Beliefs; Biases; Search interaction; Health search.

1. INTRODUCTION

Information scientists have analyzed the cognitive mechanisms behind the search for information, including the development of models for how information needs emerge [4][37] and how they evolve during search [23][24]. The models developed typically focus on a cognitive actor, and that actor's interactions with information objects and systems, within a context [17][30]. Although they may model historic search interests, these models do not consider prior *beliefs* about outcomes and associated likelihoods, or biases arising from those beliefs. Biases in cognition may lead people to create beliefs based on false premises and behave in a seemingly irrational manner [21], e.g., exhibiting preference for information in support of their position over information refuting it, irrespective of factual correctness [2][3][21]. For example, although there is a definite answer to the yes-no question *Can tea tree oil treat canker sores?*, and that answer is *yes*, a health seeker may favor a particular outcome in light of their beliefs about the value of the oil, and seek or unconsciously prefer disaffirming information.

SIGIR '13, July 28–August 1, 2013, Dublin, Ireland.

Biases can be observed in information retrieval (IR) in situations *where searchers seek or are presented with information that significantly deviates from true likelihoods.* In IR, the term "bias" has been associated with search engine functionality (e.g., caption generation [47]) and user preferences (for higher ranked results [20] or particular domains [16]), but not seemingly irrational behaviors or skewed result lists as we focus on here. Although the motivation between previous studies and ours differs, the impact of the biases can be similar: both types cause searchers to be interested in particular results for reasons beyond relevance. As such, biased beliefs can also affect aggregated behavioral signals (e.g., result click-through) used by search engines for ranking [1][19]. As we show here, when an answer to a yes-no medical question is provided in the top result from a search engine, more than half of the time that answer is incorrect. Search engines need to consider both satisfying users (by surfacing results that reinforce biases, but could also be factually incorrect) and providing correct answers (e.g., performing bias mitigation to provide more rational result sets that accurately reflect background probabilities). For important searches such as those in the health domain—where people have been shown to interpret the result ranking as an ordering of condition likelihoods [44]—search engines may wish to favor accuracy over satisfaction given the potentially-serious ramifications of an incorrect answer.

In this paper we present the first comprehensive study of beliefs and biases in search, highlighting the potentially counterproductive effects of biases on answer accuracy. Focused on the health domain, we demonstrate the large extent to which bias is evident in search behaviors and results, and we argue that biases need to be considered by the IR community in ranking and interaction support. To study these biases we employ a range of methods, including an initial exploratory survey to gain insight into prior beliefs and how they change as a result of search, human labeling (by crowd-sourced judges as well as physicians), and a log analysis of Web search behavior. We study biases in the context of yes-no questions because we can attain direct ground truth answers via expert consensus, allowing us to study answer accuracy, central to our definition of bias. As we show, yes-no questions are also popular (2% of the queries in our search engine log sample were yes-no questions) and they offer an excellent opportunity for search engines to help users since there is often a likely answer. This study answers the following research questions: (i) Do people's beliefs in different outcomes (*yes* versus *no* in this case) change (and how) as a result of searching? (ii) To what extent are search engine results biased in favor of particular outcomes? (iii) To what extent do biases appear to affect search behaviors? and (iv) What is the impact of these factors on search outcomes, specifically answer accuracy? Answers to these questions help us better understand the role of biases in search and can inform the design of IR methods to consider biases, e.g., in deciding when accuracy should feature in result ranking, or when systems should diversify the result set to expose new perspectives.

The remainder of the paper is structured as follows. Section 2 describes related work in the psychology and IR research communities. Section 3 presents the results of a large exploratory survey of biases in beliefs during the search process. Section 4 describes the identification of yes-no question content labels and definitive answers necessary for our analysis. Section 5 describes the extent to which search engine result pages (SERPs) and the result ranking is skewed toward a particular answer for the yes-no questions we select. Section 6 focuses on search behavior, including the accuracy of the answers that searchers appeared to find. We discuss the findings and their implications in Section 7 and conclude in Section 8.

2. RELATED WORK

Research in a number of areas is relevant to the work described here, namely: (i) cognitive biases and decision making, (ii) utilizing search behavior to rank results, (iii) biases in search interaction, and (iv) personalization and diversity. We consider each area in turn.

Numerous models of the search process have been developed over the past few decades [4][17][23][24][30]. These models primarily focus on information need formulation, search interaction, resolving uncertainty, and contextual influences on the search process. However, these models largely ignore situations when seemingly irrational search behavior is observed, e.g., people accepting factually incorrect or unsupported information because it reinforces a particular belief they hold. Cognitive biases are defined as a pattern of deviation in judgment occurring in particular situations, where a deviation may refer to a difference from what is normatively expected, either by the judgment of people outside of the situation or by independently verifiable facts [21]. Biases play a central role in human judgment and decision making and span a number of different dimensions (see [2][3][21] for summaries). Other models of irrational human behavior are plentiful, including related concepts such as bounded rationality [33]. Biases can be difficult to distinguish and are not necessarily negative. For example, they can form information-processing shortcuts leading to more effective actions in a given context or enable faster decisions when timeliness is more valuable than accuracy, e.g., the availability heuristic allows rapid assessments of likelihoods based on ease of recall [15][21].

Confirmation bias describes people's unconscious tendency to prefer confirmatory information [26][41]. This can make searchers more likely to employ positive test strategies, where people seek evidence that supports their hypothesis and disregard evidence that refutes it [22]. Moving beyond behavior, biases in the *results* returned toward one perspective can reinforce existing beliefs and leave searchers susceptible to the effects of information availability [33][39], where people's ability to make rational decisions is limited by the information that they have access to [33] and the ease with which information is recalled (via the engine in this case) maps to likelihood estimates [39]. Although there has been extensive research on cognitive processes in search, we are the first to present a detailed investigation of beliefs and biases in search. The role of biases in search were discussed in previous studies on "cyberchondria" [44], but were not studied as directly as we do in this paper.

Over the past decade, a number of authors have proposed methods for using behavioral data of various forms—including queries, result clicks, and post-click navigation behavior—to improve result relevance [1][4][19]. Despite its utility for ranking, search behavior can still be affected by biases related to the ordering or presentation of results on the SERP, or user preferences for particular resources. Joachims et al. [20] analyzed searchers' decision processes via gaze tracking and compared implicit feedback from search-result clicks against manual relevance judgments. They found that clicks are informative but biased (favoring results at higher rank positions), yet relative result preferences derived from clicks mirror searchers' true preferences. Searcher models can capitalize on this consistent behavior to infer search result attractiveness and document relevance (e.g., [10]). Over time, searchers' focus of attention on top-ranked content can create a vicious cycle whereby clicks reinforce popular results [8], although this popularity bias may be offset somewhat by the heterogeneity of searchers' topical interests [14].

Other factors beyond rank position can introduce bias into search. Clarke and colleagues [9] introduced click inversions to study features of the captions that increase caption attractiveness. Yue and colleagues [47] studied the effect of caption attractiveness, defined for their study as the presence and absence of bolded terms in the titles and snippets of the caption. They show via experiments conducted on the Google Web search engine substantial evidence of presentation bias in clicks towards results with more attractive titles. Beyond captions, Ieong and colleagues [16] studied the effect of domain biases, whereby a result is believed to be more relevant because of its source domain. They show that this bias exists in click behaviors as well as human judgments, and that domain can flip caption preferences around a quarter of the time, independent of rank or relevance. However, these biases are unrelated to biased beliefs about task outcomes and the role of search engines in reinforcing those beliefs, as we target in this study.

Beyond aggregating search behavior across all users, search engines can also cater to the individual needs of their users via personalization, presenting the opportunity to model their preferences within the current session [42][46] and across multiple sessions [34][38][45]. However, these models focus on term or topic level interests rather than degrees of belief in particular outcomes. This provides a limited view on factors that could affect preferences, and considering beliefs and biases could improve personalization. Research on result diversity (e.g., [25][40][48]) is also relevant but typically focuses on aspects such as topical variance, rather than results skewed toward one perspective or biased search behaviors.

The research presented in this paper extends previous work in a number of ways. First, we are the first, to our knowledge, to examine biased beliefs and skewed search engine result lists in IR. Second, through a detailed study of yes-no questions (involving a survey, human labeling, and large-scale log analysis – the latter two focused on the important domain of health search) we empirically demonstrate and quantify the effect of biases in results and search behaviors. Finally, we establish the effects of biases on search outcomes, specifically the accuracy of answers that people find.

3. BELIEFS DURING SEARCH

We begin by describing the retrospective survey that we performed to better understand the role of biased beliefs in Web search. This provided us with insight into people's beliefs before searching as well as afterwards, their perceptions of the process, and their rationales for their actions. An invitation to complete an online survey was distributed via email to a sample of employees within Microsoft Corp. The sample comprised employees in a range of technical and non-technical roles. We were particularly interested in those who had recently pursued yes-no answers using search engines. Since there are only two opposing outcomes, such questions provide a means of quickly and easily measuring degrees of belief. A total of 198 respondents (23.1% of all respondents) reported issuing such a question to any Web search engine during two weeks immediately prior to survey distribution. We asked participants to recall that particular searching episode, and provide the yes-no

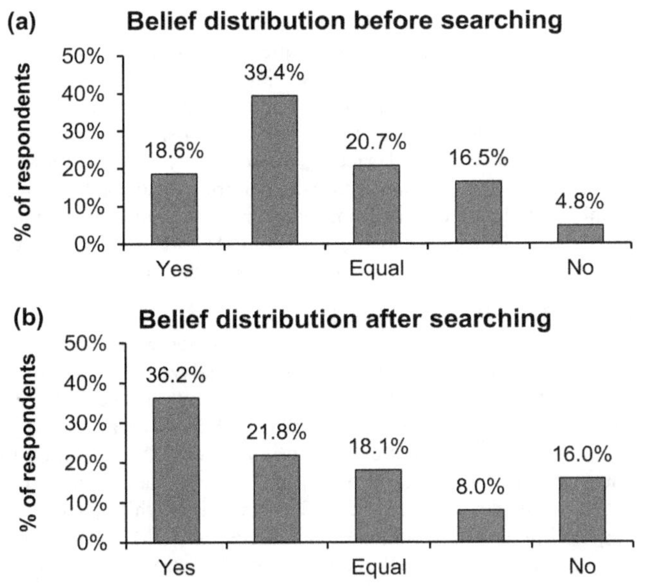

Figure 1. Distribution of (a) prior and (b) posterior reported recalled beliefs about the answer (ranging from Yes to No).

query issued, as well as the motivation behind the search. Question queries reported by respondents included "*Does chocolate contain caffeine?*" and "*Are shingles contagious?*". We also asked respondents questions about their experience during their recalled search.

We believe that there is value in using retrospective analysis to explore search beliefs, even though our method depends on participant recollections and they already knew the outcome of the recalled search episode. Alternative methods such as in-situ judging are intrusive and may draw undue attention to beliefs at query time, asking respondents to create yes-no questions at survey time lacks realism, and third-party judges issuing these questions as queries could not accurately consider searchers' true beliefs or motivations.

3.1 Belief Dynamics

The focus of our study was on how participant beliefs changed as a result of performing the search that they recalled. To do this, we asked participants to quantify their level of belief in each of the outcomes (*yes* and *no*) before and after the search.

Before searching: Given that they recalled a recent yes-no question searching episode, survey respondents were then asked to "*Rate your relative prior belief about the likelihood of each outcome before you used the search engine*" on a nine-point scale, where extreme values corresponded to the response options *yes* and *no*, and the mid-point corresponded to an equal belief in *yes* and *no*. This allowed us to obtain a precise distribution of beliefs across the range of response options. Given small counts in some cells, and to more easily identify trends, we created five response groups: *yes*, *lean yes*, *equal*, *lean no*, and *no*. The *lean yes* and *lean no* groups comprise the three ratings between *equal* and *yes* and *no* respectively. Figure 1a has the distribution of reported recalled beliefs.

Figure 1a provides evidence of a positive skew in respondents' beliefs before they search. Specifically, 58% of respondents leaned toward *yes* and only 21% leaned toward *no* (the remaining 21% reported an equal belief in both outcomes). This corroborates prior research on confirmation discussed earlier in the related work section (e.g., [26][41]). In addition, analysis of the explanations offered for leaning *yes* or *no* revealed that 47% of respondents explicitly cited *confirmation* of their beliefs as the primary search activity they were performing (e.g., "I was verifying", "I wanted to check").

Table 1. Fraction of respondents reporting different beliefs following search (columns) given the belief before (rows).

Belief before search	*Belief after search*: Yes		Equal		No
Yes	77.1%	8.6%	8.6%	2.9%	2.9%
	35.1% ❶	40.5%	9.5%	2.7% ❷	12.2%
Equal	23.1%	12.8%	43.6%	15.4%	5.1%
	16.1%	9.7%	19.4%	19.4% ❶	35.5%
No	11.1%	–	11.1%	–	77.8%

After searching: We also wanted to understand the impact of search on respondents' beliefs. To do so we asked respondents to "*Rate your relative posterior belief about the likelihood of each outcome once you finished searching*" The distribution of responses appears in Figure 1b. This distribution shows less uncertainty, with more responses at *yes* and *no*. One possible explanation for this is that people were more informed after they examined results. There is more of a split between *yes* and *no*, with less than half of respondents still exhibiting some uncertainty (i.e., 48% believed *lean yes*, *equal*, or *lean no*) compared to more than three quarters of respondents (77%) before searching. The fraction of searchers who believed *yes* after the search is more than double that of any other outcome, suggesting that respondents mostly shifted their prior beliefs from *lean yes* to *yes*. However, this analysis is insufficient to understand the belief dynamics in individual respondents.

Table 1 shows the fraction of users transitioning to a particular belief after they search (columns) conditioned on their beliefs with respect to *yes* and *no* before they searched (rows). For example, 77% of searchers who strongly believed *yes* beforehand, still believe this afterwards, with a similar value (78%) for *no*. These findings suggest that if searchers are certain about their beliefs initially then they are likely to remain unchanged following the search. Research on anchoring-and-adjustment has shown that people typically perform little revision to their beliefs, especially if those beliefs are strongly held [21]. To our knowledge, our work is the first demonstration of this heuristic being applied in a search setting.

There are other noteworthy findings from Table 1:

1. Respondents leaning *yes* or *no* before searching either retain that belief, or become more certain (i.e., ① in Table 1).
2. Respondents with a belief in *yes* or *no* (definite or lean) at the outset are unlikely to dramatically change their opinion to the opposing perspective after the search (e.g., ② in Table 1).
3. Respondents who are uncertain at the outset (*equal*) are likely to either remain uncertain (44%) or be more likely to lean positive following the search, e.g., 36% of respondents (23.1% + 12.8%) who believed equal beforehand believed *yes* afterward, versus 21% who believed *no* (15.4% + 5.1%).

There are a few possible explanations for these findings: (i) searchers are drawn to information supporting or confirming their prior beliefs (as suggested in survey remarks) and are therefore unlikely to change their opinion as they are not exposed to contradictory evidence, (ii) search engines rank results with *yes* higher in the list leading searchers to be more likely to view those results, or (iii) the prior distribution of correct answers to the yes-no questions submitted to search engines is skewed positive. We answer the first question using survey responses and later log analysis. The others require an assessment of the content of the SERPs and landing pages, and a correct answer to the questions posed. We do not address these directly in the survey, since respondents may not be able to make the assessments objectively. However, later in the paper we describe how we obtained direct labels for SERPs and results and answers for a subset of yes-no question queries.

Table 2. Reported motivations for considering other answers once candidate answer was found. Multiple reasons permitted.

Reason	*Percentage of responses*
Confirmation of the current best answer from another source	83.9%
Information that contradicted the current best answer (e.g., to assess its validity)	43.4%
Direct comparisons of the two outcomes (*yes* and *no*) in the same Web page	16.9%

3.2 Answer Perceptions and Follow-on Search

Answers found using search engines can affect action in the world. It is therefore important to understand whether people report finding answers and how confident they are in the accuracy of those answers. Overall, 85% of respondents reported finding an answer to their yes-no question by searching, with 92% of those who found an answer reporting that they were *confident* or *extremely confident* in answer accuracy. These high percentages are encouraging if the search engine is correct, but as we show this is not always the case.

Since searchers frequently examine multiple results [11], we were also interested in the motivation behind additional seeking once an initial answer was found. We asked respondents: "*If you found an answer early in your search, did you still consider multiple results before settling on your final answer?*" In total, 49% of our respondents reported viewing multiple answers. We then asked them to explain the motivation behind that additional searching (Table 2). The findings in the table demonstrate that once a searcher finds an initial answer their follow-up searching is likely to be related to seeking confirmatory information. Overall, 84% of respondents reported that confirmation of the initial answer was their motivation, compared to the 43% and 17% who provided reasons linked to testing the robustness of the initial answer with contradictory information.

3.3 Summary

The survey was part of an initial exploration of belief dynamics and their impact on search behavior. There are two main takeaways from the findings that are relevant to our focus in this paper:

1. Respondents reported confirmatory search behaviors by sticking to an answer if they strongly believed *yes* or *no*, transitioning to a stronger belief if they leant toward *yes* or *no* initially, respondents favored information supporting their belief, and sought confirmation once an answer was found.
2. If people are unsure (i.e., have equal belief in *yes* and *no*) they are almost twice as likely to move toward a positive answer rather than negative following searching.

Search engines may be supporting these biased processes and we need to explore this further as part of our study. While the survey findings provide motivation to study search-related biases, to study them in detail we need ground truth answers for the questions that people pose and judgments reflecting the results surfaced by search engines. We performed an extensive follow-up study using human labeling of SERPs and results, and a log analysis of search behavior for yes-no questions. Focusing on the medical domain, given its importance and since we could gather ground truth answers, we obtained answers from physicians and judgments from crowdworkers.

4. QUESTIONS, ANSWERS, JUDGMENTS

We first describe the automatic identification of yes-no questions from logs, the process of obtaining answers to a subset of those questions from physicians, and the process of gathering judgments about answers in SERP captions and landing pages for that subset.

4.1 Searcher Questions

We automatically extracted yes-no questions from a random sample of the logs of queries issued by 2.3M users of Microsoft Bing during a two-week period from September 2012. The data includes user identifiers, timestamps, queries, result clicks, and the captions (titles, snippets, URLs) of each of the top 10 results. To remove variability from cultural and linguistic variation in search behavior, we only include log entries from searchers in the English-speaking United States locale. We also obtained the HTML content of each of the top 10 results from the engine index during the same period.

4.1.1 Extracting Questions

Yes-no questions are an interrogative construction where an answer of *yes* or *no* is required. We automatically analyze the logs searching for questions asked as queries using variants of "be," "have," "do", or a modal verb (e.g., "can," "will"). We also created a list of stop phrases (e.g., "do not call," "do it yourself," "will smith") to remove frequent non-yes-no questions from our data. During extraction, we normalized queries via lowercasing, whitespace trimming, and punctuation removal. We identified 3.4M yes-no question queries using this method. The yes-no question queries in our set comprised around 2% of the total query volume in our sample and covered a wide range of topics. Since we are interested in the assessment of answer accuracy, we needed to filter the yes-no questions to a topic where we could obtain reliable answers. To this end, we restricted the questions to those with a medical intent and sought answers to them from trained medical professionals (physicians). To help ensure data quality, we did the following additional filtering: (i) selected SERPs with same 10 results and same result ordering across all instances of the query in the two weeks, and; (ii) focused on query instances that were either the only query in the session or the terminal query in the session with no preceding queries with query-term overlap. Filter #2 gave us more certainty that users had terminated their search with that query. This is important in later analysis when we infer answer attainment from clicked results.

4.1.2 Labeling Questions with Medical Intent

Given the large number of questions selected as described in the previous section, we needed a way to automatically label whether questions had medical intent. To do this we used a proprietary classifier from Bing. The classifier labeled 2.5% of yes-no questions as having strong medical intent (threshold > 0.8). This aligns with prior analysis of query topics, which showed that approximately 3% of search queries are medical [45]. From this set, we randomly selected 1000 medical yes-no questions. To remove noisy queries and provide sufficient data from which to analyze search behavior, selected questions had to be issued by at least 10 users. Examples of the questions selected include "*Do food allergies make you tired?*", "*Is congestive heart failure a heart attack?*", and "*Can aspirin cause blood in urine?*". We restricted the size of the question set to 1000 questions since we wanted to obtain answer labels from medical professionals, who were time constrained.

4.2 Physician Answers

As stated earlier, to measure biases we needed ground truth answers to the yes-no questions in our set. We employed two practicing physicians as judges. Each judge reviewed the same set of 1000 medically-focused yes-no questions and provided an answer on a three-point scale: *yes*, *50/50*, *no*. The judges worked independently and there was no opportunity for discussion between them to resolve disagreements. Judges were encouraged to apply their knowledge and think of the most common scenario/circumstances that could apply when a user types such a question on the Internet. The middle rating (50/50) was only to be used if: (i) there really was an equal split between *yes* and *no* in the most common scenario or circumstances, and/or (ii) more information would certainly be needed to provide an answer. Two other response options were provided: (i) *don't know*: if the judge did not know the answer, and (ii) *n/a*: if the query was not medical or was not a yes-no question (possible given the automated identification of yes-no questions from logs).

Overall, 4% of the questions were labeled by at least one of the two judges as not being a yes-no question. These questions were excluded from further analysis. Of the remaining 960 questions, the judges agreed on either *yes* or *no* as the answer to the question for 674 (70.2%) of them. Seeking a second opinion is common practice in medicine and the 30% disagreement between physicians is similar to that reported in medical literature [18]. However, if we consider the disagreement in more detail, we see that for 14.0 % of the questions (roughly half of the disagreement), judges completely disagreed on the answer (i.e., one labeled *yes* and the other chose *no*). For 15.8% of the questions, one judge was unsure (13.6%) or both were unsure (2.2%). The agreement matrix is in Table 3.

The percent of overall agreement across all of the four answer options was 72.2%. The Cohen's free-marginal kappa (κ) inter-rater agreement, considering chance agreement between raters is 0.630, signifying substantial agreement. Note that we use the free-marginal kappa because our raters were not forced to assign a certain number of cases to each category [7]. If we only focus on the questions where both judges provided a *yes* or *no* response, the percent of overall agreement rises to 83.4%, with κ=0.668, signifying even more substantial agreement. The only discernible difference between the questions where the physicians disagreed directly on *yes* and *no*, was that those with disagreement were much more likely to start with "can" (e.g., "*Can a pinched nerve in neck cause throat pain?*"). Overall, 49.3% of questions with disagreement started with "can," vs. 34.0% of questions with agreement. Since the usage of "can" denotes *possibility*, these questions may be more subjective and dependent on the knowledge and experience of the judges.

Since there is a high amount of uncertainty for the *50/50* and the *don't know* categories, and they occur infrequently (e.g., only 12 cases where the experts both believed that more information was definitely required), we focus on the cases where both judges were sufficiently confident to assign a rating of *yes* or *no*. Because the questions with yes-no disagreement might highlight contentious, subjective, or difficult questions, we focused on the 674 questions where both judges agreed that the answer was *yes* or *no*. Within this set, 55.2% of answers were *yes* and 44.8% *no*. These particular percentages are important because they provide the background probabilities, or *base rates*, of each answer across our data set.

Returning to our earlier discussion of why post-search beliefs tend positive (Section 3), this provides supporting evidence that the questions being posed are more likely to be answered affirmatively, although the difference is not as large as the 2:1 ratio between *yes* and *no* shown in Figure 1b, perhaps because the question sets differ. Using search logs, we have the ability to analyze results and behaviors in detail. If search engines or users lean toward *yes*/*no* significantly more than the 55/45 split, this offers direct evidence of bias.

4.3 Crowdsourced Judgments

So that we could assess the level of skew in SERPs and results, and also study which captions and results people selected, we required judgments on the perspectives offered by captions and results. For this task we used crowd-sourced judges from a pool provided under contract to our organization by Clickworker.com. To suit the geographic and linguistic filtering performed on the question queries, all judges resided in the United States and were fluent in English.

Table 3. Agreement matrix in the responses from the two physicians. Highlighted = yes-no agreement between judges.

Physician 1	*Physician 2*: *Yes*	*No*	*50/50*	*Don't know*	*Total*
Yes	**38.8%**	8.2%	3.7%	0.5%	51.2%
No	5.7%	**31.5%**	1.2%	0.2%	38.5%
50/50	1.8%	2.0%	1.3%	0.0%	5.0%
Don't know	1.3%	3.1%	0.2%	0.7%	5.3%
Total	47.5%	44.8%	6.3%	1.5%	100.0%

The judges were required to read task guidelines and successfully complete a qualification test similar before they could start judging.

4.3.1 SERP Caption Judgments

The task required judges to assess whether a caption (title, snippet, and URL) presented on a SERP suggested an answer to the current yes-no question. Judges were provided with a yes-no query such as "*Can Flonase make you tired?*" and a single caption. The caption may answer the question with *yes* or *no* directly (e.g., "*... can Flonase make you tired? Yes ...*") or suggest an answer somewhat indirectly (e.g., "*... Flonase is unrelated to tiredness ...*"). Captions can also contain contradictory answers, and no answer. Judges were required to review the caption with respect to the question and provide one of the following ratings about answers to the question:

1. Yes only (affirmative): Caption *only contains* content answering the yes-no question affirmatively.
2. No only (negative): Caption *only contains* content answering the yes-no question negatively.
3. Both (affirmative *and* negative): Caption contains content answering the yes-no question affirmatively *and* content answering the yes-no question answering negatively.
4. Neither: Caption contains neither affirmative nor negative answers to the yes-no question.

Figure 2 shows examples of each of the caption labels for a variety of queries. These examples are taken from the guidelines provided to crowd-sourced judges to help them understand the task.

Between three and five judges rated each of the 6,740 captions under consideration to achieve a consensus comprising at least three judges with the same rating. In total, consensus was reached for 96% of captions, with 85% of captions attaining agreement with only three judges. We only use those captions with agreement.

4.3.2 Landing Page Judgments

In addition to judging the captions that the search engine presented on the SERP, we employed a similar methodology to judge the full text of the results returned by the search engine. As mentioned earlier, the results were retrieved from the search engine's index at the time that the query logs were recorded. We once again used crowd-sourced judges from the same pool, between three and five judges (three needed to attain consensus), as with the captions. Judges labeled each page based on whether it contained an answer and the type of answer it contained. The judges provided one of the same four ratings as they provided for the captions. Judges could provide an error label if the page could not be loaded, although this was seldom used (for < 2% pages). In total, consensus was achieved for 92% of pages (excluding errors); 81% of results had agreement among three judges and did not need further judgments. This labeling task was slightly more difficult than caption labeling because the full page had to be inspected and some answers may be missed.

4.3.3 Validating Crowdsourced Judgments

We suspected that these tasks (which were recognition oriented) would not require the specialized medical training. To verify the correctness of this decision we asked our medical experts and our

Suggests AFFIRMATIVE answer (Yes only):
Question: [can i take l carnitine while pregnant]
Is it safe to **take L-Carnitine while pregnant** - The Q&A wiki
http://wiki.answers.com/Q/Is_it_safe_to_take_L-Carnitine_while_pregnant
Is **l-carnitine** safe to **take while pregnant**? yes. Is it safe to **take** zithromax **while pregnant**? yes it is safe to **take while pregnant**. A doctor would not prescribe it ...

Suggests NEGATIVE answer (No only):
Question: [does robaxin show up on drug tests]
Does robaxin show up on drug tests? | Answerbag
http://www.answerbag.com/q_view/1239474
Does robaxin show up on drug tests? no... More Questions. Additional questions in this category. Can you have a DUI & work at a school in Pennsylvania?

Suggests BOTH affirmative and negative:
Question: [is tooth a bone]
Is **tooth** consider as a **bone** - The Q&A wiki
http://wiki.answers.com/Q/Is_tooth_consider_as_a_bone
What does the **bone** in the **tooth** do? It helps u chew. Is a **tooth** a **bone**? Yes. Is your **tooth** a **bone**? No, teeth are not **bones**. Is the "skin" lining your stomach skin?

Suggests NEITHER affirmative nor negative:
Question: [does crestor cause bloating]
Does Crestor Cause Bloating? – HealthCentral
http://www.healthcentral.com/cholesterol/h/does-crestor-cause-bloating.html
Everything you need to know about **does crestor cause bloating**, including common uses, side effects, interactions and risks.

Figure 2. Examples of each of the caption ratings. The answer text is highlighted in the first three captions.

crowd-sourced judges to label the same sample of 100 captions and 100 landing pages with the labels described above, and we assessed the agreement between them. We found a high level of agreement between the physicians (both $\kappa \geq 0.886$), as well as between the two physicians and the consensus labels provided by the crowd-sourced judges (both Fleiss' multi-rater $\kappa \geq 0.853$ [13]). The findings suggest that for these tasks, the crowd-sourced judges provide similar rating quality to trained physicians (mirroring [34]). There were only 6% labeling discrepancies between captions and their associated landing pages (e.g., caption label = *both*, page label = *yes*-only). Explanations for these differences include caption generation effects or differences in judges used for caption and result labeling.

The data described in this section allows us to study the distribution of answers on SERPs and in the results themselves, as well as search interaction. Given the physician answers, we can also analyze the accuracy of the answer pages found and condition analyses of SERPs, results, and behaviors on the ground truth answers.

5. BIASED SERPS & SEARCH RESULTS

Given the data described in the previous section we can analyze the SERPs generated by the search engine (using the caption judgments) and the top-ranked results returned by the engine (using the landing-page judgments). In this analysis we focus on the presence and distribution of *yes* and *no* answers across the 674 queries in the agreement set. Recall from earlier that we focused on queries where the SERP was unchanged over the two weeks of logs, giving us exactly one SERP per query. Studying the role of captions is particularly important as they play a critical role in searchers' decision making [9][47]. We used the physician answer to study significance in two ways: (i) changes in the distributions across answer types when conditioned on the answer types (e.g., does fraction of *yes*-only top-ranked results increase when the ground truth (from expert consensus) is *yes*?), and (ii) how closely does the distribution of answer types model the truth? For (ii), if there was no bias, the distribution of *yes* and *no* would resemble the 55/45 split in our data.

5.1 Answer Presence and Result Distributions

We first wanted to determine what fraction of the results (SERP captions and landing pages) contained an answer of *yes*, *no*, *both*, and *neither* to the yes-no question posed by the user. Table 4 shows the fraction of SERPs that contain each type of answer, in terms of occurrences in captions and occurrences in the full-text of the results. The table clearly shows a bias toward *yes*. Since these are per-SERP statistics they do not reveal much about the concentration of the answers in the SERP or their relative ordering by the search engine. Table 5 presents the fraction of all captions and results for the yes-no question containing an answer. The findings show that results and captions containing *yes* are much more likely to appear in the results than those with no; around 3-4 times more likely across all captions and all SERPs. There were no significant variations in those percentages when we conditioned using the physician answer, suggesting that for these questions the search engine is insensitive to the truth (very little change in the values as we varied the physician answer). Focusing on yes-only and no-only captions and results, McNemar's chi-squared tests and Z-tests of proportions showed differences between yes-only and no-only in all cases (all $p < 0.01$) and differences from the base rates (i.e., 55/45) at $p < 0.01$ in all cases other than *no*-only in Table 5 ($p = 0.54$), which was similar to the *no* answer prior in our dataset (i.e., 45%).

Table 4. Percentage of SERPs with at least once instance of each type of answer in captions or results. N=674. SERPs can contain multiple answers so rows do not sum to one.

Source	*Yes only*	*No only*	*Both*	*Neither*
Caption	75.5%	43.0%	17.1%	85.6%
Result	74.5%	46.1%	34.5%	95.5%

Table 5. Percentage of captions/results with answer. N=6491.

Source	*Yes only*	*No only*	*Both*	*Neither*
Caption	28.7%	8.4%	2.7%	60.2%
Result	35.0%	12.7%	6.3%	41.0%

Table 6. Average rank of the highest-ranked result with each answer type, including standard deviation. Top rank=1.

Source	*Yes only*	*No only*	*Both*	*Neither*
Caption	2.66±1.72	2.98±2.01	4.02±2.35	2.15±2.00
Result	2.17±1.65	2.98±1.98	3.93±2.35	3.11±2.17

Table 7. Percentage of SERPs where top *yes* caption or result appears above (nearer the top of the ranking than) the top *no*.

Source	*Yes above No*	*No above Yes*
Caption	65.1%	34.9%
Result	62.4%	37.6%

5.2 Distribution of Highest-Ranked Answers

The previous section examined answer *presence* on SERPs and in results. In this section we examine the distribution of answers in captions and results as a function of *rank* position within the top 10 results. Table 6 presents the average rank position of the first answer of each type in the result list. We focus on the first answer to help ameliorate the effects from different volumes of answer types in the top 10 results. Since people inspect the results from top to bottom [20], the first occurrence of each answer in the captions is particularly important anyway. The table shows that the topmost captions and the results with *yes* are ranked above those with *no* and other answer labels. We performed one-way analyses of variance (ANOVA) for each of the two sources (captions and results), and the findings revealed significant differences between the rank of *yes* and *no* and all of the other answers for both captions and the full text of the results (both $F(1,4665) \geq 6.85$, both $p < 0.01$). The analysis also shows that that results with *yes*-only appear higher in the ranking (rank=2.15) than captions (rank=2.66) ($p < 0.001$).

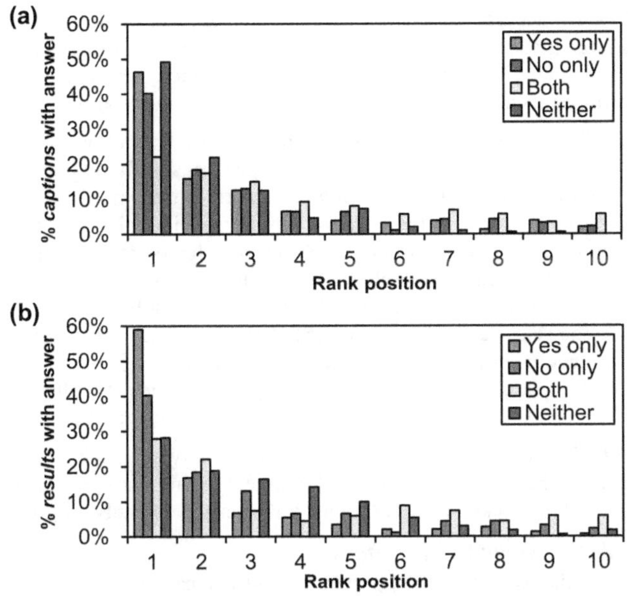

Figure 3. Distribution of *highest-ranked* answers of each type across (a) top 10 captions and (b) top 10 results.

We also computed the *distribution* of ranks for highest-ranked answers and report this in Figure 3 for answers of each type and for captions and results. The presence of an answer at ranks 2-10 is conditioned on the absence of the same type of answer at higher ranks. Figure 3a shows that the distributions of highest-ranked *yes* and *no* captions was similar across all ranks, with 40-45% occurring at the top of the list. The distribution of top-ranked answers in *results*, shown in Figure 3b, was more skewed toward the top of the ranking for *yes* than for other types, and *yes* was significantly more likely to appear in the top position than *no* (59.1% *yes* vs. 40.2% *no*, $Z = 5.00, p < 0.001$), once again illustrating positive rank bias.

5.3 Relative Ordering of Yes and No

Despite the evidence of bias toward *yes* answers presented in the previous section, a more direct comparison of *yes* and *no* comes from their relative ordering when both are present in the results. Our analysis also shows that around 35% of SERPs contained both a *yes* and a *no* answer. Table 7 presents the fraction of captions and results that have the top *yes* above the top *no*, and vice versa. The results show that the captions with *yes* are ranked well above those with *no* for both captions and results. The results also show that captions exhibit this bias slightly more than the results themselves (65% for captions vs. 62% for results), highlighting possible skew in the caption generation methods or rankings associated with caption clickthrough. There were no significant effects on the distribution from physician answers. However, *yes* was ranked above *no* more often than the 55% that would be expected given the base rates (both $Z \geq 2.00$, both $p \leq 0.02$), further confirming a positive bias in SERPs and results for the queries in our dataset.

5.4 Summary

Overall, we have shown that search engines are more likely to present captions/results answering a yes-no question positively (*yes*) in the top results, and they are more likely to rank results with positive answers at the top of the list, and above *no* (when both are shown on the SERP). We also showed that the distribution of answer content was insensitive to the ground truth answers provided by medical professionals; the positive bias persists irrespective of the ground truth. Finally, we showed that distributions were skewed more positive than expected from base rates. It might be argued that

Table 8. SERP click likelihoods for different captions given variations in answer presence in SERPs/captions, and rank.

Condition(s)	*All*	*Physician Answer*	
		Yes	*No*
$SERP_Y$	80.0%	83.6%	74.4%
$SERP_N$	75.9%	80.6%	69.6%
$SERP_{BOTH}, Caption_Y$	45.6%	58.2%	41.1%
$SERP_{BOTH}, Caption_N$	14.2%	13.4%	21.8%
$Caption_Y$	41.1%	47.1%	37.7%
$Caption_N$	16.3%	12.9%	20.2%
$Caption_{Y,r=1}$	47.4%	60.0%	40.9%
$Caption_{N,r=1}$	12.6%	11.1%	17.6%

Table 9. Distribution of clicks and skips by answer. *N*=245.

Click	*Skip*	
	Yes only	*No only*
Yes only	33.3%	41.5%
No only	8.5%	16.7%

this bias is reasonable if searchers are satisfied. However, if search engines lead users to incorrect answers, then this requires corrective action. We examine answer accuracy at the end of the next section.

6. BIASED BEHAVIORS & OUTCOMES

We now study biases in behavior, linking SERP caption judgments with clicks, and using page judgments to study answer accuracy.

6.1 SERP Behaviors

From our search logs, we extracted all instances of the 674 yes-no queries that resulted in at least one click on a result: 496 (83%) of our yes-no question queries met this criterion. In this analysis, we focus on the *first* click that users perform and the content of the captions that they click. We do this to help reduce the effects of learning during search. We consider a number of aspects of click behavior, namely all clicks, clicks controlled for position and the distribution of yes-no results, and we also examine caption skips.

6.1.1 Result Clicks

Across all observed clicks in our set, 41.1% are on a caption labeled yes-only and 16.3% are on a caption labeled no-only (*note: the other clicks are on captions with both or neither*). Focusing solely on the clicks on *yes* and *no* that means 71.6% of clicks were on *yes*, whereas only 28.4% of clicks were on *no*. This strongly suggests that people are more likely to click on captions with positive outcomes. Table 8 provides a series of click likelihoods computed empirically from the data depicting the relationship between properties of the SERP and SERP captions, and click likelihoods (in the *All* column). The presence of *yes* or *no* in the caption is denoted as *Y* or *N* respectively, and the rank of the click is denoted r. $SERP_{BOTH}$ means that captions with yes-only and no-only answers appear on the SERP. The table also breaks down the clicks by physician answer, to help us understand the effect of the truth on click behavior as we did in previous sections. A number of conclusions can be drawn from the findings. The first is that people are more likely to click when the SERP contains *yes*, and also are more likely to click when the physician answer is *yes*, irrespective of the SERP content (top two rows of Table 8), although this difference was not significant ($p = 0.63$). Focusing on captions, people appear 2-4 times as likely to click on captions with positive content (rows 3-6), even though *yes* is only marginally more likely in our ground truth data. Considering physician answers we see that likelihoods shift as expected (e.g., clicking *no* becomes more likely when answer is *no*), but clicking *yes* is still around twice as likely (all $Z \geq 3.16$, all $p \leq 0.001$) and far exceeds what is expected given our base rates.

Table 10. Breakdown in correctness by answer definition.

Answer defn.	*All*	*Physician Answer*	
		Yes	*No*
Top result	45.0%	57.1%	22.9%
First click	50.0%	59.1%	27.9%
Last click	52.3%	66.2%	29.4%

Table 11. Distribution of changes in the answer rating for first click versus the last click for the yes-no query instance.

First click	*Last click*	
	Yes only	**No only**
Yes only	70.2%	0.0%
No only	7.2%	22.6%

6.1.2 Controlling for Rank Position

One major factor that could explain the strong preference for positive information is the tendency of the search engine to return positive search results above negative results (as shown in Section 5). Given how searchers typically examine result lists (top-to-bottom), this could lead to an *apparent* preference for positive information caused by the search engine, even if one did not exist for searchers. Since we were performing our analysis retrospectively, we could not use methods such as FairPairs [29] to counteract positional bias. To do this in our study, we focused only on the result at the top position in the list (r=1) and assume that it is always examined (a hypothesis supported by gaze tracking studies [20]). Although the distribution of *yes* and *no* answers in these captions was very similar there were still more *yes* than *no* captions at the first position (see Figure 3a for the distribution). To ensure that the distribution was equal, we randomly down-sampled the *yes* instances. This gave us the same number of *yes* and *no* captions on which to study clicks (N=357). The findings appear in the last two rows of Table 8. The trends are similar to the original analysis, and the differences are still significant (all $p < 0.001$), although the effects of the physician answer are amplified when removing position effects (e.g., click *yes* is five times as likely as click *no* when physician answer is *yes*, and still more than twice as likely when the answer is *no*).

6.1.3 Skips and Clicks

Beyond clickthrough behavior, it is also worth considering the nature of the results that users *skipped* over prior to clicking on a particular caption. This provides additional insight into searcher preferences that is not available in clicks alone. To study this in our context, we targeted SERPs with both yes-only and no-only answers in captions, and identified clicks on a caption with a *yes* or *no* answer where the user had skipped over another caption prior to clicking (e.g., skip *yes*, click *no*). Table 9 shows the percentage of all skip-click pairs in each combination. A McNemar's chi-squared test shows significant differences between the outcomes ($\chi^2(1)$ = 16.99, $p < 0.001$). The table shows that it is common to skip over a caption and click on another caption with the same answer. However, what is most interesting is that on 42% of observed skip events, people skip over a caption with *no* to click on a caption with *yes*. This happens more frequently (five times) than it occurs in the opposite direction (skip *yes*, click *no*) and offers more evidence that people are drawn to information related to positive (*yes*) answers.

6.2 Answer Accuracy

Moving beyond search behavior, we now focus on whether searchers found the correct answer to their yes-no question and try to better understand the role of the engine in getting them to that answer.

6.2.1 Identifying Answers

To study accuracy in our logs, we first had to identify the particular answer that searchers found. Since we did not have direct judgments about if and where an answer was located, we inferred that from results and behavior. We devised three answer definitions:

1. Top result provided by the search engine. This allows us to study how well the search engine performs in finding answers. Note that even though the search engine may not be trying to answer the question directly, positional biases mean that searchers are more likely to select the top result [20].
2. First satisfied result click for the query instance. A satisfied click has a subsequent dwell time of 30 or more seconds, or the last click in the session [5]. This allows us to study the accuracy of the answers that searchers initially find.
3. Last satisfied result click for the query instance. This helps study the effect of user experience during the query session.

Note that since most of the impressions had only one click, then the first and the last clicks are often the same. For this analysis, we only focused on clicked pages assigned a *yes*-only or *no*-only judgment.

6.2.2 Answer Correctness

Given that we know the physician answer to each of the questions in the set (which we regard as our ground truth), and we know the answer rating for the page that searchers clicked on, or the top-ranked search result provided by the engine, we can calculate the *correctness* of the answer that the user found. Table 10 presents the breakdown of correctness by our three answer types. The findings summarized in the table show that if searchers trust the top-ranked result of the search engine, they will obtain the correct answer less than half of the time (45%). Analyzing results by physician answer, we can better understand its effect on answer correctness. In all cases, the answer was more likely be correct if the physician answer was *yes* (all $Z \geq 4.23$, all $p \leq 0.001$). If the physician answer is *yes*, then searchers settled on *yes* 66% of the time, perhaps because results with *yes* are more likely to be ranked higher in the list making them more likely to be chosen. Importantly, if the physician answer is *no*, then users attain the correct answer 23-29% of the time, showing that the focus is still on positive information.

In analyzing the results that searchers select rather than the top result that the search engine returns, we see that there is a small increase in correctness (45% to 50-52%) that can be attributed to searchers overriding the search engine ranking. The gains are small, perhaps because choices are limited to the results available in the top 10. Further analyzing the questions with high and low accuracy in the answer provided by the top result, we see that those questions starting with the terms "is" and "does" have the highest answer accuracy (61% and 59% respectively). However, questions starting with "can" (e.g., "*Can acid reflux cause back pain?*") had the lowest accuracy (38%). As mentioned earlier in the analysis of the expert labels, "can" denotes possibility and as such, for a question of this type base rates may need to factor in result ranking.

6.2.3 Answer Transitions

The findings in the survey suggested that there may be some interesting dynamics between the first and last clicks for a query (e.g., people reported being much more likely to search for confirmatory information than for information that challenged their hypothesis). We studied the changes in outcomes between queries where there were multiple clicks and different URLs at first and last click. Table 11 shows that people focus on a particular answer and stick with it as they review other resources ($\chi^2(1) = 70.01, p < 0.001$). The table also shows that no one transitioned from *yes* to *no*. These findings align with our survey, which showed that confirmation was the primary motivation for pursuing information after the initial answer.

6.3 Summary

Our findings have shown that people are more likely to target results with positive content than expected given base rates. They also show that users are much more likely to skip over captions containing no-only answers to click on those with yes-only (42%) than vice versa (9%). We studied answer accuracy and showed that around half of the time people found the correct answer to our questions. Although the search engine is not trying to answer directly, biases limit selection options and previous studies have shown that people can interpret result order as a likelihood ordering [44]. In addition, we also see strong evidence to support our survey findings that people seek confirmatory information and rarely change answer focus.

7. DISCUSSION AND IMPLICATIONS

We have shown evidence of biases in how people seek information and in search engine rankings toward particular outcomes. Our mixed methods approach used a survey, log analysis, and analysis of labeled data from crowdworkers and physicians. The survey provided insight into people's belief dynamics during search, and the role of search engines and their search behavior in finding information that supports those beliefs. As we have shown, biases in the results provided by the search engine may lead users to incorrect answers; on average people were likely to find the wrong answer half of the time. However, there were also marked differences in accuracy related to the nature of the queries, with questions denoting answer *possibility* resulting in lower answer accuracy.

There are limitations of the research that we should acknowledge. First, we focused on a small set of carefully-selected queries of a particular question type. Such focus was necessary given the scale of the human labeling effort (over 2000 person-hours of judgment time for the crowd-sourced caption/content judging alone) and to simplify our analysis. Different types of questions, such as those with a subjective or exploratory focus, are also worth examining. It is also worth considering situations where biases in beliefs could be significant (e.g., diagnostic scenarios, controversial topics). Second, although there are similarities between the survey and our later analysis, the survey did not specifically focus on health. Finally, we focused on the questions with physician agreement. The questions with diverging opinions may represent challenging or difficult topics, or cases where more information is needed prior to answering.

The research has implications for improving the design of search systems and raises important points for discussion on the role of search engines. Overall, a better understanding of how search engines rank answer pages is needed. Our findings show that the results that search engines offer are heavily skewed toward particular answers (usually positive), irrespective of the truth. As suggested earlier, this may be a consequence of search engines learning from biased, aggregated user behavior [1]. It may also relate to how users frame their queries. Studies have shown that people are more likely to frame questions positively when testing hypotheses [41]. Indeed, almost all of the yes-no queries in our dataset were framed in this way (e.g., "*Can acid reflux cause back pain?*" and not "*Is acid reflux unrelated to back pain?*"). As a result, ranking methods such as vector-space similarity [30] may consider a result with a *yes*-oriented answer (e.g., "Acid reflux can cause back pain") to be more similar to the query than a *no*-oriented answer (e.g., "Acid reflux cannot cause back pain"). Although text similarity is only one component of sophisticated search engine ranking algorithms, the higher query similarity with confirmatory content may be evident in other sources such as anchor text and document titles, and needs further investigation.

Although search results may not reflect the truth, they may reflect the dominant opinions of page authors or searchers, in which case on average people may well be satisfied with the answers provided, even if they are strictly inaccurate. Research on the "filter bubble" [27] suggests that search engines have a duty of care and that personalization filters out information that disagrees with user viewpoints. In this work, we show that related effects are observed beyond personalization; search engines exhibit positive biases in result ordering irrespective of the truth. Rank ordering is important given that people may interpret ranked lists of results as a ranking of likelihoods [44]. We also show that users are more likely to engage with positively-leaning content, important because it confirms their beliefs and biases (as our survey shows). The tradeoff between helping users validate beliefs and providing accurate information, and the incorporation of likelihood information should be explored at a query, domain, user, or cohort level. Other effects such as source reliability, the ease with which people can confirm versus refute their beliefs (conclusively falsifying hypotheses can be challenging [28]), and the distribution of positive and negative answers in online content, also need to be considered. Although the general online availability of *yes* and *no* content needs to be studied, we did show in Table 7 that even when both answers are available in the top 10 results, *yes* is ranked above *no* much more frequently.

Exploring accuracy depends critically on the availability of reliable truth data. Technology developed for Web-scale question answering (e.g., [12]) may be applied in the ranking of search results to help search engines consider base rates, especially for particular queries or query classes (e.g., as we demonstrate in our analysis with yes-no questions beginning with "can"). Search engines using learning-to-rank algorithms could consider the nature of the terminology in captions associated with clicks and downweight clicks that appear to be driven by known biases, e.g., those associated with health anxiety. Focused crawling strategies, proposed in the medical domain [36], could improve the reliability of the content in the engine index, since that may affect answer correctness. Long-term models to better represent beliefs, preferences, and perspectives of users beyond topical or term-level interests may also be useful. Tools and other search support could also be provided to introduce diversity into the results, highlight more trustworthy content [32], and prominently display base rates (e.g., in answers on SERPs).

8. CONCLUSIONS

Biases affect judgment and decision making. Although these biases can impact search behavior and result ranking, they have largely been ignored in IR. We have described a detailed study of biases in search, in the context of yes-no questions in the medical domain. We employed a retrospective survey, log analysis, content labeling by human judges, and answers from physicians. We showed that people seek to confirm their beliefs with their searches and that search engines provide positively-skewed search results, irrespective of the truth. We also showed that people are more likely to select positive (*yes*) information on SERPs, even when we control for rank, and are likely to skip negative results to reach positive ones (when the opposite is not true). Perhaps the most concerning insight from our analysis is that the combination of system and searcher biases lead people to settle on incorrect answers around half of the time (and that this inaccuracy is amplified when the physician answer, used as our ground truth, is *no*). The findings highlight a tradeoff between bias and accuracy that search engines need to consider. In future work we will study biases in domains beyond health search, and on different question types. We will also investigate bias-sensitive ranking methods to tackle challenges such as when accuracy should factor in ranking, and how base rates should be accurately determined, represented, and used by search engines.

ACKNOWLEDGMENTS
The author is grateful to Peter Bailey, Susan Dumais, Eric Horvitz, and Resa Roth for feedback and discussions around related ideas.

REFERENCES
[1] Agichtein, E., Brill, E., and Dumais, S. (2006). Improving web search ranking by incorporating user behavior information. *Proc. SIGIR*, 19–26.

[2] Ariely, D. (2008). *Predictably Irrational: The Hidden Forces that Shape Our Decisions*. Harper Collins.

[3] Baron, J. (2007). *Thinking and Deciding*. Cambridge Press.

[4] Belkin, N.J., Oddy, R.N., and Brooks, H.M. (1982). ASK for information retrieval: Part I - background and theory. *J. Documentation*, 38(2): 61–71.

[5] Bennett, P.N. et al. (2012). Modeling the impact of short- and long-term behavior on search personalization. *Proc. SIGIR*, 185–194.

[6] Bilenko, M. and White, R.W. (2008). Mining the search trails of the surfing crowds: identifying relevant websites from user activity. *Proc. WWW*, 51–60.

[7] Brennan, R.L. and Prediger, D.J. (1981). Coefficient Kappa: Some uses, misuses, and alternatives. *Educational and Psychological Measurement*, (41): 687–699.

[8] Cho, J. and Roy, S. (2004). Impact of search engines on page popularity. *Proc. WWW*, 20–29.

[9] Clarke, C., Agichtein, E., Dumais, S., and White R.W. (2007). The influence of caption features on clickthrough patterns in Web search. *Proc. SIGIR*, 135–142.

[10] Craswell, N., Zoeter, O., Taylor, M., and Ramsey, B. (2008). An experimental comparison of click position-bias models. *Proc. WSDM*, 87–94.

[11] Dou, Z., Song, R., and Wen, J.R. (2007). A large-scale evaluation and analysis of personalization search strategy. *Proc. WWW*, 581–590.

[12] Dumais, S. et al. (2002). Web question answering: Is more always better? *Proc. SIGIR*, 291–298.

[13] Fleiss, J.L. (1971). Measuring nominal scale agreement among many raters. *Psychological Bulletin*, 76(5): 378–382.

[14] Fortunato, S., Flammini, A., Menczer, F., and Vespignani, A. (2006). Topical interests and the mitigation of search engine bias. *PNAS*, 103(34): 12684–12689.

[15] Gigerenzer, G. and Todd, P.M. (2000). *Simple Heuristics That Make Us Smart*. Oxford University Press.

[16] Ieong, S., Mishra, N., Sadikov, E., and Zhang, I. (2012). Domain bias in Web search. *Proc. WSDM*, 413–422.

[17] Ingwersen, P. (1994). Polyrepresentation of information needs and semantic entities: Elements of a cognitive theory for information retrieval interaction. *Proc. SIGIR*, 101–110.

[18] Inlander, C.B. (1993). *Good operations, Bad operations: The People's Medical Society's Guide to Surgery*. Viking Adult.

[19] Joachims, T. (2002). Optimizing search engines using clickthrough data. *Proc. SIGKDD*, 132–142.

[20] Joachims, T. et al. (2007). Evaluating the accuracy of implicit feedback from clicks and query reformulations in web search. *ACM TOIS*, 25(2).

[21] Kahneman, D. and Tversky, A. (1974). Judgment under uncertainty: heuristics and biases. *Science*, 185(4157): 1214–1231.

[22] Klayman, J. and Ha, Y. (1987). Confirmation, disconfirmation, and information in hypothesis testing. *Psychological Review*, 94: 211–228.

[23] Kuhlthau, C. (1991). Inside the search process: Information seeking from the user's perspective. *JASIST*, 42(5): 361–371.

[24] Marchionini, G. (1995). *Information Seeking in Electronic Environments*. Cambridge University Press.

[25] Mowshowitz, A. and Kawaguchi, A. (2002). Bias on the Web. *CACM*, 45(9): 56–60.

[26] Nickerson, R.S. (1998). Confirmation bias: a ubiquitous phenomenon in many guises. *Rev. Gen. Psych.*, 2(2): 175–220.

[27] Pariser, E. (2011). *The Filter Bubble: What is the Internet Hiding from You*? Penguin Press.

[28] Popper, K. (1959). *The Logic of Scientific Discovery*. Basic Books.

[29] Radlinski, F. and Joachims, T. (2006). Minimally invasive randomization for collecting unbiased preferences from clickthrough logs. *Proc. AAAI*.

[30] Salton, G., Wong, A., and Yang, C.S. (1975). A vector space model for automatic indexing. *CACM*, 18(11): 613–620.

[31] Saracevic, T. (1997). The stratified model of information retrieval interaction: Extensions and applications. *Proc. ASIS*, 34: 313–327.

[32] Schwarz, J. and Morris, M.R. (2011). Augmenting Web pages and search results to help people find trustworthy information online. *Proc. SIGCHI*, 1245–1254.

[33] Simon, H. (1991). Bounded rationality and organizational learning. *Organization Science*, 2(1): 125–134.

[34] Snow, R., O'Connor, B., Jurafsky, D., and Ng, A.Y. (2008). Cheap and fast – but is it good? Evaluating non-expert annotations for natural language tasks. *Proc. EMNLP*, 254–263.

[35] Sontag, D. et al. (2012). Probabilistic models for personalizing web search. *Proc. WSDM*, 433–442.

[36] Tang, T.T., Hawking, D., Craswell, N., and Griffiths, K. (2005). Focused crawling for both topical relevance and quality of medical information. *Proc. CIKM*, 147–154.

[37] Taylor, R.S. (1968). Question-negotiation and information seeking in libraries. *College and Res. Libraries*, 29: 178–194.

[38] Teevan, J., Dumais, S.T., and Horvitz, E. (2005). Personalizing search via automated analysis of interests and activities. *Proc. SIGIR*, 449–456.

[39] Tversky, A. and Kahneman, D. (1973). Availability: A heuristic for judging frequency and probability. *Cognitive Psychology*, 5(1): 207–233.

[40] Vaughn, L. and Thelwall, M. (2004). Search engine coverage bias: evidence and possible causes. *IP&M*, 40(4): 693–707.

[41] Wason, P.C. (1960). On the failure to eliminate hypotheses in a conceptual task, *Q. J. of Exp. Psychology*, 12: 129–140.

[42] White, R.W., Bennett, P.N., and Dumais, S.T. (2010). Predicting short-term interests using activity-based search context. *Proc. CIKM*, 1009–1018.

[43] White, R.W. and Drucker, S.M. (2007). Investigating behavioral variability in Web search. *Proc. WWW*, 21–30.

[44] White, R.W. and Horvitz, E. (2009). Cyberchondria: Studies of the escalation of medical concerns in web search. *ACM TOIS*, 27(4): 23.

[45] White, R.W. and Horvitz, E. (2012). Studies on the onset and persistence of medical concerns in search logs. *Proc. SIGIR*, 265–274.

[46] Xiang, B. et al. (2010). Context-aware ranking in web search. *Proc. SIGIR*, 451–458.

[47] Yue, Y., Patel, R., and Roehrig, H. (2010). Beyond position bias: Examining result attractiveness as a source of presentation bias in clickthrough data. *Proc. WWW*, 1011–1018.

[48] Zhai, C., Cohen, W.W., and Lafferty, J. (2003). Beyond independent relevance: Methods and evaluation metrics for subtopic retrieval. *Proc. SIGIR*, 10–17.

Improving Search Result Summaries by Using Searcher Behavior Data

Mikhail Ageev*
Moscow State University
mageev@yandex.ru

Dmitry Lagun
Emory University
dlagun@emory.edu

Eugene Agichtein
Emory University
eugene@mathcs.emory.edu

ABSTRACT

Query-biased search result summaries, or "snippets", help users decide whether a result is relevant for their information need, and have become increasingly important for helping searchers with difficult or ambiguous search tasks. Previously published snippet generation algorithms have been primarily based on selecting document fragments most similar to the query, which does not take into account which parts of the document the searchers actually found useful. We present a new approach to improving result summaries by incorporating post-click searcher behavior data, such as mouse cursor movements and scrolling over the result documents. To achieve this aim, we develop a method for collecting behavioral data with precise association between searcher intent, document examination behavior, and the corresponding document fragments. In turn, this allows us to incorporate page examination behavior signals into a novel Behavior-Biased Snippet generation system (BeBS). By mining searcher examination data, BeBS infers document fragments of most interest to users, and combines this evidence with text-based features to select the most promising fragments for inclusion in the result summary. Our extensive experiments and analysis demonstrate that our method improves the quality of result summaries compared to existing state-of-the-art methods. We believe that this work opens a new direction for improving search result presentation, and we make available the code and the search behavior data used in this study to encourage further research in this area.

Categories and Subject Descriptors

H.4 [**Information Systems Applications**]: Miscellaneous

Keywords

Result summary generation, searcher behavior, mouse cursor movement

1. INTRODUCTION

While web search engines have been rapidly evolving, one constant in the search result pages has been the presence of some form of a document summary, or "snippet", provided to help a user to select the best result documents. For some queries, the generated snippets already contain the desired information, either by design (e.g., Google's "Instant Answers"[1] or Wolfram Alpha[2]) or by serendipity. Search engines have been increasingly successful at this, as evidenced by work on "good abandonment" [25] and others. Nevertheless, for a large class of queries where the desired information need is either ambiguous or cannot be answered succinctly, result snippets play a crucial role in guiding the users to the needed documents.

Our aim is to improve snippet generation for *informational* queries [7]. Specifically, our goal is twofold: If possible, the snippet text should include the desired information directly. Otherwise, the snippet should provide sufficient information for the user to distinguish the useful from the non-useful results. Fortunately, millions of users search daily, clicking on results and examining the documents. Our key insight is that by capturing such examination data, we could relate the *areas of interest* in the document to the *search intent*, subsequently generating more useful snippets for future searchers.

As a concrete example, consider an information need, specified as "How many pixels must be dead on a iPad 3 before Apple will replace it.". After issuing the search query "how many dead pixels ipad 3 replace", the user examined the document to find the answer, as shown in Figure 1 (the eye gaze positions were collected by using infra-red eye tracking). Note that while the user examined both useful and non-useful document fragments, she eventually focused on the best fragment containing the answer to the question. Hence, for this search intent and this document, an ideal snippet would include the text fragment where the user focused her attention. In contrast, if a document was *not* relevant, a good snippet should also include the area of most interest, as it could help users with the same intent to avoid visiting this result in the future.

This example intuitively motivates our goal to generate *Behavior-Biased* Snippets, or BeBS, which, as we show experimentally, can significantly improve snippet quality, which has been shown in eye-tracking studies to significantly affect search behavior (e.g. [10]). While putting an eye-tracker on every desk is not yet feasible, we can still *infer* searcher interest in particular page regions from their mouse cursor and scrolling behavior (e.g., following the ideas of [18] and [24]), and then incorporate this evidence to make the snippets more useful. To the best of our knowledge, our work is the first to successfully incorporate such behavior data into result snippet generation.

*Work done at Emory University.

SIGIR'13, July 28–August 1, 2013, Dublin, Ireland.
Copyright 2013 ACM 978-1-4503-2034-4/13/07 ...$15.00.

[1] http://googleblog.blogspot.com/2010/09/google-instant-behind-scenes.html
[2] http://www.wolframalpha.com/

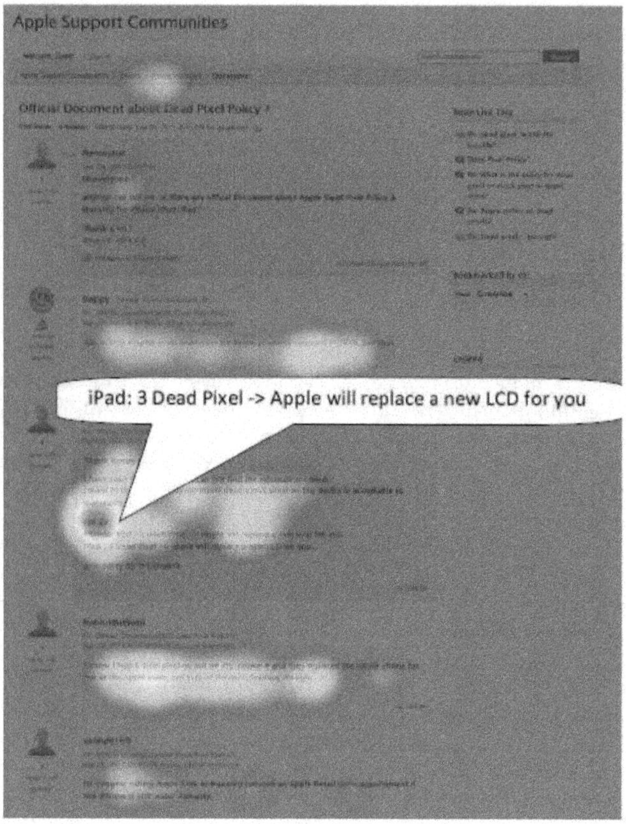

Figure 1: Attention heatmap of result document examination for the search intent "How many pixels must be dead on a iPad 3 before Apple will replace it." The user's attention is focused on a text fragment (highlighted in the callout box), containing the answer.

Specifically, our contributions include:

- A novel *behavior-biased* approach to snippet generation, that naturally integrates textual and behavioral evidence to improve snippets for informational queries (Section 3).
- A robust infrastructure for precisely associating fine-grained searcher behavior with document content (Section 3.3).
- Thorough experiments over hundreds of search sessions and thousands of page views, demonstrating significant improvements to snippet quality by harnessing searcher behavior data (Section 6).

Next, we describe related work to place our contributions in context.

2. RELATED WORK

Our work touches on three areas of research: search result summary (or snippet) generation, document summarization, and modeling searcher behavior and examination data.

Document Summarization and Search Snippet Generation Automatic summarization has been explored in many research areas including natural language processing, artificial intelligence and information retrieval. In particular, summaries desired in information retrieval application are mostly short, succinct text fragments informing user about document's relevance to the user's information need. Among various approaches for generating such summaries, the most popular is extracting sentences or sentence fragments from a document. Early work of Kupiec et al. [29] addressed sentence selection problem, using a Naive Bayes classifier to predict whether a sentence should be included in a static, query-independent document summary. Subsequently, Tombros and Sanderson [37] demonstrated that query-biased summaries are more advantageous than static or query independent summaries in allowing users to identify relevant documents with higher accuracy. One approach is to use linguistic and relevance features (e.g., Goldstein et al. [16]). Another related area is automatic question answering, where a system could perform deep semantic analysis to identify the question or query intent, and attempt to return an answer directly (e.g., [6, 21, 12]. Our approach is complimentary, as it could be used to improve selecting candidate answers by any of the text-based snippet generation systems. Most closely related to our goal is the research on query-focused summarization (e.g., [4, 13, 14]), which uses a variety of document- and query text features to generate a document summary focused on a given query. These ideas were further extended in machine learning-based approaches to web search snippet generation (e.g., [33, 26, 27]). Our work builds on these ideas by adding a radically different type of evidence –search behavior data– to make the result summaries more useful to the searcher.

Eye Tracking for Web Search Result and Document Examination: There is a rich history of using eye tracking technology to identify areas of interest and attention, and to study reading behavior. In the context of web search document examination, Buscher et al. [9] extracted subdocuments by tracking eye movements as implicit feedback and expanded search queries to improve the search result ranking. Buscher et al. also studied the prediction of salient Web page regions using eye-tracking [8]. This work, and others, have shown that user attention can help identify regions of documents of particular relevance or usefulness for the query. While eye tracking equipment limits the applicability of these findings, these studies served as inspiration to our work on biasing snippet generation to privilege the *inferred* areas of interest.

Mouse Cursor Tracking in Web Search: Recently, mouse cursor tracking has been proposed as a natural proxy for user's attention, to replace the requirement for eye tracking equipment. One of the earliest work of correlating cursor and gaze position in web search was by Rodden et al. [35], where the authors discovered the coordination between a user's eye movements and mouse movements when scanning a web search results page. Guo and Agichtein [18] extended this work to predict eye-mouse coordination (i.e., whether the mouse cursor is in close proximity to eye gaze at any given point in time) by modeling mouse movements. This work was further extended by Huang et al. to directly predict the gaze position from mouse cursor movement [23], with over 70% accuracy. Thus, there is mounting evidence that searcher attention in web search can be approximated by using mouse cursor, scrolling, and other interaction data.

Modeling Cursor Movement on Landing Pages: In addition to studying cursor movement on Search Engine Result Pages (or SERPs), mouse cursor analysis work has been recently applied to examination of the clicked documents, or landing pages. Hijikata et al. [22] proposed a method to extract text fragments of Web pages based on the user's mouse activity and found that the extracted fragments based on mouse activity such as *text tracing, link pointing, link clicking and text selection* enable more accurate extraction of key words of interest than using the whole text of the page. More recently, White and Buscher [39] proposed a method that uses text selections as implicit feedback, while Guo and Agichtein [19] proposed a *Post Click Behavior (PCB)* model to estimate the "intrinsic" document relevance by modeling post-click behavior such as mouse cursor movements and scrolling. Our method extends this approach to identify specific regions, or fragments of the page, of particular interest to the users for including in the result summary.

In summary, our work extends previous state-of-the-art in snippet generation by considering a radically new source of evidence, namely the user examination data, in order to bias the resulting summaries towards the most "interesting" or "useful" parts of the document, as we describe next.

3. PROBLEM STATEMENT AND APPROACH

First, we formalize the problem of generating "useful" snippets. Then, we describe the key parts of our approach (Section 3.2), and the infrastructure we developed to accomplish the required data collection (Section 3.3).

3.1 Problem Statement

Following the literature on snippet quality [31], snippets must satisfy the aspects of *Representativeness*, *Readability*, and *Judgeability*:

1. *Representativeness*: measures how well the snippet summarizes parts of the web page relevant to the search query. A representative snippet would clearly show why the page was found by a search engine in response to the query.

2. *Readability* measures the ease with which the text of the snippet can be read and understood. Note, that readability does not depend on the search query [27].

3. *Judgeability* measures how well the snippet helps a user to understand whether the page is helpful for the specific search intent, and to decide whether to click on a link or not. An ideal snippet would either contain an answer to a user's information need (or a clear indication that an answer is present in the document), or else clearly show that the page is not relevant .

Our primary goal is to optimize the Representativeness and the Judgeability criteria by *biasing* the selected snippets towards the regions of most interest to the user, as inferred from the page examination data. That is, our goal is not to replace the existing text-based snippet generation approaches, but rather to add additional evidence (when available) about the parts of the document to privilege.

3.2 Approach

Our approach operationalizes the snippet quality criteria above by incorporating both textual and behavioral evidence using a robust machine learning-based approach. Specifically, we combine together the traditional text-based snippet generation features, and the inferred user interest in specific parts of a document.

First, following [27], a fragment scoring system is trained based on text-based features, using human judges, resulting in a strong text-only baseline that generates *candidate fragments* to be included into the snippet (Section 4.1). Separately, examination behavior data is collected over the landing pages, using our logging infrastructure described in the next section. Then, a behavior model is trained to infer the document fragments of interest to the user, based on user examination data (Section 4.3). Finally, the behavior-based prediction of interest in each candidate fragment is combined with the original (text-based) fragment score, in order to generate the final *behavior-biased* snippet candidate ranking (Section 4.4). Note that by decoupling the behavior modeling from the candidate generation method, our approach can be used with any other snippet generation approach that provides scores for the candidate fragments, which could be combined with the behavior scores for the final ranking step.

While general and flexible, our approach makes three key assumptions. First, our method is primarily targeted (and evaluated for) informational queries – that is, queries for which the user expects to find an answer in the text of the page, and optimizes the snippets accordingly. Second, we assume that document visits can be grouped by query intent, so that behavior features on the landing pages can be aggregated together for all the searchers with the same information need. While a number of methods have been proposed to cluster queries (and results clicks) by intent (e.g., [34]), we acknowledge that these techniques are not perfect, and may introduce noise in practice. Finally, we assume that user interactions on landing pages can be collected by a search engine or a third party. While this naturally introduces potential privacy concerns, this assumption is not far-fetched: already, browser plug-ins and toolbars collect user interactions on web pages; major organizations can (and often do) use proxies for external web access; and common page widgets like banner ads and visit counters inject JavaScript code to monitor basic user interactions and can be easily extended to collect more detailed data. While the privacy and security considerations of these methods are beyond the scope of this paper, we merely point out that these behavior gathering tools already exist and are widely deployed. We will discuss these issues and potential solutions in more depth in Section 7.

3.3 Page Examination Behavior Logging

A key component of our system is a mechanism for collecting searcher interactions on web pages, and tying them precisely to the page content at the word level. As a starting point, we adapt the publicly available EMU toolbar for the Firefox browser [17], that is able to collect mouse cursor movements over any visited webpage. Unfortunately, out-of-the-box EMU functionality is not sufficient, as the user interactions are not connected to the underlying page content: the available JavaScript API does not provide the text position under the cursor, which could depend on screen resolution, size of browser window, browser version, and personal browser settings.

To associate the tracked mouse cursor positions with corresponding text fragments we employed the following technique. After the HTML page is rendered in the browser window, our JavaScript code modifies the document DOM tree, so that each word is wrapped by a separate DOM element tags. Then for each DOM Element, the window coordinates of that element are evaluated and saved in the Element's attributes. Then, the processed HTML page with the coordinates of each DOM Element is saved to the server by an asynchronous request. The saved coordinates are updated if the page layout is changed due to a *resize* window event or an AJAX action.

Thus, for each page visit we know the searcher's intent (question), the search engine query that the user issued, the URL, the contents of the document, the bounding boxes of each word in the HTML text, and the log of behavior actions: mouse cursor coordinates, mouse clicks, scrolling, and an answer to the question that the user found in a page and submitted in the game interface. Next, we show how to use this information to infer patterns of browsing behavior that capture portions of document that are of most interest to the user.

4. BEHAVIOR-BIASED SNIPPET GENERATION

We now present the details of our Behavior-Biased snippet generation system (BeBS). First, we describe the text-only snippet generation system (Sections 4.1 and 4.2). Then, we introduce the method for inferring the most interesting or useful parts of the document from user behavior (Section 4.3), to incorporate into the combined snippet generation process (Section 4.4).

4.1 Text-Based Snippet Generation

In order to generate snippets, we extend the approach presented in Metzler and Kanungo [33]. The downloaded HTML pages are pre-processed and indexed with Natural Language Tool Kit (NLTK [3]). Extracted text is divided into sentences using *Punk* unsupervised sentence splitter [28]. We index the text of the web page excluding the <script> and <style> tags.

For a given query we first select all the sentences that have at least one match of query terms for further snippet fragment generation. Once the set of sentences is selected, our system generates all possible snippet fragment candidates by applying a sliding window moving along each sentence. We vary fragment length from 3 words to a maximum character length provided as an input parameter. We discard all fragments that do not contain any query term matches. Along with fragment generation our system scores each fragment using *TextScore* function described in Section 4.2. This score is used to generate the final snippet.

The problem of summary generation has been studied extensively in natural language processing and summarization research communities. It has been shown in [36] that this problem is equivalent to a weighted set cover problem which is, in turn, known to be NP-Hard. There are several possible approaches, including greedy weighted set cover and relaxations, primarily based on integer linear programming. We resort to a greedy algorithm, due to relative simplicity of implementation. Our system can easily be extended with more advanced set cover solver if needed. As the set cover algorithm requires score computation for the set of selected fragments, we recompute the scoring function for the union of selected candidate fragments to find a set that greedily maximizes the score for the entire snippet.

4.2 Fragment Scoring

The fragment scoring required for snippet generation relies on a machine learning approach based on set of text features representing various quality aspects of fragment candidate. We extend the method of [33] by adding additional features capturing relevance of the fragment (relevance group), properties of query match (query match group) and readability of the fragment (readability group). These features are summarized in Table 1. For *TextScore* score computation we used the Gradient Boosting Regression Tree model [15] (GBRT). GBRT is a powerful family of models that has been successfully used in many applications including sentence selection for search result summarization [33] and search result snippet readability assessment [27]. We train a GBRT model on a subset of training query-URL pairs to predict snippet fragment scores.

Gradient Boosting Regression Tree performs a numerical optimization in function space instead of parameter space. We provide a brief overview of the algorithm and refer to the original paper for detailed information [15]. A regression tree model $f(x), x \in R^n$, partitions the space of covariates into disjoint intervals $R_k, k = 1, 2, ..., K$ associated with leaf nodes of the tree. Each interval is assigned a value ϕ_k, such that $f(x) = \phi_k$ if $x \in R_k$. Thus, the tree model can be written in

$$T(x; \Theta) = \sum_{j=k}^{K} \phi_k I(x \in R_k)$$

where $\Theta = \{R_k, \phi_k\}_{k=1}^{K}$, and I is an indicator function. For a given loss function $L(y_i, \phi_i)$ the parameters Θ are result of the following optimization problem:

$$\hat{\Theta} = argmin_{\Theta} \sum_{k=1}^{K} \sum_{x_i \in R_k} L(y_i, \phi_k)$$

In our experiments we employ the squared loss function to train the regression trees. A gradient boosted regression tree is an ensemble model [15] that incorporates a series of regression trees, and can be written as:

$$f_M(x) = \sum_{m=1}^{M} T(x; \Theta_m)$$

where at each stage m, Θ_m is estimated to fit the residuals from the $m-1$th stage:

$$\hat{\Theta}_m = argmin_{\Theta_m} \sum_{i=1}^{N} L(y_i, f_{m-1}(x_i) + \phi_{k_m})$$

and M is the number of stages (regression trees) in the model. In practice, one adds $T(x; \Theta_m)$ multiplied by ρ – the learning rate input parameter specified for the algorithm, resulting in the final predictor:

$$f_M(x) = \sum_{m=1}^{M} \rho T(x; \Theta_m)$$

In our implementation we used $M = 200$ regression trees, and $\rho = 0.01$ to train the GBRT model for fragment scoring.

4.3 Inferring Relevant Text Fragments from Search Behavior

To infer the text fragment importance from the user's browsing behavior, we again apply supervised machine learning, namely the Gradient Boosting Regression Tree (GBRT) algorithm [15], trained to identify "interesting" text fragments. Specifically, for each page visit of a user, the document is represented as a set of short text *fragments*. We consider a particular fragment to be "interesting" (attractive), if the user submitted an answer in the current session,

Feature	Description	Feature Group
ExactMatch	1 if fragment contains query as a substring, otherwise 0	Metzler - Kanungo
TermOverlap	Overlap of query terms and the fragment	
SynOverlap	Overlap of query terms expanded with synonyms and the fragment	
LanguageModelScore	Fragment score under the language model as in [33]	
Length	Total number of terms	
Location	Relative location of the fragment in the document	
BM25ScoreFragment	BM25 score of the fragment	Relevance
BM25ScoreSentence	BM25 score of the sentence from which fragment was extracted	
BM25ScorePerWord	BM25 of the fragment divided on number of words in the fragment	
NumMatches	Absolute count of query terms matched in the fragment	Query Match
SentenceBegDistance	Number of words between beginning of the sentence and first word in the fragment	
SentenceEndDistance	Number of words between end of the sentence and last word in the fragment	
QueryTermDistanceAvg	Average distance of query terms in the fragment measured in words	
QueryTermDistanceMin	Minimum distance of query terms in the fragment measured in words	
QueryTermDistanceMax	Maximum distance of query terms in the fragment measured in words	
NumDistinctTerms	Number of distinct terms in the fragment	Readability
NumPunctChar	Number of punctuation characters	
PercentPunctChar	Percent of punctuation characters	
NumLetterChar	Number of letter ([a-zA-Z]) characters	
NumWordsCap	Number of words with first letter capitalized	
PercentWordsCap	Percent of words with first letter capitalized	
PunctPerWord	Number of punctuation characters per word in the fragment	

Table 1: Text-based features for text fragments

and the answer shares words with the fragment (after stemming and stopword removal). Other fragments are labeled to be not interesting.

For each fragment we create a set of behavior features that could capture fragment interestingness. One key feature is the duration of time when the mouse cursor was placed over the text fragment, or very close to the fragment. We also adapt the features to measure scrollbar and event activity from references [11] and [19], in order to detect "reading" vs. "skimming" behavior. The complete list of the fragment behavior features is presented in Table 2. Note that these features are exclusively focused on capturing user's behavior associated with focused attention, and, by design, do not contain any document or query information, in order for the learned behavior model to be applicable to unseen documents and queries.

The feature generation algorithm joins a sequence of behavior events and a set of bounding boxes for each word and DOM Element of a page. To speed up this join, our implementation uses a spatial R-Tree index of element bounding boxes, which allows for each logged event to be efficiently matched to the matching DOM Elements in the specified coordinate range.

We then train the GBRT model on the training set of the labeled document fragments, each represented using the behavior features described above. The data is stratified by the original document URLs, so that the URLs of the fragments in the training and test sets are disjoint. The training set is created from only those page visits where the document text has a non-empty intersection with the user's answer, and the answer is correct. The trained prediction model is then applied to all page visits in the test set. Note that when the predictor is applied on the test set, it has no information about the user's intent, answer, or the current query, and uses only the behavioral features of the current page visit. The predicted behavior-based fragment interestingness score, is then used as a key evidence for the final snippet generation algorithm, described next.

Feature	Description
MouseOverTime	Time duration when the mouse cursor was over the text fragment
MouseNearTime	Time duration when the mouse cursor was close to the text fragment in the window ($x \pm 100px$, $y \pm 70px$)
MouseOverEvents	The number of mouse events during *MouseOverTime*
MouseNearEvents	The number of mouse events during *MouseNearTime*
DisplayTime	Time duration when the text fragment has been visible in the browser window (depends on scrollbar position)
DispMiddleTime	Time duration when the text fragment was visible in the the middle part of the browser window

Table 2: Behavior features for text fragments

4.4 Combining Text and Examination Evidence

The final step in our approach is to *combine* the text-based score $TextScore(f)$ for a candidate fragment (Section 4.1) with the behavior-based interestingness score $BScore(f)$ (Section 4.3), inferred from the examination data. In our current implementation we combine these scores by linear combination:

$$FScore(f) = \lambda \cdot BScore(f) + (1 - \lambda) \cdot TextScore(f)$$

Note that $TextScore(f)$ is not normalized, and could have values in the range $[1, 5]$, while $BScore(f)$ is normalized to be between 0 and 1.

The parameter λ affects two characteristics of the algorithm: snippet *coverage* and *quality*. Snippet *coverage* is defined as the ratio of the snippets produced by the behavior-biased algorithm that differ from the snippets produced by the text-only baseline. Snippet *quality* is measured by judgeability, readability, and representativeness metrics, via manual assessments. As λ approaches zero, coverage would also approach zero (as text-based features would dominate candidate selection), and the algorithm effectively backs off to the baseline. In contrast, when λ is large, snippet *quality* might decrease by weighing the behavior-based score too highly compared to the text-based score. We performed manual assessments for five different parameter values of $\lambda \in [0, 1]$ to select the best value. Other more sophisticated ways to combine text and behavior evidence are possible, such as jointly learning over both text and behavior features, as could be explored in the future. However, we chose to follow the simpler linear approach for better interpretability of the results (e.g., by analyzing the results of varying the λ parameter).

5. DATA COLLECTION AND EXPERIMENTAL SETUP

This section presents the methodology used for acquiring search behavior data for training our system (Section 5.1), describes the resulting behavioral data (Section 5.2), the explicit snippet judgments dataset used for training and validating the text-based snippet generation baseline (Section 5.3). Note that the code and the data used for experiments are available from `http://ir.mathcs.emory.edu/intent/`.

5.1 Acquiring Search Behavior Data

To collect the search behavior data, we used the infrastructure created and published by [1], and modified it for our task. The participants played a search contest "game" consisting of 12 search tasks (questions) to solve. The stated goal of the game was to submit the highest possible number of correct answers within the allotted time. After the searcher decided that they found the answer, they were instructed to type the answer together with the supporting URL, into the corresponding fields in the game interface. Each search session (for one question) was completed by either submitting an answer, or by clicking the "skip question" button to pass to the next question.

Participants were recruited through the Amazon Mechanical Turk (MTurk) website. As a first step, the workers had to solve a ReCaptcha puzzle to verify that they are human and not an automated "bot". A browser verification check was performed to verify that the browser is compatible with our JavaScript tracking code. During the data postprocessing stage, we filtered out the users who did not answer even the easy, trivial questions, as it indicated either poor understanding of the game rules, or an attempt to make a quick buck without effort.

To capture all of the participants' search actions, they were instructed to use only our search interface. Our search interface performs web search using the public API of a popular web search engine (we used Bing for our experiments), and displays the result pages using the original page design, layout and stylesheets, so the user's search experience is not affected. The Apache Web server proxy functionality was used by configuring the modules *mod_proxy*, *mod_proxy_html*, and *mod_sed* so that the users could search and browse the Web as usual, while the URLs in the HTML links were automatically replaced to request the document through our proxy. As the requested documents were returned through our proxy, JavaScript logging code was injected into the document, as described in Section 3.3.

5.2 Browsing Behavior Dataset

A total of 109 MTurk participants finished their tasks. After filtering out the users who did not follow the game rules, we obtained 1175 search sessions, performed by 98 users. Our data for these users consists of 3,294 queries, 1,598 unique queries, and 2,997 SERP clicks on 662 distinct URLs. Of these, the document behavioral data was collected for 2,289 page visits (76%) and 508 distinct URLs, comprising the final dataset for our experiments described below[3]. For each page view there were on average 400 atomic browsing events (mouse movements, scrolling, key pressing) on average. Note that a document might be visited from different queries, and for each query-URL pair, the snippet generation algorithm would produce a snippet independently. So the comparative experiments for snippet quality evaluation were performed on a set of 707 different query-URL pairs.

The set of the documents with collected behavior data was divided randomly into equal-sized training and test set, stratified by the document URLs to ensure no snippets derived from the same document to be included in both the training and test set. The training set was used to train the regression algorithm for predicting fragment interestingness, and the test set was used to evaluate the generated snippets.

5.3 Text Fragment Quality Judgments

In order to train the text-based baseline snippet generation algorithm (Section 4.1), we require a set of labeled text fragments. For this, we collected 949 text fragment quality judgments through the Amazon MTurk service. The assessors were asked to re-rank 10 text fragments randomly chosen by our fragment generator system to obtain a reliable training set. Each fragment was judged by 3 assessors. The fragments used in for this data collection were generated from query-URL instances taken from our training set, and do not overlap with our test set. We specifically asked assessors to re-rank fragments to avoid potential inaccuracies caused by using an absolute scale. In order to train the fragment scorer, we performed rank aggregation by computing the average rank of the fragment among the rankings produced by different judges.

6. RESULTS

We now present the main results of our study. First, we report the intermediate result of using the behavior data to infer the interesting (useful) fragments in the document. Then, we report the main results of the paper where the quality of the generated snippets, with and without using behavior data, compared using human judgments (Section 6.2).

6.1 Prediction of Fragment Interestingness

This experiment evaluates how well we can predict interesting fragments by observing the user's document examination behavior. We define the fragment to be interesting if it is related to the answer for the question. For each visited page we collect the user's answer (if submitted), and all the correct answers from all the users who answered this question. Then we automatically compare those answers to each text fragment in the document.

[3]For the remaining 24% of the page visits, the behavioral data was missing due to conflicts between our JavaScript tracking code and other JavaScript code already present on the page, and these documents were omitted from the dataset.

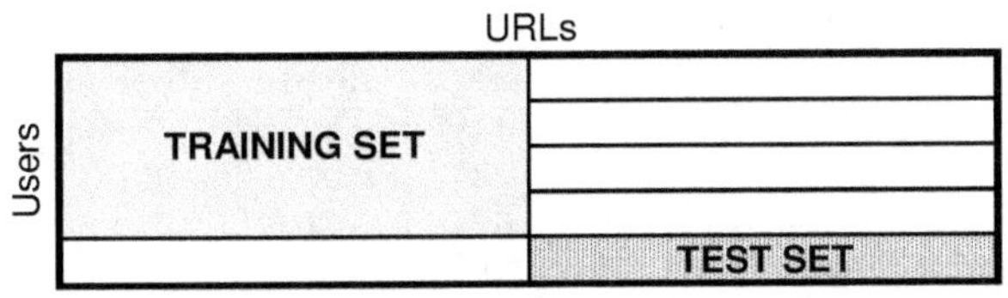

Figure 2: Illustration of the cross-validation setup: the training and test sets are disjoint by both users and URLs.

For this experiment, the document text is represented as a set of short text fragments, each consisting of five words. Those 5-word sequences are, on one hand, almost unique in a typical web document, and thus could be used as an identifier of a text position in a document, and on the other hand are short enough to match to local behavior patterns. For each fragment a set of behavior features is computed as described in section 4.3.

The cross-validation experiment set up as illustrated in Figure 2. The set of users and URLs are divided into a training set and a test set, so that the training set and the test set are disjoint for both sets of users and URLs. 10-fold cross-validation was performed, so that each user-URL pair appeared in a test set for some cross-validation split.

In the training set, a fragment's label is set to $label(fragment_i) = 1$ if the user submitted an answer in the current session, the answer is correct, and the answer has common words with the fragment. If the user submitted a correct answer, but the answer shares no words with a document fragment, then $label(fragment_i) = 0$. If the user did not submit an answer, or the answer is incorrect, we excluded the fragment from the training set. The answer and the fragment were compared after stemming and stopword removal. Similarly, in the test set we use for evaluation only those fragments that share words with the submitted search query.

The Gradient Boosting Regression Tree algorithm was trained on the training set of fragments, and applied to the test set. So each fragment in the test set receives a *fragment interestingness* $BScore(fragment_i) \in \mathbb{R}$.

We evaluate the interestingness of fragments by comparing the fragment's text with user's answer (if it exists), and to all the correct answers submitted by all users for the same question. We use the standard ROUGE-1 and ROUGE-2 metrics [32] for evaluation of the fragment intersection with answers, as these metrics are commonly used for evaluation of automatic summarization and annotation algorithms.

ROUGE-N metric for a fragment and a set of answers A, is computed as the recall of the answer set covered by the fragment word N-grams:

$$\text{ROUGE-N}(fragment, A) = \frac{\sum_{a\in A}\sum_{gram_n \in fragment} \text{Count}_{match}(gram_n)}{\sum_{a\in A}\sum_{gram_n \in fragment} \text{Count}(gram_n)}$$

Figure 3 shows the relationship between the interestingness of a fragment and the behavior score. The graph shows that when the score is high (≥ 0.5), the average intersection between the fragment and user's answer is much higher than those when the fragment score is low. All ROUGE-N metrics increase when the behavior score increases, but the ROUGE-2 values over all correct answers are always very small (changing from 0.003 to 0.007). We note that

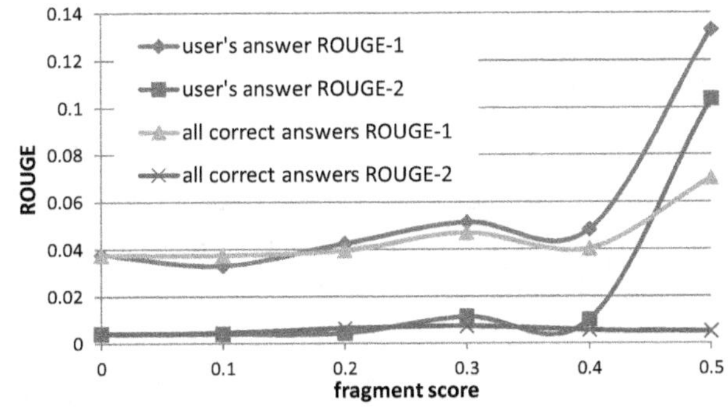

Figure 3: Fragment ROUGE-1 and ROUGE-2 values vs. behavior-based interestingness score ***BScore*****.**

ROUGE-1 is much greater than ROUGE-2 for high scores, as the interesting fragment might contain useful information for the answer, but the user reformulates the obtained information and submits reformulated answer. The ROUGE-N values for a user's answer are much greater than those for all correct answers, as other users might obtain valuable information from other documents, and some questions have distinct correct answers.

This experiment shows that we can predict fragment interestingness by using behavior features only. In the next section, we apply the computed behavior scores for a practical task of improving search result summaries.

6.2 Snippet Quality Evaluation

Evaluation Setup: Our evaluation follows the snippet quality desiderata outlined in Section 3.1. Specifically, the snippet quality is evaluated by performing blind paired preference tests. For each query and URL, a pair of snippets produced by two different algorithms were evaluated by an assessor. A pair of snippets were presented on a page in random order, so the assessors did not know which algorithm produced which snippet.

Each assessor was asked to examine the web page, the search query, and the pair of snippets, and to answer three questions that correspond to our snippet quality criteria:

- Which of the snippets better summarize the parts the web page relevant to the search query? You need to read the web page before answering this question.
- Which of the snippets is written better – and is more readable?
- Imagine that you have the following search intent: "*question*". Which snippet helps you to identify relevant content better, and helps you decide whether to click on this result or not? You must consult the list of the correct answers for this question before answering.

For each question there were three possible answers: "Snippet 1 is better", "Both snippets are similar for this criterion", and "Snippet 2 is better".

We hired 14 pre-qualified Amazon MTurk workers, who have previously shown accurate results and high agreement with our "gold standard" subset of snippets labeled by the authors. As an additional test, we also included a small portion of exactly the same snippets to check the quality of MTurk workers, to verify that for the *same* snippets the worker submitted "Both snippets are similar" label for each criterion. As a result, we collected pairwise preference

Feature Group	NDCG@10
Single Feature Group	
Metzler-Kanungo	0.719
Relevance	0.741
Readability	**0.743**
QueryMatch	0.719
All Except One Feature Group	
All-Metzler-Kanungo	0.725
All-Relevance	0.736
All-Readability	**0.743**
All-QueryMatch	0.717
All	**0.764**

Table 3: Feature ablation results for fragment text scoring (10-fold cross validation)

labels for 2959 snippet pairs, 8525 atomic judgements (three judgements for each snippet pair, excluding "no answer" responses). The total amount paid to the MTurk workers was \$217. One half of the obtained judgements were used for development and debugging purposes, and the other half were used for testing and reporting the results in the next section.

Evaluation Metrics: As a main evaluation metric we use the fraction of labels that give *preference* to the BeBS system, compared to the baseline. The preference ratio metric is evaluated for each criterion in (judgeability, readability, representativeness). The reason is that we found that the snippet quality criteria are difficult for assessors to judge absolutely, but can be easily compared as relative preferences.

6.3 Analysis of the Text-based Baseline

Before studying the benefits of behavior-based snippet generation, we optimized the text-based baseline method (Section 4.1) by varying the combination of features used. The results of the feature ablation experiments are reported in Table 3. As this table shows, using *all* of the text-based features achieves highest judge preference for the resulting snippets, thus, we use all of the features described in Table 1 for the baseline system performance in subsequent experiments.

6.4 Evaluation of the BeBS System

This experiment compares the text-based baseline with our BeBS system. Recall, that the λ parameter (the relative weight of the behavior score) affects two characteristics of the algorithm: coverage and snippet quality, as described in Section 4.4. To explore the resulting trade-offs, Figure 4 reports the judgeability, readability, representativeness, and coverage for five values of λ. The binomial distribution two-sided statistical significance test with confidence level 0.9 was computed, and the corresponding confidence intervals are presented on the graph. The graph shows that setting of $\lambda = 0.7$ provides significant improvement on all three snippet quality metrics. For this value, the coverage is 40%, which means that the behavior features provide improvement in representativeness for $0.4 * 0.68 = 27\%$ of all snippets, and produce worse snippets for $0.4 * (1 - 0.68) = 13\%$ of all snippets. When $\lambda = 0.5$, judgeability and readability also improve, but the improvement in representativeness is small and not statistically significant. When $\lambda = 0.9$, coverage grows up to 53%, but results in more noise and degrades snippet quality. When λ is set to a low value, the coverage drops, and we have too few modified snippets from the baseline to observe statistically significant differences in snippet

Baseline vs. behavior with $\lambda = 0.7$			
	Judg.	Read.	Repr.
baseline is better	44	35	34
similar	23	27	29
behavior is better	67	71	71
no answer	0	1	0
ratio of improved	0.60*	0.67*	0.68*
p-value	0.018	0.0003	0.0002
Baseline vs. behavior with $\lambda = 0.5$			
	Judg.	Read.	Repr.
baseline is better	108	107	122
similar	160	149	207
behavior is better	162	142	140
no answer	41	73	2
ratio of improved	0.60*	0.57*	0.53
p-value	0.0006	0.0015	0.14

Table 4: Pairwise preference tests for snippets with behavior features added, number of judgements

quality. The graph shows that for $\lambda \in \{0.1, 0.3\}$, the confidence intervals cross $y = 0.5$ axis, and this means that the difference in snippet quality is not statistically significant. The Table 4 reports the detailed assessment data for the two best runs.

Finally, we show two examples that demonstrate how incorporating behavior features can affect the resulting snippets. The first example (Figure 5, left) compares two snippets, the first produced by the baseline algorithm (top), and the second by using BeBS (bottom), for the query "sports invented in australia", corresponding to the question "What sports did Britain get from Australia?". The example shows that the snippet produced by BeBS is substantially more useful than the baseline, in clearly indicating to the searcher that the answer is present in the document. Note that this document is a difficult case for traditional snippet generation approaches: the landing page contains 8 matches for the query word "sport", and more than 50 matches for each of words "invent", and "Australia". Furthermore, the relevant fragment is located near the bottom of the document (three scrolling screens down), yet it is included into the snippet because several users scrolled near the end of the page and inspected the text near this fragment thoroughly, resulting in a high behavioral score.

The second example shows a case where the BeBS produced an inferior snippet compared to the baseline. The searcher issued a query "metals less dense than water", and the baseline algorithm produced a good snippet that contains the correct answer "Potassium and Lithium", relevant to both search query and search intent. But many users did not found the answer on the landing page, and instead examined the attractive section of the page corresponding to "Popular Searches", with the list of suggested queries. That resulted in a high behavior scores for that fragment, and consequently BeBS produced a snippet with poorly readable and irrelevant text. Additional behavior data, and further tuning of the behavior score prediction may alleviate these errors, as we plan to explore in future work.

6.4.1 Behavior Feature Importance Analysis

To estimate relative importance of behavior features for snippet generation, we analyzed the Gini importance index [5] for each behavior feature from the table 2. The table 5 shows that the most important features are *DispMid-*

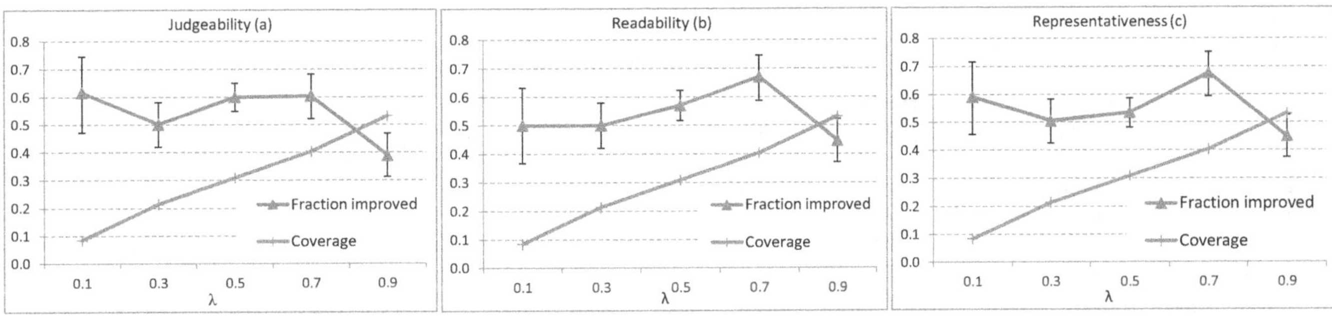

Figure 4: Snippet judgeability (a), readability (b), and representativeness (c) vs. coverage for varying values of λ.

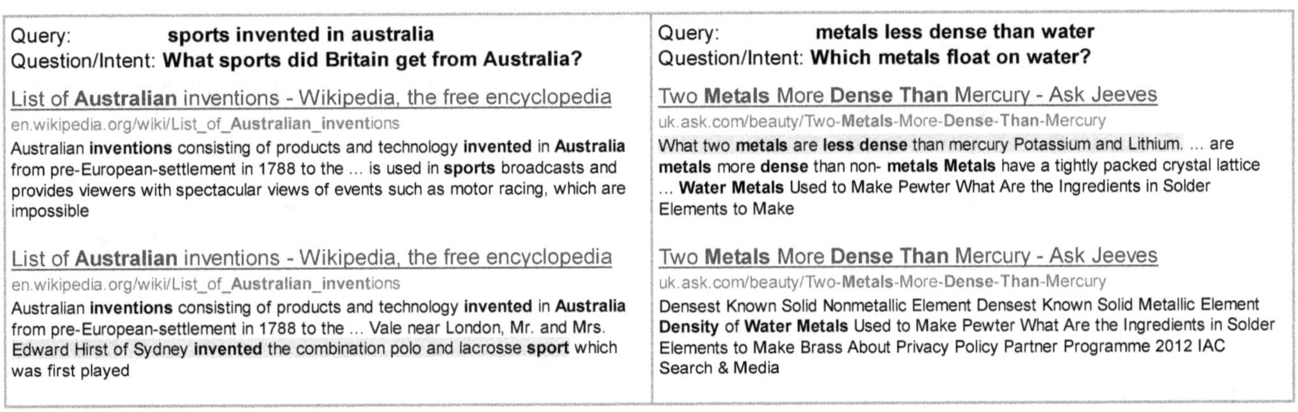

Figure 5: Comparison of snippets produced by a baseline algorithm (top), and by the BeBS system (bottom) for two different queries. The relevant snippet parts are highlighted in yellow.

Feature	Gini coefficient
DispMiddleTime	0.51
MouseOverTime	0.34
DisplayTime	0.12
MouseNearTime	0.02
MouseOverEvents	0.01
MouseNearEvents	0.01

Table 5: Feature importance for behavioral features

dleTime - the time duration when the text fragment was visible in the middle of the browser window, and *MouseOverTime*, the time duration when the mouse cursor hovered over the text fragment. While the first feature has been previously shown [11] to be beneficial for re-ranking search results, we are encouraged to find it to be also helpful for snippet generation. The *MouseOverTime* feature has been shown to be correlated with user interest [18], thus confirming our hypothesis that searcher interest can be helpful for generating better snippets.

7. CONCLUSIONS AND FUTURE WORK

We presented a novel way to generate *behavior-biased* search snippets that privilege the document fragments examined by the users. To our knowledge, our work is the first to incorporate search examination behavior data into snippet generation result summary generation. To accomplish this, we developed a robust methodology to acquire precise document examination data at scale using mouse cursor movement and scrolling, and to associate these interactions with the fragments of the underlying document. Our results show significant quantitative improvements over a strong text-based snippet generation baseline. We complement the results with qualitative observations about the cases where examination behavior can be helpful or harmful to the generated snippets. Our code is based on the freely available EMU plug-in for the Firefox browser [17], and the search behavior data used for experiments is shared with the research community to encourage further work in this area.

While our work makes significant advances to search snippet generation, it also opens many directions for future improvements and extensions. While our method was primarily targeted (and evaluated for) informational queries, an important consideration is how to generalize our approach to a wider class of queries. For other query classes (e.g., navigational), snippets might be optimized using a different criteria, but snippet generation could still take advantage of the search examination data. We have also assumed that document visits can be grouped by query intent. A number of methods have been proposed to cluster queries (and result clicks) by intent (e.g., [34, 30, 38]), and one future direction is to extend our method to work with automated query clustering techniques, which might introduce additional noise. Another key assumption is that user interactions on landing pages can be collected by a search engine. As we pointed out earlier, commercially deployed methods already exist to collect interaction data on landing pages, for applications such as advertising. While addressing the privacy issues inherent in search behavior logging is beyond the scope of this paper, research in privacy-preserving data mining [2] could potentially alleviate these concerns. Furthermore, as efficient machine learning methods and computational capabilities of personal and mobile devices continue to advance, mining searcher interactions could be performed directly on the user's device, only sharing the less detailed predictions with the search engine. Finally, our approach is not necessarily limited to desktop-based computers with a mouse. Modeling interactions on mobile and touch-enabled devices also allows to infer searcher interest and attention [20], and incorporating this richer searcher behavior data into result summary generation is another promising future research direction.

ACKNOWLEDGMENTS

This work was supported by the National Science Foundation grant IIS-1018321, the DARPA grant D11AP00269, and by the Russian Foundation for Basic Research Grant 12-07-31225.

8. REFERENCES

[1] M. Ageev, Q. Guo, D. Lagun, and E. Agichtein. Find it if you can: A game for modeling different types of web search success using interaction data. In *Proc. of SIGIR*, 2011.

[2] C. C. Aggarwal and S. Y. Philip. *A general survey of privacy-preserving data mining models and algorithms*. Springer, 2008.

[3] S. Bird. Nltk: the natural language toolkit. In *Proc. of the COLING/ACL.*, pages 69–72, 2006.

[4] S. Blair-Goldensohn and K. McKeown. Integrating rhetorical-semantic relation models for query-focused summarization. In *Proc. of DUC*, 2006.

[5] L. Breiman and L. Breiman. Bagging predictors. In *Machine Learning*, pages 123–140, 1996.

[6] E. Brill, S. Dumais, and M. Banko. An analysis of the askmsr question-answering system. In *Proc. of ACL*, EMNLP '02, pages 257–264, Stroudsburg, PA, USA, 2002. Association for Computational Linguistics.

[7] A. Broder. A taxonomy of web search. *SIGIR Forum*, 36(2):3–10, Sept. 2002.

[8] G. Buscher, E. Cutrell, and M. R. Morris. What do you see when you're surfing?: using eye tracking to predict salient regions of web pages. In *Proc. of CHI*, CHI '09, pages 21–30. ACM, 2009.

[9] G. Buscher, A. Dengel, and L. van Elst. Query expansion using gaze-based feedback on the subdocument level. In *Proc. of SIGIR*, 2008.

[10] G. Buscher, S. T. Dumais, and E. Cutrell. The good, the bad, and the random: an eye-tracking study of ad quality in web search. In *Proc. of ACM SIGIR*, SIGIR '10, pages 42–49, New York, NY, USA, 2010. ACM.

[11] G. Buscher, L. van Elst, and A. Dengel. Segment-level display time as implicit feedback: a comparison to eye tracking. In *Proc. of SIGIR*, 2009.

[12] H. Dang, D. Kelly, and J. Lin. Overview of the trec 2007 question answering track. In *Proc. of TREC-2007*, 2007.

[13] H. Daumé III and D. Marcu. Bayesian query-focused summarization. In *Proc. of ACL*, 2006.

[14] S. Fisher and B. Roark. Query-focused summarization by supervised sentence ranking and skewed word distributions. In *Proc. of DUC*, 2006.

[15] J. H. Friedman. Greedy function approximation: A gradient boosting machine. *The Annals of Statistics*, 29(5):pp. 1189–1232, 2001.

[16] J. Goldstein, M. Kantrowitz, V. Mittal, and J. Carbonell. Summarizing text documents: sentence selection and evaluation metrics. In *Proc. of SIGIR*, pages 121–128. ACM, 1999.

[17] Q. Guo and E. Agichtein. Exploring mouse movements for inferring query intent. In *Proc. of SIGIR*, 2008.

[18] Q. Guo and E. Agichtein. Towards predicting web searcher gaze position from mouse movements. In *Proc. of CHI*. ACM, 2010.

[19] Q. Guo and E. Agichtein. Beyond dwell time: estimating document relevance from cursor movements and other post-click searcher behavior. In *Proc. of WWW*, 2012.

[20] Q. Guo, H. Jin, D. Lagun, S. Yuan, and E. Agichtein. Mining touch interaction data on mobile devices to predict web search result relevance. In *Proc. of SIGIR*, 2013.

[21] S. Harabagiu and F. Lacatusu. Using topic themes for multi-document summarization. *ACM Trans. Inf. Syst.*, 28(3):13:1–13:47, July 2010.

[22] Y. Hijikata. Implicit user profiling for on demand relevance feedback. In *Proc. of IUI*, pages 198–205. ACM, 2004.

[23] J. Huang, R. White, and G. Buscher. User see, user point: gaze and cursor alignment in web search. In *Proc. of CHI*, pages 1341–1350, New York, NY, USA, 2012. ACM.

[24] J. Huang, R. W. White, G. Buscher, and K. Wang. Improving searcher models using mouse cursor activity. In *Proc. of SIGIR*, 2012.

[25] J. Huang, R. W. White, and S. Dumais. No clicks, no problem: using cursor movements to understand and improve search. In *Proc. of CHI*. ACM, 2011.

[26] T. Kanungo, N. Ghamrawi, K. Y. Kim, and L. Wai. Web search result summarization: title selection algorithms and user satisfaction. In *Proc. of CIKM*, 2009.

[27] T. Kanungo and D. Orr. Predicting the readability of short web summaries. In *Proc. of WSDM*, 2009.

[28] T. Kiss and J. Strunk. Unsupervised multilingual sentence boundary detection. *Computational Linguistics*, 32(4):485–525, 2006.

[29] J. Kupiec, J. Pedersen, and F. Chen. A trainable document summarizer. In *Proc. of SIGIR*, SIGIR '95, pages 68–73, New York, NY, USA, 1995. ACM.

[30] X. Li, Y.-Y. Wang, and A. Acero. Learning query intent from regularized click graphs. In *Proc. of SIGIR*, 2008.

[31] S. Liang, S. Devlin, and J. Tait. Evaluating web search result summaries. *Advances in Information Retrieval*, pages 96–106, 2006.

[32] C.-Y. Lin. ROUGE: A Package for Automatic Evaluation of Summaries. pages 74–81, Barcelona, Spain, July 2004. Association for Computational Linguistics.

[33] D. Metzler and T. Kanungo. Machine learned sentence selection strategies for query-biased summarization. In *SIGIR Learning to Rank Workshop*, 2008.

[34] F. Radlinski, M. Szummer, and N. Craswell. Inferring query intent from reformulations and clicks. In *Proc. of WWW*, 2010.

[35] K. Rodden, X. Fu, A. Aula, and I. Spiro. Eye-mouse coordination patterns on web search results pages. In *Proc. of CHI*, 2008.

[36] H. Takamura and M. Okumura. Text summarization model based on maximum coverage problem and its variant. In *Proc. of the 12th Conf. of the European Chapter of the ACL*, pages 781–789, 2009.

[37] A. Tombros and M. Sanderson. Advantages of query biased summaries in information retrieval. In *Proc. of SIGIR*, pages 2–10. ACM, 1998.

[38] J.-R. Wen, J.-Y. Nie, and H.-J. Zhang. Clustering user queries of a search engine. In *Proc. of WWW*, 2001.

[39] R. W. White and G. Buscher. Text selections as implicit relevance feedback. In *Proc. of SIGIR*, 2012.

How Query Cost Affects Search Behavior

Leif Azzopardi
School of Computing Science,
University of Glasgow
Glasgow, United Kingdom
leif@dcs.gla.ac.uk

Diane Kelly
School of Information and
Library Science, University of
North Carolina
Chapel Hill, NC, USA
dianek@email.unc.edu

Kathy Brennan
School of Information and
Library Science, University of
North Carolina
Chapel Hill, NC, USA
knb11@live.unc.edu

ABSTRACT

We investigate how the cost associated with querying in the context of information retrieval affects how users interact with a search system. Microeconomic theory is used to generate the *cost-interaction hypothesis* that states as the cost of querying increases, users will pose fewer queries and examine more documents per query. A between-subjects laboratory study with 36 undergraduate subjects was conducted, where subjects were randomly assigned to use one of three search interfaces that varied according to the amount of physical cost required to query: Structured (high cost), Standard (medium cost) and Query Suggestion (low cost). Results show that subjects who used the Structured interface submitted significantly fewer queries, spent more time on search results pages, examined significantly more documents per query, and went to greater depths in the search results list. Results also showed that these subjects spent longer generating their initial queries, saved more relevant documents and rated their queries as more successful. These findings have implications for the usefulness of microeconomic theory as a way to model and explain search interaction, as well as for the design of query facilities.

Categories and Subject Descriptors

H.3.3 [**Information Storage and Retrieval**]: Information Search and Retrieval:Search Process; H.3.4 [**Information Storage and Retrieval**]: Systems and Software:Performance Evaluation

General Terms

Theory, Experimentation, Economics, Human Factors

Keywords

Search Behavior, Economic Models, Production Theory, Interactive Information Retrieval, Query Interfaces, Query Cost

SIGIR'13, July 28–August 1, 2013, Dublin, Ireland.

1. INTRODUCTION

During interactive information retrieval (IIR), users perform various interactions, such as posing queries, examining snippets and evaluating documents. Each action requires a certain amount of effort and comes at a cost, whether mental, physical, temporal, fiscal, or a combination thereof. In the early days of search system research, cost and utility figured prominently in both systems-centered and user-centered evaluation frameworks [6, 36]; however, less attention has been devoted to costs in contemporary information search research. Fiscal costs are presumed to be less important because search tools and information are freely available online. Mental and physical costs have been incorporated into evaluation measures as fixed parameters (for example, by introducing discounting based on rank [24]) and used to characterize interactions [25], but they have rarely been studied as independent variables because they are difficult to manipulate and measure. While many interactive search studies incorporate effort-based measures, such as the number of documents examined, number of queries issued and amount of time spent performing different actions [35, 25], few studies have attempted to model how interaction costs shape search behavior [27]. There have been some exceptions, though, where information seeking and retrieval behavior has been formally modeled using a cost-benefit framework [2, 31, 34].

In this work, we explore how the costs associated with querying affect search behaviors in the context of IIR. This is an important question to address because understanding the relationship between cost, behavior and performance might help explain how and why users interact with search systems in particular ways, and subsequently, enable designers of such systems to influence user interaction and search behavior. We ground our experiment using the recently proposed Search Economic Theory [2], which uses microeconomics to model the search process and provides a means to reason about interaction, cost and performance. Using this theory, we formulated the *cost-interaction hypothesis* that states: as the cost of querying increases, users will pose fewer queries and examine more documents per query. We conducted a laboratory experiment with 36 subjects and three interfaces that varied according to query cost, where cost was operationalized as time required to submit a query. Our findings show that subjects who used the more costly query interface submitted significantly fewer queries and examined significantly more documents per query than subjects who used the interfaces with lower querying cost.

2. BACKGROUND

Cost has had a long history in IR research and has figured prominently in both systems-centered and user-centered research. Cost have been defined in a number of ways, including as mental, physical, temporal and fiscal cost. In the pre-Web era, research often focused on fiscal costs since search tools and online information were not free; many measures of fiscal costs focused on the amount users were willing to pay for search results [6, 9, 41]. For example, Cooper [10] proposed that users associate dollar amounts with search results as a way to understand subjective utility and Salton [36] proposed a number of cost-based measures related to the operational environment and response times. Today, only a few IR measures attempt to incorporate some type of cost into their computation, including nDCG [24], RBP [28], and time-biased gain [40].

While fiscal costs are no longer investigated as much, temporal cost, and more specifically response time, continues to be an important variable in research [12]. Since the late 1990s, a number of studies have demonstrated that network latency and download speeds impact how people interact with Web pages and their evaluations of information and website quality (e.g., [14, 23, 29]). In a recent study of time delays and search behavior, Taylor et al. [42] investigated the relationship between the amount of time Web pages take to load, the number of pages people viewed and the amount of information examined per page. Taylor et al. hypothesized that as response time increased, the number of pages searched would decrease and the amount of information examined per page would increase. The researchers hypothesized a step relationship between response time and search behavior rather than a linear or curvilinear relationship (that is, changes in behavior would only occur after a critical time delay point). Results showed partial support for the hypothesis related to response time and number of pages examined, and full support for the hypothesis related to response time and the amount of information examined per page. While these results provide evidence that cost, as measured by response time, impacts search behavior, the task explored in this study presented participants with a set of static Web pages, and query cost and participants' interactions with result pages were not examined.

There is some evidence that introducing time delays and query constraints can impact search behavior. Brutlag [7] reports in a blog about research conducted at Google that the time taken to return search results impacts the number of searches conducted by users. An increase in 400 milliseconds was shown to reduce the number of searches by 0.59% across a six week period on the Google search engine. Fujikawa et al. [19] constrained the number of queries a user could issue, ostensively making queries more valuable, and found that participants whose querying was constrained posed fewer queries and examined more documents per query, while participants who were not constrained submitted more queries and examined fewer documents per query. While this study was not focused on query cost, the results suggest that limitations on people's abilities to input queries can impact search behavior. Several studies have examined how query input facilities impact the types and properties of queries entered by users, and how this subsequently impacts search outcomes [1, 5, 17], but these relationships were not investigated in a cost-benefit framework. Furthermore, these studies have mainly focused on encouraging different querying behaviors, rather than understanding how the query facility and the cost of querying shapes the entire search interaction.

Recently, Baskaya et al. [3] used a simulation to study the cost of querying on two different devices. Query cost was measured as time and set to different speeds related to how long it takes the average person to enter a query using a desktop computer and smart phone. Baskaya et al. found that increasing the time to enter a query resulted in a reduction in the number of queries submitted across a variety of querying strategies and across sessions of different lengths. Essentially, this simulation suggests that as query cost increases, the number of queries issued will decrease. However, the findings have yet to be empirically validated.

Researchers have also used physical costs, or the amount of effort a person exerts during search, as a way to evaluate IR systems and user interaction. These effort-based measures include number of queries issued, number of result pages evaluated and documents viewed [27]. However, few laboratory studies have attempted to model behavior or understand if and how different costs shape behavior, or how different interfaces are associated with different costs. Studies using large scale search log data have made some progress on modeling effort and search behavior (e.g., [16, 46]), but since physical cost cannot always be manipulated in operational environments, these studies present only a partial view of search behavior under particular circumstances. In addition, while these studies indicate how people act with a given technology, they do not show how people might act given different interface costs.

Researchers have also tried to model search costs by examining mental effort. This represents a much smaller body of work (but no less important, since searching is, by nature, a mental activity) presumably because of the difficulty of measuring mental effort. Both Dennis et al. [15] and Gwizdka [20] have examined the cognitive costs of different interfaces using cognitive load theory. In these works, the authors conducted experiments to estimate the mental effort required to undertake various search interactions during the search process. However, the relationship among cost, performance and interaction was not explored.

In terms of theoretical research there has been a number of proposals that model costs and search behavior within a cost-benefit framework [2, 18, 4, 31, 32, 33, 34]. Bates [4], for example, suggests one of the search tactics users adopt while interacting with a system is to make decisions about whether to pursue the current strategy or to change strategy, depending on a cost-benefit analysis. While Bates did not formally pursue this idea, Russell et al. explored this in their work on the cost of sense-making [34]. Here they analyzed the possible actions a user could take during the information seeking process in terms of the gain that would be accumulated over time. Then actions could be compared under the assumption that users would try to maximize gain while minimizing total cost. In this process, gain can be seen as the amount of relevant information found (or the value of the relevant information found). Information Foraging Theory (IFT) [31] provides a theoretical grounding for these ideas. IFT models how users would act and behave within heterogeneous information environments in ecologically valid ways. Specifically, it proposes that information seekers aim to minimize effort and maximize gain as they move between information patches, follow scents and assume a particular information diet. In experiments using a clustering interface based on the Scatter-Gather principle, it was shown that users tend to act in an ecologically valid manner (that is, they conserve effort while seeking the most gain) [33].

Another way to formally model the information seeking process is through microeconomics. Azzopardi [2] proposes Search Economic Theory (SET) as a way to predict and explain search behavior. The model consists of a gain function and a cost function, which are parameterized by the type and number of interactions performed during the search process. Like the other formal models, the model assumes people will seek to minimize costs and maximize gain. Unlike the previous work, the theory was specifically developed to model the interaction between a user and an information retrieval system. As a result, the theory may provide useful insights into search behavior and can guide empirical investigation. In this paper, we explore how query costs affect search behavior under SET and then describe an empirical study that investigates this theory.

3. SEARCH ECONOMIC THEORY

In Azzopardi [2], the search process was modeled using an analogy to Production Theory [44]. In Production Theory, a firm takes inputs (i.e., capital and labor) and converts them to output (i.e., widgets). When applied to search, a user with a search engine is considered the firm, the user's interactions are considered inputs and the relevant information found is considered as the output (and measured by Cumulative Gain (**CG**) [24]). Azzopardi defined the inputs as the number of queries posed (**Q**) and the number of documents assessed per query (**A**). A functional relationship was proposed such that performance was related to interaction as follows: $\mathbf{CG} = g(\mathbf{Q}, \mathbf{A})$. This function (referred to as the search production function) denoted the upper bound on output given a specific input combination (i.e., the maximum that can be produced with the given inputs). It was shown that for several standard information retrieval models (such as Boolean, VSM with TFIDF and BM25 [11]) the function $g(\mathbf{Q}, \mathbf{A})$ could be modeled closely with a Cobbs-Douglas production function [44]:

$$g(\mathbf{Q}, \mathbf{A}) = \mathbf{k}.\mathbf{Q}^{\mathbf{b}}.\mathbf{A}^{(1-\mathbf{b})} \quad (1)$$

where **k** denoted how well the hypothetical user could convert actions into relevant documents using the search system, and **b** was a mixing parameter which regulated the interplay between querying and assessing. The following cost model $c(\mathbf{Q}, \mathbf{A})$ was then used to ascribe a total cost to the interactions undertaken [2]:

$$c(\mathbf{Q}, \mathbf{A}) = \mathbf{a}.\mathbf{Q} + \mathbf{Q}.\mathbf{A} \quad (2)$$

where **a** denoted the relative cost of querying to assessing. The cost of assessing documents was assumed to be 1 (where the total number of documents assessed was **Q** multiplied by **A**).

Given this model of interaction defined by the gain and cost functions, it is possible to explore how the search behavior of a user would change when different variables are manipulated. We conducted a simulation to illustrate what changes in search behavior we could expect to see when query cost increases under the proposed model. We explored a range of relative querying costs ($\mathbf{a} = 0.5, 1, 2, 4$) across various search production functions where **b** was varied from 0.5 to 0.6 and **k** was set to 3. Then we set $\mathbf{CG} = g(\mathbf{Q}, \mathbf{A}) = 30$

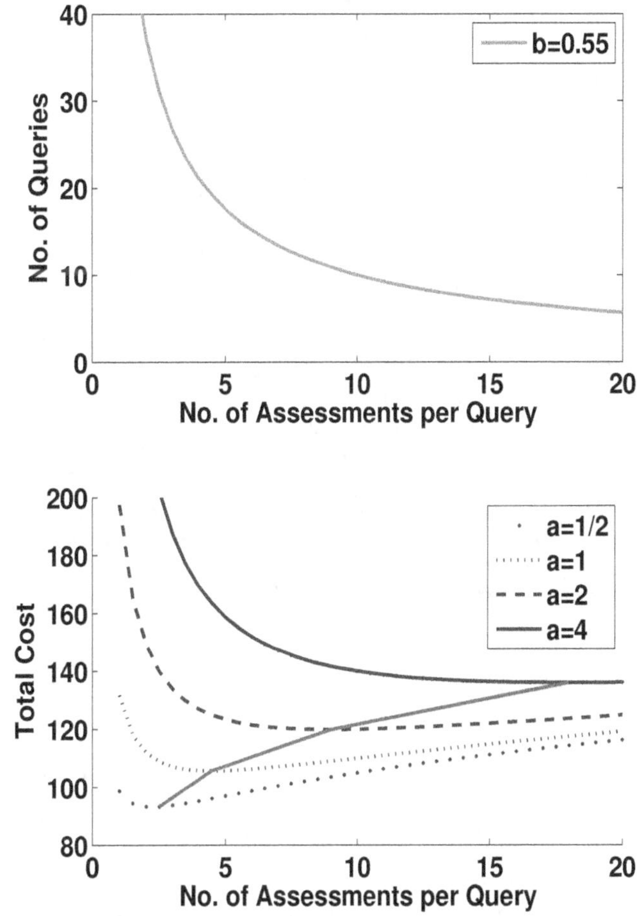

Figure 1: An example production function when b=0.55 (top), and the corresponding cost curves for different levels of a (bottom). The red line indicates the minimum cost point on each cost curve.

which models the situation where users are looking for 30 relevant documents (assuming binary relevance for computing cumulative gain)[1].

Figure 1 shows the search production function when $\mathbf{b} = 0.55$ (top plot) and the corresponding cost curves (bottom plot). Each point on the production curve represents the number of queries (**Q**) and the number of assessments per query (**A**) required to find 30 relevant documents. When $\mathbf{b} = 0.55$, there exists a number of possible combinations of inputs that would yield the desired output: a user could, for example, issue approximately 10 queries and assess 10 documents per query, or issue approximately 4 queries and assess 20 documents per query to obtain the same gain.

The bottom plot shows the corresponding cost curves associated with the gain function when $\mathbf{b} = 0.55$. The red line indicates the minimum cost point on each cost curve (i.e., the combination of inputs which minimizes the cost given the relative cost of querying). It is clear from this plot that as the relative query cost increases, the number of assessments per query also increases (and this results in a corresponding decrease in the number of queries issued). This trend

[1] Note that when we varied **k** this only affected the number of queries required not the number of assessments per query. So as **k** increased, **Q** decreased.

	Query Cost				
	a	0.5	1.0	2.0	4.0
	A	12.5	24.5	49.0	98.0
b=0.51	Q	8.1	4.2	2.2	1.1
	mc	104.9	107.8	110.8	113.8
	A	4.0	8.0	15.5	31.5
b=0.53	Q	22.5	12.2	6.8	3.6
	mc	101.4	109.7	118.6	128.3
	A	2.5	4.5	9.0	18.0
b=0.55	Q	31.1	19.2	10.9	6.2
	mc	93.3	105.7	119.9	136.0
	A	1.5	3.0	6.0	12.5
b=0.57	Q	41.8	24.8	14.7	8.5
	mc	83.7	99.2	117.6	139.4
	A	1.0	2.5	4.5	9.0
b=0.59	Q	49.5	26.2	17.4	10.8
	mc	74.3	91.7	113.2	139.9

Table 1: For different production curves characterized by b, the A and Q that result in the minimum cost (mc) for the relative query cost a is shown. As a increases, Q decreases and A increases.

is similar for different values of **b**. Table 1 shows a number of outcomes where **b** is varied between 0.51 and 0.59. The combination of **Q** and **A** that minimizes the total cost for each **a** is shown for each gain function with value **b**. These results show more generally that the model predicts the following: as relative query cost increases (i.e. $\mathbf{a} = 0.5 \rightarrow 4$), to minimize overall cost, a user should decrease the number of queries issued and increase the number of documents assessed per query.

It should be noted that as **b** decreases, assessing documents becomes more productive (i.e. there are more relevant documents in the ranked list) and so assessing will begin to dominate the production process. That is, at some point the best strategy is to keep looking at more documents, rather than querying. This is because as **b** decreases the gain derived from assessing documents increases. Put more formally, as **b** tends to zero, then $\mathbf{A}^{1-\mathbf{b}}$ tends to **A**. For the above cost function, this point is when $\mathbf{b} \leq 0.5$, where from then on, the combination of inputs that minimizes the total cost is to issue one query, and then continue assessing until the desired level of gain is obtained. This can be seen as a boundary case. On the other hand, if **b** increases, then the combination of inputs that minimizes costs tends towards issuing many queries and assessing only one document per query (again this depends on the cost model). That is, if high precision queries are very cheap then it makes sense to keep issuing them until the desired level of gain is achieved. However, as the cost of a query increases there will be a point where it is better to substitute querying for more assessments per query. The **b** values shown in Table 1 show this trade-off. Note the **b** values shown are representative of standard IR algorithms [2].

This model of search behavior follows the basic economic principle that if cost goes up, consumption goes down [44]. It also reflects some of the empirical and simulated observations made in prior work [3, 7]. While this is promising, the model and its predictions are based on a number of assumptions which need to be considered.

Modeling Caveats and Assumptions Firstly, the model assumes that users are rational and will behave such that they would minimize interaction costs, and maximize performance. This is a common modeling assumption often employed (*c.f.* [4, 31, 32, 33, 34]). In the context of searching, an operation that users repeat and practice often, it has been shown that users adapt their behavior to systems [38], and that users do *try* to minimize effort and maximize performance [33] (i.e. they subscribe to Zipf's Principle of Least Effort). While the model may overestimate how well users could use an IR system, the assumption that they will try to optimize their behavior is, at least, reasonable. On an operational level, the model assumes that users will assess a fixed number of documents per query. However a user is likely to examine a different number of documents per query depending on the performance of the query. Given this assumption, it means that the model is rather coarse grained, considering the average number of documents assessed per query. A second operational point is that the cost model seems to ignore other costs, like viewing snippets, and how the costs of certain interactions may increase or decrease during the information seeking process. For example, a user may begin to run out of ideas for queries, and thus, increase the amount of time to generate subsequent queries. Ultimately, these simplifying assumptions reduce the problem to only the most salient factors, enabling us to reason about the relationship between the two main interactions within the search process: querying and assessing. The model generates a testable hypothesis, which we shall refer to as the *cost-interaction hypothesis*:

> As the relative cost of querying increases the average number of queries issued will decrease and the average number of documents assessed per query will increase.

4. METHOD

To test this hypothesis, we conducted an experiment, where we operationalized cost in terms of query time as done in [40]. Three interfaces were created that required different amounts of time to enter queries. Subjects were randomly assigned to use one of these interfaces (Figure 2):

1. Structured Query Interface (high cost);
2. Standard Query Interface (medium cost);
3. Query Suggestion Interface (low cost).

Aside from the different query facilities, these interfaces were similar and displayed 10 search results per page. Each query facility occupied the same amount of vertical space. To approximate the query cost in terms of time, we employed the GOMS Keystroke Level Model [8] using the timings from a search experiment by [39] (shown in Table 2). For this approximation, we assumed that the average length of a query was three terms, and each term was, on average, seven characters in length. A summary of the GOMS analysis for these query interfaces is provided in Table 3. This analysis is discussed in more detail in each sub-section below.

4.1 Standard Query Interface

The Standard interface functioned as the baseline and is similar to what is provided by modern search engines. We estimated that this interface would require a medium amount of query effort relative to the other interfaces. To issue a query using the Standard interface subjects need to: (1) Go

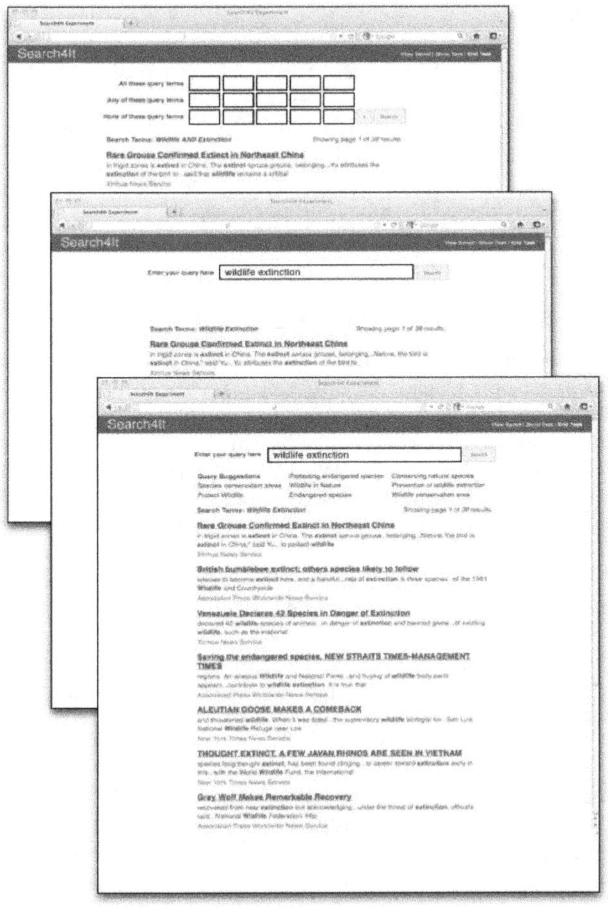

Figure 2: The Structured query interface (behind), the Standard query interface (middle) and the Query Suggestion interface (front).

to the search box, (2) Enter 3 query terms of seven characters in length (plus two spaces), (3) Submit the query by pressing the return key and then wait for a response. With respect to the GOMS analysis, the corresponding low-level actions for each of these steps are (1) MHPCH, (2) 3*7K+2K, (3) KR. Using the estimates shown in Table 2, the total amount of time is 10.9 seconds per query.

4.2 Structured Query Interface

The Structured interface consisted of 15 query boxes (3 rows x 5 columns), a search button and a plus button. Subjects could enter one term per box, but could not press the tab or enter keys to move among boxes. Each row of search boxes provided different Boolean functionality: AND, OR and NOT. While this interface might seem overly cumbersome, such search interfaces are common in commercial services; for example, EBSCO Host and ERIC provide a structured query interface similar to the one used in this study (see Hearst [22] for other examples). The plus button allowed query term boxes to be added. For this interface the GOMS analysis is as follows: (1) Go to a search box (MHPCH), (2) Type in the first query term (7K), (3) Go to the next search box (MHPCH), (4) type in the second query term (7K), (5) type in third query term (MHPCH + 7K),

Action	Time	Description
K	0.28	Press a key or button
P	1.1	Point with a mouse (excluding click)
H	0.4	Move hands to keyboard from mouse or vice versa
M	1.35	Mentally Prepare
R	0.8	System Response
C	0.2	Click

Table 2: GOMS Keystroke Level Model (time in seconds for each low level interaction)[8].

	Number of Queries Issued				
Interface	1	2	3	4	5
Structured	17.6	35.2	52.8	70.4	88.0
Standard	10.9	21.8	32.7	43.6	54.5
Suggestion	10.9	14.7	18.5	22.3	26.1

Table 3: Estimated GOMS total time spent querying in seconds for each interface.

and then (6) Submit the query - which requires the user to click the submit button (HC) and wait for response (R). The estimated total time required to enter each query is 17.6 seconds. To ensure that the physical costs associated with the Structured interface were as close to the GOMS model as possible, subjects had to retype query terms if they wanted to modify their previous query, i.e., query terms were removed from the boxes once the query was submitted, but the query was displayed on the screen. We assumed that this interface would also increase mental effort because subjects would have to understand how to enter terms.

4.3 Query Suggestion Interface

The Suggestion interface was identical to the Standard interface except query suggestions were presented after subjects entered their initial queries. For each topic, eight query suggestions were provided. These queries were collected in a previous study [26] and led to good results, where the queries retrieved between two and five TREC relevant documents in the top ten results. To issue a query using the Suggestion interface subjects needed to perform the same actions as for the Standard interface. However, for subsequent queries, subjects could select query suggestions, rather than type in queries. This resulted in the action sequence MHPCR taking approximately 3.8 seconds per suggestion. The Suggestion interface, while decreasing the amount of time to issue a query, should also reduce the mental effort associated with querying as it provides useful predefined suggestions. The query suggestions can be considered as a type of externalization, which is generally believed to reduce cognitive load in human-computer interactions [37]. Gwizdka's study of cognitive load in search found that an interface that displayed category terms reduced participants' cognitive load during query modification [20]. Thus, we anticipated that the query suggestion interface would also require less mental effort than the other two interfaces.

4.4 Corpus, Search Topics and System

A 3GB Text Retrieval Conference (TREC) test collection of over one million newspaper articles was used [45]. We selected three search topics from this collection: 344 (Abuses of E-mail); 347 (Wildlife Extinction) and 435 (Curbing Population Growth). We selected topics that had some contemporary relevance, that we thought would be of interest to our target subjects and had a similar number of relevant documents available (123, 165 and 152, respectively). Our selection was also based on evidence from previous user studies with a similar system setup [26] where it was shown that the difficulty of these topics did not significantly differ. Subjects searched all three topics, where the topics were rotated with a Latin-square. The Whoosh IR Toolkit was used as the core of the retrieval system, with BM25 as the retrieval algorithm, using standard parameters, but with an implicit ANDing of query terms to restrict the set of retrieved documents to only those that contain all the query terms (similar to BM25A used in [2]). Subjects were not provided with a tutorial of the system.

4.5 Search Behaviors

To measure the impact of the cost variations on search behavior, the following signals were logged as subjects searched: start time of search tasks, end time of search tasks, queries issued, query suggestions used, results pages viewed, documents viewed, documents marked relevant, and task descriptions viewed. From the log it was possible to calculate the amount of time subjects spent issuing queries; examining search results pages and reformulating queries at this page; and viewing documents. It was also possible to examine features of the search interaction, such as, the number of terms per query, the depth of the last document viewed in the rank list, the number of queries issued and the number of documents saved.

4.6 Overall Workload: NASA TLX

The NASA Task Load Index (TLX) questionnaire was used to elicit subjects' perceptions of: Mental Demand, Physical Demand, Temporal Demand, Performance, Effort and Frustration. After finishing the three search tasks, subjects completed a NASA TLX questionnaire to rate their overall experience with the system, and then completed another NASA TLX questionnaire focused specifically on querying (Table 7). We reduced the number of scale points from 21 to 7 (the number of points on the computer version of the scale were difficult to distinguish and psychometric research shows that there is little gain in reliability beyond 11 points [30]) and we modified the factor statements so they matched the target task (in Hart's 2006 review of the usage of the NASA TLX it was noted that this modification was often performed by researchers [21]).

4.7 Subjects

Subjects were recruited from the University of Glasgow, UK[2]. Thirty-six undergraduate student subjects participated (12 subjects per interface). Twenty-one subjects were female and fifteen were male. Their average age was 21.8 (SD=4.4). Forty-seven percent were science majors and 53% were humanities majors. Subjects' search experience was measured using a modified version of the Search Self-Efficacy scale [13]. This instrument contains 14-items describing different search-related activities. Subjects respond to each item by indicating their confidence in completing each activity on a 10-point scale (1=totally unconfident; 10=totally confident). Subjects reported fairly high search self-efficacy [M=7.26 (SD=1.69)].

[2]Ethical Approval to conduct this study was obtained from the College of Science and Engineering, Reference No. CSE00913.

4.8 Instructions and Incentives

Subjects were instructed to imagine they were newspaper reporters and needed to gather documents to write stories about the provided topics. Subjects were told that there were over 100 relevant documents in the collection for each topic and they should try to find as many of these as possible during the allotted time (10 minutes per topic). To incentivize subjects, monetary bonuses were given to the top three performers for each topic per condition. Each subject was compensated with £10 and could earn an extra £2.50 per topic as a bonus.

5. RESULTS

Results are presented in three sections. The first two sections show how the search interface affected subjects' search behaviors, including the amount of time they spent engaged in different search processes. The third section presents results of the NASA TLX. We used ANOVA and post-hoc tests with Bonferroni's correction for analysis.

5.1 Search Behavior

The mean number of queries submitted by subjects, documents assessed per query, relevant documents found and assessment depth per query is shown in Table 5. Depth is the average position at which the last document was viewed in the search results list when at least one document was viewed.

	Interface		
Interactions	**Structured**	**Standard**	**Suggestion**
Queries (Q)	19.4 ± 10.6	35.0 ± 8.9	31.2 ± 10.4
Query Len.	3.7 ± 1.49	3.5 ± 0.7	3.2 ± 0.5
Assess. / Q	4.7 ± 4.2	1.6 ± 0.5	2.5 ± 1.5
Depth / Q	14.9 ± 12.2	5.0 ± 3.7	9.3 ± 10.1
Rels. Saved	47.7 ±24.1	34.7 ± 18.5	43.2 ± 18.7
TREC Rels.	17.3 ±8.1	11.5 ± 7.3	15.3 ± 6.7

Table 5: Search behavior and performance recorded per interface.

Subjects who used the Structured interface issued significantly fewer queries than those using the Standard and Suggestion interfaces ($F(2,33) = 7.59$, $p < 0.01$). There was no difference in query length across different interfaces. Subjects who used the Structured interface viewed significantly more documents per query and went to greater depths to view these documents. Both the number of documents examined per query ($F(2,33) = 3.26$, $p = 0.05$) and the depth per query were significantly different ($F(2,33) = 4.45$, $p < 0.01$), but only between the Structured and Standard interfaces. Subjects who used the Structured interface saved the most documents, followed by those who used the Suggestion interface and those who used the Standard interface, but these differences were not significant. Of these saved documents, the number relevant was determined by using the relevance judgments included in the TREC test collection. Subjects who used the Structured interface found more relevant documents than those who used the Suggestion and Standard interfaces. However, these differences were not significant.

5.2 Time Spent Engaged in Search Processes

Table 6 displays the average amount of time subjects spent issuing their first query, on search results pages (QSERPs)

Factors	Questions for: (a) System (b) Query
Mental Demand	How mentally demanding was it to (a) use this system to complete the search tasks?, (b) query?
Physical Demand	How physically demanding was it to: (a) use this system to complete the search tasks?, (b) query?
Temporal Demand	How hurried or rushed did you feel when (a) using this system to complete the search tasks?, (b) querying?
Effort	How hard did you have to work to (a) accomplish your level of performance with this system?, (b) query?
Performance	How successful were (a) you using this system to complete the search tasks?, (b) your queries?
Frustration Level	How insecure, discouraged, etc. were you while (a) using this system?, (b) submitting queries?

Table 4: Modified NASA TLX factor definitions for overall system load and query load.

and on document pages. The average amount of time spent on QSERPs includes the time spent viewing snippets and formulating queries. Subjects who used the Structured interface spent approximately 20 seconds longer formulating their first query than subjects who used the Standard and Suggestion interfaces ($F(2,33) = 4.05$, $p = 0.027$). Follow-up tests confirm that subjects who used the Structured interface took significantly more time to construct their initial queries than subjects who used the other two interfaces. These subjects also spent significantly more time on QSERPs, viewing snippets and reformulating queries ($F(2,33) = 8.149$, $p < 0.01$). There were no statistically significant differences in the amount of time subjects spent viewing documents among interface conditions, although subjects who used the Standard interface spent slightly more time per document.

	Interface		
Interactions	**Structured**	**Standard**	**Suggestion**
First Query	44.1 ± 35.7	22.9 ± 11.3	19.9 ± 12.3
QSERPs.	62.1 ± 32.9	28.6 ± 7.7	34.7 ± 16.1
Documents	15.1 ± 7.9	17.4 ± 5.1	15.3 ± 6.5

Table 6: Mean (SD) time (in seconds) spent formulating first queries, on search results pages viewing snippets and reformulating queries (QSERP) and viewing documents.

5.3 NASA TLX

Table 7 (top) displays the overall NASA TLX scores for each factor for each interface. These results capture the overall workload experienced by subjects as they engaged in all search behaviors (querying, viewing snippets and assessing documents). Subjects using the Standard interface reported experiencing the highest mental demand, followed by those using the Structured and Suggestion interfaces. This ordering was consistent for physical demand and temporal demands. Subjects indicated similar levels of success (performance), effort and frustration. None of the differences identified above were statistically significant.

Individual factor scores were summed to arrive at a total workload score. The Standard interface received the highest overall workload score, followed by the Structured and the Suggestion interfaces. These differences were also not significant. Table 7 also provides information about the relative contributions of each factor to overall workload for each interface. For example, effort was rated as the highest contributor to load by those who used the Structured and Suggestion interfaces, while mental demand was rated highest by those using the Standard interface. More interestingly, physical demand received the lowest scores regardless of interface. It was also the case that temporal demand was evaluated as the second highest contributor to load by subjects who used the Structured and Standard interfaces, but as the second lowest for those using the Suggestion interface.

Table 7 (bottom) displays the NASA TLX ratings for query load. These results help us understand the load experienced by subjects as they queried. Subjects using the Standard interface reported experiencing the highest mental demand when querying, followed by those using the Structured and Suggestion interfaces. There were no differences among interfaces according to physical demand. With respect to temporal demand, subjects using the Structured and Standard interfaces reported higher demands than those using the Suggestion interface. Subjects who used the Structured interface described their queries as more successful (performance) than those using the Standard and Suggestion interfaces. Subjects using the Standard interface reported greater levels of frustration and effort. None of the differences identified above were statistically significant. With respect to overall query load, the Structured and Standard interfaces received similar scores, which were higher than overall query load for the Suggestion interface. These differences were not significant.

System Load		**Interface**	
Factor	**Structured**	**Standard**	**Suggestion**
Mental	4.5 ± 1.4	5.1 ± 0.9	3.9 ± 1.6
Physical	2.3 ± 1.3	2.7 ± 1.1	1.9 ± 1.4
Temporal	4.6 ± 1.8	5.0 ± 1.4	3.6 ± 1.9
Performance	4.0 ± 1.4	4.1 ± 1.4	4.2 ± 1.4
Effort	4.8 ± 1.5	4.9 ± 1.4	4.7 ± 1.6
Frustration	3.5 ± 1.4	3.7 ± 1.7	3.8 ± 1.8
Total	23.7 ± 5.2	25.5 ± 5.9	22.1 ± 5.1

Query Load		**Interface**	
Factor	**Structured**	**Standard**	**Suggestion**
Mental	4.2 ± 1.4	4.8 ± 1.3	3.7 ± 1.9
Physical	2.2 ± 1.3	2.1 ± 1.2	2.2 ± 1.6
Temporal	4.2 ± 1.9	4.1 ± 1.8	3.0 ± 2.0
Performance	4.2 ± 2.0	3.1 ± 1.6	3.9 ± 2.0
Effort	4.4 ± 1.3	4.9 ± 1.6	4.5 ± 1.6
Frustration	4.0 ± 1.7	4.3 ± 1.5	3.1 ± 2.0
Total	23.2 ± 5.1	23.3 ± 7.0	20.4 ± 8.6

Table 7: Mean (SD) of NASA TLX Factors

6. DISCUSSION

We found that subjects who used the Structured (high cost) interface submitted significantly fewer queries, examined more documents per query and went to greater depths in the search results list than subjects who used the lower cost Standard and Suggestion interfaces. This finding supports the *cost-interaction hypothesis* we generated from the microeconomic theory: as the cost of querying increases, the number of queries issued will decrease and the number of documents evaluated will increase. However, counter to what we expected, we found that subjects who used the Standard interface, which was constructed to represent medium cost, issued the most queries, viewed the fewest documents per query and were the shallowest in their evaluation of the search results list. Our expectation was that these behaviors would be associated with the Suggestion interface since the cost of querying was considered lowest.

One possible explanation for this finding is that subjects who used the Suggestion interface may not have experienced any meaningful differences with respect to cost since they did not always click on the available suggestions. On average, subjects selected 7.31 query suggestions out of 24 query suggestions, which were available to them during their search sessions. The initial GOMS analysis assumed a greater uptake of suggestions, which would have resulted in much lower querying costs. If we revise our GOMS estimate, based on the actual usage statistics, then the time spent per query on the Suggestion interface would have been approximately, 9.24 seconds, on average[3]. This indicates that in terms of querying, the costs between these interfaces was very similar (and not as great as we originally anticipated). The empirical findings also confirmed that there was no significant difference in querying time between the Suggestion and Standard interface. However, the Suggestion interface may have introduced some added costs since subjects needed to examine and make decisions about the query suggestions. This is partially supported by the differences in the amount of time subjects spent on QSERPs evaluating snippets and formulating queries. Subjects who used the Suggestion interface spent slightly longer on QSERPs than subjects who used the Standard interface (34.7 and 28.6 seconds, respectively) and this increased time might have reflected time spent evaluating query suggestions. Though, here, the differences were not significant, which implies that the querying cost between these conditions was not different.

This raises a number of issues when applying the microeconomic theory in practice: (1) what costs are at play and how do we estimate them within the cost function, and (2) if the query costs were not significantly different, why do we observe different behavior between the Standard and Suggestion interfaces. Regarding costs, our research has shown that cost and how it is operationalized within the economic model needs to be reconsidered. Is the querying cost inclusive of the time spent viewing snippets or not, and if not, is it a document cost? If we use the QSERP estimates to denote the query cost (i.e. time spent querying and viewing snippets per query) then the Standard interface would be the least expensive: and our findings would be consistent with the cost-interaction hypothesis. However, the theory and the cost models employed would need to be refined, perhaps, redefined, to determine whether this is appropriate. We leave this to further work, and consider alternative explanations regarding the differences in search behavior between these two interfaces below.

We first considered whether the results with regard to the Standard and Suggestion interfaces were caused by differences in query quality and search result quality. Since the Suggestion interface provided good quality queries that had reasonably high precision, differences in query quality might explain why subjects who used the Suggestion interface tended to assess more documents per query and issue fewer queries than subjects using the Standard interface (i.e., they might have seen better search results). It is important to note that query quality differences would not

[3]Revised GOMS estimate: (23.89 queries entered manually * 10.9 seconds per query + 7.31 suggestions clicked * 3.8 seconds per suggestion) / (31.2 total queries) = 9.24 seconds per query issued.

	Structured	Standard	Suggestion
#Q	232	420	374
P@5	0.159	0.191	0.239**
P@10	0.139	0.171	0.217**
P@15	0.121	0.162*	0.196**

Table 8: Mean precision of queries issued across each interface. * (**) indicates significantly better than Structured (Structured and Standard).

have been caused by individual ability since subjects were randomly assigned to interface condition.

To determine whether there was a difference in query quality, subjects' queries were submitted to the retrieval system and evaluated using TREC relevance judgements to better understand what types of performance subjects encountered. Table 8 reports the precision values at 5, 10 and 15 documents along with the number of queries issued in each group. The results show that the quality of the queries on the Suggestion interface was higher than the other two interfaces. Statistical testing revealed that system performance was significantly better across these three precision measures ($p < 0.05$). This finding suggests that subjects who used the Suggestion interface issued better quality queries and potentially encountered more TREC relevant documents in the ranked lists, but we note that there were no significant differences in the number of documents subjects saved or the number of TREC-relevant saved, so we cannot conclude that subjects using the Suggestion interface experienced better performance, especially considering the work of Turpin and Hersh [43] who have shown that system performance evaluated in this way does not always map to user performance.

The results from the NASA TLX also provide additional insights about how subjects experienced these interfaces, and the extent to which cost, as we have manipulated it in this study, impacted their experiences. Although many interesting differences are discussed below, it is important to keep in mind that none of these were statistically significant, so this discussion is primarily presented in the service of future research.

The NASA TLX was administered twice: once to focus on system load and once to focus on query load. The system load allowed us to understand the entire experience (querying, evaluating snippets and results, search result quality), while query load isolated the load introduced by the query facilities. One of the most interesting and consistent findings was that physical demand contributed the least to subjects' overall loads. For query load, the Structured, Standard and Suggestion interfaces were rated nearly the same for this factor (2.2, 2.2, and 2.1, respectively). There were greater differences in subjects' ratings of physical demand for system load, with the Standard interface receiving a rating of 2.7, followed by Structured (2.3) and Suggestion (1.9) interfaces. These ratings were, in general, low, when compared to the other factors, which suggests that our manipulation of physical demand may not have been as extreme as expected.

Results also showed that subjects associated the most mental demand with the Standard interface (4.8), followed by the Structured (4.2) and Suggestion (3.7). This ordering was consistent for the mental demand associated with system load, although the values were slightly larger (5.1, 4.5 and 3.9, respectively). Compared to the ratings for physical demand, it is clear that mental demand contributed more to subjects' overall workloads. The Suggestion interface received the lowest ratings for mental demand as expected, but the Standard received higher ratings than the Structured, which was unexpected. We believe that the higher mental demand associated with the Standard interface was a result of subjects creating more queries while searching.

While one might argue that the Structured interface is clunky and less usable than the other interfaces, subjects did not report high levels of frustration with the query facility. Rather, the highest levels of frustration were reported by subjects who used the Standard interface. This suggests that subjects did not find the added time costs associated with the Structured interface annoying and that subjects were more frustrated by having to enter more queries with the Standard interface. The Suggestion interface, as expected, received the lowest frustration rating for query load. These results make us question how subjects would have rated the usability or aesthetics of the interfaces. We hypothesize that subjects would rate the Structured interface the lowest, which is interesting since they actually performed better with it. We leave this for future work.

A final difference we observed in the NASA TLX was with respect to the temporal factor, which gauged how hurried or rushed subjects felt when doing the search tasks. Subjects who used the Standard interface reported experiencing the highest levels of temporal demand (5.0), followed by those who used the Structured interface (4.6) and those who used the Suggestion interface (3.6). This difference suggests that a system that encourages the type of search behavior that subjects who used the Standard interface engaged in - issuing more queries, evaluating fewer documents per query and shallowly evaluating search results lists - might have negative psychological consequences, assuming that feeling hurried and rushed generates stress. There were no differences between the Standard and Structured interfaces for temporal demand for query load, which seems to further suggest that it was the total search strategy engaged in by those who used the Standard interface that contributed to the differences in overall temporal demand.

7. CONCLUSIONS AND FUTURE WORK

In this paper, we investigated how query cost affects search behavior. We used microeconomic theory to motivate our study and conducted a theoretical analysis, which generated the *cost-interaction hypothesis*. A laboratory study with 36 subjects was conducted to evaluate this hypothesis using three interfaces: Structured, Standard and Suggestion. We found partial support for this hypothesis: subjects who used the high cost Structured interface submitted fewer queries, spent more time on search results pages, examined more documents per query, and went to greater depths in the search results list than subjects who used the lower cost Standard and Suggestion interfaces.

Our results have both theoretical and practical implications. Attempts to formally model search interaction are promising, but the results of this study suggest that refinements to the microeconomic theory are required to improve the realism of the model. Our results also imply that at least one additional factor should be included in the gain and cost functions to account for viewing snippets, and that more sophisticated cost functions may be more appropriate. We found that in testing the theory, care needs to be taken to control each of the factors involved. Changing the costs may change other aspects of the interaction and these need to be accounted for when testing hypotheses generated by the model.

Future work will focus on further refining the search economic theory/models and exploring how alternative designs for query facilities and other search interface features might encourage users to engage in and adopt more positive and successful search behaviors.

Acknowledgments We would like to thank Kelly Marshall for her help in conducting the user experiments.

8. REFERENCES

[1] E. Agapie, G. Golovchinsky, and P. Qvardordt. Encouraging behavior: A foray into persuasive computing. In *Proceedings on the Symposium on Human-Computer Information Retrieval*, 2012.

[2] L. Azzopardi. The economics in interactive information retrieval. In *Proceedings of the 34th ACM conference on research and development in information retrieval (SIGIR)*, pages 15–24, 2011.

[3] F. Baskaya, H. Keskustalo, and K. Järvelin. Time drives interaction: simulating sessions in diverse searching environments. In *Proceedings of the 35th ACM conference on research and development in information retrieval (SIGIR)*, pages 105–114, 2012.

[4] M. J. Bates. Training and education for online. chapter Information search tactics, pages 96–105. Taylor Graham Publishing, London, UK, UK, 1989.

[5] N. J. Belkin, D. Kelly, G. Kim, J.-Y. Kim, H.-J. Lee, G. Muresan, M.-C. Tang, X.-J. Yuan, and C. Cool. Query length in interactive information retrieval. In *Proceedings of the 26th ACM conference on research and development in information retrieval (SIGIR)*, pages 205–212, 2003.

[6] N. J. Belkin and A. Vickery. *Interaction in Information Systems*. University Press, 1985.

[7] J. Brutlag. Speed matters for google web search. In *Technical Report, Retrieved online at http://googleresearch.blogspot.com/2009/06/speed-matters.html, on May 11, 2013*, 2009.

[8] S. K. Card, T. P. Moran, and A. Newell. The keystroke-level model for user performance time with interactive systems. *Communications of the ACM*, 23(7):396–410, 1980.

[9] M. D. Cooper. A cost model for evaluating information retrieval systems. *Journal of the American Society for Information Science*, pages 306–312, 1972.

[10] W. S. Cooper. On selecting a measure of retrieval effectiveness, part 1: The subjective philosophy of evaluation. *Journal of the American Society for Information Science*, 24:87–100, 1973.

[11] B. Croft, D. Metzler, and T. Strohman. *Search Engines: Information Retrieval in Practice*. 2009.

[12] J. Dabrowski and E. V. Munson. 40 years of searching for the best computer system response time. *Interacting with Computers*, 23:555–564, 2011.

[13] S. Debowski, R. Wood, and A. Bandura. The impact of guided exploration and enactive exploration on self-regulatory mechanisms and information

acquisition through electronic enquiry. *Journal of Applied Psychology*, 86:1129–1141, 2001.

[14] A. R. Dennis and N. J. Taylor. Information foraging on the web: The effects of acceptable internet delays on multi-page information search behavior. *Decision Support Systems*, 42:810–824, 2006.

[15] S. Dennis, P. Bruza, and R. McArthur. Web searching: a process-oriented experimental study of three interactive search paradigms. *Journal of the American Society for Information Science and Technology*, 53(2):120–133, Jan. 2002.

[16] G. Dupret and B. Piwowarski. A user behavior model for average precision and its generalization to graded judgments. In *Proceedings of the 33rd ACM conference on research and development in information retrieval (SIGIR)*, pages 531–538, 2010.

[17] K. Franzen and J. Kalgren. Verbosity and interface design. In *SICS Technical Report: T2000:04, Retrieved online at http://soda.swedish-ict.se/2623/2/irinterface.pdf on May 11, 2013*, 1997.

[18] N. Fuhr. A probability ranking principle for interactive information retrieval. *Information Retrieval*, 11(3):251–265, 2008.

[19] K. Fujikawa, H. Joho, and S. Nakayama. Constraint can affect human perception, behaviour, and performance of search. In *Proceedings of the 14th International Conference on Asia-Pacific Digital Libraries (ICADL)*, pages 39–48, 2012.

[20] J. Gwizdka. Distribution of cognitive load in web search. *Journal of the American Society for Information Science and Technology*, 61(11):2167–2187, Nov. 2010.

[21] S. G. Hart. Nasa-task load index (nasa-tlx); 20 years later. In *Proceedings of the Human Factors and Ergonomics Society 50th Annual Meeting*, pages 904–908, 2006.

[22] M. A. Hearst. *Search User Interfaces*. New York, NY: Cambridge University Press, 2009.

[23] J. A. Jacko, A. Sears, and M. S. Borella. The effect of network delay and media on user perceptions of web resources. *Behaviour and Information Technology*, 19(6):427–439, 2000.

[24] K. Järvelin and J. Kekäläinen. Cumulated gain-based evaluation of information retrieval technology. *ACM Trans. on Information Systems*, 20(4):422–446, 2002.

[25] D. Kelly. Methods for evaluating interactive information retrieval systems with users. *Foundations and Trends in Information Retrieval*, 3:1–224, 2009.

[26] D. Kelly, K. Gyllstrom, and E. W. Bailey. A comparison of query and term suggestion features for interactive searching. In *Proceedings of the 32nd ACM conference on research and development in information retrieval (SIGIR)*, pages 371–378, 2009.

[27] D. Kelly and C. Sugimoto. A systematic review of interactive information retrieval evaluation studies, 1967-2006. *Journal of the American Society for Information Science and Tech.*, 64(4):745–770, 2013.

[28] A. Moffat and J. Zobel. Rank-biased precision for measurement of retrieval effectiveness. *ACM Trans. on Information Systems*, 27(1):2:1–2:27, 2008.

[29] F. F. H. Nah. A study on tolerable waiting time: How long are web users willing to wait? *Behaviour and Information Technology*, 23(3):153–163, 2004.

[30] J. C. Nunnally. *Psychometic Theory*. McGraw, 1978.

[31] P. Pirolli and S. Card. Information foraging. *Psychological Review*, 106:643–675, 1999.

[32] P. Pirolli and W. T. Fu. Snif-act: a model of information foraging on the www. In *Proceedings of the 9th International Conference on User Modeling*, pages 45–54, 2003.

[33] P. Pirolli, P. Schank, M. Hearst, and C. Diehl. Scatter/gather browsing communicates the topic structure of a very large text collection. In *Proceedings of the ACM SIGCHI Conference*, pages 213–220, 1996.

[34] D. M. Russell, M. J. Stefik, P. Pirolli, and S. K. Card. The cost structure of sensemaking. In *Proceedings of the INTERACT and SIGCHI Conference*, pages 269–276, 1993.

[35] I. Ruthven. Interactive information retrieval. *Annual Review of Information Science and Technology (ARIST)*, 42:43–92, 2008.

[36] G. Salton. Evaluation problems in interactive information retrieval. *Information Storage and Retrieval*, 6:29–44, 1970.

[37] M. Scaife and Y. Rogers. External cognition: How do graphical representations work? *International Journal of Human-Computer Studies*, 45:185–213, 1996.

[38] C. L. Smith and P. B. Kantor. User adaptation: good results from poor systems. In *Proceedings of the 31st ACM conference on research and development in information retrieval (SIGIR)*, pages 147–154, 2008.

[39] M. D. Smucker. Towards timed predictions of human performance for interactive information retrieval evaluation. In *Proceedings of the Symposium on Human-Computer Information Retrieval*, 2009.

[40] M. D. Smucker and C. L. Clarke. Time-based calibration of effectiveness measures. In *Proceedings of the 35th ACM conference on research and development in information retrieval (SIGIR)*, pages 95–104, 2012.

[41] L. T. Su. Evaluation measures for interactive information retrieval. *Information Processing and Management*, 28:503–316, 1992.

[42] N. J. Taylor, A. R. Dennis, and J. W. Cummings. Situation normality and the shape of search: The effects of time delays and information presentation on search behavior. *Journal of the American Society for Information Science and Tech.*, 64(5):909–928, 2013.

[43] A. Turpin and W. Hersh. Why batch and user evaluations do not give the same results. In *Proceedings of the 24th ACM conference on research and development in information retrieval (SIGIR)*, pages 225–231, 2001.

[44] H. R. Varian. *Intermediate microeconomics: A modern approach*. W.W. Norton, New York:, 1987.

[45] E. M. Voorhees. Overview of the trec 2005 robust retrieval track. In *Proceedings of TREC-14*, 2006.

[46] E. Yilmaz, M. Shokouhi, N. Craswell, and S. Robertson. Expected browsing utility for web search evaluation. In *Proceedings of the 19th ACM conference on Information and knowledge management (CIKM)*, pages 1561–1564, 2010.

Search Engine Switching Detection Based on User Personal Preferences and Behavior Patterns

Denis Savenkov, Dmitry Lagun, Qiaoling Liu
Mathematics & Computer Science
Emory University
Atlanta, US
{denis.savenkov, dlagun, qiaoling.liu}@emory.edu

ABSTRACT

Sometimes, during a search task users may switch from one search engine to another for several reasons, e.g., dissatisfaction with the current search results or desire for broader topic coverage. Detecting the fact of switching is difficult but important for understanding users' satisfaction with the search engine and the complexity of their search tasks, leading to economic significance for search providers. Previous research on switching detection mainly focused on studying different signals useful for the task and particular reasons for switching. Although it is known that switching is a personal choice of a user and different users have different search behavior, little has been done to understand how these differences could be used for switching detection. In this paper we study the effectiveness of learning personal behavior patterns for switching detection and present a personalized approach which uses user's session history containing sessions with and without switches. Experiments show that users' personal habits and behavior patterns are indeed among the most informative signals. Our findings can be used by a search log analyzer for engine switching detection and potentially other log mining problems, thus providing valuable signals for search providers to improve user experience.

Categories and Subject Descriptors

H.3.3 [**Information Storage and Retrieval**]: Information Search and Retrieval

Keywords

search engine switching

1. INTRODUCTION

Search engines such as Google, Bing, Yandex, etc. facilitate access to enormous amount of information available on the Word Wide Web. Among many available search engines, users typically prefer to use one or two, performing majority of their searches on a primary search engine. Decision on which search engine to use as a primary search provider could be based on many factors including search quality, locale, satisfaction, usability of search interface and popularity of a search engine [9]. Sometimes users switch from one search engine to another during a search task. As the majority of switching cases (57%) arise from users' dissatisfaction with the search engine [9], information on when users switch provides a valuable signal for search providers to improve user search experience in such cases. For some search sessions, the fact of switching can be easily detected, for instance via a web browser (maintained by a search engine), a browser toolbar or search logs (e.g. some users ask navigational query in the current search engine to open a new one). However, in reality only a fraction of switches can be monitored. The same users may switch in a way that cannot be detected by a search engine, e.g. by opening a new tab. Detecting the fact of switching, when such events cannot be monitored directly is difficult, but it is important for understanding users' satisfaction and the complexity of search. It also has the economic significance to search providers as switching is a low-level signal related to the market share.

Previous work [20, 21, 9] identified the most popular reasons for switching as dissatisfaction with search results, desire to get more relevant results for coverage and verification or users' personal preferences to use a particular search engine for some types of searches. This suggests that decision to switch search engines depends not only on a task, but also on user's personal behavior patterns and habits. For example, some users are more persistent than others and can make more effort exploring the search results. Previous research made progress in detecting search engine switching, but information on user's typical behavior didn't get enough attention.

In this paper, we focus on learning users' search behavior patterns and habits and using it for search engine switching detection. Our experiments show, that a state-of-the-art existing model (semi-supervised generative model proposed in [10]) benefits from using this information. In addition, we built a model based on multiple gradient boosting regression trees, which utilizes more than 400 features based on user preferences, search tasks, user behavior patterns, etc.

In our work we used publicly available dataset, which contains search logs for 1 month period, collected by Yandex for the Switching detection challenge[1] (Oct 23, 2012 - Dec 22, 2012) . The logs have search engine switching actions detected either by a browser toolbar or by clicks on URL of

SIGIR'13, July 28–August 1, 2013, Dublin, Ireland.

[1]http://switchdetect.yandex.ru/en

a different search engine from the result page of the source search engine.

The main contributions of this paper include:

- a personalized version of the generative model for web search success prediction [10]. We show that learning user's personal action transition patterns significantly improves the performance of the model.
- machine learning based switching prediction model, based on an ensemble of decision trees, which utilizes over 400 features, including users' personal search behavior information. We show that the personalized model outperforms algorithms that do not use this information. This model outperformed other competitors on the Yandex switching detection challenge.
- in-depth feature importance analysis, which shows that users' statistics are actually among the best predictors in the feature set.

The rest of the paper is organized as follows: Section 2 briefly discusses the related work, Section 3 describes the dataset we used and explains why personalization is important. Section 4 presents our personalized versions of the recently proposed Markov model based algorithm [10] and our machine learning based approach that harnesses rich personalized behavior features for switching detection. In Section 5 the results of the prediction experiments are presented and Section 6 provides some discussions and implications of the results. Finally, Section 7 concludes the paper.

2. RELATED WORK

Understanding and detecting search engine switching has recently attracted much research attention [13][14][20][9]. Heath and White [13] proposed the task of predicting search engine switching in a real-time setting, i.e. whether a user's next action during a search will be an engine switch. The algorithm used in the paper is based on a string matching idea, i.e., user's most recent actions performed and pages visited in the session so far are encoded as a character sequence and prediction is based on the number of times this sequence was previously followed by a switch or a non-switch action. Laxmant et al. [14] later improved the idea by identifying frequent predictive subsequences and estimating their associated Hidden Markov Models. Since a sequence could not catch all session information, White and Dumais [20] used a richer set of features to predict switching, which were derived from the user's most recent query, session interaction observed so far, and user search history. Guo et al. [9] investigated the reasons causing search engine switching based on in-situ feedback from users and developed models to predict the rationale for a given switching event. The above work (especially [13][14][20]) are the closest to ours, which also inspired us on the features to start with; yet several differences exist in between. First, we aim at offline detection of user switching using complete session information instead of online scenario where only partial session information is available. Second, we focus on using personalization for learning to detect search engine switching and we compare different personalization approaches, which have been little studied in previous works.

As the most popular switching rationale is dissatisfaction with search results, another relevant research area is predicting search success [10][1][8][11][12]. Field et al. [8] worked on predicting user-reported frustration, and found a few simple query log features performed better than physical sensor features. Ageev et al. [1] worked on modeling search success via a game-like infrastructure and used Conditional Random Field (CRF) models for prediction. Hassan et al. [11][12] proposed to use two Markov models for predicting search success, and found that user behavior based models are more predictive than document relevance based models. Hassan [10] recently proposed a semi-supervised approach based on a generative model and EM estimation to model search satisfaction and found that adding unlabeled data improves the effectiveness. Other relevant work include using query logs and user behavior to predict relevance of search results [7][2] as well as studying the change in user behavior when search becomes more difficult [3]. User preference is another reason causing search engine switching, e.g. sometimes a user prefers one search engine to another for some types of search tasks. Numerous researches show that user differences influence their search strategies and behavior [5][22][17] and personalization is effective to improve user experience in web search [4][18] [6].

In our work, we take a close look at the main reasons for engine switching, derive features shown useful for identifying such scenarios and focus on learning users' personal behavior models. The results of this work show that such models significantly improve the performance of switching detection and the approach can be applied to other similar tasks.

3. DATASET ANALYSIS

3.1 Dataset

For our work we used a publicly available dataset, provided by Yandex for its recent switching detection challenge. The dataset contains a subset of search logs of 30 days, which are about 1.5 years old and do not contain sessions with queries that have commercial intent detected with Yandex proprietary query classifier. Search sessions contain unique user identifier and a sequence of records for search actions, such as queries, result clicks and search engine switching actions, which were detected by a browser toolbar or by clicks on a link to open another search engine from the search engine results page. The information provided along with search actions includes for each record the time elapsed from the beginning of the session, for a click action the clicked url, or for a query action the query and the urls shown to the user. To allay privacy concerns the logs were fully anonymized, so only meaningless query, user and url ids are available. Also the dataset doesn't contain any information on the search engine the user switched to. The elapsed time for all actions are specified in time units with unknown relation to seconds. In total, the dataset includes 8,595,731 sessions, 1,457,533 sessions with switch action, 10,139,547 unique queries, 49,029,185 unique URLs, and 956,536 unique users. According to the challenge setting, the data in the last 3 days are used as the test set, and all users who don't have switches in the first 27 days were removed from the dataset.

3.2 Switching Behavior Analysis

Previous research [20] [9] showed that the main reasons for search engine switching are: dissatisfaction in 57% of the cases, verifying or finding additional information in 26% of the cases and user preferences (e.g. a user prefers one engine to another for some particular search tasks) in 12% of

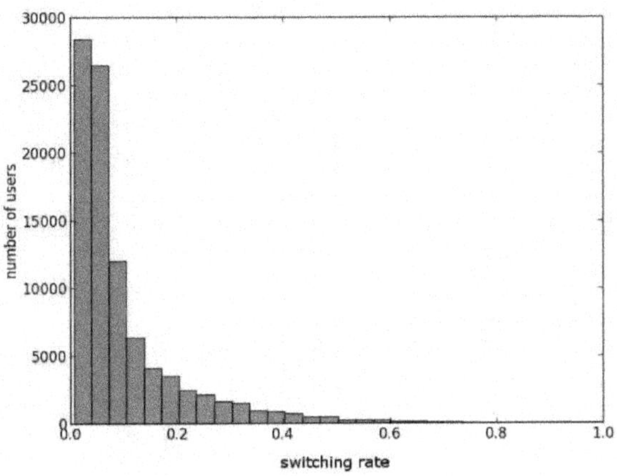

Figure 1: Histogram of switching rates for users with $\geq$ 20 sessions in the first 27 days

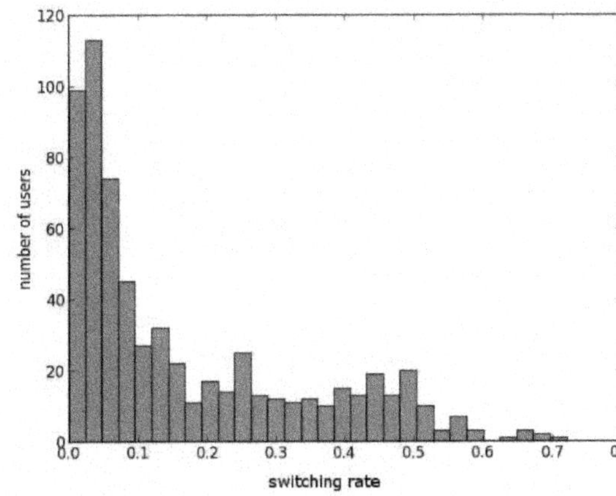

Figure 2: Histogram of switching rates for users with $\geq$ 20 sessions in the first 27 days, considering only sessions with 7 to 30 queries

the cases. This suggests that switching behavior highly depends on a search task, e.g. for an easy task the user is less likely to switch to another search engine. In [20] a histogram of probability of switching given session length is provided, suggesting that search sessions with more queries are more likely to contain a switch. But on the other hand switching behavior also depends on users' personal habits. Some users might not switch search engines even when they are not satisfied with the search results while some other users might have a habit of verifying results by opening another search engine even when the current results are relevant. Figure 1 shows the histogram of switching rates for users with at least 20 sessions in the training period (first 27 days). As you can see, some users switch more often than others. To reduce the influence of task difficulty on switching probability, the histogram on Figure 2 considers only sessions with 7 to 30 queries, as for these sessions the probability of switching is relatively more stable. Nevertheless, the histogram shows that even in this case different users still have varying switching rates. This supports the hypothesis that switching behavior have a strong personal component. Some users are more experienced with using multiple search engines, and others do this only occasionally. Another aspect relates to the search task itself. For example, a user may switch more frequently because he/she performs difficult searches more often, for which the results are more likely to be non-relevant, or because he/she asks more queries of research type and needs more search results. This means that personalization can help learn more about both users' behavior patterns and their search tasks.

As shown by White and Dumais [20], the likelihood that a switch happens in a session increases as the session length increases. We also found this result with our data by comparing the average number of queries in switching and non-switching sessions across all users (the blue line in Figure 3 shows that on average more queries are issued in sessions with a switch). However, another interesting observation is that this effect is actually different for different users. As a session gets longer, the likelihood of switching increases much more for some users than for others. Moreover, for some users the switching likelihood even decreases when more queries are issued (the left gray part in Figure 3). Therefore, to better detect switching for these users it is necessary to understand and model their personal behavior patterns.

3.3 Task and Metric Description

In this paper we are focusing on detecting search sessions that contain switch/switches to another search engine. Following the setting of Yandex switching detection challenge, we use the AUC (Area Under Curve) measure [15] to evaluate the performance of our switching prediction models. AUC is a popular measure used for evaluating classifiers, which represents the probability that a classifier will rank a randomly chosen positive instance higher than a randomly chosen negative one. To allow easier interpretation of the performance of our models, we also present the corresponding precision-recall curves in the evaluation.

4. PERSONALIZED SWITCH MODELING

4.1 Evaluation Set

The dataset contains sessions collected for 30 day period from users who switched at least once in the first 27 days. Since sessions in days 28-30 were used as the test set in Yandex switching detection challenge and the labels were not available at the time of our experiments, we held out the sessions in days 25-27 as our validation set. The rest of the data (sessions in days 1-24) were used for training. To make a validation set similar to the challenge test set, we filtered out sessions from users who didn't switch in the first 24 days.

4.2 Personalized Generative Models to Switch Detection

Search trails, i.e. sequences of actions a user performs with the search engine (e.g. queries, clicks on a search result) were shown to be very useful signals for predicting user satisfaction and search engine switching. For example, in [20] pre- and post-switch motifs were studied and shown to be useful for switching prediction. In [10] a semi-supervised generative model for search success prediction was proposed, which learns probabilities of transitions from one action to

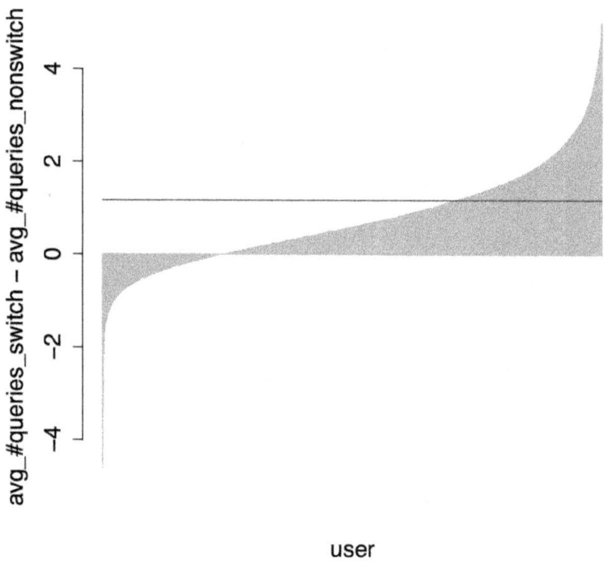

Figure 3: Difference between average number of queries in switch and non-switch sessions for each user

Table 1: Alphabets for search trails (type-I, type-II)

Action	Description
Q	query submission
C	click on a search result
E	end of the session
q	query with a short pause before next action
Q	query with a long pause before next action
K	other query
D	short dwell-time click on a search result
S	long dwell-time click on a search result
P	other clicks on a search result
E	end of the session

another and uses this data for prediction. Unfortunately, in our dataset only query and search result click actions are available, thus we could not exploit other actions such as clicks on ads or on spelling suggestions as used in previous work. As a result, the basic (type-I) alphabet for search trail encoding consists of {Q, C, E} as shown in Table 1. Inspired by previous work, we also introduce an advanced search trail encoding by distinguishing between short- and long-dwell time clicks. In addition, we felt that queries with different pause until the next action may be also helpful, so we encoded them as well. Finally, the advanced (type-II) alphabet is {q, Q, K, D, S, P, E}, as shown in Table 1. Note that, "short" is defined by less than 200 time units while "long" is defined by more than 500 time units.

A key part of the model defined in [10] for user satisfaction prediction is the action transition parameters for the switch and non-switch class respectively. Therefore, we presents the estimated transition probabilities for switch and non-switch sessions in Table 2. As you can see sessions with switches are more likely to end after a query action than sessions without switches (Note that switch actions were only used to split

Table 2: Markov model transition probabilities

	Non-switch sessions				Switch sessions		
	Q	C	E		Q	C	E
Q	0.217	0.750	0.033	Q	0.316	0.621	0.063
C	0.207	0.470	0.323	C	0.288	0.521	0.191

Table 3: Markov model transition probabilities for a particular user

	Non-switch sessions				Switch sessions		
	Q	C	E		Q	C	E
Q	0.417	0.527	0.056	Q	0.506	0.430	0.065
C	0.219	0.352	0.428	C	0.397	0.354	0.249

sessions into the two classes, not considered in transitions). Moreover, in switch sessions users tend to ask more queries.

However, we were also aware that some users have very different behavior from the average. For example, Table 3 shows the transition probabilities estimated on sessions from a particular user (who has 50 switching and 77 non-switching sessions). The differences in the estimated probabilities for this user and the general model (e.g., this user in general asks more queries) suggests that taking personal transition habits into account may improve the prediction performance.

Unfortunately, most users have just a few sessions and hence the estimated transition models can be unreliable. In this consideration, we smoothed each personalized model with the global model for final prediction. To get a good smoothing, we used a machine learning approach. Three features were generated for each session: prediction of the global model, prediction of the user's personal model, and number of sessions in the history of the user. Then a logistic regression was applied to get a combined prediction[2].

The results of our experiments with generative models are presented in Table 4. The personalized models significantly outperform the global models and other baselines. In our experiment, the semi-supervised approach proposed in [10] incorporating the EM algorithm did not improve the performance of the supervised models, perhaps due to the large amount of labeled data available. Unfortunately, encoding time information into action sequences did not help the personalized models, probably because the larger alphabet makes the action transitions more sparse and therefore the derived personalized model more unreliable.

Another interesting observation is the performance of the baseline using user switching rate compared to other baselines. Despite the fact that this predictor did not use any information about the session, it outperforms other baselines, supporting our hypothesis that switching highly depends on users' habits and behavior patterns.

4.3 Personalized Machine Learning Approach to Switch Detection

Machine learning approaches have been shown to be successful for predicting search engine switching [13][14][20] as it allows to combine various signals into a single model. Inspired by these efforts, we developed a broad set of features that cover different aspects of search behavior, including the ones described in previous work and some new ones.

[2]We also tried other models, including decision trees, but in this setup the results of different models did not differ much.

Table 4: Generative model search prediction results

Model	AUC
Baseline using query length	0.6710
Baseline using session duration	0.7257
Baseline using user switching rate (smoothed)	0.7306
Generative model (type-I sequences)	0.7058
Generative model (type-II sequences)	0.7081
Semi-supervised model (type-I sequences)	0.7064
Prediction of per-user model only (type-I)	0.6707
Personalized generative model (type-I)	**0.7725**
Personalized generative model (type-II)	0.7624

To build a personalized model we tried several approaches:

- training a separate model for each user and using its prediction as a new feature for a global training;
- encoding information about the user directly into the feature set as binary "user id" features (the total number of features becomes very large);
- calculating different statistics based on each user's sessions and using these statistics in the feature set separately as well as for normalizing other features (e.g. query clickthrough rate normalized by the average query clickthrough rate for this user). Statistics can be further calculated for users' switch and non-switch sessions separately to learn more about user behavior in both cases. Yet we need to use a separate set from the training set for computing such statistics to avoid overfitting. Therefore, we splitted the sessions from days 1-24 into two sets: a statistics set (sessions from days 1-21) and a training set (sessions from days 22-24). Then, from the training set we removed sessions by users who never switched during the statistics period, similarly as how the test set was created in the challenge setting.

4.3.1 Feature Description

The feature set we developed includes 414 features. Some of them are very similar to each other, only with different smoothing, normalization or other variations. Table 5 provides a summary of the features (not a complete list). The Python code generating the features is available online[3].

The features belong to one of the three groups:

1. features based on the current session only, e.g. session duration (in time units, in queries and in clicks), number of unique and abandoned queries (queries without clicks), average/min/max click dwell time and pause between actions (pause between issuing a query and the next action was also considered), average click position, number of SAT/DSAT clicks (as defined in Table 1), and some more.
2. features based on statistics computed from all switch/non-switch sessions in the statistics period.
3. features based on statistics computed from user-specific switch/non-switch sessions in the statistics period.

The later two groups of features are calculated on the statistics dataset. They can be grouped into three subsets:

[3]http://mathcs.emory.edu/~dsavenk/switch_detect/

- all features in group 1 normalized by the corresponding average statistics calculated across all switching/non-switching sessions (features in group 2) and across user-specific switching/non-switching sessions (features in group 3). This gives us four differently normalized versions for each feature in group 1.
- switching probability of a user/query/url. Different users have different switching probabilities. The same is true for different search tasks. To include search task related switching probability we considered queries and urls separately. For each query we calculated the number of times the query was issued before (immediately or earlier in a session) a switch in a session.
- features based on action sequences or search trails, including probabilities of this sequence appearing in switch/non-switch sessions, probabilities of this sequence under the Markov model with transition probabilities estimated on switch/non-switch sessions, and finally statistics based on all n-grams (2,3,4-grams) of this sequence, namely average ratio of their frequencies in switch and non-switch sessions.

4.3.2 Learning Algorithms

For our experiments we used the logistic regression algorithm (scikit-learn[4] implementation [16]) and the gradient boosting tree algorithm (pGBRT[5] implementation [19]).

5. EVALUATION

5.1 Personalization Performance

To test the performance we used the holdout validation set, which covers the sessions in days 25-27. Sessions in the previous 3 days (days 22-24) were used for training and the rest of the dataset (days 1-21) was used to calculate the aggregated statistics[6].

The results of the personalization approaches described in Section 4.3 are presented in Table 6. When building a model per user in the first approach we used the logistic regression (with L1-regularization and parameter C=1.0). In the second approach the number of features becomes very large and we were unable to train a gradient boosting model, so the result reported was also obtained by training a logistic regression model. In the third approach a gradient boosting tree algorithm was applied (with 400 iterations, maximum tree depth = 5 and learning rate = 0.1). For comparison purposes we also provided the performance of the logistic regression model in the same setting.

The first and second personalization methods (per-user model prediction as a feature and user ids as features) are prone to overfitting. The dataset contains a lot of users with just a few sessions (which is also true in general) and thus such models do not have good generalization properties. On the other hand, the third approach which utilizes statistics aggregated over user-specific switch and non-switch sessions significantly outperforms the other two. This model is also easier to implement in practice. It does not require building a separate model whenever a new user arrives and not

[4]http://scikit-learn.org/

[5]http://machinelearning.wustl.edu/pmwiki.php/Main/Pgbrt

[6]Increasing the size of the training set by reducing the statistics period did not improve the performance of the models.

Table 5: Features used for switching detection (not a complete list)

Features based on current session only
q_count - number of queries
c_count - number of clicks
time_to_1click - time to first click in a session (or large value if no clicks)
q_abandoned - number of abandoned queries
dwell - average, max, min dwell times of clicks
duration - session duration (in time units and in actions - queries and clicks)
pause - mean, min, max pause between actions in session
unique_queries - number of unique queries issued in a session
(d)sat_clicks - number of sat/dsat clicks
ave_click_pos - average click position (11 if no clicks)
time_between_clicks - average time between clicks
last_action - is the last action a query or a click
Features based on all switch/non-switch sessions
all above features normalized by the corresponding average statistics calculated across all switching/non-switching sessions
q_switch_freq - frequency of a query occuring before switch in a session (max, mean, min over queries in a session)
q_ctr - ctr (sat, dsat, last) of a query (max, mean, min over queries)
q_ave_clickpos - average click position for a query (max, mean, min over queries)
q_freq - query frequency (max, mean, min over queries)
clicked_url_ctr - ctr (sat, dsat, last) of a clicked url (max, mean, min over all clicked urls in a session)
url_switch_freq - frequency of a clicked url apperaring before switch in a session (max, mean, min over all clicked urls)
markov_models - probability of the action sequence by Markov models estimated on switch/non-switch sessions
n-grams - average ratio of frequencies of the sequence n-grams in switch and non-switch sessions
seq_prob - probability of this exact action sequence appearing in switch/non-switch sessions
Features based on user-specific switch/non-switch sessions
all session-based features normalized by the corresponding average statistics calculated across all user's switch/non-switch sessions
all average statistics of session features computed over this user's switch/non-switch sessions
user_switch_prob - number of user sessions with a switching + 1 divided by the total number of user sessions + 10
user_switch_prob_periods - similar to *user_switch_prob* but computed for each 3-day period within the statistics period
user_last(middle,toolbar,serp)_switch_prob - number of user sessions with a switch (last/middle in session or of toolbar/serp type) divided by the total number of user sessions
user_session_count - number of sessions of this user in the statistics period
ave_time_to_switch - average time to switch for this user

Table 6: Performance of different personalization approaches

Method	AUC
Overall statistics used in feature set (boosting)	0.7782
Per-user model prediction as feature	0.7753
User ids as binary features	0.7587
User statistics used in feature set (boosting)	**0.8413**
User statistics used in feature set (logistic)	0.8348

require rebuilding a model to add a new user id. Note that the gradient boosting algorithm performed better than the logistic regression algorithm in this same setting, thanks to the power of the former algorithm to catch the non-linear interactions between the features.

Figure 4 shows how the prediction quality depends on the size of user's history (number of sessions), for personalized and non-personalized approaches. We chose the best-performing third personalization method using the gradient boosting algorithm and its non-personalized counterpart (the only difference is that all features depending on user-specific statistics are ignored) for this comparison. As we can see the personalized approach improves prediction performance for all kinds of users and the more information we have the better the result we can achieve. We do not have users without history in our dataset, but even if we have just one session we can still learn something from it and improve the results. The performance of the non-personalized approach also improves as the number of sessions in user history grows. The reasons could be that users who rarely use the search engine have different behavior from users who frequently use the search engine, and that sessions by different user groups have different level of individual differences in behavior.

5.2 Individual Feature Importance

Table 7 presents the importance scores for some of the features. We chose two scores: information gain and Gini index based score calculated on the boosting trees ensemble (denoted as boosting score). Only a couple of features from each group are presented in the table. The ranks of the features in the list are computed by the boosting score.

The analysis shows that the most important signals for switch detection are sequence n-gram statistics, user switching frequency, and average click position. Interestingly, the average click position feature is ranked 3rd by the boosting score but much worse (123th) by the information gain. This feature can be an indicator of both difficult search tasks and tasks requiring more coverage. Sequence features

Table 7: Feature importance scores (ranks are computed based on the boosting score)

Rank	Feature	Information gain	Boosting score
1	*user_typeII_3gram* - a ratio of 3-gram (type-II, see above) counts in user's switch and non-switch sessions averaged over all 2-grams in a search trail	0.0350	0.0230
2	*user_switches_count* - total number of switches in user's sessions during the statistics period	0.0194	0.0222
3	*ave_click_pos* - average position of clicks in a session	0.0149	0.0219
4	*user_switch_prob* - smoothed user's switching rate in sessions from the statistics period	0.0309	0.0184
11	*typeII_3gram* - a ratio of 3-gram counts in all switch and non-switch sessions from the statistics period averaged over all 3-grams in a search trail	0.0290	0.0134
12	*time_to_1click_user_normalized* - time to the first click in a session normalized by average time to the first click in user's non-switch sessions	0.0103	0.0129
14	*abandoned_to_ave_abandoned* - number of abandoned queries normalized by average number of abandoned queries in user's non-switch sessions	0.0229	0.0114
15	*unique queries* - number of unique queries in a session	0.0204	0.0114
21	*ave_clickedurl_switchprob* - number of times a user switched after (later in a session) clicking on the given url divided by the total number of clicks on this url averaged over all clicked urls in the session	0.0100	0.0103
22	*min_pause_user_switch* - minimum pause in a session normalized by average minimum pause in user's switch sessions	0.0016	0.0101
27	*ave_time_to_switch* - average time before switching in user's sessions	0.0026	0.0092
30	*time_1click* - time to first click in a session	0.0078	0.0082
42	*sat_clicks* - number of sat clicks in a session	0.0046	0.0069
51	*user_ave_query_switchprob* - number of times the user switched after issuing the given query divided by the total number of times the query was asked averaged over all queries in the session	0.0013	0.0059
64	*session_duration* - duration of the session in time units	0.0182	0.0050
291	*query_nonswitchprob* - number of time a query was asked and there was no switch afterwards in the session divided by the total number of times the query was asked averaged over all queries in a session	0.0001	0.0000

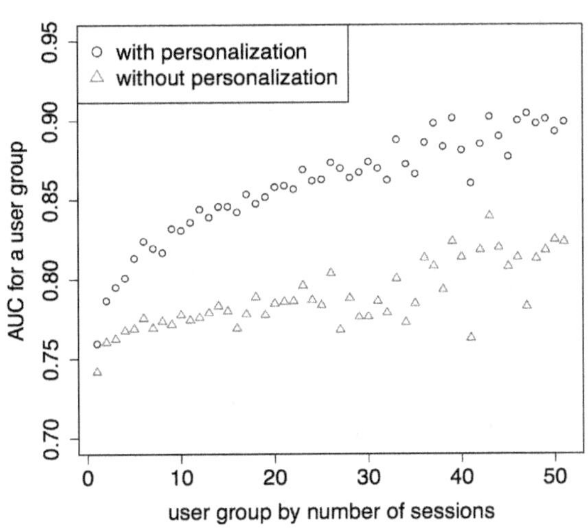

Figure 4: AUC for users with different size of search history (number of sessions)

placed at the top of the ranked list, suggesting that Markov models, whole sequence frequencies and n-gram statistics are all useful. Comparing the two types of sequences, we found that features calculated based on type-II sequences are ranked best, which means that encoding different dimensions of time information (i.e., distinguishing different lengths of pause after a query and of pause after a click separately) is useful, which supports the previous researches. It was surprising that url switching statistics (probability that a session contains a switch after a click on the given url) are more important than query switching statistics. The possible explanation is that some urls "suggest" users to try another search engine. Unfortunately we couldn't explore this deeper because the dataset is anonymized and actual urls are not available. Another reason could be sparsity of the statistics: only $\sim$ 48 % of the queries shown in sessions from the validation period were also asked at least once in the training/statistics period, and $\sim$ 67% of urls clicked during the validation period were also clicked at least once during the training period.

As the analysis showed that n-gram features are among the most useful predictors, we decided to look at some n-grams in more details. Table 8 shows some 3-grams over type-II sequences ranked by the ratio of their frequencies in switch and non-switch sessions. We can see that 3-grams with Q (queries with long pause) tend to occur more frequently in switch sessions, and on the contrary 3-grams with S (SAT clicks) are indicators of non-switch sessions.

5.3 Feature Group Importance

To investigate how features interact with each other we analyzed the prediction performance for each of the feature groups described in Chapter 4.3.1. A special interest is to see which of the following is the most important: frequency of switches for users, queries, urls or search trails. Therefore, we considered another way to group features into five dis-

Table 8: 3-grams ranked by the ratio of frequencies to appear in switching and non-switching sessions

3-gram	Ratio	3-gram	Ratio
QKQ	1.6332	qSS	0.2096
KQQ	1.5983	SSS	0.2107
QQQ	1.5895	SSP	0.2449
QQK	1.5259	SPS	0.2568
KQK	1.4143	SSD	0.2649
KKQ	1.4041	PSS	0.2697
...	...	...	...
qqq	0.4384	DDD	0.4194

joint sets: 1) features based on session statistics[7] (duration, number of queries, number of clicks, etc); 2) features based on user statistics[8] (user switch probability and some modification); 3) features based on query statistics (frequency of switches after a given query, ctr of queries in a session, etc); 4) features based on url statistics (frequency of switches after a given url is clicked in a session, ctr of clicked urls in a session, etc); and 5) features based on action sequence statistics (Markov model probabilities, n-gram statistics, etc).

Based on the above two ways of feature grouping, we conducted a series of feature ablation experiments. Table 9 shows the prediction performance when providing a single feature group or when providing all feature groups except the given one. Among the first set of feature groups, overall statistics features alone are more effective than session features alone, which verifies our intuition that aggregated statistics on a separate period helps with switching prediction. Moreover, user-specific statistics features gave even more signals for predicting switches. This single feature group run achieved 98.1% of the validation AUC obtained by training on all features. And removal of this feature group resulted in a significant drop in prediction quality (from 0.8413 to 0.7782).

Among the second set of feature groups, the most effective ones are session statistics features and sequence features. Here we also see that url switching statistics features alone obtained better AUC than user statistic features alone (e.g. user switching frequency). Query statistic features alone resulted in significantly worse performance in predicting switches. On the other hand, results of runs with a feature group removed are very close to each other, indicating that signals in each of the five feature groups could be covered to a certain extent by other four feature groups.

In Figure 5 we plotted the precision and recall curve for the positive class (switch sessions) for models with different subsets of features. It shows that for the switching detection task, high precision (e.g., 0.78) could be achieved at the cost of recall (e.g., 0.1). Also the figure suggests that adding personalized statistics improves the prediction quality significantly as you can see a gap between curves with and without personalized statistics.

5.4 Model Tuning

Considering the training set is imbalanced (only 10% of the sessions contain switches and the rest are sessions without a switch), we tried two approaches to balance the dataset, namely increasing the weight of positive examples and subsampling the negative examples. The results for both approaches are summarized in Table 10. In addition, to reduce the variance of the prediction model, an averaging approach was applied. Models for seven different time splits (e.g., days 1-3 as training period while days 4-24 as statistics period, days 4-6 as training period while days 1-3,7-24 as statistics period, etc) were built and average of the individual model predictions was used as the final score. As the results show, these strategies improve the prediction performance.

[7]Note that session statistics features here included all the normalized versions by the corresponding average statistics computed in the statistics period.

[8]Note that user statistics features here did not include those relying on queries, urls, or action sequences in the session.

Table 9: Feature ablation experiments

Feature group	Training AUC	Validation AUC
Single feature group runs		
Session features	0.7563	0.7491
Overall statistics features	0.7853	0.7777
User-specific statistics features	0.8381	0.8253
Session statistics features	0.8298	0.8183
User statistics features	0.7503	0.7273
Query statistics features	0.6480	0.6352
Url statistics features	0.7488	0.7396
Sequence statistics features	0.8062	0.7952
Without feature group runs		
Session features	0.8532	0.8326
Overall statistics features	0.8371	0.8290
User-specific statistics features	0.7882	0.7782
Session statistics features	0.8453	0.8348
User statistics features	0.8490	0.8289
Query statistics features	0.8529	0.8380
Url statistics features	0.8466	0.8273
Sequence statistics features	0.8517	0.8397
All features	0.8534	0.8413

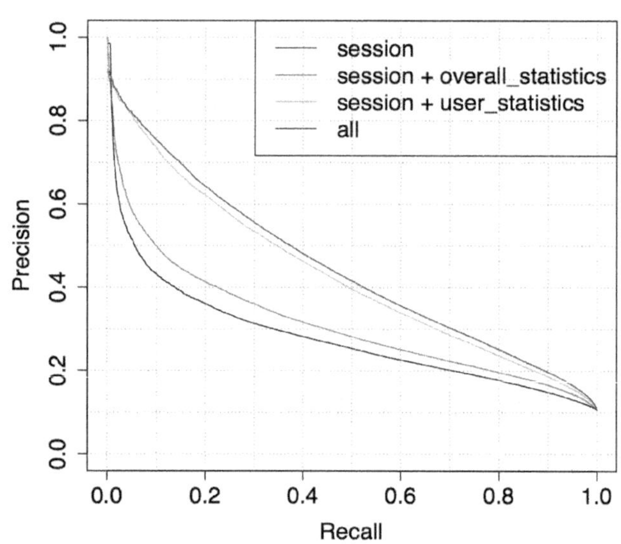

Figure 5: Precision-Recall curve for the positive class (switch sessions)

Table 10: Results for dataset balancing and model averaging

	Train AUC	Validation AUC
No balancing	0.8473	0.8403
Pos weight = 4	0.8534	0.8413
Subsampling	0.8490	0.8412
Model trained on d22-24	0.8534	0.8413
Averaging 8 models	-	**0.8450**

5.5 Comparison with Other Models

As baselines we decided to use the following algorithms: ranking by session length in queries, by session duration in time and by user switching rate on a separate period. Table 11 compares results of our model with other known algorithms. Unfortunately, some of the features described in [10] and [20] cannot be calculated base on our fully anonymized dataset, thus we included just a subset of the described features. Most of them were already a part of the feature set used for this work. We should mention that in [20] the online switch prediction problem is solved, i.e. given a part of a session predict if the next action is a switch. This problem is different from (probably more difficult than) the offline detection of switching, and thus we were unable to get high AUC score with this online model. To train it we used gradient boosting tree algorithm (200 iterations, depth = 5 and learning rate = 0.1).

Table 11: Comparison of different switching detection algorithms

Model	AUC
Baseline using query length	0.6710
Baseline using session duration	0.7257
Baseline using user switching rate (smoothed)	0.7306
Semi-supervised model from [10]	0.7081
Personalized generative model (type-I)	0.7725
Online prediction model trained on subset of features from [20]	0.7206
Our personalized model	**0.8450**

The results in Table 11 show that the developed personalized switching prediction model outperforms other known models for the switching detection task. Another interesting observation is the performance of the baselines. On our task and dataset, session duration and user switch rate predictors show better performance than the generative model. And user switching rate is the strongest baseline, which proves that switching behavior depends highly on user habits. Yandex Switching detection challenge also proved competitiveness of the presented personalized model as this method placed 1st out about $\sim$ 100 teams.

6. DISCUSSION AND IMPLICATIONS

A primary focus of this research has been a better detection of search engine switches inside a session using personalized models. We showed that users have different behavior patterns and habits when using web search and mostly ignored personal statistics information is very useful for understanding search logs. Tables 2 and 3 show an example of differences between "average" search behavior and behavior of a particular user. There are other examples, which support the idea that users do have different search behavior and we can benefit from learning behavior of each individual user. A simple baseline model, which predicts probability of a session to contain switching action based on how frequent the given user switched before performed as good as some other more complicated models. Learning more about user's behavior can also help improve performance of existing models. As an example, we trained a personalized version of one of the recently proposed models [10] - a generative model for satisfaction prediction and applied it to switching detection. Personalized model allows to achieve 9.45% improvement over non-personalized model.

Another common approach to switching detection is a machine learning based approach. To learn how personalization would affect such models we developed a set of features which include some of previously studied signals as well as some other predictors and applied a gradient boosting tree algorithm to learn a detector for session containing switching actions. In this paper we presented 3 possible personalization approaches, namely training a model for each user as well as a global model, using user id as a feature and calculating rich aggregated statistics based on user-specific sessions as both independent features and normalizers for other features. Unfortunately the first two approaches didn't show any improvement as models became overfitted, but the last approach allowed us to get a 8.1% improvement over a similar model trained on unpersonalized feature set. Our analysis showed that features based on user's statistics are among the most important features. The features ablation experiments also support the conclusion on usefulness of user's statistics. The group of features obtained by considering statistics collected on user's previous switching and non-switching sessions performed better than the others and removal of this group leads to significant decline in prediction quality.

A possible problem with this approach is the sparsity of the statistics, as just a small fraction of users have good search history. But as Figure 4 suggests even for users with small history the model still does good prediction which is even better then for non-personalized model. The same experiment shows that the more history we have the better (we only had enough data to look at users with up to 50 sessions), but the grows in the prediction performance stabilizes after as few as 10 sessions in user's history.

We believe that the features we designed and the personalization approach we used can be useful in some other tasks, like user satisfaction prediction, relevance prediction from click logs, etc. For example, some users click on more results without paying too much attention to snippets and some may examine results longer than others. This means that the clicks of these users may weight differently when estimating results relevance.

7. CONCLUSIONS

In this paper we presented a personalized approach to search engine switching prediction. The approach allows a model to learn user's personal behavior patterns in switching and non-switching sessions and use this information to improve the prediction performance. We showed that some existing models can benefit from using personalized information, e.g. the recently proposed generative markov model for user satisfaction prediction, when applied to switching detection problem, can be improved by learning per-user models. We also designed a machine learning approach which utilizes several kinds of personalized and aggregated statistics, collected on a period separate from the training set. All the features were designed to help learning different users' switching habits and behavior patterns as well as different reasons for switching (i.e. dissatisfaction and necessity in better coverage). We demonstrated that personalized statistics and session feature normalization allow to improve switching prediction quality significantly. We believe that our approach can also be used in other log mining tasks such as search success prediction and document relevance prediction.

8. ACKNOWLEDGMENTS

This work was supported by the NSF grant IIS-1018321, the DARPA grant D11AP00269, and the Yahoo! Faculty Research Engagement Program.

9. REFERENCES

[1] M. Ageev, Q. Guo, D. Lagun, and E. Agichtein. Find It If You Can: A Game for Modeling Different Types of Web Search Success Using Interaction Data. In *Proc. of SIGIR'11*, pages 345–354, New York, New York, USA, July 2011. ACM Press.

[2] E. Agichtein, E. Brill, and S. Dumais. Improving web search ranking by incorporating user behavior information. In *Proceedings of the 29th annual international ACM SIGIR conference on Research and development in information retrieval*, SIGIR '06, pages 19–26, New York, NY, USA, 2006. ACM.

[3] A. Aula, R. M. Khan, and Z. Guan. How does search behavior change as search becomes more difficult? In *Proceedings of the SIGCHI Conference on Human Factors in Computing Systems*, CHI '10, pages 35–44, New York, NY, USA, 2010. ACM.

[4] P. N. Bennett, R. W. White, W. Chu, S. T. Dumais, P. Bailey, F. Borisyuk, and X. Cui. Modeling the impact of short- and long-term behavior on search personalization. In *Proceedings of the 35th international ACM SIGIR conference on Research and development in information retrieval*, SIGIR '12, pages 185–194, New York, NY, USA, 2012. ACM.

[5] G. Buscher, R. W. White, S. Dumais, and J. Huang. Large-scale analysis of individual and task differences in search result page examination strategies. In *Proceedings of the fifth ACM international conference on Web search and data mining*, WSDM '12, pages 373–382, New York, NY, USA, 2012. ACM.

[6] H. Cao, D. Jiang, J. Pei, Q. He, Z. Liao, E. Chen, and H. Li. Context-aware query suggestion by mining click-through and session data. In *Proceedings of the 14th ACM SIGKDD international conference on Knowledge discovery and data mining*, KDD '08, pages 875–883, New York, NY, USA, 2008. ACM.

[7] G. Dupret and C. Liao. A model to estimate intrinsic document relevance from the clickthrough logs of a web search engine. In *Proceedings of the third ACM international conference on Web search and data mining*, WSDM '10, pages 181–190, New York, NY, USA, 2010. ACM.

[8] H. A. Feild, J. Allan, and R. Jones. Predicting searcher frustration. In *Proc. of SIGIR'10*, pages 34–41, New York, New York, USA, July 2010. ACM Press.

[9] Q. Guo, R. White, Y. Zhang, B. Anderson, and S. Dumais. Why searchers switch: understanding and predicting engine switching rationales. In *Proc. of SIGIR'11*, pages 335–344, 2011.

[10] A. Hassan. A semi-supervised approach to modeling web search satisfaction. In *Proc. of SIGIR'12*, pages 275–284, New York, NY, USA, 2012. ACM.

[11] A. Hassan, R. Jones, and K. L. Klinkner. Beyond DCG: User Behavior as a Predictor of a Successful Search. In *Proc. of WSDM'10*, pages 221–230, New York, New York, USA, Feb. 2010. ACM Press.

[12] A. Hassan, Y. Song, and L.-w. He. A task level metric for measuring web search satisfaction and its application on improving relevance estimation. In *Proc. of CIKM'11*, pages 125–134, New York, New York, USA, Oct. 2011. ACM Press.

[13] A. Heath and R. White. Defection detection: Predicting search engine switching. In *Proc. of WWW'08*, pages 1173–1174, 2008.

[14] S. Laxman, V. Tankasali, and R. W. White. Stream prediction using a generative model based on frequent episodes in event sequences. In *Proc. of SIGKDD'08*, pages 453–461, New York, New York, USA, Aug. 2008. ACM Press.

[15] C. Ling, J. Huang, and H. Zhang. Auc: a statistically consistent and more discriminating measure than accuracy. In *International Joint Conference on Artificial Intelligence*, volume 18, pages 519–526, 2003.

[16] F. Pedregosa, G. Varoquaux, A. Gramfort, V. Michel, B. Thirion, O. Grisel, M. Blondel, P. Prettenhofer, R. Weiss, V. Dubourg, J. Vanderplas, A. Passos, D. Cournapeau, M. Brucher, M. Perrot, and E. Duchesnay. Scikit-learn: Machine Learning in Python . *Journal of Machine Learning Research*, 12:2825–2830, 2011.

[17] S. Shen, B. Hu, W. Chen, and Q. Yang. Personalized click model through collaborative filtering. In *Proceedings of the fifth ACM international conference on Web search and data mining*, WSDM '12, pages 323–332, New York, NY, USA, 2012. ACM.

[18] D. Sontag, K. Collins-Thompson, P. N. Bennett, R. W. White, S. Dumais, and B. Billerbeck. Probabilistic models for personalizing web search. In *Proceedings of the fifth ACM international conference on Web search and data mining*, WSDM '12, pages 433–442, New York, NY, USA, 2012. ACM.

[19] S. Tyree, K. Weinberger, K. Agrawal, and J. Paykin. Parallel boosted regression trees for web search ranking. In *Proc. of WWW'11*, pages 387–396. ACM.

[20] R. White and S. Dumais. Characterizing and predicting search engine switching behavior. In *Proc. of CIKM'09*, pages 87–96. ACM, 2009.

[21] R. White, A. Kapoor, and S. Dumais. Modeling long-term search engine usage. *User Modeling, Adaptation, and Personalization*, pages 28–39, 2010.

[22] R. W. White and S. M. Drucker. Investigating behavioral variability in web search. In *Proceedings of the 16th international conference on World Wide Web*, WWW '07, pages 21–30, New York, NY, USA, 2007. ACM.

Emerging Topic Detection for Organizations from Microblogs

Yan Chen[*]
State Key Laboratory of Software Development Environment
Beihang University, China
chenyan@cse.buaa.edu.cn

Hadi Amiri
School of Computing
National University of Singapore, Singapore
hadi@comp.nus.edu.sg

Zhoujun Li
State Key Laboratory of Software Development Environment
Beihang University, China
lizj@buaa.edu.cn

Tat-Seng Chua
School of Computing
National University of Singapore, Singapore
chuats@comp.nus.edu.sg

ABSTRACT

Microblog services have emerged as an essential way to strengthen the communications among individuals and organizations. These services promote timely and active discussions and comments towards products, markets as well as public events, and have attracted a lot of attentions from organizations. In particular, emerging topics are of immediate concerns to organizations since they signal current concerns of, and feedback by their users. Two challenges must be tackled for effective emerging topic detection. One is the problem of real-time relevant data collection and the other is the ability to model the emerging characteristics of detected topics and identify them before they become hot topics. To tackle these challenges, we first design a novel scheme to crawl the relevant messages related to the designated organization by monitoring multi-aspects of microblog content, including users, the evolving keywords and their temporal sequence. We then develop an incremental clustering framework to detect new topics, and employ a range of content and temporal features to help in promptly detecting hot emerging topics. Extensive evaluations on a representative real-world dataset based on Twitter data demonstrate that our scheme is able to characterize emerging topics well and detect them before they become hot topics.

*This work was done when the first author was a visiting scholar in the National University of Singapore.

SIGIR'13, July 28–August 1, 2013, Dublin, Ireland.

Categories and Subject Descriptors

H.0 [**Information Systems**]: General; H.3.5 [**Information Storage and Retrieval**]: Online Information Services

General Terms

Algorithms, Experimentation

Keywords

Microblog Service, Emerging Topic Detection, Brand Monitoring, Organization Monitoring

1. INTRODUCTION

Microblog services such as Twitter and Weibo provide an essential platforms for users to convey their thoughts, exchange their opinions and share their experiences. One key reason leading to their popularity is their real-time nature. On these platforms, individuals update their status regarding various topics, spanning from "what are they doing" (Twitter), to " what are on their mind" (Facebook), and this is conveyed instantaneously to their friends. This greatly strengthens inter-personal exchange and cooperation.

Besides facilitating communications among individuals, microblog services also explicitly or implicitly contain rich information towards organizations, such as banks, universities, and government organizations, etc. Many organizations are keen on continually mining and analyzing these user-generated social data due to the following reasons. First, social data contains the interests, concerns and criticisms of their users, and provides pointers for organizations to improve their products or services. Second, social data implicitly contains invaluable market insights for the organizations. The primary foundation of these high-level applications is based on topic monitoring and tracking. Specifically, organizations would like to: (1) track the evolution of any identified relevant topics about them; and (2) be informed of any new emerging topics which are fast gathering momentum in microblogs.

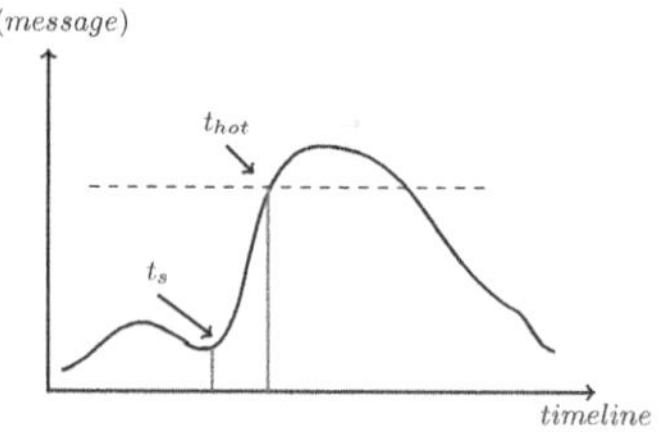

Figure 1: The key phases of an hot emerging topic.

Several threads of research have been done on emerging topic detection. They can roughly be grouped into three categories. The first is based on traditional topic detection methods to identify new terms [12, 6, 21]. The second is to utilize topic model to learn a dynamic word distribution or topic transition [24]. The last is to detect novel topic-related words by dictionary learning methods [11, 19]. However, the definition of "emerging" in previous literature focuses only on the novelty of topics, and they mainly model the novel words based on word co-occurrences within the topics. In this work, we extend the definition of "emerging" to incorporate temporal aspect of timeliness. In other words, we want to detect emerging topics that are not only novel, but also those that will become hot and viral in the near future. This presents an additional challenge to model the temporal characteristics of topics in real-time.

Figure 1 presents the evolution of a hot topic starting from the time that it is detected (t_s), to the time that it becomes hot (t_{hot}). The period from t_s to t_{hot} is known as the emerging phase. We expect to identify this topic as hot and emerging before t_{hot}.

However, emerging topic detection for organizations from microblog context faces several challenges. The first challenge is the dilemma of relevant data collection. This is a challenging issue as most live microblog services impose limits on the amount and frequency of data that can be crawled[1]. This, in conjunction with the low ratio of relevant data in microblog content, results in missing relevant data about the organizations. The second challenge is on modeling of topics with effective features to facilitate the detection of hot topics during the emerging phase.

To address these two challenges, we design a novel scheme to monitor and collect microblog messages (tweets) about organizations as well as detect the hot emerging topics promptly. It comprises two stages as illustrated in Figure 2. The first stage aims to gather rich social data with good coverage for a designated organization. Specifically, given a specific organization, we collect data in multiple aspects from four sources including fixed keywords, emerging keywords, known accounts and key users of the organization. All the crawled data is then sent to a binary SVM classifier, which discriminates the relevant tweets from the huge amount of irrelevant ones. During this process, an organization user network is also maintained based upon the existing relationships[2] between users within the organization. The second stage first employs the well-known incremental clustering algorithms [25, 2] to discover topics in real time. It then analyzes the emerging topic-related features including user authority, tweets influence, and organization attributes such as the emerging keywords. These features are then incorporated into the topic learner to identify hot emerging topics in a timely manner.

[1]This limit is, for each request, "up to 1%" of Firehose tweets for the streaming API of Twitter.

[2]The existing relationship includes the follower, followee and friends, etc.

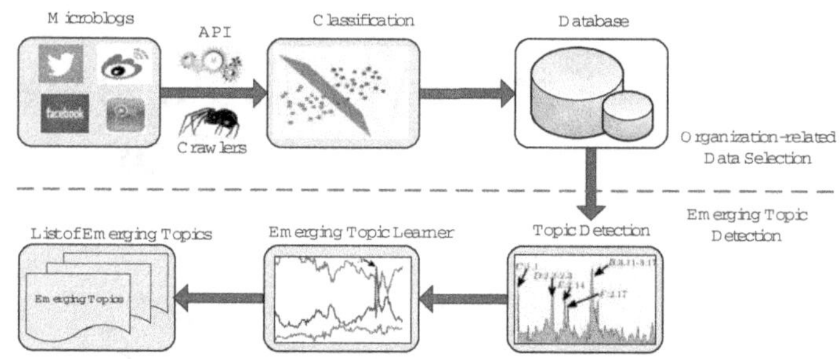

Figure 2: The overview of our framework.

The main contributions of this paper are as follows:

- We design a crawling strategy that incorporates multiple aspects of microblog data to obtain more comprehensive organization related data. Based on the collected data, we detect organization related topics.
- We build two effective semi-supervised models to detect hot emerging topics for an organization in a timely manner. To the best of our knowledge, this is the first that targets effective feature extraction for hot emerging topics detection.

The rest of this paper is organized as follows: Section 2 introduces the related work of emerging topic detection. Sections 3 and 4 respectively detail organization-related data selection and emerging topic detection. Our experimental results are presented in Section 5, followed by concluding remarks in Sections 6.

2. RELATED WORK

The popularity of microblog portals like Twitter has enabled hot topics to be quickly propagated to a large number of users over wide geographical regions. Research on detecting emerging and evolving [8, 25] topics[3] of live tweet streams has gained much interest in recent years, and has been applied to a wide variety of applications [7], such as detecting emergencies like earthquakes [20], predicting political election outcomes [22], mining topic and evolution [9], discovering controversial topics from twitter [17], and so on. There are several lines of research in this direction.

One line of research is based on the traditional topic detection approach. From the feature pivot aspects, some keywords based approaches [12] work well on mining tweets about specific topics. While high frequency of terms may be a good indicator for hot topics or trends, it does not identify new of emerging trends. Cataldi et al. [6] defined emerging keywords as those which are frequently used in a given time period, but not in previous ones. They presented an approach to identify emergent keywords and utilized them together with frequently co-occurring words as emerging topics. From the document-pivot aspects, Sayyadi et al. [21] created a keyword graph, and used it to cluster tweets based on various distance and similarity metrics.

Probabilistic latent semantic analysis (PLSA) and Latent Dirichlet Allocation (LDA) [5] are probabilistic methods

[3]Here, topic can be exchangeable with event.

that have found remarkable success in building topic models of static text. Variants of PLSA and LDA have been proposed for online and dynamic topic modeling [4].Wang et al. [23] took advantage of temporal information, and tried to model the topics continuously over time. They learned the dynamic word distributions and trends of topics over time. Wang et al. [24] proposed a Temporal-LDA or TM-LDA method to mine streams of social text such as the Twitter stream for an author, by modeling the topics and topic transitions that naturally arise in such data. Different from the work of [23], TM-LDA focuses more on learning the relationship among topics.

Another line of related research is on dictionary learning and non-probabilistic matrix factorizations based methods. Kasiviswanathan et al. [11] proposed a two stage approach based on the detection and clustering of novel user-generated content. They derived a scalable approach by using the alternating directions method to effectively solve the resulting optimization problems. By extending the above work, Saha and Sindhwani [19] adapted Non-negative Factorization to learn trending topics in the context of social media. They showed that better topic modeling performance can be achieved, when the continuity between topics matrices in consecutive time stamps is taken into account.

Previous research on emerging topic [18, 1] detection mainly focused on keywords and textual content, whereas we aim to find emerging topics with respect to an organization. The major difference is that for entities like organizations, in addition to textual content, user association to the organization and social relations among users of the organization will greatly affect the detection of emerging topics for the organization. These features have not been utilized before due to the focus on general emerging topics.

3. ORGANIZATION-RELATED DATA SELECTION

To perform high-order analytics, it is desirable to collect a relatively complete set of relevant data for the target organization in an effective way. However, such a task is often overwhelmed by the tremendous amount of relevant as well as irrelevant data. To ensure comprehensive data collection, two interconnected observations can be made: (a) users related to organizations are more likely to post tweets related to the organization; and (b) tweets on organization often contain organization related keywords. These two observations enable us to generate descriptive keywords and cues, such as fixed keywords, dynamic keywords, known accounts, and organization keyusers. Accordingly, we design four intelligent crawlers to comprehensively crawl organization relevant data from multiple aspects, as shown in Figure 3. The generation of four aspects of sources are detailed in the following subsections.

3.1 Fixed and Dynamic Keywords Sources

Given the name of the organization, we first manually select a few fixed keywords that uniquely identify the organization, such as the name of the organization, the key terms of its brands, and the name of its CEO, etc. These fixed keywords are used in the streaming based *Fixed Keyword Crawler*.

To elicit a live and more diverse set of relevant tweets about the organization, typically those that do not contain

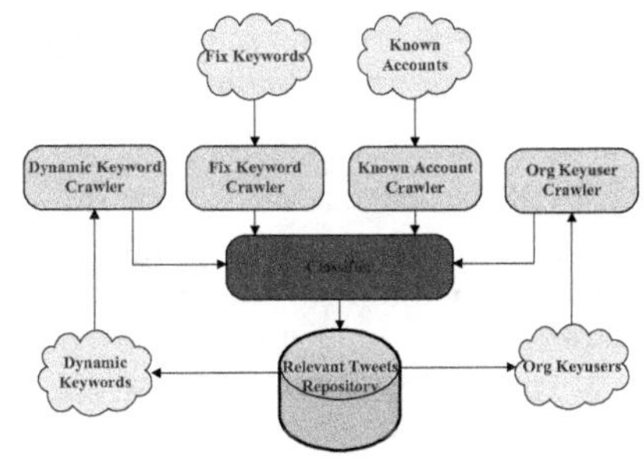

Figure 3: Crawling of data from multi-aspect sources.

the organization keywords, we extract a list of temporally relevant emerging terms about the organizations at each time point t. Emerging terms are defined as those newly introduced terms that are able to represent emerging topics about the organization. To identify these terms, two sets of foreground (S^t_{for}) and background (S^t_{bak}) tweets at each time point t are constructed. All the relevant tweets in the current time slot $[t-T, t]$ are regarded as S^t_{for} tweets, where T is the time interval. While S^t_{bak} covers all the tweets sent during the three time slots of: $[t-2T, t-T]$ of current day, $[t-T, t]$ of previous day, as well as $[t-T, t]$ of one week ago. This definition aims to filter out the time related periodical terms, such as morning, Friday, etc. The vocabulary sets of these two sets of tweets are respectively denoted as, $W^{for} = \{w^{for}_1, w^{for}_2, ...\}$ and $W^{bak} = \{w^{bak}_1, w^{bak}_2, ...\}$. Our goal is to identify the terms that have distinctively different distributions in S^t_{for} and S^t_{bak}. This signals that the term is changing its behavior over time. Specifically, in terms of statistics, given two distributions of a term w_i in S^t_{for} and S^t_{bak}, we expect to disprove the null hypothesis that the two distributions are drawn from the same distribution function to a certain level of significance. Those terms with rising frequencies are the potential emerging keywords, whereas those with decreasing frequencies will gradually disappear. In this work, we use the chi-square test [14] to compare two distributions due to its efficiency and ability to handle rapidly evolving microblog contents. Formally, for each word $w_i \in W^{for}$, its chi-square distribution is:

$$\chi^2_i = \begin{cases} \frac{(f_i-b_i)^2}{b_i} + \frac{[(100-f_i)-(100-b_i)]^2}{100} & \text{if } f_i > b_i; \\ 1 & \text{if } otherwise. \end{cases} \quad (1)$$

where f_i and b_i are the normalized word frequency values of w_i in S^t_{for} and S^t_{bak} respectively, defined as:

$$f_i = 100 \times \frac{w^{for}_i}{\sum_{\forall i} w^{for}_i}, \quad and \quad b_i = 100 \times \frac{w^{bak}_i}{\sum_{\forall i} w^{bak}_i}.$$

Based on the value of χ^2, a list of ordered terms is generated, and the terms in the top N positions are truncated as the dynamic keywords. Each dynamic keyword will be concatenated with the acronym of the target organization to form a specific query for data collection.

3.2 Known Accounts Source

Similar to fixed keywords, we manually identify a set of organization related accounts. These are typically official accounts of the organization on microblog platform that often post relevant tweets about the target organization, such as news about the target organization. These known accounts are monitored by the streaming based *Known Accounts Crawler*.

3.3 Org Keyusers Source

The above mentioned three kinds of crawlers explicitly identify and collect data about the target organization. However, they overlook some important tweets posted by the users related to the organization. The tweets are relevant to the target organization, but in implicit form, i.e., not containing the fixed or emerging keywords. *Org Keyusers Crawler* intends to plug this gap by exploring the sources from the perspective of users. At time t, given a time interval T (such as 24 hours), we obtain a subset of users $U_{\Delta t}$ who post at least one relevant tweets in the time window $\Delta t = [t-T, t]$. Here, we regard org keyusers as those people who post more about the organization and have many followers (a larger influence) in the time window Δt. As mentioned before, an organization user relationship graph G_O is constructed in real time. Nodes of G_O are obtained from the known accounts, and contain all the users who posted at least one organization relevant tweets, as well as their friends and followers. Edges of G_O are obtained by crawling the social relationships between them. In addition, we want to incorporate their activity degree during Δt. The activity degree of a user is proportional to the number of tweets the user sent during Δt. We can compute the authority score of user u_i by incorporating the activity degree of user into graph G_O as follows.

$$auth^k(u_i) = \alpha \sum_{u_j \in follower(u_i)} \frac{auth^{k-1}(u_j)}{|following(u_j)|} + (1-\alpha)\frac{|Tw_{\Delta t}^{u_i}|}{|Tw_{\Delta t}|}. \tag{2}$$

where $\alpha \in (0,1)$ is a damping factor, $following(u_j)$ stands for a set of users that u_j follows, $Tw_{\Delta t}$ represents the relevant tweets in Δt time slot, and $Tw_{\Delta t}^{u_i}$ is the relevant tweets of u_i in Δt. We calculate users' authority score in an iterative manner, i.e., when we calculate the authority value of u_i in the kth iteration, we utilize u_j's $(k-1)$th authority score. We then rank users in $U_{\Delta t}$ by their authority scores and the top N users are selected as the org keyusers.

3.4 Two-class SVM Classification

The data collected from the four sources are a mix of relevant and irrelevant tweets to the organization. In order to filter out the noisy data, we utilize a standard two-class SVM classifier. For the training data, we regard all the tweets from known account source and fixed keyword (rule based to select) source as relevant.

4. EMERGING TOPIC DETECTION

We first present an incremental clustering method to discover topic collections. Through extracting features from topic and organization views, we train two semi-supervised hot emerging topic learners.

4.1 Topic Detection

For our real-time scenario, we need to handle live and large volume of tweets about an organization to detect topics without any prior knowledge of the number of topics, since the topics are constantly evolving and growing in size. Online or incremental clustering algorithms, which are able to handle a constant stream of new tweets, are desirable in our setting, where new tweets are continually being produced. We employ a single-pass incremental clustering algorithm [3] with a threshold τ. At each time t, and within a time interval T, we obtain all tweets D during [t-T, t] in a time order. Such a clustering algorithm considers each tweet in turn and determines the suitable cluster assignment based on a similarity function. The algorithm considers each tweet d_i in order, and computes its similarity $(d_i, Center_j)$ against each existing cluster C_j. If the maximum similarity value is greater than τ, the tweet will be distributed to the cluster, meanwhile the clustering center will be updated. Otherwise, we will generate a new cluster and cluster center. The details of this algorithm are shown in Algorithm 1.

Algorithm 1 Incremental Clustering for Topic Discovery

```
Input: tweet sets D, topic cluster set C, cluster center set Center, and threshold τ.
Output: update topic clusters C, and update cluster centers Center.
Process:
if C = ∅ then
    random select N tweets from D and add into C and Center.
end if
initialize max, tmp_C, tmp_center.
for d_i ∈ D do
    for center_j ∈ Center do
        compute Cosine Similarity sim between center_j and d_i.
        if sim > max then
            max = sim, tmp_C = C_j, tmp_center = center_j.
        end if
    end for
    if max > τ then
        distribute d_i to cluster tmp_C, and update tmp_center.
    else
        new cluster and centroid and add to C and Center.
    end if
end for
return C and Center.
```

4.2 Topic Related Features

In Section 3, we have extracted emerging keywords and org keyusers for the target organization from a global view point. To infer the importance of a topic within an organization, we need to examine also the influence of tweets and users at the local (topic) level.

4.2.1 Topical User Authority

Given a topic tp, there is a set of users related to tp, which is denoted as $U_{tp} = \{u_1, u_2, ..., u_i, ..., u_m\}$. We observe that the authority score of a user with respect to a specific topic $u_i \in U_{tp}$ is related to three factors. u_i will have a larger influence on topic tp if u_i has: (a) posted many tweets about topic tp; (b) posted more tweets retweeted by other users in U_{tp}; and (c) more followers in U_{tp}. Based on this observation, at time t, we can compute the authority score for each topic user $u_i \in U_{tp}$ as follows.

$$auth_{tp}(u_i) = \beta \frac{r_{u_i}}{\sum_j r_{u_j}} + \varphi \frac{f_{u_i}+1}{\sum_j f_{u_j}} + \omega \frac{q_{u_i}+1}{\sum_j q_{u_j}}, \tag{3}$$

where r_{u_i} is the total number of relevant tweets posted by u_i; f_{u_i} is the total number of u_i's followers who exist in U_{tp}; q_{u_i} is the total number of u_i's relevant tweets that has been retweeted by other users; and β, φ and ω are weighting parameters i.e., $\beta + \varphi + \omega = 1$.

4.2.2 *Topical Tweet Influence*

We can also find a set of tweets related to a topic tp, which are defined as $Tw_{tp} = \{tw_1, tw_2, ..., tw_i, ..., tw_n\}$. These tweets are posted by users U_{tp}. There are two intuitions: (a) if a tweet tw_i has a strong influence, it should be propagated to a large scope and be retweeted by a relatively higher number of times; and (b) if the tweet is posted by a topic authority user, it should also have the potential to influence more users. Thus, given a tweet tw_i in topic tp, we employ the number of retweets and authority of users to evaluate its influence, defined as follows.

$$auth_{tp}(tw_i) = \log(1 + auth_{tp}(u_{tw_i})) + \sum_{u \in U_{rtw_i}} \log(1 + auth_{tp}(u)), \tag{4}$$

where $auth_{tp}(tw_i)$ is the influence of tweet tw_i; $auth_{tp}(u_{tw_i})$ is the author of tw_i's authority; and U_{rtw_i} represents the user group that retweets tw_i.

Let $W_{tp} = \{w_1, ..., w_i, ..., w_r\}$ be the set of words that appear in topic tp. For each word w_i in topic tp, we compute its weight $Weight_{tp}(w_i)$ through the influence of tweets that it appears in, as:

$$Weight_{tp}(w_i) = \frac{\sum_{\forall tw_j \in Tw_{tp} \wedge w_i \in tw_j} auth_{tp}(tw_j)}{\sum_{\forall w \in W_{tp}} \sum_{\forall tw \in Tw_{tp} \wedge w \in tw} auth_{tp}(tw)}. \tag{5}$$

We use $Weight_{tp}(w_i)$ to rank the list of topic-related keywords.

4.3 Hot Emerging Topic Learner

In order to identify the hot emerging topics from the topic collection at each time t, we should analyze and extract the emerging features of topics. Given a target organization at time t, from an organization view point, we extract key users and emerging keywords for the target organization, and from a local topic view point, we calculate the authority of users, tweets and keywords for a specific topic. By combining these two views, we extract six representative features for each topic at time t to train the emerging topic learner. The six features with respect to topic tp are defined as follows.

- f_1 is the rate of increase of user number,

$$f_1 = \frac{|U^t|}{\sum_{x=0}^{t} \frac{1}{t-x+1} |U^x|}. \tag{6}$$

- f_2 is the rate of increase of tweets number,

$$f_2 = \frac{|Tw^t|}{\sum_{x=0}^{t} \frac{1}{t-x+1} |Tw^x|}. \tag{7}$$

- f_3 is the rate of increase of re-tweets number,

$$f_3 = \frac{|Rtw^t|}{\sum_{x=0}^{t} \frac{1}{t-x+1} |Rtw^x|}. \tag{8}$$

- f_4 is the overlap between org keyusers and top N influential topic users,

$$f_4 = \frac{\#(ku_{tp} \cap ku)}{\#ku_{tp}}. \tag{9}$$

- f_5 is the overlap between org keywords and top N influential topic keywords, and

$$f_5 = \frac{\#(kw_{tp} \cap kw)}{\#kw_{tp}}. \tag{10}$$

- f_6 represents the rate of increase of influence of the accumulated weight of tweets,

$$f_6 = \frac{|A^t|}{\sum_{x=0}^{t} \frac{1}{t-x+1} |A^x|}, \tag{11}$$

where $A = \frac{\sum_{tw \in Tw_{tp}} auth_{tp}(tw)}{|Tw_{tp}|}$.

These six features were chosen to discriminate an hot emerging topic from the topic collection. For an emerging topic, the number of participating users, the increasing rate of tweets, and the number of retweets are expected to be distinctively higher than the normal topics and that of previous time. Moreover, there are some clues that the key topic users and keywords would have a large overlap with the current org keyusers and dynamic keywords. As tweets are likely to be retweeted, the increasing rate of accumulated weight of tweets are comparatively higher than those in previous time period too.

The design of our learners considers two factors in the microblog domain. (1) Since there are hundreds of clusters for an organization at each time t, the labeling process can be time consuming and labor intensive for all training data. Hence there will be the problem of insufficient training data. (2) There is a problem of imbalance of positive (emerging phase) and negative (not emerging topics or not emerging phase for emerging topics) data, since the vast majority of data are negative instances. Hence the learner must be able to achieve good accuracy in the face of imbalance training data. The above two factors require that the chosen learners should work well under the conditions of sparse and imbalance training data scenario. Thus, we adopt a co-training learner and a semi-supervised ensemble learner for our learning task. We define the training data as $TrainSet = \{(X_l, Y), X_u\}$, where X_l and X_u denote the labeled and unlabeled dataset respectively; and Y represents the label set ($positive(p)$ and $negative(n)$). Our aim is to learn a learner $c : X \mapsto Y$.

4.3.1 *Co-training Learner*

Algorithm 2 Co-training Learner

Input: $TrainSet = \{(X_l, Y), X_u\}$, let $L_1 = L_2 = \{\{(X_l, Y_p)\}, \{(X_l, Y_n)\}\}$ and $|\{(X_l, Y_p)\}| = |\{(X_l, Y_n)\}|$.
Output: $TrainSet = \{(X_l, Y), (X_u, Y)\}$ and two learners c_1 and c_2.
Process:
while Unlabeled dataset $\{X_u\} \neq \emptyset$ **do**
  Train two classifiers: v(1) c_1 from L_1, and v(2) c_2 from L_2.
  Classify unlabeled data with c_1 and c_2 separately.
  Add c_1's k-most-confident (x, c_1(x)) to labeled data L_2.
  Add c_2's k-most-confident (x, c_2(x)) to labeled data L_1.
  Remove these from the unlabeled dataset $\{X_u\}$.
  Update L_1, sampling removing negative instances to keep $|\{(X_{l:L_1}, Y_p)\}| = |\{(X_{l:L_1}, Y_n)\}|$.
  Update L_2, sampling removing negative instances to keep $|\{(X_{l:L_2}, Y_p)\}| = |\{(X_{l:L_2}, Y_n)\}|$.
end while
return c_1 and c_2.

Features of topic tp at time t are divided into two orthogonal views: v(1) the number increasing rate features (f_1, f_2, and f_3); and v(2) the overlap features (f_4 and f_5) and the accumulated weights of increasing rate feature (f_6). We assume that both v(1) and v(2) are orthogonal to each other, and they are sufficient to train reasonably strong classifiers. We then train two basic SVM classifiers based on these two views. The training process is described in Algorithm 2. It is worth noting that in order to account for the imbalance data scenario, the construction of training instance set L (L_1 and L_2) are different from the previous co-training approaches. Here we keep all the positive instances in L, while sample only an equal number of labeled negative instances from the training data into L at each iteration.

4.3.2 *Semi-supervised Ensemble Learner*

As an alternative to co-training, we employ the voting based ensemble learning to train a semi-supervised classifier. Three classifiers (Decision Tree, SVM, and Naive Bayesian) are chosen to learn from the labeled training data to predict the unlabeled training data independently. Their results are used to vote for each unlabeled data instance. The consistent data will be added to the next training iteration, until convergence. Algorithm 3 describes the training process.

Algorithm 3 Ensemble Learner

Input: $TrainSet = \{(X_l, Y), X_u\}$, $L_1 = \{\{(X_l, Y_p)\}, \{X_l : L_1, Y_n\}\}$, $L_2 = \{\{(X_l, Y_p)\}, \{X_l : L_2, Y_n\}\}$, $L_3 = \{\{(X_l, Y_p)\}, \{X_l : L_3, Y_n\}\}$ and if $|\{(X_l, Y_p)\}| = N$, $|\{(X_l : L_1, Y_n)\}| = |\{(X_l : L_2, Y_n)\}| = |\{(X_l : L_3, Y_n)\}| = N$.
Output: $TrainSet = \{(X_l, Y), (X_u, Y)\}$ and ensemble learner c.
Process:
while Unlabeled dataset X_u is used up **do**
  Train three classifiers: c_1 from L_1, c_2 from L_2 and c_3 from L_3.
  Classify unlabeled data with c_1, c_2 and c_3 separately.
  Voting.
  Add consistent results set to L_1, L_2 and L_3.
  Remove these from the unlabeled dataset X_u.
  Update L_1, sampling removing negative instances to keep $|\{(X_{l:L_1}, Y_p)\}| = |\{(X_{l:L_1}, Y_n)\}|$.
  Update L_2, sampling removing negative instances to keep $|\{(X_{l:L_2}, Y_p)\}| = |\{(X_{l:L_2}, Y_n)\}|$.
  Update L_3, sampling removing negative instances to keep $|\{(X_{l:L_3}, Y_p)\}| = |\{(X_{l:L_3}, Y_n)\}|$.
end while
return c.

4.4 Overall Algorithm for Hot Emerging Topic Detection

The overall process of hot emerging topic detection schema is detailed in Algorithm 4. At each time t, topics are discovered by Algorithm 1. For each topic, we extract the desired features and classify it using algorithm 2 or 3. If it is an emerging topic and the cluster id does not exist in $ETSet$, we will record the id and t into $ETSet$, which holds the list of emerging topic candidates.

Algorithm 4 Overall Algorithm of Emerging Topic Detection

Input: Start time point t_0.
Output: Emerging topic list $ETSet$.
Process:
$t = t_0$, and get tweets during $t - \Delta t$ as D.
while $D \neq \emptyset$ **do**
  Detect topic using algorithm 1, and get topic cluster set C at t.
  for each topic $C_i, i = 1, \ldots$ **do**
    Extract features of C_i.
    Label C_i using algorithm 2 or 3 into p or n.
    if C_i labeled with p and $id \notin ETSet$ **then**
      Add id and time point t of C_i into $ETSet$.
    end if
  end for
  $t = t + \Delta t$.
  Get tweets as D from $t - \Delta t$.
end while
return $ETSet$.

5. EXPERIMENTS

5.1 Datasets, Ground Truth and Settings

In order to evaluate our approach, experiments were conducted on a real life dataset crawled for three organizations of different nature in Singapore. They are *StarHub*[4], Development Bank of Singapore (*DBS*)[5] and National University of Singapore (*NUS*)[6]. These three organizations cover local telecommunication company (*StarHub*), the university (*NUS*), and a cross-border bank (*DBS*). We use twitter API[7] to collect the datasets that contain 51K, 130K, and 142K tweets from 15K, 44K and 36K users for the above three organizations respectively. Because there is no benchmark for our emerging topic detection task, we generate the ground truth of hot emerging topics by adopting the following procedures.

(1) We manually align the topics with online news and labeled the topic as hot emerging topic if its relevant tweets number at least doubled in the future 24 hours after its detection. Finally we obtain 24, 17 and 5 hot emerging topics respectively for the three organizations.

(2) For each hot emerging topic, we label two time points: t_s and t_{hot}, the start of the topic and the time when topic becomes hot, respectively (see Figure 1). t_s is the first time slot in which the emerging topic is detected. t_{hot} represents a time slot in which tweets number exceeds a threshold. A middle point t_{mid} between t_s and t_{hot} is also computed automatically.

The statistics about the datasets for the three organizations are detailed in Table 1. We list the time duration of data collection as well as hot emerging topic numbers. Table 1 also lists the initial period of data that we used for training. In our system, the numbers of org keyusers and dynamic keywords are set to 100 and 50 respectively, in order to limit the crawling resources required to monitor the keyusers and keywords. We empirically set the thresholds $\tau = 0.7$, $\alpha = 0.6$ and $\beta = \varphi = \omega = 0.33$. The two-class SVM and dynamic keywords mining are performed at intervals of every half an hour, while the org keyusers mining are performed at every 24 hour intervals. The time interval used for topic and emerging topic detection (Algorithm 4) is 1-hour.

5.2 Results and Analysis

Because of the lack of space, we only detail our experi-

[4]http://www.starhub.com/
[5]http://www.dbs.com.sg/
[6]http://www.nus.edu.sg/
[7]https://dev.twitter.com/docs/api

Table 1: Statistics for organizations

Organization	Time Duration	#Tweets	#Users	#Emerging Topic	Training Time Duration	#Training Emerging Topic
StarHub	10 Oct-9 Nov, 2012	51,708	15,792	24	10-22 Oct, 2012	10
DBS	15 Oct-14 Nov, 2012	130,791	44,454	17	15-28 Oct, 2012	8
NUS	14-27 Oct, 2012	142,091	36,973	5	14-20 Oct, 2012	2

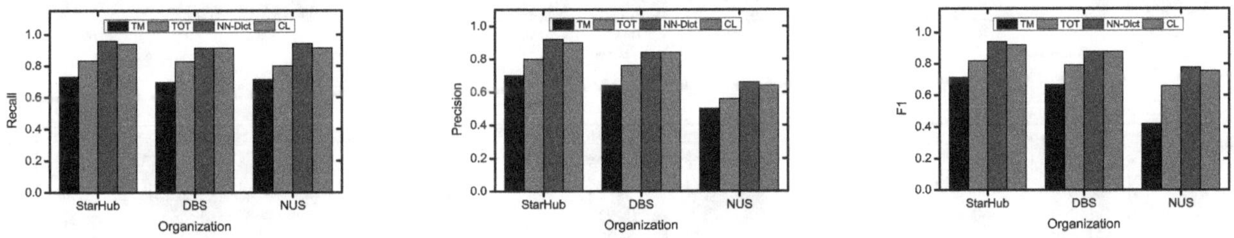

(a) *Recall* (b) *Precision* (c) F_1

Figure 4: Performance of topic Detection

ments on topic detection and emerging topic detection only. The effectiveness of our data collection strategy will not be discussed here. It is tested indirectly through the accuracy of hot emerging topic detection experiments.

5.2.1 Performance of Topic Detection

The performance of emerging topic detection model is based on the premise that the approach can fetch more organization related topics. In this work, we compare our topic detection approach with several baselines to demonstrate its effectiveness:

- **TwitterMonitor (TM)** [15]: It is a system that performs trending topic detection over the Twitter stream. We implemented two core algorithms of this paper (finding and grouping bursty keywords). Here we set the value of k in this method to 50, and the window size is set to $W = 1h$.
- **Topics over Time (TOT)** [23]: This is a LDA-based topic model that explicitly models the time jointly with word co-occurrence patterns. Here we set the topic number $|T| = 50$, hyper-parameter $\alpha = 1$, and $\beta = 0.1$.
- **NN-Dict** [11]: This is a dictionary learning based scheme. It utilizes the nearest neighbor approach to detect novel documents and then create emerging topic clusters by a dictionary learning technique. Here we set the topic numbers to 50, and the parameter $\lambda = \frac{1}{100}$.

For ease in evaluation, we utilize two sources of information to construct the ground truth for topic detection. The first is the emerging topics as shown in Table 1. The second is based on the idea of pooling by aggregating all the new topics detected by the four methods (CL, TM, TOT, and NN-Dict). We asked three people to evaluate the new topics detected and come up with the final set as the ground truth. The ground truth contain 34, 31 and 24 topics for *StarHub*, *DBS*, and *NUS*. In this work, we use several widely-used classifier performance metrics for evaluation [13]: recall, precision and F_1. Figure 4 presents the performance of CL and three baselines for three organizations.

It can be seen from the Figure that NN-Dict and CL achieve better performance than TOT and TM across all evaluation metrics for all organizations. The main reason for the poor performance of TM is that it constructs an undirected graph and groups bursty keywords by maximum connected components. This probably leads to multiple semantically separate topics being merged together and therefore produces very large topics that reflect very little about the real world topics. For TOT, it discovers topics clusters and their evolution over time. However, it often identifies old or non-informative topics as compared to the previously appearing ones. Overall, our method and NN-Dict can detect over 90% of topics with a F_1 measure of 70%. Finally, it is worth noting that the higher recall but lower F_1 of *NUS* suggests that there are not many topics happened in *NUS* as compared to *StarHub* and *DBS*.

5.2.2 Performance of Emerging Hot Topic Detection

This subsection aims to detect whether a newly found topic is emerging and will become a hot topic at a later stage. Hence there is a temporal dimension to this task, that the hot topic should be detected during the emerging phase as shown in Figure 1. Here we want to test the ability of the method to identify a topic as "hot topic" before a time T_L. For evaluation purpose, we select two time limits: a stringent one with $T_L = t_{mid}$, and a more relax one with $T_L = t_{hot}$ (see Figure 1). If the topic is identified as hot topic before T_L, it is considered a positive detection; otherwise it is considered a failure.

As our baselines are designed for novel topic detection, but not emerging topic detection, we need to incorporate time dimension into these methods. Here, we incorporate our two emerging topic learners, Co (Co-training learner) and En (Semi-supervised ensemble learner) with our proposed incremental learning method (CL) and the three baselines, giving rise to 8 combination of methods as shown in Figure 5, which list the F_1 measure of hot emerging topic detection when $T_L = t_{hot}$. Three main observations can be drawn from Figure 5. First, the topic detection methods incorporating semi-supervised ensemble learner (CL+En, TM+En, TOT+En, and NN-Dict+En) generally perform much better than those incorporating the co-training learner (CL+Co, TM+Co, TOT+Co, and NN-Dict+Co). The reason for the poor performance of Co is because the emerging features are split into two views with each view being weaker than the overall combined feature set. Second, NN-Dict and our proposed CL incorporating the emerging topic learners perform much better than the other two methods. This shows that

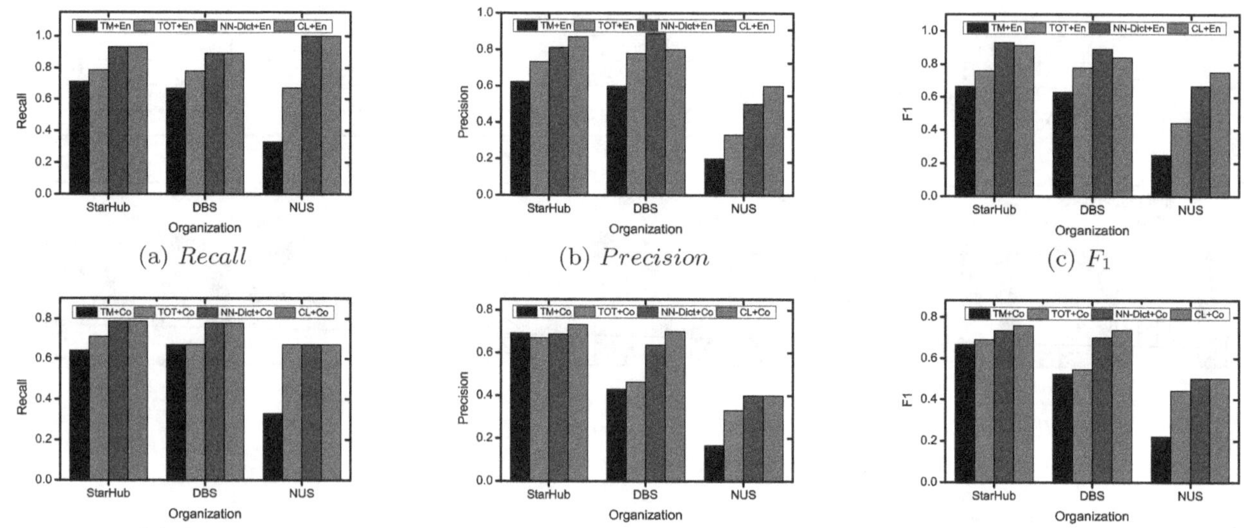

(a) *Recall* (b) *Precision* (c) F_1

(d) *Recall* (e) *Precision* (f) F_1

Figure 5: Performance of emerging topic Detection when $T_L = t_{hot}$

Table 2: Performance of emerging topic detection when $T_L = t_{hot}$

Methods	Organization	recall	precision	F_1
CL+En	*StarHub*	**0.93**	**0.87**	**0.90**
CL+TSVM		0.86	0.75	0.80
CL+Semi-NB		0.86	0.71	0.77
CL+En	*DBS*	**0.89**	**0.80**	**0.84**
CL+TSVM		**0.89**	0.73	0.80
CL+Semi-NB		**0.89**	0.67	0.70
CL+En	*NUS*	**1.00**	**0.60**	**0.75**
CL+TSVM		**1.00**	0.50	0.67
CL+Semi-NB		**1.00**	0.42	0.73

Table 3: Performance of emerging topic detection when $T_L = t_{mid}$

Methods	Organization	recall	precision	F_1
CL+En	*StarHub*	**0.71**	**0.83**	**0.77**
CL+TSVM		**0.71**	0.71	0.71
CL+Semi-NB		**0.71**	0.67	0.69
CL+En	*DBS*	**0.78**	**0.78**	**0.78**
CL+TSVM		**0.78**	0.70	0.74
CL+Semi-NB		**0.78**	0.64	0.70
CL+En	*NUS*	**0.67**	**0.50**	**0.57**
CL+TSVM		**0.67**	0.40	0.50
CL+Semi-NB		**0.67**	0.40	0.50

a strong topic detection baseline is needed to achieve good performance in hot emerging topic detection. Here we also observe that the recall performance is better than precision for most cases. This is important as in real applications, the ability to flag all possible hot topics is essential for organizations to handle all possible eventualities. Third, it is observed that our CL performs comparably in recall as compared to NN-Dict method but much better in precision, resulting in superior F_1 measure. In general, our method can detect close to 90% of hot topics with a precision of over 70%. This is an encouraging results for hot emerging topic detection.

5.2.3 Efficiency Analysis

The efficiency problem is very important for a real-time schema. In this subsection, we evaluate the average run time with different sizes of incoming tweets for different methods. We run the algorithms on a computer with 2.83GHz Intel(R) Core 2 Quad CPU, and 4GB memory. The experimental result of logarithm deviation of run time varying with increasing tweets size is shown in Figure 6. It can be seen from the figure that the run time increases with rising incoming tweet number. TOT performs poorly as it needs to sample the tweets and iterate to convergence in several steps in each iteration. For TM, it spends much time on bursty keyword graph mining. The main cost of NN-Dict is to maintain and update the term dictionaries and to find novel clusters by clustering methods. Overall, incremental clustering is the most efficient for real-time scenarios, as it explicitly maintains topics and related tweets for further analysis of emerging topic features.

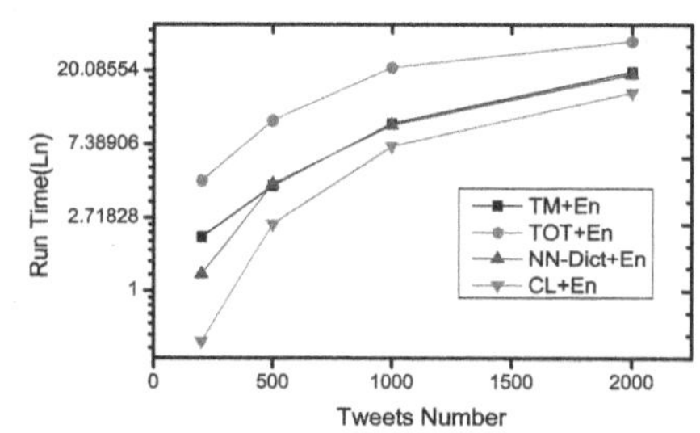

Figure 6: The impact of incoming tweets size on Run Time

5.2.4 Comparison with State-of-the Arts Methods

Because of the poor performance of CL+Co, it will not be included in further experiments. Here we conduct further experiments to compare the performance of CL+En against two start-of-the-arts methods: Transductive SVM (TSVM) [10] and Semi-supervised Naive Bayesian classifiers (Semi-NB) [16]. As with the previous approaches, the parameters of the methods are carefully tuned. And we test the ability of the methods to detect emerging topic at $T_L = t_{hot}$ and $T_L = t_{mid}$.

Tables 2 and 3 show the precision, recall and $F1$ measure of the methods for $T_L = t_{hot}$ and $T_L = t_{mid}$ respectively.

From the Tables, it is observed that our proposed incremental clustering with ensemble learner (CL+En) performs the best against all the other methods, with a high F_1 of 0.90. The results show that our semi-supervised ensemble learner can inherit the advantages of each learner to make up for the shortcomings of a single learner. It is also observed that the recall is higher than precision generally, which is an important attribute of emerging topic detection methods. Table 3 presents the comparison results when $T_L = t_{mid}$, which has a much more stringent criterion than that in Table 2. It naturally shows a performance reduction for all the learners. Finally, it is observed that performance of *StarHub* and *DBS* is better than that of *NUS* for the classification based metrics shown in Tables 2 and 3. The poorer performance of *NUS* is mainly due to the low number of tweets and lack of labeled data during the emerging phase.

5.2.5 Emerging Feature Analysis

In this subsection, experiments are carried out to investigate the influence of various emerging features on F_1. We progressively remove one feature for our semi-supervised ensemble learner. The experimental results on *StarHub*, *DBS*, and *NUS* are illustrated in Figure 7. Here, "f" on x-axis means all the features are used for the learner, and "-f*" means that all the features except feature "f*" are used in the ensemble learner. It is observed that the performance of F_1 on the three organizations are all degraded to a certain degree with the absence of some features. This observation verifies that all features have some contributions to the learners towards achieving good performance. However, it can be observed that the absence of features f_2, f_3 and f_6 cause the most degradation in performance. This shows that the rates of increasing tweets number (f_2), re-tweets number (f_3), and overall accumulated influence of tweets (f_6) are very important, and comparatively, user factors are less influential. This could be due to the fact that topic has only a small number of users. More testing needs to be done for future work. Finally, as compared to the other two organizations, *NUS* shows a much larger performance degradation with the absence of the above three factors. This is again due to the small training size for *NUS*.

5.2.6 Imbalance Impact

As mentioned in Section 4.3, training data imbalance is also a challenging problem in our task. In this section, we briefly look into the impact of imbalance training data for the two semi-supervised learners. The F_1 performance of two learners for the balance and imbalance settings is shown in Figure 8. It can be seen from the Figure that the F_1 performance of the two learners for the imbalance data degrades greatly as compared to that with balance data. As imbalance data makes our learners bias towards negative instances, which will increase the false positive errors for the methods. This is worse for the co-training learner. As false positive error will be accumulated into the next iteration, the co-training classifier is more easily affected by the noisy data.

6. CONCLUSIONS

In this paper, we proposed a real-time framework for detecting hot emerging topics for organizations in social media context. First, we introduced four sources of crawling organization data from multiple perspectives to ensure a more complete set of dataset for the target organization. Second, we discovered emerging topics and extracted emerging features from both the organization and topic perspectives. Thirdly, we developed semi-supervised learners to facilitate timely identification of hot emerging topics for organizations. We demonstrated the effectiveness of our proposed framework by comparing them with the state-of-the-arts methods. Empirical evaluation on the Twitter datasets on three organizations (*StarHub*, *DBS* and *NUS*) illustrated the effectiveness of the proposed emerging topic detection framework.

One can envision several directions for future work. While the current work is based on organizations to detect emerging and evolving topics, we can extend our framework to more general entities, such as the people and location, etc. The other important direction is to build human readable emerging topic summarization for organization users.

7. ACKNOWLEDGMENTS

This work was supported by the National Natural Science Foundation of China (60973105, 90718017, 61170189, and 61202239), the Research Fund for the Doctoral Program of Higher Education (20111102130003), the Fund of the State Key Laboratory of Software Development Environment (SKLSDE-2013ZX-19), and the Innovation Foundation of Beihang University for Ph.D. Graduates (YWF-13-T-YJSY-024). This research was also supported by the Singapore National Research Foundation under its International Research Center @ Singapore Funding Initiative and administered by the IDM Programme Office.

8. REFERENCES

[1] C. G. Akcora, M. A. Bayir, M. Demirbas, and H. Ferhatosmanoglu. Identifying breakpoints in public opinion. In *Proceedings of the 1st Workshp on Social Media Analytics*, 2010.

[2] J. Allan, R. Papka, and V. Lavrenko. On-line new event detection and tracking. In *Proceedings of the 21st annual International ACM SIGIR Conference on Research and development in information retrieval*, 1998.

[3] H. Becker, M. Naaman, and L. Gravano. Learning similarity metrics for event identification in social media. In *Proceedings of the 3rd ACM International Conference on Web Search and Data Mining*, 2010.

[4] D. M. Blei and J. D. Lafferty. Dynamic topic models. In *Proceedings of the 23rd International Conference on Machine Learning*, 2006.

[5] D. M. Blei, A. Y. NG, and M. I. Jordan. Latent dirichlet allocation. *Journal of Machine Learning Research*, pages 993–1022, 2003.

[6] M. Cataldi, L. D. Caro, and C. Schifanella. Emerging topic detection on twitter based on temporal and social terms evaluation. In *Proceedings of the 10th International Workshop on Multimedia Data Mining*, 2010.

[7] Y. Chen, Z. Li, L. Nie, X. Hu, X. Wang, T. S. Chua, and X. Zhang. A semi-supervised bayesian network model for microblog topic classification. In *Proceedings of the 24th International Conference on Computational Linguistics*, 2012.

[8] Q. He, K. Chang, and E.-P. Lim. Analyzing feature trajectories for event detection. In *Proceedings of the*

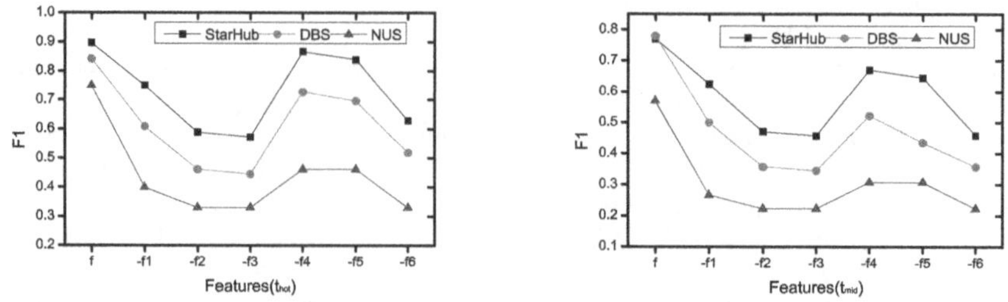

(a) $T_L = t_{hot}$ (b) $T_L = t_{mid}$

Figure 7: The impact of emerging features on F_1 measure

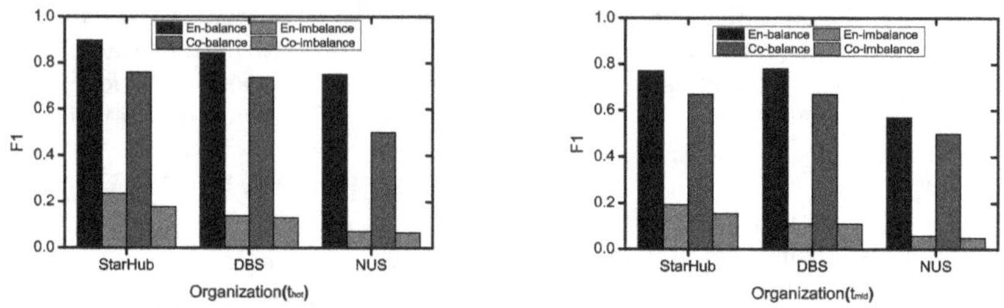

(a) $T_L = t_{hot}$ (b) $T_L = t_{mid}$

Figure 8: The impact of imbalance data on F_1 measure

30th annual International ACM SIGIR Conference on Research and Development in Information Retrieval, 2007.

[9] L. Hong and B. D. Davison. Empirical study of topic modeling in twitter. In *Proceedings of the 1st workshop on Social Media Analytics*, 2010.

[10] T. Joachims. Transductive inference for text classification using support vector machines. In *Proceedings of the 16th International Conference on Machine Learning*, 1999.

[11] S. P. Kasiviswanathan, P. Melville, A. Banerjee, and V. Sindhwani. Emerging topic detection using dictionary learning. In *Proceedings of the 20th ACM International Conference on Information and knowledge management*, 2011.

[12] A. Kotov, C. Zhai, and R. Sproat. Mining named entities with temporally correlated bursts from multilingual web news streams. In *Proceedings of the 4th ACM International Conference on Web Search and Data Mining*, 2011.

[13] S. B. Kotsiantis. Supervised machine learning: A review of classification techniques. *Informatica*, pages 249–268, 2007.

[14] H. O. Lancaster and E. Seneta. Chi-square distribution. *Encyclopedia of Biostatistics*, 2005.

[15] M. Mathioudakis and N. Koudas. Twittermonitor: trend detection over the twitter stream. In *Proceedings of the 2010 ACM SIGMOD International Conference on Management of data*, 2010.

[16] K. Nigam, A. K. Mccallum, S. Thrun, and T. Mitchell. Text classification from labeled and unlabeled documents using EM. In *Machine Learning - Special issue on information retrieval*, pages 103–134, 2000.

[17] A.-M. Popescu and M. Pennacchiotti. Detecting controverisal events from twitter. In *Proceedings of the 19th ACM International Conference on Information and Knowledge Management*, 2010.

[18] K. Randinsky, S. Davidovich, and S. Markovitch. Learning causality for news events prediction. In *Proceedings of the 21st International Conference on World Wide Web*, 2012.

[19] A. Saha and V. Sindhwani. Learning evolving and emerging topics in social media: a dynamic nmf approach with temporal regularization. In *Proceedings of the 5th ACM International Conference on Web Search and Data Mining*, 2012.

[20] T. Sakaki, M. Okazaki, and Y. Matsuo. Earthquake shakes twitter users: real-time event detection by social sensors. In *Proceedings of the 19th International Conference on World Wide Web*, 2010.

[21] H. Sayyadi, M. Hurst, and A. Maykov. Event detection and tracking in social streams. In *Proceedings of the 3rd International AAAI Conference on Weblogs and Social Media*, 2009.

[22] A. Tumasjan, T. O. Sprenger, P. G. Sandner, and I. M. Welpe. Predicting elections with twitter: What 140 characters reveal about political sentiment. In *Proceedings of the 4th International AAAI Conference on Weblogs and Social Media*, 2011.

[23] X. Wang and A. McCallum. Topics over time: a non-markov continuous-time model of topical trends. In *Proceedings of the 12th ACM SIGKDD International Conference on Knowledge Discovery and Data Mining*, 2006.

[24] Y. Wang, E. Agichtein, and M. Benzi. Tm-lda: efficient online modeling of latent topic transitions in social media. In *Proceedings of the 18th ACM SIGKDD International Conference on Knowledge Discovery and Data Mining*, 2012.

[25] Y. Yang, T. Pierce, and J. Carbonell. A study on retrospective and online event detection. In *Proceedings of the 21st annual International ACM SIGIR Conference on Research and development in information retrieval*, 1998.

Pseudo Test Collections for Training and Tuning Microblog Rankers

Richard Berendsen
r.w.berendsen@uva.nl

Manos Tsagkias
e.tsagkias@uva.nl

Wouter Weerkamp
w.weerkamp@uva.nl

Maarten de Rijke
derijke@uva.nl

ISLA, University of Amsterdam, Amsterdam, The Netherlands

ABSTRACT

Recent years have witnessed a persistent interest in generating pseudo test collections, both for training and evaluation purposes. We describe a method for generating queries and relevance judgments for microblog search in an unsupervised way. Our starting point is this intuition: tweets with a hashtag are relevant to the topic covered by the hashtag and hence to a suitable query derived from the hashtag. Our baseline method selects all commonly used hashtags, and all associated tweets as relevance judgments; we then generate a query from these tweets. Next, we generate a timestamp for each query, allowing us to use temporal information in the training process. We then enrich the generation process with knowledge derived from an editorial test collection for microblog search.

We use our pseudo test collections in two ways. First, we tune parameters of a variety of well known retrieval methods on them. Correlations with parameter sweeps on an editorial test collection are high on average, with a large variance over retrieval algorithms. Second, we use the pseudo test collections as training sets in a learning to rank scenario. Performance close to training on an editorial test collection is achieved in many cases. Our results demonstrate the utility of tuning and training microblog search algorithms on automatically generated training material.

Categories and Subject Descriptors

H.3.3 [**Information Search and Retrieval**]: Retrieval Models

Keywords

Simulation, pseudo test collections, learning to rank, microblog retrieval

1. INTRODUCTION

Modern information retrieval (IR) systems have evolved from single model based systems to intelligent systems that learn to combine uncertain evidence from multiple individual models [10, 22]. The effectiveness and flexibility of such systems has led to wide adoption in IR research. A key contributor to the success of such systems is the learning phase, i.e., the training set they are given for learning. Training sets have to be tailored to the task at hand and, in contrast to the systems themselves, do not generalize to other tasks. This characteristic requires compiling task-specific training sets, which is a time consuming and resource intensive process, as it usually involves human labor. Automating the process of compiling training sets has obvious advantages in reducing costs, while it simultaneously increases the size of the training set. This observation has led to a persistent interest in finding ways for generating so-called *pseudo test collections*, which consist of a set of queries, and for each query a set of relevant documents (given some document set). In this paper, we consider the problem of generating pseudo test collections for microblog search.

Microblog search is the task of finding information in microblogs, such as Facebook status updates, Twitter posts, etc. The task became popular with the advent of social media and is distinct from web search and from blog search due mainly to its real-time nature, the very limited length of microblog posts and the use of "microblog language," e.g., hashtags, mentions, which can provide useful information for retrieval purposes. In 2011 the Text REtrieval Conference (TREC) launched the Microblog track aimed at developing a test collection from Twitter data and evaluating systems' performance on retrieving—given a query and time-stamp—relevant and interesting tweets in a simulated real-time scenario. Several participants approached the task using learning to rank methods for combining evidence from multiple rankers [21]. This approach to microblog search comes natural because of the many dimensions available for ranking microblog posts, e.g., recency, user authority, content, existence of hyperlinks, hashtags, retweets. For training a learning to rank-based system at the TREC 2011 Microblog track, participants used a traditional supervised method: many manually labeled data for compiling a training set. What if we could generate the required training sets automatically? In 2012 a second edition of the Microblog track was organized. This gives us the opportunity to compare what yields better learning to rank performance: training on the 2011 relevance assessments, or training on automatically generated ground truth?

Our starting point is the following intuition, based upon the observation that hashtags tend to represent a topic in the Twitter domain: *From tweets T_h associated with a hashtag h, select a subset of tweets $R_h \subseteq T_h$ that are relevant to an unknown query q_h related to h.* We build on this intuition for creating a training set for microblog rankers. To this end, we take several steps, each raising research questions. First, we select hashtags h and associated relevant tweets R_h. Can we just select all hashtags and use all their associated tweets? In microblog search, time is important: what is considered relevant to a query may change rapidly over time. A

SIGIR'13, July 28–August 1, 2013, Dublin, Ireland.

microblog query, then, has a timestamp, and relevant tweets must occur prior to this timestamp. As for a query, the topic a *hashtag* is associated with may change over time. Can we exploit this analogy, and label hashtags with a timestamp, regarding tweets prior to this timestamp as relevant? Another well-known aspect of microblog posts is that they often contain casual conversation that is unlikely to be relevant to a query. Can we improve generated training sets by selecting interesting tweets and hashtags associated with such tweets? Once we have selected a hashtag h and a set of tweets R_h, how do we generate a query q_h related to h?

The main contribution of this paper is a set of methods for creating pseudo test collections for microblog search. These collections are shown to be useful as training material for tuning well-known retrieval methods from the literature, and for optimizing a learning to rank method. In particular, we contribute: (1) unsupervised pseudo test collection generation methods; (2) a supervised pseudo test collection generation method, where we learn what are interesting tweets from TREC Microblog track assessments; (3) insights into the sensitivity of our methods to parameter settings.

2. PROBLEM DEFINITION

Below, we consider a number of instantiations of our pseudo test collection generator. For the purposes of the TREC Microblog track, a *test collection for microblog search* consists of queries with timestamps and a set of relevant documents for these queries. A *pseudo test collection for microblog search* consists of a set of queries $\mathcal{Q}$, in which each query $q \in \mathcal{Q}$ is associated with a timestamp q_t and a set of relevant documents R_q. Given this definition, there are three main steps for generating a pseudo test collection for microblog search: generating (a) the query; (b) the query timestamp; and (c) a set of relevant tweets for the query.

We start from the following intuition: *From the tweets T_h that contain a hashtag h, we can select tweets R_h that are relevant to an unknown query q_h related to h.* In the next section, we present three methods to generate a pseudo test collection. Each method selects hashtags and for every hashtag h it selects tweets R_h from T_h that will act as relevant tweets to a suitable query related to h. In §4, we present a technique for generating queries from R_h.

3. SELECTING HASHTAGS AND TWEETS

We propose four solutions to selecting hashtags and tweets for inclusion in a pseudo test collection. **(A) Random:** A sanity check baseline against our hypothesis that hashtags are good sources for generating pseudo test collections. Collections are created by randomly sampling a set of relevant tweets for each topic, without replacement. All these random collections are of a fixed size, equal to our largest hashtag-based pseudo test collection. **(B) Hashtags:** A naive method that serves as baseline in our experiments and that considers all hashtags and tweets to be equally important (§3.1). **(C) Hashtags-T:** A method that creates a test collection in the microblog retrieval sense, in which queries have timestamps (§3.2). **(D) Hashtags-TI:** A method that aims at capturing interestingness in tweets. Interesting tweets should contain good candidate terms for a query. We present a method with which we can estimate from example queries and relevant tweets the probability of interestingness of a tweet (§3.3).

3.1 Hashtags: All hashtags, tweets are equal

We select all hashtags, with a single requirement: that they are mentioned in a reasonable amount of tweets, m (Algorithm 1). There are three reasons for this lower bound: (i) it reflects a certain consensus about the meaning of a hashtag; (ii) we generate our queries based on word distributions in these tweets: for this to work reliably, we need a reasonable amount of tweets, see §4; (iii) we train a learning to rank retrieval algorithm on our pseudo test collection; we hypothesize that it would benefit from a relative large set of positive training examples, see §5. We normalize hashtags by lowercasing them and removing any non-alphanumeric characters. In all our experiments, we set $m = 50$. The pseudo test collection generated by Algorithm 1 is called *Hashtags*.

Algorithm 1: Generating collection *Hashtags*

```
H ⟵ {h : |T_h| >= m};
for h ∈ H do
    R_h ⟵ T_h;
    Generate query q_h from R_h;                 // See §4
end
```

3.2 Hashtags-T: Generating timestamps

Microblog search is sensitive to the query issue time because of the real time nature of tweets. To generate a timestamp for a query related to a hashtag h, we make an analogy between search volume over time for a query and publishing volume over time for tweets with h. Our assumption is that users often issue queries for trending topics because they want to monitor developments, similar to certain types of blog search [28]. We generate a timestamp for hashtag h just after peaks in publishing volume. In this way, our generated queries will be about trending topics. In addition, we keep a large amount of tweets from T_h, while discarding a limited number, after h stops trending. In collections that span a considerable period of time, re-occurring topics, such as Christmas or Super Bowl, may quite likely be observed. In this case, one may want to assign multiple issue times for a query, depending on the number of observed peaks. Our corpus (see §5) covers a relatively short period, and we assign only one issue time to every query sampled.

In detail, our query issue time generation works as follows. First, we group the time span of the collection in 8-hours bins. Then, for each hashtag, we count how many relevant documents belong to each bin; this results in generating the hashtag's timeseries. In our setting, timeseries are short and sparse; our peak detection method aims at coping with this challenge. We find the bin with the most counts and resolve ties by taking the earliest date. This approach allows us to return a peak even for very sparse timeseries. We call the pseudo test collection generated by Algorithm 2: *Hashtags-T*.

3.3 Hashtags-TI: Selecting interesting tweets

Consider the following tweet: "Hey follow me here #teamfollowback #justinbieber." We hypothesize that this tweet would not be useful for sampling terms for topics labeled #teamfollowback or #justinbieber or as a relevant document for these topics. To avoid selecting such tweets, we rank tweets by their probability of interestingness and keep the best X percent. We think of a tweet

Algorithm 2: Generating collection *Hashtags-T*

```
H' ⟵ {h : |T_h| ≥ m};
for h ∈ H' do
    Generate timestamp t(h);                     // See §3.2
    R_h ⟵ {τ : τ ∈ T_h and t(τ) ≤ t(h)};
end
H ⟵ {h : h ∈ H' and |R_h| ≥ m};
for h ∈ H do
    Generate query q_h from R_h;                 // See §4
end
```

as interesting if it carries some information and could be relevant to a query. We use a set of criteria to capture interestingness and present a method to learn from example queries and relevant documents from an editorial collection.

Let $C_1, C_2, \ldots, C_n$ be random variables associated with the criteria and let $I_\tau := I(\tau) = 1$ be the event that a tweet is interesting. We estimate $P(I_\tau | C_1 = c_1, \ldots, C_n = c_n)$, or, shorthand: $P(I_\tau | c_1, \ldots, c_n)$. Following Bayes' rule, we have

$$P(I_\tau | c_1, \ldots, c_n) = \frac{P(c_1, \ldots, c_n | I_\tau) P(I_\tau)}{P(c_1, \ldots, c_n)}, \quad (1)$$

where $P(I_\tau)$ is the a-priori probability that a tweet is interesting, $P(c_1, \ldots, c_n | I_\tau)$ is the likelihood of observing the evidence given that a tweet is interesting, and $P(c_1, \ldots, c_n)$ is the probability of observing the evidence. The crucial step is to estimate $P(c_1, \ldots, c_n | I_\tau)$. We hypothesize that tweets that are known to be relevant to a query are interesting and estimate $P(c_1, \ldots, c_n | I_\tau)$ with $P(c_1, \ldots, c_n | R_\tau)$, where R_τ is the event that a tweet is relevant to a query in an editorial collection. We use the TREC Microblog 2011 qrels for this estimation. Since we do not have enough relevant tweets to estimate the full joint probability, we assume conditional independence of c_i given that a tweet is relevant:

$$P(I_\tau | c_1, \ldots, c_n) \approx \frac{\left(\prod_i P(c_i | R_\tau)\right) P(I_\tau)}{P(c_1, \ldots c_n)}. \quad (2)$$

Since we rank tweets by interestingness we do not have to estimate $P(I_\tau)$. Instead, we have:

$$\text{rank}_\tau(P(I_\tau | c_1, \ldots, c_n)) = \text{rank}_\tau \left(\frac{\sum_i \log(P(c_i | R_\tau))}{P(c_1, \ldots, c_n)} \right). \quad (3)$$

Most of the criteria we use have discrete distributions. For those that do not, we bin their values in B bins; we set $B = 10$. To avoid rejecting a tweet on the basis of one measurement that did not occur in any of the relevant tweets, we add one observation to every bin of every $P(c_i | R_\tau)$ distribution. For $P(c_1, \ldots, c_n)$ we use the empirical distribution of all tweets in the collection. After selecting the best X percent of tweets, we again filter out hashtags that have less than 50 interesting tweets. We build this method on top of our pseudo test collection *Hashtags-T*, only ranking the tweets in this collection and keeping the best 50% of them. We call the pseudo test collection generated by Algorithm 3 *Hashtags-TI*.

Algorithm 3: Generating collection *Hashtags-TI*

```
H'' ⟵ {h : |T_h| ≥ m};
for h ∈ H'' do
    Generate timestamp t(h);                        // See §3.2
    T_{h,t} ⟵ {τ : τ ∈ T_h and t(τ) ≤ t(h)};
end
H' ⟵ {h : h ∈ H'' and |T_{h,t}| ≥ m};
T ⟵ ∪_{h∈H'} T_{h,t};
// Rank tweets by probability of being
   interesting
Rank T by P(I_τ|c_1, ..., c_n(τ));                // See eq. 3
Let T_I be the top X percent of this ranking;
for h ∈ H' do
    R_h ⟵ T_{h,t} ∩ T_I;
end
H ⟵ {h : h ∈ H' and |R_h| ≥ m};
for h ∈ H do
    Generate query q from R_h;                      // See §4
end
```

The criteria we use build on textual features (*density* and *capitalization*) and microblog features (*links*, *mentions*, *recency*). Each criterion is discussed below. The marginal distributions $P(c_i | R_\tau)$ of three criteria are shown in Fig. 1 as white histograms. They overlap with black histograms of all tweets in our *Hashtags* pseudo test collection. These criteria have different distributions over relevant tweets and over tweets that have a hashtag, which motivates our idea to keep tweets with high probability of interestingness.

Links. The existence of a hyperlink is a good indicator of the content value of a tweet. TREC Microblog 2011 defines interestingness of a tweet as whether a tweet contains a link [21]. Also, a large fraction of tweets are pointers to online news [19]. Tweets with links are likely to include terms that describe the linked web page, rendering them good surrogates for query terms [5].

Mentions. Tweets with mentions (@username) signify discussions about the hashtag's topic. This type of tweet is likely to be noisy because of their personal character. They may, however, bring in query terms used by a niche of people.

Tweet length. Document length has been shown to matter in retrieval scenarios [35]. Short tweets are less likely to contain terms useful for query simulation, see Fig. 1 (Center) for the distribution of tweet length.

Density. A direct measure for probing a tweet's content quality is the density score [20]. Density is defined as the sum of tf-idf values of non-stopwords, divided by the number of stopwords they are apart, squared:

$$Density(\tau) = \frac{K}{K-1} \sum_{k=1}^{K-1} \frac{weight(w_k) + weight(w_{k+1})}{distance(w_k, w_{k+1})^2},$$

where K is the total number of non-stopwords terms in tweet τ, w_k and w_{k+1} are two adjacent keywords in τ. $weight(\cdot)$ denotes the term's tf-idf score, and $distance(w_k, w_{k+1})$ denotes the distance between w_k and w_{k+1} in number of stopwords. Fig. 1 (Left) shows the distribution of density scores of tweets.

Capitalization. The textual quality of tweets can partially be captured through the use of capitalization [41]. Words in all capitals are considered shouting and an indication of low quality. The ratio of capitals may indicate the quality of the text. Fig. 1 (Right) shows the distribution of the fraction of capital letters over tweet length.

Direct. A tweet is *direct* if it is meant to be a "private" message to another user (i.e., the tweets starts with *@user*).

4. GENERATING QUERIES

Sampling query terms is a challenging step in the process of automatically generating pseudo test collections. Azzopardi et al. [3] propose several methods for sampling query terms from web documents for known-item search, while Asadi et al. [2] avoid the problem by using anchor texts. Neither approach is applicable in the microblog setting due to a lack of both redundancy in the tweets and anchor texts. Terms in tweets usually occur at most once, but if not, this is often a signal for spam [26]. Probabilistic sampling methods that boost terms occurring with high probability are less likely to return good candidates for query terms. Tf-idf methods emphasize rare terms, which are likely to be spelling mistakes or descriptive of online chatter (e.g., "loooooool") in our setting.

The log-likelihood ratio (LLR) is suitable for our problem of sampling terms from (tweets associated with) a given hashtag [25]. LLR is defined as the symmetric Kullback-Leibler divergence of the expected and observed term probabilities in two corpora. Terms are ranked by how discriminative they are for both corpora. For

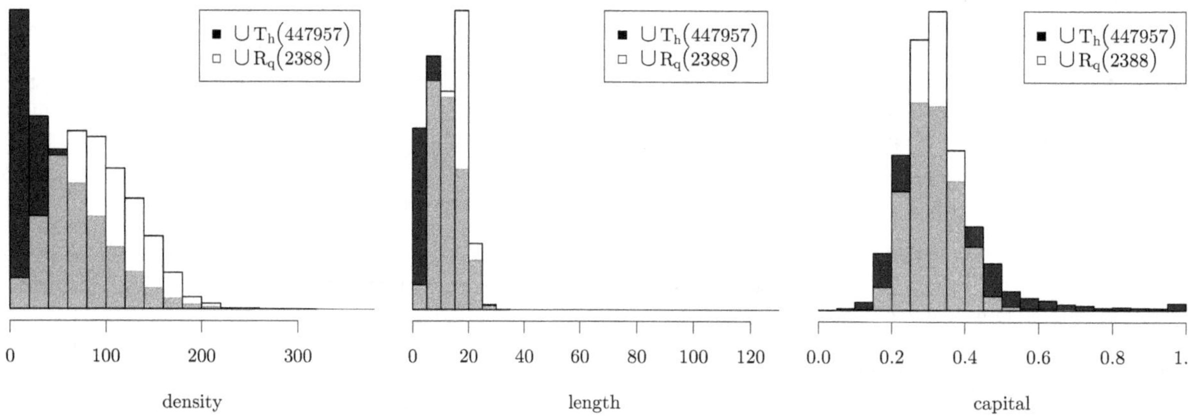

Figure 1: Distribution of (Left) density scores, (Center) tweet length, and (Right) capitalization. Where the histograms for the tweets associated with hashtags (dark grey) and for the TREC MB 2011 relevant tweets (white) overlap, the color is light grey.

our purposes, we set one corpus to be a set of tweets associated with hashtag h and the other to consist of the rest of the tweets in the collection. Stopwords, spam terms, or terms indicative of online chatter will rank lower because they occur in both corpora with roughly the same frequency.

Let T be a collection of tweets τ, R_h a set of relevant tweets associated with a hashtag h resulting from one of the sampling methods described in §3, and w a term in τ. For every $w \in \bigcup_{\tau \in R_h} \tau$ we compute LLR(w), given corpora R_h and $B = T \setminus R_h$:

$$LLR(w) = 2 \cdot \left[O_{R_h}(w) \log \frac{O_{R_h}(w)}{E_{R_h}(w)} + O_B(w) \log \frac{O_B(w)}{E_B(w)} \right],$$

where $O_{R_h}(w) = tf(w, R_h)$ and $O_B(w) = tf(w, B)$ are the observed term frequencies of w in R_h and B, respectively. $E_{R_h}(w)$ and $E_B(w)$ are the expected values of the term frequency of w in R_h and B, respectively.

For every hashtag h, terms are ranked in descending order of their log-likelihood ratio score. We remove terms if one of the following pertains: (1) The term is equal to the hashtag up to the '#' character. In this case, all tweets in T_h contain the hashtag, making the query very easy for all rankers, which then leads to a learning to rank method having a hard time distinguishing between rankers. (2) The term occurs in fewer than 10 documents. We generate queries that consist of the top-K ranked terms. For all pseudo test collections described in §3 we set $K = 10$. For our most promising method, we examine the impact of this parameter by generating queries of length 1, 2, 3, 5, and 20.

5. EXPERIMENTAL SETUP

The main research question we aim to answer is: *What is the utility of our test collection generation methods for tuning retrieval approaches and training learning to rank methods?*

Parameter tuning. We do parameter sweeps for some retrieval runs on different (pseudo) test collections, see Table 1 for details. We ask: (a) What is better in terms of retrieval performance: tuning on a different editorial test collection or tuning on a pseudo test collection? We answer by calculating how far performance obtained by tuning on either collection is from optimal performance for each retrieval model. (b) Do scores between a pseudo test collection and an editorial test collection correlate better than scores between editorial test collections? We answer by calculating Kendall's tau and expected loss in effectiveness.

Learning to rank. We compare the utility of test collections as training material for a learning to rank algorithm. We ask: (a) What is better in terms of retrieval performance: training on a different editorial test collection, or training on a pseudo test collection? We answer by calculating the difference in retrieval performance between training on each. (b) Which of our pseudo test collections is most useful? (c) Do learning to rank algorithms trained on pseudo test collections outperform the best individual feature?

Parameter sensitivity. We also analyze parameter sensitivity of our methods, focusing on two parameters. First, in generating *Hashtag-TI* (§3), we keep the best $X = 50\%$ percent of tweets. How sensitive are our results to this method to different values for X? We try these values: 20, 40, 60, and 80. In all our experiments,

Algorithm 4: Training an LTR system on a pseudo test collection, and testing it on an editorial collection

for $i = 1 \rightarrow N$ **do**
  `// -- Training phase: --`
  Generate the pseudo test collection;
  for *each ranker* **do**
    Sweep parameters on the pseudo test collection;
    Randomly sample parameter vector to use from winners;
  end
  for $q \in Q$ **do**
    Merge the ranked lists into M_q;
    Let positive training examples $\leftarrow R_{q,h} \cap M_q$;
    Randomly sample $|R_{q,h}|$ negative training examples from $M_q \setminus R_{q,h}$;
  end
  Learn a LTR model on the training set;
  `// -- Testing phase: --`
  for *each ranker* **do**
    Run on test topics using the sampled parameter vector;
  end
  Run the learned LTR model on the test set;
end

Table 1: Retrieval algorithms tuned.

	Ranker	Description	Parameter	Values	cf. Literature
Indri 5.1	LM	Language modeling with Dirichlet smoothing	μ	$\{50, 150, \ldots, 10050\}$	[42]
	Tf-idf	Indri's implementation of tf-idf	k1 b	$\{0.2, 0.4, \ldots, 3\}$ $\{0, 0.05 \ldots, 1\}$	[33]
	Okapi	Okapi, also known as BM25 [35]	k1 b k3	$\{0, 0.2, \ldots, 3\}$ $\{0, 0.05 \ldots, 1\}$ $\{0\}$	[33]
	BOW	Boolean ordered window	Window size	$\{1, 2 \ldots, 15, \text{inf}\}$	
	BUW	Boolean unordered window	Window size	$\{1, 2 \ldots, 15, \text{inf}\}$	
Terrier 3.5	Tf-idf	Terrier's implementation of tf-idf	b	$\{0, 0.05 \ldots, 1\}$	[33]
	PL2	A Divergence from Randomness (DFR) model [1]	c	$\{0.5, 1, 5, 10\}$	[9]
	DFR-FD	Terrier's DFRee model with a document score modifier that takes into account co-occurence within a window	Window size	$\{2, 3 \ldots, 15\}$	[31]
	QE	Terrier's implementation of query expansion	No. documents No. terms	$\{1, 5, 10, 20, 30, 50\}$ $\{1, 5, 10, 20, 30, 50\}$	[23]

when we generate queries, we keep the top 10 terms of the ranking produced by LLR (§4). For our best pseudo test collection, we ask how parameter tuning results and learning to rank performance is influenced by different query length. We try query lengths 1, 2, 3, 5, and 20.

5.1 Dataset and preprocessing

We use the publicly available dataset from the TREC 2011 and 2012 Microblog tracks. It covers two weeks of Twitter data, from January 24, 2011–February 8, 2011, consisting of approximately 16 million tweets. We perform a series of preprocessing steps on the content of tweets. We discard non-English tweets using a language identification method for microblogs [6]. Exact duplicates are removed; among a set of duplicates the oldest tweet is kept. Retweets are discarded; in ambiguous cases, e.g., where comments were added to a retweet, we keep the tweet. Punctuation and stop words are removed using a collection-based stop word list, but we keep hashtags without the '#' character. After preprocessing we are left with 4,459,840 tweets, roughly 27% of all tweets. Due to our aggressive preprocessing, we miss 19% of the relevant tweets per topic, on average. Our 10 retrieval models avoid using future evidence by using per topic indexes. For completeness, we note that our stopword list and the idf-weights in the density feature were computed on the entire collection. Pseudo test collections and both TREC microblog test collections also contain tweets from the entire collection. For generating queries, we index the collection with Lucene without stemming or stopword removal.

Table 2 lists statistics of the pseudo test collections generated with the methods described in §3, as well as statistics of the collections generated by choosing different values for X. The Hashtags-TI-QL{1,2,3,5,20} pseudo test collections are of the same proportions as *Hashtags-TI*, apart from the query length. We have listed only one of fifteen Random collections, but these are all of the same proportions: about as large as the *Hashtags* collection.

Table 2: Statistics for pseudo test collection generated from our methods and the TREC Microblog 2011 track.

Collection	Topics #	Max length	Min length	Avg. length	Relevant documents #	Max	Min	Avg.
TREC MB 2011	49	6	1	3.4	2,965	178	1	60.5
TREC MB 2012	59	7	1	2.9	6,286	572	1	106.5
Random-1	1,888	10	10	10	462560	245	245	245.0
Hashtags	1,888	10	10	10	462,013	16,105	50	244.7
Hashtags-T	891	10	10	10	212,377	9,164	50	238.4
Hashtags-TI	481	10	10	10	98,586	4,949	50	205.0
H-TI-X20	175	10	10	10	32,221	3661	50	184.1
H-TI-X40	392	10	10	10	75,287	4804	50	192.1
H-TI-X60	576	10	10	10	121,639	5277	50	211.2
H-TI-X80	740	10	10	10	166,489	6956	50	225.0

5.2 Learning to rank

We follow a two-step approach to learning to rank, outlined in Algorithm 4. First, we run several retrieval algorithms, then we rerank all retrieved tweets. For retrieval, we use the retrieval algorithms listed in Table 1, optimized for MAP [24, 34] after tuning on a training collection. In case of ties among parameter vectors for a ranker, we randomly sample a parameter vector. We also use a parameter free retrieval algorithm, DFRee [1]. For re-ranking, we compute three groups of features.

Query-tweet features. These are features that have different values for each query-tweet pair. We subdivide these as follows. *Rankers*: the raw output of each retrieval algorithm. For LM, BOW and BUW we transform the raw output X by taking the exponent: $\exp(X)$. *Ranker meta features*: the number of rankers that retrieved the tweet, the maximal, average, and median reciprocal rank of the tweet over all rankers. *Recency*: query-tweet time difference decay, computed as $\exp(t(\tau) - q_t)$, where $t(\tau)$ is the timestamp of the tweet and q_t the timestamp of the query. We linearly normalize query-tweet features over all retrieved tweets for the query.

Query features. These are features which have the same value for every retrieved tweet within the same query. We use *Query clarity*, a method for probing the semantic distance between the query and the collection [11]. We linearly normalize query features over the set of retrieved tweets for all queries.

Tweet features. These are features that have the same value for each tweet independent of the query. We use the *Quality criteria* listed in §3: *link*, *mentions*, *tweet length*, *density*, *capitalization*, and *direct*. We linearly normalize tweet features over the set of retrieved tweets for all queries.

To build a training set, one needs positive and negative training examples. Let $q \in Q$ be a query from the training collection, R_q the set of relevant tweets for query q, and M_q the set of all retrieved tweets for q. Then, for each query in the training collection we use $R_q \cap M_q$ as positive examples. To have a balanced training set, we randomly sample $|R_q|$ tweets as negative training examples from $M_q \setminus R_q$.

Next, we feed the training set to four state of the art learners: (a) Pegasos SVM[1] [36, 37], (b) Coordinate ascent [27], (c) RankSVM [17], and (d) RT-Rank [29]. We set Pegasos SVM to optimize the area under the ROC curve using indexed sampling of training examples, with regularization parameter $\lambda = 0.1$ for a maximum of 100,000 iterations. We set coordinate ascent to optimize for MAP with $\epsilon = 0.0001$ and maximum step size of 3. We use line search to optimize each feature with uniform initialization and consider only positive feature weights without projecting points on the manifold. For RankSVM we set the cost parameter to 1 per query. In preliminary experiments, RT-Rank performed poorly and therefore we choose to leave it out from our report.

Recall that training sets are compiled using tuned rankers and that in case of ties between different parameter vectors for a ranker, a random vector is selected. When compiling test sets for TREC MB 2011 and TREC MB 2012 to evaluate the utility of a training set, we use the exact same parameter vectors, so that the same set of features are used for training and testing.

Algorithm 4 has randomness in several stages: (i) when generating the pseudo test collection (only in the case of the Random collections), (ii) when sampling a winning parameter setting for each feature, (iii) when randomly sampling negative training examples, and (iv) during model learning. To obtain a reliable estimate of of the performance when training on a pseudo test collection, this procedure is repeated $N = 10$ times, each time generating a new pseudo test collection (in the case of the Random test collection), selecting random parameter vectors, selecting random negative training examples, and training an LTR model.

5.3 Evaluation

We report on precision at 30 (P30) on binary relevance judgments. We choose P30 because it has been one of the main metrics in both the TREC 2011 and 2012 Microblog track. We also report on MAP, as it is a well understood and commonly used evaluation metric in information retrieval, allowing us to better understand the behavior of our pseudo test collections. Note that in the 2011 task, tweets had to be ordered by their publication date instead of by their relevance. Many top performing systems treated the task as normal relevance ranking and cut off their ranked lists at rank 30 [21]. In the 2012 track organizers decided to focus on ranking by relevance again, which is what we will focus on.

Testing for statistical significance. For each training collection, we run Algorithm 4 $N = 10$ times, giving rise to N scores for each topic, for each collection. We report average performance and sample standard deviation over these iterations. To also gain insight if any differences between a pair of training collections would be observed on different microblog topics from the same hypothetical population of topics, we proceed as follows. We pick for each collection the iteration of Algorithm 4 which had the smallest *training* error on that collection. Then, we do a paired t-test over differences per topic as usual and report the obtained p-values. Statistically significant differences are marked as $^{\blacktriangle}$(or $^{\blacktriangledown}$) for significant differences for $\alpha = .001$, or $^{\vartriangle}$(and $^{\triangledown}$) for $\alpha = .05$.

6. RESULTS AND ANALYSIS

First, we report on our parameter tuning results; then on our learning to rank results. We also analyze parameter sensitivity with regard to the percentage of interesting tweets kept and query length.

6.1 Parameter tuning results

The main outcomes in this section will be correlations, to answer the question whether relative performance of parameter values on pseudo test collections correlates with relative performance of the same values on an editorial collection. We begin with two case studies to gain a better understanding of the behavior of our pseudo text collections. We sweep (a) the document length normalization parameter b for Terrier's tf-idf implementation (Fig. 2(a)), and (b) μ for Indri's implementation of language modeling with Dirichlet smoothing (Fig. 2(b)). We only include one of our ten random pseudo test collections; all random collections behave similarly, for all retrieval systems and metrics.

Fig. 2(a) shows that on the TREC MB 2011 collection there is a general trend to prefer lower values of b, possibly because of the very small average document length, which, in turn, renders the deviation from the average length close to one. All pseudo test collections capture this trend, including the Random-1 pseudo test collection. The curves of the pseudo test collections are smoother than the curve obtained when tuning on the TREC MB 2011 topics; this is because the pseudo test collections have far more test topics. Pseudo test collections show differences in absolute scores, but most importantly, we are interested in whether pseudo test collection predictions that one parameter vector is better than another correlate to such predictions of editorial collections. Kendall's tau expresses exactly that correlation, see Table 3. In addition, we want to know the following: if we sample a random parameter vector from those predicted to yield optimal performance on a pseudo test collection, what will be the expected loss with regard to optimal performance on an editorial collection? Table 5 provides these quantities. Correlations are high across the board, and expected loss is low. All pseudo test collections can be used to reliably tune the b parameter of Terrier's TF-IDF, even the Random-1 collection.

Turning to a second case study, Indri's language modeling algorithm with Dirichlet smoothing, we see a different picture (Fig. 2(b)). The TREC MB 2011 topics show a slightly decreasing trend for larger μ values. We believe this is due to the short document length; tweets after processing are few terms long, and therefore even small μ values overshadow the document term probability with the background probability. This trend is not entirely captured by the pseudo test collections. All have a short increase for low values of μ which is much less pronounced in the TREC MB 2011 curve. After that, all except the Random-1 collection show a decline, if only in the third digit. Correlations are fair (Table 4), but the Random-1 collection fails here. Expected loss is low across the board (Table 6).

Looking at the big picture, we average the correlations and expected loss figures in Tables 7 and 8 over all nine retrieval models from Table 1. For the hashtag based collections, correlations are high, with a large variance over systems. Expected loss is low. This indicates that pseudo test collections can be used to reliably and profitably tune parameters for a variety of well established retrieval algorithms, with more or less success depending on which model is being tuned. Tuning retrieval models on all hashtag based pseudo test collections is about as reliable as tuning on editorial test collections. For most retrieval algorithms, a Random collection cannot be recommended for tuning. Thus, the idea of grouping tweets by hashtag has value for creating pseudo test collections for tuning retrieval algorithms.

6.2 Learning to rank results

In this section we evaluate the usefulness of our pseudo test collections (PTCs) by training several learning to rank algorithms on them. In Tables 9 and 10, we report P30 and MAP performance on the TREC 2011 Microblog track topics. We compare training on our PTCs with training on the TREC 2012 Microblog track top-

[1] http://code.google.com/p/sofia-ml/

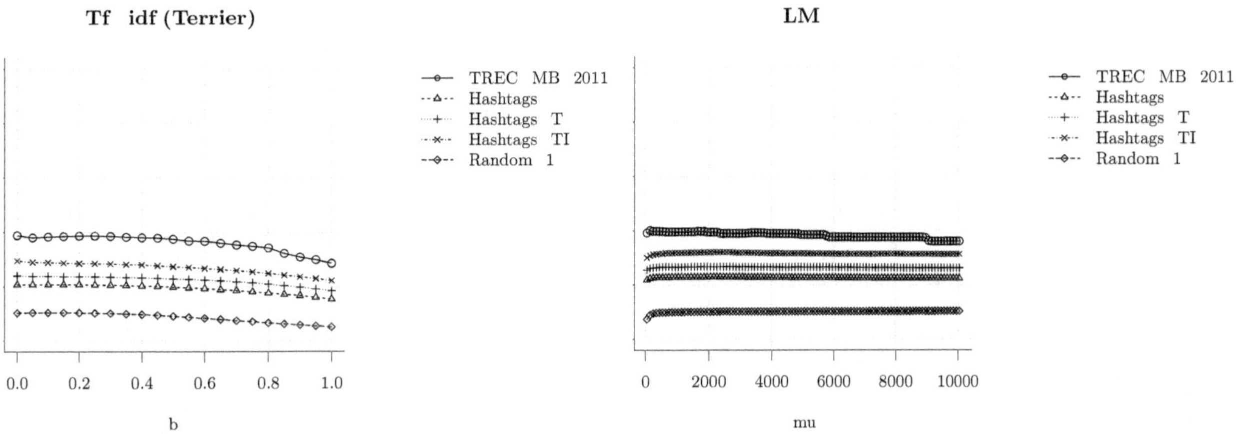

Figure 2: Sweeping the b parameter of Tf-idf (Terrier) (2(a)) and the μ parameter of LM (2(b)). The x-axes have parameter values, the y-axes average P30 over the topics of the respective tuning collection.

Table 3: For Tf-idf (Indri), and P30, Kendall's tau correlations of parameter sweeps on several pseudo test collections with sweeps on TREC MB 2011 and 2012 collections. Kendall's tau between sweeps over TREC MB 2011 and 2012 is 0.85.

Tune on	TREC MB 2011	TREC MB 2012
Random-1	0.18	0.20
Hashtags	0.87	0.86
Hashtags-T	0.90	0.86
Hashtags-TI	0.90	0.86

Table 4: For language modeling (LM), and P30, Kendall's tau correlations of parameter sweeps on several pseudo test collections with sweeps on TREC MB 2011 and 2012 collections. Kendall's tau between sweeps over TREC MB 2011 and 2012 is 0.61.

Tune on	TREC MB 2011	TREC MB 2012
Random-1	-0.87	-0.65
Hashtags	0.65	0.78
Hashtags-T	0.69	0.77
Hashtags-TI	0.58	0.79

ics and indicate significant differences. In Tables 11 and 12, we report P30 and MAP performance on the TREC 2012 Microblog track topics, and compare training on our PTCs with training on the TREC 2011 Microblog track topics.

A first brief glance at all four tables tells us that training on an editorial test collection is in most cases (but not all) the best strategy. Still, if training on a PTC is not substantially and significantly worse, we may conclude that in the abscence of training data, pseudo test collections are a viable alternative.

A second glance at all four tables shows us that training on the Random PTC is always significantly outperformed by training on editorial collections. Still, in most cases, there is a hashtag based PTC on which training yields performance on par with training on editorial collections. This shows that there is added value in our idea of using hashtags to group tweets by topic.

Another phenomenon we can observe in all tables is that Pegasos has remarkably stable performance over pseudo test collections, compared to the other two learning to rank algorithms. With the exception of Hashtags-TI-QL1 and Random, it seems to be able to exploit the structure in any PTC to learn a function that yields performance comparable to a function learned on editorial training data. RankSVM, on the other hand, has unstable performance. Especially in Table 12 it refuses to work on anything but manually obtained ground truth. Coordinate Ascent, a remarkably simple learning to rank algorithm holds the middle ground. When queries are

Table 5: For Tf-idf (Indri), expected loss in P30 performance of parameter sweeps on several training collections compared to optimal performance on TREC MB 2011 and 2012 collections.

Tune on	TREC MB 2011	TREC MB 2012
TREC MB 2011	-	0.003
TREC MB 2012	0.006±0.005 (3)	-
Random-1	0.029	0.024
Hashtags	0.012±0.002 (2)	0.002±0.002 (2)
Hashtags-T	0.002	0.000
Hashtags-TI	0.002	0.000

Table 6: For language modeling (LM), expected loss in P30 performance of parameter sweeps on several training collections compared to optimal performance on TREC MB 2011 and 2012 collections.

Tune on	TREC MB 2011	TREC MB 2012
TREC MB 2011	-	0.010
TREC MB 2012	0.006	-
Random-1	0.039±0.001 (11)	0.014±0.001 (11)
Hashtags	0.010	0.001
Hashtags-T	0.013±0.004 (2)	0.001±0.001 (2)
Hashtags-TI	0.014	0.002

too short, as in Hashtags-TI-QL1, Hashtags-QL2 and Hashtags-TI-QL3 performance detoriates. When subsamples of tweets become too small (Hashtags-TI-X20) the same happens.

So which PTC is the best? All PTCs are significantly outperformed by training on an editorial collection in at least one of the conditions. Hashtags-TI-X60 and Hashtags-TI-X80 both yield best results in one case. Also, like Hashtags, Hashtags-T and Hashtags-TI are significantly outperformed in only a small number of cases.

Learning to rank only makes sense if improvements over individual retrieval algorithms can be obtained. Tables 13 and 14 show performance of the retrieval models we use as features. In the great majority of cases our hashtag based PTCs outperform the best feature. The Random collection never achieves this.

7. RELATED WORK

We describe two types of related work: (i) searching microblog posts and (ii) pseudo test collections.

Searching microblog posts. Microblog search is a growing research area. The dominant microblogging platform that most research focuses on is Twitter. Microblogs have characteristics that introduce new problems and challenges for retrieval [12, 40]. Massoudi et al. [26] report on an early study of retrieval in microblogs, and introduce a retrieval and query expansion method to account for

Table 7: For all systems, and P30, Kendall's tau correlations of parameter sweeps on several pseudo test collections with sweeps on TREC MB 2011 and 2012 collections. Kendall's tau between sweeps over TREC MB 2011 and 2012 is 0.80.

Tune on	TREC MB 2011	TREC MB 2012
Random-1	0.27±0.62 (2 NA)	0.32±0.56 (1 NA)
Hashtags	0.78±0.20 (1 NA)	0.70±0.35 (1 NA)
Hashtags-T	0.80±0.20 (1 NA)	0.78±0.30 (1 NA)
Hashtags-TI	0.75±0.26 (1 NA)	0.81±0.23 (1 NA)

Table 8: Over all retrieval models, average expected loss in P30 performance of parameter sweeps on several training collections compared to optimal performance on TREC MB 2011 and 2012 collections.

Tune on	TREC MB 2011	TREC MB 2012
TREC MB 2011	-	0.003±0.006
TREC MB 2012	0.003±0.003	-
Random-1	0.021±0.021	0.013±0.012
Hashtags	0.005±0.006	0.004±0.006
Hashtags-T	0.004±0.005	0.002±0.005
Hashtags-TI	0.004±0.005	0.002±0.005

microblog search challenges. Efron and Golovchinsky [13] investigate the temporal aspects of documents on query expansion using pseudo relevance feedback. Naveed et al. [30] develop a retrieval model that takes into account document length and interestingness defined over a range of features.

In 2011, TREC launched the microblog search track, where systems are asked to return relevant and interesting tweets given a query [21]. The temporal aspect of Twitter and its characteristics, e.g., hashtags and existence of hyperlinks, were exploited by many participants, for query expansion, filtering, or learning to rank [21]. Whereas teams depended on self-constructed training data to train learning to rank systems during TREC 2011, most of these systems were successfully trained on the 2011 queries during TREC 2012. Teevan et al. [40] find that over 20% of Twitter queries contain a hashtag, an indication that hashtags may be good topical surrogates, which can be leveraged for building pseudo test collections.

Pseudo test collections. The issue of creating and using pseudo test collections is a longstanding and recurring theme in IR, see, e.g., [38, 39]. Several attempts have been made to either simulate human queries or generate relevance judgments without the need of human assessors for a range of tasks. Azzopardi et al. [3] simulate queries for known-item search and investigate term weighting methods for query generation. Their main concern is not to develop training material, but to determine whether their pseudo test collection generation methods ultimately give rise to similar rankings of retrieval systems as manually created test collections. Kim and Croft [18] generate a pseudo test collection for desktop search. Huurnink et al. [15] use click-through data to simulate relevance assessments. Later, they evaluate the performance of query simulation methods in terms of system rankings [16] and they find that incorporating document structure in the query generation process results in more realistic query simulators. Hofmann et al. [14] try to smooth noise from click-through data from an audio-visual archive's transaction log using purchase information of videos. We extend previous work on pseudo test collection generation [4] with a principled method to obtain good quality training material, using knowledge derived from editorial judgements.

Asadi et al. [2] describe a method for generating pseudo test collections for training learning to rank methods for web retrieval. Their methods build on the idea that anchor text in web documents is a good source for sampling queries, and the documents that these anchors link to are regarded as relevant documents for the anchor text (query). Our work shares analogies, but in the microblog setting, there is no anchor text to sample queries. Moreover, the temporal aspect of relevance plays a bigger role in microblog search.

Table 9: P30 performance on TREC MB 2011 topics for various LTR algorithms, trained on different collections. Features are tuned on MAP. Best run in bold. Indicated statistically significant differences are with regard to training on TREC-MB-2012. The best individual tuned ranker, DFR-FD, achieved 0.416.

Train on	Pegasos	RankSVM	CA
TREC-MB-2012	**0.446±0.001**	**0.436±0.004**	**0.447±0.004**
Random	0.401±0.004▽	0.356±0.011▼	0.378±0.006▼
Hashtags	0.437±0.002	0.430±0.004	0.434±0.002
Hashtags-T	0.438±0.001	0.426±0.002	0.434±0.003
Hashtags-TI	0.437±0.001	0.406±0.007▽	0.429±0.002▽
Hashtags-TI-X20	0.432±0.001	0.265±0.016▼	0.383±0.016▼
Hashtags-TI-X40	0.435±0.001	0.361±0.006▼	0.427±0.001▽
Hashtags-TI-X60	0.438±0.001	0.415±0.004▽	0.431±0.003▽
Hashtags-TI-X80	0.438±0.001	0.427±0.003	0.435±0.002
Hashtags-TI-QL1	0.189±0.135▼	0.034±0.015▼	0.293±0.107▼
Hashtags-TI-QL2	0.435±0.002	0.244±0.024▼	0.421±0.047▼
Hashtags-TI-QL3	0.443±0.001	0.240±0.012▼	0.427±0.023▼
Hashtags-TI-QL5	0.443±0.001	0.259±0.008▼	0.428±0.005▽
Hashtags-TI-QL20	0.438±0.001	0.320±0.007▼	0.432±0.004

Table 10: MAP performance on TREC MB 2011 topics for various LTR algorithms, trained on different collections. Features are tuned on MAP. Best performance per LTR algorithm in bold. Indicated statistically significant differences are with regard to training on TREC-MB-2012. The best individual tuned ranker, Tf-idf (Indri), achieved 0.357.

Train on	Pegasos	RankSVM	CA
TREC-MB-2012	**0.388±0.001**	0.362±0.003	**0.387±0.003**
Random	0.348±0.004▼	0.294±0.009▼	0.319±0.009▼
Hashtags	0.374±0.001	0.360±0.005	0.385±0.001
Hashtags-T	0.379±0.000	0.362±0.005	0.386±0.000
Hashtags-TI	0.383±0.001	0.344±0.003	0.377±0.002
Hashtags-TI-X20	0.376±0.001▽	0.198±0.015▼	0.332±0.013▼
Hashtags-TI-X40	0.380±0.001	0.300±0.007▽	0.373±0.001▽
Hashtags-TI-X60	0.383±0.001	0.352±0.005	0.381±0.003
Hashtags-TI-X80	0.381±0.000	**0.363±0.002**	0.384±0.002
Hashtags-TI-QL1	0.141±0.125▼	0.020±0.009▼	0.202±0.119▼
Hashtags-TI-QL2	0.370±0.001▽	0.185±0.019▼	0.360±0.046▼
Hashtags-TI-QL3	0.379±0.000	0.166±0.011▼	0.366±0.026▼
Hashtags-TI-QL5	0.383±0.001	0.165±0.007▼	0.372±0.006▽
Hashtags-TI-QL20	0.383±0.001	0.231±0.008▼	0.381±0.002

Carterette et al. [7] investigate what the minimal judging effort is that must be done to have confidence in the outcome of an evaluation. Rajput et al. [32] present a method for extending the recall base in a manually created test collection. Carterette et al. [8] find that test collections with thousands of queries with fewer relevant documents considerably reduce the assessor effort with no appreciable increase in evaluation errors. This finding inspired us to come up with pseudo test collection generators that are able to produce large numbers of queries: while the signal produced by an individual query may be noisy, the volume will produce a signal that is useful for learning and parameter tuning.

8. DISCUSSION AND CONCLUSION

Following the results of our experiments we list three main observations: (1) The Random pseudo test collection performs significantly worse than editorial collections in the retrieval experiments and shows low correlation to these collections in the tuning phase. (2) The top pseudo test collections are not significantly worse than editorial collections and show high correlation when tuning parameters. (3) Differences between various pseudo test collections on retrieval effectiveness are small.

Table 11: P30 performance on TREC MB 2012 topics for various LTR algorithms, trained on different collections. Features are tuned on MAP. Best performance per LTR algorithm in bold. Indicated statistically significant differences are with regard to training on TREC-MB-2011. The best individual tuned ranker, DFR-FD, achieved 0.351.

Train on	Pegasos	RankSVM	CA
TREC-MB-2011	**0.392±0.001**	**0.391±0.007**	0.392±0.007
Random	0.341±0.003$^\blacktriangledown$	0.289±0.008$^\blacktriangledown$	0.314±0.006$^\blacktriangledown$
Hashtags	0.379±0.001	0.330±0.011$^\triangledown$	0.378±0.001$^\triangledown$
Hashtags-T	0.372±0.001$^\triangledown$	0.336±0.005$^\triangledown$	0.382±0.001
Hashtags-TI	0.381±0.001	0.326±0.007$^\triangledown$	0.393±0.002
Hashtags-TI-X20	0.377±0.001	0.248±0.013$^\blacktriangledown$	0.353±0.008
Hashtags-TI-X40	0.379±0.001$^\triangledown$	0.294±0.009$^\blacktriangledown$	0.389±0.001
Hashtags-TI-X60	0.379±0.001	0.348±0.003$^\triangledown$	**0.394±0.006**
Hashtags-TI-X80	0.373±0.001$^\triangledown$	0.337±0.006$^\triangledown$	0.388±0.007
Hashtags-TI-QL1	0.198±0.089$^\blacktriangledown$	0.047±0.016$^\blacktriangledown$	0.291±0.059$^\blacktriangledown$
Hashtags-TI-QL2	0.374±0.002$^\triangledown$	0.231±0.016$^\blacktriangledown$	0.377±0.035$^\blacktriangledown$
Hashtags-TI-QL3	0.381±0.001	0.218±0.007$^\blacktriangledown$	0.382±0.016$^\blacktriangledown$
Hashtags-TI-QL5	0.385±0.001	0.248±0.005$^\blacktriangledown$	0.391±0.004
Hashtags-TI-QL20	0.380±0.001	0.302±0.005$^\blacktriangledown$	0.388±0.002

Table 12: MAP performance on TREC MB 2012 topics for various LTR algorithms, trained on different collections. Features are tuned on MAP. Best performance per LTR algorithm in bold. Indicated statistically significant differences are with regard to training on TREC-MB-2011. The best individual tuned ranker, DFR-FD, achieved 0.220.

Train on	Pegasos	RankSVM	CA
TREC-MB-2011	**0.245±0.000**	**0.245±0.004**	**0.246±0.004**
Random	0.207±0.001$^\blacktriangledown$	0.159±0.005$^\blacktriangledown$	0.176±0.006$^\blacktriangledown$
Hashtags	0.231±0.000$^\triangledown$	0.181±0.008$^\blacktriangledown$	0.224±0.001$^\triangledown$
Hashtags-T	0.227±0.001$^\triangledown$	0.193±0.004$^\blacktriangledown$	0.227±0.001$^\triangledown$
Hashtags-TI	0.234±0.001$^\triangledown$	0.172±0.005$^\blacktriangledown$	0.233±0.001$^\triangledown$
Hashtags-TI-X20	0.233±0.001$^\triangledown$	0.143±0.007$^\blacktriangledown$	0.210±0.005$^\blacktriangledown$
Hashtags-TI-X40	0.233±0.000$^\triangledown$	0.158±0.005$^\blacktriangledown$	0.230±0.001$^\triangledown$
Hashtags-TI-X60	0.233±0.000	0.196±0.002$^\blacktriangledown$	0.234±0.003$^\triangledown$
Hashtags-TI-X80	0.230±0.000$^\triangledown$	0.189±0.004$^\blacktriangledown$	0.230±0.004$^\triangledown$
Hashtags-TI-QL1	0.106±0.060$^\blacktriangledown$	0.026±0.008$^\blacktriangledown$	0.165±0.048$^\blacktriangledown$
Hashtags-TI-QL2	0.229±0.001$^\triangledown$	0.123±0.011$^\blacktriangledown$	0.233±0.021$^\blacktriangledown$
Hashtags-TI-QL3	0.234±0.000	0.106±0.004$^\blacktriangledown$	0.231±0.015$^\blacktriangledown$
Hashtags-TI-QL5	0.235±0.000	0.118±0.004$^\blacktriangledown$	0.233±0.003$^\triangledown$
Hashtags-TI-QL20	0.231±0.000$^\triangledown$	0.162±0.003$^\blacktriangledown$	0.228±0.001$^\triangledown$

Combining the top two observations leads us to conclude that our approach to constructing pseudo test collections works. We can successfully use pseudo test collections, as long as we find appropriate surrogate relevance labels. Why are these findings important? To train learning to rank methods on microblog retrieval tasks we do not have to invest in manual annotations but can use hashtags for creating training examples. Pseudo test collections can also be used successfully for tuning parameters of retrieval models.

The third observation is that the differences between our pseudo test collections are limited. More advanced methods for selecting tweets and hashtags result in performance that is only sporadically better than the naive baseline method, which treats all tweets and hashtags equally. We can look at this from two angles. (i) Collection construction: We can limit time spent on constructing a smooth and interesting pseudo test collection by substituting more advanced methods (Hashtags-T and -TI) with the naive Hashtags method. Using the naive method is faster and results in a larger collection, with similar results. (ii) Training volume: Investing in obtaining more interesting tweets and hashtags using our more advanced methods substantially reduces the number of queries in our collections. While the naive Hashtags uses over 1,800 queries and 460,000 relevant tweets, the other methods use only 890 (Hashtags-T) and 480 (Hashtags-TI) queries and equally reduced sets of relevant tweets. Training efficiency improves substantially by limiting

Table 13: P30 performance on 2011 and 2012 topics for retrieval models for which MAP was tuned on 2011 topics, ordered by 2012 performance. The only parameter free retrieval model, DFRee, achieved 0.416 on the 2011 topics, and 0.346 on the 2012 topics.

Model	2011	2012
DFR-FD (Terrier)	0.416	0.351
Tf-idf (Terrier)	0.397	0.348
PL2 (Terrier)	0.406	0.336
PRF (Terrier)	0.391	0.335
Tf-idf (Indri)	0.413	0.331
Okapi (Indri)	0.409	0.329
LM (Indri)	0.404	0.325
BUW (Indri)	0.128	0.154
BOW (Indri)	0.094	0.134

Table 14: MAP performance on 2011 and 2012 topics for retrieval models for which MAP was tuned on 2011 topics, ordered by 2012 performance. The only parameter free retrieval model, DFRee, achieved 0.351 on the 2011 topics, and 0.216 on the 2012 topics.

Model	2011	2012
DFR-FD (Terrier)	0.352	0.220
Tf-idf (Terrier)	0.352	0.215
PL2 (Terrier)	0.348	0.209
PRF (Terrier)	0.335	0.201
Tf-idf (Indri)	0.357	0.194
Okapi (Indri)	0.354	0.191
LM (Indri)	0.346	0.188
BUW (Indri)	0.075	0.069
BOW (Indri)	0.060	0.061

the number of queries in the collections. In other words, we can choose between spending more time on constructing our collections, while reducing training time, or take a naive collection construction approach that results in larger collections and thus longer training times. A similar observation holds for the editorial collections, which are the smallest collections (50–60 queries), but (supposedly) with the highest quality.

Summarizing, we have studied the use of pseudo test collections for training and tuning LTR systems for microblog retrieval. We use hashtags as surrogate relevance labels and generate queries from tweets that contain the particular hashtag. These pseudo test collections are then used for (1) tuning parameters of various retrieval models, and (2) training learning to rank methods for microblog retrieval. We explore three ways of constructing pseudo test collections, (i) a naive method that treats all tweets and hashtags equally, (ii) a method that takes timestamps into account, and (iii) a method that uses timestamps and selects only interesting microblog posts. We compare their performance to those of a randomly generated pseudo test collection and two editorial collections.

Our pseudo test collections have high correlation with the editorial collections in the parameter tuning phase, whereas the random collection has a significantly lower correlation. In the LTR phase we find that in most cases our collections do not perform significantly worse than the editorial collections, while the random collection does perform significantly worse.

Looking forward, we are interested in training on a mixture of editorial and generated ground truth. Our work is related to creating ground truth in a semi-supervised way and we also aim to further explore this relation.

Acknowledgements

This research was partially supported by the European Community's Seventh Framework Programme (FP7/2007-2013) under grant agreements nr 258191 (PROMISE Network of Excellence) and 288-024 (LiMoSINe project), the Netherlands Organisation for Scientific Research (NWO) under project nrs 640.004.802, 727.011.005, 612.001.116, HOR-11-10, the Center for Creation, Content and

Technology (CCCT), the BILAND project funded by the CLARIN-nl program, the Dutch national program COMMIT, the ESF Research Network Program ELIAS, the Elite Network Shifts project funded by the Royal Dutch Academy of Sciences (KNAW), and the Netherlands eScience Center under project number 027.012.105.

9. REFERENCES

[1] G. Amati and C. van Rijsbergen. Probabilistic models of information retrieval based on measuring the divergence from randomness. *ACM Trans. Inf. Syst.*, 20(4):357–389, 2002.

[2] N. Asadi, D. Metzler, T. Elsayed, and J. Lin. Pseudo test collections for learning web search ranking functions. In *SIGIR '11*, pages 1073–1082, 2011.

[3] L. Azzopardi, M. de Rijke, and K. Balog. Building simulated queries for known-item topics: an analysis using six european languages. In *SIGIR '07*, pages 455–462, 2007.

[4] R. Berendsen, M. Tsagias, M. de Rijke, and E. Meij. Generating pseudo test collections for learning to rank scientific articles. In *CLEF '12*, 2012.

[5] M. Bron, E. Meij, M. Peetz, M. Tsagkias, and M. de Rijke. Team COMMIT at TREC 2011. In *TREC 2011*, 2011.

[6] S. Carter, W. Weerkamp, and E. Tsagkias. Microblog language identification. *Language Resources and Evaluation Journal*, 47(1), 2013.

[7] B. Carterette, J. Allan, and R. Sitaraman. Minimal test collections for retrieval evaluation. In *SIGIR '06*, pages 268–275, 2006.

[8] B. Carterette, V. Pavlu, E. Kanoulas, J. A. Aslam, and J. Allan. Evaluation over thousands of queries. In *SIGIR '08*, pages 651–658, 2008.

[9] S. Clinchant and E. Gaussier. Bridging language modeling and divergence from randomness models: A log-logistic model for ir. In *ECIR '09*, pages 54–65, 2009.

[10] B. Croft, D. Metzler, and T. Strohman. *Search Engines: Information Retrieval in Practice*. Addison Wesley, 2009.

[11] S. Cronen-Townsend and W. B. Croft. Quantifying query ambiguity. In *HLT '02*, pages 104–109, 2002.

[12] M. Efron. Information search and retrieval in microblogs. *J. Am. Soc. Inf. Sci. Technol.*, 62:996–1008, 2011.

[13] M. Efron and G. Golovchinsky. Estimation methods for ranking recent information. In *SIGIR '11*, pages 495–504, 2011.

[14] K. Hofmann, B. Huurnink, M. Bron, and M. de Rijke. Comparing click-through data to purchase decisions for retrieval evaluation. In *SIGIR '10*, pages 761–762, 2010.

[15] B. Huurnink, K. Hofmann, and M. de Rijke. Simulating searches from transaction logs. In *SIGIR 2010 Workshop on the Simulation of Interaction*, 2010.

[16] B. Huurnink, K. Hofmann, M. de Rijke, and M. Bron. Validating query simulators: an experiment using commercial searches and purchases. In *CLEF '10*, pages 40–51, 2010.

[17] T. Joachims. Training linear SVMs in linear time. In *KDD '06*, pages 217–226, 2006.

[18] J. Kim and W. B. Croft. Retrieval experiments using pseudo-desktop collections. In *CIKM '09*, pages 1297–1306, 2009.

[19] H. Kwak, C. Lee, H. Park, and S. Moon. What is Twitter, a social network or a news media? In *WWW '10*, pages 591–600, 2010.

[20] G. G. Lee et al. SiteQ: Engineering high performance QA system using lexico-semantic pattern matching and shallow NLP. In *TREC 2001*, pages 442–451, 2001.

[21] J. Lin, C. Macdonald, I. Ounis, and I. Soboroff. Overview of the TREC 2011 Microblog track. In *TREC 2011*, 2012.

[22] T.-Y. Liu. Learning to rank for information retrieval. *Found. and Trends in Inf. Retr.*, 3:225–331, 2009.

[23] C. Lundquist, D. Grossman, and O. Frieder. Improving relevance feedback in the vector space model. In *CIKM '97*, pages 16–23, 1997.

[24] C. Macdonald, R. Santos, and I. Ounis. The whens and hows of learning to rank for web search. *Inf. Retr.*, pages 1–45, 2012.

[25] C. D. Manning and H. Schütze. *Foundations of statistical natural language processing*. MIT Press, 1999.

[26] K. Massoudi, E. Tsagkias, M. de Rijke, and W. Weerkamp. Incorporating query expansion and quality indicators in searching microblog posts. In *ECIR '11*, pages 362–367, 2011.

[27] D. Metzler. *A Feature-Centric View of Information Retrieval*. Springer, 2011.

[28] G. Mishne and M. de Rijke. A study of blog search. In *ECIR '06*, pages 289–301, 2006.

[29] A. Mohan, Z. Chen, and K. Q. Weinberger. Web-search ranking with initialized gradient boosted regression trees. *J. Mach. Learn. Res., Workshop and Conf. Proc.*, 14:77–89, 2011.

[30] N. Naveed, T. Gottron, J. Kunegis, and A. C. Alhadi. Searching microblogs: coping with sparsity and document quality. In *CIKM '11*, pages 183–188, 2011.

[31] J. Peng, C. Macdonald, B. He, V. Plachouras, and I. Ounis. Incorporating term dependency in the DFR framework. In *SIGIR '07*, pages 843–844, 2007.

[32] S. Rajput, V. Pavlu, P. B. Golbus, and J. A. Aslam. A nugget-based test collection construction paradigm. In *CIKM '11*, pages 1945–1948, 2011.

[33] S. Robertson and K. Jones. Simple, proven approaches to text retrieval. Technical report, U. Cambridge, 1997.

[34] S. Robertson and H. Zaragoza. On rank-based effectiveness measures and optimization. *Inf. Retr.*, 10(3):321–339, 2007.

[35] S. Robertson, S. Walker, S. Jones, M. Hancock-Beaulieu, and M. Gatford. Okapi at trec-3. In *TREC '94*, pages 109–109, 1995.

[36] D. Sculley. Large scale learning to rank. In *NIPS Workshop on Advances in Ranking*, 2009.

[37] S. Shalev-Shwartz, Y. Singer, and N. Srebro. Pegasos: Primal estimated sub-gradient solver for SVM. In *ICML '12*, pages 807–814, 2012.

[38] J. Tague and M. Nelson. Simulation of user judgments in bibliographic retrieval systems. In *SIGIR '81*, pages 66–71, 1981.

[39] J. Tague, M. Nelson, and H. Wu. Problems in the simulation of bibliographic retrieval systems. In *SIGIR '80*, pages 236–255, 1980.

[40] J. Teevan, D. Ramage, and M. R. Morris. #twittersearch: a comparison of microblog search and web search. In *WSDM '11*, pages 35–44, 2011.

[41] W. Weerkamp and M. de Rijke. Credibility-based reranking for blog post retrieval. *Inf. Retr.*, 15(3–4):243–277, 2012.

[42] C. Zhai and J. Lafferty. A study of smoothing methods for language models applied to ad hoc information retrieval. In *SIGIR '01*, pages 334–342, 2001.

Learning Latent Friendship Propagation Networks with Interest Awareness for Link Prediction*

Jun Zhang[1,2,3,4] Chaokun Wang[2,3,4] Philip S. Yu[5] Jianmin Wang[2,3,4]
[1] Department of Computer Science and Technology, Tsinghua University
[2] School of Software, Tsinghua University
[3] Tsinghua National Laboratory for Information Science and Technology
[4] Key Laboratory for Information System Security, Ministry of Education, P. R. China
[5] Department of Computer Science, University of Illinois at Chicago
zhang-jun10@mails.thu.edu.cn, chaokun@tsinghua.edu.cn, psyu@uic.edu, jimwang@tsinghua.edu.cn

ABSTRACT

It's well known that the transitivity of friendship is a popular sociological principle in social networks. However, it's still unknown that to what extent people's friend-making behaviors follow this principle and to what extent it can benefit the link prediction task.

In this paper, we try to adopt this sociological principle to explain the evolution of networks and study the latent friendship propagation. Unlike traditional link prediction approaches, we model link formation as results of individuals' friend-making behaviors combined with personal interests. We propose the Latent Friendship Propagation Network (LFPN), which depicts the evolution progress of one's egocentric network and reveals future growth potentials driven by the transitivity of friendship based on personal interests. We model individuals' social behaviors using the Latent Friendship Propagation Model (LFPM), a probabilistic generative model from which the LFPN can be learned effectively. To evaluate the power of the friendship propagation in link prediction, we design LFPN-RW which models the friend-making behavior as a random walk upon the LFPN naturally and captures the co-influence effect of the friend circles as well as personal interests to provide more accurate prediction.

Experimental results on real-world datasets show that LFPN-RW outperforms the state-of-the-art approaches. This convinces that the transitivity of friendship actually plays important roles in the evolution of social networks.

Categories and Subject Descriptors

H.2.8 [**DATABASE MANAGEMENT**]: Database Applications—*Data mining*; J.4 [**SOCIAL AND BEHAVIORAL SCIENCES**]: Sociology

Keywords

Link Prediction; Social Networks; Transitivity of Friendship; Friendship Propagation; Interest Awareness

*Corresponding authors: Chaokun Wang and Jianmin Wang.

SIGIR'13, July 28–August 1, 2013, Dublin, Ireland.
Copyright 2013 ACM 978-1-4503-2034-4/13/07 ...$15.00.

1. INTRODUCTION

The evolution of social networks has attracted considerable attention recently. Since the seminal work of Liben-Nowell and Kleinberg [18], it has been formulated as the link prediction task which studies the formation and variation of the links in the network. Both unsupervised and supervised approaches have been proposed, based on the current observations of the network, utilizing the structural or vertex-intrinsic features [19][9][20][1]. Most approaches treat the network as an evolving graph and each individual as a general vertex in the graph, while ignoring the initiative of individuals as active participants in the evolution of the social network.

From another point of view, people's social behaviors have been studied by sociologists long ago [28]. They have found many interesting and popular phenomena [23][21][26][8], which are also verified in online social networks by computer scientists [12][5][24][11][27]. Among these phenomena is triadic closure [26][8], which states that two persons with common friends will likely become friends in the future. The sociological principle under this phenomenon is the transitivity of friendship [26][15]. Although researchers have found that most of new links close an open triangle [16], not all open triangles will be closed with equal probabilities. It's still unknown how this principle works in real world, and to what extent it can promote the evolution of social networks and furthermore benefit the link prediction task.

In this paper, we study the evolution of social network based on one of the well-known sociological principles, i.e. the transitivity of friendship. We address the above problems by positing that there is some underlying unknown network over which friendships propagate, and the evolution of social networks can be regarded as results of the friendship propagation based on common user interests. We formulate such network as the Latent Friendship Propagation Network (LFPN), which depicts the growth process of one's ego-centric social network driven by the friendship propagation via the co-influence effect of the friend circles with common user interests, and also captures the trend of friendship propagation on the whole network. In LFPN, we assume one, denoted by the *ego*, expands her social circles mainly via her existing friends, who act as *intermediaries* and introduce new friends to the ego explicitly or implicitly based on common interests.

We demonstrate the proposed LFPN with a toy example. Fig. 1(a) shows an egocentric network with a as the ego, which we mark as purple. The blue vertices are a's friends; the green ones show the friends of a's friends. The connections among the blue and green vertices are omitted for brevity. Given the plain structure of an egocentric network, we can hardly observe the implicit intrinsic

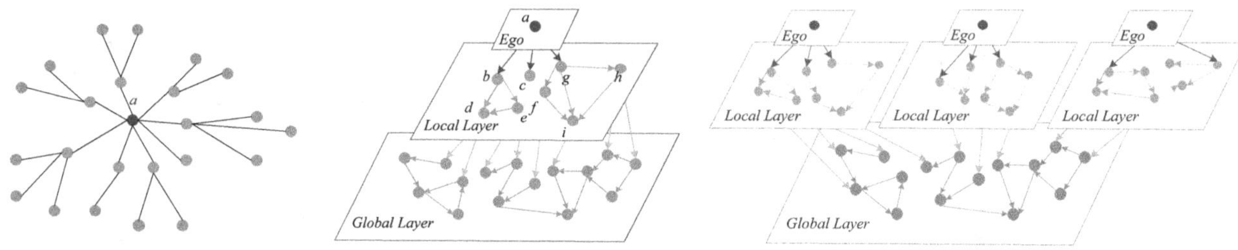

(a) Egocentric network of a (b) a's partial view of the LFPN (c) More complete view of the LFPN

Figure 1: An LFPN is composed of three layers: the ego layers, the local layers for each ego, and the global layer for the whole network. In this figure, the purple vertex *a* is the ego, the blue vertices are the friends of the ego and the green ones show other individuals in the network.

structures and relations within it. The LFPN shows a 3-layer hierarchical network for the original network. Fig. 1(b) shows the partial view of the ego a. While the first layer is the ego herself, the second layer, the *local layer*, consists of all her current friends and the directed edges as representation of the friendship propagation traces along which a created relationships with each one. In this figure we can see that a made friends with b directly, and via b she became friends of e, and furthermore she created friendship with d via b and e. Through the *local layer* as intermediaries a can make more new friends in the *global layer* in which the edges among individuals represent the potential friendship propagation directions in the whole network. While the *local layer* is defined for each ego and visualizes the growth of one's friend circles by showing the intermediaries for each of her friends, the *global layer* is inferred based upon all the *local layers* and defined for the whole network. A more complete LFPN with multiple egos is shown in Fig. 1(c).

However, learning the LFPN is challenging because the network over which friendship propagation takes place is usually unknown and unobserved. Thus, the first challenge is, *how we can leverage one's social behaviors to infer all the potential intermediaries and furthermore learn the structure of the friendship propagation network?*

While traditional approaches for link prediction are usually based on the topological features, LFPN provides a hierarchical view of one's friend circles from which we can observe the evolution of networks from the perspective of the ego, who drives this evolution progress. This leaves us the second challenge: *to what extent the transitivity of friendship influences the network evolution, whether there is a co-influence effect of the friend circle, and how they can be utilized to predict future shapes of the network?*

Along with the transitivity of friendship, another factor which affects one's social behaviors is the personal interests. In this study, we're also interested in the challenge that *how the personal interests, along with the friendship propagation, affect the creation of friendships?*

1.1 Contributions

To address these challenges we study how the LFPN can be inferred based on behavior modeling, and further utilized for predicting or recommending new links. To the best of our knowledge, this is the first time that the transitivity of friendship is deeply investigated and the link formation is studied based on the behavior modeling. The main contributions of this paper can be summarized as follows.

Firstly, we formulate the **LFPN**, which depicts the evolution traces of one's egocentric social network and potential friendship propagation traces on the whole network based on the transitivity of friendship with interest awareness.

We design **LFPM** (Latent Friendship Propagation Model), a probabilistic generative model for the friend-making behaviors of individuals in social networks. LFPM models the interest-aware friendship propagation driven by the transitivity of friendship. Given the time-stamped individuals' social behavior histories, we can learn the hidden LFPN based on LFPM effectively. It should be noted that both the friendship propagation and personal interests are inferred from the social behaviors only, and no other evidences are included.

Furthermore, we put forward a new method for link prediction utilizing the transitivity of friendship and personal interests based on the LFPN. We simulate the link creation using a random walk of an ego on the two layers of the LFPN. Firstly, she seeks for a preferred intermediary in her *local layer* of the LFPN, and via this intermediary she goes to the *global layer* where she makes new friends. We name this process as **LFPN-RW** (Random Walk upon LFPN), in which the random walk is guided by the friendship propagation based on the co-influence effect of friend circles and personal interests.

We conduct extensive experiments on real-world datasets. Experimental results show that the inferred LFPN actually contains important knowledge about the network evolution and can benefit the link prediction significantly.

1.2 Roadmap

The rest of this paper is organized as follows. We formulate the LFPN in Section 2. Methods for inferring the LFPN are developed in Section 3. Afterwards we present LFPN-RW, the new approach for link prediction upon LFPN in Section 4. In Section 5, we discuss the experimental results. We review related work in Section 6 and conclude this study in Section 7.

2. LFPN DEFINITION

In this section, we introduce the concepts related to LFPN. As shown in Fig. 1(c), the LFPN $\mathcal{G}$ is composed of three layers: the ego, the local layer and the global layer. In the following we first define the local layer and global layer respectively, and then give the definition of the LFPN.

Let $\mathbb{G} = \{G_1, G_2, \cdots, G_T\}$ denote an evolving social network where $G_t = (V_t, E_t)$ is a directed graph denoting the snapshot of the network at time t. Each vertex in V_t represents an individual in the network, and the edges in E_t indicate the friendships among them. ΔG_t denotes the new vertices and edges appearing during the period t (i.e. the time from $t-1$ to t), and thus we have $G_t = G_{t-1} \cup \Delta G_t$. We'll use G to denote any snapshot of the evolving $\mathbb{G}$ for simplicity. Furthermore, for each snapshot G_t we have a corresponding interaction set $X_t \subset V_t \times V_t$ which denotes the interactions among individuals in t. The interactions include co-authoring a paper in scholar collaboration network, leaving a message on Facebook, etc.

It should be noted that although the network G is directed here, the problem discussed in this paper is also applicable to undirected networks which can be transformed to directed networks.

In this paper, we study how E grows in social networks, i.e. the formation of friendships. Based on the transitivity of friendship, when two individuals become friends, we assume their common friends act as the role of "*intermediaries*".

Definition 1. **Latent Friendship Propagation Triple** (*LFP Triple*). For three vertices u, z and v in G, (u, z, v) is named as an **LFP Triple** if u makes friends with v via z. u is called the initiator of this tuple and z is the intermediary.

Each LFP Triple (u, z, v) is associated with an **intermediation probability** $p(z|\langle u, v\rangle)$ which denotes the probability that z has acted as the intermediary for u to makes friends with v.

We use $F_t(u)$ to denote the set of friends of u at time t, and $F_t(u, v)$ to denote the set of common friends of u and v at time t. As each common friend in $F_t(u, v)$ may act as the intermediary, the intermediation probability satisfies:

$$\sum_{z \in F_t(u,v)} p(z|\langle u, v\rangle) = 1. \tag{1}$$

If u doesn't have any common friends with v, we assume u makes friends with v directly.

Definition 2. The **local layer** of ego u on an LFPN $\mathcal{G}$, denoted as $\mathcal{G}^{L(u)}$, consists of all the friends of u. For each LFP Triple (u, z, v) initiated by u there is a corresponding *local LFP edge* $\langle z, v\rangle$ in $\mathcal{G}^{L(u)}$, whose weight $w^{L(u)}_{z,v} = p(z|\langle u, v\rangle)$.

The *local layer* of the LFPN is defined for each ego u. Each friend of the ego $u \in \mathcal{G}^{L(u)}$ can play the role of intermediary for u to make more new friends. We use the **intermediary preference probability** $p(u \rightarrowtail z)$ to measure u's preference for each friend z as the intermediary.

We define the cross-layer edges from the *ego* to the *local layer* as *intermediary preference edges.*

Definition 3. For each friend $z \in \mathcal{G}^{L(u)}$, there's an **intermediary preference edge** $\langle u, z\rangle$ pointing from the ego u to z in the local layer, whose weight $w^{E}_{u,z} = p(u \rightarrowtail z)$.

Definition 4. Each LFP Triple (u, z, v) derives an **LFP Pattern** $z \twoheadrightarrow v$, indicating that one's friendship with z is likely to propagate to v.

Each LFP Pattern is associated with a **friendship propagation probability** $p(z \twoheadrightarrow v)$ which denotes the extent to which z is willing to recommend v to her friends and the friends of z are likely to make friends with v in the future.

Definition 5. The **global layer** of an LFPN $\mathcal{G}$, denoted as $\mathcal{G}^G$, consists of all the individuals of the given social network. For each LFP Pattern $z \twoheadrightarrow v$ there's a corresponding *global LFP edge* $\langle z, v\rangle$ in $\mathcal{G}^G$, whose weight $w^{G}_{z,v} = p(z \twoheadrightarrow v)$.

The *global layer* is defined for the whole network based on the LFP Patterns. It can be interpreted as the aggregation of all the *local layers*. Each vertex has its direct projection on the *global layer* so we don't define the cross-layer from the *local* to *global* layer again.

Now we can give the definition of LFPN.

Table 1: The notations for the LFPM

U, K	# of individuals and topics
N_u, V_u	# of new friends and interactions of u
$F(u)$	The current friend set of individual u
$Y(u)$	The new friend set of individual u
$X(u)$	The interaction collection of individual u
θ_u	The intermediary preference distribution of u
ϕ_u	The friendship strength distribution of u
χ_u	The interest preference distribution of u
ψ_c	The reputation distribution of topic c
$z_{u,y}$	The intermediary assignment of the friendship $u \rightarrow y$
$\alpha, \beta, \delta, \gamma$	The prior parameters for θ, ϕ, χ, ψ, respectively
$\Omega^{(cz)}_{c_i,z_i}$	# that z_i has acted an intermediary in topic c_i
$\Omega^{(cy)}_{c_i,y_i}$	# that y_i has been recommended and accepted as a new friend in topic c_i
$\Omega^{(uc)}_{u_i,c_i}$	# that u_i has selected friends in topic c_i
$\Omega^{(uz)}_{u_i,z_i}$	# that u_i has selected z_i as an intermediary
$\Omega^{(zy)}_{z_i,y_i}$	# that z_i has recommend y_i for others
$\Omega^{(uv)}_{u_i,y_i}$	# that u_i has interacted with y_i

Definition 6. The **Latent Friendship Propagation Network** (LFPN) $\mathcal{G}$ for a given social network G is a weighted 3-layer network consisting the *ego layers* $\{u\}$, the *local layers* for each ego $\{\mathcal{G}^{L(u)}\}$, and the *global layer* $\mathcal{G}^G$.

The *local layer* shows the inferred traces for the evolution history of one's current egocentric network, while the *global layer* indicates the possible traces for the friendship propagation on the whole social network in the future. The *global layer* can also be regarded as a friend-recommendation network, as in some sense it's the recommendation among people that promotes the friendship propagation.

3. LFPN INFERENCE

In this section, we develop effective algorithms for the inference of LFPN for the given social network. Before proceeding, we formulate our problem as follows:

LFPN Inference Problem. Given an evolving social network $\mathbb{G} = \{G_1, G_2, \cdots, G_t\}$ and the associated interaction sets $\mathbb{X} = \{X_1, X_2, \cdots, X_t\}$, the LFPN inference problem is to infer the LFPNs $\mathcal{G}_1, \mathcal{G}_2, \cdots, \mathcal{G}_t$, where $\mathcal{G}_t$ is the LFPN for G_t.

As each snapshot is a subgraph of any of later snapshots, each LFPN also contains the structures of the LFPN inferred from the earlier snapshots. However, the weights of the same edges are not necessarily equal because the network is evolving and the propagation patterns are also varying.

In the remainder of this section, we first introduce the LFPM model for learning the LFPN on a single snapshot, and then present the inference framework for LFPM. We discuss the inference of LFPN on an evolving network at last.

3.1 The LFPM Model

Each LFP Triple (u, z, v) implies the assumption that the friend-making behavior is a 2-step process: u selects z as an intermediary first and then via z she makes friends with v. Meanwhile this process is inevitably influenced by the interests of u. LFP Patterns are the aggregation of LFP Triples, and both of them are the basic elements for LFPN. Thus the preliminary problem for the LFPN inference is to find all the LFP Triples. In other words, given each friendship between u and v, we need to infer the intermediary z.

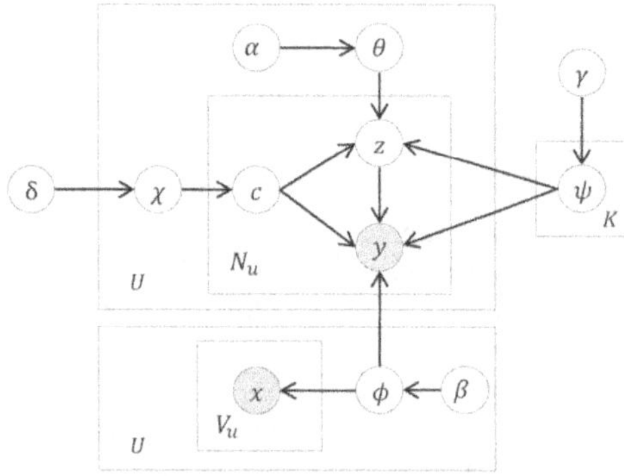

Figure 2: The graphical representation of LFPM

To model this process and infer the intermediaries of each friendship, we propose the Latent Friendship Propagation Model (LFPM), a probabilistic generative model for the social behaviors in social networks. In this paper we only consider the social behaviors like friend-making and interactions. LFPM models the generative process for individuals' social behaviors as follows:

1. Sample the number of individuals $U \sim$ Poisson (ϵ).
2. For each of the K interest areas c, sample its *reputation distribution* $\psi_c \sim$ Dir(γ)
3. For each individual u:
   (a) Sample her *friendship strength distribution* $\phi_u \sim$ Dir(β_u).
   (b) Sample the number of her interactions, $V_u \sim$ Poisson(ξ).
   (c) For each of the V_u interactions:
      i. Sample one of her existing friends, $x \sim \phi_u$, as another participant of the interaction
4. For each individual u:
   (a) Sample her *interest preference distribution* $\chi_u \sim$ Dir(δ).
   (b) Sample her *intermediary preference distribution* $\theta_u \sim$ Dir(α_u).
   (c) Sample the number of her new friends, $N_u \sim$ Poisson(ζ).
   (d) For each of the N_u new friends:
      i. Sample an interest area $c \sim \chi_u$
      ii. Sample an intermediary $z \sim \theta_u \cdot \psi_c$
      iii. Sample a new friend $y \sim \phi_z \cdot \psi_c$

We draw the graphical representation of LFPM in Fig. 2. In LFPM, each interest area is modelled as a distribution over individuals. Each ego is modelled as a distribution of her intermediaries, i.e. the individuals that may make recommendations to her, and each intermediary as a distribution over the friends of this intermediary. Thus, the set of new friends of an ego can be modelled as the mixture of her intermediaries and interest areas. Specifically, the *intermediary preference distribution* θ describes through whom an ego prefers to make new friends, and *friendship strength distribution* ϕ models the closeness of an ego with each of her friends. Such closeness can be reflected by both the frequency of their interactions and the willingness of the ego to recommend her friends to others. We use the *interest preference distribution* χ to model one's interest preference in friend-making behaviors, and regard the *reputation distribution* ψ as a global reputation ranking of all individuals in each interest area. It's natural to assume that one prefers to make friends with someone with higher reputation in her preferred area. It should be noted that the interests here are learned only from the social behavior histories, rather than external profiles.

To improve the inference performance, we adopt heuristic pruning by constraining that for each individual her intermediary preference distribution and friendship strength distribution are only defined over her current friends, based on the assumption that only the current friends of ego u may act as u's intermediaries, and that an intermediary z can only recommend and interact with the current friends of z. This is different from traditional topic models like LDA[2], which defines the distributions over the whole space. Thus in our model, each individual maintains a unique sampling space for herself. Correspondingly, the prior distributions for θ and ϕ are also required to be defined on the corresponding pruned space for each individual. That's why the priors α and β need to be defined for each individual u and are placed within the big box labelled U in the graphical model shown in Fig. 2.

LFPM applies to a snapshot G_t and tries to infer the friendship propagation in the expansion of one's egocentric network in period t. For the social behaviors that happen in period t, the hidden distributions θ and ϕ of LFPM can be naturally interpreted as the intermediary preference probabilities w^E of each ego and friendship propagation probabilities w^G in the LFPN in period t, respectively. Each possible intermediary assignment for each friendship is an LFP Triple and the sampling probability can be regarded as the intermediation probabilities w^L. With the inferred LFP Triples and the weights w^E, w^L and w^G we can construct the LFPN $\mathcal{G}_t$.

3.2 Inference Framework for LFPM

Exact inference for LFPM is generally intractable. In this subsection we present the framework for LFPM inference using Gibbs sampling, a special case of Markov-Chain Monte Carlo (MCMC) simulation, which can emulate high-dimensional probability distributions by the stationary behavior of a Markov chain.

Firstly, the joint probability of all observed and unobserved data can be stated as follows (with the distributions integrated out):

$$P(C,Z,X,Y;\alpha,\beta,\gamma,\delta) = \Big(\prod_{u=1}^{U}\frac{B(\Omega_u^{(uz)}+\alpha_u^{(\theta)})}{B(\alpha_u^{(\theta)})}\Big)\Big(\prod_{k=1}^{K}\frac{B(\Omega_k^{(cz)}+\Omega_k^{(cy)}+\gamma)}{B(\gamma)}\Big) \cdot\Big(\prod_{u=1}^{U}\frac{B(\Omega_u^{(uv)}+\Omega_u^{(zy)}+\beta_u^{(\phi)})}{B(\beta_u^{(\phi)})}\Big)\Big(\prod_{u=1}^{U}\frac{B(\Omega_u^{(uc)}+\delta)}{B(\delta)}\Big), \quad (2)$$

where $B(\cdot)$ is the multinomial Beta function. For the details of other notations please refer to Table 1.

We infer the model by updating the estimation for unobserved variables c and z iteratively. In each iteration, we sample c and z for each new friendship i according to the conditional probability $p(c_i|C_{-i},Z,X,Y;\alpha,\beta,\gamma,\delta)$ and $p(z_i|C,Z_{-i},X,Y;\alpha,\beta,\gamma,\delta)$. Y and X are the new friendship and the interaction data, respectively. C and Z are estimations for the interest area and intermediary for each friendship, respectively. C_{-i} is the current estimations except c_i and Z_{-i} is that except z_i.

The sampling probabilities can be estimated by

$$p(c_i|C_{-i},Z,X,Y;\alpha,\beta,\gamma,\delta)=\frac{P(C,Z,X,Y)}{P(C_{-i},Z,X,Y)} \propto \frac{(\Omega_{c_i,z_i}^{(cz)}+\Omega_{c_i,y_i}^{(cy)}+\gamma_{c_i,z_i}-1)}{\sum_{v\in F(u_i)}(\Omega_{c_i,v}^{(cz)}+\Omega_{c_i,v}^{(cy)}+\gamma_{c_i,v})-1} \cdot\frac{\Omega_{u_i,c_i}^{(uc)}+\delta_{u_i,c_i}-1}{\sum_{k=1}^{K}(\Omega_{u_i,k}^{(uc)}+\delta_{u_i,k}-1)}, \quad (3)$$

$$p(z_i|C,Z_{-i},X,Y;\alpha,\beta,\gamma,\delta)=\frac{P(C,Z,X,Y)}{P(C,Z_{-i},X,Y)} \propto \frac{\Omega_{u_i,z_i}^{(uz)}+\alpha_{u_i,z_i}^{(\theta)}-1}{\sum_{v\in F(u_i)}(\Omega_{u_i,v}^{(uz)}+\alpha_{u_i,v}^{(\theta)})-1} \cdot\frac{\Omega_{z_i,y_i}^{(uv)}+\Omega_{z_i,y_i}^{(zy)}+\beta_{z_i,y_i}^{(\phi)}-1}{\sum_{v\in F(u_i)}(\Omega_{z_i,v}^{(uv)}+\Omega_{z_i,v}^{(zy)}+\beta_{z_i,v}^{(\phi)})-1} \cdot\frac{\Omega_{c_i,z_i}^{(cz)}+\Omega_{c_i,z_i}^{(cy)}+\gamma_{c_i,z_i}-1}{\sum_{v\in F(u_i)}(\Omega_{c_i,v}^{(cz)}+\Omega_{c_i,v}^{(cy)}+\gamma_{c_i,v})-1}. \quad (4)$$

Algorithm 1 LFPM Inference using Gibbs Sampling

Require:
The snapshot network G_{t-1} at time $t-1$
The increment of the network in period t, ΔG_t
The interaction set in period t, X_t
Ensure:
The hidden distributions θ, ϕ, χ, ψ
The sampling distributions P^c, P^z
1: Initialize F, Y using $G_{t-1}, \Delta G_t$, respectively
2: Assign interest areas for each new friendship randomly
3: Assign intermediaries for each new friendship randomly
4: **while** not finished **do**
5:   **for** each individual u who has new friends **do**
6:     **for** each new friend $v \in Y(u)$ **do**
7:       Sample interest area using Eq. 3
8:       Sample intermediary using Eq. 4
9:     **end for**
10:   **end for**
11: **end while**
12: Update distributions θ, ϕ, χ, ψ using Eq. 5 – 8
13: Record all the sampling distributions for topics and intermediaries in the last iteration with P^c and P^z
14: **return** $\theta, \phi, \chi, \psi, P^c, P^z$

Given the estimations for all unobserved data, we can estimate the hidden distributions:

$$\theta_{u_i,z_i} = \frac{\Omega^{(uz)}_{u_i,z_i} + \alpha^{(\theta)}_{u_i,z_i}}{\sum_{v\in F(u_i)}(\Omega^{(uz)}_{u_i,v} + \alpha^{(\theta)}_{u_i,v})}, \quad (5)$$

$$\phi_{z_i,y_i} = \frac{\Omega^{(uv)}_{z_i,y_i} + \Omega^{(zy)}_{z_i,y_i} + \beta^{(\phi)}_{z_i,y_i}}{\sum_{v\in F(u_i)}(\Omega^{(uv)}_{z_i,v} + \Omega^{(zy)}_{z_i,v} + \beta^{(\phi)}_{z_i,v})}, \quad (6)$$

$$\chi_{u_i,c_i} = \frac{\Omega^{(uc)}_{u_i,c_i} + \delta_{u_i,c_i}}{\sum_{k=1}^{K}(\Omega^{(uc)}_{u_i,k} + \delta_{u_i,k})}, \quad (7)$$

$$\psi_{c_i,u_i} = \frac{\Omega^{(cz)}_{c_i,u_i} + \Omega^{(cy)}_{c_i,u_i} + \gamma_{c_i,u_i}}{\sum_{u=1}^{U}(\Omega^{(cz)}_{c_i,u} + \Omega^{(cy)}_{c_i,u} + \gamma_{c_i,u})}. \quad (8)$$

Algorithm 1 presents the inference framework. Firstly, it initializes the friends set F before period t, and the new friendships Y that emerge in t. The interest area and intermediary for each new friendship are initialized randomly before the iteration. Next in Line 4–11 the interest and intermediary are updated for each new friendship using Eq. 3 and 4, iteratively. The iteration is repeated until converge or the count of iterations reaches a given threshold. The hidden distributions can be estimated using Eq. 5 - 8.

3.3 Learning Evolving LFPN in Cascade

In LFPM all behaviors are assumed to be independent with each other, and the correlation among the behaviors is ignored, which will lead to the loss of knowledge carried by the temporal behavior sequence. To minimizing this loss, we can split the evolving social network $\mathbb{G}$ into fine-grained snapshots $G_1, G_2, \cdots, G_t$ and infer the LFPM model on each snapshot, and thus we can build the corresponding LFPN $\mathcal{G}_1, \mathcal{G}_2, \cdots, \mathcal{G}_t$ respectively. However, each $\mathcal{G}_t$ is also a snapshot of the evolving $\mathcal{G}$ and only carries the information of the behaviors in t, but ignores the knowledge of the previous behavior history. For learning the complete evolving LFPN, we apply the LFPM in cascade, during which the later models can inherit the knowledge learned from the previous models.

The knowledge accumulation in cascade LFPM is achieved by the prior parameters, which can significantly influence the behaviour of the model by bringing important priori knowledge[10]. Via the priors, the knowledge in the previous period can be transferred into the next period successively. We define the priors of the LFPM at time t as the linear combination of the accumulated knowledge from previous models encoded by the priors and the new knowledge encoded by the statistics in the last period $t-1$ as follows:

$$\alpha^t_{u,z} = \lambda \cdot \alpha^{t-1}_{u,z} + \Omega^{(u,z)(t-1)}_{u,z} \quad (9)$$

$$\beta^t_{u,y} = \lambda \cdot \beta^{t-1}_{u,y} + \Omega^{(u,v)(t-1)}_{u,y} + \Omega^{(z,y)(t-1)}_{u,y} \quad (10)$$

$$\delta^t_{u,c} = \lambda \cdot \delta^{t-1}_{u,c} + \Omega^{(u,c)(t-1)}_{u,c} \quad (11)$$

$$\gamma^t_{c,u} = \lambda \cdot \gamma^{t-1}_{c,u} + \Omega^{(c,y)(t-1)}_{c,u} \quad (12)$$

where λ is a cascade damping factor. A higher λ means to inherit more priori information from the earlier models. For the first model the priors are initialized with the default values $\alpha_0, \beta_0, \delta_0, \gamma_0$.

While cascade LFPM allows knowledge accumulation in the model inference on the sequential snapshots, the LFPN can also inherit the structures from previous periods. By adding the new structures and updating the weights learned from the LFPM for each period, we can always get the up-to-date evolving LFPN for the evolving social network. The details are given in Algorithm 2.

Algorithm 2 Building Evolving LFPN

Require:
The evolving network $\mathbb{G}$
Ensure:
The evolving LFPNs $\{\mathcal{G}_t\}$ for $\mathbb{G}$
Split $\mathbb{G}$ into T subgraphs by discrete periods
for each period $t \in T$ **do**
  Initialize the priors for t using the previous model according to Eq. 9 – 12
  Infer the LFPM on G_t
  Initialize LFPN $\mathcal{G}_t$ using the structure of $\mathcal{G}_{t-1}$
  {In the following we omit the subscript t of weights and distributions for brevity}
  for each ego $u \in G_t$ **do**
    Add new friends of u in t to $\mathcal{G}^{L(u)}_t$
    for each friend $z \in \mathcal{G}^{L(u)}_t$ **do**
      Add cross-layer edge $\langle u, z\rangle$ and set $w^E_{u,z} \leftarrow \theta_{u,z}$
    end for
    for each LFP Triple (u, z, v) initiated by u **do**
      Add local LFP edge $\langle z, v\rangle$ to $\mathcal{G}^{L(u)}_t$
      Set $w^{L(u)}_{z,v} \leftarrow p(z|\langle u, v\rangle)$
    end for
  end for
  Add new individuals to $\mathcal{G}^G_t$
  for each LFP Pattern (z, v) derived from the LFP Triples **do**
    Add global LFP edge $\langle z, v\rangle$ to $\mathcal{G}^G_t$
    Set $w^G_{z,v} \leftarrow \phi_{z,v}$
  end for
end for
return $\mathcal{G}_1, \mathcal{G}_2, \cdots, \mathcal{G}_t$

4. LFPN-BASED LINK PREDICTION

LFPN adopts the transitivity of friendship to explain the evolution of social networks and shows the potential friendship propagation in the network. An interesting problem is, to what extent the LFPN can model the hidden power which drives the growth of social networks. We study this by applying LFPN in the traditional link prediction problem in social networks. We formulate the problem as follows:

LFPN based Link Prediction Problem. Given an LFPN $\mathcal{G}_t$ inferred from a snapshot G_t of the evolving social network G at

Table 2: The statistics of the datasets. V, E: number of existing nodes and edges in each dataset, S: number of egos for prediction, D: total number of candidate friends for the egos, R: total number of candidate friendships for prediction, E/V: average degree of each node, R/S: average candidate friendships of each ego.

Dataset	V	E	S	D	R	E/V	R/S
cond-mat	27,348	72,119	465	21,266	274,817	2.637	1,182.009
hep-ex	5,667	60,425	45	3,476	85,447	10.663	3,797.644
hep-lat	3,804	13,331	216	3,059	74,189	3.504	686.935
hep-ph	17,615	78,932	601	14,943	529,623	4.481	1,762.473
hep-th	14,751	27,299	113	11,608	100,717	1.851	1,782.603
nucl-ex	4,425	59,769	167	3,396	132,803	13.507	1,590.455

time t, our problem is to predict the new friendships in period $t+1$, i.e. ΔE_{t+1}.

Here we don't consider the new-coming vertices in the network. Random Walk (RW) provides an effective node proximity measure for predicting new links [31][1]. However, traditional RW regards the social network as a plain graph while ignoring the motivation of individuals. Unlike them, we predict new links based on behavior modeling. We design a new random walk upon the LFPN, **LFPN-RW**. In LFPN-RW, we treat the creation of new friendship as the result of friendship propagation in the network. In this way, LFPN-RW captures the co-influence effect of the friend circles on one's friend-making behaviors, rather than considering them as independent events. Furthermore, the personal interests are also taken into consideration by being incorporated within the weights of edges.

To predict the new friends of u, consider a random walker who starts the LFPN-RW from the ego u. Then LFPN-RW operates on the *local* and *global* layer of the LFPN successively, modeling the 2-step friend-making process. The walk on *local layer* allows one to find an intermediary first, and to make new friends via this intermediary on the *global layer* next. The basic assumption for the random walk on the *local layer* is that one should prefer the intermediary whom she knows via her preferred intermediaries; and that for the random walk on the *global layer* is that one should be likely to make friends with those recommended by important people.

We introduce the process of LFPN-RW for u as follows. Firstly, the walker goes to any vertex $z \in \mathcal{G}^{L(u)}$ with the intermediary preference probability $w^{E}_{u,z}$, and walks in $\mathcal{G}^{L(u)}$ randomly. At each vertex, the walker can go to next vertex along any local LFP edge with probability $1-\mu$, or go back to the ego u with probability μ and then restart the walk.

When the walker stops at some vertex $z \in \mathcal{G}^{L(u)}$, before jumping to the ego u, she jumps to the projection of z in the global layer $\mathcal{G}^{G}$, and starts the random walk on $\mathcal{G}^{G}$ to find a new friend. Arriving at any vertex in $\mathcal{G}^{G}$, the walker may go to any of its neighbors along the global LFP edges with probability $1-\mu$, or just stop there with probability μ and then jump back to the ego u directly.

Before proceeding, we revise the weight definition of the edges in LFPN to combine the global propagation probabilities and personal interests in the random walk from u:

$$w^{L(u)}_{z,v} = \phi_{z,v} \cdot p(z|\langle u, v\rangle), \quad (13)$$

$$w^{G(u)}_{v,y} = \phi_{v,y} \cdot \sum_{c \in C} (\chi_{u,c} \cdot \psi_{c,y}), \quad (14)$$

where C is the collection of interest areas. Eq. 13 biases the local layer using global propagation probabilities. Meanwhile, Eq. 14 biases the global layer by incorporating the personal interests, and thus ensures that the friendship is more likely to propagate to those with higher reputation in u's preferred interest areas in the random walk of u.

Let $r^{L(u)}(z)$ and $r^{G(u)}(v)$ denote the steady-state probabilities of the random walk initialized from the ego u in $\mathcal{G}^{L(u)}$ and $\mathcal{G}^{G(u)}$, respectively. They satisfy: (assuming all the weights in LFPN are normalized)

$$r^{L(u)}(z) = (1-\mu) \cdot \sum_{z' \in F(u,z)} w^{L(u)}_{z',z} \cdot r^{L(u)}(z') + \mu \cdot w^{E(u)}_{u,z} \quad (15)$$

$$r^{G(u)}(v) = (1-\mu) \cdot \sum_{v' \in F(v)} w^{G(u)}_{v',v} \cdot r^{G(u)}(v') + \mu \cdot r^{L(u)}(v) \quad (16)$$

where μ is the restart probability in the walk. $r^{L(u)}(z)$ can be regarded as the probability that u will select z as the intermediary in a friend-making behavior, and $r^{G(u)}(v)$ as the probability that u decides to make friends with v finally. This can be used to predict or recommend new friends for u.

5. EXPERIMENTAL EVALUATION

In this section, we demonstrate the effectiveness of our model through comprehensive experiments on multiple real-world datasets. We introduce our experimental settings in the first two subsections, and afterwards present and discuss the details of the experimental results.

5.1 Datasets

We construct 6 real-world datasets from Arxiv[1], an archive for electronic preprints of scientific papers in the fields of mathematics, physics, etc. The datasets include **cond-mat** (Condensed Matter), **hep-ex** (High Energy Physics - Experiment), **hep-lat** (High Energy Physics - Lattice), **hep-ph** (High Energy Physics - Phenomenology), **hep-th** (High Energy Physics - Theory) and **nucl-ex** (Nuclear Experiment). For each dataset, we use the network evolution history in 1998–2000 as the training set and predict the new links emerging in 2001–2003. Here we only make predictions for the egos who have been in the network up to 1998. And then for each ego, we select her/his 2-hop neighbors as candidate friends for prediction, because it's found that most of the new links connect two individuals with common friends[16][1]. The statistics of the datasets are shown in Table 2.

5.2 Baselines and Evaluation Methodology

Baselines. We compare our method with other 9 popular link prediction methods, which can be classified into 5 sorts.

- Local neighbourhood based measures, including *Jaccard Coefficient* and *Adamic / Adar*, two best measures reported in [19].
- Variants of random walk based on global network structures, including *Random Walk with Restarts (RWR)* [25] , *SimRank* [13] and *Maximum Entropy Random Walk (MERW)* [4]. *R-WR* measures the proximity between two nodes by the probability that one arrives at another in a random walk. *SimRank*

[1]Arxiv: http://arxiv.org/

Table 3: The performance of various link prediction methods on the six datasets.

Dataset	Metric	AdamicAdar	Jaccard	LaFT-Proximity	SimRank	MF	MF-BL	RWR	MERW	SRW	LFPN-RW
cond-mat	MAP	0.20119	0.1743	0.20796	0.12685	0.09929	0.09266	0.25933	0.2165	**0.26378**	0.24867
	P@10	0.08782	0.07815	0.07438	0.05363	0.04761	0.04524	0.1089	0.10901	0.10428	**0.11191**
	AUC	0.69089	0.62261	0.70027	0.5658	0.53794	0.50567	0.74899	0.59948	0.75552	**0.76101**
hep-ex	MAP	0.23527	0.23922	0.23388	0.20722	0.10362	0.12034	**0.26752**	0.20549	0.21131	0.26608
	P@10	0.10001	0.11556	0.07667	**0.12222**	0.06444	0.06667	0.08667	0.05111	0.08889	0.09778
	AUC	0.65977	0.6738	0.67723	0.66678	0.47561	0.47822	0.6697	0.64236	0.66543	**0.67919**
hep-lat	MAP	0.19878	0.15381	0.20324	0.10139	0.06187	0.08202	0.25117	0.19337	0.25893	**0.27711**
	P@10	0.11574	0.08287	0.09083	0.05046	0.02685	0.04352	0.14444	0.08093	0.09028	**0.16019**
	AUC	0.73988	0.67935	0.74152	0.61405	0.51185	0.48524	0.78936	0.61661	0.80564	**0.83025**
hep-ph	MAP	0.17418	0.16228	0.17627	0.09455	0.07149	0.07835	0.24014	0.1994	0.22646	**0.27212**
	P@10	0.08587	0.07056	0.05775	0.03729	0.04344	0.06837	0.11566	0.09274	0.11141	**0.12830**
	AUC	0.71379	0.66339	0.72125	0.59292	0.53282	0.61038	0.76727	0.6312	0.75767	**0.81268**
hep-th	MAP	0.19384	0.16609	0.11209	0.09864	0.08205	0.11605	**0.25992**	0.21746	0.23688	0.25668
	P@10	0.06903	0.06814	0.07918	0.03717	0.02655	0.03982	0.10088	0.10133	0.09425	**0.11239**
	AUC	0.68021	0.63403	0.69231	0.53306	0.51608	0.51852	0.74719	0.60993	0.72813	**0.78204**
nucl-ex	MAP	0.18049	0.17826	0.22870	0.1858	0.09074	0.09723	0.28525	0.29525	0.25826	**0.31502**
	P@10	0.12216	0.10599	0.12994	0.11018	0.0521	0.06527	0.16826	0.16581	0.18497	**0.22515**
	AUC	0.71581	0.67474	0.75488	0.68996	0.49876	0.53021	0.76803	0.72169	0.76481	**0.79627**

estimates how soon two random walkers will meet each other in the graph. While both assume the graph is unweighted, *MERW* assigns the propagation probabilities proportional to the eigenvector centrality of nodes [17].

- A state-of-the-art supervised link prediction approach, *Supervised Random Walk (SRW)* [1], which performs random walk on a weighted graph with the weights learned as a function of features.
- Matrix Factorization methods, including the basic *MF* [30] which considers the hidden features as the recommendation of intermediaries, and an improved method, denoted as *MF-BL* here, which tries to overcome the imbalance problem [22].
- *LaFT-Proximity*, a proximity measure based on the LaFT-Tree, our previous work which studies the transitivity of friendship in social networks[32].

All of the above methods are based on link structures while *SRW* utilizes more external features.

Evaluation Metrics. We evaluate the prediction performance of the above algorithms using 3 metrics: MAP (Mean Average Precision), P@10 and AUC (Area Under the ROC Curve). Generally, MAP measures how well the algorithm ranks positive instances above negative instances, P@10 measures the precision of the top 10 predictions given by the algorithm, and AUC measures how well the algorithm distinguishes positive instances from negative instances.

Parameter Settings. For LFPM, we set the default priors $\alpha_0 = \beta_0 = 1, \delta_0 = \gamma_0 = 0.1$, and the number of interest areas $K = 10$, as they are shown appropriate in our experiments. For each LFPM, we run Gibbs sampling for 20 iterations at most. The cascade damping factor for LFPM $\lambda = 0.5$.

In *LFPN-RW*, *RWR*, *MERW* and *SRW*, we set the restart probability $\mu = 0.15$, and the number of iterations of random walk is limited to 100. For *SimRank*, we set the decay factor $C = 0.8$ and the maximum number of iterations as 6, as in [13]. For *MF* and *MF-BL*, we set the number of hidden features as 20.

For *SRW*, we select the Wilcoxon-Mann-Whitney (WMW) loss function and logical edge strength function, as reported the best in [1]. We select the two-hop neighbors of each ego as the negative instances for that in our settings only the two-hop neighbors are considered as the candidate friends for prediction. We apply the gradient descent method to solve the optimization problem and the iteration is executed at most 20 times. The features for *SRW* include number of friends of the two individuals, number of their common friends, Jaccard coefficient and Adamic/Adar score.

5.3 Performance Comparison

We present the evaluation results in Table 3. As highlighted in bold, *LFPN-RW* consistently outperforms other methods on most datasets and most metrics.

LaFT-Proximity is a proximity measure based on the LaFT-Tree, another work which tries to explain link formation using the transitivity of friendship. Though *LaFT-Proximity* shows better performance than other local neighbourhood based measures, including *Jaccard* and *Adamic/Adar*, it fails when compared with more complex algorithms which can utilize more global network information. *LaFT-Proximity* is always worse than our *LFPN-RW*, demonstrating the importance and effectiveness of modeling interests in LFPM and capturing the co-influence of friend circles in *LFPN-RW*.

By utilizing the global network topological structure for proximity measure, random walk based methods, including *RWR*, *MERW* and *SRW*, show better performance than other baselines. In most occasions their performance exceeds *Adamic/Adar* and *Jaccard*, the two best local measures reported in [19]. However, the variants of *RWR*, *MERW* and *SRW*, are not always better than *RWR* as expected. *SRW* outperforms the *RWR* on **cond-mat** and **hep-lat** on MAP and AUC, but becomes worse on **hep-ph**. *MERW* fails to improve the performance of *RWR* on most of our datasets. Both *MERW* and *SRW* try to weight the edges in the graph based on the topological features; on the contrary, *LFPN-RW* weights the edges by modeling the behaviors of individuals and capturing the co-influence of friend circles based on the common user interests, and thus achieves better improvement over *RWR* than *MERW* and *SRW*. On **hep-lat**, **hep-ph** and **nucl-ex**, *LFPN-RW* achieves on average 0.04 higher AUC and 0.03 higher MAP as compared to *RWR*. Furthermore, we notice that *LFPN-RW* is not only accurate but also more stable than others. This convinces us that the LFPN can capture the important information about the network growth and people's friend-making behaviors.

It is important to note that, unlike *SRW* which requires feature extraction from both positive and negative instances, *LFPN* estimates the weighted network from only the "positive instances", and no other features are considered.

The performance of *LFPN-RW* far exceeds that of *MF* which tries to capture the effect of intermediary by matrix factorization, and that of its improved version *MF-BL*. While in matrix factorization we can explain the latent feature space as the intermediation effect, these methods cannot utilize the internal relations among individuals' friend-making behaviors and thus the intermediation effect cannot be modelled well.

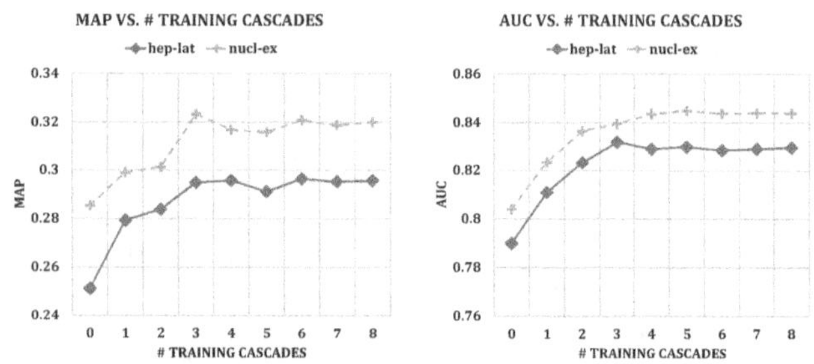

Figure 3: The effect of knowledge accumulation in Cascade LF-PM on the link prediction performance of LFPN-RW.

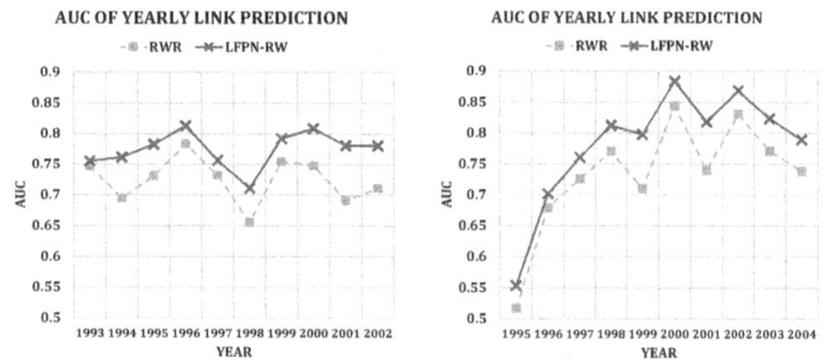

(a) hep-lat (b) nucl-ex

Figure 4: The performance of dynamic link prediction for each year.

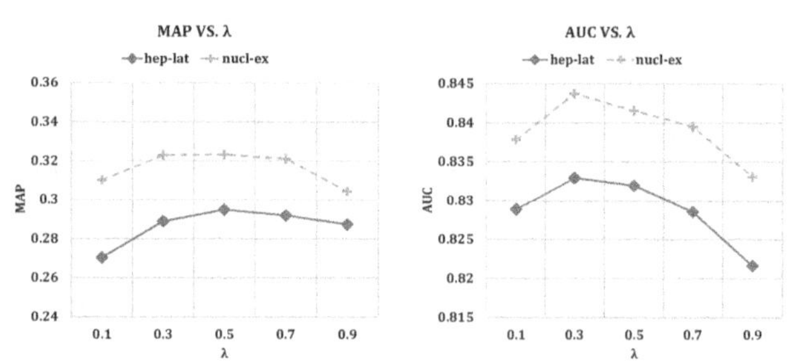

Figure 5: The variance of link prediction performance of LFPN-RW with different damping factor λ in Cascade LFPM.

5.4 Effect of Knowledge Accumulation

In this subsection, we study to what extent the knowledge accumulation in Cascade LFPM can influence the learned LFPN and the link prediction performance based on LFPN. We conduct this study by three questions: (1) Does a longer training time mean more accumulated knowledge and thus promise better performance in link prediction? (2) As time goes by, with more knowledge accumulated in cascades, will the prediction performance increase continuously? (3) How should we control the amount of the accumulated knowledge that be passed from one period to the next?

We answer the first question by examining the performance variance of *LFPN-RW* on the LFPNs with different length of training time. Longer training time means more earlier knowledge is learned and accumulated, and afterwards reflected in the final LFPN. Fig. 3 shows the experimental results. Here we split the training data into multiple cascades by year and each cascade corresponds to one year. For the sake of readability we only show the results on **hep-lat** and **nucl-ex**, and similar results are observed on other datasets. When the number of training cascades is 0, our *LFPN-RW* decays to *RWR*. *LFPN-RW* with one training cascade only utilizes

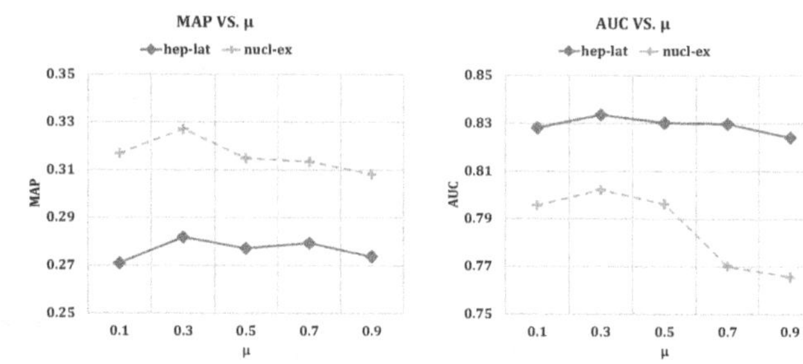

Figure 6: The variance of link prediction performance of LFPN-RW with different μ in LFPN-RW.

the knowledge of the current period and outperforms that with no training cascade, i.e. *RWR*, on both datasets and both metrics. The AUC of *LFPN-RW* increases with the number of training cascades in the beginning, and then tends to be stable after 4 training cascades. This indicates that the accumulated knowledge in the recent time can really improve the performance; however, the knowledge too far in the past has little effect because people's behaviors and interests are changing with time. This finding proves that our approach is more feasible as when only little training data are given it can still show promising performance.

To answer the second question, we conduct dynamic link prediction tasks on the datasets. For fixed individuals in the first year in each dataset, we make yearly link prediction which predicts the new links for the next year given the network in each year, and study how the performance will vary. As time goes by and the number of friends of each individual keeps growing, there will be more candidate friendships than new emerging friendships in each year, so it's difficult to compare the performance on a sequential basis. Thus we compare *LFPN-RW* with *RWR* in each year. The results are presented in Fig. 4. The curves of *RWR* and *LFPN-RW* are quite similar on both datasets. We observe that *LFPN-RW* is not only always better than *RWR*, but also more stable, as shown in the more smooth curve. *RWR* will perform worse if there exist outliers in the network; however, LFPN becomes increasingly robust with continuous knowledge accumulation. Furthermore, in **nucl-ex** and later time of **hep-lat**, we see the improvement of *LFPN-RW* over *RWR* increases with time.

Finally, we study how we can control the extent of knowledge accumulation by the cascade damping factor λ in LFPM inference for better link prediction performance. The choice of λ faces the trade-off between the knowledge learned in the new period and that accumulated from previous models. Just think of the extreme cases. When $\lambda = 0$, each LFPM is trained in each period independently, without the accumulated knowledge; however, when $\lambda = 1$, all previous knowledge is passed to the next model, with equal importance as the new knowledge. Typically, we set a higher λ when less data is observed in the specific period. Otherwise, if we observe sufficient data for the current model, we can lower the influence of the previous models on the current one by setting a smaller λ. When evaluating on real data we observe that λ plays an important role in the cascade inference procedure. For the sake of readability, we only show some representative curves in Fig. 5. We can see λ in the range from 0.3 to 0.5 seems to be most appropriate.

5.5 Effect of Co-influence of Friend Circles

In LFPN-RW, we treat the creation of a new friendship as a result of friendship propagation in the network and model the link prediction as a random walk upon the LFPN, taking the co-influence ef-

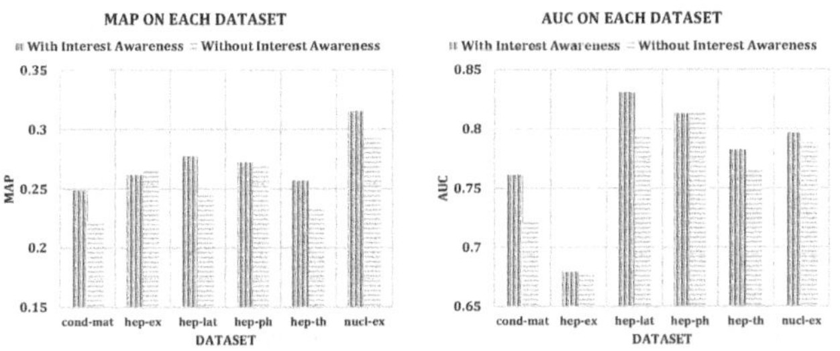

Figure 7: Comparison of link prediction performance of LFPN-RW with/without interest awareness.

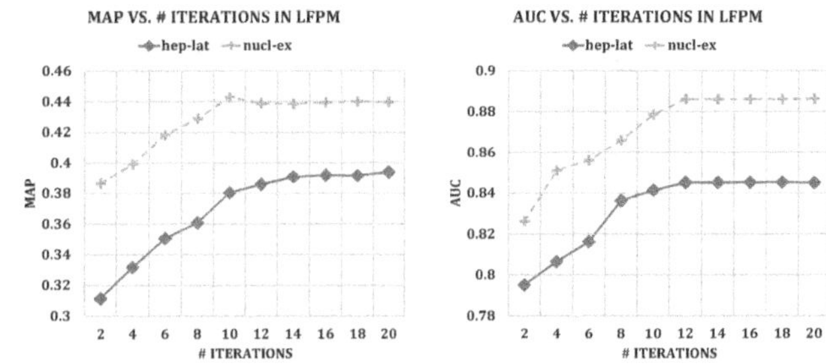

Figure 8: The variance of link prediction performance of LFPN-RW with increasing number of iterations in LFPM.

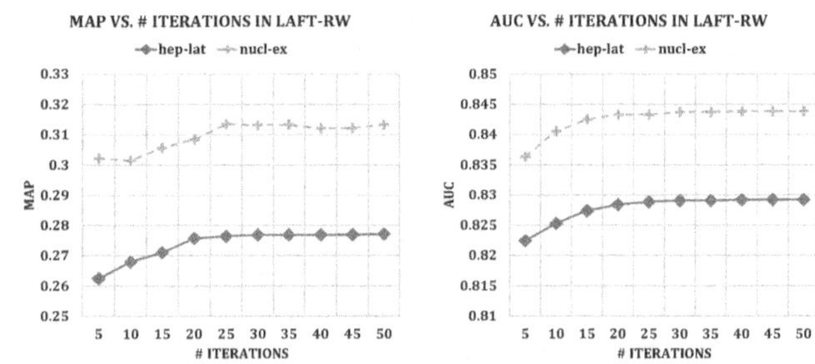

Figure 9: The variance of link prediction performance of LFPN-RW with increasing number of iterations in LFPN-RW.

fect of the friend circles on one's friend-making behaviors into consideration naturally. In this subsection we study how we can benefit from the co-influence effect. In the LFPN-RW, the restart probability μ controls how "far" the walker wanders on the network; a smaller value allows the walker to walk farther and increases the co-influence of the friend circles on one's friend-making behaviors, and a larger value enhances the direct influence of one's current friends. As shown in Fig. 6, in our evaluations we see the lower value of μ tends to achieve better performance. This demonstrates the importance of the co-influence captured in our LFPN-RW. Furthermore, the performance will decrease if $\mu < 0.3$ because the direct influence from the current friends is reduced too much. To achieve better performance, one needs to make trade-off between the influence from current friends and the co-influence of friend circles in specific networks.

5.6 Effect of Interest Awareness

In LFPM and LFPN-RW, we assume that the creation of friendship is the result of friendship propagation, which would be influenced by both the transitivity of friendship and the personal interests. In this subsection, we investigate how personal interests will influence the link prediction performance. We remove the interest factors, including χ and ψ, from LFPM and LFPN-RW, and get a new algorithm denoted by *LFPN-RW without Interest Awareness*. Correspondingly, our original algorithm can be denoted by *LFPN-RW with Interest Awareness*. We compare the performance of the new algorithm with our original algorithm on all the datasets and the results are shown in Fig. 7. We can see the latter outperforms the former on most datasets. It should be noted that we don't introduce external personal profiles to learn the personal interests. This convinces us that the personal interests can be well captured from the social behaviors of the individuals and the topological structure of the network, and furthermore can benefit the link prediction using LFPN-RW, i.e. the *LFPN-RW with Interest Awareness* here, which models the friendship propagation with interest awareness.

5.7 Convergence Analysis

In this subsection we study the convergence speed of our LFPM inference and LFPN-RW.

In Fig. 8 we investigate how the performance of LFPN-RW varies with the number of iterations of LFPM. From the two representative curves on **hep-lat** and **nucl-ex**, we see the performance increases quickly, and then LFPM converges in nearly 15 iterations.

Fig. 9 shows the performance variance with the number of iterations in LFPN-RW. Experimental results on **hep-lat** and **nucl-ex** demonstrate the LFPN-RW converges in about 30 iterations.

6. RELATED WORK

Link prediction is a classical problem which attracts many attentions. The general approach for link prediction is based on the proximity measuring in the network. One branch of this method is based on the local neighbourhood structures, such as *common neighbors*, *Jaccard coefficient* and *Adamic/Adar*, all of which were surveyed by Liben-Nowell and Kleinberg [19]. Another popular approach utilizes the random walk to measure the node proximity on the whole network, including *Random Walk with Restarts (R-WR)* [25], *SimRank* [13] and *Katz* [14]. Approaches have also been proposed to improve the traditional random walk by adjusting the transition probabilities , including *randomized shortest-path (RSP) dissimilarity* [29] and *Maximum Entropy Random Walk(MERW)* [4][17]. *Supervised Random Walk(SRW)* was proposed to learn the transition probabilities with a supervised method [1]. However, supervised methods face the imbalance problem [20][22] and require elaborate feature extraction; on the contrary, our LFPN-RW models personal behaviors depending only on the positive instances. Furthermore, we identify personal interests from their social relations only, without other node-specific attributes.

It's also interesting to study how the network evolves [16] and how people make friends [12]. Researchers have found many interesting patterns, such as *preferential attachment* [23], *triadic closure* [27], *reciprocity*[24][11] and *homophily* [5]. The transitivity of friendship has been noticed long ago [26][28] and used to explain the phenomenon of triadic closure in social networks [15]. Recently, the role of triadic closure in the link formation in social networks was further verified [7][27][3][6]. However, it hasn't been studied that how the triadic closure and the transitivity of friendship drive the microscopic evolution of social networks. Yin et al. proposed a matrix factorization approach for link prediction by considering the hidden features as the recommendation of intermediaries [30]. Their work is a bit similar with ours; however, they ignore the sequential relationship among the social behaviors and cannot model the actual contribution of each intermediary on the link formation.

Our previous work [32] primarily focuses on how to capture the expansion traces of one's social network. It does not explore the dimension of personal interest and model its impact on network expansion. Neither does it utilize the concept of friend circles to capture the co-influence effect of one's friends based on interest awareness as in our paper.

7. CONCLUSION

Modeling people's social behaviors and furthermore understanding their motivations are important for us to know how the social network emerges, evolves and vanishes eventually, as the people are the dominant players in social networks. In this paper, we model people's friend-making behaviors using the LFPM, a generative model driven by the famous sociological principle of the transitivity of friendship and personal interests. The inferred LFPN incorporates rich knowledge about the patterns of individuals's behaviors and the growth potentials of the social network, with the co-influence of friend circles and personal interest well modeled. Furthermore, we propose LFPN-RW, which treats the link prediction task as a random walk on the LFPN, guided by the interest-aware friendship propagation. Our approach achieves promising performance in experimental studies, which leads us to draw the conclusion that the transitivity of friendship really plays important roles in the evolution of social networks and can be utilized to analyze the network evolution if well modeled with interest awareness.

8. ACKNOWLEDGMENTS

We would like to thank the anonymous reviewers for their valuable comments and suggestions to improve this paper. This work is supported in part by the National Natural Science Foundation of China (No. 61170064, No. 61073005, No. 61133002), the National High Technology Research and Development Program of China (No. 2012AA011002), US NSF through grants IIS-0905215, CNS-1115234, IIS-0914934, DBI-0960443, and OISE-1129076, and Huawei grant.

9. REFERENCES

[1] L. Backstrom and J. Leskovec. Supervised random walks: predicting and recommending links in social networks. In *WSDM '11*, pages 635–644, 2011.

[2] D. M. Blei, A. Y. Ng, and M. I. Jordan. Latent dirichlet allocation. *J. Mach. Learn. Res.*, 3:993–1022, Mar. 2003.

[3] M. J. Brzozowski and D. M. Romero. Who should I follow? recommending people in directed social networks. In *ICWSM'11*, 2011.

[4] Z. Burda, J. Duda, J. M. Luck, and B. Waclaw. Localization of the maximal entropy random walk. *Phys Rev Lett*, 102(16):160602, 2009.

[5] M. De Choudhury. Tie formation on twitter: Homophily and structure of egocentric networks. In *SocialCom/PASSAT '11*, pages 465 –470, 2011.

[6] M. Doroud, P. Bhattacharyya, S. F. Wu, and D. Felmlee. The evolution of ego-centric triads: A microscopic approach toward predicting macroscopic network properties. In *SocialCom/PASSAT '11*, pages 172 –179, 2011.

[7] S. A. Golder and S. Yardi. Structural predictors of tie formation in twitter: Transitivity and mutuality. In *SocialCom/PASSAT '10*, pages 88–95, 2010.

[8] M. S. Granovetter. The Strength of Weak Ties. *The American Journal of Sociology*, 78(6):1360–1380, 1973.

[9] M. A. Hasan, V. Chaoji, S. Salem, and M. Zaki. Link prediction using supervised learning. In *SDM '06 workshop on Link Analysis, Counterterrorism and Security*, 2006.

[10] G. Heinrich. Parameter estimation for text analysis. Version 2.9, Fraunhofer IGD, 2009.

[11] J. Hopcroft, T. Lou, and J. Tang. Who will follow you back?: reciprocal relationship prediction. In *CIKM '11*, 2011.

[12] H. Hu and X. Wang. How people make friends in social networking sites - a microscopic perspective. *Physica A: Statistical Mechanics and its Applications*, 391(4):1877 – 1886, 2012.

[13] G. Jeh and J. Widom. Simrank: a measure of structural-context similarity. In *KDD '02*, 2002.

[14] L. Katz. A new status index derived from sociometric analysis. *Psychometrika*, 18:39–43, 1953.

[15] D. Krackhardt and M. S. Handcock. Heider vs simmel: emergent features in dynamic structures. In *ICML'06*, 2006.

[16] J. Leskovec, L. Backstrom, R. Kumar, and A. Tomkins. Microscopic evolution of social networks. In *KDD '08*, 2008.

[17] R.-H. Li, J. X. Yu, and J. Liu. Link prediction: the power of maximal entropy random walk. In *CIKM '11*, 2011.

[18] D. Liben-Nowell and J. Kleinberg. The link prediction problem for social networks. In *CIKM '03*, 2003.

[19] D. Liben-Nowell and J. Kleinberg. The link-prediction problem for social networks. *J. Am. Soc. Inf. Sci. Technol.*, 58(7), 2007.

[20] R. N. Lichtenwalter, J. T. Lussier, and N. V. Chawla. New perspectives and methods in link prediction. In *KDD '10*, 2010.

[21] M. McPherson, L. Smith-Lovin, and J. M. Cook. Birds of a feather: Homophily in social networks. *ANNUAL REVIEW OF SOCIOLOGY*, 27:415–444, 2001.

[22] A. K. Menon and C. Elkan. Link prediction via matrix factorization. In *ECML PKDD'11*, 2011.

[23] M. E. J. Newman. Clustering and preferential attachment in growing networks. *PHYS.REV.E*, 64:025102, 2001.

[24] V.-A. Nguyen, E.-P. Lim, H.-H. Tan, J. Jiang, and A. Sun. Do you trust to get trust? a study of trust reciprocity behaviors and reciprocal trust prediction. In *SDM '10*, 2010.

[25] J.-Y. Pan, H.-J. Yang, C. Faloutsos, and P. Duygulu. Automatic multimedia cross-modal correlation discovery. In *KDD '04*, pages 653–658, 2004.

[26] A. Rapoport. Spread of information through a population with socio-structural bias: I. assumption of transitivity. *Bulletin of Mathematical Biology*, 15:523–533, 1953.

[27] D. M. Romero and J. Kleinberg. The directed closure process in hybrid social-information networks, with an analysis of link formation on twitter. In *ICWSM '10*, 2010.

[28] G. Simmel and K. H. Wolff. *The Sociology of Georg Simmel*. Free Press, 1964.

[29] L. Yen, M. Saerens, A. Mantrach, and M. Shimbo. A family of dissimilarity measures between nodes generalizing both the shortest-path and the commute-time distances. In *KDD '08*, 2008.

[30] D. Yin, L. Hong, and B. D. Davison. Structural link analysis and prediction in microblogs. In *CIKM '11*, 2011.

[31] Z. Yin, M. Gupta, T. Weninger, and J. Han. A unified framework for link recommendation using random walks. In *ASONAM '10*, pages 152–159, 2010.

[32] J. Zhang, C. Wang, J. Wang, and P. S. Yu. LaFT-Tree: Perceiving the expansion trace of one's circle of friends in online social networks. In *WSDM '13*, 2013.

An Experimental Study on Implicit Social Recommendation

Hao Ma
Microsoft Research
One Microsoft Way
Redmond, WA 98052
haoma@microsoft.com

ABSTRACT

Social recommendation problems have drawn a lot of attention recently due to the prevalence of social networking sites. The experiments in previous literature suggest that social information is very effective in improving traditional recommendation algorithms. However, explicit social information is not always available in most of the recommender systems, which limits the impact of social recommendation techniques. In this paper, we study the following two research problems: (1) In some systems without explicit social information, can we still improve recommender systems using implicit social information? (2) In the systems with explicit social information, can the performance of using implicit social information outperform that of using explicit social information? In order to answer these two questions, we conduct comprehensive experimental analysis on three recommendation datasets. The result indicates that: (1) Implicit user and item social information, including similar and dissimilar relationships, can be employed to improve traditional recommendation methods. (2) When comparing implicit social information with explicit social information, the performance of using implicit information is slightly worse. This study provides additional insights to social recommendation techniques, and also greatly widens the utility and spreads the impact of previous and upcoming social recommendation approaches.

Categories and Subject Descriptors

H.3.3 [**Information Search and Retrieval**]: Information Filtering

General Terms

Algorithm, Experimentation

Keywords

Matrix Factorization, Recommender Systems, Implicit Social Information, Singular Value Decomposition

SIGIR'13, July 28–August 1, 2013, Dublin, Ireland.

1. INTRODUCTION

Due to the rapid growth of information on the Web, especially on the social Web, recommender system has become an indispensable technique for filtering and recommending online information. In order to satisfy Web users' ever-increasing information needs, traditional recommendation techniques have been widely adopted by various products in industrial companies, including but not limited to Amazon, Netflix, Apple iTunes, Yahoo! News, etc.

Traditional recommendation techniques normally only take into account the user-item rating matrix for computing recommendations. Recently, based on the intuition that users' social network information can be utilized to improve recommendation qualities, the research of social recommender systems becomes popular. Several social recommendation approaches [8, 9, 20, 21] have been proposed in the literature. These methods suggest that the explicit social information is very helpful in improving the traditional methods, especially when the user-item rating matrix is sparse.

In general, most of the social recommendation methods are based on the matrix factorization framework, which is both effective and efficient in generating recommendations. Typically, social information is utilized to better shape the user latent space. Different intuitions on interpreting these social information will result in different objective functions or learning models. In [20], a social recommendation approach is proposed by adding the social regularization term to the matrix factorization objective function. In this method, the additional social regularization term ensures that the distance of the latent feature vectors of two friends will become closer if these two friends share similar tastes. The experimental results illustrate that social recommendation approaches are very effective at improving traditional recommendation techniques, especially when few ratings are available.

Although social recommendation methods have been extensively studied in the literature, many problems are still left unexplored.

The essence of social recommendation methods is utilizing users' explicit social connections to improve recommendation results. However, explicit social connection information is not always available in real-world recommender systems. Only few Web sites have implemented the social or trust mechanisms, like Epinions (http://www.epinions.com, a general consumer review site that was established in 1999, where users can also add other users into their trust list) and Doudan (http://www.douban.com, the largest Chinese Web 2.0 site devoted for movies, books, and music reviews

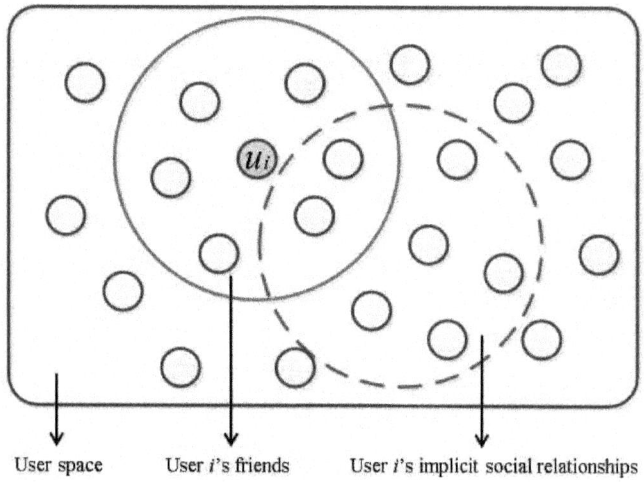

Figure 1: Explicit and Implicit Social Relationships

that was launched in 2005). Lacking of social recommendation data greatly limits the impact and utilization of social recommendation methods.

Fortunately, in case that we do not have explicit social information, we can always compute a set of implicit social information for each user. We summarize the relationships between users' explicit social information and implicit social information in a toy example illustrated in Figure 1. In this figure, users within the blue solid circle represent explicit social connections of user u_i, while users within the purple dashed circle represent this user's implicit social information, which is calculated using some similarity metrics.

Thus, in this paper, based on the example shown in Figure 1, we are interested in exploring the following two research problems:

1. Can we take advantages of implicit social information in case we do not have explicit social connection information?
2. When the explicit social information is available, can the performance of using implicit social information outperform that of using explicit social information?

In order to answer the questions, in this paper, we conduct comprehensive experiments on three datasets: the MovieLens and EachMovie datasets, which do not have explicit social information, as well as the Douban dataset, which has a social network in addition to the user-item rating matrix. Based on our analysis, we have the following conclusions:

- When explicit social information is **unavailable**:
  - In the absence of *explicit* user social information, we find that using *implicit* user social information (i.e., the most similar users), can also improve the recommendation qualities under the matrix factorization framework.
  - Besides the most *similar* users, for each user, the list of most *dissimilar* users is another ideal source to further improve recommender systems.
  - We extend the idea of computing implicit *user* social information, and conclude that the implicit *item* social information is also very helpful in increasing the recommendation performance.
- When explicit social information is **available**:
  - We find that using implicit social information performs slightly worse than using explicit social information.
  - We also conclude that a social network with larger friend diversity is more effective in improving recommendation quality.

The remainder of this paper is organized as follows. Section 2 introduces previous methods that are related to this work. Section 3 details one popular matrix factorization method in the literature. Section 4 presents how to incorporate implicit social information. The results of an empirical analysis are presented in Section 5, followed by the conclusion in Section 6.

2. RELATED WORK

In this section, we review several popular approaches for recommender systems in the literature, including: (1) traditional recommender systems, especially matrix factorization based methods, and (2) social recommendation methods.

2.1 Traditional Recommender Systems

Traditional recommender systems normally only utilize the user-item rating information for recommendation. One of the the most popular techniques in recommender systems is collaborative filtering.

Typically, collaborative filtering approaches include two types of methods: memory-based methods as well as model-based approaches. Memory-based methods focus on using predefined similarity calculation functions to find similar users or items for generating predictions. Memory-based methods can be further classified as user-based [2, 4, 10] and item-based approaches [3, 16, 27] based on whether similar users or similar items are used.

In contrast to the memory-based methods, the model-based approaches use the observed ratings to train a predefined learning model. The ratings are then predicted via the trained model instead of directly manipulating the original rating database as the memory-based approaches [17]. Algorithms in this category include but not limited to clustering model [11], the aspect models [5, 6, 28], the Bayesian hierarchical model [33], the ranking model [17], etc. Hofmann in [5] proposed an algorithm based on a generalization of probabilistic latent semantic analysis to continuous-valued response variables. Kohrs et al. [11] presented an algorithm for collaborative filtering based on hierarchical clustering, which tried to balance both robustness and accuracy of predictions, especially when few data were available. Recently, due to the effectiveness and efficiency in dealing with very large user-item rating matrices, several low-dimensional matrix factorization techniques [15, 24, 25, 26, 29, 31] have been proposed.

Matrix factorization methods in recommender systems normally seek to factorize the user-item rating matrix into two low rank user-specific and item-specific matrices, and then utilize the factorized matrices to make further predictions. Low-rank matrix approximations based on minimizing the sum-squared errors can be easily solved using Singular Value

Decomposition (SVD), and a simple and efficient Expectation Maximization (EM) algorithm for solving weighted low-rank approximation is proposed in [29]. In [30], Srebro et al. proposed a matrix factorization method to constrain the norms of U and V instead of their dimensionality. Salakhutdinov et al. presented a probabilistic linear model with Gaussian observation noise in [25]. The user and item latent factors can be learned by maximize the proposed probabilistic likelyhood function. The proposed method is very effective and efficient, and this method is essentially equivalent to the Regularized SVD method. In their following work proposed in [26], Salakhutdinov et al. placed the Gaussian-Wishart priors on the user and item hyperparameters, which can further improve the prediction accuracy. More recently, Koren et al. [12, 13, 14] proposed several enhanced matrix factorization methods which illustrate promising results by incorporating heterogeneous information. In [12], the authors discussed the possibility to improve recommender systems using neighborhood information, which is quite related to our work. However, in this paper, we focus on very different aspect of recommender system, i.e., social recommendation. Moreover, we provide many additional insights that previous work ignored.

2.2 Social Recommendation

The above mentioned traditional recommendation techniques are all based on working on the user-item rating matrix, and ignore the abundant relationships among users. Recently, due to the prevalence of Web 2.0 social networking sites, many researchers have started studying social recommender systems [1, 7, 8, 9, 20, 21, 22, 23, 32].

Due to the nature of each method, the social recommendation techniques can also be classified into two types: memory-based [1, 8, 21, 22, 23] and model-based [7, 9, 20, 32].

The memory-based methods normally directly or indirectly use the degree of social trust to represent the similarity between two users. In [21], a trust-aware method for recommender system is proposed. In this work, the collaborative filtering process is replaced by the reputation of users, which is computed by propagating trust. The degrees of trust are calculated to replace the similarity value between two users. The experiments on a large social recommendation dataset - Epinions, show that this work increases the coverage (number of ratings that are predictable) while not decreasing the accuracy (the error of predictions). In [23], two trust-aware methods are proposed to improve standard collaborative filtering methods. The experimental results indicate that the user trust information can help improve recommendation quality.

More recently, by taking advantages of the effectiveness and efficiency of matrix factorization framework, several novel model-based methods have been proposed to enhance traditional matrix factorization methods by incorporating user social information. In [20], two Social Regularization methods have been proposed by constraining the matrix factorization objective function with user social regularization terms. Different with previous methods, the proposed methods are very general, they not only work with user trust relationships, but also perform well with user social friend relationships. The experimental analysis indicates that the proposed framework outperforms other state-of-the-art methods.

Although the aforementioned matrix factorization based social recommendation methods move a nice step forward in the research of recommender systems, their utilities are limited since these methods require using explicit user social information, which is not always available in most of the recommender systems. In [18], the idea of using implicit information is briefly introduced, however, many interesting problems are left unattended. In this paper, we present an comprehensive experimental study on implicit social recommendation which provides many useful insights to current social recommendation techniques.

3. MATRIX FACTORIZATION

In this subsection, we review one popular matrix factorization method that is widely studied in the literature.

Considering an $m \times n$ matrix R describing m users' ratings on n items, a low-rank matrix factorization approach seeks to approximate the frequency matrix R by a multiplication of d-rank factors $R \approx U^T V$, where $U \in \mathbb{R}^{d\times m}$ and $V \in \mathbb{R}^{d\times n}$ with $d << \min(m,n)$. The matrix R in the real-world is usually very sparse since most of the users only visited a few Web sites.

Traditionally, the Regularized Singular Value Decomposition (RSVD) method is employed to estimate a matrix R by minimizing

$$\begin{aligned} L &= \min_{U,V} \frac{1}{2}\sum_{i=1}^{m}\sum_{j=1}^{n} I_{ij}(r_{ij} - \mathbf{u}_i^T\mathbf{v}_j)^2 \\ &+\frac{\lambda_1}{2}||U||_F^2 + \frac{\lambda_2}{2}||V||_F^2, \end{aligned} \quad (1)$$

where $\mathbf{u}_i$ and $\mathbf{v}_j$ are column vectors with d values, I_{ij} is the indicator function that is equal to 1 if user i rated item j and equal to 0 otherwise, and λ_1, λ_2 represent the regularization parameters. The optimization problem in Equation 1 minimizes the sum-of-squared-errors objective function with quadratic regularization terms.

By adopting a simple stochastic gradient descent technique, for each observed rating r_{ij}, we have the following efficient updating rules to learn latent variables $\mathbf{u}_i$, $\mathbf{v}_j$:

$$\begin{aligned} \mathbf{u}_i &\leftarrow \mathbf{u}_i + \gamma_1(\Delta_{ij}\mathbf{v}_j - \lambda_1\mathbf{u}_i), \\ \mathbf{v}_j &\leftarrow \mathbf{v}_j + \gamma_2(\Delta_{ij}\mathbf{u}_i - \lambda_2\mathbf{v}_j), \end{aligned} \quad (2)$$

where

$$\Delta_{ij} = r_{ij} - \mathbf{u}_i^T\mathbf{v}_j,$$

and γ_1, γ_2 are the learning rates.

The Regularized SVD algorithm introduced in this section is both effective and efficient in solving the collaborative filtering problem and it is perhaps one of the most popular methods in collaborative filtering. In this paper, we use this approach as the baseline method.

4. INCORPORATING IMPLICIT SOCIAL INFORMATION

In this section, we first introduce a matrix factorization-based social recommendation method proposed in the literature. Then we illustrate how to leverage the implicit user social information in the case that explicit user social information is not available. Finally, we demonstrate how to utilize dissimilar users as well as item social information to further improve recommender systems.

Note that the main focus of this paper is designing a scientific experimental study to explore several interesting research problems by borrowing and extending previous social recommendation techniques. Developing brand new social recommendation techniques is out of the scope of this paper. Also, we will only briefly describe the techniques if they are borrowed from previous work.

4.1 Social Regularization

In [20], in order to model the social recommendation problems more accurately, a general social recommendation approach, Social Regularization (SR), is proposed.

The objective function of this approach is formulated as:

$$\begin{aligned} L &= \min_{U,V} \frac{1}{2}\sum_{i=1}^{m}\sum_{j=1}^{n} I_{ij}(r_{ij} - \mathbf{u}_i^T\mathbf{v}_j)^2 \\ &+\frac{\alpha}{2}\sum_{i=1}^{m}\sum_{f\in\mathcal{F}^+(i)} s_{if}\|\mathbf{u}_i - \mathbf{u}_f\|_F^2 \\ &+\frac{\lambda_1}{2}\|U\|_F^2 + \frac{\lambda_2}{2}\|V\|_F^2, \end{aligned} \tag{3}$$

where α is the regularization parameter, s_{if} indicates the similarity between user i and user f, and $\mathcal{F}^+(i)$ represents user i's outlink friends.

In this method, the social network information is employed in designing the social regularization term to constrain the matrix factorization objective function. The social regularization term also indirectly models the propagation of tastes. More specifically, if user i has a friend f and user f has a friend user g, this regularization term actually indirectly minimizes the distance between latent vectors $\mathbf{u}_i$ and $\mathbf{u}_g$. The propagation of tastes will reach a harmonic status once the learning is converged.

Similarly, for each observed rating r_{ij}, we have the following stochastic gradient descent updating rules to learn the latent parameters:

$$\begin{aligned} \mathbf{u}_i &\leftarrow \mathbf{u}_i + \gamma_1\Big(\Delta_{ij}\mathbf{v}_j - \alpha\sum_{f\in\mathcal{F}^+(i)} s_{if}(\mathbf{u}_i - \mathbf{u}_f) \\ &\quad -\alpha\sum_{g\in\mathcal{F}^-(i)} s_{ig}(\mathbf{u}_i - \mathbf{u}_g) - \lambda_1\mathbf{u}_i\Big), \\ \mathbf{v}_j &\leftarrow \mathbf{v}_j + \gamma_2(\Delta_{ij}\mathbf{u}_i - \lambda_2\mathbf{v}_j), \end{aligned} \tag{4}$$

where

$$\Delta_{ij} = r_{ij} - \mathbf{u}_i^T\mathbf{v}_j, \tag{5}$$

and $\mathcal{F}^-(i)$ represents user i's inlink friends.

4.2 Implicit User Social Relationships

As mentioned in Section 1, all the social recommendation approaches need to utilize the additional explicit user social information, which may limit the impact and utilization of these approaches. In this section, we seek an alterative way to compute implicit user social information once the explicit user social relationships are unavailable.

The essence of social recommendation approaches lies in the additional explicit social information of each user. The information of these social friends can then be utilized to help model a user's taste more accurately. In the case of missing explicit social information, as shown in Figure 1, we can always compute another set of Top-N similar users and then plug in those similar users to the aforementioned social recommendation matrix factorization framework.

There are several methods we can borrow in the literature to compare the similarity between two users. In this paper, we adopt the most popular approach Pearson Correlation Coefficient (PCC) [2], which is defined as:

$$s_{if} = \frac{\sum_{k\in I(i)\cap I(f)} (r_{ik} - \overline{r}_i)\cdot(r_{fk} - \overline{r}_f)}{\sqrt{\sum_{k\in I(i)\cap I(f)} (r_{ik} - \overline{r}_i)^2}\cdot\sqrt{\sum_{k\in I(i)\cap I(f)} (r_{fk} - \overline{r}_f)^2}}, \tag{6}$$

where $I(i)$ is a set of items that rated by user i, and $\overline{r}_i$ represents the average rate of user i. From this definition, user similarity s_{if} is ranging from $[-1, 1]$, and a larger value means users i and f are more similar. We employ a mapping function $f(x) = (x + 1)/2$ to bound the range of PCC similarities into $[0, 1]$.

Based on the PCC similarity, the computed Top-N similar users can then be injected into the objective function detailed in Equation 3.

4.3 Dissimilar Users

So far in this paper, we only consider utilizing similar users to improve recommender systems. In the social regularization term $s_{if}||u_i - u_f||_F^2$ employed in Equation 3, if user i is similar to user f, the distance between latent vectors u_i and u_f will become closer since the similarity s_{if} is a relatively large value.

Motivated by the similar users, we can actually endow the social regularization term more modeling power if we also include the most dissimilar users. If user i is dissimilar with user f, the ideal property we want is to make the distance between u_i and u_f larger or in other words, maximize the distance between them. Inspired by the work in [19], we can easily achieve this property by turning the similarity $s_{if} = -s_{if}$. Hence, in this case, the social regularization term $s_{if}||u_i - u_f||_F^2$ will actually lead to make the distance between u_i and u_f larger. This is an ideal property we desire to include those dissimilar users.

Hence, in this paper, in addition to the Top-N similar users, we also include the Top-N dissimilar users for each user. This will not change the objective function mentioned in Equation 3. It will only increase the size of the implicit social neighbors specified in the set $\mathcal{F}^+(i)$ and change the signs of the similarity values for dissimilar users.

4.4 Item Social Relationships

In the original social recommendation problems, there are only social relationships among users due to the reason that normally, social network only refers to the social relationships between people.

In this paper, since we define the implicit user social information as the similar or dissimilar users, we can naturally extend this idea to also take advantages of the implicit item social information, which can be found through the similar or dissimilar items.

The Social Regularization method described in Section 4.1 is a very general approach, and it can be easily extended to incorporate the item social information. The objective function can be formulated as:

$$L = \min_{U,V} \frac{1}{2}\sum_{i=1}^{m}\sum_{j=1}^{n} I_{ij}(r_{ij} - \mathbf{u}_i^T\mathbf{v}_j)^2 + \frac{\beta}{2}\sum_{j=1}^{n}\sum_{q\in\mathcal{Q}^+(j)} s_{jq}\|\mathbf{v}_j - \mathbf{v}_q\|_F^2 + \frac{\lambda_1}{2}\|U\|_F^2 + \frac{\lambda_2}{2}\|V\|_F^2, \quad (7)$$

where $Q^+(j)$ represents item j's implicit social information (i.e., the Top-N items similar to item j and the Top-N items dissimilar to item j).

The similarity between item j and item q can be calculated by the item-based PCC method:

$$s_{jq} = \frac{\sum_{k\in U(j)\cap U(q)} (r_{kj} - \overline{r}_j)\cdot(r_{kq} - \overline{r}_q)}{\sqrt{\sum_{k\in U(j)\cap U(q)} (r_{kj} - \overline{r}_j)^2}\cdot\sqrt{\sum_{k\in U(j)\cap U(q)} (r_{kq} - \overline{r}_q)^2}}, \quad (8)$$

where $U(j)$ denotes a set of users that rated item j.

Similarly, we have the following updating rules to learn the latent parameters:

$$\begin{aligned} \mathbf{u}_i &\leftarrow \mathbf{u}_i + \gamma_1(\Delta_{ij}\mathbf{v}_j - \lambda_1\mathbf{u}_i), \\ \mathbf{v}_j &\leftarrow \mathbf{v}_j + \gamma_2\Big(\Delta_{ij}\mathbf{u}_i - \beta\sum_{q\in\mathcal{Q}^+(j)} s_{jq}(\mathbf{v}_j - \mathbf{v}_q) \\ &\quad -\beta\sum_{h\in\mathcal{Q}^-(j)} s_{jh}(\mathbf{v}_j - \mathbf{v}_h) - \lambda_1\mathbf{v}_j\Big), \end{aligned} \quad (9)$$

where

$$\Delta_{ij} = r_{ij} - \mathbf{u}_i^T\mathbf{v}_j. \quad (10)$$

4.5 A Unified Model

From Section 4.2 to Section 4.4, we demonstrate how to utilize implicit user social information, dissimilar users, and item social information, respectively. We can then design the following integrated model to take into account all the possible information that will potentially benefit the recommender systems:

$$L = \min_{U,V} \frac{1}{2}\sum_{i=1}^{m}\sum_{j=1}^{n} I_{ij}(r_{ij} - \mathbf{u}_i^T\mathbf{v}_j)^2 + \frac{\alpha}{2}\sum_{i=1}^{m}\sum_{f\in\mathcal{F}^+(i)} s_{if}\|\mathbf{u}_i - \mathbf{u}_f\|_F^2 + \frac{\beta}{2}\sum_{j=1}^{n}\sum_{q\in\mathcal{Q}^+(j)} s_{jq}\|\mathbf{v}_j - \mathbf{v}_q\|_F^2 + \frac{\lambda_1}{2}\|U\|_F^2 + \frac{\lambda_2}{2}\|V\|_F^2, \quad (11)$$

For every observed rating r_{ij}, we have the following stochastic updating rules to learn the all the latent parameters:

$$\begin{aligned} \mathbf{u}_i &\leftarrow \mathbf{u}_i + \gamma_1\Big(\Delta_{ij}\mathbf{v}_j - \alpha\sum_{f\in\mathcal{F}^+(i)} s_{if}(\mathbf{u}_i - \mathbf{u}_f) \\ &\quad -\alpha\sum_{g\in\mathcal{F}^-(i)} s_{ig}(\mathbf{u}_i - \mathbf{u}_g) - \lambda_1\mathbf{u}_i\Big), \\ \mathbf{v}_j &\leftarrow \mathbf{v}_j + \gamma_2\Big(\Delta_{ij}\mathbf{u}_i - \beta\sum_{q\in\mathcal{Q}^+(j)} s_{jq}(\mathbf{v}_j - \mathbf{v}_q) \\ &\quad -\beta\sum_{h\in\mathcal{Q}^-(j)} s_{jh}(\mathbf{v}_j - \mathbf{v}_h) - \lambda_1\mathbf{v}_j\Big), \end{aligned} \quad (12)$$

where

$$\Delta_{ij} = r_{ij} - \mathbf{u}_i^T\mathbf{v}_j.$$

The unified model is constrained by four types of information: similar user regularization, dissimilar user regularization, similar item regularization and dissimilar item regularization. We use the aforementioned information to help better shape the user and item latent spaces, hence generate more accurate recommendation results.

5. EXPERIMENTAL ANALYSIS

In this section, we conduct several experiments to compare different recommendation methods using implicit social information. Our experiments are intended to address the following questions:

- When explicit social information is **unavailable**:
  1. Is implicit user social information effective in improving traditional matrix factorization methods?
  2. Can dissimilar users be used to further improve the recommendation quality?
  3. Can we also take advantages of implicit item social information in addition to the implicit user social information?
  4. What is the performance comparison on users with different observed ratings?
- When explicit social information is **available**:
  1. Can the performance of using implicit social information outperform that of using explicit social information?

We use the popular Mean Absolute Error (MAE) and Root Mean Square Error (RMSE) metrics to measure the prediction quality of all the mentioned algorithms. MAE is defined as:

$$MAE = \frac{\sum_{i,j}|r_{ij} - \widehat{r}_{ij}|}{N}, \quad (13)$$

where r_{ij} denotes the rating user i gave to item j, $\widehat{r}_{ij}$ denotes the related predicted rating, and N denotes the number of tested ratings. RMSE is defined as:

$$RMSE = \sqrt{\frac{\sum_{i,j}(r_{ij} - \widehat{r}_{ij})^2}{N}}. \quad (14)$$

From the definitions, we can see that a smaller MAE or RMSE indicates a better performance.

Table 1: Statistics of Dataset MovieLens

Statistics	User	Item
Min. Num. of Ratings	20	1
Max. Num. of Ratings	737	583
Avg. Num. of Ratings	106.04	59.45

Table 2: Statistics of Dataset EachMovie

Statistics	User	Item
Min. Num. of Ratings	1	1
Max. Num. of Ratings	1,455	32,868
Avg. Num. of Ratings	37.78	1,706.30

5.1 Without Explicit Social Information

5.1.1 Description of Datasets

When the explicit social information is not available, we evaluate all the algorithms on two popular datasets: MovieLens[1] and EachMovie[2].

The MovieLens dataset we adopt in this paper is a relatively small dataset contains 100,000 user-item ratings (scale from 1 to 5) rated by 943 users on 1,642 items. The EachMovie data set is a relatively large dataset includes 74,424 users, 1,648 movies, and 2,811,718 ratings in the range from 0 to 5.

Other statistics of these two datasets are summarized in Table 1 and Table 2, respectively.

5.1.2 Performance Analysis

In this section, we will compare the following different methods described in this paper as well as some baseline methods.

1. **UserMean**: this is a baseline method uses the mean value of every user to predict the missing values.

2. **ItemMean**: this is a baseline method utilizes the mean value of every item to predict the missing values.

3. **RSVD**: this is the Regularized SVD method. It is equivalent with the method proposed by Salakhutdinov and Minh in [25]. The underlining distribution is assumed as Gaussian distribution. The details of this method are also introduced in Section 3.

4. $\mathbf{SR}^{u+}$: this is the Social Regularization method using implicit similar user information. The notation u in the superscript denotes that implicit user social information is used in this method, while the notation "+" indicates only similar users are included.

5. $\mathbf{SR}^{u+-}$: this is the Social Regularization method using both implicit similar and dissimilar user information. The notation "−" indicates dissimilar information is included.

6. $\mathbf{SR}_{i+}$: this is the Social Regularization method using implicit similar item information. We use the subscript to describe item related information.

7. $\mathbf{SR}_{i+-}$: this is the Social Regularization method using both implicit similar and dissimilar item information.

8. $\mathbf{SR}^{u+-}_{i+-}$: this is the final integrated model that using similar and dissimilar user information as well as similar and dissimilar item information.

Data Preparation.

For all the experiments conducted in this section, we utilize 80% as training data in both datasets. Training data 80%, for example, means we randomly select 80% of the ratings from the MovieLens or the EachMovie dataset as the training data to predict the remaining 20% of ratings.

Top-N Neighbors Generation.

The methods we study in this paper also involve the calculation of the Top-N similar and Top-N dissimilar users or items. We adopt the following rules to generate Top-N similar and dissimilar users or items. In order to reduce the noises when computing the similarities using PCC method between two users i and f, we require that user i and user f should at least co-rated 10 items, otherwise, we will ignore user f when computing user i's Top-N similar or dissimilar neighbors, and vice versa. Furthermore, for all the similar neighbors, the similarity between two users should be greater than 0.75, while for all the dissimilar neighbors, the similarity between two users should be less than 0.25. The same rules are also adopted when calculating similar and dissimilar items.

Parameter Settings.

In order to fairly compare every method, we employ similar parameter settings for those common parameters adopted in all the approaches. In this paper, for RSVD, SR^{u+}, SR^{u+-}, SR_{i+}, SR_{i+-} and SR^{u+-}_{i+-}, we use the setting $\lambda_1 = \lambda_2 = 0.01$. At the same time, all the learning rates γ_1 and γ_2 are set to 0.005. For all the Social Regularization based methods, α and β are set to 0.015 in the MovieLens dataset, while in the EachMovie dataset, they are set to 0.001.

Performance Analysis.

The experimental results using 10 and 50 dimensions to represent the latent factors in two different datasets are shown in Table 3 and Table 4, respectively. The percentages in the results are the improvements of our SR^{u+-}_{i+-} method over the corresponding approaches. In all our methods, the number of implicit user or item social neighbors are set to 10.

The following summarizes the key conclusions we observe from the results:

- We first notice that approach SR^{u+} outperforms the RSVD method, which only utilizes the user-item rating matrix. This observation coincides with our intuition that, at the absence of the explicit user social network, employing implicit user social information can help increase the recommendation quality.

- Secondly, besides the implicit user social information, the implicit item social information can also be used to improve the recommendation quality, as demonstrated by the method SR_{i+}. Among SR^{u+} and SR_{i+}, we observe that SR_{i+} generates better results than SR^{u+} in both datasets. A possible reason is that the rating styles of items typically have less diversities that those of users. Hence, the similarity calculation based on

[1]http://www.grouplens.org/system/files/ml-100k.zip.
[2]http://www.research.digital.com/SRC/EachMovie/. It is now retired by Hewlett-Packard (HP).

Table 3: Performance Comparisons (MovieLens)

Dataset	Dimension	Metrics	UserMean	ItemMean	RSVD	SR^{u+}	SR^{u+-}	SR_{i+}	SR_{i+-}	SR^{u+-}_{i+-}
MovieLens	10D	MAE	0.8389	0.8274	0.7525	0.7411	0.7400	0.7409	0.7398	**0.7333**
		Improve	12.59%	11.37%	2.55%					
		RMSE	1.0466	1.0359	0.9540	0.9421	0.9406	0.9403	0.9391	**0.9284**
		Improve	11.29%	10.37%	2.68%					
	50D	MAE	0.8389	0.8274	0.7416	0.7330	0.7321	0.7329	0.7320	**0.7281**
		Improve	13.21%	12.00%	1.82%					
		RMSE	1.0466	1.0359	0.9413	0.9298	0.9291	0.9292	0.9280	**0.9221**
		Improve	11.90%	10.99%	2.04%					

Table 4: Performance Comparisons (EachMovie)

Dataset	Dimension	Metrics	UserMean	ItemMean	RSVD	SR^{u+}	SR^{u+-}	SR_{i+}	SR_{i+-}	SR^{u+-}_{i+-}
EachMovie	10D	MAE	1.1409	1.1020	0.8854	0.8737	0.8725	0.8701	0.8690	**0.8681**
		Improve	23.91%	21.23%	1.95%					
		RMSE	1.4278	1.3851	1.1678	1.1520	1.1506	1.1491	1.1487	**1.1440**
		Improve	19.88%	17.41%	2.04%					
	50D	MAE	1.1409	1.1020	0.8751	0.8631	0.8614	0.8597	0.8588	**0.8571**
		Improve	24.88%	22.22%	2.06%					
		RMSE	1.4278	1.3851	1.1579	1.1413	1.1401	1.1389	1.1374	**1.1333**
		Improve	20.63%	18.18%	2.12%					

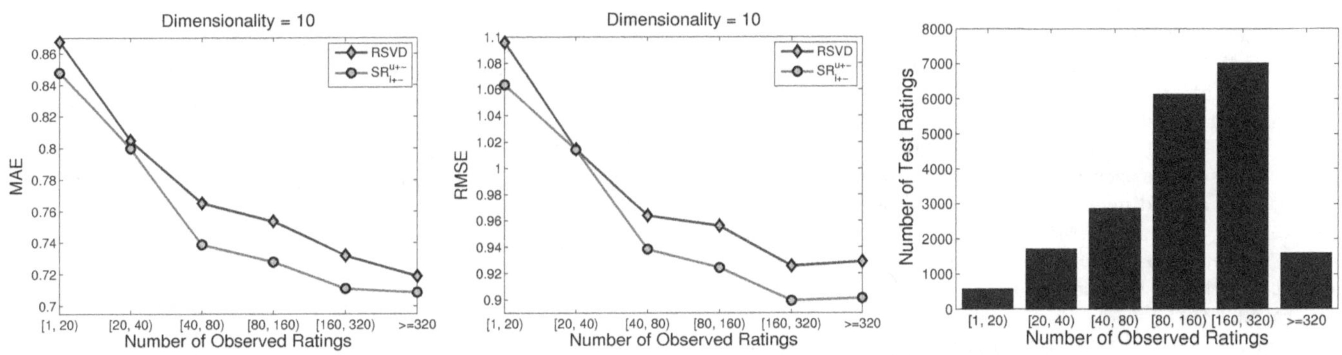

(a) MAE Comparison on Different User Rating Scales (MovieLens) (b) RMSE Comparison on Different User Rating Scales (MovieLens) (c) Distribution of Testing Data (MovieLens)

Figure 2: Performance Comparison on Different Users (MovieLens)

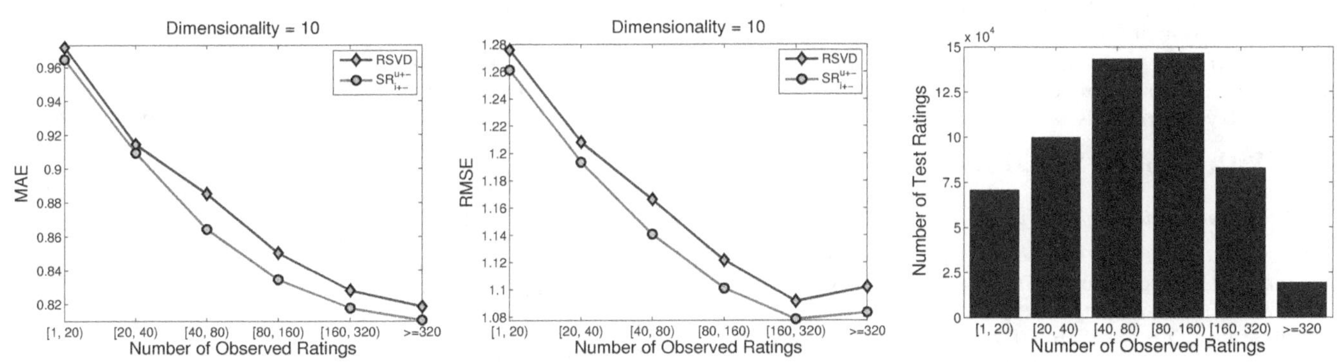

(a) MAE Comparison on Different User Rating Scales (EachMovie) (b) RMSE Comparison on Different User Rating Scales (EachMovie) (c) Distribution of Testing Data (EachMovie)

Figure 3: Performance Comparison on Different Users (EachMovie)

items is probably more accurate than the calculation based on users.

- Thirdly, another key observation we find through the experiments is that dissimilar user or item information can be used to further improve the recommender systems, as presented by the approaches SR^{u+-} and SR_{i+-}. They generate slightly better results than SR^{u+} and SR_{i+}, respectively.
- Fourthly, an integrated model SR^{u+-}_{i+-} demonstrates the best performance by incorporating all the useful implicit social information, including similar and dissimilar users as well as similar and dissimilar items. In general, the experimental results not only prove the effectiveness of incorporating implicit social information, but also demonstrate the flexibility of social regularization framework.

5.1.3 *Prediction Accuracy on Different Users*

In order to analyze the experiments thoroughly, in this section, we evaluate how different methods perform on different users based on how many ratings the users rated in the training datasets. We first group all the users in the training datasets based on the number of observed ratings, and then measure the prediction accuracies of different user groups. The experimental results conducted in both MovieLens and EachMovie datasets are illustrated in Figure 2 and Figure 3, respectively. In these two figures, in order to interpret the results more intuitively, we include the baseline method RSVD for comparison since it does not include any social information.

Users are grouped into 6 classes: "[1, 20)", "[20, 40)", "[40, 80)", "[80, 160)","[160, 320)" and ">=320". Figure 2(c) and Figure 3(c) summarizes the distributions of the number of testing data according to the groups in the training data. For example, in the EachMovie dataset, there are a total of 70,677 user-item pairs need to be predicted in the testing dataset in which the related users in the training dataset have rated 1 to 19 items.

From Figure 2(a), Figure 2(b), Figure 3(a) and Figure 3(b), we can see that the method SR^{u+-}_{i+-} with implicit social information consistently outperforms the RSVD method in all the user groups. We also notice an interesting phenomenon, that is, the method SR^{u+-}_{i+-} performs much better than RSVD when more ratings are observed. Actually, when more ratings are observed for a user, the similarity calculation process will find more accurate similar or dissimilar neighbors for this user since we have more information to represent or interpret this user. Hence, it will perform better than RSVD especially when more ratings are observed.

5.2 With Explicit Social Information

5.2.1 *Description of Dataset*

We use the Douban[3] dataset in this subsection since in addition to the user-item rating matrix, it also contains a social friend network between users.

Douban is a Chinese Web 2.0 Web site providing user rating, review and recommendation services for movies, books and music. Users can assign 5-scale integer ratings (from 1 to 5) to movies, books and music. It also provides Facebook-like social networking services, which allows users to find their friends through their email accounts. This means that most of the friends on Douban actually know each other offline.

[3]http://www.douban.com

Table 5: Statistics of User-Item Matrix of Douban

Statistics	User	Item
Min. Num. of Ratings	1	1
Max. Num. of Ratings	6,328	49,504
Avg. Num. of Ratings	129.98	287.51

Table 6: Statistics of Friend Network of Douban

Statistics	Friends per User
Max. Num.	986
Avg. Num.	13.07

Table 7: Performance Comparisons (5D)

Training Data	Metrics	SR_{exp}	SR_{imp}	SR^{top10}_{imp}
40%	MAE	**0.5698**	0.5707	0.5705
	RMSE	**0.7214**	0.7223	0.7222
60%	MAE	**0.5640**	0.5648	0.5645
	RMSE	**0.7133**	0.7142	0.7139

The Douban dataset we study in this paper contains 129,490 unique users and 58,541 unique movies with 16,830,839 movie ratings. As to the social friend network, the total number of friend links between users is 1,692,952. The statistics of the Douban user-item rating matrix and social friend network are summarized in Table 5 and Table 6, respectively.

5.2.2 *Performance Analysis*

We compare the following three methods using Douban datasets:

1. $\mathbf{SR}_{exp}$: this is the social regularization method described in Equation 3, which utilizes the explicit social information in improving recommender systems.
2. $\mathbf{SR}_{imp}$: this is the social regularization method that uses the implicit social information. Suppose that user u_i has n explicit social connections in the Douban dataset, then we will choose the most similar n users as the implicit social connections in this method. This setting is employed to fairly compare the method SR_{imp} with SR_{exp}.
3. $\mathbf{SR}^{top10}_{imp}$: this is also a social regularization method uses implicit social information. Different with SR_{imp}, for each user, we use the top-10 most similar users as the implicit connections.

All the parameters of the above three methods are identical for fairly comparison.

The results are summarized in Table 7. In this table, we evaluate three methods using different percentages of training data, i.e., 40% and 60%. From the results, we surprisedly find that for all the settings, the SR_{exp} method performs slightly better than both SR_{imp} and SR^{top10}_{imp} approaches, which indicates that in recommender systems, using user-established explicit social connections are better than computer-generated implicit social information.

In order to find out why using explicit social connections is more effective, we conduct the consistence analysis on

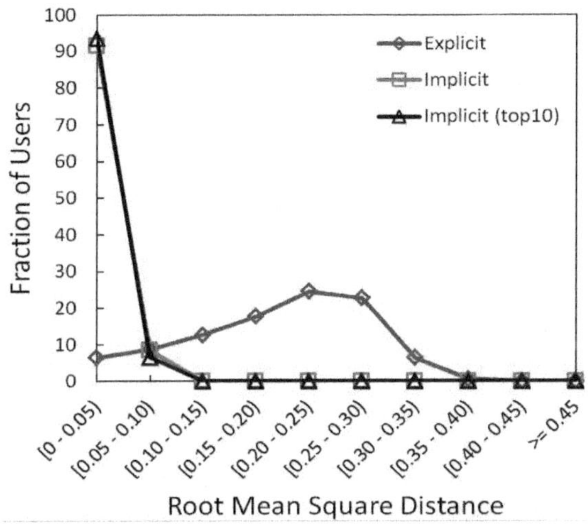

Figure 4: Similarity Consistence Analysis

three social networks we have, including one explicit (used in SR_{exp} method), and two implicit social networks (used in SR_{imp} and SR_{imp}^{top10} methods). The questions we address in this analysis are: How consistent are one user's social peers? Do the similarities between a user and his/her social peers vary a lot?

In order to answer the above questions, we evaluate the consistences based on the following metric, i.e., Root Mean Square Distance (RMSD). The definitions of user i are:

$$RMSD = \sqrt{\frac{\sum_{f \in S(i)} (s_{if} - \overline{s}_i)^2}{|S(i)|}}, \quad (15)$$

where s_{ik} is the similarity between user i and user k defined in Equation 6, $\overline{s}_i$ is the average social similarity of user i, while $S(i)$ represents the list of social peers of user i.

From the definitions, we can see that we are actually measuring in what extent a user's social similarity s_{if} will deviate from his/her average social similarity $\overline{s}_i$. If a user's social peer similarities all fall into a small range, then his/her RMSD will be relatively small, which indicates this user's social peers are very consistent with this user. If we observe a large RMSD value, then this user's social peers are relatively diverse. Figure 4 shows the analysis results of RMSD.

We notice that the curves of these three social networks illustrate different patterns. The figure reveals that a very large portion of users in the generated two implicit networks have very small RMSD values, which implies that users' social peers are relatively more consistent in these two implicit social networks. The RMSD values in Douban explicit friend communities are relatively larger, which presents that users' social peers in this network are more diverse.

Combining the results we obtain from Table 7, this observation actually suggests that social network with larger friend diversity is more effective in improving recommendation quality. This conclusion also coincides with the intuition we propose in Section 4.3, i.e., dissimilar users can also be utilized to improve recommender systems.

6. CONCLUSION

This paper studies a research problem on how to improve recommender systems using implicit social information. A very general matrix factorization framework is employed to incorporate different implicit social information. The experimental analysis suggests that similar user information, dissimilar user information, similar item information and dissimilar item information can be effectively used to improve recommender systems. Our work not only provides in-depth insights to social recommendation techniques, but also will greatly extend the impact of previous and upcoming social recommendation approaches.

7. REFERENCES

[1] P. Bedi, H. Kaur, and S. Marwaha. Trust based recommender system for the semantic web. In *Proceedings of the 20th international joint conference on Artifical intelligence*, IJCAI'07, pages 2677–2682, Hyderabad, India, 2007.

[2] J. S. Breese, D. Heckerman, and C. Kadie. Empirical analysis of predictive algorithms for collaborative filtering. In *Proceedings of the Fourteenth conference on Uncertainty in artificial intelligence*, UAI'98, pages 43–52, Madison, Wisconsin, 1998.

[3] M. Deshpande and G. Karypis. Item-based top-n recommendation. *ACM Transactions on Information Systems*, 22(1):143–177, 2004.

[4] J. L. Herlocker, J. A. Konstan, A. Borchers, and J. Riedl. An algorithmic framework for performing collaborative filtering. In *Proceedings of the 22nd annual international ACM SIGIR conference on Research and development in information retrieval*, SIGIR '99, pages 230–237, Berkeley, California, USA, 1999.

[5] T. Hofmann. Collaborative filtering via gaussian probabilistic latent semantic analysis. In *Proceedings of the 26th annual international ACM SIGIR conference on Research and development in informaion retrieval*, SIGIR '03, pages 259–266, Toronto, Canada, 2003.

[6] T. Hofmann. Latent semantic models for collaborative filtering. *ACM Transactions on Information Systems*, 22(1):89–115, 2004.

[7] J. Huang, X.-Q. Cheng, J. Guo, H.-W. Shen, and K. Yang. Social recommendation with interpersonal influence. In *Proceedings of the 19th European Conference on Artificial Intelligence*, ECAI '10, pages 601–606, Amsterdam, The Netherlands, 2010.

[8] M. Jamali and M. Ester. Trustwalker: a random walk model for combining trust-based and item-based recommendation. In *Proceedings of the 15th ACM SIGKDD international conference on Knowledge discovery and data mining*, KDD '09, pages 397–406, Paris, France, 2009.

[9] M. Jamali and M. Ester. A matrix factorization technique with trust propagation for recommendation in social networks. In *Proceedings of the fourth ACM conference on Recommender systems*, RecSys '10, pages 135–142, Barcelona, Spain, 2010.

[10] R. Jin, J. Y. Chai, and L. Si. An automatic weighting scheme for collaborative filtering. In *Proceedings of the 27th annual international ACM SIGIR conference on Research and development in information retrieval*, SIGIR '04, pages 337–344, Sheffield, United Kingdom, 2004.

[11] A. Kohrs and B. Merialdo. Clustering for collaborative filtering applications. In *Proceedings of CIMCA '99*, 1999.

[12] Y. Koren. Factorization meets the neighborhood: a multifaceted collaborative filtering model. In *Proceedings of the 14th ACM SIGKDD international conference on Knowledge discovery and data mining*, KDD '08, pages 426–434, Las Vegas, Nevada, USA, 2008.

[13] Y. Koren. Collaborative filtering with temporal dynamics. In *Proceedings of the 15th ACM SIGKDD international conference on Knowledge discovery and data mining*, KDD '09, pages 447–456, Paris, France, 2009.

[14] Y. Koren, R. M. Bell, and C. Volinsky. Matrix factorization techniques for recommender systems. *IEEE Computer*, 42(8):30–37, 2009.

[15] M. Kurucz, A. A. Benczur, and K. Csalogany. Methods for large scale svd with missing values. In *Proceeding of KDD CUP '07*, San Jose, CA, USA, 2007.

[16] G. Linden, B. Smith, and J. York. Amazon.com recommendations: Item-to-item collaborative filtering. *IEEE Internet Computing*, pages 76–80, Jan/Feb 2003.

[17] N. N. Liu and Q. Yang. Eigenrank: a ranking-oriented approach to collaborative filtering. In *Proceedings of the 31st annual international ACM SIGIR conference on Research and development in information retrieval*, SIGIR '08, pages 83–90, Singapore, Singapore, 2008.

[18] H. Ma, I. King, and M. R. Lyu. Learning to recommend with explicit and implicit social relations. *ACM Transactions on Intelligent Systems and Technology*, 2(3):29:1–29:19, May 2011.

[19] H. Ma, M. R. Lyu, and I. King. Learning to recommend with trust and distrust relationships. In *Proceedings of the third ACM conference on Recommender systems*, RecSys '09, pages 189–196, New York, New York, USA, 2009.

[20] H. Ma, D. Zhou, C. Liu, M. R. Lyu, and I. King. Recommender systems with social regularization. In *Proceedings of the fourth ACM international conference on Web search and data mining*, WSDM '11, pages 287–296, Hong Kong, China, 2011.

[21] P. Massa and P. Avesani. Trust-aware collaborative filtering for recommender systems. In *Proceedings of CoopIS/DOA/ODBASE '04*, pages 492–508, 2004.

[22] P. Massa and P. Avesani. Trust-aware recommender systems. In *Proceedings of the 2007 ACM conference on Recommender systems*, RecSys '07, pages 17–24, Minneapolis, MN, USA, 2007.

[23] J. O'Donovan and B. Smyth. Trust in recommender systems. In *Proceedings of the 10th international conference on Intelligent user interfaces*, IUI '05, pages 167–174, San Diego, California, USA, 2005.

[24] J. D. M. Rennie and N. Srebro. Fast maximum margin matrix factorization for collaborative prediction. In *Proceedings of the 22nd International Conference on Machine Learning*, pages 713–719, Bonn, Germany, 2005.

[25] R. Salakhutdinov and A. Mnih. Probabilistic matrix factorization. In *Proceedings of Advances in Neural Information Processing Systems*, NIPS '07, 2007.

[26] R. Salakhutdinov and A. Mnih. Bayesian probabilistic matrix factorization using markov chain monte carlo. In *Proceedings of the 25th international conference on Machine learning*, ICML '08, pages 880–887, Helsinki, Finland, 2008.

[27] B. Sarwar, G. Karypis, J. Konstan, and J. Riedl. Item-based collaborative filtering recommendation algorithms. In *Proceedings of the 10th international conference on World Wide Web*, WWW '01, pages 285–295, Hong Kong, Hong Kong, 2001.

[28] L. Si and R. Jin. Flexible mixture model for collaborative filtering. In *Proceedings of the 20th International Conference on Machine Learning*, ICML '03, pages 704–711, 2003.

[29] N. Srebro and T. Jaakkola. Weighted low-rank approximations. In *Proceedings of the 20th International Conference on Machine Learning*, pages 720–727, Washington, DC, USA, 2003.

[30] N. Srebro, J. D. M. Rennie, and T. Jaakkola. Maximum-margin matrix factorization. In *Proceedings of Advances in Neural Information Processing Systems*, NIPS '04, 2004.

[31] K. Yu, S. Zhu, J. Lafferty, and Y. Gong. Fast nonparametric matrix factorization for large-scale collaborative filtering. In *Proceedings of the 32nd international ACM SIGIR conference on Research and development in information retrieval*, SIGIR '09, pages 211–218, Boston, MA, USA, 2009.

[32] Q. Yuan, L. Chen, and S. Zhao. Factorization vs. regularization: fusing heterogeneous social relationships in top-n recommendation. In *Proceedings of the fifth ACM conference on Recommender systems*, RecSys '11, pages 245–252, Chicago, Illinois, USA, 2011.

[33] Y. Zhang and J. Koren. Efficient bayesian hierarchical user modeling for recommendation system. In *Proceedings of the 30th annual international ACM SIGIR conference on Research and development in information retrieval*, SIGIR '07, pages 47–54, Amsterdam, The Netherlands, 2007.

Task-Aware Query Recommendation

Henry Feild and James Allan
Center for Intelligent Information Retrieval
School of Computer Science
University of Massachusetts
Amherst, MA 01003
{hfeild,allan}@cs.umass.edu

ABSTRACT

When generating query recommendations for a user, a natural approach is to try and leverage not only the user's most recently submitted query, or reference query, but also information about the current search context, such as the user's recent search interactions. We focus on two important classes of queries that make up search contexts: those that address the same information need as the reference query (on-task queries), and those that do not (off-task queries). We analyze the effects on query recommendation performance of using contexts consisting of only on-task queries, only off-task queries, and a mix of the two. Using TREC Session Track data for simulations, we demonstrate that on-task context is helpful on average but can be easily overwhelmed when off-task queries are interleaved—a common situation according to several analyses of commercial search logs. To minimize the impact of off-task queries on recommendation performance, we consider automatic methods of identifying such queries using a state of the art search task identification technique. Our experimental results show that automatic search task identification can eliminate the effect of off-task queries in a mixed context.

We also introduce a novel generalized model for generating recommendations over a search context. While we only consider query text in this study, the model can handle integration over arbitrary user search behavior, such as page visits, dwell times, and query abandonment. In addition, it can be used for other types of recommendation, including personalized web search.

Categories and Subject Descriptors

H.3.3 [**Information Storage and Retrieval**]: Information Search and Retrieval—*search process, query formulation*

Keywords

Query recommendation, context-aware recommendation, search task identification

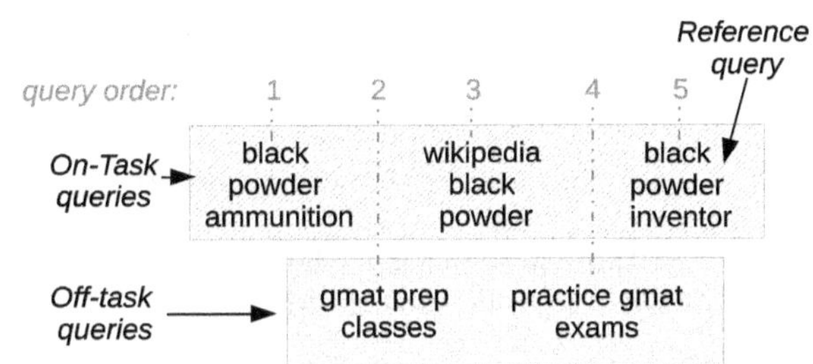

Figure 1: A search context with interleaved tasks.

1. INTRODUCTION

Query recommendation is a common tool used by search engines to assist users in reformulating queries. When an information need, or *task*, requires multiple searches, the sequence of queries form a context around which new queries can be recommended. Figure 1 illustrates a series of queries issued by a user consisting of two tasks: 1) finding information about the history of black powder firearms and 2) preparing for the GMAT standardized test. Given this sequence, our goal is to generate a list of query suggestions with respect to the most recently submitted query, or *reference query*, which is "black powder inventor" in this example. Notice, however, that the user has *interleaved* the two tasks such that no two adjacent queries are part of the same task. If we use the entire context to generate recommendations, two of the queries will be *off-task* with respect to the reference query and three (including the reference query) will be *on-task*. This paper explores the effects that on- and off-task contexts have on query recommendation. While previous work has considered task-aware query recommendation over logged user data, we are not aware of any work that systematically explores the effects of on-task, off-task, and mixed contexts on recommendation performance.

Though the example in Figure 1 may seem an extreme case, consider that Lucchese et al. found 74% of web queries were part of multi-tasking search sessions [15] in a three-month sample of AOL search logs; Jones and Klinkner observed that 17% of tasks were interleaved in a 3-day sample of Yahoo! web searches [10]; and Liao et al. [14] found 30% of sessions contained multiple tasks and 5% of sessions contained interleaved tasks in a sample of half a billion sessions extracted from Bing search logs. In addition, in a labeled sample of 503 AOL user sessions, we found 44% of search tasks consisted of two or more queries (see Figure 2), but there was only a 45% chance that any two adjacent queries

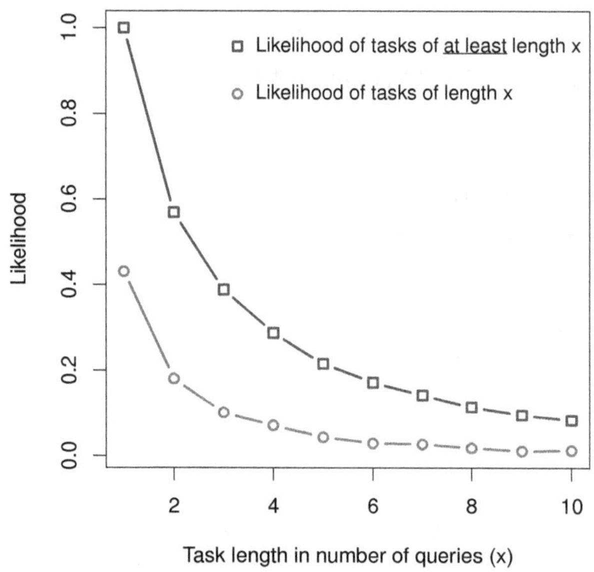

Figure 2: Distribution of tasks lengths observed in a labeled sample of the AOL query log.

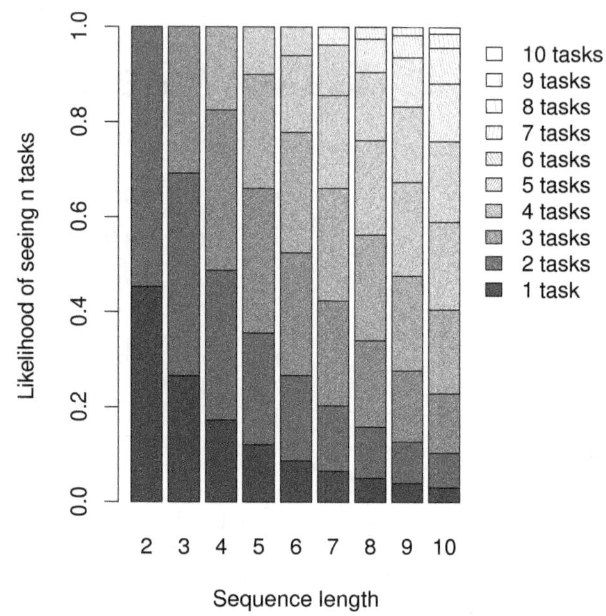

Figure 3: The distribution of seeing n tasks in a sequence of x queries as observed in a labeled sample of the AOL query log.

were part of the same task. Figure 3 shows the likelihood of seeing n tasks in any sequence of x queries, e.g., 10-query sequences typically consist of 3–7 search tasks. This means that a context consisting of the most recent n queries is very likely to consist of sub-contexts for several disjoint tasks, none of which may be a part of the same task as the reference query.

The goal of this paper is to better understand the effects of on-task, off-task, and mixed contexts on query recommendation quality. We also present and analyze several methods for handling mixed contexts. We address four questions concerning query recommendation:

RQ1. How does on-task context affect query recommendation performance?

RQ2. How does off-task context affect query recommendation performance?

RQ3. How does mixed context (on- *and* off-task queries) affect query recommendation performance?

RQ4. How do the following three methods affect query recommendation performance in a mixed context? (a.) using only the reference query, (b.) using the most recent m queries, or (c.) using the most recent m queries with same-task classification scores to weight the influence of each query.

To answer these questions, we perform a number of experiments using simulated search sequences derived from the TREC Session Track. For recommendation, we rely on random walks over a query flow graph formed from a subset of the 2006 AOL query log. We measure query recommendation performance by the quality of the results returned for a recommendation, focusing primarily on mean reciprocal rank (MRR). Our results show that on-task context is usually helpful, while off-task and mixed contexts are extremely harmful. However, automatic search task identification is a reliable way of detecting and discarding off-task queries.

There are four primary contributions of this paper: (1) an analysis of task-aware query recommendation demonstrating the usefulness of on-task query context, (2) an analysis of the impact of automatic search task identification on task-aware recommendation, in which we show the state of the art works very well, (3) an open source data set for evaluating context-aware query recommendation, and (4) a generalized model of combining recommendations across a search context, regardless of the recommendation algorithm.

2. RELATED WORK

Huang, Chien, and Oyang [9] introduced a search log-based query recommendation algorithm that extracts suggestions from search sessions in a query log that appeared similar to the user's current session, thereby incorporating the surrounding search context. They found it outperformed methods that extract suggestions from retrieved documents in many aspects.

Filali et al. [8] presented a probabilistic model for generating rewrites based on an arbitrarily long user search history. Their model interpolates the same-task similarity of a rewrite candidate to the reference query with the average similarity of that candidate to all on-task queries from a user's history, weighted by each query's similarity to the reference query. They found that giving some weight to the history, but most weight to the reference query, did best on a set of manually and automatically labeled data.

Liao et al. [14] explored the effect of task-trails on three applications, including query recommendation. They compare two session-based, two task-based, and two single-query recommendation models and found they retrieve complementary sets of suggestions, though the task-based models provided the higher quality suggestions. To identify tasks, they used an SVM model using features similar to Jones and Klinkner [10], and the weighted connected components clustering method described by Lucchese et al. [15]. Unlike Liao et al., we focus on the effects of on- and off-task context in various mixtures and evaluate on publicly accessible data. Their work is complementary to ours and our findings support theirs concerning the quality of recommendations using on-task recommendations.

Cao et al. [4] introduce a context-aware recommendation system that converts a series of user queries into concept sequences and builds a suffix tree of these from a large query log. To produce recommendations, a concept sequence is looked up in the suffix tree and the common next queries are given as suggestions.

Cao et al. [5] explored an efficient way to train a very large variable length Hidden Markov Model (vlHMM), which considers sequences of queries and clicks in order to produce query and URL recommendations as well as document reranking. The authors trained the vlHMM on a large commercial search log. However, they did not analyze the effects of on- and off-task contexts on recommendation and the vlHMM technique is tied to large search logs, limiting its portability.

Boldi et al. [2] presented a technique for building a query reformulation graph over user sessions, called a query flow graph. They considered two edge weighting techniques: one uses the threshold weight output by a same-task classifier and the other uses the observed likelihood of one query being submitted after the other. They looked at two applications of query flow graphs: (1) identifying sequences of queries that share a common search task and (2) generating query recommendations. The query suggestion component involves random walks and can be configured to consider the most recent n queries.

Several groups have investigated automatic methods for segmenting and clustering user search interactions into search tasks [2, 10, 13, 15, 18]. Most of these depend on machine learning algorithms—logistic regression, support vector machines, and decision trees—trained over large amounts of manually or automatically labeled user data to classify a pair of queries as belonging to the same task or not. We decided to use the Lucchese et al. method [15], which is a heuristic model that depends on lexical and semantic features of the pair of queries being classified. This method is the most recent and was shown to out-perform machine learned models on a sample of AOL data. The other methods are, however, equally applicable to the analysis we conduct.

3. QUERY RECOMMENDATION

We only consider one query recommendation algorithm based largely on the query flow graph (QFG) work of Boldi et al. [2] and the term-query graph (TQGraph) work of Bonchi et al. [3]. We use a query flow graph G in which the vertices V are queries from a query log L and the edges E represent reformulation probabilities. For any vertex $v \in V$, the weights of all outgoing edges must sum to 1. A *reformulation* is defined as an ordered pair of queries (q_i, q_j) such that the pair occurs in a user search session in that order, though not necessarily adjacent. A *session* is defined to be the maximal sequence of queries and result clicks such that no more than t seconds separate any two adjacent events. The outgoing edges of v are normalized across all sessions and users in L.

While we do not require reformulations to be adjacent, Boldi et al. did. By considering all reformulations—adjacent and otherwise—within a session, we expand the coverage of G beyond using adjacent query reformulations only but avoid incorporating as many off-task reformulations as when the scope is a user's entire search history. We assume that reformulations in which q_i and q_j are from different tasks, q_j will be an infrequent follower of q_i, and therefore statistically insignificant among q_i's outgoing edges. In addition, Boldi et al. used a thresholded and normalized chaining probability for the edge weights, but we do not due to the sparseness of our data (the AOL query logs).

To generate recommendations, we rely on a slight adaptation of the query flow graph, called the term-query graph [3]. This adds a layer to the QFG that consists of all terms that occur in queries in the QFG, each of which points to the queries in which it occurs. Given a query q, we find recommendations by first producing random walk scores over all queries in Q for each term $t \in q$.

To compute the random walk with restart for a given term t, we must first create a vector $\mathbf{v}$ of length $|V|$ (i.e., with one element per node in Q). Each element corresponding to a query that contains t is set to 1 and all others are set to 0. This is our *initialization vector*. Next, we must select the probability, c, of restarting our random walk to one of the queries in our initialization vector. Given the adjacency matrix of G, A, and a vector $\mathbf{u}$ that is initially set to $\mathbf{v}$, we then compute the following until convergence:

$$\mathbf{u} = (1 - c)A\mathbf{u} + c\mathbf{v} \tag{1}$$

After convergence, the values in $\mathbf{u}$ are the random walk scores of each corresponding query q' for t. We denote this as the term-level recommendation score $\widehat{\mathbf{r}}_{\text{term}}(q'|t)$.

One issue with using the random walk score for a query is that it favors frequent queries. To address this, Boldi et al. used the geometric mean $\mathbf{r}_{\text{term}}$ of the random walk score $\widehat{\mathbf{r}}_{\text{term}}$ and its normalized score $\overline{\mathbf{r}}_{\text{term}}$. Given an initial query q, the scores for an arbitrary query q' can be computed by:

$$\overline{\mathbf{r}}_{\text{term}}(q'|q) = \frac{\widehat{\mathbf{r}}_{\text{term}}(q'|q)}{\widehat{\mathbf{r}}_{\text{uniform}}(q')} \tag{2}$$

$$\begin{aligned} \mathbf{r}_{\text{term}}(q'|q) &= \sqrt{\widehat{\mathbf{r}}_{\text{term}}(q'|q) \cdot \overline{\mathbf{r}}_{\text{term}}(q'|q)} \\ &= \frac{\widehat{\mathbf{r}}_{\text{term}}(q'|q)}{\sqrt{\widehat{\mathbf{r}}_{\text{uniform}}(q')}} \end{aligned} \tag{3}$$

where $\widehat{\mathbf{r}}_{\text{uniform}}(q')$ is the random walk score produced for q' when the initialization vector $\mathbf{v}$ is uniform.

The final query recommendation vector is computed using a component-wise product of the random walk vectors for each term in the query. Specifically, for each query $q' \in V$, we compute the query-level recommendation score $\mathbf{r}_{\text{query}}(q'|q)$ as follows:

$$\mathbf{r}_{\text{query}}(q'|q) = \prod_{t \in q} \mathbf{r}_{\text{term}}(q'|t) \tag{4}$$

4. CONTEXT AWARE RECOMMENDATION

In this section, we introduce formal definitions of general and task-based contexts as well as the automatic search task identification algorithm used for the experiments.

4.1 Generalized context model

The recommendation models described above, and recommendation algorithms in general, that generate suggestions with respect to a single query can be easily extended to handle additional contextual information. The basic idea is simple: when generating recommendations for a query, consider the search context consisting of the m most recently submitted queries from the user, weighting the influence of each according to some measure of importance. Many functions can be used to measure the importance of a context query. The two we consider in this paper are how far back in a user's search history a query occurs and whether the query appears to be related to a user's current task. However, others may include whether a context query was quickly abandoned or spell corrected, how many results the user visited, the time of day they were visited, and other behavioral aspects. In this section, we introduce a generalized model that makes it easier for us to talk about the various importance functions we are interested in and can be used with additional functions explored in future work.

Assume that we have a search context C that contains all the information about a user's search behavior related to a sequence of m queries, with the mth query, $C[m]$, being the most recently submitted query. Also assume that we have a set of n importance functions, $\boldsymbol{\theta}_1, \boldsymbol{\theta}_2, \ldots, \boldsymbol{\theta}_n$ and corresponding weights $\lambda_1, \lambda_2, \ldots, \lambda_n$ that tell us how much weight to give to each of the importance functions. We will represent corresponding functions and weights as tuples in a set $F = \{\langle\lambda_1, \boldsymbol{\theta}_1\rangle \langle\lambda_2, \boldsymbol{\theta}_2\rangle \ldots, \langle\lambda_n, \boldsymbol{\theta}_n\rangle\}$. We compute the context-aware recommendation score for a query suggestion q' as follows:

$$\mathbf{r}_{\text{context}}(q'|C, F) = \sum_{i=1}^{m} \mathbf{r}_{\text{query}}(q'|C[i]) \sum_{\langle\lambda, \boldsymbol{\theta}\rangle \in F} \lambda \cdot \boldsymbol{\theta}(i, m, C) \tag{5}$$

Each importance function $\boldsymbol{\theta}$, takes three parameters: i, m, C, where i is the position of the query within context C for which importance is being measured and m is the position of the reference query. In this work, the reference query is always the last query of C, but the model does not make the assumption that this is always the case. The $\mathbf{r}_{\text{context}}$ recommendation scoring function scores q' with respect to each query in the context ($C[i]$) and adds that score to the overall score with some weight that is computed as the linear combination of the importance function values for that query.

4.2 Decaying context model

One of the importance functions we consider in this paper is a decaying function, where queries earlier in a user's context are considered less important than more recent queries. As such, queries submitted more recently have a greater influence on recommendation scores. This has the intuitive interpretation that users are less interested in older queries, otherwise they would not have moved on to new queries.

Boldi et al. [2] discussed a decay weighting method for entries in the random walk initialization vector ($\mathbf{v}$ in Eq. 1). They proposed that each query in a search context receive a weight proportional to β^d, where d is the distance in query count from the current query. For example, the second most recent query would get a weight of β^1, because it's one query away from the most recent query.

While the Boldi et al. method is specific to recommendations using random walks, we can transfer their exponential decay function to our model as follows:

$$\mathbf{decay}(i, j, C) = \beta^{j-i} \tag{6}$$

$$\mathbf{r}_{\text{decay}}(q'|C) = \mathbf{r}_{\text{context}}(q'|C, \{\langle 1.0, \mathbf{decay}\rangle\}) \tag{7}$$

4.3 Task context model

While decaying the influence of queries earlier in a search context is a natural importance function, we are also interested in functions that incorporate the degree to which a query is on the same task as the reference query. It is reasonable to assume (an assumption we test) that queries from a search context that are part of the same task should be more helpful in the recommendation process than queries that are not.

As we have stated earlier, Lucchese et al. observed that 74% of web queries are part of multi-task search sessions [15] while Jones and Klinkner found that 17% of tasks are interleaved in web search [10]. Using a labeled sample of the AOL query log, we observed an exponential decrease in the likelihood that the previous m queries are part of the same task as m increases (see Figure 3). This suggests that using the m most recent queries as the the search context for generating recommendations will likely introduce off-topic information, causing recommendations that seem out of place. Therefore, it may be beneficial to identify which queries from that context share the same task as the reference query.

Formally, given a search context C with m queries, we define a task context T to be the maximal subset of queries in C that share a common task to $C[m]$:

$$T \subseteq C \mid \forall\, i \in [1, m], C[i] \in T \iff \mathbf{sametask}(i, m, C) > \tau \tag{8}$$

where $\mathbf{sametask}(i, m, C)$ is a function that outputs a prediction in the range [0,1] as to how likely $C[i]$ and $C[m]$ are to be part of the same search task given C and τ is the decision threshold.

Once we have T, the natural question to pose is how do we use it? One method would be to treat T just as C and use it with the $\mathbf{r}_{\text{decay}}$ function, i.e., $\mathbf{r}_{\text{decay}}(q'|T)$. However, it may be that the off-task context is still useful, just not as useful as T. To support both of these points of view, we can use the following *hard task* recommendation scoring functions:

$$\mathbf{taskdecay}(i, j, C) = \beta^{\mathbf{taskdist}(i,j,C)} \tag{9}$$

$$\mathbf{hardtask}(i, j, C) = \begin{cases} \mathbf{taskdecay} & \text{if } \mathbf{sametask} > \tau, \\ 0 & \text{otherwise.} \end{cases} \tag{10}$$

$$\mathbf{r}_{\text{hardtask}}(q'|C) = \mathbf{r}_{\text{context}}(q'|C, \{\langle\lambda, \mathbf{hardtask}\rangle, \langle 1-\lambda, \mathbf{decay}\rangle\}) \tag{11}$$

where λ can be used to give more or less weight to the task context and **taskdist** is the number of on-task queries between $C[i]$ and $C[j]$. If we set $\lambda = 1$, we only use the task context, whereas with $\lambda = 0$, we ignore the task context altogether. If we use $\lambda = 0.5$, we use some of the task information, but still allow the greater context to have a presence. Note that we have left off the parameters to **decay** and **sametask** in Eq. 16 for readability.

This approach may work well if one is comfortable with setting a hard threshold τ on the output of the **sametask** function. If, however, we want to provide a mechanism by which we use the output of **sametask** as a confidence, we can use the following *soft task* recommendation scoring functions:

$$\textbf{softtask}(i, j, C) = \textbf{sametask} \cdot \textbf{decay} \tag{12}$$

$$\mathbf{r}_{\text{softtask}}(q'|C) = \mathbf{r}_{\text{context}}(q'|C, \{\langle\lambda, \textbf{softtask}\rangle, \langle 1-\lambda, \textbf{decay}\rangle\}) \tag{13}$$

Here, λ smooths between using and not using the same-task scores to dampen the decay weights. As before, we have left off the parameters to **sametask** and **decay** in Eq. 12.

Two additional models we consider are both variations of what we call *firm task* recommendation, as they combine aspects of both the hard and soft task models. The first, called **firmtask1**, behaves similarly to the soft task model, except that the weight given to any queries with a same task score at or below the threshold τ are weighted as 0. The second, called **firmtask2**, is identical to the hard task model, except that the task classification score is used in addition to the **taskdecay** weight. Mathematically, the firm task recommendation models are described by:

$$\textbf{firmtask1}(i, j, C) = \begin{cases} \textbf{sametask} & \text{if } \textbf{sametask} > \tau, \\ \times \textbf{ decay} & \\ 0 & \text{otherwise.} \end{cases} \tag{14}$$

$$\mathbf{r}_{\text{firmtask1}}(q'|C) = \mathbf{r}_{\text{context}}(q'|C, \{\langle\lambda, \textbf{firmtask1}\rangle, \langle 1-\lambda, \textbf{decay}\rangle\}) \tag{15}$$

$$\textbf{firmtask2}(i, j, C) = \begin{cases} \textbf{sametask} & \text{if } \textbf{sametask} > \tau, \\ \times \textbf{ taskdecay} & \\ 0 & \text{otherwise.} \end{cases} \tag{16}$$

$$\mathbf{r}_{\text{firmtask2}}(q'|C) = \mathbf{r}_{\text{context}}(q'|C, \{\langle\lambda, \textbf{firmtask2}\rangle, \langle 1-\lambda, \textbf{decay}\rangle\}) \tag{17}$$

Note that unlike the hard task model, the decay component of the **firmtask1** model is affected by every query, not just those above the threshold.

For example, suppose we have a context C with five queries, $q_1, \ldots, q_5$. Relative to the reference query, q_5, suppose applying **sametask** to each query produces the same-task scores [0.4, 0.2, 0.1, 0.95, 1.0]. If we set $\tau = 0.2$, then $T = [q_1, q_4, q_5]$. Using $\beta = 0.8$, notice in Figure 4 how the importance weight of each query in the context changes between using only the decay function (a.) and setting $\lambda = 1$ for the task-aware recommendations (b.–e.). Note that when $\lambda = 0$, the hard, firm, and soft task recommendation scores are equivalent (they all reduce to using the decay-only scoring function).

There are two primary differences between using hard- and soft task recommendation. First, hard task recommendation does not penalize on-task queries that occur prior to a sequence of off-task queries, e.g. in Figure 4, we see that q_1 is on-task and **hardtask** treats it as the first query in a sequence of three: $\beta^{n-1} = 0.8^2$. Conversely, the soft task recommendation model treats q_1 as the first in a sequence of five: $\beta^{m-1} = 0.8^4$.

Second, soft task recommendation can only down-weight a query's importance weight, unlike-hard task recommendation, which we saw can significantly increase the weight of an on-task query further back in the context. At the same time, however, soft task recommendation only allows a query to be given a zero weight if its same-task score is zero. The two firm task models balance these aspects in different ways.

	sametask	=	[.8, .2, .1, .9, 1.0]
a.	$\mathbf{r}_{\text{decay}}$	≈	[.4, .5, .6, .8, 1.0]
b.	$\mathbf{r}_{\text{softtask}}$	≈	[.3, .1, .1, .7, 1.0]
c.	$\mathbf{r}_{\text{firmtask1}}$	=	[.3, .0, .0, .7, 1.0]
d.	$\mathbf{r}_{\text{firmtask2}}$	=	[.5, .0, .0, .7, 1.0]
e.	$\mathbf{r}_{\text{hardtask}}$	≈	[.6, .0, .0, .8, 1.0]

Figure 4: An example of the degree to which each query in a context contributes (right column) given its predicted same-task score (top row) for: (a.) decay only, (b.) soft task, (c.) firm task-1, (d.) firm task-2, and (e) hard task recommendation. We set $\beta = 0.8$ for all, and $\lambda = 1, \tau = 0.2$ for b.–e.

4.4 Automatic search task identification

In Section 3, we discussed how to use information about tasks for query recommendation, but we did not say how to generate the scores. We use the search task identification heuristic described by Luccehse et al. [15]. In deciding if two queries q_i and q_j are part of the same task, we calculate two similarity measures: a lexical and a semantic score, defined as follows.

The lexical scoring function $\mathbf{s}_{\text{lexical}}$ is the average of the Jaccard coefficient between term trigrams extracted from the two queries and one minus the Levenshtein edit distance of the two queries. The score is in the range [0,1]. Two queries that are lexically very similar—ones where a single term has been added, removed, or reordered, or queries that have been spell corrected—should have an $\mathbf{s}_{\text{lexical}}$ score close to one.

The semantic scoring function $\mathbf{s}_{\text{semantic}}$ is made of up two components. The first, $\mathbf{s}_{\text{wikipedia}}(q_i, q_j)$, creates the vectors v_i and v_j consisting of the tf·idf scores of every Wikipedia document relative to q_i and q_j, respectively. The function then returns the cosine similarity between these two vectors. The second component, $\mathbf{s}_{\text{wiktionary}}(q_i, q_j)$ is similarly computed, but over Wiktionary entries. We then set $\mathbf{s}_{\text{semantic}}(q_i, q_j) = \max\left(\mathbf{s}_{\text{wikipedia}}(q_i, q_j), \mathbf{s}_{\text{wiktionary}}(q_i, q_j)\right)$. As with the lexical score, the range of the semantic score is [0,1].

The combined similarity score, $\mathbf{s}$, is defined as follows:

$$\mathbf{s}(q_i, q_j) = \alpha \cdot \mathbf{s}_{\text{lexical}}(q_i, q_j) + (1 - \alpha) \cdot \mathbf{s}_{\text{semantic}}(q_i, q_j)$$

We can define a same-task scoring function to use s directly, as follows:

$$\textbf{sametask}_1(i, j, C) = \mathbf{s}(C[i], C[j]) \tag{18}$$

Alternatively, we can run one extra step: single-link clustering over the context C using s as the similarity measure. Clustering allows us to boost the similarity score between two queries that are only indirectly related. Similar to Liao et al. [14], our choice of clustering follows the results of Lucchese et al. [15], who describe a weighted connected components algorithm that is equivalent to single-link clustering with a cutoff of η. After clustering, we use the notation $K_C[q]$ to represent the cluster or task associated with query q in context C; if two queries $q, q' \in C$ are part of the same task, then $K_C[q] = K_C[q']$, otherwise $K_C[q] \neq K_C[q']$. A

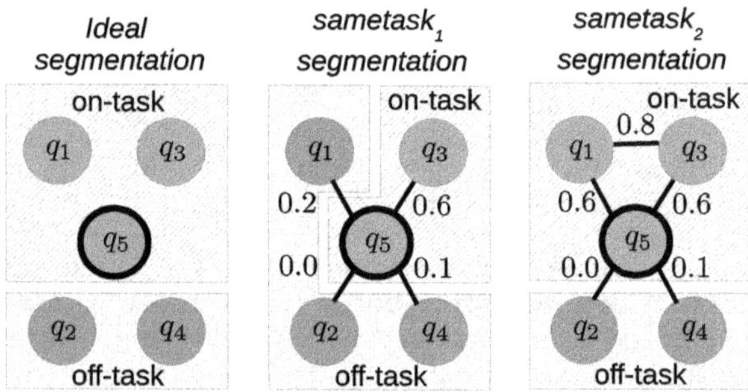

Figure 5: Examples of on-task/off-task segmentations using sametask$_1$ and sametask$_2$ scoring. The reference query, q_5, sits in the bolded center node. Note that the edge (q_1, q_5) goes from 0.2 using sametask$_1$ to 0.6 under sametask$_2$ due to q_1's strong similarity to q_3, which has a similarity score of 0.6 with q_5.

scoring function that uses task clustering is the following:

$$\mathbf{sametask}_2(i, j, C) = \max_{\substack{k \in [1,|C|]: \\ k \neq i \wedge \\ K_C[C[k]] = K_C[C[j]]}} \mathbf{s}(C[i], C[k]) \quad (19)$$

Note that **sametask$_2$** will return the highest similarity between $C[i]$ and any member of $C[j]$'s tasks, excluding $C[i]$. Figure 5 illustrates a case in which **sametask$_2$** improves over **sametask$_1$**; note, however, that **sametask$_2$** can also be harmful when an off-task query is found to be similar to an on-task query.

5. EXPERIMENTAL SETUP

In this section, we describe the data, settings, and methodology used for the experiments.

5.1 Constructing a query flow graph

We extracted query reformulations from the 2006 AOL query log, which includes more than 10 million unique queries making up 21 million query instances submitted by 657,426 users between March–April 2006. Considering all ordered pairs from a 30-query sliding window across sessions with a maximum timeout of 26 minutes, we extracted 33,218,915 distinct query reformulations to construct a query flow graph (compared to 18,271,486 if we used only adjacent pairs), ignoring all dash ("-") queries, which correspond to queries that AOL scrubbed or randomly replaced. The inlink and outlink counts of the nodes in the graph both have a median of 2 and a mean of about 5. If we were to use only adjacent reformulations from the logs, the median would be 1 and the mean just under 2.

5.2 Task data

We used the 2010 and 2011 TREC Session Track [11, 12] data to generate task contexts. The 2010 track data contains 136 judged sessions, each with two queries (totaling 272 queries), covering three reformulation types: drift, specialization, and generalization relative to the first search. We ignore the reformulation type. The 2011 track data consists of 76 variable length sessions, 280 queries (average of 3.7 queries per session), and 62 judged topics. Several topics have multiple corresponding sessions. In total, we use all 212 judged sessions from both years. The relevance judgments in both cases are over the ClueWeb09 collection. Our goal is to provide recommendations to retrieve documents relevant to the last query in each session, thus we mark the last query as the reference query.

Each session constitutes a single task, and henceforth we refer to the sessions as tasks. Since the TREC data consists of single tasks, we need some way of simulating the case that multiple tasks are interleaved. We describe our approach for this next.

5.3 Experiments

To answer our four research questions, we use the following set of experiments. Throughout all of these experiments, the baseline is to use only the reference query for generating query recommendations.

Experiment 1. For RQ1, which seeks to understand the effect of including relevant context on recommendation performance, we use each task T from the TREC Session Track and recommend suggestions using the most recent m queries for $m = [1, |T|]$. If incorporating context is helpful, then we should see an improvement as m increases. Note that $m = 1$ is the case in which only the reference query is used.

Experiment 2. To address RQ2, which asks how off-task context affects recommendation performance, we modify the experiment described above to consider a context of $m = [1, |T|]$ queries such that queries 2–$|T|$ are off-task. To capture the randomness of off-task queries, we evaluate over R random samples of off-task contexts (each query is independently sampled from other tasks, excluding those with the same TREC Session Track topic) for each task T and each value of $m > 1$. If off-task context is harmful, we should see a worsening trend in performance as m increases.

Experiment 3. To address RQ3, which asks how query recommendation performance is affected by a context that is a mix of on- and off-task queries, we rely on a simulation of mixed contexts. As we saw in Figure 3, the probability that a sequence of m queries share the same task decreases exponentially as m increases, and so the mixed context assumed in RQ3 is realistic if not typical. We simulate mixed contexts by taking each task T of length n and considering a context window of length $m = [1, n + R]$, where R is the number of off-task queries to add into the context. The last query in the context q_m always corresponds to the last query q_n in T. Queries $q_1, \ldots, q_{m-1}$ consist of a mix of the queries from T and other tasks from the TREC Session Track. The queries from T will always appear in the same order, but not necessarily adjacent.

To incorporate noise, we initially set $C = []$. We select R off-task queries as follows: first, we randomly select an off-topic task, O, from the TREC Session Track and take the first R queries from that task. If $|O| < R$, we randomly selected an addition off-topic task and concatenate its first $R-|O|$ queries to O. We continue the process until $|O| = |R|$. We now randomly interleave T and O, the only rule being that T_n—the reference query—must be the last query in C (an easy rule to adhere to by simply removing T_n before the randomized interleaving, and then concatenating it to the end). For a given value of R, we can perform many randomizations and graph the effect of using the most recent $n + R$ queries to perform query recommendation.

Experiment 4. The final research question, RQ4, asks

how mixed contexts should be used in the query recommendation process. We have limited ourselves to consider three possibilities: (a.) using only the reference query (i.e., our baseline throughout these experiments), (b.) using the most recent $n + R$ queries (i.e., the results from Experiment 3), or (c.) incorporating same-task classification scores. Experiment 4 concentrates on (c.) and analyzes the effect of incorporating same-task classification scores during the search context integration process. This is where we will compare the task-aware recommendation models described in the previous section.

5.4 Technical details

For the query recommendation using the TQGraph, we used a restart probability of $c = 0.1$, as was found to be optimal by Bonchi et al. [3]. Note that they refer to the restart value α, where $c = 1 - \alpha$. To increase the speed of our recommendation, we only stored the 100,000 top scoring random walk results for each term. Bonchi et al. [3] found this to have no or very limited effects on performance when used with $c = 0.1$.

For task classification, we used the parameters found optimal by Lucchese et al. [15]: $\eta = 0.2$ (used during task clustering) and $\alpha = 0.5$ (used to weight the semantic and lexical features). We also set $\tau = \eta$ since τ is used in much the same way in the task-aware recommendation models.

To evaluate recommendations, we retrieved documents from ClueWeb09 using the default query likelihood model implemented in Indri 5.3 [17].[1] We removed spam by using the Fusion spam score dataset [6] at a 75th percentile, meaning we only kept the least spammy 25% of documents.[2]

6. RESULTS

In this section, we cover the results of each of the experiments described in Section 5.3. We then discuss the meaning of our findings as well as their broader implications.

6.1 Experimental results

In all experiments, we measured recommendation performance using the mean reciprocal rank (MRR) of ClueWeb09 document retrieved for the top scored recommendation averaged over the 212 TREC Session Track tasks. We found similar trends using normalized discounted cumulative gain (nDCG) and precision at 3, 5, and 10. There are several ways one can calculate relevance over the document sets retrieved for recommendations, such as count any document retrieved in the top ten for any of the context queries as non-relevant (rather harsh), indifferently (resulting in duplicate documents), or by removing all such documents from the result lists of recommendations. We elected to go with the last as it is a reasonable behavior to expect from a context-aware system. We removed documents retrieved for any query in the context, not just those that are on-task. This is a very conservative evaluation and is reflected in the performance metrics.

Experiment 1. With this experiment, our aim was to quantify the effect of on-task query context on recommendation quality. Focusing on the top line with circles in Figure 6, the MRR of the top scored recommendation averaged over the 212 tasks performs better than using only the ref-

[1] http://www.lemurproject.org/indri/

[2] http://plg.uwaterloo.ca/~gvcormac/clueweb09spam/

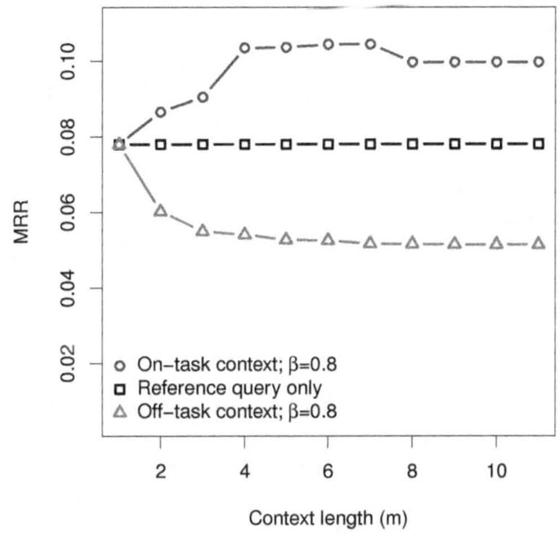

Figure 6: The effect of adding on-task (blue circles) and off-task (red triangles) queries versus only the reference query on recommendation MRR (black squares). MRR is calculated on the top scoring recommendation.

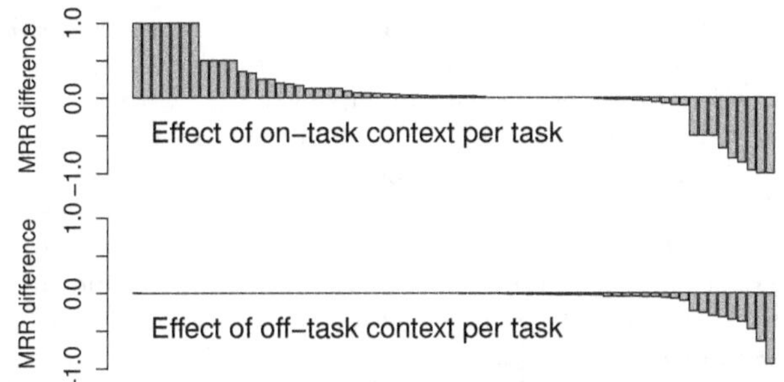

Figure 7: The per session effect of on- and off-task context on the change in MRR of the top scoring recommendation. The y-axis shows the difference between the MRR of using context and using only the reference query. A higher value means context improved MRR. Note that 145 tasks were removed as neither on- nor off-task context had an effect. The bars are not necessarily aligned between the two plots and should not be compared.

erence query (middle line with squares). To generate these scores, we used the $\mathbf{r}_{\text{decay}}$ model with $\beta = 0.8$, as set by Boldi et al. [2] in their decay function. For each value of m, if a particular task T has fewer than m queries, the value at $|T|$ is used. The MRR scores are low because for a large number of tasks, none of the methods provide any useful recommendations. We performed evaluations where such tasks were ignored and found that the MRR does indeed increase and the relationship between the methods plotted stays the same. However, in order to ensure comparability with future work, we elected to report on all tasks.

While performance is better on average in Figure 6, the top bar chart in Figure 7 breaks the performance down by the TREC search tasks and we can see that there are many tasks for which on-task context is very helpful, as well as several where it hurts. Note that some of the tasks are not displayed for readability.

Experiment 2. The goal of the second experiment was to ascertain the effect of off-task context on query recommendation. We generated 50 random off-task contexts for each task and report the micro-average across all trials. The bottom line with triangles in Figure 6 shows that adding off-task queries under the $\mathbf{r}_{\text{decay}}$ model with $\beta = 0.8$ rapidly decreases recommendation performance for low values of m before more or less leveling off around $m = 5$ (it still decreases, but much slower). Its performance is well below that of the baseline of using only the reference query, making it clear that off task context is extremely detrimental.

Turning to the bottom plot in Figure 7, we see that off-task context has an almost entirely negative effect (there is an ever so slight increase in performance for the task represented by the far left bar). Interestingly, for the severely compromised tasks on the far right, the effect is not as negative as when on-task context hurts. We have not conducted a full analysis to understand this phenomena, but one possible cause is the averaging over 50 trials that takes place for the off-task contexts. We leave investigations into this for future work.

Experiment 3. With Experiment 3, we wanted to understand the effect of mixed contexts—consisting of both on- and off-task queries—on query recommendation performance. As explained earlier, the experiment explores the performance of tasks when R noisy queries are added to the entire set of on-task queries. The bottom line with triangles in Figure 8 shows just this, using $\mathbf{r}_{\text{decay}}$ with $\beta = 0.8$. The far left point, where $R = 0$, lines up with the far right point of the on-task line in Figure 6. We randomly generated 50 noisy contexts per task for each value of R. The solid line shows the micro-averaged MRR over all tasks' samples. The dotted lines on either side show the minimum and maximum values for the micro-average MRR on a set of 1,000 sub-samples (with replacement) of the original 50. As you can see, the bounds indicate relatively low variance of the micro-average across the 212 tasks. There are still certain tasks for which performance is very high or very low (that is, the bounds on the micro-average do not inform us of the variance among tasks).

An important observation from this experiment is that performance dips below that of the baseline when even a *single* off-task query is mixed in. This is quite startling when you consider that the chances of three queries (at $R = 1$, all contexts are of at least length three) in a row belonging to a single task are below 30% (see Figure 3) and that roughly 40% of tasks in the wild are of length three or more (see Figure 2). These results clearly show that blindly incorporating mixed context is a poor method of incorporating context.

Experiment 4. In the final experiment, we hoped to determine the effects of using recommendation models that consider the reference query only, the entire context, or the entire context, but in a task-aware manner. The first two were addressed in the previous experiments, where we learned that using the reference query is more effective than blindly using the entire context. Figure 8 shows the results of using the models we introduced in Section 4.3. We used the same randomizations as in Experiment 3 and likewise generated the minimum and maximum bounds around each model's performance line. For these experiments, **sametask**$_1$ scores were used to produce same-task scores. We also performed the experiment using **sametask**$_2$ and found it was comparable. We used $\lambda = 1$ for all task-aware models; setting it to anything less resulted in an extreme degradation of performance.

There are several interesting observations. First, the firm-

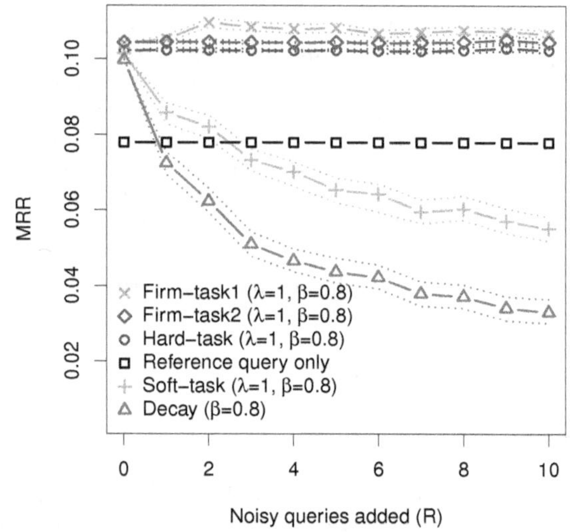

Figure 8: The effect of adding off-task queries to a task context on MRR when same task classification is used and is not used versus only using the reference query (black squares). The sametask$_1$ scoring method is used for all task-aware recommendation models. MRR is calculated on the top scoring recommendation.

task models performed best, though it is likely that the performance of the $\mathbf{r}_{\text{firmtask1}}$ model (the top line with x's) would decrease with larger amounts of noise because the decay function depends on the length of the context, not the number of queries predicted to be on-task. Thus, for on-task queries occurring early on in very large contexts, the decay weight will effectively be 0. You may notice that this model also increases for a bit starting at $R = 2$. This is likely due to the decay function used: since every query in the context, and not just the on-task queries, count toward the distances between an on-task query and the reference query under $\mathbf{r}_{\text{firmtask1}}$, on-task queries are actually down-weighted to a greater degree than in the $\mathbf{r}_{\text{firmtask2}}$ and $\mathbf{r}_{\text{hardtask}}$ models. The graph indicates that this change in weighting is helpful. This also suggests that setting β differently may improve the performance of the other models.

The $\mathbf{r}_{\text{firmtask2}}$ model (diamonds) comes in at a close second and narrowly outperforms $\mathbf{r}_{\text{hardtask}}$ (circles). All three models outperform the baselines—using only the reference query (squares) and $\mathbf{r}_{\text{decay}}$ over the entire context (triangles).

The $\mathbf{r}_{\text{softtask}}$ model, however, performs rather poorly. While it can offer some improvement over using just the reference query for a small amount of noise, once the noise level reaches four off-task queries, it is not longer viable. It does, however, outperform the decay model applied in a task-unaware manner.

Another interesting point is that the performance of the task-aware models is actually better at $R = 0$ than if the known tasks are used. The likely explanation is that the same-task scores prevent on-task queries that are quite different from the reference query from affecting the final recommendation. These kinds of queries may introduce more noise since their only recommendation overlap with the reference query may be generic queries, such as "google". This is not always the case, however. For example, one task consists of the queries ["alan greenspan", "longest serving Federal Reserve Chairman"]. The first query is detected to be

Rank	Reference query	RR	Decay	RR	Hard task ($\lambda = 1$)	RR
1.	google		history of films		black powder sabots	1.00
2.	ebay		the history of european culture of drinking		black powder cannons	0.33
3.	yahoo		the history of european alcohol drinking...		google	
4.	yahoo.com		the history of european alcohol drinking		marlin firearms	
5.	google.com		aircraft crash testing		black powder weapons for sale	0.08

Figure 9: The top 5 suggestions generated from three of the models for the randomly generated context shown in Figure 10. Reciprocal rank (RR) values of 0 are left blank.

No.	Query context	sametask_1
5.	**black powder inventor**	**1.00**
4.	**wikipedia black powder**	**0.52**
3.	us geographic map	0.06
2.	**black powder ammunition**	**0.75**
1.	us political map	0.03

Figure 10: An example of a randomly generated mixed context along with the same-task scores. The top query (No. 5) is the reference query. The bolded queries are on-task.

off-task, however, it is imperative to generate decent recommendations since the reference query generates generic Federal Reserve-related queries and not ones focused on Alan Greenspan.

Overall, though, the same-task classification with a threshold $\tau = 0.2$ worked well. The same-task classification precision relative to the positive class was on average 80%. The precision relative to the negative class varied across each noise level, but was on average 99%. The average accuracy was 93%. The decent same-task classification is why the three models at the top of Figure 8 are so flat.

6.2 Discussion

The results of our experiments demonstrate not only the usefulness of on-task context, but also the extreme impact of off-task and mixed contexts. The results from Experiment 4 suggest that the appropriate model is one that balances a hard threshold to remove any influence from context queries predicted to be off-task, and to weight the importance of the remaining queries by both their distance to the reference query and by the confidence of the same-task classification. Based on the results, we recommend the $\mathbf{r}_{\text{firmtask2}}$ model, since its performance will be consistent regardless of how far back in a user's history we go, unlike $\mathbf{r}_{\text{firmtask1}}$.

We did not see any substantial effects from using task clustering, as Liao et al. [14] used. However, other task identification schemes may perform differently; after all, as we saw in Experiment 4, our task identification method actually caused slight improvements over using the true tasks.

To get a feel for the quality of the recommendations produced generally with the AOL query logs and specifically by different models, consider the randomly generated mixed context in Figure 10. The top five recommendations from three methods for this context are shown in Figure 9. Notice that using only the reference query produces popular queries, none of which are related to the context in the least. Meanwhile, blindly using the context produces suggestions that are swamped by the off-task queries. This is in stark contrast to using the hard task model, which suggests four decent looking suggestions, three of which have non-zeros reciprocal rank values.

Another observation from this example is the amount of noise: very popular queries such as "google" appear in the suggestion lists. This is in part due to not finely tuning the various parameters of the underlying recommendation algorithm we used—something we avoided since the recommendation algorithm was not the focus of this work. It is likely also due to the age and scope of the AOL query log, which is not large compared to the commercial logs commonly used in query recommendation research. Nonetheless, the context-aware recommendation models we presented in Section 4 are compatible with any recommendation algorithm that supplies a sufficiently long, scored list of suggestions. We leave the investigation as to whether performance follows for future work.

Many of the tasks for which task-aware recommendation performed well involved specialization reformulations. Some examples include: *heart rate→slow fast heart rate*, *bobcat tractor→bobcat tractor attachment*, *disneyland hotel→disneyland hotel reviews*, and *elliptical trainer→elliptical trainer benefits*. One possible reason for this is that incorporating recommendations for a context query that is a subset of the reference query focuses the final recommendations on the most important concepts.

None of the experiments used notions of temporal sessions or complete user histories. We did this mainly because the mixed contexts were generated and not from actual user logs where context windows could be tied to temporal boundaries, e.g., two-day windows. We believe that by focusing on factors such as on- and off-task queries, we struck at the core questions in this space. We leave testing whether the results from these experiments port to real user data to future work, but we believe they will, especially given the results of related studies, such as those conducted by Liao et al. [14] and Filali et al. [8].

7. SUMMARY AND FUTURE WORK

In this work, we investigated four key research questions surrounding context-aware query recommendation and the effects of on- and off-task recommendation: (RQ1) How does on-task context affect recommendation quality relative to using only the most recently used query? (RQ2) How does off-task context affect recommendation quality? (RQ3) How does mixed context consisting of on- and off-task queries affect recommendation quality? and (RQ4) How do task-aware recommendation models affect performance given a mixed context?

We designed four sets of experiments that used random walks over a term-query graph of the 2006 AOL query logs for recommendations and the 2010–2011 TREC Session Track data for tasks. We evaluated all models using micro-averaged mean reciprocal rank (MRR) over the 212 TREC tasks and used 50 trials when randomization was needed. The results of our experiments show that on-task context is, on average, very helpful, but can sometimes degrade performance substantially. On the other hand, off-task context only degrades performance. We found that leveraging mixed contexts, when used without regard of the task corresponding to each of its constituent queries, reduced the quality of recommendations. Finally, we demonstrated the effectiveness of four task-aware models, which rely on a state-of-the-art search task identification algorithm. Three of the four models out-performed using only the most recently submitted query when up to ten off-task queries were added. Results suggest that two of those models would maintain their accuracy at large levels of noise since their weighting schemes completely ignore any query classified as off-task.

In many ways these results are not surprising: incorporating relevant queries improves query accuracy just as relevance feedback improves document ranking. What is surprising, though, is the extraordinary sensitivity of these approaches to off-task queries. Even making a single mistake and including an off-task query can shift many approaches in the wrong direction, away from relevant documents. This work takes a methodical look at the relative impact of on- and off-task queries and provides a deeper understanding of their inter-relationships than had been reported previously.

In addition, our findings rely on publicly accessible datasets, which eases others' efforts in validating and reproducing our results. Furthermore, it allows others to compare directly with our results if they so desire. The simulated contexts and corresponding recommendations used in our experiments are available on our website.[3]

There are many avenues of future work. One element to explore is the portability of our findings to real user search behavior over many more tasks. Another is to consider other recommendation algorithms, including ones not dependent on query logs [1] and ones that use other user behavior [7, 19]. We only considered the effectiveness of query recommendations to address the current task, but other measures of suggestion quality exists [16], such as attractiveness and diversity; exploring these other evaluations would provide a fuller picture of the value of task-aware recommendation. Other future directions include expanding the analysis to other applications, such as website or task recommendation [20].

8. ACKNOWLEDGMENTS

This work was supported in part by the Center for Intelligent Information Retrieval and in part by NSF grant #IIS-0910884. Any opinions, findings and conclusions or recommendations expressed in this material are those of the authors and do not necessarily reflect those of the sponsor.

References

[1] S. Bhatia, D. Majumdar, and P. Mitra. Query suggestions in the absence of query logs. In *Proc. of SIGIR*, pages 795–804, 2011.

[2] P. Boldi, F. Bonchi, C. Castillo, D. Donato, A. Gionis, and S. Vigna. The query-flow graph: model and applications. In *Proc. of CIKM*, pages 609–618, 2008.

[3] F. Bonchi, R. Perego, F. Silvestri, H. Vahabi, and R. Venturini. Efficient query recommendations in the long tail via center-piece subgraphs. In *Proc. of SIGIR*, pages 345–354, 2012.

[3] `http://ciir.cs.umass.edu/downloads/task-aware-query-recommendation`

[4] H. Cao, D. Jiang, J. Pei, Q. He, Z. Liao, E. Chen, and H. Li. Context-aware query suggestion by mining click-through and session data. In *Proceeding of KDD*, pages 875–883, 2008.

[5] H. Cao, D. Jiang, J. Pei, E. Chen, and H. Li. Towards context-aware search by learning a very large variable length hidden Markov model from search logs. In *Proc. of WWW*, pages 191–200, 2009.

[6] G. Cormack, M. Smucker, and C. Clarke. Efficient and effective spam filtering and re-ranking for large web datasets. *Information retrieval*, 14(5):441–465, 2011.

[7] S. Cucerzan and R. W. White. Query suggestion based on user landing pages. In *Proc. of SIGIR*, pages 875–876, 2007.

[8] K. Filali, A. Nair, and C. Leggetter. Transitive history-based query disambiguation for query reformulation. In *Proc. of SIGIR*, pages 849–850, 2010.

[9] C. Huang, L. Chien, and Y. Oyang. Relevant term suggestion in interactive web search based on contextual information in query session logs. *JASIST*, 54(7):638–649, 2003.

[10] R. Jones and K. L. Klinkner. Beyond the session timeout: automatic hierarchical segmentation of search topics in query logs. *Proceedings of CIKM 2008*, 2008.

[11] E. Kanoulas, P. Clough, B. Carterette, and M. Sanderson. Session track at TREC 2010. In *Proc. of the SIGIR Workshop on the Simulation of Interaction*, pages 13–14, 2010.

[12] E. Kanoulas, B. Carterette, M. Hall, P. Clough, and M. Sanderson. Overview of the TREC 2011 Session Track. In *Proc. of TREC*, 2011.

[13] A. Kotov, P. N. Bennett, R. W. White, S. T. Dumais, and J. Teevan. Modeling and analysis of cross-session search tasks. In *Proc. of SIGIR*, pages 5–14, 2011.

[14] Z. Liao, Y. Song, L.-w. He, and Y. Huang. Evaluating the effectiveness of search task trails. In *Proc. of WWW*, pages 489–498, 2012.

[15] C. Lucchese, S. Orlando, R. Perego, F. Silvestri, and G. Tolomei. Identifying task-based sessions in search engine query logs. In *Proc. of WSDM*, pages 277–286, 2011.

[16] Z. Ma, Y. Chen, R. Song, T. Sakai, J. Lu, and J. Wen. New assessment criteria for query suggestion. In *Proc. of SIGIR*, pages 1109–1110, 2012.

[17] D. Metzler and W. Croft. Combining the language model and inference network approaches to retrieval. *Information processing & management*, 40(5):735–750, 2004.

[18] F. Radlinski and T. Joachims. Query chains: learning to rank from implicit feedback. In *Proc. of KDD*, pages 239–248, 2005.

[19] Y. Song and L.-w. He. Optimal rare query suggestion with implicit user feedback. In *Proc. of WWW*, pages 901–910, 2010.

[20] G. Tolomei, S. Orlando, and F. Silvestri. Towards a task-based search and recommender systems. In *ICDEW*, pages 333–336, 2010.

Extracting Query Facets from Search Results

Weize Kong and James Allan
Center for Intelligent Information Retrieval
School of Computer Science
University of Massachusetts Amherst
Amherst, MA 01003
{wkong, allan}@cs.umass.edu

ABSTRACT

Web search queries are often ambiguous or multi-faceted, which makes a simple ranked list of results inadequate. To assist information finding for such faceted queries, we explore a technique that explicitly represents interesting facets of a query using groups of semantically related terms extracted from search results. As an example, for the query "baggage allowance", these groups might be different airlines, different flight types (domestic, international), or different travel classes (first, business, economy). We name these groups query facets and the terms in these groups facet terms. We develop a supervised approach based on a graphical model to recognize query facets from the noisy candidates found. The graphical model learns how likely a candidate term is to be a facet term as well as how likely two terms are to be grouped together in a query facet, and captures the dependencies between the two factors. We propose two algorithms for approximate inference on the graphical model since exact inference is intractable. Our evaluation combines recall and precision of the facet terms with the grouping quality. Experimental results on a sample of web queries show that the supervised method significantly outperforms existing approaches, which are mostly unsupervised, suggesting that query facet extraction can be effectively learned.

Categories and Subject Descriptors

H.3.3 [**Information Storage and Retrieval**]: Information Search and Retrieval—*Clustering, Query formulation*

General Terms

Algorithms, Experimentation

Keywords

Query Facet, Semantic Class Extraction, Multi-faceted Query

1. INTRODUCTION

Web search queries are often ambiguous or multi-faceted [27]. Current popular approaches try to diversify the result list to account for different search intents or query subtopics [24]. A weakness of this approach is that the query subtopics are hidden from the user, leaving him or her to guess at how the results are organized.

In this work, we attempt to extract query facets from web search results to assist information finding for these queries. We define a query facet as a set of coordinate terms – i.e., terms that share a semantic relationship by being grouped under a more general hypernym ("is a" relationship). For example, for the query *mars landing*, three possible query facets are shown in Table 1.

Table 1: Example query facets

Query: mars landing
1. Curiosity, Opportunity, Spirit
2. USA, UK, Soviet Union
3. video, pictures, news
Query: baggage allowance
1. Delta, Jetblue, AA, Continental, ...
2. domestic, international
3. first class, business class, economy class
4. weight, size, quantity
Query: mr bean
1. comics, movies, tv, books
2. the curse of mr bean, mr bean goes to town, ...
3. rowan atkinson, richard wilson, jean rochefort, ...
4. mr bean, irma gobb, rupert, hubert, ...

The first query facet, {*Curiosity, Opportunity, Spirit*}, includes different Mars rovers. The second query facet, {*USA, UK, Soviet Union*}, includes countries relevant to Mars landings. These are both facets where the terms are instances of the same semantic class. Somewhat differently, the last facet, {*video, pictures, news*}, includes labels for different query subtopics. These labels can be viewed as instances of a special semantic class, the subtopics of the query *mars landing*.

Query facets can be used to help improve search experience in many ways. Like in faceted search [6], query facets can help users to navigate through different topics of the search results by applying multiple filters. Using the examples in Table 1, for query *baggage allowance*, a user can select *Delta, international, business class, quantity* from each of its facets, to find pages discussing the number of bags allowed on Delta's international business class flights. Query facets can also be used as query suggestions or clarification questions to help users specify search intent. For example, for the query *mars landing*, a system might suggest the query facet {*video*, *pictures*, *news*} or generate clarification questions like "*Which Mars rover are you looking for? a) Curiosity, b) Opportunity, c) Spirit*". Query facets are also useful for exploratory search since they succinctly summarize interesting facts for the issued query. For example, facets for the query *mr bean* list episodes titles, characters and casts for the Mr. Bean television series.

In this paper we develop a supervised method based on a graphical model for query facet extraction. The graphical model learns how likely it is that a term should be selected and how likely it is that two terms should be grouped together in a query facet. Further, the model captures the dependencies between the two factors. We propose two algorithms for approximate inference on the graphical model since exact inference is intractable. Also, we design an evaluation metric for query facet extraction, which combines recall and precision of the facet term, with the grouping quality.

The rest of this paper is organized as follows. We discuss related work in Section 2, and then present the problem formulation in Section 3. Section 4 describes the general framework we use for query facet extraction. Section 5 describes our graphical model based approach in detail. Section 6 briefly describes two alternate approaches that we use as baselines. We describe the dataset as well as the metrics we used for evaluation in Section 7, and report experimental results in Section 8. Finally, we conclude the work in Section 9.

2. RELATED WORK

Related work of query facet extraction can be divided into the following topics.

2.1 Search Results Diversification

Search result diversification has been studied as a method of tackling ambiguous or multi-faceted queries while a ranked list of documents remains the primary output feature of Web search engine today[24]. It tries to diversify the ranked list to account for different search intents or query subtopics. A weakness of search result diversification is that the query subtopics are hidden from the user, leaving him or her to guess at how the results are organized. Query facet extraction addresses this problem by explicitly presenting different facets of a queries using groups of coordinate terms.

2.2 Search Results Clustering/Organization

Search results clustering is a technique that tries to organize search results by grouping them into, usually labeled, clusters by query subtopics [4]. It offers a complementary view to the flat ranked list of search results. Most previous work exploited different textual features extracted from the input texts and applied different clustering algorithms with them. Instead of organizing search results in groups, there is also some work [14, 15, 16] that summarizes search results or a collection of documents in a topic hierarchy. For example, Lawrie et al. [14, 15] used a probabilistic model for creating topical hierarchies, in which a graph is constructed based on conditional probabilities of words, and the topic words are found by approximately maximizing the predictive power and coverage of the vocabulary. Our work is different from these work in that our target is to extract different facets of a query from search results, instead of organizing the search results.

2.3 Query Subtopic/Aspect Mining

To address multi-faceted queries, much previous work studied mining query subtopics (or aspects). A query subtopic is often defined as a distinct information need relevant to the original query. It can be represented as a set of terms that together describe the distinct information need [29, 31, 5] or as a single keyword that succinctly describes the topic [28]. Different resources have been used for mining query subtopics, including query logs [30, 11, 32, 29, 31, 33], document corpus [2] and anchor texts [5].

A query subtopic is different from a query facet in that the terms in a query subtopic are not restricted to be coordinate terms, or have peer relationships. Query facets, however, organize terms by grouping "sibling" terms together. For example, {*news*, *cnn*, *latest news*, *mars curiosity news*} is a valid query subtopic for the query *mars landing*, which describes the search intent of Mars landing news, but it is not a valid query facet, given our definition, since the terms in it are not coordinate terms. A valid query facet that describes Mars landing news could be {*cnn*, *abc*, *fox*}, which includes different news channels. In a recent work [7], Dou et al. developed a system to extract query facets from web search results and showed the potential of doing so. However, the unsupervised method they proposed is far from optimal, and it does not improve by having human labels available. Also, to the best of our knowledge, their evaluation can be problematic in some cases, which will be discussed in Section 7.2.3.

2.4 Semantic Class Mining

Semantic class mining can be used to help query facet extraction. **Class attribute extraction** [17, 18] aims to extract attributes for a target semantic class usually specified by as a set of representative instances. For example, given a semantic class *country*, together with some instances like *USA*, *UK*, *China*, some class attributes can be *capital city*, *president*, *population*. Those extracted class attributes can be used as query subtopics. However, class attribute extraction targets semantic classes, not general search queries.

Semantic class extraction aims to automatically mine semantic classes represented as their class instances from certain data corpus. Existing approaches can be roughly divided into two categories: distributional similarity and pattern-based [25]. The distributional similarity approach is based on the distributional hypothesis [8], that terms occurring in analogous contexts tend to be similar. Different types contexts has been studied for this problem, including syntactic context [20] and lexical context [21, 1, 19]. The pattern-based approach applied textual patterns [9, 22], HTML patterns [26] or both [34, 25] to extract instances of a semantic class from some corpus. The raw semantic class extracted can be noisy. To address this problem, Zhang et al. [34] used topic modeling to refine the extracted semantic classes. Their assumption is that, like documents in the conventional setting, raw semantic classes are generated by a mixture of hidden semantic class. In this paper, we apply pattern-based semantic class extraction on the top-ranked Web documents to extract candidates for finding query facets.

2.5 Faceted Search

Faceted search is a technique for accessing information organized according to a faceted classification system, allowing users to digest, analyze and navigate through multidimensional data. It is widely used in e-commerce and digital libraries [6]. Faceted search is similar to query facet extraction in that both of them use sets of coordinate terms to represent different facets of a query. However, most existing works for faceted search are build on as specific domain or predefined categories [7], while query facet extraction does not restrict queries in a specific domain, like products, people, etc.

3. PROBLEM FORMULATION

Query facet extraction is the problem of finding query facets for a given query q from available resources, such as web search results. A **query facet** $F = \{t\}$ is a set of coordinate terms, terms that are part of a semantic set, which we call **facet terms**. These facet terms can be instances of a semantic class, for example *Curiosity*, *Opportunity*, *Spirit* are all Mars rovers. They can be labels for query subtopics, such as *video*, *pictures*, *news* for the query *mars landing*. We use $\mathcal{F} = \{F\}$ to denote the set of query facets. $T_{\mathcal{F}} = \{t | t \in F, F \in \mathcal{F}\}$ is the set of all the facets terms that appear in $\mathcal{F}$.

Query facets can be extracted from a variety of different resources, such as a query log, anchor text, taxonomy and social folksonomy. In this work, we only focus on extracting query facets from the top k web search results $\mathcal{D} = \{D_1, D_2, \ldots, D_k\}$. We intend to explore the use of other information sources for this problem in future work.

4. GENERAL FRAMEWORK

In this section, we describe the general framework we use for extracting query facet from web search results. Given a query q, we retrieve the top k search results, $\mathcal{D}$, as input to our system. Then query facets $\mathcal{F}$ are extracted by, first, extracting candidates from search results $\mathcal{D}$ and then finding query facets from the candidates.

4.1 Extracting candidate lists

Similar to Dou et al. [7], we use pattern-based semantic class extraction approach [25] to extract lists of coordinate terms from search results as candidates for query facets. In pattern-based semantic class extraction, patterns are applied on the corpus to discover specific relationships between terms. For example, the pattern "*NP* such as *NP*, *NP*, ..., and *NP*" can be used to extract coordinate terms and their hypernyms from text. Besides lexical patterns, HTML patterns are often used on HTML documents to extract coordinate terms from some HTML structures, like <UL>, <SELECT> and <TABLE>.

Table 2: Semantic class extraction patterns

Type	Pattern
Lexical	*item*, {,*item*}*, (and|or) {other} *item*
HTML	<select><option>*item*</option>...</select>
	<ul><li>*item*</li>...</ul>
	<ol><li>*item*</li>...</ol>
	<table><tr><td>*item*<td>...</table>

We use both of the two types of patterns, summarized in Table 2. In the table, all *items* in each pattern are extracted as a candidate list. For example, from the text sentence "*... Mars rovers such as Curiosity, Opportunity and Spirit*", according to the lexical pattern, we will extract a candidate list {*Curiosity*, *Opportunity*, *Spirit*}. For the lexical pattern, we also restrict those *items* to be siblings in the parse tree of that sentence. We use the PCFG parser [12] implemented in Stanford CoreNLP[1] for parsing documents. For HTML tables, following Dou et al. [7], lists from each column and each row are extracted.

After extracting the lists from the top ranked results $\mathcal{D}$, we further process them as follows. First, all the list items are normalized by converting text to lowercase and removing non-alphanumeric characters. Then, we remove stopwords and duplicate items in each lists. Finally, we discard all lists that contain fewer than two item or more than 200 items. After this process, we have a set of candidate lists $\mathcal{L} = \{L\}$, where each list $L = \{t\}$ is a set of list items.

4.2 Finding query facets from candidate lists

The candidate lists extracted are usually noisy [34], and could be non-relevant to the issued query, therefore they cannot be used directly as query facets. Table 3 shows four candidate lists extracted for the query *mars landing*. L_1 contains list items that are relevant to *mars landing*, but they are not coordinate terms. L_2 is a valid query facet, but it is incomplete – another Mars rover *Spirit* appears in L_3. L_3 is extracted from the sentence, "*It is bigger than the 400-pound Mars Exploration rovers, Spirit and Opportunity, which landed in 2004*". The list item "*the 400 pound mars exploration rovers*" is an extraction error.

Table 3: Four candidate lists for query *mars landing*

L_1:	curiosity rover, mars, nasa, space
L_2:	curiosity, opportunity
L_3:	the 400 pound mars exploration rovers, spirit, opportunity
L_4:	politics, religion, science technology, sports, ...

Since the candidate lists are frequently noisy, we need an effective way to find query facets from extracted candidate lists. More formally, given a set of candidate lists $\mathcal{L} = \{l\}$, the task is to find a set of query facets $\mathcal{F}$, where $T_{\mathcal{F}} \subseteq T_{\mathcal{L}}$. Similar to $T_{\mathcal{F}}$, $T_{\mathcal{L}} = \{t | t \in L, L \in \mathcal{L}\}$ is the set of all list items in $\mathcal{L}$. To address this problem, we develop a graphical model, which learns how likely a list item is a facet term, how likely two list items should be grouped in a query facet, and capture the dependencies between the two factors.

5. A GRAPHICAL MODEL FOR FINDING QUERY FACETS

In this section, we describe the directed graphical model we use to find query facts form noisy candidate lists. A directed graphical model (or Bayesian network) is a graphical model that compactly represents a probability distribution over a set of variables [23]. It consists of two parts: 1) a directed acyclic graph in which each vertex represents a variable, and 2) a set of conditional probability distributions that describe the conditional probabilities of each vertex given its parents in the graph.

We treat the task of finding query facets from candidate lists as a labeling problem, in which we are trying to predict

[1]http://nlp.stanford.edu/software/corenlp.shtml

1) whether a list item is a facet term, and 2) whether a pair of list items is in one query facet. Then, we used a directed graphical model to exploit the dependences that exist between those labels. Similar to conditional random fields [13], we directly model the conditional probability $P(y|x)$, where y is the label we are trying to predict and x is the observed data – list items and item pairs. Thus, it avoids modeling the dependencies among the input variables x, and can handle a rich set of features. For our graph model, exact maximum a posteriori inference is intractable; therefore, we approximate the results using two algorithms.

5.1 The Graphical Model

5.1.1 Graph

First we define all the variables in our graphical model. Let $Y = \{y_i\}$, where $y_i = 1\{t_i \in T_{\mathcal{F}}\}$ is a label indicating whether a list item t_i is a facet term. Here $1\{\cdot\}$ is an indicator function which takes on a value of 1 if its argument is true, and 0 otherwise. $p_{i,j}$ denotes the list items pair (t_i, t_j), and $P_{\mathcal{L}} = \{p_{i,j}|p_{i,j} = (t_i, t_j), t_i, t_j \in T_{\mathcal{L}}, t_i \neq t_j\}$ denotes all the items pairs in $T_{\mathcal{L}}$. Let $Z = \{z_{i,j}\}$, where $z_{i,j} = 1\{\exists F \in \mathcal{F}, t_i \in F \wedge t_j \in F\}$ is a label indicates whether the corresponding item pair $p_{i,j}$ should be grouped together in a query facet. The vertices in our graphical model are $V = T_{\mathcal{L}} \cup P_{\mathcal{L}} \cup Y \cup Z$. Note that the list items $T_{\mathcal{L}}$, and item pairs $P_{\mathcal{L}}$ are always observed.

As shown in Figure 1, there are three types of edges in the graph: 1) edges from each list item t_i to its corresponding labels y_i; 2) edges that point to each item pair label $z_{i,j}$ from the two corresponding list items y_i and y_j; 3) edges from each item pair $p_{i,j}$ to its corresponding label $z_{i,j}$.

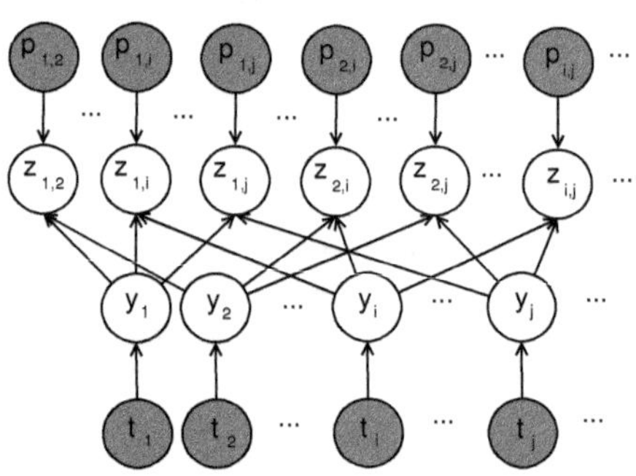

Figure 1: A graphical model for candidate list data

5.1.2 Conditional Probability Distribution

We use logistic-based conditional probability distributions (CPDs) for variable y_i and $z_{i,j}$, defined as in Equation 1 and Equation 2.

$$P(y_i = 1|t_i) = \frac{1}{1 + \exp\{-\sum_k \lambda_k f_k(t_i)\}} \quad (1)$$

$$P(z_{i,j} = 1|p_{i,j}, y_i, y_j) = \frac{y_i y_j}{1 + \exp\{-\sum_k \mu_k g_k(p_{i,j})\}} \quad (2)$$

f_k and g_k are features that characterize a list item and a item pair respectively. λ and μ are the weights associated with f_k and g_k respectively. Compared to a conventional logistic function, Equation 2 has an extra term, $y_i y_j$, in the numerator. When $y_i = 0$ or $y_j = 0$, we have $P(z_{i,j} = 1|p_{i,j}, y_i, y_j) = 0$. This means when either of the two list items is not a facet term, the two items can never appear in a query facet together. When both of the t_i and t_j are facet terms, $P(z_{i,j} = 1|p_{i,j}, y_i, y_j)$ becomes a conventional logistic function, which models the probability of t_i and t_j being grouped together in a query facet, given the condition that both t_i and t_j are facet term.

The joint conditional probability for the graphical model is calculated as

$$P(Y, Z|T_{\mathcal{L}}, P_{\mathcal{L}}) = \prod_{y_i \in Y} P(y_i|t_i) \prod_{z_{i,j} \in Z} P(z_{i,j}|p_{i,j}, y_i, y_j) \quad (3)$$

where the CPDs are defined in Equation 1 and Equation 2.

5.1.3 Parameter Estimation

The training set for the graphical model can be denoted as $\{T_{\mathcal{L}}, P_{\mathcal{L}}, Y^*, Z^*\}$, where Y^*, Z^* are the ground truth labels for the list items $T_{\mathcal{L}}$ and item pairs $P_{\mathcal{L}}$. The conditional probability of the training set can be calculated according to Equation 4.

$$P(\lambda, \mu) = \prod_{T_{\mathcal{L}}, P_{\mathcal{L}}} P(Y^*, Z^*|T_{\mathcal{L}}, P_{\mathcal{L}}) \quad (4)$$

The log-likelihood $l(\lambda, \mu)$, can be calculated as follows,

$$l(\lambda, \mu) = l_t(\lambda) + l_p(\mu) \quad (5)$$

$$l_t(\lambda) = \sum_{T_{\mathcal{L}}} \sum_{y_i \in Y} \log P(y_i|t_i) - \frac{\sum_k \lambda_k^2}{2\sigma^2} \quad (6)$$

$$l_p(\mu) = \sum_{T_{\mathcal{L}}} \sum_{z_{i,j} \in Z} \log P(z_{i,j}|p_{i,j}, y_i, y_j) - \frac{\sum_k \mu_k^2}{2\gamma^2} \quad (7)$$

$l(\lambda, \mu)$ is separated into two parts, $l_t(\lambda)$ and $l_p(\mu)$. The last terms of Equation 6 and Equation 7 are served as regularizers which penalize large values of λ, μ. σ and γ are regularization parameters that control the strength of penalty. Notice that, in the train set, for those item pairs $p_{i,j}$ with any of its list item not being a facet term, their labels $z_{i,j} = 0$. According to Equation 2, for those item pairs, $\log P(z_{i,j}|p_{i,j}, y_i, y_j) = 0$, which makes no contribution to $l_p(\mu)$, and thus $l_p(\mu)$ can be simplified as

$$l_p(\mu) = \sum_{T_{\mathcal{L}}} \sum_{z_{i,j} \in Z'} \log P(z_{i,j}|p_{i,j}, y_i, y_j) - \frac{\sum_k \mu_k^2}{2\gamma^2} \quad (8)$$

where Z' is a subset of Z, which contains only the labels for item pairs with both of its list items being facet terms.

We can see that Equations 6 and 8 are exactly the same as log-likelihoods for two separated logistic regressions. In fact, Equation 6 learns a logistic regression model for whether a list item is a facet term, and Equation 8 learns a logistic regression model for whether two facet terms should be grouped together. The parameter λ and μ can be learned by maximizing the log-likelihood using gradient descent, exactly same as in logistic regression.

5.2 Inference

When given a new labeling task, we could perform maximum a posteriori inference - compute the most likely labels Y^*, Z^* by maximizing the joint conditional probability $P(Y, Z|T_{\mathcal{L}}, P_{\mathcal{L}})$. After that, the query facet set $\mathcal{F}$ can be easily induced from the labeling Y^*, Z^*. (Collect list items with $y_i = 1$ as facet terms, and group any two of them into a query facet if the corresponding $z_{i,j} = 1$.) Note that the graphical model we designed does not enforce the labeling to produce strict partitioning for facet terms. For example, when $Z_{1,2} = 1$, $Z_{2,3} = 1$, we may have $Z_{1,3} = 0$. Therefore, an optimal labeling results may induce an overlapping clustering. To simplify the problem, we add the strict partitioning constraint that each facet term belongs to exactly one query facet. Also, to directly produce the query facets, instead of inducing them after predicting labels, we rephrase the optimization problem as follows. First, we use the following notations for log-likelihoods,

$$\begin{aligned}
s_t(t_i) &= \log P(y_i = 1|t_i) \\
\overline{s_t}(t_i) &= \log(1 - P(y_i = 1|t_i)) \\
s_p(t_i, t_j) &= \log P(p_{i,j} = 1|p_{i,j}, y_i = 1, y_j = 1) \\
\overline{s_p}(t_i, t_j) &= \log(1 - P(p_{i,j} = 1|p_{i,j}, y_i = 1, y_j = 1))
\end{aligned}$$

Using the notations above, the log-likelihood $l(\mathcal{F})$ for a particular query facet set $\mathcal{F}$ formed from $\mathcal{L}$ can be written as

$$\begin{aligned}
l(\mathcal{F}) &= l_t(\mathcal{F}) + l_p(\mathcal{F}) \\
l_t(\mathcal{F}) &= \sum_{t \in T_{\mathcal{F}}} s_t(t_i) + \sum_{t \notin T_{\mathcal{F}}} \overline{s_t}(t_i) \\
l_p(\mathcal{F}) &= \sum_{F \in \mathcal{F}} \sum_{t_i, t_j \in F} s_p(t_i, t_j) + \sum_{\substack{F, F' \\ \in \mathcal{F}}} \sum_{\substack{t_i \in F, \\ t_j \in F'}} \overline{s_p}(t_i, t_j) \quad (9)
\end{aligned}$$

In the right hand side of Equation 9, the first term is the intra-facet score, which sums up $s_p(\cdot, \cdot)$ for all the item pairs in each query facet. The second term is the inter-facet score, which sums up the $\overline{s_p}(\cdot, \cdot)$ for each item pair that appears in different query facets. Then the optimization target becomes $\mathcal{F} = \arg\max_{\mathcal{F} \in \mathfrak{F}} l(\mathcal{F})$, where $\mathfrak{F}$ is the set of all possible query facet sets that can be generated from $\mathcal{L}$ with the strict partitioning constraint.

This optimization problem is NP-hard, which can be proved by a reduction from the Multiway Cut problem [3]. Therefore, we propose two algorithms, **QF-I** and **QF-J**, to approximate the results.

5.2.1 QF-I

QF-I approximates the results by predicting whether a list item is a facet term and whether two list items should be grouped in a query facet independently, which is accomplished two phases. In the first phase, QF-I selects a set of list items as facet terms according to $P(y_i|t_i)$. In this way, the algorithm predicts whether a list item t_i is a facet term independently, ignoring the dependences between y_i and its connected variables in Z. In our implementation, we simply select list items t_i with $P(t_i) > w_{min}$ as facet terms. (For convenience, we use $P(t_i)$ to denote $P(y_i = 1|t_i)$.) In the second phase, the algorithm clusters the facet terms $T_{\mathcal{F}}$ selected in the first phase into query facets, according to $P(t_i, t_j)$. ($P(t_i, t_j)$ is used to denote $P(z_{i,j} = 1|p_{i,j}, y_i = 1, y_j = 1)$). Many clustering algorithm can be applied here, using $P(t_i, t_j)$ as the distance measure. For our implementation, we use a cluster algorithm based on WQT [7], because it considers the importance of nodes while clustering. We use $P(t_i)$ as the measure for facet term importance, and $d_t(t_i, t_j) = 1 - P(t_i, t_j)$ as the distance measure for facet terms. The distance between a cluster and a facet term is computed using complete linkage distance, $d_f(F, t) = max_{t' \in F} d(t, t')$, and the diameter of a cluster can be calculated as $dia(F) = \max_{t_i, t_j \in F} d_t(t_i, t_j)$. The algorithm is summarized in Algorithm 1. It processes the facet terms in decreasing order of $P(t)$. For each facet term remaining in the pool, it builds a cluster by iteratively including the facet term that is closest to the cluster, until the diameter of the cluster surpasses the threshold d_{max}.

Algorithm 1 WQT for clustering facet term used in QF-I

Input: $T_{\mathcal{F}}, P(t), d_f(F, t), dia(F), d_{max}$
Output: $\mathcal{F} = \{F\}$
$T_{pool} \leftarrow \mathcal{F}$
repeat
  $t \leftarrow \arg\max_{t \in T_{pool}} P(t)$
  $F \leftarrow \{t\}$
  iteratively include facet term $t' \in T_{pool}$ that is closest to F, according to $d_f(F, t')$, until the diameter of the cluster, $dia(F)$, surpasses the threshold d_{max}.
  $\mathcal{F} \leftarrow \mathcal{F} \cup \{F\}$, $T_{pool} \leftarrow T_{pool} - F$
until T_{pool} is empty
return $\mathcal{F}$

5.2.2 QF-J

QF-I finds query facets based on the graphical model by performing inference of y_i and $z_{i,j}$ independently. The second algorithm, QF-J, instead tries to perform joint inference by approximately maximizing our target $l(\mathcal{F})$ with respect to y_i and $z_{i,j}$ iteratively. The algorithm first guesses a set of list items as facet terms. Then it clusters those facet terms by approximately maximizing $l_p(\mathcal{F})$, using a greedy approach. After clustering, the algorithm checks whether each facet term "fits" in its cluster, and removes those that do not fit. Using the remaining facet terms, the algorithm repeats the process (clustering and removing outliers) until convergence.

QF-J is outlined in Algorithm 2. The input to the algorithm are the candidate list item set $T_{\mathcal{L}}$, and the log-likelihoods $l(\mathcal{F})$, $l_p(\mathcal{F})$. In the first step, we select top n list items according to $s_t(t)$ as the initial facet terms, because it is less sensitive to the absolute value of the log-likelihood. In our experiment, n is set to 1000 to make sure most of the correct facet terms are included. Then, the algorithm improves $l(\mathcal{F})$ by iteratively performing functions CLUSTER and REMOVEOUTLIERS. CLUSTER performs clustering over a given set of facet terms. In step 10 to 12, it puts each facet terms into a query facet by greedily choosing the best facet, or creates a singleton for the list item, according to the resulting log-likelihood, $l_p(\mathcal{F})$. We choose to process these list items in decreasing order of $s_t(t)$, because it is more likely to form a good query facet in the beginning by doing so. REMOVEOUTLIERS removes facet terms according to the joint log-likelihood $l(\mathcal{F})$. In step 20 to 22, it checks each facet term to see if it fits in the facet, and removes outliers. F' is the set of facet terms the algorithm selected when processing each facet F.

5.2.3 Ranking Query Facets

The output of QF-I and QF-J is a query facet set $\mathcal{F}$. To produce ranking results, we defined a score for a query facet as $score_F(F) = \sum_{t \in F} P(t)$, and rank the query facets according to this scoring, in order to present more facet terms in the top. Facet terms within a query facet are ranked according to $score_t(t) = P(t)$.

Algorithm 2 QF-J

```
Input: T_L = {t}, l, l_p
Output: F = {F}
T_F ← top n list items from T_L according to s_t(·)
repeat
    F ← CLUSTER(T_F, l_p)
    T_F ← REMOVEOUTLIERS(F, l)
until converge
return F

function CLUSTER(T_F, l_p)
    F ← ∅
    for each t ∈ T_F in decreasing order of s_t(t) do
        Choose to put t into the best facet in F or add
        t as a singleton into F, whichever that has the highest
        resulting l_p(F).
    end for
    return F
end function

function REMOVEOUTLIERS(F, l)
    T_F ← all facet terms in F
    for each F ∈ F do
        F' = ∅
        for each t ∈ F in decreasing order of s_t(·) do
            choose to add t into F' or not, whichever has
            the highest resulting l({F'})
            if not, T_F ← F − {t}
        end for
    end for
    return T_F
end function
return F
```

Table 4: Two types of features

Item Features for list item t	
length	Number of words in t
clueIDF	IDF of t in ClueWeb09 collection
TF	Term frequency of t in $\mathcal{D}$
DF	Document frequency of t in $\mathcal{D}$
wDF	Weighted DF. Each document count weighted by $1/\sqrt{docRank}$
SF	Site frequency. Number of unique websites in $\mathcal{D}$ that contain t
titleTF	TF of t for the titles of $\mathcal{D}$
titleDF	DF of t for the titles of $\mathcal{D}$
titleSF	SF of t for the titles of $\mathcal{D}$
snippetTF	TF of t for the snippets of $\mathcal{D}$
snippetDF	DF of t for the snippets of $\mathcal{D}$
snippetSF	SF of t for the snippets of $\mathcal{D}$
listTF	Frequency of t in candidate lists extracted from $\mathcal{D}$
listDF	Number of documents that contain t in their candidate lists
listSF	Number of unique websites that contain t in their candidate lists
listIDF	IDF of t in a general candidate list collection
TF.clueIDF	TF × clueIDF
listTF.listIDF	listTF × lisIDF
Item Pair Features for item pair $p_{i,j} = (t_i, t_j)$	
lengthDiff	Length difference, $\lvert len(t_i) - len(t_j)\rvert$
listCooccur	Number of candidate lists extracted from $\mathcal{D}$, in which t_i, t_j co-occur
textContextSim	Similarity between text contexts
listContextSim	Similarity between list contexts

5.3 Features

There are two types of features used in our graphical model, summarized in Table 4.

Item features, $f_k(t)$ in the graphical model, characterize a single list item. To capture the relevance of item t to the query, we use some TF/IDF-based features extracted from the top k search results, $\mathcal{D}$. For example, *snippetDF* is the number of snippets in top k search results that contain item t. *snippetDF* and other frequency-based features are normalized using $log(frequency + 1)$. To capture how likely item t is to be an instance of a semantic class, we use features extracted from candidate lists. For example, *listTF* is the frequency of t in the candidate lists extracted from $\mathcal{D}$. Some list items occur frequently in candidate lists across different queries, such as *home*, *contact us* and *privacy policy*. They are treated as stopwords, and removed from the candidate lists. We also use *listIDF* to cope with this problem. *listIDF* is the IDF of a list item in a general collection of candidate lists we extracted (see Section 7.1). It is calculated as $listIDF(t) = \log \frac{N - N_t + 0.5}{N_t + 0.5}$, where N is the total number of lists in the collection, N_t is the number of lists contain t. The same form is used for *clueIDF*, IDF in ClueWeb09[2] collection.

Item Pair Features, $g(p_{i,j})$ in the graphical model, are used to capture how likely a pair of list items should be grouped into a query facet, given that the two list item both are facet terms. This can be measured by context similarity [25]. For *textContextSim*, we use window size 25, and represent text context as a vector of TF weights. Cosine similarity is used as the similarity measure. Similarly, we use the candidate lists that contain the list item as its list context, and calculate *listContextSim* in the same way as *textContextSim*.

[2]http://lemurproject.org/clueweb09

6. OTHER APPROACHES

In this section, we describe two alternative approaches for finding query facets from candidate lists. They are used as baselines in our experiments.

6.1 QDMinder

Dou et al. [7] developed QDMiner/QDM for query facet extraction, which appears to be the first work that addressed the problem of query facet extraction. To solve the problem of finding query facets from the noisy candidate lists extracted, they used an unsupervised clustering approach. It first scores each candidate list by combining some TF/IDF-based scores. The candidate lists are then clustered with bias toward important candidate lists, using a variation of the Quality Threshold clustering algorithm [10]. After clustering, clusters are ranked and list items in each clusters are ranked/selected based on some heuristics. Finally, the top k clusters are returned as results. This unsupervised approach does not gain by having human labels available. Also, by clustering lists, they lose the flexibility of breaking a candidate list into different query facets.

6.2 Topic modeling

In semantic class extraction, Zhang et al. [34] proposed to use topic models to find high-quality semantic classes from a large collection of extracted candidate lists. Their assumption is, like documents in the conventional setting, candidate lists are generated by a mixture of hidden topics, which are the query facets in our case. pLSA and LDA are used in their experiments. We find this approach can be directly used for finding query facets from candidate lists. The major change we need to make is that: in semantic class extraction, topic modeling is applied globally on the candidate lists (or a sample of them) from the entire corpus; in query facet extraction, we apply topic modeling only on the top k search results $\mathcal{D}$, assuming the coordinate terms in $\mathcal{D}$ are relevant to the query. Then, the topics are returned as query facets, by using the top n list items in each topic (according to the list item's probability in the topic). Though this topic modeling approach is more theoretically motivated, it does not have the flexibility of adding different features to capture different aspects such as query relevance.

7. EVALUATION

7.1 Data

Queries. We constructed a pool of 232 queries from different sources, including random samples from a query log, TREC 2009 Web Track queries [3], example queries appearing in related publications [32, 29] and queries generated by our annotators. Annotators were asked to select queries that they are familiar with from the pool for annotating. Overall, we collect annotations for 100 queries (see Table 5).

Table 5: Query statistics

Source	#queries collected	#queries annotated
query log	100	30
related publications	20	10
TREC 2009 Web Track	50	20
annotators generated	62	40
sum	232	100

Search results. For each query, we acquire the top 100 search results from a commercial Web search engine. A few search results are skipped due to crawl errors, or if they are not HTML Web pages. For the 232-query set, we crawled 22,909 Web pages, which are used for extracting feature *listIDF* described in Section 5.3. For the 100 annotated queries, the average number of crawled Web pages is 98.7, the minimum is 79, both the maximum and the median are 100.

Query facet annotations. We asked human annotators to construct query facets as ground truth. For each query, we first constructed a pool of terms by aggregating facet terms in the top 10 query facets generated by different models, including two runs from QDM, one run from each of pLSA and LDA using top 10 list items in each query facets, and one run for our graphical model based approach. Then, annotators were asked to group terms in the pool into query facets for each query they selected. Finally, the annotator was asked to give a rating for each constructed query facet, regarding how useful and important the query facet is. The rating scale of good=2/fair=1 is used. Annotation statistics are given in Table 6. There are 50 query facets pooled per query, with 224.8 distinct facet terms per query.

[3]http://trec.nist.gov/data/web/09/wt09.topics.queries-only

Table 6: Annotation statistics

	fair	good	pooled
#terms per query	26.6	55.8	224.8
#facets per query	3.1	4.8	50.0
#terms per facet	8.6	11.6	8.8

7.2 Evaluation Metrics

Query facet extraction can be evaluated from different aspects. We use standard clustering and classification evaluation metrics, as well as metrics designed for this particular task to combine different evaluation aspects.

Notation: we use "$*$" to distinguish between system generated results and human labeled results, which we used as ground truth. For example, $\mathcal{F}$ denotes the system generated query facet set, and $\mathcal{F}^*$ denotes the human labeled query facet set. For convenience, we use T to denote $T_{\mathcal{F}}$ in this section, omitting subscript $\mathcal{F}$. T^* denotes all the facet terms in human labeled query facet set. We use r_{F^*} to denote the rating score for a human labeled facet F^*.

7.2.1 Effectiveness in finding facet terms

One aspect of query facet extraction evaluation is how well a system finds facet terms. This can be evaluated using standard classification metrics as follows,

- facet term precision: $P(T,T^*) = \frac{|T \cap T^*|}{|T|}$
- facet term recall: $R(T,T^*) = \frac{|T \cap T^*|}{|T^*|}$
- facet term F1: $FT(T,T^*) = \frac{2|T \cap T^*|}{|T|+|T^*|}$

where facet term F1 is denoted as FT (the T stands for facet *term*) to avoid confusion with a query facet F and clustering F1 defined below. These metrics do not take clustering quality into account.

7.2.2 Clustering quality

To evaluate how well a system groups facet terms correctly, similar to Dou et al. [7], we use several existing cluster metrics, namely, Purity, NMI/Normalized Mutual Information and F1 for clustering. To avoid confusion with facet term F1, FT, we call F1 for facet term clustering *facet clustering F1*, and denote it as FP (with P standing for term *pair*).

In our task, we usually have $T \neq T^*$. The facet terms in the system generated and human labeled clustering results might be different: the system might fail to include some human identified facet terms, or it might mistakenly include some "incorrect" facet terms. These standard clustering metrics cannot handle these cases properly. To solve this problem, we adjust $\mathcal{F}$ as if only facet terms in T^* were clustered by the system, since we are only interested in how well the "correct" facet terms are clustered from these metrics. The adjusting is done by removing "incorrect" facet terms ($t \in T - T^*$) from $\mathcal{F}$, and adding each missing facet term ($t^* \in T^* - T$) to $\mathcal{F}$ as singletons. By this adjusting, we do not take into account the effectiveness of finding correct facet terms.

7.2.3 Overall quality

To evaluate the overall quality of query facet extraction, Dou et al. [7] proposed variations of nDCG (Normalized Discounted Cumulative Gain), namely fp-nDCG and rp-nDCG. It first maps each system generated facet F to a human labeled facet F^* that covers the maximum number of terms in F. Then, it assigns the rating r_{F^*} to F, and evaluates $\mathcal{F}$ as a ranked list of query facets using nDCG. The discounted gains are weighted by precision and/or recall of facet terms in F, against its mapped human labeled facet F^*. For fp-nDCG, only precision are used as weight, $\frac{|F^* \cap F|}{|F|}$. For rp-nDCG, precision and recall are multiplied as weight, $\frac{|F^* \cap F|^2}{|F^*||F|}$. However, to the best of our understanding, this metric can be problematic in some cases. When two facets F_1 and F_2 are mapped to a same human labeled facet F^*, only the first facet F_1 is credited and F_2 is simply ignored, even if it is more appropriate to map F_2 to F^* (e.g. F_2 is exactly same as F^*, while F_1 contain only one facet term in F^*).

The quality of query facet extraction is intrinsically multi-faceted. Different applications might have different emphasis in the three factors mentioned above - precision of facet terms, recall of facet terms and clustering quality of facet terms. We propose a metric $PRF_{\alpha,\beta}$ to combine the three factors together, using weighted harmonic mean. Let $p = P(T, T^*)$, $r = R(T, T^*)$, $f = FP(\mathcal{F}, \mathcal{F}^*)$, then $PRF_{\alpha,\beta}$ can be expressed as follows,

$$PRF_{\alpha,\beta}(\mathcal{F}, \mathcal{F}^*) = \frac{(\alpha^2 + \beta^2 + 1)prf}{\alpha^2 rf + \beta^2 pf + pr} \quad (10)$$

where α and β are used to adjust the emphasis between the three factors. When $\alpha = \beta = 1$, we omit the subscript part for simplicity, i.e. $PRF \equiv PRF_{1,1}$.

While $PRF_{\alpha,\beta}$ has the flexibility to adjust emphasis between the three factors, it does not take into account the different ratings associated with query facets. To incorporate ratings, we use a weighted version of $P(T, T^*)$, $R(T, T^*)$ and $FP(\mathcal{F}, \mathcal{F}^*)$ in $PRF_{\alpha,\beta}$. We call the new metric $wPRF_{\alpha,\beta}$. The weighted facet term precision, recall and FT are defined as follows

- weighted facet term precision: $wP(T, T^*) = \frac{\sum_{t \in T \cap T^*} w(t)}{\sum_{t \in T} w(t)}$
- weighted facet term recall: $wR(T, T^*) = \frac{\sum_{t \in T \cap T^*} w(t)}{\sum_{t^* \in T^*} w(t^*)}$
- weighted facet term F1: $wFT(T, T^*) = \frac{2wP(T,T^*)wR(T,T^*)}{wP(T,T^*)+wR(T,T^*)}$

where $w(t)$ is the weight for facet term t, and assigned as follows

$$w(t) = \begin{cases} r_{F^*} & \text{if } t \in T^* \\ 1 & \text{otherwise} \end{cases}$$

Similarly, $wFP(\mathcal{F}, \mathcal{F}^*)$ is computed by weighting its pairwise precision and recall in the same fashion as the weighted facet term precision and recall above. Instead of $w(t)$, we need weight for a pair of facet terms $w(t_1, t_2)$ in this calculation. We assign weight for facet term pair $w(t_1, t_2)$ using their sum, $w(t_1) + w(t_2)$.

8. EXPERIMENT RESULTS

8.1 Experiment settings

We compare effectiveness of the five models, QDM, pLSA, LDA and QF-I, QF-J, on the 100-query data set. All the models take the same candidate lists extracted/cleaned (see Section 4.1) as input. We perform 10-fold cross validation for training/testing and parameter tuning in all experiments and for all models (if applicable). When training the graphical model, we standardize features by removing the mean and scaling to unit variance. We set both of the two regularizers σ and γ in Equation 5 to be 1. There are too many negative instances ($y_i = 0$, $z_{i,j} = 0$) in the training data, so we stratify samples by labels with the ratio of positive:negative to be 1:3. For QDM, we tune the two parameters used in the clustering algorithm Dia_{max} (the diameter threshold for a cluster) and W_{min} (the weight threshold for a valid cluster), as well as two parameters used for selecting facet terms in each facet ($S_{t|F} > \alpha|Sites(F)|$ and $S_{t|F} > \beta$). For pLSA and LDA, we tune the number of facet terms in a query facet. For QF-I, we tune the weight threshold for facet terms, w_{min}, and the diameter threshold, d_{max}. For QF-J, there are no parameter need to be tuned. We returned top 10 query facets from all the five models in all evaluation.

8.2 Finding Facet terms

To evaluate effectiveness in finding facet terms, we tune all the models on wFT, which combines both precision and recall, and takes into account facet term weighting.

Table 7: Facet term precision, recall and F1 tuned on wFT

Model	P	wP	R	wR	FT	wFT
pLSA	0.284	0.385	0.562	0.561	0.351	0.430
LDA	0.292	0.394	0.595	0.593	0.364	0.446
QDM	0.407	0.523	0.378	0.388	0.360	0.420
QF-I	0.347	0.458	**0.644**	**0.652**	0.427	**0.514**
QF-J	**0.426**	**0.534**	0.525	0.526	**0.449**	0.511

Table 8: Average number of facet terms in output per query for different models

Model	#terms/query
pLSA	153.1
LDA	154.8
QDM	68.0
QF-I	153.7
QF-J	97.8

Table 7 shows facet term precision, recall and F1 and their weighted version described in Section 7.2. QF-I and QF-J perform relatively well for both precision and recall. Their improvements over the other three models shown are all significant ($p < 0.05$, using paired t-test), except the improvements of QF-J over QDM for P and wP. The two topic model based approaches, pLSA and LDA, have relatively high recall and low precision. Contrarily, QDM has high precision and low recall. This difference can be explain by Table 8, which gives the number of facet terms output per query from each models. QDM only outputs 68 facet terms per query, while pLSA and LDA both output over twice that number. One possible reason for the low precision of pLSA and LDA is that they select facet terms solely according to term probabilities in the learned topics (query facets in our case) and do not explicitly incorporate query relevance. We find most of their facet terms are frequently-occurring list items, which are not necessary relevant to the query.

While the number of facet terms QF-I outputs is similar to pLSA and LDA, QF-I obtain much higher precision and recall, likely due to the rich set of features used. Table 9 shows the five most important item features according to the absolute values of learned weights. Not surprisingly, list TF/IDF features which are used to capture the likelihood of being a coordinate term have relatively high weights, as well as some features that are used to capture query relevance, e.g. *TF.clueIDF*.

Table 9: Top 5 item features, ranked by absolute weights

Feature	Weight
listTF.listIDF	2.6424
listSF	2.1374
wDF	-1.0754
TF.clueIDF	1.0115
SF	0.6873

From Table 7, we also find the the weighted metrics are usually consistent with their corresponding unweighted metric. One exception is that QF-J performs better than QF-I in FT, but it does slightly worse than QF-J in wFT. This is likely to be caused by the high recall for QF-I, which may include more highly rated facet terms.

8.3 Clustering Facet terms

Table 10 shows clustering performance of the five models, which are tuned on wFP. The improvements of QF-I and QF-J over the other three models shown are all significant ($p < 0.05$, using paired t-test). pLSA and LDA do not perform well in clustering, which could be caused by data sparsity. There are on average 5159 candidate lists per query, but only 3.9 items per list.

Table 10: Facet clustering performance tuned on wFP

Model	Purity	NMI	FP	wFP
pLSA	0.793	0.524	0.230	0.229
LDA	0.773	0.511	0.227	0.226
QDM	0.871	0.565	0.367	0.380
QF-I	0.843	0.606	**0.408**	**0.410**
QF-J	**0.922**	**0.631**	0.352	0.346

Table 11: Weights learned for item pair features

Feature	Weight
listContextSim	1.4944
textContextSim	0.7186
listCooccur	0.0817
lengthDiff	0.0563

The better performance in clustering for QF-I and QF-J can be explained by their incorporating factors other than list item co-occurrence information. In Table 11, we list the weights learned for item pair features. Besides one item co-occurrence related feature, *listContextSim*, we also find that *textContextSim* has a relatively high weight. *textContextSim* is used to capture the similarity of the two list items using their surrounding text, so it can help to group two facet terms together even if they might not co-occur a lot in candidate lists. As an example, for the query *baggage allowance*, we find different airlines do not co-occur a lot in candidate lists, (e.g. *delta* and *jetblue* only co-occur twice), but they tend to have high *textContextSim* (e.g. $textContextSim(delta, jetblue) = 0.81$), and are therefore grouped together by QF-I and QF-J.

8.4 Overall Evaluation

To compare overall effectiveness of the five models, we tune all the models on wPRF, and the results are reported in Table 12.

Table 12: Overall performance tuned on wPRF

Model	wP	wR	wFP	wPRF
pLSA	0.353	0.630	0.229	0.309
LDA	0.358	**0.670**	0.225	0.311
QDM	0.523	0.388	0.253	0.319
QF-I	0.450	0.667	**0.399**	**0.444**
QF-J	**0.534**	0.526	0.346	0.417

Unweighted metrics are very similar to their corresponding weighted metrics in terms of conclusions, and are omitted due to space limitation. Results here are consistent with the results that were tuned on wFT or wFP. pLSA and LDA have high recall, but low precision and FP. QDM has relatively high precision, but low recall and FP. It has on average 68 facet terms per query as output, and fails to improve the overall effectiveness when including more facet terms in its output. QF-I and QF-J are among the best two models according to both PRF and wPRF.

Since wPRF does not account for facet ranking effectiveness, we also report fp-NDCG and rp-NDCG tuned on themselves in Table 13. QF-J gives the best performance for both fp-NDCG and rp-NDCG. The improvements of QF-I and QF-J over the other three models shown in the Table 12 and 13 are all significant ($p < 0.05$, using paired t-test), except the improvements of QF-J over QDM for wP and QF-I over QDM for fp-nDCG.

Table 13: fp-nDCG and rp-nDCG tuned on themselves

Model	fp-nDCG	rp-nDCG
pLSA	0.250	0.071
LDA	0.238	0.063
QDM	0.257	0.093
QF-I	0.290	0.157
QF-J	**0.336**	**0.193**

9. CONCLUSIONS

In this paper, we studied the problem of extracting query facets from search results. We developed a supervised method based on a graphical model to recognize query facets from the noisy facet candidate lists extracted from the top ranked search results. We proposed two algorithms for approximate inference on the graphical model. We designed a new evaluation metric for this task to combine recall and precision of facet terms with grouping quality. Experimental results showed that the supervised method significantly outperforms other unsupervised methods, suggesting that query facet extraction can be effectively learned.

10. ACKNOWLEDGMENTS

This work was supported in part by the Center for Intelligent Information Retrieval and in part under subcontract #19-000208 from SRI International, prime contractor to DARPA contract #HR0011-12-C-0016. Any opinions, findings and conclusions or recommendations expressed in this material are those of the authors and do not necessarily reflect those of the sponsor.

11. REFERENCES

[1] E. Agirre, E. Alfonseca, K. Hall, J. Kravalova, M. Paşca, and A. Soroa. A study on similarity and relatedness using distributional and wordnet-based approaches. In *Proceedings of NAACL-HLT'09*, pages 19–27, 2009.

[2] J. Allan and H. Raghavan. Using part-of-speech patterns to reduce query ambiguity. In *Proceedings of SIGIR'02*, pages 307–314, 2002.

[3] N. Bansal, A. Blum, and S. Chawla. Correlation clustering. In *MACHINE LEARNING*, pages 238–247, 2002.

[4] C. Carpineto, S. Osiński, G. Romano, and D. Weiss. A survey of web clustering engines. *ACM Comput. Surv.*, 41(3):17:1–17:38, July 2009.

[5] V. Dang, X. Xue, and W. B. Croft. Inferring query aspects from reformulations using clustering. In *Proceedings of CIKM '11*, pages 2117–2120, 2011.

[6] D. Dash, J. Rao, N. Megiddo, A. Ailamaki, and G. Lohman. Dynamic faceted search for discovery-driven analysis. In *Proceedings of CIKM '08*, pages 3–12, 2008.

[7] Z. Dou, S. Hu, Y. Luo, R. Song, and J.-R. Wen. Finding dimensions for queries. In *Proceedings of CIKM '11*, pages 1311–1320, 2011.

[8] Z. Harris. Distributional structure. *The Philosophy of Linguistics*, 1985.

[9] M. A. Hearst. Automatic acquisition of hyponyms from large text corpora. In *Proceedings of COLING '92*, pages 539–545, 1992.

[10] L. Heyer, S. Kruglyak, and S. Yooseph. Exploring expression data: identification and analysis of coexpressed genes. *Genome research*, 9(11):1106–1115, 1999.

[11] Y. Hu, Y. Qian, H. Li, D. Jiang, J. Pei, and Q. Zheng. Mining query subtopics from search log data. In *Proceedings of SIGIR '12*, pages 305–314, 2012.

[12] D. Klein and C. D. Manning. Accurate unlexicalized parsing. In *Proceedings of ACL '03*, pages 423–430, 2003.

[13] J. D. Lafferty, A. McCallum, and F. C. N. Pereira. Conditional random fields: Probabilistic models for segmenting and labeling sequence data. In *Proceedings of ICML '01*, pages 282–289, 2001.

[14] D. Lawrie, W. B. Croft, and A. Rosenberg. Finding topic words for hierarchical summarization. In *Proceedings of SIGIR '01*, pages 349–357, 2001.

[15] D. J. Lawrie and W. B. Croft. Generating hierarchical summaries for web searches. In *Proceedings of SIGIR '03*, pages 457–458, 2003.

[16] C. G. Nevill-manning, I. H. Witten, and G. W. Paynter. Lexically-generated subject hierarchies for browsing large collections. *International Journal on Digital Libraries*, 2:111–123, 1999.

[17] M. Paşca. Organizing and searching the world wide web of facts – step two: harnessing the wisdom of the crowds. In *Proceedings of WWW '07*, pages 101–110, 2007.

[18] M. Paşca and E. Alfonseca. Web-derived resources for web information retrieval: from conceptual hierarchies to attribute hierarchies. In *Proceedings of SIGIR '09*, pages 596–603, 2009.

[19] P. Pantel, E. Crestan, A. Borkovsky, A.-M. Popescu, and V. Vyas. Web-scale distributional similarity and entity set expansion. In *Proceedings of EMNLP '09*, pages 938–947, 2009.

[20] P. Pantel and D. Lin. Discovering word senses from text. In *Proceedings of KDD '02*, pages 613–619, 2002.

[21] P. Pantel, D. Ravichandran, and E. Hovy. Towards terascale knowledge acquisition. In *Proceedings of COLING '04*, 2004.

[22] M. Pasca. Acquisition of categorized named entities for web search. In *Proceedings of CIKM '04*, pages 137–145, 2004.

[23] J. Pearl. *Probabilistic reasoning in intelligent systems: networks of plausible inference.* 1988.

[24] T. Sakai and R. Song. Evaluating diversified search results using per-intent graded relevance. In *Proceedings of SIGIR '11*, pages 1043–1052. ACM, 2011.

[25] S. Shi, H. Zhang, X. Yuan, and J.-R. Wen. Corpus-based semantic class mining: distributional vs. pattern-based approaches. In *Proceedings of COLING '10*, pages 993–1001, 2010.

[26] K. Shinzato and K. Torisawa. Acquisition of categorized named entities for web search. In *Proceedings of RANLP '05*.

[27] C. Silverstein, H. Marais, M. Henzinger, and M. Moricz. Analysis of a very large web search engine query log. *SIGIR Forum*, 33(1):6–12, Sept. 1999.

[28] R. Song, M. Zhang, T. Sakai, M. Kato, Y. Liu, M. Sugimoto, Q. Wang, and N. Orii. Overview of the ntcir-9 intent task. In *Proceedings of NTCIR-9 Workshop Meeting*, pages 82–105, 2011.

[29] X. Wang, D. Chakrabarti, and K. Punera. Mining broad latent query aspects from search sessions. In *Proceedings of KDD '09*, pages 867–876, 2009.

[30] X. Wang and C. Zhai. Learn from web search logs to organize search results. In *Proceedings of SIGIR '07*, pages 87–94, 2007.

[31] F. Wu, J. Madhavan, and A. Halevy. Identifying aspects for web-search queries. *J. Artif. Int. Res.*, 40(1):677–700, Jan. 2011.

[32] X. Xue and X. Yin. Topic modeling for named entity queries. In *Proceedings of CIKM '11*, pages 2009–2012, New York, NY, USA, 2011. ACM.

[33] X. Yin and S. Shah. Building taxonomy of web search intents for name entity queries. In *Proceedings of WWW '10*, pages 1001–1010, 2010.

[34] H. Zhang, M. Zhu, S. Shi, and J.-R. Wen. Employing topic models for pattern-based semantic class discovery. In *Proceedings of ACL '09*, pages 459–467, 2009.

Learning to Personalize Query Auto-Completion

Milad Shokouhi
Microsoft
Cambridge, United Kingdom
milads@microsoft.com

ABSTRACT

Query auto-completion (QAC) is one of the most prominent features of modern search engines. The list of query candidates is generated according to the *prefix* entered by the user in the search box and is updated on each new key stroke. Query prefixes tend to be short and ambiguous, and existing models mostly rely on the past popularity of *matching* candidates for ranking. However, the popularity of certain queries may vary drastically across different demographics and users. For instance, while *instagram* and *imdb* have comparable popularities overall and are both legitimate candidates to show for prefix *i*, the former is noticeably more popular among young female users, and the latter is more likely to be issued by men.

In this paper, we present a supervised framework for personalizing auto-completion ranking. We introduce a novel labelling strategy for generating offline training labels that can be used for learning personalized rankers. We compare the effectiveness of several user-specific and demographic-based features and show that among them, the user's long-term search history and location are the most effective for personalizing auto-completion rankers. We perform our experiments on the publicly available AOL query logs, and also on the larger-scale logs of Bing. The results suggest that supervised rankers enhanced by personalization features can significantly outperform the existing popularity-based baselines, in terms of mean reciprocal rank (MRR) by up to 9%.

Categories and Subject Descriptors

H.3.3 [**Information Storage and Retrieval**]: Query formulation, Web search

General Terms

Algorithms

Keywords

Query auto-completion, autosuggest, Personalized search

SIGIR'13, July 28–August 1, 2013, Dublin, Ireland.

1. INTRODUCTION

Auto-completion is among the first services that the users interact with as they search and form their queries. Following each new character entered in the query box, search engines filter suggestions that match the updated *prefix*, and suggest the top-ranked candidates to the user. The first step (filtering) is often facilitated by using data structures such as prefix-trees (tries) that allow efficient lookups by prefix matching [Chaudhuri and Kaushik, 2009]. In the second step (ranking), those suggestions that match the prefix are ordered according to their expected *likelihood*. The likelihood values are often approximated with respect to aggregated *past* frequencies [Bar-Yossef and Kraus, 2011] although other approaches that rank suggestions according to their predicted *future* popularities have been also explored [Shokouhi and Radinsky, 2012].

In majority of previous work, the likelihood of QAC suggestions are computed globally and are considered to be the same for all users. Hence for a given prefix, all users are presented with the same set of suggestions. The two exceptions are the work by Bar-Yossef and Kraus [2011], and Weber and Castillo [2010]. Bar-Yossef and Kraus [2011] added a session bias parameter in auto-completion ranking by comparing candidates with the queries recently submitted by the user. However, the notion of likelihood for a query does not vary across users, or demographic groups, plus their work is not applicable on single-query sessions that account for no less than 50% of the search traffic [Jansen et al., 2007]. Weber and Castillo [2010] discussed the differences in query distributions across various demographics and briefly covered query completion by focusing on predicting the *second query term*. In essence, they build a conditional probabilistic model for common phrases based on a set of demographic features. Their model is based on simple aggregation over different demographics and does not address the sparsity issues as more features are added. Weber and Castillo [2010] do not consider any user-specific feature (as their focus is not on personalization), and do not report the results for more general scenarios where only the first few characters of queries are entered.

In this paper, we propose a novel supervised framework for learning to personalize auto-completion rankings. We are motivated by the previous studies that demonstrated that the query likelihoods vary drastically between different demographic groups [Weber and Castillo, 2010] and individual users [Teevan et al., 2011]. Inspired by these observations we develop several features based on users age, gender, location, short- and long-history for personalizing auto-completion

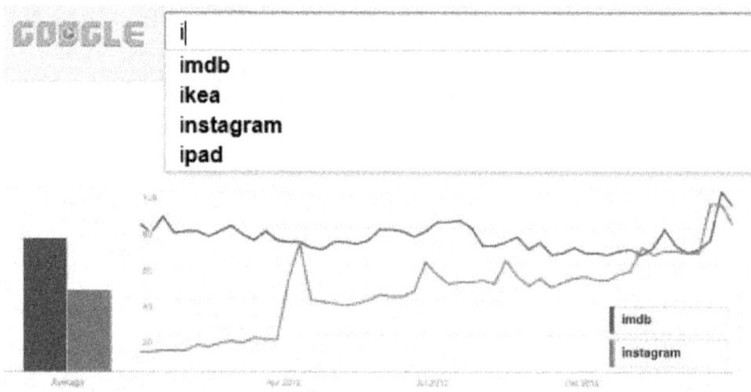

Figure 1: (Top) The default auto-completion candidates for prefix *i*, according to the US market version of `google.com`. The prefix was typed in private browsing mode and the snapshot was taken on Wed, Jan 16, 2013. (Bottom) The query frequencies of *instagram* and *imdb* according to Google Trends.

rankings. For instance, consider the auto-completion candidates returned by Google for prefix *i* in Figure 1 (top).[1] All four suggestions are popular (head) queries with comparable historical frequencies. In particular, the frequency distributions for *instagram*, and *imdb* are demonstrated in Figure 1 (bottom) according to Google Trends.[2] The depicted trends suggest similar likelihoods for both *imdb* and *instagram*, although the popularity of the latter is rising.

In general, in the absence of any information about the user, the ranking of QAC candidates in Figure 1 look reasonable – although models based on temporal query frequency trends [Shokouhi and Radinsky, 2012] may boost the position of *instagram*. The question we are addressing in this work, is how this ranking can be further improved if there are some additional information available about the user. Figure 2 (top) compares the likelihood of *instagram* and *imdb* among different demographics of users according to Yahoo! Clues.[3] At the bottom of Figure 2 the same analysis is repeated using the query logs of Bing search engine which we use as one of the testbeds in our experiments. The overall trends are remarkably similar; *instagram* is mostly popular among young female users below the age of 25. In contrast, the query *imdb* is issued more often by male users particularly those between the age of 25 to 44. Hence, going back to Figure 1, if we knew that the person issuing the query was an under-25 female user, perhaps the original order of QAC candidates could be improved by boosting *instagram*. Then again, if the previous query submitted by the user in the session was about *ipad covers* boosting *ipad* could be possibly better. We investigate how such additional information can be used in a supervised framework for personalizing auto-completion. To train personalized auto-completion rankers, we introduce a new strategy for generating training labels from previous queries in the logs. Our experiments on two large-scale query logs suggest that integrating demographic and personalized features can significantly improve the effectiveness of auto-completion.

The remainder of this paper is organized as follows; we continue by covering the related work in Section 2. Our new framework for personalized auto-completion is described in Section 3. Section 4 discusses our testbed data, and the features used for personalization. The evaluation results are presented in Section 5. Finally, we conclude in Section 6 and suggest a few directions for future work.

[1]The prefix was submitted to the US market version of `google.com` on January 16, 2013, in private browsing mode.
[2]`http://www.google.com/trends`
[3]`http://clues.yahoo.com`, discontinued in March 2013

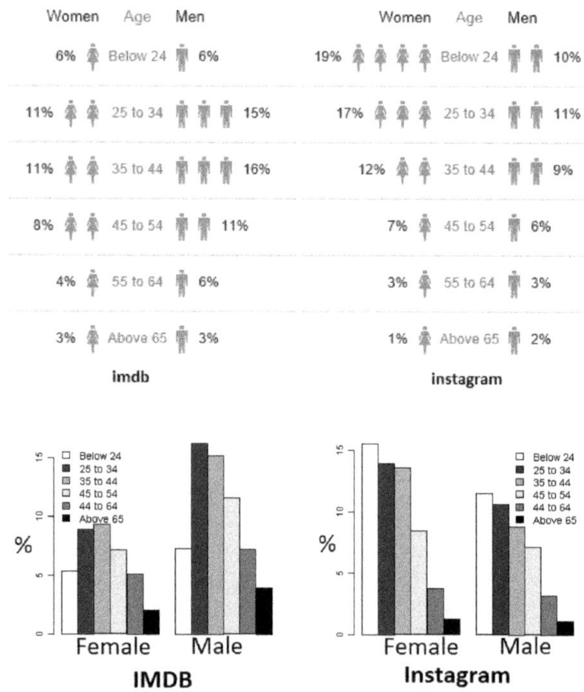

Figure 2: (Top) The likelihood of *instagram* and *imdb* in queries submitted by different demographics according to Yahoo! Clues. (Bottom) The likelihood of *instagram* and *imdb* in queries submitted by the logged-in users of Bing.

2. RELATED WORK

Query auto-completion. Auto-completion has been widely adopted in most modern text editors, browsers and search engines. In *predictive auto-completion* systems, the candidates are matched against the prefix on-the-fly using information retrieval and NLP techniques [Darragh et al., 1990; Grabski and Scheffer, 2004; Nandi and Jagadish, 2007]. For example, Grabski and Scheffer [2004] deployed an index-based retrieval algorithm and a cluster-based approach for their sentence-completion task. Bickel et al. [2005] learned a linearly interpolated n-gram model for sentence completion. Fan et al. [2010] proposed a generative model that incorporates the topical coherence of terms based on Latent Dirichlet Allocation (LDA) [Blei et al., 2003]. White and Marchionini [2007] proposed a real-time query expansion model that generates new expansion terms as the user types in search box. The results suggested that their real-time query-expansion system helps users to form better queries for their information needs. Bhatia et al. [2011] mined frequently occurring phrases and n-grams from text collections and deployed them for generating and ranking auto-completion candidates for partial queries in the absence of search logs.

In *pre-computed auto-completion* systems, the list of matching candidates for each prefix are generated in advance and stored in efficient data structures such as prefix-trees (trie) for fast *lookups*. As the user types more characters, the list of candidates is updated by exact prefix matching although more relaxed lookups based on fuzzy matching have been also explored [Chaudhuri and Kaushik, 2009; Ji et al., 2009].

Once the matching candidates are filtered, they can be ranked according to different criteria. For instance, in an online store such as `amazon.com`, suggestions may be ordered according to price or review scores of products [Chaudhuri and Kaushik, 2009]. In web search scenarios, the common approach is to rank suggestions according their past popularity. Bar-Yossef and Kraus [2011] referred to this type of ranking as the *MostPopularCompletion* (MPC) model and argued that it can be regarded as an approximate maximum likelihood estimator. Given a search log of previous queries $\mathcal{Q}$, a prefix $\mathcal{P}$, and the list of query-completion candidates that match this prefix $\mathcal{C}(\mathcal{P})$, the MPC algorithm is essentially applying the following *Maximum Likelihood Estimation* for ranking:

$$MPC(\mathcal{P}) = \arg\max_{q \in \mathcal{C}(\mathcal{P})} w(q), \quad w(q) = \frac{f(q)}{\sum_{i \in \mathcal{Q}} f(i)} \qquad (1)$$

Here, $f(q)$ represents the past query frequency for q in the $\mathcal{Q}$ logs. Shokouhi and Radinsky [2012] later extended the MPC model and replaced the past frequency values $f(q)$ in Equation (1) with predicted frequency values $\hat{f}(q)$. They showed that the predicted values produced by applying time-series on query history are more effective for ranking auto-completion candidates. Strizhevskaya et al. [2012] also modelled the frequency trends of queries by time-series for improving the auto-completion ranking.

In the context of query auto-completion, the closest studies to ours are done by Bar-Yossef and Kraus [2011] and Weber and Castillo [2010]. The *NearCompletion* method [Bar-Yossef and Kraus, 2011] considers the user's recent queries as *context* and takes into account the similarity of QAC candidates with this context for ranking. Their hybrid model computes the final score of each candidate by linearly combining the popularity-based (MPC) and context-similarity scores. We go beyond session-based features and explore the effectiveness of considering users' age, gender, location and longer search history in auto-completion ranking. Further, in contrast to the NearCompletion model that uses a linear combination of two features for ranking, we propose a supervised framework for ranking, and define a novel objective function for optimizing it. It is also worth noting that while the NearCompletion approach is not applicable to single-query search sessions (more than 50% of traffic [Jansen et al., 2007]), our personalized model can be applied on all search queries. Weber and Castillo [2010] mostly focused on showing differences in query likelihoods across different demographics. They briefly discussed a special case of auto-completion for predicting the second term in a query based on an unsupervised probabilistic model generated according to phrase counts across different demographics. They did not discuss the effectiveness of individual features (e.g. age versus gender), and did not report any results for more general cases where only the first few characters of queries are available. Their work is still based on *aggregation* over different demographic groups and they do not address how such features can be combined with other user-specific features (e.g. session history) in a unified framework for ranking auto-completion candidates.

Query Suggestion. Query suggestion and auto-completion are closely related. Apart from differences in *matching* that are largely imposed by stricter latency constrains in auto-completion, the main distinction is in the type of user input – a query in query suggestion and a prefix in auto-completion. Query prefixes are by definition shorter than submitted queries and hence they are more ambiguous. Thus, the potential for disambiguation using personalized features is arguably higher in auto-completion. Nevertheless, the problems are sufficiently similar that covering some of the related work on query suggestions might be worthwhile.

Mei et al. [2008] generated query suggestions by running a random-walk on a bipartite click graph. They suggested that personalized subsets of this bipartite graph can be used for generating personalized suggestions. Song and He [2010] combined both click and skip information in random-walk for improving estimations on relatedness of queries. To remedy the data sparsity issues in click graphs, Cao et al. [2008] and Liao et al. [2011] first clustered the queries in the click graph into a smaller set of virtual *concepts*. In the second step, they matched the users' context captured based on their recent queries against these clusters for ranking query suggestions. Guo et al. [2011] proposed a similar two-step approach, in which the user's session context is matched against pre-generated topic models for ranking query suggestions. Song et al. [2011] re-ranked the original order of query suggestions promoting those that increase diversity and return documents from different topics.

Santos et al. [2012] extracted queries that frequently co-appeared in the same sessions to generate query suggestions. They took a learning-to-rank approach and evaluated the quality of suggestions with respect to their performance at ranking relevant documents. In a similar vein, Liu et al. [2012] learned to rank query suggestions based on their predicted performance focusing on difficult queries mainly. Ozertem et al. [2012] also presented a learning-to-rank framework for ranking query suggestions. They regarded the query co-occurrences in search logs as positive examples and trained a model based on lexical (e.g. edit-distance) and result set features (e.g. number of overlapping URLs). In the same manner Reda et al. [2012] combined several lexical and result set features for query suggestion on LinkedIn.[4] Song et al. [2012] built a term-transition graph from search logs and used it to learn a model for generating query suggestions by term replacement.

Personalized search. Our study is also related to a large body of previous work on search personalization. Noteworthy among them, Bennett et al. [2012b] investigated how short-term and long-term user behavior interact, and how can they be used for personalizing search results. They observed that long term history is particularly useful at the beginning of search session, while short-term history becomes more useful as the session evolves. Teevan et al. [2005] indexed all information copied or viewed by users over a limited period to form their profiles, and used that information to personalize (re-rank) their search results. Comparably Matthijs and Radlinski [2011] collected users browsing his-

[4] `http://www.linkedin.com`

Table 1: The process of assigning labels to auto-completion candidates offline. For a given query submitted by the user – in this case *australian open* – all prefixes are first extracted. For each prefix $\mathcal{P}$ the top-ranked candidates matched in the auto-completion trie are collected. The query which was eventually submitted by the user is considered as the only right (relevant) candidate and is assigned a positive label. The other candidates are all regarded as non-relevant and get zero labels. In the example below, the first line represents the prefix while c_1, c_2, c_3 and c_4 respectively denote the top-4 auto-completion candidates returned for the prefix. The relevant candidate in each list is specified by a checkmark (✓), and the Mean-Reciprocal-Rank (MRR) values computed with respect to these offline labels are presented in the last row.

$\mathcal{P}$	a	⇒	au	⇒	aus	···	australian open
c_1	amazon		autotrader		australia		australian open ✓
c_2	alaska airlines		autozone		austerity		australian open 2013
c_3	apple		audacity		australian open ✓		australian open tennis
c_4	aol		audible		australian shepherd		australian open 2012
MRR	0.00		0.00		0.33		1.00

tory by a browser add-on and used the language model of captured pages for personalizing search results.

Teevan et al. [2011] analysed the result re-visitation pattern of users and classified at least 15% of all clicks as *personal navigation* in which the user repeatedly searches for the same page. They showed that boosting the position of personal navigation pages in search results is effective for personalization. Xiang et al. [2010] captured the users' context according to their latest queries and used those contextual features for ranking the results of subsequent queries in the session. Cheng and Cantú-Paz [2010] used demographic-based and user-specific features for better click-prediction and personalizing the ranking of sponsored search results. Similarly, Kharitonov and Serdyukov [2012] used users age and gender for re-ranking and personalizing search results.

In the next section, we introduce a novel approach for personalizing query auto-completion. To the best of our knowledge, this is the first study that applies a supervised model for QAC ranking. We are also unaware of any other work that considers user-specific and demographic features for personalizing auto-completion in a unified framework.

3. PERSONALIZED AUTO-COMPLETION

Learning to personalize auto-completion ranking of query suggestions for prefixes, is analogous to learning to personalize search results for queries. In typical learning to rank frameworks in information retrieval [Liu, 2009], the training data consists of a set of *labeled* query-document pairs, and the goal is to learn a ranking model by optimizing a cost function that is expected to be correlated with user satisfaction. The same models can be applied for learning to rank auto-completion rankings. Here, the "query" is a prefix and the goal is learn a model for ranking query candidates ("documents"). The key missing piece is deciding on a strategy for assigning labels to auto-completion candidates for training.

Manual labelling of *relevance* for personalized search scenarios is notoriously difficult. Relevance assessors are often instructed to rate relevance according to the most likely intent(s). However as described earlier, the most likely intent may differ between users and demographic groups. To overcome this issue, Fox et al. [2005] introduced a new scheme for inferring personalized labels according to user implicit feedback which was later widely adopted for training personalized rankers [Bennett et al., 2011, 2012a; Collins-Thompson et al., 2011; Kharitonov and Serdyukov, 2012]. First, a set of unique *impressions* are sampled from the logs. Each impression consists of a unique user-ID, a time-stamp, the submitted query, and the set of results presented to the user along with information about implicit measures such as clicks and dwell time on those results. In the second step, documents that received a satisfied click (SAT clicks) are annotated with relevant labels and others are regarded as irrelevant. The definition of a SAT-Click could be subjective, but it is typically assumed that the last result click in the session, or clicks with longer than 30 seconds dwell time are SAT [Bennett et al., 2011; Fox et al., 2005].

We propose a similar labelling strategy for personalized auto-completion; we start by sampling a set of impressions from search logs. For each sampled impression, we assume that the query that was eventually submitted by the user is the only *right* (or the most relevant) suggestion that should have been suggested right after the first key-stroke and all the way until submission. With this assumption in mind, we decompose each sampled query into all prefixes that lead to it and for each case we obtain all query candidates that match in the auto-completion trie. In practice – and also for all experiments in this paper – we can restrict the list of candidates to the top-ranked auto-completion suggestions that are returned by a default context-free model such as MPC [Bar-Yossef and Kraus, 2011]. For each pair of prefix and auto-completion list constructed this way, we assign positive label to the query submitted by the user at the end (if it appears in the list) and zero label to others.

Table 1 provides an example: here we sampled an impression from search logs in which the user had submitted *australian open* as query. We split the query into prefixes and for each case obtain the top-ranked candidates from an auto-completion trie.[5] For each prefix, the only suggestion that is assigned a positive label is specified with a checkmark (✓). The last row contains the Mean-Reciprocal-Rank (MRR) value of each ranking computed according to the assigned labels. Note that for the same user-prefix pair, depending on the submitted query, the candidate labels may vary in different impressions. For example, if the same user issues

[5]The candidates in this example were obtained from `google.com` in private browsing mode on January 19, 2013.

amazon as query in another impression, with the exception of *amazon* all QAC candidates including *australian open* will be regarded as non-relevant for that impression.

Learning to rank. Once the training data is collected as described above, we can apply virtually any existing learning-to-rank algorithm for training a personalized auto-completion ranker. We chose Lambda-MART [Burges et al., 2011] as our learning algorithm. Lambda-MART is an extension of Lambda-Rank [Burges et al., 2006] based on boosted decision trees. It is one of the most effective state-of-the-art learning algorithms, and was chosen as the winner of the Yahoo! 2010 *Learning to Rank Challenge* (Track 1).[6] We used a fixed number of 200 trees across all experiments and tuned the learning parameters through standard training and validation on separate sets.

We consider the MostPopularCompletion (MPC) method [Bar-Yossef and Kraus, 2011] that ranks candidates according to their past popularity as our baseline. Other extensions of MPC such as the time-sensitive models [Shokouhi and Radinsky, 2012] are orthogonal to our technique and can be used alternatively without loss of generality. Any potential gains from temporal modelling is expected to also benefit our framework. We use the top-10 candidates returned by the MPC model as input to our ranker. Therefore in all experiments the rankers are compared against exactly the same set of candidates and gains and losses are solely due to personalized re-ranking. Given that there is only one relevant candidate per prefix in each impression, we use the Mean-Reciprocal-Rank of relevant candidates as our evaluation metric and report the average values over all our sampled impressions.

4. DATA & FEATURES

We conducted our experiments on two sets of query logs, one publicly available sampled from AOL search logs in 2006 [Pass et al., 2006], and one proprietary dataset consisting of queries sampled from the logs of Bing search engine. We respectively refer to these two datasets as AOL, and Bing testbeds hereafter.

AOL testbed. The queries in this dataset were sampled between 1 March, 2006 and 31 May, 2006. In total there are 16,946,938 queries submitted by 657,426 unique users. Each query has a time-stamp and we follow the common practice [Jansen et al., 2007] and group queries submitted within 30 minute window of each other to form sessions.

We used the queries submitted before 15 April 2006 as *background data* for generating the tries and forming the long-term history of users. The remaining data was split into two sets according to the user IDs. Users with even IDs were grouped together for training and validation, and those with odd IDs were used for testing.

Bing testbed. Our other experimental dataset consists of a sample of several million queries submitted by those Bing users who were *signed-in* with their Microsoft Live account when issuing their queries. The data was collected between 1 January, 2013 and 9 January, 2013. In total there are 196,190 unique users in this dataset, and each user-ID is associated with an age, gender and zip-code based on the user's profile information.[7] As in the previous dataset, we determine the session boundaries by applying the same 30 minute threshold. Sessions initiated before 7 January, 2013 were used as *background data* for generating the tries and forming the long-term history of users. The users in the remaining sessions were split based on their user-IDs – as described above – for training, validation and testing.

In both datasets, we filtered queries that appeared less than 10 times. A lot of these queries were rare, misspelled, and not popular enough to rank high in auto-completion lists anyway. The MPC auto-completion trie which we use as baseline and foundation for personalized re-ranking was constructed after this filtering and contained respectively $128,620$, and $699,862$ unique queries in the AOL and Bing datasets.

Next, we describe the user-specific and demographic-based features that we developed for personalizing auto-completion on these datasets.

User history features. We investigate the effectiveness of features developed based on both short-term and long-term search history of users for personalizing auto-completion. In addition to the raw historical frequency numbers, we also measured the n-gram similarity of auto-completion candidates with the past queries issued by the user. To generate the short-history features, only queries submitted previously in the same session are considered. For long-history, the entire search history of the user is considered. Similar features have been used in previous work for re-ranking search results [Bennett et al., 2012a; Teevan et al., 2011; Xiang et al., 2010] and query suggestions [Cao et al., 2008; Mei et al., 2008].

Demographic features. In the Bing dataset, we have access to users age, gender and zip-codes based on their Microsoft Live profile information. We split the users into five age groups {Below 20, 21-30, 31-40, 41-50, and above 50}. Suppose that for a given user-prefix pair in our testing set we would like to generate the age-specific ranking features for all matching auto-completion candidates; we first assign the user to one of the age groups above according to the profile information. Once the user's age group is determined, for each candidate, we count the number of times it has been issued as a query by all users that belong to the same age group in the *background data*. We follow the same procedure for computing our gender-specific features. We also generated similar location-specific features based on users zip-code information in their profiles. To reduce sparsity, we collapse the US zip-codes into 10 *regions* according to their first digits. Figure 3 depicts the regional groups formed this way in different colors.

MPC features. Our personalized auto-completion ranker is built on top of the MPC algorithm. That is, the matching candidates are first ranked according to their past popularity and the top-ranked ones – that otherwise would be presented directly to the user in the absence of personalization – will go through re-ranking. The original order before personalization provides rich insights about queries popularity that could be valuable to the ranker. Therefore, we use the position of each candidate in the original list, and also

[6] `http://learningtorankchallenge.yahoo.com`

[7] All user-IDs are annoymized in such way that the actual user-names could not be identified.

Table 2: **The list of features used in our experiments for personalizing auto-completion. The aggregated features are computed in a cross-validation fashion. That is, to generate the features for candidates in the testing set, the numbers are aggregated over all (or subset of) users in the the training and validation sets.**

Feature	Feature Group	Description
PrevQueryNgramSim	Short history	n-gram similarity with the previous query in the session ($n = 3$).
AvgSessionNgramSim	Short history	Average n-gram similarity with all previous queries in the session ($n = 3$).
LongHistoryFreq	Long history	The number of times a candidate is issued as query by the user in the past.
LongHistorySim	Long history	Average n-gram similarity with all previous queries in the user's search history.
SameAgeFrequency	Demographics	Candidate frequency over queries submitted by users in the same age group.
SameAgeLikelihood	Demographics	Candidate likelihood over queries submitted by users in the same age group.
SameGenderFrequency	Demographics	Candidate frequency over queries submitted by users in the same gender group.
SameGenderLikelihood	Demographics	Candidate likelihood over queries submitted by users in the same gender group.
SameRegionFrequency	Demographics	Candidate frequency over queries submitted by users in the same region group.
SameRegionLikelihood	Demographics	Candidate likelihood over queries submitted by users in the same region group.
SameOriginalPosition	MPC	The position of candidate in the MPC ranked list.
SameOriginalScore	MPC	The score of candidate in the MPC ranked list computed based on past popularity.

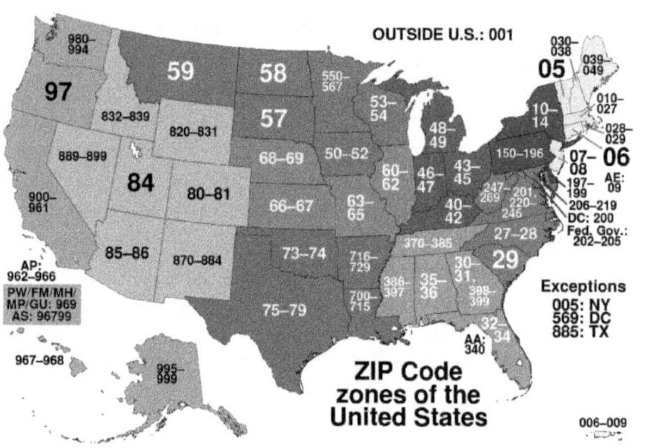

Figure 3: The zip code zones in the United States (Source: Wikipedia). In our experiments, we collapsed all the zip-codes that start with the same digit together. The colour codes above correspond to these collapsed regions.

its overall past popularity (total frequency across all users in the other sets) as two additional ranking features.

More details about the features used in our re-ranking experiments are provided in Table 2.

5. EXPERIMENTS

We begin our analysis by investigating effectiveness of each feature group and subgroup listed in Table 2 separately. After providing a number of re-ranking examples for each case we report the final results from a ranker that is trained by all features. Given the propitiatory nature of our Bing dataset, we do not report the absolute MRR values on that dataset and instead the relative wins and losses against the no-reranking baseline are presented.

In all our experiments, the list of candidates are generated from the top-10 queries ranked by MPC [Bar-Yossef and Kraus, 2011]. Instances in which the *right* query does not appear among the top-10 candidates are removed from the analysis. Note that this does not change any of the conclusions as the MRR is going to be zero before and after personalization (re-ranking) for such cases.

Table 3: The effectiveness of auto-completion personalization according to the user's short session history in terms of MRR. All differences are detected to be statistically significant by the t-test ($p < 0.01$).

Testbed	Baseline	Personalized (Short, MPC)	MRR (Gain/Loss)
AOL	0.666	0.679	+1.95%
Bing	-	-	+0.91%

Short history features. Table 3 contains the result of auto-completion personalization based on features generated from users short-term search history (session). Here, we compare the lexical similarity of candidates with the previous queries submitted by the user in the same session and use that for re-ranking. We always keep the MPC features (default score and position) in our rankers, as they are the most effective features in general, and allow the rankers to learn a safe backoff strategy.

The NearCompletion model [Bar-Yossef and Kraus, 2011] also relied on the user's session history for re-ranking. While we trained our ranker based on decision-trees, the NearCompletion model is based on a linear combination of MPC and session-similarity scores. In addition, NearCompletion expands candidates and previous queries and map them into a higher dimensional vector space for computing the lexical similarities, while we simply rely on n-gram matching. Despite these differences, the numbers for Personalized ranker in Table 3 can be regarded as reference points for the performance of session-based re-ranking techniques such as NearCompletion. The MRR numbers show about 2% improvement on the AOL dataset, and just less than 1% improvement on the Bing dataset. The example provided below is based on a session taken from our testing subset of the AOL dataset. Here, the user (52822) had already issued the following queries in the session, and has typed d in the search box as prefix.

```
52822  ryans pet supplies   2006-05-24 19:13:49
52822  dell computer        2006-05-24 20:04:46
52822  circut city          2006-05-24 20:05:20
```

The default order of auto-completion candidates matching

Table 4: The effectiveness of auto-completion personalization according to the user's long history in terms of MRR. All differences are detected to be statistically significant by the t-test ($p < 0.01$).

Testbed	Baseline	Personalized (Long, MPC)	MRR (Gain/Loss)
AOL	0.666	0.696	+4.45%
Bing	-	-	+5.57%

d based on their MPC scores is respectively: *dictionary*, *driving directions*, *deal or no deal*, *delta airlines* and *dell*. The personalized auto-completion ranker boosts the ranking of dell by 4 positions and places it at position one, while keeping the original order for the rest of candidates. Here, the personalization model has picked up on the high lexical similarity between *dell* (candidate), and *dell computer* (2nd last query in the session) for re-ranking.

Long history features. The re-ranking results based on the long history features are reported in Table 4. The first thing to notice compared to the previous experiment based on short-term features is that the MRR gains are higher. Bennett et al. [2012a] compared the impact of long-term and short-term user behaviour features on personalizing search results and found the former to be more effective early in the session when the intents are more ambiguous and relatively less exploratory. Given that by definition prefixes are more ambiguous than queries and also given that more than 50% of sessions in both our datasets have only single queries, the trends observed here are to be expected.

As an example, consider the long search history of user (46669) in the AOL dataset. Note that for brevity, the entire history is not presented here. According to the AOL data, the same user started typing *n* on 2006-05-31 at 08:54:22. The MPC ranking of matching candidates based on past popularity would be: *nascar*, *netflix*, *nick.com*, *nascar.com*, *nextel*, *northwest airlines* and so forth. After personalization however, the top-3 candidates were respectively: *netflix*, *nascar*, and *northwest airlines*. The other candidates were ranked lower in their respective original order. The personalization model realizes that *netflix* has appeared twice in user's search history before and boosts it to position one. This is analogous to the Personal-Navigation model for search result personalization [Teevan et al., 2011]. It is also interesting to note that *northwest airlines* has moved from position six to three after personalization due to its high n-gram similarities with some of the previous queries in user's search history (e.g. *united airlines* and *american airlines*).

```
46669  netflix             2006-03-05 17:31:56
46669  greentortoise       2006-03-05 17:42:14
46669  united airlines     2006-03-08 12:16:25
46669  american airlines   2006-03-08 12:40:44
46669  bank one            2006-03-08 16:51:50
46669  google              2006-03-09 22:23:57
46669  british airways     2006-03-10 08:56:23
46669  netflix             2006-04-24 20:01:20
46669  apple               2006-04-26 09:58:20
```

Table 5: The effectiveness of auto-completion personalization according to the user's age group in terms of MRR. The users age groups are obtained from their profiles in the Bing dataset. The MRR gain is detected as statistically significant by the t-test ($p < 0.01$).

Testbed	Baseline	Personalized (Age, MPC)	MRR (Gain/Loss)
Bing	-	-	+3.80%

Table 6: The biggest movers in personalized auto-completion rankings when the ranker is trained by age features. Each column includes the candidates that were boosted most frequently in the personalized auto-completion rankings for users of the specified age groups.

Below 20	21-30	31-40
taylor swift	piers morgan	bank of america
justin bieber	richard nixon	worldstarhiphop
deviantart	weather	alex jones
full house	beyonce	indeed
harry styles	movies	national weather service
41-50		**Above 50**
national cathedral		mapquest
target		fedex tracking
chase		florida lottery
microsoft		pogo
traductor google		jigsaw puzzles

Age features. Table 5 contains the results of personalized auto-completion by a ranker trained based on age-specific and MPC features. The AOL dataset does not have any information about users age groups but users in the Bing dataset were *signed-in* when issuing their queries, and their age information were collected from their profiles at the time. The results show statistically significant improvements in MRR when the user's age information is used for personalization. To better understand the type of auto-completion suggestions that are boosted for each age group, we have provided the list of *big movers* in Table 6. For each age group, we extracted queries that were promoted most frequently in personalized auto-completion rankings. As expected, the under-20 group list is dominated by teen's favorite stars, and celebrities. Most of the top movers in the other groups are also intuitive; online banking and stores for users between 30-50, and online games for those above 50 are noteworthy examples.

Gender features. The QAC personalization results based on the gender features are included in Table 7. The personalization gains are comparable to those achieved by using the gender features. Once again we have listed the top movers in Table 8. These are the suggestions that were boosted by personalization and their positions in the auto-completion rankings differed most across the two gender groups before and after personalization. For male users the list was dominated by the names of popular pornographic websites, and car related suggestions. For females, job seeking websites, kids games and shopping related suggestions were among big movers.

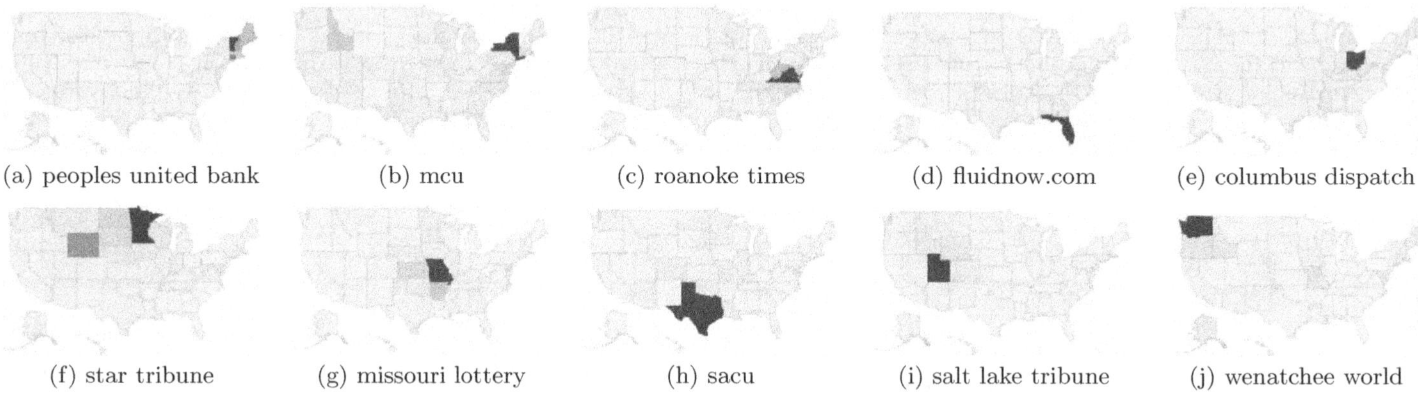

(a) peoples united bank (b) mcu (c) roanoke times (d) fluidnow.com (e) columbus dispatch

(f) star tribune (g) missouri lottery (h) sacu (i) salt lake tribune (j) wenatchee world

Figure 4: The top movers in each region. These are queries that their average positions in rankings with and without personalization differ the most in each region. The regions are specified by collapsing the first zip-code digits and the users in each region are grouped accordingly. The counters (a)–(j) respectively refer to regions in Figure 3. Each map shows the distribution of query popularity across different US states according to Google Trends, and the colors range between light blue (rare) and dark blue (popular).

Table 7: The effectiveness of auto-completion personalization according to the user's gender group in terms of MRR. The users age groups are obtained from their profiles in the Bing dataset. The MRR gain is detected as statistically significant by the t-test ($p < 0.01$).

Testbed	Baseline	Personalized (Gender, MPC)	MRR (Gain/Loss)
Bing	-	-	+3.59%

Table 8: The biggest movers in personalized auto-completion rankings when the ranker is trained by gender features. Each column includes the candidates that were boosted most frequently in the personalized auto-completion rankings for users of the specified gender groups.

Male	imdb, *pornographic-related*[8], drudge, autotrader, usaa
Female	indeed.com, poptropica, daily mail, victoria secret

Region features. We also investigate the effectiveness of using user's location for auto-completion personalization. According to the results in Table 9, the *location-aware* ranker shows statistically significant improvement over the baseline, and the location features show the highest gain among all demographic-based features.

The top movers in each region are displayed in Figure 4. These are queries that their average positions in rankings with and without personalization differ the most in each region. The regions are determined by collapsing the users zip-codes by their first digits and correspond to the color codes illustrated in Figure 3. The counters (a)–(j) in Figure 4 respectively refer to regions in Figure 3. Each map shows the distribution of query popularity across different US states, and the colors range between light blue (rate) and dark blue (popular). While our experiments are conducted on the Bing dataset, we show the popularity distribution of big movers according to Google Trends so that they can be verified externally. The query popularity trends in the Bing dataset are remarkably similar. For instance, 83% of users searching for *peoples united bank* were from region 0, while 9.5% of them were from region 1, which are comparable statistics with those in Figure 4 (a). Similarly, 89% of users search for *mcu* in our Bing dataset are from region 1, which is consistent with distributions from Google Trends in Figure 4(b).

Table 9: The effectiveness of auto-completion personalization according to the user's region group in terms of MRR. The users region groups are obtained from their profiles in the Bing dataset. The MRR gain is detected as statistically significant by the t-test ($p < 0.01$).

Testbed	Baseline	Personalized (Region, MPC)	MRR (Gain/Loss)
Bing	-	-	+4.58%

Table 10: The effectiveness of auto-completion personalization according to all user-specific and demographic-based features in terms of MRR. Note that there are no demographic information available in the AOL dataset. The MRR gain is detected as statistically significant by the t-test ($p < 0.01$).

Testbed	Baseline	Personalized (All)	MRR (Gain/Loss)
AOL	0.666	0.709	+6.45%
Bing	-	-	+9.42%

Overall, the list of top movers is mainly dominated by queries with significant local intent particularly, regional news agencies (e.g. *columbus dispatch*, *star tribune*, *salt lake tribune*, *wentachee world*) and various local financial agencies (e.g. *peoples united bank* and *mcu*).

All features. So far, we demonstrated that each of our user-specific and demographic-based feature groups can contribute to significant MRR gains when used individually for

for personalization. Here, we report the results of a ranker which is trained with combinations of all these features. The results are presented in Table 10 and as expected, the MRR gains when using all features are substantially higher than all individual feature groups. The best performing individual feature group was long history that achieved +5.57% MRR improvements on the Bing testbed (+4.45% on AOL), followed by the location features that improved MRR by 4.58%. On the Bing dataset, using all user-specific and demographic features together, the MRR gains can be almost doubled to reach 9.42%. On the AOL dataset, using both short- and long-history features increases the gains to +6.45.

We also performed an A/B testing evaluation on the live traffic of a commercial search engine. We performed this evaluation for 16 days in January 2013, over approximately 3.1 million users. While further details cannot be shared due to their sensitivity, we can confirm that MRR and other user-engagement metrics were significantly improved by the personalized ranker.

6. CONCLUSIONS

We proposed a new approach for learning to personalize auto-completion rankings. While previous auto-completion models rely on aggregated statistics across all (or demographic groups of) users, we showed that user-specific and demographic-based features can be used together under the same framework. We introduced a novel strategy for extracting training labels from previous logs and showed that it can be used for training auto-completion rankers. We also compared the effectiveness of various user-specific and demographic features and showed that certain demographic features such as location are more effective than others for personalization, and as expected, adding more features based on users demographics and search history leads to further boost in personalization effectiveness.

There are several directions for future work; while we considered our labels to be binary, it would be interesting to investigate how multi-graded labels (perhaps based on user's interactions with landing pages) may change the results. Along similar lines, our model can be extended by allowing more than one relevant candidate per ranking if they are closely related. For instance, if a sampled impression has *facebook* as query, both *facebook* and *facebook.com* may be regarded as relevant candidates for prefix *f*.

In addition, investigating the impact of personalization on different types of suggestions (e.g. informational, navigational) may reveal interesting insights about those segments that are more likely to benefit from personalization. Last but not least, we sampled our training impressions at random and that may introduce a slight bias towards longer queries as the match more prefixes. Other sampling strategies for generating training data may lead to more balanced training and potentially bigger gains.

Acknowledgements

The author is grateful to Sebastian Blohm for proof reading the first draft of this work.

References

Z. Bar-Yossef and N. Kraus. Context-sensitive query auto-completion. In *Proc. WWW*, pages 107–116, Hyderabad, India, 2011.

P. N. Bennett, F. Radlinski, R. W. White, and E. Yilmaz. Inferring and using location metadata to personalize web search. In *Proc. SIGIR*, pages 135–144, Beijing, China, 2011. ISBN 978-1-4503-0757-4.

P. N. Bennett, R. W. White, W. Chu, S. T. Dumais, P. Bailey, F. Borisyuk, and X. Cui. Modeling the impact of short- and long-term behavior on search personalization. In *Proc. SIGIR*, pages 185–194, Portland, OR, 2012a. ISBN 978-1-4503-1472-5.

P. N. Bennett, R. W. White, W. Chu, S. T. Dumais, P. Bailey, F. Borisyuk, and X. Cui. Modeling the impact of short- and long-term behavior on search personalization. In *Proc. SIGIR*, SIGIR '12, pages 185–194, Portland, OR, 2012b. ISBN 978-1-4503-1472-5.

S. Bhatia, D. Majumdar, and P. Mitra. Query suggestions in the absence of query logs. In *Proc. SIGIR*, pages 795–804, Beijing, China, 2011. ISBN 978-1-4503-0757-4.

S. Bickel, P. Haider, and T. Scheffer. Learning to complete sentences. In *Proc. ECML*, volume 3720 of *Lecture Notes in Computer Science*, pages 497–504. Springer, 2005. ISBN 3-540-29243-8.

D. M. Blei, A. Y. Ng, and M. I. Jordan. Latent dirichlet allocation. *J. Mach. Learn. Res.*, 3:993–1022, Mar. 2003.

C. Burges, R. Ragno, and Q. V. Le. Learning to rank with nonsmooth cost functions. In *Proc. NIPS*, pages 193–200, Vancouver, BC, 2006. MIT Press.

C. Burges, K. Svore, P. Bennett, A. Pastusiak, and Q. Wu. Learning to rank using an ensemble of lambda-gradient models. *Journal of Machine Learning Research - Proceedings Track*, 14:25–35, 2011.

H. Cao, D. Jiang, J. Pei, Q. He, Z. Liao, E. Chen, and H. Li. Context-aware query suggestion by mining click-through and session data. In *Proc. SIGKDD*, pages 875–883, Las Vegas, NV, 2008. ISBN 978-1-60558-193-4.

S. Chaudhuri and R. Kaushik. Extending autocompletion to tolerate errors. In *Proc. SIGMOD*, pages 707–718, Providence, Rhode Island, USA, 2009.

H. Cheng and E. Cantú-Paz. Personalized click prediction in sponsored search. In *Proc. WSDM*, pages 351–360, New York, NY, 2010. ISBN 978-1-60558-889-6.

K. Collins-Thompson, P. N. Bennett, R. W. White, S. de la Chica, and D. Sontag. Personalizing web search results by reading level. In *Proc. CIKM*, pages 403–412, Glasgow, UK, 2011. ISBN 978-1-4503-0717-8.

J. J. Darragh, I. H. Witten, and M. L. James. The reactive keyboard: A predictive typing aid. *Computer*, 23:41–49, November 1990.

J. Fan, H. Wu, G. Li, and L. Zhou. Suggesting topic-based query terms as you type. In *Proc. APWEB*, pages 61–67, Washington, DC, 2010.

S. Fox, K. Karnawat, M. Mydland, S. Dumais, and T. White. Evaluating implicit measures to improve web search. *ACM Transactions on Information Systems*, 23 (2):147–168, Apr. 2005. ISSN 1046-8188.

K. Grabski and T. Scheffer. Sentence completion. In *Proc. SIGIR*, pages 433–439, Sheffield, United Kingdom, 2004.

J. Guo, X. Cheng, G. Xu, and X. Zhu. Intent-aware query similarity. In *Proc. CIKM*, pages 259–268, Glasgow, UK, 2011. ISBN 978-1-4503-0717-8.

B. J. Jansen, A. H. Spink, C. Blakely, and S. Koshman. Defining a session on web search engines. *Journal of the American Society for Information Science and Technology*, 58(6):862–871, 2007.

S. Ji, G. Li, C. Li, and J. Feng. Efficient interactive fuzzy keyword search. In *Proc. WWW*, pages 371–380, Madrid, Spain, 2009.

E. Kharitonov and P. Serdyukov. Demographic context in web search re-ranking. In *Proc. CIKM*, pages 2555–2558, 2012. ISBN 978-1-4503-1156-4.

Z. Liao, D. Jiang, E. Chen, J. Pei, H. Cao, and H. Li. Mining concept sequences from large-scale search logs for context-aware query suggestion. *ACM Transactions on Intelligent Systems and Technology*, 3(1):17:1–17:40, Oct. 2011. ISSN 2157-6904.

T.-Y. Liu. Learning to rank for information retrieval. *Foundation and Trends in Information Retrieval*, 3(3):225–331, Mar. 2009. ISSN 1554-0669.

Y. Liu, R. Song, Y. Chen, J.-Y. Nie, and J.-R. Wen. Adaptive query suggestion for difficult queries. In *Proc. SIGIR*, pages 15–24, Portland, OR, 2012. ISBN 978-1-4503-1472-5.

N. Matthijs and F. Radlinski. Personalizing web search using long term browsing history. In *Proc. WSDM*, pages 25–34, 2011. ISBN 978-1-4503-0493-1.

Q. Mei, D. Zhou, and K. Church. Query suggestion using hitting time. In *Proc. CIKM*, pages 469–478, Napa Valley, CA, 2008. ISBN 978-1-59593-991-3.

A. Nandi and H. V. Jagadish. Effective phrase prediction. In *Proc. VLDB*, pages 219–230, Vienna, Austria, 2007.

U. Ozertem, O. Chapelle, P. Donmez, and E. Velipasaoglu. Learning to suggest: a machine learning framework for ranking query suggestions. In *Proc. SIGIR*, pages 25–34, Portland, OR, 2012. ISBN 978-1-4503-1472-5.

G. Pass, A. Chowdhury, and C. Torgeson. A picture of search. In *Proc. InfoScale*, New York, NY, USA, 2006. ACM. ISBN 1-59593-428-6.

A. Reda, Y. Park, M. Tiwari, C. Posse, and S. Shah. Metaphor: a system for related search recommendations. In *Proc. CIKM*, pages 664–673, Maui, HI, 2012. ISBN 978-1-4503-1156-4.

R. Santos, C. Macdonald, and I. Ounis. Learning to rank query suggestions for adhoc and diversity search. *Information Retrieval*, pages 1–23, 2012. ISSN 1386-4564.

M. Shokouhi and K. Radinsky. Time-sensitive query auto-completion. In *Proc. SIGIR*, pages 601–610, Portland, Oregon, USA, 2012. ISBN 978-1-4503-1472-5.

Y. Song and L.-w. He. Optimal rare query suggestion with implicit user feedback. In *Proc. WWW*, pages 901–910, Raleigh, NC, 2010. ISBN 978-1-60558-799-8.

Y. Song, D. Zhou, and L.-w. He. Post-ranking query suggestion by diversifying search results. In *Proc. SIGIR*, pages 815–824, 2011. ISBN 978-1-4503-0757-4.

Y. Song, D. Zhou, and L.-w. He. Query suggestion by constructing term-transition graphs. In *Proc. WSDM*, WSDM '12, pages 353–362, 2012. ISBN 978-1-4503-0747-5.

A. Strizhevskaya, A. Baytin, I. Galinskaya, and P. Serdyukov. Actualization of query suggestions using query logs. In *Proc. WWW*, pages 611–612, Lyon, France, 2012. ISBN 978-1-4503-1230-1.

J. Teevan, S. T. Dumais, and E. Horvitz. Personalizing search via automated analysis of interests and activities. In *Proc. SIGIR*, SIGIR '05, Salvador, Brazil, 2005. ISBN 1-59593-034-5.

J. Teevan, D. J. Liebling, and G. Ravichandran Geetha. Understanding and predicting personal navigation. In *Proc. WSDM*, pages 85–94, 2011. ISBN 978-1-4503-0493-1.

I. Weber and C. Castillo. The demographics of web search. In *Proc. SIGIR*, pages 523–530, Geneva, Switzerland, 2010. ISBN 978-1-4503-0153-4.

R. W. White and G. Marchionini. Examining the effectiveness of real-time query expansion. *Inf. Process. Manage.*, 43:685–704, May 2007.

B. Xiang, D. Jiang, J. Pei, X. Sun, E. Chen, and H. Li. Context-aware ranking in web search. In *Proc. SIGIR*, pages 451–458, 2010. ISBN 978-1-4503-0153-4.

Leveraging Conceptual Lexicon: Query Disambiguation using Proximity Information for Patent Retrieval

Parvaz Mahdabi[†] Shima Gerani[†] Jimmy Xiangji Huang[‡] Fabio Crestani[†]
[†]University of Lugano, Faculty of Informatics, Lugano, Switzerland
{parvaz.mahdabi, shima.gerani, fabio.crestani}@usi.ch
[‡] School of Information Technology, York University, Toronto, Canada
jhuang@yorku.ca

ABSTRACT

Patent prior art search is a task in patent retrieval where the goal is to rank documents which describe prior art work related to a patent application. One of the main properties of patent retrieval is that the query topic is a full patent application and does not represent a focused information need. This query by document nature of patent retrieval introduces new challenges and requires new investigations specific to this problem. Researchers have addressed this problem by considering different information resources for query reduction and query disambiguation. However, previous work has not fully studied the effect of using proximity information and exploiting domain specific resources for performing query disambiguation.

In this paper, we first reduce the query document by taking the first claim of the document itself. We then build a query-specific patent lexicon based on definitions of the International Patent Classification (IPC). We study how to expand queries by selecting expansion terms from the lexicon that are focused on the query topic. The key problem is how to capture whether an expansion term is focused on the query topic or not. We address this problem by exploiting proximity information. We assign high weights to expansion terms appearing closer to query terms based on the intuition that terms closer to query terms are more likely to be related to the query topic. Experimental results on two patent retrieval datasets show that the proposed method is effective and robust for query expansion, significantly outperforming the standard pseudo relevance feedback (PRF) and existing baselines in patent retrieval.

Categories and Subject Descriptors

H.3.3 [**Information Storage and Retrieval**]: Retrieval Models, Query Formulation

General Terms

Experimentation, Performance, Measurement

SIGIR'13, July 28–August 1, 2013, Dublin, Ireland.

Keywords

Patent Search, Query Expansion, Proximity Information

1. INTRODUCTION

For any new invention, in order to be granted a valid patent, the owner of the idea needs to ensure that the invention is novel, i.e., it has not been previously patented by someone else or has not been described in a scientific paper. To this end, a search for documents relevant to the invention is carried out to see if the idea in the patent application is invalidating on some existing ideas. This type of search is called *prior art search*.

This search is executed by the author himself or (someone else hired by the author) using keyword-based searches from the claims of the patent application prior to filing the patent application. The same type of search is performed by the patent examiner in the patent office after the application is filed, to ensure if the filed patent application can be granted a valid patent.

These keyword-based searches are then completed using other metadata associated with the patent applications such as (International Patent Classification) IPC classes[1] and date tags. Bibliographic information such as citations, both backward and forward, can also be used to perform prior art searches. These searches made from different sources are then merged to compose a unique rank list. The goal of combining these complementary searches is to solve the term mismatch problem which is due to the obscure style of writing a patent (patentese) and often leads to low retrieval effectiveness [11].

Prior art search can take a very long time (days or weeks) because the searcher needs to ensure he is not missing on any relevant documents as infringing on some existing patents might result in a multi-million dollar lawsuit. Therefore, prior art search is considered as a recall-oriented application.

Patent retrieval, similar to other domain specific IR tasks [17, 19], has the following three major problems: the frequent usage of non-standardized acronyms which are invented by patent applicants, the presence of homonyms (the same word referring to two or more different entities), such as bus[2] and closet[3], and synonyms (two or more words referring to the same entity) such as signal and wave.

[1]http://www.wipo.int/classifications/ipc/en/

[2]i) motor vehicle, ii) an electronic subsystem transferring plurality of digits bits in group.

[3]i)water closet (flush toilet), ii) a small cupboard used for storing things.

Previous research [15, 9] has tackled this term mismatch problem by first forming a keyword query from the patent application (query patent) based on the frequency information, and then enhancing the query through a knowledge base such as Wikipedia or WordNet, exploiting this enhanced query to disambiguate the occurrences of query terms in the documents.

Using external resources has been shown to be more effective compared to the performance of the initial query and pseudo relevance feedback (PRF). In fact, the retrieval effectiveness of PRF has been shown to be disappointing in patent retrieval mainly due to the low MAP of the initial rank list [5].

Patent examiners use term proximity heuristics in their searches in Boolean retrieval model in order to reward a document where the matched query terms occur close to each other. Two forms of adjacency operators are used in Boolean retrieval model to address proximity. "ADJn" operator which searches for terms within n words proximity in the order specified, and"NEARn" operator, which searches for the terms within n words, in either order. This usage shows that proximity information plays an important role in patent searching.

Previous work [15, 9] which uses external resources for query expansion did not take into account proximity information between query terms and related expansion concepts to form high quality expansions. Expansion terms extracted from these external resources are often general terms. Thus, it is necessary to condition their occurrences on their neighboring query terms which are more precise and consequently ignore their appearance in isolation from a query term.

In this paper, our aim is to address the term mismatch problem in the patent retrieval through query expansion. Different from previous research [15, 9], we intend to use a domain-dependent resource. We believe that using a domain-dependent resource leads to the extraction of more relevant expansion concepts. To do this, we first constructed a lexicon from IPC definition pages[4]. Definition of IPC classes consists of the explanations regarding each IPC class which can be used to identify the important concepts and subtopics of the query. We extract expansion concepts specific to each query from this lexicon for query expansion. We then use term proximity information to calculate reliable importance weights for the expansion concepts.

We propose a proximity-based query propagation method to calculate the query term density at each point in the document. Our proximity-based framework incorporates positional information into the estimation of importance of expansion concepts so that we can reward expansion concepts occurring close to query terms. This way we can concentrate on the terms that are associated with the query terms and avoid the topic drift which is caused by taking into account irrelevant terms.

Our proposed model consists of four steps. In the first step, we shorten the query document by taking the first claim of the document itself. We use the first claim as the source for building the initial query since it contains the core of the invention and serves as a source for extracting precise initial query terms.

In the second step, a query-specific lexicon is built. In the third step, query expansion is performed by deriving expansion concepts from the query-specific lexicon and positional information is used to calculate weights for insuring high quality expansions. To this end, we utilize kernel functions to keep track of the distance of the expansion concepts from the query terms. Thus words appearing within the neighborhood of a given query term are more likely to be associated with that query term. In the fourth step, the initial query and feedback runs (made using proximity information) are combined together to generate a unique rank list.

[4]http://web2.wipo.int/ipcpub/

Our contributions are:

- Presenting an approach to construct a domain-dependent lexicon for identifying expansion concepts.
- Presenting a proximity-based method for estimating the probability that a specific query expansion term is relevant to the query term.
- Investigating different strategies for extracting concepts from domain-dependent lexicon for query reformulation.

We evaluate our work on two patent retrieval corpora, CLEF-IP 2010 and CLEF-IP 2011, using baselines which employ external resources for query expansion. The experimental results show that our model achieves significant improvement over these baselines in terms of recall. The results show the advantage of deploying a domain-dependent resource for selecting expansion candidate terms in contrast to systems which deploy external resources that are not dependent to the domain.

The results also confirm that our model outperforms systems which perform query expansion via PRF. Besides, the results demonstrate that utilizing the proximity information leads to the calculation of reliable weights for the expansion concepts in the process of query expansion.

2. RELATED WORK

Patent retrieval faces many challenges among which we focus on the following two. The first challenge is to reduce the original query topic in order to find a focused information need and remove the ambiguous and noisy terms. In previous work, researchers explored different sections of the query patent to perform the query reduction [18, 4]. Some of the previous work reported that effective queries were built from the query patent [18], while others obtained better results using single fields of the query patent such as claims or description [4].

The second challenge is related to query disambiguation. Previous work used different external resources for query expansion such as Wikipedia [9] and WordNet [15] with the goal of query disambiguation. The goal of this task is to alleviate the term mismatch problem by expanding the query with all words related to the concept of the query or synonyms of the query terms.

Our proximity-based framework is inspired by the original work of Lv and Zhai on positional language model and positional relevance model [12, 13]. An advantage of Lv and Zhai's work is that they can capture passage level evidence in a "soft" way by modeling proximity information via density functions. Their experiments confirmed that such approach works better than applying a "hard" boundary of passages.

Proximity information has shown to be useful in different IR tasks such as opinion mining [6]. Authors investigate proximity information for capturing the opinion density at each point in the document.

Term position and proximity cues were mostly ignored in previous work in patent retrieval. Recently, Ganguly et al.'s work on reducing query patent using PRF captures term position and proximity evidence indirectly through the use of appropriate passages [5]. This work provides a general model for query reduction using PRF. In fact, this passage-based feedback model is orthogonal to our approach, in the sense that it can be used as a pre-processing for our query expansion method. Our proximity-based query expansion framework can be applied on their reduced query. This way we can ensure a more precise set of query terms as the initial query.

Another recent study, Bashir and Rauber's work on improving retrievability of patent documents [3], combined term proximity heuristics with other features to select good query expansion terms in the context of PRF. In this work different distance functions were considered from different windows surrounding query term occurrences. They reported an increase in terms of retrievability [2] of individual patents using proximity heuristics compared to the standard PRF. However, they did not evaluate directly the performance of their approach in terms of retrieval effectiveness.

Finally, Mahdabi et al.'s work used a learning approach to predict the quality of a query [16]. This work uses proximity information loosely through the use of noun phrases. This work is complementary with our ideas as our proximity-based method for estimating the probability of query relatedness of an expansion term can be integrated as a feature in their learning-based model to improve their performance.

3. MULTIPLE INFORMATION SOURCES

We identify different information sources that can be used as additional knowledge for query reformulation in patent retrieval. In this section we summarize and categorize them.

- **Query patent**: This document is a structured document which is composed of the following sections: *title*, *abstract*, *description*, and *claims*. A claim which does not reference any other claim is called an *independent claim* and others are called *dependent claims* [10]. The independent items in the claims of the patent document comprise the kernel of the technical innovation of a patent document. Among the claims the most important claim is the first independent claim which represents the essence of the technology of the patent document. The other parts of the patent document illustrate the reason, background, implementation and advantages, of the invention being described [11].
- **IPC classification**: The International Patent Classification (IPC classification) provides a hierarchical categorization over different technological fields such as computer science, electronics, mechanics, materials science, and bio-chemistry. Such classes are language independent keywords assigned as metadata to the patent documents. They categorize the content of a patent document and describe the field of technology that a patent document belongs to. These IPC classes can be seen as conceptual tags assigned to the documents [11]. For each conceptual tag there is textual descriptions (IPC definition pages) available which is an additional source of information, providing contextual cues about different technical fields.
- **Retrieval corpus**: Our retrieval corpus can be used as another source for extracting expansion concepts via the procedure of PRF.

The above sources have different vocabulary usage. The query patent itself has an obscure style of writing (patentese) [11]. This characteristic might create term mismatch problem for finding relevant documents in the existing filed patents, such that a query term may not be a good indicator in referring to a technological concept as it is not frequently used in the given context by other authors.

However, the two other resources provide a more established vocabulary usage. The descriptions of IPC classification represent the standard vocabulary usage related to different domains. This source provides a general but accepted vocabulary usage for explaining technological concepts. Performing query expansion via PRF allows extracting a set of terms which are not used by the author but are frequent in the retrieval corpus. Thus, the vocabulary usage of the two latter sources are complementary to the query itself.

It is worth to mention that previous work [8] used the conceptual tags for filtering the patent documents. In this work, we propose to exploit the textual description of such conceptual tags in addition to the tags themselves.

4. BUILDING DOMAIN-DEPENDENT LEXICON

We now explain the process of building a lexicon from IPC definition pages. We refer to this lexicon as a *conceptual lexicon*. We first perform stop-word removal on the text of IPC definition pages. We then build a language model for each IPC class and detect terms with document frequency higher than 10 (based on experiments). We refer to these terms as patent-specific stop-words and we filter them out to increase the accuracy of our lexicon. Examples of these patent-specific stop-words are "method", "device", "apparatus", "process".

Each entry in our lexicon is composed of a key and a value. The key is an IPC class and the value is a set of terms representing the mentioned class. These terms are extracted from the IPC definition pages as previously described. An example of an entry in the conceptual lexicon is presented in Table 1.

IPC Class	Representing Terms
C07D 279/24	hydrocarbon, radicals, amino, ring, nitrogen, atom

Table 1: An entry in the conceptual lexicon.

The lexicon can be used to extract expansion concepts related to the context of the information need of a given query patent. To this end, the IPC class of the query is searched in the lexicon and the terms matching this class are considered as candidate expansion terms.

Query expansion using the lexicon will help us solve the two following problems: The first problem is related to the fact that the usage of words is sensitive to the topic domain; In different domains, the same word may be used to indicate different meanings. We aim at finding the correct sense of a word, by associating relevant terms from the topic domain to the given query terms for each query patent.

The second problem is related to the term mismatch. The vocabulary of the query patent is tailored by the language usage of the author (a non-standard terminology), while conceptual lexicon provides a more standard terminology. We try to combine these two complementary vocabularies, as we believe this will help alleviate the term mismatch problem.

In the next sections we will explain with more detail how the lexicon is used for query expansion.

5. A PROXIMITY-BASED FRAMEWORK

Our hypothesis is that an author will use standard terminology from a conceptual lexicon for clarifying his invented concepts. We note that a query term might belong to the author terminology or some terminology that is commonly used in a domain but is not as conventional as the vocabulary of the conceptual lexicon.

We now focus our attention to identify expansion concepts in the document that are referring to the concepts in the query. These expansion concepts can be extracted from one of the sources explained in the previous section. We need to estimate the probability that an expansion term is referring to a query term. To do this, we rely on the structure of the document. We assume that an expansion term refer with higher probability to the query terms closer to its position. We thus regard the distance of an expansion term to the query term as a measure of relatedness.

5.1 Estimating the Query Relatedness

In this section, we explain our method for estimating the probability that an expansion term e at position i, is related to the query term q. We calculate this probability as follows:

$$P(q|i,d) = \sum_{j=1}^{m} P(q|t_j)P(j|i,d) \quad (1)$$

where d denotes a document, i denotes an expansion term position and $J = \{1, 2, ..., m\}$ denotes a set of query term positions. $P(q|i,d)$ indicates the probability that the expansion term at position i in document d is about the query term q. We refer to this probability as the *query relatedness probability*. To find the query relatedness at position i, we calculate the accumulated probability from all query positions at that position. For every position j in a document we consider the query weight of the term at that position, denoted by $P(q|t_j)$, and weight it by the probability that the term at position j is about the expansion term at position i, denoted by $P(j|i,d)$. This probability is estimated as follows:

$$P(j|i,d) = \frac{k(j,i)}{\sum_{j'=1}^{|d|} k(j',i)} \quad (2)$$

where $K(i,j)$ is the kernel function which determines the weight of propagated query-relatedness from t_j to t_i. We model the query relatedness by placing a density kernel function around query terms. We use the same notation throughout the paper.

In the following, we present different kernels used in our experiments. We study three different density functions, namely Gaussian, Laplace, and Rectangle kernel. We selected Gaussian and Laplace kernels as they have been shown to be the best performing kernels among the kernel functions tested in the previous work [12, 6]. We also chose Rectangle kernel to simulate the effect of imposing a hard boundary over passages in contrast to the soft boundary introduced by other kernels.

- **Gaussian Kernel**

$$k(i,j) = \frac{1}{\sqrt{2\pi\sigma}} \exp\left[\frac{-(i-j)^2)}{2\sigma^2}\right]$$

- **Laplace Kernel**

$$k(i,j) = \frac{1}{2b} \exp\left[\frac{-|i-j|}{b}\right]$$

$$\text{where } \sigma^2 = 2b^2$$

- **Rectangle Kernel**

$$k(i,j) = \begin{cases} \frac{1}{2a} & \text{if } |i-j| \leqslant a \\ 0 & \text{otherwise} \end{cases}$$

$$\text{where } \sigma^2 = \frac{a^2}{3}$$

Our aim is to investigate whether it is better to use kernels which favor expansion term occurrence in close proximity of query terms or not.

5.2 Calculating Document Relevance Score

In this section, we intend to calculate the overall probability that relevant expansion concepts (inside the document) are directed towards the technical concept of the query. This probability is denoted by $P(q|d,e)$. $P(q|d,e)$ is defined as:

$$P(q|d,e) = \sum_{i=1}^{|d|} P(q,i|d,e) = \sum_{i=1}^{|d|} P(q|i,d,e)P(i|d,e) \quad (3)$$

We assume e and q are conditionally independent given the position in the document. Thus, $P(q|i,d,e)$ reduces to $P(q|i,d)$ which can be estimated using the query relatedness probability. We now need to estimate the probability $P(i|d,e)$. We suggest two different methods for estimating $P(i|d,e)$.

- **Avg Position Strategy**: All positions of expansion concepts are equally important:

$$\begin{cases} P(i|d,e) = 1/|pos(e)| & \text{if } t_i \in e \\ 0 & \text{otherwise} \end{cases}$$

by substituting this in Equation 3 we have:

$$P(q|d,e) = 1/|pos(e)| \sum_{i \in pos(e)} P(q|i,d) \quad (4)$$

- **Max Position Strategy**: As an alternative, we can assume that only the expansion term position where $P(q|i,d)$ is maximum is important:

$$P(q|d,e) = \max_{i \in pos(e)} P(q|i,d) \quad (5)$$

Example 1 (Topic ID: pac-1474)
Patent title: "Optical information recording medium" Query terms extracted from first independent item of claims: optical, layer, record, lens, light, interlay, irradiation, wavelength Expansion concepts selected from the conceptual lexicon related to the query: organic, dielectric, sensitizing, record, reproduction
Retrieved docs for example 1 Number of retrieved relevant documents in the baseline run: 15/42 Number of retrieved relevant documents after using proximity-based method: 24/42
Example 2: (Topic ID: pac-552) Patent title: "Power supplying apparatus, design method of the same, and power generation apparatus" Query terms extracted from first independent item of claims: power, supply, boost, transformer, switch, resonance Expansion concepts selected from the conceptual lexicon related to the query: conversion, semiconductor, electrode, light, push-pull
Retrieved docs for example 2 Number of retrieved relevant documents in the baseline run: 6/15 Number of retrieved relevant documents after using proximity-based method: 12/15

Table 2: Examples where using proximity-based information with IEC method improves recall in patent retrieval.

6. QUERY REFORMULATION

In this section, given an input query $Q = \{q_1, q_2, ..., q_n\}$, we can identify a set of concepts $C_E = \{e_1, e_2, ..., e_m\}$ which are selected from the conceptual lexicon. The set of C_E is associated to the query Q as the conceptual lexicon contains explanations about the IPC classes to which a patent document is assigned. Once the set of concepts C_E is identified, we determine the concept importance weights according to their distance from the query terms based on the intuition that concepts closer to query terms are more related to the query. Equation 1 demonstrates the process for calculating the importance weight for expansion concepts. We can then re-rank documents in the original rank list $\mathbb{R}$ using a weighted combination of the matches of concepts in C_E and our original keyword query Q based on Equation 3.

We use four different strategies for the expansion concept selection process. We categorize and summarize these strategies below.

Explicit Expansion Concepts In this setting, we use the concepts in our conceptual lexicon which match against the IPC classification of the query. However, we restrict our attention to concepts that appear in D_Q. This provides a set of explicit expansion concepts (a subset of C_E) which serves as candidate expansion terms. We refer to this set as X_E. We utilize the proximity of query terms and expansion terms inside query document D_Q to assign importance weights to the explicit expansion concepts. These weights are then used to re-rank documents in the list $\mathbb{R}$.

Implicit Expansion Concepts In this strategy, the expansion terms are not limited to the set of explicit expansion concepts X_E which were defined previously. Instead, our query expansion method includes all expansion concepts in C_E. In this setting we extract proximity information from the documents inside $\mathbb{R}$ for computing the importance weights associated with the expansion terms. The advantage of this strategy compared to the previous one is that we are able to make use of all terms available in the C_E and we are not limited to the query document.

Query Document	Conceptual Lexicon	Retrieval Corpus
acrylate, ink, jet, acid, polymer, pigment, record, ...	light-sensitive, duplicate, printer, ink, sheet, mark, ...	record, liquid, surface, composition, polymer, cartridge, ...

Table 3: Comparison between the list of expansion terms derived from the information sources for the query with title "inkjet recording ink".

Combining Search Strategies In this strategy, instead of query expansion, we first calculate a relevance score based on the original keyword query Q. We then calculate an IPC score based on the expansion concepts in C_E. We linearly combine the two scores together. Our goal is to compare whether having a unified query, as exists in the query expansion, is better than constructing two separate queries and combining their results at the end. We introduce this setting for the experiments in order to simulate the specific search strategies taken by professional searchers for retrieving relevant documents [11]. In such a search strategy, searchers perform separate searches based on different information sources, such as the query document and IPC classification, and then combine the results of the runs together to produce a unique rank list.

Proximity-based Pseudo Relevance Feedback As a comparison baseline we also used the retrieval corpus as a source for PRF where we used the feedback set for selecting expansion terms and identifying their weights. We use the distance between the query terms and the candidate expansion concepts inside the feedback documents to calculate the weight for the expansion concepts.

As an example, Table 3 shows the terms selected from different information resources. The terms from the query document is selected from the first item of the claims. The terms from the retrieval corpus are selected via the procedure of PRF.

7. EXPERIMENTAL SETUP

In this section we first explain our experimental setup for evaluating the effectiveness of our proposed approach.

Testing Collections We used Terrier Information Retrieval System[5] to index the collection with the default stemming and stop-word removal. We removed patent-specific stop-words such as "device" and "method".

We conducted our experiments over two years worth of CLEF Intellectual Property (CLEF-IP) task, including CLEF-IP 2010 and CLEF-IP 2011 datasets. CLEF-IP 2010 contains 2.6 million patent documents and CLEF-IP 2011 consists of 3 million patent documents. In our experiments we used the English subsection of both collections. The English test set of CLEF-IP 2010 corresponds to 1348 topics. The English test set of CLEF-IP 2011 consists of 1351 topics. We used the training topics of CLEF-IP 2010 for tuning some parameters of our model. This training set consists of 300 topics.

Evaluation We used the relevance judgment for the English language provided by CLEF-IP for evaluation. We report the Recall, Mean Average Precision, and Patent Retrieval Evaluation Score [14] which combines MAP and Recall in one single score. We report the evaluation metrics on the top 1000 results. In the remainder of our experiments we used the Wilcoxon signed ranked matched pairs test with a confidence level of 0.05 level for testing statistical significance improvements.

8. EXPERIMENTAL RESULTS

8.1 Building the Initial Query

We built keyword queries by extracting distinguishing terms from the query patent document. To this end, we estimated the importance of each term according to a weighted log-likelihood based approach, as in [16]. We used the claims and the first independent claim for selecting query terms. Table 4 summarizes the results we obtained for the topics in the training and test set of CLEF-IP 2010 and the test set of CLEF-IP 2011. We used top-10 query terms with higher weights from the estimated query model in our experiments. Results marked with † and ‡ achieve statistically significant improvement in terms of MAP and recall, respectively. Note that this comparison is performed among runs belonging to the same experimental settings.

The results of Table 4 demonstrate that the performance of the runs obtained by issuing the query built from the first-claim is always stronger than the performance of the runs where the query is built from the claims in terms of MAP. However, the opposite holds for recall. The reason for the high MAP is because the first independent item of claims is focused on the core invention of the patent document. However, we are losing some information by ignoring the text of the rest of the claims and this explains the low recall of this setting.

To guarantee the assignment of reliable importance weights to the expansion concepts in our proximity-based framework, we need to start with a set of precise query terms. This is because we rely on the distance between query terms and expansion concepts to calculate importance weights for

[5] http://ir.dcs.gla.ac.uk/terrier/

CLEF-IP 2010 (training topics)				
Method	Run description	MAP	Recall	PRES
C10TR	claims	0.1211	0.6302 ‡	0.5492
FC10TR	first-claim	0.1530 †	0.6015	0.5479
CLEF-IP 2010 (test topics)				
Method	Run description	MAP	Recall	PRES
C10TE	claims	0.1293	0.6067 ‡	0.5140
FC10TE	first-claim	0.1445 †	0.5624	0.4911
CLEF-IP 2011 (test topics)				
Method	Run description	MAP	Recall	PRES
C11TE	claims	0.0823	0.5905 ‡	0.4850
FC11TE	first-claim	0.1198 †	0.5360	0.4538

Table 4: Choosing baseline on the two retrieval collections.

expansion concepts. Obviously starting with focused and less noisy query terms has a direct effect on the quality of calculated importance weights. Thus, in the remainder of this paper, we focus on selecting query terms from the first independent item of the claims.

We used the Language Modeling approach with Dirichlet smoothing [20] to score documents from both collections and build the initial rank lists. We empirically set the value for the smoothing parameter μ to1500. We also used Language Modeling for the re-ranking of the results. We note that we do not use citation information in our experiments.

8.2 Choosing the Baseline

In terms of our comparison baseline, we chose the strongest configuration in terms of PRES from Table 4, the retrieval run where query terms are selected from the claims section of the patent document. C10TR is chosen as the baseline on the training topics of CLEF-IP 2010. C10TE is chosen as the baseline on the test topics of CLEF-IP 2010 and C11TE is chosen as the baseline over test topics of CLEF-IP 2011. Note that the training set of CLEF-IP 2010 is only used for tuning the parameters of the model, thus we will refer to C10TR in such comparisons.

Table 5 shows the performance of strong baselines of the previous work [5, 15] over CLEF-IP 2010. We presented their performance evaluation in terms of MAP and PRES as the recall values were not reported for the two baselines.

method	MAP	PRES
baseline1 [5]	0.1278	0.4604
baseline2 [15]	0.1399	0.4860

Table 5: Strong baselines of the previous work

As we can see from the results of Table 5, C10TE is as strong as the baseline1 and baseline2 in terms of PRES. This ensures the selection of a strong baseline which will be used in evaluating the performance of our proposed model in the rest of the paper.

8.3 Motivation for Using Proximity Information

In order to test if closeness of expansion concepts to the query terms is correlated with relevance, we carry out preliminary experiments on the CLEF-IP 2010 collection. In these experiments, we selected 100 random queries.

For each query, we first retrieved the top 100 documents

IEC				
kernel \ σ	25	75	125	150
Gaussian	**0.6443**	**0.6561** †	**0.6676** †	**0.6795** †
Laplace	0.6422	0.6556 †	0.6588 †	0.6709 †
Rectangle	0.6398	0.6523	0.6559 †	0.6678 †

EEC				
kernel \ σ	25	75	125	150
Gaussian	**0.6388**	**0.6418**	0.6669 †	**0.6637** †
Laplace	0.6362	0.6390	**0.6685** †	0.6516
Rectangle	0.6339	0.6375	0.6642 †	0.6497

Table 6: Recall results of different settings of the kernel functions using query reformulation methods (IEC and EEC) on the training topics of CLEF-IP 2010.

using a Language Modeling retrieval method. We separated relevant and non-relevant documents according to relevance judgements (qrels). We then looked at the average distance between query terms and expansion concepts inside the set of relevant documents, denoted by R, and the set of non-relevant documents, denoted by $\bar{R}$. The distance in each of the two mentioned sets is calculated as follows:

$$DIS(Q,R) = \sum_{D \in R} \frac{\sum_{q \in Q} min_{e \in E}(Dis(q,e))}{|Q||R|}$$

$$DIS(Q,\bar{R}) = \sum_{D \in \bar{R}} \frac{\sum_{q \in Q} min_{e \in E}(Dis(q,e))}{|Q||\bar{R}|}$$

where q denotes a query term drawn from the set of query terms, denoted by Q, e denotes an expansion term, and E denotes the set of expansion concepts selected from the conceptual lexicon. The distance between two terms is calculated in terms of the number of terms between them. The minimum is calculated among all the occurrences of each pair of query term and expansion term.
Figure 1 shows the average distance for relevant and non-relevant documents for each query topic. For clarity purposes, topics are sorted by the average distance DIS of their relevant documents.

It can be seen from Figure 1 that the minimum distance between an expansion term and a query term in relevant documents is less than their respective distance in non-relevant documents. Therefore we can use this proximity information to differentiate the relevant documents from non-relevant documents and to improve the ranking of relevant documents.

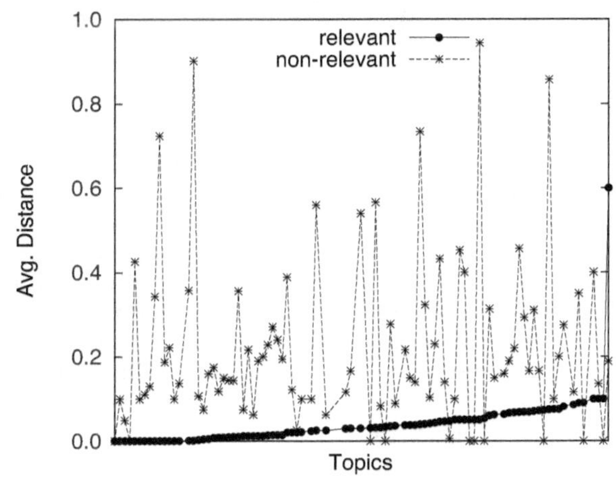

Figure 1: ***AverageDIS*** **value for each topic using qrels and top-retrieved non-relevant documents.**

8.4 Effect of Density Kernel

We are interested to investigate the effectiveness of different query reformulation methods proposed in Section 6 for scoring documents in our proximity-based framework. The results of this comparison are summarized in Table 6.

In all the comparisons, our query expansion method which uses *explicit expansion concept* is denoted as EEC. The query expansion method which uses *implicit expansion concept* is referred to as IEC.

Since the performance of these methods is directly determined by the effectiveness of the kernel function used to estimate the propagated query relatedness probabilities for the expansion concepts, we first need to compare three different proximity-based kernel functions to see which one performs the best.

We place a density kernel around each occurrence of query term positions in the document as previously explained in Section 5. The query relatedness at each expansion term position is then calculated by counting the accumulated query relatedness density from different query terms at that position. Therefore, an expansion term which occurs at a position close to many query terms will receive high query relatedness and thus will obtain a higher importance weight.

Our proximity-based framework has two parameters: the type of kernel function and its bandwidth parameter σ which controls the degree of query relatedness propagation throughout the entire document. To tune the parameters of our model we used the training topics of CLEF-IP 2010.

The results of comparing different kernel functions on the training topics of CLEF-IP 2010 are shown in Table 6. A † denotes statistical significant improvement over C10TR and the best result for each kernel type is highlighted. The results show that the performance of EEC and IEC with all kernel functions improve over C10TR.

It is also clear that among all the kernel functions, the Gaussian kernel outperforms other types of kernels in most cases. Since the Gaussian kernel performed the best in most of the carried experiments, we use this kernel function for our system evaluation in the rest of our experiments.

In order to find the best value for the parameter σ we tried a set of fixed values in the range of [25, 200] with a step of 25 similar to the previous work [12, 13]. Table 6 reports the performance of different kernel functions using varying values of σ. The results show that selecting a value of 125 or 150 usually gives the best retrieval performance.

Overall, the results of Table 6 clearly demonstrate that the results obtained with the σ value of 150 achieved better performance in most cases, although the difference among different settings was not significant. We thus use the σ value of 150 in the rest of our experiments. In Section 8.5 we further study the performance of the query reformulation

Collection	metric	IEC	EEC	CSS	PPRF
CLEF-IP 2010	MAP	0.1050	0.1026	0.0982	0.0705
	Recall	0.6595 †	0.6437 †	0.6241	0.5877
	PRES	0.5540	0.5498	0.5354	0.5023
CLEF-IP 2011	MAP	0.0772	0.0761	0.0738	0.0629
	Recall	0.6371 ‡	0.6254 ‡	0.6088	0.5632
	PRES	0.5288	0.5249	0.5127	0.4945

Table 7: The performance results of query reformulation approaches on two patent retrieval datasets on the test topics of CLEF-IP 2010 and CLEF-IP 2011.

methods.

Comparison of Max and Avg Strategy We are interested to evaluate the two strategies for calculating the probability of relevance of a document as proposed in Section 5.2. Table 8 shows the result of using avg and max strategies for different sigma values on the training topics of CLEF-IP 2010 using the IEC reformulation method.

The results show that max strategy is statistically better than the avg strategy. Thus, we use the max strategy in all configurations of our experiments throughout this paper. A † denotes the statistical significant improvement over avg method.

method \ σ	25	75	125	150
max	0.6443 †	0.6561 †	0.6676 †	0.6795 †
avg	0.6164	0.6198	0.6207	0.6238

Table 8: Recall of the Max and Avg method using Gaussian kernel with IEC reformulation method on training topics of CLEF-IP 2010.

8.5 Effect of Query Reformulation

In this section, we present the evaluation results of our proposed approaches on the topics in the test set of CLEF-IP 2010 and CLEF-IP 2011.

Table 7 reports the retrieval performance of query reformulation methods described in Section 6. The symbols † and ‡ denote statistical significant improvements over C10TE and C11TE, respectively.

We now compare the performance of our query formulation methods. In addition to EEC and IEC which were introduced earlier, the results of the two other query reformulation methods (described in Section 6) are presented in Table 7. Our method which *combines search strategies* is denoted as CSS. The last method in our comparisons is the *positional-based pseudo relevance feedback*, which is denoted by PPRF.

The main observation from Table 7 is that IEC is always more effective than the other three methods. In addition, IEC improves the baseline in terms of recall on both collections significantly.

Table 7 shows that a method which uses a conceptual lexicon for selecting expansion terms outperforms a method which uses feedback documents for identifying expansion terms. This is evident by comparing the performance of EEC, IEC and CSS to the performance of PPRF, as the first three methods use the conceptual lexicon for query expansion. This result is consistent on both corpora used for evaluation.

In addition, the results of Table 7 demonstrate that IEC obtains improvement over EEC. In contrast to IEC, EEC extracts a limited set of expansion terms from the conceptual lexicon, the ones which are present in the query document itself. This diminishes the power of EEC in contrast to IEC, and explains the advantage of IEC. Results confirm that the unlimited usage of the conceptual lexicon is superior to the limited usage of it.

Another observation which can be made from Table 7 is that CSS attains worst results compared to both EEC and IEC. This is perhaps due to the fact that some information is lost during the combination of two separate runs made from the query terms and expansion terms. While, in EEC and IEC we use a unified query which is composed of query terms and expansion terms.

Overall, the results of Table 7 show that using the conceptual lexicon as a domain-dependent external resource is effective in terms of recall, although this improvement does not hold for precision. Table 2 shows some queries where using IEC reformulation method improved the recall.
We used 40 expansion terms (based on initial experiments) in each of the query reformulation methods. We studied the effect of the number of expansion terms on the performance of each method. We report the result of this study in Section 8.7.

8.6 Comparison to Standard PRF

Table 9 reports the retrieval performance of PPRF compared to PRF. A ‡ indicates the statistical significant improvement over the baseline which is built from the first-claim presented in Table 4. A † denotes the statistical significant improvement over standard PRF in terms of recall.

As previously explained in Section 6, PPRF is similar to PRF since they both use feedback set for expansion term selection. However, PPRF uses proximity information inside feedback set to calculate weight for expansion terms in contrast to standard PRF.

The results show that PPRF performs significantly better than the standard PRF. This result confirms the usefulness of proximity information for identifying importance weights for expansion terms as previously was shown in [13].

Note that PPRF and PRF does not achieve improvement over the baseline, but a fair comparison is to compare the retrieval effectiveness after query expansion with the retrieval effectiveness before query expansion. We thus need to compare the results of Table 9 with the results of FC10TE and FC11TE which correspond to the performance of the initial query built from the first claim.

Our results show that the performance obtained with PPRF method achieves statistical significant improvements in terms

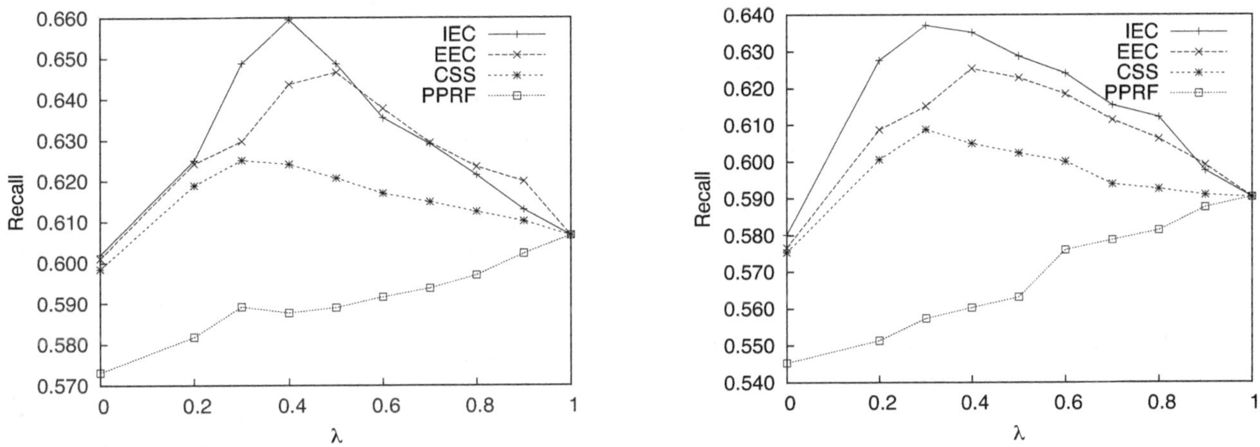

a) CLEF-IP 2010

b) CLEF-IP 2011

Figure 2: Sensitivity to the λ coefficient in the linear combination of results made from the initial and the expanded query

of recall over the initial query (before expansion). This result is interesting as a recent study [5] pointed out that often standard PRF method fails on the patent prior art search. This poor performance is associated to the low MAP of the initial rank list from which feedback documents are selected. This comparison demonstrates the usefulness of aggregating the proximity information in the calculation of the expansion weights as performed in our proximity-based framework.

We fixed the number of feedback documents used in both PPRF and PRF to 10.

8.7 Influence of Different Parameter Settings

In this section, we are interested to study the influence of different parameters on the effectiveness of our proposed methods. We used the test topics of both corpora during the evaluations.

Collection	metric	PPRF	PRF
CLEF-IP 2010	MAP	0.0705	0.0650
	Recall	0.5877 ‡†	0.5630
	PRES	0.5023	0.4961
CLEF-IP 2011	MAP	0.0629	0.0617
	Recall	0.5632 ‡†	0.5346
	PRES	0.4945	0.4792

Table 9: The comparison of performance results of PRF and PPRF.

Number of Expansion Terms To see the effect of the number of expansion terms on the effectiveness of our proposed methods we plot the sensitivity of different query reformulation methods to the number of expansion terms over CLEF-IP 2010 test topics. We change the number of expansion terms from 1 to 50. The recall results are shown in Figure 3. We observe that all four methods achieve effective performance using around 40 expansion terms.

Effect of Combination In all configurations of our experiments we linearly combined the results we got from each

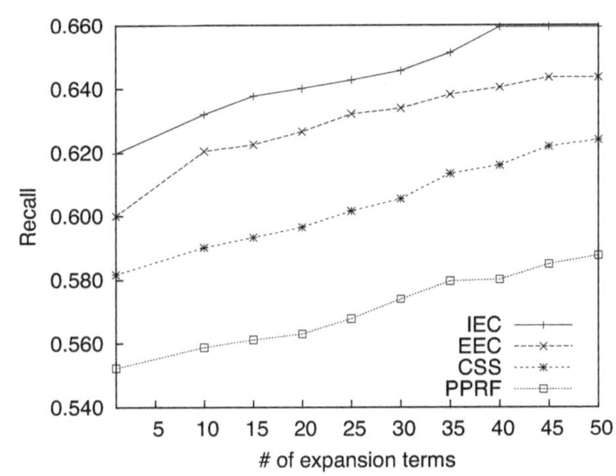

Figure 3: Sensitivity to the effect of number of expansion terms on CLEF-IP 2010

of the reformulation methods with the initial query. The weight of the interpolation λ controls the weight of the initial query. When $\lambda = 0$, the query expansion model is used and when $\lambda = 1$ the initial query is used. λ was tuned based on the training topics of CLEF-IP 2010.

Figure 2 shows the results of the sensitivity analysis over the coefficient λ on the test topics of CLEF-IP 2010 and CLEF-IP 2011. We notice that IEC is more effective than other query reformulation methods for different λ values. The optimal value for the parameter λ seems to be in a range around 0.4.

Effect of Normalization

We now compare the effect of different normalization methods prior to linear combination using two score normalization methods, MinMax [7] and HIS normalization [1], which are used in distributed information retrieval or meta-search.

MinMax normalization method shifts and scales scores to be between zero and one. While, HIS normalization estimates a single cumulative density function (CDF) for every search engine based on historical queries.

We also experimented with a variation of score normalization where we first applied MinMax and then we applied HIS normalization. We refer to this method as MinMax-HIS throughout the experiments.

Table 10 shows the comparison among different normalization methods. These results correspond to the final performance of each run after the combination over test topics of CLEF-IP 2010. The results are obtained with the IEC method. The best results are highlighted although the difference is not statistically significant.

metric	MinMax	HIS	MinMax-HIS
MAP	0.0924	0.0991	**0.1050**
Recall	0.6520	0.6568	**0.6595**
PRES	0.5473	0.5522	**0.5540**

Table 10: The comparison of different normalization methods over CLEF-IP 2010 using IEC method

We observe that IEC achieves the best performance using MinMax-HIS normalization. The results of other methods were also confirming that applying normalization using MinMax-HIS was better compared to either MinMax or HIS alone, although not significantly. We thus presented the results of normalization using MinMax-HIS method throughout the paper.

9. CONCLUSION AND FUTURE WORK

In this paper we introduced a proximity based framework for query expansion which utilizes a conceptual lexicon for patent retrieval. To this end, we constructed a domain-dependent conceptual lexicon which can be used as an external resource for query expansion. Our proximity-based retrieval framework provides a principled way to calculate the importance weight for expansion terms selected from the conceptual lexicon. We showed that proximity of expansion terms to query terms is a good indicator of the importance of the expansion terms. In this paper we focused on performing query expansion with single terms to ensure the efficiency of the expansion concept selection process.

We have evaluated our proposed method on two patent retrieval corpora, namely CLEF-IP 2010 and CLEF-IP 2011. Our query formulation method, IEC, was shown to outperform the strong baselines of CLEF-IP and a standard pseudo relevance feedback method in terms of recall. Further analysis of the performance of the query reformulation methods proposed in this paper showed the high quality of expansion terms extracted from the conceptual lexicon.

10. ACKNOWLEDGMENTS

The work of Parvaz Mahdabi was funded by the Information Retrieval Facility, through the research project "Interactive Patent Search (IPS)". This research is also supported in part by the research grant from Natural Sciences and Engineering Research Council (NSERC) of Canada. We thank anonymous reviewers for their thorough review comments on this paper.

11. REFERENCES

[1] A. Arampatzis and J. Kamps. A signal-to-noise approach to score normalization. In *CIKM*, pages 797–806, 2009.

[2] L. Azzopardi and V. Vinay. Retrievability: an evaluation measure for higher order information access tasks. In *CIKM*, pages 561–570, 2008.

[3] S. Bashir and A. Rauber. Improving retrievability of patents in prior-art search. In *ECIR*, pages 457–470, 2010.

[4] S. Cetintas and L. Si. Effective query generation and postprocessing strategies for prior art patent search. *JASIST*, 63(3):512–527, 2012.

[5] D. Ganguly, J. Leveling, W. Magdy, and G. J. F. Jones. Patent query reduction based on pseudo-relevant documents. In *CIKM*, pages 1953–1956, 2011.

[6] S. Gerani, M. J. Carman, and F. Crestani. Aggregation methods for proximity-based opinion retrieval. *TOIS*, 30(4):26, 2012.

[7] J.-H. Lee. Analyses of multiple evidence combination. In *SIGIR*, pages 267–276, 1997.

[8] P. Lopez and L. Romary. Patatras: Retrieval model combination and regression models for prior art search. In *CLEF (Notebook Papers/LABs/Workshops)*, pages 430–437, 2009.

[9] P. Lopez and L. Romary. Experiments with citation mining and key-term extraction for prior art search. *CLEF (Notebook Papers/LABs/Workshops)*, 2010.

[10] M. Lupu and A. Hanbury. Patent retrieval. *Foundations and Trends® in Information Retrieval*, 7(1):1–97, 2013.

[11] M. Lupu, K. Mayer, J. Tait, and A. Trippe. *Current Challenges in Patent Information Retrieval.* Springer, 2011.

[12] Y. Lv and C. Zhai. Positional language models for information retrieval. In *SIGIR*, pages 299–306, 2009.

[13] Y. Lv and C. Zhai. Positional relevance model for pseudo-relevance feedback. In *SIGIR*, pages 579–586, 2010.

[14] W. Magdy and G. J. F. Jones. PRES: A score metric for evaluating recall-oriented information retrieval applications. In *SIGIR*, pages 611–618, 2010.

[15] W. Magdy and G. J. F. Jones. A study on query expansion methods for patent retrieval. In *PAIR 2011 - CIKM*, pages 19–24, 2011.

[16] P. Mahdabi, L. Andersson, M. Keikha, and F. Crestani. Automatic refinement of patent queries using concept importance predictors. In *SIGIR*, pages 505–514, 2012.

[17] P. Sondhi, V. G. V. Vydiswaran, and C. Zhai. Reliability prediction of webpages in the medical domain. In *ECIR*, pages 219–231, 2012.

[18] X. Xue and W. B. Croft. Automatic query generation for patent search. *CKIM*, pages 2037–2040, 2009.

[19] X. Yin, X. Huang, and Z. Li. Promoting ranking diversity for biomedical information retrieval using wikipedia. In *ECIR*, pages 495–507, 2010.

[20] C. Zhai and J. D. Lafferty. A study of smoothing methods for language models applied to ad hoc information retrieval. In *SIGIR*, pages 334–342, 2001.

Aggregated Search Interface Preferences in Multi-Session Search Tasks

Marc Bron
ISLA, University of Amsterdam
m.m.bron@uva.nl

Jasmijn van Gorp
TViT, Utrecht University
j.vangorp@uu.nl

Frank Nack
ISLA, University of Amsterdam
nack@uva.nl

Lotte Belice Baltussen
Netherlands Institute for Sound & Vision
lbbaltussen@beeldengeluid.nl

Maarten de Rijke
ISLA, University of Amsterdam
derijke@uva.nl

ABSTRACT

Aggregated search interfaces provide users with an overview of results from various sources. Two general types of display exist: tabbed, with access to each source in a separate tab, and blended, which combines multiple sources into a single result page. Multi-session search tasks, e.g., a research project, consist of multiple stages, each with its own sub-tasks. Several factors involved in multi-session search tasks have been found to influence user search behavior. We investigate whether user preference for source presentation changes during a multi-session search task.

The dynamic nature of multi-session search tasks makes the design of a controlled experiment a non-trivial challenge. We adopt a methodology based on triangulation and conduct two types of observational study: a longitudinal study and a laboratory study. In the longitudinal study we follow the use of tabbed and blended displays by 25 students during a project. We find that while a tabbed display is used more than a blended display, subjects repeatedly switch between displays during the project. Use of the tabbed display is motivated by a need to zoom in on a specific source, while the blended display is used to explore available material across sources whenever the information need changes.

In a laboratory study 44 students completed a multi-session search task composed of three sub-tasks, the first with a tabbed display, the second and third with blended displays. The tasks were manipulated by either providing three task about the same topic or about three different topics. We find that a stable information need over multiple sub-tasks negatively influences perceived usability of the blended displays, while we do not find an influence when the information need changes.

Categories and Subject Descriptors

H.3.3 [**Information Search and Retrieval**]: Search process; H.5.2 [**User Interfaces**]: Evaluation/methodology

Keywords

Search interface preferences, search behavior, aggregated search, multi-session search tasks

1. INTRODUCTION

In today's information society, organizations such as census bureaus, news companies, and archives, are making their collections of high quality information accessible through individual search interfaces [22]. As these sources are rarely indexed by major web search engines, seeking for information across these sources requires users to sequentially go through each of them individually. Aggregated search interfaces are a solution to this problem; they provide users with an overview of the results from various sources (verticals) by collecting and presenting information from multiple collections. Two general types of aggregated search interfaces exist: *tabbed* and *blended*. Tabbed interfaces provide access to each source in separate tabs, while blended interfaces combine multiple sources into a single result page [20].

The focus of previous work on aggregated search interfaces has been on selecting which vertical to present given a query and where to present it in the result list based on click logs [24], judgements [2, 3, 23] or on simulations [18]. Others have investigated how users interact with aggregated search interfaces, i.e., how verticals influence user search behavior [1] or the influence of tabbed and blended interfaces on user behavior and preferences in single-session tasks of varying complexity [4, 28, 29].

A multi-session search task, such as writing a report, consists of multiple information seeking tasks, each of which might be composed of its own sub-tasks [10]. Several factors involved in multi-session search tasks have been found to influence user search behavior. Such factors include: stages in the overall task, user search experience, user knowledge of the search topic, and complexity of individual sub-tasks [5, 9, 14, 17, 31, 34, 35].

Research also shows that users apply the display which they feel will be most effective and efficient in solving their task [19]. For multi-session research tasks this means that the preference for a tabbed or blended interface might alter between sub-tasks, depending on the user's idiosyncratic needs. This potential alteration is problematic for interface designers, because the prediction of which vertical to show, where, and how, requires an understanding of the relationship between the presentation options of each interface type, the user needs, and the performed sub-tasks.

We investigate whether user preference for source presentation changes during a multi-session search task with the following research questions: (1) Do users switch between tabbed and blended display types during a multi-session search task and what is the motivation to switch between display types? (2) Do changes in users' information need across sub-tasks influence preference for a particular display type? And (3) what other factors are related to changes in display preference during a multi-session search task?

We focus our investigation on research tasks in the humanities, as the data sources investigated in this domain can be very diverse and the behavior of repeatedly re-visiting sources that one encounters here naturally requires multi-session search. Importantly, while there is a general focus on text-based media, the domain increasingly makes use of other media types too. An example here is the field of media studies, where finding answers to hypotheses as part of the paper writing process relies on the inspection of audio-visual media, (through metadata or content-based), related metadata and secondary literature [8].

The dynamic nature of multi-session search tasks make the design of a controlled experiment a non-trivial challenge. For the research presented in this paper we adopt a methodology based on triangulation [11] and conduct two types of studies: a longitudinal study and a laboratory study. In our *longitudinal* study we follow 25 students during a four week research project. We provide students with an interface that allows switching between a tabbed display, blended display, and blended display with a find-similar functionality. This allows for the study of display use and switching in a naturalistic setting. Through questionnaires and focus group discussions we elicitate the motivation for using a particular display.

In a *laboratory* study we present 44 students with a multi-session search task consisting of three complex sub-tasks. Each sub-task is carried out with a different display: the first task with the tabbed display; the second task with the blended display; and the third task with the blended display with a find-similar feature. We zoom in on the influence of changes in information need associated with recurring search sessions by manipulating whether a subject is assigned three sub-tasks about the same topic or three sub-tasks about different topics. This allows us to investigate the factors associated with changes in information need and whether these influence preference for a tabbed or blended display in different stages of a multi-session search task.

In Section 2 we describe the three variants of the aggregated interface; Section 3 and 4 describe the experimental setup and results of the longitudinal and laboratory study, respectively; in Section 5 we discuss the results of both studies in light of our research questions; Section 6 describes related work; we conclude in Section 7.

2. AGGREGATED SEARCH DISPLAYS

An aggregated search interface provides access to multiple, often heterogeneous collections. In building an aggregated search interface there are three aspects to consider: (i) how to retrieve relevant information from each vertical; (ii) which verticals to show; and (iii) where to place the verticals on the screen. Below we first give details of the back-end of our aggregated search interface and then describe three types of aggregated search interface displays: a tabbed display, a blended display and a blended display with find-similar functionality.

2.1 Data and Retrieval Back-end

The theme of the course selected for our longitudinal study is television history and the research projects carried out by the students are centered around television personalities between 1900 and 2010. To provide students with relevant material we obtained six collections from several archives and libraries: (i) a television program collection (metadata records for .5M programs); (ii) a photo collection (20K photos); (iii) a Wiki dedicated to television programs and presenters (20K pages); (iv) scanned television guides (25K pages); (v) scanned news papers starting from 1900 till 1995 (6M articles); (vi) digital news papers starting from 1995 till 2010 (1M articles). Each collection was indexed using Lucene SOLR 4.0 and the retrieval model used was BM25.

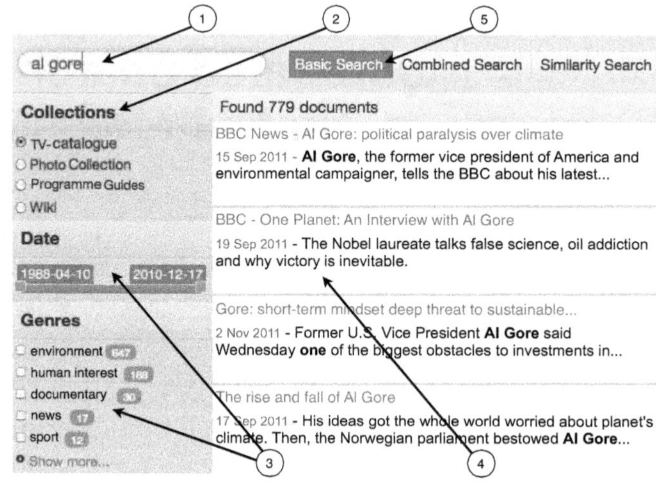

Figure 1: Tabbed display.

A single retrieval model may not be equally effective for each collection due to differences in term statistics and the presence of specific metadata fields in different collections [26]. To overcome this issue we provide faceted search and query preview capabilities in the aggregated search displays. These enable users to explore and learn about the characteristics of individual collections [32]. We did not optimize a retrieval model for each collection as depending on the size of the test set and type of queries a bias may be introduced towards particular types of documents, which is unwanted in a research task. The available facets depend on the collection as documents in some collections have rich metadata while others do not. The interaction model behind the facet values operates as follows: values within a single facet are combined using an OR operator, while values across facets are combined using an AND operator [30].

2.2 Tabbed Display

The tabbed display mimics the functionality and layout of a typical web search engine and is the default display presented to the user when opening the search interface. The tabbed display is shown in Figure 1; we use numbers 1, ..., 5 to reference specific components in the display. It consists of: (1) a search box; (2) a collection selection menu; (3) values for several facets; (4) a result list; and (5) an option to select the tabbed or blended interface.

A search is initiated by submitting a query via the search box (1). The television program collection is selected by default (2). In response to a query 10 document snippets are shown for the selected collection on the result page (4). At the top of the result list the number of documents found is displayed and at the bottom of the page a pagination button enables moving to the next and further result pages. To further refine the results the top 5 values for several facets are available (3). Pressing on the *show more* button extends the list of facets up to the top 100. By selecting a different collection (2) results for this collection are displayed for the current query. Each tab displays the same number of results (ten) as a ranked list, five of which are generally visible above the fold depending on the size of the display.

A document can be viewed by clicking on a result snippet. The search result page is covered by an overlay and the content and metadata of a document are displayed. There are two special cases where the displayed information depends on the type of document, i.e., image and Wiki. Records form the photo or tv-guide collections consist of several images; in the overlay the photo and its

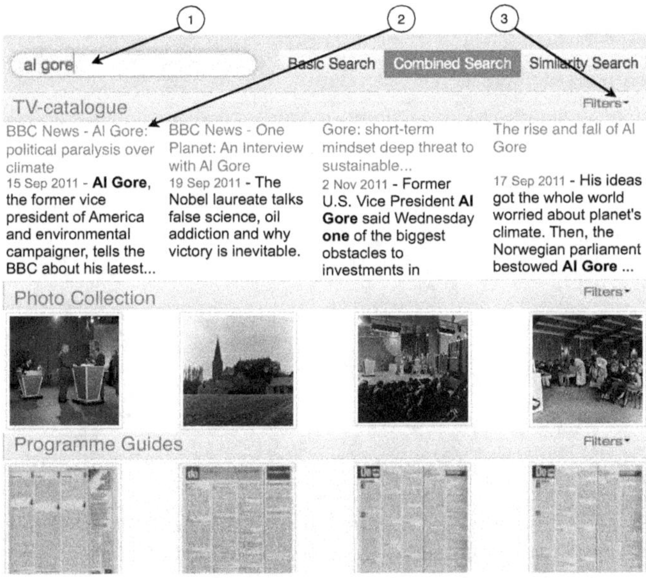

Figure 2: Blended display.

metadata are show with the additional option of viewing the next or previous photo without leaving the overlay. Wiki page content is not shown in the overlay, only the metadata and a link that opens the page in a new tab. To save a particular document a bookmark button is available, when hovering over a search results and in the document view overlay. Clicking the bookmark button saves the title of the document to a bookmark list available as a drop down list at the top of the screen. Selecting a title from the drop down list triggers an overlay with the document.

2.3 Blended Display

The blended display is based on the layout of interfaces typically used within digital libraries [25]. The blended display is shown in Figure 2; we use numbers 1, . . . , 3 to reference specific components in the display. It consists of: (1) a search box; and six horizontally orientated rectangular panes one for each collection. The vertical order in which the six collections are displayed is fixed and is the same as the order of the collection selection menu in the tabbed display, e.g., the top most pane shows results for the television program collection. Within a collection pane four results are shown ordered from left (most relevant) to right (less relevant) (2). To free up screen space for displaying results horizontally the facets for each collection are hidden. A button is available to toggle the display of facet values (3). The facets, bookmark options and document views are all the same as in the tabbed interface.

The blended display presents six by four results of which eight are generally visible above the fold depending on display size. More results are available as each source provides an independent pagination button. By scrolling down more results are available than in the tabbed display, however, only four results are available from each source. This is a trade-off between the two display types. The tabbed display supports searching through a single source, while the blended display supports searching through multiple sources.

In our blended display we use a fixed order and fixed number of results. This is in contrast to a trend seen in current web search engines, which is to display a variable number of results from a variable number of collections in a vertically oriented ranked list in a query dependent manner. The latter display method requires careful tuning, either on large numbers of users or on log data, both of which are unavailable for complex or multi-session search tasks.

2.4 Similarity Search

An additional feature was added to the blended display and provided as an additional screen, i.e., similarity search. By clicking on a document the user submits the current query and the first 100 words of the clicked document as an OR query [7, 27]. This type of explicit feedback is often implemented in a digital library context to discover related material across multiple sources [20]. However, the additional effort of using this feature and lack of understanding of how it works limits the use of find-similar like features [6, 33]. We add this feature to the blended display in order to explore its use in multi-session search tasks.

By clicking the find-similar button a query is issued and the document used for the query is placed in the query history pane appearing as a new row above the first row of search results. There are four slots, one of which is filled each time the find-similar button is clicked ordered from newest to oldest. When all slots are occupied the oldest document is removed and the others shifted to the right to free up space for the new document. Whenever a new query is issued the query history is emptied by removing the top row. Note that without clicking the find-similar button the similarity search display is exactly the same as the blended display.

3. A LONGITUDINAL STUDY

The goal of our first, longitudinal study was to investigate in which way people change between interfaces for a given work task in a natural setting and how this swapping behavior can be motivated, if it happens at all. The type of multi-session work task we make use of is a scholarly task, i.e., the task of writing a paper, which covers multiple search tasks to be carried out to collect and investigate the material that finally contributes to the paper [15]. Below we first describe the details of our experimental setting followed by an analysis of the data and discussion of the findings.

3.1 Study Setting

Through inquiries among staff at the humanities department of our university we searched for a course suitable for our study, one in which students complete the cycle of a research project including the development of a research question, searching for and interpreting materials, and reporting about their findings. The course that offered this structure and on which we finally settled is entitled: "Reception of media in historical perspective." The lecturer is experienced in teaching the course and used the same course schedule and assignments as in previous years. The course consists of two parts, we only focus on the first five weeks in which students conclude the following research project: "reconstruct the historical context of the 1950's (start of television) or 1920's (start of film) in order to explain the emancipatory role of a famous female television/film personality. Write a photo essay in which you incorporate primary and secondary sources that place the photos in context." The research project is split into four assignments, one due each week: (i) "familiarize yourself with the television/film personality of your choice and compose a list of five additional television/film personalities that fit your theme;" (ii) "start collecting images centered around your theme and collect material that motivates choosing these images;" (iii) "select ten images and add keyword descriptions to create a coherent story;" (iv) "prepare a presentation explaining the theme of your project, using the collected material." These assignments provide structure for the students as well as a natural separation of the research project into four parts.

Subjects. In total twenty-five students participated in the course and all were at the postgraduate level in the area of media studies. The sample consists of 12 men and 13 women, aged in terms of median (MD) and interquartile range (IQR) around twenty-three years ($MD = 23$, $IQR = 22$–24). We asked subjects background questions using a 5 point Likert-type scale, where a one indicates no agreement and a five indicates extreme agreement. Subjects reported high levels of experience in general computer use ($MD = 4$, $IQR = 4$–5) and using online search tools ($MD = 4$, $IQR = 4$–5),

Procedure. At the end of the first lecture the experimenters presented the aggregated search system, explained how the three displays work and described the available data sources. After the presentation subjects were invited to sign up for the experiment, fill in a consent form and create a login. Subjects who signed up were not required to use the interface but were encouraged to use the system as a supplement to the sources normally used in the class. The incentive for using the system was the availability of unique sources otherwise unavailable. The experiment lasted 4 weeks.

Data collection. In conducting a naturalistic study there is a tension between collecting as much data as possible and affecting the environment through this data collection process. After negotiating with the lecturer we settled on three points of interaction with the subjects: at the end of the first lecture, once during the project and at the end of the final lecture (of the first part of the course). Participation of the students in all parts of the study was optional and no requests were made to use any specific features or to complete specific tasks with the aggregated search system, e.g., bookmarking. It was not deemed appropriate to collect the project grades of the students for use in the experimental analysis.

Two methods were used to collect qualitative data: open question surveys, and focus group discussions. In preparation of the focus group, subjects were asked to complete two online questionnaires, one before the second class and one before the fourth class. Questions focussed on the motivation to use a particular type of display. At the end of the second lecture and the final lecture a 15 minute focus group discussion was conducted. The discussion focussed on the motivation for using a particular type of display and switching between displays. The discussion was tape recorded and transcribed for later analysis. In addition, we collected quantitative data by logging all actions with the aggregated search system. See [12] for further details about subjects' browsing behavior.

3.2 Analysis

To investigate what type of display subjects use and whether they switch between display types in a multi-session search task, we first analyze the log data and then place our findings in the context of the qualitative data collected.

Log analysis. We first investigate whether there is a change in the amount that each of the three displays was used during the project. We considered three alternative indicators for the amount of use of a display. First, the amount of time that a subject spent logged into the system may overestimate the time a subject actually spent using the system. Similarly, clicks may underestimate the use of the system as inspection of result pages does not necessarily lead to clicks. We finally settled on the number of mouse hovers within a particular display as an indication for the amount of use of a display. A mouse hover is recorded when the cursor remains in the same position for 40ms and is only recorded again if the position changes [13]. Figure 3 shows the cumulative number of hovers with each of the three displays per day. We observe a sharp increase in the number of hovers recorded for each display before the 7th, 14th, 21th, and 28th day of the project, followed by a plateau of inactivity. These days coincide with the lecture and assignment deadline for each week and provides a natural separation of the course project into four stages. We further observe that most hovers are recorded for the tabbed display (solid) throughout the 28 days of the project. The blended display (dashed) receives less hovers, and the similarity display (crossed) receives the least hovers. In the second week more hovers are recorded for the tabbed and blended display compared to the first and last week. This may be due to the assignment of that week or the focus group after the second lecture. We return to this issue in the discussion of the qualitative analysis.

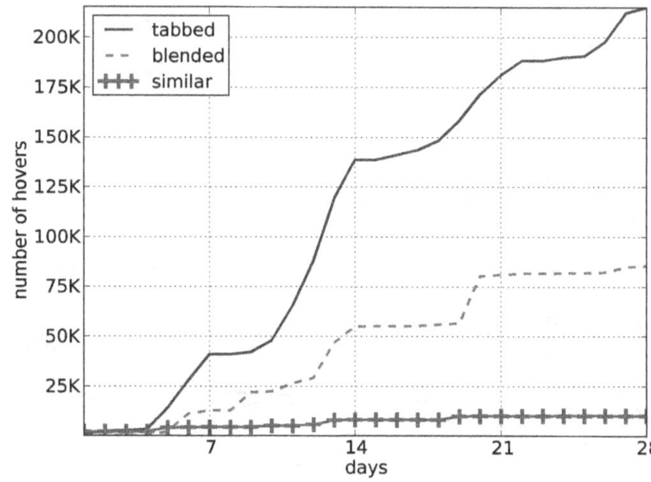

Figure 3: Cumulative number of mouse hovers recorded per day for the tabbed display (solid line), blended display (dashed line) and similarity display (cross marked).

Next, we investigate whether individual subjects differ in the amount of use of each display. In the log data we find that not all subjects used all of the displays provided by the aggregated search interface. For all 25 subjects, hovers are recorded for the tabbed display, for 18 subjects hovers are recorded for the blended display, and for 11 subjects hovers are recorded for the similarity display. Figure 4 shows the total number of hovers recorded per user during the project on the tabbed display (solid bar), blended display (dashed bar), and similarity display (crossed bar) ordered by the total number of hovers. We observe that for 23 out of 25 subjects most hovers are recorded for the tabbed display, while for 2 subjects most hovers are recorded for the blended display. The

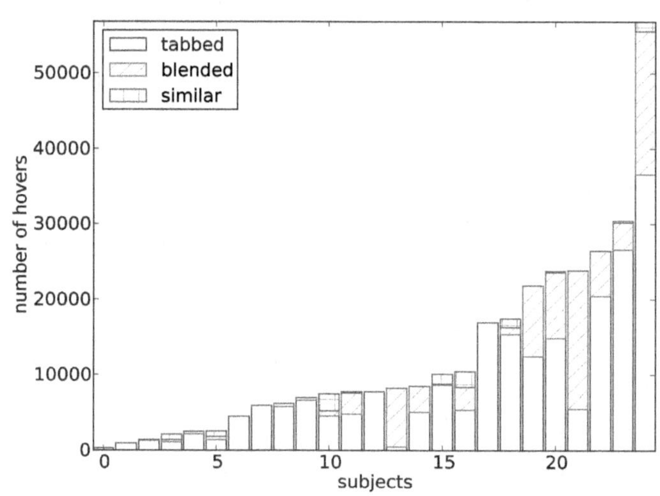

Figure 4: Total number of hovers received per user during the project on the tabbed display (solid bar), blended display (dashed bar), and similarity display (crossed bar).

blended interface is used notably by 8 subjects for which 25% or more of their total hovers occur with the blended display.

Finally, we investigate whether individual subjects differ in the amount of use of each display per week. Figure 5 shows the number of hovers recorded for each subject per week of the project with the tabbed display (solid bar), blended display (dashed bar), and similarity display (crossed bar). We observe that during the first week (bottom row in Figure 5) out of the 25 subjects 11 make no or limited use of the displays. Of the remaining subjects' most have at least 75% of their hovers in the first week recorded with the tabbed display (12/25). For the remaining subjects (2/25) one predominantly uses the blended display, the other the find-similar display. In the second week (second row Figure 5, use of all displays increases. Out of 25 subjects 10 have around 100% of their hovers recorded for the tabbed display. The blended displays are used more than in the first week as for 8 subjects about 50% or more of their hovers are recorded with the blended display and two with the find-similar display. The remaining 5 subjects have no or hardly any hovers recorded for any of the displays. In the third week no or a limited number of hovers are recorded for most subjects (17/25) with the aggregated search system. The remaining subjects (8/25), however, continue to use the system with an intensity comparable to that of week 2. In the fourth week use drops to a level similar to that of week 1 with (13/25) active subjects. Of these subjects, one uses the tabbed and blended display equally, the remaining subjects predominantly use the tabbed display.

We perform a Chi square test to investigate whether these differences in display usage per week are due to chance and find that there is significant association between project week and use of display ($\chi^2(df = 6, N = 311061) = 14458.8, p < 0.001$). Table 1 shows a cross-tabulation of display type and project week. We find that in the second and third week relatively more attention is spent to the blended display (50% and 30%) than the tabbed display (45% and 20%), which receives attention more throughout the project. The standardized residuals of the hover values that most contribute to the significant effect are highlighted in boldface. Especially the amount of use of the similarity display in the first week is surprising, as well as the increased use of the blended display in the third and diminished use in the fourth week. Use of the tabbed display dominates the fourth week.

The absolute number of hovers provides an indication of the amount of use. Whether subjects switch between displays, how-

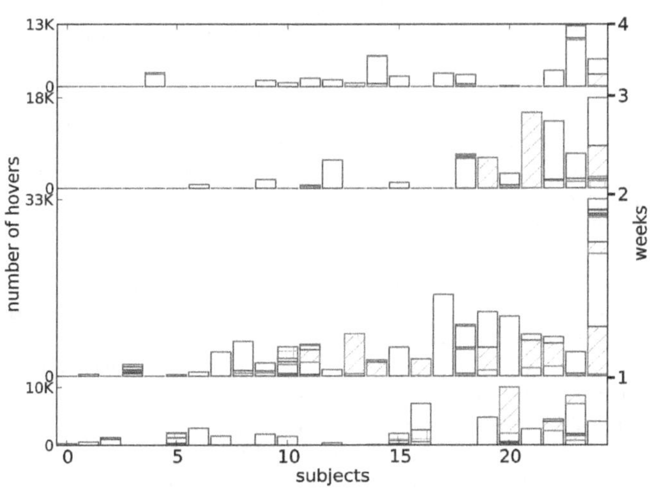

Figure 5: Number of hovers per user for each of the four stages of the project with the tabbed display (solid bar), blended display (dashed bar), and similarity display (crossed bar).

Table 1: Cross-tabulation of display type and project week, in percentages of both the week marginals and the interface marginals. The number of hovers are distributed as: tabbed $N = 215284$, blended $N = 85488$, and similarity $N = 10289$. Standardized residuals are show in brackets, the largest are highlighted in boldface

	tabbed	blended	similarity	
	70.4%	22.1%	7.5%	100%
week 1	19.0% (3.5)	15.0% (-24.7)	42.4% (**55.5**)	
	67.7%	29.5%	2.7%	100%
week 2	45.3% (-6.7)	49.7% (14.8)	38.3% (-11.8)	
	60.5%	36.9%	2.6%	100%
week 3	19.9% (-27.9)	30.5% (**47.8**)	17.9% (-10.2)	
	89.1%	10.5%	0.4%	100%
week 4	15.8% (**46.7**)	4.7% (**-63.2**)	1.4% (-31.7)	
	100%	100%	100%	

ever briefly, and in what sequence remains unclear. Figure 6 shows the same data as Figure 5—the number of hovers recorded for each subject per week of the project with the tabbed display (solid bar), blended display (dashed bar), and similarity display (crossed bar)—on a log scale. We observe that 6 out of 25 subjects only use the tabbed display and 4 out of 25 subjects only switch once to another display during the 4 weeks of the study. The remaining 15 subjects switch 2 or more times between displays and switching occurs in all 4 weeks. The tabbed display is the default whenever subjects login to the system and switching between displays takes a conscious effort. It is to be expected that in the first week subjects explore the system and try the various options. That switching between displays occurs in any of the weeks and for some subjects several times within a week indicates that subjects have a function for each display during the project.

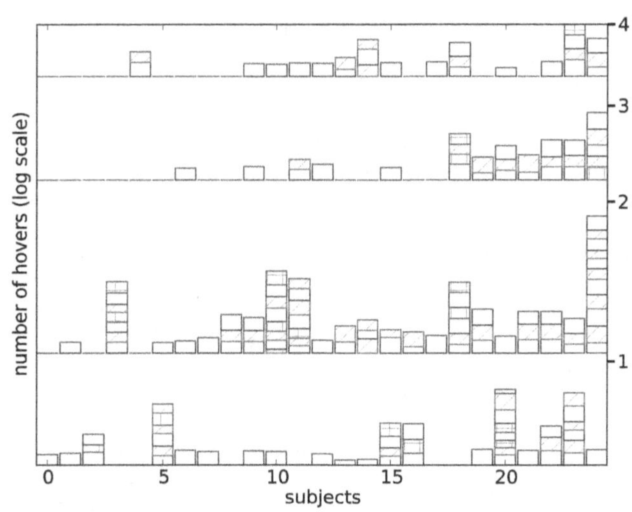

Figure 6: Number of hovers log scaled per user for each of the four stages with the tabbed display (solid bar), blended display (dashed bar), and similarity display (crossed bar).

Qualitative analysis. The above analysis shows that a majority of the subjects switches display during the weeks of the research project. In the first week subjects predominantly use the tabbed display, while a minority prefers to use another display. In the second and third week of the project usage of the blended display increases over that of the first week. The number of subjects using the system, however, decreases. Below we summarize the qualitative data gathered from two surveys and two focus group discussions and discuss subjects' motivation to switch between displays.

Before the second lecture 15 subjects completed a survey with open questions about the use of the three displays during the first week. On the question why subjects did or did not use the tabbed display all subjects indicated to have used the system: 8 subjects indicated to use the display to explore the collections and to get an impression of the available material; 5 subjects used the display to try out the system; 1 subject used the display but provided no motivation; and 1 subject liked the ability to specify in which collection to search. On the question why subjects did or did not use the blended display 10 subject indicated not to use the blended display: 5 subjects indicated not to have decided on a specific topic for their project yet and that they preferred the tabbed display to explore available material; and 5 subjects did not provide a motivation. Of the remaining 5 subjects that did use the blended display: 3 subjects indicated to like the blended display as it provided them with a better overview than the tabbed display; 1 subject found the blended display confusing; and 1 subject was trying out the display. On the question why subjects did or did not use the similarity display 8 subjects indicated not to use this display: 4 subjects indicated not to have decided on a specific topic; and 4 provided no motivation. Of the remaining 7 subjects that did use the similarity display: 3 subjects expected to find related television personalities; 2 subjects found that the similarity display did not provide relevant information; and 2 subjects were trying out the display.

In a 15 minute focus group discussion with 25 participants conducted at the end of the second lecture we focussed on the motivation for using or not using the system with a particular display. The consensus among participants is that the information provided by most of the sources is too specific for the current stage of the project: "in this phase I want general information, now when I search for photos of her I would get very specific information." Due to the stage of the project the tabbed display, with which a single collection can be explored, was preferred: "I found the Wiki interesting, because of our assignment this week" and "next week I will search differently, as this week was for exploration." In the similarity and blended display all collections are presented at the same time which subjects found less useful: "you get results with which you can not get an overview of the topic." Subjects also noted to prefer other resources, e.g., Wikipedia, and web search engines in order to get an overview of the possible topics for their project.

In summary, the above qualitative data suggests several reasons why subjects preferred the tabbed display during the first week and why use of the system was lower compared to the second week. First, the search behavior in this stage was of an exploratory nature as subjects tried to get an overview of available information and to decide on a topic for their project. Second, the information in most sources other than the Wiki was too specific. For example, a photo of a presenter and a guest during a specific broadcast of a television show provides little background information necessary to get oriented on a topic, for this purpose Wikipedia and similar sources are more useful. Finally, subjects preferred to use other resources such as Wikipedia and web search engines.

Before the fifth lecture 15 students again completed a survey with open questions about the use of the three displays during the second third and fourth week. Regarding the use of the tabbed display 6 subjects remarked that they liked to use it to find specific information in a specific collection, while 3 subjects preferred it to get an overview, and 1 provided no motivation. Subjects that did not use the tabbed interface favored the use of external sources (3 subjects) or preferred the overview of multiple collections (2 subjects). Regarding the blended display 7 subjects remarked that it was useful to find additional information: "to find next to images, more specific information about a person or event" or "get an as complete as possible overview of what is available about a specific program." To search for images 2 subjects preferred the blended display and 1 subject preferred the overview without searching for anything specific. The remaining 4 subjects did not find the blended display useful as it was confusing or did not provide relevant material. The similarity display was used by 2 subjects that mentioned being curious about the material that would be found. The remaining 13 subjects did not use the similarity display because they did not get around to using it or because results were irrelevant.

We conducted a second 15 minute focus group discussion with 25 students at the end of the fourth week. We focused again on the motivation for using a particular display and centered the discussion around three points: (i) did becoming more familiar with the search system affect display choice; (ii) did increased knowledge of the research topic affect display choice; and (iii) did the assignment each week affect display choice. Subjects did not experience difficulties in using the displays:"it is a reasonably intuitive system, I understand it." They did not associate any changes in display use with an increase in familiarity with the search system. Both increasing knowledge of the research topic and type of assignment are factors that subjects associate with changes in display use. Two groups emerged in this discussion. One group that changed from using the tabbed display to using the blended display: "I started to use the combined display more, because I know what I need, and then I want to see everything that is available about her." The other group changed from using the blended display to using the tabbed display:"I felt the same, that my search started to become more focussed, but then I preferred using the tabbed display because in the first week you do not know how to use photos and program guides, and now I wanted to know what was said in those sources about a specific person." Some subjects remarked that they did not use the system in later weeks of the project as it did not contain any relevant material for the theme they had chosen. There were two options for a project theme, i.e., female role models in television or film, see section 2. The material in the repositories is predominaltly focussed on television and does not contain as much relevant material for the second theme.

In summary, the second survey and focus group suggests that after the first week subjects' use of the system increased as their search topic became more concrete and the various sources became more relevant. We find several motivations for the switching behavior between displays throughout the project. The use of the tabbed display is motivated in the first week by an exploratory information need, where the Wiki was the only suitable source. In later weeks searching a single source is motivated by a more specific information need, e.g., photos for the essay. The use of the blended display is initially motivated by a need to explore the content of the various sources. Later the blended display provides a way to explore multiple sources simultaneously for material about a specific entity. We observed several switching patterns in Figure 6 that can be explained using the above motivations. Whether subjects engaged in a particular pattern seemed to depend on the individual subject. Some subjects indicated to have searched with the blended display in the first week and preferred to continue searching with the tabbed display in the second week. In this case the blended display is only used for an initial exploration of the sources. Other subjects repeatedly switched between the tabbed and blended display during the project. In these cases the blended display is likely used to search for additional information about a specific entity across sources.

Limitations. The setup of the longitudinal study involved that subjects were asked several times, i.e., focus group and surveys, about their use of and switching between displays. This may have influenced the behavior of the subjects. To avoid influencing subjects two measures were taken. First, subjects do not get a reward and have no obligation to use the tool. Their priority is to finish the assignment for each week and pass the course. To this end subjects choose to use the display which they feel will be most effective in solving their task [19]. As one subject remarked: "I have to search longer before I find something [with the aggregated search system] and I notice that I want to be efficient and then I quickly switch to a web search engine. I want to use the [aggregated search system] because I know you [the experimenters] need that, but at some point I think [insert expletive] I need to find my material and then I choose for something that quickly gives me results..." Although use of the system diminished in the third and fourth week, a number of subjects used the system and switched displays throughout the project. This suggests that the tabbed and blended displays are both found useful by some of the subjects and that each display supports a recurring need. Second, subjects were encouraged to use the system and explore all of its functionality with equal emphasis. The find similar and blended displays were both mentioned in the first focus group as being used less than the tabbed display in order to elicit a discussion about why this is. If the focus group discussion had any influence on the use of the find-similar display than this had a diminishing effect on its use.

4. A LABORATORY STUDY

In our first, longitudinal study we observed that the majority of subjects switched between displays and that use of the blended display was motivated by a need to explore the content of the sources available in the aggregated search system. Initially subjects desired an overview of the sort of information generally available in the sources, later the blended display was used to obtain an overview whenever a new specific information need arose, i.e., what is available in each source about a specific entity. We are interested in whether user preferences change in later stages of the multi-session search task depending on whether there are changes in the users' information need. We recreated this process in a laboratory study by assigning subjects three tasks to complete: the first task with a tabbed display, the second with a blended display, and the third with the similarity display. We compare two conditions: (i) one in which the three tasks are about the same topic allowing subjects to become increasingly familiar with the topic; and (ii) one in which tasks are about different topics simulating changes in information need. In this setting we investigate whether subjects preferences for displays deviate as some become more familiar with a topic, while others encounter new topics.

4.1 Study setting

The study uses a mixed methods design with 3 search tasks as within subject factor and the (in)dependency of the tasks as between subject factor. This design is similar to other work on multi-session search tasks [16] The following 3 sub-tasks emulate a multi-session search task: (i) imagine that you work at the editorial office of a current affairs program and are asked to collect information about [celebrity]. Collect at least 5 items deemed to be relevant for this collection, (ii) search for events that were key in the career of [celebrity]. Collect at least 5 items for this collection, for example articles and photographs, about these events, (iii) key in the career of [celebrity] was [event]. Collect at least 5 items about the run-up to the program, the program itself, and the aftermath. In this experiment [celebrity] stands for one of three television personalities and [event] represents an event related to the corresponding celebrity. The tasks are modeled after the assignments subjects received in the longitudinal study, i.e., starting out broad and gradually becoming more specific. Randomizing this order would obfuscate the simulation of a multi-session search task.

A subject completes 3 sub-tasks that are either dependent or parallel [16]. In a dependent series of sub-tasks all tasks are performed with respect to the same celebrity, while in a parallel series of sub-tasks each task has a different celebrity as topic simulating changes in a users information need. In the parallel condition the celebrities are randomized across tasks and in the dependent condition celebrities are randomized across subjects. In this manner each celebrity and task combination is seen an equal amount of times in each condition. All subjects are presented with the same display for each task. To complete the first task subjects are provided with the tabbed display, for the second task with the blended display, and for the third task with the similarity display.

We used a fixed order for the displays as we are interested in the preference of the blended display in later stages of the multi-session search task. In this way subjects are able to become familiar with the repositories using the tabbed display before encountering the blended display.

Subjects. A group of 44 undergraduate students participated in the study. For two of the subjects a technical failure prevented recording the pre-experiment questionnaire data. All analyses reported in the results section are excluding these two subjects and are conducted on the remaining 42 subjects. The students (30 female, 12 male) were around nine-teen years of age ($MD = 19.0$, $IQR = 19\text{–}21.75$). Random assignment to conditions resulted in two groups. The dependent task group contained 23 students (6 male and 17 female), where the parallel condition group contained 19 subjects (6 male and 13 female). We asked subjects of both groups to answer background questions using a 5 point Likert-type scale, where a one indicates no agreement and a five indicates extreme agreement. Subjects generally reported high levels of experience in general computer use ($MD = 4$, $IQR = 4\text{–}5$).

We additionally measured topic knowledge (1 item scale) and search experience (7 item scale) to make sure that these characteristics were balanced over the two groups. We found no significant difference between the two groups in terms of topic knowledge (Z=.68, p=.50), general computer use (Z=.18, p=.86) or search experience (Z=.20, p=.84) using Wilcoxon rank-sum tests.

Procedure. The study was conducted on two separate occasions in a computer lab equipped with 30 computers. Subjects could sign up for one of two time slots to participate in the study. Subjects of the first slot were asked not to communicate about the experiment until the second run had been finished. Each occasion of the study started with an introduction to the research project and a viewing of a 5-minute tutorial video explaining the use of the search displays. After the viewing of the tutorial, subjects were invited to fill in a consent form and create a login. Subjects were not allowed to talk, use mobile phones or open any other browsers. Four experimenters invigilated each of the experiments. After completing a background questionnaire eliciting demographics subjects were randomly assigned to either the dependent or parallel condition and presented with a pre-experiment questionnaire to collect information about search experience and prior knowledge about the task topic(s). Next, subjects started on the multi-session search task. For every task the subjects were given 10 minutes after which they were redirected to a post-task questionnaire asking about the topic difficulty, the perceived usability of the display, and the search effectiveness of the display. After the final search task a post-experiment questionnaire was presented that asked subjects to order the dis-

Table 2: Search effectiveness scale.

1	The display has supported me in solving the search task.
2	The display provided enough information for every collection to solve the search task.
3	The display provided surprising search results relevant to the search task.
4	The display supported me in finding relevant search results.

plays by preference, and to express any remarks they might have about the experiment. In total an experiment lasted 1.5 hours.

Data collection. We use two Likert-scales to measure subjects' preference for a particular type of display. For each item in the scales subjects indicated their agreement with the statement on a scale from one to five, where a one indicates no agreement and a five indicates extreme agreement. To arrive at a single score for each Likert-scale the mean of the responses was taken. To measure perceived usability we use an adaptation of the perceived usability sub-scale of the O'Brien Engagement Scale [21]. We modified the scale to apply to an aggregated search setting by substituting the word "shopping" and "website" by "searching" and "display" in the items. Additionally, we rephrased some of the items to a positive wording to arrive at an alternating 10 item scale.

To measure search effectiveness we used the items in Table 2. A final 3 items were devoted to subjects' perception of the task: (i) "the task was difficult to complete;" (ii) "there was one collection most useful in solving the search task;" and (iii) "to get an overview of the results in different collections is important in solving the task." These were not combined and are analyzed separately. All actions with the aggregated search interface were logged.

4.2 Results

We first investigate whether subjects' preferences differ within conditions in terms of relations between task and the dependent variables usability, task difficulty, and search effectiveness. We use non-parametric tests as data is collected on ordinal scales, and not all variables meet the assumption of normality. Table 3 shows the median (M) and inter quartile range (IQR) for each of the dependent variables split over each topic and the two conditions, i.e., dependent and parallel. We observe that there is a significant interaction between task and perceived usability of the display in the within subject dependent condition (Kruskal-Wallis H(2, N = 42) =17.7, p<.001), top part of Table 3). Post hoc comparisons show a significant difference between task 1-task 2 (Mann-Whitney U(N =42) =155, p=.008) and between task 1-task 3 (Mann-Whitney U(N =42) =81.5, p=<.001) at the Bonferroni corrected significance level of $\alpha = .05/3$. These results show that when the topic of the search task remains the same, subjects find the tabbed display easiest to use, and that the blended displays provided in later stages are considered more difficult to use. In the parallel condition we do not find a significant interaction between topics and usability. The median and IQR values are stable for the first two topics and decreases for the third topic. With this result we are unable to determine whether users find the blended display easier to use to explore a new topic.

We further observe that there is a significant interaction between task and task difficulty in the within subject parallel condition (Kruskal-Wallis H(2, N = 42) =6.45, p=.04), second row of Table 3). Post hoc comparisons show a significant difference between task 1-task 3 (Mann-Whitney U(N=42) =94.5, p=.006). In the dependent condition we do not find a significant interaction, although in terms of the median values the first and third task are considered more difficult than the second task. This suggests that in the parallel

Table 3: Interaction effects of the perceived usability, search effectiveness, topic difficulty, one collection is important and an overview is important responses in terms of median (interquartile range) across conditions (dependent and parallel) and across topics. The Kruskal Wallis hypothesis test is used to test for significant within subject effects, the Mann-WhitneyU hypothesis test is used to test for significance between subjects.

condition	task 1	task 2	task 3	K-W (H,p)
		perceived usability		
dependent	3.9 (3.8-4.1)	3.6 (3.3-4.1)	3 (2.7-4)	**(17.7, <.001)**
parallel	3.7 (2.9-4)	3.7 (3.1-4.1)	3.4 (2.9-3.7)	(2.90, .24)
M-W (U,p)	**(108,<.001)**	(197, .30)	(190, .24)	
		task difficulty		
dependent	3 (2-3)	2 (2-3)	3 (2-4)	(5.95, .051)
parallel	3 (3-4)	3 (2-3)	2 (2-3)	**(6.45, .040)**
M-W (U,p)	**(134, .017)**	**(151, .045)**	(155, .054)	
		search effectiveness		
dependent	3.3 (3.3-3.8)	3.3 (2.8-3.9)	3.3 (2.4-3.9)	(2.68, .26)
parallel	3.3 (3.3-3.8)	3.3 (3.0-3.6)	3.3 (2.6-3.6)	(3.21, .20)
M-W (U,p)	(194, 0.27)	(201, 0.33)	(194, 0.27)	
		overview important		
dependent	4 (3-4)	3 (3-4)	3 (3-4)	(4.02, .13)
parallel	4 (3-4)	4 (3-4)	3 (3-4)	(2.75, .25)
M-W (U,p)	(214, .46)	**(149, .040)**	(183, .19)	
		one collection important		
dependent	4 (3.5-4)	3 (2-3.5)	3 (2-3.5)	**(16.4, <.001)**
parallel	4 (3-4)	3 (2-4)	3 (2-4)	(2.70, .26)
M-W (U,p)	**(148, .038)**	(211, .43)	(218, .50)	

condition subjects find that the tasks become easier as they search material for new topics with the blended displays, while in the dependent condition task difficulty first decreases and then increases. This seems counter intuitive as subjects in the dependent condition have encountered more material on the topic and during the first two search tasks and should have a better idea of what search terms and which sources to use.

We find no relation between topics and the search effectiveness that subjects experience with the displays.

Two possible factors that moderate the preference of subjects for a certain display are: (i) whether for a particular task a subject considers a single collection as the most important source to search for material; and (ii) whether a subject considers it important to get an overview of the material available in different collections for a certain task. We do not find any interaction between the tasks and the importance of getting an overview. We do find a significant interaction between tasks and the fact that a single collection is considered to be the most important in solving a task (Kruskal-Wallis H(2, N = 42) =16.4, p<.001). Post hoc comparisons show a significant difference between task 1-task 2 (Mann-Whitney U(N =42) =109.5, p=<.001) and between task 1-task 3 (Mann-Whitney U(N =42) =103.5, p<.001). Subjects in the dependent conditions initially consider a single collection important to solve the search task, while in later tasks more collections become important.

Next, we investigate between subject effects in terms of relations between topic knowledge and the dependent and moderating variables. We find that in the first task there is a significant difference between the perceived usability reported by subjects from the dependent and parallel condition (Mann-Whitney U(N=42)=108, p<.001). We further observe that in the first and second task there

Table 4: **Cross tabulation of search moves in stage 1 for the dependent and parallel conditions. Search moves are given in percentages with the standardized residuals in brackets.**

move	dep.%(N=926)		par.%(N=728)	
paginate	6.48	(-1.38)	9.34	(1.55)
bookmark	11.77	(-1.37)	15.52	(1.55)
filter	17.93	(1.21)	14.29	(-1.36)
change tab	21.38	(1.14)	17.58	(-1.29)
queries	11.23	(-0.55)	12.64	(0.62)
view docs	22.14	(0.28)	21.15	(-0.32)
delete bookmark	0.32	(-0.46)	0.55	(0.52)
unique queries	8.75	(-0.08)	8.93	(0.09)

is a significant difference between the task difficulty reported by subjects from the dependent and parallel condition (Mann-Whitney U(N=42)=134, p=.017), i.e., in the dependent condition the first and second task are considered easier.

Regarding the moderating variables we find that in the second task subjects in the parallel condition consider getting an overview more important than subjects in the dependent condition (Mann-Whitney U(N=42)=149, p=.40). With respect to the importance of a single collection to solve the first search task, subjects in the dependent condition consider this more important than subjects in the parallel condition.

During the first stage subjects are assigned the same task and possess the same level of prior knowledge. Subjects were randomly assigned to the dependent and parallel conditions and no significant differences were found in terms of subjects' background, i.e., prior knowledge, search experience, and computer use. Finding significant effects in the first stage indicates the presence of additional factors that possibly interact with the dependent variables. Table 3 shows that subjects in the dependent condition consider the first task easier, a single collection more important, and find the tabbed display easier to use than subjects in the parallel condition.

We also investigate to what extend search strategy is involved in the effects between the two conditions. Table 4 shows a cross tabulation of the search moves with the tabbed display recorded within the dependent and parallel condition. We find that there is a significant relation between the moves made in a display and the conditions ($\chi^2(df$=7,N=1654)=16.2, p=.022). From the standardized residuals we find that especially the following search actions contribute to the significant effect: paginating, bookmarking, using filters and changing collection (tab). Subjects in the dependent condition tend to switch between collections and use the facet filters, while subjects in the parallel condition tend to paginate and bookmark more frequently. This suggests that subjects in the dependent condition initially explore more of the collections while subjects in the parallel condition dig deeper into material of a single source.

5. DISCUSSION

Regarding our first research question, we find that the majority of subjects switch between displays during the project. The main motivation to use the tabbed display is to zoom in on a single source as other sources are not considered relevant at that stage of the project, e.g., Wiki documents are relevant at the start of the project to gather general background information, while photos of specific events become relevant at a later point. The use of the blended display is initially motivated by a need to explore the content of various sources. Later the blended display provides a way to explore multiple sources simultaneously for material related to a specific information need.

With respect to our second research question, we find that when subjects are completing search tasks about the same topic there is a negative influence on the usability of a blended display when switching from a tabbed to a blended display. We also find that when subjects are completing search tasks about different topics there is a decrease in perceived task difficulty when switching from tabbed to blended displays. These findings suggest that subjects are more likely to switch to a blended display when their information need changes since switching is then associated with decreasing task difficulty. While switching to a blended display is less likely when subjects are engaged in a sequence of search tasks related to the same topic because of a negative influence on usability.

Turning to our third research question, we find that there are several factors that influence the preferences of subjects for the tabbed display, i.e., whether subjects find the tabbed display easy to use, whether they find the first search task easy, and whether they find that one of the collections is most important in solving the first search task. These factors limit the generalizability of our findings as the observed interactions between changes in information need and usability (information need and task difficulty) may be specific to our sample with this particular configuration of these factors.

In general, both studies suggest reasons for subjects to change preferences and switch displays during a multi-session search task.

6. RELATED WORK

The work described in this paper expands on work from two fields of study: aggregated search and multi-session tasks. Studies in aggregated search have investigated whether users prefer tabbed or blended displays for single-session search tasks of varying complexity. Most closely related to our study is work by [28] who find that for complex tasks users prefer blended displays. A later study shows that indeed more verticals are clicked when task complexity increases, but that users do not necessarily prefer a blended or tabbed display [4]. As a possible explanation the search experience of the subjects is suggested. We find that the users actually change interface preference during a specific type of multi-session search task depending on changes in information need.

Regarding studies on multi-session search tasks, there is work that shows that increasing topic knowledge affects dwell time [16], which can be used as a predictor for document usefulness. We did not analyze the effect of increasing topic knowledge at this level of granularity and foccussed on the effect of changes in information need rather then the increase of topical knowledge. Other work on understanding multi-session search task is focussed on describing the factors involved [9, 14, 31] and the search patterns of users with existing systems [17, 35]. Our work is different in that it attempts to compare the usefulness of a new type of system to an existing system within the context of a multi-session task.

7. CONCLUSION

Aggregated search interfaces are a promising way to provide users with an overview of results from various sources. In this paper we investigated the use and preferences of users for a tabbed and blended display within the context of a multi-session search tasks. In our first, longitudinal study we observed that the tabbed display is predominantly used motivated by a need to zoom in on specific sources. The majority of subjects, however, switched between the tabbed and blended displays. Use of the blended display was motivated by a need to explore the content of the sources available in the aggregated search system. Initially, subjects desired an overview of the sort of information generally available in the sources, later the blended display was used to obtain an overview whenever a new specific information need arose.

In a laboratory study a multi-session search task was recreated, composed of three tasks with either a tabbed or blended display. The tasks were manipulated by either providing three tasks about the same topic or about three different topics. We found that a stable information need across multiple sub-tasks negatively influences perceived usability of the blended displays, while we do not find an influence when the information need changes.

The combined results from both studies suggest that subjects change display preference during a specific type of multi-session search task, i.e., seeking archival materials across multiple heterogeneous sources during a research project.

Acknowledgements. This research was supported by the European Community's Seventh Framework Programme (FP7/2007-2013) under grant agreements nr 258191 (PROMISE Network of Excellence) and 288024 (LiMoSINe project), the Netherlands Organisation for Scientific Research (NWO) under project nrs 640.004.802, 727.011.005, 612.001.116, HOR-11-10, the Center for Creation, Content and Technology (CCCT), the BILAND project funded by the CLARIN-nl program, the Dutch national program COMMIT, the ESF Research Network Program ELIAS, the Elite Network Shifts project funded by the Royal Dutch Academy of Sciences (KNAW), and the Netherlands eScience Center under project number 027.012.105.

8. REFERENCES

[1] J. Arguello and R. Capra. The effect of aggregated search coherence on search behavior. *CIKM'12*, 2012.

[2] J. Arguello, F. Diaz, and J. Callan. Learning to aggregate vertical results into web search results. In *CIKM'11*, pages 201–210. ACM, 2011.

[3] J. Arguello, F. Diaz, J. Callan, and B. Carterette. A methodology for evaluating aggregated search results. In *Adv. in Inf. Retr.*, pages 141–152. Springer, 2011.

[4] J. Arguello, W. Wu, D. Kelly, and A. Edwards. Task complexity, vertical display and user interaction in aggregated search. In *SIGIR'12*, pages 435–444. ACM, 2012.

[5] A. Aula, R. Khan, and Z. Guan. How does search behavior change as search becomes more difficult? In *SIGCHI'10*, pages 35–44, 2010.

[6] N. J. Belkin. Helping people find what they don't know. *Communications of the ACM*, 43(8):58–61, 2000.

[7] M. Bron, B. Huurnink, and M. de Rijke. Linking archives using document enrichment and term selection. In *TPDL '11*, pages 360–371. Springer, 2011.

[8] M. Bron, J. van Gorp, F. Nack, M. de Rijke, and S. de Leeuw. A subjunctive exploratory search interface to support media studies researchers. In *SIGIR '12*, pages 425–434. ACM, 2012.

[9] K. Byström. Information and information sources in tasks of varying complexity. *JASIST*, 53(7):581–591, 2002.

[10] K. Byström and P. Hansen. Conceptual framework for tasks in information studies. *JASIST*, 56(10):1050–1061, 2005.

[11] N. Denzin. *The research act: A theoretical introduction to sociological methods.* Aldine De Gruyter, 2009.

[12] J. He, M. Bron, and A. de Vries. Characterizing stages of a multi-session complex search task through direct and indirect query modifications. In *SIGIR '13*. ACM, 2013.

[13] J. Huang, R. White, and S. Dumais. No clicks, no problem: using cursor movements to understand and improve search. In *CHI 2011*, pages 1225–1234. ACM, 2011.

[14] C. Kuhlthau. Inside the search process: Information seeking from the user's perspective. *JASIS*, 42(5):361–371, 1991.

[15] Y. Li. Exploring the relationships between work task and search task in information search. *JASIST*, 60(2):275–291, 2008.

[16] J. Liu and N. Belkin. Personalizing information retrieval for multi-session tasks: The roles of task stage and task type. In *SIGIR '10*, pages 26–33. ACM, 2010.

[17] J. Liu, N. Belkin, X. Zhang, and X. Yuan. Examining users' knowledge change in the task completion process. *Information Processing & Management*, 2012.

[18] W. Lu, Q. Wang, and B. Larsen. Simulating aggregated interfaces. *Workshop on Aggregated Search*, pages 24–28, 2012.

[19] J. McGrenere, R. M. Baecker, and K. S. Booth. A field evaluation of an adaptable two-interface design for feature-rich software. *ACM Trans. Comput.-Hum. Interact.*, 14(1), 2007.

[20] M. Melucci and R. Baeza-Yates. *Advanced topics in information retrieval*, volume 33. Springer, 2011.

[21] H. O'Brien and E. Toms. The development and evaluation of a survey to measure user engagement. *JASIST*, 61(1):50–69, 2009.

[22] S. Raghavan and H. Garcia-Molina. Crawling the hidden web. *Stanford Digital Libraries Technical Report*, 2000.

[23] R. Santos, C. Macdonald, and I. Ounis. Aggregated search result diversification. In *Adv. in Inf. Retr.*, pages 250–261. Springer, 2011.

[24] J. Seo, W. Croft, K. Kim, and J. Lee. Smoothing click counts for aggregated vertical search. In *Adv. in Inf. Retr.*, pages 387–398. Springer, 2011.

[25] A. Shiri. Metadata-enhanced visual interfaces to digital libraries. *JIS*, 34(6):763–775, 2008.

[26] M. Shokouhi and L. Si. Federated search. *Found. & Trends in Inf. Retr.*, 2011.

[27] M. D. Smucker and J. Allan. Find-similar: similarity browsing as a search tool. In *SIGIR '06*, pages 461–468. ACM, 2006.

[28] S. Sushmita, H. Joho, and M. Lalmas. A task-based evaluation of an aggregated search interface. In *SPIRE '09*, pages 322–333. Springer, 2009.

[29] S. Sushmita, H. Joho, M. Lalmas, and R. Villa. Factors affecting click-through behavior in aggregated search interfaces. In *CIKM'10*, pages 519–528. ACM, 2010.

[30] D. Tunkelang. Faceted search. *Synthesis Lectures on Information Concepts, Retrieval, and Services*, 1(1):1–80, 2009.

[31] P. Vakkari, M. Pennanen, and S. Serola. Changes of search terms and tactics while writing a research proposal: A longitudinal case study. *Information processing & management*, 39(3):445–463, 2003.

[32] R. White and R. Roth. Exploratory search: Beyond the query-response paradigm. *Synthesis Lectures on Information Concepts, Retrieval, and Services*, 1(1):1–98, 2009.

[33] R. W. White, I. Ruthven, and J. M. Jose. The use of implicit evidence for relevance feedback in web retrieval. In *Adv. in Inf. Retr.*, pages 93–109. Springer, 2002.

[34] T. Wilson. Models in information behaviour research. *J. Doc.*, 55(3):249–270, 1999.

[35] I. Xie and S. Joo. Factors affecting the selection of search tactics: Tasks, knowledge, process, and systems. *Information Processing & Management*, 48(2):254–270, 2012.

An Effective Implicit Relevance Feedback Technique Using Affective, Physiological and Behavioural Features

Yashar Moshfeghi
School of Computing Science
University of Glasgow
Glasgow, UK
Yashar.Moshfeghi@glasgow.ac.uk

Joemon M. Jose
School of Computing Science
University of Glasgow
Glasgow, UK
Joemon.Jose@glasgow.ac.uk

ABSTRACT

The effectiveness of various behavioural signals for implicit relevance feedback models has been exhaustively studied. Despite the advantages of such techniques for a real time information retrieval system, most of the behavioural signals are noisy and therefore not reliable enough to be employed. Among many, a combination of dwell time and task information has been shown to be effective for relevance judgement prediction. However, the task information might not be available to the system at all times. Thus, there is a need for other sources of information which can be used as a substitute for task information. Recently, affective and physiological signals have shown promise as a potential source of information for relevance judgement prediction. However, their accuracy is not high enough to be applicable on their own. This paper investigates whether affective and physiological signals can be used as a complementary source of information for behavioural signals (i.e. dwell time) to create a reliable signal for relevance judgement prediction. Using a video retrieval system as a use case, we study and compare the effectiveness of the affective and physiological signals on their own, as well as in combination with behavioural signals for the relevance judgment prediction task across four different search intentions: seeking information, re-finding a particular information object, and two different entertainment intentions (i.e. entertainment by adjusting arousal level, and entertainment by adjusting mood). Our experimental results show that the effectiveness of studied signals varies across different search intentions, and when affective and physiological signals are combined with dwell time, a significant improvement can be achieved. Overall, these findings will help to implement better search engines in the future.

Categories and Subject Descriptors: H.3.3 Information Storage and Retrieval - *Information Search and Retrieval - Search Process*

SIGIR'13, July 28–August 1, 2013, Dublin, Ireland.
Copyright 2013 ACM 978-1-4503-2034-4/13/07 ...$15.00.

General Terms: Performance, Experimentation

Keywords: Implicit Relevance Feedback, Affective, Physiological, Behavioural, Dwell Time, Search Intentions

1. INTRODUCTION

It has been understood for some time that the formulated queries in an information seeking process do not always provide an adequate description necessary to retrieve relevant documents [39], since it is only an approximation of the actual information need [33]. Likewise, queries formulated may not adequately define the characteristics of relevant documents, or indeed any relevant information because of an *ill-defined* information need situation. Since more complete representations generally lead to more precise search results, supplementing textual queries with additional sources of information, such as documents users have found relevant [26], can be advantageous [37]. Research has shown that searchers can specify the relevance of a document to their needs more easily than explicitly specifying their information needs [31]. Therefore, in order to help the searcher, IR systems have previously employed a range of relevance feedback techniques, where feedback is gathered through explicit [20], implicit [37], and/or affective feedback [1].

Despite the robustness of explicit feedback in improving retrieval effectiveness [20], it is not always applicable or reliable due to the cognitive burden that it places on users [38]. To overcome this cognitive burden, implicit relevance feedback (IRF) is proposed; with relevance inferred instead from behaviour signals (i.e. interactional data) in an indirect and unobtrusive manner [18]. For example, researchers try to understand how dwell time (the time spent by a user on a retrieved document) [19] and task [37] relate to relevance. Dwell time on a document has got a particular interest since it can be detected in real-time [22]. Recent studies have shown that dwell time combined with task information can improve IRF algorithm performance [37]. However, in a real-time situation, task information might not be apparent or easy to obtain in many cases. Hence, there is a need for other sources of information which can be used as a substitute for the task information.

Due to recent advances in technology, new sensory devices have been developed. It is now possible to leverage affective and physiological signals from user while they are interacting with a system. For instance, facial expression recognition, galvanic skin response, heart rate monitoring and electroencephalography provide more information about interaction than ever before. Currently, there are numerous efforts in disciplines that extend beyond IR to understand how such information can be used to improve human-machine interactions, e.g., [29]. The output of these sensory devices has gained notable attention from the IR community, in particular for their effectiveness in predicting relevance. As a result of such studies, affective feedback has been proposed [1] where the intention is to capture facial expression [4], and physiological signals [3] (such as skin temperature) and use them as implicit relevance judgement. Despite the great potential of this information for IRF techniques, the accuracy of such information in the past was not high enough to be used on its own in a real time system.

Our hypothesis is that signals obtained from sensory channels can be considered as a suitable replacement of task information for IRF techniques based on dwell time information. This hypothesis is motivated by the findings of recent studies from both Poddar et al. [30] where they show that tasks with different characteristics stimuli different emotions in the searcher, and Arapakis et al. [1] where they show that relevance information that derives from the selected sensory channels is correlated to user affective behaviour. They investigated whether they can deduce topical relevance by measuring physiological signals taken from the participants, in the context of online information seeking. However, the effect of combining signals obtained from sensory devices with behavioural data has yet to be studied. Successful results steer the situation for using IRF in a real-time system. This paper is an attempt in this vein of research.

To further investigate our hypothesis, we study the effectiveness of such IRF techniques for search tasks with different intentions. Recent advances in query log analysis for search engines such as Google, Yahoo! and Bing has shown that Web searchers' intentions do not always fit into the typical taxonomy of informational, navigational or transactional intentions [34]. Although informational (i.e. to acquire information present on one or more sites), navigational (i.e. to reach a particular site) and transactional (i.e. to perform some Web-mediated activity) intentions are all commonly found in query logs [7], there is an increasing body of evidence showing that re-finding and re-retrieving the visited information is a regular activity by searchers [34, 12]. In addition, there is also recent interest in the notion of entertainment, where the searchers do not have any particular information need [13] and the prime motivation behind their search is to satisfy an emotion need [27]. Thus the effectiveness of these sources of information on their own and in combination with behavioural data (i.e. dwell time) has yet to be studied for search processes with different intentions, i.e. information seeking, re-finding information and/or entertainment.

Therefore, two important questions emerge. First, whether combining sensory channels and behavioural signals provide a reliable set of features for IRF techniques. Second, what would be the effect of different search intentions (e.g. seeking information, re-finding or entertainment) on the relevance judgement predictability of this set of features. In order to investigate our research questions, we use an interactive information retrieval evaluation framework. In particular, we devised four search tasks each of which cover a search intention. We then capture affective and physiological signals of the participants while they were performing the tasks along with their relevance assessment for the visited videos. Finally, we investigate the discriminative power of the captured signals with and without dwell time for predicting the relevance of the assessed videos across different search intentions.

This paper has three novel contributions. First, we studied and compared the discriminative power of multitude sensory channels (i.e. EEG, heart rate, facial expression, skin temperature, etc.) for relevance judgement prediction task. Second, we investigated the possibility of substituting task information with these sensory signals for dwell time based IRF techniques. Finally, we investigated the prediction accuracy of these signals for search processes with different intentions. The rest of the paper is organised as follows: related work is presented in Section 2, the experiment methodology is described in Section 3. Results and discussion are presented in Section 4, and finally, the paper is concluded in Section 5.

2. RELATED WORK

Dwell Time and IRF: Much past research has attempted finding a reliable set of features for IRF techniques [18]. One of the main features investigated researchers is dwell time, due to its applicability for real time systems [22]. Despite early studies by Morita et al. [25] and Claypool et al. [8] where they proposed dwell time as a reliable behavioural signal for IRF, later studies conducted by Kelly and Belkin [19] show that dwell time by its own is not reliable and that it can differ significantly according to specific task, and according to specific user. More recent studies in this path by White and Kelly [37] show that a combination of dwell time and task information is a reliable source of information for IRF techniques. However, information about the search task is not available all the time. Thus many approaches try to predict this information. One of the common way to do so is to use the behavioural signals such as dwell time [21]. However, this approach cannot be useful if the predicted task information is required to be combined with the dwell time itself for IRF. Therefore, clearly there is a need for other sources of information that can be substituted with the task information for dwell time based IRF techniques. This paper is an attempt to investigate this research question.

Task and Emotion: In recent years the relation between the search tasks within an information seeking process (ISP) and emotion has gained much attention. For example, several works studied the emotional impact of search tasks within the ISP [30, 2, 23]. Poddar and Ruthven [30] examined how participants emotion responses are influenced by tasks of different natures. In particular, their results indicate that (i) artificial tasks have higher uncertainty and less sense of ownership than genuine search tasks, and (ii) more complex search tasks have lower positive emotions and more uncertainty before and after searching. Similar findings were earlier reported also by [2] in an information seeking activity. They concluded that users' emotions progressively transit from positive to negative valence as the degree of task difficulty increases. They also found that emotions both interweave with different physiological, psychological and cognitive processes during an information seeking process, and form distinctive patterns according to specific tasks. However, [23] reported no significant relationship between searchers' mood and search tasks due to the complexity involved in such studies. In another study, [17] investigated the relationship between the subjective (e.g. happiness levels, feeling lost during search, etc.) and objective (e.g. search outcomes and search task characteristics, etc.) factors in the ISP. Their results show that "higher happiness levels before the search and during the search correlate with better feelings after the search, but also correlate with worse search outcomes and lower satisfaction, suggesting that, perhaps, it pays off to feel some 'pain' during the search in order to 'gain' quality outcomes" [17]. These valuable insights into the relation between emotion and search task motivated our research. This paper investigates the possibility of substituting task information with experienced emotion to be combined with dwell time in order to have a reliable real time features for IRF techniques. The question that might be raised is how one can capture human emotion.

Affective Relevance Feedback: Recent advances in information technology have facilitated the development of sensory channels to capture human emotion [28, 29, 11]. The argument is that such changes are often expressed through a psycho-physiological mobilisation that is reflected by a series of more or less observable cues, such as facial expressions, body movements, localised changes in the electrodermal activity, variations in the skin temperature, and many more [3]. The affective and physiological (A&P) signals obtained from such devices have provided researchers with additional sources of information not previously available. Thus these A&P signals have gained significant attention in the IR community, and their effectiveness has been studied for numerous tasks and purposes, e.g [1, 3, 4].

The most related work to this paper are the studies conducted by Arapakis and his colleagues on the effectiveness of A&P information for relevance judgment prediction (known as affective feedback) [2]. For example, Arapakis et al. [4] show that affective features captured from facial expression during an information seeking process can be used to develop a multimodal recommendation system. In another study, Arapakis et al. [3] explored the role of affective (captured via facial expression) and physiological signals (captured via skin temperature and body movement) in designing multimedia search systems. They investigated whether topical relevance could be deduced by measuring key physiological signals taken from the user. Finally, In a more recent study, the role of affective signals was studied in a personalised system [1] for topical relevance.

However, two main limitations can be associated with these studies. First, the accuracy of A&P information in the past was not high enough to be used by its own in a real time system. For example, Feild [16] found little benefit from the physiological signals when they tried to used them for searcher frustration prediction where three physical sensors were used: a mental state camera, a pressure sensitive mouse, and a pressure sensitive chair. Given the relation between task characteristics and stimulated emotion in the searcher (explained above) and the possibility of extracting emotion using A&P sensory channels, we hypothesis that a combination of A&P signals with behavioural signals (in particular dwell time) can lead to a reliable set of features for IRF. Second, the effectiveness of A&P information was only investigated for information seeking scenarios where a clear information need is defined (i.e. topical relevance). Thus the effectiveness of such sensory channels for a more realistic representation of real life search process has yet to be studied, where variety of tasks with different intentions are proposed. This paper is an attempt to investigate this research problem.

Seeking Information on the Web: Traditionally, the general belief of the Information Retrieval (IR) community was that the dominant intention of people engaging in search processes was informational [7]. However, Broder [7] shows the existence of search intents other than the assumed informational intent, i.e. navigational and transactional. In more recent studies, researchers have identified a wider range of search intents that go beyond Broader's taxonomy of intentions, i.e. re-finding [34] and entertainment [13]. Re-finding the visited information has been shown to be a regular activity by searchers [34, 12]. Teevan et al. [34], by analysing Yahoo! Web query logs showed that up to 40% of the submitted queries were re-finding queries. Elsweiler et al. [12], in an empirical study, showed that it is possible to isolate re-finding behaviour in search logs through various qualitative and quantitative analyses. Given this evidence, it is important to study the effect of affective, physiological and behavioural signals in the re-finding intention.

In addition, recently there is an increased effort in the research community to explore search processes with entertainment intents, e.g. "Entertain Me" [5] and "Search4FUN" [14] workshops. Besides the works published in these workshops, [13] attempted to understand the needs and motivation underlying leisure-based activities in the context of television viewing. They reported that the nature of the need and motivation are different between leisure-based and work-based situations where most of the needs reported for leisure-based situation are motivated by a desire to change mood, emotion, or arousal level. Further research related to leisure-based activity is the work by [32] which studies pleasure reading behaviour. Their results show that pleasure readers find information without having any prior information need. In addition, [40] and in a more in-depth study, [15], reported that in casual search, the motivation is not to resolve an information need, but hedonistic, e.g. entertainment driven.

Given the emergence of entertainment seeking intentions on the Web and their unexplored characteristics, it is also important to study the effect of affective, physiological and behavioural signals in entertainment seeking intentions. The defined entertainment seeking intentions in this paper are based on research done by Zillmann [36], who was instrumental in the establishing a range of theories in this domain. Zillmann and his colleagues posit that entertainment choices are a reflection of a basic human need to enhance or retain positive states, and to lessen or steer clear of negative ones [27]. They have suggested two possible states in which there may be a need for regulation: physiological arousal and affect. In the case of physiological arousal, their study suggests that users might be over-stimulated (i.e., stressed) or under-stimulated (i.e., boredom). In the case of affect states, it suggests that users might be in negative (i.e. dysphoric) or positive (i.e. upbeat) moods. An individual experiencing such states will choose their entertainment content according to their expectations of what would lead them back to an optimal state [27]. Thus, we investigate two entertainment seeking intentions: entertainment by adjusting arousal level and entertainment by adjusting mood.

3. EXPERIMENTAL METHODOLOGY

3.1 Experiment Design

This study used a within subject design. The independent variable was the search intents (with four levels: "Information Seeking" (INS), "Information Re-finding" (INF), "Entertainment by adjusting Arousal" (ENA), "Entertainment by adjusting Mood" (ENM)), which was controlled by the simulated search task given to the participants (see Section 3.2). We did not perform any control on the number of relevant and irrelevant results, in order to simulate a real search scenario situation as much as possible. The dependent variables were: (i) task perception and (ii) relevance judgment prediction accuracy.

3.2 Tasks

Four search tasks were devised, each simulating a search intent. The structural framework of simulated need situations [6] were used to present search tasks. By doing so, short cover stories were introduced that helped us describe to our participants the source of their information need, the problem to be solved and the environment of the situation. This facilitated a better understanding of the search objective and introduced a layer of realism, while preserving well-defined relevance criteria. In the following, each of the search tasks is explained in detail.

INS Task: This search task simulates the information seeking search intent. Information seeking is the most studied search intent in the information seeking and retrieval domain. This task is designed as a control group since the majority of studies on relevance judgement prediction in the past were based on a similar search task intent. For this search task, we prepared a number of search topics that covered a variety of contexts in order to capture participants' interests as best as possible. The topics, presented in Table 1, were all checked manually prior to the experiment, to ensure the availability of relevant documents. The simulated search scenario for INS task was as follows: *"Imagine you have graduated recently and are going to interview for a job in a local company. As part of the interview process, you are asked to explain and expand on the area you will be working on. You feel very enthusiastic about the interview; however, due to your lack of knowledge you would like to find out more about this particular topic before taking part in the interview."* Each participant was then asked to choose one of the topics that they were unfamiliar with but consider interesting. Using the video retrieval system, they had to find as many relevant videos as possible so that they could acquire a good knowledge about their selected topic.

Table 1: Search topics for the information seeking task scenario.

Obtaining information regarding contraception methods.
Investigating new knowledge on global warming.
Formulating an opinion about existing social networking sites.

INF Task: This search task simulates the information re-finding search intent. There are two differences between this task and the previous one: (i) there is only one document that can satisfy the information need of the searcher, and (ii) the searcher has seen the relevant documents at some point before initiating the search process and is now attempting to re-find it. The similarity between this task and the previous one is that in both cases searchers have an information need. For this search task, we prepared a number of videos that covered a variety of contexts in order to capture participants' interests as best as possible. The videos were intentionally selected as they would likely be very hard to find because they lacked textual description. The motivation was to simulate a challenging information re-finding process where the recalled terms are very ambiguous and do not lead directly to the relevant item. This would better represent many realistic re-finding tasks, when the user cannot recall the exact description of the item they are looking for. The simulated search scenario for INF task was as follows: *"Imagine you are discussing a video which you have seen few days ago with your friends. They are interested in seeing the video and have asked you to send them a link to it. You can remember the content of the video but you cannot remember its title or any textual information which can help you in retrieving it."* Each participant was then asked to select and watch one of the three videos presented to them (an animal[1], martial arts[2], or a science video[3]) that they are unfamiliar with and consider interesting. Once participants watched the video, they were asked to find it as fast as possible.

ENA Task: This search task simulates the entertainment-based search intent where searchers adjust their arousal level. The main difference between this task and the two tasks before is that the primary need is hedonistic rather than informational. Therefore, to accurately simulate such search processes, we avoid introducing any explicit information need. Thus, for this search task, we did not prepare any specific search topic. This decision is motivated by the literature in sociology [27] and the information seeking and retrieval domain on entertainment [13]. The simulated search scenario for the ENA task was as follows: *"Imagine you are working in a factory as a night-guard. You have just finished your routine checks and will be taking out more checks shortly. You are tired so you decide to watch some videos to wake yourself up and make yourself ready for your next round of checks."* Each participant was asked to find as many relevant videos as possible that make them feel excited.

ENM Task: This search task simulates the entertainment-based search intent where searchers adjust their mood. Similar to ENA task, searchers engage in such search processes with hedonistic rather than informational needs. Therefore, to accurately simulate this search process, we avoid introducing any explicit information need. Thus, similar to the ENA task, we did not provide any pre-prepared search topic. The simulated search scenario for the ENM task was as follows: *"Imagine your boyfriend/girlfriend is travelling and communication access is very limited. It is now a few days since he/she has gone and you are missing him/her very much. You are feeling very sad and in order to change your mood, you have decided to watch some videos."* Each participant was asked to find as many relevant videos as possible that make them feel happy.

Questionnaires: At the beginning of the experiment, the participants were given an *entry questionnaire*. This gathered background and demographic information, and inquired about previous experience with online videos, in particular, browsing and searching habits including their inten-

[1] www.youtube.com/v/wx7rY1lqb0k&showinfo=0

[2] www.youtube.com/v/pEUeP7hx8fs&showinfo=0

[3] www.youtube.com/v/P8Cs2t05w74&showinfo=0

tions. At the end of each task, the participants completed a *post-task questionnaire* to elicit the subject's viewpoint on certain aspects of the search process, in particular their perception of the encountered task. All of the questions included in these questionnaires were a forced-choice type. Finally, an *exit questionnaire* was introduced at the end of the study. In this questionnaire we gathered information about the encountered system as well as the user study in general: which task they preferred and why, and their general comments about the user study.

Procedure: The user study was carried out in the following manner. The formal meeting with the participants took place in a laboratory setting. At the beginning of the session the participants were given an information sheet which explained the conditions of the experiment. They were then asked to sign a Consent Form and were notified about their right to withdraw at any point during the study, without affecting their legal rights or benefits. Then, they were given an Entry Questionnaire to fill in.

The session proceeded with a brief tutorial on the use of the search interface. Then participants were helped to wear the sensory devices, followed by a calibration of the web-camera. After completion of this step, each participant had to complete four search tasks (explained in Section 3.2), one for each level of search process intentions (see Section 3.1). To negate the order and fatigue effects we counter-balanced the task distribution using a Latin Square design. The subjects were asked every time to provide judgment for any video that they watch, and were given 10 minutes to complete their task, during which they were left unattended to work. At the end of each task, the subjects were asked to complete a post-task questionnaire. Questions in the post-task questionnaire were randomised to avoid the effect of fatigue. Between each task, a cooling-off period was applied to minimise the carry-over effect. An exit questionnaire was administered at the end of the session. Finally, the participants were asked to sign a payment form, prior to receiving the payment of £12.

Each study took approximately 120 minutes to complete; this is from the time they accepted the conditions until they signed the payment receipt. Users could only participate once in the study. The total cost of the evaluation was £348, including the cost of the pilot studies. A user study with the procedure explained above was conduced over a period of 10 days from 16th to 26th of July 2012. The results of these studies are presented in Section 4.

Apparatus: For our experiment we used one desktop computer, equipped with a monitor, keyboard, and mouse. The computer provided access to a custom-made video retrieval system explained in Section 3.4. The web-camera (Creative Live! Cam Optia AF with a 2.0 megapixels sensor) was used in combination with eMotion [35], for real-time facial expression analysis. In addition, we used three unobtrusive wearable devices to capture participants' physiological signals: (i) Polar RS800 Heart Rate Monitor, and (ii) BodyMedia SenseWear® Pro3 Armband (iii) NeuroSky MindKit-EM™headset. All devices and systems were logging using a common system time. Finally, we used entry, post and exit questionnaires in each session.

3.3 Sensory Channels

Affective Signals: In this study we considered facial expression as our affective signal. This decision was motivated by the findings of previous studies in IR related to this paper [1] as well as findings from other domains showing that emotions are primarily communicated through facial expressions [28] and facial expressions can be associated with universally distinguished emotions, e.g. happiness, sadness, anger, fear, disgust, and surprise [11]. We applied a real-time facial expression analysis using an automatic facial expression recognition system with emotion-detection capabilities (i.e. eMotion) [35]. The process of recognition occurred as follows: initially, eMotion would locate certain facial landmark features (eyebrows, corners of the mouth, etc.) and construct a 3-dimensional wireframe model of the face, consisting of surface patches wrapped around it. After construction of the model, head motion or any other facial deformation would be tracked and measured in terms of motion-units (MU's), and, finally, classified into one of the six detectable emotion categories plus neutral. eMotion applies a generic classifier that has been trained on a diverse data set, combining data from the Cohn-Kanade database. The main advantage of this system is its reasonable performance across all individuals, irrespective of the variation introduced from mixed-ethnicity groups. Results of the person-dependent and person-independent tests presented in [35] support our performance-related assumptions. For additional information regarding the advantages and limitations of eMotion the reader is referred to [35].

Physiological Signals: In order to capture physiological signals we consider multiple sensory channels including heart rate monitoring, skin temperature, and neural activity. This decision was also motivated by the findings of previous studies in IR related to this paper [3]. Emotions can be expressed through several sensory channels and are reflected by a series of more or less observable cues, such as localised changes in the electrodermal activity, variations in skin temperature, neural activity and many more. It has been shown that transitions between emotional states are correlated with temporal changes in physiological states [9], which cannot be easily faked. In this work we monitor participants' physiological responses by using three sensory devices: Polar RS800, BodyMedia SenseWear® Pro3 Armband and NeuroSky's MindKit-EM™.

Polar RS800 Heart Rate Monitor consists of the Polar RS800 Running Computer, a wrist-watch that displays and records the heart rate data, an elastic strap with two electrodes and Polar WearLink® 31, a wireless transmitter. The elastic strap is worn around the chest (below the chest muscles), allowing the built-in soft textile electrodes to detect the heartbeat and then transmit the heart rate signal to the running computer, via the Polar WearLink R 31, which is attached to the strap.

BodyMedia SenseWear® Pro3 Armband is an unobtrusive, lightweight, multi-sensor hub, which is worn above the triceps area of the right arm. It can simultaneously measure five low-level physiological metrics: (i) galvanic skin response, (ii) skin temperature, (iii) near-body ambient temperature, (iv) heat flux, and (v) motion, via a 3-axis accelerometer. From those vital sign streams it can produce accurate statements about the human body states and behaviours. Moreover, the existence of multiple sensors allows for the disambiguation of contexts, which a single sensor would have not interpreted accurately.

NeuroSky MindKit-EM™ consists of hardware and software components for simple integration of bio-sensor tech-

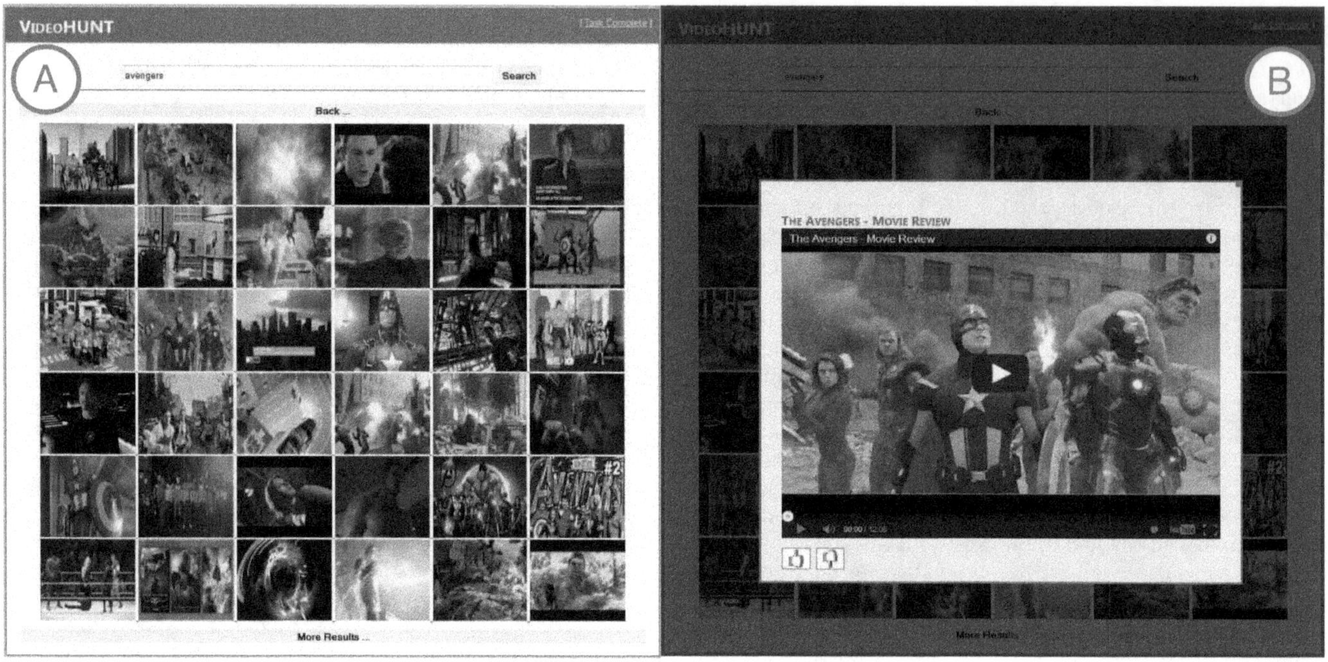

Figure 1: A snapshot of the video retrieval system for query "avengers".

nology into consumer and industrial end-applications. NeuroSky MindKit-EM™ features two key technologies: (i) ThinkGear-EM™ headset and (ii) eSense-EM™ software (i.e. brainwave interpretation software). The headset is used to extract, filter, and amplify brainwave (EEG) signals and convert that information into digital mental state outputs for eSense-EM™ software. The EEG signals read by the MindKit-EM™ are detected on the forehead via points Fp1 (electrode placement system by the International Federation in Encephalography and Clinical Neurophysiology). The headset has three dry active sensors: one sensor located on the forehead and two sensors are located behind the ears as ground/reference sensors. It also has electronic circuitry that filters and amplifies the brainwaves. The eSense-EM™ software further processes and analyses the obtained brainwave signals into two useful neuro-sensory values: the user's Attention[4] and Meditation[5] levels at any given moment. The output of eSense-EM™ software has been tested over a wide population and under different environmental conditions, to work across a wide spectrum of individuals.

3.3.1 Features

For our affective features, we considered 19 features (referred to as "FX") extracted from the output of eMotion: 7 features related to the classified emotions (i.e. happiness, sadness, anger, fear, disgust, and surprise) plus neutral and 12 features related to the motion units (MU's) data, which is a low-level category of features very similar to Ekman's action-units (AU's) [10]. For our physiological features, we considered the heart rate data (referred to as "HR") from the output of the Polar RS800 Heart Rate Monitor; the galvanic skin response, skin temperature, near-body ambient temperature, heat flux, and motion data (referred to as "AB") from the output of the BodyMedia SenseWear® Pro3 Armband; and the Attention or Meditation data (referred to as "NV") from the output of the eSense-EM™ software. For our behavioural signal, we considered the dwell time (referred to as "DT") logged by the system as our dwell time feature. Finally the task intention was considered as task feature (referred to as "Task").

Preprocessing: For each visited video, the value of each sensory feature (for both affective and physiological features) was calculated by averaging the data logged by its sensory device during the dwell time period. Since none of the instruments we used normalised the data, we scaled signal values before applying any classification method, to avoid having attributes in greater numeric ranges dominating those in smaller numeric ranges.

3.4 Video Retrieval System

For the completion of the search tasks we used a custom-made search environment (named *VideoHunt*) that was designed to resemble the basic layout of existing video retrieval services, while retaining a minimum of graphical elements and distractions. VideoHunt works on top of the Bing Video Search API. For every query submitted, it returned a list of 100 results (36 results on each page), stripped of their title, snippet and any other metadata. This layout was intentional to ensure that the participants would judge the relevance of videos only after they have examined them. Even though this approach introduced our participants into artificial search situations which differ from real-life experiences, it was a necessary trade-off for capturing affective responses exhibited towards the viewed content.

Search Interface: The layered architecture approach of VideoHunt interface is shown in Figure 1. The first layer of the interface is dedicated to supporting any interaction that occurs during the early stages of the search process (such as query formulation and search execution). Any output generated during this phase is presented in the second layer (shown in Figure 1 - A). From there, participants could

[4]Attention Meter: Combination of waves associated with being in a state of readiness and thinking. It relates to mental arithmetic, concentration and creative thinking.

[5]Meditation Meter: Combination of waves associated with a state of calm and tranquility.

easily select and preview any of the retrieved clips. The content of a clip is shown on a separate panel, in the foreground (shown in Figure 1 - B), which corresponds to the third layer of our system. The main reason behind this layered architecture was to isolate the viewed content from all possible distractions that reside on the desktop screen; therefore, establishing additional ground truth that allowed us to relate participants' affective responses to the source of stimuli (in our case, the perused videos). This was an important aspect of our experimental methodology, since we were interested in isolating content-specific emotions. In addition, in the context of video retrieval, we would expect less interaction with the system during the dwell time making the captured physiological signals particularly valuable in this type of environment. Upon viewing the clip, the participants had to explicitly indicate the relevance of the video. Finally, the length of time a user spent watching a clip (dwell time) was monitored and logged by the search interface.

Pilot Studies: Prior to running the actual user study, a pilot study was performed using 5 participants to confirm that the process worked correctly and smoothly. A number of changes were made to the system based on feedback from the pilot study. The changes consisted of modifications to the system to improve logging capabilities and improvements to the tasks. After the final pilot, it was determined that the participants were able to complete the user study without problems and that the system was capturing all necessary data.

Participants: Participants consisted of 24 healthy people with equal gender distribution (12 female and 12 male) all under the age of 41, with the largest group between the ages of 18-23 (45.8%) followed by the group between ages of 24-29 (36%). Participants tended to have a high school diploma or equivalent (4.16%), college degree (4.16%), bachelors (41.66%) or graduate degree (50%). They were primarily students (62.5%), though there were a number of self-employed (16.6%), not employed (4.16%) and employed by a company or organisation (16.6%).

4. RESULTS AND DISCUSSION

In this section we present the experimental findings of our study, based on the 96 search sessions that were carried out by 24 subjects. We first discuss the task perception expressed in the questionnaire. Following this, we discuss the predictability of search intentions based on features derived from the user interaction with the system in Section 4.1.

Task Perception: Figures 2 shows the box plots for the qualitative analysis of users' perception of the four tasks (i.e. INS, INF, ENA, and ENM). Each box plot reports data aggregated from 24 participants, along with five key statistics: the minimum, first, second (median), third, and maximum quartiles.[6] We performed an ANOVA test between measures obtained at each phase, across four search tasks for each user to check the significance of the difference among them. The test is suitable for this data as we have four groups of data, therefore we need to compare four means and variances. We use (*) and (**) to denote the fact that a measure had results different across four search tasks with the confidence levels ($p < 0.05$) and ($p < 0.01$), respectively.

In the post-task questionnaire we measured participants' perception of their performed task in terms of the difficulty of the task, the familiarity of the participant with the task, the extent to which they found the task stressful, interesting and clear by asking the following question *"The task we asked you to perform was [easy/stressful/interesting/ clear/familiar] (answer: 1: "Strongly Disagree", 2: "Disagree", 3: "Neutral", 4: "Agree", 5: "Strongly Agree")".* The results shown in Figure 2 indicate that participants found the INF task difficult and stressful, followed by the INS task, whereas they found other two tasks easy and not-stressful (the differences were statistically significant). The difference in the answer provided by the participants for interesting, clear and familiar measures is not statistically significant. In the post-task questionnaire we also asked the opinion of the participants with respect to the following statement *"I had enough time to do an effective search.] (answer: 1: "Strongly Disagree", 2: "Disagree", 3: "Neutral", 4: "Agree", 5: "Strongly Agree")".* The results show that they found the time given enough to do an effective search task, (INS: M=4.0 SD=0.88, INF: M=3.8 SD=0.96, ENA: M=4.0 SD=0.97, ENM: M=4.3 SD=0.56, the differences are however not statistically significant across the tasks).

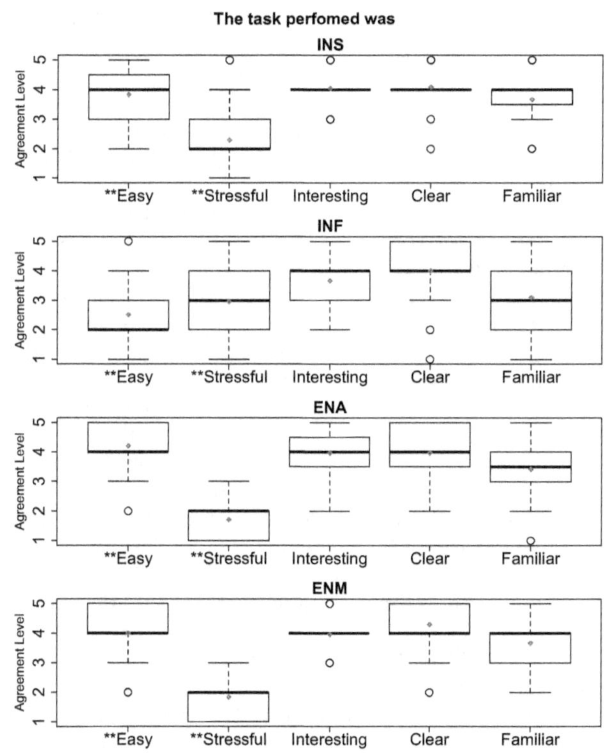

Figure 2: Box plot of the task perception based on the information gathered from 24 participants questionnaires. The diamond represents the mean value. (*) and (**) indicate confidence levels ($p < 0.05$) and ($p < 0.01$) respectively.

4.1 Relevance Prediction

In this section, we investigate our research questions introduced in Section 1. We first study the main effect of using affective, physiological and behavioural signals for the relevance judgement prediction task, by combining the relevance judgement obtained from our four search intents. We then study the interaction effect of these signals with search intents for the relevant judgment prediction task. For this

[6] Further information can be found in [24].

purpose, the features explained in Section 3.3.1 were used. In total, participants judged 488 videos (with 247 relevant, 50.60%), of which 141 (with 82 relevant, 64.53%), 128 (with 91 relevant, 64.06%), 133 (with 73 relevant, 54.88%), and 86 (with 1 relevant, 1.17%) videos belong to "ENM", "ENA", "INS", and "INF" respectively. Due to the ratio of relevant to non-relevant videos for INF task, we consider two combination scenarios: one where the relevance judgments of all tasks are combined (referred to as "ALL") and another one where the relevance judgments of all tasks are combined, except those for the INF task (referred to as "ALL - INF").

For relevance prediction, we have a binomial classification problem where the classes are "+1" (relevant) and "-1" (non-relevant). We used SMO, an implementation of SVM in Weka,[7] to discriminate between the two classes explained above. We trained our models using a polynomial kernel which in the majority of cases outperformed other SVM kernels (e.g. radial-basis) based on our analysis, not presented due to the space limits. For each classification method we present only the model which achieved the best performance among the rest in its category.

Table 2 shows the classification performance averaged over the 24 participants of the study across four different search tasks. It reports the accuracy of the model (i.e. fraction of items in the test set for which the models' predictions were correct) using 10-fold cross-validation.

For the scenarios where only sensory signals are used to train a model, the baseline represents an untrained model where all its predictions are biased to a dominant class (referred to as "BL1"). This baseline is more realistic than a baseline which is based on a random choice (i.e. where its accuracy is set to 50%). Any feature set that results in higher accuracy than what is reported for BL1 is as a result of the discriminative power of the set itself. For the scenarios where dwell time and sensory signals are used to train a model, the baseline represents a model trained on the dwell time feature only (referred to as "BL2"). Finally, for the scenarios where dwell time, task and sensory signals are used to train a model, the baseline represents a model trained based on dwell time and task features (referred to as "BL3"). We also performed a paired Wilcoxon test between the predictions obtained for each model to check the significance of the difference with its baseline. We use [(*) and (**)], [(†) and (††)], and [(‡) and (‡‡)] to denote the fact that a model trained on a set of features had results different from that of "BL1", "BL2", and "BL3" with the confidence levels [($p < 0.05$) and ($p < 0.01$)] respectively.

Main Results: The key findings which emerged from the results are that combining dwell time with sensory signals provides a reliable set of features for IRF techniques. This means that sensory signals can be used as a good substitution for task information for dwell time based IRF techniques. We also observed that the effectiveness of dwell time as well as sensory channel signals vary across the search intentions. In the remainder of this section we discuss each of our research questions in more detail.

RQ1: which combination of affective, physiological and behavioural signals provide a reliable set of features for IRF techniques? In order to answer this research question we study the main effect of these signals for the relevance prediction task. This is an attempt to simulate a real life scenario where the system has to predict the relevance judgement for search processes with different (and in the majority of the cases, unidentified) intentions. Therefore, we only consider the results obtained for the scenarios where the model has to predict the relevance judgement gathered from multiple search intentions (i.e. "All - INF" and "ALL" columns).

Behavioural and Sensory Signals: Considering dwell time with only one sensory signal at a time as a feature set, the findings show that the combination of facial expression features and dwell time results in the highest accuracy (i.e. "DT+FX" row). The findings show that a higher accuracy can be achieved when the model has been trained on a feature set that has dwell time and all the sensory signals (i.e. "DT+FX+AB+HR+NV" row). This finding suggests the complementary nature of the information obtained through various behavioural and sensory signals. Furthermore, they also outperform the scenario where dwell time and task features are used to train a model, showing that this set of features is a reliable substitute for IRF techniques

Sensory Signals: Considering each sensory signal individually as a feature set, the findings show that for the situation where the model has to predict the relevance judgement gathered for all studied search intentions (i.e. "ALL" column), facial expression features results in the highest accuracy (i.e. "FX" row). However such an observation cannot be made for the situation where the model has to predict the relevance judgement gathered for multiple search intentions except those of the re-finding intention (i.e. "All - INF" column). The difference in the accuracy of facial expression features between "ALL" and "All - INF" situations suggest that facial expression features can discriminate relevance judgments of the tasks which have a significant difference in their difficulty. The results indicate that if there is no significant difference in the task difficulty, the heart rate feature provides the highest accuracy in relevance judgement prediction (i.e. "HR" row). The findings show that a higher accuracy again can be achieved when the model has been trained on a feature set that is based on all sensory signals (i.e. "FX+AB+HR+NV" row).

Behavioural Signals: Considering only dwell time, the findings show that for the situation where the model has to predict the relevance judgement gathered for all studied search intentions (i.e. "ALL" column), the dwell time feature results in a high accuracy level. However, once the model has to predict the relevance judgements gathered for multiple search intentions except those of re-finding intention (i.e. "All - INF" column), its effectiveness decreases. Our findings also show that the combination of dwell time and task information improves the accuracy of the relevance judgement prediction significantly, only if the performed tasks varies in some aspect, such as difficulty (as it is in our case). This finding supports the results obtained by Kelly and Belkin [19]. We observe that if the performed tasks does not vary significantly in their characteristics, task information do not provide any additional value and it can also significantly harm the accuracy.

In the Presence of Task Information: Finally, we investigated the effect of having task information along with dwell time and all the sensory signals on the accuracy of relevance judgment prediction (i.e. "DT+Task+FX+AB+HR+NV" row). The findings show that the prediction accuracy of a model trained on these features is significantly higher than

[7] http://www.cs.waikato.ac.nz/ml/weka/

Table 2: This table shows the prediction accuracy of a model trained on different sets of features (presented as rows), given different search intentions (presented as columns). The best performing set of features for each condition and search intention is highlighted in bold.

	INS	*ENA*	*ENM*	*INF*	*ALL - INF*	*ALL*
Random [BL1](*)	54.88%	64.06%	64.53%	98.83%	61.19%	50.60%
DT [BL2](†)	62.40%	65.62%	66.16%	98.83%	71.31%	72.74%
DT+Task [BL3](‡)	-%	-%	-%	-%	69.65%	76.63%
FX	55.63%* (+1.3%)	**66.4%** (+3.6%)**	64.53% (+0%)	98.83% (+0%)	62.43%** (+2.0%)	**64.54%** (+27.4%)**
AB	54.88% (+0%)	64.06% (+0%)	64.53% (+0%)	98.83% (+0%)	61.19% (+0%)	50.60% (+0%)
HR	**57.89%** (+5.4%)**	64.06% (+0%)	64.53% (+0%)	98.83% (+0%)	**62.93%** (+2.8%)**	53.27%** (+5.2%)
NV	55.63%* (+1.3%)	64.06% (+0%)	64.53% (+0%)	98.83% (+0%)	61.19% (+0%)	55.73%** (+10.1%)
FX+AB+HR+NV	55.63%* (+1.3%)	**69.53%** (+8.5%)**	64.53% (+0%)	98.83% (+0%)	**67.16%** (+9.7%)**	**65.98%** (+30.3%)**
DT+FX	**67.66%†† (+8.4%)**	68.75%†† (+4.7%)	71.63%†† (+8.2%)	98.83% (+0%)	**72.88%†† (+2.2%)**	**77.04%†† (+5.9%)**
DT+AB	66.91%†† (+7.2%)	67.96%†† (+3.5%)	81.56%†† (+23.2%)	98.83% (+0%)	71.64% (+0.4%)	76.22%†† (+4.5%)
DT+HR	63.15%† (+1.2%)	**73.43%†† (+11.9%)**	**82.26%†† (+24.3%)**	98.83% (+0%)	72.13%† (+1.1%)	76.22%†† (+4.5%)
DT+NV	64.41%†† (+3.2%)	70.31%†† (+7.1%)	74.46%†† (+12.5%)	98.83% (+0%)	72.13%† (+1.1%)	75.40%†† (+5.6%)
DT+FX+AB+HR+NV	66.16%†† (+6.0%)	**75%†† (+14.2%)**	80.14%†† (+21.1%)	98.83% (+0%)	**75.37%†† (+5.6%)**	**77.04%†† (+5.9%)**
DT+Task+FX+AB+HR+NV	-%	-%	-%	-%	**76.36%‡‡ (+9.6%)**	**78.89%‡‡ (+2.9%)**

the prediction accuracy of a model trained on dwell time and task features significantly (i.e. "DT+Task" row). The results also show that the prediction accuracy of such a model is even higher than a model trained on all features except task one (i.e. "DT+FX+AB+HR+NV" row). This show that researches on task prediction are complementary to this study rather than contradictory.

RQ2: What would be the accuracy of these feature sets with respect to different search intentions? In order to answer this research question we study the interaction effect of these signals with search intentions for relevance prediction task. Therefore, we consider the results obtained for the scenarios where the model has to predict the relevance judgement gathered from one search intention at a time (i.e. "INS", "ENM", "ENA" and "INF" columns). Overall, the results do not show any general pattern, meaning that the effectiveness of different signals are task dependent. We exclude the "INF" intention from our further analysis, since for "INF" intention, almost all of the judged videos were non-relevant, additionally the accuracy of "BL1" model is too high to be outperformed by any of our models.

The findings suggests that sensory channels combined with dwell time performs better for the search intentions which do not have a clear information need (i.e. "ENM" and "ENA") than the ones that do (i.e "INS"). For search processes with entertainment-based intentions, a combination of heart rate and dwell time features results in the highest accuracy. For search processes with information seeking intention, combination of facial expression and dwell time feature is the highest accuracy. In particular, the results suggest that for the ENM task, heart rate and skin temperature; for ENA task, heart rate and EEG; for INS task, facial expression and skin temperature are the best two sensory signals, once they are combined with dwell time. Search processes for which the purpose is to satisfy an information need, facial expression and skin temperature are the best two sensory channels once they are combined with dwell time information.

An interesting finding is that the discriminative power of sensory signals changes once they are combined with dwell time, even though they show no such power individually. For example, a sensory feature that was not discriminative on its own for a task (e.g. "HR" feature for "ENM" task), when combined with dwell time, can result in the highest prediction accuracy (i.e. "DT+HR" features for "ENM" task). In addition, the findings suggest that across all search tasks, combining each sensory signal with dwell time results in a higher accuracy compared to the situation where only either of them is used. The combination of all the sensory channels does not result in the highest accuracy, except for the "ENA" task. Similar behaviour is observed when these features are combined with dwell time one.

Finally, comparison of the accuracy obtained from BL2 (dwell time) and BL1 show that dwell time performs better for tasks based on information needs (i.e. "INS") than tasks based on hedonistic needs (i.e. "ENA" and "ENM"). However, the findings show that the accuracy of the dwell time feature and sensory channels by themselves is not high and is task dependent. This finding supports the results obtained by previous studies, i.e. [19] for dwell time feature and [3] for sensory features.

5. CONCLUSIONS

In this paper we investigated the discriminative power of different sensory channel signals as a reliable substitute for task information for IRF techniques based on dwell time, given different search intentions. In order to do so, we devised four search tasks, each simulating one of the following search intentions: information seeking, re-finding, entertainment adjusting arousal level and entertainment adjusting mood. Using a video retrieval system as a use case, we conducted a user study with 24 participants. We then studied two research questions: (1) which combination of affective, physiological and behavioural signals provide a reliable set of features for IRF techniques? and (2) what would be the accuracy of these feature sets with respect to different search intentions? The findings show that combining dwell time with sensory signals provides a reliable set of features for IRF techniques, and the sensory signals can be used as a good substitution of task information for dwell time based IRF techniques. We also observed that the effectiveness of both the dwell time feature as well as sensory channel signals vary across different search intentions. The major implication of our work is in developing real time interactive systems.

Finally, although the findings of this paper are limited to the video retrieval domain and not generalizable, they motivate the exploration of similar hypotheses in other domains. Even though significant improvement in relevance prediction were achieved by adding affective and physiological measures across different search task types, we acknowledge the following limitations: first, the experiment was conduced in an artificial situation (i.e. a laboratory setting) which lacks the ecological validity of a naturalistic study. Second, only one behavioural signal (i.e. dwell time) was considered in this experiment. Our positive findings encourage us to explore more exhaustively behavioural signals such as click-through and mouse movement as well as eye movement in combination with affective, physiological signals for future work. Finally, it will be some time before physiological signals can be used by practical applications. Therefore, the study in this area is in its infancy. There are still many research questions left to be answered. The findings of this paper lay the foundation for further studies to address these areas.

6. ACKNOWLEDGEMENT

This work was supported by the EU FP7 LiMoSINe project (288024).

7. REFERENCES

[1] I. Arapakis, K. Athanasakos, and J. M. Jose. A comparison of general vs personalised affective models for the prediction of topical relevance. In *SIGIR*, pages 371–378, 2010.

[2] I. Arapakis, J. M. Jose, and P. D. Gray. Affective feedback: an investigation into the role of emotions in the information seeking process. In *SIGIR*, pages 395–402, 2008.

[3] I. Arapakis, I. Konstas, and J. M. Jose. Using facial expressions and peripheral physiological signals as implicit indicators of topical relevance. In *ICMR*, pages 461–470, 2009.

[4] I. Arapakis, Y. Moshfeghi, H. Joho, R. Ren, D. Hannah, and J. M. Jose. Enriching user profiling with affective features for the improvement of a multimodal recommender system. *CIVR*, 2009.

[5] N. Belkin, C. Clarke, N. Gao, J. Kamps, and J. Karlgren. Report on the sigir workshop on entertain me: supporting complex search tasks. *ACM SIGIR Forum*, 45(2):51–59, 2012.

[6] P. Borlund and P. Ingwersen. The development of a method for the evaluation of interactive information retrieval systems. *Journal of documentation*, 53(3):225–250, 1997.

[7] A. Broder. A taxonomy of web search. *ACM Sigir forum*, 36(2):3–10, 2002.

[8] M. Claypool, P. Le, M. Wased, and D. Brown. Implicit interest indicators. In *IUI*, pages 33–40, 2001.

[9] R. Cornelius. Theoretical approaches to emotion. In *ISCA Tutorial and Research Workshop (ITRW) on Speech and Emotion*, 2000.

[10] P. Ekman. Facial expressions. *Handbook of cognition and emotion*, pages 301–320, 1999.

[11] P. Ekman. *Emotions revealed: Recognizing faces and feelings to improve communication and emotional life.* Times Books, 2003.

[12] D. Elsweiler, M. Harvey, and M. Hacker. Understanding re-finding behavior in naturalistic email interaction logs. In *SIGIR*, pages 35–44. ACM, 2011.

[13] D. Elsweiler, S. Mandl, and B. Kirkegaard Lunn. Understanding casual-leisure information needs: a diary study in the context of television viewing. In *IIiX*, pages 25–34, 2010.

[14] D. Elsweiler, M. Wilson, and M. Harvey. Searching4fun. *ECIR workshop*, 2012.

[15] D. Elsweiler, M. Wilson, and B. Lunn. Understanding casual-leisure information behaviour. *Library and Information Science*, 211:241, 2011.

[16] H. A. Feild, J. Allan, and R. Jones. Predicting searcher frustration. In *SIGIR*, pages 34–41, 2010.

[17] J. Gwizdka and I. Lopatovska. The role of subjective factors in the information search process. *JASIST*, 60(12):2452–2464, 2009.

[18] T. Joachims, L. Granka, B. Pan, H. Hembrooke, and G. Gay. Accurately interpreting clickthrough data as implicit feedback. In *SIGIR*, pages 154–161, 2005.

[19] D. Kelly and N. J. Belkin. Display time as implicit feedback: understanding task effects. In *SIGIR*, pages 377–384, 2004.

[20] J. Koenemann and N. J. Belkin. A case for interaction: a study of interactive information retrieval behavior and effectiveness. In *SIGCHI*, pages 205–212, 1996.

[21] J. Liu, M. J. Cole, C. Liu, R. Bierig, J. Gwizdka, N. J. Belkin, J. Zhang, and X. Zhang. Search behaviors in different task types. In *JCDL*, pages 69–78, 2010.

[22] J. Liu, J. Gwizdka, C. Liu, and N. J. Belkin. Predicting task difficulty for different task types. In *ASIS&T*, volume 47, pages 16:1–16:10, 2010.

[23] I. Lopatovska. Searching for good mood: Examining relationships between search task and mood. *ASIST*, 46(1):1–13, 2009.

[24] R. McGill, J. W. Tukey, and W. A. Larsen. Variations of box plots. *American Statistician*, 32(1):12–16, 1978.

[25] M. Morita and Y. Shinoda. Information filtering based on user behavior analysis and best match text retrieval. In *SIGIR*, pages 272–281, 1994.

[26] R. Oddy. Information retrieval through man-machine dialogue. *Journal of documentation*, 33(1):1–14, 1977.

[27] M. B. Oliver. Mood management and Selective Exposure. *Communication and Emotion: Essays in honor of Dolf Zillmann*, pages 85–106, 2003.

[28] M. Pantic and L. Rothkrantz. Expert system for automatic analysis of facial expressions. *Image and Vision Computing*, 18(11):881–905, 2000.

[29] M. Pantic and L. Rothkrantz. Toward an affect-sensitive multimodal human-computer interaction. *IEEE*, 91(9):1370–1390, 2003.

[30] A. Poddar and I. Ruthven. The emotional impact of search tasks. In *IIiX*, pages 35–44, 2010.

[31] Y.-W. Seo and B.-T. Zhang. Learning user's preferences by analyzing web-browsing behaviors. In *Agents*, pages 381–387, 2000.

[32] C. Sheldrick Ross. Finding without seeking: The information encounter in the context of reading for pleasure. *IPM*, 35(6):783–799, 1999.

[33] R. Taylor. Question-negotiation an information-seeking in libraries. Technical report, DTIC Document, 1967.

[34] J. Teevan, E. Adar, R. Jones, and M. Potts. Information re-retrieval: repeat queries in yahoo's logs. In *SIGIR*, pages 151–158, 2007.

[35] R. Valenti, N. Sebe, and T. Gevers. Facial expression recognition: A fully integrated approach. In *ICIAP Workshop*, pages 125–130, 2007.

[36] P. Vorderer. Entertainment theory. *Communication and emotion: Essays in honor of Dolf Zillmann*, pages 131–153, 2003.

[37] R. White and D. Kelly. A study on the effects of personalization and task information on implicit feedback performance. In *CIKM*, pages 297–306, 2006.

[38] R. W. White. *Implicit Feedback for Interactive Information Retrieval.* PhD thesis, University of Glasgow, 2004.

[39] R. W. White, J. M. Jose, and I. Ruthven. A task-oriented study on the influencing effects of query-biased summarisation in web searching. *IPM*, 39(5):707–733, 2003.

[40] M. Wilson and D. Elsweiler. Casual-leisure searching: the exploratory search scenarios that break our current models. In *HCIR*, pages 28–31, 2010.

How Do Users Respond to Voice Input Errors? Lexical and Phonetic Query Reformulation in Voice Search

Jiepu Jiang
School of Information Sciences,
University of Pittsburgh
jiepu.jiang@gmail.com

Wei Jeng
School of Information Sciences,
University of Pittsburgh
wej9@pitt.edu

Daqing He
School of Information Sciences,
University of Pittsburgh
dah44@pitt.edu

ABSTRACT

Voice search offers users with a new search experience: instead of typing, users can vocalize their search queries. However, due to voice input errors (such as speech recognition errors and improper system interruptions), users need to frequently reformulate queries to handle the incorrectly recognized queries. We conducted user experiments with native English speakers on their query reformulation behaviors in voice search and found that users often reformulate queries with both lexical and phonetic changes to previous queries. In this paper, we first characterize and analyze typical voice input errors in voice search and users' corresponding reformulation strategies. Then, we evaluate the impacts of typical voice input errors on users' search progress and the effectiveness of different reformulation strategies on handling these errors. This study provides a clearer picture on how to further improve current voice search systems.

Categories and Subject Descriptors

H.3.3 [**Information Storage and Retrieval**]: Information Search and Retrieval – *query formulation, relevance feedback.*

General Terms

Measurement, Experimentation, Human Factors.

Keywords

Query reformulation; voice search; voice input errors.

1. INTRODUCTION

Supporting query reformulation has long been recognized as an important strategy to help users further their search progress [3]. Users may need to reformulate queries several times until their information needs are fully satisfied. The need for reformulation may be attached to the users themselves. As users may have limited understanding of their information needs, the retrieval system and the collection, it is difficult for them to develop one single query to complete the search. At the same time, the need for reformulation may come from search problems being explorative where relevant documents may be scattered among different subtopics, so that it is impossible to retrieve all relevant documents with a single query. Therefore, many studies [7, 22] concentrated on supporting reformulation of textual queries.

Along with the rapidly increasing usage of mobile devices and the improvement of speech processing, voice search becomes an alternative search mode. During voice search, users can vocalize their queries and the retrieval system utilizes the voice recognition results for retrieval [6, 19]. Though previous studies found that query reformulation plays an important role in conventional textual search systems, to the best of our knowledge, there are very limited studies on voice search, especially concerning users' query reformulation in voice search.

In this paper, we therefore focus on explaining query reformulation behaviors in the context of *voice search.* The term *voice query*[1] refers to the query in voice search. It contains not only the lexical contents, but also the phonetic characteristics such as the speaker's stress, speed, and intonation. In comparison, we refer to those searches in which users need to type queries on a keyboard as *conventional searches.*

We mainly concentrate on three research objectives in this study. First, voice search relies on users' vocalization of queries and systems' automatic speech recognition to transcribe voice queries, which may result in various *voice input errors.* Voice input errors include not only the errors from automatic speech recognition but also the system's interruptions during users' vocalization of queries. Therefore, our first objective is to characterize the types of voice input errors in voice search and evaluate their impacts on voice search.

Second, upon recognition of voice input errors, users will take actions in their subsequent query reformulation to overcome the errors. As voice queries involve both lexical and phonetic characteristics, users' reformulation choices and preferences would also be different from those in conventional searches. Therefore, our second objective is to identify and characterize users' query reformulation patterns in voice search.

Third, as the ultimate goal of this study is to shed light on how to support query reformulation in voice search, it is important to analyze users' preferences of using different reformulation patterns and examine the effectiveness of the reformulation patterns in handling voice input errors. In this study, we evaluate the effectiveness of the reformulation patterns by how they overcome the voice input errors and improve the retrieval performance.

To meet our research objectives, we conducted a series of voice search experiments involving native English speakers working on TREC search topics using the Google voice search app on the iPad. The participants were only permitted to speak voice queries to initiate searches and reformulate queries. Within a certain time limit, the participants could freely issue multiple voice queries, read or click on returned search results, and use Google's query suggestions. Users' voice queries, the system's transcription

SIGIR'13, July 28–August 1, 2013, Dublin, Ireland.

[1] In this paper, we use voice queries to refer to *spoken queries* and *speech queries*, which were used in previous studies [5]. Our rationale is to keep a consistency with Google Voice Search, the platform used in our experiment.

results to the voice queries, and the clicked documents were all recorded for analysis.

The rest of the paper is organized as follows: Section 2 reviews related studies in query reformulation and voice-based search; Section 3 introduces our methods for experimentation and analysis; in Section 4, we characterize voice query input errors and voice query reformulation patterns; Section 5 evaluates the impacts of voice input errors on voice search; Section 6 evaluates the effectiveness of each type of voice query reformulation; finally, we discuss suggestions for future development of voice-based search systems and outline our conclusions.

2. RELATED WORKS

2.1 Voice Search

Voice search [8, 23] or voice-enabled search [2, 20] refer to the search systems that allow users to input search queries in a spoken language and then retrieve the relevant entries based on system-generated transcriptions of the voice queries. Currently, voice search is commonly applied via mobile devices. Researchers examined the scenario of using voice search compared with traditional desktop search. For example, Schalkwyk et al. [19] analyzed Google's search logs and found that users utilized Google Voice Search more frequently when they tried to find information such as food and local geographical information (e.g. city names and local restaurants). However, it remains unclear whether the location-related information needs are intrinsically related to voice search, or are due to the fact that the current devices supporting voice search are mostly mobile devices.

Existing studies on voice search are very limited, especially those related to users' voice queries and query reformulations. Schalkwyk et al. [19] reported statistics of queries from Google Voice's search logs which found that voice queries are statistically shorter than desktop search queries. Crestani et al. [6] conducted a user experiment based on collections of users' voice queries. However, the experiment environment did not involve a real search system. Participants were asked to formulate voice queries without knowing whether their voice queries could be recognized, or if they would retrieve meaningful results. In comparison, in our experiments, participants freely interacted with the voice search systems, so that the participants' interactions, particularly their responses to voice input errors, could be collected and studied.

2.2 Query Reformulation

The lexical query reformulation patterns we adopted in this paper come from the summarization of many previous studies, including [9–11, 18, 21]. As we did not aim to create a systematic taxonomy of the reformulation patterns in voice search, we simplified the patterns to only four types: addition, substitution, removal, and re-ordering. However, our substitution pattern involved many other patterns defined in previous works, such as stemming [9, 21] and acronyms [9]. Also, many textual reformulation patterns that do not exist in voice search were removed, including: punctuation [21], URL stripping [9], substring [9], spelling correction [1], and capitalization [21].

3. METHODS

3.1 Settings and Experiment System

As stated, we are interested in users' query reformulation behaviors in voice search, especially how they utilize query reformulations to cope with voice input errors. Admittedly, as currently voice search is mostly used on mobile devices, an ideal experiment setting for our study should simulate mobile search environment, including many issues previously found to have an impact on automatic speech recognition (ASR) and voice search, such as the background noise [19]. However, after consideration, we decided to conduct our study in a controlled laboratory experiment setting for the following reason: our focus is on how users change their queries when voice input errors happen in voice search. Therefore, automatic speech recognition (ASR) errors and the often concerned noise and vocabulary issues in ASR [19], though important in voice search, are just part of the problem and have secondary importance in our study.

Among the state-of-the-art web search engines that support voice search, we adopted the Google search app on the iPad for our experiment because of the popularity of Google in conventional web search. We believed that users with Google search experience could more easily understand its voice search function. In addition, using the iPad for experiment also replicated some form of mobile search environment.

As our study focus on query reformulation behaviors in voice search, we simply adopted Google voice search as an out-of-box system, despite it is unclear how the voice search system and its ASR were implemented. Although the voice search system and the effectiveness of ASR can influence experiment results, we believe that Google voice search system is probably the best choice for this experiment and the experiment results would be still representative of users in other voice search systems.

Figure 1 contains screenshots of the system[2]. As shown in Fig.1 (a), a user can touch the voice search icon to issue voice queries. If the user stops speaking or pauses for a while, the system concludes that the user has completed the voice query. Then it starts the recognition of the voice query and uses the transcribed query to search (see Fig.1 (b)).

Google voice search system provides different audio cues to indicate its various statuses, which includes: starting or stopping "listening" a voice query; displaying the transcribed query; and failing to generate the transcribed query. These audio cues are very useful in our transcriptions of the experiment recordings.

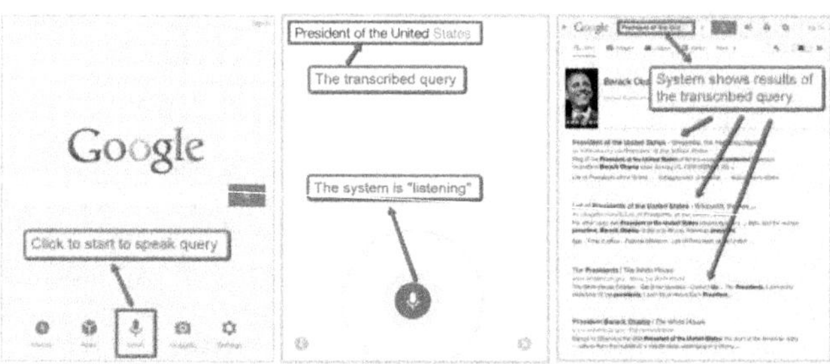

(a) (b) (c)

Figure 1. Screenshots of the Google search app on iPad.

3.2 Search Tasks and Topics

Our experiment setting is similar to the one adopted by the TREC session track [17], in which users can issue multiple queries to work on one search topic.

Ideally, search topics should be representative of users' information needs in the mobile search environment. However, as discussed in Section 3.1, our experiment setting was not a real mobile environment, therefore we selected conventional TREC ad hoc search topics in our experiments. On the one hand, we could not find many mobile search topics due to limited resources. On the other hand, we also wanted to study the connections between query reformulation in voice search and those in conventional

[2] The screenshots were made in January 2013, 6 months after the experiments. However, the main system features did not change.

textual queries as part of our future study. Therefore, we selected 50 TREC topics for our study, of which 30 are from the TREC robust track in 2004, and 20 are from the TREC web track in 2009 and 2010. The selected topics were representative of informational search problems [4]. Table 1 shows the selected TREC topic numbers.

Although the literature shows that many searches on mobile devices involve location-related information needs [19], we did not want to restrict our findings by not including other types of information needs. The first reason is that there is no absolute demarcation line between mobile devices and portable computers. The second is that many voice search systems such as Google can be used on laptop and desktop computers.

Table 1. Selected topics for experiments.

Datasets	Selected Topics
Robust Track 2004	301, 302, 303, 307, 309, 311, 313, 314, 316, 318, 321, 322, 338, 348, 351, 356, 365, 380, 404, 406, 608, 628, 630, 637, 647, 651, 654, 672, 683, 698
Web Track 2009, 2010	51, 52, 54, 56, 68, 70, 72, 73, 74, 91, 94, 100, 104, 107, 108, 110, 112, 113, 122, 141

3.3 Experiment Procedure

We recruited 20 participants (14 females and 6 males). The majority of them were college students (13) and graduate students (3). All 20 participants were native English speakers, and their average age is 23.7 with standard deviation being 4.72.

Each participant was compensated financially for their involvement in the experiment, which lasted for about 1.5 hours. At the beginning of the experiment, each participant was trained to work on one TREC topic (other than the 50 topics in table 1) to make sure that they knew how to use the voice search system, and were clear about what operations they were allowed to do during the experiments.

They then each worked on 25 of the 50 topics listed in Table 1. We alternated the topic assignments to reduce learning and fatigue bias. For each topic, the participant first read the topic description on a computer screen and then worked on each topic using the Google voice search app on iPad for 2 minutes. The participant could only vocalize queries, browse and click the search results, and use Google's query suggestions. The participant was not allowed to type queries on the iPad touch screen. After each topic, the participants were asked to answer a short questionnaire regarding their perceptions of topic difficulty and familiarity.

The experiment paused for a 5-minute break after the participant finished 15 topics. When all 25 topics were completed, each participant was interviewed for about 10 minutes on his/her perceptions of the voice search and query reformulation. The whole experimental process was recorded for later transcription and analysis of users' voice queries and interviews.

3.4 Data

Two coders manually transcribed the voice queries and agreed on 100% of the transcribed texts except for the use of plurals and prepositions (which are difficult to identify and usually do not affect search results after stemming and stopword removal).

Google's search history automatically records the system's transcribed queries and the users' click-through pages. For each participant, we created a Google user account and recorded the user's search history during the experiments.

Each participant went through a semi-structured interview at the end of the experiments on their opinions of using voice search systems and especially on how they constructed and reformulated voice queries. Some of the interview questions were based on our own experience of using voice search and a pilot study. As the study was highly exploratory, we also developed new interview questions for the experiments. We hired a professional transcription company to transcribe the interview texts.

The experiment was conducted in July 2012. In total, we collected 1,650 voice queries and 32 cases of using query suggestions. On average, each subject issued 3.30 voice queries per topic (SD=2.50). Among the 1,650 voice queries, 742 were correctly recognized. Voice input error happened in 908 voice queries, of which 810 were caused by speech recognition error and 98 by system interruption. We also found 42 voice queries for which the system could not provide any transcription results. For these queries, we simply counted their transcribed queries as empty strings and their search results as empty lists. These voice queries and query suggestions provided us with 1,182 query reformulation pairs. The average number of results clicked by a user throughout the session of a search topic were 1.41 (SD=1.14). On average, for each topic, 9.76 unique clicked results were aggregated as qrels (SD=3.11).

3.5 Search Effectiveness Evaluation

For each topic, we assume that a set of topic-level relevant results can be collected to evaluate each query in the search sessions dealing with that topic. Such evaluation method was widely adopted in multi-query search session evaluation, e.g. [12–14, 16]. Due to the time limitation of the experiments, we did not ask the participants to make relevance judgments, but relied on the clicked results as relevant documents for evaluation. Similar methods were widely adopted in web search [15].

Due to the voice input errors, sometimes a participant will not be able to find any meaningful results within the 2-minute session. Thus, for each topic, we aggregated the results clicked by any of the participants when they were working on that topic. Each clicked result was assigned a relevance score of 1 for that topic. Other results were considered non-relevant (relevance score is 0). On such a basis, we can calculate standard evaluation metrics such as nDCG of the queries.

Note that this method will be biased toward the transcribed queries in evaluation, because only those results retrieved by the transcribed queries have the chance to being clicked upon (i.e. some of the voice queries' results were not clicked upon because they were never shown to the participants). Thus, the evaluated effectiveness of the voice queries may be underestimated. However, this problem does not affect the validity of our study. As will be shown in Section 6, even if they are underestimated, voice queries still outperform their corresponding transcribed queries in nearly all the cases.

Google search history only records clicked results of queries. Thus, we crawled the first page of Google results for each of the voice queries and system transcribed queries. These results were accessed 5 months after our experiments. Although these results may be somewhat different from those at the time we conducted the experiments, we assume they do not influence the comparison between queries.

4. VOICE INPUT ERRORS AND REFORMULATION PATTERNS

4.1 Voice Input Error Identification

In voice search, a user speaks a *voice query* (q_v), and the search system generates the transcription of q_v for search, which is referred to as the *transcribed query* (q_{tr}). We say a *voice input error* occurs when the actual content of a voice query q_v differs from its transcribed query q_{tr}. Let $\{q_v^{(1)}, \ldots, q_v^{(n)}\}$ be n voice queries, and $\{q_{tr}^{(1)}, \ldots, q_{tr}^{(n)}\}$ be the corresponding n transcribed queries. The transition from $q_v^{(i)}$ to $q_v^{(i+1)}$ is referred to as a *voice query reformulation*.

Through comparison of manually transcribed voice queries with system transcribed voice queries, we can obtain recognition errors, which include:

Missing words: words in q_v that do not appear in q_{tr}.

Incorrect words: words in q_{tr} that do not appear in q_v.

When identifying recognition errors in this experiment, we did not consider the word differences caused by letter case (e.g. "United States" and "united states" are considered as equivalent) and plurals (e.g. "neil young tickets" is considered as equivalent to "neil young ticket"). The reason for this is that these types of errors do not have a significant impact on search results.

In addition to the system's speech recognition errors, voice input errors can also be caused by the system's interruption of the participants' voice inputs. While vocalizing a query, if the participant pauses for a certain amount of time, the system will "think" that the participant has completed the query. So the system will stop listening to the participant's voice input and directly transcribe the unfinished voice query for search. This type of error can be reliably identified by listening to the recording. The participant would pause and then start to talk again but the system had already issued the audio cue for stopping listening. Therefore, we manually annotated each voice query with one of the following four categories, two of which indicate the voice input error type:

Speech Recognition Error: the participant completed a query without any interruption, but the voice query was not recognized correctly. This error can be characterized by missing words or/and incorrect words as mentioned earlier.

System Interruption: the participant was improperly interrupted by the system and failed to speak all of the query words.

No Error: no voice input error.

Query Suggestion: the participant used a Google's query suggestion. If the search history recorded that the participant searched for a query while we did not hear it in the recording, we consider that to be a case of using Google's query suggestion.

During the annotation of voice input errors, the two coders agreed on 100% of the voice queries' category types. Because the participants usually stopped speaking when system interruption happened, we cannot determine the unspoken contents of the queries (i.e. for queries with system interruption, we can only have information on q_{tr} but not q_v). Thus, in much of the later analysis that requires the information on q_v, we mainly focus on queries without voice input errors and those with speech recognition errors.

4.2 Voice Query Reformulation Patterns

As voice queries have both lexical and phonetic characteristics, voice query reformulation can incorporate not only textual changes to the query but also phonetic changes. Thus, voice query reformulation can have *lexical query reformulation*, *phonetic query reformulation* or both. In the remainder of this section, we will discuss the patterns of voice query reformulation, which were summarized from previous works [9] and our observations on the experiment's results.

4.2.1 Lexical Query Reformulation

Expanded from previous studies [9], we characterized lexical query reformulation into addition, substitution, removal, and re-ordering of words, or the combination of these patterns. Although these patterns also exist in conventional search, users may utilize them for different reasons in voice search.

Addition (ADD): adding new words to the query. We refer to the newly-added words as *ADD words*. For example:

	Voice Query	Transcribed Query	ADD words
q_1	the sun	the son	
q_2	the sun solar system	the sun solar system	solar system

Substitution (SUB): replacing words with semantically-related words. In voice search, we noticed that users may substitute the words that were incorrectly recognized with other words of similar meanings. We refer to the words being replaced and the new words as *SUB words*. For example:

	Voice Query	Transcribed Query	SUB words
q_1	art theft	test	
q_2	art embezzlement	are in Dublin	theft→embezzlement
q_3	stolen artwork	stolen artwork	embezzlement→stolen art→artwork

Different from the substitution pattern in [9], we also count "acronym", "abbreviation", and "word stemming" in [9] as word substitution patterns, for example:

avp → association of volleyball professionals
united states → us
ireland peace talk interruption → ireland peace talk interrupted

Removal (RMV): removing words from the query. In voice search, we noticed that the participant may remove a part of a voice query, if the part was not correctly recognized and was not essential to the search topic. The words being removed are referred to as *RMV words*. For example:

	Voice Query	Transcribed Query	RMV words
q_1	advantages of same sex schools	andy just open it goes	
q_2	same sex schools	same sex schools	advantages of

Re-ordering (ORD): changing the order of the words in a query. The words being re-ordered are referred to as *ORD words*. In voice search, we noticed that the words being re-ordered are usually those wrongly recognized. For example:

	Voice Query	Transcribed Query
q_1	interruptions to ireland peace talk	is directions to ireland peace talks
q_2	ireland peace talk interruptions	ireland peace talks interruptions

4.2.2 Phonetic Query Reformulation

Phonetic query reformulation is unique in voice search. During our transcription of experiment recordings, we found the following human recognizable phonetic query reformulation patterns:

Partial Emphasis (PE). Partial emphasis refers to the behavior of phonetically emphasizing a part of the current query that also appeared in the previous query. Typically, the users can put stress (STR) on certain words, or slow down (SLW) at these words, or use both. Sometimes the users may only emphasize a vowel or consonant in the word. We also noticed other ways of emphasizing words when speaking voice queries. For example, some users spell out each letter in the word (SPL), or try different pronunciations (DIF) for some non-English words (e.g. Puerto Rico). Overall, STR and SLW are the two primary patterns of partial emphasis, whereas SPL and DIF occurred rarely in our experiments. The recurring words being emphasized during speaking are referred to as *PE words*. We use the following methods to represent the PE methods:

PE	Example	Explanation
STR	***rap*** and crime	put stress on "rap"
SLW	rap and c-r-i-m-e	slow down at "crime"
SPL	P·u·e·r·t·o Rico	spell out each letter in "Puerto"
DIF	Puerto Rico	pronounce "Puerto" differently

In voice search, we notice that the part of the query being emphasized is usually that part being incorrectly recognized in previous searches. For example:

	Voice Query	Transcribed Query	PE words
q_1	rap and crime	rap and crying	
q_2	rap and c-r-i-m-e	rob and crime	crime
q_3	***rap*** music influence	rap music influence	rap

Whole Emphasis (WE). Whole emphasis is to place emphasis on every part of the query, usually by putting stress or slow down on each of the words. It usually happens when the majority of the previous query was wrongly recognized. For example:

	Voice Query	Transcribed Query
q_1	art embezzlement	are in dublin
q_2	a-r-t e-m-b-e-z-z-l-e-m-e-n-t	art embezzlement

We did not find other meaningful phonetic reformulation patterns other than PE and WE in our transcription.

4.2.3 *Recognition of Query Reformulation Types*

We recognize lexical query reformulation types by automatic and manual methods. Let $q_1 \rightarrow q_2$ be a lexical query reformulation, then the procedures of recognizing the patterns are:

Step 1: automatically check whether all words in q_1 also appear in q_2. If yes, any extra words in q_2 are recognized as ADD words, and q_2 is an ADD of q_1. Similarly, if all q_2's words are in q_1, any extra words in q_1 are recognized as RMV words, and q_2 is an RMV of q_1.

Step 2: For the rest of the query pairs, check manually whether q_2 contains SUB words of q_1. The two coders agreed on 93.9% of the cases at the beginning, and finally came to agreements on the remaining 6.1% after further discussion.

Step 3: Compared with q_1, if some newly appeared words in q_2 are not recognized as SUB words, we mark them as ADD words and q_2 as an ADD of q_1. Similarly, if q_2 removed some words in q_1 and the removed words are not substituted by other words, we mark them as RMV words and q_2 as an RMV of q_1.

Step 4: Finally, if two words appeared in both q_1 and q_2, and their sequence was changed, we mark q_2 as an ORD of q_1.

Note that ADD, RMV, SUB, and ORD are not exclusive of each other. For example:

Reformulation	q_1: information retrieval system q_2: search system development
Reformulation Type & Words	ADD: development SUB: retrieval → search RMV: information

The phonetic query reformulation types and the PE words were manually recognized. In transcribing the recordings, we found that STR and SLW almost always happened together. Thus, we mark STR and SLW as one type "STR/SLW". Finally, we come to four exclusive phonetic reformulation patterns: STR/SLW, SPL, DIF, and WE. The two coders agreed on 87.6% of the cases at the beginning, and finally came to agreement on the remaining 12.4% after further discussion.

5. INFLUENCE OF VOICE INPUT ERROR

5.1 Voice Input Errors in Individual Queries

RQ1*: How do speech recognition errors affect voice queries?*

Speech recognition error is the major type of voice input error. It occurred in 810 voice queries (89.2% of all 908 queries with voice input errors in our study). We found that speech recognition error can greatly change the content and results of voice query, most likely hurting the performance of voice search.

At the word level, we calculated the average percentage of missing words in voice queries and the average percentage of incorrect words in transcribed queries. As shown in Table 2, when speech recognition error occurred, about half of the words (49.7%) in voice queries were missing in the transcribed queries. Similarly, about half of the words (49.3%) in transcribed queries were incorrect transcriptions. On average there were 1.77 missing words and 1.84 incorrect words per query.

Such high proportions of missing words and incorrect words greatly affected the results of voice search. For each of the 810 voice queries with speech recognition errors, we calculated the Jaccard similarity of Google's first pages of results between voice query and transcribed query (i.e. Jaccard(q_v, q_{tr}) in Table 2). As shown in Table 2, the average Jaccard similarity was only 0.118, indicating very low overlap between those retrieved by the transcribed queries and those that should have been retrieved by the voice queries' true content. Figure 2(a) further illustrated the low overlap by showing the distribution of Jaccard similarity, which indicated that, for 69% (556 out of 810) of voice queries with speech recognition errors, the search results will be totally different from users' expectations (i.e. Jaccard similarity is 0).

Table 2. Comparison of voice queries that contained no errors, speech recognition errors, or system interruptions.

	No Errors 742 Queries		**Speech Recognition Errors 810 Queries**		**System Interruptions 98 Queries**	
	mean	**SD**	**mean**	**SD**	**mean**	**SD**
nDCG@10 of q_v	0.275	0.20	0.264	0.22	-	-
nDCG@10 of q_{tr}	0.275	0.20	$\mathbf{0.083}^{*\downarrow}$	0.16	$\mathbf{0.061}^{\dagger}$	0.14
Length of q_v	3.82	1.68	$\mathbf{4.14}^{*}$	1.99	-	-
Length of q_{tr}	3.82	1.68	$\mathbf{4.21}^{*}$	2.31	$\mathbf{2.34}^{\dagger}$	1.41
# missing words	-	-	1.77	1.09	-	-
# incorrect words	-	-	1.84	1.44	-	-
% missing words	-	-	49.7%	29%	-	-
% incorrect words	-	-	49.3%	31%	-	-
Jaccard(q_v, q_{tr})	-	-	0.118	0.27	-	-
ΔnDCG@10	-	-	-0.182	0.23	-	-

*: the difference between queries with no errors and recognition errors is significant at 0.01 level according to Welch t-test; †: the difference between queries with no errors and system interruptions is significant at 0.01 level according to Welch t-test; $^{\downarrow}$: the difference between q_v and q_{tr} under the same error conditions is significant at 0.01 level according to paired t-test.

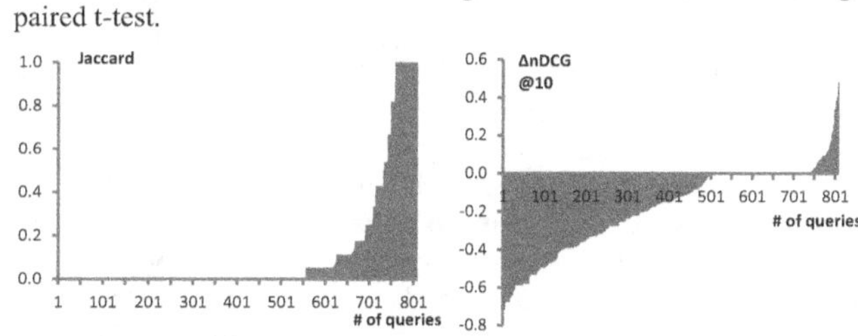

(a) (b)

Figure 2. Jaccard similarity and ΔnDCG@10 of the top 10 results of q_v and q_{tr} for 810 queries with recognition errors.

In addition, speech recognition errors hurt the performance of voice search significantly. As shown in Table 2, the average nDCG@10 of the 810 voice queries with speech recognition errors was 0.084. However, if all the speech recognition errors were corrected, the average nDCG@10 could be significantly improved to as high as 0.264, comparable to the average nDCG@10 of voice queries with no voice input errors (0.275).

Figure 2(b) further shows the distribution of ΔnDCG@10 for the 810 queries (i.e. the difference of nDCG@10 between the transcribed query and the voice query). For 500 queries (62% of the 810), nDCG@10 declined. The remaining 310 queries, whose search performance was not hurt, were intrinsically inefficient queries. Even inputted correctly, these queries could only have an average nDCG@10 value of 0.117, which is significantly less than other queries. Therefore, these queries' performance was not hurt probably because there was not much room to degrade their search performance.

***RQ2**: How do system interruptions affect voice queries?*

System interruptions occurred in 98 queries (10.8% of all 908 queries with voice input errors), which also greatly altered the content of queries and hurt the performance of voice search. When system interruption occurred, it was impossible to determine the real content of the voice queries. Therefore, we calculated statistics only for the transcribed queries.

Compared with the 742 correctly recognized voice queries, the 98 queries with system interruptions performed significantly worse (0.061 vs. 0.275 in average nDCG@10). When system interruption occurred, the transcribed queries were also significantly shorter than those of the correctly recognized queries (2.34 vs. 3.82 words), probably because the users were interrupted improperly and were not able to vocalize the entire query words.

***RQ3**: When do speech recognition errors happen?*

We found that query length may be one factor related to speech recognition errors. As shown in Table 2, queries with speech recognition errors were significantly longer than those correctly recognized queries (4.14 vs. 3.82 words). On the one hand, this is not surprising: as recognition error may happen in any word of a voice query, the more words spoken, the more likely an error happens. On the other hand, the longer the query, the richer the context it provides, which may help the speech recognition. Therefore, further study is needed on whether or not query length can affect speech recognition errors.

We also explored the relationship between speech recognition errors and certain types of words. We calculated recognition error rates for the words used by the participants, which is defined as the number of times a word was not recognized correctly divided by the total number of times the word was used in voice queries. We only calculated error rates for words being used at least 10 times. Table 3 shows the categorization of the 20 words with the highest recognition error rate.

The first recognizable category of words with high recognition error rates are acronyms, such as "ER" (emergency room, a TV show), "AVP" (the Association of Volleyball Professionals), US and USA. One can hardly expect the system to recognize certain obscure acronyms, such as "ER" and "AVP".

Our interviews showed that more than half of the participants (N=14) reported their concerns about the use of acronyms. When the acronyms were not recognized, they tended to reformulate queries using the full words. For example, participant S14 said that "I was a little concerned … Like how I said AVP, and it pops up APP, which would be a totally different topic. I was a little worried about that … Once I realized what AVP was, I tried to use association, the full name. [sic]". Participant S20 said that "When I did the NRA, instead of giving me a single letter, N-R-A, it spelled out 'in' like that. Then I just switched over to actually saying the National Rifle Association because that was quicker."

Acronyms, named entities and non-English words comprise half of the top 20 words with the highest error rates. Examples of the uncategorized words are also listed in Table 3 as "other words".

5.2 Voice Input Errors in Search Sessions

***RQ4**: How do voice input errors influence search sessions?*

We collected 500 search sessions (20 participants with each working on 25 topics). We divided the 500 sessions into two groups by whether or not voice input errors occurred in the session. As shown in table 4, voice input errors occurred in 187 sessions.

Table 3. Categorization of 20 words with the highest recognition error rates.

Type	Examples (# NOT recognized correctly / # used)
Acronym	ER(29/29), AVP(11/11), US(57/61), USA(6/11)
Named Entity	Owen(25/26), Culpeper(18/27), Ralph(22/36), Gulf(13/24), Falkland(14/27)
Non-English	Nino(31/46)
Other words	theft(14/14), achievement(10/10), taxing(18/21), fraud(12/14), violence(19/27), talk(9/15), sun(24/41), aspirin(23/43), embezzlement(9/18), maglev(8/16)

Table 4. Comparison of session-level statistics between sessions with and without voice input errors.

	187 Sessions w/o Voice Input Errors		313 Sessions w/ Voice Input Errors	
	mean	SD	mean	SD
# voice queries	1.44	0.82	**4.41***	2.51
# unique voice queries	1.44	0.82	**3.30***	1.87
# queries w/o voice input errors	1.44	0.82	1.51	1.36
# queries w/ recognition errors	0	0	**2.59***	2.14
# queries w/ system interruptions	0	0	**0.31***	0.65
# unique results by q_v	13.38	6.66	**26.69***	13.90
# unique results by q_{tr}	13.38	6.66	**37.95***↑	21.00
# unique relevant results by q_v	2.90	1.56	3.04	1.59
# unique relevant results by q_{tr}	2.90	1.56	**2.78**↓	1.71
# clicked results in the session	1.39	1.01	1.34	1.23
% sessions user clicked results	84.49%	-	69.97%	-
% sessions q_{tr} found relevant results	95.72%	-	92.01%	-

*: the difference between sessions w/ and w/o voice input errors is significant at 0.01 level according to Welch t-test; ↑ and ↓: the difference between q_v and q_{tr} is significant at 0.01 level according to paired t-test.

We found that, within the same period of time (a 2-minute search session), the participants issued significantly more voice queries when voice input errors occurred in the search session. As shown in Table 4, the average number of voice queries in sessions with errors was 4.41 and 1.44 without errors (the difference is significant). When voice input errors occurred in the search session, on average 1.11 queries in the session were repeating previously used queries, whereas when no errors occurred, users seldom repeated used queries. After removing the repeated queries, the participants still issued significantly more unique voice queries when voice input error occurred (3.30 vs. 1.44).

One consequence of the increased number of voice queries in sessions with voice input errors was that the participants had to spend more efforts to browse and examine the extra returned results. As showed in Table 4, the unique number of results returned by the transcribed queries in sessions with voice input errors was significantly higher than that of those without voice input errors. Although some of the participants could immediately reformulate the voice query without looking at any results, the increased number of returned results at least would not reduce the participants' search efforts.

We further looked into retrieval effectiveness of search sessions. In sessions with voice input errors, although more results were returned within a session, on average less unique relevant results were actually found. In the 313 sessions with voice input errors, on average the transcribed queries returned only 2.78 unique relevant results within a session. Whereas, if no voice input errors occurred, those sessions' voice queries should result in on average 3.04 relevant results (the difference is significant). Compared with the 313 sessions with voice input errors, the transcribed queries also returned more relevant results in the 187 sessions without any voice input error (2.90 vs. 2.78) and triggered more clicks (1.39 vs. 1.34), but the differences are not statistically significant.

Voice input error also has a higher likelihood of causing a failed search session, in which no relevant result were found. On average, 95.72% of the sessions without voice input errors returned at least one relevant result and in 84.49% of the sessions the participants clicked at least one result. In comparison, when voice input error occurred, only 92.01% of the sessions returned at least one relevant result and in 69.97% of the sessions the participants clicked at least one result.

In addition, voice input errors can also affect the participants' affective feelings. In our interviews, 90% of our participants reported frustration with their search experience when voice input error occurred. For example, participant S15 reported: "It's frustrating! I know I'm saying the word right and I know what I'm looking for, but it's just not connecting, and that disconnection is like arrgh! … (hope I can) just type it. [sic]".

To summarize, our results demonstrated that voice input errors significantly affected the performance of voice queries, and consequently made the whole search process more difficult and less effective. In response, users utilized both lexical and phonetic reformulations to handle the errors, which will be analyzed in the next section.

Table 5. Change in nDCG@10 after query reformulation.

			$q_v^{(2)}$				
			No Error	**Recognition Error**	**System Interruption**	**Query Suggestion**	**All**
			ΔnDCG@10	**ΔnDCG@10**	**ΔnDCG@10**	**ΔnDCG@10**	**ΔnDCG@10**
$q_v^{(1)}$	**No Error**	q_v	0.266 → **0.218** ↓	0.255 → 0.204	-	-	-
		q_{tr}	0.266 → **0.218** ↓	0.255 → **0.095** ↓	0.256 → **0.059** ↓	0.290 → 0.244	0.262 → **0.164** ↓
		# cases	209	143	27	15	394
	Recognition Error	q_v	0.248 → 0.248	0.261 → 0.267	-	-	-
		q_{tr}	0.053 → **0.248** ↑	0.058 → 0.074	0.096 → 0.062	0.099 → 0.226	0.059 → **0.135** ↑
		Frequency	231	392	44	14	681
	System Interruption	q_{tr}	0.071 → **0.237** ↑	0.038 → 0.085	0.134 → 0.012	-	0.056 → **0.128** ↑
		Frequency	30	56	7	0	93
	Query Suggestion	q_{tr}	0.299 → 0.100	0.189 → 0.020	0.235 → 0.000	0.233 → 0.110	0.233 → **0.061** ↓
		Frequency	4	6	1	3	14
	All	q_{tr}	0.150 → **0.233** ↓	0.104 → **0.079** ↓	0.156 → 0.056	0.201 → **0.223** ↑	0.129 → **0.143** ↑
		Frequency	474	597	79	32	1,182

↑ and ↓: the difference between $q_v^{(1)}$ and $q_v^{(2)}$, or between $q_{tr}^{(1)}$ and $q_{tr}^{(2)}$, is significant at 0.01 level according to paired t-tests.

6. VOICE QUERY REFORMULATION

In this section, we focus on users' query reformulations. In the following discussion, we use $q_v^{(1)}$ and $q_{tr}^{(1)}$, $q_v^{(2)}$ and $q_{tr}^{(2)}$ for the voice query and transcribed query both before and after query reformulation, respectively.

6.1 Effectiveness

***RQ5**: Can users' query reformulations improve search performance of voice queries?*

We found that query reformulation in voice search led to overall improvements in performance, but the magnitude depends on whether voice input errors occurred before or after reformulation.

Table 5 shows the comparison of search performance before and after query reformulation when different types of voice input errors occurred in $q_v^{(1)}$ and $q_v^{(2)}$. If counting all 1,182 cases of reformulation, search performance (as measured by nDCG@10) improved significantly from 0.129 to 0.143 (+10.85%) because of query reformulation. However, the improvements mainly occurred in the cases where voice input error occurred in $q_v^{(1)}$ and $q_v^{(2)}$ was correctly recognized, e.g. "Recognition Error" → "No Error" and "System interruption" → "No Error". If no voice input error occurred in $q_v^{(1)}$ or voice input error occurred in $q_v^{(2)}$, query reformulation resulted in limited improvements and it sometimes even hindered search performance.

Since results in Section 5 demonstrated the great influence of voice input errors on search performance, it is not surprising that the effectiveness of query reformulations also largely relied on whether or not voice input errors occurred in $q_v^{(2)}$.

***RQ6**: Can users' query reformulation correct the speech recognition errors in previous queries?*

We found that when recognition error occurred in $q_v^{(1)}$, users' query reformulation corrected some of the missing words in $q_v^{(1)}$. However, at the same time, new voice input errors could also happen in $q_v^{(2)}$, which may counteract the corrected errors and finally lead to degradation in search performance.

Table 6 shows the missing and incorrect words before and after query reformulation for 681 query reformulation cases in which speech recognition errors occurred in $q_v^{(1)}$. We separately calculated the statistics by the different types of queries and voice input errors in $q_v^{(2)}$. As showed in Table 6, when no voice input error occurred in $q_v^{(2)}$ (231 out of 681 cases), it is not surprising that the number of missing and incorrect words both dropped to 0 after query reformulation. When speech recognition errors occurred in $q_v^{(2)}$ (392 out of 681), the number of missing words only dropped slightly from 1.89 to 1.74 (the difference is significant at 0.05 level of significance) and the number of incorrect words slightly increased (the difference is not significant).

Does this mean users' query reformulations can only correct voice input errors when the reformulated queries are correctly recognized? On the contrary, in further analysis, we found that even when speech recognition errors occurred again in $q_v^{(2)}$, users' query reformulation did correct parts of the errors in $q_v^{(1)}$. However, at the same time, new errors also appeared in $q_v^{(2)}$.

To better explain the case, we calculated: the number of missing words in $q_v^{(1)}$ that were correctly recognized in $q_{tr}^{(2)}$; the number of missing words in $q_v^{(1)}$ that were removed in $q_v^{(2)}$; and the number of new missing words in $q_v^{(2)}$ (those are missing words in $q_v^{(2)}$ but not in $q_v^{(1)}$). As shown in Table 6, when speech recognition error occurred in $q_v^{(2)}$, 27.5% (0.52 out of 1.89) of the missing words in $q_v^{(1)}$ were corrected after query reformulation and 18.0% (0.34 out of 1.89) were simply removed. However, on average, 0.72 new missing words were produced in $q_v^{(2)}$, which still impeded the performance.

When system interruption occurred in $q_v^{(2)}$, on average, only 0.23 missing words in $q_v^{(1)}$ were corrected, which is significantly less than the 0.52 missing words corrected in the cases in which speech recognition error occurred in $q_v^{(2)}$.

Table 6. Comparison of the missing and incorrect words before and after query reformulation for the 681 query pairs in which speech recognition error happened in $q_v^{(1)}$.

$q_v^{(2)}$	# missing words	# incorrect words	# missing words in $q_v^{(1)}$ corrected in $q_{tr}^{(2)}$	# missing words in $q_v^{(1)}$ removed in $q_v^{(2)}$	# new missing words in $q_v^{(2)}$
	$q_v^{(1)} \rightarrow q_v^{(2)}$	$q_{tr}^{(1)} \rightarrow q_{tr}^{(2)}$			
No Errors	1.75 → 0.00**	1.81 → 0.00**	1.13	0.61	0.00
Rec Errors	1.89 → 1.74*	1.72 → 1.78	0.52	0.34	0.72
Sys Interrupt	1.71	-	0.23	-	-
Suggestion	1.14	-	0.86	-	-

* and **: the difference of $q_v^{(1)}$ and $q_v^{(2)}$ is significant at 0.05 and 0.01 level.

Table 7. The frequencies of using reformulation patterns.

$q_v^{(1)}$	ADD	SUB	RMV	ORD	Lexical	Lexical & Phonetic
No Errors	90.50 %	15.04 %	66.75 %	33.51 %	99.74 %	0.26 %
Rec Errors	32.98 %	16.34 %	37.93 %	43.03 %	77.36 %	11.99 %
Overall	53.82 %	14.87 %	48.37 %	39.58 %	85.47 %	7.74 %
$q_v^{(1)}$	STR/ SLW	SPL	DIF	WE	Phonetic	Repeat w/o PE or WE
No Errors	0 %	0 %	0 %	0.26 %	0.26 %	0 %
Rec Errors	14.84 %	0.60 %	0.90 %	9.30 %	25.64 %	20.54 %
Overall	9.46 %	0.39 %	0.57 %	6.02 %	16.44 %	13.58 %

6.2 Use of Reformulation Patterns

***RQ7**: How do users utilize different query reformulate patterns in voice search? Do voice input errors influence the use of query reformulation patterns?*

Table 7 shows the frequency of using different reformulation patterns in voice search. Despite how the query input mechanism changes dramatically in voice search, lexical reformulations were still the primary forms of query reformulation. No matter if speech recognition errors occurred, lexical reformulations were consistently used much more frequently than phonetic reformulations.

However, speech recognition errors did significantly affect the use of specific lexical query reformulation patterns. When speech recognition errors occurred, the participants tended to reformulate queries using more substitution (SUB) and re-ordering (ORD) patterns but dramatically less addition (ADD) and removal (RMV) patterns. As further examined in RQ8, this is probably because substitution and re-ordering can effectively correct the missing words in previous queries, whereas addition and removal cannot.

The use of phonetic reformulation patterns is almost always associated with speech recognition errors. As shown in Table 7, when no voice input error occurred in $q_v^{(1)}$, only 0.26% of the query reformulations adopted phonetic reformulation patterns. In comparison, 25.64% of the query reformulations adopted phonetic reformulation patterns when speech recognition errors happened in $q_v^{(1)}$. In addition to the phonetic reformulation patterns, repeating is also closely connected with speech recognition errors. When speech recognition errors occurred in $q_v^{(1)}$, we found that 20.54% of the reformulations were simply repeating $q_v^{(1)}$ without any recognizable phonetic changes.

Among all of the phonetic reformulation patterns, partial emphasis (PE) was used more frequently than whole emphasis (WE). As we mentioned in Section 4, stressing (STR) and slowing down (SLW) were the most frequent patterns for partial emphasis, while spelling (SPL) and using different pronunciations (DIF) rarely happened. Repeating was used as frequently as phonetic reformulation patterns when recognition errors happened in $q_v^{(1)}$.

To conclude, our results indicate that in voice search, a user's adoption of both lexical and phonetic query reformulation patterns were greatly impacted by voice input errors. As further illustrated in RQ8, many of the reformulation patterns were used specifically to correct the missing words occurred in previous queries.

***RQ8**: How do users utilize different reformulation patterns to handle speech recognition errors? Are these patterns effective in correcting speech recognition errors?*

When speech recognition errors happen, it is very common for some of the words spoken by the users to be incorrectly recognized or missing from the system's transcribed queries. Solutions to speech recognition errors should be able to effectively correct these errors. Among the lexical and phonetic query reformulation patterns summarized in our paper, four patterns can be used specifically related to the missing words: substitution (SUB), removal (RMV), re-ordering (ORD), and partial emphasis (PE). Users can substitute other words for the missing words, or remove the missing words, or re-order the missing words and other words, or phonetically emphasize the missing words. In comparison, the other patterns affect equally the missing words and other words in the query.

We evaluate the reformulation patterns by their effectiveness of correcting the missing words in voice queries. Similarly, we can evaluate by their effectiveness of reducing the incorrect words in transcribed queries. However, due to space limitation, we only reported the following measures regarding the missing words:

(1) For each of the four patterns that can be used specifically for handling the missing words (i.e. SUB, RMV, ORD, and PE), we calculated the percentage that the pattern was used specifically related to the missing words (i.e. the missing words were substituted, removed, re-ordered, or emphasized) out of all the cases that the reformulation pattern was used.

(2) The success rate of each pattern in correcting the missing words. For re-ordering (ORD) and partial emphasis (PE) patterns, the success rate was calculated as the percentage of missing words being corrected out of all the cases that the missing words were re-ordered or specifically emphasized. For addition (ADD), whole emphasis (WE), and repeating patterns, the success rate was calculated as the percentage of missing words being corrected out of all the cases that ADD, WE, or repeating was used (since it is difficult to identify whether these patterns were used specifically on the missing words). For substitution, the success rate was calculated as the percentage of the replaced words being correctly recognized out of all the cases that the missing words were replaced.

(3) The improvement in nDCG@10 between $q_{tr}^{(1)}$ and $q_{tr}^{(2)}$ when each pattern was used.

As shown in Table 8, the percentage of the patterns used specifically related to the missing words indicates users' adoption of the pattern to solve speech recognition errors. Among all of the patterns, partial emphasis (PE) has most usage. When PE was used, it was nearly always (93.69%) the case that the words emphasized were the missing words from $q_v^{(1)}$. In comparison, substitution (SUB), removal (RMV), and re-ordering (ORD) patterns have fewer but still considerably high usage (84.30%, 62.82% and 75.23%). Results indicate that, when recognition errors happened, these lexical patterns were primarily used to correct speech recognition errors, which is different from the intention to use these patterns in conventional searches.

Table 8 also reveals the effectiveness of different reformulation patterns in correcting speech recognition errors. As indicated in the results, different reformulation patterns vary widely in their success rates in correcting missing words in previous queries. Among these patterns, substitution (SUB) and re-ordering (ORD) had the two highest success rates (73.5% and 69.1%). In comparison, partial emphasis (PE) was less effective (62.5%). It is indicated that when recognition errors happened, it was usually more effective to modify the missing words into others (SUB) or to change the contexts around the missing words (ORD), rather than emphasizing with phonetic changes (PE).

Table 8. Effectiveness of reformulation patterns in correcting speech recognition errors that occurred in previous queries.

	% used specifically related to the missing words in $q_v^{(1)}$	Success rate of correcting missing words	nDCG@10 $q_{tr}^{(1)} \rightarrow q_{tr}^{(2)}$
ADD	-	40.73 %	0.085 → 0.119
SUB	84.30 %	73.53 %	0.052 → **0.156** †
RMV	62.82 %	-	0.077 → 0.111
ORD	75.23 %	69.14 %	0.062 → **0.147** †
PE	93.69 %	62.50 %	0.022 → **0.150** †
WE	-	60.94 %	0.028 → **0.110** †
Repeat w/o PE and WE	-	59.73 %	0.051 → **0.142** †
Overall	-	47.45 %	0.058 → **0.132** †

†: the difference of nDCG@10 is significant at 0.01 level according to paired t-tests.

We suspect that users' adoption of partial emphasis (PE) is directly related to their everyday life experience: when others miss your words, it is natural to repeat and emphasize the missing part. However, it seems that this method cannot work well for automatic speech recognition systems. The speech recognition algorithms are usually trained with samples of the normal way of speaking, but the phonetic query reformulations may make the queries quite different from the normal way of speaking.

According to the success rates, partial emphasis (PE), whole emphasis (WE), and repeating effectively helped to correct the missing words (compared to the overall success rate of only 47.45%). However, we suspect that the effectiveness of the phonetic reformulation patterns is over-estimated. Compared with repeating, the phonetic patterns emphasized either certain parts of the queries or the entire queries. Therefore, we can use repeating as a baseline to evaluate the effectiveness of phonetic emphasis. However, as partial emphasis (PE) and whole emphasis (WE) had only slightly higher success rates compared to repeating, it is arguable whether or not phonetic emphasis was truly useful.

Finally, we looked into the improvement of the transcribed queries' search performance (by nDCG@10) after each pattern had been used in reformulated queries. Except for addition (ADD) and removal (RMV), we observed significant improvements with other patterns. In addition, the magnitude of nDCG@10 improvements for other patterns was also greater than those of ADD and RMV patterns. This indicates that ADD and RMV are less effective solutions to speech recognition errors.

To conclude, we found that substitution, re-ordering, partial emphasis, whole emphasis, and repeating were five effective reformulation strategies in voice search to handle recognition errors. Among these patterns, substitution and re-ordering are lexical patterns, but they outperformed the other three phonetic patterns in solving speech recognition errors.

7. DISCUSSION AND FUTURE WORK

(1) Should we use and support long and natural language queries or short and keyword queries in voice search?

Our results show that query length is an important factor associated with speech recognition errors (see Table 2 and discussion in RQ3). Long queries are prone to speech recognition errors. This reminds us of the different findings in previous studies: Schalkwyk et al. found that voice search queries were tend to be shorter than in conventional searches [19], whereas Crestani et al. found that voice queries tend to longer and more similar to natural language [6].

Since we did not conduct conventional search experiments for comparison, we cannot come to an answer to this disputable issue. We suggest that further studies are needed to identify the characteristics of queries in voice search. We believe that users' adoption of short or long queries depends on various factors. On the one hand, as voice search may be closer to people's normal ways of speaking, voice queries are probably also closer to natural language queries. On the other hand, as long queries may have more speech recognition errors, users may also prefer shorter and simpler keyword queries in voice search.

(2) Query suggestion in voice search.

Although the participants were told explicitly that they could use Google's query suggestions in our experiment, we did not observe many cases of them doing so (see Table 5). We tried some cases in Google and found that currently, Google's query suggestion in voice search is simply suggesting queries based on the transcribed queries' texts. Therefore, it is not surprising that the suggestions are ineffective when the transcribed texts are likely to be incorrect (due to voice input errors). For example, we submitted an incorrect transcription "rap and crying" (the correct one is "rap and crime") to Google and obtained two suggestions that are irrelevant to "rap and crime" but probably relevant to "rap and crying": "rapper crying at bet awards" and "soulja boy crying". This shows that query suggestion is more challenging in voice search.

In addition, we believe that query suggestion is more important for users in voice search than in conventional search. As shown in our results, despite various query reformulation methods have been developed, users' voice query reformulations might not totally resolve the old recognition errors, and at the same time could introduce new errors. In comparison, it may be a better solution for users to accept a good query suggestion for query reformulation. This calls for studies on query suggestion algorithms specifically designed for voice search. Probably a promising solution is to develop effective query suggestion algorithms considering not only the transcribed texts, but also speech recognition results.

(3) Interface for supporting voice query inputs and voice query reformulation.

Considering the effort and risk of issuing a voice query, voice search systems should employ proper methods to reduce the efforts and risks of constructing and reformulating voice queries. Based on our observation, one suggestion is to design a voice query reformulation interface that frees users from having to speak the whole voice query again if they only intend to correct one or two error words. For example, the users should be given the ability to specify and repeat the part of the query that they want to modify and let the search system recompose a new voice query based on the updated information.

In addition, our experiments also shown that system interruptions greatly harmed the performance of voice search, even though they occurred less frequently (see Table 2 & 5). The participants could not finish their voice queries, and sometimes became really frustrated after several consecutive interruptions. Voice query generation may impose higher cognitive load on the users than typing textual queries. Therefore, voice search systems should better manage their interruptions. For example, systems can allow users to control whether or not they will be interrupted while speaking voice queries.

8. CONCLUSION

In this paper, we studied two significant and closely related issues in voice search. First, what is the influence of voice input errors on search effectiveness in voice search? Second, how do users utilize different query reformulation patterns, including both lexical and phonetic query reformulation patterns, to handle these voice input errors? We conducted a controlled laboratory experiment for voice search, which helped answer these questions.

Our study systematically evaluated the influence of voice input errors on voice search from the aspects of individual queries and overall search sessions. We found that voice input errors greatly changed the content and results of queries, resulting significant decline of search performance for individual queries. This in turn led to increased efforts and negative feelings of users, hindering overall performance of the search session. In addition, current query suggestion algorithms may fail to generate effective suggestions due to voice input errors in transcribed queries.

Then, we characterized users' query reformulation patterns in voice search and evaluated the effectiveness of those patterns in handling voice input errors and improving search effectiveness. We found that users utilized both lexical query reformulation patterns that exist in conventional search and phonetic query reformulation patterns newly found in voice search. Despite some of the patterns effectively corrected voice input errors, users' query reformulation resulted in limited overall improvements in search performance, because voice input errors occurred frequently in reformulated queries.

Our study suggested voice input errors as the essential issue to be resolved in voice search. A possible solution is to better support users' query reformulation, which includes designing better interface supporting voice query reformulation and developing query suggestion algorithms using both lexical and phonetic information. To a broader extent, our study explored the influence of query input devices on user behaviors and search systems. Our methods and results may shed light on user behaviors and search systems in similar situations, such as when handwriting is used for input.

Admittedly, our study has one limitation in that the experiment setting did not fully replicate mobile search environment and tasks. This may influence the occurrences of the different types of voice input errors and users' adoption of the voice query reformulation patterns. However, it is very likely that the impacts of voice input errors on voice search systems and the effectiveness of different voice query reformulation patterns are representative of the cases in other voice search systems.

9. REFERENCES

[1] Anick, P. 2003. Using terminological feedback for web search refinement: a log-based study. In Proceedings of the 26th annual international ACM SIGIR conference on Research and development in informaion retrieval (SIGIR '03): 88-95.

[2] Ballinger, B. et al. 2010. On-Demand Language Model Interpolation for Mobile Speech Input. Interspeech (2010): 1812–1815.

[3] Bates, M.J. 1979. Information search tactics. Journal of the American Society for Information Science, 30(4): 205–214.

[4] Broder, A. 2002. A taxonomy of web search. SIGIR Forum 36(2): 3-10.

[5] Crestani, F. 2002. Spoken query processing for interactive information retrieval. Data Knowl. Eng. 41, 1 (April 2002): 105-124.

[6] Crestani, F. et al. 2006. Written versus spoken queries: A qualitative and quantitative comparative analysis. J. Am. Soc. Inf. Sci., 57: 881–890.

[7] Dang, V. and Croft, W.B. 2010. Query reformulation using anchor text. In Proceedings of the third ACM international conference on Web search and data mining (WSDM '10): 41-50.

[8] Feng, J. and Bangalore, S. 2009. Effects of word confusion networks on voice search. (Mar. 2009): 238–245.

[9] Huang, J. and Efthimiadis, E. N. 2009. Analyzing and evaluating query reformulation strategies in web search logs. In Proceedings of the 18th ACM conference on Information and knowledge management (CIKM '09): 77-86.

[10] Jansen, B.J. et al. 2005. A temporal comparison of AltaVista Web searching. J. Am. Soc. Inf. Sci., 56(6): 559–570.

[11] Jansen, B.J. et al. 2009. Patterns of query reformulation during Web searching. J. Am. Soc. Inf. Sci., 60(7): 1358–1371.

[12] Järvelin, K. et al. 2008. Discounted Cumulated Gain Based Evaluation of Multiple-Query IR Sessions. LNCS 4956: Proceedings of the 30th European Conference on Information Retrieval (ECIR '08): 4–15.

[13] Jiang, J. et al. 2012. Contextual evaluation of query reformulations in a search session by user simulation. In Proceedings of the 21st ACM international conference on Information and knowledge management (CIKM '12): 2635-2638.

[14] Jiang, J. et al. 2012. On Duplicate Results in a Search Session. Proceedings of the 21st Text REtrieval Conference, (TREC 2012).

[15] Joachims, T. 2002. Optimizing search engines using clickthrough data. In Proceedings of the eighth ACM SIGKDD international conference on Knowledge discovery and data mining (KDD '02): 133-142

[16] Kanoulas, E. et al. 2011. Evaluating multi-query sessions. Proceedings of the 34th international ACM SIGIR conference on Research and development in Information Retrieval (SIGIR '11): 1053–1062.

[17] Kanoulas, E. et al. 2011. Session Track 2011 Overview. The 20th Text REtrieval Conference Notebook Proceedings (TREC 2011).

[18] Rieh, S.Y. et al. 2006. Analysis of multiple query reformulations on the web: The interactive information retrieval context. Information Processing & Management. 42(3): 751–768.

[19] Schalkwyk, J. et al. 2010. "Your Word is my Command": Google Search by Voice: A Case Study. Advances in Speech Recognition SE - 4. A. Neustein, ed. Springer US. 61–90.

[20] Song, Y.-I. et al. 2009. Voice search of structured media data. 2009 IEEE International Conference on Acoustics, Speech and Signal Processing (Apr. 2009): 3941–3944.

[21] Teevan, J. et al. 2007. Information re-retrieval: repeat queries in Yahoo's logs. In Proceedings of the 30th annual international ACM SIGIR conference on Research and development in information retrieval (SIGIR '07): 151-158.

[22] Wang, X. et al. 2008. Mining term association patterns from search logs for effective query reformulation. In Proceedings of the 17th ACM conference on Information and knowledge management (CIKM '08): 479-488.

[23] Wang, Y.-Y. et al. 2008. An introduction to voice search. Signal Processing Magazine, IEEE.

Mining Touch Interaction Data on Mobile Devices to Predict Web Search Result Relevance

Qi Guo*
Microsoft
One Microsoft Way
Redmond, WA 98052 USA
qiguo@microsoft.com

Haojian Jin
Emory University
400 Dowman Drive
Atlanta, GA 30322 USA
haojian.jin@emory.edu

Dmitry Lagun
Emory University
400 Dowman Drive
Atlanta, GA 30322 USA
dlagun@emory.edu

Shuai Yuan
Emory University
400 Dowman Drive
Atlanta, GA 30322 USA
syuan3@emory.edu

Eugene Agichtein
Emory University
400 Dowman Drive
Atlanta, GA 30322 USA
eugene@mathcs.emory.edu

ABSTRACT

Fine-grained search interactions in the desktop setting, such as mouse cursor movements and scrolling, have been shown valuable for understanding user intent, attention, and their preferences for Web search results. As web search on smart phones and tablets becomes increasingly popular, previously validated desktop interaction models have to be adapted for the available touch interactions such as pinching and swiping, and for the different device form factors. In this paper, we present, to our knowledge, the first in-depth study of modeling interactions on touch-enabled device for improving Web search ranking. In particular, we evaluate a variety of touch interactions on a smart phone as implicit relevance feedback, and compare them with the corresponding fine-grained interactions on a desktop computer with mouse and keyboard as the primary input devices. Our experiments are based on a dataset collected from two user studies with 56 users in total, using a specially instrumented version of a popular mobile browser to capture the interaction data. We report a detailed analysis of the similarities and differences of fine-grained search interactions between the desktop and the smart phone modalities, and identify novel patterns of touch interactions indicative of result relevance. Finally, we demonstrate significant improvements to search ranking quality by mining touch interaction data.

Categories and Subject Descriptors

H.3.3 [**Information Storage and Retrieval**]: Information Search and Retrieval – relevance feedback, search and selection process.

*Work was done as a Ph.D. student at Emory University

SIGIR'13, July 28–August 1, 2013, Dublin, Ireland.

Keywords

Mobile search behavior; touch interaction models; implicit relevance feedback

1. INTRODUCTION

Accurately estimating document relevance is at the core of Web search or information retrieval in general. Implicit feedback from users are good indicators of document relevance, among which, dwell time, or the time user spends on visiting the clicked Web search result document, has been found to be indicative of document relevance [9, 36] and has been successfully applied in various other Web search applications [35, 18, 10]. However, dwell time may be misleading – a user may spend 30 seconds reading a relevant paragraph in a document or struggling finding the information and skimming through during the 30 seconds.

In previous studies [33, 14, 23, 16, 22], fine-grained interactions such as mouse cursor movements and scrolling were found to be indicative of searcher interests and preferences. In particular, post-click behavior were found to capture the different viewing patterns of relevant and non-relevant document, resulting in a more accurate prediction of intrinsic document relevance [16], compared to using dwell time information alone. For example, extensive and slow mouse movements were found to correlate with reading a relevant document while fast scrolling are found to correlate with skimming a non-relevant document.

Recently, touch-enabled mobile devices, such as smart phones and tables, have become an increasingly popular modality for users to search and browse the Web. Despite the success of modeling fine-grained interactions on a personal computer with a mouse and a keyboard as the primary input devices, fine-grained Web search interactions on these new devices, where users zoom and swipe instead of using a mouse, are less understood. While these touch interactions may also provide additional signals of document relevance beyond dwell time, we are not aware of any reports of modeling these fine-grained touch interactions as implicit relevance feedback. Thus, we explore the following two research questions:

- Do users view search result documents differently on a *touch-enabled mobile device* compared to using a *desktop computer* with a mouse and keyboard as the primary input device?
- Do users behave differently on a *touch-enabled mobile de-*

vice when viewing a *relevant* search result document compared to a *non-relevant* document?

To answer these research questions, we analyzed searcher behavior on a smart phone and a desktop computer in two user studies, which involved 56 participants in total and hundreds of unique Web search queries and page examinations. In particular, we identify behavioral patterns that correspond to viewing relevant and non-relevant documents. Using these insights, we design a variety of touch interaction features to capture these patterns, and analyze the correlations of these feature values with the document relevance. We also compare the differences and similarities of the interaction patterns across these two modalities. Finally, we develop relevance prediction models based on the touch interaction features, and demonstrate significant improvements over using dwell time information alone.

In summary, our contributions include:

- A characterization of patterns of examination and touch interactions that correspond to viewing a relevant or non-relevant Web search result document (Section 4).
- MTI, a novel model of relevance prediction that captures fine-grained Web search interactions on touch-enabled mobile devices (Section 5).
- A comparison of the differences and similarities of fine-grained Web search interactions on a touch-enabled mobile device and a desktop PC (Section 6).
- Empirical evidence that MTI is more effective than using dwell time information alone, for ranking Web search result documents using the estimated relevance (Section 7).

Next, we briefly survey the background and related work to put our contribution in context.

2. RELATED WORK

Using page dwell time for inferring relevance has a long history in the information retrieval community, with mixed conclusions about its utility. Some of the early research done in the area of implicit feedback in information retrieval was that of Morita and Shinoda [30]. They conducted a study where participants were asked to provide explicit feedback about interestingness of news articles that they have read. The study focused on the correlation between reading time and explicit feedback, while considering document length and additional textual features. They noted that there is a strong tendency to spend more time on interesting articles rather than on uninteresting ones. Similar findings have also been reported in [9] and [11]. Furthermore, Morita and Shinoda found only a weak correlation between the lengths of articles and associated reading times, indicating that most articles are only read in parts, not in their entirety.

Interestingly, dwell time does not always correlate with relevance. Kelly and Belkin [27] tried to reproduce the results of Morita and Shinoda in a different, more complex information retrieval scenario, yet found no correlations between display time and explicit relevance ratings for a document. In a subsequent, naturalistic study, Kelly and Belkin [28] found again no general relationship between display time and the users' explicit ratings of the documents' usefulness. Instead, they observed high variation of display time with respect to different users and different tasks. Recently, White and Kelly [36] reported that adjusting display time thresholds for implicit feedback according to task type leads to improved retrieval performance, while adjusting the thresholds according to individual users degraded performance. This stands in contrast to findings of a prior study by Rafter and Smyth [32] who showed for one specific task type that display time is correlated with user interest, especially after individually adjusting the measure. In summary, while dwell time does appear to contain relevance information, previous studies have found many different interpretations of it, with no clear consensus of the relationship to document relevance.

Additional implicit measures have been examined on the object level (e.g., document paragraph or page item) as well. On one hand, it has been found that good indicators of interest include the amount of scrolling on a page [9], click-through [11, 25], and exit type for a Web page [11]. On the other hand, mouse cursor movements and mouse clicks while viewing a document do correlate with user interest [9]. Furthermore, user behavior on the Search Engine Result Pages (SERPs), when combined with page dwell-time and session level information, can significantly improve result ranking in the aggregate (e.g., [1]), and can be further improved by personalizing these measures (e.g., [29]).

Other previous efforts focused on modeling more explicit user interactions. Golovchinsky et al. [12] focused on user-created annotations on documents such as highlightings, underlinings, circles, and notes in margin. They used this kind of feedback to infer relevance of document passages. In a document search scenario utilizing query expansion, they reported a significant improvement of the annotation-based feedback technique over explicit relevance feedback on the document level. Ahn et al. [2] followed a similar idea but used the concept of a personal notebook where users could paste text passages worth remembering. The two previous approaches require some form of explicit and therefore rare user interactions (e.g., annotating, copying and pasting) to work properly. In contrast, Buscher et al. [5] only rely on implicit data, and determine which parts of a document have been read, skimmed, or skipped by interpreting eye movements. The read and skimmed parts of the document were taken as relevant, while skipped document parts were ignored. The authors report considerable improvements for re-ranking of result lists, when including gaze-based feedback on the segment level compared to relevance feedback on the document level.

Our work builds on the previous research on connecting searcher examination patterns to user interest and document relevance. In particular, mouse cursor tracking has emerged as a useful tool for understanding searcher behavior. Previous research has shown the coordination between the searcher gaze position and mouse movement over the search results [33, 15, 21], as well as association between mouse cursor movements and searcher attention [13, 14, 31] and result preferences [23, 16, 22]. Most closely related to our work, Guo and Agichtein [16] found correlations between fine-grained interactions such as mouse cursor movements and document relevance, and showed that better relevance prediction can be achieved by incorporating these additional fine-grained behavioral signals compared to using dwell time information alone.

Recently, with the increasing popularity of touch-enabled devices, there have been a number of recent studies aiming to characterize and understand mobile search intent (e.g., [8]) and behavior (e.g., [26, 7]). Yet, the new types of interactions available on these touch-enabled devices are not yet sufficiently understood for optimizing the mobile searcher experience. In a recent position paper, Huang and Diriye argue for modeling of touch interactions for Web users [20]. However, to the best of our knowledge, there has been little empirical research on mining touch interactions for improving Web search. One exception is the recent work by Guo et al. [17], where the authors studied the problem of predicting search suc-

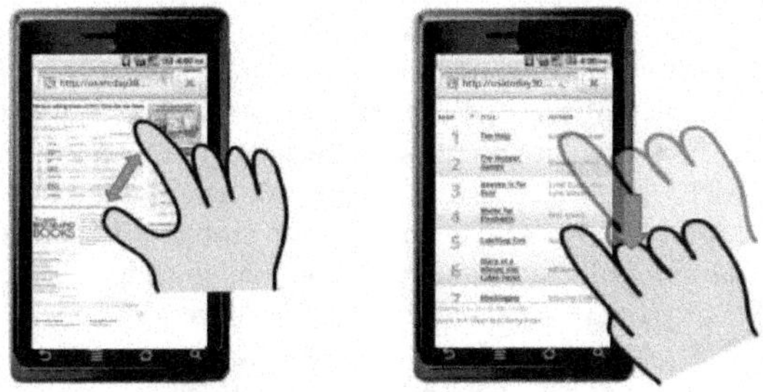

(a) (b)

Figure 1: (a) A searcher uses two fingers to pinch out (zoom in) a Web page on a smart phone touch screen; (b) A searcher uses one finger to swipe the page down to see the upper part of the page.

1	What was the best selling book (title and author) of 2011 in the US? How many copies of the book were sold in 2011 in the US?
2	Find three vegetarian restaurants near the Lenox Square.
3	What is the average temperature for the Dallas,SD for winter? Summer?"
4	How many pixels must be dead on a iPad 3 before Apple will replace it? Assume the tablet is still under warranty.
5	In what year did the USA experience its worst drought? What was the average precipitation in the country that year?
6	Is the band State Radio coming to Atlanta,GA within the next year? If not, when and where will they be playing closest?
7	Find the working hours of the Target store nearest to Emory University.

Table 1: Tasks descriptions

cess and satisfaction on a smart phone, and found that by modeling the amount of touch interactions more accurate predictions can be achieved.

In summary, our work extends previous research by offering the first in-depth study of modeling touch interactions for web search. We focus on the core problem of predicting document relevance for improving search result ranking. We present the first comprehensive analysis of touch interactions in search, with the aim of distinguishing the examination patterns of viewing a relevant or a non-relevant search result document.

3. USER STUDY

In this section, we introduce the two user studies conducted in the mobile and desktop settings respectively, and the interaction data collected in these studies.

3.1 Web Search on a Smart Phone

In the first user study, we capture the touch interactions during Web search on a smart phone, such as zooming and swiping (two examples are shown in Figure 1). To capture such interactions, we developed a modified version of the Chrome browser application for an Android phone, due to the popularity of this mobile operating system. All user actions, including clicks, touches, swiping, zooming, bookmarking page navigation and other interactions were logged with timestamps, and sent to a remote server via HTTP for further analysis. Similar instrumentation can be implemented for iPhones or Windows phones, as the types of touch interactions for viewing Web pages are largely shared across these platforms.

For each touch event, we additionally recorded the following information:

- Action type (namely, down, move and up)
- Number of touch points (i.e., number of fingers with contact with the screen)
- X and Y coordinates of the touch points
- Touch pressure, with a normalized value between 0.0 (no touch) and 1.0 (full force)
- Touch "size" with a normalized value between 0.0 (the smallest detectable size) to 1.0 (largest detectable size).

A gesture (a sequence of touch events starting with "down" and ends with "up"), may result in specific browser actions. For example, a pinch-out (or pinch-in) gesture with two fingers would result in zooming – an enlargement (or shrinkage) of a Web page (Figure 1 (a)) while a continued sequence of touch movements would result in swiping – a change of the viewing content ((Figure 1 (b)). Both zooming and swiping events are recorded in addition to the primitive touch events, with the former storing additional information about the new and old display scales, while the latter type providing additional information about the current vertical and horizontal page offsets.

Twenty-six subjects were recruited for this user study (fifteen females and eleven males). The mean age of participants was 21.7. All the subjects were undergraduate and graduate students from Emory University, with a variety of majors (e.g., psychology, economics, computer science, history and business), and all had some experience with Web search on a mobile device with a touch screen.

We designed the search tasks for this study to be representative of common Web search tasks on mobile devices. Table 1 reports the search tasks, together with the descriptions provided to the participants. As we can see, the tasks are a mixture of different topics, and highlight some geographical intents that are identified as significant part of mobile information needs in previous research [8, 26]. The search tasks were also designed to be difficult to solve with a search engine (i.e., the answer was not easily found on a single page). This is particularly valuable, since these more difficult and long-tailed search tasks are the main challenge for the state-of-the-art search engines. To distinguish oneself from the others, a search engine provider need to ensure that they do a good job on such search tasks.

Prior to starting the study, participants were given a tutorial on using the phone, including clicking, zooming, swiping, and changing the screen orientation. Next, a "warm-up" task was given to each participant to familiarize her with the procedure. Following the warm-up task, seven search tasks were given to each participant. To begin each task, the participants were presented a task description and an initial query to ensure starting with the same first set of result. After launching the initial query using the Google search engine, the participants were free to use the search engine however they chose in order to complete the task. Although participants generally agreed that the initial queries were reasonable for each task, they reformulated queries as needed.

Each time the participants navigated away from a non-search result document, or "landing page", they were asked (through a pop-up window) the degree to which the document satisfied the task. The rating was on a five point scale, with "1" indicating the page was "Bad", meaning it "did not satisfy the information need at all", and "5" indicating that the page was "Perfect", meaning it "completely satisfied the information need". The participants had the option to skip the rating, if they had not viewed the page.

In total, we obtained 393 unique Web page views, associated with explicit relevance judgments by the 26 participants. Our modified version of the browser application and the data used in this paper is available for the research community at `http://ir.mathcs.emory.edu/data/SIGIR2013/`.

3.2 Web Search on a Desktop PC

For the desktop setting, the data set we used was collected in a user study conducted by researchers at the University of Massachusetts [10]. The search behavior data of the participants was tracked, containing the URLs the searchers visited, the fine-grained interactions with the browsed pages, such as clicks, mouse cursor movements, and scrolling, the time-stamp of each page view and interaction was also recorded. The user population and search tasks in this second study are similar to that of the first user study we conducted to analyze mobile Web search behavior. The original dataset of the second user study is publicly available online [1] (additional information can be found along with the original dataset).

Similar to the first study, upon leaving a non-search page, the searchers were asked the degree to which their information need of the task was satisfied by the page on a five point scale. In total, 666 unique Web page views are provided, associated with explicit relevance judgments by the 30 participants.

4. TOUCH INTERACTION PATTERNS ON LANDING PAGES

In this section, we analyze the patterns of landing page examination and touch interactions. In general, we observed that the examination is typically a mixture of "reading" and "skimming" behavior, as found in previous research for the desktop setting [16]. In particular, "skimming" typically happens when the user is still searching the needed information, while "reading" typically happens when the user found the (seemingly) relevant information and is examining it more thoroughly.

The corresponding observable behavior, however, on a touch-enabled mobile device is different from a desktop personal computer due to the difference in the input and output device form factors. On a desktop personal computer, users scroll to change the content of the page (if the page is long enough to scroll), and may use the mouse cursor to focus attention (e.g., vertical coordination or text highlighting) [15, 16]. In contrast, on a touch-enabled mobile device, users use their fingers to swipe to change the displayed content, and stop touching the screen to read; they may pinch-out (zoom) to enlarge the web page if the content is not readable, or if they found something particularly interesting to examine more closely.

Based on analyzing the replays of touch interactions on hundreds of page views, we found that fast swiping behavior appears to indicate "skimming" behavior, while slow swiping/inactivity, and zooming suggest "reading" behavior or focused attention, where the former is an indicator of viewing non-relevant content, and the latter is an indicator of viewing relevant content. Figure 2 provides some illustrative examples of these interactions. Figure 2 (a) and (b) present two landing page examinations by a study participant, each of which is represented by the upper vertical coordinates of the smart phone view port (gray lines) as a result of swiping, and the corresponding view port scales (red lines) and zooming occurrences (red dots) over time. As we can see, both of the two page views have roughly 30 seconds dwell time, which would be considered relevant based on previous research [9, 11]. However, from the interaction patterns, we can tell that the two cases are actually different. As shown in Figure 2 (a), the user briefly paused, swiped down, briefly paused (possibly finding something seemingly relevant), and then swiped up again, without stopping to spend a significant amount of time reading any particular region of the page. Upon leaving the page, the user rated the page as "Bad". In contrast, in Figure 2 (b), the same user swiped down a little before a zoom-in, followed by a long period of inactivity (possibly indicating reading the content carefully). Upon leaving the page, the user rated the page as "Perfect". If we had only considered the dwell time information, we would predict the document of Figure 2 (a) as relevant due to the long dwell time. In contrast, in Figure 2 (b), the touch interactions data indicate that the user spends less time to find the needed information (i.e., less extensive swiping for changing the view port), while spending more time on "reading" or consuming the information (i.e., by observing the longer inactivity period following the zoom-in gesture), thus suggesting the document to be relevant.

The left part of Figure 2 (c) shows the corresponding heat map of the page examination shown in Figure 2 (b), where the darker the shade of green, the longer is the time that the user remained inactive or spent on reading the content that is presented in the corresponding view port. The right part of Figure 2 (c) shows the enlargement of the corresponding region where the user spent most of the time on after the zoom-in gesture. As we can see, the region indeed contains the needed information for the user (i.e., the worst drought year of the US history and the corresponding yearly average precipitation of that year, needed for completing Task 5 of Table 1). This further demonstrates that inactivity and zoom-in may be good indicators of user's reading behavior and, in turn, document relevance.

In addition to the amount of swiping, zooming and inactivity, a closer look at Figure 2 (a) and (b) reveals the potential of behavioral sequences in distinguishing viewing a relevant or a non-relevant document. For example, the periods of inactivity in Figure 2 (a) are followed by extensive swiping gestures, suggesting the dissatisfaction of the user after "reading"; in contrast, the inactivity in Figure 2 (b) is followed by the end of the page view, suggesting that the user was satisfied with the information she read about.

Next, we present our proposed approach of capturing these behavioral patterns and empirical results to demonstrate the utility of such modeling, which would provide further support to our observations about the "reading" and "skimming" behavior. However, to more comprehensively verify these assumptions, an eye-tracking study of searching on a mobile device (similar to the one reported in [3]) would be needed, suggesting a promising future extension of this work.

5. MODELING TOUCH INTERACTIONS

In this section, we describe our proposed *Mobile Touch Interaction (MTI)* features to capture the page examination patterns on a touch-enabled mobile device, with the goal of estimating document relevance. The full list of MTI features with brief descriptions is reported in Table 2, and expanded below.

5.1 Dwell Time

Dwell time, or document viewing time, has been extensively used as an indicator of document relevance – the longer the dwell time, the more likely the document is relevant. As typically done, dwell time is defined as the interval, in seconds, between the time the page is loaded and the time the searcher leaves the page. We use

[1] `http://ciir.cs.umass.edu/~hfeild/downloads.html`

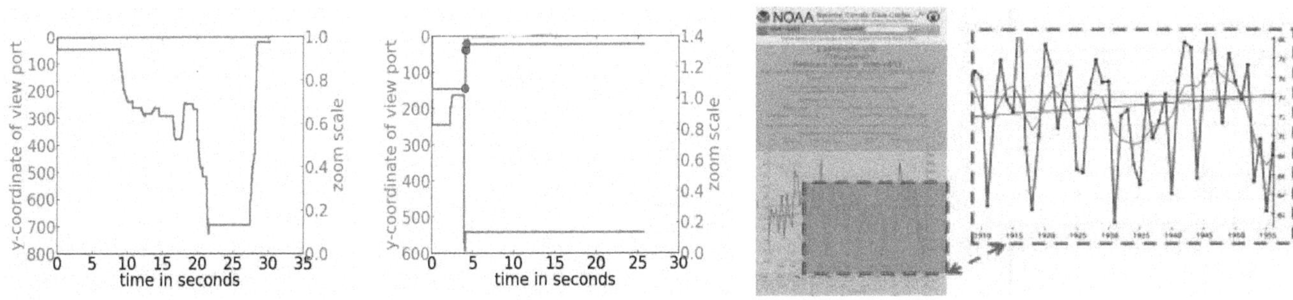

(a) $dwell: 30s\ (rel: 1)$ (b) $dwell: 25s\ (rel: 5)$ (c)

Figure 2: Two example landing page examinations, represented by the vertical swipe coordinates (gray lines), the view port scales (red lines) and zooming occurrences (red dots) over time. The x-axis represents the time from page load in seconds, and the y-axes represent the vertical page offset (i.e., upper vertical coordinate of the corresponding view port) resulted from the swipe event and the zooming scale: (a) a user viewing an non-relevant document; (b) the same user viewing a relevant document; (c) the heat map for the page examination shown in (b) and the corresponding enlargement of the page region that received the most attention from the user (i.e., the long period of inactivity or "reading" after a zoom-in). The darker the green in (c) the longer the time the user remained inactive or spent on reading the content that is presented in the corresponding view port.

Group	*Feature Description*
Dwell	*dwell:* time of the page view in seconds
Gestures	*gestcnt:* number of touch gestures *gestfreq:* gestcnt/dwell *pressure:* average touch pressure, normalized to the range of 0 and 1 *touchsize:* average touch size, normalized to the range of 0 and 1
Zooming	*zoomcnt:* number of zooming gestures *zoomfreq:* zoomcnt / dwell *zoomdist:* accumulated zooming scale changes *zoomspeed:* zoomdist / dwell *zoommax:* maximum zooming scale
Swiping	*swipecnt:* number of vertical swipes *swipefreq:* swipecnt / dwell *swipedist:* total vertical swipe distance *swipespeed:* swipedist / dwell *swipemax:* maximum vertical swipe coordinate
Inactivity	*inactive_total:* accumulated inactive time *inactive_pct:* inactive_total / dwell *inactive_avg:* average inactive time *inactive_max:* maximum inactive time
Transitions	*s_i-s_j_cnt:* number of transitions from state s_i to observation s_j during the page view *transitions_cnt:* total number of observation transitions during the page view *s_i-s_j_prob:* s_i-s_j_cnt / transitions_cnt
User	*user_id:* the ID of the user who viewed the page

Table 2: Feature descriptions

dwell time both as a baseline to compare against and as a feature in our full model.

5.2 Gestures

As mentioned in Section 3, a gesture is a sequence of touches with x and y coordinates, starting with a "down" touch and ends with an "up" touch. A gesture may trigger effects such as zooming (pinching) and view port changing (swiping). The modeling of zooming and swiping are moved to their own feature groups. This group of features aim to capture the overall amount of efforts of the user (on a "syntactical" level) without knowing the "semantic" meaning of the gesture. Features include the number and frequency of the gestures, which were found to be negatively correlated with task-level searcher satisfaction in previous preliminary study of touch interactions [17]. In addition, we also capture the average pressure and touch sizes of the gestures, assuming they correlate with searcher's frustration level and could be indicative of document relevance. That is, viewing non-relevant document may cause users to become frustrated and thus change the touch pressure and size. Similar features such as mouse pressure were identified as frustration indicator in previous research [10].

5.3 Zooming

The zooming behavior typically occurs when users would like to take a closer look at the Web page, which happens relatively frequently on a mobile device with a limited screen size (especially, when users are viewing a Web page that is not optimized for mobile devices [17]), and infrequently happens on a desktop computer where screen sizes are typically much bigger. Zooming scale, as we noted in Section 4, can be indicative of degree of user interest. As pointed out by Huang and Diriye in their position paper [20], zooming may correspond to the mouse cursor movements in the desktop setting, such as text highlighting [34, 16] and hovering [23], which were found to be indicators of searcher interest. In this feature group, we capture the count, frequency of the zooming behavior, as well as the maximum zooming scale, the accumulated changes in zooming scale and the speed of the scale changing, following the representation of mouse cursor movements of the PCB model proposed by Guo and Agichtein [16].

5.4 Swiping

The swiping behavior on a touch screen results in the change of the view port similar to the scrolling behavior on a desktop computer. Due to the small screen sizes of mobile devices, users tend to swipe more often on such devices compared to scrolling on a desktop computer. Nevertheless, the change of view port on both of the modalities (as shown in Section 4 and previous research [16], respectively) tend to indicate that the user is still in the searching mode, thus extensive swiping when viewing a Web page is likely to suggest non-relevance. Following the previous research in the desktop setting [16], we focus on modeling the vertical swipe for this group, capturing the overall amount, the frequency, and speed of the swiping behavior, as well as the overall swipe distance and its maximum in pixels.

5.5 Inactivity

As noted in Section 4, a period of inactivity on a touch-enabled mobile device seems to be a good indicator of "reading" behavior. This is in part due to the touch nature of the device – as a result, inactivity is typically needed to keep the screen still for careful reading (after adjustment of the view port through zooming and swiping). In contrast, inactivity was not found to be a good indicator of relevance in the desktop setting with a mouse and a keyboard as the primary input devices [16]. In the desktop setting, some users remain inactive when reading, while some other users use mouse cursor as the reading-aid [33, 15, 21, 34] and remain inactive when nothing interest them. The effectiveness of the inactivity may also attribute to the smaller screen sizes of the mobile devices – a long period of inactivity on a large PC screen may correspond to reading a specific area or skimming through the whole view port while a long period of inactivity on a small mobile device screen is less likely to correspond to skimming behavior (as it would take much less time). Empirical evidence would be provided in the next section to illustrate the difference of inactivity in these two modalities. For this feature group, we define inactivity as the time period of more than one second between a pair of consecutive touch behavior, and compute the total inactive time, and average and maximum time of inactive periods.

5.6 Sequence

Section 4 sheds some light on the potential of modeling behavioral sequence. For example, inactivity followed by the end of the page view is an indicator of viewing a relevant page while inactivity followed by swiping before ending may suggest that the document were seemingly relevant but actually not. The features in this group aim to capture these sequential patterns. We define the fine-grained interactions during a page view as a sequence of observed states $S = s_0 \rightarrow s_1 \rightarrow ... \rightarrow s_n$, where $s_i \in \{ZI, ZO, SD, SU, SS, IS, IM, IL\}$. The possible states are summarized in Table 3.

Given a sequence of states, we then count the occurrences of transitions $s_i \rightarrow s_j$ to characterize the behavioral sequence when viewing the page. We also normalize the transition counts by the total transition count of each page view to generate another set of transition features.

5.7 User Variability

Previous research has discovered significant variations in behavioral patterns among different users [15, 6]. For example, some users are found to be more "active" in examination than others [6]. Modeling such user variations was shown useful in improving estimating document relevance [16] and other Web search applications [15]. In this paper, we consider a simple modeling of user variation through incorporating participant IDs as additional features, which were shown effective in previous research [15].

6. CHARACTERIZING MTI FEATURES

We first characterize the "atomic" (non-sequential) MTI features, and evaluate their utilities as implicit relevance feedback through calculating their correlations with self-reported relevance judgements. We also compare MTI features with the corresponding fine-grained interaction features for the desktop setting (e.g., the PCB features presented in [16]), when available. Then, we characterize and evaluate the utility of the Markov transitions between features, for implicit feedback.

State	*Description*
START	start of the page view
ZI	zoom in
ZO	zoom out
SD	swipe down
SU	swipe up
SS	swipe still (i.e., horizontal swipe)
IS	short period of inactivity (1 to 5 secs)
IM	medium period of inactivity (5 to 20 secs)
IL	long period of inactivity (longer than 20 secs)
END	end of the page view

Table 3: Possible states used in sequence modeling.

Feature	*Mobile*	*PC*
dwell time	44.3 (36.2)	31.2 (29.9)
swipe/scroll distance	2808.8 (4007.6)	570.2 (1770.7)
swipe/scroll speed	66.9 (96.1)	17.8 (45.1)
swipe/scroll maximum	1352.6 (1915.4)	275.4 (835.4)
inactive percentage	0.59 (0.21)	0.57 (0.22)
total inactive time	28.0 (27.2)	19.1 (22.5)
average inactive time	4.3 (6.2)	4.7 (4.3)
maximum inactive time	14.8 (18.5)	9.2 (13.0)
zoom count	0.89 (2.71)	n/a
touch size	0.15 (0.06)	n/a
cursor ymax	n/a	595.5 (236.1)
cursor xspeed	n/a	108.5 (120.4)

Table 4: Means and standard deviations of representative fine-grained interaction features on the two different modalities

6.1 Comparing the Two Modalities

In Section 4 and Section 5, we compare the fine-grained interactions on the two modalities qualitatively. This section presents some statistics to demonstrate the similarities and differences in a more quantitative way.

First, we compare the overall statistics between the two modalities, including means and standard deviations of the features, which are summarized in Table 4. As we can see, some features are primarily used for the desktop PC setting, such as the wide variety of features that aim to capture mouse cursor movements [16]. Some representative examples include the maximum y-coordinate and the horizontal mouse moving speed. Similarly, some other features are primarily for touch-enabled mobile devices, such as zooming counts and touch sizes.

Despite the obvious differences in the types of common interactions, the two modalities also share some interaction features, such as dwell time, view port changing (i.e., swiping vs. scrolling) and periods of inactivity. While these shared interaction features can be considered as similarities of the two modalities, a closer look reveals noticeable differences. For example, dwell time and inactive time overall tend to be longer for the mobile setting, which may be explained by the slower searching and reading on this modality due to the relatively small screen size. Also likely due to partly the smaller screen size and partly the easiness in changing the view port through swiping, we can see that mobile users swipe much more and faster compared to scrolling on a desktop PC.

Second, we evaluate the MTI feature utility by computing the correlation with explicit relevance judgements provided by the users and compare with the feature utility for the counterpart fine-grained interaction features for the desktop setting. The findings for representative features of the two modalities are summarized in Table 5.

As we can see, the dwell time information is consistently effective, exhibiting significant, but weak positive correlations around 0.17 for both modalities. Gesture count and frequency, in accordance with previous research [17], were found to be indicators of searcher dissatisfaction, both exhibiting negative correlations with the explicit relevance judgements. This makes sense as more efforts the user needs to make to find the information the more likely the user is dissatisfied and the document is more likely to be not relevant. In contrast, the touch size and touch pressure were found to be only weak indicators of document relevance, exhibiting insignificant correlations, which is in line with what has been reported previously [10] about pressure of using mouse on desktop computer. Somewhat surprising was the positive correlation (instead of negative correlation as assumed), which may be explained by the association of interaction speed with touch size/pressure – for example, when users swipe faster, the touch sizes of their fingers tend to be smaller compared to leaving their fingers on the screen to slowly swipe.

Similar to the scrolling behavior on a PC, the swiping behavior on touch-enabled mobile device also exhibits negative correlations with the document relevance – the faster the users swipe, the more likely the user was still searching and not satisfied by the document content. One subtle difference appear to be the decreased importance of knowing the actual number of pixels the user swipe. For example, the swipe speed on a mobile device exhibits only -0.165 correlation compared to the -0.212 correlation of its counterpart scroll speed on a PC, while the swipe and scroll frequency on the two modalities exhibit both around -0.210 negative correlations with document relevance. One explanation is the effects brought in by zooming behavior on the mobile device – with a zoomed-in view of the Web page, the same amount of swiping effort may only translate to smaller change in terms of pixels for the view port.

Zooming behavior, as expected, are mostly positively correlated with document relevance, but not in a significant way. The strongest correlation from this group is the insignificant positive correlation of 0.039 from the zoom distance features, which captures the accumulated amount of zooming scale changes. One explanation of the insignificance of zooming behavior is its relatively rare occurrences – with more and more Web sites provide mobile customized views of their page contents, zooming behavior may become less and less needed. Another factor that may contribute to the insignificance is the noise brought in by zooming on a mobile unfriendly non-relevant document, in which case, similar to the perception bias in click signals that are found in previous research [16], zooming is just a necessity for being able to view the seemingly relevant document and is not sufficient to reveal the actual relevance by itself.

The features of inactivity, which aim to capture the "reading" behavior on a touch-enabled mobile device, exhibit significant and positive correlations with document relevance. This accords with our intuition that inactivity on such device is indicative of "reading" and, in turn, indicative of relevance. Interestingly, while the overall statistics of inactivity features for the two modalities appear similar (in Table 4), the correlations for the same set of features on the desktop PC setting are mostly insignificant (except for the total inactive time, which may borrow strength from the overall dwell time as it has strongest correlation with the overall dwell time among all the features in the group). The maximum inactive time is among the strongest features in the group for mobile, exhibiting a significant positive correlation of 0.284. Its counterpart for the desktop PC, however, only has an insignificant correlation of 0.059. This observation supports our assumption that inactivity on a desktop PC

Feature	*Mobile*	*PC*
dwell time	0.171*	0.167*
gesture count	-0.042	n/a
gesture frequency	-0.201*	n/a
touch size	0.032	n/a
touch pressure	0.020	n/a
swipe/scroll count	-0.043	-0.008
swipe/scroll frequency	-0.210*	-0.206*
swipe/scroll distance	-0.065	-0.092*
swipe/scroll maximum	-0.052	-0.025
swipe/scroll speed	-0.165*	-0.212*
zoom count	0.026	n/a
zoom frequency	-0.008	n/a
zoom distance	0.039	n/a
zoom maximum	0.021	n/a
inactive percentage	0.244*	-0.044
total inactive time	0.232*	0.124*
average inactive time	0.276*	0.016
maximum inactive time	0.284*	0.059
cursor count	n/a	0.164*
cursor frequency	n/a	-0.082*
cursor ymax	n/a	0.243*
cursor xspeed	n/a	-0.143*

Table 5: Pearson's correlation between individual implicit feedback feature and the actual explicit judgments of document relevance (* indicates $< .05$ statistical significance).

(with bigger screen size, and mouse and keyboard as primary input devices) does not necessarily correspond to the reading behavior.

Even though inactivity features are not good relevance indicators for the desktop PC setting, we found that its exclusive features of mouse cursor movements instead provide substantial utility as implicit relevance feedback. In accordance with the previous research [16], we found that the amount of mouse cursor movements (e.g., cursor ymax) indicates user's interest level of the document, exhibiting significant positive correlation with document relevance, while faster mouse movements seems to suggest "skimming" behavior, exhibiting significant negative correlation with document relevance.

In summary, we have identified interesting similarities and differences of the fine-grained interactions between the two modalities, both in terms of their overall characteristics and utility as implicit relevance feedback. Next, we will characterize and evaluate the utility of modeling behavioral sequence as Markov transitions.

6.2 Evaluating Markov Transitions

Figure 3 summarizes the Markov state transitions for viewing a document on a touch-enabled mobile device, estimated from our dataset. In the figure, the nodes represent the possible states, and the directed edges represent the transitions between the two connected states with the width of the edge signifying the likelihood of the corresponding transitions. The figure reveals some interesting sequential patterns. For example, the START state is most likely to be followed by IM (Inactivity Medium), suggesting users tend to remain inactive for a intermediate period of time in the beginning to get themselves familiar with the page content in this initial view port before deciding the next step (e.g., swipe, zoom or end). The heaviest outgoing edge for IM, interestingly, is SD (i.e., swipe down), which is much thicker compared to the outgoing edge to END, suggesting that in most cases, users would not find the rele-

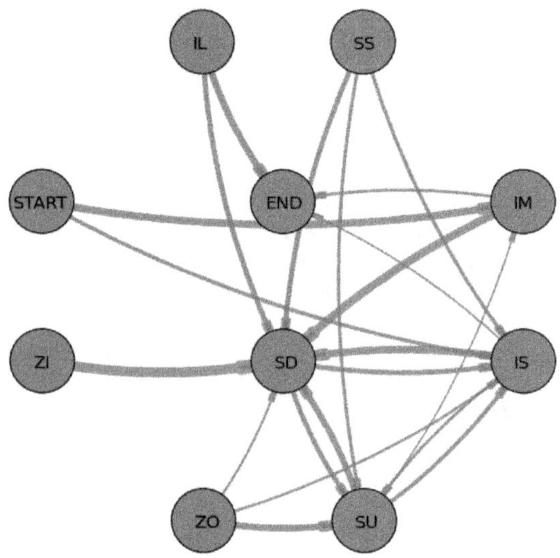

Figure 3: Markov state transitions for interactions of viewing a document on a touch-enabled mobile device. The transition probabilities are indicated by the line width; transitions with probabilities of less than 0.1 are not shown.

vant information in the very first view port (neither would exit the page view immediately) and tend to swipe down to view further. As a matter of fact, SD is the largest receiving state, with many dominant edges pointing from other states. This may also be explained by the relatively small screen size and the easiness of swiping on a touch-enabled mobile device – it is not hard to imagine, users often need to swipe down to continue reading no matter whether they have found something promising (e.g., transitioning from state IL or ZI), or have not found something interesting (e.g., transitioning from IS), or would like to re-examine (e.g., transitioning from SU). Another two interesting prominent transitions are ZO to SU and IL to END, where the former signifies the typical pattern of going back (e.g., to revisit previously seen content) while the latter signifies a typical "happy ending" where the user ends the page view after a long period of "reading".

Table 6 highlights example state transitions that are particularly indicative of document relevance, with each row reporting the likelihoods of a particular transition under the relevant and non-relevant Markov models and the corresponding likelihood ratio. Self-reported judgments greater or equal to 3 ("good") were considered "relevant" while "Fair" and "Bad" were considered "non-relevant" in this analysis. IL-END is one of the most interesting transitions: the chance of seeing such "happy ending" is 1.6 times more likely to happen for viewing a relevant document as compared to reading a non-relevant document. Its counterpart IS-END, in contrast, signifies an opposite trend, exhibiting a 0.558 likelihood ratio. Interestingly, a swipe down after IL (i.e., IL-SD) turns out to be a strong negative indicator of relevance. This makes sense as a continued searching after a long read is likely to suggest that the user was not (completely) satisfied. Another interesting example is START-IS, which is 1.4 times more likely to happen when viewing a relevant document. This may correspond to cases where users found something interesting or promising and quickly react thus shorten the period of time for the initial orienteering. Regarding swiping, SS-SU (i.e., horizontal swipe followed by a upward swipe), which signifies the re-examination, also appears to be a strong indicator of non-relevance. Zooming-related transition features, while hav-

Transition	*Relevant Lik.*	*Non-relevant Lik.*	*Lik. Ratio*
IL-SD	0.255	0.488	0.522
SS-SU	0.145	0.265	0.546
IS-END	0.095	0.170	0.558
ZO-IM	0.034	0.059	0.586
SU-IS	0.311	0.278	1.118
SD-ZO	0.003	0.002	1.414
IM-END	0.267	0.187	1.429
SU-ZO	0.049	0.030	1.609
START-IS	0.372	0.266	1.400
SS-IS	0.362	0.230	1.575
IL-END	0.638	0.395	1.615

Table 6: Relevant and Non-relevant Likelihoods (*Lik.*), Likelihood Ratio (*Lik. Ratio*) for Example Markov State Transitions

ing relative big likelihood ratios (e.g., SU-ZO), are not necessarily good predictors as they occur rarely.

In summary, we have characterized the common behavioral sequences using Markov transition probabilities, and demonstrated the potential of modeling these transitions for estimating document relevance.

7. PREDICTING DOCUMENT RELEVANCE

Next, we describe our experiments on predicting document relevance, and re-ranking documents based on the predicted relevance scores.

7.1 Prediction Model

We treat the relevance prediction as a regression problem, and use a learning algorithm based on an ensemble of regression trees, which is representative of what major search engines tend to use for training ranking algorithms. In particular, similar to the previous research [16], we used Bagging (Bootstrap Aggregation) [4], which outputs a numerical outcome as prediction by aggregating multiple versions of a single predictor through plurality voting. The multiple versions of the single predictor are formed by making bootstrap replicates of the learning set, and using these as new learning sets. The single predictor, or weak learner, used was the C4.5 regression tree, which splits the tree at each node by choosing the attribute that is most effective in terms of normalized information gain. The advantages of this non-linear ensemble regressor include its expressiveness, which can capture complex interactions among a variety of features, resistance to over-fitting, and the relative computational efficiency compared to other non-linear learning algorithms such as neural networks.

7.2 Evaluation Metric

We evaluated the performance of predicting document relevance by computing the standard information retrieval measure of NDCG (Normalized Discounted Cumulative Gain) for the corresponding re-ranking of the search results. Specifically, given a ranked list of documents for a search task, $NDCG_k$ [24] measures the quality of a ranked list at position k, as follows:

$$NDCG_k = \frac{DCG_k}{IDCG_k}, DCG_k = \sum_{i=1}^{k} \frac{2^{rel_i} - 1}{\log_2(1+i)}$$

where $IDCG_k$ is the DCG_k value of the ideal ranking with respect to the actual document relevance, and the rel_i is the relevance judgment, which is at a five point scale. DCG_k aims to penalize the ranked list with highly relevant documents appearing at lower positions, with the graded relevance value reduced proportionally to the position of the result in the list. $NDCG_k$ of 1.0 indicates a perfect ranking that is identical to $IDCG_k$, with smaller values indicating worse rankings. We first compute $NDCG_k$ for each individual search task, and then average the scores into one $NDCG_k$ to summarize the quality of the ranked list provided by each method. We evaluate this score for various k values and highlight $k = 1, 3, 10$, which are the values reported to be used by commercial search engines.

7.3 Methods Compared

We consider the following methods for estimating document relevance, including three variants of the MTI model, and two baseline models using dwell time information and the original search result rank, respectively. All the models are trained with Bagging with regression trees (Section 7.1).

ResultRank: This model uses the original search result rank as the feature to predict document relevance, which encodes the belief in relevance that the search engine holds and is typically derived from thousands of ranking signals. Presumably, the smaller the rank value (i.e., the higher the document was ranked), the more relevant the document is likely to be. However, if the search engine fails in accurately estimating the relevance, the rank would become uninformative. For the viewed documents in the search trail that were not ranked in the SERP, the rank of the landing page (i.e., the origin of the search trail the document was on) is used.

DwellTime: This model uses dwell time information as the feature to predict document relevance, which has been widely used in previous research as implicit relevance feedback [36, 16], and successfully applied to addressing a variety of real-world Web search applications [35, 18, 10, 19].

MTI_P: A variant of the MTI model that adapts the feature representations proposed by the PCB model [16] – for example, MTI_P incorporates features for swiping behavior that are similar to the PCB scrolling features, features for zooming and raw gestures similar to PCB features for mouse cursor movements that aim to capture user degree of interest, efforts and engagements. In other words, the features from the Dwell Time, Gesture, Swiping and Zooming groups that are described in Section 5 are used to train this model.

MTI_PI: A variant of the MTI model that adapts the feature representations proposed by the PCB model and adds the newly proposed inactivity features. In other words, the features from Gesture, Swiping, Zooming, and Inactivity groups that are described in Section 5 are used.

MTI_PIM: A variant of the MTI model that adapts the feature representations proposed by the PCB model and adds the newly proposed inactivity and Markov transition features that are described in Section 5.

MTI_PIM_U: A variant of the MTI model that incorporates User Variability features (Section 5) in addition to all MTI_PIM features, aiming to model variations in user behavior.

7.4 Results

We now report our results on re-ranking the viewed documents using the estimated relevance. For training and testing, we use 10-fold cross-validation, with 10 randomized experimental runs. We report $NDCG_k$, averaged over all the search tasks across different users.

The overall experimental results are summarized in Figure 4 across multiple K values. As we can see, all of the four variants of the MTI model substantially and significantly outperform the two baseline models across all K values. The relatively poor performance of the ResultRank baseline is expected due to the difficulty of the assigned search tasks, which was also observed in previous research [16]. Among the MTI variants, the simplest version in MTI_P already results in significant gains, on top of which, adding inactivity features MTI_P results in another substantial lift. Adding Markov transition features (MTI_PIM) and user features (MTI_PIM_U) achieve further incremental gains with smaller yet statistically significant margins. Interestingly, all the models based on implicit feedback seem to perform particularly well at the top positions (e.g., $K < 3$). One explanation is that the search interaction patterns are more consistent for viewing very relevant documents (e.g., with "perfect" rating on the five point scale), thus resulting in more accurate estimation. The improvements over the stronger DwellTime baseline are further summarized in Table 7 for $K = 1, 3, 10$. As we can see, the improvements are around 20% and are substantially higher for top positions, which is desirable as these are the ranking positions that matters most to Web searchers and are of particular interest to search engines.

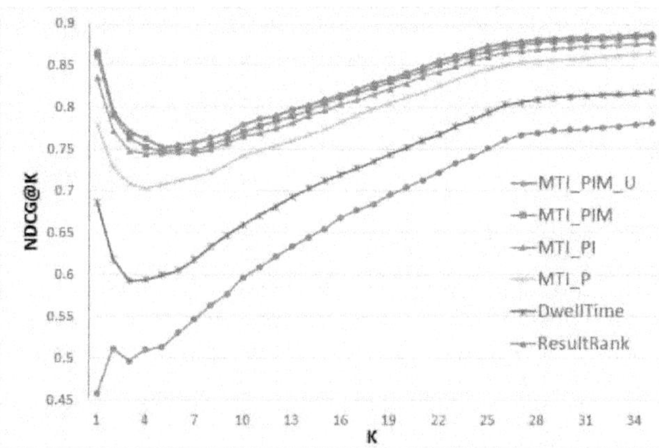

Figure 4: NDCG at K (K=1, 2, ..., 35) for the different variants of the MTI model compared to the dwell time and result rank baseline models. The differences between the different methods are statistically significant at p < .05 level.

Method	*K=1*	*K=3*	*K=10*
MTI_PIM_U	0.866 (+26%)	0.771 (+30%)	0.780 (+18%)
MTI_PIM	0.862 (+25%)	0.764 (+29%)	0.771 (+17%)
MTI_PI	0.835 (+22%)	0.749 (+26%)	0.766 (+16%)
MTI_P	0.780 (+14%)	0.709 (+19%)	0.743 (+13%)
DwellTime	0.687	0.593	0.659

Table 7: NDCG at K (K=1, 3, 10) for the different variants of the MTI model compared to the dwell time baseline model. The differences between the different methods are statistically significant at p < .05 level.

8. CONCLUSIONS

In this paper we introduced a new model for representing Web search interactions on touch-enabled mobile devices, which captures not only dwell time information, but also fine-grained user interactions, such as zooming, swiping and inactivity. To our knowledge, our proposed Mobile Touch Interaction (MTI) model is the first successful attempt to exploit such "low-level" behavioral signals to identify the basic patterns of "reading" and "scanning" behavior, as well as more complex combinations of these on a touch-enabled mobile device, represented by expressive features to capture these examination patterns automatically. We also presented in-depth comparative analyses of the fine-grained interaction modeling for the mobile and the desktop Web search settings, identifying interesting similarities and differences.

Our experimental results show that the proposed behavioral signals indeed correlate with searchers' explicit judgments of document relevance, and provide additional valuable information beyond dwell time alone. For example, we found that periods of inactivity, as being indicative of "reading" behavior on a touch-enabled mobile device, are among the most predictive signals of document relevance on this new Web search modality, but not for the desktop PC setting. We also found that swiping behavior, being similar to the scrolling behavior in their functionality of changing view port, are indicative of information searching or "skimming" and can be used as negative implicit feedback. Furthermore, we found that incorporating the behavioral sequence and user information can additionally improve document relevance estimation. In combination, these signals enable MTI to exhibit substantial improvements on relevance prediction accuracy, consequently improving document ranking by up to 30% compared to using dwell time data alone.

In summary, we have laid the groundwork for exploiting fine-grained search behavior for improving relevance estimation and search result ranking for touch-enabled devices, providing a significant advance towards improving the mobile search experience.

9. ACKNOWLEDGMENTS

This work was supported by the National Science Foundation grant IIS-1018321. The authors also thank Henry Feild for sharing the data of the second user study for the desktop PC setting and the reviewers for valuable comments to help improve the paper.

10. REFERENCES

[1] E. Agichtein, E. Brill, and S. Dumais. Improving web search ranking by incorporating user behavior information. SIGIR '06, pages 19–26, 2006.

[2] J.-w. Ahn, P. Brusilovsky, D. He, J. Grady, and Q. Li. Personalized web exploration with task models. In *Proceeding of the 17th international conference on World Wide Web*, WWW '08, pages 1–10, 2008.

[3] R. Biedert, A. Dengel, G. Buscher, and A. Vartan. Reading and estimating gaze on smart phones. ETRA '12, pages 385–388, New York, NY, USA, 2012. ACM.

[4] L. Breiman. Bagging predictors. *Mach. Learn.*, 24(2):123–140, Aug. 1996.

[5] G. Buscher, A. Dengel, and L. van Elst. Query expansion using gaze-based feedback on the subdocument level. SIGIR '08, pages 387–394, 2008.

[6] G. Buscher, R. W. White, S. Dumais, and J. Huang. Large-scale analysis of individual and task differences in search result page examination strategies. WSDM '12, pages 373–382, 2012.

[7] K. Church and N. Oliver. Understanding mobile web and mobile search use in today's dynamic mobile landscape. In *Proc. of the 13th International Conference on Human Computer Interaction with Mobile Devices and Services*, 2011.

[8] K. Church and B. Smyth. Understanding the intent behind mobile information needs. In *Proceedings of the 14th international conference on Intelligent user interfaces*, IUI '09, pages 247–256, 2009.

[9] M. Claypool, P. Le, M. Wased, and D. Brown. Implicit interest indicators. IUI '01, pages 33–40, 2001.

[10] H. A. Feild, J. Allan, and R. Jones. Predicting searcher frustration. SIGIR '10, pages 34–41.

[11] S. Fox, K. Karnawat, M. Mydland, S. Dumais, and T. White. Evaluating implicit measures to improve web search. *ACM Transactions on Information Systems*, 23(2), 2005.

[12] G. Golovchinsky, M. N. Price, and B. N. Schilit. From reading to retrieval: freeform ink annotations as queries. SIGIR '99, pages 19–25.

[13] Q. Guo and E. Agichtein. Exploring mouse movements for inferring query intent. SIGIR '08, pages 707–708, 2008.

[14] Q. Guo and E. Agichtein. Ready to buy or just browsing?: detecting web searcher goals from interaction data. SIGIR '10, pages 130–137, 2010.

[15] Q. Guo and E. Agichtein. Towards predicting web searcher gaze position from mouse movements. CHI EA '10, pages 3601–3606, 2010.

[16] Q. Guo and E. Agichtein. Beyond dwell time: estimating document relevance from cursor movements and other post-click searcher behavior. WWW '12, 2012.

[17] Q. Guo, S. Yuan, and E. Agichtein. Detecting success in mobile search from interaction. SIGIR '11, 2011.

[18] A. Hassan, R. Jones, and K. L. Klinkner. Beyond dcg: user behavior as a predictor of a successful search. WSDM '10, pages 221–230.

[19] A. Hassan, Y. Song, and L.-w. He. A task level user satisfaction metric and its application on improving relevance estimation. CIKM '11, 2011.

[20] J. Huang and A. M. Diriye. Web user interaction mining from touch-enabled mobile devices. HCIR '12, 2012.

[21] J. Huang, R. White, and G. Buscher. User see, user point: gaze and cursor alignment in web search. CHI '12, pages 1341–1350, 2012.

[22] J. Huang, R. W. White, G. Buscher, and K. Wang. Improving searcher models using mouse cursor activity. SIGIR '12, pages 195–204, 2012.

[23] J. Huang, R. W. White, and S. Dumais. No clicks, no problem: using cursor movements to understand and improve search. CHI '11, pages 1225–1234, 2011.

[24] K. Järvelin and J. Kekäläinen. Ir evaluation methods for retrieving highly relevant documents. SIGIR '00, pages 41–48, 2000.

[25] T. Joachims, L. Granka, B. Pan, H. Hembrooke, F. Radlinski, and G. Gay. Evaluating the accuracy of implicit feedback from clicks and query reformulations in web search. *ACM Trans. Inf. Syst.*, 25(2), 2007.

[26] M. Kamvar, M. Kellar, R. Patel, and Y. Xu. Computers and iphones and mobile phones, oh my!: a logs-based comparison of search users on different devices. WWW '09, pages 801–810, 2009.

[27] D. Kelly and N. J. Belkin. Reading time, scrolling and interaction: exploring implicit sources of user preferences for relevance feedback. SIGIR '01, pages 408–409, 2001.

[28] D. Kelly and N. J. Belkin. Display time as implicit feedback: understanding task effects. SIGIR '04, pages 377–384, 2004.

[29] M. Melucci and R. W. White. Discovering hidden contextual factors for implicit feedback. In *CIR'07*, pages –1–1, 2007.

[30] M. Morita and Y. Shinoda. Information filtering based on user behavior analysis and best match text retrieval. SIGIR '94, pages 272–281, 1994.

[31] V. Navalpakkam and E. Churchill. Mouse tracking: measuring and predicting users' experience of web-based content. CHI '12, pages 2963–2972, 2012.

[32] R. Rafter and B. Smyth. Passive profiling from server logs in an online recruitment environment. In *Proc. of ITWP*, 2001.

[33] K. Rodden, X. Fu, A. Aula, and I. Spiro. Eye-mouse coordination patterns on web search results pages. CHI EA '08, pages 2997–3002, 2008.

[34] R. W. White and G. Buscher. Text selections as implicit relevance feedback. SIGIR '12, pages 1151–1152, 2012.

[35] R. W. White and S. T. Dumais. Characterizing and predicting search engine switching behavior. CIKM '09, 2009.

[36] R. W. White and D. Kelly. A study on the effects of personalization and task information on implicit feedback performance. CIKM '06, pages 297–306, 2006.

An Information-Theoretic Account of Static Index Pruning

Ruey-Cheng Chen
National Taiwan University
1 Roosevelt Rd. Sec. 4
Taipei 106, Taiwan
rueycheng@turing.csie.ntu.edu.tw

Chia-Jung Lee
University of Massachusetts
140 Governors Drive
Amherst, MA 01003-9264
cjlee@cs.umass.edu

ABSTRACT

In this paper, we recast static index pruning as a model induction problem under the framework of Kullback's principle of minimum cross-entropy. We show that static index pruning has an approximate analytical solution in the form of convex integer program. Further analysis on computation feasibility suggests that one of its surrogate model can be solved efficiently. This result has led to the rediscovery of *uniform pruning*, a simple yet powerful pruning method proposed in 2001 and later easily ignored by many of us. To empirically verify this result, we conducted experiments under a new design in which prune ratio is strictly controlled. Our result on standard ad-hoc retrieval benchmarks has confirmed that uniform pruning is robust to high prune ratio and its performance is currently state of the art.

Categories and Subject Descriptors

H.1.1 [**Systems and Information Theory**]: Information theory; H.3.1 [**Content Analysis and Indexing**]: Indexing methods; H.3.4 [**Systems and Software**]: Performance evaluation (efficiency and effectiveness)

Keywords

Static index pruning; principle of minimum cross-entropy; model induction; uniform pruning

1. INTRODUCTION

Kullback discussed one famous problem in his seminal work [14] about inducing a probability measure based on some previous measurement. When one has some initial hypothesis about a system and seeks to update this measurement incrementally, she needs to choose a new hypothesis from a set of feasible measures that best approximates her current belief. Here, the difficulty lies in defining the notion of closeness in the probability space. While at the time this was an important issue in everyday probabilistic modeling, a genuine solution had yet to come.

SIGIR'13, July 28–August 1, 2013, Dublin, Ireland.

To answer the question he had raised, Kullback introduced a method called "minimum discrimination information," or in the recent literature known as the *principle of minimum cross-entropy*. This approach has later become one of the most influential inductive principles in statistics, and also has benefited numerous fields, including some subareas in information retrieval [15,20]. Kullback's solution was simple and elegant: One shall choose a measure that most closely resembles the previous measurement in terms of Kullback-Leibler divergence. Specifically, this is equivalent to solving the following optimization problem, given some prior measure p and a set of feasible measures $\mathcal{F}$:

$$\begin{array}{ll} \text{minimize} & \mathrm{D}(q\|p) \\ \text{subject to} & q \in \mathcal{F}. \end{array} \tag{1}$$

In this paper, we apply this induction framework to a classic problem in information retrieval, called *static index pruning*. Static index pruning is a task that reduces the index size for improving disk usage and query throughput [1]. Size reduction is done by removing index entries. Generally, the aim in static index pruning is to find a subset of index entries that best approximates the full index in terms of retrieval performance. This aspect, as we will show later, is closely related to model induction.

One key assumption in this paper is that an inverted index is a nonparametric, conditional distribution of document D given term T, i.e., $p(D|T)$. This follows directly from Chen et al.'s definition [10], which allows us to measure the resemblance between two versions of inverted indexes the way we do probability distributions. Here, the following definitions put static index pruning into the framework of Equation (1):

- The prior distribution p is defined as the full (unpruned) inverted index.
- The set of feasible hypotheses $\mathcal{F}$ contains all the possible pruned indexes of p that have reached some given prune ratio ρ. In other words, each element $q \in \mathcal{F}$ is a pruned version of the original inverted index p.

This conception marks the very beginning of our quest for developing an efficient solution of static index pruning. Through analysis, we first show that static index pruning is essentially a combinatorial optimization problem. Nevertheless, in Section 3, we manage to obtain a weaker analytical solution that is practically operable by trading off some mathematical rigor. We found that, under appropriate assumptions, static index pruning reduces to a convex integer program. But this is not a good solution in general, since the number of variables in the convex program is linear to the number of postings in the inverted index, which may easily exceed a few millions on any medium-sized text collection. That means this solution does not scale at all, even with the latest super-efficient convex solver.

We further attacked this problem using an alternative approach, called surrogate modeling. We created a surrogate problem that is easier to solve. As we will show in later sections, this analytical solution has pointed us to a general version of a simple pruning method called *uniform pruning*. Sharp-eyed readers might notice that uniform pruning is by no means a new invention. Uniform pruning was originally introduced to static index pruning in Carmel et al.'s paper as a baseline approach [9]. In a preliminary experiment, Carmel et al. compared this method with their term-based pruning method. Using TF-IDF as the score function, they found that, even though term-based method performed slightly better, in general the performance for both approaches was roughly comparable. While this was indeed a very interesting finding, the exploration was discontinued as they went ahead to study other important issues.

To the best of our knowledge, since then uniform pruning has not been studied in any follow-up work. It is easy to see why this has been the case. The lack of control on one experiment variable, prune ratio, has made the performance result difficult to interpret. When we make comparisons between methods, this variable needs to be strictly controlled so that the comparisons make sense. Nevertheless, very few in the previous work adopted this design. As a result, there was no obvious way to conduct any form of significance testing to static index pruning. Without serious scrutiny—by which we mean significance assessment—it is only reasonable to dismiss uniform pruning, for that it seemed like an ad-hoc and maybe inferior approach.

In our study, the rediscovery of uniform pruning has gained us a second chance to rethink this issue. Our answer was a redesigned empirical study, in which prune ratio for each experimental method is strictly controlled to minimize the experimental error, and the performance is analyzed using multi-way repeated-measure analysis of variance. As we will shortly cover, the experiment result suggests that uniform pruning with Dirichlet smoothing significantly outperformed the other term-based methods under diverse settings.

The rest of the paper is structured as follows. Section 2 covers an overview to static index pruning and the relevant research. In Section 3, we motivate static index pruning in the minimum cross-entropy framework and show that the analytical solution leads to the uniform pruning method. An empirical study is given in Section 4. We put the theoretical and empirical evidence together and discuss the implication in Section 5. Section 6 delivers the concluding remarks.

2. RELATED WORK

In the coming subsections, we briefly review the literature and discuss the recent development of static index pruning. Following an overview, some notable pruning methods will be treated in slightly more details. Note that this is only aimed at providing enough background knowledge for the reader. A complete coverage is not attempted here.

2.1 Overview

The idea of static index pruning first appeared in the groundbreaking work of Carmel et al. [9] and has since garnered much attention for its implication to Web-scale retrieval [8, 11]. Static index pruning is all about reducing index size—by removing index entries from the inverted index. This technique was proposed to mitigate the efficiency issue caused by operating a large index, for that a smaller index loads faster, occupies less disk space, and has better query throughput. But since only partial term-document mapping is preserved, a loss in retrieval performance is inevitable.

Much effort has been driven towards developing importance measures of individual index entries, so that one can easily prioritize index entries on their way out of the index. Many such measures have been proposed and tested in various retrieval settings. One simple example is *impact*, the contribution of a term-document pair to the final retrieval score [8, 9]. Other approaches in this line include probability ranking principle (PRP) [7], two-sample two proportion (2P2N) [19], and information preservation (IP) [10]. Some measures assess only term importance [6], so the corresponding pruning algorithms can only choose between keeping the entire term posting list or not at all. Some others assess only documents importance [21].

2.2 Methodologies

Term-based pruning (or *term-centric pruning*) is proposed by Carmel et al. [9]. It was so named because it attempts to reduce the posting list for each term in the index. The basic idea is to compute a cutting threshold for each term, and throw away those entries with smaller impact values. Since the cutting threshold depends on some order statistics (i.e., the k-th largest impact value) about the posting list, term-based pruning is less efficient than the other methods.

In contrast to the aforementioned term-centric approach, *document-centric pruning* seeks to reduce the posting list for each document. Büttcher and Clarke [8] considered the contribution for term t to the Kullback-Leibler divergence $\mathrm{D}(d||C)$ between document d and the collection model C. This quantity is used to measure the importance of a posting. Analogously, for each document, a cutting threshold has to be determined based on some order statistics.

There are also other pruning strategies that focus on removing an entire term posting list (whole-term) or an entire document (whole-document) all at once. Blanco and Barreiro [6] presented four term-importance measures, including inverse document frequency (idf), residual inverse document frequency (ridf), and two others based on term discriminative value (TDM). They adopted a whole-term pruning strategy. Analogously, Zheng and Cox [21] proposed an entropy-based measure in a whole-document pruning setting. Both parties have reported comparable performance to term-based pruning on some standard benchmark.

Blanco and Barreiro [7] developed a decision criterion based on the probability ranking principle [18]. The idea is to take every term in the index as a single-word query and calculate the odd-ratio of relevance $p(r|t,d)/p(\overline{r}|t,d)$. This quantity is used in prioritizing all the term-document pair. Since there is only one cutting threshold determined globally, the implementation is relatively easy and efficient.

Thota and Carterette [19] used a statistical procedure, called *two-sample two-proportion* (2P2N), to determine if the occurrence of term t within document d is significantly different from its occurrence within the whole collection. Chen et al. [10] developed a method called *information preservation*. They suggest using the innermost summand of the conditional entropy $H(D|T)$ to measure predictive power contributed by individual term-document pairs to the index model. This quantity is claimed easier to compute than the probability ranking principle.

Altingovde et al. [2] proposed an interesting *query-view* technique that works orthogonally with the aforementioned measure-based approaches. The general idea is to count the number of time a document falls within the top-k window of any given query collected from the query log. The count collected from a query is then evenly distributed to individual query terms. Thus the larger this number, the greater importance the posting is. The query view algorithm would later use this information to prune the entries.

Our work in this paper departs from the previous effort in three major ways. First, our approach is model-based, meaning that we infer a pruned model as a whole rather than partially. This is a novel approach in contrast to all the previous methods. Second, other information-theoretic approaches, such as Zheng and Cox [21] and Chen et al. [10], focused on minimizing the loss of information, while ours focused on minimizing the divergence from the full index. These are entirely different concepts in information theory. Three, our result on the uniform pruning method is more general than Carmel et al.'s description because we considered the query model $p(t)$. Our take of uniform pruning is a weighted version, which may be useful when such a query model (e.g., session logs) is available.

3. MINIMUM CROSS-ENTROPY AND STATIC INDEX PRUNING

3.1 Problem Definition

Let us first develop some notation for describing an inverted index. Let T denote the set of terms and D denote the set of documents. We define an index entry (*posting*) as a 3-tuple of the form (t, d, n), where $t \in T$, $d \in D$, and $n \in \mathbf{N}_+$ (i.e., n is a positive integer.) This means that "term t appears n times in document d." We further consider an inverted index as a probabilistic model $p(D|T;\theta)$ that takes a set of index entries θ as parameters. This model is therefore *nonparametric* because the number of its parameters is not fixed. For brevity, in this paper we sometimes abuse the notation and use one symbol, e.g., θ, to represent both a distribution and its parameters.

In static index pruning, one seeks to induce a pruned model θ from a full model θ_0 such that the following two constraints are satisfied: (i) θ is a subset of the full model θ_0, and (ii) the size of θ is $1-\rho$ times the size of θ_0. Here, $0 < \rho < 1$ denotes the *prune ratio*. Note that these constraints only specify what we need as the output from static index pruning, not how pruning shall be done. As there are exponentially many ways to prune an index down to a given ratio, it is natural to ask how does one engineer this decision to avoid excessive performance loss.

Now, to illustrate this point, let us assume the existence of a function $g(\theta)$ that measures the retrieval performance of model θ. With this hypothetical construct, we formally define static index pruning as follows.

$$\begin{array}{ll} \text{maximize} & g(\theta) \\ \text{subject to} & \theta \subseteq \theta_0 \\ & |\theta|/|\theta_0| \text{ reaches } 1-\rho. \end{array} \tag{2}$$

It is not difficult to envision static index pruning being formulated this way, as a constrained optimization problem.

For now, we shall focus on estimation of this hypothetical function. The conventional approach, as discussed in Section 2.2, is to devise an importance measure to take the role of $g(\cdot)$, which is expected to capture certain properties of an index relevant to retrieval performance. Yet one caveat is that sometimes we risk being arbitrary: The importance measure may only be empirically tested and does not necessarily come with any theoretical guarantee.

One simple idea that we had failed to see casted away all these doubts. We noticed the similarity between this formulation and Kullback's famous induction framework. As we replace $g(\cdot)$ in Equation (2) with the negative Kullback-Leibler divergence (KL divergence), the static index pruning problem reduces to a model induction problem, written in a minimization form:

$$\begin{array}{ll} \text{minimize} & \mathrm{D}(\theta||\theta_0) \\ \text{subject to} & \theta \subseteq \theta_0 \\ & |\theta|/|\theta_0| \text{ reaches } 1-\rho. \end{array} \tag{3}$$

In the following subsections, we shall develop a procedure to practically solve this optimization problem. For brevity, we write $p(\cdot)$ and $p_0(\cdot)$, respectively, to denote the models parametrized by inverted indexes θ and θ_0. The probability measures that we consider here are conditional distributions of D given T. To make this explicit, we define:

$$\mathrm{D}(\theta||\theta_0) \equiv \mathrm{D}(p(D|T)||p_0(D|T)). \tag{4}$$

3.2 Assumptions

Before diving into the full analysis, we need to make explicit two important assumptions.

ASSUMPTION 1 (QUERY AND INDEX MODELS). *We can separate a joint distribution of D and T into a product of two models: (1) a distribution of T, called the query model, and (2) a conditional distribution of D given T, called the index model. We assume there is only one query model $q(t)$ and it is independent of the index model in use. In other words, we have:*

$$p(d,t) = p(d|t)q(t), \qquad p_0(d,t) = p_0(d|t)q(t).$$

Sometimes, we simply write $p(t)$ or $p_0(t)$ to denote the query model when the meaning is clear in the context.

Assumption 1 simply states that the query model $q(t)$ (or $p(t)$) has to be estimated from somewhere else. It makes little sense to infer a query model from the index.

ASSUMPTION 2 (NORMALIZATION FACTOR). *Let $p(t|d)$ and $p_0(t|d)$ be the conditional distributions of T given D for the induced and the original models, respectively. Let $\mathbb{I}_{t,d}$ be a binary variable that indicates whether an index entry (t,d,n) (for some $n \in \mathbb{N}_+$) in the original model is retained in the induced model. We have $p(t|d) \equiv \mathbb{I}_{t,d}p_0(t|d)/Z_d$, where Z_d is the normalization factor for document d.*

In Assumption 2, we introduce a normalization factor Z_d for each document d. As we shall address later, setting an appropriate value for Z_d is the key step in the subsequent analysis. To correctly normalize $p(t|d)$, we need to set:

$$Z_d = \sum_t \mathbb{I}_{t,d}p_0(t|d).$$

But this would make the resulting formula intractable, since the value of $\mathbb{I}_{t,d}$ depends on other variables in the same document, i.e., $\mathbb{I}_{\cdot,d}$. To deal with this issue, we suggest setting $Z_d = k$ for all $d \in D$, where $k > 0$ is some constant. Using this normalization trick results in weak inference and inevitably sacrifices mathematical rigors. We want to emphasize that this is a necessary compromise, without which the following analysis would not have been possible.

3.3 Analysis

Now, we shall go ahead and analyze the objective function. First of all, let us write out the objective in full:

$$\mathrm{D}(p(D|T)||p_{\mathrm{O}}(D|T)) \equiv \sum_{t,d} p(d,t) \log \frac{p(d|t)}{p_{\mathrm{O}}(d|t)}. \quad (5)$$

We use Assumption 1 to dissect the joint distribution $p(d,t)$ into the product of the query model $p(t)$ and the index model $p(d|t)$. Applying Bayes Theorem to $p(d|t)$ and $p_{\mathrm{O}}(d|t)$ and assuming uniform $p(d)$ and $p_{\mathrm{O}}(d)$, we have the objective organized as follows:

$$\sum_t p(t) \sum_d \frac{p(t|d)}{\sum_{d'} p(t|d')} \log \frac{p(t|d)}{p_{\mathrm{O}}(t|d)} \frac{\sum_{d'} p_{\mathrm{O}}(t|d')}{\sum_{d'} p(t|d')}. \quad (6)$$

Observe that, since in this optimization framework we look for a subset of θ_{O}, we are essentially dealing with a combinatorial problem ("assignment problem"). Each index entry $(t,d,n) \in \theta_{\mathrm{O}}$ either stays within the induced model θ or gets removed. This combinatorial nature is best characterized via the indicator variables $\mathbb{I}_{\cdot,\cdot}$ in Assumption 2.

Let us now replace all the occurrences of $p(t|d)$. Note that, under the setting $Z_d = k$ (suggested), all the normalization factors cancel out. We have:

$$\sum_t p(t) \sum_d \frac{\mathbb{I}_{t,d} p_{\mathrm{O}}(t|d)}{\sum_{d'} \mathbb{I}_{t,d'} p_{\mathrm{O}}(t|d')} \log \mathbb{I}_{t,d} \frac{\sum_{d'} p_{\mathrm{O}}(t|d')}{\sum_{d'} \mathbb{I}_{t,d'} p_{\mathrm{O}}(t|d')}. \quad (7)$$

As we separate the support of the inner summation over d into two subsets according to whether $\mathbb{I}_{t,d}$ is switched on, i.e., one over $\{d|\mathbb{I}_{t,d} = 1\}$ and the other over $\{d|\mathbb{I}_{t,d} = 0\}$, the latter sub-summation disappears since $0 \log 0 = 0$. The resulting equation becomes:

$$\sum_t p(t) \sum_{d:\mathbb{I}_{t,d}=1} \frac{p_{\mathrm{O}}(t|d)}{\sum_{d'} \mathbb{I}_{t,d'} p_{\mathrm{O}}(t|d')} \log \frac{\sum_{d'} p_{\mathrm{O}}(t|d')}{\sum_{d'} \mathbb{I}_{t,d'} p_{\mathrm{O}}(t|d')}. \quad (8)$$

Notice that the innermost logarithm does not depend on d anymore. We can therefore move that entire term out of the inner summation. From there, we have the inner summation over d canceled out. The equation is now written as:

$$\sum_t p(t) \log \frac{\sum_{d'} p_{\mathrm{O}}(t|d')}{\sum_{d'} \mathbb{I}_{t,d'} p_{\mathrm{O}}(t|d')}. \quad (9)$$

We can get rid of the numerator, i.e., $\sum_{d'} p_{\mathrm{O}}(t|d')$, in the logarithm when minimizing this equation, because the numerator does not depend any combinatorial choice we make. Once again, we rewrite it as a maximization problem by taking the negation. The final form of static index pruning is expressed as the following:

$$\begin{array}{ll} \text{maximize} & \sum_t p_{\mathrm{O}}(t) \log \sum_d \mathbb{I}_{t,d} p_{\mathrm{O}}(t|d) \\ \text{subject to} & \mathbb{I}_{t,d} \text{ is binary, for all } (t,d,\cdot) \in \theta_{\mathrm{O}}, \\ & \sum_{t,d} \mathbb{I}_{t,d} = (1-\rho)|\theta_{\mathrm{O}}|. \end{array} \quad (10)$$

```
Input: a global threshold ε
begin
    for t ∈ T do
        for d ∈ postings(t) do
            compute A(t,d) = p(t)p(t|d)
            if A(t,d) < ε then
                remove d from postings(t)
            end
        end
    end
end
```

Algorithm 1: The weighted uniform pruning algorithm.

Equation (10) is in general ill-posed even though it can be solved with a convex integer program solver. This is because the number of index entries can easily exceed a few millions in any production retrieval system. Solving this exactly is only possible for very small test collections. To tackle this issue, we resort to a technique called *surrogate modeling* (or optimization transfer), which approximates the original objective using a majorization/minorization function that is analytically or numerically efficient to compute. See Lange et al. [16] for a comprehensive treatment.

To the best of our knowledge, there are two major approaches for inducing such surrogate models: taking the first-order Taylor approximation, or using the Jensen's inequality. In this paper, we stick with the second approach[1]. Recall that Jensen's inequality states that the following properties hold for any convex (or concave) function f:

$$\begin{array}{ll} \mathbb{E}f(X) \geq f(\mathbb{E}X) & (f \text{ is convex}) \\ \mathbb{E}f(X) \leq f(\mathbb{E}X) & (f \text{ is concave}). \end{array}$$

Let f be the logarithmic function. The original objective in our problem (Equation 10) now corresponds to the left-hand side $\mathbb{E}f(X)$. Since the logarithmic function is concave, we have the surrogate model $f(\mathbb{E}X)$ an upper bound of the original objective:

$$\text{maximize} \quad \log \sum_{t,d} \mathbb{I}_{t,d} p_{\mathrm{O}}(t) p_{\mathrm{O}}(t|d), \quad (11)$$

or equivalently:

$$\text{maximize} \quad \sum_{t,d} \mathbb{I}_{t,d} p_{\mathrm{O}}(t) p_{\mathrm{O}}(t|d). \quad (12)$$

This surrogate model has a simple analytical solution: Sort the index entries according to weighted query likelihood, i.e., $p(t)p(t|d)$, and keep only the top $(1-\rho)N$ entries. It can be shown that a simple maneuver such as Algorithm 1, called *weighted uniform pruning*, guarantees to maximize the objective. This corresponds to a weighted version of Carmel et al.'s uniform pruning method. This algorithm would fall back to the unweighted form when we supply a uniform $p(t)$ and a plug-in estimate of the query likelihood. Note that the plug-in approach is valid only when the score function is proportional to the true likelihood.

For simplicity, we take a very loose definition of query likelihood in this paper so as to cover the well-known BM25 function. As we shall present shortly, the empirical result

[1]In our case, the first-order Taylor expansion leads to an even more sophisticated objective.

shows that the performance of BM25 is no worse than that of a rigorously defined language model (with Jelinek-Mercer smoothing). What is left unsettled is how to estimate ϵ given a target prune ratio ρ. This issue is treated in Section 4.2.

4. EXPERIMENT

Thus far, we have established the theoretical ground for uniform pruning. Our next quest is to find empirical evidence that supports this result. In the coming subsections, we shall briefly describe the experiment settings and present the experimental result in greater detail.

4.1 Setup

We used three test collections in this experiment: TREC disks 4 & 5, WT2G, and WT10G. The first two collections are tested against topics 401-450 and the latter against topics 451-550. For each topic, we tested both short (title) and long (title + description) queries. Details about the benchmark are summarized in Table 1. All three collections were indexed using the Indri toolkit[2]. To preprocess the documents, we applied the porter stemmer and used the standard 411 InQuery stoplist. No additional text processing is done to the test collections.

According to how index traversal is preferred, a pruning method can be either term-centric or document-centric. Since different traversal strategies rely on different index creation procedures, it is difficult to have both sets implemented in one place. For simplicity, in this experiment we focused only on term-centric methods. Specifically, we tested the following methods:

1. Uniform pruning (UP) [9]: This method is the subject of this experiment. In this experiment, we tested three variations of uniform pruning, each using a different score function. These functions are BM25 (UP-bm25), language model using Dirichlet smoothing (UP-dir), and language model using Jelinek-Mercer smoothing (UP-jm). For BM25, we used the standard setting provided by Indri. For language models, we set $\mu = 2500$ in Dirichlet smoothing and $\lambda = 0.6$ for the Jelinek-Mercer smoother.

2. Top-k term-centric pruning (TCP) [9]: We set $k = 10$ as suggested to maximize the top-10 precision and used BM25 as the score function. Note that other score functions such as language models may also apply to this pruning method. Here, we simply comply with the previous work.

3. Probability ranking principle (PRP) [7]:
$$\frac{p(r|t,d)}{p(\overline{r}|t,d)} \equiv \frac{p(t|D)p(r|D)}{p(t|\overline{r})(1-p(r|D))}.$$
As suggested, we use the following equations to estimate these probabilities:
$$p(t|D) = (1-\lambda)p_{\mathrm{ML}}(t|D) + \lambda p(t|C), \quad (13)$$
$$p(r|D) = \frac{1}{2} + \frac{1}{10}\tanh\frac{dl - \overline{X_d}}{S_d}, \quad (14)$$
$$p(t|\overline{r}) = p(t|C). \quad (15)$$
Note that dl is the document length. X_d and S_d respectively are the sample mean and sample standard deviation of document length. For query likelihood, we set $\lambda = 0.6$.

4. Information preservation, with uniform document prior (IP-u) [10]:
$$-\frac{p(t|d)p(d)}{\sum_{d'} p(t|d')p(d')}\log\frac{p(t|d)p(d)}{\sum_{d'} p(t|d')p(d')}.$$
In this formula, the query likelihood $p(t|d)$ is estimated using Jelinek-Mercer smoothing. Here, We set $\lambda = 0.6$ and assumed uniform document prior $p(d)$.

[2]http://www.lemurproject.org/indri.php

Collection	# Documents	Query Topics
Disks 4 & 5	528k	401-450
WT2G	247k	401-450
WT10G	1692k	451-550

Table 1: Test collections and the corresponding query topics.

We are aware that document-length update may improve the TCP and PRP retrieval performance [5,7]. Nevertheless, in this study we did not implement this feature. This shall be addressed in the future work.

4.2 Prune Ratio

In this experiment, we settled on 9 fixed prune levels at $\rho = 0.1, 0.2, \ldots, 0.9$. To control the prune ratio, comparison is only allowed between experimental runs at the same prune level. In each reference method, the true prune ratio depends on some parameter (e.g., ϵ in TCP and PRP), which we called the *threshold parameter*. To reduce the index down to the right size, we employed two different approaches to determine this cutting threshold:

1. Sample percentile: Collect the prune scores on top of a sample of index entries and use the percentile estimates to determine the right cutting threshold. This is mostly useful when the prune score is globally determined. Here, we used Definition 8 from Hyndman and Fan [13] to estimate percentiles.

2. Bisection: Take an interval of feasible parameter values $[a, b]$, and test-prune using the median value $(a+b)/2$. Return the current median if the test-prune reached the expected ratio; otherwise shrink the interval in half and repeat. This method is useful when the prune score for each index entry depends on the others in the same posting list, as in TCP.

Bisection requires several test-prune runs into the entire index and is therefore more time-consuming. Sample percentile needs only one pass through the index, but the resulting prune ratio can be less precise than that with the values learned using bisection. In this paper, we applied bisection to TCP to learn the parameter ϵ, and applied sample percentile to the rest of methods. Specifically, we used a sample size of 10% of the entire index. For either case, the prune ratio error is controlled to within $\pm 0.2\%$.

MAP (t)	.1	.2	.3	.4	.5	.6	.7	.8	.9
TCP	160	157	152	145	139	134	127	118	095
UP-bm25	159	158	154	148	144	140	135	127	102
UP-dir	160	157	153	149	145	143	142	137	120
UP-jm	160	158	153	146	140	133	126	110	085
PRP	156	152	148	142	133	123	110	088	045
IP-u	156	153	148	140	135	123	107	092	046

MAP (td)	.1	.2	.3	.4	.5	.6	.7	.8	.9
TCP	203	197	187	177	163	147	142	130	091
UP-bm25	204	189	177	170	160	158	141	141	116
UP-dir	204	199	191	183	177	175	174	164	136
UP-jm	204	199	185	179	164	150	137	103	074
PRP	186	174	160	150	136	123	112	090	050
IP-u	189	171	165	149	143	124	116	095	051

P10 (t)	.1	.2	.3	.4	.5	.6	.7	.8	.9
TCP	260	256	252	246	245	236	209	201	174
UP-bm25	259	258	254	239	226	225	204	192	168
UP-dir	261	257	254	248	249	242	241	236	222
UP-jm	261	259	253	249	243	237	225	190	168
PRP	256	250	239	224	201	182	157	125	107
IP-u	257	248	243	214	202	193	164	133	106

P10 (td)	.1	.2	.3	.4	.5	.6	.7	.8	.9
TCP	347	347	339	332	315	290	279	267	231
UP-bm25	351	339	336	309	295	287	264	248	209
UP-dir	347	350	341	338	327	317	316	311	291
UP-jm	347	350	341	335	319	299	267	229	191
PRP	344	324	300	281	249	222	181	169	127
IP-u	340	329	310	280	253	233	186	175	122

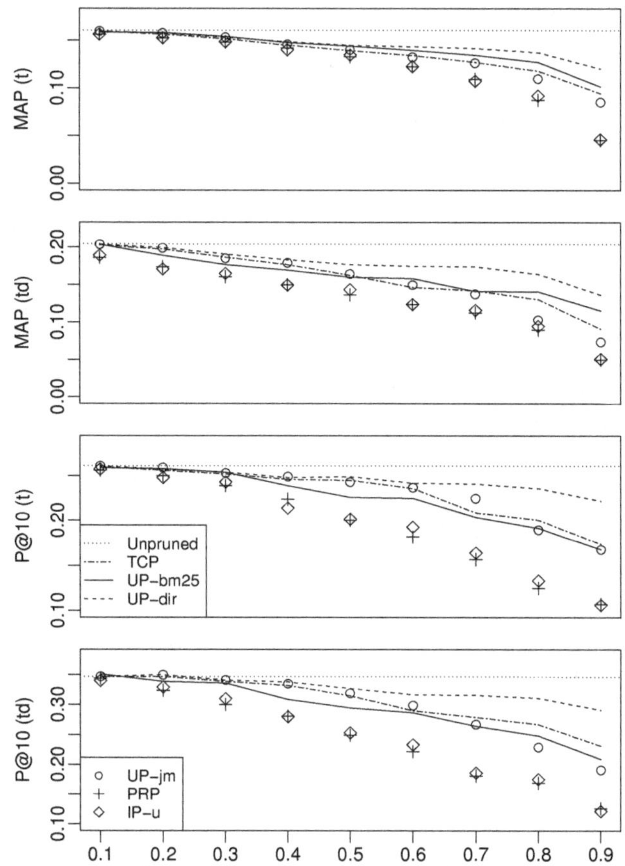

Figure 1: The overall performance result on WT10g. All the measurements are rounded to the 3rd decimal place, with preceding zero and decimal point removed. The best raw performance at each prune level is underlined. The unpruned baseline has achieved 0.160/0.204 (t/td) in MAP and 0.261/0.347 (t/td) in P@10.

4.3 Retrieval Performance

We followed Blanco and Barreiro [7] for using BM25 as the post-pruning retrieval method. Retrieval performance is measured in mean average precision (MAP) and precision-at-10 (P@10). The result on the largest set WT10G is summarized in Figure 1 (see Figures 2 and 3 at the very end of this paper for results on the smaller sets). Each figure has four sets of measure-to-query-type combinations, and the result for each combination is given both as a table on the left and a plot on the right. These combinations from top to bottom, respectively, are MAP-t, MAP-td, P@10-t, and P@10-td. Table columns and x-axes in the plots indicate prune levels, from 0.1 to 0.9 (10% to 90%). Rows and curves indicate pruning methods.

Our result shows that, at small prune levels (≤ 0.5), all these methods differ little in performance, and the difference at larger prune levels seems more evident. Both PRP and IP-u, whose performance was nearly identical, have consistently achieved the bottom performance in all settings. In general, the performance for the UP family and TCP is comparable, though UP-dir performed slightly better than the other. We noticed that the performance of UP-dir is also robust to high prune ratio. On WT10G, when tested under an extreme setting with 90% prune ratio, UP-dir still managed to retain 75% of the baseline MAP for short queries, and 66.7% for long queries. Of the baseline P@10, UP-dir retained 85.1% for short queries and 83.9% for long queries. Under a less aggressive setting such as 50% prune ratio, UP-dir have done even better by retaining 90.6% and 86.8% of baseline MAP, and 95.4% and 94.2% of baseline P@10, respectively for short and long queries.

4.4 Significance Tests

We further conducted an analysis of variance (ANOVA) to check if the performance difference is significant. Due to the unbalanced size of measurement, we tested each corpus independently. Here, we assume a fixed-effect, 4-way no interaction, repeated measure design, expressed as:

$$Y_{i,j,k,l} = a_i + b_j + c_k + d_l + \epsilon_{i,j,k,l},$$

where $Y_{i,j,k,l}$ is the measured performance, a_i is the query-type effect, b_j the prune-level effect, c_k the method effect, and d_l the topic effect, and $\epsilon_{i,j,k,l}$ denotes the error.

The result is covered in Table 2. Each row indicates a measure-effect combination and each column a test corpus. Test statistics, such as degrees of freedom (DF) and F-values (F), are given for every test case. We used partial eta-square (η_p^2) to measure the effect size [17]. We first ran an omnibus test to see if any main effect is significant. Of all three collections, all the main effects were tested significant for

Response	Main Effect	Disks 4 & 5 DF	F	η_p^2	WT2G DF	F	η_p^2	WT10G DF	F	η_p^2
MAP	Query Type	F(1, 5336)	74.10	.01	F(1, 5336)	42.57	.01	F(1, 10686)	192.25	.02
	Prune Ratio	F(8, 5336)	240.30	.26	F(8, 5336)	306.17	.31	F(8, 10686)	193.26	.13
	Method	F(5, 5336)	11.00	.01	F(5, 5336)	40.20	.04	F(5, 10686)	61.47	.03
	Query Topic	F(49, 5336)	885.35	.89	F(49, 5336)	335.89	.76	F(49, 10686)	422.46	.80
P@10	Query Type	F(1, 5336)	66.16	.01	F(1, 5336)	10.89	.00	F(1, 10686)	622.34	.06
	Prune Ratio	F(8, 5336)	105.00	.14	F(8, 5336)	133.98	.17	F(8, 10686)	122.43	.08
	Method	F(5, 5336)	20.34	.02	F(5, 5336)	44.06	.04	F(5, 10686)	71.01	.03
	Query Topic	F(49, 5336)	484.06	.82	F(49, 5336)	296.88	.73	F(49, 10686)	226.31	.68

Table 2: The 4-way no-interaction ANOVA result. Each cell indicates a combination of performance measure (row) and test collection (column). Degrees of freedom and F-values are given for testing all the main effects. Effect size is given in η_p^2. In our experiment, all the main effects are significant for $p < 0.001$.

	Disks 4 & 5 Method	Mean	Group	WT2G Method	Mean	Group	WT10G Method	Mean	Group
MAP	UP-bm25	.204	a..	UP-dir	.223	a...	UP-dir	.162	a..
	UP-dir	.200	a..	UP-bm25	.211	.b..	UP-bm25	.151	.b.
	TCP	.196	ab.	TCP	.204	.b..	TCP	.148	.b.
	UP-jm	.191	.bc	UP-jm	.192	..c.	UP-jm	.145	.b.
	PRP	.187	..c	IP-u	.181	...d	IP-u	.129	..c
	IP-u	.187	..c	PRP	.179	...d	PRP	.127	..c
P@10	UP-dir	.433	a..	UP-dir	.404	a...	UP-dir	.286	a..
	TCP	.433	a..	TCP	.385	ab..	TCP	.268	.b.
	UP-jm	.424	a..	UP-jm	.367	.bc.	UP-jm	.265	.b.
	UP-bm25	.417	a..	UP-bm25	.359	..c.	UP-bm25	.259	.b.
	PRP	.392	.b.	IP-u	.322	...d	IP-u	.222	..c
	IP-u	.389	.b.	PRP	.319	...d	PRP	.219	..c

Table 3: The overall result for Tukey's HSD test. For each combination of performance measure (row) and test collection (column), pruning methods are ordered in descending mean and tested for group difference. Methods that differ significantly do not share the same group label.

$p < 0.001$. Further analysis shows that query type and prune method have relatively small effect sizes, suggesting that query topic and prune ratio have much greater influence on the retrieval performance than the others do.

Post-hoc tests are then called for to examine the difference caused by different factor values. Since our experimental setting involves multiple comparison, we employed Tukey's honest significance difference (HSD) to control the overall Type I error [12]. Note that since Tukey's HSD is a one-way test, only one effect is tested in each run. In the following paragraphs, we summarize the HSD results for all the main effects. Here, since our focus is on the method effect, we shall briefly cover the other three for the sake of completeness.

Method Effect. Table 3 summarizes this HSD result for the method effect. For each measure-corpus combination, we assigned group labels, e.g., "a" to "d", to individual methods based on the pairwise differences in their means. The difference between two methods is significant if and only if they share no common group label.

The result is briefly summarized as follows. First, the UP family and TCP consistently achieved top performance in both MAP and P@10 across different test settings. In the leading group, UP-dir delivers slightly better performance than the others. This is even more pronounced under the Web settings, in which UP-dir significantly outperformed the rest of methods in MAP (on both corpora) and in P@10 (on WT10G only). Second, the performance for the rest of UP family and TCP is in general comparable. Take UP-bm25 and TCP. The performance difference between the two is subtle: UP-bm25 was shown superior in MAP on Disks 4 & 5 but inferior in P@10 on WT2G. Third, PRP and IP-u are inferior to all the other methods. This result is consistent with our analysis on the raw performance measurements.

Query Type Effect. Long queries (td) achieve better performance than short queries (t), which is expected because short queries are less precise than longer ones. This difference is confirmed on all three test collections, and appears more evident in the largest set WT10G.

Prune Ratio Effect. Small prune levels do better than large ones in both metrics, which is also expected since more aggressive pruning results in less information in the index. According to the pairwise comparison made within the HSD test, this result is generally true except for a few small pairs such as 0.1-against-0.2. Specifically, WT10G has many such insignificant small pairs, suggesting that retrieval on larger Web collections is less sensitive to information loss.

Topic Effect. The result is difficult to interpret due to the size of topic pairs, e.g., topics 451-551 on WT10G has produced 4950 such pairwise comparisons. In general, only a small number of queries have significantly deviated from the average performance, meaning that most queries are designed to be about equally difficult.

5. DISCUSSION

The experiment result for uniform pruning is generally in line with our understanding to impact, much of this was contributed by the previous work in index compression and dynamic pruning. Since many ideas come from the same outlet in the indexing pruning community, it is no surprise that uniform pruning is related to many existing impact-based methods. For example, Anh et al. [3] concluded that impact-sorted indexes combined with early termination heuristics can best optimize retrieval system performance. This technique is conceptually equivalent to uniform pruning. Further work in this line investigated impact-based pruning, an application of impact-sorting to dynamic query pruning [4]. And again, this is a dynamic version of uniform pruning. Adding to these results, our analysis shows that impact-based methods are good approximate solutions to the proposed model induction problem.

One further question that invites curious eyes is why Dirichlet smoothing worked so well with uniform pruning that it significantly outperformed all the other variations on our Web benchmark WT2G and WT10G. So far the answer is still unclear to us. Here, let us discuss a few possibilities:

- BM25 might be a poor approximation to the probability $p(t|d)$ since the framework presented in this paper was tailored specifically for language models. While this may explain why BM25 was inferior to Dirichlet smoothing in our experiments, it does not tell us why the performance for Jelinek-Mercer smoother and for BM25 were comparable.

- Another possibility is that, since parameter optimization is lacking in our experiment, we might have failed in producing the most competitive result for BM25 and Jelinek-Mercer smoother. If this theory is true, score functions will need task-specific fine-tuning in their further use. But for that to make sense, one needs to point out in what major way the role of a score function in index pruning departs from that in ordinary ad-hoc retrieval. This may point to an interesting direction for future work, but based on the evidence collected so far this claim is difficult to verify.

With the argument given in Section 3 about the convex integer program, one may argue that it is important to prevent depleting any term posting since doing so would take the objective in Equation 10 to minus infinity. In other words, an additional constraint, called "no depletion", shall be added into the index pruning guideline. This is because, even though we do not attempt to solve the convex program, the constraint still needs to be enforced to guarantee that information loss is bounded. In this respect, it is necessary to adopt a top-k preserving strategy (i.e., skip any term posting that has less than k entries), such as the one in TCP, to avoid depleting term postings.

6. CONCLUSION

In this paper, we review the problem of static index pruning from a brand new perspective. Given the appropriate assumptions, we show that this problem can essentially be tackled within a model induction framework, using the principle of minimum cross-entropy. The theory guarantees that the induced model best approximates the full model in terms of probability divergence. We show that static index pruning can be written as a convex integer program. Yet exact inference, though possible as it might be, is generally computationally infeasible for large collections. So we further propose a surrogate model to address the computation issue, and show that uniform pruning is indeed an optimal solution to the formalism. To verify the correctness of our result, we conducted an extensive empirical study. The experiment was redesigned to take two factors, variable control and significance testing, into consideration. This setup has helped us reduce possible experimental bias or error.

Our result confirms that, when paired with the Dirichlet smoother, the performance of uniform pruning is state of the art. Significant improvement over the other methods were observed across diverse retrieval settings. Uniform pruning also exhibits an advantage in robustness with respect to large prune ratio. Specifically, our result on WT10G for short queries suggests that uniform pruning with the Dirichlet smoother retains at least 90% of the baseline performance at 50% prune ratio and 85% at 80% prune ratio. To the best of our knowledge, this is by far the best performance ever reported for static index pruning on the standard benchmark.

This research work has given rise to many technical issues, some have been addressed in Section 5 and some remain unsettled. It shall be interesting to see how uniform pruning responds to other test environments, such as different retrieval engines, corpora, or tasks. Document-length update and pseudo relevance feedback have been two landmark issues that we are ready to explore. Since we did not fine-tune the baseline performance, testing pruning methods against optimized, strong baseline shall provide more insight about this art. Besides all these possibilities, one promising direction is to extend the model induction idea to other type of structured data, such as lexicons or language models. Further investigation into the theory may shed us some light in the role that impact plays in different IR tasks.

7. ACKNOWLEDGMENT

We would like to thank Wei-Yen Day, Ting-Chu Lin, and the anonymous reviewers for their useful comments.

8. REFERENCES

[1] I. S. Altingovde, R. Ozcan, and O. Ulusoy. A practitioner's guide for static index pruning. In M. Boughanem, C. Berrut, J. Mothe, and C. Soule-Dupuy, editors, *Advances in Information Retrieval*, volume 5478 of *Lecture Notes in Computer Science*, chapter 65, pages 675–679. Springer Berlin / Heidelberg, Berlin, Heidelberg, 2009.

[2] I. S. Altingovde, R. Ozcan, and O. Ulusoy. Static index pruning in web search engines: Combining term and document popularities with query views. *ACM Transactions on Information Systems*, 30(1), Mar. 2012.

[3] V. N. Anh, O. de Kretser, and A. Moffat. Vector-space ranking with effective early termination. In *Proceedings of the 24th annual international ACM SIGIR conference on Research and development in information retrieval*, SIGIR '01, pages 35–42, New York, NY, USA, 2001. ACM.

[4] V. N. Anh and A. Moffat. Pruned query evaluation using pre-computed impacts. In *Proceedings of the*

MAP (t)	.1	.2	.3	.4	.5	.6	.7	.8	.9
TCP	225	221	213	206	198	186	172	149	109
UP-bm25	227	226	223	218	208	194	168	166	143
UP-dir	225	222	213	206	197	190	178	157	117
UP-jm	224	221	211	202	192	180	163	140	103
PRP	227	224	219	209	194	168	148	149	108
IP-u	227	225	220	211	195	173	147	147	108

MAP (td)	.1	.2	.3	.4	.5	.6	.7	.8	.9
TCP	251	246	239	232	219	201	184	162	117
UP-bm25	250	246	235	229	222	202	179	176	158
UP-dir	251	247	239	232	220	210	196	173	133
UP-jm	250	246	238	228	216	194	173	148	110
PRP	253	246	228	212	195	168	148	146	129
IP-u	252	240	230	215	195	173	145	138	125

P10 (t)	.1	.2	.3	.4	.5	.6	.7	.8	.9
TCP	438	434	434	430	428	426	424	384	326
UP-bm25	438	440	436	438	438	412	370	358	294
UP-dir	438	434	432	428	426	434	416	398	344
UP-jm	438	434	432	428	424	416	410	370	318
PRP	436	442	444	452	428	400	340	284	204
IP-u	438	440	440	450	430	406	338	278	190

P10 (td)	.1	.2	.3	.4	.5	.6	.7	.8	.9
TCP	476	468	478	474	468	460	462	432	358
UP-bm25	470	486	482	470	444	420	400	390	324
UP-dir	474	468	472	462	458	450	440	442	386
UP-jm	476	470	470	468	466	442	430	412	336
PRP	486	486	468	470	428	388	350	316	236
IP-u	474	478	474	464	436	400	340	292	226

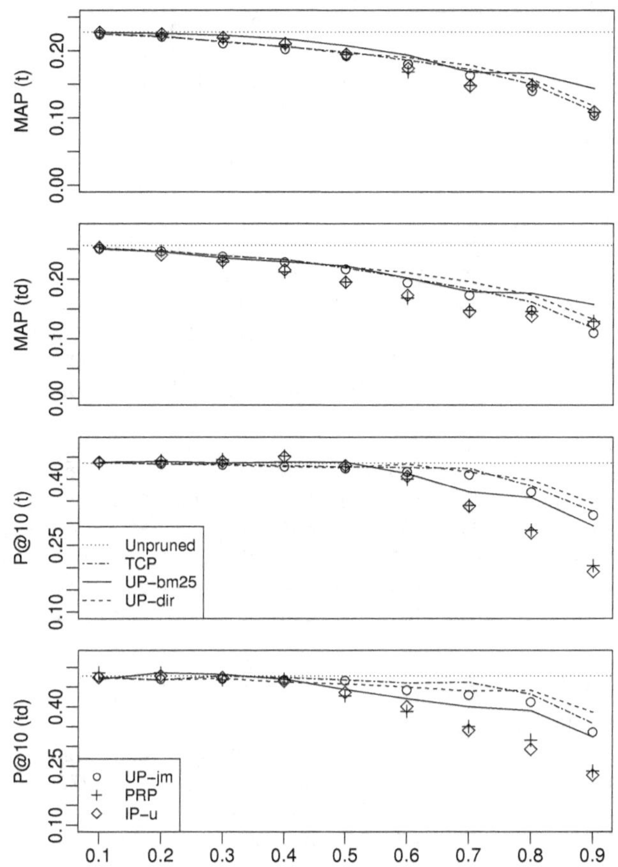

Figure 2: The performance result on Disk 4 & 5, with all measurements rounded to the 3rd decimal place, preceding zero and decimal point removed. The best raw performance at each prune level is underlined. The unpruned baseline has has achieved 0.228/0.256 (t/td) in MAP and 0.436/0.478 (t/td) in P@10.

29th annual international ACM SIGIR conference on Research and development in information retrieval, SIGIR '06, pages 372–379, New York, NY, USA, 2006. ACM.

[5] R. Blanco and A. Barreiro. Boosting static pruning of inverted files. In *Proceedings of the 30th annual international ACM SIGIR conference on Research and development in information retrieval*, SIGIR '07, pages 777–778, New York, NY, USA, 2007. ACM.

[6] R. Blanco and A. Barreiro. Static pruning of terms in inverted files. In G. Amati, C. Carpineto, and G. Romano, editors, *Advances in Information Retrieval*, volume 4425 of *Lecture Notes in Computer Science*, chapter 9, pages 64–75. Springer Berlin Heidelberg, Berlin, Heidelberg, 2007.

[7] R. Blanco and A. Barreiro. Probabilistic static pruning of inverted files. *ACM Transactions on Information Systems*, 28(1), Jan. 2010.

[8] S. Büttcher and C. L. A. Clarke. A document-centric approach to static index pruning in text retrieval systems. In *Proceedings of the 15th ACM international conference on Information and knowledge management*, CIKM '06, pages 182–189, New York, NY, USA, 2006. ACM.

[9] D. Carmel, D. Cohen, R. Fagin, E. Farchi, M. Herscovici, Y. S. Maarek, and A. Soffer. Static index pruning for information retrieval systems. In *Proceedings of the 24th annual international ACM SIGIR conference on Research and development in information retrieval*, SIGIR '01, pages 43–50, New York, NY, USA, 2001. ACM.

[10] R.-C. Chen, C.-J. Lee, C.-M. Tsai, and J. Hsiang. Information preservation in static index pruning. In *Proceedings of the 21st ACM international conference on Information and knowledge management*, CIKM '12, pages 2487–2490, New York, NY, USA, 2012. ACM.

[11] E. S. de Moura, C. F. dos Santos, D. R. Fernandes, A. S. Silva, P. Calado, and M. A. Nascimento. Improving web search efficiency via a locality based static pruning method. In *Proceedings of the 14th international conference on World Wide Web*, WWW '05, pages 235–244, New York, NY, USA, 2005. ACM.

[12] D. Hull. Using statistical testing in the evaluation of retrieval experiments. In *Proceedings of the 16th annual international ACM SIGIR conference on Research and development in information retrieval*, SIGIR '93, pages 329–338, New York, NY, USA, 1993. ACM.

MAP (t)	.1	.2	.3	.4	.5	.6	.7	.8	.9
TCP	248	242	233	222	208	195	176	143	090
UP-bm25	249	250	249	236	225	213	188	133	108
UP-dir	247	240	234	226	207	195	198	181	139
UP-jm	247	239	229	220	199	173	143	107	080
PRP	253	249	237	226	196	166	114	092	063
IP-u	250	247	240	225	205	164	126	081	074

MAP (td)	.1	.2	.3	.4	.5	.6	.7	.8	.9
TCP	288	278	258	241	222	206	183	147	096
UP-bm25	288	276	260	237	226	209	193	151	122
UP-dir	290	279	268	258	238	225	224	209	161
UP-jm	289	281	262	245	217	187	149	113	078
PRP	284	262	233	214	189	166	119	093	067
IP-u	284	263	236	216	190	161	124	087	079

P10 (t)	.1	.2	.3	.4	.5	.6	.7	.8	.9
TCP	416	410	408	398	400	380	374	338	268
UP-bm25	414	420	418	386	380	384	340	238	210
UP-dir	414	402	402	404	380	386	392	374	332
UP-jm	414	404	402	402	378	348	336	306	248
PRP	418	418	408	394	362	342	250	126	144
IP-u	410	408	400	390	380	338	268	138	126

P10 (td)	.1	.2	.3	.4	.5	.6	.7	.8	.9
TCP	464	446	428	410	410	388	356	328	302
UP-bm25	464	446	412	370	378	384	326	268	218
UP-dir	460	446	432	436	422	428	422	408	346
UP-jm	460	446	430	420	388	354	340	276	260
PRP	442	434	392	382	340	334	260	142	146
IP-u	450	430	402	392	348	324	258	158	170

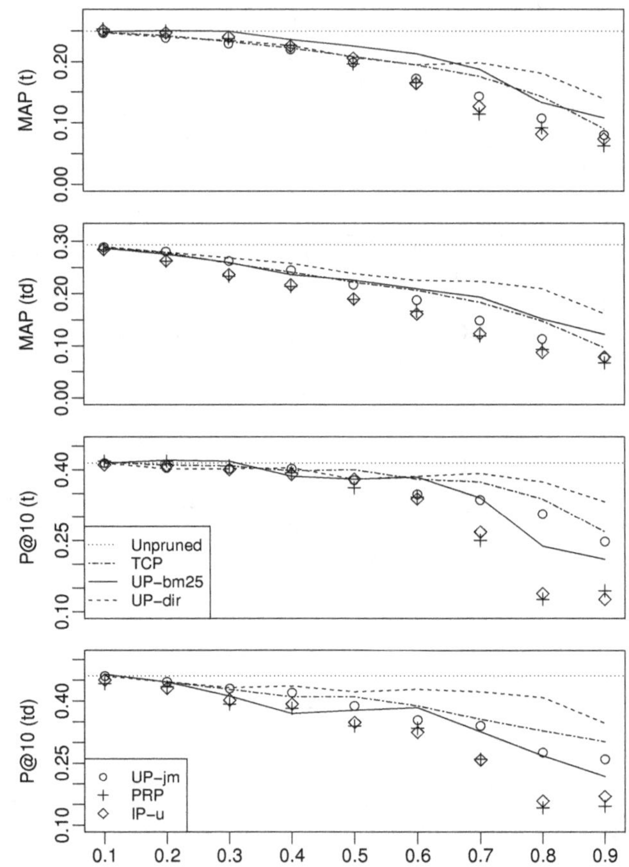

Figure 3: The performance result on WT2G. All measurements were rounded to the 3rd decimal place, and preceding zero and decimal point removed. The best raw performance at each prune level is underlined. The unpruned baseline has has achieved 0.249/0.293 (t/td) in MAP and 0.414/0.460 (t/td) in P@10.

[13] R. J. Hyndman and Y. Fan. Sample quantiles in statistical packages. *The American Statistician*, 50(4):361–365, Nov. 1996.

[14] S. Kullback. *Information Theory and Statistics.* Wiley, New York, 1959.

[15] J. D. Lafferty and C. Zhai. Document language models, query models, and risk minimization for information retrieval. In W. B. Croft, D. J. Harper, D. H. Kraft, J. Zobel, W. B. Croft, D. J. Harper, D. H. Kraft, and J. Zobel, editors, *SIGIR*, SIGIR '01, pages 111–119, New York, NY, USA, 2001. ACM.

[16] K. Lange, D. R. Hunter, and I. Yang. Optimization transfer using surrogate objective functions. *Journal of Computational and Graphical Statistics*, 9(1), 2000.

[17] D. C. Montgomery. *Design and analysis of experiments (6th ed.).* Wiley, 2004.

[18] S. Robertson. The probability ranking principle in IR. In K. S. Jones and P. Willett, editors, *Reading in Information Retrieval*, chapter The probability ranking principle in IR, pages 281–286. Morgan Kaufmann Publishers Inc., San Francisco, CA, USA, 1997.

[19] S. Thota and B. Carterette. Within-Document Term-Based index pruning with statistical hypothesis testing. In P. Clough, C. Foley, C. Gurrin, G. Jones, W. Kraaij, H. Lee, and V. Mudoch, editors, *Advances in Information Retrieval*, volume 6611 of *Lecture Notes in Computer Science*, chapter 54, pages 543–554. Springer Berlin Heidelberg, Berlin, Heidelberg, 2011.

[20] C. Zhai and J. Lafferty. Model-based feedback in the language modeling approach to information retrieval. In *Proceedings of the tenth international conference on Information and knowledge management*, CIKM '01, pages 403–410, New York, NY, USA, 2001. ACM.

[21] L. Zheng and I. J. Cox. Entropy-Based static index pruning. In M. Boughanem, C. Berrut, J. Mothe, and C. Soule-Dupuy, editors, *Advances in Information Retrieval*, volume 5478 of *Lecture Notes in Computer Science*, chapter 72, pages 713–718. Springer Berlin / Heidelberg, Berlin, Heidelberg, 2009.

Document Identifier Reassignment and Run-Length-Compressed Inverted Indexes for Improved Search Performance

Diego Arroyuelo*
Dept. of Informatics,
Univ. Técnica F. Santa María.
Yahoo! Labs Santiago, Chile
darroyue@inf.utfsm.cl

Senén González
Department of Computer Science, University of Chile.
Yahoo! Labs Santiago, Chile
sgonzale@dcc.uchile.cl

Mauricio Oyarzún
University of Santiago.
Yahoo! Labs Santiago, Chile
mauricio.silvaoy@usach.cl

Victor Sepulveda
Yahoo! Labs Santiago, Chile
vsepulve@dcc.uchile.cl

ABSTRACT

Text search engines are a fundamental tool nowadays. Their efficiency relies on a popular and simple data structure: the *inverted indexes*. Currently, inverted indexes can be represented very efficiently using index compression schemes. Recent investigations also study how an optimized document ordering can be used to assign document identifiers (docIDs) to the document database. This yields important improvements in index compression and query processing time. In this paper we follow this line of research, yet from a different perspective. We propose a docID reassignment method that allows one to focus on a given subset of inverted lists to improve their performance. We then use run-length encoding to compress these lists (as many consecutive 1s are generated). We show that by using this approach, not only the performance of the particular subset of inverted lists is improved, but also that of the whole inverted index. Our experimental results indicate a reduction of about 10% in the space usage of the whole index (just regarding docIDs), and up to 30% if we regard only the particular subset of list on which the docID reassignment was focused. Also, decompression speed is up to 1.22 times faster if the runs must be explicitly decompressed and up to 4.58 times faster if implicit decompression of runs is allowed. Finally, we also improve the Document-at-a-Time query processing time of AND queries (by up to 12%), WAND queries (by up to 23%) and full (non-ranked) OR queries (by up to 86%).

Categories and Subject Descriptors

H.3.3 [**Information Storage and Retrieval**]: Information Search and Retrieval; H.2.4 [**Systems**]: Textual databases

*Partially funded by Fondecyt Grant 11121556.

SIGIR'13, July 28–August 1, 2013, Dublin, Ireland.
Copyright 2013 ACM 978-1-4503-2034-4/13/07 ...$15.00.

General Terms

Algorithms, Experimentation, Performance

Keywords

Inverted index compression, document reordering, query processing.

1. INTRODUCTION

Inverted indexes are the *de facto* data structure to support the high-efficiency requirements of a text search engine [29, 4, 10, 18, 31]. This includes, for instance, providing fast response to thousands of queries per second and using as less space as possible, among others. Given a document collection $\mathcal{D}$ with vocabulary $\Sigma = \{w_1, \ldots, w_V\}$ of V different words (or terms), an inverted index for $\mathcal{D}$ stores a set of *inverted lists* $I_{w_1}[1..n_1], \ldots, I_{w_V}[1..n_V]$. Every list $I_{w_i}[1..n_i]$ stores a *posting* for each of the n_i documents that contain the term $w_i \in \Sigma$. Typically, a posting stores the document identifier (docID) of the document that contains the term, the number of occurrences of the term in this document (the term frequency) and, in some cases, the positions of the occurrences of the term within the document. The inverted index also stores a *vocabulary table*, which allows us to access the respective inverted lists.

The space required by the inverted lists is dominant in the space of the index. Therefore, lists are kept compressed, not only to reduce their space usage but also to reduce the transference time from disk—which can be up to 4–8 times slower if the disk-resident lists are not compressed [10, see Table 6.9–page 213]. To answer a query, the involved lists must be decompressed—fully or partially. Hence, fast decompression is a key issue to support quick answers.

Inverted index compression has been studied in depth in the literature [29, 18, 4, 10]. Usually, docIDs, frequencies and positions are stored separately, hence they can be compressed independently. Even though it is important to compress each of these components, this paper is devoted to compressing just the docIDs. Frequencies and term positions can be usually compressed using similar techniques to that used for docIDs. However, the improvements obtained in this paper will be tailored to docIDs. According to [30, 3], docIDs correspond to about 65% of a docIDs+frequencies index. If we also consider positional information, docIDs correspond to about 20% of the overall space [3].

The docIDs of list I_{w_i} are compressed sorting them by increasing docID, to then represent the list using gap encoding: the first docID of the list is represented as it is, whereas the remaining docIDs are represented as the difference with the previous docID. We call DGap this difference. For instance, given the inverted list $\langle 10, 30, 65, 66, 67, 70, 98\rangle$, its DGap encoding is $\langle 10, 20, 35, 1, 1, 3, 28\rangle$. This generates a distribution with smaller numbers, in particular for long lists. As we shall see through this paper, many of these DGaps are actually 1s, which correspond to terms that appear in documents whose docIDs are consecutive. To support searching, inverted lists are logically divided into blocks of, say, 128 DGaps each. This allows us skipping blocks at search time, decompressing just the blocks that are relevant for a query, not necessarily the whole list. Among the existing compression schemes for inverted lists, we have classical encodings like Elias [13] and Golomb/Rice [14], as well as the more recent ones VByte [28], Simple 9 [1], Interpolative [19] and PForDelta [32] encodings. All these methods benefit from sequences of small integers.

The assignment of docIDs to a given document database is not trivial. This task—usually known as *document reordering*—consists in ordering the documents in $\mathcal{D}$, to then assign the docIDs following this order. For instance, a simple and effective method consists in ordering the documents according to their urls [23]. These are called *ordered document collections* and will be the focus of this paper. Document reordering is not always feasible, as discussed in [30]. However, there are many applications where this can be used. The advantage of assigning docIDs in an optimized way is that it yields smaller DGaps in the inverted lists, hence better compression can be achieved [5, 6, 21, 23, 24] and in general a much better inverted index performance [30, 26]. Reductions of up to 50% both in space usage and *Document at a Time* (DAAT) query processing have been reported [30, 26]. The main reason of this improvement in the query processing time is that the docIDs that are relevant to a query tend to be clustered within the same inverted lists blocks, hence less blocks need to be decompressed.

A remarkable feature of ordered document collections is that the number of 1 DGaps is increased. For instance, after reordering the TREC GOV2 document collection, the distribution of DGaps has almost 60% of 1s, whereas a random ordering yields just 11% of 1s. Actually, these 1s tend to form long runs in the inverted lists. Having runs of equal symbols in a sequence allows us to use run-length encoding [14]: we simply encode a run writing its length. There are, nowadays, five main ways to take advantage of these runs in the lists, namely:

1. To use compression approaches that have been particularly tuned to compress small DGaps [30].
2. To use compression approaches like *Interpolative Encoding* [19], which is suitable to compress small DGaps.
3. To use compression approaches like *Interval Encoding* [7], able to compress the runs in the lists.
4. To use compression approaches like the one proposed in [2] to compress long runs of 1s.
5. To use compression approaches like *VSEncoding* [25], which computes the optimal block partitioning to improve both compression ratio and decompression speed.

Approach (1) above compresses every 1 in a run *explicitly*. If one uses the OptPFD approach [30] and a given run of 1s is large enough, we can encode each 1 using one bit. Approach (2), on the other hand, is able to represent the runs *implicitly*, which is a desirable feature: when the integer encoding process gets into a run, it will encode the extreme values of the run and then each 1 within the run is not represented. That is, interpolative encoding deals with the runs in a natural way. The only detail is that, depending on where a run lies within the list, it could be split into several consecutive runs by the encoding process. This may be not optimal, yet efficient enough in most cases. The main drawback of approach (2) is that both the decoding and query-processing performance are not competitive [10, 30]. Approach (3) also encodes the intervals of consecutive docIDs (i.e., the runs of 1s in the DGap-encoded lists), storing the initial docID in the run, followed by the length of the run. All runs in a list are stored in a separate storage. The remaining docIDs (i.e., those that are not in any run) are called *residuals*. These are encoded using DGaps, as usual. Even though approach (3) is effective for web graph compression, it has two potential drawbacks in our information retrieval setting. First, the separate storage of the docIDs (i.e., intervals and residuals) is not adequate for DAAT query processing. Second, after removing the intervals from the list, bigger DGaps are generated, which is similar to the effect seen in [17]. Unfortunately, this worsens the compression ratio achieved. Approach (4) suggests that their method can compress runs of 1s in inverted lists. Yet, it is not studied in depth [2]. Finally, approach (5) could be used along with the techniques proposed in this paper to implicitly compress runs of 1s.

In this paper we study in depth how the inverted index compression and DAAT query processing are affected by the runs of 1s that are generated in ordered document collections. We conclude that properly managing these runs can lead to improvements in the space usage and query processing time. See Section 3 for a summary of our contributions.

2. PREVIOUS CONCEPTS

2.1 Inverted List Compression Schemes

We study here the basic compression schemes for inverted lists, which shall be used throughout this paper.

2.1.1 Variable-Byte Encoding

VByte encodes an integer using an integral number of bytes [28]. As the encoding is byte-aligned, it can be decoded faster. To obtain this encoding, the binary representation of the integer to be encoded is split into 7-bit chunks, adding an extra continuation bit (or flag) to every chunk. This flag indicates whether the current chunk is the last one in the representation of the integer or not. The compression ratio of VByte is not efficient when the inverted lists have small DGaps like 1, 2 or 3 (which are relatively frequent in large inverted lists, particularly for ordered collections).

2.1.2 Simple 9 Encoding

The *Simple 9* encoding (S9 for short) [1] aims at a fast decompression, yet achieving a competitive compression ratio. Assuming a machine word of 32 bits, we divide it into as many chunks of equal size as we can, storing a DGap in each chunk. We use a 4-bit header to indicate the decoder how many DGaps have been stored in that word. Hence, we have 28 bits left to store the DGaps. There are 9 ways—hence its name—of dividing the remaining 28 bits into equal-size chunks: 1 chunk of 28 bits; 2 chunks of 14 bits; 3 chunks of 9 bits, 1 unused bit; 4 chunks of 7 bits; 5 chunks of 5 bits, 3 unused bits; 7 chunks of 4 bits; 9 chunks of 3 bits, 1 unused bit; 14 chunks of 2 bits; and 28 chunks of 1 bit.

To decompress an S9 word, its header is used to determine the case using a `switch` statement in C, where the 9 cases are hard-coded to improve decompression speed. In practice, the decompression speed is slightly better than VByte, and it has a better compression ratio in general.

2.1.3 PForDelta *Encoding*

The PForDelta encoding [32] divides an inverted list into *blocks* of, usually, 128 DGaps each. To encode the DGaps within a given block, it gets rid of a given percentage—usually 10%—of the largest DGaps within the block, and stores them in a separate memory space. These are the *exceptions* of the block. Next, the method finds the largest remaining DGap in the block, let us say x, and represents each DGap in the block in binary using $b = \lceil \log x \rceil$ bits. Though the exceptions are stored in a separate space, we still maintain the slots for them in their corresponding positions. This facilitates the decoding process. For each block we maintain a *header* that indicates information about the compression used in the block, e.g., the value of b.

To retrieve the positions of the exceptions, we store the position of the first exception in the header. In the slot of each exception, we store the offset to the next exception in the block. This forms a linked list with these slots. In case that b is too small and cannot accommodate the offset to the next exception, the algorithm forces to add extra exceptions between two original exceptions. This increases the space usage when the lists contain many small numbers.

To decompress a block, we first take b from the header, and invoke a specialized function that obtains the b-bit DGaps. Each b has its own extracting function, so they can be hard-coded for high efficiency. Once we decode the DGaps, we traverse the list of exceptions of the block, storing the original DGaps in their corresponding positions. This step can be slower, yet it is carried out just for 10% of the block. In typical implementations of PForDelta, the header is implemented in 32 bits, since we only need to store the values of b (in 6 bits, since $1 \leq b \leq 32$) and the position of the first exception (in 7 bits, since the block has 128 positions). PForDelta has shown to be among the most efficient compression schemes [30], achieving a high decompression speed.

2.2 Document Reordering

The *document reordering* problem (or, equivalently, the *document identifier assignment* problem) consists in assigning similar docIDs—ideally, consecutive docIDs—to documents that contain similar terms [5, 6, 21, 23, 24]. This generates smaller DGaps in the inverted lists. As discussed in [30], document reordering is not always feasible. In particular, when global measures of page ranking (e.g., PageRank [8] and Hits [16]) are used for early termination. However, some applications benefit from document reordering.

Previous work [30] studies the performance of different compression schemes for ordered document collections. One of the main conclusions from [30] is that some compression schemes are not suitable for these cases, e.g., PForDelta, since most DGaps are small numbers, like 1 and 2. Hence, small values of b should be used in each block (e.g., $b = 1$ or $b = 2$). However, recall that PForDelta forces to add extra exceptions when b is not enough to represent an offset, which makes it unsuitable in these cases.

Two new alternative are introduced in [30]. The first one is called New PForDelta (NewPFD from now on), which supports using any value of $b \geq 1$ without adding any extra exception. The trick is to use the b-bit slot to store just b bits of the offset, while the remaining bits of the offset are stored in a separate space of memory. At decompression time, the original offsets are reconstructed using bit masks. The second alternative, called Optimized PForDelta (OptPFD from now on), allows us to use a variable number of exceptions in each block. Hence, one can choose either to minimize the space usage or to maximize the decompression speed, yielding also different trade-offs. One of the main results from [30] is that, given a target decompression speed, NewPFD and OptPFD have a better space usage than PForDelta.

3. OUR CONTRIBUTIONS

In this paper we show that by properly representing the runs of 1s that appear in inverted lists when document reordering is used, relevant improvements in space usage and query time can be achieved. In particular, we introduce a method for focusing the generation of runs of 1s to a particular set of lists and then show how to compress these runs using methods that support efficient query processing. Overall, our results are:

1. We reduce the space usage of the most efficient alternatives in [30] by about 10%.
2. The decompression speed is up to 1.22 faster if the runs must be explicitly decompressed and up to 4.58 times faster if implicit decompression of runs is allowed.
3. We improve the DAAT query processing time of AND (by up to 12%), WAND (by up to 23%), and full OR queries (by up to 86%).
4. We show that by using our approaches, the number of docIDs and the list blocks that are decompressed at query time can be reduced by up to 55%.
5. We show that our approaches are more suitable to compress static caches of inverted lists.

4. DOCUMENT REORDERING METHODS TO GENERATE RUNS OF 1S

Inverted list compressors benefit from distributions with small DGaps. Document reordering (Section 2.2) yields small DGaps in the resulting inverted lists. E.g., in the inverted index of the TREC GOV2 collection under random document order, just 10.75% of DGaps have value 1. If, on the other hand, we sort the documents by urls [23], we obtain 60.30% of DGaps with value 1. Thus, the ordered case generates many 1 DGaps [12]. Actually, it can be observed that many of these 1s are grouped into long runs. Instead of regarding these 1s separately (as in previous work [30]) we deal with the runs. We aim at improving the space usage and query processing time of current alternatives. Runs can be encoded more efficiently, e.g., using *run-length compression* [14]: a run of repeated symbols can be encoded indicating the symbol and then writing the length of the run. This approach has been successfully used in many areas [14, 20].

The existing document reordering methods are mainly based on the document collection to carry out the ordering. This yields smaller indexes with enhanced query time [30, 26] since, after reordering, the documents that are relevant to a query tend to group into a few inverted-list blocks. Thus, less blocks need to be decompressed at query time. However, typically in practice some inverted lists are more important than others. Hence, one would want to focus on improving their particular performance, as opposed to improving the whole index. A particular such application is that of static inverted-list caches: the aim is to maintain in main memory the most-frequently-queried inverted lists, as well as other big inverted lists that are eventually queried and whose big size makes prohibitively expensive to transfer them from secondary storage. This effect cannot be achieved if we use methods that first assign docIDs and then construct the index following this assignment.

We develop next a heuristic to assign docIDs such that it improves the compression of a particular set of inverted lists. Our method uses the inter-list dependencies (i.e., the list intersections) to assign docIDs. As a result, these intersections become runs when encoded as DGaps. This will improve the compression ratio of these lists, avoiding the space-usage problems of [17] in cases where document reordering is allowed. Also, in Section 6 we will show that the resulting run (i.e., the intersection) will be stored inside a single block, reducing the number of blocks that are decompressed at query time. In general, finding the docID assignment that optimizes the amount of runs in the lists is known to be an NP-hard problem [15]. Thus, our technique is a heuristic that attempts just to improve the distribution and quality of runs, though it may not be the optimal one.

4.1 A Flexible docID Assignment Method for Focusing the Creation of Runs

Let $\mathcal{I}$ be the inverted index for a given document collection $\mathcal{D}$, where docIDs have been assigned arbitrarily. Let $\mathcal{L} = \langle I_{i_1}, I_{i_2}, \ldots, I_{i_m}\rangle$ be an ordered subset of the inverted lists of $\mathcal{I}$, such that I_{i_j} is the jth list in $\mathcal{L}$. The document ordering process will be based on this ordered set of lists. Let $F : \mathbb{Z} \mapsto \mathbb{Z}$ be a function such that $(i, j) \in F$ iff docID i has been already reenumerated as docID j.

Initially, we set $F \leftarrow \emptyset$, and start the process from I_{i_1}, which stores docIDs $d_1, d_2, \ldots, d_l$. A simple approach could be to rename $d_1 \to 1$, $d_2 \to 2$, …, $d_l \to l$. For each such d_i, we set $F \leftarrow F \cup \{(d_i, i)\}$. Notice how this transforms I_{i_1} into a single run when representing the list as DGaps. Now, we go on to reenumerate I_{i_2}, with the restriction that every docID i such that $(i, j) \in F$ (for a given j) cannot be reenumerated anymore during the process. These are called *fixed* docIDs. Hence, we assign consecutive docIDs (starting from $l+1$) to any docID i in I_{i_2} such that $(i, j) \notin F$, for any j, and add the corresponding pair to F. For instance, let us consider the following example: $I_{i_1} = \langle 10, 30, 65, 66, 67, 70, 98\rangle$ and $I_{i_2} = \langle 20, 30, 66, 70, 99, 101\rangle$. The first step reenumerates I_{i_1} assigning $10 \to 1$, $30 \to 2$, $65 \to 3$, $66 \to 4$, $67 \to 5$, $70 \to 6$, $98 \to 7$. Now we reenumerate I_{i_2}, having into account that docIDs 30, 66 and 70 are now fixed. Hence, we assign $20 \to 8$, $99 \to 9$, $101 \to 10$. After the process, the result is $I_{i_1} = \langle 1, 2, 3, 4, 5, 6, 7\rangle$ and $I_{i_2} = \langle 2, 4, 6, 8, 9, 10\rangle$.

Notice from the previous example that after the first step, all docIDs in the intersection $I_{i_1} \cap I_{i_2}$ are fixed docIDs, hence they cannot be changed when processing I_{i_2}. Notice also how the inter-list dependencies complicate the run generation in I_{i_2}, as the documents in $I_{i_1} \cap I_{i_2}$ could have been reenumerated in any order when processing I_{i_1}.

We can fix this problem as follows. We instead start by reenumerating the docIDs in $I_{i_1} \cap I_{i_2}$, renaming them from 1 to $|I_{i_1} \cap I_{i_2}|$ and add them as fixed docIDs in F. Next, and since the remaining of both lists do not intersect each other, we can reenumerate them to generate a run in each list. In this way, one of the lists will become a single run when DGap encoded, whereas the other will contain two runs. For the previous example, we start reenumerating the intersection $I_{i_1} \cap I_{i_2}$ as $30 \to 1$, $66 \to 2$, $70 \to 3$. Then, we reenumerate the remaining elements in I_{i_1} as $10 \to 4$, $65 \to 5$, $67 \to 6$, $98 \to 7$. Finally, we reenumerate the remaining elements in I_{i_2} as $20 \to 8$, $99 \to 9$, $101 \to 10$. The resulting lists are $I_{i_1} = \langle 1, 2, 3, 4, 5, 6, 7\rangle$ and $I_{i_2} = \langle 1, 2, 3, 8, 9, 10\rangle$. This generates more runs than the previous approach.

In general, we start from I_{i_1} and compute $I_{i_1} \cap I_{i_2}$. If $|I_{i_1} \cap I_{i_2}| \geq M$, for a given threshold M, we compute $I_{i_1} \cap I_{i_2} \cap I_{i_3}$, and repeat the process until $|I_{i_1} \cap \cdots \cap I_{i_{j+1}}| < M$. At this point, we take the d documents in $I_{i_1} \cap \cdots \cap I_{i_j}$ and assign them consecutive docIDs (e.g., from 1 to d). Next, we add them as fixed docIDs in F. This will generate a run of length d when computing the DGap encoding of I_{i_j}. Then, we go back and assign consecutive docIDs to the d' documents in $I_{i_1} \cap \cdots \cap I_{i_{j-1}}$. Notice that d of these docIDs are already fixed from the previous step, hence we only assign docIDs from $d+1$ to d' to the remaining ones. This generates a run of length d' in $I_{i_{j-1}}$. Eventually, this process gets back to I_{i_1}, where all documents in $I_{i_1} \cap I_{i_2}$ are fixed and will form a run. Next, the inverted lists $I_{i_1}, I_{i_2}, \ldots, I_{i_j}$ are removed from $\mathcal{L}$, and their non-yet-fixed docIDs are re-inserted into $\mathcal{L}$ as independent lists, following some well-defined order. This process is repeated until $\mathcal{L} = \emptyset$.

We call *intersection-based docID assignment* (IBDA) this process. It is important to note that the intersections:

- $I_{i_1} \cap I_{i_2}$ in either I_{i_1} and I_{i_2};
- $I_{i_1} \cap I_{i_2} \cap I_{i_3}$ in I_{i_3};
- …;
- $I_{i_1} \cap \cdots \cap I_{i_j}$ in I_{i_j}

are transformed into respective runs in each of these lists after the first step of IBDA. As we shall learn through this paper, this gives us a way to precompute intersections as runs. We just need to be careful in setting a suitable initial order for the lists in $\mathcal{L}$: if, for some reason, we want to transform the intersection between two given inverted lists into a run, these lists must be consecutive in $\mathcal{L}$. This can have many advantages at query time (see Section 6).

To summarize, notice the flexibility of our method, because of the following:

- It allows any initial order in the lists to be processed.
- It is based on just an initial inverted index; no information about the underlying documents is needed.

- It allows any initial docID assignment.
- It allows any re-insertion order for the tails of the lists.

This allows us to adapt the method to different situations.

5. RUN-LENGTH COMPRESSION OF INVERTED LISTS

Instead of using Interpolative Encoding [19] or Interval Encoding [7] to deal with the runs, we adapt some of the most effective compression schemes to run-length encode runs of 1s in inverted lists. We aim at efficient query processing time and improved compression ratios.

5.1 Run-Length Encoded VByte

To run-length encode the runs of 1s with VByte, we need to set a special mark that indicates, at decompression time, that we are in the presence of a run. Since we are encoding DGaps > 0, we use the byte 00000000 as the special mark The idea is to replace $x \geq 3$ consecutive 1s in an inverted list by the 00000000 mark, followed by the VByte encoding of x. We call RLE VByte this scheme. RLE VByte is able to detect and handle very small runs (of length ≥ 3). We restrict the minimum length to be 3, because this yields the same space as for runs of minimum length 2 (in both cases the minimum run uses 2 bytes), yet the former has better decompression times. Indeed, this will be the only method in this paper able to deal with small runs of length $3 \leq \ell \leq 27$.

We introduce now an alternative implementation of the original VByte scheme, on which will be based the RLE VByte implementation. The idea is to take advantage, at decompression time, of several consecutive small DGaps. Assuming that 0 is used as terminator flag in VByte, we take 4 consecutive bytes from the encoding (i.e., a 32-bit word) and carry out a bitwise AND with 0X80808080. This allows one to determine at once the 4 terminator flags of these bytes. In particular, if the bitwise AND results in a 0, it means that the terminator flags are all 0, hence we have 4 DGaps encoded in 4 bytes. We can then hard-code all cases, which can make a difference if most DGaps use 1 byte.

A potential drawback of RLE VByte is that, at decompression time, we need to make an extra comparison per element in the list, to know whether it is the mark of a run or not. However, to decode a run, the original VByte has to make one comparison for every 1. RLE VByte, on the other hand, is able to decode the run more efficiently, as we shall see in our experiments.

5.2 Run-Length Encoded S9

S9 can be easily adapted to run-length encode the runs of 1s, as it is suggested for a variant of this scheme [2]. We only need to add a new S9 case, which will be used to encode runs—recall that we use just 9 out of 16 cases available for the 4-bit headers. The remaining bits of the S9 word are used to represent the length of the run. It is rather common in practice to find S9 words that encode 28 ones, followed by a different S9 case (indeed, this is one of the most frequent cases for GOV2 inverted lists).

We define RLE S9 as follows, in order to compress runs of 1s: **(C1)** 1 chunk of 28 bits; **(C2)** 2 chunks of 14 bits each; **(C3)** 3 chunks of 9 bits each, 1 unused bit; **(C4)** 4 chunks of 7 bits each; **(C5)** 7 chunks of 4 bits each; **(C6)** 9 chunks of 3 bits each, 1 unused bit; **(C7)** 14 chunks of 2 bits each; **(C8)** 28 chunks of 1 bit each followed by C1; **(C9)** 28 chunks of 1 bit each followed by C2; **(C10)** 28 chunks of 1 bit each followed by C3; **(C11)** 28 chunks of 1 bit each followed by C4; **(C12)** 28 chunks of 1 bit each followed by C5; **(C13)** 28 chunks of 1 bit each followed by C6; **(C14)** 28 chunks of 1 bit each followed by C7; **(C15)** 28 chunks of 1 bit each followed by 5 chunks of 5 bits each; **(C16)** there are two cases still missing. The first one consists of a word storing 5 chunks of 5 bits each. The second case corresponds to runs of 1s longer than 28. Since the case of 5 chunks of 5 bits each has 3 bits unused, we use one of them to make the difference between these cases. If the bit is a 0, then we have 5 chunks of 5 bits each. If the bit is 1, then we use the remaining 27 bits to represent the length of the run.

Cases 1 to 15 are identified with 4-bit headers from 0000 to 1110. The remaining two cases use 5-bit headers 11110 and 11111. These variable-length headers can be uniquely decoded very efficiently using a `switch` statement in C, checking just 4-bit headers as usual. If the 4-bit header is 1111, we check the following bit to determine the 5-bit header.

The compression process is carried out in two steps: *(1)* We first compress the list using the original S9 algorithm; *(2)* we traverse the S9 words generated in the previous step, and replace the S9 words that store 28 ones by one of the new cases defined above: if there are multiple consecutive such S9 words, we replace them by case 11111; if instead we have one such word followed by a different case, we replace it by the corresponding case 8 to 15.

5.3 Run-Length Encoded PForDelta

We define now RLE PFD, which adds run-length-encoding capabilities to PForDelta, with minor changes to the original scheme. We define two kind of blocks: *(1)* *normal blocks*, containing 128 DGaps (as usual), and prefixed by a 32-bit block header; *(2)* *run blocks*, which encode a run storing its length within the 32-bit header. We need an extra bit in the header to indicate whether it corresponds to a normal block or encodes a run length. Fortunately, the original PForDelta leaves a unused bit in the header. At decompression time, the flag is checked to see whether one must decompress a normal block or a run.

This scheme is unable to encode relatively short runs. First, we use 32 bits (the header) to represent the run length. Hence, we define run blocks as encoding runs of length ≥ 32 (hence, we use at most 1 bit to encode each 1 in the run). Second, it is very likely that some of the 1s lying at the beginning of a run will be used to fill the preceding normal block. Just the remaining 1s could be used to form a run—provided they are 32 or more. Hence, runs of moderate length ($\approx$ 100–200)—which are rather frequent in practice—are easy to detect. We can have, for instance, that the first docID in an inverted list is $i \neq 1$, and next it has a run of 158 1-DGaps. RLE PFD will not be able to encode the run as such: the first block will be a normal block storing i and then 127 1-DGaps. The next will be also a normal block storing the 31 remaining 1-DGaps (which cannot be regarded as a run, as we already said).

5.4 Experimental Evaluation

For our experiments we use an HP ProLiant DL380 G7 (589152-001) server, with a Quadcore Intel(R) Xeon(R) CPU E5620 @ 2.40GHz processor, with 128KB of L1 cache, 1MB of L2 cache, 2MB of L2 cache, and a 96GB RAM, running version 2.6.34.8-68.fc13.i686.PAE of Linux kernel.

We index the 25.2 million documents from the TREC GOV2 collection. We implement our RLE schemes using C++. We compile our codes with `g++ 4.4.5`, with optimization flag `-O5`. For PForDelta, NewPFD, and OptPFD we use the highly-efficient implementations from [30]. We base our implementation of RLE PFD on OptPFD. VByte and S9 implementations are from ourselves. For VByte, S9, PForDelta, NewPFD and OptPFD, we subtract 1 to each DGap in the index, so they start from zero.

5.4.1 Document Reordering Methods

In our experiments, we use the following document orders to assign the docIDs to the TREC GOV2 collection: (1) the original order given to the documents in the collection ("Unsorted" in our tables); (2) the URL sorting ("URL" in our tables); (3) the IBDA ("IBDA" in our tables) method introduced in Section 4.1.

In our experiments, we found out that IBDA works better on inverted indexes for already-sorted document collections. Thus, we apply IBDA to the inverted index constructed for the URL-sorted document collection. In our particular implementation of IBDA, we sort the inverted lists of the index according to the following procedure (recall from Section 4.1 that we need an ordered set of list $\mathcal{L}$). We take the 10,000 first queries from the TREC 2006 query log and compute the pairs of terms that are most frequently queried. We then sort the inverted lists such that if the most-frequently-queried pair of terms is w_i and w_j, hence the inverted lists I_{w_i} and I_{w_j} are the first lists in $\mathcal{L}$. We then take the second most-frequent pair of terms and add their inverted lists to $\mathcal{L}$ (just in case they have not being added before). This procedure is repeated until all frequent pairs have been added. Notice how in this way we force the inverted lists of the most-frequently-queried pairs of terms to be in consecutive positions of $\mathcal{L}$. The result is that the intersection of these pairs is transformed into a run by IBDA. This precomputes these intersections to speed-up query processing. All lists that do not appear among the most frequent pairs are sorted by length, from longest to shortest. In each step of the algorithm, the non-processed list tails are re-inserted according to their lengths.

5.4.2 Space Usage

Table 1 shows the experimental space usage of the docID data of the whole inverted index, for different compression schemes and the various docID assignment schemes we tested.

The main conclusions are the following:

- The space usage of either interpolative encoding, VByte, S9 and OptPFD is slightly improved when using our IBDA enumeration method, rather than just sorting by URL.
- When we use the RLE-encoded schemes on docIDs assigned by URL and IBDA, the space usage improves considerably compared with the corresponding normal schemes. The best improvement is achieved by RLE VByte: a reduction in space usage of 44.58%. This is because relatively-short runs are rather frequent in inverted indexes and, unlike other schemes, RLE VByte is able to encode runs of length ≥ 3.

Table 1: Overall space usage (in MB) of the TREC GOV2 inverted index, for different compression schemes and docID assignment methods. The space includes just the docIDs.

Compression Scheme	Reorder Method: Unsorted	URL	IBDA
Interpolative Encoding	5,507	2,712	2,641
VByte	7,526	6,726	6,754
S9	6,687	3,777	3,735
OptPFD	6,348	4,600	4,504
RLE VByte	7,418	3,861	3,743
RLE S9	6,687	3,455	3,392
RLE PFD	6,384	4,264	4,137

- Disregarding interpolative encoding, the smallest space usage is achieved by RLE S9 on docIDs assigned by IBDA. The improvement over S9 on docIDs assigned by URL (the previously-known best performer [30]) is of about 10.19%.
- Finally, RLE S9 uses between 25.82% and 28.44% extra space on interpolative encoding, depending on the docID assignment scheme used.

5.4.3 Decompression Speed

To test decompression speed, we use the TREC 2006 query log and decompress the inverted lists corresponding to the query terms. Table 2 shows the average decompression speed (in millions of DGaps per second) for the different compression schemes and docID assignment methods we have studied. All RLE methods *implicitly* decompress the runs.

Table 2: Average decompression speed (in millions of DGaps per sec.) for different compression schemes and docID assignment methods, on the TREC GOV2 inverted index.

Compression Scheme	Reorder Method: Unsorted	URL	IBDA
Interpolative Encoding	43.94	43.05	64.44
VByte	818.81	827.98	917.47
S9	749.28	983.84	1199.61
OptPFD	927.02	857.48	852.65
RLE VByte	446.58	1,313.03	1,988.86
RLE S9	779.52	1,812.22	2,691.09
RLE PFD	989.74	2,026.54	3,931.73

The main conclusions are the following:

- Except for OptPFD, using IBDA (instead of just URL) increases the decompression speed of either interpolative (49.67%), S9 (21.93%) and VByte (10.81%).
- The decompression performance of our VByte variant (recall Section 5.1) is faster than the original implementation of VByte (which in our tests decompresses 571 million docIDs per second for Unsorted, 576 millions for URL, and 594 millions for IBDA). This is because 1-byte DGaps are the most frequent in inverted indexes and our implementation takes advantage of

this fact. Notice that the decompression speed of our VByte implementation is competitive with S9. Dean [11] shows similar approaches to group the flag bits to decode them fast. We think that our implementation can be also useful to speed-up the decompression of text snippets [27].

- RLE S9 on URL yields an enhancement of 84.19% over S9 on URL. For RLE PFD on URL the improvement is of 136.34%. RLE S9 on IBDA, on the other hand, increases the decompression speed by 173.53% over S9 on URL. Finally, for RLE PFD on IBDA the decompression speed is improved by 358.52%.

- RLE PFD shows an enhancement of decompression speed of 34.22% compared to PForDelta on URL. If, on the other hand, we consider RLE PFD on IBDA rather than PForDelta on IBDA, the improvement is of 45.32%.

The results in Table 1 and Table 2 indicate that RLE S9 on IBDA offers the best space vs. decompression-time trade-off. We can conclude that IBDA by itself is able to improve decompression speed by up to 22% on URL. However, using the RLE encodings on IBDA data is the key to obtain the remarkable speedups that we mention above.

6. RUNS OF 1S AND DAAT PROCESSING

Document-at-a-Time (DAAT) and *Term-at-a-Time* (TAAT) are the usual ways to support efficient query processing in inverted indexes [10]. DAAT is generally faster and uses less memory than TAAT. Next we adapt DAAT query processing to efficiently handle the runs of 1s in the lists.

6.1 DAAT Query Processing

DAAT processes simultaneously—and from left to right—the inverted lists $I_{w_{i_1}}, \ldots, I_{w_{i_q}}$ of the query terms. This process is carried out with function $\texttt{nextGEQ}(I_{w_j}, d)$, which yields the smallest docID d' in the inverted list I_{w_j} such that $d \leq d'$. Since `nextGEQ` will be invoked with increasing values of d, every inverted list maintains a *cursor* `curr` with the current position in that list. Thus, function `nextGEQ` moves the cursor forward and each invocation to `nextGEQ` starts from the position where the previous invocation stopped.

To support DAAT, inverted lists are compressed using a block layout: each list is divided into blocks of a given amount of DGaps—typically, 128 DGaps per block. For each block, a *block header* is maintained. Each such header stores, among other things, the largest absolute docID of the block. This is used for skipping at query time. Assume that we must search for docID d in inverted list I_{w_j}. Hence, we invoke $\texttt{nextGEQ}(I_{w_j}, d)$. This function starts from position `curr` and moves through the block headers comparing d with the last docID in each block, skipping all non-relevant blocks. Once we arrive at the block that potentially stores d, we fully decompress it into an auxiliary `Buffer`. (This is not completely true if the block has been compressed using VByte, where a DGap per DGap decompression and checking is more efficient.) Next, we move `curr` through `Buffer` from left to right, looking for d.

6.2 DAAT and Implicit Run Decompression

As in Section 5.4.3, we do implicit decompression of runs, this time to support DAAT query processing. That is, if when decompressing a block we detect that a run has been compressed, we do not write every such 1 in `Buffer`. Instead, we just write the special mark 0 in the corresponding position of `Buffer`, followed by the length of the run. In other words, the time needed to decompress the whole run will be that needed to decompress just its length (i.e., a single integer) from our RLE schemes.

Assume that, at query time, we invoke $\texttt{nextGEQ}(I_{w_j}, d)$ and that the block that potentially stores d has been decompressed into `Buffer`. Suppose that, looking for d, we reach position j of `Buffer` and it holds that $\texttt{Buffer}[j] = 0$. That is, we have reached a run of 1s of length $\ell = \texttt{Buffer}[j+1]$. Let d' denote the docID stored at position $j-1$ in `Buffer`. Notice that the docIDs represented in the run lie in the interval $[d'+1, d'+\ell]$. If it holds that $d'+\ell < d$, we can safely skip the run and go on from position $k+2$ in `Buffer`. Otherwise, if $d'+\ell \geq d$ holds, the sought docID lies within the run, hence we cannot skip it. Notice that $p = d - d'$ is the position within the run corresponding to docID d. In this case we set $d' = d$ (indicating to the subsequent `nextGEQ` invocation that we have processed up to docID d) and return to the caller. We maintain the values of p and d' for the next search on the list. Assume now that we invoke $\texttt{nextGEQ}(I_{w_j}, d'')$, for $d'' > d$. Assuming that d'' lies within the same block as d, we check whether $d'+\ell-p < d''$ holds. If that is the case, we can skip the run and go on form position $k+2$ in `Buffer`. Otherwise, d'' also lies within the run, hence we act as before, updating d' and p.

This approach can be seen as an abstract optimization of inverted lists, since we only need to change the way in which function `nextGEQ` is implemented. Hence, this approach can in principle be used by any DAAT-like algorithm [9, 22], obtaining the gains in space usage of Table 1.

6.3 Redefining the Block Layout of the Lists

We need to redefine the block structure of the lists, since they store long segments that have been implicitly represented—the runs. If, as usual, we force the blocks to store a fixed number of DGaps, then we would need to break some long runs in order to accommodate them within a block. This would dilute the benefits of having long runs. Lists are divided into blocks of fixed size because whole blocks must be decompressed to search inside then (as we saw before). Hence, a block cannot store too many DGaps. However, we do not need to decompress runs explicitly, thus the cost of decompressing a run is actually the same as decompressing a single integer. Also, handling a run in `Buffer` does not incur in considerable extra costs, just checking whether we can skip the run or not. Thus, we define blocks of fixed size, say 128 DGaps, and regard every run as if it were a single DGap. For RLE S9, if it happens that the 128th DGap lies in the middle of an S9 word, then we include the whole S9 word within the block. Hence, S9 blocks can have slightly more than 128 DGaps. In the case of RLE PFD, as we already saw in Section 5.3, it handles runs of length ≥ 32.

Notice that in this way the number of blocks in the lists could be reduced, except for RLE PFD. As a result, we would need to store less block headers, thus reducing the space usage. Also, we will see in the experiments below that the number of blocks decompressed at query time is reduced when compared to the results in [30], improving the decompression effectiveness.

6.4 Experimental Evaluation

We test now the efficiency of our approaches at query time. We use the original TREC 2006 query log for the GOV2 collection.

6.4.1 Space Usage

Table 3 shows the space usage of the TREC GOV2 inverted index. This time we include the space required by the block headers. Disregarding interpolative encoding, the smallest space is achieved by RLE S9 on docIDs assigned by IBDA. The space is about 11.08% smaller than S9 on URL and uses 21.70% extra space on that of interpolative encoding.

Table 3: Space usage (in MB) of the TREC GOV2 inverted index, for different compression schemes and docID assignment methods. The space includes the docIDs and the block headers.

Compression Scheme	Reorder Method		
	Unsorted	URL	IBDA
Interpolative Encoding	6,551	3,756	3,685
VByte	8,264	7,464	7,497
S9	7,524	4,601	4,572
OptPFD	6,835	5,087	5,105
RLE VByte	8,448	4,626	4,485
RLE S9	7,524	4,147	4,091
RLE PFD	7,267	5,003	4,850

6.4.2 AND Queries

Table 4 shows the experimental query time (in milliseconds per query) for different query processing algorithms (in particular, AND, WAND and OR). We compare different compression schemes and reordering methods.

For AND queries, S9 on URL sorting (the best existing trade-off from [30]) achieves 5.53 msec/q (according to our experiments). Using our IBDA technique to order the document collection and then our RLE PFD approach to compress the resulting docID inverted lists, we obtain 4.84 msec/q (an improvement of 12.11%). If, alternatively, we use RLE S9 on IBDA, we obtain 5.14 msec/q (an improvement of 7.05% over S9 on URL). Notice also the following: if we consider S9 and RLE S9, both on URL assignment, the query times changes just slightly: from 5.53 to 5.52, respectively. If, on the other hand, we consider using IBDA instead of URL to assign docIDs, the reduction of query time is bigger. This shows again the effectiveness of IBDA, as it is able to improve the already highly-efficient query times of AND queries [30] (recall, from Section 5.4.1, that we have used a query log to carry out IBDA).

6.4.3 WAND Queries

We also test with the WAND query-processing algorithm [9], which is rather popular in current search engines. We use tf-idf ranking and look for top-10 results. As it can be seen in Table 4, we are able to speed-up the query processing by using IBDA and the RLE compression methods. For instance, by using RLE S9 on IBDA docIDs we can enhance the query time from about 60 msec/q to about 47 msec/q (an improvement of about 20.84%). For RLE PFD on IBDA, the improvement is of about 23.44%. Table 5 shows the average

Table 4: Experimental query time for the different query processing algorithms we tested.

Query Algorithm	Compression Scheme	Reorder Method		
		Unsorted	URL	IBDA
AND	VByte	42.85	22.88	28.88
	S9	11.97	5.53	5.43
	OptPFD	11.90	5.57	5.56
	RLE VByte	19.73	7.49	6.91
	RLE S9	12.67	5.52	5.14
	RLE PFD	12.46	5.34	4.84
WAND (top-10)	VByte	175.71	76.93	75.27
	S9	145.99	59.50	50.34
	OptPFD	152.03	60.73	52.87
	RLE VByte	184.74	66.95	54.57
	RLE S9	150.87	59.14	47.10
	RLE PFD	153.14	58.77	46.49
OR	VByte	330.39	292.07	288.38
	S9	380.90	331.88	327.30
	OptPFD	357.28	323.90	319.15
	RLE VByte	340.29	83.99	41.62
	RLE S9	475.70	141.58	59.97
	RLE PFD	465.35	177.10	66.03

number of docIDs (in millions) that are decoded per query (runs are regarded as single integers) and average number of blocks (in thousands) that are decompressed per query. Our

Table 5: Millions of docIDs decoded on average per query ("Ints.") and thousands of blocks decompressed on average per query ("Blks.") for WAND. The processing is carried out for top-10 results.

Comp. Scheme	Reorder Method					
	Unsorted		URL		IBDA	
	Ints.	Blks.	Ints.	Blks.	Ints.	Blks.
VByte	10.07	63.29	5.34	24.04	6.23	18.24
S9	10.98	82.42	4.70	34.53	4.50	33.00
OptPFD	10.91	85.30	4.62	36.11	4.42	34.51
RLE VByte	6.93	60.53	1.71	15.51	1.30	11.58
RLE S9	10.89	81.85	3.21	24.21	2.09	15.87
RLE PFD	10.91	85.44	3.60	31.90	2.22	18.24

results indicate that the number of docIDs decoded (as well as the number of decompressed blocks) is reduced in two ways: first, by using an RLE compression scheme; second, by using IBDA rather than URL sorting. For instance, if we use RLE S9 on URL sorting instead of S9 on URL, we obtain a reduction of about 30% in decoded docIDs (the same figure can be observed for decompressed blocks). If we now use RLE S9 on IBDA sorting, we obtain a further reduction of about 34% over RLE S9 on URL. This shows that we are able to improve the decompression effectiveness, as we can process the same queries decompressing less blocks and docIDs. This is not only effective to reduce the query time (as we can see in Table 4) but also in cases where accessing blocks is expensive (for instance, when blocks need to be transferred from secondary storage).

Finally, we think that this query-time reduction can be also achieved by the Block-Max WAND algorithm from [22].

6.4.4 Full-OR Queries

We use now the run-length encoding of inverted lists to improve the performance of OR queries. In particular, full OR queries, where the full result (rather than a ranking) must be obtained. The main application is the offline merging of inverted lists.

Let I_1 and I_2 be the involved inverted lists. The search algorithm proceeds as usual for DAAT OR queries. However, if while processing I_1 we arrive at a run whose docIDs define the interval $[d', d' + \ell']$, we switch to I_2 and look for $d' + \ell' + 1$ in it. If we find that $d' + \ell' + 1$ also lies within a run $[d'', d'' + \ell'' + 1]$ in I_2, then we switch to I_1 again and look for $d'' + \ell'' + 1$ in it. We keep repeating this process until the current docID d^* we are looking for is not within a run. In this case, we can report the run-length encoding of the interval $[d', d^* - 1]$. This allows us to compute the union of these intervals without decompressing them. Notice also that runs are written in the output already encoded. We call RLE OR this process.

Table 4 shows the experimental results. For VByte, S9 and PForDelta we use the traditional DAAT OR processing. As it can be seen, RLE OR introduces relevant improvements. In particular, for RLE VByte on IBDA, where we obtain a reduction of 85.75% compared to VByte on URL. The rationale behind this exceptional performance of RLE VByte is that it is the only RLE scheme able to catch short runs. These are rather frequent in practice, which explains the good performance.

6.5 Inverted List Caching

We study now how the RLE compression methods and the IBDA docID assignment behave when compressing static inverted-list caches [17]. We show that the RLE compression schemes on docIDs assigned with IBDA are more suitable for compressing a small set of inverted lists, rather than using the classic compression schemes on a global docID assignment method, such as URL sorting.

In our experiments, we use as a building block the TREC GOV2 inverted index with docIDs assigned by URL sorting. We use the TREC 2006 query log to compute the frequency of the query terms. We then sort the inverted lists according to this frequency (from most frequent to least frequent). Next, we consider the top-Q lists in this sorting, for $Q = 1$ thousand, 2 thousands, ..., 10 thousands. For each such Q, we apply IBDA on the resulting set of lists, using the order we already mentioned.

Figure 1 shows the space usage as a function of the number of lists considered in each case. We also show a table with the cache hit ratio achieved for every Q. We include just S9 compression, since similar results are obtained for the remaining methods (yet, S9 yields the smallest space usage among all other schemes). As it can be seen, RLE S9 compression yields a considerable reduction of space usage, either on URL and IBDA sorting. For instance, we can conclude that 10 thousand lists compressed with RLE S9 on IBDA sorting use about the same amount of space than 2 thousand lists compressed with S9 on URL. In other words, within the same space used by S9 on URL to achieve a 24% hit ratio, RLE S9 on IBDA is able to achieve a 51% hit ratio.

An important feature that must be noted is that the re-

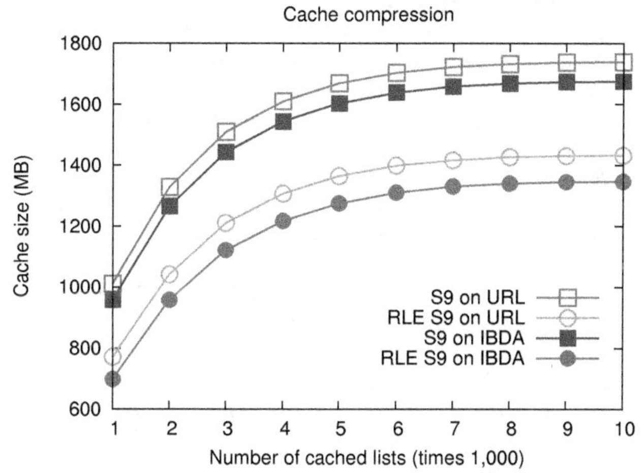

Lists:	1	2	3	4	5	6	7	8	9	10
% Hit ratio:	13	24	31	37	40	42	44	46	49	51

Figure 1: (Above) Cache space usage as a function of the number of inverted lists compressed, using variants of S9. (Below) Cache hit ratio achieved for the different number of lists.

duction of space usage degrades as we compress more lists. In our experiments, for 1,000 lists and using RLE S9 on IBDA the reduction is of about 31%. For 10,000 lists, on the other hand, the reduction is of about 23% (recall that for the whole index we obtain a reduction of about 10%, recall Tables 1 and 3).

7. CONCLUSIONS AND FUTURE WORK

We have shown that using our docID assignment scheme IBDA (for focusing the generation of run on a given set of inverted list) and then run-length encoding these lists yields better general performance. This reinforces and improves the results obtained in previous related work [30]. We obtain an improvement of about 10% in space usage compared with the (already very efficient) results from [30]. If we compare our decompression speed with that of [30], we are up to 1.22 times faster if the runs must be explicitly decompressed and up to 4.58 times faster if implicit decompression of runs is allowed. DAAT query processing can be also improved using our approaches: AND queries can be improved by up to 12%, WAND queries by up to 23% and full OR queries by up to 86%. Finally, we have shown that our approaches are useful for the efficient caching of inverted lists, achieving a reduction in space usage of up to 31%.

As future work, we plan to test our approaches to improve the performance of the Block-Max WAND algorithm of [22]. It would be also interesting to use the approach of [25] along with our approaches. Also, it would be interesting to adapt our schemes to graph compression [7]. That is, adapting our IBDA scheme to generate runs in the adjacency lists to then run-length encode these lists.

8. ACKNOWLEDGEMENTS

The authors want to thank the thorough comments from the anonymous referees, which definitely helped to improve the quality of this paper.

9. REFERENCES

[1] V. N. Anh and A. Moffat. Inverted index compression using word-aligned binary codes. *Information Retrieval*, 8(1):151–166, 2005.

[2] V. N. Anh and A. Moffat. Improved word-aligned binary compression for text indexing. *IEEE Trans. Knowl. Data Eng.*, 18(6):857–861, 2006.

[3] D. Arroyuelo, S. González, M. Marin, M. Oyarzún, and T. Suel. To index or not to index: time-space trade-offs in search engines with positional ranking functions. In *Proc. of 35th Annual Int. ACM SIGIR Conf. on Research and Development in Information Retrieval*, pages 255–264. ACM, 2012.

[4] R. Baeza-Yates and B. Ribeiro-Neto. *Modern Information Retrieval - the Concepts and Technology Behind Search, Second Edition.* Pearson Education Ltd., Harlow, England, 2011.

[5] R. Blanco and A. Barreiro. Document identifier reassignment through dimensionality reduction. In *Proc. of 27th European Conference on IR Research (ECIR)*, LNCS 3408, pages 375–387. Springer, 2005.

[6] D. Blandford and G. Blelloch. Index compression through document reordering. In *Proc. of 2002 Data Compression Conference (DCC)*, pages 342–351. IEEE Computer Society, 2002.

[7] P. Boldi and S. Vigna. The webgraph framework I: compression techniques. In *Proc. of 13th Int. Conference on World Wide Web (WWW)*, pages 595–602. ACM, 2004.

[8] S. Brin and L. Page. Reprint of: The anatomy of a large-scale hypertextual web search engine. *Computer Networks*, 56(18):3825–3833, 2012.

[9] A. Broder, D. Carmel, M. Herscovici, A. Soffer, and J. Zien. Efficient query evaluation using a two-level retrieval process. In *Proc. of 2003 ACM CIKM Int. Conf. on Information and Knowledge Management*, pages 426–434. ACM, 2003.

[10] S. Büttcher, C. Clarke, and G. Cormack. *Information Retrieval: Implementing and Evaluating Search Engines.* MIT Press, 2010.

[11] J. Dean. Challenges in building large-scale information retrieval systems: invited talk. In *Proc. of 2nd Int. Conf. on Web Search and Web Data Mining (WSDM)*, page 1. ACM, 2009.

[12] S. Ding, J. Attenberg, and T. Suel. Scalable techniques for document identifier assignment in inverted indexes. In *Proc. of 19th Int. Conference on World Wide Web (WWW)*, pages 311–320. ACM, 2010.

[13] P. Elias. Universal codeword sets and representations of the integers. *IEEE Transactions on Information Theory*, 21(2):194–203, 1975.

[14] S. Golomb. Run-length encoding. *IEEE Transactions on Information Theory*, 12(3):399–401, 1966.

[15] D. Johnson, S. Krishnan, J. Chhugani, S. Kumar, and S. Venkatasubramanian. Compressing large boolean matrices using reordering techniques. In *Proc. of 30th Int. Conf. on Very Large Data Bases (VLDB)*, pages 13–23. Morgan Kaufmann, 2004.

[16] J. Kleinberg. Authoritative sources in a hyperlinked environment. *Journal of the ACM*, 46(5):604–632, 1999.

[17] H. T. Lam, R. Perego, N. T. M. Quan, and F. Silvestri. Entry pairing in inverted file. In *Proc. of 10th Int. Conf. on Web Information Systems Engineering (WISE)*, LNCS 5802, pages 511–522. Springer, 2009.

[18] C. Manning, P. Raghavan, and H. Schütze. *Introduction to Information Retrieval.* Cambridge University Press, 2008.

[19] A. Moffat and L. Stuiver. Binary interpolative coding for effective index compression. *Information Retrieval*, 3(1):25–47, 2000.

[20] D. Salomon. *Data compression - The Complete Reference, 4th Edition.* Springer, 2007.

[21] W.-Y. Shieh, T.-F. Chen, J. J.-J. Shann, and C.-P. Chung. Inverted file compression through document identifier reassignment. *Information Processing and Management*, 39(1):117–131, 2003.

[22] D. Shuai and T. Suel. Faster top-k document retrieval using block-max indexes. In *Proc. of 34th Annual Int. ACM SIGIR Conf. on Research and Development in Information Retrieval*, pages 993–1002. ACM, 2011.

[23] F. Silvestri. Sorting out the document identifier assignment problem. In *Proc. of 29th European Conference on IR Research (ECIR)*, LNCS 4425, pages 101–112. Springer, 2007.

[24] F. Silvestri, S. Orlando, and R. Perego. Assigning identifiers to documents to enhance the clustering property of fulltext indexes. In *Proc. of 27th Annual Int. ACM SIGIR Conf. on Research and Development in Information Retrieval*, pages 305–312. ACM, 2004.

[25] F. Silvestri and R. Venturini. Vsencoding: efficient coding and fast decoding of integer lists via dynamic programming. In *Proc. of 19th ACM Conf. on Information and Knowledge Management (CIKM)*, pages 1219–1228, 2010.

[26] N. Tonellotto, C. Macdonald, and I. Ounis. Effect of different docid orderings on dynamic pruning retrieval strategies. In *Proc. of 34th Annual Int. ACM SIGIR Conf. on Research and Development in Information Retrieval*, pages 1179–1180. ACM, 2011.

[27] A. Turpin, Y. Tsegay, D. Hawking, and H. Williams. Fast generation of result snippets in web search. In *Proc. of 30th Annual Int. ACM SIGIR Conf. on Research and Development in Information Retrieval*, pages 127–134, 2007.

[28] H. Williams and J. Zobel. Compressing integers for fast file access. *The Computer Journal*, 42(3):193–201, 1999.

[29] I. Witten, A. Moffat, and T. Bell. *Managing Gigabytes: Compressing and Indexing Documents and Images, 2nd Edition.* Morgan Kaufmann, 1999.

[30] H. Yan, S. Ding, and T. Suel. Inverted index compression and query processing with optimized document ordering. In *Proc. of 18th Int. Conference on World Wide Web (WWW)*, pages 401–410. ACM, 2009.

[31] J. Zobel and A. Moffat. Inverted files for text search engines. *ACM Comput. Surveys*, 38(2), 2006.

[32] M. Zukowski, S. Héman, N. Nes, and P. Boncz. Super-scalar RAM-CPU cache compression. In *Proc. of 22nd Int. Conf. on Data Engineering (ICDE)*, page 59. IEEE Computer Society, 2006.

Fast Document-at-a-time Query Processing using Two-tier Indexes

Cristian Rossi
Univ. Federal do Amazonas
Manaus,AM, Brazil
cristian.infor@gmail.com

Edleno Silva de Moura
Univ. Federal do Amazonas
Manaus,AM, Brazil
edleno@icomp.ufam.edu.br

Andre Luiz Carvalho
Univ. Federal do Amazonas
Manaus,AM, Brazil
andre@icomp.ufam.edu.br

Altigran Soares da Silva
Univ. Federal do Amazonas
Manaus,AM, Brazil
alti@icomp.ufam.edu.br

ABSTRACT

In this paper we present two new algorithms designed to reduce the overall time required to process top-k queries. These algorithms are based on the document-at-a-time approach and modify the best baseline we found in the literature, Blockmax WAND (BMW), to take advantage of a two-tiered index, in which the first tier is a small index containing only the higher impact entries of each inverted list. This small index is used to pre-process the query before accessing a larger index in the second tier, resulting in considerable speeding up the whole process. The first algorithm we propose, named *BMW-CS*, achieves higher performance, but may result in small changes in the top results provided in the final ranking. The second algorithm, named *BMW-t*, preserves the top results and, while slower than BMW-CS, it is faster than BMW. In our experiments, BMW-CS was more than 40 times faster than BMW when computing top 10 results, and, while it does not guarantee preserving the top results, it preserved all ranking results evaluated at this level.

Categories and Subject Descriptors

H.4 [**Information Systems Applications**]: Miscellaneous; D.2.8 [**Software Engineering**]: Metrics—*complexity measures, performance measures*

Keywords

Top-k Query Processing, Efficiency, Two-tier indexes

SIGIR'13, July 28–August 1, 2013, Dublin, Ireland.

1. INTRODUCTION

Computing ranking of results by using information retrieval (IR) models is one of the core tasks of search systems. While search systems often index a massive number of documents, usually their users are not interested in an in-depth list of results related to a query, but rather to a small list of highly relevant documents that will satisfy their informational needs. Thus, part of the recent research related to search systems is aimed at improving the quality of the top results presented to users, instead of the overall quality of the presented list. This focus on a narrower set of high quality results has led to the development of a number of technologies to improve the efficiency of methods to compute the top results in search systems.

When determining the best results for a given query, a search system usually deploys a number of different sources of relevance evidence. For instance, web search engines use information such as titles of the pages, URL tokenization, and link analysis, among others. These sources of relevance evidence may be combined using a myriad of approaches, such as the adoption of learning to rank techniques. Even in these cases, the initial process of computing the ranking consists of applying a basic IR model, such as BM25 [11] or the Vector Space Model [12], to compute an initial rank of top results, typically limited to the size of just about one thousand documents [5].

In this paper we propose two new algorithms which reduce the overall time required to compute the final query ranking. The algorithms modify the best baseline we found in the literature, the *Blockmax WAND* (*BMW*) [6], to take advantage of a two-tiered index. The first algorithm we proposed, named *BMW-CS*, from BMW using the first tier as a candidate selector, uses the first tier to select candidate documents that are taken into account to compute the final ranking when processing the second tier. It achieves higher performance, but may result in small changes in the top results provided in the final ranking. In BMW-CS, the entries of the first tier are not present in the second tier. The second algorithm, named *BMW-t*, from BMW using the first tier as a threshold selector, preserves the top results and, while slower compared to BMW-CS, it is faster than BMW. The first tier is used only to compute a safe initial threshold to be adopted when processing the second tier, thus allowing a slightly faster query processing when compared to BMW. The price paid is that the second tier in BMW-t should contain the full index and the first tier is an extra index.

While there were previous approaches based on using a smaller index tier to improve efficiency, our proposed algorithms are designed to take advantage of dynamic pruning techniques, not to minimize the effort of processing answers from the first tier, but to reduce the time required to read and process entries from the second tier.

The remainder of this article is structured as follows. Section 2 presents the background and related research necessary to better understand the proposed methods. Section 3 presents our methods, BMW-CS and BMW-*t*. Section 4 presents the experimental results. Finally, Section 5 presents the conclusion and prospective future work.

2. BACKGROUND AND RELATED WORK

Usually, most of the data needed by a search system to process user queries is stored in data structures known as *inverted files* [3]. They contain, for each term t, the list of documents where it occurs and an *impact factor*, or weight, associated with each document. This list of pairs of document and term impacts is called the *inverted list* of t and it is used to measure the relative importance of terms in the stored documents. Each document is represented in these lists by a value named *document id*, referred to as *docId* in this article. The inverted files may become huge in some systems, thus they are usually stored in a compressed format.

2.1 TAAT approach

In a query processing approach named Term-At-A-Time (TAAT), the inverted lists are sorted by term impact in non-increasing order. The query results are obtained by sequentially traversing one inverted list at a time. As an advantage, we can mention the fact that a sequential access behavior to inverted lists may speed up the process.

As the main disadvantage, we can mention that this strategy requires the usage of large amounts of memory to store partial scores achieved by each document when traversing each inverted list. These partial scores should be stored to accumulate the score results obtained by each document when traversing each inverted list. The final ranking can be computed only when all the inverted lists are processed. Several authors proposed methods to discard partial scores, thus reducing the amount of memory required to process queries in the TAAT mode [15, 2, 1]. Despite the significant reduction of required memory for query processing, the space required to store the partial scores remains one of the drawbacks of the TAAT query processing approach.

Anh and Moffat [1] studied the application of dynamic pruning over inverted indexes where the entries are sorted by impact, thus adopting a TAAT approach. In their work, a first phase processes blocks containing entries with higher impact in a disjunctive mode. Once all documents that might be present in the top-k results, k being a parameter, are found, the method starts a second phase applying a conjunctive mode query processing where only documents included as results by the first phase are considered. They also present a modified version of their algorithm, named as method B, where the top results may be changed, thus giving approximate results. In method B, only a percentage of the results obtained in the first phase are taken into account in the second phase. This modified version results in even faster query processing, but does not guarantee top k results of the ranking will not be modified.

Strohman and Croft [15] proposed a new method for efficient query processing when documents are stored in main memory that modifies the method presented by Anh and Moffat [1]. In their proposal, a dynamic pruning is applied in each phase of query processing over the candidate documents with the goal of obtaining the final query results without requiring a full evaluation of all candidates. The query processing is performed over impact sorted inverted lists and the impact values are discretized in a small range of integer values.

2.2 DAAT approach

Another approach to process queries is to adopt a Document-At-A-Time (DAAT) query processing. In this alternative, the inverted lists are sorted by *docIds*, which allows the algorithms to traverse all the inverted lists related to a query in parallel. As a consequence, the final scores of documents can be computed while traversing the lists and the system may store only the top results required by the user, so the memory requirements are fairly smaller. On the other hand the fragmented access may slow down the query processing and, since the inverted lists are sorted by *docIds*, important entries are spread along the inverted lists, making the pruning of entries more complex in this query processing approach.

As in the TAAT approach, several authors have presented algorithms and data structures to accelerate the query processing in the DAAT approach. For instance, data structures to allow fast jumps in the inverted lists, named as skiplists [7], are adopted to accelerate the query processing. Skiplists divide the inverted lists into blocks of entries and provide pointers for fast access to such blocks, so that a scan in the skiplist determines in which block a document entry may occur, if it does, in the inverted list.

The problem of efficiently computing the ranking of results for a given user query has been largely addressed in the literature in several research articles. We here detail the ones closer to our research, focusing on DAAT, which is the approach adopted by our algorithms.

2.2.1 WAND

Broder et al [4] proposed a successful strategy for query processing, known as WAND, which allows fast query processing for both conjunctive and disjunctive queries, with the possibility of configuring the method for preserving the top k documents in the query answer or not. In the case where the top answers are not guaranteed to be preserved, the method leads to even faster query processing.

WAND processes the queries using DAAT approach, so the inverted lists of the query terms are traversed in parallel. A heap of scores is created to keep the top k documents with larger scores at each step of the query processing, k being the number of documents requested to the search system. The smaller score in the heap at each moment is taken as a *discarding threshold* to accelerate the query processing. A new document is evaluated and inserted in the heap only if it has a score higher than this *discarding threshold.*

The WAND has a two level evaluation approach. In the first level, a document pivot has its *maximum possible score* evaluated using the information of *maximum score* of each list where the document may occur. If the *maximum possible score* is greater than the actual *discarding threshold*, the document has its actual score evaluated. Otherwise, the document is discarded and a new pivot is selected.

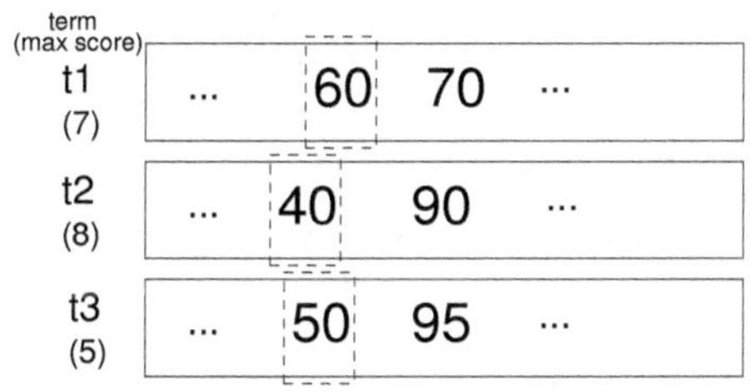

Figure 1: Inverted lists when processing query with terms t1, t2, and t3. Marked entries are the ones currently processed.

At each moment in the DAAT query processing, there is a pointer to the next document to be processed in each inverted list associated with the query. For instance, if we have a query with terms $t1$, $t2$ and $t3$, there will be a pointer to the next document processed in each of their lists, as illustrated in Figure 1. In the Figure, documents 60, 40 and 50 are currently pointed in lists $t1$, $t2$ and $t3$, respectively. The WAND algorithm assures that previous occurrences in each list were already examined and that each of the pointed documents represents the smaller *docId* in the list that was not yet processed [4]. Thus, since the lists are organized by *docIds*, at this point we know the smaller *docId* (40) occurs only in the list of term $t2$, while document 50 occurs in $t3$ and might occur in $t2$. Finally, document 60 occurs in the list of $t1$ and might occur in the other two lists.

At this point, knowing the maximum score a document may reach in each list, we can estimate the maximum scores each of the currently pointed documents can obtain when processing the query: 40 can reach *maximum possible score* equal to the maximum score a document may achieve in the list of $t2$; 50 can reach the sums of maximum scores of $t2$ and $t3$, and 60 can reach the sum of maximum scores of the three terms as its *maximum possible score*. Using this information, we may discard the documents which are not able to reach the *discarding threshold*, i.e., cannot achieve a score higher than the minimum score among the top k results already processed at this moment.

So, to discard documents, we check the current documents pointed in each inverted list associated with the query and estimate their *maximum possible score*. The entry with smaller *docId* among the ones that reach a maximum possible score higher than the current *discarding threshold* is then chosen as a candidate to be included in the answer. This entry is known as the pivot. We then move all posting lists so that they point to *docIds* of at least the same as the pivot. Notice only pointers of lists where the current *docIds* are smaller than the pivot require a movement. If one of the posting lists with *docId* smaller than the pivot does not have the pivot document, the document is discarded, a new pivot is selected and the process repeated. Otherwise, if all these lists contain the document, its actual score is then computed. If the actual score of the pivot is higher than the *discarding threshold*, it is included in the answer set and the *discarding threshold* is updated. After processing the pivot, we move all the lists to the next document with *docId* bigger than the pivot and start the process again.

An interesting feature of the WAND method is that it can be configured as a more or less aggressive pruning method by either applying a reduction in the max score values of each list or by increasing the pruning threshold so that fewer documents will be accepted in the top results. When the pruning threshold is increased, there is no guarantee of preserving the exact top result set. Further details about the WAND method can be found in the article where it was first proposed [4].

2.2.2 Blockmax WAND

Ding and Suel [6] have recently revisited the ideas presented in the WAND method, and proposed an even faster solution named the *Blockmax* WAND (BMW). In BMW, the entries of the inverted lists are grouped into compressed blocks that may be jumped without any decompression of their content. Each block contains information about the maximum impact among the entries found in it. Whenever such maximum impact is not relevant to change the results for a given query, the whole block is discarded, which avoids important query processing costs.

Authors present experiments which indicate BMW results in significant reduction of query processing times when compared to previous work, being currently the fastest query processing method found by us.

The BMW is based on the WAND algorithm and uses the same approach for selecting a document pivot during the query processing. In BMW, the pruning of entries is performed using two main pieces of information: (i) the maximum impact found inside an inverted list, which is also adopted in WAND; and (ii) The maximum impact found in each block pointed by the skiplist entries, known as the *block max score*, so that before accessing a block it is possible to predict the maximum impact of an entry among those found in such a block.

The basic idea of BMW is to take advantage of information (ii) to speedup query processing. Once a candidate document is selected to have its score computed, the algorithm uses the *block max score* information to accelerate the query processing by discarding documents with no chance of being in the top answers. The algorithm also allows skipping entire blocks of inverted list entries based on the *block max score* present on the skiplists, a procedure that they call shallow movement. Contrary to the regular movement present on the inverted lists, the shallow movement accesses only the skiplist entries, which avoids costs to decompress blocks of the inverted lists when processing queries.

The BMW algorithm starts with a pivoting phase, where a document is selected as a candidate to be inserted in the answer. Its pivoting phase is similar to the one performed in the WAND algorithm. Using the global max score of each list and the lists ordered by the value of the current *docId* pointed in each of them.

Before decompressing and evaluating the pivot document, BMW makes a shallow movement to align the inverted lists over the blocks that possibly have the document. After the alignment, the algorithm uses the information of *block max score*, stored in the skiplists, to estimate a local upper bound score of the candidate document. If this upper bound score is lower than a given pruning threshold, the document is discarded and one of the lists is advanced.

As in WAND, the pruning threshold is dynamically updated according to the score of the evaluated candidate. As the processing is DAAT, each evaluated candidate has its complete score calculated, since all inverted lists are processed in parallel. Further details about the BMW algorithm can be found in the article where it was proposed [6].

Shan et al [13] show that the performance of BMW is degraded when static scores, such as Pagerank, are added in the ranking function. They study efficient techniques for Top-k query processing in the case where a page's static score is given and propose a set of new algorithms based on BMW which outperform the existing ones when static scores are taken into account when computing the final ranking. Their study can also be applied to our proposal as a future work, being orthogonal to the study presented here.

2.3 Multi-tier indexes

Some authors proposed the splitting of the inverted index in more than one tier in an attempt to accelerate query processing. In these architectures, the query processing starts in a small tier and only if necessary proceeds to larger tiers. Risvik and Aasheim [10] divided the index into three tiers with the goal of achieving better scaling when distributing the index. According to static and dynamic sources of evidence, documents considered as more relevant are selected to compose the smaller tier. The query processing starts in the higher tier and only if the result set is not satisfactory, according to an evaluating algorithm, the query processing proceeds to the next tier. Performance gains are achieved when the processing does not visit the larger tiers. There is no guarantee that the result set is the exact set if compared to the exhaustive query processing.

In our proposed algorithms, we also kept the documents considered more important, in our case those with higher impact, in the smaller tier. However, in this paper we use each tier as part of the query processing. Our algorithms could, for instance, be applied to each tier proposed by Ravisk and Aesheim [10], being then ortoghonal to their proposal.

Ntoulas and Cho [8] presented a two-tiered query processing method that avoids any degradation of the quality of results, always guaranteeing the exact top-k results set. The first tier contains the documents considered the most important to the collection, selecting the entries by using static and dynamic pruning strategies that remove non-relevant documents and terms. The second tier contains the complete index. Their proposal uses the first tier as a cache level to accelerate query processing. Whenever the method detects that the results of the first tier assures that the top results will not be changed, it does not access the second tier, basing its results only on the first tier. Otherwise, they process the query using the second tier.

To guarantee that their method preserves the top answer results when compared to a system without pruning, the method evaluates the ranking function when processing the first tier, assigning the maximum possible score that could be achieved when processing the full index for entries that are not present in the first tier. The authors show how to determine the optimal size of a pruned index and experimentally evaluate their algorithms in a collection of 130 million Web pages. In their experiments, the presented method achieved good results for first tier index sizes varying from 10% to 20% of the full index. The two-tier strategy is also adopted in our article, but instead of using the first tier as a cache, we use it as a candidate selection layer as part of our algorithms to compute the top results of a given query. Another important difference is that we always process the queries using both tiers, and we do not guarantee the exact top-k results.

Skobeltsyn et al [14] evaluate the impact of including a cache in the system when using the two-tier method presented by Ntoulas et al [8] and shows the query distribution workload is affected by the cache system. When using the cache, queries with a few terms, which would be the ones that would benefit more from the two-tier strategies, are usually solved by the cache system. As a consequence, the queries with more terms, which are difficult to process with pruning strategies, become more important in the workload when considering a system that adopts a cache of results.

3. BMW-CS AND BMW-T

In this section, we present the details of the algorithms we proposed to accelerate the query processing when computing the ranking of results, which are named *BMW-CS*, from BWW with candidate selection, and *BMW-t*, from BMW with a threshold selection. These algorithms are based on a two-tiered index organization in which the first tier is a small index created using the entries with the highest impact from each term list, while the second tier is a larger index. The idea of relying on a high-quality tier is similar to the one adopted by Ntoulas et. al. [8].

The main objective of our algorithms is to use the first tier to accelerate the query processing in the second tier (i.e., the larger index) when computing the final ranking. In *BMW-CS*, the two tiers are disjointed, that is, the high-impact entries in the small index in first tier are not present in the second one. In *BMW-t*, the second tier contains the full index. Thus, even the high-impact entries in the first tier are also present in it.

In both cases, to select the entries for the first tier, we compute a global threshold to select entries so that the size of the first tier is about $\Delta\%$ of the full index. The parameter Δ provides an estimation of the final size of the first tier index. We adopted a minimum size of 1000 entries in each inverted list to prevent any individual list from becoming too small.

In our index organization, we used skiplists in both tiers in order to accelerate the query processing. For each block of 128 document entries, a skiplist entry is created that keeps the information of the current *docId* and the highest impact among the documents of the block. Also, for each term in the collection, the highest impact (max score) in the whole inverted list and the lowest impact found in this list in the first tier are computed and stored along with the term information. The lowest impact in the list at the first tier can be seen as an upper bound for the impact of the document entries that were not included in this list. Using this information, we can set the upper bound of contribution for the entries that are not present in the first tier, but appear in the inverted list in the second tier.

3.1 BMW-CS

Listing 1 presents our first algorithm called *BWM with candidate selection*, or *BMW-CS*. In its first phase, BMW-CS uses the first tier to select documents that are candidates to be present in the top results. Initially, the set of candidate documents, denoted by $\mathcal{A}$, is generated by the function

Listing 1: Algorithm BMW-CS

```
BMW-CS(queryTerms[1..q], k)
  𝒜 ← SelectCandidates(queryTerms, k)

  sort 𝒜 by score
  min_score ← 𝒜_k.score

  //Remove the candidates with low upper_score
  for (i = 0 to |A|)
    if(𝒜_i.upper_score < min_score) remove 𝒜_i
  end for

  ℛ ← CalculateCompleteScore(𝒜, queryTerms, k)

  return ℛ
```

SelectCandidates, which computes the candidates for the top k results of a query composed of a set of terms (Listing 2). Then, the algorithm trims this set of documents, removing all candidates that cannot be present in the top-k results. This trimming decreases the cost of the second phase. In the second phase, the second tier is processed to compute the final ranking of the top k results. This phase is performed by the function *CalculateCompleteScore* (Listing 6).

The main idea behind BMW-CS is to take advantage of the fact that the first tier has entries with higher impact in order to significantly reduce the amount of documents analyzed in the second tier. We show in the experiments that this approach yields a quite competitive query processing algorithm.

3.1.1 Candidates Selection

BMW-CS selects candidate documents from the first tier. However, the inverted lists in the first tier are not complete, which means, for instance, that a document which appears only in the list of one of the terms of a query in the first tier, may appear in lists of other terms of this query when considering the entries present in the second tier. Thus, during the candidate selection phase, the algorithm may discard a document that could have a high enough score when the full inverted lists are evaluated.

To reduce the possible negative impacts of this incompleteness of the lists in the first tier, we modified the BMW algorithm so that it considers the possibility of a missing pair $(term, docId)$ in the first tier to occur in the second tier. During the pivoting phase and the upper boundary score checking, a lower boundary score is added for each missing term of the document that might be absent in the first tier, thus avoiding the possibility of discarding high score candidates due to incompleteness in the first tier.

This lower boundary score represents the max score that a document can achieve after processing the inverted list in the second index. With these two values, we can adjust the *discarding threshold* used to prune documents in BMW. A minimum heap is used to store the top-k documents with a higher score. The smallest score of the heap is used as the *discarding threshold* for BMW to dynamically prune entries with no chance to be part of the final top-k results. All evaluated documents that have a score higher than the *discarding threshold* when processing the first tier are added to the set of candidate documents.

We can see the detailed algorithm for the candidate selection phase in Listing 2. The algorithm starts by selecting

Listing 2: Algorithm SelectCandidates

```
1  SelectCandidates (queryTerms[1..q], k)
2    Let ℋ be the minimum heap to keep the top k results
3    Let 𝒜 be the list of candidates
4    Let ℐ_cand be the first tier index
5
6    lists ← ℐ_cand(queryTerms);// Gets inverted lists
7    θ ← 0;
8    //Point to the first docId in  each list
9    for each  {0 ≤ i < |lists|} do Next(lists[i], 0);
10
11   repeat
12     sortByCurrentPointedDocId(lists);
13     p ← Pivoting(lists, θ);
14     if (p == −1) break; //No more candidates
15     d ← lists[p].curDoc;
16     if(d == MAXDOC) break; //End of the list
17
18     //Move only the skip pointers
19     for each {0 ≤ i ≤ p} do NextShallow(lists[i], d);
20
21     if( CheckBlockMax(θ, p) == TRUE)
22       if(lists[0].curDoc == d)
23         doc.docId ← d;
24         doc.score ← Σ_{i=0}^{p} BM25(lists[i]);
25         doc.upper_score ← doc.score +
26                           Σ_{i=p+1}^{|lists|} lists[i].min_score;
27
28         if (|ℋ| < k) ℋ ← ℋ ∪ doc;
29         else if (ℋ_0.score < doc.score)
30           remove ℋ_0; // the one with smallest score
31           ℋ ← ℋ ∪ doc;
32           θ ← ℋ_0.score; //Update the threshold
33         end if
34
35         //Insert only documents with possible score > θ
36         if (θ <= doc.upper_score)
37              doc.terms ← queryTerms[0..p];
38              𝒜 ← 𝒜 ∪ doc;
39              if ({∃dLow ∈ 𝒜| dLow.upper_score < θ})
40                  𝒜 ← 𝒜 − dLow;
41              endif
42         endif
43         //Advance all evaluated lists
44         for each {0 ≤ i ≤ p} do Next(lists[i], d+1);
45       else
46         j ← {x|lists[x].curDoc < d ^
47              |lists[x]| < |lists[y]|, ∀0 ≤ y < p};
48         Next(lists[j], d);
49       end if
50     else
51       d_next ← GetNewCandidate(lists[j], p);
52       j ← {x| |lists[x]| < |lists[y]|, ∀0 ≤ y ≤ p};
53       Next(lists[j], d_next);
54     end if
55   end repeat
56
57   return 𝒜
```

the inverted lists to be processed (Line 6), which are the lists that represent each query term. The *discarding threshold*, Θ, is initially set to 0(Line 7) and is updated to the minimum score stored in the heap $\mathcal{H}$ if it is full (Line 32). Line 9 makes each of the inverted lists point to their first document. The function $Next(l, d)$ searches in the skiplist associated with list l for the block where there is the first occurrence of a *docId* equal or bigger than d, setting *l.current_block* to the found position. Then, it moves the pointer to the current document of the list, *l.curDoc*, to the smallest entry with value greater than d.

The lists shown in Listing 2 are represented by vector *lists* and each list has an internal pointer to the docId being processed at each moment, the current *docId*. In Line 12 we sort this vector into increasing order according to the current *docId* pointed by each of these lists. We then compute in Line 13 the next document that has a chance to be present in the top results, performing the pivoting, which is

Listing 3: Algorithm Pivoting

```
Pivoting (lists, θ)
  accum ← 0;
  for each 0 ≤ i < |lists| do
    accum ← accum + lists[i].max_score;
    accum_min ← Σ_{j=i+1}^{|lists|} lists[j].min_score
    if (accum + accum_min >= θ)
       while(i+1<|lists| AND
             lists[i+1].curDoc == lists[i].curDoc) do
               i ← i + 1;
       end while
       return i
    end if
  end for
  return −1;
```

Listing 4: Algorithm CheckBlockMax

```
CheckBlockMax (lists, p, θ)

  //Sum the max score of each block, that d can appear
  max ← Σ_{i=0}^{p} lists[i].getBlockMaxScore();

  //Add the min score of the lists that d may appear in
       the full index
  max ← max + Σ_{i=p+1}^{|lists|} lists[i].min_score;
  if(max > θ) return true
  return false
```

Listing 5: Algorithm GetNewCandidate

```
GetNewCandidate (lists, p)
  mindoc ← MAXDOC

  //Selects the lower docId between the blocks boundaries
  // of the lists already checked
  for each {0 ≤ i ≤ p} do
    if(mindoc > lists[i].getDocBlockBoundary())
      mindoc ← lists[i].getDocBlockBoundary();
    end if
  end for

  //Select the lower docId between the lists not checked
  for each {p + 1 ≤ i < |lists|} do
    if(mindoc > lists[i].curDoc)
      mindoc ← lists[i].curDoc;
    end if
  end for

  return mindoc; //Return the smallest docId found
```

the main step of the BMW heuristic. Our pivoting, however, is computed taking into consideration the possibility of some of the entries of a document being not included in the first tier, which let us add this information to compute the *upper_score*, which is the maximum score when selecting the pivot. This procedure is described in Listing 3. Lines 15 to 17 test break conditions and set the current document to be analyzed by the algorithm.

Line 19 adopts the function NextShallow to move the current documents pointer in each list. The function NextShallow is the same presented in the original BMW proposal, and differs from function Next because it does not need to access the documents, accessing only the skiplists of the inverted lists to move their pointers and set a new current block in each inverted list. Using this function, we can skip entries without needing to access or decompress them. Line 21 calls function CheckBlockMax, detailed in Listing 4, which is also modified when compared to the original one proposed in BMW, since it also needs to deal with the incompleteness of the first tier.

The remaining algorithm checks whether a document has enough score to be included in the answer. Line 25 takes the incompleteness of the first tier into consideration when computing the *upper_score*. The score of each document is used to include it in heap $\mathcal{H}$, Lines 28 to 33. $\mathcal{H}$ is maintained to control the discarding threshold θ. The upper_score of each document is used in Line 36 to check whether a document should be included in the candidate documents set $\mathcal{A}$.

The threshold θ changes as more documents are processed, so, whenever we add a document to $\mathcal{A}$, we also check if there is at least one document in $\mathcal{A}$ with an upper_score value lower than the current value of θ. In such cases, we remove the document (Lines 39 to 40). This procedure avoids wasting memory by keeping elements in $\mathcal{A}$ which will be discarded at the end of the process. By the end of the candidate selection algorithm, the list of candidate documents $\mathcal{A}$ is returned, so that the final result can be obtained by processing the remainder of the index in the second tier.

3.1.2 Computing the Final Ranking

In function *CalculateCompleteScore* (Listing 6), the scores of candidates with missing terms are evaluated using the larger index in the second tier, which contains the index entries not present in the first tier. To avoid unnecessary costs with decompression, the shallow movement described in [6] is used to align all the term lists. Then, a second BlockMaxScore check is made to verify whether the document can be part of the top k results or not. Each document is evaluated only if it has a high enough score, otherwise it is discarded. As in the first phase, we keep a minimum heap with the documents with the greatest scores evaluated, and the minimum score of this set is used as a *discarding threshold* to prune candidates.

As the candidate set is small, and only documents with incomplete scores are evaluated, this phase is expected to be performed extremely fast, even considering that it processes a the larger tier.

In *BWM-CS*, the first tier may not contain enough information to assure all top documents are considered as candidate documents. Since only candidate documents can be included in the final results, it does not guarantee exact results in the final ranking. For instance, a document which contains entries for all three terms of a query, but whose entries are present only in the second tier, will not be included in the candidate selection. However, this document may achieve scores higher than the ones in the top documents found by the candidate selection, in cases where there are top results that do not contain all query terms. Notice however that such a situation tends to occur for documents that would be included in the final positions of the top results and, as we show in our experiments, is it does not affect the final results very much.

3.2 BMW-t

In our second algorithm, *BMW with threshold selection*, or *BMW-t*, we use just the first tier to set the initial discarding threshold adopted by methods WAND and BMW. In these methods, this initial discarding threshold is set to 0 at the beginning, and grows as the documents with higher scores

Listing 6: Algorithm CalculateCompleteScore

```
CalculateCompleteScore( 𝒜, queryTerms[1..q], k)
  Let ℋ be the minimum heap to hold the k most relevant
        candidates
  Let ℐ_second_tier be the second index
  lists ← ℐ_second_tier(queryTerms) //Select the terms lists
  θ ← 0
  ℋ ← ∅
  sort 𝒜 by docId;

  for each {0 ≤ i < |A|} do
    if (𝒜_i.score < 𝒜_i.upper_score)
     local_upper_score ← 𝒜_i.score;

     for each {0 ≤ j < |lists|} do
      if (queryTerm[j] ∉ 𝒜_i.terms)
       NextShallow(lists[j], 𝒜_i.docId);
       local_upper_score ← local_upper_score +
                               lists[j].getBlockMaxScore();
      end if
     end for

     if (local_upper_score > θ)
      for each {0 ≤ j < |lists|} do
       if (queryTerm[j] ∉ 𝒜_i.terms)
        Next(lists[j], 𝒜_i.docId);
       end if
      end for
      //Complete the score with the missing lists
      for each {0 ≤ x < |lists||lists[x].curDoc = 𝒜_i.docId} do
        𝒜_i.score ← 𝒜_i.score + BM25(lists[x]);
      end for
     end if
    end if

    if (θ < 𝒜_i.score)
     if (|ℋ| < k)
       ℋ ← ℋ∪ 𝒜_i;
     elseif (ℋ_0.score < 𝒜_i.score)
       remove ℋ_0;
       ℋ ← ℋ∪ 𝒜_i;
       θ ← ℋ_0.score;
     end if
    end if
  end for

  sort ℋ by score;
  return ℋ;
end
```

are found and included in the answer. As a consequence, the query processing discards fewer documents at the beginning of the process, since the discarding threshold starts with a small value. We thus propose the usage of the first tier of the index to support a pre-processing stage just to compute an initial discarding threshold that is higher than 0. This simple strategy naturally may speed up the process if the gains when processing the full index are worth the cost of computing the initial discarding threshold when processing the first tier.

We then experiment with a variation of BMW, we named BMW-t, and a variation of WAND, we named WAND-t. These variations use the first tier to select an initial *discarding threshold* when processing the queries. This new usage of the two tier index presents the advantage of preserving the top k results, which does not happen in BMW-CS. The WAND-t performed worse than the BMW-t, thus we report only BMW-t in the experiments.

4. EXPERIMENTAL EVALUATION

We used the TREC GOV2 collection for the experiments in this paper. The collection has 25 million web pages crawled from the .gov domain in early 2004. It has 426 gigabytes of text, composed of HTML pages and the extracted content of pdf and postscripts documents. The full index has about 7 gigabytes of inverted lists and a vocabulary of about 4 million distinct terms. We applied the Porter Stemmer [9] when indexing the collection. Our indexes use the frequency of the terms as the impact information. To evaluate the quality of query results, we randomly selected a set of 1000 queries from the TREC 2006 efficiency queries set and removed the stop-words from these queries. During the query processing, the entire index is loaded to memory, to avoid any possible bias in the query processing time. | All these setup options were chosen for being similar to those adopted in the baseline [6] and previous studies [15]. We ran the experiments in a 24-cores Intel(R) Xeon(R), with X5680 Processor, 3.33GHz and 64 GB of memory. All the queries were processed in a single core.

We used Okapi BM25 as the rank function, but our method can be adopted to compute other ranking functions. The generated skiplists have one entry for each block of 128 documents. Each skiplist entry keeps the *docId*, to help the random decompression, and the *maximum impact* registered in the block. We also experimented with blocks of 64 entries, and the results and conclusions were about the same, thus we decided to report only results with 128. We varied the first tier $\Delta\%$ from 1 to 20 percent of the full index in the experiments.

Another parameter evaluated in the experiments was the size of the top results required by the algorithms. We evaluated the algorithms requesting 10 and 1000 results. Retrieving top 1000 results was included to simulate an environment where the top results are computed to feed a more sophisticated ranking method that performs a re-rank of results. The top 10 results was included to simulate a more common scenario where the user is interested in getting only a small list of results.

We evaluated the methods in terms of query response time, the amount of accumulators required to process the queries, amount of decoded entries from the inverted lists, and finally the mean reciprocal rank Distance (MRRD), presented in Equation 1, which was the measure adopted by Broder et al [4] to evaluate the distance between the results when preserving top results to rankings that do not preserve the top results. Using the MRRD distance, we are able to know how much an approximated rank differs from the one that preserves the top results. This measure returns a value between 0 and 1, where identical results provide MRRD=0, and completely distinct results provide MRRD=1.

$$MRRD(B,P) = \frac{\sum_{i=1, d_i \in B-P}^{k} 1/i}{\sum_{i=1}^{k} 1/i} \quad (1)$$

4.1 Baselines

One of the implemented baseline algorithms was BMW [6]. As one of our methods may not preserve the top ranking results, we also have considered including as a baseline the version of WAND that does not preserve the top results, proposed by Broder et al [4]. However, the results achieved by the approximate WAND were even slower than the BMW. We thus removed it from the baselines, and modified the method BMW to implement the same approximation strategy proposed to WAND. As a result, we transformed BMW to an approximated top-k query processing algorithm, which does not guarantee preserving top results, but may be faster

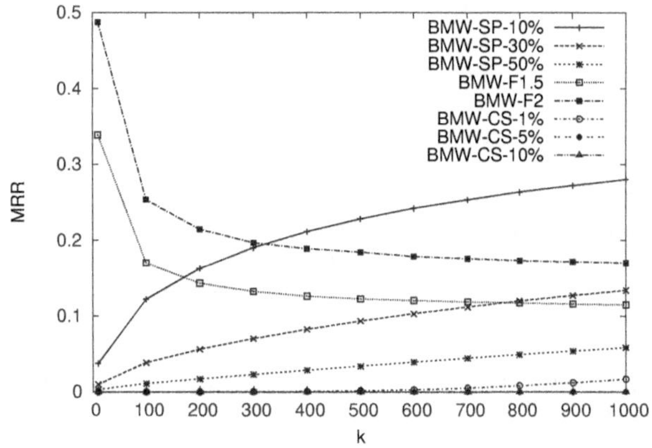

Figure 2: MRRD values compared to a exact rank for baselines BMW-SP and BMW-f

than original BMW. Basically, we artificially increase the pruning threshold during the query processing by multiplying this threshold for a pruning factor f. If f is 1, the exact top-k is guaranteed. When f is greater than 1, there is no guarantee of preserving the exact rank, but less entries will be evaluated, resulting in performance gains.

Finally, a reader could wonder if the results would also be good if we had adopted just the first tier for processing queries, considering the first tier as a statically pruned index. Thus, in order to avoid these doubts, we included a naive method using only the first tier for processing queries. We named it *BMW-SP* (applying BMW with static pruning).

4.2 Results

We begin the report of our experimental results by answering the possible doubts about the advantage of using the BMW-CS algorithm, which does not guarantee that all the top results are preserved, when compared to a simple static pruning strategy that adopts only the first tier to compute the ranking. Figure 2 presents the MRRD results when computing the top k results by using our method with the first tier of 1%, 5% and 10% compared to the usage of the static pruning approach, named BMW-SP. As can be seen in Figure 2, even when using BMW-SP with the first tier with 50% of the full index, the error level (MRRD) obtained by BMW-CS with 1% is still smaller than it. Even considering this observation, for the sake of completeness, we still report the time efficiency results obtained when using the BMW-SP with the first tier being 50%.

Figure 2 also presents the BMW-f MRRD results when varying parameter f. As can be seen in Figure 2, BMW-f achieves error levels worse than BMW-CS even when setting the factor f to the low value of 1.5. Lower factor values would slow down the performance of the method, thus we adopt this factor in our efficiency experiments, even considering that its error level is higher than those achieved by our method. We stress that both BMW-f and BMW-SP are included in the experiments to avoid doubts about these possible variations in the usage of BMW. These methods were not explicitly proposed in the literature.

Next we present the percentage of entries we included in the first tier of BMW-CS. This choice affects three main factors: the time for processing queries, the MRRD results of our methods and the amount of memory required to process queries. Variation of these parameters are illustrated in Figure 3. As can be seen, when computing the top 1000 results, the MRRD results decrease as the size of the first tier increases, being almost zero for first tier sizes higher than 8%. When computing the top 10 results, MRRD was always zero for all sizes of first tier experimented. Time tends to increase as the first tier increases in both cases. On the other hand, the number of accumulators presents more complex behavior. In the top 1000, it first increases as the size of the first tier increases. Then, at some point, it starts to decrease, since the candidate selection procedure starts to perform better pruning, thus reducing the set of candidate documents.

When looking to the general results presented in Figure 3, we conclude that a good size for the first tier in BMW-CS is 2% when tuning the method to compute the top 10 results and 10% when tuning the method to top 1000 results. These parameters provide a good combination of a low number of candidate documents, low query processing times and low MRRD. Notice however that even if choosing other first tier sizes among the ones presented in the experiments, still our method would be quite fast and competitive.

Figure 3 (c) and (d) also indicates how much memory our algorithm needs to store the candidate documents. We can see the requirement is not so high in both the top 10 and top 1000 scenarios, being limited to a few times greater than the size of top results required to be computed.

Finally, regarding the MRRD error level achieved by BMW-CS it is noteworthy that a user would almost not perceive the differences in top k results when using BMW-CS even when considering higher values of k. For instance, as $k = 1000$, the error of BMW-CS is still smaller than 0.0001 in terms of MRRD for the 10% first tier size. To better illustrate what this error level means, analyzing the results in detail, we perceived that BMW-CS with a 10% first tier resulted in no changes in the top 1000 results for 90% of the evaluated queries. Further, in all experimented first tier sizes, the top 10 results were preserved for all queries. Changes in the ranking, when they occur, are more common in the bottom results. For instance, we preserved the top 100 results for all queries, and preserved the top 200 results for 99.9% of the queries.

We also studied the MRR variation of method BMW-t, but do not present the variation due to space restrictions. Its performance is close to the best when using 1% for the first tier, becoming slower as the partition increases and not improving so much when it decreases. We report the results on the remaining experiments with our methods using 2% and 10% first tier sizes in case of BMW-CS, and 1% in case of BMW-t.

In Tables 1 and 2, we can observe the performance of the algorithms in terms of MRRD, decoded integers and query time when processing the top-10 and top-1000. The results of time are presented with confidence level of 95%. BMW-CS provides extremely low MRRD results, which means these answers are almost the same as the correct top k results. On the other hand, its performance is considerably better than BMW and BMW-f, which do not have a preprocessing phase during query evaluation, and thus are performed directly over the full index.

We can see the performance of BMW-t, which preserves the top results, presents an improvement of around 10% in

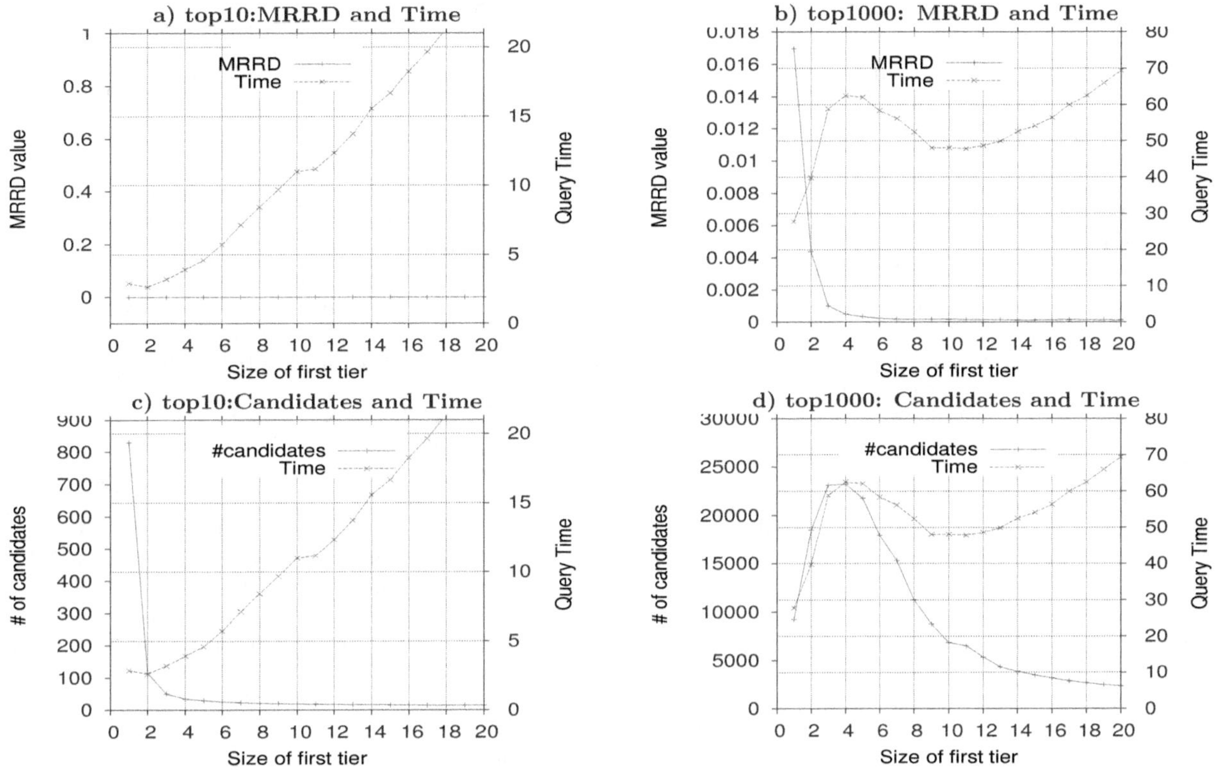

Figure 3: Variation in time and MRRD(a and b); and between time and number of candidate documents stored in (c and d) when processing first tier for method BMW-CS when using distinct sizes of first tier.

query processing times when compared to BMW. The approximated version BMW-f, using the factor f=1.5, processes query 20% faster than the exact BMW. However, BMW-CS is not only faster than BMW-f, but also presents lower MRRD values.

Still regarding Tables 1 and 2, we can see that BMW-CS preserves the result set more than the other approximated methods implemented and is about 40 times faster than BMW when computing the top 10 results (using a 2% tier), and about 4.75 times faster when computing the top 1000 results(using a 10% tier). These gains can also be seen when analyzing the number of decoded integers, which is one of the main costs when elements are stored in memory.

	top 10		
Algorithm	MRRD	Decoded	time
BMW	0	2353066	100.1 ± 9.9
BMW-f1.5	0.3386	1797451	78.5 ± 7.8
BMW-SP-50	0.0032	1700488	79.8 ± 8.0
BMW-t	0	2082782	89.5 ± 8.8
BMW-CS-2	0	48989	2.4 ± 0.4
BMW-CS-10	0	217627	10.4 ± 0.5

Table 1: MRRD, number of decoded entries, and time(ms) efficiency achieved by the experimented methods when computing top 10 results.

Table 3 presents the performance of the algorithms when processing distinct query sizes for both the top 10 and top 1000 results computation. BMW-CS was the fastest option for all query sizes. Although the gain is smaller for queries with more than 5 terms, our method still results in

	top 1000		
Algorithm	MRRD	Decoded	time
BMW	0	5032834	226.0 ± 18.0
BMW-f1.5	0.1149	4463099	193.7 ± 15.4
BMW-SP-50	0.0584	3495885	174.8 ± 13.0
BMW-t	0	4799477	205.7 ± 16.9
BMW-CS-2	0.0043	1258859	39.8 ± 4.6
BMW-CS-10	0.0001	921687	47.6 ± 4.2

Table 2: MRRD, number of decoded entries, and time(ms) efficiency achieved by the experimented methods when computing top 1000 results.

impressive gains when compared to all baselines even for long queries.

One explanation for the smaller gain in long queries is that in the first phase of the process, as we have many terms in the query, the *upper_score* of a candidate will be higher because it sums the *minimum score* of the missing lists. Thus, as we have an index with only a small fraction of the full index, the number of documents in the first phase with a complete score will be lower according to the number of terms in the query, making the threshold values lower when compared to the estimated *upper_scores*. This configuration will lead to a less effective pruning during the candidate selection, increasing the costs of the whole process.

We observed differences in time results when comparing our experiments to the ones presented by Ding et al [6]. While we adopt exactly the same dataset, the query processing times we obtained are lower than the ones presented in their article. However we see that the number of decoded

Algorithm	Query time (ms)				
	2	3	4	5	>5
	top 10				
BMW	12.0	46.6	100.5	197.9	442.7
BMW-f1.5	7.8	34.0	77.3	155.5	367.7
BMW-SP-50	10.3	38.7	82.4	160.1	331.6
BMW-t	10.4	41.1	87.7	179.3	401.7
BMW-CS-2	0.58	1.42	2.42	3.74	9.96
BMW-CS-10	2.3	5.7	11.6	19.7	36.8
	top 1000				
BMW	37.9	122.3	243.6	437.9	848.6
BMW-f1.5	29.9	102.5	206.3	390.1	725.0
BMW-SP-50	32.6	102.1	192.0	333.5	610.3
BMW-t	29.8	104.6	220.9	406.5	803.5
BMW-CS-2	8.49	20.62	44.58	79.07	139.1
BMW-CS-10	14.6	29.3	51.8	82.2	160.8

Table 3: Time achieved by the experimented methods when processing queries with distinct sizes and computing top 10 and top 1000 results.

integers still similar. The final difference in times can be due to the choice of the queries, since we do not know the exact set of queries adopted by them, the architecture of the implemented system, and the machines used for the experiments. These differences do not affect the conclusions presented in our study because they affect all the experimented methods.

Acknowledgements

This work is partially supported by INWeb (MCT/CNPq grant 57.3871/2008-6), DOMAR (MCT/CNPq 476798/2011-6), TTDSW (FAPEAM), by CNPq fellowship grants to Edleno Moura (307861/2010-4) and Altigran Silva (308380/2010-0), and FAPEAM scholarship to Cristian Rossi.

5. CONCLUSION

The algorithms proposed and studied by us outperform the existent state-of-the-art algorithms for DAAT query processing. BMW-CS presents the advantage of being about 40 times faster than BMW when computing top 10 results and 4.75 times faster when computing top 1000 results. While it does not guarantee to preserve the top results, we show through experiments that the application of the algorithm does not change the results very much. The MRRD error level is quite small and the algorithm provides an impressive gain in performance. Thus, in situations where preserving the top results is not mandatory, the BMW-CS algorithm is an interesting alternative.

The price paid for this fast query processing is the necessity of more memory for processing queries. As we show, the number of candidate documents stored by the algorithm, which is the extra memory required by it, is not prohibitive, being, for instance, around 10 times the size of the final results in our experiments. Further, in practice a search system usually processes queries in multiple threads per machines, and the reduction in the query processing times cooperates to increase the throughput, thus compensating for the extra memory required by each thread. We intend to better study this question in future studies, since this was not the focus of this current study.

The second algorithm proposed by us, BMW-t, presents the advantage of preserving the top results. It delivers smaller, but significant gains when compared to the application of plain BMW, being about 10% faster.

Finally, in the future, we also want to study the combination of our algorithm BMW-CS to ranking strategies that take more information into account. In this regard, we plan to study how our algorithms can be adapted to strategies as those presented by Shan et al [13], where the authors study the impact of including external sources of relevance evidence into the performance of query processing algorithms, and such as [5], in which the authors show how to encode several features into a single impact value.

6. REFERENCES

[1] V. Anh and A. Moffat. Pruned query evaluation using pre-computed impacts. In *ACM SIGIR*, pages 372–379, 2006.

[2] V. N. Anh, O. de Kretser, and A. Moffat. Vector-space ranking with effective early termination. In *ACM SIGIR*, pages 35–42, 2001.

[3] R. Baeza-Yates and B. Ribeiro-Neto. *Modern Information Retrieval*. Addison-Wesley Publishing Company, USA, 2nd edition, 2011.

[4] A. Z. Broder, D. Carmel, M. Herscovici, A. Soffer, and J. Zien. Efficient query evaluation using a two-level retrieval process. In *ACM CIKM*, pages 426–434, 2003.

[5] A. Carvalho, C. Rossi, E. S. de Moura, D. Fernandes, and A. S. da Silva. LePrEF: Learn to Pre-compute Evidence Fusion for Efficient Query Evaluation. *JASIST*, 55(92):1–28, 2012.

[6] S. Ding and T. Suel. Faster top-k document retrieval using block-max indexes. In *ACM SIGIR*, pages 993–1002, 2011.

[7] A. Moffat and J. Zobel. Self-indexing inverted files for fast text retrieval. *ACM TOIS*, 14(4):349–379, 1996.

[8] A. Ntoulas and J. Cho. Pruning policies for two-tiered inverted index with correctness guarantee. In *ACM SIGIR*, pages 191–198, 2007.

[9] M. Porter. An algorithm for suffix stripping. *Program: electronic library and information systems*, 40(3):211–218, 2006.

[10] K. Risvik, Y. Aasheim, and M. Lidal. Multi-tier architecture for web search engines. In *First Latin American Web Congress*, pages 132–143, 2003.

[11] S. E. Robertson and S. Walker. Some simple effective approximations to the 2-poisson model for probabilistic weighted retrieval. In *ACM SIGIR*, pages 232–241, 1994.

[12] G. Salton, A. Wong, and C. S. Yang. A vector space model for automatic indexing. Technical report, Ithaca, NY, USA, 1974.

[13] D. Shan, S. Ding, J. He, H. Yan, and X. Li. Optimized top-k processing with global page scores on block-max indexes. In *WSDM*, pages 423–432, 2012.

[14] G. Skobeltsyn, F. Junqueira, V. Plachouras, and R. Baeza-Yates. ResIn: a combination of results caching and index pruning for high-performance web search engines. In *ACM SIGIR*, pages 131–138, 2008.

[15] T. Strohman and W. B. Croft. Efficient document retrieval in main memory. In *ACM SIGIR*, pages 175–182, 2007.

Faster and Smaller Inverted Indices with Treaps *

Roberto Konow
Dept. of Computer Science
Univ. of Chile, Chile
EIT, Univ. Diego Portales

Gonzalo Navarro
Dept. of Computer Science
Univ. of Chile, Chile

Charles L. A. Clarke
Alejandro López-Ortíz
School of Computer Science
Univ. of Waterloo, Canada

ABSTRACT

We introduce a new representation of the inverted index that performs faster ranked unions and intersections while using less space. Our index is based on the treap data structure, which allows us to intersect/merge the document identifiers while simultaneously thresholding by frequency, instead of the costlier two-step classical processing methods. To achieve compression we represent the treap topology using compact data structures. Further, the treap invariants allow us to elegantly encode differentially both document identifiers and frequencies. Results show that our index uses about 20% less space, and performs queries up to three times faster, than state-of-the-art compact representations.

Categories and Subject Descriptors

H.3.3 [**INFORMATION STORAGE AND RETRIEVAL**]: Information Search and Retrieval

General Terms

Algorithms, Performance

Keywords

Treap, Inverted Index, Top-k, Query Processing

1. INTRODUCTION

Modern Web search engines, and other information retrieval systems, face two competing challenges. On the one hand, they have to manage huge amounts of data. On the other hand, they have to provide very precise results in response to user queries, often identifying a few relevant documents among increasingly larger collections. These requirements can be addressed via a two-stage ranking process [37, 16]. In the first stage, a fast and simple filtration procedure extracts a subset of a few hundreds or thousands of candidates from the possibly billions of documents forming the collection. In the second stage, more complex learned ranking algorithms are applied to the reduced candidate set in order to obtain a handful of high-quality results. In this paper, we focus on improving the efficiency of the first stage, freeing more resources for the second stage and increasing the overall performance. In contexts where traditional ranking methods are sufficient, the goal of the first stage is to directly convey a few top-quality results to the final user.

The first stage aims to return either a set of the highest ranked documents containing all the query terms (a ranked intersection) or some of the most important query terms (a ranked union). In most cases, ranked intersections are solved via a Boolean intersection, followed by the computation of scores for the resulting documents. Ranked unions are generally solved only in approximate form, avoiding a costly Boolean union. However, Ding and Suel [21] showed that ranked intersections can be processed faster than Boolean intersections. They also obtained the best known performance for ranked unions, giving exact, rather than approximate results, and demonstrating the feasibility of their approach.

In this paper, we introduce a new compressed representation for posting lists that performs ranked intersections and (exact) unions directly. This representation is based on the *treap* data structure [34], a binary tree that simultaneously represents a left-to-right and a top-to-bottom ordering. We use the left-to-right ordering for document identifiers (which supports fast Boolean operations) and the top-to-bottom ordering for term weights (which supports the thresholding of results simultaneously with the intersection process). Using this data structure, we can obtain the top-k results for a ranked intersection/union without having to first produce the full Boolean result.

Additionally, the treap representation allows us to differentially encode both document identifiers and weights, which is crucial for the space-efficient representation of inverted indexes. Posting lists have been compressed for decades [38] to handle very large collections within minimal space. Using other representations we must choose either identifiers or weights for differential encoding, but not both.

Our experiments show that the space usage of our treap-based inverted index representation is less than the state-of-the-art compressed representations: around 22% less space than Block-Max [21] and 18% less space than Dual-Sorted [25]. As for the time, treaps outperform previous techniques for k up to 30 on intersections, and up to 130 on unions,

*Partially funded by Fondecyt grant 1-110066 , by the Conicyt PhD Scholarship Program, Chile and by the Emerging Leaders in the Americas Program, Government of Canada.

SIGIR'13, July 28–August 1, 2013, Dublin, Ireland.

being up to three times faster than the alternatives in some cases. Those ranges of k values make this result of particular interest both in applications where a limited result set is of interest, and in large-scale distributed systems in which each node contributes a limited set to the global result.

2. BASIC CONCEPTS

The *inverted index* plays a central role in the efficient processing of ranked and Boolean queries [38, 41, 18, 16, 5]. It can be seen as an array of *lists* or *postings*, where each entry of the array corresponds to a different *term* or *word* in the collection, and the lists contain one element per distinct document where the term appears. For each document, the index stores the *document identifier (docid)* and the *weight* of the term in the document. The set of terms is called the *vocabulary* of the collection, which is comparatively small in most cases [24].

In the first stage of query processing, a simple metric is used to assign a *score* to a document with respect to a query. In the classical *bag-of-words* model, the query Q is seen as a set of q terms $t \in Q$, and the score of a document d is computed as $score(Q, d) = \sum_{t \in Q} w(t, d)$, where $w(t, d)$ is the weight of term t in document d. For example, in the well-known tf-idf scoring scheme, this weight is computed as $w(t, d) = tf_{t,d} \cdot idf_t$. Here, $tf_{t,d}$ is the *term frequency* of t in d, that is, the number of times t occurs in d. The second term is $idf_t = \log \frac{D}{df_t}$, where df_t is the *document frequency*, that is, the number of documents where the term t appears, and D is the total number of documents. Since idf_t (or df_t) depends only on t, an efficient way to store $w(t, d)$ in an inverted index is to store idf_t or df_t together with each distinct vocabulary term, and store the values $tf_{t,d}$ in the posting list of term t, together with each docid d. In this paper we will assume that term frequencies are stored in the posting lists, but any other integer measure, such as impacts [2] could be used.

In the *bag-of-words* model we are given Q and k, and asked to retrieve k documents d with the highest $score(Q, d)$ values. In the two-stage model, typical values of k are hundreds to thousands, as discussed earlier. In simpler one-stage systems, typical values of k are below 20. Note that it is not necessary for all the terms of Q to appear in a returned document d; a missing term t simply implies that $w(t, d) = 0$. This problem is frequently called *ranked union*. A variant of the problem, popularized by Web search engines to favor precision over recall, is the *ranked intersection*, where only documents containing all the terms are returned. Nowadays, ranked intersections are more common than unions.

The Boolean intersection problem, without ranking, aims at retrieving all the documents d where all the terms of Q appear. A typical way to solve a ranked intersection is to first compute a Boolean intersection, then compute the scores of all the resulting documents, and finally keep the documents with the k highest scores. This approach has triggered much research on the Boolean intersection problem [20, 6, 32, 8, 25]. This approach is, of course, suboptimal, since in principle one could use weight information to filter out documents that belong to the intersection but one can ensure will not make it to the top-k list. Only recently some schemes specifically aimed at solving ranked intersections have appeared [21]. All these schemes store the posting lists in increasing docid order, which is convenient for skipping documents during intersections.

Ranked unions, instead, cannot be efficiently solved through a Boolean union, as this returns too many results. In this case, most research has aimed at returning an *approximate* answer within good time bounds [30, 2]. Most of these techniques order the posting lists by decreasing weight values, not by docids. Recently, it has been shown that ranked unions can be solved in exact form within reasonable time [15, 35, 21] by using increasing docid order for the posting lists in the best solution [21].

Traditionally, the posting lists were stored on disk. With the availability of large amounts of main memory, this trend has changed to use the main memory of a cluster of machines, and many intersection algorithms have been designed for random access [20, 6, 32, 19, 33, 35, 8, 25]. In distributed main-memory systems, usually documents are distributed across independent inverted indexes, and each index contributes with a few results to the final top-k list. Therefore, it is most interesting that an individual inverted index solves top-k queries efficiently for k values in the range 10–100 [16].

Both when stored on disk and in main memory, reducing the size of the inverted index representation is crucial. On disk, it reduces transfer time. In main memory, it increases the size of the collections that can be managed within a given RAM budget, or alternatively reduces the amount of servers that must be allocated in a cluster to hold the index, the energy they consume, and the amount of communication. Compression of inverted indexes is possibly the oldest and most successful application of compressed data structures (e.g., see [38]). The main idea to achieve compression is to differentially encode either the document identifers or the weights (depending on how the lists are sorted), whereas the other value (weight or docid, respectively) becomes harder to compress. The problem of this duality in the sorting, and how it affects compression and query algorithms, has been discussed in past work [38, 4, 25].

In this context, our contribution is a new in-memory posting list representation that, on the one hand, achieves improved compression because it allows differential encoding of both docids and frequencies, and on the other hand, performs exact ranked intersections and unions directly and natively without having to first intersect/merge and then rank.

3. RELATED WORK

3.1 Query Processing Strategies

Two kinds of approaches are used for unions and intersections (ranked or Boolean): Term-at-a-time (TAAT) and Document-at-a-time (DAAT) [16].

TAAT processes one posting list after the other. The lists are considered from shortest to longest, starting with the first one as a candidate answer set, and refining it as we consider the next lists. TAAT is especially popular for processing ranked unions [30, 2, 35], as the successive lists have decreasing idf_t value and thus a decreasing impact on the result, not only for the tf-idf model, but also for BM25 and other models. The documents in each list are sorted by decreasing weight. Thus heuristic thresholds can be used to obtain an approximate ranked union efficiently, by pruning the processing of lists earlier, or avoiding lists completely, as we reach less relevant documents and our candidate set becomes stronger [30, 2]. A more sophisticated approach based on similar ideas can be used to guarantee that the answer is exact [35].

DAAT processing is more popular for Boolean intersections and unions. Here the q lists are processed in parallel, looking for the same document in all of them. Posting lists must be sorted by increasing docid, and we keep a pointer to the current position in each of the q lists. Once a document is processed, the pointers move forward. Much research has been carried out on Boolean intersections [20, 6, 32, 19, 8]. While a DAAT processing is always used to intersect two lists, experimental results suggest that the most efficient way to handle more lists is to intersect the two shortest ones, then the result with the third, and so on. This can be seen as a TAAT strategy.

Many ranked intersection strategies employ a full Boolean intersection followed by a postprocessing step for ranking. However, recent work has shown that it is possible to do better [21]. The advantage of DAAT processing is that, once we have processed a document, we have complete information about its score, and thus we can maintain a current set of top-k candidates whose final scores are known. This set can be used to establish a threshold on the scores other documents need to surpass to become relevant for the current query. Thus the emphasis on ranked DAAT is not on terminating early but on skipping documents. This same idea has been successfully used to solve exact (not approximate) ranked unions [15, 21].

The strategies we use to solve ranked union and intersection queries in this paper are best classified as DAAT. We use sophisticated mechanisms to skip documents using the current threshold given by the current top-k candidate set.

3.2 Compressed Posting List Representations

A list $\langle p_1, p_2, p_3, \ldots p_\ell \rangle$ is usually represented as a sequence of d-gaps $\langle p_1, p_2 - p_1, p_3 - p_2, \ldots, p_\ell - p_{\ell-1} \rangle$, and uses a variable-length encoding for these differences, for example δ-codes, γ-codes or Rice/Golomb codes [38], the latter usually giving the best compression. Recent proposals make use of byte-aligned [33, 19] or word-aligned [39, 1] codes, which are faster at decoding at a small loss in compression. Extracting a single list or merging lists is done optimally by traversing the lists from the beginning, but intersections can be done much faster if random access to the sequences is possible. A typical solution to provide random access is to perform a sampling of the sequences, cutting them into *blocks* that are differentially encoded, while storing in a separate sequence the absolute values of the block headers and pointers to the encoded blocks. Different sampling strategies have been used [19, 32] and the intersection algorithms have been tailored to them.

When lists are sorted by decreasing weight (for approximate ranked unions), the differential compression of docids is not possible, in principle. Instead, term weights can be stored differentially. When storing *tf* values, one can take advantage of the fact that long runs of equal *tf* values (typically low ones) are frequent, and thus not only run-length encode them, but also sort the corresponding docids increasingly, so as to encode them differentially [4, 41].

3.3 State of the Art for Exact Ranked Queries

The following two approaches have recently displayed the best performance for exact ranked intersections and unions.

3.3.1 *Block-Max*

Block-Max [21] is a special-purpose structure for ranked intersections and unions. It sorts the lists by increasing docid, cuts the lists into blocks, and stores the maximum weight for each block. This enables them to skip whole blocks whose maximum possible contribution is very low, by comparing its maximum weight with a threshold given by the current candidate set. Block-Max obtains considerable performance gains over the previous techniques for exact ranked unions [15, 35], and also over the techniques that perform ranked intersections via a Boolean preprocessing.

The basic concept is as follows: Suppose the next document of interest, d, belongs to blocks $b_1, \ldots, b_q$ in the q lists. Compute an upper bound to $score(Q, d)$ using the block maxima instead of the weights $w(t, d)$. If even this upper bound does not surpass the kth best score known up to now, no document inside the current blocks can make it to the top-k list. So we can safely skip some blocks.

Our technique can be seen as a generalization of the Block-Max idea, in which we use the treap concept to naturally define a hierarchical blocking scheme. The generalization is algorithmically nontrivial, but it is practical and beats the flat Block-Max. In addition, the treap structure allows us to differentially encode both docids and weights, which translates into space savings with respect to Block-Max.

3.3.2 *Dual-sorted inverted lists*

Dual-Sorted inverted lists [29, 25] represent the posting lists sorted by decreasing frequency, using a wavelet tree data structure [23, 28]. The wavelet tree efficiently simulates ordering by increasing docids. TAAT processing is used for approximate ranked unions and DAAT-like processing for (exact) ranked intersections. The latter, although building on Boolean intersections, is implemented in native form on wavelet trees, which makes it particularly fast, even faster than Block-Max. Basically, the wavelet tree can recursively subdivide the universe of docids and efficiently determine that some list has no documents in the current interval.

Our technique shares with Dual-Sorted the ability to maintain the lists sorted by both docids and weights simultaneously, and is able to perform a similar kind of native intersection, that is, determine that in an interval of documents there is a list with no elements. In contrast, Dual-Sorted does not know the frequencies until reaching the individual documents, whereas our treaps give an upper bound to the frequencies in the current interval. This allows us to perform ranked intersections faster than the Boolean intersections of Dual-Sorted. In addition, the treap uses less space, since Dual-Sorted cannot use differential encoding on docids.

4. DIFFERENTIALLY ENCODED TREAPS

We describe our data structure in this section. First, we survey the treap data structure and show it can be used to represent a posting list. Then we describe how we represent the resulting data structure using little space. In addition, we describe some practical improvements on the basic idea. At the end, we describe how query processing is carried out on the final representation.

4.1 The Treap Data Structure

A *treap* [34] is a binary tree where nodes have two attributes: a *key* and a *priority*. The treap satisfies the invariants of a binary search tree with respect to the keys: the root key is larger than those of its left subtree and smaller

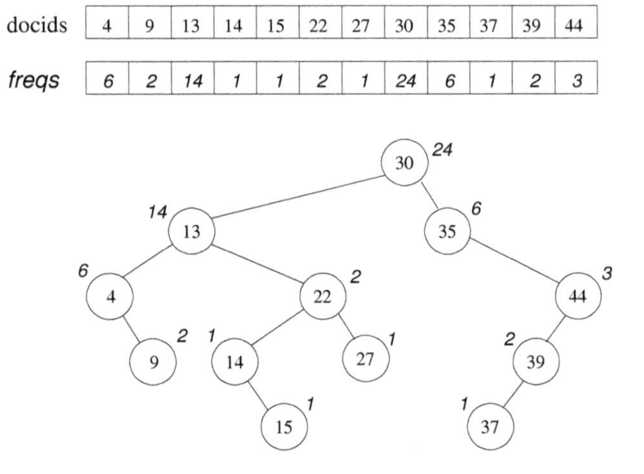

Figure 1: An example posting list (with docids and frequencies) and the corresponding treap representation in our scheme. Note that docids (inside the nodes) are sorted inorder and frequencies (outside the nodes) are sorted top to bottom.

than those of its right subtree. Furthermore, the treap satisfies the invariants of a binary heap with respect to the priorities: the priority of the parent is larger than those of its descendants.

Given its invariants, a treap can be searched for a key just as a binary search tree, and it can be simultaneously used as a binary heap. While in the literature it has mostly been used with randomly assigned priorities [34, 26, 13] to ensure logarithmic expected height independently of the order of insertions, a treap can also be seen as the *Cartesian tree* [36] of the sequence of priorities once the values are sorted by keys. Such Cartesian tree can be built in $O(n)$ time from a sequence of n elements already sorted by key, even in compressed form [10, 9, 22].

Treaps are a particular case of *priority search trees* [27], which can guarantee balancedness but are unlikely to be as compressible as Cartesian trees. There has been some work on using priority search trees for returning top-k elements from suffix trees and geometric range searches [12, 11] but, as far as we know, our use of treaps for ranked queries on inverted indexes, plus their differential compression, is novel.

4.2 Inverted Index Representation

We consider the posting list of each term as a sequence sorted by docids (which act as keys), each with its own term frequency (which act as priorities). Term impacts, or any other term weights, may also be used as priorities. We then use a treap to represent this sequence. Therefore the treap will be binary searchable by docid, whereas it will satisfy a heap ordering on the frequencies. This means, in particular, that if a given treap node has a frequency below a desired threshold, then all the docids below it in the treap can be discarded as well.

Figure 1 illustrates a treap representation of a posting list. This treap will be used as a running example.

4.3 Compressing the Treap

In order to compete with existing compressed representations of posting lists, we represent the treap data (topology, docids, and frequencies) in compact form. The key issue is that we choose a representation where all the treap operations can be carried out efficiently, so as to exploit the treap properties at query time.

4.3.1 Compact topology representation

Given a posting list of n documents, the treap will be a binary tree of n nodes. We represent it as a general tree using a well-known isomorphism: First, a fake root node v_r is created. The children of v_r become the nodes in the rightmost path of the treap, from the root to the leaf. Then each of those nodes are converted recursively.

With this transformation, the treap root is the first child of v_r. The left child of a treap node v is its first child in the general tree. The right child of v is its next sibling in the general tree. An inorder traversal of the treap corresponds to a postorder traversal of the general tree.

There are $\Theta(4^n/n^{3/2})$ general trees of n nodes, and thus one needs $\log_2(4^n/n^{3/2}) = 2n - \Theta(\log n)$ bits to represent any such tree. There exist various compact tree representations using $2n+o(n)$ bits that can in addition carry out many tree operations efficiently, including taking the first child, next sibling, computing postorder of a node, and so on. We will use a recent representation that has proven to be efficient in practice [31, 3]. It is based on a balanced parentheses representation of the tree, obtained by a preorder traversal where we append an opening parenthesis when reaching a node and a closing parenthesis when leaving it.

4.3.2 Differentially encoded trees

In addition to the tree topology, we must represent docids and term frequencies. Our plan is not to access the posting lists in sequential form as in classical schemes, thus a differential encoding each docid with respect to the previous one is not directly applicable. Instead, we make use of the invariants of the treap data structure.

Let $id(v)$ be the docid of a treap node v, and $f(v)$ its frequency. We represent $id(v)$ and $f(v)$ for the root in plain form, and then represent those of its left and right children recursively. For each node v that is the left child of its parent u, we represent $id(u) - id(v)$ instead of $id(v)$. If, on the other hand, v is the right child of its parent u, we represent $id(v) - id(u)$ [17]. In both cases, we represent $f(u) - f(v)$ instead of $f(v)$. Those numbers get smaller as we move downwards in the treap.

The sequence of differentially encoded $id(v)$ and $f(v)$ values is represented according to an inorder traversal of the treap. As we move down the treap, we can easily maintain the correct $id(v)$ and $f(v)$ values for any node arrived at, and use it to compute the values of the children as we descend.

For this sake we need to randomly access a differential value in the sequence, given a node. We store those values in an array indexed by node preorders (in the general tree), which we can easily compute in our topology representation. Furthermore, we need a storage mechanism for the differences that: *i*) can access any value in the sequence directly, while *ii*) uses fewer bits to represent smaller numbers. We use Direct Addressable Codes (DACs) [14], which are designed precisely with this aim.

DACs encode a sequence of numbers $x_1, \ldots, x_n$ as follows. The $\lceil \log_2(\max\{x_i\}+1) \rceil$ bits needed to represent any x_i are divided into chunks of varying size. Then the first chunk of lowest bits of all the numbers are represented in

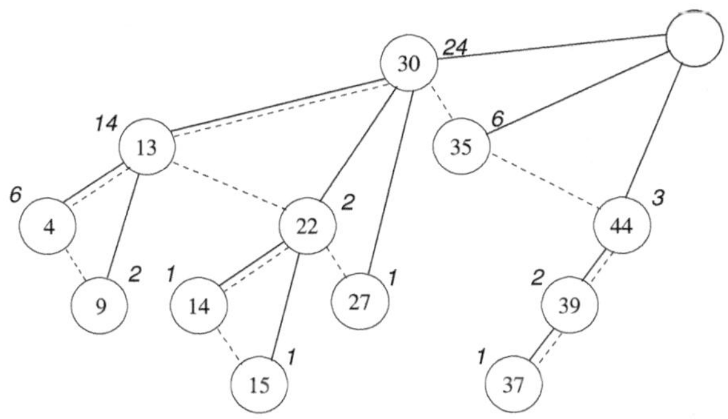

Topology (((()())(()())())()((())))

diff ids	9	5	17	8	1	9	5	30	5	2	5	9
diff freqs	*8*	*4*	*10*	*1*	*0*	*12*	*1*	*24*	*18*	*1*	*1*	*3*

Figure 2: The compressed representation of the example treap. The original binary tree edges (dashed) are replaced by a general tree, whose topology is represented with parentheses. Docids and frequencies are sorted inorder and represented in differential form with respect to their parent.

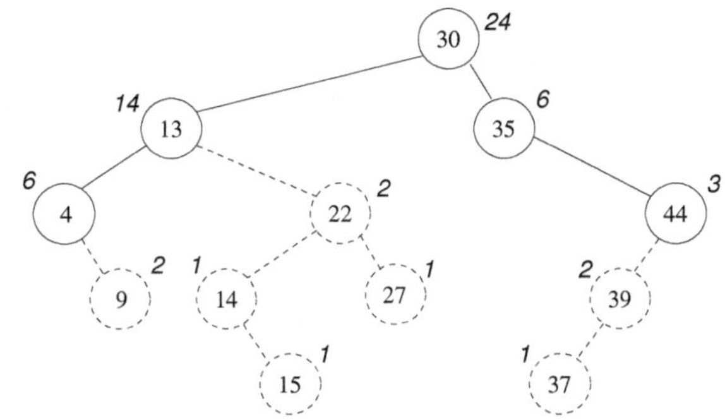

ids1	14	15	27	37
ids2	9	22	39	

diff ids1	14	1	12	10
diff ids2	9	13	17	

Figure 3: Separating frequencies below $f_0 = 2$ in our example treap. The part that is removed from the treap is dashed. For the documents with frequencies 1 and 2, we show the absolute docids on the left and their differential version on the right.

a first sequence, the second chunks in a second sequence, and so on. Some numbers x_i will only participate in the first sequences because they are smaller than others. Compact bitmap representations are used to drive the extraction process for any x_i through the different sequences where its chunks are represented. DACs can tune the block sizes so as to use minimum space, given the sequence of x_i values.

Figure 2 illustrates our compressed treap representation.

4.4 Practical Improvements

The scheme detailed above would not be so successful without two important improvements. First, because many posting lists are very short, it turns out to be more efficient to store two single DAC sequences, with all the differential docids and all the differential frequencies for all the lists together, even if using individual DACs would have allowed us to optimize their space for each sequence separately. The overhead of storing the chunk lengths and other administrative data overweights the benefits for short sequences.

A second improvement is to break ties in frequencies so as to make the treap as balanced as possible, by choosing the maximum that is closest to the center of each interval. This improves the binary searches for docids.

The third, and more important, improvement is to omit from the treap representation all the elements of the lists where the frequency is below some threshold f_0. According to Zipf's law [40, 18, 16, 5], a large number of elements will have low frequencies, and thus using a separate posting list for each frequency below f_0 will save us from storing those frequencies wherever those elements would have appeared in the treap. Further, the docids of each list can be differentially encoded in classical sequential form, which is more efficient than in treap order.

It turns out that many terms do not have to store a treap at all, as they never occur more than f_0 times in any document. We represent the gap-encoded lists using Rice codes and take an absolute sample every 128 values (which form a block). Samples are stored separately and explicitly in an array, with pointers to the block [19]. Searches in these lists will ask for consecutively larger values, so we remember the last element found and exponentially search for the next query starting from there. Figure 3 illustrates the separation of low-frequency elements from our example treap.

A neat feature of these lists is that often we will not need to access them at all during queries, since ranked queries aim at the highest frequencies.

4.5 Query Processing

4.5.1 *General procedure*

Let Q be a query composed of q terms $t \in Q$. To obtain the top-k documents from the intersection or union of q posting lists we proceed in DAAT fashion: We traverse the q posting lists in synchronization, identifying the documents that appear in all or some of them, and accumulating their weights $w(t,d)$ into a final $score(Q,d) = \sum_t w(t,d) = \sum_t tf_{t,f} \cdot idf_t$. Those documents are inserted in a min-priority queue limited to k elements, where the priority is the score. Each time we insert a new element and the queue size reaches $k+1$, we remove the minimum. At the end of the process, the priority queue contains the top-k results. Furthermore, at any stage of the process, if the queue has reached size k, then its minimum score L is a lower bound to the scores we are interested in for the rest of the documents.

4.5.2 *Intersections*

Let d be the smallest docid not yet considered (initially $d=1$). All the treaps t maintain a stack of nodes (initially holding just a sentinel value element u_t with $id(u_t) = +\infty$ and $f(u_t) = +\infty$), and a cursor v_t (initially the treap root). The stack will contain the nodes in the path from the root to v_t where we descend by the left child. We will always call u_t the top of the stack, thus u_t is an ancestor of v_t and it holds $id(u_t) > id(v_t)$.

We advance in all the treaps simultaneously towards a node v with docid $id(v) = d$, while skipping nodes using the current lower bound L. In all the treaps t we maintain the invariant that, if v is in the treap, it must appear in the subtree rooted at v_t. In particular, this implies $d < id(u_t)$.

Because of the decreasing frequency property of treaps, if d is in a node v within the subtree rooted at v_t, then $f(v) \leq f(v_t)$. Therefore, we can compute an *upper bound* U to the score of document d by using values $f(v_t)$ instead of $f(v)$, for example $U = \sum_{t \in Q} f(v_t) \cdot idf_t$ for a tf-idf scoring[1]. If this upper bound is $U \leq L$, then there is a valid top-k answer where d does not participate, so we can discard d. Further, no node that is below all the current v_t nodes can qualify. Therefore, we can safely compute a new target $d \leftarrow \min_t(id(u_t))$. Each time the value of d changes (it always increases), we must update the stack of all the treaps t to restore the invariants: While $id(u_t) \leq d$, we assign $v_t \leftarrow u_t$ and remove u_t from the stack. We then resume the global intersection process with this new target d. The upper bound U is recomputed incrementally each time any v_t value changes (U may increase or decrease).

When $U > L$, it is still feasible to find d with sufficiently high score. In this case we have to advance towards the node containing d in some treap. We obtained the best results by choosing the treap t of the shortest list. We must choose a treap where we have not yet reached d; if we have reached d in all the treaps then we can output d as an element of the intersection, with a known score (the current U value is the actual score of d), insert it in the priority queue of top-k results as explained (which may increase the lower bound L), and resume the global intersection process with $d \leftarrow d + 1$ (we must update stacks, as d has changed).

In order to move towards $d \neq id(v_t)$ in a treap t, we proceed as follows. If $d < id(v_t)$, we move to the left child of v_t, l_t, push v_t in the stack, and make $v_t \leftarrow l_t$. Instead, if $d > id(v_t)$, we move to the right child of v_t, r_t, and make $v_t \leftarrow r_t$. We then recompute U with the new v_t value.

If we have to move to the left and there is no left child of v_t, then d does not belong to the intersection. We stay at node v_t and redefine a new target $d \leftarrow id(v_t)$. If we have to move to the right and there is no right child of v_t, then again d is not in the intersection. We make $v_t \leftarrow u_t$, remove u_t from the stack, and redefine $d \leftarrow id(u_t)$. In both cases we adjust the stacks of the other treaps to the new value of d, as before, and resume the intersection process.

Algorithm 1 gives pseudocode for the intersection.

4.5.3 Handling low-frequency lists

We have not yet considered the lists of documents with frequencies up to f_0, which are stored separately, one per frequency, outside the treap. While a general solution is feasible (but complicated), we describe a simple strategy for the case $f_0 = 1$, which is the case we implemented.

Recall that we store the posting lists in gap-encoded blocks. Together with the treap cursor, we will maintain a *list cursor*, which points inside some block that has been previously decompressed. Each time there is no left or right child in the treap, we must search the list for potential elements omitted in the treap. More precisely, we look for elements in the range $[d, id(v_t) - 1]$ if we cannot go left, or in the range $[d, id(u_t) - 1]$ if we cannot go right. Those elements must be processed as if they belonged to the treap before proceeding

[1]Replacing $f(v)$ by $f(v_t)$ will yield an upper bound whenever the scoring function is monotonic with the frequencies. This is a reasonable assumption and holds for most weighting formulas, including tf-idf and BM25.

Algorithm 1 Top-k of intersection using treaps.

```
Intersect(Q, k)
  results ← ∅ // priority queue of pairs (key, priority)
  for t ∈ Q do
    stack_t ← ⟨⊥⟩ // stack of treap t, id(⊥) = f(⊥) = +∞
    v_t ← root of treap t
  end for
  compute score U using f(v_t) values, e.g. Σ_{t∈Q} f(v_t) · idf_t
  d ← 1
  L ← −∞
  while d < +∞ do
    while U ≤ L do
      changed(min_{t∈Q} id(top(stack_t)))
    end while
    if ∀t ∈ Q, d = id(v_t) then
      report(d, U)
      changed(d + 1)
    else
      t ← treap of shortest list such that d ≠ id(v_t)
      if d < id(v_t) then
        l_t ← left child of v_t
        if l_t is not null then
          push(stack_t, v_t)
          changev(t, l_t)
        else
          changed(id(v_t))
        end if
      else
        r_t ← right child of v_t
        if r_t is not null then
          changev(t, r_t)
        else
          changev(t, pop(stack_t))
          changed(id(v_t))
        end if
      end if
    end if
  end while
  return results

changed(newd)
  d ← newd
  for t ∈ Q do
    v ← v_t
    while d ≥ id(top(stack_t)) do
      v ← top(stack_t)
      pop(stack_t)
    end while
    changev(t, v)
  end for

report(d, s)
  results ← results ∪ (d, s)
  if |results| > k then
    remove minimum from results
    L ← minimum priority in results
  end if

changev(t, v)
  remove contribution of f(v_t) from U, e.g. U − f(v_t) · idf_t
  v_t ← v
  add contribution of f(v_t) to U, e.g. U + f(v_t) · idf_t
```

in the actual treap. Finding this new range $[l, r]$ in the list may imply seeking and decompressing a new block.

The cleanest way to process range $[l, r]$ is to search as if it formed a subtree fully skewed to the right, descending from v_t. If we descended to the left of v_t towards the range, we push v_t into the stack. Since all the elements in the list have the same frequency, when we are required to advance towards (a new) d we simply scan the interval until reaching or exceeding d, and the docid found acts as our new $id(v_t)$ value. When the interval $[l, r]$ is exhausted, we return to the treap. Note that the interval $[l, r]$ may span several physical list blocks, which may be subsequently decompressed.

4.5.4 Unions

The algorithm for ranked unions requires a few changes on the algorithm for intersections. First, in the two lines that call **changed**$(id(v_t))$, we do not change the d for all the treaps when the current treap does not find it. Rather, we keep values $nextd_t$ where each treap stores the minimum $d' \geq d$ it contains, thus those lines are changed by $nextd_t \leftarrow id(v_t)$. Second, we will choose the treap t to advance only among those where $id(v_t) \neq d$ and $nextd_t = d$, as if $nextd_t > d$ we cannot find d in treap t. Third, when all the treaps t where $id(v_t) \neq d$ satisfy $nextd_t > d$, we have found exactly the treaps where d appears. We add up $score(Q, d)$ over those treaps where $id(v_t) = d$, report d, and advance to $d+1$. If, however, this happens but no treap t satisfies $id(v_t) = d$, we know that d is not in the union and we can advance d with **changed**$(\min_{t \in Q} nextd_t)$. Finally, **changed**$(newd)$ should not only update d but also update, for all the treaps t, $nextd_t$ to $\max(nextd_t, newd)$.

5. EXPERIMENTS AND RESULTS

5.1 Experimental Setup

We use the TREC GOV2 collection, parsed using Porter's stemming algorithm. The collection contains about 25.2 million documents and about 32.8 million terms in the vocabulary. The inverted lists contain about 4.9 billion postings in total. We used the TREC2006 Efficiency Queries dataset using distinct amounts of terms, from $q = 2$ to 5.

We compare our results with two baselines: (1) Block-Max [21], using their implementation and modifying it to use tf-idf scoring, and (2) Dual-Sorted [25], using their implementation. As additional baselines, we implemented (3) our own version of a traditional docid-sorted inverted index using Rice encoding of the gaps, sampling values every 128 values to support random access via exponential search, and Rice encoding of absolute frequencies, and (4) our own version of a traditional frequency-sorted inverted index, using gap- and run-length encoding for the frequencies, and Rice encoding of absolute docids (except within equal frequencies, where docids are sorted and differentialy encoded).

Our experiments were performed on an Intel(r) Xeon(r) model E5620 running at 2.40 GHz with 96GB of RAM and 12,288KB of cache, running version 2.6.31-41 64 bits of the Linux kernel. All solutions were implemented in C++, compiled with g++ version 4.4.3 and -O3 optimization.

5.2 Space Usage

Figure 4 shows the space usage of the main structures compared, for increasing subsets of GOV2. The line "Treap w/o f_0" shows the space of our basic treap mechanism without representing the low-frequency lists separately. As it can be seen, the treap mechanism to encode both docids and frequencies in partially differential form is not sufficient by itself to beat a representation like Block-Max (which does not encode frequencies differentially, but encodes docids differentially much better, in left-to-right order) or Dual-Sorted (which does not encode docids differentially, but encodes frequencies differentially and with run-length encoding).

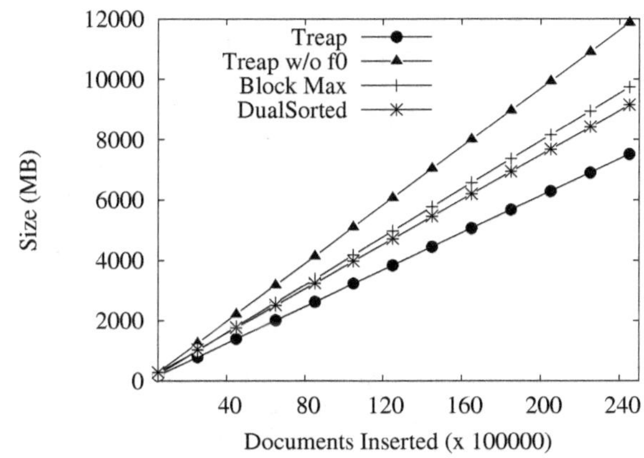

Figure 4: Space usage per document inserted.

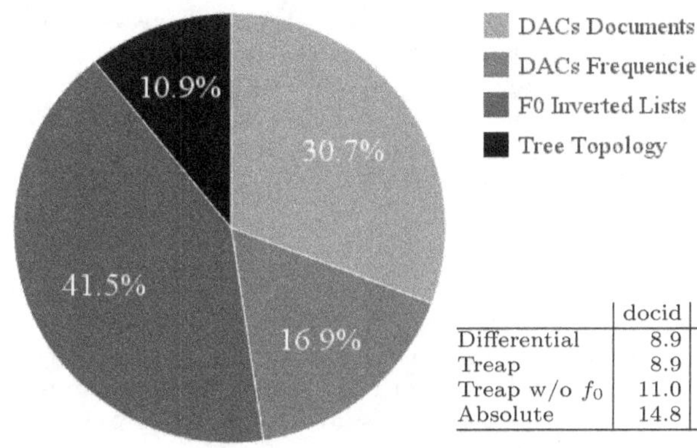

	docid	freq
Differential	8.9	1.6
Treap	8.9	2.1
Treap w/o f_0	11.0	5.6
Absolute	14.8	5.7

Figure 5: Pie chart with fraction of space used by the structures in our index. Bottom right: bpp for different representations of docids and frequencies.

When we separate the low-frequency lists ("Treap" in the figure), the situation is much better, as this is roughly equivalent to run-length compressing consecutive postings with frequency 1, and in addition the overhead of the tree topology and of non-left-to-right differential encoding of documents disappears within those lists. With this improvement, our compressed treap structures offer a space gain of 22% over Block-Max and of 18% over Dual-Sorted. While the idea of low-frequency lists could be applied to Block-Max and Dual-Sorted, it would probably make them slower (unlike our treaps, which become faster when processing low-frequency lists) and the impact in their space would not be as high as on the treaps (e.g., they have no tree topology and their differential encoding of docids would not improve).

Our tree representation (with low-frequency lists) requires about 12.3 bits per posting (bpp). Figure 5 shows how that space distributes across our structures. Almost half of the space is used for the treap DACs, the docids using about twice the space of the frequencies. The docids for frequency

	Docid	Freq	Topology	Total
Docid sorted	8.9	5.7		14.6
Freq sorted	14.8	1.6		16.4
Treap	8.9	2.1	1.3	12.3
Treap w/o f_0	11.0	5.6	2.4	19.0
Block-Max				15.8
Dual-Sorted				15.0

Table 1: Bpps of main components of the indexes.

$f_0 = 1$ (F0), differentially encoded, use more than 40% of the space, which shows again how large is their impact on the space. Finally, the compressed treap topologies require about 10% of the space. Adding DACs and F0, we use 8.9 bpp for the docids, plus 2.1 bpp for the frequencies and 1.3 bpp for the topology. Our version without separating low-frequency lists, instead, uses 11 bpp for the docids, 5.6 bpp for the frequencies, and 2.4 bpp for the topology, adding up to 19 bpp. This is compared in the figure (bottom right) with differential and absolute encodings of docids and frequencies (as detailed in Section 5.1), showing how treaps achieve intermediate results. Table 1 shows how the space of the various indexes adds up from those components.

5.3 Ranked Intersection

Figure 6 gives ranked intersection times for varying k, averaging over all the queries, and for $k = 10$ and $k = 20$, separating the queries by number of words (q). As noted in previous work [25], Dual-Sorted is unique in that it improves for longer queries, taking over for queries of 4–5 words or more. Averaged over all the queries, it performs similarly to Block-Max, and both are superior to a Boolean intersection followed by a ranking (labeled "Intersection") implemented over our docid-sorted inverted index. None of these methods is much affected by k (which is expected for Dual-Sorted and Intersection since they always produce the full intersection and then rank the resulting documents).

Our treaps are more affected by the value of k, achieving larger speedups over a plain intersection for smaller k. Indeed, they are much faster than all the alternatives for small k values, and become similar to them for $k = 30$. For $k = 10$, treaps outperform the others by a wide margin (up to 3 times faster than Block-Max, its closest competitor) for queries up to 4 words. For more than 4 words, as explained, Dual-Sorted takes over. The scenario is similar, yet less sharp, for $k = 20$.

To explain the improved times of the treap representation compared to a plain intersection, Figure 7 shows the number of documents accessed in both cases. It can be seen that the treap data structure is very effective to prune the number of documents that must be considered, starting examining about 2.6% of the documents considered by a Boolean intersection for $k = 10$, and becoming ineffective only at $k = 1000$. On the other hand, the compact data structures of the treap (namely the compressed representation of the topology and the DAC representation of the docids and frequencies) are significantly slower than a plain representation: both require about 300 nanoseconds per basic operation [3, 14], whereas a plain memory access costs 15–30 nanoseconds. This 10–20-fold slowdown makes the final time competitive only up to $k = 30$. The figure also shows the number of docids accessed at the low-frequency lists (F0), which increases with k but stays around 20% of the total.

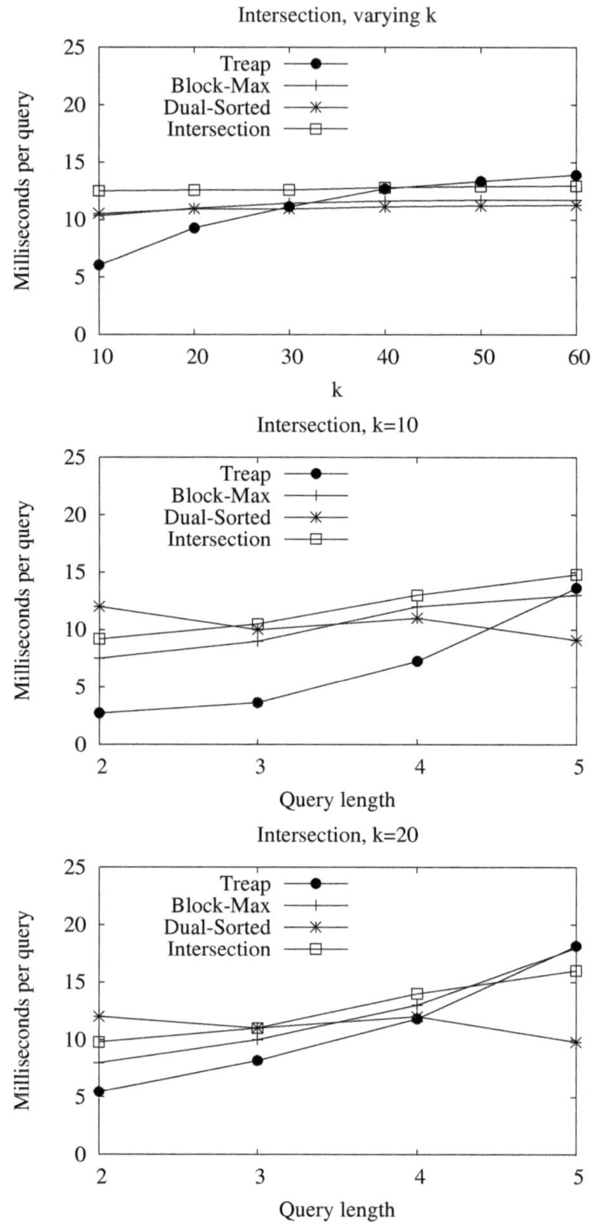

Figure 6: Time performance for ranked intersections. On top, for all the queries and increasing k. The other two discriminate by number of words in the query and use fixed $k = 10$ and $k = 20$.

5.4 Ranked Union

Figure 8 shows the results for ranked union queries. Using a Boolean union as a filter for these queries is ineffective, so we use our frequency-sorted inverted index to implement an approximate ranked union, Persin et al.'s [30] (labeled "Persin" in the plots). Dual-Sorted also implements Persin et al.'s algorithm, so both report only approximate results. Only Block-Max and our treaps give exact results.

It can be seen that all the times worsen as k and q increase, more than linearly on q and sublinearly on k. Our treaps outperform Block-Max and Dual-Sorted for all k values up to 130. They are 2.5 times faster, for example for 3-word

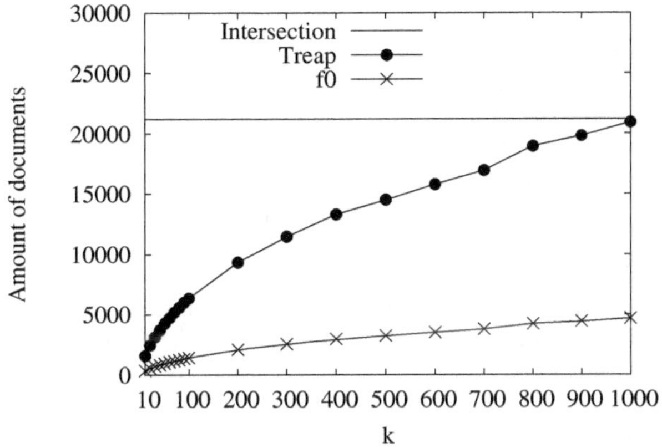

Figure 7: Documents evaluated during a ranked intersection query.

queries. Treaps are only outperformed by the native Persin implementation, which however is not exact.

6. EXTENSIONS

It is not hard to adapt our algorithm for unions to the ranked version of the more general *thresholded* queries [7], which in addition to Q give a value $q' < q$, so that at least q' of the q query terms must appear in the reported documents. In this more general view, ranked unions correspond to $q' = 1$ and ranked intersections to $q' = q$. The more general Weak-AND operator [15] can also be easily supported. When we find which treaps t reach value $id(v_t) = d$, we can evaluate document d and determine whether it qualifies.

On the other hand, approximate answers for ranked union queries have been the norm for decades, and our treap data structures can efficiently implement those as well. For example, we could easily implement Persin et al.'s [30] TAAT processing, even better than classical frequency-sorted lists. We could maintain the candidate set as a list sorted by docid. Each new treap that is processed is traversed in docid order, stopping at nodes where the threshold for considering documents is reached. As we produce the qualifying documents in docid order, we can simply merge them with the candidate set, without the need of more sophisticated structures. Furthermore, for subtrees of treap nodes whose frequency is below the threshold for inserting new documents in the candidate set, we can switch to a mode where the subtree is intersected with the candidates, using the next candidate docid to skip treap nodes.

7. CONCLUSIONS AND FUTURE WORK

We have introduced a new inverted index representation based on the treap data structure. Treaps turn out to be an elegant and flexible tool to represent simultaneously the docid and the weight ordering of a posting list. We use them to design efficient ranked intersection and union algorithms that simultaneously filter out document by docid and frequency. The treap also allows us to represent both docids and frequencies in differential form, thus enabling better compression of the posting lists. Our experiments show significant gains in space and time compared to the state of the art: not only our structure uses about 20% less space than previous ones, but also it is faster (sometimes as much as

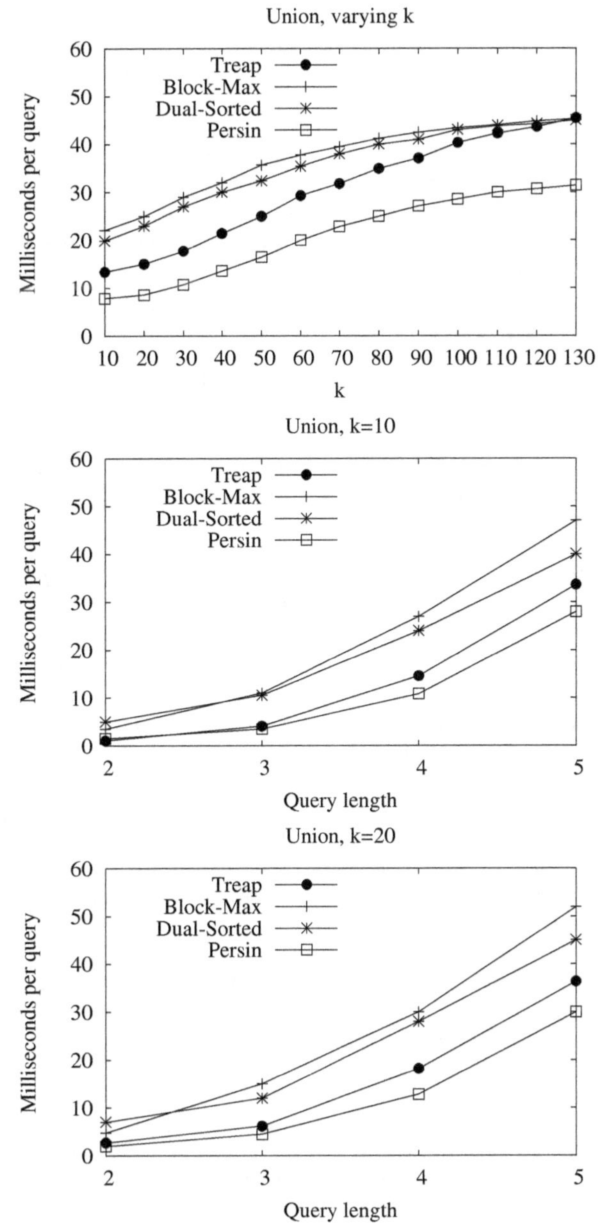

Figure 8: Time performance for ranked unions. On top, for all the queries and increasing k. The other two discriminate by number of words in the query and use fixed $k = 10$ and $k = 20$.

three times faster) for up to $k = 30$ on ranked intersections and $k = 130$ on ranked unions.

A first future work question is how the scheme performs with other scoring formulas. We have used simple tf-idf, but we could use BM25, impacts, etc. Some require to adapt the way we compute the upper bound U, such as considering document sizes in BM25 (but this has been solved [15, 21]).

A second question is what would be the impact of reassigning docids. There is much recent research on this topic (see, e.g., [21]) that shows that reassignment can significantly improve both space and processing time. How much would treaps improve with such schemes? Can we optimize the reassignment for a treap layout?

An important part of our gain owed to separating lists with frequency $f_0 = 1$. How to efficiently separate lists with higher frequencies is a challenge, and it can lead to substantial further gains. It is also interesting to test how this idea impacts on schemes like Block-Max and Dual-Sorted.

Finally, our performance degrades sharply with q, an effect already noted before in Block-Max [21]. We believe the time would become almost nonincreasing with q if we used treaps under a TAAT scheme where the longer lists were processed after determining good lower bounds with the shorter lists.

8. REFERENCES

[1] V. Anh and A. Moffat. Inverted index compression using word-aligned binary codes. *Inf. Retr.*, 8(1):151–166, 2005.

[2] V. Anh and A. Moffat. Pruned query evaluation using pre-computed impacts. In *Proc. 29th SIGIR*, pages 372–379, 2006.

[3] D. Arroyuelo, R. Cánovas, G. Navarro, and K. Sadakane. Succinct trees in practice. In *Proc. 11th ALENEX*, pages 84–97, 2010.

[4] R. Baeza-Yates, A. Moffat, and G. Navarro. Searching large text collections. In *Handbook of Massive Data Sets*, pages 195–244. Kluwer, 2002.

[5] R. Baeza-Yates and B. Ribeiro-Neto. *Modern Information Retrieval.* Addison-Wesley, 2nd edition, 2011.

[6] R. Baeza-Yates and A. Salinger. Experimental analysis of a fast intersection algorithm for sorted sequences. In *Proc. 12th SPIRE*, pages 13–24, 2005.

[7] J. Barbay and C. Kenyon. Adaptive intersection and t-threshold problems. In *Proc. 13th SODA*, pages 390–399, 2002.

[8] J. Barbay, A. López-Ortiz, T. Lu, and A. Salinger. An experimental investigation of set intersection algorithms for text searching. *ACM J. Exp. Alg.*, 14:art. 7, 2009.

[9] M. Bender and M. Farach-Colton. The LCA problem revisited. In *Proc. 9th LATIN*, pages 88–94, 2000.

[10] O. Berkman and U. Vishkin. Recursive star-tree parallel data structure. *SIAM J. Comp.*, 22(2):221–242, 1993.

[11] I. Bialynicka-Birula. *Ranked Queries in Index Data Structures.* PhD thesis, University of Pisa, 2008.

[12] I. Bialynicka-Birula and R. Grossi. Rank-sensitive data structures. In *Proc. 12th SPIRE*, pages 79–90, 2005.

[13] G. Blelloch and M. Reid-Miller. Fast set operations using treaps. In *Proc. 10th SPAA*, pages 16–26, 1998.

[14] N. Brisaboa, S. Ladra, and G. Navarro. DACs: Bringing direct access to variable-length codes. *Inf. Proc. Manag.*, 49(1):392–404, 2013.

[15] A. Broder, D. Carmel, M. Herscovici, A. Soffer, and J. Zien. Efficient query evaluation using a two-level retrieval process. In *Proc. 12th CIKM*, pages 426–434, 2003.

[16] S. Büttcher, C. Clarke, and G. Cormack. *Information Retrieval: Implementing and Evaluating Search Engines.* MIT Press, 2010.

[17] F. Claude, P. Nicholson, and D. Seco. Differentially encoded search trees. In *Proc. 22nd DCC*, pages 357–366, 2012.

[18] B. Croft, D. Metzler, and T. Strohman. *Search Engines: Information Retrieval in Practice.* Pearson Education, 2009.

[19] J. Culpepper and A. Moffat. Compact set representation for information retrieval. In *Proc. 14th SPIRE*, pages 137–148, 2007.

[20] E. Demaine, A. López-Ortiz, and J. Munro. Adaptive set intersections, unions, and differences. In *Proc. 11th SODA*, pages 743–752, 2000.

[21] S. Ding and T.Suel. Faster top-k document retrieval using block-max indexes. In *Proc. 34th SIGIR*, pages 993–1002, 2011.

[22] J. Fischer and V. Heun. Space-efficient preprocessing schemes for range minimum queries on static arrays. *SIAM J. Comp.*, 40(2):465–492, 2011.

[23] R. Grossi, A. Gupta, and J. Vitter. High-order entropy-compressed text indexes. In *Proc. 14th SODA*, pages 841–850, 2003.

[24] H. Heaps. *Information Retrieval - Computational and Theoretical Aspects.* Academic Press, NY, 1978.

[25] R. Konow and G. Navarro. Dual-sorted inverted lists in practice. In *Proc. 19th SPIRE*, pages 295–306, 2012.

[26] C. Martínez and S. Roura. Randomized binary search trees. *J. ACM*, 45(2):288–323, 1997.

[27] E. McCreight. Priority search trees. *SIAM J. Comp.*, 14(2):257–276, 1985.

[28] G. Navarro. Wavelet trees for all. In *Proc. 23rd CPM*, pages 2–26, 2012.

[29] G. Navarro and S. Puglisi. Dual-sorted inverted lists. In *Proc. 17th SPIRE*, pages 309–321, 2010.

[30] M. Persin, J. Zobel, and R. Sacks-Davis. Filtered document retrieval with frequency-sorted indexes. *J. Am. Soc. Inf. Sci.*, 47(10):749–764, 1996.

[31] K. Sadakane and G. Navarro. Fully-functional succinct trees. In *Proc. 21st SODA*, pages 134–149, 2010.

[32] P. Sanders and F. Transier. Intersection in integer inverted indices. In *Proc. 9th ALENEX*, 2007.

[33] F. Scholer, H. Williams, J. Yiannis, and J. Zobel. Compression of inverted indexes for fast query evaluation. In *Proc. 25th SIGIR*, pages 222–229, 2002.

[34] R. Seidel and C. Aragon. Randomized search trees. *Algorithmica*, 16(4/5):464–497, 1996.

[35] T. Strohman and B. Croft. Efficient document retrieval in main memory. In *Proc. 30th SIGIR*, pages 175–182, 2007.

[36] J. Vuillemin. A unifying look at data structures. *Comm. ACM*, 23(4):229–239, 1980.

[37] L. Wang, J. Lin, and D. Metzler. A cascade ranking model for efficient ranked retrieval. In *Proc. 34th SIGIR*, pages 105–114, 2011.

[38] I. Witten, A. Moffat, and T. Bell. *Managing Gigabytes.* Morgan Kaufmann, 2nd edition, 1999.

[39] H. Yan, S. Ding, and T. Suel. Inverted index compression and query processing with optimized document ordering. In *Proc. 18th WWW*, pages 401–410, 2009.

[40] G. Zipf. *Human Behaviour and the Principle of Least Effort.* Addison-Wesley, 1949.

[41] J. Zobel and A. Moffat. Inverted files for text search engines. *ACM Comp. Surv.*, 38(2):art. 6, 2006.

An Unsupervised Topic Segmentation Model Incorporating Word Order*

Shoaib Jameel and Wai Lam
Department of Systems Engineering and Engineering Management,
The Chinese University of Hong Kong,
Hong Kong.
{msjameel, wlam}@se.cuhk.edu.hk

ABSTRACT

We present a new unsupervised topic discovery model for a collection of text documents. In contrast to the majority of the state-of-the-art topic models, our model does not break the document's structure such as paragraphs and sentences. In addition, it preserves word order in the document. As a result, it can generate two levels of topics of different granularity, namely, segment-topics and word-topics. In addition, it can generate n-gram words in each topic. We also develop an approximate inference scheme using Gibbs sampling method. We conduct extensive experiments using publicly available data from different collections and show that our model improves the quality of several text mining tasks such as the ability to support fine grained topics with n-gram words in the correlation graph, the ability to segment a document into topically coherent sections, document classification, and document likelihood estimation.

Categories and Subject Descriptors

H.3.3 [**Information Storage and Retrieval**]: Information Search and Retrieval - Clustering

Keywords

Topic Modeling, Topic Segmentation, N-gram words, Gibbs Sampling, Document Classification

1. INTRODUCTION

Simplicity may not always lead to greatness! Topic models such as Latent Dirichlet Allocation (LDA) [5] have been widely used to find topics in a document collection. Typically, a topic is a probability distribution over words. But the LDA model has been criticized for its bag-of-words assumption [32] as the model does not consider the structural information inherent in the text which could help tap extra knowledge from the text. It is well known that the bag-of-words assumption is mainly a simplifying assumption to reduce the complexity of the model [24].

Some recent topic models have demonstrated better qualitative and quantitative performance when the bag-of-words assumption is relaxed [18], [20], [1], and [23]. Maintaining the word order during the processing of documents introduces some computational overhead, but it allows us to achieve what the bag-of-words models cannot do in general [15]. In order to address the shortcoming inherent in the LDA model, the authors in [39] introduced the Topical N-gram model (TNG) to find n-gram words in topics. By n-gram we mean a word can be a unigram, a bigram, a trigram word, etc. The TNG model has the ability to decide whether to form a unigram or a bigram during the topic discovery process. The TNG model mainly extends the LDA Collocation model [14] (LDACOL) and the Bigram Topic Model [35] (BTM). All these models advocate that the word order in a document is essential. But one shortcoming of these models is that they lack the ability to consider the document's structure such as paragraphs and sentences. Thus they cannot segment a document into coherent topics. This sometimes becomes essential in tasks such as tackling the word sense disambiguation problem as shown in [15], segmenting news articles and finding topics in each segment [30], topic detection and tracking [40], and a plethora of other tasks which motivate us to explore deeper into the topic segmentation model with n-gram topic word discovery.

We propose a new unsupervised topic discovery model, called NTSeg, for a collection of text documents. NTSeg maintains the segment structure of the document such as paragraphs and sentences. In addition, it preserves the word order in the document. NTSeg can help capture topical changes in the document from one segment to another. As a result, it can generate two levels of topics of different granularity, namely, segment-topics and word-topics. In addition, it can generate n-gram words in each word-topic. We also conduct extensive experiments on publicly available datasets to demonstrate the superiority of NTSeg in comparison to the state-of-the-art models in solving several text mining tasks such as the ability to support fine grained topics with n-gram words in the correlation graph, the ability to segment

*The work described in this paper is substantially supported by grants from the Research Grant Council of the Hong Kong Special Administrative Region, China (Project Code: CUHK413510) and the Direct Grant of the Faculty of Engineering, CUHK (Project Codes: 2050476 and 2050522). This work is also affiliated with the CUHK MoE-Microsoft Key Laboratory of Human-Centric Computing and Interface Technologies. The authors would like to thank Xiaojun Qian for his help with the experiments and some discussions related to the technical content in the paper.

SIGIR'13, July 28–August 1, 2013, Dublin, Ireland.

ACM 978-1-4503-2034-4/13/07 ...$15.00.

a document into topically coherent sections, document classification, and document modeling.

2. RELATED WORK

Topic models: Some previous works have considered the order of the words in a document during the topic discovery process. For example, in [35], the author described the Bigram Topic Model (BTM) which incorporates the hierarchical Dirichlet language model into the unigram based topic model in order to capture the dependencies between the words in sequence. One drawback of this model is that it only generates bigram words in a topic. This limitation was addressed in the LDA Collocation model (LDACOL) [14] which introduces a new set of status variables in the model called the bigram status variable. This variable indicates whether two consecutive words form a bigram or not. One limitation of the LDACOL model is that it cannot decide whether to form a unigram or a bigram for the same two consecutive words depending on their nearby context. Another issue with the model is that only the first term in a bigram has a topic assignment. One needs to make some assumptions in order to give the topic assignment to every term in a bigram [38], and [37]. The limitations inherent in the LDACOL model have been addressed in the Topical N-gram model, TNG [39]. The TNG model allows for consecutive words in a topic model to depend on each other in that they can be selected either to come from a unigram term distribution or from a bigram distribution. However, one limitation of the Topical N-gram model is that it cannot segment a document into topically coherent units, known as topic segmentation task. There are also other limitations and they have been addressed recently in [23] where the authors gave the same topic assignment to every term in a phrase and the words share the same probability mass in the phrase by introducing the hierarchical Pitman-Yor processes (HPYP) [34] in their model named PDLDA. The PDLDA model also cannot perform topic segmentation. Incorporating the HPYP model in our NTSeg model to capture phrasal terms would make our model NTSeg overly complex leading to inefficient processing of large text corpora.

Recently in [26] the authors proposed a topic model where n-gram words are viewed as random variables. The authors manually generated n-gram words from the dataset and considered those n-grams as part of the vocabulary. This model focuses on handling discussions or debates. In [19], the author proposed another topic n-gram model which mines sentiments from text corpora. Wang et al. [36] proposed an n-gram topic model for academic retrieval. They apply an online inference algorithm and find unigrams and bigrams in a topic. In [42], the authors presented an n-gram based news thread extraction model that uses the TNG model with a background distribution. A method which has adopted a different approach to n-gram topic modeling is [20]. It combines the paradigms of frequent pattern mining and topic modeling. All the topic models proposed above do not employ topic segmentation. In [41], the authors proposed an Auto Topic Number LDA (ATNLDA) model for topic segmentation and apply the model on stem cell research literature. This model can automatically calculate the optimal topic number. A difference between ATNLDA and ours is that ATNLDA does not consider the word order.

Topic Correlations: Shafiei et al. in [31] described a latent Dirichlet co-clustering method, known as LDCC, which captures correlation between word-topics and document-topics (or super-topics). The LDCC model is a hierarchical topic model where unigram words are assigned to the word-topics and paragraphs are assigned to the document-topics. The model can also find correlations between the word-topics and the document-topics. In [3], the authors proposed correlated topic model (CTM) that can capture the evolution of topics over time without considering the word order. In [22], the authors proposed Pachinko Allocation Model (PAM) where the concept of topic is extended to not only including distributions over words, but also distributions over topics. This model assumes the structure of an arbitrary DAG in which each leaf is associated with a word and each non-leaf node is a distribution over its children. The interior nodes are distributions over topics called super-topics. Recently, in [6], the authors presented a new model to find correlation among topics in a corpus using the Generalized Dirichlet distribution model instead of the Dirichlet distribution.

One similarity between our work and the topic correlation models is that our work also introduces two levels of topic assignments. For example, word-topics and document-topics as described in Shafiei et al. [31] share the same notion as the word-topics and segment-topics described in our proposed approach. We adopt the name segment-topics because known text segments such as paragraphs or sentences are assigned to the segment-topics. However, all the correlation topic models mentioned above assume exchangeability among the words in a document. The importance of capturing n-gram words is that it reduces the ambiguity in the mind of the reader as to what the word is referring to in the correlation graph. For example, presenting the word "networks" in a topic is ambiguous especially for a person who is not a domain expert. In contrast, showing the word "neural networks" in a topic significantly reduces ambiguities. In addition, all the topic correlation models mentioned above cannot conduct topic segmentation.

Topic segmentation: In [16], the author presented the TextTiling algorithm for segmenting a textual discourse into coherent segments. TextTiling is a domain-independent text segmentation technique that assigns a score to each segment boundary candidate based on a cosine similarity measure between chunks of words appearing to the left and right of the candidate. Then the segment boundaries are placed at the locations of valleys under this measure, and are then adjusted to coincide with known paragraph boundaries. TextTiling algorithm does not find topics. In [12], the authors presented a topic segmentation based approach which takes into account the lexical cohesion. The authors modeled lexical cohesion in a Bayesian context and obtained significant improvement against the existing models. They assumed that words are drawn from a multinomial language model. Our work is significantly different from the above two models in that ours is a domain-independent topic segmentation method based on a topic model. Apart from finding a low-dimensional representation of the original vector space, our model also segments a document and finds n-gram words in each topic.

In [25], the authors presented a method for topic segmentation based on topic modeling where the authors used the LDA model to segment texts into coherent topics that assume exchangeability among the words in a document. In [4], the authors described another topic segmentation method by unifying the segmenting hidden Markov model in [27] and

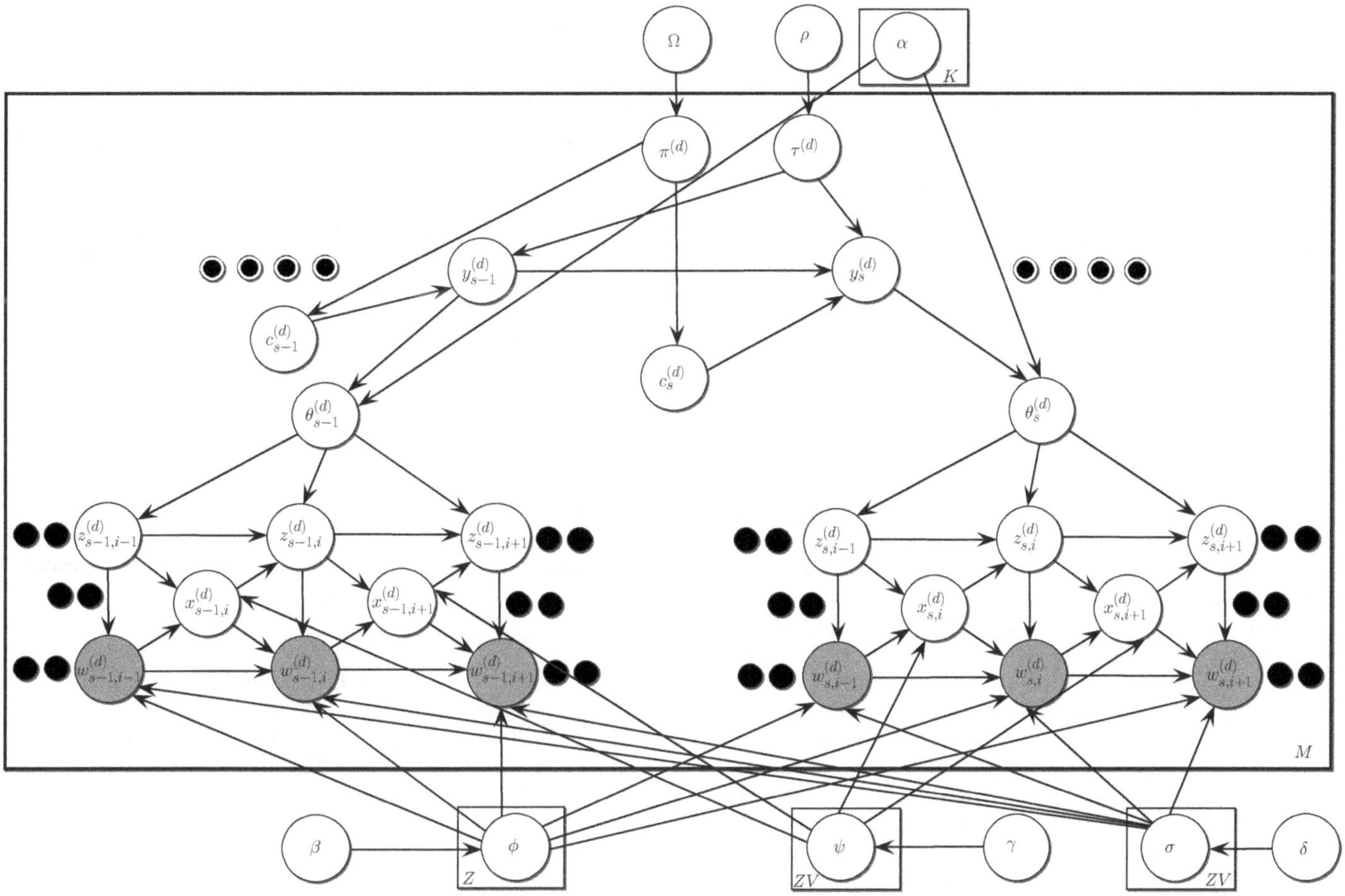

Figure 1: Our proposed model NTSeg in plate notation.

the aspect model in [17]. Recently, in [30], the authors presented `TopicTiling` based on `LDA`. Their algorithm is very similar to the `TextTiling` algorithm, and segments documents using the `LDA` topic model. Also, in [29], the authors presented methods in which topic models can help segmentation based methods by extending their own `TopicTiling` model. Similarly, in [32] the authors proposed a topic segmentation based topic model, known as `LDSEG`, where they assumed that the word order is not important. The authors introduced the notion of topic hierarchy where sentences are assigned to the document-topics and unigrams are assigned to the word-topics. The `LDSEG` model represents documents as a distribution over document-topics or super-topics in such a way that each segment is assigned a super-topic or document-topic, which is then used to choose the parameters of a document independent Dirichlet distribution from which the word-topics for the segment is drawn. In order for consecutive segments to have similar word-topic distributions, an additional binary variable per segment encodes whether the document-topic is forced to be the same as that of the previous segment. In [9], the authors proposed a topic model based hierarchical segmentation approach where they assumed that the word order within the segment is not important and apply variational Bayesian Expectation-Maximization procedure for computing the posterior inference. This model has been designed for segmenting the speech data. In [11], the authors proposed a collapsed Gibbs sampler for the topic segmentation problem for a faster posterior inference. They employ a hierarchical Pitman-Yor processes to handle hierarchical modeling, which our model does not incorporate. In [33], the authors presented a topic segmentation model which does not find topics in a segment. In contrast to the above models, our model does not assume exchangeability among the words in a document. In [8], the authors proposed a subsequence based topic segmentation approach which uses a suffix tree model for representing text and measures coherence between sentences based on subsequence. Their model maintains the order of the words in each segment, but the model does not find collocations in that text segment.

3. OUR PROPOSED MODEL (NTSeg)

We depict our proposed `NTSeg` model in Figure 1 using a graphical model in plate notation where shaded circles represent observed variables and unshaded ones are the latent variables. Each document, in general, is organized as atomic segments such as paragraphs or sentences. Our model preserves this structure. One characteristic of our model is that a document comprises of several topically coherent segments. Another characteristic of our model is due to the preservation of the ordering of the words it is able to capture word-collocations. Thus our proposed model is no longer invariant to the reshuffling of the words in each segment.

For a properly written discourse comprehension, documents are generally composed of coherent segments which are semantically linked to one another so that a reader could relate the storyline as one moves forward in the discourse [21]. Our model comprises of two levels of topic of different granularity. One is the segment-topic to which atomic segments in a document are assigned and the ordering of segments as they appear in the document defines the topic change-points in the document. The other is the word-topic to which n-gram words in the segment are assigned. Segment-topics come from a predefined number of segment-topics K. Each segment-topic comprises of a mixture of several word-topics where the mixture coefficients uniquely specify the segment-topic. Word-topics come from a predefined number of word-topics Z. In general, the number of segment-topics will be less than the number of word-topics. The reason is that the number of segments in a document is less than compared to the number of words [31].

In the graphical model shown in Figure 1, M denotes the number of documents in the collection and V denotes the number of words in the vocabulary. In each atomic segment s, NTSeg finds n-gram words in a word-topic $\mathbf{z}$. It can also find correlations between both kinds of topics i.e. word-topics $\mathbf{z}$ and segment-topics $\mathbf{y}$. The segments of each document are assumed to follow a Markov structure on the topic distributions of each segment. We assume that there will be a high probability that the topic for the segment s in the document will be the same as that of the segment $s-1$. A segment binary switching variable $c_s^{(d)}$ for the segment-topic in the document d indicates whether there is a change of topic between the segments. The states of the switching variable correspond to the segmentation of the document into coherent topical units. Apart from the segment switching binary variable, NTSeg also incorporates another random variable known as the bigram status variable $\mathbf{x}$ which indicates the bigram status i.e. whether a word w at position i in the segment s in the document d, denoted as $w_{si}^{(d)}$, forms a bigram with the previous word $w_{s,i-1}^{(d)}$. The mechanism is that if $x_{si}^{(d)} = 1$, then $w_{s,i-1}^{(d)}$ and $w_{si}^{(d)}$ form a bigram else they do not.

It can be observed that the existing topical n-gram model (TNG) [39], LDSEG, [32], and LDCC, [31] are special cases derived from our model. For example, consider only a segment, for instance segment s, in Figure 1. Removing the segmentation scheme along with a set of arrows pointing from $z_{s,i-1}^{(d)} \rightarrow z_{si}^{(d)}$ and $x_{si}^{(d)} \rightarrow z_{si}^{(d)}$ reduces to the TNG model. One can observe that our model, NTSeg, has the capability of deciding whether to generate a unigram or a bigram in a topic and the topic assignment for the words in a bigram are the same. This aspect differentiates NTSeg from TNG. Similar to TNG, NTSeg assumes a first order Markov assumption i.e. it is mainly a bigram model, but the basic generation process produces unigram or bigram words. However, NTSeg has the ability to produce higher order n-grams (i.e. $n > 2$) by concatenating consecutive n-grams (unigram or bigram words) having the same topic and the bigram status variable between them is 1. In this way, the words in the n-gram share the same topic. This again contrasts NTSeg from TNG where TNG analyzes each n-gram post hoc as if the topic of the final word in the n-gram was the topic assignment of the entire n-gram. But it violates the principle of non-compositionality [23]. Removing the bag-of-words assumption in each segment of our proposed NTSeg model reduces to the LDSEG model. Relaxing both bag-of-words and removing the segmentation switch variable of NTSeg reduces to the LDCC model. NTSeg has the ability to decide whether to form a unigram or bigram based on context which the LDSEG model cannot achieve.

The following generative process of our model, NTSeg, helps better understand the graphical model shown in Figure 1:

1. Draw ϕ_z from **Dirichlet**(β) for each word-topic z, where ϕ_z is the word (unigrams only) distribution for the word-topic z; β is the parameter of the Dirichlet prior on the per-word-topic word (unigrams only) distribution

2. Draw ψ_{zw} from **Beta**(γ) for each word-topic z and each word w, where ψ_{zw} is the Bernoulli distribution for the bigram status variables for the word-topic z and the word w; γ is the parameter of the Beta prior

3. Draw σ_{zw} from **Dirichlet**(δ) for each word-topic z, and each word w, where σ_{zw} is the bigram word distribution for bigrams; δ is the parameter of the Dirichlet prior on word-topic bigram word distribution

4. For each document d in the collection
   (a) Draw $\tau^{(d)}$ from **Dirichlet**(ρ), where $\tau^{(d)}$ is the mixing proportion of the segment-topics in the document d; ρ is the parameter of the Dirichlet prior on the segment-topics
   (b) Draw $\pi^{(d)}$ from **Beta**(Ω), where $\pi^{(d)}$ defines the parameter of the Bernoulli distribution for the segment switch variable in the document d; Ω is the parameter of the Beta prior
   (c) For each segment s in the document d
      i. Draw $c_s^{(d)}$ from **Bernoulli**($\pi^{(d)}$)
      ii. Draw the segment-topic $y_s^{(d)}$ for s from **Multinomial**($\tau^{(d)}$) if $c_s^{(d)} = 0$ else $y_s^{(d)} = y_{s-1}^{(d)}$, where $y_s^{(d)}$ is the segment-topic that is assigned to the segment s in the document d
      iii. Draw $\theta_s^{(d)}$ for s in the document d from **Dirichlet**($\alpha_{y_s^{(d)} z}$); α is a $K \times Z$ matrix where each row represents the mixing proportion of the word-topics in a segment-topic; $\theta_s^{(d)}$ is the mixing proportion of the word-topics in the segment s in the document d
      iv. For each of $N_s^{(d)}$ words in the segment s in the document d, where $N_s^{(d)}$ denotes the number of words in the segment s in the document d
         A. Draw $x_{si}^{(d)}$ from **Bernoulli**($\psi_{z_{s,i-1}^{(d)} w_{s,i-1}^{(d)}}$), where $x_{si}^{(d)}$ is the bigram status variable between words $w_{s,i-1}^{(d)}$ and $w_{si}^{(d)}$ in the segment s of the document d
         B. Draw $z_{si}^{(d)}$ from **Multinomial**($\theta_s^{(d)}$) if $x_{si}^{(d)} = 0$ else $z_{si}^{(d)} = z_{s,i-1}^{(d)}$, where $z_{si}^{(d)}$ is the word-topic assignment for the word $w_{si}^{(d)}$ in the segment s in the document d.
         C. Draw $w_{si}^{(d)}$ from **Multinomial**($\sigma_{z_{si}^{(d)} w_{s,i-1}^{(d)}}$) if $x_{si}^{(d)} = 1$ else draw $w_{si}^{(d)}$ from **Multinomial**($\phi_{z_{si}^{(d)}}$)

$c_s^{(d)}$ indicates whether there is a change in the segment-topic between the segments $s-1$ and s in the document d. If $c_s^{(d)}=1$ then it means that $y_s^{(d)}=y_{s-1}^{(d)}$ i.e. segment-topic does not change between the segments in the document d. However, when $c_s^{(d)}=0$, then $y_s^{(d)}$ is drawn from a Multinomial distribution parameterized by $\tau^{(d)}$. The computation of the probability $P(y_s^{(d)}|c_s^{(d)},\tau^{(d)},y_{s-1}^{(d)})$ is done based on two conditions i.e. $\rho(y_s^{(d)},y_{s-1}^{(d)})$ when $c_s^{(d)}=1$ or sampling from **Multinomial** $(\tau^{(d)})$ when $c_s^{(d)}=0$.

The segment distribution $P(y_s^{(d)}|c_s^{(d)},\tau^{(d)},y_{s-1}^{(d)})$ is not properly defined for the first segment of every document. Therefore, $c_s^{(d)}=1$ is defined for the first segment which is drawn from **Multinomial**$(\tau^{(d)})$. Similarly we assume that $x_{s1}^{(d)}$ is observed and only unigram is allowed at the beginning of every segment.

4. POSTERIOR INFERENCE

The inference problem is related to computing the posterior probability of the hidden variables when the input parameters $\beta,\gamma,\delta,\rho,\Omega$ and the observed variable $\mathbf{w}$ are given. Also, an estimate of the α hyperparameter has to be made. It can be shown that computing the exact inference in our model is intractable. Hence, we need to resort to approximation techniques such as Gibbs sampling [7]. Adoption of Bayesian methods results in some hidden parameters being integrated out instead of being explicitly estimated. Assuming conjugate priors on the model parameters also eases the inference algorithm significantly. Algorithm 1 depicts the Gibbs sampling used in our approximate inference for `NTSeg`

We need to compute the two conditional distributions:

$$P(z_{si}^{(d)},x_{si}^{(d)}|z_{\neg si}^{(d)},x_{\neg si}^{(d)},\mathbf{w},\mathbf{c},\mathbf{y},\mathbf{x},\alpha,\beta,\gamma,\delta,\rho,\Omega) \quad (1)$$

$$P(y_s^{(d)},c_s^{(d)}|\mathbf{z},y_{\neg s}^{(d)},c_{\neg s}^{(d)},\mathbf{w},\mathbf{x},\alpha,\beta,\gamma,\delta,\rho,\Omega) \quad (2)$$

Note that $w_{\neg si}^{(d)}$ defines all the words in the segment except the current word $w_{si}^{(d)}$ in segment s in the document d. $z_{\neg si}^{(d)}$ is the word-topic assignment for all other words except the current word $w_{si}^{(d)}$. In Equations 3 and 4, n_{zw} is the number of times the word w is assigned to the word-topic z as a unigram. m_{wvz} is the number of times the word w appears as a second word of a bigram with a previous word v and both words in the bigram are assigned to the same word-topic z. p_{zwt} denotes the number of times the status variable $x=t$ (0 or 1) given the previous word w and the previous word's word-topic z. $h_{sz}^{(d)}$ is the number of times a word in segment s of document d is assigned to word-topic z. $\kappa_{c_s,0}^{(d)}$ and $\kappa_{c_s,1}^{(d)}$ is the number of times the switching variable $c_s^{(d)}$ is set to 0 and 1 in the document d, respectively. $\rho_{y_s^{(d)}}$ is the corresponding Dirichlet parameter for the segment-topic $y_s^{(d)}$. $b_k^{(d)}$ is the number of times a segment in the document d has been assigned to the segment-topic k. $y_{\neg s}^{(d)}$ is the segment-topic assignments for all the segments except the current segment s in the document d.

Beginning with the joint probability of a dataset, and using the chain rule, we obtain the conditional probabilities conveniently. We obtain the following equations:

$$\begin{aligned}&P(z_{si}^{(d)},x_{si}^{(d)}|\mathbf{w},z_{\neg si}^{(d)},x_{\neg si}^{(d)},\mathbf{y},\mathbf{c},\alpha,\beta,\gamma,\delta,\rho,\Omega)\propto\\&(\alpha_{y_s^{(d)}z_{si}^{(d)}}+h_{sz_{si}^{(d)}}^{(d)}-1)\times(\gamma_{x_{si}^{(d)}}+p_{z_{s,i-1}^{(d)}w_{s,i-1}^{(d)}x_{si}^{(d)}}-1)\\&\times\begin{cases}\frac{\beta_{w_{si}^{(d)}}+n_{z_{si}^{(d)}w_{si}^{(d)}}-1}{\sum_{v=1}^{V}\left(\beta_v+n_{z_{si}^{(d)}v}\right)-1} & \text{if } x_{si}^{(d)}=0\\ \frac{\delta_{w_{si}^{(d)}}+m_{w_{si}^{(d)}w_{s,i-1}^{(d)}z_{si}^{(d)}}-1}{\sum_{v=1}^{V}\left(\delta_v+m_{w_{s,i-1}^{(d)}vz_{si}^{(d)}}\right)-1} & \text{if } x_{si}^{(d)}=1\ \&\ z_{si}^{(d)}=z_{s,i-1}^{(d)}\end{cases}\end{aligned} \quad (3)$$

$$\begin{aligned}&P(y_s^{(d)},c_s^{(d)}|\mathbf{z},y_{\neg s}^{(d)},c_{\neg s}^{(d)},\mathbf{w},\mathbf{x},\alpha,\beta,\gamma,\delta,\rho,\Omega)\propto\\&\begin{cases}(\rho_{y_s^{(d)}}+b_{y_s^{(d)}}^{(d)}-1)\times(\alpha_{y_s^{(d)}z_{si}^{(d)}}+h_{sz_{si}^{(d)}}^{(d)}-1)\times\\ \left(\frac{\kappa_{c_s,0}^{(d)}+\Omega_0}{\sum_{x=0}^{1}\kappa_{c_s,x}^{(d)}+\Omega_0+\Omega_1}\right) & \text{if } c_s^{(d)}=0\\ (\alpha_{y_s^{(d)}z_{si}^{(d)}}+h_{sz_{si}^{(d)}}^{(d)}-1)\times\left(\frac{\kappa_{c_s,1}^{(d)}+\Omega_1}{\sum_{x=0}^{1}\kappa_{c_s,x}^{(d)}+\Omega_0+\Omega_1}\right)\\ \qquad\qquad \text{if } c_s^{(d)}=1\ \&\ s>1\ \&\ y_s^{(d)}=y_{(s-1)}^{(d)}\end{cases}\end{aligned} \quad (4)$$

Note that in our model the hyperparameter α captures the relationships between the segment-topics and word-topics. This hyperparameter must be estimated from the data. Although there are many ways to estimate this hyperparameter [31], we adopt the moment matching method which is computationally less expensive [31], and [22]. Therefore at each iteration of the Gibbs sampling (Line 37 of Algorithm 1), we update:

$$\overline{\lambda}_{kz}=\frac{1}{q_k}\sum_{s\in S_k}\frac{h_{sz}^{(d)}}{N_s^{(d)}} \quad (5) \qquad \overline{\nu}_{kz}=\frac{1}{q_k}\sum_{s\in S_k}\left(\frac{h_{sz}^{(d)}}{N_s^{(d)}}-\overline{\lambda}_{kz}\right)^2 \quad (6)$$

$$\alpha_{kz}\propto\overline{\lambda}_{kz} \quad (7) \qquad \lambda_{kz}=\frac{\overline{\lambda}_{kz}(1-\overline{\lambda}_{kz})}{\overline{\nu}_{kz}}-1 \quad (8)$$

$$\sum_{z=1}^{Z}\alpha_{kz}=\exp\left(\frac{\sum_{z=1}^{Z}\log(\lambda_{kz})}{Z-1}\right) \quad (9)$$

where S_k is the set of segments assigned to the segment-topic k. q_k is the number of segments assigned to the segment-topic k. $\overline{\lambda}_{kz}$ and $\overline{\nu}_{kz}$ are the sample mean and sample variance, respectively, of the number of times the word-topic z is assigned to the segment-topic k.

The posterior estimates for θ, ϕ, ψ, π, τ, σ are:

$$\hat{\theta}_{s,yz}^{(d)}=\frac{\alpha_{yz}+h_{sz}^{(d)}}{\sum_{z=1}^{Z}(\alpha_{yz}+h_{sz}^{(d)})} \quad (10) \qquad \hat{\phi}_{z,w}=\frac{\beta_w+n_{zw}}{\sum_{v=1}^{V}(\beta_v+n_{zv})} \quad (11)$$

$$\hat{\psi}_{zw,x}=\frac{\gamma_x+p_{zwx}}{\sum_{t=0}^{1}(\gamma_t+p_{zwt})} \quad (12) \qquad \hat{\sigma}_{zw,v}=\frac{\delta_w+m_{wvz}}{\sum_{v=1}^{V}(\delta_v+m_{wvz})} \quad (13)$$

$$\hat{\pi}_r^{(d)}=\frac{\Omega_r+\kappa_{c_s,r}}{\sum_{r=0}^{1}(\Omega_r+\kappa_{c_s,r})} \quad (14) \qquad \hat{\tau}_y^{(d)}=\frac{\rho_y+b_y^{(d)}}{\sum_{k=1}^{K}(\rho_k+b_k^{(d)})} \quad (15)$$

The target distribution is the posterior distribution of the word-topics, the segment-topics, the topic switching variables of the segments, and the bigram status variables. When we use the Gibbs sampling technique, at each iteration, we sample from the conditional distribution of the word-topics in a document conditioned on the word-topic assignments for all other words except the current word (Line 23 in Algorithm 1). In addition, we also sample the bigram status variable (Line 24). We sample from the conditional distribution of a segment-topic for a segment (Line 14) and also the corresponding switching variable given the segment-topic assignments (Line 14).

At each iteration of the Gibbs sampling procedure, we only sample a subset of the variables which are directly related to the conditional probability. We perform this step repeatedly until we arrive at some approximation. A variable is sampled from the conditional distribution given that the assignments for all other variables are known which is a standard procedure in a Gibbs sampler. As the list of words is being scanned along with the bigram status variables, the sampler keeps track of any new segment being encountered. For each new segment, the sampler decides about the topic assignment of the segment i.e., whether it should assign the current segment to the same topic as the previous segment or a new segment-topic. If the segment has to be assigned to a new segment-topic, the sampler estimates the probability of assigning the segment to the segment-topic. These probabilities are computed from the conditional distribution for a segment given all other topic assignments to every other segment and all words in the segment as depicted in Algorithm 1.

5. EXPERIMENTS AND RESULTS

Evaluation of topic models is a challenging task. Simply showing the highly probable n-gram words obtained from each topic may not be able to portray the underlying strengths or weaknesses of a topic model. Therefore, we evaluate our model on several text mining tasks including the ability to support fine grained topics with n-gram words in the correlation graph, the ability to segment a document into topically coherent sections, document classification, and document likelihood estimation.

In each experiment, we chose several existing closely related comparative methods for comparison purpose. We will describe those comparative methods in the subsections that follow. For our proposed framework, `NTSeg`, the segment granularity is basically a paragraph because topical changes typically occur at paragraph boundary and this strategy is also used in [31]. Note that `NTSeg` can also work at the granularity of a sentence which has also been used in one of our experiments (refer Section 5.2). In our experiments, the number of iterations for the Gibbs sampler is 1000 which is the value of the $MaxIteration$ used in Algorithm 1. We have chosen the following hyperparameter values $\beta = 0.01$, $\gamma = 0.1$, $\delta = 0.1$, $\Omega = 0.1$, and $\rho = 0.1$. Other topic models such as `TNG`, `LDSEG` etc, also assume fixed hyperparameter values. We did not perform any stemming, but removed stopwords[1] from the collection.

5.1 Correlation Graph

`NTSeg` produces two levels of topics, namely, segment-topics and word-topics. A word-topic is comprised of n-grams. We show the correlation graph for the purpose of depicting how our model finds correlations among various

[1]http://jmlr.csail.mit.edu/papers/volume5/lewis04a/a11-smart-stop-list/english.stop

Input : $\gamma, \delta, Z, K, \rho, \Omega, \beta, Corpus, MaxIteration$
Output: N-gram words derived from the word-topic assignments; assignments of segment-topics to segments in documents; an estimate of α

1 Initialize count variables in Equations 3 and 4 to 0;
2 Initialize $b_k^{(d)}$, $\kappa_{c_s,0}^{(d)}$ and $\kappa_{c_s,1}^{(d)}$ for all values of $k \in \{1, \cdots, K\}$ in all documents;
3 Initialize $h_{sz}^{(d)}$ for all values of $z \in \{1, \cdots, Z\}$ in all documents and their segments;
4 Initialize n_{zw} and p_{zwt} for all values of $z \in \{1, \cdots, Z\}$ and for all words in the collection;
5 Initialize m_{wvz} for all values of $z \in \{1, \cdots, Z\}$ and for all bigrams in the collection;
6 Randomly initialize word-topic assignments, segment-topic assignments, segment-topic switch variables, and bigram status variables;
7 **if** *performing parameter value estimation* **then**
8   Initialize α using Equations 5, 6, 7, 8, 9;
9 **end**
10 **for** *iter* $\leftarrow$ *1* **to** $MaxIteration$ **do**
11   **foreach** *document* $d \in [1, M]$ *in the collection* **do**
12   **foreach** *segment* s *in the document* d **do**
13   Exclude segment s and its assigned topic k from the count variables;
14             $(new_k, new_c) \leftarrow$ sample new segment-topic and segment switching variable for segment s using Equation 4;
15   **if** $(new_c == 0)$ **then**
16   Assign new_k as the new segment-topic for segment s;
17   Update variables $b_k^{(d)}$, and $\kappa_{c_s,0}^{(d)}$ using the new segment-topic new_k for segment s;
18   **end**
19   **if** $(new_c = 1)$ **then**
20   Update variable $\kappa_{c_s,1}^{(d)}$;
21   **end**
22   **foreach** *word* i *in segment* s *in the document* d*, according to order* **do**
23   Exclude word i and its assigned word-topic z from the count variables;
24                 $(new_z, new_x) \leftarrow$ sample new word-topic for word i and bigram status variable using Equation 3;
25   **if** $(new_x == 0)$ **then**
26   Assign new_z as the new word-topic;
27   Update n_{zw}, $h_{sz}^{(d)}$, p_{zw0} using word-topic new_z for word i;
28   **end**
29   **if** $(new_x == 1)$ **then**
30   Update $h_{sz}^{(d)}$, p_{zw1}, m_{wvz} for word i;
31   **end**
32   **end**
33   Update the posterior estimate for $\theta_s^{(d)}$ for each segment using Equation 10;
34   **end**
35   Update the posterior estimates for $\pi^{(d)}$ and $\tau^{(d)}$ for each document using Equations 14, and 15;
36   **end**
37   **if** *performing parameter value estimation* **then**
38   Update α using Equations 5, 6, 7, 8, and 9;
39   **end**
40 **end**
41 Update the posterior estimates for ϕ_{zw}, ψ_{zwt} and σ_{zw} using Equations 11,12, and 13,;

Algorithm 1: Inference algorithm for `NTSeg`.

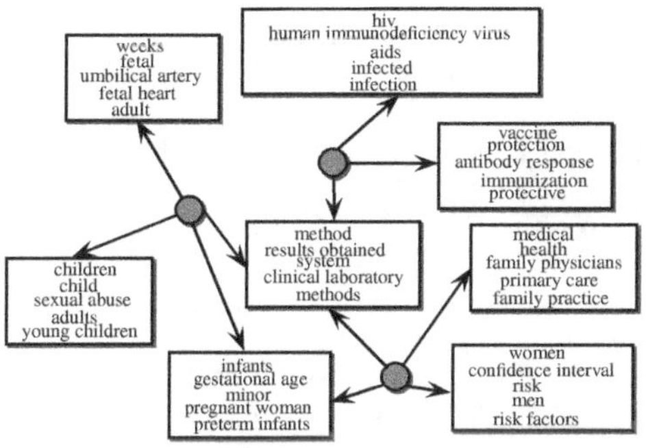

Figure 2: Correlation identified by `NTSeg` between the word-topics and the segment-topics on OHSUMED collection considering $Z = 200$ and $K = 100$. Each circle shows a segment-topic and each box corresponds to a word-topic. We can notice that a segment-topic can capture correlations between several word-topics.

segment-topics and word-topics. Details regarding constructing and interpreting such correlation graphs can be found in [22], and [31].

We have used the OHSUMED[2] collection to show the correlation graph. The collection is composed of 348,566 documents with 154,711 words in the vocabulary without stop-words.

We have experimented by varying both number of the word-topics Z and the number of the segment-topics K. Z was varied from 50 to 200 in steps of 50 whereas K was varied from 50 to 150 in steps of 50. However, we did not observe significant difference in the quality of the results. The resulting correlation graph is shown in Figure 2 which is obtained by setting $Z = 200$ and $K = 100$. Due to space constraint, we only show the graph obtained from our `NTSeg` model. Note that other models such as `PAM`, `LDCC`, `LDSEG`, `GD-LDA` [6] and `CTM`, only form unigrams in a topic leading to ambiguous interpretation. For example, presenting the unigram "confidence" will not be that insightful in a correlation graph. In contrast, presenting the term "confidence interval" is more meaningful as shown in Figure 2.

5.2 Topic Segmentation Experiment

The purpose of this experiment is to show how well `NTSeg` generates segmentation of documents corresponding to coherent topical units. The segmentation information is obtained via the segmentation switch variable $c_s^{(d)}$ which gives the segment topic change-points in the document. In our problem setting we know the segment boundaries in advance such as paragraphs or sentences, but we do not know the word and segment topics. Our purpose is thus to learn the segment and word topics from the document collection. The prediction output of the segment status variable will define the segmentation of a document. To evaluate the performance, we make use of the annotated segmentation information. We use two standard metrics, namely, Pk and WinDiff which are widely used in the topic segmentation literature [32]. As described in [32], Pk is defined as the probability that two segments drawn randomly from a document are incorrectly identified as belonging to the same topic [2]. WinDiff [28] moves a sliding window across the text and counts the number of times the hypothesized and reference segment boundaries are different from within the

[2]http://ir.ohsu.edu/ohsumed/ohsumed.html

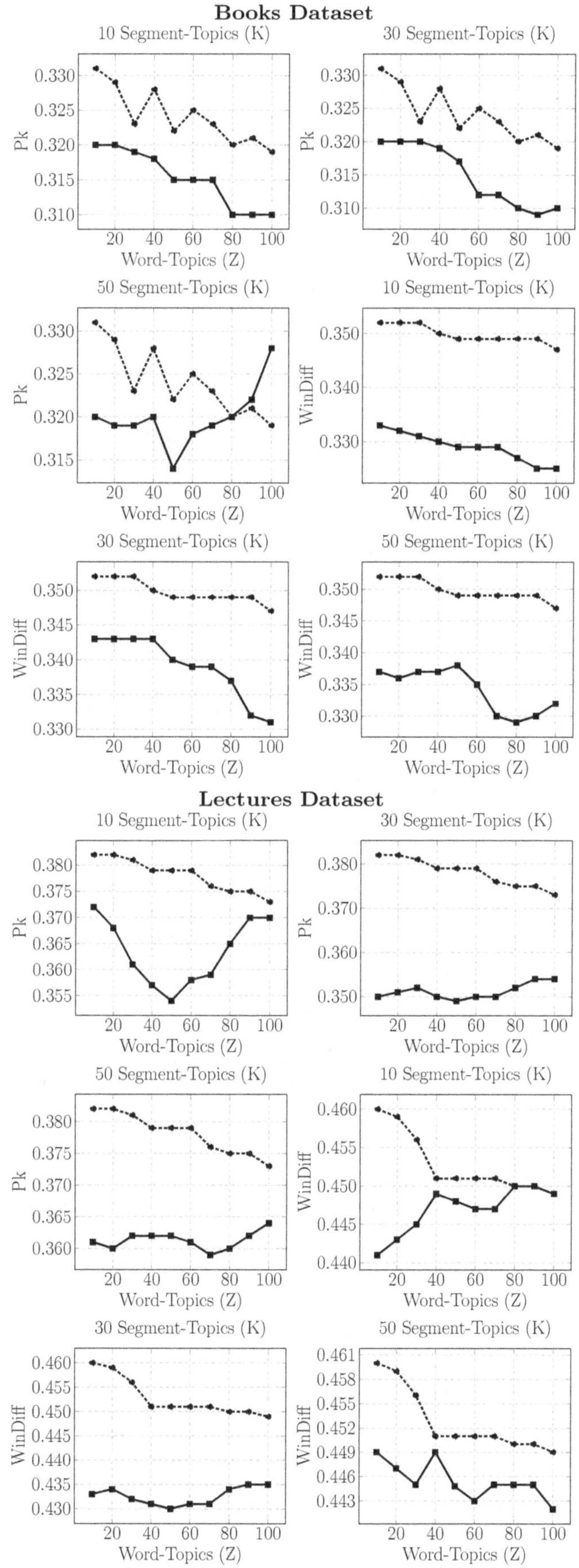

Figure 3: Comparison of `NTSeg` (depicted by —■— marker) against `TopicTiling` (depicted by -◆- marker) on topic segmentation task.

	Precision	Recall	F-Measure
LDSEG	0.580	0.420	0.487
PAM	0.550	0.450	0.495
LDACOL	0.400	0.300	0.343
TNG	0.490	0.420	0.452
PDLDA	0.580	0.500	0.537
NTSeg	**0.640**	**0.520**	**0.574**

Table 1: Document classification results for the Computer Dataset of the 20 Newsgroups corpus.

	Precision	Recall	F-Measure
LDSEG	0.440	0.400	0.419
PAM	0.500	0.330	0.398
LDACOL	0.420	0.370	0.393
TNG	0.560	0.470	0.511
PDLDA	0.580	0.510	0.543
NTSeg	**0.620**	**0.560**	**0.588**

Table 2: Document classification results for the Science Dataset of the 20 Newsgroups corpus.

	Precision	Recall	F-Measure
LDSEG	0.390	0.320	0.352
PAM	0.540	0.490	0.514
LDACOL	0.550	0.410	0.470
TNG	0.550	0.450	0.495
PDLDA	0.590	0.410	0.484
NTSeg	**0.620**	**0.570**	**0.594**

Table 3: Document classification results for the Politics Dataset of the 20 Newsgroups corpus.

	Precision	Recall	F-Measure
LDSEG	0.330	0.320	0.325
PAM	0.368	0.360	0.363
LDACOL	0.200	0.180	0.189
TNG	0.340	0.290	0.313
PDLDA	0.380	0.210	0.271
NTSeg	**0.420**	**0.380**	**0.399**

Table 4: Document classification results for the Sports Dataset of the 20 Newsgroups corpus.

window. The lower the values obtained for these two metrics, the better is the segmentation result.

We use two publicly available datasets that contain segment boundaries corresponding to the topic changes. The first dataset, called Lectures in our experiment, consists of spoken lecture transcripts from an undergraduate physics class and a graduate artificial intelligence class. The transcripts consist of a 90 minute lecture recording and have 500 to 700 sentences with about 9000 words. Note that here the segment granularity is a sentence. More details about this dataset can be obtained from [32]. Our second dataset, called Books in our experiment, is the books[3] dataset in which each document is a chapter extracted from a medical textbook.

We chose a recently proposed topic segmentation method `TopicTiling` [30] which has outperformed many state-of-the-art text segmentation models proposed in the literature and chose the best performing variant of `TopicTiling` from [30]. Note that `TopicTiling` only has the notion of word-topics. For each of the segment and word-topics, we run the Gibbs sampler five times and take the average of the Pk and WinDiff values at the end of the fifth run.

We illustrate the segmentation results in Figure 3. From the results, we note that our model performs extremely well in both datasets compared to the state-of-the-art topic segmentation model. Using a two-tailed significance test, our results are statistically significant with $p < 0.05$ against `TopicTiling`. In the Books dataset, `NTSeg` performs reasonably better, but the improvement obtained is not very high considering both Pk and WinDiff metrics. However, good improvement is obtained in the Lectures dataset using both metrics.

5.3 Document Classification Experiment

We conduct document classification experiment using topic models. In the training phase, a topic model is learned for each class using the set of training documents in that class. In testing, to conduct document classification for a testing document, we compute the likelihood of the testing document against each trained topic model for each class. The testing document is classified to the model that produces the highest likelihood. Note that this procedure is also used in [22].

We measure the classification performance using precision, recall and F-measure. The meaning of precision for a class is the number of true positives divided by the total number of documents predicted to that class. Recall is defined as the number of true positives divided by the total number of elements that actually belong to that class in the gold standard. F-measure is the harmonic mean of precision and recall.

We use the 20 Newsgroups corpus[4] and generated four datasets. The first dataset comprises of documents related to computer technology (the "comp" directory in the dataset). It is composed of several classes such as "graphics", "windows", "hardware", etc. Each of these classes consists of 1000 documents. We split the documents in each of these classes into 75% training and 25% test documents. For each class, we trained and tested the model by varying the number of word-topics from 10 to 100 in steps of 10 and the number of segment-topics from 10 to 50 in steps 20. We compute precision and recall using the test set for each class for each word-topic and segment-topic values and then we compute the average result for one class across all word-topics and segment-topics. Similarly, we follow the same precision and recall computation for all classes. Finally we compute the average over all precision and recall values for all the classes. We then compute F-measure from the obtained precision and recall values. The experimental setup is similar for the other three datasets, namely, "sci" (called Science Dataset), "politics" (called Politics Dataset), and "sports" (called Sports Dataset).

The comparative methods include `LDSEG`, `PAM`, `LDACOL`, `TNG`, and `PDLDA`. All these models are described in Section 2. Note that some of the comparative methods such as `TNG`, `PDLDA`, and `LDACOL` have no notion of segment-topics.

The classification performance results are presented in Tables 1, 2, 3 and 4. We can observe that in all the datasets our model, `NTSeg`, has outperformed all the comparative methods. Compared to all the comparative methods, our results are also statistically significant using the sign test with $p < 0.05$. Gain obtained in the Computer and Science datasets is more when compared to the gain in Sports and

[3]http://groups.csail.mit.edu/rbg/code/bayesseg/

[4]http://qwone.com/~jason/20Newsgroups/

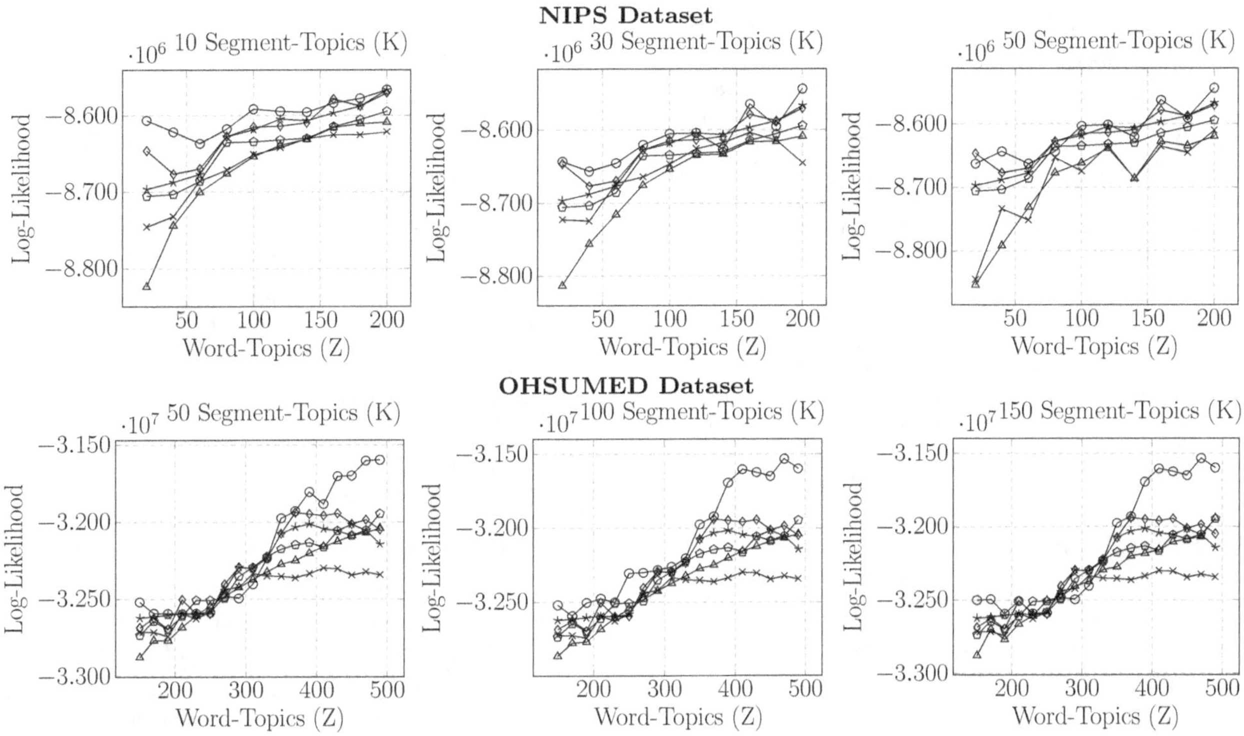

Figure 4: Performance of NTSeg (depicted by —⊖—) in terms of generalizing on the new data. We can see that our model NTSeg generalizes better than other comparative methods which are: LDSEG (depicted by —△—), PAM (depicted by —×—), LDACOL (depicted by —⊖—), TNG (depicted by —★—), and PDLDA (depicted by —◇—).

Politics datasets. PDLDA also proved to be a better model in comparison to the other comparative methods.

5.4 Document Likelihood Experiment

Another evaluation scheme to compare the relative performance of topic models is to study how the models generalize on an unseen data. The entire corpus in this method is first split into training and testing set. The training set generally contains more number of documents as compared to the testing set. A model is first learned on the training data, and the testing set is used to measure the generalization performance of the topic models. In the topic modeling literature, metrics such as perplexity computation or log-likelihood have often been used. For example, PAM uses empirical log-likelihood [10] as an evaluation metric and so does a recently proposed method GD-LDA [6]. Log-likelihood has also been widely used as one of the evaluation metrics, for example in [3]. We chose log-likelihood metric for comparing the topic models. The comparative methods here are LDSEG, PAM, LDACOL, TNG, and PDLDA.

We use the NIPS dataset[5]. The NIPS collection is widely used in the topic modeling literature. Note that the original raw NIPS dataset consists of 17 years of conference papers. But we supplemented this dataset by including some new raw NIPS documents[6] and it has 19 years of papers in total. Our NIPS collection consists of 2741 documents comprising of 453,606,9 non-unique words and 94961 words in the vocabulary. In addition to the NIPS collection we also use the OHSUMED collection.

In order to calculate the likelihood of held-out data, we must integrate out the sampled multinomials and sum over all possible topic assignments which has no closed-form solution. Griffiths et al. [13] have used Gibbs sampling for computing such approximations. First, we randomly split each of the datasets into 80% training and 20% testing. We trained each of the topic models on the training set. We then tested the models on the testing set by running the inference algorithms five times for each word-topic and segment-topic pair. We then took average value for all five runs. We varied the number of segment-topics from 10 to 50 in steps of 20 and the number of word-topics from 20 to 200 in steps of 20 in the NIPS collection. As the OHSUMED collection is larger compared with the NIPS collection, so we varied the number of segment-topics from 50 to 150 in steps of 50 and word-topics from 150 to 490 in steps of 20.

From the results in Figure 4 we can see that in the NIPS collection, NTSeg performs better than the comparative methods especially when the number of segment-topics is 10. However, its performance deteriorates a bit when the number of segment-topics is increased, but still remains competitive with the comparative methods. Moreover, we notice that as the number of word-topics increases, the performance of NTSeg deteriorates to some extent in the NIPS collection. However, in the OHSUMED collection, NTSeg again performs better against the comparative methods when the number of word-topics is increased. We can observe that NTSeg outperforms the comparative methods considerably when the number of segment-topics is 100. The results suggest that NTSeg can perform very well on large document collections as large collections provide richer information about word co-occurrences.

[5]http://www.cs.nyu.edu/~roweis/data.html
[6]http://ai.stanford.edu/~gal/Data/NIPS/

6. CONCLUSIONS AND FUTURE WORK

We have developed a generative topic discovery model, known as NTSeg, which maintains the document's structure such as paragraphs and sentences and also keeps the order of the words in the document intact. NTSeg incorporates the notion of word-topics and segment-topics. We have conducted extensive experiments and shown results using both qualitative analysis where we show the n-gram words in the correlation graph and quantitative performance. Experimental results demonstrate that by relaxing the bag-of-words assumption in each segment improves the performance of the model.

Giving an arbitrary number of word-topics and segment-topics to the model is one issue that we would look into for future work. We would attempt to work towards a model which could automatically find out the desirable number of word-topics and segment-topics in the collection.

7. REFERENCES

[1] B. Adams, D. Phung, and S. Venkatesh. Discovery of latent subcommunities in a blog's readership. *ACM Trans. on the Web*, 4(3):12:1–12:30, 2010.

[2] D. Beeferman, A. Berger, and J. Lafferty. Statistical models for text segmentation. *Machine Learning*, 34:177–210, 1999.

[3] D. Blei and J. Lafferty. Correlated topic models. *Proc. of NIPS*, pages 147–155, 2006.

[4] D. M. Blei and P. J. Moreno. Topic segmentation with an aspect Hidden Markov model. In *Proc. of SIGIR*, pages 343–348, 2001.

[5] D. M. Blei, A. Y. Ng, and M. I. Jordan. Latent Dirichlet Allocation. *JMLR*, 3:993–1022, 2003.

[6] K. L. Caballero, J. Barajas, and R. Akella. The Generalized Dirichlet Distribution in enhanced topic detection. In *Proc. of CIKM*, pages 773–782, 2012.

[7] G. Casella and E. I. George. Explaining the Gibbs sampler. *The American Statistician*, 46(3):pp. 167–174, 1992.

[8] X. Chen and S. Chen. Subsequence-based text segmentation and labeling. In *Proc. of ECTS*, pages 582–587, 2009.

[9] J. Chien and C. Chueh. Topic-based hierarchical segmentation. *IEEE Transactions on Audio, Speech, and Language Processing*, 20(1):55–66, 2012.

[10] P. Diggle and R. Gratton. Monte Carlo methods of inference for implicit statistical models. *Journal of the Royal Statistical Society*, pages 193–227, 1984.

[11] L. Du, W. Buntine, and H. Jin. A segmented topic model based on the two-parameter Poisson-Dirichlet process. *Machine Learning*, 81(1):5–19, 2010.

[12] J. Eisenstein and R. Barzilay. Bayesian unsupervised topic segmentation. In *Proc. of EMNLP*, pages 334–343, 2008.

[13] T. L. Griffiths and M. Steyvers. Finding scientific topics. *National Academy of Sciences of the United States of America*, 101(Suppl 1):5228–5235, 2004.

[14] T. L. Griffiths, M. Steyvers, and J. B. Tenenbaum. Topics in semantic representation. *Psychological Review*, 114(2):211, 2007.

[15] A. Gruber, Y. Weiss, and M. Rosen-Zvi. Hidden topic Markov models. In *Proc. of AI and Statistics*, pages 163–170, 2007.

[16] M. A. Hearst. TextTiling: Segmenting text into multi-paragraph subtopic passages. *Comput. Linguist.*, 23(1):33–64, 1997.

[17] T. Hofmann. Unsupervised learning by Probabilistic Latent Semantic Analysis. *Machine Learning*, 42:177–196, 2001.

[18] S. Jameel and W. Lam. An N-gram topic model for time-stamped documents. In *Proc. of ECIR*, pages 292–304. 2013.

[19] N. Kawamae. Identifying sentiments over n-gram. In *Proc. of WWW*, pages 541–542, 2012.

[20] H. D. Kim, D. H. Park, Y. Lu, and C. Zhai. Enriching text representation with frequent pattern mining for probabilistic topic modeling. *Journal of American Society for Information Science and Technology*, 49(1):1–10, 2012.

[21] W. Kintsch. The role of knowledge in discourse comprehension: A construction-integration model. *Psychological Review*, 95(2):163, 1988.

[22] W. Li and A. McCallum. Pachinko allocation: DAG-structured mixture models of topic correlations. In *Proc. of ICML*, pages 577–584, 2006.

[23] R. V. Lindsey, W. P. Headden, and M. J. Stipicevic. A phrase-discovering topic model using hierarchical Pitman-Yor processes. In *Proc. of EMNLP*, pages 214–222, 2012.

[24] D. Metzler and W. B. Croft. A Markov Random Field model for term dependencies. In *Proc. of SIGIR*, pages 472–479, 2005.

[25] H. Misra, F. Yvon, J. M. Jose, and O. Cappe. Text segmentation via topic modeling: An analytical study. In *Proc. of CIKM*, pages 1553–1556, 2009.

[26] A. Mukherjee and B. Liu. Mining contentions from discussions and debates. In *Proc. of KDD*, pages 841–849, 2012.

[27] P. V. Mulbregt, I. Carp, L. Gillick, S. Lowe, and J. Yamron. Text segmentation and topic tracking on broadcast news via a hidden markov model approach. In *Proc. of ICSLP*, pages 2519–2522, 1998.

[28] L. Pevzner and M. A. Hearst. A critique and improvement of an evaluation metric for text segmentation. *Comput. Linguist.*, 28(1):19–36, 2002.

[29] M. Riedl and C. Biemann. How text segmentation algorithms gain from topic models. In *Proc. of NAACL HLT*, pages 553–557, 2012.

[30] M. Riedl and C. Biemann. TopicTiling: A text segmentation algorithm based on LDA. In *Proc. of ACL 2012 Student Research Workshop*, pages 37–42, 2012.

[31] M. Shafiei and E. Milios. Latent Dirichlet Co-Clustering. In *Proc. of ICDM*, pages 542 –551, 2006.

[32] M. Shafiei and E. Milios. A statistical model for topic segmentation and clustering. In *Proc. of Advances in Artificial Intelligence*, pages 283–295, 2008.

[33] A. Tagarelli and G. Karypis. A segment-based approach to clustering multi-topic documents. In *Proc. of SDM*, pages 1–33, 2008.

[34] Y. Teh, M. Jordan, M. Beal, and D. Blei. Hierarchical Dirichlet processes. *JASA*, 101(476):1566–1581, 2006.

[35] H. M. Wallach. Topic modeling: Beyond bag-of-words. In *Proc. of ICML*, pages 977–984, 2006.

[36] H. Wang and B. Lang. Online Ngram-enhanced topic model for academic retrieval. In *Proc. of ICDIM*, pages 137–142, 2011.

[37] L. Wang, B. Wei, and J. Yuan. Topic discovery based on LDACOL model and topic significance re-ranking. *Journal of Computers*, 6(8):1639–1647, 2011.

[38] X. Wang and A. McCallum. A note on Topical N-grams. Technical report, DTIC Document, 2005.

[39] X. Wang, A. McCallum, and X. Wei. Topical N-Grams: Phrase and topic discovery, with an application to Information Retrieval. In *Proc. of ICDM*, pages 697 –702, 2007.

[40] Y. Wang, E. Agichtein, and M. Benzi. TM-LDA: Efficient online modeling of latent topic transitions in social media. In *Proc. of KDD*, pages 123–131, 2012.

[41] Q. Wu, C. Zhang, and X. An. Topic segmentation model based on ATNLDA and co-occurrence theory and its application in stem cell field. *Journal of Information Science*, pages 1–14, 2012.

[42] Z. Yan and F. Li. News thread extraction based on Topical N-gram model with a background distribution. In *Proc. of ICONIP*, pages 416–424, 2011.

Semantic Hashing using Tags and Topic Modeling

Qifan Wang
Computer Science Department
Purdue University
West Lafayette, IN 47907, US
wang868@purdue.edu

Dan Zhang
Facebook Incorporation
Menlo Park, CA 94025, US
danzhang@fb.com

Luo Si
Computer Science Department
Purdue University
West Lafayette, IN 47907, US
lsi@purdue.edu

ABSTRACT

It is an important research problem to design efficient and effective solutions for large scale similarity search. One popular strategy is to represent data examples as compact binary codes through semantic hashing, which has produced promising results with fast search speed and low storage cost. Many existing semantic hashing methods generate binary codes for documents by modeling document relationships based on similarity in a keyword feature space. Two major limitations in existing methods are: (1) Tag information is often associated with documents in many real world applications, but has not been fully exploited yet; (2) The similarity in keyword feature space does not fully reflect semantic relationships that go beyond keyword matching.

This paper proposes a novel hashing approach, Semantic Hashing using Tags and Topic Modeling (SHTTM), to incorporate both the tag information and the similarity information from probabilistic topic modeling. In particular, a unified framework is designed for ensuring hashing codes to be consistent with tag information by a formal latent factor model and preserving the document topic/semantic similarity that goes beyond keyword matching. An iterative coordinate descent procedure is proposed for learning the optimal hashing codes. An extensive set of empirical studies on four different datasets has been conducted to demonstrate the advantages of the proposed SHTTM approach against several other state-of-the-art semantic hashing techniques. Furthermore, experimental results indicate that the modeling of tag information and utilizing topic modeling are beneficial for improving the effectiveness of hashing separately, while the combination of these two techniques in the unified framework obtains even better results.

Categories and Subject Descriptors

H.3.1 [**Information Storage and Retrieval**]: Content Analysis and Indexing; H.3.3 [**Information Storage and Retrieval**]: Information Search and Retrieval; I.2.6 [**Artificial Intelligence**]: Learning

General Terms

Algorithms, Performance, Experimentation

Keywords

Hashing, Tags, Topic Modeling

1. INTRODUCTION

Similarity search identifies similar information objects given a query object, which has many information retrieval applications such as similar document detection, content-based image retrieval and collaborative filtering. Due to the explosive growth of the internet, a huge amount of data such as texts, images and videos has been generated, which indicates that nearest neighbor methods for similarity search are becoming more reliable. Therefore, it is important to design effective and efficient nearest neighbor methods for similarity search with large scale data.

Two major challenges have to be addressed for using similarity search in large scale datasets such as storing the data efficiently and retrieving the large scale data in an effective and efficient manner. Traditional text similarity search methods in the original keyword vector space are difficult to be used for large datasets, since these methods utilize the content vectors of the documents in a high-dimensional space and are associated with high cost of float/integer computation.

Semantic hashing (e.g., [9, 22, 34]) has been proposed as a promising technique for addressing these two challenges, which designs compact binary code in a low-dimensional space for each document so that similar documents are mapped to similar binary codes. Query documents can also be efficiently transformed into hashing codes so that similarity search can be conducted. The retrieval process of similarity search can be simply conducted by calculating the Hamming distances between the hashing codes of available documents and a query and selecting documents within small Hamming distance. Therefore, this method addresses the two major challenges of large scale similarity search in the following ways: (1) The encoded data is highly compressed within a low-dimensional binary space, and thus can often be dealt with in main memory and stored efficiently; (2) The retrieval process is very efficient, since the distance between two codes is simply the number of bits that they differ.

Existing semantic hashing approaches generate promising results and are successful in addressing the two challenges of storage and retrieval efficiency. However, two major issues are not addressed in the existing methods: (1) Tag information is not fully utilized in previous methods. Most existing methods only deal with the contents of documents without utilizing the information contained in tags. Actually, in many real-world applications, documents are often associated with multiple tags, which provide useful knowledge in learning effective hashing codes. For instance, in some big corporations, their employees often assign tags to some webpages in the intranet, such that they can find these webpages again more easily through these tags. Another example is microblog, usually each tweet is associated with multiple tags such as 'stock', 'business', 'sports', etc.; (2) Document similarity in the original keyword feature space is used as guidance for generating hashing codes in previous methods, which may not fully reflect the semantic relationship. For example, two documents in the same topic may have low document content similarity in keyword space due to the vocabulary gap, although their semantic similarity can be high.

Based on the above observations, this paper proposes a novel hashing approach, Semantic Hashing using Tags and Topic Modeling (SHTTM). The SHTTM approach integrates available tag information and document similarity in semantic topics for generating effective hashing codes. There are three main challenges for designing this method: (1) How to incorporate the tag information? (2) How to preserve the similarity between documents based on semantic topics? (3) How to obtain the hashing code for a query document as no tag information is available for the query document?

A unified framework is proposed to address the above challenges, which ensures the consistency of hashing codes with tag information by a latent factor model and preserves document semantic similarity based on topic modeling. An iterative optimization procedure is proposed for learning the optimal hashing codes. An extensive set of experiments on four real world datasets has been conducted to demonstrate the advantages of the proposed method over several state-of-the-art methods. More specifically, a set of experiments clearly demonstrates the benefits of utilizing tag information and topic modeling separately, while the combination of these two methods in the unified framework generates the best results. To our best knowledge, this is the first piece of research work on semantic hashing that integrates both tag information and semantic topic modeling, which generates more effective hashing codes than several other state-of-the-art methods.

2. RELATED WORK

Efficiency is a crucial issue for large scale information retrieval applications with a huge amount of text documents. When there is only a low-dimensional feature space, similarity search can be carried out by some space partitioning index structures, such as TF-IDF methods [23, 24], KD-tree, or data partitioning index structures, like R-tree [5]. Several types of structures and operations of inverted indexing are also proposed [6, 26, 40] for traditional ad-hoc text search with relatively short user queries. However, traditional similarity search may fail to work efficiently within a high-dimensional vector space [33], which is often the case for many real world information retrieval applications.

Semantic hashing [22] is proposed to address the similarity search problem within a high-dimensional feature space. In particular, semantic hashing methods try to represent each document by using a small fixed number of binary bits so that the queries can be answered in a short time [27]. The hashing based fast similarity search can be viewed as a strategy to transform documents from a high-dimensional space into a low-dimensional binary space, and at the same time preserve the semantic similarity between documents as much as possible. Hashing methods generate binary codes for efficient search, which is different from traditional dimensionality reduction methods such as Principal Component Analysis (PCA) and Latent Semantic Indexing (LSI) [8, 12].

Locality-Sensitive Hashing (LSH) [2, 7] is one of the most popularly used hashing methods. It simply utilizes random linear projections to map documents from a high-dimensional Euclidean space to a low-dimensional one. It has already been shown that the Hamming distance between different documents will asymptotically approach their Euclidean distance in the original feature space with the increase of the hashing bits. LSH has been extended to Kernelized Locality-Sensitive Hashing (KLSH) [16] by exploiting kernel similarity for better retrieval efficacy. Recently, the work in [35] further extends the KLSH to the scheme of Boosting Multi-Kernel Locality-Sensitive Hashing (BMKLSH) that improves the retrieval performance of KLSH by making use of multiple kernels.

Several machine learning approaches have been proposed to solve the hashing problem. For example, the PCA Hashing [19] method projects each example to the top principal components of the training set, and then binarizes the coefficients by setting a bit to 1 when its value is larger than the median value seen for the training set, and -1 otherwise. The work in [22] uses stacked Restricted Boltzman Machine (RBM) [10, 11] to generate compact binary hashing codes, which can be viewed as binarized LSI. Recently, Spectral Hashing (SH) [34] is proposed to learn compact binary codes that preserve the similarity between documents by forcing the balanced and uncorrelated constraints into the learned codes, which be viewed as an extension of spectral clustering [37]. A graph-based hashing method has been proposed in work [21] to automatically discover the neighborhood structure inherent in the data to learn appropriate compact codes. More recently, the work [38] proposes a Composite Hashing with Multiple Information Sources (CHMIS) method to integrate information from different sources. In another recent work [15], an isotropic hashing (IsoHash) method is proposed to learn projection functions of individual hashing codes with equal variances.

In the following two sections, we mainly discuss two state-of-the-art hashing methods that are most related to the proposed research as Self-Taught Hashing [39] and Semi-Supervised Hashing [31].

2.1 Self-Taught Hashing(STH)

Self Taught Hashing (STH) [39] generally provides more effective hashing solutions than LSH [7] and SH [34]. STH combines an unsupervised learning step with a supervised learning step to learn hashing codes.

In the unsupervised learning step, STH constructs a similarity graph using a fix number of nearest neighbors for the given dataset, and then embeds all the documents into a k dimensional space through spectral analysis, and finally uses simple thresholding to obtain the binary hashing code for each document. This step can be formulated as follows:

$$\min \sum_{i,j} \boldsymbol{S}_{ij} ||y_i - y_j||^2$$
$$s.t. \quad y_i \in \{-1,1\}^k, \sum_i y_i = 0, \frac{1}{n} \sum_i y_i y_i^T = \boldsymbol{I} \tag{1}$$

$\boldsymbol{S}_{ij}$ is the pairwise similarity between document i and document j, y_i is the hashing code for document i, k is the number of hashing bits. The objective function incurs a heavy penalty if two similar documents are mapped far away, which preserves the similarity between documents. The constraint $\sum_i y_i = 0$ requires each bit to be balanced and $\frac{1}{n}\sum_i y_i y_i^T = \boldsymbol{I}$ forces the hashing bits to be uncorrelated with each other.

In the supervised learning step, a set of k SVM classifiers are trained based on existing documents and their binary hashing codes learned from the previous step. Then, the k classifiers can be used to generate the hashing codes for the query documents as a classification problem. STH does not assume that data are uniformly distributed in a hyper-rectangle as requested by SH, which is often too restrictive for real world applications. STH often generates more effective hashing codes than SH.

However, there are two main limitations for STH. Firstly, STH does not utilize tag information, which is often available with documents in many real world applications. Secondly, the similarity matrix in STH is calculated in the original feature (keyword vector) space, which may not reflect the semantic similarity beyond simple keyword matching. Topic modeling (e.g., [4]) has been shown as an effective approach for capturing semantic meanings in text documents. In the proposed new research, we address both of the two problems of STH through integrating the tag information and topic modeling into one unified framework so that the semantic similarity between documents can be better preserved in the learned hashing codes.

2.2 Semi-Supervised Hashing(SSH)

The work in [31] proposes a Semi-Supervised Hashing (SSH) approach for incorporating the pairwise relationships between documents into the semantic hashing problem. More precisely, these pairwise similarity constraints are also called Must-Link and Cannot-Link, which could be partially generated from tags. For example, a Must-Link is created when two documents share a common tag and a Cannot-Link is created when two documents share no tag. Their basic motivation is that the hashing codes of the document pairs with Must-Link should be as close as possible, while the hashing codes of document pairs with Cannot-Link should be as different as possible. This motivation is then incorporated into the objective function for learning the hashing codes. A sequential projection method is utilized to solve the resulting optimization problem.

The SSH has shown promising results for improving hashing effectiveness by leveraging the pairwise information, but there are several limitations for SSH. Firstly, the SSH method only utilizes the pairwise similarity constraints as the summary of tag information, which is suboptimal with respect to the complete information in the tags. Secondly, the pairwise link information may not be accurately generated when tags are missing, incomplete or mismatched, which is often the case for many real world applications. Furthermore, SSH also directly works in the original keyword feature space for modeling content similarity of documents. These problems may potentially limit the performance of the hashing methods based on pairwise constraints. Different from SSH, the proposed method utilizes the complete tag information as well as semantic information from topic modeling for building more effective hashing codes.

3. ALGORITHM DESCRIPTION

3.1 Problem Setting

We first introduce the problem of SHTTM. Assume there are total n training documents in the dataset, denoted as: $\boldsymbol{X} = \{x_1, x_2, \ldots, x_n\} \in \boldsymbol{R}^{m \times n}$, where m is the dimensionality of the content feature. Denote their tags as: $\boldsymbol{T} = \{t_1, t_2, \ldots, t_n\} \in \{0,1\}^{l \times n}$, where l is the total number of possible tags associated with each document. A tag with label 1 means a document is associated with a certain tag/category, while a tag with label 0 means a missing tag or the document is not associated with that tag/category. The main purpose of SHTTM is to obtain optimal binary hashing codes $\boldsymbol{Y} = \{y_1, y_2, \ldots, y_n\} \in \{-1,1\}^{k \times n}$ for the training documents $\boldsymbol{X}$, and a hashing function $f : \boldsymbol{R}^m \to \{-1,1\}^k$, which maps each document to its hashing code with k bits (i.e, $y_j = f(x_j)$).

3.2 Approach Overview

The proposed SHTTM approach is a general learning framework that consists of two stages. In the first stage, the hashing codes are learned in a unified framework by simultaneously ensuring hashing codes to be consistent with tag information by a formal latent factor model and preserving the document topic/semantic similarity. In particular, the objective function of SHTTM is composed of two components: (1) Tag consistency component, which ensures that the hashing codes are consistent with tag information; (2) Similarity preservation component, which aims at preserving the topic/semantic similarity in the learned hashing codes. An iterative algorithm is then derived based on the objective function using a coordinate descent optimization procedure. In the second stage, the hashing function is learned with respect to the hashing codes for training documents.

The rest of this section first presents the two stages of the proposed SHTTM approach respectively, and then addresses the corresponding optimization problem. Finally, this section discusses connections and distinctions of the proposed approach with some related research work.

3.3 Tag Consistency

In many real world applications, documents are associated with tag information, which can provide useful knowledge in learning effective hashing codes. There are two main challenges for utilizing tags: (1) We have no knowledge about how the tags are related to the hashing codes. Therefore, we need to explore the correlation between them in order to bridge tags with hashing codes; (2) Tags may be missing, we need to deal with the situation of incomplete tags.

The first problem of exploring the correlation between tags and hashing codes can be addressed by matrix factorization with a latent factor model. A latent variable u_i for each tag t_i is first introduced, where u_i is a $k \times 1$ vector indicating the correlation between tags and hashing codes. Then a tag consistency component can be formulated as follows:

$$\sum_{i=1}^{l}\sum_{j=1}^{n} ||\boldsymbol{T}_{ij} - u_i^T y_j||^2 + \alpha \sum_{i=1}^{l} ||u_i||^2 \quad (2)$$

where $\boldsymbol{T}_{ij}$ is the binary label of the *i-th* tag on the *j-th* document. $u_i^T y_j$ can be viewed as a weighted sum that indicates how the *i-th* tag is related to the *j-th* document, and this weighted sum should be consistent with the observed label $\boldsymbol{T}_{ij}$ as much as possible. The second regularization component, $\sum_{i=1}^{l} ||u_i||^2$, is introduced to avoid the overfitting issue (e.g., [28, 29]). α is a meta parameter that explores the trade-off between the tag consistence and regularization.

The second problem of dealing with missing tags can be addressed by introducing a confidence matrix $\boldsymbol{C} \in \boldsymbol{R}^{l \times k}$. If the value of $\boldsymbol{C}_{ij}$ is large, we trust the tag information $\boldsymbol{T}_{ij}$ more. As discussed before, $\boldsymbol{T}_{ij} = 0$ can be interpreted in two ways: tag i on the *j-th* document is either missing or not related. We will use a similar strategy as in [14] for a different application to set $\boldsymbol{C}_{ij}$ a higher value when $\boldsymbol{T}_{ij} = 1$ than $\boldsymbol{T}_{ij} = 0$ as follows,

$$\boldsymbol{C}_{ij} = \begin{cases} a, \; if \; \boldsymbol{T}_{ij} = 1 \\ b, \; if \; \boldsymbol{T}_{ij} = 0 \end{cases} \quad (3)$$

where a and b are parameters satisfying $a > b > 0$[1]. Then the whole component of tag consistency becomes:

$$\sum_{i=1}^{l}\sum_{j=1}^{n} \boldsymbol{C}_{ij}||\boldsymbol{T}_{ij} - u_i^T y_j||^2 + \alpha \sum_{i=1}^{l} ||u_i||^2 \quad (4)$$

The above equation can be rewritten in a compact matrix form as:

$$||\boldsymbol{C}^{\frac{1}{2}} \cdot (\boldsymbol{T} - \boldsymbol{U}^T\boldsymbol{Y})||_F^2 + \alpha||\boldsymbol{U}||^2 \quad (5)$$

where $\boldsymbol{C}^{\frac{1}{2}}$ is the element-wise square root matrix of $\boldsymbol{C}$, and $\cdot$ is the element-wise matrix multiplication. $|| ||_F$ is the matrix Frobenius norm. By minimizing this component, the consistency between tags and the learned hashing codes can be ensured.

3.4 Topic Modeling and Similarity Preservation

One of the key problems in semantic hashing methods is similarity preserving, which indicates that semantically similar documents should be mapped to similar hashing codes within a short Hamming distance. A popular criterion of similarity preservation is to minimize the objective value in Eqn.1, where $\boldsymbol{S}$ is the document similarity matrix. This criterion incurs a heavy penalty if two similar documents are mapped far away in the dataset.

There are many different ways of defining the similarity matrix. In SH [34], the authors used the global similarity structure of all document pairs, while in STH [39] and CHMIS [38], the local similarity structure,*i.e.*, k nearest neighborhood, is used. However, all these methods compute the similarity matrix $\boldsymbol{S}$ within the original keyword feature space and thus may not reflect the document semantic similarity that goes beyond simple keyword matching.

To address the limitation of calculating semantic similarity in existing approaches, features from topic modeling are used to measure the semantic similarity between documents instead of features from the original keyword space. Topic modeling algorithms (e.g., [3, 36]) are used to discover a set of "topics" from a large collection of documents and provide an interpretable low-dimensional representation of the documents associated with the topics. Topic modeling has been widely used in many information retrieval applications such as document clustering and classification. Here we exploit the Latent Dirichlet Allocation (LDA) [4] approach of topic modeling to extract k latent topics from the document corpus. Each document x_j corresponds to a distribution θ_j over the topics where two semantically similar documents have similar topic distributions. In this way, document semantic similarity is preserved in the extracted topic distributions $\boldsymbol{\theta}$. Since we require the hashing codes to reflect the topic distributions, a document similarity preservation component can be naturally defined as follows:

$$\sum_{j=1}^{n} ||y_j - \theta_j||^2 = ||\boldsymbol{Y} - \boldsymbol{\theta}||^2 \quad (6)$$

By minimizing this component, the similarity between different documents is preserved in the learned hashing codes.

3.5 Overall Objective and Optimization Algorithm

The entire objective function of the proposed SHTTM approach integrates two components such as the tag consistency component in Eqn.5 and the semantic similarity preservation component given in Eqn.6 as follows:

$$\begin{aligned} \min_{\boldsymbol{Y},\boldsymbol{U}} \; & ||\boldsymbol{C}^{\frac{1}{2}} \cdot (\boldsymbol{T} - \boldsymbol{U}^T\boldsymbol{Y})||_F^2 + \alpha||\boldsymbol{U}||^2 + \gamma||\boldsymbol{Y} - \boldsymbol{\theta}||^2 \\ s.t. \quad & \boldsymbol{Y} \in \{-1,1\}^{k \times n}, \;\; \boldsymbol{Y}\mathbf{1} = 0 \end{aligned} \quad (7)$$

where α and γ are trade-off meta parameters to balance the weight between the components. The constraint $\boldsymbol{Y}\mathbf{1} = 0$ requires each bit to appear 50% of the time (with equal probability as positive or negative). Note that one advantage of our method is that we do not need the bits-uncorrelated constraint $\boldsymbol{Y}\boldsymbol{Y}^T = \boldsymbol{I}$ while many previous methods do. This is because we assign each hashing bit a semantic meaning (a latent topic), which is learned from topic modeling and latent topics can be assumed to be highly uncorrelated. Therefore, by imposing the semantic similarity term between $\boldsymbol{Y}$ and $\boldsymbol{\theta}$, the uncorrelated property among $\boldsymbol{Y}$ is preserved.

Directly minimizing the objective function in Eqn.7 is intractable because of the discrete constraints. Therefore, we propose to relax this constraint and drop the constraint $\boldsymbol{Y}\mathbf{1} = 0$ first (we will discuss this constraint later). However, even after the relaxation, the objective function is still non-convex with respect to $\boldsymbol{Y}$ and $\boldsymbol{U}$ jointly, which makes it difficult to optimize. Fortunately, this relaxed problem is convex with respect to either one of the two sets of parameters when the other one is fixed, and therefore can be

[1]In our experiments, we set the confidence parameters a=1 and b=0.01 consistently throughout all experiments.

Training procedure:
Input:
1. A set of n training documents, $\boldsymbol{X} = \{x_1, x_2, \dots, x_n\}$ associated with tags $\boldsymbol{T} = \{t_1, t_2, \dots, t_n\}$.
2. Meta parameters: Tag consistency parameter α, Similarity preservation parameter γ and Hashing function parameter λ.
Output:
Hashing codes $\boldsymbol{Y}$ for the training documents, Hashing function matrix $\boldsymbol{W}$, Tag-Hashing code correlation matrix $\boldsymbol{U}$ and Median vector $\boldsymbol{m}$.
Initialization:
1. Topic modeling: learning topic distribution of training documents $\boldsymbol{\theta} = LDA(\boldsymbol{X})$.
2. Construct confidence matrix $\boldsymbol{C}$ by Eqn.3.
3. Initialize $\boldsymbol{Y} = \boldsymbol{\theta}$.
4. Coordinate Descent Optimization: obtain the optimal $\boldsymbol{Y}$ and $\boldsymbol{U}$ by iteratively solving Eqn.9 and Eqn.11 and updating $\boldsymbol{U}$ and $\boldsymbol{Y}$ respectively.
5. Optimizing Eqn.13 to obtain the hashing function matrix $\boldsymbol{W}$.
6. Get the median vector by $\boldsymbol{m} = median(\boldsymbol{Y})$.
7. Generating the hashing codes by thresholding $\boldsymbol{Y}$ to the median vector $\boldsymbol{m}$.
Predicting procedure:
Input:
A query document q, Hashing function matrix $\boldsymbol{W}$ and Median vector $\boldsymbol{m}$.
Output:
The binary hashing code y_q for q.
1. Calculate the regression output by hashing function $f(q) = \boldsymbol{W}q$.
2. Obtain the hashing code y_q by thresholding $f(q)$ to the median vector $\boldsymbol{m}$.

Table 1: The algorithm description of the complete SHTTM approach.

solved by coordinate descent optimization with guaranteed convergence similar to [32]. In particular, after initializing $\boldsymbol{Y}$, the optimization problem can be solved by doing the following two steps iteratively, until convergence.

Step 1: Fix $\boldsymbol{Y}$, optimize:

$$\min_{\boldsymbol{U}} \|\boldsymbol{C}^{\frac{1}{2}} \cdot (\boldsymbol{T} - \boldsymbol{U}^T\boldsymbol{Y})\|_F^2 + \alpha\|\boldsymbol{U}\|^2 \tag{8}$$

By taking the derivative of Eqn.8 with respect to u_i and setting it to 0, we can obtain the close form solution of this optimization below:

$$u_i = (\boldsymbol{Y}\boldsymbol{C}_i\boldsymbol{Y}^T + \alpha\boldsymbol{I})^{-1}\boldsymbol{Y}\boldsymbol{C}_i\boldsymbol{T}_i \tag{9}$$

where $\boldsymbol{C}_i$ is a $n \times n$ diagonal matrix with $\boldsymbol{C}_{ij}, j = 1, 2, \dots, n$ as its diagonal elements and $\boldsymbol{T}_i = (\boldsymbol{T}_{ij}), j = 1, 2, \dots, n$ is a $n \times 1$ label vector of i-th tag.

Step 2: Fix $\boldsymbol{U}$, optimize:

$$\min_{\boldsymbol{Y}} \|\boldsymbol{C}^{\frac{1}{2}} \cdot (\boldsymbol{T} - \boldsymbol{U}^T\boldsymbol{Y})\|_F^2 + \gamma\|\boldsymbol{Y} - \boldsymbol{\theta}\|^2 \tag{10}$$

By taking the derivative of Eqn.10 with respect to y_j and setting it to 0, we can obtain the optimal y_j:

$$y_j = (\boldsymbol{U}\boldsymbol{C}_j\boldsymbol{U}^T + \gamma\boldsymbol{I})^{-1}(\boldsymbol{U}\boldsymbol{C}_j\boldsymbol{T}_j + \gamma\boldsymbol{\theta}_j) \tag{11}$$

where $\boldsymbol{C}_j$ is a $l \times l$ diagonal matrix with $\boldsymbol{C}_{ij}, i = 1, 2, \dots, l$ as its diagonal elements and $\boldsymbol{T}_j = (\boldsymbol{T}_{ij}), i = 1, 2, \dots, l$ is a $l \times 1$ label vector of the j-th document. By solving Eqns.8 and 10 iteratively, optimal $\boldsymbol{Y}$ and $\boldsymbol{U}$ can be obtained.

3.6 Hashing Function

In the previous section, the optimal hashing codes $\boldsymbol{Y}$ are obtained after relaxing the binary constraint and the bit balance constraint $\boldsymbol{Y}\boldsymbol{1} = 0$. In this section, we will discuss how to obtain the hashing function that maps the data into binary hashing codes and how to binarize the optimal $\boldsymbol{Y}$ in order to satisfy the constraints.

In this paper, we utilize a linear hashing function to generate binary hashing code, which is consistent with previous hashing methods (e.g., [30, 31, 38]) as:

$$y_j = f(x_j) = \boldsymbol{W}x_j \tag{12}$$

where $\boldsymbol{W}$ is a $k \times m$ parameter matrix representing the hashing function. Then the optimal hashing function can be obtained by minimizing the following objective:

$$\begin{aligned} \boldsymbol{W}^* &= \arg\min_{\boldsymbol{W}} \sum_{j=1}^{n} \|y_j - \boldsymbol{W}x_j\|^2 + \lambda\|\boldsymbol{W}\|_F^2 \\ \Rightarrow \boldsymbol{W}^* &= \boldsymbol{Y}^T\boldsymbol{X}(\boldsymbol{X}^T\boldsymbol{X} + \lambda\boldsymbol{I})^{-1} \end{aligned} \tag{13}$$

Here λ is a weight parameter for the regularization term to avoid overfitting.

The binary hashing codes for the training set can be obtained by thresholding $\boldsymbol{Y}$. Then, a natural question is how to pick these thresholds? In [19] and [37], the authors pointed out that a good semantic hashing should also maximize the entropy to ensure efficiency. Following the maximum entropy principle, a binary bit that gives balanced partitioning of the whole dataset always provides maximum information. Therefore, we set the threshold for binarizing the p-th bit to be the median of y^p. We denote the median of all bits by vector $\boldsymbol{m}$. Thus, if the p-th bit of document y_j is larger than $\boldsymbol{m}_p$, then y_j^p is set to +1, otherwise y_j^p is set to -1. In this way, the binary code achieves the best balance and the constraint $\boldsymbol{Y}\boldsymbol{1} = 0$ in Eqn.7 can also be satisfied. The hashing code of a query document q can be obtained by first computing the hashing function $f(q) = \boldsymbol{W}q$. Then, the

	ReutersV1					*Reuters*				
Methods	8 bits	16 bits	32 bits	64 bits	128 bits	8 bits	16 bits	32 bits	64 bits	128 bits
SHTTM	**0.559**	0.636	**0.712**	**0.781**	**0.815**	0.716	**0.741**	**0.755**	**0.758**	**0.753**
SSH [31]	0.531	**0.641**	0.664	0.722	0.727	**0.718**	0.722	0.724	0.731	0.739
STH [39]	0.507	0.568	0.643	0.646	0.694	0.703	0.715	0.731	0.740	0.734
SH [34]	0.514	0.556	0.617	0.631	0.658	0.641	0.694	0.711	0.703	0.716
PCAH [19]	0.431	0.557	0.601	0.638	0.641	0.652	0.687	0.693	0.646	0.631
LSH [7]	0.289	0.382	0.444	0.557	0.652	0.569	0.592	0.624	0.653	0.678
	20Newsgroups					*WebKB*				
Methods	8 bits	16 bits	32 bits	64 bits	128 bits	8 bits	16 bits	32 bits	64 bits	128 bits
SHTTM	**0.576**	**0.644**	**0.648**	**0.684**	**0.697**	**0.546**	**0.558**	**0.581**	**0.611**	**0.625**
SSH [31]	0.557	0.576	0.624	0.649	0.665	0.514	0.536	0.543	0.562	0.583
STH [39]	0.526	0.585	0.615	0.623	0.651	0.421	0.449	0.495	0.532	0.538
SH [34]	0.510	0.579	0.574	0.607	0.622	0.504	0.513	0.536	0.541	0.547
PCAH [19]	0.471	0.513	0.541	0.568	0.616	0.471	0.524	0.531	0.568	0.570
LSH [7]	0.389	0.431	0.474	0.557	0.646	0.339	0.377	0.389	0.387	0.401

Table 2: Precision of the top 100 retrieved documents on four datasets with different hashing bits.

corresponding binary hashing code can be obtained through thresholding the hashing function output, *i.e.*, set the *j-th* code for q to be +1, if $f(q)_j > \boldsymbol{m}_j$, and -1 otherwise.

The whole training procedure and predicting procedure of the proposed method is described in Table 1. For hashing methods, the training process is always conducted off-line. Therefore, our focus of efficiency is on the predicting process. This process of generating hashing code for a query for prediction only involves some dot products and comparisons between two binary vectors, which can be done in $O(m * k + k)$ time.

3.7 Discussion

The formulation of the proposed SHTTM approach is related to the traditional collaborative filtering methods (e.g., [14, 25, 13]) by treating each document as an item and the label of each tag as a rating from a user (i.e., tag) on this item (i.e., document). From this perspective, the proposed method is related to Collaborative Topic Modeling (CTM) [29], in which both the rating scores and the content of items are incorporated into one topic modeling framework. However, several major differences exist between the proposed work and CTM: (1). CTM is designed for collaborative filtering, while the proposed method investigates how tags and topic modeling can be integrated to improve the performance of hashing; (2). in the proposed research, one focus is on out-of-sample query examples, which do not exist in the training dataset. Therefore, the proposed research designs hashing function to convert query examples to their corresponding hashing codes, while this is not considered in CTM.

As for the speed issue, the major off-line computational costs of the proposed method come from LDA and the latent factor model parts. For LDA, we can use parallel LDA (e.g., [1]) to accelerate the computational speed. For optimizing the unified framework, it normally converges within 20 iterations and only some simple updates are necessary in each iteration. For the more important issue of calculating hashing codes of the query examples for similarity search, it is very efficient since only some linear transformations are necessary.

4. EXPERIMENTS

This section presents an extensive set of experiments to demonstrate the advantages of the proposed research.

4.1 Datasets

A set of datasets are utilized in evaluation as follows:

1. *ReutersV1* (Reuters-Volume I): This dataset contains over 800,000 manually categorized newswire stories [18]. There are in total 126 tags associated with this dataset. A subset of 365001 documents of ReutersV1 is used in our experiment. 328501 documents are randomly selected as the training data, while the remaining 36500 documents are used as testing queries. 106 tags are selected for training and 20 for testing.

2. *Reuters* (Reuters21578)[2] is a collection of documents that appeared on Reuters newswire in 1987. It contains 21578 documents, and 135 tags/categories. In our experiments, documents corresponding to the top 57 categories are kept[3], with approximately 10376 documents. 9339 documents are randomly chosen as the training set, while 1037 for testing. 47 tags are utilized in training and 10 left for testing.

3. *20Newsgroups*[4] corpus is collected and originally used for document categorization in [17]. We use the popular '18828' version which contains 18828 documents. The data is organized into 20 different newsgroups, each corresponding to a different topic. Since some of the newsgroups are very closely related to each other (*e.g.* comp.sys.ibm.pc.hardware / comp.sys.mac.hardware), while others are highly unrelated (*e.g.* misc.forsale / soc.religion.christian). Therefore, we partition these documents according to subject matter into 6 categories, which are denoted as 6 different tags. 16946 documents are randomly chosen

[2]http://daviddlewis.com/resources/textcollections/reuters21578/.

[3]we removed the tags which only have a limited number of examples.

[4]http://people.csail.mit.edu/jrennie/20Newsgroups/

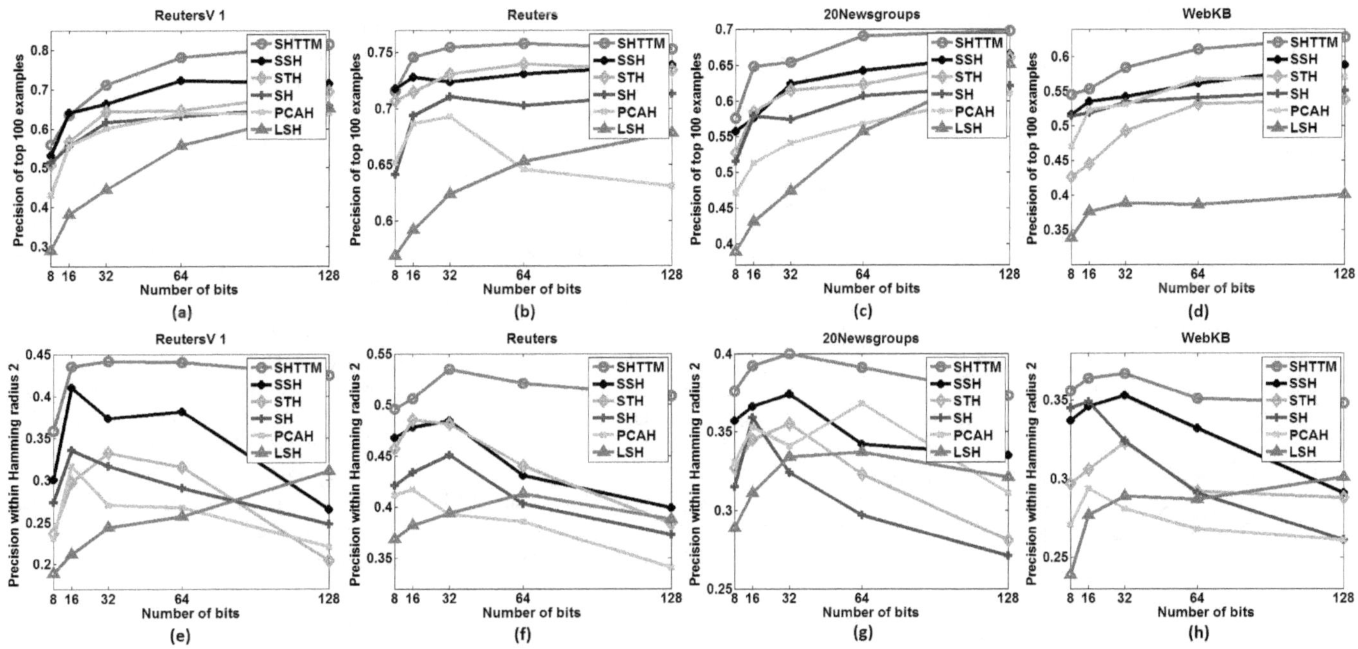

Figure 1: Results of precision of top 100 examples and Precision within Hamming radius 2 on four datasets with different hashing bits. (a)-(d): Precision of the top 100 retrieved examples. (e)-(h): Precision of the retrieved examples within Hamming radius 2.

for training and the rest 1882 documents are used for testing. 3 tags are utilized in training process and 3 for testing.

4. $WebKB$[5] consists of 6883 webpages, collected from four universities, and is divided into 7 categories/tags. 90% documents (6195) are randomly selected as training data, while the remaining (688) documents are used for testing. 4 tags are used in training while 3 for testing.

In all datasets, term frequency (i.e. tf) features are used as content features and also used for learning topic distributions. Note that tags in each dataset are divided into two groups, one set is used only in training and the other is treated as ground truth only for testing.

4.2 Evaluation Metrics

To conduct similarity search, each document in the testing set is used as a query document to search for similar documents in the corresponding training set based on the hamming distance of their hashing codes. The performance is measured with standard information retrieval performance metrics: precision as the ratio of the number of retrieved relevant documents to the number of all retrieved documents and recall as the ratio of the number of retrieved relevant documents to the number of all relevant documents. The performance is averaged over all test queries in the dataset.

There are several methodologies to determine whether a retrieved document is relevant to the given query document. In SH [34], the k closest documents in the original feature space are considered as the relevant documents. In STH [39] and CHMIS [38], the documents with the same tag as the query document are considered as the most relevant ones. The former metric is not suitable since the similarity in the original feature space may not well reflect the document semantic similarity (as discussed in section 3.3). The latter metric is also questionable since documents with more than one tag are discarded in STH and CHMIS, while documents are allowed to have multiple tags in our experiments. Therefore, we adopt a similar metric as in [20] and [31] in our experiments. In particular, a retrieved document that shares any common test tag with the query document is regarded as a relevant document.

4.3 Experiment Settings

The proposed SHTTM approach is compared with five different methods on these datasets such as Semi-Supervised Hashing (SSH) [31], Self Taught Hashing (STH) [39], Spectral Hashing (SH) [34], PCA Hashing (PCAH) [19], and Latent Semantic Hashing (LSH) [7] by using the evaluation metric described above.

The parameters α, γ and λ in SHTTM are tuned by 3-fold cross validation on the training set through the grid $\{0.01, 0.1, 1, 10, 100\}$. The number of nearest neighbors is tuned to be 7 when constructing the graph Laplacians for STH in all experiments. For LSH, we randomly select projections from a Gaussian distribution with zero-mean and identity covariance to construct the hash tables. For SSH, we sample $2k$ random points from the training set to construct the pairwise constraint matrix. We evaluate the performance of different methods by varying the number of hashing bits in the range of $\{8, 16, 32, 64, 128\}$ and calculate the average result by repeating each experiment 10 times.

[5]CMU world wide knowledge base (WebKB) project. Available at http://www.cs.cmu.edu/ WebKB/.

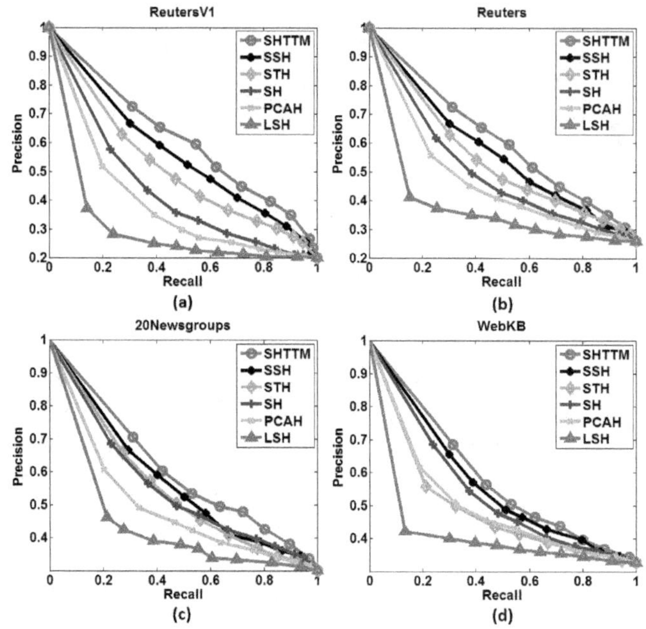

Figure 2: Results of Precision-Recall curve with 32 hashing bits on four datasets.

4.4 Results and Discussions

Four sets of experiments are conducted on each dataset to measure the performance of the proposed SHTTM approach and the five alternative methods to answer the following questions: (1) Whether SHTTM can outperform other methods in high-precision results such as the precision for the top 100 retrieved documents based on the hamming distance ranking and the precision for retrieved documents within a fixed hamming distance 2; (2) How does the SHTTM compare with other methods with recall-related metrics as the precision-recall curve? In particular, for each query document, we vary the number of retrieved documents from 0 to the number of all training documents while fixing the number of hashing bits to 32; (3) How do the two components of the SHTTM approach work that only utilize the tag information or the topic modeling information? These two variants are compared with corresponding baseline methods and the SHTTM approach that combines both tag and topic modeling information; (4) Whether SHTTM has robust performance with respect to different values of meta model parameters.

In the first set of experiments, we report the precision for the top 100 retrieved documents with different numbers of hashing bits in Fig.1(a)-(d) and Table 2. The precisions for the retrieved documents within hamming radius 2 are shown in Fig.1(e)-(h). From these comparison results, it can seen that SHTTM gives the overall best performance among all six hashing methods on all four datasets.

In Fig.1(e)-(h), the precision of most compared methods decreases when the number of hashing bits increases from 16 to 128 This is because when using longer hashing bits, the Hamming space becomes increasingly sparse and very few data points fall within the Hamming ball of radius 2, resulting in even queries with precision 0. Similar behavior is also observed in [20] and [31]. In this situation, the precision results of top 100 documents from Fig.1(a)-(d) provide better performance measurement, while the precision results of SHTTM are still consistently better than other methods.

In the second set of experiments, the precision-recall curves of different methods with 32 hashing bits on different datasets are reported in Fig.2. It can be seen that among all of these comparison methods, SHTTM shows the best performance.

From these figures, we can see that LSH does not perform well in most cases, especially its precision of the top 100 documents is not satisfactory. This is because LSH method is data-oblivious and may lead to inefficient codes in practice as also observed in [22] and [34]. For methods SH and STH, although these methods try to preserve the similarity between documents in their learned hashing codes, they do not utilize the supervised information contained in tags. Moreover, the similarity matrices in both methods are computed from the original keyword feature space, which may not fully reflect the semantic similarity between documents that goes beyond keyword matching. Therefore, the SHTTM method substantially outperforms these two methods by leveraging tag information and topic modeling. SSH achieves better results than SH and STH due to the incorporation of pairwise similarity constraints. However, as pointed out in Section 2.2, these coarse pairwise constraints generated from tags may lose detailed tag information and may not be reliable. On the other hand, the tag information is fully exploited in the SHTTM approach via modeling the semantic correlation between tags and hashing codes through a latent factor model and thus SHTTM generates higher quality hashing codes than SSH.

In the third set of experiments, the effectiveness of the two components of the proposed SHTTM such as tag modeling and topic modeling are evaluated separately. In particular, the component of tag modeling is obtained by setting γ to 0 in Eqn.7, which means we do not utilize topic models. This method is named SHTTM-TagOnly in our experiment. SHTTM-TagOnly is compared with SSH which incorporates summary tag information as pairwise constraints into learning hashing codes. the component of topic modeling is obtained by setting the tag matrix $\boldsymbol{C} = \boldsymbol{0}$ in Eqn.7, which means we do not utilize any tag information in learning hashing codes. This method is called SHTTM-TopicOnly and it is compared with STH that calculates the document similarity in the original keyword feature space.

The precision results of top 100 retrieved documents of SHTTM-TagOnly, SHTTM-TopicOnly, SHTTM and the corresponding baseline methods are shown in Fig.3 when different numbers of hashing bits are used. The experimental results in Fig.3 indicate that the modeling of tag information and utilizing topic modeling are beneficial for improving the effectiveness of hashing separately as SHTTM-TagOnly is more effective than SSH while SHTTM-TopicOnly is more effective than STH. In particular, the SHTTM-TagOnly method incorporates the complete tag information into learning hashing codes via a latent factor model, while SSH only utilizes the partial tag information in pairwise constraints. The SHTTM-TopicOnly method preserves the document similarity in the topic/semantic, while the original keyword feature space used by STH may not fully reflect the semantic relationships that go beyond keyword matching. Finally, combining these two components together, the proposed SHTTM achieves even better performance, which is consistent with our expectation.

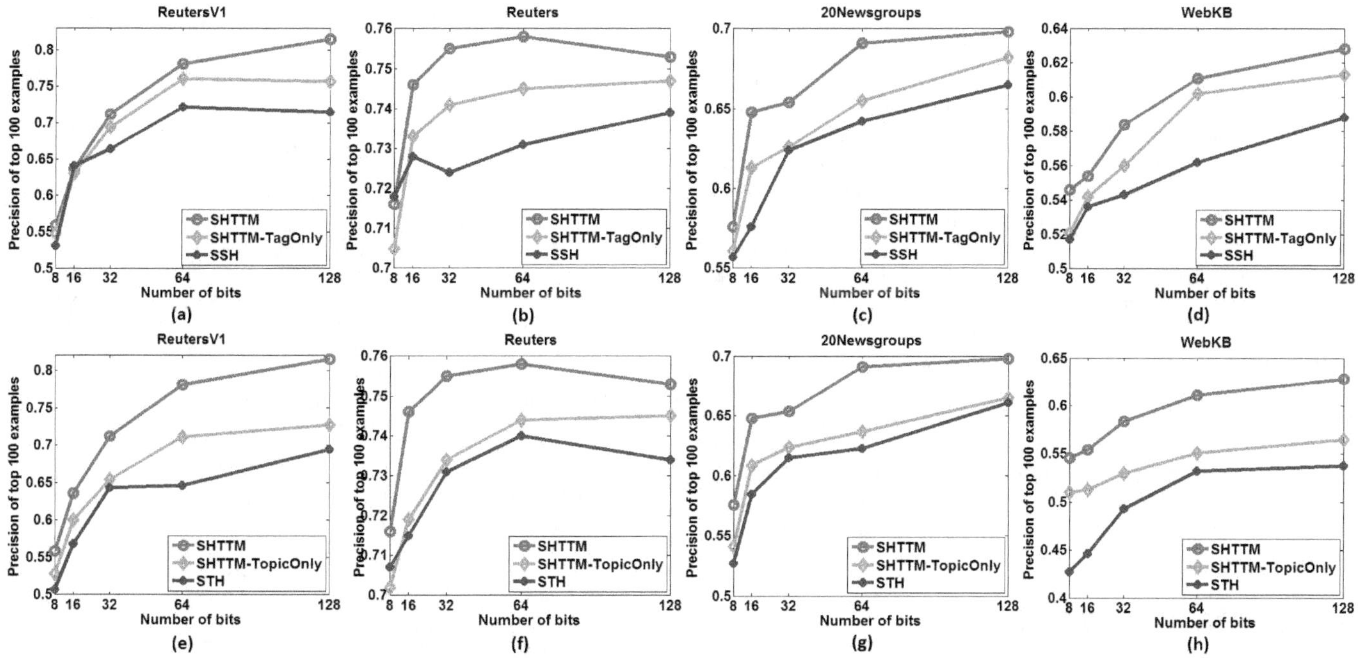

Figure 3: Precision of the top 100 retrieved documents of SHTTM-TagOnly, SHTTM-TopicOnly and SHTTM on four datasets with different hashing bits. (a)-(d): Comparison results of using tag model only. (e)-(h): Comparison results of using topic model only.

The fourth set of experiments study the performance of SHTTM with respect to the meta parameters α, γ and λ. To prove the robustness of the proposed method, we conduct parameter sensitivity experiments on all datasets. In each experiment, we tune only one parameter from $\{0.5, 1, 2, 4, 8, 16, 32, 128\}$, while fixing the other two to the optimal values obtained from the first set of experiments. We report the results on $ReutersV1$ and $20Newsgroups$ in Fig.4. It is clear from these experimental results that the performance of SHTTM is relatively stable with respect to α, γ and λ. We also observe similar results of the proposed method in the other two datasets. But due to the limit of space, they are not presented here.

The prediction procedure for generating hashing codes is very fast. The linear hashing function allows a quick mapping of a query document from the original high-dimensional feature space to the low-dimensional space of hashing codes. We implement our method using Matlab on a PC with Intel Duo Core i5-2400 CPU 3.1GHz and 4GB RAM. It takes 0.0002 second average per query document for the prediction procedure (Table 1) on all datasets.

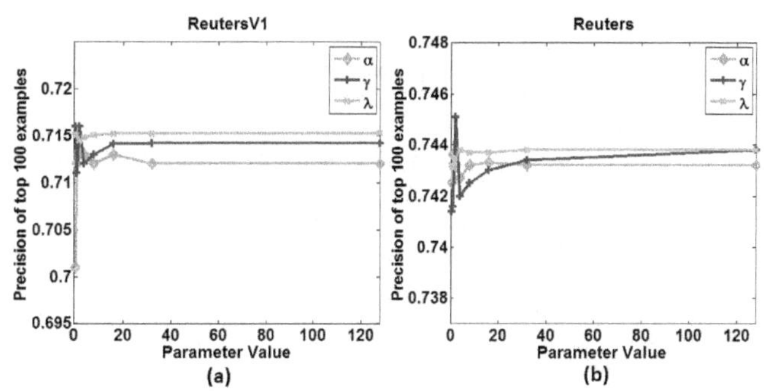

Figure 4: Parameter Sensitivity for α, γ and λ. Results of precision of the top 100 retrieved documents with 32 hashing bits.

5. CONCLUSIONS

Similarity search has become an important technique in many information retrieval applications such as search and recommendation. Many applications with similarity search often involve a large amount of data, which demands effective and efficient solutions. Semantic hashing has been proposed for the problem to map data examples like documents in a high-dimensional space (e.g., a vector space of keywords in the vocabulary) into a low-dimensional binary vector space, which at the same time preserves the semantic relationship of the data examples as much as possible. Valuable prior research has been conducted in this direction for learning hashing codes and mapping function with techniques such as unsupervised learning and supervised learning. However, most existing research on semantic hashing is only based on content similarity computed in the original keyword feature space. Moreover, tag information is not fully utilized in existing research, although they are often available in many information retrieval applications.

This paper proposes novel research for semantic hashing that jointly considers tag information and semantic similarity in generating hashing codes. The proposed research utilizes topic modeling to explore semantic similarity between documents that goes beyond keyword matching. The new SHTTM approach incorporates two components as tag consistency and topic consistency together into a joint objective function for learning desired tag representation and topic representation simultaneously. An iterative coordinate descent method is proposed to obtain the optimal hashing codes by solving the objective function. An extensive set of experiments has shown that the proposed new research can generate more accurate hashing codes than several other state-of-the-art hashing methods. In particular, the experiments clearly demonstrate the benefits of utilizing tag information and topic modeling information separately, and further show that the joint approach generates the best results by combining both two types of information.

There are several possible directions to explore in the future research. For example, the research in this paper only utilizes a fixed number of topics, which may not be optimal for different types of datasets. We plan to explore new research for automatically adjusting the number of topics with either model selection methods or a nonparametric Bayesian approach.

6. ACKNOWLEDGMENTS

This work is partially supported by NSF research grants IIS-0746830, CNS- 1012208 and IIS-1017837. This work is also partially supported by the Center for Science of Information (CSoI), an NSF Science and Technology Center, under grant agreement CCF-0939370.

7. REFERENCES

[1] A. Ahmed, M. Aly, J. Gonzalez, S. Narayanamurthy, and A. J. Smola. Scalable inference in latent variable models. In *WSDM*, pages 123–132, 2012.

[2] A. Andoni and P. Indyk. Near-optimal hashing algorithms for approximate nearest neighbor in high dimensions. In *FOCS*, pages 459–468, 2006.

[3] D. Blei and J. Lafferty. Topic models. *Text Mining: Theory and Applications*, 2009.

[4] D. M. Blei, A. Y. Ng, and M. I. Jordan. Latent dirichlet allocation. *Journal of Machine Learning Research*, 3:993–1022, 2003.

[5] T. Cormen, C. Leiserson, R. Rivest, and C. Stein. *Introduction to algorithms*. The MIT press, 2001.

[6] J. S. Culpepper and A. Moffat. Efficient set intersection for inverted indexing. *ACM Trans. Inf. Syst.*, 29(1):1, 2010.

[7] M. Datar, N. Immorlica, P. Indyk, and V. S. Mirrokni. Locality-sensitive hashing scheme based on p-stable distributions. In *Symposium on Computational Geometry*, pages 253–262, 2004.

[8] S. C. Deerwester, S. T. Dumais, T. K. Landauer, G. W. Furnas, and R. A. Harshman. Indexing by latent semantic analysis. *JASIS*, 41(6):391–407, 1990.

[9] A. Gionis, P. Indyk, and R. Motwani. Similarity search in high dimensions via hashing. In *VLDB*, pages 518–529, 1999.

[10] G. E. Hinton, S. Osindero, and Y. W. Teh. A fast learning algorithm for deep belief nets. *Neural Computation*, 18(7):1527–1554, 2006.

[11] G. E. Hinton and R. R. Salakhutdinov. Reducing the dimensionality of data with neural networks. *Science*, 313(5786):504–507, 2006.

[12] T. Hofmann. Probabilistic latent semantic indexing. In *SIGIR*, pages 50–57, 1999.

[13] T. Hofmann. Collaborative filtering via gaussian probabilistic latent semantic analysis. In *SIGIR*, pages 259–266, 2003.

[14] Y. Hu, Y. Koren, and C. Volinsky. Collaborative filtering for implicit feedback datasets. In *ICDM*, pages 263–272, 2008.

[15] W. Kong and W.-J. Li. Isotropic hashing. In *NIPS*, pages 1655–1663. 2012.

[16] B. Kulis and K. Grauman. Kernelized locality-sensitive hashing for scalable image search. In *ICCV*, pages 2130–2137, 2009.

[17] K. Lang. Newsweeder: Learning to filter netnews. In *ICML*, pages 331–339, 1995.

[18] D. D. Lewis, Y. Yang, T. G. Rose, and F. Li. Rcv1: A new benchmark collection for text categorization research. *Journal of Machine Learning Research*, 5:361–397, 2004.

[19] R.-S. Lin, D. A. Ross, and J. Yagnik. Spec hashing: Similarity preserving algorithm for entropy-based coding. In *CVPR*, pages 848–854, 2010.

[20] W. Liu, J. Wang, R. Ji, Y.-G. Jiang, and S.-F. Chang. Supervised hashing with kernels. In *CVPR*, pages 2074–2081, 2012.

[21] W. Liu, J. Wang, S. Kumar, and S.-F. Chang. Hashing with graphs. In *ICML*, pages 1–8, 2011.

[22] R. Salakhutdinov and G. E. Hinton. Semantic hashing. *Int. J. Approx. Reasoning*, 50(7):969–978, 2009.

[23] G. Salton. Developments in automatic text retrieval. *Science*, 253(5023):974–980, August 1991.

[24] G. Salton and C. Buckley. Term-weighting approaches in automatic text retrieval. *Inf. Process. Manage.*, 24(5):513–523, 1988.

[25] L. Si and R. Jin. Flexible mixture model for collaborative filtering. *In ICML*, pages 704–711, 2003.

[26] F. Silvestri and R. Venturini. Vsencoding: efficient coding and fast decoding of integer lists via dynamic programming. In *CIKM*, pages 1219–1228, 2010.

[27] B. Stein. Principles of hash-based text retrieval. In *SIGIR*, pages 527–534, 2007.

[28] V. Vapnik. *The nature of statistical learning theory*. Springer Verlag, 2000.

[29] C. Wang and D. M. Blei. Collaborative topic modeling for recommending scientific articles. In *KDD*, pages 448–456, 2011.

[30] J. Wang, S. Kumar, and S.-F. Chang. Sequential projection learning for hashing with compact codes. In *ICML*, pages 1127–1134, 2010.

[31] J. Wang, S. Kumar, and S.-F. Chang. Semi-supervised hashing for large-scale search. *IEEE Trans. Pattern Anal. Mach. Intell.*, 34(12):2393–2406, 2012.

[32] Q. Wang, L. Si, and D. Zhang. A discriminative data-dependent mixture-model approach for multiple instance learning in image classification. In *ECCV (4)*, pages 660–673, 2012.

[33] R. Weber, H.-J. Schek, and S. Blott. A quantitative analysis and performance study for similarity-search methods in high-dimensional spaces. In *VLDB*, pages 194–205, 1998.

[34] Y. Weiss, A. Torralba, and R. Fergus. Spectral hashing. In *NIPS*, pages 1753–1760, 2008.

[35] H. Xia, P. Wu, S. C. H. Hoi, and R. Jin. Boosting multi-kernel locality-sensitive hashing for scalable image retrieval. In *SIGIR*, pages 55–64, 2012.

[36] X. Yi and J. Allan. Evaluating topic models for information retrieval. In *CIKM*, pages 1431–1432, 2008.

[37] L. Zelnik-Manor and P. Perona. Self-tuning spectral clustering. In *NIPS*, 2004.

[38] D. Zhang, F. Wang, and L. Si. Composite hashing with multiple information sources. In *SIGIR*, pages 225–234, 2011.

[39] D. Zhang, J. Wang, D. Cai, and J. Lu. Self-taught hashing for fast similarity search. In *SIGIR*, pages 18–25, 2010.

[40] J. Zobel and A. Moffat. Inverted files for text search engines. *ACM Comput. Surv.*, 38(2), 2006.

Incorporating Popularity in Topic Models for Social Network Analysis

Youngchul Cha Bin Bi Chu-Cheng Hsieh Junghoo Cho
UCLA Computer Science Dept
Los Angeles, CA 90095
{youngcha, bbi, chucheng, cho}@cs.ucla.edu

ABSTRACT

Topic models are used to group words in a text dataset into a set of relevant topics. Unfortunately, when a few words frequently appear in a dataset, the topic groups identified by topic models become noisy because these frequent words repeatedly appear in "irrelevant" topic groups. This noise has not been a serious problem in a text dataset because the frequent words (e.g., *the* and *is*) do not have much meaning and have been simply removed before a topic model analysis. However, in a social network dataset we are interested in, they correspond to popular persons (e.g., *Barack Obama* and *Justin Bieber*) and cannot be simply removed because most people are interested in them.

To solve this "popularity problem", we explicitly model the popularity of nodes (words) in topic models. For this purpose, we first introduce a notion of a "popularity component" and propose topic model extensions that effectively accommodate the popularity component. We evaluate the effectiveness of our models with a real-world Twitter dataset. Our proposed models achieve significantly lower perplexity (i.e., better prediction power) compared to the state-of-the-art baselines.

In addition to the popularity problem caused by the nodes with high incoming edge degree, we also investigate the effect of the outgoing edge degree with another topic model extensions. We show that considering outgoing edge degree does not help much in achieving lower perplexity.

Categories and Subject Descriptors

H.3.3 [**Information Storage and Retrieval**]: Information Search and Retrieval—*clustering*; D.2.8 [**Software Engineering**]: Metrics—*performance measures*

General Terms

Experimentation, Algorithms

Keywords

topic model, social-network analysis, popularity bias, handling popular users, Latent Dirichlet Allocation

1. INTRODUCTION

Microblogging services such as Twitter are popular these days because they empower users to broadcast and exchange information or thoughts in realtime. Distinct from other social network services, relationships on Twitter are unidirectional and often interest-oriented. A user may indicate her interest in another user by "following" her, and previous studies [16, 23] show that users are more likely to follow people who share common interests, even though "following relationships" among users look unorganized and haphazard at first glance. Thus, if we can correctly identify the shared hidden interests behind users' following relationships, we can recommend more relevant users and group users sharing common interests in the social network services.

In this paper, we refine topic models to correctly identify the hidden interests behind users' following relations (instead of their tweets as in [30]). A topic model is a statistical model originally developed for discovering hidden topics from a collection of documents. It postulates that every document is a mixture of topics, and words in a document are attributable to these hidden topics. Here, we posit that the following relations are not random but are interest-attributable. Then, we can discover the hidden interest behind each following relation by regarding a user's following list as a document, and each person in the user's following list as a word. Now, topic models can easily help us correctly identify the hidden interests and derive a low dimensional representation of the observed following lists.

However, simply applying topic models to the follow-relation analysis may cause some problems. Our previous study [7] reported significant clustering quality degradation when the authors directly applied Latent Dirichlet Allocation (LDA) [5] to Twitter's following relation dataset. As LDA is built on an assumption that every word in a document should be of roughly equal popularity, stop words like *the* and *is* must be removed in preprocessing stages. However, keeping popular persons like *Barack Obama* and *Justin Bieber* in a user's following list can be beneficial for the following reasons: (1) These well-known users can work as an effective labels of identified topic groups. For example, when a group contains well-known politicians like Barack Obama, we may immediately identify that the group is likely to be on politics.[1] (2) Many new Twitter users do not know who is on Twitter and who is not, so they often fail to follow popular users of potential interest, not knowing their presence. If the system can recommend interesting and well-known users of interest, it can significantly improve the users' return rate and stickiness [31].

In this work, we propose refined topic models specialized in handling the quality degradation caused by a limited number of popular users, which we call "popularity bias". For this, we introduce a notion of a "popularity component" and explore various ways to effectively incorporate it. We also evaluate the effectiveness of our proposed topic models with the widely used "perplexity" [2] calculated over the real-world Twitter following relation dataset.

Note that the popularity bias is not limited to social network datasets. This bias often appears in datasets showing user's preference over some popular items (or nodes) such as webpage visit logs, advertisement click logs, product purchase logs, etc. We believe our proposed models can effectively improve the quality of recommendations and clusterings in the web services generating such logs.

In summary, we make the following contributions in this paper:

- We propose topic models appropriate for social-network analysis. We introduce a popularity component, which explicitly models popularity of users, and explore various ways to incorporate it step by step.
- We conduct extensive experiments using a real-world Twitter dataset. Through these experiments, we demonstrate that our models are very effective in recommending more relevant users with significantly lower perplexity than the state-of-the-art baselines.
- We show that there is no clear relationship between how many persons a user follows (i.e., outgoing edge degree) and how topic sensitive she is. It is quite different from the popularity bias which shows that if a user is followed many times (i.e., high incoming edge degree), many users follow her because she is just popular.

2. RELATED WORK

In this section, we briefly review topic models related to social-network analysis in three categories: topic models for authorship, hypertexts, and edges.

The topic models in the first category were proposed to analyze documents (texts) with their authors. As these models incorporate authors and their relationships in the model, they can be viewed as early forms of social-network topic models. They attempt to group documents and authors by assuming that a document is created by authors sharing common topics. The concept of authors (users) was initially introduced by Steyvers et al. [34] in the Author-Topic (AT) model. With the additional co-author information, they could successfully extract hidden research topics and trends from CiteSeer's abstract corpus. The AT model was extended to the the Community User Topic (CUT) model by Zhou et al. [41] to capture semantic communities. McCalum et al. [24] also extended the AT model and proposed the Author-Recipient-Topic (ART) model and the Role-Author-Recipient-Topic (RART) model to analyze e-mail networks. Pathak et al. [29] modified the ART model and suggested the Community-Author-Recipient-Topic (CART) model, which is similar to the RART model. In addition to these AT model family, other LDA extensions and probabilistic topic models were also proposed to analyze chat data [36], voting data [38], annotation data [22], and tagging data [17].

The topic models in the second category are more closely related to social-network analysis and analyze documents with their citations (i.e., hypertexts). Cohn et al. [10] initially introduced a topic model combining PLSI [20] and PHITS [9]. Later, PLSI in this model was replaced with LDA [5] by Erosheva et al. [13]. Nallapati et al. [27] extended Erosheva's model and proposed Link-PLSA-LDA model which applies PLSI and LDA to cited and citing documents, respectively. Chang et al. [8] also proposed the Relational Topic Model (RTM) which models a citation as a binary random variable. Dietz et al. [12] proposed a topic model to analyze topical influence of research publications. More sophisticated models were proposed by Gruber et al. [15] and Sun et al. [35]. Hybrid approaches were also attempted. Mei at al. [25] introduced a regularized topic modeling framework incorporating a graph structure and Nallapati et al. [26] combined network flow and topic modeling.

The topic models in the last category only uses linkage (edge) information. Since they only focus on the graph structure, they can be easily applied to a variety of datasets. However, there has been relatively less research in this category. Our work belongs to this category and focuses on solving the issue caused by popular nodes in the graph structure. Airoldi et al. [3] proposed the Mixed Membership Stochastic Block (MBB) model to analyze pairwise measurements such as social networks and protein interaction networks. Zhang et al. [40] and Henderson et al. [18] dealt with the issues in applying LDA to academic social networks. The former focused on the issue of converting the co-authorship information into a graph, and proposed edge weighting schemes based on collaboration frequency. The latter addressed the issue of a large number of topic clusters generated due to "low popularity" nodes in the network. The "high popularity" issue was initially addressed by Steck [32]. He defined a new metric called Popularity-Stratified Recall and suggested a matrix factorization method optimizing it. In our previous study [7], we investigated the issue in more detail and proposed effective solutions based on probabilistic topic models. However, our previous solutions are rather heuristic and more about how to tune topic models to handle the high popularity issue. In this paper, we take a more principled approach to this issue and propose more effective topic models.

3. FOLLOW-RELATION ANALYSIS USING LDA

In this section, we explain how to apply topic models to social network analysis. After briefly explaining two probabilistic topic models, Probabilistic Latent Semantic Indexing (PLSI) and Latent Dirichlet Allocation (LDA), we introduce

[1]Existing topic models simply identify a group of words (or users) that belong to a topic group, not the semantic labels of each group.

[2]It measures prediction power of a trained model. The definition is given in Section 5.2

the challenge of a "popularity bias" which we address in this study.

3.1 Topic Models

Topic models are built on the assumption that there are latent variable(s) behind each observation in a dataset. In the case of a document corpus, the usual assumption is that there is a hidden topic behind each word. PLSI [20] introduced a probabilistic generative model to Latent Semantic Indexing (LSI) [11], one of the most popular topic models. Equation (1) represents its document generation process based on the probabilistic generative model:

$$p(d,w) = p(d)p(w|d) = p(d)\sum_{z\in Z} p(z|d)p(w|z). \quad (1)$$

$p(d,w)$ denotes the probability of observing a word w in a document d and can be decomposed into two parts: $p(d)$, the probability distribution of documents, and $p(w|d)$, the probability distribution of words given a document. This equation describes a word selection process for a document, where an author first selects a document then a word in that document. By repeating this selection process sufficiently, we can generate a full document and eventually a whole document corpus. Based on the assumption that there is a latent topic z for each word w, the equation above can be rewritten with the multiplication of $p(w|z)$, the probability distribution of words given a topic, and $p(z|d)$, the probability distribution of topics given a document. In this way, an additional topic selection step is added between the document selection step and the word selection step. We sum the multiplication over a set of all independent topics Z because there exist a number of possible topics from which a word may be derived.

The goal of the topic model analysis is to accurately infer $p(w|z)$ and $p(z|d)$. Given the probabilistic generative model explained above, we can effectively infer $p(w|z)$ and $p(z|d)$ by maximizing the log-likelihood function L of observing the entire corpus as in Equation (2):

$$\begin{aligned} L &= \log[\prod_{d\in D}\prod_{w\in W} p(d,w)^{n(d,w)}] \\ &= \sum_{d\in D}\sum_{w\in W} n(d,w)\log p(d,w), \end{aligned} \quad (2)$$

where $n(d,w)$ denotes the word frequency in a document. The inferred $p(w|z)$ and $p(z|d)$ measure the strength of association between a word w and a topic z and that between a topic z and a document d, respectively. For example, if $p(w_{vehicle}|z_{car}) > p(w_{technology}|z_{car})$, the word *vehicle* is more closely related to the topic *car* than the word *technology*, though they are all related to the topic *car*. In this way, PLSI and other probabilistic topic models support multiple memberships and produce more reasonable clustering results.

Although PLSI introduced a sound probabilistic generative model, it showed a poor performance when predicting unobserved words and documents. To solve this "overfitting" problem, LDA [5] introduced Dirichlet priors α and β to PLSI, to constrain $p(z|d)$ and $p(w|z)$, respectively. α is a vector of dimension $|Z|$, the number of topics, and each element in α is a prior for a corresponding element in $p(z|d)$. Thus, a higher α_i implies that there are more frequent prior observations of topic z_i in a corpus. Similarly, β is a vector of dimension $|W|$, the number of words, and each element in β is a prior for a corresponding element in $p(w|z)$. By placing Dirichlet priors α and β on the multinomial distributions $p(z|d)$ and $p(w|z)$, these posterior distributions are smoothed by the amount of priors α and β, and the model becomes safe from PLSI's overfitting problem. As a conjugate prior for the multinomial distribution, the Dirichlet distribution also simplifies the statistical inference and enables the use of the collapsed Gibbs sampling [33]. It is also known that PLSI emerges as a specific instance of LDA under Dirichlet priors [14, 19].

3.2 LDA on Recommending Who to Follow

In a social network service, a user r's following another user w can be intuitively interpreted as the user r (acting as a "reader") expresses her interest in tweets written by the user w (acting as a "writer"). We believe this interest plays a role in the establishment of the following relation (or edge) as the topic does in the document generation process explained in Section 3.1. In this study, we assume that there exists a follow edge generative model: a reader first chooses an interest, and based on the chosen interest, the reader chooses a writer to follow. In this model, a document in a corpus becomes a reader's following list, and a word becomes a writer in the list.

Analyzing Twitter follow edges using LDA delivers two estimates: $p(z|r)$ and $p(w|z)$. $p(z|r)$ indicates a reader r's interest distribution and $p(w|z)$ indicates a writer w's importance in an interest group z. Thus, $p(w|z)$ can be used in clustering Twitter users having the same interest. From Equation (1), we can easily estimate $p(w|r)$, the likelihood of a reader r's following a writer w, which can be used for recommendation.

When we apply topic models to a social network dataset, we notice the following differences [7]:

1. In a document generative model, a word is sampled *with replacement*. However, in our follow edge generative model, a reader cannot follow the same writer twice. Thus, a writers should be sampled *without replacement*.

2. When analyzing a textual dataset, common entries like *the* and *is* are simply ignored because they do not have important meaning. Thus, they are called "stop words". However, in a social network dataset, these entities correspond to "celebrities" like *Barack Obama* and *Justin Bieber* who attract more followers than others. Thus, they cannot be simply ignored but should be carefully handled.

Because of the first difference, some probability distributions in our model follow *multivariate hypergeometric distributions* instead of *multinomial distributions*. This difference is important because LDA benefits from Dirichlet priors, which are conjugate priors of multinomial distributions. However, it is known that a multivariate hypergeometric distribution converges to a multinomial distribution as the population size grows large [1]. Since millions of users are included in our Twitter dataset, we can disregard the consequence caused by the sampling *without replacement*.

The second difference affects the quality of a topic model analysis. When celebrities are simply included without any special handling, they appear even in irrelevant topic groups and make the topic analysis severely biased to them. Such a "popularity bias" can be seen everywhere, from purchase logs to movie rating data. In the next section, we propose refined topic models which address this popularity bias.

4. REFINED TOPIC MODELS

In this section, we introduce a notion of a "popularity component" using a *simple model*, which acts as a base of our later models. We propose three refined models, and discuss how they may ease the popularity bias. At the end of this section, we explore various extensions to these refined models.

4.1 Simple Model

As described in Section 3.2, in our follow edge generative models, a reader first selects an interest (a topic) from a distribution $p(z|r)(\theta)$, and then selects a writer from a distribution $p(w|z)(\phi)$. The θ and ϕ are constrained by Dirichlet priors α and β, respectively. This process is depicted in a plate notation in Figure 1(a). We formulate the probability for a reader a to follow a writer b based on an interest z (or $z_{a,b}$) as follows:

$$p(z_{a,b}|\cdot) = p(z|r_a)p(w_{a,b}|z). \quad (3)$$

Note that this equation is equivalent to Equation (1), and we use $w_{a,b}$ to indicate a follow edge between a reader a to a writer b. By considering the Dirichlet priors α and β, the same probability can be represented in LDA as follows:

$$p(z_{a,b}|\cdot) \propto \int p(z|\theta)p(\theta|\alpha)d\theta \times \int p(w_{a,b}|z,\phi)p(\phi|\beta)d\phi. \quad (4)$$

In a *simple model*, we incorporate a "popularity component" into LDA, as in Figure 1(b). The popularity component (in a dotted box) consists of a multinomial distribution π, which represents an in-corpus writer distribution, and a Dirichlet prior γ constraining π. Note that γ is a vector of length J, the number of unique writers, and each element has a value of $\gamma_w = \frac{f_w}{f_*}$, where f_w denotes an in-corpus frequency of a writer w (i.e., the number of followers to the writer), and f_* denotes a total frequency ($\sum_w f_w$). Thus, in the *simple model*, when a reader follows a writer, the writer selection probability ϕ is multiplied by π so that popular writers are weighted accordingly. We formulate this change (from Equation (4)) into the following equation:

$$p(z_{a,b}|\cdot) \propto \int p(z|\theta)p(\theta|\alpha)d\theta$$
$$\times \iint p(w_{a,b}|z,\phi,\pi)p(\phi|\beta)p(\pi|\gamma)d\phi d\pi. \quad (5)$$

4.2 Polya-Urn Model

Although the *simple model* incorporates the popularity component in LDA, this incorporation is too simple. Whenever a reader follows a writer, the model favors a popular writer according to her in-corpus distribution π. However, the in-corpus writer distribution can be largely different from a in-topic writer distribution. For example, though *Barack Obama* is more popular than *Justin Bieber* in general, *Justin Bieber* is more popular than *Barack Obama* among people who like music. Thus, the writer should be picked up from the in-corpus distribution or the in-topic distribution. When every topic is assumed to be equally likely (as in LDA's symmetric prior assumption), the in-corpus writer distribution is the sum of per-topic (in-topic) writer distributions ($p(w) = \sum_z p(w|z)p(z)$), and we may consider the former as a global writer distribution and the latter as a local writer distribution. Since a writer is picked up from her global (in-corpus) distribution or local (per-topic) distribution, we may represent a popularity-incorporated writer distribution as a mixture of the global distribution and the local distribution. This interpretation leads us to a *polya-urn model* depicted in Figure 1(c). In [2], the authors took a similar approach for a topic distribution θ to capture global topics as well as local topics.

Figure 1(c) depicts how the global and local distribution are populated with the popularity component depicted in the dotted box. In addition to the γ and π in the *simple model*, the popularity component in the *polya-urn model* has a concentration scalar λ. Initially, the multinomial distribution π is generated from the Dirichlet prior γ. Then, π works as a Dirichlet prior for ϕ, together with the concentration scalar λ. As λ works as a weight to the prior observation π, ϕ becomes similar to π when λ has a high value. On the other hand, ϕ deviates from π when λ has a low value. Since π works as a base distribution and ϕ deviates from π per topic, π can be considered as a global (in-corpus) writer distribution, and ϕ can be considered as a local (per-topic) writer distribution.

To derive a collapsed Gibbs sampling equation for the *polya-urn model*, we define $c_{k,m,j}$ as the number of associations between a topic z_k and a writer w_j followed by a reader r_m (or a follow edge from a reader r_m to a writer w_j) as in Equation (6) [33]:

$$c_{k,m,j} = \sum_{n=1}^{N_m} I(z_{m,n} = k \& w_{m,n} = j). \quad (6)$$

We also define $c_{k,m,j}^{-(a,b)}$ as the count when we exclude the edge from a reader r_a to a writer w_b. Then the collapsed Gibbs sampling equation of LDA (derived from Equation (4)) becomes:

$$p(z_{a,b}|\cdot) \propto \frac{c_{z_{a,b},a,*}^{-(a,b)} + \alpha_{z_{a,b}}}{c_{*,a,*}^{-(a,b)} + \alpha_*} \times \frac{c_{z_{a,b},*,w_{a,b}}^{-(a,b)} + \beta_{w_{a,b}}}{c_{z_{a,b},*,*}^{-(a,b)} + \beta_*}, \quad (7)$$

where the symbol * denotes a summation over all possible subscript variables. As we select a writer from a mixture of a global and a local writer distribution, the topic assignment probability of the *polya-urn model* should be extended to:

$$p(z_{a,b}|\cdot) \propto \frac{c_{z_{a,b},a,*}^{-(a,b)} + \alpha_{z_{a,b}}}{c_{*,a,*}^{-(a,b)} + \alpha_*} \times$$
$$\left(\frac{c_{z_{a,b},*,w_{a,b}}^{-(a,b)}}{c_{z_{a,b},*,*}^{-(a,b)}} + \lambda\frac{c_{*,*,w_{a,b}} + \gamma_{w_{a,b}}}{c_{*,*,*} + \gamma_*}\right). \quad (8)$$

Note that the global distribution dominates in the mixture as the concentration parameter λ increases. On the other hand, as λ decreases, the local distribution dominates and the whole equation becomes similar to that of LDA.

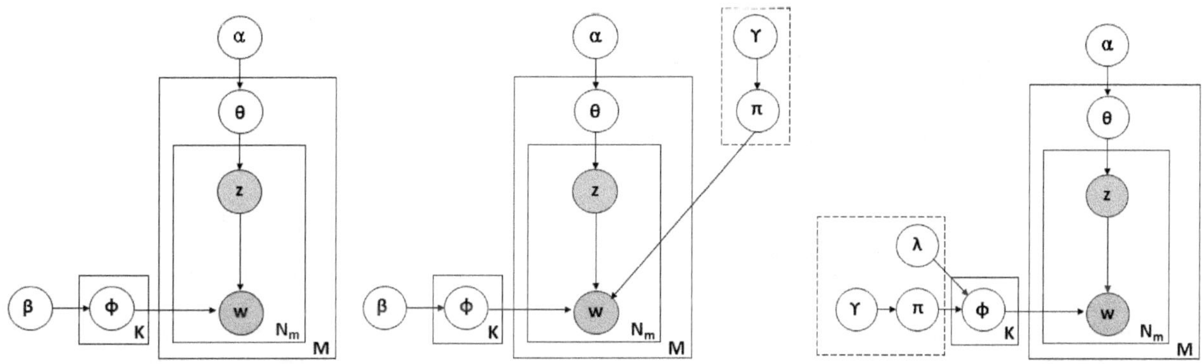

(a) LDA (b) Simple model (c) Polya-urn model

(d) Two-path model (e) Weight model

Figure 1: LDA and proposed topic models

4.3 Two-Path Model

In the *polya-urn model*, when a reader follows a writer, she first selects a topic, and then selects a writer from the mixture of a global and a local writer distribution for the selected topic. Although the mixture explains non-topic related (popularity-based) following relations as well as topic related (interest-based) ones, the initial topic selection process is common in both cases. In a *two-path model*, we clearly separate the non-topic related following relations from the topic related ones by assuming that there are two separate paths from which a writer can come. This separation in early stage is expected to help generate more clear topics. For this separation, we introduce a new binary latent variable t which indicates the path the writer comes from. $t = 1$ means that the writer comes from a "topic path" and $t = 0$ means that she comes from a "popularity path". Now, we do a "path-labeling" as well as a "topic-labeling" for a follow edge, and our goal is to accurately infer t as well as z (when $t = 1$).

Figure 1(d) depicts this *two-path model*. The variable t follows a Bernoulli distribution τ which is constrained by a Beta prior δ. As a more popular writer may have a higher probability of being followed through the popularity path than a less popular writer, we pose an asymmetric prior according to the writer's popularity. For example, larger portion of edges to *Barack Obama* will be labeled with the popularity path because he has lower δ and τ. We extend Equation (6) with the new path indicator variable t:

$$c_{k,m,j,s} = \sum_{n=1}^{N_m} I(z_{m,n} = k \& w_{m,n} = j \& t_{m,n} = s). \qquad (9)$$

Then, the path-labeling and the topic-labeling probability are derived as:

$$p(t_{a,b}|\cdot) \propto \frac{c^{-(a,b)}_{*,*,w_{a,b},t_{a,b}} + \delta_{w_{a,b},t_{a,b}}}{c^{-(a,b)}_{*,*,w_{a,b},*} + \delta_{w_{a,b},*}}, \qquad (10)$$

$$p(z_{a,b}|\cdot) \propto \frac{(c^{-(a,b)}_{z_{a,b},a,*,1} + \alpha_{z_{a,b}})}{(c^{-(a,b)}_{*,a,*,1} + \alpha_*)} \times \frac{(c^{-(a,b)}_{z_{a,b},*,w_{a,b},1} + \beta_{w_{a,b}})}{c^{-(a,b)}_{z_{a,b},*,*,1} + \beta_*} \qquad (11)$$

where δ is defined with a scaling constant C_1 as:

$$\delta_{w_n,1} = \frac{C_1}{\log f_{w_n}}, \qquad (12)$$

$$\delta_{w_n,0} = \max(0, 1 - \frac{C_1}{\log f_{w_n}}). \qquad (13)$$

The two latent variables are inferred simultaneously in every Gibbs sampling iteration. The topic-labeling process is performed only when $t_{a,b} = 1$. When $t_{a,b} = 1$ for all edges, the *two-path model* becomes equivalent to the standard LDA.

4.4 Weight Model

In the *two-path model*, we assumed that there are two paths from which a writer can come. Then, we introduced the path indicator t to denote the path from which the writer comes. While a writer from the topic path is assigned with a topic, a writer from the popularity path is ignored and not assigned with a topic. We generalize this binary topic indicator t to a non-negative weight (confidence) in a *weight model*. For example, when $\tau_{obama} = 0.7$ in the *two-path model*, seven out of ten w_{obama} observations (follow edges), likely come from the topic path and the three likely come from the popularity path. Instead of probabilistically selecting which w_{obama} observation comes from which path, we may uniformly assign the τ_{obama} value to each w_{obama} observation. This τ value can be viewed as a weight or a confidence value. When we are very confident that a writer observation comes from the topic path, we may assign a value 1 to the writer observation. In the opposite case, we may assign 0 to it. If we are 70% confident, we may assign 0.7 to each writer observation.

Figure 1(e) depicts the newly introduced weight value ρ in the dotted box. ρ is associated with each writer observation and has a non-negative real number. If we strongly believe a writer is from the topic path, we may assign a high weight (even bigger than 1). Otherwise, we assign a value close to 0 or 0. Equation (14) is a ρ-incorporated version of Equation (6):

$$c_{k,m,j} = \sum_{n=1}^{N_m} I(z_{m,n} = k \& w_{m,n} = j) \cdot \rho_n, \tag{14}$$

where ρ_n is defined with a scaling constant C_2 as:

$$\rho_n = \frac{C_2}{\log f_{w_n}} \tag{15}$$

As in the *two-path model*, we believe that popular writers more likely come from the popularity path and should be assigned lower weights. When $\rho_n = 1$ for all writers, the equation becomes equivalent to that of LDA. While the *two-path model* requires the additional path-labeling process, the *weight model* is free from it and has the same complexity as LDA. The confidence and weight approach on observations can be found in the literature on recommender systems [21, 28, 32]. Especially, Steck [32] defined a new metric called Popularity-Stratified Recall by assigning lower weights to popular items, and suggested a matrix factorization method optimizing the metric. The term weighting scheme for LDA was also proposed for cross-language retrieval [39].

4.5 Other Extensions

We may further extend our models by considering reader-side popularity (in a sense that edges from a reader are more frequent in a dataset) as well as the writer-side popularity discussed so far. The reader-side popularity shows how "active" she is because it represents the length of her following list. We expect that an active reader who follows more writers can be considered less "topic-sensitive" (topic-focused) than one who follows fewer writers. If we include the reader-side popularity in the previous models, Equation (8), (10), and (15) should be accordingly extended into:

$$\begin{aligned} p(z_{a,b}|\cdot) &\propto \left(\frac{c^{-(a,b)}_{z_{a,b},*,w_{a,b}}}{c^{-(a,b)}_{z_{a,b},*,*}} + \lambda_1 \frac{c_{*,*,w_{a,b}} + \gamma_{w_{a,b}}}{c_{*,*,*} + \gamma_*}\right) \\ &\quad \times \left(\frac{c^{-(a,b)}_{z_{a,b},a,*}}{c^{-(a,b)}_{*,a,*}} + \lambda_2 \frac{c_{*,a,*} + \alpha_{z_{a,b}}}{c_{*,*,*} + \alpha_*}\right), \end{aligned} \tag{16}$$

$$\begin{aligned} p(t_{a,b}|\cdot) &\propto \frac{c^{-(a,b)}_{*,*,w_{a,b},t_{a,b}} + \delta_{w_{a,b},t_{a,b}}}{c^{-(a,b)}_{*,*,w_{a,b},*} + \delta_{w_{a,b},*}} \\ &\quad \times \frac{c^{-(a,b)}_{*,a,*,t_{a,b}} + \epsilon_{r_a,t_{a,b}}}{c^{-(a,b)}_{*,a,*,*} + \epsilon_{r_a,*}}, \end{aligned} \tag{17}$$

$$\rho_{m,n} = \frac{C_3}{\log(f_{w_n} \times f_{r_m})}, \tag{18}$$

where ϵ is a prior for reader's path indicator distribution and defined as:

$$\epsilon_{r_m,1} = \frac{C_4}{\log f_{r_m}}, \tag{19}$$

$$\epsilon_{r_m,0} = \max(0, 1 - \frac{C_4}{\log f_{r_m}}). \tag{20}$$

For the *two-path model*, we also try posing hyper priors δ' and ϵ' over δ and ϵ, respectively, similar to the approach in [37]. Then, Equation (17) should be extended to:

$$\begin{aligned} p(t_{a,b}|\cdot) &\propto \frac{c^{-(a,b)}_{*,*,w_{a,b},t_{a,b}} + \delta_* \times \frac{c_{*,*,*,t_{a,b}} + \delta'_{t_{a,b}}}{c_{*,*,*,*} + \delta'_*}}{c^{-(a,b)}_{*,*,w_{a,b},*} + \delta_*} \\ &\quad \times \frac{c^{-(a,b)}_{*,a,*,t_{a,b}} + \epsilon_* \times \frac{c_{*,*,*,t_{a,b}} + \epsilon'_{t_{a,b}}}{c_{*,*,*,*} + \epsilon'_*}}{c^{-(a,b)}_{*,a,*,*} + \epsilon_*}. \end{aligned} \tag{21}$$

We also combine the *polya-urn model* with *weight model*. There are many possible combinations in mixing two models. We report only the meaningful results in the next section.

Before moving to the next section, we summarize the symbols used in this paper in Table 1.

Table 1: Symbols used throughout this paper and their meanings

Symbol	Meaning
r	Reader (follower)
w	Writer (followed user)
z	Topic (interest)
$w_{a,b}$	Writer b in reader a's following list (follow edge)
$z_{a,b}$	Topic assigned to edge from reader a to writer b
t	Binary topic-path indicator
M	Number of unique readers
J	Number of unique writers
K	Number of unique topics
N_m	Number of writers reader m follows
f_w	In-corpus frequency of writer w
$\alpha, \beta, \gamma, \delta, \epsilon$	Dirichlet (Beta) priors
θ	Topic distribution for reader ($p(z\|r)$)
ϕ	Writer distribution for topic ($p(w\|z)$)
π	In-corpus writer distribution ($p(w)$)
τ	Topic-path distribution for writer ($p(t\|w)$)
ρ	Weight (confidence) on edge (observation)
λ	Concentration scalar

5. EXPERIMENTS

In this section, we evaluate the proposed models based on the perplexity value calculated using a real-world Twitter dataset. As baselines, we use LDA and the best performer in our prior work [7] [3]. The experimental results show that our proposed models are very effective in lowering perplexity. We also discuss why and how they perform better than the baselines.

5.1 Dataset and Experiment Settings

We use the Twitter dataset we used in our previous work [7]. It has 10 million follow edges from 14,015 reader to

[3] As perplexity is only available for probabilistic topic models, we limited our baselines to probabilistic topic models.

2, 427, 373 writers. The dataset is sampled to ensure that all the outgoing edges from a randomly sampled reader are preserved. The average number of outgoing edges for a reader is 713.52.

Table 2 summarizes the 12 representative experimental cases we report in this section. We have two baselines: *base-lda* [4], the standard LDA experiment, and *base-f2step*, the best performer in our previous work [7]. *polya-w/r/wr* denotes the *polya-urn model* experiment considering writer popularity, reader popularity (activeness), and both side popularity, respectively. *2path-w/r/wr* are cases from the *two-path model* experiments, and *wlda-w/r/wr* are from the *weight model* experiments. *p-w&w-r* denotes a combination of *polya-w* and *wlda-r*. Though we ran a lot more experiments than reported ones here, we only report some meaningful ones for clarity and to save space [5]. Other cases like the *simple model*, the *two-path model* with hyper priors, and various combination models did not show much improvements. For the *weight model*, we tested various weighting schemes based on frequency, probability, PageRank [6], pointwise mutual information (PMI) [39], etc. We only report the best weighting schemes in this section. The best weighting scheme might be different for a different corpus. In all of our experiments, we ran 100 Gibbs sampling iterations and generated 100 topic groups because they turned out reasonable in our previous experiments [7]. We also define a popular writer as a writer having more than 100 followers in our experiments [6]. We ran multiple runs to find the following optimal parameter values: $\lambda = 0.1$, $\lambda_1 = 0.2$, $\lambda_2 = 20.0$, $C_1 = 4.2$, $C_2 = 2.0$, $C_3 = 2.0$, and $C_4 = 8.6$.

Table 2: Experimental cases and descriptions

Case	Experiment Description
base-lda	LDA
base-f2step	Two-step labeling with filtering
polya-w/r/wr	Polya-urn model for writer/reader/both
2path-w/r/wr	Two-path model for writer/reader/both
wlda-w/r/wr	Weight model for writer/reader/both
p-w&w-r	*polya-w* + *wlda-r*

5.2 Perplexity Analysis

We evaluate our proposed models using the widely-used perplexity metric [5, 7, 18, 19, 40] defined as:

$$perplexity(W_{test}) = \exp^{-\frac{\sum_{w \in W_{test}} \log p(w)}{|W_{test}|}}, \quad (22)$$

where W_{test} denotes all the writers (edges) in a test dataset. The perplexity quantifies the prediction power of a trained model by measuring how well the model handles unobserved test data. Since the exponent part of Equation (22)is a minus of the average log prediction probability over all the test edges, a lower perplexity means stronger prediction power of the model. In our previous study [7], slightly lower (3.27%) perplexity led to significant (64%) improvement on human-perceived clustering quality [7]. Thus, we believe that we can significantly improve the clustering quality of the model by further lowering its perplexity. We calculated the perplexity for two separate 10% randomly held-out datasets after training a model on the remaining 80% dataset. We averaged results from ten runs (five runs for each held-out dataset with different random seeds). As the standard LDA (*base-lda*) is designed to minimize perplexity, it is not easy to achieve lower perplexity than *base-lda*.

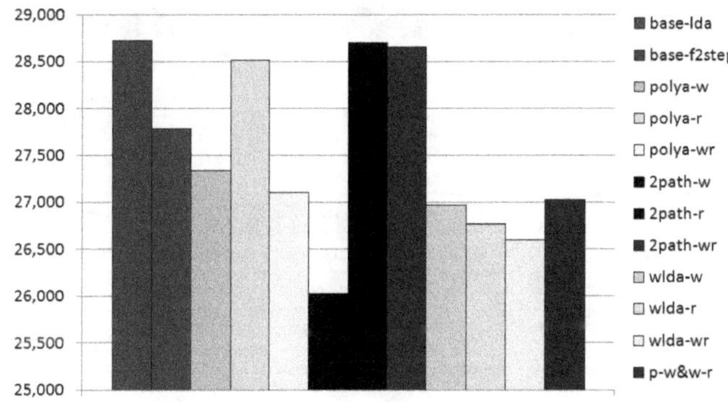

Figure 2: Perplexity comparison

We report the perplexity values from the 12 representative test cases in Figure 2, where we observe:

1. All our proposed models seem very effective in achieving lower perplexity than *base-lda*. However, the reader-side models of the *polya-urn model* and the *two-path model* show quite high perplexity compared to their counterparts (writer-side models).

2. *2path-w* shows the lowest perplexity. It shows 9.41% lower perplexity than *base-lda* (6.35% lower than *base-f2step*). However, *2path-r* and *2path-wr* show no improvements.

3. Different from the *polya-urn model* and the *two-path model*, the *weight model* shows low perplexity when the reader-side popularity is considered. It seems to conflict with our explanation that the *weight model* can be viewed as an extension to the *two-path model* in Section 4.4. We discuss this issue in Section 5.4

4. The combination models do not perform better than other models. Even *p-w&w-r*, the best performer among various combination models, shows higher perplexity than the *two-path model* and the *weight model*

If we pick the best performers in each group, the performance order would be: *two-path model* > *weight model* > combination model > *polya-urn model* > *base-f2step* > *base-lda*. In the two following sections, we investigate the *two-path model* and the *weight model* in detail.

5.3 Popularity vs. Activeness

To visualize the effect of the path-labeling, we compare the top-10 writers in two example topic groups related to *technology* from *base-lda* and *2path-w* in Figure 3. In the left

[4]We implemented our models based on the LDA implementation in [4].

[5]We tested *simple/polya/2path/wlda-w/r/wr*, *p-w/r/wr&w-w/r/wr*, and *hyperprior-w/r/wr*.

[6]We also tested 50 and 500 as the boundary value instead of 100 and the results were similar.

[7]The correlation between the perplexity and the human-perceived clustering quality was −0.806 in our previous work (excluding HLDAs).

writer	f_w	Bio
barackobama	7410	This account is run by #Obama2012 campaign staff. ...
whiteafrican	111	Where Africa and technology collide... Co-founder of Ushahidi, iHub ...
kiwanja	57	Mobile technologist. Anthropologist. Conservationist | Tech Awards ...
mrtweet	3697	We recommend awesome people to you!
stephenfry	3384	British Actor, Writer, Lord of Dance, Prince of Swimwear & Blogger
ushahidi	64	We are a non-profit tech company that specializes in developing free ...
hashtags	1862	How-to knowledge to improve your social media branding ...
stii	38	Code monkey. Love Django, Python, PHP, Surfing, Longboard ...
zoopedup	49	Zoopedup is an automotive social network that allows you ...
appfrica	41	Innovative international software development and design firm ...

(a) Example topic group from *two-path model*

writer	f_w	Bio
laughingsquid	1998	An online resource for interesting art, culture and technology. Founder ...
chrismessina	1078	Bachelor of Arts. UX designer on Google+. #godfather ...
jason	3382	LAUNCH Festival March 4-6, Hackathon March 2-4th: ...
davemorin	824	... Husband. Entrepreneur. Skier. Co-Founder and CEO of @Path
jack	1923	A sailor, a tailor *[Comment: Twitter creater Jack Dorsey]*
sarahcuda	886	I'm a reporter/author in silicon valley
dsifry	561	... Founder of Offbeat Guides, Technorati, Linuxcare, others...
anildash	1051	I love NYC, tech & funk. Cofounder of @activateinc & @thinkup. ...
joi	724	Director, MIT Media Lab
monstro	331	Co-founder Get Satisfaction, Adaptive Path, & Original. Co-author. ...

(b) When popularity-path edges are re-labeled with topics

Figure 3: Effect of path-labeling

figure, we see two highlighted writers who are not related to *technology*: *barackobama* and *stephenfry*. These celebrities are included in this group because they are so popular and followed by the people who are interested in *technology* as well. The standard LDA labels the follow edges from these people as *technology*-related even though those edges are purely generated from the popularity path. On the other hand, all the writers in the right figure are closely related to *technology*. The path-labeling reduces the chance of celebrities' appearing in irrelevant topic groups by labeling non-topic-driven follow edges with the popularity path as explained in Section 4.3.

Table 3: Path-labeling result from *2path-w*

Edge (from r to w)	*Group-p*	*Group-t*	*G-p/G-t*
Portion of edges	8.72%	91.28%	-
Avg. num. of edges to w	387.41	71.94	5.39
Avg. num. of edges from r	509.90	846.06	0.60
Avg. entropy of $p(z\|w)$	2.86	1.60	1.79
Avg. entropy of $p(z\|r)$	3.78	4.01	0.94

To measure the effect of the path-labeling, we gathered some statistics from *2path-w* and report them in Table 3. We observe that 8.72% of the test edges were processed by the popularity component (*group-p*) and 91.28% of them were processed by the topic component (*group-t*). We also calculated the average writer/reader popularity (number of incoming/outgoing edges) for the edges in both groups. The second and the third row of Table 3 tell us that each edge in *group-p* is from a reader following 509.90 writers on average [8] to a writer having 387.41 followers on average. We observe that the edges in *group-p* belong to much more popular writers than those in *group-t*. However, the edges in *group-p* seem to belong to less active readers. This finding contradicts our initial expectation on the "activeness", explained in Section 4.5, that a more active reader would be less topic sensitive. To more closely investigate this contradiction, we measured average entropy of $p(z|r)$ and $p(z|w)$. The intuition behind this measurement is that the higher

[8]We excluded the readers who follow less than 10 writers from our dataset because they may contain follow edges generated by pure curiosity and reciprocity. The same approach was used in [30].

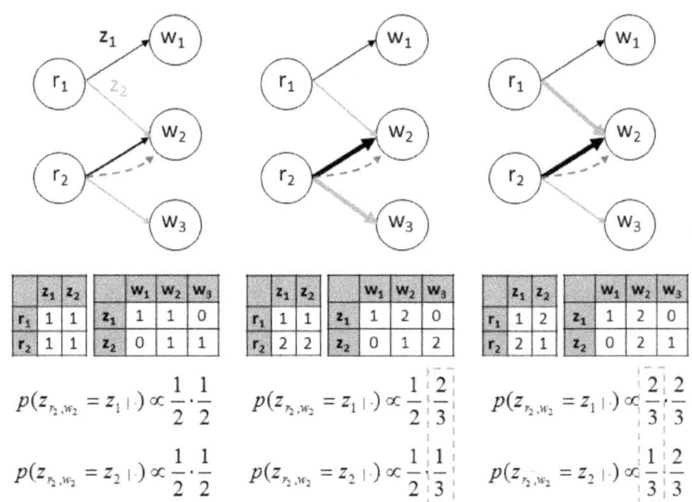

Figure 4: Reader weight vs. writer weight

entropy (uncertainty) of $p(z|r)$ or $p(z|w)$ of an edge (from reader r to writer w) may indicate that the edge has a lower probability to be labeled with a specific topic. Thus, it may have a higher chance of being labeled with the popularity path than one with a lower entropy. The fourth row of Table 3 [9] reports that the edges in *group-p* belong to the writers having much higher topic uncertainty. On the other hand, both groups show similar topic uncertainty in terms of reader-side topic entropy [10]. Thus, the reader-side popularity (activeness) does not seem to be useful in the correct path/topic-labeling. This finding also explains why *polya-r* and *2path-r* produced results with higher perplexity than their counterparts. However, we see the opposite results in the *weight model* experiments. The writer-side model (*wlda-w*) performs worse than the reader-side model (*wlda-r*). We discuss more about this anomaly in the next section.

5.4 Two-Path Model vs. Weight Model

To explain the reason why the anomaly explained in the

[9]We used a reduced 1M-edge dataset to calculate entropy due to the limited memory size of our machine.

[10]We also observe that the reader-side entropy is much higher than the writer-side entropy.

previous section happens in the results from the *two-path model* and the *weight model*, we devise a very simple social network edge-labeling example. The upper section of Figure 4 illustrates following edges among two readers and three writers. We assume that, among the four following edges, two of them are labeled with topic z_1 (darker one), and the other two are labeled with topic z_2 (lighter one). We also assume that edges have different weights and denote an edge with a weight 1 as a narrow edge and an edge with a weight 2 as a thick edge. Thus, the bi-partite graph in the left shows the standard LDA and the one in the center shows a *wlda-r* case where edges from a reader r_2 have higher weights. The bi-partite graph in the right shows a *wlda-w* case where edges to a writer w_2 have higher weights. Each pair of tables in the middle section show a pair of count matrices (reader-topic and topic-writer) for each bi-partite graph. Each value in a count matrix is a weight assigned to each edge. Now, let's think about the case we want to label a new edge from the reader r_2 to the writer w_2 (the dotted arrow) [11]. Each bottom section shows the probability of labeling the new edge with topic z_1 or z_2 for each case according to Equation (7) [12]. Unlike the standard LDA in the left, the probabilities between topic z_1 and z_2 are different in the dotted boxes in the bottom section. Interestingly, when we assign different weights to edges from different "readers" (*wlda-r* in the center) we find that the right part of the topic-labeling probability, which corresponds to the "writer" distribution for a topic ($p(w|z)$), changes instead of the topic distribution for a reader ($p(z|r)$), and vice versa. In the topic-labeling formula given in Equation (7), the numerator in the right part is a sum of weights of the edges from many readers to a certain writer. Thus, if the weights of the edges from a reader are changed, topics associated with those edges get different association probability. However, since the numerator in the left part is a sum of weights of edges from a reader, even though those weights are changed, the sum remains the same for all topics. This aspect explains why *wlda-r* performs better than *wlda-w*. While *wlda-w* affects the topic distribution for a reader ($p(z|r)$), *wlda-r* changes the writer distribution for a topic ($p(w|z)$), which is related to writer's popularity distribution.

Though the *weight model* produces results with higher perplexity, it has the same computational complexity as the standard LDA since it does not introduce a new hidden variable. Also, we may use various weighting schemes according to the nature of application domains. Though we only reported the result from the best weighting scheme in this paper, there were many candidate weighting schemes producing results with competitive perplexity values.

6. CONCLUSION

In this paper, we proposed topic models appropriate to analyze social network graphs. Different from a textual dataset, a popular user has very important meaning in a social network dataset and should be carefully handled. We started with the *simple model* which introduces the concept of the popularity component and explored various ways to effectively incorporate it in probabilistic topic models.

In extensive experiments with a real-world Twitter dataset, our models achieved significant improvements in terms of lowering *perplexity*. Particulary, our *two-path model* showed 9.41% lower perplexity than that of LDA. Given that a 3.27% lower perplexity led to 64% higher human-perceived clustering quality in our previous work [7], we believe that our *two-path model* can also significantly improve the clustering quality. With the *two-path model*, we also showed that the reader-side popularity (activeness) is not effective in judging the reader's topic sensitivity. We extended the *two-path model* into the *weight model* and explained why the latter behaves differently from what we have expected. The *weight model* is very flexible in selecting its weighting schemes and does not increase the complexity of LDA.

Since the popularity bias is universal in various datasets including webpage visit logs, advertisement click logs, and product purchase logs, our models can effectively provide more relevant recommendations in many web services.

7. ACKNOWLEDGEMENTS

We would like to thank Christopher Moghbel, and Sunghoon Ivan Lee for their help and feedback throughout this research. We are also very grateful for valuable comments from the anonymous reviewers.

8. REFERENCES

[1] Multinomial distribution. `http://en.wikipedia.org/wiki/Multinomial_distribution`.

[2] A. Ahmed, Y. Low, M. Aly, V. Josifovski, and A. J. Smola. Scalable distributed inference of dynamic user interests for behavioral targeting. In *KDD*, pages 114–122, 2011.

[3] E. M. Airoldi, D. M. Blei, S. E. Fienberg, and E. P. Xing. Mixed membership stochastic blockmodels. In *J. Mach. Learn. Res.*, 2008.

[4] D. Andrzejewski and X. Zhu. Latent dirichlet allocation with topic-in-set knowledge. In *Proceedings of the NAACL HLT 2009 Workshop on Semi-Supervised Learning for Natural Language Processing*, SemiSupLearn '09, pages 43–48, Stroudsburg, PA, USA, 2009. Association for Computational Linguistics.

[5] D. M. Blei, A. Y. Ng, and M. I. Jordan. Latent dirichlet allocation. *Journal of Machine Learning Research*, 3:993–1022, 2003.

[6] S. Brin and L. Page. The anatomy of a large-scale hypertextual web search engine. *Computer Networks*, 1998.

[7] Y. Cha and J. Cho. Social-network analsys using topic models. In *SIGIR*, 2012.

[8] J. Chang and D. Blei. Relational topic models for document networks. In *AIStats*, 2009.

[9] D. Cohn and H. Chang. Learning to probabilistically identify authoritative documents. In *Proceedings of the Seventeenth International Conference on Machine Learning*, ICML '00, pages 167–174, San Francisco, CA, USA, 2000. Morgan Kaufmann Publishers Inc.

[10] D. Cohn and T. Hofmann. The missing link - a probabilistic model of document content and hypertext connectivity. In *NIPS '00: Advances in Neural Information Processing Systems*. MIT Press, Cambridge, MA, 2000.

[11] S. Deerwester, S. T. Dumais, G. W. Furnas, T. K. Landauer, and R. Harshman. Indexing by latent

[11] We allow multiple edges in this example to make it simple.

[12] For simplicity, we ignored $-(a, b)$ and priors (α and β).

semantic analysis. *Journal of the American Scociety for Information Science*, 1990.

[12] L. Dietz, S. Bickel, and T. Scheffer. Unsupervised prediction of citation influences. In *In Proceedings of the 24th International Conference on Machine Learning*, pages 233–240, 2007.

[13] E. Erosheva, S. Fienberg, and J. Lafferty. Mixed membership models of scientific publications. In *Proceedings of the National Academy of Sciences*, page 2004. press, 2004.

[14] M. Girolami and A. Kaban. On an equivalence between plsi and lda. In *SIGIR*, 2003.

[15] A. Gruber, M. Rosen-Zvi, and Y. Weiss. Latent topic models for hypertext. In *UAI 2008, Proceedings of the 24th Conference in Uncertainty in Artificial Intelligence, July 9-12, 2008, Helsinki, Finland*, pages 230–239. AUAI Press, 2008.

[16] J. Hannon, M. Bennett, and B. Smyth. Recommending twitter users to follow using content and collaborative filtering approaches. In *RecSys*, pages 199–206. ACM, 2010.

[17] M. Harvey, I. Ruthven, and M. J. Carman. Improving social bookmark search using personalised latent variable language models. In *WSDM*, 2011.

[18] K. Henderson and T. Eliassi-Rad. Applying latent dirichlet allocation to group discovery in large graphs. In *Proceedings of the 2009 ACM symposium on Applied Computing*, 2009.

[19] M. D. Hoffman, D. M. Blei, and F. Bach. Online learning for latent dirichlet allocation. In *In NIPS*, 2010.

[20] T. Hofmann. Probabilistic latent semantic indexing. In *SIGIR*, 1999.

[21] Y. Hu, Y. Koren, and C. Volinsky. Collaborative filtering for implicit feedback datasets. In *Proceedings of the 2008 Eighth IEEE International Conference on Data Mining*, ICDM '08, pages 263–272, Washington, DC, USA, 2008. IEEE Computer Society.

[22] T. Iwata, T. Yamada, and N. Ueda. Modeling social annotation data with content relevance using a topic model. In *NIPS*, 2009.

[23] A. Java, X. Song, T. Finin, and B. L. Tseng. Why we twitter: An analysis of a microblogging community. In *WebKDD/SNA-KDD*, volume 5439 of *Lecture Notes in Computer Science*, pages 118–138. Springer, 2007.

[24] A. Mccallum, X. Wang, and A. Corrada-Emmanuel. Topic and role discovery in social networks with experiments on enron and academic email. *Journal of Artificial Intelligence Research*, 30:249–272, 2007.

[25] Q. Mei, D. Cai, D. Zhang, and C. Zhai. Topic modeling with network regularization. In *Proceedings of the 17th international conference on World Wide Web*, WWW '08, pages 101–110, New York, NY, USA, 2008. ACM.

[26] R. Nallapati, D. A. McFarland, and C. D. Manning. Topicflow model: Unsupervised learning of topic-specific influences of hyperlinked documents. *Journal of Machine Learning Research - Proceedings Track*, 15:543–551, 2011.

[27] R. M. Nallapati, A. Ahmed, E. P. Xing, and W. W. Cohen. Joint latent topic models for text and citations. In *Proceedings of the 14th ACM SIGKDD international conference on Knowledge discovery and data mining*, KDD '08, pages 542–550, New York, NY, USA, 2008. ACM.

[28] R. Pan, Y. Zhou, B. Cao, N. N. Liu, R. Lukose, M. Scholz, and Q. Yang. One-class collaborative filtering. *2008 Eighth IEEE International Conference on Data Mining*, 57:502–511, 2008.

[29] N. Pathak, C. DeLong, A. Banerjee, and K. Erickson. Social topic models for community extraction. In *The 2nd SNA-KDD Workshop*, 2008.

[30] M. Pennacchiotti and S. Gurumurthy. Investigating topic models for social media user recommendation. In *Proceedings of the 20th international conference companion on World wide web*, WWW '11, pages 101–102, New York, NY, USA, 2011. ACM.

[31] J. B. Schafer, J. Konstan, and J. Riedi. Recommender systems in e-commerce. In *Proceedings of the 1st ACM conference on Electronic commerce*, EC '99, pages 158–166, New York, NY, USA, 1999. ACM.

[32] H. Steck. Item popularity and recommendation accuracy. In *Proceedings of the fifth ACM conference on Recommender systems*, RecSys '11, pages 125–132, New York, NY, USA, 2011. ACM.

[33] M. Steyvers and T. L. Griffiths. Probabilistic topic models. *Handbook of Latent Semantic Analysis*, 2007.

[34] M. Steyvers, P. Smyth, M. Rosen-Zvi, and T. Griffiths. Probabilistic author-topic models for information discovery. In *SIGKDD*, 2004.

[35] C. Sun, B. Gao, Z. Cao, and H. Li. Htm: a topic model for hypertexts. In *Proceedings of the Conference on Empirical Methods in Natural Language Processing*, EMNLP '08, pages 514–522, Stroudsburg, PA, USA, 2008. Association for Computational Linguistics.

[36] V. Tuulos and H. Tirri. Combining topic models and social networks for chat data mining. In *In Proc. of the 2004 IEEE/WIC/ACM International Conference on Web Intelligence*, 2004.

[37] H. Wallach, D. Mimno, and A. McCallum. Rethinking lda: Why priors matter. In *NIPS*, 2009.

[38] X. Wang, N. Mohanty, and A. Mccallum. Group and topic discovery from relations and text. In *In Proc. 3rd international workshop on Link discovery*, pages 28–35. ACM, 2005.

[39] A. T. Wilson and P. A. Chew. Term weighting schemes for latent dirichlet allocation. In *Human Language Technologies: The 2010 Annual Conference of the North American Chapter of the Association for Computational Linguistics*, HLT '10, pages 465–473, Stroudsburg, PA, USA, 2010. Association for Computational Linguistics.

[40] H. Zhang, B. Qiu, C. L. Giles, H. C. Foley, and J. Yen. An lda-based community structure discovery approach for large-scale social networks. In *In IEEE International Conference on Intelligence and Security Informatics*, pages 200–207, 2007.

[41] D. Zhou, E. Manavoglu, J. Li, C. L. Giles, and H. Zha. Probabilistic models for discovering e-communities. In *World Wide Web Conference*, 2006.

Topic Hierarchy Construction for the Organization of Multi-Source User Generated Contents

Xingwei Zhu[1]*, Zhao-Yan Ming[2]†, Xiaoyan Zhu[1], Tat-Seng Chua[2]
[1]State Key Laboratory of Intelligent Technology and Systems, Tsinghua National Laboratory for Information Science and Technology, Department of Computer Sci. and Tech., Tsinghua University
[2]Department of Computer Science, School of Computing, National University of Singapore, Singapore
etzhu192@hotmail.com, mingzhaoyan@nus.edu.sg, zxy-dcs@tsinghua.edu.cn, chuats@nus.edu.sg

ABSTRACT

User generated contents (UGCs) carry a huge amount of high quality information. However, the information overload and diversity of UGC sources limit their potential uses. In this research, we propose a framework to organize information from multiple UGC sources by a topic hierarchy which is automatically generated and updated using the UGCs. We explore the unique characteristics of UGCs like blogs, cQAs, microblogs, *etc.*, and introduce a novel scheme to combine them. We also propose a graph-based method to enable incremental update of the generated topic hierarchy. Using the hierarchy, users can easily obtain a comprehensive, in-depth and up-to-date picture of their topics of interests. The experiment results demonstrate how information from multiple heterogeneous sources improves the resultant topic hierarchies. It also shows that the proposed method achieves better F_1 scores in hierarchy generation as compared to the state-of-the-art methods.

Categories and Subject Descriptors

H.0 [**Information Systems**]: General; H.3.2 [**Information Storage and Retrieval**]: Information Storage

Keywords

User Generated Contents, Information Organization, Topic Hierarchy

1. INTRODUCTION

With the rapid development of Web 2.0, user generated contents (UGCs) on the internet are becoming important sources for information navigation and knowledge acquisition. For example, when a user wants to know Barack Obama's performance in the 2012 presidential campaign, he may refer to blogs on Blog sites like *Blogger*[1] for authoritative criticisms, ask questions on community question answering (cQA) sites like *Yahoo! Answers*[2] for specific information and read tweets from *Twitter*[3] to follow up with his friends' opinions.

However, the volume of UGCs is huge and increasing every day. Even for a specific topic, it is usually impossible for users to go through all the contents and manually identify the newly emerging and important sub-topics. On the other hand, though in some UGC sources like *Wikipedia*[4], the data is well organized into structured format which can be easily accessed, they cannot catch up with the ever changing internet since they rely on human to compile and update.

The characteristics of different kinds of UGCs are diversified. Information in any single source is always limited and domain specific. For example, if a user requires a technical report for "IPhone 5", it is better to refer to blogs or cQAs instead of tweets in Twitter. But when he wants to know how his friends like "IPhone 5", Twitter turns out to be a better place. As a result, in order to have an overall picture of the topic, users have to refer to multiple UGC sources, which further increases their burdens to integrate these heterogeneous contents together.

To address the above problems, in this paper, we propose to organize information from multiple UGC sources using an automatically generated topic hierarchy. The task is not trivial due to the following three challenges:

- Instead of merely constructing a hierarchy [8] or organizing contents according to an existing hierarchy [12], our task requires the two problems to be solved at the same time, which requires a seamless integration of state-of-the-art techniques in both fields.
- Though there have been many works proposed to organize information from individual UGC sources like blogs [4], cQAs [12] or tweets [14], *etc.*, integrating information from multiple sources is a new and difficult problem since they are heterogeneous and may contain different kinds of noise and errors.
- In order to keep up with the ever changing internet, a novel framework is required to enable real time update on the hierarchies with newly obtained data. The real

* This work was done when the first author was a visiting student in National University of Singapore.
† Corresponding author.

SIGIR'13, July 28–August 1, 2013, Dublin, Ireland.
Copyright 2013 ACM 978-1-4503-2034-4/13/07 ...$15.00.

[1]http://www.blogger.com/
[2]http://answers.yahoo.com/
[3]https://twitter.com/
[4]http://en.wikipedia.org/wiki/Main_Page

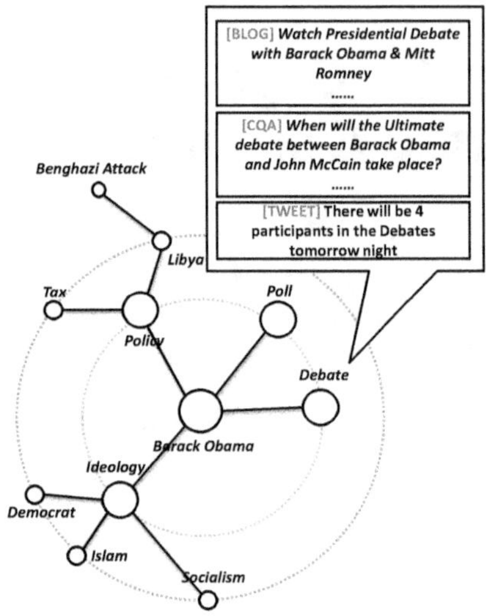

Figure 1: The topic hierarchy for "Barack Obama". It organizes 119 blogs, 476 cQAs and 49749 tweets. Due to the space limit, we only illustrate the title of one blog, one cQA and one tweet for one of its sub-topics, *debate*.

time requirement is very different from previous approaches [8] [13], where a hierarchy is built using static data set and requires no further update.

In view of the above challenges, a three step framework is proposed to organize UGCs using automatically generated topic hierarchies. Given a collection of UGCs such as blogs, cQAs and tweets on a specific topic, we first identify potential topic terms from these sources. Then assisted by external knowledge from Wikipedia, *WordNet*[5] and search engine results, we propose a novel scheme to identify sub-topic relations between topic terms using multiple evidences. Finally, by treating topic terms as nodes and sub-topic relations between them as edges, a graph-based algorithm is used to incrementally generate a topic hierarchy. Each time new data is available, the same framework can also be used to update the previously generated hierarchy with newly emerging sub-topics. Using the resultant topic hierarchy, the UGCs can be organized to nodes on the hierarchy according to their relevant sub-topics. In Figure 1, we show an example topic hierarchy for the topic "Barack Obama". It contains 11 sub-topics, under which a total of 119 blogs, 476 cQAs and 49749 tweets are organized. The contributions of our work can be summarized as:

- We propose a novel framework to organize UGCs by automatically generated topic hierarchies with real time update. The experimental results demonstrate its superior performance over the state-of-the-art methods.

- We leverage heterogeneous information from multiple sources by exploring their unique characteristics, and propose a novel scheme to combine the evidences extracted from these sources to enhance the framework.

The remainder of this paper is organized as follows: In section 2 we present the related work and in Section 3 we formally define the problem. Section 4 presents the framework of our approach, followed by detailed description on the three main modules, *i.e.*, topic term identification, topic relation identification and topic hierarchy generation including the real time hierarchy updating algorithm. In section 5, we discuss our evaluation method, experiments and results. Finally Section 6 concludes the paper.

[5]http://wordnet.princeton.edu

2. RELATED WORK

Topic Term Detection: TF-IDF weighting has been found to be very effective [2] [6] for topic term extraction from documents. To avoid the need to estimation IDF, which requires huge document collections, Matsuo et al.[11] employed a sentence-level word co-occurrence matrix to find the keywords in a single document. NLP tools such as TextRunner [20] has also been applied to extract keyword terms, however, since these tools are linguistics-based, it is hard to use them to analyze UGCs which usually contain multiple languages and are ill grammar. In some recent works [10], the hierarchical cluster structure of documents (e.g., Wikipedia) is also adopted to improve the keyword selection performance.

Taxonomy Induction: Given a small document set, Lawrie et al. [9] proposed to extract its intrinsic topic hierarchy by estimating the topicality of terms and co-occurrence probability between them using only the given documents. Given a candidate term set, Navigli et al. [13] trained classifiers to detect is-a relations between terms and utilized a graph-based algorithm to optimize the term taxonomy. Besides, Snow et al.[16] introduced a probabilistic model to determine the most possible hierarchy for a set of concepts. Using both statistics-based and pattern-based features, Yang et al.[19] further proposed the metrics of information function and created hierarchies by an insert process, in which nodes are inserted onto the hierarchy to minimize the change of information functions. A recent work [21] extended this approach by employing more objective functions, *i.e.*, minimum Hierarchy Discrepancy and minimum Semantic Inconsistency to achieve a better insertion decision.

Approaches using Multiple Sources: Information from multiple sources provides researchers clues in different views and helps to achieve better results by overcoming the bias of any single information source [3] [5] [17]. Han et al.[3] used information from Wikipedia, WordNet and a NE co-occurrence corpus to measure the semantic relatedness between words. Although they just chose the conditionally most confident source to estimate the relatedness, instead of integrating the three sources together, the results have already outperformed the methods which only used single source. On the other hand, Hoffart et al.[5] proposed to integrate information from Wikipedia, WordNet, Geo-Name corpus, *etc.*, to build Yago2, an open domain structured knowledge base.

3. PROBLEM FORMULATION

We define the *root topic* $\mathcal{C}$ as a word or phrase which indicates the users' search intends. It can be an entity (*e.g.*, "Barack Obama"), an event (*e.g.*, "Benghazi Attack") or other informative concept. Given a root topic, we define its *information source set* S_c as $S_c = \{s_i\}_{i=1}^{N}$, in which s_i indicates a collection of documents from the ith information source. They are collected for $\mathcal{C}$ and can be automatically updated when new data is available.

The data in S_c is usually unstructured and contains noise and errors. We define a *topic hierarchy* as $H = \{T, M, R\}$, in which all useful information in S_c is organized using the following three components:

- **Topic Set** $T = \{t_1, t_2, ..., t_i, ...\}$, where t_i indicates a topic term. T includes the root topic $\mathcal{C}$ and the potential sub-topics of $\mathcal{C}$ for the documents in S_c.
- **Document-Topic Mapping** $M : d \to 2^T$, where d indicates a document in S_c. M assigns each document with terms in T as its relevant topics. For some noisy documents, the mapping results may be ϕ.
- **Sub-topic Relation Set** R: Denote $r(t_A, t_B)$ as a sub-topic relation, which means t_B is a sub-topic of t_A. $R = \{r_1, r_2, ..., r_i, ...\}$ is a set of sub-topic relations between the topics in T. It links all the topics into a hierarchy rooted at $\mathcal{C}$.

Formally, we define our task as follows:
Information Organization Task: Given a root topic $\mathcal{C}$ and its information source set S_c, we aim to build and continuously update a topic hierarchy H for $\mathcal{C}$ in order to organize the information in S_c according to their relevant topics.

4. APPROACH

4.1 Information Sources

Inevitably, every single UGC source has flaws. Take blog as an example, although well-written, blog usually focuses on narrow points (*e.g.*, technical reports for "IPhone 5" or big events for "Barack Obama") and takes a long time work before being published online. On the other hand, tweets can provide timely information (*e.g.*, release date for "IPhone 5" in Europe), while they also contain a huge amount of noises (*e.g.*, *"should I buy a IPhone 4S or IPhone 5?"*). These drawbacks limit the potential uses of the UGCs.

In this paper, we will tackle the above problem by combining the power of three prevailing UGCs, *i.e.*, Blogs, cQA and Twitter as our information sources. we also utilize domain-independent factoid knowledge from Wikipedia, WordNet, *etc.* to supplement the limited and specific UGC sources.

4.2 Framework

To address the information organization task, we introduce a three step framework as illustrated in Figure 2. For a given root topic $\mathcal{C}$, we first identify potential sub-topic terms from S_c. Then we identify the sub-topic relations between the sub-topics. Finally we generate the topic hierarchy and assign UGCs in S_c onto the hierarchy. The following three sections will describe the details for each module. We will also show how the framework can be used to update an existing hierarchy when new data is available.

4.3 Topic Term Identification

We collect potential sub-topics for $\mathcal{C}$ in two steps: (1) we extract keywords from documents in S_c to obtain an initial topic set; and (2) we extend the topic set with more abstract and general topics using knowledge from external sources.

4.3.1 Grounding Topic Extraction

The documents in S_c contains many potential sub-topic terms. Since these terms directly reflect people's focuses and interests, we denote them as *grounding topics*, t_g. To characterize a potential grounding topic, we first adopt four heuristic rules from [7], *i.e.,the pos-tag heuristic, length heuristic, frequency heuristic* and *linguistic-alteration heuristic.* In Table 1, we present a brief introduction of them.

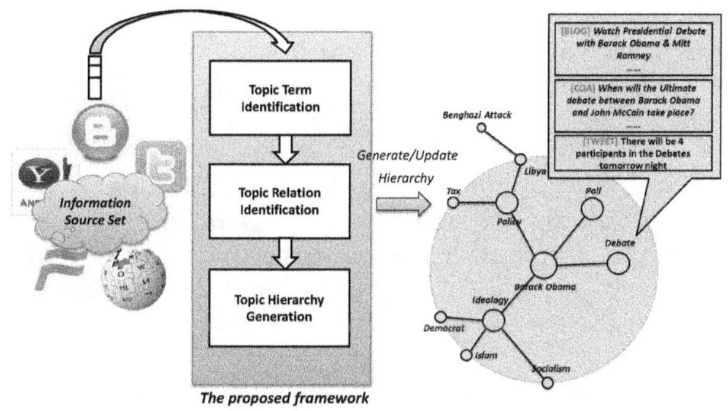

Figure 2: The proposed method: maintaining a Topic Hierarchy using real-time data from multiple heterogeneous UGC sources by a three step framework.

Heuristic	Details
POS-tag	A topic term must be a NP[6]("battery") or a NP phrase("battery life").
Length	A topic term contains at least 1 word and at most 3 words.
Frequency	A topic term must occurs in at least 3 documents in the corpus.
Linguistic-Alteration	If a phrase is like "NP_1 of NP_2"("life of battery") or "NP_2's NP_1"("battery's life"), it will be converted to "NP_2 NP_1"("battery life"). Rules about *plural* and *abbreviation* are also used.

Table 1: Heuristic rules used in topic identification

Next, for each source in S_c, we separately estimate the *TF-IDF* scores for the potential grounding topics and obtain topic terms for each document as follows.
Blogs: We use the blog title and content to compute the TF-IDF scores for terms in blogs. Since the title of a blog usually indicates its main topics, we double the weights of terms in titles. For each blog, the top 5 ranked terms by TF-IDF are selected as its topic terms.
cQAs: We use the question title, description and the best answers to compute the TF-IDF scores. For each cQA, the top 5 ranked terms are selected as its topic terms.
Tweets: We use the content and the words surrounded by hash tags to compute the scores. Since tweets are short and cover fewer topics, we only collect the top ranked term as their topic terms.

Simply putting the topic terms of documents together may bring lots of noise. In order to select high quality and popular topic terms for the root topic, we adopt the following two assumptions:

*Assumption 1: A topic term is of **high quality** only if it can be extracted from documents in different information sources.*

*Assumption 2: A topic term is **popular** only if it can be extracted from many different documents.*

[6]We use the Stanford CoreNLP toolkit (http://nlp.stanfo-rd.edu/software/corenlp.shtml) to get the POS-tags.

We thus only collect the topic terms that are among the top 200 frequent topic terms in at least 2 different information sources into the *grounding topic set*, $T_G = \{t_{g1}, t_{g2}, ...\}$.

4.3.2 Topic Set Extension

Although T_G contains many low-level topic terms (*e.g.*, ***siri***, ***battery*** for "IPhone 5"), it lacks middle level topic terms (*e.g.*, ***software*** and ***device***) partly because they are too abstract and general for UGCs. Since these middle level terms are also useful in topic hierarchy generation, we investigate external information sources to obtain them.

Search Engine: For each term in T_G, we use two patterns, *i.e.*, "** such as <slot>*" and "*<slot> of **" to obtain its higher level topic terms. We first fill the term into the slot and submit it to a search engine like *Bing*[7]. Then we collect the noun phrases in the position of the wildcard on the returned search pages as middle level topics.

WordNet: WordNet contains hypernym relations between concepts. If a topic term in T_G is included in WordNet, we collect the terms in its direct hypernym synset as middle level topics.

Wikipedia: If a topic term in T_G is a Wikipedia title, its category tags are also collected as middle level topics.

The middle level topics shared by at least 2 sources are collected into the *extended topic set*, T_E. Then the final candidate topic set $T = \{\mathcal{C}\} \cup T_G \cup T_E$.

4.4 Topic Relation Identification

The sub-topic relation between topic terms provides essential information to organize the topics. Take "Barack Obama" as an example, if we know that there is a sub-topic relation between two of its sub-topics, *e.g.*, ***policy*** $\rightarrow$ ***tax***, which indicates that ***tax*** is a sub-topic of ***policy***, it will be very probable that there is a path between the two topic terms on the topic hierarchy.

To infer a sub-topic relation $r(t_A, t_B)$, we need to estimate the probability that the topic t_B is a sub-topic of t_A. Inspired by [18], we approximate this probability with an empirical score $e(r(t_A, t_B))$ which is estimated by evidences from multiple sources. The evidences are summarized in Table 2 and the details are listed as follows:

Evidences from the Information Source Set: If there is a sub-topic relation between two topic terms, they must be highly related, where contextual distribution can be used to measure this relatedness. More specifically, for each topic term, the nouns, verbs and adjectives that co-occur with it in the documents/sentences in S_c are collected as its document/sentence level contexts. For each term pair t_A and t_B, the document and sentence level contextual evidences, *i.e.*, $e_{distr_{doc}}(t_A, t_B)$[8] and $e_{distr_{sen}}(t_A, t_B)$ are defined as the cosine similarity between the corresponding contexts of them.

Evidences from Wikipedia: *Pointwise Mutual Information (PMI)* is also a measurement for the relatedness between two terms. We compute the PMI over a subset of Wikipedia corpus, which only includes pages that are not redirect pages and contain more than 1000 words. For t_A and t_B, we compute the normalized PMI as $npmi(t_A, t_B) = \frac{pmi(t_A, t_B)}{-log[p(t_A, t_B)]}$, where $pmi(t_A, t_B) = log\frac{p(t_A, t_B)}{p(t_A)p(t_B)}$. Then the pmi evidence $e_{pmi}(t_A, t_B) = \frac{1 + npim(t_A, t_B)}{2}$.

[7]http://www.bing.com

[8]We do not use tweets in generating document level contextual evidence since they are relatively too short.

We also use the category and sub-title evidences from Wikipedia, *i.e.*, $e_{wcate(t_A, t_B)}$ and $e_{wtitle}(t_A, t_B)$, which can be estimated as follows, respectively:

$$e_{wcate}(t_A, t_B) = \begin{cases} 1 & : \text{ wikipage } t_B \text{ has category tag } t_A \\ 0 & : \text{ otherwise.} \end{cases} \tag{1}$$

$$e_{wtitle}(t_A, t_B) = \begin{cases} 1 & : \ t_B \text{ is a subdirectory of } t_A \text{ on a wikipage} \\ 0 & : \text{ otherwise.} \end{cases} \tag{2}$$

Evidences from WordNet: If t_A and t_B can be found in WordNet and t_A is an ancestor of t_B, then it is very probable that t_B is a sub-topic of t_A. In practice, if t_A is an ancestor of t_B in WordNet, we use the WordNet similarity [15] to estimate the WordNet evidence as $e_{wnet}(t_A, t_B) = \frac{1}{WNDis(t_A, t_B)}$, where $WNDis(t_A, t_B)$ denotes the length of the shortest path between t_A and t_B in WordNet. Otherwise we just let $e_{wnet}(t_A, t_B) = 0$.

Evidences from Search Engine Results: We also use patterns like "*<topic>* such as *<subtopic>* and" to collect evidences from the internet. For each term pair t_A and t_B, we generate a query by filling them into the pattern (*e.g.*, "t_A *such as* t_B and") and submit it together with the root topic [9] to the search engine. Denote $pattern_i$ as the i_{th} pattern, we can obtain a 0/1 pattern-based evidence $e_{spattern_i}(t_A, t_B)$, whose value is set to 1 only if the search engine returns more than ζ results that contain this query; otherwise it is set to 0. In practice, we select 6 patterns as listed in Appendix *A* and ζ is set to 10 empirically.

To combine the above evidences, instead of simply adding or multiplying them together like [19][21], we first divide the evidences into two sets as shown in Table 2, *i.e.*, the **directed-evidence** set E_{dir} which includes the evidences that can determine the direction of the sub-topic relation and the **undirected-evidence** set E_{und} in which the evidences bear no directionality information.

For the directed-evidences, we use a linear combination to combine them together as follows:

$$e_{dir}(t_A, t_B) = \sum_{e_k \in E_{dir}} w_k \cdot e_k(t_A, t_B) \tag{3}$$

where w_k is the weight of the kth evidence in determining the direction of the sub-topic relation and $\sum_k w_k = 1$.

Since the training data is not always available for open domain topics, supervised methods used in previous works [21] on weight estimation cannot be used to calculate w_k. In this paper, we propose an unsupervised method to meet this challenge. The basic idea of our method is that since sub-topic relation is directed, it is not possible that both $r(t_A, t_B)$ and $r(t_B, t_A)$ exist. Therefore, if a directed-evidence e_k supports both $r(t_A, t_B)$ and $r(t_B, t_A)$, which happens when the difference between $e_k(t_A, t_B)$ and $e_k(t_B, t_A)$ is not significant, e_k should be less weighted. More specifically, we estimate the weight w_k for each directed-evidence e_k as $w_k = \frac{dif_k}{\sum_k dif_k}$, in which dif_k is calculated as follows:

$$dif_k = \frac{1}{p_k} \sum_{\substack{t_A, t_B \in T \\ t_A \neq t_B}} |e_k(t_A, t_B) - e_k(t_B, t_A)| \cdot l_{k, t_A, t_B}$$

[9]The root topic is used to filter out irrelevant search results.

directed-evidences in E_{dir}	**Source**
$e_{spattern_0}$ - $e_{spattern_5}$	*search engine*
e_{wtitle}	*wikipedia*
e_{wcate}	*wikipedia*
e_{wnet}	*wordnet*
undirected-evidences in E_{und}	**Source**
$e_{distr_{doc}}$	*information set*
$e_{distr_{sen}}$	*information set*
e_{pmi}	*wikipedia*

Table 2: The sources of evidences we use to estimate the probability of a sub-topic relation

where $l_{k,t_A,t_B} = \max\{e_k(t_A,t_B), e_k(t_B,t_A)\}$ gives higher weights to the evidences with high values and $p_k = \sum_{t_A,t_B \in T, t_A \neq t_B} |e_k(t_A,t_B) + e_k(t_B,t_A)|$ punishes the evidences that are too general. Then the final score $e((r(t_A,t_B))$ is estimated using the following equation:

$$e(r(t_A,t_B)) = e_{dir}(t_A,t_B) \cdot \prod_{e_s \in E_{und}} e_s(t_A,t_B) \quad (4)$$

where $\prod_{e_s \in E_{und}} e_s(t_A,t_B)$ combines all the undirected-evidences for the two topic terms.

4.5 Topic Hierarchy Generation

By treating the sub-topics in T as nodes, sub-topic relations between them as edges, we can generate a sub-topic graph. Next, we estimate the weight for each edge using the scores estimated in section 4.4 using the following equation:

$$w(r(t_A,t_B)) = \begin{cases} |e(r(t_A,t_B)) - e(r(t_B,t_A))| \cdot e(r(t_A,t_B)), & \text{if } e(r(t_A,t_B)) > e(r(t_B,t_A)) \text{ and } t_A \neq t_B \\ 0, & \text{if } e(r(t_A,t_B)) < e(r(t_B,t_A)) \text{ and } t_A \neq t_B \\ 1, & \text{if } t_A = t_B \end{cases} \quad (5)$$

in which $w(r(t_A,t_B))$ is proportional to both $e(r(t_A,t_B))$ and the difference between $e(r(t_A,t_B))$ and $e(r(t_B,t_A))$, indicating the strength of the edge from the node t_A to t_B. By removing the zero weighted edges, equation 5 also guarantees that there is only one directed edge between two nodes, which is essential for a valid hierarchy.

Next, we need to prune this graph into a hierarchy. Inspired by [13], we employ a graph based method to tackle this problem. Different from this work, we take an iterative approach: at each step we only add one sub-topic into the hierarchy, which makes our method amendable to incrementally update the hierarchies. In general, the proposed hierarchy generation algorithm can be formalized as Algorithm 1.

Given a candidate topic set T for $\mathcal{C}$, the algorithm functions as follows. Let T_i and R_i be the resultant topic set and sub-topic relation set of the hierarchy after the ith iteration, we initialize them as $T_0 = \{\mathcal{C}\}$ and $R_0 = \phi$ (line 1). In the ith iteration, we first add a topic term t in $T - T_{i-1}$ into T_{i-1} (line 3 - 9) using the following function:

$$t = \underset{t_s \in T - T_{i-1}}{\text{argmax}} \sum_{t_k \in T_{i-1}} (w(r(t_k,t_s)) + w(r(t_s,t_k))) \quad (6)$$

where t is the topic term that maximizes $score(t) = \sum_{t_k \in T_{i-1}} (w(r(t_k,t_s)) + w(r(t_s,t_k)))$, which indicates the overall relatedness between t_s and topic terms in T_{i-1}. Note that *NIL* will be returned if $T - T_{i-1} = \phi$ or *score*(t) is 0.

Once we have added t into T_{i-1} to form T_i, we also add all the edges between t and topics in T_{i-1} into R_{i-1}, resulting in R_i (line 10 - 15). In order to guarantee that edges in R_i make up a valid hierarchy, next we use a graph based method to prune the edges in R_i as follows.

Algorithm 1 Hierarchy Generation Algorithm

Input:
  T: the candidate topic set;
Output:
  R_{ret}: the sub-topic relation set of the resultant hierarchy;
  T_{ret}: the topic set of the resultant hierarchy;
  Initialize $T_0 = \{\mathcal{C}\}$, $R_0 = \phi$
  for i = 1 TO ∞ **do**
    $t \leftarrow$ selectTermFrom($T - T_{i-1}$)
    if t is NIL **then**
      $R_{ret} \leftarrow R_{i-1}$
      $T_{ret} \leftarrow T_{i-1}$
      break
    end if
    $T_i \leftarrow t \cup T_{i-1}$
    $R_i \leftarrow R_{i-1}$
    for all t_k IN T_{i-1} **do**
      if edgeBetween(t_k, t) exists **then**
        $R_i \leftarrow R_i \cup$ edgeBetween(t_k, t)
      end if
    end for
    edgeWeighting(R_i)
    R_i = hierarhcyPruning(R_i)
  end for

Edge Weighting using Topic Relatedness (line 16): Edge weighting assigns score to each edge in R_i, indicating its importance in constructing the hierarchy. Our method generalizes that of [13] by weighting each edge in R_i with the estimated weights instead of simple 0/1 values. The process is as follows:

- If a topic term is related to many grounding topics in T_G, it could be important in the hierarchy. Let $w_t(t_k)$ denotes the weight of a topic term t_k in T_i, we estimate it as $w_t(t_k) = \sum_{t_g \in T_G} w(r(t_{root}, t_g)) \cdot w(r(t_k, t_g))$, in which $w(r(t_{root}, t_g))$ gives the importance of the grounding topics, and $w(r(t_k, t_g))$ reflexes the relatedness between t_k and the grounding topics.
- Then for each node $t_k \in T_i$, by denoting $L = \{t_u \rightarrow t_{u+1}\}_{u=0}^{|L|}$ as a path that connects t_{root} and t_k, its score is calculated as: $score_L = \sum_{u=0}^{|L|-1} w_t(t_u) \cdot w(r(t_u, t_{u+1}))$. Next, for each edge $t_s \rightarrow t_k$, its weight is estimated as follows:

$$w_r(t_s \rightarrow t_k) = \max_{\substack{L \text{ ends} \\ \text{with } t_s \rightarrow t_k}} score_L \quad (7)$$

Hierarchy Pruning using Optimum Branching (line 17): Given the edge weighting results, we can use the *Chu-Liu/Edmond's optimum branching algorithm* [1] to find a subset of the current edge set R_i, which is the optimized hierarchy for the given topic terms where *every non-root node has only one parent and the sum of the edge weights are maximized.*

When the iteration terminates at the Nth iternation, the resultant topic set T_{N-1} and sub-topic relation set R_{N-1} will be collected for the final topic hierarchy. To guarantee that the hierarchy is specifically related to the given topic $\mathcal{C}$ and the documents in S_c, we further remove (1) the nodes that are not reachable for the root topic and (2) the leaf nodes that are not in the grounding topic set. Finally, for each topic term t in the topic set, we assign the documents in S_c whose topic terms contain t to the corresponding node, resulting in M, the document-topic mapping function of the resultant topic hierarchy.

4.6 Topic Hierarchy Update

For a given topic, the information on the internet is ever-changing. Different from many previous approaches that work on static corpus, we find it useful and necessary to dynamically sketch evolving topic hierarchies for users. For example, assume we have built a topic hierarchy for "Barack Obama" before the presidential campaign; when people start to talk about his inauguration ceremony on the internet, we need to detect the corresponding new sub-topic ***inauguration*** and insert it and its relevant documents to the correct place on "Barack Obama"'s topic hierarchy.

To this end, we make it a key function for our proposed framework to be able to incrementally update the topic hierarchy by using the newly obtained data. Let $H_{old} = \{T_{old}, M_{old}, R_{old}\}$ be the existing hierarchy and S_{new} the newly obtained data set, a new hierarchy $H_{new} = \{T_{new}, M_{new}, R_{new}\}$ can be obtained by updating H_{old} using the following process:

Update the candidate topic set:
$T_{add} \leftarrow$ topic term identified from S_{new};
$T_{new} \leftarrow T_{old} \cup T_{add}$;
Update the topic hierarchy:
$R_{new}, T_{new} \leftarrow$ generate hierarchy using Algorithm 1 in which $R_0 = R_{old}$, $T_0 = T_{old}$ and $T = T_{new} - T_{old}$, thus adding new nodes in T_{add} and edges between terms in T_{add} and T_{old} into T_{old} and R_{old}.
Update the document-topic mapping function:
$M_{add} \leftarrow$ new mapping results between terms in T_{new} and documents in S_{new};
$M_{new} \leftarrow M_{old} \cup M_{add}$;

This update process is robust. This is evidenced from the fact that, when there are mistakes in the existing hierarchy, the newly obtained information can be used to correct the wrong relations. For example, the sub-topic relation set $R_{old} = \{$***barack obama*** $\rightarrow$ ***tax***$\}$ contains a very ambiguous relation[10]. When a new topic term ***policy*** is discovered from the new data set, instead of just adding it as a child to any of the two existing nodes, our method can further break the original ambiguous relation and create a better structure for the three topic terms; thus $R_{new} = \{$***barack obama*** $\rightarrow$ ***policy***, ***policy*** $\rightarrow$ ***tax***$\}$.

5. EVALUATION

5.1 Experimental Setup

We collect UGCs from the internet to form a corpus of four categories: Digital Products, Politicians, Cosmetics and Corporations. In each category, two to three topics are selected, resulting in 11 root topics. For each topic, blogs, cQAs and tweets are collected. We crawl blogs for a topic by submitting the topic name as the query into the Google Blog search engine[11] and collect the first 200 returned blogs. For cQAs and tweets, we use the Yahoo! Answer API and Twitter API to obtain the data stream on the target topic. A brief statistics of our corpus can be found in Table 3.

Category	Topic	blog	cQA	tweet
Digital Products	IPhone 5	182	1,523	411,826
	IPad mini	192	797	2,782
	Xbox kinect	195	1,476	30,261
Politicians	Barack Obama	193	1,043	426,811
	Mitt Romney	188	1,024	2,759
	Hillary Clinton	190	1,050	811
Cosmetics	Chanel	179	985	2,782
	Estee Lauder	194	1,049	17,816
Corporations	Facebook Inc.	190	973	429,979
	Microsoft Corp.	175	1,034	429,483
	Blizzard Inc.	192	999	2,022

Table 3: Statistics on the collected data sets in each information source

Topic	Sub-topics
IPhone 5	game, siri, battery, cost, software, jailbreak, wifi, update, ...
Barack Obama	policy, debate, law, islam, benghazi, poll, democrat, tax, ...
Chanel	perfume, watch, bags, sunglass, toiletry, mall, event, advert, ...
Microsoft Corp.	bing, surface, os, partner, outlook, windows phone 8, office 2013, ...

Table 4: Resultant candidate topic sets for four exemplar root topics

Note that the data in all the three information sources are tagged with time stamps. For blogs, they can be obtained from the snippets in Google Blog search results which indicate when the blogs are published. The data from Yahoo! Answer and Twitter APIs also contains time stamps on when the questions are asked or the tweets are created.

5.2 Topic Term Identification

In this section, we will first analysis the candidate topic sets generated by the method described in section 4.3. Next we will demonstrate how the use of different UGC sources improve its performance.

Table 4 shows a portion of identified topic terms for four exemplar root topics. From the results we can see that UGCs contain very rich and diversified information. For "Barack Obama", sub-topics on different aspects like politics (e.g., ***law***), personal information (e.g., ***islam***) and latest events (e.g., ***debates***) can be precisely extracted. We even obtain more comprehensive product-related topics (e.g., ***sunglass***) for "Chanel" than those in Wikipedia.

Define the ***coverage*** of the candidate topic set T as the ratio of the documents in the information source set that contain at least one term in T as its relevant topics, the average coverage is 18.4% for all root topics. Although twitter contains a huge amount of noise (more than 85% are noise from statistics on a randomly selected data set that contains 550 tweets), the proposed method can effectively filter out most of them, hence only 18.2% high-quality tweets are covered. On the other hand, higher coverage is observed for blogs (54.7%) and cQAs (40.4%).

From the covered documents, we sample 20 blogs, 20 cQAs and 50 tweets for each topic. Three annotators are asked to

[10] It may means ***barack obama***'s ***policy*** on ***tax*** or ***barack obama***'s own ***tax***.

[11] http://www.google.com/blogsearch

determine whether the topic terms we found are relevant to the corresponding documents. Only the documents that have agreement among all annotators are used for the statistics. The result shows that for all UGC sources and topic categories, our method can achieve a precision of 73.2% to 90.4%.

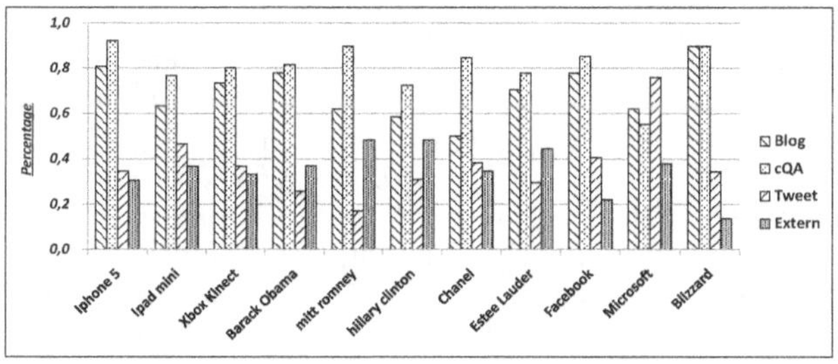

Figure 3: The percentage of topic terms supported by each information source on the topic set

Figure 3 shows the contribution of different UGC sources in topic term identification. We can see that all sources are indispensable. Although cQAs and blogs provide the majority of the topic terms, tweet tends to contribute timely and popular topics such as ***release date*** of ***iphone 5*** and ***price*** of ***ipad mini***. Though very limited, external sources provide middle-level topics such as ***os*** of ***microsoft*** and ***policy*** of ***barack obama***, which are essential when organizing the topics into a hierarchy.

5.3 Topic Hierarchy Generation

5.3.1 Evaluation Metrics

We evaluate our results against manually created gold standards. For each topic, three annotators are employed to create hierarchies independently using terms from the candidate topic set according to the following three rules.
Rule 1: Relevancy. All nodes on the hierarchy must be reasonable sub-topics of the root topic. It guarantees that users won't get noisy information from the topic hierarchy.
Rule 2: Maximum coverage. All relevant nodes should be included into the hierarchy. Hence users won't miss any useful information about the root topic.
Rule 3: Hierarchical structure. Each two connected nodes must be directly related that no other nodes in the candidate topic set can be inserted between them. This makes the hierarchy completely structured for users to quickly find their interested contents.

For example, given the candidate topic set {***barack obama***, ***policy***, ***tax***, ***medic care***, ***friday***} for "Barack Obama". First, only ***friday*** will be removed according to rule 1 and 2. Then according to rule 3, the gold standard hierarchy should be {***barack obama*** → ***policy***, ***policy*** → ***tax***, ***policy*** → ***medic care***}, which provides users a completely hierarchical view of the available UGCs about "Barack Obama".

Next, the three annotators compare their resultant candidate hierarchies and come up with the gold standards through discussions. On average, the gold standard hierarchies contain 22.3 nodes and 21.3 edges with an average depth of 3.64.

We use the precision, recall and F_1 scores to measure the hierarchy generation performance. Denote R and R_{gold} as the sub-topic relation sets of our output and the gold standard, respectively, the metrics can be calculated as follows:

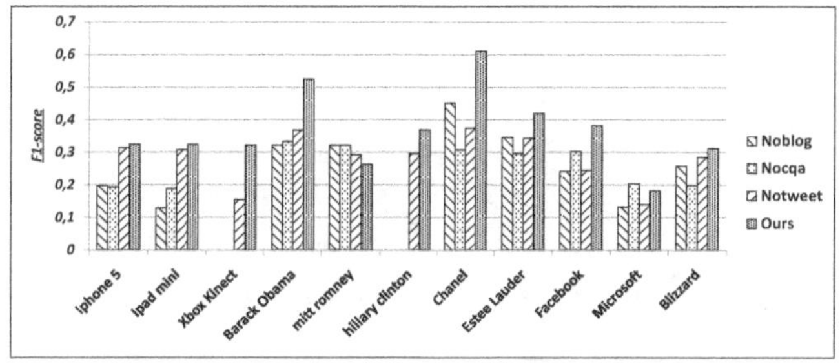

Figure 4: Performance on topic hierarchy generation when using different information source set

$$\text{precision (pre.)} = \frac{|R \cap R_{gold}|}{|R|)}$$

$$\text{recall (rec.)} = \frac{|R \cap R_{gold}|}{|R_{gold}|}$$

$$F_1 \text{ score } (F_1) = 2 \cdot \frac{\text{precision} \cdot \text{recall}}{\text{precision} + \text{recall}}$$

5.3.2 Ablation Study on the Contribution of Information Sources

In Figure 4, we first compare the performance of our proposed methods when using different information source set, which consists of (1) only cQAs and tweets (*noBlog*), (2) blogs and tweets (*noCQA*), (3) blogs and cQAs (*noTweet*), and (4) all the three sources (*All*). The results show that the more the sources we use, the better the performance we can achieve, where the improvements of around 31.2% - 74.8% are observed on the average F_1 scores of *All* against those of the other three combinations. There are mainly two reasons. First, since multiple sources provide more topic terms (as shown in Figure 3), the recall is improved by 39% - 124%. Second, though not for all the topics, the average precision is also improved. This is partly because more UGCs help to estimate better evidences which result in building more optimal topic hierarchies.

On the other hand, when comparing the results of *noBlog*, *noCQA* and *noTweet*, we can see that *noBlog* performs the poorest for most topics (for topics like "Xbox Kinect", the F_1 score is even 0.). It indicates that blogs play a critical role in our method, partly because blogs are usually well-written and contain rich contents. For topics like "Chanel", the performance does not drop that much when removing the blog data. This is partly because many of the crawled blogs are about fashion events and product comparison instead of focusing on real sub-topics like ***perfume*** and ***lipstick***. Once we can collect more appropriate blogs for these topics, even higher performances can be expected.

5.3.3 Evaluation on Effectiveness of Evidence Combination Schemes

The proposed evidence combination scheme plays an important role in our method. In this section, we compare it with three baseline methods: (1) *Linear*, which simply combines all evidences linearly and has been used in [19] [21]. For each topic, we adopt ridge regression [19] to optimize the weight vector using the training data from the other topics in the topic category. (2) *No undirect*, a variation of the proposed scheme which does not use undirected-evidences. (3) *Equal direct*, a variation of the proposed scheme in which

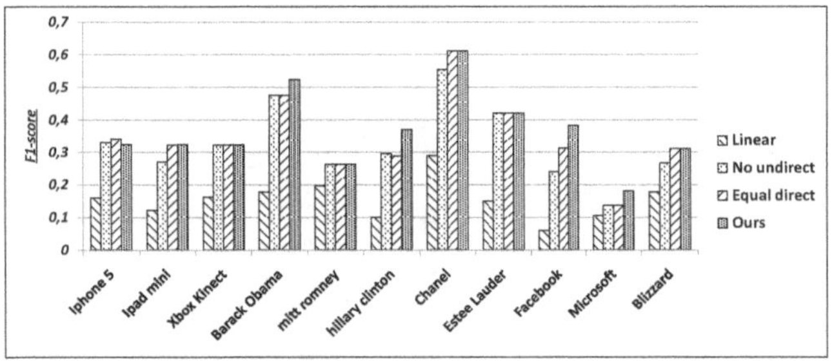

Figure 5: Performance on topic hierarchy generation when using different evidence combination schemes

the weights of all the directed-evidences are set to be equal. All methods run on the same topic sets as those used in generating the gold standards [12].

The result is shown in Figure 5. Compared to the *Linear* method, all the three methods that adopt our proposed scheme perform significantly better on the F_1 scores (t-test, p-value<0.05). This indicates that considering the directed and undirected evidences separately is a better way to estimate the probability of sub-topic relations than putting all the evidences together undistinguishedly. The use of undirected-evidences also significantly improve the performance (t-test, p-value<0.05). Since we only adopt nine carefully selected directed-evidences, the effect of weights is limited. However, as shown in Table 5, the weight vector indeed reflexes the quality of different evidences. For example, the Wikipedia-based evidences (e.g., e_{wcate}, e_{wtitle}) usually obtain higher weights since they are from high quality sources. Stricter patterns (e.g., $e_{spattern0}$) are also higher weighted than general patterns (e.g., $e_{spattern2}$). As the result, more improvement could be observed when more evidences of varied qualities [21] are introduced.

evidence	$e_{spattern_0}$ [a]	$e_{spattern_2}$ [b]	e_{wcate}	e_{wtitle}
weight	0.116	0.099	0.129	0.129

[a] <*topic*> such as <*subtopic*> and

[b] <*subtopic*> on <*topic*> and

Table 5: Part of the weight vector of directed-evidences for "IPhone 5"

5.3.4 Comparison with State-of-the-art Methods

Based on the results in previous two sections, our method performs the best when using all information sources and adopting the proposed combination scheme. We now compare our best method with three state-of-the-art methods: (1) *Yang's Method* [19], which organizes concepts into a hierarchy according to a information function. For each topic, the information function employs all the evidences in Table 2 and is trained using the gold standard of this topic. (2) *Navigli's Method* [13], a graph based method which only employs a classifier-based 0/1 evidence and does not support real time update. Since the evidence used in this paper only provides clues for *is-a* relation, we extend it with extra directed-evidences from our evidence set for the sake of fair comparison. (3) *Snow's Method* [16], which uses a probability model to obtain the most probable hierarchy for the concepts in a given concept set. For fair comparison, we use the probability of a sub-topic relation approximated for our method here.

[12]In fact, since these methods (including those presented in the following section) use the same topic identification process, they all share the same candidate topic sets.

In Table 6, we can see that our proposed method achieves the best performance on all metrics for most topics and significantly outperforms the state-of-the-art methods on the averaged F_1 score (t-test, p-value<0.05). Compared to Yang's method, the proposed graph based method makes better use of the relations among three or more topics. Taking the root topic "Chanel" as an example, given its sub-topic set {***chanel***, ***product***, ***perfume***, ...}, while Yang's method returns the relation set {***chanel*** → ***product***, ***chanel*** → ***perfume***, ...} by considering only the strongness of pairwise sub-topic relations, our method can further detect the sub-topic chain along the three topics, *i.e.*, ***chanel*** → ***product*** → ***perfume***, ,which better captures the global relation. Moreover, the proposed method outperforms Snow's method in term of F_1 score by about 12%. It is partly because the results of Snow's method are strongly affected by the insertion order of the topics. Once an insertion error occurs in one step, it cannot be corrected in the following steps. But our incremental updating mechanism can naturally solve this problem. Navigli's method tends to generate very deep hierarchies [13], where errors occur sometimes (e.g., ***iphone 5*** → ***camera*** → ***cost***, where the cost of IPhone 5's camera does not make sense). This type of errors can be solved by our method through the use of multiple evidences. As for the iphone 5 example, we will determine that the relatedness between ***iphone 5*** and ***cost*** is much stronger than that between ***camera*** and ***cost*** in term of evidences like PMI, thus a direct connection is established between ***iphone 5*** and ***cost***.

5.3.5 Case Study on Topic Hierarchy Generation

In this section, we analyse the strength and weakness of our method using a few examples. First, rather than simply assigning all sub-topics as direct children of the root topic, our method tends to generate completely structured hierarchies (average depth is 5.27). For example, (***facebook*** → ***application*** → ***business*** → ***marketing*** → ***ads***) is a sub-topic chain in the resultant hierarchy of "Facebook Inc.". Evidences from all sources contribute to this result. Pattern-based evidences support the relations that frequently occurs on web pages like ***facebook*** → ***application***. On the other hand, Wikipedia-based and WordNet-based evidences help to find many novel relations (rather than traditional *is-a* or *has-a* relation), such as ***marketing*** → ***ads*** for the given example and ***policy*** → ***tax*** for "Barack Obama". The undirected-evidences are also important. For the given example, both contextual-based and pmi-based evidences suggest that ***marketing*** and ***ads*** are more relevant than ***business*** and ***ads***. Based on all these evidences, our method can best capture the relations among all the sub-topics of a given root topic.

However, multiple sources also bring in different errors. For pattern-based evidences, when a pattern "<*topic*> such as <*subtopic*> and" matches a string " *... as well as other companies/brands/**games** such as **Bing** and Gears of War ...*", a sub-topic relation between ***game*** and ***bing*** will be detected. This is obviously wrong but is hard to be corrected by NLP tools. On the other hand, for an error sub-topic relation (***event*** → ***lipstick***) for "Chanel", we found that

Topic	*Yang's Method*			*Navigli's Method*			*Snow's Method*			*Our Method*		
	pre.	rec.	F_1	pre.	rec.	F_1	pre.	rec.	F_1	pre.	rec.	F_1
Iphone 5	0.16	0.15	0.16	0.36	0.30	**0.33**	0.30	0.27	0.28	0.36	0.31	**0.33**
Ipad mini	0.14	0.16	0.15	0.41	0.20	0.27	0.26	0.20	0.22	0.50	0.24	**0.33**
Xbox Kinect	0.10	0.14	0.12	0.50	0.23	**0.32**	0.36	0.24	0.28	0.50	0.24	**0.32**
Barack Obama	0.19	0.23	0.20	0.50	0.45	0.47	0.55	0.50	**0.52**	0.55	0.50	**0.52**
Mitt Romney	0.07	0.10	0.08	0.29	0.23	**0.26**	0.26	0.23	0.25	0.30	0.24	**0.26**
Hillary Clinton	0.21	0.40	0.28	0.33	0.27	0.30	0.41	0.33	**0.37**	0.42	0.33	**0.37**
Chanel	0.16	0.22	0.18	0.55	0.55	0.55	0.61	0.61	**0.61**	0.61	0.61	**0.61**
Estee Lauder	0.23	0.33	0.27	0.40	0.44	**0.42**	0.35	0.38	0.37	0.40	0.44	**0.42**
Facebook Inc.	0.20	0.22	0.21	0.32	0.36	0.34	0.32	0.36	0.34	0.36	0.41	**0.39**
Microsoft Corp.	0.18	0.19	0.18	0.18	0.19	**0.21**	0.14	0.18	0.15	0.14	0.15	0.18
Blizzard Inc.	0.18	0.22	0.20	0.26	0.27	0.26	0.22	0.22	0.22	0.30	0.32	**0.31**

Table 6: Performance comparison between our method and state-of-the-art methods. The bold face indicates the best F_1 performance for each topic. Our method achieves significant improvements on F_1 scores (t-test, p-value<0.05) compared to all three baseline methods.

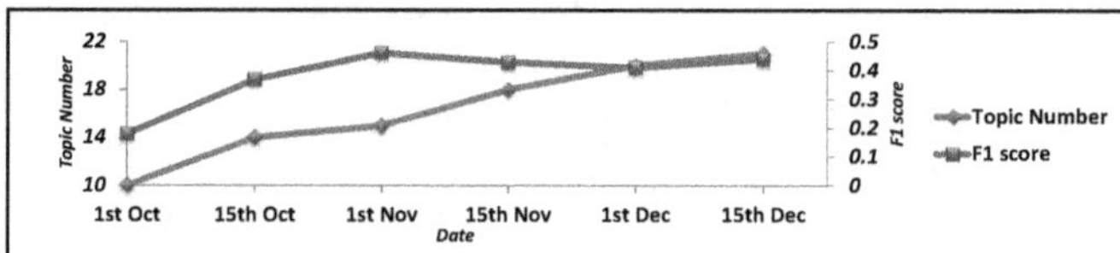

1st Oct ~ 15th Oct: ***debate*** (Barack Obama →election →***debate***), ***Benghazi***, ...
15th Oct ~ 1st Nov: ***policy*** (Barack Obama →***policy*** →taxes)
1st Nov ~15th Nov: ***democrats*** (Barack Obama →voters → ***democrats***), ...
15th Nov ~ 1st Dec: ***Israel*** (Barack Obama → ***Israel***), ***medicare***, ...
1st Dec ~ 15th Dec: ***inauguration*** (Barack Obama → ***inauguration***)

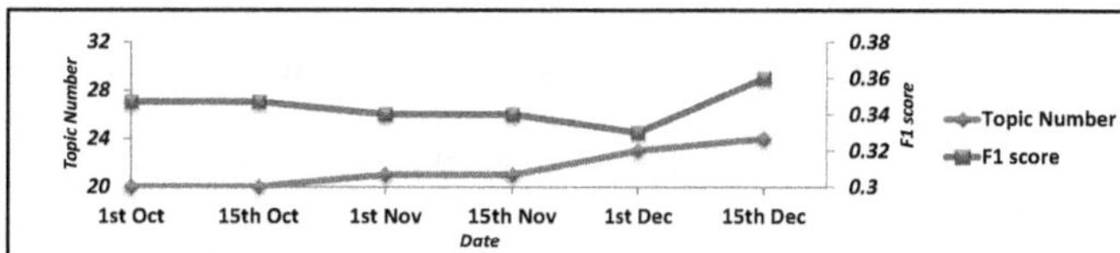

1st Oct ~ 15th Oct: *N/A*
15th Oct ~ 1st Nov: ***decision*** (IPhone 5→accessory →... →device → ***decision***)
1st Nov ~ 15th Nov: *N/A*
15th Nov ~ 1st Dec: ***jailbreak*** (IPhone 5 →***jailbreak***), ***Itune***, ...
1st Dec ~ 15th Dec: ***siri*** (IPhone 5→ accessory →... → software → ***siri***)

Figure 6: Hierarchy update on "IPhone 5" and "Barack Obama" between 1st Oct and 15th Dec: The trend map shows how the F_1 score changes when the topic set grows along time; the table illustrates some examples of the newly detected topics (indicated by *Bold Italic* face) and their position in the hierarchies (shown in brackets) in each period.

the only evidence that supports it is from WordNet, since there is a WordNet path[13] between the two words.

5.4 Hierarchy Update

Online UGCs increase every minute. In this section, we demonstrate how the proposed method can be used to update the topic hierarchies incrementally with real time information. We use the data of blogs, cQAs and tweets published before 15th Dec, 2012 on two example topics, *i.e.*, "Barack Obama" and "IPhone 5". According to their published date, we split the data into 7 sub sets. We initiate the hierarchy using the data before 1st Oct and update it using the data in the other 6 sub sets, each indicates a duration of 15 or 16 days. As our baselines are not designed for real time data, we only show our results for the hierarchy updating experiments here.

The result in Figure 6 offers us a close look of this process. We can see that as time passes and new topics emerge, our method can effectively detect these topics and merge them into the hierarchy. As the results, topics like ***jailbreak*** for "IPhone 5", ***debate***, ***inauguration*** for "Barack Obama" are updated onto the appropriate positions of the topic hierarchy shortly after they become popular on the internet. From the results, we can also find that "Barack Obama" is a more time-sensitive topic, which brings in new sub-topics in each period. On the contrary, the change of topics on "IPhone 5" is very small during the two and a half months.

[13]The WordNet path: ***event*** → ***makeup*** → ***lipstick***.

6. CONCLUSION

In this paper, we proposed an automatic method for incremental information organization for multiple UGC sources. Given a root topic, we used evidences from multiple UGCs to identify topic terms and sub-topic relations between them. With these topic terms, a graph-based algorithm was applied to generate and update the topic hierarchies, on which the UGCs can be organized according to their relevant topics. Comprehensive experiments on 11 root topics demonstrated the effectiveness of our method. For future work, we will explore more UGC sources such as forums and try to find available initial topic hierarchies to enhance our system. It is also interesting to apply the generated topic hierarchy in more sophisticated text analysis tasks.

7. ACKNOWLEDGMENTS

This research is supported by the Singapore National Research Foundation under its International Research Centre @ Singapore Funding Initiative and administered by the IDM Programme Office and The National Key Basic Research Program (also called 973 Program), No.2012CB316301 and NSFC under project No.61272227.

8. REFERENCES

[1] J. Edmonds. Optimum branchings. *Journal of Research of the National Bureau of Standards B*, 71:233–240, 1967.

[2] Y. HaCohen-Kerner, Z. Gross, and A. Masa. Automatic extraction and learning of keyphrases from scientific articles. *Computational Linguistics and Intelligent Text Processing*, pages 657–669, 2005.

[3] X. Han and J. Zhao. Structural semantic relatedness: a knowledge-based method to named entity disambiguation. In *Proceedings of the 48th Annual Meeting of the Association for Computational Linguistics*, pages 50–59. Association for Computational Linguistics, 2010.

[4] C. Hayes, P. Avesani, and U. Bojars. An analysis of bloggers, topics and tags for a blog recommender system. *From Web to Social Web: Discovering and Deploying User and Content Profiles*, pages 1–20, 2007.

[5] J. Hoffart, F. Suchanek, K. Berberich, and G. Weikum. Yago2: a spatially and temporally enhanced knowledge base from wikipedia. *Artificial Intelligence*, 2012.

[6] A. Hulth. Improved automatic keyword extraction given more linguistic knowledge. In *Proceedings of the 2003 conference on Empirical methods in natural language processing*, pages 216–223. ACL, 2003.

[7] S. N. Kim and M.-Y. Kan. Re-examining automatic keyphrase extraction approaches in scientific articles. In *Proceedings of the Workshop on Multiword Expressions: Identification, Interpretation, Disambiguation and Applications*, pages 9–16. Association for Computational Linguistics, 2009.

[8] Z. Kozareva and E. Hovy. A semi-supervised method to learn and construct taxonomies using the web. In *Proceedings of the 2010 Conference on Empirical Methods in Natural Language Processing*, pages 1110–1118. ACL, 2010.

[9] D. J. Lawrie and W. B. Croft. Generating hierarchical summaries for web searches. In *Proceedings of the 26th annual international ACM SIGIR conference*, pages 457–458. ACM, 2003.

[10] X. Mao, Z. Ming, Z. Zha, T. Chua, H. Yan, and X. Li. Automatic labeling hierarchical topics. 2012.

[11] Y. Matsuo and M. Ishizuka. Keyword extraction from a single document using word co-occurrence statistical information. *International Journal on Artificial Intelligence Tools*, 13(01):157–169, 2004.

[12] Z. Ming, K. Wang, and T. Chua. Prototype hierarchy based clustering for the categorization and navigation of web collections. In *Proceedings of the 33rd international ACM SIGIR conference*, pages 2–9. ACM, 2010.

[13] R. Navigli, P. Velardi, and S. Faralli. A graph-based algorithm for inducing lexical taxonomies from scratch. In *Proceedings of the Twenty-Second international joint conference on Artificial Intelligence - Volume Three*, pages 1872–1877. AAAI Press, 2011.

[14] K. Nishida, R. Banno, K. Fujimura, and T. Hoshide. Tweet classification by data compression. DETECT '11, pages 29–34. ACM, 2011.

[15] T. Pedersen, S. Patwardhan, and J. Michelizzi. Wordnet:: Similarity: measuring the relatedness of concepts. In *Demonstration Papers at HLT-NAACL 2004*, pages 38–41. ACL, 2004.

[16] R. Snow, D. Jurafsky, and A. Ng. Semantic taxonomy induction from heterogenous evidence. In *Proceedings of the 21st International Conference on Computational Linguistics and the 44th annual meeting of the Association for Computational Linguistics*, pages 801–808. ACL, 2006.

[17] X. Wang, K. Zhang, X. Jin, and D. Shen. Mining common topics from multiple asynchronous text streams. In *Proceedings of the Second ACM International Conference on Web Search and Data Mining*, pages 192–201. ACM, 2009.

[18] H. Yang and J. Callan. Feature selection for automatic taxonomy induction. In *Proceedings of the 32nd international ACM SIGIR conference*, pages 684–685. ACM, 2009.

[19] H. Yang and J. Callan. A metric-based framework for automatic taxonomy induction. In *Proceedings of the Joint Conference of the 47th Annual Meeting of the ACL and the 4th International Joint Conference on Natural Language Processing of the AFNLP: Volume 1-Volume 1*, pages 271–279. ACL, 2009.

[20] A. Yates, M. Cafarella, M. Banko, O. Etzioni, M. Broadhead, and S. Soderland. Textrunner: Open information extraction on the web. In *Proceedings of Human Language Technologies: The Annual Conference of NAACL: Demonstrations*, pages 25–26. ACL, 2007.

[21] J. Yu, Z. Zha, M. Wang, K. Wang, and T. Chua. Domain-assisted product aspect hierarchy generation: towards hierarchical organization of unstructured consumer reviews. In *Proceedings of the Conference on Empirical Methods in Natural Language Processing*, pages 140–150. ACL, 2011.

APPENDIX

A. SEARCH ENGINE-BASED EVIDENCES

In Table 7, we list the patterns we use in estimating the pattern-based evidences.

Pattern
<*topic*> such as <*subtopic*> and
<*topic*>'s <*subtopic*>
<*subtopic*> on <*topic*> and
<*topic*> including <*subtopic*> and
<*subtopic*> of <*topic*>
<*subtopic*> and other <*topic*>

Table 7: Patterns used to estimate the pattern-based evidences

Looking Ahead: Query Preview in Exploratory Search

Pernilla Qvarfordt, Gene Golovchinsky, Tony Dunnigan
FX Palo Alto Laboratory, Inc.
3174 Porter Drive, Palo Alto, CA 94304
{pernilla, gene, tonyd}@fxpal.com

Elena Agapie
Harvard University
33 Oxford St, Cambridge, MA 02138
eagapie@seas.harvard.edu

ABSTRACT
Exploratory search is a complex, iterative information seeking activity that involves running multiple queries and finding and examining many documents. We designed a query preview control that visualizes the distribution of newly-retrieved and re-retrieved documents prior to running the query. When evaluating the preview control with a control condition, we found effects on both people's information seeking behavior and improved retrieval performance. People spent more time formulating a query and were more likely to explore search results more deeply, retrieved a more diverse set of documents, and found more different relevant documents when using the preview.

Categories and Subject Descriptors
H.5.m [**Information interfaces and presentation (e.g., HCI)**]: Miscellaneous.

Keywords
Information seeking, exploratory search, information retrieval, HCIR

1. INTRODUCTION
Exploratory search plays an important role in many domains such as academic research, intelligence analysis, e-discovery and pharmaceutical research. Information seeking in these fields typically involves long sessions consisting of many queries, evolving information needs as searchers learn about the topic of interest and about the collection, and a focus on finding many pertinent documents (not just one "best match").

Exploratory search is a complex, cognitively demanding activity that places a heavy load on memory and on sense-making processes. Forcing people to use external tools that are poorly integrated or requiring them to rely on memory for significant periods of time may make a difficult task even harder. On the other hand, an overly complex interface may impose its own cognitive burden, distracting from the real task. Thus one challenge in building tools to support exploratory search involves finding a sweet spot in the design space: making tools that help more than they distract.

In this paper, we describe a visualization that is designed to help people understand the relationship between the documents a query *will* retrieve and documents *already found* within in a search session. While searchers are formulating their query (e.g. typing in query terms or adding a document to the query as relevance feedback), a preview control displays the outcome of the query by aggregating the counts of new documents, of documents already retrieved, and of seen documents. This preview control helps people reformulate queries on the fly, without having to wait for the results to be incorporated into the workspace.

The contributions of this work are a description and implementation of a novel interface widget for facilitating exploratory search, and an experimental evaluation of the widget that assessed its impact on user behavior and system performance.

Below, after covering the related work, we describe the preview control, and report the results of a controlled study to assess its effectiveness. We conclude with a discussion of our findings and their implications for interface design for information seeking.

2. RELATED WORK
Exploratory search is often recall-oriented, as searchers seek a more complete description of particular ideas or phenomena [15]. The notion that recall-oriented information seeking activity spans multiple cycles of interaction with the system is rooted in early research in library and information science (e.g., [4, 5, 6, 14, 15]). The notion that the query history should be represented in search systems dates back to at least the 1970s with systems such as DIALOG (see [22] for an example) that kept track of a searcher's queries and allowed those queries to be reused by reference. In the 1990s, web browsers quickly converged on the idea of using link color to reflect recent link traversal. A more modern example can be found in Ancestry.com [1], a commercial search engine for genealogical data that allows people to document family trees using historical records. It annotates search results with badges that show whether a particular record has already been associated with a person in the searcher's family tree.

These issues have also been explored in a range of research systems. VOIR [9] displayed the retrieval history of documents using histograms that represented rank information. Ariadne [21] created a visual representation of a search trajectory to review earlier actions. SearchPad [7] let people save and revisit queries and documents while conducting web search. Spoerri [20] showed overlap among search results submitted to different search engines, but these techniques could also be applied to queries in the same search task. Komolodi *et al.* [13] described a number of interface designs involving query histories after studying information seeking in the legal environment.

Reasons for including histories of interaction in information seeking interfaces include allowing searchers to review what has been done, and to try alternative formulations of queries to better approximate the latent information need. But there is more to history than just the list of queries and saved documents. NRT [19] implemented a more comprehensive history mechanism that recorded not only previously-run queries, but also the documents retrieved by them, making it possible for the searcher to scan the results list visually for new or for re-retrieved documents. Querium [10] implemented a principled framework for recording queries, and retrieved, viewed, opened, and saved documents to

SIGIR'13, July 28–August 1, 2013, Dublin, Ireland.

keep track of searchers' entire information seeking activity as it spanned multiple engagements with the system. It then made this *process* metadata available to the searcher via faceted filters for restricting query results to select documents that were as yet unexplored, newly-retrieved, etc.

All of these systems look at various aspects of earlier search activity and make it possible to use that information in some way to help with sense making or query formulation. Auto-completion interfaces give searchers a preview of what they might want to look for through a query completion (e.g., [11, 3]) based on aggregations of prior queries collected from other searchers typing similar text. Google Instant [11] also shows the results of the most common expansion without having to press the Enter key to evaluate the query. Autosuggestion of keywords (e.g., [2, 12]) is another form of interactive query formulation assistance.

While query auto-completion is quite useful for precision-oriented, commonly occurring information needs, it does not translate as well to exploratory search in which a particular searcher's information need may be sufficiently different from those of others to make quality recommendation difficult. In situations that involve proprietary data (e.g., e-discovery, patentability searches, intelligence analysis, etc.), query histories to make accurate recommendations may not be available at all.

3. QUERY PREVIEW

One of the challenges of dealing with complex information needs through multiple queries is that queries can exhibit considerable overlap in terms of the documents retrieved. This makes it difficult for searchers to understand whether they are simply re-retrieving the same documents at different ranks, or whether they are in fact finding new information. These duplicates can impair a user's understanding of the search results and can interfere with an accurate sense of progress toward the search goal.

To address this problem, we developed a novel interface component to preview search results before the query is run. We wanted to bring the fluid style of interaction of Google Instant to the more complex expressions of information need typical of exploratory search. We designed a query preview widget that helps searchers understand what a query *will* retrieve before its results are seen. The system evaluates a searcher's query continuously as it is being typed (similar to Google Instant query completion), but rather than suggesting alternative queries, the system generates a visualization of the documents that would be retrieved if the query were executed, and contrasts these results with the documents that have been previously retrieved in the current search context.

The preview control is a stacked bar chart with ten bars. Each bar represents ten documents: the first bar represents documents ranked 1-10, the second represents documents 11-20, etc. Each bar is subdivided into three parts. These represent counts of documents that that will be: newly-retrieved (a bright teal blue), re-retrieved but have not yet been seen by the searcher (medium blue), and documents previously seen by the searcher (dark blue).

The goal of this control is to create a visual preview that indicates whether significant numbers of new documents will be retrieved by the query being constructed, and, if so, how these documents will be distributed throughout the overall ranked list. This is another important difference between the precision-oriented design of Google Instant and the recall-oriented design of Querium: here, the top 100 documents are represented, rather than just the top 10 shown in Google Instant.

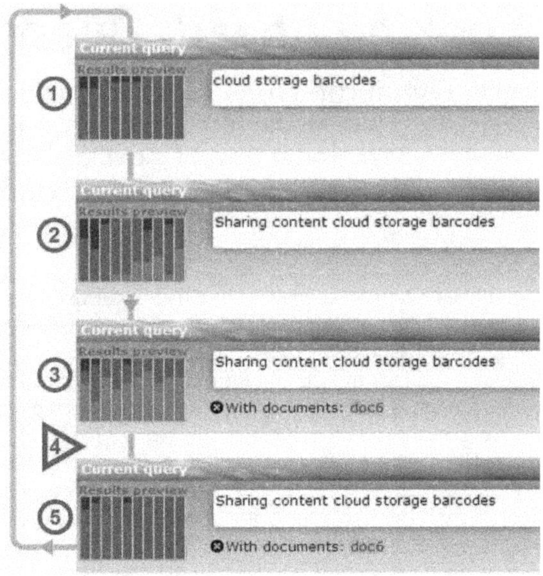

Figure 1. Example of the preview control as the searcher adds search terms (2), selects a document for relevance feedback (3), runs the query (4), and sees the final results (5)

Figure 1 shows changes in the bar colors representing the types of documents that will be retrieved by a query. Step 1 shows the control prior to modifying the query: some documents have been opened (dark blue, pages 1, 2, 4, 5, 6), while all others are marked as retrieved (medium blue) but not seen. As the searcher adds new search terms (step 2), the preview changes to reflect the types of documents the current query will return if submitted. The term "sharing content," will cause more previously-opened documents to be re-retrieved at higher ranks, but will also retrieve some new documents (teal) in the lower ranks. When the searcher adds a document as relevance feedback (doc6 in step 3), the preview control changes again to reflect that more new documents will be now be retrieved. When the searcher chooses to run the query (step 4) the preview control updates to show that all documents have either been opened or retrieved (step 5).

The preview is computed when the user pauses typing for about 300 msec, or when a document is selected or removed for relevance feedback [16]. Computation takes well under a second. Transitions between preview states are animated by adjusting bar component heights, producing an effect similar to spectral power displays in some audio equipment.

The design goal of this widget is to give searchers some insight into whether the query reformulation (e.g., adding a keyword or selecting documents for relevance feedback) will be effective at identifying new documents. It was also designed to increase the information scent [17] of documents in the lower parts of the result list, potentially giving incentive to explore the results in more depth. We also wanted to keep the interaction light-weight and modeless to avoid disrupting the searcher.

4. EVALUATION OF QUERY PREVIEW

To evaluate the impact of the preview on user behavior and search performance, we designed a study with two versions of an exploratory search user interface; one containing the preview control and one without. We used a simplified version of the Querium interface [10], described in more detail below, as the experimental interface. We were interested in testing three hypotheses related to recall-oriented search tasks:

Hypothesis One: The preview control affects searchers' attention and behavior during query formulation. People often look away while thinking [8], avoiding visual stimuli that may distract their cognitive processes; we wanted to assess whether people would be paying attention to the preview control as it was providing potentially useful information during query formulation.

Hypothesis Two: The preview control causes searchers to create queries that retrieve more different documents. Diversity of results is one key to more effective recall-oriented search. Would this control work as designed to increase the range of different documents people identify during a search task?

Hypothesis Three: The preview encourages deeper exploration of the search results. By definition, recall-oriented search relies less on the quality of the ranking function than precision-oriented search does. Would this control get people to look deeper?

4.1. Experimental design

The experiment was a one-factor within-subjects design. It compared two interface conditions, one with the preview, and one without (see Figure 2 and Figure 3), over a total of six different search topics (three in each condition). Topics were assigned to experimental conditions in a counter-balanced manner. Each participant performed three topics in each condition; each topic was performed once by each participant. Participants were randomly assigned to the counter-balanced configuration of topics, half starting with the preview condition and half starting with the control condition. The study was divided into two sessions, one for each condition usually run on separate days.

Figure 2. Query input area for the preview condition.

Figure 3. Query input area for the control condition

4.2. Search Topics

We designed experimental search topics to be as realistic as possible. Topics were framed as searches for relevant literature that might constitute prior or sufficiently-related art for proposed patent applications, a task requiring finding as many relevant documents as possible. In this context, not finding many relevant documents is not a bad outcome, as it may indicate that the research idea is a good candidate for a patent.

To construct the topics, we used summary descriptions of existing invention proposals and modified them to contain uniformly-detailed information and be of equal length. Some topics were updated to include modern technological components; overly technical terminology was simplified to allow us to include as many participants as possible and to leave room for query formulation. None of the participants in our study had specialized knowledge of the search topics, as these invention proposals had been created by people who did not participate in the study. However, participants had general knowledge about the research areas so that they could judge the relevance of the search results.

Each topic description included a title, a brief summary of the invention proposal (110-120 words), and eight keywords at the end of the description. A fragment of a topic description is shown in Figure 4 (5).

For each topic, we constructed two queries to seed the information seeking process: one query was derived from the topic title, and the other from three keywords in the topic description. Examples of two seed queries for a topic are shown in the query history in Figure 4 (4). Our motive, unknown to the participants, for providing the these two seed queries was to have some snippets to view when starting the topic, since this would allow the preview control to provide useful information from the participant's first query, and to focus their attention on query formulation. Participants were told that their partner had previously run a couple of queries to explore the search space. Since our participants often work with others on these kinds of tasks, picking up where someone left off was not unusual.

The following six topics were used in the study: "Text-reading support on handheld devices," "Creating movies of media streams on small devices," "Detecting and acting on multiple people crowding a small display for information sharing," "Improving interactions on mobile devices using large displays," "Sharing content using cloud storage and barcodes," and "Semi-Automatic Document Scanning with Digital and Video Cameras."

4.3. Search UI: Querium

We used Querium [10] as a platform to study the effects of the preview control in exploratory search tasks. Querium is an asynchronous collaborative search tool that organizes search activities into tasks; each task contains its own queries, retrieved documents, comments, and assessments of relevance. Within each task, a searcher can run multiple queries, examine results, save documents, perform relevance feedback (RF), etc. Querium makes it possible to perform relevance feedback by checking one or more checkboxes next to document snippets in the results list, and re-running the search. Terms drawn from selected documents are used to expand the query [16].

For the purpose of these experiments, we connected Querium to a snapshot of the CiteSeer database of academic papers, containing about two million documents. CiteSeer automatically extracts metadata such as author, title, and date from the PDF or Postscript files that it crawls, and also extracts the full text of the document. We used a snapshot of the CiteSeer corpus (including text and metadata) from June 2012, and built our own index of this collection using Lucene.

The Querium interface was simplified to focus participants' search behavior on query formulation. The study UI (Figure 4) organizes the display into several regions: the query area, the search results, a query history, and the document display area. PDF documents were replaced with their extracted text because iBrowser, the browser instrumented to collect eye-tracking browser data used for the study, could not display PDFs.

4.4. Participants

Thirteen participants completed the study. As search topics required domain knowledge, we recruited researchers and other members of the technical staff of our company to participate in the study. They did not receive any additional compensation. Five participants had used the full version of Querium previously; one had received a tutorial on the full version of Querium, and seven participants had not used Querium previously. All participants were familiar with the kind of search task involved in the study since similar tasks are part of their job assignment. None of the participants was actively involved in the development of the preview or of Querium.

It is worth noting that the interface of the experimental version of Querium shared only a few characteristics with the full version used previously by some of our participants. Most novel features had been removed to simplify the interface and to make the experiment more interpretable. In addition, all participants were given a 15 minute introduction on the experimental system. We believe that prior experience with Querium did not give those participants a material advantage, and, as the experiment had a within-subject design, the differences, if any, would cancel out.

Participants rated the two versions of Querium to support their search activities equally well (preview: 5.2, SD=1.36 vs. control: 5.2, SD=1.42 on scale 1-7 where 1 was very bad and 7 very good), indicating that they were equally satisfied with both.

4.5. Procedure and Instructions

The study was divided into two sessions, one for each condition with three search topics in each. Both sessions followed the same procedure. First, participants were given an introduction to Querium, after which the eye tracker was calibrated and the calibration was tested. Participants were then shown one of the three topic descriptions before using Querium. They were encouraged to read the description carefully so that they would not need to refer to it frequently while working on the topic, although the task description was available onscreen during the study (Figure 4 (5)).

Participants were instructed to quickly review what was done by their colleague, and then to run additional queries to find pertinent documents. To focus participants' activity on query formulation rather than on document review, they were told that they did not necessarily need to read the documents, but only to mark interesting documents by pressing the "thumbs up" button (See Figure 4 (2)). They were encouraged to work on the task until they felt they had exhausted the search space, or for at most 15 minutes. The maximum time was set to avoid fatigue and to assure that each search topic, independent of order, got about the same exposure in the study. Participants pressed the "done" button to move to the next topic. They were allowed to take short breaks between topics. Remember that for these search topics, not finding any relevant documents was not considered a bad outcome, so participants were not under pressure to find a large volume of relevant documents.

After a participant had completed the three search topics, the calibration of the eye tracker was tested again and the person was asked to fill in a short post-test questionnaire. Each of the two study sessions lasted in total 30 minutes to one hour; the second session was generally faster as the participants were now familiar with Querium and could skip most of the introduction.

4.6. Data collection and analysis

4.6.1. Log analysis

Querium was instrumented to report all significant user events (e.g., running a query, selecting a relevance feedback document, clicking on links, etc.) to the server, which kept a detailed log of these events. The log contained all queries that were run, and all documents that were retrieved, viewed, and saved by storing the data into a relational database. These logs and database records were also used in the following analysis to characterize searchers' behavior and results.

4.6.2. Ground truth

We created a set of ground-truth documents for each topic by pooling participants' results, sampling documents from the pooled set, and assessing these sampled documents in terms of relevance

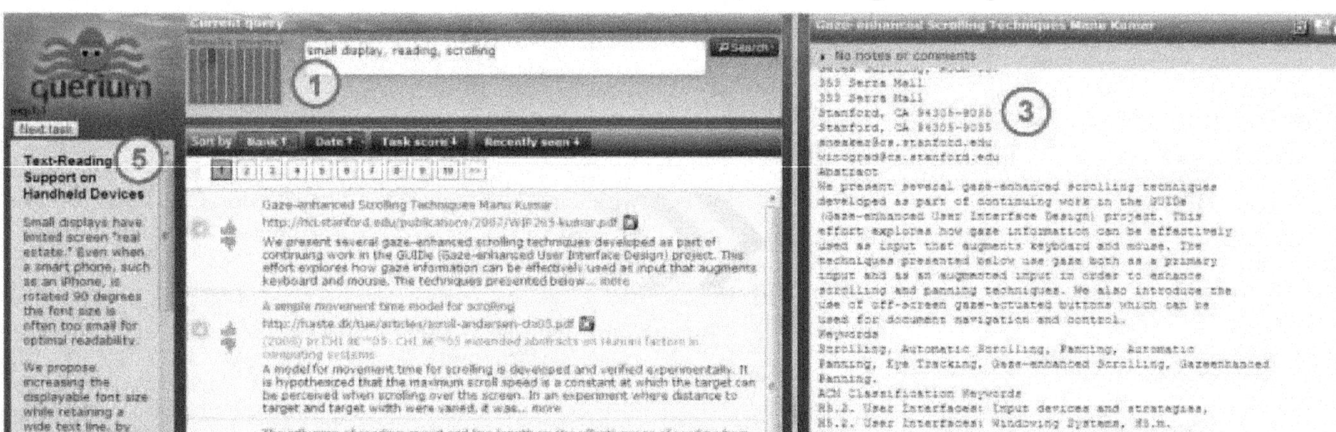

Figure 4. Querium interface for preview experiment.

to the task. Two assessors created the assessments independently. For each topic, each assessor rated 20 top-ranked documents. They then reviewed each other's decisions to arrive at a shared understanding of what constituted relevance for each topic. Finally, the assessors judged a random sample of documents drawn from the set of all documents at least one experimental participant had interacted with. In this context, "interacted with" means that the document was retrieved and either opened for reading, or the participant moved the mouse over its snippet.

Table 1. Total number of retrieved, assessed and relevant documents by topic

Topic	Retrieved in study	Assessed	Relevant
Topic 1	527	220	27
Topic 2	554	243	32
Topic 3	701	249	11
Topic 4	400	229	50
Topic 5	517	237	22
Topic 6	536	236	23

This set of documents judged relevant for each topic was used to score participants' performance in the experiment. Table 1 shows the total number of documents participants interacted with, the total number of documents assessed, and the total number of relevant documents for each topic.

4.6.3. Eye tracker

We recorded the participants' eye movements using a Tobii X120 eye tracker run at 60Hz. The gaze data was recorded by a custom piece of software (internally called iBrowser). iBrowser is a web browser that records eye tracker data synchronized with user initiated events such as key presses and mouse positions and clicks. iBrowser exposed a JavaScript API that the experimental Querium system used to communicate positions of UI elements as they changed based on searchers' interactions. This allowed us to track which controls and documents the searcher looked at relative to the logical structure of the interface during the search session. In addition to logging UI elements and eye tracking data, iBrowser also logged key presses and mouse interaction.

Fixations were identified in the eye-tracking data using a dispersion-based fixation detection algorithm [18]. When reporting on attention on different UI elements, attention data is based on the total fixation duration on that particular UI element. We used the following UI elements in the analysis: query (query input area excluding the preview and the search button), the preview control (when shown), search button, results, task description, query history, and document viewer.

We included only valid gaze data samples when calculating gaze durations. A valid gaze sample is when the eye tracker is correctly tracking at least one of the participant's eyes, and an invalid sample is when the eye tracker fails to track either eye. The average ratio of valid gaze samples was 0.82 (SD=0.094) over all conditions and topics. Only data samples with a ratio of 0.75 or higher valid gaze points for a specific time period (such as query formulation) were used in our analysis.

4.6.4. Data Analysis

For most of the analyses, unless noted, we used a one-way, repeated measures ANOVA with two conditions (control and preview). In cases where we expected that the participants would not display a consistent behavior, we used the t-test to compare the two conditions. This method was commonly used when analyzing queries and behavior during query formulation.

We used the ratio of valid gaze data samples as an indication of whether participants were looking at the display or away from it. This use of eye tracker accuracy is unconventional; other factors besides looking away from the display, such as rapid head movements, may cause loss of gaze data. However, we observed that many participants frequently looked away from the display as part of their natural movement pattern while interacting with Querium, (e.g., moving hand from mouse to keyboard, etc.). This loss of valid gaze data would be similar in both conditions, so any discrepancy in the ratio of valid gaze data samples in one condition over another could be assumed to arise from the participants looking away more frequently from the display.

When analyzing user behavior, we were particularly interested in participants' query formulation strategies. Using the mouse interaction and keyboard logs, we identified events representing query start (clicking in the search input area, adding a document to a query) and end (pressing the "enter" key or clicking the search button). Next, we analyzed fixations five seconds before the event, during the event, and five seconds after running the query.

For all analyses, we removed outliers that exceeded the mean by five standard deviations. The few points removed in this manner are reflected in the different numbers of degrees of freedom reported in tests of statistical significance.

5. RESULTS

The goal of this experiment was to characterize participants' behavior when using the preview control, and to understand its effect on overall system performance. We split the analysis into three parts: first, we characterize participants' behavior as observed through the eye tracker. Second, we describe the patterns of retrieval, viewing, and saving based on the data logged in Querium sessions. Finally, we compare participants' performance between conditions in terms of recall and precision.

5.1. Attention during query formulation

To test the first hypothesis, we examined participants' gaze patterns and behavior during the query formulation phase. The query formulation phase was initiated by activating the query box to type keywords or selecting documents for relevance feedback, and ended when the participant submitted the query. In the analysis, we included a five second time period *before* and *after* the query formulation phase to be able to compare behavior *before*, *during* and *after* query formulation.

Participants submitted on average 7.7 queries per topic in the control condition and 6.4 queries per topic in the preview condition ($F(1, 12) = 5.55$, $p < 0.05$). The time to formulate a query varied greatly, from 0.4 seconds to 7 minutes. The average query formulation duration was 21.4 seconds (SD=50.1) for the control condition and 27.2 seconds (SD=45.9) for the preview condition. Querium allows searchers to specify queries using a combination of keywords and documents for relevance feedback. We anticipated that the preview would be most useful for keyword queries (without documents) as these queries give searchers the most control over how a query is constructed. For these queries, the average query formulation duration was 12.4 sec (SD=20.1) for the control condition and 20.2 sec (SD=36.3) for the preview condition, which makes the query formulation on average 7.8 sec longer in the preview condition, a borderline statistically significant difference ($F(1, 12) = 4.43$, $p = 0.057$).

To investigate participants' attention during query formulation, we first examined the ratio of valid gaze samples in our data. We found that this ratio of valid gaze samples was different before, during and after query formulation ($F(2, 22) = 40.13$, $p < 0.001$), and we saw an interaction between the time periods and the conditions ($F(2, 24) = 7.31$, $p < 0.01$). Further analysis showed that the time period *after* query formulation had a significantly higher ratio of valid gaze samples compared to gaze samples collected *during* query formulation (During vs. After: $F(1, 12) = 44.69$, $p < 0.001$, Bonferroni adjusted for multiple comparisons), as shown in Figure 5. The time period *before* query formulation was not quite significant (Before vs. During: $F(1, 12) = 6.47$, $p < 0.0774$, Bonferroni adjusted). The *before* and *after* time periods ratio did not significantly differ. A possible explanation of this curious result is that participants looked away from the stimuli rich display to collect their thoughts during query formulation, a behavior observed by the experimenter and consistent with research on gaze behavior during cognitively demanding tasks [8].

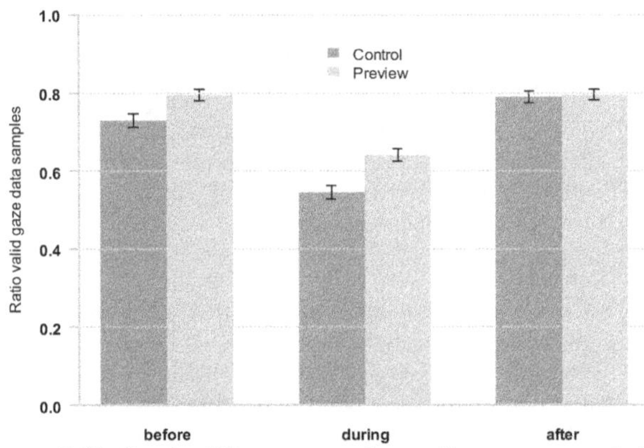

Figure 5. Ratio of valid gaze samples on the query area before, during and after query formulation.

The difference in the ratio of valid gaze samples during query formulation for the two conditions was significant ($F(1,12) = 8.18$, $p < 0.05$). These results show that participants looked at the display significantly more during query formulation when the preview control was available than in the control condition.

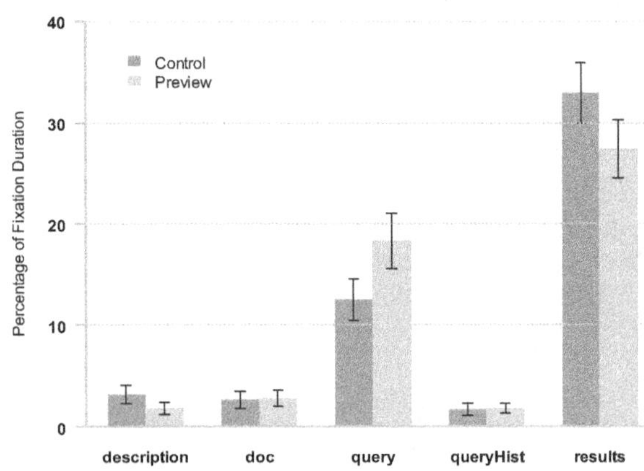

Figure 6. Percentage of attention on UI elements *during* query formulation (total fixation duration on UI element).

To further test the hypothesis that the preview control affects the participants' attention and behavior, we investigated the UI regions that participants looked at when formulating queries. Since the duration of query formulation varied considerably, we used the percentage of the total fixation duration during query formulation that was spent on the five major parts of Querium UI as the dependent variable (Figure 6). The biggest difference in attention is clearly related to the query input area; the second largest difference is in the results area. The difference in percentage of fixation duration on the query input area was statistically significant (Wilcox Rank Sum Test; W=3767.5, $p<0.05$). In absolute numbers, participants spent 6.1 sec (SD=8.08) looking at the query input area in the preview condition vs. 3.5 sec (SD=5.27) in the control condition. This result suggests that participants appeared to spend more effort at formulating queries in this condition compared to the control.

In the preview condition, in addition to spending 28% (SD=61.8) of the query formulation duration looking at the query area, participants spent on average 4% (SD=11.2) of the query formulation duration inspecting the preview control. We also found that participants spent on average 8% (SD=17.3) of the time period *before* starting on a query looking at the preview control and 7% (SD=15.3) *after* submitting the query. This corresponds to an average total fixation time of 391 ms (SD=865) looking at the preview *before*, 1021 ms (SD=2224) *during* query formulation and 362 ms (SD=764) *after* query formulation. The average fixation duration, when fixations were found on the preview control, was 297 ms (SD=139) which was not different from the average fixation duration on the query box (327 ms, SD=256). Considering the extra 7.8 seconds for query formulation in the preview condition, the ratio of that extra time spent on inspecting the preview is quite low. The additional time used for query formulation in the preview condition was more likely spent on formulating the query than interpreting the preview.

To understand the extra time participants spent on formulating queries in the preview condition, we investigated whether the query length differed between the two conditions. However, we found that query lengths were essentially equal: in the control condition, queries contained on average 5.3 words (SD=3.06) vs. 5.5 words (SD=2.62) in the preview condition. We also investigated if the participants made more edits, i.e. deleting or replacing query terms, to their queries. We found that in the control condition participants made 5.4 edits per topic (SD=4.46) vs. 6.6 edits per topic (SD=4.39) in the experimental condition. Due to the sparse sample of edits, the difference between conditions were not significant ($F(1, 12)=1.63$, *ns.*).

We also looked at individual differences in how participants spent their attention during query formulation. Some of the participants appeared to look for a longer time at the preview control than others. Of the 13 participants, nine looked at the preview control for at least 8% of the time period before, during or after query formulation. Of these, four participants looked at the preview control for at least 6% of the time period during query formulation. We did not find any differences in the use of the preview due to previous experience with Querium.

One interesting observation from the analysis of attention on the query box before, during, and after query formulation was that participants continued to look at the query box and the preview control after submitting the query. In the control condition participants' attention was shifted towards the search results, where it was 9% higher compared to the preview ($F(1, 11)=5.32$, $p<0.05$). The experimenter observed that participants seemed to try to use the preview control as a tool for navigating to newly retrieved material by placing the mouse on the preview control to count the bars and remember the location after the preview was flushed when new documents were retrieved. This was confirmed by participants' comments.

5.2. Query overlap

One of the motivations for the design of Querium was the observation that exploratory search tasks often involve queries that retrieve many of the same documents as searchers struggle to represent their information needs. We wanted to quantify this phenomenon in our data to validate some of the assumptions that underlie the system design.

In an on-going information seeking task, results overlap can be measured in a number of ways: it's possible to compare the results of each query to the union of the results of all preceding queries to assess its contribution to the entire task. It's also possible to measure query-to-query differences only, emphasizing incremental gains. Of course it's also possible to blend the two by discounting documents retrieved longer in the past. For our initial analysis, we chose the two extremes: the global uniqueness count and the incremental uniqueness count. For this analysis, we categorized queries as being based on keywords only, or a combination of keywords and documents for relevance feedback.

Table 2. Average percent of new documents per query by query type (QT), query overlap measure (global & incremental uniqueness) and experimental condition.

Query overlap	Condition	QT: Keyword M	QT: Keyword SD	QT: Document (RF) M	QT: Document (RF) SD
Global	Control	52.5	31.6	33.8	28.9
	Preview	58.0	29.8	41.8	27.8
Incremental	Control	71.6	27.8	48.0	30.7
	Preview	73.7	27.5	52.4	28.8

We calculated global uniqueness for a query by computing the number of documents it retrieved that had not been found up to that point in the search task. Note that some of these documents would likely be re-retrieved by subsequent queries. The numbers range from about 34% to about 58% for global uniqueness, and from 48% to 74% for incremental uniqueness (Table 2). While the query type effect is wildly significant ($F(1, 536) = 45.609$, $p < 0.001$), this is not surprising: relevance feedback queries produced lower results because some of the documents these queries retrieved had been previously found by keyword queries, as it is not possible to run a document query without first retrieving a document through some other query.

The difference in global uniqueness due to experimental conditions was significant ($F(1, 536) = 7.918$, $p < 0.01$). But differences in incremental uniqueness were not. Thus we clearly demonstrated that the initial assumptions regarding query overlap for exploratory tasks were valid, and also found support for hypothesis two (that the experimental condition would have less overlap). We take up that hypothesis again later in the performance analysis section.

5.3. Interaction results

We used several dependent measures to assess the impact of the preview on user behavior. The preview was designed to encourage people to look deeper in the results lists. Thus we used the rank of the document with which searchers interacted as an indicator of depth of exploration of the results. To test hypothesis three (that the preview control encourages people to explore more of the result set), we looked at the number of queries run, and at the rates at which participants viewed, opened, and saved documents in each condition. The only reliable difference between conditions was the number of queries per topic (Table 3).

Table 3. Summary statistics per topic. *p < 0.05.

	Control M	Control SD	Preview M	Preview SD	Sig. Test F(1, 12)
Topic duration (min)	12.2	3.16	11.7	3.18	< 1
No. Queries	7.7	3.54	6.4	2.52	5.55 *
Retrieved docs	525	186	522	123	< 1
Viewed snippets	76.9	39.3	73.4	37.7	< 1
Open documents	5.4	6.21	4.4	5.75	< 1
Saved documents	5.6	5.28	6.4	5.28	< 1

To explore participants' behavior in more detail, we broke down the viewed, opened, and saved document distributions by retrieval rank. To make the data easier to understand and to discount slight changes in rank (since a difference of a few rank places is not very important in recall-oriented search), we binned ranks into groups of 10, corresponding to the pages of results displayed by the preview control. As Querium retrieves up to 100 documents per query, each set of search results was divided into ten bins.

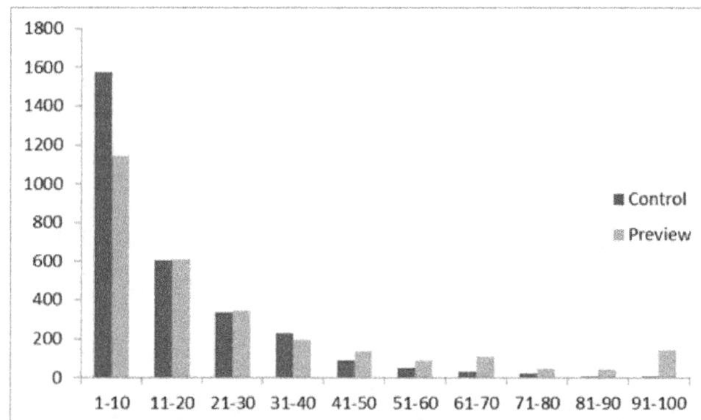

Figure 7. Distribution of viewed snippets by retrieval rank.

Figure 7 shows counts of ranks of viewed snippets for each interface condition. In the preview condition (light grey), participants examined many more documents at middle to lower ranks compared to the control. A Kruskal-Wallis test showed a significant effect of condition on viewed rank ($\chi^2(1)=132$, $p < 0.001$). This distribution suggests that in the preview condition participants devoted less attention to documents retrieved on the first page, and more to lower-ranked documents.

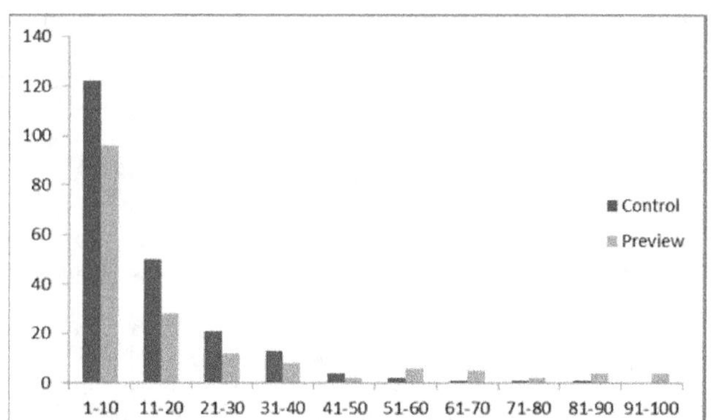

Figure 8. Distribution of opened documents by retrieval rank.

From eye tracking data we found that participants looked at each document snippet on average for 3.3 seconds in both conditions (Control: SD=20.53; Preview: SD=20.18). The number of unique documents per search topic that participants viewed for more than three seconds was 30.3 (SD=13.83) in the control condition, and

28.9 (SD=13.79) in the preview condition. These results show that participants allocated about the same resources to review the search results independent of condition.

We then compared the rates at which participants actually opened the documents to look at them, rather than relying on snippets alone. As can be seen from Figure 8, participants tended to open fewer documents in the preview condition in the top half of the ranks, and more in the bottom half. A Kruskal-Wallis test revealed a significant effect of condition on opened rank ($\chi^2(1)=4.0$, $p < 0.05$). While this effect is weaker than the viewed snippet rate discussed above, it does show a shift from opening documents from the top half of the ranked list to the lower half.

Finally, we examined the rate at which participants marked documents as being pertinent to their task. Pertinence was defined by participants' judgment rather than through an externally-imposed gold standard. The preview condition shows increased rates of documents being saved in the 11 to 100 rank range; a Kruskal-Wallis test revealed a significant effect of condition on saved rank ($\chi^2(1)=8.5$, $p < 0.001$), as shown in Figure 9.

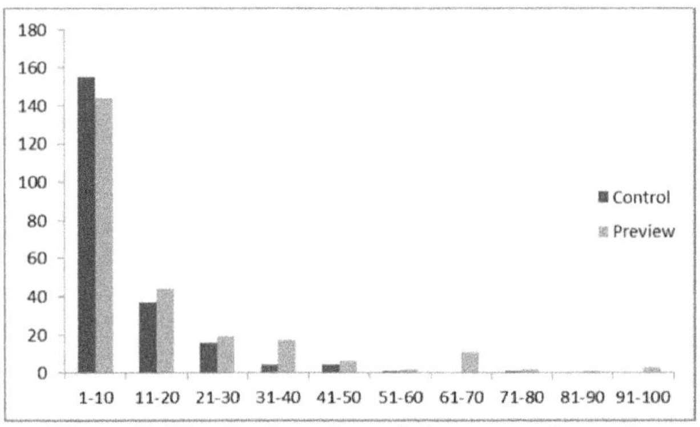

Figure 9. Distribution of saved documents by rank.

These analyses suggest that the preview encouraged participants to explore query results more thoroughly rather than running more queries. In addition, these explorations yielded more useful documents in the same amount of time as the control condition.

5.4. Retrieval performance

We assessed participants' performance by measuring residual recall (RR) and residual precision (RP) using the ground truth we had created. For each participant query in a topic session, we computed the number of *new* relevant documents retrieved, and used the presence of these documents to calculate RP and RR. Documents retrieved by the two seed queries in each topic were excluded from this analysis. Once a document was counted as being relevant to a query, it was not counted as being relevant when re-retrieved by subsequent queries within that topic. The goal was to measure how many new documents each subsequent query found, rather than simply re-retrieving the same documents.

The preview control was designed to facilitate deeper exploration of the results, a tactic we found our participants made use of in exploratory search. As can be seen in Figure 9, participants found and saved pertinent documents throughout the ranked lists returned by the queries. Thus to compare the experimental condition with the control using the ground truth, we wanted to compare the entire curve rather than just one or two points on it.

We computed the Average Residual Precision (ARP) metric by averaging RP computed at rank cutoffs of 10, 20, …, 100, and compared Mean ARP (MARP) between the experimental and control conditions. Three of 540 data points were excluded from RP analysis, and two were excluded from the analysis of RR because they were outliers.

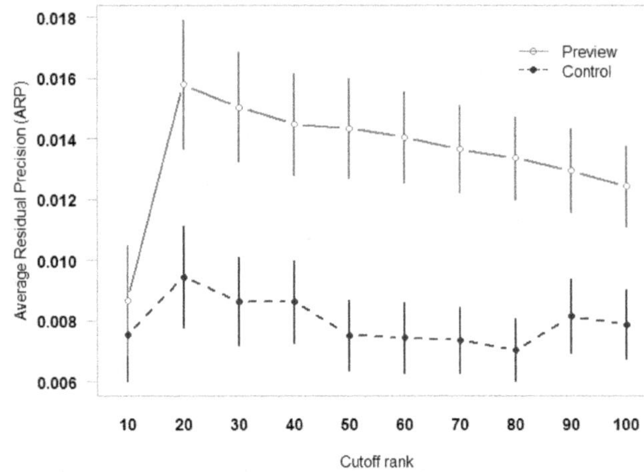

Figure 10. Average Residual Precision (ARP) vs. cutoff rank.

Figure 10 summarizes ARP over the cutoff range. Even without the statistical test, it is obvious that in the preview condition (upper curve), participants found significantly more relevant documents throughout ranks 20-100 compared with the control ($t(468.28)=3.553$, $p < 0.001$).

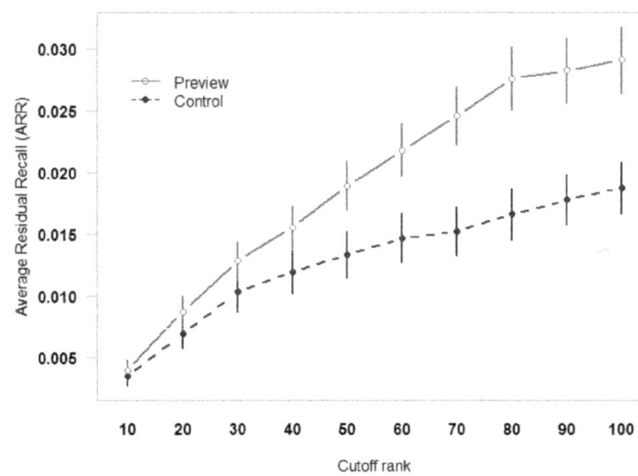

Figure 11. Average Residual Recall (ARR) vs. cutoff rank.

In an analogous manner, we computed Average Residual Recall (ARR), as shown in Figure 11. Here we see participants retrieving significantly more unique relevant documents over most of the ranked list ($t(536)=2.554$, $p < 0.01$). Thus not only was there no precision-recall tradeoff, but instead both RP and RR increased in when the participants had access to the preview control.

When comparing regular (not residual) recall and precision of the queries the two conditions, we find no statistically-significant differences (both $t(538) < 1$). We also find that the diversity of search results (the number of relevant unique documents retrieved per query) is significantly higher in the experimental condition (52 (SD=30.0) vs. 44 (SD=31.8), $t(538) = 2.7$, $p < 0.01$).

We conclude that in the control condition participants ran queries that tend to re-retrieve the same relevant documents, whereas in the preview condition they tended to retrieve a more diverse set of documents. This diversity caused an increase in the residual precision and recall rates.

6. DISCUSSION

We demonstrated that a small change in the interface produced a significant increase in the diversity, precision, and recall of search results in an interactive search environment without changes to the underlying search algorithms. Instead the system provided searchers with appropriate and timely feedback on the characteristics of the queries they were constructing, and gave them an opportunity to revise queries prior to viewing the results.

Interestingly, the tactics participants used to revise queries are hard to pin down. The average number of terms did not change; participants did not engage in trial-and-error tactics to select terms, as the average number of edits made to a query was about the same. Instead, it seems that improvements in retrieval performance were due to qualitative differences in how the queries were created. Our results suggest that participants put more thought into the search terms when the preview was present; they looked more at the user interface while formulating queries, and used on average 7.8 sec (29%) longer to formulate queries. This longer duration cannot be explained solely by participants looking at the preview. While participants looked at the preview for about one second on average, they looked about two and half seconds longer per query at the query input area. There seemed to be no advantage, however, to looking at other parts of the UI: participants spent more time looking at the results list, more time looking at documents, etc., in the control condition, but this did not result in better outcomes. This indicates that the preview control was working as we had intended, nudging people toward retrieving more diverse result sets and toward exploring these results more completely. It seems that people were engaged in more sense-making behavior both during query construction and when examining search results.

One effect of the search engine retrieving better results was that participants needed to submit fewer queries to find a satisfactory number of relevant documents. We saw a change in tactics in the experimental condition: participants looked deeper into the results lists, presumably due to the preview visualization. Participants tried to use the preview as a navigation tool, although it was not designed as such. As discussed earlier, examining lower ranked documents during exploratory search is important since the object is to find as many relevant document about a topic as possible rather than finding just one document. Residual precision and recall metrics underscore this as well: fewer unique documents were found in the ten top ranked documents than in the lower ranked documents. If these lower ranked documents had not been examined, they might not have been identified.

These results are encouraging. The design of the preview control is simple and requires little additional capability in the system; yet it prompted participants to formulate more effective queries. Our analyses of three independent aspects – gaze, interaction, and performance – all indicated that the preview had an effect on participants' behaviors and on outcomes. The consistency of these findings gives us some confidence that the effects are robust.

This work illustrates how interaction design can complement retrieval algorithm improvements. Empowering people's decision-making in complex search tasks can yield better outcomes for the combined human-computer system.

7. NEXT STEPS

In this study, we showed that the preview control helps searchers to make sense of the results a query is going to retrieve. Here we discuss how this control can be improved further.

7.1. Usability

While most of our participants understood the purpose of the preview, they described two main usability issues with the control: lack of visible change for some queries, and the resetting of the visualization when results are loaded.

The first problem occurs if the profile of the preview is identical to the profile of the current query. Participants perceived this lack of change as an error because they were biased to expect changes.

The second problem occurs when the preview resets after the results of the newly-run query are incorporated into the task workspace. While this is, in a sense, consistent behavior, it leads to poor usability due to a mismatch with user expectations. Also, resetting the display loses the opportunity to use the preview as a navigation mechanism to explore the new results, something that participants actively attempted during the experiment.

The design challenge is to represent these system states in a consistent, predictable, usable, and useful manner:

1. Query construction or reformulation: while it is working, the system should reflect that it is computing the preview.
2. Once the preview is computed, the system should indicate that the widget is displaying a preview. Even if the distribution of documents has not changed, the system should indicate clearly that it has recomputed the results.
3. After a query is run, the preview display should retain the previewed distribution and should act as a navigation mechanism into the document set retrieved by the query.

We are designing a new version of the control that preserves the visualization when the query is executed, and makes it possible to click on bars to navigate to corresponding pages of search results. The computation state is represented by a halo around the control; when results are available, the halo starts to pulsate gently, suggesting that the system is waiting for the searcher to react.

Figure 12. Mockup of alternative preview design.

Another possible design is to project the distributions of seen, unseen, and new documents directly onto the pagination controls, as shown in Figure 12. This solution decouples the preview from the display of retrieved documents. While this simplifies the individual widgets, it introduces additional complexity by representing related information in two different ways, and by complicating the design of the familiar pagination control. We are exploring this design space further.

7.2. Extensions in design

The preview control displayed three categories of information regarding documents that would be retrieved by the query being composed: whether or not the document had been retrieved previously, and if had been viewed or saved. It is possible to display other kinds of preview information as well.

Novelty could be defined in a fuzzy way based on significant rank promotion: when a document that has been previously retrieved at a low rank but has not been seen is retrieved at a significantly higher rank (e.g., a difference of 20 or more positions), its promotion could be indicated in the preview. This blurring of the distinction between new and as-yet-unseen documents is probably a useful simplification but requires additional testing. Another variant could represent the amount of time that has passed since a document has been retrieved. This temporal expiration of whether a document has been found might be useful to remind people about early decisions in a long-standing information need. Time could be measured in absolute terms, or by including only the periods during which the searcher is interacting with the system.

7.3. Broader application

Querium was designed as an integrated information seeking environment that is, while web-based, a closed system. Yet some of the interactivity described in this paper can be applied beyond Querium to more generic search engines. One obvious application of the preview widget is a web browser plugin that monitors search activity and keeps track of found documents. The goal of this light-weight approach is to focus specifically on the task of managing the retrieval history in a nuanced and useful way. We are currently building a browser extension that tracks and visualizes re-retrieval patterns that occur during web search.

8. CONCLUSIONS

In this paper, we described a novel widget for helping searchers make sense of search results for complex information seeking tasks. We evaluated this widget in a controlled experiment to assess is impact on searchers' behavior. We found that it increases the rates at which participants examined documents at middle ranks in query results, and thus helped discover more useful documents in those middle ranks than without the preview widget. We also found that the preview control can increase the diversity of documents found in a search session, which can in turn lead to better performance in terms of recall and precision.

This exploration suggests that appropriately-designed interactive displays can be used to improve searchers' effectiveness in conducting searches for complex information needs. These kinds of visualizations use structural information collected during the search session to allow searchers to reason about the incremental result set. By making it easier for searchers to explore the results in more depth, we can reduce reliance on ranking algorithms that are only partially effective at predicting useful documents.

9. ACKNOWLEDGMENTS

We thank our participants for their efforts and Frank Shipman for some early discussions and insight. We thank Maribeth Back for her feedback on this paper.

10. REFERENCES

1. Ancestry.com http://www.ancestry.com
2. Bast, H., Majumdar, D., and Weber, I. (2007). Efficient interactive query expansion with complete search. In *Proc. CIKM '07*. ACM, New York, NY, USA, 857-860.
3. Bast, H. and Weber, I. (2006) Type less, find more: fast autocompletion search with a succinct index. In *Proc. SIGIR '06*. ACM, New York, NY, USA, 364-371.
4. Bates, M. (1989) The design of browsing and berrypicking techniques for the online search interface. *Online Review*, 13(5):407–424. Online: http://gseis.ucla.edu/faculty/bates/berrypicking.html
5. Belkin, N.J. (1980) Anomalous states of knowledge as a basis for information retrieval. *Canadian Journal of Information Science*, 5:133–143.
6. Belkin, N. J., Oddy, R. and Brooks, H. (1982) ASK for Information Retrieval. *Journal of Documentation*, 38, 61-71 (part 1) & 145-164 (part 2).
7. Bharat, K. (2000) SearchPad: Explicit Capture of Search Context to Support Web Search. In *Proc. WWW2000*, pp. 493-501.
8. Doherty-Sneddon, G., & Phelps, F. G. (2005) Gaze aversion: A response to cognitive or social difficulty? *Memory & Cognition*, 33, 727-733.
9. Golovchinsky, G. (1997) Queries? Links? Is there a difference? In *Proc. CHI 1997*. ACM Press.
10. Golovchinsky, G., Diriye, A., and Dunnigan, T. (2012) The future is in the past: Designing for exploratory search. In *Proc. IIiX 2012* (Nijmegen, The Netherlands). ACM Press.
11. Google Instant. http://www.google.com/insidesearch/features/instant/about.html
12. Hoeber, O. and Yang, X.D. (2006). Interactive Web Information Retrieval Using WordBars. In Proc *WI '06*. IEEE Computer Society, Washington, DC, USA, 875-882.
13. Komlodi, A., Marchionini, G., and Soergel, D. (2007) Search history support for finding and using information: user interface design recommendations from a user study. *IP&M*, 43, 1 (Jan. 2007), 10-29
14. Kuhlthau, C. (1991) Inside the search process: Information seeking from the user's perspective. *JASIS* 42,5, 361-371.
15. Marchionini, G. (1995). *Information Seeking in Electronic Environments*. Cambridge University Press.
16. Pickens, J., Cooper, M., and Golovchinsky, G. (2010) Reverted Indexing for Feedback and Expansion. In Proc. *CIKM 2010*.
17. Pirolli, P. and S. K. Card. (1999) Information foraging. Psychological Review, 106, 643-675.
18. Salvucci, D. and Goldberg, J. (2000) Identifying Fixations and Saccades in Eye-Tracking Protocols. In Proceedings of *ETRA'10*. ACM, 2000, 283-290.
19. Sanderson, M. and van Rijsbergen, C.J. (1991) NRT: News Retrieval Tool. *Electronic Publishing*, vol. 4(4), pp. 205-217.
20. Spoerri, A. (2004) How Visual Query Tools Can Support Users Searching the Internet. In *Proc ICIV'04*, London, UK, July 14-16 2004.
21. Twidale, M. and Nichols, D. M. (1998) Designing interfaces to support collaboration in information retrieval. *Interacting with Computers* 10(2), pp. 177-193.
22. Walker, G. & Janes, J. (1993) *Online retrieval: A dialogue of theory and practice*. Libraries Unlimited: Englewood, CO. p. 100.

News Vertical Search: When and What to Display to Users

Richard McCreadie, Craig Macdonald, and Iadh Ounis
{firstname.lastname}@glasgow.ac.uk
University of Glasgow
G12 8QQ, Glasgow, UK

ABSTRACT

News reporting has seen a shift toward fast-paced online reporting in new sources such as social media. Web Search engines that support a news vertical have historically relied upon articles published by major newswire providers when serving news-related queries. In this paper, we investigate to what extent real-time content from newswire, blogs, Twitter and Wikipedia sources are useful to return to the user in the current fast-paced news search setting. In particular, we perform a detailed user study using the emerging medium of crowdsourcing to determine when and where integrating news-related content from these various sources can better serve the user's news need. We sampled approximately 300 news-related search queries using Google Trends and Bitly data in real-time for two time periods. For these queries, we have crowdsourced workers compare Web search rankings for each, with similar rankings integrating real-time news content from sources such as Twitter or the blogosphere. Our results show that users exhibited a preference for rankings integrating newswire articles for only half of our queries, indicating that relying solely on newswire providers for news-related content is now insufficient. Moreover, our results show that users preferred rankings that integrate tweets more often than those that integrate newswire articles, showing the potential of using social media to better serve news queries.

Categories and Subject Descriptors: H.3.3 [Information Storage & Retrieval]: Information Search & Retrieval

General Terms: Experimentation, Performance

Keywords: News Vertical, Web Search, User-generated Content

1. INTRODUCTION

Major universal Web search engines serve around a billion of user queries each day [25]. It has been reported that up to 11% of these Web search queries are related to current news [8]. We refer to these queries as *news-related queries*. When a news-related query is submitted to a Web search engine, a news-vertical is used to identify relevant news-related content from one or more providers, traditionally e-newspapers. If relevant content is found, then this content can be integrated into the Web search ranking, normally within a vertical result block, as illustrated in Figure 1.

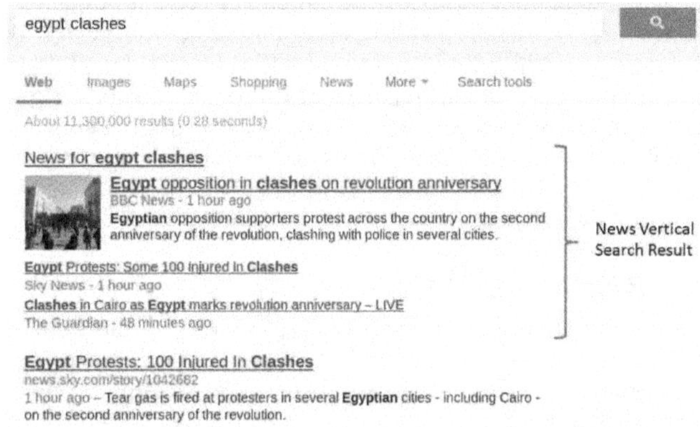

Figure 1: Example of vertical search result integration for the query 'egypt clashes' on the 25/01/2013.

The online news landscape has been greatly affected by the emergence of *user-generated content* sources such as Twitter. In particular, the role of the public in the online news space has shifted from static consumers to real-time reporters and commentators. Indeed, current events are now summarised and discussed in real-time [7, 27] using a variety of diverse media [21], driven by user interaction and user-generated content, e.g. news reporting in Twitter [26].

This shift has had important consequences for Web search engines when tackling news-related queries. In particular, users are now searching for information about events mere seconds after those events have occurred [14]. Moreover, new and potentially valuable content is being produced outside of the normal newswire providers that are used by news verticals. Indeed, we argue that relying solely on newswire providers is no longer sufficient to satisfy news-related queries.

In this paper, we investigate three questions with regard to real-time news vertical search, namely: Is newswire article integration still sufficient given the increasing pace of news-reporting? To what extent can content from user-generated sources also satisfy the end-user? How does the age of an event affect the types of content that users prefer? To answer these questions, we perform a large-scale user study. In particular, we first develop an evaluation interface for performing preference assessment between pairs of rankings. We then sample almost 300 queries relating to recent news events in real-time using the Google Trends and Bitly APIs.

SIGIR'13, July 28–August 1, 2013, Dublin, Ireland.
Copyright 2013 ACM 978-1-4503-2034-4/13/07 ...$15.00.

For each query and time, we also collect individual rankings of Web pages, newswire articles, blogs, tweets and Wikipedia pages for them. Using our proposed interface in conjunction with the crowdsourcing marketplace Amazon's Mechanical Turk, we employ workers (acting as surrogates for end-users) to compare Web page rankings with the same rankings enhanced with additional news content from newswire, the blogosphere, Twitter or Wikipedia. In this way, we evaluate the extent to which different sources can be used to better satisfy news-related queries. Indeed, this is the first user study examining the integration of different content types for news vertical search.

The remainder of this paper is structured as follows. In Section 2, we provide a background into prior works that have examined news vertical search and crowdsourcing. Section 3 describes our methodology, including the design of the crowdsourcing interface we use in our user study. In Section 4, we detail our experimental setup in terms of topic development and crowdsourcing/worker statistics. Section 5 describes the results of our crowdsourced user study with respect to our three research questions. Concluding remarks are provided in Section 6.

2. RELATED WORK

This paper builds upon two areas related to the field of information retrieval (IR), namely news vertical search and crowdsourcing. We discuss prior works that examined news vertical search in Section 2.1, while we provide a background on crowdsourcing for IR in Section 2.2.

2.1 News Vertical Search

The field of news vertical search has seen little investigation to date, with prior works focusing on how to predict when a user will click on a news-related document added into the Web search ranking. In particular, Diaz [12] proposed a machine learning approach for click prediction on newswire articles. This approach trains an initial model using features extracted from the news articles along with additional query features from past Web and news vertical query-logs. The approach then incorporates click-feedback, in that it allows a user's subsequent clicks to enhance the model over time. Arguello *et al.* [4] expanded upon the approach by Diaz for multiple verticals, extracting features from each vertical considered to build a classification model. Later, König *et al.* [20] also examined a learned approach for click prediction for news-related queries. They propose the use of additional features from the query, in addition to features describing the distribution of the query terms in blog, newswire and Wikipedia corpora, with the aim of better estimating the proportion of users that will click on a newswire article if displayed. Importantly, these works only examine the integration of newswire articles into the Web search results, not the integration of user-generated content (in König's case blogs and Wikipedia are used to better determine when newswire articles should be displayed, not as a source of content). In contrast, in this paper, we examine the integration of blogs, tweets and Wikipedia articles in addition to newswire articles. Moreover, rather than predicting document clicks to estimate when to integrate content (which requires access to large proprietary query logs), we perform a user study to ascertain from a user perspective when integrating additional content is useful. Furthermore, an added value of this work is that the assessments produced as part of our user study could be used to train machine learned models for news vertical search, like those described above.

Relatedly, in the context of search over multiple verticals (including the news vertical), Zhou *et al.* [31], proposed a general evaluation framework for aggregate search. However, their framework pre-supposes that relevance assessments for each document are available, which is not the case in our scenario. Hence, we take an alternative evaluation approach in this paper. Arguello *et al.* [5] performed a user study using 29 people from a nearby town to examine the relationship between task complexity and the use of integrated search results from multiple. However, their study focused on the user cognitive process for general tasks, rather than news-specific search tasks. Indeed, to the best of our knowledge, our user study is the first that examines news vertical search to date.

2.2 Crowdsourcing in IR

Crowdsourcing in general is the act of outsourcing tasks, traditionally performed by a specialist person or group, to a large undefined group of people or community (referred to as the "crowd"), through an open call [16]. There are many motivations for crowdsourcing tasks. For example, simple tasks can be completed at a relatively small cost, and often very quickly [3]. Moreover, by employing a crowd of 'users' to perform assessments as opposed to a few 'experts', a wider range of talent can be accessed and expert bias avoided [15]. However, crowdsourcing has also been the subject of much controversy as to its effectiveness. In particular, the work produced by crowdsourced workers is known to sometimes be of low quality [6] and results can be affected by random or malicious work [13].

In an IR setting, crowdsourcing has been used as an alternative method for evaluating search system performance. Alonso *et al.* [3] first suggested crowdsourcing as a cheap, fast, effective and flexible alternative to using specialist assessors when creating relevance assessments for ad-hoc test collections. Indeed, crowdsourcing was later used to generate relevance assessments for larger collections [2], in addition to being both the subject of one track[1] and used to support other tracks [24] at the Text REtrieval Conference (TREC). Relatedly, Zhu and Carterette [32] also used crowdsourcing to perform a successful pilot study examining the integration of images into the Web search results.

In this paper, we use crowdsourced workers from the Amazon's Mechanical Turk marketplace to compare Web search rankings to those enhanced with additional news-related content for news queries. Indeed, crowdsourcing is particularly suitable to use in our user study for three reasons. First, workers can act as surrogates of end-users on the assumption that those same workers also use Web search engines. Second, the worker-base is large and diverse [17] meaning that our results are less likely to suffer from demographic bias, in contrast to using students or co-workers. Third, assessments are quick, cheap and reproducible by other researchers.[2]

Prior works in the field of crowdsourcing have identified effective *validation* approaches for the identification of poor quality work, with the aim of increased accuracy. Snow *et*

[1] `https://sites.google.com/site/treccrowd/`

[2] Subject to implementation of the same assessment interface and access to the dataset described later in Section 4.1, which is available at `http://terrierteam.dcs.gla.ac.uk/vertical/`.

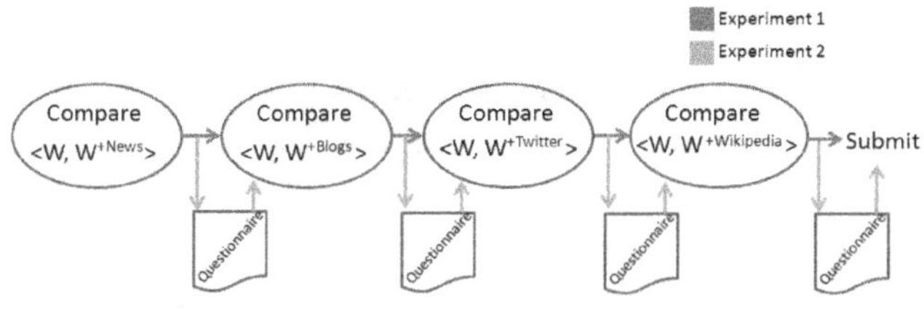

Figure 2: Workflow of a single assignment.

al. [29] and Callison-Burch [10] investigated the accuracy of crowdsourced labels generated for natural language processing tasks, concluding that 'expert' quality labels can be achieved by having three or five workers complete each crowdsourcing task and taking the majority (most commonly selected) label. Kittur *et al.* [19] proposed the introduction of questions with verifiable, quantitative answers, often referred to as 'gold judgements' or a 'honey-pot' to identify poorly performing workers. However, subsequent research by Ipeirotis [18] has indicated that within a Web page classification context, gold judgements are unnecessary when larger numbers of assessors work on each task. In particular, their results indicate that when 10 assessors work on each task and a majority result is taken, then no appreciable gains in accuracy are observed when further adding a gold judgement validation, i.e. crowdsourced work can be validated through redundancy. Following this prior work, as part of our user study, we use 10 redundant workers to compare each of our rankings. The majority vote is used to ensure quality.[3] Our assessment interface (described later in Section 3.1) also contains an in-built form of validation, to identify bots and users that randomly click on answers. In the next section, we describe our experimental methodology, including how we designed the interface we show to our crowdsourced workers.

3. METHODOLOGY

In an IR setting, rankings are usually evaluated using incomplete Cranfield-style relevance assessments [11] pooled from multiple systems [30]. However, such an approach is not suitable for evaluation of vertical search rankings because documents within a ranking cannot be judged independently of one another. In particular, whether the news-related results added by the news vertical improve the initial Web search ranking depends both upon the documents added and the extent to which the Web search ranking already satisfied the user's news need. Moreover, each ranking contains multiple types of documents, which from a pair-wise perspective may not be directly comparable. For instance, how can the value of a tweet be directly compared to a newswire article? Furthermore, the real-time nature of news-related queries mean that the value that each news-related document brings to the ranking is dependant upon both its relevance and also its recency/timeliness with regard to the event underlying the query.

Instead, inspired by prior works by Thomas and Hawking [28] and Carterette [9], we propose a comparative evaluation approach, where the top ten documents from each ranking are considered as a single evaluation unit (rather than evaluating the individual documents). For this type of evaluation, multiple different rankings are displayed to the user, who then selects the one that he/she prefers. In our scenario, for a news-related query, the user is shown both the unmodified Web search ranking and a ranking with content from either newswire, the blogosphere, Twitter or Wikipedia integrated. In particular, for each news-related query, we have users compare the Web search ranking to rankings enhanced with content from each of the aforementioned sources in turn, such that they can identify those cases where integrating additional content is useful. The advantage of this approach is that it avoids the issues of pair-wise document comparability and redundancy by having end-users compare both document rankings as single units.

Formally, our approach takes as input a Web search ranking W and a set of news and user-generated content rankings $e \in E$ for a news-related query Q and a given point in time t. For our experiments, E is comprised of four rankings, namely rankings of newswire articles, blogs, tweets and Wikipedia pages. Each ranking is ranked by relevance to Q and with respect to the query time t, i.e. only documents from before t are ranked. For each query, the Web search ranking W is combined with each of the four news and user-generated content rankings in E to form four *enhanced rankings*. We denote an enhanced ranking as W^{+e}, e.g. W^{+Blogs}.

Our strategy for generating the enhanced rankings is as follows. For W^{+News}, W^{+Blogs} and $W^{+Twitter}$, we select the top three documents ranked for Q and add them to the top of W within a special result box. This simulates the look and feel of current news vertical search results, like those shown previously in Figure 1. For $W^{+Wikipedia}$, we include only the top ranked Wikipedia page for the query, based on the observation that Web search engines typically only return one page from Wikipedia in their top 10 results.

Finally, we combine the Web search ranking W with its four enhanced rankings to form four document ranking pairs, e.g. $<W, W^{+Blogs}>$. During our user study, for each query, a user is shown each of the four ranking pairs for that query in turn, selecting the one that they would prefer to see for Q and time t in each case. Figure 2 illustrates the workflow for a single assignment. As described later in Section 4.1, we evaluate using two datasets. For the second dataset, after the user selects a ranking, we also give the user a multiple-choice questionnaire about why they selected each ranking.

If the majority of users that compare a ranking pair for a query Q select the enhanced ranking W^{+e}, we say that W^{+e} *better satisfies* Q (the query topic) for time t. In Section 3.1, we describe the interface we show to the users, while Section 3.2 describes of the questionnaire that we use.

3.1 Crowdsourcing Interface

To facilitate our comparative evaluation approach, we develop an assessment interface to perform the presentation of document ranking pairs to the user, and record the results. Figure 3 provides an illustration of the assessment interface for the query 'mariangela melato' made on January 12th 2013. We enlarge the enhanced ranking for easy viewing in Figure 3. At the top of the interface, the title of the task is displayed along with a button that reveals the instructions for the task (hidden in Figure 3). The instructions are divided into two separate components, namely: the main instruction block that describes what the user is being asked to do; and the guidelines block that provides additional clarifications about the task. When a user first views the task

[3]Tie-breaking assessments are unneeded when using many (10 in our case) workers.

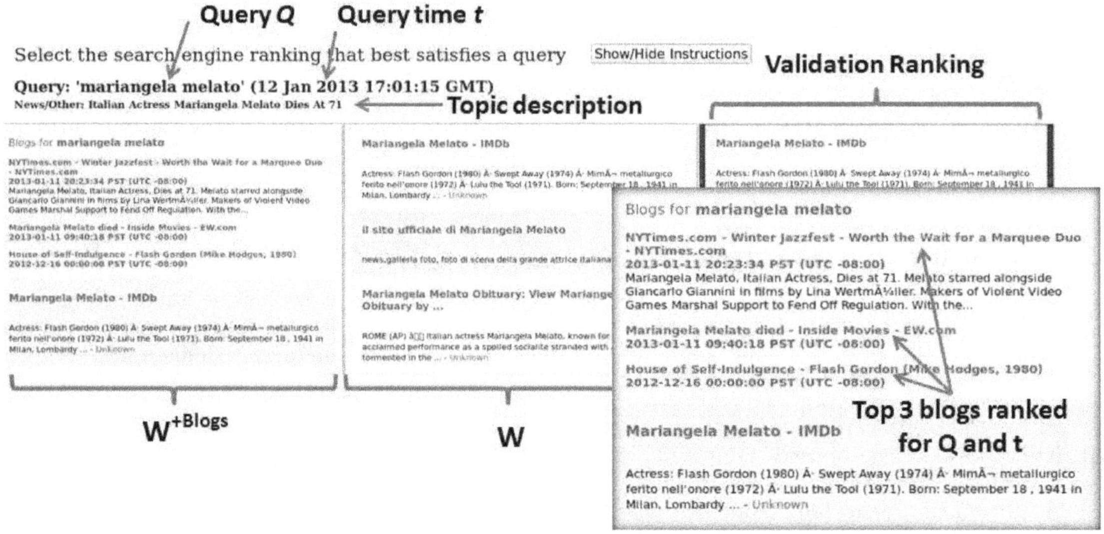

Figure 3: Illustration of our ranking interface produced for the query 'mariangela melato' on the 12/01/13 at 5:01pm. The first ranking is W^{+Blogs}, while the second ranking is W. The third (red bordered) ranking is a validation ranking designed to catch workers that are randomly clicking.

(before accepting it) the instructions are displayed to them. When actively attempting the task, the instructions are automatically closed by default to save screen real-estate.

Below the instructions, the news-related user query is displayed along with a short topic description. For the example in Figure 3, the user was searching for information about the death of Italian cinema and theatre actress Mariangela Melato. Below the query Q and topic description, the document rankings W and W^{+e} from the current pair are rendered (W^{+Blogs} in Figure 3). Users are instructed to select the ranking that best satisfies the query, while the guidelines instruct the user to focus on whether the additional results added to one of the rankings make it better or worse. To enable users to state their preference for one of the displayed rankings, each ranking is clickable. Clicking a ranking records the user's preference for that ranking. Recall that the rankings are produced with respect to the query time t, i.e. only documents published before the time of the query are ranked. Both the timestamp of the query and the publication time of each post (if available) are rendered as part of the interface. Users are instructed to consider recency as well as relevance when assessing using these timestamps.

The four ranking pairs for each query topic are assessed by a single user in sequence to increase efficiency [23]. After a user clicks on a ranking, if there are any ranking pairs remaining for the current query topic (of the four total), then the next ranking pair is rendered for assessment, else a link is displayed to enable the user to submit their assessments. If any of the news and/or user-generated content sources did not return documents for the query, e.g. because no relevant documents had yet been published, then both of the rankings in the associated pair would be identical. In these cases, the interface automatically skips to the next pair to be assessed.

As described in Section 2.2, one of the criticisms of crowdsourcing is a susceptibility to poor quality work. In addition to having 10 unique users assess each ranking pair, our assessment interface also integrates one method for validating user work. In particular, the interface renders the Web result ranking twice, creating three rankings. One of these rankings has a red border (as shown in Figure 3). The users are instructed never to select the red bordered ranking. We use this ranking to identify bots or malicious users that are randomly selecting rankings. Any set of assessments where a red-bordered ranking has been clicked is automatically rejected without payment. The three rankings are randomly ordered to avoid click bias for any one position.

3.2 Questionnaire

When assessing the topics in our second dataset (see Section 4.1), we show a questionnaire to the user after they select each ranking. Depending upon which ranking the user selected, a different questionnaire is displayed. In particular, for the enhanced ranking, the user is asked to select one or more statements that apply to the content added (either newswire articles, blogs, tweets or Wikipedia pages). The six statements are listed below:

```
> Relevant to the query
> Relate to a recent event (at the time of the query)
> Appear to be about breaking news
> Better satisfy the query by being included
> Are informative based upon the title/snippet shown
> Provide useful general information, unrelated to a
  recent event
```

In contrast, if the user selected the Web search ranking, they are asked to select one of the following reasons why the additional content did not better satisfy the query:

```
> Partially relevant, but I still preferred the basic
  ranking.
> Out-of-date, new information was added, but it was old.
> Redundant, no information was added that was not in the
  basic ranking.
> Completely irrelevant, the added documents were
  unrelated to the query.
> Spam, the added documents appear to be spam or
  advertising.
```

In this way, we first have users decide whether a ranking is improved by the integration of news or user-generated content and then have them elaborate as to why this is the case.

Table 1: Statistics for the two datasets used in this paper and the number of query topics belonging to each temporal class within each.

	2012_{Apr}	2013_{Jan}
Topic Source	Google Trends	Bitly Bursting Phrases
Time-Period	11/04/12 → 23/04/12	10/01/13 → 16/01/13
# Breaking	74	64
# Recent	38	7
# Long-Running	29	15
# Other	58	0
Total Topics	199	98

We use the interface and questionnaire described above in conjunction with Amazon's Mechanical Turk to perform our user study. In the next section, we describe our experimental setup for the user study.

4. EXPERIMENTAL SETUP

Due to a lack of publicly available datasets upon which we could evaluate ([12] and [20] described in Section 2.1 used private Yahoo! and Microsoft data for instance) we develop two new datasets for evaluation. In Section 4.1, we describe the creation of two new datasets that we use for evaluation. Section 4.2 summaries the structure of our user study. In Section 4.3, we detail the statistics of our crowdsourcing experiments, while Section 4.4 provides information about our MTurk workers.

4.1 Topic Development

We develop two new datasets to facilitate our evaluation using publicly available resources. Our first dataset, referred to as 2012_{Apr}, spans the period of the 11th to the 23rd of April 2012. The second dataset, referred to as 2013_{Jan} spans the period of the 10th to the 16th of January 2013. Each dataset contains a set of <query,timestamp> pairs and rankings of Web pages, newswire articles, blogs, tweets and Wikipedia pages for each.

To generate our news-related queries, we use the Google Trends[4] and the Bitly Data API[5]. In particular, for the 2012_{Apr} dataset, we sampled the queries that were reported trending by Google Trends on an hourly basis for that period. At the end of each day, we manually identified those queries that matched a reported news event, while all other queries were discarded. This left a set of 199 queries known to be news-related over the 12 day period. For the 2013_{Jan} dataset, we instead crawled the 'Bursting Phrases' service of Bitly's Data API at 30 minute intervals, since Bitly updates its bursting phrases more frequently than Google Trends. The bursting phrases service returns phrases that were receiving a consistently high volume of click traffic at the time. From this set of bursty phrases returned, we manually identified 98 that referred to news events, using these as our news-related queries for the second dataset. For both datasets, the timestamp of the query is the time when it was crawled using either API. Hence, this timestamp corresponds to a period when the query/phrase was either receiving high traffic as recorded by Google or Bitly. We also manually created topic descriptions for each query with reference to the main news stories around the time of each query.

To collect rankings for each topic, we again used publicly available API's. For the time of each query as recorded by that query's timestamp, we downloaded Bing Web search results[6], newswire articles and blogs from the Blekko API[7], Twitter tweets[8] and Wikipedia pages[9] for that query. These rankings are real-time in nature, i.e. they contain only documents published before the query timestamp t. The documents are ranked by relevance with respect to the query Q. Recall from Section 3 that the top three newswire articles, blog posts and tweets are selected for integration into the Web search ranking, while for Wikipedia, only the top ranked Wikipedia page is integrated.

[4] `http://www.google.co.uk/trends/hottrends`
[5] `http://dev.bitly.com/`

Table 2: Types of data collected from the two crowdsourcing tasks.

Data Subject	Data Type	2012_{Apr}	2013_{Jan}
Document Rankings	Ranking Preference	✔	✔
Document Rankings	Questionnaire	✗	✔
Worker	Work Submitted	✔	✔
Worker	Time Taken	✔	✔
Worker	Geo-Location	✗	✔

To aid our later analysis, we also divide our queries into four classes, representing the time elapsed between the event underpinning each query and that query's timestamp:

- **Breaking**: Queries related to events that have broken within the prior 12 hours.
- **Recent**: Queries related to a recent news event that occurred between 12 and 48 hours previously.
- **Long-Running**: Queries relating to older events that are still of interest.
- **Other**: The time of the originating event could not be accurately identified.

Table 1 summarises the statistics of our two datasets and the number of query topics belonging to each query class within them.

4.2 Experiment structure

Following best practices in crowdsourcing [1], we adopt an iterative design methodology. In particular, we separate our crowdsourced user study into two separate crowdsourcing experiments, one for each of the two datasets described in the previous section. Based upon worker feedback from the first experiment (2012_{Apr}), we improved the assessment interface, user behaviour logging and the provided instructions before crowdsourcing the second experiment (2013_{Jan}). Most notably, the questionnaires were added to enable users to better articulate why one ranking might be better than another, while IP-address logging was enabled to estimate the location of workers. Table 2 summaries the data that was collected from the two crowdsourcing experiments.

4.3 Crowdsourcing Configuration

We use the crowdsourcing marketplace Amazon's Mechanical Turk (MTurk) to recruit workers for our evaluation. Following [18], as described in Section 2.2, we have ten individual workers assess each document ranking pair. Each MTurk

[6] `http://www.bing.com/developers/`
[7] `http://blog.blekko.com/2012/10/15/powering-web-apps-with-the-blekko-api/`
[8] `https://dev.Twitter.com/`
[9] `http://www.mediawiki.org/wiki/API:Main_page`

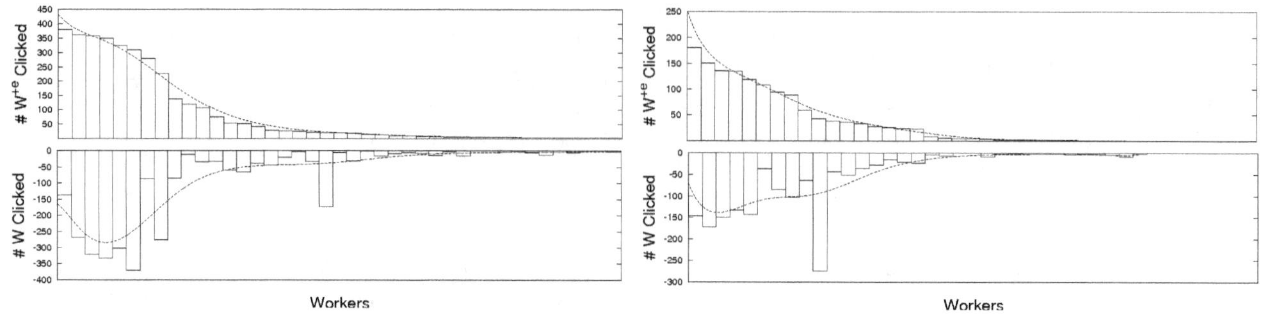

(a) 2012_{Apr} (b) 2013_{Jan}

Figure 4: The distribution of enhanced and Web search rankings selected by workers for each experiment.

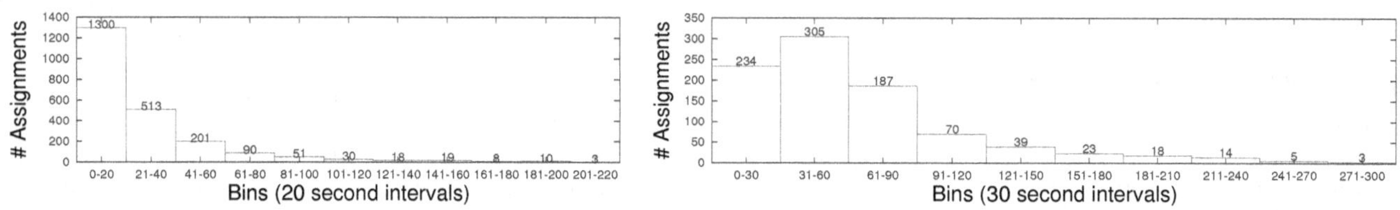

(a) 2012_{Apr} (b) 2013_{Jan}

Figure 5: Assignments binned by the time they took to complete for each of the two experiments.

assignment involves the assessment of 4 document pairs (the Web search ranking in comparison to 4 different enhanced rankings). The second experiment also added the questionnaires after each assessment was made. We paid US $0.05 for each set of 4 document pairs assessed, since assessment requires that the user browses the two rankings and makes a single click. For the second experiment, an additional $0.05 was paid for completion of the questionnaires. We use the in-built worker validation described in Section 3.1 to detect bots and spammers. Any assignment where a red-bordered ranking was selected was rejected without payment and re-submitted for another user to complete. The total cost of running the two experiments was US $217.25, including MTurk's 10% fee.

In terms of the two experiments, the 199 topics from the first dataset translate into 1990 assignments (199x10), while the 98 topics from the second dataset translate into 980 assignments (98x10). Both experiments were completed individually in under 48 hours. Automatic validation (based on clicking of red-bordered rankings) resulted in the rejection of 9.5% and 3.05% of assignments for each of the two datasets respectively. Inter-worker agreement was 0.33 using Cohen κ for the first experiment and 0.23 using Cohen κ for the second experiment. Note that a low agreement is expected in this case due to both the large number of workers attempting each task and a greater scope for disagreement between workers due to individual preferences.

4.4 Worker Statistics

In total, 98 unique workers completed one or more assignments over our two experiments, 57 workers during the first experiment and 41 during the second experiment. Figures 4 (a) and (b) show the distribution of enhanced (W^{+e}) and Web search rankings (W) selected by workers. As is typical for crowdsourced tasks [2, 24], we see that the completed work follows a long-tail distribution, with a few workers completing many assignments and a long tail of workers that completed only a few assignments. Furthermore, we

Table 3: Work statistics broken down by country for the second dataset.

Country	# of Page Requests	# Unique IP-Addresses	Proportion of Work Done	Proportion of IP-Addresses
India	6,479	41	68%	39%
United States	1,484	40	16%	38%
Macedonia	843	3	9%	3%
Philippines	242	1	3%	1%
Romania	210	3	2%	3%
United Kingdom	141	3	2%	3%
Pakistan	122	1	1%	1%
Bangladesh	10	1	0.1%	1%
Japan	8	5	0.1%	5%
Singapore	8	2	0.1%	2%
Hungary	6	1	0.1%	1%
Ireland	6	1	0.1%	1%
Albania	4	1	>0.1%	1%
Australia	3	1	>0.1%	1%
Canada	3	1	>0.1%	1%

also observe that the majority of workers show no clear bias toward selecting either type of ranking. Note that because 10 individual workers assess each topic, the impact that a single worker can have on the final result is limited.

The time taken by the workers to complete each assignment varies. Figures 5 (a) and (b) show the amount of time that assignments (4 assessments) took, separated into 20/30 second bins (for readabilty). From Figure 5, we observe that for the first experiment (2012_{Apr}), to assess four ranking pairs took the majority of the workers (57%) under 20 seconds, with a further 23% of assignments taking between 21 and 40 seconds. In contrast, for the second experiment (2013_{Jan}), assessment took longer on average, with 33% of workers taking between 31 and 60 seconds and a further 20% taking between 61 and 90 seconds. This is because the second experiment also required workers to fill in the questionnaire after each of the four ranking pairs per assignment.

Finally, for the second experiment (2013_{Jan}), we also logged the IP-addresses of the workers. From this information, we identified the county of origin that each worker comes from. Table 3 reports the number of page requests, unique IP-addresses and their proportions for each country made during the second experiment. From Table 3, we observe that 39% of IP-addresses and hence workers came from India, followed by 38% from the U.S. However, while the number of unique workers is similar between these two countries, the volume of work done is much higher for Indian workers. This indicates that Indian workers completed more assignments on average than US workers.

4.5 Measures

In our subsequent experiments, we report the majority preference over the ten workers that compared each ranking pair. Recall from Section 3.1 that not all sources return content for all of the topics. In these cases, both rankings in a pair would be identical, hence we remove these cases from our dataset. For this reason, the click counts can be lower than the total number of assignments.

5. RESULTS

In this section, we investigate to what extent integrating newswire articles, blogs, tweets and Wikipedia pages into the search results for news-related queries can better satisfy the user. In particular, we examine the following three research questions, each in a separate subsection:

- Is newswire article integration still sufficient given the increasing pace of news-reporting? (Section 5.1)
- To what extent can content from user-generated sources better satisfy the end-user in comparison to returning the Web search ranking or integrating newswire articles? (Section 5.2)
- How does the age of a event affect the types of content that users prefer? (Section 5.3)

5.1 Integrating Newswire Articles

We begin by examining our first research question, i.e. is news article integration still sufficient to satisfy news-related queries in real-time. We report on the number of users that clicked (stated a preference for) rankings enhanced with newswire articles (W^{+News}) in comparison to the Web search ranking unaltered (W). If the users prefer the newswire-enhanced rankings, then this would indicate that newswire articles are still sufficient. On the other hand, if there are many topics where users do not prefer the newswire-enhanced ranking, then this would indicate that we need to look to other sources of content to satisfy the user for these queries.

Table 4 reports the raw number of users that clicked on the newswire-enhanced or Web search ranking, i.e. when $<W,W^{+News}>$ pairs were compared. Recall that we have ten users (workers) assess each ranking pair to counteract any noise introduced by poorly performing workers. Table 4 also reports the majority preference over the ten workers, i.e. the number of real-time news topics where the majority preferred either ranking. From Table 4, we observe the following. First, comparing the raw click counts for each of the newswire-enhanced and Web search rankings (rows 3 and 5), we observe that for 28.9% of topics the users preferred the Web search ranking, while 48.5% preferred the newswire enhanced ranking (aggregating both datasets). Second, when taking the majority vote (rows 4 and 6), we similarly see that the Web search ranking was preferred by the majority of users for 17.8% of topics, while for 44.4% of the topics, the news-enhanced rankings were preferred by the majority of users. These results show that only around half of

Table 4: Number of topics for which the majority of end-users preferred either the Web search ranking or the rankings enhanced with user-generated content.

Ranking Preferred	Majority Vote?	2012_{Apr}	2013_{Jan}	Total	Proportion
Web	✗	828	418	860	28.9%
Web	✔	24	29	53	17.8%
News	✗	1002	442	1444	48.5%
News	✔	98	34	132	44.4%

our real-time news-related topics could be better satisfied by integrating newswire articles.

To investigate why newswire article integration was not able to satisfy many of our real-time news-related topics, we examine the reasons selected by our users in the questionnaire from our second experiment (see Section 3.2). Of the 418 Web search rankings clicked by our users in the second experiment, Figure 6 reports the percentage of those clicks that were attributed to the added documents in the newswire-enhanced ranking being either partially relevant, out-of-date, redundant, unrelated or spam. From Figure 6, we see that the main reason that users gave was that the results added were partially relevant, but did not make the enhanced ranking better. This result is interesting, since it indicates that the newswire sources were providing related content to the query, but that this content was not useful to the majority of our users. One example where the majority of users selected the Web search ranking was the query 'game industry', with the topic description 'News/Politics: Biden meeting with representatives from the video game industry'. For this query, the top two added newswire articles discussed violence relating to the video game industry, but did not specifically mention Joe Biden or the topic. The third integrated article was directly relevant to the topic. However, the original Web search ranking already contained two relevant Associated Press articles about the topic. Hence, the Joe Biden article was redundant, but the two other added articles were deemed by our users to be useful – even though they do not mention the topic directly.

Next, we examine the 442 instances from the second experiment where integrating newswire articles did improve the Web search ranking. Figure 7 illustrates the percentage of newswire-enhanced search rankings selected because they were more relevant, recent, reported breaking news, better satisfied the query, were particularly informative or provided general (background) information on the topic.[10] From Figure 7, we observe the following. First, as expected, we see that over 77.2% of the enhanced rankings were selected because they contained more relevant documents than the Web search ranking. We also see that over 63.3% of the enhanced rankings were selected because the added documents related to the recent event described in the topic description. Note the distinction between documents being relevant and documents relating to the event referred to by the query, i.e. some users may find that adding background articles for longer-running events is enough to improve over the Web search ranking. On the other hand, a much lower percentage of users (28.2%) indicated that they selected the enhanced ranking because the added documents were about breaking news. Also of note is that only 41.2% of users indicated that the introduction of newswire articles better satisfy the query

[10]Note that because a user can select multiple reasons for a single ranking, the percentages do not sum to one.

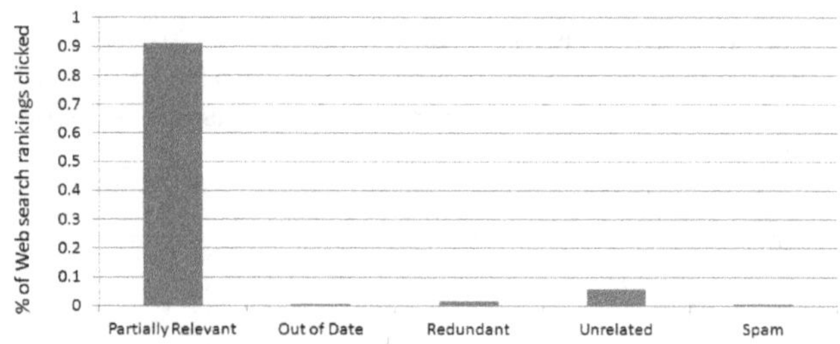

Figure 6: The percentage of Web search rankings clicked that were attributed to the added documents in the newswire-enhanced ranking being either partially relevant, out-of-date, redundant, unrelated or spam.

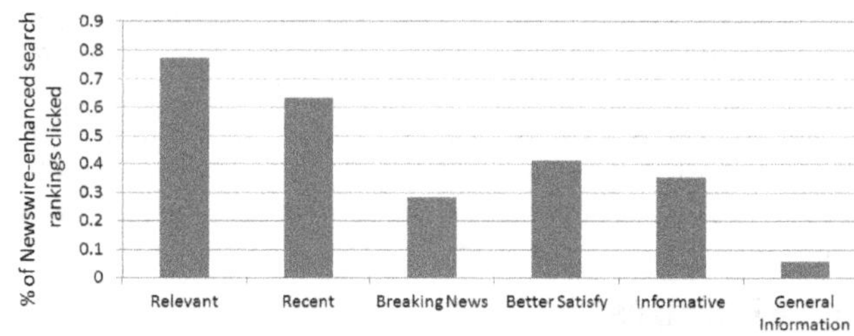

Figure 7: The percentage of newswire-enhanced search rankings selected because they were more relevant, recent, report breaking news, better satisfy the query, were particularly informative or provide general (background) information.

by being included, even though they stated a preference for the enhanced ranking. This indicates that either our users disagreed upon the meaning of 'satisfy' in the questionnaire, or that users can prefer the enhanced ranking for a topic, even if it does not better satisfy that topic. Indeed, almost all users selected the 'relevant' but not the 'better satisfied' choice for one or more topics.

To answer our first research question, newswire articles were not sufficient to satisfy the majority of topics in our two datasets, primarily because while some relevant content is added for most queries, users did not find that it improved the ranking. For the assignments where users preferred the newswire-enhanced ranking, users indicated that they preferred them because the added content was about the event underlying the query or was simply relevant to the query topic. In the next section, we investigate whether the integration of user-generated content can better satisfy users.

5.2 Integrating User-Generated Content

Next, we examine our second research question, i.e. to what extent can content from user-generated sources also satisfy the end-user? To this end, we begin by reporting on the number of users that clicked (stated a preference for) rankings enhanced with either blog posts, tweets or Wikipedia pages in comparison to the Web search rankings unaltered. If the number of topics where the majority of users selected the user-generated content-enhanced rankings is greater than for the number of topics that were similarly enhanced by integrating newswire articles (132 topics – see Table 4 row 6) then we can conclude that user-generated content sources may be more effective for news vertical integration than the traditional newswire sources used today.

Table 5 row 3 reports the number of topics where the majority of users preferred rankings enhanced with either blogs, tweets or Wikipedia pages to the Web search ranking unaltered. We report both the number of topics for each of the two datasets (2012_{Apr} and 2013_{Jan}), as well as the summation over the two. From Table 5 row 3, we observe that in total, the blog-enhanced rankings were preferred for 56.9% of the topics over the unaltered Web search rankings, while tweet-enhanced rankings were preferred for 71.2% of topics and Wikipedia pages for 52.1% of topics. Moreover, these proportions are consistent across both datasets. This result shows that all three of the user-generated content sources tested can enhance the Web search ranking for a substantial proportion of the 297 (see Table 1) real-time news-related topics tested. Most notably, the rankings including tweets were particularly favoured by our users, indicating that Twitter is a good source of real-time news content to integrate. Indeed, integrating tweets satisfied more query topics (168 – see Table 5 row 3, column 7) than integrating newswire articles (132 topics – see Table 4 row 6), indicating that Twitter is a better overall news source than traditional news providers.

However, if at the time t of each topic there exists relevant newswire articles, then user-generated content may not be required to satisfy the user, i.e. the extra content may be redundant. Indeed, in the previous section, we showed that approximately half of our topics could be better satisfied by integrating newswire articles than returning the Web search ranking unaltered. To examine this, we contrast the query topics that benefited from the integration of news articles to those that benefited by the integration of user-generated content. For a given query, if relevant user-generated content was found, integrated and the ranking was preferred by the majority of users, then user-generated content can be said to better satisfy that query than when integrating nothing. However, that same query may be equally or better satisfied by the integration of newswire articles. On the other hand, if there are news-related queries that user-generated content can satisfy, but newswire articles cannot (at the time those queries were made), then we can show that user-generated content is necessary to satisfy those queries.

Table 5 rows 4-6 report the number of topics for which integrating user-generated content aided but that integrating newswire did not (# Topics Better than Newswire). For comparison, we also report the reverse case (where integrating newswire articles aided but integrating user-generated content did not) and where integrating either newswire articles or user-generated content was equivalent (either both better satisfied the user or neither did). The total number of topics where integrating user-generated content aided but integrating newswire did not is highlighted in bold. From Table 5, we see the following two points of interest. First, each of our three user-generated content sources were able to satisfy topics which were not already satisfied by newswire articles. For instance, 22.2% of all topics could be better satisfied by integrating blogs but not newswire articles (row 4, column 4). Second, of the three user-generated content sources tested, we again see that Twitter is the most effective, improving 84 topics (34%), which were not better satisfied by integrating newswire articles. The query 'lionel richie' (issued on the 13th of April 2012) was one example where integrating tweets better satisfied our users but integrating newswire articles did not. For this query, the Twitter stream returned tweets reporting that music star

Table 5: The number of topics where users preferred rankings enhanced with either blogs, tweets or Wikipedia pages and comparison against those topics that could also be enhanced with newswire articles.

	Blogs			Twitter			Wikipedia		
	2012_{Apr}	2013_{Jan}	Total	2012_{Apr}	2013_{Jan}	Total	2012_{Apr}	2013_{Jan}	Total
# Topics Enhanced	86 (58.9%)	29 (51.8%)	115 (56.9%)	121 (73.8%)	47 (71.2%)	168 (71.3%)	66 (55.4%)	21 (43.8%)	87 (52.1%)
# Topics Better than Newswire	39 (22.2%)	15 (23.8%)	**54 (22.6%)**	53 (29.1%)	31 (47.0%)	**84 (33.9%)**	29 (17.3%)	12 (17.6%)	**41 (17.4%)**
# Topics Worse than Newswire	51 (29.0%)	20 (31.7%)	71 (29.7%)	30 (16.5%)	18 (27.3%)	48 (19.4%)	25 (36.8%)	25 (36.8%)	86 (36.4%)
# Topics Equal to Newswire	86 (48.9%)	28 (44.4%)	114 (47.7%)	99 (54.3%)	17 (25.7%)	116 (46.8%)	78 (46.4%)	31 (45.6%)	109 (46.2%)
# Topics Better than Blogs	—	—	—	66 (48.5%)	33 (48.5%)	99 (48.5%)	40 (26.8%)	16 (23.2%)	41 (20.2%)
# Topics Worse than Blogs	—	—	—	31 (22.8%)	15 (22.1%)	46 (22.5%)	60 (40.3%)	24 (44.4%)	84 (41.4%)
# Topics Equal to Blogs	—	—	—	39 (28.7%)	20 (29.4%)	59 (28.9%)	49 (32.9%)	29 (53.7%)	78 (38.4%)
# Topics Better than Twitter	31 (22.8%)	15 (22.1%)	46 (22.5%)	—	—	—	19 (14.1%)	10 (15.6%)	29 (14.6%)
# Topics Worse than Twitter	66 (48.5%)	33 (48.5%	99 (48.5%)	—	—	—	74 (55.2%)	36 (56.3%)	110 (55.6%)
# Topics Equal to Twitter	39 (28.7%)	20 (29.4%)	59 (28.9%)	—	—	—	41 (30.6%)	18 (28.1%)	59 (29.8%)
# Topics Better than Wikipedia	60 (40.3%)	24 (34.7%)	84 (38.5%)	74 (55.2%)	36 (56.2%)	110 (55.6%)	—	—	—
# Topics Worse than Wikipedia	40 (26.8%)	16 (23.2%)	56 (25.7%)	19 (14.2%)	10 (15.6%)	29 (14.6%)	—	—	—
# Topics Equal to Wikipedia	49 (32.9%)	29 (42.0%)	78 (35.8%)	41 (30.6%)	18 (28.1%)	59 (29.8%)	—	—	—

Lionel Richie was facing a large tax bill over allegations he owed more than $1 million to the U.S. government. On the other hand, our newswire stream returns no relevant articles for that query and time.

Having shown that integrating user-generated content can be more effective than integrating newswire articles, we now investigate whether the three user-generated content sources predominantly aid for the same or different topics. Indeed, even if Twitter is the most effective of the three user-generated sources overall, it may be that blogs and Wikipedia can aid for other topics. Table 5 rows 7-15 report the number of topics for which the rankings enhanced with content from each user-generated source were preferred over the rankings enhanced with another user-generated source. From Table 5, we observe the following. First, the three user-generated content sources appear to aid for different topics. For example, blog-enhanced rankings were preferred for 46 topics where rankings integrating tweets were not. However, there were similarly 99 topics for which the Twitter-enhanced rankings were preferred, where the blog-enhanced rankings were not. Second, the proportion of topics where integrating two different user-generated content sources were equivalent (both aided or neither did) is quite small, e.g. 22.5% of topics when considering tweets and blog posts. This indicates that user-generated content sources are useful for tackling different types of queries and that by effectively using multiple types of content, a larger proportion of news-related queries might better be satisfied. For instance, the topic 'james holmes' about a plea extension in the Aurora movie theatre shooting court case was only better satisfied by integrating tweets, while the topic 'baby lion' about a dog being mistaken for baby lion in Virginia was better covered by local newswire outlets.

To answer our second research question, integrating user-generated content into the Web search results can better satisfy many of our news-related topics. Moreover, many of these topics could not be similarly satisfied by integrating newswire articles published at the time. The most effective user-generated content source tested was Twitter, highlighting its usefulness for real-time news vertical search.

5.3 Content Integration and Event Age

In this section, we investigate our final research question, i.e. how does the age of a event affect the types of content that users prefer. To this end, we examine the query topics for which the integration of user-generated content aided when we break down our topics by the time between the originating event and the topic time. The aim is to determine whether different sources are better to integrate at different points during an event's life cycle.

Figures 8 (a) and (b) report the proportion of query topics where users preferred the enhanced ranking in comparison to the Web search ranking divided into three time classes (see Section 4.1) for each dataset, respectively. From Figure 8 (a) and (b) we observe the following. First, the proportion of topics improved by integrating newswire articles shows a downward trend as the time elapsed from the event increases. This indicates that newswire articles are less useful to return for long-running events, possibly because newswire providers tend to publish a burst of articles around the time of the event, with little content published later. Secondly, in contrast, we see that integrating blogs satisfied a larger proportion of long-running queries than breaking or recent queries. This supports prior observations that for some types of events bloggers tend to lag behind newswire when publishing [22]. Next, we see that integrating Tweets was most effective for satisfying queries relating to breaking events. Indeed, on the first dataset, 52% of the breaking news queries could be better satisfied by integrating tweets into the Web search ranking. For example, one such query was 'levon helm', referring to American rock multi-instrumentalist and actor who was fighting cancer at the time. When this query was issued on the 19th of April 2012, Twitter returned tweets reporting his death, while our newswire stream only returned articles reporting that he was in the final stages of cancer. This illustrates the value that Twitter can bring from a content integration perspective for breaking news queries where no newswire articles have yet been published.

To answer our third research question, we find that users prefer rankings that integrate tweets or newswire articles soon after an event breaks. As an event matures, tweets and newswire articles become less effective, while integrating blogs becomes more effective.

6. CONCLUSIONS

In this paper, we examined to what extent integrating news and user-generated content for real-time news-related queries could better satisfy end-users. We performed a novel user study using the emerging medium of crowdsourcing, where we had ten different users compare Web search rankings for 297 news-related queries against rankings that integrate newswire articles, blog posts, tweets and Wikipedia pages. From this user study, we showed that newswire articles were not sufficient to satisfy the majority of news-related queries tested, highlighting the need to examine new

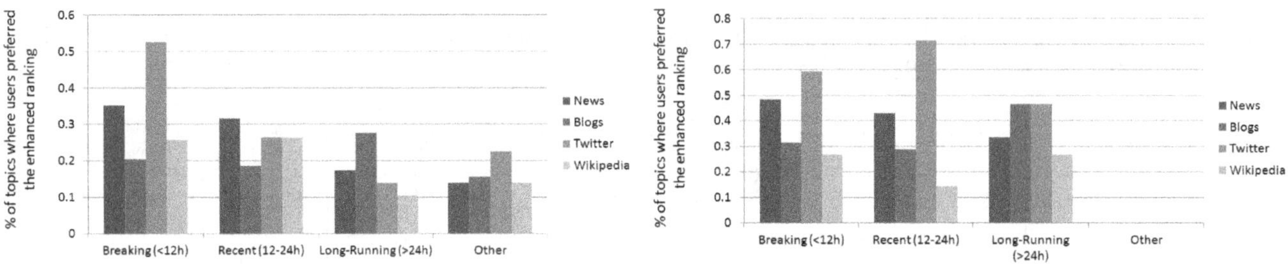

(a) 2012_{Apr} (b) 2013_{Jan}

Figure 8: The percentage of topics where the enhanced rankings were selected divided by topic temporal class (the amount of time between the originating event and topic time).

sources of content. We also showed that integrating blog posts, tweets and Wikipedia pages instead can satisfy many of the queries where integrating newswire articles did not. Finally, our results indicate that users tend to prefer rankings that integrate tweets or newswire articles soon after an event breaks, with blogs becoming more useful over time.

From the results of this study, we believe that new approaches that effectively integrate both newswire articles and user-generated content based upon a combination of relatedness, novelty and timeliness will be able to better serve news-related queries in real-time than using newswire articles alone. For future work, we aim to investigate machine learned approaches to automatically select user-generated content to integrate for news-related queries, as well as further examining what documents are useful to return for such real-time news-related information needs.

7. REFERENCES

[1] O. Alonso. Crowdsourcing for relevance evaluation. In *Tutorial at ECIR'10.*

[2] O. Alonso and R. Baeza-Yates. Design and implementation of relevance assessments using crowdsourcing. *Information Retrieval Journal* 2011.

[3] O. Alonso, D. E. Rose, and B. Stewart. Crowdsourcing for relevance evaluation. *SIGIR Forum*, 2008.

[4] J. Arguello, F. Diaz, J. Callan, and J.-F. Crespo. Sources of evidence for vertical selection. In *Proc. of SIGIR'09.*

[5] J. Arguello, W.-C. Wu, D. Kelly and A. Edwards. Task Complexity, Vertical Display and User Interaction in Aggregated Search. In *Proc. of SIGIR'12.*

[6] J. Atwood. Is Amazon's Mechanical Turk a failure? `http://www.codinghorror.com/blog/2007/04/is-amazons-mechanical-turk-a-failure.html`, accessed on 28/01/2013.

[7] R. Bandari, S. Asur, and B. Huberman. The pulse of news in social media: Forecasting popularity. In *Proc. of ICWSM'12.*

[8] J. Bar-Ilan, Z. Zhu, and M. Levene. Topic-specific analysis of search queries. In *Proc. of WSDM'09 workshop on Web Search Click Data.*

[9] B. Carterette. *Low-Cost and Robust Evaluation of Information Retrieval Systems.* PhD thesis, University of Massachusetts Amherst, 2009.

[10] C. Callison-Burch. Fast, cheap, and creative: Evaluating translation quality using Amazon's Mechanical Turk. In *Proc. of EMNLP'09.*

[11] C. W. Cleverdon. The significance of the Cranfield tests on index languages. In *Proc. of SIGIR'91.*

[12] F. Diaz. Integration of news content into Web results. In *Proc. of WSDM'09.*

[13] J. Downs, M. Holbrook, S. Sheng, and L. Cranor. Are your participants gaming the system? Screening Mechanical Turk workers. In *Proc. of CHI'10.*

[14] S. Hansell. Google keeps tweaking its search engine. `http://www.nytimes.com/2007/06/03/business/yourmoney/03google.html`, accessed on 28/01/2013.

[15] J. Howe. *Crowdsourcing: Why the Power of the Crowd Is Driving the Future of Business.* Three Rivers Pr, 2009.

[16] J. Howe. The rise of Crowdsourcing. `http://www.wired.com/wired/archive/14.06/crowds.html`, accessed on 28/01/2013.

[17] P. G. Ipeirotis. Demographics of Mechanical Turk. Tech Report, New York University, 2010.

[18] P. G. Ipeirotis. Crowdsourcing using Mechanical Turk: Quality Management and Scalability. In *Proc. of the WSDM'11 workshop on Crowdsourcing for Search and Data Mining.*

[19] A. Kittur, E. H. Chi, and B. Suh. Crowdsourcing user studies with Mechanical Turk. In *Proc. of CHI'08.*

[20] A. C. König, M. Gamon, and Q. Wu. Click-through prediction for news queries. In *Proc. of SIGIR'09.*

[21] H. Kwak, C. Lee, H. Park, and S. Moon. What is Twitter, a Social Network or a News Media. In *Proc. of WWW'10.*

[22] L. Levon, P. Kaulgud, and S. Skiena. Newspapers vs. blogs: Who gets the scoop. In *Proc. of the AAAI Spring Symposium on Computational Approaches to Analyzing Weblogs*, 2006.

[23] R. McCreadie, C. Macdonald, and I. Ounis. Crowdsourcing Blog Track Top News Judgments at TREC. In *Proc. of the WSDM'11 workshop on Crowdsourcing for Search and Data Mining.*

[24] R. McCreadie, C. Macdonald, and I. Ounis. Identifying Top News using Crowdsourcing. *Information Retrieval Journal*, 2013.

[25] J. Norman. Google processes 1,000,000,000 search queries per day. `http://www.historyofinformation.com/index.php?id=3276`, accessed on 28/01/2013.

[26] T. O'Brien. Twitter breaks news of plane crash in the Hudson. `http://www.switched.com/2009/01/15/twitter-breaks-news-of-plane-crash-in-the-hudson/`, accessed on 28/01/2013.

[27] T. O'Reilly and S. Milstein. *The Twitter Book.* O'Reilly Media, Inc., May 2009.

[28] P. Thomas and D. Hawking. Evaluation by comparing result sets in context. In *Proc. of CIKM'06.*

[29] R. Snow, B. O'Connor, D. Jurafsky, and A. Y. Ng. Cheap and fast—but is it good?: Evaluating non-expert annotations for natural language tasks. In *Proc. of EMNLP'08.*

[30] K. Sparck-Jones and C. J. van Rijsbergen. Report on the need for and provision of an "ideal" judgements retrieval test collection. Technical Report, British Library Research and Development, 1975.

[31] K. Zhou, R.Cummins, M. Lalmas and J. M. Jose. Evaluating Aggregated Search Pages. In *Proc. of SIGIR'12.*

[32] D. Zhu and B. Carterette. An Analysis of Assessor Behavior in Crowdsourced Preference Judgments. In *Proc. of SIGIR'10.*

Toward Self-Correcting Search Engines: Using Underperforming Queries to Improve Search

Ahmed Hassan
Microsoft Research
Redmond, WA 98052 USA
hassanam@microsoft.com

Ryen W. White
Microsoft Research
Redmond, WA 98052 USA
ryenw@microsoft.com

Yi-Min Wang
Microsoft Research
Redmond, WA 98052 USA
ymwang@microsoft.com

ABSTRACT

Search engines receive queries with a broad range of different search intents. However, they do not perform equally well for all queries. Understanding where search engines perform poorly is critical for improving their performance. In this paper, we present a method for automatically identifying poorly-performing query groups where a search engine may not meet searcher needs. This allows us to create coherent query clusters that help system designers generate actionable insights about necessary changes and helps learning-to-rank algorithms better learn relevance signals via specialized rankers. The result is a framework capable of estimating dissatisfaction from Web search logs and learning to improve performance for dissatisfied queries. Through experimentation, we show that our method yields good quality groups that align with established retrieval performance metrics. We also show that we can significantly improve retrieval effectiveness via specialized rankers, and that coherent grouping of underperforming queries generated by our method is important in improving each group.

Categories and Subject Descriptors

H.3.3 [**Information Storage and Retrieval**]: Information Search and Retrieval – *selection process, search process.*

Keywords

Dissatisfied query groups; Search satisfaction; Specialized rankers.

1. INTRODUCTION

Search engines are emerging as the primary resource through which people find information. As a result, they are expected to handle a broad range of different types of requests. However, search engines may only apply a single ranking function over all queries they receive [35]. Inevitably in such circumstances, there are queries that search engines do not handle well, leading to user dissatisfaction (DSAT). Automatically identifying groups of underperforming DSAT queries could help search designers decide where to focus resources to improve performance.

There has been work on studying searcher success and frustration as well as measuring query performance through human labels or via automatic methods [13][14][20]. Those methods have focused on identifying individual instances of user dissatisfaction from log data. However, from the search engine's perspective it is not cost effective to simply identify particular queries where the engine performs poorly. Commercial search engines are trained over very large sets of queries. When a poorly performing query is identified, this signal can be difficult to use for improving ranking quality. First, it is only a single example, among millions of others, so even if it is added to the training data, it is unlikely that it will have any effect on the training model. Moreover, machine learned models are difficult to debug or interpret and hence we will most likely be unable to determine why a particular query fails. Finally, human intervention, either for the generation of new interface, for ranking features, or for manually labeling more examples of queries, is costly and it is not prudent to make these investments on a per-query basis. Therefore, we must be able to combine the queries into coherent groups to take action and improve them.

In this paper we present an approach for identifying groups of queries where search engines perform poorly and develop methods to automatically improve retrieval quality for groups of failing queries. Dissatisfied query groups are identified automatically from search engine logs. The resulting groups have a strong correlation with two established measures of search performance: search-result click-through rate (CTR) and normalized discounted cumulative gain (NDCG) [26]. The query groups that our method identifies therefore comprise queries that are likely to result in searcher dissatisfaction. The queries in these groups share common attributes and are coherent in a way that makes them susceptible to ranking improvements. As such, we also trained a specialized ranker that is optimized to a particular dissatisfaction group that yielded significant relevance gains over our baselines.

This paper makes the following research contributions:

- Proposes the automatic identification of underperforming (dissatisfaction) query groups as a means for search engines to better understand and improve their performance.
- Introduces a novel method for automatically identifying such dissatisfaction groups given interaction log data.
- Validates that the groups that our method identifies are indeed correlated with dissatisfaction estimates made via established measures of search performance.
- Develops specialized rankers that leverage the coherence of the queries in the dissatisfaction groups to improve the search engine's retrieval quality.
- Demonstrates through experimentation that: (i) our learned specialized ranker outperforms a general ranker trained on a diverse set of queries, and (ii) the coherence of the groups identified by our method leads to larger relevance gains over a specialized ranker trained only on underperforming queries.

The remainder of this paper is structured as follows. Section 2 describes relevant related work in the areas of search success and query performance. Section 3 defines our problem and Section 4 describes how we extract instances of dissatisfaction from log data. We describe our method for automatically grouping dissatisfaction instances in Section 5. In Section 6 we describe the training of a specialized ranker to target a typical DSAT group identified using our method. Experiments and associated results are presented in

SIGIR'13, July 28–August 1, 2013, Dublin, Ireland.

Section 7. We discuss the findings and their implications in Section 8 and conclude in Section 9.

2. RELATED WORK

There are two areas of work related to the research presented in this paper: (i) search satisfaction, success, and frustration, and (ii) query performance. We cover each of the two areas in turn.

2.1 Satisfaction, Success, and Frustration

Extensive literature exists on deriving indicators of task success or failure from online user behavior. In search specifically, several fruitful approaches have been tried. One approach is to correlate behavior with either self-reported success [14] or labels of success provided by expert judges [13][20]. Early investigations correlated self-reported measures of search satisfaction with implicit signals, such as search-result clicks and dwell time for clicks [14].

Fox et al. [14] used an instrumented browser to determine whether there was an association between explicit ratings of satisfaction and implicit measures of searcher interest and identified the measures that were most strongly associated with user satisfaction. They found that there was a link between user activity and satisfaction ratings, and that clickthrough, dwell time, and session termination activity combined to make good predictors of satisfaction for Web pages. Fox et al. found that short dwell times and clicking many (four or more) search results for a query were both indicators of dissatisfaction. Behavioral patterns were also used to predict user satisfaction for search sessions. Feild et al. [13] developed methods to predict user frustration. They assigned users difficult information seeking tasks and monitored their degree of frustration via query logs and physical sensors. One behavior that can be associated with dissatisfaction is search engine switching – the voluntary transition between different engines. Guo et al. [16] characterized the reason that searchers switch between search engines. Using a browser plugin, they captured switching rationales in-situ. They showed that one of the primary reasons that searchers changed engine was dissatisfaction with the results provided by the pre-switch engine. Using the labeled switching events gathered from the plugin, they also showed that there was sufficient consistency in searchers' interaction behaviors before and after the switching event to accurately predict switching rationales. This predictor can be used to dynamically adapt the search experience and derive more accurate competitive metrics. Indeed, Feild et al. showed that features capable of accurately predicting switching events were also highly predictive of searcher frustration.

Huffman and Hochster [25] found a relatively strong correlation with session satisfaction using a linear model encompassing the relevance of the first three results returned for the first query in a search task, whether the information need was navigational, and the number of events in the session. Hassan et al. [20] developed models of user behavior to accurately estimate search success on a session level, independent of the relevance of documents retrieved by the search engine. Ageev et al. [1] propose a formalization of different types of success for informational search, and presented a scalable game-like infrastructure for crowdsourcing search behavior studies, specifically targeted towards capturing and evaluating successful search strategies on informational tasks with known intent. They show that their model can predict search success effectively on their data and on a separate set of log data comprising search engine sessions. Going beyond individual search sessions to study the effects of satisfaction over time, Hu et al. [23] performed a longitudinal study of the relationship between search satisfaction and search engine re-use. They showed that satisfaction with a search engine can contribute to users' propensity to use and re-use its service over time.

2.2 Query Performance

Search engine performance for a particular query is typically measured using relevance metrics such as NDCG [26]. NDCG can be calculated based on manual judgments on the relevance of documents in the result list, or estimated using models derived from user click behavior (e.g., [2]). Session discounted cumulative gain (SDCG) [27] applies a discount to relevant results found in response to queries later in the session. This considers that multiple queries can be part of a search goal, but still requires manual relevance judgments, which can be costly to obtain and do not scale to unseen queries. Al-Maskari et al. [4] found a reasonable correlation between many information retrieval (IR) metrics and user satisfaction with result rankings (although surprisingly not NDCG, given the small numbers of judgments available per query). They advocated for a combination of different measures in evaluating the effectiveness of IR systems.

Research on predicting query performance has been conducted to understand differences in the quality of search results provided by search systems for different queries. Measures such as Jensen-Shannon divergence [8], query clarity [10], and weighted information gain 0 have been developed to predict the retrieval performance on a query (as measured by average precision, for example). He and Ounis [23], and Hauff et al. [22] also developed automatic methods for predicting query difficulty (i.e., how good the search results are for a query). Leskovec et al. [29] used graphical properties of the link structure of the result set to predict the quality of the result set and the likelihood of query reformulation. Teevan et al. [31] developed methods to predict which queries could most benefit from personalization. Research has also been conducted on predicting query performance using searcher interactions. Carterette and Jones [9] used clickthrough behavior to evaluate the quality of search advertising results, but they did not study other interaction features, and their focus was on search advertising not general Web search. Guo et al. [14] used interaction features, including switching features, to predict query performance. However, that was on a per-query basis rather than on the basis of query groups that lead to searcher dissatisfaction.

The research presented in this paper extends this previous work in a number of ways: (i) rather than predicting the performance of individual queries, we focus on identifying underperforming query *groups* that share attributes such as length or domain; (ii) we validate that the groups represent likely searcher dissatisfaction via established performance measures such as clickthrough rate and NDCG, and; (iii) we train a specialized ranker for groups identified and show that (a) we can obtain relevance gains by targeting specific DSAT groups, and (b) training a specialized ranker tailored to the coherent DSAT groups identified by our method is better than simply targeting the broad set of all underperforming queries (e.g., only those queries with low CTR).

3. PROBLEM DEFINITION

We start by defining some terms used throughout the paper:

DEFINITION. A *query group* is a set of queries sharing a set of common factors and can be characterized using binary attributes. For example "Queries about movies with 5 or more words".

DEFINITION. A *DSAT query group* is a set of queries for which the search engine performs poorly in comparison to its average performance over all queries.

DEFINITION. A *specialized ranker* is a ranking model that is built to handle a specific query group. The specialized ranker has a local effect because it only provides the search results for queries belonging to a specific query group.

Given a stream of queries submitted by search engine users, we seek to: (i) automatically identify poorly-performing groups of queries suggestive of searcher dissatisfaction (DSAT), and (ii) train a specialized local ranker capable of addressing the DSAT through relevance gains. To identify the underperforming query groups we construct attribute sets that cover DSAT instances and correlate highly with dissatisfaction.

Commercial search engines rely on features of log data. They also need humans to define these features and to generate relevance labels from which the ranking algorithms can learn [2]. In theory, a search engine that adopts a framework capable of doing both (i) and (ii) above could improve with little need for human involvement in generating additional features which could result in a self-correcting search engine. The development of such a framework motivates our research. We now describe its implementation in our context.

The input to our method is the search log interaction data gathered from consenting users of a toolbar deployed by a commercial search engine. Search logs are usually organized in the form of search sessions. A *search session* is a sequence of user activities that begin with a query, includes subsequent queries and URL visits, and ends with a period of inactivity. A session ends if the user was idle for more than 30 minutes on a page. The 30-minute cutoff to determine session boundaries has been commonly used in previous work, e.g., [12]. In our case, search sessions can span multiple search engines since we are interested in transitions between engines as evidence of searcher dissatisfaction. More discussion on this issue is provided in the next section of the paper.

We use the data from search sessions to automatically identify queries that resulted in searcher dissatisfaction. This step is the first step in our process. This module uses log data (from the search engine or in our case a toolbar from the search provider) to generate a large number of individual dissatisfaction instances. For each instance, we collect information about the query, time and market where it was submitted, and the search engine results page (SERP). Individual dissatisfaction instances were used to identify poorly performing groups of queries.

Specialized rankers specifically targeting the identified groups are then trained to improve the search experience. One specialized ranker is trained for each dissatisfaction group. The specialized ranker can use the same features used by the original ranker, but trained using a group-specific dataset. Alternatively, additional investment may be involved to further improve these groups. For example, once the groups have been identified, additional features may need to be generated to help the ranker learn how to perform better for this query group. This activity is labor intensive and time consuming, meaning that an automated alternative such as the method proposed in this paper can be extremely valuable.

Finally the specialized ranker is combined with the general ranker and the resultant ranker can be used to replace the original. The specialized ranker has a local effect because it will be used for queries that belong to the corresponding group only. The general ranker will be used for the remainder of the query traffic. If gains are achieved through the specialized ranker and all other queries are treated in the same way as before, then overall relevance gains will be observed. *The primary challenge is therefore in identifying dissatisfaction groups because enumerating all possible ways of combining attributes to form groups is prohibitively expensive. Addressing this challenge is our focus in this paper.*

We begin by describing how we identify the individual DSAT instances that are used to construct the DSAT query groups.

4. MINING DSAT INSTANCES

We mine instances of searcher dissatisfaction based on search engine switching events. Search engine switching is the process describing a user's voluntary transition from one Web search engine to another. A search engine switching event is a pair of consecutive queries that are issued on different search engines within a single session. Note that in identifying pre-switch queries, if the user issued a navigational query for a target search engine (e.g., search for "yahoo" on Google, or "google" on Bing), this query is regarded as part of the switching action and the preceding query in the pre-switch engine is used as the "pre-switch" query.

Search logs contain a large and varied set of search behaviors that could be associated with searcher dissatisfaction (e.g., clickthrough rate, abandonment, short dwell time or quick back clicks). We use search engine switching to identify user dissatisfaction instances for two main reasons: (i) search engine switching is a rare but important event that has been shown to correlate with dissatisfaction in prior research [16][32], and we have a reliable classifier that can distinguish switches caused by dissatisfaction from others; (ii) other query performance measures such as clickthrough data or editorial judgments could be used, but we abstained from using them in this phase in order to be able to use them later to validate our results. After the validity of our dissatisfied query groups is established through our study, these query performance measures could be used to generate more dissatisfaction instances.

Users switch from one search engine to another for various reasons. One of the most common reasons is dissatisfaction with the results they received from the pre-switch engine [33], which accounts for around 60% of engine switching events. Guo et al. [16] proposed a method for estimating the cause behind an observed switch given recent search behavior such as queries and SERP clicks on the source and destination search engines. They gathered ground truth data through the deployment of a plugin to around 200 Web searchers. The plugin captured switching rationales in-situ when a switch occurred and also logged search behavior before and after the switch. The cause of the switch could be one of: (i) dissatisfaction (the searcher was unhappy with the pre-switch engine), (ii) coverage (the searcher wanted to check the information they had found on the other search engine), (iii) preferences (they usually used the target engine or the target engine was better for the current task type), (iv) unintentional (browser defaults or homepage settings), and (v) other. They found that they could accurately predict when the reason for an engine switch was dissatisfaction-related.

Inspired by the work of Guo and colleagues, we built a classifier to distinguish dissatisfaction-related engine switches. The dissatisfaction engine switching classifier learns to predict the switch cause from training data of switching instances from [16]. The dataset contained 562 labeled switches from 107 different users.

We merged all switching causes into two classes: dissatisfaction and everything else, and trained a logistic regression classifier to identify dissatisfaction instances.

DEFINITION. A *dissatisfaction instance* in our study is a switch between search engines where the pre- and post-switch queries are the same and has been labeled by our classifier as DSAT-related. We assume that a dissatisfaction instance represents dissatisfaction with the pre-switch engine.

We represent search behavior by adapting and extending a subset of the features presented in previous studies that we believed were particularly likely to be associated with dissatisfaction [16]. We also

Table 2. Features to identify dissatisfied engine switches.

Feature	Description
	Query features
$char\_len$	Num. characters in query
$word\_len$	Num. words in query
$time\_diff$	Time in seconds between pre-switch and post switch queries
	Pre- and Post-switch features
$num\_queries$	Num. queries in session
$uniq\_queries$	Num. unique queries in session
num_reform	Num. query reformulations
num_clicks	Num. clicks
num_sat_clicks	Num. clicks with dwell time > 30s
num_quick_backs	Num. clicks with dwell time < 15s
num_term_clicks	Num. clicks on URLs containing a query term in their title
$trail\_len$	Length of the trail from search engine result page, defined as the number of clicks made after leaving SERP
a_{ij}_count	Num. transitions between every action pair $a_i \rightarrow a_j$ for every $a_i \in A$ where A = {Query, SERPClick, AdClick, Answer, etc.}
a_{ij}_time	Avg. dwell time for every action pair $a_i \rightarrow a_j$

added features describing the action transition of users (e.g., query-click, query-query, etc.), and the time difference between every pair of actions. It has been shown in previous work that action transitions are a very good descriptor of user behavior when modeling satisfaction [20][21]. An action could be a query submission, a click on a SERP, or a click on any other SERP feature. For example, submitting a query followed by reformulating and resubmitting a related query is a sign of dissatisfaction. The features used in our classifier are summarized in Table 1. We only considered switching instances that had the same query before and after the engine switch since these have been shown to be more strongly associated with dissatisfaction in previous work [16].

Later in our experiments, we will use only query-related features and post-switch features to identify switches resulting from DSAT. Excluding pre-switch features allows us to validate the results of our DSAT group identification using measures such as SERP click-through rate without introducing any bias.

We evaluated the performance using the F-score, with β set to 0.5. This gives twice as much weight to precision than to recall. We are interested in a highly precise set of dissatisfaction cases that we can reliably use as input for the following steps. There are a large number of switching instances in the logs. We need to precisely identify some of them, rather than finding many of them with lower precision. We evaluated the performance using 10-fold cross validation which resulted in an $F_{0.5}$ score of 81.2 when we use query and post-switch features. This exceeds the 79.0 reported by Guo et al. [16], attributable to the extra features we added.

5. IDENTIFYING DSAT GROUPS

Many previous studies have addressed the problem of measuring query performance [10][26][29]. Individual instances where users are dissatisfied with search result quality can be identified using a number of methods. One such method was presented in the previous section. Given a set of DSAT instances, the more challenging problem is how to take actions to improve search relevance based on these observations. This is challenging because it may be difficult to tweak the search engine ranking algorithm to handle a dissatisfaction case in an isolated context. To provide richer context to dissatisfaction cases, we seek to find frequently-occurring patterns that define dissatisfaction *groups*.

In the remainder of this section we describe the methods that we use to identify dissatisfaction groups. We begin with how we represent the individual DSAT instances, then describe the frequent pattern mining approach that we used to identify frequent attribute sets, and conclude by describing the method used to create the dissatisfaction groups from these attribute sets.

5.1.1 Representation

We describe every dissatisfaction instance with a vector of binary attributes. Each attribute describes a specific characteristic of the dissatisfaction instance. Let $A = \{a_1, a_2, \dots, a_n\}$ be a set of n binary attributes. Let $D = \{d_1, d_2, \dots, d_n\}$ be a set of dissatisfaction instances. Every DSAT instance in D has a subset of attributes in A.

We use several types of attributes to describe each dissatisfaction instance. We summarize them below:

Query Attributes: This is a set of attributes that describe the query itself. Several categories are used to describe the intent behind the query. It is impractical to use the text in Web pages to draw conclusions about the topicality of the query. Conversely, we could look at URLs or domains but that would be very limited due to data sparseness. Instead, we used the Open Directory Project (ODP), also referred to as dmoz.org. ODP is an open Web directory maintained by a community of volunteer editors. It uses a hierarchical scheme for organizing URLs into categories and subcategories. We use the top two ODP categories and assign labels to URLs automatically using an approach similar to [34]. URLs that exist in the directory were classified according to the corresponding categories. Missing URLs were incrementally pruned one path level at a time until a match was found or a miss declared. A query is assigned the plurality label of the labels of its top 10 results. In addition to these categories, we also include the query length, language, query phrase type (noun phrase, verb phrase or a question) as determined by the Stanford parser [28].

SERP Attributes: We also added a set of attributes to describe the SERP that was displayed to the user as a response to submitting the query. Examples of these attributes include whether a direct answer was displayed for that query, and if so, then what type of answer (e.g. Weather, Stocks, etc.), whether a query suggestion was shown, and whether a spelling correction was shown.

Impression Attributes: An impression is a single instance of a particular query. We used another set of attributes to describe each dissatisfaction impression. We use the market from which the query was issued (e.g., US, UK, etc.), the vertical used to issue the query (e.g., Web, News, Images, etc.) and the search engine used to issue the query (Bing, Google or Yahoo). This allows us to identify DSAT groups for specific markets, verticals, and engines as well as DSAT groups that span multiple markets, verticals, or engines. We also added some temporal attributes such as day of the week, time of day (morning, afternoon, evening, night), and month of the year.

This yields a set A with 140 attributes. Every dissatisfaction instance d is represented with a subset of attributes in A.

5.1.2 Frequent Patterns

a	b	c	d	e
1	1	0	0	0
0	1	1	0	1
1	0	1	1	1
1	0	0	1	1
1	1	0	1	0
1	1	1	0	0
1	0	0	0	0
1	1	1	0	0
1	1	0	0	0
0	1	1	1	0

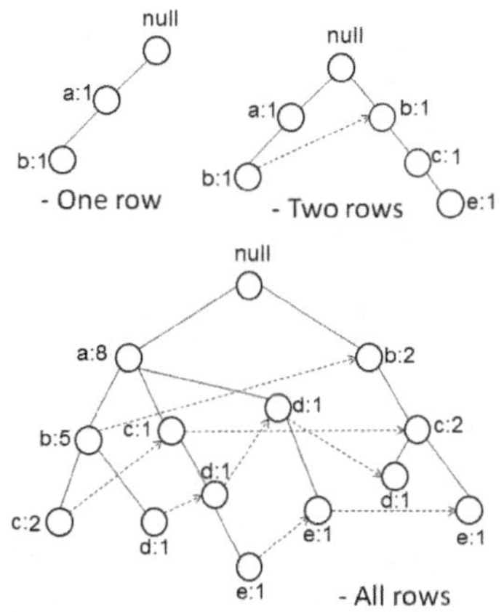

Figure 1. An example illustrating how the FP-tree is constructed in the FP-Growth algorithm.

Identifying frequent patterns in transactional or relational data sets is a well-studied problem in the data mining literature [18]. The problem was motivated by the massive amounts of data continuously collected and stored by many businesses. The discovery of frequent patterns in this huge amount of data was found useful for many decision making processes. A typical example of this scenario is the market basket analysis problem. The objective of this analysis is to find associations between the different items that customers purchase. This information is valuable for designing marketing plans and product catalogs.

The problem of mining dissatisfaction groups can be approached from a similar perspective. To find dissatisfaction groups, we look for frequent patterns of attributes that correlate with user dissatisfaction. The representation we described in the previous subsection aligns well with this approach. In the proposed representation, every dissatisfaction instance is represented by a row, and every attribute is presented by a column. All values are binary; indicating whether the corresponding attribute is present in a particular row or not. Multi-valued attributes are replaced with multiple variables corresponding to the different values. An attribute in our case is analogous to an item in the market basket analysis case. Note that we use the terms "attribute" and "item" interchangeably throughout the remainder of the paper.

There are several algorithms for discovering frequent patterns from relational databases. For example, Apriori [5] is a seminal algorithm for finding frequent itemsets. It employs a level-wise search process where frequent itemsets of size l are used to discover frequent itemsets of size $l+1$. It starts by finding the counts of single items, then itemsets with size 2 and so on. Finding each set of itemsets with a certain size requires a full scan of the dataset. To reduce the search space, it discards all itemsets that are supersets of previously found infrequent itemsets.

The main disadvantage of Apriori is that it employs a generate-and-test method which may result in the generation of a huge number of candidate sets. Additionally, it may need to repeatedly scan the database for every itemset size. The FP-Growth algorithm [19] overcomes these problems via a divide-and-conquer strategy. FP-Growth only needs to scan the dataset twice, and unlike Apriori, it does not involve any candidate itemset generation. We use the Weka [17] implementation of FP-Growth [19]. There are also variants of FP-Growth that were designed to be run in parallel on a distributed cluster of machines, allowing large volumes of log data to be processed using this algorithm [11][30].

Table 2. Examples of frequent attribute sets.

Frequent Attribute Sets
{English Query, Local, Navigational, NumWords >10}
{English Query, Locations, Questions, NumWords >10}
{English Query, US Market}
{NumWords >10}

Table 3. Dataset contains satisfaction and dissatisfaction.

Attribute_1	Attribute_2	...	Attribute_n	(D)SAT
True	False	...	True	DSAT
True	False	...	False	DSAT
False	True	...	True	DSAT
....	....	...	....	....
False		...	True	SAT
True	True	...	False	SAT
True	False	...	True	SAT
....	....	...	....	....

The FP-Growth algorithm consists of two main steps. In the first step, a compact data structure, the FP-tree, is built to represent the data. In the second step, frequent patterns are extracted from the FP-tree. To build the FP-tree, the data are scanned twice. In the first scan, it counts the frequencies of every attribute and discards infrequent attributes. The attributes are then sorted in decreasing order based on their frequencies. This fixed order is used so paths can overlap when records share items. So, paths overlap when they share the same prefix.

In the second scan, the FP-tree is constructed. The FP-tree is a compact way to retain information about itemset association [19]. Nodes in the tree represent attributes and each node has a counter. The algorithm reads one row at a time and maps it to a path. Paths overlap when rows share attributes and node counters are incremented. Special pointers are used to link nodes representing the same attribute. An example illustrating the FP-tree construction is shown in Figure 1. The algorithm starts by creating the root of the tree and labeling it "null". For each row in the dataset, the items in that row are sorted according to their frequency and a branch is created to represent the row. Every node in the branch corresponds to an item and is labeled with the item identifier and its count; which is initialized to 1 at creation. This process is repeated for every row. A pointer is created to connect any two nodes with the same identifier and the node count is updated accordingly. Figure 1 shows the tree after reading the one row, two rows and all rows. After reading the first row, where only a and b are set to 1, two nodes are added to the tree corresponding to a and b and the counter is set to *1* in both cases. The second row has b, c, and d set to *1*. The second row does not share the same prefix with the first one, hence a new path is created and the counters of all nodes are set to *1*. When the algorithm reads the third row, it finds out that the prefix {a} overlaps with the prefix for the first row. Hence, the counter of node a is increased and new nodes are created to represent c, d, and e. This process continues until all rows are scanned. Pointers are maintained between nodes representing the same item (dotted lines in the figure). As explained earlier, the algorithm needs to scan the dataset only twice. In the first scan, the number of occurrences of every attribute is computed and infrequent attributes are discarded. The FP-tree is created in the second scan.

After constructing the FP-tree, we proceed to the second step. To extract frequent patterns, FP-Growth applies a bottom-up algorithm using a divide-and-conquer strategy starting at the leaves and moving toward the root, building frequent patterns as it ascends the tree. For example, it starts with frequent attribute sets ending in *e* and then ending in *de* and so on so forth.

We apply the FP-Growth algorithm to the dataset described in the previous section. Table 2 presents a few examples of some of the identified frequent attribute sets. Some sets consist of a single attribute, while others have many attributes. In the next subsection, we describe how dissatisfaction groups can be identified using these frequent attribute sets.

5.1.3 From Frequent Patterns to DSAT Groups

Frequent attribute sets discovered from a set of dissatisfaction instances do not necessarily define a dissatisfaction group. It could be the case that a set of attributes defines a large query group, and even though the percentage of dissatisfaction cases resulting from this group is very small, it could still be overrepresented in the dissatisfaction dataset. For example, FP-Growth reported that the group $\{English\ Query, US\ Market\}$ is frequent. This occurred because most of the queries in the dataset are English queries coming from the US market, not because this is a dissatisfaction group.

To address this problem, we built a new data set, the *satisfaction dataset*, and define a measure to identify groups correlated with dissatisfaction. We build this dataset by randomly sampling a number of queries from L where: (i) the query received many clicks and the last one had dwell time greater than 30 seconds, or (ii) the query received a single click with dwell time greater than 30 seconds. Dwell time greater than 30 seconds has been widely used to denote satisfaction as in previous work [14].

Table 3 shows an example illustrating the appearance of the combined dataset. The dataset contains both satisfaction (SAT) and DSAT instances. Every instance is represented by a row in the dataset. The same set of attributes is used to describe both types of instances. An additional attribute is added to show whether the instance is associated with satisfaction or dissatisfaction.

We apply the FP-Growth algorithm to the data to generate sets of attributes that co-occur frequently with one another. Unlike the market basket analysis, we are not concerned with the correlation between all kinds of attributes. We are mainly interested in attribute sets that correlate highly with dissatisfaction. As a result, we restrict the generated sets to those that include the attribute "DSAT" and ignore all other patterns.

To distinguish attribute sets that are highly correlated with dissatisfaction and attribute sets that are highly represented in both satisfaction and dissatisfaction instances, we define "*DSAT correlation*". *DSAT correlation* is a simple measure that estimates the correlation/dependence between an attribute set and dissatisfaction. It is defined as follows for any attribute set $A = \{a, \dots, a_n\}$:

$$DSAT\ correlation = \frac{P(A, DSAT)}{P(A)P(DSAT)}$$

where $P(X)$ is the probability of observing the set of attributes $P(X)$. $P(A, DSAT)$ is estimated by dividing the number of instances that belong to both the group defined by A and the dissatisfaction set by the total number of SAT and DSAT instances. $P(A)$ is estimated by dividing the number of instances that belong to the group defined by A by the total number instances. Finally $P(DSAT)$ is the proportion of dissatisfaction instances in the dataset. The number of occurrences of A and $A \cap DSAT$ are computed using the FP-Growth algorithm as explained earlier.

If the resulting value of the *DSAT correlation* is less than 1, then the occurrence of A is negatively correlated with dissatisfaction. If the resulting value is greater than 1, then A is positively correlated with dissatisfaction. If the value is exactly 1, then A and dissatisfaction are independent. This value is sometimes referred to as the *lift* in the data mining literature [18]. In our case, it implies that the occurrence of the set of attributes in A "lifts" the occurrence of dissatisfaction.

Now let us revisit the group that was defined by the attribute set $\{English\ Query, US\ Market\}$. Even though this set frequently co-occurs with dissatisfaction, its DSAT correlation is 0.98 showing that it is nearly independent of SAT or DSAT. This allows us to identify more interesting groups and gives us a metric to evaluate how every group correlates with dissatisfaction.

Other measures of correlation could be used as well for the same purpose (e.g., χ^2). Correlation measures are better than confidence (i.e., the number of occurrences of $A \cap DSAT$ divided by the number of occurrences of A). Confidence could be misleading if the dataset is unbalanced with respect to the proportion of satisfaction and dissatisfaction instances. This imbalance is typical in any random sample of query impressions because most users achieve their search goals and dissatisfaction is usually the exception. For example, Ageev et al. [1] performed a study where users were asked to find answers to specific questions using Web search. In 87% of the tasks, users reported success, and in 75% of these cases, the answer was correct. Hassan et al. [21] collected firsthand success labels from users using several search engines and reported a 80% satisfaction rate. Notice that the DSAT correlation is also insensitive to the distribution of SAT vs. DSAT cases in the dataset. Hence, it will find attribute sets statistically correlated with dissatisfaction regardless of whether the sample follows the original underlying distribution of satisfaction or not.

6. A SPECIALIZED RANKER

A specialized ranker can be trained for each dissatisfaction group. DSAT groups are easier to learn than individual DSAT instances because they provide more context for the learning algorithm than single instances. Additionally, and importantly, the coherence of the DSAT groups we identify makes them more susceptible to ranking improvements than a potentially broad and heterogeneous set of underperforming queries. We show later in this section that the coherence is important for training specialized rankers.

Attributes of the group can be used to determine for each query whether to apply the method. In practice, the specialized ranker is used for all queries where the group's membership criteria applies and the general ranker is used for all other traffic. If we observe gains through applying the specialized ranker and do not change the general ranker used for all other queries, we will see the overall search effectiveness of the search engine improve. In the remainder of this section we describe how we train a specialized ranker for one such DSAT group identified through the analysis in the previous section and show that we can obtain significant relevance gains over strong baselines by targeting that group.

In a learning-to-rank framework, each query document pair is represented by a feature vector. The performance of any ranking function depends on feature selection and training data. We fix the set of features used for both the general and the specialized rankers. Our feature set contains several hundred features including query, document, and query-document features. It includes many content-based features, click-based features, static rank-based features, and many others. Note that the features that were used to characterize the DSAT groups (i.e., the attributes used by the DSAT group identification step) were also available to the general ranker, giving it an opportunity to learn to use DSAT information on its own and potentially removing the need to identify DSAT groups. The general ranker therefore represents a strong baseline against which to compare our specialized ranking approach.

We employ a re-ranking framework to create a specialized ranker optimized to perform well on the DSAT group. We use a cascade approach where the output of the *General Ranker* is used as a feature for training a Specialized Ranker. The specialized ranker is trained on the DSAT group data only using the same features as the general ranker. The output of the general ranker is added to the training and testing data of the specialized ranker as an additional feature. This allows the specialized ranker to benefit from the signals in the general data, and at the mean time optimize the performance over the specialized data.

Notice that we cannot simply combine the general dataset with the specialized dataset and train a single ranker. By doing this, we are altering the true underlying distribution of queries and the general traffic will be under-represented compared to the natural query distribution. Even though, this ranker may have a better performance on the DSAT group, it will alter the performance of the rest of the traffic. This is an undesirable effect because our objective is to improve the performance on the DSAT group without affecting the general traffic.

By changing the training data for the specialized ranker to only use in-group queries, we show that identifying an underperforming group is a fundamental step toward improving the performance of search engines on queries belonging to this group. We will also show that we can achieve relevance gains (perhaps attributable to group coherence) by simply targeting that group even when the feature set is held constant. Note that the training and testing data does not overlap with the data used to learn the underperforming query groups.

7. EXPERIMENTS AND RESULTS

7.1 Validating DSAT Groups

7.1.1 Data and Experimental Setup

In this subsection, we describe the data we used to identify individual DSAT instances and DSAT groups. We obtained millions of records of interaction logs (from July to September 2011) for hundreds of thousands of consenting users through a widely-distributed Web browser toolbar. Log entries include a unique identifier for the user, a timestamp for each page view, and the URL of the Web page visited. Intranet and secure (https) URL and any personally identifiable information were removed from the logs prior to analysis. From these logs, we identified switching instances where the same query has been issued on different search engines. This set of logs is referred to as L.

We applied the DSAT classifier described earlier to a random set of switches observed in L, setting recall low to boost precision. The classifier predicted that approximately 100,000 of the instances were caused by dissatisfaction with the pre-switch engine results. We randomly sampled a set of another 100,000 satisfaction instances as described in Section 5 to construct the satisfaction dataset and applied the method in Section 5 to generate DSAT groups. We generated around 200 groups; 50% of them were either negatively correlated or uncorrelated with DSAT and were discarded.

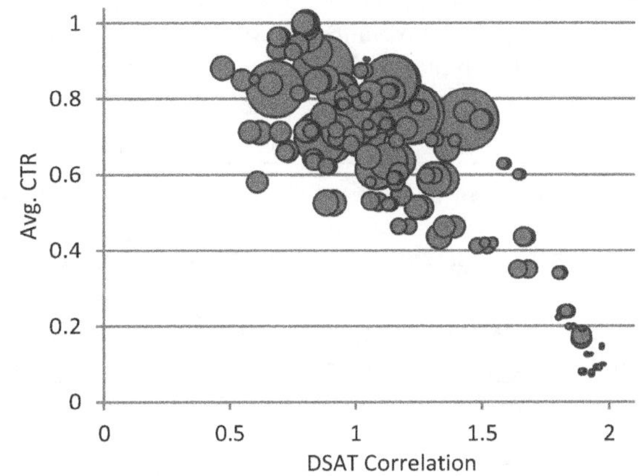

(a)

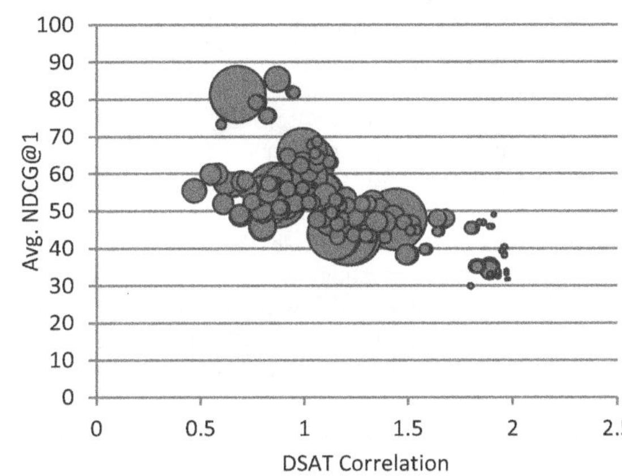

(b)

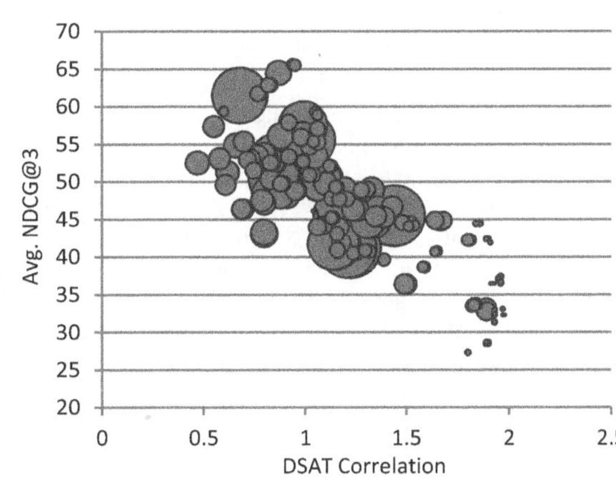

(c)

Figure 2. (a) Relation between average clickthrough rate and DSAT correlation for every DSAT group. (b) Relation between average NDCG@1 and DSAT correlation for every DSAT group. (c) Relation between average NDCG@3 and DSAT correlation for every DSAT group. Note that in all figures the size of the circle denotes the number of DSATs that belong to every group.

Table 4. Correlation between *DSAT correlation* and different query performance measures averaged over queries belonging to the corresponding group.

	Avg. CTR	Avg. NDCG@1	Avg. NDCG@3
DSAT Correlation	−0.87	−0.72	−0.80

Table 5. NDCG improvements for a DSAT query group using a specialized ranker.

NDCG@ 1 Gain	NDCG@ 2 Gain	NDCG@ 3 Gain	NDCG@ 4 Gain	NDCG@ 5 Gain
1.52%	0.58%	0.86%	0.94%	0.77%

Table 6. NDCG improvements for low CTR group using a ranker trained on low CTR data.

NDCG@ 1 Gain	NDCG@ 2 Gain	NDCG@ 3 Gain	NDCG@ 4 Gain	NDCG@ 5 Gain
0.51%	0.39%	0.12%	0.05%	0.03%

The average number of attributes describing every group was 3.4. The average fraction of dissatisfaction instances in a group was 5.5% of the total number of DSAT instances. We divided the groups into three bins according to DSAT correlation: less than 0.8, 0.8 to 1.2, and greater than 1.2. These correspond to groups with negative correlation, no correlation, and positive correlation to dissatisfaction. We noticed that groups with no correlation to dissatisfaction have lower average number of attributes (3.2), and higher average number of instances (7.6%) compared to the other two groups that had a number of attributes of 3.4 and 3.6 and a percentage of instances of 3.8% and 3.7% for the negative correlation and the positive correlation groups respectively.

Once we had the groups generated, we wanted to establish whether they were in fact related to searcher dissatisfaction. To validate that the groups that we identify do actually represent likely searcher dissatisfaction, we used established measures of search engine performance, namely result clickthrough rate (CTR) and NDCG.

For every identified group, we compute the average clickthrough rate for queries belonging to this group. Average clickthrough rate is computed using a separate set of queries that does not overlap with the datasets described in the previous section. Every group is defined using a set of attributes. To compute the average clickthrough rate, we identify all queries that have all those attributes, compute the clickthrough rate for every query and then compute the average over all such queries. We abstained from using any pre-switch features (i.e., only used query and post-switch features; see Section 4) while generating dissatisfaction switches to avoid any bias in the clickthrough rate experiment.

7.1.2 Results

Figure 3a shows the relation between average clickthrough rate and *DSAT correlation* for every group. We included all frequent groups even those who were found to be uncorrelated or negatively correlated with dissatisfaction. Every group is represented by a bubble. The size of the bubble represents the number of dissatisfaction instances that belong to this group. Groups are not orthogonal and hence the same dissatisfaction instance may belong to more than one group. The size of the attribute set defining every group can range from 1 to arbitrary large numbers. In practice, the largest attribute set had no more than six attributes. Groups with size less than 0.5% of the size of the entire dissatisfaction set are ignored. We have to set a lower limit on the size of a group; otherwise every dissatisfaction instance will result in a group.

We can observe from Figure 3a that groups with high *DSAT correlation* have low clickthrough rate, while groups with low *DSAT correlation* have higher clickthrough rate resulting in a high correlation between the two measures. We also notice that most of the large groups are either negatively correlated or uncorrelated with dissatisfaction. Many of those groups are defined by a single attribute such as long queries or informational queries.

Similarly, we compared *DSAT correlation* to NDCG@1 and NDCG@3 in Figures 3b and 3c, respectively. NDCG at a particular rank position k is defined as:

$$NDCG@k = \frac{DCG@k}{IDCG@k} = \frac{1}{IDCG@k}\sum_{i=1}^{k}\frac{2^{rel(i)}}{\log(1+i)}$$

where $rel(i)$ is the relevance of the ith document in the ranked list. NDCG is computed by normalized DCG using the DCG of the ideal ranking (IDCG). We used a large query set with editorial relevance judgments labeled as part of a separate search engine assessment effort to identify a set of queries that belong to each group. Every query-document pair was judged on a five-point grade scale: *Bad*, *Fair*, *Good*, *Excellent*, or *Perfect*, giving us a value for $rel(i)$ for each result. The dataset was constructed using pooled relevance judgments and query-document pairs were judged by trained human assessors. Comparison against NDCG yields very similar results to comparison against CTR.

To quantify the correlation with established query level metrics, we computed the Pearson correlation coefficient between *DSAT correlation* and: (i) average clickthrough rate, (ii) average NDCG@1, and (iii) average NDCG@3. Correlations were measured using the Pearson's correlation coefficient. The results are shown in Table 4. The table shows a strong negative correlation between *DSAT Correlation* and the three other metrics validating that the groups do seem to represent likely searcher dissatisfaction.

In summary, we defined a process and a metric for identifying query groups associated with dissatisfaction. The process uses search interaction logs and does not involve any human intervention. The identified groups show high correlation with established query-level performance metrics such as CTR or NDCG. One important advantage of these groups is that they are coherent in a way that provides a rich context for isolated queries. This coherence allows us to use these groups to improve Web search performance, as we will demonstrate in the next section.

7.2 Specialized Ranker Performance

7.2.1 Data and Experimental Setup

We used the learning-to-rank algorithm presented in [35] and compared different ranking functions using NDCG (defined earlier). In this subsection we present the results of two comparisons: (i) a specialized ranker trained on one of our groups versus general ranker trained over all queries, and (ii) specialized ranker trained on one of our groups versus a ranker trained on a potentially-diverse set of underperforming queries.

The group that we selected represented approximately 2% of the dissatisfaction instances, and had a *DSAT correlation* of 1.3. We selected this group because we were able to use existing query-document relevance judgments to quickly build a dataset with queries with document relevance judgments that belong to this group. Collecting query-document relevance judgments for thousands of queries and hundreds of documents per query is a costly and time consuming process. Crowdsourcing could be used to create more labeled datasets to target other DSAT groups.

We compare the results of three experiments. First, we use a general queryset to train a learning-to-rank algorithm. The general queryset contains queries that belong to the specific group among many other queries. Second, we train a specialized ranker using a queryset with queries that only belong to the selected group. If targeting specific underperforming groups is a good strategy, then the ranking function trained using a specialized query set will be better than the one using a general query set. Finally, to measure the value of coherence in our groups, we compare the performance of our specialized ranker with a ranker trained specifically for a set of poorly-performing queries, with low CTR.

The general ranker baseline is trained using a general queryset with 10,000 queries; some of them belong to the selected group. As noted above, the general ranker had access to attributes used in identifying DSAT groups, allowing it to learn to use DSAT information. Note that the general ranker is a state-of-the-art heavily optimized ranker using hundreds of features including clickthrough rate, link based features and content based features.

The specialized ranker is trained using a specialized dataset. The dataset contains queries that belong to the selected group only. The size of the specialized dataset is 2,000 queries. The size of the specialized dataset is much less than the size of the general dataset. This is not intentional and we believe that increasing the size of the specialized dataset could even lead to larger gains. The data used to train both rankers does not overlap with the data used to identify the underperforming query groups.

7.2.2 *Effect of Specialized Ranker*

We evaluated both the general and the specialized rankers using the specialized data using 10-fold cross validation. We evaluate the performance of both rankers using specialized data only because we are only altering the ranking on queries belonging to the selected group. The performance on all other queries will remain unchanged. The rationale behind this is that the all queries will go to the general ranker except for queries belonging to the selected group which will go to the specialized ranker. Note that these are not the same underperforming queries we identified earlier. Rather, they are new queries that belong to the underperforming group (i.e. all the attributes defining the group fire for them).

In Table 5, we report NDCG@1 through NDCG@5 improvements over the general ranker. Improvements are statistically significant at the 0.05 level according to the Wilcoxon *p-value.* The table shows that we observe a 1.52% NDCG@1 improvement and NDCG@5 improvement of 0.77%.

7.2.3 *Effect of Group Coherence*

We performed another experiment to measure the effect that the *coherence* of the identified dissatisfaction groups has in improving relevance when a specialized ranker is trained. We wanted to understand whether the relevance gains we achieved were specific to dissatisfaction groups, or if they can be obtained if we train a ranker on any set of poorly-performing queries. We construct a new data set with poorly performing queries (clickthrough rate less than 0.2), and with the same number of queries as the specialized dataset described earlier. We train a ranker using the same set of features on the low CTR dataset. We measure the performance using NDCG gain compared to the general ranker. The results are shown in Table 6. The results show that the gain is much smaller than the specialized ranker case and often not significant. The NDCG@1 gain is the only gain that is significant at the 0.05 level. This shows the value of the dissatisfaction groups and supports our hypothesis that group coherence is important for ranking.

8. DISCUSSION AND IMPLICATIONS

Identifying groups of queries where search engines underperform is an important research challenge. We have described a novel method to automatically identify dissatisfaction groups comprising queries where a search engine appears to be failing. For one such group identified by our method, we trained a specialized ranking algorithm and showed significant relevance gains over a state-of-the-art general ranker.

We validated our DSAT group identification approach by showing that groups identified were correlated with established measures of search engine performance, namely clickthrough rate and NDCG. However, unlike subsets of the queries identified by those metrics, queries were grouped so that they shared common attributes. As we showed through an experiment, such coherence is important for ranking. In particular, we showed that the specialized ranker performed better for our coherent groups than groups containing a broad range of queries that were just filtered based on a measure of retrieval effectiveness (low CTR in our case).

The methods presented combine to form an end-to-end framework capable of automatically identifying dissatisfied query groups and the adapting the ranking algorithm to them. However, the framework does not have to be used in its entirety. It may be desirable to first identify the groups of queries on which the search engine is underperforming and then triage those groups to make a determination regarding how to proceed. Deploying a specialized ranker may not always be appropriate depending on the nature of the group identified. For example, in DSAT groups where the searcher may benefit from interactive support rather than ranking improvements (e.g., a specialized direct answer on the SERP), interface modifications may be more appropriate.

We should also acknowledge some limitations of our study. The framework is limited by the need to gather dissatisfaction data before specialized rankers can be trained. New rankers that are released based on this data then need to wait some time (days or weeks) for new data to arrive. The method can only work on groups of sufficient size to provide a sufficient number of queries to train the ranker. This approach does not work for the smaller groups. One solution is to create group hierarchies to combine multiple smaller groups into a single large group based on shared attributes.

There are a number of important areas of future work. For the training and evaluation of our specialized ranking algorithms we used human relevance judgments. However, obtaining these judgments may be costly and we may not have such judgments readily available for the query groups identified by our algorithm. Prior work has shown that judgments may be obtained implicitly from search interaction [3][7] and we will explore the use of such judgments to further lessen the any remaining dependencies on human involvement in our framework (reducing additional costs where possible). We will also investigate the cost-benefit tradeoffs of adding more features tailored to the group of interest, rather than simply re-training the ranker for the current set of features. To handle smaller query groups for which we may lack sufficient training data to train a dedicated ranker, we will investigate how to combine multiple groups in a way that still maintains the group coherence that contributes to the success of our approach.

9. CONCLUSIONS AND FUTURE WORK

Search engines try to satisfy all users' needs and inevitably do not perform well for all queries. In this paper, we described and validated a method for automatic identification of dissatisfaction groups comprising queries where an engine is underperforming. Knowledge of these DSAT groups can help search engines since it can offer insights that inform engine design decisions and resource allocation. Importantly, rather than only identifying underperforming groups, we closed the loop and investigated automatically learning a specialized ranking algorithm that outperforms a general ranker with access to the same features. Our findings also show the benefit of group coherence in training specialized rankers. The method we describe in this paper can help search engines learn from evidence of searcher dissatisfaction and directly improve their search performance for troublesome queries. Future work will expand this research to target learning new ranking algorithms for multiple DSAT groups simultaneously and develop new methods to combine many smaller query groups to improve coverage.

REFERENCES

[1] Ageev, M., Guo, Q., Lagun, D., and Agichtein, E. (2011). Find it if you can: a game for modeling different types of web search success using interaction data. *Proc. SIGIR*, 345–354.

[2] Agichtein, E., Brill, E., and Dumais, S.T. (2006). Improving web search ranking by incorporating user behavior information. *Proc. SIGIR*, 19–26.

[3] Agichtein, E., Brill, E., Dumais, S.T., and Ragno, R. (2006). Learning user interaction models for predicting web search result preferences. *Proc. SIGIR*, 3–10.

[4] Agrawal, R., Imielinski, T., and Swami, A. (1993). Mining association rules between sets of items in large databases. *Proc. SIGMOD*, 207–216.

[5] Agrawal, R., and Srikant, R. (1994). Fast algorithms for mining association rules. *Proc. VLDB*, 487–499.

[6] Al-Maskari, A., Sanderson, M., and Clough, P. (2007). The relationship between IR effectiveness measures and user satisfaction. *Proc. SIGIR*, 773–774.

[7] Bennett, P.N., Radlinski, F., Yilmaz, E. and White, R.W. (2011). Inferring and using location metadata to personalize web search. *Proc. SIGIR*, 135–144.

[8] Carmel, D., Yom-Tov, E., Darlow, A., and Pelleg, D. (2006). What makes a query difficult? *Proc. SIGIR*, 390–397.

[9] Carterette, B. and Jones, R. (2007). Evaluating search engines by modeling the relationship between relevance and clicks. *Proc. NIPS*, 217–224.

[10] Cronen-Townsend, S., Zhou, Y., and Croft, W. B. (2002). Predicting query performance. *Proc. SIGIR*, 299–306.

[11] Dan, O., Dmitriev, P., and White, R.W. (2012). Mining for insights in the search engine query stream. *Proc. WWW*, 489-490.

[12] Downey, D., Dumais, S., and Horvitz, E. (2007). Model of searching and browsing: Languages, studies and applications. *Proc. IJCAI*, 2740–2747.

[13] Feild, H., Allan, J., and Jones, R. (2010). Predicting searcher frustration. *Proc. SIGIR*, 34–41.

[14] Fox, S., Karnawat, K., Mydland, M., Dumais, S.T., and White, T. (2005). Evaluating implicit measures to improve the search experience. *ACM TOIS*, 23(2): 147–168.

[15] Guo, Q., White, R.W., Dumais, S.T., Wang, J., and Anderson, B. (2010). Predicting query performance using query, result, and user interaction features. *Proc. RIAO.*

[16] Guo, Q., White, R.W., Zhang, Y., Anderson, B., and Dumais, S.T. (2011). Why searchers switch: understanding and predicting engine switching rationales. *Proc. SIGIR*. 335–344.

[17] Hall, M., Frank, E., Holmes, G., Pfahringer, B., Reutemann, P., and Witten, I. (2009). The WEKA data mining software: an update, *SIGKDD Explorations*, 11(1).

[18] Han, J. and Kamber, M. (2006). Data Mining: Concepts and Techniques, Second Edition. *Morgan Kaufmann.*

[19] Han, J., Pei, J., Yin, Y., and Mao, R. (2004). Mining Frequent Patterns without Candidate Generation: A Frequent-Pattern Tree Approach. *Data Mining and Knowledge Discovery,* 8(1), 53–87.

[20] Hassan, A., Jones, R., and Klinkner, K.L. (2010). Beyond DCG: user behavior as a predictor of a successful search. *Proc. WSDM*, 221–230

[21] Hassan, A., Song, Y., and He, L. (2011). A task level user satisfaction model and its application on improving relevance estimation. *Proc. CIKM*, 125–134.

[22] Hauff, C., Murdock, V., and Baeza-Yates, R. (2008). Improved query difficulty prediction for the web. *Proc. CIKM*, 439–448.

[23] He, B. and Ounis, I. (2004). Inferring query performance using pre-retrieval predictors. *Proc. SPIRE*, 43–54.

[24] Hu, V., Stone, M., Pedersen, J., and White, R.W. (2011). Effects of search success on search engine re-use. *Proc. CIKM*, 1841–1846.

[25] Huffman, S. and Hochster, M. (2007). How well does result relevance predict session satisfaction? *Proc. SIGIR*, 567–574.

[26] K. Järvelin and Kekalainen. J. (2002). Cumulated gain-based evaluation of IR techniques. *ACM TOIS*, 20(4), 422–446.

[27] K. Järvelin, S.L. Price, L.M.L. Delcambre, and M.L. Nielsen. (2008). Discounted cumulated gain based evaluation of multiple-query IR sessions. *Proc. ECIR*, 4–15.

[28] Dan Klein and Christopher D. Manning. (2003). Accurate unlexicalized parsing. *Proc. ACL*, 423–430

[29] Leskovec, J., Dumais, S., and Horvitz, E. (2007). Web projections: Learning from contextual subgraphs of the Web. *Proc. WWW*, 471–480.

[30] Li, H., Wang, Y., Zhang, D., Zhang, M., and Chang, E. (2008). PFP: parallel FP-growth for query recommendation. *Proc. RecSys*, 107–114.

[31] Teevan, J., Dumais, S., and Liebling, D. (2008). To personalize or not to personalize: Modeling queries with variation in user intent. *Proc. SIGIR*, 620–627.

[32] White, R.W. and Drucker, S.M. (2007). Investigating behavioral variability in Web search. *Proc. WWW*, 21–30.

[33] White, R.W. and Dumais, S. (2009). Characterizing and predicting search engine switching behavior. *Proc. CIKM*, 87–96.

[34] White, R.W. and Huang, J. (2010). Assessing the scenic route: measuring the value of search trails in web logs. *Proc. SIGIR*, 587–594.

[35] Xu, J., and Li, H. (2007). AdaRank: A boosting algorithm for information retrieval. *Proc. SIGIR*, 391–398.

[36] Zhou, Y. and Croft, W.B. (2007). Query performance prediction in Web search environments. *Proc. SIGIR*, 543–550.

Fighting Search Engine Amnesia: Reranking Repeated Results

Milad Shokouhi
Microsoft
milads@microsoft.com

Ryen W. White
Microsoft Research
ryenw@microsoft.com

Paul Bennett
Microsoft Research
pauben@microsoft.com

Filip Radlinski
Microsoft
filiprad@microsoft.com

ABSTRACT

Web search engines frequently show the same documents repeatedly for *different* queries within the same search session, in essence forgetting when the same documents were already shown to users. Depending on previous user interaction with the repeated results, and the details of the session, we show that sometimes the repeated results should be promoted, while some other times they should be demoted.

Analysing search logs from two different commercial search engines, we find that results are repeated in about 40% of multi-query search sessions, and that users engage differently with repeats than with results shown for the first time. We demonstrate how statistics about result repetition within search sessions can be incorporated into ranking for personalizing search results. Our results on query logs of two large-scale commercial search engines suggest that we successfully promote documents that are more likely to be clicked by the user in the future while maintaining performance over standard measures of non-personalized relevance.

Categories and Subject Descriptors

H.3.3 [**Information Search and Retrieval**]: Information Search and Retrieval—*Search Process, selection process*

General Terms

Algorithms, Measurement, Experimentation

Keywords

Repeated Results, User History, User Sessions, Click Prediction, User Modelling, Re-finding Queries

1. INTRODUCTION

When interacting with Web search engines, people frequently encounter the same results for different queries, both within a single session and across multiple sessions [33]. There are times when this repetition may be intentional, as is the case with re-finding, where users purposely seek the same Web document [30, 32]. However, as we will show, repeated results are shown to users much more often than can be explained by re-finding alone. Rather, results are often shown multiple times as users try to find the solutions to satisfy information needs – and most Web search engines exhibit a form of amnesia, without taking longer interactions with users into account. Previous research has largely treated sequences of queries independently [2, 20], or as weakly interacting by building models of user tasks or interests [37], rather than as a single continuing conversation between the user and search engine. Making this problem even more interesting, repetition of results can intuitively be interpreted in a few distinct ways.

Consider a document shown twice to a user for two related queries. The first time it was returned, the document must have been (1) not noticed, (2) noticed and considered but not clicked, or (3) clicked. If we can detect the first case, we may want to promote the document to help the user notice it as recurring and potentially relevant. If we can detect the second case, we may want to demote it. The third case is most interesting, as the user may be attempting to re-find the document (in which case it should be aggressively promoted), or the user may have decided that it is non-relevant (in which case it should be aggressively demoted). This leads us to the two key challenges we address in this paper: First, how do we know when a later query is similar enough to an earlier query to warrant inclusion considering previous displays of repeated documents? Second, how do we differentiate between re-finding and non-relevance?

Before describing our approach, it is important to verify that Web results are often shown repeatedly, and that behavior on them is different. Our analysis shows that repetition is both frequent, and has a substantial effect on user behavior. About 40% of multi-query sessions include at least one result being shown in the top-10 results more than once. When a result is skipped once, depending on position, it is 20% to 50% less likely to be clicked later – compared to the expected clickthrough rate (CTR) at the same position. But unnoticed results are about 10% more likely to be clicked when shown again later. Conversely, results previously clicked *once* are 10% to 50% less likely to be clicked when shown again while results previously clicked *three times* are up to 30% more likely to be clicked when shown again.

We conjecture that a method that can leverage the skip and click behavior of users to automatically promote and

SIGIR'13, July 28–August 1, 2013, Dublin, Ireland.

demote results could lead to better ranking. We therefore propose R-cube, a *context-aware* ranker enhanced by features generated from a user's interaction with repeatedly-displayed search results. We evaluate R-cube *offline* using log data from two large commercial search engines (one proprietary and one publicly available), and *online* via A-B testing with users of a commercial search engine. The results show significant gains from R-cube over competitive baselines.

After presenting related work in Section 2, and based on an analysis of logs in Section 3, we build models that leverage features of these repeated results and other features such as query similarity to predict click preferences between result pairs. Section 4 presents our re-ranking approach, and describes our evaluation data and metrics. We follow that by discussing our experimental results in Section 5, and providing concluding remarks in Section 6.

2. RELATED WORK

There is substantial prior research that relates to this work in a number of areas. We review each in turn.

Repeated Queries and Results. Searchers repeat queries and revisit the same results often. Previous research has shown that well over half of all of the Web pages a person visits are pages that they have visited previously (with some estimates of re-visitation volume reaching 80%) [8, 29], and a third of the queries issued to search engines involve a user re-finding a previously-found result [30]. Teevan *et al.* [30] explored how queries used to re-find changed and how well future clicks could be predicted following repeat queries. In a similar study and perhaps the most related to our work, Teevan *et al.* [32] proposed a model for *personal navigation*. The authors monitored the user's long-term history and showed that when the user repeatedly submits the same query and clicks on the same single result over time, the target URL can be regarded as a personal navigation destination. That is, if the user issues the same query again, it is likely that the same result gets clicked. Similarly, Dou *et al.* [12] consider re-ranking for identically repeated queries.

In our analysis, the click patterns on exactly repeated queries and results are a special case. In contrast to personal navigation [32] that only focuses on singleton clicked results over a long user history, we cover several classes of user feedback (click, skip, missed) based on the short session history. We model user behaviour on any repeated result, regardless of whether it was clicked or not, or even shown for the same query before.

Other studies have looked at temporal properties of an individual's repeated searches and clicks and aspects of repeat queries related to time [25], and how people re-find previously viewed Web pages across multiple sessions and within an individual session [30, 33].

Interpreting Clicks. In general, search engine result page clicks provide informative signals of when users are attracted to a search result. Joachims *et al.* [21] analysed users' decision processes using gaze tracking and compared implicit feedback from search-result clicks against manual relevance judgements. They found that clicks are informative but biased: Clicks as an absolute signal are biased by rank, but relative preferences derived from clicks are fairly accurate. Agichtein *et al.* [2] also used search and browsing data from a Web search engine to predict search result preferences but generalized the approach to model user behaviour beyond clicks, resulting in more accurate preference predictions.

Searcher models (e.g., [7, 10, 34]) track the user's state as they examine search results and use the observable events (e.g., clickthrough) to infer search result attractiveness and document relevance. The examination hypothesis [13] states that the likelihood that the user will click on a search result is influenced only by (i) whether the user examined the search result snippet and (ii) its attractiveness. Since users are biased towards clicking search results that are higher ranked, the examination hypothesis is used to isolate a search result's attractiveness from its position. The cascade hypothesis [10] assumes that a user always examines search results sequentially from top-to-bottom, and is used to determine whether a user examined the result. We use this approach here. Under this assumption, a user decides whether to click a result before examining the next result, preventing scenarios where the user returns to a higher-ranked search result after passing it by. Therefore, if users do not examine a particular search result, they will not examine any search results below it. Extensions of the cascade hypothesis allow for query sessions to comprise multiple clicks [17] or represent the probability that a user abandons a query session without clicking [7, 16]. Other searcher models avoid the cascade hypothesis entirely, allowing the user to examine results non-sequentially via modelling user browsing behaviour [14, 34], or modelling tasks, via the sequence of queries and clicks in a session [40].

Learning from Clicks. In addition to modeling search behavior, clicks have also been used to improve the quality of search engine ranking. Joachims [20] presents a method for automatically optimizing the retrieval quality of search engines using implicit feedback gathered from clickthrough data. He shows that his method is both effective and scalable, outperforming a state-of-the-art search engine given only limited training data. Radlinski and Joachims [23] study connected query chains to generate preference judgements from search engine logs. These judgements are used to learn search result rankings that outperform a static ranking function. Agichtein *et al.* [1] extend this work beyond search engine result pages (SERPs). Incorporating later user behaviour data, they show that it can be used to improve search engine performance.

User Interest Modelling. Knowledge of a particular user's interests and search context has been used to improve search. Short-term interests, expressed by actions such as recent queries or clicks, can improve retrieval performance [11, 27, 39]. They have also been used by White *et al.* [36, 37] to construct models of searchers' recent interests, and predict future interests. Teevan *et al.* [31] constructed user profiles of long-term interests from desktop documents, showing that this information could be used to re-rank results and improve relevance for individuals. Matthijs and Radlinski [22] constructed user profiles using users' browsing history, and evaluated their approach using an interleaving methodology. Bennett *et al.* [4] compared the effectiveness of features based on short-term and long-term history of the user for personalization, and found the latter particularly effective at the start of search sessions.

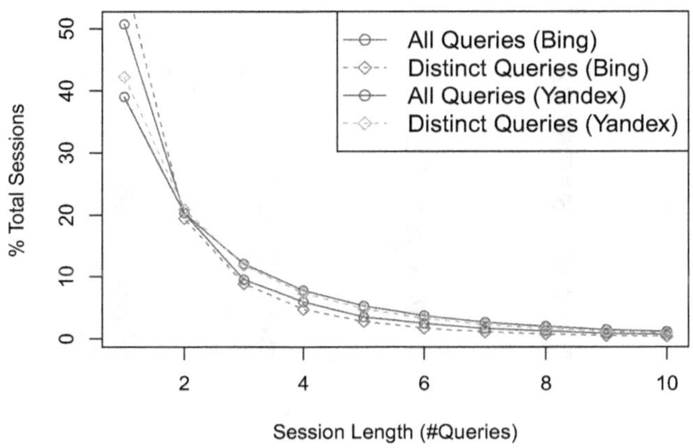

Figure 1: The distribution of the number of queries in sessions (session length). For distinct columns, repeated queries in each session are ignored.

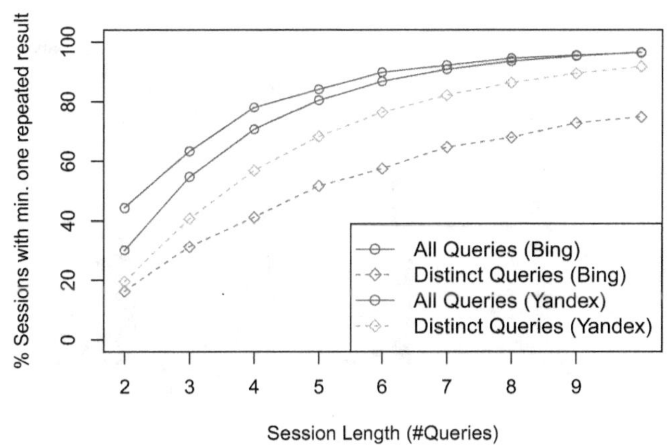

Figure 2: Fraction of sessions that include a repeated result as a function of length of session.

Our Contributions. Our research extends previous work in a number of ways. First, we focus specifically on repeatedly-displayed search results, arguing for treating the session as a continuous interaction. Second, we characterize the role that repeat results play within search sessions and the potential benefit from targeting repetition. This serves to motivate our work. Third, we focus on interpreting how users engage with results to determine whether to promote or demote repeated results. Previous work has only looked at repetition in identical repeated queries [12, 32]. Our proposal is more general, targeting the promotion or demotion of any repeat result from any position for any query, related to the current query or not. Finally, we demonstrate significant improvements in result re-ranking performance using our methods over competitive baselines on search logs from two large commercial search engines, including one dataset that is publicly available.

3. MOTIVATION AND HYPOTHESES

As a first step, we must verify that repetition happens frequently in search sessions, and that repeated results are treated differently by users. We perform this analysis on sample logs of two large commercial search engines. The first one consists of three weeks of log data from Bing sampled in November 2012. The logs contain a search session identifier, the query and the top 10 results returned by the engine. We take search sessions to comprise a sequence of queries and clicks, terminated by a 30-minute inactivity time-out, as in previous work (e.g. [23]). To facilitate reproducibility of our experiments and results, we also evaluate on a more readily available log. This second log consists of approximately 340 million queries in 44 million sessions from Yandex. These logs were shared by Yandex for participants of the Relevance Prediction Challenge[1] held in the scope of the WSDM-WSCD workshop in 2012 [26]. The Bing log contains anonymized user IDs, and preserves the full text of submitted queries. In Yandex data however, the user IDs are not available and query texts are replaced by unique numerical identifiers. Note that Bing and Yandex datasets were collected not only from different search engines, but also from users of different markets and languages.

Sessions and Repetition. Figure 1 shows that between 40 and 60% of sessions (depending on whether we focus on distinct[2] queries, and depending on the search engine) have single queries only, and the remaining 40%-60% have two queries or more. These numbers are comparable to the 46-54% split reported elsewhere [18]. Figure 2 shows that 16-44% of sessions (depending on the search engine) with two queries have at least one repeated result. This is large when we consider that the user in such short sessions is usually shown not more than 20 results. Repetition increases to almost all sessions with ten or more queries (or up to 75% when only distinct queries in the session are considered). Clearly repetition is frequent.

Classes of Repetition. For a given query and its results (subsequently referred to as an *impression*), each result must either be displayed for the first time in the session (new), or must have been shown for a previous query. For analysis, we split the repeated class into three groups[3]:

- Results previously displayed and *clicked.*
- Results previously displayed but *skipped.* We consider a result skipped when it was not clicked by the user, but at least one lower ranked result was clicked.
- Results previously displayed but *missed.* We consider a result missed when it was not clicked by the user and there were no clicked results at lower positions.

The clickthrough rates (CTR) for the Bing dataset in Figure 3 demonstrate that users interact with the results in each of these classes differently. The x-axis represents the result position, while the y-axis shows the average normalized CTR for all results in this class.[4] The numbers in the top plot are

[1] `http://imat-relpred.yandex.ru/en/`

[2] Repeated queries in the session are discarded.

[3] Note that a particular result may belong to more than one category when it appears more than twice in the session.

[4] We rescale all clickthrough graphs, based on the overall CTR@1 value averaged across all queries and impressions.

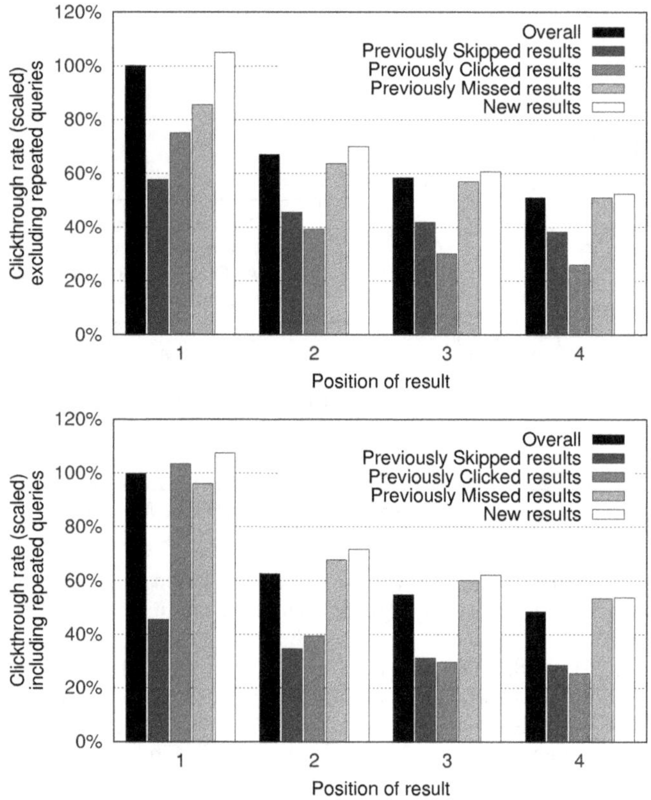

Figure 3: The clickthrough rates for different classes of results for the Bing dataset (scaled with respect to the overall CTR@1 rates across all queries and impressions). In the top plot, repeated queries in each session are excluded before calculating clickthrough rates. In the bottom plot, they are not.

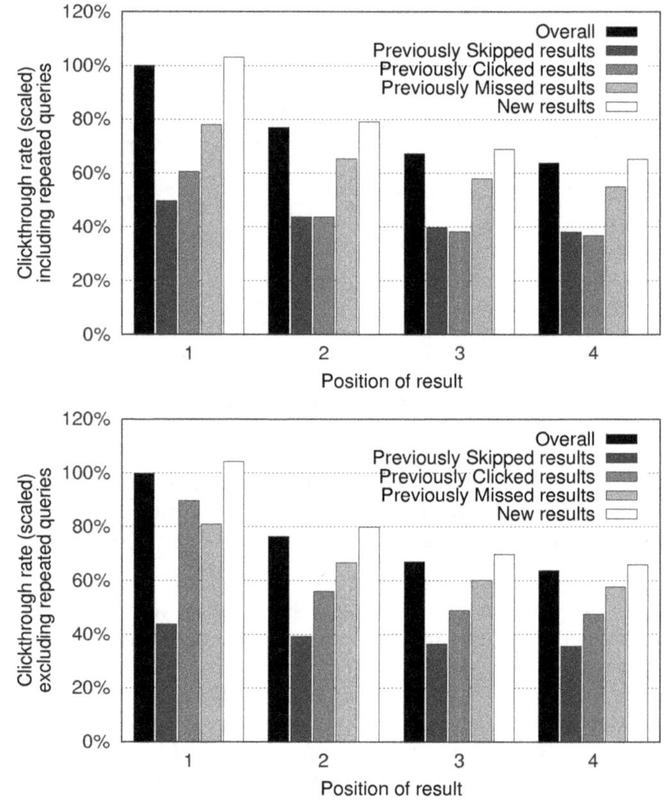

Figure 4: The clickthrough rates for different classes of results for the Yandex dataset (scaled with respect to the overall CTR@1 rates across all queries and impressions). In the top plot, repeated queries in each session are excluded before calculating clickthrough rates. In the bottom plot, they are not.

generated after excluding identical repeated queries to reduce the impact of personal navigation, while in the bottom plot all impressions are retained. The overall trends in the top plot are intuitive: repeated results have substantially lower CTR than those displayed for the first time in the session. Among the repeated classes, those that are likely to have been missed by the user for the earlier impressions are more likely to be clicked, followed by those that have been displayed but skipped. The only exception is the CTR at position 1. This is due to personal navigation [32], where users frequently re-find the same URL but with a different query. Note that although personal navigation was strictly defined for identical query-result pairs, users sometimes use different reformulations in a session to navigate to the same target. This is particularly common for popular navigational destinations (e.g. using `facebook` and `facebook login` interchangeably to navigate to `www.facebook.com`). Similar observations were reported by Teevan *et al.* [30] suggesting that in about 5% of queries, users re-find their navigational destination by issuing different queries.

The bottom plot in Figure 3 shows the impact of including repeated queries on CTR. It reveals two main differences compared to the top chart, where repeated queries were excluded. First, there is an increase in the CTR at the top rank position for previously-clicked results. This can be attributed to within-session personal navigation behaviour using identical queries. Second, there is a consistent drop in CTR across all four rank positions for results that were previously skipped. From this observation we can infer that once a user has skipped a result for a particular query, it is unlikely that they will click on it when it is returned again for the same query. Equivalent analysis on Yandex data shows very similar trends in Figure 4.

We continue by studying the repetition categories separately. First, consider results that have been skipped. Figure 5 based on the Bing (top) and Yandex (bottom) datasets shows that, the more often a result has been skipped in a session, the less likely it is to be clicked when repeated again. As before, the x-axis is the position, and the CTR curves are scaled with respect to the average CTR across all impressions. The results show that the expected CTR@1 drops by almost 60% when a result is skipped once in the session. That is, the conditional click probability of a document displayed at position one given that is skipped once before in the session, is 60% lower than the overall CTR figures at position one. We repeated the analysis for distinct queries in the session and the trends remained the same, hence are not presented here separately. Likewise, we noticed that skipped and missed results have similar CTR distributions across different positions, with the CTR values being generally higher for the latter category. In addition, the missed results have a relatively less skewed CTR distribution, and

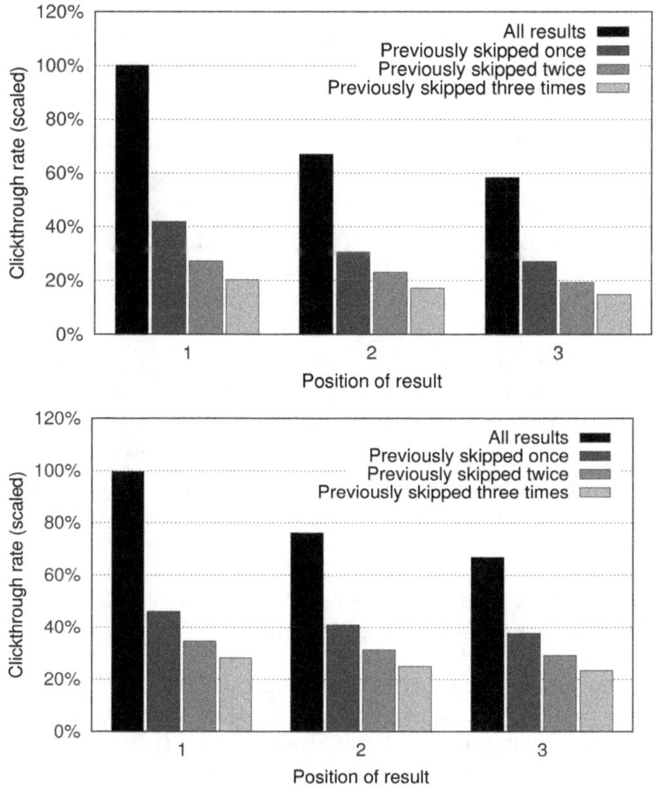

Figure 5: Clickthrough rate of repeated results as a function of the number of times they have been skipped before in the session, based on the Bing (top) and Yandex (bottom) logs.

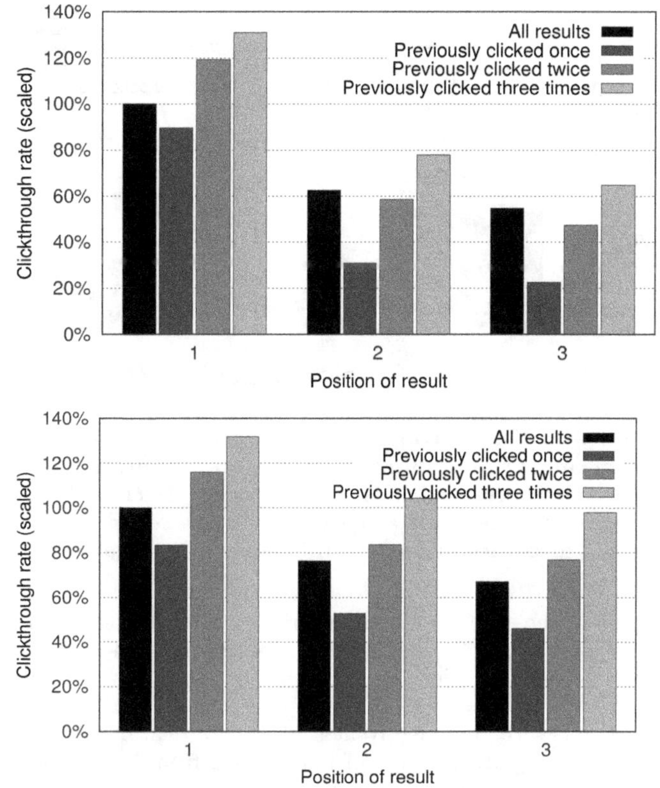

Figure 6: Clickthrough rate of repeated results as a function of the number of times they have been clicked before in the session, based on the Bing (top) and Yandex (bottom) logs.

are substantially more likely to be clicked at lower positions (the plots are omitted for brevity).

Figure 6 shows the conditional click probability of results given their position and the total number of prior clicks they have received in the session. We see that the more a result is clicked in the session, the more likely it is going to be clicked again. If a result was previously clicked just once, its expected CTR is lower than the average. However, once a result is clicked for the second time, the CTR increases substantially as it is more likely to fall in the personal navigation category. Excluding repeated queries (not shown here) led to lower CTR values for the clicked results overall but the general trends remained the same.

Beyond the scenarios covered here, there could be several other factors that affect the click probability of repeated results. For instance, in Figure 7 we can find a clear positive correlation between the amount of time spent on a result when it has been clicked once previously in the session, and the likelihood of it being clicked again. The unit of time is not specified in Yandex logs, hence the dwell time analysis is based on the Bing data only. Here, each column represents the total amount of time *dwelled* on the result. Shorter dwell times may reflect dissatisfaction with the content of the result [15] and make re-visitation less likely. We now take the insights obtained from this analysis, and develop features that can be used to improve the ranking of repeated results.

4. RE-RANKING REPEATED RESULTS

Thus far, we have demonstrated that repeated results have different click likelihoods than those that are shown for the first time in a session. We also showed that depending on the number of previous clicks, number of prior displays, and the total dwell time, the click probability of repeated results may vary significantly. In this section we describe how such features can be used to train a model for re-ranking search results in sessions. We will refer to this trained model as R-cube, as it involves Re-ranking Repeated Results.

Collecting relevance labels for evaluating *context-sensitive* rankers such as R-cube is not trivial. We need a personalized set of judgements in which the same query-result pair may be assigned with different labels depending on the search context and preferences of each user. Fox *et al.* [15] proposed using implicit measures such as satisfied clicks (SAT-Clicks) for evaluation and since then, this approach has become a common practice for evaluating personalized search systems [3, 4, 9]. We follow the same *log-based* approach for generating training data and assigning labels. First we sample a set of *impressions* from query logs. Each impression consists of a query $\mathcal{Q}$, the unique identifier of the user who issued $\mathcal{Q}$, and the set of results that were returned for $\mathcal{Q}$ on that impression. Additionally, click statistics for that impression are collected for assigning labels, and contextual features such as previous queries and clicks are used for generating ranking features. As in previous work [3, 4], in each impression, we assign positive labels to results that had SAT-Clicks, and

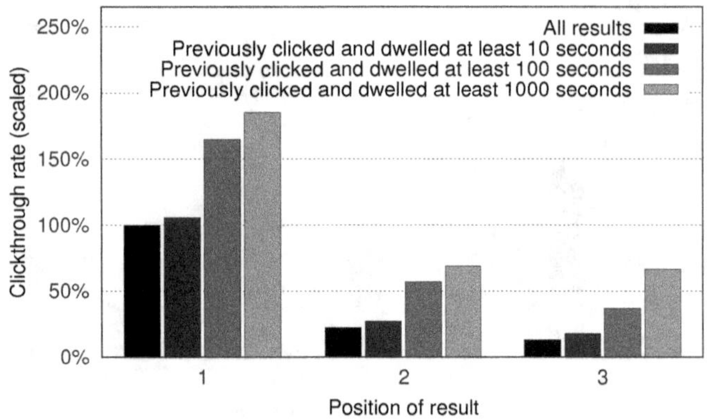

Figure 7: Clickthrough rate of repeated results as a function of the amount of dwell time spent on them after their first click in the session. Each column represents the total amount of time *dwelled* on the result in common logarithmic scale (Bing dataset).

consider the other results as non-relevant. To define a SAT-Click, we follow the definition suggested in previous work [28, 35] and consider last clicks in the session, and clicks with at least 30 seconds dwell time as SAT-Clicks.[5]

To measure the effectiveness of R-cube features for re-ranking, we sample a set of impressions from logs, generate the features for each impression, assign the labels as described above, and finally train a ranker. We chose to use LambaMART [38] for the preference learning. LambdaMART is an application of the LambdaRank approach [5], which gives a methodology for optimizing a variety of non-continuous ranking objective functions, to gradient-boosted decision trees. LambdaMART and generally gradient-boosted decision trees have been successful over a number of information retrieval problems – most notably the Yahoo! Learning to Rank challenge Track 1 [6] where LambdaMART was a key component of the winning entry.

We used our implementation's default settings for key parameters. These were, number of leaves=70, minimum documents per leaf = 2000, number of trees = 500, learning rate = 0.3 and used 10% of the training set as validation data. Note that for this study, neither the particular choice of learning algorithm nor the parameters are crucial. Our primary concern is the demonstration that it is possible to capture improved accuracy by using a learned model over the key factors we have described.

As our evaluation metrics, we compute the *mean reciprocal rank* (MRR) and *mean average precision* (MAP) of search results with respect to the log-based labels over all impressions. The Yandex dataset was released with limited set of generic (context-sensitive) relevance labels. In the following sections we also measure the impact of re-ranking with respect to those labels.

R-Cube Features. Our observations in the previous sections highlighted unique characteristics of repeated results. Those inspired us to develop several features that capture various properties of repeated results. Detailed description of our features are provided in Table 1. In general, we have four groups of features:

- (♢) Click features : These features are developed based on the number and position of previous clicks on the results (e.g. PrevClicked).
- (♡) Display features: These are similar to the click features except that they focus on the display positions regardless of whether the repeated result was previously clicked or not (e.g. PrevShown).
- (♣) Query similarity features: These features are designed to distinguish between repeated queries, personal navigation, re-finding, and query reformulation for exploring new information (e.g. RepeatQuery).
- (♠) Other features: These are features that do not belong to any of the categories above (e.g. Position).

Data. To evaluate our approach quantitatively, we use the Bing and Yandex query logs described in Section 3. For Bing analysis, we use the second week of logs (from November 8th to November 15th, 2011) for training, and the third week (between November 16th and November 23rd) for testing. The first week was used for analysing the CTR patterns that we covered in earlier sections. In total, there were $6,672,701$ impressions in the testing subset of Bing dataset from which $1,273,577$ had R-cube features (19.1%). Other impressions were either the first query of their sessions or did not have any repeated results. We report the result on this segment, and the overall impact across the entire traffic can be re-scaled accordingly.

Similarly, on the Yandex testbed, we split the dataset into two sets for training and testing. Splitting is done according to the SessionID meta-data in the logs. We sampled sessions with SessionID smaller than $3E+07$ and assigned them to the training set, and sampled from the remainder to generate our testing set. In total, there were $31,814,133$ impressions in our testing subset dataset from which $5,580,720$ had R-cube features (17.5%).

Baselines. In our experiments, we use three baselines. The first baseline (*Default*) involves no re-ranking: This is just the default order that search results were retrieved by Bing and Yandex search engines.

For our second baseline (*ClickHistory*) we train a ranker with three features: {Score, Position, and Click-history}. The former two features are common among all our experiments. The Click-history feature represents the overall long-term click counts for each result on a per query basis (without regard to which user clicked which result). Hence, for each result pair in our test data, the document that was historically clicked most by all users for the current query gets the highest Click-history value. Note that this baseline only affects queries that have been observed previously, and where the same results returned currently were previously clicked. In other cases, the default ordering is preserved. This is slightly different than simply re-ranking results according to their past click frequency. Here, the ranker may *choose* not to apply such re-ranking depending on the differences in the original Scores.

[5]Each query in the Yandex dataset is assigned with a numerical value as time-stamp. However, no extra information is disclosed about how these values were computed. We therefore relax our positive labelling criteria from SAT-Clicks to Clicks on this dataset.

Table 1: **The features used in R-cube for re-ranking search results. The suit in each bracket represents the experimental group the corresponding feature belongs too. Note that *query similarity* features (♣) are not available in experiments using the Yandex data.**

Feature	Description
PrevClicked (♢)	How many times the document is clicked earlier in the session.
PrevClickedMRR (♢)	Similar to PrevClicked, but with a reciprocal rank discount determined according to the clicked positions.
PrevShown (♡)	How many times the result is shown earlier in the session.
PrevShownMRR (♡)	Similar to PrevShown, but with a reciprocal rank discount determined according to the display positions.
PrevMissed (♡)	How many times the result is *missed* earlier in the session.
PrevMissedMRR (♡)	Similar to PrevMissed, but with a reciprocal rank discount determined according to the display positions.
PrevSkipped (♡)	How many times the result is *skipped* earlier in the session.
PrevSkippedMRR (♡)	Similar to PrevSkipped, but with a reciprocal rank discount determined according to the display positions.
MaxQSim (♣)	Max. n-gram similarity of current query with any of the previous queries in the session.
AvgQSim (♣)	Average n-gram similarity of current query with previous queries in the session.
PrevQSim (♣)	n-gram similarity of current query with the previous query in the session.
MaxClkQSim (♣)	Max. n-gram similarity of current query with any previous query in the session where the same URL is clicked.
AvgClkQSim (♣)	Average n-gram similarity of current query with previous queries in the session where the same URL is clicked.
PrevClkQSim (♣)	n-gram similarity of current query with the previous query in the session where the same URL is clicked.
RepeatQuery (♣)	1 if the query has appeared before in the session and 0 otherwise.
QueryNo (♠)	Number of queries submitted in the session including the current query.
Position (♠)	Display rank of the URL before re-ranking.
Score (♠)	Original score of the URL before re-ranking.
NumSessionClicks (♠)	Total number of clicks in the previous impressions of the session.
NumRepAbove (♠)	Number of repeated documents in the current impression that are ranked at or above the current position.
PrevDwell (♠)	Total amount of dwell time spent on this URL on previous clicks.

Finally, in our third baseline (*Personal Navigation*) [32], we train a re-ranking model based on the original Score, Position, and a Personal Navigation feature. The *Personal Navigation* feature is only applicable on repeated queries, and counts the number of times a particular result has been clicked for the same query previously in the session.[6]

Our last two baselines can respectively be regarded as a proxy for non-personalized re-ranking models based on aggregated click frequencies, and repetition-aware state-of-the-art models for search personalization.

5. EXPERIMENTS

We compare the effectiveness of R-cube features in personalizing search results against the three baselines. The results on the Yandex and Bing datasets are respectively summarized in Tables 2 and 3. We evaluate each model in terms of *mean average precision* (MAP) and *mean reciprocal rank* (MRR). These are computed based on the SAT-Click labels generated offline as described in Section 4.

On Yandex data (Table 2) R-cube significantly outperforms all baselines on both metrics ($p < 0.01$). Compared to the no re-ranking (Default) baseline, R-cube improves MRR by 2.1% and increases MAP by 3.2%. Other re-ranking baselines also outperform the default ranker but their gains are significantly smaller. In contrast to the ClickHistory and Personal-Navigation baselines, R-cube considers all types of repetition including *misses* and *skips* in the session. To investigate the impact of such features on the effectiveness of R-cube we train a ranker without them, using the click-based (♢) features only. The evaluation results for this ranker are shown in the last row of Table 2. While R-cube still manages to outperform all baselines by using the click features only, the gains are reduced by half, confirming that modelling other types of repetition is indeed useful for re-ranking.

[6]In the original *Personal Navigation* paper [32], re-ranking rules are hard-coded and require clicks to be *the only clicks* in impression. Given that we use a supervised model for re-ranking, we relax the only click rule to improve coverage.

The results on Bing data are presented in Table 3. Due to proprietary nature of this dataset, we only report the relative gains and losses against the default no-reranking baseline and the absolute MAP and MRR values are not disclosed. Overall, the trends are similar to those on the Yandex dataset. R-cube significantly outperforms all other baselines ($p < 0.01$) on both MAP and MRR. One interesting observation is that the ClickHistory baseline does not show any improvement over the Default ranker. This is to some extent expected since the Default ranker – which is the production ranker of a commercial search engine – is already trained to take clicks into account. We also suspect that the Yandex data has been sampled over a longer period compared to our Bing dataset which is sampled over three weeks. The details of sampling have not been disclosed by Yandex, but their dataset is considerably larger than our Bing data in terms of the number of sessions and impressions.

As in the previous testbed, we investigate the performance of R-cube when only the Click-based (♢) features are used for training and we show the results in the bottom section of the Table 3. The overall trends are similar; R-cube remains as the most effective re-ranking model but the gains are substantially reduced.

While the Yandex data does not contain the text of queries, that information is available in our Bing dataset and allows us to measure the importance of *query similarity features* (♣) separately. The last row in Table 3 includes the MRR and MAP values of a R-cube ranker that is trained without the query similarity features. The results suggest that while the query similarity features contribute positively to the gains, their importance is less significant than the *display features* (♡).

Win-Loss analysis. In addition to the overall evaluation numbers presented above, we investigate the average number of positions that the SAT-Clicked results are moved by R-cube in the ranking. Promoting SAT-Clicks is consid-

Table 2: The MRR and MAP of the baselines and our approach (R-cube) on Yandex data. The differences between the baselines and R-cube are all statistically significant according to a t-test ($p < 0.01$). The lower part shows impact Click features on R-cube effectiveness. The numbers in the brackets show the relative gain/loss against the Default (no-reranking) baseline.

Model	MRR		MAP	
Default	0.696		0.536	
Personal Nav. [32]	0.700	(▲0.4%)	0.540	(▲0.7%)
ClickHistory	0.698	(▲0.3%)	0.537	(▲0.2%)
R-cube	0.711	(▲2.1%)	0.553	(▲3.2%)
R-cube (◇ feats.)	0.704	(▲1.1%)	0.544	(▲1.5%)

Table 3: The MRR and MAP of the baselines and our approach (R-cube) on the Bing dataset. All differences between the baselines and R-cube are statistically significant according to a t-test ($p < 0.01$). The lower part shows impact of different feature groups on R-cube effectiveness. The numbers in the brackets show the relative gain/loss against the Default baseline. Due to the proprietary nature of the dataset, only the relative gains and losses are shown.

Model	MRR		MAP	
Personal Nav. [32]	-	(▲1.2%)	-	(▲3.3%)
ClickHistory	-	(0.0%)	-	(0.0%)
R-cube	-	(▲3.4%)	-	(▲7.1%)
R-cube (◇ feats.)	-	(▲1.4%)	-	(▲3.7%)
R-cube (◇, ♡ feats.)	-	(▲3.0%)	-	(▲6.3%)

ered as a win and contributes positively to MAP and MRR while demoting a SAT-Click would have the opposite effect. Figure 8 depicts the percentage of SAT-Clicks that moved up, or down, by the given number of positions. The x-axis represents the number of positions moved while the y-axis shows the percentage of SAT-Clicks moved by that many positions. The blue bars are used for specifying the promoted SAT-Clicks (good re-ranking), and the red bars are used to represent demoted (loss) cases.

One both testbeds, the great majority of changes are by one position. On the Bing dataset (top), 63% of SAT-Click moves are by one position, from which 46% are correctly promoted while 17% are incorrectly demoted – 2.7 win/loss ratio. On Yandex data (bottom) the win/loss ratio for one-position changes is 1.6 (43% promotion versus 26% demotion). On both datasets, about 90% of changes are by three positions or less and the total win/loss ratio is about 2 to 1.

Click history as re-ranking feature. R-Cube takes advantage of result repetition patterns in session history and uses them for re-ranking. In contrast, ClickHistory is based on aggregated click statistics across all users. Here, we investigate whether combining these two signals would lead to further improvements. Table 4 includes the results of this analysis on the Bing and Yandex datasets where we train a ranker with both ClickHistory and R-cube features for comparison. The original performance numbers for R-cube from Tables 2 and 3 are added as reference. As expected, the results show that combining short-term session repetition and

Table 4: The impact of adding *historical clicks* to R-cube on MRR. All differences compared to the default baseline are statistically significant ($P < 0.01$).

Model	MRR		MAP		
R-cube	-	(▲3.4%)	-	(▲7.1%)	Bing
+ historical clicks	-	(▲3.5%)	-	(▲7.2%)	
Default	0.696		0.536		Yandex
R-cube	0.711	(▲2.1%)	0.553	(▲3.2%)	
+ historical clicks	0.716	(▲2.9%)	0.559	(▲4.2%)	

Table 5: Evaluation results based on relevance labels using the subset of Yandex testing data for queries with relevance judgements present. Except for Personal Navigation, all differences compared to the default baseline are statistically significant ($P < 0.01$).

Model	DCG@3	DCG@10
Default	5.5	7.1
Personal Nav. [32]	5.5	7.1
ClickHistory	5.4	7.0
R-cube	5.4	7.0

long-term aggregate history features improves performance even further. The gains on the Yandex testbed are more noticeable. This is consistent with the trends observed earlier in Tables 2 and 3 that suggested that the ClickHistory features were relatively more effective on the Yandex dataset.

Relevance-based Evaluation. In our experiments so far, we have only focused on click-based and personalized evaluation. The Yandex dataset provides binary relevance judgements for a subset of query-result-region triples, which allows us to evaluate using typical non-personalized relevance metrics. Note that clicks are inherently specific to each user and many of our improvements are due to users' personal feedback based on what they have already seen. Judges were not asked what should change in a ranking if a user previously skips or clicks particular results, hence we do not expect to see large relevance improvements here. However, we do need to validate that re-ranking does not tend to demote many relevant documents for later queries.

We filter the sessions in our Yandex testing dataset to only include queries for which have at least one result judged as relevant. We use the R-cube model learned based on click preference labels explained earlier to do full re-ranking of the results for all queries in the testing set. The DCG [19] results in Table 5 show that R-cube does not substantially degrade the ranking quality in terms of relevance metrics (although the 1.8% and 1.4% drops in DCG@3 and DCG@10 are statistically significant by the t-test). Since significance may relate to large sample sizes, we measured effect size with Cohen's d and found that all $d \leq 0.04$, suggesting almost no effect. Overall, these results are encouraging as they show that although R-cube is trained towards a click-based metric, the impact on relevance metrics is minimal.

A-B test on live traffic. We performed a second evaluation of R-cube using interleaving whereby results from different

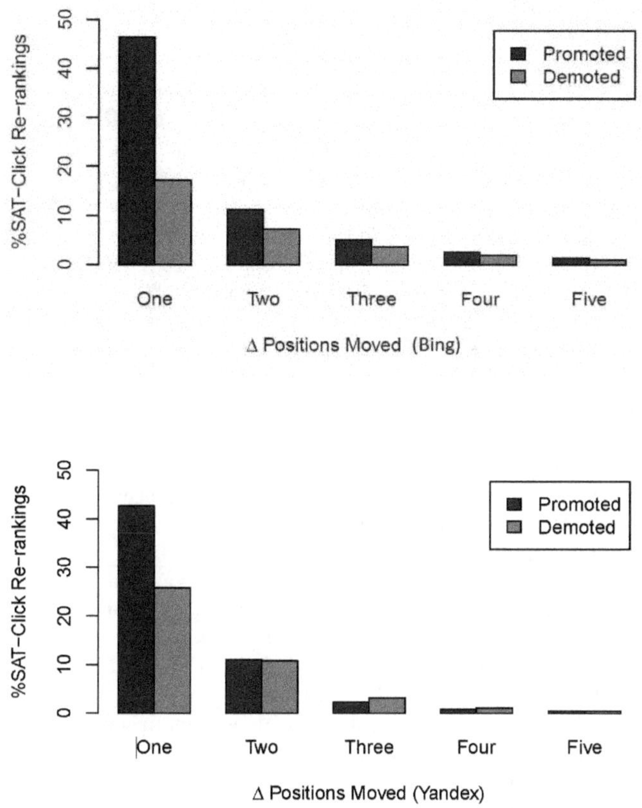

Figure 8: The distribution of re-ranked SAT-Click results with respect to their original positions on the Bing (top) and Yandex (bottom) datasets. The x-axis shows the number of positions moved and the y-axis represent the percentage of re-ranked SAT-Clicks that fall into that category. The blue bars show cases where as SAT-Click result was promoted (good re-ranking), while the red bars denote cases where the SAT-Click result was demoted (loss) with respect to its original position.

rankers are interwoven [24]. The results produced by re-ranking the top-10 Web results based on R-cubed scores were interleaved with those produced by a current commercial ranker and shown to a small, randomly selected, fraction of users of the Bing search engine. The Team Draft interleaving algorithm [24] was used, randomly allocating each result position to R-cube or the baseline. Whenever a user clicked on a result, the click was credited to the approach that had selected that result for that position. For each query, the number of clicks credited to each ranker was compared, with the ranker with more clicks receiving credit for the query (unless there was a tie due to an equal number of clicks). The random allocation of positions to rankers ensures that Team Draft interleaving produces an unbiased preference for one of the two alternatives (or a tie) [24].

We performed this evaluation for five days in June 2012, presenting the interleaved ranking for approximately 370,000 queries. We found that when the two rankers differed at or above the clicked rank, the R-cubed ranking was preferred for 53.8% of queries, and the baseline was preferred for 46.2% of queries. This preference is statistically significantly different from 50% ($p<0.001$) using a binomial sign test. The two rankers differed by the clicked position for 5.8% of queries, and the baseline and R-cubed returned a different top result for 4.5% of queries. We note that differences in rank order between R-cubed and the baseline occurred for roughly one third of queries, however Web search users predominantly click on higher-position results thus the fraction of queries affected is small. Overall, the results from live traffic indicate a statistically significant user preference for the ranker which is enhanced by R-cube features.

6. CONCLUSIONS

In this paper, we observed that the same results are often shown to users multiple times during search sessions. We showed that there are a number of effects at play, which can be leveraged to improve information retrieval performance. In particular, previously skipped results are much less likely to be clicked, and previously clicked results may or may not be re-clicked depending on other factors of the session.

We presented a number of features and a learning framework that targets the repeated results in the session for re-ranking. We conducted our experiments over query logs of two large commercial search engines (one proprietary and on publicly-available, for repeatability) and demonstrated that R-cube outperforms our experimental baselines. We showed that combining the long-term click-statistic signals in our re-ranking model increased the gains further, and also reported that the overall impact of re-ranking according to non-personalized relevance metrics is minimal. Although the R-cube model was optimized for personal, click-based judgements, demonstrating that it does not harm general relevance in the process is also important. In addition, we also performed an online interleaving analysis on the live traffic of a commercial search engine, and the results suggested a significant user preference towards the ranker enhanced by R-cube features versus the default production ranker that did not have these features.

Overall, our findings demonstrate the utility of the R-cube approach via multiple evaluation methods. It is clear from these findings that modeling different aspects of repetition (not just clicks, but also misses and skips), as well as other contextual features such as query similarity, are important in leveraging repetition and the behaviors associated with it. Future work will consider richer feature sets and long-term repetition of search results in, for example, cross-session search tasks. In addition, it would be interesting to explore repetition in other datasets such as those released with the TREC session track.[7]

7. REFERENCES

[1] E. Agichtein, E. Brill, and S. T. Dumais. Improving web search ranking by incorporating user behavior information. In *Proc. SIGIR*, pages 19–26, 2006.

[2] E. Agichtein, E. Brill, S. T. Dumais, and R. Ragno. Learning user interaction models for predicting web search result preferences. In *Proc. SIGIR*, 2006.

[7] `http://ir.cis.udel.edu/sessions`

[3] P. Bennett, F. Radlinski, R. White, and E. Yilmaz. Inferring and using location metadata to personalize web search. In *Proc. SIGIR*, pages 135–144, 2011.

[4] P. N. Bennett, R. W. White, W. Chu, S. T. Dumais, P. Bailey, F. Borisyuk, and X. Cui. Modeling the impact of short- and long-term behavior on search personalization. In *Proc. SIGIR*, pages 185–194, Portland, OR, 2012.

[5] C. Burges, R. Ragno, and Q. Le. Learning to rank with non-smooth cost functions. In *Proc. NIPS*, 2006.

[6] C. J. C. Burges, K. M. Svore, P. N. Bennett, A. Pastusiak, and Q. Wu. Learning to rank using an ensemble of lambda-gradient models. *JMLR*, 14:25–35, 2011.

[7] O. Chapelle and Y. Zhang. A dynamic bayesian network click model for web search ranking. In *Proc. WWW*, pages 1–10, 2009.

[8] A. Cockburn, S. Greenberg, S. Jones, B. Mckenzie, and M. Moyle. Improving web page revisitation: Analysis, design and evaluation. *IT & Society*, 1(3):159–183, 2003.

[9] K. Collins-Thompson, P. N. Bennett, R. W. White, S. de la Chica, and D. Sontag. Personalizing web search results by reading level. In *Proc. CIKM*, pages 403–412, Glasgow, UK, 2011.

[10] N. Craswell, O. Zoeter, M. Taylor, and B. Ramsey. An experimental comparison of click position-bias models. In *Proc. WSDM*, pages 87–94, 2008.

[11] M. Daoud, L. Tamine-Lechani, M. Boughanem, and B. Chebaro. A session based personalized search using an ontological user profile. In *Proc. SOC*, 2009.

[12] Z. Dou, R. Song, and J. R. Wen. A large-scale evaluation and analysis of personalized search strategies. In *Proc. WWW*, pages 581–590, 2007.

[13] G. E. Dupret and C. Liao. A model to estimate intrinsic document relevance from the clickthrough logs of a web search engine. In *Proc. WSDM*, pages 181–190, 2010.

[14] G. E. Dupret and B. Piwowarski. A user browsing model to predict search engine click data from past observations. In *Proc. SIGIR*, pages 331–338, 2008.

[15] S. Fox, K. Karnawat, M. Mydland, S. Dumais, and T. White. Evaluating implicit measures to improve web search. *ACM TOIS*, 23:147–168, 2005.

[16] F. Guo, C. Liu, A. Kannan, T. Minka, M. Taylor, Y.-M. Wang, and C. Faloutsos. Click chain model in web search. In *Proc. WWW*, pages 11–20, 2009.

[17] F. Guo, C. Liu, and Y. M. Wang. Efficient multiple-click models in web search. In *Proc. WSDM*, pages 124–131, 2009.

[18] B. J. Jansen, A. Spink, C. Blakely, and S. Koshman. Defining a session on web search engines: Research articles. *JASIST*, 58(6):862–871, Apr. 2007.

[19] K. Järvelin and J. Kekäläinen. Cumulated gain-based evaluation of IR techniques. *ACM TOIS*, 20(4):422–446, 2002.

[20] T. Joachims. Optimizing search engines using clickthrough data. In *Proc. KDD*, pages 132–142, 2002.

[21] T. Joachims, L. Granka, B. Pan, H. Hembrooke, F. Radlinski, and G. Gay. Evaluating the accuracy of implicit feedback from clicks and query reformulations in web search. *ACM TOIS*, 25(2), 2007.

[22] N. Matthijs and F. Radlinski. Personalizing web search using long term browsing history. In *Proc. WSDM*, pages 25–34, 2011.

[23] F. Radlinski and T. Joachims. Query chains: Learning to rank from implicit feedback. In *Proc. KDD*, pages 239–248, 2005.

[24] F. Radlinski, M. Kurup, and T. Joachims. How does clickthrough data reflect retrieval quality? In *Proc. CIKM*, pages 43–52, 2008.

[25] M. Sanderson and S. Dumais. Examining repetition in user search behavior. In *Proc. ECIR*, 2007.

[26] P. Serdyukov, N. Craswell, and G. Dupret. Wscd 2012: workshop on web search click data 2012. In *Proc. WSDM*, pages 771–772, 2012.

[27] X. Shen, B. Tan, and C. Zhai. Context-sensitive information retrieval using implicit feedback. In *Proc. SIGIR*, pages 43–50, 2005.

[28] B. Tan, X. Shen, and C. Zhai. Mining long-term search history to improve search accuracy. In *Proc. KDD*, pages 718–723, 2006.

[29] L. Tauscher and S. Greenberg. How people revisit web pages: Empirical findings and implications for the design of history systems. *International Journal of Human-Computer Studies*, 47(1):97–137, 1997.

[30] J. Teevan, E. Adar, R. Jones, and M. Potts. Information re-retrieval: Repeat queries in yahoo's logs. In *Proc. SIGIR*, pages 151–158, 2007.

[31] J. Teevan, S. T. Dumais, and E. Horvitz. Personalizing search via automated analysis of interests and activities. In *Proc. SIGIR*, pages 449–456, 2005.

[32] J. Teevan, D. Liebling, and G. R. Geetha. Understanding and predicting personal navigation. In *Proc. WSDM*, 2011.

[33] S. Tyler and J. Teevan. Large scale query log analysis of re-finding. In *Proc. WSDM*, 2010.

[34] K. Wang, N. Gloy, and X. Li. Inferring search behaviors using partially observable markov (pom) model. In *Proc. WSDM*, pages 211–220, 2010.

[35] K. Wang, T. Walker, and Z. Zheng. Pskip: estimating relevance ranking quality from web search clickthrough data. In *Proc. KDD*, pages 1355–1364, 2009.

[36] R. White, P. Bailey, and L. Chen. Predicting user interests from contextual information. In *Proc. SIGIR*, pages 363–370, 2009.

[37] R. White, P. Bennett, and S. Dumais. Predicting short-term interests using activity-based search context. In *Proc. CIKM*, pages 1009–1018, 2010.

[38] Q. Wu, C. Burges, K. Svore, and J. Gao. Adapting boosting for information retrieval measures. *Journal of Information Retrieval*, 13:254–270, 2009.

[39] B. Xiang, D. Jiang, J. Pei, X. Sun, E. Chen, and H. Li. Context-aware ranking in web search. In *Proc. SIGIR*, pages 451–458, 2010.

[40] Y. Zhang, W. Chen, D. Wang, and Q. Yang. User-click modeling for understanding and predicting search-behavior. In *Proc. KDD*, pages 1388–96, 2011.

Addressing Cold-Start in App Recommendation: Latent User Models Constructed from Twitter Followers

Jovian Lin[1,2] Kazunari Sugiyama[1] Min-Yen Kan[1,2] Tat-Seng Chua[1,2]
[1]School of Computing, National University of Singapore, Singapore
[2]Interactive and Digital Media Institute, National University of Singapore, Singapore
jovian.lin@gmail.com
{sugiyama,kanmy,chuats}@comp.nus.edu.sg

ABSTRACT

As a tremendous number of mobile applications (apps) are readily available, users have difficulty in identifying apps that are relevant to their interests. Recommender systems that depend on previous user ratings (*i.e.*, collaborative filtering, or CF) can address this problem for apps that have sufficient ratings from past users. But for apps that are newly released, CF does not have any user ratings to base recommendations on, which leads to the *cold-start* problem.

In this paper, we describe a method that accounts for nascent information culled from Twitter to provide relevant recommendation in such cold-start situations. We use Twitter handles to access an app's Twitter account and extract the IDs of their Twitter-followers. We create *pseudo-documents* that contain the IDs of Twitter users interested in an app and then apply latent Dirichlet allocation to generate latent groups. At test time, a target user seeking recommendations is mapped to these latent groups. By using the transitive relationship of latent groups to apps, we estimate the probability of the user liking the app. We show that by incorporating information from Twitter, our approach overcomes the difficulty of cold-start app recommendation and significantly outperforms other state-of-the-art recommendation techniques by up to 33%.

Categories and Subject Descriptors

H.3.3 [**Information Search and Retrieval**]: Information filtering, Search process

General Terms

Algorithms, Experimentation, Performance

Keywords

Recommender systems, Collaborative filtering, Cold-start problem, Mobile apps, Latent user models, Twitter

1. INTRODUCTION

Mobile applications (apps) for smartphones are soaring in popularity and creating economic opportunities for app developers, companies, and marketers. At present, users are able to access a substantial number of apps via *App Stores*; furthermore, the selection available in app stores is growing rapidly as new apps are approved and released daily (Apple recently reported that more than 40 billion apps have been downloaded for its devices[1]). While this growth has provided users with a myriad of unique and useful apps, the sheer number of choices also makes it more difficult for users to find apps that are relevant to their interests.

Historically, recommender systems have been introduced to alleviate this type of information overload by helping users find relevant items (*i.e.*, apps). One effective and widely used recommender system technique, collaborative filtering (CF), employs user ratings to recommend items. However, CF is ineffective in the case of new apps as they have no prior ratings to base recommendations on. This is an important manifestation of the *cold-start* problem, in which the performance of CF systems suffers for items with few or no prior ratings. The only way for the systems to provide automatic recommendation is to either wait for sufficient ratings to be supplied by users—which will take some time—or use content-based filtering (CBF).

CBF algorithms seek to recommend items based on similar content. For apps, this would be the metadata such as textual descriptions and genre information. An obvious drawback of CBF is that the recommended items are similar to the user's previously-consumed items [23]. For example, if a user has only downloaded weather-related apps, CBF would recommend other apps that are related to weather. This lack of diversity results in unsatisfactory recommendations.

With the rise of social networking services (SNS), people broadcast and message friends, colleagues, and the general public about many different matters in a short and informal manner [25]. They do it often as the overhead of broadcasting such short messages is low. For instance, Twitter experienced several record-breaking events in 2012, such as having one million accounts created daily and having 175 million tweets sent out per day[2]. Additionally, SNS often include rich information about its users [33], such as posted user-generated content, user logs, and user-to-user connections (*e.g.*, Alice *follows* Bob).

People use SNS to talk about many subjects—including apps. An interesting possibility thus arises: Can we merge information

[1] App Store Tops 40 Billion Downloads with Almost Half in 2012. Retrieved Jan 10, 2013, from `http://goo.gl/fvND9`.

[2] 100 Fascinating Social Media Statistics and Figures From 2012. Retrieved Jan 10, 2013, from `http://goo.gl/IvSJW`.

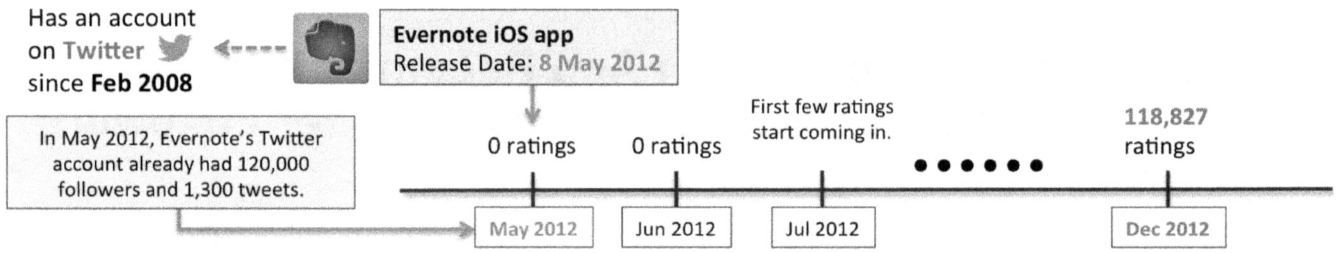

Figure 1: For two months since its release on the iTunes App Store, the Evernote app did not have any ratings. However, its Twitter account already had active tweets and followers. This shows that despite the cold-start, there is still information out there about the app, particularly on social networking services like Twitter.

mined from the rich data in SNS to enhance the performance of app recommendation? More formally, can we address the cold-start weaknesses of the proprietary user models of recommender systems (*e.g.*, the *user profiles* in an app store) by using nascent signals about apps from SNS (*e.g.*, the *user profiles* in Twitter)?

Through our case studies on the correlation and lag between SNS and formal reviews in app stores, we verified that the answer to this question is indeed "yes." How then, would one go about capturing and encoding data from SNS? Through our observation of app stores, we note that the descriptions of some apps contain references to their Twitter accounts; by having a Twitter account, an app's developer or the organization can interact with its users on Twitter and market themselves, such as announcing new apps or updates. For example, within the descriptions in its Google Play[3] and iTunes[4] app stores, the "Angry Birds Star Wars" app has a line that says "follow @angrybirds[5] on Twitter."

We also observed that app mentions in SNS can precede formal user ratings in app stores. This is important as it asserts that an early signal for app ranking (and thus recommendation) can be present in SNS. For example, Figure 1 shows that the "Evernote" app that was released in May 2012 had no ratings in the iTunes App Store for two months. It was only until July 2012 that the first few ratings started coming in. However, even before May 2012, Evernote's Twitter account[6] already had more than 120,000 followers and 1,300 tweets. We take advantage of this active yet indirect information that is present in Twitter and use it to alleviate the cold-start problem that besets newly released apps.

We integrate these findings into a novel approach to app recommendation that leverages on information from SNS (in specific, Twitter) to drive recommender systems in cold-start situations. By extracting *follower* information from an app's (official) Twitter account, we create a set of *pseudo-documents* that contains Twitter-follower information; these pseudo-documents are different from the standard documents written in natural language. We then utilize latent Dirichlet allocation (LDA) [6] to construct latent groups of "Twitter personalities" from the pseudo-documents. By harnessing information from the linked topology of Twitter accounts, we can infer a probability of how likely a target user will like a newly released app—even when it has no official ratings.

We conduct extensive experiments and compare the usage of Twitter-follower information with other types of features, such as app genres, app developers, and text from app descriptions. In order to show that our approach excels not because of the use of Twitter information alone, we compare our approach with a non-LDA technique that also employs the same information from Twitter. Finally, we combine our Twitter-follower feature with other features gleaned from app metadata through the use of gradient boosted trees (GBT) [10] and compare our approach with other state-of-the-art techniques. We show that our approach significantly outperforms these techniques.

[3] "Angry Birds Star Wars" in Google Play Store. Retrieved Jan 10, 2013, from http://goo.gl/DnOT1.

[4] "Angry Birds Star Wars" in iTunes App Store. Retrieved Jan 10, 2013, from http://goo.gl/9ov2K.

[5] http://twitter.com/angrybirds

[6] http://twitter.com/evernote

2. RELATED WORK

2.1 Addressing the Cold-Start

As the lack of ratings (*i.e.*, the cold-start) hinders the use of CF techniques [29], various alternatives have been employed to overcome the problem. For example, Zhou *et al.* [35] experimented with eliciting new user preferences by using decision trees with collaborative filtering. Moshfeghi *et al.* [21] proposed a method for combining content features such as semantic and emotion information with ratings information for the recommendation task. Liu *et al.* [19] identified representative users whose linear combinations of tastes are able to approximate other users. Likewise, many other works attempt to overcome the cold-start by finding radical ways of using proprietary user models and content.

2.2 Latent Factor Models

Another effective approach to the cold-start is to use latent factor models [17] that map users and items into a dense and reduced latent space that captures their most salient features. These models provide better recommendations than traditional neighborhood methods [11] as they reduce the level of sparsity and improve scalability [16]. Notable latent factor models include probabilistic latent semantic analysis (PLSA) [12], principal component analysis (PCA) [15], neural networks such as the restricted Boltzmann machine (RBM) [27], and singular vector decomposition (SVD) [30]. However, latent factor models have the following two major disadvantages in recommendation tasks: Firstly, the learned latent space is not easy to interpret. Secondly, many latent factor models rely on other user ratings, which may be lacking if the dataset is sparse.

2.3 Probabilistic Topic Models

In order to better understand learned latent groups, a few recent recommender systems employ probabilistic topic models. These topic models [5] discover a set of "topics" from a large collection of documents, where a topic is a distribution over terms that is biased around those associated under a single theme [31]. One of the widely used probabilistic topic models is latent Dirichlet allocation (LDA) [6], which can be seen as a dimensionality reduction technique like latent factor models, but with proper underlying generative probabilistic semantics that make sense for the type of data that it models.

Topic models provide an interpretable, low-dimensional representation of the documents [7] and may aid in the recommendation process. In recent works, Ramage *et al.* [24] used a variant of LDA to characterize microblogs in order to recommend which users to follow. They used both tweets and hashtags to help identify prominent topics for Twitter users, and used these topics to characterize the users. Wang and Blei [31] combined CF based on latent factor models and content based on probabilistic topic modeling to recommend scientific papers. LDA is also employed in [21], which we described in Section 2.1.

2.4 User Profiling Using Social Networks

With the emergence of social networks, recommender systems that rely on SNS have started to gain popularity. For example, Said *et al.* [26] explored movie recommendations based on user ratings and a social network (that comes with the user ratings data) where users can befriend one another. Jamali and Ester [14] incorporated trust propagation mechanisms into the matrix factorization technique in order to recommend items. We note that the aforementioned works rely on social networks within the dataset itself; that is, they do not rely on external SNS. As many domains and datasets do not incorporate a social network of their own, it is more realistic if we can glean useful data from an external and ubiquitous source, such as Twitter.

In addition, given an external social network, a standard way of profiling users is through the identification of *influence* [3], which can be measured in a number of ways. Kwak *et al.* [18] compared three different measures of influence on Twitter (number of followers, PageRank [22], and number of retweets) and found that the ranking of the most influential users differed depending on the measure. Similarly, Cha *et al.* [9] also compared three different measures of influence (number of followers, number of retweets, and number of mentions) and found that all three captured different perspectives of influence. We note that "following" information has generally been a popular indicator for measuring influence.

Our work differs from the ones mentioned in Section 2.1 in that instead of using proprietary user models and content, we use information from Twitter (*i.e.*, non-proprietary content from SNS) and construct latent groups of "Twitter personalities" to predict recommendations under the cold-start. Although textual features have generally been a popular source of alternative data to substitute for the lack of ratings—such that even state-of-the-art techniques (Section 2.2 and 2.3) are primarily dependent on—it is not a universal solution as not all domains contain reliable textual data. Additionally, as mentioned in Section 2.4, it is more realistic to rely on external SNS. Therefore, our work is unique in that it uses the "who *follows* whom" information on Twitter as its primary source of data, as textual features in the app domain are inherently noisy and unreliable (in contrast to the cases of movies or scholarly papers).

3. OUR APPROACH

We first explain the kind of problem we address. Then we describe the relation between apps and Twitter-followers, and how we use them in our work. Next, we construct *pseudo-documents* and *pseudo-words* using data from users, apps, users' preferences, and Twitter-followers. Thereafter, we generate *latent groups* from the pseudo-documents, whereby a latent group represents the combined "interests" of various Twitter-followers. Finally, the set of latent groups is used as a crucial component of our algorithm to estimate the probability of a target user liking an app.

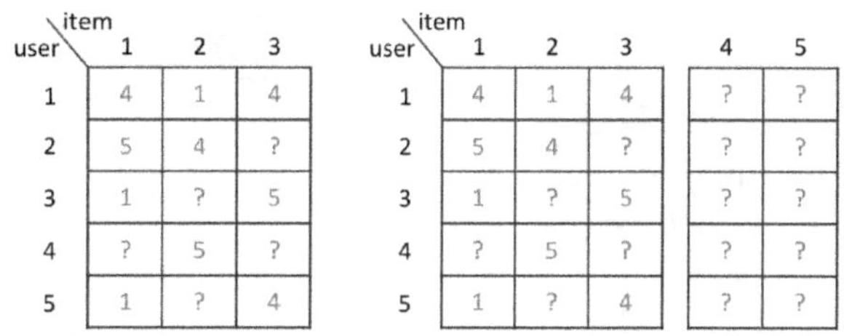

(a) In-matrix prediction (b) Out-of-matrix prediction

Figure 2: Difference between (a) in-matrix prediction and (b) out-of-matrix prediction.

3.1 Targeting the Cold-Start Problem

There are two types of cold-start problems in CF: in-matrix prediction and out-of-matrix prediction [31]. Figure 2(a) illustrates in-matrix prediction, which refers to the problem of recommending items that have been rated by at least one user in the system. This is the task that CF researchers have often addressed [8, 1, 13, 28, 34, 4, 27, 17].

On the other hand, Figure 2(b) illustrates out-of-matrix prediction, where newly released items (*e.g.*, items 4 and 5) have never been rated. Traditional CF algorithms cannot predict ratings of items in the out-of-matrix prediction as they rely on user ratings, which are unavailable in this scenario.

Our work focuses on this second, more challenging problem. Hereafter, we use "cold-start problem" to refer to "out-of-matrix prediction," for ease of reference.

3.2 Apps and their Twitter-Followers

Apps have textual descriptions displayed in their app store entries; some of these descriptions further contain links to the apps' official Twitter account (*i.e.*, *Twitter handle*). For example, the "Angry Birds" franchise contains a link to its Twitter handle (@angrybirds). From the handle, we can identify the IDs of Twitter-followers who follow the app. We note that by following an app's Twitter handle, the Twitter-followers subscribe to the tweets that are related to the particular app, which can be seen as an indicator of interest [9]. Figure 3 illustrates the relation between users, apps, and Twitter-followers. By using information from the apps' Twitter-followers, we can construct "latent personalities" from two sources of data: the app store and Twitter. Using these latent personalities, our algorithm is able to recommend newly released apps in the absence of ratings[7] as shown in Figure 2(b).

Given that an app has a set of Twitter-followers, our approach estimates the probability that user u—defined by his or her past ratings—likes app a that is *followed* by Twitter-follower t (*i.e.*, Twitter-follower t follows app a's Twitter account):

$$p(+|t, u), \qquad (1)$$

where "+" denotes the binary event that a user likes an app.

Furthermore, as an app is represented by a set of its Twitter-followers, it is necessary to aggregate the probability in Equation (1) over the various Twitter-followers of app a. This allows us to estimate the probability of how likely the target user will like the app:

$$p(+|a, u). \qquad (2)$$

[7]Note that although other types of information can be extracted from Twitter, such as the textual tweets and hashtags, we only focus on the Twitter-followers in this work as early experiments have shown that other types of information are noisy and potentially ambiguous.

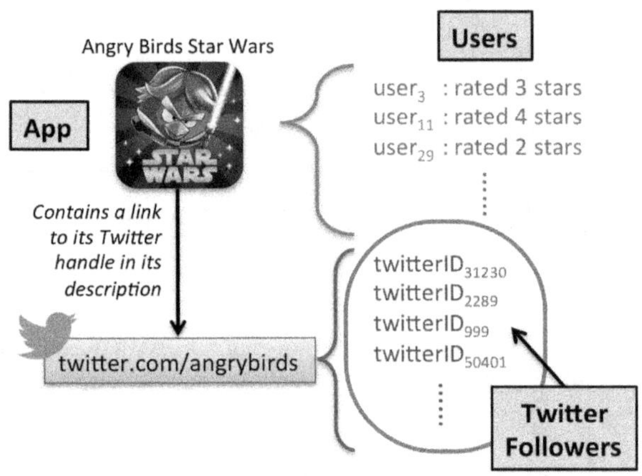

Figure 3: Instead of solely relying on the ratings of users, our approach also makes use of the Twitter IDs that *follow* the apps (red oval).

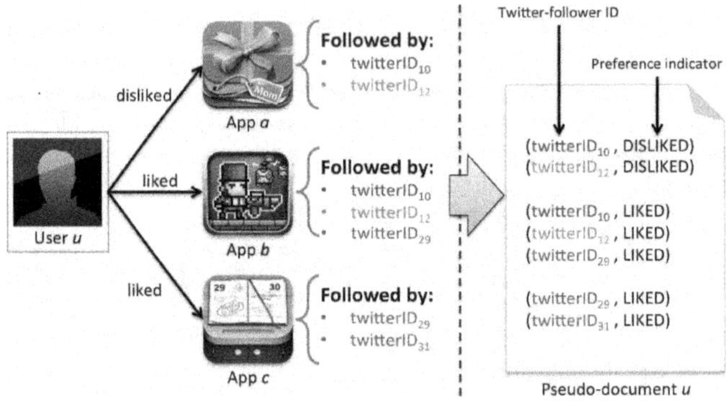

Figure 4: A *pseudo-document* is constructed based on information from a user, apps, Twitter-followers, and binary ("liked" or "disliked") preference indicators. A pseudo-document contains *pseudo-words*; each pseudo-word is represented as a *tuple* containing a Twitter-follower ID and a binary preference indicator.

3.3 Pseudo-Documents and Pseudo-Words

In order to estimate the probability $p(+|a, u)$ in Equation (2), we build upon latent Dirichlet allocation (LDA)—a generative probabilistic model for discovering latent semantics that has been mainly used on textual corpora. Given a set of textual documents, LDA generates a probability distribution over latent "topics" for each document in the corpus, where each topic is a distribution over words. Documents that have similar topics share the same latent topic distribution.

We adapt LDA for the purpose of collaborative filtering. As mentioned in Section 3.2, users download apps and apps may have Twitter-followers. Hence, user u and the Twitter-followers (of the apps that user u has downloaded) are analogous to a document and the words in the document, respectively. For the sake of clarity, we will call them *pseudo-documents* from now on as our "documents" actually do not contain natural language words in our work.

Drawing on the parallelism, we formally define the following terms:

- We first assume that user u likes app a, and app a has a set of Twitter-followers $\{t_1, \ldots, t_n\}$ following its Twitter handle.
- A *pseudo-document* represents user u. Because of this, we use u to represent both pseudo-document and user.
- A *pseudo-word* is a "word" in pseudo-document u that corresponds to the ID of a Twitter-follower t. If user u has liked the apps a_1, a_2, and a_3, the pseudo-document u will then contain all the IDs of the Twitter-followers that are following the Twitter handles of apps a_1, a_2, and a_3. Note that there may be duplicated *pseudo-words* as a Twitter-follower t may be following more than one app's Twitter handle.

However, the problem of only considering the "liked" apps is in that LDA will indirectly assign higher probabilities to apps that many users liked. In other words, LDA will indirectly give high probabilities to popular apps. For example, suppose that two apps are judged the same number of times. The probability given by LDA will rank the two apps in order of their probability to be "liked," which we desire. In contrast, if the first app has been judged by all the users and half of them liked the app, it will have the same probability as another app that was judged by only half of the users but liked all the time, which is undesirable.

To address this popularity problem, we incorporate the magnitude of negative information as it indirectly allows us to account for the frequency of the whole judging group (*i.e.*, "liked" apps + "disliked" apps = total apps). In addition, this solution allows user groups to not only reflect the Twitter-followers that appear in the apps that they like, but also in the apps that they dislike, thus providing richer information. We now formally define a pseudo-word:

- A *pseudo-word* is a "word" in pseudo-document u that contains the ID of a Twitter-follower t and its associated binary ("liked" or "disliked") preference indicator.

Figure 4 illustrates how a *pseudo-document* is constructed based on *pseudo-words*, which in turn are constructed based on the IDs of Twitter-followers and the binary preference indicators from users. Furthermore, in order to obtain the binary preferences, it is mandatory to convert the user ratings (*i.e.*, the 5-point Likert scale) into binary like/dislike indicators (see Section 4.2).

Note that the concept of pseudo-documents and pseudo-words does not apply exclusively to Twitter-followers; it can also be applied to other sources of information such as the app genres, app developers, and the words in the app descriptions. For example, instead of using the IDs of Twitter-followers, we can also construct pseudo-words based on the IDs of app developers. We focus on Twitter-followers as our goal is to assess the effectiveness of this new source of data. In Section 5.1, we will create different sets of pseudo-documents based on different features (*i.e.*, Twitter-followers, app genres, app developers, and words) and identify the most effective feature in the recommendation of apps.

3.4 Constructing Latent Groups

Given the set of pseudo-documents $\{u_1, \ldots, u_m\}$, LDA can generate a probability distribution over *latent groups* for each pseudo-document, where each latent group is represented as a distribution over Twitter-follower IDs and binary preference indicators. Figure 5 illustrates this framework.

By using the information on "which apps are followed by which Twitter-followers," we can estimate the probability of target user u liking app a by taking into account the IDs of the Twitter-followers following app a, and marginalizing over the different latent groups of pseudo-document u.

Formally speaking, given the set of tuples of pseudo-words $T_u = \{(t_1, d_1), \ldots, (t_n, d_n)\}$, where t_i and d_i are a Twitter-follower ID

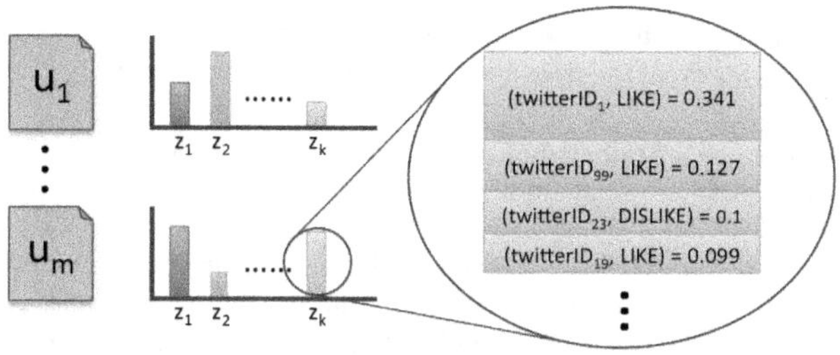

Figure 5: Given the set of pseudo-documents $\{u_1, \ldots, u_m\}$, LDA generates a probability distribution over *latent groups* for each pseudo-document, where each latent group z is represented as a distribution over pseudo-words. A pseudo-word is represented as a tuple containing a Twitter-follower ID and a binary preference indicator.

and its associated binary ("liked" or "disliked") preference indicator, respectively, we define LDA as a generative process that creates a series of tuples:

$$p(T_u|\alpha, \beta) = \int p(\theta|\alpha) \left(\prod_{i=1}^{n} \sum_{z=1}^{K} p(z|\theta) p(t_i, d_i|\beta_z) \right) d\theta,$$

where K is the number of latent groups, θ follows the Dirichlet distribution of hyper-parameters α, and the latent group z follows a multinomial distribution given by β_z. The model is fully specified by α and β_z for each possible latent group z. Those hyper-parameters are learned by maximizing the likelihood of the dataset.

The LDA model is used to compute the probability that the presence of a Twitter-follower t indicates that it is "liked" $(+)$ (or "disliked" $(-)$) by user u, given user u's past interaction T_u and the learned parameters α and β. Hence, we get the following equation:

$$\begin{aligned} p(\pm, t|u) &= p(\pm, t|T_u, \alpha, \beta) \\ &= \sum_{z \in Z} p(\pm, t|z) p(z|u), \end{aligned} \tag{3}$$

where Z is the set of latent groups, $p(\pm, t|z)$ is computed from the per-topic word distribution of LDA, and $p(z|u)$ is computed from the per-document topic distribution of LDA.

3.5 Estimation of the Probability of How Likely the Target User Will Like the App

Our approach is based on a simple "averaging" method where the probability of how likely the target user will like the app is the expectation of how the Twitter-followers like the app. Given a set of Twitter-followers T, the probability that user u likes app a is defined as follows:

$$\begin{aligned} p(+|a, u) &= \sum_{t \in T(a)} p(+, t|a, u) \\ &= \sum_{t \in T(a)} p(+|t, u) P(t|a), \end{aligned} \tag{4}$$

where $T(a)$ is the set of possible Twitter-followers following app a, in which we assume that: (i) Twitter-followers are examined one at a time to make a decision about whether an app is liked or disliked. In this case, t and t' are disjoint events whenever $t \neq t'$; (ii) when the Twitter-follower is known, the judgement does not depend on the app any more, *i.e.*, $p(+|t, a, u) = p(+|t, u)$; (iii) the fact that given a user and an app, there is no judgement involved, *i.e.*, $p(u, a) = p(u)p(a)$; (iv) the fact that an app has a given Twitter-follower is independent from the user, *i.e.*, $p(t|a, u) = p(t|a)$.

Equation (4) is then reduced to the estimation of two quantities:

1. the probability that user u likes app a given that app a has Twitter-follower t, *i.e.*, $p(+|t, u)$, and
2. the probability of considering Twitter-follower t given app a, *i.e.*, $p(t|a)$.

$p(+|t, u)$ is straightforward to estimate as it can be rewritten as:

$$p(+|t, u) = \frac{p(+, t|u)}{p(+, t|u) + p(-, t|u)},$$

where $p(+, t|u)$ and $p(-, t|u)$ are derived from LDA in Equation (3), which is the probability that Twitter-follower t occurs in an app that is liked (or disliked) by user u.

As for the probability $p(t|a)$, we explore the following two ways:

(I) Assume a uniform distribution over the various Twitter-followers present in app a

This framework is defined as follows:

$$p(t|a) = \begin{cases} \frac{1}{\#T(a)} & \text{if } t \text{ is a Twitter-follower of app } a \\ 0 & \text{otherwise,} \end{cases} \tag{5}$$

where $T(a)$ and $\#T(a)$ denote the set of Twitter-followers following app a and the set cardinality, respectively.

(II) Give more importance to influential Twitter-followers

In this alternative framework, we compute the influence of Twitter-followers by using TwitterRank [32]. Let $TR(t)$ be the TwitterRank score of Twitter-follower t. With that, for each Twitter-follower t, we retrieve its TwitterRank score and normalize it with the scores obtained by the other Twitter-followers following app a. That is:

$$p(t|a) = \begin{cases} \frac{TR(t)}{\sum_{t' \in T(a)} TR(t')} & \text{if } t \text{ is a Twitter-follower of app } a \\ 0 & \text{otherwise,} \end{cases} \tag{6}$$

where $T(a)$ denotes the set of Twitter-followers following app a.

Prior tests on our dataset have shown that there is no significant difference in performance between (I) and (II) above. This is because the Twitter-followers that we get (note that each latent group consists of Twitter-followers) are generally not prominent, influential people. Rather, they are the average users on Twitter. Therefore, even if we use TwitterRank, the influence of each Twitter-follower eventually converges into the uniform distribution. We thus adopt the uniform distribution defined by Equation (5) in our evaluation for its simplicity.

4. EVALUATION PRELIMINARIES

We preface our evaluation proper by detailing how we constructed our dataset, our settings for the dataset and the LDA model, and how we chose our evaluation metric.

4.1 Dataset

We constructed our dataset by crawling from Apple's iTunes App Store and Twitter during September to December 2012. The dataset consists of the following three elements:

1. *App Metadata.* These include an app's ID, title, description, genre, and its developer ID. The metadata is collected by first getting all the app IDs from the iTunes App Store, and then retrieving the metadata for each app via the iTunes Search API. The metadata is the source for the genre, developer, and word features mentioned at the end of Section 3.3.

2. *Ratings*. For each app, we built a separate crawler to retrieve its reviews from the iTunes App Store. A review contains the app's ID, its rating, the reviewer's ID, the subject, and the review comments. This is the source of the rating feature.

3. *Related Twitter IDs*. We used two methods to collect app-related Twitter IDs. The first way is to get the IDs that follow an app's Twitter account. We scanned through each app's description to identify its Twitter handle. For each app's Twitter handle, we used Twitter's API to search for every Twitter ID following its handle. The second method uses Twitter's Streaming API to receive tweets in real-time. To retrieve tweets that are related to apps, we only kept tweets that contain hyperlinks to apps in the iTunes App Store, and stored the Twitter IDs (who wrote the tweet) as well as the app IDs that were mentioned in the tweets.

Altogether, we collected 1,289,668 ratings for 7,116 apps (that have accounts on Twitter) from 10,133 users. The user-item ratings matrix has a sparsity of 98.2%. We also collected 5,681,197 unique Twitter IDs following the apps in our dataset. With respect to app ratings and the number of related Twitter-followers per app, we restrict that each user gives at least 10 ratings and each Twitter ID is related to at least 5 apps, respectively. On average, each user has rated 26 apps—ranging from a minimum of 10 rated apps to a maximum of 271.

4.2 Experimental Settings

In order to train the LDA model, we require binary relevance judgements to convert the user ratings to binary preference indicators, as well as two sets of hyper-parameters—namely, the number of latent groups K and the priors α and β.

We performed per-user normalization of the 5-point Likert scale ratings when converting them to the binary like/dislike values required by our LDA application. This is because the average rating for different users can vary significantly [16].

Let $r_{avg(u)}$ and $r_{u,a}$ be user u's average rating among all apps and user u's rating for app a, respectively. The normalized rating is thus $r_{n(u,a)} = r_{u,a} - r_{avg(u)}$, where if $r_{n(u,a)} \geq 0$, the rating is converted to a "like" (+), or "dislike" (−), otherwise.

We set the priors α and β as proposed in [20]. The number of latent groups has a crucial influence on the performance of the LDA approach. We used the likelihood over a held out set of training data to find the relevant number of latent groups. We tried several settings for K (*i.e.*, the number of latent groups), namely 10, 20, 35, 50, 80, 100, 120, 150, and 200. The final number of latent groups was selected by maximizing the likelihood of observations over the development set.

In order to simulate the cold-start, we selected 10% of the apps which were then the held out set for all users (*i.e.*, we removed their ratings in the training set). Therefore, each user has the same set of within-fold apps and we can guarantee that none of these apps are in the training set of any user.

We performed 10-fold cross validation where in each fold, we used 70% of the apps to train the LDA model, 20% to identify the number of latent groups for LDA (*i.e.*, the development set), and the remaining 10% as test data.

4.3 Evaluation Metric

Our system outputs M apps for each test user, which are sorted by their probability of liking. We evaluate the algorithms based on which of these apps were actually downloaded and liked (*i.e.*, the normalized rating of the test user).

This methodology leads to two possible evaluation metrics: precision and recall. However, a missing rating in training is ambiguous as it may either mean that the user is not interested in the app (negative), or that the user does not know about the app (truly missing). This makes it difficult to accurately compute precision [31]. But since the known ratings are true positives, we feel that recall is a more pertinent measure as it only considers the positively rated apps within the top M, *i.e.*, a high recall with a lower M will be a better system. We thus chose Recall@M as our primary evaluation metric. Let n_u and N_u represent the number of apps the user likes in the top M and the total number of apps the user likes, respectively. Recall@M is then defined as their ratio: n_u/N_u. We compare systems using average recall, where the average is computed over all test users.

5. EXPERIMENTS

As our approach specifically attempts to address the cold-start, we work on the specific scenario when a new set of apps is released and users have yet to rate them (shown in Figure 2(b)). The goal of our experiments is to answer the following research questions:

RQ1 How does the performance of the Twitter-followers feature compare with other features, such as the app genres, app developers, and words in the app descriptions? Can we obtain better recommendation accuracy by combining them?

RQ2 How does our proposed method compare with other state-of-the-art techniques?

RQ3 Do the latent groups make any sense? If so, what can we learn from them?

5.1 Comparison of Features (RQ1)

We benchmark how the signal from Twitter-followers affects performance in comparison to other sources of data. We compare the Twitter-followers feature (hereafter, T) with the other features: app genres (G), app developers (D), and words in the app descriptions (W). To perform this comparison in a fair manner, for each of these four features, we constructed a set of pseudo-documents that contains a set of *feature-related* pseudo-words (see Section 3.3).

Additionally, we assessed the effectiveness of these features in combination; we combine multiple features (*i.e.*, Twitter-followers, genres, developers, and words) through the use of gradient boosted trees (GBT) [10]. We also performed ablation testing where we removed features from the combined feature set to determine the importance of each feature. The features given to GBT are a set of probabilities defined by Equation (4). In GBT, we set the maximum number of trees and maximum tree depth to 2000 and 3, respectively, and used the least-squares regression as a cost function.

Results. Figure 6 shows the results of the first experiment, which compares the overall performance between features (words (W), developers (D), genres (G), Twitter-followers (T), and all features (All) combined) when we vary the number of returned apps $M = 20, \ldots, 200$. Fixing $M = 100$, we ablated individual features from our combined method and show the results in Table 1.

The results are quite consistent. In the overall comparison over all ranges of M, the individual feature of Twitter-followers gives the best individual performance, followed by genres, developers, and words in the app descriptions. From the combination and ablation study in Table 1, we see that all features are necessary for the optimal results. Matching the results in Figure 6, Table 1 also shows that the removal of the best (worst) individual features leads to the corresponding largest (smallest) drop in recall.

It may be surprising that the developer (D) and genre (G) features are more effective than words in the app description (W).

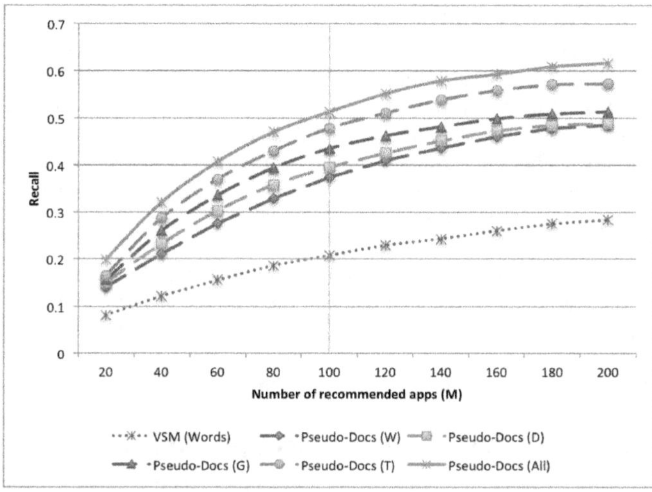

Figure 6: Recall obtained by different individual features (dashed lines), as well as our method that combines all features (solid). The baseline vector space model (VSM), using the app description word vocabulary is also shown (dotted). The vertical line marks model performance at $M = 100$ (*cf.* Table 1).

Table 1: Recall levels in our feature ablation study at $M = 100$. TGDW and individual feature (T, G, D, W) performances in Figure 6 are also shown.

Feature	R@100
All features (TGDW)	**0.513**
All, excluding Twitter-followers (GDW)	0.452
All, excluding Genres (TDW)	0.491
All, excluding Developers (TGW)	0.498
All, excluding Words (TGD)	0.507
Twitter-followers (T)	0.478
Genres (G)	0.435
Developers (D)	0.395
Words (W)	0.373

We observe that users may favor developer brands; possible causes could be that the user recognizes the brand, or that the apps themselves may promote sister apps that are made by the same developer. In addition, some apps complement one another. For example, "Google Chrome," "Gmail," and "Google Maps" form a complementary set. Also, the genres of apps may correlate with download behavior. Figure 7 shows the distribution of app genres, and indeed we observe that the "Games" genre dominates the distribution. This indicates that users often download apps that belong to the "Games" genre.

From a practical standpoint, the most straightforward way to recommend apps in a cold-start would be to use the textual descriptions in a content-based filtering system, as in our (W) system. But it performs the worst among the four individual features. Why do words in app descriptions (W) perform the least well?

Carrying out a more detailed inspection, we find that app descriptions do not give informative hints about the app's role; rather, they are more focused on self-promotion as many apps boast about the reviews that they have received in their app descriptions. Figure 8 is a screenshot of an app description that demonstrates this fact. In addition, according to [2], users pay more attention to screenshots instead of descriptions, which suggests that the information from

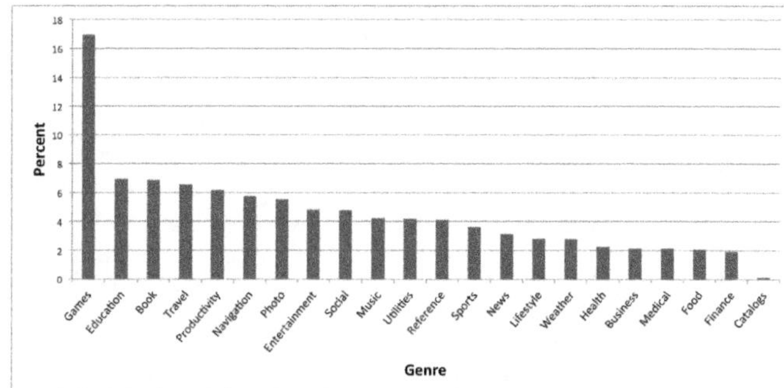

Figure 7: Distribution of app genres within our dataset.

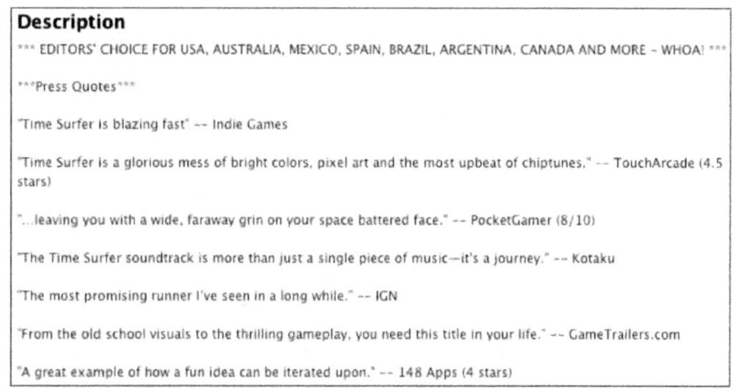
Description

*** EDITORS' CHOICE FOR USA, AUSTRALIA, MEXICO, SPAIN, BRAZIL, ARGENTINA, CANADA AND MORE - WHOA! ***

Press Quotes

"Time Surfer is blazing fast" -- Indie Games

"Time Surfer is a glorious mess of bright colors, pixel art and the most upbeat of chiptunes." -- TouchArcade (4.5 stars)

"...leaving you with a wide, faraway grin on your space battered face." -- PocketGamer (8/10)

"The Time Surfer soundtrack is more than just a single piece of music—it's a journey." -- Kotaku

"The most promising runner I've seen in a long while." -- IGN

"From the old school visuals to the thrilling gameplay, you need this title in your life." -- GameTrailers.com

"A great example of how a fun idea can be iterated upon." -- 148 Apps (4 stars)

Figure 8: A screenshot of an app description that illustrates why word features may not be effective as it largely boasts about endorsements received.

app descriptions is not as useful. This result also further explains why text-dependent baselines such as CTR and LDA did not perform much better (*cf.* the next section on RQ2).

Features aside, we also assessed whether our use of the LDA-based pseudo-document method is an important factor in recall performance. We compared a straightforward use of the same data with a standard vector space model (VSM) where we used the same app description words (W) to build a vector of standard $tf.idf$ weighted words to represent each app.

Figure 6 also shows this result in the bottom two lines. We see that the pseudo-document use of words (W) greatly outperforms the VSM-based version (VSM). A two-tailed t-test at $M = 100$ shows that the improvement is statistically significant ($p < 0.01$). This validates our LDA-based pseudo-document approach.

5.2 Comparison Against Baselines (RQ2)

As we focus on the cold-start problem, we did not consider other well-known recommender techniques that require user ratings, such as matrix factorization or latent factor models. We compare our approach with four baselines. The first two baselines are VSM-based—the first is the app description-based VSM recapped from RQ1 (*i.e.*, "VSM (Words)") while the second uses the IDs of Twitter-followers as its vocabulary (*i.e.*, "VSM (Twitter)"). The VSM (Twitter) baseline evaluates whether our LDA-based approach of using the Twitter-follower data betters the simpler VSM method. The third baseline is the LDA model, which is equivalent to using our pseudo-documents model on words in app descriptions. Lastly, as a much stronger baseline, we show the performance of a re-implementation of Wang and Blei's [31] collaborative topic regression (CTR) model—a state-of-the-art CF algorithm that can also make predictions in cold-start scenarios.

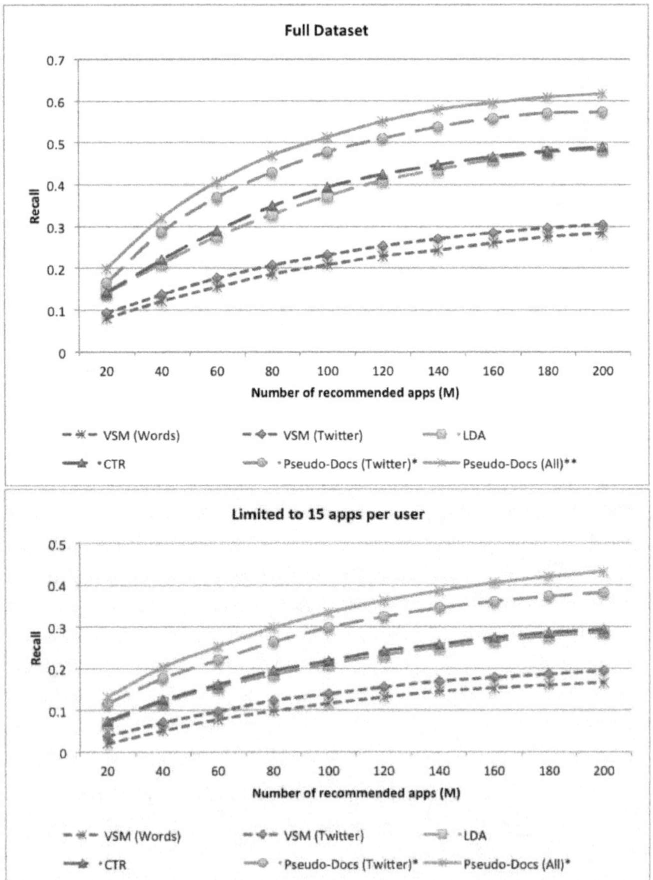

Figure 9: Recall varying the number of recommendations on the full (top) and sparse (bottom) datasets. "*" and "" denote statistically significant improvements over the best baseline (CTR) at $p < 0.05$ and $p < 0.01$, respectively.**

Additionally, in order to study the impact of sparsity on our models, in a separate experimental condition, we randomly removed some ratings from the training set so that the maximum number of rated apps per user was 15, which represents a sparser environment.

Results. Figure 9 plots the results of this set of experiments when we vary the number of returned apps $M = 20, \ldots, 200$. We observe that our approach that combines various pseudo-documents using GBT consistently and significantly outperforms other models (at $p < 0.01$ on the full dataset), particularly the CTR model that is the best among all baselines. This shows that we can achieve significant improvement in recommendation accuracy by integrating multiple sources of information. We also observe that our model of using pseudo-documents with Twitter data alone (*i.e.*, "Pseudo-Docs (Twitter)" in Figure 9) outperforms other models. This validates our observation that Twitter is indeed a good source of information to address the cold-start in app recommendation. It also indirectly points out that the textual features are less effective in the app domain, which is obvious from the performances of the CTR and LDA models that solely rely on textual data. We also note that the performance of CTR is fairly similar to LDA. This is due to the fact that the matrix-factorization component of CTR cannot perform recommendation in the cold-start. Therefore, like LDA, its recommendation is based entirely on content.

We also observe that between the two models that only use Twitter features (*i.e.*, "VSM (Twitter)" and "Pseudo-Docs (Twitter)"), our model significantly outperforms the VSM model. This again validates our earlier findings that our method's performance is not just due to the use of new data, but also how we make use of it.

Another important observation is that under a sparser cold-start environment where we limit our training data to 15 apps per user at maximum, there is an overall drop in recall, which is expected. However, we note that our model (both using Twitter feature alone and multi-features) still outperforms all of the baselines. This indicates that using Twitter features is more robust than using app descriptions under sparse conditions, as the IDs of the Twitter-followers are independent from the apps—misleading or absent app descriptions do not directly influence the Twitter-followers.

5.3 Analysis of Latent Groups (RQ3)

We use LDA and the notion of Twitter users as pseudo-words to achieve good recall. A natural question to ask is whether the latent groups discovered by LDA (from the individual features of Twitter-followers, genres, and developers) have any meaning. We observe interesting points for the developer (D) and Twitter-follower (T) features.

For the developer feature, in most latent groups, the developers who have received a substantial number of ratings for all their apps are different from the independent ("indie") developers. This is due to the fact that these developers usually have apps that users "liked," whereas the indie developers sometimes have apps that users "disliked" as well as apps that users "liked." This coincides with our hypothesis about brand loyalty, as the developers with a substantial number of ratings either have created a large number of apps (such as EA Games) or have created a small number of well-received apps (such as the apps by Google). We also observe that the clustered developers are classified into the same genre or strong competitors like Facebook and Twitter.

In order to understand why Twitter-followers work best, we scrutinized the latent groups discovered by LDA at the optimal performance point of $K = 120$. Each group consists of Twitter-followers; and each Twitter-follower follows at least 5 apps in our dataset. We then manually visited the Twitter pages of the top 5 Twitter-followers in each of the 120 latent groups, and then verified their profile descriptions and their latest tweets. We observe that more than 95% of these Twitter-followers exhibit consistent interest in apps. This shows that our approach accurately distinguishes between Twitter users who have implicit/explicit interest in apps and regular Twitter users. Our approach assigns low probabilities to Twitter users who have little or no correlation to apps, effectively filtering out their influence as noise.

To illustrate the quality of the latent groups, we performed an additional level of micro-analysis. We selected the 3 most important latent groups among the 120 groups based on the expectation of the probability of each latent group over the set of training data (*i.e.*, the pseudo-documents), along with their corresponding top 5 Twitter individuals' public profile (Figure 10). The top-most row in Figure 10 shows the top genres and examples of apps in each of the top 3 latent groups. We see that the apps in each group coincides with the Twitter profiles of the top 5 individuals in the same group. Latent Group 1 is composed of family-oriented Twitter users who also download family-oriented apps. Such a latent group would be difficult to describe if we were to use genres alone, as this group consists of a non-discrete mix of children-friendly apps. In Latent Group 2, we see that this group consists of professional music-creation apps, which also coincides with the type of Twitter users who are either actual musicians or people interested

Latent Group 1	Latent Group 2	Latent Group 3
Top genres: • Books (45%) • Education (33%) • Games (13%) **Example apps:** • The Cat in the Hat (Books) • Christmas Cutie (Books) • Happy Earth Day, Dear Planet (Books) • Friendly Shapes (Education) • There's No Place Like Space! (Education) • Pasta Crazy Chef (Games) • Gingerbread Dress (Games)	**Top genres:** • Music (92%) **Example apps:** • BeatStudio (Music) • AmpKit+ (Music) • GuitarStudio (Music) • Everyday Looper (Music) • Mixr DJ (Music) • KORG iELECTRIBE (Music) • KORG iPolysix (Music) • Pro Metronome (Music) • Chord Detector (Music)	**Top genres:** • Games (77%) • Photo & Video (12%) **Example apps:** • Another World 20th Anniversary (Games) • Paper Monsters (Games) • Stickman Cliff Diving (Games) • Lili (Games) • Snoopy's Street Fair (Games) • Gizmonauts (Games) • InstaBooth+ (Photo & Video) • ArtStudio for iPad (Photo & Video)
Nosy Crow Apps (twitter.com/nosycrowapps) Nosy Crow creates children's books and apps. You may know our 3-D Fairytale apps, The Three Little Pigs & Cinderella.	Derek Jones (twitter.com/MusicInclusive) Indie music publishing label, studio & brand. Blues&Rock, Progressive&Funk, Jazz&Fusion, Alternate&Christian, Classical, Education & a lot in-between too!	Sarah Thomson (twitter.com/SarahLuvsVGames) Video games warrior, lover of life, eternal student of the universe, drinker of Kombucha, Baroness of PlayStation Mobile.
The iMums (twitter.com/TheiMums) Four mums dedicated to reviewing apps and technology products for children to help educate their parents about the variety available. Loads of giveaways too!	Chip Boaz (twitter.com/iosmusicandyou) I'm a musician based in the San Francisco Bay Area with an interest in using my iPad, iPhone, & iPod to make music. Follow my iOS adventures @ iOS Music And You	JasonLeeNester (twitter.com/JasonNester) I am a Multimedia developer working at Kent State University! I also do art services for the game industry as well as run a small indie game company, True Media.
Mums with Apps (twitter.com/momswithapps) Supporting family-friendly developers seeking to promote quality apps for kids and families.	Dave Gibson (twitter.com/MicroTrackdB) Creator of MicroTrack dB, a music making app for iOS and Samsung bada. Musician, writer, audio engineer and synth nerd. http://www.facebook.com/microtrackdb	Agalag iOS Games (twitter.com/AgalagGames) Agalag Games is an independent iOS game studio. Our aim is to create fun innovative and casual iPhone games which we really like and want to play. Publisher.
Charly James (twitter.com/CharlyJames2) Div. Mom of 2 w/varying SN & medical d/x. dandelion moms; A4 Free Apps @CharlyJames4; Ellie's Games; Fernandez Design.	Ashley Elsdon (twitter.com/IamAshleyElsdon) Everything from Mobile Music Creation, geekery, tech, art and Doctor Who! http://www.ashleyelsdon.com	Samadhi Games (twitter.com/SamadhiGames) Hi! Samadhi Games LLC is an Indie Developer of iOS, Android and Desktop Apps. Arizona · http://www.samadhigames.com
Next is Great (twitter.com/nextisgreat) We create and develop brain teasing educational iOS apps for kids and teenagers. Check out Pirate Trio Academy and Geek Kids.	Andrew Wardell (twitter.com/andrewwardell) Nostalgic futurist, amateur photographer, sax-playing synthesist, musical mountain-biking metacomic. More than just a bag of salty water...	Finger Arts: App Dev (twitter.com/fingerartsgames) We develop cool & innovative iPhone, iPod Touch & iPad Games. Rocking the charts in iTunes: Sudoku 2, Hangman RSS, 4 in a Row & now Solitaire :)

Figure 10: The top 3 latent groups; each group shows the top 5 Twitter-followers and their public profile.

in creating music. This is in contrast with the "Music" genre in app stores, which is in some sense too diverse as it may refer to music-player apps, music-streaming apps, or trivial music-making apps. Lastly, Latent Group 3 captures games that are of a light-hearted, indie nature. We can also relate the Twitter users to the downloaded apps, which are difficult to describe using genres or words alone. In short, our Twitter-follower feature is able to capture the personalities of Twitter-individuals. Therefore, even when an app does not have user ratings, our system can still provide relevant recommendation based on information about *who is following* the app's Twitter account.

6. CONCLUSION

By taking advantage of the unique property of apps and their corresponding Twitter profiles, we identify Twitter-followers of the Twitter profiles of apps. Pseudo-documents are then created to represent users, where each pseudo-document contains the IDs of Twitter-followers of the apps that a user has previously downloaded. Thereafter, LDA is applied to the set of pseudo-documents to generate latent groups which is then used in the recommendation process. By combining the feature of Twitter-followers with other features based on various app metadata such as genre, developer, and the words in the app description, we can generate a much more accurate estimation of how likely a target user will like an app. Experimental results show that features extracted from Twitter consistently and significantly outperform state-of-the-art baselines which rely on (potentially misleading) textual information distilled from app descriptions. This also shows that *follower* information from Twitter helps us discover valuable signals that is effective in alleviating the cold-start situation.

In our future work, we plan to expand the use of data from SNS. For instance, second-degree relationships such as Twitter-followers *following* the current set of Twitter-followers may be useful, as would using data from other SNS, such as Facebook. Finally, we note that apps have a unique trait—they can be *updated*, which usually improves the app by incorporating new features or bug fixes. We plan to explore the use of this kind of temporal information to enhance our app recommender system.

7. ACKNOWLEDGEMENTS

This research is supported by the Singapore National Research Foundation under its International Research Centre @ Singapore Funding Initiative and administered by the IDM Programme Office.

8. REFERENCES

[1] C. C. Aggarwal, J. L. Wolf, K.-L. Wu, and P. S. Yu. Horting Hatches an Egg: A New Graph-theoretic Approach to Collaborative Filtering. In *Proc. of the 5th ACM SIGKDD International Conference on Knowledge Discovery and Data Mining (KDD'99)*, pages 201–212, 1999.

[2] R. Ayalew. *Consumer Behaviour in Apple's App Store.* PhD thesis, Uppsala University, 2011.

[3] E. Bakshy, J. M. Hofman, W. A. Mason, and D. J. Watts. Everyone's an Influencer: Quantifying Influence on Twitter. In *Proc. of the 4th ACM International Conference on Web Search and Data Mining (WSDM'11)*, pages 65–74, 2011.

[4] R. Bell, Y. Koren, and C. Volinsky. Modeling Relationships at Multiple Scales to Improve Accuracy of Large Recommender Systems. In *Proc. of the 13th ACM SIGKDD International Conference on Knowledge Discovery and Data Mining (KDD'07)*, pages 95–104, 2007.

[5] D. M. Blei and J. D. Lafferty. Topic Models. *Text mining: Classification, Clustering, and Applications*, 10:71, 2009.

[6] D. M. Blei, A. Y. Ng, and M. I. Jordan. Latent Dirichlet Allocation. *Journal of Machine Learning Research*, 3:993–1022, 2003.

[7] J. Boyd-Graber, J. Chang, S. Gerrish, C. Wang, and D. M. Blei. Reading Tea Leaves: How Humans Interpret Topic Models. In *Proc. of the 23rd Annual Conference on Neural Information Processing Systems (NIPS'09)*, 2009.

[8] J. S. Breese, D. Heckerman, and C. Kadie. Empirical Analysis of Predictive Algorithms for Collaborative Filtering. In *Proc. of the 14th Conference on Uncertainty in Artificial Intelligence (UAI'98)*, pages 43–52, 1998.

[9] M. Cha, H. Haddadi, F. Benevenuto, and K. P. Gummadi. Measuring User Influence in Twitter: The Million Follower Fallacy. In *Proc. of the 4th International AAAI Conference on Weblogs and Social Media (ICWSM'10)*, pages 10–17, 2010.

[10] J. H. Friedman. Greedy Function Approximation: A Gradient Boosting Machine. *The Annals of Statistics*, 29:1189–1232, 2001.

[11] J. L. Herlocker, J. A. Konstan, A. Borchers, and J. Riedl. An Algorithmic Framework for Performing Collaborative Filtering. In *Proc. of the 22nd Annual International ACM SIGIR Conference on Research and Development in Information Retrieval (SIGIR'99)*, pages 230–237, 1999.

[12] T. Hofmann. Latent Semantic Models for Collaborative Filtering. *ACM Transactions on Information Systems (TOIS)*, 22:89–115, 2004.

[13] T. Hofmann and J. Puzicha. Latent Class Models for Collaborative Filtering. In *Proc. of the 16th International Joint Conference on Artificial Intelligence (IJCAI'99)*, pages 688–693, 1999.

[14] M. Jamali and M. Ester. A Matrix Factorization Technique with Trust Propagation for Recommendation in Social Networks. In *Proc. of the 4th ACM Conference on Recommender Systems (RecSys'10)*, pages 135–142, 2010.

[15] D. Kim and B.-J. Yum. Collaborative Filtering Based on Iterative Principal Component Analysis. *Expert Systems with Applications*, 28(4):823–830, 2005.

[16] Y. Koren. Factorization Meets the Neighborhood: A Multifaceted Collaborative Filtering Model. In *Proc. of the 14th ACM SIGKDD International Conference on Knowledge Discovery and Data Mining (KDD'08)*, pages 426–434, 2008.

[17] Y. Koren and R. Bell. Advances in Collaborative Filtering. *Recommender Systems Handbook*, pages 145–186, 2011.

[18] H. Kwak, C. Lee, H. Park, and S. Moon. What is Twitter, a Social Network or a News Media? In *Proc. of the 19th International Conference on World Wide Web (WWW'10)*, pages 591–600, 2010.

[19] N. N. Liu, X. Meng, C. Liu, and Q. Yang. Wisdom of the Better Few: Cold-Start Recommendation via Representative based Rating Elicitation. In *Proc. of the 5th ACM Conference on Recommender Systems (RecSys'11)*, pages 37–44, 2011.

[20] H. Misra, O. Cappé, and F. Yvon. Using LDA to Detect Semantically Incoherent Documents. In *Proc. of the 12th Conference on Computational Natural Language Learning (CoNLL'08)*, pages 41–48, 2008.

[21] Y. Moshfeghi, B. Piwowarski, and J. M. Jose. Handling Data Sparsity in Collaborative Filtering using Emotion and Semantic-based Features. In *Proc. of the 34th International ACM SIGIR Conference on Research and Development in Information Retrieval (SIGIR'11)*, pages 625–634, 2011.

[22] L. Page, S. Brin, R. Motwani, and T. Winograd. The PageRank Citation Ranking: Bringing Order to the Web. Technical Report SIDL-WP-1999-0120, Stanford Digital Library Technologies Project, 1998.

[23] S.-T. Park and W. Chu. Pairwise Preference Regression for Cold-Start Recommendation. In *Proc. of the 3rd ACM Conference on Recommender Systems (RecSys'09)*, pages 21–28, 2009.

[24] D. Ramage, S. Dumais, and D. Liebling. Characterizing Microblogs with Topic Models. In *Proc. of the 4th International AAAI Conference on Weblogs and Social Media (ICWSM'10)*, pages 130–137, 2010.

[25] R. Recuero, R. Araujo, and G. Zago. How Does Social Capital Affect Retweets. In *Proc. of the 5th International AAAI Conference on Weblogs and Social Media (ICWSM'11)*, pages 305–312, 2011.

[26] A. Said, E. W. De Luca, and S. Albayrak. How Social Relationships Affect User Similarities. In *Proc. of the 2010 Workshop on Social Recommender Systems*, pages 1–4, 2010.

[27] R. Salakhutdinov, A. Mnih, and G. Hinton. Restricted Boltzmann Machines for Collaborative Filtering. In *Proc. of the 24th International Conference on Machine Learning (ICML'07)*, pages 791–798, 2007.

[28] B. Sarwar, G. Karypis, J. Konstan, and J. Riedl. Item-based Collaborative Filtering Recommendation Algorithms. In *Proc. of the 10th International Conference on World Wide Web (WWW'01)*, pages 285–295, 2001.

[29] A. I. Schein, A. Popescul, L. H. Ungar, and D. M. Pennock. Methods and Metrics for Cold-Start Recommendations. In *Proc. of the 25th Annual International ACM SIGIR Conference on Research and Development in Information Retrieval (SIGIR'02)*, pages 253–260, 2002.

[30] G. Takács, I. Pilászy, B. Németh, and D. Tikk. Matrix Factorization and Neighbor based Algorithms for the Netflix Prize Problem. In *Proc. of the 2nd ACM Conference on Recommender Systems (RecSys'08)*, pages 267–274, 2008.

[31] C. Wang and D. M. Blei. Collaborative Topic Modeling for Recommending Scientific Articles. In *Proc. of the 17th ACM SIGKDD International Conference on Knowledge Discovery and Data Mining (KDD'11)*, pages 448–456, 2011.

[32] J. Weng, E.-P. Lim, J. Jiang, and Q. He. TwitterRank: Finding Topic-sensitive Influential Twitterers. In *Proc. of the 3rd ACM International Conference on Web Search and Data Mining (WSDM'10)*, pages 261–270, 2010.

[33] S. Wu, J. M. Hofman, W. A. Mason, and D. J. Watts. Who Says What to Whom on Twitter. In *Proc. of the 20th International Conference on World Wide Web (WWW'11)*, pages 705–714, 2011.

[34] G.-R. Xue, C. Lin, Q. Yang, W. Xi, H.-J. Zeng, Y. Yu, and Z. Chen. Scalable Collaborative Filtering using Cluster-based Smoothing. In *Proc. of the 28th Annual International ACM SIGIR Conference on Research and Development in Information Retrieval (SIGIR'05)*, pages 114–121, 2005.

[35] K. Zhou, S.-H. Yang, and H. Zha. Functional Matrix Factorizations for Cold-Start Recommendation. In *Proc. of the 34th Annual International ACM SIGIR Conference on Research and Development in Information Retrieval (SIGIR'11)*, pages 315–324, 2011.

A Location-Based News Article Recommendation with Explicit Localized Semantic Analysis

Jeong-Woo Son A-Yeong Kim Seong-Bae Park
School of Computer Science and Engineering
Kyungpook National University
Daegu, Korea
[jwson, aykim, sbpark]@sejong.knu.ac.kr

ABSTRACT

The interest of users in handheld devices is strongly related to their location. Therefore, the user location is important, as a user context, for news article recommendation in a mobile environment. This paper proposes a novel news article recommendation that reflects the geographical context of the user. For this purpose, we propose the Explicit Localized Semantic Analysis (ELSA), an ESA-based topical representation of documents. Every location has its own geographical topics, which can be captured from the geo-tagged documents related to the location. Thus, not only news articles but locations are also represented as topic vectors. The main advantage of ELSA is that it stresses only the topics that are relevant to a given location, whereas all topics are equally important in ESA. As a result, geographical topics have different importance according to the user location in ELSA, even if they come from the same article. Another advantage of ELSA is that it allows a simple comparison of the user location and news articles, because it projects both locations and articles onto an identical space composed of Wikipedia topics. In the evaluation of ELSA with the New York Times corpus, it outperformed two simple baselines of Bag-Of-Words and LDA as well as two ESA-based methods. Rt10 of ELSA was improved up to 46.25% over other methods, and its NDCG@k was always higher than those of the others regardless of k.

Categories and Subject Descriptors

H.3.3 [**Information Storage and Retrieval**]: Information Search and Retrieval—*Information filtering*

General Terms

Algorithm, Experimentation, Performance

Keywords

Localized recommender system; Explicit localized semantic analysis; Geographical context; Local topic distribution

SIGIR'13, July 28–August 1, 2013, Dublin, Ireland.

1. INTRODUCTION

Content-based news article recommendation aims to offer news articles to a reader based on his/her interests. To reflect the interests of a specific reader into article recommendation, the interests are predicted from the user profile that is a collection of articles he/she has read in the past or explicit information about the reader such as age and gender. This kind of user profile is static or at least almost static. The profile remains same regardless of the user location, even if a large number of users of handheld devices (i.e. smart phone or tablet PC) access online news providers anywhere, and their interests depend on their location.

The fact that the interests of a user are strongly related to their location, implies that his/her geographical context is important for localized news article recommendation. For instance, assume that a user is reading an article "After Delays, Wireless Web Comes to Parks" of The New York Times. This article delivers news about establishing wireless networks at the prominent parks in New York city. Therefore, it has two major topics, a new facility of public parks and a company that won a contract for the wireless network service. The people who are strolling at a public park will focus on the former, while those working at Wall Street would prefer the latter.

The key of news article recommendation is obviously a representation of the articles. Word frequencies or topics are the most widely used representation of articles [11, 18], but recently, topic representation is preferred because a topic is a good proxy for article contents [23]. For instance, Wang and Blei proposed a collaborative topic model using Latent Dirichlet Allocation (LDA) to recommend scientific articles [2]. Egozi et. al [5] projected articles onto a topic space constructed with Explicit Semantic Analysis (ESA) [7]. In ESA, each Wikipedia concept is regarded as a possible topic, and an article is represented as a topic vector with Wikipedia concepts. Because Wikipedia has a large volume of concepts, articles can be expressed efficiently and accurately. On the other hand, such topic representations of articles are geo-neutral. Therefore, a topic model that reflects the geographical context of a user is needed to localize an article recommendation.

When the location at which a user is standing is the only information available for the user profile, the geographical context of a user is equivalent to the geographical context of his/her location. The geographical context of a location can also be expressed as a topic vector, because most locations have their own geographical topics that are defined as spatially coherent meaningful themes [25]. Most topic models proposed for extracting geographical topics from a location identify topics actually from a set of geo-tagged documents associated with the location [13]. Nevertheless, they have a problem in that the geo-tagged documents include not only the topics that are related directly to the location but also some other topics that have no relationship with the location.

This paper proposes a novel method for the topical representation of documents, Explicit Localized Semantic Analysis (ELSA). ELSA basically represents news articles as topic vectors considering the geographical context of a location. It inherits all the advantages of ESA as an extension of ESA, but overcomes the drawback in that ESA is geo-neural. That is, the topic vectors of the articles in ELSA are biased to the geographical context of the location. For this purpose, ELSA estimates the distribution of local topics for a given user location. All topics for a location are found from the geo-tagged documents of the location, but they are generally dependent on one another. For instance, the topics 'FC Barcelona' and 'Lionel Messi' are somehow dependent from each other, as they are related to *Camp Nou*, a football stadium in Barcelona. To express the topic dependency, the link information within Wikipedia concepts is adopted. All Wikipedia concepts, which are related to the location, are expressed as a graph with their link information. The hub nodes of this topic dependency graph are the actual *local* topics associated with the location.

Another advantage of ELSA is that it can be used to represent not only articles but also locations. This is because the user location is also expressed with the topics from a set of geo-tagged documents retrieved with that location. That is, the articles and locations are all represented as vectors in identical topic space. This leads to a simple comparison of articles and locations, and efficient recommendation of the articles that are relevant to the user location.

A series of experiments were carried out to verify the recommendation performance of ELSA. In the experiments, the articles were recommended for fifteen locations in three distinguished categories: Airport, Baseball stadium, and National park. The New York Times corpus was used as the recommendation candidates, and the performance of ELSA was compared with four other methods: Bag-of-Words, Latent Dirichlet Allocation (LDA) [2], Explicit Semantic Analysis (ESA) [7], and Probabilistic Explicit Semantic Analysis (PESA) [21]. According to the experimental results, ELSA outperformed the others in both Rt10 (Rating of Top 10) [15] and NDCG@k. These results highlight the effectiveness of ELSA in the localized article recommendation.

2. RELATED WORK

2.1 Localized Recommendation

The popularity of handheld devices with a GPS makes the user location available for various kinds of recommendations [12, 17, 19]. Most previous studies on localized recommendation have focused on the physical attributes of locations. Dao et al. proposed a context-aware collaborative filtering for location-based advertising [4]. In their study, the item scores for a specific user are determined by considering user's location. That is, the user-item matrix of this method is expanded with the user locations. Thus, the user similarity can be obtained using the items shared by other users at the same location.

Zheng et al. proposed the user-centered collaborative location and activity filtering (UCLAF) to recommend tourism spots and activities [27]. In UCLAF, the similar users of a specific user are obtained based on their GPS trajectories and activities at tourism spots. UCLAF recommends tourism spots for the user by analyzing similar users. CityVoyager system proposed by Takeuchi and Sugimoto [22] uses the shops previously visited by a user to recommend new shops for him/her. Ye et al. proposed Geo-Measured Friend-based Collaborative Filtering (GM-FCF) to recommend places such as stores, movie theaters, etc [24]. The recommendation by GM-FCF is made using the places visited by his/her friends in the social network. GM-FCF ranks the places by their physical distance from his/her location. Yu and Chang suggested a tour planning system [26]. This system also recommends sightseeing spots, hotels, and restaurants based on user's location.

As shown in these studies, the user's location helps recommendation systems improve their performance. This is because it reveals valuable information of the user. This was recently taken into account for news recommendation. GeoFeed is a location-aware news feed system [1]. This system provides its users with the news that are spatially related with the users. The spatial relationship between the user and a news in GeoFeed is determined using the distances from his/her to the locations tagged in the news. Mokbel et al. employed user locations to recommend *local* news [14]. In their study, they considered the distance between the user and location in which the news article was published. Although these studies proved the feasibility of their idea by implementing practical localized recommender systems, only the physical attributes of the user location was considered but its latent attributes are ignored. To the best of our knowledge, no study has used the latent attributes of the user locations in news article recommendation.

2.2 Geographical Topic Model

A location is described physically by its longitude and latitude. This is because it is difficult to transform a location into other forms but the coordinate of the longitude and latitude, even though most locations have their own geographical context and the context can be expressed with topics at these locations. For instance, the topics '*shopping*' at a department store and '*trip*' at a sightseeing spot describe their locations well. One of the efforts to extract the geographical topics of a location is the geographical topic model. Therefore, range of geographical topic models have been proposed [20, 28].

The main issue in geographical topics is how to associate topics with locations. Eisenstein et al. proposed a generative model to determine the topics of a set of geo-tagged documents and the regions corresponding to the topics simultaneously [6]. In order to determine them simultaneously, they assumed that a document is generated from two latent variables of geographical topics and regions. Yin et al. proposed Latent Geographical Topic Analysis (LGTA) [25] to solve the same problem. The contribution of LGTA is that it allows geographical topics to be associated with multiple regions. Hong et al. proposed a generative model to discover geographical topics in the tweet stream [9]. They made a similar assumption using the above-mentioned methods, but the idiosyncracy of their method comes from the fact that the method attempts to reflect the preferences of twitter users and the dependency between regions and topics.

These geographical topic models were applied successfully to geographical topic discovery. On the other hand, it is difficult to apply them to news article recommendation. In order to recommend articles for a specific location, all the topics at the location should be identified first. However, the topic models for topic discovery try to find major topics for the location. As a result, some topics are ignored, even if they deliver some information for the location. Thus, a topic model that utilizes all topics of a given location is needed.

One candidate to represent a location with all its topics is Probabilistic Explicit Semantic Analysis (PESA) [21]. PESA is a probabilistic topic model based on Explicit Semantic Analysis (ESA) [7], and is designed to compare locations with their topics. For this, it maps locations onto a topic space spanned by Wikipedia concepts. Because all Wikipedia concepts are employed in representing locations, there are no missing topics associated with a location in PESA.

PESA aims to compare locations, and its performance in location comparison is high. However, it has a critical problem when being applied to localized article recommendation. PESA computes the topic prior distribution to reflect the dependency among topics. This prior distribution forces the locations in the same geographical category to be similar locations. It is global in that it comes from the dependency relations of all possible topics. Nevertheless, the topics relevant only to a specific location are more influential than those observed at almost all locations in the localized recommendation. For instance, assume two baseball stadiums, Rangers Ballpark and Angel Stadium. They share many topics regarding baseball games. Hence, PESA considers them to be similar locations. However, they should be treated differently in localized article recommendation because they are physically far and can have different geographically-affected topics. That is, Rangers Ballpark could have topics about Texas, whereas Angel Stadium could have topics about Los Angeles or California.

3. LOCALIZED NEWS ARTICLE RECOMMENDATION

Assume that a user is specified only by his/her location $l = \{longitude, latitude\} \in R^2$. The localized news article recommendation then ranks a set of articles, $\mathbf{A} = \{a_1, a_2, \ldots, a_n\}$ so that the order between ranks $a_1 \succ a_2 \succ \ldots \succ a_n$ satisfies the geographical preference of the user at l. The preference relation is determined by a score function $f(a, l)$ that always meets $f(a_i, l) > f(a_j, l)$ if $a_i \succ a_j$. That is, the top k ($k \leq n$) articles from $\mathbf{A}$ scored by this function are suggested as appropriate news articles according to the location l.

The score function $f(a, l)$ measures the appropriateness of each a to l. If both a and l are represented as vectors in the same topic space, it can be replaced by a similarity function [3]. That is, the score function $f(a, l)$ can be defined as

$$f(a, l) = \frac{\Phi(a) \cdot \Phi(l)}{|\Phi(a)| \cdot |\Phi(l)|}, \quad (1)$$

where Φ is a mapping function of news articles and locations into a topic space.

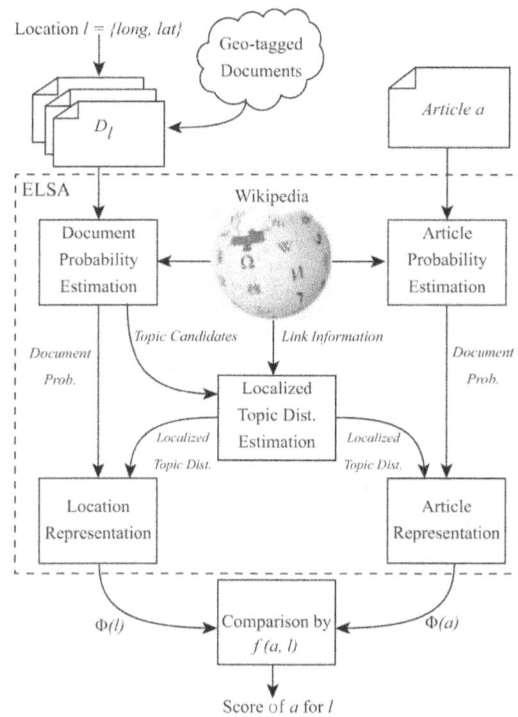

Figure 1: Overall process of the localized article recommendation.

Figure 1 depicts the overall process of measuring how appropriate a news article a is to a specific location l by Explicit Localized Semantic Analysis (ELSA). When l, the location of a user is given, D_l, a set of documents for l, is crawled from geo-tagged documents such as Twitter, Facebook, and Flickr tags. Each document d in D_l is represented as a topic vector of which dimension is the number of concepts in Wikipedia as done in ESA. Then, the location l is represented as a product of all d's in D_l. The concepts with non-zero values in this product vector are the possible topics for l, even though some non-relevant topic are also included at this step.

We assume that the topic would be dependent on one another if they are actually related to l. In order to reflect this dependency into the recommendation, a dependency graph of the topics is constructed using the link information in Wikipedia, and the local topic distribution is estimated from this graph using PageRank [16]. This local topic distribution explains which topics are actually important with respect to l when the topics are related to each other. Therefore, it is used as a weight vector for the product vector of D_l. Then, the final mapping $\Phi(l)$ of a location l into the Wikipedia topic space is the multiplication of the product vector and the local topic distribution.

News articles are also projected onto the Wikipedia topic space in the same way. A news article a is first expressed as a topic vector as ESA does. Then, the final mapping $\Phi(a)$ of a is a multiplication of the topic vector of a and the local topic distribution. Note that even the same article would be represented differently according to the location, because every different location has a different local topic distribu-

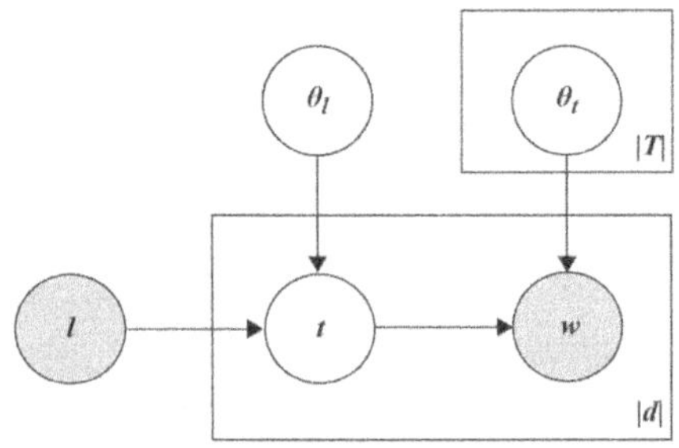

Figure 2: Graphical representation of ELSA.

tion. At last, the appropriateness of a to l is determined by $f(a, l)$.

4. EXPLICIT LOCALIZED SEMANTIC ANALYSIS

4.1 Location Representation

Explicit Semantic Analysis (ESA) [7] is a topical representation of unrestricted natural language documents. When a set of geo-tagged documents D_l for a location l is given, it maps, for the representation of l, D_l onto a topic space which is explicitly defined with Wikipedia concepts. The dimensionality of the topic space is equivalent to the number of Wikipedia concepts. Let T be a set of Wikipedia concepts. Then, D_l is expressed as a topic vector

$$D_l = \langle \phi_1(D_l), \phi_2(D_l), \ldots, \phi_{|T|}(D_l) \rangle.$$

Here, $\phi_i(D_l)$ is the weight of the i-th topic for D_l and is given as

$$\phi_i(D_l) = \sum_{d \in D_l} \sum_{w \in d} tfidf(w, d, D_l) \cdot tfidf(w, c_i, T)), \quad (2)$$

where c_i is an article of a Wikipedia concept $t_i \in T$, and $tfidf(w, d, D_l) = tf(w, d) \cdot idf(w, D_l)$. Here, $tf(w, d)$ is the term frequency of w in d and $idf(w, D_l)$ is the inverse document frequency of w in D_l. That is, the location is represented as a topic vector through the geo-tagged documents related to the location.

Because news articles, themselves are documents, they can also be represented as topic vectors by ESA. Thus, ESA provides an identical semantic representation for both locations and articles. In addition, this is a fine-grained representation of locations and articles due to the rich world-knowledge of Wikipedia. However, some topics that are irrelevant to l can be included in D_l. Since ESA does not consider any geographical context of a location, it is affected by those irrelevant topics.

ELSA is different from ESA in that it considers the geographical context of a location in expressing the locations and articles. ELSA reinforces ESA with a local topic distribution. Figure 2 shows the graphical representation of ELSA. Here, a document $d \in D_l$ depends on topics $t \in T$, and the topics are dependent on a location l. Note that l and d are the observed variables, while t is the unobserved one. θ_l denotes the local topic distribution at l and θ_t is the word distribution of the topic t. Both are also unobserved variables.

ELSA represents a location l as

$$\Phi(l) = \left\langle p(D_l, t_1, l|\theta_l, \theta_{t_1}), \ldots, p(D_l, t_{|T|}, l|\theta_l, \theta_{t_{|T|}}) \right\rangle, \quad (3)$$

where $p(D_l, t_i, l|\theta_l, \theta_{t_i})$ is the probability of the i-th topic. Since l is independent of θ_l and θ_t, $p(D_l, t_i, l|\theta_l, \theta_t)$ becomes $p(D_l, t_i|l, \theta_l, \theta_{t_i}) \cdot p(l)$. Note that only l is related directly to t in Figure 2. Therefore,

$$\begin{aligned} p(D_l, t_i, l|\theta_l, \theta_{t_i}) &= p(D_l, t_i|l, \theta_l, \theta_{t_i}) \cdot p(l) \\ &= p(D_l|t_i, \theta_{t_i}) \cdot p(t_i|l, \theta_l) \cdot p(l) \\ &= p(t_i|l, \theta_l) \cdot p(l) \cdot \prod_{d \in D_l} p(d|t_i, \theta_{t_i}). \end{aligned}$$

If $p(l)$ is assumed to be uniform for all locations,

$$p(D_l, t_i, l|\theta_l, \theta_{t_i}) \propto p(t_i|l, \theta_l) \cdot \prod_{d \in D_l} p(d|t_i, \theta_{t_i}).$$

Then, for the scalability,

$$\begin{aligned} p(D_l, t_i, l|\theta_l, \theta_{t_i}) &\propto \log(p(D_l, t_i, l|\theta_l, \theta_{t_i})) \\ &\propto \log p(t_i|l, \theta_l) + \sum_{d \in D_l} \log p(d|t_i, \theta_{t_i}). \end{aligned}$$

Therefore, $p(d|t_i, \theta_{t_i})$ and $p(t_i|l, \theta_l)$ should be estimated for each topic t_i.

When we assume all words are independent, $\log p(d|t_i, \theta_{t_i})$ can be expressed as

$$\log p(d|t_i, \theta_{t_i}) = \sum_{w \in d} \log p(w|t_i, \theta_{t_i}).$$

Because Wikipedia concepts are adopted as topics, each topic has its own Wikipedia article. $p(w|t_i, \theta_{t_i})$ then measures how w is possibly generated from c_i, which is the Wikipedia article for t_i. Thus, after add-one smoothing, $p(w|t_i, \theta_{t_i})$ is

$$p(w|t_i, \theta_{t_i}) = \frac{1 + n_{c_i}(w)}{|W_{c_i}| + \sum_{w \in c_i} n_{c_i}(w)}, \quad (4)$$

where W_{c_i} is a set of words in c_i and $n_{c_i}(w)$ is the frequency of w in c_i.

4.2 Estimating Local Topic Distribution

The local topic distribution $p(t_i|l, \theta_l)$ denotes the probability of a topic t_i at the location l. However, most topics at l are often coherent so that they are dependent on one another. This dependency among topics makes it difficult to estimate $p(t_i|l, \theta_l)$ directly. Thus, ELSA first constructs the dependency structure of local topics of l, and then approximates $p(t_i|l, \theta_l)$ with it.

As a first step to derive $p(t_i|l, \theta_l)$, all topics related to l should be identified. Because $p(D_l|t_i, \theta_{t_i})$ is the probability that topic t_i generates geo-tagged documents D_l of l, the actual topics of l are those with non-zero $p(D_l|t_i, \theta_{t_i})$. We denote the set of these actual topics as T_l. Then, the dependency structure of the topics of T_l is constructed using the link information within Wikipedia articles. Wikipedia articles often contain hyperlinks to other articles. These hyperlinks have semantics because all Wikipedia articles are published and managed carefully and manually by massive users, According to Kamps and Kollen [10], the hyperlinks in Wikipedia articles reflect semantic relationships among Wikipedia concepts. Because ELSA uses Wikipedia concepts as its geographical topics, it is natural to use these link

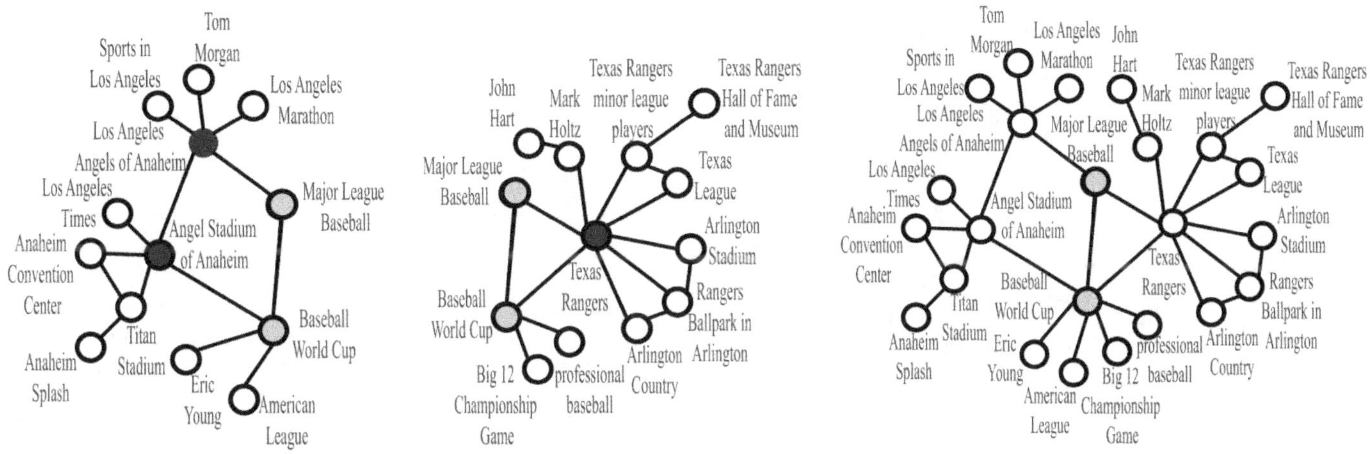

(a) Topic graph for *Angel Stadium* (b) Topic graph for *Rangers Ballpark* (c) Combined topic graph for both locations

Figure 3: Different major topics of ELSA and PESA at two baseball stadiums.

information among topics in T_l for the dependency structure of the topics. ELSA represents the dependency structure as a directed graph. For instance, when *Central park* has a hyperlink to *National historic landmark*, the corresponding dependency exists from *Central park* to *National historic landmark*.

When the dependency structure of T_l is given, ELSA approximates $p(t_i|l, \theta_l)$ from it according to the PageRank algorithm [16], because the values obtained from PageRank can be regarded as probabilities of the graph nodes in a complicated link structure [8]. That is, $p(t_i|l, \theta_l)$ is

$$\begin{aligned} p(t_i|l, \theta_l) &\approx PR(t_i) \\ &= \frac{1-\alpha}{|T_l|} + \alpha \cdot \sum_{t' \in in(t_i, T_l)} \frac{PR(t')}{L(t')}, \end{aligned} \quad (5)$$

where α is a damping factor, $in(t_i, T_l)$ is the set of topics in T_l with a link to t_i, and $L(t')$ is the number of outbound links from t'.

4.3 Article Representation

ELSA projects a location onto the topic space of Wikipedia concepts through a set of geo-tagged documents. Therefore, when a set of news articles, $\mathbf{A} = \{a_1, a_2, \ldots, a_n\}$ is given, all articles of $\mathbf{A}$ can be projected onto the topic space because news articles are also documents. Thus, the projection of an article $a \in \mathbf{A}$ can be written as

$$\Phi(a) = \left\langle p(a, t_1, l|\theta_l, \theta_{t_1}), \ldots, p(a, t_{|T|}, l|\theta_l, \theta_{t_{|T|}}) \right\rangle .$$

Since we assume that the location probability $p(l)$ is uniform,

$$\begin{aligned} p(a, t_i, l|\theta_l, \theta_{t_i}) &= p(a, t_i|l, \theta_l, \theta_{t_i}) \cdot p(l) \\ &\propto p(a, t_i|l, \theta_l, \theta_{t_i}). \end{aligned}$$

According to Figure 2, $p(a, t_i|l, \theta_l, \theta_{t_i}) = p(a|t_i, \theta_{t_i}) \cdot p(t_i|l, \theta_l)$. Thus,

$$\begin{aligned} p(a, t_i, l|\theta_l, \theta_{t_i}) &\propto p(a|t_i, \theta_{t_i}) \cdot p(t_i|l, \theta_l) \\ &= p(t_i|l, \theta_l) \cdot \prod_{w \in a} p(w|t_i, \theta_{t_i}) \\ &\propto \log p(t_i|l, \theta_l) + \sum_{w \in a} \log p(w|t_i, \theta_{t_i}) \\ &= \log p(t_i|l, \theta_l) \cdot \sum_{w \in a} \log \left(\frac{1 + n_{c_i}(w)}{|W_{c_i}| + \sum_{w \in c_i} n_{c_i}(w)} \right), \end{aligned}$$

where $n_a(w)$ denotes the frequency of a word w in a. The term $p(t_i|l, \theta_l)$ is the local topic distribution given in Equation (5). Because this term depends on l, it becomes different for every different l. As a result, even the same news article is represented differently if the location changes.

4.4 Comparison with PESA

The probabilistic ESA (PESA) is another topical representation of documents based on ESA [21], and is designed to compare locations through geo-tagged documents. It assigns high similarity to the pairs of locations in the same geographical category, while assigning very low similarities to the pairs of locations from different categories. For this, it regards, as geographical topics, the Wikipedia concepts of which a Wikipedia article has geo-tags or hyperlinks to other geo-tagged Wikipedia articles. Then, PESA uses these geographical topics to estimate a topic distribution.

PESA also estimates a topic distribution to reflect dependencies among topics. Because it considers the dependency of almost all topics, the global topics shared by most locations in a geographical category have high probabilities in the topic distribution of PESA. These global topics are important in PESA, since PESA focuses on location comparison in which similar locations share geographical topics. On the other hand, the task of a localized news article recommendation aims to offer appropriate articles for each specific location. That is, the local characteristics are more important in this task than the global characteristics. Many

Table 1: Locations used in the experiments and their categories

Geographical category	Locations
Airport	George Bush Airport John F. Kennedy Airport La Guardia Airport Phoenix Sky Harbor Airport Washington Dulles Airport
Baseball stadium	Angels Stadium of Anaheim Busch stadium Citizens Bank Park Rangers Ballpark Turner Field
National park	Arches Grand Canyon Hawaii Volcanoes Rocky Mountain Yellowstone

topics that are important globally are often not important locally. Therefore, PESA is unsuitable for this task.

ELSA estimates the distribution of only local topics. In the topic distribution of ELSA, the topics directly associated with a given location have high probabilities. As a result, even the locations from the same category have different topic distributions. This is reasonable because the locations could have different geographical context even if they belong to the same category.

The advantage of ELSA can be addressed by a simple example. Figure 3 shows the topic structures of two locations: *Angel Stadium* at Anaheim, CA (Figure 3(a)) and *Rangers Ballpark* at Arlington, TX (Figure 3(b)). In these graphs, the nodes are topics and the edges are their dependencies. The top thirteen topics were chosen from each location according to the probabilities over its D_l.

ELSA assigns high probabilities to the black nodes in each graph, because the nodes are local hubs. When the location is *Angel Stadium*, "Los Angeles, Angels of Anaheim" and "Angel Stadium of Anaheim" have high probabilities. On the other hand, the highest probability is assigned to the topic of "Texas Rangers" in the topic distribution of *Rangers Ballpark*. As a result, even the same article would be represented differently due to these different local topics.

PESA uses the dependency structure of all topics. Thus, it determines the topic distribution from the combined graph in Figure 3(c). After the graphs of Figure 3(a) and 3(b) are combined, the topics such as "Major League Baseball" and "Baseball World Cup" (gray nodes in this graph) are considered as hubs. These topics shared by two locations force the topic vectors of the locations to be similar. Therefore, PESA is effective in location comparison. However, the emphasis on global topics is adverse to localized news article recommendation in which local topics are preferable.

5. EXPERIMENTS

5.1 Experimental Settings

For the evaluation of ELSA, fifteen locations in USA are selected manually. Table 1 lists the locations and their categories. All locations belong to one of three geographical categories: 'Airport', 'Baseball stadium', and 'National park'. The keywords of the Flickr images are used as a set of geo-tagged documents, D_l for location l. These are adopted as geo-tagged documents because the keywords are often a description of the location. For each location, l in Table 1, the images that are closely associated with l are crawled through Flickr API (`http://www.flickr.com/services/api`). The GPS information attached to the images is used to determine their association with l. We determined that the image would be associated with l if the distance from l to the image location is within a predefined threshold. The threshold used was 0.2 km for 'Baseball stadium', 1 km for 'Airport', and 10 km for 'National park'. The keywords tagged to an image are regarded as a geo-tagged document.

Table 2: Statistics of the Flickr data

Category	Avg. documents	Avg. keywords	Unique keywords
Airport	177.8	7.49	1,895
Baseball stadium	179.0	8.66	900
National park	201.0	6.74	1,010

Table 2 describes the Flickr data set used in the experiments. The locations in the category of 'Airport' have 177.8 documents on average, whereas those in 'Baseball stadium' and 'National park' have 179 and 201 documents, respectively. The average number of keywords in a document is 7.49 in 'Airport', 8.66 in 'Baseball stadium', and 6.74 in 'National park'. The last attribute is the number of unique keywords. 'Airport' has 1,895 unique keywords, and 'Baseball stadium' and 'National park' have 900 and 1,010 unique keywords respectively.

A Wikipedia snapshot as of May 2, 2012 was used to generate geographical topics. A preprocessing described in [21] was adapted to the snapshot to exclude irrelevant topics, such as digit, time, and so on. After preprocessing, 1,116,275 concepts remain, and they are used for a topic set T in all the experiments below. The number of unique terms in this Wikipedia snapshot was 1,498,045.

The New York Times (NYT) corpus was adopted as a pool of news articles. This corpus contained 1,841,402 articles published by the New York Times from 1987 to 2007. Among them, the articles from January 1, 2006 to June 19, 2007 were actually used as a set of news articles, $\mathbf{A}$. This set contained 127,005 articles composed of 356,595 distinct words.

ELSA was compared using four baseline methods: BOW, LDA, ESA, and PESA. BOW is the bag-of-words model that represents locations and articles with the frequency of words. Thus, the need for a topic model in a localized article recommendation can be shown by a comparison with BOW. Three topic-based models, LDA, ESA, and PESA were prepared to evaluate the effectiveness of ELSA. LDA is the Latent Dirichlet Allocation that is used widely in the various applications to extract topics from documents. ESA and PESA both use Wikipedia concepts as their topics, but PESA additionally models the prior distribution of geographical topics.

The performance of these methods were compared with two metrics: (i) Rt10 (Rating of Top 10), the average score of recommended articles, and (ii) Normalized Discounted Cumulative Gain at top k (NDCG@k) which is widely used

Table 3: Kappa values of the articles scores by the human evaluators and actual number of news articles per location.

Category	Kappa value	Avg. distinct articles per location
Airport	0.510	32.8 ± 2.2
Baseball stadium	0.677	28.0 ± 6.5
National park	0.680	31.0 ± 3.7
Overall	0.623	30.6 ± 4.6

Table 4: Rt10 of the experimental methods

Category	BOW	LDA	ESA	PESA	ELSA
Airport	1.490	1.620	1.710	1.700	**2.119**
Baseball stadium	2.110	1.940	1.290	1.800	**2.400**
National park	1.470	0.700	**1.620**	1.490	1.560
Overall	1.690	1.420	1.540	1.663	**2.026**

for measuring the rank accuracy. Two human evaluators are employed to label the scores of news articles manually. Since there are too many articles in the data set, the evaluation was done only for the recommended articles. That is, for a given location, all five methods including ELSA select their own top ten articles. Accordingly, the number of news articles per location is at most 50. Since two or more methods can recommend the same articles, the evaluators score normally less than 50 articles per each location. The guidelines of scoring news articles are as follows.

- 0 point: The article has nothing to with the geographical category.
- 1 point: The article is weakly related to the geographical category.
- 2 point: The article belongs to the geographical category, but is not related to the location.
- 3 point: The article is strongly related to the location.

Table 3 lists the Kappa values of the scores by the evaluators. As shown in this table, Kappa values for 'Baseball stadium' and 'National park' were approximately 0.68, and approximately 30 distinct articles are recommended for each location. These values corresponded to *substantial agreement*. For 'Airport', the Kappa value was 0.51, which falls in *moderate agreement*, and the average distinct articles per location was 32.8.

5.2 Experimental Results

Table 4 shows the Rt10 values of the five methods. As shown in this table, LDA achieved 1.420, which was the worst performance. This Rt10 was obtained when LDA shows the best performance with 500 topics. The fact that LDA was worst among the five methods implies that it fails to capture diverse topics of news articles and locations. On the other hand, all methods based on Wikipedia concepts outperform LDA. This result highlights the effectiveness of the Wikipedia concepts as geographical topics.

BOW showed the second best performance with 1.69 of Rt10. This is an unexpected result, because BOW does not adopt topics to represent articles and locations. The good performance of BOW originates mostly from the locations of 'Baseball stadium'. Most geo-tagged documents for baseball stadiums contain the name of home teams, which allows a simple lexical matching to work well. As a result, the Rt10 score of BOW for 'Baseball stadium' was very high. However, its performance in other categories was lower than ESA-based topic models. Therefore, from the results of LDA and BOW the topical representation leads to high performance in localized article recommendation, if the topic space is rich enough to cover the entire topics.

ELSA was found to be the best method in this experiment. ELSA achieved significantly higher performance than the other methods. Its Rt10 in 'Airport' and 'Baseball stadium' was much higher than those of others. In 'National park', ESA showed the best Rt10 of 1.620, but the difference between ELSA and ESA was only 0.06. As a result, ELSA outperformed all other methods with an overall Rt10 of 2.026, and was the only method of which the overall Rt10 was more than 2.0. The outperformance of ELSA over other methods was statistically significant with a confidence interval of 95%. The p-values of the T-test against the null hypothesis that ELSA does not outperform other methods were all below 0.05. The essential factor of ELSA that distinguishes it from ESA and PESA is the use of the *local* topic distribution as the geographical context of a location, Therefore, the best performance of ELSA proves the importance of a geographical context of locations in location and article representation.

The overall quality of the recommended articles can be verified by Rt10. However, the quality of a method can be poor, even if the method achieves a high Rt10. This occurs when a large number of recommended news articles receive 1 or 2 point by human evaluators. Therefore, it is important to determine how many articles receive 2 or 3 point. Figure 4 shows the number of recommended articles for each score. As shown in this figure, the quality of ELSA is best in that most of the articles recommended by it received 2 or 3 point. In particular, an examination of the overall category (Figure 4-(d)) showed that, the number of articles with 3 point recommended by ELSA exceeded those by other methods. Note that most articles recommended by PESA received 2 point. This is because PESA uses the distribution of all topics, which makes it difficult for the locations within the same category to be distinguished. On the other hand, even though ELSA shares topics with PESA, it effectively characterizes the geographical context of each location by its local topic distribution. As a result, ELSA recommends the articles that match the given location better than the other methods.

The Rt10 scores and number of articles with high scores have a tendency to decrease, as the location boundary becomes larger. The Rt10 score for 'National park' that has a boundary of 10 km was the worst, whereas that for 'Baseball stadium' with a boundary of 0.2 km was the best. This is because a location has a range of geographical topics as its boundary becomes large, and this variety of topics decreases the locality effect of the topics. However, ELSA outperformed the other methods regardless of how large the location boundary was.

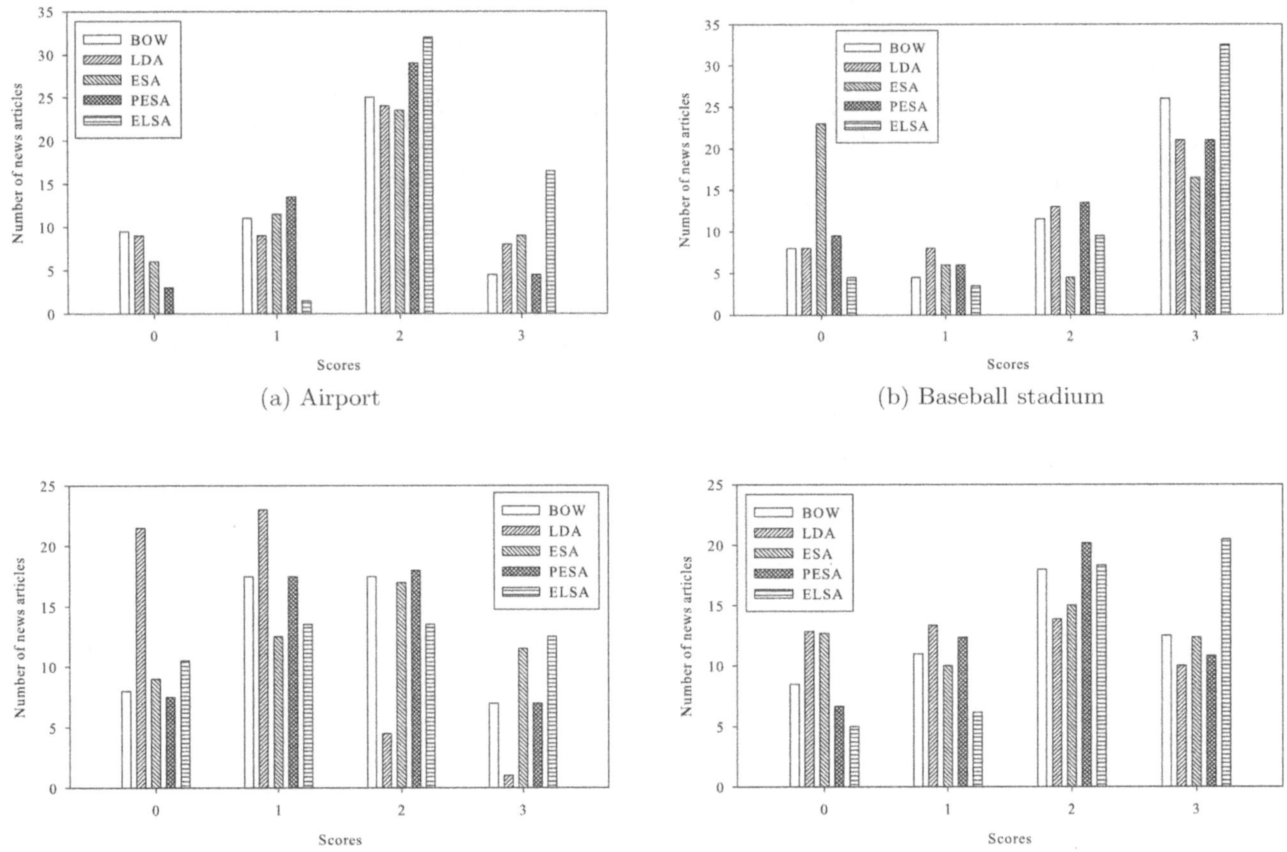

(a) Airport (b) Baseball stadium (c) National park (d) Overall category

Figure 4: Number of news articles for each score.

The ranking performance of the methods was also measured with NDCG@k. Figure 5 shows the NDCG@k values with k from 1 to 10. Even with this metric, ELSA outperformed the others for all geographical categories. Although PESA achieved a similar performance in 'Baseball stadium', its performance was lower than ESA and BOW in 'National park'. BOW showed the lowest NDCG@k when k was less than 3. Because it considers only the shared words by the news articles and geo-tagged documents, it recommends many irrelevant articles with some general words. For instance, many articles with a word, *angel* are irrelevant to Angel Stadium, and those with *bush* are irrelevant to George Bush Airport.

ELSA outperformed the others consistently for all k's. All improvements in NDCG@k of ELSA over the other methods are also statistically significant, because the p-values against the null hypothesis were less than 0.05. In particular, when $k \leq 3$, a large gap between ELSA and other methods was observed. As k was increased up to 10, this gap became smaller but was still higher than others. This result suggests that ELSA recommends news articles successfully that are appropriate to the geographical context.

PESA was the second best and also reflected the distribution of geographical topics in representing articles with topics. Thus, the superiority of ELSA and PESA over other methods proves the importance of geographical topics in the localized news article recommendation. Interestingly, ELSA and ESA showed a similar tendency in NDCG@k for all categories as k increased even though NDCG@k of ELSA was always higher than that of ESA. This fact implies that ELSA improves ESA successfully and substantially as its expansion for localized news article recommendation by adopting the *local* topic distribution.

6. CONCLUSION

This paper proposed a localized news article recommendation with the Explicit Localized Semantic Analysis (ELSA). The location of a user provides valuable information as user context, because each location has its own geographical topics, which are often strongly related to the user context at that location. Therefore, the proposed method recommends the news articles that are appropriate to the location by reflecting the geographical context of user. For this, ELSA represents news articles as the topic vectors of Wikipedia concepts. The weight of each topic for an article is adjusted to reflect the geographical context of the user. The user location is also expressed as a topic vector through the geo-tagged documents of the user location. Because the concerns of the user are affected by his/her location, even the same article should be represented differently according to

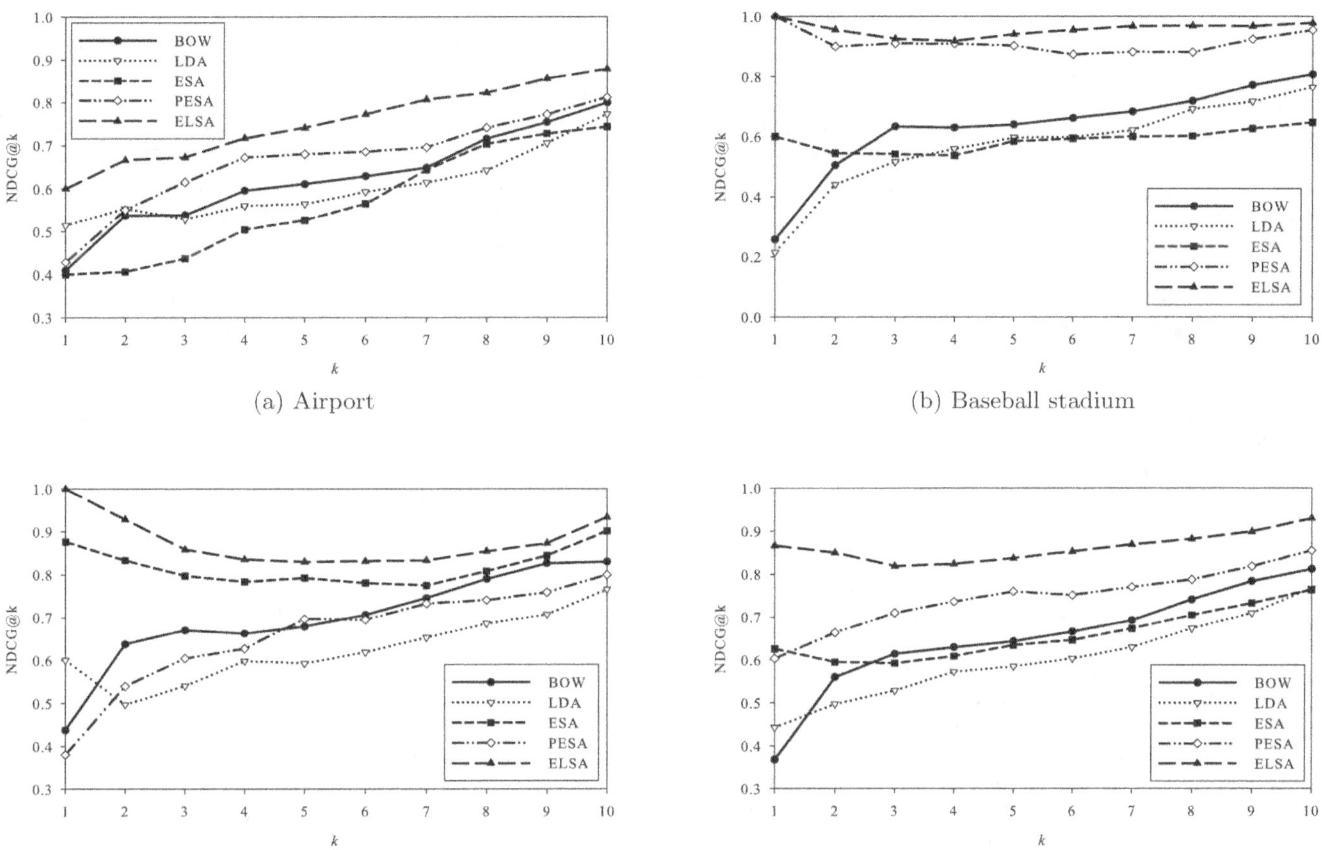

(a) Airport (b) Baseball stadium

(c) National park (d) Overall categories

Figure 5: NDCG@k scores with various k.

the user's location. To reflect it into article recommendation, ELSA models the dependencies of local topics. Then, the local topic distribution estimated from the topic dependencies is applied to represent both locations and news articles.

ELSA was evaluated with the New York Times corpus for fifteen famous locations. It was compared with four other methods: BOW, LDA, ESA, and PESA. All the methods were evaluated with two kinds of metrics: Rt10 and NDCG@k. According to the experimental results, ELSA outperformed all other methods substantially. The superiority of ELSA over BOW and LDA implies the effectiveness of the topic space by the Wikipedia concepts. PESA, another ESA-based topic model achieved higher performance than other methods including ESA, itself. Although both ELSA and PESA adopt the topic space by Wikipedia concepts, they are different in that ELSA uses a local topic distribution whereas PESA uses a global topic distribution. The performance of ELSA was superior to that of PESA in both metrics, because the local topic distribution is more appropriate than the global topic distribution in localized article recommendation.

The contributions of this paper are two-fold. First, this is the first effort to recommend articles according to user locations. Although every location has its own geographical topics, most legacy localized recommendation systems focused on their physical attributes. In this paper, by considering topics of a location as its geographical context, the articles that match the geographical context of a location could be recommended. Second, we manually constructed a data set for localized article recommendation. 459 news articles out of approximately 120,000 articles of the New York Times were tagged with scores from 0 to 3 with respect to their relevance to fifteen locations. Because this is the first data set for localized article recommendation, it can be used for further developments.

Acknowledgement

This work was supported by the Industrial Strategic Technology Development Program (10035348, Development of a Cognitive Planning and Learning Model for Mobile Platforms) funded by the Ministry of Knowledge Economy (MKE, Korea).

7. REFERENCES

[1] J. Bao, M. Mokbel, and C. Chow. GeoFeed: A location-aware news feed system. In *Proceedings of the 28th IEEE International Conference on Data Engineering*, pages 54–65, 2012.

[2] D. Blei, A. Ng, and M. Jordan. Latent Dirichlet Allocation. *Journal of Machine Learning Research*, 3:993–1022, 2003.

[3] T. Bogers and A. Bosch. Comparing and evaluating information retrieval algorithms for news recommendation. In *Proceedings of ACM conference on Recommender systems*, pages 141–144, 2007.

[4] T. Dao, S. Jeong, and H. Ahn. A novel recommendation model of location-based advertising: Context-aware collaborative filtering using ga approach. *Expert Systems with Applications*, 39(3):3731–3739, 2012.

[5] O. Egozi, S. Markovitch, and E. Gabrilovich. Concept-based information retrieval using Explicit Semantic Analysis. *ACM Transactions on Information Systems*, 29(2):8:1–8:34, 2011.

[6] J. Eisenstein, B. O'Connor, N. A. Smith, and E. P. Xing. A latent variable model for geographic lexical variation. In *Proceedings of the 2010 Conference on Empirical Methods in Natural Language Processing*, pages 1277–1287, 2010.

[7] E. Gabrilovich and S. Markovitch. Computing semantic relatedness using Wikipedia-based Explicit Semantic Analysis. In *Proceedings of the 20th International Joint Conference on Artificial Intelligence*, pages 1606–1611, 2007.

[8] T. Griffiths, M. Steyvers, and A. Firl. Google and the mind: Predicting fluency with PageRank. *Psychological Science*, 18(12):1069–1076, 2007.

[9] L. Hong, A. Ahmed, S. Gurumurth, A. Smola, and K. Tsioutsiouliklis. Discovering geographical topics in the twitter stream. In *Proceedings of the 21st International Conference on World Wide Web*, pages 769–778, 2012.

[10] J. Kamps and M. Koolen. The importance of link evidence in Wikipedia. In *Proceedings of the 30th European Conference on IR Research*, pages 270–282, 2008.

[11] R. Krestel, P. Fankhauser, and W. Nejdl. Latent Dirichlet Allocation for tag recommendation. In *Proceedings of the 6th ACM Conference on Recommender Systems*, pages 61–68, 2009.

[12] Y. Li, A. Guo, S. Liu, Y. Gao, and Y. Zheng. A location based reminder system for advertisement. In *Proceedings of the 18th International Conference on Multimedia*, pages 1501–1502, 2010.

[13] Q. Mei, C. Liu, and H. Su. A probabilistic approach to spatiotemporal theme pattern mining on weblogs. In *Proceedings of the 15th International Conference on World Wide Web*, pages 533–542, 2006.

[14] M. Mokbel, J. Bao, A. Eldawy, J. Levandoski, and M. Sarwat. Personalization, socialization, and recommendations in location-based services 2.0. In *Proceedings of the International Workshop on Personalized Access, Profile Management, and Context Awareness in Databases 2011, collocated with VLDB*, pages 1–6, 2011.

[15] R. Mooney and L. Roy. Content-based book recommending using learning for text categorization. In *Proceedings of the SIGIR-99 Workshop on Recommender Systems: Algorithms and Evaluation*, 1999.

[16] L. Page, S. Brin, R. Motwani, and T. Winograd. *The pagerank citation ranking: Bringing order to the web.* Technical report, Computer Systems Laboratory, Stanford University, 1998.

[17] M. Park, J. Hong, and S. Cho. Location-based recommendation system using bayesian user's preference model in mobile devices. In *Proceedings of the 4th International Conference on Ubiquitous Intelligence and Computing*, pages 1130–1139, 2007.

[18] D. Ramage, D. Hall, R. Nallapati, and C. Manning. Labeled LDA: a supervised topic model for credit attribution in multi-labeled corpora. In *Proceedings of the 2009 Conference on Empirical Methods in Natural Language Processing*, pages 248–256, 2009.

[19] N. Savage, M. Baranski, N. Chavez, and T. Höllerer. I'm feeling loco: A location based context aware recommendation system. In *Advances in Location-Based Services*, pages 37–54, 2012.

[20] S. Sizov. GeoFolk: Latent spatial semantics in web 2.0 social media. In *Proceedings of the 3rd ACM International Conference on Web Search and Data Mining*, pages 281–290, 2010.

[21] J. Son, Y. Noh, H. Song, S. Park, and S. Lee. Location comparison through geographical topics. In *Proceedings of the 2012 IEEE/WIC/ACM International Conference on Web Intelligence*, pages 311–318, 2012.

[22] Y. Takeuchi and M. Sugimoto. CityVoyager: An outdoor recommendation system based on user location history. In *Proceedings of the 3rd International Conference on Ubiquitous Intelligence and Computing*, pages 625–636, 2006.

[23] X. Wei and B. Croft. LDA-based document models for ad-hoc retrieval. In *Proceedings of the 29th Annual International ACM SIGIR Conference on Research and Development in Information Retrieval*, pages 178–185, 2006.

[24] M. Ye, P. Yin, and W. Lee. Location recommendation for location-based social networks. In *Proceedings of the 18th SIGSPATIAL International Conference on Advances in Geographic Information Systems*, pages 458–461, 2010.

[25] Z. Yin, L. Cao, J. Han, C. Zhai, and T. Huang. Geographical topic discovery and comparison. In *Proceedings of the 20th International Conference on World Wide Web*, pages 247–256, 2011.

[26] C. Yu and H. Chang. Personalized location-based recommendation services for tour planning in mobile tourism applications. In *Proceedings of the 10th International Conference on E-Commerce and Web Technologies*, pages 38–49, 2009.

[27] V. Zheng, B. Cao, Y. Zheng, X. Xie, and Q. Yang. Collaborative filtering meets mobile recommendation: A user-centered approach. In *Proceedings of the 24th AAAI Conference on Artificial Intelligence*, pages 236–241, 2010.

[28] Y. Zhou and J. Luo. Geo-location inference on news articles via multimodal pLSA. In *Proceedings of the 20th ACM International Conference on Multimedia*, pages 741–744, 2012.

Opportunity Models for E-commerce Recommendation: Right Product, Right Time

Jian Wang, Yi Zhang
School of Engineering
University of California, Santa Cruz
Santa Cruz, CA 95060 USA
{jwang30, yiz}@soe.ucsc.edu

ABSTRACT

Most of existing e-commerce recommender systems aim to recommend the right product to a user, based on whether the user is likely to purchase or like a product. On the other hand, the effectiveness of recommendations also depends on the time of the recommendation. Let us take a user who just purchased a laptop as an example. She may purchase a replacement battery in 2 years (assuming that the laptop's original battery often fails to work around that time) and purchase a new laptop in another 2 years. In this case, it is not a good idea to recommend a new laptop or a replacement battery right after the user purchased the new laptop. It could hurt the user's satisfaction of the recommender system if she receives a potentially right product recommendation at the wrong time. We argue that a system should not only recommend the most relevant item, but also recommend at the right time.

This paper studies the new problem: how to recommend the right product at the right time? We adapt the proportional hazards modeling approach in survival analysis to the recommendation research field and propose a new *opportunity model* to explicitly incorporate time in an e-commerce recommender system. The new model estimates the joint probability of a user making a follow-up purchase of a particular product at a particular time. This joint purchase probability can be leveraged by recommender systems in various scenarios, including the zero-query pull-based recommendation scenario (e.g. recommendation on an e-commerce web site) and a proactive push-based promotion scenario (e.g. email or text message based marketing). We evaluate the opportunity modeling approach with multiple metrics. Experimental results on a data collected by a real-world e-commerce website(shop.com) show that it can predict a user's follow-up purchase behavior at a particular time with descent accuracy. In addition, the opportunity model significantly improves the conversion rate in pull-based systems and the user satisfaction/utility in push-based systems.

Categories and Subject Descriptors

H.3.3 [**Information Storage and Retrieval**]: Information Search and Retrieval

General Terms

Algorithms, Design, Experimentation

Keywords

Recommender System; Opportunity Model; E-commerce

1. INTRODUCTION

As online shopping becomes popular, e-commerce recommendation is an increasingly important business tool for promoting sales. Researchers and industry practitioners are looking for all possible approaches to improve the recommendation performance. Even a minor improvement could lead to a big business return.

Traditional recommender systems focus on finding the right item to recommend. Major approaches include content-based methods, collaborative filtering methods and hybrid methods. For example, if a user viewed or purchased some camera(s) in the website, the system recommends more similar items (e.g. similar cameras) to the user. Recent research [19] proposed that recommender systems should recommend items that maximize the users' marginal utility, instead of only items that a user likes. As the marginal utility of a camera decreases immediately after a user purchased a camera, a system's follow-up recommendation should include camera accessories instead of similar cameras.

On the other hand, the user satisfaction/utility depends on both the relevance and the time of the recommendation. While an irrelevant recommendation results in a negative utility, the opportunity cost of recommending a relevant item at the wrong time could also be high, as we wasted the space while giving the user a negative impression. This is especially a problem for email or message based recommendations, as it wastes a user's time and effort to receive product recommendation emails/messages that are full of products she does not need to purchase at the time. In the long term, the user may have negative impression about the company, unsubscribe from the marketing email list, label the emails as spams, or uninstall the message application.

To address these issues, recommender systems need to answer the following question: when is the *right time* for the system to make recommendations of the *right product(s)*? For example, after a user purchased a camera, whether and when should the system recommend related accessories including camera lenses, batteries, digital photo frames, etc.?

Multiple heuristic approaches [18, 24] have been proposed to tackle this problem. In this paper, we propose a theoretical model to learn the probability of a user making a follow-up purchase at a particular time. The model is inspired by the hazards model in survival analysis in statistics. The purchase time would be influenced by multiple factors, such as the user's characteristics, the user's purchase history, the product promotion information, the global environment and so on. Thus we propose to leverage the proportional hazards modeling approach which incorporates related factors as covariates(i.e., features). We further extend the model with the hierarchical Bayesian framework to handle the data sparsity issue. The new model is denoted as the *Opportunity Model* in this paper. It predicts the joint purchase probability, i.e., the probability of a user purchasing a product at a particular time. It helps to promote a right item at the right time which further enhances the user satisfaction. Experimental results are performed with a dataset from a real-world e-commerce website. Detailed analysis shows that the opportunity model could help to significantly improve the conversion rate and the user satisfaction.

The major contribution of this paper includes:

- We propose a new research problem in recommender systems: When is the right time to make recommendation of the right product in the e-commerce domain?
- To solve this problem, we propose a principled approach, (i.e. the**opportunity model**), to predict the joint probability of purchasing a product and the time of the event. We extend the proportional hazards model in statistics with the hierarchical Bayesian framework as part of the solution, and derive detailed inference steps based on the variational Bayesian algorithm.
- We leverage the joint probability in both the zero-query pull-based recommendation scenario and the proactive push-based email/message promotion scenario [1]. In particular, the probability enables a proactive recommendation agent to decide whether to send recommendations of certain items to a user at a particular time based on a solid utility optimization framework. Experimental results show that the opportunity modeling approach significantly improve the user satisfaction and the conversion rate of the system.

2. RELATED WORK

To provide recommendations to a user, recommendation systems usually predict a user's ratings for each item or probability of purchasing, then rank all items in the descending order. There are two major recommendation approaches: content-based filtering and collaborative filtering. Content-based filtering [12]assumes that descriptive features of an item indicate a user's preferences. Thus a recommender system estimates the score of each item based on descriptive features of other items the user likes or dislikes. Usually, the system recommends items that are similar to what the user liked before. On the other hand, collaborative filtering [7, 18, 13, 5] assumes that users with similar tastes on some items may also have similar preferences on other items. Thus the main idea is to use the behavior history from other like-minded users to provide the current user with good recommendations. Research on collaborative filtering algorithms reached a peak due to the 1 million dollar Netflix movie recommendation competition. Factorization-based collaborative filtering approaches [3, 9, 19, 17], such as the regularized Singular Value Decomposition, performed well on this competition. A common characteristic of these models is the introduction of user latent factors and/or item latent factors to solve the data sparsity issue. In the field of recommender systems, the effect of time [10, 18, 24] has received some research attention recently. One focus is about the drift of the user's preference over time [10, 23, 15]. Koren [10] revamped two popular collaborative filtering methods by modeling the time drifting factor of user preferences. Rendel et al. [15] proposed a factorized personalized model that subsumes both a common Markov chain and the normal matrix factorization model.

Recommendation in the e-commerce domain is a topic that has been studied in the IR community [8, 20]. Several methods have been tried in this domain, including neighborhood-based method, graph models [6], MDP-based methods [16], multi attribute utility theory based methods [11] and so on. In general, most of these existing methods, directly or indirectly, only estimate whether a user would like an item or purchase an item. Some recent work studied modeling the time interval between purchase orders in the e-commerce domain [18, 24]. Wang et al. [18] discovered different post-purchase behavior in different time windows after purchasing. Zhao et al. [24] used the purchasing time interval to improve the temporal diversity of recommendations [15]. The time interval and the corresponding purchase probability is modeled inside the framework of a utility-based recommender system [19]. The hybrid system takes the time interval into consideration when ranking all candidate items. Compared to the prior work about time, our work explicitly models the joint probability of purchasing the product at the time based on a solid theoretical foundation. We explicitly model the conditional probability as a white box by leveraging Weibull distribution with various covariates to estimate the time-based probabilistic density. These covariates enable us to capture various time-dependent patterns such as local changes, cyclic behavior, seasonable pattern, general trend of follow-up purchase behaviors, which are not captured by the prior work. Besides, the joint probability of product and time enables us to improve the recommendation accuracy.

3. OPPORTUNITY MODEL IN E-COMMERCE

To recommend the right product at the right time, we exam each candidate product for each user at a particular decision time. We propose to build an opportunity model to estimate the probability of a user purchasing the product at a particular time interval (i.e. $(y, y+\Delta t]$). That is the joint probability $P(p\_product, T \in (y, y+\Delta t])$, where T is the purchasing time. Let $P(p\_product)$ represent the probability of the user purchasing the product, and $P(T \in (y, y+\Delta t] | p\_product)$ represent the conditional probability of the user purchasing the product at a particular time period conditioned on that the user will purchase the product.

[1]In the pull-based scenario, a user comes to the website and views some recommendation. In the push-based scenario, a system sends promotion emails or messages to the user.

Based on the chain rule, we have the joint probability:

$$P(p\_product, T \in (y, y + \Delta t]) = P(T \in (y, y + \Delta t] | p\_product) P(p\_product) \quad (1)$$

We propose to adapt hazards models in survival analysis to estimate $P(T \in (y, y + \Delta t] | p\_product)$, and adapt existing recommendation algorithms to estimate $P(p\_product)$.

3.1 Hazards Model in Survival Analysis

Survival analysis is a heavily studied topic in statistics, which is named as duration modeling in economics or reliability analysis in engineering. One major part of survival analysis is to estimate the time of an event, such as when a machine fails to work or when a patient fails to survive. In the e-commerce domain, we can view the task of conditional opportunity model as predicting the time of the follow-up purchase event of the product. Follow-up purchases may include repurchases that happen regularly or new purchases that are triggered by the previous purchase. Given the similar nature of survival analysis and our e-task, we propose to use the hazards model in survival analysis to estimate $p(y|p\_product)$ in this paper.

Let us review basic hazards models in survival analysis. Let $p(y)$ denote the density function of the time distribution of an event. Let y be a value of time and T be a random variable representing the event time. The cumulative distribution function is denoted as $P(y) = Pr(T \leq y)$ and survival function is denoted as $S(y) = Pr(T > y) = 1 - P(y)$. The hazards function is $h(y) = \frac{p(y)}{S(y)}$. It indicates the instantaneous potential per unit time for the event to occur at time y given that the event has not occurred up to time y.

The survival analysis further extends the model with covariates. Covariates are features that would affect the survival time. For example, if a product is on promotion, it might shorten the time before a user waits to purchase it. The covariates could include different types of features, including time independent variables (user age, gender, household income, product brand etc.), time dependent internal variables (time since last purchase of the same product, recent user search queries or clicks etc.) and time dependent external variables (global economy, seasonal index, day of the week, etc.). There are two common approaches to incorporate covariates $\mathbf{x}$(a vector of features) in a hazards model. The first approach is the *Cox proportional hazards model* [14]. It assumes that covariates are multiplicatively related to the hazards. The second approach is the *Accelerated life model* [22]. It assumes that covariates are multiplicatively related to the survival time. Research in statistics discovered that the Weibull distribution satisfies assumptions in both directions. The density function of the basic Weibull distribution is shown in Equation 2 [21].

$$p(y) = \gamma \theta y^{\gamma-1} exp\{-\theta y^{\gamma}\} \quad (2)$$

where γ is sometimes called the shape parameter and held fixed. If $\gamma = 1$, the Weibull model reduces to the exponential model and the hazard is constant. If $\gamma > 1$, the hazard increases as time increases. If $\gamma < 1$, the hazard decreases over time. θ is the scale parameter and can be re-parameterized based on a regression parameter β and covariates $\mathbf{x}$ as follows:

$$p(y) = \gamma exp\{\beta^T \mathbf{x}\} y^{\gamma-1} exp\{-exp\{\beta^T \mathbf{x}\} y^{\gamma}\} \quad (3)$$

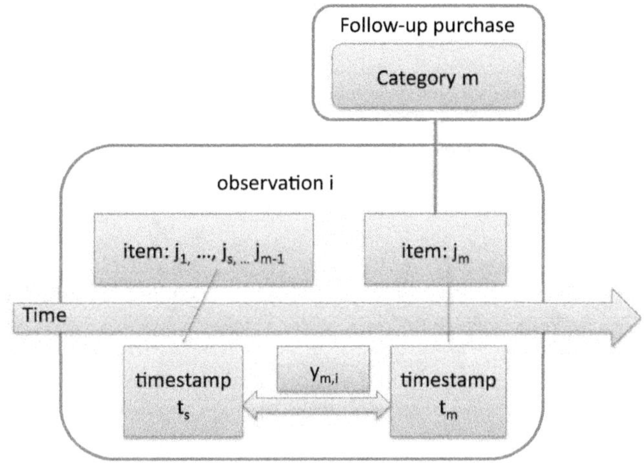

Figure 1: Illustration of the relationship of variables. The user first makes a series of product purchases before timestamp t_m. Then the user makes a purchase of item j_m in category m at timestamp t_m. This follow-up purchase in category m is the ith observation in category m. Suppose that the purchase of j_m is triggered by item j_s at timestamp t_s. Purchase time $y_{m,i} = t_m - t_s$ is the time gap between t_m and t_s. An observation i is associated with two major variables: 1) purchase time $y_{m,i}$ and 2) covariates $\mathbf{x_{m,i}}$ (which is not shown in the figure).

where $exp\{\beta^T \mathbf{x}\}$ represents the new scale parameter θ'. This density function represents the basic proportional hazards model that models the event time with associated covariates. The corresponding hazards function is simply $h(y) = \gamma \theta' y^{\gamma-1}$.

3.2 Notations

Here we describe notations in the e-commerce domain in this paper. The relationship between different variables is shown in Figure 1.

- $u = 1, 2, ..., U$: the index of users.
- $m = 1, 2, ..., M$: the index of item categories. In the e-commerce domain, it is the category of the product, such as *Apparel & Accessories|Swimwear*, *Baby|Car Seats*, *Sports and Fitness|Football*, etc.
- $j_m = 1_m, 2_m, ..., J_m$: the index of items in category m. In this paper, an item is a product.
- t_m: the purchase timestamp of item j_m.
- Δt: the window size of the purchase time in consideration (such as 3 days or 1 hour)
- D: The observed data of all follow-up purchases from all users. Each category m has N_m follow-up purchase observation from all users. Each follow-up purchase observation $i = 1, ..., N_m$ in category m is associated with the purchase time $y_{m,i}$ and covariates $\mathbf{x_{m,i}}$.
- $y_{m,i}$: the purchase time of the ith observation in category m. $y_{m,i} = t_m - t_s$ is the time distance between

the user's purchase timestamp t_m of item j_m and the user's purchase timestamp t_s of the triggering item j_s.

- $\mathbf{x_{m,i}}$: the k-dimensional vector of covariates associated with the ith observation in category m. Covariates could be associated with user u who makes the purchase, the user's purchase history $j_1, ..., j_{m-1}$, the purchase item j_m, the global environment, etc.

- $P(p\_product = yes)$: the probability of a user purchasing the product. The probability is calculated for each user-product pair.

- *Opportunity model*: density function/model to predict the joint purchase probability $p(y, p\_product)$, i.e., the probability of a user purchasing of the product at the particular time.

- *Conditional opportunity model*: density function/model to predict the conditional time probability $p(y|p\_product)$, i.e., the probability of a user purchasing the product at the particular time, given that the user will purchase the product.

3.3 Conditional Opportunity Model

In this paper we propose to adapt the Cox proportional hazards model to the e-commerce domain and use it to estimate $P(T \in (y, y+\Delta t]|p\_product)$. To do that, we learn the *conditional opportunity model* $p(y|p\_product)$, which is the density function/model of the purchasing time. We can either learn one model per product or one model per product category. Without loss of generality, we describe the model by assuming one model per category in this paper.

In the real world, a small number of categories are often purchased while most categories have few purchases. To solve the data sparsity issue, we follow a common practice and extend the conditional opportunity model with a hierarchical Bayesian framework as illustrated in Figure 2. This framework helps the category with few observations by borrowing information from other categories through a common prior for parameters of all proportional hazards models.

For each category m, β_m is sampled from a Gaussian distribution: $\beta_m \sim N(\mu_\beta, \mathbf{\Sigma}_\beta)$ and γ_m is sampled from the Gamma distribution: $\gamma_m \sim Gamma(a_\gamma, b_\gamma)$. We denote $\phi = (\mu_\beta, \mathbf{\Sigma}_\beta, \mathbf{a}_\gamma, \mathbf{b}_\gamma)$. For each ith observation in category m with its observed covariates $\mathbf{x_{m,i}}$, its purchase time $y_{m,i}$ is sampled from the conditional opportunity model

$$p(y_{m,i}|\beta_m, \gamma_m) \\ = \gamma_m exp\{\beta_m^T \mathbf{x_{m,i}}\} y_{m,i}^{\gamma_m - 1} exp\{-exp\{\beta_m^T \mathbf{x_{m,i}}\} y_{m,i}^{\gamma_m}\} \tag{4}$$

Consider that data D consists of a series of observations from all categories. Purchase times in the observations are generated by using a set of hidden variables $\theta = \{\theta_1, \theta_2 ..., \theta_M\}$ ($\theta_m = \{\beta_m, \gamma_m\}$). The likelihood can be written as a function of $\phi = (\mu_\beta, \mathbf{\Sigma}_\beta, \mathbf{a}_\gamma, \mathbf{b}_\gamma)$. We use y_m to represent $\{y_{m,1}, ..., y_{m,i}, ..., y_{m,N_m}\}$, i.e., observation times in category m.

$$p(D|\phi) = \prod_{m=1}^{M} p(y_m|\phi) = \prod_{m=1}^{M} \int p(\theta_m, y_m|\phi) d\theta_m \tag{5}$$

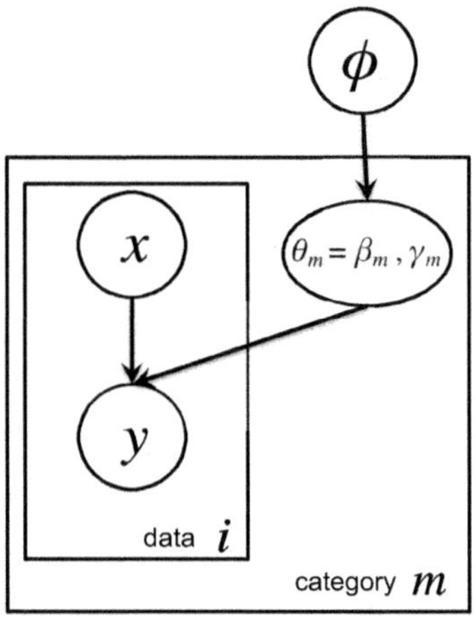

Figure 2: Illustration of dependencies of variables in the hierarchical conditional opportunity model. It shows the ith observation of category m. $y_{m,i}$ is the purchase time which is dependent on the conditional opportunity model $\theta_m = \{\beta_m, \gamma_m\}$ of category m, as wells the observed covariates $\mathbf{x_{m,i}}$ of this purchase. Each category m has its own parameters of the conditional opportunity model β_m, γ_m. Models of each category share information through the prior, $\phi = (\mu_\beta, \mathbf{\Sigma}_\beta, \mathbf{a}_\gamma, \mathbf{b}_\gamma)$.

3.4 Parameter Inference with Variational Bayesian

There is no closed-form solution for the estimation of the model parameters. We follow the variational Bayesian method[1] for constrained (approximate) optimization to derive an iterative process to find the approximate solution. Maximizing the likelihood in Equation 5 is equivalent to maximizing the log likelihood $L(\phi)$.

$$L(\phi) = \ln p(D|\phi) = \sum_{m=1}^{M} \ln p(y_m|\phi) = \sum_{m=1}^{M} \ln \int p(\theta_m, y_m|\phi) \mathrm{d}\theta_m$$

We can simplify the problem by introducing an auxiliary distribution $q(\theta_m)$ for each hidden variable θ_m [1]. In the variational approach, we constrain $q(\theta_m)$ to be a particular tractable form for computational efficiency. In particular, we assume that $q(\beta_m) = N(\mu_{\beta_m}, \Sigma_{\beta_m})$ and $q(\gamma_m) = Gamma(a_{\gamma_m}, b_{\gamma_m})$. The process to infer parameters is to iterate between the following E-step and M-step until convergence.

3.4.1 E-Step

In the **E-step**, we infer the posterior distributions over hidden variables θ_m given the current parameter setting ϕ. There is no closed-form solution. Instead, we find a tractable approximation of the posterior distribution of θ_m given ϕ (i.e, $q(\theta_m)$ that maximizes $L(\phi)$).

$$L(\phi) = \sum_{m=1}^{M} \ln \int q(\theta_m) \frac{p(\theta_m, y_m|\phi)}{q(\theta_m)} d\theta_m$$
$$\geq \sum_{m=1}^{M} \int q(\theta_m) \ln \frac{p(\theta_m, y_m|\phi)}{q(\theta_m)} d\theta_m$$
$$= \sum_{m=1}^{M} \int q(\theta_m) \ln p(y_m|\phi) d\theta_m - \sum_{m=1}^{M} \int q(\theta_m) \ln \frac{q(\theta_m)}{p(\theta_m|y_m, \phi)} d\theta_m$$
$$\equiv \boldsymbol{F}(q(\theta_1), ..., q(\theta_M), \phi) \quad (6)$$

To maximize $L(\phi)$, it is the same as minimize the following equation to find each distribution $q(\theta_m)$:

$$q(\theta_m)^{(t)} = \arg \min_{q(\theta_m)} \int q(\theta_m) \ln \frac{q(\theta_m)}{p(\theta_m|y_m, \phi)} d\theta_m \quad (7)$$

Given that $p(\theta_m|y_m, \phi) = \frac{p(y_m|\theta_m)p(\theta_m|\phi)}{p(y_m|\phi)}$, we have:

$$q(\theta_m) = \arg \min_{q(\theta_m)} KL[q(\theta_m)||p(\theta_m|\phi)] - \int q(\theta_m) \ln p(y_m|\theta_m) d\theta_m \quad (8)$$

The first part in Equation 8 is the KL-divergence between the posterior distribution $q(\theta_m)$ and the prior distribution $p(\theta_m|\phi)$.

$$KL[q(\theta_m)||p(\theta_m|\phi)] = KL[q(\beta_m)||p(\beta_m|\phi)] + KL[q(\gamma_m)||p(\gamma_m|\phi)]$$

The KL-divergence between two Gaussian distributions is

$$KL[q(\beta_m)||p(\beta_m|\phi)]$$
$$= \frac{1}{2}[tr(\Sigma_\beta^{-1}\Sigma_{\beta_m}) + (\mu_\beta - \mu_{\beta_m})^T \Sigma_\beta^{-1}(\mu_\beta - \mu_{\beta_m})$$
$$- \ln(\frac{\det \Sigma_{\beta_m}}{\det \Sigma_\beta}) - k]$$

The KL-divergence between two gamma distributions is

$$KL[q(\gamma_m)||p(\gamma_m|\phi)]$$
$$= (a_{\gamma_m} - a_\gamma)\Psi(a_{\gamma_m}) - \log\Gamma(a_{\gamma_m}) + \log\Gamma(a_\gamma)$$
$$+ a_\gamma(\log b_{\gamma_m} - \log b_\gamma) + a_{\gamma_m}\frac{b_\gamma - b_{\gamma_m}}{b_{\gamma_m}}$$

where $\Psi(*)$ is the digamma function.

The second part in Equation 8 is to maximize the data likelihood of $y_m = \{y_{m,1}, ..., y_{m,i}, ..., y_{m,N_m}\}$ with the current $\theta_m = \{\beta_m, \gamma_m\}$.

$$\sum_{i=1}^{N_m} \int q(\theta_m) \ln p(y_{m,i}|\theta_m) d\theta_m \quad (9)$$
$$= \sum_{i=1}^{N_m} \int \int q(\beta_m) q(\gamma_m) \ln p(y_{m,i}|\beta_m, \gamma_m) d\beta_m d\gamma_m$$
$$= \sum_{i=1}^{N_m} [E(\ln \gamma_m) + E(\beta_m)^T \mathbf{x_{m,i}} + (E(\gamma_m) - 1) \ln y_{m,i}$$
$$- E(exp(\beta_m^T \mathbf{x_{m,i}})) E(y_{m,i}^{\gamma_m})]$$

The expectations in the above equation are

$$E(\ln \gamma_m) = \Psi(a_{\gamma_m}) - \ln(b_{\gamma_m})$$
$$E(\beta_m) = \mu_{\beta_m}$$
$$E(\gamma_m) = \frac{a_{\gamma_m}}{b_{\gamma_m}}$$
$$E(exp(\beta_m^T \mathbf{x_{m,i}})) = exp\{\mu_{\beta_m}^T \mathbf{x_{m,i}} + \frac{1}{2}\mathbf{x_{m,i}}^T \Sigma_{\beta_m} \mathbf{x_{m,i}}\}$$
$$E(y_{m,i}^{\gamma_m}) = \frac{b_{\gamma_m}^{a_{\gamma_m}}}{(b_{\gamma_m} - \ln y_{m,i})^{a_{\gamma_m}}}$$

We can combine the above derivations with Equation 8, then find $q(\theta_m)$ using the conjugate gradient descent method.

3.4.2 M-Step

In the **M-step**, the goal is to maximize $\boldsymbol{F}(q(\theta_1), ..., q(\theta_M), \phi)$ in Equation 6 with respect to ϕ given all θ_m. It is same as to maximize the following quantity:

$$\phi^{(t+1)} \leftarrow \arg \max_{\phi} \sum_{m=1}^{M} \int q(\theta_m) \ln p(y_m|\phi) d\theta_m \quad (10)$$

The optimal ϕ at this step can be estimated with the following closed form:

$$\mu_\beta = \frac{\sum_m^M \mu_{\beta_m}}{M}$$
$$\Sigma_\beta = \frac{\sum_m^M [\Sigma_{\beta_m} + (\mu_{\beta_m} - \mu_\beta)(\mu_{\beta_m} - \mu_\beta)^T]}{M}$$
$$a_\gamma = \Psi^{-1}(\ln b_\gamma + \frac{\sum_m^M \Psi(a_{\gamma_m}) - \ln(b_{\gamma_m})}{M})$$
$$b_\gamma = \frac{M a_\gamma}{\sum_m^M \frac{a_{\gamma_m}}{b_{\gamma_m}}}$$

where $\Psi^{-1}(*)$ is the inverse digamma function.

3.5 Joint Purchase Probability

At a time y, we can decide whether to recommendation a particular product in category m to a particular user or not based on the following estimation: whether a user is likely to purchase the product in the near future (i.e. between time y and time $y + \Delta t$), given that the user has not purchased the product since a triggering time point. To do so, we need to estimate $P(p\_product = yes, T \in (y, y + \Delta t]) = P(p\_product = yes)P(y < T \leq y + \Delta t | T > y, p\_product = yes)$, where

$$P(y < T \leq y + \Delta t | T > y, p\_product = yes)$$
$$= \frac{P(T \leq y + \Delta t) - P(T \leq y)}{1 - P(T \leq y)} \quad (11)$$

where:

$$P(T \leq y) \quad (12)$$
$$= 1 - E_{\beta_m, \gamma_m}[exp\{-y^{\gamma_m} exp\{\beta_m^T \mathbf{x_i}\}\}]$$
$$\approx 1 - exp\{E_{\beta_m, \gamma_m}[-y^{\gamma_m} exp\{\beta_m^T \mathbf{x_i}\}]\}$$
$$= 1 - exp\{E_{\gamma_m}[-y^{\gamma_m}] E_{\beta_m}[exp\{\beta_m^T \mathbf{x_i}\}]\}$$
$$= 1 - exp\{-\frac{b_{\gamma_m}^{a_{\gamma_m}}}{(b_{\gamma_m} - \ln y)^{a_{\gamma_m}}} exp\{\mu_{\beta_m}^T x_i + \frac{1}{2}x_i^T \Sigma_{\beta_m} \mathbf{x_i}\}\}$$

The approximation is used because there is no closed-form solution of the integration for calculating the expectation.

To estimate $P(p\_product = yes)$, i.e., the probability of the user purchasing the product, we can use any existing recommender systems through the logistic regression model:

$$P(p\_product = yes) = \frac{1}{1 + e^{-\mathbf{f}^T \mathbf{x}}}$$

where $\mathbf{x}$ is a vector of features that are associated with the purchasing, which includes the score/output of the existing recommender system(such as SVD), as well as other features that might help to predict the user's purchase probability. $\mathbf{f}$ is a vector of coefficients that can be learnt by maximizing the likelihood of the training data.

3.6 Implementation Details

The purchase time y_m is determined by the purchase timestamp of product j_m and that of the triggering product j_s. The triggering product is not necessarily the product in the most recent purchase. There are multiple heuristic approaches to find the triggering item j_s in the user's purchase history. Here we leverage the transition probability $P(j_s, j_m)$ in Equation 13.

$$P(j_a, j_b) = \frac{\#\ (j_a, j_b) + \lambda}{\sum \#\ (j_a, *) + J \cdot \lambda} \tag{13}$$

where $\#\ (j_a, j_b)$ is the number of follow-up purchases of j_b that happened after j_a. $\sum \#\ (j_a, *)$ is the number of follow-up purchases after j_a. J is the number of products and λ is the smoothing factor, which is set as 0.1.

We first rank all items $\{j_1, ..., j_s, ..., j_{m-1}\}$ that happened less than k_t days before j_m and have $P(j_s, j_m) > Thres_{tran}$. Then we use the top one as the triggering item. Other approaches can be explored in the future work. Although other purchases $\{j_1, ..., j_{s-1}, j_{s+1}, ..., j_{m-1}\}$ in the user history are not treated as the triggering item, they are incorporated into the opportunity model as covariates $\mathbf{x_{m,i}}$.

In this paper, we use the following covariates for each purchase of product j_m made by user u at timestamp t_m: whether user u purchased any product in category m in time bin $t_{b1}, ..., t_{bk}$; how many times the user u purchased any product in category m in time bin $t_{b1}, ..., t_{bk}$; whether the user purchased the product j_m in time bin $t_{b1}, ..., t_{bk}$; how many times the user u purchased the product j_m in time bin $t_{b1}, ..., t_{bk}$; which season t_m is in, whether t_m is in the holiday season, etc. Time bins $t_{b1}, ..., t_{bk}$ are set as one day, one week, one month, two months, three months, six months, one year, etc. We choose these covariates to show the effect of incorporating covariates in the conditional opportunity model. These covariates capture the change of the time distribution with the user's purchase history, the seasonal change, the cyclic pattern, etc. All covariates are normalized in the scale of $[0, 1]$.

4. EVALUATION METHODOLOGY

As we are studying a new problem of recommending the right product at the right time, there is no standard evaluation methodology. We design various experiments to evaluate the performance of the opportunity model. Major research questions that we aim to answer are:

Predictability of the conditional opportunity model How accurate is the conditional time probability that is predicted by the conditional opportunity model? How accurate is the predicted purchase time, compared to the actual purchase time? Are covariates useful?

Predictability of the opportunity model Is the joint purchase probability a good signal of making recommendations? Does it generate a better ranking in traditional zero-query pull-based recommendation systems? Can it help to improve the user satisfaction/utility in proactive push-based recommendation systems?

4.1 Evaluation of Conditional Opportunity Model

4.1.1 Metrics

It is a relatively new research topic to predict the purchase time and evaluate the performance of such model. We introduce the following two metrics to evaluate the performance of the conditional opportunity model.

The first metric is the perplexity of the model. It is motivated by the perplexity metric used to evaluate language models and speech recognition [2]. The perplexity measures how well a model predicts the testing data. It is defined as follows:

$$perplexity = \left(\prod_{m=1}^{M}\prod_{i=1}^{N_m} \frac{1}{P(T \in (y, y + \Delta t]|p\_product)}\right)^{\frac{1}{\sum_{m=1}^{M} N_m}} \tag{14}$$

$$= 2^{-\sum_{m=1}^{M}\sum_{i=1}^{N_m}\frac{1}{\sum_{m=1}^{M} N_m} log_2 P(T \in (y, y+\Delta t]|p\_product)}$$

where $P(T \in (y, y{+}\Delta t]|p\_product)$ is defined in Equation 11, and i is the index for a testing data point. A better model tend to give a higher data likelihood to the actual follow-up purchase time in the testing data, thus they have lower *perplexity*, which means they are less surprised by the testing data.

The second metric focuses on the difference between the estimated time $y_{m,i}$ and the actual time $\hat{y}_{m,i}$. After a model predicts the distribution $p(y_{m,i}|p\_purchase)$ of the purchase time, we use the median of the distribution as the estimated purchase time $\hat{y}_{m,i}$. The median of the distribution is $exp(\beta_m \mathbf{x_{m,i}})^{-\frac{1}{r_m}} (\ln 2)^{\frac{1}{r_m}}$. The error across all testing data can then be used to analyze and compare. The smaller the error, the better the model. Here we use three types of errors: mean absolute error(MAE), mean squared error(MSE) and mean absolute percentage error($MAPE = \frac{1}{\sum_{m=1}^{M} N_m}\sum_{m=1}^{M}\sum_{i=1}^{N_m}\frac{|\hat{y}_{m,i} - y_{m,i}|}{y_{m,i}}$).

4.1.2 Conditional Opportunity Models to Compare

In our experiments, we compare the following four conditional opportunity models.

Uniform assigns a uniform distribution to all time. $p(y_{m,i} |p\_purchase) = \frac{1}{T_{uniform}}$ where $T_{uniform}$ is the maximum time in consideration. We set $T_{uniform} = 500$, i.e., 500 days, arbitrarily in this paper.

O-One is a conditional opportunity model that fits a **single** set of parameters with no covariates (i.e., a basic Weibull distribution) to the purchase data. All follow-up purchases in different category m use the same model.

O-Dest is a hierarchical conditional opportunity model that fits one Weibull distribution per product category, with no covariates.

O-DestCov further incorporates covariates into *O-Dest*. In this case, the probability density function changes for each user and product as values of the associated covariates change over time.

All models smooth the conditional probability estimation $P(T \in (y, y + \Delta t]|p\_product) = \max(P(\text{minThres}, T \in (y,$

Table 1: The utility set of the recommender system. There are four types of utilities, depending on whether the system recommends the item to the user and whether the user purchases the item.

	show:Y	show:N
accept:Y	u_{TP}	u_{FN}
accept:N	u_{FP}	u_{TN}

$y + \Delta t]|p\_product))$ to avoid having a probability that is too low (such as when there is no triggering item before the purchase). minThres is set as 0.001. Δt in Equation 11 is set as 7 (i.e., 7 days) for all models during the prediction step. The threshold for the transition probability to consider the an item j_s as the triggering item is set as 0.01.

4.2 Evaluation of Opportunity Model

4.2.1 Metrics

Here we evaluate the predictability of the opportunity model with the joint purchase probability in two scenarios.

1) **[Zero-query pull-based scenario]** assumes the user comes to the site to look for products to purchase without issuing any search query. In this scenario, the goal is to discover products that the user would purchase and recommend them to the user proactively. The system ranks all products by their joint purchase probability and recommends top K products to the user.

The evaluation metric in this scenario is the conversion rate which reflects whether a user receives at least one good recommendation. Each testing time corresponds to the time when a user comes to the site and makes purchases. Let $S_{purchased}$ contain all unique products in the order. Let $C_{purchased}$ contain all unique categories in the order. Let $S_{K,recommended}$ contain top K unique product recommendations. Let $C_{K,recommended}$ top K unique category recommendations. $CR_{product}$ is the conversion rate at the product level and $CR_{category}$ is the conversion rate at the category level. Significance level of 0.05 with the paired two-tailed t-test is used to compare two models.

$$CR_{product}@K = \begin{cases} 1 & S_{purchased} \cap S_{K,recommended} \neq \varnothing \\ 0 & otherwise \end{cases}$$

$$CR_{category}@K = \begin{cases} 1 & C_{purchased} \cap C_{K,recommended} \neq \varnothing \\ 0 & otherwise \end{cases}$$

2) **[Push-based email promotion scenario]** assumes that recommender systems send email/message proactively to a user regularly regardless of whether the user comes to the site or not.

The evaluation metric in this scenario is the average utility/user satisfaction. The utility for each type of recommendations is shown in Table 1. The $utility_g$ for each email of recommendations is calculated by Equation 15.

$$utility_g = \sum (u_{TP} I_{show,accept} + u_{FP} I_{show,\bar{accept}} + u_{FN} I_{\bar{show},accept} + u_{TN} I_{\bar{show},\bar{accept}}) \quad (15)$$

I_* is the indicator function where $I_* = 1$ if $*$ is true. Unlike traditional metrics such as conversion rate@K, the utility metric considers both the positive effect for *good* recommendations and the negative effect for *bad* recommendations. The higher the utility, the better the model.

To achieve a better utility, the system with a filtering component should send emails only if the expected utility of adding the product is higher than zero (i.e. the joint probability is higher than the threshold). The recommendation threshold is automatically determined by the following equation [4]: $\frac{u_{FP}-u_{TN}}{u_{FP}-u_{TN}+u_{FN}-u_{TP}}$.

We don't have a real push-based email promotion system for a user study. Instead, we create an evaluation dataset with the purchase data from a pull-based e-commerce website. The goal is to evaluate each model's predictability of discovering the "real opportunity" and avoiding the "fake opportunity" in the email marketing. For each purchase at time t in the testing dataset, we let each model consider two opportunities: sending a recommendation email the weekend right before t and sending an email on some other random weekend before t. Since existing models can not tell whether to send an email or not, they always send an email with top K recommendations for each opportunity. The opportunity model with a filtering component will add a product to the email if the expected utility of adding the product is higher than zero. If no product is added to the email, the opportunity model would skip this opportunity and do not send an email. Recommendations in the email are compared with actual products that the user purchases in the week after the email is sent. Assume that there are G opportunities to send recommendation emails in the testing period. The average utility/user satisfaction $utility$ can be calculated as following: $utility = \frac{\sum_{g=1}^{G} utility_g}{G}$.

4.2.2 Recommendation Models to Compare

We choose the following recommendation models to compare:

TopPop recommends most popular products to the user.

SVD is a widely-used recommendation algorithm with a decent performance on the well-known Netflix competition. It is the basis of several recommendation algorithms based on latent factors.

SVD.util is the state-of-art recommendation algorithm in the e-commerce domain without time consideration. It modifies SVD with the marginal net utility framework [19].

Regression.Model is an alternative new approach to predict the probability of a user purchasing a product at a particular time using a logistic regression model, with various important time-dependent features. This model contains features such as the SVD score of the product, whether the product/category has been purchased t days ago, how many time the product/category has been purchased t days ago, etc.

Conditional.Opportunity.Model recommends products based on $P(T \in (y, y + \Delta t])$, which is estimated by the hierarchical conditional opportunity model with covariates.

Opportunity.Model recommends products based on the joint probability of a user making a purchase of a product in the near future($P(p\_product, T \in (y, y + \Delta t])$).

Opportunity.Model.Filtering adds a filtering component to *Opportunity.Model*. In the push-based email scenario, it adds a product to the promotion email only if the expected utility of adding the product is higher than zero.

4.3 Dataset

The purchase history from 2004-01-01 to 2009-03-08 collected on a real-world e-commerce website, shop.com, is used for our experiments. We use all purchases that have category information of the product. Tail users that made less than 5 product purchases are filtered out in the training data, which follows the similar pre-processing in related work [19, 24]. In addition, 10 possible spam users that made more than 200 product purchases are filtered out as well. The remaining data contains 11,351 users and 67,291 products. There are 105,550 unique (user, product) pairs. This user-product matrix is quite sparse, with only 0.014% density. There are 380 categories in total.

To evaluate the conditional opportunity model as in Section 4.1, 10-fold cross validation is used. To evaluate the opportunity model with the joint purchase probability as in Section 4.2, we sort all purchase history by time. The first 90% is used as the training data (data before 2008-11-24) and the last 10% is used as the testing data (data after 2008-11-24). There are 7,014 testing cases in total. At the product level, there are 1,143 repurchase cases(16.29%) and 6,269 new purchase cases(89.37%). At the categorical level, there are 2,850 repurchase cases(i.e. 40.63% cases with purchase from the same category) and 4,850 new purchase cases(i.e. 69.14% cases with purchase from a new category).

To train the regression model with SVD as one of the features, the first half training data is used to train the SVD model and the second half training data is used to learn coefficients in the regression model. The number of latent factors for all SVD-related models is set to 50. In the recommendation step, all models recommend top K (K=5) products to the user. To save the computation time, $Regression.Model$, $Conditional.Opportunity.Model$ and $Opportunity.Model$ rank among top N recommendations from SVD and selects top K to recommend, where $N = 100$ and $K = 5$.

The time density plots of some common transitions from products in the *Baby|Feeding* category to the target item j_m are shown in Figure 3. This supports our motivation of identifying triggering items in the user history. For example, users who purchased from *Baby|Feeding* would purchase items in other *Baby* related categories in the future. The purchase time of the follow-up purchase does follow different distributions for different products or different covariates (take the triggering product as a covariate). For example, users who purchased from the *Baby|Feeding* category would purchase products from this category again in one month. Later on when the baby grows up, they would purchase products from *Toys|Board, Card&Dice Games.*

5. EXPERIMENTAL RESULTS

5.1 Analysis of Conditional Opportunity Model

The perplexity of all conditional opportunity models in Section 4.1.2 are compared in Table 2. All conditional opportunity models have lower perplexity than the baseline model *Uniform*. This demonstrates that conditional opportunity models have better predictability of the time-based purchase probability in the data. Among all conditional opportunity models, *O-DestCov* achieves the lowest perplexity, followed by *O-Dest*, and *O-One*. *O-DestCov* incorporates related covariates in addition to fitting parameters of a conditional opportunity model for each category m. It shows the importance of considering covariates when modeling the purchase time of a follow-up purchase.

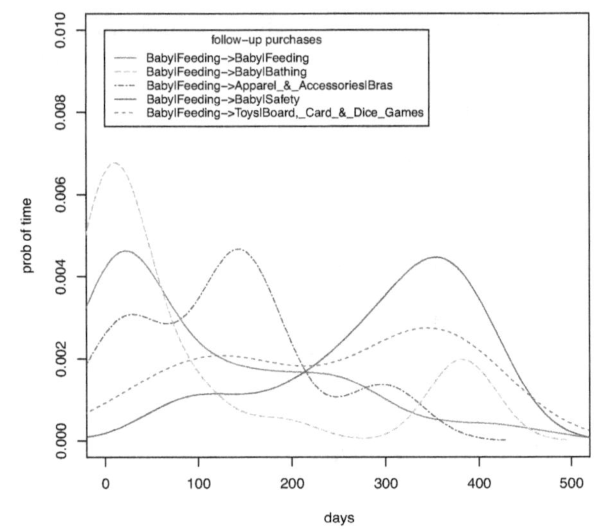

Figure 3: Density plot of the purchase time between different follow-up purchases from Baby|Feeding

Table 2: Perplexity of different conditional opportunity models in 10-fold cross validation.

Data	Uniform	O-One	O-Dest	O-DestCov
All purchases	46.95	23.75	22.45	**18.95**
repurchases	58.99	16.68	14.80	**9.75**
new purchases	44.25	26.04	25.01	**22.48**

To further analyze the effect of covariates, we compare the perplexity of all models in the repurchase data and the new purchase data in Table 2. As expected, the major gain is in reducing the perplexity of repurchases. More feature exploration would be useful to improve the prediction of new purchases in the future.

Now we compare the estimated purchase time with the actual time of a follow-up purchase in Table 3. All conditional opportunity models perform better than the baseline model $Uniform$. *O-DestCov* gives the most accurate estimation of the purchase time, followed by *O-Dest*, and *O-One*. According to MAE, the estimated purchase time from *O-DestCov*

Table 3: Error between the estimated purchase time and the actual purchase time. MAE stands for mean absolute error. MSE stands for mean squared error. MAPE stands for mean absolute percentage error.

Data	Error rate	Uniform	O-One	O-Dest	O-DestCov
All Purchases	MAE	159.74	105.279	102.617	**77.695**
	MSE	30859.346	23322.373	21920.462	**14335.505**
	MAPE	16.592	3.796	3.763	**2.434**
Repurchases	MAE	183.337	63.7	62.119	**34.536**
	MSE	37728.853	9406.591	8799.832	**4456.393**
	MAPE	27.895	6.165	5.631	**0.658**
New Purchases	MAE	154.244	114.956	112.042	**87.736**
	MSE	29260.204	26560.746	24973.753	**16634.239**
	MAPE	13.964	3.246	3.329	**2.847**

Table 4: Conversion rate of recommendation models in the zero-query pull-based scenario. Numbers in bold are significantly better than the corresponding value in baseline models.

Product level						
	All purchases		Repurchases		New purchases	
Model	CR@1	CR@5	CR@1	CR@5	CR@1	CR@5
TopPop	0.0	0.0155	0.0	0.0936	0.0	0.0003
SVD	0.0134	0.0344	0.0822	0.2073	0.0	0.0011
SVD.util	0.0287	0.0369	0.1750	0.2248	0.0002	0.0003
Regression.Model	**0.0339**	**0.0525**	**0.2082**	**0.3202**	0.0	0.0003
Conditional.Opportunity.Model	0.0160	0.0282	0.0962	0.1706	0.0003	0.0006
Opportunity.Model	0.0289	**0.0452**	**0.1750**	**0.2712**	0.0005	0.0011
Category level						
	All purchases		Repurchases		New purchases	
Model	CR@1	CR@5	CR@1	CR@5	CR@1	CR@5
TopPop	0.0204	0.0848	0.0130	0.1382	0.0219	0.0435
SVD	0.0577	0.1688	0.1309	0.3267	0.0066	0.0540
SVD.util	0.0751	0.1344	0.1779	0.2453	0.0041	0.0511
Regression.Model	**0.0999**	**0.1792**	**0.2330**	**0.3646**	0.0076	0.0472
Conditional.Opportunity.Model	**0.1102**	**0.2154**	**0.2467**	**0.3856**	0.0144	**0.0907**
Opportunity.Model	**0.1313**	**0.2345**	**0.3091**	**0.4495**	0.0082	**0.0816**

is 77 days away(higher or lower) from the actual time. It is a decent performance given that the total time range is 500 days. Further analysis shows that *O-DestCov* predicts more accurately in both the repurchase and the new purchase data.

5.2 Analysis of Opportunity Model

5.2.1 Pull-based Scenario

Now we evaluate the performance of the opportunity model with the joint purchase probability. The conversion rate of different recommendation models in the zero-query pull-based scenario is compared in Table 4.

The opportunity model achieves higher conversion rate at both the product level and the category level. Further analysis shows that the contribution of the conditional opportunity model is mainly at the category level. It is not surprising because the model is designed at the category level. Product-level models can be explored in the future. The key challenge is to solve the sparsity and scalability issues.

We further analyze the performance of the conversion rate in different purchase scenarios. In Table 4, we show the conversion rate of repurchases and new purchases. It is clear that the major contribution of the opportunity model is in the repurchase scenario. The observation is consistent with the evaluation of the conditional opportunity model in Section 5.1: the conditional opportunity model predicts more accurately in repurchases.

5.2.2 Push-Based Scenario

Now we evaluate all models in the push-based scenario. In the *Opportunity.Model.Filtering* model, a product is recommended only if its joint purchase probability is higher than the threshold. We evaluate the model with three sets of utility at both the product level (i.e. true positive means that the user purchased the exact product) and the category level (i.e. a true positive means that the user purchased a product in same category as the recommendation). The results are shown in Table 5. There are 3,014 email opportunities in the testing period. 55% of them have follow-up

Table 5: Average utility of email recommendations in the push-based scenario. *Coverage* is the percentage of emails that are sent among all possible opportunities. *Rec count* is the average number of unique recommendations in a email when the email is sent.

utility set 1: $u_{TP} = 3$, $u_{FN} = 0$, $u_{FP} =$ -1, $u_{TN} = 0$, Threshold = 0.25					
Product level					
Model	TopPop	SVD	SVD.util	Opportunity.Model	Opportunity.Model Filtering
Utility	-4.994	-4.862	-4.768	-4.810	**-0.048**
Coverage	1	1	1	1	0.023
Rec count	5	5	5	5	2.432
category level					
Model	TopPop	SVD	SVD.util	Opportunity.Model	Opportunity.Model Filtering
Utility	-4.823	-4.515	-4.570	-4.255	**0.006**
Coverage	1	1	1	1	0.023
Rec count	5	5	5	5	1.081
utility set 2: $u_{TP} = 10$, $u_{FN} = 0$, $u_{FP} =$ -1, $u_{TN} = 0$, Threshold = 0.09					
Product level					
Model	TopPop	SVD	SVD.util	Opportunity.Model	Opportunity.Model Filtering
Utility	-4.983	-4.621	-4.363	-4.477	**-0.399**
Coverage	1	1	1	1	0.180
Rec count	5	5	5	5	3.007
Category level					
Model	TopPop	SVD	SVD.util	Opportunity.Model	Opportunity.Model Filtering
Utility	-4.514	-3.667	-3.819	-2.951	**0.282**
Coverage	1	1	1	1	0.180
Rec count	5	5	5	5	1.880
utility set 3: $u_{TP} = 3$, $u_{FN} =$ -1, $u_{FP} =$ -1, $u_{TN} = 0$, Threshold = 0.20					
Product level					
Model	TopPop	SVD	SVD.util	Opportunity.Model	Opportunity.Model Filtering
Utility	-4.992	-4.828	-4.710	-4.762	**-0.066**
Coverage	1	1	1	1	0.033
Rec count	5	5	5	5	2.356
Category level					
Model	TopPop	SVD	SVD.util	Opportunity.Model	Opportunity.Model Filtering
Utility	-4.779	-4.394	-4.463	-4.069	**0.015**
Coverage	1	1	1	1	0.033
Rec count	5	5	5	5	1.115

purchases in the following week. Among those with follow-up purchases, the average number of purchases is 2.227.

In the *first* utility set, the utility u_{TP} for a good recommendation that the user purchases is set to 3. When the system shows a product and the user does not purchase it, the utility u_{FP} is -1. The resulting filtering threshold is 0.25. In this case, *Opportunity.Model.Filtering* has a better utility than other models by filtering out many false alarms. The average utility at the category level is higher, which is expected. It rewards a recommendation if it matches the user's purchase at the category level, which is an easier task. In general, the model with higher conversion rate in the pull-based scenario has high utility in the push-based scenario.

In the *second* utility set, the utility u_{TP} is set to 10, indicating that the user is more tolerant to **bad** recommendations. Thus the threshold is lower, being 0.09. The coverage of *Opportunity.Model.Filtering* increases while the average utility drops. There is a tradeoff between the utility and the recommendation coverage, which can be tuned in a real-world application by a user or the system designer.

In the *third* utility set, u_{FN} is set to -1. It is the penalty for not recommending a product that would be purchased by the user in the following week. Thus the coverage of *Opportunity.Model.Filtering* is higher to avoid missing good recommendations with the threshold being 0.02. It still achieves the highest utility among all models.

6. CONCLUSION AND FUTURE WORK

In this paper, we propose to develop the *opportunity model* to predict the probability of a user purchasing a product at a particular time. This is achieved by modeling the joint probability of time and product, which can be calculated by combining a proportional hazards model and a logistic regression model. The joint probability guides the system to make the right product recommendation at the right time.

This is just the first step to tackle the research problem of capturing the time-based recommendation opportunity. Besides Weibull distribution, other distributions such as Exponential, Log-logistic, Lognormal, Generalized gamma, can be explored. Further improvements could be achieved with better covariates. More systematic approaches of discovering the triggering item could be explored. It would be helpful to carry out experiments with a real push-based system to evaluate the effectiveness of the opportunity model in a real user study. Due to the limited number of research data available and our own computational limits, we only learn the category-level conditional opportunity model, which clearly work well at the category level prediction. Another follow-up work is to evaluate this approach on a large-scale system to learn the product-level models, which might lead to better prediction at the product level.

Acknowledgments

We would like to thank shop.com for sharing the data. This work was funded by National Science Foundation IIS-0713111 and IIS-0953908. Any opinions, findings, conclusions or recommendations expressed in this paper are the authors, and do not necessarily reflect those of the sponsors.

7. REFERENCES

[1] M. Beal. *Variational algorithms for approximate Bayesian inference.* PhD thesis, University of London, 2003.

[2] S. Chen, D. Beeferman, and R. Rosenfeld. Evaluation metrics for language models. In *DARPA Broadcast News Transcription and Understanding Workshop (BNTUW)*, Lansdowne, Virginia, USA, Feb. 1998.

[3] P. Cremonesi, Y. Koren, and R. Turrin. Performance of recommender algorithms on top-n recommendation tasks. In *Proceedings of the 4th ACM Recommender systems*, pages 39–46, 2010.

[4] C. Elkan. The foundations of cost-sensitive learning. In *Proceedings of the 17th international joint conference on Artificial intelligence - Volume 2*, IJCAI'01, pages 973–978, 2001.

[5] N. Golbandi, Y. Koren, and R. Lempel. Adaptive bootstrapping of recommender systems using decision trees. In *Proceedings of the fourth ACM WSDM'11.*

[6] Z. Huang, W. Chung, and H. Chen. A graph model for e-commerce recommender systems. *J. Am. Soc. Inf. Sci. Technol.*, 55:259–274, February 2004.

[7] R. Jin, L. Si, C. Zhai, and J. Callan. Collaborative filtering with decoupled models for preferences and ratings. In *Proceedings of the twelfth CIKM*, pages 309–316, New York, NY, USA, 2003. ACM.

[8] Y. S. Kim, B.-J. Yum, J. Song, and S. M. Kim. Development of a recommender system based on navigational and behavioral patterns of customers in e-commerce sites. *Expert Syst. Appl.*, 28:381–393, February 2005.

[9] Y. Koren. Factorization meets the neighborhood: a multifaceted collaborative filtering model. In *Proceeding of the 14th ACM SIGKDD KDD'08.*

[10] Y. Koren. Collaborative filtering with temporal dynamics. In *KDD*, 2009.

[11] S. li Huang. Designing utility-based recommender systems for e-commerce: Evaluation of preference-elicitation methods. *Electronic Commerce Research and Applications.*

[12] R. J. Mooney and L. Roy. Content-based book recommending using learning for text categorization. In *DL '00*, pages 195–204, 2000.

[13] D. Parra-Santander and P. Brusilovsky. Improving collaborative filtering in social tagging systems for the recommendation of scientific articles. *Web Intelligence and Intelligent Agent Technology*, 1:136–142, 2010.

[14] C. D. R. Regression models and life tables. *Journal of the Royal Statistic Society*, B(34):187–202, 1972.

[15] S. Rendle, C. Freudenthaler, and L. Schmidt-Thieme. Factorizing personalized markov chains for next-basket recommendation. In *Proceedings of the 19th WWW.*

[16] G. Shani, D. Heckerman, and R. I. Brafman. An mdp-based recommender system. *J. Mach. Learn. Res.*, 6:1265–1295, 2005.

[17] E. Shmueli, A. Kagian, Y. Koren, and R. Lempel. Care to comment?: recommendations for commenting on news stories. In *Proceedings of the 21st international conference on World Wide Web*, WWW '12, pages 429–438, New York, NY, USA, 2012. ACM.

[18] J. Wang, B. Sarwar, and N. Sundaresan. Utilizing related products for post-purchase recommendation in e-commerce. In *Proceedings of the 5th ACM Recommender systems.*

[19] J. Wang and Y. Zhang. Utilizing marginal net utility for recommendation in e-commerce. In *Proceedings of the 34th ACM SIGIR'11*, pages 1003–1012, 2011.

[20] J. Wang, Y. Zhang, and T. Chen. Unified recommendation and search in e-commerce. In *Information Retrieval Technology*, pages 296–305. Springer Berlin Heidelberg, 2012.

[21] J. Wang, Y. Zhang, C. Posse, and A. Bhasin. Is it time for a career switch? *Proceedings of the 22nd International World Wide Web Conference*, 2013.

[22] L. J. Wei. The accelerated failure time model: A useful alternative to the cox regression model in survival analysis. *Statistics in Medicine*, 11(14-15):1871–1879, 1992.

[23] L. Xiang, Q. Yuan, S. Zhao, L. Chen, X. Zhang, Q. Yang, and J. Sun. Temporal recommendation on graphs via long- and short-term preference fusion. In *Proceedings of the 16th ACM SIGKDD KDD'10.*

[24] G. Zhao, M. L. Lee, W. Hsu, and W. Chen. Increasing temporal diversity with purchase intervals. In *Proceedings of the 35th ACM SIGIR.*

Improve Collaborative Filtering Through Bordered Block Diagonal Form Matrices

Yongfeng Zhang, Min Zhang, Yiqun Liu, Shaoping Ma
State Key Laboratory of Intelligent Technology and Systems
Tsinghua National Laboratory for Information Science and Technology
Department of Computer Science & Technology, Tsinghua University, Beijing, 100084, China
zhangyf07@gmail.com {z-m,yiqunliu,msp}@tsinghua.edu.cn

ABSTRACT

Collaborative Filtering-based recommendation algorithms have achieved widespread success on the Web, but little work has been performed to investigate appropriate user-item relationship structures of rating matrices. This paper presents a novel and general collaborative filtering framework based on (Approximate) Bordered Block Diagonal Form structure of user-item rating matrices. We show formally that matrices in (A)BBDF structures correspond to community detection on the corresponding bipartite graphs, and they reveal relationships among users and items intuitionally in recommendation tasks. By this framework, general and special interests of a user are distinguished, which helps to improve prediction accuracy in collaborative filtering tasks. Experimental results on four real-world datasets, including the Yahoo! Music dataset, which is currently the largest, show that the proposed framework helps many traditional collaborative filtering algorithms, such as User-based, Item-based, SVD and NMF approaches, to make more accurate rating predictions. Moreover, by leveraging smaller and denser submatrices to make predictions, this framework contributes to the scalability of recommender systems.

Categories and Subject Descriptors

H.3.3 [**Information Storage and Retrieval**]: Information Filtering; H.3.5 [**Online Information Services**]: Web-based services

Keywords

Collaborative Filtering; Community Detection; Block Diagonal Form; Graph Partitioning

1. INTRODUCTION

Recommender Systems play an important role on the Web which is becoming more and more personalized. With their ability to discover various items of potential interest to users, recommender systems benefit users by saving time when the users are looking for what they want, and they benefit online shops that seek to expand their marketing efforts.

Collaborative Filtering (CF) [22] recommendation algorithms based on user-item rating matrices have achieved great success in recommender systems. Typically, they take a rating matrix (Figure 1(a)) as input to make rating predictions, where each row/column/cross represents a user/item/rating. An important advantage of CF-based algorithms is their ability to make recommendations without clear content descriptions of the items, which is the reason why they are widely applied in recommender systems thus far [22].

However, CF-based recommendation algorithms also suffer from several drawbacks. First is the data sparsity problem, which usually decreases the accuracy of the rating predictions. Second is the problem of scalability, which is usually caused by the presence of computationally expensive training components. Finally, the lack of distinguishing users and items from different communities, which makes them incapable of detecting users' special interests and decreases their abilities to make long tail recommendations.

Some previous research has been performed attempting to address these problems, which mainly focus on various matrix-clustering [11, 26, 27, 39, 34] or community detection [6, 36, 23] techniques. Clustering-based approaches cluster users and/or items for CF. However, in real-world applications, clusters are usually difficult to interpret. Moreover, they usually assume that a user or an item should fall into one particular cluster, which might not be a reasonable assumption in reality. Community detection approaches based on user-item bipartite graphs attempt to improve accuracy and diversity by detecting user-item communities. Distinguishing the general and special interests of a given user helps to make better recommendations, but it is difficult for them to take advantage of various successful CF techniques on rating matrices in real-world recommender systems.

In fact, rating matrices and bipartite graphs can be equivalently transformed into each other. Before problem formalization, we would like to use an intuitional example to introduce the matrix structures that are leveraged in this framework. Figure 1(a) shows a rating matrix, and its corresponding bipartite graph is shown in Figure 1(d), where each row/column/non-zero of the matrix is represented as an R-node/C-node/Edge in the graph. Figure 1(b) is a *Bordered Block Diagonal Form (BBDF)* structure of the original matrix, where Row4, Row9 and Column7 are permuted to 'borders', and the remaining parts are thus permuted into two 'diagonal blocks'. The permuting procedure is conducted recursively on the first diagonal block. The *Approximate*

SIGIR'13, July 28–August 1, 2013, Dublin, Ireland.

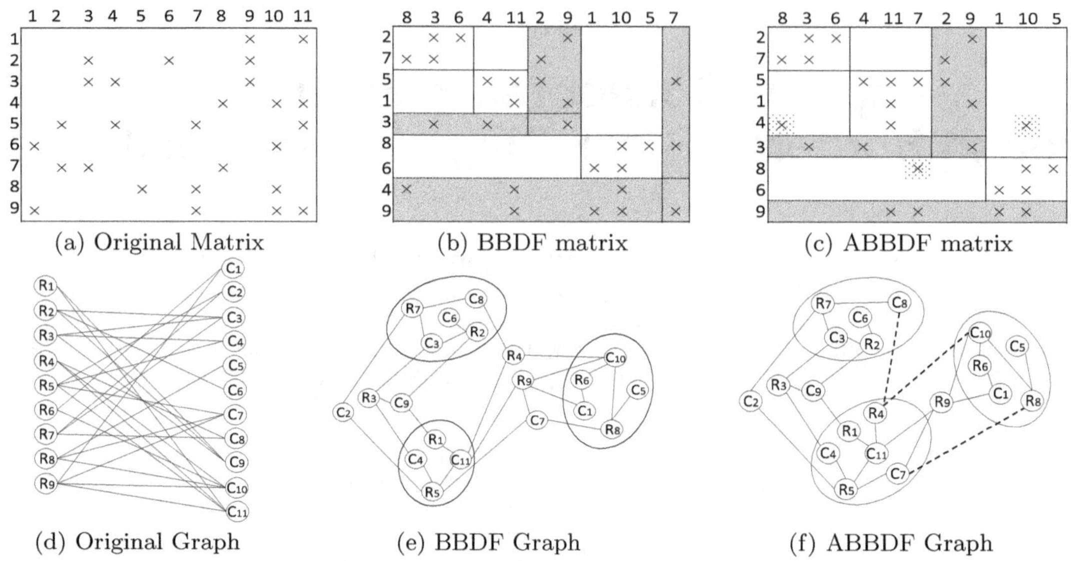

Figure 1: An example of User-Item Rating Matrices and their corresponding Bipartite Graphs.

Bordered Block Diagonal Form (ABBDF) structure is a generalization of BBDF where scattered non-zeros are allowed in off-diagonal blank areas, as shown in Figure 1(c).

It is important to note that the ABBDF structure of rating matrices is capable of representing community detection results on the corresponding bipartite graphs. In Figure 1(f), for example, each community in the graph corresponds to a diagonal block in Figure 1(c); nodes out of communities constitute borders, and dotted inter-community edges correspond to the non-zeros in off-diagonal blank areas. In this sense, BBDF structure is a special case of ABBDF when the community detection result contains no inter-community edge, as shown by the example in Figure 1(e) and 1(b).

The CF framework based on (A)BBDF structures of rating matrices proposed in this paper is capable of combining the advantages of community detection and matrix clustering techniques as well as making use of various CF algorithms. An important advantage of this framework is that it does not rely on a specific CF algorithm. Any CF algorithm that is based on rating matrices can be integrated into this framework, such as User-based, Item-based, SVD and NMF. Experimental results show that this framework helps these CF algorithms to improve the prediction accuracy and, at the same time, benefits system scalability.

In summary, the contributions of the paper are four-fold:

- The relationship between (A)BBDF structures of rating matrices and community detection on the corresponding bipartite graphs is investigated formally.
- Two density-based algorithms are designed to transform sparse rating matrices into (A)BBDF structures.
- We propose a general collaborative filtering framework based on these structures to make rating predictions in recommendation tasks.
- Both the efficiency and effectiveness of the proposed framework are verified through experimental studies on four benchmark datasets.

In the remaining part of this paper, section 2 reviews some related work, and section 3 introduces some definitions and theorems. Section 4 presents the proposed algorithms and framework. Experimental settings and results are shown in section 5. In section 6, we present a discussion, and section 7 concludes the work and provides future directions.

2. RELATED WORK

Collaborative Filtering (CF) [22, 2] algorithms based on user-item rating matrices focus on the core task of making rating predictions. They attempt to discover and leverage the knowledge of users' preferences when making recommendations. Unlike Content-Based Filtering (CBF) [28], which makes recommendations by analyzing the item features of a user's historical items, CF algorithms take advantage of the wisdom of crowds, and they usually have no special requirements on items or domains.

One of the most widely used forms of CF is the nearest neighbor approach [22]. User-based [29] and Item-based [31] CF algorithms are two best-known methods that fall into this category. Nearest neighbors can be determined by various similarity measures, such as Pearson correlation and cosine similarity. User-based CF attempts to find the neighborhood of like-minded users for each user and predicts a user's ratings according to the ratings given by the user's neighbors. Similarly, Item-based CF takes advantage of the similar items of each item, and predictions for a user are determined by the user's historical ratings. Nearest neighbor approaches are usually unable to detect item synonymies and are also computationally expensive in real-world recommender systems.

The Matrix Factorization (MF) [16] approaches attempt to factorize a rating matrix into products of real-valued component matrices. A reconstruction error objective function is usually defined, and gradient descent optimization procedures are usually conducted [25]. SVD [33, 37] and NMF [17, 40, 19] methods are typical algorithms that are investigated. However, computationally intensive training components of these techniques make them not scalable enough and impractical to conduct frequent model re-training. Incremental and distributed versions of SVD and NMF algorithms [4, 37, 32, 21, 10] partially alleviate this problem, but they are still not efficient enough because the effects of small updates to the rating matrix are not localized.

Various matrix clustering techniques have been investigated in an attempt to address the problems of efficiency, scalability and sparsity. User clustering and item clustering methods [26] cluster user or item vectors first, and nearest neighbors of a user or item are restricted to its cluster. Some other matrix clustering techniques, such as co-clustering [7, 18, 11], ping-pang algorithm [27] and clustered low-rank approximation [35], cluster users and items at the same time, and the procedure of rating prediction takes advantage of these user-item clusters. By utilizing clusters, the scalability of recommender systems is usually improved, but clusters are usually difficult to interpret. In addition, these approaches usually force a user or item to fall into a single cluster, which might not be a reasonable assumption in real-world applications.

Recently, community detection techniques based on graphs have been investigated extensively with the rapid growth of social networks [20, 24, 23, 6], which helps to improve both the accuracy and diversity of the recommender systems by extracting user or item communities.

In fact, user-item rating matrices can be equivalently transformed into bipartite graphs [1, 3], and community detection results on the bipartite graphs can be represented as (A)BBDF structures on the corresponding rating matrices. Any CF method can still be applied to the permuted matrix without any modification, but by leveraging user-item community information therein, more accurate and specific recommendations can be made.

3. DEFINITIONS AND THEOREMS

Several definitions and theorems are presented in this section, which will be the basis of the (A)BBDF permutation algorithms and the collaborative filtering framework to be proposed in Section 4.

DEFINITION 1. **Bordered Block Diagonal Form (BBDF).** *Matrix A is in Bordered Block Diagonal Form if:*

$$A = \begin{bmatrix} A_{11} & A_{12} & \cdots & A_{1k} & A_{1B} \\ A_{21} & A_{22} & \cdots & A_{2k} & A_{2B} \\ \vdots & \vdots & \ddots & \vdots & \vdots \\ A_{k1} & A_{k2} & \cdots & A_{kk} & A_{kB} \\ A_{B1} & A_{B2} & \cdots & A_{Bk} & A_{BB} \end{bmatrix} = \begin{bmatrix} D_1 & & & & C_1 \\ & D_2 & & & C_2 \\ & & \ddots & & \vdots \\ & & & D_k & C_k \\ R_1 & R_2 & \cdots & R_k & B \end{bmatrix} \quad (1)$$

Namely, $A_{ij} = \mathbf{0}$ $(i \neq j, 1 \leq i, j \leq k)$. Each D_i $(1 \leq i \leq k)$ is a 'diagonal block'; $R = [R_1 \cdots R_k B]$ and $C = [C_1^T \cdots C_k^T B^T]^T$ are 'borders'. Recursively, each of the diagonal blocks D_i can also be in the BBDF structure. □

BBDF structure is a generalization of Block Diagonal Form (BDF) matrices, for example, $A = \mathrm{diag}(D_1 D_2 \cdots D_k)$, where the latter has no border.

DEFINITION 2. **Approximate Bordered Block Diagonal Form (ABBDF).** *Matrix A is in Approximate Bordered Block Diagonal Form if:*

$$A = \begin{bmatrix} A_{11} & A_{12} & \cdots & A_{1k} & A_{1B} \\ A_{21} & A_{22} & \cdots & A_{2k} & A_{2B} \\ \vdots & \vdots & \ddots & \vdots & \vdots \\ A_{k1} & A_{k2} & \cdots & A_{kk} & A_{kB} \\ A_{B1} & A_{B2} & \cdots & A_{Bk} & A_{BB} \end{bmatrix} = \begin{bmatrix} D_1 & A_{12} & \cdots & A_{1k} & C_1 \\ A_{21} & D_2 & \cdots & A_{2k} & C_2 \\ \vdots & \vdots & \ddots & \vdots & \vdots \\ A_{k1} & A_{k2} & \cdots & D_k & C_k \\ R_1 & R_2 & \cdots & R_k & B \end{bmatrix} \quad (2)$$

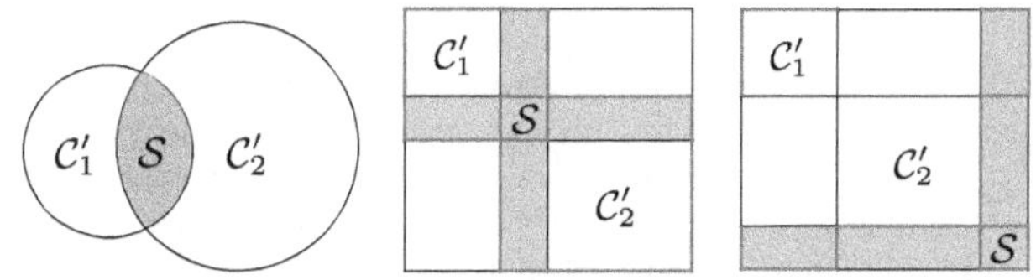

(a) Communities (b) Middle result (c) ABBDF

Figure 2: Community detection and ABBDF, $k = 2$

Namely, A_{ij} $(i \neq j, 1 \leq i, j \leq k)$ can also contain scattered non-zeros compared with the BBDF structure. $D_1 D_2 \cdots D_k$ might also be in the ABBDF structure. □

ABBDF is a generalization of BBDF in that scattered non-zeros are allowed in off-diagonal blank areas. We also refer to BBDF as Accurate BBDF to distinguish it from Approximate BBDF.

DEFINITION 3. **Community Detection.** *Given a graph $\mathcal{G} = (\mathcal{V}, \mathcal{E})$, a community in $\mathcal{G}$ is a set of vertices $\mathcal{C}_i \subseteq \mathcal{V}$, and a community detection with k $(k \geq 1)$ communities is $\mathcal{C} = \{\mathcal{C}_1 \mathcal{C}_2 \cdots \mathcal{C}_k\}$, witch satisfies the following:*

i. $\mathcal{C}_i \neq \emptyset$ $(1 \leq i \leq k)$

ii. $\mathcal{C}_i \cap \Big(\bigcup_{j=1, j\neq i}^{k} \mathcal{C}_j \Big) \neq \mathcal{C}_i$ $(1 \leq i \leq k)$

The second requirement means that each community contains at least one monopolized node. It's important to clarify that no definition of community detection is universally accepted until now because definitions often depend on a specific application and algorithm [9]. This definition is solely for introducing the relationships between the (A)BBDF structure and community detection in this paper. Even so, Definition 3 is general enough to describe the output of many frequently used community detection algorithms, including both independent and overlapping communities, depending on $\mathcal{C}_i \cap \big(\bigcup_{j=1,j\neq i}^{k} \mathcal{C}_j\big) = \emptyset$ $(1 \leq i \leq k)$ or not.

THEOREM 1. *Any community detection result with k communities $\mathcal{C} = \{\mathcal{C}_1 \mathcal{C}_2 \cdots \mathcal{C}_k\}$ on a bipartite graph $\mathcal{G} = (\mathcal{V}, \mathcal{E})$ can be represented as an ABBDF structure with k diagonal blocks on its corresponding rating matrix A.*

PROOF. Without loss of generality, we assume that $\bigcup_{i=1}^{k} \mathcal{C}_i = \mathcal{V}$, in other words, that each node belongs to at least one community. Otherwise, we permute the nodes in $\mathcal{V} - \bigcup_{i=1}^{k} \mathcal{C}_i$ to the borders first. We will make a proof by induction.

If $k = 1$, then the property holds naturally, and the matrix is viewed as a single diagonal block.

If $k = 2$, then permute the nodes in $\mathcal{S} = \mathcal{C}_1 \cap \mathcal{C}_2$ to borders, followed by permuting the nodes in $\mathcal{C}_1' = \mathcal{C}_1 - \mathcal{S}$ and $\mathcal{C}_2' = \mathcal{C}_2 - \mathcal{S}$ to construct two diagonal blocks, shown in Figure 2.

Suppose that the property holds for $k = n - 1$. When $k = n$, as shown in Figure 3, let $\mathcal{S}_1 = \mathcal{C}_1 \cap \big(\bigcup_{i=2}^{n} \mathcal{C}_i\big)$ and $\mathcal{C}_i' = \mathcal{C}_i - \mathcal{S}_1$ $(1 \leq i \leq n)$. Note that $\mathcal{C}_i' \neq \emptyset$ $(1 \leq i \leq n)$,

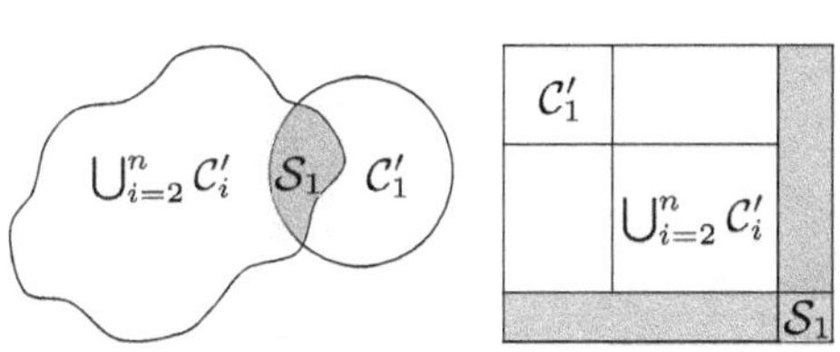

Figure 3: Community detection and ABBDF, $k = n$

according to Definition 3. Permute the vertices in $\mathcal{S}_1$ to the borders, permute $\mathcal{C}_1'$ to the upper-left corner and permute $\bigcup_{i=2}^{n}\mathcal{C}_i'$ to the bottom-right corner. According to the inductive assumption, $\bigcup_{i=2}^{n}\mathcal{C}_i'$ can be permuted into an ABBDF structure with $n-1$ diagonal blocks in the same manner. As a result, the final matrix is an ABBDF structure with n diagonal blocks, and the final border is $\mathcal{S}=\bigcup_{i=1}^{n-1}\mathcal{S}_i$. □

It is helpful to look at the case of $k=3$, as shown in Figure 4. First, let $\mathcal{S}_1=\mathcal{C}_1\cap(\mathcal{C}_2\cup\mathcal{C}_3)$ and $\mathcal{C}_i'=\mathcal{C}_i-\mathcal{S}_1$ $(i=1,2,3)$. Permute $\mathcal{S}_1$ to the borders, and there will be two diagonal blocks in the matrix, corresponding to vertex sets $\mathcal{C}_1'$ and $\mathcal{C}_2'\cup\mathcal{C}_3'$. Moreover, let $\mathcal{S}_2=\mathcal{C}_2'\cap\mathcal{C}_3'$ and $\mathcal{C}_i''=\mathcal{C}_i'-\mathcal{S}_2$ $(i=2,3)$. By recursively permuting $\mathcal{S}_2$ to the borders, one of the diagonal blocks is again permuted into an ABBDF structure, which gives us two new diagonal blocks that correspond to $\mathcal{C}_2''$ and $\mathcal{C}_3''$. The final number of diagonal blocks is 3, and the border is $\mathcal{S}=\mathcal{S}_1\cup\mathcal{S}_2$.

Corollary 1. *Given a community detection result $\mathcal{C}=\{\mathcal{C}_1\mathcal{C}_2\cdots\mathcal{C}_k\}$ on a bipartite graph, let $\mathcal{S}_i=\mathcal{C}_i\cap\big(\bigcup_{j=1,j\neq i}^{k}\mathcal{C}_j\big)$ and $\mathcal{C}_i'=\mathcal{C}_i-\mathcal{S}_i$ for each $1\le i\le k$. Then, $\mathcal{C}$ corresponds to an Accurate BBDF structure if and only if there is no edge from $\mathcal{C}_i'$ to $\mathcal{C}_j'$ when $i\neq j$.*

Proof. The result follows from the fact that a non-zero in the off-diagonal blank areas in an ABBDF structure corresponds to an edge that connects two nodes, u and v, from two communities, $\mathcal{C}(u)$ and $\mathcal{C}(v)$, where u and v are monopolized by $\mathcal{C}(u)$ and $\mathcal{C}(v)$, correspondingly. □

Intuitionally, a diagonal block in an (A)BBDF matrix is a 'user-item community', with its users and items being its 'dominant' users and items. The borders can be viewed as 'super' users and items among communities. Super users are users whose tastes are relatively broad and fall into different communities. Super items are items favored by users from different communities. Users might indeed focus their main attentions on certain fields, but they do step into other fields occasionally, which is important when detecting the potential interests of a user. In this sense, an Approximate BBDF structure is more natural than an Accurate BBDF structure.

The following definitions and theorems concern how to permute a sparse rating matrix into accurate and approximate BBDF structures.

Definition 4. **Graph Partitioning by Vertex Separator (GPVS)-based Community Detection.**
Consider an undirected graph $\mathcal{G}=(\mathcal{V},\mathcal{E})$. $Adj(v)$ denotes the set of vertices adjacent to v. For a vertex subset $\mathcal{V}'\subset\mathcal{V}$, $Adj(\mathcal{V}')=\{v_j\in\mathcal{V}-\mathcal{V}':\exists v_i\in\mathcal{V}' s.t.\ v_j\in Adj(v_i)\}$.
$\mathcal{V}_S\subset\mathcal{V}$ is a vertex separator if the subgraph induced by $\mathcal{V}-\mathcal{V}_S$ has $k\ge 2$ connected components. Formally, GPVS is defined as $\Gamma_v=\{\mathcal{V}_1\mathcal{V}_2\cdots\mathcal{V}_k;\mathcal{V}_S\}$, where $\mathcal{V}_i\neq\emptyset$, $\mathcal{V}_i\cap\mathcal{V}_S=\emptyset$, $Adj(\mathcal{V}_i)\subset\mathcal{V}_S$ for $1\le i\le k$, $\mathcal{V}_i\cap\mathcal{V}_j=\emptyset$ for $1\le i<j\le k$, and $(\bigcup_{i=1}^{k}\mathcal{V}_i)\cup\mathcal{V}_S=\mathcal{V}$. Note that $\mathcal{V}_S=\emptyset$ is allowed.
$\mathcal{C}=\{\mathcal{C}_1\mathcal{C}_2\cdots\mathcal{C}_k\}$ is the community detection result, where $\mathcal{C}_i=\mathcal{V}_i\cup\mathcal{V}_S$ $(1\le i\le k)$. □

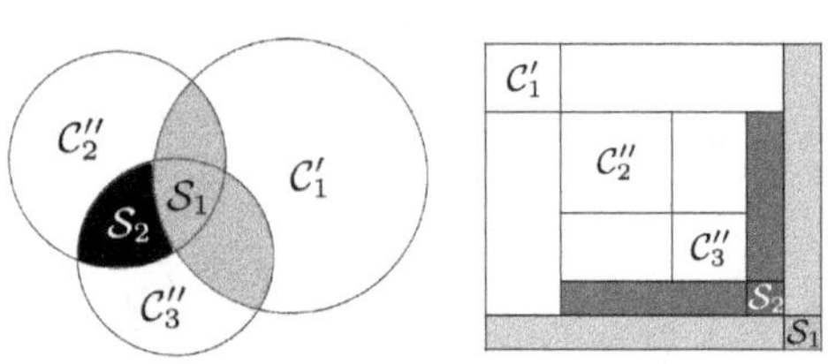

Figure 4: Community detection and ABBDF, $k=3$

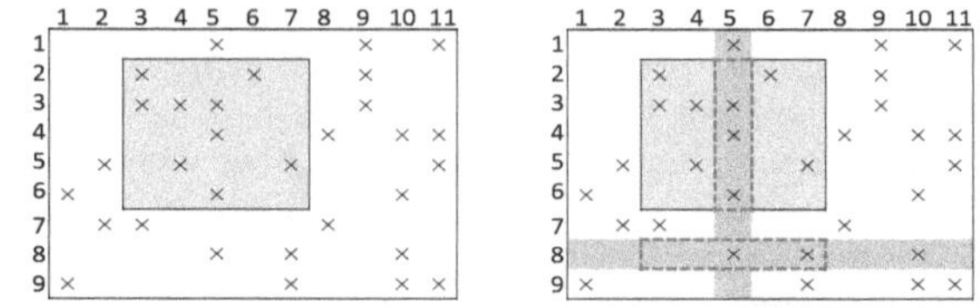

(a) A block in matrix (b) Restricted lines

Figure 5: Block, Line and Line Density

Intuitively in GPVS, the removal of a vertex separator splits the graph into k connected components. GPVS is a type of community detection algorithm that corresponds to accurate BBDF structures. This conclusion can be derived directly from Corollary 1 and Definition 4 because $\mathcal{S}_i=\mathcal{C}_i\cap\big(\bigcup_{j=1,j\neq i}^{k}\mathcal{C}_j\big)=\mathcal{V}_S$ and $\mathcal{C}_i'=\mathcal{C}_i-\mathcal{S}_i=\mathcal{V}_i$ are disconnected when $i\neq j$.

The reader can refer to Figure 1(b) and 1(e) for an example. By first removing nodes R_4 R_9 and C_7 which are represented by shaded borders, the remaining nodes are partitioned into two parts, corresponding to the two main diagonal blocks in the rating matrix. Furthermore, by removing nodes R_3 C_2 and C_9, one of the diagonal blocks is again permuted into the BBDF structure with two diagonal blocks.

Definition 5. **Graph Partitioning by Edge Separator (GPES)-based Community Detection.**
Consider the undirected graph $\mathcal{G}=(\mathcal{V},\mathcal{E})$.
$\mathcal{E}_S\subset\mathcal{E}$ is an edge separator if the removal of $\mathcal{E}_S$ gives $\Gamma_e=\{\mathcal{V}_1\mathcal{V}_2\cdots\mathcal{V}_k\}$ $(k\ge 2)$, where $\mathcal{V}_i\neq\emptyset$ for $1\le i\le k$, $\mathcal{V}_i\cap\mathcal{V}_j=\emptyset$ for $1\le i<j\le k$, $\bigcup_{i=1}^{k}\mathcal{V}_i=\mathcal{V}$, and the subgraphs induced by $\mathcal{V}_i$ and $\mathcal{V}_j$ are disconnected for $i\neq j$.
$\mathcal{C}=\{\mathcal{C}_1\mathcal{C}_2\cdots\mathcal{C}_k\}$ is the community detection result, where $\mathcal{C}_i=\mathcal{V}_i$ $(1\le i\le k)$. □

GPES-based community detection corresponds to an ABBDF structure with no border because $\mathcal{S}_i=\mathcal{C}_i\cap\big(\bigcup_{j=1,j\neq i}^{k}\mathcal{C}_j\big)=\emptyset$. This structure can be used to further construct an ABBDF structure with borders when necessary, which will be presented by the algorithms in the following sections.

Definition 6. **Density.** *Let A be an $m\times n$ $(m,n\ge 1)$ matrix, let $\mathrm{n}(A)$ be the number of non-zeros in A, and let $\mathrm{area}(A)=m\times n$ be the area of A.*
The density of A is $\rho(A)=\frac{\mathrm{n}(A)}{\mathrm{area}(A)}$, and the average density of k matrices $A_1\cdots A_k$ is $\bar{\rho}(A_1\cdots A_k)=\frac{\sum_{i=1}^{k}\mathrm{n}(A_i)}{\sum_{i=1}^{k}\mathrm{area}(A_i)}$. Let $\mathcal{G}$ denote the bipartite graph of A; then, $\rho(\mathcal{G})=\rho(A)$, $\bar{\rho}(\mathcal{G}_1\cdots\mathcal{G}_k)=\bar{\rho}(A_1\cdots A_k)$.
A row or a column of matrix A is referred to as a 'line'. The density of line l restricted to a block B is $\rho(l(B))$, where $l(B)$ denotes the sub-vector on line l that is restricted to block B, shown as the red dashed rectangles in Figure 5(b). □

The density of graphs or matrices has been widely used in various community detection algorithms and tasks [9]. Taking Figure 5 as an example, the density of the shaded block is $\frac{9}{25}$ in Figure 5(a). In Figure 5(b), the density of column 5 is $\frac{5}{9}$, and the density of row 8 restricted to the shaded block is $\frac{2}{5}$.

4. ALGORITHMS

4.1 Accurate BBDF Permutation

4.1.1 Basic Procedure of BBDF Permutation

In accurate BBDF permutation, a basic procedure is performed recursively, which is to permute some lines to borders and to permute the remaining part to construct several diagonal blocks. This recursive framework is known as *George's nested dissection approach* [3, 14], which has been widely used in fill-reducing ordering of sparse matrices. This basic procedure is investigated in this subsection, and the accurate BBDF permutation algorithm in the following subsection leverages this procedure.

The basic step is equivalent to GPVS [1] on the corresponding user-item bipartite graph, which has been shown in preliminaries. It is typical that a graph has more than one vertex separator, and a proper GPVS algorithm attempts to find the one with the least number of vertices, namely, the *minimum vertex separator*. Unfortunately, the minimum vertex cut problem is known to be NP-hard [5], but this problem has been investigated extensively, and many efficient and high-quality heuristic-based methods have been proposed [15], such as the multilevel approach, spectral partitioning and kernel-based methods. It has been verified both theoretically and experimentally that multilevel approaches usually provides both fast execution time and very high quality partitions [15, 30, 1, 3]. Perhaps the most widely known and used package for graph partitioning is Metis by Karypis [13], which is based on a multilevel approach, and we chose the core multilevel graph partitioning routine implemented in Metis as the basic GPVS algorithm.

In this study, we utilize the *density* of user-item communities to control the procedure of BBDF permutation because dense subgraphs are usually interpreted as actual communities. This approach has been widely used in community detection tasks [9]. Algorithm 1 shows the basic procedure.

Algorithm 1 Basic-BBDF-Permutation($A, \mathcal{G}$)

Require:
User-Item rating matrix A.
Bipartite graph $\mathcal{G} = (\mathcal{V}, \mathcal{E}) = (\mathcal{R} \cup \mathcal{C}, \mathcal{E})$ of A. ▷ $\mathcal{R}/\mathcal{C}$ are row/column vertex sets of $\mathcal{V}$ correspondingly.
Ensure:
Average density of resulting diagonal blocks $\bar{\rho}$.
$\Gamma_{\mathcal{V}} \leftarrow \{\mathcal{V}_1\mathcal{V}_2\cdots\mathcal{V}_k; \mathcal{V}_S\} \leftarrow$ GPVS($\mathcal{G}$)
Permute rows of A in order of $\mathcal{R}_1\mathcal{R}_2\cdots\mathcal{R}_k\mathcal{R}_S$
Permute columns of A in order of $\mathcal{C}_1\mathcal{C}_2\cdots\mathcal{C}_k\mathcal{C}_S$
return $\bar{\rho}(D_1D_2\cdots D_k)$ ▷ D_i denotes the i-th diagonal block which corresponds to vertex set $\mathcal{V}_i = \mathcal{R}_i \cup \mathcal{C}_i$

We expect the average density of diagonal blocks to be improved compared with the density of the original matrix A after permutation; we discuss the relevant issues here.

Taking the notations in Definition 6, we have:

$$\rho(A) = \frac{\mathrm{n}(A)}{\mathrm{area}(A)}, \quad \bar{\rho}(D_1\cdots D_k) = \frac{\sum_{i=1}^{k}\mathrm{n}(D_i)}{\sum_{i=1}^{k}\mathrm{area}(D_i)}$$

Let $n = \mathrm{n}(A), n_1 = \sum_{i=1}^{k}\mathrm{n}(D_i), n_2 = n - n_1$; $s = \mathrm{area}(A)$, $s_1 = \sum_{i=1}^{k}\mathrm{area}(D_i), s_2 = s - s_1$. We have:

$$\rho_A = \rho(A) = \frac{n}{s}, \quad \rho_1 = \bar{\rho}(D_1\cdots D_k) = \frac{n_1}{s_1}, \quad \rho_2 = \frac{n_2}{s_2}$$

where ρ_2 represents the average density of off-diagonal blank areas plus borders. Let $\bar{\rho}(D_1\cdots D_k) > \rho(A)$, namely, $\rho_1 > \rho_A$; then, we have:

$$\frac{n_1}{s_1} > \frac{n}{s} = \frac{n_1 + n_2}{s_1 + s_2} \quad \Leftrightarrow \quad \frac{n_1}{s_1} > \frac{n_2}{s_2} \quad \Leftrightarrow \quad \rho_1 > \rho_2$$

This statement means that the average density of the resulting diagonal blocks will increase if and only if it is greater than the average density of the remaining parts. This relationship is usually satisfied because the GPVS algorithm attempts to find a separator with the minimum number of vertices. Furthermore, the total area of off-diagonal blocks plus borders tends to be much larger than the area of the diagonal blocks [1]. For this reason, we choose the average density to be an important controller in the algorithm.

4.1.2 Accurate BBDF Permutation Algorithm

The density-based BBDF permutation algorithm requires a parameter ρ as an input, which is a pre-defined requirement on the minimum average density of diagonal blocks. It conducts Basic-BBDF-Permutation on a matrix and recurses on each of the resulting diagonal blocks until the density of a diagonal block has reached the density requirement ρ or the Basic-BBDF-Permutation cannot improve the average density any more. Algorithm 2 shows the procedure.

Algorithm 2 BBDF-Permutation($A, \mathcal{G}, \rho$)

Require:
User-Item rating matrix A.
Bipartite graph $\mathcal{G} = (\mathcal{V}, \mathcal{E})$ of A.
Density requirement ρ.
Ensure:
Matrix A permuted into BBDF structure.
1: $\rho_A \leftarrow \rho(A)$
2: **if** $\rho_A < \rho$ **then** ▷ else do nothing
3: $\bar{\rho} \leftarrow$ Basic-BBDF-Permutation($A, \mathcal{G}$)
4: **if** $\bar{\rho} > \rho_A$ **then** ▷ else do nothing
5: **for each** diagonal block D_i in A **do**
6: BBDF-Permutation($D_i, \mathcal{G}_{\mathcal{V}_i}, \rho$) ▷ $\mathcal{V}_i$ denotes the vertex set of D_i, $\mathcal{G}_{\mathcal{V}_i}$ is the subgraph induced by $\mathcal{V}_i$
7: **end for**
8: **end if**
9: **end if**

Note that, in the 4-th line, we do nothing if the average density of the resulting diagonal blocks is not improved compared with the original matrix, although some diagonals might not have reached the density requirement ρ. Such a diagonal D is viewed as a sparse user-item community, and such a case occurs when the density requirement ρ is set too high. An important reason for using the average density to prevent such diagonals from recursion is that they would result in many small scattered communities with only a few users and items. Proper density requirements give better BBDF structures, and this issue will be discussed with the experimentation below.

4.2 Approximate BBDF Permutation

Approximate BBDF can be achieved by GPES, and we also make use of the multilevel graph partitioning approach that is implemented in Metis. The ABBDF permutation algorithm also has a density requirement of ρ, as input. It computes a GPES on the bipartite graph of a rating matrix

A, and by ignoring the non-zeros corresponding to the edge separator, matrix A is permuted to several diagonal blocks.

Unlike an accurate BBDF permutation, which accomplishes nothing if the average density is not improved after the permutation, the approximate BBDF permutation algorithm moves lines from diagonal blocks to borders to further improve their average density, unless the average density is greater than the original matrix. Note that this goal can always be reached because the density of a single non-zero is one. This procedure is performed recursively in each diagonal block until the density requirement is reached, as shown in Algorithm 3.

Algorithm 3 ABBDF-Permutation($A, \mathcal{G}, \rho$)

```
Require:
    User-Item rating matrix A.
    Bipartite graph G = (V, E) = (R ∪ C, E) of A.
    Density requirement ρ.
Ensure:
    Matrix A permuted into ABBDF structure.
if ρ(A) ≥ ρ then
    return
else
    Γ_e ← {V_1 V_2 ··· V_k} ← GPES(G)
    Permute rows of A in order of R_1 R_2 ··· R_k
    Permute columns of A in order of C_1 C_2 ··· C_k
    {V'_1 V'_2 ··· V'_k; V'_S} ←Improve-Density(A, G, Γ_e)
    for each diagonal block D_i in A do
        ABBDF-Permutation(D_i, G_{V'_i}, ρ)
    end for
end if
```

The sub-procedure Improve-Density selects the specific line whose removal improves the average density the most from the diagonal blocks at each time and inserts it into the borders. This process is shown in Algorithm 4.

Algorithm 4 Improve-Density($A, \mathcal{G}, \Gamma_e$)

```
Require:
    User-Item rating matrix A.
    Bipartite graph G = (V, E) = (R ∪ C, E) of A.
    GPES resultΓ_e = {V_1 V_2 ··· V_k} of G.
Ensure:
    Average density of diagonal blocks greater than ρ(A).
{V'_1 V'_2 ··· V'_k; V'_S} ← {V_1 V_2 ··· V_k; ∅}
while ρ̄(D_1 D_2 ··· D_k) < ρ(A) do
    l', i' ← 0, ρ̄' ← 0
    for each diagonal block D_i do
        for each line l in D_i do
            ρ̄ ← (Σ_{j=1}^{k} n(D_j) − n(l(D_i))) / (Σ_{j=1}^{k} area(D_j) − area(l(D_i)))
            if ρ̄ > ρ̄' then
                l' ← l, i' ← i, ρ̄' ← ρ̄
            end if
        end for
    end for
    Permute line l' to borders
    V'_{i'} ← V'_{i'} − {node(l')}
    V'_S ← V'_S ∪ {node(l')}  ▷ node(l') denotes the node in V'_{i'} corresponding to line l'
end while
return {V'_1 V'_2 ··· V'_k; V'_S}
```

Note that, when looking for the line that improves the average density the most, there is no need to check all of the lines in each diagonal block in a real implementation. In each diagonal block, we only need to check the line with the minimum density restricted to it, namely the line that contains the fewest non-zeros in it.

4.3 (A)BBDF-based Rating Prediction

A great advantage of the CF framework based on the accurate or approximate BBDF structure is that any CF algorithm can be used on a submatrix that is made up of diagonal blocks and borders. In this paper, we do not propose new CF algorithms on (A)BBDF structures but instead propose a general CF framework, which makes use of user-item communities. By utilizing the community information, the prediction accuracy tends to be improved. Furthermore, conducting collaborative filtering on smaller and denser submatrices contributes to the scalability of CF algorithms.

The intuitive example shown in Figure 6 will be used to introduce the framework. For each diagonal block, we reconstruct its corresponding community by combining it with borders from different levels. Specifically, we use dominant users and items together with the corresponding super users and items to make predictions. In Figure 6, three submatrices are constructed, which correspond to the diagonal blocks A, B and C. Note that, in the ABBDF structure, scattered non-zeros in off-diagonal areas are ignored because they are viewed as special interests or unprofessional ratings of users.

On each submatrix, any CF algorithm can be conducted to make rating predictions. There could be more than one prediction for user-item pairs from border crosses because they are shared by different submatrices. These predictions are averaged as the final prediction. It is a natural idea that the predictions can be averaged with different weights, but in this paper, we take only the average value. The averaging strategy could be investigated in future work.

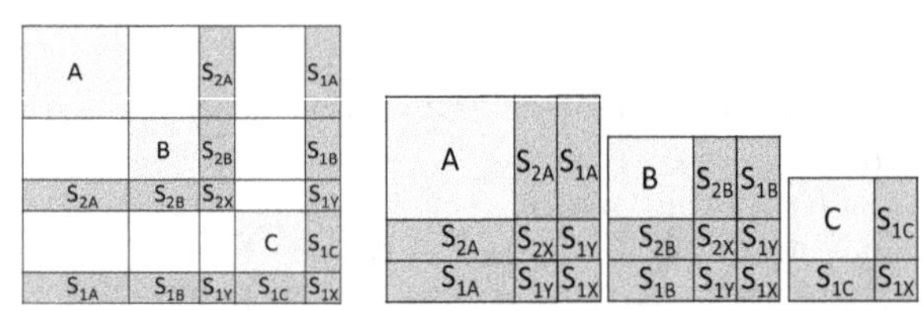

(a) BBDF matrix (b) Submatrices extracted

Figure 6: A toy example for extracting communities

5. EXPERIMENTS

5.1 Dataset Description

We conducted a series of experiments on four real-world datasets: MovieLens-100K, MovieLens-1M, Dianping and Yahoo! Music to validate the effectiveness of the proposed framework. Among these datasets, MovieLens-100K and MovieLens-1M are from the well-known MovieLens dataset.

Table 1: Statistics of the four datasets

	ML-100K	ML-1M	Dianping	Yahoo! Music
#users	943	6,040	11,857	1,000,990
#items	1,682	3,952	22,365	624,961
#ratings	100,000	1,000,209	510,551	262,810,175
#ratings/user	106.045	165.598	43.059	262.550
#ratings/item	59.453	253.089	22.828	420.523
average density	0.0630	0.0419	0.00193	0.000421

Table 2: Community analysis for Approximate BBDF on Dianping when density requirement is 0.005

Community	1	2	3	4	5	6	7	8	9
City	Chengdu	Shenzhen	Tianjin	Beijing	Nanjing	Suzhou	Hangzhou	Guangzhou	Shanghai
#users	323	288	922	2903	684	262	295	845	4531
#restaurants	1189	1359	2548	5011	1327	1443	1309	1274	4586
%accuracy	89.6	90.4	92.6	94.4	91.6	88.7	89.2	90.7	91.1

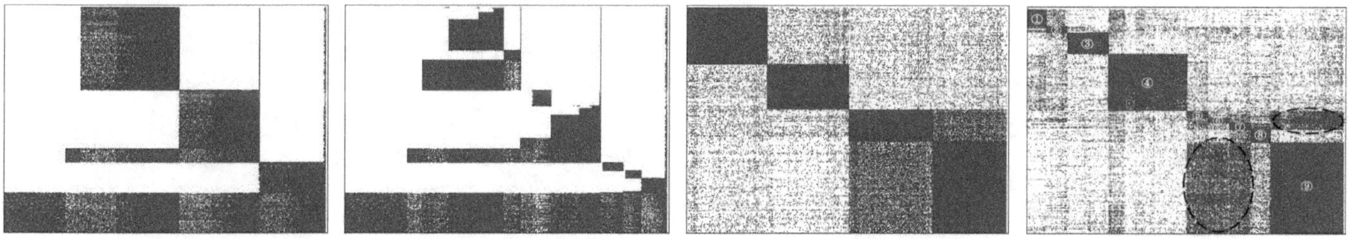

(a) BBDF $\rho = 0.005$ (b) BBDF $\rho = 0.01$ (c) ABBDF $\rho = 0.005$ (d) ABBDF $\rho = 0.01$

Figure 7: Accurate BBDF (BBDF) and Approximate BBDF (ABBDF) structures on Dianping dataset

Besides, we also collected a year's data from a famous restaurant rating web site *Dianping.com* (http://www.dianping.com) in China, and selected those users who made 20 or more ratings. The ratings also range from 1 to 5 like the MovieLens dataset. The Yahoo Music dataset [8] is from KDD Cup 2011, and its ratings range from 1 to 100. Statistics on these four datasets are presented in Table 1.

These datasets are chosen because they have different sizes and densities. Additionally, two of them have more users than items, and the other two are the opposite. We expect to verify whether the framework works regardless of the size or density of the matrix. A significant difference between Dianping and other frequently used datasets is that Dianping is a location-based service in which the longitude and latitude of each restaurant is recorded. By analyzing the locations of user-item communities discovered by (A)BBDF algorithms, we expect to obtain an intuitional observation of their effects.

5.2 Algorithms and Evaluation Metrics

Four popular CF algorithms were experimented on using the framework. The User-based and Item-based CF algorithms are famous memory based approaches, while SVD and NMF are known to be famous matrix factorization approaches.

User-based: The Pearson correlation was used for user similarities, as suggested in [29]. The neighborhood size is $k = 100$.

Item-based: Adjusted cosine similarity was used because it is reported to give the best performance in [31], and $k = 100$ is also used for neighborhood size.

SVD: We use the popular SVD prediction strategy presented in [16]. Here, the number of factors k is 100, and the regularization coefficient λ is 0.015.

NMF: The most commonly used non-negative matrix factorization algorithm in [17] was used to make predictions, and we also used $k = 100$ and $\lambda = 0.015$.

To make a comparison with the literature, we used the Root Mean Square Error (RMSE) to measure the prediction accuracy in this work. Five-fold cross validation was conducted on the MovieLens and Dianping datasets, and the average RMSE was calculated. For the Yahoo! Music dataset, we used its training set and validation set for training and evaluation, respectively.

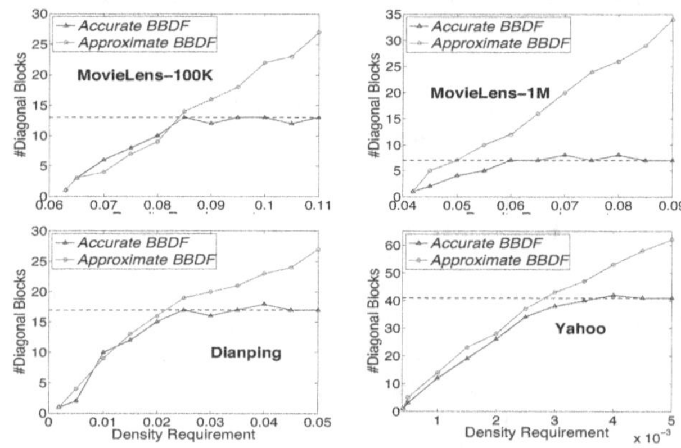

Figure 8: #communities v.s. density requirement

5.3 Community Analysis

The most important parameter in the density-based BBDF and ABBDF permutation algorithms is the density requirement ρ. Low density requirements lead to fewer and larger user-item communities, and high density requirements result in more and smaller communities, as shown in Figure 7, where $\rho = 0.005$ and $\rho = 0.01$ are applied to the accurate and approximate BBDF algorithms on the Dianping dataset. Note that the matrix is not as dense as it appears to be in these figures; The appearance of density arises because more than half a million points are restricted to a small canvas.

An appropriate density requirement is important. If the density requirement is too low, then the user-item communities hidden in the original rating matrix cannot be extracted properly and completely. However, if the density requirement is too high, then it will result in many small scattered communities, which could lead to over-fitting problems.

An appropriate density requirement gives reasonable and meaningful communities. See the ABBDF structure in Figure 7(d), for example. Nine communities are extracted, numbered 1 through 9, from the upper-left to bottom-right corner. It is interesting to note that they represent nine main cities in China. Table 2 presents these cities and shows how high a percentage of restaurants in each community truly belong to that corresponding city.

One can find that communities 5, 6, 7 and 9 are highly related to each other by the dense pseudo-blank areas marked by circles. By viewing the dense areas horizontally, we know

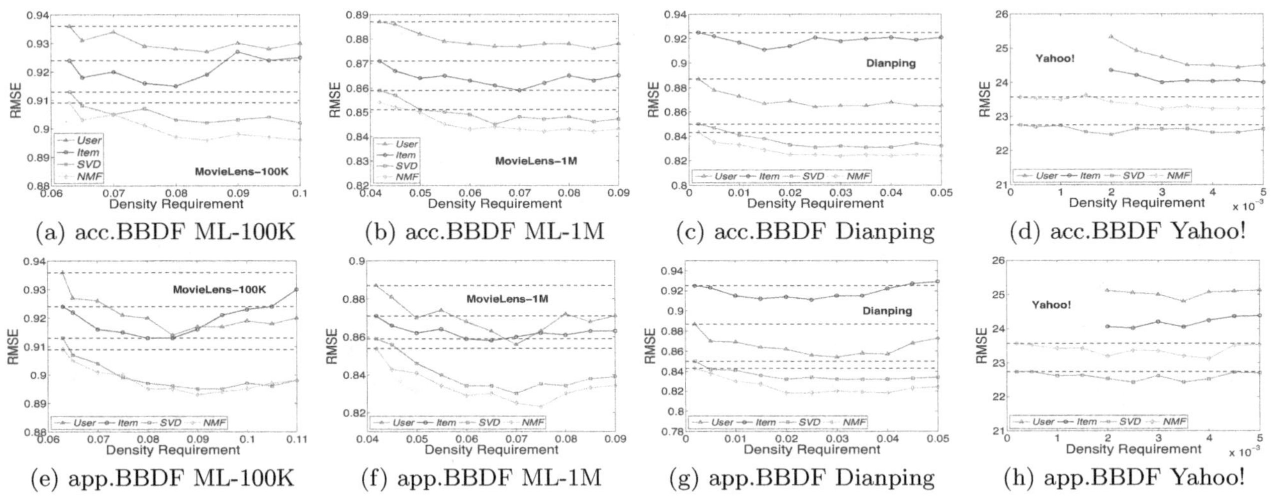

(a) acc.BBDF ML-100K (b) acc.BBDF ML-1M (c) acc.BBDF Dianping (d) acc.BBDF Yahoo!

(e) app.BBDF ML-100K (f) app.BBDF ML-1M (g) app.BBDF Dianping (h) app.BBDF Yahoo!

Figure 9: RMSE on the four datasets based on accurate (acc.) and approximate (app.) BBDF structures

that users in one city can usually go to restaurants in another city, and vertically we know that restaurants in the other city can be frequently visited by users from the first city. These observations are reasonable in reality because these four cities are geographically very close to each other, as shown in Figure 10. Traffic among these cities is developed, and their business relationships are close. In fact, this area is exactly the famous Yangtze River Delta of China.

Figure 8 shows the relationship between the number of extracted communities and the density requirement on the four datasets, respectively. For accurate BBDF, the number of communities rises first, and then tends to be stable after a certain density requirement is met because a diagonal block will not be permuted recursively if its average density does not increase after graph partitioning. However, for approximate BBDF, the number of communities increases consistently because it moves lines to borders to increase the average density in such cases. This strategy makes the algorithm more flexible but could also lead to too many small scattered communities if the density requirement is too high. The impact of the density requirement on the prediction accuracy will be analyzed next.

5.4 Prediction Accuracy

Experimental results on four datasets show that the proposed CF framework helps existing CF algorithms to improve their accuracy in a large range of density requirements.

The experimental results on the RMSE versus the density requirement is shown in Figure 9. Each sub-figure presents the performance of all of the four CF algorithms on the corresponding dataset. Note that the beginning point of each curve represents the base performance of the CF method on the dataset, and the density requirement of this point is set to the density of the whole rating matrix. As a result, points on a curve below its beginning point mean an improvement on the prediction accuracy, and vice versa.

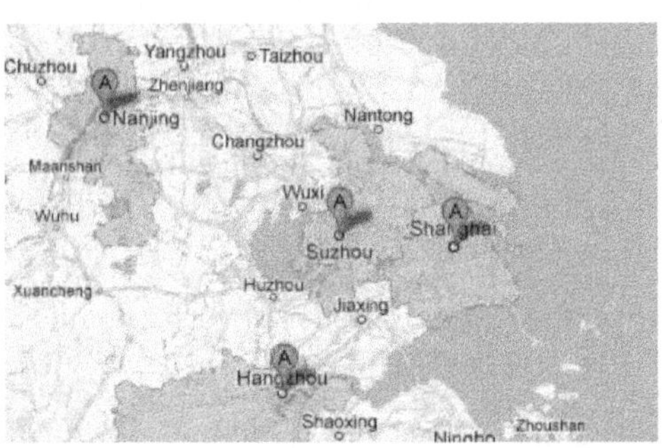

Figure 10: Location of the four highly related cities.

We must note the fact that the very large number of users and items in the Yahoo! Music dataset makes it unrealistic for current hardware to conduct memory-based CF algorithms. To the best of our knowledge, there is no report of direct user-based or item-based collaborative filtering on this dataset. Strategies such as KNN with SVD features [12] or parallelization [38] were attempted in KDD cup, but these strategies would make the results incomparable with other datasets. As a result, we did not perform KNN on the whole dataset. However, we found that our CF framework makes it possible to run KNN predictions on a standalone machine when the number of communities is more than 27, and experiments were performed in such cases.

Experimental results show that the proposed CF framework on accurate BBDF benefits user-based, SVD, and NMF algorithms consistently on all of the four datasets. However, mixed results were obtained on the item-based CF method. On MovieLens-1M, Dianping and Yahoo! Music datasets, its performance is slightly improved, but on the MovieLens-100K dataset, its accuracy rises at first and begins to drop while the density requirement continues to rise. Furthermore, a negative effect can even be introduced if the density requirement is too high.

This effect could be the reason that the item-based algorithm utilizes historical ratings of a user, which is different from other CF algorithms that take advantage of neighborhood relationships. A user's historical ratings are reduced in the BBDF framework, especially on small datasets, which introduces bad predictions. However, it still benefits from BBDF structure given reasonable density requirements.

For approximate BBDF structure, prediction accuracy improves at first but tends to drop when the density requirement is too high, in almost all of the cases. The reason for the performance improvement could be that approximate BBDF plays a role in data denoising, and user-item communities help to extract professional ratings. However, small

Table 3: Best RMSE of the CF framework based on Accurate (Acc.) and Approximate (App.) BBDF structures on the four datasets and the corresponding density requirement ρ. The standard deviations are $\leq$ 0.006 on MovieLens and DianPing dataset and $\leq$ 0.05 on Yahoo! Music dataset.

Method	MovieLens-100K					MovieLens-1M					Dianping					Yahoo! Music				
	base	Acc.BBDF		App.BBDF		base	Acc.BBDF		App.BBDF		base	Acc.BBDF		App.BBDF		base	Acc.BBDF		App.BBDF	
	RMSE	ρ	RMSE	ρ	RMSE	RMSE	ρ	RMSE	ρ	RMSE	RMSE	ρ	RMSE	ρ	RMSE	RMSE	ρ	RMSE	ρ	RMSE
User-based	0.936	0.085	0.927	0.085	**0.914**	0.887	0.070	0.876	0.070	**0.856**	0.887	0.025	**0.864**	0.030	**0.854**	-	0.0045	24.443	0.0035	24.798
Item-based	0.924	0.080	0.915	0.080	0.913	0.871	0.070	0.859	0.065	0.858	0.925	0.015	0.911	0.025	0.911	-	0.0030	24.002	0.0025	24.020
SVD	0.913	0.085	0.902	0.090	0.895	0.859	0.065	0.845	0.070	**0.830**	0.850	0.025	0.831	0.020	0.832	22.746	0.0020	22.469	0.0025	22.434
NMF	0.909	0.085	0.896	0.090	0.893	0.854	0.075	0.842	0.075	**0.823**	0.843	0.030	0.824	0.020	**0.818**	23.572	0.0030	23.223	0.0040	**23.124**

scattered communities could give bad predictions because of over-fitting problems, which leads to a decrease in the performance when high density requirements are used.

Table 3 presents the best performance of each CF method on each dataset for accurate and approximate BBDF frameworks. A bold number indicates an obvious improvement, where the RMSE is reduced more than 0.02 on MovieLens and Dianping or more than 0.4 on Yahoo! Music.

When calculating the average RMSE on each dataset, five-fold cross-validation was conducted on MovieLens and DianPing, and experiments were conducted five times on Yahoo!Music. Standard deviations were $\leq$ 0.006 on MovieLens and DianPing and were $\leq$ 0.05 on Yahoo! Music.

We see that both accurate and approximate BBDF benefits CF algorithms in the best cases, and approximate BBDF tends to achieve better performance.

5.5 Scalability and Efficiency

Experiments were conducted on a linux server with 8 core 3.1GHz CPU and 64GB RAM. For both accurate and approximate BBDF algorithms on each dataset, we averaged the computational time consumed under different density requirements, as shown in Table 4.

Table 4: Computational time of the BBDF and ABBDF algorithms on the four datasets.

Dataset	ML-100K	ML-1M	Dianping	Yahoo!
accBDF	85.6ms	1.61s	21.2s	42.6min
appBDF	521.8ms	6.43s	80.3s	103.4min

Experiments show that the computational time of the BBDF algorithms increases along with the scale of rating matrices, but the time used for BBDF permutation is small compared with the CF prediction algorithms. Moreover, once BBDF structures have been constructed, they help to decrease the total prediction time by conducting collaborative filtering on smaller submatrices, especially for user-based and item-based methods. We calculated the average speedups for each CF algorithm on each dataset, as shown in Table 5, where speedup is defined as:

$$Sp = \frac{T_{CF}}{T_{BBDF} + T_{BBDF\_CF}}$$

T_{CF} is the time used by a CF prediction algorithm on the whole matrix, T_{BBDF} is the time of accurate or approximate BBDF permutation algorithms, and T_{BBDF_CF} is the time of CF prediction algorithms on (A)BBDF structures.

The experimental results show that in almost all of the cases, (A)BBDF structures speed up rating prediction; the speedup is obvious especially for nearest neighbor CF methods and large datasets.

Table 5: Speedups of conducting collaborative filtering based on (A)BBDF structures on four datasets.

Dataset	ML-100K		ML-1M		Dianping		Yahoo!	
	acc.	app.	acc.	app.	acc.	app.	acc.	app.
User	1.28	1.25	1.24	1.21	1.33	1.21	-	-
Item	1.15	1.19	1.21	1.18	1.39	1.29	-	-
SVD	1.10	1.11	1.16	1.28	1.30	1.28	1.46	1.34
NMF	1.07	1.02	1.20	1.17	1.26	1.32	1.54	1.47

6. DISCUSSION

In practical real-world recommender systems, rating matrices are usually changing continuously as new ratings are made by users. However, (A)BBDF structures make it possible to re-predict the submatrices that are truly in need of re-prediction, for example, those whose RMSE have reached a criterion, rather than to re-predict the whole matrix, which might further contribute to the scalability in real-world recommender systems.

The cold-start problem has long been an important issue in the research of collaborative filtering. By inserting a new user or item into a proper community and making recommendations there, the framework could benefit the cold-start recommendation. Additionally, ABBDF structure distinguishes a user's special interests from the general interests of his or her community, which could contribute to the serendipity of the recommendations, and these issues will be investigated in future work.

Although the (A)BBDF permutation algorithms have only one tunable parameter density requirement ρ, it could be difficult to determine a proper ρ given a new dataset in real applications because too low or too high density requirements might both not give the best performance, which is currently a shortcoming of the algorithms. Further work will be performed to investigate the possibility of learning proper density requirements automatically.

7. CONCLUSIONS

In this paper, we investigated the relationship between (A)BBDF structures and community detection on user-item bipartite graphs, and we proposed algorithms that, in fact, need only one intuitional parameter density requirement to permute a matrix into (A)BBDF structures. We further proposed a general collaborative filtering framework that is based on (A)BBDF structures to make rating predictions.

Experimental results show that, by utilizing user-item communities contained in these structures, the proposed framework benefits many CF algorithms improving their prediction accuracies, and at the same time contributes to system scalability, which means that (A)BBDF structures tend to be a general and promising framework to improve the performance of existing CF algorithms.

8. ACKNOWLEDGEMENT

The authors thank the anonymous reviewers for their constructive reviews and suggestions. This work was supported by Natural Science Foundation (60903107,61073071) and National High Technology Research and Development (863) Program (2011AA01A205) of China.

9. REFERENCES

[1] C. Aykanat, A. Pinar, and U. V. Catalyurek. Permuting Sparse Rectangular Matrices into Block-Diagonal From. *SISC*, 2004.

[2] R. M. Bell and Y. Koren. Scalable Collaborative Filtering with Jointly Derived Neighborhood Interpolation Weights. *Proc. ICDM*, 2007.

[3] E. Boman and M. Wolf. A Nested Dissection approach to Sparse Matrix Partitioning for Parallel Computations. *Proc. AMM*, 2007.

[4] M. Brand. Fast online SVD revisions for lightweight recommender systems. *Proc. SIAM SDM*, 2003.

[5] T. N. Bui and C. Jones. Finding Good Approximate Vertex and Edge Partitions is NP-hard. *Inform. Process. Lett.*, 1992.

[6] J. Chen and Y. Saad. Dense Subgraph Extraction with Application to Community Detection. *TKDE*, 2012.

[7] I. S. Dhillon, S. Mallela, and D. S. Modha. Information Theoretic Co-clustering. *Proc. SIGKDD*, pages 89–98, 2003.

[8] G. Dror, N. Koenigstein, Y. Koren, and M. Weimer. The Yahoo! Music Dataset and KDD-Cup'11. *KDDCUP*, 2011.

[9] S. Fortunato. Community Detection in Graphs. *Physics Reports*, 486:75–174, 2010.

[10] R. Gemulla, E. Nijkamp, P. J. Haas, and Y. Sismanis. Large-scale Matrix Factorization with Distributed Stochastic Gradient Descent. *KDD*, 2011.

[11] T. George and S. Merugu. A Scalable Collaborative Filtering Framework based on Co-clustering. *Proc. ICDM*, 2005.

[12] M. Jahrer and A. Toscher. Collaborative Filtering Ensemble. *KDDCUP*, 2011.

[13] G. Karypis. Metis-A Software Package for Partitioning Unstructured Graphs, Meshes, and Computing Fill-Reducing Orderings of Sparse Matrices-Version 5.0. *University of Minnesota*, 2011.

[14] G. Karypis and V. Kumar. A Fast and High Quality Multilevel Scheme for Partitioning Irregular Graphs. *SISC*, 1998.

[15] J. Kim, I. Hwang, Y. H. Kim, and B. R. Moon. Genetic Approaches for Graph Partitioning: A Survey. *Proc. CECCO*, pages 473–480, 2011.

[16] Y. Koren, R. Bell, and C. Volinsky. Matrix Factorization Techniques for Recommender Systems. *Computer*, 42:30–37, 2009.

[17] D. D. Lee and H. S. Seung. Algorithms for Non-negative Matrix Factorization. *NIPS*, 2001.

[18] K. W. Leung, D. L. Lee, and W. Lee. CLR: A Collaborative Location Recommendation Framework based on Co-Clustering. *Proc. SIGIR*, 2011.

[19] T. Li, C. Gao, and J. Du. A NMF-based Privacy-Preserving Recommendation Algorithm. *Proc. ICISE*, 2009.

[20] W. Lin, X. Kong, P. S. Yu, Q. Wu, Y. Jia, and C. Li. Community Detection in Incomplete Information Networks. *Proc. WWW*, pages 341–349, 2012.

[21] C. Liu, H. Yang, J. Fan, L. He, and Y. Wang. Distributed Nonnegative Matrix Factorization for Web-scale Dyadic Data Analysis on MapReduce. *Proc. WWW*, pages 681–690, 2010.

[22] J. Liu, M. Z. Q. Chen, J. Chen, F. Deng, H. Zhang, Z. Zhang, and T. Zhou. Recent Advances in Personal Recommender Systems. *Jour. Info. and Sys. Sci.*, 5:230–247, 2009.

[23] F. Luo, J. Z. Wang, and E. Promislow. Exploring Local Community Structures in Large Networks. *Proc. WI*, 2006.

[24] T. Nakahara and H. Morita. Recommender System for Music CDs Using a Graph Partitioning Method. *Proc. KES*, 2009.

[25] J. Noel, S. Sanner, K. Tran, P. Christen, and L. Xie. New Objective Functions for Social Collaborative Filtering. *Proc. WWW*, pages 859–868, 2012.

[26] M. O'Connor and J. Herlocker. Clustering Items for Collaborative Filtering. *Proc. SIGIR Workshop*, 1999.

[27] S. Oyanagi, K. Kubota, and A. Nakase. Application of Matrix Clustering to Web Log Analysis and Access Prediction. *Proc. WEBKDD*, pages 13–21, 2001.

[28] M. J. Pazzani and D. Billsus. Content-Based Recommendation Systems. *The Adaptive Web LNCS*, pages 325–341, 2007.

[29] P. Resnick, N. Iacovou, M. Suchak, P. Bergstrom, and J. Riedl. GroupLens: An Open Architecture for Collaborative Filtering of Netnews. *CSCW*, 1994.

[30] P. Sanders and C. Schulz. Engineering Multilevel Graph Partitioning Algorithms. *ESA*, 2011.

[31] B. Sarwar, G. Karypis, J. Konstan, and J. Riedl. Item-Based Collaborative Filtering Recommendation Algorithms. *Proc. WWW*, pages 285–295, 2001.

[32] B. Sarwar, G. Karypis, J. Konstan, and J. Riedl. Incremental Singular Value Decomposition Algorithms for Highly Scalable Recommender Systems. *Proc. ICCIT*, 2002.

[33] B. M. Sarwar, G. Karypis, J. A. Konstan, and J. T. Riedl. Application of Dimensionality Reduction in Recommender Systems - a case study. *WebKDD*, 2000.

[34] B. Savas and I. S. Dhillon. Clustered Low Rank Approximation of Graphs in Information Science Applications. *Proc. SIAM SDM*, pages 164–175, 2011.

[35] B. Savas and I. S. Dhillon. Clustered Low Rank Approximation of Graphs in Information Science Applications. *Proc. SIAM SDM*, pages 164–175, 2011.

[36] F. Wang, T. Li, X. Wang, S. Zhu, and C. Ding. Community Discovery using Nonnegative Matrix Factorization. *Journal of DMKD*, 22, 2011.

[37] Q. Wang, J. Xu, H. Li, and N. Craswell. Regularized Latent Sematic Indexing. *Proc. SIGIR*, 2011.

[38] Y. Wu, Q. Yan, D. Bickson, et al. Efficient Multicore Collaborative Filtering. *KDDCUP*, 2011.

[39] B. Xu, J. Bu, and C. Chen. An Exploration of Improving Collaborative Recommender Systems via User-Item Subgroups. *WWW*, pages 21–30, 2012.

[40] S. Zhang, W. Wang, J. Ford, and F. Makedon. Learning from Incomplite Ratings Using Non-negative Matrix Factorization. *Proc. SIAM SDM*, 2006.

Personalized Ranking Model Adaptation for Web Search

Hongning Wang
Department of Computer Science
University of Illinois at Urbana-Champaign
Urbana IL, 61801 USA
wang296@illinois.edu

Xiaodong He[1], Ming-Wei Chang[1],
Yang Song[1], Ryen W. White[1], Wei Chu[2]
[1]Microsoft Research, Redmond WA, 98052 USA
[2]Microsoft Bing, Bellevue WA, 98004 USA
{xiaohe,minchang,yangsong,ryenw,wechu}
@microsoft.com

ABSTRACT

Search engines train and apply a single ranking model across all users, but searchers' information needs are diverse and cover a broad range of topics. Hence, a single user-independent ranking model is insufficient to satisfy different users' result preferences. Conventional personalization methods learn separate models of user interests and use those to re-rank the results from the generic model. Those methods require significant user history information to learn user preferences, have low coverage in the case of memory-based methods that learn direct associations between query-URL pairs, and have limited opportunity to markedly affect the ranking given that they only re-order top-ranked items.

In this paper, we propose a general ranking model adaptation framework for personalized search. Using a given user-independent ranking model trained offline and limited number of adaptation queries from individual users, the framework quickly learns to apply a series of linear transformations, e.g., scaling and shifting, over the parameters of the given global ranking model such that the adapted model can better fit each individual user's search preferences. Extensive experimentation based on a large set of search logs from a major commercial Web search engine confirms the effectiveness of the proposed method compared to several state-of-the-art ranking model adaptation methods.

Categories and Subject Descriptors

H.3.3 [**Information Systems**]: Information Search and Retrieval—*Retrieval Models*

Keywords

Learning to rank, model adaptation, personalization

1. INTRODUCTION

Search engine users' information needs are diverse. Even for the same query, different users might express different preferences over the retrieved documents, resulting in distinct ranking requirements for search results [11, 27, 29]. For example, for the seemingly unambiguous query "facebook," some people might search for the login page of the social networking service, i.e., `www.facebook.com`; while others might be more interested about the recent news reports of the public company, stock quotes, and suchlike. However, the deployed ranking function in search engines is usually tuned according to general relevance judgments for a generic population of users [2, 19]; as a result, one globally-optimized ranking model cannot satisfy such diverse search preferences. In this scenario, it is preferable for the search engine to adapt the global ranking function to accommodate each individual user's result preference, i.e., personalized search.

Prior research has demonstrated that users' aggregated clicks are informative for learning their preferences and developing global search result ranking models [1, 17]. However, these models only reflect the common preferences across all searchers. Adapting the global ranking model towards each individual's search preferences to maximize search utility for each single user is more desirable. Existing personalization methods require rich user history information to learn user preferences [24, 25] (meaning that they are slow to adapt to user interests and interest dynamics), have low coverage in the case of memory-based methods that learn direct associations between query-URL pairs [28], and have limited opportunity to affect the ranking given that they frequently only re-order the top-ranked items [3]. In this paper, we proposed a method that effectively learns to adapt a generic ranking algorithm on a per-user basis, and overcomes many of the aforementioned challenges faced by existing personalization approaches.

Beside the adapted model's ranking accuracy, adaptation *efficiency* is also a primary consideration in this work. Existing work of ranking model adaptation in information retrieval (IR) mainly focuses on domain adaptation, e.g., from Web search to image search, where the goal of adaptation is to estimate a new ranking model for a target domain using information from a related source domain [6, 12, 13, 14]. Rooted in the classifier adaptation problem in transfer learning (c.f. [21]), the general assumption of domain adaptation in IR is that in the target domain there are insufficient labeled queries to accurately estimate a ranking model, but there is adequate supervision in the source domain. Therefore, to help model learning in the target domain, the adaptation methods need to effectively exploit supervision from the source domain. However, since most of existing methods estimate the adapted model in an offline manner, adaptation efficiency has received little attention in prior research. Nevertheless, in the scenario of adapting a generic ranking model for personalized search (our focus here), adaptation

SIGIR'13, July 28–August 1, 2013, Dublin, Ireland.

efficiency becomes an equally important criterion for two main reasons: 1) such an operation must be executable on the scale of all the search engine users; 2) due to the dynamic nature of users' search intent and the need to offer searchers a great experience quickly, search engines cannot wait weeks or even days to collect adaptation data, since by then user preferences may have already shifted or they may have switched to another search engine. Our specific emphasis on adaptation efficiency prohibits us from directly applying most of existing domain adaptation methods.

Inspired by the linear regression based model adaptation methods widely studied in automatic speech recognition (e.g., maximum likelihood linear regression [18], minimum classification error linear regression [15]), we propose a general framework of ranking model adaptation, which enables rapid personalization. In particular, we assume that in a parametric ranking model different users' ranking preferences can be fully characterized by different settings of model parameters. For example, some users might prefer high authority websites, i.e., larger weight on the static rank score (page quality independent of query); while other users would emphasize query-term matching in documents, e.g., larger weight on retrieval-score features such as BM25. As a result, adjustment of the generic ranking model's parameters with respect to individual user's ranking preferences, e.g., click feedback, is necessary to satisfy their distinct ranking requirements. In our framework, such adjustment is achieved via linear transformations; and to meet the efficiency requirement for fast adaptation, we restrict such transformations to be simple and shared across features in a group-wise manner.

In this paper, based on the proposed framework for ranking model adaptation at the level of individual users, we aim to answer the following two research questions:

1) Under efficiency constraints, how should we effectively perform ranking model adaptation for each individual user? and;

2) What type of queries/users will benefit most from the proposed ranking model adaptation?

The first question is answered by the proposed ranking model adaptation framework, in which the parameters of a global ranking model are updated via a series of linear transformations, e.g., scaling and shifting, for each individual user. In the per-user basis ranking model adaptation scenario, the lack of adaptation data is a serious problem leading to sparse observations of ranking features for each user. To alleviate the sparsity problem, transformations are shared across features in a group-wise manner, such that it is possible to adapt the parameters of features that are not observed in the adaptation data. The proposed framework is general, and we demonstrated the detailed instantiation of the framework to three frequently used learning-to-rank algorithms, i.e., RankNet [4], LambdaRank [22] and RankSVM [16], where several important properties of the proposed adaptation framework is unveiled. To answer the second question, we collected a large set of search logs from Bing.com, and compared the proposed method against several state-of-the-art ranking model adaptation methods. Through extensive comparisons, our proposed method achieved significant improvement, not only in adaptation efficiency (measured in terms of the number of queries until reaches a performant state), but also in terms of the adapted model's ranking accuracy, against the baseline methods.

2. RELATED WORK

There are two major types of research closely related to our work in this paper, namely, ranking model adaptation and personalized search.

The major body of ranking model adaptation study in IR focuses on domain adaption, which can be categorized into three classes. One popular class is instance-based adaptation [6, 10, 13], which assumes certain parts of the data in the source domain can be reused for the target domain by re-weighting. Chen et al. [6] weighted the queries in the source domain by a heuristically defined utility function. In [13], Gao et al. employed a binary classifier to separate the documents in target domain from those in source domain, and then defined the importance of each source-domain document by the output of this classifier. The second category of work is feature-based [5], where a new feature representation is learned for the target domain and used to transfer knowledge across domains. Chen et al. proposed CLRank in [5], which constructs a new ranking feature representation so as to reduce the distributional difference between source and target domains. The third category is model-based [12, 14], which assumes the source and target ranking models share some parameters or priors. Geng et al. [14] regularized target-domain ranking model training using a given model from the source domain. Gao et al. [12] updated the source-domain model by the training errors on the adaptation data via stochastic gradient boosting algorithm.

To the best of our knowledge, few work attempts to adapt a generic ranking model for each individual user. Under efficiency constraints, both instance-based and feature-based methods are infeasible for this task, because they have to operate on numerous instances in the source domain, which is prohibitively expensive to perform for each single user. To avoid costly operation for each user, our proposed method falls in the class of model-based adaptation: we update the parameters of global ranking model for each individual user according to the observed click feedback. To alleviate the problem of sparse observation in adaptation data, transformations are shared across features so that parameters of unseen features can also be effectively updated.

The task of personalized search aims at leveraging information about an individual to identify the most relevant search results for them. Mainstream of personalization techniques target the extraction of user-centric profiles or features, e.g., location, gender and click history, and incorporating such information into the original ranking function. Teevan et al. encoded user profiles extracted from relevance feedback to re-rank the retrieved documents [26]. Dou et al. [9] performed a large-scale evaluation of several personalized search strategies, e.g., user profile based re-ranking [7], and revealed that personalization has mixed effects on the ranking performance. These and other personalization models (e.g., [24, 25]) use significant quantities of search history to learn interest profiles for each user, requiring sufficient data available to perform personalization effectively.

Memory-based personalization techniques learn direct associations between query-URL pairs [28] (e.g., given this query, the current user consistently selects a particular URL), which can perform well given high revisitation likelihoods, but have limited query coverage. Shen et al. [23] developed a context-sensitive language model by introducing both click feedback and preceding queries for short-term personalization. However, these short-term models are specific to the current context and cannot generalize well to accommodate user's general preferences. Once a model is learned, a common strategy for the *application* of personalization is to re-rank the top-n results [3, 9]. This means the personalized models do not have the opportunity to promote results of low general interest (i.e., outside of the top n), but of high interest to the current user, into the top-ranked results.

In our approach, we quickly adapt the search engine's generic ranking function on a per-user basis, and therefore overcome many of these shortcomings.

3. RANKING MODEL ADAPTATION

Inspired by the linear regression based model adaptation methods in speech recognition [15, 18], we propose a general framework to perform ranking model adaptation. We assume that a global ranking model is trained based on a large user-independent training set. For each user, an adapted model is obtained by applying a set of learned linear transformations, e.g., scaling and shifting, to the parameters of the global model based on each individual user's adaptation data, e.g., query with corresponding clicks.

In the following discussions, we first describe our general framework of ranking model adaptation, and then we take three frequently used learning to rank algorithms, i.e., RankNet [4], LambdaRank [22] and RankSVM [16], as examples to demonstrate the detailed procedures of applying the proposed adaptation framework.

3.1 General Framework

For a given set of queries $Q^u = \{q_1^u, q_2^u, \dots, q_m^u\}$ from user u, each query q_i^u is associated with a list of document-label pairs $\{(x_{i1}^u, y_{i1}^u), (x_{i2}^u, y_{i2}^u), \dots, (x_{in}^u, y_{in}^u)\}$, where x_{ij}^u denotes a retrieved document represented by a V-dimensional vector of ranking features, and y_{ij}^u is the corresponding relevance label indicating if the document x_{ij}^u is relevant to user u (e.g., clicks). Since our focus of this work is on user-level ranking model adaptation, in the following discussions we ignore the superscript u to make the notations concise when no ambiguity is involved.

A ranking model f is defined as a mapping from a document x_{ij} to its ranking score s_{ij}, i.e., $f : x_{ij} \to s_{ij}$, such that when we order the retrieved documents for query q by f, a certain ranking metric, e.g., mean average precision (MAP) or precision at k (P@k) [2], is optimized. Such ranking model can be manually set, or estimated by an automatic algorithm based on a collection of annotated queries [19]. In this work, we focus on *linear* ranking models, which can be characterized by a parametric form of linear combination of ranking features, i.e., $f(x) = w^{\mathsf{T}}x$, where w is the linear coefficients for the corresponding ranking features.

Denoting $f^s(x) = {w^s}^{\mathsf{T}}x$ as the given global ranking model estimated in a user-independent manner, the adaptation of $f^s(x)$ for each individual user is performed via the linear transformations defined by a $V \times (V+1)$ dimensional matrix A^u, by which three linear operations, i.e., scaling, shifting and rotation, can be encoded. More precisely,

$$f^u(x) = (A^u \tilde{w}^s)^{\mathsf{T}} x \tag{1}$$

where $\tilde{w}^s$ is an augmented vector of w^s, i.e., $\tilde{w}^s = (w^s, 1)$, to facilitate the shifting operation for parameter adaptation.

There are two major considerations in designing such a transformation matrix A^u. First, a full transformation matrix has the number of $O(V^2)$ free parameters, which is redundant and even larger than the number of parameters needed to estimate a new ranking model for each user (i.e., $O(V)$). As a result, it is infeasible for us to estimate a full transformation matrix for every user. To reduce the size of free parameters in A^u, we decide to only focus on the scaling and shifting operations for adapting the parameters in $f^s(x)$. This reduces the size of free parameters in A^u from $O(V^2)$ to $O(V)$. Second, a more important consideration is how to alleviate the problem of sparse observation of ranking features in the limited adaptation data. Because some advanced ranking features used in modern search engines, e.g., topic category of documents, might not be trigged in the scattered adaptation queries, one will encounter missing feature values. In order to properly update the parameters for unseen features during adaptation, we organize the features in groups and share the same shifting and scaling transformations to the parameters within the same group.

Based on the above considerations, we design the transformation matrix A^u to be the following specific form,

$$\mathbf{A}^u = \begin{pmatrix} a^u_{g(1)} & 0 & \cdots & b^u_{g(1)} \\ 0 & a^u_{g(2)} & \cdots & b^u_{g(2)} \\ \vdots & \vdots & \ddots & \vdots \\ 0 & \cdots & a^u_{g(V)} & b^u_{g(V)} \end{pmatrix}_{V \times (V+1)}$$

where $g(\cdot)$ is a feature grouping function, which maps V original ranking features to K different groups, a_k^u and b_k^u denote the scaling and shifting operations applied to the linear coefficients w^s of the source model $f^s(x)$ in group k. As a result, Eq (1) can be realized as,

$$f^u(x) = \sum_{k=1}^{K} \sum_{g(i)=k} (a_k^u w_i^s + b_k^u) x_i \tag{2}$$

The grouping function $g(\cdot)$ defines the transformation sharing among the original ranking features. It enables the observations from seen features to be propagated to unseen features within the same group during adaptation, which is critical in addressing the problem of sparsity in the limited adaptation data. However, defining the optimal grouping of ranking features is non-trivial; we postpone the discussion of constructing $g(\cdot)$ to Section 3.4.

Once the grouping function $g(\cdot)$ is given, another important component in our adaptation framework is the criterion to estimate the optimal transformation matrix A^u. An ideal transformation should be able to adjust the generic ranking model to meet each individual's ranking preference, i.e., maximizing the search utility for each user. In the study of learning-to-rank algorithms in IR, various types of objective functions, e.g., pairwise and listwise, have been proposed to realize the goal of optimizing ranking metrics [19]. Therefore, to make the proposed framework generally applicable, we do not restrict our adaptation objective to any specific form, but instantiate it with the objective function from the ranking algorithm we choose to adapt.

We want to emphasize that although in our framework we utilize the objective function from the ranking algorithm to be adapted as the criterion to estimate the transformation matrix A^u, it does not necessarily restrict the global model to being estimated by the same ranking algorithm. As long as the global model and adapted model share the same model structure, e.g., neural network structure in RankNet and linear model in RankSVM, the proposed adaptation framework is applicable.

To summarize, our general framework for ranking model

adaptation can be formalized as follows,

$$\min_{A^u} \quad L_{\text{adapt}}(A^u) = L(Q^u; f^u) + \lambda R(A^u) \tag{3}$$
$$\text{where } f^u(x) = (A^u \tilde{w}^s)^\mathsf{T} x \text{ and } \tilde{w}^s = (w^s, 1)$$

in which $L(Q^u; f^u)$ is the objective function defined in the ranking algorithm we choose to adapt, e.g., cross-entropy in RankNet or hinge loss in RankSVM, $R(A^u)$ is a regularization function defined on the transformation matrix A^u, λ is a trade-off parameter, and w^s is the linear coefficients for ranking features in the global ranking model.

3.2 Adapting RankNet & LambdaRank

RankNet [4] is a probabilistic learning-to-rank algorithm, which models the probability that a document x_{ij} is ranked higher than x_{il} for query q_i, i.e., $P(y_{ij} > y_{il})$. A logistic function is employed to map the predicted ranking scores of two documents, e.g., s_{ij} and s_{il}, to probability of ordering,

$$P(y_{ij} > y_{il}) = \frac{1}{1 + e^{-(s_{ij} - s_{il})}}.$$

The training objective function in RankNet is defined as the cross-entropy between the predicted pairwise ordering probabilities and the observed pairwise preferences in the training data, i.e.,

$$L_{\text{RankNet}} = \sum_{q_i} \sum_{y_{ij}, y_{il}} -\bar{P}(y_{ij} > y_{il}) \log P(y_{ij} > y_{il}) - (1 - \bar{P}(y_{ij} > y_{il})) \log(1 - P(y_{ij} > y_{il})) \tag{4}$$

where $\bar{P}(y_{ij} > y_{il})$ is the empirically estimated probability that x_{ij} is ranked higher than x_{il}.

RankNet is usually optimized via a neural network. Because in each layer of a neural network, every neuron's output is linearly combined to feed into the next layer, our adaption framework can be smoothly applied to the linear weights for each neuron (e.g., different transformation matrices for each neuron in the hidden layers). In order to understand the effect of the proposed adaptation in RankNet, we will use a RankNet with no hidden layers for discussion, but the same procedure can be applied to general RankNet with an arbitrary number of hidden layers.

To adapt RankNet, we take the same cross-entropy function defined in Eq (4) as our adaptation objective, and define the following regularization function on matrix A^u,

$$R(A^u) = \frac{1}{2} \sum_{k=1}^{K} (a_k^u - 1)^2 + \frac{\sigma}{2} \sum_{k=1}^{K} {b_k^u}^2 \tag{5}$$

where we penalize the transformation which increases the discrepancy between the adapted model and the global model, and σ is a parameter that controls the balance between the penalty on shifting and scaling operations.

As a result, the gradient with respect to the scaling parameter a_k^u can be calculated as,

$$\frac{\partial L_{\text{adaptRankNet}}(A^u)}{\partial a_k^u} \tag{6}$$
$$= \sum_{q_i \in Q_u} \sum_{y_{ij} > y_{il}} [P(y_{ij} > y_{il}) - 1] \frac{\partial (A^u \tilde{w}^s)^\mathsf{T} \Delta x_{ijl}}{\partial a_k^u} + \lambda \frac{\partial R(A^u)}{\partial a_k^u}$$
$$= \sum_{q_i \in Q_u} \sum_{y_{ij} > y_{il}} [P(y_{ij} > y_{il}) - 1] \sum_{g(v)=k} w_v^s \Delta x_{ijlv} + \lambda (a_k^u - 1)$$

where Δx_{ijl} is a V-dimensional vector defined as $\Delta x_{ijl} = x_{ij} - x_{il}$. Accordingly, the gradient with respect to b_k^u is,

$$\frac{\partial L_{\text{adaptRankNet}}(A^u)}{\partial b_k^u} \tag{7}$$
$$= \sum_{q_i \in Q_u} \sum_{y_{ij} > y_{il}} [P(y_{ij} > y_{il}) - 1] \sum_{g(v)=k} \Delta x_{ijlv} + \lambda \sigma b_k^u$$

The above gradients induce a new neural network defined over the linear transformations, where the connection among neurons is specified by the grouping function $g(\cdot)$: the term $P(y_{ij} > y_{il}) - 1$ in Eq (6) and Eq (7) represents the prediction error of the global ranking model on the adaptation data; and based on this error, the gradients specify the direction in which the adaptation should take. We can note that the gradients for a_k^u and b_k^u are estimated based on all the observations of ranking features in the same group; as a result, the parameters for the unseen features can also get updated, by sharing such jointly estimated transformations.

To generalize this procedure to RankNet with multiple hidden layers, we only need to replace the error term defined by $P(y_{ij} > y_{il}) - 1$ with the corresponding back-propagation error in each hidden layer in Eq (6) and Eq (7), and the original optimization procedure for RankNet can be directly applied to the adapted problem. One thing we should note is that since one can set different number of neurons in each hidden layer, to apply the proposed adaptation in a RankNet with multiple layers, we need to specify the grouping function $g(\cdot)$ for each neuron in the hidden layers. This can be achieved via the clustering method proposed in Section 3.4.

Based on the discussion of adapting RankNet within the proposed framework, it is straightforward to adapt LambdaRank [22] in a similar manner. As a listwise learning-to-rank algorithm, LambdaRank modifies the error term in RankNet by adding an additional correction term and names such modified error as lambda function,

$$\lambda_{ijl} = [P(y_{ij} > y_{il}) - 1] |\Delta_{\text{IR-Metric}}| \tag{8}$$

where $|\Delta_{\text{IR-Metric}}|$ is the change of any specific ranking metric, e.g., MAP or NDCG, given by swapping the rank positions of document x_{ij} and x_{il} while leaving the rank positions of all other documents unchanged.

Therefore, to adapt LambdaRank within our framework, we only need to replace the error function of the output layer in RankNet with the lambda function defined in Eq (8), and all the other procedures remain the same as in RankNet.

3.3 Adapting RankSVM

RankSVM [16] is a classic pairwise learning-to-rank algorithm, in which the learning problem is formalized as,

$$\min_{w, \xi_{ijl}} \quad \frac{1}{2} ||w||^2 + C \sum_{q_i} \sum_{j,l} \xi_{ijl} \tag{9}$$
$$\text{s.t.} \quad w^\mathsf{T} \Delta x_{ijl} \geq 1 - \xi_{ijl}, \forall q_i, x_{ij}, x_{il}$$
$$\xi_{ijl} \geq 0$$
$$\text{where } y_{ij} > y_{ij} \text{ and } \Delta x_{ijl} = x_{ij} - x_{il}$$

where C is a trade-off parameter to control the balance between model complexity and empirical hinge loss over the identified preference pairs from the training data.

To adapt RankSVM, we keep the hinge loss defined in Eq (9) as our adaptation objective, and use the same regularization function for A^u defined in Eq (5). By taking the linear transformation $w^u = A^u \tilde{w}^s$ into Eq (9), we get the adapted problem for RankSVM as,

$$\min_{\mathbf{a}^u,\mathbf{b}^u,\xi_{ij}} \frac{1}{2}\sum_{k=1}^{K}(a_k^u-1)^2+\frac{\sigma}{2}\sum_{k=1}^{K}(b_k^u)^2+C\sum_{q_i}\sum_{j,l}\xi_{ijl} \quad (10)$$
$$\text{s.t. } {w^u}^{\mathsf{T}}\Delta x_{ijl}\geq 1-\xi_{ijl},\forall q_i,x_{ij},x_{il}$$
$$\xi_{ijl}\geq 0$$
$$\text{where } w^u=A^u\tilde{w}^s,\ y_{ij}>y_{il}, \text{ and } \Delta x_{ijl}=x_{ij}-x_{il}$$

Since the input for RankSVM training is document pairs, in the following discussion, we briefly denote Δx_{ijl} as $\vec{x}_t$, in which the subscript t ranges over all the preference pairs in the adaptation set, to simplify the notations. Following the conventional derivation of RankSVM, we get the dual problem of Eq (9) by introducing a set of Lagrange multipliers α,

$$\max_{\alpha}\sum_{t}\Big[1-f^s(\vec{x}_t)\Big]\alpha_t-\frac{1}{2}\alpha^{\mathsf{T}}\Big[K_1(\vec{\mathbf{x}},\vec{\mathbf{x}})+K_2(\vec{\mathbf{x}},\vec{\mathbf{x}})\Big]\alpha \quad (11)$$
$$s.t.\ 0\leq\alpha_t\leq C,\forall t$$
$$\text{where } K_1(\vec{x}_t,\vec{x}_r)=\sum_{k=1}^{K}\Big(\sum_{g(v)=k}w_v^s\vec{x}_{tv}\Big)\Big(\sum_{g(v)=k}w_v^s\vec{x}_{rv}\Big)$$
$$K_2(\vec{x}_t,\vec{x}_r)=\frac{1}{\sigma}\sum_{k=1}^{K}\Big(\sum_{g(v)=k}\vec{x}_{tv}\Big)\Big(\sum_{g(v)=k}\vec{x}_{rv}\Big)$$

By solving the above dual problem, we can get the optimal transformations as,

$$a_k^u=1+\sum_t\alpha_t\sum_{g(v)=k}w_v^s\vec{x}_{tv}$$
$$b_k^u=\frac{1}{\sigma}\sum_t\alpha_t\sum_{g(v)=k}\vec{x}_{tv}$$

The effect of the proposed adaptation on RankSVM is clearly depicted in its dual form. First, as we know that the linear coefficients in front of the Lagrange multipliers α in Eq (11) correspond to the separation margin for each training instance in SVM. In the adapted problem, the margin is rescaled according to the global model $f^s(\vec{x}_t)$'s prediction on the adaptation data: if the global model can well separate the adaptation pair $\vec{x}_t$, i.e., $f^s(\vec{x}_t)>0$, the margin decreases, indicating this case is not crucial for adaptation; if the global model fails to correctly predict the order for this pair, i.e., $f^s(\vec{x}_t)\leq 0$, the margin increases, and $\vec{x}_t$ becomes a more important instance in adaptation for this particular user. This precisely interprets the effect of model-based adaptation: we only update the global model when it makes a mistake on the adaptation data; otherwise keep it intact. Second, the proposed linear transformations induce two new kernels in a compressed space: $K_1(\vec{x}_t,\vec{x}_s)$, corresponding to the scaling operation, defines a compound polynomial kernel over the ranking features projected by the global ranking model w^s; and $K_2(\vec{x}_t,\vec{x}_s)$, corresponding to the shifting operation, defines another compound polynomial kernel over the original ranking features. Both kernels work in a compressed K-dimensional space determined by the feature group mapping function $g(\cdot)$, and are interpolated by the balance parameter σ between the regularizations for shifting and scaling operations. As a result, non-linearity is introduced to the original linear RankSVM model, and such non-linearity helps the model to leverage the observations from seen features to the unseen ones in the same group.

3.4 Feature Grouping

In the proposed framework, a feature grouping function $g(\cdot)$ is used to organize the ranking features so that shared transformation is performed on the parameters of features in the same group. This grouping can be given *a priori* according to the design of ranking features, or be determined by data-driven approaches based on a given set of queries and documents. In this work, we proposed and compared three possible ways of creating such feature groups.

The first grouping method is based on the name of ranking features. Ranking features are usually described by the way they are generated, e.g., *BM25 of Body*, *BM25 of Title* [20], such that the name of a ranking feature provides informative indication of its functionality. Given the naming scheme of features in a collection, we can manually define patterns to cluster the features into groups. We denote this grouping method *Name*.

The second method is based on the co-clustering algorithms in document analysis. Similar to [8], we first project the document-feature matrix into a lower dimensional space by singular value decomposition (SVD), and then perform k-means clustering to group the features into K clusters based on this low dimensional representation. We name this grouping method *SVD*.

The third method groups features by the corresponding learned parameters in the ranking models. We first evenly split the training collection into N non-overlapping folds, and train a single ranking model, e.g., RankSVM, on each fold. Then, we create a $V\times N$ matrix by putting the learned parameters from those N independent models together, on which k-means clustering is applied to extract K feature groups. We name this grouping method *Cross*.

The *Name* method requires the collection to have a reasonable feature naming scheme; if the ranking features are arbitrarily named, e.g., named by ID, such method cannot be used. The *SVD* method is generally applicable since it only requires a collection of query-document pairs represented by the ranking features. In the *Cross* method, besides a set of documents, a relevance judgment for each document with respect to a given query is also needed to estimate the grouping of features. In particular, for RankNet with multiple layers, the *Cross* method can be used to estimate the grouping function for each neuron in the network based on the learned weights of connections.

3.5 Discussion

There are four advantages of the proposed adaptation framework. First, it is a general framework for ranking model adaptation, which is applicable to a majority of existing learning-to-rank algorithms [19]. Second, since the proposed adaptation framework is model-based, unlike the instance-based or feature-based adaptation methods, it does not need to operate on the numerous data from the source domain, which makes the per-user basis ranking model adaptation feasible. Third, the same optimization technique for the original learning algorithm can be directly applied with little change, so that it does not increase the complexity of solving the adaptation problem. And in the adaptation phase, we only need to solve the optimization problem over a small amount of adaptation data, which ensures the computational efficiency for performing the adaptation on the scale of all search engine users. Fourth, and most importantly, transformation is shared across features in the proposed adaptation framework. According to Eq (2), the same transformation is applied onto the parameters of features in the same group, which renders several important properties in the adapted ranking models: in RankNet, the gradients for scaling (in Eq (6)) and shifting (in Eq (7)) operations are estimated based on all the observations in the same group; while in RankSVM, two new non-linear kernels are induced over the original linear function space. As a result, even though we might not observe a specific feature occurring in the adaptation data, we can still propagate the information from other features in the same group to update it properly.

4. EXPERIMENT

In order to evaluate the proposed adaptation framework, we performed a series of experiments on large-scale search query logs sampled from Bing.com. A set of state-of-the-art ranking model adaptation methods were included as baselines to validate the effectiveness of the proposed method.

4.1 Dataset and Settings

We extracted five days' search logs from May 27, 2012 to May 31, 2012 from Bing.com for our experiments. During this period, a subset of users were randomly selected and all their search activities were collected, including the anonymized user ID, query string, timestamp, top 10 returned document lists and the corresponding clicks. The queries were ordered by their timestamp in each user, and the documents were sorted by their original order returned by the search engine under each query.

To apply the proposed adaptation method and compare with the baselines according to user click feedback, we can only use the queries with clicks. Therefore, in our experiment, we filtered out the queries without clicks and required each user to have at least two queries with clicks, i.e., one for adaptation and one for testing.

We also sampled a large set of manually annotated query logs from our existing data collection as the user-independent training set for adaptation. Each query-document pair in this annotation set is labeled with a five-grade relevance score, i.e., from 0 for "bad" to 4 for "perfect." Documents in both the selected user data set and annotation data set are represented by a set of 1,830 ranking features selected from their overlapped feature set, including frequently used ranking features such as BM25, language model score and PageRank. Using the language of domain adaptation, we treat the collection of annotated queries as our source domain and each user's queries with clicks as target domain. This setting provides a good simulation for real Web search scenario, where the generic rankers in use are usually trained on offline annotated data, and thus it helps us compare the effectiveness of different ranking model adaptation methods. The basic statistics of the annotation set and selected user set are summarized in Table 1.

Preference pairs are extracted from user's clicks to reflect their unique search requirements. In order to ameliorate the positional biases inherent in click data [1], we followed Joachims et al.'s method to extract the click preference pairs [17]. In particular, we employed two click heuristics: for a given query q with a ranked document list $\{(x_1, y_1), (x_2, y_2), \ldots, (x_n, y_n)\}$ returned by the search engine,

1. "*Click* $\succ$ *Skip Above*": extract preference pair $x_i \succ x_j$ for all pairs $1 \leq j < i$ with $y_i > y_j$.
2. "*Click* $\succ$ *Skip Next*": extract preference pair $x_i \succ x_{i+1}$ for all $y_i > y_{i+1}$.

Table 1: Statistics of annotation and user data set.

	# Users	# Queries	# Documents
Annotation Set	-	49,782	2,320,711
User Set	34,827	187,484	1,744,969

In order to avoid defining different feature grouping functions for different ranking algorithms we selected to adapt, e.g., in RankNet each neuron in the hidden layers needs a possibly different grouping function but in RankSVM only one grouping function is needed for the original features, we decided *not* to use hidden layers in the neuron networks for RankNet and LambdaRank in our experiment. As a result, the same grouping function defined on the original ranking features can be directly used in RankNet, LambdaRank and RankSVM. A LambdaRank model optimizing NDCG@10 is trained on the annotation set and used as the global ranking model for adaptation in the following experiments (denoted as *Source-Only*)[1]. The trade-off parameter λ (in Eq (3)) and σ (in Eq (5)) in our method are selected by 5-fold cross validation on the whole user set in advance.

To quantitatively compare different adaptation methods' performance, we employed a set of standard IR evaluation metrics: by treating all the clicked documents as relevant, we calculated Mean Average Precision (MAP), Precision at 1 (P@1), Precision at 3 (P@3) and Mean Reciprocal Rank (MRR). Definitions of these metrics can be found in [2].

4.2 Analysis of Feature Grouping

The grouping of features has a substantial impact on the adaptation performance in our method, since transformations will be shared for the parameters of features in the same group. Ideally, we should put parameters that need to be updated synchronously in the same group. In this experiment, we evaluated the three feature grouping methods, i.e., *Name*, *SVD*, and *Cross*, proposed in Section 3.4. For comparison purposes, we also included two trivial grouping methods: 1) "*Full*," which creates a group for every single feature, i.e., no transformation is shared across features; 2) "*RND*," which randomly allocates features into K groups.

In our data set, according to the naming scheme of features, i.e., *featureType_source_seqID*, 413 feature groups are extracted by the *Name* method. The two data-driven approaches, *SVD* and *Cross*, were performed on the annotation set, but we have to specify the group size K for them in advance. To analyze the effect of group size K in our proposed adaptation framework, we evaluated the adaptation performance of RankNet by varying the setting of K. To control the number of adaptation queries in each user, which influences the adaptation performance, we selected a subset of users, where each user has at least six queries with clicks (close to the average number of queries with clicks per user in our collection), and used the first three queries for adaptation and last three queries for testing in each user. This leads to a collection of 8,879 users with 112,069 queries.

The MAP ranking performance of adapted RankNet with different feature grouping methods is shown in Figure 1 (a). First, it is clear that a properly set K is crucial for both *SVD* and *Cross* methods. The more groups we set, the more adaptation parameters need to estimate based on the limited adaptation data; but if we set too few feature groups, the

[1]Since we only used a subset of annotated queries and features, the results here do not reflect the actual performance of the search engine.

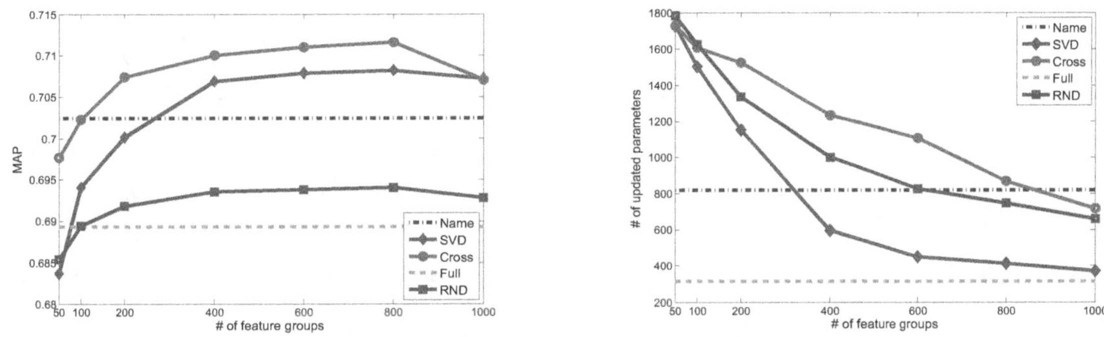

(a) Adaptation performance with different K (b) Number of updated parameters with different K

Figure 1: Analysis of feature grouping in RankNet adaptation.

discriminations among the features will be lost due to inaccurate parameter updating by adaptation sharing. Besides, Figure 1 (a) also shows that the adaptation performance is less sensitive to K around its optimal value, i.e., the performance as indicated by MAP is stable in a wide range of K from 400 to 800, for both *SVD* and *Cross*.

Another observation in Figure 1 (a) is that *Cross* performed consistently better than the other grouping methods under the same setting of K. Because in the *Cross* method features with similar contributions (i.e., linear coefficients) to document ranking are grouped together, and they tend to update synchronously. Sharing transformations among such features is more desirable. In contrast, other grouping methods cannot exploit such relationship among the features, e.g., *SVD* only exploits the co-occurrence relationship between features, and thus they achieved worse results.

In order to understand the in-depth effect of feature grouping in our adaptation framework, we computed the average number of updated parameters in the adapted ranking model for each user with respect to different group size K and illustrated the results in Figure 1 (b). We can note that on average only 316 features (with a standard deviation of 214) can be observed in the adaptation data according to the result of *Full* method. However, because of adaptation transformation sharing across features in our framework, the number of parameters that have been actually adjusted is much larger. For example, with 800 groups, about 870 parameters (with a standard deviation of 220) on average are effectively updated by the *Cross* method, indicating that more than 60% of updated parameters are adapted without actual observations. On the other hand, when K becomes smaller, the number of updated parameters increases rapidly. Consequently, using too fewer groups forces less relevant features get updated by the shared transformations, which in turn degrades the overall adaptation performance.

Similar adaptation results with respect to group size K were also observed in LambdaRank and RankSVM. In the following experiments, to avoid selecting K for each individual user and the variation of performance introduced by this factor, we fix K to be 800 for both *SVD* and *Cross*.

4.3 Comparison of Adaptation Performance

4.3.1 Baselines

To make a thorough evaluation of the proposed adaptation method, we included several state-of-the-art ranking model adaptation methods as baselines, covering instance-based, feature-based and model-based methods, for comparisons. We describe the employed baselines briefly in text below.

TransRank [6] is an instance-based ranking model adaptation method, in which a utility function is defined to select the top k important queries from the source domain into target domain for model training. IW-RankSVM [13] is another instance-based adaptation method, which re-weights the instances in source domain by measuring its distance to the classification hyperplane between source and target domain, and only uses those re-weighted instances from source domain for target-domain model training. CLRank [5] is a feature-based adaptation method, which constructs a new joint feature representation for both source and target domains to reduce the distributional difference between them.

However, it would be prohibitively expensive if we directly applied these baselines for every user, because such methods need to access all the offline training data during adaptation. To make these methods applicable in our application scenario, we pooled all the user's adaptation data together to form a combined user collection, on which the above baseline methods are applied. In addition, we also trained a new LambdaRank model optimizing MAP on this integrated user collection as a baseline, and named it Target-Only.

RA-RankSVM [14] is a model-based adaptation method, which treats the source-domain ranking model as an additional regularization for model training in the target domain. Based on RA-RankSVM, we used the same regularization idea in RankNet and LambdaRank to get the corresponding RA-RankNet and RA-LambdaRank baselines. Besides, without knowledge about the global model, we estimated a ranking model only based on each individual user's adaptation data, and denoted such method as Tar, e.g., Tar-RankSVM, accordingly.

All baseline methods' hyper-parameters, e.g., trade-off parameter C in RA-RankSVM, are tuned by 5-fold cross validation on the full user data set in advance.

4.3.2 Adaptation Accuracy

We performed the experiment on all user data in our collection, in which the first 50% of queries from each user are used for adaptation and the rest are used for testing.

• **Comparison in per-user basis adaptation:** we first compared the ranking performance of our proposed adaptation methods (under all the three grouping methods) with the model-based adaptation baseline methods, e.g., RA-RankSVM, RA-RankNet and RA-LambdaRank, and the baseline methods solely depend on the adaptation data, i.e., Tar-RankSVM, Tar-RankNet and Tar-LambdaRank. These are the only baselines applicable in the scenario of per-user basis ranking model adaptation. In particular, MAP metric is chosen to be optimized in the adapted LambdaRank model.

Table 2: Comparison of per-user basis ranking model adaptation performance.

	MAP	P@1	P@3	MRR
Tar-RankSVM	0.6240	0.4905	0.2335	0.6282
RA-RankSVM	0.6366	0.4809	0.2510	0.6410
Name-RankSVM	0.6544	0.5078	0.2546	0.6585
SVD-RankSVM	**0.6643**	**0.5209**	**0.2579**	**0.6687**
Cross-RankSVM	0.6638	0.5200	0.2574	0.6681
Tar-RankNet	0.6342	0.5051	0.2360	0.6384
RA-RankNet	0.6577	0.5267	0.2481	0.6619
Name-RankNet	0.6709	0.5425	0.2535	0.6750
SVD-RankNet	0.6751	0.5412	0.2581	0.6796
Cross-RankNet	**0.6781**	**0.5450**	**0.2593**	**0.6826**
Tar-LambdaRank	0.6436	0.5182	0.2384	0.6477
RA-LambdaRank	0.6616	0.5341	0.2479	0.6657
Name-LambdaRank	0.6814	0.5556	0.2569	0.6859
SVD-LambdaRank	0.6878	0.5590	0.2616	0.6925
Cross-LambdaRank	**0.6922**	**0.5662**	**0.2629**	**0.6969**

In Table 2, we can observe significant improvements in ranking performance from the model-based adaptation methods, i.e., our methods and RA methods, against the methods solely depending on the adaptation data, i.e., Tar methods. As discussed before, sparsity is a serious problem in the per-user basis model estimation. Tar methods cannot estimate the parameters for the unseen features, and thus their ranking capability is limited. RA methods alleviate such deficiency by using the global model as back-off: for features not observed in the adaptation data, the parameters from the global model would be used. In our proposed method, besides back-off to the global model when no observation is available (as shown in Eq (5)), we also propagate the observations from seen features to unseen features by transformation sharing to help the model better estimate the parameters of those unseen features. As a result, our adaptation methods, under all grouping methods, outperformed the corresponding RA adaptation methods (all the improvements are significant with p-value<0.01 under paired t-test).

Another observation in Table 2 is that the adapted LambdaRank performed consistently better than the adapted RankNet and RankSVM within our framework. In LambdaRank the lambda function helps the model directly optimize the IR-related metrics, e.g., MAP in our case, while RankNet and RankSVM can only minimize pairwise loss. LambdaRank has shown better performance than those pairwise learning-to-rank algorithms in many classical ranking tasks [22]. In our adaptation framework, such advantage of LambdaRank is preserved since the same lambda function and optimization procedure are applied as in the original LambdaRank. This demonstrates the flexibility of our adaptation framework, in which we can choose to adapt any specific ranking algorithm according to the property of the task.

• **Comparison with integrated adaptation:** according to the results in Table 2, we compared our best performing method *Cross*-LambdaRank with the instance-based and feature-based ranking model adaptation methods, and list the results in Table 3.

First of all, we can notice that in Table 3 the global ranking model trained on the annotation set (i.e., Source-Only) did not perform well on the user testing set; while the model trained on the integrated user data improved most of the ranking metrics over 10%. This indicates evident distributional difference between the generic annotation set and user click set. Through instance re-weighting, i.e., IW-RankSVM and TransRank, or feature construction, i.e., CLRank, all baseline adaptation methods achieved improved results against the global model. For these baseline methods, since we have pooled all the users' adaptation data together, sparsity is no longer a serious problem. However, individual user's specific ranking preferences will be overwhelmed once we pooled different users' clicks together. In our adaptation method, e.g., *Cross*-LambdaRank, the global model is adapted for each individual user towards maximizing the search utility based on their own adaptation data. As a result, *Cross*-LambdaRank outperformed all these baseline adaptation methods, which are originally designed for domain adaptation, in this user-oriented evaluation.

Table 3: Comparison of adaptation performance.

	MAP	P@1	P@3	MRR
Source-Only	0.5637	0.3356	0.2503	0.5679
Target-Only	0.6258	0.4667	0.2468	0.6298
IW-RankSVM	0.6427	0.4865	0.2506	0.6470
TransRank	0.6468	0.5202	0.2400	0.6512
CLRank	0.6590	0.5090	0.2561	0.6594
Cross-LambdaRank	**0.6922**	**0.5662**	**0.2629**	**0.6969**

• **Query-/User-level improvement analysis:** the results shown in Table 2 and Table 3 are averaged over all the users' testing queries. It is necessary to further investigate to what extent and what types of users/queries can benefit from the proposed adaptation method. We analyzed the detailed ranking results given by *Cross*-LambdaRank against those from the global ranking model and RA-LambdaRank, which is the best baseline according to Table 2 and Table 3.

Table 4: Ranking performance gain against the global model from *Cross*-LambdaRank and RA-LambdaRank on repeated and non-repeated queries.

Query Type	Method	ΔMAP	ΔP@1	ΔP@3	ΔMRR
Repeated	RA	0.2329	0.4082	0.0249	0.2331
	Cross	0.2375	0.4129	0.0273	0.2379
Non-repeated	RA	-0.0337	-0.0050	-0.0292	-0.0342
	Cross	0.0204	0.0498	-0.0024	0.0206

Query repetition is a common phenomenon in user's query log, and it is crucial for many memory-based personalization methods [9, 28]. First, we categorized the testing queries as repeated queries, if it occurred in the corresponding user's adaptation query set, and the rest as non-repeated ones; and then computed the improvement of ranking performance against the global model from *Cross*-LambdaRank and RA-LambdaRank on these two types of testing queries. As shown in Table 4 (all the differences are significant with p-value<0.01 under paired t-test), both methods achieved notably improvements against the global model on the repeated queries, but only *Cross*-LambdaRank attained improved results on the non-repeated queries. For the repeated queries, both methods can simply "memorize" and "promote" the documents clicked by the user; while for the non-repeated queries, because RA-LambdaRank did not get any direct observations to adjust the relevant ranking features, it could not generalize well from the adaptation data. In *Cross*-LambdaRank, the unseen features can also be updated via transformation sharing, which affords the model a better ranking capability on those non-repeated queries.

In addition, we also applied a proprietary multi-label classifier to annotate the query intent into 63 categories, e.g., navigational, commerce and etc., and found that the major improvement of our method against the global model comes from the navigational queries. In detail, comparing to the global model 44.9% navigational queries get improved MAP results and only 10.2% of them become worse. "HowTo," "Health" and "Q&A" are the major categories of queries on which our method failed to generate better ranking than the global model. We investigated such kind of queries in the user data set and found the users' clicks are mostly for exploration purposes in these kinds of informational queries (diverse clicked documents), since they might not have a clear mind of answers for these queries yet. As a result, such clicks are less reliable for updating the ranking model.

To understand what types of users can benefit from our adaptation method, we categorized the users in our collection into three classes by the number of adaptation queries they have: 1) *heavy* user, who has more than 10 adaptation queries; 2) *medium* user, who has 5 to 10 adaptation queries; and 3) *light* user, who has less than 5 adaptation queries. We calculated the ranking performance gain from *Cross*-LambdaRank against the global model averaged over the users in these three classes in Table 5. Besides, we also included the improvement from RA-LambdaRank against the global model in the table for comparison.

Table 5: User-level ranking performance gain over global model from *Cross*-LambdaRank and RA-LambdaRank.

Method	User Class	ΔMAP	ΔP@1	ΔP@3	ΔMRR
RA	Heavy	0.1843	0.3309	0.0120	0.1832
	Medium	0.1102	0.2129	0.0025	0.1103
	Light	0.0042	0.0575	-0.0221	0.0041
Cross	Heavy	0.1998	0.3523	0.0182	0.1994
	Medium	0.1494	0.2561	0.0208	0.1500
	Light	0.0403	0.0894	-0.0021	0.0406

All the differences in Table 5, except the *Cross*/Light/ΔP@3 with the value of -0.0021, are significant with p-value<0.01 under paired t-test. We can observe that on the heavy users, who only cover 6.8% population in our collection, *Cross*-LambdaRank and RA-LambdaRank achieved similar improvements against the global model; while on the medium and light users, who consist 14.9% and 78.3% of the whole collection, *Cross*-LambdaRank achieved much more remarkably improvement than RA-LambdaRank. On the heavy users, both methods get relatively sufficient observations from each user to adapt the global model; while on the medium and light users, the observations become scattered and many features are not observed during adaptation. RA-LambdaRank failed to adjust the unseen features properly and only achieved modest improvement over the global model. By sharing transformation across features, *Cross*-LambdaRank better exploited the information conveyed in the limited adaptation data, and obtained better improvement against the global model. Besides, we also found that on the light users, both methods gave degraded P@3 results (the degradation of the *Cross*-LambdaRank is insignificant). We analyzed the results and found that with limited observations in this group of users, the adapted models tend to overfit the original top ranked documents due to positional biases. As a result, the diversity of user preferences might not be properly captured in this type of users.

4.3.3 Adaptation Efficiency

We have discussed different adaptation methods' computation complexity in Section 4.3.1, from which we concluded that the instance-based methods, e.g., TransRank and IW-RankSVM, and feature-based methods, e.g., CLRank, cannot be applied in the per-user basis adaptation scenario, due to the need to frequently access source-domain data during adaptation. Therefore, in this experiment, we will only compare with the model-based adaptation method, i.e., RA method. Besides, we also included the ranking model solely estimated on each user's adaptation data as a baseline. In particular, we will only illustrate the comparison results based on LambdaRank due to its superior ranking performance shown in Section 4.3.2. (Similar results also obtained in RankNet and RankSVM, but due to space limit we cannot include them.) Since all the three methods share similar computational complexity, we evaluated their adaptation efficiency by varying the number of adaptation queries and examining which method can adapt to a user's preferences with fewer number of adaptation queries. To make the results comparable across different settings of adaptation queries, we selected a subset of users who have at least 15 queries in total, in which we fixed the last 5 queries in each user as testing queries. This gives us a collection of 2,743 users with 42,595 queries.

First, we gradually increased the size of adaptation queries from 1 to 10 in each user, and re-estimated the adapted models every time accordingly. The relative improvement of MAP metric for all the methods against the global ranking model on the testing set are shown in Figure 2 (a).

As shown in Figure 2 (a), by leveraging knowledge from the global model, the adapted ranking models outperformed the model only estimated on the adaptation data; and, with only a small amount of adaption data, e.g., 1 or 2 queries, the adapted models can already achieve encouraging improvement (over 15%) against the global model. Comparing with the RA method, our proposed adaptation method achieved more rapid improvement: *Cross*-LambdaRank achieved 25% improvement by using three queries, while RA-LambdaRank slowly climbed to 23% improvement only after 10 queries. Such efficient adaptation credits to the transformation sharing across features in our framework, which helps the model better handle the sparsity problem during adaptation.

The settings in Figure 2 (a) simulate a situation in which batch update is performed, i.e., update the models for each user once we have collected sufficient adaptation data. However, in a more practical setting, we cannot wait too long to collect sufficient adaptation data, so that *online* updating is required. In this experiment, we used the same set of users as in Figure 2 (a), but updated the ranking models for every adaptation query we collected from the user in an online manner, in which we treated the previously updated model as the base model for the next iteration of model updating. The results are shown in Figure 2 (b).

We can clearly notice the advantage of our adaptation method against the baseline methods from the online adaptation results. Because Tar-LambdaRank cannot leverage any knowledge from the global model about the unseen features, its performance fluctuated due to the variance in the adaptation queries. Although RA-LambdaRank appeals to the global model for estimating the unseen features, in the online setting, the knowledge from global model gets diminished rapidly as adaptation evolves, because it only treats the model from last iteration as regularization. As a result, its performance is worse than that in the batch mode (in Figure 2 (a)). In our method, observations in the adaptation data can be fully exploited via transformation sharing, so that unseen features can also be properly updated during online adaptation, which leads to consistent improvement of ranking performance in both batch and online settings.

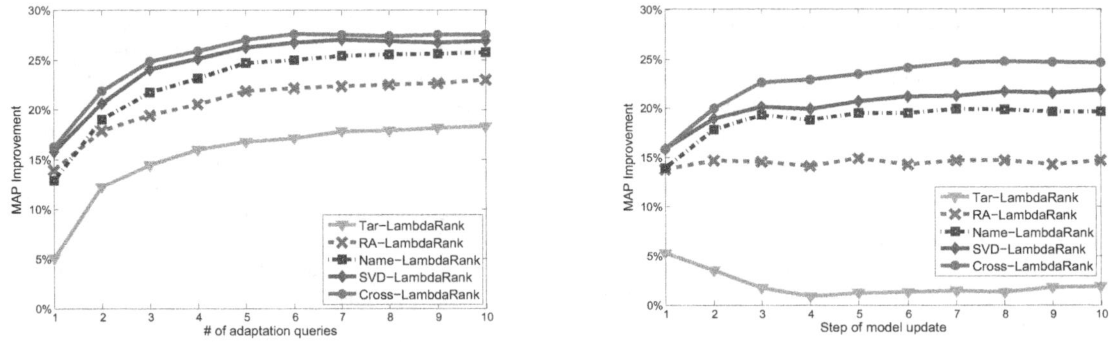

(a) Batch adaptation for LambdaRank (b) Online adaptation for LambdaRank

Figure 2: Adaptation efficiency comparisons.

5. CONCLUSIONS

In this work, we proposed a general ranking model adaptation framework for personalized search. A series of learned linear transformations, e.g., scaling and shifting, were performed on the parameters of a generic linear ranking model in a per-user basis, such that the adapted model can better fit each individual user's search result ranking preferences. By sharing transformations across features in a group-wise manner, unseen features can also be properly updated given only limited number of adaptation queries. We instantiated the proposed framework with three frequently used learning-to-rank algorithms, i.e., RankNet, LambdaRank and RankSVM, and the adaptation method achieved significant improvement in, not only adaptation efficiency, but also ranking performance of the adapted ranking models, against several state-of-the-art ranking model adaptation methods in extensive experimentation.

In our current solution, the feature grouping function and transformation matrix are estimated independently. It would be meaningful to jointly estimate the two components for better adaptation performance. Besides, the proposed linear transformation based ranking model adaptation framework opens an interesting new direction for personalization: rich signals, e.g., user-specific profiles and features, could also be included to affect the transformation in order to better reflect users' individual search interests.

6. REFERENCES

[1] E. Agichtein, E. Brill, S. Dumais, and R. Ragno. Learning user interaction models for predicting web search result preferences. In *SIGIR'06*, 2006.

[2] R. Baeza-Yates, B. Ribeiro-Neto, et al. *Modern information retrieval*, volume 463. ACM press New York, 1999.

[3] P. N. Bennett, R. W. White, W. Chu, S. T. Dumais, P. Bailey, F. Borisyuk, and X. Cui. Modeling the impact of short- and long-term behavior on search personalization. In *SIGIR'12*, pages 185–194, 2012.

[4] C. Burges, T. Shaked, E. Renshaw, A. Lazier, M. Deeds, N. Hamilton, and G. Hullender. Learning to rank using gradient descent. In *ICML'05*, pages 89–96. ACM, 2005.

[5] D. Chen, Y. Xiong, J. Yan, G. Xue, G. Wang, and Z. Chen. Knowledge transfer for cross domain learning to rank. *Information Retrieval*, 13(3):236–253, 2010.

[6] D. Chen, J. Yan, G. Wang, Y. Xiong, W. Fan, and Z. Chen. Transrank: A novel algorithm for transfer of rank learning. In *ICDMW'08*, pages 106–115. IEEE, 2008.

[7] P. Chirita, W. Nejdl, R. Paiu, and C. Kohlschütter. Using odp metadata to personalize search. In *SIGIR'05*, pages 178–185. ACM, 2005.

[8] I. Dhillon. Co-clustering documents and words using bipartite spectral graph partitioning. In *KDD'01*, pages 269–274. ACM, 2001.

[9] Z. Dou, R. Song, and J. Wen. A large-scale evaluation and analysis of personalized search strategies. In *WWW'07*, pages 581–590. ACM, 2007.

[10] K. Duh and K. Kirchhoff. Learning to rank with partially labeled data. In *SIGIR'08*, pages 251–258. ACM, 2008.

[11] R. Fidel and M. Crandall. Users' perception of the performance of a filtering system. In *SIGIR'97*, volume 31, pages 198–205. ACM, 1997.

[12] J. Gao, Q. Wu, C. Burges, K. Svore, Y. Su, N. Khan, S. Shah, and H. Zhou. Model adaptation via model interpolation and boosting for web search ranking. In *EMNLP'09*, pages 505–513, 2009.

[13] W. Gao, P. Cai, K. Wong, and A. Zhou. Learning to rank only using training data from related domain. In *SIGIR'10*, pages 162–169. ACM, 2010.

[14] B. Geng, L. Yang, C. Xu, and X. Hua. Ranking model adaptation for domain-specific search. *Knowledge and Data Engineering, IEEE Transactions on*, 24(4):745–758, 2012.

[15] X. He and W. Chou. Minimum classification error linear regression for acoustic model adaptation of continuous density hmms. In *ICME'03*, pages I–397. IEEE, 2003.

[16] T. Joachims. Optimizing search engines using clickthrough data. In *KDD'02*, pages 133–142, 2002.

[17] T. Joachims, L. Granka, B. Pan, H. Hembrooke, and G. Gay. Accurately interpreting clickthrough data as implicit feedback. In *SIGIR'05*, pages 154–161. ACM, 2005.

[18] C. Leggetter and P. Woodland. Maximum likelihood linear regression for speaker adaptation of continuous density hidden markov models. *Computer speech and language*, 9(2):171, 1995.

[19] T. Liu. Learning to rank for information retrieval. *Foundations and Trends in Information Retrieval*, 3(3):225–331, 2009.

[20] T. Liu, J. Xu, T. Qin, W. Xiong, and H. Li. Letor: Benchmark dataset for research on learning to rank for information retrieval. In *SIGIR'07 workshop on learning to rank for information retrieval*, pages 3–10, 2007.

[21] S. Pan and Q. Yang. A survey on transfer learning. *Knowledge and Data Engineering, IEEE Transactions on*, 22(10):1345–1359, 2010.

[22] C. Quoc and V. Le. Learning to rank with nonsmooth cost functions. In *NIPS'07*, volume 19, page 193, 2007.

[23] X. Shen, B. Tan, and C. Zhai. Context-sensitive information retrieval using implicit feedback. In *SIGIR'05*, pages 43–50. ACM, 2005.

[24] D. Sontag, K. Collins-Thompson, P. N. Bennett, R. W. White, S. Dumais, and B. Billerbeck. Probabilistic models for personalizing web search. In *WSDM'12*, pages 433–442, 2012.

[25] B. Tan, X. Shen, and C. Zhai. Mining long-term search history to improve search accuracy. In *KDD'06*, pages 718–723, 2006.

[26] J. Teevan, S. Dumais, and E. Horvitz. Personalizing search via automated analysis of interests and activities. In *SIGIR'05*, pages 449–456. ACM, 2005.

[27] J. Teevan, S. Dumais, and D. Liebling. To personalize or not to personalize: modeling queries with variation in user intent. In *SIGIR'08*, pages 163–170. ACM, 2008.

[28] J. Teevan, D. J. Liebling, and G. Ravichandran Geetha. Understanding and predicting personal navigation. In *WSDM'11*, pages 85–94, 2011.

[29] R. W. White and S. M. Drucker. Investigating behavioral variability in web search. In *WWW'07*, pages 21–30, 2007.

Ranking Document Clusters Using Markov Random Fields

Fiana Raiber
fiana@tx.technion.ac.il

Oren Kurland
kurland@ie.technion.ac.il

Faculty of Industrial Engineering and Management, Technion
Haifa 32000, Israel

ABSTRACT

An important challenge in cluster-based document retrieval is ranking document clusters by their relevance to the query. We present a novel cluster ranking approach that utilizes Markov Random Fields (MRFs). MRFs enable the integration of various types of cluster-relevance evidence; e.g., the query-similarity values of the cluster's documents and query-independent measures of the cluster. We use our method to re-rank an initially retrieved document list by ranking clusters that are created from the documents most highly ranked in the list. The resultant retrieval effectiveness is substantially better than that of the initial list for several lists that are produced by effective retrieval methods. Furthermore, our cluster ranking approach significantly outperforms state-of-the-art cluster ranking methods. We also show that our method can be used to improve the performance of (state-of-the-art) results-diversification methods.

Categories and Subject Descriptors: H.3.3 [Information Search and Retrieval]: Retrieval models

General Terms: Algorithms, Experimentation

Keywords: ad hoc retrieval, cluster ranking, query-specific clusters, markov random fields

1. INTRODUCTION

The cluster hypothesis [33] gave rise to a large body of work on using query-specific document clusters [35] for improving retrieval effectiveness. These clusters are created from documents that are the most highly ranked by an initial search performed in response to the query.

For many queries there are query-specific clusters that contain a very high percentage of relevant documents [8, 32, 25, 14]. Furthermore, positioning the constituent documents of these clusters at the top of the result list yields highly effective retrieval performance; specifically, much better than that of state-of-the art retrieval methods that rank documents directly [8, 32, 25, 14, 10].

As a result of these findings, there has been much work on ranking query-specific clusters by their presumed relevance to the query (e.g., [35, 22, 24, 25, 26, 14, 15]). Most previous approaches to cluster ranking compare a representation of the cluster with that of the query. A few methods integrate additional types of information such as inter-cluster and cluster-document similarities [18, 14, 15]. However, there are no reports of fundamental cluster ranking frameworks that enable to effectively integrate various information types that might attest to the relevance of a cluster to a query.

We present a novel cluster ranking approach that uses Markov Random Fields. The approach is based on integrating various types of cluster-relevance evidence in a principled manner. These include the query-similarity values of the cluster's documents, inter-document similarities within the cluster, and measures of query-independent properties of the cluster, or more precisely, of its documents.

A large array of experiments conducted with a variety of TREC datasets demonstrates the high effectiveness of using our cluster ranking method to re-rank an initially retrieved document list. The resultant retrieval performance is substantially better than that of the initial ranking for several effective rankings. Furthermore, our method significantly outperforms state-of-the-art cluster ranking methods. Although the method ranks clusters of similar documents, we show that using it to induce document ranking can help to substantially improve the effectiveness of (state-of-the-art) retrieval methods that diversify search results.

2. RETRIEVAL FRAMEWORK

Suppose that *some* search algorithm was employed over a corpus of documents in response to a query. Let $\mathcal{D}_{\text{init}}$ be the list of the initially highest ranked documents. Our goal is to re-rank $\mathcal{D}_{\text{init}}$ so as to improve retrieval effectiveness.

To that end, we employ a standard cluster-based retrieval paradigm [34, 24, 18, 26, 15]. We first apply *some* clustering method upon the documents in $\mathcal{D}_{\text{init}}$; $Cl(\mathcal{D}_{\text{init}})$ is the set of resultant clusters. Then, the clusters in $Cl(\mathcal{D}_{\text{init}})$ are ranked by their presumed relevance to the query. Finally, the clusters' ranking is transformed to a ranking of the documents in $\mathcal{D}_{\text{init}}$ by replacing each cluster with its constituent documents and omitting repeats in case the clusters overlap. Documents in a cluster are ordered by their query similarity.

The motivation for employing the cluster-based approach just described follows the cluster hypothesis [33]. That is, letting similar documents provide relevance status support to each other by the virtue of being members of the same clusters. The challenge that we address here is devising a (novel) cluster ranking method — i.e., we tackle the second step of the cluster-based retrieval paradigm.

SIGIR'13, July 28–August 1, 2013, Dublin, Ireland.

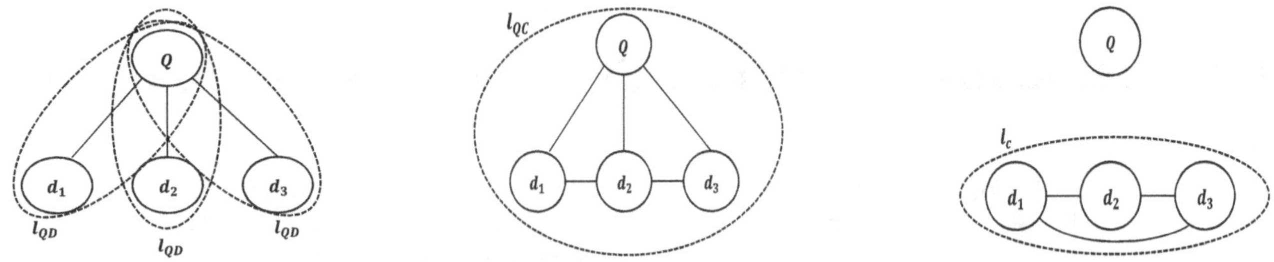

Figure 1: The three types of cliques considered for graph G. G is composed of a query node (Q) and three (for the sake of the example) nodes (d_1, d_2, and d_3) that correspond to the documents in cluster C. (i) l_{QD} contains the query and a single document from C; (ii) l_{QC} contains all nodes in G; and, (iii) l_C contains only the documents in C.

Formally, let C and Q denote random variables that take as values document clusters and queries respectively. The cluster ranking task amounts to estimating the probability that a cluster is relevant to a query, $p(C|Q)$:

$$p(C|Q) = \frac{p(C,Q)}{p(Q)} \overset{rank}{=} p(C,Q). \quad (1)$$

The rank equivalence holds as clusters are ranked with respect to a fixed query.

To estimate $p(C,Q)$, we use Markov Random Fields (MRFs). As we discuss below, MRFs are a convenient framework for integrating various types of cluster-relevance evidence.

2.1 Using MRFs to rank document clusters

An MRF is defined over a graph G. Nodes represent random variables and edges represent dependencies between these variables. Two nodes that are not connected with an edge correspond to random variables that are independent of each other given all other random variables. The set of nodes in the graph we construct is composed of a node representing the query and nodes representing the cluster's constituent documents. The joint probability over G's nodes, $p(C,Q)$, can be expressed as follows:

$$p(C,Q) = \frac{\prod_{l \in L(G)} \psi_l(l)}{Z}; \quad (2)$$

$L(G)$ is the set of cliques in G and l is a clique; $\psi_l(l)$ is a potential (i.e., positive function) defined over l; $Z = \sum_{C,Q} \prod_{l \in L(G)} \psi_l(l)$ is the normalization factor that serves to ensure that $p(C,Q)$ is a probability distribution. The normalizer need not be computed here as we rank clusters with respect to a fixed query.

A common instantiation of potential functions is [28]:

$$\psi_l(l) \overset{def}{=} \exp(\lambda_l f_l(l)),$$

where $f_l(l)$ is a feature function defined over the clique l and λ_l is the weight associated with this function. Accordingly, omitting the normalizer from Equation 2, applying the rank-preserving log transformation, and substituting the potentials with the corresponding feature functions results in our **ClustMRF** cluster ranking method:

$$p(C|Q) \overset{rank}{=} \sum_{l \in L(G)} \lambda_l f_l(l). \quad (3)$$

This is a generic linear (in feature functions) cluster ranking function that depends on the graph G. To instantiate a specific ranking method, we need to (i) determine G's structure, specifically, its clique set $L(G)$; and, (ii) associate feature functions with the cliques. We next address these two tasks.

2.1.1 Cliques and feature functions

We consider three types of cliques in the graph G. These are depicted in Figure 1. In what follows we write $d \in C$ to indicate that document d is a member of cluster C.

The first clique (type), l_{QD}, contains the query and a single document in the cluster. This clique serves for making inferences based on the query similarities of the cluster's constituent documents when considered *independently*. The second clique, l_{QC}, contains all nodes of the graph; that is, the query Q and all C's constituent documents. This clique is used for inducing information from the *relations* between the query-similarity values of the cluster's constituent documents. The third clique, l_C, contains only the cluster's constituent documents. It is used to induce information based on query-independent properties of the cluster's documents.

In what follows we describe the feature functions defined over the cliques. In some cases a few feature functions are defined for the same clique, and these are used in the summation in Equation 3. Note that the sum of feature functions is also a feature function. The weights associated with the feature functions are set using a train set of queries. (Details are provided in Section 4.1.)

The l_{QD} clique. High query similarity exhibited by C's constituent documents can potentially imply to C's relevance [26]. Accordingly, let d ($\in C$) be the document in l_{QD}. We define $f_{\mathbf{geo-qsim};l_{QD}}(l_{QD}) \overset{def}{=} \log sim(Q,d)^{\frac{1}{|C|}}$, where $|C|$ is the number of documents in C, and $sim(\cdot,\cdot)$ is *some* inter-text similarity measure, details of which are provided in Section 4.1. Using this feature function in Equation 3 for all the l_{QD} cliques of G amounts to using the *geometric mean* of the query-similarity values of C's constituent documents. All feature functions that we consider use logs so as to have a conjunction semantics for the integration of their assigned values when using Equation 3.[1]

The l_{QC} clique. Using the l_{QD} clique from above results in considering the query-similarity values of the cluster's documents independently of each other. In contrast, the l_{QC} clique provides grounds for utilizing the relations between these similarity values. Specifically, we use the log

[1]Before applying the log function we employ add-ϵ ($= 10^{-10}$) smoothing.

of the minimal, maximal, and standard deviation[2] of the $\{sim(Q,d)\}_{d\in C}$ values as feature functions for l_{QC}, denoted **min-qsim**, **max-qsim**, and **stdv-qsim**, respectively.

The l_C clique. Heretofore, the l_{QD} and l_{QC} cliques served for inducing information from the query similarity values of C's documents. We now consider query-independent properties of C that can potentially attest to its relevance. Doing so amounts to defining feature functions over the l_C clique that contains C's documents but not the query. All the feature functions that we define for l_C are constructed as follows. We first define a query-independent document measure, $\mathcal{P}$, and apply it to document d ($\in C$) yielding the value $\mathcal{P}(d)$. Then, we use $\log \mathcal{A}(\{\mathcal{P}(d)\}_{d\in C})$ where $\mathcal{A}$ is an aggregator function: minimum, maximum, and geometric mean. The resultant feature functions are referred to as min-$\mathcal{P}$, max-$\mathcal{P}$, and geo-$\mathcal{P}$, respectively. We next describe the document measures that serve as the basis for the feature functions.

The cluster hypothesis [33] implies that relevant documents should be similar to each other. Accordingly, we measure for document d in C its similarity with all documents in C: $\mathcal{P}_{\mathbf{dsim}}(d) \stackrel{def}{=} \frac{1}{|C|}\sum_{d_i\in C} sim(d,d_i)$.

The next few query-independent document measures are based on the following premise. The higher the breadth of content in a document, the higher the probability it is relevant to *some* query. Thus, a cluster containing documents with broad content should be assigned with relatively high probability of being relevant to *some* query.

High entropy of the term distribution in a document is a potential indicator for content breadth [17, 3]. This is because the distribution is "spread" over many terms rather than focused over a few ones. Accordingly, we define $\mathcal{P}_{\mathbf{entropy}}(d) \stackrel{def}{=} -\sum_{w\in d} p(w|d)\log p(w|d)$, where w is a term and $p(w|d)$ is the probability assigned to w by an unsmoothed unigram language model (i.e., maximum likelihood estimate) induced from d.

Inspired by work on Web spam classification [9], we use the inverse compression ratio of document d, $\mathcal{P}_{\mathbf{icompress}}(d)$, as an additional measure. (Gzip is used for compression.) High compression ratio presumably attests to reduced content breadth [9].

Two additional content-breadth measures that were proposed in work on Web retrieval [3] are the ratio between the number of stopwords and non-stopwords in the document, $\mathcal{P}_{\mathbf{sw1}}(d)$; and, the fraction of stopwords in a stopword list that appear in the document, $\mathcal{P}_{\mathbf{sw2}}(d)$. We use INQUERY's stopword list [2]. A document containing many stopwords is presumably of richer language (and hence content) than a document that does not contain many of these; e.g., a document containing a table composed only of keywords [3].

For some of the Web collections used for evaluation in Section 4, we also use the PageRank score [4] of the document, $\mathcal{P}_{\mathbf{pr}}(d)$, and the confidence level that the document is not spam, $\mathcal{P}_{\mathbf{spam}}(d)$. The details of the spam classifier are provided in Section 4.1.

We note that using the feature functions that result from applying the geometric mean aggregator upon the query-independent document measures just described, except for dsim, could have been described in an alternative way. That is, using $\log \mathcal{P}(d)^{\frac{1}{|C|}}$ as a feature function over a clique containing a single document. Then, using these feature functions in Equation 3 amounts to using the geometric mean.[3]

[2]It was recently argued that high variance of the query-similarity values of the cluster's documents might be an indicator for the cluster's relevance, as it presumably attests to a low level of "query drift" [19].

3. RELATED WORK

The work most related to ours is that on devising cluster ranking methods. The standard approach is based on measuring the similarity between a cluster representation and that of the query [7, 34, 35, 16, 24, 25, 26]. Specifically, a geometric-mean-based cluster representation was shown to be highly effective [26, 30, 15]. Indeed, ranking clusters by the geometric mean of the query-similarity values of their constituent documents is a state-of-the-art cluster ranking approach [15]. This approach rose as an integration of feature functions used in ClustMRF, and is shown in Section 4 to substantially underperform ClustMRF.

Clusters were also ranked by the highest query similarity exhibited by their constituent documents [22, 31] and by the variance of these similarities [25, 19]. ClustMRF incorporates these methods as feature functions and is shown to outperform each.

Some cluster ranking methods use inter-cluster and cluster-document similarities [14, 15]. While ClustMRF does not utilize such similarities, it is shown to substantially outperform one such state-of-the-art method [15].

A different use of clusters in past work on cluster-based retrieval is for "smoothing" (enriching) the representation of documents [20, 16, 24, 13]. ClustMRF is shown to substantially outperform one such state-of-the-art method [13].

To the best of our knowledge, our work is first to use MRFs for cluster ranking. In the context of retrieval tasks, MRFs were first introduced for ranking documents directly [28]. We show that using ClustMRF to produce document ranking substantially outperforms this retrieval approach; and, that which augments the standard MRF retrieval model with query-independent document measures [3]. MRFs were also used, for example, for query expansion, passage-based document retrieval, and weighted concept expansion [27].

4. EVALUATION

4.1 Experimental setup

corpus	# of docs	data	queries
AP	242,918	Disks 1-3	51-150
ROBUST	528,155	Disks 4-5 (-CR)	301-450, 600-700
WT10G	1,692,096	WT10g	451-550
GOV2	25,205,179	GOV2	701-850
ClueA ClueAF	503,903,810	ClueWeb09 (Category A)	1-150
ClueB ClueBF	50,220,423	ClueWeb09 (Category B)	1-150

Table 1: Datasets used for experiments.

The TREC datasets specified in Table 1 were used for experiments. AP and ROBUST are small collections, composed mostly of news articles. WT10G and GOV2 are Web

[3]Similarly, we could have used the geometric mean of the query-similarity values of the cluster constituent documents as a feature function defined over the l_{QC} clique rather than constructing it using the l_{QD} cliques as we did above.

collections; the latter is a crawl of the .gov domain. For the ClueWeb Web collection both the English part of Category A (ClueA) and the Category B subset (ClueB) were used. ClueAF and ClueBF are two additional experimental settings created from ClueWeb following previous work [6]. Specifically, documents assigned by Waterloo's spam classifier [6] with a score below 70 and 50 for ClueA and ClueB, respectively, were filtered out from the initial corpus ranking described below. The score indicates the percentage of all documents in ClueWeb Category A that are presumably "spammier" than the document at hand. The ranking of the residual corpus was used to create the document list upon which the various methods operate. Waterloo's spam score is also used for the $\mathcal{P}_{spam}(\cdot)$ measure that was described in Section 2.1. The $\mathcal{P}_{spam}(\cdot)$ and $\mathcal{P}_{pr}(\cdot)$ (PageRank score) measures are used only for the ClueWeb-based settings as these information types are not available for the other settings.

The titles of TREC topics served for queries. All data was stemmed using the Krovetz stemmer. Stopwords on the INQUERY list were removed from queries but not from documents. The Indri toolkit (www.lemurproject.org/indri) was used for experiments.

Initial retrieval and clustering. As described in Section 2, we use the ClustMRF cluster ranking method to re-rank an initially retrieved document list $\mathcal{D}_{\text{init}}$. Recall that after ClustMRF ranks the clusters created from $\mathcal{D}_{\text{init}}$, these are "replaced" by their constituent documents while omitting repeats. Documents within a cluster are ranked by their query similarity, the measure of which is detailed below. This cluster-based re-ranking approach is employed by all the reference comparison methods that we use and that rely on cluster ranking. Furthermore, ClustMRF and *all* reference comparison approaches re-rank a list $\mathcal{D}_{\text{init}}$ that is composed of the 50 documents that are the most highly ranked by *some* retrieval method specified below. $\mathcal{D}_{\text{init}}$ is relatively short following recommendations in previous work on cluster-based re-ranking [18, 25, 26, 13]. In Section 4.2.7 we study the effect of varying the list size on the performance of ClustMRF and the reference comparisons.

We let all methods re-rank three different initial lists $\mathcal{D}_{\text{init}}$. The first, denoted **MRF**, is used unless otherwise specified. This list contains the documents in the corpus that are the most highly ranked in response to the query when using the state-of-the-art Markov Random Field approach with the sequential dependence model (SDM) [28]. The free parameters that control the use of term proximity information in SDM, λ_T, λ_O, and λ_U, are set to 0.85, 0.1, and 0.05, respectively, following previous recommendations [28]. We also use MRF's SDM with its free parameters set using cross validation as one of the re-ranking reference comparisons. (Details provided below.) All methods operating on the MRF initial list use the exponent of the document score assigned by SDM — which is a rank-equivalent estimate to that of $\log p(Q,d)$ — as $sim_{MRF}(Q,d)$, the document-query similarity measure. This measure was used to induce the initial ranking using which $\mathcal{D}_{\text{init}}$ was created. More generally, for a fair performance comparison we maintain in all the experiments the invariant that the scoring function used to create an initially retrieved list is rank equivalent to the document-query similarity measure used in methods operating on the list. Furthermore, the document-query similarity measure is used in all methods that are based on cluster ranking (including ClustMRF) to order documents within the clusters.

The second initial list used for re-ranking, **DocMRF** (discussed in Section 4.2.4), is created by enriching MRF's SDM with query-independent document measures [3].

The third initial list, **LM**, is addressed in Section 4.2.5. The list is created using unigram language models. In contrast, the MRF and DocMRF lists were created using retrieval methods that use term proximity information. Let $p_z^{Dir[\mu]}(\cdot)$ be the Dirichlet-smoothed unigram language model induced from text z; μ is the smoothing parameter. The LM similarity between texts x and y is $sim_{LM}(x,y) \stackrel{def}{=} \exp\left(-CE\left(p_x^{Dir[0]}(\cdot) \;\middle\|\; p_y^{Dir[\mu]}(\cdot)\right)\right)$ [37, 17], where CE is the cross entropy measure; μ is set to 1000.[4] Accordingly, the LM initial list is created by using $sim_{LM}(Q,d)$ to rank the entire corpus.[5] This measure serves as the document-query similarity measure for all methods operating over the LM list, and for the inter-document similarity measure used by the dsim feature function.

Unless otherwise stated, to cluster *any* of the three initial lists $\mathcal{D}_{\text{init}}$, we use a simple nearest-neighbor clustering approach [18, 25, 14, 26, 13, 15]. For each document d ($\in \mathcal{D}_{\text{init}}$), a cluster is created from d and the $k-1$ documents d_i in $\mathcal{D}_{\text{init}}$ ($d_i \neq d$) with the highest $sim_{LM}(d,d_i)$; k is set to a value in $\{5, 10, 20\}$ using cross validation as described below. Using such small overlapping clusters (all of which contain k documents) was shown to be highly effective for cluster-based document retrieval [18, 25, 14, 26, 13, 15]. In Section 4.2.6 we also study the performance of ClustMRF when using hierarchical agglomerative clustering.

Evaluation metrics and free parameters. We use MAP (computed at cutoff 50, the size of the list $\mathcal{D}_{\text{init}}$ that is re-ranked) and the precision of the top 5 documents (p@5) and their NDCG (NDCG@5) for evaluation measures.[6] The free parameters of our ClustMRF method, as well as those of *all* reference comparison methods, are set using 10-fold cross validation performed over the queries in an experimental setting. Query IDs are the basis for creating the folds. The two-tailed paired t-test with $p \leq 0.05$ was used for testing statistical significance of performance differences.

For our ClustMRF method, the free-parameter values are set in two steps. First, SVM^{rank} [12] is used to learn the values of the λ_l weights associated with the feature functions. The NDCG@k of the k constituent documents of a cluster serves as the cluster score used for ranking clusters in the learning phase[7]. (Recall from above that documents in a

[4]The MRF SDM used above also uses Dirichlet-smoothed unigram language models with $\mu = 1000$.

[5]Queries for which there was not a single relevant document in the MRF or LM initial lists were removed from the evaluation. For the ClueWeb settings, the same query set was used for ClueX and ClueXF.

[6]We note that statAP, rather than AP, was the official TREC evaluation metric in 2009 for ClueWeb with queries 1–50. For consistency with the other queries for ClueWeb, and following previous work [3], we use AP for all ClueWeb queries by treating prel files as qrel files. We hasten to point out that evaluation using statAP for the ClueWeb collections with queries 1–50 yielded relative performance patterns that are highly similar to those attained when using AP.

[7]Using MAP@k as the cluster score resulted in a slightly less effective performance. We also note that learning-to-

		Init	TunedMRF	ClustMRF
AP	MAP	10.1	9.9	**10.8**
	p@5	50.7	48.7	**53.0**
	NDCG@5	50.6	49.4	**54.4**$_t$
ROBUST	MAP	19.9	20.0	**21.0**^i_t
	p@5	51.0	51.0	**52.4**
	NDCG@5	52.5	52.7	**54.7**
WT10G	MAP	15.8	15.4	**18.0**^i_t
	p@5	37.5	36.9	**44.9**^i_t
	NDCG@5	37.2	35.3^i	**42.8**^i_t
GOV2	MAP	12.7	12.7	**14.2**^i_t
	p@5	59.3	60.8	**70.1**^i_t
	NDCG@5	48.6	49.5	**56.2**^i_t
ClueA	MAP	4.5	4.9^i	**6.3**^i_t
	p@5	19.1	21.1	**44.6**^i_t
	NDCG@5	12.6	15.6^i	**29.4**^i_t
ClueAF	MAP	8.6	8.7	**8.9**
	p@5	46.3	47.8	**50.2**
	NDCG@5	32.4	33.1	**33.9**
ClueB	MAP	12.5	13.5^i	**16.1**^i_t
	p@5	33.1	35.5	**48.7**^i_t
	NDCG@5	24.4	27.0	**37.4**^i_t
ClueBF	MAP	15.8	16.3^i	**17.0**
	p@5	44.8	46.8	**48.5**
	NDCG@5	33.2	34.3	**36.9**

Table 2: The performance of ClustMRF and a tuned MRF (TunedMRF) when re-ranking the MRF initial list (Init). Boldface: the best result in a row. 'i' and 't' mark statistically significant differences with Init and TunedMRF, respectively.

		ClustMRF	stdv-qsim	max-sw2	geo-qsim	min-sw2
AP	MAP	**10.8**	9.4	9.7	10.6	9.6
	p@5	**53.0**	43.7^c	44.6^c	50.9	49.1
	NDCG@5	**54.4**	45.0^c	45.8^c	52.0	50.4
ROBUST	MAP	**21.0**	19.0^c	17.7^c	20.6	16.8^c
	p@5	**52.4**	50.7	46.9^c	50.4	44.7^c
	NDCG@5	**54.7**	52.4	49.1^c	52.4	45.9^c
WT10G	MAP	**18.0**	15.4^c	12.2^c	16.3^c	14.2^c
	p@5	**44.9**	38.4^c	31.7^c	39.3^c	33.9^c
	NDCG@5	**42.8**	37.8^c	28.6^c	39.0^c	32.4^c
GOV2	MAP	**14.2**	12.7^c	12.9^c	13.2^c	**14.2**
	p@5	**70.1**	59.3^c	62.3^c	58.0^c	66.3
	NDCG@5	**56.2**	48.2^c	48.8^c	46.6^c	52.3

		ClustMRF	max-sw2	max-sw1	max-qsim	geo-qsim
ClueA	MAP	**6.3**	5.4^c	5.3^c	4.5^c	4.8^c
	p@5	**44.6**	28.7^c	29.3^c	18.7^c	20.9^c
	NDCG@5	**29.4**	20.3^c	20.5^c	12.4^c	14.0^c
ClueAF	MAP	**8.9**	8.6	7.8^c	8.3	8.6
	p@5	**50.2**	47.2	40.4^c	49.3	48.7
	NDCG@5	33.9	32.5	28.9^c	**34.3**	33.9
ClueB	MAP	**16.1**	14.2^c	15.4	12.8^c	12.9^c
	p@5	**48.7**	41.9^c	42.9^c	33.9^c	34.2^c
	NDCG@5	**37.4**	30.1^c	32.5^c	25.5^c	25.6^c
ClueBF	MAP	**17.0**	16.3	15.7^c	14.8^c	15.9
	p@5	**48.5**	45.0	42.3^c	42.9^c	43.2
	NDCG@5	**36.9**	35.5	32.8	32.8	33.6

Table 3: Using each of ClustMRF's top-4 feature functions by itself for ranking the clusters so as to re-rank the MRF initial list. Boldface: the best performance per row. 'c' marks a statistically significant difference with ClustMRF.

cluster are ordered based on their query similarity.) A ranking of documents in $\mathcal{D}_{\text{init}}$ is created from the cluster ranking, which is performed for each cluster size k ($\in \{5, 10, 20\}$), using the approach described above; k is then also set using cross validation by optimizing the MAP performance of the resulting document ranking. The train/test split for the first and second steps are the same — i.e., the same train set used for learning the λ_l's is the one used for setting the cluster size. As is the case for ClustMRF, the final document ranking induced by any reference comparison method is based on using cross validation to set free-parameter values; and, MAP serves as the optimization criterion in the training (learning) phase.

Finally, we note that the main computational overhead, on top of the initial ranking, incurred by using ClustMRF is the clustering. That is, the feature functions used are either query-independent, and therefore can be computed offline; or, use mainly document-query similarity values that have already been computed to create the initial ranking. Clustering of a few dozen documents can be computed efficiently; e.g., based on document snippets.

4.2 Experimental results

4.2.1 Main result

Table 2 presents our main result. Namely, the performance of ClustMRF when used to re-rank the MRF initial list. Recall that the initial ranking was induced using MRF's SDM with free-parameter values set following previous recommendations [28]. Thus, we also present for reference the re-ranking performance of using MRF's SDM with its three free parameters set using cross validation as is the case for the free parameters of ClustMRF; **TunedMRF** denotes this method. We found that using exhaustive search for finding SDM's optimal parameter values in the training phase yields better performance (on the test set) than using SVM^{rank} [12] and SVM^{map} [36]. Specifically, λ_T, λ_O, and λ_U were set to values in $\{0, 0.05, \ldots, 1\}$ with $\lambda_T + \lambda_O + \lambda_U = 1$.

We first see in Table 2 that while TunedMRF outperforms the initial MRF ranking in most relevant comparisons (experimental setting × evaluation measure), there are cases (e.g., for AP and WT10G) for which the reverse holds. The latter finding implies that optimal free-parameter values of MRF's SDM do not necessarily generalize across queries.

More importantly, we see in Table 2 that ClustMRF outperforms both the initial ranking and TunedMRF in all relevant comparisons. Many of the improvements are substantial and statistically significant. These findings attest to the high effectiveness of using ClustMRF for re-ranking.

4.2.2 Analysis of feature functions

We now turn to analyze the relative importance attributed to the different feature functions used in ClustMRF; i.e., the λ_l weights assigned to these functions in the training phase by SVM^{rank}. We first average, per experimental setting and cluster size, the weights assigned to a feature function using the different training folds. Then, the feature function is assigned with a score that is the reciprocal rank of its corresponding (average) weight. Finally, the feature functions are ordered by averaging their scores across experimental settings and cluster sizes. Two feature functions, pr and spam, are only used for the ClueWeb-based settings. Hence, we perform the analysis separately for the ClueWeb and non-ClueWeb (AP, ROBUST, WT10G, and GOV2) settings.

rank methods [23] other than SVM^{rank}, which proved to result in highly effective performance as shown below, can also be used for setting the values of the λ_l weights.

		Init	Inter	AMean	GMean	CRank	CMRF
AP	MAP	10.1	10.4	10.6	10.6	10.0	**10.8**
	p@5	50.7	**55.9**^{i}	51.1	50.9	50.0	53.0
	NDCG@5	50.6	**56.0**^{i}	52.2	52.0	50.5	54.4
ROBUST	MAP	19.9$_c$	20.8^i	20.3$_c$	20.6^i	19.7$_c$	**21.0**^{i}
	p@5	51.0	52.2	49.1$_c$	50.4	46.6^i_c	**52.4**
	NDCG@5	52.5	53.9	51.2$_c$	52.4	49.1^i_c	**54.7**
WT10G	MAP	15.8$_c$	15.1$_c$	16.6^i_c	16.3$_c$	14.5$_c$	**18.0**^{i}
	p@5	37.5$_c$	38.0$_c$	39.6^i_c	39.3$_c$	34.2$_c$	**44.9**^{i}
	NDCG@5	37.2$_c$	36.8$_c$	38.5$_c$	39.0$_c$	32.7^i_c	**42.8**^{i}
GOV2	MAP	12.7$_c$	12.9$_c$	13.1^i_c	13.2^i_c	12.7$_c$	**14.2**^{i}
	p@5	59.3$_c$	62.9$_c$	58.8$_c$	58.0$_c$	62.3$_c$	**70.1**^{i}
	NDCG@5	48.6$_c$	50.2$_c$	47.8$_c$	46.6$_c$	48.4$_c$	**56.2**^{i}
ClueA	MAP	4.5$_c$	5.3$_c$	4.6$_c$	4.8$_c$	5.2$_c$	**6.3**^{i}
	p@5	19.1$_c$	24.3$_c$	19.3$_c$	20.9$_c$	24.3$_c$	**44.6**^{i}
	NDCG@5	12.6$_c$	17.8$_c$	13.2$_c$	14.0$_c$	18.5^i_c	**29.4**^{i}
ClueAF	MAP	8.6	**8.9**	8.8	8.6	8.3	**8.9**
	p@5	46.3	44.8	49.8^i	48.7	41.5$_c$	**50.2**
	NDCG@5	32.4	32.6	**35.0**^{i}	33.9	30.0	33.9
ClueB	MAP	12.5$_c$	14.9^i	13.0^i_c	12.9$_c$	16.0^i	**16.1**^{i}
	p@5	33.1$_c$	44.5^i	34.7$_c$	34.2$_c$	46.6^i	**48.7**^{i}
	NDCG@5	24.4$_c$	34.3^i	26.1^i_c	25.6$_c$	35.3^i	**37.4**^{i}
ClueBF	MAP	15.8	16.7	15.9	15.9	**17.7**^{i}	17.0
	p@5	44.8	48.2	45.6	43.2	**50.3**	48.5
	NDCG@5	33.2	36.4	34.4	33.6	**38.0**^{i}	36.9

Table 4: Comparison with cluster-based retrieval methods used for re-ranking the MRF initial list. (CMRF is a shorthand for ClustMRF.) Boldface marks the best result in a row. 'i' and 'c' mark statistically significant differences with the initial ranking and ClustMRF, respectively.

For the non-ClueWeb settings, the feature functions, in descending order of attributed importance, are: stdv-qsim, max-sw2, geo-qsim, min-sw2, max-sw1, max-qsim, min-dsim, geo-sw2, min-icompress, min-qsim, min-sw1, geo-icompress, max-dsim, geo-dsim, max-icompress, geo-entropy, min-entropy, geo-sw1, max-entropy. For the ClueWeb settings the feature functions are ordered as follows: max-sw2, max-sw1, max-qsim, geo-qsim, max-spam, geo-sw2, min-icompress, min-sw2, geo-sw1, min-sw1, min-qsim, stdv-qsim, max-pr, min-dsim, min-entropy, max-entropy, min-spam, geo-icompress, geo-entropy, max-icompress, geo-spam, geo-pr, geo-dsim, min-pr, max-dsim.

Two main observations rise. First, each of the three types of cliques used in Section 2.1 for defining the MRF has at least one associated feature function that is assigned with a relatively high weight. For example, the geo-qsim function defined over l_{QD}, the max-qsim function defined over l_{QC}, and the max-sw2 function defined over l_C, are among the 4, 6 and 2 most important functions in both cases (non-ClueWeb and ClueWeb settings). Second, for the ClueWeb settings, the feature functions defined over the l_C clique and which are based on query-independent document measures (e.g., max-sw1, max-sw2, max-spam) are attributed with high importance. In fact, among the top-10 feature functions for the ClueWeb settings only two (max-qsim and geo-qsim) are not based on a query-independent measure. This is not the case for the non-ClueWeb settings where different statistics of the query-similarity values are among the top-10 feature functions. We note that using *some* of the query-independent document measures utilized here was shown in work on Web retrieval to be effective for ranking documents directly [3]. We demonstrated the merits of using such measures for ranking document clusters.

In Table 3 we present the performance of using each of the top-4 feature functions (for the non-ClueWeb and ClueWeb settings) by itself as a cluster ranking method. As in Section 4.2.1, we use the cluster ranking to re-rank the MRF initial list. We see in Table 3 that in almost all relevant comparisons ClustMRF is more effective — often to a substantial and statistically significant degree — than using one of its top-4 feature functions alone. Thus, we conclude that ClustMRF's effective performance cannot be attributed to a single feature function that it utilizes.

We also performed ablation tests as follows. ClustMRF was trained each time without one of its top-10 feature functions. This resulted in a statistically significant performance decrease with respect to at least one of the three evaluation metrics of concern (MAP, p@5 and NDCG@5) for all top-10 feature functions for the ClueWeb settings. (Actual numbers are omitted as they convey no additional insight.) Yet, there was no statistically significant performance decrease for any of the top-10 feature functions for the non-ClueWeb settings. These findings attest to the redundancy of feature functions when employing ClustMRF for the non-ClueWeb settings and to the lack thereof in the ClueWeb settings.

Finally, we computed the Pearson correlation of the learned λ_l's values (averaged over the train folds and cluster sizes) between experimental settings. We found that for pairs of non-ClueWeb settings, excluding AP, the correlation was at least 0.5; however, the correlation with AP was much smaller. For the ClueWeb settings, the correlation between ClueB and ClueBF was high (0.83) while that for other pairs of settings was lower than 0.5. Thus, we conclude that the learned λ_l values can be collection, and setting, dependent.

4.2.3 Comparison with cluster-based methods

We next compare the performance of ClustMRF with that of highly effective cluster-based retrieval methods. All methods re-rank the MRF initial list.

The InterpolationF method (**Inter** in short) [13] ranks documents directly using the score function: $Score(d;Q) \stackrel{def}{=} (1-\lambda)\frac{sim(Q,d)}{\sum_{d' \in \mathcal{D}_{\text{init}}} sim(Q,d')} + \lambda \frac{\sum_{C \in Cl(\mathcal{D}_{\text{init}})} sim(Q,C) sim(C,d)}{\sum_{d' \in \mathcal{D}_{\text{init}}} \sum_{C \in Cl(\mathcal{D}_{\text{init}})} sim(Q,C) sim(C,d')}$. This state-of-the-art re-ranking method represents the class of approaches that use clusters to "smooth" document representations [13].

In contrast to Inter, ClustMRF belongs to a class of methods that rely on cluster ranking. Accordingly, the next reference comparison methods represent this class. Section 4.1 provided a description of how the cluster ranking is transformed to a ranking of the documents in $\mathcal{D}_{\text{init}}$. The **AMean** method [26, 15], for example, scores cluster C by the arithmetic mean of the query similarity values of its constituent documents. Formally, $Score(C;Q) \stackrel{def}{=} \frac{1}{|C|} \sum_{d \in C} sim(Q,d)$.

Scoring C by the geometric mean of the query-similarity values of its constituent documents, $Score(C;Q) \stackrel{def}{=} \sqrt[|C|]{\prod_{d \in C} sim(Q,d)}$, was shown to yield state-of-the-art cluster ranking performance [15]. This approach, henceforth referred to as **GMean**, results from aggregating several feature functions (geo-qsim) that are used in our ClustMRF method. (See Section 2.1 for details.)

An additional state-of-the-art cluster ranking method is ClustRanker (**CRank** in short) [15]. Cluster C is scored by $Score(C;Q) \stackrel{def}{=} (1-\lambda)\frac{sim(Q,C)p(C)}{\sum_{C' \in Cl(\mathcal{D}_{\text{init}})} sim(Q,C')p(C')} +$

		DocMRF	ClustMRF
AP	MAP	9.9	**11.0**
	p@5	50.7	**53.5**
	NDCG@5	51.0	**53.5**
ROBUST	MAP	20.3	**21.2**^{d}
	p@5	52.1	**53.2**
	NDCG@5	54.0	**55.3**
WT10G	MAP	17.1	**17.7**
	p@5	42.0	**42.5**
	NDCG@5	**40.4**	40.3
GOV2	MAP	15.0	**15.3**
	p@5	66.3	**68.7**
	NDCG@5	54.0	**55.8**
ClueA	MAP	9.8	**10.0**
	p@5	42.4	**49.3**^{d}
	NDCG@5	28.4	**33.4**^{d}
ClueAF	MAP	**9.5**	**9.5**
	p@5	**52.6**	49.6
	NDCG@5	**35.7**	**35.7**
ClueB	MAP	16.6	**18.9**^{d}
	p@5	45.6	**52.9**^{d}
	NDCG@5	33.6	**39.9**^{d}
ClueBF	MAP	17.6	**19.4**^{d}
	p@5	50.3	**55.3**^{d}
	NDCG@5	37.5	**41.9**^{d}

Table 5: Using ClustMRF to re-rank the DocMRF [3] list. Boldface: best result in a row. 'd' marks a statistically significant difference with DocMRF.

$\lambda \frac{\sum_{d \in C} sim(Q,d) sim(C,d) p(d)}{\sum_{C' \in Cl(\mathcal{D}_{\text{init}})} \sum_{d \in C'} sim(Q,d) sim(C',d) p(d)}$; $p(C)$ and $p(d)$ are estimated based on inter-cluster and inter-document (across clusters) similarities, respectively. These similarities, computed using the language-model-based measure $sim_{LM}(\cdot,\cdot)$, are not utilized by ClustMRF that uses inter-document similarities only within a cluster.

Following the original reports of Inter [13] and CRank [15], we estimate $sim(Q,C)$ and $sim(C,d)$ in these methods using $sim_{LM}(\cdot,\cdot)$; C is represented by the concatenation of its constituent documents. For a fair comparison with ClustMRF, $sim(Q,d)$ is set in all reference comparisons considered here to $sim_{MRF}(\cdot,\cdot)$, which was used to create the initial MRF list that is re-ranked.

All free parameters of the methods are set using cross validation. Specifically, λ which is used by Inter and CRank is set to values in $\{0, 0.1, \ldots, 1\}$. The graph out degree and the dumping factor used by CRank are set to values in $\{4, 9, 19, 29, 39, 49\}$ and $\{0.05, 0.1, \ldots, 0.9, 0.95\}$, respectively. The cluster size used by each method is selected from $\{5, 10, 20\}$ as is the case for ClustMRF. Table 4 presents the performance numbers.

We can see in Table 4 that in a vast majority of the relevant comparisons ClustMRF outperforms the reference comparison methods. Many of the improvements are substantial and statistically significant. In the few cases that ClustMRF is outperformed by one of the other methods, the performance differences are not statistically significant.

4.2.4 *Using ClustMRF to re-rank the DocMRF list*

Heretofore, we studied the performance of ClustMRF when used to re-rank the MRF initial list. The analysis presented in Section 4.2.2 demonstrated the effectiveness — especially for the ClueWeb settings — of using feature functions that utilize query-independent document measures. Thus, we now turn to explore ClustMRF's performance when employed over a document ranking that is already based on using query-independent document measures.

To that end, we follow some recent work [3]. We re-rank the 1000 documents that are the most highly ranked by MRF's SDM that was used above to create the MRF initial list. Re-ranking is performed using an MRF model that is enriched with query-independent document measures [3]. We use the same document measures utilized by ClustMRF, except for dsim which is based on inter-document similarities and which was not considered in this past work that ranked documents independently of each other [3]. The resultant ranking, induced using SVM^{rank} for learning parameter values, is denoted **DocMRF**. (SVM^{rank} yielded better performance than SVM^{map}.) We then let ClustMRF re-rank the top-50 documents. In doing so, we use the exponent of the score assigned by DocMRF to document d, which is a rank equivalent estimate to that of $\log p(Q,d)$, as the $sim(Q,d)$ value used by ClustMRF. Thus, we maintain the invariant mentioned above that the scoring function used to induce the ranking upon which ClustMRF operates is rank equivalent to the document-query similarity measure used in ClustMRF. We note that ClustMRF is different from DocMRF in two important respects. First, by the virtue of ranking clusters first and transforming the ranking to that of documents rather than ranking documents directly as is the case in DocMRF. Second, by the completely different ways that document-query similarities are used.

Comparing the performance of DocMRF in Table 5 with that of the MRF initial ranking in Table 2 attests to the merits of using DocMRF for re-ranking. We can also see in Table 5 that applying ClustMRF over the DocMRF list results in performance improvements in almost all relevant comparisons. Many of the improvements for the ClueWeb settings are substantial and statistically significant.

4.2.5 *Using ClustMRF to re-rank the LM list*

The third list we re-rank using ClustMRF is LM, which was created using unigram language models. For reference comparison we use the cluster-based Inter method which was used in Section 4.2.3. Experiments show — actual numbers are omitted due to space considerations — that for re-ranking the LM list, the GMean cluster ranking method is more effective in most relevant comparisons than the other two cluster ranking methods used in Section 4.2.3 for reference comparison (AMean and CRank). Hence, GMean is used here as an additional reference comparison.

ClustMRF, Inter and GMean use the $sim_{LM}(\cdot,\cdot)$ similarity measure, which was used for inducing the initial ranking, for $sim(Q,d)$. All other implementation details are the same as those described above. As a result, ClustMRF, as well as Inter and GMean, use *only* unigram language models in the LM setting considered here. This is in contrast to the MRF-list setting considered above where term-proximities information was used.

An additional reference comparison that uses unigram language models is relevance model number 3 [1], **RM3**, which is a state-of-the-art query expansion approach. RM3 is also used to re-rank the LM list. All (50) documents in the list are used for constructing RM3. Its free-parameter values are set using cross validation. Specifically, the number of expansion terms and the interpolation parameter that controls the reliance on the original query are set to values in $\{5, 10, 25, 50\}$ and $\{0.1, 0.3, \ldots, 0.9\}$, respectively. Dirichlet-smoothed language models are used with $\mu = 1000$.

		Init	Inter	GMean	RM3	ClustMRF
AP	MAP	9.9	10.6^{i}	$\mathbf{10.8}^{i}$	9.9	10.5
	p@5	49.6	$\mathbf{56.1}^{i}_{c}$	50.7	49.1	51.3
	NDCG@5	49.9	$\mathbf{55.6}^{i}$	51.8	49.3	51.7
ROBUST	MAP	19.3_{c}	20.1^{i}	$\mathbf{20.6}^{i}$	19.7^{i}_{c}	20.5^{i}
	p@5	49.5_{c}	50.9	52.1	49.7_{c}	$\mathbf{52.9}^{i}$
	NDCG@5	51.6_{c}	53.1	53.8	52.1_{c}	$\mathbf{55.6}^{i}$
WT10G	MAP	**15.0**	14.9	14.9	14.5	14.6
	p@5	36.4_{c}	37.5	37.5	36.6_{c}	$\mathbf{42.2}^{i}$
	NDCG@5	35.8	37.1	35.5	35.9	**39.3**
GOV2	MAP	11.8_{c}	12.6^{i}_{c}	12.4^{i}_{c}	12.7^{i}_{c}	$\mathbf{13.5}^{i}$
	p@5	56.6_{c}	62.4^{i}_{c}	60.8^{i}_{c}	60.4^{i}_{c}	$\mathbf{68.4}^{i}$
	NDCG@5	46.5_{c}	50.4^{i}	48.8_{c}	49.1_{c}	$\mathbf{54.3}^{i}$
ClueA	MAP	3.3_{c}	5.0^{i}	3.7^{i}_{c}	3.8^{i}_{c}	$\mathbf{5.5}^{i}$
	p@5	16.1_{c}	24.6^{i}_{c}	17.2_{c}	17.4_{c}	$\mathbf{43.3}^{i}$
	NDCG@5	10.7_{c}	17.9^{i}_{c}	11.5_{c}	11.0_{c}	$\mathbf{27.7}^{i}$
ClueAF	MAP	8.0_{c}	8.5^{i}	8.2	$\mathbf{8.7}^{i}$	$\mathbf{8.7}^{i}$
	p@5	47.4	46.7	45.7	47.6	**51.5**
	NDCG@5	32.3	32.6	32.3	34.3	**35.6**
ClueB	MAP	11.4_{c}	13.8^{i}_{c}	12.0^{i}_{c}	13.9^{i}_{c}	$\mathbf{16.0}^{i}$
	p@5	29.0_{c}	40.5^{i}	31.6^{i}_{c}	40.2^{i}	$\mathbf{46.0}^{i}$
	NDCG@5	21.2_{c}	29.6^{i}	23.4^{i}_{c}	30.0^{i}	$\mathbf{34.8}^{i}$
ClueBF	MAP	14.7_{c}	15.6	15.5	16.4^{i}	$\mathbf{16.8}^{i}$
	p@5	42.9_{c}	46.3	43.4	48.9^{i}	$\mathbf{49.2}^{i}$
	NDCG@5	32.1_{c}	34.6	33.4_{c}	36.6^{i}	$\mathbf{38.7}^{i}$

Table 6: Re-ranking the LM initial list. Boldface: the best result in a row. 'i' and 'c' mark statistically significant differences with the initial ranking and ClustMRF, respectively.

We see in Table 6 that ClustMRF outperforms the reference comparisons in a vast majority of the relevant comparisons. Many of the improvements are substantial and statistically significant. These results, along with those presented in Sections 4.2.1 and 4.2.4, attest to the effectiveness of using ClustMRF to re-rank different initial lists.

4.2.6 *Varying the clustering algorithm*

Thus far, we used ClustMRF and the reference comparisons with nearest-neighbor (**NN**) clustering. In Table 7 we present the retrieval performance of using hierarchical agglomerative clustering (**HAC**) with the complete link measure. This clustering was shown to be among the most effective hard clustering methods for cluster-based retrieval [24, 13]. We use $\frac{1}{sim_{LM}(d_1,d_2)} + \frac{1}{sim_{LM}(d_2,d_1)}$ for an inter-document dissimilarity measure; and, cut the clustering dendrogram so that the resultant average cluster size is the closest to a value k ($\in \{5, 10, 20\}$). Doing so somewhat equates the comparison terms with using the NN clusters whose size is in $\{5, 10, 20\}$. Cross validation is used in all cases for setting the value of k.

The MRF initial list is clustered and serves as the basis for re-ranking. Experiments show (actual numbers are omitted due to space considerations) that among the three cluster ranking methods which were used above for reference comparison (AMean, GMean, and CRank) CRank is the most effective when using HAC. Hence, CRank serves as a reference comparison here.

We see in Table 7 that in the majority of relevant comparisons, ClustMRF improves over the initial ranking when using HAC. In contrast, CRank is outperformed by the initial ranking in most relevant comparisons for HAC. Indeed, ClustMRF outperforms CRank in most cases for both NN and HAC. We also see that ClustMRF is (much) more effective when using the overlapping NN clusters than the hard clusters created by HAC. The improved effectiveness of using NN in comparison to HAC echoes findings in previous work on cluster-based re-ranking [13]. For CRank, the performance of using neither NN nor HAC dominates that of using the other.

		Init	HAC		NN	
			CRank	ClustMRF	CRank	ClustMRF
AP	MAP	10.1	**9.9**	9.6^{i}	10.0	$\underline{\mathbf{10.8}}$
	p@5	50.7	**49.8**	46.5^{i}	50.0	$\underline{\mathbf{53.0}}$
	NDCG@5	50.6	**50.5**	46.8^{i}	50.5	$\underline{\mathbf{54.4}}$
ROBUST	MAP	19.9	19.1	**19.6**	19.7	$\underline{\mathbf{21.0}}^{i}_{c}$
	p@5	51.0	50.1	**50.4**	46.6^{i}	$\underline{\mathbf{52.4}}_{c}$
	NDCG@5	52.5	51.7	**51.9**	49.1^{i}	$\underline{\mathbf{54.7}}_{c}$
WT10G	MAP	15.8	14.8	**15.8**	14.5	$\underline{\mathbf{18.0}}^{i}_{c}$
	p@5	37.5	36.6	**38.2**	34.2	$\underline{\mathbf{44.9}}^{i}_{c}$
	NDCG@5	37.2	34.4	**37.0**	32.7^{i}	$\underline{\mathbf{42.8}}^{i}_{c}$
GOV2	MAP	12.7	13.2^{i}	$\mathbf{13.6}^{i}$	12.7	$\underline{\mathbf{14.2}}^{i}_{c}$
	p@5	59.3	61.5	**63.9**	62.3	$\underline{\mathbf{70.1}}^{i}_{c}$
	NDCG@5	48.6	49.7	**51.5**	48.4	$\underline{\mathbf{56.2}}^{i}_{c}$
ClueA	MAP	4.5	5.6^{i}	$\mathbf{5.8}^{i}$	5.2	$\underline{\mathbf{6.3}}^{i}_{c}$
	p@5	19.1	23.7	$\mathbf{31.7}^{i}_{c}$	24.3	$\underline{\mathbf{44.6}}^{i}_{c}$
	NDCG@5	12.6	16.9^{i}	$\mathbf{21.0}^{i}$	18.5^{i}	$\underline{\mathbf{29.4}}^{i}_{c}$
ClueAF	MAP	8.6	8.4	$\underline{\mathbf{9.2}}$	8.3	**8.9**
	p@5	46.3	43.9	**48.9**	41.5	$\underline{\mathbf{50.2}}_{c}$
	NDCG@5	32.4	32.0	**33.4**	30.0	$\underline{\mathbf{33.9}}$
ClueB	MAP	12.5	14.4^{i}	$\mathbf{14.5}^{i}$	16.0^{i}	$\underline{\mathbf{16.1}}^{i}$
	p@5	33.1	39.5^{i}	$\mathbf{39.7}^{i}$	46.6^{i}	$\underline{\mathbf{48.7}}^{i}$
	NDCG@5	24.4	$\mathbf{30.6}^{i}$	30.3^{i}	35.3^{i}	$\underline{\mathbf{37.4}}^{i}$
ClueBF	MAP	15.8	**15.3**	15.2	$\underline{\mathbf{17.7}}^{i}$	17.0
	p@5	44.8	**43.9**	43.1	$\underline{\mathbf{50.3}}$	48.5
	NDCG@5	33.2	**32.7**	32.5	$\underline{\mathbf{38.0}}^{i}$	36.9

Table 7: Using nearest-neighbor clustering (NN) vs. (complete link) hierarchical agglomerative clustering (HAC). The MRF initial list is used. Boldface: the best result in a row per clustering algorithm; underline: the best result in a row. 'i' and 'c': statistically significant differences with the initial ranking and CRank, respectively.

4.2.7 *The effect of the size of the initial list*

Until now, ClustMRF and all reference comparison methods were used to re-rank an initial list of 50 documents. Using a short list follows common practice in work on cluster-based re-ranking [18, 25, 26, 13] as was mentioned in Section 4.1. We now turn to study ClustMRF's performance when re-ranking longer lists. To that end, we use for the initial list the n ($\in \{50, 100, 250, 500\}$) documents that are the most highly ranked by MRF's SDM [28] which was used above for creating the MRF initial list. For reference comparisons we use TunedMRF (see Section 4.2.1); and, the AMean and GMean cluster ranking methods described in Section 4.2.3. Nearest-neighbor clustering is used.

We see in Figure 2 that in almost all cases — i.e., experimental settings and values of n — ClustMRF outperforms both the initial ranking and TunedMRF; often, the performance differences are quite substantial. Furthermore, in most cases (with the notable exception of AP) ClustMRF outperforms AMean and GMean.

4.2.8 *Diversifying search results*

We next explore how ClustMRF can be used to improve the performance of search-results diversification approaches. Specifically, we use the MMR [5] and the state-of-the-art xQuAD [29] diversification methods.

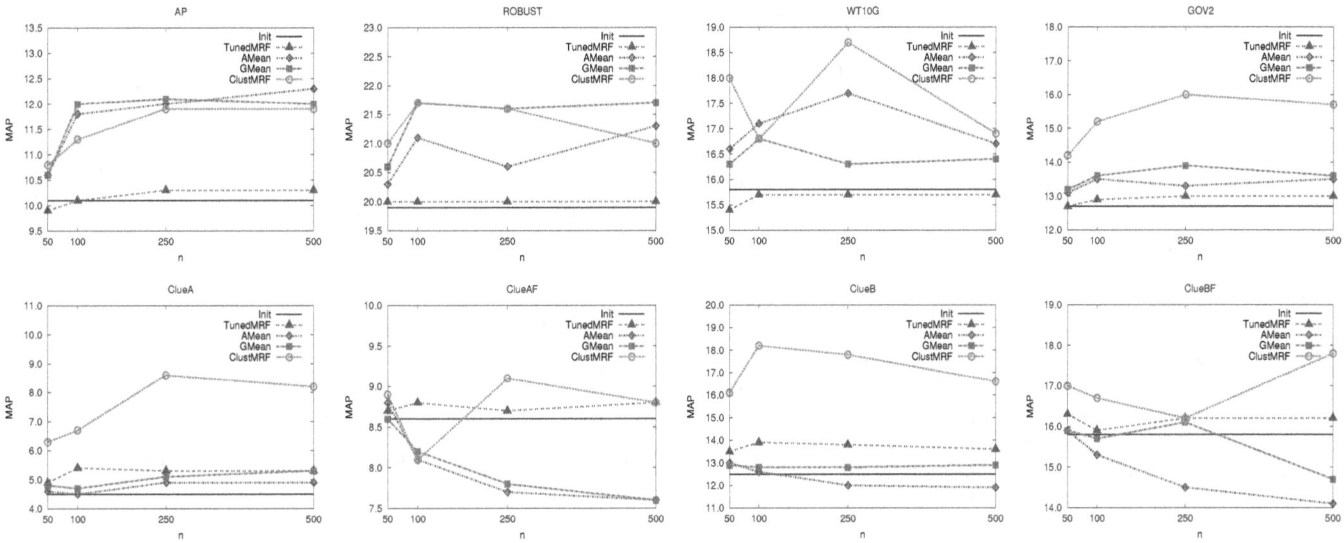

Figure 2: The effect on MAP(@50) performance of the size n of the MRF initial list that is re-ranked.

		Init	MMR			xQuAD		
			MRF	QClust	ClustMRF	MRF	QClust	ClustMRF
ClueA	α-NDCG	24.5	26.2_c	25.4_c	$\mathbf{38.7}^i$	27.4^i_c	28.9^i_c	$\underline{\mathbf{38.8}}^i$
	ERR-IA	16.0	17.3_c	17.5_c	$\mathbf{30.5}^i$	17.9^i_c	19.6^i_c	$\underline{\mathbf{30.6}}^i$
	P-IA	11.8	10.3_c	9.6^i_c	$\mathbf{16.7}^i$	13.3_c	13.6^i_c	$\underline{\mathbf{17.2}}^i$
ClueAF	α-NDCG	42.6	42.9	39.0^i_c	**43.8**	44.3^i	43.7	$\underline{\mathbf{45.5}}^i$
	ERR-IA	32.0	32.3	29.8_c	**34.2**	33.4^i	33.1	$\underline{\mathbf{34.9}}^i$
	P-IA	$\underline{21.0}$	$\mathbf{20.2}_c$	14.9^i_c	17.6^i	$\underline{\mathbf{21.0}}$	20.0	20.6
ClueB	α-NDCG	33.2	33.6_c	33.9_c	$\mathbf{43.7}^i$	39.7^i_c	39.3^i_c	$\underline{\mathbf{45.5}}^i$
	ERR-IA	21.1	21.3_c	21.5_c	$\mathbf{32.0}^i$	25.9^i_c	25.3^i_c	$\underline{\mathbf{32.9}}^i$
	P-IA	15.4	14.4^i_c	12.8^i_c	$\mathbf{17.4}^i$	19.4^i_c	19.2^i_c	$\underline{\mathbf{21.0}}^i$
ClueBF	α-NDCG	41.6	42.6^i_c	38.7^i_c	$\mathbf{45.4}^i$	46.1^i_c	44.2^i_c	$\underline{\mathbf{48.1}}^i$
	ERR-IA	29.7	30.2^i_c	27.0^i_c	$\mathbf{33.3}^i$	33.2^i	31.2_c	$\underline{\mathbf{34.8}}^i$
	P-IA	18.9	**18.4**	14.5^i_c	17.8	21.4^i_c	20.9^i_c	$\underline{\mathbf{22.0}}^i$

Table 8: Diversifying search results. Underline and boldface mark the best result in a row, and per diversification method in a row, respectively. 'i' and 'c' mark statistically significant differences with the initial ranking (Init) and ClustMRF, respectively. The MRF initial list is used.

MMR and xQuAD iteratively re-rank an initial list $\mathcal{D}_{\text{init}}$. In each iteration the document in $\mathcal{D}_{\text{init}} \setminus \mathcal{S}$ assigned with the highest score is added to the set $\mathcal{S}$; $\mathcal{S}$ is empty at the beginning. The final ranking is determined by the order of insertion to $\mathcal{S}$.

The score MMR assigns to document d ($\in \mathcal{D}_{\text{init}} \setminus \mathcal{S}$) is $\beta sim_1(Q,d) - (1-\beta) \max_{d_i \in \mathcal{S}} sim_2(d, d_i)$; β is a free parameter; $sim_1(\cdot,\cdot)$ and $sim_2(\cdot,\cdot)$ are discussed below. In contrast to MMR, xQuAD uses information about Q's subtopics, $\mathcal{T}(Q)$, and assigns d with the score $\beta p(d|Q) +$ $(1-\beta) \sum_{t \in \mathcal{T}(Q)} \left[p(t|Q) p(d|t) \prod_{d_i \in \mathcal{S}} (1 - p(d_i|t))\right]$; $p(t|Q)$ is the relative importance of subtopic t with respect to Q; $p(d|Q)$ and $p(d|t)$ are the estimates of d's relevance to Q and t, respectively.

The parameter β controls in both methods the tradeoff between using relevance estimation and applying diversification. Our focus is on improving the former and evaluating the resulting (diversification based) performance. This was also the case in previous work that used cluster ranking for results diversification [11]. Hence, this work serves for reference comparison below.[8]

We study three different estimates for $sim_1(Q,d)$ (used in MMR) which we also use for $p(d|Q)$ (used in xQuAD).[9] The first, $sim_{MRF}(Q,d)$, is that employed in the evaluation above to create the MRF initial list that is also used here for re-ranking. (Further details are provided below.) The next two estimates are based on applying cluster ranking and transforming it to document ranking using the approach described in Section 4.1. In these cases, $\frac{1}{r(d)}$ serves for $sim_1(Q,d)$, where $r(d)$ is the rank of d in the document result list produced by using the cluster ranking method. The first cluster ranking method is ClustMRF. The second, **QClust**, was used in the work mentioned above on utilizing cluster ranking for results diversification [11]. Specifically, cluster C is scored by $sim_{LM}(Q,C)$ (see Section 4.1 for de-

[8]There is work on using information induced from clusters for the diverisification itself (e.g., [21]). Using ClustMRF for cluster ranking in these approaches is future work.

[9]For scale compatibility, the two resultant quantities that are interpolated (using β) in MMR and xQuAD are sum normalized with respect to all documents in $\mathcal{D}_{\text{init}}$ before the interpolation is performed.

tails of $sim_{LM}(\cdot,\cdot)$); C is represented by the concatenation of its documents.

We use MMR and xQuAD to re-rank the MRF initial list that contains 50 documents. $sim_{LM}(\cdot,\cdot)$ serves for the $sim_2(\cdot,\cdot)$ measure used in MMR and for $p(d|t)$ that is used in xQuAD. The official TREC subtopics, which are available for the ClueWeb settings that we use here, were used for experiments. Following the findings in [29], we set $p(t|Q) \stackrel{def}{=} \frac{1}{|\mathcal{T}(Q)|}$. The value of β is selected from $\{0.1, 0.2, \ldots, 0.9\}$ using cross validation; α-NDCG (@20) is the optimization metric. In addition to α-NDCG (@20), ERR-IA (@20) and P-IA (@20) are used for evaluation.

Table 8 presents the results. We see that using the MRF similarity measure in MMR and xQuAD outperforms the initial ranking, which was created using this measure, in most relevant comparisons. This attests to the diversification effectiveness of MMR and xQuAD. Using QClust outperforms the initial ranking in most cases, but is consistently outperformed by using the MRF measure and our ClustMRF method. More generally, the best performance for each diversification method (MMR and xQuAD) is almost always attained by ClustMRF, which often outperforms the other methods in a substantial and statistically significant manner. Thus, although ClustMRF ranks clusters of similar documents, using the resultant document ranking can help to much improve results-diversification performance.

5. CONCLUSIONS

We presented a novel approach to ranking (query specific) document clusters by their presumed relevance to the query. Our approach uses Markov Random Fields that enable the integration of various types of cluster-relevance evidence. Empirical evaluation demonstrated the effectiveness of using our approach to re-rank different initially retrieved lists. The approach also substantially outperforms state-of-the-art cluster ranking methods and can be used to substantially improve the performance of results diversification methods.

6. ACKNOWLEDGMENTS

We thank the reviewers for their comments. This work has been supported by and carried out at the Technion-Microsoft Electronic Commerce Research Center.

7. REFERENCES

[1] N. Abdul-Jaleel, J. Allan, W. B. Croft, F. Diaz, L. Larkey, X. Li, M. D. Smucker, and C. Wade. UMASS at TREC 2004 — novelty and hard. In *Proc. of TREC-13*, 2004.

[2] J. Allan, M. E. Connell, W. B. Croft, F.-F. Feng, D. Fisher, and X. Li. INQUERY and TREC-9. In *Proc. of TREC-9*, 2000.

[3] M. Bendersky, W. B. Croft, and Y. Diao. Quality-biased ranking of web documents. In *Proc. of WSDM*, pages 95–104, 2011.

[4] S. Brin and L. Page. The anatomy of a large-scale hypertextual web search engine. In *Proc. of WWW*, pages 107–117, 1998.

[5] J. G. Carbonell and J. Goldstein. The use of MMR, diversity-based reranking for reordering documents and producing summaries. In *Proc. of SIGIR*, pages 335–336, 1998.

[6] G. V. Cormack, M. D. Smucker, and C. L. A. Clarke. Efficient and effective spam filtering and re-ranking for large web datasets. *Informaltiom Retrieval Journal*, 14(5):441–465, 2011.

[7] W. B. Croft. A model of cluster searching based on classification. *Information Systems*, 5:189–195, 1980.

[8] D. R. Cutting, D. R. Karger, J. O. Pedersen, and J. W. Tukey. Scatter/Gather: A cluster-based approach to browsing large document collections. In *Proc. of SIGIR*, pages 318–329, 1992.

[9] D. Fetterly, M. Manasse, and M. Najork. Spam, damn spam, and statistics: Using statistical analysis to locate spam web pages. In *Proc. of WebDB*, pages 1–6, 2004.

[10] N. Fuhr, M. Lechtenfeld, B. Stein, and T. Gollub. The optimum clustering framework: implementing the cluster hypothesis. *Information Retrieval Journal*, 15(2):93–115, 2012.

[11] J. He, E. Meij, and M. de Rijke. Result diversification based on query-specific cluster ranking. *JASIST*, 62(3):550–571, 2011.

[12] T. Joachims. Training linear svms in linear time. In *Proc. of KDD*, pages 217–226, 2006.

[13] O. Kurland. Re-ranking search results using language models of query-specific clusters. *Journal of Information Retrieval*, 12(4):437–460, August 2009.

[14] O. Kurland and C. Domshlak. A rank-aggregation approach to searching for optimal query-specific clusters. In *Proc. of SIGIR*, pages 547–554, 2008.

[15] O. Kurland and E. Krikon. The opposite of smoothing: A language model approach to ranking query-specific document clusters. *Journal of Artificial Intelligence Research (JAIR)*, 41:367–395, 2011.

[16] O. Kurland and L. Lee. Corpus structure, language models, and ad hoc information retrieval. In *Proc. of SIGIR*, pages 194–201, 2004.

[17] O. Kurland and L. Lee. PageRank without hyperlinks: Structural re-ranking using links induced by language models. In *Proc. of SIGIR*, pages 306–313, 2005.

[18] O. Kurland and L. Lee. Respect my authority! HITS without hyperlinks utilizing cluster-based language models. In *Proc. of SIGIR*, pages 83–90, 2006.

[19] O. Kurland, F. Raiber, and A. Shtok. Query-performance prediction and cluster ranking: Two sides of the same coin. In *Proc. of CIKM*, pages 2459–2462, 2012.

[20] K.-S. Lee, Y.-C. Park, and K.-S. Choi. Re-ranking model based on document clusters. *Inf. Process. Manage.*, 37(1):1–14, 2001.

[21] T. Leelanupab, G. Zuccon, and J. M. Jose. When two is better than one: A study of ranking paradigms and their integrations for subtopic retrieval. In *Proc. of AIRS*, pages 162–172, 2010.

[22] A. Leuski. Evaluating document clustering for interactive information retrieval. In *Proc. of CIKM*, pages 33–40, 2001.

[23] T.-Y. Liu. *Learning to Rank for Information Retrieval.* Springer, 2011.

[24] X. Liu and W. B. Croft. Cluster-based retrieval using language models. In *Proc. of SIGIR*, pages 186–193, 2004.

[25] X. Liu and W. B. Croft. Experiments on retrieval of optimal clusters. Technical Report IR-478, Center for Intelligent Information Retrieval (CIIR), University of Massachusetts, 2006.

[26] X. Liu and W. B. Croft. Evaluating text representations for retrieval of the best group of documents. In *Proc. of ECIR*, pages 454–462, 2008.

[27] D. Metzler. *A feature-centric view of information retrieval.* Springer, 2011.

[28] D. Metzler and W. B. Croft. A Markov random field model for term dependencies. In *Proc. of SIGIR*, pages 472–479, 2005.

[29] R. L. T. Santos, C. Macdonald, and I. Ounis. Exploiting query reformulations for web search result diversification. In *Proc. of WWW*, pages 881–890, 2010.

[30] J. Seo and W. B. Croft. Geometric representations for multiple documents. In *Proc. of SIGIR*, pages 251–258, 2010.

[31] J. G. Shanahan, J. Bennett, D. A. Evans, D. A. Hull, and J. Montgomery. Clairvoyance Corporation experiments in the TREC 2003. High accuracy retrieval from documents (HARD) track. In *Proc. of TREC-12*, pages 152–160, 2003.

[32] A. Tombros, R. Villa, and C. van Rijsbergen. The effectiveness of query-specific hierarchic clustering in information retrieval. *Inf. Process. Manage.*, 38(4):559–582, 2002.

[33] C. J. van Rijsbergen. *Information Retrieval.* Butterworths, second edition, 1979.

[34] E. M. Voorhees. The cluster hypothesis revisited. In *Proc. of SIGIR*, pages 188–196, 1985.

[35] P. Willett. Query specific automatic document classification. *International Forum on Information and Documentation*, 10(2):28–32, 1985.

[36] Y. Yue, T. Finley, F. Radlinski, and T. Joachims. A support vector method for optimizing average precision. In *Proc. of SIGIR*, pages 271–278, 2007.

[37] C. Zhai and J. D. Lafferty. A study of smoothing methods for language models applied to ad hoc information retrieval. In *Proc. of SIGIR*, pages 334–342, 2001.

A Novel TF-IDF Weighting Scheme for Effective Ranking

Jiaul H. Paik
Indian Statistical Institute, Kolkata, India
jia.paik@gmail.com

ABSTRACT

Term weighting schemes are central to the study of information retrieval systems. This article proposes a novel TF-IDF term weighting scheme that employs two different within document term frequency normalizations to capture two different aspects of term saliency. One component of the term frequency is effective for short queries, while the other performs better on long queries. The final weight is then measured by taking a weighted combination of these components, which is determined on the basis of the length of the corresponding query.

Experiments conducted on a large number of TREC news and web collections demonstrate that the proposed scheme almost always outperforms five state of the art retrieval models with remarkable significance and consistency. The experimental results also show that the proposed model achieves significantly better precision than the existing models.

Categories and Subject Descriptors

H.3.3 [**Information Systems**]: Information Search and Retrieval : Retrieval Models

General Terms

Algorithm, Experimentation, Performance

Keywords

Document ranking, Retrieval model, Term weighting

1. INTRODUCTION

Term weighting schemes are the central part of an information retrieval system. Effectiveness of IR systems are thus crucially dependent on the underlying term weighting mechanism. Almost all retrieval models integrate three major variables to determine the degree of importance of a term for a document: (i) within document term frequency, (ii) document length and (iii) the specificity of the term in the collection. Term frequency and document length combination is used to infer the saliency of a term in a document, and when a query contains more than one term, term specificity is used to reward the documents that contain the terms rare in the collection.

Retrieval models can be broadly classified into two major families based on their term weight estimation principle. Vector space model casts queries and documents as finite dimensional vectors, where the weight of an individual component is computed using numerous variations of tf-idf scores. On the other hand, probabilistic models [16, 17] primarily focus on estimating the probabilities of the terms in the documents, and the estimation techniques differ from one approach to the other. But in essence all of them use the same basic principles that we have outlined before.

Most of the existing models (possibly all) employ a single term frequency normalization mechanism that does not take into account various aspects of a term's saliency in a document. For example, frequency of a term in a document relative to the frequency of the other terms in the same document gives us an important clue that can not be achieved by the commonly used document length based normalization scheme. On the contrary, length based normalization can restrict the likelihood of retrieval of extremely long documents which can not be taken care of by the relative frequency based term weighting.

Another major limitation of the present models is that they do not balance well in preferring short and long documents. Such limitation makes a system to retrieve low quality documents at the top of the ranked list when they face queries of varying length. For example, in pivoted document length normalization scheme, if the parameter is set to a smaller value, it performs better for shorter queries, and when the parameter value is larger, longer queries are benefited more than the shorter queries [10]. Similar observation can be made for other models such as BM25, language model or relatively recent divergence from randomness based models [13, 10].

The main reason is that when the parameter is set to a static value, most of the models prefer either short documents or long documents. If a weighting scheme prefers long documents, it pulls up extremely long documents when longer queries are encountered, since the longer documents have higher verbosity level it matches more query terms[28]. On the other direction, preference of short documents may degrade the overall retrieval performance, since it violates the likelihood of relevance versus retrieval pattern suggested by Singhal et al. [28].

SIGIR'13, July 28–August 1, 2013, Dublin, Ireland.
Copyright 2013 ACM 978-1-4503-2034-4/13/07 ...$15.00.

This article proposes a term weighting scheme that can address these weaknesses in an effective way. In particular, we argue that the two aspects of term frequencies, when combined appropriately, leads to significant performance benefit. In this article we make the following contributions.

- It introduces a two aspect term frequency normalization scheme, that combines relative tf weighting and the tf normalization based on document length. One component of the term frequency tends to prefer long documents, while the other component prefers short documents and therefore, it maintains a good balance in preferring short and long documents.
- It uses the query length information to emphasize the appropriate component. In particular, when the system faces a long query, it down-weights the part that prefers long documents in order to compensate the effect and vice versa.
- It modifies the usual term discrimination measure (idf) by integrating mean term frequency of a term in the set of documents the term is contained in.
- Finally, we use asymptotically bounded function (similar to Robertson and Walker [22]) to transform the tf factors that better handles the term coverage issues in the documents and also helps to combine the two tf factors more easily. As a bi-product of such transformation, the ranking function easily produces the similarity values in the range of [0-1].

In order to assess the effectiveness of the proposed model we carry out a set of experiments on a large number of standard test collections containing news and web data. The experimental results show that the proposed weighting function consistently and significantly outperforms five state of the art retrieval models (from vector space as well as probabilities families) measured in terms of the standard metrics such as MAP and NDCG. The experimental outcomes also attest that the model achieves significantly better precision than all the other models when measured in terms of a recently popularized metric, namely, expected reciprocal rank (ERR) [6].

The remainder of the article is organized as follows. In Section 2 we review the state of the art. Section 3 describes the proposed weighing scheme. Description about the test collections, evaluation metrics and the details of the baselines are given in Section 4. Experimental results are presented in Section 5, where we compare the performance of the proposed model with the state of the art vector space models, followed by the comparison with the probabilistic models. Finally, we conclude in Section 6.

2. STATE OF THE ART

Information retrieval systems, when encounter a query, tries to rank documents by their likelihood of relevance. Most IR systems assign a numeric score to the documents and then they are ranked based on these scores. Three widely used models in IR are the vector space model [26, 25], the probabilistic models [21] and the inference network based model [30]. In this section we review some of the state of the art models.

In vector space model, queries and documents are represented as the vector of terms. To compute a score between a document and a query the model measures the similarity between the query and document vector using cosine function. The central part of the vector space model is to determine the weight of the terms that are present in the query and the documents. Three main factors that come into play to compute the weight of a term are: (i) frequency of the term in the document, (ii) document frequency of the term in the collection (first proposed in [29]) and (iii) the length of the document that contains the term. Fang et al. [10] give a comprehensive analysis of four retrieval models by defining a set of constraints that needs to be satisfied for effective retrieval. Using these constraints the strengths and weaknesses of some well known models are analyzed and some of the models are modified. There are also a number of recent works that focus on the constraint based analysis of the retrieval models [8, 9].

Salton and Buckley [24] summarize a number of term weighting approaches which use various types of normalization. It is evident that document length is an important component in effective term weighting. Singhal et al. [28] identify a number of weaknesses of cosine and maximum tf normalization and they observe that a weighting formula that retrieves documents *with chances similar to their probability of relevance* performs better. Following this observation, they propose a pivoted normalization scheme that acts as a correction factor of old normalization and is one of the most effective term weighting schemes in the vector space framework. The pivoted length normalization scheme computes the term weight as follows [27]:

$$\sum_{t \in Q \cap D} \frac{1 + ln(1 + ln(TF(t,D)))}{1 - s + s\frac{len(D)}{ADL(C)}} \cdot TF(t,Q) \cdot ln\frac{N+1}{df(t)} \quad (1)$$

The parameter s controls the extent of normalization with respect to the document. Typically, the term weighting functions in vector space model are designed heuristically, which are based on the researchers experience. Several work tried to use the data to learn the patterns that satisfy the data. For example, Greiff [11] uses exploratory data analysis to uncover some important relationship between the document frequency and the relevance of a document.

The key part of the probabilistic models is to estimate the probability of relevance of the documents for a query. This is where most probabilistic model differs from one another. Binary independence model is perhaps the most widely accepted technique in the classical probabilistic model. A number of weighting formula have been developed and BM25 [20] has been the most effective among the formulae. The major differences between BM25 and the other commonly used TF-IDF models are the slightly variant IDF formulation and the use of the query term frequency. The length normalization factor uses the average document length and a parameter has been introduced to control the relative length effect.

Probabilistic language modeling technique [19, 14] is another effective ranking model that is widely used today. Typically, language modeling approaches compute the probability of generating a query from a document, assuming that the query terms are chosen independently. Unlike TF-IDF models, language modeling approaches do not explicitly use document length factor and the *idf* component. It seems that the length of the document is an integral part of this formula and that automatically takes care of the length normalization issue. However, smoothing is crucial and it has very similar effect as the parameter that controls the length normalization components in pivoted normalization or BM25 model. Three major smoothing techniques (Dirichlet, Jelinek-Mercer and Two-stage) are commonly used in this model [31].

Relatively recent, another probabilistic model is proposed in [3] that computes the weight of a term by measuring the informative content of a term by computing the amount of divergence of the term frequency distribution from the distribution based on a random process. Like most of the well known models, they also use the same basic components. However, the integration of various component are derived theoretically. This family of formula also uses the average document length as an ideal length of the documents and the term frequencies are normalized with respect to the average document length.

In inference network, document retrieval is modeled as an inference process [30]. A document instantiates a term with a certain strength and given a query the credit from multiple terms is accumulated to compute a relevance that is very equivalent to the similarity score of vector space model. From an operational angle, the strength of instantiation of a term for a document can be considered as weight of the term in a document. The strength of instantiation of a term can be computed using any reasonable formula.

3. PROPOSED WORK

3.1 Preliminaries

Given a query Q and a document D, the main task of a ranking function is to assign a score to D with respect to the query Q. The main objective of a term weighting scheme is to quantify the saliency of the query terms in the document. This section describes a novel TF-IDF term weighting scheme that serves above purpose. En-route to the development, we are guided by a number of hypotheses that are commonplace in quantifying the importance of a term. Thus, before we give the main motivation behind our work, let us first revisit the three key hypotheses.

1. **Term Frequency Hypothesis (TFH)**: The weight of term in a document should increase with the increase in term frequency (TF). However, it seems unlikely that the importance of a term grows linearly with the increase in TF. Therefore, researchers have used dampened TF instead of the raw TF for ranking. The most widely used damping function has been $log(TF)$ and the basis of this damping can be best captured by the following advanced hypothesis.

   Advanced TF Hypothesis (AD-TFH): The modified term frequency hypothesis captures the intuition that the rate of change of weight of a term should decrease with the larger TF. For example, the change in the weight caused by increasing TF from 2 to 3 should be higher than that caused by increasing TF from 25 to 26 [10]. Thus, the raw TF has to be transformed to fulfill the above goal. Formally, we hypothesize that, a function $F_t(TF)$, that maps the original TF to the resultant value (which will be used for final weighting), should possess the following two properties.

   (a) $F'_t(TF) > 0$

   (b) $F''_t(TF) < 0$

2. **Document Length Hypothesis (DLH)**: This hypothesis captures the relationship between the term frequency and the document length. Long documents tend to use a term repeatedly, thus term frequency can be higher in a long document. Therefore, if TF is considered in isolation (disregarding the document length), long documents are given undue preference. Thus, it is necessary to regulate the TF value in accordance with the document length. The general principle is that if two documents have different lengths and the same TF values for a term t, then the contribution of TF (of t) should be higher for the shorter document.

3. **Term Discrimination Hypothesis (TDH)**: If a query contains more than one term, then a good weighting scheme should prefer a document that contains the rare term (in the collection).

3.2 Two Aspects of TF

Most existing weighting schemes employ the above heuristics to quantify the term importance. However, they generally normalize the term frequency that captures a single aspect of the saliency of the terms and hence disregards another important aspect that we detail next. In particular, we consider the following two aspects:

1. **Relative Intra-document TF (RITF)** : In this factor, the importance of a term is measured by considering its frequency relative to the average TF of the document. Thus, a natural formulation for this could be

   $$RITF(t, D) = \frac{TF(t, D)}{Avg.TF(D)} \qquad (2)$$

   where $TF(t, D)$ and $Avg.TF(t, D)$ denote the frequency of the term t in D and average term frequency of D respectively. However, Equation 2 may too much prefer excessively long documents, since the denominator is close to 1 for a very long document [28]. Hence, a sublinear damping of TF seems to be a better choice over the raw TF and thus we use the following function.

   $$RITF(t, D) = \frac{log_2(1 + TF(t, D))}{log_2(1 + Avg.TF(D))} \qquad (3)$$

   Indeed, such a formula has been used by Singhal et al. [28] in the pivoted length normalization framework to normalize the tf values in accordance with the number of unique terms in the document.

2. **Length Regularized TF (LRTF)** : This factor normalizes the term frequency by considering the number of terms present in a document. Similar to Robertson's [22] notion, we assume that the appropriate length of a document should be the average document length of the collection and the frequency of the terms of an average length document should remain unchanged. Thus, a reasonable starting point could be $TF(t, D) \times \frac{ADL(\mathcal{C})}{len(D)}$, where $ADL(\mathcal{C})$ is the average document length of the collection and $len(D)$ is the length of the document D. But once again, it seems unlikely that the increase in term frequency follows a linear relationship with the document length, and thus the above formula over-penalizes the long documents. To overcome this

bias, we employ the following function (used in [3]) to achieve the length dependent normalization.

$$LRTF(t, D) = TF(t, D) \times log_2 \left(1 + \frac{ADL(C)}{len(D)}\right) \quad (4)$$

Equation 4 still punishes the long documents but with diminishing effect.

However, we believe that any document length normalization can be used to achieve this purpose. Some of the possible alternatives might be the length normalization component of BM25 or that of the pivoted normalization scheme.

3.2.1 Motivation

In order to motivate the use of two TF factors, let us consider the following two somewhat toy examples. We use these examples just to introduce the basic idea.

Example 1 Let D_1 and D_2 be two documents of equal lengths, with the following statistics.

1. $len(D_1) = 20$, # distinct term of $D_1 = 5$, $TF(t, D_1)$=4
2. $len(D_2) = 20$, # distinct term of $D_2 = 15$, $TF(t, D_2)$=4

In both of the cases, $LRTF$ considers t equally important. A little thought will convince us that this is not appropriate, since the focus of the document D_1 seems to be divided equally among 5 terms and therefore t should not be considered salient, while t seems to be important for D_2. Thus, in the later case $RITF$ seems to be a better choice to $LRTF$.

Let us now turn to the other direction and consider the second example.

Example 2 Let D_1 and D_2 be two documents with the following statistics.

1. $len(D_1) = 20$, # distinct term of $D_1 = 15$, $TF(t, D_1)$=4
2. $len(D_2) = 200$, # distinct term of $D_2 = 150$, $TF(t, D_2)$=4

For this instance however, $RITF$ considers the term t equally important for both D_1 and D_2, which is not right, since D_2 contains more distinct terms and thus seems to cover many other topics (also possibly uses t repeatedly). Therefore, in this case, the use of $LRTF$ seems to be a potential choice over $RITF$.

Motivated by the above examples, our main goal now is to integrate the above two factors into our weighting scheme. However, we do not use the TF factors as defined in the Equations 3 and 4. We transform these TF values for our final use that in some sense makes use of the hypothesis **AD-TFH**. The next section details the transformation procedure and the underlying motivation.

3.2.2 Transforming TF Factors

Recall that the main motivation behind the advanced hypothesis on term frequency (AD-TFH) is that a good weighting function, while emphasizing on term frequencies and term discrimination factors, should also pay attention to the term coverage issue (i. e number of match). For example, if a document D_1 contains a query term 10 times and another document D_2 contains two query terms (of the same query) 5 times each, then the assigned score should be higher for D_2 (assuming that both the query terms have equal term discrimination values). That is probably the most important reason why raw TF does not work well in practice. Second, another common trait of many weighting schemes (for example, pivoted normalization) is that they use the TF functions that are not bounded above. We transform the TF factors using a function $f(x)$ that possesses the following properties: (i) vanishes at 0, (ii) satisfies the two conditions of **AD-TFH** hypothesis ($f'(x) > 0$ and $f''(x) < 0$), and (iii) asymptotically upper bounded to 1.

One of the simplest functions that satisfies the above properties is $f(x) = \frac{x}{1+x}$. Indeed, similar functions have been employed before in [22] and in [3]. Using this function, we now transform the two TF factors as follows:

$$BRITF(t, D) = \frac{RITF(t, D)}{1 + RITF(t, D)} \quad (5)$$

$$BLRTF(t, D) = \frac{LRTF(t, D)}{1 + LRTF(t, D)} \quad (6)$$

3.2.3 Combining Two TF Factors

Now the key question that we face: how should we combine $BRITF(t, D)$ and $BLRTF(t, D)$? A natural way to do this is as follows:

$$TFF(t, D) = w \times BRITF(t, D) + (1 - w) \times BLRTF(t, D) \quad (7)$$

where $0 < w < 1$. The next important issues that arise out of Equation 7 are the following:

- Should we prefer $BRITF(t, D)$ $(w > 0.5)$?
- Should we prefer $BLRTF(t, D)$ $(w < 0.5)$?

In order to answer these questions, we now analyze the properties of the two TF components. From Equation 5, it is clear that $BRITF(t, D)$ has a tendency to prefer long documents, since for long documents the denominator part of $RITF(t, D)$ is close to 1, and TF is usually larger. On the other hand, $BLRTF(t, D)$ tends to prefer short documents, since $LRTF(t, D) \to 0$ as $len(D) \to \infty$. Therefore, when a query is long, $BRITF(t, D)$ heavily prefers extremely long documents, since the number of matches is more or less proportional to the length of the document [28]. On the contrary, since $BLRTF(t, D)$ prefers short documents it can penalize extremely long documents when it faces longer queries, and thus it is preferable when longer queries are encountered. Another interesting property of $BRITF(t, D)$ is that it emphasizes on the number of matches, since the main component of this formula $RITF(t, D)$ heavily punishes the term frequency, and thus important for the short queries. Hence, the foregoing discussion suggests that, for short queries $BRITF(t, D)$ should be preferred, while for longer queries, $BLRTF(t, D)$ should be given more weight

Based on the discussion given in the previous section, we now turn to incorporate the query length information into our weighting formula. The value of w should decrease with the increase in query length, while it must lie between [0-1]. Specifically, we characterize the query length factor ($QLF(Q)$) by the following variables. (i) $QLF(Q) = 1$ for $|Q| = 1$, (ii) $QLF'(Q) < 0$ and (iii) $0 < QLF(Q) < 1$. Numerous different functions can be constructed that satisfy the above conditions. We used the following three different functions.

$$QLF_1(Q) = \frac{1}{log_2(1+|Q|)} \quad (8)$$

$$QLF_2(Q) = \frac{2}{1+log_2(1+|Q|)} \quad (9)$$

$$QLF_3(Q) = \frac{3}{2+log_2(1+|Q|)} \quad (10)$$

The first function descends more rapidly than the second function, while the second function descends more rapidly than the third function. Our experiments suggest that function 9 performs consistently better than the other two functions on all the collections. Hence, we set $w = QLF_2(Q)$. We leave this issue for further investigation.

3.3 Term Discrimination Factor

The goal of the term discrimination factor in weighting is to assign higher score to the documents that contain the terms which are rare in the collection. Inverse document frequency (IDF) is a well known measure that serves the above purpose. A number of IDF formulation are prevalent in the IR literature, all of which essentially quantify the above intuition. We use the following standard *idf* measure.

$$IDF(t, \mathcal{C}) = log\left(\frac{CS(\mathcal{C})+1}{DF(t,\mathcal{C})}\right) \quad (11)$$

The above IDF measure considers only the presence or absence of a term in a document and does not take into account the document specific term occurrence. We hypothesize that the term discrimination is a combination of the above two factors. In particular, we hypothesize that if two terms have equal document frequencies, then the term discrimination should increase with the increase in average elite set term frequency. The average elite set term frequency (AEF) is defined as $\frac{CTF(t,\mathcal{C})}{DF(t,\mathcal{C})}$, where $CTF(t, \mathcal{C})$ denotes the total occurrence of the term t in the entire collection. In fact, Kwok [18] used AEF for term weighting, but the purpose was different. However, the combination of raw AEF with IDF may disturb the overall term discrimination value, since the IDF values are obtained by dampening through *log* function. Hence, we employ a slowly increasing function to transform the AEF values for this combination. Once again, we use the function $f(x) = x/(1+x)$ to transform the AEF values for the final use. The final term discrimination value of term t is computed as

$$TDF(t, \mathcal{C}) = IDF(t, \mathcal{C}) \times \frac{AEF(t,\mathcal{C})}{1+AEF(t,\mathcal{C})} \quad (12)$$

Our experiments reveal that the use of the above term discrimination has not very significant effect on the overall performance. However, it is observed that the improvements, although are small, consistent across the collections.

3.4 Final Formula

Integrating the above factors we now obtain the following final scoring formula.

$$Sim(Q, D) = \sum_{i=1}^{|Q|} TFF(q_i, D) \times TDF(q_i, \mathcal{C}) \quad (13)$$

Again, since $TFF(q_i, D) < 1$, we obtain the following relationship.

$$Sim(Q, D) < \sum_{i=1}^{|Q|} TDF(q_i, \mathcal{C}) \quad (14)$$

Therefore, we can easily modify Equation 13 to get the normalized similarity scores ($0 < Sim(Q, D) < 1$) as follows:

$$Sim_{norm}(Q, D) = \frac{\sum_{i=1}^{|Q|} TFF(q_i, D) \times TDF(q_i, \mathcal{C})}{\sum_{i=1}^{|Q|} TDF(q_i, \mathcal{C})} \quad (15)$$

Equations 13 and 15 are equivalent in the sense that they produce the same ranked lists. However, an application that requires normalized scores, Equation 15 can be used as a suitable alternative.

4. EXPERIMENTAL SETUP

In this section we describe the details of our.experimental setup. First, in Section 1 we give the details of the test collections used in our experiments. In Section 4.2 and Section 4.3 we describe the evaluation measures and the baseline retrieval models respectively.

4.1 Data

Table 1 summarizes the statistics on test collections used in our experiments. The experiments are conducted on a large number of standard test collections, that vary both by type, the size of the document collections and the number of queries.

TREC 6,7,8 and ROBUST are news collections containing 528,155 documents and supplemented by 150 (queries 301-450) and 100 (601-700) queries respectively. WT10G is a web collection of moderate size supplemented by 100 queries (451-550), while GOV2 is another web collection of larger size, which is crawled from .gov domain. There are 150 (queries 701-850) queries attached with GOV2 collection which were used in TREC terabyte [4] track for three years.

Table 1: Test Collection Statistics

Name	# of docs	# of queries
TREC 6,7,8	528,155	150
ROBUST	528,155	100
WT10G	1,692,096	100
GOV2	25,205,179	150
MQ-07	25,205,179	1778
MQ-08	25,205,179	784

The MQ-07 and MQ-08 set of queries are based on the Million Query Track 2007 [2] and 2008 [1] respectively. This track was designed to serve two purposes. First, it was an exploration of ad-hoc retrieval on a large collection of documents. Second, it investigated questions of system evaluation, particularly whether it is better to evaluate using many shallow judgments or fewer thorough judgments. Both million query track use GOV2 as document collection. Topics for this task were drawn from a large collection of queries that were collected by a large Internet search engine. The queries also vary by their length, with short (2-3 words) to long (6-10 words). Specifically, MQ-07 and MQ-08 collections contain 505 and 433 queries of length higher than 5 respectively. Therefore, the test collections provide us a diverse experimental setup for assessing the effectiveness of the proposed weighting method.

Except TREC-6,7,8, all the test collections have three scale graded relevance assessment. The grades are 0, 1 and 2- meaning non-relevant, relevant and highly relevant respectively. TREC-6,7,8 collection uses binary relevance assessment.

4.2 Evaluation Measures and IR System

All our experiments are carried out using TERRIER[1] retrieval system (version 3.5). Terrier is a flexible Information retrieval system which provides the implementation of many well known models. We use title field of the topics (note that two million query data contain more than 1000 queries that contain more than 5 terms). From all the collections we removed stopwords during indexing. Documents and queries are stemmed using Porter stemmer. Statistical significance tests are done using two sided paired t-test at 95% confidence level (i,e $p < 0.05$).

We use the following metrics to evaluate the systems.

- Mean Average Precision (MAP): This is a standard metric for binary relevance assessment.

- Normalized DCG at k (NDCG@k) [15]: Discounted cumulative gain (DCG) is an evaluation measure that can leverage the relevance judgment in terms of multiple grades, and has an explicit position-wise discount factor. NDCG is the normalized version of DCG.

- Expected Reciprocal Rank at k (ERR@k) [6]: To relax the additive nature and the underlying independent assumption in NDCG, another evaluation measure, namely, Expected Reciprocal Rank (ERR) is proposed in [6]. It discounts the documents which are shown below very relevant documents, and is defined as the expected reciprocal length of time that a user will take to find a relevant document. ERR@k is computed as follows:

$$ERR@k = \sum_{i=1}^{k} \frac{R(g_i)}{i} \prod_{j=1}^{i-1} (1 - R(g_i)) \qquad (16)$$

where $R(g) = \frac{2^g - 1}{2^{hg}}$, hg is the highest grade and $g_1, g_2 \ldots g_k$ are the relevance grades associated with the top k documents. The value of mg is 2 for all the collections, except TREC 6,7&8 (for this $mg = 1$).

The first two metrics are used to reflect the overall performance of the systems, while the last evaluation measure reflects better the precision of search results, thereby making more important for the precision oriented systems. ERR has been chosen as one of the official metrics for recent TREC web tracks [7].

Note that, two million query collections (MQ-07 and MQ-08) have incomplete relevance assessment. Therefore, for the sake of more reliable conclusions, we evaluate the million query sets in two different ways. First, we skip the unjudged documents from the ranked lists to compute the values of well known metrics following the recommendation made in [23]. Additionally, we also present the statistical average precision[2] [5] which was one of the official metrics for the million query tracks [2].

4.3 Baselines

We have compared the performance of the proposed weighting scheme with five state of the art retrieval models. Since the proposed weighting function is a TF-IDF based formula, we have taken two well known state of the art TF-IDF models. We have also chosen BM25, language model with Dirichlet smoothing (LM), and relatively recent divergence from randomness based formula (PL2) as the other state of the art baselines. The choice of our baselines are primarily motivated by [10], which provides a thorough and detailed description of all the state of the art models along with the parameter sensitivity issues.

The performances of all the baseline models are dependent on the parameters they contain. Therefore, for the sake of more reliable comparisons with the baselines, we carry out two experiments by taking first 50 judged queries from MQ-07 and MQ-08 collections. We search parameters by optimizing NDCG@20. The parameters values are given in the description of the corresponding baselines. Our experiments mostly agree with the findings reported by Fang et al. [10]. In particular, we find that the performances of Pivoted TF-IDF and PL2 are very sensitive with the variation of the parameters. For example, the parameter value ($s = 0.2$) suggested for pivoted TF-IDF in the original paper [28] gives 12% poorer MAP than that we find here by training. Similarly, the default PL2 parameter ($c = 1$) is 14% poorer than the one we find. Therefore, for fair comparisons, we use these optimal parameter values for the baselines. The details of the baselines are given below.

1. Pivoted length normalized TF-IDF model: This model is one of the best performing TF-IDF formula in the vector space model framework. The value of the parameter s is set to 0.05.

2. Lemur TF-IDF model: This model is another TF-IDF model that uses Robertson's tf and the standard idf. The parameter of this model is set to its default value, 0.75.

3. Classical Probabilistic model (BM25): BM25 is chosen as a state of the art representative of the classical probabilistic model. The main differences with this model and the previous model are that BM25 uses query term frequency in a different way and the *idf* also differs with the standard one. The parameters of this model is set to $k_1 = 1.2$, $b = 0.6$ and $k_3 = 1000$. Note that we found (on training data) slightly better results for $b = 0.6$ than the default 0.75.

4. Dirichlet smooth language model (LM): Language model is another probabilistic model that performs very effectively. For this model we set the value of Dirichlet smoothing (μ) to 1700.

5. Divergence from Randomness model (PL2): Finally, PL2 [12] represents the recently proposed non-parametric probabilistic model from divergence from randomness

[1]http://terrier.org/

[2]the code available at TREC million query page is used to compute stat AP

(DFR) family. Similar to the previous models, its performance also depends on a parameter value (c in the formula). We conduct experiments for this model by setting $c = 13$.

5. RESULTS

In this section we present the experimental results of our proposed work and compare them with the state of the art retrieval models. In Section 5.1 we compare the performance of the proposed model (MATF for Multi Aspect TF) with the two TF-IDF models, followed by the comparison with three probabilistic models- BM25, language model (LM) and PL2. We use three evaluation measures to evaluate the performance of all the methods.

5.1 Comparison with TF-IDF Models

In this section we focus on to compare the performance of the proposed model (MATF) with the Lemur TF-IDF and and Pivoted TF-IDF models. Table 2 presents the experimental results for six test collections measured in terms MAP, NDCG@20 and ERR@20.

First, we describe the results in terms of MAP. Table 2 clearly shows that MATF gains significantly better MAP than both of the TF-IDF models on two news collections. MATF performs 12% and 15.7% better than Lemur TF-IDF model on TREC-678 and ROBUST respectively. MATF is also significantly surpasses the Pivoted TF-IDF model on these collections with a margin of 8.8% and 6.3% respectively.

The behavior of MATF is similar when we see the results for two web collections, namely, WT10G and GOV2. Once again, MATF outperforms Lemur TF-IDF model by a margin of more than 20% in both of the occasions, which is clearly highly significant as confirmed by the paired t test. Like the previous two news collections, MATF maintains its superior behavior over Pivoted TF-IDF in these web collections also. In particular MATF gains more than 8% and 19% average precision than Pivoted TF-IDF for both of the collections and paired t test once again attests the significance.

We now turn to describe the results on two million query data sets. These two collections are particularly interesting, since they contain real search queries collected from a commercial search engine and also because of their variations in length. Table 2 once again demonstrates that MATF unequivocally outperforms the two TF-IDF models with significantly large margin. The MAP achieved by MATF is nearly 11% and 7% better than that achieved by Lemur TF-IDF on MQ-07 and MQ-08 collections respectively. Similarly, MATF surpasses the Pivoted TF-IDF by more than 10% margin on both of the occasions. Significance tests show that the performance differences are always statistically significant.

Among the two TF-IDF models, Lemur TF-IDF often seems to perform poorer than Pivoted (except MQ-08 where Lemur TF-IDF is nearly 4% better than pivoted). One potentially interesting outcome that we can see from Table 2 is that, when the document collection is larger MATF outperforms Pivoted TF-IDF with larger margin. In particular, MATF gains a MAP on GOV2 collection which is almost 20% better than the pivoted TF-IDF, which is a clear sign of effectiveness of MATF over the state of the TF-IDF models.

So far our discussion of experimental outcomes primarily confined on the basis of the binary relevance assessment. Note that five out of six test collections used in our evaluation have graded assessment in three scales (0,1,2). Therefore, we now turn to describe the results measured in terms of NDCG, that leverages the graded assessment.

The middle segment of Table 2 presents the results in terms of NDCG@20. It is once again clear that the performances are more or less consistent with MAP. Specifically, MATF surpasses the Lemur TF-IDF models with consistently and significantly large margin on all six collections and often the differences are higher or close to 10%, which once again clearly demonstrates the effectiveness of MATF. Performance of pivoted TF-IDF is once again very similar under the graded assessment and it achieves larger NDCG than Lemur TF-IDF except in one occasion. MATF once again is significantly better than the pivoted TF-IDF on all the collections and the differences are larger for larger web collections.

Our final comparison between the proposed model and the TF-IDF models focus on precision enhancing capabilities measured in terms of a metric ERR, that consider three things simultaneously: rank of the document, quality conveyed by the assessor assigned grade (non-relevant, relevant and highly relevant) and the quality of the documents that have been seen before the document of our focus.

The last segment of Table 2 reports the ERR@20 values achieved by the competing models on six collections. We can easily infer that MATF once again unanimously beats the two TF-IDF models. Only on WT10G, pivoted TF-IDF performs slightly better than MATF. Consistent with the previous measures, ERR@20 results demonstrate that on larger web collections the performance differences between MATF and the two TF-IDF models are larger.

Table 3: Comparison with TF-IDF models (statAP). Lemur means Lemur TF-IDF. Superscripts have their usual meaning.

	Lemur	pivot	MATF (% improv)
MQ-07	29.0	29.7	$\mathbf{34.4}^{lp}$ (18.2, 15.8)
MQ-08	28.4	27.6	$\mathbf{32.5}^{lp}$ (14.9, 17.8)

The performances of MATF and the two TF-IDF models on two million query data, measured by statistical average precision, are shown in Table 3. MATF transcends Lemur TF-IDF by a margin of 18% and 15% on MQ-07 and MQ-08 respectively, while it is better than pivoted TF-IDF with more than 15% on both of the collections.

In summary, based on the results shown in Table 2 and Table 3 we can infer that MATF outperforms two state of the art TF-IDF models with remarkable significance and consistency, and the performance differences are often noticeably large. The performance measured by three evaluation metrics unequivocally demonstrate that MATF is highly effective in ranked retrieval. Moreover, the results also show that MATF is more effective for larger web collections.

5.2 Comparison with Probabilistic Models

In the last section we compare the performance of our model with two TF-IDF models. In this section we compare the performance of MATF with three well known state of the

Table 2: Comparison with the TF-IDF models measured in terms of MAP, NDCG@20 and ERR@20. MATF denotes the proposed model. The best results are boldfaced. Superscripts l and p denote that the performance difference is statistically significant ($p < 0.05$) compared to Lemur TF-IDF and Pivot TF-IDF respectively.

Metric	Method	TREC-678	ROBUST	WT10G	GOV2	MQ-07	MQ-08
MAP	Lemur.TF-IDF	20.9	26.1	18.4	24.8	39.6	42.8
	Pivot.TF-IDF	21.5	28.4	20.5	26.5	40.0	41.2
	MATF	**23.4**^{lp}	**30.2**^{lp}	**22.2**^{lp}	**31.7**^{lp}	**44.2**^{lp}	**45.7**^{lp}
% better than Lemur.TF-IDF		12.0	15.7	20.7	27.8	11.6	6.8
% better than Pivot.TF-IDF		8.8	6.3	8.3	19.6	10.5	10.9
NDCG@20	Lemur.TF-IDF	40.0	37.5	31.6	43.8	46.8	50.1
	Pivot.TF-IDF	41.5	40.2	33.4	46.8	48.3	48.7
	MATF	**44.6**^{lp}	**41.5**^{lp}	**34.6**^{l}	**51.0**^{lp}	**51.1**^{lp}	**52.6**^{lp}
% better than Lemur.TF-IDF		11.5	10.7	9.5	16.4	9.2	5.0
% better than Pivot.TF-IDF		7.5	3.2	3.6	9.0	5.8	8.0
ERR@20	Lemur.TF-IDF	40.7	45.7	34.7	48.3	40.6	44.5
	Pivot.TF-IDF	41.9	46.3	**37.9**	49.4	42.9	44.6
	MATF	**43.9**^{lp}	**48.5**^{lp}	37.1^{l}	**53.4**^{lp}	**44.9**^{lp}	**47.3**^{lp}

art probabilistic retrieval models. Our evaluation strategy is once again similar to the previous section. We compare the performances of the models under MAP, NDCG@20 and ERR@20.

First we compare the performance of MATF with the BM25 model. Table 4 shows the summary of the retrieval results on six test collections. It is clear from the table that MATF is superior to BM25 model. This result holds for all the collections and for all three evaluation measure. When the performance differences between them are measured in terms of MAP, we notice that MATF is significantly effective for news as well as web corpora compared to BM25. In fact, MATF is nearly 10% better than BM25 on two news data, while on two web collections (WT10G and GOV2), MATF achieves 17% and 12% more MAP than BM25. The differences on MQ-07 and MQ-08 are similarly significant with substantial margins. The performance differences between MATF and BM25 revealed by NDCG metric are consistent with that revealed by MAP and once again, all the differences are statistically significant. ERR@20 depicts that for all the collections, MATF remains consistently superior to BM25, which clearly confirms that MATF is very effective for precision oriented systems.

We now compare the effectiveness of MATF and language model with Dirichlet prior language model. From Table 4 we clearly see that the performance differences between MATF and LM are larger in three out of six cases than that we had observed when comparing the performance of MATF and BM25. Specifically, MATF achieves close to or more than 10% MAP than LM on four out out six instances (except WT10G). The performance measured on graded relevance assessment also demonstrates that MATF unequivocally beats the Dirichlet prior language model based approach, and the differences are substantially large. On GOV2, MQ-07 and MQ-08 data, MATF surpasses LM with a margin of 14%, 8% and nearly 9% respectively. The comparison of precision enhancing abilities of MATF and LM also clearly indicates that MATF is always better than LM, which is very concordant with the experimental findings captured by MAP and NDCG.

We now compare the performance of the proposed model with another probabilistic model from the divergence from randomness family, namely, PL2. This model is relatively recent compared to the previous two probabilistic models and was also found to be better than BM25 in the experiments reported in [3]. Table 4 reflects two major facts. First, it appears from the table that PL2 is most effective among the probabilistic models and in particular only on MQ-08 data it performs worse than BM25 as reflected by both MAP and NDCG. The second major observation that can be made from Table 4 is that MATF beats this model also with harmonious consistency and performance differences are statistically significant on TREC-678, GOV2, MQ-07 and MQ-08 data. Similar to the previous outcomes, on web collections the performance differences between MATF and PL2 are larger than that for the news collections. Lastly, ERR metric depicts that MATF is better than PL2 across all six collection.

Table 5: Comparison with probabilistic models (statAP).

	BM25	LM	PL2	MATF (% improvement)
MQ-07	30.6	29.7	30.4	**34.4**^{blp} (12.8, 15.8, 13.2)
MQ-08	29.6	27.6	27.4	**32.5**^{blp} (10.5, 17.8, 18.6)

Table 5 compares the performance of four models for million query collections measured in terms of statistical average precision. It is once again clearly evident that MATF is consistently better than all three models and all the differences are very large and it is very consistent with the performance measured in terms other metrics presented in Table 4.

Overall, the comparative analysis clearly shows that MATF is the most effective retrieval model, which unequivocally outperforms all three probabilistic models, when the performances are measured in terms of MAP, NDCG and a precision biased metric, namely, ERR. Also, the relative per-

Table 4: Comparison with probabilistic models measured in terms of MAP, NDCG@20 and ERR@20. MATF denotes the proposed model. The best results are boldfaced. Superscripts b, l and p denote that the performance differences are statistically significant compared to BM25, LM and PL2 respectively.

Metric	Method	TREC-678	ROBUST	WT10G	GOV2	MQ-07	MQ-08
MAP	BM25	21.3	27.7	18.9	28.3	41.2	43.6
	LM	21.3	28.4	21.3	29.1	40.1	41.0
	PL2	22.7	29.5	21.3	29.7	40.9	41.5
	MATF	$\mathbf{23.4}^{blp}$	$\mathbf{30.2}^{bl}$	$\mathbf{22.2}^{b}$	$\mathbf{31.7}^{blp}$	$\mathbf{44.2}^{blp}$	$\mathbf{45.7}^{blp}$
% better than BM25		9.9	9.0	17.5	12.1	7.3	4.8
% better than LM		9.9	6.9	4.2	8.9	10.2	11.5
% better than PL2		3.1	2.4	4.2	6.7	8.1	10.1
NDCG@20	BM25	41.2	39.3	32.4	45.2	48.1	50.9
	LM	40.2	39.3	32.5	44.6	47.2	48.3
	PL2	42.9	41.1	33.1	46.1	48.0	49.0
	MATF	$\mathbf{44.6}^{blp}$	$\mathbf{41.5}^{bl}$	$\mathbf{34.6}^{bl}$	$\mathbf{51.0}^{blp}$	$\mathbf{51.1}^{blp}$	$\mathbf{52.6}^{blp}$
% better than BM25		8.3	5.6	6.8	12.8	6.2	3.3
% better than LM		10.9	5.6	6.5	14.3	8.3	8.9
% better than PL2		4.0	1.0	4.5	10.6	6.5	7.3
ERR@20	BM25	41.1	45.6	34.7	48.2	41.3	44.8
	LM	41.2	46.5	35.4	47.6	39.9	42.7
	PL2	43.0	47.0	35.2	47.7	40.7	42.7
	MATF	$\mathbf{43.9}^{blp}$	$\mathbf{48.5}^{b}$	$\mathbf{37.1}^{b}$	$\mathbf{53.4}^{blp}$	$\mathbf{44.9}^{blp}$	$\mathbf{47.3}^{blp}$

Table 6: Performance of two TF factors on short and long query. The values are MAP.

	short		long	
	MQ-07	MQ-08	MQ-07	MQ-08
LRTF	43.5	43.3	39.9	44.3
RITF	45.4	45.0	37.7	41.8

formance differences are often substantially large and the differences are even larger for the web collections that contain large number of queries. Among the three probabilistic models, PL2 and Dirichlet prior language model perform almost equally, with PL2 having a marginal edge over LM.

5.3 Analysis

In this section we analyze the effect of the two TF factors on short and long queries. For this analysis we choose the two million query collections, primarily because the collections have large number of queries. We divide the queries in two sets. The queries having at least 5 terms are denoted as short, while the rest of the queries (longer than 5 words) are treated as long. The main goal of this section is to validate the hypothesis made in the proposed section that relative intra-document based TF (RITF) performs better on short queries, while length regularized TF (RLTF) performs better on long queries.

Table 6 presents the experimental results on two million query data. The results seem to confirm our aforesaid assumption. LRTF always performs better than RITF on both of the collections, while RITF does better for short queries. However, the performance differences between the methods on longer queries are noticeably better than that for shorter queries.

6. CONCLUSION

In this paper, we present a novel TF-IDF term weighting scheme. The proposed term weighting scheme employs two aspects of within document term frequency normalization to determine the importance of a term. One component of the term frequency tends to prefer short documents, while the other tends to prefer long documents. We then combine these two TF components using the query length information, that maintains a balanced trade-off in retrieving short and long documents, when the ranking function faces queries of varying lengths.

Experiments carried out on a set of news and web collections show that the proposed model outperforms two well known state of the art TF-IDF baselines with significantly large margin, when measured in terms of MAP and NDCG. The model also surpasses three state of the art probabilistic models with remarkable significance almost always. Moreover, the proposed model is also significantly better than all of the five baselines in improving precision.

Acknowledgments

I would like to thank Dipasree Pal, Mandar Mitra and Swapan Parui for their comments, suggestions and help.

7. REFERENCES

[1] J. Allan, B. Carterette, J. A. Aslam, V. Pavlu, and E. Kanoulas. Million query track 2008 overview. In E. M. Voorhees and L. P. Buckland, editors, *The Sixteenth Text REtrieval Conference Proceedings (TREC 2008)*. National Institute of Standards and Technology, December 2009.

[2] J. Allan, B. Carterette, B. Dachev, J. A. Aslam, V. Pavlu, and E. Kanoulas. Million query track 2007 overview. In *TREC*, 2007.

[3] G. Amati and C. J. Van Rijsbergen. Probabilistic models of information retrieval based on measuring the divergence from randomness. *ACM Trans. Inf. Syst.*, 20(4):357–389, Oct. 2002.

[4] S. Büttcher, C. L. A. Clarke, and I. Soboroff. The trec 2006 terabyte track. In *TREC*, 2006.

[5] B. Carterette, V. Pavlu, E. Kanoulas, J. A. Aslam, and J. Allan. Evaluation over thousands of queries. In *Proceedings of the 31st annual international ACM SIGIR conference on Research and development in information retrieval*, SIGIR '08, pages 651–658, New York, NY, USA, 2008. ACM.

[6] O. Chapelle, D. Metlzer, Y. Zhang, and P. Grinspan. Expected reciprocal rank for graded relevance. In *Proceedings of the 18th ACM conference on Information and knowledge management*, CIKM '09, pages 621–630, New York, NY, USA, 2009. ACM.

[7] C. L. A. Clarke, N. Craswell, I. Soboroff, and E. M. Voorhees. Overview of the trec 2011 web track. In *TREC*, 2011.

[8] S. Clinchant and E. Gaussier. Retrieval constraints and word frequency distributions a log-logistic model for ir. *Inf. Retr.*, 14(1):5–25, Feb. 2011.

[9] R. Cummins and C. O'Riordan. A constraint to automatically regulate document-length normalisation. In *Proceedings of the 21st ACM international conference on Information and knowledge management*, CIKM '12, pages 2443–2446, New York, NY, USA, 2012. ACM.

[10] H. Fang, T. Tao, and C. Zhai. Diagnostic evaluation of information retrieval models. *ACM Trans. Inf. Syst.*, 29(2):7:1–7:42, Apr. 2011.

[11] W. R. Greiff. A theory of term weighting based on exploratory data analysis. In *Proceedings of the 21st annual international ACM SIGIR conference on Research and development in information retrieval*, SIGIR '98, pages 11–19, New York, NY, USA, 1998. ACM.

[12] B. He and I. Ounis. A study of the dirichlet priors for term frequency normalisation. In *Proceedings of the 28th annual international ACM SIGIR conference on Research and development in information retrieval*, SIGIR '05, pages 465–471, New York, NY, USA, 2005. ACM.

[13] B. He and I. Ounis. On setting the hyper-parameters of term frequency normalization for information retrieval. *ACM Trans. Inf. Syst.*, 25(3), July 2007.

[14] D. Hiemstra, S. Robertson, and H. Zaragoza. Parsimonious language models for information retrieval. In *Proceedings of the 27th annual international ACM SIGIR conference on Research and development in information retrieval*, SIGIR '04, pages 178–185, New York, NY, USA, 2004. ACM.

[15] K. Järvelin and J. Kekäläinen. Cumulated gain-based evaluation of ir techniques. *ACM Trans. Inf. Syst.*, 20(4):422–446, Oct. 2002.

[16] K. S. Jones, S. Walker, and S. E. Robertson. A probabilistic model of information retrieval: development and comparative experiments - part 1. *Inf. Process. Manage.*, 36(6):779–808, 2000.

[17] K. S. Jones, S. Walker, and S. E. Robertson. A probabilistic model of information retrieval: development and comparative experiments - part 2. *Inf. Process. Manage.*, 36(6):809–840, 2000.

[18] K. L. Kwok. A new method of weighting query terms for ad-hoc retrieval. In *Proceedings of the 19th annual international ACM SIGIR conference on Research and development in information retrieval*, SIGIR '96, pages 187–195, New York, NY, USA, 1996. ACM.

[19] J. M. Ponte and W. B. Croft. A language modeling approach to information retrieval. In *Proceedings of the 21st annual international ACM SIGIR conference on Research and development in information retrieval*, SIGIR '98, pages 275–281, New York, NY, USA, 1998. ACM.

[20] S. Robertson and H. Zaragoza. The probabilistic relevance framework: BM25 and beyond. *Found. Trends Inf. Retr.*, 3(4):333–389, Apr. 2009.

[21] S. E. Robertson. Readings in information retrieval. chapter The probability ranking principle in IR, pages 281–286. Morgan Kaufmann Publishers Inc., San Francisco, CA, USA, 1997.

[22] S. E. Robertson and S. Walker. Some simple effective approximations to the 2-Poisson model for probabilistic weighted retrieval. In *Proceedings of the 17th annual international ACM SIGIR conference on Research and development in information retrieval*, SIGIR '94, pages 232–241, New York, NY, USA, 1994. Springer-Verlag New York, Inc.

[23] T. Sakai. Alternatives to bpref. In *Proceedings of the 30th annual international ACM SIGIR conference on Research and development in information retrieval*, SIGIR '07, pages 71–78, New York, NY, USA, 2007. ACM.

[24] G. Salton and C. Buckley. Term-weighting approaches in automatic text retrieval. *Inf. Process. Manage.*, 24(5):513–523, Aug. 1988.

[25] G. Salton and M. J. McGill. *Introduction to Modern Information Retrieval*. McGraw-Hill, Inc., New York, NY, USA, 1986.

[26] G. Salton, A. Wong, and C. S. Yang. A vector space model for automatic indexing. *Commun. ACM*, 18(11):613–620, Nov. 1975.

[27] A. Singhal. Modern information retrieval: A brief overview. *IEEE Data Eng. Bull.*, 24(4):35–43, 2001.

[28] A. Singhal, C. Buckley, and M. Mitra. Pivoted document length normalization. In *Proceedings of the 19th annual international ACM SIGIR conference on Research and development in information retrieval*, SIGIR '96, pages 21–29, New York, NY, USA, 1996. ACM.

[29] K. Sparck Jones. Document retrieval systems. chapter A statistical interpretation of term specificity and its application in retrieval, pages 132–142. Taylor Graham Publishing, London, UK, UK, 1988.

[30] H. Turtle and W. B. Croft. Evaluation of an inference network-based retrieval model. *ACM Trans. Inf. Syst.*, 9(3):187–222, July 1991.

[31] C. Zhai and J. Lafferty. A study of smoothing methods for language models applied to information retrieval. *ACM Trans. Inf. Syst.*, 22(2):179–214, Apr. 2004.

Retrieving Documents With Mathematical Content

Shahab Kamali
David R. Cheriton School of Computer Science
University of Waterloo, Waterloo, ON, Canada
skamali@cs.uwaterloo.ca

Frank Wm. Tompa
David R. Cheriton School of Computer Science
University of Waterloo, Waterloo, ON, Canada
fwtompa@uwaterloo.ca

ABSTRACT

Many documents with mathematical content are published on the Web, but conventional search engines that rely on keyword search only cannot fully exploit their mathematical information. In particular, keyword search is insufficient when expressions in a document are not annotated with natural keywords or the user cannot describe her query with keywords. Retrieving documents by querying their mathematical content directly is very appealing in various domains such as education, digital libraries, engineering, patent documents, medical sciences, etc. Capturing the relevance of mathematical expressions also greatly enhances document classification in such domains.

Unlike text retrieval, where keywords carry enough semantics to distinguish text documents and rank them, math symbols do not contain much semantic information on their own. In fact, mathematical expressions typically consist of few alphabetical symbols organized in rather complex structures. Hence, the structure of an expression, which describes the way such symbols are combined, should also be considered. Unfortunately, there is no standard testbed with which to evaluate the effectiveness of a mathematics retrieval algorithm.

In this paper we study the fundamental and challenging problems in mathematics retrieval, that is how to capture the relevance of mathematical expressions, how to query them, and how to evaluate the results. We describe various search paradigms and propose retrieval systems accordingly. We discuss the benefits and drawbacks of each approach, and further compare them through an extensive empirical study.

Categories and Subject Descriptors

H.3.3 [**Information Storage And Retrieval**]: Information Search and Retrieval– Retrieval models

Keywords

Mathematics retrieval, Search, Math queries, Documents with math content.

SIGIR'13, July 28–August 1, 2013, Dublin, Ireland.
Copyright 2013 ACM 978-1-4503-2034-4/13/07 ...$15.00.

1. INTRODUCTION

Many collections of documents contain mathematical expressions. Examples include technical and educational web sites, digital libraries, and other document repositories such as patent collections. Currently, due to the lack of an effective mathematics retrieval system, such rich mathematical knowledge is not fully exploited when searching for such documents. Querying with mathematical expressions, and consequently retrieving relevant documents based on their mathematical content, is not straightforward:

- Mathematical expressions are objects with complex structures and rather few distinct symbols and terms. The symbols and terms alone are usually inadequate to distinguish among mathematical expressions. For example $\sum_{i=1}^{n} i$ and $\sum_{j=1}^{m} j$ are quite similar, but 2^n and n^2 are quite dissimilar even though they share the same symbols.

- Relevant mathematical expressions might include small variations in their structures or symbols. For example, $1 + \sum_{i=1}^{n} i^2$ and $\sum_{j=1}^{n} j^k$ might both be useful matches to a query.

- Each mathematical expression has two sides: *i*) its appearance (or *presentation*) and *ii*) its mathematical meaning (often termed its *content*). The majority of the published mathematical expressions are encoded with respect to their appearance, and most instances do not preserve much semantic information.

As is true for other retrieval systems, a mathematics search engine should be evaluated based on its usefulness, that is, how well it can satisfy users' needs. What makes mathematics retrieval distinct is the difficulty of judging which mathematical expressions are relevant and which are not. For example, a user who is interested in $\sin^2(x)$ might also be interested in $\sin^3(x)$ but not in $\cos^2(x)$. We know of no consensus for similarity of mathematical expressions in general. On the other hand, if we were to limit the search to exact matches only, many relevant expressions will be missed, and the user might need to issue too many queries to find a useful answer. For example if the user is looking for $\sum_{i=1}^{10} \frac{1}{(i+1)^2}$, then pages that contain $\sum_{j=1}^{10} \frac{1}{(j+1)^2}$, $\sum_{i=1}^{n} \frac{1}{(i+1)^2}$, and $\sum_{x=1}^{n} \frac{1}{x^2}$ probably also address her needs.

Mathematics retrieval is still at an early stage. Unfortunately, content-based mathematics retrieval systems [7, 15] are limited to resources that encode the semantics of mathematical expressions, and they do not perform well with presentation markup. The lack of content information within web pages forces a retrieval system to rely mostly on the presentation of expressions, and it is often hard to judge whether a similar-looking expression is relevant to a query.

Some systems rely on the presentation of mathematical expressions [3, 9, 20, 26, 27, 28], but they either find exact matches only or they use models that ignore the whole or parts of the structure and usually return many irrelevant results. They do not define how to measure the relevance of matched mathematical expressions, and there has not been much effort to evaluate such systems in terms of the usefulness of search results.

In this paper we focus on the problem of matching mathematical expressions, and hence we assume that a query consists of a single expression. Systematically addressing this problem is a prerequisite for developing systems that handle more complex queries, such as ones that consist of multiple expressions or a combination of expressions and keywords.

Because mathematical expressions are often distinguished by their structure rather than relying merely on the symbols they include, we describe two search paradigms that incorporate structure:

1. Structural similarity: The similarity of two expressions is defined as a function of their structures and the symbols they share. The similarity is used as an indication of how relevant a document containing an expression is when given another expression as a query. We propose an algorithm based on tree edit distance to calculate the similarity of two expressions. Documents are ranked with respect to the similarity of their contained mathematical expressions to the query.

2. Pattern match: As an alternative approach, a query can be represented as a pattern or template. The added expressivity of such a query language provides the user with tools to specify more details, which allows more accurate and complete results in return. On the other hand, the richness and variety of mathematical concepts implies that the query language is potentially difficult to learn and use.

If the two mentioned approaches perform equally well, the simpler query language is probably preferred; the extra cost of forming a query with the expressive query language is justified only when this expressive power results in higher-quality answers. We discuss the advantages and disadvantages of each approach, and we report on an extensive empirical study to evaluate them in terms of their ability to predict the relevance of pages containing mathematical expressions. We also describe other alternative algorithms (e.g. keyword search only, etc.) and compare them against the proposed algorithms.

The contributions of this paper are as follows:

- We categorize existing approaches to match mathematical expressions, concentrating on two paradigms that consider the structure of expressions.

- We propose a representative system for each search paradigm.

```
<apply>
    <times/>
    <cn>
        2
    </cn>
    <apply>
        <plus/>
        <ci>
            x
        </ci>
        <apply>
            <times/>
            <cn>
                3
            </cn>
            <ci>
                y
            </ci>
        </apply>
    </apply>
</apply>
```

```
<mrow>
    <mn>
        2
    </mn>
    <mfenced>
        <mi>
            x
        </mi>
        <mo>
            +
        </mo>
        <mn>
            3
        </mn>
        <mi>
            y
        </mi>
    </mfenced>
</mrow>
```

Figure 1: Content MathML (left) vs. Presentation MathML (right) for $2(x+3y)$

- We evaluate and compare the described approaches through detailed user studies in real scenarios.

This is the first attempt to describe and evaluate possible solutions in a principled way. Understanding the effectiveness of approaches to matching mathematical expressions is necessary for evaluating the further development of any mathematics retrieval algorithm. Hence, we believe the result of this study is an important step towards building a useful mathematics retrieval system.

In this paper we focus on the quality of results when matching mathematical expressions. Indexing and other optimization techniques to reduce query processing time or index size is out of the scope of this paper (Elsewhere, we extensively discuss such optimization techniques [14].). In this paper, we also do not address the problem of evaluating mathematical expressions, which is the goal of systems such as Wolfram Alpha [1], or Bing Math [11].

The rest of this paper is organized as follows. After formulating the mathematics retrieval problem more precisely in the next section, we describe related work in more detail in Section 3. In Section 4 we describe an approach based on matching structurally similar expressions, and in Section 5 we describe an approach based on matching expressions to templates. We present the results of our experiments and the comparison of alternative search approaches in Section 6. We finally conclude the paper with an indication of future work.

2. THE FRAMEWORK

In this section we present definitions for some general concepts. We also describe the search problem and any assumptions we make about the query and the results.

2.1 Definitions

Math Expression: A mathematical expression is a finite combination of symbols that is formed according to some context-dependent rules. Symbols can designate numbers (constants), variables, operations, functions, and other mathematical entities.

There are various ways to encode and represent a mathematical expression. Such approaches can be divided into two main groups:

1. Content-based: Semantics of symbols and their interactions are encoded. *Content MathML* [6] and *Open-*

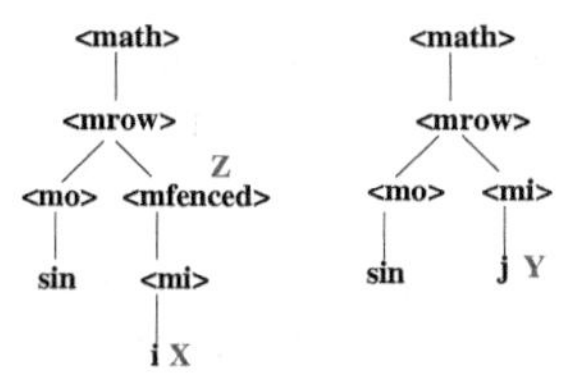

Figure 2: Two trees representing $sin(i)$ (left) and $sin\ j$ (right) in Presentation MathML.

Math [5] are XML-based markup languages that belong to this group.

2. Presentation-based: Expressions are encoded with respect to their appearance. Examples include images of expressions, *Presentation MathML* [6], and LaTeX.

EXAMPLE 1. *Consider* $2(x + 3y)$ *as a simple expression. The Content MathML encoding for this expression is shown in Figure 1 (left), and the Presentation MathML is shown in Figure 1 (right). Presentation MathML contains some surface semantic information. For example, <mn> and <mi> indicate that* 2 *and* 3 *are numbers and* x *and* y *are variables, respectively. However, the multiplication operator is represented by the <times> tag in content markup, but it is invisible and hence not shown in presentation markup. On the other hand, parentheses are not encoded in content markup because they do not carry semantic information. The plus operator is represented by the <plus> tag in content markup, and its operands (*x *and* $3y$*) are also clearly specified. Using presentation markup, the "+" symbol is shown where it appears in the expression, and even though it is marked as an an operator, its operands are not explicitly indicated.*

Presentation MathML is part of the W3C recommendation that is increasingly used to publish mathematics information on the web, and many web browsers support it [18]. There are various tools to translate mathematical expressions from other languages, including LaTeX, into Presentation MathML. Moreover, Presentation MathML expressions can be processed by parsers and other applications for XML documents. Hence, in this paper we assume mathematical expressions are encoded with Presentation MathML unless otherwise is specified.

DOM Tree: Documents with XML markup can be naturally expressed as ordered labelled trees, also called Document Object Model (DOM) trees. A DOM tree T is represented by $T = (V, E)$, where V represents the set of vertices and E represents the set of edges of T. A label $\lambda(n)$ is assigned to each node n, and Σ is the set of all possible labels. Two examples are shown in Figure 2.

A text document, such as a web page, that contains a mathematical expression is a *document with mathematical content*. The search goal is to retrieve such documents by querying their mathematical content.

2.2 Problem Formulation

Here we present a general definition for the search problem and the query language. Details of the query language and the way a match is defined are specific to a mathematics retrieval system. We describe several possible approaches in the following sections.

Query: The aim of a query is to describe a mathematical expression. Hence, a query is either a mathematics expression, or it specifies a pattern that describes one or more expressions.

Search problem: Given a query, the search problem is to find a list of relevant documents with mathematical content. A document is relevant if it contains an expression that matches the query.

The query and all mathematical expressions are encoded with Presentation MathML. Because forming queries directly with Presentation MathML is difficult, input devices such as pen-based interfaces and tablets [17, 25] or more widely-known languages such as LaTeX could be used instead to enter a query. Automatic tools can then be applied to translate queries to Presentation MathML. Hence, regardless of the user interface, we assume the query is eventually represented in the form of Presentation MathML. Thus, this approach is appropriate for the majority of the available mathematics information on the web.

2.3 Discussion

In the case of text retrieval, syntactic variants of query terms can be matched through stemmers and semantic variants can be matched through ontologies. These and similar tools can improve the results of search systems. Similarly, for mathematics retrieval using mathematical equivalence rules and transforming expressions to canonical forms accordingly (e.g. "$ab + ac$" and "$a(b + c)$") can improve search results. Nevertheless, such approaches are orthogonal to our algorithms and out of the scope of this paper.

Extending the query language to cover more complex cases can increase the usefulness of a search system. For example, allowing a query to consist of multiple mathematical expressions or a combination of mathematical expressions and text keywords can increase its expressive power. Including a (symbolic) mathematics engine to calculate the answer to a mathematical query can also be used to address some users' needs. However, in this paper our primary goal is to study the usefulness of the basic search paradigms and to compare them. While such extensions are potentially useful, the effectiveness of the basic search primitives should be proved first. Hence, in this paper we only focus on the basic search paradigms. An extended query language can then be studied by leveraging our findings.

3. RELATED WORK

In this section, we describe existing algorithms for mathematics retrieval systems in a framework that classifies them based on how they attempt to match expressions.

3.1 Exact Match

Some algorithms assume expressions are available only in images, and they try to match a given query by calculating the similarity of images [30, 31]. In the best case, the performance of such algorithms is similar to *ExactMatch* algorithms, which allow for very limited variation among the expressions returned. We describe and evaluate ExactMatch algorithms further in Section 6.

TexSN [27] is a textual language that can be used to normalize mathematical expressions into canonical forms. After that a search is performed to find mathematical expressions that exactly match a (normalized) query. MathQL [9] and MML Query [3] propose very detailed and formal query languages through which mathematical expressions are presented as sets of symbols. To perform a search, sets of expressions containing specific symbols are selected and then intersected using relational database operations. Einwohner and Fateman [7] propose a data structure and an algorithm for searching integral tables. In this approach, pre-calculated integrals are stored in a table. A requested integral matches an entry in the table if its integrand agrees with that of the table entry up to a choice of parameters, e.g. $\frac{1}{x^2+1}$ matches $\frac{1}{x^2+a}$. We characterize all of these approaches as *NormalizedExactMatch* algorithms, which we describe and evaluate further in Section 6.

As shown in Section 6, ExactMatch and NormalizedExactMatch perform poorly in retrieving web pages with mathematical content.

3.2 Approximate match

3.2.1 Substructure match

Sojka and Liska [26] propose another algorithm that first tokenizes expressions, where a token is a subtree of the expression. Each token is next normalized with respect to various rules (e.g. variables names are removed, number values are removed, or both), and multiple normalized copies are preserved. The resulting collection of tokens is then indexed with a text search engine. A query is similarly normalized (but not tokenized) and then matched against the index. Similarly, Egomath [19] tranforms math expressions into tokens (that represent subexpressions), and uses a text search system to index and query them. Regardless of the tokenization details, some structure information is missed by transforming an expression into bags of tokens, which affects the accuracy of results as shown later in this paper. MathWebSearch [15] is a semantic-based search engine for mathematical expressions. The query language is an extension to OpenMath, with some added tags and attributes, e.g. *mq:not, mq:and, mq:or.* Mathematical expressions are interpreted as prefix terms and are stored in a tree data structure called a substitution tree, where common prefixes are shared. A search is performed by traversing the tree. MathWebSearch can only process and index expressions encoded with Content MathML and OpenMath; presentation-based encoding is not well suited for use by this system. Schellenberg et al. [24] propose extending substitution trees to expressions with LaTeX encoding. Such approaches support exact matching of expressions well, but they support partial matching only when expressions share a common part at the top of the tree. Kamali and Tompa [12] propose to allow the common parts of two expressions to appear anywhere in the trees. We characterize such algorithms as *SubexprExactMatch* algorithms, and we show in Section 6 that their performance remains relatively poor.

3.2.2 Structure Similarity

Pillay and Zanibbi [23] propose an algorithm based on tree edit distance for combining the results of different math recognition algorithms. The goal of this approach is to enhance such algorithms to recognize hand-written expressions. Algorithms for retrieving general XML documents based on tree-edit distance have been proposed [16], and these could be adapted to match XML-encoded mathematical expressions. However, these approaches have not been thoroughly investigated for retrieving mathematical expressions. We propose an algorithm in this *SimSearch* class in Section 4 and show in Section 6 that it has a much better performance than other approaches such as exact match.

An alternative for matching based on structural similarity is to express a query in the form of a template, much as QBE does for querying relational data [33]. We describe how templates may be used to specify precisely where variability is permitted. We review our previous work on *PatternMatch* algorithm [13] in more detail in Section 5 and evaluate its performance in Section 6.

3.2.3 Keyword Similarity

The maturity of keyword search algorithms has motivated some researchers to use them for mathematics retrieval [28, 31]. Such approaches typically represent a mathematics expression as a bag of words, where each word represents a mathematics symbol or function. Youssef [28] proposes an algorithm based on the vector space model to rank mathematical expressions in response to a given query. To try to accommodate the specific nature of mathematics, alternative weighting schemes are considered instead of term frequency and inverse document frequency. Nguyen et al. [21] propose another algorithm that considers a semantic encoding (Content MathML) of expressions. Each expression is represented by several textual tags, after which standard keyword search algorithms are used to search mathematical expressions. This allows supporting queries that contain both keywords and mathematical expressions and using existing IR optimizations. As shown in Section 6, ignoring the structure significantly affects the performance.

3.3 Evaluating Math Retrieval Systems

Very few studies consider the problem of evaluating math retrieval systems in terms of satisfying user needs. This is partly due to the lack of a consensus on the definition of the relevance of math expressions, and partly due to the lack of a clear understanding of users' needs. Zhao et al. [32] report on the interviews of a small group of potential users to ascertain their needs. They conclude that users prefer to use keywords that describe an expression to search for it rather than specifying the expression (e.g. "binomial coefficient" instead of $\binom{n}{k}$). As we mentioned earlier, in many cases an expression is not described with keywords or the user is not aware of such keywords. Moreover, with math expressions more details can be specified (e.g. $\binom{n^2}{n}$). Finally, user-friendly interfaces for entering math expressions, such as pen-based devices, were not widely available at the time of the interview. Some search algorithms that compare images of expressions evaluate their systems in terms of success rate [31, 29]. In such cases, the success rate mostly captures the correctness of recognizing math expressions rather than their relevance. In other words, if an expression or subexpression is returned as the search result, and they exactly match, it is counted as a successful search.

To date, mathematics retrieval systems that perform approximate matching and then rank expressions based on their similarity to a query have not been analyzed in terms of their effectiveness: there are no experimental results comparing their ability to find relevant matches. However, the lack of their popularity may be a sign that in many situations they do not perform well.

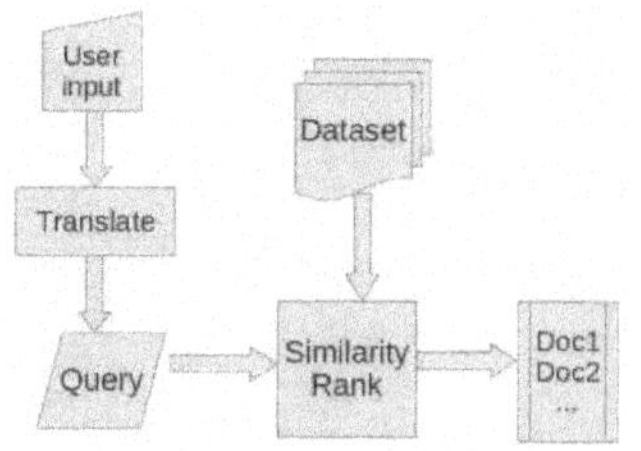

Figure 3: The flow of data in a mathematics retrieval system based on similarity ranking.

4. SIMILARITY SEARCH

The similarity function for mathematics considers only the mathematical content of a document, where each potentially relevant document contains at least one mathematics expression that matches the query. After the user inputs a query through a user interface, it is translated into Presentation MathML to be processed by the ranking algorithm. The result consists of a list of ranked documents sorted with respect to the similarity of their mathematical content to the query. Figure 3 shows the flow of data in this approach.

A general sketch for similarity search is presented in Algorithm 1. The definition of similarity between two mathematical expressions (Line 6) is a key concept that significantly affects such systems.

Just like other information retrieval systems, semantic similarity ranking is generally very useful, as it can better capture the intention of a user. Thus, the limited semantic information that is available (i.e., whether a symbol is a number, a variable, or an operator) should also be considered to calculate similarity in order to broaden the set of potentially matching expressions.

Unfortunately, a ranking function based on more expressive semantic similarity requires that the query and the expressions be semantically encoded using a markup language such as OpenMath or Content MathML. Hence, it requires more effort from the user to form a query semantically and also requires that content markup be used to publish mathematical expressions. As stated earlier, this is generally unavailable for retrieval from the web.

Algorithm 1 Similarity Search

```
1: Input: Query q and collection D of documents.
2: Output: A list of documents ranked with respect to
   their similarity to q.
3: Define list L that is initially empty
4: for each document d ∈ D do
5:     for each math expression E in d do
6:         Calculate the similarity of E and q and store the
           result
7:     end for
8:     Calculate the similarity of d and q and store the result
       in L
9: end for
10: Sort documents in L with respect to the calculated similarities in descending order
11: return L
```

We now propose a similarity function that is based on tree edit distance [4], and define the similarity of a document to a math query accordingly. More specifically, we propose appropriate similarity functions to be used in Lines 6 and 8 of Algorithm 1.

Consider two ordered labelled trees $T_1 = (V_1, E_1)$ and $T_2 = (V_2, E_2)$ and two nodes $N_1 \in V_1 \cup P_\phi$ and $N_2 \in V_2 \cup P_\phi$ where P_ϕ is a special node with label ϵ. An edit operation is a function represented by $(N_1 \rightarrow N_2)$ where $(\lambda(N_1), \lambda(N_2)) \in (\Sigma \cup \epsilon) \times (\Sigma \cup \epsilon) - \{(\epsilon, \epsilon)\}$. The operation is a relabelling if $\lambda(N_1),\ \lambda(N_2) \neq \epsilon$. It is a deletion if N_1 is not the root of T_1 and $\lambda(N_2) = \epsilon$, where deleting N_1 makes the children of N_1 become the children of the parent of N_1 in place of node N_1. Finally, the operation is an insertion if $\lambda(N_1) = \epsilon$, where insertion is the mirror image of deletion. A transformation τ from T_1 to T_2 is a sequence of edit operations that transforms T_1 to T_2. To each edit operation $N_1 \rightarrow N_2$ we assign a cost $\omega(N_1 \rightarrow N_2)$. The cost of a transformation is the sum of the costs of its edit operations. The edit distance of T_1 and T_2 is defined as follows:

$$dist(T_1, T_2) = min\{cost(\tau) | \tau(T_1) = T_2\} \tag{1}$$

We customize the cost of an edit operation $N_1 \rightarrow N_2$ for mathematical expressions as follows:

1. If $\lambda(N_1) = \lambda(N_2)$ then $\omega(N_1 \rightarrow N_2) = 0$.
2. If N_1, N_2 are leaf nodes and $\lambda(N_1) \neq \lambda(N_2)$ and $\lambda(parent(N_1)) = \lambda(parent(N_2))$ then $\omega(N_1 \rightarrow N_2) = C_{PL}(\lambda(parent(N_1)), \lambda(N_1), \lambda(N_2))$.
3. If N_1, N_2 are leaf nodes and $\lambda(N_1) \neq \lambda(N_2)$ and $\lambda(parent(N_1)) \neq \lambda(parent(N_2))$ then $\omega(N_1 \rightarrow N_2) = C_L(\lambda(N_1), \lambda(N_2))$.
4. If N_1, N_2 are not both leaf nodes and $\lambda(N_1) \neq \lambda(N_2)$ then $cost(N_1 \rightarrow N_2) = C_I(\lambda(N_1), \lambda(N_2))$.

In the above definition, C_I and C_L, and C_{PL} are static functions that assign values to an edit operation. Their values for various inputs are shown in Table 1. In this table, "<mi>", "<mn>", and "<mo>" represent variables, numbers, and operators respectively; α, β, and γ are constants whose values are set based on the following observations about math expressions (Some math retrieval systems normalize math expressions based on similar observations [19].). Typically, renaming variables affects the semantics less than changing math operators. Similarly, renaming a variable should be less costly than changing a variable to a number, and renaming non-leaf nodes should be more costly that renaming leaf nodes. Therefore, we set $\alpha \leq \beta \leq \gamma$.

EXAMPLE 2. *Consider nodes X and Y in Figure 2. $X \rightarrow Y$ is a relabelling. The label of their parents, <mi>, states that they are variables. According to Table 1, C_{PL}(" <mi> ", "i", "j") $= \alpha$. Hence, $\omega(X \rightarrow Y) = \alpha$. Also, $Z \rightarrow P_\phi$ is a deletion and $\omega(Z \rightarrow P_\phi) = \gamma$. The edit distance between the two trees is equal to $\alpha + \gamma$.*

Consider two mathematical expressions E_1 and E_2 represented by trees T_1 and T_2. The similarity of the two expressions is calculated as follows:

$$sim(E_1, E_2) = 1 - \frac{dist(T_1, T_2)}{|T_1| + |T_2|} \tag{2}$$

where $|T|$ is the number of nodes in tree T.

There are many algorithms for calculating the edit distance between two trees. We use RTED [22] to calculate the tree edit distance.

Value of C	Condition
$C_{PL}(``<mi>", x, y) = \alpha$	$x \neq y$
$C_{PL}(``<mn>", x, y) = \alpha$	$x \neq y$
$C_{PL}(``<mo>", x, y) = \alpha$	$x \neq y$ and $\{x, y\} \in \{+, -\}$
$C_L(\epsilon, x) = \beta$	
$C_L(x, \epsilon) = \beta$	
$C_L(x, y) = 2\beta$	$x \neq y$
$C_I(\epsilon, x) = \gamma$	
$C_I(x, \epsilon) = \gamma$	
$C_I(x, y) = 2\gamma$	$x \neq y$

Table 1: Examples of various cost values assigned to edit operations

Assume document d contains mathematical expressions $E_1 \ldots E_n$. The rank of d for a query Q is calculated with the following formula:

$$docRank(d, Q) = max\{sim(E_i, Q) | E_i \in d\} \quad (3)$$

that is, a document's score is equal to the similarity of the most similar expression in that document.

5. PATTERN SEARCH

An alternative to similarity ranking is to specify a template as the query and return expressions that match it as the search result [13]. This allows flexible matching of expressions but in a controlled way (as distinct from the similarity ranking where the user has less control on approximate matching of expressions). For example, the user can specify that she is looking for $[E]^n$ where n is a number and $[E]$ is an expression that contains $\sin(x)$. This capability is not supported by any exact matching algorithm, and the similarity search may not rank relevant expressions high enough. The approach is analogous to querying a collection of strings by specifying a partial context-free grammar, and returning strings that can be parsed by the grammar. Similarly, a template can be defined using wildcards as non-terminals, and regular expressions to describe their relationships. For example, $\sqrt{[V]}$, where $[V]$ is a wildcard that matches any variable, can be used to search for expressions that consist of the square root of a variable.

According to this paradigm, the user has more power to direct the search; hence the results are expected to be more relevant. However, the variety of wildcards and operations that are available to specify a template may result in a complex query language, which requires more effort from the user.

To find a relevant document, the user starts with a pattern to be searched. It may be necessary to tune the query, as the initial pattern may not correctly model the expression the user is looking for or it may be too general or too specific. After the results are shown, she tunes the pattern until she finds a relevant answer. A diagram of the data flow for this search paradigm is shown in Figure 4. Algorithm 2 presents a general sketch for this search paradigm.

In some cases, combining similarity ranking and structured search is useful. For example, assume a user is looking for expressions that contain the square root of an expression E such that E is similar to $sin(x)$. In this case, $\sqrt{sin(x)}$ is a better match than $\sqrt{sin(\frac{x}{2}+1)}$, and while the latter still complies with the pattern, $\sqrt{sin(x)}+1$ is not match. This search paradigm has been adopted in other contexts. Examples include XQuery with full-text capability [2] and other

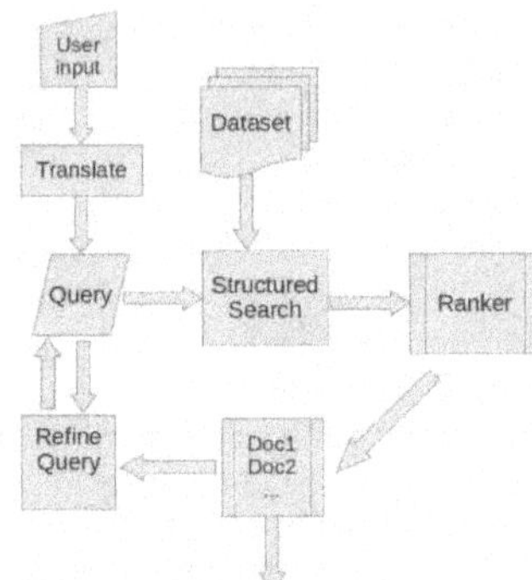

Figure 4: The flow of data in a mathematics retrieval system based on pattern matching.

keyword search features on structured data [10]. Adding this capability to a search system can increase its flexibility to capture relevant results.

In conclusion, this search paradigm is suitable for specialized search where the user can be expected to put more effort to form a query and get better results in return.

Algorithm 2 Structured Search

1: **Input:** Query q and collection D of documents.
2: **Output:** A ranked list of documents that match the query.
3: Define list L that is initially empty
4: **for each** document $d \in D$ **do**
5:   **for each** math expression E in d **do**
6:     **if** E matches q **then**
7:       put d in L
8:     **end if**
9:   **end for**
10: **end for**
11: Sort documents in L with respect to ranking criteria
12: **return** L

5.1 A Model Query Language

A query is expressed as a pattern consisting of a mathematical expression augmented with *wild cards*, optional parts, and constraints in the form of *where clauses*. A query matches an expression (Algorithm 2-Line 6) as follows. A wild card represents a slot that will match any subtree of the appropriate type, where $[V_i]$ matches any variable, $[N_i]$ matches any number, $[O_i]$ matches any operator, and $[E_i]$ matches any expression. A wild card's index i is an optional natural number such that if two or more wild cards share the same type and index, they must match identical subtrees. Wild cards with no index are unconstrained.

EXAMPLE 3. *The query $x^{[N_1]} - y^{[N_1]}$ matches $x^2 - y^2$ and $x^5 - y^5$ but not $x^2 - y^3$, whereas either of the queries $x^{[N_1]} - y^{[N_2]}$ or $x^{[N]} - y^{[N]}$ matches all three.*

Optional parts are enclosed by braces and they may appear in some matching expressions.

EXAMPLE 4. *$x^2\{+[N]\}$ matches x^2 and $x^2 + 1$ but not $x^2 + y$ or $x^2 - 1$.*

Constraints can be specified for wild cards in a query using a "where" clause, as follows:

- Number wild cards can be constrained to a specific range or to a domain, which can be specified using a context-free grammar.
- Variable wild cards can be constrained to a restricted set of possible names.
- Operator wild cards can be constrained to a restricted set of operators.
- Expression wild cards can be constrained to contain a given subexpression, which can in turn include further wild cards and constraints.

EXAMPLE 5.

- *Query "*$[E]^2[O1]3$ **where** $O \in \{+,-\}$*" matches* x^2+3 *and* $(x+1)^2-3$ *but not* $x^2 \times 3$.
- *Query "*$x^{[N1]}$ **where** $1 \leq N1 \leq 5$*" matches* x^2 *but not* x^9 *or* x^{-1}.
- *Query "*$[E1]-2$ **where** $[E1]$ *contains* x^2*" matches* x^2-2 *and* $\log(x^2+3y)-2$ *but not* $x-2$ *or* y^2-2.
- *Query "*$[E1]$ **where** $E1$ *contains* $\log_2([V])$*" matches all expressions that include a base 2 logarithm of a variable.*

In our experiments we assume a pattern does not contain a similarity constraint. Otherwise, pattern search would be a generalized form of the similarity search approach, which makes it hard to compare them. Moreover, ranking documents with respect to a pattern query that contains multiple similarity constraints is a complex problem that should be addressed after the more basic problem of capturing the similarity of two math expressions (discussed in this paper) is addressed. This problem is a direction of our future work.

5.2 Query Processing

A query is processed by trying to match it against the stored expressions by parsing them with respect to the query. Each document that contains a match is included in the search result.

While similarity ranking is in fact an information retrieval approach to the problem, pattern search resembles a database look-up. Therefore, the result of this search paradigm is a list of documents with expressions that match the query. To rank documents in the list (Algorithm 2-Line 11), a ranking criterion should be considered. In our implementation we sort results with respect to the sizes of the matched expressions in increasing order.

6. EXPERIMENTS

In this section we present the results of our empirical evaluation of the described approaches.

6.1 Alternative Algorithms

In our experiments we consider the following specific algorithms:

- *TextSearch:* The query and expressions are treated as bags of words (nodes' labels in their DOM trees). A standard text search algorithm is used for ranking documents according to a given query[1].

[1]We used Apache Lucene in our implementation.

- *ExactMatch:* An expression is reported as a search result only if it matches a given query exactly. Results are ranked with respect to the alphabetic order of the name of their corresponding documents.
- *NormalizedExactMatch:* Some normalization is performed on the query and on the stored expressions: in particular, we ignore specific numbers, variables, and operators by removing all leaf nodes. The normalized expressions are searched and ranked according to the ExactMatch algorithm.
- *SubexprExactMatch:* An expression is returned as a search result if at least one of its subexpressions exactly matches the query. Results are ranked by increasing sizes of their DOM trees.
- *NormalizedSubExactMatch:* Normalization is done on the query and on the stored expressions as for NormalizedExactMatch, and an expression is returned as a search result if one of its normalized subexpressions matches the normalized query.
- *MIaS*: As described in Section 3, subtrees are normalized and transformed into tokens and a text search engine is used to index and retrieve them [26].
- *SimSearch:* Expressions are matched against a query according to the algorithm described in Section 4.
- *PatternSearch:* Expressions are matched against a pattern according to the algorithm described in Section 5. Like SubexprExactMatch, results are ranked with respect to the sizes of their DOM trees.

Note that among the above algorithms, the results of ExactMatch are subsets of the results of TextSearch, NormalizedExactMatch, and SubexprExactMatch.

6.2 Experiment Setup

6.2.1 Data Collection

For our experiments we use a collection of web pages with mathematical content. We collected pages from the Wikipedia and DLMF (Digital Library of Mathematics Functions) websites. Wikipedia pages contain images of expressions annotated with equivalent LaTeX encodings of the expressions. We extracted such annotations and translated them into Presentation MatchML using Tralics [8]. DLMF pages use Presentation MathML to represent mathematical expressions. Statistics summarizing this dataset are presented in Table 2.

6.2.2 Queries

To evaluate the described algorithms we prepared two sets of queries as follows.

- *Interview:* We invited a wide range of students and researchers to participate in our study. They were asked

	Wikipedia	DLMF	Total
Number of pages	44,368	1,550	45,918
Number of expressions	611,210	252,148	863,358
Average size of expressions	28.3	17.6	25.2
Maximum size of expressions	578	223	578

Table 2: Dataset statistics

to try our system and search for mathematical expressions of potential interest to them in practical situations. They could also provide us with their feedback about the quality of results after each search.

- *Mathematics forum:* People often use mathematics forums in order to ask a questions or discuss math-related topics. Many discussion threads can be described with a query that consists of a single math expression. Usually, by reading the rest of the thread and responses, the exact intention of the user is clear. This allows us to manually judge if a given expression, together with the page that contains it, can answer the information need of the user who started the thread. We manually read such discussions and gathered a collection of queries.

The precise query formulations for PatternSearch were created by one of the authors. Thus the experimental results reflect search environments in which queries are formed reasonably well by an experienced user.

Table 3 summarizes statistics about the queries, where the number of nodes in the query tree is used to represent query size. For the sake of reproducibility and as a basis for further evaluation of various search paradigms, both the dataset and the complete set of queries can be obtained from the authors upon request[2].

6.2.3 Methodology

For each query we use each algorithm to search the dataset, and only consider the top 10 results.

The way we collected queries ensures that a user's information needs are clear, which allows us to judge if a match is actually relevant or not. Searches for which we do not have a user's relevance feedback (i.e., Forum queries) require that we manually judge results. Hence, for Forum queries we consider discussion threads that clearly describe an information need with no ambiguity. For example a discussion thread might start with this question: "prove that $F_n^2 - F_{n-1}F_{n-2} = (-1)^{n-1}$ where F_n is the nth Fibonacci number". A search result page is considered relevant if it satisfies the information need that is inferred from the thread. If a page contains data that can be clearly used to answer the query, we judge it as relevant. Note that a page may contain an exact match to a query, but it still does not answer the information need, hence we assume it is irrelevant (e.g. if a page contains the same expression as in the previous example, but F_n is not a Fibonacci number, or it does not contain any information that helps to prove it.).

As mentioned earlier, for PatternSearch the query may be refined repeatedly unless appropriate results are returned or the query is refined a certain number of times and the user gives up (Figures 4). Hence, unless otherwise specified, the results for PatternSearch are presented with respect to the final refined query. For other algorithms however, refining a query is often not necessary or effective, and the results are shown for the original query.

6.2.4 Evaluation measures

NFR: A search fails if fewer than 10 results are returned (including nothing returned), and none of them is relevant.

[2]The query collections with examples of matching documents are publicly available at *http://db.uwaterloo.ca/mathretrieval/queries.xhtml.*

	Interview	Math Forum	Total
Number of queries	45	53	98
Average size of queries	14.2	23.8	19.4

Table 3: Query statistics

Non-Failure-Rate (NFR) is the number of searches that do not fail divided by the total number of searches:

$$NFR = \frac{|\{q \in Q | searching\ q\ does\ not\ fail\}|}{|Q|} \quad (4)$$

MRR: The rank of the first correct answer is a representative metric for the success of a mathematics search. Hence, for each search we consider the *Reciprocal Rank* (RR), that is, the inverse of the rank of the first relevant answer. For example if the first correct answer is ranked second, the reciprocal rank of the search is $\frac{1}{2}$. The *Mean Reciprocal Rank* (MRR) is the average reciprocal rank for all queries:

$$MRR = \frac{1}{|Q|} \sum_{q \in Q} \frac{1}{C(q)} \quad (5)$$

where Q is the collection of queries, and $C(q)$ is the rank of the first relevant answer for query q.

If no relevant document is among the top 10 results, we optimistically assume the search did not fail, and the rank of the first relevant document is 11. If a search fails, we do not include it for calculating MRR.

Rewrite-Rate: It often happens that a search is not successful, and a user must rewrite the query to find a relevant result. For each search algorithm, starting from an initial query, we logged how many times a query was rewritten to obtain a relevant answer among the top 10 results. We assume that the user gives up after five tries, and the search fails or no relevant result is found. The average number of rewrites for all queries is the *rewrite rate* of an algorithm.

Other measures such as *Mean Average Precision* (MAP) could alternatively be considered. However, for our data and query collections, MRR seems to be a better choice. In most cases, there are a few (often one) relevant documents for the query. Hence, MRR can better reflect the accuracy of algorithms. Recall that some of the baselines (e.g. pattern search and substructure search) deploy database operators to perform a search, while some other ones (e.g. structural similarity and keyword search) use IR techniques. Hence, because such approaches are inherently different, it is important to consider measures that fairly compare them. MRR and NFR together provide an indicative measure of the accuracy of such algorithms.

6.3 Evaluation Results

6.3.1 Correctness

The NFR and MRR for each algorithm are presented in Tables 4 and 5 for the Forum and Interview queries, respectively. As the results suggest, PatternSearch and SimSearch have high NFR and also high MRRs. PatternSearch has a higher MRR because irrelevant expressions are less likely to match a carefully formed pattern. On the other hand, SimSearch has a slightly higher NFR because in some cases even an experienced user may not be able to guess the pattern that will yield a correct answer. Furthermore, the next section shows that a template pattern may need to be modified several times to capture a relevant result.

Algorithm	NFR	MRR	p-value
SimSearch	100%	0.74	-
PatternSearch	90%	0.86	0.171
MiaS	94%	0.46	*0.002*
TextSearch	100%	0.19	*0.000*
ExactMatch	13%	1	0.186
NormalizedExactMatch	34%	0.46	*0.007*
SubexprExactMatch	18%	0.94	0.173
NormalizedSubExactMatch	41%	0.43	*0.004*

Table 4: Algorithms' performance for Forum Queries.

Algorithm	NFR	MRR	p-value
SimSearch	100%	0.78	-
PatternSearch	76%	0.96	0.084
MiaS	90%	0.63	*0.014*
TextSearch	100%	0.23	*0.000*
ExactMatch	15%	1	0.211
NormalizedExactMatch	50%	0.58	*0.005*
SubexprExactMatch	30%	0.62	*0.044*
NormalizedSubExactMatch	60%	0.44	*0.009*

Table 5: Algorithms' performance for Interview Queries.

Because MRR is only calculated when the search does not fail, ExactMatch has a high (in fact, perfect) MRR. However, in most cases, there is no expression that exactly matches the query, and hence no result is produced and this algorithm fails. SubexprExactMatch has a slightly better NFR, but it is still too low to satisfy many users' needs. This implies that often there are no relevant expressions or subexpressions that exactly match the query. However, in instances where a matching expression or subexpression exists, it is ranked highly by ExactMatch and SubexprExactMatch. Normalizing expressions, as done in NormalizedExactMatch and NormalizedSubExactMatch, further increases the NFR, but it also increases the chances that irrelevant expressions are matched. Because such algorithms do not offer an effective ranking algorithm, in many cases the most relevant results are not among the top 10 results.

Note that although the MRR of SimSearch is lower than ExactMatch and SubexprExactMatch, it has a much higher NFR as it produces some results for all queries. If we only consider queries for which there is an exact match (so ExactMatch produces at least one answer), SimSearch has an MRR that is not significantly different from that of ExactMatch. The reason is that in such cases, the structural similarity for documents that contain exact matches is 1, and such documents are ranked at the top of the results.

TextSearch has a very low MRR. Because this algorithm ignores the structure, it often does not rank a correct answer highly enough against many irrelevant expressions with similar MathML tags and symbols but different structures.

Note that, although we reformulate queries only for pattern search, the structural similarity search produces results that are comparable with the results of well-formulated pattern queries. ExactMatch or NormalizedExactMatch are essentially pattern search with poorly formed queries. As shown, such algorithms produce poor results.

To show the statistical significance of the results, we use a Student's t-test on the reciprocal ranks of the queries. For each algorithm, we test whether there is a statistical difference between the reciprocal ranks of its produced results and that of SimSearch. We consider a one-tailed t-test for paired samples (i.e. only non-failed searches are considered). As the data in Tables 4 and 5 suggest, there are significant differences (at the 0.05 significance level) between the results of SimSearch and all algorithms except PatternSearch, ExactMatch, and SubexprExactMatch (for Forum queries). The reason is that in cases that such algorithms do not fail, SimSearch ranks relevant results equally well.

6.3.2 *Query Rewriting*

To compare how much effort is required from the user to perform a search, we look at PatternSearch in terms of its rewrite rates. Assume a user is looking for $\sum_{i=1}^{10} 2^i$, and suppose the only relevant match to this query is $\sum_{i=1}^{n} a^i$. The edit distance between the corresponding DOM trees is relatively low, and thus this answer is ranked highly by the SimSearch algorithm. For PatternSearch, however, if the user forms a query with no wild cards, it performs similarly to ExactMatch, and the correct answer is not found. The following is a plausible sequence of query refinements before an answer is found:

$\sum_{i=1}^{10} 2^i \rightarrow \sum_{[V1]=1}^{10} 2^{[V1]} \rightarrow \sum_{[V1]=1}^{[N1]} [N2]^{[V1]} \rightarrow \sum_{[V1]=1}^{[N1]} [V2]^{[V1]}$

While the rewrite rate of SimSearch is always 1 (as no query rewriting is required), PatternSearch has an average rewrite rate of 2.2 and 1.45 for the Forum and Interview queries respectively. As the results suggest, when using PatternSearch, each query may well be refined to obtain relevant results, and hence the user must invest more effort to find relevant documents.

6.3.3 *Summary*

In summary, simply viewing mathematics expressions as if they were conventional document fragments, as represented by TextSearch, or not allowing variations in matched expressions or subexpressions, as represented by ExactMatch and SubexprExactMatch, leads to extremely poor search results. On the other hand, SimSearch and PatternSearch perform very well: much better than the other algorithms that ignore the structure or perform exact matching only. PatternSearch may perform slightly better than SimSearch, but the user will likely need to spend more time to tune a query pattern when using this algorithm. Reassuringly, these results are consistent across the two sources of queries.

7. CONCLUSIONS AND FUTURE WORK

Given a mathematics expression, finding pages with relevant mathematical content is an important problem that is the basis of many mathematics retrieval systems. Correctly predicting the relevance of mathematical expressions is a core problem that should be addressed in order to develop useful retrieval systems.

We characterized several possible approaches to this problem, and we elaborated two working systems that exploit the structure of mathematical expressions for approximate match: structural similarity search and pattern matching. We empirically showed that these two search paradigms outperform other search techniques, including the ones that perform exact matching of (normalized) expressions or subexpressions and the one that performs keyword search. We also showed that it takes more effort from the user to form queries when doing pattern search as compared to similarity search, but when relevant matches are found they are ranked somewhat higher. So in conclusion, structural similarity search seems to be the best way for general users to search for mathematical expressions, but we hypothesize that pattern search may be the preferred approach for experienced users in specific domains.

In this paper we focussed on the usability of answers and how well a search system can find relevant documents for a given query. Others may wish to re-evaluate these results using more controlled methods for assessing relevance. The study should next be extended in an ongoing effort to include new approaches as they are developed. Optimizing the proposed search techniques in terms of query processing time and index size is a separate direction [14]. Based on the results of this paper, more complex query languages can also be developed to accommodate queries that consist of multiple mathematical expressions supplemented by textual keywords that might match other parts of relevant documents, or pattern queries with one or more similarity constraints.

NTCIR is an international initiative to create a public and shared infrastructure to facilitate research in Math IR. It aims to provide a test collection and a set of math tasks. As a part of our future research, we plan to use this data (which is not yet available) to further evaluate the discussed algorithms.

8. ACKNOWLEDGEMENTS

We acknowledge financial support from NSERC, Mprime, and the University of Waterloo, and we thank the referees for their suggestions.

9. REFERENCES

[1] www.wolframalpha.com.

[2] S. Amer-Yahia, C. Botev, and J. Shanmugasundaram. TeXQuery: a full-text search extension to XQuery. In *WWW*, pages 583–594, 2004.

[3] G. Bancerek. Information retrieval and rendering with MML Query. In *MKM*, pages 266–279, 2006.

[4] P. Bille. A survey on tree edit distance and related problems. *Theor. Comput. Sci.*, 337(1-3):217–239, 2005.

[5] S. Buswell, O. Caprotti, D. P. Carlisle, M. C. Dewar, M. Gaëtano, and M. Kohlhase, editors. *The OpenMath Standard, Version 2.0.* The OpenMath Esprit Consortium, 2004.

[6] D. Carlisle, P. Ion, and R. Miner. *Mathematical Markup Language (MathML) Version 3.0.* W3C Recommendation, 2010.

[7] T. H. Einwohner and R. J. Fateman. Searching techniques for integral tables. In *ISSAC*, pages 133–139, 1995.

[8] J. Grimm. *Tralics, A LaTeX to XML Translator.* INRIA, 2008.

[9] F. Guidi and I. Schena. A query language for a metadata framework about mathematical resources. In *MKM*, pages 105–118, 2003.

[10] V. Hristidis, L. Gravano, and Y. Papakonstantinou. Efficient IR-style keyword search over relational databases. In *VLDB*, pages 850–861, 2003.

[11] S. Kamali, J. Apacible, and Y. Hosseinkashi. Answering math queries with search engines. In *WWW*, pages 43–52, 2012.

[12] S. Kamali and F. W. Tompa. Improving mathematics retrieval. In *DML*, pages 37–48, 2009.

[13] S. Kamali and F. W. Tompa. A new mathematics retrieval system. In *CIKM*, pages 1413–1416, 2010.

[14] S. Kamali and F. W. Tompa. Structural similarity search for mathematics retrieval. In *CICM*, 2013.

[15] M. Kohlhase and I. A. Sucan. A search engine for mathematical formulae. In *AISC*, pages 241–253. Springer, 2006.

[16] C. Laitang, M. Boughanem, and K. Pinel-Sauvagnat. XML information retrieval through tree edit distance and structural summaries. In *AIRS*, pages 73–83, 2011.

[17] S. Maclean and G. Labahn. A new approach for recognizing handwritten mathematics using relational grammars and fuzzy sets. *IJDAR*, pages 1–25, 2012.

[18] B. Miller. 3 years of DLMF: Web, math & search. In *CICM*, 2013.

[19] J. Misutka and L. Galambos. System description: Egomath2 as a tool for mathematical searching on wikipedia.org. In *Calculemus/MKM*, pages 307–309, 2011.

[20] R. Munavalli and R. Miner. Mathfind: a math-aware search engine. In *SIGIR*, pages 735–735, 2006.

[21] T. T. Nguyen, K. Chang, and S. C. Hui. A math-aware search engine for math question answering system. In *CIKM*, pages 724–733, 2012.

[22] M. Pawlik and N. Augsten. RTED: A robust algorithm for the tree edit distance. *PVLDB*, 5(4):334–345, 2011.

[23] A. Pillay and R. Zanibbi. Intelligent combination of structural analysis algorithms: Application to mathematical expression recognition. In *PenMath*, 2009.

[24] T. Schellenberg, B. Yuan, and R. Zanibbi. Layout-based substitution tree indexing and retrieval for mathematical expressions. In *DRR*, 2012.

[25] E. S. Smirnova and S. M. Watt. Communicating mathematics via pen-based interfaces. In *SYNASC*, pages 9–18, 2008.

[26] P. Sojka and M. Líska. The art of mathematics retrieval. In *ACM Symposium on Document Engineering*, pages 57–60, 2011.

[27] A. Youssef. Search of mathematical contents: Issues and methods. In *IASSE*, pages 100–105, 2005.

[28] A. Youssef. Methods of relevance ranking and hit-content generation in math search. In *Calculemus/MKM*, pages 393–406, 2007.

[29] R. Zanibbi and D. Blostein. Recognition and retrieval of mathematical expressions. *IJDAR*, 15(4):331–357, 2012.

[30] R. Zanibbi and L. Yu. Math spotting: Retrieving math in technical documents using handwritten query images. In *ICDAR*, pages 446–451, 2011.

[31] R. Zanibbi and B. Yuan. Keyword and image-based retrieval of mathematical expressions. In *DRR*, pages 1–10, 2011.

[32] J. Zhao, M.-Y. Kan, and Y. L. Theng. Math information retrieval: user requirements and prototype implementation. pages 187–196, 2008.

[33] M. M. Zloof. Query-by-Example: the invocation and definition of tables and forms. In *VLDB*, pages 1–24, 1975.

Time-aware Point-of-interest Recommendation

Quan Yuan, Gao Cong, Zongyang Ma, Aixin Sun, Nadia Magnenat-Thalmann
School of Computer Engineering, Nanyang Technological University, Singapore 639798
{qyuan1@e., gaocong@, zma4@e., axsun@, nadiathalmann@}ntu.edu.sg

ABSTRACT

The availability of user check-in data in large volume from the rapid growing location-based social networks (LBSNs) enables many important location-aware services to users. Point-of-interest (POI) recommendation is one of such services, which is to recommend places where users have not visited before. Several techniques have been recently proposed for the recommendation service. However, no existing work has considered the temporal information for POI recommendations in LBSNs. We believe that time plays an important role in POI recommendations because most users tend to visit different places at different time in a day, *e.g.,* visiting a restaurant at noon and visiting a bar at night. In this paper, we define a new problem, namely, the *time-aware POI recommendation*, to recommend POIs for a given user at a specified time in a day. To solve the problem, we develop a collaborative recommendation model that is able to incorporate temporal information. Moreover, based on the observation that users tend to visit nearby POIs, we further enhance the recommendation model by considering geographical information. Our experimental results on two real-world datasets show that the proposed approach outperforms the state-of-the-art POI recommendation methods substantially.

Categories and Subject Descriptors

H.3.3 [**Information Storage and Retrieval**]: Information Filtering

Keywords

Recommendation; Point-of-interest; Location-based Social Networks; Spatio-Temporal

1. INTRODUCTION

Location-based social networks (LBSNs) such as Foursquare, Gowalla, Facebook Places, *etc.*, have been growing rapidly in recent years. As of January 2013, Foursquare had over 3 billion check-ins made by 30 million users[1]. In these LBSNs, users can post their physical locations in the form of "check-in" (see Figure 1 for an example), and share their experiences and tips for points of interest (POI), such as restaurants, sightseeing sites, *etc.* The availability of user check-in data in large volume makes it possible to recommend unvisited POIs to users. *POI recommendation* is of great value to both users and the business owners of POIs. Several techniques have been exploited for POI recommendations. Since *user-based collaborative filtering* method has performed well for POI recommendations according to a recent work [23], in this paper, we aim to further enhance the user-based collaborative filtering method by considering the important factors that have been neglected in earlier studies.

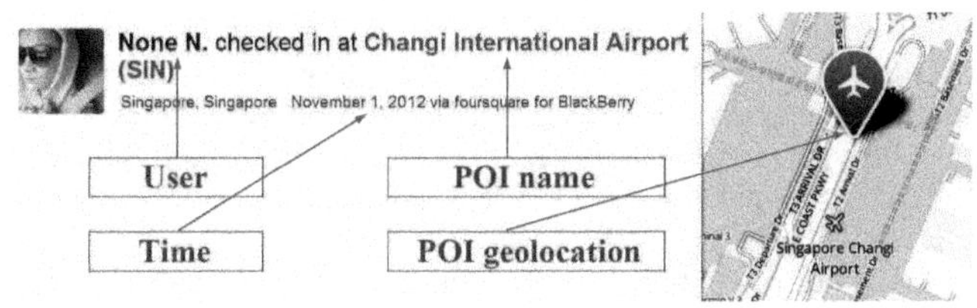

Figure 1: An example of check-in

Users' activities are often influenced by time. For example, a user is more likely to go to a restaurant rather than a bar for lunch at noon, and is more likely to go to a bar rather than a library at midnight. Therefore, the recommendation results should be time-aware or time-oriented. However, to the best of our knowledge, *no existing work has considered the time factor* for POI recommendations in LBSNs. In this paper, we define a new problem for POI recommendations, namely, the *time-aware POI recommendation*, which aims to return a set of POIs for a user to visit at a specified time in a day. We believe that this is a natural and useful extension to the conventional POI recommendation problem which has not considered the time factor.

To address the POI recommendation problem, we explore the following two human behaviors, namely, *temporal behavior* and *spatial behavior* for POI recommendations. Note that these two human behaviors are not applicable to most of the recommendation tasks over conventional purchase or rating data (*e.g.,* for movies, books or other products).

1. **Temporal behavior**: Temporal influence plays an important role in analyzing users' daily activities [16]. In LBSNs, the temporal behavior of a user is reflected by the check-ins of the user to POIs over time. We can therefore mine the temporal behaviors of users by analyzing their historical check-ins, and make use of the mined temporal behaviors for time-aware POI recommendations. For example, if many users visit a bar at midnight but very few users visit a library at the same time, then the bar should be given a higher priority

[1] `https://foursquare.com/about/`

SIGIR'13, July 28–August 1, 2013, Dublin, Ireland.

than the library when we recommend POIs for a user to visit at midnight.

2. **Spatial behavior**: Spatial influence is another important factor in analyzing users' daily activities [13, 23]. Intuitively, users tend to visit nearby POIs, and thus the POIs visited by users often form spatial clusters. Hence, the spatial behaviors of users can be utilized to enhance POI recommendations.

To exploit the temporal behavior in POI recommendations, we propose an approach incorporating temporal influence. Intuitively, if two users have similar temporal behavior, they are likely to visit similar POIs at the same time. Thus, we perform collaborative filtering by exploiting other user's temporal preferences to POIs. Since most people maintain a relatively fixed routine of their daily mobility (*e.g.,* go to office in the morning and have dinner at restaurants after work) [5, 13], we split time into hourly-based slots and model the temporal preference to POIs of a user in a time slot by the POIs visited by the user in the time slot. However, splitting time into slots will make the check-in data sparser. To tackle this problem, we enhance the proposed method with *smoothing* by taking advantage of user's temporal preference at other time slots. Given a user and a specific time, we first find the users sharing similar temporal preference with him or her, and then produce the time-specific recommendations based on their historical check-ins made around the time.

We also propose a new method to exploit the spatial behavior. We assume the willingness of a user moving from one POI to another POI is influenced by the distance between the two POIs. Based on the assumption, we calculate the conditional probability that a user will visit another POI given a POI. By applying the Bayes rule, we derive that the probability that a user will visit a candidate POI is determined by both the popularity of the candidate POI and the conditional probability of visiting the historical check-in POIs of the user given the candidate one. We further extend the model to accommodate the temporal factor. Note that spatial behavior has been exploited in [23] with a different assumption from ours. A detailed discussion on the differences between our method and that in [23] is given in Section 2.

Finally, we employ a unified framework to combine the aforementioned two approaches, *i.e.*, integrating the spatial and temporal influences, to make the time-aware POI recommendation. The contributions of this paper are threefold:

- We define a new time-aware POI recommendation problem, which aims at recommending time-specific POIs for a user.
- We analyze the temporal influence and spatial influence from historical check-in data, and develop POI recommendation methods that exploit the two kinds of influences. Moreover, we fuse the spatial and temporal influences with a framework to make the time-aware POI recommendation.
- We evaluate the proposed POI recommendation method by comprehensive experiments on two real world LBSN datasets collected from Foursquare and Gowalla, respectively. Experimental results show that: (1) Time has a significant influence on the accuracy of POI recommendations, improving on the recommendation accuracy by 37% to 51% over the baseline collaborative filtering method without considering time; (2) The proposed method of utilizing the spatial influence outperforms the state-of-the-art POI recommendation approach [23] that also considers the spatial influence; and (3) The proposed unified method substantially outperforms the baseline methods in terms of recommendation accuracy.

The rest of this paper is organized as follows. In Section 2, we review related work. In Sections 3 and 4, we describe the proposed recommendation methods incorporating temporal influence and spatial influence, respectively. Section 5 presents the unified framework. We present experimental results in Section 6. Finally Section 7 concludes this paper.

2. RELATED WORK

Collaborative Filtering. Collaborative filtering (CF) technique is widely adopted for recommender systems and many collaborative filtering recommendation methods (*e.g.*, [8, 12, 17]) have been proposed. The CF methods can be divided into two categories, namely *memory-based CF* and *model-based CF*. Memory-based CF methods can be further divided into user-based CF and item-based CF. User-based CF first finds similar users based on their ratings on items using a similarity measure, such as cosine similarity. Then the recommendation score for an item is computed by a weighted combination of historical ratings on the item from similar users. We will detail the user-based CF for POI recommendations in Section 3. In contrast, item-based CF works by finding items that are similar to other items the user has liked or rated. Model-based CF builds models using data mining techniques, such as clustering, on user ratings and the models are used to make recommendations [18]. The model building algorithms are usually computationally expensive.

POI Recommendation. The work by Ye *et al.* [23] is the most closely related to our work. Ye *et al.* tailor the CF model for POI recommendations, aiming at improving the recommendation accuracy. The work considers the social influence under the framework of user-based CF, and models the spatial influence by model-based method (a Bayesian CF algorithm). Specifically, the work employs user-based CF to compute the recommendation score of a candidate POI for a user. To exploit the social influence, the work makes use of the user's friends for recommendation rather than all the users by following the approach in [15]. To explore the geographical influence, this work assumes that the probability that a user visits two POIs is determined by their distance, and that the probability of a user visiting a set of POIs is the product of probabilities of visiting all the pairwise POIs in the set. The probability that a user checks in a new POI is estimated by the product of the probabilities of visiting all the pairwise POIs, each pair consisting of the new POI and each previously visited POI. This work reports three findings: (i) Geographical influence has a significant impact on the accuracy of POI recommendations; (ii) The social friend links themselves contribute little for the accuracy of POI recommendations; and (iii) Random walk based method and item-based CF perform much worse than user-based CF for POI recommendations.

In light of these findings, we develop our method based on user-based CF. We also investigate the geographical influence for POI recommendations and propose a new method to exploit the geographical influence. We make a different assumption from that in [23]. Specifically, we assume that the willingness that a user moves from a POI to another POI is a function of their distance. Based on the Bayes rule, we develop a method with a sound probabilistic foundation to recommend POIs. Because of the different assumptions made in [23] and our work, the techniques are significantly different. An additional advantage of our method is that the temporal information can be easily incorporated into our probabilistic model, which can further improve the recommendation accuracy.

In their earlier work [22], Ye *et al.* aim to improve recommendation efficiency for POI recommendations in LBSNs by exploiting the social and geospatial information in recommendation. Nevertheless, the work focuses on efficiency instead of effectiveness.

There exists other work that incorporates social link information into POI recommendations, such as the probabilistic generative model-based method [21], and matrix factorization-based method [4]. The focus of [4, 21] is to explore social link information for POI recommendations and their problem setting is different from ours.

POI Prediction. The recent work on POI prediction in LBSNs [5] is also related, in which any POI, irrespective of whether it has been visited by a user, can be suggested to the user as the next-to-visit POI. The authors report that the movement of human is periodic between "work" and "home" states, and the Gaussian mixture model is employed to predict the POI to be visited next. Specifically, given a user and the previously visited POIs of the user, the method [5] first calculates the probability of the user being in either of the two states in the next time point, and then uses the Gaussian models of the two states to estimate the visiting probability for each POI. Although the method is developed for POI prediction, it can be adapted for POI recommendations by disregarding the POIs that have been visited by the user in the prediction results. We implemented the method [5] and applied it for time-aware POI recommendations, but it performed much worse than user-based CF method. One reason is that the method is not developed for recommendation, and another potential reason could be: the method requires that each user have a number of check-ins (more than 10 used in [5]) on each day to estimate the parameters of Gaussian models. However, the datasets used in this paper are much sparser in which less than 15% of users have at least 10 check-ins per day (see Section 6.1 for more details about the data).

Clements *et al.* propose a kernel convolution method to predict similar locations for a given location based on users' travel behavior [6]. The problem settings of this work is different from the above studies that focus on location prediction for users.

Location Identification and Recommendation. There exists work on location identification and recommendation from the GPS trajectories of a number of users over a long period. Zheng *et al.* [24] mine interesting locations and travel sequences, which can be recommended to users as they are popular among many users. Cao *et al.* [3] develop a technique capable of extracting semantic locations from GPS data. The outcome of the extraction can serve as location recommendations that takes the significance of location and the distance from the user to the location into account. Leung *et al.* [14] perform co-clustering on a graph consisting of users, locations and activity entities to find similar users, locations and activities from the GPS trajectories, and make location recommendation based on the cluster results. Our work differs from these studies in that our work aims to provide personalized time-aware recommendation results for a specific user while the results in these studies are not personalized.

Our work is also related to the work on location recommendation in location-based services. Horozov *et al.* [9] propose a user-based CF method to recommend restaurants for a user. The method first finds candidate POIs close to the user, and then makes recommendation based on the similarities between users who have rated these POIs and the user, and their ratings to these POIs.

Recommendation with Temporal Information. Ye *et al.* [20] present a tagging approach to recommending semantic tags for POIs in LBSNs, and the tagging method considers the temporal information as features. However, both the problem and the approach in the work [20] are different from ours. Existing work on POI recommendations does not take into account the time factor. In other domains time factor is considered for recommendation in several studies, including using item-based CF method [7], matrix factorization method [11] and random walk based method [19]. However, the time factor in these studies is different from the periodic time factor considered in this paper. In these studies, the time gap between the occurring time of a previous rating and the recommendation time is used as a decaying factor to weight the rating—earlier rating will be given a smaller weight. In contrast, we divide time into periodic time slots (*e.g.*, by hour) and make use of the periodic temporal property in our method.

Table 1: Symbols

Symbol	Description
U, L, T	user set, POI set, time slot set
u, v, l, t	user $u, v \in U$, POI $l \in L$, time slot $t \in T$
$c_u, c_{u,t}$	the binary check-in vector of u over L, and the binary check-in vector u over L at t
$c_{u,l}, c_{u,t,l}$	element of c_u and $c_{u,t}$, respectively
$w_{u,v}$	the similarity between u and v
$w^{(t)}_{u,v}, w^{(ts)}_{u,v}$	time-enhanced similarity, smoothed similarity
$dis(l_i, l_j)$	distance between l_i and l_j
$wi(dis)$	the willingness a user visits a dis far away POI
$CI_l, CI_{l,t}$	the set of check-ins at l, CI_l at time t

Context-aware Recommendation. Our work is related to the existing work [1] on integrating context into recommender systems. The approach proposes a reduction-based algorithm that uses only the ratings that pertain to the recommendation context. The approach suffers from rating sparsity. The general motivation of using only context-pertinent data is similar to that of our method to be presented in Section 3.2. However, we address the sparsity problem in our proposed method in Section 3.3.

Summary. Our study differentiates itself from all these existing studies in that the study of both temporal influence and spatial influence under a unified framework for time-aware POI recommendations in LBSNs is unexplored in previous work.

3. UTILIZING TEMPORAL INFLUENCE

In this section, we first present the baseline user-based CF method in Section 3.1. We then present the method of incorporating time influence in the user-based CF in Section 3.2. The enhancement to the method by smoothing is then presented in Section 3.3. All the notations used in this paper are listed in Table 1.

3.1 User-based Collaborative Filtering

Given a user, user-based CF first calculates the similarities between the user and other users, and then produces a prediction for a POI by taking a weighted combination of the other users' check-in records on the POI. More specifically, let $v \in U$ denote a user in the user set U, and $l \in L$ denote a POI in the POI set L. We set $c_{v,l} = 1$, if v has checked in (or visited) l before; and $c_{v,l} = 0$ otherwise. Given a user u, the recommendation score that u will check-in a POI l that she has not visited before is computed by the following equation, where $w_{u,v}$ is the similarity between user u and user v.

$$\widehat{c}_{u,l} = \frac{\sum_v w_{u,v} c_{v,l}}{\sum_v w_{u,v}}$$

The similarity between two users $w_{u,v}$ can be computed with various measures. Among these measures, cosine similarity is a widely adopted measure for implicit data (check-in records are implicit data and $c_{u,l}$ takes either 1 or 0 value). The cosine similarity between u and v is defined in Equation 1, where each user is represented by a binary check-in vector over all POIs L.

$$w_{u,v} = \frac{\sum_l c_{u,l} c_{v,l}}{\sqrt{\sum_l c_{u,l}^2}\sqrt{\sum_l c_{v,l}^2}} \quad (1)$$

3.2 Incorporating Temporal Influence

3.2.1 Check-in Representation

As reported in [5], human show strong periodic behavior throughout a day. For example, people tend to check-in restaurants during daily lunch hours.

We split a day into multiple equal time slots based on hour (We can also split the time based on the day of a week). For ease of presentation, *time* and *time slot* are used interchangeably in this paper unless noted otherwise. Then, we represent the behavior of a user at a specific time by the set of check-ins that user has made at that time.

To represent the temporal check-in behavior of users, we introduce the the time dimension into the conventional user-POI matrix. Specifically, we use user-time-POI cube (UTP) to represent the temporal check-in records. In the UTP cube, each element $c_{u,t,l}$ represents the check-in activity of a user u, at a POI l at time slot t, where $c_{u,t,l} = 1$ if user u has checked in POI l at time t, and $c_{u,t,l} = 0$ otherwise.

3.2.2 Recommendation

To make use of the time influence for time-aware POI recommendations, we extend the user-based CF model in two aspects: (i) we leverage the time factor when computing the similarity between two users (to be presented in Section 3.2.3); (ii) we consider the historical check-ins at time t in the repository, rather than at all time, during recommendation.

Given a user u and time t, the recommendation score that the user will check-in an unvisited POI l at t is:

$$\hat{c}_{u,t,l}^{(t)} = \frac{\sum_v w_{u,v}^{(t)} c_{v,t,l}}{\sum_v w_{u,v}^{(t)}},$$

where $w_{u,v}^{(t)}$ is the temporal behavior similarity between u and v. Next, we detail the computation of the temporal behavior similarity $w_{u,v}^{(t)}$.

3.2.3 Similarity Estimation

In our method, the similarity between two users is estimated based on their temporal behaviors over all time. Specifically, if two users always check-in the same POIs at the same time, the similarity value between the two will be high, and one user's check-in history has a large impact on the POI recommendation for the other user. Therefore, we extend the cosine similarity measure to calculate the similarity between u and v as follows:

$$w_{u,v}^{(t)} = \frac{\sum_{t=1}^{T}\sum_{l=1}^{L} c_{u,t,l} \cdot c_{v,t,l}}{\sqrt{\sum_{t=1}^{T}\sum_{l=1}^{L} c_{u,t,l}^2}\sqrt{\sum_{t=1}^{T}\sum_{l=1}^{L} c_{v,t,l}^2}} \quad (2)$$

Note that, the similarity might be calculated in an alternative manner based on the check-in history at the *exact time*, which is similar to the general idea of context-aware recommendation [1]. We did not adopt this approach because of two reasons: (i) There is a high possibility that the user has never made any check-in at the time. In our two datasets (Foursquare check-ins in Singapore, and Gowalla check-ins in California and Nevada, see Section 6.1 for more details), on average the check-ins of each user fail into 9.97 and 13.58 hour slots, respectively. Thus, if we only consider the time, no similar users may be found for the user; (ii) Even if the user has check-ins at the time, the number of these check-ins is still too small for meaningful similarity computation (on average, only 4.17 and 5.81 check-ins in each hour for the two datasets, respectively).

3.3 Enhancement by Smoothing

The straightforward extension of incorporating temporal influence presented in Section 3.2 has its weakness in handling data sparsity. In this section, we first explain the reason of the weakness and then present two enhancements to overcome this weakness. First, we smooth the similarity estimation using the similarity values of the other time slots. Second, we consider the POIs visited by similar users at different time slots, and weight them with the estimated similarity for recommendation.

The similarity incorporating temporal influence in Equation 2 is estimated based on the UTP cube, which is much sparser than the user-POI matrix. The sparsity could easily make it fail to characterize the users' similarity when a POI is visited at different time slots by different users. For example, consider two POIs and two time slots. User u checked in l_1 and l_2 at t_1 and t_2, respectively, while user v checked in l_1 and l_2 at t_2 and t_1, respectively. If we do not consider time, the similarity between the two users will be 1 by Equation 1, since both users checked in both POIs. However, if the time is taken into account, their similarity becomes 0 according to Equation 2, since their check-ins to the two POIs are made at different time. Obviously, the time-aware similarity is not desirable in the case, particularly when t_2 is very close to t_1, *e.g.*, the next hour to t_1.

We proceed to discuss how to address this problem caused by data sparsity. A straightforward method is to use a decaying parameter to give a higher weight to the POIs checked in at close time slots, and a smaller weight to those checked in at distant time slots. However, this method faces the following challenge: A user's behavior at a time is described by the check-in records of the user at that time, and the user behavior at different time may be similar. For example, the check-in behavior of a user at 9-10AM might be similar to the check-in behavior of the user at 3-4PM, because the user is likely to stay at workplace and make check-ins around it. Such similarity cannot be easily captured by a decaying parameter.

To further illustrate the point, we analyze the check-in data in Foursquare made within Singapore for the similarity patterns between check-in behaviors of users at different time. Note that, the results on the other data used in our experiment arequalitatively similar to this dataset, and thus are omitted here.

Let $c_{u,t} = \{c_{u,t,1}, c_{u,t,2}, ..., c_{u,t,L}\}$ be the check-in vector of user u at time t, which is extracted from the UTP cube. For each user u, we calculate the cosine similarity between every pair of check-in vectors c_{u,t_i} and c_{u,t_j} at time t_i and t_j respectively. Then, we calculate the similarity value between two time slots t_i and t_j to be the average of the similarity values of all users between these two time slots t_i and t_j.

Figure 2 shows the similarity curves for three time slots (6:00, 8:00, and 16:00) over the Singapore data. The similarity curve for 6:00 shows the check-in similarity between 6:00 and every other hour in a day, similarly for the other two curves. Observe that the check-in behavior at a time is similar to the check-in behavior of its close time slots. For example, the check-in similarity between

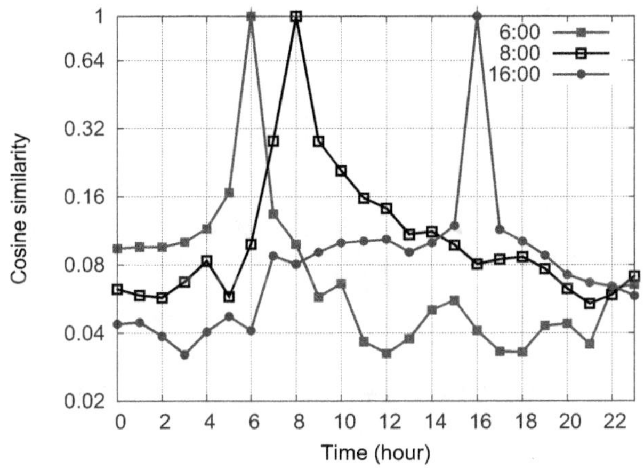

Figure 2: User behavior similarities between a given hour (6:00, 8:00, and 16:00) and other hours

6:00 and 5:00 is much higher than the similarity between 6:00 and 4:00. Nevertheless, although 6:00 and 8:00 are close to each other in terms of time, their *similarity curves* are in quite different shapes. For instance, the check-in behavior of 6:00 is similar to that at its previous hours (0:00 – 5:00), but quite different from the behavior at the later hours (8:00 – 23:00). The curve of time 8:00 displays an opposite shape. In contrast, the curve of 16:00 drops with equal speed on both sides. Observe that the curve of 16:00 almost does not decrease from 8:00 to 14:00, and it even increases around 12:00 to 13:00. This is, users might stay at workplace during that period, and hence have similar check-ins (while people tend to have lunch about 12:00, making the curve drops to some extent). Instead of using cosine similarity to compute the user check-in behavior, we have also tried other metrics, such as Pearson correlation and Total Variation Distance, but observed similar results. In summary, the check-in behavior at one time may be more similar to some time slots than others. This motivates us to develop a method to utilize the check-in behavior similarity for POI recommendations.

We propose to smooth the UTP cube based on the check-in similarity between different time slots. For each check-in vector in the cube, we smooth it using the vectors of those similar time slots. Specifically, we compute a new value for element $c_{u,t,l}$ using Equation 3, where $\rho_{t,t'}$ is the similarity between time slots t and t'. Accordingly, the smoothing enhanced similarity between two users u and v is calculated using Equation 4.

$$\widetilde{c}_{u,t,l} = \sum_{t'=1}^{T} \frac{\rho_{t,t'}}{\sum_{t''=1}^{T} \rho_{t,t''}} c_{u,t',l} \tag{3}$$

$$w_{u,v}^{(te)} = \frac{\sum_{t=1}^{T} \sum_{l=1}^{L} \widetilde{c}_{u,t,l} \cdot \widetilde{c}_{v,t,l}}{\sqrt{\sum_{t=1}^{T} \sum_{l=1}^{L} \widetilde{c}_{u,t,l}^{2}} \sqrt{\sum_{t=1}^{T} \sum_{l=1}^{L} \widetilde{c}_{v,t,l}^{2}}} \tag{4}$$

With the similarity formulation in Equation 4, if two users u and v have visited the same POIs at *the same* or *similar* time slots, their similarity value will be high. Otherwise, if they have visited the same POIs at dissimilar time slots, their similarity value will be low.

The check-in behavior similarity between two time slots also enables us to introduce another enhancement in recommending POIs for user u at a given time t. Recall that in the method described in Section 3.2, only the POIs visited by a similar user v at the time t are considered in recommendation. The check-in behavior similarity between time slots makes it possible to consider any candidate POI l visited by a similar user v, irrespective if the check-in time t' by v is the same as the time t. More specifically, in the enhancement method, a candidate POI l is weighted by the similarity value between two time slots, t' and t, if the historical check-ins are in different from the time t. The recommendation score, denoted by $\widetilde{c}_{u,t,l}^{(te)}$, that user u will check-in l at t is then updated as follows:

$$\widetilde{c}_{u,t,l}^{(te)} = \frac{\sum_{v} w_{u,v}^{(te)} \sum_{t'} \widetilde{c}_{v,t',l} \cdot \rho_{t,t'}}{\sum_{v} w_{u,v}^{(te)}} \tag{5}$$

4. UTILIZING SPATIAL INFLUENCE

The geolocation of POI is an important factor affecting human's check-in behavior and has been exploited in earlier studies [23]. In this work, we however make a different assumption from the work in [23] and show that POI recommendation can be improved by considering spatial influence in an alterative manner. In our experiments, we shall compare the performance of different approaches of incorporating spatial influence.

We first analyze the effect of distance on user's check-in behavior, and then propose a new POI recommendation method by exploiting the spatial influence. In our work, we assume that *human tend to visit nearby POIs to their previous locations, and their willingness to visit a POI decreases as the distance increases.* To verify this assumption, we perform a data analysis on two datasets (see Section 6.1 for more details on the datasets) to study the impact of distance on users' check-in behaviors.

For each user, we sort the user's check-ins by time. For the check-ins made within a day, we calculate the distance between two POIs of every two adjacent check-ins. We aggregate the results of all users, and plot the number of check-ins as a function of the distance in Figure 3. Note that a larger probability value implies that users are more willing to check in POIs at that distance. Observe from Figure 3, the distribution of the probability values follows a power law, suggesting that users are more willing to check in nearby POIs to their current places. Moreover, observe that the slop of the curve of Singapore (Figure 3(a)) drops quickly after 10KM. Similar observation holds for the curve of California and Nevada (Figure 3(b)). That is, the willingness of people visiting a faraway POI (*e.g.*, 10KM) drops significantly.

4.1 Incorporating Spatial Influence

To incorporate spatial influence in POI recommendations, we use a power law distribution to model the willingness of a user moving from one place to another as a function of their distance. Defined in Equation 6, $wi(dis)$ is the willingness of a user to visit a dis km far away POI, and a, k are parameters of the power law function.

$$wi(dis) = a \cdot dis^{k} \tag{6}$$

Maximum likelihood estimation [2] is used to estimate the two parameters a and k. More specifically, we take logarithmic on both side of Equation 6, and get the following equation.

$$\ln(wi(dis)) = \ln(a) + k\ln(dis). \tag{7}$$

The above linear function over $\ln(dis)$ can be easily learned by the least-square regression. As the result, we learn the parameters in Equation 6. Note that, in learning the two parameters, irregular portion in Figures 3(a) and 3(b) (*i.e.*, data points having distance larger than 10km) is not considered. These data points represent fewer than 15% of the total number of check-ins.

Consider a user is currently at POI l_i and POI l_j is a candidate POI to check in next, at distance $dis(l_i, l_j)$ from l_i. We model the

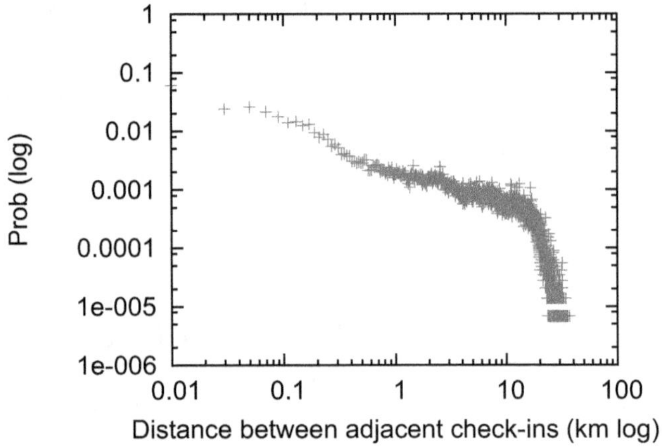

(a) Singapore

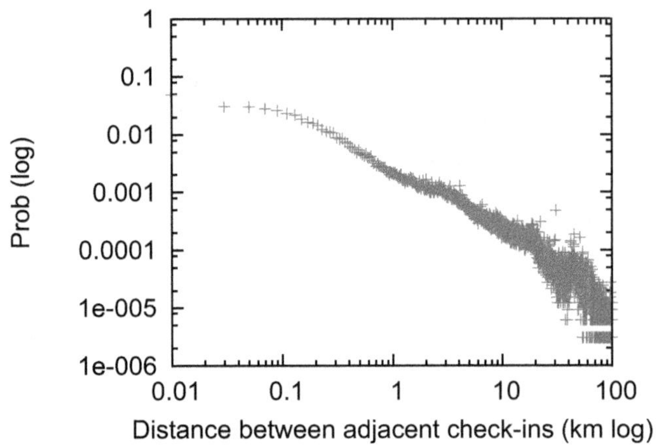

(b) California and Nevada

Figure 3: Distribution of distance between successive check-ins

probability that the user will check in l_j to be proportional to the user's willingness to check in a POI at distance $dis(l_i, l_j)$. The conditional probability is computed using the following equation.

$$p(l_j|l_i) = \frac{wi(dis(l_i, l_j))}{\sum_{l_k \in L, l_k \neq l_i} wi(dis(l_i, l_k))} \tag{8}$$

Observe that, as the distance increases, the conditional probability decreases, which reflects that the user is less likely to visit a faraway candidate POI.

Given a user u, and his/her historical POIs L_u, we calculate $P(l|L_u)$ as the ranking score for each candidate POI l, and then recommend the top ranked POIs to the user. Based on the Bayes rule, this score is calculated as follows.

$$\widetilde{c}^{(s)}_{u,l} = P(l|L_u) \propto P(l)P(L_u|l) \tag{9}$$

$$= P(l) \prod_{l' \in L_u} P(l'|l) \tag{10}$$

Note that the derivation from Equation 9 to Equation 10 is based on the assumption that for a given l, the check-in probabilities of POIs in L_u are independent from each other.

4.2 Enhancement by Temporal Popularity

In Equations 9 and 10, $P(l)$ is the prior probability that POI l is checked in by all users in the dataset. However, the popularity of a POI varies over time, *e.g.*, a restaurant is more popular around noon and evening, and a workplace is more popular during working hours. To illustrate this point, we plot the check-in probabilities of the top-5 most popular POIs in Figure 4, based on the check-in data of Singapore, collected from Foursquare. The check-in probability at a given time is computed by the ratio of the number of check-ins at that time to the total number of check-ins at the POI. Observe that the popularity of each POI varies greatly over time, and different POIs become popular at different time.

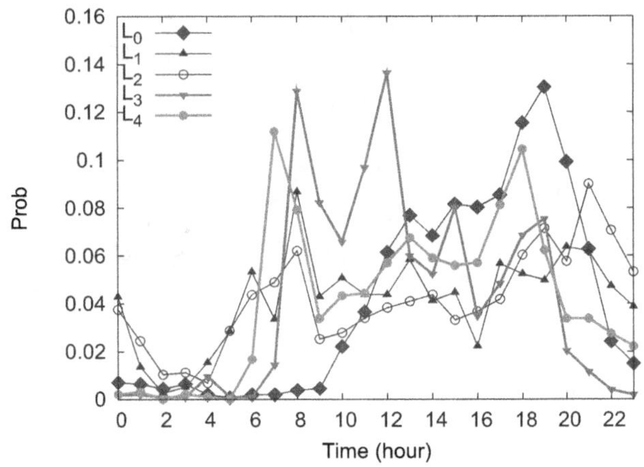

Figure 4: The distribution of 5 popular POIs over time

Reconsider Equations 9 and 10. The probability of checking in a POI should reflect both its popularity at the specific time and the distance to the user's current location. In other words, the probability user u will check in POI l at time t depends on the probability (or popularity) of l at t, along with the distance between l and u's visited POIs. It provides us a way to enhance this model by adjusting $P(l)$ with the temporal popularity of POI l, denoted by $P_t(l)$.

$$P_t(l) = \beta \frac{|CI_{l,t}|}{\sum_{l' \in L} |CI_{l',t}|} + (1-\beta) \frac{|CI_l|}{\sum_{l' \in L} |CI_{l'}|} \tag{11}$$

In the above equation, $|CI_l|$ is the number of check-ins at l; $|CI_{l,t}|$ is the number of check-ins at l at time t, and β tunes the weight between l's temporal popularity and long-term popularity.

By replacing $P(l)$ in Equation 10 with $P_t(l)$, the resultant method incorporates the temporal popularity. The recommendation score, denoted by $\widetilde{c}^{(se)}_{u,t,l}$, is then computed by the following equation.

$$\widetilde{c}^{(se)}_{u,t,l} \propto P_t(l) \prod_{l' \in L_u} P(l'|l)$$

We emphasize that the temporal information here is used in a different way from what we do in Section 3. In Section 3, the temporal information is employed to discover personalized temporal preference on POIs. In contrast, here we use the temporal preference on POIs in a collective manner (*i.e.*, by all users).

5. A UNIFIED FRAMEWORK

Given a user u, time t and a candidate POI l, we can get a recommendation score $\widetilde{c}^{(t)}_{u,t,l}$ that user u will check in l at t using either of the two methods incorporating temporal influence in Section 3 (*i.e.*, with or without smoothing). Similarly, we can also compute a score $\widetilde{c}^{(s)}_{u,t,l}$ using either of the two methods incorporating spatial influence in Section 4 (*i.e.*, with or without considering temporal popularity).

Table 2: Statistics on the datasets (after pre-processing)

Dataset	No. of Check-ins	No. of Users	No. of POIs
Foursquare	194,108	2,321	5,596
Gowalla	456,988	10,162	24,250

We use linear interpolation to weight the two scores to compute the final recommendation score for POI l. However, the two scores are measured by different methods, and have different value ranges. Thus, we first normalize the two scores using min-max normalization before we combine them.

$$\overline{c}^{(t)}_{u,t,l} = \frac{\widetilde{c}^{(t)}_{u,t,l} - min_{l'}(\widetilde{c}^{(t)}_{u,t,l'})}{max_{l'}(\widetilde{c}^{(t)}_{u,t,l'}) - min_{l'}(\widetilde{c}^{(t)}_{u,t,l'})} \quad (12)$$

$$\overline{c}^{(s)}_{u,t,l} = \frac{\widetilde{c}^{(s)}_{u,t,l} - min_{l'}(\widetilde{c}^{(s)}_{u,t,l'})}{max_{l'}(\widetilde{c}^{(s)}_{u,t,l'}) - min_{l'}(\widetilde{c}^{(s)}_{u,t,l'})} \quad (13)$$

In the above equations, $max_{l'}(\cdot)$ and $min_{l'}(\cdot)$ denote the maximum and minimum check-in scores of u at t across all POIs.

After normalization, we compute the combined score that user u will check-in POI l at time t using the following equation, where α is a tuning parameter.

$$c_{u,t,l} = \alpha \times \overline{c}^{(t)}_{u,t,l} + (1 - \alpha) \times \overline{c}^{(s)}_{u,t,l'}, \quad (14)$$

By this framework, we calculate the check-in score for each candidate POI, and return the top ranked POIs as the recommendation results.

6. EXPERIMENTS

We evaluate the accuracy of the proposed methods, including the recommendation methods utilizing temporal influence (presented in Section 3), the methods utilizing spatial influence (presented in Section 4), and the unified method (presented in Section 5). We also study the effect of the length of time slot on the recommendation accuracy.

6.1 Experimental Setup

We first introduce the datasets used in our experiments and the metrics. We then list the methods to be evaluated and explain the design of the experiments.

Dataset. Two datasets are used in our experiments. We collect 342,850 check-ins from Foursquare which were made within Singapore between Aug. 2010 and Jul. 2011. We also set a bounding box and extracted 736,148 Gowalla check-ins from the dataset provided by [5], which were made within California and Nevada between Feb. 2009 and Oct. 2010. Each check-in contains user, time and POI ID information. For both datasets, we removed users who have checked in fewer than 5 POIs, and then removed POIs which fewer than 5 users checked in. After pre-processing, the Foursquare dataset (Foursquare) contains 194,108 check-ins made by 2,321 users at 5,596 POIs, and the Gowalla dataset (Gowalla) contains 456,988 check-ins made by 10,162 users at 24,250 POIs (see Table 2). The two datasets have different scales in terms of the size of entities (*i.e.*, users, POIs, and check-ins) and geographical range. For each user, we randomly mark off 12.5% of his or her visited POIs as development data to tune parameters, and mark off another 25% of POIs as testing data to evaluate the effectiveness of the recommendation methods. The two datasets are available online [2].

[2]`http://www.ntu.edu.sg/home/gaocong/datacode.htm`

The densities of the training data of Foursquare and Gowalla are 6.35×10^{-3} and 9.85×10^{-4}, respectively. As expected, after splitting a day into 24 slots by hours, the data becomes much sparser. The densities of the two datasets after splitting become 4.82×10^{-4} and 6.65×10^{-5}, respectively.

Metrics. To study the effectiveness of the proposed methods, *i.e.*, how well the methods can recover the hold-off POIs in the testing data for a given user at a given time, we use two metrics, namely, precision@N and recall@N (denoted by pre@N and rec@N, respectively), where N is the number of recommendation results, following the work [23].

The pre@N measures how many POIs in the top-N recommended POIs correspond to the hold-off POIs in the testing data, and the rec@N measures how many POIs in the hold-off POIs in the testing set are returned as top-N recommended POIs. Given an user u and a time t (a time slot), we denote by $T_{u,t}$ the set of corresponding groundtruth POIs in the testing data, and by $R_{u,t}$ the set of recommended POIs by a method. We divide the POIs in the two sets, and get the following three values: $tp_{u,t}$, $tn_{u,t}$, and $fp_{u,t}$.

$tp_{u,t}$	: the number of POIs contained in both $T_{u,t}$ and $R_{u,t}$
$tn_{u,t}$	: the number of POIs contained in $T_{u,t}$ but not in $R_{u,t}$
$fp_{u,t}$	: the number of POIs contained in $R_{u,t}$ but not in $T_{u,t}$

Then, the precision and recall for time slot t are calculated as follows:

$$precision(t) = \frac{\sum_{u'\in U} tp_{u',t}}{\sum_{u'\in U}(tp_{u',t} + np_{u',t})} \quad (15)$$

$$recall(t) = \frac{\sum_{u'\in U} tp_{u',t}}{\sum_{u'\in U}(tp_{u',t} + tn_{u',t})} \quad (16)$$

The overall precision and recall are calculated by averaging the precision and recall values over all time slots, respectively:

$$precision = \frac{1}{T}\sum_{t'\in T} precision(t') \quad (17)$$

$$recall = \frac{1}{T}\sum_{t'\in T} recall(t') \quad (18)$$

Equations 17 and 18 actually compute the macro-precision and recall over all time slots. We also considered other ways to calculate the overall precision and recall, such as micro-precision and recall. We found that the results from these variant measures are very similar and we choose to report the results calculated by Equations 17 and 18. For each metric, we consider three values of N (*i.e.*, 5, 10, 20) in our experiments, where 5 is the default value.

Recall that both the Foursquare and Gowalla datasets have a low density, which usually results in relatively low precision and recall values [10, 23]. In addition, the POIs in the test data of each user may represent only a small portion of POIs that the user may be interested in. Thus, although the relatively low precision and recall values are common and reasonable, in this paper, *we focus on the relative improvements we achieved, instead of the absolute values.*

Recommendation Methods. We evaluated 9 recommendation methods as listed in Table 3. Among the 9 methods, User-based CF with time function (UTF) is a baseline method that has not been discussed before. We detail it in the following.

UTF is the user-based version of the algorithm proposed in [7]. It estimates the similarity between users as does the conventional user-based CF, but weights the check-ins of a similar user according to the gaps between their time slots and the recommendation time slot. The rationale is that with a larger time gap the check-in would

Table 3: Methods for comparison

Method	Description
U	User-based CF (Section 3.1)
UTF	U with Time Function [7]
UT	U with Temporal preference (Section 3.2.2)
UTE	UT with smoothing Enhancement (Section 3.3)
SB	Spatial influence based Baseline [23] (Section 2)
S	Spatial influence based recommendation (Sec. 4.1)
SE	S with popularity Enhancement (Section 4.2)
U+SB	Combination of U and SB [23]
UTE+SE	Combination of UTE and SE (Section 5)

be less useful for the POI recommendation. Formally, given a user u and time t, the recommendation score that u will check in POI l at time t is:

$$\overrightarrow{c}_{u,l} = \frac{\sum_v w_{u,v} f(t_{v,l}, t)}{\sum_v w_{u,v}}$$

where the time function $f(t_{v,l}, t) = e^{-\frac{1}{H}|t-t_{v,l}|}$; $|t - t_{v,l}|$ is the time gap between the time slot v checked in l and the time of recommendation, and H is a parameter controlling the decaying factor of the time gap. We tune H on the development data by varying H from 1 to 5, and found the best recommendation accuracy is always reached when $H = 1$ on both datasets. We also tried the original item-based method [7], but its results were much worse.

We conduct three groups of experiments. The first group is to evaluate the accuracy of the proposed recommendation methods utilizing temporal influence, and we compare methods U, UTF, UT and UTE.

The second group is to evaluate the effectiveness of the proposed methods utilizing spatial influence, and we compare methods SB, S, SE, among which SB is the state-of-the-art method utilizing spatial influence.

The third group is used to evaluate the effectiveness of the proposed unified method, and we compare methods U, U+SB, and UTE+SE. Among them, U is the baseline method, and U+SB is the unified method proposed in [23].

6.2 Performance of Methods

Methods Utilizing Temporal Influence. We compare the effectiveness of the methods utilizing the temporal influence on the two datasets. The precision and recall of the 4 methods (U, UTF, UT, and UTE) are reported in Figure 5.

Observe that the methods that make use of the time information always outperform the baseline method U, which does not take time into account. In terms of pre@5, UT outperforms U by 40% and 20% on Foursquare data and Gowalla data, respectively. UTE outperforms U by 51% on Foursquare data and 37% on Gowalla data, respectively. This result suggests that, taking time into consideration is essential for time-aware POI recommendations.

Compared to U, the UTF baseline method always exhibits better results in terms of all measures. This is because UTF exploits the time information, and recommends POIs which have been visited by users who have similar visiting history with the user.

Compared to UTF, UT performs better on the Foursquare data, but poorer on the Gowalla data. This is because the Gowalla data is much sparser than the Foursquare data. When data is sparse, the similarity between users in UT becomes less accurate because the similarity only considers exact matching on the UTP cube.

Among all 4 methods, UTE always achieves the best results in terms of both precision and recall at different N values on both

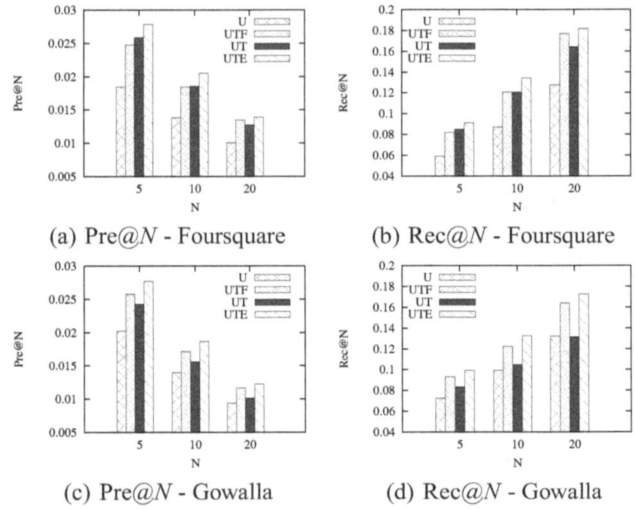

(a) Pre@N - Foursquare (b) Rec@N - Foursquare

(c) Pre@N - Gowalla (d) Rec@N - Gowalla

Figure 5: Performance of Methods Utilizing Temporal Influence

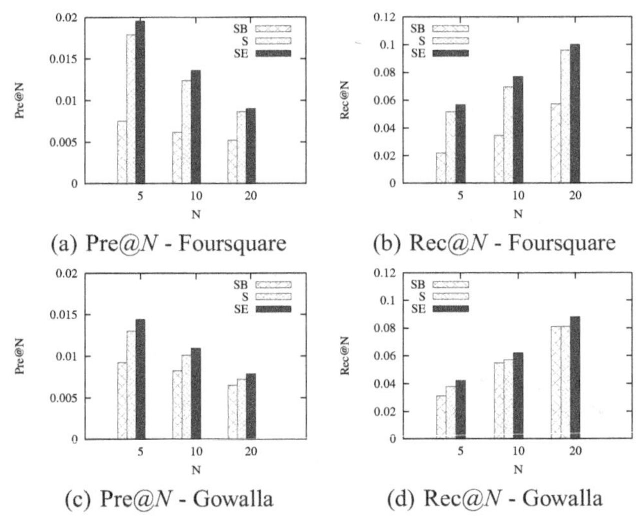

(a) Pre@N - Foursquare (b) Rec@N - Foursquare

(c) Pre@N - Gowalla (d) Rec@N - Gowalla

Figure 6: Performance of Methods Utilizing Spatial Influence

datasets. The superior performance is due to the smoothing enhancement, which addresses the sparsity problem. The detailed results of each time slot on the Foursquare data are provided in Section 6.4 as a case study.

Methods Utilizing Spatial Influence. We compare the effectiveness of the proposed methods utilizing spatial influence with the state-of-the-art method utilizing spatial influence [23]. The precision and recall are plotted in Figure 6.

Observe from Figure 6, S achieves much better recommendation accuracy than SB in terms of both precision and recall, on both datasets. This clearly demonstrates the effectiveness of the proposed method. Moreover, the integration of temporal popularity (SE) further improves the precision and recall of the recommendation. Recall that in method SE, parameter β (Equation 11) tunes the weight between a POI's temporal popularity and long-term popularity. We tune β on the development data by varying it from 0.0 to 1.0, and observe that the best recommendation accuracy is achieved when $\beta = 0.5$ and 0.9 on Foursquare and Gowalla, respectively.

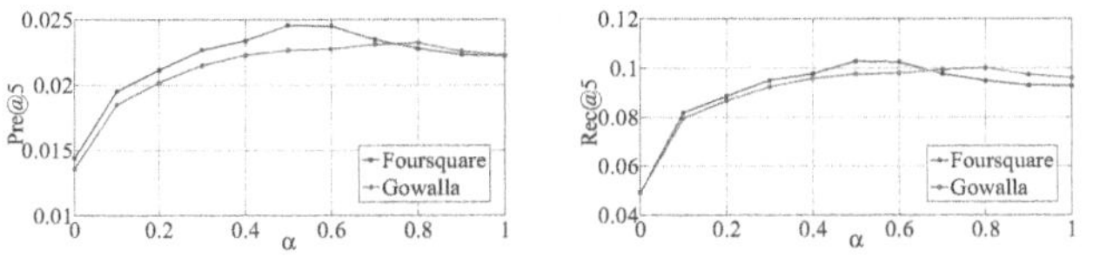

(a) Pre@5 (b) Rec@5

Figure 7: Tuning parameter α

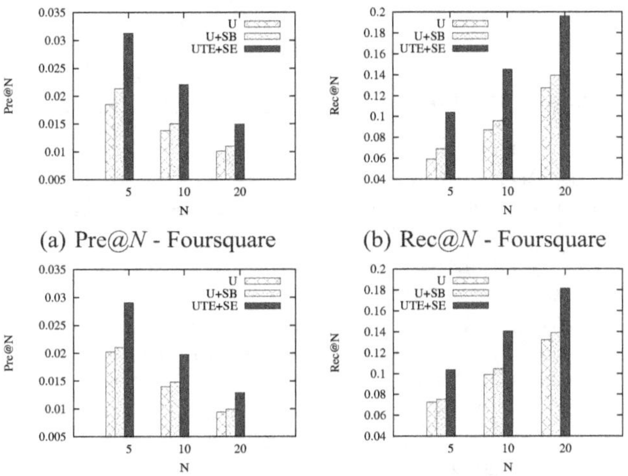

(a) Pre@N - Foursquare (b) Rec@N - Foursquare

(c) Pre@N - Gowalla (d) Rec@N - Gowalla

Figure 8: Performance of Unified Methods

Unified Methods. The unified method (UTE+SE) combines the method utilizing temporal influence and the method utilizing spatial influence for time-aware POI recommendations. We select the state-of-the-art method U+SB as the baseline.

For UTE+SE, a parameter α is used to control the weights of the temporal part UTE and the spatial part SE (Equation 14). We tune α on the development data, and plot the average pre@5 and rec@5 on both datasets with different α values in Figure 7. From the figures, it is observed that best precision and recall are reached when $\alpha = 0.5$ and 0.8 on Foursquare and Gowalla, respectively. For method U+SB, the best results are achieved when $\alpha = 0.6$. Due to the space limitation, we omit the tuning results.

Setting α to the optimal values for both methods UTE+SE and U+SB, the precision and recall of the three methods (U, UTE+SE, and U+SB) on both datasets are reported in Figure 8. As shown in the figure, both U+SB and UTE+SE outperform U, indicating that exploiting spatial information can help improve the accuracy of time-aware POI recommendations. More importantly, observe that in terms of both precision and recall, UTE+SE outperforms U+SB by around 45% on Foursquare data, and around 38% on Gowalla data. This result demonstrates that our proposed method is superior to the state-of-the art method in terms of effectiveness.

6.3 Effect of the Length of Time Slot

This experiment is to study the effect of the length of time slot. The length of time slot controls the time granularity of time-aware POI recommendations. A larger length of time slot implies that the recommendation results will be less time-specific. Here we only consider the methods utilizing temporal influence to focus on the effect of the length of time slot. We report the prec@5 and rec@5 on the Foursquare data in Figure 9, since the results on the Gowalla data are similar. From Figure 9, we make two observations.

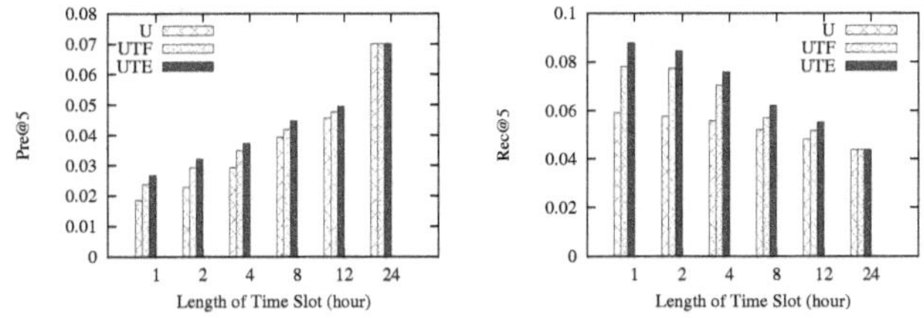

(a) Pre@5 - Foursquare (b) Rec@5 - Foursquare

Figure 9: Performance of varying length of time slot

- The first observation is that as the time slot length increases, the precision of all methods increases as well, but the recall drops. The reason for better precision is, increasing the length makes the data denser, leading to better precision. Nevertheless, increasing the length of time slots will bring in more groundtruth POIs for each user at each time slot. With the number of recommendations (*i.e.*, *N*) unchanged, poorer recall values are observed with increasing the length of time slot.
- A more important observation is that, for all lengths of time slots, the proposed method UTE outperforms the baseline method U. However, the amount of improvement decreases as the length of time slot getting larger, because increasing the length of time slot reduces the temporal influence. When the length is increased to 24-hour, the proposed method UTE reduces to the user-based CF method U.

6.4 Case Study

As a case study, using the Foursquare data, we study the recommendation accuracy at different time slots in a day, (*i.e.*, at what time of a day, the POI recommendation is more accurate). We first show the check-in count distribution over time in Figure 10(a). From the figure, we find that users have more check-ins during 13:00–20:00 than in the morning or midnight. The curve reaches its peaks at 13:00 and 19:00, respectively, indicating that users are more active during or slightly after lunch and dinner hour.

The pre@5 and rec@5 of methods U and UTE are plotted in Figures 10(b) and 10(c) respectively. Observe from the figures, the proposed method UTE outperforms the baseline U over all the time slots and the percentage of relative improvement is quite stable. For both methods, the best recommendation accuracies (in terms of pre@5 and rec@5) are obtained between 5:00 and 6:00 as well as between 17:00 and 18:00. However, in these two periods, users are likely involved in very different activities and check-in different kinds of POIs. This is an interesting phenomenon that needs further study.

7. CONCLUSION AND FUTURE WORK

The availability of historical check-in data in LBSNs enables the POI recommendation service. In this paper, we define a new problem of time-aware POI recommendation as an extension of the conventional POI recommendation problem by considering the temporal influence in user activities. To the best of our knowledge, this is the first work on time-aware POI recommendations. The proposed solutions exploit both the temporal influence and spatial influence, which are specific for POI recommendations. We start with a new method that utilizes the temporal influence for POI recommendations. We then propose a new approach exploring the spatial influence. Lastly, we combine the two approaches through a unified framework. We conduct extensive experiments over two real-world

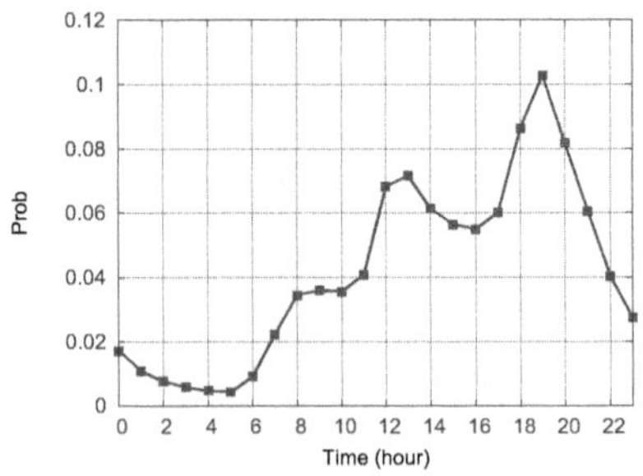

(a) Distribution of check-in in a day

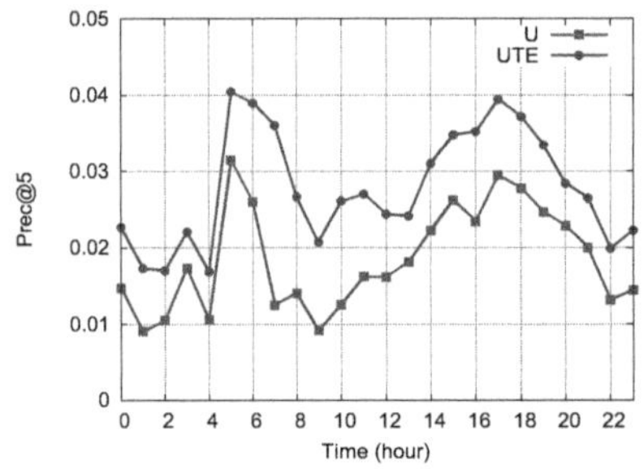

(b) Pre@5 - Foursquare

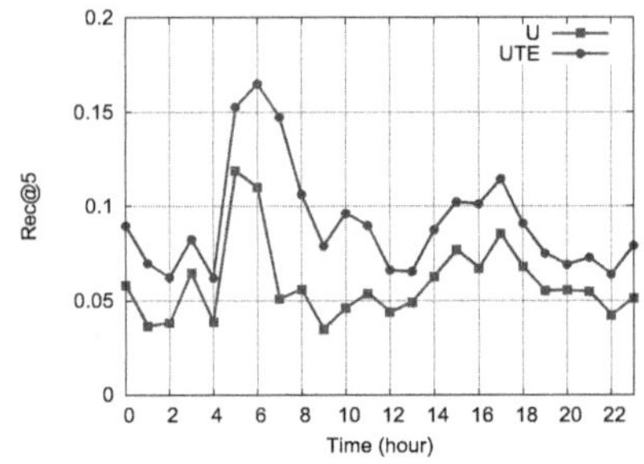

(c) Rec@5 - Foursquare

Figure 10: Performance of different time of a day

LBSN datasets. The experimental results show that the proposed methods beat all baselines, and improve the accuracy of POI recommendations by more than 37% over the state-of-art method.

Several interesting directions exist for further exploration. First, in addition to hour, humans' check-in behavior is also influenced by the day of a week and even the month of a year. Hence we plan to exploit other time dimensions in POI recommendations. Second, POIs are often associated with category information in LBSNs. It would be promising to exploit category information in recommendation. In addition, we are also interested in incorporating the temporal influence and spatial influence in the POI prediction task.

8. ACKNOWLEDGEMENTS

This work is supported in part by a grant awarded by a Singapore MOE AcRF Tier 2 Grant (ARC30/12), a Singapore MOE AcRF Tier 1 Grant (RG66/12), and a grant awarded by Microsoft Research Asia. Quan Yuan would like to acknowledge the Ph.D. grant from the Institute for Media Innovation, Nanyang Technological University, Singapore.

9. REFERENCES

[1] G. Adomavicius, R. Sankaranarayanan, S. Sen, and A. Tuzhilin. Incorporating contextual information in recommender systems using a multidimensional approach. *ACM Trans. Inf. Syst.*, 23(1):103–145, 2005.

[2] B. Arnold. *Pareto Distribution*. International Cooperative Publishing House, Fairland, Maryland, 1983.

[3] X. Cao, G. Cong, and C. S. Jensen. Mining significant semantic locations from gps data. *PVLDB*, 3(1):1009–1020, 2010.

[4] C. Cheng, H. Yang, I. King, and M. R. Lyu. Fused matrix factorization with geographical and social influence in location-based social networks. In *AAAI*, 2012.

[5] E. Cho, S. A. Myers, and J. Leskovec. Friendship and mobility: user movement in location-based social networks. In *KDD*, pages 1082–1090, 2011.

[6] M. Clements, P. Serdyukov, A. P. de Vries, and M. J. T. Reinders. Finding wormholes with flickr geotags. In *ECIR*, pages 658–661, 2010.

[7] Y. Ding and X. Li. Time weight collaborative filtering. In *CIKM*, pages 485–492, 2005.

[8] J. L. Herlocker, J. A. Konstan, A. Borchers, and J. Riedl. An algorithmic framework for performing collaborative filtering. In *SIGIR*, pages 230–237, 1999.

[9] T. Horozov, N. Narasimhan, and V. Vasudevan. Using location for personalized poi recommendations in mobile environments. In *SAINT*, pages 124–129, 2006.

[10] I. Konstas, V. Stathopoulos, and J. M. Jose. On social networks and collaborative recommendation. In *SIGIR*, pages 195–202, 2009.

[11] Y. Koren. Collaborative filtering with temporal dynamics. In *KDD*, pages 447–456, 2009.

[12] Y. Koren, R. M. Bell, and C. Volinsky. Matrix factorization techniques for recommender systems. *IEEE Computer*, 42(8):30–37, 2009.

[13] K. Lee, S. Hong, S. J. Kim, I. Rhee, and S. Chong. Slaw: A new mobility model for human walks. In *INFOCOM*, pages 855–863, 2009.

[14] K. W.-T. Leung, D. L. Lee, and W.-C. Lee. Clr: a collaborative location recommendation framework based on co-clustering. In *SIGIR*, pages 305–314, 2011.

[15] H. Ma, M. R. Lyu, and I. King. Learning to recommend with trust and distrust relationships. In *RecSys*, pages 189–196, 2009.

[16] A. Noulas, S. Scellato, C. Mascolo, and M. Pontil. An empirical study of geographic user activity patterns in foursquare. In *ICWSM*, 2011.

[17] B. M. Sarwar, G. Karypis, J. A. Konstan, and J. Riedl. Item-based collaborative filtering recommendation algorithms. In *WWW*, pages 285–295, 2001.

[18] X. Su and T. M. Khoshgoftaar. A survey of collaborative filtering techniques. *Adv. Artificial Intellegence*, 2009, 2009.

[19] L. Xiang, Q. Yuan, S. Zhao, L. Chen, X. Zhang, Q. Yang, and J. Sun. Temporal recommendation on graphs via long- and short-term preference fusion. In *KDD*, pages 723–732, 2010.

[20] M. Ye, K. Janowicz, C. Mülligann, and W.-C. Lee. What you are is when you are: the temporal dimension of feature types in location-based social networks. In *GIS*, pages 102–111, 2011.

[21] M. Ye, X. Liu, and W.-C. Lee. Exploring social influence for recommendation: a generative model approach. In *SIGIR*, pages 671–680, 2012.

[22] M. Ye, P. Yin, and W.-C. Lee. Location recommendation for location-based social networks. In *GIS*, pages 458–461, 2010.

[23] M. Ye, P. Yin, W.-C. Lee, and D. L. Lee. Exploiting geographical influence for collaborative point-of-interest recommendation. In *SIGIR*, pages 325–334, 2011.

[24] Y. Zheng, L. Zhang, X. Xie, and W.-Y. Ma. Mining interesting locations and travel sequences from gps trajectories. In *WWW*, pages 791–800, 2009.

Modeling User's Receptiveness Over Time For Recommendation

Wei Chen Wynne Hsu Mong Li Lee
School of Computing, National University of Singapore, Singapore
{weichen,whsu,leeml}@comp.nus.edu.sg

ABSTRACT

Existing recommender systems model user interests and the social influences independently. In reality, user interests may change over time, and as the interests change, new friends may be added while old friends grow apart and the new friendships formed may cause further interests change. This complex interaction requires the joint modeling of user interest and social relationships over time. In this paper, we propose a probabilistic generative model, called *Receptiveness over Time Model* (RTM), to capture this interaction. We design a Gibbs sampling algorithm to learn the receptiveness and interest distributions among users over time. The results of experiments on a real world dataset demonstrate that RTM-based recommendation outperforms the state-of-the-art recommendation methods. Case studies also show that RTM is able to discover the user interest shift and receptiveness change over time.

Categories and Subject Descriptors

H.3.3 [**Information Storage and Retrieval**]: Search and Retrieval-*Information Filtering*

General Terms

Algorithms, Experimentation, Measurement, Performance

Keywords

Recommendation, Social trust, Personalization, Collaborative Filtering

1. INTRODUCTION

Recommender systems are fast becoming the tools of choice for a user to sieve through tons of online materials in order to find information that is relevant to him/her. Many of these recommender systems employ collaborative filtering (CF) techniques to identify similar users based on their purchased history or past ratings to generate personalized recommendation. This works well when the users have long term interests that do not change from time to time. However, for users with short term interests, modeling the shift in users' interests has been shown to improve recommendation accuracy. This is achieved by introducing a personalized time factor for each user to capture the shift in users' interests over time [18, 7, 5, 8]. With the advent of online social networks, social network based CF approaches to recommendation have emerged [4, 17, 11]. The assumption is that friends tend to influence their friends to exhibit similar likes and dislikes. Hence, we can further improve recommendation accuracy by taking into account the social relationships.

Let us consider the snapshots of users' item ratings and their social relationships at time points T_1 and T_2 in Figure 1. Suppose our target user is U_2. At time point T_1, both users U_1 and U_2 have watched and rated the movie "$Movie2$". Traditional CF methods [15, 16, 13] will group U_1 and U_2 as similar users and recommend "$Movie1$" to U_2 since U_1 has watched "$Movie1$" previously. Yet, U_2's interest does not remain static. We observe that at time point T_2, his interest has shifted from movies to kids as he rates a new item "$Kids1$". Recognizing this, CF with temporal dynamics will recommend "$Kids2$" to U_2 instead. On the other hand, looking at the social relationships among users, we realize that U_2 and U_3 are friends. Hence, social network based CF will conclude that U_2 is likely to like "$Book1$" and "$Book2$" since his friend U_3 have read and rated these books. Each of the different methods arrive at different items to recommend. How do we reconcile the different recommendations? To complicate matter, social relationships are not static but evolve over time as a user can make new friends and old friends do grow apart. We observe that at time point T_1, U_2 has only one friend U_3, whereas at time point T_2, his friends are $\{U_3, U_4\}$. Now if we want to give a recommendation to U_2 at time point T_2, what item should we recommend so that it is most likely to be accepted by U_2?

To answer this question, we must be able to quantify the degree of influence on a user's decision making process from his/her long term and short term interests, as well as his/her social trust relationships over time. Note that these two factors are not independent. We advocate that when two users' long term and short term interests are aligned, they are likely to become friends, and they will tend to be more receptive towards each other's preferences. Conversely, if the users' interests are not aligned, they will grow apart after some time and become less receptive towards the preferences of the other user.

SIGIR'13, July 28–August 1, 2013, Dublin, Ireland.

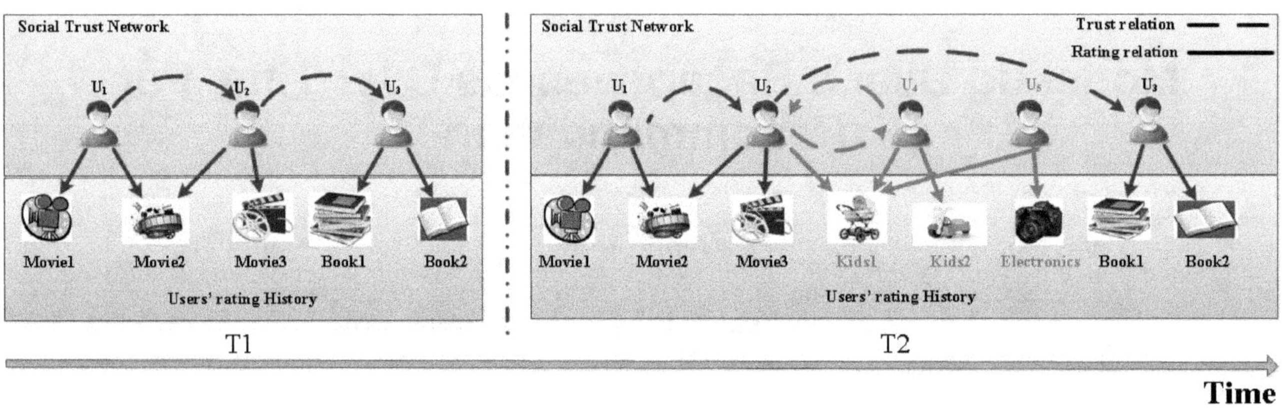

Figure 1: Example of Users' Rating History and their Social Trust Network.

In this paper, we propose a model called the *Receptiveness over Time Model* (RTM), to quantify the dynamic interaction between user interest and social trust. This model utilizes a probabilistic generative approach to leverage on the information embedded in a users' social trust network, and the users' rating history. The RTM captures (1) the degree of receptiveness for each user over time (modeling receptiveness change), (2) the distribution of personal preference over the latent topics for each user over time (modeling users' interests change), (3) the distribution of items for each topic over time. The estimation of the RTM model parameters is performed using Gibbs sampling MCMC procedure. To overcome the data sparsity problem, we design a special Bayesian treatment to the latent variable to ensure that the evolution of latent parameter is smooth and share the topic-level rating knowledge across different time points. We carry out experiments on a real world Epinions dataset to demonstrate the effectiveness of our proposed approach. We also demonstrate how RTM can be used to explicitly track and visualize the change in users' interests and their receptiveness to other users.

The rest of the paper is organized as follows. Section 2 gives the related work. Section 3 describes our problem formulation and the proposed RTM model. Section 4 presents the experimental results, and we conclude in Section 5.

2. RELATED WORK

Existing recommender systems for item recommendation can be roughly divided into two major categories. Content-based systems [1, 12] make use of explicitly stated profiles of users or products to characterize their nature. On the other hand, collaborative filtering (CF) based systems [16, 15] do not exploit such explicit user profiles. Instead, they infer the user profiles through their past activities, such as their transaction history or product satisfaction expressed in ratings. The earliest studies [16, 15] on collaborative filtering automatically predict relevant items ratings for a given user by referencing item rating information from other similar users. Recently, [13] propose a Bayesian model that applies LDA to cluster users and items into groups and model ratings using group membership. Bi-LDA further extends this model to allow users or movies to belong to several groups, one for each rating.

Temporal modeling has largely been neglected in the collaborative filtering community until Koren et.al [7] propose their time-aware algorithm timeSVD++. This work extends the standard matrix factorization model by introducing time dependent user/item biases and user latent factors to cope with changing user and item characteristics. Xiong et. al [8] view the temporal domain as a third dimension and use tensor factorization to factorize the temporal components so that a user's rating on an item within a particular time step depends not only on the user and item factors but also on the latent factors associated with the time step. To cope with temporal dynamics in implicit user feedback data, [18] proposes a random walk model where the user-item edges are weighted such that a user's more recent preferences would be more strongly emphasized during the random walk. [14] combines the latent factor model and Markov chain model to predict the next items a user may be interested in. While all these methods are able to model users' preferences and their shift of interests over time, they have not taken social influences from friends into account.

Independently, a number of researchers have realized that social trust plays a great role in user acceptance of the recommendation [6, 3]. The works in [9, 10, 11] propose to use matrix factorization method to learn the user latent vectors and item latent vectors and integrate social trust network into their model through different social regularization term. [4] develop a generative approach with trust propagation based on [11]. [17] develop a joint personal and social latent factor (PSLF) model which combines the collaborative filtering and social network modeling approaches for social recommendation. [19] propose the probabilistic model called social influenced selection (SIS), to model the decision making of item selection. However, all these works assume that the social relationships are static and they do not consider users' changing interests. To the best of our knowledge, this is the first work that models both the shift in user interests and change in social relationships for recommendation.

3. PROPOSED METHOD

In this section, we first give our problem formulation. Then we describe the RTM model and show how the model can be used for various tasks such as rating prediction, tracking receptiveness between friends and user interest change.

3.1 Problem Formulation

In recommender systems, we have a set of users $U = \{ u_1, \ldots u_a \}$ and a set of items $M = \{ m_1, \ldots m_b \}$. At time t, a user u expresses his/her preference for an item m by giving a rating in the range of 1 to 5 with 1 being the least preferred and 5 being the most preferred. These ratings are represented using the matrix $R^{(t)}$ with dimensions $|U| \times |M|$. Each entry in this matrix, $r^{(t)}(u, m)$, corresponds to the rating provided by user u on item m at time point t.

Besides the rating information, we also represent the social relationships among the users at time t in the form of a matrix $S^{(t)}$ with dimensions $|U| \times |U|$ such that its entry $s^{(t)}(u, v) = 1$ if u issues trust statement towards user v at time point t. Otherwise $s^{(t)}(u, v) = 0$. Note that $S^{(t)}$ is asymmetric in general.

We formulate our task as follows: Given a user $u \in U$ at time t and an item $m \in M$, we want to predict the rating that u will give to m at time t based on the past rating history and social relationships, i.e. $R^{(t')}$ and $S^{(t')}$ for all $t' \in [1, t)$.

3.2 Receptiveness over Time Model

In order to capture the dynamic interactions between long term and short term interests as well as friendships for recommendation, our model has two parts. The first part models user receptiveness at a single time point. The second part incorporates temporal information to allow for modeling over time.

3.2.1 *Single Time Point Receptiveness Modeling*

Receptiveness captures the dynamic interaction between user interest and social trust. Existing social CF filtering approaches [11, 10, 4, 17] incorporate social trusts as auxiliary data to regulate user preferences for recommendation. In other words, if two users are friends, social CF approaches will assign greater weights to their corresponding preferences. However, we realize that a user's decision making process is not so simplistic. A person may be his/her friend, however, if that friend's interests are not aligned with him/her, the receptiveness to that friend's interest will not be high and vice versa.

Among the approaches that model user's interests for recommendation, Bi-LDA has proven to work well in practice [13]. It is a generative model with several advantages that are suitable for our work:

1. It models the distribution of users' interest within a probabilistic framework, thus allowing a more interpretable explanation compared to the matrix factorization approach.

2. It allows the inclusion of prior knowledge into the generative process and a principled framework to select model structure. This proves to be useful in linking consecutive time points to avoid the data sparsity problem in the second part of RTM.

However, Bi-LDA does not incorporate social relationships. For this reason, we extend Bi-LDA to incorporate social relationships and call it Bi-LDA^{social}. Table 1 summarizes the symbols used in describing the Bi-LDA^{social} model. In Bi-LDA^{social}, each user u follows a preference distribution π_u^{friend} that depicts how likely u's friend will contribute to u's item rating decision. The probability for a friend of u to influence the item rating decision is proportional to the receptiveness of u to this friend. Note that, we assume u is a special friend of himself/herself (i.e.,$u \in F(u)$).

Table 1: Meanings of symbols used

Symbol	Meaning
u	A user
U	The set of all users
m	A item
M	The set of all items
f	Friend of user
$F(u)$	The set of user u's friends
K	Number of user topic
L	Number of item topic
Dir	Dirchlet
x	The observed rating for user u on item m
$z_{u,m}^{friend}$	The receptive friend picked for rating given by user u on item m
$z_{u,m}^{user}$	The user topic picked for rating given by user u on item m
$z_{u,m}^{item}$	The item topic picked for rating given by user u on item m
π_u^{friend}	Distribution of user u over users' friend
π_u^{user}	Distribution of user u over users' topics
π_m^{item}	Distribution of item m over items' topics
$\Phi_{z_{u,m}^{user}, z_{u,m}^{item}}$	Rating-scale mixing proportion of user-item topic joint distribution over values $\{1...R\}$ for topic $z_{u,m}^{user}$, $z_{u,m}^{item}$

In addition, each user u and item m follow the topic distribution parameters π_u^{user} and π_m^{item} respectively. To rate an item m, a user u first draws a user topic $z_{u,m}^{user}$ and the item m draws a item topic $z_{u,m}^{item}$ from the corresponding distributions. $\Phi_{z_{u,m}^{user}, z_{u,m}^{item}}$ is the rating-scale mixing proportion of user-item topic joint distribution over values $\{1...R\}$ for topic $z_{u,m}^{user}$, $z_{u,m}^{item}$.

During the generative process, ratings are generated as follows:

1. Choose a $K \times L$ distribution over ratings $\Phi \sim Dir(\beta)$

2. Choose a distribution over friends for each user $\pi_u^{friend} \sim Dir(\alpha^{friend})$

3. Choose a distribution over K users' topic for each user $\pi_u^{user} \sim Dir(\alpha^{user})$

4. Choose a distribution over L items' topic for each item $\pi_m^{item} \sim Dir(\alpha^{item})$

5. For each rating $r_{u,m}$:
   - Choose receptive friend $z_{u,m}^{friend} \sim Multinomial(\pi_u^{friend})$
   - Choose user topic $z_{u,m}^{user} \sim Multinomial(\pi_f^{user})$
   - Choose item topic $z_{u,m}^{item} \sim Multinomial(\pi_m^{item})$
   - Choose a rating $r_{u,m} \sim \Phi_{z_{u,m}^{user}, z_{u,m}^{item}}$

The graphical model is shown in Figure 2. We note that the decision of rating given by user u on item m is based on the receptiveness of a friend (including u himeself/herself).

The receptive friend $z^{friend}_{u,m}$ can be drawn from $Multinomial$ (π^{friend}_u). Once the receptive friend $z^{friend}_{u,m}$ is picked, we randomly draw a topic $z^{user}_{u,m}$ from user $z^{friend}_{u,m}$'s preference based on $Multinomial(\pi^{user}_u)$. Similarly, a topic $z^{item}_{u,m}$ from item m is also drawn based on $Multinomial(\pi^{item}_m)$. The user and item topics $z^{user}_{u,m}$ and $z^{item}_{u,m}$ together with user-item topic joint distribution Φ jointly specify the rating, that is, $r_{u,m} \sim \Phi_{z^{user}_{u,m}, z^{item}_{u,m}}$.

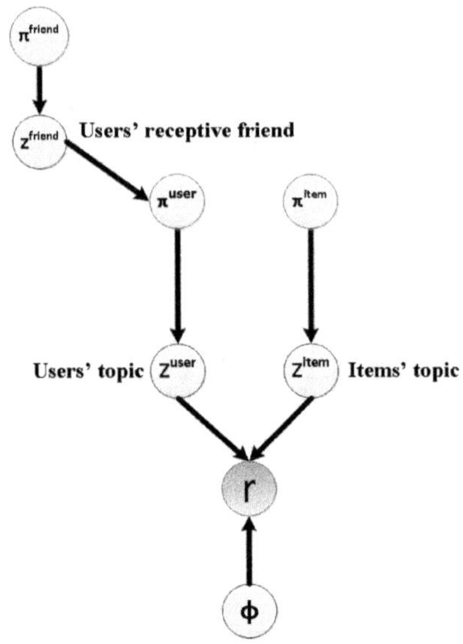

Figure 2: Graphical model representation of Bi-LDA^{social}

In order to compute the rating $r_{u,m}$, we need to obtain a number of model parameters, $\Theta = \{ \pi^{friend}_u, z^{friend}_{u,m}, \pi^{user}_u, \pi^{item}_m, z^{user}_{u,m}, z^{item}_{u,m}, \Phi_{z^{user}_{u,m}, z^{item}_{u,m}} \}$. Among them, $\pi^{friend}_u \in \mathbb{R}^{1 \times |U|}$ with Dirchlet priors α^{friend} captures distribution of the receptiveness of user u to his/her friends, $\pi^{user}_u \in \mathbb{R}^{1 \times K}$ with Dirchlet priors α^{user} depicts the distribution of user u's preferences on the K users' topics, $\pi^{item}_m \in \mathbb{R}^{1 \times L}$ with Dirchlet priors α^{item} captures the distribution of an item m on the L items' topics, $\Phi \in \mathbb{R}^{K \times L}$ with Dirchlet priors β is rating-scale mixing proportion of user-item joint topic, $z^{friend}_{u,m}$ represents the receptive friend whom user u has picked for the rating given by user u on item m, $z^{user}_{u,m}$ represents the topic user u has picked and $z^{item}_{u,m}$ represents the topic item m has picked. The hyper-parameters of the Dirichlet priors α^{friend}, α^{user}, α^{item} and β can be simply set to 1 [13].

Let x be the observed rating for user u on item m. Putting everything together, we obtain the joint probability distribution for the Bi-LDA^{social} as follows:

$$\begin{aligned} & Pr(x, z^{friend}, z^{user}, z^{item}, \Phi, \pi^{user}, \pi^{item}) \\ & = Pr(x|z^{user}, z^{item}, \Phi)\ Pr(\Phi|\beta)\ Pr(z^{user}|\pi^{user}) \times \\ & Pr(\pi^{user}|\alpha^{user}, z^{friend})\ Pr(z^{friend}|\pi^{friend}) \times \\ & Pr(\pi^{friend}|\alpha^{r})\ Pr(z^{item}|\pi^{item})\ Pr(\pi^{item}|\alpha^{item}) \end{aligned} \tag{1}$$

Solving this equation is intractable, instead we adapt the collapsed Gibbs sampler [2] to learn the model parameters. In particular, we analytically marginalize out all the conjugate distributions Φ, π^{user}, π^{item} and π^{friend} and obtain an expression for the joint probability $P(x, z^{user}, z^{item}, z^{friend})$. With this, we can compute the conditional distributions necessary for Gibbs sampling. We give the explicit forms for the following conditional distributions where $x = r_{u,m}$ is the observed rating, $k = z^{user}_{u,m}$ and $l = z^{item}_{u,m}$:

$$\begin{aligned} & P(f = z^{friend}_{u,m} | \Theta \backslash z^{friend}_{u,m}, x) \propto \left((n^{friend}_{u,f})^{\neg(u,m)} + \alpha^{friend} \right) \\ & \times \left((n^{user}_{f,k})^{\neg(u,m)} + \alpha^{user} \right) \left(\frac{N^{\neg(u,m)}_{k,l,x} + \beta}{\sum_r (N^{\neg(u,m)}_{k,l,r} + \beta)} \right) \end{aligned} \tag{2}$$

where $n^{friend}_{u,f}$ denotes the number of times that user u is receptive to f in all the ratings , $(n^{friend}_{u,f})^{\neg(u,m)}$ denotes the number of times that user u is receptive to f in all the ratings excluding $r_{u,m}$, $(n^{user}_{f,k})^{\neg(u,m)}$ denotes the number of times user f will be assigned to user topic k in all the ratings except for $r_{u,m}$, $N_{k,l,r}$ represents the number of times the user with user topic k has rated item with item topic l with the rating r, and $N^{\neg(u,m)}_{k,l,x}$ represents the number of times the observed rating x has been given by user with user topic k on item with item topic l excluding $r_{u,m}$.

Similarly, we define the conditional distribution for user topic $z^{user}_{u,m}$:

$$\begin{aligned} & P(z^{user}_{u,m} = k | \Theta \backslash z^{user}_{u,m}, x) \\ & \propto \left((n^{user}_{f,k})^{\neg(u,m)} + \alpha^{user} \right) \left(\frac{N^{\neg(u,m)}_{k,l,x} + \beta}{\sum_r (N^{\neg(u,m)}_{k,l,r} + \beta)} \right) \end{aligned} \tag{3}$$

The conditional distribution is the same for the item topic with the role of user and item reversed.

$$\begin{aligned} & P(z^{item}_{u,m} = l | \Theta \backslash z^{item}_{u,m}, x) \\ & \propto \left((n^{item}_{m,l})^{\neg(u,m)} + \alpha^{item} \right) \left(\frac{N^{\neg(u,m)}_{k,l,x} + \beta}{\sum_r N^{\neg(u,m)}_{k,l,r} + \beta} \right) \end{aligned} \tag{4}$$

where $(n^{item}_{m,l})^{\neg(u,m)}$ denotes the number of times that an item m is assigned to item topic l in all the ratings except for $r_{u,m}$, and $N_{k,l,r}$ represents the number of times that a user with user topic k has rated an item with item topic l with the rating r.

The parameter π^{friend}, π^{user}, Φ and π^{item} can be obtained as follows:

$$\begin{aligned} \pi^{friend}_{u,f} &= \frac{n^{friend}_{u,f} + \alpha^{friend}}{\sum_{f \in F(u)} (n^{friend}_{u,f} + \alpha^{friend})} \\ \Phi_{k,l,x} &= \frac{N_{k,l,x} + \beta}{\sum_r (N_{k,l,r} + \beta)} \\ \pi^{user}_{u,k} &= \frac{n^{user}_{u,k} + \alpha^{user}}{\sum_k (n^{user}_{u,k} + \alpha^{user})} \\ \pi^{item}_{m,l} &= \frac{n^{item}_{m,l} + \alpha^{item}}{\sum_l (n^{item}_{m,l} + \alpha^{item})} \end{aligned} \tag{5}$$

The algorithm of the collapsed Gibbs sampler for inferring these latent variables $\{z^{friend}, z^{user}, z^{item}\}$ is shown in Algorithm 1.

Algorithm 1: Gibbs sampling for Bi-LDA^{social}

input : Users' rating histories X, users' trust relation S, K and L

output: π^{user}, Φ, π^{item} and π^{friend}

/*Initialization of the latent variables and counters*/

Random initialize z^{friend}, z^{user} and z^{item}

Initialize n^{friend}, n^{user}, n^{item} and N as 0

foreach $x = r_{u,m} \in X$ **do**

  $f = z^{friend}_{u,m}$, $k = z^{user}_{u,m}$ and $l = z^{item}_{u,m}$

  Increase the counter of $n^{friend}_{u,f}$, $n^{user}_{u,k}$, $n^{item}_{m,l}$ and $N_{k,l,x}$

for *index=1 to Iter* **do**

  /* for each rating $x = r_{u,m}$ in X */

  foreach $x = r_{u,m} \in X$ **do**

    /* Sample Friends */

    $f = z^{friend}_{u,m} \sim P(z^{friend}_{u,m}|\Theta \backslash z^{friend}_{u,m}, x)$ according to Equation (2)

    /* Sample Users' Topics */

    $k = z^{user}_{u,m} \sim P(z^{user}_{u,m}|\Theta \backslash z^{user}_{u,m}, x)$ according to Equation (3)

    /* Sample Items' Topics */

    $l = z^{item}_{u,m} \sim P(z^{item}_{u,m}|\Theta \backslash z^{item}_{u,m}, x)$ according to Equation (4)

    $f = z^{friend}_{u,m}$, $k = z^{user}_{u,m}$, $l = z^{item}_{u,m}$, $x = r_{u,m}$

    /* Update Counter */

    Update the counter $n^{friend}_{u,f}$, $n^{user}_{u,k}$, $n^{item}_{m,l}$ and $N_{k,l,x}$

/* Get the mean estimate for π^{friend}, π^{user}, Φ and π^{item} */

π^{friend}, π^{user}, Φ and π^{item} can be calculated according to Eq. (5).

3.2.2 *Receptiveness over Time*

The second part of RTM is to model the dynamic interaction of users' interest along with the receptiveness among friends over time. Given the users' rating histories at T different time points, a naive approach is to fit a Bi-LDA^{social} model at each time point and learn the receptiveness and user interest distribution at the various time points, denoted as $\{\pi^{friend\ (1)}, \cdots, \pi^{friend\ (T)}\}$ and $\{\pi^{user\ (1)}, \cdots, \pi^{user\ (T)}\}$, respectively. However, using this approach, the latent topics learnt at time point t_1 may be totally different from that at time point t_2. Furthermore, since we regard each user in the different time point as independent, we are unable to make use of his/her ratings in the past. This worsens the data sparsity problem.

To overcome the shortcomings, we assume that the overall interest distribution of the whole user population should remain stable. This enable us to share the Φ across the different time points. In addition, we impose constraints on π^{user} and π^{friend} by assuming dependency between two consecutive snapshots as follows:

$$\pi^{friend\ (t)} \sim P(\pi^{friend\ (t)}|\pi^{friend\ (t-1)})$$

In other words, we introduce a prior from $\pi^{friend\ (t-1)}$ to $\pi^{friend\ (t)}$ so that at time t, we are drawing from the Dirichlet prior parameterized by $\pi^{friend\ (t-1)}$ where

$$\pi^{friend(t)} \sim Dirchlet(\lambda\pi^{friend\ (t-1)})$$

The intuition of $\lambda_{\pi^{friend\ (t-1)}}$ can be interpreted as the prior observed counts that user is receptive to his/her friends before any friend from the current time points is observed. Similarly, we introduce the parameterized prior for both user and item topic distributions:

$$\pi^{user\ (t)} \sim Dirchlet(\lambda\pi^{user\ (t-1)}),$$
$$\pi^{item\ (t)} \sim Dirchlet(\lambda\pi^{item\ (t-1)})$$

The graphical representation of the RTM model is shown in Figure 3. With this change, the conditional distribution of Equation (2) is now

$$P(f = z^{friend}_{u,m}|\Theta \backslash z^{friend}_{u,m}, x) \propto \left((n^{friend}_{u,f,t})^{\neg(u,m,t)} + \lambda\pi^{friend\ (t-1)}\right) \times \left((n^{user}_{f,k,t})^{\neg(u,m,t)} + \lambda\pi^{user\ (t-1)}\right)\left(\frac{N^{\neg(u,m,t)}_{k,l,x} + \beta}{\sum_r (N^{\neg(u,m,t)}_{k,l,r} + \beta)}\right) \quad (6)$$

where $(n^{friend}_{u,f,t})^{\neg(u,m,t)}$ denotes the number of times that user u is receptive to f in all the ratings at time t excluding $r^{(t)}_{u,m}$. $(n^{user}_{f,k,t})^{\neg(u,m,t)}$ denotes the number of times user f will be assigned to user topic k in all the ratings at time t except for $r^{(t)}_{u,m}$. $N_{k,l,r}$ represents the number of times the user with user topic k has rated item with item topic l with the rating r, $N^{\neg(u,m,t)}_{k,l,x}$ represents the number of times the observed rating x has been given by user with user topic k on item with item topic l excluding $r^{(t)}_{u,m}$ Similar change can be applied to the Equation (3) and (4) by introducing an additional temporal dimension for the counter, that is:

$$P(z^{user}_{u,m} = k|\Theta \backslash z^{user}_{u,m}, x) \propto \left((n^{user}_{f,k,t})^{\neg(u,m,t)} + \lambda\pi^{user\ (t-1)}_{u,k}\right)\left(\frac{N^{\neg(u,m,t)}_{k,l,x} + \beta}{\sum_r (N^{\neg(u,m,t)}_{k,l,r} + \beta)}\right) \quad (7)$$

$$P(z^{item}_{u,m} = l|\Theta \backslash z^{item}_{u,m}, x) \propto \left((n^{item}_{m,l,t})^{\neg(u,m,t)} + \lambda\pi^{item\ (t-1)}_{u,k}\right)\left(\frac{N^{\neg(u,m,t)}_{k,l,x} + \beta}{\sum_r N^{\neg(u,m,t)}_{k,l,r} + \beta}\right) \quad (8)$$

With this, based on the Eq. (5), the parameter π^{friend}, π^{user}, Φ and π^{item} can be constructed as:

$$\begin{aligned}
\pi^{friend\ (t)}_{u,f} &= \frac{n^{friend}_{u,f,t} + \lambda\pi^{friend\ (t-1)}_{u,f}}{\sum_{f \in F(u)} (n^{friend}_{u,f,t} + \lambda\pi^{friend\ (t-1)}_{u,f})} \\
\pi^{user\ (t)}_{u,k} &= \frac{n^{user}_{u,k,t} + \lambda\pi^{user\ (t-1)}_{u,k}}{\sum_k (n^{user}_{u,k,t} + \lambda\pi^{user\ (t-1)}_{u,k})} \\
\pi^{item\ (t)}_{m,l,t} &= \frac{n^{item}_{m,l,t} + \lambda\pi^{item\ (t-1)}_{m,l}}{\sum_l (n^{item}_{m,l,t} + \lambda\pi^{item\ (t-1)}_{m,l})} \\
\Phi_{k,l,x} &= \frac{N_{k,l,x} + \beta}{\sum_r (N_{k,l,r} + \beta)}
\end{aligned} \quad (9)$$

The process of generating time series ratings is summarized as follows:

1. Choose a $K \times L$ distribution over ratings $\Phi \sim Dir(\beta)$

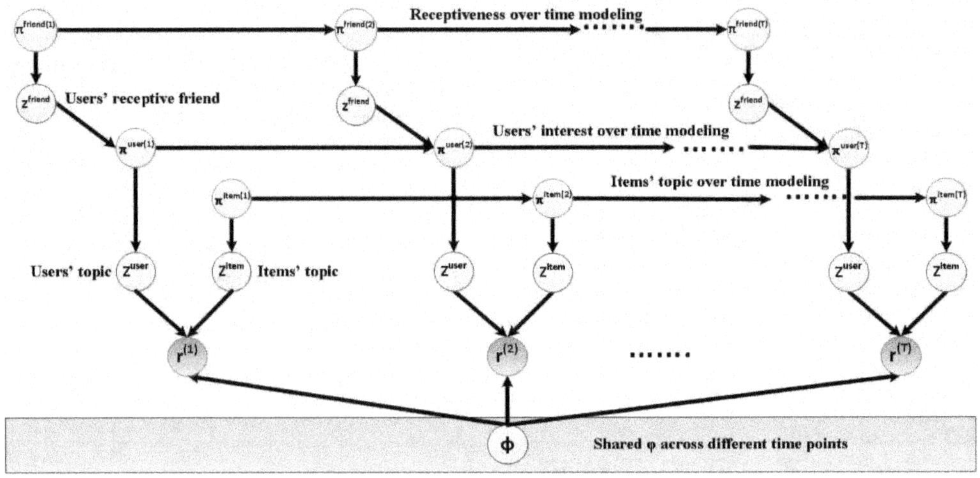

Figure 3: Graphical model representation of RTM Model

2. For time $t = 1$, choose a distribution over friends $F(u)$ for each user $\pi_u^{friend\ (1)} \sim Dir(\alpha^{friend})$;
   For time $t > 1$, choose a distribution over friends $F(u)$ for each user $\pi_u^{friend\ (t)} \sim Dir(\lambda \pi^{friend\ (t-1)})$
3. For time $t = 1$, choose a distribution over K users' topic for each user $\pi_u^{user\ (1)} \sim Dir(\alpha^{user})$.
   For time $t > 1$, choose a distribution over K users' topic for each user $\pi_u^{user\ (t)} \sim Dir(\lambda \pi^{user\ (t-1)})$.
4. For time $t = 1$, choose a distribution over L items' topic for each item $\pi_m^{item\ (1)} \sim Dir(\alpha^{item})$.
   For time $t > 1$, choose a distribution over L items' topic for each item $\pi_m^{item\ (t)} \sim Dir(\lambda \pi^{item\ (t-1)})$.
5. For each rating $x = r_{u,m}^{(t)}$:
   - Choose user friend $f = z_{u,m}^{friend} \sim Multinomial(\pi_u^{friend\ (t)})$
   - Choose user topic $k = z_{u,m}^{user} \sim Multinomial(\pi_f^{user\ (t)})$
   - Choose item topic $l = z_{u,m}^{item} \sim Multinomial(\pi_m^{item\ (t)})$
   - Choose a rating $r_{u,m}^{(t)} \sim \Phi_{k,l}$

Based on the generative process, we can design Gibbs sampling to infer the latent variables as shown in Algorithm 2.

Note that that the cost of running a full Gibs iteration is $\mathcal{O}(p)$ where p is the total number of rating observations.

3.3 Applications of RTM

In this section, we discuss how the RTM model can be used for rating prediction, tracking receptiveness over time, and analyzing users interest change.

- **RTM-based Rating Prediction**
  Having obtained the RTM model, we predict the rating made by user u on item m at time point t as follows:

$$\hat{r}_{u,m}^{(t)} = \sum_{f \in F(u)} \pi_{u,f}^{friend\ (t)} \, [\pi_u^{user\ (t)}]^\top \Phi \pi_m^{item\ (t)}$$

Algorithm 2: Gibbs sampling for RTM

input : Users' rating histories over time $R=\{R^{(1)},...R^{(T)}\}$, users' trust relation over time $S=\{S^{(1)},...,S^{(T)}\}$, K, L and λ

output: $\pi^{user\ (t)}$, Φ, $\pi^{item\ (t)}$ and $\pi^{friend\ (t)}$

/*Initialization of the latent variables and counters*/

Random initialize z^{friend}, z^{user} and z^{item}

Initialize n^{friend}, n^{user} and n^{item} and N as 0

foreach $x = r_{u,m}^{(t)} \in X$ **do**

  $f = z_{u,m}^{friend}$, $k = z_{u,m}^{user}$ and $l = z_{u,m}^{item}$

  Increase the counter of $n_{u,f,t}^{friend}$, $n_{u,k,t}^{user}$, $n_{m,l,t}^{item}$ and $N_{k,l,x}$

/* for each rating $x = r_{u,m}^{(t)}$ in X */

for *index=1 to Iter* **do**

  foreach $x = r_{u,m}^{(t)} \in X$ **do**

    /* Sample Friends */

    $f = z_{u,m}^{friend} \sim p(z_{u,m}^{friend} | \Theta \backslash z_{u,m}^{friend}, x)$ according to Equation (6)

    /* Sample Users' Topics */

    $k = z_{u,m}^{user} \sim P(z_{u,m}^{user} | \Theta \backslash z_{u,m}^{user}, x)$ according to Equation (7)

    /* Sample Items' Topics */

    $l = z_{u,m}^{item} \sim P(z_{u,m}^{item} | \Theta \backslash z_{u,m}^{item}, x)$ according to Equation (8)

    /* Update Counter */

    Update the counter $n_{u,f,t}^{friend}$, $n_{u,k,t}^{user}$, $n_{m,l,t}^{item}$ and $N_{k,l,x}$

/* Get the mean estimate for $\pi^{friend\ (t)}$, $\pi^{user\ (t)}$, Φ and $\pi^{item\ (t)}$*/

$\pi^{friend\ (t)}$, $\pi^{user\ (t)}$, Φ and $\pi^{item\ (t)}$ can be calculated according to Eq. (9).

Table 2: Summary of methods.

Data used	*No social trust*	*Static social trust*	*Social trust over time*
Static rating	Bi-LDA, PMF	SocialMF	RTM-StaticInterest
Rating over time	TimeSVD++	RTM-StaticSocial	RTM

- **Receptiveness Change Analysis**
For a given user u, the receptiveness of u to his/her friends (including user u) at time point t is $\pi_u^{friend\ (t)}$. By constructing the receptiveness of other users to user u in T time points, we can track the receptiveness of other users on user u over time:

$$C_u^{friend} = \left[\pi_u^{friend\ (1)}, ..., \pi_u^{friend\ (t)}\right]$$

where C_u^{friend} is an $|U| \times T$ matrix. Each column in C_u^{friend} can be interpreted as the expected probability where user u may be receptive to the other $|U|$ users at time point t. In other words, we can discover who are the users that u is most receptive to at the particular time point.

- **User Interest Change Analysis**
For a given user u, we compute the user u's preference over item topic at time point t as $[\pi_u^{user\ (t)}]^\top \Phi$. By constructing u's preference over item topic for all T time points, we can track u' s interest change over time:

$$C_u = \left[[\pi_u^{user\ (1)}]^\top \Phi, ..., [\pi_u^{user\ (t)}]^\top \Phi\right]$$

where C_u is a $L \times T$ matrix. Each column in C_u can be interpreted as the expected ratings provided by user u on all the L item topic at time point t. By sorting the columns, we can discover what kind of items are preferred by a user at a certain time point.

4. EXPERIMENTAL RESULTS

In this section, we evaluate the effectiveness of the proposed RTM model that utilizes both time-stamped rating data and trust over time for recommendation. We also implement two variants of RTM:

- **RTM-StaticSocial**: this variant assumes that the social trust does not change over time while user interest may shift over time as reflected by the time-stamped rating data. This is achieved by using the same social trust information for all the time points.

- **RTM-StaticInterest**: this variant assumes that the user interest does not change over time and only the social trust changes over time. This is achieved by using the same rating information for all the time points.

We compare the proposed models with the following state-of-the-art recommender methods for rating prediction:

1. **Probabilistic Matrix Factorization (PMF)** [15]. This is a matrix factorization based CF algorithm that utilizes static user ratings on items. No social trust information is used.

2. **Bi-LDA** [13] This is a generative model that also utilizes static ratings for prediction. Again no social trust information is employed.

3. **TimeSVD++**[7] This is temporal CF algorithm that assumes user interests change over time and is the baseline of temporal CF methods. This method does not incorporate social trust information.

4. **SocialMF** [4]. This is a social CF algorithm that utilizes the social trust information and is the baseline of social CF methods. This method does not consider the shift in user interest.

Table 2 gives a summary of the various methods. All the experiments are carried out on an Intel Core i7-2600 CPU with 8GB RAM, running Windows 7-64 bit.

4.1 Experimental Dataset

We use the Epinions dataset[1] in our experiments. This dataset comprises of two files. The first file contains 717, 667 user trust statements with time-stamps, while the second file contains 13, 668, 319 users' ratings provided by 120, 492 users on 755, 760 articles on a scale of 1 to 6, with 1 being not helpful and 6 being most helpful. Each rating is associated with a time-stamp over the period from February 2001 to July 2002.

We sort the data according to the time-stamps and split the data into 6 equal time slices. Each time slice corresponds to about 3 months. We use the first 5 time slices of data as the training data, and the last time slice for testing. We also filter out users that have made less than 10 unique ratings. After pre-processing, we obtain 5, 077, 392 users' ratings with 9, 149 users and 116, 697 articles and 236, 878 social relations. Table 3 summarizes the statistics of the rating dataset.

Table 3: Statistics of rating dataset.

Statistics	Users	Movies
Min. # of ratings	10	1
Max. # of ratings	39,467	1134
Mean. # of ratings	554.96 ± 1681.11	43.50 ± 41.04

[1] *http : //www.trustlet.org/wiki/Extended$_E$pinions$_d$ataset*

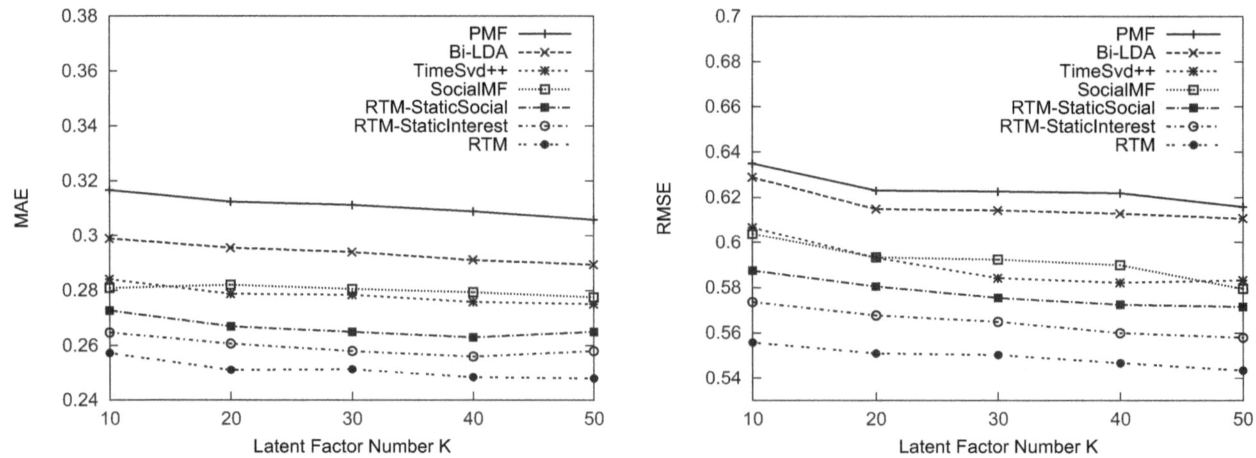

(a) MAE (b) RMSE

Figure 4: Accuracy of Rating Prediction

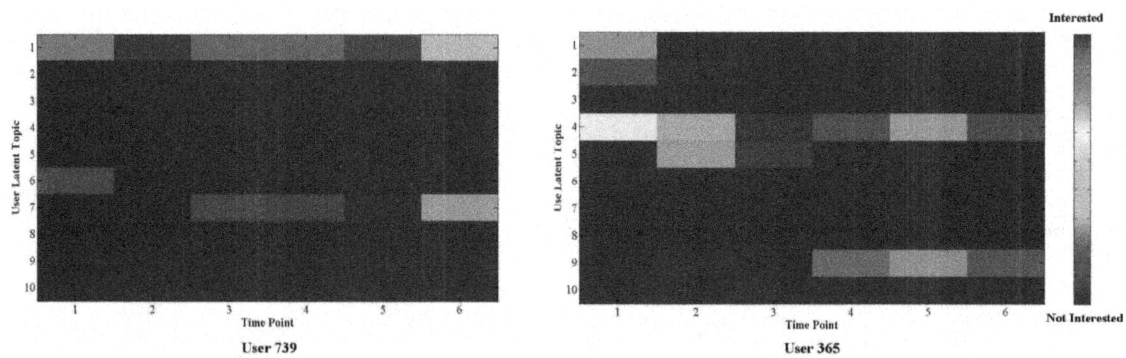

Figure 5: User interest change over time

4.2 Rating Prediction Analysis

In this set of experiments, we compare the performance of the various methods. We use the standard evaluation metrics Mean Absolute Error (MAE) and Root Mean Square Error (RMSE) defined as follows:

$$MAE = \frac{\sum_{r_i \in D} |r_i - \hat{r_i}|}{|D|}$$

$$RMSE = \sqrt{\frac{\sum_{r_i \in D} (r_i - \hat{r_i})^2}{|D|}}$$

where D denotes the test dataset, r_i is the actual rating and $\hat{r_i}$ is the predicted rating. A smaller value of MAE or RMSE indicates a better performance.

Figure 4 shows the results when we vary the number of user/item dimensions from 10 to 50. We observe that the proposed RTM model has the lowest MAE and RMSE, demonstrating that capturing the dynamic interest between user interest and social trust can improve the rating prediction accuracy. In particular, RTM model lowers the RMSE (MAE) by as much as 7.71% (8.26%) compared to the SocialMF model, and 8.14% (9.29%), compared to TimeSVD++.

Both SocialMF and RTM-StaticInterest outperform conventional CF models that do not incorporate trust information, namely, Bi-LDA and PMF. This indicates that social trust can help improve the rating prediction accuracy. Both TimeSVD++ and RTM-StaticSocial model user interest over time and thus perform better than Bi-LDA and PMF.

4.3 User Interest Change Case Study

Here, we visualize the user interest profile obtained from the RTM model over time. Figure 5 shows the interest profiles of 2 users from the Epinions dataset. We observe that the user 739's interests remains stable over the time, as indicated by his/her high preference for user latent topic 1 throughout the 6 time points. User 365's main interest is in the latent topic 4 from time points 1 to 3, and changes to latent topics 9 from time point 4 to 6, showing a shift in his/her interest.

On closer examination, we find that user 739 has rated a lot of reviews in the topic with id 72 for all the time points.

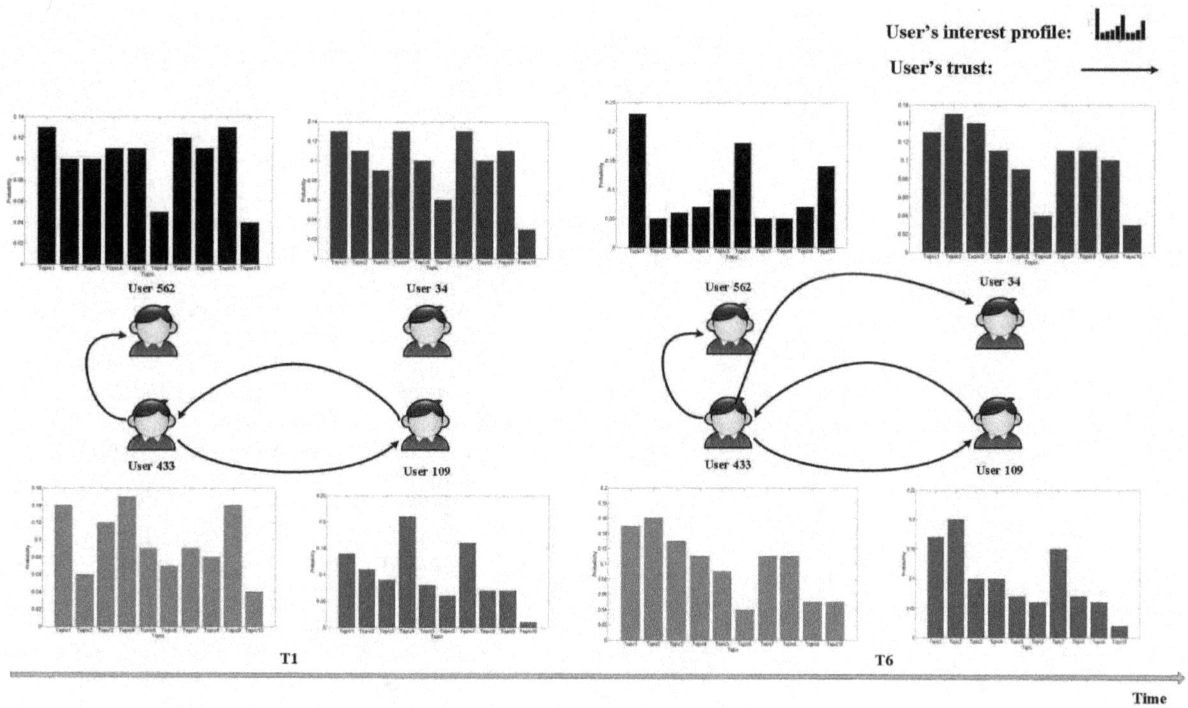

Figure 6: User interest profiles and their trust relationships

On the other hand, user 365 mainly rated reviews on the topic with id 549 from time points 1 to 3, and then change to rate reviews on the topic with id 447 from time points 4 to 6. This confirms that the interest profiles obtained from the RTM model can capture user interest change.

4.4 User Receptiveness Case Study

Next, we analyze the user interest profiles and their social trust relationships over time. Figure 6 shows the interest profiles of 4 users and their social trust relationships at time points T1 and T6. Suppose user 433 is our target user. We note that at time point T1, user 433 does not know user 34 and their interest profiles are quite different. However at time point T6, user 34 has become user 344's friend and his/her interest profile has shifted to become similar to that of user 344. Looking at Figure 7 which shows the receptiveness of user 433 towards the other 3 users over time, we observe that the receptiveness of user 433 to user 34 increases sharply at T6. This indicates that the RTM model captures the dynamic interaction between user interests and social relationships faithfully.

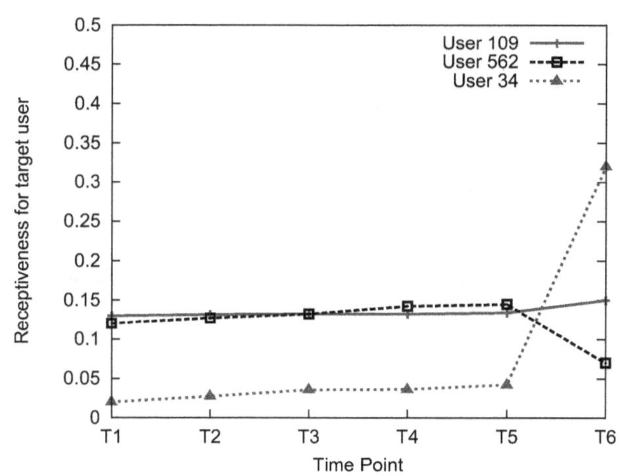

Figure 7: Receptiveness change over time

4.5 Sensitivity Experiments

In this section, we examine the effect of various parameters on the performance of the RTM model.

4.5.1 Effect of varying K and L

Table 4 shows the RMSE of RTM as we vary the number of user topic K and the number of item topic L from 10 to 50. We observe that RMSE does not vary much. The best performance is achieved by setting $K = 40$ and $L = 50$.

Table 4: Effect of K and L on RMSE

K \ L	10	20	30	40	50
10	0.5572	0.5512	0.543	0.5419	0.5420
20	0.5532	0.5473	0.5447	0.5428	0.5443
30	0.5718	0.5518	0.5428	0.5434	0.5417
40	0.5534	0.5417	0.5412	0.5431	0.5367
50	0.5521	0.5447	0.5401	0.5414	0.5439

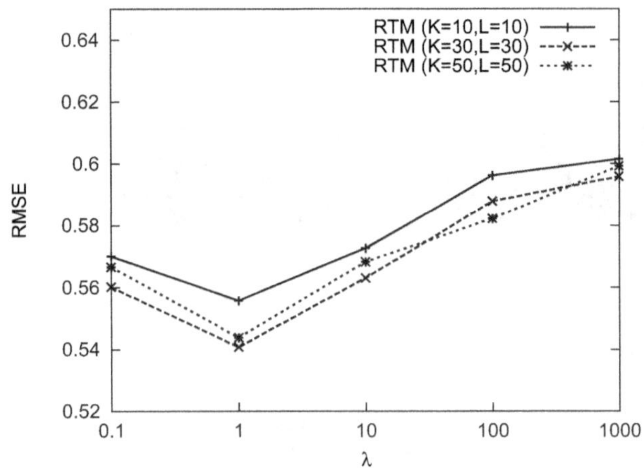

Figure 8: Effect of λ on RMSE

4.5.2 *Effect of varying λ*

Recall that the parameter λ control how much the prior information is transferred from the previous time slice to the current time slice. When $\lambda = 0$, no prior information is used.

Figure 8 shows the RMSE obtained for varying λ values. We observe that the best performance is obtained when $\lambda = 1$, indicating that prior information helps to improve item rating prediction.

5. CONCLUSIONS

In this paper, we have motivated the need to capture the dynamic interaction between trust and user interest for recommendation. We have designed the RTM generative model that incorporates user interest and social trust relationships over time. We have also devised efficient algorithms to learn the latent variables in the RTM model using Gibbs sampling. Experimental results have shown that RTM-based recommendation outperforms state-of-the-art CF methods. In addition, the model provides easy interpretations to allow easy visualization of users' receptiveness and interest change over time.

6. REFERENCES

[1] M. Balabanović and Y. Shoham. Fab: content-based, collaborative recommendation. *Communications of the ACM*, pages 66–72, March 1997.

[2] G. Casella and E. I. George. Explaining the Gibbs sampler. *The American Statistician*, 46:167–174, 1992.

[3] M. Jamali and M. Ester. Trustwalker: a random walk model for combining trust-based and item-based recommendation. In *Proceedings of the 15th ACM SIGKDD international conference on Knowledge discovery and data mining*, KDD, pages 397–406, 2009.

[4] M. Jamali and M. Ester. A transitivity aware matrix factorization model for recommendation in social networks. In *Proceedings of the 22nd international joint conference on Artificial Intelligence*, IJCAI, pages 2644–2649, 2011.

[5] N. Koenigstein, G. Dror, and Y. Koren. Yahoo! music recommendations: modeling music ratings with temporal dynamics and item taxonomy. In *Proceedings of the fifth ACM conference on Recommender systems*, RecSys, pages 165–172, 2011.

[6] I. Konstas, V. Stathopoulos, and J. M. Jose. On social networks and collaborative recommendation. SIGIR, pages 195–202, 2009.

[7] Y. Koren. Collaborative filtering with temporal dynamics. In *Proceedings of the 15th ACM SIGKDD international conference on Knowledge discovery and data mining*, KDD, pages 447–456, 2009.

[8] T.-K. H. J. S. J. G. C. Liang Xiong, Xi Chen. Temporal collaborative filtering with bayesian probabilistic tensor factorization. In *Proceedings of SIAM Data Mining*, 2010.

[9] H. Ma, I. King, and M. R. Lyu. Learning to recommend with social trust ensemble. SIGIR, pages 203–210, 2009.

[10] H. Ma, M. R. Lyu, and I. King. Learning to recommend with trust and distrust relationships. In *Proceedings of the third ACM conference on Recommender systems*, RecSys, pages 189–196, 2009.

[11] H. Ma, D. Zhou, C. Liu, M. R. Lyu, and I. King. Recommender systems with social regularization. In *Proceedings of the fourth ACM international conference on Web search and data mining*, WSDM, pages 287–296, 2011.

[12] R. J. Mooney and L. Roy. Content-based book recommending using learning for text categorization. In *Proceedings Of 5th ACM Conference On Digtal Libraries*, pages 195–204, 1999.

[13] I. Porteous, E. Bart, and M. Welling. Multi-hdp: A non parametric bayesian model for tensor factorization. In *Proceedings of the 23rd national conference on Artificial intelligence*, AAAI, pages 1487–1490, 2008.

[14] S. Rendle, C. Freudenthaler, and L. Schmidt-Thieme. Factorizing personalized markov chains for next-basket recommendation. WWW, pages 811–820, 2010.

[15] R. Salakhutdinov and A. Mnih. Probabilistic matrix factorization. *Advances in Neural Information Processing Systems*, pages 1257–1264, 2008.

[16] B. Sarwar, G. Karypis, J. Konstan, and J. Riedl. Item-based collaborative filtering recommendation algorithms. WWW, pages 285–295, 2001.

[17] Y. Shen and R. Jin. Learning personal + social latent factor model for social recommendation. In *Proceedings of the 18th ACM SIGKDD international conference on Knowledge discovery and data mining*, KDD, pages 1303–1311, 2012.

[18] L. Xiang, Q. Yuan, S. Zhao, L. Chen, X. Zhang, Q. Yang, and J. Sun. Temporal recommendation on graphs via long- and short-term preference fusion. In *Proceedings of the 16th ACM SIGKDD international conference on Knowledge discovery and data mining*, KDD, pages 723–732, 2010.

[19] M. Ye, X. Liu, and W.-C. Lee. Exploring social influence for recommendation: a generative model approach. SIGIR, pages 671–680, 2012.

Query Representation for Cross-Temporal Information Retrieval

Miles Efron
Graduate School of Library and Information Science
University of Illinois, Urbana-Champaign, USA
mefron@illinois.edu

ABSTRACT

This paper addresses the problem of long-term language change in information retrieval (IR) systems. IR research has often ignored lexical drift. But in the emerging domain of massive digitized book collections, the risk of vocabulary mismatch due to language change is high. Collections such as Google Books and the Hathi Trust contain text written in the vernaculars of many centuries. With respect to IR, changes in vocabulary and orthography make 14th-Century English qualitatively different from 21st-Century English. This challenges retrieval models that rely on keyword matching. With this challenge in mind, we ask: given a query written in contemporary English, how can we retrieve relevant documents that were written in early English? We argue that search in historically diverse corpora is similar to cross-language retrieval (CLIR). By considering "modern" English and "archaic" English as distinct languages, CLIR techniques can improve what we call *cross-temporal IR* (CTIR). We focus on ways to combine evidence to improve CTIR effectiveness, proposing and testing several ways to handle language change during book search. We find that a principled combination of three sources of evidence during relevance feedback yields strong CTIR performance.

Categories and Subject Descriptors

H.3.3 [**Information Storage and Retrieval**]: Information Search and Retrieval; H.3.7 [**Digital Libraries**]: Systems Issues

Keywords

Information retrieval, temporality, digital libraries, book search

1. INTRODUCTION

Today, digitized book collections are growing in size and scope. This raises new challenges for information retrieval (IR) research. Repositories such as Google Books[1] and the Hathi Trust[2] collect millions of scanned volumes with the aim of improving readers' access to the range of information stored in academic libraries. To meet this goal, these collections must support appropriate search interactions.

This paper tackles a specific problem in book search: long-term language change. Though many books in, say, the Hathi Trust are written in English, 20th-Century authors used English very differently than authors did during the 14th- or even the 17th-Centuries. This presents a challenge to retrieval models that rank documents based on the distribution of query words observed in documents. In Google Books, a query term *work* may imply a user's interest in *werk, woork, wyrke* or even *swyinkinge*. All textual IR suffers from the vocabulary mismatch problem, where searchers and authors use different terms for similar ideas. But in historically diverse collections, this mismatch is exacerbated by centuries of linguistic evolution.

Our aim in this paper is to allow a query written in contemporary English to retrieve documents written in the vernacular of older centuries. Thus a person interested in the pedigree of the proverb *many hands make light work* will be able to find a broad range of variants on this theme, from a range of historical periods using a single query. This task is similar to cross-language information retrieval (CLIR), and so we will refer to it as cross-temporal retrieval (CTIR).

This paper's main contribution is a novel approach to CTIR. We present a model that imagines contemporary queries as translations of archaic statements. Given a query in modern English Q^M we attempt to recover terms from the "true" archaic version Q^A. The model yields a distribution over terms that fits naturally into a structured query for the inference network retrieval model. While we describe and test several techniques, the paper's main contribution (described in Section 6.4.2) is a relevance feedback method that combines information from a bilingual dictionary, orthographic evidence and feedback probabilities in a principled way.

2. EXAMPLE USE CASE

Though book search has a strong research community – especially in the INEX book track – many issues that impact the effectiveness of IR in digitized book collections have yet to be articulated clearly. In particular, realistic use cases and their attendant demands on a system are non-obvious for search over digitized book collections. Who would use these collections, and for what purposes? What would realistic queries look like? What constitutes relevance in peoples' interactions with a scanned and OCR'd library?

[1] http://books.google.com

[2] http://hathitrust.org

In this paper, we limit our attention to a fairly narrow hypothetical use case. Our imagined user – probably a humanities scholar, perhaps a general-interest reader – is interested in a particular phrase or historically durable idea. Examples of such interests include:

- A phrase from a literary work
- A proverb or saying
- A famous literary device such as a metaphor.

Thus our user might be interested in finding variants of the opening lines of Chaucer's *Canterbury Tales*. These lines vary from manuscript to manuscript and edition to edition, each with different spellings and vocabulary. They were also adapted into increasingly modern English as critics and writers influenced by Chaucer echoed his text. To get a sense of the range of these lines' deployment in literature over the years, a searcher would need to use a typical IR system very carefully, relying on a great deal of expert knowledge.

In other cases, there is no canonical text to retrieve. The proverb *many hands make light work* has changed over the years; it has no "true" version. *A communitie maketh the werk lesse* is clearly related to this proverb, though neither rendition is in any sense more authoritative than the other.

We imagine that a user of our system is a person with an interest in finding historical variants of a textual seed which we call the searcher's *exemplar*. We aim to retrieve items that contain *renditions* of that exemplar – appropriations, variants, in-line quotations, etc. This suggests that topical relevance is not a suitable criterion for optimizing our system. Searches like those described here seek variants of an exemplar, not necessarily documents that are about that exemplar. A critic's quote of Chaucer's opening lines would be relevant to this searcher. But so would a 15th-Century play by an author who borrows from *The Canterbury Tales* in the course of his own work. We will operationalize this notion of relevance when we describe our experimental evaluation.

Though this use case is narrow, we believe that it is realistic. It speaks to the diachronic focus that has driven much earlier work on information access in scanned book repositories, [3, 27, 28].

3. PREVIOUS WORK

To the best of our knowledge, the cross-temporal IR problem has not been studied before. However, cognate problems have seen a good deal of attention. Much of this earlier work relates to this paper, both in terms of the problems we approach and the ways we propose solving them.

Historical linguists have lent sophistication and rigor to the study of language change. Most notable in our context is Edward Sapir's theories on "language drift," the process by which a language changes over time to such an extent that earlier texts become unintelligible to contemporary readers [30]. However, although historical linguistics could surely help with the problem of CTIR, its focus on the analysis of linguistic genealogies is only indirectly useful here.

In domains closer to IR, work on document date identification relates to our study. In [11], [17], and [5], variations on language modeling have been brought to bear on the problem of identifying when a given document was written. As in these studies, our approaches to CTIR are based on language models, resting on the assumption that resolving differences among distant centuries' vernaculars is tractable via a high-level estimation of word probabilities.

From a conceptual and practical standpoint, CTIR is similar to two active IR research areas: cross-language IR and IR over noisy text (typically due to OCR errors).

If we consider archaic English and Modern English to be two distinct languages, then the CTIR problem as we have presented it *is* a cross-lingual retrieval problem. Certainly, CLIR methods as surveyed in [10] have a role to play in CTIR. For instance, reliance on dictionary-based and corpus-based translation tools enter into our analysis. Additionally, the approach to structuring queries that we adopt is common in the CLIR literature (cf. [4]). Efforts to solve the vocabulary mismatch problem have brought CLIR methods into monolingual retrieval, as well. Work such as [2] and [12] considers query-document matching as an English-to-English translation process.

The CTIR problem also echoes challenges faced by retrieval over modern OCR'd text. Of course, much of the research on IR for scanned documents is situated in the domain of cultural heritage [6], as is our work. But the similarity is more substantive that this. Foundational work such as [8] presents n-gram methods for supporting search over degraded texts. Additionally, variants of the n-gram methods that followed this work (particularly in the TREC confusion track) will form one of our experimental baselines in Section 8. Of particular interest is [18], where Lam-Adesina et al. note that many IR methods are quite robust against OCR-introduced noise; but relevance feedback is more brittle. Our feedback technique presented in Section 6.4.2 was developed in part due to this observation.

Finally, the task of CTIR is not constrained to search over digitized books. But these collections do make the problem of language drift particularly keen. A good deal of work in the INEX book track has treated OCR-related problems in book search (cf. [13] for an overview). However, the focus of INEX topics have left linguistic change as a relatively minor problem in most previous studies of book search.

Perhaps the most important fact about the literature on book search is that while digitized book data is plentiful, what people will want to do with these data is still largely unknown. We intend this paper to complement recent efforts to expand the scope of interaction design for large book repositories [14, 15, 16].

4. CROSS-TEMPORAL INFORMATION RETRIEVAL FOR BOOK SEARCH

Whatever the nature of users' information needs, repositories of digitized books present a novel challenge for IR systems: massive language drift. A corpus such as Google Books or the Hathi Trust contains texts that are nominally written in the same language (e.g. English), but whose vocabularies are nonetheless dissimilar due to long-term language change. The first line of the famous poem *Sir Gawain and the Green Knight* [32] reads: *Sithen the sege and the assaut watz sesed at Troye*, which translates into contemporary English as *Since the siege and the assault was ceased at Troy*. Seeing this equivalence is easy for scholars of Middle English, but it is difficult for many English speakers, let alone for a computational system.

In this paper, our goal is to support a query issued in contemporary English, retrieving documents that are relevant but that are written in the vernacular of earlier centuries. For convenience, we refer to the user's language as *modern* English, with all old forms of English called *archaic*. This is a simplification in the sense that "modern" has technical implications in certain disciplines of the humanities. Likewise, our umbrella term "archaic" refers to many eras such as Middle English and early modern English. While operationally, we have divided English into two classes – *modern* and *archaic* – the fluidity between these classes will be apparent later in our discussion.

5. QUERY STRUCTURE AND RETRIEVAL MODEL

Though not strictly necessary, in this paper we rely on the inference network retrieval model implemented in the Indri search engine [24, 31] . Given a query Q and a document D, the inference network allows us to compute $P(\mathcal{I}|Q, D, \Theta)$ where $\mathcal{I}$ is the information need that generated Q and Θ contains the parameters of the underlying joint distribution over indexing features. The inference network approach is helpful here because it admits operations on structured queries. The belief operators in the Indri query language have been widely used for cross-language IR in a way that we adopt directly. Consider the user-supplied modern query Q^M, *april showers*. For cross-temporal IR, we might rewrite this as Q^S, `#combine(#wsyn(0.5 april 0.3 aprile 0.2 aprylle) #wsyn(0.7 showers 0.2 shours 0.1 rain))` where the `wsyn` operator treats word variants as weighted synonyms. Of course, finding proper synonyms and weights is hard; it is the task that comprises the contribution of this paper.

Given a modern query $Q^M = \{m_1, m_2, \ldots, m_n\}$, we will build a structured query Q^S that consists of n `wsyn` clauses such that the ith clause contains k archaic translations of the ith modern term. For retrieval we use the "Boolean and" (`band`) belief operator to calculate

$$P(\mathcal{I}|Q, D, \Theta) = \prod_{i=1}^{n} \sum_{j=1}^{k} P(a_j|D)^{w_{ij}} \tag{1}$$

where we have k translations for each of our n observed terms and w_{ij} is the weight of the jth translation for the ith observed term. We use Indri's default parameters such that the probabilities are estimated using Dirichlet smoothing of multinomial language models with a hyperparameter of $\mu = 2500$. In other words $\Theta = \{\mu P(t_1|C), \mu P(t_2|C), ..., \mu P(t_V|C)\}$ where $P(t|C)$ is the probability of term t in the collection and V is the size of the vocabulary.

6. QUERY TRANSLATION

Given the retrieval model given by Eq. 1, a core challenge of CTIR lies in finding archaic synonyms for each modern query term and assigning weights to them. To accomplish this, we pose the problem as a variation on cross-language retrieval, where modern and archaic English are considered to be two distinct languages. We assume that a modern query Q^M is generated by an underlying information need $\mathcal{I}$. Our goal is to rephrase Q^M as a query Q^S that will retrieve documents useful to $\mathcal{I}$ but expressed in a way that will retrieve documents written in archaic English[3].

We begin by assuming that an observed modern query Q^M is a translation of an unknown archaic query Q^A. Our goal is to recover Q^A from Q^M. To simplify this process we further assume that an observed query word m_i translates to 0 or more archaic terms $\{a_{i1}, a_{i2}, \ldots, a_{ik}\}$. In this paper we estimate the probability of each archaic translation of a modern term m_i in isolation from all other observed terms $m_j \neq m_i$, leaving non-independencies for future work.

For a modern term m_i, we can rank the V terms in the vocabulary $\{a_1, a_2, \ldots, a_V\}$ in decreasing order of $P(a|m_i)$. Those archaic terms whose $P(a|m_i)$ exceeds some threshold τ are added as a synonym for m_i in the final query, with $P(a|m_i)$ as their weight in the `wsyn` clause.

For the modern query $Q^M = \{m_1, m_2, \ldots, m_n\}$ we choose elements for the `wsyn` query clause associated with term m_i by taking the top k terms from $P(a|m_i)$. This gives the clause: `#wsyn(`$P(a_{i1}|m_i)\, a_{i1}\; P(a_{i2}|m_i)\, a_{i2} \ldots P(a_{ik}|m_i)\, a_{ik}$`)`.

Our final query has an analogous clause for each of the n observed modern query terms. For simplicity we assume that all observed terms (i.e. all `wsyn` clauses) are given equal weight in the final query.

6.1 Translation in CTIR

All of the models we present are based on a simple probabilistic form, which we present here. Let T be a body of text such as a document, a corpus or a dictionary. We define $P(a|m, T)$, the probability that in a text T, the term a acts as a translation of m. By the definition of conditional probability, we have:

$$P(a|m, T) = \frac{P(a, m, T)}{P(m, T)}. \tag{2}$$

We can think of $P(.|m, T)$ as a multinomial characterized by Θ_m, the probability that m is a translation of $\{a_1, a_2, \ldots, a_V\}$ for a vocabulary of size V. To estimate Θ_m, the maximum likelihood estimator is:

$$\hat{P}^{ml}(a|m, T) = \frac{|a, m, T|}{\sum_{i=1}^{|T|} |t_i, m, T|} \tag{3}$$

where $|a_i, m, T|$ is the number of times that term a_i acts as a translation of m in T.

The following sections will define several approaches to determining if an occurrence of a in T is acting as a translation of m. Thus, Eq. 2 is generic. To make it useful we need a method of calculating the strength of the translational relationship between a and m. For any source of evidence $\mathcal{E}$, we will define an indicator function $\varphi_{\mathcal{E}}(a, m)$ that evaluates to 1 if criteria specific to $\mathcal{E}$ are met by a and m, or 0 otherwise, allowing us to obtain the counts specified in Eq. 3. The precise way to define φ will depend on the type of evidence we are using.

6.2 Dictionary Evidence

Bilingual dictionaries are a mainstay of cross-language IR [1, 20]. Researchers in the humanities have created similar resources that are helpful for cross-temporal IR. Of course many machine-readable dictionaries of Old and Middle English are available[4]. But these are often small, with commentary that makes using them in automated settings difficult.

[3]Of course, a search engine would retrieve both archaic *and* modern documents relevant to $\mathcal{I}$. However, retrieving modern versions is a problem that is at least conceptually distinct from our focus here.

[4]`http://archive.org/details/ElementaryMiddleEnglishGrammar`, `http://www.gutenberg.org/ebooks/10625`, e.g.

However, one resource stands out in this field. The digital humanities MorphAdorner project[5] contains a list of $\langle archaic, modern \rangle$ word pairs. After case-folding this "dictionary" contains 202,285 pairs. The MorphAdorner lexicon is helpful for CTIR due to its high quality. In personal correspondences, project developers explained that compiling the list took substantial work by subject experts. Because it was built by human experts there are very few false positives in the dictionary. Likewise, from its inception, the dictionary was intended to support automated systems. Thus using it requires no disambiguation or other data cleaning.

But like any bilingual dictionary, the MorphAdorner word list presents problems for use during CTIR:

1. **Translation weights.** Word pairs in the list are simple tuples, lacking a measure of translation quality. For instance, the modern term *authority* maps to 46 archaic variants in the list. Some of these terms appear often in archaic English, such as *auctoritee* and *authorite*. But *uthority* is rare. During IR, it would be helpful to let the strength of an *archaic* ↔ *modern* term association inform our query model.
2. **Out of vocabulary terms.** Even a list of 202,285 term pairs will suffer a sparse data problem due to the long-tailed distribution of terms in text.

Despite these issues, the structure and high quality of the MorphAdorner dictionary makes a simple translation indicating function obvious. Given a dictionary D of archaic-modern term pairs:

$$\varphi_D(a, m) = \begin{cases} 1 & \text{if } \langle a, m \rangle \in D \\ 0 & \text{otherwise.} \end{cases} \tag{4}$$

Plugging Eq. 4 into Eq. 3 we have the estimator:

$$\hat{P}_D^{ml}(a|m, D) = \frac{|a, m, D|}{|m, D|} \tag{5}$$

where $|m, D|$ is the number of tuples in the dictionary with m as their modern entry, and $|a, m, D|$ is the number of these $|m, D|$ tuples that have a as their archaic entry.

Eq. 5 allows us to specify a "dictionary" query Q^D. For an n-term modern query Q^M, Q^D has $\nu \leq n$ `wsyn` clauses. The elements of each `wsyn` clause are simply the archaic terms with non-zero $\hat{P}_D^{ml}(a|m, D)$, with all archaic terms weighted uniformly, in accordance with Eq. 5.

6.3 Orthographic Evidence

Cross-temporal IR invites us to supplement dictionary-based evidence with a second source of information. Unlike, say, English and French, where cognates are rare, word spellings in 20th-Century English and Early Modern or even Middle English are often similar. Most English readers are familiar with the addition of a terminal *e* when translating a modern term to an archaic version, as in *april* ↔ *aprile*. It is likewise easy to recognize that *aperil* is a "cognate" for *april*. These similarities are common, and thus provide obvious leverage for translating modern terms into archaic terms. We refer to this as *orthographic*, or *spelling* evidence.

Orthographic evidence is attractive because it relieves the problem of out-of-dictionary terms. Spelling evidence might also be useful in determining translation weights for structured queries. However, several problems impinge on using orthographic evidence in cross-temporal IR.

- A few patterns such as adding a terminal *e* are common in modern-archaic word pairs. But most orthographic distortions are idiosyncratic, making it hard use spelling systematically.
- The risk of false positives is high. Adding a terminal *e* to a modern word is often safe. But it can easily lead to errors; e.g. adding an *e* to *man* yields the (incorrect) modern term *mane*.
- Combining dictionary and spelling information is non-trivial. How to combine these sources of evidence in a sensible way is a challenge.

Regardless of these difficulties, we hypothesize that if handled properly, orthographic modern-archaic word similarity should improve the quality of query translations. Our goal in this regard is to induce a model that gives $P_S(a|m)$, the spelling-related probability that archaic word a is a viable translation of modern word m. Intuitively, $P_S(aprile|april)$ should be large, as should $P_S(avril|april)$. But $P_S(peril|april)$ should be small, with $P_S(man|april)$ still smaller.

The appeal of using orthography to identify translations is that it frees us from our dictionary's limitations. Instead of D, we will now use the entire text of the corpus C as T in Eq. 2. That is, we simply consider C to be a very large document. Referring to Eq. 3 we have the spelling probability:

$$\hat{P}_S^{ml}(a|m, C) = \frac{|a, m, C|}{\sum_{i=1}^{V} |t_i, m, C|} \tag{6}$$

where the number of translation events between a and m is determined by a function $\varphi_S(a, m)$ which we define in the following subsection.

6.3.1 Stochastic Edit Distance

To assess whether a and m are "close enough" to be archaic-modern translations with respect to orthography, we need a measure of string similarity. A good deal of prior work has treated this problem. Much of this work focuses on variants of the edit distance. Given given two strings a and m, a set of permissible edit operations, and a cost function ℓ, the edit distance $d(a, m)$ between a and m is the minimum cost of transforming a into m via our allowed operations[6].

If all costs equal 1, then this definition gives the well-known Levenshtein distance. But the Levenshtein distance has two drawbacks. First, it has no ready probabilistic interpretation that would help us integrate it into CTIR. Also, in CTIR, some operations intuitively merit different costs.

Several probabilistically motivated edit distances that address these issues have been proposed in the literature. We rely on results by Oncina and Sebban [26] and Ristad and Yianilos [29]. In particular, we make use of the model developed by Oncina and Sebban which finds the maximum likelihood estimator of the cost matrix via the EM algorithm[7]. Since we use this algorithm without alteration, we omit explicating it here, referring readers to [26, Appendix

[5] `http://morphadorner.northwestern.edu/morphadorner/`

[6] We use the common edit operations, insert, delete and replace.

[7] Our results rely on the open-source SEDIL software, `http://labh-curien.univ-st-etienne.fr/SEDiL/`.

A] for a full treatment. For our purposes, two details of the algorithm are important. First, it operates without any domain knowledge aside from the training tuples. Second, based on a corpus of archaic-modern term tuples, we obtain a translation model $t(a|m)$ by normalizing the results of the EM algorithm such that $t(.|m_i)$ sums to one for all m_i.

We trained $t(a|m)$ on the MorphAdorner dictionary. This leads to the spelling indicator function:

$$\varphi_S(a,m) = \begin{cases} 1 & \text{if } t(a|m) > \tau_S \\ 0 & 0, \text{otherwise.} \end{cases} \quad (7)$$

for an empirically determined threshold τ_S which governs how similar a term a must be to m to be considered a viable translation for m.

6.4 Combining Evidence

The previous two subsections introduced sources of evidence that might help cross-temporal IR. But combining these sources would presumably improve effectiveness of CTIR, much as evidence combination has aided CLIR [25]. This section presents two methods of combining dictionary and spelling evidence in the framework given by Eq. 2.

6.4.1 Naive Combination

It is tempting simply to assume that strong evidence on both dimensions – dictionary and spelling – should increase our confidence in a translation. We refer to this approach as *naive combination.*

We can combine dictionary and spelling evidence by using the dictionary model $P_D(a|m,D)$ as the basis for a prior to find the maximum a posteriori (MAP) estimate of the spelling model. Because $P_S(a|m,C)$ is a multinomial, we use the Dirichlet distribution (the multinomial's conjugate prior) with parameters $\{\mu_S P_D(a_1|m,D), \mu_S P_D(a_2|m,D), \ldots, \mu_S P_D(a_V|m,D)\}$ as our prior, with a smoothing hyperparameter μ_S.

The maximum *a posteriori* estimate is thus:

$$\hat{P}_N^{map}(a|m,C) = \frac{|a,m,C| + \mu_S P_D(a|m,D)}{\sum_{i=1}^{V} |t_i,m,C| + \mu_S} \quad (8)$$

where $P_N(a|m,C)$ is the "naive" translation model.

6.4.2 Relevance Feedback

Eq. 8 alleviates the constraints of dictionary-based translation, but at the cost of a huge increase in the size of the search space. Because Eq. 8 operates in a completely unsupervised way over the entire vocabulary, it is likely that a query populated with all terms with non-zero probability according to Eq. 8 will contain many false positives.

Thus, we hypothesize that weak orthographic similarity is a strong indicator that a is a bad translation of m. But it is not the case that high orthographic similarity implies a good translation. If this is true, while Eq. 8 allows us to ignore many low-similarity terms, it will still suffer from a high false positive rate.

To overcome this problem, a logical approach is to constrain the search space of translation discovery. Relevance feedback accomplishes this. Given R, a set of k (pseudo-) relevant documents obtained by the dictionary-based query Q^D, we will limit consideration of translation to terms that occur in R, aiming for two effects:

1. **Term identification.** The set of relevant documents may contain translations of m that were not present in the dictionary. We can add these to the final query.
2. **Term weighting.** The dictionary gives deterministic evidence about the relationship between a and m. But with respect to a particular information need, some translations of m may be preferable to others. Feedback lets us update the weights of translations.

The central idea in our feedback approach is that we only allow terms that appear in the pseudo-relevant documents to alter our query model based on orthographic similarity to observed modern query terms.

This approach uses intuition similar to He's work on CLIR [9]. However, our approach is unique in several senses. Aside from the obvious difference in focus (CTIR vs. CLIR) and the attendant differences in evidence, our approach differs from He's mathematically and algorithmically. He used feedback to improve a translation model learned from parallel corpora, linearly interpolating model weights with dictionary probabilities. We have no parallel corpus. This invites a Bayesian approach, considering the dictionary model as a prior over translations which we use to smooth the probabilities estimated during feedback.

In the remainder of this section, we assume that based on our initial, dictionary-built query, we have retrieved $k = 20$ pseudo-relevant documents. We concatenate these k documents into a large pseudo-document R.

Continuing with our earlier notation, we have the relevance feedback probability of a given m:

$$\hat{P}_R^{ml}(a|m,R) = \frac{|a,m,R|}{\sum_{i=1}^{V} |t,m,R|}. \quad (9)$$

Again, we enumerate the translation events between a and m in R via the indicator function:

$$\varphi_R(a,m) = \begin{cases} 1 & \text{if } t(a|m) < \tau_R \\ 0 & \text{otherwise} \end{cases} \quad (10)$$

where $t(a|m)$ is the orthographic probability (i.e. string similarity) and τ_R is a threshold that governs how similar a term a in the feedback documents must be to m to be considered a viable translation for m.

As in the case of our naive combination model, in this case we update our feedback probabilities by considering the dictionary model as the basis for a Dirichlet prior: $\{\mu_R P_D(a_1|m,D), \mu_R P_D(a_2|m,D), \ldots, \mu_R P_D(a_V|m,D)\}$, giving:

$$\hat{P}_R^{map}(a|m,R) = \frac{|a,m,R| + \mu_R P_D(a|m,D)}{\sum_{i=1}^{V} |t_i,m,R| + \mu_R}. \quad (11)$$

6.5 Summary of Models

We have presented four models for building CTIR queries. Table 1 summarizes them and lists an abbreviated name for each. A few points about these models are worth stressing:

- Orthographic evidence operates as a binary variable via the indicator functions φ_*. That is, a term a is classified as a translation of m if $t(a|m)$ exceeds a threshold τ_*. The thresholds τ_S and τ_R differ because the CFB model searches for translations over an elite set of documents, while SPELL and CNAIVE search all

Table 1: Summary of Baseline and Experimental Query Models. Baseline methods are shown with a gray background, with more novel models shown against a white background.

Name	Definition	Parameters	Description
DICT	$P_D(a,\|m,D)$	none	Simple dictionary lookup of candidate translations. Uniform weights.
USER	NA	unigrams=0.85, #owl=0.1 #uw8=0.05	Judges cut-and-paste a relevant passage to create a query. Queries formed via sequential dependency model [23].
RM3	NA	k = 20 documents, n = 20 terms, $\lambda = 0.5$ interpolation	Relevance model 3 of [19]. Feedback terms interpolated with Q^D (Eq. 5).
SPELL	$\hat{P}_S^{ml}(a,\|m,C)$	$\log \tau_S$ =-2.1	Includes all terms from the vocabulary whose string probability $t(a\|m) < \tau_S$.
CNAIVE	$\hat{P}_N^{map}(a,\|m,C)$	$\log \tau_S = -4.2$, $\mu_S = 20000.0$	Naive evidence combination. Uses Bayesian updating to improve the spelling model based on dictionary evidence. Considers all terms in the collection. Weights terms by dictionary evidence and collection frequency.
CFB	$\hat{P}_R^{map}(a,\|m,R)$	$\log \tau_R = -9.0$, $\mu_R = 10.0$, k = 20 documents	Same as CNAIVE but the set of possible translations is constrained to the vocabulary of k feedback documents. Weights terms by dictionary evidence and frequency in feedback documents.

documents. Thus CFB can tolerate a wider range of spelling variation than SPELL and CNAIVE can.

- The Dirichlet hyperparameters μ_* govern the extent to which we trust dictionary evidence versus spelling evidence observed in texts (either the whole collection or feedback documents).
- CNAIVE and CFB are identical except for the documents they consider – the full corpus versus only feedback documents – and their parameterization.

7. EXPERIMENTAL DATA

To evaluate our approaches, we built a new test collection. We did not use a pre-existing collection such as the INEX book track's corpora due two considerations:

1. We needed to ensure a high degree of historical diversity in our collection.
2. The types of information needs (and queries) needed for our use case were not present in existing collections.

This section details our test collection.

7.1 Documents

Documents came from two sources. Members of the Google Books team (not affiliated with the authors) made the text of 3,690 volumes available to us. These were a random sample of out-of-copyright texts by the authors listed on three Wikipedia pages in October 2010[8]. These samples had many redundancies, with duplicate and near-duplicate pages being common; these were retained. Documents resulted from OCR on scanned pages, leading to typographical noise.

Besides the Google Books data, we harvested 34,806 full-text books from Project Gutenberg in October 2010. These books were selected by requesting all titles labeled as being in English, Middle English, or Old English.

[8] http://en.wikipedia.org/wiki/List_of_English_writers, http://en.wikipedia.org/wiki/Classical_Latin, http://en.wikipedia.org/wiki/Classical_Greek

For our experiments, we set the page (as opposed to the book, chapter, etc.) as the unit of retrieval. For the Google Books data, page-breaks were already present. The Gutenberg data, however, were simply long text files. We split these files into non-overlapping passages of no more than 300 words to form retrievable "documents." The 300-word window was intended to mimic the length of book pages, though it was chosen without rigorous estimation.

All metadata was removed from documents, and texts were indexed using Indri, with no stemming or stoplists applied at index time. This yielded an index containing 25,845,101 documents and a vocabulary size of 6,657,631 terms. We did not perform any language identification to learn which documents were indeed modern and which were archaic; we preferred to let our models tackle this problem.

7.2 Topics

Topics were developed by two hired subject experts in digital humanities – one masters and one doctoral student. The students self-identified as users of Google books. As they created queries, topic developers explored the collection using a simple web interface to the index described above.

Each topic developer was given a page-long description of the proposed CTIR use case. Based on this, they were asked to imagine exemplars that they would like to learn about. Developers were free to choose exemplars that are very common (such as famous Biblical passages) or rarer ones. The main imperative was for them to identify exemplars that would plausibly be of interest to digital humanists in the context of CTIR.

For each exemplar, the developer was asked to write a single version of it in modern English. These were used as queries during experimentation. The developers were instructed to choose a modern phrasing that would be a plausible starting point for a searcher interested in the exemplar. Finally, topic authors wrote a description of the exemplar that their query referred to as a basis for relevance judging.

This process raises at least two objectionable points. First, in some sense, our topic development was done backwards from a more realistic scenario. Generating modern renditions of a known archaism is artificial. Second, with no "correct" way to write an archaic exemplar as a modern query, subjectivity entered the process of query creation. However, we argue that the first point – artificial order of operations in query-building – is tolerable; developers were asked to consider the overarching problem, and their expertise in the field put them in a good position to handle this ambiguity. As for the latitude in query expression, this is little different than any other topic development, where an abstract information need must be couched in a particular phrasing.

Developers created a total of 53 topics. Two topics were later found to have zero highly relevant documents and were removed. Five topics were chosen with uniform probability to be used for model training. The remaining 46 topics were used for testing.

Queries ranged in length from 3 to 23 words, with a median of 6 and mean 7.65 terms. Figure 1 shows that the MorphAdorner dictionary provides good coverage of the queries, with only six queries having more than one out-of-dictionary term. Based on this, we believe that the simple dictionary-based query is likely to perform well for these data.

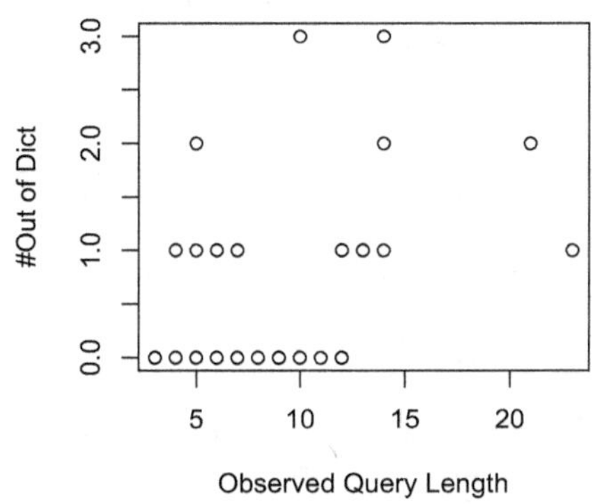

Figure 1: Length of Test Queries and each Query's Number of Out-of-dictionary Terms.

7.3 Relevance Judgments

Unfortunately, the topic authors were not available to serve as relevance assessors. So four Ph.D. students in Medieval Studies were hired to perform relevance judgments. These students were all self-identified experts in early English. Assessors were shown the same topic development guidelines that query authors had read. In addition, assessors were given instructions on how they were to judge document relevance. They then completed an initial trial of 25 judgments, after which they raised any questions before moving on to the bulk of their work.

Judging was done on a three-point scale: 0=not relevant, 1=somewhat relevant, 2=relevant. Assessors were also allowed to say "I don't know," though this option was never used. In Section 8, all effectiveness measures except NDCG treat judgments of 1 and 2 as relevant. NDCG leaves the three-point scale intact.

The criteria for relevance in the context of CTIR are not obvious. Judges were instructed to consult query-document pairs and ask *does the document contain language that intentionally echoes the query*? By *intentionally*, we did not mean that the author needed to know his source. Instead, he needed to know that he was using language that has the history referenced by the query.

Novelty and document quality were not taken into account during the judging process.

Pooling was conducted by running methods DICT, RM3, CNAIVE, and CFB described in Table 1 over the queries (with parameters chosen empirically) . These results were then pooled at a depth of 50 documents per query per model, yielding a total of 8,791 judgments.

Because our assessors were paid domain experts, we only assigned one assessor per judgment, yielding more judgments than multiple assessments per pair would allow. Nevertheless, we wanted some sense of inter-rater reliability. Thus we sampled 50 query-document pairs: 5 queries taken uniformly from our 53, with 10 documents sampled uniformly from those documents that were in at least three of our pools. All assessors rated these query-document pairs. On the three-point relevance scale, this gave a Fleiss kappa agreement of 0.638. Conflating ratings of 1 and 2 to a single *relevant* class, increased kappa to 0.752. Both of these statistics gave $p < 0.001$, suggesting that our assessors largely agreed on the criteria for assigning relevance judgments.

8. EMPIRICAL EVALUATION

Because CTIR is largely an unstudied problem, defining a reasonable baseline for comparing approaches is non-trivial. We define three baselines, shown in the gray rows of Table 1. The run DICT is the simple dictionary lookup described in Eq. 5. The USER run is in some sense an oracle condition; relevance assessors were asked to cut and paste a single, highly relevant passage from a document to form the query verbatim. This text was then represented using the sequential dependency variant of the Markov Random Field model [22]. The USER run is thus not strictly comparable to the others we report because it is based on explicit feedback. But it isn't a pure oracle condition since USER queries stem from a single relevant document and are not expanded in any way. USER queries are high-quality but narrow.

8.1 Omitted Results

Due to space constraints, we do not report results from several models because they were unsuccessful; we list them here for completeness. As additional baselines, we used the character n-gram model described in [8]. We also implemented several ad hoc models based on soundex query transformation (cf. [33]). These methods did not approach the effectiveness of the simple DICT run, so we did not pursue them further. Of course, this is not a defect in the approaches themselves. Rather it simply means that they did not transfer from their original domains to CTIR. Finally, standard Rocchio and BM25 pseudo-feedback were less successful than the reported relevance models.

8.2 Model Effectiveness

Table 2 summarizes the outcomes of our experimental assessment. Results are based on retrievals of 100 documents per query. In the table, statistically significant changes via a permutation test are shown as follows. $\triangle$: improvement over DICT has $p < 0.05$, $\blacktriangle$: improvement over DICT has $p < 0.01$, $\uparrow$: improvement over USER has $p < 0.05$, $\Uparrow$: improvement over USER has $p < 0.01$, $\downarrow$: decline wrt USER has $p < 0.05$, $\Downarrow$: decline wrt USER has $p < 0.01$.

Table 2: Summary of Retrieval Effectiveness. Statistics are mean average precision (MAP), number of relevant retrieved (Rel Ret), R-precision (Rprec) and normalized discounted cumulative gain (NDCG).

Model	MAP	Rel Ret	Rprec	NDCG
DICT	$0.1702^{\downarrow}$	542	$0.1932^{\downarrow}$	$0.2932^{\Downarrow}$
USER	$0.2793^{\vartriangle}$	554	$0.2944^{\vartriangle}$	$0.4606^{\blacktriangle}$
RM3	$0.1753^{\Downarrow}$	$532^{\Downarrow}$	$0.195^{\Downarrow}$	$0.2787^{\Downarrow}$
SPELL	$0.1316^{\Downarrow}$	521	$0.1543^{\Downarrow}$	$0.2175^{\Downarrow}$
CNAIVE	$0.1688^{\downarrow}$	$551^{\downarrow}$	0.1961	$0.2869^{\Downarrow}$
CFB	$0.3025^{\blacktriangle\uparrow}$	$870^{\blacktriangle\uparrow}$	$0.3143^{\blacktriangle\uparrow}$	$0.4528^{\blacktriangle}$

A few results are unsurprising: The dictionary-based queries (DICT) do seem like a reasonable baseline. The condition with known relevant text as queries (USER) performs very strongly. And in the bottom three rows, adding increasing amounts of structure to our dictionary-orthography combinations improves effectiveness.

The most obvious point of interest in Table 2 is the strong performance by our orthographically informed feedback method, CFB. Except for the semi-oracle USER run's NDCG, CFB outperforms all methods on all effectiveness measures.

By comparing CFB to DICT and RM3 we can see another interesting result. Pseudo-relevance feedback helps when it is used to alter a query by combining feedback and orthographic evidence via CFB. In contrast, standard feedback did not improve over the simple dictionary method. It is important to note that our implementation of RM3 interpolated the feedback model with the dictionary model; i.e. RM3 it did not give up the query structure of the other models. Also, the RM3 run used a custom stoplist with words added to the standard Indri stoplist to improve performance.

Figure 2 helps us assess the relationship between the two highest-performing runs – USER and CFB. In Figure 2 we see that both methods give higher MAP than the DICT run on most queries. However, CFB is "safer" than the USER run insofar as CFB's queries whose effectiveness decline with respect to DICT do so less than comparable declines seen for USER. This is not surprising, as the USER run puts all of the query burden on the words obtained from a *single* relevant document. Thus USER is very good at retrieving some relevant documents. But it does this at the cost of overfitting the supplied relevant text. Not surprisingly, if we remove the documents from which the judges extracted the query text for USER, its MAP declines to 0.2096.

Though CFB performed well, Table 2 shows that using spelling evidence is risky. The purely orthographic SPELL model was significantly inferior to the simple dictionary lookup. And CNAIVE saw a small, though not significant decline as well. This suggests that there is information in orthographic information, but that using it well is difficult.

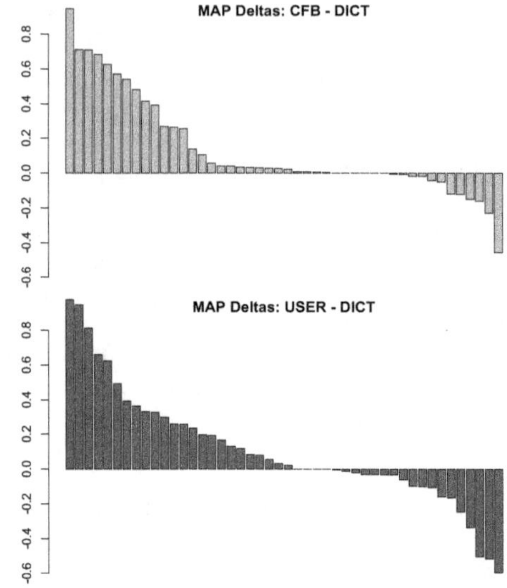

Figure 2: Query-by-Query Difference in MAP between DICT and CFB (Gray) & USER (Blue). Each bar corresponds to one test query. Bar height is MAP under an experimental condition minus MAP of DICT.

8.3 Feedback for CTIR, Further Analysis

The CFB feedback method aims to improve a simple DICT query in two ways: by discovering candidate translations that were not in the dictionary and by learning weights for query terms. The formalism given in Section 6.4.2 dictates how these goals are combined in CFB. But a logical question is: which aspect – term discovery or term weighting – is most responsible for the improvements over DICT seen in Table 2? To pursue this question, we created two variants of CFB that isolate these effects (at the expensive of becoming heuristic in motivation). CFB-W reweights terms from the dictionary query as Eq. 11 dictates but does not add any query terms. Conversely, CFB-T adds all feedback terms to the model that constitute "translations" according to Eq. 10. But in CFB-T, all terms from the dictionary receive a weight of 1.0, while added terms are weighted at 0.5.

Table 3: Retrieval Effectiveness Measures for variants of CFB Feedback Method. Statistically significant changes via a permutation test are shown as follows. ▼: decline wrt CFB has $p < 0.01$.

Model	MAP	Rel Ret	Rprec	NDCG
CFB-W	$0.1603^{\blacktriangledown}$	$523^{\blacktriangledown}$	$0.1817^{\blacktriangledown}$	$0.2932^{\blacktriangledown}$
CFB-T	0.3106	907	0.3176	0.4631

Table 3 suggests that the crucial mechanism for CFB is its ability to discover new terms. If we disable this behavior (yielding CFB-W) performance declines significantly. But if we ignore the induced term weights of CFB (yielding CFB-T) we actually see an increase in effectiveness.

9. DISCUSSION AND FUTURE WORK

Our experiments suggest that methods for handling language change have a strong effect on the success of the types of queries studied in this paper. Without a canonical baseline, it is difficult to say if our methods are performing "well." However, the MorphAdorner dictionary is an unusually large and clean knowledge base by CLIR standards. Thus we argue that the DICT model gives a reasonable baseline.

To improve on this performance, it is logical to enlist orthographic evidence, since it often provides a clear path from a modern term to its historical variants. But our hypothesis that orthographic evidence can only help CTIR in a limited way was borne out experimentally. If a term a is orthographically similar to m, that does not imply that a is a good substitute for m in a CTIR query. But it is also the case that if we fail to see orthographic similarity between a and m, it is unlikely that we have a match that we should trust without further corroboration.

We anticipated a benefit from using feedback to moderate string similarity's influence during retrieval. The strength of the CFB model bears out this hypothesis. By constraining the domain of possible orthographic matches to those in high-quality documents, we avoid the high false positive problem that the purely string-based approach such as SPELLING encountered.

Several limitations of this study are worth noting. We omitted discussion of the sensitivity of the parameters μ_* and τ_* because sweeps on our training queries showed little interesting change. But the poor performance of the CNAIVE model suggests that closer attention to parameterization would be helpful. More importantly, using only five training queries limited our ability to assess parameterization robustly.

Another limitation hinges on temporal diversity. Between "archaic" and "modern" English there is a spectrum of vernaculars. Effective CTIR should retrieve documents across this spectrum. But without a clear metric for assessing such diversity, we have not reported our success in finding documents from diverse periods.

Finally, a fourth type of evidence could be used for CTIR: translation models learned from parallel corpora. We built such a model using Biblical translations, but found that the high number of out-of-vocabulary query terms made its use infeasible. Perhaps an approach based on the less restrictive notion of comparable corpora will allow us to incorporate such evidence. In future work we plan to pursue this.

Two other avenues will inform our future work on CTIR. First, Table 3 suggests that our feedback model performs well but not optimally. Though probabilistically convenient, Eq. 11 is not an optimal way to combine dictionary, spelling and feedback information. In future work we will pursue how to exploit the strengths of CFB more fully.

Our second avenue for future work lies in expanding the domains in which we study cross-temporal IR. This paper has focused on book search. But techniques for handling language change have a role to play in other types of IR. In particular, social media such as microblogs see rapid shifts in discursive conventions [7]. While the temporal dynamics of relevance (e.g. [21]) have seen a good deal of attention recently, the problem of temporality as an invitation for vocabulary mismatch deserves increased scrutiny.

10. CONCLUSION

The growing opportunity for digitized book repositories to impact peoples' use of information suggests that language evolution will be an increasingly important challenge for modern IR. Without prompting, all four of the Medieval Studies Ph.D. candidates who performed our relevance judgments said that they wished that a system capable of cross-temporal search were available to them.

In light of this change, this paper proposed techniques for handling vocabulary mismatch due to temporal shifts in language. From a conceptual standpoint, our contribution entails a generic way of considering the use of texts (dictionaries, corpora, relevant documents) to inform CTIR. More pragmatically, the paper's main contribution is a novel feedback technique that combines several types of evidence to improve cross-temporal retrieval.

11. ACKNOWLEDGEMENTS

This work was supported by a Google Digital Humanities Award and NSF Grant # 1217279. Any opinions, findings, and conclusions or recommendations expressed in this material are those of the author and do not necessarily reflect the views of the funders. The author thanks Jon Orwant for his help in the early stages of this research.

12. REFERENCES

[1] Lisa Ballesteros and W. Bruce Croft. Dictionary methods for cross-lingual information retrieval. In *Proceedings of the 7th International Conference on Database and Expert Systems Applications*, DEXA '96, pp. 791–801, London, UK, 1996. Springer-Verlag.

[2] Adam Berger and John Lafferty. Information retrieval as statistical translation. In *SIGIR '99: Proceedings of the 22nd Annual International ACM SIGIR Conference on Research and Development in Information Retrieval*, pages 222–229, New York, NY, USA, 1999. ACM.

[3] Dan Cohen. Is google good for history?, January 7, 2010. http://hdl.handle.net/1920/6101.

[4] Kareem Darwish and Douglas W. Oard. Probabilistic structured query methods. In *Proceedings of the 26th annual international ACM SIGIR conference on Research and development in informaion retrieval*, SIGIR '03, pp. 338–344, New York, NY, USA, 2003. ACM.

[5] F.M.G. de Jong, H. Rode, and D. Hiemstra. Temporal language models for the disclosure of historical text. In *Humanities, Computers and Cultural Heritage: Proceedings of the XVIth Intl. Conf. of the Assn. for History and Computing (AHC 2005)*, pages 161–168, Amsterdam,, September 2005. Royal Netherlands Academy of Arts and Sciences.

[6] Michael Droettboom. Correcting broken characters in the recognition of historical printed documents. In *Proceedings of the 3rd ACM/IEEE-CS Joint Conference on Digital Libraries*, JCDL '03, pages 364–366, Washington, DC, USA, 2003. IEEE Computer Society.

[7] Miles Efron. Information search and retrieval in microblogs. *Journal of the American Society for Information Science and Technology*, 62(6):996–1008, 2011.

[8] S. Harding, W. Croft, and C. Weir. Probabilistic retrieval of OCR degraded text using n-grams. In Carol Peters and Costantino Thanos, editors, *Research and Advanced Technology for Digital Libraries*, Volume 1324 of *Lecture Notes in Computer Science*, pages 345–359. Springer Berlin / Heidelberg, 1997.

[9] Daqing He and Dan Wu. Enhancing query translation with relevance feedback in translingual information retrieval. *Inf. Proc. and Mgmt.*, 47(1):1 – 17, 2011.

[10] Daniel Jurafsky and James H. Martin. *Speech and Language Processing, 2nd Edition.* Prentice Hall, New York, 2008.

[11] Nattiya Kanhabua and Kjetil Nørvåg. Improving temporal language models for determining time of non-timestamped documents. In *Proceedings of the 12th European Conference on Research and Advanced Technology for Digital Libraries*, ECDL '08, pages 358–370, Berlin, Heidelberg, 2008. Springer-Verlag.

[12] Maryam Karimzadehgan and ChengXiang Zhai. Estimation of statistical translation models based on mutual information for ad hoc information retrieval. In *Proceedings of the 33rd International ACM SIGIR Conference on Research and Development in Information Retrieval*, SIGIR '10, pages 323–330, New York, NY, USA, 2010. ACM.

[13] Gabriella Kazai and Antoine Doucet. Overview of the INEX 2007 Book Search Track (Booksearch'07). In *INEX*, pages 148–161, 2007.

[14] Gabriella Kazai, Carsten Eickhoff, and Peter Brusilovsky. Report on Booksonline'11: 4th Workshop on Online Books, Complementary Social Media, and Crowdsourcing. *SIGIR Forum*, 46(1):43–50, 2012.

[15] Marijn Koolen, Jaap Kamps, and Gabriella Kazai. Social book search: comparing topical relevance judgements and book suggestions for evaluation. In *Proceedings of the 21st ACM International Conference on Information and Knowledge management*, pages 185–194, 2012.

[16] Marijn Koolen, Gabriella Kazai, Jaap Kamps, Michael Preminger, Antoine Doucet, and Monica Landoni. Overview of the INEX 2012 Social Book Search Track. In *CLEF (Online Working Notes/Labs/Workshop)*, 2012.

[17] Abhimanu Kumar, Matthew Lease, and Jason Baldridge. Supervised language modeling for temporal resolution of texts. In *Proceedings of the 20th ACM International Conference on Information and Knowledge management*, CIKM '11, pages 2069–2072, New York, NY, USA, 2011. ACM.

[18] Adenike M. Lam-Adesina and Gareth J. F. Jones. Examining and improving the effectiveness of relevance feedback for retrieval of scanned text documents. *Inf. Proc. Mgmt.*, 42(3):633–649, 2006.

[19] Victor Lavrenko and W. Bruce Croft. Relevance based language models. In *SIGIR '01: Proceedings of the 24th Annual International ACM SIGIR Conference on Research and Development in Information Retrieval*, pages 120–127, New York, NY, USA, 2001. ACM.

[20] Gina-Anne Levow, Douglas W. Oard, and Philip Resnik. Dictionary-based techniques for cross-language information retrieval. *Inf. Proc. Mgmt.*, 41(3):523–547, 2005.

[21] Xiaoyan Li and W. Bruce Croft. Time-based language models. In *CIKM '03: Proceedings of the 12th International Conference on Information and Knowledge Management*, pages 469–475, New York, NY, USA, 2003. ACM.

[22] Donald Metzler and W. Bruce Croft. A markov random field model for term dependencies. In *SIGIR '05: Proceedings of the 28th Annual International ACM SIGIR Conference on Research and Development in Information Retrieval*, pages 472–479, New York, NY, USA, 2005. ACM.

[23] Donald Metzler and W. Bruce Croft. Latent concept expansion using markov random fields. In *SIGIR '07: Proceedings of the 30th Annual International ACM SIGIR Conference on Research and Development in Information Retrieval*, pages 311–318, New York, NY, USA, 2007. ACM.

[24] Donald Metzler, Victor Lavrenko, and W. Bruce Croft. Formal multiple-bernoulli models for language modeling. In *Proceedings of the 27th Annual International ACM SIGIR Conference on Research and Development in Information Retrieval*, SIGIR '04, pages 540–541, New York, NY, USA, 2004. ACM.

[25] Jian-Yun Nie, Michel Simard, Pierre Isabelle, and Richard Durand. Cross-language information retrieval based on parallel texts and automatic mining of parallel texts from the web. In *Proceedings of the 22nd Annual International ACM SIGIR Conference on Research and Development in Information Retrieval*, SIGIR '99, pages 74–81, New York, NY, USA, 1999. ACM.

[26] J. Oncina and M. Sebban. Learning stochastic edit distance: Application in handwritten character recognition. *Pattern Recognition*, 39(9):1575–1587, 2006.

[27] Marc Parry. The humanities go google. *The Chronicle of Higher Education*, May 2010. http://chronicle.com/article/The-Humanities-Go-Google/65713/.

[28] Matjaz Perc. Evolution of the most common English words and phrases over the centuries. *Journal of the Royal Society: Interface*, 1:3323–3328, 2010.

[29] Eric Sven Ristad and Peter N. Yianilos. Learning string edit distance. *IEEE Transactions on Pattern Recognition and Machine Intelligence*, 20(5):522–532, May 1998.

[30] Edward Sapir. *Language: And Introduction to the Study of Speech.* Harcourt, Brace, New York, 1921.

[31] Trevor Strohman, Donald Metzler, Howard Turtle, and W. Bruce Croft. Indri: a language-model based search engine for complex queries. Technical report, in *Proceedings of the International Conference on Intelligent Analysis*, 2005.

[32] J. R. R. Tolkien and E. V. Gordon, editors. *Sir Gawain and the Green Knight.* Clarendon Press, Oxford, 1967.

[33] Justin Zobel and Philip Dart. Phonetic string matching: lessons from information retrieval. In *Proceedings of the 19th Annual International ACM SIGIR Conference on Research and Development in Information Retrieval*, SIGIR '96, pages 166–172, New York, NY, USA, 1996. ACM.

On the Measurement of Test Collection Reliability

Julián Urbano[*] jurbano@inf.uc3m.es

Mónica Marrero[*] mmarrero@inf.uc3m.es

Diego Martín[†] dmartin@dit.upm.es

[*]University Carlos III of Madrid
Department of Computer Science
Leganés, Spain

[†]Technical University of Madrid
Department of Telematics Engineering
Madrid, Spain

ABSTRACT

The reliability of a test collection is proportional to the number of queries it contains. But building a collection with many queries is expensive, so researchers have to find a balance between reliability and cost. Previous work on the measurement of test collection reliability relied on data-based approaches that contemplated random *what if* scenarios, and provided indicators such as swap rates and Kendall tau correlations. Generalizability Theory was proposed as an alternative founded on analysis of variance that provides reliability indicators based on statistical theory. However, these reliability indicators are hard to interpret in practice, because they do not correspond to well known indicators like Kendall tau correlation. We empirically established these relationships based on data from over 40 TREC collections, thus filling the gap in the practical interpretation of Generalizability Theory. We also review the computation of these indicators, and show that they are extremely dependent on the sample of systems and queries used, so much that the required number of queries to achieve a certain level of reliability can vary in orders of magnitude. We discuss the computation of confidence intervals for these statistics, providing a much more reliable tool to measure test collection reliability. Reflecting upon all these results, we review a wealth of TREC test collections, arguing that they are possibly not as reliable as generally accepted and that the common choice of 50 queries is insufficient even for stable rankings.

Categories and Subject Descriptors

H.3.4 [**Information Storage and Retrieval**]: Systems and Software—*Performance evaluation.*

General Terms

Experimentation, Measurement, Reliability.

Keywords

Test Collection, Evaluation, Reliability, Generalizability Theory, TREC.

SIGIR'13, July 28–August 1, 2013, Dublin, Ireland.

1. INTRODUCTION

The purpose of evaluating the effectiveness of an Information Retrieval (IR) system is to assess how well it would satisfy real users. The main tool used in these evaluations are test collections, which comprise a collection of documents to search, a set of queries $\mathcal{Q}$, and a set of relevance judgments that contains information as to what documents are relevant, and to which degree, to the queries [16]. Given the results returned by a system A for one of the queries $q \in \mathcal{Q}$, an effectiveness measure uses the information in the relevance judgments to compute a score $\lambda_{q,\mathsf{A}}$ that represents the effectiveness of the system for that query. After running the system for all queries in the collection, the average $\overline{\lambda}_{\mathcal{Q},\mathsf{A}} = \frac{1}{|\mathcal{Q}|}\sum \lambda_{i,\mathsf{A}}$ is usually reported as the main measure of system effectiveness, representing the expected behavior of the system for an arbitrary new query. When comparing two systems A and B, the main measure reported is the average effectiveness difference $\overline{\Delta\lambda}_{\mathcal{Q},\mathsf{AB}} = \overline{\lambda}_{\mathcal{Q},\mathsf{A}} - \overline{\lambda}_{\mathcal{Q},\mathsf{B}}$. Based on this difference, we conclude which system is better.

The immediate question to ask is: *how reliable are those conclusions about system effectiveness?* Ideally, researchers would evaluate the system with the set of all possible queries that a user might request. In such a case, we could be sure that the true average performance of the system corresponds to the score we computed with the collection. The problem is that building such a collection is either impractical for requiring an enormous amount of queries and relevance judgments, or just impossible if the potential query set is not defined, which use to be the case because we can not account for future queries that do not yet exist. Therefore, the query set $\mathcal{Q}$ in a test collection must be regarded as a sample from the universe of all queries, and the sample mean $\overline{\lambda}_{\mathcal{Q},\mathsf{A}}$ as an estimate of the *true* effectiveness mean λ_{A}. But because we are estimating this score with a sample of queries, our estimates are erroneous to some degree. The results may change drastically with a different query set $\mathcal{Q}'$, so much that differences between systems could be reversed.

An evaluation result is reliable if it can be replicated with another collection: if the set of queries $\mathcal{Q}$ suggests that system A outperforms system B, we can be very sure that the conclusion would hold for a different set of queries $\mathcal{Q}'$, and in the end, for the universe of all queries. A simple way to make a collection reliable is to include many queries; the more we employ the smaller the variance of the estimates and thus the more reliable the conclusion. The problem is that more queries also means more cost to create the collection, so researchers have to find a balance between the reliability of the results and the cost of the collection. To this end, it is necessary to develop indicators of test collection reliability.

Several works in the last fifteen years have studied the problem of reliability in IR evaluation experiments. The basic methodology consisted in evaluating a series of systems with two different and random sets of queries, computing several reliability indicators that measured how similar those evaluations were. Using different query sample sizes and randomizing query selection, researchers were able to map query set size to reliability and extrapolate results to larger query sets. The data used consisted in runs submitted to several TREC tracks (mostly the Ad Hoc tracks), and the sets of queries employed in each edition. While these approaches are clearly faithful to the data, they are limited in that the full query set had to be partitioned in two disjoint sets to comply with the assumption that they were independent.

In 2007 Bodoff and Li [6] proposed Generalizability Theory (GT) as an alternative [7, 18]. GT is grounded on analysis of variance components, which allows to dissect the variability in effectiveness scores and figure out how much of it is due to system differences, query difficulty, assessors, etc. In an ideal evaluation setting, we would like all variance to be due to actual differences between systems and not due to query variability; if the queries in the collection are too varied, or differences between systems too small, then we need many queries to ensure that our estimates are reliable. From these variance components GT allows researchers to estimate the reliability of a test collection even before it has been created. Based on some previous data, GT can estimate the reliability of a collection with a larger number of queries, more than one assessor providing judgments for each query, etc. GT provides indicators for the stability of both the absolute scores and the relative differences by computing different variance ratios.

The main advantages of GT against the traditional data-based approaches are that 1) it is based on statistical theory, 2) it is easy to employ because it does not require tedious and repetitive *what if* scenarios, and 3) it allows us to estimate the reliability of a collection or experimental design that does not exist yet. But it has disadvantages too: 1) it is unknown the extent to which reliability indicators are affected by the data used to estimate variance components, and 2) it is very hard to interpret them in practical terms.

We address these two problems of GT applied to the measurement of test collection reliability. In the next section we review past work following data-based approaches and the reliability indicators used. We then review the use of GT and discuss the motivation for this work. In Section 3 we show how the initial data used in GT studies has a very large effect on the results, discussing minimum sample sizes and interval estimators. Section 4 reports a study to provide an empirical mapping between GT-based indicators of reliability and the well known data-based ones. Next we discuss the reliability of several TREC collections based on the results from previous sections, presenting conclusions in Section 6.

2. INDICATORS OF RELIABILITY

Several indicators of test collection reliability have been proposed in the literature. This section reviews traditional indicators found in the early data-based studies and the GT-based indicators more recently proposed.

2.1 Data-based Indicators

Given a query set $\mathcal{Q}$ and a similar set $\mathcal{Q}'$ of the same size, we can define the following data-based reliability indicators:

- **Kendall correlation (τ),** compares the order in which systems are ranked according to $\mathcal{Q}$ and $\mathcal{Q}'$, regardless of the magnitude of the differences $\overline{\Delta\lambda}_{\mathsf{AB}}$. It ranges from 1 (same rankings) to -1 (reversed rankings), counting the number of system pairs that are swapped between the two rankings. For $\mathcal{Q}$ to be reliable, τ must therefore tend to 1.
- **AP correlation (τ_{AP}),** adds a top-heaviness component to Kendall τ, such that swaps between systems towards the top of the rankings are more penalized than swaps towards the bottom [23].
- **Power ratio (β),** is the fraction of pairwise system differences that result statistically significant according to query set $\mathcal{Q}$. If the difference $\overline{\Delta\lambda}_{\mathcal{Q},\mathsf{AB}}$ between two systems is deemed as statistically significant, it serves as further evidence that the true difference $\Delta\lambda_{\mathsf{AB}}$ has the same sign. For $\mathcal{Q}$ to be reliable, β must therefore tend to 100%. In this paper we compute standard 2-tailed t-tests at the 0.05 level [19].
- **Minor Conflict ratio (α_-),** is the fraction of statistically significant differences with $\mathcal{Q}$ that have a sign swap with $\mathcal{Q}'$ but are not statistically significant there. α_- is therefore the fraction of *uncertain* conclusions when measuring statistical significance, so for $\mathcal{Q}$ to be reliable α_- must therefore tend to 0%.
- **Major Conflict ratio (α_+),** is the fraction of statistically significant differences with $\mathcal{Q}$ that are also significant with $\mathcal{Q}'$ but have a sign swap. α_+ is therefore the fraction of *incorrect* conclusions when measuring statistical significance, so for $\mathcal{Q}$ to be reliable α_+ must therefore tend to 0% as well.
- **Absolute Sensitivity (δ_a),** is the minimum *absolute* difference $\overline{\Delta\lambda}_{\mathcal{Q},\mathsf{AB}}$ that need be observed between any two systems such that the differences with $\mathcal{Q}'$ have the same sign at least 95% of the times. For $\mathcal{Q}$ to be reliable, δ_a must therefore tend to 0, meaning that even small differences can be trusted.
- **Relative Sensitivity (δ_r),** is the minimum *relative* difference $\overline{\Delta\lambda}_{\mathcal{Q},\mathsf{AB}}/\max\left(\overline{\lambda}_{\mathcal{Q},\mathsf{A}}, \overline{\lambda}_{\mathcal{Q},\mathsf{B}}\right)$ that need be observed with $\mathcal{Q}$ such that the differences with $\mathcal{Q}'$ have the same sign at least 95% of the times. For $\mathcal{Q}$ to be reliable, δ_r must therefore tend to 0% too.
- **Root Mean Squared Error (ε),** measures the difference between the absolute scores with $\mathcal{Q}$ and with $\mathcal{Q}'$. Thus, for $\mathcal{Q}$ to be reliable ε must tend to 0 too.

One of the first reliability studies was conducted in 1998 by Voorhees [20], who analyzed the effect of having different assessors provide relevance judgments. Employing a methodology based on randomization, she concluded that the absolute scores could suffer wide variations between assessors, but that the ranking of systems was seldom altered, establishing $\tau = 0.9$ as the de facto minimum on ranking similarity. She also studied swap rates as a function of $\overline{\Delta\lambda}$ and suggested a minimum of 25 queries to have a somewhat stable ranking. Also in 1998, Zobel [24] studied the effect of pool depth on absolute system scores, extrapolating trends to larger pool depths. He also compared different statistical procedures in terms of power and conflict ratios.

Buckley and Voorhees [8] compared in 2000 the reliability of various effectiveness measures by mapping effectiveness differences to error rates. Extrapolating to 50 queries, they concluded that $\overline{\Delta\lambda} \geq 0.05$ produced less than 1.5% system swaps when computing Average Precision (AP), while other measures such as Precision at cutoff 10 (P@10) produced 3.6% of swaps. In 2002, Voorhees and Buckley [22] extended their work with other collections and methods, but again extrapolating trends. They concluded that with 50 queries the sensitivity of AP was $\delta_a = 0.05$, while increasing the query set size to 100 would yield $\delta_a = 0.03$. They also reported large differences across collections and effectiveness measures. Lin and Hauptmann [13] showed that the empirical model used by Voorhees and Buckley can be derived theoretically, and that the three factors affecting reliability are query set size, mean effectiveness scores, and variability of scores. Sanderson and Zobel [17] also revisited this work by computing relative sensitivity and incorporating statistical procedures to account for score variability. They concluded $\delta_r = 10\%$ with AP if coupled with statistical significance, and $\delta_r = 25\%$ if not. They observed very similar relative sensitivity between AP and P@10, arguing the use of more queries with fewer judgments as previous work suggested that much of the score variability is due to queries [4].

In 2007 Sakai [15] used similar methods to compare the reliability of several effectiveness measures, though he did not extrapolate to larger query sets. He computed τ correlations, absolute sensitivity δ_a and a variation of δ_r, and observed that these indicators were not very correlated with statistical significance, arguing the importance of considering score variability rather than just means. Voorhees revisited in 2009 [21] the use of statistical procedures with the TREC Robust 2004 collection, computing reliability indicators with an unprecedented set of 100 queries, therefore avoiding the need to extrapolate to the usual size 50. When using AP, she observed power $\beta = 47\%$ and conflict ratios $\alpha_- = 2.7\%$ and $\alpha_+ = 0.04\%$. She showed again that P@10 is less reliable than AP also in these terms; and that nDCG showed higher reliability (agreeing with Sakai [15]). She also found that minor conflicts were usually coupled with large relative differences, thus suggesting that researchers employ several large collections to draw general conclusions.

2.2 GT-based Indicators

Bodoff and Li [6] proposed Generalizability Theory [7, 18] as an alternative to measure test collection reliability that directly addresses variability of scores rather than just the mean as was common before. GT has two stages: a Generalizability study (G-study) to estimate variance components based on previous data, and a Decision study (D-study) that subsequently computes reliability indicators for a different experimental design. We consider a fully crossed design and decompose variability of scores into three components: variance due to actual differences among systems (σ_s^2), variance due to differences in difficulty among queries (σ_q^2), and variance due to the system-query interaction effect whereby some systems are particularly good (or bad) for some queries ($\sigma_{s:q}^2$). The variance due to other effects, such as assessors, is in our case confounded with the interaction effect.

Using Analysis of Variance (ANOVA) procedures, these variance components can be estimated from previous data:

$$\hat{\sigma}_{s:q}^2 = \hat{\sigma}_e^2 = \mathrm{E}M_{residual} \tag{1}$$

$$\hat{\sigma}_s^2 = \frac{\mathrm{E}M_s - \hat{\sigma}_e^2}{n_q} \tag{2}$$

$$\hat{\sigma}_q^2 = \frac{\mathrm{E}M_q - \hat{\sigma}_e^2}{n_s} \tag{3}$$

where $\mathrm{E}M_\nu$ is the expected Mean Square of component ν, and n_s and n_q are the number of systems and queries [7, 18]. These estimates can be used to compute the proportion of total variance that is due to each of the effects, such as how much of it is due to actual differences between systems.

In the D-study, we can use the variance estimates from the G-study to compute the reliability of a larger query set. To this end, two reliability indicators are usually employed:

- **Generalizability Coefficient ($\mathrm{E}\rho^2$),** is the ratio of system variance to itself plus relative error variance:

$$\mathrm{E}\rho^2\left(n_q'\right) = \frac{\sigma_s^2}{\sigma_s^2 + \frac{\sigma_e^2}{n_q'}} \tag{4}$$

  and it provides a measure of the stability of relative differences between systems $\overline{\Delta\lambda}$. By extension, it measures the reliability of the ranking. For a collection to be reliable, $\mathrm{E}\rho^2$ must therefore tend to 1.
- **Index of Dependability (Φ),** is the ratio of system variance to itself plus absolute error variance:

$$\Phi\left(n_q'\right) = \frac{\sigma_s^2}{\sigma_s^2 + \frac{\sigma_q^2+\sigma_e^2}{n_q'}} \tag{5}$$

  and it provides a measure of the stability of absolute effectiveness scores $\overline{\lambda}$. For a collection to be reliable, Φ must therefore tend to 1 as well.

The main advantage of these indicators is that they allow us to estimate the reliability of an arbitrary query set size n_q', so there is no need to follow the traditional methodologies based on random *what if* scenarios and extrapolation. From equations (4) and (5) it can be seen that the reliability of the collection increases as n_q' increases, because the estimates of query difficulty (i.e. average system performance per query) are more precise. These indicators were used by Kanoulas and Aslam [12] to derive the gain and discount functions of nDCG that yield optimal reliability when n_q' is constant.

With simple algebraic manipulation, we can calculate the minimum number of queries needed to reach some level of relative or absolute stability π:

$$n_{\mathrm{E}\rho^2}'(\pi) = \left\lceil \frac{\pi \cdot \sigma_e^2}{\sigma_s^2(1-\pi)} \right\rceil \tag{6}$$

$$n_\Phi'(\pi) = \left\lceil \frac{\pi\left(\sigma_q^2+\sigma_e^2\right)}{\sigma_s^2(1-\pi)} \right\rceil \tag{7}$$

which can be used to estimate how many more queries we need to add to our collection for it to be reliable. The main use of this approach can be found in the TREC Million Query Track [2, 1], which set out to study whether many queries with a few judgments yield more reliable results than a few queries with many judgments. The conclusion was that $n_q' \approx 80$ queries are sufficient for a reliable ranking, while $n_q' \approx 130$ are needed for reliable absolute scores.

2.3 Motivation

The two problems of GT can be clearly spotted at this point. First, equations (1) to (3) show that we do not compute the *true* σ_ν^2 variance components, but just *estimates* $\hat{\sigma}_\nu^2$ based on some previous data. If we use a different, yet similar set of systems or queries to estimate these variance components, the resulting $\mathrm{E}\hat{\rho}^2$ and $\hat{\Phi}$ scores might be very

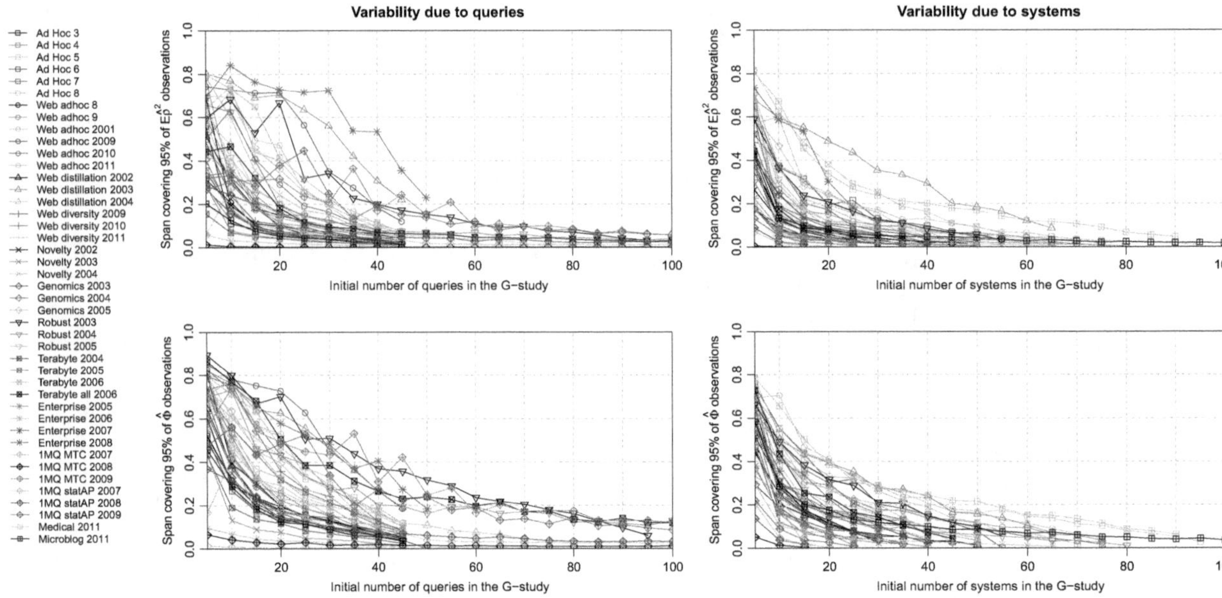

Figure 1: Variability in $E\hat{\rho}^2$ (top) and $\hat{\Phi}$ (bottom) scores as a function of the initial number of queries (left) and number of systems (right) used in the G-study to estimate variance components.

different. In a revised paper, Bodoff [5, §4.6] briefly discussed this issue and argued that differences are marginal. However, he reports the results when randomly selecting only one system per research group instead of all of them, and only one trial of such experiment. We argue that this situation is not representative because the full set of systems and the reduced set after removing runs by the same groups are actually very similar to begin with, so it is expected that reliability scores do not change much. Also, only one such randomly reduced set is compared, so there is really no evidence to support that claim. Likewise, he further suggests that as few as five queries or systems are often enough to provide stable estimates of the variance components in the G-study [5, §3.1]. We further analyze this issue in Section 3.

Second, equations (6) and (7) allow us to estimate the minimum number of queries n'_q to reach some stability level π, but the greater question is: *how much is stable enough?* Bodoff [5] mentions that in most Social Science applications a stability coefficient of 0.8 is acceptable, but there is no similar standard for Engineering applications. Kanoulas and Aslam [12] set $\Phi = 0.95$ as the target in their experiments, but this choice is arbitrary. In their analysis of the Million Query Track 2007 [2] and 2008 [1], Allan et al. [1] and Carterette et al. [9, 10] also set $E\rho^2 = 0.95$ as the target. They mention in a footnote that in their experiments $E\rho^2 = 0.95$ approximately corresponded to $\tau = 0.9$, but details are omitted. We study this issue in Section 4 by empirically mapping GT-based indicators onto data-based indicators that are easier to understand and use in practice.

3. VARIABILITY OF GT INDICATORS

To measure the effect of the number of queries and number of systems used in the G-study to estimate variance components, we use data from 43 TREC collections covering 12 tasks across 10 tracks, from TREC 3 to TREC 2011 (see Table 1). As in previous studies [22, 17, 6, 21], we remove the bottom 25% of systems so that our results are not obscured by possibly buggy implementations. For each collection, we randomly selected $n_q = 5$ queries and computed the variance components using the full set of systems. We then calculated $E\rho^2$ and Φ for the full query set size, and the required number of queries to reach 0.95 stability. This was repeated with increments in n_q of 5 queries, up the maximum permitted by the collection or 100. For each query set size, we ran 200 random trials, each of which can be considered as the possible data available for a G-study when analyzing a test collection design. The same process was followed by varying the initial number of systems n_s and using the full set of queries instead.

Figure 1 shows the variability in G-study results[1]. For each collection and initial number of queries used, the y-axis plots the length of the span covering 95% of the $E\hat{\rho}^2$ and $\hat{\Phi}$ observations in the 200 random trials. The right hand side plots show the same span lengths, but for different number of systems used in the G-study. As expected, the queries have a larger effect. Most importantly, we see that the average span length with just 5 queries is about 0.5 across collections. That is, the stability estimates could be as low as 0.3 or as high 0.8, for example, just depending on the particular set of queries we use in the G-study. In fact, estimates of the minimum number of queries required can vary in orders of magnitude if not using enough data. For example, with as many as 30 initial queries and all 184 systems from the Microblog 2011 collection, GT may suggest from 63 to 133 queries to reach $E\rho^2 = 0.95$. Similarly, from 40 initial systems and all 34 queries from the Medical 2011 collection, GT may suggest from 109 to 566 queries. In general, at least 50 queries and 50 systems seem necessary for 95% of estimates to be within a 0.1 span. This means that GT may be trusted to measure the reliability of an existing collection, but that

[1]Given the amount of datapoints displayed in this paper, we recommend to access the full-color version available online.

$$\left(\frac{L_\zeta-1}{n_q},\frac{U_\zeta-1}{n_q}\right),\text{ where} \quad (8)$$
$$L_\zeta=\frac{M_s}{M_e F_{\alpha:df_s,df_e}}$$
$$U_\zeta=\frac{M_s}{M_e F_{1-\alpha:df_s,df_e}}$$

$$\left(\frac{n_s L_\Lambda}{n_s L_\Lambda+n_q},\frac{n_s U_\Lambda}{n_s U_\Lambda+n_q}\right),\text{ where} \quad (9)$$
$$L_\Lambda=\frac{M_s^2-F_{\alpha:df_s,\infty}M_sM_e+\left(F_{\alpha:df_s,\infty}-F_{\alpha:df_s,df_e}\right)F_{\alpha,df_s,df_e}M_e^2}{(n_s-1)F_{\alpha:df_s,\infty}M_sM_e+F_{\alpha:df_s,df_q}M_sM_q}$$
$$U_\Lambda=\frac{M_s^2-F_{1-\alpha:df_s,\infty}M_sM_e+\left(F_{1-\alpha:df_s,\infty}-F_{1-\alpha:df_s,df_e}\right)F_{1-\alpha,df_s,df_e}M_e^2}{(n_s-1)F_{1-\alpha:df_s,\infty}M_sM_e+F_{1-\alpha:df_s,df_q}M_sM_q}$$

researchers should be cautious when planning a collection based on the results of a handful of systems and queries.

These results clearly evidence the need for a measure of confidence on GT indicators. Bodoff [5] suggests the use of confidence intervals to account for this variability, but only computes them for the variance components in the G-study. Confidence intervals for the ultimately more useful D-study can be worked out from various variance ratios (see equations (8) and (9)[2]). Feldt [11] derived exact $100(1-2\alpha)\%$ confidence intervals for the ratio $\zeta=\sigma_s^2/\sigma_e^2$ under the assumption of normally distributed scores. The confidence interval on $\mathrm{E}\rho^2(n'_q)$ is computed using the endpoints in (8):

$$\mathrm{E}\rho^2\left(n'_q\right)=\frac{n'_q\zeta}{1+n'_q\zeta} \quad (10)$$

Arteaga et al. [3] derived approximate $100(1-2\alpha)\%$ confidence intervals for the ratio $\Lambda=\sigma_s^2/\left(\sigma_s^2+\sigma_q^2+\sigma_e^2\right)$, again assuming a normal distribution of scores. The confidence interval on $\Phi\left(n'_q\right)$ is computed using the endpoints in (9):

$$\Phi\left(n'_q\right)=\frac{n'_q\Lambda}{1+\left(n'_q-1\right)\Lambda} \quad (11)$$

Brennan [7, §6] discusses different methods to compute confidence intervals in both G-studies and D-studies, showing that the above intervals work reasonably well even when the normality assumption is violated. The right hand side of Table 1 reports the point and 95% interval estimates of the stability of the 43 TREC collections we consider in this paper. These intervals provide a more suitable estimate of test collection reliability because they account for variability in the G-study. For example, researchers could use these intervals to infer the required number of queries to reach the lower endpoint of the interval instead of the point estimate:

$$n'_{\mathrm{E}\rho^2}(\pi)=\left\lceil\frac{\pi}{\zeta(1-\pi)}\right\rceil \quad (12)$$

$$n'_{\Phi}(\pi)=\left\lceil\frac{\pi(1-\Lambda)}{\Lambda(1-\pi)}\right\rceil \quad (13)$$

4. INTERPRETING GT INDICATORS

To empirically derive a mapping between GT-based and data-based reliability indicators, we again used the 43 TREC collections in Table 1. For each collection we proceeded as follows. Two random and disjoint query subsets of size $n_q=10$ were selected from the full set of queries; let these subsets be $\mathcal{Q}$ and $\mathcal{Q}'$. The full set of systems was evaluated with both query subsets, and all data-based reliability indicators in Section 2.1 were computed, along with the two GT-based indicators according to $\mathcal{Q}$ and $\mathcal{Q}'$. This was repeated with increments in n_q of 10 queries, up to the maximum permitted by the collection. For query subset size we ran 50 random trials, each trial providing us with 32 datapoints ($\mathrm{E}\hat{\rho}^2$ and $\hat{\Phi}$ according to $\mathcal{Q}$ and to $\mathcal{Q}'$, mapped to $\hat{\tau}$,$\hat{\tau}_{AP}$, $\hat{\beta}$, $\hat{\alpha}_-$, $\hat{\alpha}_+$, $\hat{\delta}_a$, $\hat{\delta}_r$ and $\hat{\varepsilon}$). Theoretically though, $\mathrm{E}\rho^2$ is better related to τ, τ_{AP}, β, α_-, α_+ and δ_a because it measures the stability of relative differences, while Φ is better related to δ_r and ε because it measures the stability of absolute scores. We thus mapped only these combinations.

Figure 2 shows the mappings. For each collection we fitted a model with all available datapoints. However, we dropped points for which $\mathrm{E}\hat{\rho}^2<0.8$ and $\hat{\Phi}<0.5$ so that the trends were not affected by mappings with such small stability to be even practical. These thresholds were chosen based on the observed stability of the 43 TREC collections; about 85% of them show larger stability scores (see Table 1). This resulted in over 28,000 points for each plot. In the top three plots (τ, τ_{AP} and β) we fitted the model $y=x^a$, where a is the parameter to fit. This resulted in the desired theoretical behavior that $\lim_{x\to1}y=1$ and $\lim_{x\to0}y=0$, that is, when all variability is due to system differences τ should be 1 because the ranking cannot be altered, and if all variance is due to queries then τ should be 0 because the rankings are completely random. Similarly, in the bottom four plots we fitted the model $y=(1-x)^a$, such that $\lim_{x\to1}y=0$ and $\lim_{x\to0}y=1$, that is, ε should for example be 0 if there is no variability due to queries.

As the first plot shows, all 43 collections do actually need $\mathrm{E}\rho^2>0.95$ to reach $\tau=0.9$. In general, $\mathrm{E}\rho^2=0.95$ corresponds to $\tau\approx0.85$, and on average $\mathrm{E}\rho^2\approx0.97$ is needed across collections to reach $\tau=0.9$. The two clear exceptions are found in the Million Query Track. The 2008 collection is the one that reaches the target $\tau=0.9$ with the lowest stability ($\mathrm{E}\rho^2\approx0.93$), while the 2007 collection needs the largest ($\mathrm{E}\rho^2\approx0.98$). Note that these were the two collections for which the $\mathrm{E}\rho^2=0.95\to\tau=0.9$ correspondence was established [1, 9, 10]. It should be noted here that these fits have an exponential-like shape, meaning that it is hard to achieve a mid level of τ, but once $\mathrm{E}\rho^2$ is large enough small improvements in stability translate into large improvements in τ. However, the relation between n'_q and $\mathrm{E}\rho^2$ has a logarithmic-like shape, meaning that it is increasingly more expensive to improve $\mathrm{E}\rho^2$ to begin with. Thus, it should be considered the required effort for slight improvements in τ.

The second plot shows quite high τ_{AP} scores at these levels of relative stability, but generally below τ. This suggests that the swaps in the rankings are still happening between systems at the top of the rankings [23]. The third plot shows that at these stability levels it is expected to observe statistical significance in about 80% of system comparisons. In the middle right plot we can see that the proportion of conflicting results is generally below the $\alpha=0.05$ significance level when $\mathrm{E}\rho^2\geq0.9$.

[2] $F_{\varphi:df_1,df_2}$ is the quantile function of the F distribution with df_1 and df_2 degrees of freedom. In our fully crossed design, $df_s=n_s-1$, $df_q=n_q-1$, and $df_e=(n_s-1)(n_q-1)$.

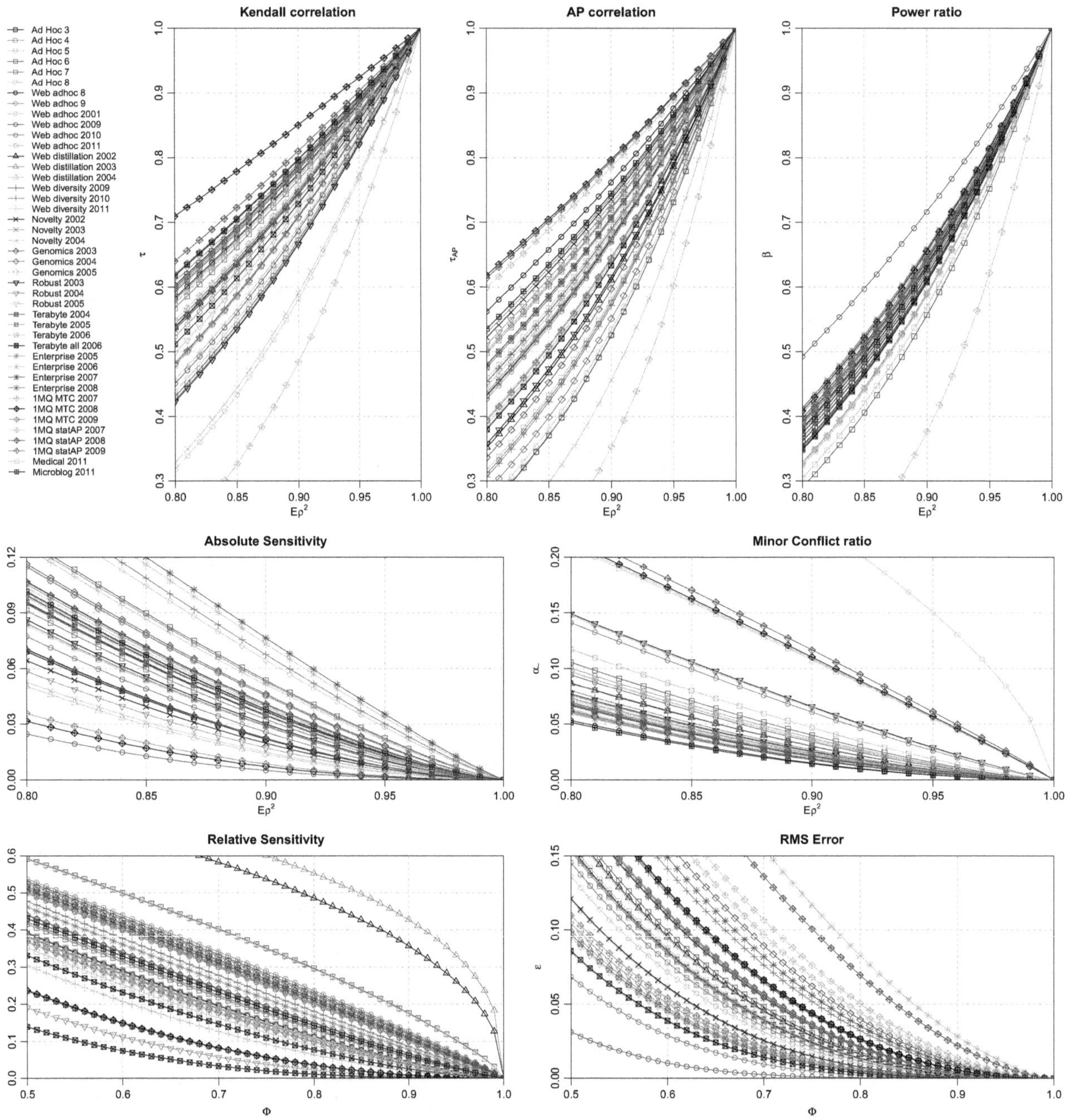

Figure 2: Mapping from GT-based to data-based reliability indicators on a per-collection basis.

Researchers interested in the particular mapping for one of these collections may use the estimates in Table 1 and the plots in Figure 2 to get a better understanding of the evaluation results and draw more informed conclusions. To assess the reliability of future collections and guide in their development process, we fitted a single model using all available data instead of one model per collection. Figure 3 shows these fits, along with 95% and 90% *prediction* intervals that theoretically cover 95% and 90% of all future observations. In terms of sensitivity, the middle left plots show that $\delta_a \approx 0.03$ for $\mathrm{E}\rho^2 \approx 0.9$, which is about 60% of what Voorhees and Buckley reported for the Ad Hoc tracks [22]; although the intervals cover their values well. In the bottom left plot we see that $\delta_r \approx 20\%$ for $\Phi \approx 0.75$, generally agreeing with Sanderson and Zobel [17]. As to statistical significance, we replicated Voorhees's [21] study with random sets of 50 queries from the Ad Hoc 7-8 topics and Robust 2004 systems. The average relative stability is $\mathrm{E}\hat{\rho}^2 \in [0.81, 0.88]$, which corresponds to $\beta \in [37\%, 54\%]$, $\alpha_- \in [3.9\%, 7.8\%]$ and $\alpha_+ \in [0.38\%, 1.3\%]$. These are again larger than she reported, but the intervals cover her values well.

Overall, these models produce a decent fit on the data, and they fill the gap between data-based methodologies and Generalizability Theory. They provide a valuable tool to rapidly assess and easily understand the reliability of a test collection design.

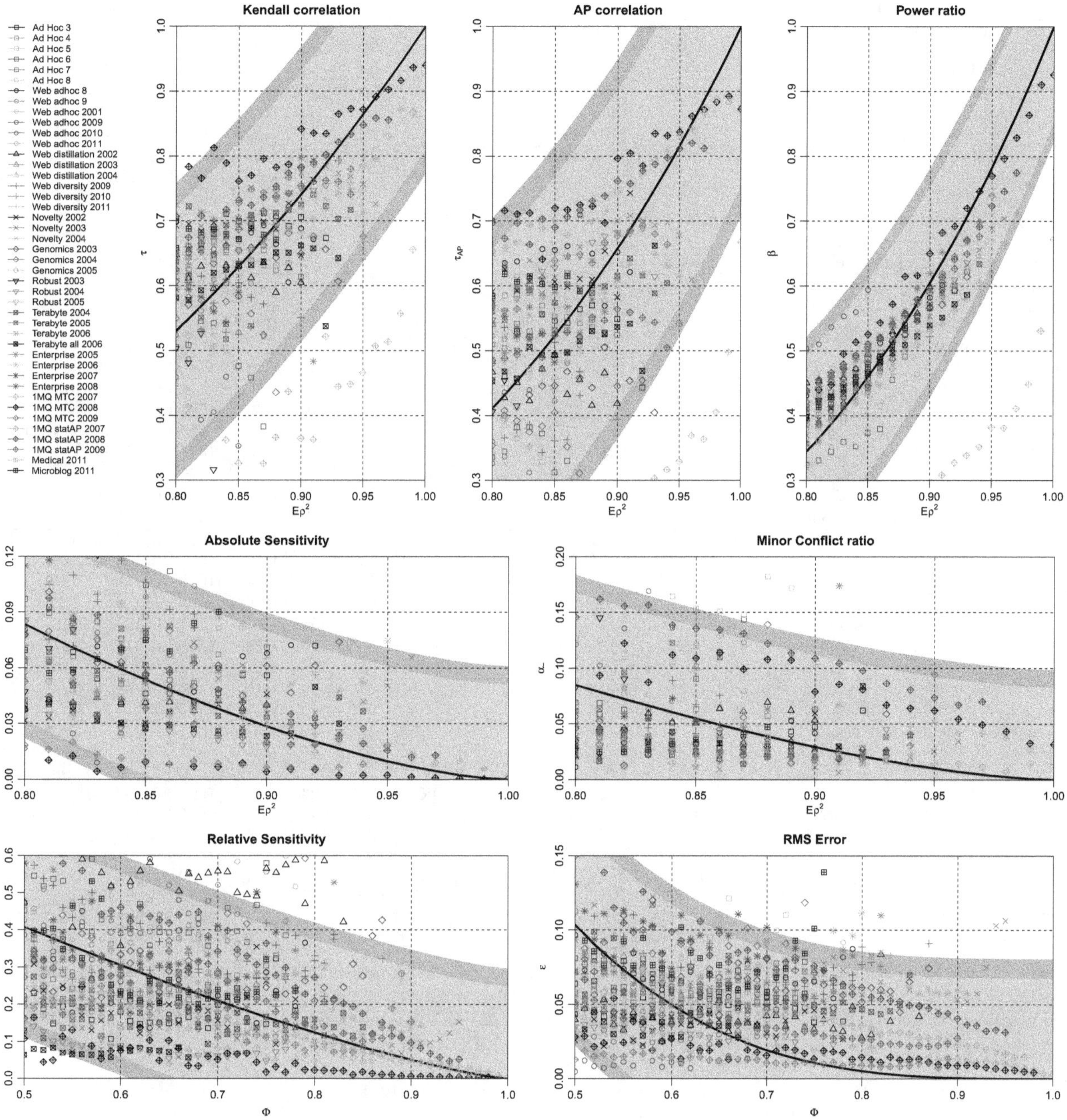

Figure 3: General mapping from GT-based to data-based reliability indicators, with 95% (dark grey) and 90% (light grey) prediction intervals.

5. DISCUSSION

The last columns in Table 1 report point and 95% interval estimates of the stability of the 43 TREC collections we considered. Collections in the same group correspond to the same tasks, providing a historical perspective on the reliability of the collections used so far since 1994 and for a variety of tasks. For example, the average relative stability in the Ad Hoc collections was $E\rho^2 \in [0.86, 0.93]$, which according to Figure 3 corresponds to $\tau \in [0.65, 0.81]$. For the Web Ad Hoc collections we find $E\rho^2 \in [0.8, 0.93]$, which would correspond to $\tau \in [0.53, 0.81]$. There are large differences within some tasks, such as Web Distillation, Genomics, Terabyte and Enterprise. This is further evidence of the variability in D-study results due to the data used in the G-study. Except for a few particular cases though, the computation of confidence intervals smooths the problem. Across collections the averages are $E\rho^2 = 0.88$ and $\Phi = 0.74$, with some tasks having very low scores. According to Figure 3 the expected τ correlation is 0.69 with variations from 0.49 to 0.95, that is, much lower than desired.

Figure 4 plots the historical trend of test collection reliability. The left plot shows that relative stability has varied in the (0.8,1) interval for the most part, but most importantly it suggests that the stability of collections has decreased very

Track	Documents	Query Set	Measure	n_s	n_q	$E\hat{\rho}^2(n_q)$		$\hat{\Phi}(n_q)$	
Ad Hoc 3	Disks 1 & 2	151-200	AP	40	50	0.933	0.893-0.963	0.786	0.661-0.88
Ad Hoc 4	Disks 2 & 3	201-250	AP	33	49	0.907	0.847-0.952	0.79	0.658-0.89
Ad Hoc 5	Disks 2 & 4	251-300	AP	94	50	0.856	0.804-0.9	0.62	0.488-0.732
Ad Hoc 6	Disks 4 & 5	301-350 *	AP	74	50	0.898	0.855-0.933	0.806	0.714-0.875
Ad Hoc 7	Disks 4 & 5	351-400 *	AP	103	50	0.919	0.891-0.943	0.799	0.71-0.864
Ad Hoc 8	Disks 4 & 5	401-450 *	AP	129	50	0.908	0.88-0.932	0.701	0.59-0.787
$\text{Web}_{\text{AdHoc}}$ 8	WT2g	401-450 *	AP	44	50	0.929	0.89-0.96	0.83	0.728-0.904
$\text{Web}_{\text{AdHoc}}$ 9	WT10g	451-500	AP	104	50	0.876	0.833-0.912	0.76	0.662-0.835
$\text{Web}_{\text{AdHoc}}$ 2001	WT10g	501-550	AP	97	50	0.862	0.813-0.904	0.711	0.598-0.801
$\text{Web}_{\text{AdHoc}}$ 2009	ClueWeb09	"W1-W50" *	AP (MTC)	71	50	0.81	0.729-0.876	0.619	0.473-0.744
$\text{Web}_{\text{AdHoc}}$ 2010	ClueWeb09	"W51-W100" *	AP	56	48	0.829	0.746-0.895	0.662	0.513-0.787
$\text{Web}_{\text{AdHoc}}$ 2011	ClueWeb09	"W101-W150" *	AP	37	50	0.804	0.685-0.895	0.702	0.537-0.835
$\text{Web}_{\text{Distillation}}$ 2002	.GOV	551-600	AP	71	49	0.901	0.858-0.935	0.84	0.762-0.898
$\text{Web}_{\text{Distillation}}$ 2003	.GOV	TD1-TD50	AP	93	50	0.45	0.249-0.619	0.315	0.144-0.492
$\text{Web}_{\text{Distillation}}$ 2004	.GOV	"WT04"	AP	74	75	0.89	0.844-0.927	0.747	0.643-0.832
$\text{Web}_{\text{Diversity}}$ 2009	ClueWeb09	"W1-W50" *	α-nDCG@20	48	50	0.903	0.852-0.943	0.847	0.759-0.911
$\text{Web}_{\text{Diversity}}$ 2010	ClueWeb09	"W51-W100" *	α-nDCG@20	32	50	0.882	0.803-0.94	0.804	0.676-0.899
$\text{Web}_{\text{Diversity}}$ 2011	ClueWeb09	"W101-W150" *	α-nDCG@20	25	50	0.844	0.725-0.929	0.719	0.535-0.865
Novelty 2002	Disks 4 & 5	50 from 300-450 *	F	42	49	0.919	0.873-0.955	0.792	0.671-0.883
Novelty 2003	AQUAINT	N1-N50	F	55	50	0.966	0.949-0.979	0.944	0.91-0.967
Novelty 2004	AQUAINT	N51-N100	F	60	50	0.801	0.708-0.876	0.181	0.1-0.301
$\text{Genomics}_{\text{AdHoc}}$ 2003	MEDLINE	"G1-G50"	AP	49	50	0.94	0.909-0.965	0.87	0.792-0.925
$\text{Genomics}_{\text{AdHoc}}$ 2004	MEDLINE	"G51-G100"	AP	43	50	0.903	0.848-0.945	0.768	0.64-0.868
$\text{Genomics}_{\text{AdHoc}}$ 2005	MEDLINE	"G101-150"	AP	62	49	0.77	0.664-0.855	0.422	0.269-0.586
Robust 2003	Disks 4 & 5	50 from 301-450 & 601-650 *	AP	78	100	0.846	0.784-0.897	0.509	0.384-0.636
Robust 2004	Disks 4 & 5	301-450 & 601-700 *	AP	110	249	0.95	0.934-0.964	0.824	0.768-0.872
Robust 2005	AQUAINT	50 from 301-700 *	AP	74	50	0.864	0.807-0.911	0.693	0.564-0.797
Terabyte 2004	GOV2	701-750 *	bpref	70	49	0.953	0.933-0.97	0.877	0.809-0.924
Terabyte 2005	GOV2	751-800 *	bpref	58	50	0.875	0.815-0.923	0.648	0.501-0.774
Terabyte 2006	GOV2	801-850 *	bpref	80	50	0.762	0.668-0.841	0.427	0.283-0.575
$\text{Terabyte}_{\text{All}}$ 2006	GOV2	701-850 *	bpref	61	149	0.94	0.913-0.962	0.719	0.617-0.812
$\text{Enterprise}_{\text{Expert}}$ 2005	W3C	EX01-EX50	AP	37	50	0.916	0.864-0.955	0.824	0.713-0.905
$\text{Enterprise}_{\text{Expert}}$ 2006	W3C	EX51-EX105	AP	91	49	0.965	0.952-0.976	0.939	0.909-0.96
$\text{Enterprise}_{\text{Expert}}$ 2007	CERC	CE001-CE050	AP	55	50	0.884	0.827-0.929	0.785	0.674-0.87
$\text{Enterprise}_{\text{Expert}}$ 2008	CERC	CE051-CE127	AP	42	55	0.565	0.315-0.757	0.28	0.11-0.498
1MQ 2007	GOV2	"MQ1-MQ10000"	AP (MTC)	29	1692	0.999	0.999-1	0.998	0.997-0.999
1MQ 2008	GOV2	"MQ10001-MQ20000"	AP (MTC)	25	784	0.998	0.996-0.999	0.988	0.979-0.995
1MQ 2009	ClueWeb09	"MQ20001-MQ60000"	AP (MTC)	35	542	0.96	0.936-0.979	0.908	0.854-0.951
1MQ 2007	GOV2	"MQ1-MQ10000"	statAP	29	1153	0.992	0.986-0.996	0.982	0.97-0.991
1MQ 2008	GOV2	"MQ10001-MQ20000"	statAP	25	564	0.978	0.962-0.99	0.969	0.946-0.986
1MQ 2009	ClueWeb09	"MQ20001-MQ60000"	statAP	35	475	0.96	0.935-0.979	0.929	0.886-0.963
Medical 2011	NLP	"M101-M135"	bpref	127	34	0.774	0.704-0.835	0.497	0.348-0.628
Microblog 2011	Tweets2011	MB1-MB50	P@30	184	49	0.92	0.899-0.938	0.818	0.747-0.869

Table 1: Summary of all 43 TREC collections analyzed. Query sets with * are used in more than one collection. Query numbers in quotes are not official, but arbitrarily named for this paper. The last two columns report the point and 95% interval estimates of the GT-based reliability indicators.

slightly with the years. The clear exceptions are again the Million Query Track collections, which specifically aimed at increasing the number of queries. Within each task it appears that stability tended to decrease as the tasks got older despite that query set sizes were normally unaltered. The second plot shows that this decrease in stability could be due to system variance getting smaller with the years. That is, systems perform more similarly as the tasks get older, indicating that retrieval techniques are generally improved. The right plot shows that query difficulty also varied within tasks. Sudden peaks may be explained by changes in the document set or in the task definition. The general trend suggests that queries are getting more alike with the years, further contributing to the decrease in reliability.

Bodoff [5, §5] discusses the incorporation of the document set as another facet in Generalizability Theory, much like queries and systems, to measure variability due to documents [14]. He argues that it does not make sense in general, because we do no assign performance scores for individual documents but for sets of documents (e.g. the first k retrieved when computing $P@k$). In our case we could compare different editions of the same task but with different document sets to get a (weak) clue of the variability due to documents. For example, the Ad Hoc task of the Web Track shows quite different stability scores in the first three editions (WT2g and WT10g collections) compared to the last three editions (ClueWeb09), given that they all used the standard query set size of 50. Similarly, the Expert Search task in the Enterprise Track shows very different stability levels when using the W3C collection or the CERC collection. We must bear in mind though that these differences might actually be due to the systems and queries used, which varied from year to year.

From the confidence intervals in Table 1, we used the models fitted in Section 4 to provide in Table 2 the estimated data-based reliability scores for all 43 collections. It is evident that expected τ correlations are well below the desired 0.9 in most cases. In that line, some collections are clearly

Track	$\hat{\tau}$	$\hat{\tau}_{AP}$	$\hat{\beta}$ (%)	$\hat{\alpha}_{-}$ (%)	$\hat{\alpha}_{+}$ (%)	$\hat{\delta}_a$	$\hat{\delta}_r$ (%)	$\hat{\epsilon}$	$\hat{n}'_{E\rho^2}(.95)$	$\hat{n}'_{\Phi}(.95)$
Ad Hoc 3	0.725-0.898	0.637-0.86	58-83	0.6-3.2	0.02-0.28	0.01-0.03	6-25	0.001-0.029	37-114	130-487
Ad Hoc 4	0.622-0.87	0.515-0.823	45-79	0.9-5.6	0.03-0.72	0.01-0.06	6-25	0.001-0.03	47-169	116-484
Ad Hoc 5	0.537-0.741	0.418-0.657	35-60	2.9-8.2	0.23-1.38	0.03-0.08	18-42	0.013-0.112	106-233	348-999
Ad Hoc 6	0.641-0.821	0.537-0.758	47-72	1.6-5.2	0.08-0.62	0.02-0.05	7-20	0.001-0.017	69-161	136-381
Ad Hoc 7	0.72-0.846	0.631-0.791	58-76	1.2-3.3	0.05-0.29	0.01-0.03	8-20	0.001-0.017	58-117	150-389
Ad Hoc 8	0.695-0.819	0.6-0.756	54-72	1.6-3.9	0.08-0.38	0.02-0.04	13-31	0.006-0.054	69-130	257-662
$\text{Web}_{\text{AdHoc}}$ 8	0.718-0.89	0.629-0.849	57-82	0.7-3.4	0.02-0.3	0.01-0.03	5-18	0-0.014	40-118	102-355
$\text{Web}_{\text{AdHoc}}$ 9	0.595-0.77	0.484-0.694	42-65	2.4-6.4	0.17-0.9	0.02-0.06	10-24	0.003-0.028	92-190	189-484
$\text{Web}_{\text{AdHoc}}$ 2001	0.554-0.749	0.437-0.668	37-62	2.8-7.7	0.21-1.22	0.03-0.08	12-31	0.005-0.051	102-220	236-640
$\text{Web}_{\text{AdHoc}}$ 2009	0.406-0.686	0.283-0.59	22-53	4.1-13.5	0.41-3.24	0.04-0.13	17-44	0.011-0.122	135-354	327-1058
$\text{Web}_{\text{AdHoc}}$ 2010	0.434-0.729	0.311-0.643	25-59	3.1-12.2	0.27-2.73	0.03-0.12	13-39	0.006-0.095	107-311	247-868
$\text{Web}_{\text{AdHoc}}$ 2011	0.34-0.728	0.221-0.642	16-59	3.2-17	0.27-4.81	0.03-0.17	10-37	0.003-0.08	112-438	188-819
$\text{Web}_{\text{Distillation}}$ 2002	0.647-0.827	0.544-0.766	48-73	1.5-5	0.07-0.59	0.01-0.05	5-16	0.001-0.009	65-154	106-292
$\text{Web}_{\text{Distillation}}$ 2003	0.019-0.255	0.004-0.148	0-10	22.8-64.4	7.89-47.06	0.23-0.64	41-82	0.108-0.6	585-2862	980-5631
$\text{Web}_{\text{Distillation}}$ 2004	0.617-0.807	0.508-0.741	44-70	1.8-5.8	0.1-0.76	0.02-0.06	10-26	0.003-0.034	112-264	288-791
$\text{Web}_{\text{Diversity}}$ 2009	0.633-0.847	0.528-0.792	46-76	1.2-5.4	0.05-0.66	0.01-0.05	4-16	0-0.009	58-166	93-301
$\text{Web}_{\text{Diversity}}$ 2010	0.535-0.839	0.416-0.782	35-74	1.3-8.3	0.06-1.4	0.01-0.08	5-23	0.001-0.025	61-234	107-457
$\text{Web}_{\text{Diversity}}$ 2011	0.401-0.811	0.278-0.746	22-70	1.7-13.8	0.09-3.35	0.02-0.14	7-37	0.001-0.081	73-360	149-826
Novelty 2002	0.679-0.877	0.582-0.833	52-80	0.9-4.2	0.03-0.44	0.01-0.04	6-24	0.001-0.026	44-136	124-457
Novelty 2003	0.86-0.941	0.81-0.919	78-90	0.3-1.1	0-0.04	0-0.01	1-4	0-0	21-52	33-94
Novelty 2004	0.374-0.685	0.252-0.589	19-53	4.1-15.1	0.42-3.93	0.04-0.15	63-87	0.309-0.709	135-392	2203-8579
$\text{Genomics}_{\text{AdHoc}}$ 2003	0.762-0.903	0.684-0.867	63-84	0.6-2.5	0.02-0.18	0.01-0.02	3-13	0-0.006	35-95	78-250
$\text{Genomics}_{\text{AdHoc}}$ 2004	0.624-0.852	0.517-0.799	45-76	1.2-5.6	0.05-0.71	0.01-0.05	7-27	0.001-0.035	56-171	146-536
$\text{Genomics}_{\text{AdHoc}}$ 2005	0.311-0.641	0.195-0.537	14-47	5.2-18.8	0.62-5.69	0.05-0.19	32-67	0.055-0.358	158-472	657-2528
Robust 2003	0.5-0.734	0.379-0.649	31-60	3.1-9.6	0.25-1.78	0.03-0.09	27-53	0.036-0.204	218-525	1087-3043
Robust 2004	0.823-0.902	0.761-0.865	72-84	0.6-1.6	0.02-0.08	0.01-0.02	7-15	0.001-0.008	175-336	693-1428
Robust 2005	0.544-0.766	0.426-0.689	36-64	2.5-8	0.17-1.32	0.02-0.08	13-34	0.005-0.066	94-227	242-733
Terabyte 2004	0.82-0.916	0.758-0.884	72-86	0.5-1.6	0.01-0.08	0-0.02	4-12	0-0.004	30-68	77-220
Terabyte 2005	0.558-0.795	0.442-0.725	38-68	2-7.5	0.12-1.19	0.02-0.07	15-41	0.008-0.103	80-217	279-947
Terabyte 2006	0.316-0.61	0.2-0.5	14-44	6-18.5	0.8-5.52	0.06-0.18	33-65	0.06-0.336	181-474	702-2406
$\text{Terabyte}_{\text{All}}$ 2006	0.772-0.897	0.696-0.859	65-83	0.7-2.4	0.02-0.16	0.01-0.02	11-29	0.004-0.043	111-269	657-1761
$\text{Enterprise}_{\text{Expert}}$ 2005	0.661-0.877	0.56-0.831	50-80	0.9-4.7	0.03-0.52	0.01-0.05	5-20	0-0.017	46-149	100-383
$\text{Enterprise}_{\text{Expert}}$ 2006	0.868-0.932	0.821-0.907	79-89	0.3-1	0.01-0.03	0-0.01	2-4	0-0	24-48	39-93
$\text{Enterprise}_{\text{Expert}}$ 2007	0.582-0.812	0.468-0.746	40-70	1.7-6.8	0.09-1	0.02-0.07	7-23	0.001-0.025	73-200	143-459
$\text{Enterprise}_{\text{Expert}}$ 2008	0.037-0.453	0.01-0.33	0-26	11.4-56	2.41-37.02	0.11-0.56	41-86	0.104-0.683	335-2277	1053-8458
1MQ 2007	0.997-0.999	0.995-0.999	99-100	0-0	0-0	0-0	0-0	0-0	11-38	30-104
1MQ 2008	0.989-0.997	0.985-0.996	98-100	0-0	0-0	0-0	0-1	0-0	16-59	81-313
1MQ 2009	0.827-0.942	0.767-0.92	73-90	0.3-1.5	0-0.07	0-0.01	2-8	0-0.002	219-710	534-1756
1MQ 2007	0.962-0.989	0.947-0.984	94-98	0-0.1	0-0	0-0	0-1	0-0	88-304	196-685
1MQ 2008	0.896-0.972	0.858-0.961	83-95	0.1-0.7	0-0.02	0-0.01	0-2	0-0	107-421	156-616
1MQ 2009	0.826-0.941	0.765-0.919	73-90	0.3-1.5	0-0.08	0-0.01	1-6	0-0.001	194-628	352-1156
Medical 2011	0.368-0.598	0.246-0.486	19-42	6.3-15.5	0.88-4.08	0.06-0.15	28-57	0.039-0.246	129-273	383-1208
Microblog 2011	0.74-0.833	0.656-0.774	60-74	1.4-3	0.07-0.24	0.01-0.03	7-17	0.001-0.011	62-105	141-315

Table 2: Predicted reliability of all 43 TREC collections analyzed. All confidence intervals are based on the fits from Figure 3 at the endpoints of the 95% confidence intervals computed with equations (10) and (11).

not reliable, such as the Web Distillation 2003, Genomics Ad Hoc 2005, Terabyte 2006, Enterprise Expert Search 2008, or the very recent Medical 2011 and Web Ad Hoc 2011. Regarding the expected RMS Error of absolute scores, we can see that collections are somewhat stable, but with clear exceptions such as Web Distillation 2003, Novelty 2004 and Enterprise Expert Search 2008.

The last two columns in Table 2 report intervals on the number of queries, as per equations (12) and (13), required to achieve 0.95 stability. In general the number of queries needs to be at least doubled, and in many cases a few hundred queries seem to be needed. This is particularly interesting for the most recent collections, such as Web Ad Hoc 2010 and 2011, Medical 2011 and Microblog 2011, which stick to the traditional size of 50 queries but need about 200. What becomes clear from these figures is that the ideal size of a collection depends greatly on the task it will be used for, and thus it is not appropriate to fix some acceptable size such as 50 or 100 throughout tasks. Each task has different characteristics and should be analyzed accordingly.

6. CONCLUSIONS

In this paper we discussed the measurement of test collection reliability from the perspective of traditional data-based methodologies and of Generalizability Theory. GT is regarded as a more appropriate, easy to use, and powerful method to assess reliability, but it has two drawbacks. First, we showed that GT is very sensitive to the particular sample of systems and queries used to estimate reliability of a larger query set. We showed that about 50 systems and 50 queries are needed for robust estimates of collection reliability. Therefore, researchers should be cautious in using GT when building new collections from scratch. To account for all this variability we discussed a more robust approach based on interval estimates of the stability indicators, which helps in making more appropriate decisions regarding number of queries or different structure in the experimental design. Second, we empirically established a mapping between GT-based and traditional data-based indicators to help interpreting results from GT which, otherwise, do not have a

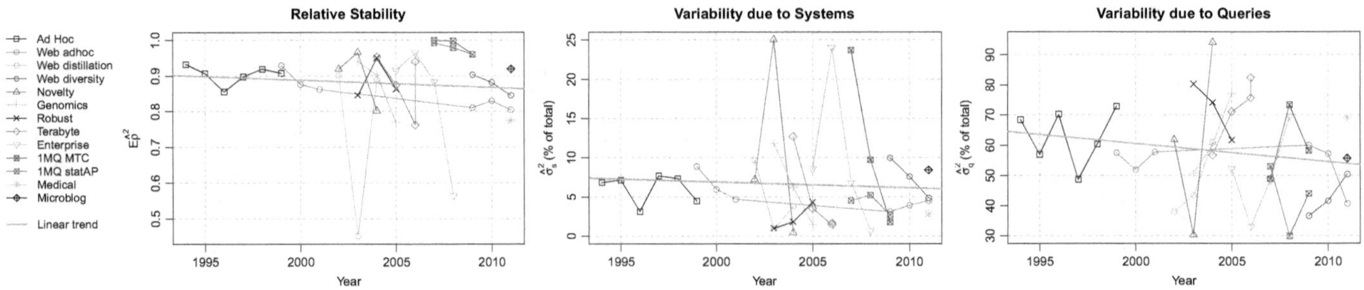

Figure 4: Historical trend of relative stability (left), variability due to systems (middle) and to queries (right).

clear and easily understandable meaning. Based on these results, we reviewed the reliability of 43 TREC test collections, evidencing that some of them are very little reliable. We show that the traditional choice of 50 queries is clearly not enough even for stable rankings, and in most cases a couple hundred queries are needed. Our results also show that the ideal query set size varies significantly across tasks, suggesting that we avoid the use of some fixed size such as 50 or 100 and that we analyze tasks and collections separately.

There are two clear lines for future research. First, we completely ignored the assessor facet in our study. It is evident that different assessors provide different results, so it would be interesting to include them in the analysis. Second, although we fitted the theoretically correct models, it is clear that they can be improved (see for instance Power and RMS Error in Figure 3). IR evaluation experiments generally violate assumptions of GT, such as normality of distributions and random sampling, so different models and features to better fit the actual data should be investigated.

We created some scripts for the statistical software `R` that can help researchers perform all these computations to easily assess the reliability of custom test collection designs. They can be downloaded from `http://julian-urbano.info`.

7. REFERENCES

[1] J. Allan, J. A. Aslam, B. Carterette, V. Pavlu, and E. Kanoulas. Million Query Track 2008 Overview. In *Text REtrieval Conference*, 2008.

[2] J. Allan, B. Carterette, J. A. Aslam, V. Pavlu, B. Dachev, and E. Kanoulas. Million Query Track 2007 Overview. In *Text REtrieval Conference*, 2007.

[3] C. Arteaga, S. Jeyaratnam, and G. A. Franklin. Confidence Intervals for Proportions of Total Variance in the Two-Way Cross Component of Variance Model. *Communications in Statistics: Theory and Methods*, 11(15):1643–1658, 1982.

[4] D. Banks, P. Over, and N.-F. Zhang. Blind Men and Elephants: Six Approaches to TREC data. *Information Retrieval*, 1(1-2):7–34, 1999.

[5] D. Bodoff. Test Theory for Evaluating Reliability of IR Test Collections. *Information Processing and Management*, 44(3):1117–1145, 2008.

[6] D. Bodoff and P. Li. Test Theory for Assessing IR Test Collections. In *ACM SIGIR*, pages 367–374, 2007.

[7] R. L. Brennan. *Generalizability Theory*. Springer, 2001.

[8] C. Buckley and E. M. Voorhees. Evaluating Evaluation Measure Stability. In *ACM SIGIR*, pages 33–34, 2000.

[9] B. Carterette, V. Pavlu, E. Kanoulas, J. A. Aslam, and J. Allan. Evaluation Over Thousands of Queries. In *ACM SIGIR*, pages 651–658, 2008.

[10] B. Carterette, V. Pavlu, E. Kanoulas, J. A. Aslam, and J. Allan. If I Had a Million Queries. In *ECIR*, pages 288–300, 2009.

[11] L. S. Feldt. The Approximate Sampling Distribution of Kuder-Richardson Reliability Coefficient Twenty. *Psychometrika*, 30(3):357–370, 1965.

[12] E. Kanoulas and J. A. Aslam. Empirical Justification of the Gain and Discount Function for nDCG. In *ACM CIKM*, pages 611–620, 2009.

[13] W.-H. Lin and A. Hauptmann. Revisiting the Effect of Topic Set Size on Retrieval Error. In *ACM SIGIR*, pages 637–638, 2005.

[14] S. Robertson and E. Kanoulas. On Per-Topic Variance in IR Evaluation. In *ACM SIGIR*, pages 891–900, 2012.

[15] T. Sakai. On the Reliability of Information Retrieval Metrics Based on Graded Relevance. *Information Processing and Management*, 43(2):531–548, 2007.

[16] M. Sanderson. Test Collection Based Evaluation of Information Retrieval Systems. *Foundations and Trends in Information Retrieval*, 4(4):247–375, 2010.

[17] M. Sanderson and J. Zobel. Information Retrieval System Evaluation: Effort, Sensitivity, and Reliability. In *ACM SIGIR*, pages 162–169, 2005.

[18] R. J. Shavelson and N. M. Webb. *Generalizability Theory: A Primer*. Sage Publications, 1991.

[19] J. Urbano, M. Marrero, and D. Martín. A Comparison of the Optimality of Statistical Significance Tests for Information Retrieval Evaluation. In *ACM SIGIR*, 2013.

[20] E. M. Voorhees. Variations in Relevance Judgments and the Measurement of Retrieval Effectiveness. In *ACM SIGIR*, pages 315–323, 1998.

[21] E. M. Voorhees. Topic Set Size Redux. In *ACM SIGIR*, pages 806–807, 2009.

[22] E. M. Voorhees and C. Buckley. The Effect of Topic Set Size on Retrieval Experiment Error. In *ACM SIGIR*, pages 316–323, 2002.

[23] E. Yilmaz, J. A. Aslam, and S. Robertson. A New Rank Correlation Coefficient for Information Retrieval. In *ACM SIGIR*, pages 587–594, 2008.

[24] J. Zobel. How Reliable are the Results of Large-Scale Information Retrieval Experiments? In *ACM SIGIR*, pages 307–314, 1998.

Deciding on an Adjustment for Multiplicity in IR Experiments

Leonid Boytsov
Language Technologies Institute
Carnegie Mellon University
Pittsburgh, PA, USA
leo@boytsov.info

Anna Belova
Abt Associates Inc.
Bethesda, MD, USA
anna@belova.org

Peter Westfall
Texas Tech University
Lubbock, TX, USA
peter.westfall@ttu.edu

ABSTRACT

We evaluate statistical inference procedures for small-scale IR experiments that involve multiple comparisons against the baseline. These procedures adjust for multiple comparisons by ensuring that the probability of observing at least one false positive in the experiment is below a given threshold. We use only publicly available test collections and make our software available for download. In particular, we employ the TREC runs and runs constructed from the Microsoft learning-to-rank (MSLR) data set. Our focus is on non-parametric statistical procedures that include the Holm-Bonferroni adjustment of the permutation test p-values, the MaxT permutation test, and the permutation-based closed testing. In TREC-based simulations, these procedures retain from 66% to 92% of individually significant results (i.e., those obtained without taking other comparisons into account). Similar retention rates are observed in the MSLR simulations. For the largest evaluated query set size (i.e., 6400), procedures that adjust for multiplicity find at most 5% fewer true differences compared to unadjusted tests. At the same time, unadjusted tests produce many more false positives.

Categories and Subject Descriptors

H.3.4 [**Information Storage and Retrieval**]: Systems and Software—*Performance Evaluation*

General Terms

Experimentation

Keywords

Statistical significance, multiple comparisons, t-test, MaxT, permutation test, randomization test, Holm-Bonferroni.

1. INTRODUCTION

1.1 Description of the Problem

Multiple comparisons/testing is a fundamental experimental issue that arises when a certain hypothesis is being repeatedly tested in different settings. For example, a researcher proposes a new retrieval algorithm and verifies its effectiveness against a baseline. In reality, this method is equivalent to the baseline, but, after exhaustive testing with different collections and parameter settings, he observes a statistically significant improvement, which has happened by chance. Most false positives arising from multiple testing can be eliminated by considering a family of tests as a whole and requiring stronger evidence, i.e., smaller p-values, in each test. This approach is commonly referred to as an adjustment for multiple comparisons (testing).

The multiple comparisons issue received a lot of attention in a bio-medical research. In clinical trials, the cost of making a wrong conclusion is high. Thus, the US Food and Drug Administration strongly recommends to employ adjustments for multiple comparisons and requires a justification if multiplicity adjustments are not performed [1]. In contrast, in IR experiments, multiplicity issues are rarely taken into account. Yet, there is a non-negligible cost related to (1) human effort in reproducing experimental results, (2) computational effort related to aggregating results from several retrieval methods. These efforts are wasted on methods whose improvement over the baseline was observed due to spurious, i.e., random effects. This is why we believe that the IR community should also adopt the practice of reporting corrected p-values.

How do we define a family of tests where p-values should be adjusted for multiple comparisons? It turns out that the choice of the family is very subjective [6, 33]. Westfall and Young state that

> ... there can be no universal agreement: statisticians have argued back and forth (sometimes vehemently) over this issue, often arriving at dramatically different conclusions [33].

They note, however, that there is more agreement on adjusting p-values in a single experiment. This is especially pertinent when results are summarized in a single conclusion [2]. For example, the researcher may compare 10 methods against a baseline, adjust p-values, and state that only 3 differences are jointly significant.

In our work we adopt this point of view and focus on adjustments that provide a strong control of a family-wise error rate (FWER) at a significance level α. In other words, the probability of observing a false positive among all tests is at most α. We also limit our attention to the case when a small number of methods are compared against a single baseline. This is a common scenario in the TREC setting, where a group submits 2-3 official runs that are evaluated by TREC organizers. Additionally, the group may evaluate several unofficial runs on their own (using relevance judgements produced by TREC assessors). There are several other approaches to deal with multiple testing that provide a weaker control: e.g., limiting the probability to observe at most $k > 1$ false positives [15, 35] or controlling a false discovery rate (FDR) [3]. We believe that these methods are less useful for the purpose of discovering and publishing significant results, but they may be appealing to practitioners, e.g., those who seek to reduce dimensionality of machine learning models [37, 21].

1.2 Related Work

There are several papers covering a wide range of reliability issues in IR experiments [22, 5, 31, 25, 38]. We encourage the reader to follow these articles and references therein.

Wilbur [34] carried out the first comprehensive assessment of methods for testing statistical significance in IR. He used several pre-TREC collections and evaluated the Wilcoxon test, the sign test, the permutation test (also known as the randomization test), and several modifications of bootstrapping. According to Wilbur, the permutation test and the bootstrapping test had comparable statistical power, superior to that of the Wilcoxon and the sign test. These findings were confirmed by Smucker et al. [27] who conducted similar experiments using several much larger TREC collections. The experiments of Cormack and Lynam [10], though, showed that both the Wilcoxon and the sign test were sufficiently accurate and powerful, but somewhat inferior to the t-test. In addition, they discovered that there was a strong agreement among the t-test, the bootstrapping test, and the permutation test. Savoy [23] recommended to use bootstrapping to estimate the sample median instead of the sample mean.

There are also several papers focusing on multiple testing adjustments in IR experiments. Tague-Sutcliffe and Blustein carried out a statistical analysis of TREC-3 results [29] and adjusted them using the Scheffé's method [24]. They found that only large differences in performance metrics could be considered significant. Blanco and Zaragoza [4] presented an experimental analysis of spurious effects in IR and advocated for adoption of multiple comparisons adjustments. Carterette [7] modeled randomness with a linear regression and adjusted p-values for multiplicity using a single-step method that relied on multivariate Student distribution. He found that in TREC-8 relative pairwise differences in the mean average precision smaller than about 50% were insignificant, which is in line with earlier findings of Tague-Sutcliffe and Blustein [29].

The focus of our paper is on permutation tests. These procedures were independently proposed by Pitman [18] and Fisher [12] in the 1930s, long before advances in computer hardware made this approach practical. A straightforward generalization of the permutation test that accounts for multiple testing is based on the closure principle proposed by Marcus et al. [16]. It entails verification of up to $2^m - 1$ null hypotheses (m is the number of tests). Westfall and Young proposed a computational shortcut, which allows one to consider only m hypotheses [33, 32]. One method of Westfall and Young, called the MaxT permutation test, was shown to have high statistical power among methods that provided a strong control of the FWER in microarray experiments [11].

2. HYPOTHESIS TESTING

We consider a standard experimental setting in IR. There is a set of queries, which represent user's information needs, ground truth relevance judgements for these queries, and several retrieval systems. Selection of queries can be thought of as a random sampling from an infinite (or very large) population. The relevance judgements are compared against ranked sets of documents (called runs) retrieved by these systems in response to q queries. Effectiveness of retrieval is characterized by scores computed separately for each query using a performance metric, such as the Expected Reciprocal Rank at depth 20 (ERR@20). The mean of query-specific scores is then used to evaluate the overall performance of retrieval systems.

Let scores of systems X and Y be represented by vectors $x = (x_1, x_2, \ldots, x_q)$ and $y = (y_1, y_2, \ldots, y_q)$ with mean values equal to $\bar{x}$ and $\bar{y}$, respectively. Even if $\bar{x}$ is substantially larger than $\bar{y}$, we cannot safely infer that Y is inferior to X in the long run. The scores are highly variable across queries [29] and it is not uncommon for an inferior system to outperform a superior system on some subpopulation of queries. Performance of X and Y in this subpopulation is not a good indication of the relative performance in the entire population of queries. There is always a chance that our test sample has a lot of queries for which the inferior system outstrips the superior one. Thus, the measured difference between X and Y could be attributed to random sampling effects.

Significance testing is a standard approach to deal with this problem. Testing involves the following steps:

1. An IR researcher formulates a null hypothesis H (or simply a null), e.g., by assuming that there is no difference in ERR@20 (or some other performance metric) between X and Y. That is, the population means are equal. In addition, he sets a significance level α that controls the rate of false rejections (i.e., false positives).

2. He chooses a test statistic $T(x, y)$ (a function of measured systems' scores) that provides evidence against the null hypothesis H. One example is the sample mean difference: $T(x, y) = \bar{x} - \bar{y}$. Small absolute values of this statistic present evidence in favor of equality of population means, while large ones may signify that H is not true. Another well-known statistic is the paired t-statistic:

$$\frac{(\bar{x} - \bar{y})\sqrt{q(q-1)}}{\sqrt{\sum_{i=1}^{q}(x_i - y_i - \bar{x} + \bar{y})^2}}. \quad (1)$$

3. The researcher quantifies the evidence provided by the test statistic. Formally, he computes a statistic value $t = T(x, y)$ from the sample data. Then, he estimates the probability of obtaining a test statistic value at least as extreme as t *under the null hypothesis* (i.e., when H is true). This probability is known as a p-value. If the p-value is less than the chosen significance level

α, the observed value of the statistic is unlikely to happen by chance (i.e., due to *randomness in selection of queries*). Thus, the researcher can reject the null hypothesis with confidence $1 - \alpha$. We discuss this approach in Section 2.2 in more detail.

To compute the p-value, we need to know the distribution of the test statistic under the null. In a parametric approach, we assume that data follows a theoretical distribution, which allows us to derive the distribution of the test statistic analytically. A widely used parametric test is the Student's t-test. In a non-parametric approach, the distribution of the test statistic is estimated through resampling of observed data (see Sections 2.2-2.3).

When, we observe an unusually small p-value this may be due to the following:

1. The null hypothesis is not true;
2. The null hypothesis is true and extreme statistic value is observed by chance;
3. Some underlying assumptions are violated.

The null hypothesis can be true even when the statistic value is extreme. Yet, if we reject the null only when the corresponding p-value is less than α, we ensure that in a series of repeated experiments the probability to incorrectly reject the true null is α. Thus, in the frequentist approach, one should avoid a temptation to interpret the p-value as the probability of the null hypothesis being true or as another measure that quantifies the veracity of the null.

Note especially the third case. If the statistical procedure relies on the distributional assumptions (such as the normality assumption for the t-test) and these assumptions are violated, this may also lead to a rejection of the null. Unfortunately, there is no good way to control a rate of false rejections due to assumption violations. Thus, it is very desirable to use tests requiring minimal assumptions such as the non-parametric randomization procedures assessed in our work.

Effectiveness of a testing procedure can be characterized by a proportion of *true positives* (correctly rejected false null hypotheses) and by a proportion of *false positives* (incorrectly rejected true null hypotheses).

2.1 Multiple Testing

The significance level α controls the probability of a false positive under the true null hypothesis only in a single test. Consider an example, where the researcher slightly modifies a baseline method 100 times and measures changes in performance. The significance level in each test is $\alpha = 0.05$. Suppose that these modifications of the baseline method did not result in any real improvements. Therefore, he may expect to obtain at least one false positive with the probability of $1 - (1 - \alpha)^{100} \approx 0.99$, and five false positives on average. If the researcher is sufficiently naïve, he may decide that merely obtaining relevance judgements for a larger set of queries will help to overcome this problem. However he would still obtain about five false positives on average, irrespective of the number of queries used. One can easily verify this statement using the simulation approach presented in Section 3.3.

This problem can be addressed by using an adjustment for multiplicity in testing. The classic adjustment method is the Bonferroni procedure. Let $p_1, p_2, \ldots, p_m$ be a set of unadjusted p-values. The Bonferroni method consists in multiplying each p_i by the number of tests m (values larger than 1 are set to 1). Then, we reject hypotheses with p-values smaller than α. This procedure is equivalent to enforcing a significance level of α/m in each of the m tests. In other words, the probability to observe a false positive in a single experiment should be α/m, assuming that the null is true. Using the union bound, we obtain that in a series of m experiments, the probability to encounter at least one false positive is controlled at the level α.

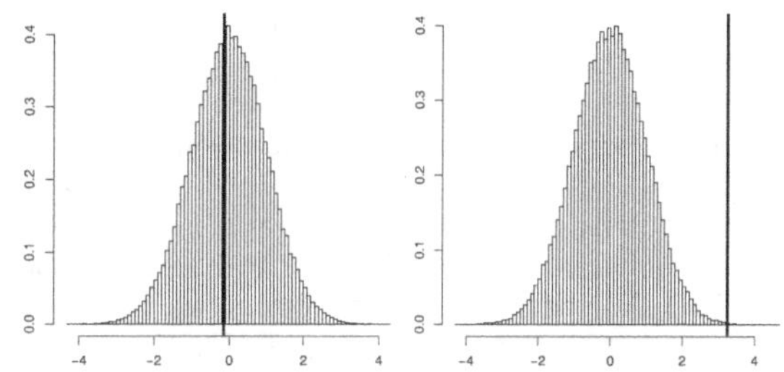
(a) Identical systems (b) Different systems

Figure 1: Distribution of statistic values obtained through random 100,000 permutations. Thick vertical lines denote statistic values computed from non-permuted system scores.

The Bonferroni adjustment provides a strong control of a family-wise error rate (FWER) at the significance level α, but it is conservative. The Holm-Bonferroni adjustment [13] is a slightly more powerful method. Let $p_1 \leq p_2 \leq \ldots \leq p_m$ be an ordered set of unadjusted p-values. The Holm-Bonferroni adjustment entails multiplying p_i by $m - i + 1$ and enforcing monotonicity of obtained values. Formally, the i-th adjusted p-value is equal to:

$$\min(1, \max_{j \leq i} p_j \cdot (m - j + 1)). \qquad (2)$$

In the subsequent sections we present several non-parametric adjustment methods based on randomization. The discussion starts with a description of the permutation test for two systems.

2.2 Permutation Test (Two Systems)

We compare two systems represented by performance scores $x = (x_1, x_2, \ldots, x_q)$ and $y = (y_1, y_2, \ldots, y_q)$. The hypothesis of interest is whether systems' mean population values of the performance metric (e.g., ERR@20) are equal. We additionally assume that under the null hypothesis H the values of x and y are outcomes of *exchangeable* multivariate random variables X and Y. This can be viewed as a combination of two random processes. The first random process generates a pair of scores in response to a query. The second process randomly labels one of the scores as belonging to X and another as belonging to Y (with equal probabilities).

From the practical perspective, this means that the distribution of the test statistic under the null hypothesis can be computed by the following randomization procedure. First, the vectors of performance scores x and y are stored in the form of the matrix with each vector representing a row:

$$\begin{vmatrix} x_1 & x_2 & \dots & x_q \\ y_1 & y_2 & \dots & y_q \end{vmatrix}.$$

Then we repeatedly obtain new pseudo-observation vectors $\widetilde{x}$ and $\widetilde{y}$ by randomly exchanging (i.e., permuting) values in the columns of this matrix. If the hypothesis H is true, all such observations are equally likely outcomes of exchangeable variables X and Y. If, in addition, we compute the value of the statistic $T(\widetilde{x}, \widetilde{y})$ for all possible 2^q permutations, we obtain an exact distribution of the test statistic (under the null). Computing all 2^q statistic values is intractable for all but very small q. Instead, the distribution could be approximated by carrying out sufficiently many random permutations B.

In Figure 1, there are two approximate distributions of the t-statistic for $B = 100,000$. The thick vertical lines indicate the values of the statistic $t = T(x, y)$ computed using non-permuted vectors x and y. The rightmost distribution in Figure 1 was computed for different systems. The value is $t \approx 3.5$ and only about one in 2,000 of computed statistic values exceeds t. The p-value is 0.0005, which means that we can reject the hypothesis that the two systems are identical at $\alpha = 0.05$. The leftmost distribution in Figure 1, was computed using very similar systems. The statistic value $t \approx 0$ and the p-value ≈ 0.5 Hence, H cannot be rejected.

The described procedure is a one-sided (one-tailed) test, because we reject the null, when the statistic value falls into the right tail of the statistic distribution. If a statistic distribution is symmetric (as distributions in Figure 1), we may choose to reject the null, when the statistic value falls into the left tail, i.e., to compute the p-value as the probability to observe a statistic value at least as low as $-T(x, y)$. If we use the paired t-statistic, the one-tailed test allows us to make statistical inference about directionality of the difference (i.e., which system has significantly better scores). For instance, if we observe a high positive value of the $T(x, y)$ we can reject the hypothesis that Y is better (has a higher average score) than X.

If we do not know a priori which method is better, we may choose only to test whether methods are different or not. To this end, one can employ a two-sided (two-tailed) test, where a p-value is computed as the probability of observing statistic values that are at least as high as $T(x, y)$ or at least as low as $-T(x, y)$. In this paper we focus on two-sided tests and leave evaluation of one-sided tests for future work. One approach to directional inference involves carrying out a two-sided test and comparing mean performance scores if the difference is significant. This approach is widespread, but not fully rigorous, because it offers no protection against choosing the wrong direction [26].

From a computational perspective, there is no need to evaluate the distribution of $T(x, y)$ explicitly. One can emulate this process using a counter C, initially set to zero. In each permutation step, we compute $T(\widetilde{x}, \widetilde{y})$ and verify if $|T(\widetilde{x}, \widetilde{y})| \geq |T(x, y)|$. When this condition is true, the counter C is incremented. For a one-sided test, one increments the counter when $T(\widetilde{x}, \widetilde{y}) \geq T(x, y)$. Finally, the p-value is computed as C/B, where B is the number permutations.

How many permutation steps are sufficient? The coefficient of variation (the standard error divided by the mean) of an estimated p-value is equal to $\sqrt{(1-p)/(pB)}$, where p is the actual p-value [12]. For $B = 20,000$ (the minimum number of permutations used in our tests) the coefficient of variation for $p = 0.05$ is approximately equal to 0.03. Using the Chebyshev's inequality, we get that the estimate is accurate within 15% for 96% of computed p-values (within 5 standard deviations).

Various test statistics can be employed with the permutation test. We use the paired t-statistic given by Equation (1), because it is asymptotically standard normal when differences in query-specific scores are independent or weekly dependent [28]. The sample mean difference does not have this property, because the variance of the statistic converges to zero when q grows. Our preliminary experiments showed that tests based on the sample mean difference sometimes suffer from subsantial loss of power.

2.3 Permutation Test (Multiple Systems)

2.3.1 Generalizing Permutation Algorithm

There are m retrieval systems and a baseline. We formulate m null hypotheses H_i by assuming that there is no difference between the system i and the baseline. Our focus is on testing all H_i jointly and controlling the FWER.

One may assume that the permutation algorithm of Section 2.2 can be generalized to deal with joint testing in the following fashion. Let $m + 1$ vectors x_i represent performance scores of $m + 1$ systems, where x_0 is the baseline. These vectors are combined in the matrix X (each vector is a row):

$$X = \begin{vmatrix} x_{01} & x_{02} & \dots & x_{0q} \\ x_{11} & x_{12} & \dots & x_{1q} \\ & \dots & & \\ x_{m1} & x_{m2} & \dots & x_{mq} \end{vmatrix}.$$

Hypothesis H_i states that there is no difference between system i and the baseline. Each H_i is associated with a test statistic $T_i(X) = T(x_i, x_0)$, where $T(x, y)$ is a paired t-statistic (Equation 1), and the counter C_i, initially set to zero. The method involves sufficiently many permutation steps, each of which includes:

- Randomly permuting values inside columns of X and obtaining a permuted matrix $\widetilde{X}$;
- Computing m statistic values $T_i(\widetilde{X}) = T(\widetilde{x}_i, \widetilde{x}_0)$ and comparing them with statistic values obtained for the original matrix X. Formally, we increment all counters C_i such that $|T_i(\widetilde{X})| \geq |T_i(X)|$.

After B iterations, we compute the i-th p-value as C_i/B. This simple procedure runs in time $O(mB)$, but it fails to produce p-values *adjusted* for multiplicity.

One can modify this method to verify the complete null hypothesis, i.e., that *all* methods are not distinguishable from the baseline. It is used as a part of the permutation-based closed testing presented in Section 2.3.3. When the complete null does not hold, there is at least one system different from the baseline. When, we reject the complete null, we are confident that not all systems are identical, but we cannot infer which systems are actually different.

To implement this modification, we need an aggregate statistic that incorporates all m individual statistics $T_i(X)$. We use the maximum of all statistics:

$$T\text{aggr}(X) = \max_{1 \leq i \leq m} |T_i(X)|.$$

Similarly to the permutation algorithm for two systems (see Section 2.2), we have one (complete) null hypothesis, one (aggregate) statistic, and a single counter C initialized with zero. We carry out B permutations steps, each of which includes random reshuffling of values inside columns of X to obtain the permuted matrix $\widetilde{X}$. If $T\text{aggr}(\widetilde{X}) \geq T\text{aggr}(X)$, we increment C. Finally, we reject the complete null if $C/B < \alpha$. To verify a partial hypothesis that methods i_1, i_2, ..., i_k are the same, one should apply this algorithm to a sub-matrix containing only rows i_1, i_2, ..., and i_k.

2.3.2 The MaxT Permutation Test

Westfall and Young proposed the MaxT permutation test, which is an extension of the generic procedure presented in Section 2.3.1. It uses the following m functions:

$$\text{MaxT}_i(X) = \max_{i \leq j \leq m} |T_j(X)|.$$

Let $t_i = |T_i(X)|$ be the statistic values computed for the *unmodified* matrix of observations X. Without a loss of generality we assume that t_i are *sorted in the non-increasing order*: $t_1 \geq t_2 \geq \ldots \geq t_m$. There are also m counters C_i (one for each hypothesis) initially set to zero.

We carry out B iterations. In each iteration, we obtain the permuted matrix $\widetilde{X}$ and compute m values $\text{MaxT}_i(\widetilde{X})$. If $\text{MaxT}_i(\widetilde{X}) \geq \text{MaxT}_i(X)$ we increment the counter C_i. In the end, we obtain p-values using the formula:

$$p\text{-value}_i = \max_{1 \leq j \leq i} C_j/B.$$

The MaxT permutation test runs in $O(mB)$ time and controls the FWER under the assumption of subset pivotality. Subset pivotality means that distributions of observed p-values under any partial null hypothesis should be the same as under the complete null hypothesis. Subset pivotality does not always hold in practice. Departure from this assumption may result in a low test power or inflated rate of false positives [35].

2.3.3 Joint Hypotheses and Closed Testing

Consider hypotheses H_1, H_2, H_3 and assume that we decided to reject at least one of them. In doing so, we express our belief that the respective joint hypothesis $H_1H_2H_3 = H_1 \cap H_2 \cap H_3$ is not true. This observation suggests that, before applying individual tests to H_1, H_2, and H_3, we could test the joint hypothesis (also known as an *intersection* hypothesis). If the intersection hypothesis is rejected, we may make additional tests to decide which individual hypotheses can be rejected. However, if $H_1H_2H_3$ is not rejected, we retain all the implied hypotheses and no further testing is needed.

This observation is the foundation of the *closed testing* procedure proposed by Marcus et al. [16]. In closed testing, *all joint* hypotheses are tested directly. If we fail to reject some joint hypothesis, we do not reject all implied hypotheses either. To test joint hypotheses, we use the permutation method from Section 2.3 and call this approach the permutation-based closed testing.

Assume now that H_1, H_2, and H_3 are true null hypotheses and, therefore, $H_1H_2H_3$ is also a true null. It is tested using an α-level test. Thus, the probability of not rejecting this *true* joint hypothesis is at least $1-\alpha$. According to the closed testing principle, if we do not reject the joint hypothesis $H_1H_2H_3$, we do not reject any of the implied hypotheses

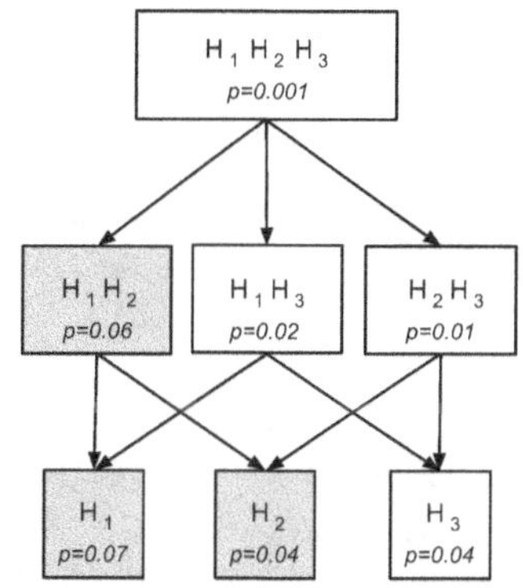

Figure 2: An example of closed testing with three hypotheses and significance level $\alpha = 0.05$. We give a p-value for each intersection hypothesis. Gray denotes hypotheses that cannot be rejected.

H_1, H_2, and H_3 either. Consequently, the probability of not rejecting any of them is at least $1-\alpha$, and the probability of rejecting at least one of them is at most α. In other words, this test controls the family-wise error rate (FWER) in the family of three hypotheses H_1, H_2, and H_3.

An example of closed testing with three hypotheses is given in Figure 2. We test 7 intersection hypotheses (including elementary hypotheses H_i as a special case) at the significance level $\alpha = 0.05$. In that, H_3 is rejected, because H_3 itself as well as all three hypotheses that include H_3, i.e., H_1H_3, H_2H_3, and $H_1H_2H_3$, have p-values smaller than α. H_1 and H_2 cannot be rejected, because we could not reject H_1H_2.

Closed testing is computationally intensive. Given that we have m individual hypotheses, there are $2^m - 1$ intersection hypotheses each of which can be tested in $O(mB)$ time. Thus, the overall runtime of the permutation-based closed testing is $O(m2^mB)$.

To reduce runtime of the complete closed testing, one could start with the narrowest intersection hypothesis (that includes all m individual hypotheses) and proceed to more generic ones. Once a hypothesis H cannot be rejected, all hypotheses implied by H need not be considered. In the example of Figure 2, we could have started with $H_1H_2H_3$ and proceeded to testing H_1H_2. Because H_1H_2 could not be rejected, H_1 and H_2 could not be rejected as well. Therefore, there is no need to test them explicitly. According to our experiments, this modification of closed-testing procedure is 10-20% faster than complete closed testing, but the overall runtime is still exponential in m.

2.4 TEST COLLECTIONS AND SYSTEMS

2.4.1 TREC Data

Similar to previous studies [27, 10, 7], we analyze data from several TREC ad hoc tasks.[1] These tasks can be divided into two groups: TRECs 3-5, 7,8, and the latest Web tasks in TRECs 19, 20. The relevance judgements in the first group are binary. They were collected through pooling to depth at least 100 [5]. The second group has 5-grade relevance judgments obtained through pooling at depth 20

[1] `http://trec.nist.gov/pubs.html`

[9]. The average number of judgements per query varies among tasks: It is roughly 2,000 in the early TRECs and is about 400 in TRECs 19, 20. The proportion of documents considered (somewhat) relevant is typically 10-20%.

The retrieval systems were represented by official runs produced by TREC participants. We downloaded raw run data and relevance judgements from the TREC website and computed the mean average precision (MAP), ERR@20 [8], and NDCG@20 using utilities `trec_eval`, and `gdeval`, which are provided by TREC organizers.

2.4.2 *Learning-to-Rank Set MSLR-WEB30K.*

This data set is provided by Microsoft[2]. It contains machine learning data with 5-grade relevance judgements, which were obtained from an obsolete training set used internally by Microsoft Bing.

MSLR-WEB30K has relevance judgments for 30,000 queries, which makes it possible to derive reliable conclusions about relative standings of retrieval systems. The judgements were collected in a way similar to a standard pooling. (Personal communication with Tao Qin, Microsoft Research Asia.)

The Microsoft data set is different from TREC collections in several important ways. First of all, it contains machine learning data, where a response of a retrieval system to a specific query is represented by a set of feature vectors such as BM25 scores [20] or document quality scores. Each document returned for a given query is represented by exactly one feature vector and a single label that expresses the degree of relevance between the document and the query.

It is not possible to access the original collection as well as to implement a system that uses data other than a set of precomputed features (stored in the MSLR-WEB30K file). In contrast to TREC runs (potentially representing thousands of documents per query), the average number of judged documents per query in MSLR-WEB30K is only 126.

Microsoft provides a rich set of 136 features, which are not scaled and have clear descriptions (i.e., they are not anonymized). This allows us to generate runs closely resembling runs obtained from a real retrieval system without actually implementing such a system. We use the following three methods or a combination thereof:

Method 1 computes a weighted sum of BM25 scores [20] as well as scores based on the language models [19] with two types of smoothing: Jelinek-Mercer and Dirichlet [36]. The value of this sum may be additionally multiplied by a linearly transformed quality score (feature 133).

Method 2 employs randomization to produce Oracle runs that improve over BM25 in a predictable way. We randomly select queries to be improved (with the probability p). A weight of each document returned in response to the selected queries is multiplied by $1+r(2^l-1)$, where r is a magnitude of improvement and l is the document relevance label.

Method 3 employs randomization to produce different runs, which nevertheless have almost identical performance scores. To make a randomized version of a run, we modify scores by adding a number drawn from a uniform distribution (with support 0–0.2) as proposed by Blanco and Zaragoza [4].

We evaluate methods using only ERR@10, which ignores documents at depths higher than 10.

[2] `http://research.microsoft.com/en-us/projects/mslr/`

Table 1: Fractions of Individually Significant Results Deemed *Insignificant* due to Adjustments for Multiplicity (smaller is better), $\alpha = 0.05$, ERR@20.

TREC	Closed test	MaxT	Holm Bonf
3	16.1%	16.4%	19.1%
4	12.7%	12.7%	15.4%
5	7.5%	8.7%	10%
7	15%	15.4%	17.3%
8	8.2%	8.2%	9.5%
19	31.1%	32.1%	32.1%
20	33.5%	33.5%	38.1%
All	16.4%	16.8%	18.8%

3. EXPERIMENTS

3.1 Statistical Tests Employed

Our experiments involve several statistical tests including permutation-based closed testing, the MaxT permutation test, and the Holm-Bonferroni adjustment (Equation 2) of the unadjusted permutation test p-values (see Section 2.2).

The permutation tests were implemented in C++. We use the Mersenne Twister generator of random numbers [17], which has a period of $2^{19937}-1$. In the analysis of the TREC data, the number of permutations $B = 50,000$; in the simulation studies with MSLR-WEB30K data, $B = 20,000$. Our code is available for download at `https://github.com/searchivarius/PermTest`.

3.2 TREC data

Our main goal is to assess (1) an agreement among different tests and (2) a degree of conservativeness of multiple comparisons adjustment procedures. To this end, we used TREC data to randomly choose retrieval systems and compare them against a randomly chosen baseline. Because closed testing run time is exponential in the number of compared systems, the number of systems is limited to 10. We carried out 50 iterations for several TREC data sets (see Table 1).

The agreement among these four statistical tests for TREC data is shown in Figure 3a. One can see that all tests that adjust for multiplicity produce larger p-values than the unadjusted permutation test. When we compare only among tests that adjust p-values for multiple comparisons, we can see that there is very little difference in p-values smaller than 0.1. The application of the Holm-Bonferroni adjustment does result in much larger p-values, but only for p-values that are already large (> 0.1). These two observations are consistent with findings by Dudoit et al. [11]. Also note that the outcomes from the permutation-based closed testing and the permutation MaxT tests are almost identical.

There is no ground truth information about relative performance of systems in TREC. This is why we can compare the power of tests only approximately, by examining the number of significant results. According to Table 1, multiple comparisons adjustments "kill" from 8 to 38 percent of results that were deemed significant by the unadjusted permutation test. In that, there is very little difference among tests. Closed testing is being slightly better than MaxT, and MaxT is slightly better than the Holm-Bonferroni adjustment. These is observed in all TRECs, but the difference

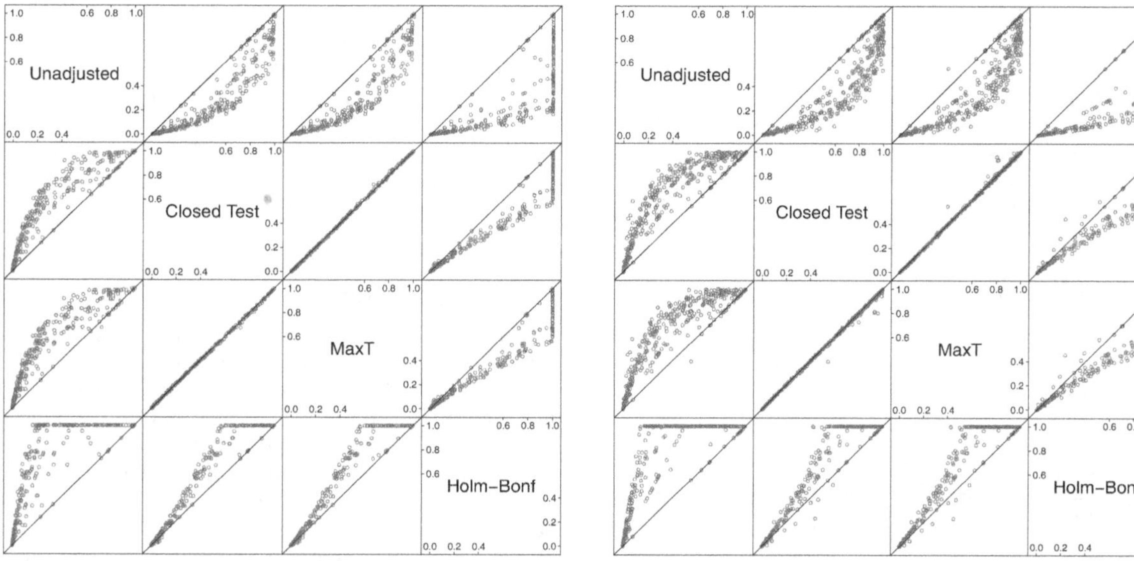

(a) TREC data, 10 runs in a comparison

(b) MSLR "Language models" data, 8 runs in a comparison

Figure 3: Agreement of p-values among adjustment methods. A performance metric is ERR@10.

is too small to be of practical importance. Note that the fraction of results that became insignificant due to multiple comparisons adjustments vary greatly among TRECs. Only about 10% of all results became insignificant in TREC-5, but in TREC-20 we lose almost half of the results, if multiple comparisons adjustments are used.

3.3 MSLR-WEB30K data

For MSLR-WEB30K we carried out a simulation study, in which we generated runs with 30,000 queries (one run for each retrieval system). These runs are "populations" that represent *long-term* performance of retrieval systems. Systems' responses to a smaller set of q queries were generated through *repeated sampling* from 30,000 queries. As a result, we obtained simulated runs representing performance of each system for selected q queries (as measured by ERR@10). In addition, mean value for each metric was computed. We evaluated several scenarios where q varied from 50 to 6,400. The sample size of 50 is intended to represent a typical TREC experimental setting, while much larger sets of queries mimic experimental environment accessible by a commercial search engine developer/researcher.

Even though the sample mean of a performance metric may vary considerably in each simulation step, the average values of ERR@10 *converge* to the mean population values (of 30,000 queries) as the number of simulation steps increases. Thus, we can use population values of performance metrics to establish ground truth relative standings among systems. To this end, we select a cutoff value $\gamma = 0.5\%$ and consider all pairs of systems with percent differences in ERR@10 (computed for the whole population) smaller than γ as identical. By repeating our analysis for $\gamma \in \{0.05, 0.1, 0.5, 1\}$, we confirmed that conclusions did not depend on the choice of this cutoff value.

The cutoff-based approach reflects a point of view that small differences in system performance may be due to sampling uncertainty of our 30,000 queries from a much larger super population. In fact, some statisticians question

> ...whether it makes sense to even consider the possibility that the means under two different experimental conditions are equal. Some writers contend that a priori no difference is ever zero (for a recent defense of this position, see Tukey 1991, 1993). Others, including this author, believe that it is not necessary to assume that every variation in conditions must have an effect [26].

The latter point is supported by studies showing that small differences may not affect user experience [30].

We generated three sets of populations: "Language Models", "Oracle 0.25", and "Oracle 0.5" (see Section 2.4). Language models were generated using Method 1. Oracle runs were generated by Method 2 with probabilities of improvement 0.25 and 0.5. The best runs in the "Language Models", "Oracle 0.25", and "Oracle 0.5" improved over the BM25 by 17%, 14%, and 27%, respectively. In each of the three population sets, we took a system with performance close to the median of the set, and replicated it 4 times using randomization (Method 3). This system is considered to be a *baseline*. Overall, each population set had 8 runs, half of which were almost identical (in terms of the mean value of ERR@10).

Given a specific sample size and a set of runs, we carried out 500 iterations of the resampling process and tested if the differences between simulated runs were significant (using selected statistical tests). Because we knew the ground truth relative standings of retrieval systems, it was possible to determine the number of false positives and negatives.

The agreement among tests is plotted in Figure 3b. The plot includes the "Language Model" runs only (all query set sizes from 50 to 6,400), because results obtained for Oracle runs are almost identical. One can see that agreement graphs are also similar to those for the TREC data:

(1) multiple comparisons adjustment procedures produce larger p-values than the unadjusted permutation test, (2) permutation-based closed testing and the MaxT permutation test agree almost ideally for the whole range of p-values, (3) the Holm-Bonferroni adjustment applied to p-values of the unadjusted permutation test is more conservative than MaxT and closed testing. Similar to TREC experiments, there is virtually no difference among all multiple comparisons methods for small p-values (< 0.1). Observation (2) is important, because we can use the MaxT permutation test instead of considerably less efficient closed testing (whose run time is exponential in the number of systems m).

Table 2: The Percent of False Negatives/Positives for different query set sizes ($\alpha = 0.05$)

	Query Set Size				
	50	100	400	1600	6400
"Lang. Models": 4 out of 8 runs same as the baseline					
Unadjusted	85.7/14.4	80.8/11.6	53.9/10.0	25.9/15.4	2.5/17.0
Closed Test	92.9/0.0	88.8/0.2	69.5/1.7	36.6/3.1	5.2/6.8
MaxT	93.9/0.0	91.8/0.2	68.0/1.2	35.7/3.0	6.3/6.6
Holm-Bonf.	94.9/2.0	92.5/1.8	69.6/2.6	37.0/3.2	6.5/6.2
"Oracle 0.25": 4 out of 8 runs same as the baseline					
Unadjusted	91.6/12.9	86.0/14.1	56.9/13.9	22.9/14.5	0.3/9.3
Closed Test	98.9/1.8	97.8/1.1	73.8/2.1	35.3/2.8	1.1/3.2
MaxT	97.3/2.0	96.4/3.0	74.4/3.0	36.1/5.5	1.0/4.6
Holm-Bonf.	98.2/2.4	97.0/3.4	74.9/2.6	37.4/4.8	1.9/4.2
"Oracle 0.5": 3 out of 8 runs same as the baseline					
Unadjusted	87.2/8.1	76.0/8.5	49.0/9.5	22.0/8.9	18.6/6.9
Closed Test	98.2/1.1	93.8/0.4	62.5/2.5	26.0/2.1	19.6/2.1
MaxT	96.9/1.2	93.3/1.6	61.4/2.6	26.5/3.2	19.4/2.8
Holm-Bonf.	97.7/1.0	91.5/2.2	62.9/2.0	27.3/2.8	19.5/2.0

Format: false negative rate (blue)/false positive rate (red).

Using ground truth relative standings for system performance, we computed the rates of false positives and false negatives for different query set sizes. In Table 2, we present results of this evaluation. Surprisingly, there is very little difference in the rate of false negatives (approximately within 10%) between the unadjusted permutation test and any test that takes multiplicity into account. However, when the number of queries is small (*as in TREC*) and the number of false negatives is close to 100%, the number of detected differences in system performance may vary greatly. For instance, in the case of 50 queries and "Language Models" runs, the unadjusted permutation test detects 14.3% of all true differences (85.7% false negative rate), while the MaxT permutation test detects only 6.1% (93.9% false negative rate). Detection of these additional 8.2% true differences comes at a price of at least one false finding in 14.4% of all experimental series. In contrast, the number of false positives for the MaxT test is zero in this case.

If the researcher does not know the true number of different systems, he may conclude that the MaxT test performs much worse than the unadjusted permutation test from the perspective of detection of true differences. Yet, in our opinion, both tests perform rather poorly in this situation. When there is a sufficient number of queries, all the tests detect more than 80-90% of true differences. In that, only the tests that adjust for multiplicity have the false positive rate close to the nominal level of $\alpha = 0.05$, i.e., they perform better than the unadjusted test, without being overly conservative.

Consider a somwehat extreme example where out of 100 systems 90 are equivalent to the baseline. For $\alpha = 0.05$, unadjusted tests may find 4-5 statistically significant differences, which represent false positives. It is possible that for small sets of queries no true difference will be detected, if false negatives rates are as high as those listed in the first column of Table 2.

3.4 Discussion

Our results indicate that multiple comparisons adjustments can be conservative when the number of queries is small. Yet, as the number of queries increases, the FWER approaches the nominal level α. When the number of queries is large, both types of tests (with and without multiplicity adjustment) detect similar number of true differences, but only adjustments for multiple comparisons allow us to control the number of false positives.

This conclusion may be affected by a small scale of our experiments (a joint test involves at most 10 systems). Yet, a small-scale experiment is not unusual for studies with both an exploratory and a confirmatory step. In the exploratory step, the researcher may "play" with a large number of systems and choose various heuristics to assess systems' performance. Multiple comparisons adjustments are typically not used in this step. The outcome is a small number of systems to be tested rigorously. During the confirmatory step, the researcher formulates the null hypotheses and carries out a statistical test using *previously unseen* data. We argue that in this step multiple comparisons adjustments are essential.

We found that the Holm-Bonferroni adjustment was only slightly more conservative than the MaxT permutation test and/or the permutation-based closed testing, which was true for both the TREC and the MSLR experiments. This is surprising, because performance scores across systems are correlated. In the presence of correlations, the MaxT permutation test and the permutation-based closed testing are expected to be more powerful than the Holm-Bonferroni adjustment.

However, permuting the data, subtracting the baseline row, and computing the t-statistic is equivalent to first subtracting the baseline row, then permuting the differences, and computing the t-statistic. Thus, it is the correlations among the deviations from the baseline that matter. We found that these correlations are small. For instance, for the TREC-8 data and ERR@20, the correlation is almost zero on average. This explains similar relative performance of the Holm-Bonferroni adjustment and the other two procedures. Yet, this may not generally hold.

We carry out an artificial experiment in which we took two vectors of performance scores such that there was a significant statistical difference between them with a p-value equal to β. Then, we replicated one of the vector several times, which is equivalent to having a number of identical systems evaluated against the baseline. The p-value computed using either the MaxT permutation test or the permutation-based closed testing procedure was approximately β in all experiments. The Holm-Bonferroni correction produced a p-value of $m\beta$, where m is the number of times the system was replicated. Thus, using the MaxT permutation test or the permutation-based closed testing can be advantageous.

While the run-time of the permutation-based closed testing procedure is exponential in the number of systems being evaluated, the run-time of the MaxT permutation test is reasonably short. For example, it takes 6 minutes to carry out 100K iterations of the MaxT permutation test to assess the joint statistical significance of 8 system runs represented by performance scores for as many as 30K queries.[3]

One may find our use of machine learning data objectionable, because it requires assumptions regarding what can be considered a retrieval system. Note, however, that the learning-to-rank community already made these assumptions and models the behavior of retrieval systems in the same fashion as we constructed "Language Model" runs. The only difference is that we designed a (semi)-linear ranking function with coefficients tuned by hand. They, instead, replace this step with a machine learning algorithm. They also evaluate performance of constructed runs using ERR@10 and employ statistical tests. Thus, it is important to show that the statistical tests work well in the learning-to-rank setting. Also note that all our tests exhibit similar behavior for both the TREC and MSLR data, which supports the hypothesis that MSLR runs are similar to those produced by real retrieval systems.

Even though permutation tests do not make strong distributional assumptions such as the normality or i.i.d, they are not assumption free. Exchangeability means that we test the equality of distributions instead of sample means. This may appear problematic, because sometimes the test may reject the null due to, e.g., a difference in variances. In particular, the simulation studies of Huang et al. [14] showed that inequality of distributions sometimes results in inflated rates of false positives. Yet, as noted by Efron and Tibshirani [12], permutation tests typically perform well in practice, even if the equality of distributions is not a reasonable assumption. They also suggest that the permutation test should be applied in all circumstances when there is "something to permute", even if other methods such, as the bootstrap test, are applicable as well. In addition, the equality of distributions is an underlying assumption for a number of statistical tests, such as the Student's t-test, already used by the IR community.

4. CONCLUSIONS

We carried out a comparative assessment of non-parametric testing procedures appropriate in the presence of multiplicity. To the best of our knowledge, such comparisons have not been done previously in the IR setting. We use only publicly available test collections and make our software available for download.

The experiments employ the realistic TREC runs and runs constructed from the Microsoft learning-to-rank dataset. The latter is a novel approach, which allows us to (1) obtain ground truth relative standings among systems, (2) experiment with much larger sets of queries and relevance assessments compared to the TREC setting.

Our recommendation is to employ adjustments for multiple comparisons in confirmatory experiments. When the number of queries is small, these procedures may, indeed, detect many fewer significant results than standard procedures such as the Student's t-test. However, the advantage of the tests without adjustments may be illusory. In this case, both the unadjusted tests and tests that adjust for multiplicity detect only a small fraction of all true differences. In that, results obtained using unadjusted tests may contain a lot of false positives, possibly, more than significant results. When there is a large query set, both types of tests may have enough power to detect true differences among systems. Yet, only the procedures adjusting for multiplicity control the rate of false positives.

The permutation-based closed testing relies on fewer assumptions than the MaxT permutation test, yet, it is impractical for all but very small sets of runs. Our recommendation is to use the MaxT permutation test, which seems to produce very similar results while being reasonably fast. In our experiments, the Holm-Bonferroni adjustments performed as well as the other adjustment methods. Yet, this may be due to specifics of our simulations, where there are small correlations among deviations from the baseline. As the example in Section 3.4 shows, permutation methods can be much more powerful when strong correlations are present.

5. ACKNOWLEDGMENTS

We thank Tao Qin (Microsoft Research Asia) for information about the MSLR collection. Leonid Boytsov was partially supported by a SIGIR Student Travel Grant. Dr. Westfall was partially supported by the following grants: NIH RO1 DK089167. Any opinions, findings, conclusions, or recommendations expressed in this material are those of the authors and do not necessarily reflect the views of any of the funding agencies.

6. REFERENCES

[1] Anonymous. Guidance for Industry - E9 Statistical Principles for Clinical Trials. Technical report, U.S. Department of Health and Human Services - Food and Drug Administration, Center for Drug Evaluation and Research, Center for Biologics Evaluation and Research, ICH, 1998.

[2] R. Bender and S. Lange. Adjusting for multiple testing—when and how? *Journal of Clinical Epidemiology*, 54(4):343 – 349, 2001.

[3] Y. Benjamini and Y. Hochberg. Controlling the False Discovery Rate: A Practical and Powerful Approach to Multiple Testing. *Journal of the Royal Statistical Society. Series B (Methodological)*, 57(1):289–300, 1995.

[4] R. Blanco and H. Zaragoza. Beware of relatively large but meaningless improvements. Technical report YL-2011-001, Yahoo! Research, 2011.

[5] C. Buckley, D. Dimmick, I. Soboroff, and E. Voorhees. Bias and the limits of pooling for large collections. *Information Retrieval*, 10:491–508, 2007.

[6] R. J. Cabin and R. J. Mitchell. To Bonferroni or not to Bonferroni: when and how are the questions. *Bulletin of the Ecological Society of America*, 81(3):246–248, 2000.

[7] B. A. Carterette. Multiple testing in statistical analysis of systems-based information retrieval experiments. *ACM Trans. Inf. Syst.*, 30(1):4:1–4:34, Mar. 2012.

[8] O. Chapelle, D. Metlzer, Y. Zhang, and P. Grinspan. Expected reciprocal rank for graded relevance. In *Proceeding of the 18th ACM conference on*

[3]The CPU is Intel Core i7 (3.4 GHz).

Information and knowledge management, CIKM '09, pages 621–630, New York, NY, USA, 2009. ACM.

[9] C. L. A. Clarke, N. Craswel, I. Soboroff, and G. V. Cormack. Overview of the TREC 2010 Web track. In *TREC-19: Proceedings of the Nineteenth Text REtrieval Conference*, 2010.

[10] G. V. Cormack and T. R. Lynam. Validity and power of t-test for comparing map and gmap. In *Proceedings of the 30th annual international ACM SIGIR conference on Research and development in information retrieval*, SIGIR '07, pages 753–754, New York, NY, USA, 2007. ACM.

[11] S. Dudoit, J. Schaffer, and J. Boldrick. Multiple hypothesis testing in microarray experiments. *Statistical Science*, 18(1):71–103, 2003.

[12] B. Efron and R. Tibshirani. *An Introduction to the Bootstrap.* Monographs on Statistics and Applied Probability. Chapman & Hall, 1993.

[13] S. Holm. A Simple Sequentially Rejective Multiple Test Procedure. *Scandinavian Journal of Statistics*, 6:65–70, 1979.

[14] Y. Huang, H. Xu, V. Calian, and J. C. Hsu. To permute or not to permute. *Bioinformatics*, 22(18):2244–2248, 2006.

[15] E. L. Lehmann and J. P. Romano. Generalizations of the familywise error rate. *Annals of Statistics*, 33(3):1138–1154, 2005.

[16] R. Marcus, P. Eric, and K. R. Gabriel. On closed testing procedures with special reference to ordered analysis of variance. *Biometrika*, 63(3):655–660, 1976.

[17] M. Matsumoto and T. Nishimura. Mersenne twister: a 623-dimensionally equidistributed uniform pseudo-random number generator. *ACM Trans. Model. Comput. Simul.*, 8(1):3–30, Jan. 1998.

[18] E. Pitman. Significance tests which may be applied to samples from any population. *Royal Statistical Society, Supplement*, 4:119–130, 1937.

[19] J. M. Ponte and W. B. Croft. A language modeling approach to information retrieval. In *Proceedings of the 21st annual international ACM SIGIR conference on Research and development in information retrieval*, SIGIR '98, pages 275–281, New York, NY, USA, 1998. ACM.

[20] S. Robertson. Understanding inverse document frequency: On theoretical arguments for IDF. *Journal of Documentation*, 60:503–520, 2004.

[21] Y. Saeys, I. n. Inza, and P. Larrañaga. A review of feature selection techniques in bioinformatics. *Bioinformatics*, 23(19):2507–2517, Oct 2007.

[22] M. Sanderson and J. Zobel. Information retrieval system evaluation: effort, sensitivity, and reliability. In *Proceedings of the 28th annual international ACM SIGIR conference on Research and development in information retrieval*, SIGIR '05, pages 162–169, New York, NY, USA, 2005. ACM.

[23] J. Savoy. Statistical inference in retrieval effectiveness evaluation. *Information Processing & Management*, 33(4):495 – 512, 1997.

[24] H. Scheffé. A method for judging all contrasts in the analysis of variance. *Biometrika*, 40(1-2):87–110, 1953.

[25] F. Scholer, A. Turpin, and M. Sanderson. Quantifying test collection quality based on the consistency of relevance judgements. In *Proceedings of the 34th international ACM SIGIR conference on Research and development in Information Retrieval*, SIGIR '11, pages 1063–1072, New York, NY, USA, 2011. ACM.

[26] J. P. Shaffer. Multiple hypothesis testing. *Annual Review of Psychology*, 46(1):561–584, 1995.

[27] M. D. Smucker, J. Allan, and B. Carterette. A comparison of statistical significance tests for information retrieval evaluation. In *Proceedings of the sixteenth ACM conference on Conference on information and knowledge management*, CIKM '07, pages 623–632, New York, NY, USA, 2007. ACM.

[28] J. Sunklodas. Approximation of distributions of sums of weakly dependent random variables by the normal distribution. In Y. Prokhorov and V. Statulevičius, editors, *Limit Theorems of Probability Theory*, pages 113–165. Springer Berlin Heidelberg, 2000.

[29] J. Tague-Sutcliffe and J. Blustein. A statistical analysis of TREC-3 data. In *Overview of the Third Text REtrieval Conference (TREC-3)*, pages 385–398, 1994.

[30] J. Urbano, J. S. Downie, B. Mcfee, and M. Schedl. How significant is statistically significant? the case of audio music similarity and retrieval. In *Proceedings of the 13th International Society for Music Information Retrieval Conference*, pages 181–186, Porto, Portugal, October 8-12 2012.

[31] W. Webber, A. Moffat, and J. Zobel. Statistical power in retrieval experimentation. In *Proceedings of the 17th ACM conference on Information and knowledge management*, CIKM '08, pages 571–580, New York, NY, USA, 2008. ACM.

[32] P. H. Westfall and J. F. Troendle. Multiple testing with minimal assumptions. *Biometrical Journal*, 50(5):745–755, 2008.

[33] P. H. Westfall and S. S. Young. *Resampling-Based Multiple Testing: Examples and Methods for p-Value Adjustment.* Wiley-Interscience, 1 edition, Jan. 1993.

[34] W. J. Wilbur. Non-parametric significance tests of retrieval performance comparisons. *J. Inf. Sci.*, 20:270–284, April 1994.

[35] H. Xu and J. C. Hsu. Applying the generalized partitioning principle to control the generalized familywise error rate. *Biometrical Journal*, 49(1):52–67, 2007.

[36] C. Zhai and J. Lafferty. A study of smoothing methods for language models applied to ad hoc information retrieval. In *Proceedings of the 24th annual international ACM SIGIR conference on Research and development in information retrieval*, SIGIR '01, pages 334–342, New York, NY, USA, 2001. ACM.

[37] J. Zhou, D. P. Foster, R. A. Stine, and L. H. Ungar. Streamwise feature selection. *Journal of Machine Learning Research*, 7:1861–1885, 2006.

[38] J. Zobel, W. Webber, M. Sanderson, and A. Moffat. Principles for robust evaluation infrastructure. In *Proceedings of the 2011 workshop on Data infrastructures for supporting information retrieval evaluation*, DESIRE '11, pages 3–6, New York, NY, USA, 2011. ACM.

Preference Based Evaluation Measures for Novelty and Diversity

Praveen Chandar and Ben Carterette
{pcr,carteret}@udel.edu
Department of Computer and Information Sciences
University of Delaware
Newark, DE, USA 19716

ABSTRACT

Novel and diverse document ranking is an effective strategy that involves reducing redundancy in a ranked list to maximize the amount of novel and relevant information available to users. Evaluation for novelty and diversity typically involves an assessor judging each document for relevance against a set of pre-identified subtopics, which may be disambiguations of the query, facets of an information need, or nuggets of information. Alternately, when expressing a *preference* for document A or document B, users may implicitly take subtopics into account, but may also take into account other factors such as recency, readability, length, and so on, each of which may have more or less importance depending on user. A *user profile* contains information about the extent to which each factor, including subtopic relevance, plays a role in the user's preference for one document over another. A preference-based evaluation can then take this user profile information into account to better model utility to the space of users.

In this work, we propose an evaluation framework that not only can consider implicit factors but also handles differences in user preference due to varying underlying information need. Our proposed framework is based on the idea that a user scanning a ranked list from top to bottom and stopping at rank k gains some utility from every document that is relevant their information need. Thus, we model the expected utility of a ranked list by estimating the utility of a document at a given rank using preference judgments and define evaluation measures based on the same. We validate our framework by comparing it to existing measures such as α-nDCG, ERR-IA, and subtopic recall that require explicit subtopic judgments We show that our proposed measures correlate well with existing measures while having the potential to capture various other factors when real data is used. We also show that the proposed measures can easily handle relevance assessments against multiple user profiles, and that they are robust to noisy and incomplete judgments.

SIGIR'13, July 28–August 1, 2013, Dublin, Ireland.

ACM 978-1-4503-2034-4/13/07 ...$15.00.

Categories and Subject Descriptors: H.3 [**Information Storage and Retrieval**]; H.3.4 [**Systems and Software**]: Performance Evaluation

Keywords: Novelty and Diversity, Evaluation

1. INTRODUCTION

The concept of relevance is the probably the most critical aspect of theoretical and practical information retrieval (IR) models. But which documents are relevant can differ from user to user depending on their exact information need, even if they start with the same keyword query. Queries can be ambiguous and/or underspecified, and the retrieval systems are required to handle these diverse information needs while providing novel information. Traditional IR evaluation also works under the assumption that documents are independently relevant separate from any user context The major drawback with this approach is that it does not penalize redundancy in rankings, potentially reducing the amount of novel information available to the user. Recently a subtopic based approach was introduced, to handle the redundancy problem and account for diverse information needs. The underlying information need for a query is decomposed into set of subtopics, and the number of novel subtopics that a document is relevant to (*i.e.* not seen earlier in the ranking) provides a measure of novelty. Various evaluation measures have been defined based on this approach [1, 9, 23, 27].

While subtopics are used to account for the diverse information needs of a query, the relation between them varies from user to user. For example, consider the query *living in India*. A person planning to visit India could be interested in *information for visitors and immigrants* & *how people live in India* whereas a student writing an essay would be more interested in *the history about life and culture in India*. Even though all of these subtopics seem relevant to the query, the importance of a subtopic is dependent on the user and the scenario in which the search was performed. It is well-known that user preferences are influenced not only by topical relevance but also by other factors such as readability, subtopic importance, completeness, etc. User profiles can be used to represent the combination of relevant subtopics and the above mentioned factors that precisely reflects the user's information need. Currently, there is no evaluation measure that (a) takes into account various factors affecting user preference, (b) handles multiple user profiles for a given query.

In this work, we propose an evaluation framework and metrics based on user preference for the novelty and diversity task. The framework revolves around the idea of assigning utility scores that reflect each set of user's preference towards each document. The document utilities are estimated using a series of preference judgments collected conditional on previously ranked documents. Document utility at a given rank implicitly accounts for the subtopic coverage, novelty, topical relevance and the other factors as well. As pointed out earlier, the utility of document could differ for each user, thus user preference are obtained across a pool of users to account for diverse information need of a query. Evaluation metrics defined based on this framework directly models a user traversing a ranking from top to bottom seeking relevant and novel information for the issued query. Therefore, our proposed measures estimate the total utility of a ranked list available to the user for a given query.

The rest of the paper is organized as follows: a detail explanation of the existing evaluation framework and the existing metrics for novelty and diversity is provided in Section 2. We point out issues with the current method and propose preference-based evaluation measures in Section 3. A description of the datasets along with the experimental design employed in our work can be found in Section 4. We analyze in detail the performance of our metrics and compare it to various existing ones in Section 5. Finally, Section 6 summarizes our findings and sketches our future directions.

2. NOVELTY/DIVERSITY EVALUATION

Search result diversification is an effective strategy to deal with the diverse information needs of the user while reducing redundancy in the ranked list [19, 28, 25]. Several methods have been proposed to produce a ranking that maximizes relevance with respect to multiple information needs for a given query, starting with the maximum marginal relevance model of Carbonell et al. [4]. In addition to new models, the task demands new evaluation metrics, as traditional IR measures are focused on relevance with respect to a single user and do not penalize redundancy in results. Zhai et al. studied the subtopic retrieval task in the context of the TREC Interactive track [17], and defined simple evaluation measures such as subtopic recall and subtopic precision based on the relevance of documents to pre-defined subtopics. Clarke et al. proposed an evaluation strategy that decomposes underlying information needs of a query into information nuggets; document utility is determined by the number of novel nuggets covered by the document. NRBP, also introduced by Clarke et al. combines ideas from α-nDCG and Rank-Biased Precision [12]. Agarwal et al. focused on the diversity problem in the web domain by taking into account the importance of user intents via a probability distribution. Each of these measures will be described in more detail below.

Almost all of the existing measures are based on the idea of explicit *subtopics*: decompositions of a given query into several pieces of information (such as facets, intents, or nuggets) that account for various underlying information needs. In this framework, novelty is solely dependent on the document's relevance to a subtopic. System effectiveness is estimated by iterating over the ranked list, penalizing relevant documents relevant to subtopic(s) seen earlier in the ranking, and rewarding documents relevant to unseen subtopic(s).

2.1 Test Collection

Test collections such as those produced for the TREC Interactive tracks [17] and the TREC Question Answering tracks [26] consist of subtopic-level judgments in documents. The TREC Web track diversity datasets created to study the problem of novelty and diversity are most suitable to our work. These datasets comprise a set of topics, and for each topic a set of subtopics that were identified semi-automatically with the help of a tool that clusters reformulations of the given query. The tool combined evidences from clicks and reformulations to obtain clusters of queries; the track organizers used these clusters to manually pick the set of subtopics for a given target query.

Binary judgments of relevance were made by NIST assessors for each subtopic to each document. Note that the use of this method means that only subtopics evidenced by a large number of users will be present in the data; interpretations that are equally "real" yet less popular will not be represented when this method is used.

2.2 Evaluation Measures

Evaluation measures for novelty and diversity must account for both relevance and novelty in rankings. It is important that redundancy caused by documents containing previously retrieved information are penalized while documents containing novel information are rewarded; as described above, this is achieved using subtopic relevance judgments. A brief description of the commonly used metrics that employ a subtopic based approach is given below:

Subtopic recall measures the proportion of unique subtopics retrieved at a given rank [27]. Given that a query q has m subtopics, the subtopic recall at rank k is given by the ratio of number of unique subtopics contained by the subset of document up to rank k to the total number of subtopics m.

$$S\text{-}recall@k = \frac{\left|\bigcup_{i=1}^{k} subtopics(d_i)\right|}{m} \tag{1}$$

α-nDCG scores a result set by rewarding newly found subtopics and penalizing redundant subtopics [13]. Computation of the gain vector and a rank discount are key to α-nDCG. The gain vector is computed by summing over subtopics appearing in the document at rank i:

$$G[i] = \sum_{j=1}^{m} (1-\alpha)^{c_{j,i}-1} \tag{2}$$

where $c_{j,i}$ is the number of times subtopic j has appeared in documents up to (and including) rank i.

The most commonly used discount function is $\log_2(1+i)$, although other discount functions are possible. Summing gains over discounts gives *discounted cumulative gain*:

$$\alpha\text{-}DCG@k = \sum_{i=1}^{k} \frac{G[i]}{\log_2(1+i)} \tag{3}$$

α-DCG must be normalized to compare the scores against various topics. This is done by finding an "ideal" ranking that maximizes α-DCG, which can be done using a greedy algorithm. The ideal ranking computation is an NP-Complete problem [5]. The ratio of α-DCG to that ideal gives α-nDCG.

Intent-aware family Agrawal et al. [1] studied the problem of evaluating ambiguous web queries. They proposed evaluating a ranking against *each* subtopic (or "intent") by any traditional IR measure, and then combining the results based on importance of subtopic. This gave rise to a family of measures that are known as *intent-aware.* Most traditional measures such as precision@k, average precision (AP), nDCG, etc. can be cast as intent-aware versions; for instance, intent-aware AP would be expressed as:

$$AP\text{-}IA = \sum_{i=1}^{m} P(i|q)AP_i \tag{4}$$

where m is the number of intents/subtopics, $P(i|q)$ is the probability that the user is interested in intent i for query q, and AP_i is average precision computed only with the documents relevant to intent i.

ERR-IA Expected Reciprocal Rank (ERR) is a measure based on "diminishing returns" for relevant documents [10]. According to this measure, the contribution of each document is based on the relevance of documents ranked above it. The discount function is therefore not just dependent on the rank but also on relevance of previously ranked documents.

$$ERR = \sum_{i=1}^{\infty} \frac{1}{i} R_i \prod_{j=1}^{i-1} (1 - R_j) \tag{5}$$

where R_i is a function of the relevance grade of the document at rank i (typically defined to be $(2^g - 1)/2^{g_{max}}$). ERR-IA is defined exactly as other intent-aware measures: a weighted average of ERR computed separately for each subtopic/intent [9]. We mention it separately because it has some appealing mathematical properties and it is one of the official measures of the TREC Web track [9].

D-Measure The D and the D# measures described by Sakai et al. [22] aim to combine two properties into a single evaluation measure. The first property is to retrieval documents covering as many intents as possible and second is to rank documents relevant to more popular intents higher than documents relevant to less popular intents.

3. PREFERENCE BASED FRAMEWORK

The subtopic-based evaluation framework focuses on estimating the effectiveness of a system based on topical and sub-topical relevance. In practice, there may be many other factors such as reading level, presentation, completeness, etc. that influence user preferences for one document over another in the context of novelty and diversity [8]. We could describe the information needs of a user that consists of various details, including specifics of pieces of information the user is interested in, reading level of the user, and so on in a *user profile.* Then we could view the goal of an evaluation measure as determining how well a ranking of documents satisfies a variety of user profiles.

In order to understand the concept of user profiles, let us consider an example query from the TREC Web track: *air travel information.* Table 1 shows the subtopics defined for the Web track's diversity task and provides the information needs of three different possible users for the given query (assuming we restrict ourselves to the TREC paradigm and represent the user's information need using only subtopics). We can think of user A as a first time air traveler looking for information on air travel tips and guidelines, user B as a journalist writing an article on the current quality of air travel and looking for statistics and reports to accomplish the task, and user C as an infrequent traveler looking restrictions and rules for check-in and carry-on luggages. Therefore, user A's profile for the above example query consists of subtopics d and e, user B's of c, and user C's of a and b. (In practice, the profiles would typically take into account other factors such as presentation, readability, and other factors as well, but none of this need be made explicit.)

Even if we restrict ourselves to modeling only subtopics, there are some issues with existing measures based on subtopics:

(a) subtopic identification is challenging and tricky as it is not easy to enumerate all possible information needs for a given query,

(b) measures often require many parameters to be set before use,

(c) measures assume subtopics to be independent of each other but in reality this is not true.

Let us refer to Table 1 to consider these issues. First, given the granularity of these subtopics, it would not be difficult to come up with additional subtopics that are not in the data. Top-ranked results from a major search engine suggest subtopics such as "Are airports currently experiencing a high level of delays and cancellations?", "I am disabled and require special consideration for air travel; help me find tips.", and "My children are flying alone, I am looking for tips on how to help them feel comfortable and safe." Are users with these needs going to be satisfied by a system that optimizes for the limited set provided?

Second, measures like α-nDCG and ERR-IA have a substantial number of parameters that must be decided on. Some are explicit, such as α (the penalization for redundancy) [15] or $P(i|q)$ (the probability of an intent/subtopic given a query[1]). Others are implicit, hidden in plain sight because they have "standard" settings: the log discount of α-nDCG or the grade value R_i of ERR-IA, for instance. Each of these parameters requires some value; it is all too easy to fall back on defaults even when they are not appropriate.

Third, some subtopics are clearly more related to each other than others (in fact, we used this similarity to create the profiles). Documents that are relevant to subtopic c are highly unlikely to also be relevant to any of the other subtopics, but it is more likely that there are pages relevant to both subtopics a and b.

In this work, we sidestep these issues by proposing an evaluation framework that simply allows users to express preferences between documents. Their preferences may be based on topical or subtopic relevance, but they may also be based on any other factors that are important to them. Preferences can be obtained over many users to capture the varying importance of topics and factors, and when a sufficiently large set of preferences has been obtained, systems can be evaluated according to how well they satisfy those users. Preference judgments have only scantly been used in IR evaluation, having been introduced by Rorvig [20] but not subject to empirical study until recently [7, 2]. Comparison studies between absolute and preference judgments show that preference judgments can often be made faster than graded judgments, with better agreement between assessors (and more consistency with individual assessors) [7] while making much finer distinctions between documents.

[1]The original definition of α-nDCG has parameters for subtopic weights as well.

	subtopic	*user A*	*user B*	*user C*
a.	What restrictions are there for checked baggage during air travel?			✓
b.	What are the rules for liquids in carry-on luggage?			✓
c.	Find sites that collect statistics and reports about airports		✓	
d.	Find the AAA's website with air travel tips.	✓		
e.	Find the website at the Transportation Security Administration (TSA) that offers air travel tips.	✓		

Table 1: An example topic (*air travel information*) along with its subtopics from the TREC Diversity dataset and three possible user profiles indicating the interests of different users.

Chandar and Carterette [8] introduced a preference-based framework similar to ours, but there exists no evaluation measure that incorporates preference judgments directly for novelty and diversity. Moreover, that work focused only on ranking novel documents, without considering the more general question of diversity—that different users will have different preferences depending on their profile.

3.1 Test Collection

Chandar and Carterette's preference-based framework is based on so-called *levels* of preference judgments. We use a similar idea; in this work, a test collection of preferences for novelty and diversity consists of two different types of preference judgments:

1. simple pairwise preference judgments, in which a user is shown two documents and asked which they prefer.
2. *conditional* preference judgments, in which a user is shown three or more documents and asked to express a preference between two of them, supposing they had read the others.

Simple pairwise preferences produce a relevance ranking: given a pair of documents, assessors select the preferred document based on some criteria. We expect topical relevance to be the primary criteria, although many criteria (such as ease of reading, completeness of information, salience of article, etc.) could factor into an assessor's choice. Since different users may have different needs and different preferences for the same query, pairs can be shown to multiple assessors to get multiple preferences. Over a large space of assessors, we would expect that documents are preferred proportionally according to the relative importance of the subtopics they are relevant to, with various other factors influencing finer-grained orderings.

Simple pairwise preferences cannot capture novelty; in fact, two identical documents should be equally preferred in all pairs in which they appear and therefore end up tied in the final ordering. Conditional preference judgments attempt to resolve this by asking for a preference for a given pair of document *conditional on* the information in other documents shown to the assessor at the same time. The assessor is asked to read those documents, then select which of the remaining two they would like to see *next*.

Figure 1 illustrates conditional preferences with a triplet of documents: the assessor would read document X, then select which of A or B they would like to see next[2] We

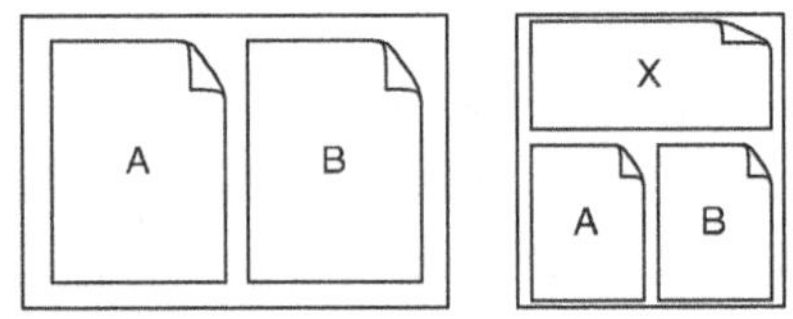

Figure 1: Left: a simple pairwise preference for which an assessor chooses A or B. Right: a triplet of documents for conditional preference judgments. An assessor would be asked to choose A or B conditional on having read X.

expect the assessor's choice to be based not only on topical relevance, but also on the amount of *new* information given what is provided in the top document. Again, they can use other factors in their preferences, but novelty should be a primary consideration: if X is identical to A, we expect them to choose B, and then a system that ranks X and A adjacent would be penalized for failing to rank B after X.

Similarly, we could obtain preferences with quadruplets of documents, quintuplets of documents, and so on. In practice it becomes increasingly difficult for assessors to make such fine distinctions, so we limit to only obtaining judgments on triplets. A triplet in our framework corresponds to Chandar and Carterette's "level 2" judgments; as they showed, these judgments capture most of the necessary information about novelty. Preferences conditional on greater numbers of other documents contribute less and less [8].

3.2 Preference-Based Evaluation Measure

We propose a model-based measure using preferences to assess the effectiveness of systems for the novelty and diversity task. Model based measures can be composed from three underlying models: *browsing model*, *document utility*, and *utility accumulation* [6]. The way users interact with the ranked list is defined by the browsing model; we rely on the most accepted model in which the user scans documents down a ranked list one-by-one and stops at some rank k. The document utility model defines the amount of utility provided by a single document, and utility accumulation models the total utility derived during browsing.

We define our utility based model for novel and diversity ranking task as follows: a user scanning documents down a ranked list derives some utility $U(d)$ from each document and stops at some rank k. We hypothesize that the utility of a document at rank i is dependent on previously ranked document (*i.e.* d_1 to d_{i-1}). Given a probability distribution for a user stoping at rank k, the utility accumulation model

[2]Note that any document may be placed at the top of a triplet; it need not be the most preferred document among the simple pairwise preferences.

can be defined as:

$$Prf = \sum_{k=1}^{n} P(k)U(d_1, ..., d_k) \quad (6)$$

where $P(k)$ is the probability that a user stops at rank k and $U(d_1, ..., d_k)$ is the total utility of the documents from ranks 1 through k.

We simplify this by formulating $U(d_1, ..., d_k)$ as a sum of individual document utilities conditional on documents ranked before:

$$Prf = \sum_{k=1}^{n} P(k) \sum_{i=1}^{k} U(d_i|S) \quad (7)$$

where $P(k)$ is the probability that a user stops at rank k, $U(d_i|S)$ gives the utility of the document at rank i conditional on a set of previously ranked document S, and the sum from $i = 1$ to k gives the total utility of all documents from ranks 1 through k. There are two main components in the above equation: the probability that a user stops at a given rank ($P(k)$) and the utility of a document conditioned of previously ranked documents ($U(d_i|S)$). Carterette demonstrated different ways to model the stopping rank from the various ad-hoc measure such as Rank Biased Precision [16], nDCG, and Reciprocal Rank [6].

1. $P_{RBP}(k) = (1-\theta)^{k-1}\theta$
2. $P_{DCG}(k) = \frac{1}{log(k+1)} - \frac{1}{log(k+2)}$
3. $P_{RR}(k) = \frac{1}{k(k+1)}$

Finally, we define the document utility model in which the document utility at a given rank is conditioned on previously ranked documents. The utility of the document at rank i is given by $U(d_i)$ for $i = 1$ since at rank 1 the user would not have seen any other documents and therefore would not be conditioning on any other documents. For subsequent ranks, utility is $U(d_i|d_{i-1}, ...d_1)$, indicating that the utility depends on documents already viewed.

Now our goal is to estimate these utilities using preference judgments. Since we have simple pairwise preferences and conditional preferences in triplets, we decompose the document utility model as follows:

$$U(d_i|S) = \begin{cases} U(d_i), & \text{if } i \text{ is } 1 \\ U(d_i|d_{i-1}), & \text{if } i \text{ is } 2 \\ F(\{U(d_i|d_j)\}_{j=1}^{i-1}), & \text{if } i > 2 \end{cases} \quad (8)$$

where the function $F()$ takes an array of conditional utilities ($U(d_i|d_j)$).

The utility $U(d_i)$ can be directly obtained using the pairwise judgments; we simply compute it as the ratio of number of times a document was preferred to the number of times it appeared in a pair. The utilities $U(d_i|d_{i-1})$ can similarly be obtained from the conditional preferences, computed as the ratio of the number of times d_i was preferred conditional on d_{i-1} appearing as the "given" document to the number of times it appear with d_{i-1} as the "given" document. Note that these utilities can be computed regardless of how many times a document has been seen, how many different assessors have seen it, how much disagreement there is between assessors, and so on. Although, a document must be shown at least few time in order to determine its relevance estimate. An estimate of the document's utility is obtain using the ratio of number of times the document was preferred to the number of time it was shown.

We experiment with two functions for $F()$: *average* and *minimum*. The intuition behind these functions can be explained with the help of an example. Consider a ranking $R = \{d_1, d_2, d_3\}$. According to equation 8 the utility of d_3 depends on $U(d_3|d_1)$ and $U(d_3|d_2)$. The minimum function assumes that d_3 cannot be any more useful conditional on both d_1 *and* d_2 than it is on either one separately, thus giving a sort of worst-case scenario. The average function assumes that the utility of d_3 conditional on both d_1 and d_2 is somewhere in between its utility conditioned on each separately, giving d_3 some benefit of the doubt that it may contribute something more when appearing after both d_1 and d_2 than it does when appearing after either one on its own.

Our measure as defined is computed over the entire ranked list. In practice, measures are often computed only to rank 5, 10, or 20 (partially because relevance judgments may not be available deeper than that). When we compute the measure to a shallower depth, we must normalize it so that it will average over a set of queries. As a final step in the computation of $nPrf$, we normalize equation 7 cut off at rank K by the ideal utility score.

$$nPrf[K] = \frac{Prf[K]}{I\text{-}Prf[K]} \quad (9)$$

where $I\text{-}Prf[K]$ is the ideal utility score that could be obtained at rank K. This can be obtained by selecting the document with the highest utility value conditioned on previously ranked documents. Document (d_1) with the highest utility value takes rank 1 and the document with highest utility when conditioned on d_1 takes rank 2 and so on.

Table 2 provides an example showing the distinction between our preference based measure and α-$nDCG$ based on the user profiles in Table 1. The document utilities are estimated by obtaining the preference judgements for all documents from all three users. We would expect the users' preferences to be consistent with their information need, for example user A would prefer d_1 and d_2 consistently to other documents that are not relevant to their needs (but relevant to other needs). Notice that α-$nDCG$ weighs all subtopics equally but the preference measure takes into account the dependency between the subtopics.

4. EXPERIMENT DESIGN

In Section 3.2, we proposed various evaluation measures based on a user model for novelty and diversity. Evaluation of the proposed metrics is challenging since there is no ground truth to compare to; there are only other measures. Approaches used in the past to validate newly introduced metrics include comparing the proposed measure to existing measures or click metrics [18, 11]; using user preferences to compare the metrics [24]; and evaluating the metric on various properties such as discriminative power [21]. While each of these approaches have their own advantages, we argue that comparison of existing measures to our measures using simulated data is suitable for this work.

Remember, our goal is to build evaluation measures for our preference based framework that assigns utility scores to a document based on user preferences. In reality, user preferences are based on various implicit factors that include

	documents	subtopics a	b	c	d	e
user A	d_1	✓				
	d_2		✓			
user B	d_3			✓		
	d_4			✓		
user C	d_5				✓	
	d_6					✓

List1	List2	
d_1	d_1	
d_2	d_3	
d_3	d_5	
1.0	1.0	α-$nDCG$
0.9	1.0	Preference Measure

Table 2: Synthetic example with 6 documents and 5 subtopics. The first ranked list does not satisfy all users where as the second one does but both rankings are scored by equally by α-nDCG, while the preference metrics are able to distinguish the difference.

subtopic relevance as well as many other properties. Since prior work [8] has suggested that presence of subtopics in a document plays a major role in user preferences, we believe it is important to validate our measures when user preferences are based solely on subtopic information. We therefore rely on the existing data with subtopic information to *simulate* user preferences.

4.1 Data

In our experiments, we used the ClueWeb09 dataset[3] consisting of one billion web pages (5 TB compressed, 25 TB uncompressed), in ten languages, crawled in January and February 2009. A subset of this collection with only English documents was used for the diversity task at TREC in 2009/10/11 [14]. A total of 150 queries have been developed and judged for the TREC Web track; the number of subtopics for each ranges from 3 to 8. For the diversity task, subtopic level judgments are available for each subtopic indicating the relevance of a document to each subtopic along with the general topical relevance. We also acquired the experimental runs submitted to TREC each year by Web track participants. A total of 48 systems were submitted by 18 groups in 2009, 32 system by 12 groups in 2010, and 62 systems by 16 groups in 2011.

4.2 Simulation of Users and Preferences

In order to verify and compare our metrics against existing measures, we acquire preferences by simulating them from subtopic relevance information. These will be based on the preferences of simulated users that are modeled by groupings of subtopics (as in Table 1). In this way we use only data that is provided as part of the TREC collection, and therefore achieve the fairest and most reproducible possible comparison between evaluation measures. In reality, our measure is well-suited for crowd-sourced assessments in a way that other measures are not, but we save that experiment for future work.

We created our user profiles by generating search scenarios for each query and marking subtopics relevant to the scenario. In Section 3, we explained our reasoning behind the user profiles in Table 1 for the query *air travel information*; we use the same approach to obtain the user profiles for all TREC queries. The user profiles were created by the authors of this paper and have been made available for public download at `http://ir.cis.udel.edu/~ravichan/data/profiles.tar`. In addition, there is a mega-user that we refer to as the "TREC profile"; this user is equally interested in all subtopics.

[3]http://lemurproject.org/clueweb09.php

These profiles are used to determine the outcome of preferences. For simple pairwise preferences, we always prefer the document with greater number of subtopics relevant to the user profile. In the case of a tie, we make a random choice between the left or right document. For conditional preferences, we have three documents (left, right, and top); between the left and the right, we prefer the document that contains the greater number of subtopics relevant to the user profile and not present in the top document. Preference judgments obtained this way are used to compute our preference measure. Finally, using the "TREC profile" to simulate preferences for our measure offers the most direct comparison to other measures.

5. ANALYSIS

We have presented a family of preference-based measures for evaluating systems based on novelty and diversity, and outlined the advantages of our metrics over existing subtopic-based measures. In this section, we demonstrate how our metrics take into account the presence of subtopics implicitly by comparing them with α-nDCG, ERR-IA, and s-recall.

5.1 System Ranking Comparisons

5.1.1 System Performance

We evaluated all experimental runs submitted to TREC in 2009, 2010, and 2011 using our proposed measure with three different stopping probabilities $P(k)$ and two different utility aggregation functions $F()$. Figure 2 shows the performance of systems with respect to both α-nDCG and our preference measure computed with $P_{RBP}(k)$ and $F_{avg}()$ functions and preferences simulated using the "TREC profile". Each point represents a TREC participant system; they are ordered on the x-axis by α-nDCG. Black circles give α-nDCG values as computed by the `ndeval` utility used for the Web track; blue x's indicate the preference measure score for the same system. In these figures we can see that the preference measure is roughly on the same scale as α-nDCG, though typically $0.1 - 0.2$ lower in an absolute sense.

Each increase or drop in the position of x's indicates disagreement with α-nDCG. The increasing trend of the curves in Figure 2 indicates that the correlation between the preference measure and α-nDCG is high. A similar trend was observed while using different $P(k)$ and $F()$ functions as well (not shown). Both α-nDCG and our preference measure agree on the top ranked system in 2009 and 2010.

We analyzed the reason behind disagreement by carefully looking at the actual ranked lists. We investigated how α-nDCG and our proposed measures reward diversified sys-

	ERR-IA@20	s-recall@20
α-nDCG@20	0.893	0.828
ERRIA@20	-	0.739

Table 3: Kendall's τ correlation values between the existing evaluation measures. Values were computed using 48 submitted runs in TREC 2009 dataset.

tems on a per topic basis. Based on our analysis, the major reason for disagreement is that α-nDCG penalizes systems that miss documents containing many unique subtopics more harshly than the preference measure does. Much of the variance in α-nDCG scores is due to differences in rank position of the documents with the greatest number of unique subtopics. In practice, this explains the lower scores returned by the preference measure as well.

5.1.2 Rank Correlation Between Measures

We measure the stability of our metrics using Kendall's τ by ranking the experimental runs under different effectiveness measures. Kendall's τ ranges from -1 (lists are reversed) to 1 (lists are exactly the same), with 0 indicating essentially a random reordering. Prior work suggest that a τ value of 0.9 or higher between a pair of rankings indicates high similarity between rankings while a value of 0.8 or lower indicates significant difference [3].

Figure 3 summarizes the rank correlations between existing subtopic-based metrics and our proposed preference metric using all three $P(k)$ (plus using no $P(k)$ at all—equivalent to a uniform stopping probability) and both $F()$ functions, simulating preferences with the "TREC profile". The correlations are fairly high across TREC datasets, $P(k)$ functions, and $F()$ functions. The $P_{DCG}(k)$ rank function fares worst, with correlations dipping quite a bit for the 2010 data in particular. Subtopic recall is a very simple non-rank based metric for diversity and thus the Kendall's τ values are expected to be slightly lower.

For comparison, Table 3 shows the Kendall's τ correlation values between α-nDCG, ERR-IA and s-recall. These correlations are similar to those in Figure 3, suggesting that the ranking of systems given by our preference measure varies no more than the rankings of systems given by any two standard measures.

There is almost no difference between the correlations for $F_{avg}()$ and $F_{min}()$ functions for aggregating utility. In fact, the correlation between preference measures computed with those two is nearly 1. Thus we can conclude that the choice of $F()$ (between those two options) does not matter. There is a great deal of difference depending on choice of $P(k)$, however, and thus this is a decision that should be made carefully based on the observed behavior of users.

5.2 Evaluating Multiple User Profiles

The experiments above are based on the "TREC profile", a user profile that considers every subtopic to be equally relevant. In this experiment, we demonstrate the ability of our methods to handle multiple, more realistic user profiles and show the stability of our metrics. Measures based on absolute subtopic judgments cannot naturally incorporate multiply-judged documents. One must average judgments, or take a majority vote, or use some other scheme. In contrast, judgments from multiple users can be incorporated easily into our preference framework in the estimation of document utilities, as the document utility is simply the ratio of number of times a document was preferred to the number of times it appeared in a pair, regardless of which user or assessor happened to see it.

We simulate preferences for each of our user profiles for each topic in the TREC set. We compute the preference measure using each profile's preferences separately (giving at least three separate values for each system: one for each user profile), and then use the full set of preferences obtained to compute a single value of the measure. Note that the latter case is *not* the same as computing the preference measure with the "TREC profile": the TREC profile user uses all subtopics to determine the outcome of a preference, while individual users would never use a subtopic that is not relevant to them to determine the outcome of a preference.

We can also compute subtopic-based measures such as α-nDCG against our profiles. To do this, we simply assume that only the subtopics that are relevant to the profile "count" in the measure computation. We will compare values of measures computed this way to our preference measures.

Our hypothesis for this experiment is twofold: 1) that the preference measure computed for a single profile will correlate well to subtopic-based measures computed against the same profile; 2) that the preference measure computed with preferences from all profiles will *not* be the same as an average of the individual profile measures, and also not the same as subtopic-based measures computed as usual. In other words, that the preference measure based on preferences from many different users is measuring something *different* than the preference measure based on preferences from one user, and also different from the subtopic measures.

Figure 4 shows the results of evaluating systems using user profile 1, 2, and 3 for each topic and averaging over topics (note that the user profile number is arbitrary; there is nothing connecting user profile 1 for topic 100 to user profile 1 for topic 110). We can see that the system ranking changes for both α-nDCG and the preference measure, as expected. The correlation between the two remains high: 0.83, 0.88, and 0.82 for user profile 1, 2, and 3 respectively. This is in the same range of correlation values that we saw in Figure 3, and supports the first part of our hypothesis.

Figure 5 shows the results of evaluating systems with all user profiles, comparing to the evaluation with the TREC profile and with α-nDCG computed with all subtopics. Note here that all three rankings are different, as evidenced by the τ correlations reported in the inset tables. This supports the second part of our hypothesis: that allowing many different users the opportunity to express their preferences can result in a different ranking of systems than treating all assessors as equivalent, as the TREC profile and α-nDCG do.

5.3 Incomplete Judgments

The test collection procedure discussed in Section 3.1 requires two sets of judgments: pairwise and conditional preferences. The number of pairwise judgments increases quadratically with increase in number of documents in the pool; it is not feasible to collect a complete set of preferences. We envision that our measure would *always* be computed with incomplete judgments. For this experiment we test the stability of our measures by comparing the system rankings obtained by using all preference judgments against a set of incomplete judgments.

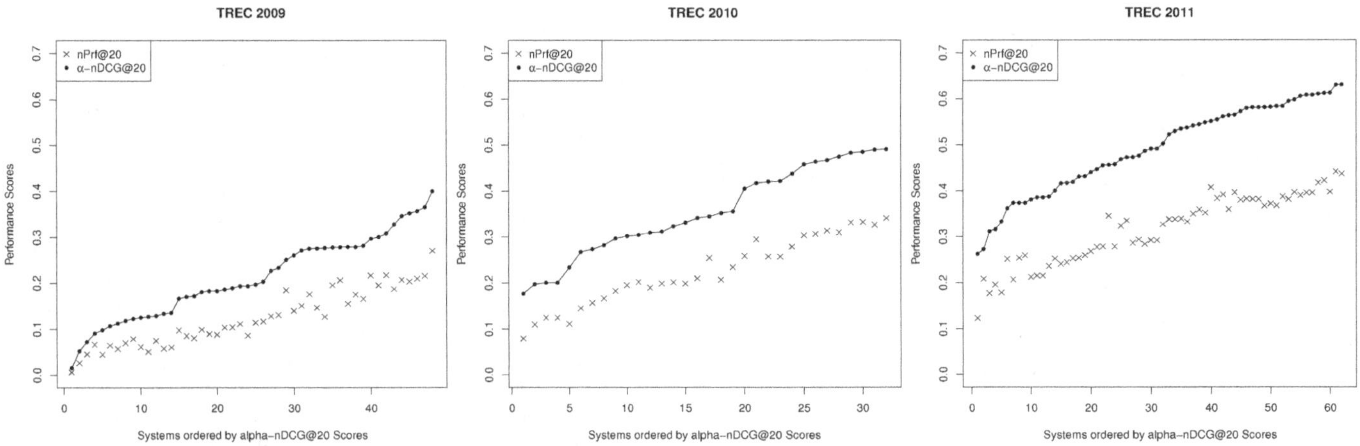

Figure 2: TREC 09/10/11 diversity runs evaluated with our preference based metric at rank 20 (nPrf@20) with P_{RBP} and $F_{Average}$. Compare to α-nDCG scores.

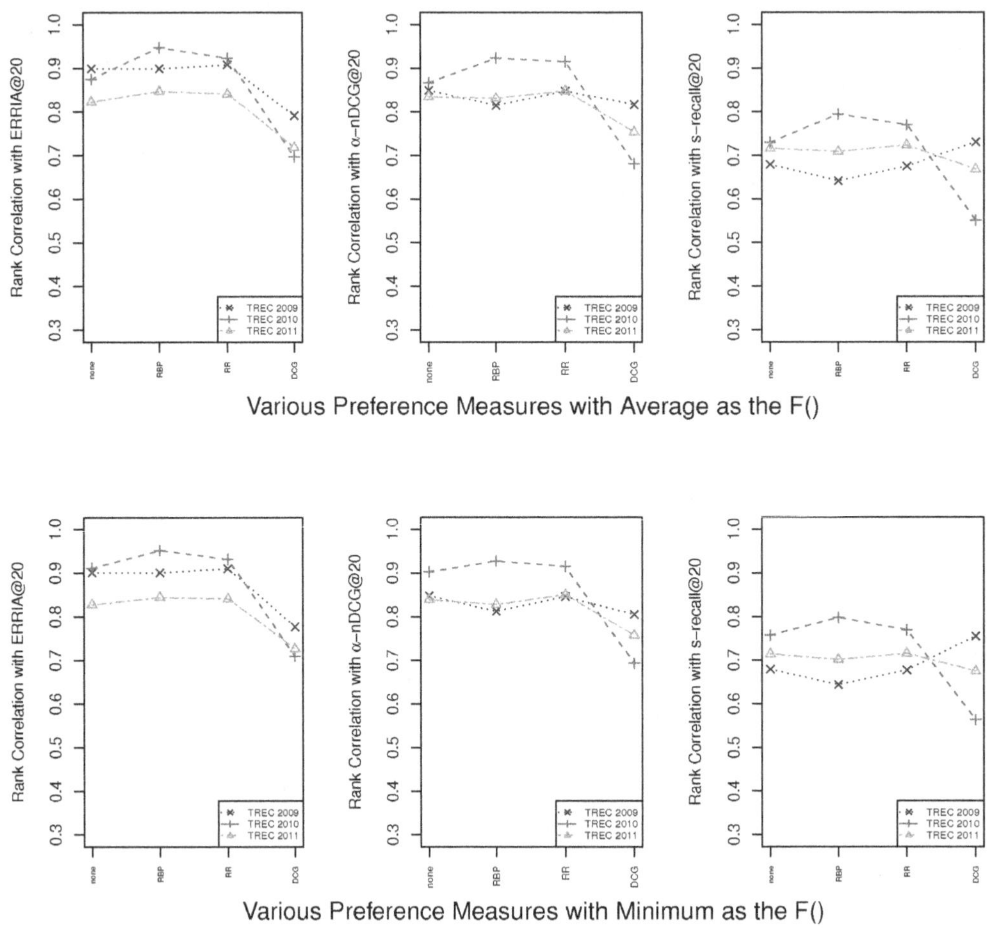

Figure 3: Kendall's τ correlation values between our proposed measures and α-nDCG, ERR-IA, s-recall. Values were computed using the submitted runs in the TREC 2009/10/11 dataset. The scores for various $P(k)$ and F() are shown.

To do this, we randomly select N triplets of documents for each query. For each triplet, one document is randomly selected to be the "top" document that the other two would be judged conditional on. Though we do not explicitly obtain simple pairwise preferences, we expect that there will be enough cases in which the top document is not relevant to the user profile that they must fall back on a simple pairwise comparison. We then sample 5 user profiles (with replacement) from those defined for the topic and simulate their preferences for the triplet. In this way we obtain $5N$ prefer-

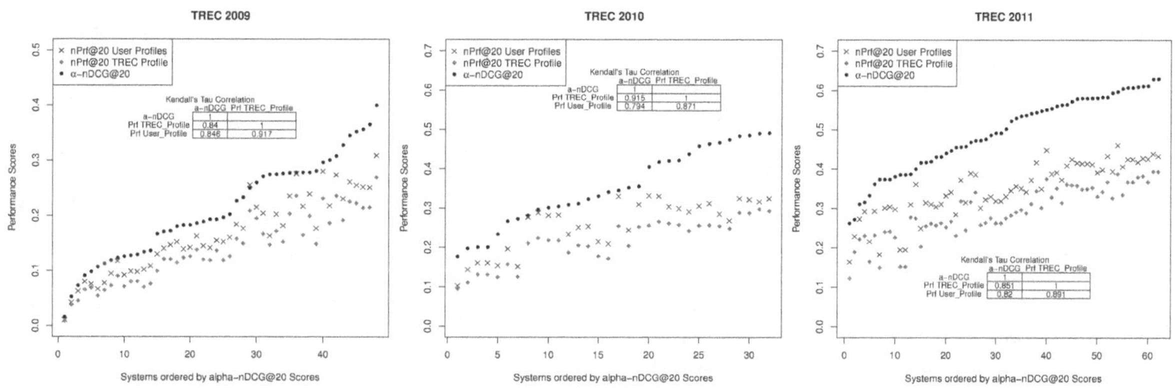

Figure 5: Comparison between α-nDCG, our preference measure computed using the TREC profile, and our preference measure computed using a mix of user profiles. Note that all three rankings, while similar, have substantial differences as well.

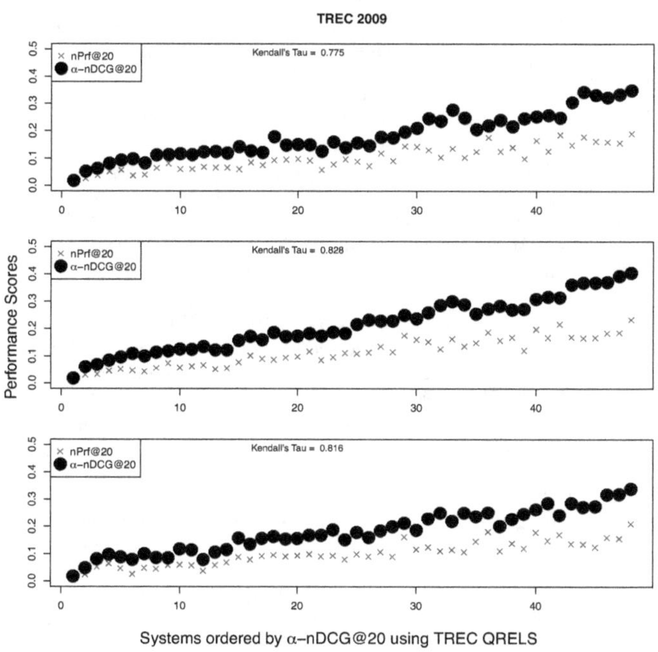

Figure 4: Comparison between α-nDCG and our preference measure computed against user profiles 1 (top), 2 (middle), and 3 (bottom) for TREC 2009 systems.

ences for each topic in a similar way as would be done in a real crowd-sourced assessment. We use those preferences to compute our measure, then compute the correlation to the measure computed with all available preferences. We repeat this 10 times for each topic, measure the correlation each time, and average the correlations.

Figure 6 shows the correlation between the system rankings when evaluated using complete judgements and increasing numbers of preferences. Correlation tends to increase as the number of preferences increases, though it does not reach 0.9. This may be partly because user profiles are not evenly represented in the preferences (which is in fact more realistic than when they are, as in the full-preference case), and

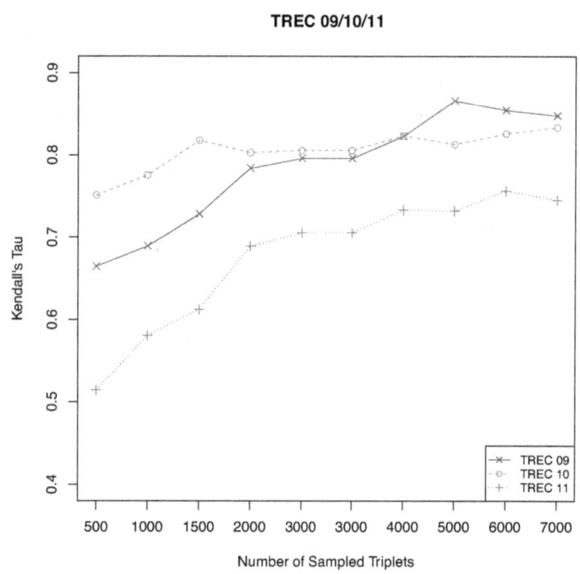

Figure 6: TREC 09/10/11 diversity runs evaluated with our preference based metric at rank 20 (nPrf@20) with P_{RR} and $F_{Minimum}$ using single assessor with complete judgments and multiple assessor with incomplete judgments.

partly because our max number of preferences is still a fairly small fraction of the total number possible: even selecting triplets from only 100 documents, there are over 161,000 possible triplets, of which we have only obtained less than 5%! Thus we expect that continuing to increase the number of triplets would continue to push the correlations higher, even though we see dips in the trend (due to variance).

6. CONCLUSION AND FUTURE WORK

In this work, we proposed a novel evaluation framework and a family of measures for IR evaluation. Our measure incorporates novelty and diversity, but can also incorporate any property that influences user preferences for one document over another. Our measure is motivated directly by a user model and has several advantage over the existing measures based on explicit subtopic judgments: it captures subtopics implicitly and at finer-grained levels, it accounts for subtopic importance and dependence as expressed by user preferences, and it requires few parameters—only a stopping probability function, for which there are several well-accepted options that can be chosen from by comparing to user log data. It correlates well with existing measures, but also clearly measures something different (which is a positive for a new measure).

This framework and measure is most well-suited for assessments done by crowd-sourcing. In a crowd-sourced assessment, we would naturally have a large user base with a wide range of preferences. Over a large number of preferences, the most important subtopics and intents would naturally emerge; documents relevant to those would become the documents with the highest utility scores. Yet the conditional judgments would prevent too many documents with those subtopics from reaching the top of the ranking. The measure is designed to handle multiple judgments, disagreements in preferences, *and* novelty of information, and as such it is novel to the information retrieval literature.

The clearest direction for future work is to perform an actual crowd-sourced assessment and determine whether our preference measure correlates better with human judgments of system performance than other measures. We plan to start this immediately. Another direction for future work is using triplets in a learning-to-rank algorithm to learn a novelty ranker. Since many learning algorithms are based on pairwise preferences, it seems a natural extension to triplets.

Acknowledgments: This work was supported in part by the National Science Foundation (NSF) under grant number IIS-1017026. Any opinions, findings and conclusions or recommendations expressed in this material are the authors' and do not necessarily reflect those of the sponsor.

7. REFERENCES

[1] R. Agrawal, S. Gollapudi, A. Halverson, and S. Ieong. Diversifying search results. *Proceedings of WSDM '09*, page 5, 2009.

[2] J. Arguello, F. Diaz, and J. Callan. Learning to aggregate vertical results into web search results. In *Proceedings of CIKM '11*, page 201, New York, USA, 2011. ACM Press.

[3] C. Buckley and E. M. Voorhees. Retrieval evaluation with incomplete information. In *Proceedings of SIGIR '04*, page 25, New York, USA, 2004. ACM Press.

[4] J. Carbonell and J. Goldstein. The use of mmr, diversity-based reranking for reordering documents and producing summaries. *Proceedings of SIGIR '98*, pages 335–336, 1998.

[5] B. Carterette. An analysis of np-completeness in novelty and diversity ranking. *Information Retrieval*, 14(1):89–106, Dec. 2010.

[6] B. Carterette. System effectiveness, user models, and user utility. In *Proceedings of SIGIR '11*, page 903, New York, USA, 2011. ACM Press.

[7] B. Carterette, P. N. Bennett, D. M. Chickering, and T. Susan. Here or there preference judgments for relevance. In *Proceedings of ECIR '08*, pages 16–27, 2008.

[8] P. Chandar and B. Carterette. Using preference judgments for novel document retrieval. *Proceedings of SIGIR '12*, page 861, 2012.

[9] O. Chapelle, S. Ji, C. Liao, E. Velipasaoglu, L. Lai, and S.-L. Wu. Intent-based diversification of web search results: metrics and algorithms. *Information Retrieval*, 14(6):572–592, May 2011.

[10] O. Chapelle, D. Metlzer, Y. Zhang, and P. Grinspan. Expected reciprocal rank for graded relevance. *Proceeding of CIKM '09*, page 621, 2009.

[11] C. Clarke, N. Craswell, I. Soboroff, and A. Ashkan. A comparative analysis of cascade measures for novelty and diversity. In *Proceedings of WSDM '11*, pages 75–84. ACM, 2011.

[12] C. Clarke, M. Kolla, and O. Vechtomova. An effectiveness measure for ambiguous and underspecified queries. *Advances in Information Retrieval Theory*, pages 188–199, 2010.

[13] C. L. Clarke, M. Kolla, G. V. Cormack, O. Vechtomova, A. Ashkan, S. Büttcher, and I. MacKinnon. Novelty and diversity in information retrieval evaluation. *Proceedings of SIGIR '08*, page 659, 2008.

[14] C. L. A. Clarke, N. Craswell, I. Soboroff, and E. M. Voorhees. Overview of the trec 2011 web track. In *Proceedings of The Eighteenth Text REtrieval Conference TREC*, pages 1–9, Gaithersburg, Maryland, 2011. NIST.

[15] T. Leelanupab, G. Zuccon, and J. M. Jose. A query-basis approach to parametrizing novelty-biased cumulative gain. In *Proceedings of the Third international conference on Advances in information retrieval theory*, ICTIR '11, pages 327–331. Springer-Verlag, 2011.

[16] A. Moffat and J. Zobel. Rank-biased precision for measurement of retrieval effectiveness. *ACM Transactions on Information Systems*, 27(1):1–27, Dec. 2008.

[17] P. Over. Trec-6 interactive track report. In *The Sixth Text Retrieval Conference (TREC-6)*, pages 57–64, 1998.

[18] F. Radlinski, M. Kurup, and T. Joachims. How does clickthrough data reflect retrieval quality? In *Proceedings of CIKM '08*, pages 43–52, New York, USA, 2008. ACM.

[19] D. Rafiei, K. Bharat, and A. Shukla. Diversifying web search results. In *Proceedings of WWW Õ10*, pages 781–790, New York, USA, Apr. 2010. ACM.

[20] M. E. Rorvig. The simple scalability of documents. *Journal of the American Society for Information Science*, 41(8):590–598, Dec. 1990.

[21] T. Sakai. Evaluating evaluation metrics based on the bootstrap. In *Proceedings of SIGIR '06*, pages 525–532, New York, USA, 2006. ACM.

[22] T. Sakai, N. Craswell, R. Song, S. Robertson, Z. Dou, and C. Lin. Simple evaluation metrics for diversified search results. In *Proceedings of the 3rd International Workshop on Evaluating Information Access (EVIA)*, 2010.

[23] T. Sakai and R. Song. Evaluating diversified search results using per-intent graded relevance. In *Proceedings of SIGIR '11*, pages 1043–1052. ACM, 2011.

[24] M. Sanderson, M. Paramita, P. Clough, and E. Kanoulas. Do user preferences and evaluation measures line up? In *Proceeding of SIGIR '10*, pages 555–562. ACM, 2010.

[25] R. L. Santos, C. Macdonald, and I. Ounis. Exploiting query reformulations for web search result diversification. *Proceedings of WWW '10*, page 881, 2010.

[26] E. M. Voorhees and H. T. Dang. Overview of the trec 2005 question answering track. In *In TREC 2005*, 1999.

[27] C. Zhai, W. Cohen, and J. Lafferty. Beyond independent relevance: methods and evaluation metrics for subtopic retrieval. In *Proceedings of SIGIR '03*, pages 10–17. ACM, 2003.

[28] W. Zheng, X. Wang, H. Fang, and H. Cheng. Coverage-based search result diversification. *Information Retrieval*, 2011.

Competence-Based Song Recommendation

Lidan Shou Kuang Mao Xinyuan Luo Ke Chen Gang Chen Tianlei Hu
College of Computer Science and Technology
Zhejiang University
Hangzhou, China
{should, mbill, wisp, chenk, cg, htl}@zju.edu.cn

ABSTRACT

Singing is a popular social activity and a good way of expressing one's feelings. One important reason for unsuccessful singing performance is because the singer fails to choose a suitable song. In this paper, we propose a novel singing competence-based song recommendation framework. It is distinguished from most existing music recommendation systems which rely on the computation of listeners' interests or similarity. We model a singer's vocal competence as singer profile, which takes voice pitch, intensity, and quality into consideration. Then we propose techniques to acquire singer profiles. We also present a song profile model which is used to construct a human annotated song database. Finally, we propose a learning-to-rank scheme for recommending songs by singer profile. The experimental study on real singers demonstrates the effectiveness of our approach and its advantages over two baseline methods. To the best of our knowledge, our work is the first to study competence-based song recommendation.

Categories and Subject Descriptors

H.3.3 [**Information Search and Retrieval**]: Information filtering; H.5.5 [**Sound and Music Computing**]: Modeling

Keywords

Song Recommendation, Singing Competence, Learning-to-rank

1. INTRODUCTION

Singing is a popular social activity and a good way of expressing one's feelings. While some people enjoy the experience of conducting a wonderful solo in a karaoke party, many others are upset by their own singing skill due to an unpleasant performance in the past. The truth is, people should blame their own skill of choosing songs rather than singing. It is extremely hard for a girl with a soft voice to sing like Mariah Carey whose songs require loud voice to express strong emotions. It is equally hard for a bass singer to perform Tristan in tenor. A good performance is only possible if a song is carefully chosen with regard to the singer's vocal competence.

However, song recommendation for singers seemed to be a task comprehensible to professionals only. Experienced singing teachers listen to find the advantages in one's voice and choose suitable songs matching one's vocal competence. Typically, they choose *challenging* songs in order to distinguish the singer from others. In other words, they tend to recommend songs which secure the best singing performance. Such selection is different from the traditional scenario of song recommendation, which typically selects songs based on the singer's interests. With the development of computational acoustic analysis, it is possible to study the vocal competence from a singer's digitized voice, and then make automatic song recommendation based on the singer's "performance caliber".

In this paper, we report our work on human *competence-based song recommendation* (CBSR). The main objective is to computationally simulate the know-how of a singing teacher – To recommend challenging but manageable songs according to the singer's vocal competence. Specifically, we develop a system which takes a singer's digitized voice recording as the input, and then recommends a list of songs relying on analysis of the singer's personal vocal competence and a subsequent search process in a song database. Although the general procedures of our approach appear similar to Music Retrieval By Humming [7], the underlying ideas and techniques are totally different from it. Our research purpose is significantly different from most existing song retrieval and recommendation systems, which focus on matching the listener's tastes or interests. To the best of our knowledge, it is the first work to study singing-song recommendation using singer's own voicing capabilities.

Competence-based song recommendation faces three main technical challenges:

First, how should competence be modeled? If we consider the singer's voicing input as a query, then a next question would be, what is the query like? As we all know, different people produce different ranges of pitches and intensity in their singing. Even for the same person, the singing performance may vary significantly depending on the pitch and intensity. The competence model and the query method must take such variations into consideration.

Second, a song database should be constructed. Likewise, we should ask, what model can be used to represent each song for the recommendation? Unlike previous work which focuses on transcription[3, 13], we attempt to discover the voice characteristics of each song, which in turn pose different requirements to the singer. For example, some songs must be sung in a soft voice while some others need to be delivered in a loud one. A good song model has to capture these features properly.

Third, a search mechanism must be provided for the database to bridge the gap between the singer's competence model and the songs. Meanwhile, a ranking method is needed to provide relevance-like ordering for the recommended songs.

To solve the first challenge, we break the ice by proposing a novel singing competence model which is instantiated as *singer profile*. To construct a singer profile, we first consider an existing vocal capability model called Vocal Range Profile (VRP), which has been proposed in the literature of medical acoustics for clinical assessment of voice diagnosis[10], voice treatment[21] and vocal training [19]. Specifically, the VRP of a person is a two-dimensional bounded area in the (pitch,intensity) space. For each pitch within the person's voicing capability, the range of intensity produced by her/him is depicted. Unfortunately, the VRP model cannot sufficiently describe one's singing competence. The main reason is that VRP overlooks a singer's *voice quality*, which largely determines how nicely a voice is produced. Our primary observation here is that, due to the fact that a person has variable performance (quality) when producing voice at different pitch and intensity, the voice quality for a person should be defined as a numerical function on the (pitch, intensity) space. As a result, the singer profile consists of two components: the singer's *VRP* and the respective *voice quality function* defined on her/his VRP area.

The above competence model (singer profile) causes a new problem – The voice quality function of a singer is not readily available. In fact, singing voice quality is an empirical value and its mathematical formulation has not been adequately studied in the acoustics community. The only obvious way to acquire a person's voice quality is manual annotation on various (pitch, intensity)-pairs. However, manual annotation at query time is apparently unacceptable. In our solution, we avoid the mathematical formulation of the voice quality function. Instead, we "learn" the function from empirical values of the population given by experts. This leads to a supervised learning method which automatically computes the voice quality function at query time.

For the second challenge, we introduce the notion *song profile*. Like a singer profile, each song profile in the database must also be annotated by the pitches of its notes and their respective intensities. While the pitches of a song are typically available, the intensity of each note cannot be easily acquired. To the best of our knowledge, extracting the singing intensity from polyphonic songs still remains an unstudied problem. We employ a number of professionals to annotate each song with a *piecewise intensity sequence* using a software tool. This process is feasible as it can be done during an offline phase.

The third challenge can seemingly be solved with a naive approach – That is to recommend songs whose pitch and intensity ranges are completely contained in one's vocal range with good quality. However, this approach tends to prioritize only "easy" songs and therefore contradict our motivation. In contrast, we propose a *competence-based song ranking* scheme to rank songs in the database for the singers. These criteria include the pitch and intensity. Nevertheless, it is possible to extend the scheme by adding other criteria.

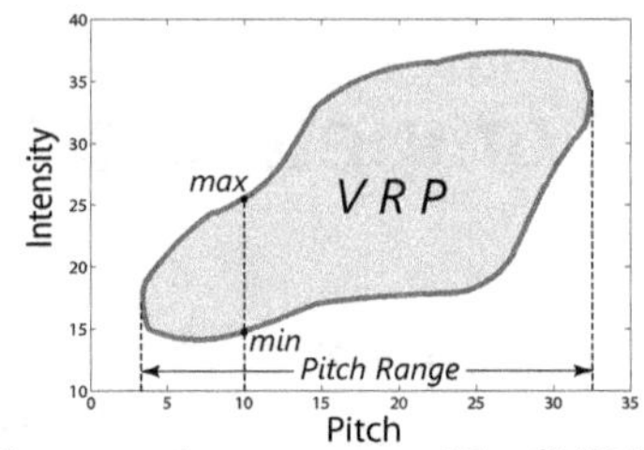

Figure 1: The vocal range profile (VRP) of a singer

In our scheme, we extract features from singer and song profiles as well as the respective rankings of experts to train a Listnet model. This model is cross-validated on our datasets

Our main contributions are summarized as follows:

(1) We propose a novel competence-based song recommendation framework.

(2) We present a singer profile to model singing competence. We illustrate the process of generating singer profiles.

(3) We also present the song profile and describe the method of generating the respective song profile from a database.

(4) The song recommendation is implemented using a multiple criteria learning-to-rank scheme.

(5) Our experiments on a group of users show promising results of the proposed framework.

The rest of our work is organized as follows: Section 2 introduces the related work. Section 3 conducts an overview of the framework. Section 4 and 5 presents the singer/song profile models and the techniques to acquire these profiles. Section 6 describes the learning-to-rank recommendation scheme. The experiments are detailed in Section 7. Finally, Section 8 concludes the paper.

2. BACKGROUND AND RELATED WORK

In this section, we shall discuss the related work in the literature and introduce some important concepts. We will look at previous studies in vocal range profile, voice quality, and song recommendation.

2.1 Vocal Range Profile

As shown in Figure 1, a *vocal range profile* (VRP), also called phonetogram, is a two-dimensional map in the pitch-intensity space (In acoustic terms, it is also called the frequency-amplitude space), where each point represents the phonation of a human being. This map depicts all possible (pitch, intensity)-pairs that one can produce. The projection of a VRP map on the pitch axis, which defines the range of pitches that one can ever produce, is called the *pitch range*. Specifically, the VRP characterizes one's voicing capability by defining the *maximum* and *minimum* vocal intensity at each pitch value across the entire pitch range.

The concept of VRP was first introduced by Wolf et al. [25] in 1935. Since then, VRP has been widely applied in objective clinical voice diagnosis and singer's vocal training. Many papers [9, 22] have studied the variation of VRP with regard to gender, age, voice training and so forth. It has been found that the VRPs of different people usually differ significantly. Therefore, it can be used as a voice signature for human being.

The recording process of VRP has been standardized and recommended by the Union of European Phoniatricians [20]. To describe it simply, the process requires the singer to traverse each pitch in her/his pitch range from the loudest to the softest through voicing vowel /a/. In our work, we employ a similar process to acquire each singer's VRP. The result is used as a basis for computing one's singer profile.

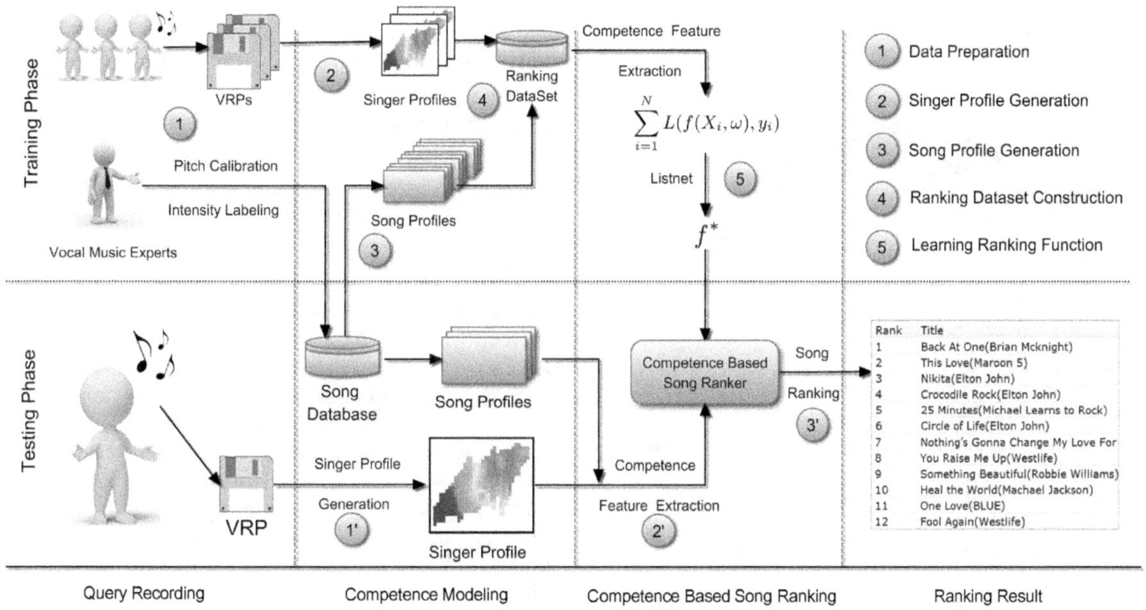

Figure 2: Overview of the competence-based song recommendation framework

2.2 Voice Quality

The technique of *objective voice quality measuring* has been widely used in voice illness diagnosis. Such techniques usually extract sound sampling features to represent voice characteristics, for example *period perturbation*, *amplitude perturbation* etc. In the field of vocal music, there are other measures that describe the voice quality of sounds. For example, singing power ratio[24] is defined upon the spectrum analyze of voice samples. This measure differs a lot between trained and untrained singers. The other similar examples include tilt[6], and ltasSlope[17]. The last two are meant to discover the singer's singing talent[24]. The above mentioned measures reveal many characteristics of the voice. However, these measures cannot adequately solve our problem, which requires detailed voice quality evaluation on a singer's VRP map.

As described in the previous subsection, VRP describes the singer's voicing area in the pitch-intensity space. Some previous studies on proprietary voice quality measures reveal that each measure may vary significantly across VRP area. [18] evaluates quality parameters such as jitter, shimmer, and crest factor over VRP, and finds that each of these quantities differs significantly across VRP. Another work in [16] analyzes the distribution of three separate acoustic voice quality parameters on VRP, and has reached a similar conclusion. In our work, we do not evaluate each single parameter. Instead, we model the voice quality as an overall function on VRP.

One study worth mentioning is [15], which incorporates the knowledge of voice diagnosis experts to train a linear model, and then predicts the overall voice quality of a patient for clinical voice diagnosis. Our method for computing voice quality on VRP area is motivated from this work. But our underlying problem and expert knowledge of singing voice quality is totally different from the previous study.

2.3 Song Recommendation

Traditional song/music recommendation focuses on recommending songs by user's listening interests. The earlier studies such as [11] explore techniques in the domain of *content based song recommendation*. These techniques aim at discovering user's favorite music in terms of music content similarity such as moods and rhythms. However, this kind of methods has its limitation because typically the low-level features cannot fully represent the user's interests. A more effective way is to employ the so-called collaborative methods[8] which recommend songs among a group of users who have similar interests.

Our work is different from the above studies as it recommends songs by singer's performance needs rather than interests. It also differs from post-singing performance appraisal[23] which requires singing to be performed in the first place. In our preliminary study[14], we demonstrated a system for karaoke song recommendation. This work significantly extends it by formulating the scientific problem of competence-based song recommendation and proposing a novel solution.

3. OVERVIEW OF CBSR FRAMEWORK

As Figure 2 shows, our competence-based song recommendation framework works in two phases, namely training phase and testing phase. During the training phase, we employ a group of singers as the subjects and a number of music experts to train a competence-based ranking function. The main procedures of training phase are listed as follows:

1. *Data Preparation*: We first record the voice of a group of singers, and generate the VRP for each singer. Meanwhile, a song database is annotated with pitch and intensity information by a few vocal music experts.
2. *Singer Profile Generation*: Each singer's voice is used to construct a singer profile which depicts (i) the singer's vocal area by a *VRP* and (ii) the singer's competence by a *voice quality function* on her/his VRP.
3. *Song Profile Generation*: The song database together with its annotated data are used to generate song profiles, which contain its note distribution and other statistical information.
4. *Construction of The Ranking Dataset*: Each training subject is asked to sing a number of songs in the song database in front of the vocal music experts. The latter will rate the song with a score for the subject. The (i) singer profiles, (ii) song profiles in the database, and (iii) the rankings given by the experts, comprise the ranking dataset.

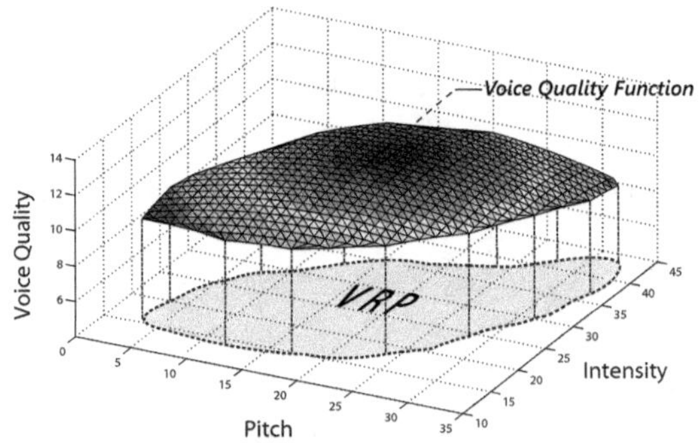

Figure 3: A Singer Profile. Colors on the surface indicate the voice quality.

5. *Learning The Ranking Function*: We extract features from the ranking dataset. These features are fed into a list-wise learning-to-rank algorithm called *Listnet* to learn the ranking function.

In the testing phase, (1') a subject is asked to record voices for singer profile generation. After (2') extracting features from the tester subject's singer profile and the song profiles in the database, we can (3') make recommendation using the ranking function learnt from the training phase.

Our main technical contributions focus on procedure 2, 3, and 5. We will give the details of the other procedures in the experimental study.

4. SINGER PROFILES

In this section, we first propose a vocal competence model called singer profile. Then we detail the process of generating singer profile. Finally, we present a simple method for per-profile analysis, which extracts some important singer profile characteristics.

4.1 Singer Profile Modeling

In our model, a singer profile contains two components: (1) VRP of the singer, and (2) a voice quality function defined over the VRP area. Given the definition of VRP in Section 2.1, we shall now formulate the definition of voice quality. If we consider each (pitch, intensity) point in VRP a *vocal point*, denoted by vp, then voice quality is defined as a function of vp.

DEFINITION 1. (Voice Quality) *Given the VRP of a singer, voice quality is a numerical function $\psi(vp) > 0$ for any vocal point $vp \in VRP$.*

Practically, voice quality indicates a quantity measuring whether the singing voice at a particular vocal point is fair-sounding.

Now a singer profile can be defined as a tuple of $< VRP, \psi >$, where VRP is the VRP of the singer and ψ is her/his respective voice quality function. In practice, however, we prefer a discretized form of singer profile, where all vocal points in a VRP are enumerated, as being defined in the following:

DEFINITION 2. (Singer Profile) *A singer profile is a set of 2-tuples, written as $<vp, \psi(vp)>$, where $vp \in VRP$ is a vocal point that the singer can voice.*

Figure 3 is a schematic diagram of a singer profile. If the VRP becomes discretized on both pitch and intensity dimensions, then the total number of vocal points in a VRP will be finite. Thus the singer profile will become a finite array of the 2-tuples.

In our system, we discretize pitches into semitone scale and intensity into units of 2 dB. This is in consistency with most vocal music requirements. However, it is a trivial task to use finer scales if necessary.

4.2 Singer Profile Generation

Generating the singer profile includes two major steps: *VRP generation* and *voice quality computation*. The first one is quite standardized and straightforward, but the second is much more complicated.

4.2.1 Step 1: VRP Generation

Before the VRP recording, the singer has to take some "warm-up" exercises such as singing. Then the singer is asked to stand 1 meter away from the microphone and start the recording procedure. The recording procedure requires the singer to pronounce each pitch in her/his pitch range from the softest intensity to the loudest. Meanwhile, a singing teacher is present to help the singer locate the pitch and guide the singer to increment the intensity while keeping the pitch steady. To help stabilizing the voice, we also provide the singer real-time visual cue of the singing pitch and intensity. However, this practice is optional.

For an untrained singer, it is difficult to increase the pitch by semitones. Therefore, singers are only requested to increase pitch by whole tone scale. Actually, by voicing each whole tone, the neighboring semitones will also be sufficiently covered. For each singer, an average number of 24 semitones are recorded in the recording procedure. Each piece of voicing is stored in a separate WAV file. The average time for recording is around 10 minutes.

Note the above procedure is in fact a sampling process in the pitch-intensity space, which results in a discrete VRP (with a number of vocal points). After this, we cut all voice files into *voice pieces* with time duration of 0.2 second. The reason for splitting voice into short pieces is that the voice pitch, intensity, and quality can be regarded as invariable in each piece. Thus, each voice piece finds its respective (pitch, intensity) value and gets associated with a vocal point in the VRP. Now the VRP can be seen as a set of vocal points, each associated with one or more voice pieces.

4.2.2 Step 2: Voice Quality Computation

As mentioned before, there exists no report on the mathematical formulation of the voice quality function, even though we need the value of this function on different vocal points. Considering the aggregated voice pieces that we collected for each vocal point in the previous step, we can take such pieces as input and manually label them with a quality value. This idea motivates a supervised learning method to learn a *quality evaluation function* from empirical voice quality annotation given by the experts. The input of this function is a voice piece, and the output is the voice quality of this voice piece (coupled by its respective vocal point, as each voice piece can be uniquely mapped to a vocal point). Thus, the quality evaluation function generates in effect a vocal point sampling for the voice quality function.

Note that the learning technique discussed here is only for generating intermediate data – the voice quality function. The reader should differentiate it from the learning-to-rank scheme proposed in Section 6 which aims at recommending songs. In the following, we will first present the method of training the quality evaluation function, and then describe how to utilize it for voice quality computation (prediction).

Supervised Learning

In order to train the quality evaluation function, a number of vocal music experts are requested to annotate the quality

Table 1: Features for voice quality evaluation

Feature Category	Feature Names
Pitch Features	*medianPitch, meanPitch, sdPitch, minPitch, maxPitch, nPulses, meanPeriod, sdPeriod*
Frequency Perturbations	*jitter_loc_abs*[1], *jitter_loc*[1], *jitter_rap*[1], *jitter_ppq5*[1]
Amplitude Perturbations	*shimmer_loc*[1], *shimmer_loc_dB*[1], *shimmer_apq3*[1], *shimmer_apq5*[1], *shimmer_apq11*[1]
Spectrum Features	*mean_nhr*[6], *mean_hnr*[26], *singing power ratio*[24], *tilt*[6], *ltasSlope*[17]

of voice pieces in each VRP recording using a software tool called *Praat* [4]. Each expert listens to the recorded WAV files and annotates the voice quality of different parts in each file. The possible annotation scores range from 1 to 5 (the lower the better quality). After an entire file becomes annotated, it will be split into voice pieces for training.

The quality evaluation function is trained as follows. First , several acoustic features are extracted for each voice piece. Table 1 shows these features classified in four categories.

- The pitch related features describe the global pitch level change of the voice piece.
- The frequency and amplitude perturbation features reflect local period's pitch perturbation and local period's amplitude perturbation within one voice piece respectively. These two classes of features indicate the sound WAV form variation with respect to pitch and intensity.
- The spectrum related features are those defined on spectrum analysis results and reflect the energy of sound along the frequency. For example, the hoarseness of the voice can be measured by HNR and NHR.

Second, we use the linear regression model to learn the quality evaluation function.

Voice Quality Prediction

The above trained linear regression model can be used for computing the voice quality of a new recorded VRP. We first split the testing sound file into voice pieces as what we did in training. Each voice piece is mapped to a vocal point vp. Meanwhile, the voice piece is fed into the regression model to obtain a voice quality value. Note that there could be multiple voice pieces being mapped to the same vocal point. In such case, the multiple predicted values will be averaged to give the final voice quality value for vp.

4.3 Singer Profile Analysis

A singer profile SP computed from the above method consists a list of tuples $t = <vp, vq>$, where each vp indicates a vocal point, vq indicates its respective voice quality. Suppose the pitch range of SP is PR, we can perform a simple profile partitioning algorithm described as following: (1) First, the vocal points whose $vq > \theta$ are marked as *good* points and those whose $vq \leq \theta$ are marked as *bad* ones. (2) Second, we look at all good points for a pitch $pt \in PR$. The one with the maximum intensity is denoted by vp_{max}, and the one with the minimum intensity is denoted by vp_{min}. Then, vocal points on pt whose intensity lie between the maximum and minimum are all marked as good ones. It is easy to see that the rest vocal points on pt are all bad ones. The detailed algorithm is given in Algorithm 1.

The output of the above partitioning algorithm will be used to derive some characteristics of a singer profile. These characteristics are important for understanding singer's competence and learning the recommendation function in Section 6.

Algorithm 1: *Singer Profile Partitioning*

```
Input: θ as the threshold;
Input: SP = {t_1, t_2, ..., t_n} as the singer profile ;
Input: PR as the pitch range of SP;
foreach t_i in SP do
    if t_i.vq<θ then
        t_i.vp is marked vp_good
    else
        mark t_i.vp as vp_bad
foreach pt in PR do
    T is the set of t_i whose pitch is pt
    vp_min = arg min_{t∈T} t.vp_good.intensity
    vp_max = arg max_{t∈T} t.vp_good.intensity
    foreach t_i ∈ T do
        if t_i.vp.intensity>vp_min.intensity and
        t_i.vp.intensity<vp_max.intensity then
            t_i.vp is marked as vp_good
        else
            t_i.vp is marked as vp_bad
```

We first define the controllable and uncontrollable areas for a singer profile.

DEFINITION 3. (Controllable Area and Uncontrollable Area) *The controllable area of a singer profile is the VRP region comprised of all good vocal points; while the uncontrollable area is the region made up of all bad vocal points.*

This definition is consistent with the fact that a singer performs good quality when the vocal point is under her/his control. A typical controllable area is a continuous region inside the VRP. This is reasonable because the voice quality produced by human vocal cords is continuous. The boundary vocal points in VRP are always voiced in one's extreme condition (e.g. highest possible pitch, strongest possible intensity), and therefore uncontrollable.

The controllable area deserves particular attention. When we look at the few leftmost or rightmost pitches of the controllable area, we find that these "pitch edges" have strong implication for singing performance. Many people feel uneasy when singing notes in these edges, as they feel themselves to be close to extreme voicing positions. However, they can actually finish a performance successfully if the song is retained within the controllable boundary. Therefore, we shall further split the controllable area into two, namely the *challenging area* and *well-performed area*.

DEFINITION 4. (Challenging Area and Well-Performed Area) *Given a singer profile, the* challenging area *is a subset of the controllable area, whose vocal points lie on either the β leftmost semitones or the β rightmost semitones of the controllable area, where β is an empirical number. The* well-performed area *is defined as the complement of the challenging area in the controllable area, or (controllable area – challenging area).*

In our implementation, $\beta = 4$. Figure 4 shows a schematic diagram of the defined areas. The challenging area indicates the "boundary pitches" which could be challenging but manageable for the singer. In contrast, the well-performed area contains vocal points which even an untrained singer would confidently produce.

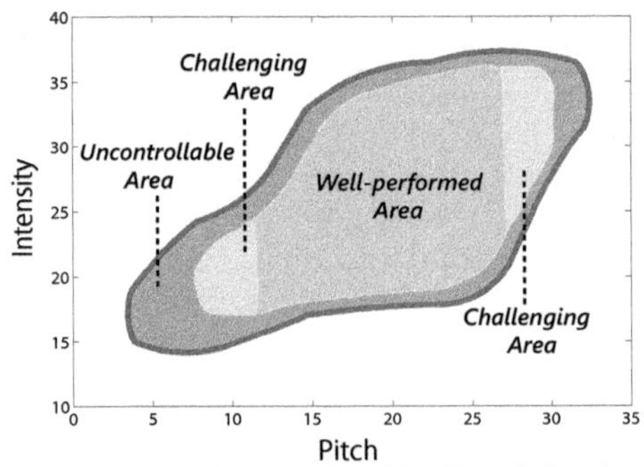

Figure 4: Singer Profile Partitioning

5. SONG PROFILES

In our solution to competence-based song recommendation, the pitch and intensity information of voices made by each singer is taken as input to generate a singer profile. Similarly, we need to build song profiles that contain singing pitch and intensity information in order to retrieve suitable singing songs for the singer. In this section, we first present the model for song profile and then describe the song profile acquisition process.

5.1 Song Profile Modeling

In our model, each song in the database contains a list of *notes*. Each note is a tuple in the form of *<pitch, duration, intensity>*, where *duration* indicates the temporal length of the note, *intensity* is the singing intensity of the note. Each *(pitch,intensity)* pair defines a *term*. In other words, notes with the same (pitch, intensity) pair are regarded as having the same *term*. For each song, we count the numbers of occurrences and aggregate the durations by terms. This results in the following definition of song profile:

DEFINITION 5. (Song Profile) *Song profile is a list of term-related quadruples as <term_pitch, term_intensity, term_freq, agg_duration>, where term_freq is the number of occurrences of the term and agg_duration is the aggregated (sum) duration of the term.*

It should be noted that each term actually determines a (pitch, intensity) pair. Therefore, the song recommendation problem derives to matching the singer profile to the set of terms.

5.2 Song Profile Acquisition

Obtaining the profile of a song mainly involves two steps: (i) to acquire the singing melody and then (ii) to obtain the singing intensity for each note. As state-of-the-art techniques in music transcription cannot accurately extract the singing melody from a polyphonic song, we choose to rely on the MIDI databases available online. A typical MIDI file contains not only the singing melody but also its accompaniment. Most melodies in MIDI files are not on the same tune with the ground-truth music scores. We perform a cleaning procedure to extract only the singing melody from a MIDI file. Then we compare some pitch characteristics (e.g. lowest/highest pitch, starting pitch etc.) of the melody against ground-truth numerical musical notation to diminish the differences in their tunes.

The singing intensity data has to be annotated manually by professionals. Each expert listens to the original song and annotates a piecewise intensity sequence using the graphical interface provided by the Cubase 5 software. The software allows one to easily annotate the intensity sequence by drawing a few lines aside the notes. Given a song melody with a note sequence in the form of $<pitch_1, duration_1>$, $<pitch_2, duration_2>$, $<pitch_3, duration_3>$, $<pitch_4, duration_4>$, $\ldots\}$, its respective piecewise intensity sequence is $\{<intensity_1, num_1>$, $<intensity_2, num_2>$, ..., $<intensity_n, num_n>\}$, where $num_i \geq 1$ indicates the number of notes that each piece of intensity covers. These intensity values are stored in the "velocity" attribute of the MIDI file and can be extracted later for constructing the song profile. The intensity values annotated by multiple experts can be averaged to give the final intensity value. Due to the simplicity of the process, the labor cost of the offline manual annotation in song profile acquisition is limited.

6. COMPETENCE-BASED SONG RANKING

We apply the *Listnet*, a listwise learning-to-rank approach, to learn our *competence-based song ranker*. In this section, we first present the Listnet-based learning method. Then we describe the features to be used in learning.

6.1 Listwise Approach

In the song ranking problem we treat a singer profile as a query, and song profiles as documents. Our aim is to learn a ranking function f which takes feature vector $\mathbf{X}$ defined on each <singer profile, song profile> pair as input and ω as parameter, and produces ranking scores of the songs. The target can be written in the form:

$$y = f(X, \omega) \tag{1}$$

The goal of the learning task is to find a function f^* that minimizes the following loss function:

$$f^* = \arg\min_f \sum_{i=1}^{N} L(f(X_i, \omega), y_i) \tag{2}$$

where N is the number of singer profiles in the training set, y_i is the human annotated relevance scores for each song profile with the i-th singer profile, X_i is the feature vector for the i-th singer profile.

We decide to learn the target function with a listwise approach. In a listwise approach, the feature vector is extracted from all possible pairs (cross-product) of singer profiles and song profiles. In addition, each feature vector is annotated with a human relevance judgement. The feature vector and its corresponding relevance annotation are considered as a learning instance in the loss function. Compared to pointwise or pairwise approaches, the listwise approach acquires higher ranking accuracy in the top ranked results according to [5], as the latter minimizes the loss of the ranking list directly.

In our solution, we employ the Listnet as the learning method. It maps each possible list of scores to a probability permutation distribution and uses the *cross entropy* between these probability distributions as the metric. Thus, the loss function is given by

$$L(y^{(i)}, z^{(i)}(f_\omega)) = -\sum_{\forall g \in \ell} P_{y^{(i)}}(g) log(P_{z^{(i)}}(g)) \tag{3}$$

where $z^{(i)} = (f_\omega(x_1^{(i)}), .., f_\omega(x_{n^{(i)}}^{(i)}))$; $f_\omega(\cdot)$ is the ranking function, and $x_j^{(i)}$ is the feature vector extracted from the i-th singer and the j-th song ($1 \leq j \leq n^{(i)}$ where $n^{(i)}$ is the number of songs relevant to the i-th singer); $y^{(i)} = (y_1^{(i)}, ..., y_{n^{(i)}}^{(i)})$ is the corresponding human annotated relevance score vector, where $y_j^{(i)}$ is the score of the j-th song for the i-th singer; ℓ indicates all possible permutations of relevant songs for i-th singer; P is the permutation probability distribution given by

$$P_{z^{(i)}(f_\omega)}(\ell(j_1, j_2, ..., j_{n^{(i)}})) = \prod_{t=1}^{n^{(i)}} \frac{exp(f_\omega(x_{j_t}^{(i)}))}{\sum_{k=t}^{n^{(i)}} exp(f_\omega(x_{j_k}^{(i)}))} \quad (4)$$

We use linear neural network as the ranking function f_ω. Parameter ω is calculated using *gradient descent.*

6.2 Competence Feature Extraction

Now we shall describe the ranking features (i.e. components of $x_j^{(i)}$ in Equation 3), which are extracted from each <singer profile, song profile> pair. Specifically, these features capture a song's *term* distribution on various characteristic areas of a singer profile. (See Section 5.1 for definition of *term.*) As discussed in Section 4.3, each singer profile can be partitioned in 2D into three areas known as the *uncontrollable area*, the *challenging area* and the *well-performed area.* In addition, we can define the 2D area outside the VRP as the *silent area.*

Given a <singer profile, song profile> pair, for any area A in the singer profile, suppose $\{term_1, term_2, ..., term_n\}$ are the song terms appearing in A, and their *term_freq* and *agg_duration* in A are denoted by $\{tf_1, tf_2, ..., tf_n\}$ and $\{dur_1, dur_2, ..., dur_n\}$ respectively, then the features on this area are defined as follows:

1. *Total TF:* This feature is defined as $\sum_{i=1}^{n} tf_i$.
2. *Total TF-IDF:* Analogous to terms in documents, song terms widely available in different song profiles are less important in distinguishing different songs. For those terms with high/low pitch or loud/soft intensity, they are more important in representing the uniqueness of the song. Thus we compute the TF-IDF value of all terms in the song profile database. If we denote the TF-IDF of $term_i$ in the current song by $tfidf_i$, then the Total TF-IDF of area A is defined as $\sum_{i=1}^{n} tfidf_i$.
3. *Total TF-IVQ (Inverse Voice Quality):* The voice quality of different areas are different. If many song terms are located in the uncontrollable or silent areas, it is really a disaster for the singer to sing that song. Thus, we incorporate the voice quality into the feature definition. The voice quality is firstly averaged on the entire area of A and then inverted (as lower value indicates higher quality). Therefore, the Total TF-IVQ is defined as $\sum_{i=1}^{n} tf_i/avq$, where avq is the *average voice quality* in area A.
4. *Total Duration:* Duration is an important factor affecting the singing performance, especially for the challenging area. Singing a term for a long time in challenging or uncontrollable areas is apparently difficult. Thus, we define the Total Duration as $\sum_{i=1}^{n} dur_i$.
5. *Total TF-IDF Duration:* The duration of each term is also affected by the term importance. The effect of the duration of less important terms should be decreased. So we define this feature as $\sum_{i=1}^{n} dur_i \cdot tfidf_i$.
6. *Total Duration-IVQ:* The effect of the duration of each term is also affected by the voice quality in the area. Therefore we define the Total Duration-IVQ as $\sum_{i=1}^{n} dur_i/avq$.

The above six features are defined in all four areas, except the two voice quality-related ones (Total TF-IVQ and Total Duration-IVQ) for the silent area. These two are undefined as their voice quality is unavailable. Table 2 shows all the defined 22 features for each area.

Table 2: Ranking features (*C-area: challenging area; W-area: well-performed area; U-area: uncontrollable area; S-area: silent area*)

Features	*C-area*	*W-area*	*U-area*	*S-area*
Total TF	√	√	√	√
Total TF-IDF	√	√	√	√
Total TF-IVQ	√	√	√	
Total Duration	√	√	√	√
Total TF-IDF Duration	√	√	√	√
Total Duration-IVQ	√	√	√	

7. EXPERIMENTS

In this section, we report the experiment setup and results. We first introduce the datasets being used in the experiments. Then we describe the baseline methods which we compare with. We also introduce the metrics which guide the evaluation of the results. Finally, the experimental results are presented and analyzed.

7.1 The Datasets

7.1.1 Singer Profile Dataset

For VRP recording, we recruit 55 volunteers including 35 males (mean age=28) and 20 females (mean age=23), with ages varying from 18 to 54. Each singer's VRP is recorded using Audition V3.0. We choose Rode M3 as the recording microphone and M-AUDIO MobilePre USB as the audio card. Before recording, each singer is requested to climb music scale to "warm-up" their voice. During the recording, a vocal music teacher helps the singers locate their pitch and guide the singer to adjust the singing intensity.

In order to build training dataset for the quality evaluation function, three experienced singing teachers (20+ years' experience) are invited to evaluate the voice quality of the recording and annotate different parts of the WAV files using Praat. We provide the recording files of all the subjects (20 females and 35 males) to the teachers for voice quality annotation. These files are then split into 6498 female and 17144 male voice pieces with human annotated voice qualities as the training data for *two* quality evaluation functions, one for women and the other for men.

7.1.2 Song Profile Dataset

We have collected 200 songs (100 for male, 100 for female) as the training dataset. All singing melodies are calibrated according to their original music scores, and the singing intensity values are annotated by the singing teachers.

7.1.3 Ranking Dataset

In order to train the Listnet for song recommendation, we need a ranking dataset which contains manually annotated relevance scores for each <singer profile, song profile> pair.

For building the male ranking dataset, we divided the 100 male's midi songs into 5 subsets. The songs in each subset cover different pitch range and intensities to avoid data skew. We divide the 35 male subjects into 5 groups for 5-fold cross validation, and ensure that their singer profiles are as equally distributed as possible. Each singer is asked to sing 20 songs in one of the 5 subsets, in front of the 3 singing teachers. Subsequently, the singer teachers choose 1 out of 5 relevance labels, namely *challenging, normal, easy, difficult, nightmare.* As a result, a total number of 700 singing performances will be scored.

The female ranking dataset is built in a similar manner. We divided the 20 female subjects and 100 songs into five subsets. In the end, 400 performances will be conducted and scored.

Our datasets are relatively small-scale due to resource constraints. However, we have observed sufficient varieties among the singers and songs. Although adding new subjects and data will for sure improve the work, we believe that research on the current datasets can already lead to interesting findings.

7.2 Baseline Methods

We compare CBSR scheme against two baseline methods:

Single pitch ranking method (SP) SP ranking method is a simplified version of our scheme. In this method, we regard each vocal point to be a single dimensional point on the pitch-axis. This is equivalent to projecting the VRP onto the pitch-axis. The voice quality of each 1D vocal point is defined as the average of those 2D points on the same pitch. As a result, we can split the 1D pitch range to obtain controllable/uncontrollable areas, challenging area, and well-performed area. The same 22 features will be extracted from the terms appearing in these areas, and then fed into the Listnet for training.

Pitch boundary ranking method (PB) PB ranking method is the most intuitive way of singing song recommendation – the one that we challenge in Section 1. This method only uses singer's pitch range of good quality corresponding to the well-performed area in VRP. The notes whose pitches are within the well-performed area is the determinant for the song ranking. We also use the Listnet to train a ranking function. The ranking features are defined for notes within or outside the well-performed area on 1D pitch range (same area as SP). These features are *Total TF*, *Total TF-IDF*, *Total Duration* and *Total TF-IDF Duration*.

7.3 Evaluation Metric

For the quality evaluation function, we use the Pearson Correlation Coefficient (ρ) as the metric measuring the distance between the human annotated voice quality score and the predicted voice quality. This metric evaluates the linear dependence between two variables. For two variables X and Y, ρ is calculated as

$$\rho_{X,Y} = \frac{cov(X,Y)}{\sigma_X \sigma_Y}. \quad (5)$$

For the competence-based song recommendation, we adopt the Normalized Discounted Cumulative Gain(NDCG) [12] and Mean Average Precision(MAP) [2] as our metrics for the ranking result. NDCG is for measuring the ranking accuracy which has more than two relevance levels and is calculated as

$$NDCG(n) = \frac{1}{Z_n} \sum_{j=1}^{n} \frac{2^{r(j)} - 1}{log_2(j+1)} \quad (6)$$

where j is the predicted rank position , $r(j)$ is the rating value of j-th document in the ground-truth rank list, Z_n is the normalization factor which is the discounted cumulative gain in the $n-th$ position of the ground-truth rank list.

MAP measures the average precision of all queries in the test set where each query's precision is the average precision computed at the point of each of the relevant documents in the predict rank list. MAP is suitable for evaluation of two level relevances. It can be computed as

$$MAP = \frac{1}{|Q|} \sum_{q \in Q} \frac{\sum_{n=1}^{N} (P@n * rel(n))}{R_q} \quad (7)$$

where Q is the test query set, R_q is q's relevant document, $rel(n)$ is a binary function on the relevance of a given rank, N is the number of retrieved documents. For MAP, we consider the top two of the five human relevance annotation levels as relevant and the remaining threes as irrelevant.

7.4 Experimental Results

We first report the results of the voice quality computation. Next, we compare the ranking accuracy of our CBSR framework against the two baseline methods. Finally, the real recommendation results for singers are demonstrated.

7.4.1 Results of Voice Quality Computation

Remember that voice quality is computed by learning the quality evaluation function. We learn the linear regression model on male-only (35 men), female-only (20 women) and hybrid (55 people) datasets. Each dataset is randomly split into 5 parts, and then go through 5-fold cross validation. In each trial, four folds are used for training and one remaining fold for testing. We apply *principle component analysis* (PCA) to conduct feature selection before learning and testing. The Pearson correlations of the predicted voice quality and human-annotated voice quality are illustrated in Table 3. The Mean and STD are the average and the standard deviation of the Pearson correlation value calculated from the five trials.

Table 3: Pearson correlation

Dataset	Without PCA		With PCA	
	Mean	STD	Mean	STD
Male	0.7281	0.0654	0.729	0.0634
Female	0.5565	0.0643	0.5068	0.0717
Hybrid	0.7115	0.0373	0.7083	0.0432

The above result shows large correlation of the predicted voice quality and human annotated voice quality. The male dataset achieves 0.7281 and the hybrid one gives 0.7115. However, the correlation value of Female is lower (0.5565). This is most probably due to the shortage of the female train data. The second finding is that PCA does not improve the voice quality prediction.

7.4.2 Singer Profile Demonstration

After learning the quality evaluation function, we are able to generate the singer profile for each subject. Figure 5 demonstrates six subjects' singer profiles (3 male and 3 female), with the color of each vocal point showing its voice quality. These singer profiles clearly illustrate the different vocal competences of the subjects.

The profiles demonstrate strong correlation between pitch and intensity. With the increase of the pitch, the intensity also becomes higher. The only exception is Figure 5(f) where the intensity does not increase by pitch in the right part of singer profile. This is because the subject changes from the modal register to the falsetto register (false voice). As an untrained singer, she cannot produce very loud voices in false voice. Figure 5(a) shows a bass who can perform the low pitch with a rich voice.

The voice quality of these profiles indicate that lower pitch or intensity are more likely to be of bad quality, while high intensity may lead to better quality. This is because in VRP recording, many subjects tend to produce soft voice, no matter whether the voice quality is good or not. When asked to

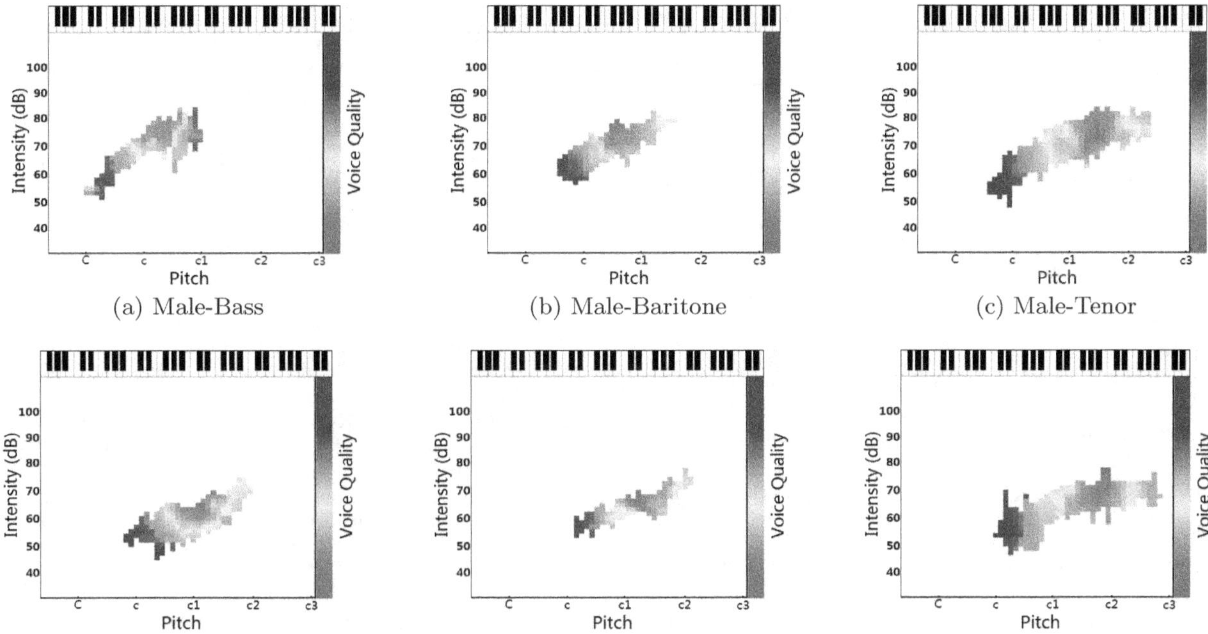

(a) Male-Bass (b) Male-Baritone (c) Male-Tenor

(d) Female-Bass (e) Female-Baritone (f) Female-Tenor

Figure 5: Singer profiles of subjects

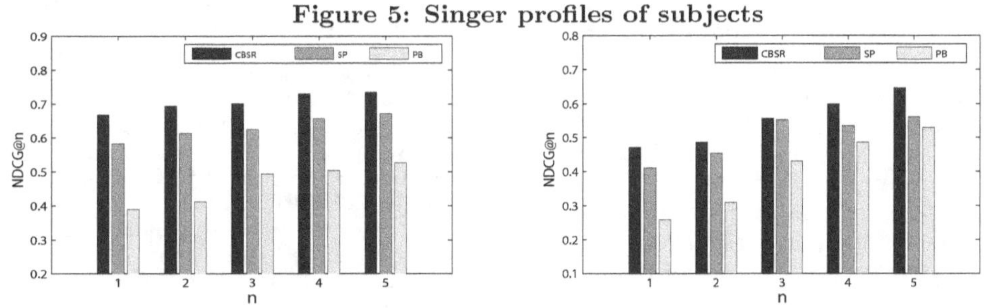

(a) Male (b) Female

Figure 6: Ranking accuracy in NDCG@n on male and female ranking datasets

produce louder voice, some of the subjects are likely to stop voicing when reaching their uncontrollable area.

Figure 5 also show clear indication of areas. The dark green and blue pixels indicate the uncontrollable area, while the light green to the yellow ones indicate the challenging area for the singer. The different areas show obvious aggregation of vocal points with similar colors, thus confirming the effectiveness of our singer profile partitioning method.

7.4.3 *Ranking Accuracy*

To study the ranking accuracy, we divide the male and female ranking datasets into five subsets for cross validation. In each trial, three subsets are used for training, one for validation, and one for testing. The validation dataset is used to tune the number of iteration in Listnet training. For feature selection, we also perform PCA to reduce the feature dimensionality to 9. The MAP and NDCG@n results reported are all averaged from the 5-fold cross validation.

Figure 6 shows the NDCG values of top 5 ranked songs on male and female ranking datasets. Apparently, our CBSR outperforms the two baseline methods. Our CBSR scheme outperforms SP (which does not consider intensity) by an average of 9%. This is a clear indication of the importance of the intensity dimension when considering song recommendation. Baseline method SP also outperforms PB, due to the effect of considering the challenging area and the voice quality. These results illustrate the superiority of CBSR scheme.

Table 5: Ranking accuracy in terms of MAP

Algorithm	CBSR	SP	PB
Male	0.682	0.521	0.503
Female	0.494	0.461	0.439

Table 5 shows the results of the MAP value for CBSR, SP, and PB on the male and female ranking datasets. The ranking accuracy of PB measured from all ranking result is satisfactory, this is because PB has a good ability of identifying "difficult" songs which contain significant number of notes outside the singer's pitch range. However, as for recommending top ranked songs that are "challenging but manageable" for the singer, then the CBSR scheme performs much better.

7.4.4 *Query Demonstration*

In this part we demonstrate the concrete recommendation results of two tenor singers using CBSR and PB. Their singer profiles are already depicted in Figure 5(c) and Figure 5(f). Their *highest voicing pitch* are f2 and #a2 for the male and female respectively. The *major singing intensity levels* are {2,3,4} and {1,2,3} for the male and female, where 1, 2, 3, 4 represent the intensity *whisper*, *soft*, *normal* and *loud* respectively. Table 4 demonstrates the top five ranking results of CBSR and PB. The Pitch/Intensity column indicates the highest pitch and major singing intensity levels of the song. The results show all songs recommended by CBSR are chal-

Table 4: Comparison of CBSR and PB Recommendation Results

Query	Top-5 CBSR Query Results			Top-5 PB Query Results		
	Song Name	Rank Value	Pitch/Intensity	Song Name	Rank Value	Pitch/Intensity
Male-Tenor	Never say goodbye	0.921	#c2/{2,3,4}	Apologize	0.986	#a1/{2,3}
	You and I	0.91	d2/{2,3,4}	My love	0.983	a1/{2,3}
	Guilty	0.909	#d2/{2,3,4}	My december	0.976	c1/{1,2,3}
	Tripping	0.905	#d2/{2,3}	I'll be there for you	0.971	d2/{2,3}
	Careless whisper	0.874	e2/{2}	As long as you love me	0.97	#g1/{3}
Female-Tenor	Memory	0.943	#f2/{1,2,3}	Listen	0.973	#f2/{2,3,4}
	I will always love you	0.938	#f2/{2,3}	Stay	0.972	d2/{2,3}
	Bleeding love	0.938	a2/{2,3}	Heartbeats	0.965	c2/{1,2}
	Time to say goodbye	0.921	a2/{2,3}	My heart will go on	0.953	#d2/{2,3,4}
	Hero	0.906	e2/{2,3}	Hero	0.952	e2/{2,3}

lenging but manageable. In contrast, those recommended by PB contain either easy-to-sing songs such as "My December" and "Heartbeats" or very tough songs in intensity such as "My heart will go on" and "Listen", because it ignores the singing intensity and challenging but manageable singing area of the singer.

8. CONCLUSIONS AND FUTURE WORK

In this paper, we broke the ice to study the competence-based song recommendation problem. We modeled singer's vocal competence as singer profile which takes voice pitch, intensity, and quality into account. We proposed a supervised learning method to train voice quality evaluation function, so that voice quality could be computed at query time. We also proposed a song model, which enabled matching with the singers. The proposed models allowed us to build a learning-to-rank scheme for song recommendation relying on human-annotated ranking datasets. The experiments demonstrated the effectiveness of our approach and its advantages compared to two baseline methods.

For future work, we plan to extend the competence model to adopt more singer characteristics, such as timbre. Another direction is to simplify the competence acquisition.

Acknowledgments

The work is supported by the National Science Foundation of China (GrantNo. 61170034).

9. REFERENCES

[1] http://www.fon.hum.uva.nl/praat/manual/Voice.html.

[2] R. Baeza-Yates and B. Ribeiro-Neto. *Modern Information Retrieval.* Addison-Wesley, 1999.

[3] E. Benetos, S. Dixon, D. Giannoulis, H. Kirchhoff, and A. Klapuri. Automatic music transcription: Breaking the glass ceiling. In *ISMIR*, pages 379–384, 2012.

[4] P. Boersma and D. Weenink. *Praat: doing phonetics by computer (Version 5.3.06) [Computer program]*, Retrieved May 1, 200. from http://www.praat.org/.

[5] Z. Cao, T. Qin, T.-Y. Liu, M.-F. Tsai, and H. Li. Learning to rank: from pairwise approach to listwise approach. In *ICML*, pages 129–136, 2007.

[6] D. Deliyski. Acoustic model and evaluation of pathological voice production. In *Proceedings of Eurospeech*, pages 1969–1972, 1993.

[7] A. Ghias, J. Logan, D. Chamberlin, and B. C. Smith. Query by humming: Musical information retrieval in an audio database. In *ACM Multimedia*, pages 231–236, 1995.

[8] D. Goldberg, D. A. Nichols, B. M. Oki, and D. B. Terry. Using collaborative filtering to weave an information tapestry. *Commun. ACM*, 35(12):61–70, 1992.

[9] L. Heylen, F. Wuyts, F. Mertens, M. D. Bodt, and P. V. de Heyning. Normative voice range profiles of male and female professional voice users. *Journal of voice*, 16:1–17, 2002.

[10] L. G. Heylen, F. L. Wuyts, F. W. Mertens, and J. E. Pattyn. Phonetography in voice diagnoses. *Acta Oto-Rhino-Laryngologica*, 50:299–308, 1996.

[11] K. Hoashi, K. Matsumoto, and N. Inoue. Personalization of user profiles for content-based music retrieval based on relevance feedback. In *ACM Multimedia*, pages 110–119, 2003.

[12] K. Järvelin and J. Kekäläinen. Ir evaluation methods for retrieving highly relevant documents. In *SIGIR*, pages 41–48, 2000.

[13] H. Kirchhoff, S. Dixon, and A. Klapuri. Multi-template shift-variant non-negative matrix deconvolution for semi-automatic music transcription. In *ISMIR*, pages 415–420, 2012.

[14] K. Mao, X. Luo, K. Chen, G. Chen, and L. Shou. mydj: recommending karaoke songs from one's own voice. In *SIGIR*, page 1009, 2012.

[15] Y. Maryn, P. Corthals, P. V. Cauwenberge, N. Roy, and M. D. Bodt. Toward improved ecological validity in the acoustic measurement of overall voice quality: combining continuous speech and sustained vowels. *Journal of voice*, 24:410–426, 2010.

[16] J. P. Pabon and R. Plomp. Automatic phonetogram recording supplemented with acoustical voice-quality parameters. *Journal of Speech and Hearing Research*, 31:710–722, 1988.

[17] G. Peeters. A large set of audio features for sound description. Technical report, IRCAM, 2004.

[18] J. Peter and H. Pabon. Objective acoustic voice-quality parameters in the computer phonetogram. *Journal of Voice*, 5:203–216, 1991.

[19] B. Schneider, M. Zumtobel, W. Prettenhofer, B. Aichstill, and W. Jocher. Normative voice range profiles in vocally trained and untrained children aged between 7 and 10 years. *Journal of voice*, 24:153–160, 2010.

[20] H. Schutte and W. Seidner. Recommendation by the union of european phoniatricians (uep): Standardizing voice area measurement/phonetography. *Folia Phoniatr (Basel)*, 35:286–288, 1983.

[21] R. Speyer, G. H. Wieneke, I. van Wijck-Warnaar, and P. H. Dejonckere. Efficacy of voice therapy assessed with the voice range profile (phonetogram). *Journal of Voice*, 17:544–559, 2003.

[22] A. M. Sulter, H. K. Schutte, and D. G. Miller. Differences in phonetogram features between male and female subjects with and without vocal training. *Journal of voice*, 9:363–377, 1995.

[23] W.-H. Tsai and H.-C. Lee. Automatic evaluation of karaoke singing based on pitch, volume, and rhythm features. *IEEE Transactions on Audio, Speech, and Language Processing*, 20:1233–1243, 2012.

[24] C. Watts, K. Barnes-Burroughs, J. Estis, and D. Blanton. The singing power ratio as an objective measure of singing voice quality in untrained talented and nontalented singers. *Journal of voice*, 20:82–88, 2006.

[25] S. K. Wolf, D. Stanley, and W. J. Sette. Quantitative studies on the singing voice. *The Journal of the Acoustical Society of America*, 6:255–266, 1935.

[26] E. Yumoto, W. Gould, and T. Baer. Harmonics-to-noise ratio as an index of the degree of hoarseness. *The Journal of the Acoustical Society of America*, 71:1544–1550, 1982.

A Low Rank Structural Large Margin Method for Cross-Modal Ranking

Xinyan Lu
College of Computer Science
Zhejiang University, China
xinyanlu@zju.edu.cn

Fei Wu
College of Computer Science
Zhejiang University, China
wufei@cs.zju.edu.cn

Siliang Tang
College of Computer Science
Zhejiang University, China
siliang@zju.edu.cn

Zhongfei Zhang
Department of Information Science & Electronic Engineering
Zhejiang University, China
zhongfei@zju.edu.cn

Xiaofei He
College of Computer Science
Zhejiang University, China
xiaofeihe@cad.zju.edu.cn

Yueting Zhuang
College of Computer Science
Zhejiang University, China
yzhuang@zju.edu.cn

ABSTRACT

Cross-modal retrieval is a classic research topic in multimedia information retrieval. The traditional approaches study the problem as a pairwise similarity function problem. In this paper, we consider this problem from a new perspective as a listwise ranking problem and propose a general cross-modal ranking algorithm to optimize the listwise ranking loss with a low rank embedding, which we call Latent Semantic Cross-Modal Ranking (LSCMR). The latent low-rank embedding space is discriminatively learned by structural large margin learning to optimize for certain ranking criteria directly. We evaluate LSCMR on the Wikipedia and NUS-WIDE dataset. Experimental results show that this method obtains significant improvements over the state-of-the-art methods.

Categories and Subject Descriptors

H.3.3 [**Information Search and Retrieval**]: Retrieval Models

General Terms

Algorithms, Theory, Experimentation

Keywords

Cross-Modal Retrieval; Ranking; Low Rank Embedding

1. INTRODUCTION

Nowadays many real-world applications involve multi-modal data. The ranking of cross-modal retrieval is imperative to many applications of the practical interest, such as finding relevant textual documents of a tourist spot that best match a given image of the spot or finding a set of images that visually best illustrate a given text description. Therefore, it is desirable to support the ranking of multi-modal data, e.g., identifying the most relevant textual documents in response to a query image or vice versa. It is obvious that a good performance of ranking multi-modal data hinges upon an appropriate learning of the similarity across different modalities. The *heterogeneity-gap* between multi-modal data has been widely understood as a fundamental barrier for the cross-modal metric learning.

In recent years, there has been a great deal of research devoted to the development of algorithms for learning an optimal direct similarity metric between different modalities. Among existing research of cross-modal metric learning, one kind of popular approaches is to map the data with multiple modalities into a common (or shared) space such that the distance between two similar objects is minimized, while the distance between two dissimilar objects is maximized. These approaches (e.g., Canonical Correlation Analysis (CCA) [12] and [33]) usually assume a training set of strictly paired data and exploit the symbiosis of multiple-modality data which is common to describe the rich literal and visual semantics, such as a web image with loosely related narrative text descriptions, and a news report with collateral text and images. Another kind of approaches for multi-modal metric learning is the extensions of Latent Dirichlet Allocation (LDA) [5] which are conducted on two or more collections of multiple-modality data in an unsupervised manner. The LDA-based approaches tend to model correlations among multi-modal documents at a latent semantic (*topic*) level across different modalities, e.g. correspondence LDA [4].

We are particularly interested in ranking the multi-modal data (i.e. *cross-modal ranking*) in this paper. Different from the two aforementioned categories of approaches which do not maximize a criterion related to the final ranking performance, recent years have witnessed the efforts in learning an optimal similarity (ranking) function between different modalities by using learning to rank techniques. These approaches (e.g. [11, 23, 2]) are supervised but do not enforce a strict assumption that the trained multi-modal data must be paired (e.g., one image is in pair-correspondence with its

SIGIR'13, July 28–August 1, 2013, Dublin, Ireland.

collateral text). They in fact need some lists of ranked data related to the queries for training where the training examples can be easily obtained from the abundance of users' clickthrough data with little overhead [18, 10]. In this way, the learned metric for ranking multi-modal data is generally optimized for a ranking-based loss function (evaluation criterion) to *preserve* the orders of the relevance instead of the purely absolute values of similarity (dis-similarity) between multi-modal data.

A discriminative kernel-based method PAMIR proposed in [11] solves the problem of cross-modal ranking by adapting the Passive-Aggressive algorithm [8]. However, PAMIR is inherently a pairwise cross-modal ranking approach; its ranking performance is limited by the distribution of the pairs of items and skewed data may even deteriorates the ranking result. These are also the same problems for another pairwise approach SSI [2] proposed by Bai et al. Moreover in the real world, a long search query (e.g., a whole document) is beneficial because users' intents can be described in more detail [31]. Therefore, it is appropriate to support long textual documents as queries in cross-modal ranking. It is obvious that PAMIR cannot easily expedite the long queries and restrains itself from a more flexible application of cross-modal ranking in the setting of uncontrolled multi-modal data involved.

This paper aims to bridge the gap between learning a latent space and ranking for multi-modal data. We consider the problem of cross-modal retrieval from a new perspective as a listwise ranking problem in this paper, and propose a general cross-modal ranking algorithm to optimize the listwise ranking loss meanwhile considering a low rank embedding, called Latent Semantic Cross-Modal Ranking (LSCMR). LSCMR employs the structural SVM [29] to support the optimizations of various ranking evaluation measures (e.g, MAP [32] and NDCG [7]) under a unified algorithmic framework. LSCMR also incorporates a low rank embedding in the learning procedure in which the latent aspect space is induced to address the curse of dimensionality and discover the correlations between different modalities.

It is worthwhile to highlight the main motivations of the proposed method. We would like the method to benefit both from the low rank embedding and the most recent advances in learning to rank techniques:

- Similar to the ideas of the latent model SSI [2] which discovers the "latent concept" from high-dimensional space, LSCMR employs the low rank embedding to eliminate textual/visual synonymy and polysemy of multi-modal data and discovers the correlations between different modalities. This is particularly appropriate to the settings where the distributions of query data and the retrieved data are intrinsically different due to the aforementioned multi-modal heterogeneity-gap. Furthermore, from a flexible retrieval point of view, LSCMR naturally supports long queries to discern users' search intentions.

- By the introduction of structural large margin learning into the optimization of a cross-modal ranking function in a *listwise* manner, LSCMR explicitly minimizes the ranking loss of a whole permutation listwise, not individuals or pairs of items. The ranking function by the maximum margin is not biased toward the queries with more data pairs, leading to a strong generalization due to its empirical risk minimization.

We show experimental results on the ranking of cross-modal data obtained from two real-world datasets. The proposed LSCMR outperforms other cross-modal ranking approaches. LSCMR is particularly appropriate for cross-modal ranking due to its structural large margin and low-rank listwise ranking pursuing.

The rest of this paper is organized as follows. In Section 2, we describe the method in detail and show its feasibility. Section 3 discusses the existing work. We compare the proposed LSCMR with other cross-modal ranking approaches on two real-world datasets in Section 4. Conclusions are given finally.

2. THE ALGORITHM OF LSCMR

The proposed method LSCMR is a general cross-modal retrieval framework in the sense that it can be applied in both directions of image-query-text retrieval and text-query-image retrieval. Consequently, a query here may be either an image or a text document. Similarly, a retrieved document can either be an image or a text document. For a clear articulation in the rest of this section, the algorithm is only derived in the case of text-query-image retrieval. We report the experiments in both scenarios.

2.1 Notation

All vectors are assumed to be column vectors and a superscript T denotes the transpose of a matrix or vector. Denote the text query as $q \in \mathbb{R}^m$ and the retrieved image as $d \in \mathbb{R}^n$, where m is the dimension of the text space (e.g., vocabulary size of bag-of-words (BoW)) and n is the dimension of the image space (e.g., vocabulary size of bag-of-visual-words (BoVW) which is quantized by clustering from low-level visual features such as SIFT [22]). We are given a training set of N samples, in which each contains a text query q_i ($i = 1, \dots, N$) as well as a set of corresponding retrieved images $\mathbf{d}_i$ with their true rankings $\mathbf{y}_i^* \in \mathcal{Y}$, where $\mathcal{Y}$ denotes the set of all possible permutations (rankings). We formulate a ranking as a matrix of pair orderings as [32] does, $\mathcal{Y} \subset \{-1, 0, +1\}^{|\mathbf{d}| \times |\mathbf{d}|}$ where the operator $|\cdot|$ denotes the number of elements in a set. For any $\mathbf{y} \in \mathcal{Y}$, $y_{ij} = +1$ if document d_i is ranked ahead of document d_j, and $y_{ij} = -1$ if d_j is ranked ahead d_i, and $y_{ij} = 0$ if d_i and d_j have equal rank. We consider only matrices with correspond to valid rankings (i.e., obeying antisymmetry and transitivity). Moreover, assume that the true ranking is a weak ranking with two rank values (*relevant* and *irrelevant*). For any textual query q_i, let $\mathbf{d}_i^+$ and $\mathbf{d}_i^-$ denote the set of relevant and irrelevant images in $\mathbf{d}_i$, respectively. For simplicity, we omit the subscript i of q_i and $\mathbf{d}_i$ when it is clear from the context.

2.2 The Low-Rank Learning Function

We consider that learning scores for ranking from a supervised manner, in which the ranking of images corresponding to a given textual query is available for training. Unlike the uni-modal data ranking, cross-modal ranking attempts to learn a similarity function $f(q, d)$ between a text query q and an image d according to a pre-defined ranking loss. The learned function f maps each text-image pair to a ranking score based on their semantic relevance.

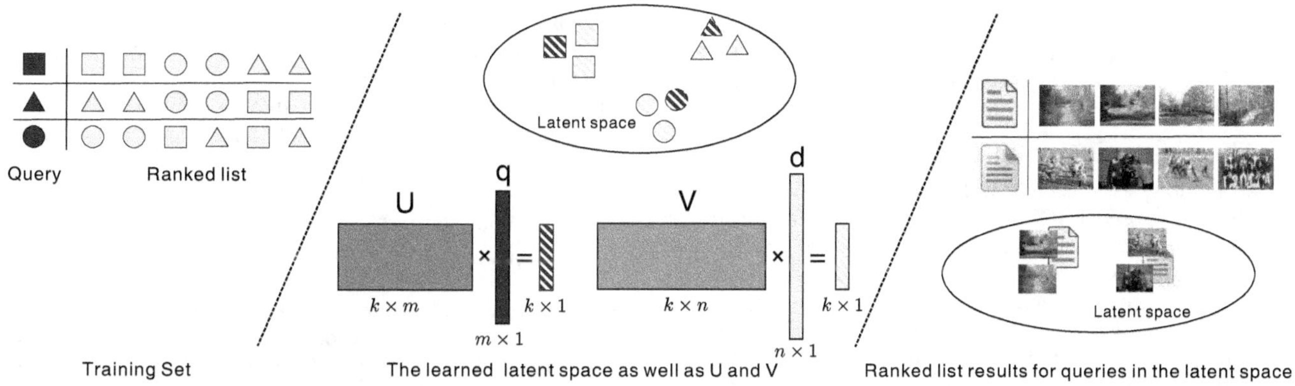

Figure 1: The algorithmic illustration of the proposed LSCMR. Shapes represent semantics (e.g., classes or categories); the same shape indicates the same (or quite relevant) semantic content. Colors represents modalities (i.e., images and text documents); the same color indicates that the data objects come from the same modality space. For simplicity in this illustration, we assume the two modalities to be text queries and image targets. Ideally, given a text query, we would like those images having the same shape (semantic content) with the query are ranked before those having different shapes in the ranking list. LSCMR tends to learn a low rank ranking function from the training set (seen queries and associated ranking lists) in a supervised manner. All the seen m-dimensional queries q and n-dimensional target documents d are mapped to a k-dimensional latent space by U and V respectively, in which those data objects with the same shape are grouped to minimize certain listwise ranking loss (e.g., MAP) directly. For unseen queries and documents, they are first mapped to the learned latent space by U and V, respectively, and then the scoring is conducted in the latent space to produce ranking results. (Figure best viewed in color)

Given a text query $q \in \mathbb{R}^m$ and an image $d \in \mathbb{R}^n$, we tend to learn a linear scoring function to measure the relevance of d given q :

$$f(q,d) = q^T W d = \sum_{i=1}^{m}\sum_{j=1}^{n} q_i W_{ij} d_j \tag{1}$$

where $f(q,d)$ is the score (or similarity) between the query q and the image d, and the only parameter $W \in \mathbb{R}^{m\times n}$ in the linear model captures the correspondence of the two different modalities of data as a weighting matrix: W_{ij} weights the correlation between the ith dimension of the text space and the jth dimension of the image space. Note that both positive values and negative values in W_{ij} are allowed in which a negative value represents a negative correlation.

Motivated by the idea of low rank embedding, a low rank prior is introduced into matrix W with $W = U^T V$ in equation (1), which results in a low rank ranking model [2]:

$$f(q,d) = q^T U^T V d = (Uq)^T V d \tag{2}$$

where $U \in \mathbb{R}^{k\times m}$ and $V \in \mathbb{R}^{k\times n}$. U refers to map the query text q from the m-dimensional text space to the k-dimensional latent space by a liner mapping, and V refers to map the retrieved image d from the n-dimensional image space to the k-dimensional latent space. Therefore, the text query and the retrieved image are mapped to a common k-dimensional latent *aspect* space, and then their similarity is measured by a dot product of the two vectors in the k-dimensional space, which is commonly used to measure the matching between textual vectors [1].

Intuitively, the low rank model in equation (2) helps us deal with the problem of textual/visual *synonymy* and *polysemy* which particularly occur in cross-modal retrieval. Note that Latent Semantic Indexing (LSI) [9] takes into account of the correlations between textual words (synonym and polysemy) in a single modality in an unsupervised manner, while the low rank model in equation (2) attempts to capture the correlation across two different modalities from a supervised manner. By constraining the form of W with a low rank form, the benefits are similar to LSI: U and V not only induce a k-dimensional latent aspect space but are also faster to compute and lead to much smaller storage requirements by representing the image documents in k dimensions instead of the original n dimensions (k is chosen much smaller than m or n). Besides, from the viewpoint of statistical learning theory, fewer parameters ($k(m+n) \ll mn$) lead to a better stability and generalization in performance.

Similar to [2], here U and V are different and there is no assumption that the query texts and the target images should be embedded to the latent space in the same way. This is appealing to cross-modal ranking since the distributions of the query texts and the target images are inherently different due to the heterogeneity-gap.

We can obtain a prediction $\mathbf{y}$ for each input query q and its corresponding ranked target images $\mathbf{d}$ by sorting the $f(q,d)$ in a descending order. The rest is to learn U and V. We aim to obtain the values of U and V by the minimization of the following empirical risk,

$$R^{\Delta}(f) = \frac{1}{N}\sum_{i=1}^{N} \Delta(\mathbf{y}_i^*, \mathbf{y}_i), \tag{3}$$

where the non-negative loss function $\Delta : \mathcal{Y}\times\mathcal{Y} \to \mathbb{R}$ quantifies the penalty for making prediction $\mathbf{y}_i$ if the correct output is $\mathbf{y}_i^*$, which is typically bounded in $[0,1]$. For example, we define the loss function Δ with the average precision (AP, detailed definition in Equation (14)) loss as follows:

$$\Delta_{ap}(\mathbf{y}^*, \mathbf{y}) = 1 - \mathrm{AP}(\mathrm{rank}(\mathbf{y}^*), \mathrm{rank}(\mathbf{y}))$$

and then to minimize the empirical risk is to maximize the Mean Average Precision (MAP). Note that one can construct different ranking objective problems by considering different ranking loss function Δ.

2.3 The Formulation of LSCMR

In this section, we present the formulation of LSCMR in details. The proposed LSCMR is inspired by the structural SVM framework [29], especially SVM^{map} [32] for optimizing the average precision. The algorithmic illustration of LSCMR is presented in Figure 1.

The motivation of LSCMR is to learn a cross-modal ranking function $h : \mathcal{X} \rightarrow \mathcal{Y}$ between an input space $\mathcal{X}$ (a text query q as well as all possible target images) and output space $\mathcal{Y}$ (rankings over the image set). Similar to SVM, we can derive a prediction by finding the ranking $\mathbf{y}$ that maximizes the following discriminant function h:

$$h(q, \mathbf{d}) = \text{argmax}_{\mathbf{y} \in \mathcal{Y}} F(q, \mathbf{d}, \mathbf{y}) \tag{4}$$

where F is considered as a compatibility function parameterized by U, V that measures how compatible the triple $(q, \mathbf{d}, \mathbf{y})$ are.

By adapting the most commonly used *partial order* combined feature representation in [19] to the cross-modal ranking, we define F as:

$$F(q, \mathbf{d}, \mathbf{y}) = \sum_{i \in \mathbf{d}^+} \sum_{j \in \mathbf{d}^-} y_{ij} \frac{(Uq)^T V(d_i - d_j)}{|\mathbf{d}^+| \cdot |\mathbf{d}^-|} \tag{5}$$

where $y_{ij} = +1$ if image d_i is more preferred (more relevant to query q) than image d_j, and $y_{ij} = -1$ otherwise since we assume that the predicted rankings are complete.

One attractive property of F is that for the fixed U and V, the ranking $\mathbf{y}$ which maximizes function F (then the predicted ranking) is simply sorted by descending $f(q, d) = (Uq)^T V d$. To see this, we note that F is a summation over the differences of all relevant/irrelevant document pairs since we assume weak rankings with two rank values. Since F decomposes linearly over the pairwise representation, we can maximize F by optimizing each y_{ij} individually: if $(Uq)^T V d_i > (Uq)^T V d_j$, y_{ij} is set to be 1, and $y_{ij} = -1$ otherwise. This is the same procedure as sorting documents by descending $f(q, d)$. More details can be obtained from [19]. We note that this simple prediction rule establishes a connection between the compatibility function F and the aforementioned low rank ranking model.

Since U and V are independent to the summation in equation (5), we rewrite F as a linear function of $U^T V$:

$$F(q, \mathbf{d}, \mathbf{y}) = < U^T V, \Psi(q, \mathbf{d}, \mathbf{y}) > \tag{6}$$

where

$$\Psi(q, \mathbf{d}, \mathbf{y}) = q \sum_{i \in \mathbf{d}^+} \sum_{j \in \mathbf{d}^-} y_{ij} \frac{d_i^T - d_j^T}{|\mathbf{d}^+| \cdot |\mathbf{d}^-|} . \tag{7}$$

Here the combined feature function $\Psi(q, \mathbf{d}, \mathbf{y})$ is a summation over the vector differences of all the relevant/irrelevant image pairs. By representing the scoring F as a Frobenius inner product of $U^T V$ and Ψ, we see that it is straightforward to extend the idea of the structural SVM to learn the cross-modal ranking function F.

For the purpose of learning to rank, the structural SVM takes a set of vector-valued features which characterize the relationship between the input query and a set of target documents as the input, and returns a ranking list $\mathbf{y} \in \mathcal{Y}$ of the target documents. The structural SVM is applied to maximize the margins between the true ranking list $\mathbf{y}^*$ and all the other possible lists $\mathbf{y}$. In this paper, LSCMR takes cross-modal ranking into consideration, for $i = 1, \ldots, N$:

$$\forall \mathbf{y} \in \mathcal{Y} : \delta F(q_i, \mathbf{d}_i, \mathbf{y}) \geq \Delta(\mathbf{y}_i^*, \mathbf{y}) - \xi_i \tag{8}$$

where for compactness, we define

$$\delta F(q_i, \mathbf{d}_i, \mathbf{y}) = F(q_i, \mathbf{d}_i, \mathbf{y}_i^*) - F(q_i, \mathbf{d}_i, \mathbf{y}) .$$

Since we assume that the query texts and the target images are embedded into a common latent space, respectively, LSCMR adapts the original structural SVM to learn the optimal U^* and V^* which maximize the margins between the true ranking and all the other possible rankings of the target images for each text query. Hence, we replace the standard quadratic regularization $\frac{\lambda}{2}\|w\|_2^2$ with $\frac{\lambda}{2}\|U\|_F^2 + \frac{\lambda}{2}\|V\|_F^2$ where $\|\cdot\|_F$ denotes the Frobenius norm. Intuitively, this extension simplifies the model complexity, thereby promoting a better generalization performance.

The optimization problem is then presented as follows:

Optimization Problem 1.

$$\min_{U,V,\xi} \quad \frac{\lambda}{2}\|U\|_F^2 + \frac{\lambda}{2}\|V\|_F^2 + \frac{1}{N}\sum_{i=1}^{N} \xi_i \tag{9}$$

$$\text{s.t.} \quad \forall i \in \{1, \ldots, N\}, \forall \mathbf{y} \in \mathcal{Y} :$$

$$\delta F(q_i, \mathbf{d}_i, \mathbf{y}) \geq \Delta(\mathbf{y}_i^*, \mathbf{y}) - \xi_i . \tag{10}$$

For each triple $(q_i, \mathbf{d}_i, \mathbf{y}_i)$ in the training set, a set of constraints (10) are added to the optimization problem. To see how these constraints indeed work, note that during the prediction the model chooses the ranking $\bar{\mathbf{y}}_i$ which maximizes $F(q_i, \mathbf{d}_i, \mathbf{y})$ given the fixed U and V. If the predicted ranking is an incorrect ranking $\bar{\mathbf{y}}$, i.e., $F(q_i, \mathbf{d}_i, \bar{\mathbf{y}}_i) > F(q_i, \mathbf{d}_i, \mathbf{y}_i^*)$ where $\mathbf{y}_i^*$ is the true ranking, the corresponding slack variable ξ_i must be at least $\Delta(\mathbf{y}_i^*, \bar{\mathbf{y}}_i)$ to satisfy the constraint. Considering all the triples $(q_i, \mathbf{d}_i, \mathbf{y}_i), i = 1, \ldots, N$, the sum of slacks (i.e., $\frac{1}{N}\sum_{i=1}^{N} \xi_i$) upper bounds the empirical risk $R^{\Delta}(f)$ defined in Equation (3). This is stated formally in Proposition 1.

Proposition 1. *Denote by $\xi^*(U, V)$ the optimal solution of the slack variables in Optimization Problem 1 for the given parameters U and V. Then $\frac{1}{N}\sum_{i=1}^{N} \xi_i^*$ is an upper bound on the empirical risk $R^{\Delta}(f)$.*

Similar to SVM, to avoid overfitting, the objective function (9) to be minimized is a tradeoff between the model complexity, and a hinge loss relaxation of Δ loss. A prechosen value of parameter λ controls this tradeoff and can be tuned to achieve a good performance via the cross validation procedure.

Note that by exploring the low rank property, the optimization problem is not convex. The well-known *kernel trick* is difficult to be applied to (9), while kernel trick is considered as one of the main benefits of the traditional support vector machine. Fortunately, a linear-SVM without using kernels has been shown to give competitive performances for textual documents classification [13]. On the other hand, according to the cross-modal retrieval approach PAMIR [11], a linear mapping of BoVW yeilds the highest performance of the other kernel mapping methods. As a result, with the multi-modal data under a certain feature representation, we argue that the model can indeed capture the linear structures of the multi-modal data to learn a cross-media semantic representation.

2.4 Algorithm and Implementation

Since $|\mathcal{Y}|$ is super-exponential in the size of the training set, our algorithm for learning U and V is adapted from the 1-slack margin-rescaling cutting-plane algorithm of Joachims et al [20]. The algorithm alternates between two steps, one optimizing the model parameters (U and V in our case) and the other updating the constraints set with a new batch of rankings $(\hat{\mathbf{y}}_1, \dots, \hat{\mathbf{y}}_N)$ ($\hat{\mathbf{y}}_i$ is one ranking for one query sample, $i = 1, \dots, N$) which most violate the current constraints. Once reaching a stopping criterion based on the accuracy of the empirical risk (the new constraint batch's empirical risk is no more than that of the current set of constraints within a tolerance $\epsilon > 0$), the algorithm terminates.

The general optimization procedure of LSCMR is listed in Algorithm 1. The code is implemented in MATLAB. The proof of the correctness can be easily extended from [20].

Algorithm 1 Latent Semantic Cross-Modal Ranking (LSCMR).

Input: ranking examples $(q_i, \mathbf{d}_i, \mathbf{y}_i^*), i = 1, \dots, N$, trade-off control parameter $\lambda > 0$, accuracy tolerance threshold $\epsilon > 0$

Output: mapping parameters U and V, slack variable $\xi \geq 0$

1: $\mathcal{W} \leftarrow \emptyset$

2: **repeat**

3: Solve for the optimal U, V and slack ξ:

$$\min_{U,V,\xi} \quad \frac{\lambda}{2}\|U\|_F^2 + \frac{\lambda}{2}\|V\|_F^2 + \xi$$

$$\text{s.t.} \quad \forall(\mathbf{y}_1, \dots, \mathbf{y}_N) \in \mathcal{W}:$$

$$\frac{1}{N}\sum_{i=1}^{N} \delta F(q_i, \mathbf{d}_i, \mathbf{y}_i) \geq \frac{1}{N}\sum_{i=1}^{N} \Delta(\mathbf{y}_i^*, \mathbf{y}_i) - \xi$$

4: **for** $i = 1$ **to** N **do**

5: $\hat{\mathbf{y}}_i \leftarrow \underset{\mathbf{y} \in \mathcal{Y}}{\text{argmax}} \Delta(\mathbf{y}_i^*, \mathbf{y}) + F(q_i, \mathbf{d}_i, \mathbf{y}_i)$

6: **end for**

7: $\mathcal{W} \leftarrow \mathcal{W} \cup (\hat{\mathbf{y}}_1, \dots, \hat{\mathbf{y}}_N)$

8: **until**

$$\frac{1}{N}\sum_{i=1}^{N} \Delta(\hat{\mathbf{y}}_i^*, \hat{\mathbf{y}}_i) - \frac{1}{N}\sum_{i=1}^{N} \delta F(q_i, \mathbf{d}_i, \hat{\mathbf{y}}_i) \leq \xi + \epsilon$$

9: **return** U, V, ξ;

To solve the optimization problem in Algorithm 1, there are two key issues to be resolved. One is searching for the most violated constraints, the so-called *separation oracle*, in Step 5. For different loss functions $\Delta(\mathbf{y}^*, \mathbf{y})$, different methods are proposed to address this issue, for example, [19] for AUC loss (defined as $1 - \text{AUC}(\mathbf{y}^*, \mathbf{y})$) and [32] for MAP loss. Recalling that F is the Frobenius inner product of $U^T V$ and Ψ, their work [19, 32] can be easily applied to this algorithm with a minor modification in implementation to reduce the computational complexity.

The other key issue is how to solve the optimization problem in Step 3. Since the problem is not a convex problem, the parameters U and V are initialized with their previous (local) optimal values while in the beginning they are randomly initialized using a normal distribution with mean zero and standard deviation one. We have implemented a subgradient descent solver adapted from Pegasos algorithm [27] originally proposed for solving a traditional support vector machine. The Pegasos algorithm is a simple iterative algorithm which alternates between stochastic subgradient descent and projection steps, and is shown to be effective to solve the primal problem of SVM. In the problem, the subgradient descent is performed by iteratively picking the most violated ranking tuple $(\hat{\mathbf{y}}_1, \hat{\mathbf{y}}_2, \dots, \hat{\mathbf{y}}_N)$ from the set $\mathcal{W}$ to minimize the slack variable.

On iteration t, the update for U is given by:

$$U_{t+\frac{1}{2}} \leftarrow (1 - \eta_t \lambda) U_t + \frac{\eta_t}{N} \sum_{i=1}^{N} V_t (\delta\Psi(q_i, \mathbf{d}_i, \hat{\mathbf{y}}_i))^T \tag{11}$$

where η_t is the learning rate on iteration t which is adjustable and $\delta\Psi(q_i, \mathbf{d}_i, \hat{\mathbf{y}}_i) \triangleq \Psi(q_i, \mathbf{d}_i, \mathbf{y}_i^*) - \Psi(q_i, \mathbf{d}_i, \hat{\mathbf{y}}_i)$. U_{t+1} is obtained by projecting $U_{t+\frac{1}{2}}$ onto the set for acceleration (see [27]):

$$B = \{U : \|U\|_F \leq 1/\sqrt{\lambda}\} \tag{12}$$

The update for V can be derived similarly except for the most violated ranking tuple which is computed using the updated U_{t+1}. The update is calculated exactly as given by:

$$V_{t+\frac{1}{2}} \leftarrow (1 - \eta_t \lambda) V_t + \frac{\eta_t}{N} \sum_{i=1}^{N} U_{t+1} \delta\Psi(q_i, \mathbf{d}_i, \hat{\mathbf{y}}_i) \tag{13}$$

followed by the projection step (12).

Moreover, our problem is a bit different from Pegasos [27]: the objective function is penalized by $\frac{\lambda}{2}(\|U\|_F^2 + \|V\|_F^2)$ to control the model perplexity. It should be noted that the optimal U and V must satisfy the condition $\|U\|_F = \|V\|_F$ since the prediction rule uses the product $U^T V$ only. Thus after each subgradient descent, the updated U and V are forced to be multiplied with a constant respectively to ensure $\|U\|_F = \|V\|_F$ while keeping $\|U^T V\|_F$ fixed. Let $\alpha = \sqrt{\|U\|_F \|V\|_F}$,

$$U \leftarrow \alpha U / \|U\|_F$$
$$V \leftarrow \alpha V / \|V\|_F$$

The experiments show that this strategy yields a much faster convergence rate. For fixing tolerance $\epsilon = 0.01$, the loop in Algorithm 1 usually terminates within 200 iterations.

3. PRIOR WORK

There has been a great deal of research devoted to the development of algorithms for learning the similarity between the data with different modalities in order to perform cross-modal retrieval. Most of cross-modal metric learning approaches tend to project multi-modal data into a common (or shared) subspace so that the correlation between multi-modal data is preserved or maximized. As one of the most popular approaches to finding a pair of linear transformations to maximize the correlations between two variables, Canonical Correlation Analysis (CCA) [15] and its extensions are applied in cross-modal similarity learning. For example, after the maximally correlated subspaces of text and image features are obtained by CCA, logistic regression is employed to cross-modal retrieval in [26]. As a supervised kernelizable extension of CCA, Generalized Multiview Analysis [28] is conducted to map data in different modality spaces to a single (non)linear subspace. Motivated by the fact that dictionary learning (DL) methods have the intrinsic power of capturing the heterogeneous features by generating different dictionaries for multi-modal data, multi-modal dictionary learning is recently applied to cross-modal metric learning [16, 24]. Following the the seminal work of Blei et al. [5], LDA has been extended to learn the joint distribution of multi-modal data (e.g., text and imagery) such as correspondence LDA [4], topic-regression multi-modal LDA [25], Multi-modal Document Random Field [17] and hierarchical Dirichlet process (HDP)-based LDA [30].

The aforementioned approaches, either optimizing the similarity (distance) between pairs of samples or optimizing the likelihood of the topic models, do not optimize for the final ranking performance directly. While bearing a resemblance to multi-modal metric learning which aims at learning the similarity or the distance measure from multi-modal data, the multi-modal ranking function is generally optimized by an evaluation criterion or a loss function defined over the *permutation* space induced by the scoring function over the target documents.

Traditionally, algorithms of learning to rank can be categorized into the pointwise approaches, the pairwise approaches, and the listwise approaches. The main differences among these three categories of approaches actually lie in the input representations and the loss functions employed in training. It is observed that the listwise and pairwise approaches usually outperform the pointwise approaches [21].

In [18] Joachims et al. trained a Ranking Support Vector Machine (RankSVM) to learn the weights of the hand-designed features in which the training set was a set of documents preference pairs obtained through the clickthrough data from the query-log of a search engine. The retrieval function is automatically learned by taking a support vector machine. The goal of RankSVM is to minimize the average number of the inversions in ranking; thus the method is considered as a pairwise preference satisfaction approach.

Unlike the pairwise approaches, Cao et al. [6] first noticed the fact that ranking was a prediction task on a list of documents and took the ranking lists as training instances. They trained two probabilistic models, respectively referred to as permutation probability and top k probability, to define a listwise loss function for learning.

Yue et al. [32] proposed another listwise approach SVM^{map} to solve the problem of learning to rank in a discriminative way. The method uses the structural SVM framework [29] with the loss function defined as MAP (mean average precision) loss that globally optimizes a hinge-loss relaxation of MAP loss. This method simplifies the process of obtaining ranking functions with a high MAP performance by avoiding the additional intermediate steps and heuristics.

Chakrabarti et al. [7] proposed almost-linear-time algorithms to optimize MRR (mean reciprocal rank) and NDCG (normalized discounted cumulative gain). Further, they folded multiple ranking loss functions into a multi-criteria max-margin optimization problem to develop a single, robust ranking model with close to the best accuracy of the learners trained on individual criterions.

Different from the aforementioned *uni*-modal learning to rank techniques, to the best of our knowledge, Passive Aggressive Model for Image Retrieval (PAMIR) is the first attempt to address the problem of ranking images by text query directly [11]. PAMIR formulates the cross-modal retrieval problem similar to RankSVM and derives an efficient training procedure by adapting the Passive-Aggressive algorithm.

The authors of [23] studied metric learning as a problem of learning to rank. They presented a general metric learning algorithm based on the structural SVM, to learn a metric such that the ranking of data induced by the distance from a query can be optimized again various ranking measures. Different from LSCMR, they focused on learning a intra-modality metric which restricts a positive semi-define matrix W (see Eq. (1)) to learn a valid metric and does not introduce a low rank embedding.

The text and imagery are usually represented as BoW and BoVW in a high-dimensional vector space. However, the high-dimensional vector space representation suffers from its inability to cope with two classic problems, i.e., synonymy and polysemy. To capture the latent semantic associations of data and to address these problems, embedding words in a low-dimensional latent space to capture the semantics is a classic approach in text retrieval such as Latent Semantic Indexing (LSI) [9] and pLSA [14]. The idea of low rank embedding is introduced into Supervised Semantic Indexing (SSI) for cross-lingual retrieval [2]. SSI defines a set of linear low rank models to take account of correlations between words (synonymy and polysemy). Related to SSI, Polynomial Semantic Indexing (PSI) [3] generalizes and extends the SSI approach to general polynomial models which could be used to capture the higher order relationships among words.

4. EXPERIMENTS AND RESULTS

The main goal of the experiments is to evaluate the effectiveness of the proposed LSCMR approach. To show its competitive performance, LSCMR is compared with other three state-of-the-art approaches (CCA, PAMIR and SSI) for cross-modal ranking.

These comparative methods are elaborately chosen for the fair comparisons. Comparing with the classical CCA method aims to test LSCMR's ability to learn a useful latent space; PAMIR has been shown to outperform pLSA and SVM [11]; however it does not consider a latent space; SSI introduces the low rank parameterizations while it minimizes a pairwise ranking loss and lacks of parameter regularization. Since LSCMR can generate low rank matrices U and V (see Eq. (2)), in the experiments, we demonstrate that the learned model also discovers the latent correlations between textual words and topics.

4.1 Experimental Setup

Two public real-world datasets are used in the comparative experiments. They are the largest available multimodal datasets that are fully paired and labeled (tagged), to the best of our knowledge. Both datasets are bi-modal with the image and the associated text modalities. The statistics of the two datasets are summarized in Table 1.

The first dataset, Wikipedia feature articles[1], consists of 2,866 images, each with a short paragraph describing the

[1] `http://www.svcl.ucsd.edu/projects/crossmodal/`

Table 1: The statistics of the datasets used.

	Wikipedia	NUS-WIDE
BoVW vocabulary size	1000	500
BoW vocabulary size	5000	1000
Avg. # of words/image	**117.5**	**7.73**
Documents Partition[a]	1,500/500 866	2,664/23,977 106,567
Queries Partition[a]	1,500/500 866	2,664/2,000 2,000

[a] Partitions are ordered by training/validation/test.

image. The images are labeled with exactly one of the 10 different semantic classes, such as art and geography. In the originally provided dataset, the text comes with a 10 dimensional feature vector representing the probabilistic distributions over the 10 topics, which are derived from a Latent Dirichlet Allocation (LDA) model [5]. We note that LSCMR and the comparative methods all resort to the raw low-level features rather than the high-level semantic features. For the training text, we extract 5,000-dimensional feature vectors using the bag of words (BoW) representation with the TF-IDF weighting scheme. For images, we first extract SIFT points from each images in the dataset. The randomly selected SIFT points are clustered by k-means to generate 1,000 centers as the visual dictionary. Then each image is quantized into a 1,000 dimensional histogram feature vector using the bag-of-visual-words (BoVW) model.

The second dataset, NUS-WIDE[2], contains 133,208 images with 1,000 tags and 81 concepts, which are pruned from the NUS dataset by keeping the images that have at least one tag and one concept. For the feature representation, we use the publicly available 1,000 dimensional text feature vector (namely tags) and 500 dimensional image feature vector based on SIFT BoVW kindly provided by the authors.

Another reason why we choose these two datasets is due to the large difference on the average number of the textual words per image and the dimensionality of the text space. In Wiki dataset the textual descriptions are based on Wikipedia surrounding paragraphs which yield a 5,000 dimension text space and in average there are 117.5 surrounding words per image. The NUS dataset, on the other hand, is based on Flickr user-provided tags which yield a 1,000 dimension text space and in average there are 7.73 words (tags) per image. A manual examination reveals that the synonymy and polysemy problem may occur more frequently in the Wiki dataset than in the NUS dataset. For their difference, first we want to examine our algorithm's ability to learn a latent space for the Wiki dataset and second we want to see whether our algorithm decays rapidly with the NUS dataset.

Note that the two datasets are both presented by pairs of text and imagery where CCA can be trained by this setting. For the other three methods (PAMIR, SSI and LSCMR), the restriction of paired correspondence of a text document and an image is not needed. On the contrary, the queries and the corresponding ranking lists are needed as training examples of the three methods. These training examples originate from both direction of the text-query-image retrieval and the image-query-text retrieval. For this purpose, we first define the relevance assessment. For the Wiki dataset, we define that a target document d is relevant to a query q if d and q belong to the same semantic class. Similarly, for the NUS dataset, a target document d is relevant if it shares at least one concept with query q. The ranking examples are generated as follows: for each text (image) query, we randomly selected 40 images (text documents) in the other modality in the training set as candidates and then the selected target documents are automatically labeled as relevant or irrelevant to form a ranking example.

[2]`http://lms.comp.nus.edu.sg/research/NUS-WIDE.htm`

For all the 2,866 generated ranking examples in the Wiki dataset, we randomly sample 1,500 examples to form the training set, of which 500 examples form the validation set. The rest are used to form the testing set. For NUS, 2,664 ranking examples are randomly selected to be the training samples and 2,000 to be validation samples (see Table 1). To be fair, all the comparative approaches are trained and tested on the same training set and testing set respectively.

For both datasets, performance evaluations are conducted using standard information retrieval metrics. We use *Mean Average Precision* (MAP) as the performance measures. Let $p^* = \text{rank}(\mathbf{y}^*)$ (true ranking with two rank value $+1$ and -1) and $p = \text{rank}(\mathbf{y})$ (predicted ranking with a total order). Given a query and a set of R retrieved target documents, the *Average Precision* (AP) is defined as

$$\text{AP}(p^*, p) = \frac{1}{L}\sum_{j=1}^{R} Prec(j) \cdot Rel(j) \tag{14}$$

where L is the number of the relevant documents in the retrieved set, $Prec(j)$ is the percentage of the relevant documents in the top j documents in predicted ranking p and $Rel(j)$ is an indicator function equaling 1 if the item at rank j in predicted ranking p is a relevant document, zero otherwise. We then average the AP values from all the queries in the query set to obtain the MAP score. The larger the MAP, the better the performance. In the experiments, R is the number of the retrieved documents to be examined, where we set $R = 50$ or $R = all$ for all the retrieved documents. Recalling that our model can be optimized for various ranking measures, we implement the greedy algorithm for optimizing the average precision proposed in [32].

We report the performance results on both directions of ranking images from text queries (*text-query-image*) and ranking text documents from image queries (*image-query-text*). Besides, to give an pictorial demonstration of an algorithm's performance, the *Precision-Recall* curves are also reported on all the approaches.

4.2 Results on the Wiki Dataset

Table 2 reports the performance of LSCMR and the other comparative models on the testing set of the Wiki dataset, showing that LSCMR outperforms all the comparative methods on both directions of the retrieval tasks. Compared to the best comparative methods, the minimum relative improvement is 9.6 percent gained by LSCMR for the image-query-text retrieval with $R = 50$ and the maximum is 25.3 percent also for the image-query-text retrieval with $R = all$.

This improvement is due to the latent semantic space. To verify this, we note that the low-rank based SSI also outperforms PAMIR in the image-query-text retrieval while PAMIR even controls the model complexity by optimizing an adapted cross-modal RankSVM model. Further, LSCMR outperforms SSI due to the structural large margin that reg-

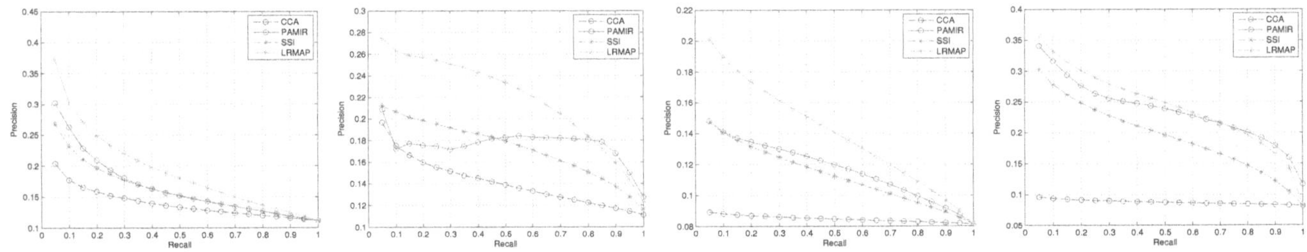

(a) Wiki Text Query (b) Wiki Image Query (c) NUS Text Query (d) NUS Image Query

Figure 2: Precision-Recall curves on the two datasets (LRMAP is short for LSCMR optimizing MAP).

Table 2: The performance comparison in terms of MAP@R scores on the Wiki dataset. Each text document is represented as 5000-D BoW and each image is presented as 1000-D BoVW. Both directions of ranking tasks are reported. The results shown in boldface are the best results.

		CCA	PAMIR	SSI	LSCMR
Text Query	$R = 50$	0.2343	0.3093	0.2821	**0.3663**
	$R = all$	0.1433	0.1734	0.1664	**0.2021**
Image Query	$R = 50$	0.2208	0.1797	0.2344	**0.2570**
	$R = all$	0.1451	0.1779	0.1759	**0.2229**

Table 3: The performance comparison in terms of MAP@R scores on the NUS dataset. Each text document is represented as 1000-D BoW and each image is presented as 500-D BovW. Both directions of ranking tasks are reported. The results shown in boldface are the best results.

		CCA	PAMIR	SSI	LSCMR
Text Query	$R = 50$	0.1497	0.2046	0.2156	**0.2781**
	$R = all$	0.0851	0.1184	0.1140	**0.1424**
Image Query	$R = 50$	0.1523	**0.5003**	0.4101	0.4997
	$R = all$	0.0883	0.2410	0.1992	**0.2491**

ularizes the model and optimizes for MAP ranking loss directly. The Precision-Recall curves on both directions are reported in Figure 2(a) and 2(b). The Precision-Recall curves further validate the superiority of LSCMR for the cross-modal ranking.

Recall that the CCA model is trained by the pairs of data objects with different modalities and learns a unified model for the retrieval tasks of both directions. Hence, CCA has achieved nearly the same performance in both image-query-text retrieval and text-query-image retrieval. On the other hand, the performances of other three approaches (including LSCMR) are noticeably different in the corresponding both directions of the retrieval.

4.3 Results on the NUS Dataset

The improvement of LSCMR on the NUS dataset is not as significant as that on the Wiki dataset. The MAP scores of all the methods are shown in Table 3 and the Precision-Recall curves are reported in Figure 2(c) and Figure 2(d). For text-query-image retrieval, LSCMR outperforms the other comparative methods again while for image-query-text retrieval LSCMR outperforms all the comparative methods in all the cases except for the case of $R = 50$ where PAMIR has a slightly better overall performance than LSCMR.

Recall that in the NUS-WIDE dataset, one image is associated with about seven annotated words in average. The low rank embedding does not help much for querying short texts in the task of image-query-text retrieval. PAMIR and LSCMR both train a regularized model, and therefore the performances of PAMIR and LSCMR is undoubtedly super to SSI in the image-query-text retrieval.

Once again, it is observed that CCA has a very similar performance in both directions of the retrieval.

4.4 The Performance Discussions

It is noted that LSCMR has a better overall performance for text-query-image retrieval than for image-query-text retrieval in the Wiki dataset and a better overall performance for image-query-text retrieval than for text-query-image retrieval in the NUS dataset. The reason exactly lies in the low-rank embedding of LSCMR that is capable of discerning the latent aspect space and consequently supports rich-semantic queries. For the Wiki dataset, each document has over one hundred words in average, resulting in a long text query which is presumably much richer in semantics than the case in the NUS dataset where each image has only about seven text words in given as the annotation that is much shorter when posed as a query. On the other hand, the overall image quality in the NUS dataset is much richer and more diverse in semantics than that in the Wiki dataset, and thus resulting in a better overall performance for image-query-text-retrieval.

As we have stated that for both datasets CCA achieves very similar performances in both directions of the retrieval tasks. The reason is that CCA learns a unified model from paired multi-modal data in which the pair-correspondence of images and text documents ensure an equal contribution to the learned metric between both modalities. However, a unified model like CCA does not give a good performance which is verified in both datasets. Our explanation is as follows: it is not the problem of unified models but the problem of taking strictly paired data as training instances; in such settings CCA can not capture the complete ranking information (e.g. dissimilarity between data in different modalities). Nevertheless, learning a unified model with ranking lists is still our interests for future work.

Overall, the results on the Wiki dataset and NUS dataset demonstrate that the use of LSCMR is advantageous for rich-semantic queries and has a superior performance in both

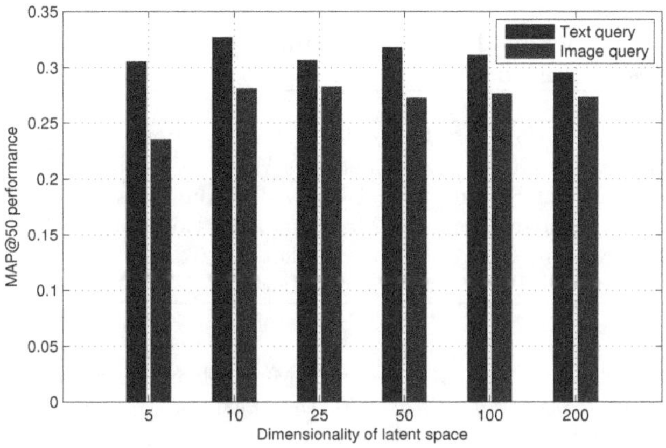

Figure 3: The performance (MAP@50) comparisons for the Wiki dataset when the dimensions of latent space are set to different values. The dimensionality of 10 is reported to be the best for the overall performance of text query and image query.

Table 4: Exemplar words along with their top 9 neighboring words from the Wiki dataset.

Fiction	Stories Manuscript Tales Language Theatre Poetry Editor Publisher Powell
Football	Teams Player NHL Goal Conference Compete Olympics Matches Yards
DVD	Moves Brand Broadcasting Movies Victims Commented Sequel Direction Producer
Airport	Passenger Oregon Democratic Communities Bring Lands Telephone Sale Coverage

directions of the cross-modal retrieval than that of the peer methods from the state-of-the-art literature.

4.5 The Embedding Latent Space

The results over the Wiki dataset outline the advantage of LSCMR over the comparative solutions, especially PAMIR. This observation is certainly due to the low rank embedding used in LSCMR. Now we look into the learned embedding latent aspect space for the Wiki dataset. Since the BoVW features used in our experiments originate from the SIFT points which are difficult to illustrate, we only demonstrate the latent space by textual words.

First, the dimensionality of the subspace (also the size of U and V) is a parameter to be determined before solving Optimization Problem 1. We tune this parameter via a validation set and the MAP@50 performance over a candidate set of the chosen dimensionalities is reported in Figure 3. It is observed that LSCMR performs the best with the optimal subspace dimensionality of 10. When the chosen dimensionality of the latent subspace is larger (even much larger) than 10, the performances do not decay rapidly at the same time it is observed that the topics overlap. But we find something interesting that though some topics overlap, some smaller but more precise topics are discovered (see the two "Biology" topics in Table 5).

Second, consider the mapping of textual words into the latent space in LSCMR. For a text query q, Uq maps q into the latent space. Note that $U \in \mathbb{R}^{k \times m}$ where k represents the dimensionality of the latent space. For each row in U, the row weights the contribution of all words to the corresponding "topic" in the latent space. The larger the number U_{ij}, the more positive correlation between topic i and word j. We then sort every row by which the most relevant words are ranked ahead. We present some topic examples in Table 5. The columns in U acts a similar way like the rows except for that each column represents the relevance between the corresponding word and all topics. We define two words are neighbors if their relevance with all topics are similar. Some examples on the neighboring words are shown in Table 4.

5. CONCLUSIONS

In this work, we have presented a new approach to solving the problem of cross-modal retrieval by casting the problem as a problem of learning to rank in a supervised manner with the idea of low rank embedding. We have demonstrated the effectiveness of our proposed method LSCMR and have shown significant improvements over the comparative methods especially on two datasets. We have also investigated the interpretability of the leaned low rank model by showing some examples on the textual topics and the neighboring words.

6. ACKNOWLEDGEMENTS

This work is supported by 973 Program (No. 2012CB316400), NSFC (61070068, 90920303), 863 program (2012AA012505), Chinese Knowledge Center of Engineering Science and Technology (CKCEST) and China Academic Digital Associative Library (CADAL). Zhongfei Zhang is also supported by US NSF (IIS-0812114, CCF-1017828).

7. REFERENCES

[1] R. Baeza-Yates and B. Ribeiro-Neto. *Modern Information Retrieval.* Addison-Wesley, 1999.

[2] B. Bai, J. Weston, D. Grangier, R. Collobert, K. Sadamasa, Y. Qi, O. Chapelle, and K. Weinberger. Learning to rank with (a lot of) word features. *Information Retrieval*, 13(3):291–314, 2010.

[3] B. Bai, J. Weston, D. Grangier, R. Collobert, K. Sadamasa, Y. Qi, C. Cortes, and M. Mohri. Polynomial semantic indexing. *Advances in Neural Information Processing Systems*, 22:64–72, 2009.

[4] D. Blei and M. Jordan. Modeling annotated data. In *Proceedings of the 26th Annual International ACM SIGIR Conference on Research and Development in Informaion Retrieval*, pages 127–134, 2003.

[5] D. Blei, A. Ng, and M. Jordan. Latent dirichlet allocation. *the Journal of Machine Learning Research*, 3:993–1022, 2003.

[6] Z. Cao, T. Qin, T. Liu, M. Tsai, and H. Li. Learning to rank: from pairwise approach to listwise approach. In *Proceedings of the 24th International Conference on Machine Learning*, pages 129–136, 2007.

[7] S. Chakrabarti, R. Khanna, U. Sawant, and C. Bhattacharyya. Structured learning for non-smooth ranking losses. In *Proceeding of the 14th ACM SIGKDD International Conference on Knowledge Discovery and Data Mining*, pages 88–96, 2008.

[8] K. Crammer, O. Dekel, J. Keshet, S. Shalev-Shwartz, and Y. Singer. Online passive-aggressive algorithms. *The Journal of Machine Learning Research*, 7:551–585, 2006.

Table 5: **Exemplar topics from the Wiki dataset. We assign each learned topic to its most probable category. Topic words are sorted by their importance values in the descending order.**

Category	Topic Words
Geography & Places	Guadalcanal Corps Sale Airport Battleships Iowa Aircraft Carriers Chicago Puerto
Biology	Subspecies Breeding Dinosaurs Fossils Wallace Genus Marsh Females Wings Virginia
Warface	Puerto Battalion Guadalcanal Oklahoma Soviet Soldier Tank Bishop Bradman Infantry
Literature & Theatre	Hamlet Theatre Gilbert Uncle Stories Shakespeare Refugees Manuscript Fiction Punk
Sports & Recreation	Tech Jordan Players Championship Tournament Olympic NHL Cricket EP Coach
Biology	Puerto Zoo Skull Nest Augustus Specimen Tail Teeth Organisms Darwin

[9] S. Deerwester, S. Dumais, G. Furnas, T. Landauer, and R. Harshman. Indexing by latent semantic analysis. *Journal of the American Society for Information Science*, 41(6):391–407, 1990.

[10] J. Gao, W. Yuan, X. Li, K. Deng, and J. Nie. Smoothing clickthrough data for web search ranking. In *Proceedings of the 32nd International ACM SIGIR Conference on Research and Development in Information Retrieval*, pages 355–362, 2009.

[11] D. Grangier and S. Bengio. A discriminative kernel-based approach to rank images from text queries. *IEEE Transactions on Pattern Analysis and Machine Intelligence*, 30(8):1371–1384, 2008.

[12] D. Hardoon, S. Szedmak, and J. Shawe-Taylor. Canonical correlation analysis: An overview with application to learning methods. *Neural Computation*, 16(12):2639–2664, 2004.

[13] C. Ho and C. Lin. Large-scale linear support vector regression. Technical report, National Taiwan University, 2012.

[14] T. Hofmann. Probabilistic latent semantic indexing. In *Proceedings of the 22nd Annual International ACM SIGIR Conference on Research and Development in Information Retrieval*, pages 50–57, 1999.

[15] H. Hotelling. Relations between two sets of variates. *Biometrika*, 28(3/4):321–377, 1936.

[16] Y. Jia, M. Salzmann, and T. Darrell. Factorized latent spaces with structured sparsity. *Advances in Neural Information Processing Systems*, 23:982–990, 2010.

[17] Y. Jia, M. Salzmann, and T. Darrell. Learning cross-modality similarity for multinomial data. In *IEEE International Conference on Computer Vision*, pages 2407–2414, 2011.

[18] T. Joachims. Optimizing search engines using clickthrough data. In *Proceedings of the 8th ACM SIGKDD International Conference on Knowledge Discovery and Data Mining*, pages 133–142, 2002.

[19] T. Joachims. A support vector method for multivariate performance measures. In *Proceedings of the 22nd International Conference on Machine Learning*, pages 377–384, 2005.

[20] T. Joachims, T. Finley, and C. Yu. Cutting-plane training of structural svms. *Machine Learning*, 77(1):27–59, 2009.

[21] H. Li. Learning to rank for information retrieval and natural language processing. *Synthesis Lectures on Human Language Technologies*, 4(1):1–113, 2011.

[22] D. Lowe. Distinctive image features from scale-invariant keypoints. *International Journal of Computer Vision*, 60(2):91–110, 2004.

[23] B. McFee and G. Lanckriet. Metric learning to rank. In *Proceedings of the 27th International Conference on Machine Learning*. Citeseer, 2010.

[24] G. Monaci, P. Jost, P. Vandergheynst, B. Mailhe, S. Lesage, and R. Gribonval. Learning multimodal dictionaries. *IEEE Transactions on Image Processing*, 16(9):2272–2283, 2007.

[25] D. Putthividhy, H. Attias, and S. Nagarajan. Topic regression multi-modal latent dirichlet allocation for image annotation. In *IEEE Conference on Computer Vision and Pattern Recognition*, pages 3408–3415, 2010.

[26] N. Rasiwasia, J. Costa Pereira, E. Coviello, G. Doyle, G. Lanckriet, R. Levy, and N. Vasconcelos. A new approach to cross-modal multimedia retrieval. In *Proceedings of the International Conference on Multimedia*, pages 251–260, 2010.

[27] S. Shalev-Shwartz, Y. Singer, and N. Srebro. Pegasos: Primal estimated sub-gradient solver for svm. In *Proceedings of the 24th International Conference on Machine Learning*, pages 807–814, 2007.

[28] A. Sharma, A. Kumar, H. Daume, and D. Jacobs. Generalized multiview analysis: A discriminative latent space. In *IEEE Conference on Computer Vision and Pattern Recognition*, pages 2160–2167, 2012.

[29] I. Tsochantaridis, T. Joachims, T. Hofmann, and Y. Altun. Large margin methods for structured and interdependent output variables. *Journal of Machine Learning Research*, 6(2):1453–1484, 2006.

[30] S. Virtanen, Y. Jia, A. Klami, and T. Darrell. Factorized multi-modal topic model. In *Proceedings of the 28th Conference on Uncertainty in Artificial Intelligence*, pages 843–851, 2012.

[31] Y. Yang, N. Bansal, W. Dakka, P. Ipeirotis, N. Koudas, and D. Papadias. Query by document. In *Proceedings of the Second ACM International Conference on Web Search and Data Mining*, pages 34–43, 2009.

[32] Y. Yue, T. Finley, F. Radlinski, and T. Joachims. A support vector method for optimizing average precision. In *Proceedings of the 30th Annual International ACM SIGIR Conference on Research and Development in Information Retrieval*, pages 271–278, 2007.

[33] Y.-T. Zhuang, Y. Yang, and F. Wu. Mining semantic correlation of heterogeneous multimedia data for cross-media retrieval. *IEEE Transactions on Multimedia*, 10(2):221–229, 2008.

Learning to Name Faces: A Multimodal Learning Scheme for Search-Based Face Annotation

Dayong Wang†, Steven C.H. Hoi†, Pengcheng Wu†,
Jianke Zhu‡, Ying He†, Chunyan Miao†
†School of Computer Engineering, Nanyang Technological University, Singapore.
‡College of Computer Science, Zhejiang University, Hangzhou, 310027, China.
{s090023, chhoi, wupe0003, yhe, ascymiao}@ntu.edu.sg, jkzhu@zju.edu.cn

ABSTRACT

Automated face annotation aims to automatically detect human faces from a photo and further name the faces with the corresponding human names. In this paper, we tackle this open problem by investigating a search-based face annotation (SBFA) paradigm for mining large amounts of web facial images freely available on the WWW. Given a query facial image for annotation, the idea of SBFA is to first search for top-n similar facial images from a web facial image database and then exploit these top-ranked similar facial images and their weak labels for naming the query facial image. To fully mine those information, this paper proposes a novel framework of Learning to Name Faces (L2NF) – a unified multimodal learning approach for search-based face annotation, which consists of the following major components: (i) we enhance the weak labels of top-ranked similar images by exploiting the "label smoothness" assumption; (ii) we construct the multimodal representations of a facial image by extracting different types of features; (iii) we optimize the distance measure for each type of features using distance metric learning techniques; and finally (iv) we learn the optimal combination of multiple modalities for annotation through a *learning to rank* scheme. We conduct a set of extensive empirical studies on two real-world facial image databases, in which encouraging results show that the proposed algorithms significantly boost the naming accuracy of search-based face annotation task.

Categories and Subject Descriptors

H.3.3 [**Information Storage and Retrieval**]: Information Search and Retrieval; I.2.6 [**Artificial Intelligence**]: Learning

General Terms

Algorithms, Experimentation

Keywords

web facial images, auto face annotation, supervised learning

1. INTRODUCTION

Automated face annotation aims to automatically detect human faces from a photo image and name the facial image with the corresponding human names, which sometimes is termed as "face naming" or "face tagging" in some existing studies. It is an important yet very challenging problem in multimedia information retrieval, which is highly desirable for many real-world applications, such as online photo management or face annotation for video summarization. One possible way is to directly apply some classical face recognition methods [3, 30, 33]. For exmaple, one can apply supervised machine learning techniques to train face classification models from a collection of well-controlled labeled facial images and then apply the models to name a new facial image. However, such kinds of "*model-based face annotation*" techniques suffer from some common drawbacks, e.g., being difficult and expensive to collect large high-quality training data and being non-trivial for adding new training data.

Recent years have witnessed an emerging promising direction to tackle the automated face annotation challenge, i.e., the "*Search-Based Face Annotation*" (SBFA) paradigm [37, 38] which attempts to explore content-based image retrieval (CBIR) techniques [16, 43] in mining massive WWW facial images freely available on the internet, such as popular social sharing web sites (e.g., Flickr or Facebook). Due to the noisy nature of web images, the raw labels of web facial images are often noisy without extra manual effort, in which some facial images are tagged with incorrect/incomplete names. We refer to such kind of raw facial image database as "weakly labeled web facial image database".

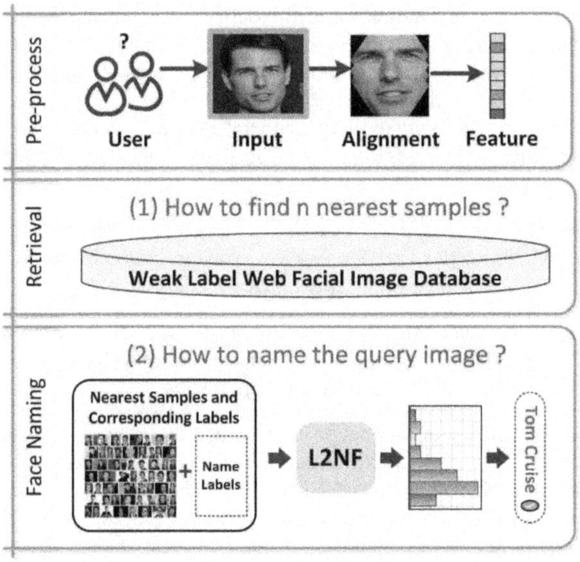

Figure 1: The framework of Search-Based Face Annotation.

Figure 1 illustrates the basic framework of the "*Search-based Face Annotation*" paradigm, which consists of three main stages: (i) given a query facial image, it typically involves a pre-processing stage, including face detection, face alignment, and facial feature extraction; consequently, the input facial image is represented as feature vectors in the facial feature space; (ii) we retrieve the top-n similar instances of the query facial image from the large-scale weakly labeled web facial image database using content-based image retrieval techniques; and (iii) finally, we aim to name the query image by mining the top-ranked similar images and the corresponding weak name labels. Such a paradigm was inspired by the search-based image annotation [39] for generic image annotation as face annotation can be generally viewed as a special case of image annotation [9, 10, 32, 36, 41, 49], which has been extensively studied, but remains still an technically challenging problem. In the following, we explain the main challenges of this task to motivate the proposed new technique.

As shown in Figure 1, there are two key challenging tasks for the search-based face annotation framework: (i) how to efficiently retrieve the top-n most similar facial images from a large facial image database given a query facial image, that is, how to develop an effective content-based facial image retrieval solution; and (ii) how to effectively exploit the short list of candidate facial images and their weak labels for naming the faces automatically. In general, these two tasks can be solved separately, though the second task can be affected by the results of the first task. As one can tackle the first task by adapting existing CBIR techniques [24, 43, 7, 42], in this paper we focus on the second challenge, which is critical due to the nature of noisily labeled web facial images.

In this paper, we propose a novel framework of "*Learning to Name Faces*" (L2NF) for search-based face annotation, which attempts to learn both the *optimal weight vector* in combining different query-neighbor similarity functions for face naming and the *refined labels* for enhancing the initial weak labels simultaneously in a unified learning framework. In particular, the key challenge of naming the query facial image is to effectively measure the similarity between the query image and its nearest instances by combining diverse facial feature representations and their proper distance measurements. To tackle this challenge, we propose a multimodal learning scheme that (i) first constructs multiple diverse facial features for representing the faces, (ii) further optimizes the distance measure on each feature space (modality) using distance metric learning, and (iii) finally learns the optimal fusion of the multiple representations by adapting the structural SVM algorithm. Besides, we suggest a graph-based label refinement scheme to enhance the weak labels of top-ranked similar facial images by exploiting the "label smoothness" assumption. The main contributions of this work include:

- We propose a novel "Learning to Name Faces" (L2NF) scheme, which tackles the face naming problem by exploring multimodal learning on weakly labeled facial image data.
- We conduct extensive experiments to evaluate the proposed algorithm for face annotation on large-scale web facial image databases and obtain encouraging results.

The remainder of this paper is organized as follows. Section 2 reviews related work. Section 3 presents the proposed algorithms of Learning to Name Faces (L2NF). Section 4 shows the experimental results of our empirical studies. Section 5 discusses the limitations, and finally Section 6 concludes this paper.

2. RELATED WORK

Automated face annotation can be directly solved by general face recognition and verification techniques, which have been extensively studied for many years [20]. However, the success of such "*model-based face annotation*" scheme often relies on a large set of high-quality facial images collected in well-controlled environments, which can be difficult and expensive to obtain. This drawback has been partially addressed in recent benchmark studies of unconstrained face detection and verification techniques on facial image testbeds collected from the web, such as LFW [18, 5].

By focusing on the facial image domain, the studies for automated face annotation can be further classified into four groups. The first group of studies aim to handle the collections of personal photos [8], where rich context clues, such as social context, GPS tags, time tamps, are available. Some techniques have already been successfully deployed in the commercial applications, e.g., Apple iPhoto,[1] Google Picasa,[2] and Facebook face auto-tagging solution.[3] The second group of works consider to refine the text-based facial image retrieval results, where a human name is used as the input query [27, 22, 17, 12, 13]. Such problems are closely related to the image re-ranking problems, and part of top-ranked facial images are tagged with the name query. For example, Ozkan and Duygulu proposed a graph-based model for finding the densest sub-graph as the most related result [27], which is improved by adding an extra constraint such that a face can only appear once in an image [12] or by introducing the images of "friends" of the query name in a query expansion scheme [26]. Following the graph-based approach, Le and Satoh [22] proposed to represent the importance of each returned image. Recently, the generative approach has also been adopted in this problem and achieved better performance [12, 13]. The third group of works have attempted to directly annotate each web facial image with the names extracted from its caption information. For example, Berg et al. [3] proposed a probability model which is combined with a clustering algorithm to estimate the relationship between the facial images and the names in their captions. Guillaumin et al. [12] proposed to iteratively update the assignment between the facial image and detected names in captions based on a minimum cost matching algorithm, which is further improved by using supervised distance metric learning techniques to grasp the important discriminative features in low dimensional spaces in their subsequent work [13]. Recently, Bu et al. [4] proposed to estimate the distance between faces and names with "commute distance". The last group of studies is the "*search-based face annotation*" (SBFA), which was inspired by the search-based image annotation and is fundamentally different from the previous three groups of research. In particular, the SBFA framework aims to solve the generic content-based face annotation problem, where facial images are directly used as the input query images and the task is to return the corresponding human names for the query images. There are rather few studies in this group. For example, by attempting to mine the large-scale noisy web facial image with weak labels, Wang et al. [37] proposed an Unsupervised Label Refinement (URL) algorithm to enhance the initial weak label matrix over the entire facial image database. In their subsequent work [38], they further proposed the Weak Label Regularized Local Coordinate Coding (WLRLCC) algorithm, which aims to fully exploit the top-ranked similar images of the query facial image via a unified optimization scheme of learning both local coordinate coding and refined labels.

[1] http://www.apple.com/ilife/iphoto/
[2] http://picasa.google.com/
[3] http://www.facebook.com/

Recently, a few of emerging works have attempted to attack the automated face annotation problem via the "*search-based face annotation*" (SBFA) paradigm [37, 38]. It was generally inspired by the *search-based image annotation* that attempts to infer the correlation or joint probabilities between query images and annotation keywords based on existing object recognition techniques and semi-supervised learning algorithms in mining massive free web images on the WWW [9, 10, 6, 32, 15, 39, 29, 35, 28]. Several studies have attempted to develop efficient content-based indexing and search techniques to facilitate image tagging tasks. For example, Russell et al. [29] developed a large collection of web images with ground truth labels to facilitate object recognition tasks. More studies in this area aim to address the final annotation process by exploring effective label propagation algorithms. For example, Wright et al. [40] proposed a classification algorithm based sparse representation technique, which predicts the label information based on the class-based feature reconstruction. Tang et al. [32] presented a sparse graph-based semi-supervised learning (SGSSL) approach to annotate web images. Wang et al. [36] proposed another sparse coding based annotation framework, where the label-based graph is used to learn a linear transformation matrix for feature dimension reduction, and sparse reconstruction is employed for the subsequent label propagation step. Wu et al. [41] proposed to select heterogeneous features with structural grouping sparsity and suggested a Multi-label Boosting scheme (denoted as "MtBGS" for short) for feature regression, where a group sparse coefficient vector is obtained for each class (category) and further used for predicting new instances. Wu et al. [43] proposed a multi-reference re-ranking scheme (denoted as "MRR" for short) for improving the retrieval process.

Our work differs from the above existing works for search-based face annotation in several aspects. First of all, the ULR algorithm aims to refine the noisy labels over the entire facial image database, which is extremely time-consuming for the large-scale database. Unlike the ULR algorithm, our work tackles such a computationally expensive task by mining only the top-ranked similar images for each query, which follows the similar approach of the WLRLCC algorithm. Further, both ULR and WLRLCC algorithms are designed to explore only one single type of facial feature descriptor, e.g., the GIST features, while our work is designed to explore more clues by constructing multiple types of facial features descriptors and further learning to optimize the fusion of the multimodal representations.

3. L2NF — LEARNING TO NAME FACES

In this section, we present the proposed "Learning to Name Faces" (L2NF) framework for search-based face annotation in detail.

3.1 Preliminaries

Throughout the paper, we denote matrixes or sets by upper case letters, e.g., X and D; we denote vectors by bold lower case letters, e.g., $\mathbf{x}$, $\mathbf{x}_i$, $\mathbf{x}_{ij}$; we denote scalars by normal letters, e.g., x_i, X_{ij}, where x_i is the i-th element of vector $\mathbf{x}$ which could also be denoted as $\mathbf{x}[i]$, and X_{ij} is the element in the i-row and j-column of matrix X, which could also be denoted as $X[i, j]$.

Let us denote by $Q = \{\mathbf{q}_i | i = 1, 2, \ldots, N_t\}$ the set of query facial images, and assume there are a total of m names (classes) in the whole retrieval database, denoted by $C = \{c_1, c_2, \ldots, c_m\}$. Each query facial image $\mathbf{q}_i \in Q$ is associated with one name (class label) $c_{\mathbf{q}_i} \in C$. Notice that we assume that there is only one name for each person. We denote by $\mathbf{y}_{\mathbf{q}_i} \in \{0, 1\}^m$ the label vector for the query instance $\mathbf{q}_i$, which contains only one non-zero item: $\|\mathbf{y}_{\mathbf{q}_i}\|_0 = 1$. If the query instance $\mathbf{q}_i$ is annotated with the k-th name ($c_{\mathbf{q}_i} = c_k$), then $\mathbf{y}_{\mathbf{q}_i}[k] = 1$. In the SBFA framework, the name (label) of the query face is predicted based on its nearest facial images. Assume the top-n retrieval results of the query image $\mathbf{q}_i$ are $\{(\mathbf{d}_{ij}, \mathbf{y}_{ij}) | j = 1, 2, ..., n\}$, where $\mathbf{d}_{ij}$ is the j-th similar image in the retrieval result and $\mathbf{y}_{ij} \in \{0, 1\}^m$ is its corresponding label vector. We denote by $Y_i = [\mathbf{y}_{i1}, \mathbf{y}_{i2}, \ldots, \mathbf{y}_{in}] \in \mathbb{R}^{m \times n}$ the label matrix for the i-th query $\mathbf{q}_i$.

For each query-neighbor pair $(\mathbf{q}_i, \mathbf{d}_{ij})$, we can create one query-neighbor similarity based feature vector:

$$\mathbf{x}_{ij} = \mathbf{\Phi}(\mathbf{q}_i, \mathbf{d}_{ij}) = [\phi_k(\mathbf{q}_i, \mathbf{d}_{ij})]_{k=1}^{N_f}$$

where $\phi_k(\cdot, \cdot)$ represents the k-th query-neighbor similarity function and N_f is the number of the query-neighbor similarity functions. Typically, the query-neighbor similarity function is related to three factors: (1) the facial feature representation, (2) the distance metric, and (3) the mapping function between the distance value and the similarity value. For example, we can extract the Local binary patterns (LBP) as the facial feature, apply the L2-norm (Euclidean) distance as the distance metric, and the radial basis function with $\gamma = 0.1$ as the similarity-mapping function:

$$\exp(-\frac{1}{\gamma^2}\|\mathbf{q}_i^{(\mathrm{lbp})} - \mathbf{d}_{ij}^{(\mathrm{lbp})}\|^2).$$

To estimate the similarity more accurately by exploring more information, we can leverage multiple diverse query-neighbor similarity functions. More details about query-neighbor similarity function construction will be presented in Section 3.4. Based on the predefined query-neighbor similarity function and the achieved query-neighbor similarity based feature vector, for the i-th query instance $\mathbf{q}_i$, we denote its query-neighbor similarity matrix by $X_i = [\mathbf{x}_{ik}]$ with $k = 1, 2, \ldots, n$ and $X_i \in \mathbb{R}^{N_f \times n}$.

3.2 Problem Overview

The basic idea of the SBFA paradigm is to exploit the weak labels of top-ranked similar facial images for naming the query face. The crux for the face naming task lies in how to effectively estimate the confidence values for the weak label vectors of the top-ranked similar instances. Given a query image $\mathbf{q}_i$ and its top-n retrieval results $\{(\mathbf{d}_{ij}, \mathbf{y}_{ij}) | j = 1, 2, \ldots, n\}$, we denote by v_{ij} the confidence value for its j-th similar image $\mathbf{d}_{ij}$. Then, the estimated label vector of $\mathbf{q}_i$, denoted as $\hat{\mathbf{y}}_{\mathbf{q}_i}$, can be generated as:

$$\hat{\mathbf{y}}_{\mathbf{q}_i} = \sum_j \mathbf{y}_{ij} * v_{ij} = Y_i \mathbf{v}_i \tag{1}$$

where $\mathbf{v}_i = [v_{i1}, v_{i2}, \ldots, v_{in}]^\top$. Obviously, the confidence value v_{ij} is related to both query $\mathbf{q}_i$ and the j-th similar instance $\mathbf{d}_{ij}$. In our problem, we assume it linearly depends on the query-neighbor similarity based feature vector $\mathbf{x}_{ij}$, that is, $v_{ij} = \mathbf{x}_{ij}^\top \mathbf{w}$. Hence, the confidence vector $\mathbf{v}_i$ can be achieved as follows:

$$\mathbf{v}_i = X_i^\top \mathbf{w} \tag{2}$$

where $\mathbf{w} \in \mathbb{R}^{N_f}$ is a weight vector for multimodal fusion, which aims to combine different features of X generated by the N_f diverse similarity functions. In other words, each confidence value v_{ij} is a weighted linear combination of the corresponding query-neighbor similarity based feature vector $\mathbf{x}_{ij}$.

Remark. This aforementioned assumption is not difficult to understand as follows: each item in $\mathbf{x}_{ij}$ (e.g. the k-th item $\mathbf{x}_{ij}[k]$) is only related to the corresponding similarity function (e.g. $\phi_k(\cdot, \cdot)$). A large $\mathbf{x}_{ij}[k]$ indicates that the j-th retrieved instance is more similar to the query instance based on the k-th similarity function. Hence, it is more possible that the query instance has the same label

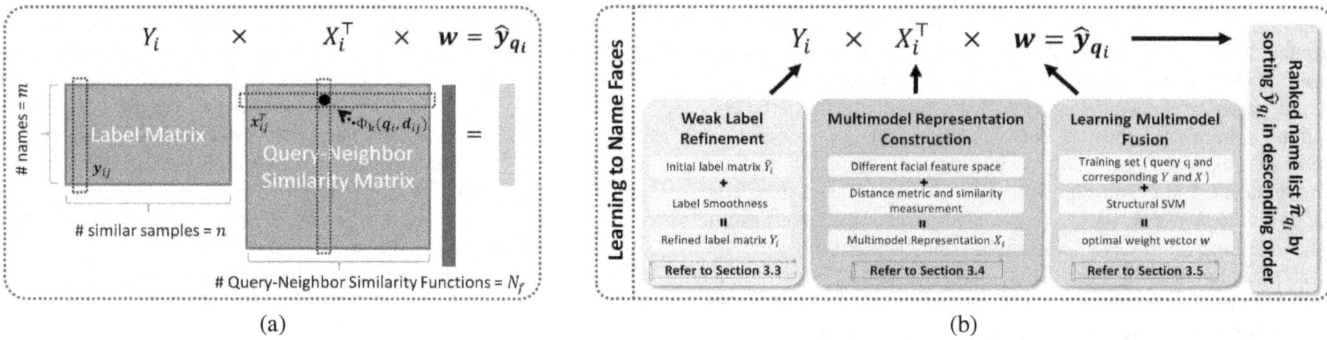

Figure 2: Introduction of face naming in "*Search-based Face Annotation*". (a) A visual explanation of Eq.(3). For a query instance $\mathbf{q}_i$, its top-n similar samples are $\{(\mathbf{d}_{ij}, \mathbf{y}_{ij})\}_{j=1,2,\ldots,n}$, and the predicted label vector is $\hat{\mathbf{y}}_{\mathbf{q}_i}$. $\mathbf{y}_{ij}$ is the label vector of the j-th nearest sample $\mathbf{d}_{ij}$. $\mathbf{x}_{ij}$ is the feature vector between the query instance $\mathbf{q}_i$ and the similar example $\mathbf{d}_{ij}$. The k-th item of $\mathbf{x}_{ij}$ is constructed with the k-th query-neighbor similarity function $\phi_k(\mathbf{q}_i, \mathbf{d}_{ij})$. The inter product value $\mathbf{x}_{ij}^\top \mathbf{w}$ is the confidence values v_{ij} for the j-th label vector $\mathbf{y}_{ij}$. (b) Three factors that affect the annotation performance of SBFA and the corresponding improvement solution.

vector with the j-th retrieved instance. As a result, the similarity value $\mathbf{x}_{ij}[k]$ is correlated with the the confidence value v_{ij}. Typically, different similarity functions can perform very differently in practice, hence they should be combined appropriately by a proper weight vector $\mathbf{w}$

By combining Eq.(1) and Eq.(2), the estimated label vector $\hat{\mathbf{y}}_{\mathbf{q}_i}$ for the query image $\mathbf{q}_i$ can be computed as follows:

$$\hat{\mathbf{y}}_{\mathbf{q}_i} = Y_i \mathbf{v}_i = Y_i X_i^\top \mathbf{w} \tag{3}$$

where Y_i and X_i vary for different query instances, and $\mathbf{w}$ is independent of the query instances. We show a visual example in Figure 2 (a) to help understand this formula.

To generate the final annotation results (a sorted candidate name list), we can rank all the m names by sorting the predicted label vector $\hat{\mathbf{y}}_{\mathbf{q}_i}$ in a descending order, as shown in Figure 2 (b). We denote by $\hat{\boldsymbol{\pi}}_{\mathbf{q}_i}$ the ranked name list, in which the item $\hat{\boldsymbol{\pi}}_{\mathbf{q}_i}[j] \in C$ is the j-th annotated name. Given the correct name of the query instance $\mathbf{q}_i$ is $c_{\mathbf{q}_i}$, a good annotation system should ensure $c_{\mathbf{q}_i}$ appears at the top-ranked position or ideally at the first position. Hence, our problem aims to minimize the ranking position of the correct name $c_{\mathbf{q}_i}$, which can be formulated as follows:

$$\min_{\mathbf{w}, Y_i, X_i} \sum_{i=1}^{N_t} \text{loss}(c_{\mathbf{q}_i}, \hat{\boldsymbol{\pi}}_{\mathbf{q}_i}) \tag{4}$$

$$\text{where } \hat{\boldsymbol{\pi}}_{\mathbf{q}_i} = \text{rank}(\hat{\mathbf{y}}_{\mathbf{q}_i}) \text{ and } \hat{\mathbf{y}}_{\mathbf{q}_i} = Y_i X_i^\top \mathbf{w}$$

In general, the loss value should be zero if the correct name $c_{\mathbf{q}_i}$ is at the first position of $\hat{\boldsymbol{\pi}}_{\mathbf{q}_i}$, and the loss value of $c_{\mathbf{q}_i}$ at the top-ranked position should be smaller than the one of $c_{\mathbf{q}_i}$ at a lower-ranked position. The goal of the whole learning to name faces scheme is to minimize the loss values over all the query instances by addressing the following three key factors: (i) the noisy label matrix Y_i, (ii) the query-neighbor similarity matrix X_i, and (iii) the combination weight vector $\mathbf{w}$, as shown in Figure 2 (b). In particular, we attempt to address each of them respectively in the following approach:

- To address the noisy nature of web images, we propose to refine the initial weak label information Y_i by a graph-based refinement scheme for exploiting the "label smoothness" assumption;
- To address the variances of web facial images captured under various conditions (illumination, position, age, and gender, etc.), we can construct multiple diverse query-neighbor similarity functions and further improve the similarity measurements by employing distance metric learning techniques;
- To find the optimal multimodal fusion, we propose a supervised learning to rank scheme to optimize the weight vector $\mathbf{w}$ by applying the structural SVM algorithms on a set of training query samples (N_t query images and their corresponding top-n retrieval results).

In the following, we will introduce the solutions of the aforementioned three problems respectively.

3.3 Weak Label Refinement

In this section, we aim to refine the initial weak label matrix for each query independently. In particular, for a query $\mathbf{q}$ (the subscript of query index value is omitted), its top-n similar samples are $\{\mathbf{d}_1, \ldots, \mathbf{d}_n\}$ and the corresponding noisy label matrix is denoted by $\tilde{Y}$. We enhance the initial label matrix $\tilde{Y}$ in a manifold learning scheme based on the key assumption of "*label smoothness*", which means that the more similar the visual contents of two facial images are, the more likely they share the same labels [37].

In particular, for two images $\mathbf{d}_i$ and $\mathbf{d}_j$ in the top-n nearest samples, we can compute their similarity value vector based on the query-neighbor similarity function: $\boldsymbol{\Phi}(\mathbf{d}_i, \mathbf{d}_j) \in \mathbb{R}^{N_f}$. By using the weight vector $\mathbf{w}$ learned in Section 3.5, we can get the similarity value between $\mathbf{d}_i$ and $\mathbf{d}_j$ as $S_{ij} = \mathbf{w}^\top \boldsymbol{\Phi}(\mathbf{d}_i, \mathbf{d}_j)$. A large value of S_{ij} indicates that $\mathbf{d}_i$ is more similar to $\mathbf{d}_j$. Hence, a larger value of S_{ij} implies that the label vectors of $\mathbf{d}_i$ and $\mathbf{d}_j$ are more likely to be the same. Based on the above motivation, we can obtain the following formulation to enhance the initial weak label matrix $\tilde{Y}$:

$$\min_{Y \geq 0} \sum_{i,j} S_{ij} * \|Y_{:i} - Y_{:j}\|^2 + \beta \|(Y - \tilde{Y}) \circ M\|_F^2 \tag{5}$$

where $\circ$ denotes the Hadamard product of two matrices, and M is the mask matrix indicating the non-zeros values in $\tilde{Y}$. In Eq.(5), the first term enforces the "*label smoothness*" assumption. Following the previous work [38], the second term is a regularization term that prevents the refined label matrix being deviated too much from the initial weak matrix $\tilde{Y}$. Notice that the label refinement problem in Eq.(5) depends on the weight vector $\mathbf{w}$ achieved by Eq.(9), while learning the weight vector $\mathbf{w}$ depends on the input data Y, as shown in Eq.(9). In our problem, we update the label matrices $Y_i, i = 1, \ldots, n$ and the weight vector $\mathbf{w}$ iteratively.

3.4 Multimodal Representation Construction

In this section, we aim to construct the multimodal representation between the query instances and their corresponding top-ranked similar samples, which is based on the query-neighbor similarity function: $\mathbf{\Phi} = \{\phi_k\}_{k=1,2,\ldots,N_f}$. Generally, we can represent one facial image in different feature space, e.g. LBP feature, GIST feature, and Gabor feature. Suppose there are $\mathcal{K}$ kinds of features in total, we can represent by $(\mathbf{q}^{(k)}, \mathbf{d}_i^{(k)})$ the query-neighbor feature pair between the query image $\mathbf{q}$ and its i-th nearest sample $\mathbf{d}_i$ in the k-th feature space. Following the existing works on distance metric learning [47, 46], we can define a distance metric $M^{(k)}$ in the k-th feature space, hence, the distance between $\mathbf{q}^{(k)}$ and $\mathbf{d}_i^{(k)}$ can be expressed by

$$d_{M^{(k)}}(\mathbf{q}^{(k)}, \mathbf{d}_i^{(k)}) = \sqrt{(\mathbf{q}^{(k)} - \mathbf{d}_i^{(k)})^\top M^{(k)}(\mathbf{q}^{(k)} - \mathbf{d}_i^{(k)})}$$

and the inner product between $\mathbf{q}^{(k)}$ and $\mathbf{d}^{(k)}$ can be expressed by

$$< \mathbf{q}^{(k)}, \mathbf{d}_i^{(k)} >_{M^{(k)}} = (\mathbf{q}^{(k)})^\top M^{(k)}(\mathbf{d}_i^{(k)})$$

Based on the k-th feature space and distance matrix $M^{(k)}$, there are two ways to compute the similarity values between two instances: one way is using the heat kernel to transform the distance value into a similarity value which is widely used in semi-supervised learning [2]. In detail, the similarity value between $\mathbf{q}^{(k)}$ and $\mathbf{d}_i^{(k)}$ can be computed as follows:

$$\phi(\mathbf{q}, \mathbf{d}_i; k, \gamma) = \exp(-d^2_{M^{(k)}}(\mathbf{q}^{(k)}, \mathbf{d}_i^{(k)})/\gamma^2), \quad \gamma \in \Gamma$$

where the query-neighbor similarity function ϕ depends on the feature type k and the parameter γ. As a result, we can obtain $k * |\Gamma|$ query-neighbor similarity functions, where Γ is the set of all possible parameters γ during the experiments.

Another way to compute the similarity value is using the sparse representation technique which has been adopted to construct adjacency matrix in some recent works [32]. In detail, in the k-th feature space with $M^{(k)}$ as the distance metric, we can obtain the sparse representation $\mathbf{s}^{(k)}$ for $\mathbf{q}^{(k)}$ based on the dictionary $D^{(k)} = [\mathbf{d}_1^{(k)}, \ldots, \mathbf{d}_n^{(k)}]$ with the kernelized sparse coding algorithm [11], which can be formulated as follows:

$$\mathbf{s}_\lambda^{(k)} = \arg\min_{\mathbf{s}^{(k)} \geq 0} < \mathbf{q}^{(k)}, \mathbf{q}^{(k)} >_{M^{(k)}} + (\mathbf{s}^{(k)})^\top K_{DD}^{(k)}(\mathbf{s}^{(k)}) - 2(\mathbf{s}^{(k)})^\top K_{D\mathbf{q}}^{(k)} + \lambda \|\mathbf{s}^{(k)}\|_1$$

where $\mathbf{s}_\lambda^{(k)}$ is the achieved sparse representation with parameter λ, $K_{DD}^{(k)}$ is an $n \times n$ matrix with $\{K_{DD}^{(k)}\}_{ij} =< \mathbf{d}_i^{(k)}, \mathbf{d}_j^{(k)} >_{M^{(k)}}$, and $K_{D\mathbf{q}}^{(k)}$ is an $n \times 1$ vector with $\{K_{D\mathbf{q}}^{(k)}\}_i =< \mathbf{q}^{(k)}, \mathbf{d}_i^{(k)} >_{M^{(k)}}$. The i-th item in the sparse represent $\mathbf{s}_\lambda^{(k)}$ presents the representative ability of the i-th dictionary instance $\mathbf{d}_i^{(k)}$ for the encoding instance $\mathbf{q}^{(k)}$. Hence, the similarity value between $\mathbf{q}^{(k)}$ and $\mathbf{d}_i^{(k)}$ is computed as follows:

$$\phi(\mathbf{q}, \mathbf{d}_i; k, \lambda) = \mathbf{s}_\lambda^{(k)}[i], \quad \lambda \in \Lambda$$

where the query-neighbor similarity function ϕ depends on the feature type k and the parameter λ. As a result, we can obtain $k * |\Lambda|$ query-neighbor similarity functions, where Λ is the set of all possible parameters Λ during the experiments.

Finally, for each feature space, we must choose a distance metric $M^{(k)}$. We can use the original feature space by setting $M^{(k)}$ with the identify matrix. To keep all the data points within the same classes close and separate all the data points from different classes far apart, it is better to adopt distance metric learning (DML) techniques to learn a better distance metric for each feature space respectively. Generally, any supervised DML algorithms can be used since the query-neighbor similarity function ϕ is independent of the DML algorithms. In our problem, we adopt "Metric Learning to Rank" (MLR) algorithm [25] that learns a metric such that rankings of data induced by the learned distance are optimized against a ranking loss measure (e.g. ROC area (AUC) or MAP). In this setting, the "relevant" results (in the same class) should lie close in space to the query, and "irrelevant" results should be pushed far away.

3.5 Optimal Fusion of Multiple Modalities

In this section, we aim to find the optimal weight vector $\mathbf{w}$ for optimizing the multimodal fusion. In particular, given a label matrix Y_i and a query-neighbor similarity matrix X_i, we can directly achieve the annotation result of $\mathbf{q}_i$ with the fusion vector $\mathbf{w}$ according to Eq.(3). Hence, finding the optimal fusion vector $\mathbf{w}$ that achieves the best ranked name list in Eq.(4) is equivalent to learning a multimodal annotation function with parameter $\mathbf{w}$ as follows:

$$f(\mathbf{w}) : \mathcal{Y} \times \mathcal{X} \to \Pi$$

based on a set of training samples $\{(\mathbf{q}_i, \mathbf{y}_{\mathbf{q}_i}, L_i, X_i)\}$ with $i = 1, 2, \ldots, N_t$ by minimizing the annotation errors. The input space contains all the multiplication results between label matrix Y_i and query-neighbor similarity matrix X_i. The output space Π contains all the possible annotation results (the ranked name list). Obviously, the result of the function f is a structural output instead of a scalar value. Hence, it could be formulated as a structural SVM problem [34, 19], which has been extensively studied in several research works and has been used for ranking problems in [48, 25, 45]. To specialize a general structure SVM algorithm for a particular problem, we define two functions: the "*loss function*" Δ and the "*feature combination function*" Ψ.

3.5.1 Loss Function

The loss function is denoted as $\Delta(\boldsymbol{\pi}, \hat{\boldsymbol{\pi}})$ in our problem, where $\boldsymbol{\pi}$ is the ground-truth ranked name list generated by the ground-truth label vector $\mathbf{y}$, while $\hat{\boldsymbol{\pi}}$ is the predicted ranked name list generated by the predicted label vector $\hat{\mathbf{y}}$. Notice that we omit the subscript for the query index for clarity. The "*hit rate*" at the top t annotated names is used as the performance metric, which measures the likelihood of having the correct name among the top t annotated names. In real world applications, we prefer a high hit rate value with a small t value, that is, the correct names are at the top-ranked position in the ranked name list $\hat{\boldsymbol{\pi}}$.

For one query facial image, suppose it has t_1 correct names ($t_1 = 1$ in our problem since we assume there is only one name for each person), all the correct names are at the top positions of the ground-truth name list $\boldsymbol{\pi}$, followed by all the incorrect names. For the predicted name list $\hat{\boldsymbol{\pi}}$, if we only consider its top t_2 names, the loss function can be formulated as follows:

$$\Delta(\boldsymbol{\pi}, \hat{\boldsymbol{\pi}}) = 1 - \sum_{i=1}^{t_1} \sum_{j=1}^{t_2} h_1(\pi_i, \hat{\pi}_j) * \frac{1}{j} \tag{6}$$

where $h_1(\cdot, \cdot)$ is a judgement function that equals 1 if the i-th name π_i in $\boldsymbol{\pi}$ is the same with the j-th name $\hat{\pi}_j$ in $\hat{\boldsymbol{\pi}}$, and 0 otherwise. For example, if $t_2 = 1$, we focus on only the first annotated name which means that if the first name in $\hat{\boldsymbol{\pi}}$ is correct, then the loss value is 0, otherwise, the loss value is 1. If $t_2 = m$, the loss function in Eq.(6) becomes a special case of MAP loss.

3.5.2 *Structural-based Feature Combination*

Typically, the feature combination function aims to combine a set of feature vectors based on a ranking result. In our problem, the ranking result is denoted by $\boldsymbol{\pi}$, which contains all the m names in the name set $C = \{c_1, \ldots, c_m\}$. For a query facial image $\mathbf{q}$, its name vector is $\mathbf{y} \in \{0,1\}^m$ with $\|\mathbf{y}\|_0 = 1$ since each facial image has only one correct name. Hence, $y_k = 1$ indicates that the k-th name c_k in C is the correct name for the query image $\mathbf{q}$. We denote by I_1 the index set of all the correct names, which contains only one item (k) according the previous case. Similarly, we denote by I_2 the index set of all the incorrect names, which contains $m-1$ items $\{1, \ldots, k-1, k+1, \ldots, m\}$. Following the previous work [48], we define the feature combination function Ψ to combine the input label matrix Y and the input query-neighbor similarity matrix X based on a ranked name list $\boldsymbol{\pi}$, as shown in Eq.(7):

$$\Psi(Y, X, \boldsymbol{\pi}) = \frac{1}{|I_1| * |I_2|} \sum_{i \in I_1} \sum_{j \in I_2} h_2(c_i, c_j, \boldsymbol{\pi})[XY_{i:}^\top - XY_{j:}^\top] \tag{7}$$

where $Y_{k:}$ is the k-th row of the label matrix L, and $h_2(\cdot,\cdot,\cdot)$ is a ranking judgement function. If the name c_i is ranked before c_j in the ranked name list $\boldsymbol{\pi}$, $h_2(c_i, c_j, \boldsymbol{\pi}) = 1$; otherwise, $h_2(c_i, c_j, \boldsymbol{\pi}) = -1$ if c_j is ranked before c_i.

Remark. For one group of input data (Y, X,$\mathbf{w}$), we can compute the label vector with Eq.(3): $\mathbf{y} = YX^\top\mathbf{w}$, which is used to generate the ranked name list $\boldsymbol{\pi}$ subsequently following the previous discussion. As shown in [45], based on the feature combination function in Eq.(7), we can obtain the same ranked name list by solving the following problem:

$$\tilde{\boldsymbol{\pi}} = \arg\max_{\boldsymbol{\pi} \in \Pi} F(\mathbf{w}, Y, X, \boldsymbol{\pi}) = \mathbf{w}^\top \Psi(Y, X, \boldsymbol{\pi}) \tag{8}$$

where $F(\mathbf{w}, Y, X, \boldsymbol{\pi})$ is the discriminant function. It indicates that we can learn the weight vector $\mathbf{w}$ by maximizing the discriminant function $F(\mathbf{w}, L, X, \boldsymbol{\pi})$ over the a set of correct ranked label lists, and predict the new label vector of the unseen query with Eq.(3).

Using the *loss function* in Eq.(6) and the *feature combination function* in Eq.(7), we can obtain the objective function to learn the weight vector $\mathbf{w}$ based on the structural SVM, which is shown as follows:

$$\min_{\mathbf{w}, \Xi = [\xi_1, \ldots, \xi_{N_t}]} \tfrac{1}{2}\mathbf{w}^\top\mathbf{w} + \tfrac{C}{N_t}\textstyle\sum_{i=1}^{N_t} \xi_i \tag{9}$$
$$s.t. \quad \forall i, \xi_i \geq 0 \quad \text{and} \quad \forall i, \forall \boldsymbol{\pi}_{\mathbf{q}_i} \in \Pi_i^\star, \forall \boldsymbol{\pi} \in \Pi \backslash \Pi_i^\star :$$
$$\mathbf{w}^\top \Psi(Y_i, X_i, \boldsymbol{\pi}_{\mathbf{q}_i}) - \mathbf{w}^\top \Psi(Y_i, X_i, \boldsymbol{\pi}) \geq \Delta(\boldsymbol{\pi}_{\mathbf{q}_i}, \boldsymbol{\pi}) - \xi_i$$

Algorithm 1: Cutting plane algorithm for Eq.(9)

Input: $(\mathbf{q}_i, \mathbf{y}_{\mathbf{q}_i}, X_i, Y_i), i = 1, 2, \ldots, N_t, C, \epsilon$
Output: weight vector $\mathbf{w}$
$\mathcal{W}_i \leftarrow \emptyset$, for all $i = 1, \ldots, N_t$
repeat
  for $i = 1$ **to** N_t **do**
    $E(\boldsymbol{\pi}; \mathbf{w}) \equiv \Delta(\boldsymbol{\pi}_{\mathbf{q}_i}, \boldsymbol{\pi}) + \mathbf{w}^\top \Psi(Y_i, X_i, \boldsymbol{\pi})$
    $\tilde{\boldsymbol{\pi}} = \arg\max_{\boldsymbol{\pi} \in \Pi} E(\boldsymbol{\pi}; \mathbf{w})$
    if $E(\tilde{\boldsymbol{\pi}}, \mathbf{w}) > \xi_i + \epsilon$ **then**
      $\mathcal{W}_i \leftarrow \mathcal{W}_i \cup \{\tilde{\boldsymbol{\pi}}\}$
      Get $(\mathbf{w}, \Xi)$ by solve Eq.(9) over $\mathcal{W} = \bigcup_i \mathcal{W}_i$
    end
  end
until *no $\mathcal{W}_i$ has changed during iteration*;

In the above formulation, the objective function of Eq.(9) is similar to that of the general SVM algorithm, where C is a regularization parameter to tradeoff between the training error and the model complexity. For the constraints, if the value of discriminant function F in Eq.(8) for an incorrect ranking $\boldsymbol{\pi} \in \Pi \backslash \Pi_i^\star$ is greater than that for one true ranking $\boldsymbol{\pi}_{\mathbf{q}_i} \in \Pi_i^\star$, the slack variable ξ_i must be at least $\Delta(\boldsymbol{\pi}_{\mathbf{q}_i}, \boldsymbol{\pi})$, which indicates the sum of slacks $\sum_i \xi_i$ upper bounds the empirical risk for the training samples based on the loss function defined in Eq.(6). Since the number of constraints in Eq.(9) is extremely large, we adopt the cutting plane algorithm [19, 48] to efficiently solve the optimization in Eq.(9), as shown in Algorithm 1. More details about the cutting plane algorithm can be found in [19].

3.6 Algorithm for Learning to Name Faces

In the above, we separately discuss the three key factors that affect the final annotation result of the proposed SBFA framework, including the label matrix Y, the query-neighbor similarity matrix X and the weight vector $\mathbf{w}$, which collectively determine the annotation result as $\mathbf{y} = YX^\top\mathbf{w}$. In this section, we will present the overall training for unifying all these three factors, and how to apply the models learned by L2NF for on-the-fly face annotation of a novel query facial image.

Algorithm 2: L2NF—Algorithm for training the models

Input: Training set $(\mathbf{q}_i, \mathbf{y}_{\mathbf{q}_i}, \mathbf{d}_{ij}, \mathbf{y}_{ij})$ in $\mathcal{K}$ feature spaces with $i = 1, \ldots, N_t$ and $j = 1, \ldots, n$, name sets C with m names, parameters β, Λ and Γ
Output: weight vector $\mathbf{w}$ and similarity function set $\mathbf{\Phi}$
for $k = 1$ **to** $\mathcal{K}$ **do**
  Learn the optimal distance metric $M^{(k)}$ in Section 3.4
end
Build query-neighbor similarity functions $\mathbf{\Phi}$ with varied combinations of $\lambda \in \Lambda, \gamma \in \Gamma$, and $M^{(k)}$, $k = 1, 2, \ldots, \mathcal{K}$
Construct query-neighbor feature matrix X_i, $i = 1, \ldots, N_t$
repeat
  Get the weight vector $\mathbf{w}$ by solving Eq.(9)
  for $i = 1$ **to** N_t **do**
    Refine the label matrix Y_i by solving Eq.(5)
  end
until *CONVERGENCE*;

Algorithm 2 shows the overall algorithmic framework for training the models by L2NF. At the beginning, we attempt to optimize each of the distance metrics for each facial feature space using the distance metric learning technique as discussed in Section 3.4. After obtaining the set of optimal distance metrics $M^{(k)}$, we can then construct the set of query-neighbor similarity functions $\mathbf{\Phi}$ based on the set of multiple diverse facial feature representations and their distance measures. Using the query-neighbor similarity functions $\mathbf{\Phi}$, we can generate the query-neighbor feature matrices X_i for each query q_i in the training query set. Finally, we optimize both the optimal weight vector $\mathbf{w}$ and the refined label matrices Y by an iterative scheme. At the end of the whole training scheme, we obtain the final model that consists of the set of query-neighbor similarity functions $\mathbf{\Phi}$ and the optimal weight vector $\mathbf{w}$ for multi-modal fusion.

The above training framework as shown in Algorithm 2 can be done in an off-line learning manner. After completing the training, we can apply the model for online face annotation for naming a novel query facial image on-the-fly. Algorithm 3 summarizes the proposed algorithm for on-the-fly annotation of an unseen query facial image. Specifically, given a new query facial image, we first find a short list of most similar faces based on CBIR techniques.

Algorithm 3: Algorithm of on-the-fly face annotation by L2NF

Input: Novel query $\mathbf{q}$ in $\mathcal{K}$ feature spaces, query-neighbor similarity function $\mathbf{\Phi}$, optimal weight vector $\mathbf{w}*$

Output: Annotation result $\boldsymbol{\pi}$

Retrieval the top-n similar images the $\{(\mathbf{d}_i, \mathbf{y}_i)\}_{i=1,2,\ldots,n}$

Construct the query-neighbor similarity matrix X based on the query-neighbor similarity function $\mathbf{\Phi}$

Obtain Y by refining the initial label matrix with Eq.(5)

$\mathbf{y} = YX^{\top}\mathbf{w}*$

Get the ranked names list $\boldsymbol{\pi}$ by sorting $\mathbf{y}$ in descending order

After that, we construct the query-neighbor similarity matrix X based on the query-neighbor similarity function $\mathbf{\Phi}$. We then refine the initial label matrix Y of the current query using Eq.(5). Finally, we compute the label vector $\mathbf{y}$ by Eq.(3) and obtain the final annotation result $\boldsymbol{\pi}$ by sorting the label vector $\mathbf{y}$ in descending order.

4. EXPERIMENTAL RESULTS

4.1 Experimental Testbed

Some web facial image databases are available on the WWW, which are used in some previous research works, e.g, LFW [18],[4] Label Yahoo!News [14],[5] and FAN-Large.[6] Although the number of persons in these three databases is large, the number of images for each person is quite small. For example, there are $13,233$ images of $5,749$ people in the LFW database. The recent database PubFig [21][7] is different from these databases. In detail, it was constructed by collecting online news sources. It contains 200 persons and $58,797$ images. Due to the copyright issue, only image URL addresses are released. As some URL links are not available any more, 41,609 images are collected by our crawler in total. For each downloaded image, we crop the face image out according the provided face position rectangle and resize all the face images into the same size (128×128). We construct the query set by randomly collecting 10 images per person from the whole PubFig database. Hence, there are a total of $2,000$ test query images used for performance evaluation, while the rest $39,609$ images are used as the retrieval database. To construct the training set, we randomly collect $2,000$ images in the same way from the retrieval database, with the rest $37,609$ images as the retrieval database for the training set. Several facial images samples are shown in the first row of Figure 3.

Figure 3: Face image examples in Pubfig database (the first row) and WDB database (the second row)

To evaluate the L2NF framework on weakly labeled web facial images, we use another western celebrity database: "weakly labeled web facial image database" (WDB for short), which has been released in [38]. There are a total of $1,600$ query images with ground truth in the WDB database. In our experiment, we divide these queries into two parts of equal size, and randomly choose one part for model training. In "WDB" database, there are a total of four retrieval databases of different sizes. In our experiment, we use two sub-databases of different scales: "WDB-040K" and "WDB-600K". "WDB-040K" is a smaller database with $53,448$ images belonging to 400 persons, while "WDB-600K" is a large-scale database with $714,454$ belonging to $6,000$ persons. All the facial images were aligned into the same well-defined positions by the face alignment algorithms in [44], as shown in the second row of Figure 3.

To construct the query-neighbor similarity functions, we adopt three kinds of features as the facial descriptors: the LBP feature [1], the GIST feature [31, 38], and the Gabor feature [23]. In particular, the 2891-dimensional LBP feature is extracted by dividing the face images into 7×7 blocks. To reduce the computation complexity, the LBP feature is further projected into a lower 500-dimensional feature space using Principal Component Analysis (PCA). Both GIST features and Gabor features are extracted over the whole aligned facial images. The parameter set for heat kernel is $\Gamma = \{-1, 0, 1, 2, 3, 4\}$, while the parameter set for sparse representation is $\Lambda = \{0.0005, 0.001, 0.005, 0.01, 0.05, 0.1, 0.5\}$. The parameters β and C of L2NF are set as 10 and 1000, respectively. For the distance metric learning algorithm (MLR), the parameter C is set as 10.

Following the previous works, we adopt the *hit rate* at top-T annotated results as the performance metric to evaluate the annotation performance, which measures the likelihood of having the true label among the top-T annotated names for a query facial image. We compare the proposed "L2NF" framework with several existing works that are proposed for web-scale face annotation or general image annotation, including "WLRLCC" [38], "SGSSL" [32], "MtBGS" [41], "MRR" [43], and a simple baseline algorithm that simply adopts the weighted majority voting "WMV". We also extend the WLRLCC algorithm and the WMV algorithm into a multimodal scheme, by equally combining the face naming results from different facial feature spaces, denoted as "WLRLCC$_{\rm mm}$" and "WMV$_{\rm mm}$".

4.2 Experiments on "WDB-040K"

This experiment aims to evaluate the face naming performance of the proposed "L2NF" framework on the database "WDB-040K" by comparing with the aforementioned seven existing algorithms. For the facial image retrieval task in L2NF, we adopt the JEC algorithm to combine the distances from different face descriptors [24], which allows each individual distance to contribute equally. The same retrieval scheme is used to find the top-ranked similar images for the multimodal extensions: "WLRLCC$_{\rm mm}$" and "WMV$_{\rm mm}$". For the single model solution, we use the GIST feature as the facial descriptor, which is similar to the experiment setting in [38]. For the $1,600$ query facial images, we randomly select half of them to learn the distance metrics of different facial features and the multimodal representation combination $\mathbf{w}$. Such a procedure is repeated 10 times and the average performance is computed over the 10 trials, as shown in Table.1.

Several observations can be drawn from the results. First, for the the single model solution, the WLRLCC algorithms achieves the best performance by using only one type of facial feature (GIST). In detail, the simple baseline WMV is about 60.9% with $T = 1$, which is boosted to 76.7% by WLRLCC. Second, if multiple facial features are available, the performance of the multimodal WLRLCC$_{\rm mm}$ increases to 80.9%, and 65.6% for the multimodal WMV$_{\rm mm}$. It indicates that using multiple facial representations is

[4] http://goo.gl/4EuIl

[5] http://goo.gl/2X1ES

[6] http://goo.gl/2baSv

[7] http://goo.gl/zlb4l

Table 1: Face naming performance on database "WDB-040K".

	T=01	T=02	T=03	T=04	T=05
WMV	0.6090 ± 0.012	0.7150 ± 0.009	0.7599 ± 0.009	0.7848 ± 0.008	0.7969 ± 0.008
SGSSL	0.7310 ± 0.011	0.7770 ± 0.010	0.8079 ± 0.011	0.8231 ± 0.013	0.8338 ± 0.012
MtBGS	0.7023 ± 0.015	0.7654 ± 0.012	0.7896 ± 0.011	0.8058 ± 0.009	0.8215 ± 0.010
MRR	0.6640 ± 0.010	0.7560 ± 0.007	0.7875 ± 0.008	0.8005 ± 0.008	0.8155 ± 0.009
WLRLCC	0.7671 ± 0.010	0.8009 ± 0.010	0.8263 ± 0.010	0.8361 ± 0.009	0.8496 ± 0.007
WMV_{mm}	0.6560 ± 0.014	0.7491 ± 0.013	0.8010 ± 0.012	0.8144 ± 0.013	0.8244 ± 0.014
$WLRLCC_{mm}$	0.8088 ± 0.011	0.8568 ± 0.014	0.8714 ± 0.015	0.8799 ± 0.012	0.8859 ± 0.011
L2NF	**0.8663** ± 0.011	**0.8918** ± 0.011	**0.8983** ± 0.010	**0.9025** ± 0.010	**0.9054** ± 0.009

helpful for the face naming task which validates the importance of this study. More specifically, the improvements of these two algorithms ($WLRLCC_{mm}$ and WMV_{mm}) in the multimodal scheme are mainly gained from two aspects: (i) the retrieval result becomes better when multiple features and distance measures are combined by JEC [24]. For example, for the WMV algorithm, if we use the multiple features for the retrieval step but only use GIST feature for the annotation step, its performance is 64.2%, which is higher than the one that uses only GIST feature for both retrieval and annotation steps(60.9%). (ii) the combination enlarges the probability that the correct name is chosen. Both of the two aspects are beneficial for the L2NF framework. Last but not least, the proposed L2NF framework can further improve the face naming performance to 86.6%, which indicates the constructed multimodal representations are discriminative and the learned fusion vector can efficiently combine various query-neighbor similarity function in different facial feature spaces. The performance improvement is mainly gained from three aspects: the refined label matrix, the constructed multimodal representation based on distance metric learning techniques, and the learned optimal combination of various query-neighbor similarity functions. More details will be further discussed in Section 4.5.

4.3 Experiments on "WDB-600K" & "PubFig"

This experiment aims to evaluate the face naming performance of the proposed L2NF framework on two different larger facial image databases: "WDB-600K" and "PubFig". The two databases were collected under very different approaches and settings, which can help us evaluate the generalization of the proposed technique on real-world data under different scenarios. For clarity, we mainly focus on the evaluation of the algorithms using multimodal representations. The experimental results are shown in Figure 4 and Table 2.

We can make several observations from the results. First of all, similar to the previous observations, the proposed L2NF framework consistently achieves the best annotation performance among all the compared algorithms. It shows that for different databases the proposed L2NF algorithm is always helpful to improve the annotation performance. Secondly, the performance on "WDB-600K" is lower than the one on "WDB-400K" which is consistent with the previous observation in [38], since increasing the number of persons leads to a larger database of more images, which makes the retrieval task more challenging. Finally, it is interesting to observe the overall annotation performance on the PubFig database is worse than the results on WDB-series databases. There are several

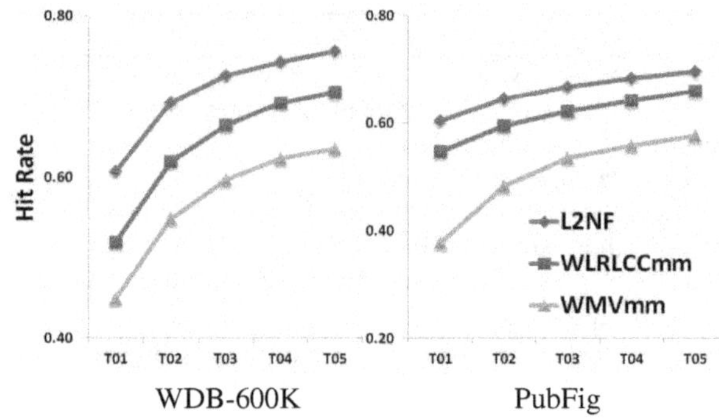

Figure 4: Face naming performance (hit rate @ top-T) on the two databases: "WDB-600K" and "PubFig".

reasons for this observation: (i) the number of images per person varies a lot in the PubFig database, in which several persons own only about 20 images. It is insufficient for the data-driven scheme, hence the annotation performance is reduced; (ii) All the facial images in the PubFig database are cropped according to the face position without adopting any face alignment algorithms, which makes the facial descriptor sensitive for face views.

4.4 Evaluation on Training Query Sizes

This experiment aims to evaluate the impact of the training query sizes in the L2NF framework based on the "WDB-040K" database. In the previous experiments, we adopt half of the 1,600 query images as the training set. In this experiment, we evaluate the annotation performance under varied number of training query images. Specifically, instead of using all the training samples (totally 800), we build three small training sets by randomly collecting 200, 400 and 600 query images, respectively. The experimental results of hit-rate @ top-1 performance are shown in Figure 5. From the results, it is obvious that the face naming performance increases when more training samples are available, and the final performance tends to become saturated when the training query size is above 600. Finally, even with a small number of queries for training, e.g., only 200 training samples, the L2NF algorithm can achieve a good performance (83.4%), which remains much better than the state-of-the-art "$WLRLCC_{mm}$" scheme.

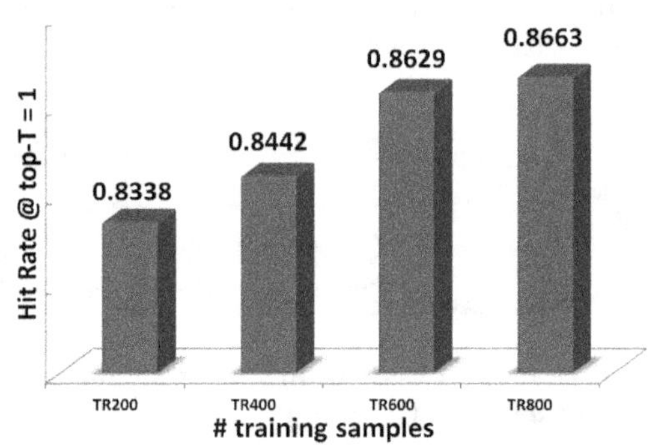

Figure 5: Face naming performance (hit rate @ top-$T = 1$) of L2NF with varied sizes of training queries.

4.5 Analysis of the Performance Gains

This experiment aims to analyze how different factors affect the face naming performance by the proposed L2NF scheme as shown in Figure 2 (b). In particular, there are three key factors: the refined

Table 2: Face naming performance (Hit Rate) on database "WDB-600K" and "PubFig"

	Database: WDB-600K					Database: PubFig				
	T=01	T=02	T=03	T=04	T=05	T=01	T=02	T=03	T=04	T=05
WLRLCC	0.5150	0.5900	0.6400	0.6675	0.6813	0.5369	0.5911	0.6213	0.6431	0.6604
WMV	0.4538	0.5500	0.5950	0.6163	0.6413	0.3572	0.4616	0.5172	0.5453	0.5650
WMV_{mm}	0.4488	0.5475	0.5963	0.6225	0.6350	0.3775	0.4830	0.5352	0.5585	0.5763
$WLRLCC_{mm}$	0.5188	0.6188	0.6638	0.6913	0.7050	0.5468	0.5948	0.6218	0.6423	0.6595
L2NF	**0.6065**	**0.6920**	**0.7258**	**0.7426**	**0.7559**	**0.6034**	**0.6449**	**0.6674**	**0.6839**	**0.6961**

label matrix, the constructed multiple representations, and the optimal weight vector for multimodal fusion.

Table 3: Evaluation and analysis of the performance gains.

	$L2NF^{w=1}_{M=I}$	$L2NF^{w=w^\star}_{M=I}$	$L2NF^{w=1}_{M=M^\star}$	$L2NF^{w=w^\star}_{M=M^\star}$
Hit Rate	0.7941	0.8120	0.8403	0.8663

First of all, to examine the efficacy of the refined label matrix Y, we compare it with the initial raw label matrix $\tilde{Y}$ using the simplest baseline algorithm WMV by excluding other factors in affecting annotation performance. Our result indicates that the refined label matrix can boost the performance from 60.9% (without refinement) to 62.0% (after refinement). Further, we examine the efficacy of another two factors as shown in Table 3. We denote by $M^\star$ the learned distance metric and $\mathbf{w}^\star$ the optimal multimodal fusion vector. When the weight vector $\mathbf{w}$ is fixed to 1 and the distance metrics are based on Euclidean distance (M is set to an identity matrix), the hit-rate @ top-1 performance of the resulting L2NF algorithm (denoted as $L2NF^{w=1}_{M=I}$) is 79.4%. This value can be boosted to 84.3% if we adopt the optimized metric $M^\star$ (denoted as $L2NF^{w=1}_{M=M^\star}$), and further boosted to 86.6% if we also use the optimal weight vector $\mathbf{w}^\star$ for multimodal fusion (denoted as $L2NF^{w=w^\star}_{M=M^\star}$). As a conclusion, the proposed L2NF framework is able to leverage all the three factors for achieving the state-the-art performance in a systematic and synergic scheme.

5. LIMITATIONS

Despite the promising results on the benchmark search-based face annotation tasks, our work still have some limitations. First, we assume each name corresponds to a unique single person. However, this is not always true for real-life scenarios. For example, it is possible that two persons have the same name or one person may have multiple names. Such kind of practical duplicate name issues may be partially solved by extending our algorithms, e.g., via learning the similarity between any two names both in the name space and visual space. Second, we assume the top retrieved web facial images are related to the query name. This is clearly true for celebrities who have many photos on the internet. However, when the query facial image is not a well-known person, there may not exist many relevant facial images on the WWW. This is a common limitation of all existing data-driven annotation techniques. Finally, although the performance of L2NF is much better, more facial feature are used which means more computational cost and storage space. We may overcome the limitation by adopting hashing techniques in our further work.

6. CONCLUSIONS

This paper investigated an emerging paradigm of search-based face annotation for automated face naming through mining large-scale web facial images freely available on the WWW. We proposed a novel framework of "Learning to Name Faces" (L2NF) by exploring multi-modal learning on weakly labeled facial image data. In particular, our framework has three major contributions: (i) we suggest enhancing the initial weak labels by a graph-based refinement scheme based on the "label smoothness" assumption; (ii) we propose to explore multiple facial feature representations, and further optimize the distance metric on each facial feature space using distance metric learning techniques; and (iii) finally, we propose to learn the optimal multimodal fusion of diverse facial features by formulating the problem as a learning to rank task, which can be efficiently solved by the existing structural SVM algorithm. We conduct a set of extensive empirical studies on two benchmark real-world facial image databases, in which encouraging results show that the proposed L2NF model significantly boosts the face annotation performance.

Acknowledgements

This research was supported in part by MOE tier 1 project grant (RG33/11), Microsoft Research grant, Interactive and Digital Media Programme Office (IDMPO) and National Research Foundation (NRF) hosted at Media Development Authority (MDA) under Grant No.: MDA/IDM/2012/8/8-2 VOL 01. Jianke Zhu was supported by National Natural Science Foundation of China under the Grant (61103105).

7. REFERENCES

[1] T. Ahonen, A. Hadid, and M. Pietikäinen. Face description with local binary patterns: Application to face recognition. *IEEE TPMAI*, 28(12):2037–2041, 2006.

[2] M. Belkin, P. Niyogi, and V. Sindhwani. Manifold regularization: A geometric framework for learning from labeled and unlabeled examples. *Journal of Machine Learning Research*, 7:2399–2434, 2006.

[3] T. L. Berg, A. C. Berg, J. Edwards, M. Maire, R. White, Y. W. Teh, E. G. Learned-Miller, and D. A. Forsyth. Names and faces in the news. In *IEEE CVPR'04*, 2004.

[4] J. Bu, B. Xu, C. Wu, C. Chen, J. Zhu, D. Cai, and X. He. Unsupervised face-name association via commute distance. In *ACM MM'12*, pages 219–228, 2012.

[5] Z. Cao, Q. Yin, X. Tang, and J. Sun. Face recognition with learning-based descriptor. In *IEEE CVPR'10*, 2010.

[6] G. Carneiro, A. B. Chan, P. Moreno, and N. Vasconcelos. Supervised learning of semantic classes for image annotation and retrieval. *IEEE TPMAI*, pages 394–410, 2006.

[7] B.-C. Chen, Y.-Y. Chen, Y.-H. Kuo, and W. H. Hsu. Scalable face image retrieval using attribute-enhanced sparse codewords. *IEEE Trans. on Multimedia*, 2012.

[8] J. Y. Choi, W. D. Neve, K. N. Plataniotis, and Y. M. Ro. Collaborative face recognition for improved face annotation

in personal photo collections shared on online social networks. *IEEE Trans. on Multimedia*, 13, 2011.

[9] P. Duygulu, K. Barnard, J. de Freitas, and D. Forsyth. Object recognition as machine translation: Learning a lexicon for a fixed image vocabulary. In *ECCV'02*, 2002.

[10] J. Fan, Y. Gao, and H. Luo. Multi-level annotation of natural scenes using dominant image components and semantic concepts. In *ACM MM'04*, pages 540–547, 2004.

[11] S. Gao, I. W.-H. Tsang, and L.-T. Chia. Kernel sparse representation for image classification and face recognition. In *ECCV'10*, ECCV'10, pages 1–14, Berlin, Heidelberg, 2010. Springer-Verlag.

[12] M. Guillaumin, T. Mensink, J. Verbeek, and C. Schmid. Automatic face naming with caption-based supervision. In *IEEE CVPR'08*, pages 1–8, 2008.

[13] M. Guillaumin, T. Mensink, J. Verbeek, and C. Schmid. Face recognition from caption-based supervision. In *IJCV'12*, 96:64–82, Jan 2012.

[14] M. Guillaumin, J. Verbeek, and C. Schmid. Multiple instance metric learning from automatically labeled bags of faces. In *ECCV'10*, pages 634–647, Sep 2010.

[15] A. Hanbury. A survey of methods for image annotation. *J. Vis. Lang. Comput.*, 19:617–627, October 2008.

[16] S. C. Hoi, R. Jin, J. Zhu, and M. R. Lyu. Semi-supervised svm batch mode active learning with applications to image retrieval. *ACM TOIS*, 27(3):1–29, July 2009.

[17] A. Holub, P. Moreels, and P. Perona. Unsupervised clustering for google searches of celebrity images. In *IEEE FG'08*, pages 1 –8, 2008.

[18] G. B. Huang, M. Ramesh, T. Berg, and E. Learned-Miller. Labeled faces in the wild: A database for studying face recognition in unconstrained environments. Technical Report 07-49, University of Massachusetts, Amherst, October 2007.

[19] T. Joachims, T. Finley, and C.-N. J. Yu. Cutting-plane training of structural svms. *Machine Learning*, 77(1):27–59, Oct. 2009.

[20] M. G. Kresimir Delac and M. S. Bartlett. *Recent Advances in Face Recognition.* I-Tech Education and Publishing, 2008.

[21] N. Kumar, A. C. Berg, P. N. Belhumeur, and S. K. Nayar. Attribute and simile classifiers for face verification. In *IEEE ICCV'09*, Oct 2009.

[22] D.-D. Le and S. Satoh. Unsupervised face annotation by mining the web. In *ICDM'08*, pages 383–392, 2008.

[23] C. Liu and H. Wechsler. Gabor feature based classification using the enhanced fisher linear discriminant model for face recognition. *IEEE TIP*, 11(4):467 –476, apr 2002.

[24] A. Makadia, V. Pavlovic, and S. Kumar. A new baseline for image annotation. In *ECCV'08*, pages 316–329, 2008.

[25] B. Mcfee and G. Lanckriet. Metric learning to rank. In *ICML'10*, 2010.

[26] T. Mensink and J. J. Verbeek. Improving people search using query expansions. In *ECCV'08*, pages 86–99, 2008.

[27] D. Ozkan and P. Duygulu. A graph based approach for naming faces in news photos. In *IEEE CVPR'06*, pages 1477–1482, 2006.

[28] X. Rui, M. Li, Z. Li, W.-Y. Ma, and N. Yu. Bipartite graph reinforcement model for web image annotation. In *ACM MM'07*, pages 585–594, Augsburg, Germany, 2007.

[29] B. C. Russell, A. Torralba, K. P. Murphy, and W. T. Freeman. Labelme: A database and web-based tool for image annotation. *IJCV*, 77(1-3):157–173, 2008.

[30] S. Satoh, Y. Nakamura, and T. Kanade. Name-it: Naming and detecting faces in news videos. *IEEE TMM*, 6(1), 1999.

[31] C. Siagian and L. Itti. Rapid biologically-inspired scene classification using features shared with visual attention. *IEEE TPMAI*, 29:300–312, February 2007.

[32] J. Tang, R. Hong, S. Yan, T.-S. Chua, G.-J. Qi, and R. Jain. Image annotation by knn-sparse graph-based label propagation over noisily tagged web images. *ACM TIST*, 2:14:1–14:15, 2011.

[33] J. Zhu, S. C. Hoi, and M. R. Lyu. Face annotation by transductive kernel fisher discriminant. *IEEE TMM*, 10(01):86–96, 2008.

[34] I. Tsochantaridis, T. Joachims, T. Hofmann, and Y. Altun. Large margin methods for structured and interdependent output variables. *Journal of Machine Learning Research*, 6:1453–1484, September 2005.

[35] C. Wang, F. Jing, L. Zhang, and H.-J. Zhang. Image annotation refinement using random walk with restarts. In *ACM MM'06*, pages 647–650, 2006.

[36] C. Wang, S. Yan, L. Zhang, and H.-J. Zhang. Multi-label sparse coding for automatic image annotation. *IEEE CVPR'09*, 0:1643–1650, 2009.

[37] D. Wang, S. C. Hoi, and Y. He. Mining weakly labeled web facial images for search-based face annotation. In *ACM SIGIR'11*, pages 535–544, 2011.

[38] D. Wang, S. C. H. Hoi, Y. He, and J. Zhu. Retrieval-based face annotation by weak label regularized local coordinate coding. In *ACM MM'11*, pages 353–362, 2011.

[39] X.-J. Wang, L. Zhang, F. Jing, and W.-Y. Ma. Annosearch: Image auto-annotation by search. In *IEEE CVPR'06*, 2006.

[40] J. Wright, A. Y. Yang, A. Ganesh, S. S. Sastry, and Y. Ma. Robust face recognition via sparse representation. *IEEE TPMAI*, 31(2):210–227, April 2008.

[41] F. Wu, Y. Han, Q. Tian, and Y. Zhuang. Multi-label boosting for image annotation by structural grouping sparsity. In *ACM MM'10*, pages 15–24, 2010.

[42] S. C. Hoi and M. R. Lyu. A multimodal and multilevel ranking scheme for large-scale video retrieval. *TMM*, 10(4):607–619, 2008.

[43] Z. Wu, Q. Ke, J. Sun, and H.-Y. Shum. Scalable face image retrieval with identity-based quantization and multi-reference re-ranking. In *IEEE CVPR'10*, pages 3469–3476, 2010.

[44] J. Zhu, S. C. Hoi, and L. V. Gool. Unsupervised face alignment by robust nonrigid mapping. In *ICCV'09*, 2009.

[45] J. Xu, T.-Y. Liu, M. Lu, H. Li, and W.-Y. Ma. Directly optimizing evaluation measures in learning to rank. In *ACM SIGIR'08*, pages 107–114, 2008.

[46] S. C. Hoi, W. Liu, M. R. Lyu, and W.-Y. Ma. Learning distance metrics with contextual constraints for image retrieval. In *CVPR'06*, volume 2, pages 2072–2078, 2006.

[47] L. Yang and R. Jin. Distance metric learning: A comprehensive survey. Technical report, MSU, 2006.

[48] Y. Yue, T. Finley, F. Radlinski, and T. Joachims. A support vector method for optimizing average precision. In *ACM SIGIR'07*, pages 271–278, 2007.

[49] L. Wu, S. C. Hoi, R. Jin, J. Zhu, and N. Yu. Distance metric learning from uncertain side information with application to automated photo tagging. In *ACM MM'09*, pages 135–144, 2009.

Utilizing Query Change for Session Search

Dongyi Guan, Sicong Zhang, Hui Yang
Department of Computer Science
Georgetown University
37th and O Street, NW, Washington, DC, 20057
{dg372, sz303}@georgetown.edu, huiyang@cs.georgetown.edu

ABSTRACT

Session search is the Information Retrieval (IR) task that performs document retrieval for a search session. During a session, a user constantly modifies queries in order to find relevant documents that fulfill the information need. This paper proposes a novel query change retrieval model (QCM), which utilizes syntactic editing changes between adjacent queries as well as the relationship between query change and previously retrieved documents to enhance session search. We propose to model session search as a Markov Decision Process (MDP). We consider two agents in this MDP: the user agent and the search engine agent. The user agent's actions are query changes that we observe and the search agent's actions are proposed in this paper. Experiments show that our approach is highly effective and outperforms top session search systems in TREC 2011 and 2012.

Categories and Subject Descriptors

H.3.3 [**Information Systems**]: Information Storage and Retrieval—*Information Search and Retrieval*

Keywords

Session search; query change model; retrieval model

1. INTRODUCTION

Session search is the Information Retrieval (IR) task that retrieves documents for a search session [4, 8, 13, 14, 15, 25, 32]. During a search session, a user keeps modifying queries in order to find relevant documents that fulfill his/her information needs. In session search, many factors, such as relevance feedback, clicked data, changes in queries, and user intentions, are intertwined together and make it a quite challenging IR task. TREC (Text REtrieval Conference) 2010-2012 Session tracks [18, 19, 20] studied session search with a focus on the "current query" task, which retrieves relevant documents for the current/last query in a session based on previous queries and interactions. Table 1 shows examples from the TREC 2012 Session track.[1]

[1]All examples mentioned in this paper are from TREC 2012. For simplicity, we use 'sx' to refer to a TREC 2012 session where x is the session identification number.

SIGIR'13, July 28–August 1, 2013, Dublin, Ireland.

Table 1: Examples of TREC 2012 Session queries.

session 6	session 28
1.pocono mountains pennsylvania	1.france world
2.pocono mountains pennsylvania hotels	cup 98 reaction
3.pocono mountains pennsylvania things to do	stock market
4.pocono mountains pennsylvania hotels	2.france world
5.pocono mountains camelbeach	cup 98 reaction
6.pocono mountains camelbeach hotel	3.france world
7.pocono mountains chateau resort	cup 98
8.pocono mountains chateau resort attractions	session 32
9.pocono mountains chateau resort getting to	1.bollywood
10.chateau resort getting to	legislation
11.pocono mountains chateau resort directions	2.bollywood law
session 85	session 37
1.glass blowing	1.Merck lobbists
2.glass blowing science	2.Merck lobbying
3.scientific glass blowing	US policy

From Table 1, we notice that queries change constantly in a session. The patterns of query changes include general to specific (*pocono mountains* → *pocono mountains park*), specific to general (*france world cup 98 reaction* → *france world cup 98*), drifting from one to another (*pocono mountains park* → *pocono mountains shopping*), or slightly different expressions for the same information need (*glass blowing science* → *scientific glass blowing*). These changes vary and sometimes even look random (*gun homicides australia* → *martin bryant port arthur massacre*), which increases the difficulty of understanding user intention. However, since query changes are made after the user examines search results, we believe that *query change is an important form of feedback*. We hence propose to study and utilize query changes to facilitate better session search.

One approach to handle query change is to classify them based on various types of explorations [20], such as specification, generalization, drifting, or slight change, then perform retrieval. Another approach is mapping queries into semantic graphical representations, such as ontologies [7] or query flow graphs developed from query logs [2], then studying how queries move in the graphs. However, ontology mapping is challenging [17], which may introduce inaccurate intermediate results and hurt the search accuracy. Moreover, relying on large scale query logs may not be applicable due to lack of such data. Therefore, although these approaches have been applied to IR tasks such as query reformulation [3] and query suggestion [2, 30], they have yet to be directly applied to session search. It is therefore necessary to explore new solutions to utilize query change for session search.

We propose to model session search as a Markov Decision Process (MDP) [16, 28], which is applicable to many human decision processes. MDP models a state space and an action space for all agents participating in the process. Actions from the agents influence the environment/states and the environment/states influence the agents' subsequent actions

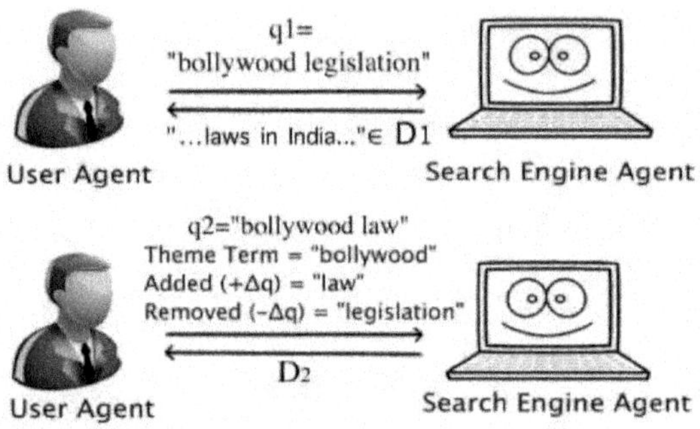

Figure 1: Session search MDP. (example is from s32)

based on certain policies. A transition model between states indicates the dynamics of the entire system. In our MDP, *queries* are modeled as states. Previous queries that the user wrote influence the search results; the search results again influence the user's decision of the next query. This interaction continues until the search stops.

As illustrated in Figure 1, we consider two agents in this entire process: the user agent and the search engine agent. The user agent's actions are mainly human actions that are able to change search results, such as adding and deleting query terms, i.e. *query change*. Clicking is a human action; however, it does not explicitly impact the retrieval. Therefore, it is not considered as a user action here. Query change is the only form of user action in this paper. Based on the user actions, we design corresponding policies for the search engine agent; which is the main focus of this paper.

It is difficult to interpret the user intent [5, 31] behind query change. For instance, for a query change from *Kurosawa* to *Kurosawa wife* (s38), there is no indication about 'wife' in the search results returned for the first query. However, *Kurosawa's wife* is actually among the information needs provided to the user by NIST's topic descriptions. Our experience with TREC Session tracks suggests that information needs and previous search results are two main factors that influence query change. However, knowing information needs before search could not easily be achieved. This paper focuses on utilizing evidence found in previous search results and the relationship between previous search results and query change to improve session search.

In this paper, we summarize various types of query changes based on potential user intents into user agent policies. We further propose corresponding policies for the search engine agent and model them in the query change retrieval model (QCM), a novel reinforcement learning [16] inspired framework. The relevance of a document to the current query is recursively calculated as the reward beginning from the starting query and continuing until the current query. This research is perhaps the first to employ reinforcement learning to tackle session search. Our experiments demonstrate that the proposed approach is highly effective and outperforms the best performing TREC 2011 and 2012 session search systems.

The remainder of this paper is organized as follows. Section 2 analyzes query change and summarizes policies for the user agent. Section 3 proposes policies for the search engine agent. Section 4 elaborates the query change retrieval model. Section 5 discusses how to handle duplicated queries. Section 6 evaluates our approach, followed by a discussion in Section 7. Section 8 presents the related work and Section 9 concludes the paper.

Table 2: Evidence that query change Δq appears in previous search results D_{i-1}.

	# in TREC'11		# in TREC'12	
	$\in D_{i-1}$	$\notin D_{i-1}$	$\in D_{i-1}$	$\notin D_{i-1}$
q_{theme}	184	20	178	21
$+\Delta q$	80	124	97	102
$-\Delta q$	141	63	112	87
Total	204 adjacent query pairs, 76 sessions		199 adjacent query pairs, 98 sessions	

2. USER AGENT: QUERY CHANGE AS A FORM OF FEEDBACK

We define a *search session* $\mathcal{S} = \{\mathcal{Q}, \mathcal{D}, \mathcal{C}\}$ as a combination of a series of queries $\mathcal{Q} = \{q_1, ..., q_i, ..., q_n\}$, retrieved document sets $\mathcal{D} = \{D_1, ..., D_i, ..., D_n\}$, and clicked information $\mathcal{C} = \{C_1, .., C_i, ..., C_n\}$, where n is the number of queries in the session (i.e., the session length) and i indexes the queries. In TREC 2010-2012 Session tracks, each retrieved document set D_i contains the top 10 retrieval results $d_{i1}, ..., d_{i10}$ ranked in decreasing relevance for q_i. Each clicked data C_i contains the user-clicked documents, clicking order, and dwell time. For instance, for s6 q_6, *pocono mountains camelbeach hotel* (Table 1), C_6 tells us that the user clicked the 4th ranked search result, followed by the 2nd, with dwell time 15 seconds and 17 seconds, respectively.

TREC 2010-2012 Session Tracks aim to retrieve a list of documents for the current query, i.e. the last query q_n in a session, ordered in decreasing relevance. Without loss of specificity, we assume that any query between q_1 to q_n could be the last query. We therefore study the problem of retrieving relevant documents for q_i, given all previous queries q_1 to q_{i-1}, previous retrieval results D_1 to D_{i-1}, and previous clicked data C_1 to C_{i-1}.

We define *query change* Δq_i as the syntactic editing changes between two adjacent queries q_{i-1} and q_i:

$$\Delta q_i = q_i - q_{i-1}$$

q_i can be written as a combination of the shared portion between q_i and q_{i-1} and query change: $q_i = (q_i \cap q_{i-1}) + \Delta q_i$.

The query change Δq_i comes from two sources. First, the added terms, which we call *positive* Δq, are new terms that the user adds to the previous query. Second, the removed terms, which we call *negative* Δq, are terms that the user deletes from the previous query. For example, in Table 1 s37, 'US' and 'policy' are the added terms; while in s28, 'stock' and 'market' are the removed terms.

We call the common terms shared by two adjacent queries *theme terms* since they often represent the main topic of a session. For example, in Table 1 s37 the theme terms are "Merck lobby".[2]

We thus decompose a query into three parts as *theme terms*, *added terms*, and *removed terms* and write it as:

$$q_i = (q_i \cap q_{i-1}) + (+\Delta q_i) - (-\Delta q_i) = q_{theme} + (+\Delta q_i) - (-\Delta q_i)$$

where q_{theme} are the theme terms, $+\Delta q_i$ and $-\Delta q_i$ represent added terms and removed terms, respectively.

Our observations suggest that documents that have been examined by the user factor in deciding the next query change. We therefore propose the following important assumption between Δq_i, the query change between adjacent

[2]We perform K-stemming to all query terms. For instance, 'lobbists' and 'lobbying' are both stemmed to 'lobby'.

Table 3: User agent's policies and actions about a query term $t \in q_{i-1}$. (Refer to sessions shown in Table 1)

	user likes D_{i-1}				**user dislikes D_{i-1}**			
	user intention	user action	example	type	user intention	user action	example	type
$t \in D_{i-1}$	1. find more information about t	add new terms t' about t	s85 $q_1 \rightarrow q_2$	specification	5. remove the wrong terms	remove t	s28 $q_1 \rightarrow q_2$	generalization
	2. satisfied & move to the next information need	remove t & add new terms t' as new focus	s6 $q_8 \rightarrow q_9$	drift	6. not satisfied & move to the next information need	remove t & add new terms t'	s6 $q_6 \rightarrow q_7$	drift
	3. satisfied	keep t	theme term	no change	7. try different expression for t	slight change of t to t'	s85 $q_2 \rightarrow q_3$	slight change
$t \notin D_{i-1}$	4. inspired by terms t' in D_{i-1}	add terms t'' about t'	s37 $q_1 \rightarrow q_2$	specification	8. try different expression for t to get more documents for t	slight change of t to t'	s32 $q_1 \rightarrow q_2$	slight change

queries q_i and q_{i-1}, and D_{i-1}, the search results for q_{i-1}:

$$\Delta q_i \leftarrow D_{i-1}.$$

The assumption basically says that *previous search results decide query change.* In fact, previous search results D_{i-1} could influence query change Δq_i in quite complex ways. For instance, the added terms in s37 (Table 1) q_1 to q_2, are 'US' and 'policy'. D_1 contains several mentions of 'policy', such as "*A lobbyist who until 2004 worked as senior policy advisor to Canadian Prime Minister Stephen Harper was hired last month by Merck*". However, these 'policy'-related mentions are about "Canada policy" whereas the user adds "US policy" in q_2. This suggests that the user might have been inspired by 'policy' in D_1, however he preferred the policy in *US*, not in *Canada*. Therefore, instead of simply cutting and pasting identical terms from D_{i-1}, the user creates related terms to add for the next search.

In another example, s28 (Table 1) q_1, 'stock' and 'market' are frequent terms that are similar to stopwords. Documents in D_1 are hence all about them and totally ignore the theme terms "france world cup 98." In q_2, the user removes "stock market" to boost rankings for documents about the theme terms. In this case, removing terms is not only about generalization, but also about document re-ranking.

To provide a convincing foundation for our approach, we look for evidence to support our assumption. We investigate whether Δq_i (at least) appears in D_{i-1}. Table 2 shows how often theme terms, added terms, and removed terms are present in D_{i-1} for both TREC 2011 and 2012 datasets. Around 90% of the time theme terms occur in D_{i-1} and most removed terms (>60%) appear in D_{i-1}.[3] Added terms are new terms for the previous query q_{i-1}; we thus expect to see few occurrences of added terms in D_{i-1}. Surprisingly, however, more than a third of them appear in D_{i-1}. It suggests that it is quite probable that previous search results motivate the subsequent query change.

Table 3 summarizes various types of query changes into possible policies for the user agent. This table mainly serves as a guide for us to design the policies for the search engine agent. We do not perform a thorough user study to validate this table. However, we believe that it is a good representative of various search scenarios and can help design a good session search agent.

Along two dimensions, Table 3 summarizes the user agent's actions and possible policies. The dimensions are whether a previous query term $t \in q_{i-1}$ appears in previous search results D_{i-1} (the left most column) and whether the user likes D_{i-1} and the occurrence of t in D_{i-1} (the top most row). Combinations of the two dimensions yield 4 main cases (as in a contingency table) and 8 sub-cases. For each case, we identify four items: a rough guess of user intention, the user's actual action, an example, and the semantic exploration type for this action. For example, query change in s6 $q_8 \rightarrow q_9$, *pocono mountains chateau resort attractions* $\rightarrow$ *pocono mountains chateau resort getting to* can be interpreted as the following. Previous query term 'attractions' appears in D_{i-1} and the user likes the returned documents D_{i-1}. One possibility is that he is satisfied with what he reads and moves to the next information need. Therefore, the user removes 'attraction' and adds new terms "getting to" as the new query focus. This is a *drift* in search focus. (case 2 in Table 3)

We further group the cases in Table 3 by types of user actions, i.e., query change, and summarize them into:

- Theme terms (q_{theme}), terms that appear in both q_{i-1} and q_i. In fact, they often appear in many queries in a session. It implies a strong preference for those terms from the user. If they appear in D_{i-1}, it shows that the user favors them since the user issues them again in q_i. If they do not appear in D_{i-1}, the user still favors towards them and insists to include them in the new query. This corresponds to t in cases 1 and 3 in Table 3.
- Added terms ($+\Delta q$), terms that appear only in q_i, not in q_{i-1}. They indicate specification, destination of drifting, or destination of slight change. If they appear in D_{i-1}, for the sake of novelty [14], they will not be favored in D_i. If they do not appear in D_{i-1}, which means that they are novel and the user favors them now. This corresponds to t' in cases 1, 2, 6, 7, and 8, and t'' in case 4 in Table 3.
- Removed terms ($-\Delta q$), terms that appear only in q_{i-1}, not in q_i. They indicate generalization, source of drifting, and source of slight change. If they appear in D_{i-1}, removing them means that the user observes them and dislikes them. If they do not appear in D_{i-1}, the user still dislikes the terms since they are not in q_i anyway. This corresponds to t in cases 2, 5, 6, 7, and 8 in Table 3.

3. SEARCH ENGINE AGENT: STRATEGIES TO IMPROVE SEARCH

The search engine agent observes query change from the user agent and takes corresponding actions. For each type of query change, *theme terms*, *added terms*, and *removed terms*, we propose to adjust the term weights accordingly for better retrieval accuracy. The search engine agent's action include

[3] A third of query terms that do not appear in D_{i-1} are removed by the user.

Table 4: Search engine agent's policy. Actions are adjustments on the term weights. ↑ means increasing, ↓ means decreasing, and → means keeping the original term weight.

	$\in D_{i-1}$	action	Example
q_{theme}	Y	↑	"pocono mountain" in s6
	N	↑	"france world cup 98 reaction" in s28, $q_1 \to q_2$
$+\Delta q$	Y	↓	'policy' in s37, $q_1 \to q_2$
	N	↑	'US' in s37, $q_1 \to q_2$
$-\Delta q$	Y	↓	'reaction' in s28, $q_2 \to q_3$
	N	→	'legislation' in s32, $q_2 \to q_3$

increasing, *decreasing*, and *maintaining* the term weights. Based on the observed query change as well as whether the query terms appeared in the previous search results D_{i-1}, we can sense whether the user will favor the query terms in the current run of search. Table 4 illustrates the policies that we propose for the search engine agent.

As shown in Section 2, theme terms q_{theme} often appear in many queries in a session and there is a strong preference for them. Thus, we propose to increase the weights of theme terms no matter whether they appeared in D_{i-1} or not (rows 1 and 2 in Table 4). In the latter case, if a theme term was not found in D_{i-1} (top retrieval results), it is likely that the documents containing them were ranked low. Therefore, the weights of theme terms need to be raised to boost the rankings of those documents (row 2 in Table 4). However, since theme terms are topic words in a session, they could appear like stopwords within the session. To avoid biasing too much towards them, we lower their term weights proportionally to their numbers of occurrences in D_{i-1}.

For added terms $+\Delta q$, if they occurred in previous search results D_{i-1}, we propose to decrease their term weights for the sake of novelty [14]. For example, in s5 $q_1 \to q_2$, "pocono mountains"→"pocono mountains park", the added term 'park' appeared in a document in D_5. If we use the original weight of 'park', this document might still be ranked high in D_2 and the user may dislike it since he read it before. We hence decrease added terms' weights if they are in D_{i-1} (row 3 in Table 4). On the other hand, if the added terms did not occur in D_{i-1}, they are the new search focus and we increase their term weights (row 4 in Table 4). In an interesting case (s37 $q_1 \to q_2$), part of $+\Delta q$, 'policy', occurred in D_1 whereas the other part, 'US', did not. To respect the user's preference, we increase the weight of 'US' while decreasing that of 'policy' to penalize documents about other 'polices' including "Canada policy".

For removed terms $-\Delta q$, if they appeared in D_{i-1}, their term weights are decreased since the user dislikes them by deleting them (row 5 in Table 4). For example, in s28 $q_2 \to q_3$, 'reaction' existed in D_2 and is removed in q_3. However, if the removed terms are not in D_{i-1}, we do not change their weights since they are already removed from q_i by the user (row 6 in Table 4).

In the sections below, we follow policies proposed for the search engine agent as shown in Table 4 and incorporate them into a novel query change retrieval model (QCM).

4. MODELING SESSION SEARCH

Markov Decision Process (MDP) [16, 28] models a state space S and an action space A. Its states $\mathcal{S} = \{s_1, s_2, ...\}$ change from one to another according to a transition model $T = P(s_{i+1}|s_i, a_i)$, which models the dynamics of the entire system. A policy $\pi(s) = a$ indicates that at a state s, what are the actions a can be taken by the agent. In session search, we employ *queries* as states. Particularly, we denote q as state, T as the transition model $P(q_i|q_{i-1}, a_{i-1})$, D as documents, and A as actions. Actions include keeping, adding, and removing query terms for the user agent and increasing, decreasing, and maintaining the term weights for the search engine agent.

In a MDP, each state is associated with a *reward function* R that indicates possible positive reward or negative loss that a state and an action may result. In session search, we consider the reward function to be the relevance function.

Reinforcement learning [16] offers general solutions to MDP and seeks for the best policy for an agent. Each policy has a value associated with the policy and denoted as $V_\pi(s)$, which is the expected long-term reward starting from state s and continuing with policy π from then on. In a MDP, it is believed that a future reward is not worth quite as much as a current reward and thus a discount factor $\gamma \in (0,1)$ is applied to future rewards. By considering the discount factor, the value function starting from s_0 for a policy π can be written as: $V_\pi(s_0) = E_\pi[R(s_0) + \gamma R(s_1) + \gamma^2 R(s_2) + ...] = E_\pi[\sum_{t=0}^{\infty} \gamma^t R(s_i)]$. The Bellman equation [16] describes the optimal value V^* for a state s in the long run and is often used to obtain the best value for a MDP:

$$V^*(s) = \max_a R(s,a) + \gamma \sum_{s'} P(s'|s,a) V^*(s')$$

where s' is the next state after s, $V^*(s)$ and $V^*(s')$ are the optimal values for s and s'.

For session search, we observe that the influence of previous queries and previous search results to the current queries, becomes weaker and weaker. The user's desire for novel documents also supports this argument. We hence propose to employ the reinforcement learning model backwards. That is, instead of discounting the future rewards, we discount the past rewards, i.e. the relevant documents that appeared in the previous search results.

We propose the query change retrieval model (QCM) as the following. We consider the task of retrieving relevant documents for q_i as ranking documents based on the reward, i.e., how relevant it is to q_i. Inspired by the Bellman equation, we model the relevance of a document d to the current query q_i as:

$$Score(q_i, d) = P(q_i|d) + \gamma \sum_a P(q_i|q_{i-1}, D_{i-1}, a) \max_{D_{i-1}} P(q_{i-1}|D_{i-1}) \quad (1)$$

which recursively calculates the reward starting from q_1 and continues with the search engine agent's policy until q_i. $\gamma \in (0,1)$ is the discount factor, $\max_{D_{i-1}} P(q_{i-1}|D_{i-1})$ is the maximum of the past rewards, $P(q_i|d)$ is the current reward, and $P(q_i|q_{i-1}, D_{i-1}, a)$ is the query transition model.

The first component in Eq.1, $P(q_i|d)$, measures the relevance between q_i and a document d that is under evaluation. This component can be estimated by the Bayesian belief network model [27]: $P(q_i|d) = 1 - \prod_{t \in q_i}(1 - P(t|d))$, where $P(t|d)$ is calculated by the multinomial query generation language model with Dirichlet smoothing [33]: $P(t|d) = \frac{\#(t,d) + \mu P(t|C)}{|d| + \mu}$, where $\#(t,d)$ denotes the number of occurrences of term t in document d, $P(t|C)$ calculates the probability that t appears in corpus C based on Maximum Likelihood Estimation (MLE), $|d|$ is the document length, and μ is the Dirichlet smoothing parameter (set to 5000).

The remaining challenges of calculating Eq.1 include maximizing the reward function $\max_{D_{i-1}} P(q_{i-1}|D_{i-1})$ and estimating the transition model $P(q_i|q_{i-1}, D_{i-1}, a)$. They are described in Section 4.1 and Section 4.2, respectively.

4.1 Maximizing the Reward Function

When considering the past/future rewards, MDP uses only the optimal (the maximum possible) values from those past /future rewards. This is reflected in $\max_{D_{i-1}} P(q_{i-1}|D_{i-1})$ as part of Eq. 1.

Prior research [10, 22] suggests that *Satisfying (SAT)* clicks, i.e., clicked documents with dwell time longer than 30 seconds [10, 22], are probably the only ones that are effective at predicting user behaviors and relevance judgments. Since the user also skims snippets in search interactions, in this work, we consider both the top 10 returned snippets and SAT clicks as *effective previous search results* and denote them as D^e_{i-1}.

To obtain an maximum reward from all possible reward functions $P(q_{i-1}|d_{i-1})$, i.e., the text relevance of previous query q_{i-1} and all previous search results $d_{i-1} \in D_{i-1}$, we propose to generate a *maximum rewarding document*, denoted as d^*_{i-1}. We further propose that the candidates for the d^*_{i-1} should only be selected from the *effective previous search results* D^e_{i-1}. We define d^*_{i-1} as the document(s) that is the most relevant to q_{i-1}. To discover d^*_{i-1}, we first rank all the documents (either a snippet or a document) $d_{i-1} \in D^e_{i-1}$ by measuring the relevance between q_{i-1} and d_{i-1} as: $P(q_{i-1}|d_{i-1}) = 1 - \prod_{t \in q_{i-1}} \{1 - P(t|d_{i-1})\}$, where $P(t|d_{i-1})$ is calculated by MLE: $P(t|d_{i-1}) = \frac{\#(t,d_{i-1})}{|d_{i-1}|}$, $\#(t, d_{i-1})$ is the number of occurrences of term t in document d_{i-1}, and $|d_{i-1}|$ is the document length. We do not apply smoothing here since $P(t|d_{i-1})$ can be zero, i.e., $t \notin D^e_{i-1}$. In fact, we rely on this property in later calculation.

After ranking documents d_{i-1} in D^e_{i-1}, we generate d^*_{i-1} by the following options: (1) using the document with the largest $P(q_{i-1}|d_{i-1})$, (2) concatenating the top k documents in D^e_{i-1} with the largest $P(q_{i-1}|d_{i-1})$, or (3) concatenating all documents in D^e_{i-1}. Experiments show that option (1) works the best and we use this setting throughout the paper. For notation simplicity, we use D_{i-1} from now on to denote effective previous search results.

4.2 Estimating the Transition Model

The transition model indicated in Eq. 1 is $\sum_a P(q_i|q_{i-1}, D_{i-1}, a)$. It includes the probabilities of query transitions under various actions. We incorporate polices designed in Table 4 to calculate it.

Search engine agent performs actions based on user agent's actions. We need to identify user's actions, i.e. query change Δq before search engine takes actions. Particularly, we recognize Δq by the following procedure. First, we generate q_{theme} based on the Longest Common Subsequence (LCS) [11] in both q_{i-1} and q_i. A subsequence is a sequence that appears in two strings in the same relative order but is not necessarily continuous. The LCS can be the common prefix or the common suffix of the two queries; it can also consist of several discontinuous common parts from the two queries. Take s6 $q_6 \rightarrow q_7$ as an example: q_6="pocono mountains camelbeach hotel", q_7="pocono mountains chateau resort", q_{theme} = LCS(q_6, q_7) = "pocono mountains". Next, we recognize added terms $+\Delta q$ and removed terms $-\Delta q$. Generally, the terms that occur in the current query but not in the previous query constitute $+\Delta q$; while the terms occur in the previous query but not in the current query constitute $-\Delta q$. In the above example, $-\Delta q_7$ = "camelbeach hotel", and $+\Delta q_7$ = "chateau resort".

The search engine actions are *decreasing, increasing,* and *maintaining* term weights. According to Table 4 rows 3 and 5, we decrease a term's weight if the query change, either $+\Delta q$ or $-\Delta q$, occurred in the effective previous search results D_{i-1}. We propose to deduct term t's weight by $P(t|d)$, i.e. t's default contribution to the relevance score between q_i and the document under evaluation (denoted as d). Furthermore, since t already occurred in D_{i-1}, for the sake of novelty, we deduct more weight that is proportional to t's frequency in D_{i-1} such that the more frequently t occurred in D_{i-1}, the more heavily t's weight is deducted from the current query q_i and d. We formulate this weight deduction for a term $t \in +\Delta q$ or $t \in -\Delta q$ as:

$$\log P_{new}(t|d) = (1 - P(t|d^*_{i-1})) \log P(t|d) \quad (2)$$

where d^*_{i-1} denotes the maximum rewarded document, d is the document under evaluation, and $P(t|d)$ is calculated by MLE. We apply the log function to avoid numeric underflow.

We notice that Eq. 2 has an interesting connection with the Kullback-Leibler divergence (KL divergence) [33]:

$$\begin{aligned} - P(t|d^*_{i-1}) \log P(t|d) &= P(t|d^*_{i-1}) \log \frac{1}{P(t|d)} \\ &\stackrel{rank}{=} P(t|d^*_{i-1}) \log \frac{P(t|d^*_{i-1})}{P(t|d)} \\ &\stackrel{rank}{=} KLD_t\left(\theta_{d^*_{i-1}} || \theta_d\right) \end{aligned} \quad (3)$$

where $KLD_t\left(\theta_{d^*_{i-1}} || \theta_d\right)$ denotes the contribution of term t to the KL divergence between two documents' language models $\theta_{d^*_{i-1}}$ and θ_d. In Eq. 3, the larger the divergence between $\theta_{d^*_{i-1}}$ and θ_d, the more novel document d is compared to D_{i-1}, and the less deduction to the relevance score. In this sense, Eq. 2 models novelty for the added terms and the removed terms during a query transition.

According to Table 4 row 4, we increase a term's weight if it is an added term and did not occur in D_{i-1}. We propose to raise the term weight proportional to its inverse document frequency (*idf*). This is to make sure that while increasing a preferred term's weight, we avoid increasing its weight too much if it is a common term in many documents. We formulate this weight increase for a novel added term t ($t \in +\Delta q$ and $t \notin D_{i-1}$) as:

$$\log P_{new}(t|d) = (1 + idf(t)) \log P(t|d) \quad (4)$$

where $idf(t)$ is the inverse document frequency of t in Corpus C and $P(t|d)$ is calculated by MLE. Note that this term weight adjustment is in a form of *tf-idf*.

The increasing in term weights also applies to theme terms, which corresponds to rows 1 and 2 in Table 4. Theme terms repeatedly appear in a session, which implies the importance of them. Similar to the novel added terms, we should avoid increasing their weights too much. We could discount the increment proportional to *idf*. However, theme terms are topical/common terms within a session, not necessarily common terms in the entire corpus. Therefore, *idf* may not be applicable here. We hence employ the negation of the number of occurrences of t in previous maximum rewarding document, $1 - P(t|d^*_{i-1})$, to substitute *idf*. We formulate this weight increase for a theme term $t \in q_{theme}$ as:

$$\log P_{new}(t|d) = (1 + (1 - P(t|d^*_{i-1}))) \log P(t|d) \quad (5)$$

where d^*_{i-1} denotes the maximum rewarded document and $P(t|d)$ is calculated by MLE.

For removed terms that did not appear in D_{i-1} (Table 4 row 6), the search agent does not change their term weights.

By considering all possible cases for the transition model as defined in Eq. 1, the relevance score between the current query q_i and a document d is represented as below:

$$\begin{aligned} Score(q_i, d) &= \log P(q_i|d) + \alpha \sum_{t \in q_{theme}} [1 - P(t|d^*_{i-1})] \log P(t|d) \\ &- \beta \sum_{\substack{t \in +\Delta q \\ t \in d^*_{i-1}}} P(t|d^*_{i-1}) \log P(t|d) + \epsilon \sum_{\substack{t \in +\Delta q \\ t \notin d^*_{i-1}}} idf(t) \log P(t|d) \\ &- \delta \sum_{t \in -\Delta q} P(t|d^*_{i-1}) \log P(t|d) \end{aligned} \quad (6)$$

where α, β, ϵ, and δ are parameters for each types of actions. Note that we apply different parameters β and δ on $+\Delta q$ and $-\Delta q$, since added terms and removed terms may affect the retrieval differently. We report the parameter selection in Section 6.

4.3 Scoring the Entire Session

It is worth noting that Eq. 6 is valid only when $i > 1$. When $i = 1$, there is no previous result for q_1. We thus use

$$Score(q_1, d) = \log P(q_1|d) \quad (7)$$

as a base case. $P(q_1|d)$ is calculated by Eq. 4.

Using Eq. 7 as the base case for the recursive function described in Eq. 1, we obtain the overall document relevance score $Score_{session}(q_n, d)$ for a session that starts at q_1 and ends at q_n by considering all queries in the session:

$$\begin{aligned} Score_{session}(q_n, d) &= Score(q_n, d) + \gamma Score_{session}(q_{n-1}, d) \\ &= Score(q_n, d) + \gamma [Score(q_{n-1}, d) + \gamma Score_{session}(q_{n-2}, d)] \\ &= \sum_{i=1}^{n} \gamma^{n-i} Score(q_i, d) \end{aligned} \quad (8)$$

where $q_1, q_2, \cdots, q_n$ are in the same session, and $\gamma \in (0, 1)$ is the discount factor. Eq. 8 provides a form of aggregation over the relevance functions of all the queries in a session.

5. DUPLICATED QUERIES

Duplicated queries sometimes occur in a search session. Prior work shows that removing duplicated queries could effectively boost the search accuracy [8, 19]. Duplicated queries often occur when a user is frustrated by irrelevant documents in search results and comes back to one of the previous queries for a fresh start. For example, in s6 (Table 1), q_2 and q_4 are duplicates and both search for *pocono mountains pennsylvania hotels*. The query between them is q_3: *pocono mountains pennsylvania things to do*. It suggests that the user might dislike the search results for q_3 and he returns to q_2 to search again ($q_2 = q_4$).

To detect query duplicates, we first remove punctuations and white spaces in queries, then apply stemming on them.

Table 5: Dataset statistics for TREC 2011 and 2012 Session.

	2011	2012		2011	2012
#topics	62	48	#queries/session	3.68	3.03
#sessions	76	98	#sessions/topic	1.23	2.04
#queries	280	297	#pages judged	19,413	17,861
#dups	16	5	#sessions w/o rel. docs	2	4

Next we determine exact string matches between every query pair. The exactly matched query pairs are identified as duplicated queries.

Since the user may dislike the queries and their corresponding search results between two duplicated queries, we propose to eliminate from the MDP the undesired queries and their interactions. We achieve this by setting the discount factor to zero for any interaction between two duplicated queries as well as that for the earlier query in the two. The new discount factor γ' can be calculated as:

$$\gamma'_i = \begin{cases} 0 & \{i | i \in [j, k), \exists q_j = q_k, j < k)\} \\ \gamma_i & \text{otherwise} \end{cases} \quad (9)$$

where γ_i is the original discount factor for the ith query, γ'_i is the updated discount factor for the ith query after deduplication.

For the above example s6, the effects from q_2 and q_3 on the session are eliminated. The entire session is now equivalent to $q_1, q_4, q_5, ..., q_{11}$.

6. EVALUATION

The evaluation datasets are from TREC 2011 and 2012 Session tracks [18, 19]. Table 5 lists the statistics about these two datasets. Each search session includes several queries and the corresponding search results. The users (NIST assessors) were given a topic description about information needs before they searched. For example, s85 (Table 1) are related to topic 43 "When is scientific glass blowing used? What are the purposes? What organizations do scientific glass blowing?" Multiple sessions can relate to the same topic. The search engine used to create the sessions was Yahoo! BOSS. The top 10 returned documents were shown to the users and they clicked documents that were interesting to them and interacted with the system. We use TREC's official ground truth and official evaluation metrics nDCG@10 and MAP.

The corpus used in this evaluation is ClueWeb09 Category B collection (CatB).[4] CatB contains the first 50 million English pages crawled from the Web during January to February 2009. We filter out the spam documents by removing documents whose WateQCMoo's "GroupX" spam ranking scores [6] are less than 70.

We compare the following systems in this evaluation:

- *Lemur*: Directly submitting the current query q_n (with punctuations removed) to the Lemur search engine [21] (language modeling + Dirichlet smoothing) and obtain the returned documents.
- *TREC best* : The top TREC system as reported by NIST [13, 14]. It adopts a query generation model with relevance feedback and handles document novelty. CatB was used in their TREC submissions. *This system is used as the baseline system in this evaluation.*
- *Nugget*: Another top TREC 2012 session search system groups semantically coherent query terms as *nuggets* and

[4]http://lemurproject.org/clueweb09/.

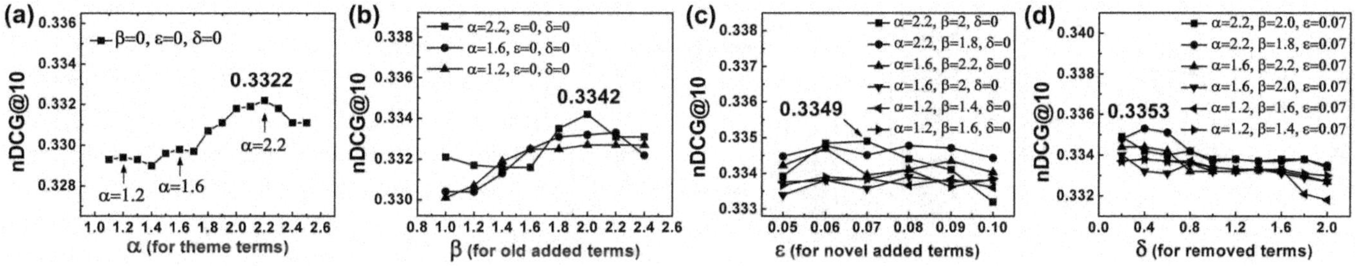

Figure 2: nDCG@10 for TREC 2012 against the parameters. (a), (b), (c), and (d) are about α, β, ϵ, and δ respectively.

Table 6: nDCG@10, MAP, and their improvements over the baseline (%chg) for TREC 2012 sessions. The runs are sorted by nDCG@10. A statistical significant improvement over the baseline is indicated with a † at $p < 0.05$ level.

Approach	nDCG@10	%chg	MAP	%chg
Lemur	0.2474	-21.54%	0.1274	-18.28%
TREC median	0.2608	-17.29%	0.1440	-7.63%
Nugget	0.3021	−4.19%	0.1490	-4.43%
TREC best	0.3221	0.00%	0.1559	0.00%
QCM	**0.3353**	**4.10%†**	0.1529	-1.92%
QCM+Dup	**0.3368**	**4.56%†**	0.1537	-1.41%

Table 7: nDCG@10, MAP, and their improvements over the baseline (%chg) for TREC 2011 sessions. The runs are sorted by nDCG@10. A statistical significant improvement over the baseline is indicated with a † at $p < 0.05$ level.

Approach	nDCG@10	%chg	MAP	%chg
Lemur	0.3378	-23.38%	0.1118	-25.86%
TREC median	0.3544	-19.62%	0.1143	-24.20%
TREC best	0.4409	0.00%	0.1508	0.00%
QCM	**0.4728**	**7.24%†**	**0.1713**	**13.59%†**
QCM+Dup	**0.4821**	**9.34%†**	**0.1714**	**13.66%†**
Nugget	0.4836	9.68%†	0.1724	14.32%†

creates structured Lemur queries [8]. We re-implement and apply it on both TREC 2011 and 2012.

- *TREC median*: The median TREC system as reported by NIST [18, 19].
- *QCM*: The proposed query change retrieval model.
- *QCM + De-Duplicate (Dup)*: The proposed query change retrieval model with duplicated queries removed.

6.1 Search Accuracy

Table 6 and Table 7 demonstrate search accuracy for all systems under comparison for TREC 2012 and TREC 2011, respectively. The evaluation metrics are nDCG@10 and MAP, the same as in the official TREC evaluations. *TREC best* serves as the baseline.

Table 6 shows that the proposed QCM approach outperforms the best TREC 2012 system on nDCG@10 by 4.1%, which is statistically significant (one sided t-test, $p = 0.05$). The search accuracy is further improved by 0.46% through removing the duplicated queries. The experimental results strongly suggest that our approach is highly effective.

Table 7 shows that for TREC 2011, our approach again outperforms the baseline by a statistically significant 7.24% (one sided t-test, $p = 0.05$) and achieves a further improvement of 9.34% by the QCM+Dup approach. For TREC 2011, the performance gain by performing de-dup is 2.1%, which is bigger than that for TREC 2012 (0.46%). The reason is probably because that TREC 2012 only has 5 duplicated queries while TREC 2011 has 16 (shown in Table 5). However, the best approach for TREC 2011 is the *nugget* approach, which is slightly better than QCM+Dup.

Table 5 illustrates the dataset differences between TREC 2011 and 2012. These differences may affect search accuracy. The average number of sessions per topic is 2.04 in 2012, that is more than that in 2011 (1.23). Moreover, on average, TREC 2012 sessions contain less queries per session (3.03) than 2011 (3.68). As a result, the shorter sessions in 2012 may make the search task more difficult than 2011 since less information are provided by previous interactions. Another difference is that 2012 sessions have fewer (sometimes even none) relevant documents than 2011 sessions in CatB ground truth. It unavoidably hurts the performance for any retrieval system. Generally, we observe lower search accuracy in 2012 (Table 6) than in 2011 (Table 7).

6.2 Parameter Tuning

We investigate good values for parameters in Eq. 6. A supervised learning-to-rank method should be able to find the optimal values for those parameters. However, in this paper, we take a step-by-step parameter tuning procedure and leave the supervised learning method as future work.

We add each component, i.e., theme terms, added terms, and removed terms, one by one into Eq. 6. The tuning is performed for QCM only and the parameters are shared between QCM and QCM+Dup.

First, we plot nDCG@10 against α while setting other parameters to 0 (Figure 2(a)). α represents the parameter for theme terms. α ranges over $[1.1, 2.5]$ by an interval of 0.1. We notice that nDCG@10 reaches its maximum at $\alpha = 2.2$. We find 2 other local maximums at 1.6 and 1.2 for α.

Next, we fix α to the above values and plot nDCG@10 against β (Figure 2(b)). β is the parameter for added terms that appeared in effective previous search results; we call them old added terms. β ranges over $[1.0, 2.4]$ by an interval of 0.2. We choose the top 2 local values from each curve and pick 6 combinations for (α, β) as indicated in Figure 2(c).

Then, we fix (α, β) and plot nDCG@10 against ϵ (Figure 2(c)). ϵ is the parameter for added terms that did not appear in effective previous search results; we call them novel added terms. ϵ ranges over $[0.05, 0.1]$ by an interval of 0.01. All the curves show similar trends and reach the highest nDCG@10 at around 0.07. We hence fix ϵ to 0.07.

Finally, we plot nDCG@10 against δ (Figure 2(d)) with the parameter combinations that we discover eerlier. Eventually, nDCG@10 reaches its peak 0.3353 at $\alpha = 2.2, \beta = 1.8, \epsilon = 0.07$, and $\delta = 0.4$. We apply this set of parameters to both QCM and QCM+Dup.

As we can see, α, β, and δ are much larger than ϵ. This is because that in Eq. 4, $idf(t) = \log(N/n_d)$ falls in the range of $[1, 10]$, while in Eq. 2 and Eq. 5, $P(t|d^*_{i-1})$ falls

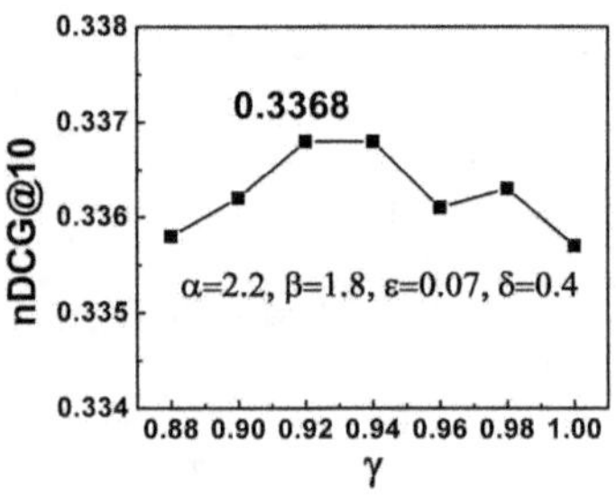

Figure 3: Discount factor γ.

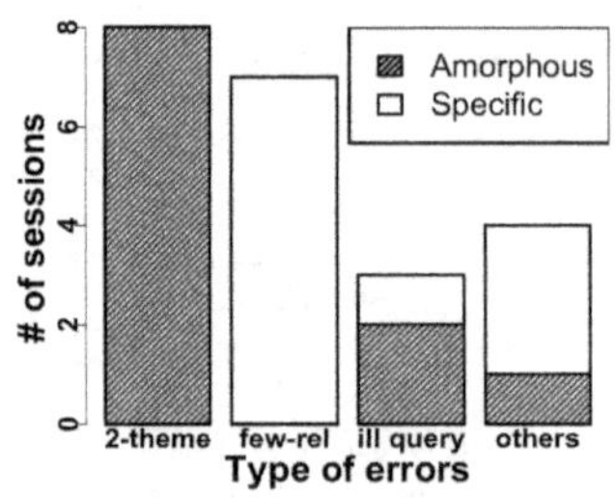

Figure 4: Error types.

Table 8: Aggregation schemes.

Approach		q_n	$q_i (i \in [1, n-1])$
Query change model		1	γ^{n-i}
Aggregation Scheme	Uniform	$\lambda_n = 1$	$\lambda_i = 1$
	PvC	$\lambda_n = 1 - \lambda_p$	$\lambda_i = \lambda_p$
	Distance-based	$\lambda_n = 1 - \lambda_p$	$\lambda_i = \frac{\lambda_p}{n-i}$

Table 9: nDCG@10 for various aggregation schemes. λ_p is 0.4 in PvC. γ is 0.92 in QCM and QCM+Dup. TREC 2012 best serves as the baseline. A significant improvement over the baseline is indicated with a † at $p < 0.05$ level.

Aggregation Scheme	TREC 2011		TREC 2012	
	nDCG@10	%chg	nDCG@10	%chg
Distance-based	0.4431	-2.40%	0.3111	−3.42%
TREC best	0.4540	0.00%	0.3221	0.00%
Uniform	0.4626	1.89%†	0.3316	2.95%†
PvC	0.4713	3.81%†	0.3351	4.04%†
QCM	**0.4728**	**4.14%†**	**0.3353**	**4.10%†**
QCM+Dup	**0.4821**	**6.19%†**	**0.3368**	**4.56%†**

in the range of [0,0.1]. Therefore, the values of ϵ are two magnitudes less than that for the other parameters. Among α, β, and δ, we find that α and β are larger than δ, which implies that theme terms and added terms may play more important roles in session search than removed terms.

6.3 Aggregation for the Entire Session

QCM proposes an effective way to aggregate all queries in a session as in Eq.8. We compare how effective it is to prior query aggregation methods. A query aggregation scheme can be represented as: $Score(session, d) = \sum_{i=1}^{n} \lambda_i \cdot Score(q_i, d)$, where $Score(q_i, d)$ is the relevance scoring function of d and q_i and λ_i is the query weight for q_i.

[8] proposed several aggregation schemes for TREC 2012 Session track. The schemes are: *uniform* (all queries are equally weighted), *previous vs. current* (known as PvC; all previous queries are discounted by λ_p, while the current query uses a complementary and higher coefficient $(1 - \lambda_p)$, and *distance-based* (previous queries are discounted based on a reciprocal function of queries' positions in the session).

We express various query aggregation schemes in terms of the discount factor γ in order to compare them with our approach. From Table 8, we find that QCM degenerates to uniform when $\gamma = 1$. Previous queries in PvC and Distance-based schemes are also discounted as they are in QCM, but with different decay functions.

The search accuracy for different aggregation schemes are compared in Table 9. QCM performs the best for both TREC 2011 and 2012. The PvC scheme is the second best scheme, which confirms what is reported in [8]. The Distance-based scheme gives the worst performance.

We explore the best discount factor γ for QCM over (0, 1) by an interval of 0.02. Figure 3 illustrates the relationship between nDCG@10 and γ. nDCG@10 climbs to its peak 0.3368 when $\gamma = 0.92$. The result suggests that a good discount factor γ is very close to 1, implying that previous queries contribute to the overall search accuracy nearly the same as the last query. It suggests that in QCM, a discount between two adjacent queries should be mild.

7. DISCUSSION

7.1 Advantages of Our Approach

A main contribution of our approach is that we treat a search session as a continuous process by studying changes among query transitions and modeling the dynamics in the entire session. Through the reinforcement learning style framework, our system provides the best aggregation scheme for all queries in a session (Table 9). This allows us to better handle sessions that demonstrate evolution and exploration in nature than most existing systems do. On the contrary, for sessions that are clear in search goals and lack of a exploratory nature, the advantage of our system over other systems looks less significant.

This can be seen in Table 10, which illustrates the search accuracy for the TREC best, Nugget, and our system for various classes of sessions. The TREC best is used as the baseline and we also show the percentile improvement over it in Table 10. TREC 2012 sessions were created by considering and hence can be classified into two facets: search target (factual or intellectual) and goal quality (specific/good or amorphous/ill) [19]. Table 10 shows that QCM works very well for all classes of sessions. Specifically, QCM works even better, i.e. outperforms the TREC best even more significantly, for sessions that search for intellectual targets as well as sessions that search with amorphous goals. In our opinion, this is due to that intellectual tasks produce new ideas or new findings (e.g. learn about a topic or make decision based on the information collected so far) while searching. Both intellectual and amorphous sessions rely more on previous search results. Thus, users reformulate queries based more on what they have retrieved, not the vague information need. This is a scenario where our approach is good at since we employ previous search results to guide the search engine's action. For specific and factual sessions, users are clearer in search goals, query changes may come less from the previous search results. In summary, our good performance on both intellectual task and amorphous task is consistent with our efforts of modeling query changes.

Moreover, we benefit from term-level manipulation in various aspects in our system. The first aspect is novelty. Both the TREC best system and our system handle novelty in a session. The TREC best system only deals with novelty at the document level. They consider documents that have been examined by the user in a previous interaction not novel and the rest are novel [14]. That is, they determine novelty purely based on document identification number, not the actual content. Through studying whether query terms appeared in previous search results, our approach evaluates and models novelty at the term level (or concept level), which we believe better represents the evolving information needs in a session. The second aspect is query handling. The Nugget approach [8] treats queries at the phrase level and formulates structured queries based on phrase-like *nuggets*. The approach achieves good performance, espe-

Table 10: nDCG@10 for different classes of sessions in TREC 2012.

	Intellectual	%chg	Amorphous	%chg	Specific	%chg	Factual	%chg
TREC best	0.3369	0.00%	0.3495	0.00%	0.3007	0.00%	0.3138	0.00%
Nugget	0.3305	-1.90%	0.3397	-2.80%	0.2736	-9.01%	0.2871	-8.51%
QCM	0.3870	14.87%	0.3689	5.55%	0.3091	2.79%	0.3066	-2.29%
QCM+DUP	0.3900	15.76%	0.3692	5.64%	0.3114	3.56%	0.3072	-2.10%

cially for TREC 2011. However, due to complexity in natural language, nugget detection is sensitive to dataset and the approach's performance is not quite as stable as ours on different datasets.

Lastly, our system benefits from trusting the user. Our approach does not use too much materials from other resources such as anchor texts, meta data, or click orders, as many other approaches do [8, 26]. We believe that the most direct and valuable feedback is the next query that the user enters. In this work, we manage to capture the query change and investigate the reasons behind it. We use ourselves as users to summarize possible human users' reasoning and actions. More detailed analysis about user intent might be useful for researchers to understand web users, however, it might be overwhelming (too fine-grained or too much semantics) for a search engine that essentially only counts words.

7.2 Error Analysis & Future Work

Our system retrieves nothing for 22 out of 98 sessions in TREC 2012. To analyze the reason for the poor performance for those sessions, we study their topic descriptions, queries, and ground truth documents. We summarize the types of errors as "two theme concepts", "ill query", "few relevant documents", and others. Figure 4 shows how many sessions that we fail to retrieve under each error type.

We call the first type of errors "two theme concepts". It comes from a type of session where the information need cover more than one concepts. For instance, s17 and s18 share the the same topic "... To what extent can decisions and policies of the Indian government be credited with these wins?". Queries in s17 and s18 ask about both concepts "indian politics' and "miss universe". Unfortunately, very few relevant documents about both theme concepts exist in the corpus. The retrieved documents are about either concept, but none is about both. Eight sessions belong to this type. As future work, we can improve our system by incorporating structures in queries, and enable more sophisticated operators such as Boolean and proximity search.

The second type of errors is "ill query", where in such sessions, queries themselves are ill formulated and do not well-represent the information needs indicated in the given topic. A common mistake is that the user misses some sub-information need. For example, the topic for s16 is: "... you want to reduce the use of air conditioning in your house ... you could protect the roof being overly hot due to sun exposure... Find information of ... how it could be done." A good query for this topic should include *roof* and *air conditioning*. However, the queries that the user issued for s60, "reduce airconditioning" and "attic insulation air conditioning costs", do not mention *roof* at all. Because of this ill query formulation, our system yields no relevant documents for s60. On the other hand, for s59, which shares the same information need with s60, our system achieves a nDCG@10 of 0.48 simply because s59 queries "cool roof". It suggests that ill queries mislead the search engine and yield poor retrieval performance. Four sessions belong to this type. As future work, we will explore effective query suggestion by studying sessions that share the same topic.

The third type of errors is "too few relevant documents". For sessions with too few relevant documents in the ground truth, our system do not perform well. In total 2,573 relevant documents exist in CatB for all 48 TREC 2012 topics; on average 53.6 relevant documents per topic. However, topics 10, 45, 47 and 48, each has no more than 2 relevant documents and topic 47 (s92 to s95) has no relevant document in CatB (Table 5). This problem could be reduced if we index the entire ClubWeb09 CatA collection.

Figure 4 also indicates in which classes of sessions these errors lie. We find that all "two theme concept" errors belong to sessions created with amorphous goals while all "too few relevant documents" errors belong to those with specific goals. Moreover, "ill queries" tend to occur more in sessions with amorphous goals. Note that "ill query" and "few relevant documents" are errors due to either the user or the data. There might not be much room for our system to improve over them. However, "two theme concepts" is where our system can certainly make further improvements.

8. RELATED WORK

Session search is a challenging IR task [4, 8, 13, 14, 25, 32]. Existing approaches investigate session search from various aspects such as semantic meanings of search tasks [23], document novelty [14], and phrase structure in queries [8]. The best TREC system [13, 14] employs an adaptive browsing model by considering both relevance and novelty; however it does not demonstrate improvement by handling novelty. In this paper, we successfully model query and document novelty by investigating the relationship between query change and previous search results. Moreover, our analysis on query change does not require knowledge of semantic types for the sessions as [23] proposed.

Our proposed work is perhaps the most similar to the problem of query formulation [1, 9, 12, 24] and query suggestion [29]. [12] showed that certain query changes such as adding/removing words, word substitution, acronym expansion, and spelling correction are more likely to cause clicks, especially on higher ranked results. The finding is generally consistent with our view of query change. However, their work only emphasized on understanding of query changes, without showing how to apply it to help session search. [24] examined the relationship between task types and how users change queries. They classified query changes by semantic types: Generalization, Specialization, Word Substitution, Repeat, and New. Similar to [12], however, [24] stopped at understanding query changes and didn't apply their findings to help session search. This probably makes us the first to utilize query changes in actual retrieval. [1] derived query-flow graph, a graph representation of user query behavior, from user query logs. The approach detected query chains in the graph and recommended queries based on maximum weights, random walk, or just the previous query. Other mining approaches [1, 29] identify the importance of query change in sessions; however, they require the luxury of large user query logs.

This research is perhaps the first to employ reinforcement learning to solve the Markov Decision Process demonstrated in session search. Reinforcement learning is complex and difficult to solve. Its solutions include model-based approaches and model-free approaches [16]. The former learn the transition model and the reward function for every possible states and actions and mainly employ MLE to estimate the model parameters. Others also use matrix inversion or *linear programming* to solve the Bellman equation. It works well when state spaces are small. However, in our case, the state space is large since we use natural language queries as the states; hence we could not easily apply model-based approaches in practice. In this work, we effectively reduce the search space by summarizing users' and search engine's actions into a few types and employ a model-free approach to learn value functions directly.

9. CONCLUSION

This paper presents a novel session search approach (QCM) by utilizing query change and modeling the dynamic of the entire session as a Markov Decision Process. We assume that query change is an important form of feedback. Based on this assumption, through studying editing changes between adjacent queries, and their relationship with previous retrieved documents, we propose corresponding search engine actions to handle individual term weights for both the query and the document. In a reinforcement learning inspired framework, we incorporate various ingredients present in session search, such as query changes, satisfactory clicks, desire for document novelty, and duplicated queries. The proposed framework provides a theoretically sound and general foundation that allows more novel features to be incorporated. Experiments on both TREC 2011 and 2012 Session tracks show that our approach is highly effective and outperforms the best session search systems in TREC. This research is perhaps the first to employ reinforcement learning in session search. Our MDP view of modeling session search can potentially benefit a wide range of IR tasks.

10. ACKNOWLEDGMENT

This research was supported by NSF grant CNS-1223825. Any opinions, findings, conclusions, or recommendations expressed in this paper are of the authors, and do not necessarily reflect those of the sponsor.

11. REFERENCES

[1] P. Boldi, F. Bonchi, C. Castillo, D. Donato, A. Gionis, and S. Vigna. The query-flow graph: model and applications. In *CIKM '08*.

[2] I. Bordino, C. Castillo, D. Donato, and A. Gionis. Query similarity by projecting the query-flow graph. In *SIGIR '10*.

[3] P. Bruza, R. McArthur, and S. Dennis. Interactive internet search: keyword, directory and query reformulation mechanisms compared. In *SIGIR '00*.

[4] B. Carterette, E. Kanoulas, and E. Yilmaz. Simulating simple user behavior for system effectiveness evaluation. In *CIKM '11*.

[5] M.-A. Cartright, R. W. White, and E. Horvitz. Intentions and attention in exploratory health search. In *SIGIR'11*.

[6] G. V. Cormack, M. D. Smucker, and C. L. Clarke. Efficient and effective spam filtering and re-ranking for large web datasets. *Inf. Retr.*, 14(5), Oct. 2011.

[7] D. Guan and H. Yang. Increasing stability of result organization for session search. In *ECIR '13*.

[8] D. Guan, H. Yang, and N. Goharian. Effective structured query formulation for session search. In *TREC '12*.

[9] J. Guo, G. Xu, H. Li, and X. Cheng. A unified and discriminative model for query refinement. In *SIGIR '08*.

[10] Q. Guo and E. Agichtein. Ready to buy or just browsing?: detecting web searcher goals from interaction data. In *SIGIR '10*.

[11] D. S. Hirschberg. Algorithms for the longest common subsequence problem. *J. ACM*, 24(4), Oct. 1977.

[12] J. Huang and E. N. Efthimiadis. Analyzing and evaluating query reformulation strategies in web search logs. In *CIKM '09*.

[13] J. Jiang, S. Han, J. Wu, and D. He. Pitt at trec 2011 session track. In *TREC '11*.

[14] J. Jiang, D. He, and S. Han. Pitt at trec 2012 session track. In *TREC '12*.

[15] R. Jones and K. L. Klinkner. Beyond the session timeout: automatic hierarchical segmentation of search topics in query logs. In *CIKM '08*.

[16] L. P. Kaelbling, M. L. Littman, and A. W. Moore. Reinforcement learning: a survey. *J. Artif. Int. Res.*, 4(1), May 1996.

[17] Y. Kalfoglou and M. Schorlemmer. Ontology mapping: the state of the art. *Knowl. Eng. Rev.*, 18(1), Jan. 2003.

[18] E. Kanoulas, B. Carterette, M. Hall, P. Clough, and M. Sanderson. Overview of the trec 2011 session track. In *TREC'11*.

[19] E. Kanoulas, B. Carterette, M. Hall, P. Clough, and M. Sanderson. Overview of the trec 2012 session track. In *TREC'12*.

[20] E. Kanoulas, P. D. Clough, B. Carterette, and M. Sanderson. Session track at trec 2010. In *TREC'10*.

[21] Lemur Search Engine. `http://www.lemurproject.org/`.

[22] C. Liu, N. J. Belkin, and M. J. Cole. Personalization of search results using interaction behaviors in search sessions. In *SIGIR '12*.

[23] C. Liu, M. Cole, E. Baik, and J. N. Belkin. Rutgers at the trec 2012 session track. In *TREC'12*.

[24] C. Liu, J. Gwizdka, J. Liu, T. Xu, and N. J. Belkin. Analysis and evaluation of query reformulations in different task types. In *ASIST '10*.

[25] J. Liu and N. J. Belkin. Personalizing information retrieval for multi-session tasks: the roles of task stage and task type. In *SIGIR '10*.

[26] A. M-Dyaa, K. Udo, N. Nikolaos, N. Brendan, L. Deirdre, and F. Maria. University of essex at the trec 2011 session track. In *TREC '11*.

[27] D. Metzler and W. B. Croft. Combining the language model and inference network approaches to retrieval. *Inf. Process. Manage.*, 40(5), Sept. 2004.

[28] S. P. Singh. Learning to solve markovian decision processes. Technical report, Amherst, MA, USA, 1993.

[29] Y. Song and L.-w. He. Optimal rare query suggestion with implicit user feedback. In *WWW '10*.

[30] Y. Song, D. Zhou, and L.-w. He. Query suggestion by constructing term-transition graphs. In *WSDM '12*.

[31] J. Teevan, S. T. Dumais, and D. J. Liebling. To personalize or not to personalize: modeling queries with variation in user intent. In *SIGIR '08*.

[32] R. W. White, I. Ruthven, J. M. Jose, and C. J. V. Rijsbergen. Evaluating implicit feedback models using searcher simulations. *ACM Trans. Inf. Syst.*, 23(3), July 2005.

[33] C. Zhai and J. Lafferty. A study of smoothing methods for language models applied to information retrieval. *ACM Trans. Inf. Syst.*, 22(2):179–214, Apr. 2004.

Toward Whole-Session Relevance: Exploring Intrinsic Diversity in Web Search

Karthik Raman
Dept. of Computer Science
Cornell University
Ithaca, NY, USA
karthik@cs.cornell.edu

Paul N. Bennett
Microsoft Research
One Microsoft Way
Redmond, USA
pauben@microsoft.com

Kevyn Collins-Thompson
Microsoft Research
One Microsoft Way
Redmond, USA
kevynct@microsoft.com

ABSTRACT

Current research on web search has focused on optimizing and evaluating single queries. However, a significant fraction of user queries are part of more complex tasks [20] which span multiple queries across one or more search sessions [26, 24]. An ideal search engine would not only retrieve relevant results for a user's particular query but also be able to identify when the user is engaged in a more complex task and aid the user in completing that task [29, 1]. Toward optimizing whole-session or task relevance, we characterize and address the problem of *intrinsic diversity* (ID) in retrieval [30], a type of complex task that requires multiple interactions with current search engines. Unlike existing work on extrinsic diversity [30] that deals with ambiguity in intent across multiple users, ID queries often have little ambiguity in intent but seek content covering a variety of aspects on a shared theme. In such scenarios, the underlying needs are typically exploratory, comparative, or breadth-oriented in nature. We identify and address three key problems for ID retrieval: identifying authentic examples of ID tasks from post-hoc analysis of behavioral signals in search logs; learning to identify initiator queries that mark the start of an ID search task; and given an initiator query, predicting which content to prefetch and rank.

Categories and Subject Descriptors

H.3.3 [**Information Storage and Retrieval**]: Information Search and Retrieval—*retrieval models, search process*

General Terms

Algorithms, Experimentation

Keywords

Search session analysis, diversity, proactive search

1. INTRODUCTION

Information retrieval research has primarily focused on improving retrieval for a single query at a time. However, many complex tasks such as vacation planning, comparative shopping, literature surveys, *etc.* require multiple queries to complete the task [20].

Initiator query	Successor queries
snow leopards	snow leopard pics where do snow leopards live snow leopard lifespan snow leopard population snow leopards in captivity
remodeling ideas	cost of typical remodel hardwood flooring earthquake retrofit paint colors kitchen remodel

Table 1: Examples of intrinsically diverse search tasks, showing the first (initiator) query and several successor queries from the same search session.

Within the context of this work, we focus on one specific type of information seeking need that drives interaction with web search engines and often requires issuing multiple queries – namely intrinsically diverse tasks [30]. Table 1 gives examples of two intrinsically diverse tasks observed in a commercial web search engine. Intrinsic diversity, where diversity is a desired property of the retrieved set of results to satisfy the current user's immediate information need, is meant to indicate that diversity is intrinsic to the need itself; this is in contrast to techniques that provide diversity to cope with uncertainty in query intent (*e.g.*, `[jaguar]`).

Intrinsically diverse tasks typically are exploratory, comprehensive, survey-like, or comparative in nature. They may result from users seeking different opinions on a topic, exploring or discovering aspects of a topic, or trying to ascertain an overview of a topic [30]. While a single, comprehensive result on the topic may satisfy the need when available, several or many results may be required to provide the user with adequate information [30]. As seen in the examples, a user starting with `[snow leopards]` may be about to engage in an exploratory task covering many aspects of snow leopards including their lifespan, geographic dispersion, and appearance. Likewise when investigating remodeling ideas, a user may wish to explore a variety of aspects including cost, compliance with current codes, and common redecoration options. Note that the user may in fact discover these aspects to explore through the interaction process itself. Thus intrinsic diversity shares overlap with both exploratory and faceted search [9, 37]. However, unlike the more open-ended paradigm provided by exploratory search, we desire a solution that is shaped by the current user's information need

SIGIR'13, July 28–August 1, 2013, Dublin, Ireland.

and is able to discover and associate relevant aspects for a topic automatically in a data-driven fashion. For example, for the query `[snow leopards]`, our goal is to enable deeper user-driven exploration of that topic, by proactively searching for the relevant information that the user might want during the course of a session on that topic, thus reducing the time and effort involved in manual reformulations, aspect discovery, and so on.

To this end, we aim to design a system that addresses two key problems needed for ID retrieval: detecting the start of an ID task, and computing an optimal set of ID documents to return to the user given engagement on an ID task. For the former, the system must be capable of predicting when a user is likely to issue multiple queries to accomplish a task, based on seeing their first "initiator query". To do this, we first develop a set of heuristic rules to mine examples of authentic intrinsic diversity tasks from the query logs of a commercial search engine. The resulting tasks provide a source of weak supervision for training classification methods that can predict when a query is initiating an intrinsically diverse task. With these predictive models, we characterize how ID initiators differ from typical queries. We then present our approach to intrinsically diversifying for a query. In particular, rather than simply considering different intents of a query, we incorporate queries that give rise to related aspects of a topic by estimating the relevance relationship between the aspect and the original query. Given the intrinsically diverse sessions identified through log analysis, we demonstrate that our approach to intrinsic diversification is able to identify more of the relevant material found during a session given less user effort, and furthermore, the proposed approach outperforms a number of standard baselines.

2. RELATED WORK

The distinction between *extrinsic* and *intrinsic* diversity was first made by Radlinski *et al.* who coined these terms [30]. In contrast to extrinsically-oriented approaches, which diversify search results due to ambiguity in user intent, intrinsic diversification requires that results are both relevant to a single topical intent as well as diverse across aspects, rather than simply covering additional topical interpretations. Existing methods like maximal marginal relevance (MMR) do not satisfy these requirements well (*cf.* Sec. 5.3). Most diversification research has focused primarily on extrinsic diversity: this includes learning [39, 34] and non-learning approaches [6, 40, 7, 8]. Recent work [2], however, indicates real-world Web search tasks are commonly intrinsically diverse and require significant user effort. For example, considering average number of queries, total time, and prevalence of such sessions, common tasks include: discovering more information about a specific topic (6.8 queries, 13.5 min, 14% of sessions); comparing products or services (6.8 q, 24.8 m, 12%); finding facts about a person (6.9 q, 4.8 m, 3.5%); and learning how to perform a task (13 q, 8.5 m, 2.5%). Thus, improvements in retrieval quality that address intrinsically diverse needs have potential for broad impact.

Some previous TREC tracks, including the Interactive, Novelty and QA tracks, studied intrinsic diversity-like problems in which retrieval effectiveness was partly measured in terms of coverage of relevant aspects of queries, along with the interactive cost to a user of achieving good coverage. However, our task and data assumptions differ from these tracks. For example, the Interactive tracks focused more on coverage of fact- or website-oriented answers, while our definition of query aspect is broader and includes less-focused subtopics. In addition to optimizing rankings to allow efficient exploration of topics, we also predict queries that initiate intrinsically diverse tasks, and show how to mine candidates for ID tasks from large-scale search log data.

Session-based retrieval is a topic that has become increasingly popular. For example, Radlinski *et al.* [31] studied the benefit of using query chains in a learning-to-rank framework to improve ranking performance. Others have proposed different session-level evaluation metrics [17, 21]. Research in this area has been aided by the introduction of the Session track at TREC [22]; this has led to papers on session analysis and classification [27]. In particular, He *et al.* use a random walk on a query graph to find other related queries, which are then clustered and used as subtopics in their diversification system [16]. In our re-ranking approach, we also use related queries to diversify the results, but maintain coherence with the original query. Specifically, we identify a common type of information need that often leads to longer, more complex search sessions. However, in contrast to previous work, rather than using the session interactions up to the current point to improve retrieval for the current query, we use a query to improve retrieval for a user's *future* session and use sessions from query logs to evaluate the effectiveness of the proposed methods. While the TREC Session track evaluated the number of uncovered relevant examples for the final query, the emphasis was on the impact of session context up to the present query; in our case, we assume no previous context, but instead are able to characterize the need for intrinsic diversity based on the single query alone.

Session data has also been used to identify and focus on complex, multi-stage user search tasks that require multiple searches to obtain the necessary information [36, 24]. This has led to research on *task-based* retrieval [14, 15] where tasks are the unit of interest (as opposed to queries or sessions). *Trail-finding* research studies the influence of factors such as relevance, topic coverage, diversity and expertise [33, 38]. While these problems are certainly related to ours, *tasks* and *trails* tend to be more specialized and defined in terms of specific structures: *e.g.* tasks are characterized as a set or sequence of sub-tasks to be accomplished, while trails are defined in terms of specific paths of user behavior on the web graph. However, intrinsically diverse search sessions, *e.g.* as in Table 1, represent a broader, less structured category of search behavior. Similarly, our approach complements work on faceted search [23] and exploratory search [37] by providing a data-driven manner of discovering common facets dependent on the particular topic.

Query suggestions are a well-established component of web search results with a large research literature: common approaches include using query similarity (*e.g.*[42]) or query-log based learning approaches (*e.g.* [19]). Query suggestions can play an important role for intrinsically diverse needs, because they provide an accessible and efficient mechanism for directing users towards potentially multiple diverse sets of relevant documents. Therefore, query suggestion techniques that do not merely provide simple reformulation of the initial query, but correctly diversify across multiple facets of a topic may be particularly helpful for intrinsically diverse needs. Thus, recent research on diversifying query suggestions [28] has partly inspired our retrieval approach.

Our approach is also motivated by recent work on *interactive ranking*. Brandt *et al.* [5] propose the notion of dynamic rankings, where users navigate a path through the search results, to maximize the likelihood of finding documents relevant to them. Our objective formulation closely relates to another recent work on two-level dynamic rankings [32], which studied the benefit of interaction for the problem of extrinsic diversity. Similarly, user interaction has been found to help in more structured and faceted search tasks [41, 13], in cases such as product search. However, while presenting interactive, dynamic rankings is one user experience that offers a way to surface the improved relevance to users, our techniques are more general: they may be used to present a summary of the topic to the user, recommend unexplored options, anticipate and then crowdsource queries to trade off latency and quality by prefetching, and more.

In contrast to previous work, we provide a way to not only identify complex search tasks that will require multiple queries but to *proactively* retrieve for future queries before the user has searched for them. Importantly, these future queries are neither simple reformulations nor completely unrelated, but are queries on the particular task that the user has started. Finally, we introduce diversification methods which, unlike previous methods, maintain coherence around the current theme while diversifying. Using these methods we demonstrate that we can improve retrieval relevance for a *task* by detecting an intrinsically diverse need and providing whole-session retrieval at that point.

3. INTRINSICALLY DIVERSE TASKS

An *intrinsically diverse task* is one in which the user requires information about *multiple, different aspects* of the *same topical* information need. In practice, a user most strongly demonstrates this interest by issuing multiple queries about different aspects of the same topic. We are particularly interested in identifying the common theme of an intrinsically diverse task *and* when a user initiated the task. We unify these into the concept of an *initiator query* where, given a set of queries on an intrinsically diverse task, the query among them that is most general and likely to have been the first among these set of queries is called the initiator query. If multiple such queries exist, then the first among them from the actual sequence (issued by the user) is considered the initiator. We give importance to the temporal sequence since the goal is to detect the initiation of the task and provide support for it as soon as possible.

While previous work has defined the concept of intrinsic diversity, there has been no further understanding of the problem or means to obtain data. We now identify and analyze authentic instances of intrinsically diverse search behavior, extracted from large-scale mining and analysis of query logs from a commercial search engine.

3.1 Mining intrinsically diverse sessions

Intuitively, intrinsically diverse (ID) tasks are topically coherent but cover many different aspects. To automatically identify ID tasks *in situ* where a user is attempting to accomplish the task, we seek to codify this intuition. Furthermore, rather than trying to cover all types of ID tasks, we focus on extracting with good precision and accuracy a set of tasks where each task is contained within a single search session. As a "session" we take the commonly used approach of demarcating session boundaries by 30 minutes of user inactivity [35]. Once identified, these mined instances could potentially be used to predict broader patterns of cross-session intrinsic diversity tasks [24, 1], but we restrict this study to mining and predicting the initiation of an ID task within a search session and performing whole-session retrieval at the point of detection.

To mine intrinsically diverse sessions from a post-hoc analysis of behavioral interactions signals with the search results, we developed a set of heuristics to detect when a session is topically coherent but covering many aspects. These can be summarized as finding sessions that are: (1) longer – the user must display evidence of exploring multiple aspects; (2) topically coherent – the identified aspects should be related to the same overall theme rather than disparate tasks or topics; (3) diverse over aspects – the queries should demonstrate a pattern beyond simple reformulation by showing diversity. Furthermore, since the user's interaction with the results will be used in lieu of a contextual relevance judgment for evaluation, we also desire that we have some "satisfied" or "long-click" results where we define a satisfied (SAT) click similar to other work as having a dwell of $\geq 30s$ or terminating the search session [11, 12].

Given these criteria, we propose a simple algorithm to collect intrinsically diverse user sessions. Our algorithm uses a series of filters, explained in more detail below. When we refer to "removing" queries, we mean they were treated as not having occurred for any subsequent analysis steps. For sessions, with the exception of those we "remove" from further analysis in Step 4, we label all other sessions as intrinsically diverse or *regular* (*i.e.*, not ID). We identify the *initiator* query as the first query that remains after all query removal steps, and likewise a *successor* query is any remaining query that follows the initiator in the session. More precisely, we use the following steps (in sequence) to filter sessions:

1. **Remove frequent queries:** Frequent queries – such as *facebook* or *walmart* – that are often interleaved with more complex tasks can obscure the more complex task the user is accomplishing. Therefore, we remove the top 100 queries by frequency as well as frequent misspellings related to these queries.
2. **Collapse duplicates:** We collapse any duplicate of a query issued later in the session as representing the same aspect but record all SAT clicks across the separate impressions.
3. **Only preserve manually entered queries:** To focus on user-driven exploration and search, we removed queries that were not manually entered, *e.g.* those obtained by clicking on a link such as by query suggestion or searches embedded on a page.
4. **Remove sessions with no SAT Document:** Since we would like to eventually measure the quality of rerankings for these session queries in a personal and contextual sense, we would like to ensure that there is at least one long-dwell click to treat as a relevance judgment. While this is not required for a session being an ID session, we simply require it for ease of evaluation. Thus, we removed sessions with no SAT clicks.
5. **Ensure topical coherence:** As ID sessions have a common topic, we removed any successor query that did not share at least one common top ten result with the initiator query. Note that this need not be the same result for every aspect. While this restricts the set of interaction patterns we identify, it enables us to be more precise, while ensuring semantic relatedness, and does not rely on the weakness of assuming one fixed static ontology.

6. **Ensure diversity in aspects:** Although we desire topical coherence across the queries, we do not want to identify simple reformulations or spelling corrections as aspects. Thus we restrict the syntactic similarity with the initiator query to avoid identifying trivial difference as substantially different aspects. To measure query similarity robust to spelling variations, we consistently use *cosine similarity with character trigrams* in this work. In particular, we remove queries where the similarity was more than 0.5.
7. **Remove long queries:** We observed a small fraction of sessions matching the above filters appear to consist of copy/paste homework questions on a common topic. While potentially interesting, we focus in this paper on completely user-generated aspects and introduce a constraint on query length, removing queries of length at least 50 characters.
8. **Threshold the number of distinct aspects:** Finally, to focus on diversity and complexity among the aspects, we threshold on the number of distinct successor queries. We identify a query as distinct when its maximum pairwise (trigram character cosine) similarity with any preceding query in the session is less than 0.6. Any session with less than three distinct aspects (including the initiator) are labeled as regular and those with three or more aspects are labeled as intrinsically diverse.

Putting everything together, we ran this algorithm on a sample of user sessions from the logs of a commercial search engine from the period April 1–May 31, 2012. We used log entries generated in the English-speaking United States locale to reduce variability caused by geographical or linguistic variation in search behavior. Starting with 51.2M sessions comprising 134M queries, applying all but the *SAT-click* filter, with the *Number of Distinct Aspects* threshold at two, led to more than 497K ID sessions with 7.0M queries. These ID tasks accounted for 1.0% of all search sessions in our sample, and 3.5% of sessions having 3 queries or more (14.4M sessions)[1]. Further applying the SAT-click filter reduced the number to 390K. Finally, focusing on the more complex sessions by setting the Number of Distinct Aspects filter to three, reduced this to 146K sessions.

Given that ID sessions require multiple queries, we hypothesize that ID sessions account for a disproportionately larger fraction of *time spent searching* by all users. To test this, we estimated the time a user spent in a session by the elapsed time from the first query to the last action (*i.e.*, query or click). Sessions with a single query and no clicks were assigned a constant duration of 5 seconds. Here, the time in session includes the whole session once an ID task was identified in that session. Our hypothesis was confirmed: while ID sessions with at least 2 distinct aspects represented 1.0% of all sessions, they accounted for 4.3% of total time spent searching, showing the significant role ID sessions play in overall search activity.

To assess the accuracy of our automatic labeling process, we sampled 150 sessions (75 each from the auto-labeled regular and intrinsic sets) of length at least 2 queries. We ignored single query sessions since those are dominated by regular intents and there may be a bias in labeling. Two assessors were given instructions similar to the description in the first paragraph of Section 3, examples of ID sessions such as those in Table 1, and all of the queries in the session and asked to label each session as regular or ID. The assessors had a 79% agreement with an inter-rater κ agreement of 0.5875. Using each assessor as a gold-standard and taking the average, on sessions of length two or greater our extraction method has a precision of 73.9% and an accuracy of 73.7% (overall accuracy is higher because of single query sessions always being regular). Thus, with both good agreement and a moderate to strong accuracy and precision, the method provides a suitable source of noisy supervised labels. With enough data, we can hope to overcome the noise in the labels (as long as it is unbiased) with an appropriate learning algorithm [3].

[1]Because we do not focus on more complex ID information seeking, such as tasks that span multiple sessions, the true percentage associated with ID tasks is likely to be larger.

4. PREDICTING INTRINSICALLY DIVERSE TASK INITIATION

Given that we may want to alter retrieval depending on whether the user is seeking intrinsic diversity or not, we ask the question whether we can identify the initiator queries for intrinsically diverse tasks and treat this as a classification problem. In particular, while in Sec. 3 we used the behavioral signals of interaction between the initiator and successor queries of a session to automatically label queries with a (weak) supervised label, here we ask if we can predict what the label would be in the absence of those interaction signals – a necessary ability if we are to detect the user's need for intrinsic diversity in an operational setting. Ultimately our goal is to enable a search engine to customize the search results for intrinsic diversity only when appropriate, while providing at least the same level of relevance on tasks predicted to be regular. Recognizing that in most operative settings, it is likely important to invoke a specialized method of retrieval only when confident, we present a precision-recall tradeoff but focus on the high precision portion of the curve.

4.1 Experimental Setting

Data: We used a sample of initiator queries from the intrinsically diverse sessions described in Sec. 3.1 as our positive examples, and the first queries (after removing common queries as in Step 1 of Sec. 3.1) from *regular* sessions were used as negative examples. Note that since the label of a query, *e.g.* `[foo]`, comes from the session context, it is possible that `[foo]` occurs in both positive and negative contexts. In order to only train to predict queries that were clearly either ID or regular, we dropped such conflicting queries from the dataset; this only occurred 1 out of every 5K ID sessions. Also to weigh each task equally instead of by frequency, we sample by type: *i.e.*, we treat multiple occurrences of a query in the positive (resp. negative) set as a single occurrence. Finally, we downsample to obtain a 1:1 ratio from the positive and negative sets to create a balanced set. Unless otherwise mentioned, the dataset was sampled to contain 61K queries and split into an 80/5/15 proportion (50000 training, 3000 validation, 8000 test) with no class bias.

Classification: We used SVMs[18] with linear kernels, unless mentioned otherwise. We varied the regularization parameter (C) over the values: $\{10^{-4}, 2\cdot 10^{-4}, 5\cdot 10^{-4}, 10^{-3}, \ldots, 500, 10^{3}\}$. Model selection was done using the validation

Feature Set	Examples	Cardinality	Coverage	Normalized?	Log?
Text	Unigram Counts	44140	100%	No	No
Stats	# Words, # Characters, # Impressions, Click Count, Click Entropy	10	81%	Yes	Yes
POS	Part-of-Speech Tag Counts	37	100%	No	No
ODP	Five Most Probable ODP Class Scores from Top Two Levels	219	25%	Yes	Yes
QLOG	Average Similarity with co-session queries, Average session length, Distribution of occurrences within session (start/middle/end)	55	44%	Yes	No

Table 2: Features used for identification of initiator queries

set by selecting the model with the best precision using the default margin score threshold (*i.e.*, 0).

Features: The features are broadly grouped into 5 classes as shown in Table 2. Apart from the text and POS tag features, all other features were normalized to zero mean, unit variance. Features with values spanning multiple orders of magnitude, such as the *number of impressions*, were first scaled down via the log function. Due to the large scale of our data, coverage of some features is limited. In particular, query classification was done similar to [4] by selecting the top 9.4M queries by frequency from a year's query logs previously in time and then using a click-based weighting on the content-classified documents receiving clicks[2]. Likewise **Stats** and **QLOG** features are built from four months' worth of query logs and have limited coverage as a result. The query logs chosen to build these features were from previous to April 2012 to ensure a fair experimental setting with no overlap with the data collection period of the intrinsically diverse or regular sessions. We found the coverage of these features to be roughly the same for both the positive and negative classes.

We also note that the cardinality of some feature sets will depend on the training set (*e.g.*,vocabulary size of *Text* grows with more training data); the values listed in Table 2 are for the default training set of 50,000 queries. Most of our experiments will use all of the 5 feature sets; the effect of using only a subset of the feature sets is explored in Sec. 4.3.

4.2 Can we predict ID task initiation?

To begin with, we would like to know the precision-recall tradeoff that we can achieve on this problem. Figure 1 shows the precision-recall curve for a linear SVM trained on 50K examples with all the features. The result is a curve with clear regions of high precision, indicating that the SVM is able to identify initiator queries in these regions quite accurately. Furthermore, performance is better than random (precision of 50% since classes are balanced) along the entire recall spectrum.

As Table 3 shows, we are able to achieve relatively high precision values at low recall values. For example, we can identify 20% of ID tasks with 80% precision.

4.3 Which features were most important?

We next investigate the effect of using different subsets of the features on performance. The results are shown in Figure 2 and Table 4. First, we note that **Stats, QLOG** and **ODP** feature sets help identify only a small fraction of the initiator queries but do so with high precision. On the other hand, the **Text** and **POS** feature sets, which have high coverage, provide some meaningful signal for all the queries, but cannot lead to high precision classification. We also find that a combination of features, such as the **Text** and **Stats** features, can help obtain higher precision as well as higher recall than either alone. In fact, such combinations perform almost as well as using all features, which is the best out of all feature combinations.

[2]For greater coverage this could be extended to a rank-weighted back-off as described in that paper.

Recall @ Precision		Precision @ Recall	
5.9	90	84.9	10
9.8	85	79.3	20
18.3	80	75	30
30.3	75	72.8	40
49.0	70	69.4	50
61.4	65	65.4	60
78.8	60	62.4	70

Table 3: Recall at different precision levels and vice-versa for predicting ID task initiation.

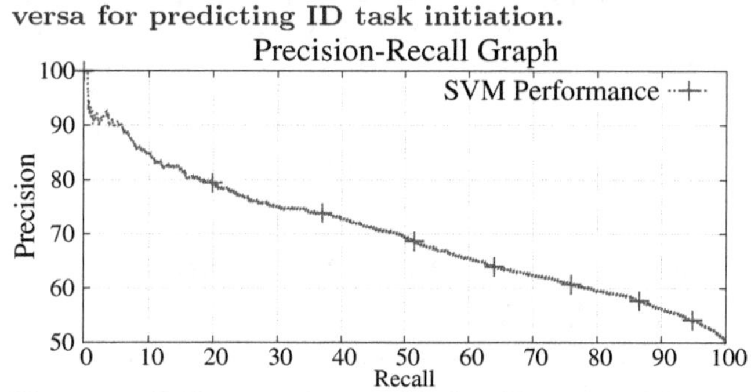

Figure 1: P-R curve for predicting ID task initiation.

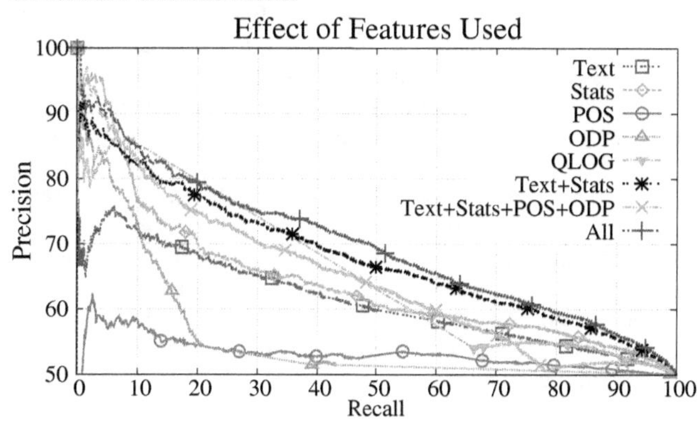

Figure 2: Change in classification performance of initiator queries as feature sets are varied.

4.4 Linguistic features of initiator queries

To further understand ID initiator queries, we identified the part-of-speech and text features most strongly associ-

Feature Set	Rec@80%Prec	Prec@40%Rec
T	0.1	62.6
S	9.2	63.7
P	0.0	52.8
O	5.6	51.6
Q	9.4	54.1
TS	13.6	69.7
TSPO	12.2	67.0
TSPOQ	18.3	72.8

Table 4: Effect of feature set on precision & recall. T=Text, S=Stats, P=POS, O=ODP, Q=QLOG

ated with them, by computing each feature's log-odds ratio (LOR)[3] compared to regular queries. Looking at the top-ranked features by LOR, we found that initiator queries are more likely to use question words (LOR=0.41); focus on proper nouns (0.40) such as places and people; use more 'filler' words (particles) found in natural language (0.27); and when they use general nouns, these tend to be plural (0.13) instead of singular (−0.052). Predominant text features indicated the importance of *list-like* nouns such as *forms, facts, types, ideas* (LOR=1.59, 1.45, 1.25, 0.92); verbs that are commonly used in questions such as *did* (1.34); and words indicating a broad need such as *information* and *manual* (1.64, 1.18). Strong negative features tend to encode exceptions – such as the most negative word *lyrics* (−2.25) used to find words to specific songs.

5. RE-RANKING FOR INTRINSIC DIVERSITY

While the previous section discusses the identification of queries that lead to ID tasks, in this section we discuss changes that can be made to the search results page to support queries for ID tasks. Specifically, we propose a re-ranking scheme that looks to satisfy not only the information need of the issued query, but also the future queries that the user is likely to issue later in the session on other aspects of the task. To the best of our knowledge, we are the first to address the problem of jointly satisfying the current query as well as future queries (unlike anticipatory search [25] which focuses solely on the latter).

We will use an interactive ranking-based paradigm here, using an approach related to the two-level rankings proposed in [32]. Given an issued query representing the start of an ID task, we consider rankings where each result can be **attributed** to some aspect of that task. We represent each aspect of the ID task by a related query of the issued query. One way this could be surfaced on a results page for a user is by placing the related query for an aspect adjacent to its corresponding search result. In such a setting, clicking on the related query could lead to results for that query being presented, thus enabling the user to explore documents for that aspect. This brings us to the question of how we find such a ranking.

5.1 Ranking via Submodular Optimization

We first describe precisely what we consider as an interactive ranking. In response to an initial query q, an interactive ranking $\mathbf{y} = (\mathbf{y}_D, \mathbf{y}_Q)$ comprises two parts: a ranking of documents $\mathbf{y}_D = d_1, d_2, \ldots$, which we refer to as the *primary* ranking; and a corresponding list of related queries $\mathbf{y}_Q = q_1, q_2, \ldots$, which represent the *aspects* associated with the documents of the primary ranking. The ith query in the list, q_i, represents the aspect associated with d_i. Structurally this can also be thought of as a ranked list of (document, related query) pairs (d_i, q_i).

Given this structure, let us consider four conditions that comprise a good interactive ranking:

1. Since the documents in the primary ranking were displayed in response to the issued query q, they should be relevant to q.
2. As document d_i is associated with the aspect represented by the related query q_i, document d_i should be relevant to query q_i.
3. Aspects should be relevant to the ID task being initiated by the query q.
4. At the same time, the aspects should not be repetitive *i.e.,* there should be diversity in the aspects covered.

We now design a ranking objective function that satisfies these four conditions to jointly optimize the selection of documents and queries $(\mathbf{y}_D, \mathbf{y}_Q)$. Suppose we have an existing interactive ranking $\mathbf{y}^{(k-1)}$ that has $k-1$ (document, related query) pairs, and our goal is to construct a new ranking $\mathbf{y}^{(k)}$ by adding an optimal (document, related query) pair to $\mathbf{y}^{(k-1)}$ – an operation we denote by $\mathbf{y}^{(k)} = \mathbf{y}^{(k-1)} \oplus (d_k, q_k)$.

Condition 1 above can be met by selecting d_k such that $R(d_k|q)$ is large, where $R(d|q)$ denotes the probability of relevance of document d given query q. Condition 2 can be met by selecting d_k such that its relevance to the related query q_k, $R(d_k|q_k)$, is large. Conditions 3 and 4 imply a standard diversification tradeoff, but here we have that the aspects q_k should be related to the initial query q and diverse. If we use a similarity function between queries to estimate the relevance between queries, Condition 3 implies that the similarity function $Sim(q, q_k)$ between q_k and q should be large. Condition 4 requires that the diversity should be maximized between q_k and all previous queries $\mathcal{Q} = q_1, \ldots, q_{k-1}$. Both Condition 3 and 4 can be jointly obtained by optimizing an MMR-like *diversity function* [6], $Div(q_k, \mathcal{Q})$, as described below. Intuitively, we would also like the change in the objective function on adding document-query pair (d_k, q_k) to the ranking $\mathbf{y}$ to be no smaller than what we would gain if adding the pair to a larger ranking $\mathbf{y} \oplus \mathbf{y}'$: that is, the objective function should be *monotone* and *submodular*. Submodular objectives are desirable because they have the property that they can be optimized using a simple and efficient *greedy* algorithm which iteratively computes the next best (d, q) pair to add to the ranking. Using the greedy algorithm ensures that the computed solution is at least $(1 - \frac{1}{e})$ times as good as the optimal.

We now consider the following objective satisfying the above conditions[4]:

$$\text{argmax}_{(d_1,q_1)\cdots(d_n,q_n)} \sum_{i=1}^{n} \gamma_i \cdot R(d_i|q) \cdot R(d_i|q_i) \cdot e^{\beta Div(q_i,\mathcal{Q})}$$

where $\mathcal{Q}$ is shorthand for the set of queries $Q = \{q_1, \ldots, q_n\}$,

[3]The LOR can be thought of as an approximation to the weight in a single-variable logistic regression.

[4]We omit the straightforward submodularity proof for space reasons.

and $Div(\cdot)$ is an MMR-like diversity function defined as

$$Div(q_i, \mathcal{Q}) = \lambda \cdot Sim(q_i, Snip(q)) - (1-\lambda) \max_{j<i} Sim(Snip(q_i), Snip(q_j)). \quad (1)$$

Here, $\lambda \in [0, 1]$ and $\beta > 0$ are parameters, where λ controls the tradeoff between related query aspect relevance and diversity while β controls the rate at which returns diminish from additional coverage. Finally, γ_i refers to the discount factor for position i: we use the common $\frac{1}{\log_2(i+1)}$ DCG discounting.

This objective can be interpreted as maximizing an expected utility (the exponential term) of covering related and diverse aspects where the expectation is over the maximum joint relevance of a document to both the initial query and the related query aspect. Furthermore, the joint probability is assumed to be conditionally independent to factor into the two relevance terms.

In this study, we define $Sim(x, y)$ as the cosine similarity between word-TF representations of x and y, and $Snip(q_j)$ is the bag-of-words representation of caption text from the top-10 search results for q_j using relevance score $R(d|q_j)$ alone. The MMR-like term appears within the exponent to ensure the objective is monotone.

Note that while the final objective optimizes for an interactive ranking, the primary ranking itself aims to present results from other aspects. We optimize this using the greedy algorithm presented in Algorithm 1, which we refer to as the **DynRR** method. In Alg. 1, the function $RelQ(q)$ denotes a function that returns related queries for query q, and $Top(\mathbf{y}_D)$ returns the top element in the ranking $\mathbf{y}_D$.

Algorithm 1 Greedy-DynRR($\beta, \lambda, P(\cdot|\cdot), q$)

$(\mathbf{y}_D, \mathbf{y}_Q) \leftarrow \phi$
for all $q' \in RelQ(q)$ **do**
  $Next(q') \leftarrow$ Document Ranking by $R(\cdot|q) \cdot R(\cdot|q')$.
for $i = 1 \rightarrow n$ **do**
  $bestU \leftarrow -\infty$
  for all $q' \in RelQ(q) / \mathbf{y}_Q$ **do**
    $d' \leftarrow Top(Next(q') / \mathbf{y}_D)$
    $v \leftarrow R(d'|q) \cdot R(d'|q') \cdot e^{\beta \cdot Div(q', \mathbf{y}_Q)}$
    if $v > bestU$ **then**
      $bestU \leftarrow v$
      $bestQ \leftarrow q'$
      $bestD \leftarrow d'$
  $(\mathbf{y}_D, \mathbf{y}_Q) \leftarrow (\mathbf{y}_D, \mathbf{y}_Q) \oplus (bestD, bestQ)$
return y

5.2 Evaluation Measures

As the problem of presenting results for both the current as well as future queries is a new one, we first discuss the evaluation methodology used. In particular, we use two kinds of evaluation metrics:

Primary ranking metrics: To compare against standard non-interactive methods of ranking, we simply evaluate the quality of the primary ranking, *i.e.*, completely ignore the related query suggestions attributed to documents. Since our goal is *whole-session relevance*, documents are considered *relevant* if and only if they are relevant to any query in the session. Given this notion of relevance, we compute the Precision, MAP, DCG and NDCG values.

Dataset	# Train	# Test
MINED	8888	2219
MIXED	4120	1027

Table 5: Datasets used in re-ranking experiments

Interactive ranking metrics: To evaluate the offline effectiveness and accuracy of the *predicted* future aspects (queries) and results (documents), we need to assume some model of human interaction. Consider the following search user model:

1. Users begin at the top of the ranking.
2. They click/expand the related query attributed to a document *if and only if* the document is relevant or the query is relevant. (We say a query is *relevant* if the top k results of the query contain a (new) relevant document.)
3. On expanding the related query, the user views the top k results for that related query, before returning to the original document ranking and continuing.
4. Users ignore previously seen documents, and click on all *new* relevant documents.

Under this user model, we can easily trace the ranking of documents that the user navigates and thus evaluate Precision@10 and DCG@10 for this ranking. We refer to these metrics as $PrecU_k$ and $DCGU_k$, and compare them with the primary Prec@10 and DCG@10 metrics.

We do not claim that this user model accurately captures all online users, nor that it is sophisticated. This is simply a well-motivated model for analyzing a rational user's actions, assuming the user is relatively accurate at predicting the relevance of an aspect based on either the top document or its related query. This in turn is intended to inform us about trends and relative differences we may see in online studies.

5.3 Experimental Setup

DATA: To evaluate the efficacy of the method, we used the data obtained from mining the search logs, as described in Section 3. We used two main datasets shown in Table 5. To analyze impact when most of the sessions are ID and more complex, the MINED dataset is obtained directly from the filtering algorithm by setting the threshold on the Number of Distinct Aspects to be 5. To determine the re-ranking impact when sessions may be a mixture of both ID and regular sessions, the MIXED dataset was obtained by predicting when a session was ID using the classifier from Sec. 4 over a mixture of the MINED dataset sessions and a random sample of regular sessions of the same size. More specifically, the combined sessions were split in a 45-10-45 split of training-validation and test sets. The trained classifier was used to classify the test set sessions as being ID or not, based on the initiator query. The sessions predicted as ID formed the *MIXED* dataset (prediction accuracy of 68.8% over the combined sessions); for those not predicted to be ID, we assume the standard ranking algorithm would be applied and thus relevance would be the same on those. The MIXED dataset is a reflection of an operational setting, where the query issued is used to predict if the resulting session will be an ID session or not, and the ones predicted to be ID are selected for re-ranking.

Obtaining Probability of Relevance: For our algorithm, we required the computation of the conditional relevance of a document given a query *i.e.*, $R(d|q)$. Thus, to en-

Query	Length
Website	Log(PageRank)
Baseline Ranker	Reciprocal Rank (if in top 10)
URL	Length # of Query Terms Covered Fraction of Query Covered TF Cosine sim LM Score(KLD) Jaccard Boolean AND Match Boolean OR Match
Anchor (Weighted)	Same as URL
Anchor (Unweighted)	TF-Cosine Sim KLD Score

Table 6: The 21 features used to train R(d|q).

able easier reproducibility by others, we learned a model using **Boosted Regression Trees**, on a dataset labeled with the relevance-values for query-document pairs with 20,000 queries using graded relevance judgments (~60 documents per query). The features used are given in Table 6. Features were all normalized to 0 mean, unit variance. To obtain the final model, we optimized for NDCG@5.

Baselines: As baselines we used the following methods:

- **RelDQ**: Ranking obtained by sorting as per $R(d|q)$.
- **Baseline**: A state-of-the-art commercial search engine ranker (also used to compute the rank feature mentioned earlier).

We also computed performance of other baselines, such as MMR and relevance-based methods such as BM-25 (using the weighted anchor text), but found them to perform far worse than RelDQ and Baseline and hence do not present the results for such other baselines.

Related Queries: To study the effect of the related queries, we used four different sources:

- **API**: We used the publicly available API of a commercial search engine (which returns 6-10 related queries)
- **Click-Graph**: Using co-click data, we obtained a set of $10-20$ related queries.
- **Co-Session Graph**: Using data of queries co-occurring in the same session, we obtained $10-20$ related queries.
- **Oracle**: As an approximate upper bound, we used the actual queries issued by the user during the session.

To ensure fairness, the graphs were constructed using data prior to April 2012. For most experiments, we only use the first 3 sources or only the second and third (which we distinguish by the suffix **C+S**).

Settings: The parameters for DynRR were set by optimizing for $DCGU_3$ on the training data[5]. All numbers reported here are for the test sets. We considered all SAT-clicked results in the session as relevant documents; since we compare *relative* to the baseline search engine, the assumption is that placing the SAT-clicked documents higher is better, rather than being an indication of absolute performance. Unless otherwise mentioned, the candidate document set for re-ranking comprises the union of the top 100 results (from the Baseline method) of the initiator query, and the top 10 results from each related query.

[5]We varied the λ parameter from 0 to 1 in increments of 0.1, while the β parameter was varied across the values $\{0.1, 0.3, 1, 3, 10\}$.

PREC	Mined	Mixed	DCG	Mined	Mixed
$PrecU_1$	1.093	1.103	$DCGU_1$	1.075	1.074
$PrecU_2$	1.247	1.223	$DCGU_2$	1.188	1.153
$PrecU_3$	1.347	1.295	$DCGU_3$	1.242	1.190
$PrecU_5$	1.401	1.345	$DCGU_5$	1.254	1.204

Table 8: Interactive Performance of DynRR for different user models (as ratios compared to the Baseline Prec@10 and DCG@10)

Set	Comp. Metric	% Gains			% Losses		
		0.2	0.5	1.0	0.2	0.5	1.0
Mined	$DCGU_3$	34.4	13.0	1.6	9.9	2.7	0.1
	DCG@10	19.6	5.2	0.3	12.7	3.8	0.3
Mixed	$DCGU_3$	29.1	12.0	1.6	10.8	3.7	0.2
	DCG@10	17.7	6.0	0.8	12.9	4.0	0.2

Table 9: % of sessions for which the metric performance of DynRR differs from the Baseline DCG@10 by more than a certain threshold.

5.4 Results

Primary Evaluation: We first study the re-ranking without any interactivity *i.e.,* using the *primary* ranking metrics to evaluate the quality of the top-level ranking. As seen in the results of Table 7, the re-ranking leads to improvements across the different metrics for both datasets. Thus, even without interactivity, the method is able to outperform the baselines in predicting future results of interest to the user, while also providing results for the current query. In particular, we found the DynRR method works best using the **C+S** related queries (which we return to later) with 9-11% gains over the baselines at position 10 across the various metrics with 3-5% relative gains. We also find that the method improves on the MIXED dataset supporting the question of whether the method can be robustly used in practical scenarios. Thus we improve an important segment of tasks while maintaining high levels of performance elsewhere; further improvements to the initiator classification model will improve the robustness further.

Interactive Evaluation: Next we evaluate the performance of the method while incorporating the interactivity. As seen in Table 8, the added interactivity leads to large increases in both the precision and DCG of the user paths navigated, across the different user models and datasets. In fact, we find 30-40% improvements in precision and 20-25% improvements in DCG, indicating that we are able to do a far better job in predicting future relevant results, and potentially, queries. These results also show that the method improvements are relatively robust to the user model.

Robustness: A key concern when comparing a new method against a baseline, is the robustness of the method. In particular, we are interested in the number of queries that are either improved or hurt, when switching from the Baseline method to the proposed re-ranking method. This is particularly crucial for the MIXED dataset, as we would want that the performance on non-ID sessions not be severely affected. Table 9 displays the % of examples for which the method either gains or loses above a certain threshold, compared to the Baseline method. We see that the number of gains far exceeds the number of losses, especially while comparing the interactive metric. We should also note that for

Set	Method	Prec			MAP			DCG			NDCG		
		@1	@3	@10	@1	@3	@10	@1	@3	@10	@1	@3	@10
Mined	RelDQ	1.00	0.94	0.97	1.00	0.97	0.98	1.00	0.97	0.99	1.00	0.97	0.99
	DynRR	**1.06**	**1.03**	**1.02**	**1.06**	**1.05**	**1.04**	**1.06**	**1.04**	**1.04**	**1.06**	**1.05**	**1.05**
	DynRR C+S	**1.10**	**1.09**	**1.09**	**1.10**	**1.10**	**1.10**	**1.10**	**1.10**	**1.11**	**1.09**	**1.10**	**1.11**
Mixed	RelDQ	1.00	0.94	0.99	1.00	0.98	0.98	1.00	0.96	0.98	1.00	0.97	0.98
	DynRR	**1.03**	**1.02**	**1.04**	**1.03**	**1.04**	**1.03**	**1.03**	**1.03**	**1.03**	**1.03**	**1.03**	**1.05**

Table 7: Primary Performance of different methods(as a ratio compared to the Baseline)

RelQ	Prec	DCG	$PrecU_3$	$DCGU_3$	$SDCG$
A	0.905	0.880	1.082	0.997	1.174
C	1.015	1.014	1.333	1.214	1.488
S	1.051	1.074	1.248	1.198	1.384
O	1.476	1.397	2.211	1.827	2.500
AS	0.961	0.961	1.271	1.157	1.452
AC	0.986	1.013	1.244	1.176	1.408
CS	1.089	1.106	1.413	1.306	1.593
ASC	1.019	1.039	1.347	1.242	1.529
ASCO	1.179	1.144	1.580	1.386	1.802

Table 10: Performance change on varying the related queries. All measures are @10 and reported as a ratio to the baseline values.

Task	Fleiss Kappa	% All agree	% 2 agree
IsTopicID?	.423	85.5	100
AreQueriesID?	.452	67.1	100
BestInitiatorQ	.694	55.3	98.7

Table 11: Annotator agreement on TREC data.

both datasets and both metrics, the DynRR method is statistically significantly better than the Baseline method, as measured by a binomial test at the 99.99% significance level.

Effect of related query set: Next we study the impact of the related queries on the method performance, using the MINED dataset. To do so, we considered different combinations of the four related query sources: API(**A**), Click-Graph(**C**), Co-Session(**S**) and Oracle(**O**). Table 10 shows the results. As we clearly see, the related query source can make a significant impact on both the primary ranking performance and the interactive performance. One thing which stands out is the extremely strong performance using the Oracle related queries, which suggest that any improvements we can make in the quality of the suggested related queries is likely to result in even better overall performance. On the other hand, we see that using the API related queries almost always hurts performance. In fact, simply using only the related queries from the click-graph and the co-session data leads to much better performance than that compared to using the API queries as well. Further analysis reveals that this is due to two reasons: (a) In many cases, the queries returned by the API are spelling corrections or reformulations, with no difference in aspect; (b) most importantly though, there is little to no diversity in the queries obtained from the API compared to those from the other sources.

5.5 TREC Session Data

We also ran experiments using the publicly available TREC 2011 Session data (which was constructed with ID topics in mind) using only publicly reproducible components. To do so, three assessors labeled the different sessions as *potentially* being intrinsically diverse or not, based: a) only on the queries issued; and b) on the narration and title of the session as well. We also asked them to label their opinion on the query best suited to be the initiator query, among the queries issued. Annotators were provided the definition of ID sessions as described at the start of Section 3. We found good agreement among the different annotators for all the different labeling tasks, as seen from Table 11. In fact, in 63 of the 76 total sessions all three annotators agreed the sessions were ID based on the narration, title, and queries. We used a 50-50 training-test split on all sets, with the training data used for selecting the parameters of the ranking methods. To obtain the conditional relevance $R(d|q)$, we trained a regularized linear regression model with features based on the scores of two standard ranking algorithms: BM25 and TFIDF. As labeled data we used the TREC Web data from 2010 and 2011, by converting the graded relevance scores for relevant and above from the $\{1,2,3\}$ scale to $\{\frac{1}{3},1,1\}$. We used related queries from the Van Dang-Croft [10] method (**Q**) on the ClueWeb '09 anchor text, where the starting seed for the random walk would use the most similar anchor text to the query by TFIDF-weighted cosine if an exact match was not available. Our candidate document pool was set similar to the previous experiments. To evaluate, we again use the same metrics as before except using the TREC assessor relevance labels instead of clicks. We considered three different candidates for the initiator query: (a) Topic; (b) First query in the session; and (c) Labeled initiator query. As a baseline, we considered the method that ranked as per $R(d|q)$. For the DynRR method, we used the titles of the top 10 results of a query (as per the baseline), as the *snippet* of the query, since snippets were not made available. The results for the primary metric comparison are shown in Table 12. As we see from the table, the method improves in precision and DCG in most cases, with particularly large improvements when the title of the *topic* is used as the initiator query. This matches feedback the assessors gave us that the titles looked much more like the general queries issued by web users; in contrast, the TREC sessions would often start with a specific query before moving to a more general query. It could be that supplying the user with a well-formulated topic description before starting the search task influences

Initiator	Method	Pr@1	Pr@3	DCG@1	DCG@3
Title	Baseline	0.58	0.60	0.84	2.13
Title	DynRR	$0.71^{\dagger}$	0.60	$1.39^{\dagger}$	2.41
First	Baseline	0.53	0.47	0.94	1.94
First	DynRR	0.5	0.48	0.92	1.97
Label	Baseline	0.55	0.51	0.87	1.95
Label	DynRR	0.61	0.5	1.13	2.09

Table 12: Absolute performance on TREC Session data. † indicates significance at $p = 0.05$ by a paired one-tailed t-test.

the user to search for a particular aspect, rather than issue a more general query as they might when no topic description is explicitly formulated.

6. CONCLUSIONS AND FUTURE WORK

In this paper, we studied *intrinsically diverse tasks* that typically require multiple user searches on different aspects of the same information need. As this is just the first step into this problem, this also opens many interesting future directions – such as iterative ways to combine the mining and query identification process or extending these techniques to other related problems like exploratory search. In this work, we motivated the problem using real-world data and presented an algorithm to mine data from search logs using behavioral interaction signals within a session. We then looked at the problem of identifying the queries that start these sessions, and treated it as a classification problem, along with an analysis of these queries. Finally, we presented an approach to alter the rankings presented to the user, so as to also provide them information on aspects of the task for which the user will search in the future. We validated our approach empirically using search log data, as well as TREC data, demonstrating significant improvement over competitive baselines in both cases.

7. REFERENCES

[1] E. Agichtein, R. White, S. Dumais, and P. Bennett. Search, Interrupted: Understanding and Predicting Search Task Continuation. In *SIGIR '12*, 2012.

[2] P. Bailey et al. User task understanding: a web search engine perspective. http://research.microsoft.com/apps/-pubs/default.aspx?id=180594, 2012.

[3] P. L. Bartlett, M. I. Jordan, and J. M. Mcauliffe. Large Margin Classifiers: Convex Loss, Low Noise, and Convergence Rates. In *NIPS 16*, 2004.

[4] P. N. Bennett, K. Svore, and S. Dumais. Classification-Enhanced Ranking. In *WWW '10*, 2010.

[5] C. Brandt, T. Joachims, Y. Yue, and J. Bank. Dynamic Ranked Retrieval. In *WSDM '11*, 2011.

[6] J. Carbonell and J. Goldstein. The use of MMR, diversity-based reranking for reordering documents and producing summaries. In *SIGIR '98*, 1998.

[7] H. Chen and D. R. Karger. Less is more: Probabilistic models for retrieving fewer relevant documents. In *SIGIR '06*, 2006.

[8] C. L. Clarke et al. Novelty and diversity in information retrieval evaluation. In *SIGIR '08*, 2008.

[9] W. Dakka et al. Automatic Discovery of Useful Facet Terms. In *SIGIR 2006 Workshop on Faceted Search*, 2006.

[10] V. Dang, M. Bendersky, and W. B. Croft. Learning to rank query reformulations. In *SIGIR '10*, 2010.

[11] S. Fox, K. Kulddep, M. Mydland, S. Dumais, and T. White. Evaluating implicit measures to improve web search. *ACM TOIS*, 23(2):147–168, 2005.

[12] J. Gao, W. Yuan, X. Li, K. Deng, and J. Nie. Smoothing clickthrough data for web search ranking. In *SIGIR '09*, 2009.

[13] S. Gollapudi, S. Ieong, A. Ntoulas, and S. Paparizos. Efficient query rewrite for structured web queries. In *CIKM '11*, 2011.

[14] A. Hassan, Y. Song, and L.-w. He. A task level metric for measuring web search satisfaction and its application on improving relevance estimation. In *CIKM '11*, 2011.

[15] A. Hassan and R. W. White. Task tours: helping users tackle complex search tasks. In *CIKM '12*, 2012.

[16] J. He et al. CWI at TREC 2011: session, web, and medical. In *TREC '11*, 2012.

[17] K. Järvelin, S. L. Price, L. M. L. Delcambre, and M. L. Nielsen. Discounted cumulated gain based evaluation of multiple-query IR sessions. In *ECIR'08*, 2008.

[18] T. Joachims. Making large-scale support vector machine learning practical. In *Advances in kernel methods*, pages 169–184. MIT Press, 1999.

[19] T. Joachims, L. Granka, B. Pan, H. Hembrooke, F. Radlinski, and G. Gay. Evaluating the accuracy of implicit feedback from clicks and query reformulations in web search. *TOIS*, 25(2), Apr. 2007.

[20] R. Jones and K. Klinkner. Beyond the session timeout: Automatic hierarchical segmentation of search topics in query logs. In *CIKM '08*, 2008.

[21] E. Kanoulas, B. Carterette, P. D. Clough, and M. Sanderson. Evaluating multi-query sessions. In *SIGIR '11*, 2011.

[22] E. Kanoulas et al. Overview of the TREC 2011 Session Track. In *TREC '11*, 2012.

[23] C. Kohlschutter, P.-A. Chirita, and W. Nejdl. Using link analysis to identify aspects in faceted web search. In *SIGIR '06*, 2006.

[24] A. Kotov, P. N. Bennett, R. W. White, S. T. Dumais, and J. Teevan. Modeling and analysis of cross-session search tasks. In *SIGIR '11*, 2011.

[25] D. J. Liebling, P. N. Bennett, and R. W. White. Anticipatory search: using context to initiate search. In *SIGIR '12*, 2012.

[26] J. Liu and N. Belkin. Personalizing information retrieval for multi-session tasks: The roles of task stage and task type. In *SIGIR '10*, 2010.

[27] J. Liu, M. J. Cole, C. Liu, R. Bierig, J. Gwizdka, N. J. Belkin, J. Zhang, and X. Zhang. Search behaviors in different task types. In *JCDL '10*, 2010.

[28] H. Ma, M. R. Lyu, and I. King. Diversifying query suggestion results. In *AAAI '10*, 2010.

[29] D. Morris, M. R. Morris, and G. Venolia. Searchbar: A search-centric web history for task resumption and information re-finding. In *CHI '08*, 2008.

[30] F. Radlinski, P. N. Bennett, B. Carterette, and T. Joachims. Redundancy, diversity and interdependent document relevance. *SIGIR Forum*, 43(2):46–52, Dec. 2009.

[31] F. Radlinski and T. Joachims. Query chains: learning to rank from implicit feedback. In *KDD '05*, 2005.

[32] K. Raman, T. Joachims, and P. Shivaswamy. Structured learning of two-level dynamic rankings. In *CIKM '11*, 2011.

[33] A. Singla, R. White, and J. Huang. Studying trailfinding algorithms for enhanced web search. In *SIGIR '10*, 2010.

[34] A. Slivkins, F. Radlinski, and S. Gollapudi. Learning optimally diverse rankings over large document collections. In *ICML '10*, 2010.

[35] R. White and S. Drucker. Investigating behavioral variability in web search. In *WWW '07*, 2007.

[36] R. W. White, P. N. Bennett, and S. T. Dumais. Predicting short-term interests using activity-based search context. In *CIKM '10*, 2010.

[37] R. W. White, G. Marchionini, and G. Muresan. Editorial: Evaluating exploratory search systems. *Inf. Process. Manage.*, 44(2):433–436, Mar. 2008.

[38] X. Yuan and R. White. Building the trail best traveled: effects of domain knowledge on web search trailblazing. In *CHI '12*, 2012.

[39] Y. Yue and T. Joachims. Predicting diverse subsets using structural SVMs. In *ICML '08*, 2008.

[40] C. X. Zhai, W. W. Cohen, and J. Lafferty. Beyond independent relevance: methods and evaluation metrics for subtopic retrieval. In *SIGIR '03*, 2003.

[41] L. Zhang and Y. Zhang. Interactive retrieval based on faceted feedback. In *SIGIR '10*, 2010.

[42] Q. Zhao et al. Time-dependent semantic similarity measure of queries using historical click-through data. In *WWW '06*, 2006.

Summaries, Ranked Retrieval and Sessions: A Unified Framework for Information Access Evaluation

Tetsuya Sakai
Microsoft Research Asia, Beijing, P.R.C.
tetsuyasakai@acm.org

Zhicheng Dou
Microsoft Research Asia, Beijing, P.R.C.
zhichdou@microsoft.com

ABSTRACT

We introduce a general information access evaluation framework that can potentially handle summaries, ranked document lists and even multi-query sessions seamlessly. Our framework first builds a *trailtext* which represents a concatenation of all the texts read by the user during a search session, and then computes an evaluation metric called *U-measure* over the trailtext. Instead of discounting the value of a retrieved piece of information based on ranks, U-measure discounts it based on its *position* within the trailtext. U-measure takes the document length into account just like *Time-Biased Gain* (TBG), and has the diminishing return property. It is therefore more realistic than rank-based metrics. Furthermore, it is arguably more flexible than TBG, as it is free from the *linear traversal* assumption (i.e., that the user scans the ranked list from top to bottom), and can handle information access tasks other than ad hoc retrieval. This paper demonstrates the validity and versatility of the U-measure framework. Our main conclusions are: (a) For ad hoc retrieval, U-measure is at least as reliable as TBG in terms of rank correlations with traditional metrics and discriminative power; (b) For diversified search, our diversity versions of U-measure are highly correlated with state-of-the-art diversity metrics; (c) For multi-query sessions, U-measure is highly correlated with Session nDCG; and (d) Unlike rank-based metrics such as DCG, U-measure can quantify the differences between linear and nonlinear traversals in sessions. We argue that our new framework is useful for understanding the user's search behaviour and for comparison across different information access styles (e.g. examining a direct answer vs. examining a ranked list of web pages).

Categories and Subject Descriptors

H.3.3 [**Information Storage and Retrieval**]: Information Search and Retrieval

Keywords

diversity, evaluation, metrics, sessions, test collections

SIGIR'13, July 28–August 1, 2013, Dublin, Ireland.

1. INTRODUCTION

Evaluation is central to the progress of Information Retrieval (IR) research. It helps researchers build better systems to achieve their ultimate goal, namely, to satisfy the user's information need. In this era of digital information overload, *system-oriented* evaluation is a necessity as a complement to *user-oriented* evaluation, as the latter is difficult to scale and to generalise. However, system-oriented evaluation in IR is facing a few serious challenges:

Challenge 1 System-oriented evaluation tends to oversimplify real search tasks in such a way that high effectiveness values may not guarantee high user performance or satisfaction. For example, whenever IR researchers rely entirely on metrics like Average Precision and Discounted Cumulative Gain (DCG), they implicitly assume that the user scans a ranked list of document IDs (not even documents) from top to bottom, like a machine; most metrics do not consider the user's actual effort for finding information from snippets and from documents of various lengths. Hence the criticism from the user-oriented camp: "*Where's the user?*"

Challenge 2 "Search" has become a commodity, and as a result, IR tasks have diversified. It is no longer just about a list of documents. We want to evaluate a system that returns a single *multi-document summary* in response to a query (e.g. [19]), a *diversified* search result page (e.g. [20]), an *aggregated* search result page (e.g. [29]), or a system that tries to satisfy the user in a *session* that accommodates query reformulations (e.g. [14]). For every new task, an appropriate evaluation methodology needs to be designed, and virtually every such methodology faces **Challenge 1**. Furthermore, the IR community lacks a "common language" across these diverse tasks, which makes it difficult for us to compare across them and to build a unified IA system.

In the present study, we tackle the above two challenges: we believe that our proposed evaluation framework is a small but significant step towards that goal.

Figure 1 introduces *trailtexts*, the central concept in our evaluation framework. Part (a) shows a single textual query-biased summary being shown to the user. Suppose that we have observed (by means of, say, *eyetracking* [13]) that the user read only the first and the last sentences of this summary. In this case, we define the trailtext as a simple concatenation of these two sentences: "`Sentence1 Sentence2`." Part (b) shows an aggregated search output: the user reads a snippet in the *news* panel, then reads an *ad*, and finally reads a snippet in the *web* panel. In this case, the trailtext is defined as "`Snippet1 Ad2 Snippet3`." Part (c) is a more traditional search engine result page: the user reads the first two snippets, and then visits the second URL to read the full text. In

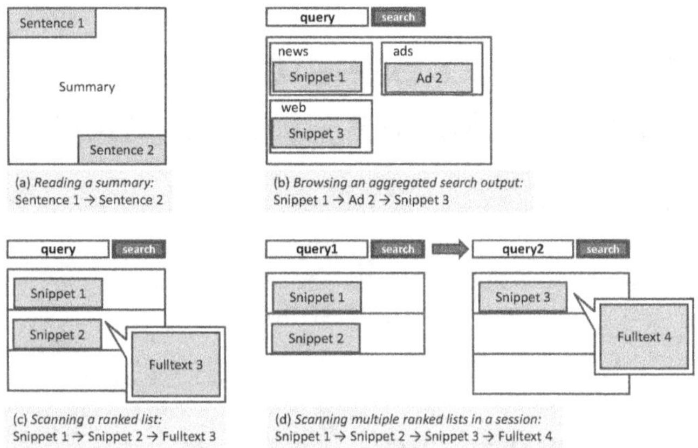

Figure 1: Constructing trailtexts for various tasks.

this case, the trailtext is "`Snippet1 Snippet2 Fulltext3`." Note that such trailtexts may possibly be constructed systematically under a certain user behaviour model instead of actual user observation. Finally, Part (d) shows a session that involves one query reformulation: the user reads two snippets in the original ranked list, reformulates the query, reads one snippet in the new ranked list, and finally visits the actual document. The trailtext is then "`Snippet1 Snippet2 Snippet3 Fulltext4`."

Our new evaluation framework comprises two steps:

Step 1 Generate a trailtext, or multiple possible trailtexts, by either observing the actual user or assuming a user model;

Step 2 Evaluate the trailtext(s), based on relevant *information units* (e.g. documents, passages, nuggets) found within it, while discounting the value of each information unit based on its *position* within the trailtext.

Our proposal was inspired by the *S-measure* framework of Sakai, Kato and Song [19], and the *Time-Biased Gain* (TBG) framework of Smucker and Clarke [23]. The S-measure framework, which only considered the evaluation of textual summaries (See Figure 1(a)), assumes that the user reads an entire summary from beginning to end at a constant speed, and that the value of an information unit wears out linearly according to its offset position in the summary. Thus, their key idea was to use *position*-based discounting, in contrast to the rank-based discounting employed by DCG for ranked retrieval. On the other hand, the TBG framework as described at SIGIR'12 was designed for ranked retrieval, and uses the *time spent by the user* as the basis for discounting the value of relevant information instead of the document rank[1].

While the work of Smucker and Clarke [23] primarily focused on estimating the *time to reach a document at rank k*, and assumed *linear traversal*, i.e., that all users scan the ranked list from top to bottom sequentially, our new framework is potentially more general. To be more specific, **Step 1** above says nothing about the user model: our framework can handle *nonlinear traversal*, i.e., cases where the user clicks a document at rank k and then one at rank $j(< k)$. Our framework is also more general in that it can handle various tasks such as Parts (a), (b) and (d) of Figure 1, and in that it provides a common language across these tasks by means of trailtexts. Potentially, this may be useful for addressing questions such as: "Given this query, which is a better IA system? One that returns a single multi-document summary, or one that returns a list of URLs with snippets?" although we leave this for future work. The objective of this paper is to demonstrate the validity and versatility of the U-measure framework.

[1]S-measure's position-based discounting is in fact a form of time-based discounting, as it assumes that the user's reading speed is constant [19].

2. RELATED WORK

2.1 Evaluating Textual Output

In summarisation and Question Answering evaluation, *comparison units* for computing precision, recall and the like are created either manually (e.g. *semantic content units* [16]) or automatically (e.g. N-grams). The matching between the system output and the gold standard may also be performed either manually or automatically: ROUGE [15] is an example of the completely automatic approach. In contrast, the S-measure framework [19] relies on manual *information unit* extraction and manual matching, and uses the *positions* of the information units for discounting their values. S-measure encourages systems to present important pieces of information first and to minimise the amount of text the user has to read.

In the present study, we borrow the idea of position-based discounting from S-measure, but devise a general framework for evaluating summaries, ranked retrieval, search sessions and other textual information seeking activities. In our *U-measure* framework, an information unit may be a nugget, a search engine snippet, or an entire document as in traditional *document* retrieval. Both automatic and manual evaluation approaches are possible with this framework, although we only consider automatic evaluation based on document relevance and clicks in this paper.

2.2 Evaluating Ranked Document Retrieval

In the evaluation of ranked document retrieval, the common assumption is that the (average) user scans the ranked list from top to bottom until he stops at a certain rank [9, 12, 13]. This *linear traversal* assumption forms the basis of virtually all existing IR metrics, including those designed for diversified search, where systems are required to achieve not only high relevance but also high diversity across possible search intents [9, 10, 20].

Unlike traditional rank-based metrics, TBG pays attention to the fact that the time spent at each rank differs, depending especially on the document length and document novelty [23]. However, TBG as described in that work relies on estimating the time to reach rank k, which in turn relies on the linear traversal assumption on a single ranked list. In contrast, our U-measure is arguably more general in that it can naturally handle multi-query sessions and nonlinear traversals. In fact, we drop the notion of "document ranks" altogether once we have constructed the trailtext (Recall Figure 1). Just like TBG, U-measure can take into account not only the documents visited but also search engine snippets, which has recently been recognised as important in search engine evaluation (e.g. [24, 28]). On the other hand, one potential advantage of TBG (and other time-based approaches [5]) over ours is that it may also be useful for evaluating retrieval of nontextual information[2].

Evaluating diversified search has received attention recently, and several diversity metrics have been proposed and compared: Chapelle *et al.* [9] and Clarke *et al.* [10] independently showed that *α-nDCG*

[2]One SIGIR reviewer commented: "*it is better to convert material read to a measure of time and stay in the TBG framework [..] TBG can be nicely adapted to non-ranked list evaluation.*" However, it is not immediately obvious to us exactly how TBG may be extended beyond "estimating the time to reach rank k" and to handle nonlinear traversal. Moreover, we argue that evaluating *textual* information access based on *texts* rather than time has benefits: for example, U-measure with information units should be useful for evaluating the quality of search engine snippets.

and *ERR-IA* (intent-aware expected reciprocal rank) have similar properties; Sakai and Song [20, 21] showed several advantages of *D-nDCG* over ERR-IA and α-nDCG. In this study, we experiment with a "D-" version and an "IA" version of U-measure for diversity evaluation, as we shall describe later.

For both traditional and diversified IR, we believe that information units that are finer than "relevant documents" are required to properly handle information novelty and redundancy (e.g. [17]). As we discussed in Section 2.1, our framework can take any textual pieces of information as information units. However, in the present study, we limit ourselves to considering snippets and relevant/clicked documents. Note that our U-measure is a generalisation of S-measure, and that the latter has already been used successfully for evaluating query-biased summaries based on information units [19].

Recently, *user simulation* has received attention as a method for bridging the gap between system-oriented and user-oriented evaluation [8, 22]. Our framework is agnostic to whether the trailtext is generated based on user observation or simulation. While the evaluation methods explored in this paper are *deterministic* in that one particular user model is considered to generate exactly one trailtext for each search scenario, it would be possible to incorporate simulation to generate a population of trailtexts that reflect different user behaviours. But this is beyond the scope of this paper[3].

2.3 Evaluating More Complex Tasks

The IR community has considered the evaluation of tasks that are more complex than returning a single ranked list of documents. Session-based IR evaluation [5, 14] is one example. Our proposed framework can evaluate sessions as well, as all user actions are encoded as a trailtext. However, unlike Baskaya, Keskustalo and Järvelin [5], we do not explicitly consider the cost of user actions such as query (re)formulation and clicking on "next page." We assume that the text read by the user is an adequate representation of the user effort. Azzopardi [4] views interactive IR applications as a stream of documents and proposes evaluation metrics such as the "frequency of observing a relevant document." His document stream is similar to our trailtext, but the latter can potentially handle arbitrary pieces of text.

Other IR tasks are something of a mix between summarisation and ranked retrieval: character-based *bpref* (binary preference) has been used for evaluating a ranked list of passages [2]; Yang and Lad [26] proposed a nugget-based evaluation method that models *utility* as *benefit* minus *cost of reading* for evaluating multiple ranked lists of passages for a standing information need. Arvola, Kekäläinen and Junkkari [3] have proposed an evaluation method for an XML retrieval task where the user first sees a list of documents and then jumps to relevant passages of a document selected from that list. Their proposal is also similar to ours in that it also considers the amount of text read by the user as well as the actual reading order (within each document). The key differences are that they treat document list scanning and document browsing as two separate modes, and that they evaluate the former by average-precision-like metrics, which assume linear traversal.

3. PROPOSED FRAMEWORK

As was mentioned in Section 1, our evaluation framework first generates a trailtext based on user observation (e.g. eyetracking or click logging) or a user model, and then defines an evaluation metric over the trailtext by applying position-based discounting. Section 3.1 defines the general U-measure framework, which computes a score for a given trailtext and relevance information associated with it. Then Section 3.2 discusses how we actually derive trailtexts from document relevance and clicks in this study.

3.1 U-measure

A trailtext tt is a concatenation of n strings: $tt = s_1 s_2 \ldots s_n$. Each string $s_k (1 \leq k \leq n)$ could be a document title, snippet, full text, or even some arbitrary part of a text (e.g. nugget). We assume that the trailtext is exactly what the user actually read, in the exact order, during an information seeking process. We define the offset position of s_k as $pos(s_k) = \sum_{j=1}^{k} |s_j|$. We measure lengths in terms of the number of *characters* [19]. Each s_k in a trailtext tt is considered either l-relevant, i.e. relevance level of $l (> 0)$, or nonrelevant. For example, in the case of summarisation evaluation based on nuggets, a relevant s_k may be a string that has been found (either manually or automatically) to be a match with a gold standard nugget [19]. Alternatively, in an evaluation environment where only document relevance assessments are available, a relevant s_k may be the full text of a relevant document, where it is assumed that the user actually read the entire document, as we shall discuss in Section 3.2. We define the *position-based gain* as $g(pos(s_k)) = 0$ if s_k is considered nonrelevant, and $g(pos(s_k)) = gv_l$ if it is considered l-relevant, where gv_l is a *gain value* for relevance level l. Note that a string s_k that is *considered* nonrelevant may in fact be relevant: for example, if the user reads duplicate documents, it is possible to count only the first one as relevant [23]; similarly, for information needs that do not require exhaustive pieces of information, it is possible to treat only the first relevant piece of information as relevant, as in the Reciprocal Rank metric.

The general form of U-measure is given by:

$$U = \frac{1}{\mathcal{N}} \sum_{pos=1}^{|tt|} g(pos) D(pos) \tag{1}$$

where $\mathcal{N}$ is a normalisation factor (which we simply set to $\mathcal{N} = 1$ in this study, following recent evaluation studies [5, 23]) and pos is an offset position within tt and $D(pos)$ is a *position-based* decay function. Following the S-measure framework [19], here we assume that the value of a relevant information unit decays with the amount of text the user has read, and adopt a linear function:

$$D(pos) = \max(0, 1 - \frac{pos}{L}) \,. \tag{2}$$

Here, L is the amount of text at which all relevant information units become worthless. Note that, if the user's reading speed is constant, Eq. 2 is also equivalent to linear discounting *by time*.

In this study, we interpret L as the largest *Maximal Trailtext Length* (MTL) across all possible search sessions, where the MTL of a session is the sum of the lengths of (a) all snippets above the lowest click and (b) all documents clicked by the user in that session. Thus, L represents the largest amount of text that the user may have had to read in one session. This is the point where we consider that all information units become worthless. Note that we do *not* rely on the linear traversal assumption: the snippets may have been read in any order, and the documents may have been clicked in any order. We simply sum up the snippet and document lengths.

To estimate L, we first obtained 21,911,694 sessions (partitioned based on 30-minute inactivities) from Microsoft's Bing (September 7, 2012, US market), under the constraint that every query in the session received at least one click. This constraint is convenient for evaluating multi-query sessions, as we shall discuss in Section 6.

[3] In our diversity experiments (Section 5), we do consider an Intent-Aware version of U-measure, which considers multiple trailtexts that represent different user intents.

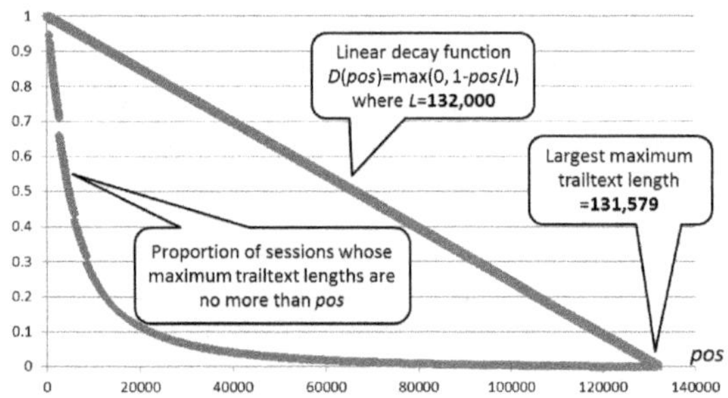

Figure 2: Proportion of sessions whose MTLs are no more than pos (after removing 0.5% of the sessions with the largest MTLs), and a linear decay function derived from it.

By assuming that every snippet is 200-character long (which on average is a valid assumption for Bing) and automatically counting the number of characters for every clicked document, we computed the MTL for each session, and discarded 0.5% sessions with the largest MTL values (extremely long sessions for some unknown reasons). As the largest MTL among the remaining 21,802,136 sessions was 131,579, we chose to set $L = 132,000$. While it is difficult to imagine a user who *actually* reads over 100,000 characters within a session, it is important that L is sufficiently large for evaluation purposes, as discussed below.

For the 21,802,136 sessions, the curve in Figure 2 shows the proportion of sessions whose MTLs are no more than x. There is a sudden drop near the 70% line, which is caused by extremely popular "navigational" sessions whose MTLs were identical (computed as the length of the first snippet plus that of the top page of the popular website). The curve seems to be in line with existing click-based studies, and that an exponential function may be a good approximation to it (e.g. [6, 23]). We leave the curve fitting for future work, and use the simple linear decay function shown in the figure: perhaps what really should be done is to segment queries into several user behaviour types (e.g. informational, navigational or even more fine-grained types), and to devise different decay functions that match these types. The raw top-heavy curve is just an average of various search behaviours, and not necessarily appropriate for evaluation purposes where, for example, we are also interested in handling informational queries. For example, the average document length computed based on our full session data is 5,445.0 characters (averged over 39,716,443 clicked web pages); that computed based on the relevant news articles of the TREC 2005 robust track test collection (which we use in Section 4 to replicate the TBG experiment by Smucker and Clarke [23]) is 3,672.0 characters (averaged over 334,079 articles). Whereas, according to the curve, the decay value is 50% when $x = 4,717$ characters. Thus, if we use the curve directly as a decay function, the value of a relevant document is halved after only one or two relevant documents have been found. In the present instantiation of U, we use the linear function to pay attention to more relevant documents. Also, since L determines the gradient of the linear function, we set it to a large value for the same reason.

For evaluating summarisation and traditional ranked retrieval, the gain value for an l-relevant information unit could be set, for example, as $gv_l = (2^l - 1)/2^H$, where H is the highest relevance level [9, 20]. Whereas, in a diversity evaluation environment where multiple possible intents i are known for each query q and per-intent relevance assessments as well as the intent probabilities $P(i|q)$ are available [20, 21], we can define the "global gain" for each relevant s_k as:

$$g(pos(s_k)) = \sum_i P(i|q) g_i(pos(s_k)) \qquad (3)$$

where $g_i(pos(s_k)) = gv_l$ if s_k is l-relevant to the i-th intent. Thus, this is the overall value of a document obtained by combining the "local" (i.e. per-intent) gain values. We plug Eq. 3 into Eq. 1 to obtain $D\text{-}U$, an extension of *D-measure* for diversity evaluation [20].

Another natural way to handle diversity is to compute a U-measure value (U_i) for each intent i separately, and finally combine them using the intent probabilities $P(i|q)$. This follows the *Intent-Aware* (IA) approach to diversity evaluation [1, 9]:

$$U\text{-}IA = \sum_i P(i|q) U_i \,. \qquad (4)$$

3.2 Deriving Trailtexts from Document Relevance and Clicks

In Section 3.1, we discussed the general case where each string s_k could be *any* piece of text that the user has read. Without eyetracking studies, however, it is difficult to construct a trailtext based on user observation. Therefore, in this paper, we consider special cases where we assume that s_k is either a search engine *snippet* or (a part of) the *full text* of the document. For each query (or a session), we construct a trailtext or several trailtexts automatically, by leveraging either *document relevance assessments* of existing test collections or *document clicks* that we obtained from a commercial search engine. In the latter case where *click order* information is available, we can drop the linear traversal assumption.

Figure 3 illustrates one way to automatically construct trailtexts based on *relevance assessments* and document rankings. Part (a) could be a ranked list from a TREC run: its second and fourth documents are relevant. (For simplicity we consider binary relevance here, although we actually leverage graded relevance.) Based on the linear traversal assumption, we can build a trailtext as shown in Part (b). Then, U can easily be computed using the relevant positions $pos(s_3)$ and $pos(s_6)$.

An important point to note here is that the U-measure computed based on trailtexts such as those described above satisfies the *diminishing return* property, similar to ERR [9]. Suppose that, in Figure 3 Part (a), the nonrelevant document at rank 3 is replaced by a relevant document. Then, since we now assume that the third document is also read, the trailtext will be longer than the one shown in Part (b), and the full text of the *fourth* document is pushed back towards the end of the new trailtext. As a result, the value of the fourth document *diminishes* according to the decay function shown in Figure 2. Whereas, many rank-based metrics such as nDCG lack this property: the value of the relevant document at rank 4 is determined absolutely by its gain value and its rank, no matter what the ranked list has above that rank.

Figure 3(c) shows a diversified ranked list of documents for a query that is known to have two intents. The second document is relevant to Intent 1 but not to Intent 2, while the fourth one is relevant to Intent 2 but not to Intent 1. In the *D-U* methodology discussed in Section 3.1, a single "global gain" value is computed for every document using Eq. 3, and a single trailtext is created as shown in Part (b). It is assumed that both of the two relevant documents are read. On the other hand, in the aforementioned *U-IA* methodology, a trailtext is created for each intent, as shown in Part (d). For example, the trailtext for Intent 1 is created by assuming that only the document at rank 2 is read.

Figure 4 illustrates one way to automatically construct trailtexts based on *click data*, which is in line with the way we compute MTLs (Section 3.1). Using click data, we can conduct session evaluation involving query reformulations and nonlinear traversals. Given the lack of eyetracking evidence, we assume that, in every session, the user reads every document he clicks, and that he reads

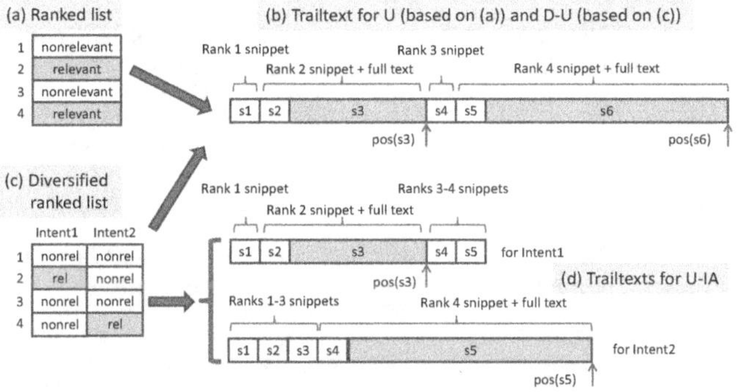

Figure 3: Automatically constructing trailtexts from relevance assessments of traditional and diversified IR test collections.

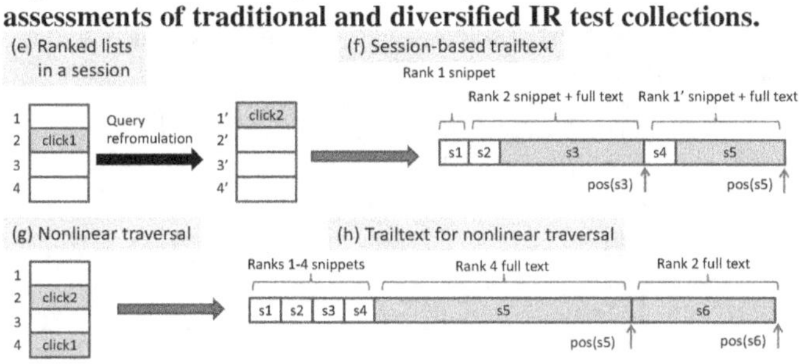

Figure 4: Automatically constructing trailtexts from clicks for nonlinear traversals and sessions.

every snippet ranked above the lowest clicked rank in every ranked list shown during the session[4]. Part (e) illustrates a session involving one query reformuation and therefore two ranked lists: the user clicks the second document in the first list and then the first document in the second list. Part (f) shows a possible trailtext for this behaviour. Part (g) shows a nonlinear traversal in which the user clicks the document at rank 4 and then one at rank 2; Part (h) shows a possible trailtext for this user, by assuming that snippets between ranks 1 and 4 are read before the full texts of the two documents are read. In this paper, we only consider sessions in which every ranked list contains at least one click: without eyetracking we cannot tell how the user examined a ranked list that did not result in any clicks [14].

So far, we have assumed that the user reads (I) all snippets above the lowest relevant or clicked document; and (II) entire full text of every relevant/clicked document. In practice, we make a more realistic assumption than (II), namely, that (II′) the user reads only $F\%$ of each relevant/clicked document. In the present study, we assume that the user reads only 20% of each clicked document (i.e. $F = 0.2$) by default. In our comparative experiments with TBG using the TREC 2005 robust data (Section 4), we show that the choice of F has a direct impact on the correlation with ranked-based metrics and on discriminative power, and that $F = 0.2$ is a reasonable choice. In Section 4.3, we show that our initial attempt at estimating F from click data also supports this choice. On the other hand, we stick to the choice of $L = 132,000$, based on the largest MTL discussed in Section 3.1. This is because, even if an *average* user reads only $F\%$ of each clicked document, we want to accommodate users who read the entire documents as well.

Figure 5 shows our instantiation of U-measure based on click data. The pseudocode reads a file where each line is a triple con-

[4]An eyetracking study by Joachims *et al.* supports this assumption [13]. For example, they report that when rank 5 is clicked, then snippets between ranks 1 and 4 are read 54.5-81.8% of the time; that at rank 5 is read 100% of the time, and that at rank 6 is read only 18.2% of the time.

$snippetlen = 200$;
$g = 0.5$; // gain of a clicked document: $(2^l - 1)/2^H = (2^1 - 1)/2^1$.
$pos = 0$; $U = 0$;
while read $< querynumber, clickedrank, doclen >$ sorted by time
  if $querynumber$ is new **then** initialise array $snippetdone[]$;
  // stores whether or not snippet at rank r has already been read.
  for($r = 1$; $r \leq clickedrank$; r++)
    if $snippetdone[r] == 0$ **then**
      pos += $snippetlen$; //reads all snippets above a click.
      $snippetdone[r] = 1$;
    end if
  pos += $F * doclen$; // reads $F\%$ of clicked document.
  U += $g * \max(0, 1 - pos/L)$;
end while
return U;

Figure 5: Algorithm for computing U-measure by reading a session data file, which consists of *querynumber*, *clickedrank* and *doclen* sorted by time.

sisting of *querynumber* (e.g. 1 for the first query in a session), *clickedrank* and *doclen* (length of clicked document), and the lines are chronologically ordered. It handles multi-query sessions and nonlinear traversals as we have illustrated in Figure 4. The use of the array *snippetdone* reflects our assumption that the user does not read the same snippet twice, although alternatives are possible.

4. EVALUATING TRADITIONAL IR

4.1 Experimental Setting

To demonstrate that U-measure is a useful alternative to TBG, we first compare them in an experimental setting very similar to that of Smucker and Clarke [23]: we evaluate 74 TREC 2005 Robust Track runs with 50 topics [25], using the document length statistics from the AQUAINT corpus[5]. Smucker and Clarke estimated several parameters required to instantiate TBG, based on a user study involving eight TREC 2005 Robust Track topics and 48 participants, where each search session ran up to 10 minutes. We copy all parameter values from their study: hence our instantiation of TBG can be described as follows.

$$TBG = \sum_{r=1}^{\infty} g(r) \exp(-T(r) \frac{\ln 2}{224}) \quad (5)$$

where the exponential factor is the time-based decay function[6] and $T(r)$ is the estimated time to reach rank r, computed as the time to read snippets plus the time to read clicked documents:

$$T(r) = \sum_{m=1}^{r-1} 4.4 + (0.018 l_m + 7.8) p_{click}(m) \, . \quad (6)$$

Eq. 6 relies on two important assumptions, namely, the linear traversal assumption (as the summation over previous ranks suggests), and that the user's reading speed is constant (the time required to read a full text is linear with respect to its length l_m as measured by the number of *words*). Also, according to Smucker and Clarke's calibration, $p_{click}(m) = 0.64$ if the document at rank m is relevant and $p_{click}(m) = 0.39$ otherwise; the gain value was estimated to be $g(r) = 0.4928$ for a relevant document and otherwise zero [23]. Thus this TBG is binary-relevance-based.

[5]http://www.ldc.upenn.edu/Catalog/docs/LDC2002T31/

[6]Smucker and Clarke [23] estimated this half-life of $h = 224$ from an MSN search engine query log that contains about five million searches.

While U and TBG are similar, we note that diminishing return is not guaranteed with TBG. Consider what happens to a relevant document at rank 2 when a 1000-word nonrelevant document at rank 1 is replaced by a 10-word relevant document. According to Eq. 6, the gain for rank 2 actually *increases*[7]. But this is not a problem if the document lengths do not vary wildly.

We note that while Smucker and Clarke used automatic duplicate document detection to account for the fact that users tend to read "redundant" documents quickly, our experiments do not employ any special treatment of such documents. As we mentioned earlier, we plan to address novelty and redundancy issues based on information units smaller than documents in our future work.

As was discussed in Section 3, we use $L = 132,000$ and $F = 0.2$ for computing U-measure by default. We compare U with TBG, AP, nDCG@10 and nDCG@1000. As U and nDCG can handle graded relevance, we used the standard gain value setting of $gv_l = (2^l - 1)/2^H$, where the highest relevance level H is 2 for the Robust test collection. In addition, we also experimented with their binary versions, which we denote by U_{bin} and $nDCG_{bin}$, as TBG and AP do not utilise graded relevance. AP and nDCG were computed using NTCIREVAL[8]; the document lengths (in words for TBG and in characters for U) were computed using the HEADLINE and TEXT fields of the AQUAINT collection.

4.2 Main Traditional IR Results

Table 1 compares the run rankings produced by different metrics in terms of Kendall's τ and symmetric τ_{ap}. The latter is similar to τ but is more sensitive to top ranks [27]. It can be observed that U is highly correlated with nDCG@1000, AP and TBG, and that it is more highly correlated with nDCG@1000 and with AP than TBG is. For example, the τ between U and nDCG@1000 is .819, while that between TBG and nDCG@1000 is .780. Whereas, TBG is more highly correlated with nDCG@10 than U is (.734 vs. .653 in τ), which is probably because the exponential decay of TBG is more top heavy than the linear decay of U. Table 2 shows the correlation results for U_{bin} and $nDCG_{bin}$, which suggest that reducing graded relevance to binary relevance has little impact on the rankings. Indeed, although not shown in these tables, the τ (τ_{ap}) between U and U_{bin} is .920 (.803).

We also compare the metrics in terms of *discriminative power* [18], which has been used in a number of recent studies for comparing the stability of metrics (e.g. [10, 20, 23]). While discriminative power does not say anything about whether the metric is right or wrong, low discriminative power means that the metric is not useful for drawing conclusions from an experiment. Table 3 compares the metrics in terms of discriminative power at the 0.05 significance level, based on a randomised version of two-sided Tukey's Honestly Significant Differences test. (This test is more conservative than standard pairwise tests, as it considers the entire set of runs [7].) Here, "required Δ" is the minimal performance difference that is usually statistically significant [18]. For example, Table 3 shows that nDCG@1000 detected a significant difference for 26.9% of the $(74*73/2 =)2,701$ run pairs, and that a difference of 0.15 in terms of Mean nDCG@1000 over 50 topics is usually statistically significant. Figure 6 provides a more general picture for some of the metrics in Table 3, in the form of *ASL (Achieved Significance Level) curves* for $0 < ASL \leq 0.1$ [18]. These results show that while U is substantially less discriminative than nDCG@1000 and AP, it is at least as discriminative as TBG, and much more discriminative than nDCG@10. Also, the results are consistent with the discriminative power experiments of Smucker and Clarke [23], who reported that TBG lies between AP and nDCG@10. The diminishing return property of U and TBG is probably one reason why they are not as discriminative as AP and nDCG@1000: once a relevant document is found, they tend to ignore additional relevant documents, which means observing fewer data points.

[7] $T(2)$ before and after the replacement are 14.5 and 9.5.

[8] `http://research.nii.ac.jp/ntcir/tools/ntcireval-en.html`

Table 1: TREC 2005 Robust τ/τ_{ap} rank correlation (74 runs; 50 topics): AP, TBG and graded-relevance metrics.

	nDCG@1000	AP	TBG	U
nDCG@10	.730/.591	.726/.592	.734/.638	.653/.531
nDCG@1000	-	.913/.843	.780/.635	.819/.680
AP		-	.792/.644	.816/.685
TBG	-	-	-	.834/.692

Table 2: TREC 2005 Robust τ/τ_{ap} rank correlation (74 runs; 50 topics): all metrics use binary relevance information.

	$nDCG_{bin}$@1000	AP	TBG	U_{bin}
$nDCG_{bin}$@10	.720/.565	.715/.561	.732/.663	.648/.494
$nDCG_{bin}$@1000	-	.903/.817	.781/.635	.825/.742
AP	-	-	.792/.644	.814/.736
TBG	-	-	-	.846/.717

Table 3: TREC 2005 Robust discriminative power at $\alpha = 0.05$ (74 runs; 50 topics).

metric	disc. power	required Δ
nDCG@1000	26.9%	0.15
$nDCG_{bin}$@1000	26.7%	0.16
AP	26.0%	0.12
U	20.0%	5.28
U_{bin}	19.6%	11.00
TBG	18.3%	1.66
$nDCG_{bin}$@10	16.4%	0.21
nDCG@10	14.6%	0.17

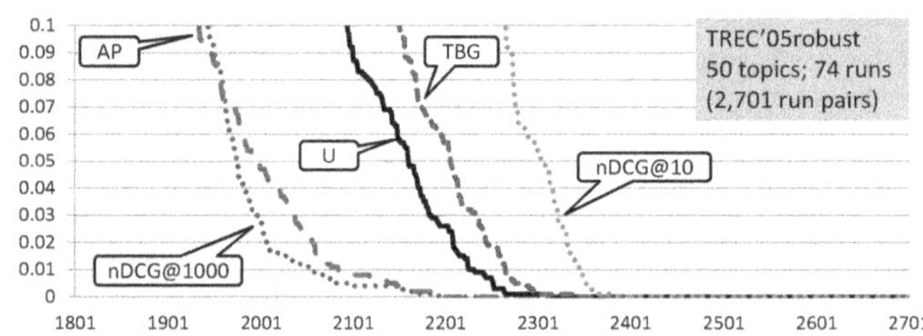

Figure 6: ASL curves for TREC 2005 Robust runs. The y axis represents the ASL and the x axis represents run pairs sorted by the ASL. nDCG and U utilise graded relevance.

To summarise our experiments with the TREC Robust Track data (following Smucker and Clarke [23]), we have shown that U is highly correlated with nDCG@1000, AP and TBG, and that it is at least as discriminative as TBG. Hence we believe that it is fair to regard U as a good alternative to TBG for the purpose of traditional ad hoc IR evaluation. In the remainder of this paper, we demonstrate the usefulness of U in other IR settings. We shall not discuss TBG any further as the instantiation of TBG we used was calibrated based on a particular user study [23], and its appropriateness for other IR settings is unknown.

4.3 Effect of F

While we have demonstrated that our default version of U performs at least as well as TBG in terms of rank correlation and discriminative power, these results are in fact dependent on the choice of F, the percentage of text that the user is expected to read for each relevant document. The main reason U and TBG are highly correlated with rank-based metrics is that they retain the rank-based penalty mechanism in the form of snippet length or snippet reading time; the main reason U and TBG differ from the ranked-based metrics is that they more realistically reflect the effort spent on reading each relevant document, and have the diminishing return property (on average for TBG). Thus, if we emphasize the snippet reading feature and suppress the document reading features of U or TBG, we get a metric that is more like a ranked-based one. As for discriminative power, a highly discriminative metric is required to (a) examine a wide range of ranks; and (b) emphasize the top ranks[9]. In the case of U, it is relatively easy to boost rank correlation with existing metrics and discriminative power at the same time, by lowering the value of F. Recall that lowering F means accumulating shorter strings s_k for trailtexts: this results in examination of deeper ranks, as illustrated below.

Given a ranked list to be evaluated, let the *Effective Measurement Depth* (EMD) be the rank at which the decay $D(pos)$ falls below 0.0001, so that the ranks further down will actually be ignored. Furthermore, let the *Average EMD* (AEMD) be the EMD averaged across all runs and all topics. In our TREC Robust experiments, the AEMD of TBD is 198.2. That is, TBD examines about top 200 documents on average. Whereas, the AEMD of U is shown in Table 4 as a function of F, together with the τ and τ_{ap} between U and other metrics: it can be observed that, as F is increased, the AEMD of U goes down monotonically. Moreover, as F is increased, the impact of the snippet reading feature (i.e. rank-based penalty) is reduced and the correlations with nDCG and AP go down monotonically as well. For example, with nDCG@1000, the τ is .876 when $F = 0.1$ but .471 when $F = 1.0$. On the other hand, $F = 0.2$, our default version of U, appears to be the most similar to TBG: the τ values with TBG for $F = 0.1$ and $F = 0.4$ are lower than that for $F = 0.2$, namely, $\tau = .834$.

Figure 7 shows the effect of F on the ASL curve of U: it can be observed that the discriminative power of U can be enhanced by setting F to a value even smaller than 0.2 (which also enhances the correlations with nDCG and AP as shown in Table 4). Interestingly, however, the relationship between F and discriminative power is not monotonic: for example, U with $F = 1.0$ appears to be a little more highly discriminative than U with $F = 0.6$.

We have also explored ways to estimate F from actual click data, but decided not to use these estimates directly in the present study for two reasons. First, we found that F is heavily dependent on clicked ranks: users spend a lot of time on top ranked documents. While the U-measure framework is open to incorporating a variable F for constructing the trailtext, this does make the metric more complex. Second, we found that the estimate of F varies considerably depending on how it is estimated. One problem we encountered is that users apparently do other things besides reading text when they dwell on a clicked page or a search engine result page.

One of the more successful methods we tried was as follows. First, to estimate the user's reading speed (SP), which we assume to be constant (as does TBG), we computed the Snippet Reading Time $SRT = t/c$ for every query q, where c is the rank of the document that received the first click and t is the time spent after issuing the query and until this first click. By averaging over 46,526,324 queries from Bing's query log (September 7, 2012, US market), we obtained $SRT = 14.002$ seconds[10]. Hence, the reading speed can be estimated as $SP = 200/14.002 = 14.283$ chars/sec. Second, to estimate F, we obtained 1,789,636 instances from the same session data where ranks k and $(k + 1)$ in the first result page were clicked consecutively, in this exact order. For each instance, let t' be the time spent between these clicks (i.e. time to read the document at rank k and then the snippet at rank $(k + 1)$), and let dl be the length of the document at rank k. Then the amount of text read at rank k can be estimated as $SP * t' - 200$, and therefore $F = (SP * t' - 200)/dl$. The average F over all instances was 0.282.

In summary, U with $F = 0.2$ is a reasonable choice, as it is highly correlated with TBG as well as with nDCG and AP, achieves relatively high discriminative power, and is supported by real click data. Hereafter, we use $L = 132,000$ and $F = 0.2$ in all of our experiments.

[9]For example, Precision@1000 satisfies (a), but not (b).

[10]This is considerably longer than 4.4 seconds in Eq. 6, the "time to evaluate a summary" in the TBG framework [23].

Table 4: τ (top row) and τ_{ap} (bottom row) with the TREC 2005 Robust data (74 runs and 50 topics): effect of F on U vs. other metrics. The $F = 0.2$ column has been copied from Table 1. Highest values across columns are shown in bold.

F	0.1	0.2	0.4	0.6	0.8	1.0
AEMD of U	462.9	384.0	281.3	221.8	182.0	155.7
nDCG@10	**.686**	.653	.590	.476	.413	.348
	.525	.531	.450	.332	.282	.235
nDCG@1000	**.876**	.819	.698	.571	.491	.471
	.776	.680	.500	.371	.302	.241
AP	**.876**	.816	.690	.562	.485	.411
	.795	.685	.506	.355	.289	.228
TBG	.811	**.834**	.801	.697	.634	.562
	.682	**.692**	.608	.489	.428	.364

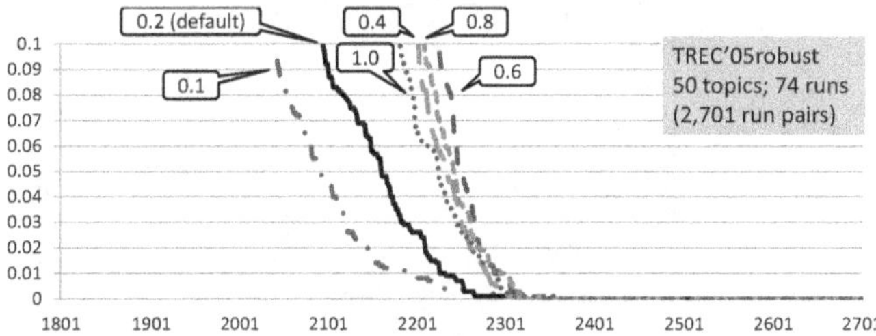

Figure 7: Effect of F on the ASL curves of U for TREC 2005 Robust runs.

5. EVALUATING DIVERSIFIED IR

In this section, we compare our trailtext-based diversity metrics *D-U* and *U-IA* with existing rank-based diversity metrics. For this purpose, we use the TREC 2011 Web Track Diversity Task data [11] as it contains per-intent *graded* relevance assessments (with $H = 3$) unlike its predessessors. We used its 50 topics and 17 Category A runs. The rank-based metrics we consider are *I-rec* (a.k.a. subtopic recall), *D-nDCG* and *D♯-nDCG* (i.e. simply an average of I-rec and D-nDCG), and per-intent-normalised version of ERR-IA [9] which we call *nERR-IA* [20, 21]. The first three are the official metrics at the NTCIR INTENT task; A version of ERR-IA was used as the primary metric at the TREC diversity task. Again, we use NTCIREVAL to compute these rank-based metrics, using the exponential gain value setting (See Section 4). Following TREC, the intent probabilities $P(i|q)$ are assumed to be uniform. As diversification concerns the very top of the ranked list, we evaluate the top ten documents (D-nDCG@10, etc.).

Table 5 compares the TREC 2011 Diversity rankings according to different metrics in terms of τ and symmetric τ_{ap}. It can be observed that D-U and U-IA are highly correlated with existing ranked-based diversity metrics (e.g. the τ between D-U and D-nDCG is .809), and that D-U and U-IA are extremely highly correlated with each other ($\tau = .985$). Below, we explain the latter observation.

As diversity metrics are generally more complex than traditional metrics, Figure 8 provides an example ranked list from an actual TREC 2011 Diversity run (Topic=137; Run=uwBA), with how D-U and U-IA are actually computed. Understanding this example should also help the reader see why D-U and U-IA are very similar.

Table 5: TREC 2011 Diveristy τ/τ_{ap} rank correlation (17 Category A runs; 50 topics).

	D-nDCG	D♯-nDCG	D-U	nERR-IA	U-IA
I-rec	.809/.761	.897/.890	.706/.560	.676/.626	.691/.551
D-nDCG	-	.912/.859	.809/.668	.779/.689	.794/.659
D♯-nDCG	-	-	.750/.610	.750/.696	.735/.601
D-U	-	-	-	.647/.528	.985/.991
nERR-IA	-	-	-	-	.632/.519

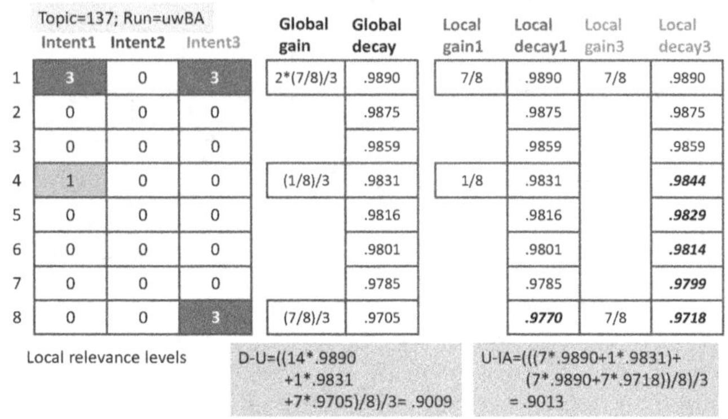

Figure 8: Examples of how D-U and U-IA are computed for the TREC 2011 Diversity runs.

This topic has three intents (i.e. subtopics), and the run returned three relevant documents: the one at rank 1 is 3-relevant to Intents 1 and 3; the one at rank 4 is 1-relevant to Intent 1 only, and so on. D-U assumes that all of the relevant documents are read, and computes "global gains" using Eq. 3 as shown in the figure. For example, for the document at rank 1, since $gv_3 = (2^3 - 1)/2^3 = 7/8$ for both Intents 1 and 3, the global gain is $2 * (7/8)/3$. On the other hand, the $D(pos)$ values are shown in the "global decay" column: for example, as the length of the document at rank 1 was found to be 6,279 characters, the estimated trailtext length after reading (a part of) this document is $200 + 0.2 * 6279 = 1455.8$. Thus $D(pos) = 1 - 1455.8/132000 = .9890$. Whereas, at rank 2, since we assume that only the snippet is read, $D(pos) = 1 - (1455.8 + 200)/132000 = .9875$. The final value of D-U is .9009. On the other hand, U-IA is computed as shown on the right of Figure 8. For Intent 1, it is assumed that only the documents at ranks 1 and 4 are read; for Intent 3, it is assumed that only the documents at ranks 1 and 8 are read. Then a U value is computed separately for Intents 1 and 3, and the final value of U-IA is .9013. Note, for example, that the local decay for Intent 3 starts deviating from the global decay at rank 4 (.9844 vs. .9831), as the document at rank 4 is not relevant to this intent.

More generally, let I be the set of known intents for a topic, and let $I'(\subseteq I)$ be the set of intents covered by a ranked list (so that $I\text{-}rec = |I'|/|I|$). We say that a document in the list is *strictly locally relevant* if it is relevant to at least one intent from I' *and* nonrelevant to at least one intent from I'. In Figure 8, the documents at ranks 4 and 8 are strictly locally relevant with respect to the ranked list. It is easy to see that if there is no strictly locally relevant document in the ranked list, then $D_i(pos) = D(pos)$ holds for any (i, x). That is, any local decay value would be identical to the global one. Whereas, $D\text{-}U = \sum_{pos}(\sum_i P(i|q)g_i(pos))D(pos) = \sum_i P(i|q)(\sum_{pos} g_i(pos)D(pos))$ from Eqs. 1 and 3, and $U\text{-}IA = \sum_i P(i|q)(\sum_{pos} g_i(pos)D_i(pos))$ from Eq. 4. Hence it is clear that *if there is no strictly locally relevant document in the ranked list, then $D\text{-}U = U\text{-}IA$ holds.* A corollary is that *if the ranked list covers only one intent (i.e. $|I'| = 1$), then $D\text{-}U = U\text{-}IA$ holds.*

Table 6: TREC 2011 Diveristy discriminative power at $\alpha = 0.05$ (17 Category A runs; 50 topics).

metric	disc. power	required Δ
D-nDCG	27.2%	0.12
D♯-nDCG	23.5%	0.15
I-rec	19.1%	0.19
nERR-IA	17.6%	0.14
D-U	14.7%	0.35
U-IA	14.7%	0.35

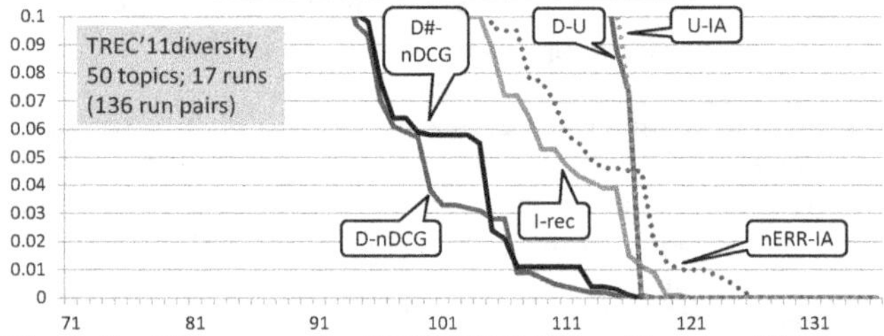

Figure 9: ASL curves for TREC 2011 Diversity runs. The y axis represents the ASL and the x axis represents run pairs sorted by the ASL.

Table 6 compares the discriminative power of the diversity metrics at $\alpha = 0.05$. Figure 9 visualises the discriminative power for $0 < ASL \leq 0.1$. From these results, it can be observed that D-U and U-IA are substantially less discriminative than D(♯)-nDCG. On the other hand, while they are less discriminative than nERR-IA at $\alpha = 0.05$, they are actually more discriminative at $\alpha = 0.01$. Again, the diminishing return property of D-U, U-IA and nERR-IA is one reason why they are not as discriminative as D(♯)-nDCG[11].

To sum up: D-U and U-IA are highly correlated with existing ranked-based diversity metrics, and are very highly correlated with each other. While they are not as discriminative as D(♯)-nDCG, they may be useful for evaluating web search result diversification from the user's perspective, as they are the only ones that take the document lengths into account.

6. EVALUATING MULTI-QUERY SESSIONS

Sections 4 and 5 discussed TREC-style evaluations using relevance assessments. In this section and in Section 7, we utilise the session data mentioned in Section 3.1 to compute U-measure based on clicks, using the algorithm shown in Figure 5.

To test the validity of U for *multi-query* session evaluation, we first constructed records of the form *sessionID, querynum, clickedrank, doclen* for the aforementioned 21,911,694 sessions. For example, a record (S1,2,3,500) indicates that in Session S1, the third URL for the second query (i.e. after one query reformulation) was clicked and that the document length is 500 characters. Moreover, within each session, the records are sorted by time. 5,178,327 of these sessions (23.6%) contained multiple queries. From these sessions, we obtained a random sample containing 50,000 sessions. The average and the maximum number of queries per session for this sample are 2.649 and 50, respectively; the average and the maximum number of clicks per session are 3.566 and 124, respectively. Sessions with many queries and clicks are often to do with pornography, as we shall discuss later.

For comparison, we also computed a version of *Session DCG* (sDCG), similar to that instantiated by Kanoulas *et al.* [14]. Although they also proposed session evaluation metrics that consider many possible browsing paths over multiple ranked lists, we do not consider them, since in our experimental setting, we can deterministically construct a trailtext based on the lowest click in each

[11] As for I-rec, its discriminative power is known to vary widely across test collections [21].

ranked list in a session. Note that sDCG and other rank-based metrics rely on the linear traversal assumption.

We compute sDCG for a given session as follows. First, construct a single ranked list by (i) truncating each ranked list at the lowest clicked rank; (ii) concatenating the ranked lists. (We do not employ any special treatment for duplicate documents [14].) Then, sDCG is computed over this concatenated ranked list:

$$sDCG = \sum_{r} \frac{isrel(r)}{\log_4(querynum(r) + 3)\log_2(r + 1)} \quad (7)$$

where $isrel(r)$ is 1 if the document at rank r in the concatenated list was *clicked* and 0 otherwise, and $querynum(r)$ returns j when the document at r comes from the ranked list for the j-th query in the session. In short, sDCG discounts relevant (or *clicked* in our case) documents not only by ranks, but also by the number of query reformulations that the user had to go through.

Figure 10 visualises the correlation between U and sDCG. As indicated in the figure, the Pearson's correlation (which takes into account the absolute scores) is .820, while kendall's τ (which compares the session rankings) is .600. **Example A** in this figure represents a session with extremely high U and sDCG values. This session actually contains two unrelated queries ("2000 Ranger 175" – a fishing boat, and "kfc in janesville wi"), but all but one of the clicks are with the former query: the user clicked 92 times to examine 39 unique documents. It is possible that (s)he was conducting a survey of the fishing boat. **Example B** is a session with 124 clicks for 4 porn queries. **Example C** represents a navigational information need: the queries are "check yahoo mail" and "check yahoo mail account," and the user clicked on the same yahoo mail page 12 times. With the first query, the user clicked the top ranked document (i.e. checked email) 11 times, which adds 11 to sDCG[12]; then, with the second query, the user clicked the top ranked document (i.e. the document at rank 2 in the concatenated list) once, which further adds $1/\log_4(2+3)\log_2(2+1) = .5435$ to sDCG. Thus $sDCG = 11.5435$. Whereas, owing to the diminishing return property, the value of a click on the yahoo mail page decays gradually with U: as the length of this page was estimated to be 539 characters, according to Figure 5, the decay value for the first click is $1 - (200 + 0.2 * 539)/132000 = .9977$, while that for the eleventh click is $1 - (200 + 11 * 0.2 * 539)/132000 = .9895$.

To sum up, click-based U is highly correlated with sDCG when used for multi-query session evaluation, but unlike sDCG, it has the diminishing return property similar to ERR [9], and can take document lengths into account. It is also possible to design trailtext-based metrics based on different browsing paths in a way similar to Kanoulas *et al.* [14], but this is beyond our current scope.

7. EVALUATING NONLINEAR TRAVERSAL

In this section, we demonstrate the potential of evaluating nonlinear traversals using click-based U. For this experiment, we first extracted a total of 2,015,311 sessions from our sample date (September 7, 2012, US market) that contained at least one nonlinear traversal somewhere in the session. From this set, we randomly sampled 50,000 sessions that contained at least one nonlinear traversal *before the first query reformulation.* Furthermore, to isolate the problem of evaluating nonlinear traversals from that of evaluating multi-query sessions, we *truncated* all records where $querynum > 1$, i.e. all clicks after the first query reformulation. The average and the

[12]Duplicate clicks can of course be filtered out, but we decided to reward every click in our experiment. In the case of **Example C**, note that the user may obtain new information every time he clicks on the yahoo mail page.

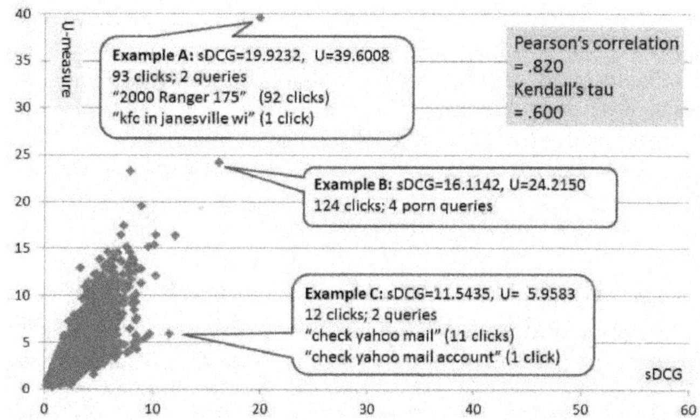

Figure 10: Correlation between U and sDCG for the 50,000 multi-query sessions.

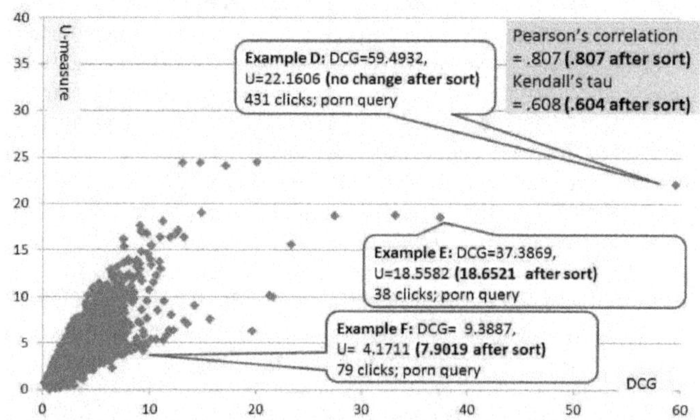

Figure 11: Correlation between U and DCG for the 50,000 truncated nonlinear traversal sessions.

maximum number of clicks per truncated session for this sample are 3.612 and 431, respectively. As we are now dealing with single ranked lists, sDCG reduces to the standard, binary-relevance version of DCG (Substitute $querynum(r) = 1$ to Eq. 7).

Figure 11 visualises the correlation between U and DCG. As shown in the figure, Pearson's correlation is .807, while Kendall's τ is .608: the values are remarkably similar to the multi-query case even though we are using a different sample here. In addition, we also computed U *after sorting each session data file by the clicked rank*, thereby obtaining artificial *linear* traversal sessions. Note that DCG cannot reflect this change as it simply discounts every clicked document based on the rank. As indicated in the figure, the effect of sorting on the correlation values is negligible, but in fact only 368 of the 50,000 sessions were unaffected by the sort in terms of U. Below, we discuss a few specific examples indicated in the figure.

Example D and **Example E** are porn queries with 431 and 38 clicks, respectively. For the latter, the value of U increases slightly after the sort. **Example F** is also a porn query, with 79 clicks, but we examine this closely as the value of U increased considerably from 4.1711 to 7.9019 after the sort. This user clicked the document at rank 426 (which was his ninth click), and then clicked one at rank 58 (his tenth click). Moreover, after clicking on the document at rank 402 (which was his 40th click), he clicked one at rank 399. Thus there were two nonlinear traversals within this truncated session. The document at rank 58 was the highest-ranked clicked document, so the artificial linear traversal file regards this as the first clicked document. This document happened to be very long: 20,044 characters. Thus, while the value of U for the original nonlinear traversal session reflects the user who examined nine relatively short documents before reaching the long document at rank 58, the U for the artificial linear traversal session represents a user who had to read this long document first. This property of encouraging systems to return *relevant and concise* information first has been inherited from S-measure for summary evaluation [19]. While other variants of U are possible, we believe that handling nonliner traversals and different document lengths as we do is a useful step towards understanding the real users' search behaviour.

8. CONCLUSIONS AND FUTURE WORK

We introduced a general information access evaluation framework that can potentially handle summaries, ranked document lists and even multi-query sessions seamlessly. Our framework first builds a *trailtext* which represents a concatenation of all the texts read by the user during a search session, and then computes *U-measure* over the trailtext, based on *position*-based discounting. U-measure takes the document length into account just like TBG, and has the diminishing return property. It is therefore more realistic than rank-based metrics. Furthermore, it is arguably more flexible than TBG, as it is free from the *linear traversal* assumption, and can handle information access tasks other than ad hoc retrieval. Our main conclusions are: (a) For ad hoc retrieval, U-measure is at least as reliable as TBG in terms of rank correlations with traditional metrics and discriminative power; (b) For diversified search, our diversity versions of U-measure are highly correlated with state-of-the-art diversity metrics; (c) For multi-query sessions, U-measure is highly correlated with Session nDCG; and (d) Unlike rank-based metrics like DCG, U-measure can quantify the differences between linear and nonlinear traversals in sessions. We argue that our new framework is useful for understanding the user's search behaviour and for comparison across different information access styles (e.g. examining a direct answer vs. examining a ranked list of web pages).

Our future work includes the following: (1) Exploring setting and varying F based on real search logs, while maintaining the simplicity of U; (2) Devising alternative decay functions for accommodating various types of information needs; (3) Comparing different information access styles, as was discussed above; (4) Combining the U-measure framework with eyetracking and/or information unit approaches, so that, for example, the difference between two search engines with similar DCG values but different snippet qualities can be quantified.

To make our work as reproducible as possible, we have made the following publicly available at `http://research.microsoft.com/u/` : (I) Length statistics for all relevant documents in the TREC 2005 Robust and 2011 Diversity data; (II) Multi-query and Nonlinear session records of the form *sessionID, querynum, clickedrank, doclen* (50,000 sessions each); and (III) Raw evaluation metric values from all experiments reported in this paper.

9. REFERENCES

[1] R. Agrawal, G. Sreenivas, A. Halverson, and S. Leong. Diversifying search results. In *Proceedings of ACM WSDM 2009*, pages 5–14, 2009.

[2] J. Allan, B. Carterette, and J. Lewis. When will information retrieval be "good enough"? In *Proceedings of ACM SIGIR 2005*, pages 433–440, 2005.

[3] P. Arvola, J. Kekäläinen, and M. Junkkari. Expected reading effort in focused retrieval evaluation. *Information Retrieval*, 13(5):460–484, 2010.

[4] L. Azzopardi. Usage based effectiveness measures. In *Proceedings of ACM CIKM 2009*, pages 631–640, 2009.

[5] F. Baskaya, H. Keskustalo, and K. Järvelin. Time drives interaction: Simulating sessions in diverse searching environments. In *Proceedings of ACM SIGIR 2012*, pages 105–114, 2012.

[6] B. Carterette. System effectiveness, user models, and user utility: A conceptual framework for investigation. In *Proceedings of ACM SIGIR 2011*, pages 903–912, 2011.

[7] B. Carterette. Multiple testing in statistical analysis of systems-based information retrieval experiments. *ACM TOIS*, 30(1), 2012.

[8] B. Carterette, E. Kanoulas, and E. Yilmaz. Simulating simple user behavior for system effectiveness evaluation. In *Proceedings of ACM CIKM 2011*, pages 611–620, 2011.

[9] O. Chapelle, S. Ji, C. Liao, E. Velipasaoglu, L. Lai, and S.-L. Wu. Intent-based diversification of web search results: Metrics and algorithms. *Information Retrieval*, 14(6):572–592, 2011.

[10] C. L. A. Clarke, N. Craswell, I. Soboroff, and A. Ashkan. A comparative analysis of cascade measures for novelty and diversity. In *Proceedings of ACM WSDM 2011*, pages 75–84, 2011.

[11] C. L. A. Clarke, N. Craswell, I. Soboroff, and E. M. Voorhees. Overview of the TREC 2011 web track. In *Proceedings of TREC 2011*, 2012.

[12] G. Dupret and B. Piwowarski. A user behavior model for average precision and its generalization to graded judgments. In *Proceedings of ACM SIGIR 2010*, pages 531–538, 2010.

[13] T. Joachims, L. Granka, B. Pan, H. Hembrooke, F. Radlinski, and G. Gay. Evaluating the accuracy of implicit feedback from clicks and query reformulations in web search. *ACM TOIS*, 25(2), 2007.

[14] E. Kanoulas, B. Carterette, P. D. Clough, and M. Sanderson. Evaluating multi-query sessions. In *Proceedings of ACM SIGIR 2011*, pages 1053–1062, 2011.

[15] C.-Y. Lin. ROUGE: A package for automatic evaluation of summaries. In *Proceedings of the ACL 2004 Workshop on Text Summarization Branches Out*, 2004.

[16] A. Nenkova, R. Passonneau, and K. McKeown. The pyramid method: Incorporating human content selection variation in summarization evaluation. *ACM Transactions on Speech and Language Processing*, 4(2):Article 4, 2007.

[17] S. Rajput, M. Ekstrand-Abueg, V. Pavlu, and J. Aslam. Constructing test collections by inferring document relevance via extracted relevant information. In *Proceedings of ACM CIKM 2012*, pages 145–154, 2012.

[18] T. Sakai. Evaluating evaluation metrics based on the bootstrap. In *Proceedings of ACM SIGIR 2006*, pages 525–532, 2006.

[19] T. Sakai, M. P. Kato, and Y.-I. Song. Click the search button and be happy: Evaluating direct and immediate information access. In *Proceedings of ACM CIKM 2011*, pages 621–630, 2011.

[20] T. Sakai and R. Song. Evaluating diversified search results using per-intent graded relevance. In *Proceedings of ACM SIGIR 2011*, pages 1043–1042, 2011.

[21] T. Sakai and R. Song. Diversified search evaluation: Lessons from the NTCIR-9 INTENT task. *Information Retrieval*, 2013.

[22] M. D. Smucker and C. L. A. Clarke. Modeling user variance in time-biased gain. In *Proceedings of HCIR 2012*, 2012.

[23] M. D. Smucker and C. L. A. Clarke. Time-based calibration of effectiveness measures. In *Proceedings of ACM SIGIR 2012*, pages 95–104, 2012.

[24] A. Turpin, F. Scholer, K. Järvelin, M. Wu, and J. S. Culpepper. Including summaries in system evaluation. In *Proceedings of ACM SIGIR 2009*, pages 508–515, 2009.

[25] E. M. Voorhees. Overview of the TREC 2005 robust retrieval track. In *Proceeings of TREC 2005*, 2006.

[26] Y. Yang and A. Lad. Modeling expected utility of multi-session information distillation. In *Proceedings of ICTIR 2009 (LNCS 5766)*, pages 164–175, 2009.

[27] E. Yilmaz, J. Aslam, and S. Robertson. A new rank correlation coefficient for information retrieval. In *Proceedings of ACM SIGIR 2008*, pages 587–594, 2008.

[28] E. Yilmaz, M. Shokouhi, N. Craswell, and S. Robertson. Expected browsing utility for web search evaluation. In *Proceedings of ACM CIKM 2010*, pages 1561–1564, 2010.

[29] K. Zhou, R. Cummins, M. Lalmas, and J. M. Jose. Evaluating aggregated search pages. In *Proceedings of ACM SIGIR 2012*, pages 115–124, 2012.

Modeling Click-through Based Word-pairs for Web Search

Jagadeesh Jagarlamudi*
Department of Computer Science
University of Maryland
College Park, USA
jags@umiacs.umd.edu

Jianfeng Gao
Microsoft Research
One Microsoft Way
Redmond, WA 98052, U.S.A.
jfgao@microsoft.com

ABSTRACT

Statistical translation models and latent semantic analysis (LSA) are two effective approaches to exploiting click-through data for Web search ranking. While the former learns semantic relationships between query terms and document terms directly, the latter maps a document and the queries for which it has been clicked to vectors in a lower-dimensional semantic space. This paper presents two document ranking models that combine the strengths of both the approaches by explicitly modeling word-pairs. The first model, called PairModel, is a monolingual ranking model based on word-pairs derived from click-through data. It maps queries and documents into a concept space spanned by these word-pairs. The second model, called Bilingual Paired Topic Model (BPTM), uses bilingual word translations and can jointly model query-document collections written in multiple languages. This model uses topics to capture term dependencies and maps queries and documents in multiple languages into a lower dimensional semantic sub-space spanned by the topics. These models are evaluated on the Web search task using real world data sets in three different languages. Results show that they consistently outperform various state-of-the-art baseline models, and the best result is obtained by interpolating PairModel and BPTM.

Categories and Subject Descriptors

H.3.3 [**Information Storage and Retrieval**]: Information Search and Retrieval; I.2.6 [**Artificial Intelligence**]: Learning; I.5.4 [**Pattern Recognition**]: Applications—*Text Processing*

General Terms

Learning, Algorithms, Experimentation

*Work done during his internship at Microsoft Research.

Keywords

Click-through Data, Latent Semantic Analysis, Topic Models, Multilingual IR, Translation Model, Web Search

1. INTRODUCTION

Web search engines till date rely strongly on matching words in a query-document pair. But very often, words tend to be either synonymous or polysemous resulting in a concept being expressed in different ways. It is well known that pure lexical matching is inaccurate and often leads to suboptimal performance [19, 32]. This problem has been addressed in mainly two ways:

- By using pairwise word associations to capture the probability of a document word translating into a query word [5]. The pairwise associations are typically learnt using document's content and its title [26], based on click-through data [3, 25, 14] or using query expansion techniques [35, 27].
- By representing documents and queries in a lower dimensional semantic space, in which words are identified by their semantics and not by their lexical form [13, 18]. Thus a query and document pair can have a non-zero similarity even though they don't share any terms.

The use of click-through data has proved to be effective in both the approaches. Statistical translation based approaches, first, learn pairwise associations between query and document words and then use these translation probabilities to rank the documents (Sec. 2.1) [14, 3]. On the other hand, topic modeling based approaches treat a document and the set of queries for which it has been clicked as an *aligned* query document pair and learn a shared topic distribution [15] (Sec. 2.2). They use the shared topic distribution to rank documents. A serious limitation of these topic modeling based approaches is that they require aligned query document pairs. But, there are lot of user queries without any click information rendering their application limited.[1] Notice that both these kinds of approaches harness different aspects of the click-through data. In specific, translation models use click-through data to mine pairwise word associations while topic modeling based approaches exploit alignment information to learn a shared topic distribution.

[1]In the literature, click-through data usually refers to clicked query document pairs. But in this paper we refer to both clicked and not-clicked query document pairs. We use aligned and unaligned to distinguish between these two sets.

1	The celebration of Thanksgiving will be incomplete without the legendary **Turkey** bird. The customary dinner reminds of the 'Four Wild Turkeys' served ···
2	**Turkey**, known officially as the Republic of **Turkey** is a Eurasian country located in Western Asia and in East Thrace in Southeastern Europe. ···

Table 1: Example documents where the term 'turkey' is used in different contexts. Relevant context words are colored in Blue.

So it is natural to investigate if exploiting these two aspects together will yield any further improvements.

With this goal, we aim to design models which can use pairwise word associations to jointly model an aligned and unaligned query-document collections. We achieve this by using word-pairs (*e.g.*, Table 2) to disambiguate the usage of terms. To understand the intuition, consider the occurrence of a term like 'turkey' in a document or a query. This term can mean the "Turkey bird" or the "Turkey country". Our approach tries to identify its most relevant concept based on its context words. For example, in the first document of Table 1, the occurrence of terms like 'thanksgiving' and 'dinner' along with 'turkey' indicates that it is used in the bird concept while the occurrence of terms like 'republic' and 'country', in the second document, indicates that it is used in the country concept. In our models, we try to disambiguate the term with the help of word-pairs. In this particular example, the bird concept is captured by associating the term to the word-pairs "turkey:thanksgiving" and "turkey:dinner" while the country concept is identified by associating it with "turkey:country" and "turkey:republic". By linking two related words, via a word-pair, we gather the evidence from both the words to make better judgements about of each of the words. Thus, we aim to build better document models which in turn lead to better ranking models.

Using this idea, we propose two models which explicitly use word-pairs to model a query-document collection. Our first model, called PairModel, is a monolingual model. It uses monolingual word-pairs derived from click-through data to model term dependencies in a query-document collection. It maps queries and documents into a concept space spanned by these word-pairs (Sec. 3). As shown in Table 2, the word-pairs capture different types of term correlations such as morphological variations, misspellings, term relatedness, *etc.*. By accounting for these different variations, PairModel builds better document models. The use of term co-occurrences to build better query or document models is not new [34], but the way we use it (*i.e.*, by combining word-pairs and topic models) is novel.

Our second model is a bilingual model called Bilingual Paired Topic Model (BPTM). It uses bilingual word-pairs, that are translations of each other say between French and English, to model a *bilingual* query-document collection (Sec. 4). Unlike PairModel, the word-pairs in BPTM are word translations and do not capture other types of semantic term correlations. So, we introduce topics to capture the semantic relatedness. This model maps queries and documents of both languages into a common lower dimensional subspace. Thus BPTM addresses the lexical gap problem and also leverages the abundant training data available in a resource rich *assisting* language (such as English) to improve ranking in a resource poor *search* language. While the use of assisting language to improve search language's ranking is not new [20, 10], the way we use it (*i.e.*, via topic modeling) is novel.

PairModel exploits term dependencies from queries and documents within the search language (French) while BPTM uses information gathered from the assisting (English) language to make better relevance judgements. So, these models are complimentary to each other and can be interpolated. Our experiments (Sec. 5) in French and German languages, using English as the assisting language, show that the combined model outperforms both the individual models and also beats various state-of-the-art baseline systems by a significant margin.[2]

2. RELATED WORK

Many strategies have been proposed to bridge the lexical gap between queries and documents using the click-through data. Click-through data is also shown to be effective in the learning to rank framework [1], but here we discuss the work that is most relevant to our problem and our approach.

2.1 Statistical Translation Based Approaches

In Language Modeling (LM) framework [29], documents are ranked based on the likelihood of generating a query. Statistical translation based approaches address the lexical gap by ranking the documents based on the likelihood of *translating* into a query. Let $\mathbf{q} = \{q_1, \ldots q_{N_q}\}$ be a query and $\mathbf{d} = \{w_1, \ldots w_{N_d}\}$ be a document, then a word based translation model [5] ranks the documents based on:

$$P(\mathbf{q}|\mathbf{d}) = \prod_{q \in \mathbf{q}} P(q|\mathbf{d}) = \prod_{q \in \mathbf{q}} \sum_{w \in \mathbf{d}} P(q|w)P(w|\mathbf{d}) \quad (1)$$

where $P(w|\mathbf{d})$ is the unigram probability of the word w in $\mathbf{d}$, and $P(q|w)$ is the probability of the document word w translating into the query word q. In these methods, a major challenge is the estimation of the translation probabilities $P(q|w)$. An ideal training data would be a large amount of aligned query-document pairs (in which each of the document is judged as relevant to the query). Due to the lack of such training data, [5] resorts to some synthetic query-document pairs while [26] uses the title-document pairs for estimating the translation probabilities. Click-through data has been explored to determine relationships between terms in queries and documents [3, 25]. However, these relationships and their probabilities are created using ad hoc similarity measures. Gao *et al.* [14] take a word alignment based approach popular in the Statistical Machine Translation community [8]. They treat an aligned query-document pair as a parallel sentence pair in two different languages and use IBM Model 1 to learn the translation probabilities. They show an improved performance by using translation probabilities learned from an year worth of click-through data.

Wei and Croft [34] discuss several co-occurrence based methods to identify term associations and their effectiveness for information retrieval. Moreover, lexical gap problem is also addressed using query expansion with automatic relevance feedback (*e.g.*, pseudo relevance feedback or PRF) [35]. Though these techniques are shown to be effective on TREC benchmark data sets [35, 27, 37, 9], their applicability to a commercial Web search engine is limited because

[2]A shorter version of this document is available at [22].

generating pseudo-relevant documents requires multi-phase retrieval, which is prohibitively expensive.

2.2 LSA Based Approaches

Latent Semantic Analysis (LSA) based approaches assume that both queries and documents lie in a lower dimensional sub-space and try to learn this space [13]. Probabilistic Latent Semantic Analysis (PLSA) [18] assumes that each document is a Multinomial distribution over T topics (called document-topic distribution) where each of the topics is in turn a Multinomial distribution over words (called topic-word distribution). Like in LM framework, the relevance of a document towards a query is assumed to be proportional to the likelihood of it generating the query. Latent Dirichlet Allocation (LDA) generalizes PLSA to unseen documents by employing a conjugate Dirichlet prior on the document-topic distributions [6]. Though, LDA is superior to PLSA in theory, its effectiveness for IR, as demonstrated in [33], has not been compared against PLSA.

Recently, Gao *et al.* [15] proposed a generative model called Bilingual Topic Model (BLTM) for Web wearch. They show that, by including the click-through data, their model achieves better performance compared to the PLSA. They assume that an aligned query and document pair share the document-topic distribution. Given this document-topic distribution, the query and the document are assumed to be independent and are generated separately. During the ranking stage, they keep the topic-word distributions fixed and fold in the unseen documents to learn their document-topic distributions. Finally, for a given query $\mathbf{q}$, they rank the documents as follows:

$$P(\mathbf{q}|\mathbf{d}) = \prod_{q \in \mathbf{q}} P(q|\mathbf{d}) = \prod_{q \in \mathbf{q}} \sum_{z=1}^{T} P(q|z)P(z|\mathbf{d}) \qquad (2)$$

Notice that this approach exploits the alignment information between queries and documents to learn the sub-space and hence it is limited to aligned data sets.

2.3 Dictionary Based Semantic Models

On the other hand, there are approaches that learn semantic sub-space using word-pairs [21, 7, 38]. These approaches usually model unaligned bilingual document collections using bilingual dictionaries, but they can be modified to model unaligned query-document collections using monolingual word-pairs. In [21], each document is assumed to be a Multinomial distribution over T bilingual topics. A bilingual topic is a Multinomial distribution over bilingual concepts (c) and each of these concepts generates a word depending on the document language. In these models, the probability of generating a string $\mathbf{s} = (w_1, \ldots, w_{N_s})$ given a document $\mathbf{d}$ is given by:

$$P(\mathbf{s}|\mathbf{d}) = \prod_{w_i \in \mathbf{s}} P(w_i|\mathbf{d}) = \prod_{w_i \in \mathbf{s}} \sum_{c,z} P(w_i|c)P(c|z)P(z|\mathbf{d}) \qquad (3)$$

where $z = 1 \ldots T$ is the bilingual topic indicator.

In this paper, we propose models that use ideas from the above mentioned approaches. More specifically, we 1) use IBM model 1 to learn word-pairs from the click-through data (Sec. 2.1), 2) exploit the association between an aligned query-document pair (Sec. 2.2) and 3) finally use the word-pairs, derived in step 1, as proxy for the concepts in the dictionary based approaches to model unaligned query-document collections as well. Thus our models combine the strengths of these individual approaches. As shown in Table 2, the word-pairs used for PairModel capture different types of semantic term correlations, so this model does not need topics. In contrast, BPTM uses bilingual word translations and can not account for the different types of variations and so it uses topics to learn the semantic space.

turkey	thanksgiving
turkey	bird
turkey	country
turkey	istanbul
government	govenment
colleges	college
university	colleges
addiction	rehab
camera	canon
camera	D3000

Table 2: Example monolingual word-pairs. The word 'govenment' is misspelled purposefully.

As explained in Sec. 1, our models use word-pairs to disambiguate the concept in which a term is used. The usage of term co-occurrences to build better document models is not new [4]. For example, most of the approaches discussed in Section 2.2 inherently use term co-occurrences in their process. But our approach uses only a subset of selected word-pairs (Sec. 5.2). As argued in [23], considering all possible pairwise associations can be noisy and hence using a pre-selected set of word-pairs is desirable.

3. PAIR MODEL

In this section, we propose our model assuming that we have monolingual pairwise word associations. An example set of word-pairs is shown in Table 2.[3] Our model is independent of the dictionary's source.

The most important aspect of our model is that we treat a word-pair as a hidden variable, *i.e.*, when we see a term we model the concept in which it is used as a hidden variable and try to infer it based on the context. The order of words in a word-pair doesn't carry any significance, *i.e.*, "addiction:rehab" is same as "rehab:addiction". By grouping two related words together we effectively combine the evidence of both words so that each word can help make an appropriate decision about the other word. Moreover, by linking evidence from related words, we move beyond bag-of-word based models and, since these words can lie anywhere in the document, our approach is different from other higher order models which consider n-gram relationships between words [30, 31].

We first describe our model for aligned query-document pairs and later discuss, briefly, on extending it to unaligned queries and documents. We assume that each aligned query-document pair is a distribution over word-pairs or concepts referred to as concept distribution. From now on, we use concept and word-pair interchangeably. Each concept is in turn a Binomial distribution over its two component words. Notice that there are no topics in this model and the only hidden variables are concepts. This is the primary difference

[3]For conciseness, we refer to this as monolingual dictionary.

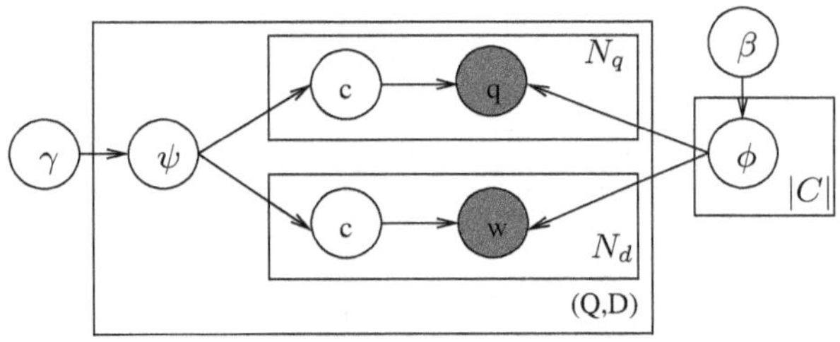

Figure 1: Graphical notation of the PairModel, the concept distribution is shared across an aligned query-document pair.

between our PairModel and other related generative models such as JointLDA [21] and BLTM [15].

Formally, we assume that an aligned query-document pair $(\mathbf{q}, \mathbf{d}) = ((q_1, \ldots, q_{N_q}), (w_1, \ldots, w_{N_d}))$ share the concept distribution $\psi_{(\mathbf{q},\mathbf{d})}$[4] which is drawn from a Dirichlet distribution with symmetric prior γ. For each word in the query-document pair, we first draw a concept (c) from the concept distribution $\psi_{(\mathbf{q},\mathbf{d})}$ and then draw a word from the words associated with the concept. Let $|C|$ be the total number of concepts, then we assume the following generative story for generating an aligned query-document pair. The corresponding graphical notation is shown in Fig. 1.

1. For each concept $c = 1 \ldots |C|$, choose $\phi_c \sim \text{Beta}(\beta, \beta)$
2. For each aligned query-document pair
   (a) Choose $\psi_{(\mathbf{q},\mathbf{d})} \sim \text{Dir}(\gamma)$
   (b) For each document term $i = 1 \ldots N_d$
      - Select a concept $c_i \sim \text{Mult}(\psi_{(\mathbf{q},\mathbf{d})})$
      - Select a word $w_i \sim \text{Bin}(\phi_{c_i})$
   (c) For each query term $i = 1 \ldots N_q$
      - Select a concept $c_i \sim \text{Mult}(\psi_{(\mathbf{q},\mathbf{d})})$
      - Select a word $q_i \sim \text{Bin}(\phi_{c_i})$

Since the size of the monolingual dictionary is limited, there will be some words that do not have any pairwise associations. For example, the word 'world' is not part of the extremely small dictionary provided in Table 2. To handle these Out-of-Dictionary words, we add dummy concepts of the form word:word ("world:world" in this particular case). Notice that this concept can generate only one word 'world' with a probability of 1. The model can be easily extended to unaligned data, in which case the generative story is limited to either a query or a document.

To understand how this model uses context words to disambiguate the concept associated with a term and improve the search ranking, consider the example documents from Table 1 and the term 'turkey'. Based on the input monolingual dictionary, the word 'turkey' has four possible concepts associated with it (as shown in Table 2). When the term 'turkey' is seen in the first document, then all the four concepts are equally likely to have generated this term, so all of them get equal probability for this document. But when we see its context words, say 'thanksgiving' then the probability of the concept "thanksgiving:turkey" increases for this document as it is triggered for both the words 'turkey' and 'thanksgiving'. Likewise, the concept "turkey:bird" also becomes more probable when the word 'bird' is seen. Similarly, in the second document, the words 'country' and 'republic' will cause the concept distribution to peak for the country sense compared to the bird sense. When we link all the terms to their most relevant concepts and gather these statistics over all queries and documents, we obtain statistics that better fit this particular data set and hence they tend to be more accurate than the translation probabilities of the original dictionary (as evidenced in our experiments in Sec. 5.2) resulting in better ranking models.

In our model, word-pairs enable us to leverage the term correlations within a document or a query. At the same time, the fact that an aligned query-document pair share concept distribution means that it also leverages term correlations across a query-document pair.

[4]We use ψ instead of the traditional θ to remind the reader that this is not a distribution over topics, instead it is a distribution over the word-pairs.

3.1 Inference

In [2], authors show that MAP inference performs comparably to the best Bayesian inference methods for generative models such as LDA. So, we use Expectation Maximization [12] algorithm to learn the MAP values for (ϕ, ψ). The E-step involves finding the posterior probabilities, *i.e.*, the probability of associating each term with a concept, as follows:

$$P(c|w, (\mathbf{q}, \mathbf{d})) = \frac{P(w|\phi_c)P(c|\psi_{(\mathbf{q},\mathbf{d})})}{\sum_{c'} P(w|\phi_{c'})P(c'|\psi_{(\mathbf{q},\mathbf{d})})} \tag{4}$$

For each concept c, $P(w|\phi_c)$ is non-zero for only the two words that are part of this concept. So, the above posterior probability is non-zero for only those concepts that can generate the given word. Because of this, although there are a total of $O(V^2)$ possible concepts, only a tiny fraction of them will have non-zero probability in a given document. Moreover, this set can be precomputed based on the document words and can be stored in an appropriate data structure for efficient processing. Again, because on an average a word has a small number of associated concepts, most of the terms in the summation term in the denominator of Eq. 4 are zeros and hence it can also be computed efficiently.

The M-step updates the parameters based on the posterior probabilities estimated in the E-step. Let $n(q, \mathbf{q})$ denote the frequency of a query word q in the query $\mathbf{q}$ and, similarly, $n(w, \mathbf{d})$ denote the frequency of a word w in the document $\mathbf{d}$. Moreover, let $N(q, c, \mathbf{q}) = n(q, \mathbf{q})P(c|q, (\mathbf{q}, \mathbf{d}))$ and $N(w, c, \mathbf{d}) = n(w, \mathbf{d})P(c|w, (\mathbf{q}, \mathbf{d}))$ then,

$$P(c|\psi_{(\mathbf{q},\mathbf{d})}) \propto (\gamma - 1) + \sum_{q \in \mathbf{q}} N(q, c, \mathbf{q}) + \sum_{w \in \mathbf{d}} N(w, c, \mathbf{d})$$

$$P(w|\phi_c) \propto (\beta - 1) + \sum_{(\mathbf{q},\mathbf{d})} \Big(N(w, c, \mathbf{q}) + N(w, c, \mathbf{d})\Big)$$

3.2 PairModel Variants

In PairModel, we force an aligned query-document pair to share the concept distribution. Instead we can allow them to have different concept distributions and then take an average of them to denote the concept distribution of the pair. The corresponding graphical notation is shown in Fig. 2. During inference, we learn $\psi_{\mathbf{q}}$ and $\psi_{\mathbf{d}}$ independently and then use $\psi = \frac{\psi_{\mathbf{q}} + \psi_{\mathbf{d}}}{2}$ as the resulting concept distribution of the document. We refer to this model as PairModel(Averaged) in the rest of the paper.

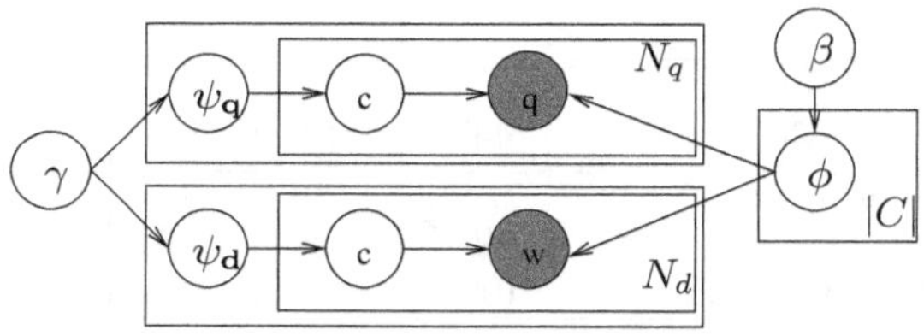

Figure 2: Graphical notation for the PairModel (Averaged), query and document do not share the concept distribution.

In another variant, we run PairModel without any word-pairs. As stated earlier, we add dummy concepts of the form "word:word" for Out-of-Dictionary words. In this variant, we use dummy concept for each word. Thus, the model reduces to a unigram language model whose parameters, shared by queries and documents, are estimated on the concatenation of queries and documents. We refer to this model as PairModel(–Pairs) in the experimental section (Sec. 5.2).

Finally, we can use posterior regularization to constrain the concepts sampled for a query and document to match with each other. But [15], shows that posterior regularization brings only a minor improvement so we skip this variant in our experimental section.

3.3 Document Ranking

We use the LM framework to rank documents. Following [36, 14], we score the relevance of documents given a query using a mixture model

$$P(\mathbf{q}|\mathbf{d}) = \prod_{q \in \mathbf{q}} \Big(\lambda_1 P_{mx}(q|\mathbf{d}) + (1-\lambda_1)P(q|\mathcal{C})\Big) \quad \text{where}$$
$$P_{mx}(q|\mathbf{d}) = \lambda_2 P_{ml}(q|\mathbf{d}) + (1-\lambda_2)P_{sys}(q|\mathbf{d}) \quad (5)$$

where $P_{ml}(q|\mathbf{d})$ is the maximum likelihood estimate of the query word q in the document and $P(q|\mathcal{C})$ is the unigram probability of the query word in the entire collection. And $P_{sys}(q|\mathbf{d})$ is the probability of q in the given document whose value varies among different ranking models. In PairModel, $P_{sys}(p|d)$ is estimated as

$$P_{sys}(q|\mathbf{d}) = \sum_{c|q \in c} P(q|c)P(c|\mathbf{d}) \quad (6)$$

where $c|q \in c$ denotes the set of all concepts that have the query word q as one of them.

4. BILINGUAL PAIRED TOPIC MODEL

Bilingual Paired Topic Model (BPTM) uses training data from an assisting language to improve ranking of documents in a search language. We assume that the assisting language (English) has richer resources, such as larger amounts of click-through data, document and query collections, that are useful for building a better Web search ranker. For concreteness, we consider the task of ranking French documents using English as an assisting language.

In what follows, we will first describe the way aligned query-document collections are modeled by BPTM. Then we extend BPTM to model unaligned query-document collections. We assume that we have aligned query-document collections (which are extracted from click-through logs) in both languages $\{(\mathbf{q}_i^e, \mathbf{d}_i^e), (\mathbf{q}_j^f, \mathbf{d}_j^f)\}$ for i=1 ... m and $j = 1 \dots n$. The queries and documents across different languages are assumed to be comparable (*e.g.*, from the same time period) but not necessarily translations of each other.

The underlying idea behind BPTM is to jointly model bilingual collections such that useful knowledge can be transferred across languages. The joint modeling is motivated by the previous study [20], which shows that training a ranker on a bilingual data is more effective than than learning a ranker in English and transferring it to French. Note that simply replacing word-pairs of PairModel with bilingual word translations does not lead to a model that is different from a document's unigram model because the model cannot capture any inter-word dependencies in documents of the same language. For example, the probability of a word-pair ("camera:caméra") in a particular French document depends only on the French word 'caméra' and is independent of other French words. Therefore, in addition to the use of bilingual translations, BPTM also uses bilingual topics. These bilingual topics map the queries and documents in different languages into a common lower dimensional semantic space. In that sense, BPTM bears resemblance to JointLDA [21] and BLTM [15] but there are some key differences. First of all, unlike BLTM where a topic is a distribution over words, a topic in BPTM is a distribution over bilingual word translation pairs (or concepts).[5] Second, unlike JointLDA which does not make use of alignment information between query and document, BPTM assumes that a query and its paired document share the same topic distribution.

We now describe BPTM more formally. We assume that an aligned query-document pair share the topic distribution $\theta_{(\mathbf{q},\mathbf{d})}$ which is a multinomial distribution over T bilingual topics and is drawn from a Dirichlet distribution with symmetric prior (α). Each bilingual topic (ψ_k) is a multinomial distribution over concepts. Finally, depending on the language of the query-document pair, these concepts generate words. Given a concept and the language, there is only one option for choosing the word and it is deterministic. To explain words that are not present in the bilingual dictionary, we add dummy translations for both Out-of-Dictionary English and French words. A dummy translation for an English word can only generate a English word and can not generate French words and vice versa. Jagarlamudi and Daumé III [21] showed that these dummy translations lead to deficient probability models and suggested adding a dependency link between the document language and the concept variable. Following their argument, let $\mathbb{I}(c_i, l_d)$ denote a binary indicator variable that denotes whether the concept c_i can generate a word from the language l_d, then the generative process of BPTM is as follows. The corresponding graphical notation is shown in Fig. 3.

1. For each topic $k = 1 \dots T$, choose $\psi_k \sim \text{Dir}(\gamma)$
2. For each aligned query-document pair
   (a) Choose $l_{(\mathbf{q},\mathbf{d})} \sim \text{Bin}(\frac{1}{2})$.
   (b) Choose $\theta_{(\mathbf{q},\mathbf{d})} \sim \text{Dir}(\alpha)$
   (c) For each document term $i = 1 \dots N_d$
      - Select a topic $z_i \sim \text{Mult}(\theta_{(\mathbf{q},\mathbf{d})})$
      - Select a concept $c_i \sim \text{Mult}(\psi_{z_i}) \cdot \mathbb{I}(c_i, l_{(\mathbf{q},\mathbf{d})})$

[5]We advise the reader to distinguish that a concept in BPTM refers to a word translation pair while it refers to a semantically related word pair in the PairModel.

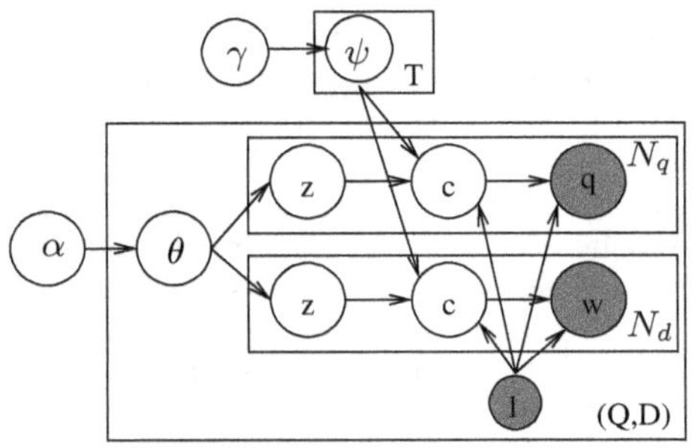

Figure 3: Graphical notation for the Bilingual Paired Topic Model (BPTM).

- Select a word $w_i \sim P(w_i|c_i, l_{(\mathbf{q},\mathbf{d})})$

(d) For each query term $i = 1 \cdots N_q$

- Select a topic $z_i \sim \text{Multi}(\theta_{(\mathbf{q},\mathbf{d})})$
- Select a concept $c_i \sim \text{Mult}(\psi_{z_i}) \cdot \mathbb{I}(c_i, l_{(\mathbf{q},\mathbf{d})})$
- Select a word $q_i \sim P(q_i|c_i, l_{(\mathbf{q},\mathbf{d})})$

To understand the generative process, consider generating an English aligned query-document pair. First, choose a topic mixture say 70% of education and 30% of sports. Then, we generate the query term by term. For the first term, choose a topic, say 'education', and then choose a concept from the education topic, let it be "university:université". We then generate the first English query term 'university' from the concept. If we were to generate the French query then we would have chosen 'université' instead. This process repeats until all words in the query and its aligned document are generated. Like in PairModel, BPTM can be trivially extended to generating queries and documents that are not aligned. In such a case, the generative process is limited to either a query or a document.

In BPTM, we use bilingual word-pairs which are translation equivalents where as in the PairModel we use monolingual word-pairs that are semantically related. Because of this distinction, BPTM doesn't inherit all the advantages of the PairModel (as evidenced in Sec. 5.3). We can use semantically related bilingual word-pairs but it is very difficult to obtain such word-pairs.

4.1 Inference

Again we use EM algorithm to derive the parameter update equations. In the E-step, we estimate the posterior probabilities and then use them to update the MAP estimates in the M-step. The E-step involves estimating:

$$P(c|z,l) = \frac{P(c|\psi_z)\mathbb{I}(c,l)}{\sum_{c'} P(c'|\psi_z)\mathbb{I}(c',l)} \quad (7)$$

$$P(c,z|w,\mathbf{d},l) = \frac{P(z|\theta_{(\mathbf{q},\mathbf{d})})P(c|z,l)}{\sum_{z',c'} P(z'|\theta_{(\mathbf{q},\mathbf{d})})P(c'|z',l)} \quad (8)$$

To compute the posterior probability for a query word, simply replace the pair $w, \mathbf{d}$ with $q, \mathbf{q}$ in Eq. 8.

As before, let $n(q, \mathbf{q})$ denote the frequency of the query word q in the query $\mathbf{q}$ and, similarly, $n(w, \mathbf{d})$ be the frequency of the word w in the document $\mathbf{d}$. Moreover, let $N(c, z, q, \mathbf{q}, l) = n(q, \mathbf{q})P(c, z|q, (\mathbf{q}, \mathbf{d}), l)$ and $N(c, z, w, \mathbf{d}, l) = n(w, \mathbf{d})P(c, z|w, (\mathbf{q}, \mathbf{d}), l)$ then the M-step involves:

		De	Fr	En	En(all)
Test	# of queries	4K	5K	5.3K	6K
	# docs	44K	54K	49K	190K
Training #($\mathbf{q}, \mathbf{d}$) pairs		128K	133K	2.1M	32M
Vocab Size		110K	76K	500K	500K
Dictionary Size		100K	82K	489K	489K

Table 3: Training and test data statistics.

$$P(z|\theta_{(\mathbf{q},\mathbf{d})}) \propto (\alpha - 1) + \sum_{q,c} N(c,z,q,\mathbf{q},l) + \sum_{w,c} N(c,z,w,\mathbf{d},l)$$

$$P(c|\psi_z) \propto (\gamma - 1) + \sum_{q|q\in c} N(c,z,q,\mathbf{q},l) + \sum_{w|w\in c} N(c,z,w,\mathbf{w},l)$$

where $w \in c$ denotes that the word w is one of the two words represented by c. Given a concept c and the language l, there is only one option for choosing the word and hence $P(w|c,l)$ need not be estimated.

4.2 Document Ranking

We first train BPTM model on the bilingual query-document collections. Then, we keep the topic-concept distributions (ψ) fixed and fold in the test documents to get their topic distributions (θ). We use the same mixture model described in Sec. 3.3 to rank the documents. Finally, the $P_{sys}(q|\mathbf{d})$ required to compute Eq. 5 is computed as follows:

$$P_{sys}(q|\mathbf{d}) = \sum_{c,z} P(q|c)P(c|z)P(z|\mathbf{d}) \quad (9)$$

5. EXPERIMENTS

In this section, we evaluate our models against state-of-the-art baseline systems in three languages: English, German and French. We first compare PairModel with different baselines on monolingual Web Search task, in Sec. 5.2, and then move on to evaluating BPTM in Sec. 5.3.

5.1 Experimental Setup

Since our ranking models rely on click-through data, we can not evaluate our models on standard TREC data sets. Therefore, following previous studies of using user log for Web search ranking [1, 14, 15], we use proprietary datasets that have been developed for building a commercial Web search engine and compare our models with state-of-the-art ranking models that are originally developed for TREC data sets [27] as well as approaches that use click-through data [14, 15]. We evaluate our models on data sets collected in three different languages, English, French, and German. The queries in all the three languages are sampled from a year of search engine query logs. Queries are "de-duped" so that only unique queries remain. To reflect a natural query distribution, we do not try to control the quality of these queries. For example, in our query sets, around 20% are misspelled queries, and around 20% are navigational queries and 10% are transactional queries, *etc.*. Second, for each query, we collect Web documents to be judged by issuing the query to Bing. Subsequently, query-document pairs are manually judged on a scale of 0 to 4, with 0 being totally irrelevant and 4 being most relevant. For all the three data sets, we filtered the queries that have less than ten relevant

	English			German			French		
	ndcg@1	ndcg@3	ndcg@10	ndcg@1	ndcg@3	ndcg@10	ndcg@1	ndcg@3	ndcg@10
JMLM	28.70	37.54	48.66	34.59	43.79	56.20	38.22	46.36	60.57
RM	31.30	40.21	50.82	36.18	45.48	57.84	40.31	48.60	62.51
WTM	31.79	40.77	51.31	36.54	46.26	*58.63*	40.09	*48.89*	**63.06**
BLTM	34.70	43.16	53.03	37.26	46.50	58.33	40.03	48.36	62.49
PairModel(–Pairs)	*34.74*	*43.46*	*53.17*	35.74	45.05	57.45	38.94	47.54	61.82
PairModel(Averaged)	34.64	43.40	53.10	*38.28*	*47.02*	*58.63*	*40.34*	48.42	62.30
PairModel	**35.02***	**43.46***	**53.26***	**39.55***	**47.64***	**58.98**	**40.94***	**48.95**	*62.58*
Δ over best baseline	+0.32	+0.30	+0.23	+2.29	+1.14	+0.35	+0.63	+0.06	-0.48

Table 4: Comparison of PairModel with state-of-the-art baseline systems. In each column, the best system is bolded, the second best system is italicized and * denotes statistical significance improvement compared to the best baseline measured by t-test at p-value of 0.05.

documents. For most of the experiments, we include documents with at least one clicked query. To evaluate the effectiveness of different systems in leveraging unaligned documents, we prepare a separate English data set, referred to as En(all), by including queries and documents that do not have any user click information. For all the data sets, the click information is extracted from query logs using a process similar to [17]. The training and test set statistics are shown in Table 3. Notice that the number of test queries is much larger than the typical 50 queries used in standard TREC evaluation settings.

We use the following baseline systems. **JMLM**: This is the unigram language model of the document with Jelinek-Mercer smoothing. **RM**: Relevance model [27], is one of the state-of-the-art PRF methods developed for the LM framework. The number of expansion terms and the number of top-ranked documents used for query expansion are optimized via cross validation. **WTM**: The third baseline is a word based translation model, a variant of statistical translation model, as implemented in [14]. We use same dictionaries for WTM and PairModel. **BLTM**: The final baseline is the Bilingual Topic Model [15].

The interpolation parameters in all the systems, λ_1 and λ_2, are estimated using 2-fold cross validation. We split the data into two halves, find the best interpolation parameters on one half using grid search and use them for testing on the other half. We report averaged results on both the splits. Finally, we use Normalized Cumulative Discounted Gain (ndcg) [24] to evaluate the ranking against the human judgements. We report ndcg at ranks 1, 3, and 10.

5.2 Monolingual Web Search Results

In this section we compare PairModel with the baseline systems. PairModel requires a monolingual dictionary of word-pairs. For English, this dictionary is learnt from a year worth of query logs (as in [14]). For German and French languages, we learn the dictionaries from the training data of aligned query-document pairs which is much smaller compared to the data used for English. For all the three languages, we run IBM Model 1 on the aligned query-document pairs and then filter all the word-pairs with conditional translation probability less than a threshold of 0.005. For quicker I/O, we keep only those word-pairs in which both the words are seen in our vocabulary and the resulting dictionary statistics are also shown in Table 3. We use the dictionary to fit PairModel and its variants and estimate the parameter values. After learning the parameter values, the documents are ranked using Eqs. 5 and 6.

Table 4 shows the results of different systems on English, German and French data sets. Across all the languages, JMLM smoothing does poorly because of the lexical gap problem. As expected, RM and WTM outperform JMLM demonstrating the effectiveness of addressing the term mismatch problem using co-occurrence statistics. BLTM performs significantly better than WTM on English but is indistinguishable on German and French. This is largely due to the size of training data we used to learn BLTM, which is considerably larger in English than in other languages as shown in Table 3. The order of the baseline systems is consistent with what has been reported in the previous literature [14, 15].

Recall that PairModel without word-pairs (PairModel(–Pairs) in Sec. 3.2) reduces to a unigram language model whose parameters are estimated from both the document title and the queries for which the document is clicked. As shown in Table 4, the performance of PairModel(–Pairs) is not consistent across different languages. It outperforms WTM and BLTM in English but underperforms in German and French. We speculate that this result is due to the fact that, on average, English documents have rich click data than German and French documents.

On the other hand, using word-pairs but neglecting the alignment between query-document pairs, as indicated by PairModel(Averaged) row of Table 4, is indistinguishable from PairModel(–Pairs) model on English, but is significantly better in other languages. This shows the effectiveness of using word-pairs especially when the click data is smaller. This model compares favorably to the state-of-the-art baselines (*i.e.*, WTM and BLTM).

Finally, PairModel which uses both the word-pairs and the alignment information between query and document pairs outperforms not only the variants, but also the baseline systems in most cases. The last row of the Table 4 shows the improvement of this model compared to the best of the four baseline systems. It achieves a significant improvement of 2.29 points at ndcg@1 for German. Overall, PairModel performed best and one of its variants performed second best.

Although PairModel and WTM use same set of word-pairs, the significantly better performance of PairModel indicates that our model seems to have the capability to adapt the translation probabilities to the data set. To verify this, we ran a separate experiment where we (re-)estimate the translation probabilities for the original pairs based on the

	English			German			French		
	ndcg@1	ndcg@3	ndcg@10	ndcg@1	ndcg@3	ndcg@10	ndcg@1	ndcg@3	ndcg@10
WTM	31.79	40.77	51.31	36.54	46.26	58.63	40.09	48.89	63.06
WTM (Adapted dict.)	**32.49**	**41.32**	**51.64**	**38.04**	**47.58**	**59.49**	**40.70**	**49.36**	**63.39**
Δ over original	+0.70	+0.55	+0.33	+1.50	+1.32	+0.86	+0.61	+0.47	+0.33

Table 5: Performance of WTM model with adapted translation dictionary.

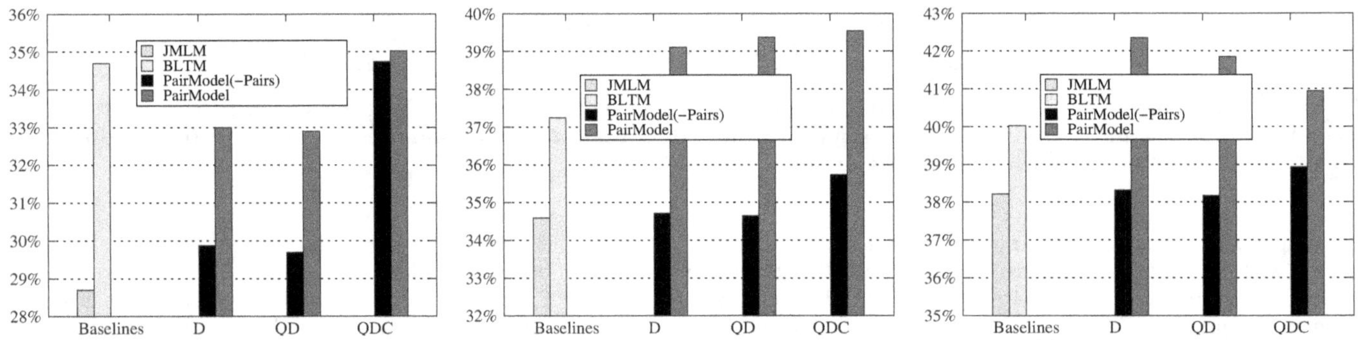

(a) English data set (b) German data set (c) French data set

Figure 4: Performance (ndcg@1) of PairModel under different resource settings. JMLM uses only titles (D) while BLTM uses titles, queries, and click data (QDC).

posterior probabilities learnt by PairModel. Let c_{12} denote the word-pair $w_1 : w_2$ and let $\{c'|w \in c'\}$ denote the set of concepts that have w as on of their words, then

$$P(w_1|w_2) = \frac{\#(w_1, w_2)}{\#(w_2)} = \frac{\#(w_1 : w_2)}{\sum_{w'} \#(w' : w_2)} = \frac{N(c_{12})}{\sum_{c'|w_2 \in c'} N(c')}$$

where $N(c)$ denote the expected number of times this concept is assigned to any of the words and is given by:

$$N(c) = \sum_{(\mathbf{q},\mathbf{d})} \Big(\sum_{q \in \mathbf{q} \; \& \; q \in c} N(q, c, \mathbf{q}) + \sum_{w \in \mathbf{d} \; \& \; w \in c} N(w, c, \mathbf{d}) \Big)$$

$N(q, c, \mathbf{q})$ and $N(w, c, \mathbf{d})$ are as defined in Sec. 3.1. For every word-pair of the input dictionary, we re-estimate its translation probability and use this re-weighted dictionary as input to WTM. Table 5 shows the results with the re-estimated dictionary. This clearly confirms that our model learns to tune the translation probabilities for this data set.

5.2.1 Variation with the Data

To better understand the model, we test the effectiveness of PairModel with varying resources. Specifically, we trained the model on document titles only (D), document titles + queries but without click information (QD) and document titles + queries + click data (QDC). Fig. 4 shows the results. The x-axis marks the resource setting and the y-axis marks the ndcg@1 scores.

Except in French, performance of PairModel increases as we add queries and their alignment information. Moreover, PairModel achieves significantly higher improvements in resource poor situations, which is justifiable as exploiting pairwise relations is expected to be more useful when there is not enough evidence for a word on its own. Another interesting observation is that, in German and French, even with only documents PairModel beats the state-of-the-art BLTM model. In the QDC setting, the performance of BLTM is closer to that of PairModel in English than in other languages, probably due to the availability of relatively larger amounts of click-through data in English.

	English (All)		
	ndcg@1	ndcg@3	ndcg@10
JMLM	26.30	31.84	43.80
WTM	28.85	34.76	47.42
BLTM	31.24	36.85	**49.36**
PairModel(−Pairs)	30.30	35.61	47.44
PairModel(Averaged)	*32.25*	*37.10*	48.88
PairModel	**32.23**	**37.13**	*48.91*
Δ over best baseline	0.99	0.28	-0.45

Table 6: Performance of all the models after adding unaligned documents and queries (in English).

In the final monolingual experiment, we evaluate the effectiveness of PairModel by adding unaligned queries and documents. Table 6 shows the results on this data set. As expected, this decreased the performance of all the systems, but notably PairModel is still able to better identify the relevant documents at rank 1. But the improvements decrease (compared to BLTM model) at higher ranks.

5.3 Bilingual Web Search Results

In this section, we report our bilingual results on German and French. Our aim is to test the effectiveness of word-pairs, in using assist language training data, to improve the accuracy in a search language and is *not* to build a competitive multilingual IR algorithm. So in this section we mainly resort to comparing with the same baselines and not with the state-of-the-art multilingual IR algorithms like [10, 11, 20].

We use the same data sets and the experimental setup as described in Sec. 5.1 and report results on Web Search task in French and German using English as the assisting

		German			French		
		ndcg@1	ndcg@3	ndcg@10	ndcg@1	ndcg@3	ndcg@10
Monolingual	BLTM	37.26	46.50	58.33	40.03	48.36	62.49
Bilingual	BPTM	37.38	46.58	58.48	40.85*	49.01*	62.73
	Δ over BLTM	+0.12	+0.08	+0.15	+0.82	+0.65	+0.24
	BPTM+PairModel	**39.66***	**47.73***	**59.04***	**42.25***	**50.01***	**63.42***
	Δ over BLTM	+2.40	+1.23	+0.71	+2.22	+1.65	+0.93

Table 7: Bilingual IR results on French and German. For comparison purposes, we have also shown the scores of best monolingual baseline system (BLTM). Again * denotes statistically significant improvement compared to BLTM as measured by t-test at p-value of 0.05.

language. For both these language pairs, we used statistical dictionaries learnt using Giza++ [28] on parallel data used for training a commercial MT system. We remove all translation pairs that have conditional translational probability less than 0.001 and keep only those pairs in which both the words are seen in our vocabularies. After the filtering, we are left with 181K and 269K word-pairs in En–De and En–Fr language pairs.

As explained in Sec. 1, PairModel exploits evidence from the search language while BPTM uses evidence from the assisting language so we also report the results of a combined model, 'BPTM+PairModel'. We use query wise interpolation to combine these models, *i.e.*, we first score the documents independently using the two models (described in sections 3.3 and 4.2) and then interpolate the document scores using a variant of Powell Search algorithm [16]. Table 7 shows the results.

We remind the reader that the major difference between BLTM and BPTM is that BPTM models query-document collections of both search and assisting languages while BLTM models only search language query-document collection. We expect the effectiveness of BPTM to depend on the coverage and quality of the bilingual word translations. Comparing BPTM with BLTM, we observe that BPTM is able to get 0.82 and 0.65 ndcg improvements at ranks 1 and 3 in French[6] but it gives almost the same performance in German. This is justifiable because of the poor quality dictionary for En–De language pair. The rich morphology and the compound word phenomenon of German limits the coverage of the En–De dictionary. The combined model, as denoted by 'BPTM+PairModel', improves over both BPTM and PairModel and the improvements are higher in French (again because of the high quality dictionary). While the reader might think that the combination of BLTM and PairModel can perform as good as BPTM+PairModel, we argue that BPTM is a better choice than BLTM since it uses assisting language query-document collection and hence is more likely to be complementary than BLTM.

6. DISCUSSION

In this paper, we proposed two models that explicitly use word-pairs to model aligned and unaligned query document collections. Our models combine the strengths of the previous click-through based approaches to lexical gap and, hence, achieve statistically significant improvements compared to the state-of-the-art baseline systems. The improvements are especially promising when the click data is small, *i.e.*, for emerging languages such as French and German. We have also observed that, significant improvements can be obtained by using a resource rich assisting language which presumably has more click-through data. To this end, our second model uses bilingual dictionaries to map queries and documents of both the languages into a common lower dimensional sub-space. Hence, it can use training data from a data rich assisting language to improve ranking in a resource poor language. Experimental analysis indicates that the performance of this model depends on the quality and the coverage of bilingual dictionaries. Since PairModel and BPTM models exploit different collections, search and assisting language resources respectively, they are complimentary to each other and hence can be combined. The combined model gave superior results compared to the individual models and also the baseline systems.

We have used word-pairs derived from click-through data for the monolingual model. Though, in principle, our model does not depend on the source of these word-pairs, its effectiveness for the Web search task will probably depend on the source. Moreover, for BPTM, we used bilingual word-pairs that are likely to be translations of each other and, again, such word-pairs may not be ideal for the Web search task. In this paper, our primarily goal is to show the utility of modeling word-pairs and is not to evaluate the suitability of the word-pairs – although the latter task is equally important. In future, we would like to study the effect of different sources on the final performance. Moreover we would like to move from word-pairs to small bilingual clusters, so that the model can effectively combine evidence from query-document pairs with-in and across languages.

[6]The improvements in French are statistically significant as measured by the t-test with p-value of 0.05

7. REFERENCES

[1] E. Agichtein, E. Brill, and S. Dumais. Improving web search ranking by incorporating user behavior information. In *SIGIR '06*, pages 19–26, New York, NY, USA, 2006. ACM.

[2] A. Asuncion, M. Welling, P. Smyth, and Y. W. Teh. On smoothing and inference for topic models. UAI '09, pages 27–34, Arlington, Virginia, United States, 2009. AUAI Press.

[3] R. Baeza-Yates and A. Tiberi. Extracting semantic relations from query logs. In *Proceedings of the 13th ACM SIGKDD*, KDD '07, pages 76–85, New York, NY, USA, 2007. ACM.

[4] J. Bai, J.-Y. Nie, G. Cao, and H. Bouchard. Using query contexts in information retrieval. In *Proceedings of the SIGIR '07*, pages 15–22, New York, NY, USA, 2007. ACM.

[5] A. Berger and J. Lafferty. Information retrieval as statistical translation. SIGIR '99, pages 222–229, New York, NY, USA, 1999. ACM.

[6] D. M. Blei, A. Y. Ng, and M. I. Jordan. Latent dirichlet allocation. *Journal of Maching Learning Research*, 3:993–1022, 2003.

[7] J. Boyd-Graber and D. M. Blei. Multilingual topic models for unaligned text. In *Uncertainty in Artificial Intelligence*, 2009.

[8] P. F. Brown, V. J. D. Pietra, S. A. D. Pietra, and R. L. Mercer. The mathematics of statistical machine translation: parameter estimation. *Comput. Linguist.*, 19:263–311, June 1993.

[9] G. Cao, J.-Y. Nie, J. Gao, and S. Robertson. Selecting good expansion terms for pseudo-relevance feedback. SIGIR '08, pages 243–250, New York, NY, USA, 2008. ACM.

[10] M. K. Chinnakotla, K. Raman, and P. Bhattacharyya. Multilingual PRF: english lends a helping hand. In *SIGIR '10*, pages 659–666, NY, USA, 2010. ACM.

[11] M. K. Chinnakotla, K. Raman, and P. Bhattacharyya. Multilingual pseudo-relevance feedback: performance study of assisting languages. In *ACL '10:*, pages 1346–1356, Morristown, NJ, USA, 2010.

[12] A. P. Dempster, N. M. Laird, and D. B. Rubin. Maximum Likelihood from Incomplete Data via the EM Algorithm. *Journal of the Royal Statistical Scociety, Series B*, 39(1):1–38, 1977.

[13] S. T. Dumais. Latent semantic analysis. *Annual Review of Information Science and Technology*, 38(1):188–230, 2004.

[14] J. Gao, X. He, and J.-Y. Nie. Clickthrough-based translation models for web search: from word models to phrase models. In *Proceedings of the CIKM '10*, pages 1139–1148, New York, NY, USA, 2010. ACM.

[15] J. Gao, K. Toutanova, and W.-t. Yih. Clickthrough-based latent semantic models for web search. In *Proceedings of the SIGIR '11*, pages 675–684, New York, NY, USA, 2011. ACM.

[16] J. Gao, Q. Wu, C. Burges, K. Svore, Y. Su, N. Khan, S. Shah, and H. Zhou. Model adaptation via model interpolation and boosting for web search ranking. In *EMNLP '09*, pages 505–513, NJ, USA, 2009.

[17] J. Gao, W. Yuan, X. Li, K. Deng, and J.-Y. Nie. Smoothing clickthrough data for web search ranking. SIGIR '09, pages 355–362, New York, NY, USA, 2009. ACM.

[18] T. Hofmann. Probabilistic latent semantic indexing. In *Proceedings of the SIGIR '99*, pages 50–57, New York, NY, USA, 1999. ACM.

[19] J. Huang, J. Gao, J. Miao, X. Li, K. Wang, F. Behr, and C. L. Giles. Exploring web scale language models for search query processing. In *Proceedings of the WWW '10*, pages 451–460, New York, NY, USA, 2010. ACM.

[20] J. Jagarlamudi and P. Bennett. Fractional similarity: Cross-lingual feature selection for search. In *Proceedings of the ECIR '11*. Springer, 2011.

[21] J. Jagarlamudi and H. Daumé III. Extracting multilingual topics from unaligned comparable corpora. In *Proceedings of the ECIR '10*, volume 5993, pages 444–456, Milton Keynes, UK, 2010. Springer.

[22] J. Jagarlamudi and J. Gao. Modeling click-through based word-pairs for web search. In *Proceedings of the WWW '12 Companion*, pages 537–538, New York, NY, USA, 2012. ACM.

[23] J. Jagarlamudi, R. Udupa, H. Daumé III, and A. Bhole. Improving bilingual projections via sparse covariance matrices. In *Proceedings of the EMNLP '11*, pages 930–940, Edinburgh, Scotland, UK., July 2011. Association for Computational Linguistics.

[24] K. Järvelin and J. Kekäläinen. IR evaluation methods for retrieving highly relevant documents. In *SIGIR '00*, pages 41–48, New York, NY, USA, 2000. ACM.

[25] H. Z. Ji-Rong Wen, Jian-Yun Nie. Query clustering using user logs. *ACM Trans. Inf. Syst.*, 20:59–81, January 2002.

[26] R. Jin, A. G. Hauptmann, and C. X. Zhai. Title language model for information retrieval. SIGIR '02, pages 42–48, New York, NY, USA, 2002. ACM.

[27] V. Lavrenko and W. B. Croft. Relevance based language models. In *Proceedings of the SIGIR '01*, pages 120–127, New York, NY, USA, 2001. ACM.

[28] F. J. Och and H. Ney. A systematic comparison of various statistical alignment models. *Computational Linguistics*, 29(1):19–51, 2003.

[29] J. M. Ponte and W. B. Croft. A language modeling approach to information retrieval. SIGIR '98, pages 275–281, New York, NY, USA, 1998. ACM.

[30] F. Song and W. B. Croft. A general language model for information retrieval. In *Proceedings of the CIKM '99*, pages 316–321, New York, NY, USA, 1999. ACM.

[31] M. Srikanth and R. Srihari. Biterm language models for document retrieval. In *Proceedings of the SIGIR '02*, pages 425–426, New York, NY, USA, 2002. ACM.

[32] K. Wang, X. Li, and J. Gao. Multi-style language model for web scale information retrieval. In *Proceeding of the SIGIR '10*, pages 467–474, New York, NY, USA, 2010. ACM.

[33] X. Wei and W. B. Croft. Lda-based document models for ad-hoc retrieval. In *SIGIR '06*, pages 178–185, New York, NY, USA, 2006. ACM.

[34] X. Wei and W. B. Croft. Modeling term associations for ad-hoc retrieval performance within language modeling framework. ECIR'07, pages 52–63, Berlin, Heidelberg, 2007. Springer-Verlag.

[35] J. Xu and W. B. Croft. Query expansion using local and global document analysis. In *Research and Development in Information Retrieval*, SIGIR '96, pages 4–11, New York, NY, USA, 1996. ACM.

[36] X. Xue, J. Jeon, and W. B. Croft. Retrieval models for question and answer archives. SIGIR '08, pages 475–482, New York, NY, USA, 2008. ACM.

[37] C. Zhai and J. Lafferty. Model-based feedback in the kl-divergence retrieval model. In *Proceedings of the CIKM '01*, 2001.

[38] D. Zhang, Q. Mei, and C. Zhai. Cross-lingual latent topic extraction. In *Proceedings of the ACL '10*, pages 1128–1137, Stroudsburg, PA, USA, 2010.

Click Model-Based Information Retrieval Metrics

Aleksandr Chuklin
Yandex & ISLA, University of Amsterdam
Moscow, Russia
A.Chuklin@uva.nl

Pavel Serdyukov
Yandex
Moscow, Russia
pavser@yandex-team.ru

Maarten de Rijke
ISLA, University of Amsterdam
Amsterdam, The Netherlands
deRijke@uva.nl

ABSTRACT

In recent years many models have been proposed that are aimed at predicting clicks of web search users. In addition, some information retrieval evaluation metrics have been built on top of a user model. In this paper we bring these two directions together and propose a common approach to converting any click model into an evaluation metric. We then put the resulting *model-based* metrics as well as traditional metrics (like DCG or Precision) into a common evaluation framework and compare them along a number of dimensions.

One of the dimensions we are particularly interested in is the agreement between offline and online experimental outcomes. It is widely believed, especially in an industrial setting, that online *A/B-testing* and *interleaving* experiments are generally better at capturing system quality than offline measurements. We show that offline metrics that are based on click models are more strongly correlated with online experimental outcomes than traditional offline metrics, especially in situations when we have incomplete relevance judgements.

Categories and Subject Descriptors

H.3.3 [**Information Storage and Retrieval**]: Information Search and Retrieval

General Terms

Human Factors, Verification

Keywords

Click models, evaluation, information retrieval measures, user behavior

1. INTRODUCTION

There are currently two orthogonal approaches to evaluating the quality of ranking systems. The first approach is usually called the Cranfield approach [17] and is done *offline*. It uses a fixed set of queries and documents judged by trained people (assessors). Ranking systems are then evaluated by comparing how good their ranked lists are—among other things, a system is expected to place relevant documents higher than irrelevant ones.

Another approach described by Kohavi et al. [28] makes use of real *online* users by assigning some portion of the users to test groups (also called *flights*). The simplest variant, called *A/B-testing*, randomly assigns some users to the "control" group (these users are presented with the existing ranking results) and the "treatment" group (these users are presented with the results of an experimental ranking system). Ranking systems are then compared by analysing the clicks of the users in the "control" against those in the "treatment" group. In the *interleaving* method by Joachims [27] users are presented with a combined list made out of two rankings. Then the system that receives more clicks is assumed to be better.

One of the main advantages of online evaluation schemes is that they are user-based and, as a result, often assumed to give us more realistic insights into the real system quality. Interleaving experiments are now widely being used by large commercial search engines like Bing and Yahoo! [11, 31] as well as studied in academia [22, 32]. However, they are harder to reproduce than offline measurements, whereas in the traditional Cranfield approach one can re-use the same set of judged documents to evaluate any ranking. This makes the use of offline editor-based evaluation methods unavoidable during the early development phase of ranking algorithms. One should take care, however, that the resulting editor-based measurements agree with the outcomes of online experiments—online comparison is often used as the final validation step before releasing a new version of a ranking algorithm.

In order to bring the two evaluation approaches closer to each other, we propose a method for building an offline information retrieval (IR) metric from a user *click model*. Click models, probabilistic models of the behavior of web search users, have been studied extensively by the IR community during the last five years. The main purpose of predicting clicks, as seen in previous works, is: (1) modeling user behavior when real users are not available (see, e.g., [23]); (2) improving ranking using relevance inferred from clicks (e.g., [10]). We hypothesize that click models can also be turned into offline metrics and the resulting *click model-based metrics* should be closely tied to the user and hence should better correlate with online measurements than traditional offline metrics. In addition, there is a growing trend to ground offline metrics in a user model and that is exactly

SIGIR'13, July 28–August 1, 2013, Dublin, Ireland.

what click modeling does—trying to propose a better user model. So, the question is why not use better user models, based on click behavior, as the basis for offline metrics?

We put our proposal for transforming click models into metrics to the test through a set of thorough comparisons with online measurements. Our comparison includes an analysis of correlations with the outcomes of interleaving experiments, an analysis of correlations with absolute online metrics, an analysis of correlations between traditional offline metrics and our new click model-based metrics, as well as an analysis of the discriminative power of the various metrics. One dimension to which we devote special attention in our comparison framework concerns unjudged documents. As was shown by Buckley and Voorhees [5], having partially-judged result pages in the evaluation pool may result in biased measurements. We examine how different offline metrics handle this problem. We also show that in situations when we cannot afford to use only fully-judged data, we can still make good use of the available data by making adjustments, by either a technique called *condensation* [34] or a new *threshold* method that we propose.

The main research questions that we address in this work are:

- How do *click model-based* IR metrics compare to the traditional offline metrics?
- How well do different offline IR metrics agree with online experiments? Do *click model-based* metrics show higher agreement?
- How well do different offline metrics perform in the presence of unjudged documents?
- How can we modify offline metrics to enhance agreement with online experiments?

Our main contributions in this paper are a method for converting click models into click model-based offline metrics. Secondly, we present a thorough analysis and comparison of specific click model-based metrics with online measurements and traditional offline metrics.

The rest of the paper is organized as follows. Section 2 presents related work. Section 3 shows how to transform a click model into a model-based offline metric. In Section 4 we examine click model-based and traditional offline metrics and report on their performance. We finish with a conclusion and discussion in Section 5.

2. RELATED WORK

Determining and comparing the quality of information retrieval systems has always been an important task in IR, both in academic and industrial research. In recent years, competition between large commercial search systems has reached the point where even a small improvement can be of great importance. As a result, a broad range of metrics to assess system performance have been proposed: Discounted Cumulative Gain (DCG) by Järvelin and Kekäläinen [26], Expected Reciprocal Rank (ERR) by Chapelle et al. [10], Expected Browsing Utility (EBU) by Yilmaz et al. [39], to name just a few. They have also been assessed from a variety of angles (see, e.g., [6, 10, 33]).

Some IR metrics have an underlying user model (e.g., ERR, EBU) or they can be viewed as such (see [6]). However, there is still a big gap between user models and metrics. For example, some of the widely used click models, such as the *User Browsing Model* (UBM) by Dupret and Piwowarski [19] and the *Dependent Click Model* (DCM) by Guo et al. [21], have so far not been used to develop an offline metric. Moreover, since the introduction of these early click models, many more click models have been developed, not only as improvements to previous models [20, 30], but also to address specific modeling issues, such as click models for diversified search [12, 14], the use of mouse movements along with clicks [24], or to model sessions [41]. We believe that all these models can be converted to evaluation measures.

The creation of traditional test collections against reduced costs has received considerable attention. Carterette and Allan [7] and Sanderson and Joho [35] discuss approaches to building test sets for evaluation at low cost. Azzopardi et al. [3], Berendsen et al. [4] go a step further and describe methods for automatically generating test collections and training material for learning-based rankers, respectively. Other works have extensively examined one particular limitation of traditional test collections: the completeness of judgments [5, 34]. Buckley and Voorhees [5] introduce a new metric called *bpref* to use in a setup where we have missing relevance judgements. Sakai [34] propose an alternative solution that does not require a new metric. We will also consider this problem when analysing metrics. Apart from evaluation metrics, there are other interesting problems arising when dealing with large query sets; these are addressed by the TREC Million Query Track [2] and further studied by Carterette et al. [8].

Another important group of extremely related studies concerns user-based experiments. Introduced by Joachims [27], the *interleaving* method is now widely used. Since its introduction, several modifications to the original method have been proposed, notably *Team-Draft Interleaving* [32] and *Probabilistic Interleaving* [22]. A thorough overview of interleaving methods can be found in [11]. Radlinski and Craswell [31] analyze and compare the sensitivity of both *interleaving* and traditional *offline* IR metrics against each other. They find that the outcomes of interleaving experiments generally agree quite well with offline metrics while data can be collected at a much lower cost. Below, we apply the same type of analysis to evaluate click model-based metrics and to compare them against traditional IR metrics. Ali and Chang [1] show that *per-query* correlation between *offline* side-by-side comparisons and online *interleaving* experiments is low even when query filtering is applied. This finding suggests that aggregating results from multiple queries as was done in [31] is less noisy than computing correlations on a per query basis. Yue et al. [40] propose ways to increase the signal of an interleaving experiment; inspired by this idea we propose to tune offline metrics through two techniques referred to as *condensation* and *thresholding* below to enhance the agreement with interleaving (see Section 4.1).

3. CLICK MODEL-BASED METRICS

From an initial focus on *precision* as a metric, the area of web search evaluation has evolved considerably. An early lesson is that we need to apply some sort of discount to the documents that appear lower in the ranking. One of the first metrics to operationalize this idea was Discounted Cumulative Gain (DCG) [26]. This metric is still widely used in the IR community. However, it has some drawbacks. One is that its discount function is not motivated by a user model. Another important issue with this metric is that it is a *static* metric, i.e., its discount values are fixed numbers. As shown in [39], a *dynamic* metric that dynamically assigns different discount values according to the relevance of the documents appearing higher in the ranking, more accurately represents real user behavior.

In this paper we introduce the notion of *click model-based* metrics. The main constituent of such a model-based metric is a *click model*—a probabilistic model aimed at predicting user clicks. Apart from click events (C_k), a click model usually has hidden variables corresponding to events such as "the user examined the snippet of the k-th document" (E_k). These hidden variables are often used to gain deeper insights into users' behavior. For example, Chapelle and Zhang [9] used a click model (DBN) to predict relevance and train a ranking function and in [19] the parameters of the click model were analysed to explain how previous user clicks influence future clicks. All click models that we study in this paper assume that users click a document only after examining the document's snippet, i.e., $P(C_k = 1|E_k = 0) = 0$.

Following Carterette [6], we distinguish between *utility-based* metrics and *effort-based* metrics. These give rise to two ways of mapping a click model to a click model-based offline metric. First, a utility-based metric uses a click model only to predict the click probability $P(C_k = 1)$ for the k-th document in the ranking. This probability is then used to calculate the metric value as the *expected utility*:

$$uMetric = \sum_{k=1}^{N} P(C_k = 1) \cdot R_k, \qquad (1)$$

where R_k is the relevance of the k-th document. It is common to use four or five relevance grades, from *Irrelevant* to *Highly Relevant* that are further mapped to numeric values. For example, the TREC 2011 Web Track [16] uses four levels of relevance: from 0 for *Irrelevant* documents to 3 for *Highly Relevant* documents.

Second, an effort-based metric requires a click model to have a notion of "user satisfaction" (S_k). A click model must have hidden variables S_k such that $P(S_k = 1|C_k = 0) = 0$ (the user can only be satisfied by the documents she clicked) and $P(E_j = 1|S_k = 1) = 0$ for $j > k$ (after being satisfied the user stops examining documents). Having this, we can define a metric to be an expected value of some *effort function*[1] at the stopping position:

$$rrMetric = \sum_{k=1}^{N} P(S_k = 1) \cdot \frac{1}{k} = \sum_{k=1}^{N} s_k P(C_k = 1) \cdot \frac{1}{k}, \qquad (2)$$

where $s_k = P(S_k = 1|C_k = 1)$ is a *satisfaction probability*.

A click model is usually *trained* using a click log. As a result we get values of the model parameters that can further be used to calculate the probability of clicks or satisfaction events to use in Equations 1 and 2. Some of the parameters are just constants, some depend on the position(s) in the ranking and some depend on the document and/or query. Parameters of the last type are the hardest ones to be used in a metric, as we want our metric to work even for previously unseen documents. But, fortunately, parameters of this type can usually be approximated from the document's relevance. In fact, when training a model we assume that these parameters only depend on the document relevance and not on the document itself. We will demonstrate this procedure for the *attractiveness* parameters in DBN, DCM, UBM and for the *satisfaction* parameters in DBN.

If a model meets the requirements listed above, it can be transformed into a click model-based metric. There is no step-by-step algorithm for such a transformation but only general guidelines. In the following sections we demonstrate the idea, using well-known click models as an example. We want to stress, however, that our framework is general enough to be applied to other click models, including those that use additional sources of information, such as recently studied session-based click models [41] or click models for vertical search [12, 14].

In Table 1 we classify previously studied metrics (ERR by Chapelle et al. [10], EBU by Yilmaz et al. [39]) and propose several new click model-based metrics: rrDBN, uDCM, rrDCM, uUBM. The left most column lists click models, the center and right most column denote derived offline metrics, utility-based and effort-based, respectively. As a recipe for naming a metric, we use the name of the underlying model and prefix it with the type metric that we are defining: *u-* for *utility-based* and *rr-* for reciprocal rank *effort-based* metrics.

Table 1: Click model-based metrics and their underlying models. Previously proposed models/metrics are followed by the reference.

	Derived metric	
Underlying click model	Utility-based	Effort-based
DBN [9]	uSDBN [10]	ERR [10]
DBN [9]	EBU [39]	rrDBN
DCM [21]	uDCM	rrDCM
UBM [19]	uUBM	–

3.1 Previously Studied Metrics

In this section we show how two previously proposed metrics, ERR and EBU, can be viewed as click model-based metrics. Despite the fact that they are different and were not in fact proposed as derivatives of a click model, they can both be viewed as metrics based on special cases of the *Dynamic Bayesian Network* click model (DBN) by Chapelle et al. [10]. In this model, the user examines document captions one by one and may be attracted by document u with probability a_u. If the user is attracted by the document, she clicks it and becomes satisfied with probability s_u. If she is not satisfied by the document she proceeds to the next document with probability γ and stops otherwise.

The Expected Reciprocal Rank (ERR) metric uses a simplified version of the DBN model [9] (we will refer to this model as SDBN) in which, as an additional constraint, all attractiveness probabilities are set to 1 ($a_{u_k} = P(C_k = 1|E_k = 1) \equiv 1$) and therefore all documents are clicked. This leads to $s_{u_k} \equiv r_{u_k}$, i.e., the satisfaction probability is equal to the probability of the document being relevant to the query. By making this assumption we obtain the probability of clicking the k-th document

$$P(C_k = 1) = \gamma^{k-1} \prod_{i=1}^{k-1} (1 - r_i) \qquad (3)$$

[1] Following [6] we use reciprocal rank $\frac{1}{k}$ as an effort function. While we are not doing it here, it would be interesting to evaluate metrics with different effort functions.

and the probability of satisfaction

$$P(S_k = 1) = r_k \gamma^{k-1} \prod_{i=1}^{k-1} (1 - r_i), \quad (4)$$

where r_i is the probability of relevance of the i-th document and γ is the continuation probability. The probability of being relevant is usually viewed as a mapping $R \to r$ from the relevance grades to the segment $[0, 1]$. In the original ERR paper [10] the authors use a mapping motivated by DCG: $r = \frac{2^R - 1}{2^{R_{max}}}$, where R_{max} is the maximum possible relevance grade ($R_{max} = 3$ in the case of TREC 2011 Web Track), but one may also fit this mapping from a click log.

Using probabilities from (3) and (4), we end up with the ERR and uSDBN metrics (cf. Equations (2), (1)):

$$\begin{aligned} \text{ERR} &= \sum_{k=1}^{N} \left(r_k \gamma^{k-1} \prod_{i=1}^{k-1} (1 - r_i) \right) \cdot \frac{1}{k} \\ \text{uSDBN} &= \sum_{k=1}^{N} \left(\gamma^{k-1} \prod_{i=1}^{k-1} (1 - r_i) \right) \cdot r_k \end{aligned}$$

In the original version of the ERR metric, the continuation probability γ of the DBN model was set to 1.[2] Conversely, for uSDBN [10, Section 7.2], we set γ ("one minus the abandonment probability") to 0.9, as suggested in [9].

The Expected Browsing Utility (EBU) metric by Yilmaz et al. [39] is also based on a variation of the DBN model. Unlike the original DBN model, their modification allows for different continuation probabilities in different situations ($p_{cont|click}$, $p_{cont|nonrel}$, $p_{cont|rel}$). While these parameters lead to greater flexibility in setting up the metric, they also represent a difficult choice for a practitioner to make. They were all set to 1 in the original paper [39] and here we do the same. By doing so we reduce the EBU model to DBN [9] with continuation probability $\gamma = 1$. One notable difference between the ERR and EBU metrics is that EBU does not set the attractiveness probabilities to 1. Instead, the attractiveness probabilities and satisfaction probabilities are both estimated from a click log using the assumptions that they are determined by the document relevance:

$$\begin{aligned} a_{u_k} &\approx P(C_k | R_{u_k}) \\ s_{u_k} &\approx P(\mathcal{L}_k | R_{u_k}), \end{aligned}$$

where C_k is the random variable corresponding to a click on the k-th document, $\mathcal{L}_k$ is the random variable corresponding to leaving the result page after clicking the k-th document and R_{u_k} is the relevance of the k-th document u_k.

3.2 New Click Model-Based Metrics

In this section we propose new offline metrics by introducing an *effort-based* variant of the EBU metric and also by converting the two popular click models, UBM and DCM, into click model-based metrics. By doing so we show that our framework of *click model-based* metrics is not only a way of viewing previously studied metrics, but also a way of deriving new metrics in a principled way.

The rrDBN metric uses essentially the same user model as the EBU metric. In fact, the parameters for EBU and rrDBN are the same. The only difference is that rrDBN is calculated using Equation (2) instead of (1).

Next, the uDCM and rrDCM metrics can be derived from the Dependent Click Model (DCM, [21]) in a way similar to how EBU and rrDBN are derived from DBN. The only difference between DCM and DBN is that the satisfaction probability $P(S_k = 1)$ depends not on the document itself but on its position k in a ranked list. Thus, the DCM model can be described with the following equations:

$$\begin{aligned} P(C_k = 1 | E_k = 0) &= 0 \\ P(C_k = 1 | E_k = 1) &= a_{u_k} \\ P(S_k = 1 | C_k = 0) &= 0 \\ P(S_k = 1 | C_k = 1) &= s_k \\ P(E_1 = 1) &= 1 \\ P(E_{k+1} = 1 | E_k = 0) &= 0 \\ P(E_{k+1} = 1 | E_k = 1, S_k) &= 1 - S_k \end{aligned}$$

As was shown by Turpin et al. [37], the attractiveness of a document's snippet can be approximated as a function of its relevance grade. A mapping from grades to attractiveness probabilities can be inferred from a click log using the click model (DCM in this case). [3] For this purpose we impose the constraint that documents with the same relevance have the same attractiveness, i.e., the attractiveness of a document is a function of its relevance grade: $a_u = a(R_u)$.

Finally, using the click model and Equations (1), (2), we can define uDCM and rrDCM metrics as follows:

$$\begin{aligned} uDCM &= \sum_{k=1}^{N} a(R_k) \prod_{i=1}^{k-1} (1 - a(R_i) s_i) \cdot R_k \\ rrDCM &= \sum_{k=1}^{N} s_k a(R_k) \prod_{i=1}^{k-1} (1 - a(R_i) s_i) \cdot \frac{1}{k} \end{aligned}$$

Chen et al. [12] report that the User Browsing Model (UBM) [19] performs better than DBN in terms of click prediction perplexity. We have also evaluated this model using a Yandex click log. We used a sample of clicks collected in November 2012. We then removed pages without clicks and split the remaining data into training and test set. In total we had 1,191,963 training and 1,292,993 test pages. To compare the models we used the *perplexity gain* [12, Section 5.2] which is a standard way of comparing perplexity values (see, e.g., [12, 20, 41]). On our data UBM outperforms DBN by 16% which is considered a big difference.

This finding motivates the idea of deriving an offline metric from UBM. In the UBM model the click probability is governed by the attraction bias and the examination bias:

$$P(C = 1 | u, q, r, d) = P(A = 1 | u, q) P(E = 1 | d, r) = a_{uq} \gamma_{rd},$$

where C stands for click, A for attraction, E for examination; u is the document URL, q is the user query, r is the document rank (position), and $d = r - \max\{j < r | C_j = 1\}$ is the distance to the previous click.[4] For convenience, we write a_r instead of a_{uq} and $\gamma_r(j)$ instead of γ_{rd}, where $d = r - j$.

Like for the EBU/rrDBN and uDCM/rrDCM metrics, we assume that the attractiveness probability a is a function of

[2]In the original paper [10, Section 3] an alternative interpretation of the ERR metric as a metric based on the *Cascade Model* by Craswell et al. [18] was also proposed.

[3]The source code for probabilistic inference is freely available at `https://github.com/varepsilon/clickmodels`.

[4]As in [19] we use a virtual zero position (which is always clicked) to simplify our equations.

the relevance of the document: $a_{uq} = a(R_{uq})$. The examination probabilities $\gamma_r(j)$ can be precomputed from click logs during the same model training process. One important difference from the previously studied models is that the UBM model relies on previous clicks and these are not available offline. To deal with this problem we factorize the probability $P(C_r = 1)$ over the position of previous clicks j:

$$P(C_r = 1) = \sum_{j=0}^{r-1} P(C_j = 1, C_{j+1} = 0, \ldots, C_{r-1} = 0, C_r = 1).$$

By applying Bayes rule we get

$$\begin{aligned} P(C_r = 1) &= \sum_{j=0}^{r-1} P(C_j = 1) \\ &\cdot \prod_{k=j+1}^{r-1} P(C_k = 0 | C_j = 1, C_{j+1} = 0, \ldots, C_{k-1} = 0) \\ &\cdot P(C_r = 1 | C_j = 1, C_{j+1} = 0, \ldots, C_{r-1} = 0) = \\ &= \sum_{j=0}^{r-1} P(C_j = 1) \left(\prod_{k=j+1}^{r-1} (1 - a_k \gamma_k(j)) \right) a_r \gamma_r(j) \end{aligned}$$

Finally, the click probability is given by a recursive formula:

$$\begin{aligned} P(C_0 = 1) &= 1 \\ P(C_r = 1) &= \sum_{j=0}^{r-1} P(C_j = 1) \left(\prod_{k=j+1}^{r-1} (1 - a_k \gamma_k(j)) \right) a_r \gamma_r(j) \end{aligned}$$

where $a_r = a(R_r)$, and $a(\cdot)$ and $\gamma_r(\cdot)$ are known functions estimated from clicks. It is important to note, that unlike Dupret and Piwowarski [19], we used all queries, not only queries with high clickthrough rate. So our resulting γ function is different from that analysed by Dupret and Piwowarski, and might be interesting on its own. For example, $\gamma_r(j)$ is much less than 1 for $j > 0$ which corresponds to the fact that most of the users click on only one document.

Given the click probability we can define the metric:

$$uUBM = \sum_{r=1}^{N} P(C_r = 1) \cdot R_r \tag{5}$$

The UBM click model does not have a notion of user satisfaction and hence we do not introduce an "rrUBM" metric.

4. ANALYSIS

In this section we analyze the click model-based metrics previously listed, both old and new, along a number of dimensions. We compare *click model-based* metrics to traditional offline metrics. As traditional metrics we consider precision, with two possible binarizations of four scale judgments (*Precision* treats the highest three relevance grades (3, 2, 1) as "relevant," while *Precision2* only treats the highest two relevance grades (3, 2) as "relevant") as well as DCG. As was shown by Chapelle et al. [10], the NDCG metric is always worse at capturing user satisfaction than DCG. We decided not to include this metric and thus to overcome potential issues with corpus-dependent NDCG normalization.

We start by determining correlations of various offline metrics to the outcomes of interleaving experiments in a way proposed by Radlinski and Craswell [31]. These correlations are then used to compare offline metrics to each other. The metric that shows the best correlation with interleaving outcomes is assumed to better represent real user behavior. We then move to more traditional comparison techniques, such as metric-to-metric correlations and discriminative power.

4.1 Correlation with Interleaving Outcomes

As was shown by Radlinski et al. [32], absolute click metrics are often unable to determine differences in IR systems. Moreover, they are always difficult to interpret and may even be misleading, because we cannot know for sure how these metrics are related to user satisfaction.

Fortunately, there is another approach, the *pairwise* or *interleaved* comparison techniques mentioned earlier [27, 32]. Following this approach, we compare two ranking systems by presenting a user with an interleaved result page, containing documents from both result lists. The winner is then determined from user clicks. We assess an offline IR metric m in terms of its agreement with the interleaving outcomes. Specifically, we use the Team-Draft Interleaving (TDI) method by Radlinski et al. [32]. In this method each document in the interleaved page is assigned to exactly one of the two ranking systems ("the teams"). We then say that a system wins a comparison if the documents it contributes to the combined list receive more clicks. The system that wins most of the comparisons is assumed to be better.

For the current experiment we used a click log of the Yandex search engine collected in October–December 2012. During this period we focus on five revisions of the core ranking functions (A, B, C, D, E), with each revision being compared to the previous one using TDI, that was run for 5-10 days. For each of our ten experiments we had at least 200,000 impressions as in the work by Radlinski and Craswell [31]. Some ranking function revisions influence more than one market (country), so in total we have 10 pairs of algorithms to compare: $\Delta_1 AB$, $\Delta_2 AB$, $\Delta_1 BC$, $\Delta_1 CD$, $\Delta_2 CD$, $\Delta_3 CD$, $\Delta_4 CD$, $\Delta_1 DE$, $\Delta_2 DE$, $\Delta_3 DE$. For each algorithm pair we recorded the *interleaving signal* value, i.e., the deviation from 50% of the number of cases where the newer system was preferred. For instance, if in the experiment labeled $\Delta_i XY$ system Y was preferred over system X in 51% of all cases, we say that the *interleaving signal* for the experiment is 1%.

Having interleaving signals, we want to compare them to the signals obtained by the offline IR measures, i.e., the average difference of the metric values. Unlike in the traditional Cranfield approach we use queries and documents from the query log. When computing an offline metric signal for a particular experiment $\Delta_i XY$, we extract queries issued by the users assigned to the experimental flight. For these queries we also extract the document lists that would have been produced by each of the systems X and Y if they had not been interleaved. By using click-log-based queries when comparing the signal of an offline metric to the interleaving signal we eliminate the effect induced by the choice of a query set that one needs to compile for a Cranfield-style evaluation. Here it also allows us to perform experiments with historical revisions of a ranking algorithm that is no longer running. Although this approach has some advantages for our research problem, it has some disadvantages for everyday usage. One notable drawback is that we use only part of the judgements available because not all the queries that we have judgements for were submitted by the users of the experimental flight. For each experiment and each metric we keep only the queries that have at least one document judged. Depending on the experiment we have from 178 to 5,815 queries per experiment (median 573). As shown in [31], it is usually sufficient to have approximately 100 queries to identify the better system in an offline comparison.

The amount of data available to the search engine is usually much larger than a human can handle. Even more important is the fact that the web corpus is constantly changing, so we cannot maintain complete judgements even for a limited set of queries. That is why it seems natural that some documents returned by the system do not have relevance judgements. In order to analyse the tradeoff between adding noise from unjudged documents and reducing the noise by allowing more queries we introduce a parameter **#unjudged**. We discard queries for which the number of unjudged documents in the top 10 is bigger than this value for either of the two systems taking part in a TDI experiment. Below, we vary this bound and see how it influences the correlation between offline metrics and interleaving.

For each offline metric m and each value of **#unjudged** from 1 to 9 we compute the weighted Pearson correlation (similar to [10]) between the metric signal and the interleaving signal. As a weight we use the number of queries participating in the calculation of the metric signal (this number is different for each experiment). The results are presented in Figure 1. We can see that the *effort-based* metrics rrDBN and rrDCM are better at dealing with unjudged documents and are remarkably different from their *utility-based* counterparts; we will confirm this difference in Section 4.3. Another interesting observation can be made about the Precision and Precision2 metrics. Their behavior differs and, moreover, Precision has a negative correlation and this is not the case for Precision2. This seems to be due to the fact that unjudged documents are treated in the same way as the lowest relevance grade 0, whereas in fact they have a higher chance to belong to one of the top relevance grades: 92% of the documents in the top 10 have a relevance grade higher than 0, while only 23% have a relevance grade higher than 1.

As we can see from Figure 1, when we increase **#unjudged**, the maximum number of unjudged documents, to 4 or higher, the correlation drops for all of the metrics studied. This means that adding queries with highly incomplete judgements adds noise to the metric signals. The problem of unjudged documents has previously been studied by Sakai [34], and his proposed solution is to exclude unjudged documents from the ranked list and *condense* the remaining documents. Despite its heuristic nature, this idea actually leads to an increase in correlation for most of the metrics as shown in Figure 2. The exceptions from this rule are rrDBN and rrDCM that supposedly suffer most from the incorrect effort function values. For example, if we miss a judgement for the first document than for the second document we apply a $\frac{1}{1}$ discount instead of $\frac{1}{2}$ (see Equation (2)).

Thresholds

Even when we apply condensation, we still have a decrease in correlation values for high values of **#unjudged**. One way of dealing with this problem is to choose an optimal value of **#unjudged** and use it to get high correlations with interleaving outcomes. We propose a different way of dealing with this noisy data. Comparing systems A and B, we discard all queries with differences in metric values less than a

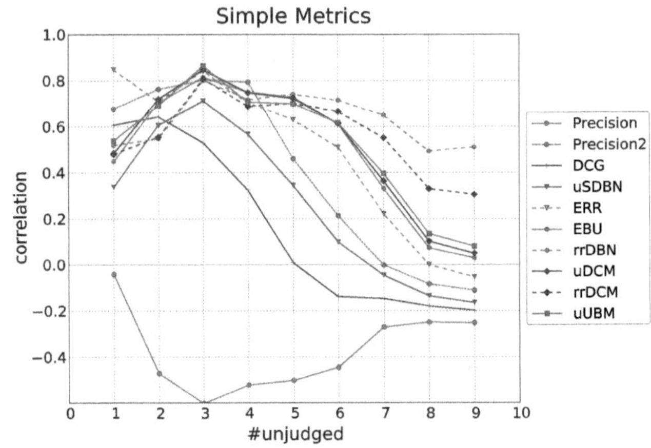

Figure 1: Pearson correlation between offline metrics and *interleaving signal*. Unjudged documents were treated as irrelevant.

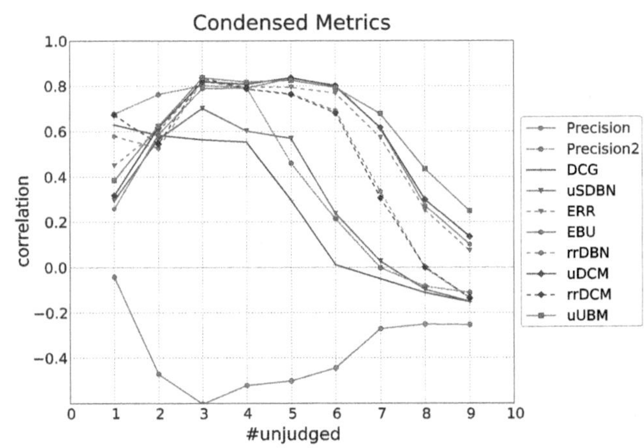

Figure 2: Pearson correlation between offline metrics and *interleaving signal*. Unjudged documents were skipped (ranked lists were condensed).

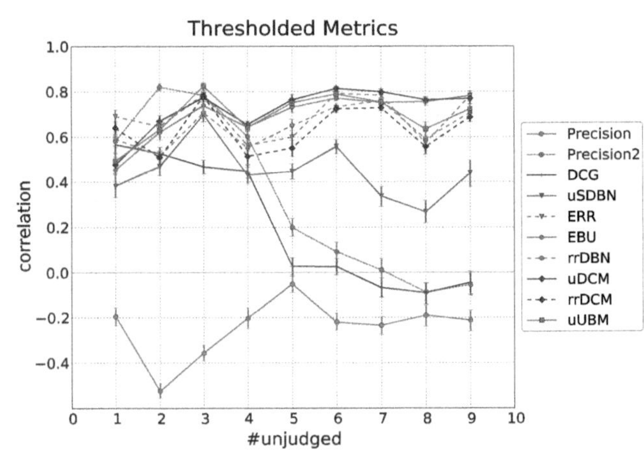

Figure 3: Pearson correlation between offline metrics with thresholds and *interleaving signal*. Unjudged documents were treated as irrelevant.

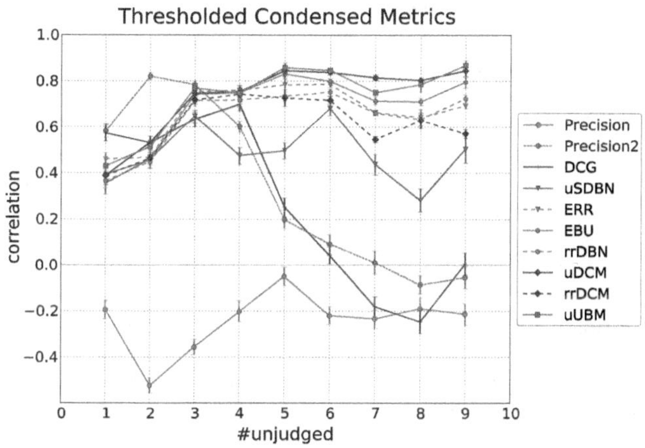

Figure 4: Pearson correlation between offline metrics with thresholds and *interleaving signal*. Unjudged documents were skipped (ranked lists were condensed).

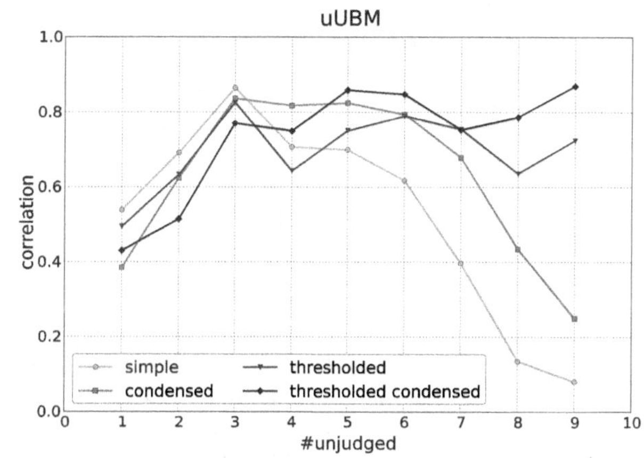

Figure 5: Pearson correlation between uUBM (in different variants) and *interleaving signal* .

threshold δ_m for each metric m:

$$MetricSignal = \frac{1}{|Q_{\delta_m}|} \sum_{q \in Q_{\delta_m}} (m(B,q) - m(A,q)),$$

where $Q_{\delta_m} = \{q \in Q \mid |m(B,q) - m(A,q)| \geqslant \delta_m\}$. This means that we use only some portion of the queries we have (up to 20%), but these are queries that strongly distinguish between systems. The idea is that by choosing an appropriate threshold δ_m we can tune a ranking system to produce the best correlation with interleaving outcomes. In order to test the idea we split our data (ten TDI experiments) into train and test set: we use the train set to choose the best threshold and the test set to compute the correlation scores.

While it would be natural to do a time-based train/test split, it appeared to be impractical with the data we have. Firstly, it was impossible to get training and test sets of reasonable sizes (either the training or the test set would consist of only 3 experiments which might give too noisy correlation values). Secondly, there are only few possible time-based splits so we are not able to assess statistical significance of the results. Instead, we used all possible 5/5 splits for our experiments, i.e., we take a subset of five experiments as a training set and the remaining five experiments as a test set. In total we had $C_{10}^5 = 252$ splits and corresponding correlation values. The correlation values were then averaged and error bars were computed using the bootstrap test at 95% confidence level and 1000 samples. Results are shown in Figures 3 and 4.

We can see in Figures 3 and 4 that the confidence intervals are quite narrow and most of the click model-based metrics continue to show high correlation scores when the value `#unjudged` is large. If we look at one of the best performing metrics, uUBM, we can see that thresholded variants are a bit worse for `#unjudged` lower than 5, while for `#unjudged` equal to 5 and higher the thresholded variants start dominating, reaching the highest point for `#unjudged` = 9 (see Figure 5).

In order to test significance of the differences in correlation values we used the 5/5 split procedure described above. Unlike what we did for *thresholded* and *thresholded condensed*, for the *simple* and *condensed* variants we only use the test set to determine the correlation and just ignored the training set as there is nothing we need to tune. The correlation values are then averaged and confidence intervals are computed using the bootstrap method with 1000 samples and 95% confidence level. Three highest correlation scores were shown by *thresholded condensed* variant of uUBM metric (for different values of `#unjudged`), while the correlation score for *thresholded condensed* uUBM (`#unjudged` = 9) is significantly higher than any other variant (*simple*, *condensed*, *thresholded*) of any metric. From Figures 1–4 we can also conclude that click model-based metrics in general show higher correlation values with the outcomes of interleaving experiments than traditional offline metrics, especially when we have many incomplete judgements (`#unjudged` > 5), which confirms the hypothesis formulated in the Introduction: *click model-based* metrics are better correlated with online measurements than traditional metrics. Another interesting observation is that for the *simple* and *condensed* variants there exist optimal values of the `#unjudged` parameter (3 and 5 respectively in our case). Conversely, for the *thresholded* and *thresholded condensed* variants it is more important to pick an appropriate metric and then use any value of `#unjudged` higher than 5.

4.2 Correlation with Absolute Online Metrics

Following the original work on ERR by Chapelle et al. [10] we also compared offline IR metrics by looking at their correlation with absolute click metrics. In our experiments we used the following metrics:

- MaxRR, MinRR, MeanRR – maximal, minimal, mean reciprocal ranks of the click. Following the work of Radlinski et al. [32] we exclude pages with no clicks to avoid correlation with UCTR.
- UCTR – binary value representing click (the opposite of abandonment).
- PLC – number of clicks divided by the position of the lowest click.

We did not include the Search Success (SS) metric considered by Chapelle et al. [10] as it uses relevances not only clicks. We also confirmed the findings of [10] that QCTR (clicks per session) has negative or close to zero correlation with all the editorial metrics and skipped it as well.

A *configuration* is a tuple that consists of a query and ten URLs of the top ranked documents presented to a user. For each configuration in our dataset we computed the values of absolute online and offline metrics. The vectors of these metric values are then used to compute Pearson correlation (unweighted). For our dataset we used clicks collected during a three-month period in 2012. Because we used a long period and hence had a sufficient amount of data, we were able to collect 12,155 configurations (corresponding to 411 unique queries) where all ten documents have relevance judgements.

The results are summarized in Table 2. A similar comparison was previously done by Chapelle et al. [10] for ERR and traditional offline metrics. The numbers they obtained are similar to ours. From the table we conclude that click model-based metrics show relatively high correlation scores while traditional offline metrics like DCG or Precision generally have lower correlations, which agrees with the results of the previous section. Using the bootstrap test (95% significance level, 1000 bootstrap samples) we confirmed that all the click model-based metrics show significantly higher correlation with all the online metrics than any of the traditional offline metrics.

As to the online metrics, we can see that the reciprocal rank family (MaxRR, MinRR, MeanRR) appears to be better correlated with the *effort-based* metrics (ERR, rrDBN, rrDCM), because the effort function used by these metrics is the reciprocal rank $\frac{1}{k}$ (see Equation 2). The same holds for PLC as it uses reciprocal rank of the lowest click that could be viewed as "satisfaction position" used by an effort-based metric. The differences between ERR and uSDBN, rrDBN and EBU, rrDCM and uDCM are statistically significant (using the same bootstrap test). Conversely, for the UCTR metric all the utility-based metrics show significantly higher correlation than corresponding effort-based metrics.

We also compared newly introduced click model-based metrics with older metrics: ERR (effort-based) and EBU (utility-based). The result of the comparison is marked as superscripts in the Table 2: the first superscript corresponds to ERR, the second one corresponds to EBU. The first (second) $\blacktriangle$ means that the metric is statistically significantly higher than ERR (EBU), $\blacktriangledown$ — significantly lower, "–" — no statistical difference can be found (95% significance level, bootstrap test). As we see, in most cases our new click metrics appear to be significantly better than the previously known ERR and EBU metrics, expect for UCTR measure, which does not account for clicks (rather for their absence) and hence obviously lacks the source of correlation with click-model based metrics. According to other metrics, rrDBN and rrDCM are better than ERR in 3 of 4 cases and better than EBU in all 4 cases, while uUBM is better than EBU in 4 of 4 cases.

Table 2: Pearson correlation between offline and absolute online metrics. Superscripts represent statistically significant difference from ERR and EBU.

	-RR				
	Max-	Min-	Mean-	UCTR	PLC
Precision	−0.117	−0.163	−0.155	0.042	−0.027
Precision2	0.026	0.093	0.075	0.092	0.094
DCG	0.178	0.243	0.237	0.163	0.245
ERR	0.378	0.471	0.469	0.199	0.399
EBU	0.374	0.467	0.464	0.198	0.397
rrDBN	$0.384^{\blacktriangle\blacktriangle}$	$0.475^{\blacktriangle\blacktriangle}$	$0.473^{\blacktriangle\blacktriangle}$	$0.194^{\blacktriangledown\blacktriangledown}$	$0.399^{-\blacktriangle}$
rrDCM	$0.387^{\blacktriangle\blacktriangle}$	$0.478^{\blacktriangle\blacktriangle}$	$0.476^{\blacktriangle\blacktriangle}$	$0.194^{\blacktriangledown\blacktriangledown}$	$0.400^{-\blacktriangle}$
uSDBN	$0.322^{\blacktriangledown\blacktriangledown}$	$0.412^{\blacktriangledown\blacktriangledown}$	$0.407^{\blacktriangledown\blacktriangledown}$	$0.206^{\blacktriangle\blacktriangle}$	$0.370^{\blacktriangledown\blacktriangledown}$
uDCM	$0.374^{\blacktriangledown\blacktriangledown}$	$0.466^{\blacktriangledown\blacktriangledown}$	$0.463^{\blacktriangledown\blacktriangledown}$	0.198^{--}	$0.396^{\blacktriangledown\blacktriangledown}$
uUBM	$0.377^{-\blacktriangle}$	$0.469^{\blacktriangledown\blacktriangle}$	$0.467^{\blacktriangledown\blacktriangle}$	0.198^{--}	$0.398^{-\blacktriangle}$

In general, all the absolute click metrics are poorly correlated with offline metrics—the correlation values are much lower than correlation with interleaving outcomes. As was shown by Radlinski et al. [32], absolute click metrics are worse at capturing user satisfaction than interleaving. That is why we propose to use the results of Section 4.1 as the main way to compare offline metrics with user behavior.

4.3 Correlation Between Offline Metrics

In order to compare offline metrics to each other in terms of ranking IR systems we used data from the TREC 2011 Web Track [16]. Participants of the TREC competition were offered a set of queries ("topics" in TREC parlance) and a set of documents for each query to rank. Each document was judged using a 4-grade scale.[5] For each metric we can build a list of system runs[6] ordered by the metric value averaged over queries. We then compute Kendall tau correlation scores between these ordered lists; they are summarized in Table 3. As was shown by Voorhees [38], metrics with correlation scores around 0.9 can be treated as very similar because this is the level of correlation one achieves when using the same metric but different judges. This level of correlation to distinguish equivalent metrics was also used in subsequent papers, for example [5, 7, 35, 37].

In Table 3 such metric pairs are marked in boldface. We see that all click model-based metrics are highly correlated within their group, *utility-based* or *effort-based*, while correlations of the two metrics based on the same model (uSDBN and ERR, EBU and rrDBN, uDCM and rrDCM) are lower.

4.4 Discriminative Power

Another measure frequently used for comparing metrics is the *discriminative power* by Sakai [33]. This measure is a bit controversial, because high values of discriminative power do not imply a good metric. Nevertheless, extremely low values of discriminative power can serve as an indication of a metric's poor ability to distinguish different rankings. As was shown in previous work (e.g., [15, 36]) discriminative power is highly consistent with respect to statistical test choice. Given this fact we focus on a bootstrap test as it makes fewer assumptions about the underlying distribution. Results based on the same TREC 2011 Web Track data as used in the previous section are summarized in Table 4. As expected, highly correlated metric pairs (e.g., (rrDBN, rrDCM) and (EBU, uDCM)) have similar discriminative power.

Another observation to be made is that the *effort-based* metrics ERR, rrDBN and rrDCM have a lower discriminative power than the *utility-based* metrics uSDBN, EBU and

[5]Initially, a 5-grade scale was listed on a TREC 2011 description page, but in the end a 4-grade scale was used for evaluation. As in the `trec_eval` evaluation tool we do not distinguish between *Irrelevant* and *Spam* documents.

[6]In total we have 62 runs submitted by 16 teams.

Table 3: Correlation between offline metrics (using the TREC 2011 runs). Values higher than 0.9 are marked in boldface.

	Precision2	DCG	ERR	uSDBN	EBU	rrDBN	uDCM	rrDCM	uUBM
Precision	0.649	0.841	0.597	0.730	0.568	0.397	0.562	0.442	0.537
Precision2	–	0.785	0.663	0.780	0.675	0.526	0.693	0.551	0.681
DCG	–	–	0.740	0.857	0.711	0.530	0.704	0.592	0.685
ERR	–	–	–	0.807	**0.919**	0.754	**0.902**	0.826	0.888
uSDBN	–	–	–	–	0.792	0.585	0.794	0.638	0.754
EBU	–	–	–	–	–	0.788	**0.970**	0.822	**0.930**
rrDBN	–	–	–	–	–	–	0.786	**0.917**	0.807
uDCM	–	–	–	–	–	–	–	0.813	**0.947**
rrDCM	–	–	–	–	–	–	–	–	0.841

Table 4: Discriminative power of different metrics according to the bootstrap test (confidence level 95%).

Metric	Discriminative Power
Precision	50.1 %
Precision2	30.8 %
DCG	48.6 %
ERR	39.3 %
uSDBN	51.1 %
EBU	35.1 %
rrDBN	21.1 %
uDCM	34.7 %
rrDCM	26.0 %
uUBM	33.3 %

uDCM, respectively. This is probably due to the fact that "position discount" for the effort-based metrics goes to zero faster than for the utility-based metrics and hence they are less sensitive to changes in the bottom of the ranked list.

5. CONCLUSION AND FUTURE WORK

In this paper we proposed a framework of *click model-based* metrics to build an offline evaluation measure on top of any click model. Answering the research questions outlined in the introduction we can say that

- *Click model-based* metrics generally differ from traditional offline metrics, while they are quite similar to each other. Moreover, *utility-based* metrics are significantly different from *effort-based* metrics in terms of system ranking.
- All *click model-based* metrics generally show high agreement with the outcomes of online *interleaving* experiments and relatively high agreement with *absolute* click measures. However, correlation with absolute metrics is low for all offline metrics (both traditional and click model-based) compared to the correlation with interleaving outcomes.
- Unjudged documents may decrease correlation with *interleaving* outcomes but by using thresholds we can overcome this issue for click model-based metrics.
- *Condensation* and *thresholding* of offline metrics are effective ways of stabilizing correlations with *interleaving* outcomes in the presence of unjudged documents.

One natural extension of our framework of *click model-based* metrics can be adding more signals from the assessors. For example, we can ask assessors to judge not only documents, but their snippets as well (a practice already in place at commercial search engines). By using this we can drop the assumption that snippet attractiveness is a function of document relevance as was assumed by the click model-based metrics. While attractiveness is highly correlated with document relevance [37], it is essential to use real attractiveness judgements when we need to evaluate a snippet algorithm, not only ranking. It might be interesting to incorporate attractiveness judgements into metrics and re-evaluate our click model-based metrics using proposed modifications.

Another interesting direction is the area of *good abandonments*. Li et al. [29] report that some snippets might be good enough to answer the user query directly on a search engine result page. As was shown in [13], one can ask human judges to indicate whether a snippet contains an answer to the user query (fully or partially). That task appeared to be relatively easy for assessors. Given such judgements, one can modify any evaluation metric by adding additional gain from the snippets that contain an answer to the user's information need. To convert this into a metric, we assign some gain to the documents that were clicked ($C_k = 1$) and some gain to the documents that were only examined, but did not attract the user ($E_i = 1$, $A_k = 0$).

Adapting click models for the unjudged/unknown documents is also an interesting direction. For example, we could modify a click model by adding probability of a document being skipped because it is unjudged. This question requires further investigation and we leave it as future work.

In our work we argued that offline metrics should be better correlated with interleaving outcomes. However, we might want to have a metric that correlates with user satisfaction. Some steps towards this problem have been taken in early work by Huffman and Hochster [25] where user studies were performed to analyse the meaning of editorial *relevance* for real users. It would be interesting to perform a study of this type to compare offline metrics.

Acknowledgements

We would like to thank Katja Hofmann, Maria-Hendrike Peetz and our anonymous reviewers for reading the paper and making useful comments and suggestions.

This research was partially supported by the European Community's Seventh Framework Programme (FP7/2007-2013) under grant agreements nr 258191 (PROMISE Network of Excellence) and 288024 (LiMoSINe project), the Netherlands Organisation for Scientific Research (NWO) under project nrs 640.004.802, 727.011.005, 612.001.116, HOR-11-10, the Center for Creation, Content and Technology (CCCT), the BILAND project funded by the CLARIN-nl program, the Dutch national program COMMIT, the ESF Research Network Program ELIAS, the Elite Network Shifts project funded by the Royal Dutch Academy of Sciences (KNAW), and the Netherlands eScience Center under project number 027.012.105.

REFERENCES

[1] K. Ali and C. Chang. On the relationship between click-rate and relevance for search engines. *WIT Trans. on Inform. and Comm. Technol.*, 1, June 2006.

[2] J. Allan, B. Carterette, J. Aslam, and V. Pavlu. Million Query Track 2007 Overview. Technical report, DTIC Document, 2007.

[3] L. Azzopardi, M. de Rijke, and K. Balog. Building simulated queries for known-item topics: an analysis using six european languages. In *SIGIR*, 2007.

[4] R. Berendsen, E. Tsagkias, M. de Rijke, and E. Meij. Generating pseudo test collections for learning to rank scientific articles. In *CLEF*, 2012.

[5] C. Buckley and E. M. Voorhees. Retrieval evaluation with incomplete information. In *SIGIR*, 2004.

[6] B. Carterette. System effectiveness, user models, and user utility: a conceptual framework for investigation. In *SIGIR*, 2011.

[7] B. Carterette and J. Allan. Incremental test collections. In *CIKM*, 2005.

[8] B. Carterette, V. Pavlu, and E. Kanoulas. If I had a million queries. In *Advances in Information Retrieval*, 2009.

[9] O. Chapelle and Y. Zhang. A dynamic bayesian network click model for web search ranking. In *WWW*. ACM, 2009.

[10] O. Chapelle, D. Metzler, Y. Zhang, and P. Grinspan. Expected reciprocal rank for graded relevance. In *CIKM*. ACM, 2009.

[11] O. Chapelle, T. Joachims, F. Radlinski, and Y. Yue. Large-scale validation and analysis of interleaved search evaluation. *ACM Trans. Inform. Systems*, 2012.

[12] D. Chen, W. Chen, and H. Wang. Beyond ten blue links: enabling user click modeling in federated web search. In *WSDM*. ACM, 2012.

[13] A. Chuklin and P. Serdyukov. Good abandonments in factoid queries. In *WWW*, 2012.

[14] A. Chuklin, P. Serdyukov, and M. de Rijke. Using Intent Information to Model User Behavior in Diversified Search. In *ECIR*, 2013.

[15] C. L. A. Clarke, N. Craswell, and I. Soboroff. A comparative analysis of cascade measures for novelty and diversity. In *WSDM*. ACM, 2011.

[16] C. L. A. Clarke, N. Craswell, I. Soboroff, and E. M. Voorhees. Overview of the TREC 2011 Web Track. In *TREC 2011*. NIST, 2012.

[17] C. W. Cleverdon, J. Mills, and M. Keen. Factors determining the performance of indexing systems. In *ASLIB Cranfield project*. 1966.

[18] N. Craswell, O. Zoeter, M. Taylor, and B. Ramsey. An experimental comparison of click position-bias models. In *WSDM*. ACM, 2008.

[19] G. Dupret and B. Piwowarski. A user browsing model to predict search engine click data from past observations. In *SIGIR*. ACM, 2008.

[20] F. Guo, C. Liu, A. Kannan, T. Minka, M. Taylor, Y.-M. Wang, and C. Faloutsos. Click chain model in web search. In *WWW*. ACM, 2009.

[21] F. Guo, C. Liu, and Y. Wang. Efficient multiple-click models in web search. In *WSDM*. ACM, 2009.

[22] K. Hofmann, S. Whiteson, and M. de Rijke. A probabilistic method for inferring preferences from clicks. In *CIKM*. ACM, 2011.

[23] K. Hofmann, A. Schuth, S. Whiteson, and M. de Rijke. Reusing Historical Interaction Data for Faster Online Learning to Rank for IR. In *WSDM*, 2013.

[24] J. Huang, R. W. White, G. Buscher, and K. Wang. Improving searcher models using mouse cursor activity. In *SIGIR*. ACM, 2012.

[25] S. B. Huffman and M. Hochster. How well does result relevance predict session satisfaction? In *SIGIR*, 2007.

[26] K. Järvelin and J. Kekäläinen. Cumulated gain-based evaluation of IR techniques. *ACM Trans. Inform. Systems*, 20(4), 2002.

[27] T. Joachims. Optimizing search engines using clickthrough data. In *KDD*. ACM, 2002.

[28] R. Kohavi, R. Longbotham, D. Sommerfield, and R. M. Henne. Controlled experiments on the web: survey and practical guide. *Data Mining and Knowledge Discovery*, 18(1), July 2008.

[29] J. Li, S. Huffman, and A. Tokuda. Good abandonment in mobile and PC internet search. In *SIGIR*, 2009.

[30] C. Liu, F. Guo, and C. Faloutsos. BBM. In *KDD*. ACM, June 2009.

[31] F. Radlinski and N. Craswell. Comparing the sensitivity of information retrieval metrics. In *SIGIR*. ACM, 2010.

[32] F. Radlinski, M. Kurup, and T. Joachims. How does clickthrough data reflect retrieval quality? In *CIKM'08*. ACM, 2008.

[33] T. Sakai. Evaluating evaluation metrics based on the bootstrap. In *SIGIR*, 2006.

[34] T. Sakai. Alternatives to Bpref. In *SIGIR*. ACM, 2007.

[35] M. Sanderson and H. Joho. Forming test collections with no system pooling. In *SIGIR*, 2004.

[36] M. D. Smucker and C. L. A. Clarke. Time-Based Calibration of Effectiveness Measures. In *SIGIR*, 2012.

[37] A. Turpin, F. Scholer, K. Jarvelin, M. Wu, and J. S. Culpepper. Including summaries in system evaluation. In *SIGIR*, 2009.

[38] E. M. Voorhees. Variations in relevance judgments and the measurement of retrieval effectiveness. *Information processing & management*, 36, 2000.

[39] E. Yilmaz, M. Shokouhi, N. Craswell, and S. Robertson. Expected browsing utility for web search evaluation. In *CIKM*. ACM, 2010.

[40] Y. Yue, Y. Gao, O. Chapelle, Y. Zhang, and T. Joachims. Learning more powerful test statistics for click-based retrieval evaluation. In *SIGIR*, 2010.

[41] Y. Zhang, W. Chen, D. Wang, and Q. Yang. User-click modeling for understanding and predicting search-behavior. In *KDD*. ACM, 2011.

Incorporating Vertical Results into Search Click Models

Chao Wang[1], Yiqun Liu[1], Min Zhang[1], Shaoping Ma[1], Meihong Zheng[2], Jing Qian[2], Kuo Zhang[1]
[1] State Key Laboratory of Intelligent Technology and Systems,
[1] Tsinghua National Laboratory for Information Science and Technology,
1 CS&T Department, Tsinghua University, Beijing, 100084, China P.R.
2 Department of Psychology, Tsinghua University, Beijing, 100084, China P.R.
chaowang0707@gmail.com

ABSTRACT

In modern search engines, an increasing number of search result pages (SERPs) are federated from multiple specialized search engines (called *verticals*, such as Image or Video). As an effective approach to interpret users' click-through behavior as feedback information, most click models were designed to reduce the position bias and improve ranking performance of ordinary search results, which have homogeneous appearances. However, when vertical results are combined with ordinary ones, significant differences in presentation may lead to user behavior biases and thus failure of state-of-the-art click models. With the help of a popular commercial search engine in China, we collected a large scale log data set which contains behavior information on both vertical and ordinary results. We also performed eye-tracking analysis to study user's real-world examining behavior. According these analysis, we found that different result appearances may cause different behavior biases both for vertical results (local effect) and for the whole result lists (global effect). These biases include: examine bias for vertical results (especially those with multimedia components), trust bias for result lists with vertical results, and a higher probability of result revisitation for vertical results. Based on these findings, a novel click model considering these biases besides position bias was constructed to describe interaction with SERPs containing verticals. Experimental results show that the new Vertical-aware Click Model (VCM) is better at interpreting user click behavior on federated searches in terms of both log-likelihood and perplexity than existing models.

Categories and Subject Descriptors

H.3.3 [Information Storage and Retrieval]: Information Search and Retrieval

General Terms

Algorithms, Measurement, Experimentation

Keywords

Federated search, Click model, User behavior analysis

1. INTRODUCTION

Millions of users submit queries to search engines every day. As the web search click logs reflect users' preferences regarding search result documents, these logs are considered to be invaluable sources of information for improving search performance. The information stored in click-through behavior data can be used in many research areas such as click-through rate (CTR) prediction, web search ranking, query recommendation, and so on. With the help of these applications, search engine can better help users to satisfy their information needs.

While analyzing click-through data, key concerns include how to construct a click model to interpret users' examination and clicking preferences and how to obtain unbiased document relevance estimations. Much effort has been made on this research topic. State-of-art click models such as user browsing model [3], click chain model [5] and dynamic Bayesian network click model [4] have shown their power in fitting the real-world data and predicting future clicks. Although these existing click models have gained much success in modeling ordinary search results, they were not designed for result lists with non-Web-page results (or *verticals*), which were provided by multiple heterogeneous vertical search engines and incorporated into a large number of SERPs. According to their appearances, we classify vertical results into three categories:

- Text vertical: The text vertical is made up of a few blue links and textual snippets, such as news search results or wiki information shown in SERPs.
- Multimedia vertical: The multimedia vertical is made up of a group of multimedia components, such as video or photo search results.
- Application vertical: The application vertical contains a button or a form embedded into SERPs to help users finish certain tasks, such as a download button or an exchange rate calculator.

Figure 1 shows examples of these verticals. We can see that the vertical results have different layout and presentation forms compared to ordinary search results. It is reasonable to suppose that they may lead to different user examination behavior and click preference. Therefore, most of previous click models, which assume all results are homogeneous, may not describe user behavior on these SERPs correctly. Chen et al. [7] made the first step to model user behavior in vertical results. They found that users were more likely to examine the vertical and the ordinary web documents nearby. They also indicated that users are more likely to be satisfied with vertical results and end the whole search session. However, although they also divided verticals into several kinds, they didn't take into account that different vertical types influence users' behavior differently.

With the help of a popular commercial search engine in China, we collected a large number of log data which contain behavior information on both vertical and ordinary results (see Section 3). By analyzing the logs we found that more than 80% SERPs of this Chinese commercial search engines contain verticals, and different result appearances caused different behavior biases both for the vertical results (local effect) and for the whole result lists (global effect). So when analyzing user behavior for modern search engines, taking verticals into account is very important. We also performed eye-tracking experiments to look into users' actual

SIGIR'13, July 28–August 1, 2013, Dublin, Ireland.

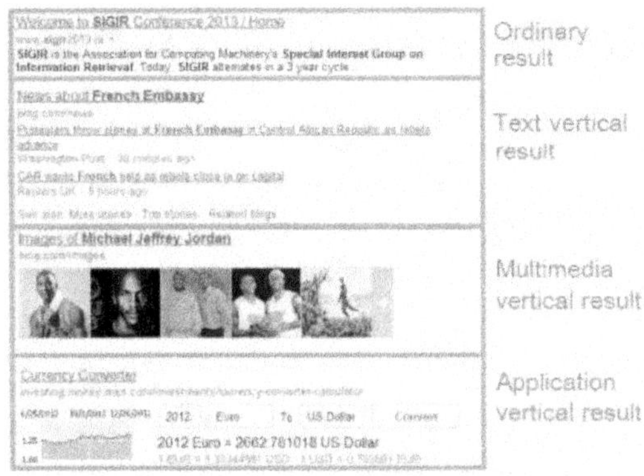

Figure 1. Different kinds of vertical results federated into SERPs (with Bing.com as an example)

examining behaviors on vertical and ordinary results. Based on these findings, a novel click model named Vertical-aware Click Model (VCM) was constructed to take these biases into consideration. The major contributions of this work include:

1. Vertical results are grouped into three categories according to their appearances on SERPs. How users interact with these vertical results and other results on a same SERP are analyzed in terms of both large scale click-through log and laboratory eye-tracking analysis.
2. User behavior bias on different kinds of vertical results are concluded which affect users' examination or click behavior either globally (for the whole SERP) or locally (for a particular vertical result).
3. A novel click model named Vertical-aware Click Model (VCM) is constructed which takes these user behavior biases into consideration. The new model is able to incorporate these biases into a calculable framework and improve click prediction performances.

The rest of the paper is organized as follows: we first provide an overview of related work in Section 2. The user behaviors in click logs are investigated in Section 3. In Section 4, an eye-tracking experiment is designed to see users' examining behavior on different vertical categories. Based on click log analysis and eye-tracking experiment, we incorporate our observations into four bias types and build Vertical-aware Click Model to model users' search behavior in Section 5. Section 6 is devoted to experimental studies. The paper is concluded in Section 7.

2. RELATED WORK

2.1 Click Model

Granka et al. [1] were among the first to carry out eye-tracking experiments to analyze users' decision process as they scan SERPs. Joachims et al. [10, 11] compared the implicit click feedbacks against the explicit relevance judgments and defined *position bias* in users' decision processes, namely, that documents appearing in higher positions always attract more clicks, even when they are less relevant than documents in lower positions. Richardson et al. [2] further proposed *examination hypothesis* to define such kind of position bias in Web search user behavior. Their hypothesis stated that a Web document must be examined before clicked, and user-perceived document relevance was defined conditional probability of being clicked. Craswell et al. [8] further proposed *cascade model* for describing where the first click happened when users linearly looked through search results. More recent works have tried to improve click models by incorporating practical behavior hypotheses. The user browsing model (UBM) [3] states that the probability of examining a document is not a constant but affected by clicks before this document. The dynamic Bayesian networks model (DBN) [4] states that users choose to examine the next document if they are unsatisfied with the clicked document. The click chain model (CCM) [5] assumes that the probability to examine the next document after a click depends on the relevance of the clicked document and user-behavior parameters. Chen et al. [6] proposed a task-centric click model (TCM) to model user click behavior in task level. They indicated that users tend to express their information needs incrementally in a task and thus tend to click fresh documents that are not included in the results of previous queries. They also found that click behavior in industrial search engines is often noisy and proposed a Noise-aware Click Model (NCM) [23] to characterize the noise degree of a click. To a certain extent, these models succeed in interpreting search users' click-through behavior and they also help improve the performance of relevance estimation based on implicit feedback information. More mathematic details of click model related to our work will be presented in section 5.

2.2 Federated Search

Federated search integrates vertical results into web searches. Heterogeneous search results are promising for promoting users' search experiences.

Most prior work focused on predicting which verticals are relevant to a query (*vertical selection*). Diaz et al. [14] first carried out a system to collect news dynamically and aggregated them into web search results. Arguello et al. [15, 16] showed that in vertical selection, query-logs are useful. They proposed a vertical ranking method by the query likelihood given the vertical's query-log language model. They also attempted to reuse training data from a set of existing verticals to obtain a predictive model for a new vertical. K Zhou et al. [19] presented an approach that considers both reward and risk within the task of vertical selection.

Some work focused on merging documents retrieved from multiple ranked lists of selected information sources into a single list (*result merging*). Arguello et al. [17, 18] proposed and three learning based approaches and concluded that the best approaches are those that allow the learning algorithm to learn a vertical-specific relationship between features and relevance. Dzung Hong et al. [20] studied on existing result merging methods and showed that learning a set of combination weights for multiple centralized retrieval algorithms is not flexible enough to deal with heterogeneous information sources. They proposed a mixture probabilistic model to learn more appropriate combination weights with respect to different types of information sources.

2.3 Web Search Biases

When using search engine on the web, a lot of potential biases will affect user's searching behavior. The most famous bias is *position bias* [10, 11] which means documents appearing in higher positions always attracted more clicks. Many click models were proposed to eliminate this influence as shown in Section 2.1. Judit et al. [21] studied user preferences for different orderings of search results and confirmed that users tend to choose one of the first results on the results page. They also observed a *site reputation bias* that pages from well-known sites are considered favorably by the subjects. Beyond the *position bias*, Y Yue et al. [22] quantified the effect of bolded keyword matches in the title and abstracts to measure the attractiveness of search results.

Most of these prior work adopted a lot of information in SERP organization and users' search behavior. However, to the best of our knowledge, few previous studies have considered federated search and user click behavior. Chen et al. [7] made the first step to construct click models for federated results. They tried to automatically infer heterogeneous documents relevance based on user click behavior. However, they didn't look into different types of vertical results as well as the examination behavior on federated results. In this paper, we make a further step to analyze the influence on users' click preference and examining sequence when adding different types of result presentation forms into SERP and build a click model that more accurately reflects users' real search behaviors.

3. CLICK-THROUGH DATA ANALYSIS

To construct an effective model for federated searches, we look into real-world search user behavior log data and compare ordinary Web results with different kinds of verticals using a number of click-through behavior features.

The adopted search log data come from one of the most popular commercial search engines in China. The data set contains 53,080,107 query sessions with 15,149,469 distinct queries during the time period from April 1st to April 3rd, 2012. At the session level, it contains 19.22% sessions with no vertical result and 80.78% with one or more vertical results. At the query level, 18.43% queries contain no vertical result while 81.57% contain one or more vertical results. We can see that a majority of SERPs contain vertical results, which makes the construction of a vertical-aware click model quite necessary. For the purpose of avoiding the combinatorial effects of multiple vertical results, in this paper we only consider the sessions with one vertical result and leave multi-vertical session processing as future work.

After manually labeling the category of most common tags which this Chinese commercial search engine uses to identify verticals, we found that most verticals fall into one of these three categories: text vertical, multimedia vertical and application vertical. Therefore, we focus our analysis on these kinds of verticals, which are also most popular ones for other search engines as far as we know. In this Chinese commercial search engine, each result page contains at most 10 results (including verticals) by default, unlike some other search engines, such as Bing, which inserts verticals into ordinary results and thus increases the number of results per page. But we don't think this will greatly affect the reliability of results in this paper.

3.1 Global Statistics

Firstly, we study the global influence of different kinds of verticals. Figure 2 shows the amount of sessions in which vertical result is placed from rank 1 to rank 10. We can see that text verticals are almost uniformly distributed to each position except that there are a bit more in position 1 and 9. The amount of sessions for multimedia and application verticals decreases when it comes to a lower ranking position, especially for application verticals. We can see that application vertical is barely placed at rank 10 (only less than 100 cases in our log data set which contains over 53 million sessions). To keep the statistical meaning of our analysis, statistics which base count is less than 1,000 are abandoned in the following part of the paper.

To confirm whether there is a global influence of vertical result to other ordinary web results on a same page, we also look into the average CTR of the first page when vertical result appears. In Figure 3, average CTR means the average click-through rate of all results on the SERP; the dotted line shows the average CTR of SERPs without verticals. From this figure, we observe that the existence of vertical results leads to differences in average CTR. When there is a multimedia vertical in a SERP, the average CTR is higher than that of SERP without verticals. On the contrary, average CTR becomes lower in the existence of application verticals. It indicates that users are more likely to click on some results when there is a multimedia vertical in SERP. The average CTR scores are even higher when multimedia results are placed at positions 6-9, which are perhaps caused by the fact that ordinary results on these relatively lower positions will not be clicked while multimedia ones attract user clicks even in these positions. The drop in average CTR of application verticals may be related with the fact that they directly help most users to finish their tasks without having to look into or clicking on other results.

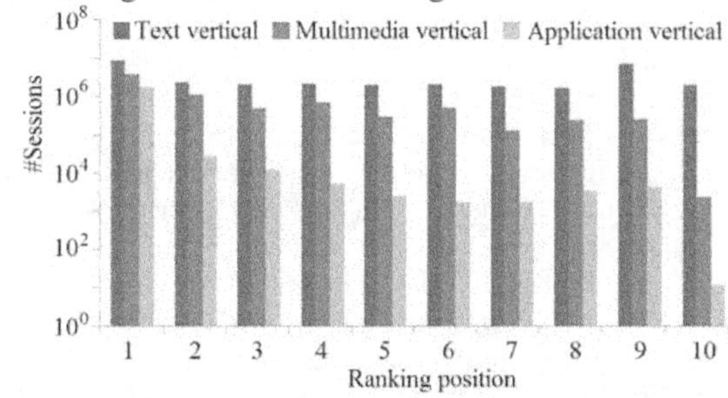

Figure 2. Amount of sessions in which different kinds of vertical results appear from rank 1 to rank 10

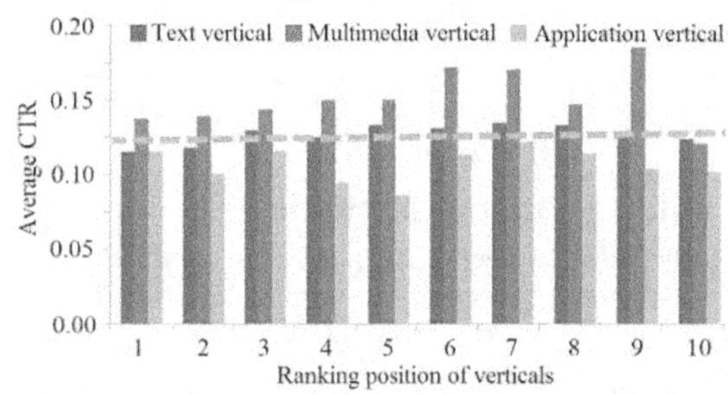

Figure 3. Average CTR of the first page when different kinds of vertical results appear from rank 1 to rank 10

3.2 Click Position Statistics

To further analyze the impact of verticals on SERPs, we compare the click distribution (CD) [9] of both vertical and ordinary results to see whether users are more willing to interact with verticals. Click distribution is defined as the degree of click concentration compared with other results on a same page at query level and it is commonly adopted in click through behavior analysis. We take the average click distribution of each result in SERPs without verticals as the baseline. For each vertical class, we calculate the average click distribution for each position and compare it with the baseline score in the same ranking position.

Heat maps in Figure 4 are used to show the differences between vertical results and baselines using brighter/darker color as a sign for larger/smaller differences, respectively. In this figure, the category axis shows where the vertical result is placed in SERP; while the value axis represents result positions in SERP. So the grid with coordinate (i, j) in this figure shows the j-th result document's CD score when a certain kind of vertical result is placed at the i-th position. Brighter color means a larger difference compared with the CD on SERP without verticals. From the Figure 4(a), we can see that the click distribution of SERP with text vertical is almost the same as SERP with no verticals. Only the CD values for text vertical results themselves (see the diagonal line from upper left to lower right) are slightly higher. Figure 4(b) shows that multimedia vertical result (also see the diagonal line) are with higher CD scores than ordinary results in the same position, which also shows a sign of user preference for this kind of vertical results. Figure 4c shows that the top-ranked application vertical results also get higher click concentration while application verticals placed at lower positions are with almost the same CD values as ordinary results.

From the above observations in Figure 4 we can see that the CD values of multimedia vertical as well as top-ranked application vertical are higher than those of ordinary results in same positions. When we look into users' click through behavior more detailed, we found that other click behaviors on vertical results are also different from ordinary ones. In Figure 5, first click distribution means how many percentages of users' first clicks are on a certain position. From Figure 5 we can see that when text or application vertical appears at the first position, it attracts a lot more first clicks than ordinary results do. For multimedia vertical, it attracts more clicks not only when it is placed at the top of the result list, but also when it is ranked among the first 5 or 6 results, which usually means in the first screen of results without scrolling.

According to the comparison of CD and first click distribution within different kinds, we can see that user behaves differently on click preference with different kinds of verticals. For multimedia class, users may pay more attention to multimedia vertical result. They are more likely to see the vertical result directly and click it. While for text class and application class, users will pay more attention to vertical result only if the vertical is placed at the top-ranking positions in SERP. This can be regarded a sign for larger examination probabilities for multimedia verticals and top-ranked text/application verticals, which we will show explicitly via eye-tracking statistics in Section 4.

3.3 Click Sequence Statistics

We have shown in Section 3.2 that multimedia verticals as well as top-ranked text/application verticals are higher in the values of either CD or first click contribution. We also want to find out what happens after users click on these vertical results. How they interact with other results on SERPs also plays an important part in the construction of a vertical aware click model.

Compared with the sequential clicking behavior which is already well-defined by existing click models, we focus on the possible revisiting behavior after users click on vertical results. From Figure 4 and 5 we can see that there are only slight chances that text/application verticals are firstly clicked when they are not placed at the 1st position. Therefore, most result revisits after clicking vertical results first should come from queries with multimedia results.

In Figure 6, revisit means that a user clicks on another higher ranked result after having clicked on a lower result. We can see from this figure that top documents before the vertical result cause higher revisit proportion. Figure 7 further shows that the second click after clicking a multimedia vertical tends to be on the 1st ranking position. It means that when users first click a multimedia vertical, there is a large chance that they continue their search session by revisiting the results that they previous skipped.

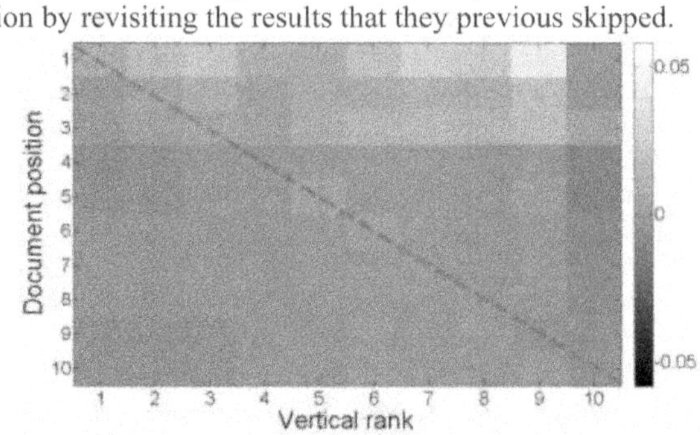

Figure 6. Revisit click distribution when vertical result appears from rank 1 to rank 10 compared with SERPs with no verticals. (Brighter color means a higher revisit probability compared with SERPs with no verticals)

According to the comparison of revisit distribution and second click position distribution to those of the ordinary class, we get a relatively clear picture on how users interact with SERPs with multimedia verticals. We may conclude that for result lists with multimedia vertical results, users have a probability to directly examine and click on the vertical result and then scan back to the top of SERP. It looks like that although multimedia results interrupt the normal search interaction process because they are attractive with image or video contents, people will resume the interrupted session by starting from the top of the result list again.

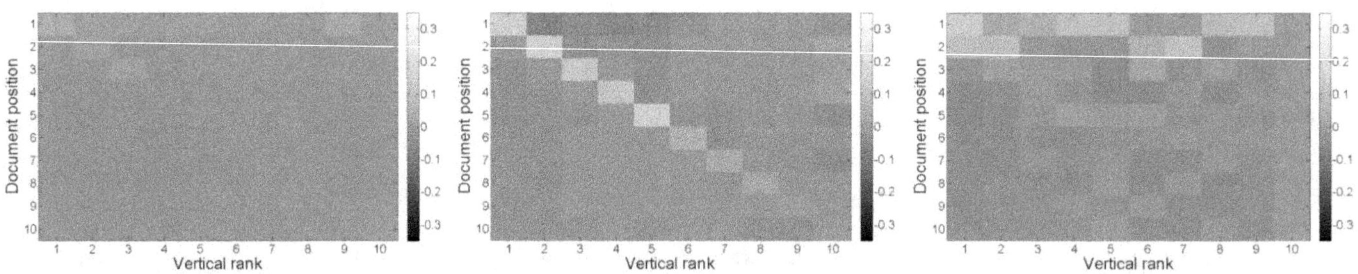

(a) (b) (c)

Figure 4. Average click distribution of SERPs with (a) text (b) multimedia (c) application vertical when vertical result appears from rank 1 to rank 10 compared with SERPs with no verticals. (Brighter color means a higher CD value)

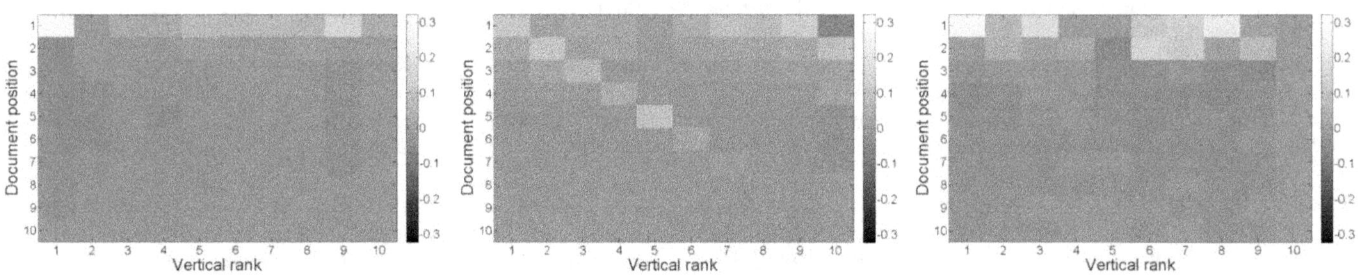

(a) (b) (c)

Figure 5. Average first click distribution of SERPs with (a) text (b) multimedia (c) application vertical when vertical result appears from rank 1 to rank 10 compared with SERPs with no verticals. (Brighter color means a higher first click probability)

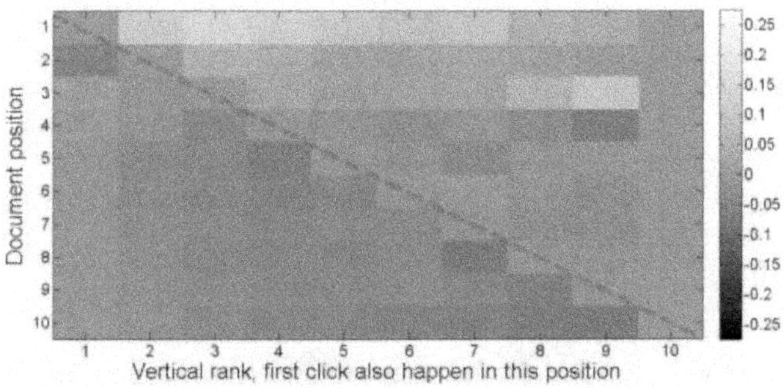

Figure 7. Average second click distribution of SERPs after first clicking a multimedia vertical. (Brighter color means a higher second click probability compared with SERPs with no verticals)

3.4 Log Data Analysis Findings

In summary, we can conclude the influence of vertical results on users' click-through behavior into four aspects:

CT 1. Different verticals have different global influence on users' clicking preference. Multimedia vertical increases global CTR while application vertical decreases global CTR.

CT 2. Click distribution of multimedia vertical results as well as top-ranked application vertical results are higher than ordinary results at same ranking positions.

CT 3. Multimedia vertical which are at the first screen and text/application vertical results which are ranked 1st attract more first clicks than ordinary results.

CT 4. After clicking a multimedia vertical result first, there is probability that users revisit results ranked higher than the vertical starting from the very beginning of the ranking list.

4. EYE-TRACKING ANALYSIS

After analyzing click-through behavior from search engine click logs, we conclude four main influences when different vertical results are federated into SERPs. However, click preference of users can be extracted directly from the click logs, while the examining behavior remains unknown from the click logs. Therefore, we designed an eye-tracking experiment to investigate how users examine SERPs with vertical results.

4.1 Eye-tracking Data Collecting

The following environment is designed to resemble the typical utilization of a WWW search engine. Subjects are asked to search 20 given queries one by one using the same search engine that helped us to collect log data as described in Section 3. Queries are selected from the same click log data set. Among these 20 queries, 5 of them contain no vertical result in their SERPs (ordinary class), the other 15 queries are assigned exactly 1 vertical result in their SERPs. Query No. 6-10 are with text verticals; 11-15 are with multimedia verticals while 16-20 are with application verticals, as shown in Table 1. Each of these queries is also assigned a description text to avoid possible ambiguities. There are no restrictions on subjects' click actions. Subjects are told that the experiment looks into how people search on the Web, but are not told that we were specifically interested in their examining behavior on vertical results of the search engine.

We recruit 23 subjects with cash compensation for their participation. All of these subjects are undergraduate students from a university and indicate at least a general familiarity with search engine interface.

Due to the inability of precisely calibrated eye tracking for one subject, comprehensive eye movement data is recorded for 22 of them. The gender distribution is split between 18 males and 5 females (typical for most departments in the university).

Table 1. Search queries adopted in the eye-tracking experiment (N, I and T represent Navigational, Informational and Transactional queries, respectively)

Query	Description	Intent	Type
4399 弹弹堂	An online game site	N	Ordinary
王立军最新消息	Recent information about Lijun Wang	I	
武道至尊免费下载	Free download of a novel	T	
大连实德总裁亲戚名单	Family information of a famous entrepreneur	I	
吞噬星空最新章节列表	Recent update of a science fiction novel	T	
重生之鸿蒙无极神诀	The name of a novel	T	Text Vertical
日本预测 9 级地震	Earthquake prediction for Japan	I	
优酷网看古装电视剧婚姻向右浪漫向左	A TV series at youku.com	T	
北京出事谣言	Political rumors in Beijing	I	
传奇私服发布网	An online game	N	
果宝特攻第二部全集	Resource of a Comic TV series	T	Multi-media vertical
马布里老婆的照片+图	Picture of a famous CBA basketball player's wife	I	
qq 头像闪图	Multimedia plugin for an online chatting software	T	
葫芦娃全集	A Chinese Comic TV series	T	
wwe 美国职业摔角 sd	Video of WWE	T	
快播播放器下载	Software download	T	Appli-cation Vertical
百度影音	Software download	T	
火车票网上订票官网	Official website for train tickets reservation	N	
vagaa	Software download	T	
飞信下载 2012 正式版官方下载	Software download	T	

The manipulations to the result pages were performed by a transfer server which shows exactly the same SERPs as the original search engine except the domain name. The server automatically eliminated all advertising content, so that the SERPs for all subjects would look as uniform as possible, with approximately the same amount of results appearing within the first scroll screen. When a subject searches for a query, if the SERP contains a vertical result, the vertical result position will be randomly placed by the server at:

1. Position 1 (top of the first screen).
2. Position 3 (middle of the first screen).
3. Position 5 (bottom of the first screen).
4. Position 10 (out of the first screen and bottom of the first SERP which can be seen only by mouse scrolling down).

None of the changes were detectable by the subjects. While being asked after their query sessions, none of the subjects suspect any manipulation. This server is also used to log all click-through behavior and all SERPs subjects visit.

All subjects' eye movements are recorded using a SMI RED250 eye-tracker, which utilizes infrared to reconstruct the subjects' eye position. BeGaze Experimental Center is used for the simultaneous acquisition and analysis of the subjects' eye movements. With this tracking device, the following indicators of ocular behaviors are recorded: fixations, saccades, pupil dilation, and scan paths [12]. Among these behaviors, we focus on eye fixation, which is the most relevant metric for evaluating information processing in online search. In this paper, eye fixation is defined as a spatially stable gaze lasting for approximately 200-300 milliseconds, during which visual attention is directed to a specific area of the visual display.

4.2 Do Users Examine Verticals First?

To analyze which result users first pay attention to, we collect subjects' first two seconds eye fixations on the screen. Figure 8 shows two samples from eye-tracking data which shows users' watching area on SERP with different kinds of verticals or no vertical results. From this figure we can see that users pay most attention to the first result when there is no vertical in SERP (which should be regarded as sign for position bias). However, when there is a multimedia vertical result at the third position, it attracts a lot of users' direct attentions.

We set 250 milliseconds as the threshold of fixation action and labeled each document's boundary manually. Then we can record each subject's eye examining sequence on document results for each SERP. This statistical result shows users' examining sequential behaviors. We compared users' first examining behavior for each vertical class using the same form with users' first click distribution we analyzed in previous section. Figure 9 shows the subjects' first examining distribution at each document position for each vertical class compared with no vertical situation. From Figure 9(b) we can see that when multimedia vertical is placed on the first screen (rank 1, 3 and 5); it actually attracts more attention than ordinary results. This conclusion is consistent with CT 2 in section 3.5. For application verticals, Figure 9(c) shows that application vertical attracts slightly more attention than ordinary result. Meanwhile Figure 9(a) shows that text vertical doesn't attract much user attention.

4.3 Behavior after Examining Verticals First

To validate the findings in Section 3 about how users behave after clicking a vertical results first. We look into the examining sequences of subjects when they examine vertical results firstly. Two typical examining sequential patterns are extracted from eye-tracking data and shown in Figure 10. We can see from this figure that users examine results above verticals either sequentially (top-down) or from the ones next to verticals first (bottom-up). Further statistics in Table 2 show that most of the subjects examine back to top results after examining a vertical first. This finding accords with our assumption in Section 3.3 that users will resume a top-down search session after being interrupted by a vertical result.

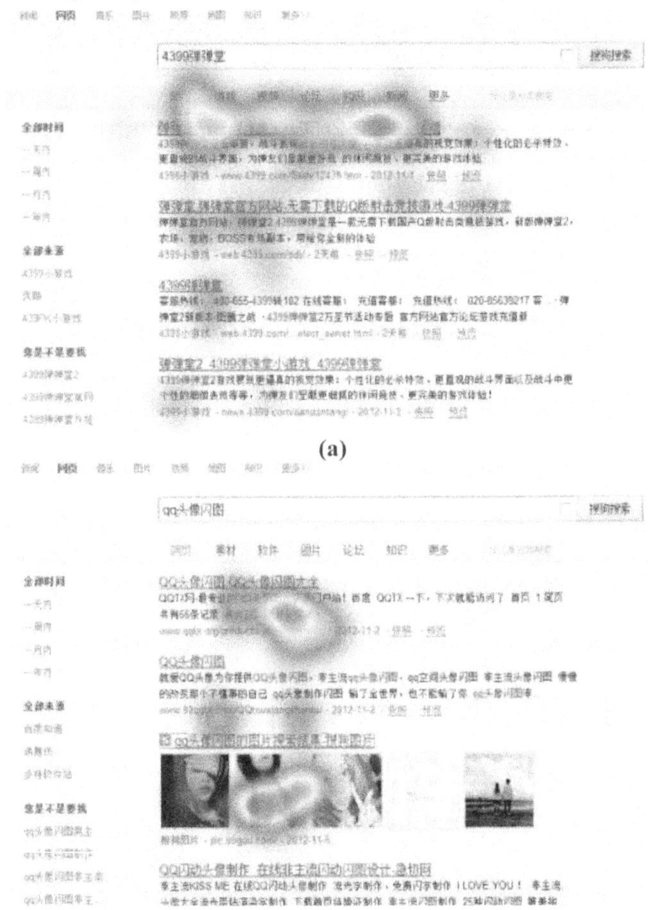

(a) (b)

Figure 8. Heat map of the subjects' eye fixation areas in first 2 seconds on (a) SERP with no vertical (b) SERP with multimedia vertical placed at the 3rd position

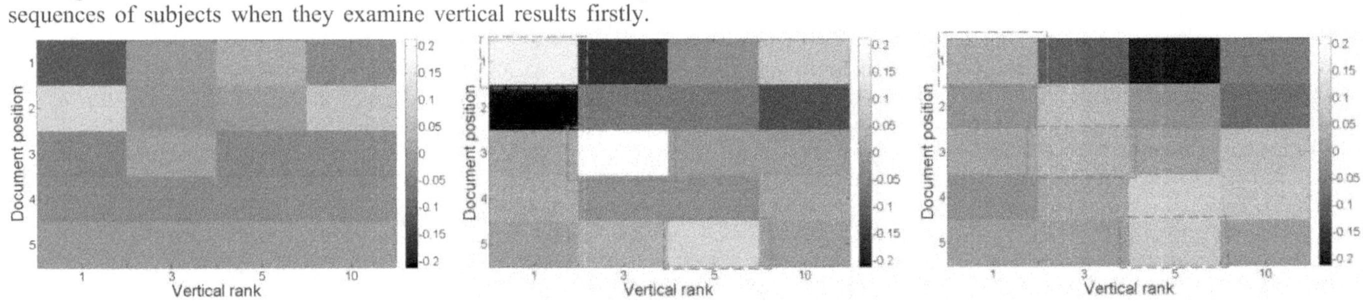

(a) (b) (c)

Figure 9. First examining distribution of SERPs with (a) text (b) multimedia (c) application vertical when vertical result is placed at rank 1, 3, 5 and 10 compared with SERPs with no verticals. (Brighter color means a higher first examining rate on document position. We don't show document positions from 6 to 10 here because almost no subjects examine results located on them first)

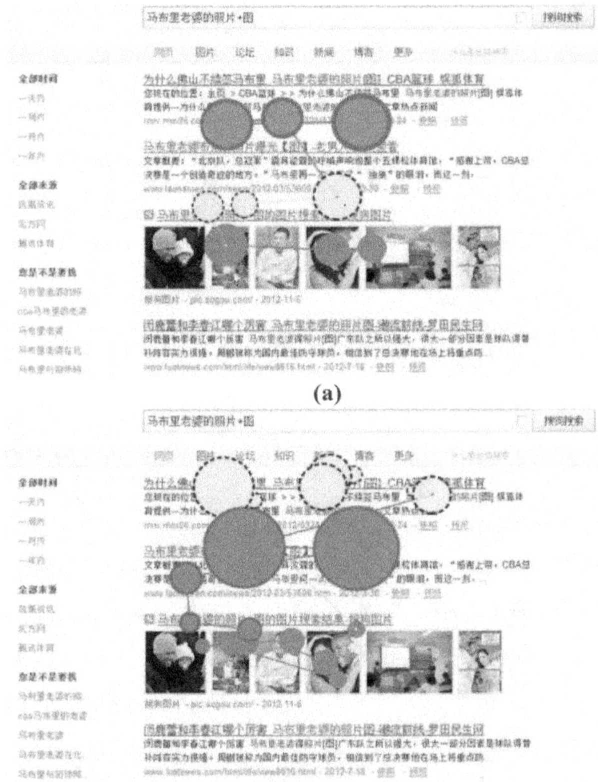

(a)

(b)

Figure 10. Typical eye-tracking cases of examining previous document (a) bottom up (b) top down after first examining verticals. The examining sequence is from green circles, yellow circles (dashed border) to red circles (solid border)

Table 2 shows the proportion of each examining patterns when user first examines verticals. We can see that after examining vertical result first, most subjects (89% users who examine 3rd result first and 100% users who examine 5th result first) scan back to the previous results. This shows that users may be attracted by the vertical's presentation and change their examination sequence; meanwhile results on top of the ranking list are always valued and not omitted by users.

Table 2. Proportion of different examining behaviors after user first examines a vertical result

Vertical Rank	#Subject[1]	Next	Previous	Back to Top
3	9	0.11	0.22	0.67
5	2	0.00	0.00	1.00

4.4 Eye-tracking Analysis Findings

In summary, we can conclude the main influence of vertical results on users' examining behavior into two aspects:

ET 1. Multimedia and application vertical results are examined more frequently compared with ordinary web results.

ET 2. After examining a vertical result first, most users will scan back to examine the previous results before the vertical either bottom-up or top-down.

[1] 11 subjects out of all 22 subjects examine vertical result first when vertical is placed at the 3rd or 5th position. We don't consider sessions in which verticals are placed at the 1st position because there would be no "previous" or "back to top" patterns.

5. VERTICAL-AWARE CLICK MODEL

We first state some definitions and notations that will be used in the following part. A search session within the same query is called a *query session*. A web search user initializes a *query session s* by submitting a *query q* to the search engine. The SERP can be represented as $D = (d_1, \ldots, d_M)$ sequentially (M = 10 if we only consider the first search result page), where d_i is document at position i from the top of the page.

Examination, click and document relevance are treated as probabilistic events. In particular, for a given query session, we use binary random variables E_i , C_i and A_i to represent the examination, click and document attractiveness events of the document at position i. The corresponding, examination and click probabilities for position i are denoted by $(E_i = 1)$, $P(C_i = 1)$ and $P(A_i = 1)$, respectively.

5.1 Preliminaries

We first introduce two important hypotheses: *examination hypothesis* and *cascade hypothesis*, which are the foundations of most existing click models.

The *examination hypothesis* [13] can be summarized as follows:

$$P(C_i = 1|E_i = 0) = 0 \quad (1)$$

$$P(C_i = 1|E_i = 1) = r_{d_i} \quad (2)$$

where $i = 1, \ldots, M$. r_{d_i} is defined as the document relevance, which is the conditional probability of a click event after examination. Given E_i, C_i is conditionally independent on previous examine/click events.

The *cascade hypothesis* in [8] assumes that users always begin the examination at the first document. The examination is strictly linear from top to bottom of the search result page, so a document is examined only if all previous documents are examined:

$$P(E_1 = 1) = 1 \quad (3)$$

$$P(E_{i+1} = 1|E_i = 0) = 0 \quad (4)$$

Given E_i , E_{i+1} is conditionally independent of all examine/click events above i, but may depend on the click C_i.

The user browsing model (UBM) [3] is based on the examination hypothesis, but it doesn't follow the cascade hypothesis. Instead, it assumes that the examination probability E_i depends on its own position and the previous clicked position l_i:

$$P(E_i = 1|C_{1:i-1}) = \gamma_{i,i-l_i} \quad (5)$$

Given click $C_{1:i-1}$, E_i is conditionally independent of all previous examination events$E_{1:i-1}$. If there is no click before i, l_i is set to 0. The probability of a query session under UBM is:

$$P(C_{i:M}) = \prod_{i=1}^{M}(r_{d_i}\gamma_{i,i-l_i})^{C_i}(1 - r_{d_i}\gamma_{i,i-l_i})^{1-C_i} \quad (6)$$

5.2 Modeling Biases

We can see from Section 3 and 4 that users treat verticals differently from ordinary results. Now, we want to develop an effective click model for federated search containing both vertical and ordinary results. Notice that we only consider the situation that only one vertical appears in the SERP. Therefore, if there are two or more verticals in SERP, we only keep the first vertical and simply regard others as ordinary results.

5.2.1 Attraction Bias

According to the conclusions of ET 1 and CT 3 described in previous sections, certain vertical result (e.g. multimedia vertical) will attract users' attention directly and cause users to examine and thus click it first. So we formalize the assumption as:

Assumption 1 (Attraction Bias): If there is a vertical placed in the SERP, there is probability that users examine it first.

We use the binary random variable F to represent the event of examining the vertical result first. Thus, the bias can be summarized as

$$P(F=1)=\phi_{t_v,l_v} \quad (7)$$

where t_v is the class of the vertical result and l_v is the position of vertical result. $\{\phi\}$ is a group of global parameters that should be estimated according to different kinds and positions of verticals.

5.2.2 Global Bias

From the conclusions of CT 1 and CT2 on user's clicking behavior described in section 3, we formalize the assumption about global preference for different vertical results as follows:

Assumption 2 (Global Bias): If there is a vertical placed in the SERP and user examines it first, the user will have a global impression on the whole page, which will affect user's examining and click probability of all results in the SERP.

This bias can be summarized as:

$$P(E_i=1|F=1)=P(E_i=1|F=0)+\theta_{q,i} \quad (8)$$

$$P(A_i=1|E_i=1,F=1)=P(A_i=1|E_i=1,F=0)+\beta_{q,i} \quad (9)$$

$\{\beta\}$ and $\{\theta\}$ are a group of parameters that represent the additional global impression of each document when users examine the vertical result first.

5.2.3 First Place Bias

From the conclusion of CT 3 in Section 3, we found that when text or application verticals are placed at the first place, users will click on these verticals much more than ordinary results. Meanwhile, because users are likely to be satisfied by the verticals, they may not click on other results any more. Therefore, we can conclude the following bias:

Assumption 3 (First Place Bias): If there is a vertical placed in the SERP and the vertical is placed at the first position, there is probability that users click more on these verticals and less on other results.

We may use another group of parameters to describe the additional influence caused by this bias. However, this group of parameters will simply occur in the same place as$\{\beta\}$ and $\{\theta\}$. Thus, $\{\beta\}$ and $\{\theta\}$ is sufficient to describe the *global bias* and the *first place bias* simultaneously.

5.2.4 Sequence Bias

In section 3 we found that users may revisit (CT 4) after clicking a vertical first. According to the eye-tracking analysis (ET 2), we also found that most users will scan back to examine the previous results either bottom-up or top-down after examining the vertical first. So we summarize the points above and make a non-sequential examining assumption as follow:

Assumption 4 (Sequence Bias): If there is a vertical placed in the SERP and user examines it first, after examining the vertical result users will scan back to the previous documents in either bottom up or top down sequence.

We use binary random variable B to represent the event of examining the previous document in bottom up sequence. Suppose that the SERP's document list $D=(d_1,\dots,d_M)$. After examining the vertical first, if the user decides to scan in top down sequence, the following examining sequence is $d_1,\dots,d_M$; if the user decides to scan in bottom up sequence, the following examining sequence of this SERP will change to $d_{l_v},\dots,d_1,d_{l_v+1},\dots,d_M$. So the bias can be summarized as:

$$P(B=1|F=0)=0 \quad (10)$$

$$P(B=1|F=1)=\sigma_{t_v,l_v} \quad (11)$$

$\{\sigma\}$ is a group of global parameters and can vary according to different kinds and positions of verticals.

We use the four biases above to represent conclusions we made in click-through log analysis and eye-tracking analysis. Then we propose a click model named Vertical-aware Click Model to take these biases into account.

5.3 Vertical-aware Click Model

The biases above can embrace the assumption of most existing click models depending on the examination hypothesis. Therefore, our Vertical-aware Click Model (VCM) can be constructed based on many existing click models (e.g., the UBM and DBN)

We choose the UBM as a basis in the following experiment. When $F=0$, the examining and click probability is the same as UBM. The global impression parameters have been introduced into the formulas for $F=1$. Thus, the VCM can now be summarized as:

$$P(C_i=1|E_i=0)=0 \quad (12)$$

$$P(C_i=1|E_i=1)=P(A_i=1|E_i=1) \quad (13)$$

$$P(F=1)=\phi_{t_v,l_v} \quad (14)$$

$$P(E_i=1|F=0,C_{1:i-1})=\gamma_{i,i-l_i} \quad (15)$$

$$P(E_i=1|F=1,C_{1:i-1})=\gamma_{i,i-l_i}+\theta_{q,i} \quad (16)$$

$$P(A_i=1|E_i=1,F=0)=\alpha_{q,i} \quad (17)$$

$$P(A_i=1|E_i=1,F=1)=\alpha_{q,i}+\beta_{q,i} \quad (18)$$

$$P(B=1|F=0)=0 \quad (19)$$

$$P(B=1|F=1)=\sigma_{t_v,l_v} \quad (20)$$

Figure 11 shows the decision-making process of VCM. When user begins with a query session, the user will have the opportunity to examine the vertical first if there is a vertical result in SERP. After examining the vertical first, the user will decide to scan back to the previous document in bottom up sequence or top down sequence.

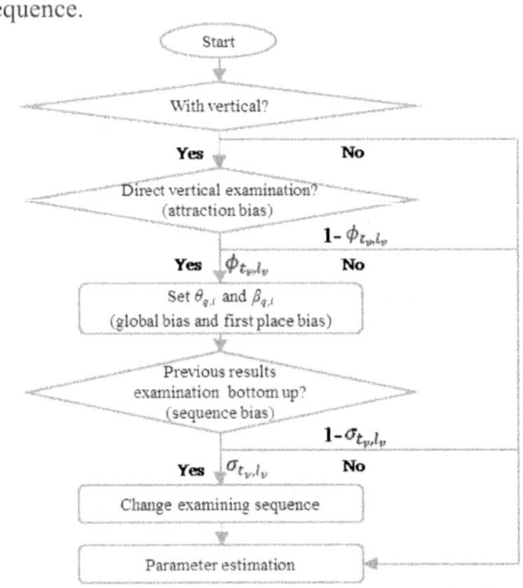

Figure 11. Decision-making process of VCM

5.4 Model Inference

We use the expectation-maximization (EM) algorithm to complete the inference step. The EM algorithm is used to find the maximum likelihood estimates of parameters, including the attraction bias parameters ϕ_{t_v,l_v}, the global bias and first place bias parameters $\beta_{q,i}$ and $\theta_{q,i}$, the sequence bias parameters σ_{t_v,l_v}, the examining probability parameters $\gamma_{i,i-l_i}$ and the document relevance parameters $\alpha_{q,i}$. The EM iteration alternates between performing an E-step, which creates a function for the expectation of the Log-Likelihood evaluated using the current estimate for the parameters, and M-step, which computes parameters maximizing the expected *Log-Likelihood* found on the E-step.

The traditional EM algorithm leads to the following updating formula, here we show how to update $\alpha_{q,i}$; the corresponding formulas for the other parameters can be derived analogously.

Supposing that there are N sessions and C_i^j denotes the click action of i-th document associated with the j-th session. q^j is the search query associated with the j-th session. A t superscript indicates the estimate at iteration t:

$$I_i^j = I(C_i^j = 1) \quad (21)$$

$$P_q^j = \prod_{i=1}^{M} \left(\alpha_{q,i}^t \gamma_{i,i-l_i}^t\right)^{I_i^j} \left(1 - \alpha_{q,i}^t \gamma_{i,i-l_i}^t\right)^{1-I_i^j} \quad (22)$$

$$A_{q,i} = \sum_{j=1}^{N} I(q^j = q)\, P_q^j \left[I_i^j + (1 - I_i^j) \times \frac{\alpha_{q,i}^t\left(1-\gamma_{i,i-l_i}^t\right)}{1-\alpha_{q,i}^t \gamma_{i,i-l_i}^t}\right] \quad (23)$$

$$B_{q,i} = \sum_{j=1}^{N} I(q^j = q)\, P_q^j \left[(1 - I_i^j) \times \frac{(1-\alpha_{q,i}^t)}{1-\alpha_{q,i}^t \gamma_{i,i-l_i}^t}\right] \quad (24)$$

where $I(\cdot)$ is the indicator function, and $\alpha_{q,i}^{t+1} = \frac{A_{q,i}}{A_{q,i}+B_{q,i}}$.

6. EXPERIMENTS AND DISCUSSIONS

In this section, we compare the VCM with UBM model with click perplexity and log-likelihood as metrics to measure the effectiveness of these two click models. UBM is selected as our baseline because we want to confirm whether the new model VCM in which four biases is added can better interpret user click behavior than the original model or not.

6.1 Experiment Setups

The click logs used for training and testing click models are sampled from a popular Chinese commercial search engine during a week in April 2012. To prevent the evaluations from being biased by extremely high-frequency queries, we allow each query at most 10^4 sessions. For each query, we sort its sessions by timestamp information and split sessions into the training and testing sets at a ratio of 4 : 1. Altogether 306,750 queries and 11,558,016 sessions were collected and their query frequency distributions are shown in Table 3.

Table 3. Query frequency distribution of experiment data set

Query Frequency	# Queries	# Sessions
1-10	228,290	688,129
10-$10^{1.5}$	43,280	777,642
$10^{1.5}$-10^2	21,060	1,157,448
10^2-$10^{2.5}$	9,103	1,573,706
$10^{2.5}$-10^3	3,341	1,802,170
10^3-$10^{3.5}$	1,140	1,980,876
$10^{3.5}$-10^4	536	3,578,045

For training the baseline model UBM, we use the inference algorithms introduced in the original paper [3]. For VCM, we use the inference method introduced in Section 5. If there are two or more verticals in SERP, we only keep the first vertical and simply regard others as ordinary results.

As for evaluation metrics, perplexity and log-likelihood were adopted by a number of previous works (e.g. [3, 5, 7]). In our experiment we also use these two metrics to show effectiveness of VCM compared with the original UBM.

Perplexity measures the accuracy for each position instead of the whole session. It is computed for binary click events at each position in a query session independently. The perplexity of the entire dataset is the average of p_i over all positions. A smaller value indicates better prediction accuracy, and perfect click prediction will have a perplexity of 1.0000. The improvement of perplexity value p_1 over p_2 is given by $(p_2 - p_1)/(p_2 - 1)$ .Log-likelihood (LL) is also widely used to measure model fitness. Given the document impression for each query session in the test data, LL is computed as the average log probability of observed click events under the trained model. A larger LL indicates better performance, and the optimal value is 0. The improvement of LL value l_1 over l_2 is computed as $(exp(l_1 - l_2) - 1)$.

6.2 Results and Discussions

Figure 12 presents perplexity scores for both UBM and VCM over different positions. Average click perplexity over all positions for VCM is 1.2792, which is 14.06% better than that of UBM (1.3249). The improvement is significant and almost adequate in all ranking positions, which indicates that biases introduced in our vertical-aware click model can learn a better accuracy at all positions compared with UBM. Table 4 also shows comparison results for different vertical types, from which we can see that the improvement of VCM in multimedia and application vertical is larger. This phenomenon is reasonable because multimedia and application vertical results have significant different appearances compared with ordinary results and user click/examination behavior on these two types of verticals are also different from ordinary ones according to Section 3 and 4. It indicates that VCM better models user behavior on these vertical results by incorporating more biases besides position bias.

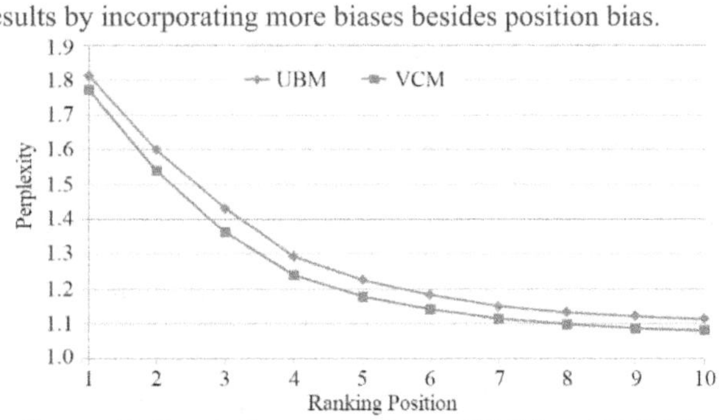

Figure 12. Perplexity comparison of UBM and VCM for results in different ranking positions

Table 4. Perplexity comparison of UBM and VCM for queries with different vertical types

	UBM	VCM	VCM Improvement
Text vertical	1.2266	1.2139	5.58%
Multimedia vertical	1.3735	1.3071	17.78%
Application vertical	1.1908	1.1601	16.09%
Without vertical	1.2388	1.2285	4.33%

Figure 13 and Table 5 present log-likelihood comparison results for VCM and UBM for queries with different frequencies. The overall LL result for VCM is -3.1128, which is 19.46% better than that of UBM (-3.3005). Similar with the perplexity results, it also shows that VCM outperforms UBM for almost all kinds of queries. Especially, Figure 13 shows that the improvement is even larger for low-frequency queries (or tailed queries). The average LL score of VCM for queries with less than 100 appearances improves UBM by 57.89%. Queries with multimedia results benefit the most among all vertical types according to Table 5, which is similar with the results shown in Table 4.

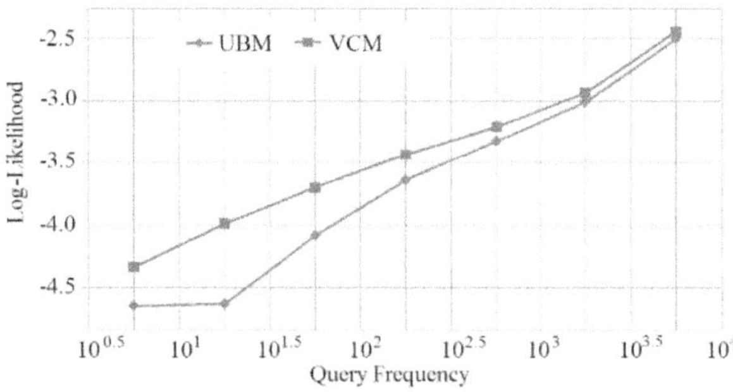

Figure 13. Log-likelihood comparison of UBM and VCM for queries with different frequencies

Table 5. Log-likelihood comparison of UBM and VCM for queries with different vertical types

	UBM	VCM	VCM Improvement
Text vertical	-2.9093	-2.7968	11.90%
Multimedia vertical	-4.1142	-3.8638	28.44%
Application vertical	-2.2671	-2.1427	13.24%
Without vertical	-3.0256	-2.9646	6.29%

The experimental results show that VCM which take four biases into consideration can better interpret user click behavior than the original UBM in terms of both perplexity and Log-likelihood. As the introduced parameters $\{\beta\}$ and $\{\theta\}$ can better interpret the additional influence brought by vertical, the original examine probability $\{\gamma\}$ is more close to the situation without vertical in SERP. Therefore, VCM can also interpret slightly better than original UBM even for session without verticals.

7. CONCLUSIONS AND FUTURE WORK

Nowadays vertical results appear in over 80% SERPs of commercial search engines. In order to solve the problem of incorporating vertical results into search click models, we look into both large scale click-through log collected from a popular search engine and laboratory based eye-tracking data of 22 participants. We found that click-through and result examining behaviors between SERPs with and without verticals are different from each other. Such behaviors are even different for verticals with different presentation forms such as text vertical, multimedia vertical and application vertical. A number of behavior differences are concluded into four biases: attraction bias, global bias, first place bias and sequence bias. A click model named Vertical-aware Click Model (VCM) is constructed and its effectiveness is evaluated in term of perplexity and log-likelihood.

In the future, we would like to extend the VCM model to cover SERPs with multiple vertical results. We will also work on incorporating VCM into a ranking model to improve ranking performance of search result lists with vertical results.

8. ACKNOWLEDGMENTS

This work was supported by Natural Science Foundation (60903107, 61073071), National High Technology Research and Development (863) Program (2011AA01A205) of China and Singapore National Research Foundation under its International Research Centre @ Singapore Funding Initiative and administered by the IDM Programme Office.

9. REFERENCES

[1] L. A. Granka, T. Joachims, and G. Gay. Eye-tracking analysis of user behavior in WWW search. In SIGIR'04, pages 478-479, 2004.

[2] M. Richardson, E. Dominowska, and R. Ragno. Predicting clicks: estimating the click-through rate for new ads. In WWW '07, pages 521–530, 2007.

[3] G. Dupret and B. Piwowarski. A user browsing model to predict search engine click data from past observations. In SIGIR'08, pages 331–338, 2008.

[4] O. Chapelle and Y. Zhang. A dynamic bayesian network click model for web search ranking. In WWW'09, pages 1–10, 2009.

[5] F. Guo, C. Liu, A. Kannan, T. Minka, M. Taylor, Y. Wang, and C. Faloutsos. Click chain model in web search. In WWW'09, pages 11–20, 2009.

[6] Y. Zhang, W. Chen, D. Wang, and Q. Yang. User-click modeling for understanding and predicting search-behavior. In KDD 2011, pages 1388-1396, 2011.

[7] D. Chen, W. Chen and H. Wang. Beyond ten blue links: enabling user click modeling in federated web search. In WSDM 2012, pages 463-472, 2012.

[8] N. Craswell, O. Zoeter, M. Taylor, and B. Ramsey. An experimental comparison of click position-bias models. In WSDM '08, pages 87–94, 2008.

[9] U. Lee, Z. Liu and J. Cho, Automatic Identification of User Goals in Web Search, in the WWW'05, pages 391-400, 2005

[10] T. Joachims, L. Granka, B. Pan, H. Hembrooke, and G. Gay. Accurately interpreting clickthrough data as implicit feedback. In SIGIR '05, pages 154–161, 2005.

[11] T. Joachims, L. Granka, B. Pan, H. Hembrooke, F. Radlinski, and G. Gay. Evaluating the accuracy of implicit feedback from clicks and query reformulations in web search. ACM Trans. Inf. Syst., 25(2):7, 2007.

[12] K. Rayner. Eye movements in reading and information processing. Psychological Bulletin, 124:372–252, 1998.

[13] M. Richardson, E. Dominowska, and R. Ragno. Predicting clicks: estimating the click-through rate for new ads. In WWW '07, pages 521–530, 2007.

[14] F. Diaz. Integration of news content into web results. In WSDM 2009, pages 182-191, 2009.

[15] J. Arguello, F. Diaz and J. Callan. Sources of evidence for vertical selection. In SIGIR'09, pages 315-322, 2009.

[16] J. Arguello, F. Diaz. Vertical selection in the presence of unlabeled verticals. In SIGIR 2010, pages 691-698, 2010.

[17] J. Arguello, F. Diaz. Learning to aggregate vertical results into web search results. In CIKM 2011, pages 201–210, 2011.

[18] J. Arguello, F. Diaz and J. Callan. A methodology for evaluating aggregated search results. In Proceedings of ECIR 2011. Springer-Verlag, pages 141–152.

[19] K. Zhou, R. Cummins. Evaluating Reward and Risk for Vertical Selection. In CIKM 2012, pages 2631-2634, 2012.

[20] D. Hong, L. Si. Mixture model with multiple centralized retrieval algorithms for result merging in federated search. In SIGIR 2012, pages 821-830, 2012.

[21] J. Bar-Ilan, K. Keenoy and M. Levene. Presentation bias is significant in determining user preference for search results—A user study. In Journal of the American Society for Information Science and Technology, pages 135–149, 2009.

[22] Y. Yue, R. Patel, H. Roehrig. Beyond position bias: examining result attractiveness as a source of presentation bias in clickthrough data. In WWW 2010, pages 1011-1018, 2010.

[23] W. Chen, D. Wang and Y. Zhang. A Noise-aware Click Model for Web Search. In WSDM 2012, pages 313-322, 2012.

Personalized Time-Aware Tweets Summarization

Zhaochun Ren
ISLA, University of Amsterdam
Amsterdam, The Netherlands
z.ren@uva.nl

Shangsong Liang
ISLA, University of Amsterdam
Amsterdam, The Netherlands
s.liang@uva.nl

Edgar Meij
Yahoo! Research
Barcelona, Spain
emeij@yahoo-inc.com

Maarten de Rijke
ISLA, University of Amsterdam
Amsterdam, The Netherlands
derijke@uva.nl

ABSTRACT

We focus on the problem of selecting meaningful tweets given a user's interests; the dynamic nature of user interests, the sheer volume, and the sparseness of individual messages make this an challenging problem. Specifically, we consider the task of time-aware tweets summarization, based on a user's history and collaborative social influences from "social circles." We propose a time-aware user behavior model, the Tweet Propagation Model (TPM), in which we infer dynamic probabilistic distributions over interests and topics. We then explicitly consider novelty, coverage, and diversity to arrive at an iterative optimization algorithm for selecting tweets. Experimental results validate the effectiveness of our personalized time-aware tweets summarization method based on TPM.

Categories and Subject Descriptors

H.3.3 [**Information Search and Retrieval**]: Information filtering

Keywords

Twitter, tweets summarization, data enrichment, topic modeling

1. INTRODUCTION

Twitter has amassed over half a billion users in 2012, who produce ("tweet") over 300 million tweets per day.[1] Twitter users can subscribe to updates from other users by following them, essentially forming a unidirectional friend relationship. Moreover, tweets can be "retweeted," basically copying a tweet posted by another user to one's own timeline. From an information retrieval point of view, the sheer volume of users and tweets presents interesting challenges. On the one hand, interesting, relevant, or meaningful tweets can easily be missed due to a large number of followed users. On the other hand, users may miss interesting tweets when none of the users they follow retweet an interesting piece of information.

[1] `http://blog.twitter.com/2012/03/twitter-turns-six.html`.

SIGIR'13, July 28–August 1, 2013, Dublin, Ireland.
Copyright 2013 ACM 978-1-4503-2034-4/13/07 ...$15.00.

One task that is aimed at addressing this dual problem is *tweets summarization* [6]: to extract a group of representative tweets from a set of tweets. The task is similar to tweet recommendation, but tweets summarization pays more attention to the *quality* of selected results, including notions such as representativeness and diversity. So far, tweets summarization methods are typically query and user-independent. How to adapt tweets summarization to a specific user is still a topic of ongoing research [4, 5, 7, 22, 31, 36]. Current methods, whether personalized or not, also neglect to explicitly model the temporal nature of the microblogging environment; time-awareness is a key feature of Twitter in general and tweets summarization in particular.

We put forward a model for personalized, time-aware tweets summarization (TaTS). We investigate three key aspects of tweets summarization: (a) novelty, preventing near-duplicate tweets to be included, (b) coverage, so as to be representative to candidate tweets, (c) diversity, covering as many aspects as possible. When working with Twitter data, several methodological challenges arise. In order to perform effective tweets summarization, we require a notion of a user's interest. Most Twitter users, however, mostly *consume* information without *producing* a lot of information. That is, they rarely post tweets of their own [22]. Hence, in order to infer a user's interest in a robust manner, we need to use other signals than just the user's tweets. To address the issue, we incorporate intuitions from the field of collaborative filtering and base our estimation of a person's interest on those of their friends on Twitter, following [5]. We assume that for each user there exist one or more "social circles," in which three or more users follow each other and form cliques. We find that people are usually connected to specific communities and assume that each user's behavior on Twitter is affected by: (a) a user's private taste, (b) a collaborative effect from social circles, and (c) a bursty component, reflecting current events.

Clearly, a user's interest can change over time. Topic modeling has proven effective for topic detection and user behavior modeling on Twitter [8, 25, 32]. As a dynamic extension of the author-topic model [26], our proposed Tweet Propagation Model (TPM) aims to track both a user's interests and any topic drift arising with the passing of time. Based on "social circles", TPM derives the user's interest from a dirichlet mixture over interests of someone who share "social circles." It does so by inferring distributions over topics and interests that change over time. Following existing topic modeling approaches for Twitter [8, 37], we extend TPM and classify the topics as (a) personal topics, (b) common topics, or (c) bursty topics. Gibbs Expectation Maximization (EM) sampling [29] is used to infer the posterior probabilities and to estimate the value of hyper-parameters in our topic models. After inferring the probabilities of each tweet, we employ an iterative algorithm to optimize the tweet selection procedure, considering coverage, novelty, and diversity.

Our contributions in this paper are as follows. (1) We propose the task of personalized time-aware tweets summarization, selecting personalized meaningful tweets from a collection of tweets. (2) We leverage a user's "collaborative influence" in order to derive the user's interests. (3) We introduce a tweet propagation model to address the potential drift in a user's interests as well as topics over time. (4) We employ a tweet selection algorithm that jointly optimizes for coverage, diversity, and novelty.

The rest of this paper is organized as follows. We introduce related work in Section 2. Our problem formulation is detailed in Section 3. Our strategy for tweet summary generation, is described in Section 4. Section 5 details our experimental setup and Section 6 presents and discusses the experimental results and Section 7 concludes the paper.

2. RELATED WORK

Our approach builds on earlier work in tweets summarization, tweet recommendation and topic modeling.

2.1 Tweets Summarization

Several publications have focused on tweets summarization: the task of selecting a list of meaningful tweets that are most representative for some topic. Most work in the literature concerns tweets as basic constituents to compose a summary. Some authors bring feature-based or graph-based summarization technologies to bear on this task [6, 27], while other methods use a term-frequency based method [28] or a strategy based on mutual reinforcement between users' influence and qualifications of tweets [9]. Recently, time-aware summarization has been studied by several authors, often in the form of timeline generation on Twitter. Chakrabarti and Punera [4] separate topic related tweets into various periods as an event evolution map, and generate an update-summarization result. Yan et al. [33] propose an evolutionary timeline summarization strategy based on dynamic programming. Evolutionary summarization approaches segment post streams into event chains and select tweets from various chains to generate a tweet summary; Nichols et al. [21] propose an effective method to separate timelines using Twitter. To the best of our knowledge, existing work on tweets summarization focuses on the extraction of representative tweets for specific topics, without considering personalization.

Other work integrates the task of selecting tweets with other web documents: Yang et al. [35] use mutual reinforcement to train both the selection of related web documents and tweets via a single graph factor model. Zhao et al. [37] extract representative keywords from tweets based on a topic model. Tweet ranking has also attracted attention: Weng et al. [31] proposed a graph-based ranking strategy for ranking tweets based on the author-topic model.

2.2 Collaborative Tweet Recommendations

In recent years, collaborative filtering on Twitter has attracted increased attention. Yang et al. [34] address recommendation and link prediction tasks based on a joint-propagation model, FTP, between social friendship and interests. Ye et al. [36] propose a generative model to describe users' behavior, given influences from social communities, for recommendation [18, 19]. To track social influence of users in a social network, Xu et al. [32] propose a graphical mixture model to describe user's behavior in posting tweets and analyze the original topic domain for a specific proposed tweet. Chen et al. [5] propose a collaborative filtering method to generate personalized recommendations in Twitter through a collaborative ranking precedure. Similarly, Pennacchiotti et al. [22] propose a method to recommend "novel" tweets to users by following users' interests and using the tweet content. However, many of these methods ignore the dynamic nature of the problem; with the change of time, user interests may also change.

Table 1: Glossary.

Symbol	Description
K	number of topics
U	number of users
V	the size of the vocabulary
T	number of time periods
$\mathcal{D}_t$	candidate tweets at time t
D_t	number of candidate tweets at time t, i.e., $\lvert\mathcal{D}_t\rvert$
u	user u on Twitter, $u \in \mathcal{U}$
$\mathcal{C}_{u,t}$	social circle for user u at t
$\mathcal{D}_{u,t}$	tweets posted by u at time t
$D_{u,t}$	number of tweets posted by u at time t, i.e., $\lvert\mathcal{D}_{u,t}\rvert$
$F_{u,t}$	number of friends of u at time t
$C_{u,t}$	number of social circles around u at time t
d_t	tweet published at time t, $d_t \in \mathcal{D}_t$
w	token/word present in some tweet, $w \in \mathcal{W}$
z_t	latent topic at t time, $z_t \in Z_t$
$c_{u,t}$	social circle around u at time t, $c_{u,t} \in \mathcal{C}_{u,t}$
$\theta_{u,t}$	distribution of u's interests over topics at time t
ϑ_t	distribution of topics within a tweet at time t
ϕ_t	distribution of words over topics at time t
Z	classification of individual topics in θ or ϑ
β, α, σ, r	hyper-parameters in TPM
N	maximum number of tweets returned
$\lambda_{u,c,t}$	weight of social circle c for user u at t

2.3 Topic Models

Topic models [2, 12] are employed to reduce the high dimensionality of terms appearing in text into low-dimensional, "latent" topics. Ever since Hofmann [12] presented probabilistic latent semantic indexing (pLSI), many extensions have been proposed. In latent Dirichlet allocation (LDA, [2]) each document is generated by choosing a distribution over topics and then each word in the document is chosen from a selected topic. To handle users' connections with particular documents and topics, the author-topic model has been proposed [26]. However, for data with topic evolution the underlying "bag of words" representation may be insufficient. To analyze topic evolution, other models have been proposed, such as the Dynamic Topic Model [1], Dynamic Mixture Models [30] and the Topic Tracking Model [13]. Topic models have not yet been considered very frequently in the setting of Twitter. Twitter-LDA is an interesting exception; it classifies latent topics into "background" topic and "personal" topics [37], while an extension of Twitter-LDA has been proved to be effective in burst detection [8].

Our work is different from the related work mentioned above in the following important ways: (1) our work focuses on personalized and time-aware tweets summarization and (2) we propose a tweet propagation model by jointly modeling time-aware propagation and collaborative filtering from "social circles," which is different from existing topic models.

3. PROBLEM FORMULATION

Before introducing our method for time-aware tweets summarization, we introduce our notation and key concepts. Table 1 lists the notation we use. Given two users u_i and u_j on Twitter, there are two main reasons for u_i and u_j to follow each other: either because

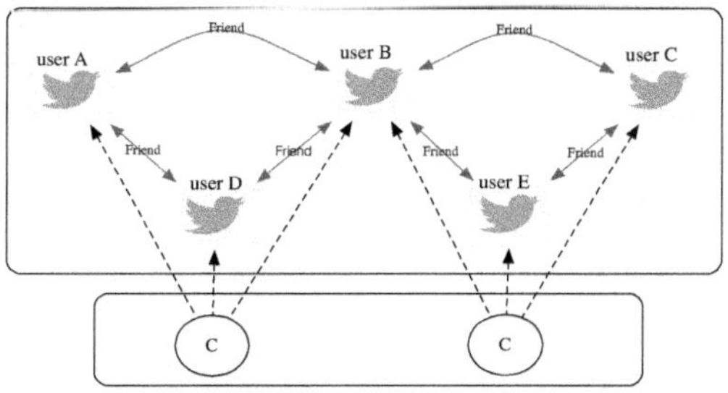

Figure 1: Example of social circles on Twitter: there are two social circles (indicated using the 'c') among the five users in this graph, where each pair of vertices in each social circle is connected through the "friend" relationship.

they have similar interests or they have some relationship outside Twitter [32]. If two users u_i and u_j follow each other, we define them to be *friends* on Twitter. Given this definition, we define a *social circle* around a user u to be a set of friends of u such that every pair of users in this set is in the *friend* relation. See Figure 1 for a schematic representation.

Similar to the author-topic model [26], we assume that each Twitter user's interests are represented by a multinomial distribution $\theta_{u,t}$, which may, however, change over time. That is, the time-aware interests of user u are represented as a multinomial distribution $\theta_{u,t}$ over topics, where each topic is represented as a probabilistic distribution over words [2]. Formally, we have $\theta_{u,t} = \{\theta_{u,t,z_1}, \cdots, \theta_{u,t,z_K}\}$, where θ_{u,t,z_i}, denotes the distribution of topic z_i for user u at time t.

We further assume that each tweet can be represented as a probabilistic distribution over topics. To cater for the phenomenon of user interests changing over time, we assume that topic distributions are dynamic and may differ between time periods. Given a user u, we split the topic set Z_t at time t into three classes: $Z_t = Z_t^u \cup Z_t^{com} \cup Z_t^B$: there exist "private" topics Z_t^u that solely depend on the user, there are common topics Z_t^{com} that are influenced by friends from shared social circles, and there are topics from event-related, bursty sources, Z_t^B. The latter type of topic will typically transfer from initially being observed at time t into Z^{com} at some later time t'.

The dynamic interests of user u at time t, reflected by $\theta_{u,t}$, evolve in different ways depending on the class that a topic $z_t \in Z_t$ belongs to. For each user, $\theta_{u,t}$ is affected by the following three classes.

(a) If $z_t \in Z_t^u$ is a "private" topic, then $\theta_{u,t,z}^u$ only depends on $\theta_{u,t-1,z}^u$ at time $t-1$.

(b) If $z_t \in Z_t^{com}$ then the topic is dependent on friends in the user's social circle(s). θ_{u,t,z_t}^{com} is computed from the collaborative effect $\theta_{ui,t-1}^{com}$ at time $t-1$ from the social circles $\{u_i | u_i \in C_{u,t-1}\}$.

(c) If $z_t \in Z_t^B$ is a "burst" topic, $\theta_{u_i,z,t}^B$ is generated according to a distribution of "burst" words in u_i's tweets at time t.

Typically, traditional summarization does not cover the evolution of a specific event. Given a split of a user's history into time periods, the task of time-aware tweets summarization is to select the most representative tweets for each time period, covering the whole event evolution on a timeline. More precisely, given a set of tweets $\mathcal{D}$, a set of time periods T, and a maximum number of tweets per period, N, time-aware tweets summarization aims to extract multiple sets of tweets RT_t $(1 \leq t \leq T)$ from $\mathcal{D}$, where for each time period t, $RT_t = \{d_{t,x_1}, d_{t,x_2}, \ldots, d_{t,x_N}\}$ is a set of representative tweets that summarize the period. Furthermore, *personalized*

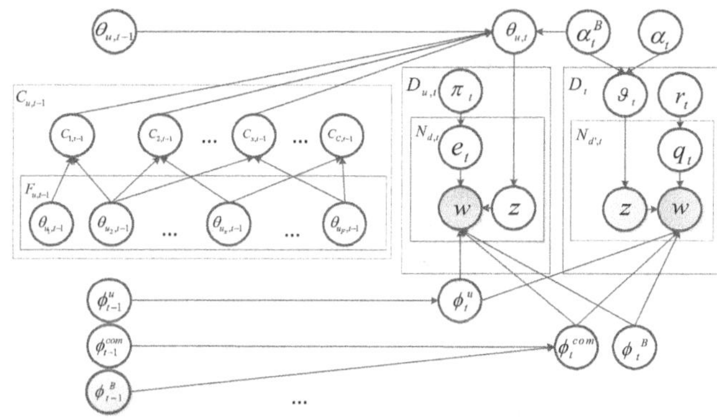

Figure 2: Graphical representation of TPM.

time-aware tweets summarization is defined similar to time-aware tweets summarization, but in this case the tweets selected for inclusion in RT_t need to be relevant based on u's interests θ_u at time t.

4. METHOD

In this section, we detail our tweets summarization method, including the required methods for joint user-tweets topic modeling, inference and parameter estimation. As input, our method has probabilistic distributions from topic modeling. The output is the time-aware tweets summary, i.e., a selection of tweets (per period) satisfying the user's interest.

4.1 Topic Modeling: Tweets Propagation

We start by proposing the tweets propagation model (TPM) to jointly track dynamic user's interests and topics. The interests of a user u are assumed to be reflected by a multinomial distribution $\theta_{u,t}$ over topics. We assume that the distribution of topics ϕ_t over words follows a dynamic propagation process with changes over time. Figure 2 provides a graphical overview of TPM.

In the graphical structure of TPM, we see a number of ingredients. Among the variables related to user u in the graph, z, θ and γ are random variables and w is the observed variable. In the candidate tweets part, ϑ, z and σ are random variables; $D_{u,t}$ and D_t indicate the number of variables in the model. As usual, directed arrows in a graphical model indicate the dependency between two variables; the variables $c_{u,t-1}$ depend on variables $\{\theta_{u_i,t-1} | u_i \in C_{u,t-1}\}$. The variables ϕ_t^{com} and ϕ_t^u depend on variables $\{\phi_{t-1}^{com}, \phi_{t-1}^B\}$ and ϕ_{t-1}^u, respectively.

Now, let us give a more detailed technical account of our model. Around user u, there exist multiple social circles. For each social circle $c_{u,t}$ in time period t, there is a random parameter $\lambda_{c_{u,t}}$ indicating the importance of $c_{u,t}$ to u at t. User u's interests $\theta_{u,t}$ are composed of three parts: the personal aspect, the common topic aspect and the bursty aspect, i.e., $\theta_{u,t} = \{\theta_{u,t}^{com}, \theta_{u,t}^u, \theta_{u,t}^B\}$, where the common topics are not only influenced by the user's social circles, but also by his own previous interests. Therefore, we use a Dirichlet distribution to derive the probability of $\theta_{u,t}^{com}$ over $x_{u,t}^{com}$ as:

$$x_{u,t}^{com} = \alpha_{u,t}\theta_{u,t-1}^{com+B} + (1 - \alpha_{u,t}) \sum_{c_i \in C_{u,t-1}} \lambda_{c_i}\theta_{c_i,t-1}^{com+B} \quad (1)$$

where $\theta_{u,t-1}^{com+B}$ refers to the set $\{\theta_{u,t-1}^{com}, \theta_{u,t-1}^B\}$ at period $t-1$, which reflects user u's interests for common and burst topics at time $t-1$, and $\theta_{c_i,t-1}^{com+B}$ refers to the set $\{\theta_{c_i,t-1}^{com}, \theta_{c_i,t-1}^B\}$ at period $t-1$. The hyperparameter $\alpha_{u,t}$ indicates the weight of $\theta_{u,t-1}^{com+B}$

1. For each topic $z, z \in Z_t^{com} \cup Z_t^B \cup Z_t^u$:
   - Draw $\phi_t^B \sim Dir(\beta_t^B)$;
   - Draw $\phi_t^{com} \sim Dir(\beta_t^{com}\{\phi_{t-1}^{com}, \phi^B{}_{t-1}\})$;
   - Draw $\phi_t^u \sim Dir(\beta_t^u \phi_{t-1}^u)$
2. For each candidate tweet $d_t \in \mathcal{D}_t$:
   - Draw $\vartheta_t \sim Dir(\alpha_t, \alpha_t^B)$; $r_t \sim Dir(\gamma_t)$;
   - For each word w in d_t
     - Draw $q \in Multi(r)$; $z_w \sim Multi(\vartheta_t)$;
       * if $q = 0$: Draw $w \sim Multi(\phi_{z,t}^{com})$;
       * if $q = 1$: Draw $w \sim Multi(\phi_{z,t}^u)$;
       * if $q = 2$: Draw $w \sim Multi(\phi_t^B)$;
3. For user $u, u \in \mathcal{U}$:
   - Draw $\theta_{u,t} \sim Dir(\{x_{u,t}^u, x_{u,t}^{com}, \alpha_t^B\})$;
   - Draw $\pi_t \sim Dir(\sigma_t)$;
   - For each word $w \in d_{u,t}$, where $d_{u,t} \in D_{u,t}$:
     - Draw $e \sim Multi(\pi)$; $z_{w,t} \sim Multi(\theta_{u,t})$
       * if $e = 0$: Draw $w \sim Multi(\phi_{z,t}^{com})$;
       * if $e = 1$: Draw $w \sim Multi(\phi_{z,t}^u)$;
       * if $e = 2$: Draw $w \sim Multi(\phi_t^B)$;

Figure 3: Generative process for the TPM model.

in Equation 1 that we use to calculate $\theta_{u,t}^{com+B}$. Here, the value of $\theta_{c_i,t-1}^{com+B}$ is equal to $\frac{1}{|\mathcal{C}_{u,t}|}\sum \theta_{u_i,t-1}$, where $u_i \in \mathcal{C}_{u,t-1}$.

For private topical aspects $\theta_{u,t}^u$, we use a Dirichlet distribution over $x_t^u = \theta_{u,t-1}^u$ that is derived from values in period $t-1$. For bursty topics in period t, we only focus on those "burst" words that have a high term frequency within period t. Similar to [32], we define a keyword to be "bursty" if its frequency $n_{w,t}$ at time t is above a threshold value. We derive $\theta_{u,t}^B$ from a Dirichlet distribution over the hyperparameter α_t^B.

For a tweet in $\mathcal{D}_t$ that is posted during time period t, a probabilistic distribution ϑ_t over topics $Z_t = Z_t^u \cup Z_t^{com} \cup Z_t^B$ is derived from a Dirichlet distribution over the hyperparameter α_t.

For each word w in tweet $d_t, d_t \in \{\mathcal{D}_{u,t}, \mathcal{D}_t\}$ proposed during period t, we assign a specific topic z from u's interests $\theta_{u,t}$ or distribution ϑ_t for candidate documents. For topic aspects z ($z \in Z_t^{com} \cup Z_t^B \cup Z_t^u$), we introduce three kinds of multinomial distribution ϕ_t^{com}, ϕ_t^u and ϕ_t^B to reflect the probability over Z^{com}, Z^B and Z^u, respectively. Based on [13, 30], we assume that the common and personal topic propagations follow a Dirichlet distribution over the value from the previous interval's distributions, with a weighted prior $\beta_t = \{\beta_t^{com}, \beta_t^u\}$: for common topics $z \in Z_t^{com}$, we use the Dirichlet distribution to infer from $\{\phi_{t-1}^{com}, \phi_{t-1}^B\}$; for private topics $z \in Z_t^u$, ϕ_t^u is derived from ϕ_{t-1}^u.

This concludes the technical account of the graphical model depicted in Figure 2. After computing the models for period t for all users in $\mathcal{U}$, we update the edge weights for the social circles ($\lambda_{u,c_i,t}$), using related users' interests θ and current social circles. Inference for our topic modeling process will then move on to period $t+1$. The generative process for the TPM model at time interval t, $0 < t < T$, is described in Figure 3.

4.2 Inference and Parameter Estimation

Sampling-based methods for LDA rarely include methods for optimizing hyper-parameters. In the TPM model, since $\alpha_{u,t}$ and $\beta_{z,t}^{f_l}$ indicate the weight of the results for period $t-1$ for computations for period t, it is necessary to find an optimized process for hyper-parameters $\alpha_{u,t}$ and $\beta_{z,t}^{f_l}$ during our posterior inference. Therefore, unlike many previous dynamic topic models, to infer weighted priors we use a Gibbs EM algorithm [29] to handle the approximate posterior inference step. For user u at time interval t, we first jointly sample topic z_i and parameter q_i from the ith word in tweet d ($d \in D_{u,t}$) over other variables. So for u's tweets we obtain:

$$p(e_i = l, z_i = z|\mathcal{W}, e_{-i}, Z_{-i}, x_{u,t}, \sigma, \beta_t^u) \propto \frac{n_{d,l,-i}^{u,t} + \sigma}{n_{d,-i}^{u,t} + 3\sigma} \cdot \frac{n_{d,z,-i}^{u,t} + x_{u,z,t}^{f_l}}{\sum_{z' \in Z^{f_l}} (n_{d,z',-i}^{u,t} + x_{u,z',t}^{f_l})} \cdot \frac{n_{w,z,-i}^{u,t} + \beta_t^{f_l}}{\sum_{w' \in N_{u,t}} n_{w',z,-i}^{u,t} + N_{u,t}\beta_t^{f_l}}, \tag{2}$$

where l indicates the possible values of variable e for the ith word in tweet p, and the f_l indicate the corresponding kind of topics when $e_i = l$. For private and common topics in u, i.e., $l = 0, 1$, in Equation 2, $n_{d,l,-i}^{u,t}$ indicates the number of times that words in d are assigned to label l except for the ith word, whereas $n_{d,-i}^{u,t}$ indicates the sum of $n_{d,l,-i}^{u,t}$ for all values of l. Furthermore, $n_{d,z,-i}^{u,t}$ is the number of times that tweet d is assigned to topic z excluding the ith word in d, whereas $n_{w,z,-i}^{u,t}$ indicates the number of times that word w is assigned by topic z excluding the ith word. According to Figure 3, if $e_i = 2$, we are dealing with a "bursty" topic, so the vocabulary only refers to the set of "bursty" keywords in $\{\mathcal{D}_{u,t}, \mathcal{D}_t\}$, then $x_{u,t}^B$ in Eq. 2 equals to α_t^B.

For the process of sampling candidate tweets from $\mathcal{D}_t$, we have a similar procedure, as follows:

$$p(q_i = l, z_i = z|\mathcal{W}, d_{-i}, Z_{-i}, \alpha_t, \gamma, \beta_t^u) \propto \frac{n_{d,l,-i}^t + \gamma}{n_{d,-i}^t + 3\gamma} \cdot \frac{n_{d,z,-i}^t + \alpha_t^{f_l}}{\sum_{z' \in Z^{f_l}} n_{d,z',-i}^t + Z^{f_l}\alpha_t^{f_l}} \cdot \frac{n_{w,z,-i}^t + \beta_t^{f_l}}{\sum_{w' \in N_t} n_{w',z,-i}^{u,t} + N_{u,t}\beta_t^{f_l}}. \tag{3}$$

Meanwhile, every time after sampling for $p(e_i = l, z_i = z)$ and $p(q_i = l, z_i = z)$, we optimize $\widehat{\alpha}_{u,t}$ and $\widehat{\beta}_{z,t,t-1}^{f_l}$ by maximizing the likelihood posterior distribution

$$p(W|\Phi_{t-1}, x_{u,t-1}, \alpha^B, \beta_t, \sigma, \gamma),$$

so we get

$$\widehat{\alpha}_{u,t} = \widehat{\alpha}_{u,t} \cdot \frac{\sum_{z \in Z_t^{com}} (\theta_{u,t-1,z} - \sum_{c_i \in C_{u,t-1}} \lambda \theta_{c_i,t-1}) A_{u,z,t}}{\Psi(n_{u,t}^{com} + \alpha_{u,t}) - \Psi(\alpha_{u,t})} \tag{4}$$

and

$$\hat{\beta}_{z,t}^{f_l} = \hat{\beta}_{z,t}^{f_l} \cdot \frac{\sum_{w \in N_t} \phi_{t-1,w}^{f_l} \left(\Psi(n_{w,z,t}^{f_l} + y_{t,t-1}^{w,z}) - \Psi(y_{t,t-1}^{w,z})\right)}{\Psi(n_{z,t}^{f_l} + \beta_{z,t}) - \Psi(\beta_{z,t})} \tag{5}$$

where $\Psi(x)$ is defined by $\Psi(x) = \frac{\partial \log \Gamma(x)}{\partial x}$, $A_{u,z,t}$ refers to

$$\Psi(n_{u,z,t}^{com} + x_{u,z,t}^{com}) - \Psi(x_{u,z,t}^{com}),$$

and $y_{t,t-1}^{w,z}$ is defined as $\beta_t^{com}\phi_{t-1}^{com+B}$.

Algorithm 1 summarizes the Gibbs EM sampling inference based on the equations that we have just derived. During the Gibbs EM

Algorithm 1: Gibbs EM Sampling Process during period t

Input: β_t, β^B, α^B, α_t, $X_{u,t}$, Φ^f_{t-1}, d_t, $\mathcal{U}$, $\mathcal{D}_t$ and R
Output: $\hat{\beta}^{fl}_t$, $\hat{\alpha}_t$, $\langle e, z\rangle$ and $\langle q, z\rangle$
Initialize β_t, β^B, α^B, α_t; *Topic assignment for all words*

```
for u ∈ U do
    r = 0;
    for r<R do
        E-Step:
        for d = 1 to D_{u,t} do
            for i = 1 to N_d do
                Draw ⟨e_i, z_i⟩ from Eq. 2
                Update n^{u,t}_{e,0,i}, n^{u,t}_{e,z,i} and n^{u,t}_{w,z,i}
            end
        end
        for d = 1 to D_t do
            for i = 1 to N_d do
                Draw ⟨q_i, z_i⟩ from Eq. 3
                Update n^t_{q,l,i}, n^t_{d,z,i} and n^t_{w,z,i};
            end
        end
        M-Step:
        Calculate θ^{fl}_{u,t}, φ^{fl}_{w,t}, ϑ^{fl}_{d,t}, and λ_{u,c_i} from Eq. 6, 8;
        Maximize α̂^{(r)}_{u,t} and β̂^{fl,(r)}_{z,t} from Eq. 4, 5;
        r = r + 1 and go to E-Step;
    end
end
```

sampling process, we estimate the parameters of user u's interests $\theta^{e=l}_{u,z,t}$, the probability of topics over candidate tweets $\vartheta^{q=l}_{d,z,t}$, topic distributions over words $\phi^{fl}_{w,z,t}$ and $\{\pi_{d,l,t}, r_{d,l,t}\}$ as follows:

$$\begin{aligned}
\theta^{fl}_{u,z,t} &= \frac{n^{u,t}_z + x^{fl}_{u,z,t}}{\sum_{z\in Z^{fl}} n^{u,t}_{z'} + x^{fl}_{u,z',t}} \\
\vartheta^{fl}_{d,z,t} &= \frac{n_{d,z,t} + \alpha_{z,t}}{\sum_{z\in Z^{fl}} n_{d,z',t} + \alpha_{z',t}} \\
\phi^{fl}_{w,z,t} &= \frac{n_{w,z,t} + \beta^{fl}_{w,t}}{\sum_{z\in Z^{fl}} n_{w,z,t} + \beta^{fl}_{w,t}} \\
\pi_{d,l,t} &= \frac{n^{u,t}_{d,l} + \sigma}{n^{u,t}_d + 3\sigma} \\
r_{d,l,t} &= \frac{n^t_{d,l} + \gamma}{n^t_d + 3\gamma}
\end{aligned} \tag{6}$$

To compute the weight $\lambda_{c_{u,t}}$, we use a Markov random walk strategy, which calculates saliency of a social circle based on "voting" from others. Since each social circle can be considered as a set of users, an interest distribution $\theta^{com+B}_{c_i,t-1}$ for each social circle c_i can be computed as $\sum_{u'\in c_i}\theta^{com+B}_{u',t-1}$. Thus we compute a $\theta^{com+B}_{u,t}$-based similarity matrix $SIM^{u,t}$ among different social circles, where each item $SIM^{u,t}_{i,j}$ is computed based on the divergence between two items:

$$div(\theta_{c_i}, \theta_{c_j}|\theta_u) = \sum_{z\in Z}\left|\theta_{c_i,z}\ln\frac{\theta_{c_i,z}}{\theta_{u,z}} - \theta_{c_j,z}\ln\frac{\theta_{c_i,z}}{\theta_{u,z}}\right| \tag{7}$$

We calculate the saliency of c_i after normalizing SIM into $\widehat{SIM}$:

$$\lambda_{u,c_i,t} = \mu\sum_{i\neq j}\widehat{sim}(\theta_{c_i,t}, \theta_{c_j,t}|\theta_{u,t})\cdot\lambda_{u,c_i,t} + \frac{(1-\mu)}{|C_{u,t}|} \tag{8}$$

4.3 Time-Aware Summarization

After Gibbs EM sampling, for each candidate tweet d_t at time t, we have two parametric distributions ϑ_t and ϕ_t that reflect the topic-tweet distribution and the word-topic distribution, respectively. I.e., $P(z_t|d_t) = \theta_{z_t,d_t}$ and $P(w|z_t) = \phi_{z,t,w}$. For user u at time t, we now derive the distribution of interests over topics $\theta_{u,t}$, i.e., $P(z_t|u,t)$.

Given the distribution $\theta_{u,t}$, one intuitive way to get the most meaningful tweets is to extract the most similar tweets with $\theta_{u,t}$ from among a candidate set $\mathcal{D}_t$. However, a high-degree relevance in latent topic distributions cannot be taken as the only criterion in our tweet selection. Thus after extracting a set of relevant tweets $\mathcal{R}_t$ from $\mathcal{D}_t$, there are three key requirements for an ideal summary [16] that we need to consider in generating a tweet summary: *novelty*, the *coverage* and the *diversity*.

Novelty calculates the semantic divergence between the currently selected set $RT_{u,t}$ and the results in previous time periods $RT_{t'}$. Our intention is to make the current results as different as possible from previous results as much as possible. Therefore, we have:

$$\mathcal{L}_N(RT_t|RT_{t'}) = \sum_{p\in RT}\min_{p'\in RT_{t'}}(div(\vartheta_p, \vartheta_{p'}|\theta_{u,t})) \tag{9}$$

where the divergence $div(\vartheta_p, \vartheta_{p'}|\theta_{u,t})$ between ϑ_p and $\vartheta_{p'}$ are calculated based on Equation 7.

Furthermore, a tweet summary should contain important aspects from all related tweets and minimize the information loss with the set of all candidate tweets. Thus, given $\theta_{u,z,t}$, the *coverage* between RT and $\mathcal{D}_t$ is calculated as follows:

$$\mathcal{L}_C(RT|\mathcal{D}_t) = \sum_{d\in RT} e^{-\min_z \sum_{d'\in\mathcal{D}_t} div(\vartheta_{d,z}, \vartheta_{d',z}|\theta_{u,z,t})} \tag{10}$$

where the divergence $div(\vartheta_{d,z}, \vartheta_{d',z}|\theta_{u,z,t})$ is calculated as follows:

$$div(\vartheta_{d,z}, \vartheta_{d',z}|\theta_{u,z,t}) = \left|\vartheta_{d,z}\ln\frac{\vartheta_{d,z}}{\theta_{u,z,t}} - \vartheta_{d',z}\ln\frac{\vartheta_{d,z}}{\theta_{u,z,t}}\right| \tag{11}$$

Diversity calculates the information divergence among all tweets within the current candidate result set. Ideally, the tweet summary results have the largest possible difference in topic distributions with each other. The equation is as follows:

$$\mathcal{L}_D(RT) = \sum_{w,w'\in RT}\max_z div(\phi_{w,z,t}, \phi_{w',z,t}|\prod_{d\in\mathcal{D}_t}\vartheta_{d,z}) \tag{12}$$

where we compute the divergence $div(\phi_{w,z,t}, \phi_{w',z,t}|\prod_{d\in\mathcal{D}_t}\vartheta_{d,z})$ in the same way as Equation 11.

The exact process for generating $RT_{u,t}$ given user u is shown in Algorithm 2. Illuminated by a previous work [33], an iterative optimization algorithm is used to select the set $RT_{u,t}$. During each iteration n, we extract tweet d_x such that $d_x \in \mathcal{R}_t \cap d_x \notin RT_{u,t}$ to substitute $d_y \in RT^{(n)}_{u,t}$ when the saliency gain $\mathcal{S}((RT_{u,t}-)\cup d_x) - \mathcal{S}(RT_{u,t})$ gets a maximum value. The algorithm will converge when $\mathcal{S}(RT_{u,t})$ reaches its maximum value.

5. EXPERIMENTAL SETUP

For our experiments we employ a Twitter dataset that includes both social relations and tweets: we crawl tweets via the Twitter

Algorithm 2: Iterative Process for $RT_{u,t}$ Generation.

Input : $\mathcal{D}_t$, $RT_{u,t'}$, $\theta_{u,t}$, ϕ_t, N;
Output: $RT_{u,t}$;

Calculate Kullback-Leibler divergence $KL(\vartheta_{d,t}, \theta_{u,t})$;
Rank and extract relevant tweets to $\mathcal{R}_t$ by $e^{-KL(\vartheta_{d,t}, \theta_{u,t})}$;
Initialize: Extract N tweets from $\mathcal{R}_t$ to $RT_{u,t}$;
repeat
  Extract $\mathcal{X}_t = \{d_x \in \mathcal{R}_t \cap d_x \notin RT_{u,t}\}$;
  for $d_x \in \mathcal{X}_t, \forall d_y \in RT_{u,t}$ **do**
    Calculate $\mathcal{S}_{RT_{u,t}} = F(\mathcal{L}_C \cdot \mathcal{L}_N \cdot \mathcal{L}_D)$;
    Calculate
    $\Delta\mathcal{S}_{d_x,d_y} = \mathcal{S}((RT_{u,t} - d_y) \cup d_x) - \mathcal{S}(RT_{u,t})$;
  end
  Get $\left\langle \hat{d_x}, \hat{d_y} \right\rangle$ that $\left\langle \hat{d_x}, \hat{d_y} \right\rangle = \arg\max_{d_x,d_y} \Delta\mathcal{S}_{d_x,d_y}$;
  $RT_{u,t} = (RT_{u,t} - \hat{d_y}) \cup \hat{d_x}$;
until $\forall\Delta\mathcal{S}_{d_x,d_y} < \varepsilon$;
return $RT_{u,t}$.

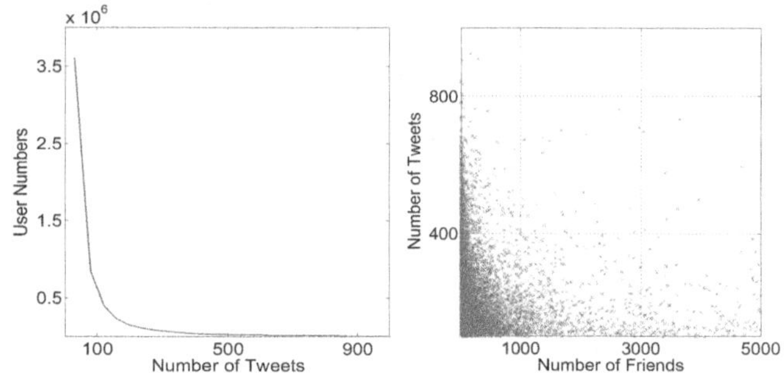

(a) (b)

Figure 4: Histograms of the number of users and tweets in our dataset: the left (a) indicates the number of tweets per user in our dataset where the y-axis denotes the number of tweets; while the right (b) indicates the number of tweets per user with its number of friends in Twitter, where y-axis indicates the number of tweets the user wrote and the x-axis indicates the number of friends.

streaming API,[2] which contains a random sample of around 10% of all items posted on Twitter. Timestamps in our dataset are from November 1, 2009 to December 31, 2010; the 2009 part contains 47,373,408 tweets and 562,361 users, while the numbers for 2010 are 295,145,421 and 5,828,356, respectively. Figure 4(a) shows the statistics of the number of tweets per user in our dataset, where we can find that most users (75.2%) in our dataset wrote fewer than 100 tweets. For crawling the social relations, we use the dataset from [15], which includes social relations for all users on Twitter until July 2009. In our experiments, we use only those tweets and users that appear in both datasets. In our experiments we assume social relations among users to remain the same over the entire time period.

Since it is impossible to evaluate the effectiveness if a user posted nothing on Twitter, sparse postings obstruct our experimental evaluation. We therefore only consider users who posted a sufficient number of tweets for our evaluation: we collect users who post over 100 tweets in our dataset. This results in a subset containing 32,659 users. Thereafter we use social relations to build the social circles around those users. Figure 4(b) shows the number of tweets of these users (y-axis) versus the number of friends on the x-axis. We further remove non-English tweets through automatic language identification [3]. We remove stop words and apply Porter stemming [23].

5.1 Data Enrichment

Since each tweet is only up to 140 characters long, the amount of textual evidence to work with is very limited. To remedy this, we employ a state-of-the-art method for *linking* tweets to Wikipedia articles [20]. In particular, we employ the so-called CMNS method that uses the prior probability that Wikipedia article c is the target of a link with anchor text q within Wikipedia:

$$CMNS(c, q) = \frac{|L_{q,c}|}{\sum_{c'} |L_{q,c'}|}, \tag{13}$$

where $L_{q,c}$ denotes the set of all links with anchor text q and target c.

After we have obtained three Wikipedia articles with the highest CMNS score, we extract the most *central* sentences from these Wikipedia articles and append them to the tweet. In particular, we apply a query-sensitive graph-based summarization method, similar to [10], to each Wikipedia article to ranking sentences, using the tweet d_t as the query. This calculates the score of each sentence via "votes" from other sentences in a document. Figure 5 shows 4 example tweets and the appended sentences. Here, the left text box in each item is a tweet and on the right we show the identified sentences from the linked Wikipedia articles.

5.2 Experimental Setup

Following existing topic models [11], we set pre-defined values for the hyperparameters α_t and β_t in our graphical model: for the weighted parameter $\alpha_{u,t}$ and β_t, we set $50/K_t^u$ to $\alpha_{u,t}$ and 0.5 to β_t respectively. And we set $50/K_t^B$ to α^B and 0.5 to β^B respectively. For the hyperparameters γ and σ in TPM, as defined in [14], we set $\sigma_u = \gamma_{com} = 0.5$ and $\gamma_u = \sigma_{com} = 0.3$. For burst topics we set $\gamma_B = \sigma_B = 0.2$ in our experiments. The initial value of $\lambda_{u,c_i,t-1}$ for each social circle of u is set to $1/C_{u,t}$, the parameter μ is set as 0.85; and ε in Algorithm 2 is set to 0.0001. For the number of topics in our topic modeling process, the default values for Z_0^u and Z_0^{com} in our experiments are set to 100, respectively. To optimize the number of topics, we compare performance in various values and discuss it latter.

Statistical significance of observed differences between two comparisons is tested using a two-tailed paired t-test. In our experiments, statistical significance is denoted using $^\blacktriangle$ for significant differences for $\alpha = 0.01$, or $^\triangle$ for $\alpha = 0.05$.

5.3 Evaluation Metrics

Evaluating the effectiveness of time-aware tweets summarization is a challenging task, especially in the absence of explicit user feedback. One possible solution is to use evidence from users themselves: we use a user's retweeted post(s) at time $t+1$ as the ground truth to evaluate performance of comparisons at time t.

We measure the quality of summaries by counting overlapping textual *units* between the generated results and the ground truth results. In our experiments, we adopt the ROUGE evaluation metrics [17], a widely-used recall-oriented metric in the task of document summarization that evaluates the overlap between a gold standard and candidate selections.[3] In our experiments, ROUGE-1 (*unigram based method*), ROUGE-2 (*bigram based method*) and ROUGE-W (*weighted longest common sequence*) are used as evaluation metrics.

[2]https://dev.twitter.com/docs/streaming-apis.

[3]Version 1.5.5 is used in this paper.

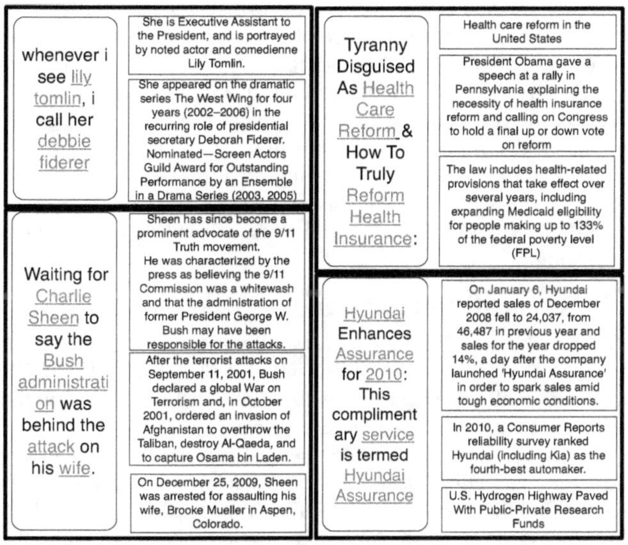

Figure 5: Four examples for entity linking and ranking corresponding to four individual tweets, where the textbox on left side indicates the original tweet while the textbox on the right side shows the extracted related sentences. A mixture of the tweet and extracted wiki sentences will replace the original tweet in our experiments.

5.4 Baseline Comparisons

Given the TPM modeling introduced in Section 4.1, our contribution is twofold: (1) we introduce collaborative influence to user's interests detection; (2) we adopt time-aware propagation to infer topics. To evaluate the influence of social circles and time-aware topics, besides our overall TPM-based strategy, we also evaluate the performance of the model that only includes (1) the collaborative influence or only the (2) time-aware propagation, respectively.

We write **TPM-ALL** for the overall process as described in Section 4.1, which includes both the social influence modeling and time-aware topic and interests tracking. We write **TPM-SOC** for the model that only considers users' social influence (so excluding time-aware topic propagation and it doesn't consider if some topic is private or not). We write **TPM-TOP** for the model that uses a user's own tweets (without social circles but considering topic and interests propagation with the time).

To evaluate our proposed method in more detail, in our experiments the baselines not only include widely-used topic models, but also recent user behavior models on Twitter. For those topic models, we use the Author-Topic Model (**AT**) [26] and the Twitter-LDA [37] as baselines for topic models: (AT) focuses on various users' interests in one static corpus. Since each tweet only has one author, AT's process on Twitter coincides with the LDA modeling process on all tweets written by a specific user. As an extension of the author-topic model, Twitter-LDA **(TLDA)** classifies topics into private topics and background topic by introducing one binomial distribution. For comparison, we use one more state-of-the-art use behavior model, **UBM** [32]; here, a user's interest is tracked by a mixture graphical model that considers background knowledge, social interests and the user's own interest. The final baseline that we consider is **TF-IDF**, which uses TF-IDF to re-calculate $\mathcal{S}_{RT_{u,t}}$ in Algorithm 2. Finally, we also use **SUM-TF**, a baseline used in [4] that extract tweets by ranking *tf* scores, and **Random**, which extracts tweets randomly in each period.

For the baseline topic models, we use a similar tweet selection method as in Algorithm 2 to select tweets in each time interval. For static topic models, results at time $t, 1 \leq t \leq T$ are calculated after re-modeling for all past data before period t.

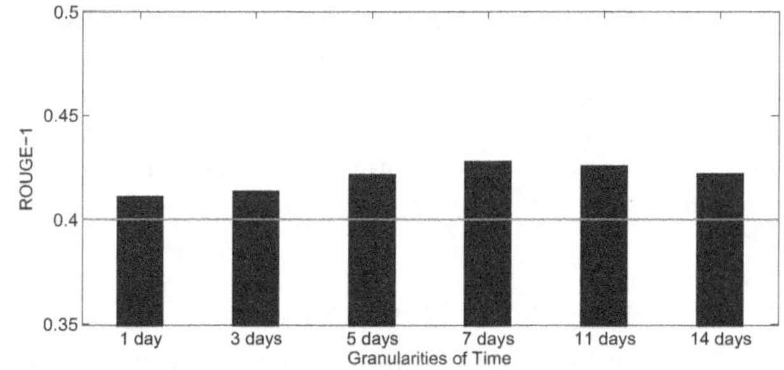

Figure 6: Performance of TPM-ALL with various granularities of time periods.

To evaluate the effectiveness of results to *personalized* aspect, we introduce several other sentence extraction procedures from the area of document summarization (without personalization) as baselines: **LexRank** and **Centroid** are two widely-used unsupervised document summarization methods, where **LexRank** [26] is a graph-based method for ranking tweet as "votes" from other tweets, and **Centroid** [24] applies the MEAD summarization method that uses statistical and structural features in tweets selection.

5.5 Granularities and Number of Topics

To test the optimal granularity of time intervals, we examine ROUGE-1 performance of TPM-ALL with different values for granularities, shown in Figure 6. The performance of TPM-ALL in terms of ROUGE-1 peaks when the granularity is set to 7 days. With fewer than 7 days, performance keeps increasing because adding more days reduces sparseness; but after 7 days, due to the increase in irrelevant and noisy tweets, the ROUGE-1 score decrease. Thus, we set the granularity to 7 days in the remainder of our experiments.

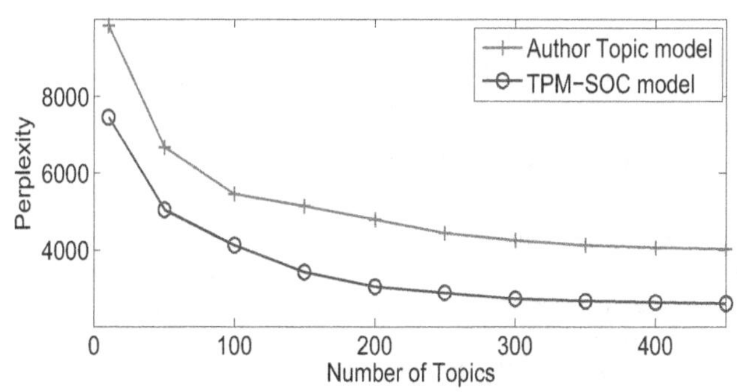

Figure 7: Perplexity performance with different number of topics in Author topic model and TPM-SOC model;

Optimizing the number of topics is a problem shared between all topic modeling approaches. Similar to previous work [2, 11, 32], we introduce the perplexity of a held-out test set to evaluate the performance of our topic models. The perplexity, usually used in language modeling, focuses on the inverse of the geometric mean per-word likelihood, which is calculated as follows:

$$Perplexity(W) = \exp\left[-\frac{\sum_{t\in T}\sum_{w\in\mathcal{D}_t}\log p(w)}{\sum_{t\in T} d_t}\right] \quad (14)$$

where $p(w)$ indicates $p(w) = p(w|z)p(z)$. Thus, a lower perplexity score indicates a better generalization performance [2]. Figure 7 shows the results of perplexity values for the author-topic model and the TPM-SOC model with differing numbers of topics on our held-out test set. After the number of topics becomes larger than 300, the perplexity of both approaches starts to flatten out. We find that TPM-SOC outperforms the author-topic model with better generalization performance. For TPM-ALL and TPM-TOP we set the number of "private" topics and "common" topics to 150, separately.

6. RESULTS AND DISCUSSION

In this section we provide an answer to the following research questions. (1) How does the TPM-based TaTS strategy perform on time-aware tweets summarization (§6.1)? (2) How does the TPM-based TaTS strategy perform on social-aware tweets summarization? (§6.2)? And (3) what is the overall performance for TPM on the task of personalized TaTS (§6.3)?

6.1 Time-Aware Comparisons

To illustrate the performance at different time periods, the evaluation results of the TPM-ALL, TPM-TOP, UBM and AT strategies at different time periods are shown in Figure 8, in terms of ROUGE-1, ROUGE-2 and ROUGE-W, respectively. We select 10 contiguous weeks from November 1, 2009 onwards as the test period and separate it into 10 periods.

In Figure 8 we observe that the AT model obtains the worst performance, while both TPM-ALL and TPM-TOP outperform all other strategies in terms of ROUGE metrics at all time intervals. This demonstrates the advantage of TPM-based strategies in time-aware comparisons. In Figure 8, we observe a "cold-start" phenomenon, which results from the sparseness of the context in the first time period. In that condition, TPM-ALL and TPM-TOP are nearly equivalent to the UBM and AT since there are neither social circles nor burst topics during the first time period. After that, the performance of the TPM based methods keeps increasing over time until it achieves a stable performance after $t = 3$. We find that TPM based strategies are sensitive to time-aware topic drifting. Meanwhile, we find that TPM-ALL performs better than TPM-TOP in Figure 8. TPM-ALL detects user's interests using social circles whereas TPM-TOP ignores them.

6.2 Social-Aware Comparisons

To evaluate the influence of social circles in our proposed strategy, we investigate the performance under various numbers of social circles. From our dataset, we extract users with different numbers of social circles and compare the performance of our methods on these data sets in terms of ROUGE. In Figure 9 we plot the values of ROUGE-1, ROUGE-2 and ROUGE-W in (a) to (c), respectively. For each figure, we compare our strategies that do consider social circles, TPM-ALL and TPM-SOC, against the TPM-TOP and UBM methods under varying number of social circles.

We observe from Figure 9(a) that the performance in terms of ROUGE-1 changes with the number of social circles, and the value increases and achieves a maximal value between 3 and 5 social circles. After that, the value decreases rapidly; redundant and irrelevant "relations" seem to enter the picture. Another plausible explanation concerns the difference of user characteristics in various social circles. Since the UBM and TPM-TOP models do not consider the social influence, their ROUGE values keep constant for different numbers of social circles. We observe a similar behavior in Figure 9(b) and 9(c) in terms of ROUGE-2 and ROUGE-W.

To evaluate the effect of collaborative filtering in TPM for various classes of users, especially for "passive" users on Twitter who rarely write a tweet, we compare the performance of different users in terms of ROUGE metrics with varying values of the number of tweets selected per period (40 or 60). We separate users into 3 classes by counting their tweets: (1) less than 400 tweets; (2) between 400 to 800; and (3) more than 800 tweets. As shown in Figure 10(a) and (c) that focusing on ROUGE-1, the difference between TPM-ALL and TPM-TOP is bigger for users with up to 400 tweets than for those with more than 400. This can be explained by the fact that the collaborative filtering used in TPM-ALL becomes more effective when there is a bigger data sparseness issue to overcome. In terms of ROUGE-2, similar results can be found in Figure 10(b) and (d).

6.3 Overall Performance

Table 2 shows the average performance of our TPM-based strategies and baselines, in terms of ROUGE-1, ROUGE-2 and ROUGE-W, based on all candidate tweets in all time periods. We find that our method outperforms the baselines in every case. Except for our TPM-based strategies, UBM get the best performance than others. Since summarization baselines are not sensitive to users' interests, thus we find that Centroid, Lex-R (short for LexRank), and SUM-TF do not perform well. Among the topic models, we found that the AT-based method yields almost the worst performance. This can be explained by the fact that the topic modeling procedure in AT does not capture topic drift and users' social circles.

We evaluated the performance of the various approaches in terms of the three ROUGE metrics for a varying number of tweets selected per period, i.e., $N = 40$ and $N = 60$. As shown in Table 2, TPM-ALL performs better than all baselines on all metrics. For $N = 40$, TPM-ALL achieves an increase of 10.6%, 11.6% and 8.9% over UBM in terms of ROUGE-1, ROUGE-2, and ROUGE-W respectively. For $N = 60$, TPM-ALL gives an increase of 11.2%, 11.2% and 10.1% over UBM. For the dynamic version without social influence, TPM-TOP outperforms all other baselines also, which indicates the effectiveness of detecting dynamic topics. We further compare TPM-TOP with UBM: for $N = 40$, TPM-TOP offers relative performance improvements of 4.1%, 6.25% and 4.8%, respectively, for the ROUGE-1, ROUGE-2 and ROUGE-W metrics, while the relative improvements are 7.8%, 6.7% and 7.3% on the same metrics for $N = 60$. We find that TPM-ALL outperforms the UBM baselines with a statistical significance difference at level $\alpha < 0.01$ in terms of all ROUGE metrics, whereas TPM-TOP and TPM-SOC outperforms UBM with a statistical significance difference at level $\alpha < 0.05$.

7. CONCLUSION AND FUTURE WORK

We have considered the task of personalized time-aware tweets summarization, based on user history and influences from "social circles." To handle the dynamic nature of topics and user interests along with the relative sparseness of individual messages, we have proposed a time-aware user behavior model. Based on probabilistic distributions from our proposed topic model, the tweets propagation model, we have introduced an iterative optimization algorithm to select tweets subject to three key criteria: novelty, coverage and diversity. In our experiments we have verified the effectiveness of our proposed method, showing significant improvements over various state-of-the-art baselines.

As to future work, we aim to employ a user-study to enhance the accuracy of interest detection, e.g., via an online evaluation. Another future direction is to take more information and features into account for our task: our current experiments ignore, e.g., URLs appearing in tweets which could enhance our entity linking setup. It will also be interesting to consider other features for modeling, such as geographic or profile information. Finally, our current model is evaluated based on fixed time intervals, which might not accurately

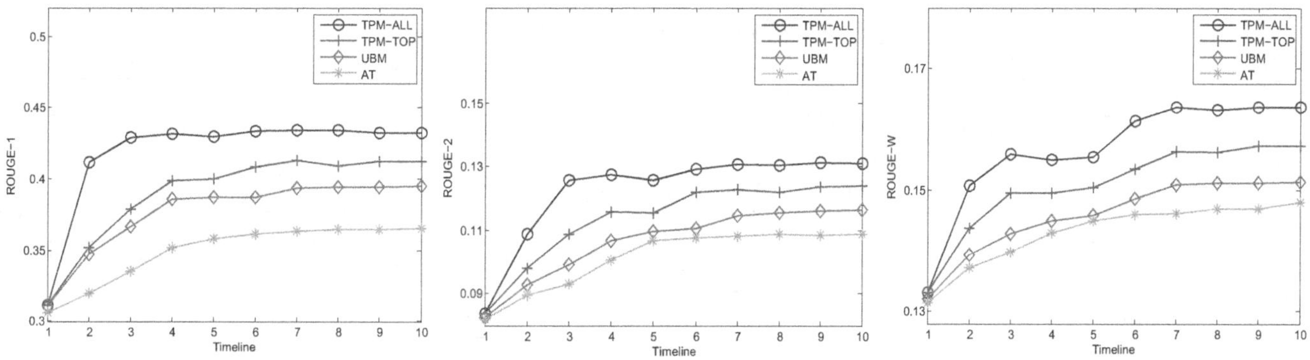

(a) ROUGE-1 (b) ROUGE-2 (c) ROUGE-W

Figure 8: Time-aware performance in terms of ROUGE metrics.

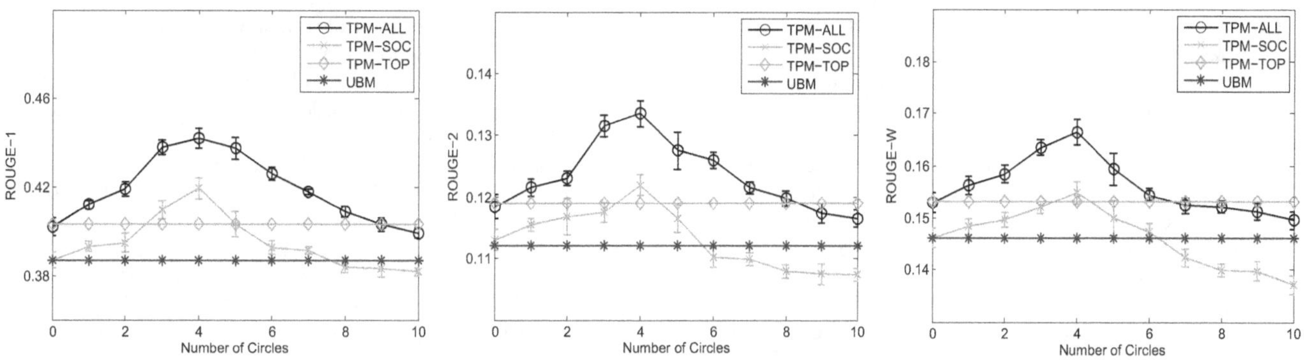

(a) ROUGE-1 (b) ROUGE-2 (c) ROUGE-W

Figure 9: ROUGE-1 and ROUGE-2 performance with increasing numbers of social circles.

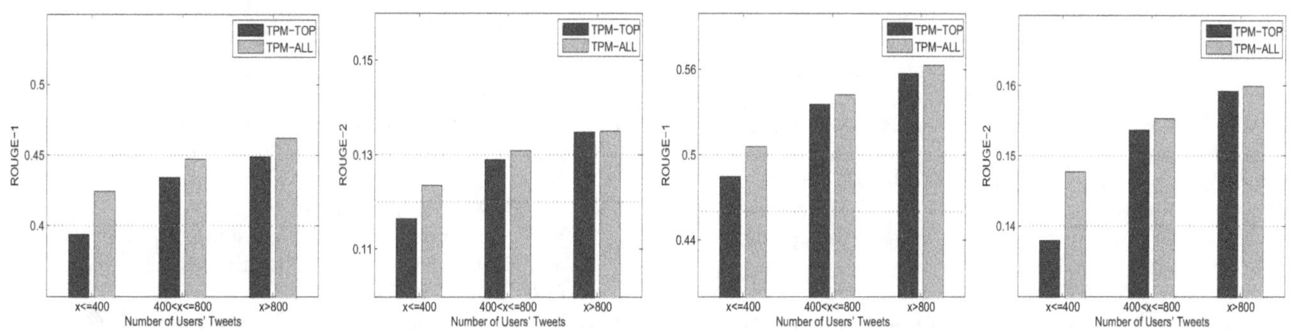

(a) ROUGE-1, N=40 (b) ROUGE-2, N=40 (c) ROUGE-1, N=60 (d) ROUGE-2, N=60

Figure 10: Performance for different kinds of users: users in our dataset are classified by their number of tweets.

reflect bursty topics on Twitter. Therefore, a novel graphical model that includes dynamic time bins instead of the fixed time granularities, will be another direction for future research.

Acknowledgements. This research was supported by the European Community's Seventh Framework Programme (FP7/2007-2013) under grant agreements nr 258191 (PROMISE Network of Excellence) and 288024 (LiMoSINe project), the Netherlands Organisation for Scientific Research (NWO) under project nrs 640.004.802, 727.011.005, 612.001.116, HOR-11-10, the Center for Creation, Content and Technology (CCCT), the BILAND project funded by the CLARIN-nl program, the Dutch national program COMMIT, the ESF Research Network Program ELIAS, the Elite Network Shifts project funded by the Royal Dutch Academy of Sciences (KNAW), and the Netherlands eScience Center under project number 027.012.105.

8. REFERENCES

[1] D. Blei and J. Lafferty. Dynamic topic models. In *ICML 2006*, pages 113–120, 2006.

[2] D. Blei, A. Ng, and M. Jordan. Latent dirichlet allocation. *Journal of machine Learning research*, 3:993–1022, 2003.

[3] S. Carter, W. Weerkamp, and M. Tsagkias. Microblog language identification: overcoming the limitations of short, unedited and idiomatic text. *Language Resources and Evaluation*, 2012.

Table 2: Overall ROUGE Performance for All Comparisons

Metrics	TPM-ALL	TPM-TOP	TPM-SOC	UBM	TLDA	AT	TF-IDF	Centroid	Lex-R	SUM-TF	Random
Cut-off of $N = 40$ tweets per period											
ROUGE-1	**0.428** $^{\blacktriangle}$	0.403 $^{\blacktriangle}$	0.395 $^{\blacktriangle}$	0.387	0.374	0.355	0.341	0.302	0.291	0.274	0.252
ROUGE-2	**0.125** $^{\blacktriangle}$	0.119 $^{\triangle}$	0.116 $^{\triangle}$	0.114	0.112	0.102	0.095	0.081	0.077	0.079	0.037
ROUGE-W	**0.159** $^{\blacktriangle}$	0.153 $^{\blacktriangle}$	0.149 $^{\triangle}$	0.146	0.142	0.144	0.137	0.118	0.115	0.105	0.076
Cut-off of $N = 60$ tweets per period											
ROUGE-1	**0.513** $^{\blacktriangle}$	0.497 $^{\blacktriangle}$	0.482 $^{\blacktriangle}$	0.461	0.457	0.423	0.411	0.362	0.369	0.329	0.281
ROUGE-2	**0.149** $^{\blacktriangle}$	0.142 $^{\triangle}$	0.139 $^{\triangle}$	0.134	0.127	0.122	0.116	0.097	0.102	0.095	0.041
ROUGE-W	**0.197** $^{\blacktriangle}$	0.191 $^{\blacktriangle}$	0.189 $^{\blacktriangle}$	0.178	0.176	0.166	0.161	0.131	0.135	0.119	0.081

[4] D. Chakrabarti and K. Punera. Event summarization using tweets. In *ICWSM 2011*, pages 66–73, 2011.

[5] K. Chen, T. Chen, G. Zheng, O. Jin, E. Yao, and Y. Yu. Collaborative personalized tweet recommendation. In *SIGIR 2012*, 2012.

[6] B. Connor, M. Krieger, and D. Ahn. Tweetmotif: Exploratory search and topic summarization for twitter. *ICWSM 2010*, pages 2–3, 2010.

[7] G. De Francisci Morales, A. Gionis, and C. Lucchese. From chatter to headlines: harnessing the real-time web for personalized news recommendation. In *WSDM 2012*, 2012.

[8] Q. Diao, J. Jiang, F. Zhu, and E. Lim. Finding bursty topics from microblogs. In *ACL 2012*, 2012.

[9] Y. Duan, Z. Chen, F. Wei, M. Zhou, and H. Shum. Twitter topic summarization by ranking tweets using social influence and content quality. In *COLING 2012*, pages 763–779, 2012.

[10] G. Erkan and D. Radev. Lexrank: Graph-based lexical centrality as salience in text summarization. *JAIR*, 22: 457–479, 2004.

[11] T. Griffiths and M. Steyvers. Finding scientific topics. *National Academy of Sciences*, 101:5228–5235, 2004.

[12] T. Hofmann. Probabilistic latent semantic indexing. In *SIGIR 1999*, pages 50–57, 1999.

[13] T. Iwata, S. Watanabe, T. Yamada, and N. Ueda. Topic tracking model for analyzing consumer purchase behavior. In *IJCAI 2009*, volume 9, pages 1427–1432, 2009.

[14] O. Jin, N. Liu, K. Zhao, Y. Yu, and Q. Yang. Transferring topical knowledge from auxiliary long texts for short text clustering. In *CIKM 2011*, 2011.

[15] H. Kwak, C. Lee, H. Park, and S. Moon. What is twitter, a social network or a news media? In *WWW 2010*, pages 591–600, 2010.

[16] L. Li, K. Zhou, G. Xue, H. Zha, and Y. Yu. Enhancing diversity, coverage and balance for summarization through structure learning. In *WWW 2009*, 2009.

[17] C. Lin. Rouge: A package for automatic evaluation of summaries. In *ACL 2004*, pages 74–81, 2004.

[18] H. Ma, I. King, and M. Lyu. Learning to recommend with social trust ensemble. In *SIGIR 2009*, pages 203–210, 2009.

[19] H. Ma, D. Zhou, C. Liu, M. Lyu, and I. King. Recommender systems with social regularization. In *WSDM 2011*, pages 287–296, 2011.

[20] E. Meij, W. Weerkamp, and M. de Rijke. Adding semantics to microblog posts. In *WSDM 2012*, pages 563–572, 2012.

[21] J. Nichols, J. Mahmud, and C. Drews. Summarizing sporting events using twitter. In *IUI 2012*, pages 189–198, 2012.

[22] M. Pennacchiotti, F. Silvestri, H. Vahabi, and R. Venturini. Making your interests follow you on twitter. In *CIKM 2012*, 2012.

[23] M. Porter. An algorithm for suffix stripping. *Program: electronic library and information systems*, 1980.

[24] D. Radev, H. Jing, M. Styś, and D. Tam. Centroid-based summarization of multiple documents. *Information Processing & Management*, 2004.

[25] D. Ramage, S. Dumais, and D. Liebling. Characterizing microblogs with topic models. In *ICWSM 2010*, pages 130–137, 2010.

[26] M. Rosen-Zvi, T. Griffiths, M. Steyvers, and P. Smyth. The author-topic model for authors and documents. In *UAI 2004*, pages 487–494, 2004.

[27] B. Sharifi, M. Hutton, and J. Kalita. Summarizing microblogs automatically. In *NAACL 2010*, 2010.

[28] H. Takamura, H. Yokono, and M. Okumura. Summarizing a document stream. *Advances in Information Retrieval*, pages 177–188, 2011.

[29] H. Wallach. Topic modeling: beyond bag-of-words. In *ICML 2006*, pages 977–984, 2006.

[30] X. Wei, J. Sun, and X. Wang. Dynamic mixture models for multiple time series. In *IJCAI 2007*, pages 2909–2914, 2007.

[31] J. Weng, E. Lim, J. Jiang, and Q. He. Twitterrank: finding topic-sensitive influential twitterers. In *WSDM 2010*, pages 261–270, 2010.

[32] Z. Xu, Y. Zhang, Y. Wu, and Q. Yang. Modeling user posting behavior on social media. In *SIGIR 2012*, pages 545–554, 2012.

[33] R. Yan, X. Wan, J. Otterbacher, L. Kong, X. Li, and Y. Zhang. Evolutionary timeline summarization: a balanced optimization framework via iterative substitution. In *SIGIR 2011*, pages 745–754, 2011.

[34] S. Yang, B. Long, A. Smola, N. Sadagopan, Z. Zheng, and H. Zha. Like like alike: joint friendship and interest propagation in social networks. In *WWW 2011*, pages 537–546, 2011.

[35] Z. Yang, K. Cai, J. Tang, L. Zhang, Z. Su, and J. Li. Social context summarization. In *SIGIR 2011*, 2011.

[36] M. Ye, X. Liu, and W. Lee. Exploring social influence for recommendation: a generative model approach. In *SIGIR 2012*, 2012.

[37] X. Zhao, J. Jiang, J. He, Y. Song, P. Achananuparp, E. LIM, and X. Li. Topical keyphrase extraction from twitter. In *ACL 2011*, 2011.

Exploiting Hybrid Contexts for Tweet Segmentation

Chenliang Li[†], Aixin Sun[†], Jianshu Weng[‡], Qi He[§]
[†]School of Computer Engineering, Nanyang Technological University, Singapore
{lich0020,axsun}@ntu.edu.sg
[‡]Independent Researcher, Singapore
jianshu@acm.org
[§]IBM Almaden Research Center, USA
heq@us.ibm.com

ABSTRACT

Twitter has attracted hundred millions of users to share and disseminate most up-to-date information. However, the noisy and short nature of tweets makes many applications in information retrieval (IR) and natural language processing (NLP) challenging. Recently, segment-based tweet representation has demonstrated effectiveness in named entity recognition (NER) and event detection from tweet streams. To split tweets into meaningful phrases or segments, the previous work is purely based on external knowledge bases, which ignores the rich local context information embedded in the tweets. In this paper, we propose a novel framework for tweet segmentation in a batch mode, called *HybridSeg*. *HybridSeg* incorporates local context knowledge with global knowledge bases for better tweet segmentation. *HybridSeg* consists of two steps: learning from off-the-shelf weak NERs and learning from pseudo feedback. In the first step, the existing NER tools are applied to a batch of tweets. The named entities recognized by these NERs are then employed to guide the tweet segmentation process. In the second step, *HybridSeg* adjusts the tweet segmentation results iteratively by exploiting all segments in the batch of tweets in a collective manner. Experiments on two tweet datasets show that *HybridSeg* significantly improves tweet segmentation quality compared with the state-of-the-art algorithm. We also conduct a case study by using tweet segments for the task of named entity recognition from tweets. The experimental results demonstrate that *HybridSeg* significantly benefits the downstream applications.

Categories and Subject Descriptors

H.3.1 [**Information Systems**]: Content Analysis and Indexing—*Linguistic processing*

Keywords

Twitter, Tweet, Tweet segmentation, Named Entity Recognition

1. INTRODUCTION

Twitter has become one of the most important channels for people to find, share, and disseminate timely information. As of March 2012, there are more than 140 million active Twitter users with over 340 million tweets posted in a day[1]. Due to its large volume of timely information generated by its millions of users, it is imperative to understand tweets' language for the tremendous downstream applications like named entity recognition (NER) [12,14,21], event detection and summarization [5,15,22], opinion mining [16,17], sentiment analysis [4,13,25], etc.

Given the limited length (*i.e.,* 140 characters) of a tweet and no restrictions on its writing styles, tweets often contain grammatical errors, misspellings, and informal abbreviations. The error-prone and short nature of tweets makes the word-level language models for tweets not reliable. For example, given a tweet "I call her, no answer. Her phone in the bag, she dancin.", there is no clue to guess its true theme with the word independent assumption. Very recently, a segment-based tweet representation model has been proposed to partially overcome the adverse features of tweets [12]. After splitting a tweet into a sequence of consecutive n-grams ($n \geq 1$), each of which is called a segment, the latent topics of the tweet can be better captured. For example, the segment "she dancin" in the previous example tweet is actually a key concept – it classifies this tweet into the family of tweets talking about the song "She Dancin", a trend topic in Bay Area in Jan, 2013.

A segment can be a named entity (*e.g.,* a movie title "finding nemo"), a semantically meaningful information unit (*e.g.,* "officially released"), or any other type of phrase which appears "more than chance" [12]. Because segments preserve more semantics of tweets than words do, they have been used as the language units for the tasks of NER and event detection [11,12]. Segment-based representation has shown its effectiveness over word-based representation particularly in the event detection task.

However, developing a high quality tweet segmentation is not trivial, because the prevalence of grammatical errors and unreliable linguistic features makes classic Natural Language Processing (NLP) techniques including part-of-speech (POS) tagging [7] and NER less applicable to tweets. For example, classic POS taggers may fail in recognizing "she dancin" as a noun phrase in the previous example tweet. The seminal tweet segmentation algorithm in [12] mainly relies on external knowledge bases (*e.g.,* Wikipedia and Microsoft Web N-Gram corpus). The main assumption is that the core semantic information is well preserved in tweets in the form of named entities or semantic phrases for information sharing, despite the noise nature of tweets, and those named entities and semantic phrases can be largely found in aforementioned external knowledge bases. We categorize this method into *global context* based solution, since it utilizes the language-generic information contained in the external knowledge bases.

SIGIR'13, July 28–August 1, 2013, Dublin, Ireland.

[1]http://blog.twitter.com/2012/03/twitter-turns-six.html

Purely relying on external knowledge bases for tweet segmentation has two major weaknesses. First, tweets are highly time-sensitive so that many recently appeared terms like "She Dancin" can not be found in external knowledge bases. Another example is "Tin Pei Ling", a new politician who gained her reputation in Singapore General Election 2011[2]. No entry about her had been created in Wikipedia until 4th, April 2011, about a week later than the time her name appeared in tweets. Second, by defining other tweets published within the same short time window (i.e., an hour/a day) as the *local context*, a tween can only be well understood within its local context. For example, "Dancin" could be a typo if it only appears in a single tweet. But it may refer to some named entity if it appears in lots of tweets in a short term.

In this paper, we propose a hybrid tweet segmentation framework incorporating local contexts into the existing external knowledge bases, and name our method *HybridSeg*. *HybridSeg* conducts tweet segmentation in batch mode. Following the same scope of [12], we only segment tweets from a targeted Twitter stream. A targeted Twitter stream receives tweets based on user defined criteria (*e.g.,* tweets containing some predefined hashtags or keywords, tweets published by a predefined list of users, or tweets published by users from a specific geographical region). Tweets from a targeted Twitter stream are grouped into batches by their publication time using a fixed time interval (*e.g.,* an hour or a day). Each batch of tweets are then segmented by *HybridSeg* collectively.

HybridSeg conducts tweet segmentation in an iterative manner. At the first iteration, *HybridSeg* segments the tweet by utilizing the local linguistic features of the tweet itself. To avoid implementation from scratch, we simply apply a set of existing NER tools trained over general English languages on tweets. These existing NER tools provide an initial collection of confident segments by voting. Initializing *HybridSeg* with a set of off-the-shelf NER tools is based on the observation that some tweets from official accounts of news agencies, organizations, advertisers, and celebrities are likely well written. A small set of named entities extracted from these tweets based on voting of classic NER tools can be a high precise yet low recall solution of tweet segmentation. For example, although "Tin Pei Ling" is a new figure, it can be recognized as people name by classic NERs with high confidence because there are many well-written tweets about her generated by news agencies.

After that, *HybridSeg* learns better segmentation iteratively based on the confident segments extracted from the batch of tweets in the last iteration. The iterative process stops when no more changes are observed from the resulted segments. The philosophy is the confident segments of one tweet can affect the segmentation of other tweets in the same batch. External knowledge bases are also integrated here to better measuring the cohesiveness of segments. To the best of our knowledge, this paper proposes a novel framework by leveraging both global and local contexts in tweet segmentation for targeted Twitter streams.

We conduct extensive experimental analysis on two tweet datasets and compare *HybridSeg* with the approach purely relying on global knowledge bases [12], known as *GlobalSeg* in this paper. Our experimental results show that *HybridSeg* achieved significant improvement on tweet segmentation quality by comparing to the set of manually labeled tweets. We further split named entities from valid segments and only compared these named entities to human labels. Again, *HybridSeg* improved the NER quality compared to *GlobalSeg*.

The rest of the paper is organized as follows. Section 2 surveys the related works such as NLP, collocation measures, noun phrase extraction, and text segmentation. Section 3 gives an overview of the global knowledge guided segmentation process. The proposed hybrid-context based segmentation algorithm is presented in Section 4. In Section 5, we conduct experimental evaluation of the proposed *HybridSeg* framework and provide detailed algorithm analysis. Section 6 concludes this paper.

[2]http://en.wikipedia.org/wiki/Tin_Pei_Ling

2. RELATED WORK

Many conventional NLP techniques are designed for formal text. Many of these techniques are supervision based and heavily rely on the local linguistic features, such as POS tags, word capitalization, trigger words (*e.g.,* Mr., Dr.), and dictionary lookup like gazetteers, etc. These linguistic features, together with effective supervised learning algorithms (*e.g.,* hidden Markov model (HMM) and conditional random field (CRF)), achieve state-of-the-art performance on formal text corpus [6,19,26]. However, these techniques cannot be directly applied to tweets because of the noisy and short nature of the latter. The error-prone and short nature of tweets (and other user-generated short text) has attracted renewed interests in conventional tasks in NLP including POS tagging [7], named entity recognition (NER) [12,14,21], etc.

To improve POS tagging on tweets, Gimple *et al.* incorporate tweet-specific features including at-mentions, hashtags, URLs, and emotions [7]. In their approach, they measure the confidence of capitalized words and apply phonetic normalization for ill-formed words to address possible peculiar writings in tweets. Normalization of ill-formed words in tweets has established itself as an important research problem. A supervised approach is employed in [8] to first identify the ill-formed words. Then, the correct normalization of the ill-formed word is selected based on a number of lexical similarity measures.

Both supervised and unsupervised approaches have been proposed for named entity recognition in tweets. T-NER is a part of the tweet-specific NLP framework in [21]. T-NER first segments named entities using a CRF model with orthographic, contextual, and dictionary features, and then labels the named entities using a LDA (Latent Dirichlet allocation) model. The NER solution proposed in [14] is also based on a CRF model. The unsupervised approach named *TwiNER* recognizes named entities with two steps: tweet segmentation and segment ranking [12]. The tweets from a Twitter stream are processed in batch mode. Member tweets in a batch are segmented and each tweet segment is a candidate named entity (see Section 3). Collocation measure between words is utilized in tweet segmentation together with the global knowledge bases. Experimental results show that the collocation measure *Symmetric Conditional Probability* (SCP) is much more effective than *Pointwise Mutual Information* (PMI). To recognize named entities from the candidate segments, a segment graph is built based on segment co-occurrences. The segments are then ranked by applying random walk on the segment graph (see Section 5.4.1). Chua *et al.* [3] propose to extract noun phrases from tweets using an unsupervised approach which is mainly based on POS tagging. Each extracted noun phrase is a candidate named entity.

Tweet segmentation is conceptually similar to the task of text segmentation despite the unit for segmentation (words vs sentences) is significantly different. Text segmentation divides a given text document into consecutive non-overlapping topically cohesive segments [1]. Each segment consists of several consecutive sentences. Most existing works follow a similar idea that the boundaries of consecutive segments correspond to a change in word usage. The boundaries between segments are often detected by monitoring the drop of the lexical similarity. The proposed solutions differ widely in the way of calculating the sentence-pair similarity (*i.e.,* topical

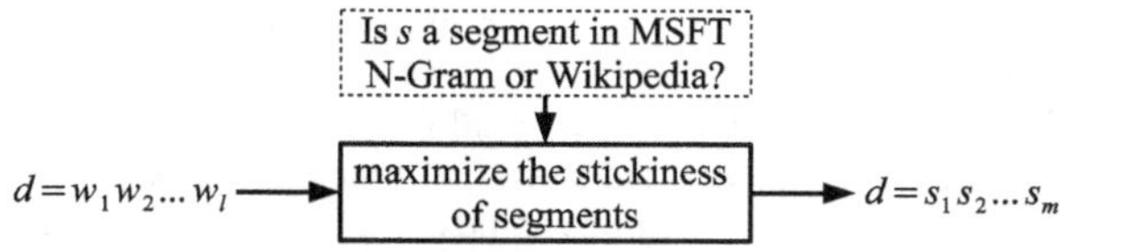

Figure 1: The framework of global knowledge bases guided tweet segmentation [12], named *GlobalSeg*.

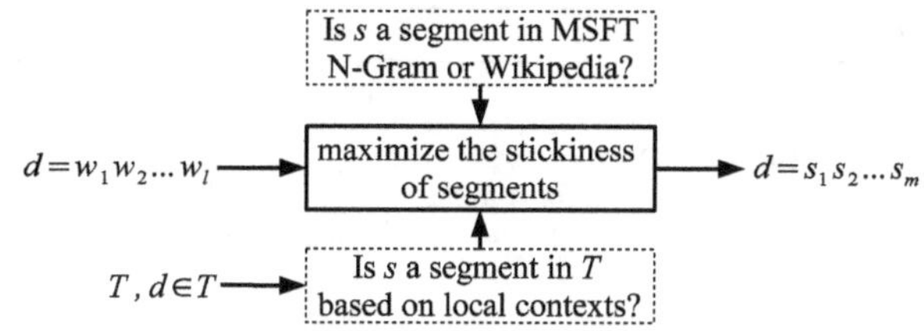

Figure 2: The framework of Hybrid-context based tweet segmentation, named *HybridSeg*.

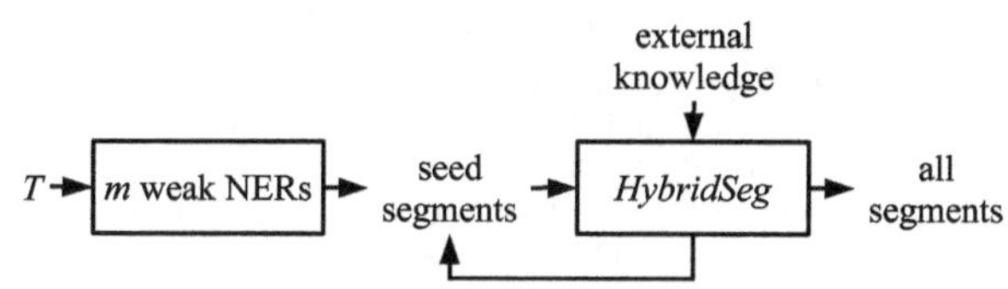

Figure 3: The iterative process of *HybridSeg*.

cohesiveness). Measures based on word co-occurrence [2, 9, 10] and generative models [1, 18, 20, 23] have been extensively studied. The determination of the segment boundaries may not only be purely based on the local sentence-pair similarities but also be based on the global information derived from the distribution of the lexical similarities of the far neighboring sentences [2,10]. Conceptually, the idea of incorporating the global information for boundary determination is similar to our idea of exploiting local context in tweets for tweet segmentation. However, the two problems (text segmentation and tweet segmentation) are different by definition and the techniques for text segmentation cannot be directly applied in tweet segmentation.

3. GLOBAL KNOWLEDGE GUIDED TWEET SEGMENTATION

Global knowledge bases like Wikipedia and Microsoft Web N-Gram corpus [24] have been successfully utilized to guide the tweet segmentation, which is named *GlobalSeg* by this paper. In this section, we briefly review its process, as illustrated by Figure 1.

The input of *GlobalSeg* is a tweet $d = w_1 w_2 \dots w_\ell$, and its output is m ($m \leq \ell$) non-overlapped segments, $d = s_1 s_2 \dots s_m$, where a segment s_i is a n-gram ($n \geq 1$). The optimal segmentation is to maximize the sum of *stickiness* scores of m segments:

$$\arg \max_{s_1,\dots,s_m} \sum_{i=1}^{m} C(s_i), \tag{1}$$

where $C(s)$ denotes a *stickiness* function, defined as:

$$C(s) = \mathcal{L}(s) \cdot e^{Q(s)} \cdot \frac{2}{1 + e^{-SCP(s)}}. \tag{2}$$

Eq. 2 encodes three factors for measuring the stickiness of each segment. They are: 1) the normalized segment length $\mathcal{L}(s) = 1$ if $|s| = 1$ and $\mathcal{L}(s) = \frac{|s|-1}{|s|}$ if $|s| > 1$ which moderately alleviates the penalty on long segments; 2) the probability that s is inside an anchor text in Wikipedia $Q(s)$; 3) the *Symmetric Conditional Probability* (SCP) measure defined by

$$SCP(s) = \log \frac{\Pr(s)^2}{\frac{1}{|s|-1} \sum_{i=1}^{|s|-1} \Pr(w_1 \dots w_i) \Pr(w_{i+1} \dots w_{|s|})}, \tag{3}$$

$Pr(s)$ is the n-gram probability provided by Microsoft Web N-Gram service. If s is a single word w, $SCP(s) = 2 \log Pr(w)$. If s contains more words, SCP tends to keep a cohesive s while all its possible binary partitions are not cohesive.

4. HYBRID-CONTEXT BASED TWEET SEGMENTATION

GlobalSeg defines a tweet segmentation method solely based on external knowledge bases (*e.g.,* Wikipedia and Microsoft Web N-Gram corpus). Its main assumption is that the external knowledge bases provide more robust segmentation features for tweets than their original natural languages which tend to be error-prone [12]. Despite its successful application in named entity recognition, it has two inherent limitations based on the below observations.

OBSERVATION 1. *Tweets are not topically independent to each other within a time window.*

In *GlobalSeg*, all tweets are segmented independently. This assumption is too strong as tweets published closely in time often talk about the same theme. These similar tweets largely share the same segments. For example, similar tweets have been grouped together to collectively detect events from tweets, and the event is usually represented by the common discriminative segments across tweets [11]. However, there is no mechanism in *GlobalSeg* to force similar tweets to be segmented consistently.

OBSERVATION 2. *Linguistic features of the tweets are not always useless.*

In *GlobalSeg*, the local linguistic features of a segment in its tweet has been abandoned completely. This assumption is mostly true especially when tweets contain many unreliable linguistic features like misspellings, informal abbreviations and unreliable capitalizations [21]. However, there indeed exist tweets composed in proper English. For example, some tweets are published by official accounts of news agencies, organizations, advertisers, and celebrities. For these tweets, the local linguistic features can be an informative source for tweet segmentation.

The two observations essentially reveal the same phenomenon: except for the external knowledge bases, local information like the other similar tweets within a time window or the linguistic features in the current tweet can also help in segmenting tweets. As both similar tweets and linguistic features refer to the *local contexts* of tweets, they lead to our novel idea of incorporating *local contexts* into the existing *external knowledge bases* for better tweet segmentation. Accordingly, we name our new method *HybridSeg*, short for a hybrid-context based segmentation for tweets.

4.1 Framework of *HybridSeg*

The general framework of *HybridSeg* is given in Figure 2. Compared to Figure 1, the major novelty is that we would examine the segment likelihood in a batch of tweets (including the tweet to be segmented) based on local contexts. That is to say, given a batch of tweets $\mathcal{T}$ within a certain time window, we are going to utilize

Algorithm 1: Tweet Segmentation by *HybridSeg*

input :
A tweet batch: $\mathcal{T} = \{t_1, t_2, ...\}$;
Off-the-shelf NERs: $r_i, r_2, ..., r_m$;
$\mu_{NER}(\lambda)$: function for learning λ from weak NERs;
$\mu_{Iter}(\lambda)$: function for learning λ from pseudo feedback;
$\mathcal{R}_\lambda$: the search space of λ;

output:
An optimal segmentation for the batch $\mathcal{T}$:
$\mathcal{S} = \{t_i = s_{i,1}s_{i,2}...s_{i,m}\}$;

`/* iteration 0: learning from weak NERs */`
1 **foreach** r_i **do**
    `/* apply NER` r_i `to the tweet batch` $\mathcal{T}$ `*/`
2     $\mathcal{S}_{r_i} \leftarrow$ recognize named entities by using NER r_i;
3 $\mathcal{M}_0 \leftarrow$ calculate $\hat{P}_{NE}(s)$ based on $\{\mathcal{S}_{r_i} | i = 1, 2, ...m\}$;
4 $\mathcal{N}_\cap \leftarrow$ extract the named entities that are recognized by all m NERs.
`/* apply` λ `learning with` $\mu_{NER}(\lambda)$ `*/`
5 $\mathcal{S}_0 \leftarrow$ segmentation with the optimal λ by using $\mu_{NER}(\lambda)$ and $\mathcal{R}_\lambda$;
`/* iteration 1,2,...: iterative learning */`
6 i=1;
7 **while** *true* **do**
8     $\mathcal{M}_i \leftarrow$ calculate $\hat{Pr}^i(s)$ based on $\mathcal{S}_{i-1}$;
    `/* apply` λ `learning with` $\mu_{Iter}(\lambda)$ `*/`
9     $\mathcal{S}_i \leftarrow$ segmentation with the optimal λ by using $\mu_{Iter}(\lambda)$ and $\mathcal{R}_\lambda$;
    `/* calculate Jensen-Shannon divergence between the segments in the last and current iterations */`
10     $jsd \leftarrow JSD(\mathcal{S}_{i-1}, \mathcal{S}_i)$
11   **if** $jsd < \varepsilon$ **then**
        `/* the stop criterion is met */`
12   break;
13     $i++$;
14 $\mathcal{S} \leftarrow \mathcal{S}_i$;
15 return $\mathcal{S}$ as the optimal segmentation;

their local linguistic features collectively for each member tweet's segmentation.

However, how to separate valid segments from the chaffs in a batch of tweets only based on local contexts is a challenging task itself. To tackle this problem, we design an iterative process in our framework, as shown in Figure 3.

Starting from a set of off-the-shelf NERs trained on classic English texts, we generate a collection of seed segments from $\mathcal{T}$ only based on local linguistic features by voting. The seed segment collection can be small yet highly confident. Then, we combine the seed segment collection with the external knowledge bases in *HybridSeg* to segment each tweet member. After that, only those segments ranked high by *HybridSeg* are used to replace the seed segment collection. The same process is then repeated until the segmentation results of *HybridSeg* do not change any more.

There are a couple of advantages in our design. First, existing NERs have already captured most known local linguistic features so that we do not need to implement from scratch. Second, most existing NERs are trained on formal texts. Applying them directly on tweets will easily cause the overfitting error. A voting algorithm can partially alleviate the error of training. Third, during each iteration, only top segments with high confidence scores are fed into *HybridSeg* in a pseudo feedback manner, further alleviating the errors caused by overfitting.

The tweet segmentation process of *HybridSeg* is outlined in Algorithm 1. In the following, we elaborate *HybridSeg* step by step.

4.2 Learning from weak NERs

In this section, we apply m weak NERs on $\mathcal{T}$ to generate the initial collection of seed segments. Based on the truth that a named entity is always a valid segment, we directly select the seed segments from the output of NERs.

Given a segment s, let f_s be its total frequency in $\mathcal{T}$. One NER r_i may recognize s as a named entity $f_{r_i,s}$ times. Note that $f_{r_i,s} \leq f_s$ since a NER may only recognize some of s's occurrences as named entity. Assuming there are multiple off-the-shelf NERs $r_1, r_2, \ldots, r_m$, we further denote f_s^R to be the number of NERs that have detected at least one occurrence of s as named entity, $f_s^R = \sum_i^m I(f_{r_i,s})$: $I(f_{r_i,s}) = 1$ if $f_{r_i,s} > 0$; $I(f_{r_i,s}) = 0$ otherwise.

We approximate the probability of s being a seed segment using a voting algorithm defined by Eq. 4:

$$\hat{Pr}(s) = w(s,m) \cdot \frac{1}{m} \sum_i^m \hat{Pr}_{r_i}(s), \quad (4)$$

$$w(s,m) = 1/\left(1 + e^{-\beta(f_s^R - m/2)}\right), \quad (5)$$

$$\hat{Pr}_{r_i}(s) = \left(1 + \frac{\alpha}{f_{r_i,s} + \varepsilon}\right)^{-\frac{f_s}{f_{r_i,s}+\varepsilon}}. \quad (6)$$

Our approximation contains two parts. The right part of Eq. 4 (rf. Eq. 6) is the average confidence that one weak NER recognizes s as named entity. A biased estimation of the right part is simply $1/m \cdot \sum_{i=1}^m f_{r_i,s}/f_s$ as each $f_{r_i,s}/f_s$ is a noisy version of the true probability. However, such simple average ignores the absolute value of $f_{r_i,s}$ which can also play an important role here. For example, for a party name in an election event, it can appear hundreds of times within a tweet batch. However, due to the free writing styles of tweets, only tens of the party name's occurrences can be recognized by weak NERs as named entity. In this case, $f_{r_i,s}/f_s$ is relatively small yet $f_{r_i,s}$ is relatively high. Thus, we design a function that can favor both $f_{r_i,s}/f_s$ and $f_{r_i,s}$. The favor scale is controlled by a factor α. When α is large, our function is more sensitive to the change of $f_{r_i,s}/f_s$; when α is small, a reasonably large $f_{r_i,s}$ can lead $\hat{Pr}_{r_i}(s)$ to be close to 1 despite of a relatively small value of $f_{r_i,s}/f_s$. In this paper we empirically set $\alpha = 0.2$ in experiments. A small constant ε is set to avoid dividing by zero.

The left part of Eq. 4, $w(s,m)$ (rf. Eq. 5) uses a sigmoid function to control the impact of the majority degree of m weak NERs on seed segments, which is tuned by a factor β. For example, in our paper we set $\beta = 10$ so that as long as more than half of weak NERs recognize s as named entity, $w(s,m)$ is close to 1. With a small β, $w(s,m)$ is getting closer to 1 only when more and more weak NERs recognize s as named entity.

The learning from weak NERs is summarized in lines 1 - 5 in Algorithm 1. Next, we discuss the combination of global knowledge bases and seed segments. The learning of λ will be detailed in Section 4.5.

4.3 Combination of knowledge bases and seed segments

After computing the probability of s being a valid segment, we can select top confident segments to be included in the seed segment collection. The next question is: how can we combine seed segments with knowledge bases for better tweet segmentation?

Recall that *GlobalSeg* encodes three factors: segment length, Wikipedia knowledge, and SCP measure based on Microsoft Web N-gram corpus, among which the text partition mainly relies on SCP measure. Now, the seed segment collection naturally provides another information source to guide the text partition. The idea can be as simple as assigning a high stickiness score to a partition in the seed segment collection. Accordingly, we modify the partition likelihood $Pr(s)$ in SCP measure using a linear combination:

$$Pr(s) = (1 - \lambda)Pr_{MS}(s) + \lambda\hat{Pr}(s), \quad (7)$$

where $\hat{Pr}(s)$ is defined by Eq. 4 with a coupling factor $\lambda \in [0, 1)$, and $Pr_{MS}(\cdot)$ is the n-gram probability provided by Microsoft Web N-Gram service.

4.4 Pseudo feedback on seed segments

The last step of *HybridSeg* is to iteratively improve the seed segments using the output of *HybridSeg*, with the final goal of improving its output in the end. The whole process will terminate until no more changes are observed in the output of *HybridSeg*.

Suppose at iteration i, *HybridSeg* outputs a set of segments $\{\langle s, f_s^i \rangle\}$, where f_s^i is the number of times s is a segment at iteration i. Then, f_s^i/f_s relatively records the segmentation confidence of *HybridSeg* on s at iteration i (recall that f_s denotes the frequency of s in current batch $\mathcal{T}$). Similar to Eq. 6, we denote

$$\hat{Pr}^i(s) = \left(1 + \frac{\alpha}{f_s^i + \varepsilon}\right)^{-\frac{f_s}{f_s^i+\varepsilon}}.$$

Following the same combination strategy defined by Eq. 7, we have the following iterative updating function:

$$Pr^{i+1}(s) = (1 - \lambda)Pr_{MS}(s) + \lambda \hat{Pr}^i(s), \quad (8)$$

Interestingly, we can treat learning weak NERs as the 0th iteration and change Eq. 7 to:

$$Pr^1(s) = (1 - \lambda)Pr_{MS}(s) + \lambda \hat{Pr}^0(s),$$

where $\hat{Pr}^0(s)$ is the voting result on m weak NERs only. The iteration process will stop when predefined criterion is met. Here, we define the stop criterion based on Jensen-Shannon divergence (JSD) of the frequency distributions of tweet segments in two consecutive iterations. Note that, in the 0th iteration, some segments may be wrongly segmented because of the errors introduced by the weak NERs. These errors could be further propagated at later iterations. For this reason, we do not consider the segments detected by weak NER whose frequency is smaller than 3 in the 0th iteration.

The learning from pseudo feedback is summarized in lines 7 - 13 in Algorithm 1.

4.5 Learning the parameter λ

Eq. 8 defines the iterative learning process of *HybridSeg*. The coupling factor λ is crucial to control the convergence of learning and the segment re-ranking performance of the next iteration. To guarantee the convergence and quality of our algorithm, we need a systematic way to learn λ.

Our idea is: a good λ must ensure that top confident segments from the previous iteration should be detected more times in the next iteration. Note that at each iteration we do not classify text partitions into binary classes (*i.e.,* segment and non-segment), but simply assign a stickiness score to each text partition and then treat segmentation as a ranking problem. Therefore, our idea is equivalent to maximizing the sum of detected frequency of top confident segments (weighted by their stickiness scores, rf. Eq. 2) extracted from the previous iteration. Accordingly, learning the parameter λ is converted to an optimization problem as follows:

$$\begin{aligned}\hat{\lambda} &= \arg\max_{\lambda} \mu_{Iter}(\lambda) \\ &= \arg\max_{\lambda} \sum_{s \in \text{top-k at iteration } i} C^i(s) \cdot f^{i+1}(s). \quad (9)\end{aligned}$$

$C^i(s)$ is the stickiness score of s output by *HybridSeg* and used for segment ranking at the previous iteration. Based on it, top-k segments can be retrieved. $f^{i+1}(s)$ is the detected frequency of s at the current iteration, which is an unknown function of the variable λ.

Table 1: Statistics of SIN and SGE datasets

Dataset	Collection period	#Tweets	#Annotations
SIN	Jun 01 - Jun 30, 2010	4,331,937	4,422
SGE	Apr 13 - May 13, 2011	226,744	3,328

Therefore, the optimal λ is intractable. In our experiments, we used brute-force search strategy to find the optimal λ for each iteration and each tweet batch. Fortunately, as the size of each tweet batch is controllable, the efficiency is not our concern in the current work.

Note that for the 0th iteration, λ must be learned differently because there do not exist top confident segments from the previous iteration. Since we use the voting results of m weak NERs as the seed segments in the 0th iteration, a good λ must ensure that the confident segments voted by m weak NERs can be detected more times by *HybridSeg*.

Let $\mathcal{N}_\cap$ be the segments that are recognized by all m NER systems (*i.e.,* $\mathcal{N}_\cap = \{s|f_s^R = m\}$). For each segment $s \in \mathcal{N}_\cap$, we consider its confident frequency to be the minimum number of times that s is recognized by a NER as named entity among all m NERs. Let the confident frequency of s be $f_{c,s}$. $f_{c,s} = min_i^m f_{r_i,s}$. Then λ is learnt as follows in the 0th iteration:

$$\hat{\lambda} = \arg\max_{\lambda} \mu_{NER}(\lambda) = \arg\max_{\lambda} \sum_{s \in \mathcal{N}_\cap} \hat{Pr}^0(s) \cdot f_{c,s} \cdot f_s^0 \quad (10)$$

In this equation, $\hat{Pr}^0(s)$ is the value computed using Eq. 4; $\hat{Pr}^0(s) \cdot f_{c,s}$ serves as a weighting factor to adjust the importance of f_s^0 in learning λ. If segment s is very likely to be a named entity (*i.e.,* $\hat{Pr}^0(s)$ is high) and it has been detected many times by all NERs (*i.e.,* $f_{c,s}$ is large), then the number of times s is successfully segmented f_s^0 has a big impact to the selection of λ. On the other hand, if $\hat{Pr}^0(s)$ is low, or $f_{c,s}$ is small, or both conditions hold, then f_s^0 is less important to λ setting.

By defining $f_{c,s} = min_i^m f_{r_i,s}$, Eq. 10 conservatively considers segments recognized by all weak NERs because of the noisy nature of tweets. This helps to reduce the possible oscillations resulted from different λ settings, since λ is a global factor (*i.e.,* not per-tweet dependent). On the other hand, we also assume that all the off-the-shelf NERs are reasonably good, *e.g.,* when they are applied on formal text. If there is a large number of NERs, then the definition of $f_{c,s}$ could be relaxed to avoid having too small values for all segments, due to one or two poor-performing NERs among them.

5. EVALUATION

In this section, we evaluate *HybridSeg* against *GlobalSeg* as the baseline. We conducted experiments on two datasets, *i.e.,* the *SIN* and *SGE* datasets that were used to evaluate *GlobalSeg* in [12]. Three weak NERs, namely, LBJ-NER, Standford-NER, and T-NER were used as input in *HybridSeg* for learning local context. We compare segmentation accuracy of *HybridSeg* against *GlobalSeg*. Because *GlobalSeg* was used to detect named entities in [12], we also report the accuracy of named entity recognition using *HybridSeg* and *GlobalSeg* respectively.

5.1 Dataset and Setting

Tweet Datasets. The *SIN* and *SGE* datasets were originally collected for simulating two targeted Twitter streams in [12]. The former was a stream consisting of tweets from users in a specific geographical region (*i.e.,* Singapore in this case), and the latter was a stream consisting of tweets matching some predefined keywords

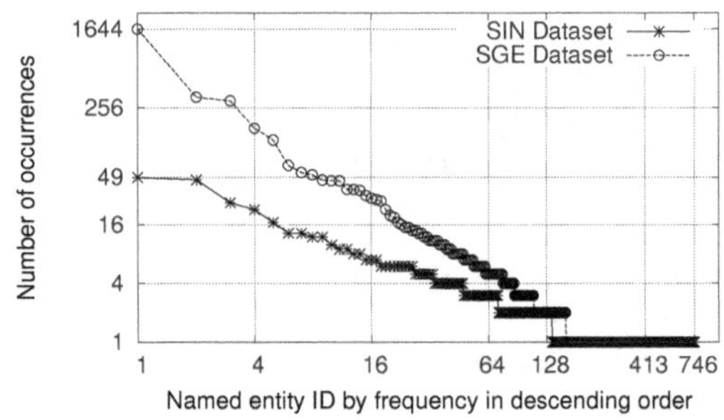

Figure 4: Frequency distribution of the annotated NEs

and hashtags for a major event (*i.e.,* Singapore General Election 2011 in this case).

Reported in Table 1, named entities in 4,422 tweets from *SIN* and 3,328 tweets from *SGE* have been manually annotated to evaluate tweet segmentation and named entity recognition performance in [12]. Table 2 reports the statistics of the annotated NEs in the two datasets where f_s^g denotes the number of occurrences (or frequency) of segment s in the annotated ground truth $\mathcal{G}$. The frequency distributions of the NEs are plotted in Figure 4.

All the annotated tweets in each dataset were published on the same day, making it possible to evaluate batch-mode tweet segmentation using a day as the time interval. To fairly compare with the results reported in [12], we conduct our experiments using all the annotated tweets in each dataset as a batch so as not to take additional context from other unlabeled tweets published in the same day.

We also used the same Wikipedia dump (released on 30 Jan, 2010[3]) as in [12]. This dump contains 3,246,821 articles and there are 4,342,732 distinct entities appeared as anchor texts in these articles.

Evaluation Metric. Recall that the task of tweet segmentation is to split a tweet into semantically meaningful segments. Ideally, a tweet segmentation method shall be evaluated by comparing its segmentation result against manually segmented tweets. However, manual segmentation of a reasonably sized data collection is extremely expensive and requires good understanding of the tweets. We therefore choose to follow [12] to evaluate a tweet segmentation method based on whether the manually annotated named entities are correctly segmented (*i.e.,* split as segments). Because each named entity is a valid segment, the annotated named entities in this case serve as partial ground truth for the evaluation. We use two measures, namely *Recall* and *Frequency-biased Recall.*

- *Recall*, denoted by *Re*, quantifies the percentage of the manually annotated named entities that are correctly split as segments. Because a segmentation method outputs *exactly one* possible segmentation for each tweet, using annotated named entities as partial ground truth, recall is the same as precision in this setting. In fact, the same measure is named as precision in [12]. Note that each named entity appearing in a specific position of a tweet is considered as one distinct instance. For example, the phrase "pap pap pap!", commonly used to express a user's strong support to the PAP party[4] in Singapore general election, consists of three distinct named entity instances "pap".

[3]http://dumps.wikimedia.org/enwiki/

[4]http://en.wikipedia.org/wiki/People's_Action_Party

Table 2: The annotated named entities in SIN and SGE datasets

Dataset	#NEs	min f_s^g	max f_s^g	$\sum f_s^g$	#NEs *s.t.* $f_s^g > 1$
SIN	746	1	49	1234	136
SGE	413	1	1644	4073	161

- *Frequency-biased Recall*, denoted by Re_F, factors in the frequency of the named entities in a batch of tweets. Because the frequent named entities are often related to hot topics or emerging events in the targeted Twitter stream, correctly identifying these named entities as segments is critical for downstream applications, like user opinion mining, topic discovery, and event detection.

  Let f_s^g be the frequency of segment s in the ground truth $\mathcal{G}$. Let $Re(s)$ be the recall of segment $s \in \mathcal{G}$ which is the percentage of segment s being correctly extracted from all occurrences of s in the annotated tweets. The frequency-biased recall is defined as follows:

$$Re_F = \frac{1}{Z} \sum_{s \in \mathcal{G}} \log(f_s^g + \varepsilon) \cdot Re(s) \tag{11}$$

  In this equation, Z is a normalization factor assuming all named entities are corrected segmented (*i.e.,* $Z = \sum_{s \in \mathcal{G}} \log(f_s^g + \varepsilon)$). The logarithm function is applied to avoid domination of few extremely frequent named entities, because of the power-law like distribution of the NEs (see Figure 4). ε is a small constant to avoid zero values for the named entities that have only single appearance ($\varepsilon = 0.001$ in our experiments).

Methods and Parameter Setting. We compare our *HybridSeg* method with *GlobalSeg* method in [12] as the baseline. Note that the method proposed in [12] is named *TwiNER* for named entity recognition and segmentation was one of its intermediate step. In this paper, *GlobalSeg* refers to the segmentation step in *TwiNER.*

The following three weak NERs are used in *HybridSeg* to derive the local context knowledge (*i.e.,* $m = 3$). Note that, we used the version downloaded from their corresponding websites. These NERs are not trained using our data.

- LBJ-NER is based on the regularized averaged perceptron approach for learning and inference. It uses gazetteers extracted from Wikipedia, word class models derived from unlabeled text corpus, and expressive non-local features [19].

- Stanford-NER is a NER system based on CRF model for learning and inference. Besides the conventional linguistic features, it also incorporates long-distance information [6].

- T-NER is a NER system designed for tweet corpus. It employs some tweet-specific features as well as the widely used conventional features for formal text [21].

For parameter settings, α in Eq. 6 is set to $\alpha = 0.2$; the top-K segments in Eq. 9 for λ adaption is set to $K = 50$. The search space for λ is set to be $[0, 0.95]$ with a step 0.05.

5.2 Segmentation Accuracy

In this section we first report the accuracy of the three weak NERs in detecting named entities. We then compare *HybridSeg* and *GlobalSeg* on segmentation accuracy.

Accuracy of three Weak NERs. The accuracy of the three weak NERs in recognizing named entities is evaluated by three standard

Table 3: Accuracy of the three weak NERs; $\mathcal{N}_\cap$ denotes the set of NEs detected by all three weak NERs. The best results are in boldface.

Method	SIN			SGE		
	Pr	*Re*	F_1	*Pr*	*Re*	F_1
LBJ-NER	0.335	0.357	0.346	0.674	0.402	0.504
T-NER	0.273	**0.523**	0.359	0.696	0.341	0.458
Stanford-NER	0.447	0.448	**0.447**	0.685	**0.623**	**0.653**
All NERs $\mathcal{N}_\cap$	**0.578**	0.233	0.332	**0.876**	0.192	0.315

metrics: Precision (*Pr*), Recall (*Re*), and F_1. *Pr* measures the percentage of the recognized named entities that are true named entities; *Re* measures the percentage of the true named entities that are correctly recognized; and $F_1 = 2 \cdot Pr \cdot Re/(Pr + Re)$ is the harmonic mean of *Pr* and *Re*. The type of the named entity (*e.g.,* person, location, and organization) is ignored as in [12]. Similar to the segmentation recall measure, each occurrence of a named entity in a specific position of a tweet is considered as one instance for the three measures *Pr*, *Re*, and F_1.

Table 3 reports the performance of the three weak NERs on the two datasets *SIN* and *SGE* respectively. Observed from the table, all three weak NERs perform poorly on the two tweets collections. The results are consistent with that reported in [12]. However, if consider the set of NEs that are recognized by all three NERs $\mathcal{N}_\cap$, the precision is much higher than any of the individual weak NER. In particular, the precision on *SGE* dataset is 0.876. That is, the set of NEs detected by all the three NERs are of good precision and can be used as local context knowledge in improving tweet segmentation. On the other hand, the recall of $\mathcal{N}_\cap$ is much lower than any of the three NERs as expected.

Segmentation Accuracy. We report two sets of results for *HybridSeg* and compare them with the baseline *GlobalSeg*. Specifically, in Table 4, we report the results of $HybridSeg_{NER}$ after learning from weak NERs, and the results of $HybridSeg_{NER+Iter}$ after the iterative learning converges in *HybridSeg*. We make three observations from the results:

1. Learning from the local context brought in by weak NERs, $HybridSeg_{NER}$ significantly improves tweet segmentation accuracy on both datasets;

2. $HybridSeg_{NER+Iter}$ further improves *Re* and Re_F on both datasets. However, the amount of improvement on top of $HybridSeg_{NER}$ is relatively small on both datasets; and

3. Compared with the baseline method *GlobalSeg*, the proposed $HybridSeg_{NER+Iter}$ improves *Re* by 13.2% and 8.2% respectively on *SIN* and *SGE* datasets. Considering segment frequency in the evaluation using Re_F measure, much larger improvements are achieved, 17.6% on *SIN* and 17.1% on *SGE*.

Our experimental results show that, incorporating local context knowledge in a batch of tweets greatly improves tweet segmentation accuracy. More importantly, the local context knowledge can be obtained with almost no cost with off-the-shelf NERs and locally derived statistics. On the other hand, the improvement made by learning from pseudo feedback is relatively small compared to the improvement made by learning from weak NERs. In the next section, we conduct a detailed analysis of *HybridSeg* for possible reasons.

Table 4: Performance of tweet segmentation algorithms, where $*$ indicates the difference against the baseline is statistically significant by paired t-test.

Method	SIN		SGE	
	Re	Re_F	*Re*	Re_F
GlobalSeg	0.758	0.799	0.874	0.756
$HybridSeg_{NER}$	0.857*	0.932*	0.942*	0.879*
$HybridSeg_{NER+Iter}$	**0.858***	**0.940***	**0.946***	**0.885***

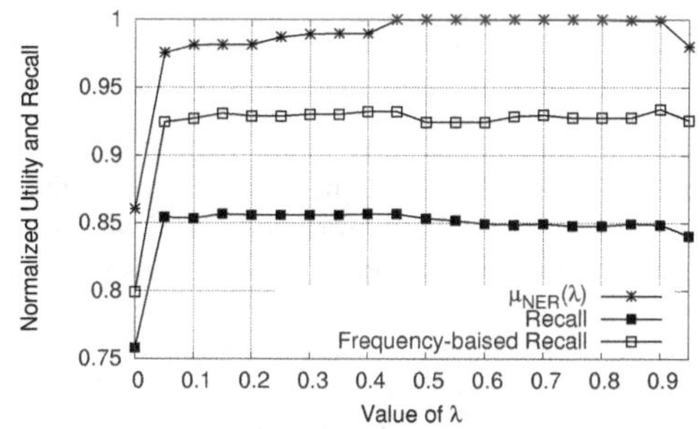

(a) *SIN* dataset

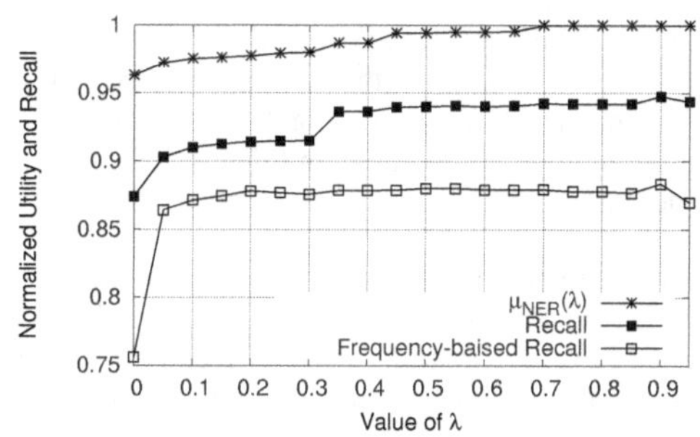

(b) *SGE* dataset

Figure 5: Re, Re_F **and** $\mu_{NER}(\lambda)$ **(%) values of** $HybridSeg_{NER}$ **with varying** λ **in the range of** $[0, 0.95]$**.**

5.3 Algorithm Analysis

Impact of λ Adaption. We exploit the local context by using linear combination in the calculation of SCP score (rf. Eq. 7 and 8). The choice of λ largely affects the performance of the tweet segmentation process. While a small λ may not sufficiently exploit the local context, a very large λ could make the local context dominate the segmentation process which may adversely affect the segments with weak local context because of their limited number of occurrences.

Figure 5 demonstrates the impact of varying λ on $HybridSeg_{NER}$ in terms of *Re* and Re_F in the 0th iteration (rf Eq. 10). For easy demonstration, we plot the normalized score obtained by Eq. 10 with different λ, denoted by $\mu_{NER}(\lambda)$ in the figure. Observe that $\mu_{NER}(\lambda)$ is positively correlated with the performance metrics *Re* and Re_F on both datasets. In our experiments, we set the parameter λ to be the smallest value leading to the best $\mu_{NER}(\lambda)$, *i.e.,* $\lambda = 0.5$ on *SIN* and $\lambda = 0.7$ on *SGE*. Because λ is a global factor for all member tweets in the batch and $\mu_{NER}(\lambda)$ is computed based on a small set of seed segments. A larger λ may not affect the segmentation of the seed segments because of their confident local context, but may cause some other segments to be wrongly split due to their noisy local context. Observe there is minor degradation for both *Re* and Re_F on *SIN* dataset when $\lambda > 0.45$ although $\mu_{NER}(\lambda)$ remains

Table 5: The performance of *HybridSeg*$_{NER+Iter}$ up to 4 iterations.

Iteration	SIN			SGE		
	Re	Re_F	*JSD*	*Re*	Re_F	*JSD*
0	0.857	0.932	–	0.942	0.879	–
1	0.857	0.940	0.0059	0.946	0.885	0.0183
2	0.858	0.940	0.0001	0.946	0.885	0.0003
3	0.858	0.940	0	0.946	0.885	0

the maximum. The impact of varying λ in the following iterations is not plotted for the interests of space. Similar observations hold.

Analysis of the Iterative Learning. *HybridSeg* employs an iterative strategy to learn from the segments produced in the previous iteration. Table 5 reports the performance of *HybridSeg* and *JSD* between the frequency distributions of the segments from two iterations.

It is observed that *HybridSeg* converges after the second iteration. To understand the possible reasons for the quick convergence, we analyze the segments detected in each iteration. There are three categories of them:

- Fully detected segments (FS): all occurrences of the segments are detected from the batch of tweets. Their *Pr*(s) is further increased by considering their local context. No more occurrences can be detected on this category of segments in the next iteration.

- Missed segments (MS): not a single occurrence of the segment is detected from the previous iteration. In this case, no local context information can be derived for them to increase their *Pr*(s). They will be missed in the next iteration.

- Partially detected segments (PS): some but not all occurrences of the segments are detected. For this category of segments, local context can be derived from the detected occurrences. Depending on the local context, *Pr*(s) will be adjusted. More occurrences may be detected or missed in the next iteration.

Table 6 reports the number of segments and their number of occurrences in each of the three sets (FS, MS, and PS). For partially detected segments, the number of detected and missed occurrences are reported.

As shown in the table, very few segments are partially detected after learning from weak NERs in 0th iteration (19 for *SIN* and 24 for *SGE*). The possible improvement can be made in the next iteration is to further detect the total 25 missed occurrences in *SIN* (resp. 67 in *SGE*), which accounts for 2.03% (resp. 1.64%) of all annotated NEs in the dataset. That is, the room for further performance improvement by iterative learning is marginal.

Consider the *SIN* dataset, on average, there are about 6 detected occurrences to provide local context for each of the 19 partially detected segments. With the local context, *HybridSeg* manages to reduce the number of partially detected segments from 19 to 11 in the next iteration and the total number of their missed instances are reduced from 25 to 14. No changes are observed for the remaining 11 partially detected segments in iteration 2. Interestingly, the number of fully detected instances increased by 2 in the last iteration. The best segmentation of a tweet is the one maximizes the stickness of its member segments (rf Eq. 1). The change in the stickness $C(s)$ of other segments leads to the detection of these two new segments in the fully detected category, each occurs once in the dataset.

In *SGE* dataset, the 24 partially detected segments reduce to 12 in the next iteration by learning from pseudo feedback. No change to these 12 partially detected segments are observed in the next iteration, despite some of these segments have very strong local context based on their detected occurrences. A manual investigation show that the missed occurrences are wrongly detected as part of some other longer segments. For example, "NSP"[5] becomes part of "NSP Election Rally" and the latter is not annotated as a named entity. A further investigation shows that, probably based on its capitalization, "NSP Election Rally" is detected by weak NERs with strong confidence (*i.e.*, all its occurrences are detected). Because of its strong confidence, "NSP" cannot be separated from this longer segment in the next iteration regardless the setting of λ. We note that although "NSP Election Rally" is not annotated in the ground truth as named entity, it is indeed a semantically meaningful phrase. On the other hand, a large portion of the occurrences for these 12 partially detected segments have been successfully detected from other tweets.

Compared to the baseline *GlobalSeg* which does not take local context, *HybridSeg* significantly reduces the number of missed segments from 195 to 152, which is 22% reduction on *SIN* dataset. On *SGE* dataset, the reduction is 20% from 140 to 112. Many of these segments are fully detected in *HybridSeg*.

5.4 Application: Named Entity Recognition

In this section, we use Named Entity Recognition as a downstream application to evaluate the impact of tweet segmentation. We first briefly review the *TwiNER* method for NER [12] and then propose our own NER method taking tweet segment as input.

5.4.1 NER by Random Walk

TwiNER recognizes named entities by applying Random Walk on the segments from a batch of tweets. The main assumption is that a named entity often co-occurs with other named entities in a batch of tweets while non-entity segments rarely co-occurs with named entities. The weight of the co-occurrence between two segments is measured by Jaccard Coefficient. A random walk model is then applied to the segment graph. Let ρ_s be the stationary probability of segment s by applying random walk, the segment is then weighted by:

$$y(s) = e^{Q(s)} \cdot \rho_s \tag{12}$$

In this equation, $e^{Q(s)}$ carry the same semantic as in Eq. 2, indicating that a segment that frequently appears in Wikipedia as an anchor text is more likely to be a named entity. With the weighting $y(s)$, the top K segments are considered as named entities.

5.4.2 NER by POS Tagger

Due to the short nature of tweets, the *gregarious* property could be very weak in tweets. As shown in Table 2, 82% of the annotated named entities appear only once in *SIN* (and 61% in *SGE*). We choose to explore the part-of-speech tags in tweets for named entity recognition by considering noun phrases as named entities.

We estimate the likelihood of a segment being a noun phrase (NP) by considering the POS tags of its constituent words. Table 7 lists three POS tags that are considered as the indicators of a segment being a noun phrase. Let $w^s_{i,j}$ be the jth word of segment s in its i-th occurrence, we calculate the probability of segment s being an noun phrase as follow:

$$\hat{P}_{NP}(s) = \frac{\sum_i \sum_j [w^s_{i,j}]}{|s| \cdot f_s} \cdot \frac{1}{1 + e^{-5\frac{(f_s - \bar{f}_s)}{\sigma(f_s)}}} \tag{13}$$

[5] http://en.wikipedia.org/wiki/National_Solidarity_Party_(Singapore)

Table 6: Fully detected, missed, and partially detected segments for *GlobalSeg* and *HybridSeg* (3 iterations). #NE: number of distinct segments, #Occur: number of occurrences, #Detect: number of detected occurrences, #Miss: number of missed occurrences.

Dataset	*SIN* dataset							*SGE* dataset						
Method/	Fully detected		Missed		Partially detected			Fully detected		Missed		Partially detected		
Iteration	#NE	#Occur	#NE	#Occur	#NE	#Detect	#Miss	#NE	#Appr	#NE	#Occur	#NE	#Detect	#Miss
0	581	944	146	152	19	113	25	295	1464	94	168	24	2374	67
1	581	959	154	163	11	98	14	291	1858	110	191	12	1996	28
2	583	961	152	161	11	98	14	289	1856	112	193	12	1996	28
GlobalSeg	504	647	195	214	47	113	85	234	708	140	336	40	2850	179

Table 7: Three POS tags as the indicator of a segment being a noun phrase, reproduced from [7]

Tag	Definition	Examples
N	common noun (NN, NNS)	books; someone
^	proper noun (NNP, NNPS)	lebron; usa; iPad
$	numeral (CD)	2010; four; 9:30

This equation considers two factors. The first factor estimates the probability as the percentage of the constituent words being labeled with an NP tag for all the occurrences of segment s, where $[w]$ is 1 if w is labeled as one of the three POS tags in Table 7, and 0 otherwise; For example, "chiam see tong", the name of a Singaporean politician and lawyer[6], is labeled as ^^^ (66.67%), NVV (3.70%), ^V^ (7.41%) and ^VN (22.22%)[7]. By considering the types of all words in a segment, we can obtain a high probability of 0.877 for "chiam see tong". The second factor of the equation introduces a scaling factor to give more preference to frequent segments, where $\bar{f}_s$ and $\sigma(f_s)$ are the mean and standard deviation of segment frequency.

The segments are then ranked by $y(s) = e^{Q(s)} \cdot \hat{P}_{NP}(s)$, *i.e.*, replacing ρ_s in Eq 12 by $\hat{P}_{NP}(s)$.

With two named entity recognition approaches, namely Random Walk (RW) and POS tagging respectively, and two segmentation methods, namely *GlobalSeg* and *HybridSeg*, we have four combinations to evaluate: $GlobalSeg_{RW}$, $HybridSeg_{RW}$, $HybridSeg_{POS}$, and $GlobalSeg_{POS}$. Note that, $GlobalSeg_{RW}$ is the same method named *TwiNER* in [12].

We introduce another baseline method $Unigram_{POS}$, which use POS Tagging without segmentation. Similar to the work in [3], we extract noun phrases from the batch of tweets by using the following regular expression.

$$NP := [\hat{}N][\hat{}N\$]*$$

The regular expression states that a noun phrase can be a combination of common noun, proper noun and numeral, which begins with common or proper noun. The confidence of a noun phrase is computed using a modified version of Eq. 13 by removing its first component.

In summary, we have five methods to evaluate: $GlobalSeg_{RW}$, $HybridSeg_{RW}$, $HybridSeg_{POS}$, $GlobalSeg_{POS}$, and $Unigram_{POS}$.

5.4.3 Experimental Results

Table 8 reports the performance of the 5 methods. The results reported is the highest F_1 of each method achieved for varying $K > 50$ following the same setting in [12]. Three observations are made.

[6] `http://en.wikipedia.org/wiki/Chiam_See_Tong`

[7] V:verb including copula, auxiliaries; for example, might, gonna, ought, is, eats.

Table 8: The performance of *GlobalSeg* and *HybridSeg* with Random Walk and POS for NER

Method	*SIN* dataset			*SGE* dataset		
	Pr	Re	F_1	Pr	Re	F_1
$Unigram_{POS}$	0.516	0.190	0.278	0.845	0.333	0.478
$GlobalSeg_{RW}$	0.576	0.335	0.423	**0.929**	0.646	0.762
$HybridSeg_{RW}$	0.618	0.343	0.441	0.907	0.683	0.779
$GlobalSeg_{POS}$	0.647	0.306	0.415	0.903	0.657	0.760
$HybridSeg_{POS}$	**0.685**	**0.352**	**0.465**	0.911	**0.686**	**0.783**

1. Tweet segmentation greatly improves NER. $Unigram_{POS}$ is the worst performer on all three evaluation metric Pr, Re, F_1 among all methods.

2. For a specific NER approach, either Random Walk or POS based, better segmentation results lead to better NER accuracy. That is, $HybridSeg_{RW}$ performed better than $GlobalSeg_{RW}$ and $HybridSeg_{POS}$ performed better than $GlobalSeg_{POS}$ on all evaluation metrics.

3. Without local context in segmentation $GlobalSeg_{POS}$ is slightly worse than $GlobalSeg_{RW}$ by F_1. However, with much better segmentation results, $HybridSeg_{POS}$ is much better than $HybridSeg_{RW}$. By F_1 measure, $HybridSeg_{POS}$ achieves the best NER result.

Figure 6 plots the *Precision@K* for the 5 methods on the two datasets with varying K from 20 to 100. The *Precision@K* reports the ratio of named entities among the top-K ranked segments by each method. Note that, *Precision@K* measures the ranking of the segments detected from a batch of tweets; the occurrences of each segment in the ranking are not considered. This is different from the measures (*e.g., Pr*) reported in Table 8 where the occurrences of the named entities are considered (*i.e.,* whether a named entity is correctly detected at a specific position in a given tweet). We made the following observations from Figure 6.

On *SIN* dataset, it is clear that all methods using POS tagging for NER enjoy much better precision. RW based methods deliver much poorer precisions due to the lack of co-occurrences in the tweets. As reported in Table 2, 82% of the annotated named entities appear only once in *SIN*. Among the three POS based methods, $HybridSeg_{POS}$ dominates the best precisions on all K values from 20 to 100. On *SGE* dataset, the differences in precisions between POS based methods and RW based methods become smaller compared to those on *SIN* dataset. The reason is that in *SGE* dataset, about 39% of named entities appear more than once, which makes a much larger chance of co-occurrences. Between the two best performing methods $HybridSeg_{POS}$ and $GlobalSeg_{POS}$, the former outperformed the latter on 6 K values plotted between 40 and 90. Without segmentation $Unigram_{POS}$ performed poorly in terms of *Precison@K* measure on *SGE* dataset.

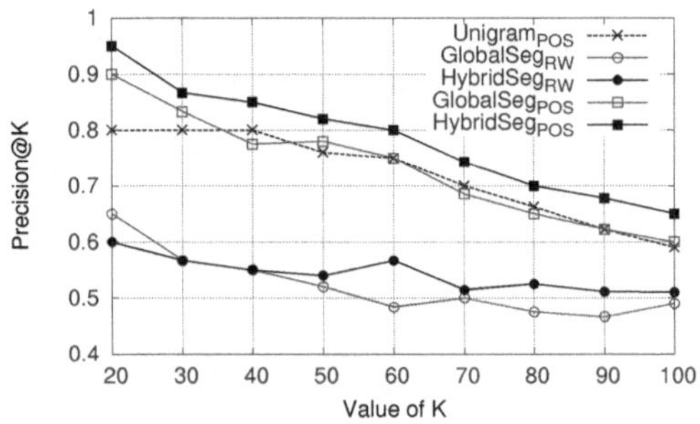

(a) SIN

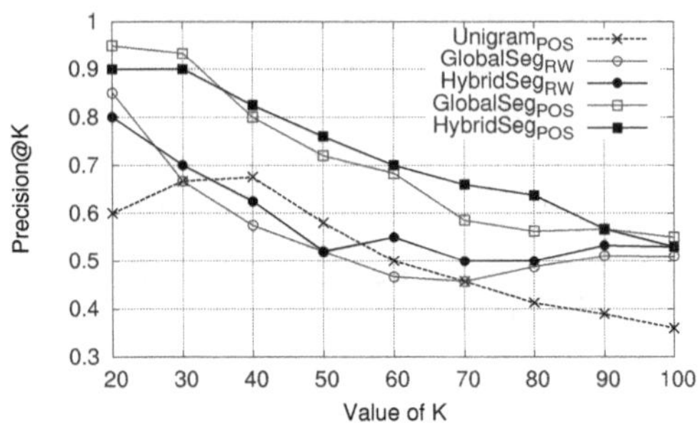

(b) SGE

Figure 6: Precision@K on two datasets

6. CONCLUSION

Recently, tweet segmentation has been proven to be effective in the tasks of NER, event detection, and summarization. In this paper, we present a novel framework *HybridSeg*, which aggregates both the local context knowledge and the global knowledge bases in the process of tweet segmentation. First, *HybridSeg* exploits the local linguistic features in a collective manner by using the existing NER tools. The recognized named entities with high confidence positively enhance the performance of tweet segmentation. Moreover, information that has not been well captured in the global knowledge bases is derived based on all segments from the tweets. Then, *HybridSeg* iteratively learns a better segmentation by considering confident seed segments in the previous iteration. Through extensive experiments, we show that *HybridSeg* significantly outperforms the existing state-of-the-art algorithm on tweet segmentation. We also show that the better segmentation benefits the named entity recognition application in tweets. In future, we plan to take more local factors into consideration for tweet segmentation, such as local word dependency.

7. REFERENCES

[1] D. Beeferman, A. Berger, and J. Lafferty. Statistical models for text segmentation. *Mach. Learn.*, 34(1-3):177–210, 1999.

[2] F. Y. Y. Choi. Advances in domain independent linear text segmentation. In *NAACL*, pages 26–33, 2000.

[3] F. C. T. Chua, W. W. Cohen, J. Betteridge, and E.-P. Lim. Community-based classification of noun phrases in twitter. In *CIKM*, pages 1702–1706, 2012.

[4] J. E. Chung and E. Mustafaraj. Can collective sentiment expressed on twitter predict political elections? In *AAAI*, 2011.

[5] A. Cui, M. Zhang, Y. Liu, S. Ma, and K. Zhang. Discover breaking events with popular hashtags in twitter. In *CIKM*, pages 1794–1798, 2012.

[6] J. R. Finkel, T. Grenager, and C. Manning. Incorporating non-local information into information extraction systems by gibbs sampling. In *ACL*, pages 363–370, 2005.

[7] K. Gimpel, N. Schneider, B. O'Connor, D. Das, D. Mills, J. Eisenstein, M. Heilman, D. Yogatama, J. Flanigan, and N. A. Smith. Part-of-speech tagging for twitter: annotation, features, and experiments. In *ACL-HLT*, pages 42–47, 2011.

[8] B. Han and T. Baldwin. Lexical normalisation of short text messages: Makn sens a #twitter. In *ACL*, pages 368–378, 2011.

[9] M. A. Hearst. Texttiling: segmenting text into multi-paragraph subtopic passages. *Comput. Linguist.*, 23(1):33–64, Mar. 1997.

[10] A. Kazantseva and S. Szpakowicz. Linear text segmentation using affinity propagation. In *EMNLP*, pages 284–293, 2011.

[11] C. Li, A. Sun, and A. Datta. Twevent: segment-based event detection from tweets. In *CIKM*, pages 155–164, 2012.

[12] C. Li, J. Weng, Q. He, Y. Yao, A. Datta, A. Sun, and B.-S. Lee. Twiner: Named entity recognition in targeted twitter stream. In *SIGIR*, pages 721–730, 2012.

[13] K.-L. Liu, W.-J. Li, and M. Guo. Emoticon smoothed language models for twitter sentiment analysis. In *AAAI*, 2012.

[14] X. Liu, S. Zhang, F. Wei, and M. Zhou. Recognizing named entities in tweets. In *ACL*, pages 359–367, 2011.

[15] X. Liu, X. Zhou, Z. Fu, F. Wei, and M. Zhou. Exacting social events for tweets using a factor graph. In *AAAI*, 2012.

[16] Z. Luo, M. Osborne, and T. Wang. Opinion retrieval in twitter. In *ICWSM*, 2012.

[17] X. Meng, F. Wei, X. Liu, M. Zhou, S. Li, and H. Wang. Entity-centric topic-oriented opinion summarization in twitter. In *KDD*, pages 379–387, 2012.

[18] H. Misra, F. Yvon, J. M. Jose, and O. Cappe. Text segmentation via topic modeling: an analytical study. In *CIKM*, pages 1553–1556, 2009.

[19] L. Ratinov and D. Roth. Design challenges and misconceptions in named entity recognition. In *CoNLL*, pages 147–155, 2009.

[20] M. Riedl and C. Biemann. Topictiling: a text segmentation algorithm based on lda. In *ACL 2012 Student Research Workshop*, pages 37–42, 2012.

[21] A. Ritter, S. Clark, Mausam, and O. Etzioni. Named entity recognition in tweets: An experimental study. In *EMNLP*, pages 1524–1534, 2011.

[22] A. Ritter, Mausam, O. Etzioni, and S. Clark. Open domain event extraction from twitter. In *KDD*, pages 1104–1112, 2012.

[23] M. Utiyama and H. Isahara. A statistical model for domain-independent text segmentation. In *ACL*, pages 499–506, 2001.

[24] K. Wang, C. Thrasher, E. Viegas, X. Li, and P. Hsu. An overview of microsoft web n-gram corpus and applications. In *HLT-NAACL*, pages 45–48, 2010.

[25] X. Wang, F. Wei, X. Liu, M. Zhou, and M. Zhang. Topic sentiment analysis in twitter: a graph-based hashtag sentiment classification approach. In *CIKM*, pages 1031–1040, 2011.

[26] G. Zhou and J. Su. Named entity recognition using an hmm-based chunk tagger. In *ACL*, pages 473–480, 2002.

Sumblr: Continuous Summarization of Evolving Tweet Streams

Lidan Shou [1,2] Zhenhua Wang [1] Ke Chen[1] Gang Chen[1]
[1]College of Computer Science and Technology
[2]State Key Lab of CAD&CG
Zhejiang University
Hangzhou, China
{should, wzh-cs, chenk, cg}@zju.edu.cn

ABSTRACT

With the explosive growth of microblogging services, short-text messages (also known as tweets) are being created and shared at an unprecedented rate. Tweets in its raw form can be incredibly informative, but also overwhelming. For both end-users and data analysts it is a nightmare to plow through millions of tweets which contain enormous noises and redundancies. In this paper, we study continuous tweet summarization as a solution to address this problem. While traditional document summarization methods focus on static and small-scale data, we aim to deal with dynamic, quickly arriving, and large-scale tweet streams. We propose a novel prototype called Sumblr (SUMmarization By stream cLusteRing) for tweet streams. We first propose an online tweet stream clustering algorithm to cluster tweets and maintain distilled statistics called Tweet Cluster Vectors. Then we develop a TCV-Rank summarization technique for generating online summaries and historical summaries of arbitrary time durations. Finally, we describe a topic evolvement detection method, which consumes online and historical summaries to produce timelines automatically from tweet streams. Our experiments on large-scale real tweets demonstrate the efficiency and effectiveness of our approach.

Categories and Subject Descriptors

H.3.1 [**Content Analysis and Indexing**]: Abstracting methods; H.3.4 [**Systems and Software**]: Performance evaluation (efficiency and effectiveness)

Keywords

Tweet stream; continuous summarization; timeline

1. INTRODUCTION

With the explosive growth of microblogging services, such as Twitter, Weibo and Tumblr, short-text messages known as tweets are being created and shared at an unprecedented rate. Take Twitter for instance, receiving over 400 million tweets per day[1], it has become an invaluable source of news, blogs, opinions, and more. Tweets in its raw form can be incredibly informative, but also overwhelming. For example, searching for a hot topic in Twitter can yield millions of tweets, which span for weeks. Even if filtering is allowed, plowing through so many tweets for interesting contents would be a nightmare, not to mention the enormous noises and redundancies that one could encounter. To make things worse, new tweets satisfying the filtering criteria may arrive continuously, at an unpredictable rate.

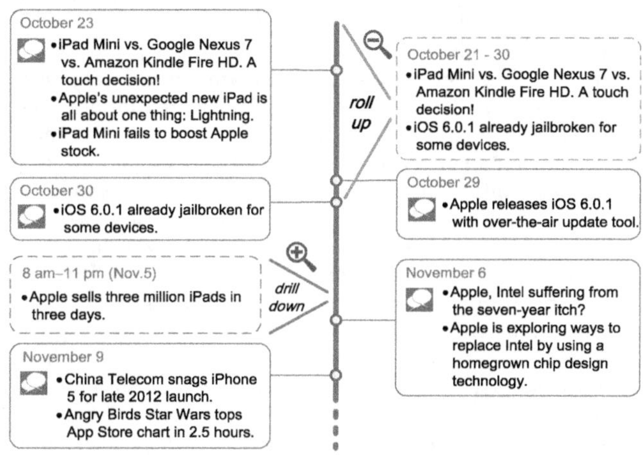

Figure 1: A timeline example for topic "Apple"

A possible solution to the above problem is *continuous tweet summarization*, which represents the massive tweets in a set of short text pieces covering the main topics (or sub-topics of course). Specifically, let us look at an example, which presumes availability of a topic-related tweet stream, for example tweets about "Apple". With a tweet summarization system, we can (i) continuously monitor "Apple"-related tweets arriving from the stream and produce a *continuous timeline* which grows by time. (ii) Suppose a user wants to learn the main happenings about "Apple" from the tweets between 22 Oct 2012 and 11 Nov 2012. The *range timeline* during that period can be provided to her, so that she understands the big picture of topic evolution in those weeks (as shown in Figure 1). (iii) After that, she may need more detailed reports for a much smaller duration (e.g. from 8 am to 11 pm on 5 Nov), which is like a *drill-down summary* on the duration. (iv) Alternatively, she may ask for a more concise report during 21 Oct to 30 Oct, in a *roll-up summary*.

[1]https://blog.twitter.com/2013/celebrating-twitter7

SIGIR'13, July 28–August 1, 2013, Dublin, Ireland.
Copyright 2013 ACM 978-1-4503-2034-4/13/07 ...$15.00.

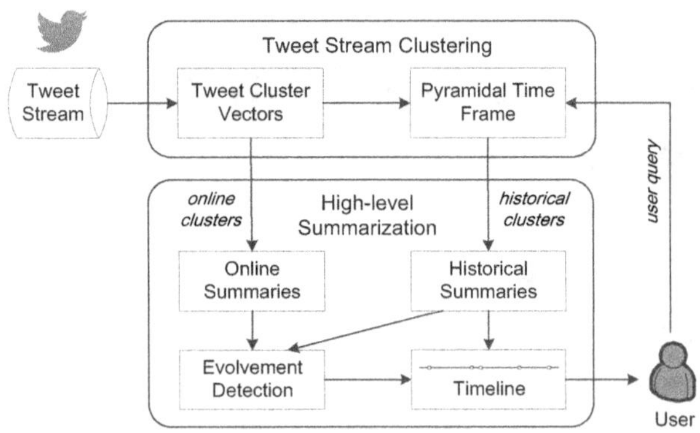

Figure 2: The framework of Sumblr

Such application would not only facilitate easy navigation in topic-relevant tweets, but also support a range of data analysis tasks such as instant reports or historical survey.

Implementing continuous tweet stream summarization is not an easy task, as the tweets are of noisy, redundant, and social nature. More importantly, tweets arrive very quickly and are strongly correlated with their posted time. A good solution to continuous tweet stream summarization has to address the following issues: (1) *Efficiency* - tweet streams always have very large scales, so their summarization should be highly efficient, with only one pass over the data; (2) *Flexibility* - the ability to provide tweet summaries of arbitrary time durations. (3) *Topic evolvement* - to automatically detect sub-topic changes and the moments that they happen.

Unfortunately, the importance of continuous summarization has long been overlooked by the research community. Although there exist numerous studies on document summarization [6, 26, 23, 13, 9, 11], these methods cannot satisfy our requirements, because: (1) They mainly focus on static and small-sized datasets, making it intractable to improve their efficiency. (2) To provide summary for arbitrary duration, these techniques will have to perform iterative/recursive summarization for every possible time duration, which is unacceptable. (3) The summary results of these algorithms are insensitive to time. Thus it is difficult for them to detect topic evolvement.

In this paper, we introduce a novel tweet summarization prototype called *Sumblr (SUMmarization By stream cLusteRing)*. To the best of our knowledge, our work is the first to study continuous tweet stream summarization. The overall structure of the prototype is depicted in Figure 2. Sumblr consists of two main components, namely a *Tweet Stream Clustering* module and a *High-level Summarization* module. In the tweet stream clustering module, we design an efficient *tweet stream clustering algorithm*, an online algorithm allowing for effective clustering of tweets with only one pass over the data. This algorithm uses two data structures to keep important tweet information in clusters. The first one is a compressed structure called *Tweet Cluster Vector (TCV)*. TCVs are considered as potential sub-topic delegates and maintained dynamically in memory during stream processing. The second structure is the *Pyramidal Time Frame (PTF)* [1], which is used to store and organize cluster snapshots at different moments, thus allowing historical tweet data to be retrieved by any arbitrary time durations.

The high-level summarization module supports the generation of two kinds of summaries: online summaries and historical ones. (1) To generate online summaries, we propose a *TCV-Rank summarization* algorithm by referring to the current clusters maintained in memory. This algorithm first computes centrality scores for tweets kept in TCVs, and selects the top-ranked ones in terms of content coverage and novelty. (2) To compute historical summaries where the user specifies an arbitrary time duration, we first retrieve two *historical cluster snapshots* from the PTF with respect to the two endpoints (the beginning and ending points) of the duration. Then, based on the difference between the two cluster snapshots, the TCV-Rank summarization algorithm is applied to generate summaries.

The summarization module also contains a topic evolvement detection algorithm, which consumes online/historical summaries to produce continuous/range timelines. A timeline is a sequence of time-stamped summaries (nodes). Both continuous and range timelines are generated by monitoring a quantity called *summary-based variation*, which is defined for summaries during the course of topic evolvement. A large variation at a particular moment implies a sub-topic change, leading to the addition of a new node on the timeline.

The main contributions of our work include: (1) A continuous tweet stream summarization framework; (2) Novel data structures and algorithms for online summarization and historical summarization of any arbitrary time interval; (3) A topic evolvement detection scheme for continuous and range timelines; (4) Extensive experiments on real Twitter datasets, showing promising results in terms of summary quality and efficiency.

The rest of the paper is organized as follows. Section 2 reviews the related work. Section 3 explains concepts including TCV and PTF. Section 4 describes our Sumblr framework in detail. The experimental settings and results are presented in Section 5. In Section 6, we conclude the paper.

2. RELATED WORK

In this section, we review the related work including *stream data clustering, traditional document summarization* and *microblog summarization and mining.*

2.1 Stream Data Clustering

Stream data clustering has been widely studied in the literature. CluStream [1] is one of the most classic stream clustering methods. It consists of an online micro-clustering component and an offline macro-clustering component. The pyramidal time frame is also proposed in [1] to recall historical micro-clusters for different time durations.

A variety of services on the Web such as news filtering, text crawling, and topic detecting etc. have posed requirements for text stream clustering. A few algorithms have been proposed to tackle the problem [7][10][27][29]. Most of these techniques adopt partition-based approaches to enable online clustering of stream data. As a consequence, these techniques fail to provide effective analysis on clusters formed over different time durations.

In [2], the authors propose to generate duration-based clustering results by extending CluStream for text and categorical data stream. However, this algorithm relies on an online phase to generate large number of "micro-clusters", leading to inefficiency and poor storage utilization.

2.2 Traditional Document Summarization

Document summarization techniques can be categorized into two types: *extractive* techniques and *abstractive* ones. The former selects sentences from the documents, while the latter may generate phrases and sentences that do not appear in the original documents. In this paper, we focus on extractive summarization.

Extractive document summarization has received a lot of recent attention. Most of them assign salient scores to sentences of the documents, and select the top-ranked sentences [3][30] [19][26] [6][22]. Some works try to extract sentences without such salient scores. A method using Singular Value Decomposition (SVD) is proposed in [8] to select highly ranked sentences. Wang et al. [23] use the Symmetric Non-negative Matrix Factorization (SNMF) to cluster sentences and choose sentences in each cluster for summarization. In [11], He et al. propose to summarize documents from the perspective of data reconstruction, and select sentences that can best reconstruct the original documents. Unfortunately, all above methods neglect the significant temporal dimension of documents, which is critical in our problem.

Yan et al. propose a technique called Evolutionary Timeline Summarization (ETS) [24] to compute evolution timelines consisting of individual but correlated component summaries. However, the dates of component summaries are determined by a pre-defined timestamp set. In contrast, our solution discovers the changing dates and generate timelines dynamically during the process of continuous summarization. More importantly, ETS does not focus on efficiency and scalability. Its task is formulated as an optimization problem via iterative substitution. Thus it does not meet our requirements.

2.3 Microblog Summarization and Mining

While document summarization has been studied for years, microblog summarization is still in its infancy. Sharifi et al. proposed the Phrase Reinforcement algorithm to summarize multiple tweet posts on the same topic with a single tweet [20]. Later, Inouye et al. proposed a modified Hybrid TF-IDF algorithm and a Cluster-based algorithm to generate multiple post summaries [13]. In [9], Harabagiu et al. introduced a framework for microblog summarization which capitalizes on a combination of two relevance models: an event structure model and a user behavior model. Takamura et al. proposed a microblog summarization method based on the p-median problem, which takes posted time of microblogs into consideration [21].

The emergence of microblogs also motivates research on other mining tasks, including topic modeling [12], storyline generation [14] and event exploration [17]. Most of these researches focus on static datasets instead of data streams. Yang et al. studied twitter stream analysis [25], but they aim at frequent pattern mining and compression, which is also a different problem from ours.

To sum up, almost all existing document/microblog summarization works mainly deal with static and small datsets, and rarely pay attention to evolvement and efficiency issues.

3. PRELIMINARIES

In this section, we first give a data model for tweets. Then we introduce two data structures used in our solution, namely the *Tweet Cluster Vector* and the *Pyramidal Time Frame*.

3.1 Tweet Representation

Generally, a document is represented as a textual vector, where the value of each dimension is the TF-IDF score of a word. However, tweets are not only textual, but also having temporal nature - a tweet is strongly correlated with its posted time. In addition, the importance of a tweet is affected by the author's social influence. To estimate the user influence, we build a matrix based on social relationships among users, and compute the UserRank as [5].

As a result, we define a tweet t_i as a tuple: $(\mathbf{tv_i}, ts_i, w_i)$, where $\mathbf{tv_i}$ is the textual vector, ts_i is the posted timestamp and w_i is the UserRank value of the tweet's author.

3.2 Tweet Cluster Vector

During tweet stream clustering, it is necessary to maintain statistics for tweets to facilitate summary generation. In this section, we propose a new data structure called *Tweet Cluster Vector*, which keeps information of tweet cluster.

DEFINITION 1. *For a cluster C containing tweets $t_1, t_2, ..., t_n$, its* ***Tweet Cluster Vector (TCV)*** *is defined as a tuple:* $TCV(C) = (\mathbf{sum\_v}, \mathbf{wsum\_v}, ts1, ts2, n, ft\_set)$, *where*

- $\mathbf{sum\_v} = \sum_{i=1}^{n} \mathbf{tv_i}/||\mathbf{tv_i}||$ *is the sum of normalized textual vectors,*
- $\mathbf{wsum\_v} = \sum_{i=1}^{n} w_i \cdot \mathbf{tv_i}$ *is the sum of weighted textual vectors,*
- $ts1 = \sum_{i=1}^{n} ts_i$ *is the sum of timestamps,*
- $ts2 = \sum_{i=1}^{n} (ts_i)^2$ *is the quadratic sum of timestamps,*
- n *is the number of tweets in the cluster, and*
- ft_set *is a focus tweet set of size m, consisting of the closest m tweets to the cluster centroid.*

The form of $\mathbf{sum\_v}$ is used for ease of presentation. In fact, we only store the identifiers and sums of values of the words occurring in the cluster. The same convention is used for $\mathbf{wsum\_v}$. To select tweets into ft_set, we use cosine similarity as the distance metric.

From the definition, we can derive the vector of cluster centroid (denoted as $\mathbf{cv}$):

$$\mathbf{cv} = (\sum_{i=1}^{n} w_i \cdot \mathbf{tv_i})/n = \mathbf{wsum\_v}/n \tag{1}$$

The definition of TCV is an extension of the cluster feature vector in [28]. Like in [28], our TCV structure can also be updated in an incremental way when new tweets arrive. We shall discuss details on updates to TCV in Section 4.1.2.

3.3 Pyramidal Time Frame

To support summarization over user-defined time durations, it is crucial to store the maintained TCVs at particular moments, which are called *snapshots*. While storing snapshots at every moment is impractical due to huge storage overhead, insufficient snapshots make it hard to recall historical information for different durations. This dilemma leads to the incorporation of the *Pyramidal Time Frame* [1]:

DEFINITION 2. *The* ***Pyramidal Time Frame (PTF)*** *stores snapshots at differing levels of granularity depending on the recency. Snapshots are classified into different* orders *which vary from 0 to $log(T)$, where T is the time elapsed since the beginning of the stream. The order of a particular class of snapshots defines the level of granularity in time at which the snapshots are maintained. The snapshots of different orders are maintained as follows:*

- *Snapshots of the i-th order occur at time intervals of α^i, where α is an integer and $\alpha \geq 1$. Specifically, each snapshot of the i-th order is taken at a moment in time when the timestamp from the beginning of the stream is exactly divisible by α^i.*
- *At any given moment in time, only the last $\alpha^l + 1$ ($l \geq 1$) snapshots of order i are stored.*

Table 1: Example of PTF with $\alpha = 3$ and $l = 2$

Order	Timestamps of snapshots in the same order
4	81
3	54 27
2	72 63 45 36 18 9
1	84 78 75 69 66 60 57 51 48 42
0	86 85 83 82 80 79 77 76 74 73

According to the definition, PTF has two properties: (1) The maximum order of any snapshot stored at T timestamps since the beginning of the stream is $log_{\alpha}(T)$; (2) The maximum number of snapshots maintained at T is $(\alpha^l + 1) \cdot log_{\alpha}(T)$. These properties are crucial for system performance. Taking more snapshots (by using a larger α or l) offers better accuracy of time duration approximation, but meanwhile causes larger storage overhead. Therefore, we need to strike a balance between duration accuracy and storage space. Note that we only maintain the current clusters in main memory, and store all historical snapshots in the PTF on disk.

To clarify how snapshots are stored, we give an example here. Let $\alpha = 3$ and $l = 2$, then there are at most $3^2+1 = 10$ snapshots stored in each order. Suppose the stream starts at timestamp 1 and the current timestamp is 86. The stored snapshots are illustrated in Table 1. Redundancy is removed by storing each snapshot only in its highest possible order.

Note that for more recent timestamps, the time interval between successive snapshots stored in PTF is smaller (finer granularity). This feature of PTF is consistent with the demand that recent summaries should be of higher quality because people usually care more about recent events.

4. THE SUMBLR FRAMEWORK

In this section, we present the details of our Sumblr framework. As shown in Figure 2, our framework includes two main modules: the tweet stream clustering module and the high-level summarization module. In what follows, we will elaborate these two modules respectively.

4.1 Tweet Stream Clustering

The tweet stream clustering module maintains the online statistical data. Given a topic-based tweet stream, it is able to efficiently cluster the tweets and maintain compact cluster statistics, with only one scan on the data.

4.1.1 Initialization

At the beginning of the stream, we collect a small number of tweets and use a k-means clustering algorithm to create the initial clusters. The value of k and the initial cluster centroids are decided via the Canopy [18] method. Once the initial clusters are established, the first set of TCVs are initialized according to Definition 1. Next, the stream clustering process starts to incrementally update the TCVs when a new tweet arrives.

4.1.2 Incremental Clustering

Suppose a tweet t arrives at time ts, and there are N active clusters at that time. First, we try to absorb t into one of the current clusters. The priority is given to the cluster whose centroid is the closest to t. Specifically, we get the centroid (denoted as co) of a cluster based on Equation (1), compute the cosine similarity between co and t, and find the cluster C_p with $MaxSim(co, t)$.

Note that although C_p is the closest to t, it does not mean t naturally belongs to C_p. The reason is that t may still be very distant from C_p. In such case, a new cluster will be created. The decision of whether to create a new cluster can be made with the following heuristic.

Algorithm 1: Incremental tweet stream clustering

```
Input: a cluster set S
while !stream.end() do
    Tweet t = stream.next();
    choose C_p in S whose centroid is the closest to t;
    if MaxSim(co_p, t) < MBS then
        create a new cluster C_new = {t};
        S = S ∪ C_new;
    else
        update C_p with t;
    if TS_current % (α^i) == 0 then
        store S into PTF;
```

HEURISTIC 1. *If $MaxSim(co, t)$ is smaller than a* ***Minimum Bounding Similarity*** *(MBS), then t is upgraded to a new cluster. Otherwise, t is added to its closest cluster.*

The MBS is defined as $\beta \cdot \overline{Sim(co, t_i)}$, where β is a bounding factor ($0 < \beta < 1$) and $\overline{Sim(co, t_i)}$ is the average cosine similarity between co and tweets included in C_p. According to Section 3.2, $\overline{Sim(co, t_i)}$ can be calculated by using the information stored in TCV:

$$\overline{Sim(co, t_i)} = \frac{1}{n}\sum_{i=1}^{n} \frac{\mathbf{tv_i} \cdot \mathbf{cv}}{||\mathbf{tv_i}|| \cdot ||\mathbf{cv}||} = \frac{\mathbf{cv}}{n \cdot ||\mathbf{cv}||}\sum_{i=1}^{n} \frac{\mathbf{tv_i}}{||\mathbf{tv_i}||}$$

$$= \frac{\frac{\mathbf{wsum\_v}}{n}}{n \cdot ||\frac{\mathbf{wsum\_v}}{n}||} \cdot \mathbf{sum\_v} = \frac{\mathbf{wsum\_v} \cdot \mathbf{sum\_v}}{n \cdot ||\mathbf{wsum\_v}||}$$

When adding a new cluster, it is hard to tell whether it is noise or a truly new sub-topic. Actually, the decision cannot be made until more tweets arrive. We discuss how noises are diminished in Section 4.4.

After applying Heuristic 1, the corresponding TCV needs to be updated. For a newly created cluster, its TCV can be initialized easily. For an existing cluster, its components in TCV can also be easily updated in an incremental manner, except the *focus tweet set*.

Recall that in Definition 1, ft_set is the set of the closest m tweets to the cluster centroid. However, as new tweets are added to the cluster during stream processing, the cluster centroid would change unpredictably. Since we can not store all tweets in the cluster, it is rather difficult to maintain exact focus tweets. For this reason, we use a heuristic strategy to choose promising candidates instead of exact focus tweets: for the newly absorbed tweet and those already in ft_set, we compute their cosine distances to *the new centroid*, and select the closest m tweets. The advantage of this strategy is that it gives a higher probability for fresh tweets to get into the focus set, which usually represent new statuses of the topic.

The above updating process is executed upon the arrival of each new tweet. Meanwhile, when the current timestamp is divisible by α^i for any integer i, we store the snapshot of the current TCVs into disk and index it by PTF. Algorithm 1 gives an overview of our incremental clustering procedure.

During incremental clustering, assume there are N active clusters, the computational cost of finding the closest cluster for every new tweet is $O(Nd)$, where d is the vocabulary size. In addition, the complexity of computing Heuristic 1 and updating TCV is $O(d)$ and $O(md)$ respectively, where m is

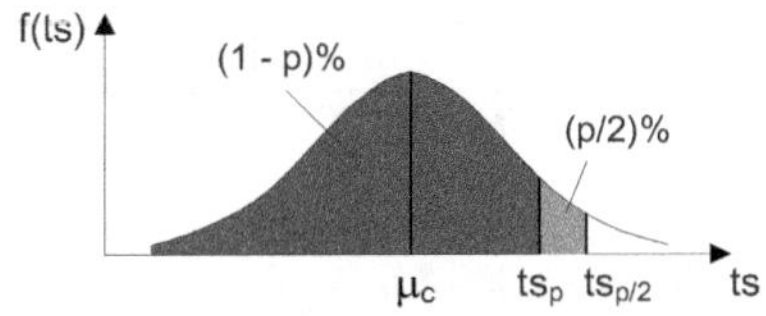

Figure 3: Probability density func. of timestamp

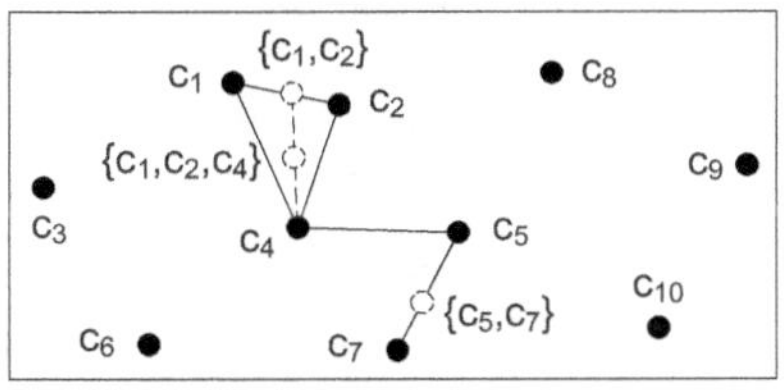

Figure 4: A running example of cluster merging

the size of focus set. Then the total cost is $O((N + m)d)$. Because m and d are static, the computational cost depends on N. Similarly, the storage costs in disk (TCV snapshots) and memory (current TCVs) also depend on N.

Given the above analysis, we need to restrict the number of active clusters. We achieve this goal via two operations: *deleting outdated clusters* and *merging similar clusters*. Since the computational complexity of deletion is $O(N)$ and that of merging is $O(N^2)$, we use the former method for periodical examination and use the latter method only when memory limit is reached.

4.1.3 Deleting Outdated Clusters

For most events (such as news, football matches and concerts) in tweet stream, timeliness is important because they usually do not last for a long time. Therefore it is safe to delete the tweet clusters representing these sub-topics when they are rarely discussed. To find out such clusters, an intuitive way is to estimate the average arrival time (denoted as Avg_p) of the last p percent of tweets in a cluster. However, storing p percent of tweets for every cluster will increase memory requirements, especially when some clusters grow big. Thus, we employ an approximate method to get Avg_p.

Note that the temporal statistics in TCV of a cluster C allow us to compute the mean and standard deviation of timestamps of tweets in C: $\mu_c = ts1/n$, $\sigma_c = \sqrt{ts2/n - (ts1/n)^2}$.

Assuming that the tweet timestamps are normally distributed, we can obtain the arrival time of the qth percentile of the tweets. The *qth percentile* is the value that cuts off the first q percent of the tweet timestamps when they are sorted in ascending order. When $q = 100 - p$, the qth percentile is the start timestamp of the last p percent of tweets (noted as ts_p in Figure 3). Then, we can approximate Avg_p using the $(100 - p/2)$-th percentile (noted as $ts_{p/2}$ in Figure 3).

Now the problem is transformed into obtaining the value of $ts_{p/2}$. Let $x = ts_{p/2}$ and $p' = (100 - p/2)\%$, we have

$$\begin{aligned} F(x) &= \Phi(\frac{x - \mu_c}{\sigma_c}) = p' \\ \Rightarrow \qquad x &= \mu_c + \sigma_c \Phi^{-1}(p') \\ &= \mu_c + \sigma_c \cdot \sqrt{2} erf^{-1}(2p' - 1) \end{aligned}$$

where $F(x)$ is the cumulative distribution function (CDF), $\Phi(x)$ is the CDF of the standard normal distribution, and $erf^{-1}(z)$ is the *inverse error function* and can be calculated using the Maclaurin series expansion [31].

The value of $ts_{p/2}$ represents the *freshness* of cluster C. We empirically set a freshness threshold as 3 days (as empirically no bursty events would last longer) and set $p = 10$. If $ts_{p/2}$ is smaller than this threshold, i.e., the average timestamp of the latest 10 percent tweets is more than 3 days old, then we regard C as an outdated cluster and remove it.

4.1.4 Merging Clusters

If the number of clusters keeps increasing and few of them are deleted, the system memory will be exhausted. To avoid this, we specify an upper limit for the number of clusters as N_{max}. When the limit is reached, a merging process starts.

The process merges clusters in a greedy way until the termination condition is satisfied. First, we sort all cluster pairs by their centroid similarities in a descending order. Then, beginning with the most similar pair, we try to merge two clusters in the pair. When both clusters are *single clusters* which have not been merged with other clusters, they are merged into a new *composite cluster*. When one of them belongs to a composite cluster (it has been merged with others before), then the other is also merged into that composite cluster. When both of them have been merged, if they belong to the same composite cluster, this pair is skipped; otherwise, the two composite clusters are merged together. This process continues until there are only mc percentage of the original clusters left (mc is a merge coefficient which provides a balance between available memory space and the quality of remaining clusters). We omit the pseudo-code of the algorithm due to space limitation.

During cluster merging, each composite cluster is given an *IDList* which consists of *ID*s of the clusters merged in it. Furthermore, its TCV is obtained by the *Aggregation operation* to combine two TCVs.

DEFINITION 3. ***(Aggregation Operation)*** *Let C_1 and C_2 be two clusters, and their TCV structures be $TCV(C_1)$ and $TCV(C_2)$. Then, when C_1 and C_2 are merged together, the composite cluster's $TCV(C_1 \cup C_2)$ is given by*

- $\mathbf{sum\_v} = \mathbf{sum\_v_1} + \mathbf{sum\_v_2}$
- $\mathbf{wsum\_v} = \mathbf{wsum\_v_1} + \mathbf{wsum\_v_2}$
- $ts1 = ts1_1 + ts1_2$
- $ts2 = ts2_1 + ts2_2$
- $n = n_1 + n_2$
- *ft_set consists of the first m tweets in $ft\_set_1 \cup ft\_set_2$, sorted by distance to the newly merged centroid.*

Figure 4 shows a running example of the process. For ease of presentation, we use cluster centroids (the black solid points) to represent clusters and use Euclidean distance instead of cosine distance. First, we calculate distances for all cluster pairs and sorted them as: $(c_1, c_2), (c_2, c_4), (c_1, c_4)$, $(c_5, c_7), (c_4, c_5), \ldots$. Suppose $mc = 0.7$, then we need to remove $10 \times (1 - 0.7) = 3$ clusters. To start with, c_1 and c_2 are merged into a composite cluster $\{c_1, c_2\}$. After that, when processing the second pair (c_2, c_4), we find that c_2 has been merged. Hence we combine c_4 into $\{c_1, c_2\}$, and the composite cluster becomes $\{c_1, c_2, c_4\}$. For next pair, c_1 and c_4 both have been merged, so this pair is skipped. Next we merge c_5 and c_7 into another composite cluster $\{c_5, c_7\}$. Now that we have reduced the number of clusters by 3, the algorithm terminates. Note that since only $N_{max} \times (1 - mc)$ (denoted as N') clusters need to be removed, we would access at most $C^2_{N'} + 1 = N'(N' - 1)/2 + 1$ pairs.

4.2 High-level Summarization

The high-level summarization module provides two types of summaries: *online* and *historical* summaries. The online summaries are retrieved directly from the current clusters maintained in the memory. For historical summaries, retrieval of the required clusters is more complicated. In what follows, we shall focus on the second type.

Suppose the length of a user-defined time duration is H, and the ending timestamp of the duration is ts_e. From PTF, we can retrieve two snapshots whose timestamps are either equal to or right before ts_e and $ts_e - H$, respectively. We denote their timestamps by ts_1 and ts_2, and their cluster sets by $S(ts_1)$ and $S(ts_2)$. Now the original duration $[ts_e - H, ts_e]$ is approximated by $[ts_2, ts_1]$.

Intuitively, we need to perform a *cluster set subtraction* between $S(ts_1)$ and $S(ts_2)$. For each cluster C in $S(ts_1)$, we acquire its ID (if it is a single cluster) or IDs in its $IDList$ (a composite cluster). For each of these IDs, we find the corresponding cluster in $S(ts_2)$, and subtract its TCV from C's TCV according to:

DEFINITION 4. ***(Subtraction Operation)*** *Given a cluster C_1 in $S(ts_1)$ and its corresponding cluster C_2 in $S(ts_2)$, when C_2 is subtracted from C_1, their difference $TCV(C_1 - C_2)$ is given by*

- **sum_v = sum_v$_1$ − sum_v$_2$**
- **wsum_v = wsum_v$_1$ − wsum_v$_2$**
- $ts1 = ts1_1 - ts1_2$
- $ts2 = ts2_1 - ts2_2$
- $n = n_1 - n_2$
- *ft_set consists of tweets which exist in ft_set_1 but not in ft_set_2.*

The above process eliminates the influence of clusters created before ts_2 on summary results. The final set of clusters after this process is the input for historical summarization.

4.2.1 TCV-Rank Summarization

Given an input cluster set, we denote its corresponding TCV set as $D(c)$. A tweet set T consists of all the tweets in the ft_sets in $D(c)$. Our tweet summarization aims to extract k tweets from T, so that they can cover as many tweet contents as possible.

We first prove it is a NP-hard problem, then we present a greedy algorithm to solve it.

LEMMA 1. *The tweet summarization problem is NP-hard.*

PROOF. Let us first describe this problem formally. $\mathcal{F} = \{T_1, T_2, ..., T_t\}$ is a collection of non-empty subsets of T, where a subset T_i represents a sub-topic and $|T_i|$ means the number of its related tweets. The subsets may have some tweets in common because one tweet can be related to more than one sub-topic. Suppose for each T_i, there is a tweet which represents the content of T_i's sub-topic. Then, selecting k tweets is equivalent to selecting k subsets.

Now, the problem can be defined as: given a number k and a collection of sets $\mathcal{F}$, find a subset $\mathcal{F}' \subseteq \mathcal{F}$, such that $|\mathcal{F}'| = k$ and $|\bigcup_{T_i \in \mathcal{F}'} T_i|$ is maximized (i.e., $\mathcal{F}'$ contains as many tweets as possible). We notice that this is the *Max-k-Cover* problem, which is NP-hard. Therefore, our summarization problem is also NP-hard. □

More generally, summary length are limited in terms of words (250 words). Since the number of words and that of tweets are linearly dependent, the problem is still NP-hard.

From the geometric interpretation, our summarization tends to select tweets that span the intrinsic subspace of candidate tweet space, such that it can cover most information of the whole tweet set.

Algorithm 2: TCV-Rank summarization

```
Input: a cluster set D(c)
Output: a summary set S
S = ∅, T = {all the tweets in ft_sets of D(c)};
Build a similarity graph on T;
Compute LexRank scores LR;
T_c = {tweets with the highest score in each cluster};
while |S| < L do
    foreach tweet t_i in T_c do
        calculate v_i according to Equation (2);
    select t_max with the highest v_i;
    S = S ∪ t_max;
while |S| < L do
    foreach tweet t'_i in T − S do
        calculate v'_i according to Equation (2);
    select t'_max with the highest v'_i;
    S = S ∪ t'_max;
return S;
```

We design a greedy algorithm to select representative tweets to form summaries (Algorithm 2). First, we gather tweets from the ft_sets in $D(c)$ as a set T, and build a cosine similarity graph. The maximum size of T is $N \times m$, where N is the number of clusters in $D(c)$ and m is the size of ft_set. It is the upper bound because ft_sets of some clusters (e.g., small clusters or clusters newly created) may not be full. Next, we apply the LexRank method [6] to compute centrality scores for tweets. LexRank is an effective static summarization method and is efficient for small-sized datasets. But when datasets become large, its efficiency drops quickly (this will be shown in the experiment). The tweet set T has at most Nm tweets (usually hundreds or thousands), so LexRank is suitable for our situation.

However, a potential problem of LexRank is that some top-ranked tweets may have similar contents. Fortunately, since the tweets are retrieved from TCVs, they have got inherent cluster information. Hence, we choose one tweet with the highest LexRank score from each TCV, and add tweet t into the summary according to:

$$t = \underset{t_i}{\text{argmax}}[\lambda \frac{n_{t_i}}{n_{max}} LR(t_i) - (1 - \lambda) \underset{t_j \in S}{\text{avg}}\, Sim(t_i, t_j)], \quad (2)$$

where λ ($0 \leq \lambda \leq 1$) is a weight parameter, n_{t_i} is the size of the cluster containing t_i, n_{max} is the size of the biggest cluster, $LR(t_i)$ is t_i's LexRank score and S is the summary set containing already chosen tweets.

The motivation of Equation (2) is analogous to that of *Maximal Marginal Relevance (MMR)* [4]. In query-oriented summarization, MMR combines query relevance and information novelty. Here, we combine coverage and novelty as our criterion: the first component on the right side of the equation favors tweets which have high scores and belong to big clusters (content coverage); the second component penalizes redundant tweets with similar contents to those already chosen (novelty).

After the first round selection, if the summary length is still not reached, then we try to select tweets globally ($t_i \in T - S$) according to Equation (2).

The computational complexity for LexRank is $O(r|T|^2)$, where r is the iteration number. In tweet selection, note that for each tweet, the first component in the righthand of Equation (2) only needs to be computed once, and the second component can be updated incrementally. So the worst-case cost of tweet selection is $O(N^2 + (|S| - N) \cdot |T|)$. Since $|S| << |T|$, the total cost for our algorithm is $O(r|T|^2 + N^2) = O(rm^2N^2)$. As mentioned before, Nm is always controlled at a relatively small number, hence the summarization procedure is very efficient.

4.3 Topic Evolvement Detection

Topic evolvment detection algorithm can produce continuous and range timelines in a similar way. We shall only describe the continuous case here.

As tweets arrive from the stream, online summaries are generated continuously by utilizing real-time cluster statistics. This allows for a continuous timeline. Generally, when an obvious variation occurs in the main contents discussed in tweets, we can expect a change of sub-topics (i.e., a time node on the timeline). To quantify the variation, we use Kullback-Leibler divergence to measure the distance between two word distributions in two successive summaries S_p and S_c, S_p is the previous summary and S_c is the current one.

$$D_{KL}(S_c||S_p) = \sum_{w \in V} p(w|S_c) ln \frac{p(w|S_c)}{p(w|S_p)}, \quad (3)$$

where

$$p(w|S_c) = \frac{tf(w, S_c)}{\sum_{w'} tf(w', S_c)}$$

$$p(w|S_p) = \frac{tf(w, S_p) + \epsilon}{\sum_{w'} (tf(w', S_p) + \epsilon)}$$

V is the vocabulary set and $tf(w, S)$ is the term frequency for word w in S. ϵ is a small positive constant for Laplace Smoothing, which is applied to avoid zero values of $p(w|S_p)$. Furthermore, we normalize the distance into interval $[0, 1)$ using $D = 1 - e^{-D_{KL}}$, for ease of comparison.

According to the summary-based variation, we determine if the current time is a sub-topic changing node by:

$$\frac{D_{cur}}{D_{avg}} > \tau,$$

where D_{cur} is the distance between current summary and its previous neighboring summary, D_{avg} is the average distance of all the previous successive summary pairs which do not produce time nodes, and τ ($\tau \geq 1$) is the decision threshold.

That is, we detect topic evolvement when there is a *burst* in distances between successive summaries. In this way, we can automatically draw a timeline as the stream proceeds.

4.4 Discussion

Handling noises The effect of clusters of noises can be diminished by two means in Sumblr. First, in tweet stream clustering, noise clusters which are not updated frequently will be deleted as outdated clusters. Second, in the summarization step, tweets from noise clusters are far less likely to be selected into summary, due to their small LexRank scores and cluster sizes.

Extension to multi-topic streams So far we have assumed a tweet stream of only one topic as the input to Sumblr. However, we should note that Sumblr can be easily extended for multi-topic streams. For example, when a new tweet arrives, we first decide its related topics by keyword matching. Then it is delivered into different groups of clusters. Clusters are grouped by their corresponding topical IDs. Consequently, Sumblr is applied within each cluster group. It is important to note that this mechanism allows for distributed system implementation.

Table 2: Basic information of 5 datasets

Topics (filtering keywords)	#Tweets	Time Span
Obama	95,055	2009.2 - 2009.10
Chelsea	438,884	2012.11 - 2012.12
Arsenal Arsene Wenger	323,555	2012.11 - 2012.12
Tablet Smartphone Cellphone	231,011	2012.11 - 2012.12
Black Friday	124,684	2012.11 - 2012.12

5. EXPERIMENTS

5.1 Experimental Setup

Datasets We construct 5 datasets to evaluate Sumblr. One is obtained by conducting keyword filtering on a Twitter dataset (from Feb. to Oct., 2009) used by [5]. The other four include more recent tweets acquired in one month via Twitter's keyword tracking API [2]. As we do not have access to the respective users' social networks for these four, we set their weights of tweets w_i to the default value of 1. Details of the datasets are listed in Table 2.

Ground truth for summaries As no previous work has conducted similar study on continuous summarization, we have to build our own ground truth (reference summaries). However, manual creation of these summaries is apparently impractical due to the huge size of the datasets.

Thus, we employ a two-step method to obtain fair-quality reference summaries without tremendous human labor:

1) Given a time duration, we first retrieve the corresponding tweet subset, and use the following three well-recognized summarization algorithms to get three candidate summaries.

ClusterSum [13]: first clusters the tweets and then summarizes each cluster by picking the most weighted post according to the hybrid TF-IDF weighting described in [13].

LexRank [6]: first builds a sentence similarity graph, and then selects important sentences based on the concept of eigenvector centrality.

DSDR [11]: models the relationship among sentences using linear reconstruction, and finds an optimal set of representative sentences to approximate the original documents, by minimizing the reconstruction error.

2) Next, for each subset, the final reference summary is manually extracted from three candidate summaries. Priority is given to those sentences appearing in at least two candidate summaries. The length of each summary is limited to 250 words.

Ground truth for timelines For the timeline generation test, the reference timelines are manually produced. We choose the "Arsenal" and "Chelsea" datasets for this experiment, as the ground truth for sport topics are relatively easier to build manually. Specifically, we read through all the related news during one month from news websites (Yahoo! and ESPN), and select those dates as nodes on the reference timeline when important events happen, e.g., football matches, players' signing of new contracts, etc. [3]

Baseline methods Most existing summarization methods are not designed to handle continuous summarization. However, they can be adapted to streaming data by using a *sliding window* scheme. As illustrated in Figure 8, each window contains a certain number (window size) of tweets which are summarized as a document. After that, the window moves forward by a *step size*, so that the oldest tweets are discarded and the new ones are added into the window.

[2]https://dev.twitter.com/docs/api/1.1/post/statuses/filter
[3]Our datasets and ground truth are available at http://db.zju.edu.cn/s/sumblr/.

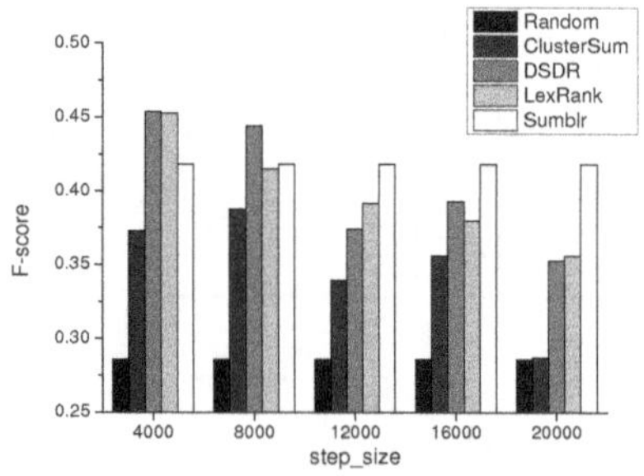

Figure 5: Quality on step size

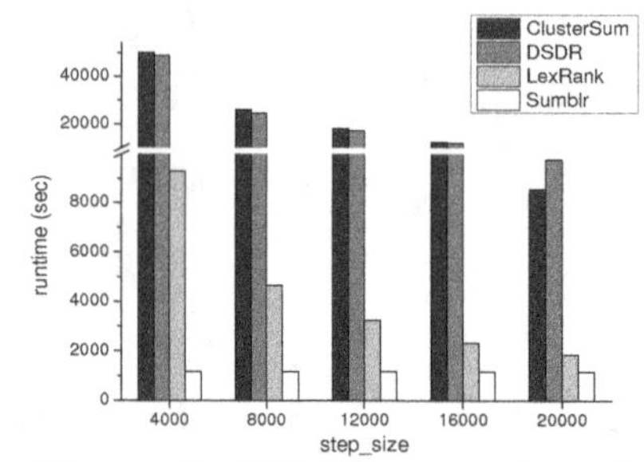

Figure 6: Efficiency on step size

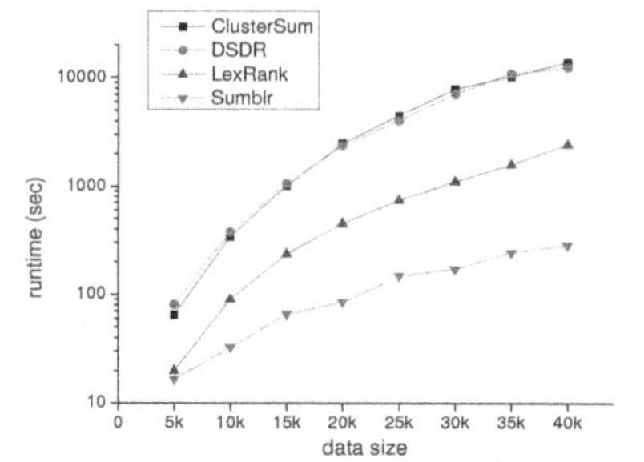

Figure 7: Scalability on data size

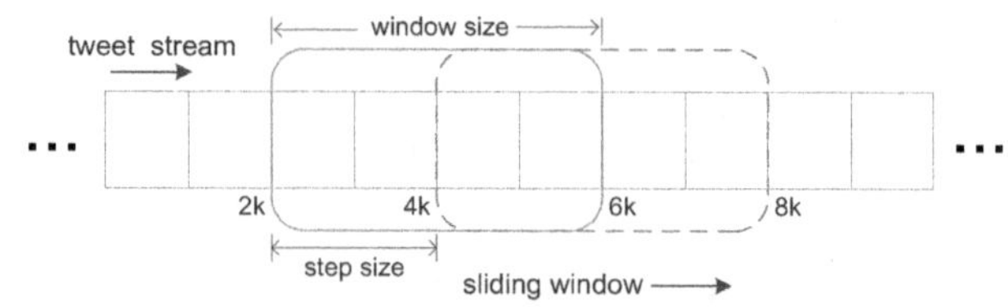

Figure 8: The sliding window mechanism

In this way, we implement the sliding window version of the above three algorithms, namely *ClusterSum*, *LexRank*, and *DSDR*. The windows are dimensioned by number of tweets instead of time duration, because the number of tweets may vary dramatically across fixed-length durations, leading to very poor performance of the baseline algorithms.

Evaluation method We apply the popular ROUGE toolkit [15] for evaluation. Among supported metrics, ROUGE-1 has been demonstrated to be the most consistent with human judgement [16]. Considering the short and informal nature of the tweet contents, we decide that ROUGE-1 is suitable for measuring tweet summaries.

To evaluate the metrics on a continuous time period $[T_0, T]$, we have to calculate the integral of the metric over the period, which is given by

$$\int_{T_0}^{T} metric(t)dt \tag{4}$$

The integral requires unaffordable number of samplings during the period. In practice, we only sample the metrics by each arrival of a certain number of new tweets. This number is called the *sampling interval*. Note the sampling interval must be no greater than the step size.

In our experiments, we find similar trends in the comparison of precision, recall and F-score between the proposed approach and the baseline methods. Therefore, we shall only report the F-score results to save space. The F-score results presented are averaged on all five datasets.

5.2 Overall Performance Comparison

In this section, we compare the F-scores and runtime cost between Sumblr and the three baseline algorithms (sliding window version). As tweets are often produced very quickly and reach a huge volume in a short while, it is hardly meaningful to summarize a small number of tweets. Thus the window size should be a relatively large one. In this experiment, we set window size to 20000, sampling interval to 2000. The step size varies from 4000 to 20000. The metrics are averaged over the whole stream.

Figure 5 and Figure 6 present the results for different step sizes. In Figure 5, we also give a baseline *Random* method, which selects tweets randomly from each window. Note that Sumblr is not affected by the step size, as it supports continuous summarization inherently.

The results show that when the step size is small (4000), DSDR and LexRank achieve better summary quality than Sumblr, at the expense of much more computation. When $step\_size \geq 12000$, Sumblr outperforms all the baseline methods in terms of both summarization quality and computation cost. Although the efficiency of LexRank is comparable with our method when $step\_size \geq 16000$, its summary quality is significantly worse.

The above results reveal a major problem with the baseline methods: These methods rely on a small step size to produce quality summaries. Unfortunately, small step size leads to very frequent and expensive computations for windows. In contrast, Sumblr strikes a good balance between summary quality and efficiency.

Another issue to note here is that, as the ground truth is generated using these baseline methods, the summary quality is to some extent biased in favor of them.

Scalability

The scalability experiment evaluates the efficiency results of a single window, while varying the window size. It simulates the case of a large burst of tweets in a short period.

Figure 7 presents the scalability results for different methods. Note that the y-axis is in the log scale. We can see that our method outperforms the others significantly. When the data size is above 15000, Sumblr is faster than LexRank by nearly an order of magnitude, and outperforms the other two by more than that. The small fluctuations in Sumblr may be caused by the cluster deletions and merges.

5.3 Parameter Tuning

In this section, we tune the parameters in our approach. In each of the following experiments, we vary one parameter and keep the others fixed.

Effect of β. In Heuristic 1 we use β to determine whether to create a new cluster. Figure 9(a) and Figure 9(b) show its effect on summary quality and efficiency. When β is small, tweets related to different sub-topics may be absorbed into the same clusters, so the input of our summarization component is of low quality. At the same time, there are many focus tweets in each cluster, thus the time cost of cluster updating and summarization is high. When β increases, too many clusters are created, causing damage to both quality and efficiency. A good choice is $\beta = 0.07$ as it gives more balanced results.

Effect of N_{max}. Figure 9(c) and Figure 9(d) depicts the performance of N_{max}. For small N_{max}s, many merging operations are conducted, which are time-consuming and produce lots of low-quality clusters. For large values, stream clustering is slow due to large number of clusters. Note that the storage overhead (both in memory and disk) is also higher for larger N_{max}s. A balanced value for N_{max} is 150.

Effect of mc. Another parameter in cluster merging is mc $(0 < mc < 1)$. It does not have significant impact on

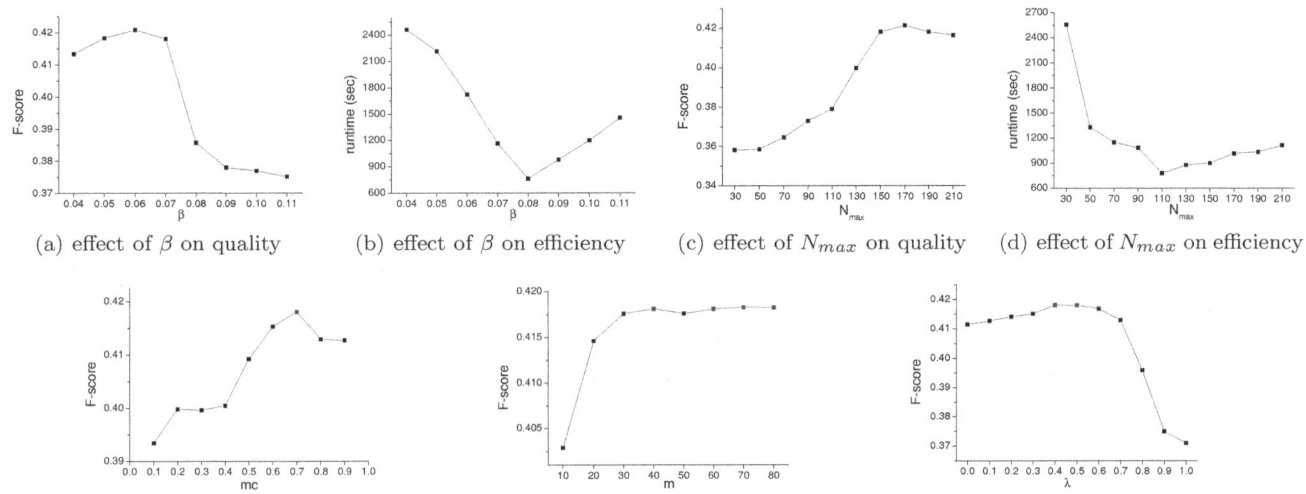

(a) effect of β on quality (b) effect of β on efficiency (c) effect of N_{max} on quality (d) effect of N_{max} on efficiency

(e) effect of mc (f) effect of m (g) effect of λ

Figure 9: Performance of different parameters

efficiency, so we only present its quality results (Figure 9(e)). Small values of mc result in low-quality clusters, while large ones lead to many merging operations, which in turn reduce the quality of clusters. An ideal value for mc is 0.7.

Effect of m. As shown in Figure 9(f), the summary quality improves when m increases. When $m \geq 40$, the improvement is not obvious. Meanwhile, a larger m incurs more storage overhead. We choose $m = 40$.

Effect of λ. Finally we check the effect of λ $(0 \leq \lambda \leq 1)$, which is a trade-off factor between content coverage and novelty. We gradually vary λ from 0 to 1 at the step of 0.1 to examine its effect, as shown in Figure 9(g). When $\lambda \geq 0.7$, the extreme emphasis on coverage causes performance loss. Therefore, we set $\lambda = 0.4$ as a balanced factor.

5.4 Flexibility

One distinguishing feature of Sumblr is the flexibility to summarize tweets over arbitrary time durations. This feature is provided by incorporating the PTF. The effectiveness of PTF depends on α and l (Section 3.3). We fix α at 2 and show the results varying l. For consistency, we extract a subset of one-month period from each dataset as the input stream. The interval between two successive snapshots (timestamp unit) is one hour. For a timestamp ts, we evaluate the results for drill-down/roll-up summaries using durations with different length len. Due to space limit, we only present the average F-score for len varying from 1 day to 10 days, and report $score(ts)$ by interval of 48 hours.

$$score(ts) = \frac{\sum_{len} F\text{-}score([ts - len, ts])}{10} \quad (5)$$

Figure 10 gives the following observations:

- There exists a common trend for all ls: as a time duration is closer to the current time, the summary quality improves. This is because PTF has finer granularity of snapshots for more recent moments. Thus the queried durations can be better approximated.
- For different values of l, the summary quality is similar for recent durations, but decreases in different degrees for early durations. The reason is that for recent moments, most of their snapshots or neighborhood snapshots are still kept in PTFs regardless of l; while for early moments, their snapshots are more likely to be removed from PTFs with smaller ls, due to smaller capacity of each order.

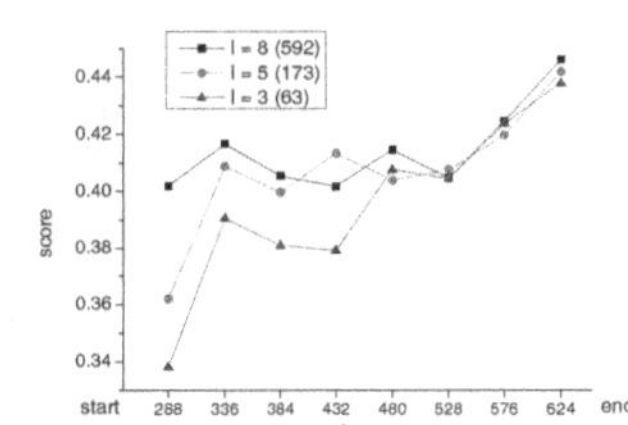

Figure 10: Quality on time duration

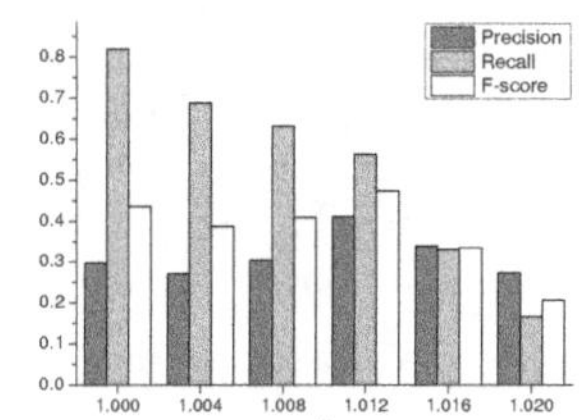

Figure 11: Effect of τ

- A larger l leads to better results but more storage cost (the numbers in the parentheses represent the amounts of snapshots in PTF). This is obvious, as a larger l enables PTF to store more snapshots, which results in more accurate approximation and heavier storage burden.

For different applications, Sumblr can be customized with different l values. For example, for real-time summarization, a small l is enough; while for historical review, a large l is needed.

5.5 Timeline Generation

In this section, we evaluate the effectiveness of topic evolvement detection. We present the precision, recall, and F-score of the timeline nodes detected by our algorithm while varying the decision threshold τ.

From Figure 11, we can see that the recall declines as τ increases. This is expected as higher threshold would exclude more promising candidates i.e., produce more false negatives. The precision and F-score both reach the highest value when $\tau = 1.012$. Although the recall drops when τ increases, precision increases further (as more false positive nodes are excluded). Surprisingly, when $\tau > 1.012$, precision also drops. This may result from the incompleteness of our manual timeline or noises in the datasets.

The output for "Arsenal" is presented in Table 3. It is interesting to find that our summary-based timeline not only detects important events (e.g. a match is called off due to a tube strike), but also contains popular public opinions (e.g. public calling for WENGER OUT).

6. CONCLUSION

We proposed a prototype called Sumblr which supported continuous tweet stream summarization. Sumblr employed

Table 3: Selected part of the timeline for "Arsenal"

12.12: 1. Yes Bradford! WENGER OUT. 2. Arsenal lose to Bradford: Should Arsene Wenger go? 3. Arsenal Chief Executive Ivan Gazidis has apologised to the club's fans, and described Arsenal's defeat to Bradford.	**12.19**: 1. Good news for Arsenal fans: Wilshere, Oxlade-Chamberlain, Ramsey, Gibbs and Jenkinson sign new contracts. 2. ♯afc Arsenal's Premier League match against West Ham on Boxing Day is called off because of a possible tube strike. 3. Five Arsenal players sign new contracts, but not one of those five is Theo Walcott. 4. Wenger: "We hope we will be capable of building a team around the young English players." ♯Arsenal ♯AFC
12.16: 1. Every arsenal fan knows how chelsea fans feel like right now. 2. Game over, we lost.. Am I sad? No are arsenal fans happy? Yes, are they gonna ever play world club cup? No. 3. RVP: "I'm sorry to Arsenal fans, I've never been happier than this. Finally I found a home and peace here. I'm happy at Man United."	**12.20**: 1. Champions League draw: Manchester United v Real Madrid, Arsenal v Bayern Munich, Celtic v Juventus. 2. So it is @Arsenal Vs Bayern Munich....good game we'll have :-)
12.18: 1. Arsenal vs Reading Come on arsenal ♯Arsenal 2. What a come back! Cazorla is a class! But I love how Wenger gave the right position for Walcott. 3. I know it's "only" Reading but still good to see Arsenal playing so well.	**12.22**: 1. Arsenal better win the game against wigan. 2. Wilshere hails Arsenal's fighting spirit after Wigan win.

a tweet stream clustering algorithm to compress tweets into TCVs and maintain them in an online fashion. Then, it used a TCV-Rank summarization algorithm for generating online summaries and historical summaries with arbitrary time durations. The topic evolvement could be detected automatically, allowing Sumblr to produce dynamic timelines for tweet streams. The experimental results demonstrated the efficiency and effectiveness of our method. For future work, we aim to develop a multi-topic version of Sumblr in a distributed system, and evaluate it on more complete and large-scale datasets.

Acknowledgments

The work is supported by the National Science Foundation of China (GrantNo. 61170034).

7. REFERENCES

[1] C. C. Aggarwal, J. Han, J. Wang, and P. S. Yu. A framework for clustering evolving data streams. In *VLDB*, pages 81–92, 2003.

[2] C. C. Aggarwal and P. S. Yu. On clustering massive text and categorical data streams. *Knowl. Inf. Syst.*, 24(2):171–196, 2010.

[3] R. Barzilay and M. Elhadad. Using lexical chains for text summarization. In *Proceedings of the ACL Workshop on Intelligent Scalable Text Summarization*, pages 10–17, 1997.

[4] J. Carbonell and J. Goldstein. The use of mmr, diversity-based reranking for reordering documents and producing summaries. In *SIGIR*, pages 335–336, 1998.

[5] C. Chen, F. Li, B. C. Ooi, and S. Wu. Ti: an efficient indexing mechanism for real-time search on tweets. In *SIGMOD*, pages 649–660, 2011.

[6] G. Erkan and D. R. Radev. Lexrank: graph-based lexical centrality as salience in text summarization. *J. Artif. Int. Res.*, 22(1):457–479, 2004.

[7] L. Gong, J. Zeng, and S. Zhang. Text stream clustering algorithm based on adaptive feature selection. *Expert Syst. Appl.*, 38(3):1393–1399, 2011.

[8] Y. Gong and X. Liu. Generic text summarization using relevance measure and latent semantic analysis. In *SIGIR*, pages 19–25, 2001.

[9] S. M. Harabagiu and A. Hickl. Relevance modeling for microblog summarization. In *ICWSM*, 2011.

[10] Q. He, K. Chang, E.-P. Lim, and J. Zhang. Bursty feature representation for clustering text streams. In *SDM*, 2007.

[11] Z. He, C. Chen, J. Bu, C. Wang, L. Zhang, D. Cai, and X. He. Document summarization based on data reconstruction. In *AAAI*, 2012.

[12] L. Hong, A. Ahmed, S. Gurumurthy, A. J. Smola, and K. Tsioutsiouliklis. Discovering geographical topics in the twitter stream. In *WWW*, pages 769–778, 2012.

[13] D. Inouye and J. K. Kalita. Comparing twitter summarization algorithms for multiple post summaries. In *SocialCom*, pages 298–306, 2011.

[14] C. Lin, C. Lin, J. Li, D. Wang, Y. Chen, and T. Li. Generating event storylines from microblogs. In *CIKM*, pages 175–184, 2012.

[15] C.-Y. Lin. Rouge: A package for automatic evaluation of summaries. In *Proc. ACL workshop on Text Summarization Branches Out*, pages 74–81, 2004.

[16] C.-Y. Lin and E. Hovy. Automatic evaluation of summaries using n-gram co-occurrence statistics. In *HLT-NAACL*, pages 71–78, 2003.

[17] A. Marcus, M. S. Bernstein, O. Badar, D. R. Karger, S. Madden, and R. C. Miller. Twitinfo: aggregating and visualizing microblogs for event exploration. In *CHI*, pages 227–236, 2011.

[18] A. McCallum, K. Nigam, and L. H. Ungar. Efficient clustering of high-dimensional data sets with application to reference matching. In *KDD*, pages 169–178, 2000.

[19] D. R. Radev, H. Jing, M. Styś, and D. Tam. Centroid-based summarization of multiple documents. *Inf. Process. Manage.*, 40(6):919–938, 2004.

[20] B. Sharifi, M.-A. Hutton, and J. Kalita. Summarizing microblogs automatically. In *HLT-NAACL*, pages 685–688, 2010.

[21] H. Takamura, H. Yokono, and M. Okumura. Summarizing a document stream. In *ECIR*, 2011.

[22] X. Wan and J. Yang. Multi-document summarization using cluster-based link analysis. In *SIGIR*, pages 299–306, 2008.

[23] D. Wang, T. Li, S. Zhu, and C. Ding. Multi-document summarization via sentence-level semantic analysis and symmetric matrix factorization. In *SIGIR*, pages 307–314, 2008.

[24] R. Yan, X. Wan, J. Otterbacher, L. Kong, X. Li, and Y. Zhang. Evolutionary timeline summarization: a balanced optimization framework via iterative substitution. In *SIGIR*, pages 745–754, 2011.

[25] X. Yang, A. Ghoting, Y. Ruan, and S. Parthasarathy. A framework for summarizing and analyzing twitter feeds. In *KDD*, pages 370–378, 2012.

[26] W.-t. Yih, J. Goodman, L. Vanderwende, and H. Suzuki. Multi-document summarization by maximizing informative content-words. In *IJCAI*, pages 1776–1782, 2007.

[27] J. Zhang, Z. Ghahramani, and Y. Yang. A probabilistic model for online document clustering with application to novelty detection. In *NIPS*, 2005.

[28] T. Zhang, R. Ramakrishnan, and M. Livny. Birch: an efficient data clustering method for very large databases. In *SIGMOD*, pages 103–114, 1996.

[29] S. Zhong. Efficient streaming text clustering. *Neural Networks*, 18(5-6):790–798, 2005.

[30] Q. Zhou, L. Sun, and J. Nie. Is_sum: A multi-document summarizer based on document index graphic and lexical chains. *DUC2005*, 2005.

[31] D. Zwillinger. *CRC standard mathematical tables and formulae.* CRC press, 2011.

Exploiting User Feedback to Learn to Rank Answers in Q&A Forums: a Case Study with Stack Overflow

Daniel Hasan Dalip,
Marcos André Gonçalves
Dept of Computer Science - UFMG
Belo Horizonte/MG, Brazil
{hasan,mgoncalv}@dcc.ufmg.br

Marco Cristo
Institute of Computing - UFAM
Manaus/AM, Brazil
marco.cristo@ic.ufam.edu.br

Pável Calado
Instituto Superior Técnico/
INESC-ID
Porto Salvo, Portugal
pavel.calado@tagus.ist.utl.pt

ABSTRACT

Collaborative web sites, such as collaborative encyclopedias, blogs, and forums, are characterized by a loose edit control, which allows anyone to freely edit their content. As a consequence, the quality of this content raises much concern. To deal with this, many sites adopt manual quality control mechanisms. However, given their size and change rate, manual assessment strategies do not scale and content that is new or unpopular is seldom reviewed. This has a negative impact on the many services provided, such as ranking and recommendation. To tackle with this problem, we propose a learning to rank (L2R) approach for ranking answers in Q&A forums. In particular, we adopt an approach based on Random Forests and represent query and answer pairs using eight different groups of features. Some of these features are used in the Q&A domain for the first time. Our L2R method was trained to learn the answer rating, based on the feedback users give to answers in Q&A forums. Using the proposed method, we were able (i) to outperform a state of the art baseline with gains of up to 21% in NDCG, a metric used to evaluate rankings; we also conducted a comprehensive study of the features, showing that (ii) review and user features are the most important in the Q&A domain although text features are useful for assessing quality of new answers; and (iii) the best set of new features we proposed was able to yield the best quality rankings.

Categories and Subject Descriptors

H.3.7 [**Information Storage and Retrieval**]: [User Issues]

Keywords

Content Quality Assessment; Q&A Forums; Answer Quality; Learning to Rank

1. INTRODUCTION

The Web 2.0 phenomena has brought deep changes to the Internet, as users are now able not only to consume, but also to produce content. This change gave rise to new ways of creating knowledge. Many web sites, such as collaborative encyclopedias, blogs, and forums, allow users to contribute to their content, thus creating large collaborative knowledge repositories. These repositories are characterized by a loose edit control, which allows anyone to freely edit almost anything. As a consequence, the varying quality of their content has raised much concern.

To deal with this problem, many collaborative sites adopt quality control mechanisms, where the users can indicate the quality and appropriateness of the content and even the reputation of the editors. However, such manual assessment not only does not scale to the current rate of growth and change of these systems, but it is also subject to human bias, which can be influenced by the varying background, expertise, and even a tendency for abuse.

Thus, many services provided by these sites, such as ranking, recommendation, and even the manual quality assessment itself, would benefit from the adoption of automated or semi-automated quality control mechanisms. Motivated by that idea, in this work, we propose new strategies for rating content, based on statistical evidences for quality and reputation. In particular, we focus on Question and Answer Forums (Q&A Forums), given their growing importance as source of specialized information on the web.

In Q&A Forums, a user (asker) can post a question about a certain topic for which he/she receives answers from other users. Normally, any user can label a particular answer as useful or not, while the asker can indicate the one he/she considers the best. Figure 1 illustrates the main elements of a Q&A Forum, here using the particular case of Stack Overflow[1]. As we can see, in Stack Overflow, any user can annotate whether an answer is useful or not, and vote for it favorably (upvote) or not (downvote). The asker can place a mark (a green "tick") on the answer he/she considers the best one.

In forums such as Stack Overflow, the answers are expected to be correct and should be ranked according to their quality. According to the Stack Overflow guide[2], a good answer, besides being correct, should be clear, provide examples, quote relevant material, be updated, and link to more information and further reading. Since "quality" is a subjective feature, it is inferred from the opinion of the asker and from the votes received from the other users. Normally, the answer at the top position is the best one, if it has already been indicated as so by the asker.

While this strategy is effective in deemphasizing the bad quality answers, it is somehow dependent on the asker's selection of the best answer. As a consequence, for many questions, a good quality ranking of the answers is not provided, since in many cases (a) the asker takes much time to choose the best answer, (b) he/she does not choose it at all or (c) after choosing it, other answers are improved to the point of becoming better than the previously selected as the best. In fact, in Q&A Forums there may not be a single

SIGIR'13, July 28–August 1, 2013, Dublin, Ireland.

ACM 978-1-4503-2034-4/13/07 ...$15.00.

[1] `http://www.stackoverflow.com`

[2] `http://meta.stackoverflow.com/questions/7656/how-do-i-write-a-good-answer-to-a-question`

Figure 1: Example of a question in the Stack Overflow Q&A Forum (*Is there a name for this: '->'*), for which one, out of seven answers, is shown. The figure also illustrates the tools users can use to indicate how good are the answers.

unique "best answer", with several of them bringing useful information to the asker (and others interested in the question). Moreover, most strategies for automatic quality assessment found in the literature expect that the answer to be ranked has already received votes from the users [32, 28]. Thus, they are unable to assess the quality of answers to new or unpopular questions, which often do not contain such information.

Since such questions would largely benefit from ranking algorithms based on automated quality assessment strategies, in this work, we propose a learning to rank approach (L2R) to rank answers in Q&A Forums according to their quality. Unlike previous work, instead of directly estimating answer quality, we try to estimate the *answer rating*, that is, the feedback a user would give regarding the quality of an answer. More specifically, we adopt an approach based on Random Forests and represent query and answer pairs using eight groups of features. Some of these features are used in the Q&A domain for the first time. Using the proposed method, we were able to outperform a state of the art baseline with gains of up to 21% in NDCG, a metric used to evaluate rankings. We also conducted a comprehensive study of the features showing that, unlike what was previously observed for collaborative encyclopedias [10], user and review features are the most important in the Q&A domain. Further, text features, which are very simple to compute, are useful for assessing quality of new answers, which did not had enough time to acquire many reviews, and the set of new features we proposed was able to yield even better quality rankings.

This paper is organized as follows. In Section 2, we present previous related work. In Section 3, we present our method and the set of pieces of evidence used to evaluate answer quality. In Section 4, we present the experiments performed to evaluate our method and the results obtained. Finally, in Section 5, we present our conclusions and directions for future work.

2. RELATED WORK

Many previous studies are related to the problem of automatic assessment of quality in Q&A Forums. These can be classified according to three distinct objectives: (1) find the best answer; (2) rank the given answers; and (3) assess the quality of the question. Since works in group 3, such as [19, 3], are less related to ours, in the following paragraphs, we discuss only groups 1 and 2.

Works in group 1, which address the problem of finding the best answer to a given question, generally follow a straightforward classification strategy. A set of questions, for which the asker has already selected the best answer, is used for training. The answers are represented using a particular set of features and a classifier is applied, to label each answer as "best" or not, according to those features. Studies in this group have suggested the use of features related to expertise [2, 34], content length [2], grammar errors [2], question topics [2], user information [28], and comments [1]. From these, we highlight the work of [28], which proposed nine different features related to the answers content and to user information, to predict the best answer in Yahoo Answers. The authors learned the best answers through a classifier based on Logistic Regression [7]. They identified features related to the users answering and asking the question are good indicators of the best answers. Similarly, the authors in [1] proposed new features related to the answer and its follow-up comments. They used an Alternating Decision Tree method [12] to classify the best answers. As a result, they achieved accuracy levels of 84% to 87% in the samples used. Furthermore, they found out that length features are not correlated with best answers for the datasets used and a feature based on the rating of the answer can be a good predictor of the best answers. Since [1] is the most recent work and the method in [28] can be easily be adapted to rank answers, we used them as our baselines.

Works in group 2, which address the problem of ranking answers, focus on matching questions to answers, using some sort of similarity measure. Examples of works in this group are the work of [31], who used an L2R method with only relevance functions as evidence; by [16], who proposed a ranking model which takes into account an answer quality estimate; and [32], which explored user expertise in the ranking. This last work deserves a more detailed description since, among those we studied, it achieved the best performance. The authors in [32] argue that a user can have different expertise levels for different topics. Thus, they proposed quality-aware methods to rank answers. First, they learn good answers by using a manually annotated corpus, where answers are identified as good or bad. Then, they use this information, combined to relevance features, to calculate an expertise value that is used to rank the answers. Their intuition is that a good answer will be provided by a user that has provided good answers to similar questions in the past. To evaluate their method, they performed a manual annotation of a set of answers regarding their relevance ("relevant" or "not relevant"). By using the proposed expertise features, along with traditional relevance features, they were able to outperform all the previously described work. Because of that, we adopt this work as our third baseline.

Note that a characteristic shared by all the methods in group 2 was the use of discrete quality taxonomies as ground truth. By doing this, they ignore the fact that, among the good answers (and among the bad answers), some are better and some are worse. To avoid this, Sakai et al. [27], extended previous efforts by using a continuous scale to evaluate answers in Q&A Forums. The proposed solution, however, requires an expensive manual annotation.

Our method is closer to those in group 2: ranking answers. However, unlike the previous methods, we do not require explicit quality rating annotations. Instead, we use the number of positive and negative votes (rating) available on a different set of questions as an implicit quality assessment. This assessment can then be used to train an L2R method, which can later be applied on new questions, even if their answers were not voted yet. Furthermore, as in [27], we use a continuous scale for answer quality. We also improve on previous proposals by studying a new set of topic-based features and textual features which were previously used to assess the quality of collaborative encyclopedia content.

3. ASSESSING ANSWER QUALITY

In this work, we adopt a point-wise Learning to Rank (L2R) method to assign a quality score for the answers in a Q&A Forum. In this section, we present the chosen L2R method and the answer and query representations used.

3.1 Learning to Rank with Random Forests

A successful approach for the task of web search result ranking is to treat it as a supervised machine learning problem [22]. In this approach, each query-document pair (d, q) is represented by a set of features and annotated with a numerical score indicating how relevant document d is to query q. The features used are usually related to the similarity between the contents of document d and the query q. A set of such pairs can then be used to train a machine learning algorithm to predict the relevance of other non annotated pairs.

L2R methods are classified into three categories: point-wise, pair-wise, and list-wise [22]. Point-wise strategies can be viewed as regression approaches that predict relevance by minimizing a loss function. Differently, pair-wise approaches learn, for any given two documents, if one is more relevant than the other. Finally, list-wise approaches iteratively optimize a specialized ranking performance measure, such as NCDG (cf. Equation 2).

From the many algorithms proposed in literature, a pointwise approach using Random Forests (RF) [6] has been shown consistently effective in several real world benchmarks [22]. Among its advantages, we cite its insensitivity to parameter choices, its resilience to overfitting, and its high degree of parallelization. In this work we adopt this method as our learning strategy.

The RF algorithm is summarized in Algorithm 1. Let $D = \{(x_1, r_1), ..., (x_n, r_n)\}$ be a set of query-document pairs x_i and their associated relevance ratings $r_i \in \mathcal{R}$. Each pair x_i is an f dimensional feature vector that incorporates statistics about queries and documents. For example, one feature could be the similarity between question and answer according to BM25 ranking function. The RF method will train a predictor $T(.)$ such that $T(x_i) \sim r_i$ and the ordering of values according to $T(.)$ is similar to that obtained according to r_i.

Algorithm 1 Random Forests Algorithm

Input: $D = \{(x_1, r_1), ..., (x_n, r_n)\}, K : 0 < K \leq f, M > 0$
Output: $T(.)$
1: **for** $i \leftarrow 1$ to M **do**
2: $\quad D_t \leftarrow sample(D)$
3: $\quad h_t \leftarrow BuildDecisionTree(D_t, K)$
4: **end for**
5: $T(.) \leftarrow \frac{1}{M} \sum_1^M h_t(.)$
6: **return** $T(.)$

The main idea of RF is to apply a decision tree regression algorithm to M subsets of D and average the results. As we can see in Algorithm 1, first, a sample D_t is extracted with replacement from D (line 2). Then, a decision tree is built for this sample using $K \leq f$ randomly chosen features (line 3). This process is repeated M times (line 1) and, at the end, the results are averaged (line 5). This process reduces overfitting by using different data sets from the same underlying distribution. Single trees are built independently from others, thus making RFs inherently parallel.

In this paper we use the RF implementation provided by the RankLib L2R tool[3]. As values for M and K, we use the default parameters of that implementation. In particular, as the decision tree regression algorithm we use *Multiple Additive Regression Trees*, an implementation of the Gradient Tree Boosting method [13], provided by RankLib. Note that this algorithm requires a validation set to define the optimal number of boosting iterations.

[3]http://people.cs.umass.edu/~vdang/ranklib.html

3.2 Question-Answer Representation

The idea of L2R can be straightforwardly used in the Q&A domain. Here, questions can take the role of queries and answers can take the role of documents. Unlike the traditional web search task, however, in this case answers are provided by users specifically to address the given questions, which makes more uncommon the presence of not relevant answers. Thus, instead of a measure of relevance, we are now interested in predicting a measure of answer quality. Likewise, statistical features used to represent questions and answers should mainly reflect this notion of quality, instead of similarity.

In this section, we will present the features used to represent the question-answer pairs. These features try to capture the quality of the answer either directly, through textual features, such as style and structure, as well as indirectly, through non-textual features, such as author reputation and relatedness to the question. In total, we studied 186 features (98 textual and 88 non-textual). Of these, 89 features have never been previously used in the Q&A domain.

To simplify our analysis, all features were organized into groups, according to the characteristics they try to capture. Thus, the non-textual features were divided into *user*, *review*, and *user-graph* features. Textual features were divided into *structure*, *length*, *style*, *readability*, and *relevance* features. All groups are described in the following.

3.2.1 User Features

The intuition behind user features is to indirectly infer the quality of the answer by examining the user who posted it. More specifically, we are interested in features related to the user profile or its behavior, captured from events such as (1) post of questions and answers; (2) suggestion of edits in questions and answers; (3) post of comments to questions and answers; and (4) gain of merit ratings and badges for questions and answers. In Table 1, we present all the features computed for each answer using its user information. This table, as all the others in this section, shows for each feature (a) its name, (b) its description, and (c) a reference to the first work using it in the Q&A domain, or 'New' if it was not used before.

Although most of the features in Table 1 are self-explanatory, some require a more detailed explanation, provided in the following paragraphs. In the table, we refer to a question for which the best answer was already selected as *solved question*.

As argued in [32], users can have different expertise levels for different topics. Thus, another important source of information is the category of the questions being answered. This can be obtained through the *tags* (e.g. "html", "C++", "database") assigned by users to the questions. We refer to the set of categories (tags) of the Q&A pair being predicted as $\mathcal{T}$. Let $Q_\mathcal{T}(u)$ be a vector with the number of questions posted by user u to each category in $\mathcal{T}$, $A_\mathcal{T}(u)$ be a vector with the number of answers posted by user u to each category in $\mathcal{T}$, and $QA_\mathcal{T}(u)$ be a vector with the number of questions and answers posted by user u to each category in $\mathcal{T}$. Features questions entropy (*u-etat*), answers entropy (*u-etqt*), and questions and answers (*u-etpt*) correspond to the entropy calculated over vectors $Q_\mathcal{T}(u)$, $A_\mathcal{T}(u)$ and $QA_\mathcal{T}(u)$, respectively.

Some user features are based on user rankings. For instance, given a user u and a list of the users sorted in decreasing order according to the number of answers they posted ($R_{answers}$), feature *u-rknq* is simply the rank of u in $R_{answers}$. Users are also ranked according to (a) the number of questions they posted ($R_{questions}$), (b) the number of answers they posted whose categories are in $\mathcal{T}$ (R_{acat}), (c) the number of questions they posted whose categories are in $\mathcal{T}$ (R_{qcat}), (d) the total rating received by asking questions (R_{rask}), (e) the total rating received by answering questions (R_{rans}), (f) the total rating received by asking questions whose categories are in $\mathcal{T}$ (R_{racat}), and (g) the total rating received by answering questions whose categories are in $\mathcal{T}$ (R_{rqcat}).

Table 1: User features.

Feature	Description	Ref.
u-dayc	n. of days since register	New
u-lac	n. of days since last access	New
u-bdg	n. of merit badges	New
u-aca	avg n. of comments per answer	New
u-xca	max n. of comments per answer	New
u-mca	min n. of comments per answer	New
u-acq	avg n. of comments per question	New
u-xcq	max n. of comments per question	New
u-icq	min n. of comments per question	New
u-aqc	n. of comments posted to answers and questions	New
u-se	n. of suggested edits	New
u-ase	n. of suggested edits approved	New
u-rse	n. of suggested edits rejected	New
u-edt	n. of edits made on answers	New
u-apq	avg answers posted per question	[2]
u-xpq	max answers posted per question	New
u-ipq	min answers posted per question	New
u-ap	n. of posted answers	[2]
u-qp	n. of posted questions	[2]
u-sela	n. of posted questions already solved	[2]
u-rknq	Rank position in $R_{questions}$	New
u-rkna	Rank position in $R_{answers}$	New
u-avqt	avg n. of questions posted in the categories of $\mathcal{T}$	New
u-xqt	max n. of questions posted in the categories of $\mathcal{T}$	New
u-mqt	min n. of questions posted in the categories of $\mathcal{T}$	New
u-aat	avg n. of answers posted in the categories of $\mathcal{T}$	New
u-xat	max n. of answers posted in the categories of $\mathcal{T}$	New
u-mat	min n. of answers posted in the categories of $\mathcal{T}$	New
u-arkat	avg rank position in R_{acat}	New
u-mrkat	max rank position in R_{acat}	New
u-xrkat	min rank position in R_{acat}	New
u-arkqt	avg rank position in R_{qcat}	New
u-xrkqt	max rank position in R_{qcat}	New
u-mrkqt	min rank position in R_{qcat}	New
u-etpt	Questions and answers entropy	[1]
u-etat	Questions entropy	New
u-etqt	Answers entropy	New
u-t3q	n. of categories user is a top-3 answerer	[32]
u-t3a	n. of categories user is a top-3 asker	[32]
u-t3qn	*u-t3q* / n. of categories user answered	New
u–t3an	*u-t3a* / n. of categories user asked	New
u-rtq	Total rating received by asking questions	[2]
u-rta	Total rating received by answering questions	[2]
u-artqt	avg rating received in the categories of $\mathcal{T}$	New
u-xrtqt	max rating received in the categories of $\mathcal{T}$	New
u-mrtqt	min rating received in the categories of $\mathcal{T}$	New
u-artat	avg rating received in the categories of $\mathcal{T}$	New
u-xrtat	max rating received in the categories of $\mathcal{T}$	New
u-mrtat	min rating received in the categories of $\mathcal{T}$	New
u-srtqt	Tot. rating got by asking questions in cats. of $\mathcal{T}$	[1]
u-srtat	Tot. rating got by answering questions in cats. in $\mathcal{T}$	[1]
u-rkq	Rank position in R_{rask}	New
u-rka	Rank position in R_{rans}	New
u-arkta	avg rank position in R_{racat}	New
u-xrkta	max rank position in R_{racat}	New
u-mrkta	min rank position in R_{racat}	New
u-arktq	avg rank position in R_{rqcat}	New
u-xrktq	max rank position in R_{rqcat}	New
u-mrktq	min rank position in R_{rqcat}	New

3.2.2 User Graph Features

User Graph Features features try to capture the expertise level of the users who answer questions by examining their relationships. While these features could be classified as *user features*, we decided to study them separately since they are particularly demanding to obtain. More specifically, we created a graph G where each node represents a user and an edge from user u to user v indicates that u answered a question posted by v. This graph was initially proposed in [34], and later used in [2], to estimate the expertise of a user, a method named as *ExpertiseRank*. ExpertiseRank is the PageRank value computed over G' (the transposed of G) [23]. As in [2], in addition to the actual PageRank value over G' (*ug-er*), we also use as feature the PageRank over G (*ug-pr*) and compute the HITS algorithm to create the authority and hub features (*ug-hu, ug-au*) [17].

3.2.3 Review Features

In collaborative digital libraries such as Wikipedia, features related to the reviewing process have been used with success to estimate the maturity level of the content [10]. In general, the more the content was reviewed, the best its quality. Similarly, in most Q&A Forums, such as those hosted by Stack Exchange, users can edit answers in order to improve them. In fact, they are encouraged to fix mistakes, include examples and further reading sources, etc. Thus, we believe that, as in the case of Wikipedia, these features may be a useful estimate of how much effort was invested in an answer. Table 2 describes the individual review features we have studied.

Features *r-count*, *r-aage*, *r-qage*, *r-sepu*, and *r-aepu* were previously proposed for assessing quality in collaborative digital libraries [10]. The general intuition behind them is that a content that received many edits has likely improved over time. In Q&A Forums, additional features with the same goal can be extracted. For instance, in Stack Exchange forums, a user can comment questions and answers and suggest edits to the author of an answer, who can accept them or not. This is a way of suggesting content improvements and providing additional information. From such comments we extracted the features *r-ase*, *r-qse*, *r-suc*, *r-qas*, *r-aas*, *r-aas*, and *r-ars*. Additionally, general information about the comments, such as *r-acc*, *r-qcc*, and *r-au* are good indicators of community engagement.

We also derived features that capture the question history by means of its answers. These are *r-ab* and *r-naq*. These features are important since they can indicate controversial topics and questions that are hard to answer.

3.2.4 Structure Features

These features attempt to describe the answer contents organization, analyzing the use of images, separation into sections, links, and HTML formatting tags. Table 3 describes the computed features.

Features *ts-ic*, *ts-sc*, *ts-ssc*, *ts-sssc*, *ts-asl*, *ts-mxsl*, *ts-misl* and *ts-ssl* were previously used in quality assessment of digital encyclopedias [24]. They are based on the idea that a good answer, specially if it is long, is organized into sections (and subsections), and contains images to improve understanding.

Several features use hints from the HTML source that indicate highlighting of concepts and ideas (*ts-boi*, *ts-quo*, and *ts-cod*), organization (*ts-lt* and *ts-lit*), and reliability by means of quotation

Table 2: Review features. Symbols *#sug* and *#ans* stand for the number of suggested edits and the number of answers, respectively.

Feature	Description	Ref.
r-count	Review count	New
r-aage	Answer age	[1]
r-qage	Question age	New
r-uedi	n. of users who edit the answer	New
r-aepu	Average n. of edits per user	New
r-sepu	Standard deviation of edits per user	New
r-ase	#sug to the answer	New
r-qse	#sug to the question	New
r-suc	n. of users who suggested edits to an ans. or qst.	New
r-qas	#sug approved by the asker	New
r-aas	#sug rejected by the asker	New
r-aas	#sug approved by the answer author	New
r-ars	#sug rejected by the answer author	New
r-ab	#ans posted before this answer	New
r-naq	#ans posted to the question	[2]
r-qcc	n. of comments posted to the question	[28]
r-acc	n. of comments posted to the answer	[28]
r-au	n. of users who commented the answer	New

of and reference to other sources (*ts-quo*, *ts-miq*, *ts-maq*, *ts-avq*, *ts-sdq*, *ts-xlc*, *ts-ilc*, and *ts-urf*).

Finally, we also used features to capture organizational hints specific of the Q&A domain, such as the use of code snippets in the answers (*ts-cod*, *ts-mic*, *ts-mac*, *ts-avc*, and *ts-sdc*). These are particularly important features in our study case since in Stack Overflow the asker is often searching for programming solutions.

3.2.5 Length Features

Length features are one of the most successful indicators of quality in collaborative encyclopedias [10]. This motivated us to test them in the domain of Q&A Forums. The general intuition behind them is that a mature and good quality text is probably neither too short, which could indicate an incomplete topic coverage, nor excessively long, which could indicate verbose content. We use three length features: word, sentences and character count (*tl-wcount*, *tl-scount*, and *tl-ccount*). These features were first used in Q&A forums by [2].

Table 3: Text Structure features.

Feature	Description	Ref.
ts-ic	Image Count	New
ts-sc	Section Count (n. of HTML H1 tags)	New
ts-ssc	Sub-section Count (n. of HTML H2 tags)	New
ts-sssc	Sub-sub-section Count (n. of HTML H3 tags)	New
ts-asl	Average section length	New
ts-mxsl	Maximum section length	New
ts-misl	Minimum section length	New
ts-ssl	Section length standard deviation	New
ts-boi	Italic plus Bold tag count	New
ts-pc	Paragraph Count	New
ts-quo	n. of quoted blocks	New
ts-cod	n. of code snippets	New
ts-lt	n. of lists	New
ts-lit	n. of list items in the text	New
ts-avc	Average code length	New
ts-mac	Maximum code length	New
ts-mic	Minimum code length	New
ts-sdc	Code length standard deviation	New
ts-avq	Average quoted text length	New
ts-maq	Maximum quoted text length	New
ts-miq	Minimum quoted text length	New
ts-sdq	Quoted text length standard deviation	New
ts-xlc	n. of links to external sources	[28]
ts-ilc	n. of links to other query/answer in the forum	New
ts-urf	n. of interactions with other forum users	New

Table 4: Text Style features. Symbols '%p' and '#p' stand for *percent of phrases* and *number of phrases*, respectively. KLD($\mathcal{D}$) stands for the Kullback-Leibner divergence [18] of a language model for dataset $\mathcal{D}$.

Feature	Description	Ref.
ty-cpc	n. of words capitalized	[2]
ty-cpe	n. of capitalization errors	[2]
ty-poc	Punctuation count	[2]
ty-pde	Punctuation density	[2]
ty-sde	Space density (n. of spaces / answer length)	[2]
ty-wse	Entropy of the text word sizes	[2]
ty-inn	Information to noise	[30]
ty-nwnt	n. of words not in WordNet	[2]
ty-typo	n. of typos	[2]
ty-slp	Size of the largest phrase	New
ty-lpr	%p where (length - avg. length) >= 10 words	New
ty-spr	%p where (avg. length - length) >= 5 words	New
ty-avc	n. of auxiliary verbs	New
ty-qc	n. of questions	New
ty-pc	n. of pronouns	New
ty-pvc	n. of passive voice sentences	New
ty-cjr	n. of words that are conjunctions	New
ty-nr	n. of nominalizations	New
ty-rpr	n. of prepositions	New
ty-ber	n. of uses of verb "to be"	New
ty-sp	#p starting with a pronoun	New
ty-sa	#p starting with an article	New
ty-scc	#p starting with a conjunction	New
ty-sscc	#p starting with a subordinating conjunction	New
ty-sipc	#p starting with an interrogative pronoun	New
ty-spr	#p starting with a preposition	New
ty-klg	KLD(good answers)	[2]
ty-klt	KLD(good answers of same category)	New
ty-klwid	KLD(Wikipedia discussion pages)	[2]
ty-klwi	KLD(Wikipedia pages classified as "Good")	[2]

3.2.6 Style Features

Style features try to capture the users writing style. The intuition is that good answers should present some distinguishable characteristics related to word usage, such as short sentences. Table 4 describes the features we use. To compute the features marked as 'New' in this table (and the Readability features in Section 3.2.7), we used the Style and Diction software[4].

Feature *ty-cpe* counts what are usually capitalization errors: the first letter of the sentence not being capitalized and the capitalization of letters that are not the first of a word. These features assume that an irregular use of capitalization may indicate a bad quality text. Features *ty-poc* and *ty-pde* try to capture the text quality through the use of punctuation, since an irregular punctuation may also be related to a bad quality text. Feature *ty-inn* measures the proportion of (stemmed) non-stopwords in the text.

We also use some vocabulary features in order to identify typos, similarly to [2]. Feature *ty-nwnt* computes the number of words that are not in the English lexical database WordNet[5]. Feature *ty-typo* counts the number of words present in a list of common misspellings, available from Wikipedia[6].

Another group of features tries to infer the difference between the language model used in the answer and other language mod-

[4] http://www.gnu.org/software/diction/

[5] http://wordnet.princeton.edu

[6] http://en.wikipedia.org/wiki/Wikipedia:Lists_of_common_misspellings

Table 5: Text Readability features.

Feature	Description	Ref.
tr-ari	Automated Readability Index [29]	New
tr-cl	Coleman-Liau [9]	New
tr-fki	Flesch-Kincaid [25]	[2]
tr-fre	Flesch reading ease [11]	New
tr-fog	Gunning Fog Index [14]	[2]
tr-lix	Läsbarhets index [5]	New
tr-sg	Smog-Grading [20]	[2]

els that can be seen as good references. The idea behind them is that an answer is more likely to be written in an inadequate manner if its generating language model is much different from language models which generate good answers. Thus, the feature *ty-klg* compares the language model of the answer to the language model of a group of answers considered good (i.e. the top 100 answers according to their rating, obtained from a sample of Stack Overflow different from the one we use for evaluation in Section 4.1). Feature *ty-klt* is similar but using only answers in the same categories of the answer being assessed (that is, categories in set $\mathcal{T}$, defined in Section 3.2.1). With the same goal, we created a sample of 100 articles, classified as Feature Articles according to the Wikipedia quality taxonomy[7], and its discussion pages in order to compare the answer language model to the language models of the Wikipedia articles and of the discussion pages, creating the features *ty-klwi* and *ty-klwid*.

Features *ty-slp*, *ty-lpr*, *ty-spr*, *ty-avc*, *ty-qc*, *ty-pc*, *ty-pvc*, *ty-cjr*, *ty-nr*, *ty-rpr*, *ty-ber*, *ty-sp*, *ty-sa*, *ty-scc*, *ty-sscc*, *ty-sipc*, and *ty-spr* were also previously used to assess content quality in collaborative encyclopedias [10]. We use them here for the first time in the Q&A domain. To calculate these features, we used the same terms used by the authors in [10]. Finally, for features *ty-spr* and *ty-lpr* we used threshold values of the Style and Diction software program.

3.2.7 Readability Features

Readability features were first used in [24] to predict quality of content in digital libraries. They aim at estimating the age or (USA) grade level necessary to comprehend a text. The intuition behind them is that good articles should be well written, understandable, and free of unnecessary complexity. The features we used are described in Table 5. Due to space constraints, we refer the interested reader to the more detailed descriptions available in the original papers, show in the table.

3.2.8 Relevance Features

Relevance features, first used in this domain in [31], try to identify the similarities between the answer and the question, in order to measure how relevant the first is to the second. These features are particularly useful to identify answers not related to the query. The features are shown in Table 6. Note that since the question has two sections, title and body, we use two features for each metric: the first one matches the title of a question to the body of the answer whereas the second one matches the body of the question to the body of the answer.

As in [31], computation of these features required different preprocessing tasks to be performed. The preprocessing tasks were stop-word removal and stemming. Content was represented using bags of terms, where terms could be words, part-of-speech (POS) tags, bi-grams, syntactic dependencies[8] and generalizations. A generalization corresponds to the transformation of each term into its corresponding category in WordNet Supersense, that is, a set of 46 categories which can be assigned to nouns and verbs (eg, "dog" is generalized to "animal", a person name is generalized to "person", a verb such as "swash" is generalized to "verb-motion"). A tagger[9] was used to extract POS tags and generalize words.

More specifically, features *tm-bm25*, *tm-bm25b*, *tm-swm*, and *tm-swmb* used stemming and content representations based on words, bi grams, dependencies, generalized bi-grams and generalized dependencies. Features *tm-span*, *tm-spanb*, *tm-swo*, and *tm-swob* used stemming and a content representation based on words. Finally, features *tm-nwad*, *tm-nwn*, *tm-nwv*, *tm-nwadb*, *tm-nwnb*, and *tm-nwvb* used a content representation based on POS tags.

4. EXPERIMENTS

Using the features described in Section 3.2, we performed a set of experiments using a Q&A test collection extracted from Stack Overflow. We now describe our experimental design, dataset, and results.

4.1 Dataset

Our dataset consists of a sample of Stack Overflow, a Q&A Forum for programmers. We chose this collection because it is freely available for download[10] and is the largest forum hosted by Stack Exchange. As any Stack Exchange forum, Stack Overflow focuses on specific topics and questions not related to these topics are removed or marked as closed. Thus, it probably has fewer spam and distractions when compared to general Q&A Forums such as Yahoo Answers.

The sample we used consists on 10,000 questions randomly extracted from the dataset. Note we extracted only questions that have, at least, 4 answers since that is the most interesting case for ranking. Questions with less than 4 answers are answers easily assessed by the users and an automatic rating is much less useful. From the resulting set, we also removed questions with no rated answers, since they could not be evaluated in a machine learning approach. These two procedures resulted in removing less than 3% of the answers in our dataset. In the end, our sample consisted of 9,721 questions with 53,263 answers[11]. To create the user graph (cf. Section 3.2.1), we considered all the Stack Overflow users and their questions and answers.

As ground truth for our machine learning approach, we use a function of the difference between upvotes and downvotes received by the answer. We refer to this function as the answer rating. r is given by Equation 1:

$$r_a = r'_a + r'_{min} \quad (1)$$

where $r'_a = u_a - d_a$ is the difference between the number of upvotes u_a and downvotes d_a received by answer a, and r'_{min} is the minimum difference between upvotes and downvotes observed in the collection, used to avoid negative values in Equation 2.

Note that the answer rating distribution follows a power law as we can see in Figure 2. Ratings vary from -16 to 505, with values from -20 to 140 corresponding to 99% of the instances in our

[7]http://en.wikipedia.org/wiki/Wikipedia:ASSESS

[8]Dependencies were detected by the tool described in [4] and available in http://sourceforge.net/projects/desr.

[9]We used a tagger based on Wordnet, described in [8] and available in http://sourceforge.net/projects/supersensetag.

[10]http://data.stackexchange.com/

[11]Data for the used sample can be downloaded at: http://www.lbd.dcc.ufmg.br/lbd/collections/ranking-q-a-forums

Table 6: Text Relevance features.

Feature	Description	Ref.
tm-bm25, tm-bm25b	BM25 ranking function, based on a probabilistic retrieval framework [26]	[31]
tm-ssm, tm-ssmb	Number of sentences shared by question and answer	[31]
tm-swm, tm-swmb	Number of words shared by question and answer	[31]
tm-swo, tm-swob	Number of words which appear in answer and question in the same order	[31]
tm-span, tm-spanb	Largest distance between two words that appear in answer and questions	[31]
tm-nwad, tm-nwn, tm-nwv, tm-nwadb, tm-nwnb, tm-nwvb	Number of new adjectives, nouns and verbs in the answer which did not appear on the question	[31]

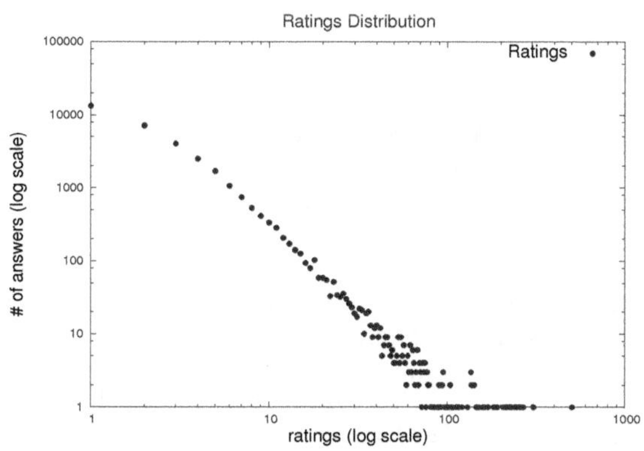

Figure 2: Ratings distribution for Stack Overflow sample.

sample. Such a skewed distribution is due to the popularity of the answers, with a few of them attracting large audiences.

4.2 Evaluation Methodology

The experiments we conduct have two main goals. First, to perform a comparative analysis between different machine learning methods in the task of ranking answers. Second, to analyze the impact of each group of features in this task.

We compare the methods using the *Normalized Discounted Cumulative Gain at top k* (NDCG@k, for short). This is a ranking evaluation metric first proposed in [15]. It allows us to measure how close the predicted answer ranking is to the ground truth ranking. More formally, NDCG@k is defined as:

$$NDCG@k = \frac{1}{N}\sum_{i=1}^{k}\left(\frac{2^{r_i}}{\log_2(i+1)}\right) \quad (2)$$

where r_i is the true rating assessment for the answer at position i in the ranking, and N is a normalization factor. The factor N is equal to the *discounted cumulative gain* (the sum part in Equation (2)) of the *ideal ranking*, i.e. the ranking where, given a pair of answers (a_i, a_j), a_i is better ranked than a_j if r'_i is greater than r'_j (cf. Equation 1).

To perform the comparative experiments, we used a five-fold cross-validation method [21] with a validation set. Thus, each dataset was randomly split into five parts, such that, in each run, one part was used as test set, one part was used as validation set, and the remaining three parts were use as training set. The split on training, validation, and test sets was the same in all experiments. The final results of each experiment represent the average of the five runs. Note that the folds were split such that answers provided to the same question belong to the same fold.

For all comparisons reported in this work, we used the signed-rank test of Wilcoxon [33] to determine if the differences in effectiveness were statistically significant. This is a nonparametric paired test that does not assume any particular distribution on the tested values. In all cases, we only draw conclusions from results that were considered statistically significant with a 95% confidence level.

In order to evaluate the impact of the chosen features, we used the information gain measure (infogain, for short) [21]. Infogain is a statistical measure of how much a given feature contributes to discriminate the class to which any given article belongs. It is normally used for feature selection but, since it provides a ranking of features based on their discriminative power, here we used to study the analyzed features. Infogain was computed for all features and the results are reported in Section 4.3.3.

4.3 Results

We now describe the experiments used to evaluate our proposed method. We first compare our method to others previously proposed in the literature and then we provide a comprehensive evaluation of the features.

4.3.1 Comparison to Previous Work

In this section we compare our method to previous work published in the literature. Since our work addresses the problem of ranking answers, our baselines are slightly modified versions of the methods proposed by Suryanto et al [32], Shah et al [28], and Burel et al [1]. In the first case, we provide the answer ratings as estimates for answer goodness and take the similarities returned by the method as rank values. In the second and third cases, we use the probability to be the best answer as rank value. We refer to our method as RF, to the method proposed by Suryanto et al as EXQD, to the method proposed by Shah et al as SHAH, and to the method proposed by Burel et al as AdTree. Note that RF uses all the features previously described.

In order to test the effectiveness of the new features proposed, we implemented a version of RF where Q&A pairs are represented only with features used by the baselines (the ones not marked as 'New' in Section 3.2). We refer to this method as RF-BaseFeatures. We also note that since SHAH uses a regression strategy, it is simple to adapt it to learn the answer rating instead the best answer. Thus, we tested several variants of the answer rating function as its target attribute. The one that achieved the best result was $\log r_a$, where r_a as given by Equation 1. We refer to this variant as SHAH-LR. Since the original implementations of these algorithms are not publicly available, we implemented them ourselves.

Figure 3 shows the NDCG@k figures for AdTree, SHAH-LR, SHAH, EXQD, RF-BaseFeatures, and RF using the best query-answer representations proposed for each method in our test dataset. All the differences pointed out between RF and the other methods were statistically significant, at all NDCG@k points, according to the Wilcoxon test.

We observe that RF and RF-BaseFeatures outperformed all the remaining methods for all values of k in our dataset. The larger gains were obtained for the top-ranked answers. The gain obtained by RF over RF-BaseFeatures indicates that our new features were able to improve the answer ranking. As for the baselines, when we compare the performance of RF and EXDQ, which was the second

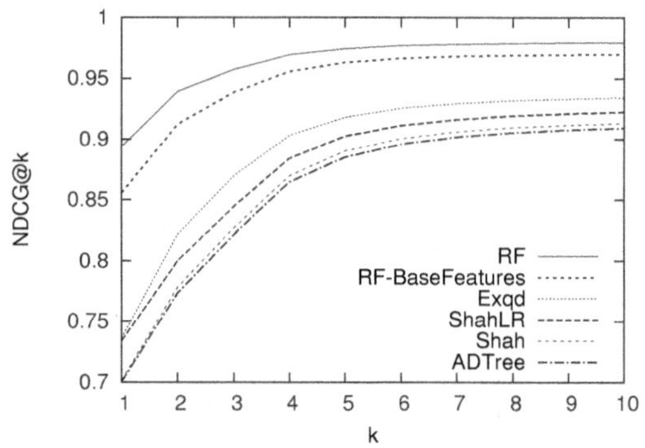

Figure 3: NDCG@k obtained for methods RF, RF-BaseFeatures, EXQD, SHAH, SHAH-LR, and AD-Tree.

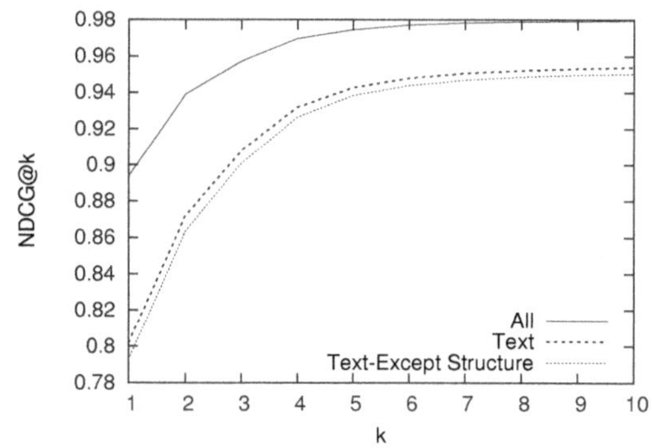

Figure 5: Random Forests effectiveness for textual features ranked according to their NDCG@k.

best method, we note gains ranging from 6% (NDCG@10) to 21% (NDCG@1). The smaller gains for the largest k values were expected since many questions have less than $k = 10$ answers then, for larger values of k, the highest rated answers are likely to be taken into account when calculating the NDCG. From the SHAH versions, the best performer was SHAH-LR. We also observe that AdTree and SHAH achieved the worst performance. Such result was expected since AdTree and SHAH were trained to find the best answers selected by the asker not those with the best ratings, which in our view may be even more informative, since the asker may have chosen the "best" one before the discussions have matured.

4.3.2 *Analysis of the Groups of Features*

To analyze the impact of each group of features, we divided our feature set into 8 groups: Structure, Length, Style, Relevance, Review History, User, User Graph, and Readability. We then conducted two series of experiments. First, we represented our question-answer pairs using only the features of each group in isolation, in order to determine the individual impact of the group. Following, we represented the Q&A pairs using all the features, leaving out one group at a time. This way, we can verify how each group is able to contribute to the results, independently from the other groups.

Figure 4 presents the results obtained for each of the feature groups. These groups are evaluated when used in isolation (Figure 4.3.2 (a)) and when excluded from the full feature set (Figure 4.3.2 (b)). For each group, we present the NDCG@k for k from 1 to 10. Note that in Figure 4.3.2 (b), feature groups whose exclusion did not result in a statistically significant loss are not shown.

As we can see in Figure 4.3.2(a), where groups are taken in isolation, no group is (statistically) significantly better than the combination of all features. Interestingly, the User features are the most relevant group. The User features are also the most important when we analyse their impact when removed (Figure 4.3.2 (b)), which highlights the importance of the profile and the history of the user to assess the quality of an answer. The second best set of features is the Review group. These features are useful to measure the engagement of the users in an answer (commenting, editing, etc.) and this engagement is probably proportional to the answer rating.

While User and Review features are the most important, text features are also useful and, more importantly, much less demanding to obtain, in terms of the preprocessing required. In addition, these features are always available from answers in any Q&A Forum, making the method more easily applicable in different forums. Thus, they are worth studying by themselves. In Figure 5, we compare the results of using all features, only textual features, and textual features excluding the structure group. Other textual feature groups are not shown since their removal did not show statistically significant differences. We can see, both in Figure 4.3.2(a) and Figure 5, that Structure features have the best performance when compared to the other textual features. Thus, we can conclude that, as previously found for collaborative encyclopedias [10], Structure is the best group of textual features.

Besides User, Review, and Structure, the remaining groups of features perform significantly worse and have no impact when removed. Relevance features have no impact probably due to the fact that most of the answers in Stack Overflow are relevant to their questions. Readability features are probably not suitable for this scenario, characterized by short text and many code snippets. Length features are probably redundant since many other features (eg, number of prepositions) are correlated to length. Finally, User Graph features presented a bad performance probably because they failed to capture user expertise in our sample dataset. This is interesting, for instance, to reduce the feature space, allowing to find even better ranking functions with less computational effort.

4.3.3 *Feature Analysis using Infogain*

To complement our previous study, we also ranked all the features according to the information gain metric. The results are summarized in Table 7, which shows the distribution of the features in groups of ten, starting from the best ranked.

Table 7: Number of features at top positions, ranked using infogain.

Group	# of features at top...					
	1-10	11-20	21-30	31-40	41-50	>50
User	7	8	2	3	3	36
Review	3	2	3	0	1	9
Structure	0	0	1	0	1	23
Length	0	0	2	1	0	0
Style	0	0	2	1	4	23
Relevance	0	0	0	5	1	34
Readability	0	0	0	0	0	7
User Graph	0	0	0	0	0	4

This table confirms the good performance of user and review features. Textual features appear only among the top-30 (length, style and structure features). Relevance features appear among the top-40. Readability and user graph features do not appear before the top-50. These two groups have already presented a bad performance in a previous work using the Yahoo! Q&A Forum [2] (User graph features) and collaborative encyclopedias [10] (Readability features).

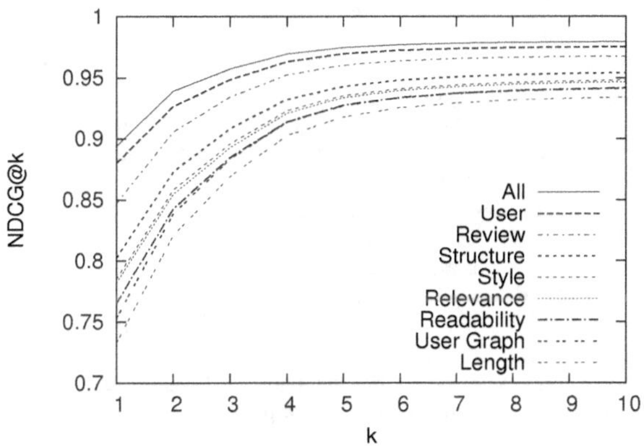

(a)

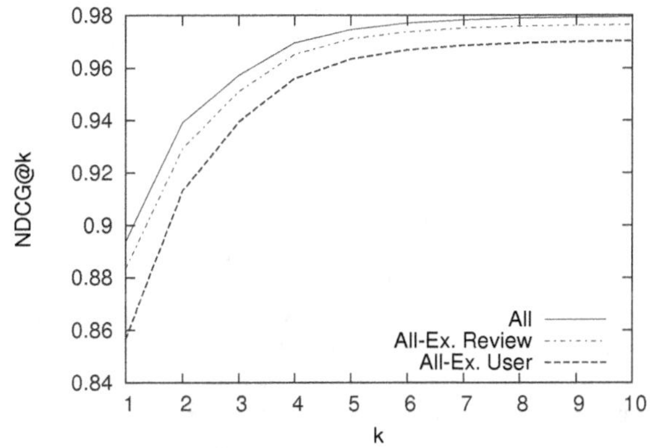

(b)

Figure 4: Random Forests effectiveness by using feature groups taken in isolation (a) or excluded from the complete set (b). Features Groups are ranked according to their NDCG@k.

Table 8: Features at top 5 positions per group and its general rank position, ranked using infogain.

User	Review	Structure	Length	Style	Relevance	Readability	User Graph
u-rka(1)	*r-au*(2)	*ts-pc*(27)	*tl-ccount*(21)	*ty-poc*(28)	*tm-nwn*(32)	*tr-sg*(74)	*ug-au*(54)
u-bdg(4)	*r-acc*(3)	*ts-cod*(49)	*tl-scount*(24)	*ty-spr*(30)	*tm-nwnb*(34)	*tr-cl*(79)	*ug-hu*(57)
u-rta(5)	*r-count*(7)	*ts-sdc*(53)	*tl-wcount*(35)	*ty-pvc*(38)	*tm-nwad*(36)	*tr-fki*(80)	*ug-pr*(73)
u-dayc(6)	*r-aepu*(17)	*ts-xlc*(62)		*ty-rpr*(41)	*tm-nwadb*(37)	*tr-ari*(81)	*ug-er*(77)
u-edt(8)	*r-aage*(20)	*ts-ilc*(65)		*ty-cpc*(47)	*tm-nwv*(39)	*tr-lix*(82)	

To better assess the best individual features, we show for each group the top-5 best features and its general rank in Table 8. As we can see, the best feature in User group is the rank position of the user according to its question answering rating (*u-rka*). This feature is evidently effective at capturing the relative expertise of the user.

The best features in the Review group are those related to comments (*r-au* and *r-acc*). These help to quantify how much attention other users have given to an answer. Other important features are the number of edits and editing users (*r-count*, *r-aepu* and *r-aepu*), also indicators of engagement, and answer age (*r-aage*). This last feature is useful because old answers have more opportunities to be voted.

The best feature of the structure group was the paragraph count (*ts-pc*), which provides hints about the answer structural organization. Other good features were related to code, links, and quotes, which indicate informative content with examples and references.

Although length features did not performed well in per-group analysis, they appear among the top 30. As in the encyclopedia domain, this probably happens because, in spite of this feature being related to quality, it carries information that is also indirectly provided by other features.

Regarding style features, the best are punctuation count and the number of short phrases (*ty-poc*, *ty-spr* respectively), which suggests that proper punctuation and well formed phrases are useful to predict quality in Q&A.

It is also interesting to note that, in the relevance group, the best features were about the new adjectives, nouns, and verbs in the answer. This shows that the appearance of new information in the answer is indicative of its quality.

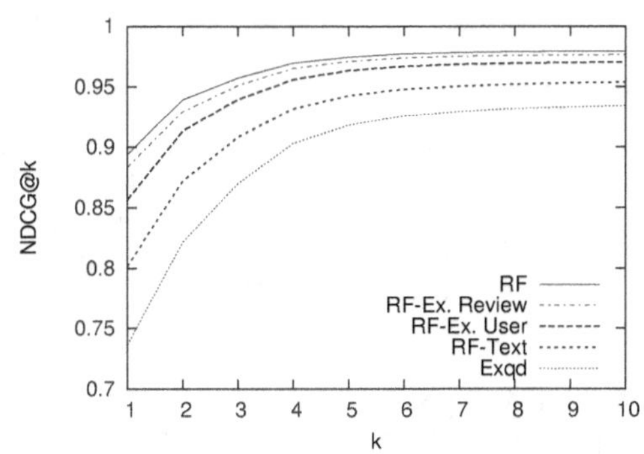

Figure 6: NDCG@k for the case of new answers and new users.

4.3.4 Rating New Answers and New Users

To finalize our evaluation, we should note that, not all the feature groups presented so far are always available to rank the answers. In particular, relatively new answers may not have any relevant Review features. Likewise, relatively new users may not have any relevant User features. For this reason, we performed experiments taking these possibilities into account.

Figure 6 shows the NDCG@k values for three cases: our approach excluding Review features, representing the case where the answer is new; our approach excluding User features, representing the case where the user is new; and our approach using only text features, representing the case where both the answer and the user are new. For comparison, we include our approach using all features (RF) and the best performing baseline (EXQD).

We can see that, even without User or Review features, we can still obtain very high NDCG@k values, close to those obtained with all features. Using only text features, on the other hand, results visibly decrease. However, they are still well above the EXQD baseline, thus showing the strength of our method, even when using much less information.

5. CONCLUSIONS

In this work we proposed an L2R approach for ranking answers in Q&A Forums. In particular, we adopted an approach based on Random Forests and represented the Q&A pairs using eight groups of features. In total, we evaluated 186 features and, to the best of our knowledge, 89 of them were not used in the Q&A domain before. These features capture several aspects of a Q&A pair which we classified in the following groups: review, user, user graph, structure, style, length, readability, and relevance. Our L2R method was trained to learn the answer rating, based on the feedback users give to answers in Q&A Forums. By using a dataset from the StackOverflow Q&A Forum, we evaluated the sets of features and compared our method to 3 other ones previously published in literature.

We found that, unlike what was previously observed for collaborative encyclopedias, review and user features are the most important in the Q&A domain. Further, text features, which are very simple to compute, are useful for assessing quality of new answers (which did not had enough time to acquire many reviews). We have shown that the set of new features proposed was able to yield even better quality rankings. We also have shown that our method was able to outperform the best baseline with statistically significant gains of up to 21% in NDCG@k.

As future work, we intend to study a multi-view combination method for this problem, based on a meta-learning stacking strategy. We also intend to study more reliable strategies to determine the expertise of the users and their importance for the forums.

Acknowledgments

This research is partially funded by InWeb - The Brazilian National Institute of Science and Technology for the Web (MCT/CNPq/ FAPEMIG grant number 573871/2008-6), FCT (Portugal) under project SMARTIS - PTDC/EIA-EIA/115346/2009, and by the authors's individual research grants from FAPEMIG, CNPq, CAPES, and Google.

6. REFERENCES

[1] Automatic identification of best answers in online enquiry communities. In G. Burel, Y. He, and H. Alani, editors, *9th Extended Semantic Web Conference*, volume 7295 of *Lecture Notes in Computer Science*, Crete, 2012. Springer Berlin Heidelberg.

[2] E. Agichtein, C. Castillo, D. Donato, A. Gionis, and G. Mishne. Finding high-quality content in social media. In *WSDM '08*, pages 183–194, Palo Alto, California, USA, 2008. ACM.

[3] A. Anderson, D. Huttenlocher, J. Kleinberg, and J. Leskovec. Discovering Value from Community Activity on Focused Question Answering Sites : A Case Study of Stack Overflow. In *KDD'12*, 2012.

[4] G. Attardi, F. dell'Orletta, M. Simi, A. Chanev, and M. Ciaramita. Multilingual dependency parsing and domain adaptation using desr. In *EMNLP-CoNLL*, pages 1112–1118, 2007.

[5] C. Björnsson. *Lesbarkeit durch Lix*. Stockholm: Pedagogiskt Centrum, 1968.

[6] L. Breiman. Random forests. *Mach. Learn.*, 45(1):5–32, Oct. 2001.

[7] S. L. Cessie and J. V. Houwelingen. Ridge estimators in logistic regression. *Journal of the Royal Statistical Society. Series C*, 41(1):191–201, 1992.

[8] M. Ciaramita and Y. Altun. Broad-coverage sense disambiguation and information extraction with a supersense sequence tagger. In *EMNLP '06*, EMNLP '06, pages 594–602, Stroudsburg, PA, USA, 2006. Association for Computational Linguistics.

[9] M. Coleman and T. L. Liau. A computer readability formula designed for machine scoring. *Journal of Applied Psychology*, 60(2):283–284, 1975.

[10] D. H. Dalip, M. A. Gonçalves, M. Cristo, and P. Calado. Automatic assessment of document quality in web collaborative digital libraries. *ACM Journal of Data and Information Quality*, 2(13), 2011.

[11] R. Flesch. A new readability yardstick. *Journal of Applied Psychology*, pages 221–235, 1948.

[12] Y. Freund and L. Mason. The alternating decision tree learning algorithm. In *ICML'99*, 1999.

[13] J. H. Friedman. Stochastic gradient boosting. *Computational Statistics & Data Analysis*, 38(4):367–378, Feb. 2002.

[14] R. Gunning. *The Technique of Clear Writing*. McGraw-Hill International Book Co, 1952.

[15] K. Järvelin and J. Kekäläinen. IR evaluation methods for retrieving highly relevant documents. In *SIGIR '00*, pages 41–48, Athens, Greece, 2000.

[16] J. Jeon, W. B. Croft, J. H. Lee, and S. Park. A framework to predict the quality of answers with non-textual features. In *SIGIR '06*, pages 228–235, Seattle, Washington, USA, 2006. ACM.

[17] J. M. Kleinberg. Hubs, authorities, and communities. *ACM Comput. Surv.*, 31(4es), Dec. 1999.

[18] S. Kullback and R. A. Leibler. On information and sufficiency. *The Annals of Mathematical Statistics*, 22(1):79–86, 1951.

[19] B. Li, T. Jin, M. R. Lyu, I. King, B. Mak, T. Chinese, and H. Kong. Analyzing and Predicting Question Quality in Community Question Answering Services Categories and Subject Descriptors. pages 775–782, 2012.

[20] G. H. McLaughlin. Smog grading: A new readability formula. *Journal of Reading*, pages 639–646, 1969.

[21] T. M. Mitchell. *Machine Learning*. McGraw-Hill Higher Education, 1997.

[22] A. Mohan, Z. Chen, and K. Weinberger. Web-search ranking with initialized gradient boosted regression trees. *JMLR Workshop and Conference Proceedings: Proceedings of the Yahoo! Learning to Rank Challenge*, 14:77–89, June 2011.

[23] L. Page, S. Brin, R. Motwani, and T. Winograd. The PageRank Citation Ranking: Bringing Order to the Web. Technical report, Stanford Digital Library Technologies Project, 1998.

[24] L. Rassbach, T. Pincock, and B. Mingus. Exploring the feasibility of automatically rating online article quality. `http://upload.wikimedia.org/wikipedia/wikimania2007/d/d3/RassbachPincockMingus07.pdf`, 2007.

[25] S. Ressler. *Perspectives on electronic publishing: standards, solutions, and more*. Prentice-Hall, Inc., Upper Saddle River, NJ, USA, 1993.

[26] S. E. Robertson and S. Walker. Some simple effective approximations to the 2-poisson model for probabilistic weighted retrieval. In *SIGIR '94*, SIGIR '94, pages 232–241, New York, NY, USA, 1994. Springer-Verlag New York, Inc.

[27] T. Sakai, D. Ishikawa, N. Kando, Y. Seki, K. Kuriyama, and C.-Y. Lin. Using graded-relevance metrics for evaluating community QA answer selection. In *WSDM '11*, page 187, New York, New York, USA, Feb. 2011. ACM Press.

[28] C. Shah and J. Pomerantz. Evaluating and predicting answer quality in community QA. In *SIGIR'10*, number March 2008, 2010.

[29] E. A. Smith and R. J. Senter. Automated readability index. *Aerospace Medical Division*, 1967.

[30] B. Stvilia, M. B. Twidale, L. C. Smith, and L. Gasser. Assessing information quality of a community-based encyclopedia. In *ICIQ'05*, pages 442–454, 2005.

[31] M. Surdeanu, M. Ciaramita, and H. Zaragoza. Learning to Rank Answers on Large Online QA Collections. *ACL '08*, 2008.

[32] M. A. Suryanto and R. H. L. Chiang. Quality-Aware Collaborative Question Answering : Methods and Evaluation. In *WSDM '09*, pages 142–151, 2009.

[33] F. Wilcoxon. Individual comparisons by ranking methods. *Biometrics*, pages 80–83, 1945.

[34] J. Zhang, M. S. Ackerman, and L. Adamic. Expertise networks in online communities. In *WWW '07*, New York, New York, USA, 2007. ACM Press.

An Incremental Approach to Efficient Pseudo-Relevance Feedback

Hao Wu
Department of Electrical and Computer Engineering
University of Delaware
Newark, DE USA
haow@udel.edu

Hui Fang
Department of Electrical and Computer Engineering
University of Delaware
Newark, DE USA
hfang@udel.edu

ABSTRACT

Pseudo-relevance feedback is an important strategy to improve search accuracy. It is often implemented as a two-round retrieval process: the first round is to retrieve an initial set of documents relevant to an original query, and the second round is to retrieve final retrieval results using the original query expanded with terms selected from the previously retrieved documents. This two-round retrieval process is clearly time consuming, which could arguably be one of main reasons that hinder the wide adaptation of the pseudo-relevance feedback methods in real-world IR systems.

In this paper, we study how to improve the efficiency of pseudo-relevance feedback methods. The basic idea is to reduce the time needed for the second round of retrieval by leveraging the query processing results of the first round. Specifically, instead of processing the expand query as a newly submitted query, we propose an incremental approach, which resumes the query processing results (i.e. document accumulators) for the first round of retrieval and process the second round of retrieval mainly as a step of adjusting the scores in the accumulators. Experimental results on TREC Terabyte collections show that the proposed incremental approach can improve the efficiency of pseudo-relevance feedback methods by a factor of two without sacrificing their effectiveness.

Categories and Subject Descriptors: H.3.3 [Information Search and Retrieval]: Search process, Relevance feedback

General Terms: Performance; Experimentation

Keywords: Pseudo-relevance Feedback; Incremental Approach; Efficiency; Query Expansion

1. INTRODUCTION

Pseudo-relevance feedback is an important technique that can be used to improve the effectiveness of IR systems. Different pseudo-relevance feedback methods have been proposed and studied for various retrieval models [8, 19, 26–28, 37, 41], but they all boil down to the problem of expanding an original query with useful term selected from a certain number of pseudo-relevant documents, i.e., top-ranked documents from an initial retrieval run. In particular, the implementation of pseudo-relevance feedback methods always require two rounds of retrieval, with the first round retrieving an initial set of documents with respect to an original query and the second round retrieving documents based on an expanded query, which is generated by expanding the original query with relevant terms selected from the previously retrieved document set.

Although pseudo-relevance feedback methods can lead to large performance gain in terms of effectiveness, there is one major downside that limits their usability in real retrieval application: its low efficiency [6, 13, 18]. In particular, the second round of retrieval could significantly slow down the performance due to the time spent on selecting terms for expansion and on executing the expanded query that are often much longer than the original one [13, 18]. It is clear that such drastically increased execution cost limits the applicability of pseudo-relevance feedback methods in real IR applications.

Compared with continual efforts on improving the effectiveness and robustness of pseudo feedback methods in the past decades [8, 10, 11, 14, 15, 19–21, 21, 22, 24, 26–28, 32, 37, 38, 41], less attention has been paid to make these methods more efficient [6, 13, 18]. Billerbeck and Zobel [6] proposed a summary based method for efficient term selection from the feedback methods. Lavrenko and Allan [18] proposed a fast relevance model, and Cartright et. al. [13] studied approximation methods to reduce the storage and computational cost for the fast relevance model. These proposed methods were designed for either a specific feedback method [13, 18] or a bottleneck in the feedback implementation, i.e., how to efficiently select expansion terms from the feedback documents [6]. However, it remains unclear whether there is a general solution to address other bottlenecks for efficient pseudo-relevance feedback implementation.

In this paper, we propose a general solution that can improve the efficiency of pseudo-relevance feedback methods. The basic idea is to reduce the execution cost for the expanded query by using the the query processing status of the original query. Existing IR systems often implement the pseudo-feedback methods as a two-round retrieval, where the second round is processed *independently* to the

SIGIR'13, July 28–August 1, 2013, Dublin, Ireland.

first round. However, since the query used in the second round retrieval is an expanded version of the original query used in the first round, it would be beneficial to leverage the results of the first round of retrieval to reduce the query processing time for the second round. Although this is an intuitive idea, we are not aware of any previous work that successfully implemented the idea. Experimental results on TREC Terabyte collections show that the proposed strategy can improve the efficiency by a factor of 2 to 4 without sacrificing the effectiveness.

The remainder of this paper is organized as follows. We first discuss related work on pseudo-relevance feedback in Section 2, and then provide background knowledge about indexing and query processing in Section 3. We then describe the motivation and details of the proposed incremental approach in Section 4. We explain the experiment set up, present experiment results and summarize our findings in Section 5. Finally, we conclude and discuss the future work in Section 6.

2. RELATED WORK

2.1 Pseudo-Relevance Feedback Methods

Pseudo-relevance feedback is an effective technique for improving retrieval accuracy. The commonly used feedback method for vector space models is the Rocchio algorithm [27,28]. In classical probabilistic models, the feedback method is based on the Robertson/Sparck-Jones weighting [26]. Two representative feedback methods for the language modeling approaches are the relevance model [19] and the model-based feedback [41].

Despite the difference in selecting expansion terms (i.e., estimating relevance models in language modeling framework), all these methods share similar implementation strategies, i.e., *initial retrieval* to find documents relevant to an original query; *term selection* to identify useful expansion terms from the feedback documents; and second-round retrieval to return documents relevant to the expanded query. This commonality in implementation makes it possible to derive a general optimization strategy that can improve the efficiency of these pseudo-relevance feedback methods, which is the focus of our paper.

More recently, continuous efforts have been put on improving the effectiveness and robustness of the pseudo-feedback methods [8,10,11,14,15,20–22,24,32,38]. For example, Tao and Zhai [32] extended model-based feedback methods using a regularized EM algorithm to reduce the parameter sensitivity, and Lv and Zhai [21] extended the relevance model to exploit term proximity.

2.2 Efficient Pseudo-Relevance Feedback

Compared with the effectiveness of an IR system, its efficiency is equally important. In particular, high query latency can decrease user satisfaction significantly [23]. Unfortunately, only a few previous studies focused on efficient pseudo-relevance feedback methods [5,6,13,18].

Billerbeck and Zobel [5,6] examined the bottlenecks of the pseudo-relevance feedback implementation and proposed to leverage tf-idf document summaries to reduce the cost of selecting expansion terms from the feedback documents. They also explored other approaches such as query association, using reduced-size collections and carrying accumulator information from the first round of retrieval to the second round, but all of them were unsuccessful. Our approach is in the same line of the third unsuccessful strategy they mentioned in the paper. However, we reach a different conclusion with our implementation, i.e., our method can improve the efficiency without obvious sacrificing the effectiveness. The main reason behind this fact is that our method allows the expanded terms to incrementally evaluate the accumulators in the initial retrieval rather than merely re-rank the top documents of the initial runs.

Lavrenko and Allan [18] proposed a fast relevance model which computes the original relevance-based ranking based on the cross-entropy between two documents (i.e., one representing the relevance model and the other representing the document to be scored). The re-arrangement used in the derivation makes it possible to shift the main computational cost from the query processing time to indexing time. Their experiment results show that the new method can reduce the query execution time significantly. However, the downside is the time taken to compute the document similarity matrix could be rather long (e.g., 90 hours for a small collection), which could makes it impractical for larger collections. Cartright et. al. [13] took one step further and propose approximation methods to reduce the storage and computational cost of this offline computing. Since these methods are specifically designed for relevance models, it remains unclear whether similar strategy can be leveraged for other feedback methods.

Cartright and Allan [12] have focused on optimizing the efficiency for interpolating subqueries. In particular, they investigated four cases of such an interpolation with varying amounts of accessibility for the original queries and expansion terms, and then proposed methods for each case. Our problem formulation is similar to the case when having access to both original queries and expansion terms, and our proposed approach bears similarity to the proposed Rewind algorithm. However, we use a different query processing technique, i.e,. score at a time (SAAT), from the one used in the previous study, i.e., document at a time (DAAT). Since SAAT makes it easier to resume the ranking status and adjust the document scores based on new terms, the improvement of our results is more significant than observed in the previous study.

Pseudo-relevance feedback is a specific type of query expansion methods where expansion terms are selected from highly-ranking documents. We now describe a couple of efforts on efficient query expansion [33,35]. Theobald et. al. [33] proposed an optimization strategy for query expansion methods that are based on term similarities such as those computed based on WordNet. Their pruning method was designed based on a similarity based scoring function, and it remains unclear how to generalize it to other query expansion methods. Wang et. al. [35] proposed a solution for efficient query expansion for advertisement search. They focused on solving a domain specific challenge, i.e., the placement of similar bid phrases. The proposed strategies in these studies are very problem-specific, and can not be directly applied to pseudo-relevance feedback methods.

3. BACKGROUND ON INDEXING AND QUERY PROCESSING

Most current IR systems are based on inverted indexes [42]. An inverted index contains one inverted list for each term in the document collection. An inverted list of a term contains a list of postings, and each posting describes the information of a document containing the term such as document ID and the term occurrence in the document. Query processing involves traversing the inverted lists of query terms, computing the relevance score for each document based on a retrieval function and then ranking the documents based on their scores.

Significant efforts have been made on making this process more efficient over the past decade [1–4,7,9,17,25,29,30,42]. Due to the limited space, we mainly provide some background about a few influential studies including those used in our system [1–4, 25, 29, 30].

3.1 Index Organization

Traditional inverted indexes are *document sorted indexing*, where the postings of an inverted list are sorted based on the document IDs [36]. The inverted lists of common terms could consist a huge number of postings. To enable faster access to the lists, various compression techniques such as delta encoding for document IDs have been used [42]. As the document IDs are usually sorted based on an increasing order, the delta codes are usually much smaller than the original IDs. It is therefore possible to reduce the space usage by storing delta codes instead of the original document IDs. Indexing compression not only saves the usage of disk and memory, but also improves the efficiency by minimizing cache/memory misses.

Another commonly used indexing organization strategy is *impact-sorted indexing*, where the postings are sorted based on their impact, i.e., their contribution to the relevance score of a document [1–4, 29]. With the impact-sorted indexing, the retrieval score of a document D for query Q can be evaluated by summing up the impact scores of D in the inverted lists of all the terms in Q. To further improve the efficiency, the impact scores are binned into a smaller number of distinct values and only the binned integer values are stored in the index. This strategy brings two benefits. First, the impact score can be stored using a very small number of bits (e.g., 6 bits for 64 distinct binned integers) instead of using 32 or 64 bits for a floating point variable. Second, with the binned scores, the number of documents with the same score is pretty large so that we can separate an inverted list into segments, one for each distinct value of the impact scores. Within each segment, documents are then ranked based on their document IDs, and the compression techniques used for document-sorted indexing can be applied here to achieve high level of compression. Formally, the retrieval score of document D for query Q is computed as follows,

$$S_{Q,D} = \sum_{w \in Q} B_{w,D}, \tag{1}$$

where $B_{w,D}$ is the binned integer score representing the impact of query term w in D. Previous studies have shown that such binning strategy would not significantly affect the retrieval accuracy [3, 29].

Skipping is another mechanism for fast accessing the information from the postings. Skips are forward pointers within an inverted list, and make it possible to pass over non-promising information on the postings with minimal efforts. They are often inserted into the indexes and stored as additional information. With the help of the skips, the system can jump to required records without going through the posting list one record by one record.

3.2 Query Processing

When processing a query, there are three different techniques to traverse the indexes and compute the relevance score for each document.

- *Document-At-A-Time (DAAT)* [7, 31, 34]: It assigns a document its final score before the next document is considered. In particular, the inverted lists of all query terms are processed in parallel. The iterators of the inverted lists need to frequently compare with each other to make sure they keep the same pace. Once all the postings of a document are accessed and processed, the system can forward the iterators to deal with the next document.

- *Term-At-A-Time (TAAT)* [9,25,42]: It starts with the inverted list of a query term, and would finish evaluating all the documents in the list before it moves to the next query term. As a result, an accumulator is required for each document to store and accumulate the retrieval scores. Once lists of all the query terms are processed, the documents with the K largest accumulated scores are returned as the retrieval results.

- *Score-At-A-Time (SAAT)* [4, 29, 30]: This strategy is only suitable for impact-based indexing. It fetches all inverted lists first (as in DAAT) and processes the postings in the decreasing order of the impact values instead of document IDs as used in TAAT. Document accumulators are still needed to accumulate partial score contributions from the different inverted lists. Since SAAT places the most promising postings close to start of the lists, early termination techniques are often used to improve the efficiency [4, 16, 39].

To reduce the computational efforts, pruning has been introduced to all these three strategies [4, 9, 34] with the goal of limiting the number of accumulators and the scan depth on the index lists. The main idea is that the process can be terminated once the system identifies that further processing will not change the ranking of top k documents.

3.3 What We Use in This Paper

We follow the previous studies [4, 29] and use a state-of-the-art four-stage SAAT query processing strategy with the impact-based indexing since it can achieve very good performance in many cases. Note that we use query generation model with Dirichlet prior smoothing as the basic retrieval model [40] (i.e., the one without using feedback) and the relevance model [19] as the pseudo-relevance feedback method. However, our proposed incremental approach can be applied to other retrieval functions and feedback methods and we plan to study it as one of our future work.

To compute the impact scores (i.e., $B_{w,D}$ in Equation (1), we use the derived equation from previous study [29]:

$$B_{w,D} = \lfloor \frac{n}{M + log(s)} (logP(w|D) - C_w) \rfloor,$$

where n is the number of distinct values used to represent impact scores and set to 64. C_w is the minimum value of $P(w|D)$ in the collection (i.e., $C_w = \min_D logP(w|D)$). M is used to ensure that the binned score is within the range, and s is a saturation parameter which makes sure that all the bin values, i.e., $[0, n]$, can be fully utilized. The details of the derivation can be found in the references [29]. Moreover, the term probability is estimated using Dirichlet Prior smoothing [40], i.e.,

$$P(w|D) = \frac{c(w;D) + \mu c(w;C)/|C|}{|D| + \mu}.$$

The parameter μ is set to 2,500 and the skip length is set to 128 bytes.

For query processing, we use the SAAT with a four-stage pruning. The four stages are: OR, AND, REFINE and IGNORE. The processing begins with the OR stage by processing the postings in the inverted lists based on the decreasing order of the impact values. Document accumulators are created whenever it is necessary, i.e., when a new document is seen in one of the inverted lists. The processing switches to AND stage when we can prove that we have created accumulators for all the documents that could possibly enter the top n. In AND stage, we ignore all the documents without an accumulator. The processing continues and we update the scores for the existing accumulators with newly processed information. The processing switches to REFINE stage as soon as we know exactly what the top n documents are without knowing their exact ranking. REFINE stage works with the accumulators of the top n documents. Once we can determine that rank order of the top n documents, the process enters the final IGNORE stage, which means that all the remaining information from the inverted list can be ignored.

The basic idea of the pruning strategy is to gradually reduce the number of active accumulators when we gain more confidence on knowing that other accumulators would not change the final top-k search results. In particular, OR stage is the only one that can add accumulators, AND stage only updates existing accumulators, and REFINE stage only process accumulators that can make to the top k results. Moreover, we further speed up the process by using skipping and accumulator trimming [29]. Skipping enables fast processing of long postings, while accumulator trimming can reduce the computational cost in the AND stage by dynamically reduce the number of enabled accumulators.

4. EFFICIENT PSEUDO-RELEVANCE FEEDBACK

4.1 Overview of Existing Implementation Strategy

As described in Section 2.1, many pseudo-relevance feedback methods have been proposed and studied. Despite the differences on how to exploit feedback information, they all require the following three-step implementation:

1. **Initial retrieval:** finding documents relevant to an original query;

2. **Term selection:** identifying useful expansion terms (i.e., relevant information in language modeling framework) from the feedback documents;

3. **Second-round retrieval:** returning documents relevant to the expanded query (i.e., updated query model in the language modeling framework).

We now provide more details on how each of these three steps is implemented in existing IR systems.

Figure 1: Processing time of the three steps in pseudo-relevance feedback implementation

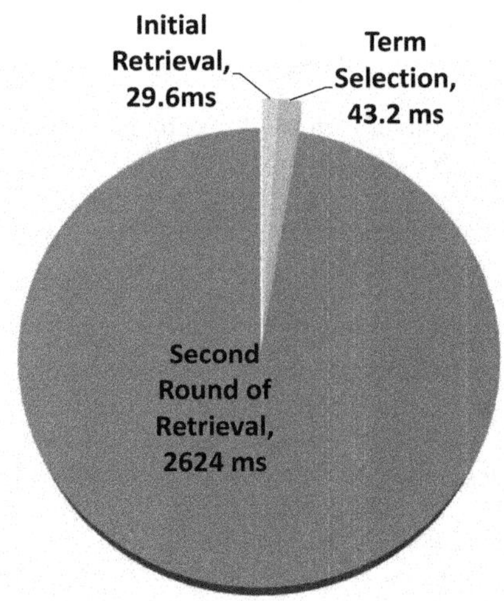

The *initial retrieval* step can be implemented with any existing top-k query processing techniques as described in Section 3. There have been significant efforts on optimizing the efficiency for this step [1–4, 7, 9, 17, 25, 29, 30, 42].

The *term selection* step is to select important terms from the feedback documents with the expectation that the selected terms can bring more relevant documents in the second round of retrieval. Traditionally, these terms are selected directly from the top ranked documents. However, this step could takes lots of time when the documents are long and the information about the documents need to be read from the disk. To solve this problem, Billerbeck and Zobel [6] proposed to generate a short tf-idf based summary for each document and select expansion terms from the summaries of the feedback documents. These summaries are small enough to be pre-loaded into the memory, and can lead to more efficient term selection. Their experimental results showed that this strategy is efficient with ignorable loss in terms of the effectiveness. In this paper, we use this strategy for term selection. One difference is that we use term probability $p(t|D)$ instead of tf-idf weighting to generate document summaries because the retrieval function used is based on language modeling approach. And we set the length of document summary to 20 terms.

The *second round retrieval* step aims to retrieve final retrieval results with the expanded query. The expanded query is often formulated as a linear interpolation of the original query and the expansion terms selected from the second step. As an example, in the relevance model [19], this step is to retrieve documents with an updated query model (i.e., θ_Q^{new}) by linearly combining the original query model (i.e., θ_Q) with the relevance model estimated from the feedback documents (i.e., $\theta_{\mathcal{F}}$) as follows:

$$\theta_Q^{new} = \lambda \cdot \theta_Q + (1 - \lambda) \cdot \theta_{\mathcal{F}}, \tag{2}$$

where the original query model θ_Q is estimated using the maximum likelihood estimation of query Q, the relevance model $\theta_{\mathcal{F}}$ estimated from the feedback documents $\mathcal{F}$ using

Figure 2: Computational flows for different implementations of pseudo-relevance feedback methods

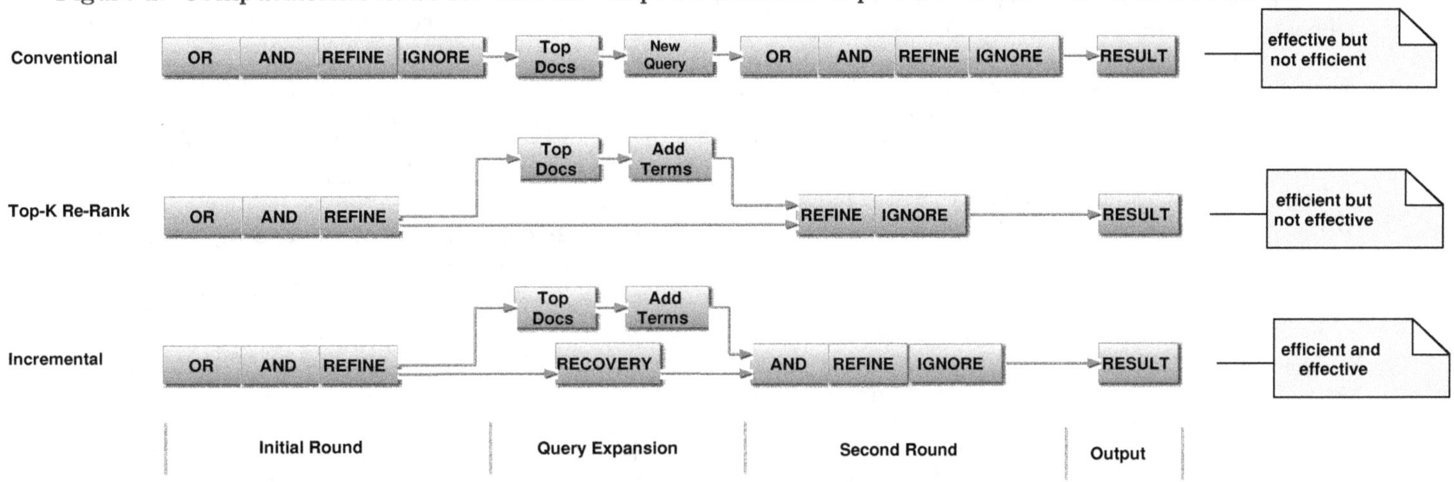

the methods described in previous study [19], and λ is to control the amount of feedback.

In the second round of retrieval, existing IR systems such as Indri would process the expanded query in the same way as a newly submitted query. In other words, the two rounds of retrieval are processed *independently*.

Figure 1 shows how much time each step takes when using the existing implementation methods described above for the relevance feedback method with 20 expansion terms. It is clear that the third step takes the most of computational time while the other two stages share a very small part the time usage. Thus, the key to efficient pseudo-relevance feedback methods is to reduce the execution time for the *second-round retrieval*, which is the focus of our paper.

4.2 Analyzing the second round retrieval

Compared with the initial retrieval, the expanded query processed in the second round is often much longer than the original query because it has much larger number of query terms to be processed. For example, the average length of Web queries is around 3, while the number of expansion terms is often set to 20. As a result, the computational cost for expanded query is significantly higher than that for the basic retrieval. Take the implementation used in our paper as an example, a longer query means that each accumulator needs to collect more postings to produce a final result and more accumulators would be created and evaluated. As a result, the system performs much more index accesses and computing, which leads to extremely long processing time compared with that for shorter queries.

One limitation of existing implementation for feedback methods is that the two rounds of retrieval are processed *independently*. Each round starts with an empty set of accumulators and gradually adds new accumulators in the OR stage. When switched to AND stage, accumulators can be updated but no new accumulated can be added. When switched to REFINE stage, only top k accumulators are processes. And in the final IGNORE stage, all the information from the inverted lists can be ignored. Note that the accumulators used the two rounds of retrieval are computed from the scratch separately. This implementation is illustrated in the upper part of Figure 2

However, unlike processing a new query, the expanded query in the second round retrieval is related to the query used in the initial retrieval. In particular, the query terms in the initial retrieval is a subset of those in the second round of retrieval, and these terms will be processed twice in this two rounds of retrieval process. Moreover, the results of these two rounds of retrieval might have a great overlap. Thus, it would be interesting to study how to leverage the results of the first round of retrieval to reduce the computational cost. But how to leverage them? This is not a simple problem without significant challenges.

The idea of exploiting the results of initial retrieval to improve the efficiency of the second round retrieval was discussed in previous study [6], but was not found useful. In the next subsection, we re-visit this basic idea and propose an incremental approach that is shown to be both efficient and effective based on the experimental results.

4.3 The Proposed Incremental Approach

Our basic idea is that the initial retrieval process should be treated as part of the query processing for the second round retrieval. Instead of processing the expanded query in the second round from the scratch, we should be able to resume the query processing results of the initial query, and continue the processing for the expanded query terms. But how to resume the results?

One possible strategy is to resume the last ranking-related stage, i.e., REFINE, in the query processing results of the initial retrieval. Recall that REFINE stage is designed to process only the accumulators of top K ranked documents. Thus, if we resume the status from the REFINE stage in the second round retrieval, it is equivalent to re-ranking those top K ranked documents using the expanded query. This strategy is illustrated in the middle part of Figure 2. Since the number of accumulators used in REFINE stage is very small, this re-ranking method would be quite efficient. However, it would suffer significant loss in terms of the effectiveness because one of the major benefits of feedback methods is to find relevant documents that were not among top ranked results for the initial retrieval and the re-ranking strategy seems to disable this nice benefit. Clearly, this is not an optimal solution. Can we do better?

Intuitively, if more document accumulators can be included in re-ranking process, the retrieval effectiveness could be improved. On the extreme case, when all the documents are considered for the re-ranking, the cost would be the same as submitting a new query. Thus, the main challenge here is how to select a set of documents to be re-ranked so that we can increase the efficiency without sacrificing the effectiveness.

Recall that the pruning technique consists of four stages: OR, AND, REFINE and IGNORE. The number of active accumulators becomes smaller as the system switches from one stage to the other. As discussed earlier, resuming from the REFINE stage is equivalent to re-ranking only top k documents, which hurts the effectiveness. On the contrary, resuming from the OR stage would not hurt the effectiveness. However, since the number of expanded terms is much larger than the number of original query terms, we might not be able to reduce the number of accumulators significantly. Thus, we propose to resume from the AND stage.

The main idea of our incremental approach is shown in the lower part in Figure 2. REFINE is the last ranking-related stage in the initial retrieval. Thus, in order to resume from the AND stage of the initial retrieval, we have to first rewind the query processing results from the end of REFINE stage back to the end of the AND stage. This new stage is referred to as RECOVERY stage in our system. The RECOVERY stage has two tasks: (1) re-enable the accumulators that were disabled at the REFINE stage; and (2) turn back the inverted list pointers to the positions where they were at the end of AND mode. Our experimental results show that this stage takes a very short ignorable time. After the RECOVERY stage, we will switch to the new AND stage to update the accumulators based on the expanded terms, and then continue to the other two stages as usual.

4.4 Discussions

Our proposed incremental approach can improve the efficiency because of the following two reasons.

First, query processing results of the original query terms can provide useful information for effective pruning in the second round retrieval. Specifically, accumulator trimming is used in the AND stage to dynamically reduce the number of active accumulators, and a threshold is used to decide whether an accumulator should be kept active or not. The threshold is to estimate a lower bound of the relevance scores for the top K ranked documents. This threshold is set to $-inf$ at the beginning of the retrieval process, and will be updated at the later stage of the retrieval when more information is gathered. Since initial value of the threshold is rather small, little pruning is applied at the early stage of the retrieval process. If the system could be informed with the range of the threshold, more pruning can be done, which would lead to shorter processing time. Since resuming the process of the initial retrieval can provide a much larger initial value for the pruning threshold, the proposed approach can reduce the query processing time.

Second, the efficiency is closely related to the number of accumulators that need to be processed. Long queries usually lead to a huge number of accumulators, which significantly hurt the efficiency. However, when resuming the query processing results of the initial query, we are able to start with a much smaller set of accumulators. Note that this strategy is not ranking safe when the expanded query is significantly different from the initial query (i.e., when λ in Equation 2 is very small). However, as shown in Section 5, the optimal value of λ is often large and this strategy does not affect the effectiveness significantly.

Table 1: Efficiency comparison using TREC Terabyte ad hoc queries (i.e., average query processing time (ms) to retrieve 1K documents)

Data sets	NoFB	FB-BL	FB-Incremental
TB04	105	5,522	3,023
TB05	77	4,502	2,462
TB06	71	4,542	2,082

Table 2: Comparison of the average size of accumulator lists per query

	FB-BL	FB-Incremental
TB04	2,368K	370K
TB05	1,805K	252K
TB06	1,901K	240K

5. EVALUATION

5.1 Experiment Design

In our study, we use three standard TREC data sets which were created for TREC Terabyte tracks in 2004 to 2006. These three sets are denoted as TB04, TB05 and TB06 in this paper. All the data sets use Gov2 collection as the document set, and the collection consists of 25.2 million web pages crawled from the .gov domain. All experiments were conducted on a single machine with dual AMD Lisbon Opteron 4122 2.2GHz processors, 8GB DDR3-1333 memory and four 2TB SATA2 disks.

The basic retrieval model used in our experiments is the Dirichlet Prior smoothing method [40], where the parameter μ was set empirically to 2500. This method is labeled as **NoFB**. We use the relevance model [19] as the pseudo-relevance feedback method. This model is chosen because of the following two reasons. First, it is a state-of-the-art pseudo-relevance feedback method that has been shown to be both effective and robust. Second, it is implemented in the Indri [1] toolkit, which makes it possible to verify the correctness of our implementation. This method is labeled as **FB**.

The implementation of our basic retrieval system (i.e., **NoFB**) is described in Section 3.3. Based on the basic retrieval system, we implemented two pseudo-relevance feedback systems: (1) **FB-BL:** traditional method of implementing pseudo-relevance feedback methods, i.e., the expanded query is processed independently to the original query; (2) **FB-Incremental:** our proposed approach that exploits the query processing results of the original query to speed up the processing of the expanded query.

Although we implemented our own indexing and query processing modules, we did not build the impact-based indexing directly from the collection. Instead, we built an initial index using Indri toolkit and use Indri API to transfer the indri index to our impact-sorted index. The size of the impact-based index for Gov2 collection is about 11.8GB with 442MB for term lookup, 7.5GB for inverted lists and

[1]http://www.lemurproject.org/indri/

Table 4: Impact of the expansion weight (i.e., λ) on the efficiency (the average execution time (ms) per query)

Data sets	Methods	λ				
		0.5	0.6	0.7	0.8	0.9
TB04	FB-BL	6,125	5,522	4,435	2,723	1,597
	FB-Incremental	3,798	3,023	2,130	1,221	826
TB05	FB-BL	5,146	4,502	3,577	2,466	1,323
	FB-Incremental	3,071	2,462	1,762	1,113	845
TB06	FB-BL	5,281	4,542	3,571	2,412	1,114
	FB-Incremental	2,664	2,082	1,406	778	560

Table 3: Effectiveness comparison using TREC Terabyte ad hoc queries (MAP@1000)

Data sets	NoFB	FB-BL	FB-Incremental
TB04	0.246	0.256	0.255
TB05	0.309	0.334	0.334
TB06	0.275	0.285	0.284

3.8GB for document summaries that are needed for the term selection step in the feedback methods. We decided to leverage the Indri index because (1) it saves our unnecessary efforts on writing codes to parse documents and count the term statistics; and (2) it enables direct comparison between our system and Indri since they now use the same information about the collection. When evaluating a query, we also leveraged Indri API to handle the tasks of converting terms/documents to their IDs.

Since we have to work with two indexes (the original Indri index and new Impact-sorted index) and all the information are read directly from disk rather than memory, our system could be slower than those using similar strategies. However, this should not affect our comparison on the two FB systems since they are implemented using the same strategy. Moreover, even working with two indexes, our developed system is still much faster than the Indri toolkit (version 5.1), which takes about 1 minute to process a query when using the relevance model on the Gov2 collection.

5.2 Experimental Results

The first two sets of experiments were conducted with the ad hoc queries used in TREC Terabyte tracks. Each data set has 50 queries, and we use title only field to formulate queries. The third set of experiments was conducted with the efficiency queries used in TREC Terabyte tracks. One data set has 50K queries while the other has 100K queries.

5.2.1 *Efficiency and Effectiveness*

We first examine whether the incremental approach can improve the efficiency. In particular, we set the number of feedback documents to 10, the number of expansion terms to 20 and the expansion weight λ is set to 0.6. These parameters are chosen because they can lead to near-optimal performance in terms of the effectiveness. Table 1 shows the average processing time (ms) for each query when 1000 documents are retrieved. The trends on the three collections are similar. Both FB systems are slower than the NoFB system. It takes around 5 seconds for FB-BL to process a query, and takes around 2.5 seconds for FB-Incremental to do so. Clearly, FB-Incremental can achieve a speed up of 2 compared with FB-BL, which shows that the proposed incremental approach can improve the efficiency. Note that we also evaluate the efficiency of the Indri toolkit, a widely used open source IR system. It takes around 1 minute for the Indri toolkit to process a query on the same collection. This suggests that the baseline system we implemented, i.e., FB-BL, is very efficient.

As discussed earlier, the speed up of FB-Incremental is achieved for two reasons. First, FB-Incremental leverages the query processing results of the initial retrieval, which avoids processing the original query terms twice. Second, the accumulator list inherited from the initial retrieval by FB-Incremental is much smaller. Table 2 shows the comparison of the accumulator list size between the two methods. Our incremental method creates only about 1/7 accumulators as those of baseline method. As a result, the new method avoids a lot of unnecessary index access and computing for those accumulators it does not include. Note that our baseline system, i.e., FB-BL, is a very strong baseline since it applied the accumulator trimming techniques which can reduce unnecessary accumulators during the process.

We also conduct experiments to examine whether the proposed approach would hurt the performance. Since our incremental approach leverages the accumulators used in the AND stage of the initial retrieval, it is possible that we may miss some relevant documents because they were not relevant to the original query and thus were not included in its accumulator lists. As a result, it is possible that the incremental approach might hurt the effectiveness, but it only happens when the expanded query is very different from the original query. Recall that the optimal value of λ is 0.6 which indeed indicates that the original query and expanded query are similar. Table 3 shows the results measured with MAP@1000. To ensure the correct implementation of our system, we compare the baseline performance with the ones reported in the previous study [30] and find that the results are similar, which confirms our implementation of $NoFB$ is correct. Moreover, we find that both FB methods can improve the retrieval accuracy about 4% to 8%, which is also similar to the performance improvement of the feedback method implemented in Indri. One interesting observation is that the effectiveness of the two FB systems are similar, which indicates that our proposed approach improve the efficiency without sacrificing the effectiveness.

5.2.2 *Impact of Parameter Values*

There are multiple parameters in the pseudo-relevance feedback methods such as the number of expansion terms, the number of feedback documents and the expansion weight (i.e., λ in Equation (2)). Since we use impact based document summary for term select, the impact of the number of feedback documents on efficiency is not very significant. Thus, we only focus on the other two parameters.

Table 5: Impact of the expansion weight (i.e., λ) on the effectiveness (MAP@1000)

Data sets	Methods	λ				
		0.5	0.6	0.7	0.8	0.9
TB04	FB-BL	0.254	0.256	0.257	0.255	0.252
	FB-Incremental	0.252	0.255	0.256	0.255	0.252
TB05	FB-BL	0.333	0.334	0.332	0.328	0.321
	FB-Incremental	0.333	0.334	0.332	0.327	0.321
TB06	FB-BL	0.284	0.285	0.285	0.284	0.281
	FB-incremental	0.282	0.284	0.283	0.282	0.280

Table 6: Average query execute time (ms) based on different expansion weights (top 10 documents for each query)

	NoFB	FB Methods	λ				
			0.5	0.6	0.7	0.8	0.9
TB04	69	FB-BL	4,731	4,016	2,786	1,756	933
		FB-Incremental	1,295	915	578	437	403
TB05	53	FB-BL	3730	2,923	1,999	1,131	547
		FB-Incremental	983	709	451	341	310
TB06	46	FB-BL	3909	3,060	2,167	1,317	573
		FB-Incremental	921	669	447	319	284

Figure 3: The speed-up rate on different expansion weight λ (top 1000 documents returned)

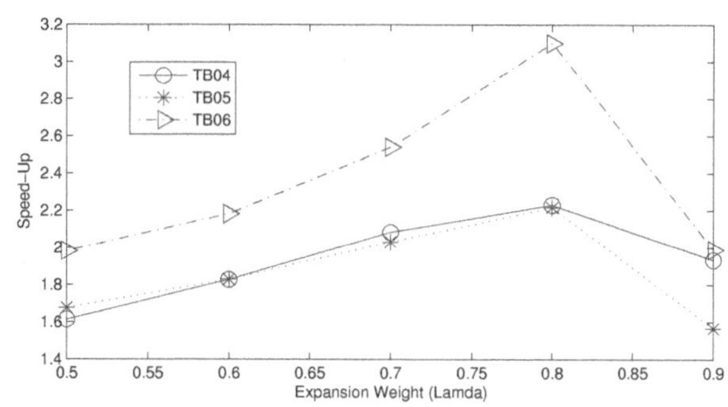

Figure 4: The speed-up rate on different number of expansion terms

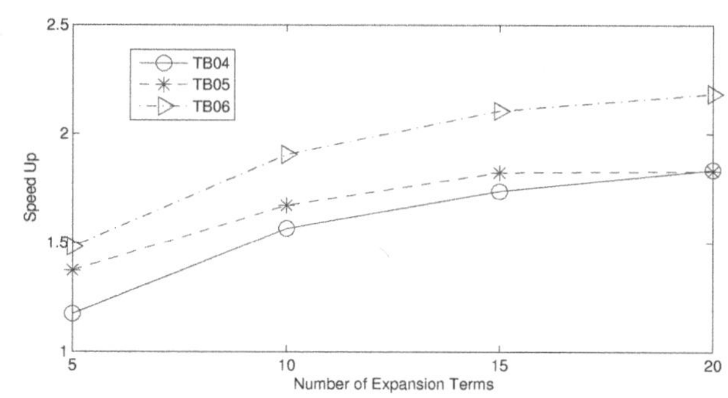

As discussed earlier, the expansion weight is an important parameter and we should examine the impact of its value on both efficiency and effectiveness. The results are shown in Table 4 and Table 5. We see that the optimal value of λ is around 0.6, which means that we should put more weights to the original query terms. According to Equation (2), the higher value of λ means that we put more trust on the original query and less weights to the expansion terms. Given the characteristics of SAAT pruning technique, postings of terms with smaller weights are more likely to be pruned. As a result, we can observe a clear trend that both methods can improve the efficiency more when the value λ is larger.

Figure 3 shows how the speed-up rate of $FB-Incremental$ compared with FB changes with the expansion weight. The higher expansion weight we choose, the more the original query determines the final ranking list and the more time the incremental method can save. However when the expansion weight is too high (e.g. 0.9), SAAT pruning technique is rather efficient and leave small room for further improvement. As a result, the speed-up rate at high expansion weight decreases.

We further test the impact of number of expansion terms on efficiency. Table 4 shows the speed up rate of $FB-Incremental$ compared with $FB-BL$. It shows that our new method benefits more when the system adds more expansion terms into the original query. The main reason of this trend is that our method efficiently controls the grows of accumulator list size when the query becomes longer.

Another important factor that could affect the retrieval speed is the number of documents retrieved for each query. Figure 5 shows how the number of retrieved documents affect the speed up of $FB-Incremental$ over $FB-BL$. The results indicate that the new method can achieve more speed-up when the system returns fewer results to users. We believe it is due to the reason that returning fewer documents brings higher cut-off threshold. And in our method, the high cut-off threshold which is got from the initial run provides a strong and efficient guidance on the accumulator selections in the resumed retrieval. As a result, the pool of candidate documents/accumulators is kept in a very small size and final result is generated soon. In opposite, the baseline method which does the second round retrieval independently cannot get the benefit from the high cut-off threshold and it still generates large number of accumulators in which most of them are unnecessary.

Figure 5: The speed-up rate on different number of retrieved documents per query

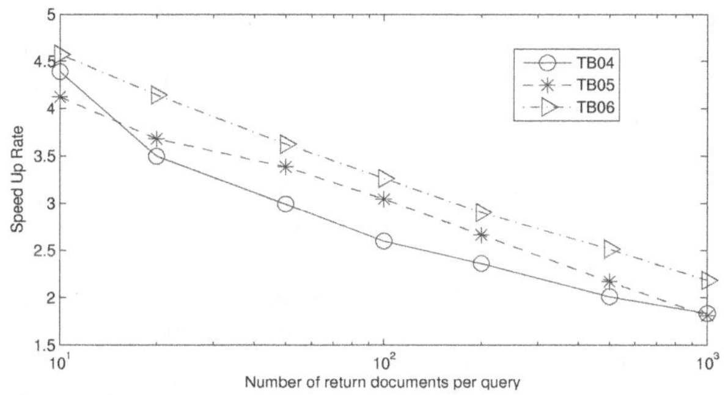

Figure 6: The speed-up rate on different expansion weight λ (top 10 documents returned)

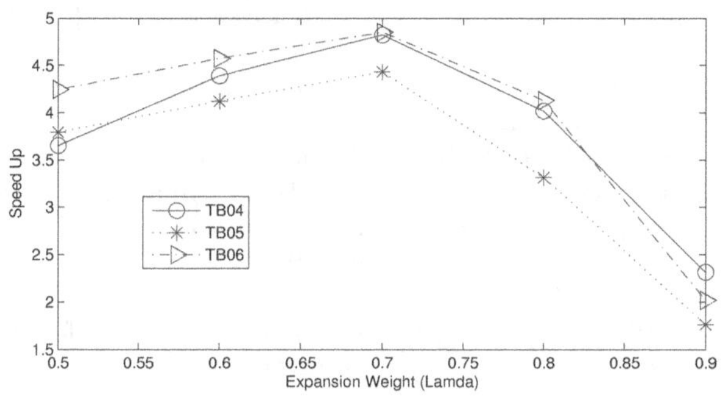

We also report the efficiency when retrieving only 10 documents for each query in Table 6. It is clear that when retrieving fewer documents, FB-Incremental can achieve a higher speed up, i.e., around four. This indicates that this method could be very useful for Web search domain since search users only need to look at 10 results per page. Finally, Figure 6 shows impact of the expansion weight on the speed-up when only 10 documents are retrieved. The trend is very similar to Figure 3.

5.2.3 Scalability

To further test the scalability of the incremental method and study how original query length affects the pseudo feedback system speed, we test both methods on 50k 2005 efficiency queries and 100k 2006 efficiency queries. For each query, 5 expansion terms are added and it only returns top 10 documents. The results show that the incremental method can stably improve the efficiency at a rate more than 2 at different original query length. For short queries, the baseline is fast and it leaves less space for further improvement. For long queries, the processing time is dominated by the original query terms and the optimizations in pseudo feedback part will not affect the total time too much. As a result, it is reasonable to observe a speed up rate summit at medium length query (i.e., 3-4 terms).

Table 7: Average query processing time (ms) on different query length (2005 50K queries)

	Avg	1	2	3	4	5	>5
NoFB	35	4	10	26	55	91	175
FB-BL	297	38	94	302	526	749	1,102
FB-Incremental	124	18	43	97	204	316	540
Speed-up	2.4	2.1	2.2	3.1	2.6	2.4	2.0

Table 8: Average query processing time (ms) on different query length (2006 100K queries)

	Avg	1	2	3	4	5	>5
NoFB	103	3	12	39	81	132	275
FB-BL	739	39	99	357	690	1,030	1,642
FB-Incremental	300	26	43	110	248	441	797
Speed-up	2.5	1.5	2.3	3.2	2.8	2.3	2.0

6. CONCLUSIONS

This paper focuses on efficient implementation of pseudo-relevance feedback methods, an important yet under-studied problem. Motivated by the fact that original query terms are often processed twice in the two-round retrieval process, we proposed an incremental approach that can exploits the query processing results of the first round retrieval for computing the document scores in the second round. Although similar idea was mentioned in a previous study [6], it was concluded as a unsuccessful strategy. On the contrary, our method has been shown to be useful and can achieve a speed up of 2 over TREC collections. This paper is one of a few studies that try to bring the gap between the continuous research efforts on improving the effectiveness of the pseudo-relevance feedback methods and the increasing efforts on efficient IR systems.

There could be many interesting directions for our future work. First, we plan to implement other pseudo feedback methods including both basic models such as model-based feedback [41] and more sophisticated models such as positional relevance model [22], and evaluate whether the proposed approach can improve their performance. Second, it would be interesting to study how to leverage the incremental approach to improve the efficiency of query processing for long queries. Finally, our system is built on impact-sorted indexing with SAAT traverse. We plan to continue our efforts and study whether it is possible to improve the efficiency for feedback methods when using other query processing strategies such as DAAT and TAAT .

7. ACKNOWLEDGMENTS

This material is based upon work supported by the National Science Foundation under Grant Number IIS-1017026. We thank the anonymous SIGIR reviewers for their useful comments.

8. REFERENCES

[1] V. N. Anh, O. de Kretser, and A. Moffat. Vector-space ranking with effective early termination. In *Proceedings of SIGIR'01*, 2001.

[2] V. N. Anh and A. Moffat. Impact transformation: efffective and efficient web retrieval. In *Proceedings of SIGIR'02*, 2002.

[3] V. N. Anh and A. Moffat. Simplified similarity scoring using term ranks. In *Proceedings of SIGIR'05*, 2005.

[4] V. N. Anh and A. Moffat. Pruned query evaluation using pre-computed impacts. In *Proceedings of SIGIR'06*, 2006.

[5] B. Billerbeck and J. Zobel. Techniques for efficient query expansion. In *Proceedings of String Processing and Information Retrieval Symposium*, 2004.

[6] B. Billerbeck and J. Zobel. Efficient query expansion with auxiliary data structures. *Information Systems*, 31(7):573–584, 2006.

[7] A. Z. Broder, D. Carmel, M. Herscovici, A. Soffer, and J. Zien. Efficient query evaluation using a two-level retrieval process. In *Proceedings of CIKM'03*, 2003.

[8] C. Buckley. Automatic query expansion using SMART: Trec-3. In D. Harman, editor, *Overview of the Third Text Retrieval Conference (TREC-3)*, pages 69–80, 1995. NIST Special Publication 500-225.

[9] C. Buckley and A. F. Lewit. Optimization of inverted vector searches. In *Proceedings of SIGIR'85*, 1985.

[10] C. Buckley and S. Robertson. Relevance feedback track overview: Trec 2008. In *Proceedings of TREC'08*, 2008.

[11] G. Cao, J.-Y. Nie, J. Gao, and S. Robertson. Selecting good expansion terms for pseudo-relevance feedback. In *Proceedings of SIGIR'08*, 2008.

[12] M.-A. Cartright and J. Allan. Efficiency optimizations for interpolating subqueries. In *Proceedings of the CIKM'11*, 2011.

[13] M.-A. Cartright, J. Allan, V. Lavrenko, and A. McGregor. Fast query expansion using approximations of relevance models. In *Proceedings of the CIKM'10*, 2010.

[14] K. Collins-Thompson and J. Callan. Estimation and use of uncertainty in pseudo-relevance feedback. In *Proceedings of SIGIR'07*, 2007.

[15] J. V. Dillon and K. Collins-Thompson. A unified optimization framework for robust pseudo-relevance feedback algorithms. In *Proceedings of CIKM'10*, 2010.

[16] S. Ding and T. Suel. Faster top-k document retreival using block-max indexes. In *Proceedings of SIGIR'11*, 2011.

[17] R. Fagin. Combining fuzzy information: an overview. *ACM SIGMOD Record*, 31(2), 2002.

[18] V. Lavrenko and J. Allan. Real-time query expansion in relevance models. Technical Report IR-473, University of Massachusetts Amherst, 2006.

[19] V. Lavrenko and B. Croft. Relevance-based language models. In *Proceedings of SIGIR'01*, pages 120–127, Sept 2001.

[20] K.-S. Lee, W. B. Croft, and J. Allan. A cluster-based resampling method for pseudo-relevance feedback. In *Proceedings of SIGIR'08*, 2008.

[21] Y. Lv and C. Zhai. Positional relevance model for pseudo-relevance feedback. In *Proceedings of SIGIR'10*, 2010.

[22] Y. Lv, C. Zhai, and W. Chen. A boosting approach to improving pseudo-relevance feedback. In *Proceedings of SIGIR'11*, 2011.

[23] M. Mayer. Scaling google for every user. In *Seattle Conference on Scalability*, 2007.

[24] J. Miao, J. Huang, and Z. Ye. Proximity-based rocchio's model for pseudo relevance. In *Proceedings of SIGIR'12*, 2012.

[25] A. Moffat and J. Zobel. Self-indexing inverted files for fast text retrieval. *ACM Transactions on Information Systems*, 14(4):349–379, 1996.

[26] S. Robertson and K. Sparck Jones. Relevance weighting of search terms. *Journal of the American Society for Information Science*, 27:129–146, 1976.

[27] J. Rocchio. Relevance feedback in information retrieval. In *The SMART Retrieval System: Experiments in Automatic Document Processing*, pages 313–323. Prentice-Hall Inc., 1971.

[28] G. Salton and C. Buckley. Improving retrieval performance by relevance feedback. *Journal of the American Society for Information Science*, 44(4):288–297, 1990.

[29] T. Strohman. *Efficient processing of complex features for information retrieval.* PhD thesis, University of Massachusetts Amherst, 2007.

[30] T. Strohman and W. B. Croft. Efficient document retrieval in main memory. In *Proceedings of SIGIR'07*, 2007.

[31] T. Strohman, H. Turtle, and W. B. Croft. Optimization strategies for complex queries. In *Proceedings of SIGIR'05*, 2005.

[32] T. Tao and C. Zhai. Regularized estimation of mixture models for robust pseudo-relevance feedback. In *Proceedings of SIGIR'06*, 2006.

[33] M. Theobald, R. Schenkel, and G. Weikum. Efficient and self-tuning incremental query expansion for top-k query processing. In *Proceedings of the SIGIR'05*, 2005.

[34] H. Turtle and J. Flood. Query evaluation: strategies and optimizations. *Information Processing & Management*, 31(1):831–850, 1995.

[35] H. Wang, Y. Liang, L. Fu, G. rong Xue, and Y. Yu. Efficient query expansion for advertisement search. In *Proceedings of SIGIR'09*, 2009.

[36] I. H. Witten, A. Moffat, and T. C. Bell. *Managing Gigabytes: Compressing and Indexing Documents and Images.* Morgan Kaufmann, 1999.

[37] J. Xu and W. B. Croft. Improving the effectivness of information retrieval with local context analysis. *ACM Transactions on Information Systems*, 18:79–112, 2000.

[38] Y. Xu, G. J. F. Jones, and B. Wang. Query dependent pseudo-relevance feedback based on wikipedia. In *Proceedings of SIGIR'09*, 2009.

[39] H. Yan, S. Shi, F. Zhang, T. Suel, and J.-R. Wen. Efficient term proximity search with term-pair indexes. In *Proceedings of CIKM'10*, 2010.

[40] C. Zhai and J. Lafferty. The dual role of smoothing in the language modeling approach. In *Proceedings of the Workshop on Language Modeling and Information Retrieval*, 2001.

[41] C. Zhai and J. Lafferty. Model-based feedback in the KL-divergence retrieval model. In *Tenth International Conference on Information and Knowledge Management (CIKM 2001)*, pages 403–410, 2001.

[42] J. Zobel and A. Moffat. Inverted files for text search engines. *ACM Computing Surveys*, 38(2), 2006.

Query Expansion Using Path-Constrained Random Walks

Jianfeng Gao
Microsoft Research, Redmond
Washington 98052, USA
jfgao@microsoft.com

Gu Xu
Microsoft Bing, Bellevue
Washington 98004, USA
guxu@microsoft.com

Jinxi Xu
Microsoft Bing, Bellevue
Washington 98004, USA
jinxixu@microsoft.com

ABSTRACT
This paper exploits Web search logs for query expansion (QE) by presenting a new QE method based on path-constrained random walks (PCRW), where the search logs are represented as a labeled, directed graph, and the probability of picking an expansion term for an input query is computed by a learned combination of constrained random walks on the graph. The method is shown to be *generic* in that it covers most of the popular QE models as special cases and *flexible* in that it provides a principled mathematical framework in which a wide variety of information useful for QE can be incorporated in a unified way. Evaluation is performed on the Web document ranking task using a real-world data set. Results show that the PCRW-based method is very effective for the expansion of rare queries, i.e., low-frequency queries that are unseen in search logs, and that it outperforms significantly other state-of-the-art QE methods.

Categories and Subject Descriptors
H.3.3 [**Information Storage and Retrieval**]: Information Search and Retrieval; I.2.6 [**Artificial Intelligence**]: *Learning*

General Terms
Algorithms, Experimentation

Keywords
Search Log, Query Expansion, Random Walk, Path Ranking Algorithm, Web Search

1. INTRODUCTION
Term mismatch is one of the fundamental challenges in Web search, where a query and its relevant documents are often composed using different vocabularies and language styles. Query expansion (QE) is an effective strategy to address the challenge. It expands a query issued by a user with additional related terms, called *expansion terms*, so that more relevant documents can be retrieved.

QE is a long-standing research topic in information retrieval (IR). The methods based on automatic relevance feedback (e.g., explicit feedback and pseudo relevance feedback (PRF)) have been proved to be useful for improving the performance of IR on TREC datasets [10, 11, 34, 36, 36, 45, 48]. However, these methods cannot be applied directly to a commercial Web search engine because the relevant documents are not always available and generating pseudo-relevant documents requires multi-phase retrieval, which is prohibitively expensive.

Recent studies demonstrate the success of exploiting search logs (i.e., clickthrough data) for QE [7, 14, 15, 19, 22, 41, 42]. These methods, called *log-based QE*, also derive expansion terms for a query from its (pseudo-)relevant document set. But, different from the methods based on automatic relevance feedback, the relevant document set is identified by user clicks recorded in search logs. For example, the set of (pseudo-)relevant documents of an input query can be formed by including the documents which have been previously clicked for the query or its similar queries [1, 7, 46]. Most state-of-the-art log-based QE methods use a global model that is pre-computed from search logs [14, 19]. The model captures the correlation between query terms and documents terms and can be used to generate expansion terms for the input query on the fly. Despite the effectiveness of log-based QE methods, they suffer from two problems. First is data sparseness. A large portion of queries have very few or no click in search logs, as stated by Zipf's law. Second is the ambiguity of search intent. For example, a term correlation model may fail to distinguish the search intent of the query term "book" in "school book" from that in "hotel booking". Although the problem can be partially alleviated by using the improved correlation models based on phrases and concepts [19], there are plenty of cases where the search intent can only be identified correctly via global context. For example, the query "why 6 bottles in one wrap" is about package, and the intent of the query "acme baked bread" is to look for the bakery in CA. In such cases, a (pseudo-)relevant document set of an input query, if available, is more likely to preserve the original search intent than any pre-computed global correlation model.

In this paper we address the two problems by proposing a new log-based QE method based on path-constrained random walks [32]. We represent the search logs, consisting of billions of clicked query-document pairs, as a labeled, directed graph, where there are three types of nodes, representing respectively queries, documents, and words (i.e., candidate expansion terms), and the edges between nodes are labeled by relations. An example graph, which will be described in detail in Section 3.1, is shown in Figure 1. For each path in the graph that links the input query Q to a candidate expansion term w, there is a path type π, defined by a sequence of edge labels. Each path type can be viewed as a particular process of generating w from Q, and the generation probability $P(w|Q,\pi)$ is computed by random walks along the paths that instantiate the path type π, as known as *path-constrained random walks* (PCRW). Many log-based QE models proposed

SIGIR'13, July 28–August 1, 2013, Dublin, Ireland.

previously can be formulated in the framework of PCRW by defining particular path types. For example, the method based on relevance feedback, where the pseudo-relevant documents D are defined as the ones that have clicks for the input query Q or its similar queries Q', can be presented using the following path type

$$\langle similar\_Q2Q', click\_Q'2D, generate\_D2w \rangle.$$

This is a three-step random walk. The first step retrieves similar queries by a random walk on edges labeled by the relation $similar\_Q2Q'$. The second follows any edges labeled by $click\_Q'2D$. The third follows any edges labeled by $generate\_D2w$. These relations are summarized in Table 1, and will be described in detail in Section 3.

We will show that PCRW provides a generic and flexible modeling framework in that it not only covers most of the popular log-based QE models as special cases, but also allows us to devise new QE models that can potentially use much richer information than that of previous models. For example, we can define a rich set of walk behaviors that support a variety of labeled edges where different information can be used at different stages of the walk. Some examples will be presented in Section 3.2.

Moreover, because different QE methods often rely on different sources and are potentially complimentary, it is desirable to combine them to address data sparseness and help disambiguate search intent. For example, while the automatic feedback methods using (pseudo-)relevant documents are good to retain search intent but suffer from data sparseness especially for rare queries, the methods based on global term correlation models can be applied equally well to both common and rare queries but, due to the limited context information it captures, may lead to an unexpected shift of search intent. We will show that PCRW provides a flexible mathematical framework in which different QE features, specified by path types π, can be incorporated in a unified way. Formally, in the PCRW-based QE method the probability of picking w for a given Q, $P(w|Q)$, is computed by a learned combination of path-constrained random walks on the graph, i.e., $P(w|Q) = \sum_{\pi \in B} \lambda_\pi P(w|Q,\pi)$, where $\lambda_\pi's$ are the combination weights learned on training data.

Our experiments (Section 4) show that the use of PCRW not only makes QE robust to data sparseness but also help disambiguate search intents, leading to a significant improvement over previous state-of-the-art QE methods.

In the rest of the paper, Section 2 reviews briefly PCRW. Section 3 describes in detail the PCRW-based QE method. Sections 4 and 5 present experiments and related work, respectively. The paper is concluded in Section 6.

2. PRELIMINARIES

This section briefly reviews the path-constrained random walk model. Readers are referred to [32] for a more detailed treatment. The model used in this study is a variant of the one described in [32, 33]. Modifications are made for the QE task.

Consider a directed, labeled graph $G = (C, T)$ where $T \subseteq C \times R \times C$ is the set of labeled edges (also known as *triples*) (c, r, c'). Each triple represents an instance $r(c, c')$ of the relation $r \in R$. For the QE task considered in this study it will be useful to introduce for each relation r a separate probabilistic model θ_r, which is used to assign a score to the edge. The score is the probability of reaching c' from c with a one-step random walk with edge type r, $P(c'|c,\theta_r)$. In Section 3 we will see how the use of relation-specific models allows us to build significantly more expressive QE models.

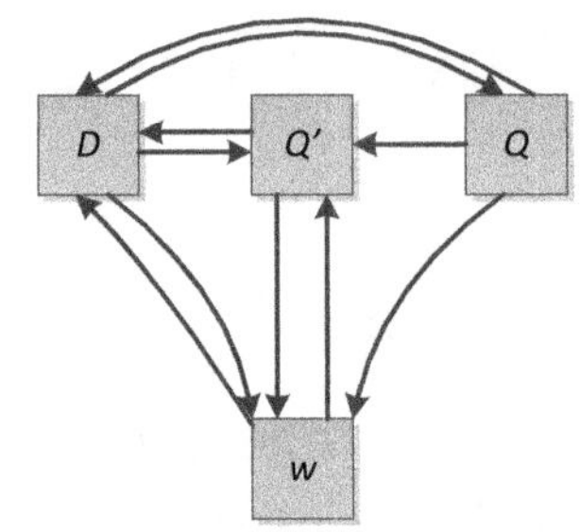

Figure 1. Search logs as a graph

A *path type* in G is a sequence $\pi = \langle r_1, \ldots, r_m \rangle$. An instance of the path type is sequence of nodes $c_0, \ldots, c_m$ such that $r_i(c_{i-1}, c_i)$. Each path type specifies a real-value feature. For a given node pair (s, t), where s is source node and t is target node, the value of the feature π is $P(t|s,\pi)$, i.e., the probability of reaching t from s by a random walk that instantiates the path type, also known as a *path-constrained random walk*. Specifically, suppose that the random walk has just reached c_i by traversing edges labeled $r_1, \ldots, r_i$ with $Q = c_0$. Then c_{i+1} is drawn at random, according to $\theta_{r_{i+1}}$, from all nodes reachable by edges labeled r_{i+1}. A path type π is *active* for pair (s, t) if $P(t|s,\pi) > 0$.

Let $B = \{\perp, \pi_1, \ldots, \pi_n\}$ be the set of all path types of length no greater than l that occur in the graph together with the dummy type $\perp$, which represents the bias feature. It is convenient to set $P(t|s,\perp) = 1$ for any nodes s, t. The score of whether target node t is related to source node s is given by

$$P(t|s) = \sum_{\pi \in B} \lambda_\pi P(t|s,\pi), \quad (1)$$

where λ_π is the weight of feature π. The model parameters to be learned are the vector $\boldsymbol{\lambda} = \langle \lambda_\pi \rangle_{\pi \in B}$. The construction of B and the estimation of $\boldsymbol{\lambda}$ are application specific. For the QE task source node is the input query to be expanded Q and target node is a candidate expansion term w. Thus, Equation (1) gives the probability of whether w is a good expansion term of Q. This is the QE model we will describe in detail in Section 3.

3. PCRW-BASED QE MODEL

3.1 Search Logs as a Graph

The search logs used in this study consist of a list of query-document pairs, also known as *clickthrough data*. Each pair contains a query and a document which has one or more user clicks for the query. We represent the search logs as a graph $G = (C, T)$, as shown in Figure 1. We define three types of nodes to represent respectively queries, documents, and words that occur in queries and documents. While a query in the search logs, denoted by Q', always has clicked document(s), an input query to be expanded, denoted by Q, could be a new, low-frequency query without clicked documents. Such a query is called a *rare query* in this paper. Q and Q' are treated as different nodes in G.

ID	Relation r	Scoring function
1	*similar_Q2Q'*	cosine similarity between the term vectors of Q and Q', where term weights are assigned using the BM25 function.
2	*translate_Q2Q'*	$\log \prod_{q' \in Q'} \sum_{q \in Q} P_{tm}(q'\vert q) \frac{tf(q;Q)}{\vert Q\vert}$
3	*click_Q2D*	$\log P(D\vert Q) = \log \frac{click(Q,D)}{\sum_{D_i \in \mathbf{D}} click(Q,D_i)}$
4	*click_D2Q*	$\log P(Q\vert D) = \log \frac{click(Q,D)}{\sum_{Q_i \in \mathbf{Q}} click(Q_i,D)}$
5	*generate_Q2w*	$\log\left((1-\alpha)\frac{tf(w;Q)}{\vert Q\vert} + \alpha\frac{cf(w)}{\vert C\vert}\right)$
6	*translate_Q2w*	$\log \sum_{q \in Q} P_{tm}(w\vert q) \frac{tf(q;Q)}{\vert Q\vert}$
7	*generate_Q'2w*	$\log\left((1-\alpha)\frac{tf(w;Q')}{\vert Q'\vert} + \alpha\frac{cf(w)}{\vert C\vert}\right)$
8	*translate_Q'2w*	$\log \sum_{q' \in Q'} P_{tm}(w\vert q') \frac{tf(q';Q')}{\vert Q'\vert}$
9	*click_Q'2D*	$\log P(D\vert Q') = \log \frac{click(Q',D)}{\sum_{D_i \in \mathbf{D}} click(Q',D_i)}$
10	*generate_D2w*	$\log\left((1-\beta)\frac{tf(w;D)}{\vert D\vert} + \beta\frac{cf(w)}{\vert C\vert}\right)$
11	*translate_D2w*	$\log \sum_{w_i \in D} P_{tm}(w\vert w_i) \frac{tf(w_i;D)}{\vert D\vert}$
12	*click_D2Q'*	$\log P(Q'\vert D) = \log \frac{click(Q',D)}{\sum_{Q'_i \in \mathbf{Q}} click(Q'_i,D)}$
13	*generate_w2D*	$\log P(D\vert w) = \log \frac{P_{lm}(w\vert D)P(D)}{\sum_{D_i \in \mathbf{D}} P_{lm}(w\vert D_i)P(D_i)}$, where $P_{lm}(w\vert D) = (1-\beta)\frac{tf(w;D)}{\vert D\vert} + \beta\frac{cf(w)}{\vert C\vert}$ and $P(D) = \frac{\sum_{Q \in \mathbf{Q}} click(Q,D)}{N}$
14	*generate_w2Q'*	$\log P(Q'\vert w) = \log \frac{P_{lm}(w\vert Q')P(Q')}{\sum_{Q'_i \in \mathbf{Q}} P_{lm}(w\vert Q_i)P(Q')}$, where $P_{lm}(w\vert Q) = (1-\alpha)\frac{tf(w;Q)}{\vert Q\vert} + \alpha\frac{cf(w)}{\vert C\vert}$ and $P(Q) = \frac{\sum_{D \in \mathbf{D}} click(Q,D)}{N}$

Table 1: Relations and their scoring functions used in the graph in Figure 1. Here, $tf(q;Q)$ is the number of times term q occurs in query Q, and $|Q|$ is the length of query Q. $tf(w;D)$ is the number of times term w occurs in D, and $|D|$ is the length of document D. The $cf(w)$ and $|C|$ values are analogously defined on the collection level, where the collection consists of all the documents in search logs. $P_{tm}(.)$ is word translation probability assigned by a translation model trained on query-title pairs derived from clickthrough data. $P_{tm}(q'|q)$ in #2 is also assigned by the same query-title translation model based on the assumption that a good expansion term q' is likely to occur in the titles of the clicked documents [19]. $click(Q',D)$ is the number of times document D is clicked for Q' in search logs. In #13, D is the full set of documents in search logs. Q in #12 and #14 is the full set of queries in search logs. N in #13 and #14 is the total number of clicks in search logs, i.e., $N = \sum_{Q \in \mathbf{Q}} \sum_{D \in \mathbf{D}} click(Q,D)$. Finally, α and β are model hyperparameters that control smoothing for query and document language models, respectively.

Each edge in the graph is labeled by a relation r, and is scored using a relation-specific model θ_r. The edge score is the probability of reaching target node t from source node s with a one-step random walk with edge type r, $P(t|s,\theta_r)$. The set of relations r and their corresponding scoring functions $score_{\theta_r}(s \to t)$, which are used in this study, are summarized in Table 1. To ensure that edge score is a probability, $P(t|s,\theta_r)$ is computed via softmax as

$$P(t|s,\theta_r) = \frac{\exp\left(score_{\theta_r}(s \to t)\right)}{\sum_{t_i} \exp\left(score_{\theta_r}(s \to t_i)\right)} \quad (2)$$

Note that in the original PCRW model [32] there is no θ_r, and the edge score is computed by

$$P(t|s,r) = \frac{\mathrm{I}(r(s,t))}{\sum_{t'} \mathrm{I}(r(s,t'))}$$

where $\mathrm{I}(r(s,t))$ is an indicator function that takes value 1 if there exists an edge with type r that connects s to t. Introducing θ_r allows us to easily incorporate well-established models that have been developed for QE and document ranking models in the IR community. The scoring functions in Table 1 lie in four categories. The first is the functions for the *similar_** relation (e.g., #1), and is based on the BM25 model [39]. The second, including functions for the relations of *generate_** (e.g., #5), uses unigram language models with Bayesian smoothing using Dirichlet priors [49]. The third, including functions for *click_** (e.g., #3), uses a click model [13]. The last category, including functions for *translation_** (e.g., #6), uses translation models [5, 17, 19], where, if clickthrough data is available for model training, the word translation probabilities P_{tm} are estimated on query-document pairs by assuming that a query is parallel to the documents clicked on for that query [17].

ID	Path type π (Comments)
TM1	$\langle translate\_Q2w \rangle$ (w is generated using clickthrough-based translation model from Q as in [19])
TM2	$\langle generate\_Q2w, generate\_w2D, generate\_D2w \rangle$ (variant of **TM1** where translation model is trained via 2-step random walks on word-document graph, as in [31])
TM3	$\langle generate\_Q2w, generate\_w2D, generate\_D2w, generate\_w2D, generate\_D2w \rangle$ (variant of **TM2** where 4-step random walks are used)
TM4	$\langle generate\_Q2w, generate\_w2Q', generate\_Q'2w \rangle$ (variant of **TM2** where random walks are performed on word-query graph)
TM5	$\langle generate\_Q2w, generate\_w2Q', generate\_Q'2w, generate\_w2Q', generate\_Q'2w \rangle$ (variant of **TM4** where 4-step random walks are used)
SQ1	$\langle similar\_Q2Q', generate\_Q'2w \rangle$ (w is generated from similar queries Q' of Q, where query similarity is based on BM25)
SQ2	$\langle translate\_Q2Q', generate\_Q'2w \rangle$ (variant of **SQ1** where query similarity is based on clickthrough-based translation model)
SQ3	$\langle similar\_Q2Q', click\_Q'2D, click\_D2Q', generate\_Q'2w \rangle$ (variant of **SQ1** where similar query set is enriched by 2-step random walks on query-document graph)
SQ4	$\langle similar\_Q2Q', click\_Q'2D, click\_D2Q', click\_Q'2D, click\_D2Q', generate\_Q'2w \rangle$ (variant of **SQ3** where 4-step random walks are used)
SQ5	$\langle translate\_Q2Q', click\_Q'2D, click\_D2Q', generate\_Q'2w \rangle$ (variant of **SQ2** where similar query set is enriched by 2-step random walks on query-document graph)
SQ6	$\langle translate\_Q2Q', click\_Q'2D, click\_D2Q', click\_Q'2D, click\_D2Q', generate\_Q'2w \rangle$ (variant of **SQ5** where 4-step random walks are used)
RD1	$\langle similar\_Q2Q', click\_Q'2D, generate\_D2w \rangle$ (w is generated from pseudo-relevant documents D clicked for similar queries Q' of Q)
RD2	$\langle translate\_Q2Q', click\_Q'2D, generate\_D2w \rangle$ (variant of **RD1** where query similarity is computed via translation model)
RD3	$\langle similar\_Q2Q', click\_Q'2D, translate\_D2w \rangle$ (variant of **RD1** where w is generated from D using translation model)
RD4	$\langle similar\_Q2Q', click\_Q'2D, click\_D2Q', click\_Q'2D, generate\_D2w \rangle$ (variant of **RD1** where set of D is enriched by 2-step random walks on query-document graph)
RD5	$\langle similar\_Q2Q', click\_Q'2D, click\_D2Q', click\_Q'2D, click\_D2Q', click\_Q'2D, generate\_D2w \rangle$ (variant of **RD1** where 4-step random walks are used)
RD6	$\langle translate\_Q2Q', click\_Q'2D, click\_D2Q', click\_Q'2D, generate\_D2w \rangle$ (variant of **RD2** where set of D is enriched by 2-step random walks on query-document graph)
RD7	$\langle translate\_Q2Q', click\_Q'2D, click\_D2Q', click\_Q'2D, click\_D2Q', click\_Q'2D, generate\_D2w \rangle$ (variant of **RD6** where 4-step random walks are used)
RD8	$\langle click\_Q2D, generate\_D2w \rangle$ (w is generated from relevant documents D clicked for query Q)
RD9	$\langle click\_Q2D, click\_D2Q, click\_Q2D, generate\_D2w \rangle$ (variant of **RD8** where the set of D is enriched by 2-step random walks on query-document graph)
RD10	$\langle click\_Q2D, click\_D2Q, click\_Q2D, click\_D2Q, click\_Q2D, generate\_D2w \rangle$ (variant of **RD9** where 4-step random walks are used)

Table 2: Some examples of path types, each used as a feature in the PCRW model for QE.

3.2 Feature as Path Type

Given a graph, any path type π that starts with the input query node Q and ends with a word node w defines a real-value feature, which can be viewed as a QE model (or QE feature). The feature value is the probability of picking w as an expansion term $P(w|Q,\pi)$ by PCRWs of type π. In what follows we illustrate the capability of the PCRW model using examples in Table 2. We focus our discussion on three categories of QE features: (1) **TM** features, which perform QE using translation models (i.e., the corresponding path types are specified by IDs from **TM1** to **TM5** in Table 2), (2) **SQ** features, which perform QE using similar queries (i.e., **SQ1** to **SQ6**), and (3) **RD** features, which perform QE using (pseudo-)relevant documents (i.e., **RD1** to **RD10**).

Many log-based QE methods use clickthrough-based translation models where term correlations are pre-computed using query-document pairs extracted from clickthrough data [14, 19, 22]. Compared to the methods that are based on thesauri either compiled manually [38] or derived from document collections [28], such log-based methods are superior in that the translation models explicitly capture the correlation between query terms and document terms. One example is the word translation model described in [19], which can be encoded by the path type **TM1**, $\langle translation\_Q2w \rangle$. In case there is not (enough) clickthrough data for model training, Lafferty and Zhai [31] present a method using Markov chains, where the translation probability between two words is computed by random walks on a document-word graph. The method can be encoded by the path types of **TM2** and **TM3** in Table 2.

Rare queries present a big challenge for Web search [45]. The expansion of a rare query Q is often performed by adding terms from common queries Q' which are similar to Q [45]. The PCRW model achieves this by a random walk that instantiates the path type **SQ1**, $\langle similar\_Q2Q', generate\_Q'2w \rangle$. [6, 21, 35] show that (more) similar queries can be retrieved by performing random walks on a query-document click graph. Thus, rare query expansion could be improved using a larger set of similar queries identified by repeatedly applying random walks following the edges with types $click\_Q2D$ and $click\_D2Q$. **SQ3** and **SQ4** in Table 2 are two examples of such improved models.

A set of relevant documents D of an input query Q that is seen in the search logs can be formed by collecting all the documents that have clicks for that query. Thus, the relevance feedback QE method can be represented as e.g., **RD8**,

$$\langle click\_Q2D, generate\_D2w \rangle.$$

If the input query is a rare query, we can form the set of pseudo-relevant documents through its similar queries Q' that are in the search logs, e.g., **RD1**,

$$\langle similar\_Q2Q', click\_Q'2D, generate\_D2w \rangle.$$

To conquer the data sparseness problem, more pseudo-relevant documents can be retrieved by performing random walks on a query-document click graph, such as **RD4** and **RD5** in Table 2.

Following previous work [12, 21, 31], in our experiments the random walks are implemented as matrix multiplication. As an example, we consider the task of retrieving similar queries by repeatedly applying random walks following $click\_Q2D$ and $click\_D2Q$. Let N be the number of query nodes in G and M be the number of document nodes. Let $\boldsymbol{A}$ be the $N \times M$ matrix with entries $\boldsymbol{A}_{Q,D} = P(D|Q)$, called query-document *transition matrix*, where the probability is calculated from clicks as in #3 in Table 1. Also, let $\boldsymbol{B}$ be the $M \times N$ matrix with entries $\boldsymbol{B}_{D,Q} = P(Q|D)$, where the probability is calculated from clicks as in #4 in Table 1. $\boldsymbol{A}$ and $\boldsymbol{B}$ are called *transition matrices*. It is easy to see that using $\boldsymbol{C} = \boldsymbol{AB}$ we can compute the probability of walking from an initial query Q_0 to any other query Q in $2k$ steps, and the corresponding probability, which is used to measure query-to-query similarity, is given by $P(Q|Q_0) = \boldsymbol{C}^k_{Q_0,Q}$. Because the matrices $\boldsymbol{A}$ and $\boldsymbol{B}$ are sparse, the matrix product $\boldsymbol{C} = \boldsymbol{AB}$ can be computed efficiently. As k increases, $\boldsymbol{C}^k$ quickly becomes dense and the powers cannot be computed efficiently. However, as k increases, the search intent shifts from the initial query, as the probability quickly spreads out over all queries. Thus, in our experiments we limit k to 1 and 2.

3.3 QE as Path Ranking

For QE, we rewrite the PCRW model of Equation (1) as

$$P(w|Q) = \sum_{\pi \in B} \lambda_\pi P(w|Q, \pi), \tag{3}$$

which is weighted linear combination of path features π in B. Thus, the PCRW model performs QE by ranking a set of combined paths, each for one pair of Q and w (i.e., a candidate expansion term). This section presents the way B is constructed and the next two sections present the way parameters λ_π are estimated.

Given a graph, the total number of path types $|B|$ grows exponentially with the increase of path length. To make the computation feasible, in our experiments we set the maximum length to 7, and only consider a small set of relations that are highly selective, as shown in Table 1. Given a path type π, due to the large number of nodes in G, even with a length limit, the total number of paths that instantiate π could be extremely large. For example, since a word could translate to any other word based on a smoothed translation model, any node pair (Q', Q) would have a non-zero-score relation $translate\_Q2Q'$ (#2 in Table 1), thus making the transition matrix extremely dense. For efficiency, we keep the (multiplication of) transition matrices sparse by retaining only top-1000 (partial) paths after each step of random walk.

3.4 Training Data Generation

The training data used for the estimation of parameters λ_π in Equation (3) is denoted as $\{(\mathbf{x}_i, y_i)\}$, where $\mathbf{x}_i$ is a vector of all the path features for the pair (Q_i, w_i). That is, the *j*-th component of $\mathbf{x}_i$ is $P(w_i|Q_i, \pi_j)$, and y_i is a Boolean variable indicating whether w_i is a good expansion term for Q_i. In our experiments D is generated using a method similar to [10], which will be described below.

Assume we have developed a relevance judgment set. The set consists of a set of queries. Each query is associated with a set of documents. Each query-document pair has a relevant label. The effectiveness of a document ranking model $Score(D, Q)$ can be evaluated on the set. We determine whether a word w is a good expansion for a query Q by examining whether expanding Q with w leads to a better document ranking result. Specifically, we use the following ranking model

$$Score(D, Q) = \alpha \log P(w|\theta_D) + \sum_{q \in Q} P(q|\theta_Q) \log P(q|\theta_D) \tag{4}$$

where w is the expansion term under consideration, α is its weight, q is a term in the original query Q, and θ_Q and θ_D are query and document models, respectively. The query model $P(q|\theta_Q)$ is estimated via MLE (maximum likelihood estimation) without smoothing as

$$P(q|\theta_Q) = \frac{tf(q; Q)}{|Q|} \tag{5}$$

where $tf(q; Q)$ is the number of times q occurs in Q, and $|Q|$ is the query length. The document model, e.g., $P(w|\theta_D)$, is estimated via MLE with Dirichlet smoothing as

$$P(w|\theta_D) = \frac{tf(w; D) + \mu P(w|C)}{|D| + \mu} \tag{6}$$

where $tf(w; D)$ is the number of times w occurs in D, $|D|$ is the document length, μ is the Dirichlet prior (set to 2000 in our experiments), and $P(w|C)$ is the probability of w on the collection C, estimated via MLE without smoothing.

Equation (4) can be viewed as a simplified form of QE with a single term. It is used to label whether w is a good expansion term for Q. To simplify the training data generation process, we assume that w acts on the query independently from other expansion terms, and each expansion term is added into Q with equal weight, i.e., $\alpha = 0.01$ or $\alpha = -0.01$.

The training data is generated as follows. For each query Q in the relevance judgment set, a set of candidate expansion terms $\{w_i\}$ is formed by collecting all terms that occur in the documents that are paired with Q but do not occur in Q. Then w_i is labeled as a good expansion term for Q if it improves the effectiveness of ranking document when $\alpha = 0.01$ and hurt the effectiveness when $\alpha = -0.01$. w_i is labeled as bad if it produces an opposite effect or produces similar effect when $\alpha = 0.01$ or $\alpha = -0.01$.

3.5 Parameter Estimation

Given training data $\{(\mathbf{x}_i, y_i)\}$, the model parameters $\boldsymbol{\lambda} = \langle \lambda_\pi \rangle_{\pi \in B}$ can be optimized by maximizing the following objective [32]

$$\mathcal{F}(\boldsymbol{\lambda}) = \sum_{(\mathbf{x},y) \in \{(\mathbf{x}_i, y_i)\}} f(\mathbf{x}, y; \boldsymbol{\lambda}) - \alpha_1 \|\boldsymbol{\lambda}\|_1 - \alpha_2 \|\boldsymbol{\lambda}\|_2^2 \tag{7}$$

where α_1 and α_2 respectively control the strength of the L_1-regularization, which helps with structure selection, and L_2-regularization which helps prevent overfitting. $f(\mathbf{x}, y; \boldsymbol{\lambda})$ is the log-likelihood of the training sample $(\mathbf{x}, y)$, and is defined as

$$f(\mathbf{x}, y; \boldsymbol{\lambda}) = y \log P(\mathbf{x}, \boldsymbol{\lambda}) + (1 - y) \log(1 - P(\mathbf{x}, \boldsymbol{\lambda})) \quad (8)$$

and

$$P(\mathbf{x}, \boldsymbol{\lambda}) \equiv P(y = 1 | \mathbf{x}, \boldsymbol{\lambda}) = \frac{\exp(\boldsymbol{\lambda}^T \mathbf{x})}{1 + \exp(\boldsymbol{\lambda}^T \mathbf{x})} \quad (9)$$

is the model-predicted probability. In our experiments the maximization is performed using the OWL-QN algorithm [2], which is a special version of L-BFGS designed to deal with non-differentiable L_1 norm.

The PCRW-based model of Equation (3) assigns each path type a weight. Such a parameterization is called *one-weight-per-path-type*. An alternative way of parameterizing the model is *one-weight-per-edge-label* [11, 37]. [32] argue that the former is superior in that it takes into account the context in which a relation appears. In our experiments we compare these two parameterization options. Following [32], we use the same objective function and optimization procedure for the parameter estimation of the one-weight-per-edge-label model. Because the model can be seen as the combination of all the PCRWs with each path having its weight set to the product of all the edge weights along the path, we can calculate the gradient of edge weights by first calculating the gradient with respect to the paths, and then applying the chain rule of derivative.

4. EXPERIMENTS

4.1 Dataset and Evaluation Method

In this study the effectiveness of a QE method is evaluated by issuing a set of queries which are expanded using the method to a search engine and then measuring the Web search performance. Better QE methods are supposed to lead to better Web search results using the correspondingly expanded query set.

Due to the characteristics of our QE methods, we cannot conduct experiments on standard test collections such as the TREC data because they do not contain related search logs we need. Therefore, following previous studies of log-based QE [e.g., 14, 19, 40], we used the proprietary datasets that have been developed for building a commercial search engine, and demonstrated the effectiveness of our methods by comparing them against several state-of-the-art QE methods that are originally developed using TREC data [45, 34, 36]. For comparison, we also reproduced on our datasets the results of several previous state-of-the-art log-based QE methods [14, 19, 41].

Our relevance judgment set consists of 12,000 rare queries in English. On average, each query is associated with 33 Web documents (URLs). Each query-document pair has a relevance label. The label is human generated and is on a 5-level relevance scale, 0 to 4, with 4 meaning document D is the most relevant to query Q and 0 meaning D is not relevant to Q.

The relevance judgment set is constructed as follows. First, the rare queries are sampled from one day of search engine logs. Adult, spam, and bot queries are all removed. To reflex a natural distribution of rare queries, we do not try to control the quality of these queries. We found that in comparison with common queries, rare queries are longer and contain more spelling errors. For example, in our rare query set, the average query length is 5 (vs. 3-word for a common query set), and there are around 20% misspelled queries (vs. 12% for a common query set). Second, for each query, we collect Web documents to be judged by issuing the query to several popular search engines (e.g., Google, Bing) and fetching top-10 retrieval results from each. Finally, the query-document pairs are judged by a group of well-trained assessors. In this study all the queries are preprocessed as follows. The text is white-space tokenized and lowercased, numbers are retained, and no stemming/inflection treatment is performed. Since all the document ranking and QE models tested in our experiments contain free parameters that must be estimated empirically on data, we used two-fold cross validation to report results: a set of results on one half of the relevance judgment set is obtained using the parameter settings optimized on the other half, and global retrieval results are combined from those of the two sets.

The search logs used in this study consist of approximately 3 billion query-document pairs sampled from the search logs of a commercial search engine. The Web document collection consists of around 730 million Web pages. In the retrieval experiments we use the index based on the content fields (i.e., body and title text) of each Web page.

The performance of Web search is evaluated by mean *Normalized Discounted Cumulative Gain* (NDCG) [26]. We report NDCG scores at truncation levels 1, 3, and 10. We also performed a significance test, i.e., a t-test with a significance level of 0.05. A significant difference should be read as significant at the 95% level.

4.2 System

We constructed the graph G using the search logs described in Section 4.1. G consists of 730 million document nodes D, 1.8 billion query nodes Q', and 100 million word nodes w. To represent the rare queries in the relevant judgment set, we extend G by generated 12,000 input query nodes Q, each for one rare query. The edges between nodes are labeled using the relations defined in Table 1. Since rare queries are unseen in search logs, the edges between Q and D, as in Figure 1, have a zero score, and all path types that include zero-score edges are inactive, such as **RD8**, **RD9** and **RD10** in Table 2.

QE is performed as follows. Given a trained PCRW model and the node of an input query Q, we perform random walks in G following all possible paths that instantiate the path types defined in B. We then generate a list of candidate expansion term nodes w together with their scores $P(w|Q)$, as computed by Equation (3). We sort all the predictions (Q, w) by the scores in descending order, and pick the top-n words that are not in the input query for QE. In our experiments we set $n = 10 \times |Q|$, where $|Q|$ is the length of the input query. The terms in the expanded query are weighted using the method described in [45]. The weights of the terms in the original query are set to 2, and the weight of a new term is set to $1.0 - 0.9 \times i/n$, where i the rank of the term in the sorted list of top-n candidates.

We use the unigram language model with Dirichlet smoothing to perform document ranking [49]. The model is defined as the second term on the right-hand-side of Equation (4).

4.3 Main Results

Table 3 summarizes the main results using different QE methods, evaluated on the relevance judgment set described in Section 4.1.

#	QE Methods	NDCG@1	NDCG@3	NDCG@10
1	**NoQE**	0.2648	0.2985	0.3905
2	**LCA (PRF)**	0.2742^{α}	0.3107^{α}	0.4075^{α}
3	**RM (PRF)**	0.2689^{α}	0.3077^{α}	0.4068^{α}
4	**LCE**	0.2695^{α}	0.3069^{α}	0.4098^{α}
5	**TC**	$0.2811^{\alpha\beta}$	$0.3198^{\alpha\beta}$	$0.4132^{\alpha\beta}$
6	**SMT**	$0.2803^{\alpha\beta}$	$0.3230^{\alpha\beta\gamma}$	$0.4199^{\alpha\beta\gamma}$
7	**TM**	$0.2837^{\alpha\beta}$	$0.3212^{\alpha\beta}$	$0.4183^{\alpha\beta\gamma}$
8	**PCRW**	$0.2959^{\alpha\beta\gamma}$	$0.3302^{\alpha\beta\gamma}$	$0.4265^{\alpha\beta\gamma}$

Table 3: Document ranking results using different QE methods. The superscripts α, β, and γ indicate statistically significant improvements ($p < 0.05$) over NoQE, LCA, and TC, respectively.

Row 1 in Table 3 (i.e., **NoQE**) is the baseline that uses the raw input queries without expansion. Rows 2 to 6 are the QE methods proposed previously. For fair comparison, the number of expansion terms for a query Q is set to $n = 10 \times |Q|$ for all QE methods.

LCA (Row 2) is local context analysis [45]. **RM** (Row 3) is relevance model [34]. LCA and RM are state-of-the-art PRF methods, developed respectively for the vector space and language modeling IR frameworks. **LCE** (Row 4) is latent concept expansion [36], which is a generalization of RM in that it explicitly models term dependencies for QE. Unfortunately, the generalization does not lead to any significant improvement in our experiments (Row 4 vs. Rows 2 and 3).

TC (Row 5) is the log-based QE method based on our implementation of the term correlation model [14]. We see that both **TC** and PRF methods improve the effectiveness of Web search significantly, and the log-based method outperforms significantly the RPF methods that do not use query logs. The results confirm the conclusion of [14].

SMT (Row 6) is a statistical machine translation (SMT) based QE system. Following Riezler et al. [41], the system is an implementation of a standard phrase-based SMT system with a set of features derived from a translation model and a language model, combined under the log-linear model framework [29]. To apply the system to QE, expansion terms of a query are taken from those terms in the 10-best translations of the query that have not been seen in the original query string. The results show that **SMT** is also effective (Row 6 vs. Row 1), outperforming significantly **TC** in NDCG at 3 and 10 (Row 6 vs. Row 5). This result is more or less consistent with what is reported in Riezler et al. [41], despite the difference in training data we used, (i.e., Riezler et al. used query-snippet pairs while we used query-title pairs).

TM (Row 7) is the QE method using a clickthrough-based translation model [17, 19]. **TM** and **TC** models are trained on the same clickthrough data that consists of 3 billion query-title pairs. The result that **TM** outperforms **TC** confirms the conclusion of [19] that a translation model trained using the EM algorithm [8, 16] is better than a correlation model estimated purely based on frequency counting as in **TC**.

TC, **SMT** and **TM**, considered as state-of-the-art QE methods, have been frequently used for comparison in related studies.

Row 8 is the PCRW-based method, described in Section 3. It outperforms significantly the baseline (Row 1) and the other QE methods we used for comparison (Rows 2 to 6). Since the PCRW model combines a wide variety of features, each encoded by a path type, it is instructive to investigate the QE performance of individual features and the impact of how these features are combined.

ID (path length)	NDCG@1	NDCG@3	NDCG@10
NoQE	0.2648	0.2985	0.3905
PCRW	0.2959	0.3302	0.4265
TM1 (1)	***0.2837***	***0.3212***	***0.4183***
TM2 (3)	0.2714	0.3101	0.3995
TM3 (5)	0.2705	0.3100	0.3989
TM4 (3)	0.2680	0.3050	0.4031
TM5 (5)	0.2688	0.3051	0.4030
SQ1 (2)	0.2768	0.3139	0.4084
SQ2 (2)	0.2793	0.3159	0.4127
SQ3 (4)	***0.2806***	***0.3164***	***0.4109***
SQ4 (6)	0.2793	0.3146	0.4103
SQ5 (4)	0.2796	0.3151	0.4107
SQ6 (6)	0.2778	0.3140	0.4102
RD1 (3)	0.2844	0.3200	0.4133
RD2 (3)	***0.2893***	***0.3242***	***0.4167***
RD3 (3)	0.2871	0.3245	0.4213
RD4 (5)	0.2873	0.3221	0.4163
RD5 (7)	0.2870	0.3234	0.4175
RD6 (5)	0.2841	0.3194	0.4122
RD7 (7)	0.2835	0.3176	0.4119

Table 4: Document ranking results using different QE features, each encoded by a path type whose ID is defined in Table 2. The IDs NoQE, PCRW and TC are defined in Table 3.

4.4 Individual Features

Recall that in Section 3.2 we group path types into three categories: (1) **TM** features, (2) **SQ** features, and (3) **RD** features. They generate expansion terms using different data sources, and thus are expected to be complimentary. Table 4 presents QE results using individual features, where the best feature in each category is in **bold** and *italic*. Comparing the results of individual features with that of the PCRW model reveals that combining features significantly improves the QE performance.

Figures 2 and 3 present respectively two example queries, where different QE features give complimentary expansion terms and the combined achieves the best result. The query "acme baked bread" in Figure 2 is issued to search for the homepage of a bakery company in Berkeley, CA. The expanded query based on clickthrough-based translation model (**TM1** in Table 2) leads to worse document ranking results than that of **NoQE** because the model generates expansion terms from query terms in a word-by-word fashion, e.g., generating "bakery" or "bread" from "baked". But, without knowing that the entire query refers to an entity (i.e., company), it cannot generate expansion terms relating to the properties of the entity (e.g., the location of the company). However, using features based on similar queries (**SQ1**) location names such as "san francisco" and "berkeley" are selected as expansion terms. It is also encouraging to see that its relevant document (www.acmebread.com) is ranked top in its pseudo-relevant document set obtained via similar queries (**RD1**).

The query "waterfall glass in dallax tx" in Figure 3 contain two common terms "waterfall" and "glass". The search intent suggested by the two terms when they occur in the same query is very different from that when only one of them occurs. As expected, the QE method using a word translation model (**TM1**) fails to improve the search performance. Neither do the similar queries retrieved via random walks (**SQ1** and **SQ3**) provide very useful expansion terms since most of the similar queries are simply different permutations of the same set of terms.

(a)	(b)	(c)
recipe 0.03239	company 0.00280	company 0.00280
recipes 0.01685	co 0.00203	markets 0.00199
bake 0.01675	berkeley 0.00203	groceries 0.00143
oven 0.00886	recipes 0.00628	coupons 0.00143
baking 0.00705	sf 0.00203	weekly 0.00143
cooks 0.00611	oven 0.00395	ad 0.00143
company 0.00598	bakery 0.00167	recipes 0.00825
html 0.00543	home 0.00280	pharmacy 0.00143
food 0.00451	recipe 0.00280	bakery 0.00143
set 0.00439	san 0.00280	grocery 0.00167
bakery 0.00432	francisco 0.00280	stores 0.00167
breads 0.00324	fresh 0.00280	homemade 0.00143
rec 0.00317	ferry 0.00203	oven 0.00395
search 0.00293	building 0.00203	baked 0.00729
make 0.00289	garlic 0.00203	yeast 0.00143
ff 0.00272	pudding 0.00280	breads 0.00239
home 0.002168	pita 0.00203	ehow 0.00333
markets 0.0018	mountain 0.00203	grandmothers 0.0017
honeybaked 0.0014	food 0.00167	recipe 0.00283
... ...	... ...	... ...

acme bread; acme bread company; acme bread co; acme bread berkeley; acme recipes; acme bread sf; baked bread recipes; oven baked bread; acme bakery; home baked bread; oven baked bread recipe; acme bread san francisco; oven baked bread recipes; home baked bread recipes;
acme bread company san francisco; acme bread ferry building
... ...

(d)

1. the acme bread company
   http://www.acmebread.com
2. acme markets groceries coupons weekly ad recipes and pharmacy
   http://www.acmemarkets.com
3. bakery acme markets grocery stores
   http://www.acmemarkets.com/departments/bakery.jsp
4. acme bread company
   http://www.ferrybuildingmarketplace.com/acme_bread_company.php
5. homemade oven baked yeast breads
   http://baking.about.com/od/yeastbreads/Yeast_Breads.htm
6. how to make home baked bread ehow com
   http://www.ehow.com/how_4794468_home-baked-bread.html
7. grandmothers oven baked bread recipe best recipes
   http://www.bestrecipes.com.au/recipe/...
8. how to bake bread bread recipes healthy breads
   http://bread-by-yia-yia.com
9. bread baking
   http://breadbaking.about.com
10. bread recipes allrecipes com
   http://allrecipes.com/Recipes/Bread

... ...

(e)

Figure 2: QE results of Q = acme baked bread. (a), (b) and (c) are top expansion terms and their scores $P(w|Q)$ generated using features TM1, SQ1 and RD1, respectively; (d) are top similar queries generated using SQ1; (e) are top pseudo relevant documents generated using RD1. Features are defined in Table 2.

(a)	(b)	(c)
texas 0.05671	lounge 3.993E-05	windsor 7.85E-05
waterfalls 0.01893	house 3.424E-05	texas 6.19E-05
falls 0.01093	club 3.424E-05	apartments 4.69E-05
water 0.00592	uptown 2.802E-05	house 4.69E-05
city 0.00401	auto 2.031E-05	communities 4.69E-05
home 0.00362	stained 2.031E-05	real 2.39E-05
dfw 0.00267	bar 2.031E-05	estate 2.39E-05
fall 0.00258	blowing 2.031E-05	travel 2.39E-05
worth 0.00255	door 2.031E-05	hotels 2.10E-05
center 0.00238	oregon 2.031E-05	profile 2.03E-05
fort 0.00220	coldplay 2.031E-05	population 2.03E-05
company 0.00191	hiking 2.031E-05	maps 2.03E-05
wikipedia 0.00187	flat 2.031E-05	averages 2.03E-05
wiki 0.00186	tile 2.031E-05	homes 2.03E-05
park 0.00186	nightclub 2.031E-05	statistics 2.03E-05
houston 0.00185	... ...	relocation 2.03E-05
county 0.00168		hospitals 2.03E-05
glasses 0.00158		restaurants 1.99E-05
north 0.00157		events 1.85E-05
... ...		... ...

glass dallas; dallas glass; glass dallas tx; waterfall glass; glass waterfall; dallas auto glass; glass house dallas; stained glass dallas; glass dallas club; glass club dallas; glass lounge dallas tx; the glass house dallas; glass bar dallas; dallas glass blowing; glass dallas uptown; dallas glass and door;
dallas glass oregon; coldplay dallas tx; hiking dallas tx; glass lounge dallas
... ...

(d)

1. welcome to the city of dallas texas city web portal
   http://dallascityhall.com/
2. dallas wikipedia the free encyclopedia
   http://en.wikipedia.org/wiki/Dallas
3. dallas hotels restaurants events and things to do dallas cvb
   http://www.visitdallas.com
4. dallas tx apartments glass house by windsor windsor communities
   http://www.windsorcommunities.com/apartments/dallas/glasshouse
5. dallas texas tx profile population maps real estate ...
   http://www.city-data.com/city/Dallas-Texas.html
6. dallas city guide hotels restaurants nightlife attractions real estate
   http://www.dallas.com
7. glass lounge uptown dallas tx
   http://www.yelp.com/biz/glass-lounge-dallas
8. glass uptown uptown dallas tx
   http://www.yelp.com/biz/glass-uptown-dallas
9. the dallas glass club dallas texas dgc home
   http://dallasglassclub.org/
10. glass uptown lounge website coming soon
   http://glassuptown.com/

... ...

(e)

Figure 3: QE results of Q = waterfall glass in dallas tx. (a), (b) and (c) are top expansion terms their scores $P(w|Q)$ generated using features TM1, SQ1 and RD1, respectively; (d) are top similar queries generated using SQ1; (e) are top pseudo relevant documents generated using RD1. Features are defined in Table 2.

Fortunately, as shown in Figure 3 (e), these permuted queries lead to a set of clicked documents (**RD1**) from which effective expansion terms are generated.

Results in Table 4 reveal the effectiveness of individual features, some of which have not been studied previously. **TM1**, which is also reported in Row 7 in Table 1, is the best among all **TM** features. Although the translation probabilities in **TM2**, **TM3**, **TM4** and **TM5** are estimated via random walks, rather than on query-document pairs as in **TM1**, these models still improve the baseline **NoQE**, although not as effective as **TM1**, thus providing an alternative way of obtaining translation models without training data.

Results of the **SQ** features suggest that (1) it is more effective to retrieve *semantically* similar queries for QE, and this can be achieved either by applying a translation model (**SQ2** vs. **SQ1**) or by applying random walks on query-document graph (**SQ3** vs. **SQ1**); and (2) taking a 2-step random walk is useful but taking longer steps is not (e.g., **SQ3** vs. **SQ1** and **SQ4**).

Parameterization	NDCG@1	NDCG@3	NDCG@10
untrained (λ_π*=1)*	0.2910	0.3263	0.4233
one-weight-per-edge-label	0.2924	0.3277	0.4249
one-weight-per-path-type	0.2959	0.3302	0.4265

Table 5: Comparison with different parameterization methods.

Results of the **RD** features show that (1) it is more effective to use a translation model to retrieve similar queries (**RD2** vs. **RD1**) or to generate expansion terms from pseudo-relevant documents (**RD3** vs. **RD1**); and (2) random walks cannot significantly improve the quality of the pseudo-relevant document set (e.g., **RD6** and **RD7** vs. **RD2**).

4.5 Impact of Parameter Estimation

Table 5 compares the PCRW model parameterized using one-weight-per-path-type with two baselines. We see that (1) the trained models outperform the untrained model; and (2) one-weight-per-path-type is slightly better than one-weight-per-edge-label, but the difference is not statistically significant, except for NDCG score at 1, indicating that capturing context information between relations in a path is useful, although the impact on QE is marginal.

5. RELATED WORK

Our work is a significant extension to the random walk models described in [11] in two aspects. First, while we use a PCRW model, [11] uses a more traditional Markov chain model, similar to [23, 37, 43], where random walks are not *constrained* by path types and their models are parameterized as one-weight-per-edge-label. As discussed in Section 3.5, paths in G provide more useful features for QE than edges since the former captures more context information. Although it is difficult for us to perform a direct comparison between our model and the model in [11] due to the dramatically different data sources that these two models are based on respectively, the result in Table 5 suggests that given the same search logs as thesauri, our model is likely to perform better. Second, while G in our model is constructed on search logs, G in [11] is constructed on thesauri that are compiled manually or derived from document collections. Our design decision of using search logs rather than pre-complied thesauri is motivated by those studies that show that log-based QE methods [e.g., 15, 19, 22, 42] often lead to a superior performance to the QE methods that use human-compiled thesauri [e.g., 24, 38] largely due to the fact that models trained on search logs explicitly capture the correlation between query terms and document terms, thus bridging the lexical gap between them more effectively. On the other hand, Web scale thesauri such as ConceptNet and Wikipedia have recently been explored for QE, leading to some promising results [30, 47]. The graph representation and the PCRW-based inference we proposed provide a flexible framework to incorporate such new thesauri. We leave it to future work.

In addition to QE, random walk models have also been applied on other Web search applications, such image search [12], query suggestion [6, 35], query translation for cross-lingual IR [9], click model smoothing [21], and email search [37]. Our method bears some resemblance to all these previous works.

Previous studies on QE can be roughly grouped into two categories: the automatic relevance feedback methods [10, 11, 34, 36, 40, 45, 48] developed mainly on TREC data and the log-based methods [14, 15, 19, 22, 41, 42] where the correlation between query terms and document terms is learned from clickthrough data. Most of the features used in our PCRW model, as in Table 2, are inspired by these QE models.

Search logs have been proved to be a valuable data source for many Web search tasks. In addition to QE, they have also been used for document ranking [1, 20, 27], query processing and spelling correction [18, 25], user query clustering [3, 4, 44], etc.

6. CONCLUSIONS

This paper exploits search logs for QE for Web search ranking. We present a QE method based on path-constrained random walks, where the search logs are represented as a labeled, directed graph, and the probability of selecting an expansion term for an input query is computed by a learned combination of constrained random walks on the graph. We show that our method is generic and flexible in that it not only represents most of popular QE models as features, but also allows us to easily devise new features, which can potentially use much richer information than previous QE models, by defining path types with a rich set of walk behaviors. The PCRW model also provides a principled mathematical framework in which different QE models, i.e., defined as path types or features, can be incorporated in a unified way, thus making it less susceptible to the sparseness issue of clickthrough data and ambiguous search intent of user queries. The evaluation on a real-world data set shows that the PCRW-based method significantly outperforms other state-of-the-art QE methods.

One area in future work is to adapt the PCRW-based method for Web document ranking directly. For example, we might model the relevance score of a query Q and a document D as the probability, computed by a learned combination of path-constrained random walks from Q to D, where different document ranking models can be incorporated as path types. In addition to clickthrough data, we need to incorporate other data source to construct G, such as link graphs and the category structure of Web documents.

7. REFERENCES

[1] Agichtein, E., Brill, E., and Dumais, S. 2006. Improving web search ranking by incorporating user behavior information. In *SIGIR*, pp. 19-26.

[2] Andrew, G., and Gao, J. 2007. Scalable training of L1-regularized log-linear models. In *ICML*.

[3] Baeza-Yates, R. 2007. Graphs from search engine queries. In Jan van Leeuwen et al. (Eds.): *SOFSEN 2007*, LNCS 4362, pp. 1-8.

[4] Baeza-Yates, R., and Tiberi, A. 2007. Extracting semantic relations from query logs. In *SIGKDD,* pp. 76-85.

[5] Berger, A., and Lafferty, J. 1999. Information retrieval as statistical translation. In *SIGIR*, pp. 222-229.

[6] Boldi, P., Bonchi, F., Castillo, C., Donato, D., and Vigna, S. 2009. Query suggestions using query-flow graphs. In *WSDM'09.*

[7] Broder, A., Ciccolo, P., Gabrilovich, E., Josifovski, V., Metzler, D., Riedel, L., and Yuan, J. 2009. Online expansion of rare queries for sponsored search. In *WWW 2009.*

[8] Brown, P. F., Della Pietra, S. A., Della Pietra, V. J., and Mercer, R. L. 1993. The mathematics of statistical machine translation: parameter estimation. *Computational Linguistics*, 19(2): 263-311.

[9] Cao, G., Gao, J., Nie, J-Y., and Bai, J. 2007. Extending query translation to cross-language query expansion with Markov chain models. In *CIKM'07*.

[10] Cao, G., Nie, J-Y., Gao, J., and Robertson, S. 2008. Selecting good expansion terms for pseudo-relevance feedback. In *SIGIR*, pp. 289-305.

[11] Collins-Thompson, K., and Callan, J. 2005. Query expansion using random walk models. In *CIKM'05*.

[12] Craswell, N., and Szummer, M. 2007. Random walks on the click graph. In *SIGIR'07*, pp. 239-246.

[13] Craswell, N. Zoeter, O., Taylor, M. J., and Ramsey, B. 2008. An experimental comparison of click position-bias models. In WSDM 2008, pp. 87-94.

[14] Cui, H., Wen, J-R., Nie, J-Y. and Ma, W-Y. 2002. Probabilistic query expansion using query logs. In *WWW*, pp. 325-332.

[15] Cui, H., Wen, J-R., Nie, J-Y. and Ma, W-Y. 2003. Query expansion by mining user log. *IEEE Trans on Knowledge and Data Engineering*. Vol. 15, No. 4. pp. 1-11.

[16] Dempster, A., Laird, N., and Rubin, D. 1977. Maximum likelihood from incomplete data via the EM algorithm. *Journal of the Royal Statistical Society*, 39: 1-38.

[17] Gao, J., He, X., and Nie, J-Y. 2010. Clickthrough-based translation models for web search: from word models to phrase models. In *CIKM*, pp. 1139-1148.

[18] Gao, J., Li, X., Micol, D., Quirk, C., and Sun, X. 2010. A large scale ranker-based system for query spelling correction. In *COLING*, pp. 358-366.

[19] Gao, J., Nie, J-Y. 2012. Towards concept-based translation models using search logs for query expansion. In *CIKM*.

[20] Gao, J., Toutanova, K., and Yih, W-T. 2011. Clickthrough-based latent semantic models for web search. In *SIGIR*, pp. 675-684.

[21] Gao, J., Yuan, W., Li, X., Deng, K., and Nie, J-Y. 2009. Smoothing clickthrough data for web search ranking. In *SIGIR*, pp. 355-362.

[22] Gao, J., Xie, S., He, X., and Ali, A. 2012. Learning lexicon models from search logs for query expansion. In *EMNLP*.

[23] Haveliwala, T. H. 2002. Topic-sensitive pagerank. In *WWW*, pp. 517-526.

[24] Hovy, E., Gerber, L., Hermjakob, U. Junk, M., and Lin, C-Y. 2000. Question answering in webclopedia. In *TREC 9*.

[25] Huang, J., Gao, J., Miao, J., Li, X., Wang, K., and Behr, F. 2010. Exploring web scale language models for search query processing. In *WWW*, pp. 451-460.

[26] Jarvelin, K. and Kekalainen, J. 2000. IR evaluation methods for retrieving highly relevant documents. In *SIGIR*, pp. 41-48

[27] Joachims, T. 2002. Optimizing search engines using click-through data. In *SIGKDD*, pp. 133-142.

[28] Jing, Y., and Croft., B. 1994. An association thesaurus for information retrieval. In *RIAO*, pp. 146-160.

[29] Koehn, P., Och, F., and Marcu, D. 2003. Statistical phrase-based translation. In *HLT/NAACL*, pp. 127-133.

[30] Kotov, A., and Zhai, C. 2012. Tapping into knowledge base for concept feedback: leveraging conceptnet to improve search results for difficult queries. In *WSDM*.

[31] Lafferty, J., and Zhai, C. 2001. Document language models, query models, and risk minimization for information retrieval. In *SIGIR'01*, pp. 111-119.

[32] Lao, N., and Cohen, W. W. 2010. Relational retrieval using a combination of path-constrained random walks. *Machine Learning*, 81:53-67.

[33] Lao, N., Subramanya, A., Pereira, F., Cohen, W. W. 2012. Reading the web with learned syntactic-semantic inference rules. In *EMNLP-CoNLL-2012*, pp. 1017-1026.

[34] Lavrenko, V., and Croft, B. 2001. Relevance-based language models. In *SIGIR*, pp. 120-128.

[35] Mei, Q., Zhou, D., and Church, K. 2008. Query suggestion using hitting time. In *CIKM'08*.

[36] Metzler, D., and Croft, B. 2007. Latent concept expansion using markov random fields. In *SIGIR'07*, pp. 311-318.

[37] Minkov, E., Cohen, W. W., and Ng, A. Y. 2006. Contextual search and name disambiguation in email using graphs. In *SIGIR'06*.

[38] Prager, J., Chu-Carroll, J., and Czuba, K. 2001. Use of Wordnet hypernyms for answering what is questions. In *TREC 10*.

[39] Robertson, S., and Zaragoza, H. 2009. The probabilistic relevance framework: BM25 and beyond. *Foundations and Trends in Information Retrieval*, Vol. 3, No. 4 (2009) 333-389.

[40] Rocchio, J. 1971. Relevance feedback in information retrieval. In *The SMART retrieval system: experiments in automatic document processing*, pp. 313-323, Prentice-Hall Inc.

[41] Riezler, S., Liu, Y. and Vasserman, A. 2008. Translating queries into snippets for improving query expansion. In *COLING 2008*. 737-744.

[42] Riezler, S., and Liu, Y. 2010. Query rewriting using monolingual statistical machine translation. *Computational Linguistics*, 36(3): 569-582.

[43] Toutanova, K., Manning, C. D., and Ng, A. Y. 2004. Learning random walk models for inducing word dependency distributions. In *ICML*.

[44] Wen, J., Nie, J-Y., and Zhang, H. 2002. Query clustering using user logs. *ACM TOIS*, 20(1): 59-81.

[45] Xu, J., and Croft, B. 1996. Query expansion using local and global document analysis. In *SIGIR*.

[46] Xu, J., and Xu, G. 2011. Learning similarity function for rare queries. In *WSDM'11*.

[47] Xu, Y. Jones, G.J.F., and Wang, B. 2009. Query dependent pseudo-relevance feedback based on Wikipedia. In *SIGIR*.

[48] Zhai, C., and Lafferty, J. 2001a. Model-based feedback in the kl-divergence retrieval model. In *CIKM*, pp. 403-410.

[49] Zhai, C., and Lafferty, J. 2001b. A study of smoothing methods for language models applied to ad hoc information retrieval. In *SIGIR*, pp. 334-342.

Efficient Query Construction for Large Scale Data

Elena Demidova
L3S Research Center
Leibniz Universität Hannover
Hannover, Germany
demidova@L3S.de

Xuan Zhou*
DEKE Lab, MOE
Renmin University of China
Beijing, China
zhou.xuan@outlook.com

Wolfgang Nejdl
L3S Research Center
Leibniz Universität Hannover
Hannover, Germany
nejdl@L3S.de

ABSTRACT

In recent years, a number of open databases have emerged on the Web, providing Web users with platforms to collaboratively create structured information. As these databases are intended to accommodate heterogeneous information and knowledge, they usually comprise a very large schema and billions of instances. Browsing and searching data on such a scale is not an easy task for a Web user. In this context, interactive query construction offers an intuitive interface for novice users to retrieve information from databases neither requiring any knowledge of structured query languages, nor any prior knowledge of the database schema. However, the existing mechanisms do not scale well on large scale datasets. This paper presents a set of techniques to boost the scalability of interactive query construction, from the perspective of both, user interaction cost and performance. We connect an abstract ontology layer to the database schema to shorten the process of user-computer interaction. We also introduce a search mechanism to enable efficient exploration of query interpretation spaces over large scale data. Extensive experiments show that our approach scales well on Freebase - an open database containing more than 7,000 relational tables in more than 100 domains.

Categories and Subject Descriptors

H.3.3 [**Information Search and Retrieval**]: Query formulation

Keywords

Query construction, Freebase, Ontology

1. INTRODUCTION

With the prevalence of Web 2.0, a number of open databases have emerged on the Web, attempting to provide a platform for users to collaboratively create and maintain structured information. A typical example is Freebase[1], which currently contains more than 22 million entities and 350 million facts from more than 100 domains, organized in 7,500 tables. Other examples include DBpedia[2], WikiTaxonomy[3], and Probase[4], whose sizes have already reached the magnitude of several GBs. Databases of this kind are intended to accommodate heterogeneous information and knowledge. It is natural that each of these datasets contains a very large schema and a large volume of data. For a typical Web user, information seeking over such large and heterogeneous database is a challenge.

The technology of interactive query construction [7] enables novice users to interactively create structured queries and retrieve desired information from a database without knowing any structured query language or studying the database schema a-priori. The existing approaches of interactive query construction work well for small or medium sized databases of a particular domain, such as IMDB[5] and Lyrics [16], which contain around 20 tables [7]. However, we found that existing approaches fail to scale on a heterogeneous Freebase database composed of several thousand tables. To this extent, the FreeQ system presented in this paper enables us to scale interactive query construction over a very large database.

The interface of interactive query construction combines the usability of keyword queries with the expressiveness of structured queries. It enables a user to start with a keyword query and refine it into a structured query by interacting with the system. Through interaction, the user can provide additional information to disambiguate the semantics of the keyword query, and finally determine the structured expression reflecting her informational need. The resulting structured queries offer enhanced expressiveness to retrieve results with complex semantics, including collective results, e.g. *"All films starring Tom Hanks"*, or results involving more than one entity, e.g. *"The role of Tom Hanks in the film The Terminal"*. In this way, interactive query construction opens the world of structured queries to unskilled users, who are not familiar with structured query languages, without actually requiring them to learn such query language. This interface is also a useful tool for expert users, who want to explore data organized in an unfamiliar and complex database schema.

Interactive query construction is especially useful for seeking information on large scale, where keyword queries become increasingly ambiguous. For instance, in Freebase, the phrase *"Jack London"* occurs in more than sixty attributes and can be matched with the entities of types *author, film, olympic athlete, tourist attraction, astronomical discovery*, and others. As a result, there can be a large number of plausible answers to the keyword query *"Jack London"*, such as author Jack London, asteroid "2625 Jack London", a British

*Corresponding author: zhou.xuan@outlook.com

[1] www.freebase.com

[2] www.dbpedia.org

[3] http://www.h-its.org/english/research/nlp/index.php

[4] http://research.microsoft.com/en-us/projects/probase

[5] www.imdb.com

SIGIR'13, July 28–August 1, 2013, Dublin, Ireland.

ACM 978-1-4503-2034-4/13/07 ... $15.00.

athlete John Edward "Jack" London, and the Jack London District in Oakland, California. To find the desired information through a keyword search interface, a user may have to scan through a long list of search results. In contrast, an interactive query construction interface suggests interaction options, such as *"Jack London is a book author"* for the user to clarify her intent. By clicking the correct options, the user helps the system to form structured queries to precisely retrieve the desired information.

There are two main reasons why existing approaches fail to scale on heterogeneous databases composed of several thousand tables. First, when the database schema is very big, the interaction options generated by the existing schemes are usually not informative enough. As a result, a user may have to go through a laborious interaction procedure to construct the desired query. For example, as the phrase *"Jack London"* appears in more than sixty Freebase attributes, this phrase can be interpreted into more than sixty meanings. Using the existing interaction schemes, in the worst case, the user may have to respond to each of the sixty interpretations to finally clarify her intent. For a more complex keyword query, the procedure of interaction can become unacceptably long. Second, the interpretation space of a keyword query on a very large database is usually too big to be materialized completely. The existing approaches to database keyword search usually rely on an entirely materialized interpretation space to retrieve top-k structured queries and interaction options. These approaches become infeasible in face of large scale databases. Thus we need new methods to explore the interpretation spaces of keyword queries.

The FreeQ system presented in this paper enables scalable interactive query construction over a very large database. First, we propose to connect a hierarchical ontology to the database schema. Using the general concepts in the ontology, we can form more informative interaction options that enable more efficient query construction. The hierarchical ontology can be a manually constructed one, such as the domain set of Freebase. It can also be a generic external ontology, such as YAGO [21]. We conducted both theoretical and experimental studies to evaluate how a hierarchical ontology can speedup interactive query construction. Second, to explore the interpretation space of keyword queries, we design a scheme that is able to efficiently generate top-k structured queries and the optimal interaction options without the complete knowledge of the search space. Finally, we conducted extensive experiments on Freebase demonstrating the effectiveness and the efficiency of our approach.

In summary, we have made the following contributions: (i) A new type of interaction options based on ontologies to enable scalable interactive query construction, and a theoretical justification about the effectiveness of these options; (ii) A scheme to enable efficient generation of top-k structured queries and interaction options, without the complete knowledge of the query interpretation space; (iii) An experimental study on Freebase to verify the effectiveness and efficiency of the proposed approach; (iv) To the best of our knowledge, this is the first attempt to enable effective keyword-based query construction on such a large scale database as Freebase, considering that most existing work on database keyword search uses only test sets of small schemas, such as DBLP, IMDB, etc.

2. PROBLEM DEFINITION

A user interface for interactive query construction is presented in Figure 1. This interface is composed of four parts: (1) an input field for keyword queries, (2) a query construction panel for presenting interaction options, (3) a query window for presenting structured queries, and (4) a result window for query results. Suppose a user, whose name is Alice, issues a keyword query to the

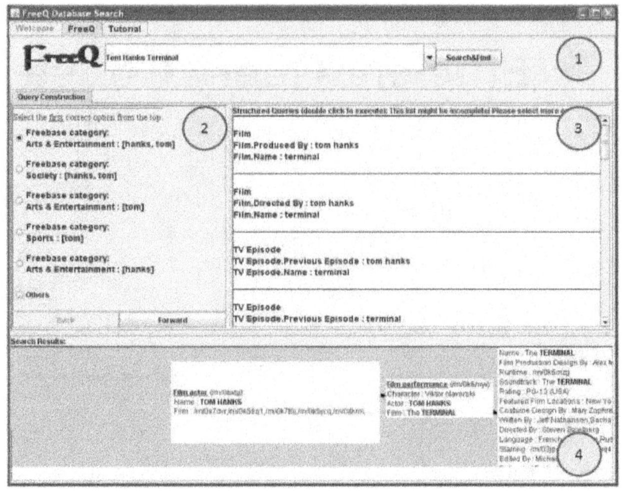

Figure 1: FreeQ GUI. Its components include: (1) an input field for keyword queries, (2) a query construction panel, (3) top-k structured queries, and (4) query results.

system. The system first tries to guess Alice's intent and generates the top-k most likely structured queries in the query window (3). If one of the top-k structured queries matches Alice's intent, she can click the query to obtain the results (4). If no query in the top-k list makes sense to Alice, she can interact with the query construction panel (2) to construct the desired structured query. Whenever Alice clicks on an interaction option in the query construction panel, the structured queries in the query window (3) are refined, such that only the queries complying with Alice's selection are preserved. Simultaneously, a new set of query construction options is presented in the query construction panel (2). The interaction continues until Alice obtains the desired structured query and results.

In this section, we introduce the basic model for enabling such interface for interactive query construction. We also elaborate on the challenges posed by large scale databases.

2.1 User Interaction Scheme

We start the discussion of the process of interactive query construction with the definition of the key concepts of this process. First of all, we model the schema of a database as a graph.

DEFINITION 2.1. *A* **schema graph** *is a graph $G=(V,E)$, where each vertex $v \in V$ represents a relational table and each edge $e \in E$ represents a foreign key relationship. In the graph, each node v is associated with a set of attributes, denoted by $A(v)$, where the ith attribute is represented by $v.a_i \in A(v)$.* □

We use the number of vertices to represent the size of a schema graph. Using the structures in a schema graph, we can create structured queries.

DEFINITION 2.2. *Given a schema graph $G=(V,E)$, a* **structured query** *is an edge preserving map $G'=(V',E')$, such that there is a function $L: V' \to V$ which satisfies: for each vertex $v' \in V'$ in the structured query, there is a vertex $L(v') \in V$ in the schema graph such that v' and $L(v')$ represent the same relational table, and for each edge $\{v'_1, v'_2\} \in E'$ in the structured query, there is an edge $\{L(v'_1), L(v'_2)\} \in E$ in the schema graph.*

In addition, each vertex v' in the structured query can be associated with a number of predicates. Each predicate is in the form $v'.a_i$ op c_i, where $v'.a_i$ is an attribute of v', op is a comparison operator, and c_i is a constant. □

For instance, given a film database, a query looking for all the actors who have collaborated with Tom Hanks can be expressed as:

Q_1= {structure:$actor_1 \bowtie acts \bowtie film_1 \bowtie acts \bowtie actor_2$, predicates:$actor_1.name =$ "*Tom Hanks*"}.

It is worth mentioning that each table in the database occurs only once in the schema graph. In contrast, a table can occur multiple times in a structured query.

In the process of interactive query construction, users express their informational needs as keyword queries.

DEFINITION 2.3. *A* **keyword query** *is a bag of terms $K = \{k_1, k_2, ..., k_n\}$, where duplicates are allowed.* □

In Definition 2.3, a term is a normalized class of tokens that is included in the system's dictionary. For token normalization, state-of-the-art Information Retrieval techniques such as case folding and word segmentation can be applied [18].

The main function of FreeQ is to translate a user's keyword query into the intended structured query. We call the structured query resulting from such translation a **query interpretation**. We say that a query interpretation is **complete** if this query interpretation contains all keywords from the initial user query. Otherwise we talk about **partial** query interpretation. We call the set of all complete query interpretations of a keyword query K an **interpretation space** of K.

For instance, the keyword query *"Tom Hanks Film"* seeking the movies starring Tom Hanks can be interpreted to:

Q_2={structure:$actor \bowtie acts \bowtie film$, predicates:$actor.name =$ "*Tom Hanks*"}.

In this interpretation, keywords *"Tom Hanks"* are mapped to the constant of a predicate, and *"Film"* is mapped to a table name. The following query is a partial interpretation of *"Tom Hanks Film"*, where only *"Tom Hanks"* is interpreted:

O_1 ={structure: *actor*, predicates: *actor.name* = "*Tom Hanks*"}.

In the process of query construction we interpret user's keywords and generate query construction options (QCOs) to assess the meaning of the keywords intended by the user. We can do that in two ways: First, we can interpret keywords very specifically as a part of a structured query (as performed in [7]). We refer to these QCOs as **query-based QCOs**. For instance, O_1 can be used as a QCO, which indicates that *"Tom Hanks"* should be interpreted as an actor's name. Second, we can also assess the general meaning of the keywords and interpret them as a generic concept representing a class of structured queries. For example, we can interpret *"Tom Hanks"* as a more generic class person, which is a superclass of actor:

O_2 ={structure: *person*, predicates: *person.name* = "*Tom Hanks*"}.

To enable efficient user interaction over large database schema, in this paper we introduce ontology-based QCOs. In a generic object-relational database, a table can be regarded as an entity type, and an attribute of the table can be regarded as a property. Using a hierarchical ontology, a set of entity types can be abstracted into a superclass, and a set of properties can be abstracted into a super-property. For instance, entity types *painter* and *musician* can be abstracted into *artist*, and their properties *painting* and *music* can be abstracted into *work*. Using these superclasses and super-properties, we can create general QCOs that subsume larger proportions of a query interpretation space than query-based QCOs.

DEFINITION 2.4. *Given a schema graph $G = (V,E)$, we use $sv \vdash v$ to denote that sv is a superclass of $v \in V$ and $se \vdash e$ to denote that se is a super-property of $e \in E$. Superclass and super-properties are partial order relationships.* □

With the concepts of superclass and super-property, we define ontology-based query interpretations and ontology-based QCOs.

DEFINITION 2.5. *Let $K = \{k_1, k_2, ..., k_n\}$ be a keyword query. Let $Q = (V,E)$ be a query interpretation of K. Let Q^o be isomorphic to Q, where the isomorphism function is $f(.)$ (that applies to the predicates too). Q^o is an* **ontology-based interpretation** *of K, iff $f(.)$ satisfies: (1) for all $v \in V$, $f(v) \vdash v$; (2) for all $e \in E$, $f(e) \vdash e$; (3) for all attributes $v.a_i \in A(v)$ in the predicates, $f(v.a_i) \vdash v.a_i$. We say that Q^o is a* **super-interpretation** *of Q.* □

When we use ontology-based interpretations as QCOs, we call them **ontology-based QCOs**. In summary, QCOs generated by our system can be either query-based or ontology-based QCOs.

DEFINITION 2.6. *A* **Query Construction Option** *(QCO) is a mapping from a subset of keyword query $K' \subseteq K$ to either:*

- *a structured query Q (a query-based QCO), or*
- *an ontology-based interpretation of K' (an ontology-based QCO).* □

In the interaction process the user is supposed to select the options that subsume her intended query interpretation.

DEFINITION 2.7. *Given a QCO O and a QCO O', we say that O* **subsumes** *O', if either:*

- *O is a subgraph of O', or*
- *O is a super-interpretation of O'.*

Subsumption relationship is transitive, i.e. if O **subsumes** *O' and O'* **subsumes** *O'', then O* **subsumes** *O''.* □

Certainly, as O_1 is a subgraph of the interpretation Q_2, O_1 subsumes Q_2. O_2 is an ontological interpretation of *"Tom Hanks"*, and it is a super-interpretation of O_1. As subsumption relationship is transitive, both O_2 and O_1 subsume Q_2, which is a complete interpretation of the query *"Tom Hanks Film"*.

With the above concepts, the conceptual process of interactive query construction can be modeled as follows:

0. Given a database whose schema is $G = (V,E)$, a user issues a keyword query $K = \{k_1, k_2, ..., k_n\}$.
1. **Initialization**: Let ζ be an interpretation space of K based on G.
2. **Top-*k* Generation**: The system retrieves the top-k interpretations from ζ, and presents them to the user. If the user finds the intended interpretation in the top-k, the query construction process terminates. Otherwise, the process continues with Step 3.
3. **QCO Generation**: The system generates a QCO O and lets the user decide whether O subsumes the intended query interpretation of K.

4. **Post Interaction**: If the user indicates that O subsumes the intended interpretation of K, then the system removes all the interpretations that cannot be subsumed by O from ζ. Otherwise, the system removes all the interpretations subsumed by O from ζ. Go back to Step 2.

Each iteration of the process requires one round of interaction with the user. As the interaction goes on, the interpretation space ζ keep shrinking. Because ζ is finite, the process guarantees to terminate at a certain point. Nevertheless, we would like the process to be short, so that users can obtain desired information as early as possible. The efficiency of query construction can be measured naturally by the number of iterations of the process. We call this measure interaction cost.

DEFINITION 2.8. *Given a process of interactive query construction, its* **interaction cost** *is the number of iterations it has been executed, which is equivalent to the number of QCOs evaluated by the user.* □

2.2 Challenges

When a database, and especially its schema graph, becomes big, it is difficult for the existing approaches to realize an efficient query construction process. This is due to the following two limitations:

PROBLEM 1. *Inefficient query-based QCOs:*

To minimize the interaction cost, the query construction process needs to shrink the query interpretation space quickly. In other words, the evaluation of each QCO should be able to remove a significant proportion of the interpretation space. Therefore, we desire the proportion of query interpretations subsumed by each QCO to fall in a certain range. This proportion should not be too small, as in this case the denial of a QCO could not reduce the interpretation space effectively. It should not be too big either, as in this case the acceptance of a QCO could not reduce the interpretation space effectively.

When the schema graph is big, a keyword can have a large number of occurrences spread across the database, resulting in a vast number of partial interpretations (query-based QCOs). The proportion of the interpretation space subsumed by each query-based QCO will be very small. As a result, query construction processes using only query-based QCOs, such as [7], cannot be efficient. Apart from query-based QCOs, we need more general QCOs to enable efficient query construction.

PROBLEM 2. *Very large query interpretation space:*

When the schema graph becomes big, it is no longer feasible to materialize the interpretation space of a complex keyword query entirely. On the one hand, with an increasing size of a schema graph, the number of its subgraphs grows very sharply. On the other hand, the occurrences of keywords are more numerous in a larger database. As a result, the number of the possible interpretations of a keyword query grows quickly with an increasing size of the schema.

The existing approaches to interactive query construction [7], [8], as well as the state-of-the-art approaches to schema-based database keyword search [2], [12], [16], [17] rely on an entirely materialized query interpretation space. These approaches can hardly work with a big schema, as it is infeasible to generate all the query interpretations at the query time. Therefore, we need a new mechanism which can enable efficient identification of the most efficient QCOs and the top-k most probable query interpretations, without the knowledge of the complete interpretation space.

Compared with the most recent approach to interactive query construction [7], in this paper we addressed the problems listed above and made the following contributions:

- We propose novel ontology-based QCOs that enable efficient query construction process over large scale data. Using these QCOs we can enable efficient query construction for ambiguous queries that have many different interpretations in a large database.
- We develop procedures and algorithms for incremental materialization of query interpretation spaces over large scale data that enables us to perform efficient query construction without materialization of the complete query interpretation space.

We present our solutions to each of these problems in Sections 3 and 4, respectively.

3. NOVEL ONTOLOGY-BASED QCOS

As pointed out by Problem 1 in Section 2.2, to minimize the interaction cost, the QCOs presented to the user need to shrink the query interpretation space quickly. In a large scale database, each single keyword can have numerous occurrences. As a result, the query-based QCOs utilized by the existing approaches [7] become inefficient in reducing interpretation spaces. In this section, we introduce a novel type of QCOs, called ontology-based QCOs. An ontology-based QCO can subsume a wider proportion of an interpretation space, such that it is usually more efficient than a query-based QCO. Intuitively, if the user provides feedback on an ontology-based QCO, we get an implicit user's feedback on multiple partial interpretations (i.e. query-based QCOs) subsumed by this ontology-based QCO within a single user interaction. Thus a query construction process using ontology-based QCOs requires less steps. In this section, we justify the efficiency of ontology-based QCOs from the perspective of information theory.

3.1 Creation of Ontology-based QCOs

Ontology-based QCOs can be created based on a hierarchical ontology or taxonomy. In order to create ontology-based QCOs, we need an ontology on top of the database schema, which defines superclasses and super-properties. This ontology can be a manually defined one, such as the domain hierarchy of Freebase. Alternatively, we can utilize external ontologies, such as e.g. WordNet [9], and YAGO [21], by mapping the elements of the database schema to the concepts in these ontologies. In this case state-of-the-art schema matching techniques can be used (see [6] for details).

With ontology-based QCOs, we can enable more efficient query construction, especially when confronted with a big database schema. To illustrate a query construction process using ontology-based QCOs, we consider the query *"Emperor Album"*, which intends to retrieve the albums of the artist Emperor from Freebase. To create the ontology-based QCOs, we make use of the domain hierarchy of Freebase. This hierarchy groups together Freebase tables such as *artist*, *album*, and *monarch* in the domains e.g. *music* and *royalty*, and further organizes these domains into the categories such as *Arts & Entertainment* and *Society*.

For this particular query, if we use only query-based QCOs (as performed by [7]), our system requires a user to interact with 74 QCOs to identify the intended interpretation. Using ontology-based QCOs, the user only needs to interact with the 10 QCOs listed in Table 1. The keyword *"album"* is not very ambiguous, as it occurs mostly in the domain of *music*. To disambiguate this keyword, FreeQ does not utilize any ontology-based QCOs. In contrast, the

QCOs (bold ones are ontology-based QCOs)	User's feed-back
Table *artist* (domain *music*): "album"	×
Table *release* (domain *music*): "album"	×
Table *recording contribution* (domain *music*): "album"	×
Table *album* (domain *music*): "album"	✓
Domain *royalty* (Category *Society*): "emperor"	×
Category *Arts & Entertainment*: "emperor"	✓
Domain *fictional universe* (Arts & Ent.): "emperor"	×
Domain *opera* (Arts & Ent.): "emperor"	×
Domain *media common* (Arts & Ent.): "emperor"	×
Query: **album** ⋈ **artist** "emperor"⊂artist.name	✓

Table 1: A Query Construction Example for the Query *"Emperor Album"* using Ontology-based QCOs

keyword *"emperor"* is very ambiguous. *"Emperor"* occurs in 221 attributes of Freebase, which are spread across multiple categories and domains. To disambiguate *"emperor"*, it is much faster if we use ontology-based QCOs. With ontology-based QCOs, we manage to first restrict the meaning of *"emperor"* to the category of *Arts & Entertainment*. Within this category, the exact meaning of *"emperor"* can be identified easily.

In what follows, we analyze how ontology-based QCOs achieve such efficiency.

3.2 A Measure of QCO Efficiency

As depicted in Section 2.2, in each round of interactive query construction, FreeQ needs to select one QCO to present to the user. For a keyword query, there is usually a large number of available QCOs. In principle, FreeQ should always select the most efficient QCO that can minimize the final interaction cost. The efficiency of a QCO can be quantified using information theory.

Let ζ denote the interpretation space of a keyword query K. Then, the uncertainty of K's interpretation can be measured by the entropy $H(\zeta)$, which can be computed as:

$$H(\zeta) = -\sum_{I \in \zeta} P(I) \times log_2 P(I), \quad (1)$$

where $P(I)$ denotes the probability that the interpretation I is the interpretation intended by the user.

The process of query construction is the process of reducing the uncertainty of K's interpretation. After one round of interaction with the user, FreeQ obtains the knowledge of one QCO, say O. Then, the uncertainty is reduced to $H(\zeta|O)$, i.e., the conditional entropy of ζ given O. The difference between $H(\zeta)$ and $H(\zeta|O)$ is known as the expected *information gain* provided by O, denoted by:

$$IG(O) = H(\zeta) - H(\zeta|O). \quad (2)$$

To minimize the interaction cost, we need maximize the information gain of each QCO presented to the user.

Obviously, the knowledge about ζ contains the knowledge of any O. In other words, the information gain provided by O is exactly the entropy of O. Therefore, we have:

$$IG(O) = H(\zeta) - H(\zeta|O) = H(O). \quad (3)$$

In turn, the entropy of O can be calculated as:

$$H(O) = -P(O)log_2 P(O) - P(\neg O)log_2 P(\neg O), \quad (4)$$

where $P(O)$ is the probability that O is accepted by the user. Let $\zeta(O)$ denote the complete set of query interpretations subsumed by O. Then, $P(O)$ can be computed as:

$$P(O) = \sum_{I \in \zeta(O)} P(I). \quad (5)$$

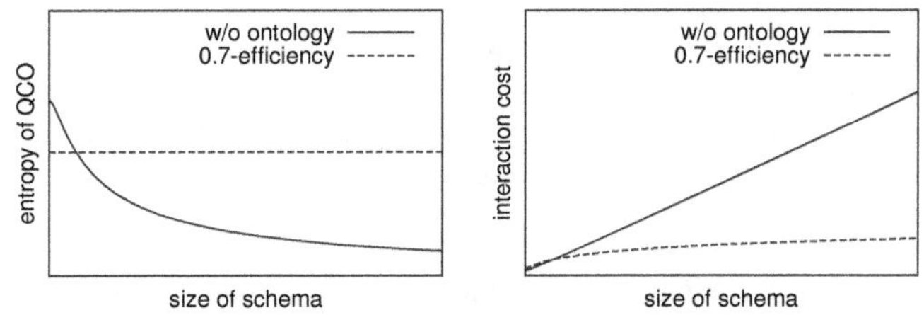

(a) Entropy of QCO (b) Interaction Cost

Figure 2: Efficiency of QCO and Interaction Cost vs. Schema Size

To summarize, the efficiency of a QCO can be measured by its entropy. Therefore, FreeQ is supposed to select the QCO with the highest entropy in each round of user interaction.

3.3 Effects of Ontology-based QCOs

As discussed in Section 3.2, to achieve fast query construction, in each round of interaction, FreeQ is supposed to present the user with an efficient QCO, i.e., a QCO whose entropy is sufficiently high. The question is whether such QCOs would be available at all. To answer this question, we first propose the following measure to quantify the efficiency of an entire query construction process.

DEFINITION 3.1. *During an interactive query construction process, if we can ensure with a high probability that the entropy of each QCO presented to the user is larger than ε ($0 < \varepsilon \leq 1$), we say that the query construction process is* **ε-efficient**.

According to Definition 3.1, to minimize the interaction cost, we should maximize the lower bound (ε) of the efficiency of the QCOs presented to the user. We can show that query-based QCOs, i.e. the QCOs used in the existing approaches [7], cannot guarantee a lower bound. In contrast, if we have an ontology with a sufficient number of concepts of diverse generality, by using ontology-based QCOs, we can achieve ε-efficient query construction with a good lower bound ε.

To simplify our analysis, we assume: (1) the number of possible interpretations of a keyword grows linearly with the size of the schema graph; (2) the number of the possible interpretations of an entire keyword query increases polynomially; (3) all the complete query interpretations are equally probable.

Let the size of the schema be x. According to (1), the number of the query-based QCOs for a keyword can be expressed as $\alpha \times x$, where α is a constant. Then the entropy of a query-based QCO for each keyword will be $H(\frac{1}{\alpha \times x})$, which can be plotted as the solid curve in Figure 2a. We can see that when the database schema grows, the efficiency of each query-based QCO will decrease. This efficiency can drop to a very small value when the database schema is big.

According to (2), the size of an interpretation space can be modeled as $\beta \times x^\gamma$, where β and γ are constants. Based on (3), the most efficient query-based QCO will be an interpretation for a single keyword, whose entropy can be modeled as: $H(\frac{1}{\alpha \times x})$. Therefore, the average interaction cost can be calculated as the entropy of the whole interpretation space divided by the maximum entropy of an QCO, i.e. $log_2(\beta \times x^\gamma)/H(\frac{1}{\alpha \times x})$, which can be plotted as the solid curve in Figure 2b. As we can see, if we use only query-based QCOs, the interaction cost can increase quickly with the size of the database schema.

In contrast, if we can achieve a 0.7-efficient query construction process, that is, the entropy of each QCO be no less than 0.7 (as illustrated by the dashed line in Figure 2a), the growth of the interaction cost can be significantly reduced (as illustrated by the dashed line in Figure 2b). This is achievable, if we utilize ontology-based QCOs.

The concepts in an ontology normally have a variety of generality. There are very specific concepts that can subsume small sets of entity types, such as *artist* and *book*. There are also very general concepts that can subsume larger proportions of entity types, such as *person* and *artifact*. As a result, no matter how big the query interpretation space is, it is always possible to find suitable concepts to form QCOs that can subsume a certain proportion of the interpretation space that would yield big entropies. As a simple analysis, we assume that the probability of a random ontology-based QCO is a random value between 0 and 1. Then, within the set of N ontology-based QCOs, the probability that we can find a QCO whose entropy is larger than ε is:

$$P_{\exists o:H(o)>\varepsilon} = 1 - \left(\frac{H^{-1}(\varepsilon)}{0.5}\right)^N, \tag{6}$$

where $H^{-1}()$ is the inverse function of the binary entropy. In this function, no matter how big ε is, we can always find a big enough N, such that the resulting probability is close to 1. (As N is an exponent in the formula, it normally does not need to be very big.) In other words, as long as there is a rich ontology with a sufficient number of concepts of diverse generality, we can achieve ε-efficiency for interactive query construction.

4. INCREMENTAL MATERIALIZATION OF QUERY INTERPRETATION SPACES

To perform query construction, FreeQ is required to quickly generate the most efficient QCOs and the most probable complete query interpretations. As mentioned in Problem 2, Section 2.2, the existing approaches to interactive query construction and schema-based database keyword search in general require a complete materialization of the query interpretation space [2], [12], [16], [17], [7]. For a large scale dataset, the interpretation space of a keyword query is usually very big, such that it is no longer feasible to materialize this space entirely. To this end, we develop new algorithms that can generate top-k most probable query interpretations and QCOs without the knowledge of the entire interpretation space.

4.1 Query Hierarchy for the QCO Generation

To enable efficient generation of QCOs and query interpretations, we organize the QCOs of a keyword query in a query hierarchy based on their subsumption relationships. Using the query hierarchy, we can materialize the interpretation space of a keyword query step-by-step by following the subsumption relationships of the QCOs. During the progress of the materialization, a lot of QCOs and interpretations can be eliminated based on the information provided by user interaction. Such progressive materialization is much less costly than the generation of an entire interpretation space.

Figure 3 illustrates a query hierarchy, in which the arrows represent the reversed subsumption relationships. The more general the QCOs, the lower their positions in the query hierarchy. The most general QCOs are the single-node QCOs, i.e. the QCOs involving only one entity type such as O_2, O_1, and O_3. These QCOs are located at the bottom of the hierarchy. The top level of the query hierarchy consists of the complete query interpretations (e.g. Q_3, and Q_4), which constitute the interpretation space of a keyword query. The entire query hierarchy looks like an upside-down trapezoid, as there are much more complete query interpretations than single-node QCOs.

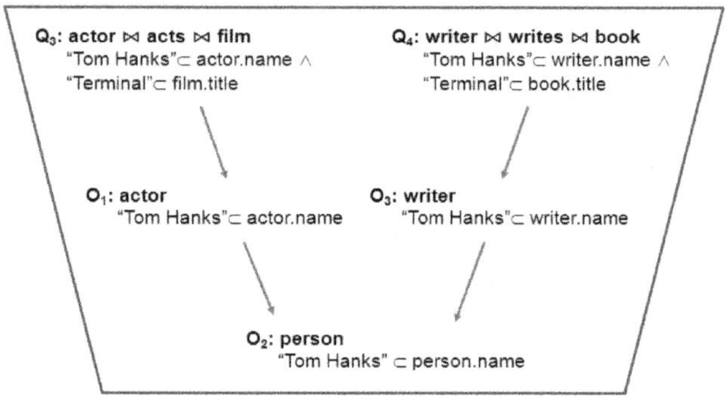

Figure 3: An Example of a Query Hierarchy for the Query "Tom Hanks Terminal" (the arrows represent reversed subsumption relationships, e.g. O_2 subsumes O_1).

As mentioned previously, it is infeasible to instantiate the complete query hierarchy at the query time. Given a big schema, the top levels of the query hierarchy can even be too big to be accommodated in the main memory. Therefore, FreeQ chooses to instantiate the query hierarchy incrementally throughout the process of query construction. The query construction process of FreeQ conforms to the generic process defined in Section 2.1, except that it does not materialize the entire query interpretation space. This process works as follows:

- **1. Initialization:** Upon receiving a keyword query, FreeQ identifies database attributes and schema elements containing keyword occurrences using an inverted index. Based on the keyword occurrences and an ontology, it generates the most general QCOs. As a result, the bottom of the query hierarchy is instantiated. As the bottom of the query hierarchy is small, its instantiation does not incur much cost.

- **2. Top-*k* Generation:** To generate the top-k complete query interpretations, FreeQ performs a **top-*k* depth first traversal (DF-*k*)** of the query hierarchy from the bottom up. All the QCOs and interpretations encountered during the DF-k are instantiated. DF-k enables FreeQ to reach the top of the query hierarchy by instantiating the minimal number of QCOs. The first k complete interpretations encountered by the DF-k are presented to the user as the top-k interpretations.

- **3. QCO Generation:** FreeQ evaluates the QCOs in the instantiated part of the query hierarchy and selects the QCO with the highest entropy. This QCO is presented to the user.

- **4. Post Interaction:** After the user provides feedback on the QCO, FreeQ truncates the query hierarchy according to the user's selection. If the user has denied the QCO, all the QCOs or query interpretations subsumed by the denied QCO are removed from the query hierarchy. If the user has accepted a QCO, only the QCOs and interpretations subsumed by the accepted QCO are preserved. After the truncation, the query hierarchy becomes smaller. If the size of the instantiated part of the hierarchy falls below a threshold, FreeQ perform a **top-*k* breadth first traversal (BF-*k*)** of the query hierarchy (from the bottom up), during which more QCOs are instantiated. The BF-k stops as the size of the instantiated part reaches a predefined upper bound.

As we can see, as the process of the interactive query construction goes on, the instantiated part of the query hierarchy remains stable in size. On the one hand, this part is truncated as the user reveals more information in the interaction process. On the other hand, the instantiated part is continuously expanded by the BF-*k* and DF-*k* to ensure that its size is sufficient to generate efficient QCOs and high quality top-*k* interpretations.

4.2 Algorithms for Efficient Top-*k* Generation

FreeQ obtains top-*k* query interpretations and query construction options by traversing the query hierarchy. To make interactive query construction smooth to the user, it is important to ensure the efficiency of the hierarchy traversal. Although in the related work the basic Breadth First (BF) and Depth First path search (DF) algorithms are typically used to materialize interpretation spaces of keyword queries [2], [12], [11], [16], these algorithms not scale on large database schemas.

The basic BF and DF path search applied in the state-of-the-art database keyword search seek to connect occurrences of the user's keywords in the database schema to materialize query interpretation spaces. For example, to materialize query interpretation space, Discover [12] explores the schema graph in a BF-manner starting from all tables containing occurrences of a keyword $k_i \in K$. The time complexity of this approach can be computed as $T_{k_i} * avg(E_t)^{r*(K-1)}$, where T_{k_i} is the number of tables containing keyword k_i, $avg(E_t)$ is an average fan-out of a table in the schema graph, K is the number of terms in the keyword query, and r is the maximum length of the path within the schema graph explored to connect occurrences of two keywords. The time complexity of this approach increases exponentially with the number of user's keywords and the length of the explored path. This makes materialization of the entire query interpretation space infeasible for longer user queries.

To address these limitations, we propose several important adaptations of the basic BF and DF path search algorithms, to enable efficient generation of the top-*k* query interpretations and QCOs over the large database schemas. We refer to these algorithms as BF-*k* and DF-*k*, respectively. Both BF-*k* and DF-*k* traverse the query hierarchy by following the subsumption relationships. Each traversal step expands a QCO to one of the QCOs it subsumes, e.g. expanding O_2 to O_1, or O_1 to Q_3 in Figure 3. Therefore, it is crucial to make the QCO expansion efficient.

In principle, a QCO can be expanded in two different ways. **The first type of QCO expansion** is to replace an entity type or a property of the QCO with its subclass or sub-property. Such expansion does not add any additional keywords to the QCO. For example, the expansion of O_2 to O_1 in Figure 3 belongs to the first type. This type of expansion requires only the knowledge of the ontology structure. Once we have indexed the ontology, such that its subclasses or sub-properties can be retrieved quickly, this type of expansion will be very efficient. **The second type of QCO expansion** is to find the paths in the schema graph to connect a QCO and an additional keyword occurrence. For instance, to expand O_1 to Q_3 in Figure 3, we need to identify the path "$actor \bowtie acts \bowtie film$" to connect O_1 and the keyword occurrence $film.title : terminal$.

To identify the paths for connecting a QCO with a keyword occurrence efficiently, FreeQ pre-indexes all the paths leading to keyword occurrences in the schema graph starting from every table in the schema graph. The index is constructed at the beginning of the query construction, as the user issues a keyword query. To ensure scalability of the indexing, we restrict the maximal size of the path connecting two keyword nodes in the structured queries that can be constructed by FreeQ and perform bi-directional search. The time complexity of the indexing procedure of FreeQ can be computed as $T * avg(E_t)^{r/2}$, where T is the number of tables in the database schema, $avg(E_t)$ is an average fan-out of a table in the schema graph, and $r/2$ is the half of the maximum length of the explored path. As we can observe, the time complexity of this approach is significantly reduced compared to Discover [12] (discussed above) and does not depend on the size of the keyword query.

To maximize the quality of the top-*k* query interpretations and QCOs generated by FreeQ, we always start the expansion with the QCOs that are most likely to be intended by the user. This applies to both DF-*k* and BF-*k*. As a result, the top-*k* interpretations generated by DF-*k* will be more likely to meet the user's requirements, and the QCOs instantiated by BF-*k* will be more likely to have high entropy. To ensure a short response time of FreeQ, we also enforce a time limit on both BF-*k* and DF-*k*. That is, we stop BF-*k* and DF-*k* once the time limit has been reached, even though the top-*k* interpretations may have not been completely generated, or the number of the instantiated QCOs has not yet reached a predefined upper bound. We demonstrate through the experiments that the resulting hierarchy traversal procedure is effective and efficient.

4.3 Probability Estimation for QCOs

The QCOs in the query hierarchy are all the candidates to be presented to the user. According to Section 3.2, the most efficient QCO is the QCO with the maximum entropy. To identify this QCO, we need to estimate the probabilities of the QCOs. These probabilities cannot be computed by Equation 5, as we do not have the entire query interpretation space materialized. Instead, we consider the frontier of the instantiated part of the query hierarchy. This frontier contains the most specific query-based QCOs (i.e. partial interpretations) that have been materialized so far. We treat all the QCOs in the frontier as samples, such that each QCO in the frontier represents the complete queries that can be derived from this QCO by further expansion of the hierarchy. For each sample represented by s, we compare this sample against each candidate QCO, say o. The comparison can end up with one of the following conclusions: (1) o subsumes s; (2) s conflicts with o (e.g. one keyword is being interpreted into two different meanings); (3) none of the above. If the conclusion is (3), s does not provide any helpful information. With (1) or (2), we can know that either $\zeta(s) \subset \zeta(o)$, or $\zeta(s) \cap \zeta(o) = \varnothing$, respectively. By applying the maximum likelihood principle, we can estimate the probability $P(o)$ using $P(s)$, that is,

$$P(o) = \frac{\sum_{\zeta(s) \subset \zeta(o)} P(s)}{\sum_{\zeta(s) \subset \zeta(o)} P(s) + \sum_{\zeta(s) \cap \zeta(o) = \varnothing} P(s)}, \quad (7)$$

where $P(o)$ and $P(s)$ are the probabilities that o and s are accepted by the user, respectively. With $P(o)$, we can obtain the entropy of o based on Equation 5. Therefore, the problem of finding the QCO with the maximum entropy is reduced to the estimation of the probabilities of (partial) query interpretations $P(s)$. FreeQ applies the probabilistic model in [7] to estimate these probabilities.

5. EXPERIMENTAL EVALUATION

We have implemented FreeQ, an interactive query construction system based on the mechanisms proposed in this paper. To evaluate the performance of FreeQ, we conducted extensive experiments. Our experiments include two parts. First, we evaluated the impact of ontology-based QCOs on the efficiency of query construction processes. Then, we evaluated the time efficiency of the proposed algorithms in handling large scale databases.

#Keywords	Avg. #nodes	Examples of keyword queries
1	1.00	location, book, event, disease, election
2	1.43	emperor album, hockey team, alpine skier
3	1.92	artist lived vancouver, founding figure kagyu
4	2.40	olympic athletes table tennis
5	2.11	canada hockey 2010 winter olympics
6	1.48	2011 san francisco international film festival
7	1.29	fictional character created by edgar allan poe
8	1.13	school type university of puerto rico at ponce

Table 2: Complexity of Keyword Queries

5.1 Dataset and Queries

Our experiments were performed on a Freebase dataset downloaded in June 2011 [10]. This dataset contains approximately 7,500 tables with more than 20 million entities in about 100 domains. We imported the dataset into a MySQL database and indexed the data and the schema using Apache Solr[6]. FreeQ was implemented as a client-server Java application. For our experiments, we used two cores and 10GB of memory on a server, which was equipped with 8x Quad-Core AMD Opteron 2.7GHz processors and 256GB of memory.

Our query set was based on the user-defined views of Freebase. Freebase allows users to create views using a dedicated query language called MQL. Each of the views is given a descriptive title in a natural language. Some examples of the view titles are: *"Lionel Richie discography"*, *"Directing Award: U.S. Dramatic - Winning Films"*, and *"TV Celebrities on Twitter"*. For evaluation, we can regard the title of each view as a keyword query and the MQL definition of the view as the structural interpretation. Then we can study how FreeQ can assist users to construct the structural interpretation from the keyword query. The ground truth is a plausible mapping between the keyword query and the structural interpretation and can be automatically established through a projection program. For our experiments, we randomly selected a set of 615 keyword queries (views). The number of keywords in each query ranges from 1 to 8 keywords. The structural interpretations of the keyword queries are of different complexity. We measure the complexity of an interpretation by the number of keyword nodes it contains. (A keyword node is a table containing at least one keyword occurrence.) The complexity of the queries in our query log ranges from 1 to 3. Table 2 presents the average complexity of queries with different number of keywords. As we can observe, the relatively complex queries mostly contain 3-5 keywords.

5.2 Effectiveness of Ontology-based QCOs

Our first set of experiments was intended to evaluate the effectiveness of the ontology-based QCOs. To this extent, we perform two sets of experiments: First, we compare our approach to that in [7], while using different ontologies to generate QCOs. Second, we compare our approach against that of ranking using different ranking functions.

For each query in our query set, its correct interpretation is already known. Thus, the correctness of each QCO generated by FreeQ can be determined without any user intervention. In [7] we evaluated accessibility of the user interface of incremental query construction in a user study, and demonstrated that the users could make the right choice of QCOs using this interface. In this paper we evaluate how big the interaction cost of query construction is, given that the user makes the right choices. In our experiments, we let the computer interact with FreeQ automatically. In this interaction, the computer will always accept the QCO presented by the system if this QCO subsumes the correct query interpretation and reject the QCO otherwise.

[6]https://lucene.apache.org/solr

Notation	Description	Size
NoOntology	no ontology is used, representing the baseline approach [7]	zero
Freebase	the ontology of Freebase, consisting of domains and categories	medium
YAGO	an external ontology YAGO	big

Table 3: Ontologies of Different Size

To evaluate the effectiveness of the ontology-based QCOs, we ran the experiments in a number of scenarios, in which different ontologies were used. The ontologies are of different size and complexity, as summarized in Table 3. *NoOntology* represents the baseline approach [7], where no ontology is used. *Freebase* represents the ontology based on the domains and categories given in the Freebase website. *YAGO* represents an external ontology known as YAGO. To associate each table of Freebase with a suitable YAGO category we used YAGO+F mapping described in [6].

In the experiments, we measured the interaction cost of query construction for the queries with different complexity in different scenarios. According to Definition 2.8, interaction cost is the number of the QCOs a user needs to evaluate to construct a structured query. The results for the 615 test queries are presented in Figure 4a.

Figure 4a presents the mean and the standard deviation of the interaction cost, with respect to query complexity (the number of keyword nodes) and number of query terms. As we can see, compared to the baseline *NoOntology* approach, the interaction cost can be significantly reduced by using the ontology-based QCOs. With a larger ontology, such as YAGO, the interaction cost tends to be smaller. For example, a 2-node query *"ami suzuki album"* requires 38 QCOs with *NoOntology*, 19 QCOs with *Freebase*, and 10 QCOs with *YAGO*. The benefits of the ontology-based QCOs become stronger with an increasing number of keyword nodes in the structural interpretation too. As we can observe, the majority of the 1-node queries, such as *"university"* and *"football game"*, can still be efficiently answered in the baseline *NoOntology* scenario, where an average cost amounts to 3. With the more complex 2-node, and 3-node queries, such as *"don shirley album"*, *"film performance tom everett", and "location leonardo da vinci lived"*, the interaction cost of *NoOntology* goes up quickly to about 30 and can occasionally exceed 70. By applying the ontology-based QCOs, this cost can be limited to a much smaller range. For example, the average cost for 2-node queries in the *YAGO* scenario is around 10. In addition, we can observe that the interaction cost tends to increase with the number of keywords, while this trend may not hold in all the cases. This is because a longer keyword query does not necessarily imply the more complex structural interpretation (see Table 2).

In the next set of experiments we compared the interaction cost of query construction using Freebase ontology against that of query ranking to evaluate the effectiveness of interactive query construction in general. To this end, we generated the top-500 interpretations using the DF-*k* algorithm of FreeQ. We ranked these interpretations using two ranking functions proposed recently: the ranking function of FreeQ described in [7], and SQAK [22]. The interaction cost of ranking corresponds to the number of interpretations a user needs to evaluate before the intended interpretation is identified, which is exactly the rank of the intended interpretation. If the intended interpretation was not contained within the top-500, we set its rank to 500. Figure 4b presents the results.

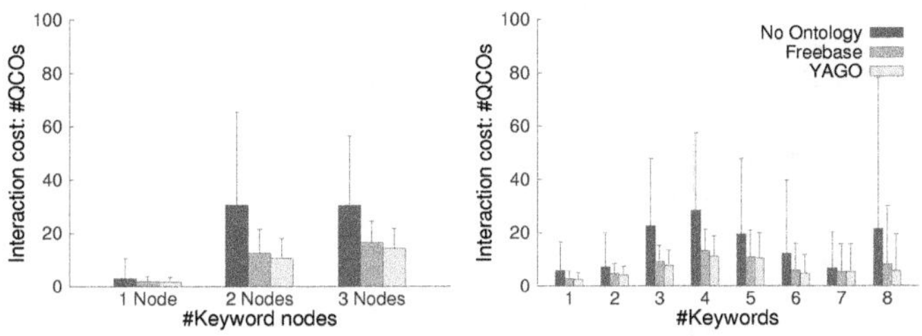

(a) Interaction Cost of Query Construction

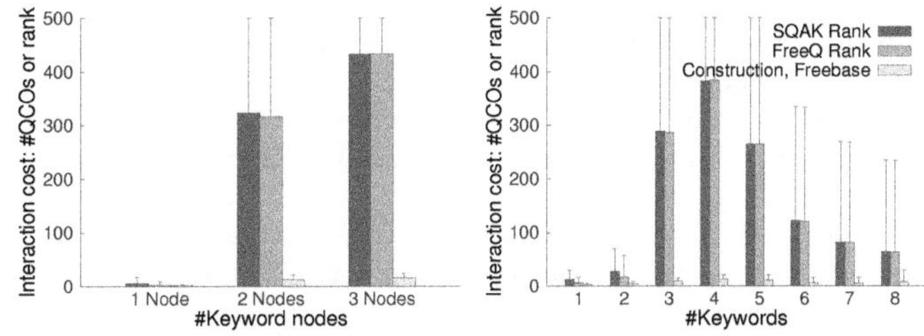

(b) Interaction Cost of Ranking vs. Query Construction

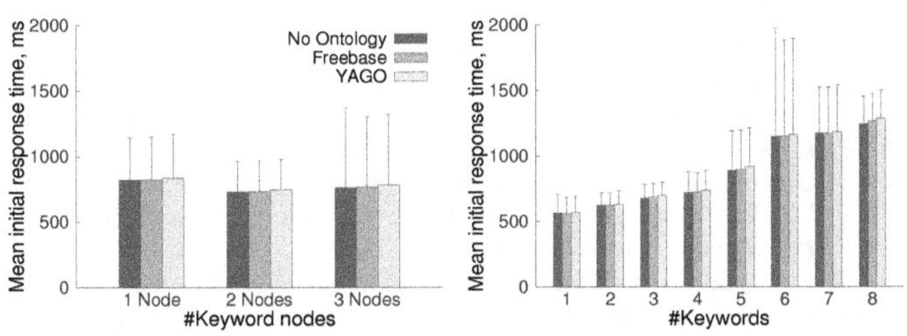

(c) Mean Initial Response Time, ms

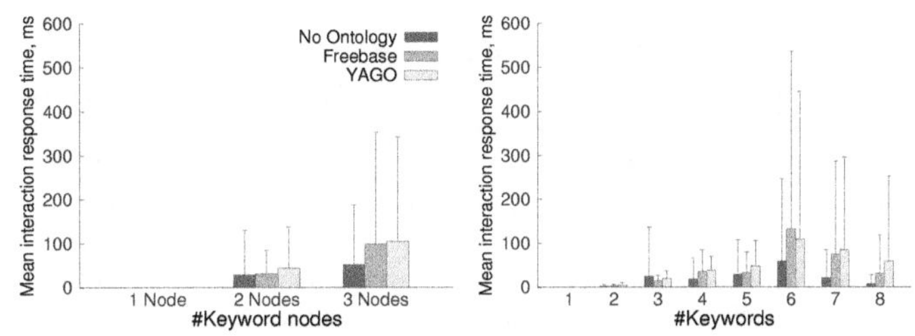

(d) Mean Interaction Response Time, ms

Figure 4: Effectiveness and Efficiency of Query Construction for Queries with Different Complexity

As we can observe, the interaction cost of both ranking and construction for the simplest queries (with 1-2 keywords or 1 keyword node) is acceptable. For the keyword queries that are relatively complex, ranking become ineffective. This is because the query interpretation space on Freebase is too big, such that there can always be a large number of non-intended interpretations that receive good ranks.

5.3 Performance of the System

Existing schema-based approaches to keyword search and interactive query construction in databases typically rely on the completely materialized interpretation space of a keyword query [2, 12, 7]. We have tried to run a number of existing algorithms, including [12], and [7] on Freebase. However, as the schema of Freebase is much bigger than the schemas these algorithms were designed for, they could not finish in a reasonable time. In contrast, the BF-k and DF-k approach allows FreeQ to explore the query interpretation space smartly. Thus it can achieve reasonable response time on a large scale dataset.

To assess the time efficiency of FreeQ, we measured its response time in two phases: (1) The *initial response time* when a user submits a query, and (2) the *interaction response time* when a user interacts with the query construction panel.

When a user issues a keyword query, FreeQ will perform a series of pre-processing, including the identification of the keyword occurrences in an inverted index and the creation of a bi-directional index for performing BF-k and DF-k expansions. The mean and the standard deviation of the initial response time for our query set are shown in Figure 4c. As we can see, the mean initialization time stays around 1 second, and its maximum does not exceed 2 seconds. With an increasing number of keywords, the initial response time increases slowly. This is because the time required for the identification of keyword occurrences in an inverted index increases with the number of query terms. This index access time ranges from 70 to 700ms for our query set. We can also see that the initialization time does not increase with the increasing query complexity. As presented in Table 2, a more complex query does not necessarily contain more query terms. The time required for the creation of a bi-directional index for DF-k and BF-k ranges from 360 to 460ms for our query set. This time mainly depends on the size and the complexity of the schema graph rather than the complexity of queries. We can also observe that the use of different ontologies has limited impact on the initial response time.

We also measured the *interaction response time*, i.e. the time required by FreeQ to present a new set of QCOs and top-k structured queries after each user interaction. This time comprises the time consumed by the BF-k and DF-k algorithms and the QCO selection. Figure 4d presents the results. As we can observe, the interaction response time of FreeQ varies from 1 to 130ms, meaning that in most cases the user would feel that the system is reacting instantaneously [20]. The interaction response time increases with an increasing query complexity. This is expected. As more keywords imply a larger query hierarchy and more QCOs to evaluate, the BF-k and DF-k algorithms and the process of QCO selection will all be more time consuming. Nevertheless, this increase does not appear steep in the results. Moreover, a larger ontology seems to incur higher interaction time too. This is because a larger ontology enables FreeQ to generate more QCOs to evaluate.

In summary, the interaction response time of our system is always below one second. Its initialization time stays within one second most of the time, except for some long queries, whose initialization time can take up to 2 seconds. While further optimization can be conducted, such performance can already ensure that the user's flow of thought stays uninterrupted [20].

6. RELATED WORK

Recently the problem of structured query generation from user's keywords has attracted a lot of research attention, e.g. [7], [22], [23]. The methods for interpreting keywords evolved from considering attribute values only, to including schema terms and operators [16], [22]. In [15], [1], the author modeled the problem as question guided search.

Demidova et al. proposed a probabilistic incremental query construction model for an interactive user interface [7]. These methods do not provide a sufficient solution to large scale datasets with flat schemas, such as the schema of Freebase. This is because these methods relied only on the database internal statistics to generate query construction options. In large scale databases, such options are not informative enough to efficiently reduce the search space. FreeQ alleviates this problem by using ontologies, such as the domain hierarchy of Freebase, and the YAGO ontology [21], in the option generation process. Furthermore, previous work on incremental query construction relied on a set of query templates generated a-priori. In contrast, FreeQ presents algorithms to generate structured queries and query construction options on the fly over a large scale database.

Database usability is a long-term research issue [13]. One of the early approaches to address this problem was the Query by Example [25]. Recent approaches include NL query interfaces [3], [5], query auto-completion, e.g. [19], and adaptive forms [14]. Some commercial DB products such as Microsoft Access offer visual query builder interfaces. Query graphs in a typical visual query builder interface have to be created starting from scratch. The user has to study the database schema and manually put together pieces of the query graph. In contrast, FreeQ enables users to focus on interpretations of keyword queries, and automatically suggests structured queries, without requiring any prior schema knowledge.

User-driven query disambiguation has been successfully applied in Information Retrieval in the context of faceted search. Faceted search engines, such as the product search engine of Google and the Yippy[7], organize search results into meaningful groups, called facets, by applying some clustering or categorization algorithms. Users can easily shrink the scope of the search by focusing on a small number of facets. Several navigational techniques, e.g. [4, 24] were proposed to support users in finding information in a hierarchy of faceted categories. The interface of FreeQ is similar to a faceted interface, whereas each facet corresponds to a query construction option.

7. CONCLUSION

In this paper, we considered the problem of scaling interactive query construction on a very large dataset, such as Freebase. To achieve this goal, we analyzed the efficiency of query construction options and extended the database schema with an ontology layer to reduce the interaction cost. Furthermore, we developed a set of algorithms to explore the interpretation spaces of keyword queries incrementally, such that top-k query interpretations and query construction options can be generated efficiently. Our results confirm the efficiency of the proposed algorithms and the effectiveness of the ontology layer created using the native taxonomy of Freebase. Furthermore, we have demonstrated that external ontologies, such as YAGO ontology, can be used to further increase the effectiveness of query construction. This is especially meaningful for the portability of the FreeQ system, as it can be applied to databases without any pre-defined ontologies.

[7]http://search.yippy.com/

8. ACKNOWLEDGMENTS

This work is partly funded by the NSFC, Project No. 61272138, the European Commission, grant agreement 270239 (ARCOMEM), BMBF ("Gute Arbeit", Re-SozIT) and KEYSTONE COST Action.

9. REFERENCES

[1] P. Adolphs, M. Theobald, U. Schäfer, H. Uszkoreit, and G. Weikum. Yago-qa: Answering questions by structured knowledge queries. In *ICSC*, 2011.

[2] S. Agrawal. Dbxplorer: A system for keyword-based search over relational databases. In *ICDE*, 2002.

[3] L. Androutsopoulos. Natural language interfaces to databases - an introduction. *Journal of Natural Language Engineering*, 1:29–81, 1995.

[4] S. Basu Roy, H. Wang, G. Das, U. Nambiar, and M. Mohania. Minimum-effort driven dynamic faceted search in structured databases. In *Proceeding of the CIKM '08*.

[5] A. Blum. Microsoft english query 7.5: Automatic extraction of semantics from relational databases and olap cubes. In *VLDB '99*.

[6] E. Demidova, I. Oelze, and W. Nejdl. Yago meets freebase: Combining a large-scale database with an ontology. Technical report, L3S Research Center, Leibniz Universität Hannover, available at: http://iqp.l3s.uni-hannover.de/yagof-TR.pdf, May 2013.

[7] E. Demidova, X. Zhou, and W. Nejdl. A probabilistic scheme for keyword-based incremental query construction. *IEEE Trans. Knowl. Data Eng.*, 24(3):426–439, 2012.

[8] E. Demidova, X. Zhou, G. Zenz, and W. Nejdl. Suits: Faceted user interface for constructing structured queries from keywords. In *DASFAA 2009*, Berlin, Heidelberg, 2009. Springer-Verlag.

[9] e. Fellbaum. *WordNet: An Electronic Lexical Database*. MIT Press, Cambridge, 1998.

[10] Google. Freebase data dumps. `http://download.freebase.com/datadumps/`, 2011.

[11] V. Hristidis, L. Gravano, and Y. Papakonstantinou. Efficient ir-style keyword search over relational databases. In *VLDB '2003*, pages 850–861. VLDB Endowment, 2003.

[12] V. Hristidis and Y. Papakonstantinou. Discover: keyword search in relational databases. In *VLDB*, 2002.

[13] H. V. Jagadish, A. Chapman, A. Elkiss, M. Jayapandian, Y. Li, A. Nandi, and C. Yu. Making database systems usable. In *SIGMOD*, 2007.

[14] M. Jayapandian and H. V. Jagadish. Expressive query specification through form customization. In *EDBT*, 2008.

[15] A. Kotov and C. Zhai. Towards natural question guided search. In *WWW '10*.

[16] F. Liu, C. Yu, W. Meng, and A. Chowdhury. Effective keyword search in relational databases. In *SIGMOD*, 2006.

[17] Y. Luo, X. Lin, W. Wang, and X. Zhou. Spark: top-k keyword query in relational databases. In *SIGMOD '07*.

[18] C. D. Manning, P. Raghavan, and H. Schütze. *Introduction to Information Retrieval*. Cambridge University Press, New York, NY, USA, 2008.

[19] A. Nandi and H. V. Jagadish. Assisted querying using instant-response interfaces. In *SIGMOD*, 2007.

[20] J. Nielsen. *Usability engineering*. Morgan Kaufmann Publishers, San Francisco, Calif., 1993.

[21] F. M. Suchanek, G. Kasneci, and G. Weikum. Yago: A Core of Semantic Knowledge. In *WWW 2007*. ACM Press, 2007.

[22] E. Tata and G. M. Lohman. Sqak: doing more with keywords. In *SIGMOD*, 2008.

[23] T. Tran, P. Cimiano, S. Rudolph, and R. Studer. Ontology-based interpretation of keywords for semantic search. In *ISWC*, 2007.

[24] P. Wu, Y. Sismanis, and B. Reinwald. Towards keyword-driven analytical processing. In *SIGMOD '07*.

[25] M. M. Zloof. Query by example. In *AFIPS '75: May 19-22, 1975, national computer conference and exposition*. ACM, 1975.

Compact Query Term Selection Using Topically Related Text

K. Tamsin Maxwell
University of Edinburgh
School of Informatics
Edinburgh EH8 9AB, UK
t.maxwell@ed.ac.uk

W. Bruce Croft
University of Massachusetts
Dept. of Computer Science
Amherst, MA 01003, USA
croft@cs.umass.edu

ABSTRACT

Many recent and highly effective retrieval models for long queries use query reformulation methods that jointly optimize term weights and term selection. These methods learn using word context and global context but typically fail to capture query context. In this paper, we present a novel term ranking algorithm, PhRank, that extends work on Markov chain frameworks for query expansion to select compact and focused terms from within a query itself. This focuses queries so that one to five terms in an unweighted model achieve better retrieval effectiveness than weighted term selection models that use up to 30 terms. PhRank terms are also typically compact and contain 1-2 words compared to competing models that use query subsets up to 7 words long. PhRank captures query context with an affinity graph constructed using word co-occurrence in pseudo-relevant documents. A random walk of the graph is used for term ranking in combination with discrimination weights. Empirical evaluation using newswire and web collections demonstrates that performance of reformulated queries is significantly improved for long queries and at least as good for short, keyword queries compared to highly competitive information retrieval (IR) models.

Categories and Subject Descriptors

H.3.3 [**Information Search and Retrieval**]: Query Formulation

Keywords

Random Walk; Verbose Queries; Query Reformulation

1. INTRODUCTION

Query reformulation is a rich area of information retrieval (IR) research, including techniques for query expansion, dependency analysis, query segmentation and term selection. For short queries, IR effectiveness is improved by smoothing and query expansion using techniques such as pseudo relevance feedback [14, 23, 34]. Conversely, long or verbose queries contain words that are peripheral or shared across many topics so expansion is prone to query drift. Reformulation instead focuses on term weighting [18, 5], term selection [3, 2] and query reduction [15]. The selection of informative terms, defined as one or many-word units, becomes critical as the number of potentially noisy terms increases.

Techniques for term selection and term weighting automatically emphasize the 'essence' of a query. Several successful techniques jointly optimize weights and term selection using both global statistics and local syntactic features [3, 33]. However, these features can fail to detect or differentiate *informative* terms, where an informative term represents the essential aspects of query meaning given a collection of documents. Global statistics are strong indicators of term importance [4] but do not reflect local query context. There is also evidence that they do not lead to significant improvement in query effectiveness [20]. Syntactic features precisely identify word relations but do not identify all the informative relations [22]. The ubiquity of global statistics and syntactic features in current methods for term selection suggests a continuing need for improved understanding of alternatives ways to estimate term informativeness [20].

In this paper, we present PhRank (phrase rank), an algorithm that uses pseudo relevance feedback for in-query term selection rather than expansion to terms not in a query. Compact and focused terms are selected from a list of candidates by ranking terms using a Markov chain framework and picking the top-ranked candidates. Candidate terms are all combinations of 1-3 words in a query that are not stopwords. Term scores are computed using the average word score for words in a term, combined with global discrimination weights. Word scores are computed using a random walk of a word co-occurrence graph constructed from pseudo relevant documents, combined with word salience weights for the query and global contexts. This approach selects terms that achieve significant gains in both recall and precision compared to the most effective techniques for query reformulation that do not use term weighting, expansion, or stratified dependencies [4]. This is achieved by focusing on a limited number of word relationships with a core concept.

PhRank has three advantages compared to previous work. First, to our knowledge PhRank is the first method to use pseudo relevance feedback for in-query term selection. Feedback was applied initially to estimate weights for independent query words without selection [8] and is predominantly used for query expansion. Previous approaches to in-query term selection use highly localized *word context*, in the form

SIGIR'13, July 28–August 1, 2013, Dublin, Ireland.
Copyright 2013 ACM 978-1-4503-2034-4/13/07 ...$15.00.

Query: *Locations of volcanic activity which occurred within the present day boundaries of the U.S. and its territories.*			
PhRank	**Sequential Dependence**	**Key Concept**	**Subset Distribution**
volcanic volcanic boundaries volcanic territories volcanic activity volcanic occurred	locations volcanic volcanic activity activity which which occurred occurred within within present present day day boundaries boundaries us us territories	present day boundaries volcanic activity	volcanic day boundaries day boundaries territories volcanic activity occurred day boundaries present day boundaries volcanic boundaries territories volcanic activity occurred activity occurred day boundaries volcanic activity occurred boundaries volcanic present day boundaries volcanic occurred boundaries + 20 bigrams (*if weights collapsed*)

Table 1: Terms selected by four highly effective query reformulation models for TREC GOV2 topic #756.

of syntactic relations and co-occurrence, and *global context* in the retrieval collection. They do not consider *query context*, such as a general query topic identified from pseudo relevant documents. The intuition behind a random walk of a query context graph is that it reinforces words that capture query 'essence' more strongly than words that are peripheral to query meaning. For this reason, informative terms are more readily apparent if query context is considered.

Second, PhRank achieves significant performance gains with a small number of compact terms while retaining the flexibility to select more and longer terms if required. Other approaches use a robust, but less effective, distribution over many imprecise but approximately relevant terms. Alternatively, they take a relatively inflexible, high-risk approach that prefers a few exact terms and is prone to mistakes. For example, Table 1 shows the terms selected for TREC topic #756 by three top performing IR models. The sequential dependence (SD) model is straightforward and *robust* [24]. The key concept (KC) model [3] aims at a highly *succinct* representation but is hampered by a requirement that terms are predefined syntactic units (noun phrase length). The subset distribution (SDist) model [33] optimizes over many term and weight variables and is *highly effective* but is biased towards longer terms of 3-6 words. PhRank demonstrates that for a majority of queries, a few precise terms, in addition to a standard query likelihood representation, are more effective than term distributions. They also result in queries that have up to 90% fewer terms, and these terms are typically only 1-2 words long.

Finally, an affinity graph captures aspects of both syntactic and non-syntactic word associations in an integrated manner. A co-occurrence affinity graph shares the same structure as a global dependency graph in which edges are defined by linguistic relations. Specifically, the most connected vertices are high frequency functional words and less frequent content-bearing words tend towards the edges of the graph [10, 11]. By consequence, the semantic significance of a word is correlated with the degree of the corresponding vertex. We infer that the shared structure of dependency and affinity graphs captures aspects of both syntactic and non-syntactic word associations. Moreover, an affinity graph can be used to estimate the semantic significance of words.

To summarize, unlike existing models of term selection, PhRank integrates three characteristics that we believe are important to accurately identify the most informative terms: query context, compactness, and integration of syntactic and semantic knowledge. We show that consolidating these characteristics delivers up to 14% performance improvement compared to highly competitive methods for TREC description topics and is comparable to the state-of-the-art for TREC keyword (title) queries.

The rest of this paper is organized as follows. In Section 2 we review related work and its connection to PhRank. Section 3 defines the problem of term selection and its key characteristics. In Section 4 we formally describe the PhRank algorithm. Section 5 presents the evaluation framework. In Section 6 we discuss the results of empirical experiments, and Section 7 concludes the paper.

2. RELATED WORK

Markov chain frameworks and spreading activation networks for a network of words are well-studied in IR with origins in associative word networks [7]. They include research on webpage authority [26], e.g. PageRank, as well as query expansion [17, 6, 23, 14]. However, they are novel for *unexpanded* term selection.

The Markov chain framework uses the stationary distribution of a random walk over an affinity graph G to estimate the importance of vertices in the graph. Vertices can represent words, in which case edges represent word associations. If the random walk is ergodic, affinity scores at vertices converge to a stationary distribution that can be used to establish a ranking, e.g. over words.

A random walk describes a succession of random or semi-random steps between vertices v_i and v_j in G. Let ℓ_{ij} be the transition probability (or edge weight) between v_i and v_j. The path of the walk is determined by a square probability matrix $H = (h_{ij})$ with size n, where n is the number of unique vertices in G. The probability $h_{ij} = \ell_{ij}$ if v_i and v_j are connected, and $h_{ij} = 0$ otherwise. Affinity scores are computed recursively. Let π_j^t be the affinity score associated with v_j at time t. Then π_j^{t+1} is the sum of scores for each v_i connected to v_j, weighted by the possibility of choosing v_j as the next step on the path from v_i:

$$\pi_j^{t+1} = \sum_i \pi_i h_{ij} \tag{1}$$

It is usual to introduce some minimal likelihood that a path from v_i at time t will randomly step to some v_j at time $t+1$ that may be unconnected to v_i. Otherwise, clusters of vertices interfere with the propagation of weight through the graph. This likelihood is often defined to be the uniform probability vector $u = 1/n$, although any other vector can be chosen [14]. A corresponding factor reflects the likelihood that a path will follow the structure of edges in G. A damping factor α controls the balance between them:

$$\pi^{t+1} = \alpha\pi^t H + (1-\alpha)u \tag{2}$$

The Markov chain framework has has been used in a principled way to smooth and expand queries in a language modeling framework [34], but application in query reformulation has been limited to selection of individual words that do not appear in the original query. By contrast, PhRank ranks terms containing one or more words that do appear in the original query. Moreover, while expansion techniques can exacerbate problems with unrelated terms, PhRank reduces the problem of query drift through improved term selection.

Markov chain processes have also been applied in text summarization for keyphrase extraction. This is a task similar to term detection for automated indexing. TextRank [25], SingleRank [32] and ExpandRank [32] use a random walk to identify salient sequences of nouns and adjectives. They improve over earlier unsupervised methods for this task but achieve only 30-40% task accuracy and may be outperformed by a *tf.idf* metric [13]. ExpandRank supplements text with pseudo relevant documents but does not improve performance compared to SingleRank [13]. PhRank is similar to these algorithms but is more flexible and better suited to IR. It uses multiple sources of co-occurrence evidence and the discriminative ability of terms in a collection. It also produces an unbiased ranking over terms of mixed lengths, does not rely on syntactic word categories such as nouns, and permits terms to contain words with long distance dependencies.

Other related work focuses on techniques for identification of dependent terms [28], key concepts [3], or sub-queries [16, 33]. This includes techniques for the removal of stop structure [15]; reduction of narrative queries to word sequences associated with part of speech blocks [19]; selection of candidate sub-queries using noun phrases [3]; query term ranking using dependency tree relations [27]; and optimized ranking over possible subqueries [33]. There is also a significant body of work on learning individual term weights [18, 5]. Much of this work incorporates syntactic and statistical features in machine learning.

3. PRINCIPLES FOR TERM SELECTION

We hypothesize that the following principles define word and term informativeness. These principles motivate the PhRank algorithm detailed in the next Section.

An informative word:

1. **Is informative relative to a query:** An informative word should accurately represent the meaning of a query. However, queries do not provide much context with which to determine meaning. Pseudo relevance used in PhRank is an established means of enhancing a query representation [29].

2. **Is related to other informative words:** The *Association Hypothesis* [31] states that, "if one index term is good at discriminating relevant from non-relevant documents, then any closely associated index term is also likely to be good at this". PhRank uses a Markov chain framework in which the value assigned to a word i is determined by the value of other words connected to i, and the number of connections to i.

An informative term:

3. **Contains informative words:** Consider a base case in which a term has only one word. It is obvious that this term must also display the properties of an informative word. We deduce that all terms must contain informative words. PhRank considers the informativeness of individual words when ranking terms.

4. **Is discriminative in the retrieval collection:** A term that occurs many times within a small number of documents gives a pronounced relevance signal. PhRank weights terms with a normalized *tf.idf* inspired weight.

4. THE PHRANK ALGORITHM

PhRank captures query context with an affinity graph constructed from stopped, stemmed pseudo-relevant documents. Vertices in the graph represent unique stemmed words (or simply, *stems*). Edges connect stems that are adjacent in the processed pseudo relevant set. Graph transition probabilities (edge weights) are computed using a weighted linear combination of stem co-occurrence, the certainty that the document in which they co-occur is relevant, and the salience of sequential bigram factors in the pseudo relevant set. The edge weights thus represent the tendency for two stemmed words w_i and $w_{j\neq i}$ to appear in close proximity in documents that that reflect a query topic.

Stems in the affinity graph are scored using a random walk algorithm. Following convergence, stem scores are weighted by a *tf.idf* style weight that further captures salience in the pseudo relevant set. This aims to compensate for potential undesirable properties of the random walk. Finally, term scores are computed using the average score for stemmed words in a term, weighted by term salience in the retrieval collection. The m highest scoring terms are employed to reformulate Q. Pseudo code for the algorithm is shown in Figure 1. The rest of this section describes the algorithm in more detail, including three heuristic weights (factors r, s and z). A number of choices for these factors could have been made and specific choices are analyzed in Section 6.1.

1) Graph construction (principle 1):

Let a query $Q = \{w_1, ...w_n\}$ and C be a document collection. The top k documents retrieved from C using Q are assumed to describe a similar topic to Q. We define C to be the retrieval collection plus English Wikipedia. We use Wikipedia since it improves IR results for query expansion using a random walk [6], but also explore the effectiveness of using the retrieval collection alone. The top k documents in C, together with Q itself encoded as a short document d_0, comprise *neighboring* documents in the neighborhood set $N = \{d_0, ...d_k\}$.

Documents in N are stopped using a minimal list of 18 words [21] and stemmed using the Krovetz stemmer. This improves co-occurrence counts for content-bearing stems and reduces the size of an affinity graph G constructed from the processed documents. Stoplisting with a longer list hurt IR effectiveness. Edges in G connect stemmed words i and j at vertices v_i and v_j if i and j are adjacent in N. Documents in N with only one word (e.g. some queries) are discarded to ensure that all vertices have at least one connecting edge.

2) Edge weights (principle 1):

Transition probabilities (edge weights) ℓ_{ij} are based on a weighted linear combination of the number of times i and

```
k = 5
resourceList = [ C, wikipedia ]

for q in queryList:

  N = set()
  for rsc in resourceList:
    N.add( retrieve_top_k( q, rsc ) )
  N = retrieve_top_k( q, N )
  N.add( q )

  # one word type per row and column
  G = arrayStruct()
  for ( doc, docRel ) in N:
    doc.stopStem()
    G.grow( buildGraph( doc, docRel ) )

  G.idfWeightEdge()          # bigram wt r
  G.normalize()
  G.iterate()
  G.weightVertex()           # word wt s

  T = q.terms
  for term in q:
    term.wt = G.score( term )
    term.wt *= term.globalWt( C ) # term wt z
  T.sortByWeight()
```

```
def buildGraph( doc, docRel ):
  docG = index( doc )
  docG.linearWt( uw2, uw10 )
  docG.weight( docRel )

  return docG


def score( term ):
  S = 0

  for w in term.wordSplit():
    S += self.affinityScore( term )

  return S /= term.length()


def globalWt( C ):
  l = self.length()
  wt = C.tfidf( self ) * l^l

  return wt
```

Figure 1: Pseudocode for the PhRank algorithm.

j co-occur in windows W of size 2 and 10. This is motivated by the idea that different degrees of proximity provide rich evidence for word relatedness in IR [25, 32, 24]. Edge weights are defined by:

$$\ell_{ij} = r * \sum_{d_k \in N} p(d_k|Q)(\lambda c_{ijW_2} + (1-\lambda)c_{ijW_{10}})$$

where $p(d_k|Q)$ is the probability of the document in which the stems i and j co-occur given Q, and c_{ijW_2} and $c_{ijW_{10}}$ are the counts of stem co-occurrence in windows of size 2 and 10 in N. λ is set to 0.6. We set the relevance of d_0 to Q to be high but reasonable (-4 for Indri log likelihood scores). The exact setting has very little effect on term ranking.

Factor r is a *tf.idf* style weight that confirms the importance of a connection between i and j in N. G includes many stemmed words, so unweighted affinity scores can be influenced by co-occurrences with highly frequent, but possibly uninformative, stems such as '*make*'. Factor r minimizes this effect. Since the *tf* component is already accounted for by $\lambda c_{ijW_2} + (1-\lambda)c_{ijW_{10}}$, we reduce r to the *idf* component:

$$r_{ij} = log_2 \frac{\sum_{ij \in N} c_{ijW_2}}{1 + c_{ijW_2}}$$

3) Random Walk (principle 2):

A random walk of G follows the standard Markov chain framework presented in Section 2. Edge weights are normalized to sum to one and π_j is the affinity score of the stem associated with v_j. π_j indicates the importance of a stem in the query context. Iteration of the walk ceases when the difference in score at any vertex does not exceed 0.0001. This translates to around 15 iterations but may be optimized for efficiency. The damping factor $\alpha = 0.85$ is equivalent to a walk along five connected edges in G before the algorithm randomly skips to a possibly unrelated vertex. The average sentence length in English is around 11-15 words so this equates to skipping at or near the boundary of a sentence around one half of the time.

4) Vertex weights (principle 3):

Following the random walk, stemmed words in G are further weighted to capture both the *exhaustiveness* with which they represent a query, and their global *saliency* in the collection [30]. Exhaustivity indicates whether a word w_1 is a sufficient representation of the query. If w_1 appears many times in N then it is less likely that a term x containing w_1 will benefit from additional words $w_2 ... w_n$. For example, the term *geysers* quite exhaustively represents the TREC query #840, '*Give the definition, locations, or characteristics of geysers*'. A term containing additional words, e.g. *definition geysers*, is not more informative. However, common stems, such as '*make*', tend to have high affinity scores because they co-occur with many words.

Factor s balances exhaustivity with global saliency to identify stems that are poor discriminators been relevant and non-relevant documents. Specifically, $s_{w_n} = w_n f_{avg} * idf_{w_n}$, where $w_n f_{avg}$ is the frequency of a word w_n in N, averaged over $k+1$ documents (the average frequency) and normalized by the maximum average frequency of any term in N. As usual, idf_{w_n} is the inverse document frequency of w_n in the collection, so $idf_{w_n} = log_2 \frac{|C|}{1+df_{w_n}}$ where $|C|$ is the vocabulary of stemmed words in the collection C, and df_{w_n} is the number of documents in C containing w_n.

An advantage of factor s is that it enables PhRank to be independent of an IR model. A model may treat the component words of terms as independent or dependent. Factor s helps to ensure that the selected terms are informative irrespective of this representation.

5) Term ranking (principles 3, 4):

To avoid a bias towards longer terms, a term x is scored by averaging the affinity scores for its component words $\{w_1, [...w_n]\}$. Term rank is determined by the average score multiplied by a factor z_x that represents the degree to which the term is discriminative in a collection:

$$z_x = f_{x_e} * idf_{x_e} * l_x$$

Let x_e be a proximity expression such that the component words of x appear in an unordered window of size $W = 4$ per word. Thus, a term with two words appears in an 8-word window, and a term with three words appears in a 12-word window. The frequency of x_e in C is f_{x_e} and idf_{x_e} is defined analogously to idf_{w_n} above. l_x is an exponential weighting factor proposed for the normalization of ngram frequencies during query segmentation [12]. This factor favors longer ngrams that tend to occur less frequently in text. Multiplication of ngram counts by l_x enables comparison of counts for terms of varying length. Let $|x|$ be the number of words in x, then $l_x = |x|^{|x|}$.

In summary, the PhRank algorithm describes how informative a term x is for Q compared to other terms. This is computed using the function:

$$f(x, Q) \stackrel{rank}{=} z_x * \frac{\sum_{w_n \in x} \pi_{w_n}}{n} \quad (3)$$

4.1 Diversity filter

PhRank often assigns a high rank to multi-word terms that contain only one highly informative word. This is due to use of an average word affinity score, and is desirable because informative terms can contain uninformative words. For example, given a query about *'the destruction of Pan Am Flight 103 over Lockerbie, Scotland'* (TREC #409), the term *'pan flight 103'* is informative even if the polysemous word *'pan'* is uninformative by itself. However, this can result in low diversity of top ranked terms used in query reformulation. To increase diversity, we apply a simple, heuristic filtering technique with top-down constraints.

Given a ranked list, all terms with a score of zero are discarded. The lowest ranked term, x_n, is checked against the list of terms with a better rank $x_{m<n}$. Let A be the set of component words in x_n and B be the set of component words in any single term $x_{m<n}$. If $\exists A : A \subset B \vee A \supset B$ then we discard x_n *iff* every component word of x_n is contained in at least one $x_{m \neq n}$ that is in the retained list of ranked words at the time B is evaluated. For example, if x_n ='*birth rate*' and we find some $x_{m<n}$ ='*birth rate china*' then we discard x_n on the assumption that the longer term better represents the information need. If x_n ='*declining birth rate*' and we find some $x_{m<n}$ ='*birth rate*' and some $x_{m<n}$ ='*declining birth*' then we discard x_n on the assumption that the shorter terms better represent the information need and the longer term is redundant. Note that the top-ranked term is always retained. This process is adequate to increase diversity in the ranked list and ensures that no vital information is lost, but clearly presents an opportunity for further improvement.

5. EVALUATION FRAMEWORK

This section describes comparative models and query reformulations used to assess the degree to which PhRank queries are robust, precise and succinct, and represent word dependency. The main point of comparison is a *robust* and highly effective IR model (SD) that uses term selection and is employed as a baseline in related work [3, 28, 33]. We also compare against the model with the highest mean average *precision* of which we are aware that is relevant to a discussion of term selection with query expansion (sDist). Finally, since compact queries are a feature of PhRank, we compare against a succinct yet competitive model that selects only two terms (KC). We note that superior IR effectiveness is possible with term weighting, but we focus on results using *unweighted terms* to more clearly demonstrate the effect of term selection alone. We also report results for query likelihood (QL) for reference even though this model uses no term selection. This is because the other models reported include a query likelihood component. We do not compare against models that use pseudo relevance feedback for expansion. Pseudo relevance feedback without expansion is a novel feature of our work that contributes to PhRank performance.

5.1 Robustness

Evaluation across three TREC collections using both description topics and title queries requires a strong, robust baseline. We use a sequential dependence (SD) variant of the Markov random field (MRF) model [24]. SD uses a linear combination of three cliques of terms, where each clique is prioritized by a weight λ_c. The first clique contains individual words (query likelihood QL), $\lambda_1 = 0.85$. The second clique contains query bigrams that match document bigrams in 2-word ordered windows ('*#1*'), $\lambda_2 = 0.1$. The third clique uses the same query bigrams as clique 2 with an 8-word unordered window ('*#uw8*'), $\lambda_3 = 0.05$. For example, the query '*new york city*' in Indri[1] query language is:

#weight(
λ_1 #combine(new york city)
λ_2 #combine(#1(new york) #1(york city))
λ_3 #combine(#uw8(new york) #uw8(york city)))

Because it is very simple to generate SD queries, this model is regularly used as a baseline. Highly effective weighted variants have also been developed [4, 33, 28]. We compare SD with a PhRank model (PR-.F) that uses the same query format, except the second and third cliques contain PhRank terms instead of query bigrams. In addition, because PhRank terms may be 1-3 words long, we adjust the unordered window operator in the manner proposed for the full dependence variant of the MRF model [24]. Namely, the window size is 4 multiplied by the number of words in a term. Note that for a term with only one word i, the operators *#1(i)* and *#uw8(i)* equate to a search for the word i in a document. So, if two terms '*york*' and '*new york city*' are selected by PhRank, the PR-.F model has the form:

#weight(
λ_1 #combine(new york city)
λ_2 #combine(york #1(new york city))
λ_3 #combine(york #uw12(new york city)))

PR-.F uses five terms for description topics and feature analysis experiments, and three terms for title queries (or less, if the required number of terms is not available after rank filtering).

5.2 Precision

Highly competitive performance compared to SD can be achieved by jointly optimizing possible subqueries and subquery weights using syntactic and statistical features. Among the models of which we are aware, the subset distribution model (sDist) [33] achieves the highest mean average precision on long queries using term selection with no higher order dependencies [4]. However, it is not entirely fair to compare sDist with PR-.F since sDist uses heavily optimized weights for ten subqueries. A subquery in sDist is a linear combination of a standard SD query and one selected term treated as a bag-of-words. This compares with the flat λ weights used in SD and PR-.F. Despite this, sDist is the most effective model we can use for stringent comparison that ensures real progress has been made. We therefore include sDist in our evaluation even though queries for Robust04 are not available from the authors.

5.3 Succinctness

Queries formulated with PhRank have few terms and a maximum of three words per term. To evaluate highly succinct queries we compare against Key Concepts (KC) [3]. KC is another succinct weighted linear feature model that combines two cliques. The first clique ($\lambda_1 = 0.8$) contains a bag-of-words query representation of the original query,

[1] http://www.lemurproject.org/

and the second clique ($\lambda_2 = 0.2$) combines a weighted bag-of-words representation for each of two selected terms. The top terms are selected from the set of query noun phrases using a decision tree with frequency-based features [3]. The model reduces to a weighted representation of the original query with word independence. If '*city*' and '*new york*' are the top two terms, it takes the following form, where δ is the decision tree confidence score associated with a term:

#weight(
λ_1 #combine(new york city)
λ_2 #weight(δ #combine(new york) δ city))

To compare against KC, we present a model (PR-zF2) that takes the same form but does not benefit from term weights δ. We use the two top terms selected by PhRank.

5.4 Word dependence

Assumptions of word dependence are an important issue in IR. To clarify the dependence assumptions made by PhRank we refer to four models of *phrase belief* presented by [9] (Figure 2, a-d). These models show how belief in a document $d_c \in C$ flows to belief in a query Q in an inference network, and thus how words and terms can be dependent. In PhRank, we do not perform inference, but by analogy these models aid interpretation of PhRank features.

Of the four models in Figure 2, the more general dependence assumption (d) is used by PhRank to score words, and term ranks are computed using an independence assumption (b). Even if component words of terms are not connected in G, weight is propagated through the graph such that word dependencies affect evidence for a term. PhRank factors z, s and r reflect Figure 2 models a, b and c respectively.

We speculate that optimal term selection occurs when 1) a high rank is assigned to terms that are important under all four interpretations of phrase belief according to evidence in N, 2) the rank of terms that have less evidence under one or more interpretation decreases gracefully, and 3) the ranking meets the principles of term selection proposed in Section 3.

6. EXPERIMENTS

We examine the performance of PhRank in three ways. First, we compare versions of the algorithm in which we omit specific features. Second, we compare performance of queries reformulated using PhRank top ranked terms against highly effective models for both TREC description topics and title queries. Third, we compare on a query by query basis the robustness and performance error for PhRank versus a distributed approach to term selection (SD).

We evaluate on three TREC collections using version 4.12 of Indri with Dirichlet smoothing, $\mu = 2500$. The Robust04, WT10G and GOV2 newswire and open web text collections have queries that vary substantially in length and known difficulty. Together they provide a diverse platform for experiments (Table 2). Topic 672 is excluded from the Robust04 evaluation as the collection contains no relevant documents. All collections and queries are stopped and stemmed using the INQUERY stoplist and Krovetz stemmer. Queries are further stopped to exclude 18 TREC stopwords such as '*describe*' [1]. Candidate terms are all units of 1-3 words in the power set $\mathcal{P}(q)$ of content-bearing words in Q. IR models are defined in Section 5. Pseudo relevant documents are retrieved using a sequential dependence model. Models '.F' exclude the feature represented by '.' and models '.T' include the feature. Thus, model rTsTzT includes all features.

Name	**# Docs**	**Topic Numbers**
ROBUST04	528,155	301-450, 601-700 (-672)
WT10G	1,692,096	451-550
GOV2	25,205,179	701-850

Table 2: TREC collections and topics

	ROBUST04		WT10G		GOV2	
	MAP	R-Pr	MAP	R-Pr	MAP	R-Pr
Description topics						
rTsTzT	26.65	30.05	0.00	0.00	28.83	34.55
zF	**27.32**	**30.32**	**23.68**	**26.71**	28.64	34.13
sF	26.03	29.61	21.00	25.10	27.93	33.67
rF	26.67	30.02	22.44	25.70	**28.93**	**34.65**
Title queries						
rTsTzT	24.87	29.04	21.78	**25.73**	31.49	37.26
zF	26.14	30.13	20.85	24.72	30.73	36.26
sF	25.90	30.03	20.72	24.30	31.30	36.91
rF	**26.32**	**30.25**	**21.81**	25.70	**31.59**	**37.42**

Table 3: Feature analysis results. Description topics perform best with omission of the global term weight z (zF). Title queries perform best with the omission of bigram salience weight r (rF).

6.1 Feature analysis

In this section we explore the impact of PhRank feature removal on IR effectiveness assessed using model PR-.F. Results in Table 3 show that PhRank is highly effective in selecting informative terms for a query. However, not all the features proposed consistently improve term ranking for IR. Description topics are most effective when factor z is omitted, and title queries are most effective when r is omitted.

1) Factor r: words dependent on term

Factor r imperfectly captures belief in component words dependent on belief in a term (Figure 2c). It uses global bigram statistics to scale edge weights in G. During a random walk, this affects the affinity scores for individual stemmed words. However, bigram statistics are only an approximate measure of term unity. More problematically, r relies on words in a term being co-occurrent in N. Highly informative terms are likely to have their component words connected in G, but this is not guaranteed. For terms with more than two words, edge weights in G also must be factored. Perhaps due to these limitations, r had minimal impact on IR effectiveness for title queries and could be omitted to improve algorithm efficiency.

However, we note that r is useful for description topics. We speculate that this is because the query words for description topics may be peripheral to the core information need. Spurious adjacent word dependencies in Q tend to appear in the pseudo relevant set because bigrams feature in the IR model employed for initial retrieval. Thus, if word co-occurrence in Q reflects query meaning, as typically occurs with title queries, the edges and weights used to initialise G are likely to be adequate. If word co-occurrence is spurious, the initialisation may be suboptimal. Factor r ameliorates misleading initial edge weights for description topics.

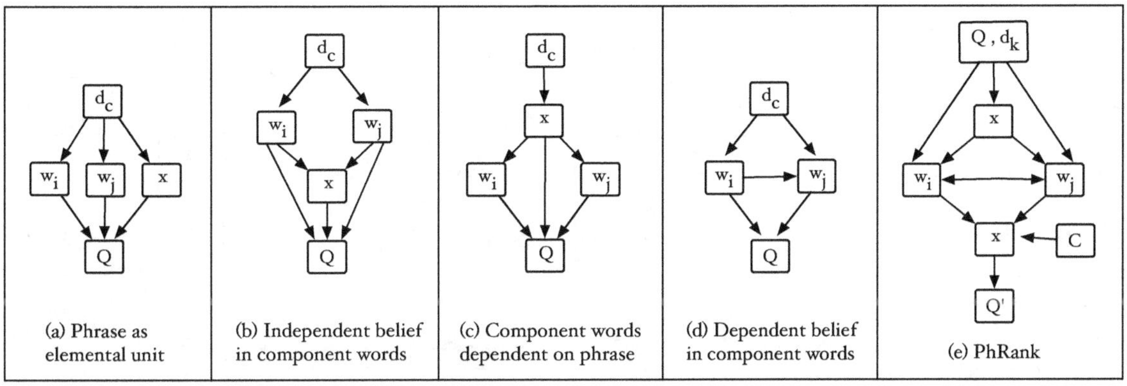

(a) Phrase as elemental unit (b) Independent belief in component words (c) Component words dependent on phrase (d) Dependent belief in component words (e) PhRank

Figure 2: Four models of phrase belief proposed by [9] (a-d). Word dependence in PhRank can be understood as a hybrid with features of all these models (e) for term $x = \{w_i, wj\}$ and documents $d_k \in N$.

2) Factor s: word independence

Factor s contributes to belief in a term dependent on belief in individual words (Figure 2b). It weights each vertex in an affinity graph by its salience in the query context N balanced by its salience in the document collection. Omission of s substantially hurt IR effectiveness. Among all the features tested it had the most impact on overall performance, perhaps because independent belief in words is the most important factor in IR effectiveness [24]. In addition, work with random walk algorithms for query expansion has found that words co-occurring with high frequency are of low value if they are not semantically close to the query [6]. We suggest that salience in N as captured by s represents semantic closeness to the query, and salience in the collection helps to identify high frequency co-occurrent words.

3) Factor z: term as elemental unit

Factor z represents belief in a term independent of belief in its component words (Figure 2a). It resembles a standard *tf.idf* weight and reflects the principle that a term should be discriminative in the retrieval collection. Given the established effectiveness of *tf.idf* weighting, it is surprising that omission of z improves IR effectiveness for description topics. However, it is based on observations of a term in an unordered proximity window in the retrieval collection. The way such observations are made implies a dependence assumption that may not provide an accurate estimate of term salience. In addition, it has recently been suggested that global statistics rarely improve retrieval performance and that local, document level evidence is sufficient [20].

We also note that both r and z account for the discrimination ability of multi-word units in the collection: r applies to bigrams and z applies to words in unordered windows. This encoding is partially redundant, so description queries may not require z because they use r, and title queries may require z because they do not use r. We remove z for our final runs for description queries, and retain it for title queries.

4) Factor k: pseudo relevant documents

Results in Table 4 show that the most improvement in IR effectiveness is achieved with 2 to 5 pseudo relevant documents. Higher k decreases effectiveness due to the introduction of non-relevant information. However, PhRank is quite robust to variation in k due to the weighting of co-occurrence relations by document relevance. Even with construction of the affinity graph from the original query only (¬PRF), PhRank performs better than sDist and comparably with SD. This suggests that most important information is retained by the term selection process.

	ROBUST04		WT10G		GOV2	
	MAP	R-Pr	MAP	R-Pr	MAP	R-Pr
¬PRF	26.44	29.59	21.88	25.36	27.85	33.28
k2	26.86	30.05	22.76	25.42	28.81	**34.38**
k5	**27.32**	**30.32**	**23.68**	**26.71**	28.64	34.13
k10	27.29	30.05	22.33	25.02	28.64	34.16
k50	27.09	30.11	23.04	26.21	**28.82**	34.27
k100	26.80	29.82	22.78	26.11	28.34	33.91

Table 4: IR effectiveness for description topics using k pseudo relevant documents. Best IR effectiveness is achieved using the top few documents only.

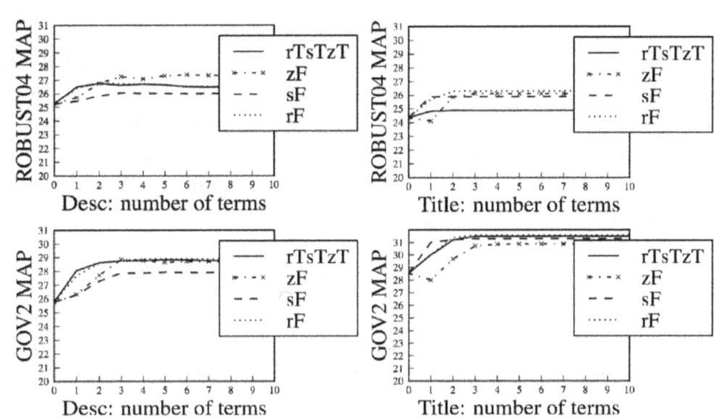

Figure 3: IR effectiveness with feature analysis and variable threshold. In many cases PhRank achieves performance gains with two terms, and is robust to variance in the number of terms selected.

6.2 Retrieval performance

We present our best results for runs using description topics and title queries on three TREC collections.

6.2.1 Robustness

For description topics, the results in Table 5 show highly significant or significant improvement in mean average precision (MAP) and R-precision compared to the SD baseline for

(a) TREC description topics

	ROBUST04		WT10G		GOV2	
	MAP	R-Pr	MAP	R-Pr	MAP	R-Pr
Robust and precise						
QL	25.25	28.69	19.55	22.77	25.77	31.26
SD	26.57	30.02	20.63	24.31	28.00	33.30
sDist	–	–	21.14	24.93	27.64	33.50
PR-zF	**27.32**	**30.32**	**23.68‡**	**26.71‡**	**28.64**†	**34.13‡**
PR¬W	27.19†	30.12	22.90†	26.57	28.18	33.77
Succinct						
KC	25.62	28.89	20.15	22.58	26.88	32.73
PR-zF2	25.91	28.92	22.02†	25.69‡	27.04	32.75
PR¬W2	25.76	28.33	21.43	25.40†	26.05	31.75

(b) TREC title queries

	ROBUST04		WT10G		GOV2	
	MAP	R-Pr	MAP	R-Pr	MAP	R-Pr
QL	24.37	28.52	19.48	23.08	28.55	34.41
SD	26.16	30.25	20.97	23.75	31.25	36.88
PR-rF	26.32	30.25	**21.81‡**	**25.70‡**	**31.59**	**37.42**
PR¬W	**26.44**	**30.40**	21.76†	25.57‡	31.50	37.14

Table 5: Retrieval results for description topics and title queries. PhRank significantly outperforms a highly effective baseline for description topics and is strongly competitive for title queries. † shows significant ($p < .05$) and ‡ highly significant ($p < .01$) results compared to SD and KC respectively as determined by a sign test.

GOV2 and WT10G. Substantial improvements in precision on Robust04 are just short of significance. For title queries, improvement is highly significant for WT10G and comparable to the baseline for other collections. Increased precision occurs for top ranked documents (top 5 and 10) as well as being a general trend in the results. Exclusion of Wikipedia has a small negative effect as shown by PR¬W and PR¬W2 corresponding to PR-.F and PR-zF2 respectively.

To assess the quality of the ranked list of terms without a measure of ground truth for term informativeness, we explore the impact of varying the number of terms included in query reformulations. The results in Figure 3 show that the quality of top terms output by PhRank are stable as more terms are selected. Further, a large part of the gain in precision is attributed to the top two terms.

To investigate performance further, for each collection we manually reviewed the ranked term lists for queries that perform significantly better or worse than SD (>100% change in MAP), and 10 queries with comparable performance. Across all queries observed, there is a strong tendency for PhRank to single out one word, or a pair of words, as the main concept of the query, and rank all terms that contain the main concept highly. Remaining terms are ranked according to the contributions of their additional words. This high risk, high reward strategy negatively affects the robustness of PhRank on a query by query basis as shown in Figure 4 for description topics. Title queries exhibit similar behavior.

For example, one of the best performing queries for GOV2 is #756 as shown in Table 1. For this query, identification of '*volcano*' as the main concept greatly helped IR. On the other hand, the same strategy for query #780, one of the worst performing queries for GOV2 (see Table 6), selected

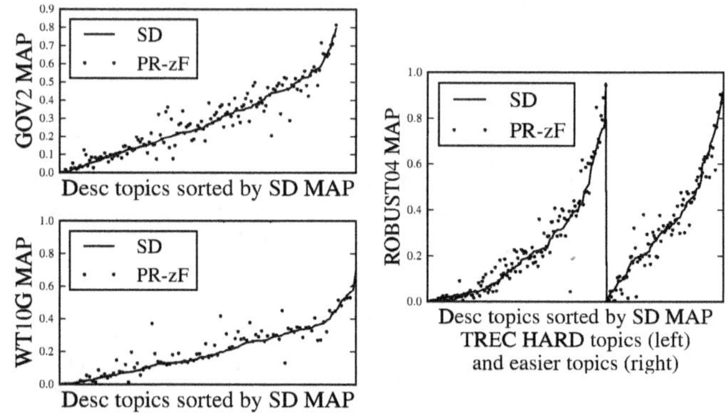

Figure 4: MAP difference compared to SD baseline per query for description topics. PhRank does slightly better on harder queries. The strategy of focus around one concept usually helps, but can significantly hurt some queries.

'*earth*' as the main concept that should be included in all top terms. This resulted in terms that were representative of the query, but not well distributed.

Nevertheless, Figure 4 shows consistent improvement for queries that are known to be harder (Robust04 HARD track) or easier (high baseline MAP). It is more likely that PhRank selects an appropriate main concept for easy queries because the pseudo relevant documents are of high quality. Difficult queries are less clearly defined and often benefit from the strong directional focus provided by PhRank terms.

In comparison, models like SD and sDist, take a more robust approach to term selection with a distribution of possibly relevant terms. This presents a very different term selection strategy, so one potential avenue for improvement is interpolation of PhRank term selection with bigrams in SD. However, the robustness of a distributed term selection approach can come with a tradeoff in overall effectiveness. Initial interpolation experiments with a weighted linear combination of SD and PhRank terms did not appear to yield any benefit over PhRank terms alone.

Alternatively, the properties of G may be turned to advantage. It has been observed that a Markov field framework selects more general and robust query expansion terms than competing methods [6]. A combination of query expansion and term selection using a Markov field framework may balance complementary high reward and robust query reformulation strategies and result in significant overall gains.

6.2.2 Precision

Results in Table 5 show significant improvement in MAP and R-precision for PhRank compared to sDist for both GOV2 and WT10G. PhRank terms are significantly more precise on average than the highest precision models for unweighted term selection. Unfortunately, the focus on one aspect of query meaning has unpredictable effects and some queries are significantly hurt by a high precision strategy.

There are two potential causes for negative results. First, PhRank may be picking a suboptimal concept. This does occur, particularly in the presence of polysemous or highly co-occurrent words in the query, or irrelevant documents in N. This is demonstrated with the high rank for '*earth*' in query #780 (Table 6). In the case of highly co-occurrent

Q: *How much of planet Earth is arable at present? Area must have plenty of water, sun and soil to support plant life.*		
PhRank terms	**SD terms**	
earth	planet earth	water sun
earth arable	earth arable	sun soil
planet earth	arable present	soil support
earth life	present area	support plant
earth water	area water	plant life

Table 6: TREC query #780: poor performance for PhRank compared to SD.

	Term Length						
	1	2	3	4	5	6	7
KC	37%	40%	15%	6%	1%	<1%	<1%
PhRank	22%	54%	24%				

Table 7: Percentage of PhRank and KC terms with various lengths.

words, these have a higher in-degree in G so they tend to accumulate weight during a random walk. A reduction in the number of iterations may help address this problem.

Irrelevant documents in G also hurt performance. The adequacy of an affinity graph G constructed using N is highly reliant on the quality of the initial query, the precision of the document similarity metric, and the adequacy of the collection being searched. If non-relevant documents occur in N there will be reduced connectivity in G, and this has an undesirable impact on the balance of word affinity scores. One solution to this problem may be to merge ranked lists computed by PhRank using different resources. The mistakes made by different instances of PhRank for the same query are likely to be less consistent than accurate assessments of term informativeness.

Second, more than one focus can occur, particularly in long queries. For example, there are two focal concepts of query #336: '*A relevant document would discuss the frequency of vicious black bear attacks worldwide and the possible causes for this savage behavior*'. The two core concepts are '*black bear*' and '*savage behavior*' but PhRank largely misses the importance of black bears. Instead, its top ranked terms for this query are {*savage, savage behavior, bear savage, vicious savage, attacks savage*}. This has a negative effect on IR effectiveness.

6.2.3 Succinctness

Results show that the performance of the top two PhRank terms in the same query structure as KC but *with no term weighting* performs comparably to KC *with term weighting.* The length of the terms is similar in both models, with around 75% of terms having a length of 1-2 words. This suggests that improved performance of unweighted PR-zF2 queries is more likely to be due to differences in the strategy for term selection than differences in term length. Note that KC shares the distributed approach to term selection with SD and sDist. KC selects two distinct concepts, whereas the top two terms selected by PhRank typically overlap.

More generally, it is observed that the succinct terms selected by PhRank are also novel. Table 8 shows that although PhRank and KC have the same number of 1-2 word terms overall, they display less than half of their potential overlap (we account for fewer terms in KC in this figure). Moreover, around 50% of PhRank terms contain two words, but only around half of them are also selected by SD.

PhRank (1-3 words)	**SD** (2 words)	**sDist** (3-6 words)	**KC** (1-7 words)
ROBUST04	23%	-	12%
WT10G	28%	11%	18%
GOV2	27%	15%	16%

Table 8: Percentage of PhRank terms selected by other models. Low figures show that PhRank is detecting novel terms with long-range dependencies.

Terms that are three words long dominate sDist (69% of all terms) yet less than half of the terms with three words in PhRank are also found in sDist queries. One likely explanation for these findings is that PhRank is not limited by syntactic or adjacency relations that are used in the other models. It detects distant word dependencies because repeat co-occurrences of word combinations reflect the associations in which they take part.

We hypothesize that distant associations may be present in queries because users condense information by relying on the ability of a search engine to infer links between words. The frequency of such textual economy was assessed in a sample of 100 queries randomly selected from Robust04 and GOV2. We assume that title queries capture a succinct information need and have informative associations between query words. By aligning description and title vocabulary, we discovered that 22% of description topics contain at least one informative word association that cannot be detected using any form of syntax or word adjacency, and a further 11% of topics contain at least one association that can only be detected using dependency relations.

7. CONCLUSION

We have presented PhRank, a novel term ranking algorithm that extends work on Markov chain frameworks for query expansion to select focused and succinct terms from within a query. PhRank captures query context with an affinity graph constructed using word co-occurrence in pseudo-relevant documents. A random walk of the graph is used for term ranking in combination with discrimination weights.

We showed that PhRank focuses on a limited number of words associated with a core query concept. Overall, this is more effective for both description topics and title queries than a distributed approach to term selection, and can generate queries with up to 90% fewer terms. However, this term selection strategy is risky and less robust than competing methods. For all collections, around 26% of queries have more than 5% decrease in MAP compared to SD (significant change is around 3-6%).

The two main issues affecting robustness are the handling queries with multiple concepts, and variation in the quality of pseudo relevance feedback. The first issue may be addressed by a diversity constraint on top ranked terms that adjusts the number of selected terms permitted to include the highest scoring query word. Improved sensitivity of the ranking algorithm may also improve results. For example, the present implementation does not consider the degree of connection between two words in the affinity graph when scoring terms. A third approach might apply a non-linear interpolation of SD and PhRank that backs off to distributed terms where required. Adaptive methods for the selection of k can address challenges with the depth of coverage in a collection or occasions when evidence for multiple concepts is widely dispersed.

Finally, the high precision strategy of term selection might be combined with the more conservative and robust expansion terms generated with a Markov chain approach to query expansion. On this point, we note that although weighted variants of an affinity graph have been proposed before, our concrete suggestion for a vertex weight s based on word salience in pseudo-relevant documents improves the informativeness of affinity scores and may benefit other techniques that use a Markov chain framework.

More generally, the work in this paper may be applicable to lexical feature selection methods for other areas of IR, including text-based image and multimedia retrieval or matching of search advertisements. Efficiency considerations surrounding the time to construct an affinity graph may be ameliorated by off-line indexing to precompute a language model for each document in a collection.

8. ACKNOWLEDGMENTS

This work was supported in part by the Center for Intelligent Information Retrieval. Any opinions, findings and conclusions or recommendations expressed in this material are those of the authors and do not necessarily reflect those of the sponsor.

References

[1] J. Allan, L. Ballesteros, J. P. Callan, W. B. Croft, and Z. Lu. Recent experiments with INQUERY. In *Fourth Text REtrieval Conference (TREC-4)*. 1995.

[2] N. Balasubramanian, G. Kumaran, and V. R. Carvalho. Exploring reductions for long web queries. In *Proc. of SIGIR 2010*, pages 571–578, New York, NY, USA, 2010. ACM.

[3] M. Bendersky and W. B. Croft. Discovering key concepts in verbose queries. In *Proc. of SIGIR 2008*, pages 491–498, New York, NY, USA, 2008. ACM.

[4] M. Bendersky and W. B. Croft. Modeling higher-order term dependencies in information retrieval using query hypergraphs. In *Proc. of SIGIR 2012*, pages 941–950, New York, NY, USA, 2012. ACM.

[5] M. Bendersky, D. Metzler, and W. B. Croft. Learning concept importance using a weighted dependence model. In *Proc. of WSDM 2010*, pages 31–40, New York, NY, USA, 2010. ACM.

[6] K. Collins-Thompson and J. Callan. Query expansion using random walk models. In *Proc. of CIKM 2005*, pages 704–711, New York, NY, USA, 2005. ACM.

[7] F. Crestani. Application of spreading activation techniques in information retrieval. *Artif. Intell. Rev.*, 11(6):453–482, Dec. 1997.

[8] W. B. Croft and D. Harper. Using probabilistic models of document retrieval without relevance information. *Journal of Documentation*, 35(4):285 – 295, 1979.

[9] W. B. Croft, H. R. Turtle, and D. D. Lewis. The use of phrases and structured queries in information retrieval. In *Proc. of SIGIR 1991*, pages 32–45, New York, NY, USA, 1991. ACM.

[10] R. Ferrer i Cancho and R. Solé. The small world of human language. In *Proc. of the Royal Society of London B*, volume 268, 2001.

[11] R. Ferrer i Cancho, R. V. Solé, and R. Köhler. Patterns in syntactic dependency networks. *Physical Review E*, 69(5), 2004.

[12] M. Hagen, M. Potthast, B. Stein, and C. Bräutigam. Query segmentation revisited. In *Proc. of WWW 2011*, pages 97–106, New York, NY, USA, 2011. ACM.

[13] K. S. Hasan and V. Ng. Conundrums in unsupervised keyphrase extraction: making sense of the state-of-the-art. In *Proc. of COLING 2010: posters*, pages 365–373, Stroudsburg, PA, USA, 2010. ACL.

[14] Y. Huang, L. Sun, and J.-Y. Nie. Query model refinement using word graphs. In *Proc. of CIKM 2010*, pages 1453–1456, New York, NY, USA, 2010. ACM.

[15] S. Huston and W. B. Croft. Evaluating verbose query processing techniques. In *Proc. of SIGIR 2010*, pages 291–298, New York, NY, USA, 2010. ACM.

[16] G. Kumaran and V. R. Carvalho. Reducing long queries using query quality predictors. In *Proc. of SIGIR 2009*, pages 564–571, New York, NY, USA, 2009. ACM.

[17] J. Lafferty and C. Zhai. Document language models, query models, and risk minimization for information retrieval. In *Proc. of SIGIR 2001*, pages 111–119, New York, NY, USA, 2001. ACM.

[18] M. Lease, J. Allan, and W. B. Croft. Regression rank: Learning to meet the opportunity of descriptive queries. In *Proc. of ECIR 2009*, pages 90–101, Berlin, Heidelberg, 2009. Springer-Verlag.

[19] C. Lioma and I. Ounis. A syntactically-based query reformulation technique for information retrieval. *Inf. Process. Manage.*, 44:143–162, January 2008.

[20] C. Macdonald and I. Ounis. Global statistics in proximity weighting models. In *Proceedings of Web N-gram 2010 Workshop at SIGIR*, 2010.

[21] C. D. Manning, P. Raghavan, and H. Schütze. *Introduction to Information Retrieval.* Cambridge University Press, 2008.

[22] K. Maxwell. *Term selection in information retrieval (forthcoming).* PhD thesis, University of Edinburgh, 2013.

[23] Q. Mei, D. Zhang, and C. Zhai. A general optimization framework for smoothing language models on graph structures. In *Proc. of SIGIR 2008*, pages 611–618, New York, NY, USA, 2008. ACM.

[24] D. Metzler and W. B. Croft. A Markov random field model for term dependencies. In *Proc. of SIGIR 2005*, pages 472–479, New York, NY, USA, 2005. ACM.

[25] R. Mihalcea and P. Tarau. Textrank: Bringing order into texts. In *Proc. of EMNLP 2004*, pages 404–411, 2004.

[26] L. Page, S. Brin, R. Motwani, and T. Winograd. The PageRank citation ranking: Bringing order to the web. Technical report, Stanford University, Stanford, CA, 1999.

[27] J. H. Park and W. B. Croft. Query term ranking based on dependency parsing of verbose queries. In *Proc. of SIGIR 2010*, pages 829–830, New York, NY, USA, 2010. ACM.

[28] J. H. Park, W. B. Croft, and D. A. Smith. A quasi-synchronous dependence model for information retrieval. In *Proc. of CIKM 2011*, pages 17–26, New York, NY, USA, 2011. ACM.

[29] J. Rocchio. Relevance feedback in information retrieval. In *The SMART Retrieval System - Experiments in Automatic Document Processing.* Prentice Hall, 1971.

[30] K. Sparck Jones. A statistical interpretation of term specificity and its application in retrieval. *J. of Documentation*, 28(1):11–21, 1972.

[31] C. J. van Rijsbergen. Information retrieval: theory and practice. In *Proceedings of the Joint IBM/University of Newcastle upon Tyne Seminar on Data Base Systems*, pages 1–14, 1979.

[32] X. Wan and J. Xiao. Single document keyphrase extraction using neighborhood knowledge. In *Proc. of AAAI 2008*, volume 2, pages 855–860. AAAI Press, 2008.

[33] X. Xue, S. Huston, and W. B. Croft. Improving verbose queries using subset distribution. In *Proc. of CIKM 2010*, pages 1059–1068, New York, NY, USA, 2010. ACM.

[34] C. Zhai and J. Lafferty. Model-based feedback in the language modeling approach to information retrieval. In *Proc. of CIKM 2001*, pages 403–410, New York, NY, USA, 2001. ACM.

Sentiment Diversification with Different Biases

Elif Aktolga and James Allan
Center for Intelligent Information Retrieval
School of Computer Science
University of Massachusetts Amherst
Amherst, Massachusetts
{elif, allan}@cs.umass.edu

ABSTRACT

Prior search result diversification work focuses on achieving topical variety in a ranked list, typically equally across all aspects. In this paper, we diversify with sentiments according to an explicit bias. We want to allow users to switch the result perspective to better grasp the polarity of opinionated content, such as during a literature review. For this, we first infer the *prior sentiment bias inherent in a controversial topic* – the 'Topic Sentiment'. Then, we utilize this information in 3 different ways to diversify results according to various sentiment biases: (1) Equal diversification to achieve a balanced and unbiased representation of all sentiments on the topic; (2) Diversification *towards* the Topic Sentiment, in which the actual sentiment bias in the topic is mirrored to emphasize the general perception of the topic; (3) Diversification *against* the Topic Sentiment, in which documents about the 'minority' or outlying sentiment(s) are boosted and those with the popular sentiment are demoted.

Since sentiment classification is an essential tool for this task, we experiment by gradually degrading the accuracy of a perfect classifier down to 40%, and show which diversification approaches prove most stable in this setting. The results reveal that the proportionality-based methods and our SCSF model, considering sentiment strength and frequency in the diversified list, yield the highest gains. Further, in case the Topic Sentiment cannot be reliably estimated, we show how performance is affected by equal diversification when actually an emphasis either towards or against the Topic Sentiment is desired: in the former case, an average of 6.48% is lost across all evaluation measures, whereas in the latter case this is 16.23%, confirming that bias-specific sentiment diversification is crucial.

Categories and Subject Descriptors: H.3.3 [**Information Search and Retrieval**]: Retrieval Models

General Terms: Experimentation, Algorithms, Measurement

Keywords: Diversity, Opinions, Sentiment, Proportionality

SIGIR'13, July 28–August 1, 2013, Dublin, Ireland.

1. INTRODUCTION

In previous work diversification has mainly been applied for better topical variety in search results [9, 25, 26, 27]. Equal preference is typically given to all aspects. How can opinionated content exhibiting sentiments be diversified? Initial approaches have been presented [10, 17, 18]; however these only consider equal diversification. In this paper, we view the problem from a high-level perspective to allow for sentiment diversification according to *different biases*, which will be vital for situations like a literature review on a controversial topic.

Consider the topic 'global warming.' In a typical use case, a user engages in a comprehensive literature review with the aim of understanding the positions on this topic. This involves – besides searching and finding relevant opinionated documents [16] – understanding and mentally categorizing opinionated content. This can be done by organizing the discussed arguments by topical content; or, they can also be grouped by sentiment, such as positive, negative, neutral, and mixed [18]. We focus on facilitating the latter approach for the user. For some topics that can clearly be generalized into 'pro' versus 'con' arguments, this sentiment categorization is more natural, whereas it can be less obvious for topics like global warming that are associated with various arguments. Focusing on the *sentiment dimension* of these arguments, we can see that negative sentiments for global warming typically express criticism and concern about it and its effects on the environment. Those with positive sentiment often claim that worries about global climate change are unjustified ("there is no such issue"), playing down the concerns in a 'calming' (i.e., positive) way. Mixed or neutral statements either express no sentiments or contain an equal amount of positive and negative arguments. Those could be "I don't care", or "It's a serious problem but we're handling it" kind of stances towards global warming.

Getting back to our use case: while a balanced and unbiased presentation of the results helps the user understand various viewpoints on a topic, discerning the topic's polarity is harder if minority opinions are 'buried' in the results [18]. Therefore, the user should be able to *switch the result perspective* as needed. This way, she can either obtain a balanced or a biased view on majority or minority opinions, make her own comparisons across the representations, and perform this task in a more informed manner. Note that this is different from showing all positive *or* all negative *or* all neutral/mixed documents at a time: with such a representation the user would still need to draw her own conclusions about which sentiments form majority or minority

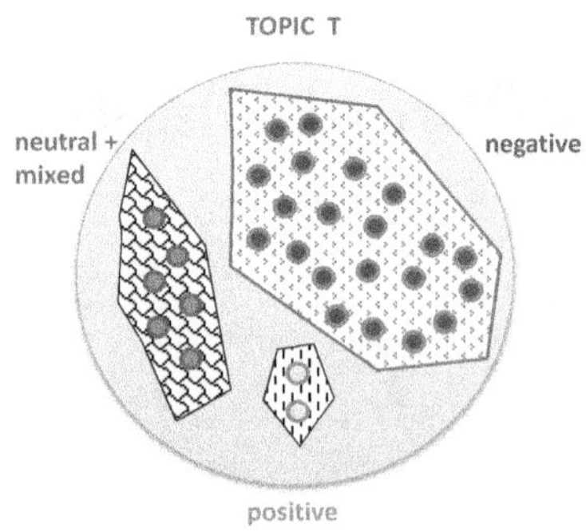

Figure 1: Topic Sentiment: Dots represent relevant documents for this topic, which are grouped according to their sentiments. The obtained sentiment distribution is used for sentiment diversification.

opinions. Our aim is to analyze this information for the user and to match the inferred trend as closely as possible in the results. For this, we need to have a good grasp of the topic a priori: we consider a large pool of relevant documents about the topic, which are grouped by sentiments as visualized in Figure 1. Then, we can infer the *topic's sentiment distribution or inherent bias* – Topic Sentiment – from this analysis. We categorize the aspects 'mixed' and 'neutral' together to represent the 'balanced' aspect, whereas 'positive' and 'negative' refer to arguments that are clearly biased towards one side only. If Figure 1 represented the Topic Sentiment for global warming, this could be interpreted as the issue being perceived with great concern since negative sentiments constitute the majority, and while there are some 'balanced' positions on it, the positive sentiments form a clear minority. By utilizing this information during diversification, three biases are emphasized in search results: (1) Equal diversification by preferring all sentiments equally. This allows for a balanced representation of all sentiments on the topic; (2) Diversification towards the Topic Sentiment, in which the resulting reranked list mirrors the actual sentiment bias in a topic. This approach highlights the general perception of a topic; (3) Diversification against the Topic Sentiment, in which documents about the minority sentiment(s) are boosted whereas those with the majority sentiment are demoted. Such a list highlights unusual and outlying opinions on the topic.

In this paper we propose different diversification models for sentiment diversity with these 3 biases, and perform experiments using the TREC Blog Track data [23]. Since sentiment classification is an essential tool for this task, we experiment by gradually reducing the accuracy of a perfect classifier down to 40%, and show which diversification approaches prove most stable in this setting. Further, in case the Topic Sentiment cannot be reliably estimated, we show how performance is affected by equal diversification when actually an emphasis either towards or against the Topic Sentiment is desired. The results reveal that particularly when highlighting minority sentiments, diversifying with the corresponding bias yields significant improvements.

2. RELATED WORK

There is a large amount of work in the area of topical diversity: the main aim is to eliminate topical redundancy in results while maximizing the number of documents containing novel information [1, 3, 6, 9, 25, 26, 27]. One of the earliest works is the maximal marginal relevance (MMR) approach [3], which employs content-based similarity measures to balance the tradeoff between novelty and relevance. More recently, researchers have shown explicit diversification approaches to be superior over implicit diversification techniques: well-known algorithms are xQuAD [25, 26, 27], IA-select [1], and more recently PM-1 and PM-2 [9]. Other approaches to topical diversity are language modeling based [31], probabilistic [4] and correlation-based [30]. Very recent research addresses personalized diversification [29], blog feed diversity [19, 28], and combined implicit and explicit aspect diversification [15].

Among these approaches, it is common to equally or uniformly diversify across all query aspects or subtopics due to the lack of data [9, 25, 26, 27]. Although the TREC Web Track diversity task provides topical query aspects [8], distributions over these aspects are not included. Agrawal et al. [1] use their own classifiers and judgments for obtaining query intent aspect distributions. Further, the NTCIR-9 Intent task provides non-uniform aspect probabilities [24]. One of our contributions in this paper is to present alternatives to the equal distribution approach (Section 3.4): a query's topic's sentiment distribution can be employed in various ways to yield an emphasis for a certain bias. Topical diversity could also benefit from these ideas.

The proportionality-based approaches PM-1 and PM-2 [9] distinguish themselves from prior research by explicitly matching the aspect distribution in the diversified list to the overall popularity of these aspects, thus yielding a proportionally diversified list. We adapt this approach to sentiment diversity, and propose a minor variation for dealing with retrieval limitations (Section 3.3).

Extensive work on opinion detection and retrieval has dealt with techniques to boost opinionated documents in retrieval [14, 28, 32, 33]. Prior work focusing on *opinion diversity* is very recent: Demartini and Siersdorfer describe a study about opinions in search results as given by popular search engines for controversial queries [11]. In later work, Demartini then tackles opinion diversification [10]: his approach is based on the xQuAD framework [25]. Retrieved search results are classified into the sentiment categories positive, negative, or objective. Diversification ensures maximum variety among these aspects with uniform preference. We implement this approach as the SCS model and combine it with the 3 biases (Section 3.2.1). The SCSF model is a further extension, presented in Section 3.2.2.

Kacimi and Gamper propose a different opinion diversification framework for controversial queries [17, 18]: three criteria are considered for diversification: topical relevance, semantic diversification, and sentiment diversification. Their model favors documents most different in sentiment direction and in the arguments they discuss. The sentiments are again one of positive, negative, and neutral. In the model the components are linearly combined; however, in order to find the documents maximizing the distances for all criteria the authors consider all subsets of documents. Our work differs from this work in several points: (1) We perform *sentiment diversification* only and not opinion diversification. Opinions refer to topical content, whereas sentiments are a non-topical aspect that we focus on in this paper. (2) This choice allows us to study sentiment diversification performance with different biases, which has not been researched in prior work.

In this context, unlike topical diversity we make a simplifying assumption that each query belongs to one topic and therefore represents one topical aspect. We avoid dealing with ambiguity by using long and specific queries in our experiments, as explained in Section 4. That is, the topical dimension is kept static so we can focus on the varied sentiment dimension. We leave it to future work to explore the interplay of topical and sentiment aspects together for diversification.

3. SENTIMENT DIVERSIFICATION

3.1 Introduction

In order to diversify a retrieved list with respect to the distribution of sentiments in a query's topic, we need to introduce a few concepts first. Let Q be a query, and let T be the query's topic $T(Q)$, abbreviated as T for simplicity. As visualized in Figure 1, we define T to include all the relevant documents that can be retrieved for Q, i.e., $T = rel(Q)$. Further, let each document D in T have a sentiment, i.e., each document is positive, negative, neutral or mixed. These can be generalized to countable sentiment criteria $\sigma \in sent(T)$. We will use this sentiment information from T in our models to diversify search results according to the distribution of sentiments in the topic.

Sentiment criteria of the form positive, negative, and neutral/mixed can take different shapes when converted into a sentiment score. In the literature [10, 17, 23] we identified a document to either have a single discrete sentiment from $\{-1, 0, 1\}$, or the sentiment is broken down into three scores *positivity*, *negativity*, and *neutrality* such that they sum to 1.0 for a single document. We refer to these latter ones as finer grained "fractional scores" in the rest of the paper. Our models are designed for these kinds of scores, but discrete scores can also be handled by simple conversion as we will show later.

Below we consider two different diversification frameworks and present several modifications to them.

3.2 Retrieval-Interpolated Diversification

Algorithm 1 Retrieval Interpolated Diversification Framework.

```
1  S = ∅
2  while|S| < τ and |R| > 0
3        do
4              D* = arg max_{D∈R} λRetC(Q) + (1 − λ)SentC(T)
5              R = R \ {D*}
6              S = S ∪ {D*}
7  return S
```

Algorithm 1 shows the Retrieval-Interpolated Diversification Framework, which is similar to xQuAD, first introduced by Santos et al. [25] for topical diversity. In this diversification framework, documents retrieved in R are iteratively added to the new ranked list S. The τ documents are chosen according to the maximization objective function in line 4:

$$D^* = argmax_{D \in R}\ \lambda \cdot \text{RetC}(Q) + (1-\lambda) \cdot \text{SentC}(T) \quad (1)$$

where RetC(Q) is the *retrieval contribution*, which is always estimated with $P(D|Q)$ – how likely D is to be relevant to Q by content, and SentC(T) is the *sentiment contribution*, which we will define in two different ways below. The scores from these two components are interpolated for diversity estimation.

3.2.1 Sentiment Contribution by Strength (SCS)

In this version of the model we estimate the sentiment contribution in the maximization objective function (Equation 1) as follows:

$$\text{SentC}(T) = P(D, \bar{S}|T) \quad (2)$$

Here $P(D, \bar{S}|T)$ measures how much D can contribute to the sentiment diversity of S. Structurally, this resembles xQuAD [25] with the difference that the estimation is conditioned on the query's topic T.

In order to make the model more flexible towards sentiment scores, we define each document to have a fractional score for each sentiment criterion $\sigma \in sent(T)$. For example, a document may be classified as positive with 75% confidence. Then, this can be converted into a trinary score $P(D|\sigma = \text{positive}) = 0.75$, $P(D|\sigma = \text{neutral}) = 0.25$, and $P(D|\sigma = \text{negative}) = 0$. Fractional classification scores directly obtained from a classifier (such as logistic regression) fit in nicely into this framework. If documents are manually judged, they are often associated with only one 'dominant' sentiment score from $\{-1, 0, 1\}$ such as -1, which can be converted into a 100% negative score. Given this information, we can further decompose $P(D, \bar{S}|T)$ as follows:

$$P(D, \bar{S}|T) = \sum_{\sigma \in sent(T)} P(D, \bar{S}|\sigma) \cdot P(\sigma|T) \quad (3)$$

$$\stackrel{rank}{=} \sum_{\sigma \in sent(T)} P(D|\sigma) \cdot P(\bar{S}|\sigma) \cdot P(\sigma|T) \quad (4)$$

where $P(\bar{S}|\sigma)$ denotes the likelihood of σ not being satisfied by the documents already chosen into S (see below for further derivation) and $P(\sigma|T)$ stands for the importance of sentiment σ to topic T. This is discussed in detail in Section 3.4. From Equation 3 to Equation 4 we make the same independence assumption as Santos et al. [25]: the diversity estimation of D with respect to the sentiments σ can be made independently of the documents already selected into S. We continue with Equation 4:

$$\sum_{\sigma \in sent(T)} P(D|\sigma) \cdot P(\bar{S}|\sigma) \cdot P(\sigma|T)$$

$$= \sum_{\sigma \in sent(T)} P(D|\sigma) \cdot P(\sigma|T) \cdot \prod_{D_j \in S} P(\overline{D_j}|\sigma)$$

$$= \sum_{\sigma \in sent(T)} P(D|\sigma) \cdot P(\sigma|T) \cdot \prod_{D_j \in S} 1 - P(D_j|\sigma) \quad (5)$$

Here we make another independence assumption for $P(\overline{D_j}|\sigma)$ as Santos et al. [25]: the likelihood of not sampling D_j's sentiment from T is independent of the sentiments of the other documents in S. Since each D_j was independently chosen into S, this is a reasonable assumption.

To summarize, Equation 5 estimates the diversity of a document D by considering how well D represents each sentiment criterion, which is weighted by how important that

Algorithm 2 Diversity by Proportionality (PM-2).

$S = \emptyset$
$\forall \sigma \;\; s_\sigma = 0$
while $|S| < \tau$ and $|R| > 0$
  do
    for $\sigma \in sent(T)$
      do
        $quotient[\sigma] = \frac{v_\sigma}{2s_\sigma + 1}$
    $\sigma^* = \arg\max_\sigma quotient[\sigma]$
    $D^* = \arg\max_{D \in R} \; \lambda \cdot quotient[\sigma^*] \cdot P(D|\sigma^*) + (1-\lambda) \sum_{\sigma \neq \sigma^*} quotient[\sigma] \cdot P(D|\sigma)$
    $R = R \setminus \{D^*\}$
    $S = S \cup \{D^*\}$
    for $\sigma \in sent(T)$
      do
        $s_\sigma = s_\sigma + \frac{P(D^*|\sigma)}{\sum_{\gamma \in sent(T)} P(D^*|\gamma)}$
return S

sentiment criterion is to T. This whole part is demoted according to how many documents of the same sentiment S already contains.

3.2.2 Sentiment Contribution by Strength and Frequency (SCSF)

We consider an alternative formulation of the sentiment contribution component above in Equation 1 in which the punish/reward factor is estimated slightly differently:

$$\text{SentC}(T) = P(D|T) \cdot (1 - P(S|T)) \tag{6}$$

where $P(D|T)$ stands for how important D's sentiment is for T, and $1 - P(S|T)$ describes how well the sentiments from T are already represented in S. We further derive:

$$\begin{aligned} & P(D|T) \cdot (1 - P(S|T)) \\ = \; & P(D|T) - P(D|T) \cdot P(S|T) \\ = \; & \sum_{\sigma \in sent(T)} P(D|\sigma) \cdot P(\sigma|T) - P(D|\sigma) \cdot P(\sigma|T) \cdot P(S|\sigma) \end{aligned} \tag{7}$$

Here we apply the Bayes' Rule to $P(S|\sigma)$:

$$P(S|\sigma) = \frac{P(\sigma|S) \cdot P(S)}{P(\sigma)} \stackrel{rank}{=} P(\sigma|S) \tag{8}$$

which is rank-equivalent since $P(S)$ is a constant across all documents in an iteration, and $P(\sigma)$, the prior probability of a particular sentiment, is equal across all sentiments. Hence we obtain from Equation 7:

$$\begin{aligned} & \sum_{\sigma \in sent(T)} P(D|\sigma) \cdot P(\sigma|T) - P(D|\sigma) \cdot P(\sigma|T) \cdot P(\sigma|S) \\ = & \sum_{\sigma \in sent(T)} P(D|\sigma) \cdot P(\sigma|T) \cdot (1 - P(\sigma|S)) \\ = & \sum_{\sigma \in sent(T)} P(D|\sigma) \cdot P(\sigma|T) \cdot P(\bar{\sigma}|S) \end{aligned} \tag{9}$$

Now we can see that the first part of Equation 9 is identical to Equation 5. We can estimate the components $P(D|\sigma) \cdot P(\sigma|T)$ the same way as described in Sections 3.2 and 3.4. However, $P(\bar{\sigma}|S)$, the likelihood of S not having sentiment σ, is new. We define its complement as follows:

$$P(\sigma|S) = \frac{sent(\sigma, S)}{|S|} \tag{10}$$

which is the number of documents in S having *dominant sentiment* σ. Each document in S can be mapped into its dominant or most confident sentiment class $\sigma \in sent(T)$, typically positive, negative, or neutral/mixed. Given this, we count the number of times a particular sentiment σ occurs in S as $sent(\sigma, S)$. We set $P(\sigma|S) = 0$ if $S = \emptyset$ to avoid zero division in the first iteration.

To summarize, this formulation calculates the punish/ reward factor directly from the *frequency* of documents present in the whole set S with certain sentiments. Contrarily, in the SCS model the *strength of sentiments* of each document in S is considered individually, whereas the frequency of such documents is implicit in the multiplication over all documents in S. In the experiments we empirically verify the effectiveness of the two models in sentiment diversification to draw conclusions about their usefulness.

3.3 Diversity by Proportionality

As a second diversification framework we consider Algorithm 2, the best-performing approach in Dang and Croft's work [9]. This framework is based on the Sante-Laguë method for seat allocation and is adapted here to sentiment diversification. In each iteration documents are chosen based on the proportionality of the diversified list. We only describe modified components due to space limitations. Instead of applying the algorithm to topical aspects, here it is employed together with sentiments $\sigma \in sent(T)$. Further, $P(D|\sigma)$ is estimated by means of fractional sentiment scores as defined in Section 3.2 instead of estimating the relevance of the document with respect to a (sub)topical aspect. Note that under this modification, a document is purely evaluated on the basis of its sentiments and not according to topical relevance.

The variables v_σ and s_σ in the quotient are important. The former is the number of relevant documents the sentiment σ should have, whereas the latter represents the estimated number of documents actually present in the list for σ. v_σ at a particular rank i can easily be inferred from $P(\sigma|T)$ as follows:

$$v_\sigma = \lfloor i \cdot P(\sigma|T) + 0.5 \rfloor \tag{11}$$

According to PM-2, s_σ is updated with the fractional sentiment scores of the chosen document, since each sentiment takes up a 'portion' of the seats in S. This denotes how well the chosen document represents each sentiment. For the relationship between document sentiments and the topic sentiment distribution, please refer to Section 3.4.

3.3.1 Diversity by Proportionality with Minimum Available Votes (PM-2M)

Unlike the seat allocation problem in a voting system, in a retrieved list of documents there is an additional constraining factor. The top K documents retrieved from a search system constitute the source for diversification, so it is possible that a particular sentiment is underrepresented in this list. Unless the system requests more documents, the desired proportionality in the diversified list may not be optimally achieved with the current set of documents. In this situation, with respect to PM-2 the given votes v_σ overestimate l_σ, the *actual number of documents* with sentiment σ in the retrieved top K set. For a large enough rank K, this may result in a suboptimally diversified list where documents with an over-emphasized sentiment are exploited early in the ranks. Therefore, we propose a small change to the quotient defined in Algorithm 2:

$$quotient[\sigma] = \frac{\min(v_\sigma, l_\sigma)}{2s_\sigma + 1} \quad (12)$$

which ensures that the quotient does not over-emphasize the importance of a sentiment if data is missing in the retrieved list. This technique has a remote resemblance to disproportionate stratified sampling in that documents are chosen slightly differently than dictated by the topic sentiment distribution in favor of improved overall diversity. We refer to this modified diversification approach as PM-2M and compare its effectiveness to PM-2, SCS and SCSF in the experimental section 4.

3.4 Favoring Different Biases in Search Results

In the presentation of the diversification models above $P(\sigma|T)$ plays a central role in defining which sentiment bias is favored in search results. Intuitively, this component stands for the importance of sentiment σ to topic T. Below we present three different possible biases in search results that the estimation of $P(\sigma|T)$ impacts.

3.4.1 Equal Sentiment Diversification (BAL)

This is our baseline approach, which does not give preference to any sentiment, but weights them equally or uniformly. Therefore, this approach does *not* utilize information from the query's topic about its prior sentiment distribution. We set

$$P(\sigma|T) = \frac{1}{|sent(T)|} \quad (13)$$

which results in each sentiment criterion $\sigma \in sent(T)$ to be considered equally important. We refer to this bias method as 'Balance' (BAL) in Section 4.

We assume that with this balanced estimation the SCS model is equivalent to Demartini's [10] approach. Since this detail is not explicitly described in their work, it is most reasonable to assume an equal bias as in prior research.

3.4.2 Diversifying Towards the Topic Sentiment (CRD)

In this approach we choose to diversify the retrieved list *towards* the distribution of sentiments in the query's topic. Such results strongly represent the crowd's opinion(s). For this, we need information about the sentiments in T. Recall from Section 3.1 that T is defined as a topic space to include all the relevant documents that can be retrieved for the query Q, i.e., $T = rel(Q)$. Then, we can map each relevant document into its dominant or most confident sentiment class $\sigma \in sent(T)$. Given this, we count the number of times a particular sentiment σ occurs in T as $sent(\sigma, T)$. This allows us to interpret $P(\sigma|T)$ as the likelihood of sentiment σ being drawn from T:

$$P(\sigma|T) = \frac{sent(\sigma, T)}{|T|} \quad (14)$$

which represents the fraction of documents in T with dominant sentiment σ; for instance the fraction of positive documents in T. We name this bias as 'Crowd' (short: CRD).

3.4.3 Diversifying Against the Topic Sentiment (OTL)

What if a user is interested in viewing minority sentiments on the topic? For favoring outlying sentiments, we need to diversify the search results *against* the Topic Sentiment. For this, we introduce one minor modification to CRD above: Let the n sentiment estimations for $\sigma \in sent(T)$ be sorted in increasing order of $P(\sigma|T)$. Then, for each σ at rank i we swap its estimation $P(\sigma|T)$ with the one at rank $n - i$. This 'reverses' the values in the topic distribution without changing the properties of the distribution. Consequently, if originally in T positive documents are strongly favored and negative documents are least favored, this trend is reversed through the value swap in T so that outlying sentiments (negative documents) will be strongly preferred during diversification. We refer to this bias as 'Outlier' (OTL) in the experiments (Section 4).

Irrespective of the preferred bias, we apply Add-1 Smoothing [5] to $P(\sigma|T)$ estimates to account for zero probabilities. In order to correct such unrealistic estimations, an unobserved sentiment class is assigned a very small probability, and the estimations for the other sentiment classes are adjusted accordingly.

4. EXPERIMENTS

4.1 Setup

Retrieval Corpus As retrieval corpus we use the TREC Blog Track data from 2006 and 2008 [23] for all our experiments. For preparation, the DiffPost algorithm is applied to the corpus for better retrieval as shown in prior work [20, 22]. Further, we perform stop word removal and Porter stemming.

Queries and Retrieval Model We split the 150 TREC Blog Track 2008 queries into 3 non-overlapping randomly chosen sets of size 50 each in order not to bias training or testing towards a specific year: split 1 is used for training and tuning parameters; the results in this paper are reported on split 2, and split 3 is reserved for sentiment classifier training. For our diversification experiments, we use a strong retrieval baseline: the queries' stopped title and description texts are combined for use with the Sequential Dependence Model in Lemur/Indri [21], smoothed using Dirichlet ($\mu = 10,000$). All diversification models are applied to the top $K = 50$ retrieved documents as determined during training. The retrieval scores are normalized to yield document likelihood scores.

Sentiment Classification The sentiment classifier is trained as a logistic regression model using Liblinear [13] with default settings. For this, we utilize the judged documents from the 50 split 3 TREC Blog Track queries. Training is done for three classes – positive, negative, and neutral to obtain probability estimates that are employed as fractional scores for sentiment estimation (Section 3.2.1). As features we extract Sentiwordnet 3.0 terms with their length-normalized term frequencies in the documents [12].

Topic Sentiment Estimation Given a query, the topic sentiment distribution can be estimated in various ways: (1) in the form of opinion relevance judgments for a pool of documents where all judged relevant documents are included in the distribution; (2) by retrieving the top M documents from a separate corpus or web search engine and tagging them with sentiment judgments. We experimented with both approaches but only present the results for (1) here due to space limitations: we use the relevance judgments from the TREC 2008 Blog Track [23], which are divided into the same sentiment aspects as required in the models.

4.2 Evaluation Measures

The sentiment diversification approaches are evaluated using standard evaluation measures that were designed for topical diversity: Precision-IA [1], s-recall [31], α-NDCG [6], ERR-IA [2], and NRBP [7]. The former two measures are set-based, whereas the remaining ones are cascade measures as described by Ashkan and Clarke [2], punishing redundancy through parameters α (α-NDCG, ERR-IA, NRBP) and additionally β (NRBP), which represents user patience. In order to measure sentiment diversity with a chosen bias, we implement all the measures in their intent-aware (or for us, 'sentiment-aware') version [1, 2]. Hence, the weighted average over the sentiment-dependent scores of a measure is computed as given by measure-IA for a query Q and topic T:

$$\text{measure-IA}(Q,T) = \sum_{\sigma \in sent(T)} P(\sigma|T) \cdot \text{measure}(Q|\sigma) \quad (15)$$

where $P(\sigma|T)$ defines the weight for the sentiment-specific result yielded by measure$(Q|\sigma)$.

Intent-aware measures can be rank-specific such as Precision-IA@k or α-NDCG@k for example, or rank-independent as NRBP. We utilize another rank-specific measure defined by Dang and Croft [9], Cumulative Proportionality (CPR) at rank K:

$$CPR@K = \frac{1}{K}\sum_{i=1}^{K} PR@i \quad (16)$$

in which $PR@i$ is computed as the inverse normalized disproportionality at rank i (see [9] for details). Here, we define the disproportionality at rank i as follows:

$$DP@i = \sum_{\sigma \in sent(T)} c_\sigma (v_\sigma - s_\sigma)^2 + \frac{1}{2} n_{NR}^2 \quad (17)$$

where v_σ is the number of relevant documents the sentiment σ should have, s_σ is the number of relevant documents actually found for σ, n_{NR} is the number of documents that are non-relevant (to any sentiment), and $c_\sigma = 1$ if $v_\sigma \geq s_\sigma$, 0 otherwise. This measure allows us to assess how proportional the diversified list is with respect to the desired topic distribution. v_σ can be inferred from the true topic sentiment distribution $P(\sigma|T)$ in the same way as detailed in Equation 11. As noted by Dang and Croft [9], CPR penalizes the under-representation of aspects (here: sentiments) and the over-representation of non-relevant documents.

4.3 Results

In this section we discuss the results of the retrieval baseline SDM and all the proposed diversification models in Section 3, SCS, SCSF, PM-2 and PM-2M, with the three biases, Crowd (CRD), Balance (BAL) and Outlier (OTL). The interpolation parameter $\lambda \in \{0.0, ..., 1.0\}$ is tuned in 0.1 steps separately for each model and bias on our training split. The results are presented with fixed parameters K and λ on test split 2, and the evaluation is performed with the TREC 2008 Blog Track judgments at rank 20. α-NDCG, ERR-IA, and NRBP require parameters, which are set to $\alpha = 0.5$ and $\beta = 0.5$.

4.3.1 *Straight-Bias Experiments*

Our primary aim in the experiments is to evaluate sentiment *diversification* performance. Sentiment classification is an important part of the system since both the to-be-diversified documents need to be tagged with sentiments, as well as those for the topic sentiment distribution estimation. Since a 'full evaluation' of sentiment diversification techniques on a publicly available dataset has not been done yet in prior work, it is important to understand how sentiment classification quality affects diversification performance. Therefore, we start with a "perfect system" in which classification accuracy is 100% for judged documents. For unjudged documents the trained sentiment classifier described in Section 4.1 is applied. We then gradually reduce the overall classification performance in 10% steps until 40% as follows: given the top $K = 50$ retrieved documents for a query, before diversification we randomly sample the ranks at which the true classification label is switched to another label randomly to achieve the desired classification error for each query.

Figure 2 shows the results for the straight-bias experiment, in which the topic sentiment distribution employed in experiment and evaluation *underlies the same favored bias.* For instance, the left-most column in Figure 2 shows the results for diversifying towards Crowd in the experiments, and measuring performance for Crowd in the evaluation (short-CRD-CRD). The middle column shows the same for Balance (short: BAL-BAL), and the right-most column is for the Outlier bias (short: OTL-OTL).

At the top-most row in the Precision-IA@20 graphs we observe a big gap between the SDM baseline and SCS model versus the rest of the models. For Crowd, the SCSF model only dominates when classification accuracy is at least 60% while it achieves the best (however not statistically significant) numbers in the Outlier graph. PM-2M and PM-2 also perform well and dominate some of the lower accuracy ranges. Statistical significance with the paired two-sided t-test (p-value$<$ 0.05) is indicated in the graphs with circles:

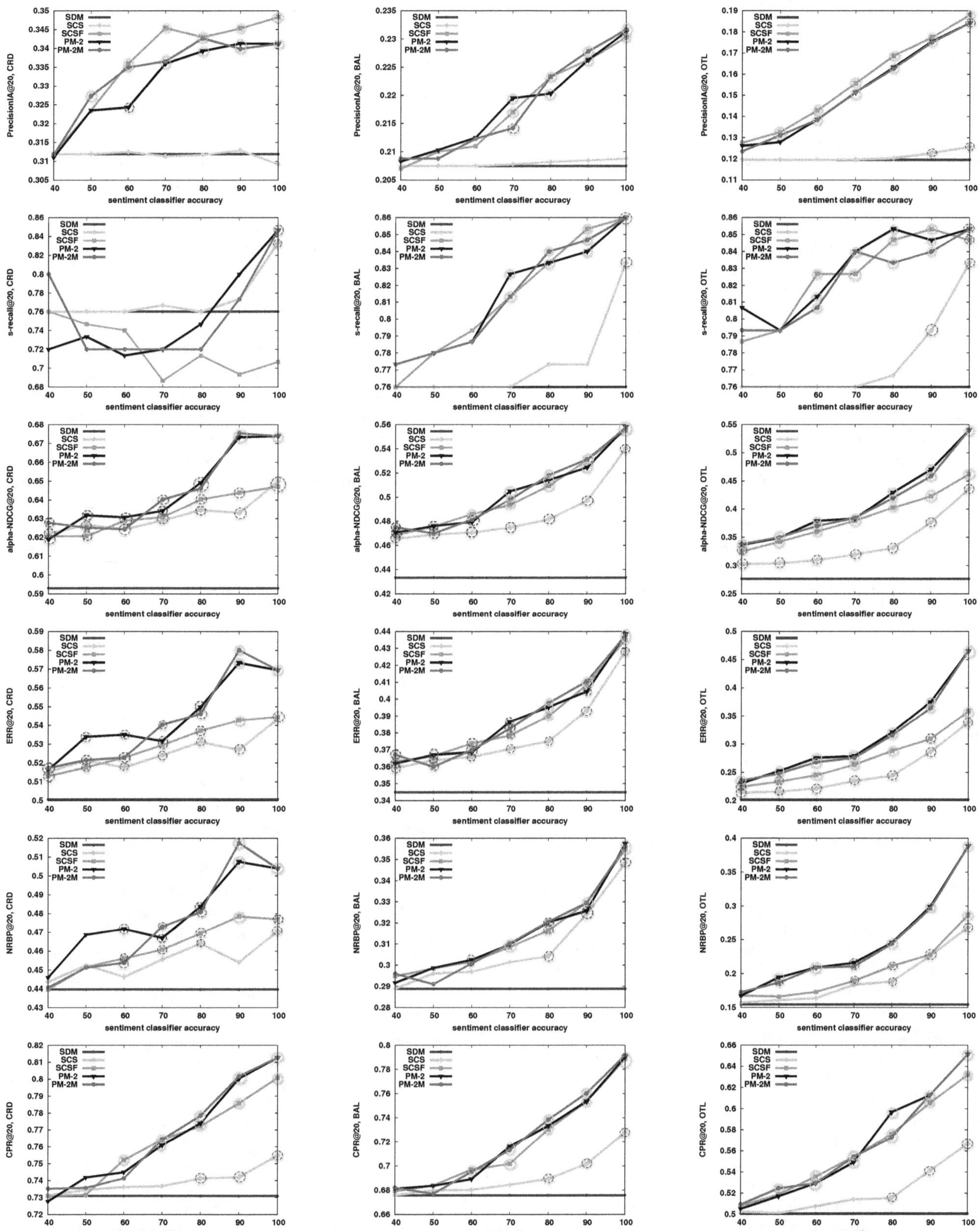

Figure 2: Straight-Bias Experiment over test split varying sentiment classifier accuracies on the x-axis and each one measure and bias on the y-axis. The leftmost column is for the Crowd bias (CRD), the middle one for Balance (BAL), and the rightmost one for Outlier (OTL). Dark purple dotted circled points indicate statistical significance over the SDM baseline with p-value < 0.05 using the paired two-sided t-test, whereas light blue circled points indicate the same over the SCS and SDM models.

Measure	Precision-IA@20		α-NDCG@20		ERR-IA@20		NRBP		CPR@20	
Exp-Eval	BAL-CRD	CRD-CRD	BAL-CRD	CRD-CRD	BAL-CRD	CRD-CRD	BAL-CRD	CRD-CRD	BAL-CRD	CRD-CRD
SDM baseline	0.312	0.312	0.593	0.593	0.501	0.501	0.440	0.440	0.731	0.731
SCS	0.308	0.309	0.642	**0.650**	0.532	**0.543**	0.453	**0.471**	0.750	**0.755**
SCSF	0.298	**0.348**	0.648	0.647	0.533	**0.545**	0.456	**0.477**	0.774	**0.801**
PM-2	0.302	**0.341**	0.642	**0.674**	0.526	**0.570**	0.446	**0.504**	0.772	**0.813**
PM-2M	0.298	**0.341**	0.639	**0.674**	0.521	**0.570**	0.440	**0.504**	0.767	**0.813**

Table 1: Cross-Bias Experiment over test split with perfect sentiment classifier to compare performance loss when diversifying equally (BAL-CRD) if actually diversification for the Crowd bias is desired (CRD-CRD). Bold entries in CRD-CRD columns are statistically significant over corresponding entries in BAL-CRD with p-value < 0.004 using the paired two-sided t-test.

the lighter blue circles refer to the result being significant over the SCS and SDM models, whereas the darker dotted circles indicate significance over the SDM model only. In the Precision-IA@20 graphs the results for SCSF and the proportionality-based methods are significant over SCS and SDM even for lower accuracies. We conclude that if precision is important, the SCSF diversification model should be used.

Among the s-recall@20 graphs the one for Crowd is the most arbitrary one. Performance drops well below the baseline for the SCSF and proportionality-based methods with medium quality classification: this indicates that the majority sentiment(s) are being emphasized too strongly, whereas minority sentiments appear much later in the ranked list for the first time, which is when the subtopic-recall measure is affected. This is expected, since we explicitly diversify in favor of majority sentiments. In the Balance and Outlier graphs for s-recall@20 there is no such trend, however precision is not as high for those biases as it is for Crowd. This is a typical precision versus recall tradeoff observation.

The next row shows results for α-NDCG@20, followed by ERR-IA@20 and NRBP: we note that the trends in these graphs look very similar, although the ranges of the values differ greatly. It is interesting to observe that the peak performance for the proportionality-based methods for the Crowd bias is not at 100% classification accuracy, but at 90%. What these three measures have in common is punishing redundancy based on the rank and sentiment criterion in addition to non-relevance. Since usually there are many documents with the majority sentiment in the retrieved list to start with, a strong emphasis on a single sentiment criterion results in more redundancy. With the 10% error in classification documents with other sentiments are slightly boosted, yielding better overall varied ranking. In the Balance and Outlier graphs this trend cannot be observed, since the Balance bias does not strongly emphasize a single sentiment criterion to begin with. Concerning the Outlier bias, there are fewer documents with minority sentiments in the retrieved list to cause the same 'clustered' ranking effect as for Crowd. Summarizing the trends across the α-NDCG@20, ERR-IA@20, and NRBP graphs we make the following conclusion: if ranking is important, the PM-2 and PM-2M methods should be chosen.

Finally, we look at the last row of graphs with the CPR@20 results: this measure evaluates how proportional the overall list is with respect to the chosen bias. PM-2 and PM-2M achieve the best results, which is closely followed by SCSF. PM-2 and SCSF are more appropriate for lower classification accuracies ($\leq 70\%$), whereas PM-2M performs slightly better with better classification quality.

Looking at the fixed values of the interpolation parameter λ during training for this experiment, the following insights can be drawn: for the SCS model, across all classifier accuracies and biases generally $\lambda \geq 0.6$ values are preferred. So this model performs best with a weaker emphasis on diversity, which pulls it closer to the SDM baseline as observed in the graphs of Figure 2. SCSF on the other hand has a good mixture of higher and lower λ values across classifier accuracies and biases, with many of them being < 0.5, particularly when the classifier is more accurate. So a heavier emphasis on the diversification part helps this model. The distinguishing feature between SCS and SCSF is the consideration of sentiment frequencies in addition to sentiment strength contributions. When the classifier is noisy however ($< 60\%$) and thus sentiment frequency counts are not accurate, SCSF also benefits from higher λ values. In the PM-2 and PM-2M models the role of λ is different: it balances the emphasis on the chosen aspect $\sigma*$ versus all the other aspects $\sigma \in sent(T), \sigma \neq \sigma*$. Here, consistently higher λ values are preferred for both models, i.e., a high emphasis on the chosen aspect and a minimal weight on the other ones seems most beneficial. The effectiveness of these two models solely relies on sentiment estimations: given our adaption of PM-2 from its original definition ([9]) to sentiment diversity, the retrieval scores are not used for building the diversified list.

4.3.2 Cross-Bias Experiments

Consider the following real-world setting: for certain topics, it may not be feasible to collect data for calculating Topic Sentiment estimations, or suitable corpora may currently not be available. This could happen if the topic is very new and the data is not substantial enough for drawing general conclusions. If judgments shall be obtained, the data tagging effort may also be a burden. In such a situation we can fall back to the Balance bias or equal diversification approach [9, 25, 26, 27]. Naturally, the next question to answer is how much performance is lost when diversifying with Balance instead of the desired bias such as Outlier. The cross-bias experiments in this section investigate this case, and enable us to draw conclusions about the value of collecting and using information about topic sentiment distributions for controversial topics.

We analyze two cases. The first, presented in Table 1 shows the results for equally diversifying for Balance, but performance is measured for the Crowd bias (BAL-CRD). This is contrasted with diversifying for the Crowd bias, and evaluating for the same (CRD-CRD). Bold entries in CRD-CRD indicate statistical significance over BAL-CRD with a p-value of < 0.004 (t-test, as before). The SDM baseline is included for comparison. We omit s-recall@20 due to space limitations. All CRD-CRD results for the proportionality-based methods are significant over BAL-CRD results, whereas for the SCSF and SCS models there are a few exceptions.

Measure	Precision-IA@20		α-NDCG@20		ERR-IA@20		NRBP		CPR@20	
Exp-Eval	BAL-OTL	OTL-OTL	BAL-OTL	OTL-OTL	BAL-OTL	OTL-OTL	BAL-OTL	OTL-OTL	BAL-OTL	OTL-OTL
SDM baseline	0.120	0.120	0.277	0.277	0.202	0.202	0.155	0.155	0.501	0.501
SCS	0.126	0.126	0.413	**0.436**	0.309	**0.338**	0.237	**0.268**	0.562	**0.567**
SCSF	0.164	**0.188**	0.433	**0.462**	0.320	**0.358**	0.243	**0.287**	0.624	0.632
PM-2	0.166	**0.184**	0.447	**0.540**	0.337	**0.465**	0.262	**0.388**	0.632	**0.651**
PM-2M	0.166	**0.184**	0.446	**0.540**	0.336	**0.465**	0.261	**0.388**	0.634	**0.651**

Table 2: Cross-Bias Experiment over test split with perfect sentiment classifier to compare performance loss when diversifying equally (BAL-OTL) if actually diversification for the Outlier bias is desired (OTL-OTL). Bold entries in OTL-OTL columns are statistically significant over corresponding entries in BAL-OTL with p-value < 0.05 using the paired two-sided t-test.

	SDM baseline		SCS	
Rank	Excerpt	Sent.	Excerpt	Sent.
1	The Religious Policeman: Mutt the Muttawa	-	The Religious Policeman: Mutt the Muttawa	-
2	Happy Feminist: PROTESTING GENDER...	o	Happy Feminist: PROTESTING GENDER...	o
3	Between tradition and demands for change	o	First women to win in Saudi elections	+
4	Saudi mobile carriers ban SMS voting...	-	Between tradition and demands for change	o
5	Saudi Arabia, Ever Our Friends And Allies	-	Saudi mobile carriers ban SMS voting...	-
6	Orientalism and Islamophobia	o	Saudi Arabia, Ever Our Friends And Allies	-
7	Laws discriminate against women...	-	Orientalism and Islamophobia	o
8	...who urged SA to improve women's rights...	o	Laws discriminate against women...	-
9	Being a Child in Saudi Arabia	o	...who urged SA to improve women's rights...	o
10	Depressing Post: ...woman filed a case against...	-	Being a Child in Saudi Arabia	o
	SCSF		PM-2	
Rank	Excerpt	Sent.	Excerpt	Sent.
1	The Religious Policeman: Mutt the Muttawa	-	The Religious Policeman: Mutt the Muttawa	-
2	Happy Feminist: PROTESTING GENDER...	o	Saudi Arabia, Ever Our Friends And Allies	-
3	Saudi Arabia, Ever Our Friends And Allies	-	First women to win in Saudi elections	+
4	Orientalism and Islamophobia	o	Happy Feminist: PROTESTING GENDER...	o
5	First women to win in Saudi elections	+	Orientalism and Islamophobia	o
6	Laws discriminate against women...	-	Laws discriminate against women...	-
7	Depressing Post: ...woman filed a case against...	-	Depressing Post: ...woman filed a case against...	-
8	Their shabby treatment of women...	-	Their shabby treatment of women...	-
9	Oprah is being smuggled into Saudi Arabia...	-	Thumbs up for the Saudi ladies.	+
10	Between tradition and demands for change	o	Between tradition and demands for change	o

Table 3: Crowd Bias: Top 10 results with 4 models for query number 1007, 'women in Saudi Arabia.' - denotes a negative document, o refers to mixed/neutral, and + to positive.

We observe a maximum loss of 16.92% for Precision-IA@20 with SCSF, and an average loss of 6.48% across all measures and diversification approaches.

The second case is presented in Table 2: we observe the results for equally diversifying for Balance, but performance is measured for the Outlier bias (BAL-OTL). This is contrasted with diversifying for the Outlier bias, and evaluating for the same (OTL-OTL). Similar to Table 1 the results are statistically significant for OTL-OTL over BAL-OTL, but the losses with equal diversification are more heavily pronounced here: there is a maximum loss of 48.79% for NRBP with PM-2M, and an average loss of 16.23% across all measures and diversification approaches. So for highlighting minority sentiments through diversification it is even more important to collect biased data about topic sentiment distributions than it is for emphasizing majority sentiments as observed in Table 1. This way diversification can be performed with the intended bias rather than with equal diversification, which yields significantly worse results.

We presented the cross-bias experiments with perfect sentiment classification to reveal the maximum performance loss. As classification accuracy degrades, the losses become smaller but remain noticeable.

4.3.3 *Analysis with Specific Queries*

To see the models in action, we look at the output for one query in Table 3, number 1007 from the TREC Blog Track: 'women in Saudi Arabia', asking for opinions about the treatment of women in Saudi Arabia. We show titles or characteristic excerpts from the documents together with their overall sentiment. The topic of this query has the following Topic Sentiment: 67% negative, 17% mixed/neutral, and 16% positive. Here we diversify for the Crowd Bias, so the aim is to mirror this distribution in the results. The top 10 retrieved results with the SDM baseline are presented at the top left: this result list does not include any positive documents, and an equal amount of negative and mixed/neutral documents, which is clearly unsatisfactory for a Crowd bias representation of the results. The SCS model includes one positive document at rank 3, since lower ranked documents through the SDM baseline can be pulled up by the diversification models. Although the documents are nicely shuffled around across ranks, the ratio of the sentiments is still not close to the Topic Sentiment. The SCSF model is able to correct this, explicitly considering the frequency of documents with their dominant sentiments: we have 6 negative documents, 3 mixed/neutral, and 1 positive. But 4 negative documents are clustered right after each other, which slightly affects measures such as α-NDCG@10. The PM-2 results (bottom right) use the overall proportionality of the sentiments in the list as a guidance for choosing further documents: here, a second positive document is pulled up from lower ranks, yielding the best CPR@10 score among the 4 models for this query at a cost of slightly lower Precision-IA@10 than SCSF. With 5 negative documents, 3 mixed/neutral ones, and 2 positive documents we are very close to the desired distribution of sentiments.

5. CONCLUSIONS & FUTURE WORK

In this paper we demonstrate how to diversify search results according to sentiments by considering a pre-defined bias. This allows us to emphasize either majority or minority sentiments during diversification, or to give an unbiased representation across all sentiment aspects. For this, we introduce several diversification models that use sentiments and topic sentiment distributions. Diversifying the output of a strong retrieval baseline, the results on the TREC Blog Track data reveal that the proportionality-based methods and the SCSF model perform best according to most measures, but an individual choice should be made based on the quality of the sentiment classifier at hand. Finally, we demonstrate the value of using biases and collecting topic sentiment distribution estimations by means of cross-bias experiments in which equal diversification is performed instead of the desired bias.

The ideas presented in this paper are not only valuable for sentiment diversity, but can also be applied to topical diversity with modifications. To what extent does it make sense to consider biases for topical diversity? For instance, with an Outlier bias-like approach underrepresented query aspects could be highlighted in search results. Further, we have proposed different extensions to existing diversification models such as xQuAD and PM-2 with the SCSF and PM-2M models, which may be effective for topical diversity as well.

There are many directions for future work: (1) Exploring other biases applicable for sentiment diversity; (2) We found that our trained 3-class sentiment classifier and ready-to-use classifiers on the web perform rather poorly at document-level sentiment classification. State-of-the-art sentiment classification works better on sentences or short text, but interpreting the overall sentiment of a document is more difficult, particularly on the web. Therefore, advances in this area would greatly benefit sentiment diversification so that it can be applied to the web beyond the TREC Blog Track; (3) In case this is difficult to realize, how can the diversification models be adapted to yield higher gains with noisy classification input; (3) Analyzing opinion or topical arguments and sentiments together with biases. One question to solve is what kind of biases could be defined to capture both, and whether more fine-grained topic-specific biases would be required.

6. ACKNOWLEDGMENTS

This work was supported in part by the Center for Intelligent Information Retrieval, in part under subcontract #19-000208 from SRI International, prime contractor to DARPA contract #HR0011-12-C-0016, and in part by NSF grant #IIS-11217281. Any opinions, findings and conclusions or recommendations expressed in this material are those of the authors and do not necessarily reflect those of the sponsor.

7. REFERENCES

[1] R. Agrawal, S. Gollapudi, A. Halverson, and S. Ieong. Diversifying search results. In *Proc. of WSDM*, 2009.

[2] A. Ashkan and C. L. Clarke. On the informativeness of cascade and intent-aware effectiveness measures. In *Proc. of WWW*, 2011.

[3] J. Carbonell and J. Goldstein. The use of mmr, diversity-based reranking for reordering documents and producing summaries. In *Proc. of SIGIR*, 1998.

[4] H. Chen and D. R. Karger. Less is more: probabilistic models for retrieving fewer relevant documents. In *Proc. of SIGIR*, 2006.

[5] S. F. Chen and J. Goodman. An Empirical Study of Smoothing Techniques for Language Modeling. In *Proc. of ACL*, 1996.

[6] C. L. Clarke, M. Kolla, G. V. Cormack, O. Vechtomova, A. Ashkan, S. Büttcher, and I. MacKinnon. Novelty and diversity in information retrieval evaluation. In *Proc. of SIGIR*, 2008.

[7] C. L. Clarke, M. Kolla, and O. Vechtomova. An effectiveness measure for ambiguous and underspecified queries. In *Proc. of ICTIR*, 2009.

[8] C. L. A. Clarke, N. Craswell, and I. Soboroff. Overview of the TREC 2009 Web Track. In *Proc. of TREC-2009*, 2009.

[9] V. Dang and W. B. Croft. Diversity by proportionality: an election-based approach to search result diversification. In *Proc. of SIGIR*, 2012.

[10] G. Demartini. Ares: a retrieval engine based on sentiments sentiment-based search result annotation and diversification. In *Proc. of ECIR*, 2011.

[11] G. Demartini and S. Siersdorfer. Dear search engine: what's your opinion about...?: sentiment analysis for semantic enrichment of web search results. In *Proc. of SEMSEARCH*, 2010.

[12] A. Esuli and F. Sebastiani. Sentiwordnet: A publicly available lexical resource for opinion mining. In *In Proc. of LREC*, pages 417–422, 2006.

[13] R.-E. Fan, K.-W. Chang, C.-J. Hsieh, X.-R. Wang, and C.-J. Lin. LIBLINEAR: A library for large linear classification. *Journal of Machine Learning Research*, 9:1871–1874, 2008.

[14] B. He, C. Macdonald, and I. Ounis. Ranking opinionated blog posts using opinionfinder. In *Proc. of SIGIR*, 2008.

[15] J. He, V. Hollink, and A. de Vries. Combining implicit and explicit topic representations for result diversification. In *Proc. of SIGIR*, 2012.

[16] X. Huang and W. B. Croft. A unified relevance model for opinion retrieval. In *Proc. of CIKM*, 2009.

[17] M. Kacimi and J. Gamper. Diversifying search results of controversial queries. In *Proc. of CIKM*, 2011.

[18] M. Kacimi and J. Gamper. Mouna: mining opinions to unveil neglected arguments. In *Proc. of CIKM*, 2012.

[19] M. Keikha, F. Crestani, and W. B. Croft. Diversity in blog feed retrieval. In *Proc. of CIKM*, 2012.

[20] Y. Lee, S.-H. Na, J. Kim, S.-H. Nam, H.-Y. Jung, and J.-H. Lee. Kle at trec 2008 blog track: Blog post and feed retrieval. In E. M. Voorhees and L. P. Buckland, editors, *Proc. of TREC, Gaithersburg, Maryland, USA, November 18-21, 2008*, volume Special Publication 500-277. National Institute of Standards and Technology (NIST), 2008.

[21] D. Metzler and W. B. Croft. A markov random field model for term dependencies. In *Proc. of SIGIR*, 2005.

[22] S.-H. Nam, S.-H. Na, Y. Lee, and J.-H. Lee. Diffpost: Filtering non-relevant content based on content difference between two consecutive blog posts. In *Proc. of ECIR*, 2009.

[23] Ounis, M. de Rijke, C. Macdonald, G. Mishne, and Soboroff. Overview of the TREC-2006 Blog Track. In *Proc. of TREC*, 2006.

[24] T. Sakai and H. Joho. Overview of ntcir-9, 2011.

[25] R. L. Santos, C. Macdonald, and I. Ounis. Exploiting query reformulations for web search result diversification. In *Proc. of WWW*, 2010.

[26] R. L. Santos, C. Macdonald, and I. Ounis. Selectively diversifying web search results. In *Proc. of CIKM*, 2010.

[27] R. L. Santos, C. Macdonald, and I. Ounis. Intent-aware search result diversification. In *Proc. of SIGIR*, 2011.

[28] R. L. T. Santos, C. Macdonald, R. McCreadie, I. Ounis, and I. Soboroff. Information retrieval on the blogosphere. *Found. Trends Inf. Retr.*, 6(1), Jan. 2012.

[29] D. Vallet and P. Castells. Personalized diversification of search results. In *Proc. of SIGIR*, 2012.

[30] J. Wang and J. Zhu. Portfolio theory of information retrieval. In *Proc. of SIGIR*, 2009.

[31] C. X. Zhai, W. W. Cohen, and J. Lafferty. Beyond independent relevance: methods and evaluation metrics for subtopic retrieval. In *Proc. of SIGIR*, 2003.

[32] W. Zhang, L. Jia, C. Yu, and W. Meng. Improve the effectiveness of the opinion retrieval and opinion polarity classification. In *Proc. of CIKM*, 2008.

[33] W. Zhang, C. Yu, and W. Meng. Opinion retrieval from blogs. In *Proc. of CIKM*, 2007.

Term Level Search Result Diversification

Van Dang and W. Bruce Croft
Center for Intelligent Information Retrieval
Department of Computer Science
University of Massachusetts
Amherst, MA 01003
{vdang, croft}@cs.umass.edu

ABSTRACT

Current approaches for search result diversification have been categorized as either *implicit* or *explicit*. The implicit approach assumes each document represents its own topic, and promotes diversity by selecting documents for different topics based on the difference of their vocabulary. On the other hand, the explicit approach models the set of query topics, or aspects. While the former approach is generally less effective, the latter usually depends on a manually created description of the query aspects, the automatic construction of which has proven difficult. This paper introduces a new approach: term-level diversification. Instead of modeling the set of query aspects, which are typically represented as coherent groups of terms, our approach uses terms without the grouping. Our results on the ClueWeb collection show that the grouping of topic terms provides very little benefit to diversification compared to simply using the terms themselves. Consequently, we demonstrate that term-level diversification, with topic terms identified automatically from the search results using a simple greedy algorithm, significantly outperforms methods that attempt to create a full topic structure for diversification.

Categories and Subject Descriptors

H.3.3 [**Information Storage and Retrieval**]: Information Search and Retrieval – retrieval models

General Terms

Algorithms, Measurement, Performance, Experimentation.

Keywords

Search result diversification, term level, topic level.

1. INTRODUCTION

Search result diversification has been studied as a task of re-ordering an initial ranking of documents retrieved for a query. The goal is to produce a more diverse ranked list with respect to some set of topics or aspects associated with this query. Existing approaches to diversification have been classified as either *implicit* or *explicit* [30]. The implicit approach includes MMR [4] and its probabilistic variants [31]. These techniques do not assume any explicit representation of the underlying topics for a query. Instead, they assume each document represents its own topic. As a result, diversity is achieved by iterating over the input ranking and selecting documents based on the difference of their vocabulary, as measured by document similarity. These methods are generally less effective [1, 30, 18] as there are no guarantees that the topics covered by the resulting documents correspond to query aspects.

The explicit approach, on the other hand, models the set of query aspects and select documents for each of them. This includes algorithms such as IA-Select [1], xQuAD [30] and Proportionality Model [18]. The success of these methods, however, has been observed mostly with descriptions of query aspects that have been created manually, either as a concise list of topics [30, 18], a larger taxonomy from which the query topics can be inferred [1], or a list of topics obtained directly from commercial search engines [30, 18].

Generating the query aspects or topic descriptions automatically, on the other hand, is not as well understood. Although there have been a number of attempts to do this [5, 27, 17], only more recent techniques that build topic descriptions by combining information from several sources have been shown to be effective on web copora [19, 20].

In the literature, a query topic or aspect is usually identified as a single phrase or unit. More generally, a topic is a coherent group of what we call topic terms. Fig. 1 shows an example TREC query: *joints* (topic 82) with two topics: *treat joint pain* and *woodwork joint type*. These topics contain five topic terms: *treat*, *joint*, *pain*, *woodwork* and *type*. The question that we address in this paper is whether diversification with respect to these topics benefits from the additional structure or grouping of terms or would diversification using the topic terms directly be just as effective?

We investigate the problem of *term level diversification* empirically. Instead of modeling the set of query aspects, each of which is a coherent group of terms, this approach directly models these terms without their topical grouping. Thus, it still explicitly models the user intents, but it uses a weaker representation of them. Our experiments on the ClueWeb collection using two existing diversification frameworks [30, 18] confirm that discarding the topic structure does not result in any significant loss in diversification effec-

SIGIR'13, July 28–August 1, 2013, Dublin, Ireland.

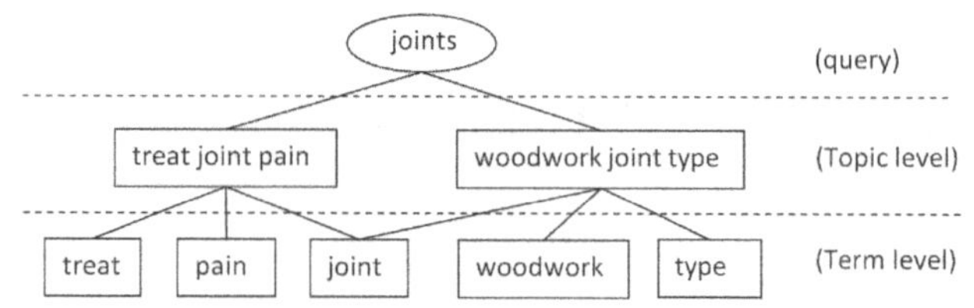

Figure 1: Two different levels for diversification: topic level and term level.

tiveness. Therefore, instead of trying to recover the topics for a query, we only need to identify a set of terms that cover most of the query topics. This is, in fact, the main task for multi-document summarization (e.g., [29, 23, 24]).

Consequently, we propose to use a simple greedy algorithm from the document summarization literature for identifying topic terms for diversification from the initial ranking of documents [23, 24]. Our results show that this simple method significantly outperforms many existing approaches for estimating the full topic structure from the same data on a wide ranges of both relevance and diversity measures. To the best of our knowledge, our method is the first one that can provide statistically significant improvement over standard relevance-based retrieval models in both relevance and diversity measures, without relying on any external data source or manually created topic set.

In summary, the main contribution of this paper is term level diversification. It simplifies the current topic level approach by taking as input a set of terms as opposed to a set of topic descriptions. This is important since automatic topic generation has proven challenging. We show that our approach with terms generated automatically, using a summarization technique [23, 24], significantly outperforms its topic level counterpart with topics generated using existing methods. When ground-truth query topics are available, our approach remains comparable to the topic level alternative.

In the next section, we briefly mention related work. Section 3 presents the current topic level diversification frameworks, which will also be used for term diversification. Section 4 describes in more detail the notion of term level diversification as well as our algorithm for identifying topic terms. Section 5 and 6 contains the experimental setup and results, as well as analysis and discussions. Finally, Section 7 concludes.

2. RELATED WORK

Search result diversification has been studied as the task of retrieving documents covering multiple possible topics, aspects, or interpretations of a query. Existing work can be categorized using two orthogonal criteria: their representation of these topics and their notion of diversity.

Query Topic Representation. Proposed techniques are usually classified as either *implicit* or *explicit*. The implicit approach, in fact, does not assume any of such representation. Instead, it assumes each document has its own topic. It promotes diversity by selecting documents that are different to one another in terms of vocabulary, as captured by document similarity such as cosine [4] or Pearson's correlation [28] between the document vectors and KL divergence between their language models [31]. As the selected documents do not necessary cover any of the query topics, this approach often fails to provide consistent improvement over standard relevance-based retrieval model on large web corpora [19, 18].

The explicit approach, on the other hand, models the set of query aspects and returns documents for each of them [5, 1, 30, 17]. Our term level diversification scheme belongs to this second category. The difference is, instead of modeling the set of query topics, each of which is a group of terms, we model these terms directly without their grouping structure. As we will show later on, the grouping provides very little benefit to diversification compared to the presence of the topic terms. This effectively reduces the task of finding a set of topics into finding a simple set of terms.

The success of the explicit approach, in fact, has been observed primarily with query topics that are either created manually (e.g. TREC subtopic descriptions [30, 18] or a larger predefined taxonomy [1]) or obtained directly from related queries provided by commercial search engines [30, 18]. Generating these aspects automatically, on the other hand, is not as well understood. For example, while clustering queries from logs [27] or anchor text and ngrams from the web [17] can produce interesting looking clusters of text, their effectiveness for diversification has yet been confirmed. Topics extracted from clustered documents, either deterministically or probabilistically via topic modeling [5], were only evaluated on a very small collection. In addition, their effectiveness is concluded to be only comparable to MMR [4], the canonical technique from the implicit approach [5]. Only more recent work [19, 20] has achieved some success, but they generally build topic descriptions by combining informations from several sources of data.

Instead of trying to generate a set of topics for a query, we apply a simple greedy algorithm [23, 24] to extract a diverse set of topic terms automatically from the input ranking. We then evaluate and compare their effectiveness for diversification (term level) with topics generated using some of the subtopic mining techniques mentioned above that utilize the same data (topic level) [5].

Notion of Diversity. There are two notions of diversity in the current literature: diversity by *redundancy* and by *proportionality*. The concepts of redundancy and novelty are based on the cascade user model which assumes users will scan the result list from top to bottom [14]. Therefore, documents at any position in the result list that provide the same information as those at earlier ranks are considered redundant. Similarly, novel documents are those that provide new information. A ranking is more diverse if it contains less redundancy, or equivalently, more novelty. Common to these techniques [4, 31, 7, 1, 5, 28, 30, 32, 18] are the greedy framework which sequentially selects documents with minimal redundancy, the measure of which is where they differ. For example, MMR [4] (implicit) measures redundancy of a document by its cosine similarity to the documents selected previously. IA-Select [1] and xQuAD [30] (explicit) measures how much it covers the query topics that have not been well covered by those chosen earlier.

On the other hand, a proportional ranking of documents with respect to a topic popularity distribution is a ranking in which the number of documents on each topic is proportional to its popularity [18]. By this definition, perfectly proportional search results would naturally be diverse. The main algorithm in this class is PM-2 [18], which selects documents in a similar greedy fashion, except that it maximizes proportionality using the Sainte-Laguë formula.

In this paper, we compare term level diversification to the topic level counterpart using both frameworks. In particular, we choose xQuAD (redundancy-based) and PM-2 (proportionality-based) simply because they have been demonstrated to be effective on the ClueWeb collection, which we also use to conduct experiments.

3. DIVERSIFICATION FRAMEWORK

In this section, we first formally describe the problem of diversification at the topic level. Then we will present the two frameworks for diversification in the current literature: redundancy-based and proportionality-based diversification. These frameworks will later be used for term diversification.

3.1 Topic Level Diversification

Let q indicate a user query and $T = \{t_1, t_2, ..., t_n\}$ indicate the set of topics for q. Let $W = \{w_1, w_2, ..., w_n\}$ denote the weights for each of the topics $t_i \in T$. These weights can be interpreted as the importance [30] or popularity [18] depending on the diversification techniques. In addition, let $R = \{d_1, d_2, ..., d_m\}$ indicate a ranked list of documents initially retrieved for q and $P(d|t)$ denote some probabilistic estimate of d's relevance to a topic t. The task of topic level diversification is to select a subset of R using $\{T, W, P(d|t)\}$ to form a diverse ranked list S of size k.

It is worth noting that the type of topics $T = \{t_1, t_2, ..., t_n\}$ will determine the relevance measure $P(d|t)$. For example, if T is a set of short textual descriptions (e.g. queries), $P(d|t)$ is often the relevance score of d to t given by some retrieval models [30, 18].

3.2 Framework

3.2.1 Diversity by Redundancy

This framework promotes diverse rankings of documents by penalizing redundancy at every rank. It does so by greedily selecting documents in R to put into S. At each step, it selects the document that is most different to those previously selected (thus minimizing redundancy), while remains relevant to the query q:

$$d^* = \arg\max_{d_j \in R} \ (1 - \lambda) \times P(d_j|q) + \lambda \times D(d_j, S) \qquad (1)$$

where $D(d_j, S)$ is a measure of novelty, which indicates the difference between the candidate document d_j and each of the documents in S. Different choices of $D(d_j, S)$ correspond to different instantiations of this framework [1, 5, 30]. In this paper, we choose xQuAD [30] simply because it has proven effective on several TREC Web Track query sets [30, 18], which we use to carry out our evaluation. Our findings, nevertheless, should apply to all techniques within this framework.

xQuAD measures the difference between documents by the topics they cover. It defines p_i to be the "portion" of the topic t_i that has not been covered by documents in S:

$$p_i = \prod_{d_j \in S} (1 - P(d_j|t_i)) \qquad (2)$$

Higher p_i indicates that most of the documents in S are not relevant to t_i. As such, t_i is less substantially covered and it should have higher "priority" in getting more documents. With this, $D(d_j, S)$ is calculated as follows:

$$D(d_j, S) = \sum_{t_i \in T} w_i \times P(d_j|t_i) \times p_i \qquad (3)$$

which means the novelty of a document is its ability to cover the topics that need covering (i.e. higher p_i) weighted by the importance of the topics w_i.

3.2.2 Diversity by Proportionality

The main algorithm in this class is the proportionality model PM-2 [18]. It is a probabilistic adaptation of the Sainte-Laguë method for assigning seats to members of competing political parties such that the number of seats for each party is proportional to the votes they receive. PM-2 starts with a ranked list S with k empty seats. For each of these seats, it computes the quotient qt_i for each topic t_i following the Sainte-Laguë formula:

$$qt_i = \frac{w_i}{2s_i + 1}$$

According the the Sainte-Laguë method, this seat should be awarded to the topic with the largest quotient in order to best maintain the proportionality of the list. Therefore, PM-2 assigns the current seat to the topic t_{i^*} with the largest quotient. The document to fill this seat is the one that is not only relevant to t_{i^*} but to other topics as well:

$$d^* = \arg\max_{d_j \in R} \ \lambda \times qt_{i^*} \times P(d_j|t_{i^*}) + (1-\lambda) \sum_{i \neq i^*} qt_i \times P(d_j|t_i) \qquad (4)$$

After the document d^* is selected, PM-2 increases the "portion" of seats occupied by each of the topics t_i by its normalized relevance to d^*:

$$s_i = s_i + \frac{P(d^*|t_i)}{\sum_{t_j \in T} P(d^*|t_j)}$$

This process repeats until we get k documents for S or we are out of candidate documents. The order in which each document is put into S determines its ranking.

4. TERM LEVEL DIVERSIFICATION

4.1 Problem Statement

Diversification at the term level is very similar to the topic level. Let $t_i = \{t_i^1, t_i^2, ..., t_i^{|t_i|}\}$ be the set of terms for topic t_i. Instead of diversifying R using the set of topics $T = \{t_1, t_2, ..., t_n\}$, we propose to perform diversification using $T' = \{t_i^1, t_i^2, ..., t_i^{|t_i|}, ..., t_n^1, t_n^2, ..., t_n^{|t_n|}\}$, in effect treating each t_i^j as a topic.

Let us reuse the example query provided in Fig. 1 earlier to illustrate this. Instead of diversifying the initial ranking for the query *joints* with respect to two of its topics: *treat joint pain* and *woodwork joint type*, we propose to perform diversification with respect to its topic terms: *treat, joint, pain, woodwork* and *type*.

We will now compare diversification at the topic level to its term level counterpart at an intuitive level, using both frameworks, to provide some justification for why one can expect similar performance from these two paradigms. This is based on the assumption that if a document is more relevant to one topic than another, it is also more relevant to the terms associated with this topic than any of the terms from the other topic. In other words, if a document is more relevant to *treat joint pain* than it is to *woodwork joint type*, we assume that it is also more relevant to *treat* and *pain* than it is to *woordwork* and *type*. Since both topics have the term *joint*, we will ignore it for the ease of explanation.

Let us first explain using the xQuAD's framework. At either the topic or term level, it follows from Eq. (1) that the first selected document d_1 is the one that is most relevant to the user query. Let us assume this document d_1 is more relevant to *treat joint pain* than it is to *woodwork joint type*. At the second step at the topic level, *woodwork joint type* will have higher "priority" (higher value for p) to get documents and thus, xQuAD will favor documents on this topic. At the same time at the term level, d_1 should be also more relevant to *treat* and *pain* than it is to *woodwork* and *type* (because of our assumption). Therefore, *woodwork* and *type* will have higher "priority" than either *treat* or *pain*. It follows that, if the topic level system is able to find a document d^* for its relevance to *woodwork joint type*, this same document should also emerge at the term level. Once this document is selected, the "priority" of *woodwork* and *type* decreases as does that of *woodwork joint type*. As the algorithm proceeds, the two approaches may select different documents due to the different numbers of "topics", each of which is down-weighted by a different amount (by Eq.(2)). Nevertheless, the general idea still applies, that if a document is selected for its relevance to any particular topic, that same document should be at least a highly potential candidate at the term level due to its relevance to the corresponding terms.

Similarly, in the framework of PM-2, let us also assume the first document d_1 is more relevant to *treat joint pain* than it is to *woodwork joint type* at both levels. As a result, the "portion" of seats occupied by *treat* and *pain* is also higher than that of both *woodwork* and *type*, just as *treat joint pain* will have a higher portion than *woodwork joint type*. At the second step, *woodwork joint type* should be assigned a higher quotient by the Sainte-Laguë formula, which again indicates *woodwork joint type* has higher "priority" similarly to what happens in the xQuAD framework.

4.2 Choice of $P(d|t)$

As mentioned earlier, diversification frameworks assume $\{T, W, P(d|t)\}$ as inputs and the choice of T will determine $P(d|t)$. An obvious choice for $P(d|t)$ for term level diversification is $P(t_i^k|d)$, the probability that the document d generates the topic term t_i^k. This is, however, highly problematic. At the term level, in addition to those true query topics which have become latent, there are also "false" latent topics formed by the wrong combinations of terms. In the context where we identify topic terms for a query automatically, some of them might be generic and ineffective. As the number of bad terms increases, the number of "false" topics will grow exponentially. Combined with the fact that there are likely many non-relevant documents in the baseline ranking, term diversification under the effects of these "false" topics might end up promoting non-relevant documents.

Assuming any document that is relevant to a true query topic should be relevant to the query itself, we propose to expand each topic term with the query. Let $\{q_1, q_2, ..., q_n\}$ be the set of terms of the query q. $P(d|t_i^k)$ is estimated as follows:

$$P(d|t_i^k) = (P(t_i^k|d)P(q|d))^{\frac{1}{|t_i^k|+|q|}} = (P(t_i^k|d)\prod_{q_j \in q} P(q_j|d))^{\frac{1}{|t_i^k|+|q|}}$$

which is essentially the query likelihood model for ranking d with respect to the query $\{t_i^k, q_1, q_2, ..., q_n\}$ [15] normalized by the query length to avoid biased towards shorter terms (i.e. terms can include both unigrams or phrases). In the case where all terms have the same length, the normalization is certainly not necessary.

Note that the inclusion of the query is not the only mechanism to keep non-relevant documents under control. Interpolating $P(t_i^k|d)$ with $P(q|d)$ as has been done in the redundancy-based framework (Eq. (1)) is another possibility. We do not do so because we do not want to introduce more parameters into the framework. In principle, any combination of $P(t_i^k|d)$ and $P(q|d)$ should be applicable. Since $P(q|d)$ can be obtained directly from the baseline rankings, this does not increase computational complexity.

4.3 Automatic Identification of Topic Terms

We now present DSPApprox, the *topic term extraction* algorithm proposed by Lawrie and Croft [23, 24] for hierarchical multi-document summarization. The goal of the algorithm is to select from a collection of documents a small set of highly representative terms that best summarize them. This algorithm is applied hierarchically, resulting in an hierarchical topic structure.

Since we only need a single diverse set of topic terms, we only apply the algorithm once on the initial ranking of documents $R = \{d_1, d_2, ..., d_m\}$ retrieved for the query q. The algorithm first identifies a set of *vocabulary* from these documents, from which it forms a set of more specific *topic terms*. It then measures for these terms their *topicality* and how well they predict the occurrences of other terms. Finally, it greedily selects a subset of topic terms, aiming to maximize both their topicality and their coverage of the vocabulary.

Vocabulary Identification. We consider as vocabulary all terms that (1) appear in at least two documents, (2) have at least two characters and (3) are not numbers. In our experiments, we test two types of terms: **unigrams** and **phrases**. We use a very simple method for phrase extraction. We scan through terms in each document and at each position, we select the longest sequence of terms that matches a wikipedia title as a phrase.

Topic Terms Identification. All vocabulary terms that co-occur with any of the query terms within a proximity window of size w is selected as topic terms.

Topicality and Predictiveness. Topicality of a term measures how informative it is at describing the set of documents. To compute topicality, a relevance model $P_R(t|q)$ [25] is first estimated from the initial set of documents R:

$$P_R(t|q) = \sum_{d_i \in R} P(t|d_i)P(d_i|q)$$

where $P(t|d)$ is the probability that d_i generates the term t and $P(d_i|q)$ is relevance of d_i to the query. The topicality $TP(t)$ of a term t is estimated as its contribution to the KL divergence between this relevance model and the language model for the entire retrieval collection:

$$TP(t) = P_R(t|q)log_2\frac{P_R(t|q)}{P_c(t)}$$

It is equivalently t's contribution to the clarity score of the query q [16].

Predictiveness, on the other hand, measures how much the occurrence of a term predicts the occurrences of others. Let $P_w(t|v)$ indicate the probability that a term t occurs within a window of size w of another term v and C_t indicate the set all such v. The predictiveness of t is estimated as follows:

$$PR(t) = \frac{1}{Z} \sum_{v \in C_t} P_w(t|v)$$

where Z is the hierarchy level specific normalization factor. In our case, we set it to the size of the vocabulary.

Greedy Algorithm. Pseudo-code for this algorithm is presented as Algorithm 1. It iteratively selects terms from the candidate topic term set T. The utility of each term is the product of its topicality and predictiveness. At each step, the algorithm selects the topic term $t^* \in T$ with maximum utility. Then, it decreases the predictiveness of other topic terms that predict the same vocabulary. This makes sure topic terms that cover the uncovered part of the vocabulary will emerge for selection in the next iteration. The algorithm stops once the utility of all candidate topic terms reaches 0, indicating that all vocabulary has been covered. Some example topic terms (both unigrams and phrases) generated by `DSPApprox` for the query *joints* are provided in Table 1.

Algorithm 1 `DSPApprox` for identifying topic terms.

$V = \{v_1, v_2, ..., v_n\}$: the set of vocabulary
$T = \{t_1, t_2, ..., t_m\}$: the set of candidate topic terms
C_{t_i}: set of terms occurring within a window to t_i
$P_w(t_i|v)$: co-occurrence (within window of size w) statistics
Compute topicality $TP(t_i), \forall t_i \in T$
Compute predictiveness $PR(t_i), \forall t_i \in T$
DTT : **the output diverse set of topic terms**
$PREDV$: vocabulary that has been predicted by DTT
$DTT \leftarrow \emptyset$
$PREDV \leftarrow \emptyset$
while $PREDV \subset V$ **and** $|T| > 0$ **do**
    $t^* \leftarrow \arg\max_{t_i \in T} TP(t_i) \times PR(t_i)$
    $DTT \leftarrow DTT \cup t^*$
    $T \leftarrow T \setminus \{t^*\}$
    $pred \leftarrow C_{t^*}$
    for all $v \in pred \setminus PREDV$ **do**
        for all $t_i \in T$ **do**
            $PR(t_i) \leftarrow PR(t_i) - P_w(t_i|v)$
        end for
    end for
    $PREDV = PREDV \cup pred$
end while

5. EXPERIMENTAL SETUP

Query and Retrieval Collection. Our query set consists of the 147 queries with relevance judgments from three years of the TREC Web Track's diversity task (2009 [10], 2010 [11] and 2011 [12]). Our evaluation is done on the ClueWeb09 Category B retrieval collection[1], which contains roughly 50 million web pages in English. This collection is stemmed using the Krovetz stemmer [22]. Stopword removal is only performed on the query using a small stopword list.

Baseline Retrieval Model. We use the standard query-likelihood model [15] implemented in Indri[2] to conduct the initial retrieval run. This run serves not only as a means to provide a set of documents for the diversification systems but also as a baseline to verify their usefulness.

[1]http://boston.lti.cs.cmu.edu/Data/clueweb09/

[2]http://www.lemurproject.org

Spam filtering is known to be an important component of web retrieval [2]. In addition, documents with too few stopwords are found to have poor readability [21, 26]. Therefore, we incorporate both of these into our baseline ranking. We use the spam filtering technique described by Cormack et al. [13], which assigns a "spamminess" percentile $S(d)$ to each document d in the collection. Let $\sigma(d)$ be the stopword to non-stopwords ratio in d and $p(d|q)$ indicate the score the retrieval model assigns to the document d. Following Bendersky et al. [2], the final score of d is given by:

$$P(d|q) = \begin{cases} p(d|q) & \text{if } S(d) \geq 60 \text{ and } \sigma(d) \geq 0.1 \\ -\infty & \text{otherwise} \end{cases}$$

Diversification Frameworks. We compare term level diversification to topic level diversification using both xQuAD [30] and Proportionality Model (PM-2) [18], which we have described in Section 3. While xQuAD obtains diversity by penalizing redundancy at every position in the ranked list, PM-2 does so by promoting proportionality at every rank.

Evaluation Metric. We report our evaluation results using several standard metrics that have been used in the official evaluation of the diversity tasks at TREC [11, 12]: α-NDCG [8], ERR-IA (a variant of ERR [6]) and NRBP [9]. These metrics penalize redundancy at each position in the ranked list based on how much of that information the user has already seen from documents at earlier ranks. In addition, we also report our results using Precision-IA [1] and subtopic recall, which indicate respectively the precision across all topics of the query and how many of those topics are covered in the search results. All of these measures are computed using the top 20 documents retrieved by each model to be consistent with official TREC evaluation. Statistically significant differences are measured using two-tailed t-test with p-value < 0.05.

Most diversification mechanisms are evaluated using only diversity measures [1, 30, 18]. It is unclear if diversity is achieved at a cost to relevance. Therefore, in addition to all diversity measures above, we also report our results using two standard relevance-based metrics for web retrieval: NDCG and ERR, which are also evaluated at the top 20 documents.

Parameter Settings. All of the diversification approaches under evaluation are applied on the top K retrieved documents. We set $K = 50$ to be consistent with existing research which found that both xQuAD and PM-2 achieve their highest performance at $K = 50$ [18]. Consequently, all topic and term extraction techniques will also operate on these top 50 documents.

Each topic and term extraction technique, as we will show later, has several *free* parameters that require tuning. xQuAD and PM-2 also have one parameter λ to tune. To enforce fair comparison, all parameters are selected via 3-fold cross validation.

We consider for λ values in the range of $[0.05, 1.0]$ with a increment of 0.05. Value ranges for parameters of the topic and term extraction methods will be presented in their respective sections.

Table 1: Some example outputs of DSPApprox for the query "joints" (topic number 82). Important terms from the original TREC subtopics for this query are also provided for easy references.

TREC Sub-topic	DSPApprox[Unigram]	DSPApprox[Phrase]
1) joints in human body	spine	elbow joint
	articulate	knee joint
2) woodworking joints types	miter	mitter joint
	planter	mitter box
3) treat joint pain	symptom	joint pain
	grease	joint anti inflamory

6. EVALUATION

6.1 Term Level Diversification: Effectiveness

We first compare the term level diversification approach to the topic level approach using the set of *true topics* associated with each query (TREC "sub-topics"). A topic is a coherent group of terms. These topics represent the oracle grouping of the oracle topic terms. By comparing the diversification effectiveness of this set of topics (topic level diversification) with that of the corresponding set of *unigram* topic terms (term level diversification), we can separate the benefit diversification algorithms get from the grouping with the benefit they get from the presence of topic terms.

In addition, related queries provided by commercial search engines have been demonstrated to be very effective for diversification [30, 18]. These queries too can be considered good underlying topics for the original query. As a result, we also compare the two diversification paradigms using this topic set. It is worth noting that the search engine provides no suggestions for *three* of the queries in our set. The query set for this experiment only contains 144 queries (out of 147).

Similar to existing work [18], the document-topic relevance function $P(d|t)$ for topic level diversification is implemented as the query-likelihood score for d with respect to t (each topic t is treated as a query). In particular, let $t_i = \{t_i^1, t_i^2, .., t_i^n\}$ indicates the set of terms for the topic t_i. $P(d|t_i)$ is computed using the geometric mean to avoid biased towards shorter topics:

$$P(d|t_i) = \left(\prod_{{t_i}^k \in t_i} P(t_i^k|d) \right)^{\frac{1}{|t_i|}}$$

For term level diversification, $P(d|t)$ is calculated as described in Section 4.2.

Table 2 compares term diversification to topic diversification using both topic sets and both diversification frameworks. The first thing to notice is that both topic and term diversification, using both PM-2 and xQuAD, significantly outperform the baseline in all metrics. This is certainly unsurprising since we are using the oracle data. Nevertheless, it confirms the effectiveness of both of these frameworks at providing relevant and diverse results.

What is more interesting from Table 2 is that the set of topic terms maintains a highly comparable level of performance to the topic structures. There are no statistically significant differences in all cases. These results are consistent across different diversification techniques and topic sets. This suggests that existing diversification frameworks are capable of returning relevant documents for topics without the explicit topical grouping.

We notice, however, that some of the query topics are different to the query itself by only one term. For example, topics for the query *"south africa"* include *"history of south africa"* and *"maps of south africa"*. Both of these topics have only one key term, which is *"history"* and *"maps"* respectively. It is possible that term level diversification is competitive with the topic level alternative because of queries like this.

To investigate this issue, we use the notion of *key term* to indicate the number of non-stopword terms in a query topic that are different to the query text. To quantify the impact the number of key terms has on our approach, we plot the number of topics where each approach is able to provide at least one relevant document against the number of key terms for these topics. In addition, we also plot the actual number of relevant documents retrieved for each topic (on log scale) against the number of key terms it contains. These plots are presented by Fig. 2 (a) and (b) respectively. Note that we only show the plots for PM-2 because the analysis with xQuAD is very similar.

Fig. 2 reveals that not only is our approach comparable with its topic counterpart on topics with a single key term, it also remains competitive consistently across different numbers of key terms. In particular, term level diversification has a slight advantage with topics that have only one single key term. With topics that have two and three key terms, although the topic level systems perform better, the difference is very small. The two approaches become comparable with larger numbers of key terms. Given that the term level systems do not need the topical structure, this very slight performance loss seems reasonable.

In summary, our experiments with the "oracle topics" show that the benefits for diversification of grouping topic terms are minimal compared to just using the terms themselves. The existing frameworks, PM-2 and xQuAD to be specific, can perform topical diversification at the term level. Together, these findings indicate that term level diversification is worth pursuing.

6.2 Automatically Generated Topics vs. Terms

We now evaluate the effectiveness of DSPApprox for automatically extracting topic terms, considering unigrams and phrases separately, from the initial ranking of documents. The total number of unigrams and phrases the algorithm returns are approximately 100 and 500 respectively. Since using too many terms is inefficient and unlikely to be effective, we use a parameter T to control the number of terms used for diversification. The second parameter is w, which determines the size of the window in which (1) a term has to co-occur with at least one query term in order to be considered a candidate topic term, and (2) prediction boundary: a term cannot predict terms that are more than w words away. We consider $w \in \{20, 30, 40, 50\}$ and $T \in \{5, 10, 20, 40, 60, 80, 100\}$.

Table 2: **Performance comparison between term level (marked as [Term]) diversification, topic level ([Topic]) and the non-diversification baseline query-likelihood (QL) using two frameworks: PM-2 and xQuAD. They are evaluated on both the oracle topic set (TREC) and the set obtained from a commercial search engine (C.S.E) using a wide range of diversity and relevance measures. Win/Loss (W/L) is with respect to α-NDCG. Q indicates statistically significant differences to QL.**

			Diversity						Relevance	
			α-NDCG	W/L	ERR-IA	Prec-IA	S-Recall	NRBP	NDCG	ERR
TREC		QL	0.3927		0.2807	0.1829	0.5824	0.2446	0.2742	0.1371
	PM-2	[Topic]	0.4742^Q	84/41	0.3536^Q	0.2021^Q	0.6341^Q	0.3212^Q	0.2979	0.1468
		[Term]	0.4635^Q	92/30	0.344^Q	0.2064^Q	0.6268^Q	0.3094^Q	0.3048^Q	0.1535^Q
	xQuAD	[Topic]	0.4447^Q	85/40	0.3207^Q	0.2035^Q	0.6259^Q	0.2856^Q	0.3002^Q	0.1490^Q
		[Term]	0.4366^Q	89/33	0.3143^Q	0.2067^Q	0.6171^Q	0.2777^Q	0.3054^Q	0.1515^Q
C.S.E.		QL	0.3884		0.2783	0.1789	0.5735	0.2428	0.2739	0.1394
	PM-2	[Topic]	0.4308^Q	62/60	0.3137^Q	0.1815	0.6084^Q	0.2784^Q	0.2790	0.1415
		[Term]	0.4305^Q	69/52	0.3162^Q	0.1874	0.6084^Q	0.2804^Q	0.2872	0.1471
	xQuAD	[Topic]	0.4024^Q	63/51	0.2888	0.183	0.5884	0.252	0.2797	0.1423
		[Term]	0.4118^Q	70/48	0.2965^Q	0.1883	0.5954^Q	0.2603^Q	0.2906	0.1464

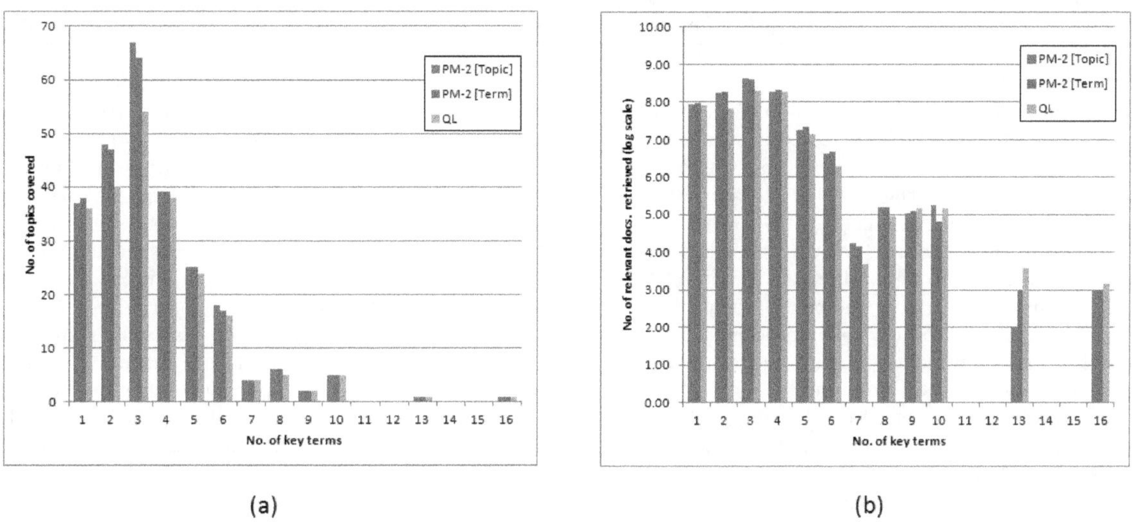

Figure 2: Figure (a) provides the total number of topics (across all queries) the term level the topic level diversification systems (under the PM-2's framework) as well as query-likelihood cover with respect to their number of key terms. Figure (b) shows the number of relevant documents (on log scale) retrieved for each of these topics.

6.2.1 Baselines

Baseline 1. Our first baseline for comparison, first proposed by Carterette and Chandar [5], estimates topic models using LDA [3] from the documents and uses the resulting clusters for diversification. This model only has one parameter, which is the number of latent topics $c \in [2..10]$. The relevance between a document to a topic is provided by the LDA framework. We use the multi-threaded implementation of LDA that is publicly available [3].

Baseline 2. Our second baseline technique, also proposed by Carterette and Chandar [5], applies k-nearest neighbor (KNN) first to cluster the documents. After that, it estimates a relevance model [25] from each of the clusters and use it as a topic model. Its parameters include $k \in [2, 10]$ and $T \in \{5, 10, 20\}$, which are the number of neighbors and the number of top terms from the relevance model to be used as topic description respectively. The topic description is treated as an Indri weighted query. The relevance between a document and this topic is obtained directly via Indri's output relevance score.

Baseline 3. MMR [4] has become a canonical baseline in the diversity literature [31, 30, 18]. Though it does not explicitly model topics, it fits into the class of algorithms that relies solely on the set of documents. The framework of MMR is very similar to the one presented in Eq. (1). The novelty component $D(d, S)$, which indicates the different between a document d and those previously selected in S, is aggregated over its difference to each of the document $d_j \in S$. The difference between two documents is implemented based on the cosine similarity. We experimented with three aggregation functions: *max*, *min* and *average* and report results with *max* since it is the most effective.

6.2.2 Results

Table 3 presents the results comparing the systems mentioned above. All of their parameters are determined using 3-fold cross validation. The letters Q, M, L, K indicate sta-

[3]https://sites.google.com/site/rameshnallapati/software

Table 3: Performance comparison among (1) topic terms (both unigrams and phrases) generated by DSPApprox (abbreviated as DSP), (2) topics generated by LDA and KNN, (3) MMR which does not explicit model query topics, and (4) the non-diversification baseline query-likelihood (QL) using two frameworks: PM-2 and xQuAD. Evaluation is done using a wide range of diversity and relevance measures. Win/Loss (W/L) is with respect to α-NDCG. *Q, M, L, K* indicate statistically significant differences (p-value $<$ 0.05) to QL, MMR, LDA and KNN respectively. Bold face indicates the best performance in each group.

		Diversity						Relevance	
		α-NDCG	W/L	ERR-IA	Prec-IA	S-Recall	NRBP	NDCG	ERR
	QL	0.3927		0.2807	0.1829	0.5824	0.2446	0.2742	0.1371
	MMR	0.393	30/39	0.2804	0.1829	0.5855	0.2445	0.2700^{Q}	0.1365
PM-2	LDA[Topic]	0.3762	56/70	0.2592^{Q}	0.1579	**0.5977**	0.2192^{Q}	0.2395^{Q}	0.1226^{Q}
	KNN[Topic]	0.3991	41/62	0.2882^{Q}	0.1808	0.5825	0.2536^{Q}	0.2711	0.1373
	DSP[Unigram]	$\mathbf{0.4161}_{L}^{Q,M}$	**71/54**	$0.3085_{L,K}^{Q,M}$	$\mathbf{0.1953}_{L,K}$	0.5789	$0.2788_{L,K}^{Q,M}$	$0.2981_{L,K}^{Q,M}$	0.1440_{L}
	DSP[Phrase]	$0.4159_{L}^{Q,M}$	68/57	$\mathbf{0.3131}_{L,K}^{Q,M}$	$\mathbf{0.1953}_{L,K}$	0.5684	$\mathbf{0.2867}_{L,K}^{Q,M}$	$\mathbf{0.3011}_{L,K}^{Q,M}$	$\mathbf{0.1480}_{L}$
xQuAD	LDA[Topic]	0.3905	55/59	0.2798	0.154^{Q}	**0.5884**	0.2453	0.2350^{Q}	0.1288^{Q}
	KNN[Topic]	0.3897	46/42	0.2786	0.1846	0.5824	0.2426	0.2752	0.1369
	DSP[Unigram]	0.3906	54/57	0.2837	0.1844_{L}	$0.5594_{L,K}^{Q,M}$	$0.252_{K}^{Q,M}$	0.2780_{L}^{M}	0.1386_{L}
	DSP[Phrase]	**0.3943**	56/63	**0.2888**	$\mathbf{0.1923}_{L}$	0.561^{M}	$\mathbf{0.2587}_{L,K}^{Q,M}$	$\mathbf{0.2889}_{L}$	$\mathbf{0.1408}_{L}$

tistically significant differences (p-value $<$ 0.05) to query-likelihood, MMR, LDA and KNN respectively. Among the three baseline techniques for topic generation, MMR's performance is the most similar to the baseline. It is interesting to see that while LDA has the best results in S-Recall, it performs poorly on all other measures, regardless of the diversification techniques. This can be explained by the fact that an LDA topic is a distribution over the entire vocabulary of the initial set of documents. Thus, each topic has a higher chance of matching its documents, but at the same time it also matches several non-relevant documents. Overall, KNN is the only technique among the three baselines that can provide some improvement over query-likelihood (with PM-2). Nevertheless, KNN has a trade-off between relevance and diversity: while KNN topics used by PM-2 help most of the diversity measures, it hurts relevance. On the other hand, the topics it generates, when used by xQuAD, helps relevance but hurt most of the diversity measures. Overall, the difference between these baselines and query-likelihood is mostly not statistically significant.

In contrast, both the unigrams and phrases generated using DSPApprox when used by PM-2 substantially outperform all other systems under comparison on many measures. Statistically significant differences are observed in many cases. In fact, it is the only system that optimizes for diversity measures yet outperforms query-likelihood in both relevance measures. Between unigrams and phrases, the former appears to be slightly more robust by improving more queries and hurting fewer, but the latter manages to retrieve more relevant results. In addition, their performance with xQuAD is still slightly higher than all three baselines on most precision-based measures.

The limited performance of our method when using xQuAD can be explained by xQuAD's vulnerability to large numbers of topics. Let us revisit Eq. (3) and assume that at the k-th step, the topic t_i has the highest "priority" p_i. We can rewrite Eq. (3) with respect to t_i as follows:

$$D(d,S) = w_i \times P(d|t_i) \times p_i + \sum_{\substack{t_j \in T \\ t_j \neq t_i}} w_j \times P(d|t_j) \times p_j$$

There is an implicit *uncontrolled* trade-off here between the relevance of a document to t_i, the topic with the highest priority, and its relevance to other lower priority topics. As the size of T increases, it becomes possible that a document d^* that is relevant to many t_j will be selected even though xQuAD should be selecting documents for t_i. This is certainly not a big problem for topic level diversification since the number of topics is relatively small. At the term level, however, our algorithm generates hundreds of terms, many of which can be very generic. As such, some non-relevant documents can appear randomly relevant to many of such terms, dominating the topic term with the highest priority.

Note that PM-2 has the same trade-off as xQuAD (Eq. (4)). The difference is that it is *controlled* by the parameter λ. If a topic term set is too noisy, cross-validation should be able to specify a larger value for λ to put more emphasis on the topic with the highest priority .

6.2.3 Improvement and Failure Analysis

We focus our analysis of DSPApprox results using PM-2. As can be seen from Table 3, although DSPApprox has slightly lower subtopic recall compared to query-likelihood (QL), the difference is not significant. Our investigation suggests that not only do DSPApprox and QL cover about the same number of topics, they cover almost the same set of topics (97% overlap). This high percentage of overlap suggests that the terms generated by DSPApprox are biased towards topics covered by the top ranked documents in the initial ranking.

We believe the cause of this bias is the way DSPApprox computes topicality. We observe that the topicality of a term is relatively proportional to the probability that it is given by the relevance model [25] estimated from the top 50 documents. This model usually assigns higher probabilities to frequent terms from higher ranked documents since they are assumed more relevant. If a document at a very low position covers topics that are different from those at early ranks, chances are their topic terms do not appear in these documents with high frequency. Therefore, their chance to be included in the resulting set of terms is relatively small, causing these topics to be excluded from the coverage of the final set. This is the main reason why subtopic recall was not improved.

Table 4: Contribution of (1) better topic coverage and (2) within topic coverage and ranking of relevant documents to the overall improvement on α-NDCG. WIN and LOSS indicate the sets of queries whose α-NDCG DSPApprox (DSP for short) improves and hurts respectively. *S.Rec* $\uparrow$ is the subset of WIN on which subtopic recall is also improved and *REST* is its complement. *S.Rec* $\downarrow$ is the subset of LOSS on which subtopic recall is also lowered and *REST* is its complement. ΔP is the difference of α-NDCG compared to query-likelihood. [U] and [P] indicate terms and phrases respectively.

		ΔP		#q	ΔP
DSP[U]	WIN	+0.2682	*S.Rec* $\uparrow$	10	+0.0652
			REST	61	**+0.2030**
	LOSS	−0.1400	*S.Rec* $\downarrow$	10	−0.0616
			REST	44	−0.0784
DSP[P]	WIN	+0.3285	*S.Rec* $\uparrow$	11	+0.0749
			REST	57	**+0.2536**
	LOSS	−0.2034	*S.Rec* $\downarrow$	14	−0.1170
			REST	43	−0.0864

Regardless, `DSPApprox` still manages to outperform `QL` in both α-NDCG and Precision-IA. This indicates that while both of them have the same topic coverage, `DSPApprox` retrieves more relevant documents for these topics as well as provides better ranking for them. More quantitative analysis on this is provided in Table 4. WIN and LOSS indicate the set of queries where `DSPApprox` helps and hurts α-NDCG compared to `QL`. ΔP denotes the performance difference in α-NDCG. *S.Rec* $\uparrow$ indicates the subset of WIN where S-Recall is also improved and *REST* indicates the remaining of the set. Similarly, *S.Rec* $\downarrow$ indicates the subset of LOSS where S-Recall is also lower and *REST* indicates the remaining. It can be seen that the increase of S-Recall contributes very little to the overall improvement on α-NDCG (the *S.Rec* $\uparrow$ sets). At the same time, they are also responsible for some performance loss (the *S.Rec* $\downarrow$ sets). On the other hand, a significant chunk of improvement is observed on the sets of queries that cover no more topics than `QL` (the *REST* sets).

The analyses above suggest that the terms provided by `DSPApprox`, though unable to recover additional topics due to the bias issue, correctly represent most of those covered by `QL`. Consequently, they help surface more documents on theses topics, significantly improving α-NDCG.

It is worth noting that, diversification with both unigrams and phrases provided by `DSPApprox` also significantly improves the relevance of the results (NDCG). Our approach, in fact, turns out to be very similar to pseudo-relevance feedback. The difference is that traditional relevance feedback uses the extracted terms to update the query model to retrieve new documents. Our approach, on the other hand, only attempts to re-order the input ranking, pushing more relevant documents to earlier ranks. As such, diversification can be considered a precision-driven framework for relevance feedback.

6.2.4 *Parameter Sensitivity*

As mentioned earlier, our topic term identification algorithm has two parameters. T controls how many of the top output terms to use for diversification and w determines how many words away can a term predict as well as how far can a topic term be from the query term. The best parameter values selected for `DSPApprox` (using 3-fold cross-validation) with unigrams is $\{T = 40, w = 20\}$ and the best values for phrases are $\{T = 80, w = 40\}$.

We first vary T from 10 to 200 and and keep $w = 20$ for unigrams and $w = 40$ for phrases. Note that the line for unigrams stops at $T = 100$ since our algorithms generates at most 100 unigram terms. Fig. 3 shows that regardless of the value of T, their is always some improvement. The set of unigrams, in particular, is very robust: it provides substantial improvement for most of T's values. As for phrases, two few (e.g. less than 50) or too many (more than 100) terms result in very minor improvement.

We then vary w from 20 to 50 and keep T constant. Fig. 3 shows the sensativity of this parameter. Similarly, improvement is observed at every value.

7. CONCLUSIONS AND FUTURE WORK

This paper introduces a new approach to topical diversification: diversification at the term level. Existing work models a set of aspects for a query, where each aspect is a coherent group of terms [30, 18]. Instead, we propose to model the topic terms directly. Our experiments, using both TREC subtopics and related queries provided by a commercial search engine, show that the two approaches achieve highly comparable results in all diversity and relevance measures. It indicates that the topical grouping provides little benefit to diversification compared to the presence of the terms themselves. The reason for this is that if a document is selected by the topic level system for its relevance to some particular topics, it is often relevant to the corresponding topic terms as well. Thus, this document also appears as a highly potential candidate to term level system. Term level diversification, in fact, works in the same principles as the topic counterpart.

This effectively reduces the task of finding a set of query topics, which has proven difficult, into finding a simple set of terms. Consequently, we propose to use a simple greedy algorithm from the literature of multi-document summarization [23, 24] to identify a diverse set of topic terms (unigrams and phrases). Our results demonstrate that, diversification using these terms significantly outperforms its topic level alternative with automatically extracted topics, as well as the standard relevance-based retrieval models on various diversity and relevance measures.

For future work, we will consider applying `DSPApprox` on not only the initial retrieved documents but also on external data such as Wikipedia and anchor text collections. We believe this will help alleviate the current bias issue, improving sub-topic recall. In addition, note that `DSPApprox` itself is a term diversification algorithm: it selects a set of terms that best cover the vocabulary. It is worth examining the possibility of replacing it with techniques such as PM-2.

8. ACKNOWLEDGMENTS

This work was supported in part by the Center for Intelligent Information Retrieval and in part under subcontract #19-000208 from SRI International, prime contractor to DARPA contract #HR0011-12-C-0016. Any opinions, findings and conclusions or recommendations expressed in this material are those of the authors and do not necessarily reflect those of the sponsor.

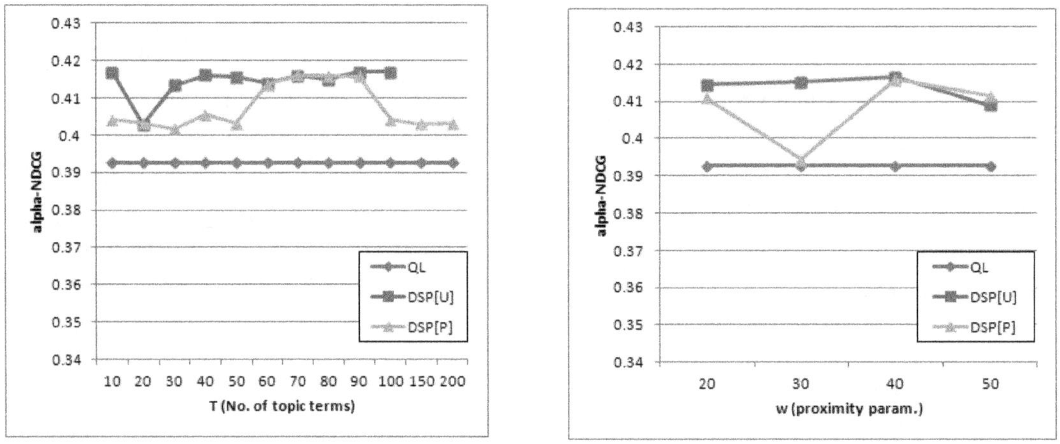

(a) (b)

Figure 3: Sensitivity of the two parameters of DSPApprox (DSP for short): T (the number of topic terms used for diversification) and w (the proximity parameter). [U] and [P] indicate unigrams and phrases respectively.

9. REFERENCES

[1] R. Agrawal, S. Gollapudi, A. Halverson, and S. Ieong. Diversifying search results. In *Proceedings of WSDM*, pages 5-14, 2009.

[2] M. Bendersky, D. Fisher, and W.B. Croft. UMass at TREC 2010 Web Track: Term dependence, spam filtering and quality bias. In *Proceedings of TREC*, 2010.

[3] D. M. Blei, A. Y. Ng, and M. I. Jordan. Latent Dirichlet allocation. In *JMLR*, (3):993–1022, 2003.

[4] J. Carbonell and J. Goldstein. The use of MMR, diversity-based reranking for reordering documents and producing summaries. In *Proceedings SIGIR*, pages 335-336, 1998.

[5] B. Carterette and P. Chandar. Probabilistic models of ranking novel documents for faceted topic retrieval. In *Proceedings of CIKM*, pages 1287-1296, 2009.

[6] O. Chapelle, D. Metlzer, Y. Zhang, and P. Grinspan. Expected reciprocal rank for graded relevance. In *Proceedings of CIKM*, pages 621-630, 2009.

[7] H. Chen and D. R. Karger. Less is more: probabilistic models for retrieving fewer relevant documents. In *Proceedings of SIGIR*, pages 429–436, 2006.

[8] C.L.A. Clarke, M. Kolla, G.V. Cormack, O. Vechtomova, A. Ashkan, S. Buttcher, and I. MacKinnon. Novelty and diversity in information retrieval evaluation. In *Proceedings of SIGIR*, pages 659-666, 2008.

[9] C.L.A. Clarke, M. Kolla, and O. Vechtomova. An effectiveness measure for ambiguous and underspecified queries. In *Proceedings of ICTIR*, pages 188-199, 2009.

[10] C.L.A. Clarke, N. Craswell, and I. Soboroff. Overview of the TREC 2009 Web track. In *TREC*, 2009.

[11] C.L.A. Clarke, N. Craswell, I. Soboroff, and G.V. Cormack. Overview of the TREC 2009 Web track. In *TREC*, 2010.

[12] C.L.A. Clarke, N. Craswell, I. Soboroff, and E.M. Voorhees. In *TREC*, 2011.

[13] G.V. Cormack, M.D. Smucker, and C.L.A. Clarke. Efficient and effective spam filtering and re-ranking for large web datasets. Apr 2010.

[14] N. Craswell, O. Zoeter, M.J. Taylor, and B. Ramsey. An experimental comparison of click position-bias models. In *Proceedings of WSDM*, pages 87-94, 2008.

[15] W.B. Croft, D. Metzler, and T. Strohman. Search Engines: Information Retrieval in Practice. *Addison-Wesley*, 2009.

[16] Predicting query performance. S. Cronen-Townsend, Y. Zhou and W.B. Croft. In *Proceedings of SIGIR*, pages 299–306, 2002.

[17] V. Dang, X. Xue, and W.B. Croft. Inferring query aspects from reformulations using clustering. In *Proceedings of CIKM*, pages 2117-2120, 2011.

[18] V. Dang and W.B. Croft. Diversity by proportionality: An election-based approach to search result diversification. In *Proceedings of SIGIR*, pages 65-74, 2012.

[19] Z. Dou, S. Hu, K. Chen, R. Song, and J.R. Wen. Multidimensional search result diversification. In *Proceedings of WSDM*, pages 475-484, 2011.

[20] J. He, V. Hollink, and A. de Vries. Combining implicit and explicit topic representations for result diversification. In *Proceedings of SIGIR*, pages 851-860, 2012.

[21] T. Kanungo and D. Orr. Predicting the readability of short web summaries. In *Proceedings of WSDM*, pages 202–211, 2009.

[22] R. Krovetz. Viewing morphology as an inference process. In *Proceedings of SIGIR*, pages 191âĂŞ-202, 1993.

[23] D. Lawrie, W.B. Croft, and A. Rosenberg. Finding topic words for hierarchical summarization. In *Proceedings of SIGIR*, pages 349–357 , 2001.

[24] D. Lawrie and W.B. Croft. Generating hierarchical summaries for web searches. In *Proceedings of SIGIR*, pages 457–458 , 2001.

[25] V. Lavrenko and W.B. Croft. Relevance-Based Language Models. In *Proceedings of SIGIR*, pages 120–127, 2001.

[26] A. Ntoulas and M. Manasse. Detecting spam web pages through content analysis. In *Proceedings of WWW*, pages 83-92, 2006.

[27] F. Radlinski, M. Szummer, and N. Craswell. Inferring query intent from reformulations and clicks. In *Proceedings of WWW*, pages 1171-1172, 2010.

[28] J. Wang and J. Zhu. Portfolio theory of information retrieval. In *Proceedings of SIGIR*, pages 115-122, 2009.

[29] M. Sanderson and W.B. Croft. Deriving concept hierarchies from text. In *Proceedings of SIGIR*, pages 206-213 1999.

[30] R. L. T. Santos, C. Macdonald, and I. Ounis. Exploiting query reformulations for web search result diversification. In *Proceedings of WWW*, pages 881-890, 2010.

[31] C. Zhai, W.W. Cohen, and J. Lafferty. Beyond independent relevance: Methods and evaluation metrics for subtopic retrieval. In *Proceedings of SIGIR*, pages 10-17, 2003.

[32] W. Zheng, X. Wang, H. Fang and H. Cheng. Coverage-based Search Result Diversification. In *Information Retrieval*, 15(5): 433-457, 2012.

Search Result Diversification in Resource Selection for Federated Search

Dzung Hong
Department of Computer Science
Purdue University
250 N. University Street
West Lafayette, IN 47907, USA
dthong@cs.purdue.edu

Luo Si
Department of Computer Science
Purdue University
250 N. University Street
West Lafayette, IN 47907, USA
lsi@cs.purdue.edu

ABSTRACT

Prior research in resource selection for federated search mainly focused on selecting a small number of information sources that are most relevant to a user query. However, result novelty and diversification are largely unexplored, which does not reflect the various kinds of information needs of users in real world applications.

This paper proposes two general approaches to model both result relevance and diversification in selecting sources, in order to provide more comprehensive coverage of multiple aspects of a user query. The first approach focuses on diversifying the document ranking on a centralized sample database before selecting information sources under the framework of Relevant Document Distribution Estimation (ReDDE). The second approach first evaluates the relevance of information sources with respect to each aspect of the query, and then ranks the sources based on the novelty and relevance that they offer. Both approaches can be applied with a wide range of existing resource selection algorithms such as ReDDE, CRCS, CORI and Big Document. Moreover, this paper proposes a learning based approach to combine multiple resource selection algorithms for result diversification, which can further improve the performance. We propose a set of new metrics for resource selection in federated search to evaluate the diversification performance of different approaches. To our best knowledge, this is the first piece of work that addresses the problem of search result diversification in federated search. The effectiveness of the proposed approaches has been demonstrated by an extensive set of experiments on the federated search testbed of the Clueweb dataset.

Categories and Subject Descriptors

H.3.3 [**Information Storage and Retrieval**]: Information Search and Retrieval

SIGIR'13, July 28–August 1, 2013, Dublin, Ireland.

Keywords

Federated Search, Resource Selection, Diversification

1. INTRODUCTION

Federated search, also known as distributed information retrieval [28, 4, 14], focuses on searching information distributed across multiple information sources such as local repositories or verticals. There are three major sub-problems in federated search: resource representation obtains information about contents and other key properties of each individual information source, resource selection selects a small number of most useful sources given a user query, and result merging integrates individual ranked lists from selected sources into a single final list. A large body of research has been conducted for resource selection in federated search [4, 28]. However, little is known about selecting a set of sources that balances relevance and novelty. This substantially limits the usability of federated search in many applications.

On the other side, search result diversification has been studied extensively in ad hoc search in order to offer more coverage for ambiguous and multifaceted queries. In several occasions, users' intents in their queries may not be expressed explicitly. For example, an ambiguous query such as "Jaguar" may refer to an animal or a car model; or a multifaceted query such as "Batman" may refer to a name of a movie, a comic character, or the comic itself. Search result diversification circumvents this problem by explicitly or implicitly considering probable aspects of the query and presenting the search results in a way that is easier for users to find the needed information. Since 2009, the TREC Web track has incorporated diversification in the evaluation of the Web track [9]. Several evaluation metrics have been developed in ad hoc search to measure the effectiveness of different approaches of search result diversification.

Search result diversification in federated search may not be as simple as diversifying the final ranked list obtained from the selected sources. In a federated environment where documents of a same source cover similar topics, selecting a set of sources that balances relevance and novelty becomes crucial. As for the example of the query "Jaguar" above, if the sources related to "Jaguar" as a car dominate the resource selection result, it will be much harder to obtain a diversified ranked list in the end.

This paper proposes new approaches in diversifying results of resource selection in federated search. To the best of our knowledge, this is the first study that tackles the issue. First, a set of new metrics is designed for measuring result diversification in resource selection. The metrics can incorporate any diversity measure that has been developed in ad hoc search, including the intent-aware expected reciprocal rank (ERR) [7], α-nDCG@k [13] and MAP-IA [1]. Second, two general approaches are proposed for diversifying resource selection. The first approach extends the ReDDE framework and utilizes a ranked list of documents on the centralized sample database. By reranking the sample documents with respect to result diversification, a better set of sources can be obtained in term of relevance and aspect coverage. The second approach offers a different view. Instead of reranking the sample documents based on their relevance to the query aspects, the information sources are reranked in a similar process. This can be done by estimating the relevance of each information source with respect to different aspects of the query by any existing resource selection algorithm. Furthermore, a learning based classification approach is proposed to combine multiple resource selection algorithms for a better estimation of source relevance with respect to query aspects. With some training data, the learning based classification approach can improve the effectiveness of resource selection for search result diversification.

An extensive set of experiments has been conducted with the federated search testbed of the Clueweb dataset to evaluate the proposed research. In many experimental settings, the new approaches can successfully improve result diversification over traditional approaches that only consider document relevance. In particular, the new approaches provide superior performance on two test levels: source-level results of resource selection and document-level results of the final ranked list of federated document retrieval. Finally, the learning based approach, which combines results from multiple resource selection algorithms, outperforms each individual algorithm in result diversification.

The rest of the paper is organized as follows. Section 2 offers the literature review on both resource selection in federated search and result diversification in ad hoc search. Section 3 discusses our proposed metric to measure the diversity of selected sources. Section 4 proposes the two result diversification approaches for resource selection in federated search. Section 5 presents the learning based classification approach. The new proposed research is examined by an extensive set of experiments in Sections 6 and 7. Section 8 concludes our work and points out some potential research directions in the future.

2. RELATED WORK

Considerable research have been conducted for all three sub-problems of federated search as resource representation, resource selection and result merging [4, 28, 15]. This section provides a discussion of prior research on resource selection, as well as a brief review on resource representation and result merging. We also discuss some popular ad hoc search algorithms for search result diversification.

Resource representation is the first step of federated search for obtaining important properties of distributed information sources such as content and size statistics. Query-based sampling [4] is a common approach as it obtains sample documents from available sources with randomly generated queries. The sample documents obtained in this process can be placed together in a *centralized sample database*.

Resource selection selects a small number of most relevant information sources for a user query. Some early resource selection algorithms such as CORI [4], CVV [37] and KL [36] treat each source as a big document and derive useful statistics to rank available sources with respect to a user query. However, these algorithms have limitation of losing the boundaries of individual documents, and thus may underestimate a big source with many relevant documents. Topic modeling has been proposed by recent work to overcome this limitation [3].

Other resource selection algorithms such as ReDDE [32], DTF [17], CRCS [27] and SUSHI [33] step away from the big document assumption by modeling individual documents of a source. Several selection algorithms in this category rely on the centralized sample database to build a ranked list of sample documents for a user query, and then assign a relevance score to available sources based on the scores of their sample documents in the list. Different algorithms use different methods for aggregating document contribution to available sources. Recent work by Markov et al. follows a similar approach, but attempts to minimize uncertainty in the centralized sample database by sampling different queries, retrieval systems, or rankings [22].

Learning based models have also been proposed for resource selection. They treat resource selection in federated search [20], or vertical search [2] as a classification problem. In particular, given a set of training queries and some relevance judgment, a classification model can learn to predict the relevance of an information source. In some experiments, the classification approaches have been shown to provide more accurate resource selection results than traditional algorithms without the training process.

Result merging is the last step in federated search, which merges documents returned by selected sources into a single ranked list. Modern methods such as SSL [31] and SAFE [30] both attempt to merge documents by approximating the centralize retrieval results in different ways.

Existing research in federated search have not explored an important issue of result novelty and diversification, which limits their abilities in representing the various information needs of users. The research work in [29] estimates the degree of document overlap among available sources, but its focus is only on duplicate documents and does not directly address the diversification problem related with multiple aspects of user queries. Other research work in [25] and [39] address diversification in aggregated search, which is similar to federated search, but operates in cooperative environments. Most importantly, those work do not target diversification in selecting relevant verticals (or sources) directly.

On the other hand, result diversification has been a popular research topic in ad hoc search. Its goal is to make a trade-off between relevance and novelty in ranking documents [38, 5, 1, 6, 26]. In order to achieve the desired effect of covering sufficient aspects of a user query (so that user will likely find the sought information), diversification algorithms target on discovering novel aspects that have not been covered in the ranked list, and reducing the redundancy information shared between multiple documents.

The earlier generation of diversification algorithms do not explicitly consider multiple aspects of a query [5, 38]. Instead, they build the ranked list from top to bottom, and make a choice of whether to include a document based on its similarity with existing documents in the list. More recent diversification algorithms directly incorporate query aspects into consideration. Agrawal et al. proposed the use of taxonomy to classify query aspects, in order to discover novel and redundant information [1]. Carterette and Chandar directly optimized the ranked list with respect to evaluation measures based on diversity [6]. Santos et al. proposed the eXplitcit Query Aspect Diversification (xQuAD) method, which estimates the surplus information that a document can add to a ranked list, using the probability of relevance with respect to all aspects of the query [26]. Recently, Dang and Croft proposed a different view on diversification by preserving the proportionality of document presence with respect to each aspect of the query [16]. Their proposed algorithm PM-2 has proven to achieve superior performance over several other algorithms of the same category. Other recent work on search result diversification include a combination of implicit and explicit topic representations [19], personalized diversification [34], and explicit relevance model [35].

3. DIVERSIFICATION METRICS IN RESOURCE SELECTION FOR FEDERATED SEARCH

There exists several standard diversification metrics for ad hoc search. However, no evaluation metric has been developed to compare the diversification results of different resource selection algorithms in federated search. This section proposes a new metric in order to fill that gap. Our metric is based on the popular R-metric [4] for resource selection in federated search. It is calculated as the ratio between the number of relevant documents contained in sources selected by a particular algorithm, over the number of relevance documents in sources selected by an ideal algorithm. In particular, the R-metric is defined as:

$$R_k = \frac{\sum_{i=1}^{k} E_i}{\sum_{i=1}^{k} B_i}$$

where E_i denotes the number of relevant documents of the i-th source according to the ranking E by a particular resource selection algorithm, and B_i denotes the same quantity with respect to the optimal ranking B. In this case, the optimal ranking B should order sources by the true number of their relevant documents. We adopt the idea to our new generic metric, which is called R-based diversification metric, as follows.

$$R_{\mathcal{M}}(\mathbf{S}) = \frac{\mathcal{M}(\text{optimal ranking of documents in } \mathbf{S})}{\mathcal{M}(\text{optimal ranking of documents in all sources})}$$

where $\mathbf{S}$ is the set of selected sources for comparison and $\mathcal{M}$ is a diversity metric of a ranked list of documents such as ERR-IA, α-nDCG, Prec-IA, S-Recall and NRBP. The optimal ranking of documents in $\mathbf{S}$ is the list that achieves the best score with respect to metric $\mathcal{M}$. For most of the aforementioned metrics, finding the optimal ranked list is an NP-hard problem, but this can be acceptably approximated by a greedy algorithm (i.e., repeatedly select the next document that maximizes the metric given the current ranking; cf. [8, 13]). The intuition of the proposed metric is that, if we can select a minimal set of sources that contains enough diversified documents to reach the optimal measure, then the R-based diversification metric is maximized to 1. Otherwise, it gives us an estimation of how far our selected sources are from the optimal ones.

Like R-metric, the proposed R-based diversification metric is independent of the retrieval algorithm utilized by each source. The R-based diversification metric returns 1 if all available sources are selected. In general, for comparison between different resource selection algorithms, the maximum number of sources is determined beforehand.

4. TWO APPROACHES FOR DIVERSIFICATION IN RESOURCE SELECTION

This section proposes two approaches for selecting diversified information sources. The first approach extends the ReDDE framework by ranking sample documents with consideration to diversity. The second approach estimates the source relevance to each aspect of the query and ranks the sources based on the estimations of their aspect relevance.

4.1 Diversification on Sample Documents under ReDDE framework

We first describe the Relevant Document Distribution Estimation (ReDDE) framework [32] for ranking sources based on the centralized sample database. In this framework, a given query is issued to the centralized sample database to retrieve a ranked list of sample documents. ReDDE makes an assumption that each sample document in this list represents a number of (unseen) documents from the source that it belongs to. Based on that, a source score is calculated by aggregating all contribution from its sample documents. The amount of contribution is scaled up depending on the source's size. Original ReDDE assigns a constant score for all documents on the top part of the returned list, and multiplies that constant with the ratio of the estimated source size over the sample size. The obtained quantity is then used for aggregating source scores. The CRCS resource selection algorithm [27] follows the same approach, but varies the amount of contribution of each document by an exponential decay function, as documents further down the ranked list have less contribution to its source.

ReDDE and many other algorithms of the same family such as CRCS and SUSHI [33] utilize a ranking on the centralized sample database to estimate the relevance of available sources. For algorithms of this family, they mostly vary in the way of defining a utility function for each document in the list. Having said that, the original ranked list from the centralized sample database plays an important role. Non-diversification algorithms target on building a centralized ranked list that covers as many relevant documents to the query as possible. In many cases, this may not pay enough attention to sources that cover multiple query aspects. For diversification purpose, we should be careful when selecting a source that mainly contains documents relevant to an aspect that has been covered before.

The above observation suggests a way to achieve good search diversification results by constructing a ranked list that covers several aspects of the query. We call this approach Diversification approach based on sample Documents (DivD). Instead of building a centralized ranked list that focuses only on relevance, we construct a ranked list that offers more diversity. The goal is to reduce the contribution of a document (on behalf of its source) that may be relevant to the query, but offers less novelty in the overall ranking.

This approach can combine a wide range of resource selection algorithms with any diversification algorithm that has been developed before, for instance, PM-2 [16] and xQuAD [26], which were mentioned in Section 2. A typical example

Algorithm 1 Diversification Approach based on Sample Documents using ReDDE and PM-2

```
Initialize scores of all sources to 0
Rank documents of the centralized sample database by
    an effective retrieval algorithm, e.g. Indri
Rerank that list by PM-2
for each document on top of the ranked list do
    Add a constant score c to the source containing the
    document
end for
return the ranked list of all sources based on their
    scores
```

Algorithm 2 Source-based Diversification using ReDDE and PM-2

```
1: Rank all sources using standard ReDDE
2: for each aspect q_i of query q and each source s_j do
3:     Estimate P(s_j|q_i), the probability of relevance of
       source s_j with respect to q_i using the ReDDE algo-
       rithm
4: end for
5: Rerank the list obtained in step 1 using PM-2 algorithm
   with the estimated P(s_j|q_i) as inputs
6: return the ranked list of all sources based on their
   diversification scores
```

of combining the standard ReDDE and PM-2 is shown in Algorithm 1.

Some resource selection algorithms utilize the relevance score of each document in the centralized sample ranked list for ranking sources (e.g. ReDDE.top [2]). In the diversification approach that has been discussed so far, this relevance score can be replaced by the diversity score given by a diversification algorithm for ad hoc search. There are different interpretations about those diversity scores, depending on the assumptions made by the diversification algorithms. In our experiments, diversity scores can be used with most resource selection algorithms effectively.

4.2 Diversification Approach based on Source-level Estimation

The second approach follows a different strategy than the first one. As presented in the previous section, the diversification approach based on sample documents works directly on the ranked list of sample documents, which is not a natural component for resource selection algorithms similar to CORI. Indeed, several resource selection algorithms utilize summary statistics of a source to estimate its relevance to a query. It is not straightforward to apply a diversification method based on individual sample documents for those kinds of algorithms.

This paper proposes another diversification approach for resource selection that operates at the source level. More specifically, many existing diversification algorithms for ad hoc search rank documents by estimating their relevance with respect to each aspect of the query, and then harvesting this information in order to produce a ranked list that balances multiple query aspects. It is possible to design a similar process that uses the *estimated source relevance* with respect to each aspect of the query. More specifically, instead of building a diversified list of documents for a given query as in ad hoc search, we can build a diversified list of available sources in a similar manner. All estimations with respect to the documents can be replaced by estimations with respect to the sources. This resource selection approach for results diversification is called Diversification approach based on Source-level estimation (DivS).

An important step in DivS is therefore to compute the probability of relevance of a source with respect to a query aspect. Many existing resource selection algorithms are able to provide such information. CORI can directly provide a relevance estimation based on the big document assumption. ReDDE and CRCS do not provide direct estimations, but it is possible to use their source scores aggregated from sample documents for such a purpose. An example of the diversification approach based on source-level estimation using ReDDE and PM-2 algorithms is presented in Algorithm 2.

Compared with diversification approach based on sample documents, the diversification approach based on source-level estimation can work with a wider range of resource selection algorithms. On the other hand, it requires multiple runs of a resource selection algorithm for all different aspects of a query, which is more time consuming than the former approach. In real-world applications, it is possible to design a parallel solution for multiple resource selection runs to speed up the process.

5. A CLASSIFICATION APPROACH FOR COMBINING DIVERSIFICATION RESULTS

The two diversification approaches based on sample documents and source-level estimation both utilize a specific resource selection algorithm and a diversification algorithm for ad hoc search. It is possible to combine the results of multiple resource selection algorithms for search result diversification, which may provide better results by modeling complementary results from different algorithms. This section proposes a learning based classification approach. With some training information, this method can learn how to combine evidence supporting available sources from different resource selection algorithms for result diversification.

In particular, we adapt the classification-based approach that has been used for both vertical search [2] and federated search [20]. For collecting training information in learning the classification model, this approach generates a pseudo-relevant judgment of a source given a query by counting the number of relevant documents that the source contains. If the number is higher than some threshold value τ, the source is considered to be relevant. In this paper, the training dataset for result diversification consists of multiple instances, each of them represents a pair of a source and a query aspect. A source is considered relevant to a query aspect if it contains at least one document relevant to that aspect of the query. For each pair of a source and a query aspect, we utilize the source score information from the following resource selection algorithms as features:

- **ReDDE.top** [2] This is quite similar to the original ReDDE algorithm, but uses the relevance scores of documents in calculating source scores, instead of a step function as in traditional ReDDE. ReDDE.top has been chosen since it provides more consistent results than ReDDE in our dataset.

- **CRCS** [27] with exponential decay function for estimating probability of relevance of sample documents. This method has been reported by several studies to be better than the linear decay version [33].
- **Big Document** This is a traditional approach that collapses all sample documents of a source into a big document, which represents this source and is used for resource selection. Our retrieval algorithm for this approach is Indri [23].
- **CORI** [4] CORI is another type of big document selection approach with a different tf.idf weighting scheme. It shares the same assumption that considers each source as a big document of its sample documents.

More specifically, the learning based approach attempts to naturally integrate evidence from two different views of resource selection algorithms, one based on big document assumption (Big Document and CORI), and the other based on aggregated information of sample documents (ReDDE.top and CRCS). In the experimental section, we will provide more analysis and some examples about why this combination strategy may outperform each individual method.

All the features provided by the above algorithms are normalized for each query in order to achieve more consistency. Given the training dataset, it is possible to design a learning method that estimates $P(s|q_k)$ for a new query aspect q_k. We choose logistic regression model as it has been shown to be among the best in many practical applications such as text categorization [18].

Let s_i^j be the binary variable that indicates the relevance of the i-th source to the query q_j, i.e. $s_i^j = 1$ indicates relevance, and $s_i^j = 0$ indicates otherwise. Let $\mathbf{f}_i^j$ be the vector of all features returned by the resource selection algorithms mentioned above. We can then represent the relevance probability of source s_i given $\mathbf{f}_i^j$ by a sigmoid function σ:

$$P(s_i^j = 1|q_j) = \frac{exp(\mathbf{f}_i^j \cdot \mathbf{w})}{1 + exp(\mathbf{f}_i^j \cdot \mathbf{w})} = \sigma(\mathbf{f}_i^j \cdot \mathbf{w})$$

where $\mathbf{w}$ denotes the combination weight vector.

Learning the combination weight $\mathbf{w}$ can be conducted by maximizing the log-likelihood function using the iterative reweighted least squares method. The learned parameter can be then used to estimate the relevance probability $P(s|q_k)$ for any particular aspect of a new user query. This probability becomes inputs for the diversification approach based on source-level estimation to rank the sources. Our hypothesis is that, if the learning model can provide a more accurate estimation than those produced by a single resource selection algorithm, we can expect the learning based approach to generate more accurate results. This approach is denoted as LR-DivS, as it applies logistic regression within the diversification approach based on source-level estimation.

6. EXPERIMENTAL METHODOLOGY

Dataset.

The experiments in the paper have been conducted on the federated search testbed of the Clueweb English dataset.

Table 1: Document statistics of the federated search testbed based on Clueweb English

# of sources	total # of docs	min # of docs	max # of docs	avg # of docs
2,780	151,161,188	48	3,417,805	54,364.27

The Clueweb dataset[1] is a large collection of web pages that has been used in several official tasks in the Text REtrieval Conference (TREC) tracks. Furthermore, the available information of queries with multiple aspects and the corresponding relevance judgment has enabled the evaluation of search result diversification. The federated search testbed derived from Clueweb is publicly available[2] as an attempt to offer a large and realistic testing environment for federated search. This collection contains 2,780 information sources and about 151 million documents, which is much larger than most other testbeds that have been previously used in federated search. Information sources are created by collecting web documents of the same domains (e.g. *blogspot.com*, *about.com*), and the Wikipedia documents are clustered into 100 collections using the K-means clustering algorithm with two passes/iterations. More statistics information of this dataset is given in Table 1. It is noticed that Clueweb has also been used in distributed environment, albeit in a different problem setting [21].

We are aware of a recent dataset that has been proposed for federated search in web search environment [24]. However, this dataset does not provide relevance judgments on multiple aspects of a query, and thus does not fully support experiments of this research at the moment.

Each information source in the testbed has been assigned a retrieval algorithm, which was chosen from a set of algorithms such as Inquery, Language Model and tf.idf in a round-robin manner. This strategy simulates the behavior that information sources in real world applications may use different types of retrieval algorithms. In order to build the centralized sample database, 300 documents have been sampled from each source via the source's specific retrieval algorithm. The Indri retrieval algorithm [23] was used in all retrieval processes on the centralized sample database.

The queries used in our experiments consist of 148 queries from the TREC Web Track 2009[9], 2010[10], and 2011[11].

Diversification Algorithm.

Diversity by Proportionality [16] (PM-2) and eXplicit Query Aspect Diversification (xQuAD) [26], which are among the state-of-the-art diversification algorithms, have been examined in our study. In particular, we notice that the performance of PM-2 tends to be better than xQuAD in most of the metrics, thus we only report our results based on PM-2. In our implementation of this algorithm, we have chosen to rerank the top $K = 500$ documents in the centralized sample database, as well as in the final step of diversifying results from the centralized complete database (i.e., all documents in available sources). The parameter λ in PM-2 is set to be 0.5 in all settings.

[1]http://boston.lti.cs.cmu.edu/Data/clueweb09

[2]http://www.cs.purdue.edu/homes/dthong/clueweb/

An important component of PM-2 and many other search result diversification algorithms is the estimation of $P(d|q_i)$, which is the relevance score of a document d with respect to a particular aspect q_i of a query. These aspects are usually not available in real-world applications. We follow the work of [16, 26] to report our results on two scenarios: all the aspects of a query are provided; or we can retrieve the aspects from a commercial search engine such as Google or Bing. For the first scenario, we use subtopics that come with TREC queries as aspects. For the second scenario, we send the original query to the search engine (Google in our experiments), and adopt its suggestions as query aspects. The second set contains 144 queries, as 6 original queries do not have search engine's suggestions at the moment of our work. We name the first scenario "Given Subtopics" and the second "Suggestions" in the results presented in Section 7.

Resource Selection Algorithms.

A set of commonly used resource selection algorithms as described in section 5 has been utilized in the new research of result diversification in resource selection. They consist of ReDDE.top, CRCS with exponential decay function, Big Document and CORI.

With CRCS, the top 500 sample documents returned by the centralized sample database are considered. The exponential decay function of CRCS makes it more stable on the Clueweb collection, which exhibits a highly skewed distribution of source sizes. On the other side, ReDDE.top is more sensitive to noise in such an environment, as a not-so-relevant sample document from a really big source may result in too much bias in favor of that source and affects the final ranked list. Therefore, for ReDDE.top, we set the number of top sample documents for each query to be smaller than CRCS's, chosen from the set $\{50, 100, 150, \cdots\}$. We report the results using top 50 documents for ReDDE.top as it provides the most consistent performance.

To name the different methods, we use a prefix "D" for a diversification resource selection algorithm to indicate an approach based on sample documents, and a prefix "S" to indicate an approach based on source-level estimation. As discussed before, the Big Document and CORI algorithms have only the S versions. For all methods reported in the next section, we select up to 10 sources for each query.

Training and Testing.

All the proposed resource selection algorithms for search result diversification do not need any training data except the final approach of combining multiple resource selection algorithms in a learning model (LR-DivS). Therefore, for the algorithms other than LR-DivS, we report the results on all 148 queries from TREC Web Track 2009-2011. For LR-DivS, since it requires a training dataset, we use queries with TREC id less than or equal to 75 for training, and the rest for testing. We also report the results on the testing set of all other algorithms for comparison. For the scenario with suggested aspects of user queries, since there is no corresponding relevance judgment, we train our model using the provided query subtopics/aspects and their corresponding relevance judgments. However, in the testing phase, the model is applied with features derived from the suggested aspects, i.e., we estimate $P(s|q_i)$ where q_i is a query aspect suggested by a commercial search engine. Finally, we evaluate all approaches with respect to TREC's provided subtopics/aspects. This strategy is consistent with the evaluation process in TREC Web Track [11].

Evaluation Metric.

The proposed new research has been evaluated at two levels: source selection and federated document retrieval.

- **Diversification results with R-based diversification metric for source selection**: We evaluate the resource selection results using the R-based diversification metric described in Section 3. In particular, five popular metrics in result diversification such as ERR-IA[7], α-nDCG[13], NRBP[12], P-IA (intent aware precision [1]) and S-Recall (subtopic recall, for the number of subtopics/aspects covered by top documents) have been adopted with the R metric in resource selection and used in the experiments.
- **Diversification results for federated document retrieval**: To make the evaluation independent from a specific result merging algorithm, the Indri algorithm is used to perform document retrieval on the centralized complete database. Only documents from the selected sources for each query have been retained, which is consistent with prior research in [32]. This ranked list of documents is reranked again using the PM-2 algorithm. We then evaluate the final ranked list by the five metrics mentioned above as ERR-IA, α-nDCG, NRBP, P-IA and S-Recall. All of these metrics are computed at the top 20 documents, which is consistent with the official TREC evaluation of search result diversification for ad hoc search [11] and consistent with the commonly used high-precision metric in federated document retrieval.

7. EXPERIMENTAL RESULTS

An extensive set of experiments has been conducted for evaluating several approaches proposed in this paper, which are: the approach based on sample documents (DivD), the approach based on source-level estimation (DivS) and the learning based approach (LR-DivS). We conduct experiments on two levels for different purposes: source-level results for resource selection and document-level results for federated document retrieval. More specifically, the first subsection compares the performance of a diversification approach with standard resource selection algorithms. The second set of experiments in 7.2 compares multiple resource selection algorithms adapting DivD and DivS approaches. The third set of experiments in 7.3 demonstrates the advantage of the learning based approach (LR-DivS) over approaches with a single resource selection algorithm. The last set of experiments in 7.4 compares the document-level diversification results across all proposed approaches.

7.1 Diversification versus Standard Resource Selection Algorithms

This subsection compares the performance of two standard resource selection algorithms ReDDE.top and CRCS with their diversification counterparts at source selection level. In particular, we choose to study the first diversification approach based on sample documents (DivD) in this subsection as they are more related with standard ReDDE.top and CRCS algorithms, while more results of both diversification approaches will be presented shortly.

Table 2 shows the performance using all the R-based diversification metrics described in the previous section. Without diversification, it can be observed that the standard CRCS significantly outperforms standard ReDDE.top in all metrics. This may be attributed to the fact that CRCS generally selects more relevant sources to the query, which leads to a wider range of aspects being covered. The advantage of CRCS may come from using the exponential decay function for document utility, which tends to be better than using document score as utility in ReDDE.top. When the document-based diversification approach is applied, it further increases the performance of the standard algorithms: D-ReDDE.top significantly outperforms ReDDE.top in its capacity of selecting diversified sources. As for CRCS, its diversification version (i.e., D-CRCS) is also consistently better than the standard CRCS algorithm. The same observation can be seen in both scenarios when the query aspects are given, or suggested by Web search.

7.2 Diversification with Different Resource Selection Algorithms

This subsection studies the performance of the two proposed resource selection approaches (i.e., DivD and DivS) using several resource selection algorithms, including ReDDE-top, CRCS, Big Document and CORI. The results are presented in Table 3. In all settings, the standard Big Document and standard CORI algorithms are outperformed by the other methods. Furthermore, both S-Big Document and S-CORI, which are under the same assumption of collapsing sample documents within a source, are inferior to S-ReDDE.top and S-CRCS. These results indicate that ReDDE-top and CRCS tend to be more effective in resource selection for result diversification than Big Document and CORI, which is consistent with previous research in federated search for resource selection without diversification.

Both DivD and DivS approaches produce comparable results when applied to ReDDE.top and CRCS. The D-CRCS version based on sample documents is better than its counterpart based on source-level estimation (i.e., S-CRCS), whereas the contrary is observed for ReDDE.top. In case of ReDDE.top, the difference is significant, which may be explained by the fact that when the original ranked list is short (only 50 for ReDDE.top), it is more difficult for the diversification algorithm to find a document that covers many query aspects, rather than finding a source that covers many aspects.

The results using the provided query aspects and suggested ones reveal an interesting observation. We notice that the performance of the two settings are quite comparable with little difference. One possible explanation is that, in federated environment, it may not need a perfect set of query aspects for selecting a diversified set of information sources, as sources are already somehow divided by different types of semantic topics. Since our goal is to select sources that can cover as many query aspects as possible, the resource selection algorithms can do a reasonably good work as long as the suggestions of query aspects provide some meaningful interpretations of different aspects of the query.

7.3 Classification Approach for Combining Diversification Results

This subsection compares the performance of the learning based classification approach with all other diversification approaches mentioned above. Since the classification approach requires a set of training queries and does the testing on another set, we also report the results of all previous methods on the testing queries for comparison. Table 4 presents the results. The performance of the standard resource selection algorithms and their diversification counterparts are better on the set of testing queries than on the set of all queries, due to the particular division of training and testing queries. The comparison between standard algorithms' performance and those of diversification approaches on the testing queries raises similar observations as mentioned in the previous subsections 7.1 and 7.2.

It can be seen that the classification approach provides the best performance over all metrics. It can be attributed to the fact that the learning based classification approach can harness the advantage of different algorithms, and combine them in an effective way. A typical example from our training set is the query "Obama family tree" with its provided subtopic "Find the TIME magazine photo essay Barack Obama's Family Tree". For ReDDE.top and CRCS, it is almost impossible to find a sample document containing all the keywords of the subtopic/aspect, if such a document does not exist in the sample database. On the other hand, Big Document and CORI can provide some useful hints for selecting sources by looking at all sample documents from each source as whole. For example, several different sample documents of a source may contain various parts of the query. This is particularly useful for sources that cover a wide range of topics, for instance, Wikipedia. Another example is the query "Volvo" with its provided subtopic "Find a Volvo dealer". Big Document and CORI can give hint to the sources that contain the words "Volvo" and "dealer" from different sample documents. For those sources, the classification approach can utilize the complementary results for improving search results diversification.

7.4 Diversification Results of Federated Document Retrieval

This subsection compares the search diversification results in document-level of federated document retrieval. Given the top ten sources selected by the proposed algorithms for each query, the final ranked list generated from the sources is evaluated. One set of results compares algorithms without training over all queries. The other set of results is included for the test queries to compare LR-DivS with other algorithms. We omit the results of Big Document and CORI on the first set due to space limitation.

Table 5 provides the results on all queries. The standard ReDDE.top algorithm falls behind the other models in its diversification capacity. Among all the methods without training, D-CRCS consistently outperforms the other methods, which is consistent with its performance on the R-based diversification metrics in the source-level.

Table 6 provides the results on the test queries. Again, the same trend with algorithms without training can be observed. When some training information is available to learn how to combine multiple evidence, the classification approach LR-DivS consistently provides the best document-level diversification performance among all models.

8. CONCLUSION AND FUTURE WORK

Resource selection is an important research problem in federated search for selecting a small number of relevance sources for a given query. Various algorithms have been pro-

Table 2: R-based diversification metric of resource selection on all 148 queries. Symbols † and ‡ indicate statistical significance under paired t-test with respect to ReDDE.top baseline and CRCS baseline ($p < 0.05$).

			R-ERR	R-α-nDCG	R-NRBP	R-P-IA	R-S-Recall
Given Subtopics	Baseline	ReDDE.top	0.549	0.529	0.566	0.406	0.545
		CRCS	$0.677^{\dagger}$	$0.652^{\dagger}$	$0.698^{\dagger}$	$0.484^{\dagger}$	$0.658^{\dagger}$
	DDiv	D-ReDDE.top	$0.624^{\dagger}$	$0.598^{\dagger}$	$0.645^{\dagger}$	$0.438^{\dagger}$	$0.612^{\dagger}$
		D-CRCS	$\mathbf{0.699}^{\dagger}$	$\mathbf{0.672}^{\dagger}$	$\mathbf{0.721}^{\dagger}$	$\mathbf{0.499}^{\dagger\ddagger}$	$\mathbf{0.674}^{\dagger}$
Suggestions	Baseline	ReDDE.top	0.542	0.522	0.558	0.396	0.541
		CRCS	$0.673^{\dagger}$	$0.649^{\dagger}$	$0.694^{\dagger}$	$0.477^{\dagger}$	$0.659^{\dagger}$
	DDiv	D-ReDDE.top	$0.614^{\dagger}$	$0.589^{\dagger}$	$0.635^{\dagger}$	$0.434^{\dagger}$	$0.604^{\dagger}$
		D-CRCS	$\mathbf{0.698}^{\dagger}$	$\mathbf{0.671}^{\dagger}$	$\mathbf{0.720}^{\dagger}$	$\mathbf{0.491}^{\dagger\ddagger}$	$\mathbf{0.677}^{\dagger}$

Table 3: R-based diversification metric on resource selection on multiple diversification approaches. Letters r, c, R, C, B, O indicate statistical significance under paired t-test to D-ReDDE.top, D-CRCS, S-ReDDE.top, S-CRCS, S-BigDoc, and S-CORI respectively ($p < 0.05$).

			R-ERR	R-α-nDCG	R-NRBP	R-P-IA	R-S-Recall
Given Subtopics	DDiv	D-ReDDE.top	0.624_{B}	0.598_{BO}	0.645_{B}	0.438_{BO}	0.612_{B}
		D-CRCS	$\mathbf{0.699}_{rBO}$	$\mathbf{0.672}_{rBO}$	$\mathbf{0.721}_{rBO}$	$\mathbf{0.499}_{rCBO}$	$\mathbf{0.674}_{rBO}$
	SDiv	S-ReDDE.top	0.680_{rBO}	0.656_{rBO}	0.701_{rBO}	0.496_{rCBO}	0.664_{rBO}
		S-CRCS	0.675_{rBO}	0.649_{rBO}	0.698_{rBO}	0.462_{rBO}	0.664_{rBO}
		S-BigDoc	0.490	0.468	0.506	0.346	0.486
		S-CORI	0.569_{B}	0.541_{B}	0.591_{B}	0.351_{B}	0.561_{B}
Suggestions	DDiv	D-ReDDE.top	0.614_{B}	0.589_{B}	0.635_{B}	0.434_{BO}	0.604_{B}
		D-CRCS	$\mathbf{0.698}_{rBO}$	$\mathbf{0.671}_{rBO}$	$\mathbf{0.720}_{rBO}$	$\mathbf{0.491}_{rCBO}$	$\mathbf{0.677}_{rBO}$
	SDiv	S-ReDDE.top	0.677_{rBO}	0.652_{rBO}	0.698_{rBO}	0.485_{rCBO}	0.666_{rBO}
		S-CRCS	0.673_{rBO}	0.647_{rBO}	0.695_{rBO}	0.458_{BO}	0.665_{rBO}
		S-BigDoc	0.490	0.469	0.508	0.342	0.490
		S-CORI	0.566_{B}	0.538_{B}	0.587_{B}	0.347_{B}	0.562_{B}

Table 4: R-based diversification metric of resource selection on multiple diversification approaches on test queries. Symbols $\dagger, \ddagger, r, c, R, C, B, O$ indicate significant improvement under paired t-test to ReDDE.top, CRCS, D-ReDDE.top, D-CRCS, S-ReDDE.top, S-CRCS, S-BigDoc, and S-CORI respectively. ($p < 0.05$).

			R-ERR	R-α-nDCG	R-NRBP	R-P-IA	R-S-Recall
Given Subtopics	Baseline	ReDDE.top	0.618	0.604	0.630	0.461	0.635
		CRCS	$0.769^{\dagger}_{rBO}$	$0.751^{\dagger}_{rBO}$	$0.783^{\dagger}_{rBO}$	$0.550^{\dagger}_{rBO}$	$0.768^{\dagger}_{BO}$
	DDiv	D-ReDDE.top	$0.711^{\dagger}_{B}$	$0.694^{\dagger}_{B}$	$0.725^{\dagger}_{B}$	$0.507^{\dagger}_{BO}$	$0.726^{\dagger}_{B}$
		D-CRCS	$0.778^{\dagger}_{rBO}$	$0.762^{\dagger}_{rBO}$	$0.791^{\dagger}_{rBO}$	$0.557^{\dagger}_{rBO}$	$0.782^{\dagger}_{rBO}$
	SDiv	S-ReDDE.top	$0.775^{\dagger}_{rBO}$	$0.757^{\dagger}_{rBO}$	$0.789^{\dagger}_{rBO}$	$0.567^{\dagger}_{rcCBO}$	$0.778^{\dagger}_{rCBO}$
		S-CRCS	$0.786^{\dagger}_{rBO}$	$0.769^{\dagger}_{rBO}$	$0.800^{\dagger}_{rBO}$	$0.544^{\dagger}_{rBO}$	$0.802^{\dagger}_{rRBO}$
		S-BigDoc	0.615	0.594	0.632	0.415	0.621
		S-CORI	0.653	0.634	0.669	0.396	0.676
	LR-DivS		$\mathbf{0.873}^{\dagger\ddagger}_{rcRCBO}$	$\mathbf{0.853}^{\dagger\ddagger}_{rcRCBO}$	$\mathbf{0.889}^{\dagger\ddagger}_{rcRCBO}$	$\mathbf{0.705}^{\dagger\ddagger}_{rcRCBO}$	$\mathbf{0.856}^{\dagger\ddagger}_{rcRCBO}$
Suggestions	Baseline	ReDDE.top	0.614	0.600	0.626	0.463	0.629
		CRCS	$0.768^{\dagger}_{BO}$	$0.751^{\dagger}_{BO}$	$0.782^{\dagger}_{BO}$	$0.555^{\dagger}_{BO}$	$0.768^{\dagger}_{BO}$
	DDiv	D-ReDDE.top	$0.724^{\dagger}_{B}$	$0.705^{\dagger}_{B}$	$0.739^{\dagger}_{B}$	$0.525^{\dagger}_{BO}$	$0.735^{\dagger}_{B}$
		D-CRCS	$0.781^{\dagger}_{rBO}$	$0.765^{\dagger}_{rBO}$	$0.794^{\dagger}_{rBO}$	$0.558^{\dagger}_{rBO}$	$0.787^{\dagger}_{rBO}$
	SDiv	S-ReDDE.top	$0.799^{\dagger}_{rBO}$	$0.779^{\dagger}_{rBO}$	$0.814^{\dagger}_{rBO}$	$0.590^{\dagger\ddagger}_{rcCBO}$	$0.800^{\dagger}_{rBO}$
		S-CRCS	$0.787^{\dagger}_{rBO}$	$0.771^{\dagger}_{rBO}$	$0.801^{\dagger}_{rBO}$	$0.550^{\dagger}_{rBO}$	$0.803^{\dagger}_{rBO}$
		S-BigDoc	0.614	0.593	0.632	0.411	0.624
		S-CORI	0.647	0.629	0.662	0.396	0.672
	LR-DivS		$\mathbf{0.821}^{\dagger\ddagger}_{rCBO}$	$\mathbf{0.805}^{\dagger\ddagger}_{rCBO}$	$\mathbf{0.834}^{\dagger\ddagger}_{rBO}$	$\mathbf{0.629}^{\dagger\ddagger}_{rcRCBO}$	$\mathbf{0.827}^{\dagger\ddagger}_{rBO}$

Table 5: Diversification results on document retrieval on all queries. The symbols $\dagger, \ddagger, r, c, R, C$ indicate statistical significance under paired t-test to ReDDE.top baseline, CRCS baseline, D-ReDDE.top, D-CRCS, S-ReDDE.top, and S-CRCS respectively ($p < 0.05$).

			ERR	α-nDCG	NRBP	P-IA	S-Recall
Given Subtopics	Baseline	ReDDE.top	0.246	0.276	0.226	0.111	0.409
		CRCS	$0.380^{\dagger}_{rR}$	$0.406^{\dagger}_{r}$	$\mathbf{0.365}^{\dagger}_{rR}$	$\mathbf{0.152}_{rR}$	$0.530^{\dagger}_{r}$
	DDiv	D-ReDDE.top	$0.319^{\dagger}$	$0.345^{\dagger}$	$0.304^{\dagger}$	$0.123^{\dagger}$	$0.477^{\dagger}$
		D-CRCS	$\mathbf{0.383}^{\dagger}_{rR}$	$\mathbf{0.410}^{\dagger}_{rR}$	$\mathbf{0.365}^{\dagger}_{rR}$	$0.151^{\dagger}_{rR}$	$\mathbf{0.535}^{\dagger}_{r}$
	SDiv	S-ReDDE.top	$0.357^{\dagger}_{r}$	$0.387^{\dagger}_{r}$	$0.340^{\dagger}_{r}$	$0.141^{\dagger}_{r}$	$0.526^{\dagger}_{r}$
		S-CRCS	$0.365^{\dagger}_{r}$	$0.395^{\dagger}_{r}$	$0.346^{\dagger}_{r}$	$0.142^{\dagger}_{r}$	$0.534^{\dagger}_{r}$
Suggestions	Baseline	ReDDE.top	0.249	0.277	0.230	0.114	0.400
		CRCS	$0.339^{\dagger}_{r}$	$0.378^{\dagger}_{r}$	$0.315^{\dagger}$	$\mathbf{0.157}^{\dagger}_{rR}$	$\mathbf{0.535}^{\dagger}_{r}$
	DDiv	D-ReDDE.top	$0.304^{\dagger}$	$0.333^{\dagger}$	$0.286^{\dagger}$	$0.129^{\dagger}$	$0.469^{\dagger}$
		D-CRCS	$\mathbf{0.356}^{\dagger}_{rR}$	$\mathbf{0.390}^{\dagger}_{rR}$	$\mathbf{0.335}^{\dagger\ddagger}_{rR}$	$\mathbf{0.157}^{\dagger}_{rR}$	$0.530^{\dagger}_{rR}$
	SDiv	S-ReDDE.top	$0.323^{\dagger}$	$0.359^{\dagger}_{r}$	$0.300^{\dagger}$	$0.144^{\dagger}_{r}$	$0.512^{\dagger}_{r}$
		S-CRCS	$0.342^{\dagger}_{r}$	$0.376^{\dagger}_{r}$	$0.320^{\dagger}$	$0.147^{\dagger}_{r}$	$0.530^{\dagger}_{r}$

Table 6: Diversification results on document retrieval on test queries. The symbols $\dagger, \ddagger, r, c, R, C, B, O$ indicate statistical significance under paired t-test to ReDDE.top baseline, CRCS baseline, D-ReDDE.top, D-CRCS, S-ReDDE.top, S-CRCS, S-BigDoc, and S-CORI respectively ($p < 0.05$).

			ERR	α-nDCG	NRBP	P-IA	S-Recall
Given Subtopics	Baseline	ReDDE.top	0.304	0.345	0.278	0.151	0.509
		CRCS	$0.478^{\dagger}_{rBO}$	$0.512^{\dagger}_{rBO}$	$0.457^{\dagger}_{rBO}$	$0.217^{\dagger}_{rRBO}$	$0.668^{\dagger}_{BO}$
	DDiv	D-ReDDE.top	$0.422^{\dagger}$	$0.457^{\dagger}$	$0.400^{\dagger}$	$0.178^{\dagger}_{O}$	$0.622^{\dagger}_{B}$
		D-CRCS	$0.485^{\dagger}_{rBO}$	$0.523^{\dagger}_{rBO}$	$0.460^{\dagger}_{rBO}$	$0.219^{\dagger}_{rRBO}$	$0.677^{\dagger}_{rBO}$
	SDiv	S-ReDDE.top	$0.463^{\dagger}_{BO}$	$0.501^{\dagger}_{rBO}$	$0.438^{\dagger}_{BO}$	$0.200^{\dagger}_{rBO}$	$0.678^{\dagger}_{rBO}$
		S-CRCS	$0.473^{\dagger}_{rBO}$	$0.515^{\dagger}_{rBO}$	$0.446^{\dagger}_{BO}$	$0.206^{\dagger}_{rBO}$	$0.687^{\dagger}_{rBO}$
		S-BigDoc	0.370	0.390	0.359	0.151	0.519
		S-CORI	0.368	0.393	0.354	0.129	0.545
	LR-DivS		$\mathbf{0.515}^{\dagger}_{rRCBO}$	$\mathbf{0.555}^{\dagger}_{rRCBO}$	$\mathbf{0.489}^{\dagger}_{rRCBO}$	$\mathbf{0.243}^{\dagger\ddagger}_{rcRCBO}$	$\mathbf{0.722}^{\dagger\ddagger}_{rRBO}$
Suggestions	Baseline	ReDDE.top	0.337	0.373	0.311	0.167	0.518
		CRCS	$0.469^{\dagger}_{rBO}$	$0.509^{\dagger}_{rBO}$	$0.445^{\dagger}_{BO}$	$0.235^{\dagger}_{rBO}$	$0.671^{\dagger}_{BO}$
	DDiv	D-ReDDE.top	$0.434^{\dagger}_{B}$	$0.471^{\dagger}_{BO}$	$0.410^{\dagger}_{B}$	$0.202^{\dagger}_{O}$	$0.637^{\dagger}_{B}$
		D-CRCS	$0.487^{\dagger}_{rBO}$	$0.524^{\dagger}_{rBO}$	$0.463^{\dagger}_{rBO}$	$0.233^{\dagger}_{rBO}$	$0.675^{\dagger}_{BO}$
	SDiv	S-ReDDE.top	$0.462^{\dagger}_{BO}$	$0.504^{\dagger}_{rBO}$	$0.435^{\dagger}_{BO}$	$0.224^{\dagger}_{BO}$	$0.674^{\dagger}_{BO}$
		S-CRCS	$0.472^{\dagger}_{BO}$	$0.512^{\dagger}_{rBO}$	$0.448^{\dagger}_{BO}$	$0.219^{\dagger}_{BO}$	$0.675^{\dagger}_{BO}$
		S-BigDoc	0.347	0.374	0.330	0.157	0.511
		S-CORI	0.370	0.400	0.349	0.150	0.560
	LR-DivS		$\mathbf{0.509}^{\dagger\ddagger}_{rRCBO}$	$\mathbf{0.543}^{\dagger\ddagger}_{rRCBO}$	$\mathbf{0.487}^{\dagger\ddagger}_{rRBO}$	$\mathbf{0.249}^{\dagger}_{rBO}$	$\mathbf{0.690}^{\dagger}_{rBO}$

posed for resource selection in federated search, but limited attention has been paid to result novelty and diversification, which affects the effectiveness of existing algorithms. As far as we know, this paper proposes the first piece of research for incorporating search result diversification in resource selection for federated search.

A family of new evaluation metrics is first proposed for measuring search result diversification in resource selection, which combines some popular diversification metrics in ad hoc search with the recall-based evaluation metric in resource selection. Two general approaches are then proposed for diversification in selecting relevant sources. The first approach is based on sample documents, which ranks sample documents with respect to result diversification, and then utilizes the ReDDE framework for ranking the sources. The second approach is based on source-level estimation, which directly ranks each information source as a whole for result diversification. Furthermore, a learning based classification approach is proposed to combine multiple resource selection algorithms for more accurate diversification results.

An intensive set of empirical studies has been conducted to evaluate the proposed research on the Clueweb federated search dataset. Both the approach based on sample documents and on source-level estimation can outperform traditional resource selection algorithms in result diversification in both source-level for resource selection and in the document-level for federated document retrieval. Moreover, the learning based approach, which combines outputs of multiple resource selection algorithms for result diversification, has been shown to generate the best results when some training data is available.

There are several possible directions to pursue in the future. The learning based method in this paper utilizes a simple model for combining outputs of multiple algorithms for result diversification, while a more sophisticated learning method may be more effective. Furthermore, it is an interesting topic to design new result merging algorithms with the focus on result diversification.

9. ACKNOWLEDGMENTS

This work is partially supported by NSF research grants IIS-0746830, CNS- 1012208 and IIS-1017837. This work is also partially supported by the Vietnam Education Foundation, the Center for Science of Information (CSoI), an NSF Science and Technology Center, under grant agreement CCF-0939370, and a travel grant from the ACM Special Interest Group on Information Retrieval. Any opinions, findings and conclusions or recommendations expressed in this material are those of the authors and do not necessarily reflect those of the sponsors.

10. REFERENCES

[1] R. Agrawal, S. Gollapudi, A. Halverson, and S. Ieong. Diversifying search results. In *Proceedings of the Second ACM International Conference on Web Search and Data Mining* pages 5–14, 2009.

[2] J. Arguello, J. Callan, and F. Diaz. Classification-based resource selection. *CIKM'09*, pages 1277–1286, 2009.

[3] M. Baillie, M. Carman, and F. Crestani. A multi-collection latent topic model for federated search. *Information Retrieval*, 14(4):390–412, 2011.

[4] J. Callan. Distributed information retrieval. *Advances in Information Retrieval*, pages 127–150, 2000.

[5] J. Carbonell and J. Goldstein. The use of MMR, diversity-based reranking for reordering documents and producing summaries. In *SIGIR'98*, pages 335–336, 1998.

[6] B. Carterette and P. Chandar. Probabilistic models of ranking novel documents for faceted topic retrieval. In *CIKM'09*, pages 1287–1296, 2009.

[7] O. Chapelle, D. Metlzer, Y. Zhang, and P. Grinspan. Expected reciprocal rank for graded relevance. In *CIKM'09*, pages 621–630. ACM, 2009.

[8] H. Chen and D. Karger. Less is more: probabilistic models for retrieving fewer relevant documents. In *SIGIR'06*, pages 429–436, 2006.

[9] C. Clarke, N. Craswell, and I. Soboroff. Overview of the TREC 2009 Web Track. *TREC*, pages 1–9, Jan. 2009.

[10] C. Clarke, N. Craswell, I. Soboroff, and G. V. Cormack. Overview of the TREC 2010 Web Track. *TREC*, pages 1–9, Jan. 2010.

[11] C. Clarke, N. Craswell, I. Soboroff, and E. Voorhees. Overview of the TREC 2011 Web Track. pages 1–9, Jan. 2011.

[12] C. Clarke, M. Kolla, and O. Vechtomova. An effectiveness measure for ambiguous and underspecified queries. *Advances in Information Retrieval Theory*, pages 188–199, 2009.

[13] C. L. A. Clarke, M. Kolla, G. V. Cormack, O. Vechtomova, A. Ashkan, S. Büttcher, and I. MacKinnon. Novelty and diversity in information retrieval evaluation. In *SIGIR'08*, pages 659–666, 2008.

[14] N. Craswell. *Methods for Distributed Information Retrieval.* PhD thesis, The Australian National University, 2000.

[15] F. Crestani and I. Markov. Distributed Information Retrieval and Applications. In *Proceedings of ECIR*, Jan. 2013.

[16] V. Dang and W. B. Croft. Diversity by proportionality: an election-based approach to search result diversification. In *SIGIR'12*, pages 65–74. ACM, 2012.

[17] N. Fuhr. Resource Discovery in Distributed Digital Libraries. In *In Digital Libraries '99: Advanced Methods and Technologies, Digital Collections*, 1999.

[18] A. Genkin, D. D. Lewis, and D. Madigan. Large-scale Bayesian logistic regression for text categorization. *Technometrics*, 49(3):291–304, 2007.

[19] J. He, V. Hollink, and A. de Vries. Combining implicit and explicit topic representations for result diversification. In *SIGIR'12*, pages 851–860. ACM, 2012.

[20] D. Hong, L. Si, P. Bracke, M. Witt, and T. Juchcinski. A joint probabilistic classification model for resource selection. *SIGIR'10*, pages 98–105, 2010.

[21] A. Kulkarni and J. Callan. Document allocation policies for selective searching of distributed indexes. *CIKM'10*, pages 449–458, 2010.

[22] I. Markov, L. Azzopardi, and F. Crestani. Reducing the Uncertainty in Resource Selection. In *Proceedings of ECIR*, 2013.

[23] D. Metzler and W. B. Croft. Combining the language model and inference network approaches to retrieval. *Information Processing and Management*, 40(5):735–750, 2004.

[24] D. Nguyen, T. Demeester, D. Trieschnigg, and D. Hiemstra. Federated Search in the Wild. In *CIKM '12*, pages 1874–1878, 2012.

[25] R. L. Santos, C. Macdonald, and I. Ounis. Aggregated search result diversification. *Advances in Information Retrieval Theory*, pages 250–261, 2011.

[26] R. L. T. Santos, C. Macdonald, and I. Ounis. Exploiting query reformulations for web search result diversification. In *Proceedings of the 19th international conference on World wide web*, pages 881–890. ACM, 2010.

[27] M. Shokouhi. Central-rank-based collection selection in uncooperative distributed information retrieval. *Advances in Information Retrieval*, 2007.

[28] M. Shokouhi and L. Si. Federated Search. 2011.

[29] M. Shokouhi and J. Zobel. Federated Text Retrieval From Uncooperative Overlapped Collections. *SIGIR'07*, pages 789–790, 2007.

[30] M. Shokouhi and J. Zobel. Robust result merging using sample-based score estimates. *ACM Transactions on Information Systems (TOIS)*, 27(3):1–29, 2009.

[31] L. Si and J. Callan. A semisupervised learning method to merge search engine results. *ACM Transactions on Information Systems (TOIS)*, 21(4):457–491, 2003.

[32] L. Si and J. Callan. Relevant document distribution estimation method for resource selection. *SIGIR'03*, pages 298–305, 2003.

[33] P. Thomas and M. Shokouhi. Sushi: Scoring scaled samples for server selection. In *SIGIR'09*, pages 419–426. ACM, 2009.

[34] D. Vallet and P. Castells. Personalized diversification of search results. In *SIGIR'12*, pages 841–850. ACM, 2012.

[35] S. Vargas, P. Castells, and D. Vallet. Explicit relevance models in intent-oriented information retrieval diversification. In *SIGIR'12*, pages 75–84. ACM, 2012.

[36] J. Xu and W. B. Croft. Cluster-based language models for distributed retrieval. In *SIGIR'99*, pages 254–261, 1999.

[37] B. Yuwono and D. L. Lee. Server ranking for distributed text retrieval systems on the internet. In *Proceedings of the Fifth International Conference on Database Systems for Advanced Applications (DASFAA)*, pages 41–50, 1997.

[38] C. X. Zhai, W. Cohen, and J. Lafferty. Beyond independent relevance: methods and evaluation metrics for subtopic retrieval. In *SIGIR'03*, pages 10–17, 2003.

[39] K. Zhou, R. Cummins, M. Lalmas, and J. M. Jose. Evaluating aggregated search pages. In *SIGIR'12*, pages 115–124, 2012.

The Effect of Threshold Priming and Need for Cognition on Relevance Calibration and Assessment

Falk Scholer
School of Computer Science
and Information Technology
RMIT University
Melbourne, Australia
falk.scholer@rmit.edu.au

Diane Kelly,
Wan-Ching Wu,
Hanseul S. Lee
School of Information and
Library Science
University of North Carolina
Chapel Hill, NC, USA
dianek@email.unc.edu

William Webber
College of Information Studies
University of Maryland
College Park, Maryland, USA
wew@umd.edu

ABSTRACT

Human assessments of document relevance are needed for the construction of test collections, for ad-hoc evaluation, and for training text classifiers. Showing documents to assessors in different orderings, however, may lead to different assessment outcomes. We examine the effect that *threshold priming*, seeing varying degrees of relevant documents, has on people's calibration of relevance. Participants judged the relevance of a prologue of documents containing highly relevant, moderately relevant, or non-relevant documents, followed by a common epilogue of documents of mixed relevance. We observe that participants exposed to only non-relevant documents in the prologue assigned significantly higher average relevance scores to prologue and epilogue documents than participants exposed to moderately or highly relevant documents in the prologue. We also examine how *need for cognition*, an individual difference measure of the extent to which a person enjoys engaging in effortful cognitive activity, impacts relevance assessments. High need for cognition participants had a significantly higher level of agreement with expert assessors than low need for cognition participants did. Our findings indicate that assessors should be exposed to documents from multiple relevance levels early in the judging process, in order to calibrate their relevance thresholds in a balanced way, and that individual difference measures might be a useful way to screen assessors.

Categories and Subject Descriptors

H.3.4 [**Information Storage and Retrieval**]: Systems and software—*performance evaluation.*

Keywords

Evaluation, assessors, relevance assessments, relevance behavior, need for cognition, threshold priming, order effects, calibration

SIGIR'13, July 28–August 1, 2013, Dublin, Ireland.

1. INTRODUCTION

Relevance is a fundamental concept in information retrieval (IR) and forms the basis of most methods of evaluating IR systems. Relevance assessments, however, are subject to human judgment. Different assessors may make different assessments of the relevance of the same document to the same topic, and one assessor may make different assessments of the same document at different times and under different conditions.

Relevance assessments are used for retrieval evaluation, either through reusable test collections such as those constructed by TREC and similar efforts, or through more ad-hoc evaluation. While differences in relevance assessments may have a limited effect on comparative system evaluation, they have a serious impact on the absolute evaluation of system effectiveness, as the level of agreement between human assessors places a practical upper bound on measurable system quality. This distortion is consequential in environments where absolute measures of retrieval completeness and accuracy are required, such as e-discovery, patent retrieval, and research literature surveys. Relevance assessments are also used to train text classifiers and learning to rank systems, and assessor variability may work to degrade the effectiveness of such systems.

While many causes of human variability in relevance assessment are inescapable, some are within the control of the evaluation designer [26]. One such factor is the order in which the assessor is asked to assess documents for relevance. A long sequence of irrelevant documents, for instance, might cause an assessor to lower their threshold of relevance, or alternatively to lose concentration and miss relevant documents—an effect evaluation designers could seek to counteract by seeding likely-relevant documents more evenly. The overall density of likely-relevant documents in the set of documents for assessment may be under the control of the evaluation designer, through sampling or pooling decisions. For instance, a uniform sampling of a document corpus will give a much lower density of relevant documents than a stratified sampling that weights samples towards retrieved or highly-ranked documents.

As assessors evaluate documents against a topic, whether of their own or of another's creation, they are building internal relevance models that guide their decision-making process about whether a document is relevant or not, and (where graded relevance is used) about the level of relevance to assign to documents. We posit that these resulting relevance models will develop differently depending on the relevance levels of documents that assessors encounter, and that this differential development of relevance models will result in different calibrations, or thresholds for relevance. We refer to this posited effect as *threshold priming*. For example, an assessor who encounters few or no relevant documents would (under our hypothesis) have a lower threshold for relevance than a person who encounters a large number of highly relevant documents. Subsequently shown the same documents, the former assessor would tend to assign a higher relevance grade than the latter.

A further factor influencing assessment reliability that may be under the evaluator's control is the choice of the assessors themselves. Studies in the e-discovery field have found that there is a great deal of variability in assessor reliability, but this does not seem to correlate with training or (at least legal) expertise (Section 2.2). Perhaps more fundamental personality traits and capacities are at play. One possible trait identified in the psychological literature is *need for cognition*, a measure of the extent to which individuals enjoy engaging in concentrated intellectual activity. We believe that assessing relevance is an example of concentrated intellectual activity, since it requires sustained attention, close and careful reading, and good memory. There are standardized scales for need for cognition; if this trait is correlated with assessor reliability, it could provide a useful filter for assessor recruitment.

We investigate the hypotheses that threshold priming and need for cognition influence assessor relevance judgments by asking the following three research questions:

1. Does threshold priming, based on the relevance level of documents that are encountered early in the judging process, affect how an assessor assigns relevance to documents that are seen later on?
2. Does threshold priming affect how well an assessor is able to form a stable conception of relevance for a topic, based on the self-consistency of ratings over time, and the level of agreement between assessors?
3. Does the need for cognition (NFC) characteristic of an assessor predict how they assign relevance to documents, or how long they take to make judgments?

2. BACKGROUND

We first review research from the information behavior literature about defining and measuring relevance. This research has primarily focused on the behaviors of searchers working on search tasks (both assigned and natural). Next, we review work examining how assessors make relevance judgments when engaged in the development of test collections or similar evaluation tasks. Finally, we review work describing individual differences and relevance behavior, and specifically need for cognition.

2.1 Relevance

A trilogy of articles by Saracevic [20, 21, 22] provide a comprehensive overview and synthesis of relevance research spanning over 30 years. Saracevic [21] conceptualized five classes of relevance: (1) system or algorithm; (2) topical; (3) pertinence or cognitive; (4) situational; and (5) motivational or affective. In our research, we focus on *topical relevance*, since this is the type of relevance that is modeled by the relevance assessments that accompany most test collections. *Topical relevance* is defined as "an intellectual assessment of how an information object corresponds to the topical area required and described by the request(s) for information" [2, p. 915]. We are also concerned with *cognitive relevance*, as our research is motivated by the theory that as people encounter documents, they are calibrating their internal relevance models of the topic, which serve as a basis for subsequent assessments. This is related to the idea of psychological relevance, which posits that relevance assessments are made in relation to a person's current psychological state: "...relevance judgments are a function of one's mental state at the time a reference is read. They are not fixed; they are dynamic" [12, p. 612]. Specifically, we are interested in how the order in which documents are encountered impacts people's relevance calibrations and subsequent assessments.

While it is generally accepted that order effects occur during document assessment, Saracevic [22] notes that only a few studies have systematically addressed this issue. The results of these studies have been inconsistent, likely due to variability in research methods. Eisenberg and Barry [9] experimented with two document orders for a set of 15 documents and a single query: one ranked high to low relevance, the other low to high. The authors found that in the high–low condition, people underestimated the relevance of documents at the higher end (assigning lower relevance scores to the highly relevant documents), while those in the low–high condition overestimated the relevance of documents in the low to middle range (assigning higher relevance scores to less relevant documents). This behavior was explained as a "hedging phenomenon" (p. 296), where participants working with a fixed scale and an unknown set of stimuli are reluctant to initially assign high or low scores to items. Purgaillis Parker and Johnson [19] did not find a systematic order effect in their study, but they used citations, rather than full-text, and like Eisenberg and Barry [9] only experimented with sets of 15 objects. Later, Huang and Wang [14] found that set size matters, with order effects being detected for sets of size 15, 30, 45 and 60, but not 5 and 75. They also found that relevance scores assigned by people in the low to high treatment were higher than those assigned by people in the high to low treatment, which is consistent with the results of Eisenberg and Barry [9].

In our research, we also focus on *degree of relevance*. Degree of relevance refers to the rating or indication of the relevance value given to documents. Borlund [2] provides an overview of different degrees of relevance including binary relevance, tripartite relevance, scale-based relevance and graded relevance. Borlund observes that degrees of relevance can also refer to whether the object as a whole is considered relevant, or only a part of it. Saracevic [22] indicates that previous research shows that people prefer to judge document relevance on a continuum, and comparatively. If people construct internal relevance models as they assess documents, then it seems reasonable to assume that the degree of relevance of the documents encountered will impact the formation of people's *relevance thresholds*, or the amount of evidence needed to associate documents with each degree of relevance.

In addition to Saracevic's conceptualizations, many researchers have also documented the various criteria (e.g., novelty, recency, depth) that people use when making relevance assessments [1, 25] and observed that the process of assigning relevance to documents is dynamic and inter-dependent, and impacted by a number of variables, including how much one knows about the topic and the search stage [6, 27]. There has also been a persistent body of research about how assessors make relevance judgments for test collections or other system evaluations. This work is reviewed in more detail in the next section.

2.2 Assessor Behavior

High levels of assessor disagreement about document relevance have been observed in a number of studies. Voorhees [29] reports a mean positive agreement between TREC assessors of 0.58. (Positive agreement can also be interpreted as the F_1 score that one assessor would achieve if evaluated by the other assessor.) Oard and Webber [18] survey a number of studies on assessor agreement, observing positive agreement between 0.33 and 0.76. Analyzing TREC assessment data, Scholer et al. [23] find that a single assessor will make at different times a different assessment of the binary relevance of the same document between 15% to 19% of the time, and 19% to 24% of the time for trinary relevance. Voorhees [29] finds that assessor disagreement has a limited effect on relative measures of system quality, but observes that it sets an upper bound on the practically measurable absolute quality. Carterette and Soboroff [5] find that (randomly simulated) optimistic assessors (those tending to mark more documents relevant) disrupt evaluation reliability more than pessimistic assessors do.

Webber [31] finds considerable variance between assessors' agreement with an authoritative assessor; nevertheless, Oard and Webber [18] conclude that assessor disagreement differs more between topics than between assessors, suggesting that topic difficulty is a major component in assessment variability. Grossman and Cormack [11] argue that assessor disagreement is due in 90% of cases to inarguable assessor error; however, their dataset has a strong selection bias towards such errors. Webber et al. [32] find that giving more detailed assessment guidelines does not improve assessor agreement or reliability. Webber et al. [32], Wang and Soergel [30], and Efthimiadis and Hotchkiss [8] all compare the reliability for e-discovery of legally trained assessors (lawyers or law students) with that of assessors who lack legal training, and find no difference between the two groups. Kazai et al. [16] find systematic biases between assessor groups in Web search towards, for instance, Wikipedia pages or documents rich in query keywords.

The impact of document order on relevance assessments has also been investigated in the context of crowd-sourcing. Le et al. [17] studied how the impact of the distribution of answers in a training set influences worker performance, and found that the accuracy of workers increases when the training set more closely reflects the underlying distribution of items that are matches or mismatches in a categorisation task. Kazai et al. [15] demonstrated that when workers are asked to assess a series of 10 documents ordered by their expected relevance (as derived from experimental IR systems) for an INEX book track, their overall accuracy compared to expert judgments is lower than when documents are ordered randomly.

Sormunen [24] investigates multi-level relevance criteria, carrying out extensive re-judging of documents for 38 topics from the TREC 7 and 8 newswire collections. Judgments were made on a 4-point relevance scale: highly relevant; relevant; marginally relevant; and non-relevant. The analysis shows that around half of the relevant documents were only marginally relevant, defined as not containing information beyond what is already available in the topic description. The assessments were made by students enrolled in a Masters degree program, and involved the pre-reading of topical documents before starting judgments. We make use of these *expert* judgments in this paper, using them as an underlying gold standard for our experiment.

2.3 Need for Cognition

While there has been some research about the impact of individual differences on search behavior (e.g., Ford et al. [10]), according to Saracevic [22] there has been little research exploring how individual differences impact relevance behavior. The exception is Davidson [7] who studied openness to information, which was measured by a number of cognitive style variables such as open-mindedness, rigidity and locus of control. Davidson [7] found that about 30% of the variance in relevance assessments was attributable to variances in openness to information.

In this study, we focus on one individual difference measure, *need for cognition* (NFC), which has been extensively studied in other fields as a way to understand differences in the extent to which people process information [3]. Cacioppo et al. [4] define NFC as "a stable individual difference in people's tendency to engage in and enjoy effortful cognitive activity" (p. 198). Empirical studies have found that individuals with high NFC are more motivated to process information, pay more attention to argument quality, perform better on cognitive tasks, react more positively to complex rules, generate more task-related and thoughtful responses, and recall more information about tasks (see Cacioppo et al. [4] for a detailed review). In this study, we seek to determine if and how NFC impacts relevance behavior.

3. METHODS

A between-subjects laboratory experiment with 82 participants was conducted. Each participant was given a single topic and asked to judge the relevance of 48 documents presented in a pre-specified order. The experimental sessions lasted approximately one hour. Participants were compensated with US$10.

3.1 Treatment

The treatment, or experimental manipulation, occurred within the lists of documents presented to participants. The document lists contained two parts: the *prologue*, consisting of the first 20 documents; and the *epilogue*, consisting of the last 28 documents. Documents in the prologue contained the experimental manipulations, while those in the epilogue were held constant for all participants for each topic. These manipulations and lists can be viewed in Table 1. Note that participants were presented with one document at a time, rather than a clickable list.

Within the prologue, one of three treatments was represented, *low*, *medium* or *high*, which corresponded to the degree of relevance of documents in the 'X' positions in the list in Table 1. In the low treatment, X was replaced by non-relevant documents. In the medium treatment, X was replaced by marginally relevant or relevant documents. In the high treatment, X was replaced by highly relevant documents. Documents shown in all positions other than those marked with an X were identical across treatments for each topic. The documents shown in positions 46-48 were duplicates of those shown in positions 21, 22 and 24. One document list was instantiated for each topic and treatment level combination; all participants who completed a specified treatment for a particular topic worked through the same list.

The documents, topics and relevance judgments came from a subset of the TREC-7 and TREC-8 test collections, which was created by Sormunen [24]. Marginally relevant and relevant documents were merged into one class and used in our treatments. However, participants were provided with the four-point relevance scale used in Sormunen [24] to make their judgments. The definitions of these various levels of relevance were:

- *Highly relevant (3)*: The document discusses the themes of the topic exhaustively. In case of a multi-faceted topic, all or most sub-themes or viewpoints are covered. Typical extent: several text paragraphs, at least 4 sentences or facts.
- *Relevant (2)*: The document contains more information than the topic description but the presentation is not exhaustive. In case of a multi-faceted topic, only some of the sub-themes or viewpoints are covered. Typical extent: one text paragraph, 2-3 sentences or facts.
- *Marginally relevant (1)*: The document only points to the topic. It does not contain more or other information than the topic description. Typical extent: one sentence or fact.
- *Not relevant (0)*: The document does not contain any information about the topic.

Prologue				Epilogue					
1	X	11	NR	21	MR-R	31	HR	41	MR-R
2	X	12	X	22	MR-R	32	MR-R	42	NR
3	NR	13	NR	23	NR	33	MR-R	43	MR-R
4	NR	14	X	24	MR-R	34	MR-R	44	NR
5	X	15	NR	25	MR-R	35	HR	45	HR
6	NR	16	X	26	HR	36	MR-R	46	MR-R, 21
7	X	17	X	27	NR	37	HR	47	MR-R, 22
8	NR	18	NR	28	HR	38	MR-R	48	MR-R, 24
9	X	19	NR	29	NR	39	NR		
10	NR	20	X	30	NR	40	HR		

Table 1: Design template for document lists. X indicates documents that differed among treatments in the Prologue. NR=non-relevant document; MR-R=relevant or marginally relevant document; HR=highly relevant document. Documents in positions 46-48 are duplicates of those in positions 21, 22, and 24.

When participants logged in to the system, they were presented with a description of what they would be doing during the experimental session. Participants were instructed: "The aim of this task is to assess the relevance of a set of documents for a particular search topic. You will be provided with a search topic to work on. You will then be presented with a series of documents, one at a time. Read each document, and decide if it is relevant for the topic." Participants were presented with the relevance definitions and scale, and were instructed to judge each document *independently* and *on its own merit* ("If a document contains information that makes it anything other than not relevant, then you should choose the appropriate relevance category, even if you have seen that information previously in another document."). Participants were further told that the documents were from the late 1980s and 1990s and that when a topic referred to "current" they should interpret this as "current to the time the article was written."

The assessment interface, which presented the search topic at the top of the screen (title, description and narrative), a document in the middle of the screen (one document was presented at a time), and the relevance assessment scale at the bottom of the screen, was also explained in the instructions. Participants were instructed that once they submitted an assessment they could not return to revise it later. During the assessment, participants could hover their mouse over each choice on the relevance scale to see the relevance definitions.

After participants finished reviewing the instructions, they completed a training task with a topic not used in the main study and two documents, so they could become familiar with the assessment process and interface. Several pilot tests were conducted during the development of the instructions and experimental infrastructure.

3.2 Topics

After completing the training task, participants were presented with one of three search topics. Our choice of topics was guided by several concerns. First, we needed to select topics for which there was a good assortment of documents at various relevance levels. Second, we needed to select topics about which most participants would know little, so that participants would start the study with the same basic models of the topics. Finally, we wanted to select topics that might interest participants. Several pilot tests were conducted during the topic and document selection phases.

Three topics were used in this study: 385 (hybrid fuel cars), 396 (sick building syndrome), and 415 (drugs, Golden Triangle). These topics were counter-balanced across the experimental treatments; that is, there were high, medium and low treatments for each topic. We understand that the inclusion of only three topics limits our ability to generalize, but including a larger number of topics was not possible since it would have required a prohibitively large number of participants to achieve statistical power.

	385	396	415
Frequency of past search	Never	Never	Never
Prior knowledge	A little	A little	Nothing
Interest	Slightly	Slightly	Somewhat
Relevance to life	Moderately	Slightly	Not at all

Table 2: Participants' Mode Responses to Topic Questions.

Participants were presented with the title, description and narrative fields and asked (1) How many times they had searched for information about the topic in the past (never, 1-2 times, 3-4 times, 5 or more times); (2) How much they knew about the topic (nothing, a little, some, a great deal); (3) How interested they were to learn more about the topic (not at all, slightly, somewhat, moderately, very); and (4) The relevance of the topic to their lives (not at all, slightly, somewhat, moderately, very). Following this, participants started the assessments.

Table 2 presents participants' mode responses to the topic items. Overall, most participants had not ever searched for information about these topics, knew little or nothing about them, were somewhat or slightly interested in learning more about them and found them moderately (385, hybrid fuel cars), slightly (396, sick building syndrome) and not at all (415, drugs, Golden Triangle) relevant to their lives. While we had hoped participants' interests in the topics might be slightly higher, our main objective was to select topics about which most participants would have no prior knowledge, so from this perspective, our topic selection was satisfactory.

3.3 Exit Questionnaire

After participants completed the main assessment task, they were directed to an exit questionnaire. The first question asked them to indicate what, if anything, was challenging about deciding which relevance levels to associate with each document. Next, they were asked to indicate their confidence in the relevance judgments they made (not at all confident, slightly confident, somewhat confident, moderately confident, very confident).

The next set of items consisted of the *Need for Cognition* scale (Cacioppo and Petty [3]). This 18-item scale contains statements such as "The notion of thinking abstractly is appealing to me," and "I like to have the responsibility of handling a situation that requires a lot of thinking." Participants indicated the extent to which the statements were characteristic of them using five choices (extremely uncharacteristic of me, somewhat uncharacteristic of me, uncertain, somewhat characteristic of me, and extremely characteristic of me).

The last part of the exit questionnaire contained demographic questions about participants' sex, age, student and occupational statuses, as well as whether English was their native language.

3.4 Participants

Participants were recruited through the mass email service at the University of North Carolina, Chapel Hill. A power analysis performed before the study indicated that approximately 25-30 participants were needed per treatment. Eighty-two people completed the experiment. Participants were randomly assigned to condition: 26 were in Treatment 1 (Low), 27 were in Treatment 2 (Medium) and 29 were in Treatment 3 (High). The majority of participants were female (85.37%). Their ages ranged from 18 to 55 years (M = 23.70, SD = 8.96). Seventy (85.36%) participants were students (57 undergraduates and 13 graduates); seven (8.54%) were university employees; four (4.88%) were both students and employees and one was neither. Student participants' majors were: social sciences (32%); professional schools (29%); sciences (19%); humanities (15%); and undecided (5%). For participants who were full- or part-time employees at the university (11, 13.42%), job titles included research assistant, IT support specialist, librarian, accountant, examiner and administrative manager/supporter. Seventy-one participants (86.59%) indicated they were native English speakers.

4. RESULTS

This paper investigates the effects of threshold priming and need for cognition on relevance assessments. In this section we present the results of our experiments as they relate to the three main research questions.

4.1 Relevance Assessments

The first research question aims to analyze how threshold priming, as operationalized by the relevance level of documents that participants see early in the judgment process, impacts how relevance scores are assigned to documents later on.

Recall that our experiments included three treatment conditions for documents in the prologue (the first 20 items that were judged): participants were shown either highly relevant (high), marginally relevant and relevant (medium), or non-relevant (low) documents. All participants then saw a consistent set of 28 documents in the epilogue. In this section, we investigate the impact of these threshold priming treatments in four ways: the impact on the relative assignment of relevance scores between study participants; the impact on relevance score assignments relative to underlying expert judgments; whether possible differences endure over time; and, whether the amount of time taken to make assessments differ according to treatment.

Before presenting these results, we first perform a treatment check to verify that participants in each of the three groups experienced the intended treatments. Participants' mean (standard deviation) ratings of prologue documents were 0.56 (0.40), 1.08 (0.34) and 1.42 (0.22) for each of the groups low, medium and high, so it appears that participants experienced the intended treatments. If participants were marking documents exactly as the underlying experts, we would expect those in the low group to have a mean of 0, those in the medium group to have a mean around 1 and those in the high group to have a mean of 1.5. These results show while participants experienced the intended treatments, those in the low group also up-marked some non-relevant documents. We explore this behavior in a subsequent section.

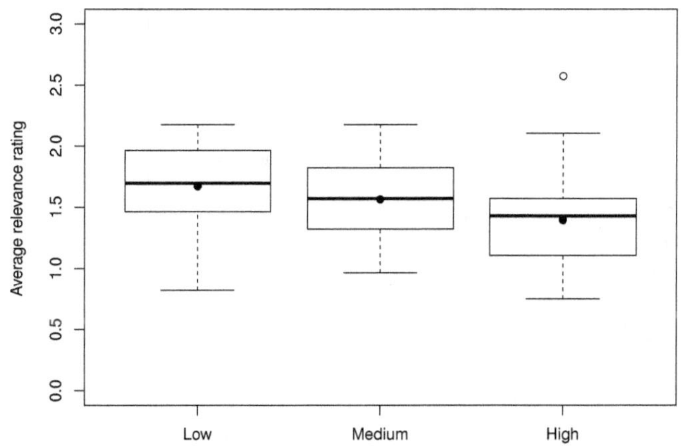

Figure 1: Distribution of mean relevance scores assigned to documents in the epilogue by participants in each of the three prologue treatments.

Impact on relative assignment of relevance scores. A convenient way to characterize the overall behavior of participants in the epilogue is to consider the mean relevance scores assigned to documents in positions 21–48. The statistic captures differences in how participants assigned relevance scores, and enables the analysis of *relative* judging behavior. (Since individual document assessments were made using a four-point ordinal scale, the mean scores should not be interpreted in absolute terms.)

A boxplot of these average relevance scores assigned by participants in each treatment is shown in Figure 1. The boxes show the data points of the 25th to 75th percentiles, with the solid black line representing the median, and mean values shown by solid black circles. The whiskers show the range of data and outlier values (data points that lie more than 1.5 times the inter-quartile range away from the box) are shown as circles. The means (and standard deviations, in parentheses) of the average relevance scores assigned to documents in the epilogue is 1.67 (0.38), 1.57 (0.33) and 1.40 (0.42) for the low, medium and high treatments, respectively.

Another possible source of variation that could impact the average relevance scores that were assigned in the epilogue comes from the search topics that participants were working on. The mean average relevance scores assigned by participants for each Topic was 1.57 (0.42) for Topic 385, 1.58 (0.37) for Topic 396, and 1.47 (0.39) for Topic 415.

A two-way ANOVA using type II sums of squares was conducted to investigate the statistical significance of both the treatment and topic effects. The treatment effect was found to be statistically significant ($F(2,73) = 3.63, p = 0.031$) while the topic effect was not significant ($F(2,73) = 0.61, p = 0.548$). The interaction effect was also not significant ($F(4,73) = 0.64, p = 0.636$). Follow-up pairwise t-tests were conducted to further investigate the treatment effect (using the Bonferroni-Holm correction for multiple comparisons [13]). The results indicated that the difference between average scores assigned by participants in the low and high treatments differed significantly ($t(53) = 2.56, p = 0.025$). The differences between the other conditions were not significant ($p > 0.05$). In terms of relative behavior, it appears that participants who initially saw no relevant documents compensated by assigning higher relevance scores to items in the epilogue, while those who were exposed to highly relevant documents assigned more moderate scores.

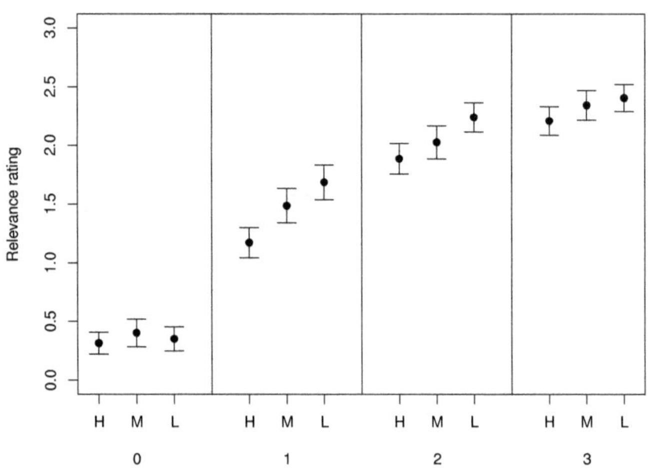

Figure 2: Mean relevance assessments of documents in the epilogue, grouped by the expert relevance rating of the document (0–3) and by prologue treatment.

Topic	Prologue			Epilogue		
	low	med	high	low	med	high
385	1.36 *0.15*	1.06 *0.12*	0.61 *0.09*	0.59 *0.07*	0.71 *0.15*	0.34 *0.11*
396	0.31 *0.11*	0.12 *0.05*	0.26 *0.09*	0.29 *0.11*	0.30 *0.11*	0.40 *0.21*
415	0.29 *0.06*	0.26 *0.13*	0.13 *0.04*	0.17 *0.06*	0.24 *0.06*	0.21 *0.06*
Total	0.67 *0.12*	0.44 *0.10*	0.33 *0.06*	0.35 *0.06*	0.40 *0.07*	0.32 *0.07*

Table 3: Mean of relevance assessments (standard error across assessors in italics) of common non-relevant prologue and epilogue documents, by topic and treatment.

Figure 2 shows the mean relevance assessments that participants assigned to documents (with a 95% confidence interval), grouped first by the expert relevance assessment and second by the experimental treatment. It can be seen that the treatment conditions had the strongest impact on ratings that participants assigned to the mid-range documents (that is, moderately relevant or relevant). These observations are supported by an analysis of the differences between the treatment conditions within each of the four expert relevance groups using a Kruskal-Wallis test ($p = 0.773$, $p < 0.001$, $p < 0.001$, and $p = 0.065$ for expert relevance levels 0 to 4, respectively).

The prologues contained ten non-relevant documents which were the same within each topic. Participants' assessments of these non-relevant documents can be seen in Table 3. The mean assessed relevances for these non-relevant documents were 0.65, 0.48, and 0.33 for the low, medium, and high treatments. A two-way ANOVA finds the difference between treatments statistically significant ($F(2, 73) = 9.78, p < 0.001$), with topic and topic–treatment interactions also being significant ($F(2, 73) = 68.01, p < 0.001$, and $F(4, 73) = 4.79, p = 0.002$). Post-hoc two-way ANOVAs between each pair of levels find significance for the contrasts of high with low treatment and medium with low treatment, but not high with medium treatment (respectively, $F(2, 49) = 20.03, p < 0.001$; $F(2, 50) = 6.91, p < 0.05$; and $F(2, 47) = 2.46, p > 0.05$). For the seven non-relevant documents in the epilogue, mean assessed relevances were 0.35, 0.42, and 0.32 for the low, medium, and high treatments, which was not significant in a two-way ANOVA, though there was still a significant topic effect ($F(2, 73) = 7.37, p = 0.001$). Assessors who saw only non-relevant documents in the prologue were disproportionately inclined to mark some of these documents as relevant; this effect disappeared in the epilogue, however, most likely due to having seen some genuinely relevant documents.

Impact on relevance scores in comparison to expert judgments. In addition to considering the impact that the treatments had on how participants in the different groups assigned relevance scores relative to each other, it is also possible to analyze how these scores compare to the underlying expert relevance judgments. As explained in Section 3, each epilogue consisted of an equal number of documents at each of the four relevance levels. The mean relevance level of each epilogue is therefore 1.5, by design. This expert mean score can be compared to the mean scores that were assigned under each of the treatment conditions; as indicated previously, these were 1.67 for low, 1.56 for medium, and 1.40 for high. Comparing each of these groups against the expert mean of 1.5 using a t-test shows that the scores of the low group differed significantly ($(t(25) = 2.31, p = 0.0293)$, while the medium and high groups did not show significant differences ($p = 0.354$ and $p = 0.193$, respectively).

A difference in the average rating that a participant assigns, relative to an expert rating, could arise due to a large difference in the assigned score for a small number of documents, or a smaller difference in the assigned score across a large set of documents. Figure 3 shows the frequency of the differences between the score that a participant assigned and the underlying expert judgment. All three treatment groups agreed with the expert judgments around 50% of the time. However, when differences occurred, the low group tended to assign relevance scores that were higher than that given by the experts, while the high group tended to assign scores that were lower than those given by the experts. Moreover, it can be seen that the observed differences in average scores were not simply due to the presence of a small number of items for which there were extreme differences of opinion.

The increase in average scores from low treatment participants on epilogue documents can be further analyzed by the expert relevance of each document. Due to bounding effects, there is a natural tendency for documents with low expert relevance to be assigned higher relevance by participants, and vice versa. We control for this by taking as the baseline the mean assessment of medium and high treatment participants for that document and topic. Compared to this baseline, low treatment participants on epilogue documents on average scored (expert-judged) irrelevant documents 0.01 points lower, marginally relevant documents 0.38 points higher, relevant documents 0.29 points higher, and highly-relevant documents 0.14 points higher. The difference between these score increases is significant in a one-way ANOVA test ($F(3, 724) = 8.47, p < 0.0001$). That is, the low treatment participants were not up-voting all documents in the epilogue, but only those with some evidence of relevance (as determined by the expert assessments). Moreover, they tended to boost the relevance of low-relevant documents by more than that of high-relevant documents.

Impact on assignment of relevance scores over time. While the prologue treatment conditions had an impact on the relative assignment of relevance scores to documents in the epilogue,

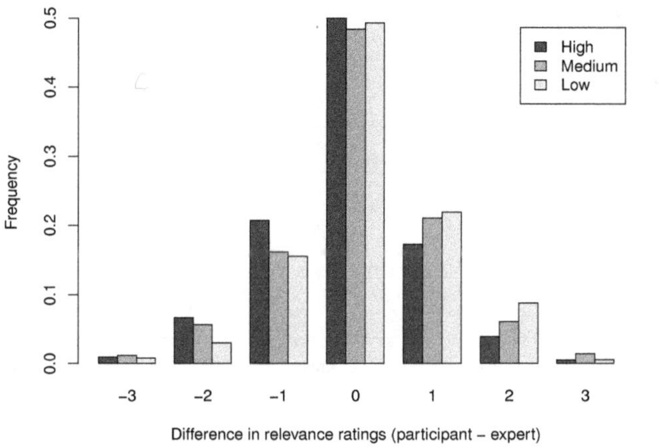

Figure 3: Frequency of the difference in relevance scores assigned by participants and experts to all epilogue documents.

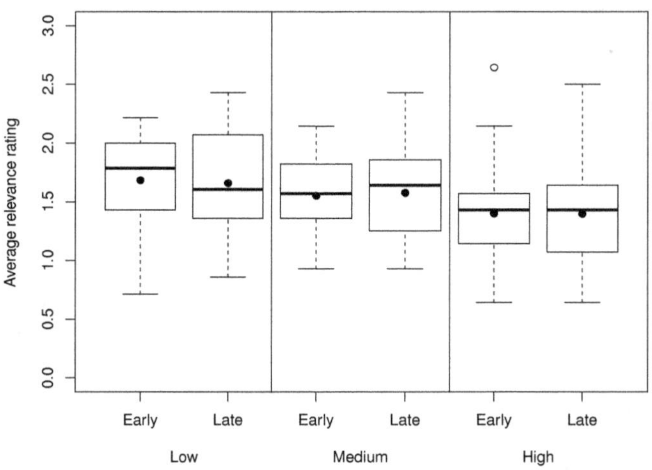

Figure 4: Distribution of mean per-participant relevance scores assigned to documents in the epilogue, for each of the three treatments.

this raises the question of whether such an effect was enduring over the entire 28 epilogue documents, or whether it changed over time. To investigate this, the epilogue was divided into halves, giving a group of 14 *early* documents and 14 *late* documents.

The results of this time-based split are shown in Figure 4, where the low, medium and high treatment conditions have been further partitioned into early and late groups. The graph suggests that variability (based on the inter-quartile range) is higher for the late documents than for the early documents. However, the differences between early and late relevance assignments within a particular treatment group are not statistically significant (t-test, $p > 0.1$).

This suggests that participants continue to refine their mental relevance models over time. Even if they do not have any reference points to begin with, they are able to re-calibrate once they begin to see documents that are relevant to different degrees.

Time taken to judge relevance. It is possible that the occurrence of documents with different levels of relevance has an effect on the amount of attention—and in particular, time—that participants devote to examining documents. For example, if an individual reads a number of documents and they are all non-relevant, the person might become disheartened, and as a result pay less attention to subsequent documents that are presented.

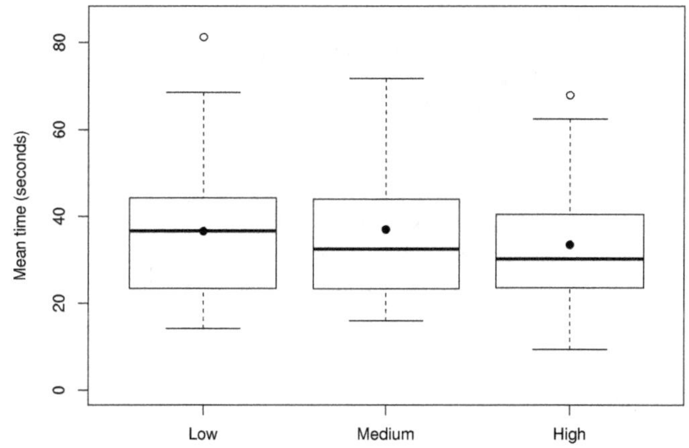

Figure 5: Distribution of the mean time that participants took to judge the relevance of documents in the epilogue, for each of the three treatments.

The boxplot in Figure 5 shows the mean time in seconds that participants took to make relevance judgments for the 28 documents in the epilogue, split by the three treatment conditions. The time was measured in seconds, from when the document was first displayed, until the participant entered and saved a response in the judging interface. While the mean judging times show slight variation (36.60, 37.02, and 33.51 seconds for the low, medium and high groups respectively), these differences are not statistically significant (one-way ANOVA, $F(2, 79) = 0.40, p = 0.669$).

4.2 Agreement

The second research question focuses on whether threshold priming affects how well participants are able to form a stable conception of relevance for a topic, based on the self-consistency of ratings over time, and the level of agreement between participants. Two types of agreement are considered: agreement among participants; and participant self-agreement when making repeat judgments of the same documents at different points in time.

Overall agreement among participants. Our experimental framework was constructed with reference to multi-level relevance judgments created by Sormunen [24], which were created through a careful assessment process.

Consider two sets of relevance judgments made by different assessors. The *overlap* (or percentage agreement) between these judgments is defined as the intersection divided by the union of the two sets (that is, the number of documents that were given the same relevance score by both assessors, divided by the total number of documents that were assessed). This mean pairwise percentage agreement among all participants is 44.80%.

When people read documents in response to a topic, their understanding of the topic changes. It is possible that exposure to different documents will influence their conception of relevance. For example, an individual who sees many relevant documents early might be able to more quickly develop a model of topical relevance; conversely, a person who has mostly seen non-relevant documents might find it more challenging to establish a stable model. To explore this issue, we investigate the relationship between study treatment and the level of agreement between participants when judging documents in the epilogue.

The treatment groups show only minor differences in mean pairwise agreement levels, with 46.45% (12.62), 45.28% (10.17) and 44.25% (12.85) for the low, medium and high groups, respectively. A two-way ANOVA was conducted to investigate the significance of treatment and topic effects. The results show that the treatment main effect was not statistically significant ($F(2, 326) = 0.99, p = 0.373$). However, differences in agreement due to the topic main effect were significant ($F(2, 326) = 5.70, p = 0.004$); the corresponding mean pairwise agreement levels were 42.76 (12.33), 44.79 (12.44), and 47.99 (10.65) for topics 385, 396, and 415, respectively.

This finding of a significant topic effect is consistent with other studies [18]. The interaction between topic and treatment was not significant.

Self-agreement over time. A second perspective on agreement is whether participants agree with their own relevance assessments, over time. Recall that the epilogue was constructed so that the first three "medium level" documents that a participant encountered in the epilogue recurred as the final three documents in the list. Self-agreement is calculated as the overlap between the relevance ratings assigned to these documents.

The average self-agreement across participants was 51.62%. Based on the different treatment levels, only slight variations were introduced, with self-agreement of 52.56%, 49.38% and 52.87% for the low, medium and high groups. The differences between the groups are not statistically significant, based on a one-way ANOVA ($F(2, 79) = 0.09, p = 0.918$).

4.3 Need for Cognition

Our third research question was whether need for cognition (NFC) influences relevance judgements. In this section, we consider the relationship between NFC and the relevance ratings participants assigned to the epilogue documents; the time taken to make relevance judgements; and the level of agreement between participants and experts.

To examine the effect of NFC, participants' responses to each of the 18 items on the NFC scale were averaged to arrive at a composite NFC score for each participant. Their composite scores from the scale ranged from 1.84 to 4.37. The mean and median of NFC composite scores were 3.16 and 3.24, respectively, and the standard deviation was .56. Participants were divided into a high need for cognition group (HNFC, n=41) and a low need for cognition group (LNFC, n=41) based on a median split [28]. The distribution of HNFC and LNFC participants across treatments was not statistically different ($\chi^2(2) = 2.741, p = 0.254$).

Impact on assignment of relevance scores. Overall, LNFC participants tended to assign lower relevance scores ($M = 1.49$, $SD = 0.39$) than HNFC ($M = 1.58$, $SD = 0.39$). A two-way ANOVA (treatment x NFC) was used to investigate the potential main and interaction effects of NFC and treatment on the relevance scores of documents in the epilogue (Figure 6). Results showed a significant main effect for treatment ($F(2, 76) = 3.89, p = 0.025$), but not NFC group ($F(1, 76) = 1.118, p = 0.294$). As the *prologue* treatment varied from *low* to *high*, the difference in relevance scores between HNFC participants and LNFC began to diverge, but not significantly ($F(2, 76) = 0.267, p = 0.767$).

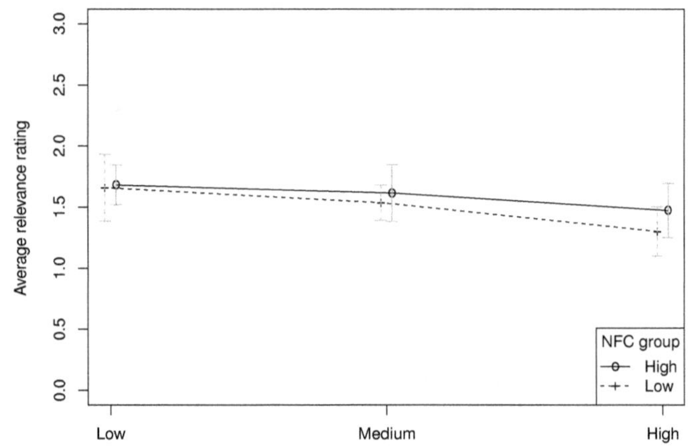

Figure 6: Main and interaction effects of NFC and prologue treatments on mean relevance scores assigned to epilogue documents.

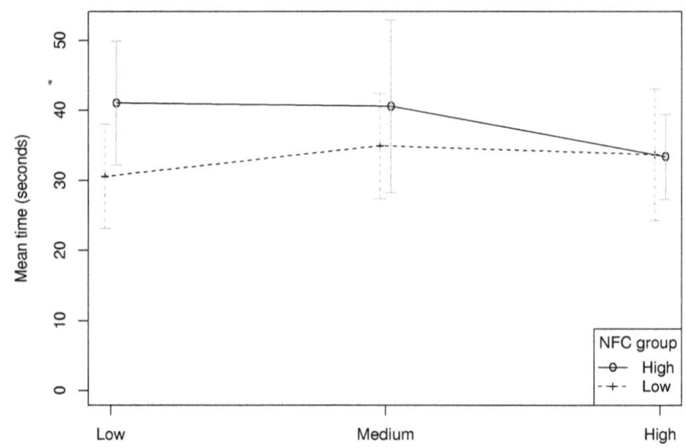

Figure 7: Main and interaction effects of NFC and Prologue treatments on mean time taken to judge the relevance of documents in the epilogue.

Impact on time to judge relevance. Results showed that HNFC participants spent more time making relevance judgements ($M = 37.97$, $SD = 16.33$) than LNFC participants ($M = 33.36$, $SD = 15.24$) (Figure 7). Results also showed that as treatment varied from *low* to *high*, the differences between the time taken by participants in the HNFC and LNFC groups converged. A two-way ANOVA found no significant differences (Treatment: $F(2, 76) = 0.473, p = 0.625$; NFC: $F(1, 76) = 2.154, p = 0.146$; Interaction: $F(2, 76) = .772, p = 0.466$).

Impact on agreement with expert judgements. Finally, the effect of NFC on participant agreement with the expert assessors was examined. Agreement was measured as the proportion of documents in the epilogue to which participant and expert assessor gave the same relevance value. HNFC participants had higher agreement ($M = 51.8\%$, $SD = 10.2\%$) with the experts than LNFC participants ($M = 46.7\%$, $SD = 9.0\%$). A three-way ANOVA (treatment x NFC group x topic) was performed to test this difference for significance. (Topic was included in the analysis due to the strong topic effect on agreement between assessors noted in Section 4.2.) The NFC effect was found to be significant ($F(1,70) = 5.48, p = 0.022$); none of the other effects or interactions achieved significance.

4.4 Assessment Challenges

At the end of the study, participants were asked what, if anything, they found challenging about deciding which relevance levels to associate with documents. The most common challenge identified by participants was related to the extent to which the topic was represented in the document. Participants noted that they struggled with documents that contained relevant terms, but no real discussion of the issues. Some mentioned difficulties assessing documents that only mentioned a single aspect of the topic and those where the topic was not the main focus. Others struggled to assess documents that only contained a few sentences about the topic. Specifically, participants commented that the proportion of the document "about" the topic was something they had a difficult time dealing with when making relevance assessments. Another frequently mentioned challenge was document length, which according to many participants made skimming difficult and also placed a burden on their memory as they moved through the document trying to identify and track relevant information. Only two participants commented about fatigue.

Although it is generally assumed that assessors will (and can) base their judgements on topical relevance alone, many participants' comments were related to other types of relevance. With respect to cognitive relevance, participants indicated that their lack of background knowledge made the assessment task challenging. One participant commented that if he did not understand a document, he categorized it as not relevant or marginally relevant. Another participant observed that it was difficult to ignore novelty when making assessments. With respect to situational relevance, several participants indicated a desire for a more thorough topic description including information about why the information was needed and how it would be used. Finally, several participants commented that they did not like some of the document genres and formats because the display was unappealing, and this was difficult to ignore when making assessments (affective relevance). Overall, these comments challenge the notion that in assessment situations, relevance judgements are based purely on external representations (i.e., topic description) and that other types of relevance can be controlled.

5. CONCLUSION AND FUTURE WORK

This study investigated threshold priming, or the extent to which the relevance of documents viewed early during the assessment process impacted subsequent assessments. This study also investigated how need for cognition, an individual difference measure, impacted relevance assessments.

Our first research question examined how threshold priming impacted participants' relevance scores. We found that participants in the low treatment group assigned significantly higher mean relevance scores to documents in the epilogue than participants in the high treatment group. In particular this change in behavior was significant for documents that were in the middle of the relevance range (marginally relevant or relevant). To investigate the impact on relevance scores over time, we sub-divided documents in the epilogue into two halves (early and late), but found that mean relevance ratings did not differ significantly. In comparing participants' assessments of identical non-relevant documents in the prologue, we found a significant difference in the scores, with those in the low treatment group assigning the highest scores, followed by those in the medium and high treatment groups. This difference disappeared in the epilogue. Taken together, these results provide evidence that people's internal relevance models are impacted by the relevance of the documents they initially view and that they can re-calibrate these models as they encounter documents with more diverse relevance scores.

With respect to agreement among scores assigned by participants and the underlying expert relevance scores, we found that scores assigned by participants in the low group significantly differed from the expert judgments, while those assigned by participants in the medium and high groups did not. In looking more closely at the disagreements, we found that participants in the high group tended to assign scores that were lower than those given by experts, while participants in the low group tended to assign scores that were higher than those given by experts. In particular, participants in the low group tended to boost the relevance of low-relevant documents more than high-relevant documents, which is consistent with past research [9, 14]. These participants were not up-voting all documents in the epilogue, but rather only those with some evidence of relevance. Given that these participants also assigned higher ratings to non-relevant documents in the prologue, it is likely that they developed lower relevance thresholds for at least some categories of relevance.

Our second research question focused on whether threshold priming impacted how well participants were able to form a consistent conception of relevance for a topic. We found no significant differences in self-agreement levels, agreement between assessors, or agreement with experts, according to treatment condition. However, regardless of treatment condition, a reasonable level of disagreement remains, indicating that making relevance assessments is a challenging task and subject to substantial variation. An interesting question for future work is to investigate whether the low self-agreement for individual assessors over time is due to a genuine change in their internal relevance model, or is representative of general inherent variability in such models, perhaps due to factors such as mental fatigue.

Our final research question focused on whether *need for cognition* (NFC) influenced relevance judgments. Although high NFC participants assigned higher relevance scores to documents, this was not significant. We also observed a divergence in mean relevance score assigned by high and low NFC participants as the treatment groups varied from low to medium to high, but this also was not significant. Similar results were found for time taken to judge relevance. Overall, high NFC participants spent more time assessing documents, and the time spent by high and low NFC participants converged as treatments varied from low to medium to high. Finally, we found that high NFC participants' level of agreement with the *expert* assessors was significantly higher than that of low NFC participants. While not all of these results are statistically significant, the results suggest that individual difference measures might provide insight into assessor variability and could be a potentially useful way to screen assessors for characteristics that are associated with more consistent judgments.

Although we did not pose a research question about the challenges participants experience when making assessments, we included a question at the close of the study about this issue. Common challenges identified by participants concerned the depth of treatment of the topic, focus of the document, and the proportion of the document devoted to the topic. We observed many comments that indicated participants struggled to base their assessments purely on topical relevance, and instead wanted to consider cognitive, situational and affective relevance as well. These results show the difficulty in trying to restrict human judgments to topical relevance.

We are conducting a follow-up study using the same design and infrastructure except that participants are asked to justify their relevance assessments explicitly after viewing each document. This will allow us to elicit and monitor the formation of participants' internal relevance models and evaluate how this procedure impacts relevance assessments. Since the study design is the same, we will be able to compare the judgments of these participants with a randomly selected subset of participants from the current study to determine how this reflective procedure impacts the judgment process across experimental treatments. If this procedure results in more consistency in judgments across treatments, then it might be included as part of assessors' initial training.

Acknowledgements

This work was supported in part by the ICT Centre of Excellence program, National ICT Australia (NICTA), and in part under the Australian Research Council's Discovery Projects funding scheme (project number DP130104007). This material is based in part upon work supported by the National Science Foundation under Grant No. 1065250. Any opinions, findings, and conclusions or recommendations expressed in this material are those of the authors and do not necessarily reflect the views of the National Science Foundation.

References

[1] Carol Barry. User-defined relevance criteria: an exploratory study. *Journal of the American Society for Information Science*, 45: 149–159, 1994.

[2] Pia Borlund. The concept of relevance in IR. *Journal of the American Society for Information Science and Technology*, 54(10): 913–925, 2003.

[3] John T. Cacioppo and Richard E. Petty. The need for cognition. *Journal of Personality and Social Psychology*, 42(1):116–131, 1982.

[4] John T. Cacioppo, Richard E. Petty, Jeffery A. Feinstein, and W. Blaire G. Jarvis. Dispositional differences in cognitive motivation: The life and times of individuals varying in need for cognition. *Psychological Bulletin*, 119(2):197–253, 1996.

[5] Ben Carterette and Ian Soboroff. The effect of assessor errors on IR system evaluation. In *Proceedings of the ACM SIGIR International Conference on Research and Development in Information Retrieval*, pages 539–546, Geneva, Switzerland, 2010.

[6] Carlos A. Cuadra and Robert V. Katter. Opening the black box of relevance. *Journal of Documentation*, 23(4):291–303, 1967.

[7] David Davidson. The effect of individual differences of cognitive style on judgments of document relevance. *Journal of the American Society for Information Science*, 28(5):273–284, 1977.

[8] Efthimis N. Efthimiadis and Mary A. Hotchkiss. Legal discovery: does domain expertise matter? *Proceedings of the American Society for Information Science and Technology*, 45:1–2, 2008.

[9] Michael Eisenberg and Carol Barry. Order effects: a study of the possible influence of presentation order on user judgments of document relevance. *Journal of the American Society for Information Science*, 39:293–300, 1988.

[10] Nigel Ford, David Miller, and Nicola Moss. Web search strategies and human individual differences: cognitive and demographic factors, internet attitudes and approaches. *Journal of the American Society for Information Science and Technology*, 56:741–756, 2005.

[11] Maura Grossman and Gordon V. Cormack. Inconsistent assessment of responsiveness in e-discovery: difference of opinion or human error? In *DESI IV: The ICAIL Workshop on Setting Standards for Searching Electronically Stored Information in Discovery Proceedings*, pages 1–11, June 2011.

[12] Stephen P. Harter. Psychological relevance and information science. *Journal of the American Society for Information Science*, 43: 602–615, 1992.

[13] Sture Holm. A simple sequentially rejective multiple test procedure. *Scandinavian Journal of Statistics*, 6(2):65–70, 1979.

[14] Mu-hsuan Huang and Hui-yu Wang. The influence of document presentation order and number of documents judged on users' judgments of relevance. *Journal of the American Society for Information Science and Technology*, 55(11):970–979, 2004.

[15] Gabriella Kazai, Jaap Kamps, Marijn Koolen, and Natasa Milic-Frayling. Crowdsourcing for book search evaluation: impact of hit design on comparative system ranking. In *Proceedings of the ACM SIGIR International Conference on Research and Development in Information Retrieval*, pages 205–214, Beijing, China, 2011. ACM.

[16] Gabriella Kazai, Nick Craswell, Emine Yilmaz, and S. M. M. Tahaghoghi. An analysis of systematic judging errors in information retrieval. In *Proceedings of the ACM International Conference on Information and Knowledge Management*, pages 105–114, Maui, Hawaii, USA, 2012.

[17] John Le, Andy Edmonds, Vaughn Hester, and Lukas Biewald. Ensuring quality in crowdsourced search relevance evaluation: The effects of training question distribution. In *SIGIR 2010 workshop on crowdsourcing for search evaluation*, pages 21–26, 2010.

[18] Douglas W. Oard and William Webber. Information retrieval for e-discovery. 2013. In submission. http://ediscovery.umiacs.umd.edu/pub/ow12fntir.pdf.

[19] Lorraine M. Purgaillis Parker and Robert E. Johnson. Does order of presentation affect users' judgment of documents? *Journal of the American Society for Information Science*, 41(7):493–494, 1990.

[20] Tefko Saracevic. Relevance: a review of and a framework for the thinking on the notion of information science. *Journal of the American Society for Information Science*, 26(6):321–343, 1975.

[21] Tefko Saracevic. Relevance: a review of the literature and a framework for thinking on the notion in information science. part II: Nature and manifestations of relevance. *Journal of the American Society for Information Science and Technology*, 58:1915–1933, 2007.

[22] Tefko Saracevic. Relevance: a review of the literature and a framework for thinking on the notion in information science. part III: Behavior and effects of relevance. *Journal of the American Society for Information Science and Technology*, 58:2126–2144, 2007.

[23] Falk Scholer, Andrew Turpin, and Mark Sanderson. Quantifying test collection quality based on the consistency of relevance judgements. In *Proceedings of the ACM SIGIR International Conference on Research and Development in Information Retrieval*, pages 1063–1072, Beijing, China, 2011.

[24] Eero Sormunen. Liberal relevance criteria of TREC – counting on negligible documents? In *Proceedings of the ACM SIGIR International Conference on Research and Development in Information Retrieval*, pages 324–330, Tampere, Finland, 2002.

[25] Anastasios Tombros, Ian Ruthven, and Joemon M. Jose. How users assess web pages for information seeking. *Journal of the American Society for Information Science and Technology*, 56(4):327–344, 2005.

[26] Christian Unkelbach, Vanessa Ostheimer, Frowin Fasold, and Daniel Memmert. A calibration explanation of serial position effects in evaluative judgments. *Organizational Behavior and Human Decision Processes*, 119:103–113, 2012.

[27] Pertti Vakkari. Changes in search tactics and relevance judgments when preparing a research proposal: a summary of the findings of a longitudinal study. *Information Retrieval*, 4(3):295–310, 2001.

[28] Bas Verplanken. Need for cognition and external information search: Responses to time pressure during decision-making. *Journal of Research in Personality*, 27(3):238–252, 1993.

[29] Ellen M. Voorhees. Variations in relevance judgements and the measurement of retrieval effectiveness. *Information Processing and Management*, 36(5):697–716, 2000.

[30] Jianqiang Wang and Dagobert Soergel. A user study of relevance judgments for e-discovery. *Proceedings of the American Society for Information Science and Technology*, 47:1–10, 2010.

[31] William Webber. Re-examining the effectiveness of manual review. In *Proc. SIGIR Information Retrieval for E-Discovery Workshop*, pages 2:1–8, Beijing, China, July 2011.

[32] William Webber, Bryan Toth, and Marjorie Desamito. Effect of written instructions on assessor agreement. In *Proceedings of the ACM SIGIR International Conference on Research and Development in Information Retrieval*, pages 1053–1054, Portland, Oregon, USA, 2012.

User Model-based Metrics for Offline Query Suggestion Evaluation

Eugene Kharitonov[†‡], Craig Macdonald[‡], Pavel Serdyukov[†], Iadh Ounis[‡]
[†]Yandex, Moscow, Russia
[‡] School of Computing Science, University of Glasgow, UK
[†]{kharitonov, pavser}@yandex-team.ru
[‡]{craig.macdonald, iadh.ounis}@glasgow.ac.uk

ABSTRACT

Query suggestion or auto-completion mechanisms are widely used by search engines and are increasingly attracting interest from the research community. However, the lack of commonly accepted evaluation methodology and metrics means that it is not possible to compare results and approaches from the literature. Moreover, often the metrics used to evaluate query suggestions tend to be an adaptation from other domains without a proper justification. Hence, it is not necessarily clear if the improvements reported in the literature would result in an actual improvement in the users' experience. Inspired by the cascade user models and state-of-the-art evaluation metrics in the web search domain, we address the query suggestion evaluation, by first studying the users behaviour from a search engine's query log and thereby deriving a new family of user models describing the users interaction with a query suggestion mechanism. Next, assuming a query log-based evaluation approach, we propose two new metrics to evaluate query suggestions, *pSaved* and *eSaved*. Both metrics are parameterised by a user model. *pSaved* is defined as the probability of using the query suggestions while submitting a query. *eSaved* equates to the expected relative amount of effort (keypresses) a user can avoid due to the deployed query suggestion mechanism. Finally, we experiment with both metrics using four user model instantiations as well as metrics previously used in the literature on a dataset of 6.1M sessions. Our results demonstrate that *pSaved* and *eSaved* show the best alignment with the users satisfaction amongst the considered metrics.

Categories and Subject Descriptors

H.3.3 [**Information search and retrieval**]: Information search and retrieval

Keywords

query suggestions, evaluation measures, user models

SIGIR'13, July 28–August 1, 2013, Dublin, Ireland.
Copyright 2013 ACM 978-1-4503-2034-4/13/07 ...$15.00.

1. INTRODUCTION

The query suggestion mechanism within a search engine is a tool aimed to help users type less while submitting a query. In its most basic form, the list of suggested queries is formed to contain queries starting with the user's input as a prefix. Similar to the evaluation of other information retrieval systems, the evaluation of query suggestions is crucial to ensure progress in this area of research. How to perform this evaluation is the general topic addressed in this paper.

The target of evaluation in information retrieval is to assess how well a retrieval system meets the needs of its users. For most web search evaluation experiments, this assessment is performed by means of measuring document ranking effectiveness, i.e. how highly relevant documents are ranked. A variety of the web search ranking evaluation approaches exist and they can be naturally divided into *user-based evaluation* and *system evaluation* classes [20]. The system evaluation paradigm originated from the Cranfield experiments [9] and is used in evaluation initiatives such as the Text REtrieval Conference (TREC). The evaluation is performed using a test collection that consists of three components: a collection of documents, a collection of queries (called "topics" in TREC terminology) and a set of document relevance assessments, usually obtained through human judgements. As a result of the evaluation, each system is associated with a value of an evaluation metric, such as Expected Reciprocal Rank (ERR) [6] and Discounted Cumulative Gain (DCG) [14]. Once the test collection is built, it can be repeatedly used to compare different retrieval systems or even adjust the system parameters in a learning-to-rank process. The results of evaluations are reproducible and easily interpretable. However, the system-based evaluation approach has several drawbacks, as discussed by Voorhees [20]. Firstly, due to the manual judgement process, it is hard to perform a large-scale evaluation. Taking that into account, special care must be taken while selecting a set of queries to be used for evaluation, since they should be representative of the users' needs. This becomes even more complicated as these needs and users' intentions behind queries tend to change and evolve over time. Apart from that, the actual users' needs expressed by a query can be significantly different from those a judge can think of and this results in additional noise in the evaluations.

On the other hand, a user-based evaluation can be performed in either online or offline manner. For instance, AB-testing and interleaving [16] are examples of the former approach. One possible way to perform the offline user-based evaluation is to use the implicit user feedback observed in historical query logs as a substitute for the human judges. For instance, in the work of Bennett et al. [3], the document that received the last satisfied click of the user was labelled as personally relevant to this user. Once the labels are generated, the test collection obtained has little differences from the system-based evaluation test collections. One can estimate the system effectiveness by means of an appropriate effectiveness metrics, e.g. Mean Reciprocal Rank (MRR) or Mean Average Precision (MAP) used by Collins-Thompson et al. [10].

We believe that the offline user-based evaluation is particularly promising for evaluation in the query suggestion domain and we support this with the arguments in Section 5. However, in order to follow this methodology an appropriate metric must be selected. A good effectiveness metric should be aligned with the user preferences, i.e. favour a system with higher level of user satisfaction. Indeed, a possible way to ensure alignment is to design the metric on top of the realistic model of the user behaviour. For evaluation in the web search domain, Expected Reciprocal Rank (ERR) [6] and Expected Browsing Utility (EBU) [21] are examples of user model-inspired efficiency metrics.

Unfortunately, to the best of our knowledge in the query suggestions domain neither a realistic model of the user interaction with the system nor an appropriate effectiveness metric based on this model were proposed. As we will discuss in the next section, a variety of evaluation metrics are used in the query suggestion literature. Often, these metrics are selected without justifying their alignment with the user satisfaction, hence it is not necessarily clear if the improvements reported would result in an actual improvement in the users' experience.

In this paper, we address these gaps and consider our contribution to be four-fold:

- We study the ways users interact with the query suggestion mechanism, as it is observed in the session logs, and propose a simple cascade model of the user behaviour on top of these observations;
- We introduce an algorithm to learn the parameters of the model;
- We propose a family of effectiveness metrics, called *Saved* parametrised by a user model and study several possible instantiations of these metrics;
- We perform a thorough experimental study of the considered user models and evaluation metrics, as well as the evaluation metrics used in the literature.

The remainder of this paper is organised as follows. After reviewing some related work in Section 2, we study the ways that users interact with a query suggestion mechanism and propose a simple user model in Section 3. In Section 4, we introduce an algorithm to learn the parameters of the user model from the session log. Next, we briefly discuss the considered evaluation framework in Section 5. Further, we introduce a novel family of evaluation metrics, called Saved, and discuss its connection to other metrics used in information retrieval in Section 6. Section 7 describes a methodology we use to compare the proposed user models and metrics. The dataset used in our experiments is presented in Section 8. We report and discuss the experimental results in Section 9. Finally, we close the paper with some conclusions and future work discussion in Section 10.

2. RELATED WORK

We consider our work to be mostly related to three areas of research: the user model-based evaluation metrics, the methods used to compare the effectiveness metrics, and the metrics used to evaluate query suggestions. Models of user search behaviour and their connection to the evaluation metrics gained a lot of attention in the web search domain and inspired us to follow this direction in our work (Section 2.1). Given a variety of metrics, the question arises how to compare them and this problem received a considerable attention in the research community (Section 2.2). We finish the overview of the related work with the discussion of the methods and metrics used in the evaluation of query suggestion previously used in the literature (Section 2.3).

2.1 User model-inspired IR metrics

One of the state-of-the-art web search evaluation metrics, Expected Reciprocal Rank (ERR), has a strong relation with a cascade model of the user behaviour and is defined as part of the cascade-based family of metrics [6]. The cascade model assumes that a user examines a list of ranked documents one-by-one, from top to bottom. After examining the document on the ith position, either the user is satisfied and stops the examination process or continues to the document on the position $i+1$. The probability of satisfying a user depends on the document's relevance. A cascade-based metric is the expectation of a utility function $\phi(r)$, where r is the rank where the user finds the document she was looking for [6]. In case of ERR, the utility function $\phi(r)$ is equal to $\frac{1}{r}$.

An extension of ERR based on the cascade model with abandonment [7] was also discussed in [6]. Apart from being based on a different user model, this extension leverages a different utility function which is equal to 1 if the user find a satisfactory result, and 0 otherwise. As a result, the value of this metric is equal to the probability of the user finding a relevant result as predicted by the underlying user model.

The Expected Browsing Utility (EBU) is another search effectiveness evaluation metric proposed by Yilmaz et al. [21], which is defined as the expected document utility a user "collects" while examining a result list. As a basis, EBU uses a more sophisticated cascade user model that accounts for snippet attractiveness.

The user model that we propose in this paper can be considered as related to the cascade family and the effectiveness metrics we introduce resemble the cascade family of the web search effectiveness metrics, but applied to the query suggestion domain with different user behaviour patterns.

2.2 Comparing IR metrics

Since the aim of the evaluation is to predict whether the retrieval system meets the user needs, it is natural to require the values of evaluation metrics to be aligned with the user preferences. A considerable effort was deployed to ensure that the metrics used in the web search evaluation setting meet this criterion. However, the papers in the literature differ in the way the user preferences are obtained.

Some authors conducted online user-based studies to address this question. For instance, Radlinski and Craswell [15] studied the agreement between Cranfield-based measures such as MAP and nDCG with results of online user-based evaluation experiments. Sanderson et al. [17] compared the outcomes of a large-scale side-by-side evaluation of retrieval systems performed by MTurkers with a preference relation over these systems imposed by Cranfield-based measures such as nDCG, MRR and Precision@10 as well as the diversity measures including α-nDCG [8], cluster recall and intent-aware precision.

The methodology considering user preference evidence in the session logs was also proposed. Chapelle et al. [6] supported ERR by a series of experiments which demonstrate that ERR shows better alignment with the user behaviour data in comparison with other widely used metrics. These experiments fall into two different categories. Firstly, the authors demonstrate that across different queries and possible rankings, ERR is better correlated with user click metrics such as search success rate. Secondly, in a simulated experiment it was shown that the difference in ERR of two ranking functions is better correlated with the difference in actual user preferences in comparison with other metrics. A similar approach to compare various metrics used to evaluate diversified result set was leveraged in Chappelle et al.'s work [5].

The evaluation methodology we use in this paper is influenced by the methods of Chapelle et al. [6], in that we compare the considered metrics in terms of their correlation with the user preferences observed in historical query logs.

2.3 Query suggestion evaluation

Shokouhi et al. [18] evaluated the quality of suggestions for a given prefix by the mean reciprocal rank of the most popular results (MRR), and the Spearman correlation between the predicted and ground-truth ranks of the selected queries. These metrics were averaged over a set of test prefixes. Considering a query as relevant if it is top-ranked according to the ground-truth query frequencies, Strizhevskaya et al. [19] reported P@3, AP@3 and nDCG@3 averaged over the observed prefixes.

Bar-Yossef and Kraus [2] used a session log-based approach for evaluation, which aimed to emulate user experience. From a session in the log, they extracted the user's context and the submitted query. After that, the suggestions are filtered to have the first character of the query as a prefix and ranked according to the user's context. The quality of the ranking is assessed as a reciprocal rank of the user's query in this ranked list of suggestions, weighted by the number of completions available for the prefix. They reported the weighted mean reciprocal rank (wMRR) averaged over the query-context pairs.

Duan and Hsu [12] used the minimal number of key presses the user has to make in order to issue the target search query (Minimal Keystrokes, MKS) to evaluate query corrections. This metric evaluates the effectiveness of the suggestion mechanism with respect to the user who always selects the optimal way of submitting a query.

As we can see from the related work, the query suggestion effectiveness metrics used in the literature are not specifically designed to reflect user satisfaction nor has their suitability been empirically shown. Following research in the web search evaluation, we address this gap by firstly modelling the user behaviour in Section 3 and devising an effectiveness metric upon it later in Section 6.

3. USER MODEL

The interface usually used to present query suggestions leads to the following process of users' interaction with the query suggestion mechanism. Let us suppose that a user is going to submit a query q to a search engine. After typing each character, the list of suggestions is changed to match the updated input and the user has a chance to examine the list before typing the next character. The examination is performed in steps and at the jth step the user either examines the query suggested on the jth position or skips it. If the query q is suggested by the system and examined by the user, she selects it from the list and that ends the interaction with the query suggestion mechanism. In the worst case, the user types the entire query q manually.

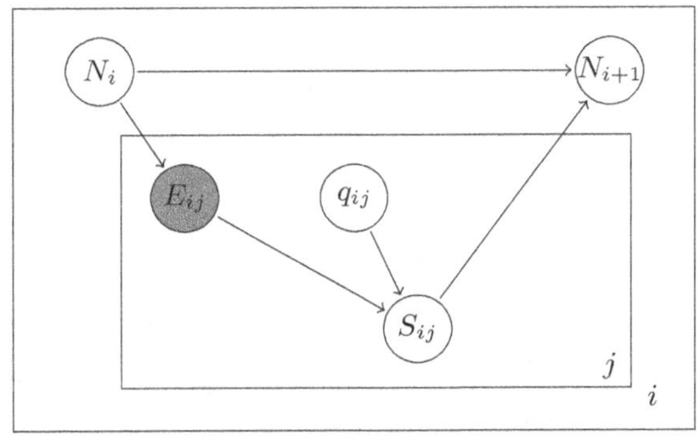

Figure 1: Graphical model of the user behaviour. Grey circles correspond to latent variables.

In order to build a user model upon this interaction schema, we assume that the user's behaviour satisfies the Markovian assumption, i.e. that given the user's current state, all of the future user's actions are independent from her earlier behaviour. The Markovian assumption is often used in the web search behaviour models, e.g. the cascade model [11] describes the user's click behaviour as a Markovian process.

The underlying graphical model is depicted in Figure 3. Denoting the prefix of the query q of length i as $q[1..i]$ and the query suggested on position j after submitting $q[1..i]$ as q_{ij}, we introduce the following random variables used in the graphical model:

- N_i: was the ith character of the query q submitted,
- E_{ij}: is the query suggested on position j for the prefix $q[1..i]$ (q_{ij}) examined,
- S_{ij}: is the user satisfied with q_{ij} after submitting $q[1..i]$,
- T_{ij}: is a variable denoting the user's state on the jth step after submitting $q[1..i]$

The model can be described using the following system of equations in terms of the random variables introduced above:

$$N_1 = 1 \tag{1a}$$
$$N_i = 0 \Rightarrow N_k = 0, k = (i+1)...|q| \tag{1b}$$
$$N_i = 0 \Rightarrow \forall j \; E_{ij} = 0 \tag{1c}$$
$$P(E_{ij}|T_{ij}) = f(T_{ij}) \tag{1d}$$

$$E_{ij} = 0 \Rightarrow S_{ij} = 0 \quad (1e)$$
$$S_{ij} = 1 \Leftrightarrow E_{ij} = 1,\ q_{ij} = q \quad (1f)$$
$$\exists j : S_{ij} = 1 \Rightarrow N_{i+1} = 0 \quad (1g)$$
$$\forall j\ S_{ij} = 0, i < |q| \Rightarrow N_{i+1} = 1 \quad (1h)$$
$$|q| = i,\ \forall j\ S_{ij} = 0 \Rightarrow N_{i+1} = 0 \quad (1i)$$

Indeed, the above equations describe the following constraints on the model: The first character is always submitted (1a); Characters are submitted sequentially (1b); Only the suggestions for the submitted prefixes can be examined (1c); The probability of examining the query suggested on the jth position is a function of the user's state (1d); A non-examined query suggestion cannot satisfy the user (1e); Examination of the query q is necessary and sufficient for the user to be satisfied, i.e. after examining the query q the user is always satisfied (1f)[1]; A satisfied user stops interaction with the query suggestion mechanism (1g); An unsatisfied user types the query until its end (1h) & (1i).

In the model described above, we do not specify the exact form of dependence of examination probabilities from the user's state and denoted it as a function $f(T_{ij})$. Varying the form of this dependence we can obtain different user models. For instance, the following functions can be considered:

1. The user always examines all the suggested queries: $f_1(T_{ij}) = 1$;
2. The examination probability depends only on position j and decays under reciprocal $f_{rr}(T_{ij}) = 1/(j+1)$ or logarithmic $f_{log}(T_{ij}) = 1/\log_2(j+2)$ laws[2];
3. The examination probability depends only on the position: $f_l^i(T_{ij}) = A_j$;
4. The examination probability depends not only on the position, but also on the prefix length: $f_l^d(T_{ij}) = B_{ij}$;

The functions $f_l^i(T_{ij})$ and $f_l^d(T_{ij})$ depend on parameters, A_j and B_{ij}. Instead of using heuristic functions such as $f_{rr}(T_{ij})$ or $f_{log}(T_{ij})$, these parameters can be learned to obtain a model that better reflects the user behaviour. In the following, we discuss an algorithm to adjust these parameters to the user behaviour observed in a session log.

The proposed model of the user behaviour is related to the cascade model [11] of the user's search click behaviour. Indeed, the user continues to type his query if and only if she is not satisfied with the current suggested queries. On the other hand, the process of examination of the list of suggestions resembles one considered in the position-based user models [11].

[1]Queries that have been seen by the user, but not selected from the suggestions list are also considered as non-examined. This do not influence generality of our proposed model.

[2]The logarithmic and reciprocal rank decays are used in DCG [14] and MRR web search metrics, respectively. We shift both functions so they start on the second rank position for two reasons: 1) the resulting probabilities are closer to those observed in our query log; 2) we avoid singularities in the user model evaluation in Section 7.1.

```
Input: Q: a set of sessions with the query suggestion
        mechanism used
Output: Examination probabilities A_j, B_ij
Initialise ∀i, j A^c_j = 0, A^s_j = 0, B^c_ij = 0, B^s_ij = 0
foreach session ∈ Q do
    foreach i ∈ 1..|q(session)|, j do
        if q_ij(session) = q(session) and q_ij not clicked
        then
            A^s_j ← A^s_j + 1
            B^s_ij ← B^s_ij + 1
        end
        if q_ij(session) = q(session) and q_ij clicked
        then
            A^c_j ← A^c_j + 1
            B^c_ij ← B^c_ij + 1
        end
    end
end
foreach j do
    A_j ← A^c_j / (A^c_j + A^s_j)
end
foreach i, j do
    B_ij ← B^c_ij / (B^c_ij + B^s_ij)
end
```

Algorithm 1: Learning the prefix length-independent A_j and the prefix length-dependent B_{ij} probabilities of examination of a query suggestion presented on position j for a prefix of length i.

4. LEARNING THE MODEL PARAMETERS

Let us consider a session with a query q submitted by selecting it from the list of queries suggested to a prefix $q[1..l]$ on position k. Before the interaction stopped, the following random events took place. The user skipped the query q each time it was suggested for a prefix shorter than l. The probability of this is equal to the following expression:

$$P_{skip} = \prod_{i=1}^{l} \left[1 - \sum_j I(q = q_{ij}) P(E_{ij})\right]$$

where $I(q = q_{ij})$ equals 1 if the query q was suggested on position j for the prefix $q[1..i]$, and 0 otherwise. Further, the user examined kth suggested query for prefix $q[1..l]$. Thus, the likelihood of the entire session is as follows:

$$L(s) = \prod_{i=1}^{l} \left[1 - \sum_j I(q = q_{ij}) P(E_{ij})\right] P(E_{lk})$$

By $l(s)$ we denote the length of the prefix typed in the session s. Substituting $P(E_{ij})$ with $f(T_{ij})$ the log-likelihood of a set of sessions Q can be represented in the following form:

$$\hat{L} = \sum_{s \in Q} \sum_{i=1}^{l(s)} \sum_j \log \left[(1 - I(q_{ij} = q) f(T_{ij}))^{1 - S_{ij}} \cdot f(T_{ij})^{S_{ij}}\right] \quad (2)$$

The log-likelihood expressed in Equation (2) can be maximised with respect to the function f to find maximum likelihood estimates (MLE) of its parameters. Assuming that $P(E_{ij})$ are binomial random variables determined by the prefix length-independent f_l^i or the prefix length-dependent

f_l^d functions, discussed in the previous section, we can find MLE estimates of their parameters, A_j and B_{ij}. These estimates can be found by means of Algorithm 1, which resembles the learning process for obtaining the parameters of the cascade model [11]. Assuming that the user's examination process is the same for sessions with the query suggestion mechanism used and for sessions where it is not used, we restrict Algorithm 1 to process only sessions with the suggestion mechanism used in order to avoid noise caused by copy-pasted queries.

The functions f_l^i and f_l^d with parameters A_j and B_{ij}, respectively optimised on a training part of a dataset described in Section 8 are reported in Table 1. We additionally report values of f_{rr} and f_{log} for comparison.

Based on an analysis of Table 1, the following conclusions can be made. Firstly, the probability of examination E_{ij} indeed shows considerable dependence on the prefix length i: for shorter prefixes, the users tend to examine the suggested queries more carefully. For instance, the probability of examination of the first position changes from $f_l^d(T_{1,1}) = 0.55$ for prefixes of length 1 to $f_l^d(T_{6,1}) = 0.33$ in case of prefixes of length 6. Another observation is that the probabilities of examination for a fixed position become almost stationary for prefixes longer than four characters, e.g. $f_l^d(T_{4,1}) = f_l^d(T_{5,1}) = f_l^d(T_{6,1})$.

Even if one considers the approximation of the probabilities of examination to be independent from the prefix length, the resulting probabilities estimated from the query logs (the function f_l^i) are different from the one imposed by the position discount functions often considered in other domains of information retrieval: the first two positions have considerably lower chances to be examined ($f_l^i(T_{1,1}) = 0.36$) than it is predicted by f_{log} ($f_{log}(T_{1,1}) = 0.63$) or f_{rr} ($f_{rr}(T_{1,1}) = 0.5$) functions. Also, it is noticeable that the reciprocal rank function decays with the suggestion rank faster than the examination probabilities learned from the user behaviour in the session log.

We have introduced the user model, its possible instantiations and the algorithm to learn their parameters from the session log. Before defining the proposed user model-based effectiveness metrics in Section 6, we firstly describe the evaluation framework we are working within and which we define in Section 5.

5. OFFLINE EVALUATION OF QUERY SUGGESTIONS

Before defining new effectiveness metrics for the query suggestion evaluation we need to discuss our evaluation framework used to evaluate a query suggestion mechanism. We use the same query log-based approach as used in [2] which falls into the user-based offline category of the evaluation approaches discussed in Section 1. In this section, we discuss the evaluation scenario imposed by the framework, its restrictions and how it compares to the experimental methodologies used in the query suggestions literature.

In the case of query suggestions domain, the considered approach implies the following evaluation algorithm. Given a query suggestion mechanism with a ranking function r and a log of user sessions Q, the evaluation is performed in three steps. At the first step, the process of submitting a query $q \in Q$ is simulated as if a user typed it. For each prefix $q[1..i]$, all of the possible candidate suggestions are ranked according to the ranking function r, i.e. the simulated user is presented with a ranked list of suggestions $r(q[1..i])$. Considering q as the only query relevant to a user, this simulated output is used to estimate the effectiveness metric. Finally, the metric is averaged over all simulated sessions.

In order to perform such an evaluation, a query log is needed. However, we consider this requirement as not restrictive in the query suggestions effectiveness assessment, since query suggestion mechanisms are often built upon the query log mining [1].

We believe that this approach is sufficiently general to cover several interesting evaluation scenarios, e.g. the minimal dataset required to evaluate the query suggestion mechanism includes only queries (and possibly their frequencies). In the more advanced setting, the same methodology is suitable to evaluate personalisation algorithms by associating each session with the context (e.g. [2, 18, 19]) or the user's long-term profile. It is also noticeable that this evaluation scenario generalises other approaches to evaluate query suggestions discussed in the literature. Strizhevskaya et al. [19], as well as Shokouhi and Radinksy [18] both sampled the test sets of prefixes and evaluated the considered systems by assessing how good the most popular prefix completion was ranked having this prefix as the user input. It is possible to consider their methodology as a special case of the evaluation approach used in this paper. Indeed, considering the set of popular queries for all the test prefixes, one can generate simulated sessions with users submitting these prefixes and measuring the system effectiveness afterwards.

Guided by this evaluation scenario, in the next section we introduce novel evaluation metrics for query suggestions.

6. PROPOSED METRICS

As we mentioned in Section 1, the family of cascade-based metrics (e.g. ERR [6]) is defined as the expectation of a utility function at a position the user finds the result she is looking for. In order to generalise this family to the query suggestion evaluation, let us recall the notation previously used in Section 3. We denote the query to be submitted as q and its length as $|q|$. A prefix of q of length i is referred to as $q[1..i]$. E_{ij} is a binary variable equal to 1 if a query suggestion for the prefix $q[1..i]$ ranked on the jth position is examined by the user, S_{ij} is a binary variable representing if the user was satisfied with the jth suggestion shown for the prefix $q[1..i]$. q_{ij} denotes a suggested query ranked on position j after submitting $q[1..i]$. T_{ij} is a variable denoting the user's state, and $U(T_{ij})$ is a utility function.

Using this notation, we can adapt the notion of the cascade-based metric $V(q)$ to the query suggestion evaluation:

$$V(q) = \sum_{i=1}^{|q|} \sum_{j} U(T_{ij}) P(S_{ij} = 1) \qquad (3)$$

where $\sum_j P(S_{ij} = 1)$ equals to the probability to stop after submitting $q[1..i]$. The question arises how to choose the utility function. In the simplest case, one can define the utility function to be a binary indicator of success: $I(S_{ij})$ equals 1 if the user used the query suggestions, and 0 otherwise. A similar utility function was used by Chapelle et al. [6] to build the modification of ERR based on the cascade model with abandonment. Given such an utility function, the metric equates to the probability of the user using the query suggestion mechanism. We refer to this metric as *pSaved*,

Table 1: Probability of examination. $f_{rr}(j)$, $f_{log}(j)$ and $f_l^i(j)$ correspond to the prefix length-independent logarithmic, reciprocal and learned examination probabilities, respectively. $f_l^d(i,j)$ denotes the prefix length-dependent probabilities of length i, as learned from the query log.

Query rank, j	1	2	3	4	5	6	7	8	9	10
$f_{rr}(j)$	0.50	0.33	0.25	0.20	0.17	0.14	0.13	0.11	0.10	0.09
$f_{log}(j)$	0.63	0.50	0.43	0.39	0.36	0.33	0.32	0.30	0.29	0.28
$f_l^i(j)$	0.36	0.24	0.20	0.19	0.17	0.16	0.16	0.16	0.16	0.15
$f_l^d(1,j)$	0.55	0.38	0.26	0.29	0.24	0.19	0.20	0.19	0.18	0.17
$f_l^d(2,j)$	0.56	0.34	0.31	0.26	0.22	0.20	0.18	0.18	0.17	0.14
$f_l^d(3,j)$	0.29	0.23	0.21	0.18	0.17	0.16	0.16	0.15	0.15	0.14
$f_l^d(4,j)$	0.33	0.27	0.23	0.21	0.19	0.18	0.18	0.18	0.18	0.16
$f_l^d(5,j)$	0.33	0.27	0.23	0.21	0.19	0.18	0.18	0.18	0.18	0.16
$f_l^d(6,j)$	0.33	0.27	0.23	0.21	0.19	0.18	0.18	0.18	0.18	0.16

and it is formally defined as follows:

$$pSaved(q) = \sum_{i=1}^{|q|}\sum_{j} I(S_{ij})P(S_{ij}=1) = \sum_{i=1}^{|q|}\sum_{j} P(S_{ij}=1) \quad (4)$$

A more complicated utility function might decrease if it takes the user more effort[3] to find the satisfactory result and thus it can be considered as a formalisation of the amount of the effort the user can avoid due to the retrieval system under consideration. In the case of a query suggestion mechanism, the user's effort can naturally be represented as the number of characters (keypresses) the user has to type to submit her query to the system. Supported by this intuition, we propose the metric *eSaved*, which is defined as the expected ratio of characters a user can skip inputting until her query is submitted. The query can be submitted either by selecting it from the suggested list of queries or by fully entering the query. Formally, *eSaved* can be calculated using the following expression:

$$eSaved(q) = \sum_{i=1}^{|q|}\left(1-\frac{i}{|q|}\right)\sum_{j} P(S_{ij}=1) \quad (5)$$

where $\left(1-\frac{i}{|q|}\right)$ is the utility function.

Both proposed metrics, *pSaved* and *eSaved* are parameterised by the user model, which defines the probability of the user satisfaction $P(S_{ij}=1)$. In the user model proposed in Section 3, this probability is defined by Equations (1d), (1e) and (1f). The user is satisfied with a suggested query q_{ij}, only if it is the target query ($q_{ij}=q$) and if it is also examined ($E_{ij}=1$):

$$S_{ij}=1 \Leftrightarrow E_{ij}=1, q_{ij}=q$$

In order to get an additional insight into the difference between the proposed metrics, we re-group Equation (5) in the following form:

$$eSaved(q) = \sum_{i=1}^{|q|}\sum_{j} P(S_{ij}=1) - \sum_{i=1}^{|q|}\frac{i}{|q|}\sum_{j} P(S_{ij}=1) \quad (6)$$

Comparing (4) and (6) we notice that *eSaved* equals to *pSaved* minus the expected part of the query the user needs to type to submit query q. As a result, *eSaved* additionally stratifies queries with equal chances to satisfy the user, according to the relative length of the query the user need to type.

This ability of *eSaved* to leverage this additional "dimension" to assess the query suggestion ranking functions can be particularly useful for longer queries where its utility function has a wide spectrum of values. We believe that improvements in the query suggestions for longer queries have a high influence on the user experience. Indeed, when submitting a long query, the suggestion mechanism can save greater effort for the user than in the case of a short query.

In this section, we proposed two novel metrics to evaluate the effectiveness of the query suggestions. However, it is unclear how one can compare effectiveness metrics and in the next section we discuss this issue.

7. EVALUATION METHODOLOGY

Our empirical study has the following goals. The first goal is to investigate the user model instantiations introduced in Section 3 compare to each other in terms of fitness to the observed user behaviour in the data. Each of these user models induces a corresponding metric from the *Saved* family and the question arises how well these metrics are aligned with the user behaviour data. It is also important to compare the proposed metrics with the ones previously used in the literature.

In order to answer these questions we perform a series of experiments with the methodology described in this section.

7.1 User model evaluation

The effectiveness of the user models is often studied by means of measuring the log-likelihood on the test data, e.g. [22]. The log-likelihood is defined as the average log probability of the events observed in the test dataset according to the probabilistic model under consideration.

Let s be a session from a dataset of sessions Q, q_s denotes the query submitted by the user in the session s and C_s^i is a binary indicator representing if the user's interaction with the query suggestions ended (i.e. no additional characters were typed) after submitting the prefix $q_s[1..i]$. By definition, $C_s^{|q_s|}=1$ if the user typed the entire query. Again, $l(s)$ denotes the number of characters submitted in session s.

In the case of the query suggestions, the log-likelihood of the user model measures how well this model predicts

[3]The utility function used in ERR degrades as the user examines more retrieved results.

a prefix which the user typed before submitting the query. More formally, the log-likelihood of the model on the session with the submitted query q is defined in the following way:

$$L(q) = \sum_{i=1}^{l(s)} \left[P(C_s^i) \log_2 P(C_s^i) + (1 - C_s^i) \log_2 (1 - P(C_s^i)) \right]$$

The overall log-likelihood is calculated as the average of the session likelihoods:

$$LL(Q) = \frac{1}{|Q|} \sum_{q \in Q} L(q)$$

Another measure widely used to evaluate the performance of click models is the average *perplexity* for top ten positions [13]. However, since the queries differ in their length and the number of suggestions available, the perplexity becomes less intuitive in the considered case.

7.2 Metrics evaluation

In order to compare the considered metrics we adapt the evaluation methodology from Chapelle et al. [6] which is also used in Chapelle et al. [5]. This methodology is aimed to show how good the tested metrics are aligned with the user satisfaction indicators. Chapelle et al. considered different click measures as indicators of the user interest, such as the search abandonment rate, the position of the first click and others. We believe that the query suggestion mechanism can be considered as useful and successful in a particular session if the user used it to submit her query. Thus we use the query suggestion mechanism's usage frequency (how often the query suggestion mechanism is used by users to submit their queries) as a ground-truth indicator of the user satisfaction. In the following, we refer to this value as *success rate* (SS). In general, other indicators of user satisfaction can be considered, e.g. mean ratio of characters a user can skip inputting until her query is submitted. The indicator selected might influence the evaluation result and should be chosen in agreement with the query suggestion mechanism's performance indicators.

Due to various personalisation algorithms, geographical contextualisation features, drifts in query popularity and changes in suggestion mechanism, different users may be presented different suggested queries while submitting the same query. We denote by configuration c a unique sequence of queries suggested for query q.

The considered metric evaluation method [5] is performed in two steps. Firstly, given a dataset of user sessions one can estimate the values of the considered metrics for each configuration observed by a user. On the other hand, for each configuration shown to the users the average value of the success rate can be calculated. In the next step, the correlation between these two values across configurations is calculated.

As discussed by Chapelle et al. [6], this approach has one possible drawback. Indeed, the correlation measures the alignment of the metrics with the user satisfaction across configurations and queries, i.e. it also measures how useful the metric is to compare the effectiveness of different queries. However, in a real-life scenario, the primary goal of a metric is to compare different ranking functions of query suggestions given a fixed set of queries. Therefore, another metric's feature is essential: if, given a *fixed* set of queries one ranking algorithm outperforms its counterpart in terms of the considered metric, does this necessarily imply that the first algorithm has higher user satisfaction once deployed? There is a possibility that a particular metric can exhibit poor performance when comparing effectiveness across queries but exhibit a good alignment with the user satisfaction from the ranking function comparison perspective.

```
Input: Q: a dataset of user sessions
Output: Correlation between query suggestion success
        rate SS and a effectiveness metric M
foreach i ∈ 1..1000 do
    foreach query q ∈ Q do
        C_q ← set of configurations of q
        if |C_q| ≥ 2 then
            c1, c2 ← two random configurations from C_q
            Assign c1 to a simulated system r1, c2 to a
            simulated system r2
        end
    end
    Compute average value of M for r1 and r2
    Compute average value of SS for r1 and r2
end
Return correlation between differences in M and SS for
all simulated pairs of r1 and r2
```

Algorithm 2: Algorithm used to evaluate if the difference in effectiveness metric values correlated with the differences in user satisfaction proposed in [6].

In order to study the metric quality from the latter point of view, we perform an experiment proposed by Chapelle et al. [6], which simulates a comparison of the ranking functions scenario. The description can be found in Algorithm 2. Informally, the idea behind the algorithm is as follows. For each query with at least two configurations in the session log, configurations c_1 and c_2 are randomly sampled. These configurations and the corresponding sessions are associated with two simulated ranking functions, r_1 and r_2, as if all sessions with c_1 and c_2 shown to the users were served by ranking algorithms r_1 and r_2, respectively. After that, the average values of the considered metric M and the user satisfaction indicator SS are calculated for both systems. Then, the differences of the user satisfaction indicator $SS(r_1) - SS(r_2)$ and the effectiveness metric values r_1 and r_2, $M(r_1) - M(r_2)$ are found. Finally, after repeating this simulation, the correlation between the metric and the satisfaction indicator differences is returned.

8. DATASET

Before discussing the experimental results in the next section, we shortly describe the dataset used in this paper. The dataset was randomly sampled from the query log of a commercial search engine. The search sessions were performed by users from a European country with two non-English languages[4] widely spoken during two consecutive workdays in January 2013. In order to reduce noise in our evaluation, we applied the following filtering procedure to the dataset. Firstly, we do not consider sessions with misspelled queries, leaving the adaptation of the proposed models to misspelled

[4]We believe that results we report in this paper generalise across different languages. However, we leave the experimental verification of this assumption as future work.

queries as a direction of future work. We also removed sessions where users selected a query from the suggested list and edited it afterwards since it is unclear if the query suggestion mechanism was useful in these sessions. All queries were normalised to the lower case, since the character capitalisation is typically ignored by query suggestion mechanisms. Finally, only query sessions with the query suggestions shown were sampled.

As a result, the dataset contains 6.1M query sessions, 3.8M unique configurations and 3.3M unique queries. The mean query length is 26.4, the median is 24.0 characters. The mean number of whitespace delimited terms is 3.3, the median is 4.0. The length of the query suggestion lists was restricted by the deployed query suggestions mechanism to be no longer than 10.

The sessions from the first day were used to estimate the user model parameters discussed in Section 3, while the evaluation of the models and the effectiveness metrics comparison were performed on the subset of sessions performed on the second day.

9. RESULTS AND DISCUSSION

We split our evaluation experiments into two parts. Firstly, we discuss the experimental evaluation of the user models (Section 9.1). After that, we report the results of the effectiveness metrics evaluation (Section 9.2).

9.1 User model evaluation

The results of the user model evaluation on the test dataset are reported in Table 2. We report the log-likelihood of the models with the following functions determining the probability of examination of the query suggestions discussed in Section 3: f_{rr}, f_{log}, f_l^i and f_l^d. The first three functions correspond to the probability examination functions which are independent from the prefix length, while the last one is the prefix length-dependent. The parameters of f_l^i and f_d^l are learned from the train dataset by means of Algorithm 1. We repeat the experiment several times, splitting queries in groups according to their absolute frequency and length. All reported differences are statistically significant according to the paired t-test, $p \leq 10^{-3}$ except for pairs labelled by $\diamond$, which do not statistically significant differ.

As seen from Table 2, the models with the probabilities of examination learned from the query log (f_l^i and f_l^d) exhibit a better fit than the models parameterised by the heuristic functions on every subset of queries considered, except for the queries of length less than 10 characters, since they are not "typical" for the training dataset (median query length is 24.0 characters). In particular, f_l^d shows the best fitness to the whole dataset.

Overall, we conclude that adjusting the model parameters to the user behaviour in the session log leads to statistically significant improvements in the model's ability to "explain" the data in the dataset. The question now is whether this improvement leads the user model-based effectiveness metrics to have a higher alignment with the user preferences. We study this issue in the next section.

9.2 Metrics evaluation

Results of the two metric evaluation experiments are presented in Tables 3 and 4. The correlation coefficients are statistically significant with $p \leq 10^{-3}$, in each column $\triangle$ denotes a group of values which statistically significantly outperform other values and do not statistically significant differ from each other with $p \leq 0.05$. We applied Holm-Bonferroni adjustment for multiple comparisons when required. To report these results, we use the following notation. *pSaved(f)* corresponds to a metric of the *pSaved* family, parameterised by function f, e.g. *pSaved*(f_l^i) is a metric obtained by assuming the model of user behaviour with probabilities of examination determined by function f_l^i. Similarly, *eSaved*(f_{rr}) is the *eSaved* metric parameterised by f_{rr}.

Table 2: Log-likelihood of the user models parameterised by different examination probability functions. A higher log-likelihood corresponds to a better fit to the data. In each row all pairwise differences are statistically significant, except for the pairs labelled with $\diamond$.

	f_{rr}	f_{log}	f_l^i	f_l^d
All queries	-3.27	-3.84	-3.16	**-3.10**
Query frequency	f_{rr}	f_{log}	f_l^i	f_l^d
1 - 10	-3.66	-4.40	**-3.46**$\diamond$	**-3.47**$\diamond$
10-10^2	-3.54	-4.23	**-3.37**$\diamond$	**-3.36**$\diamond$
10^2-10^3	-3.25	-3.76	-3.14	**-3.12**
$> 10^3$	-2.01	-2.03	-2.19	**-1.92**
Query length	f_{rr}	f_{log}	f_l^i	f_l^d
1 - 10	-1.85	**-1.68**	-2.07	-1.86
11-20	-2.74	-2.94	**-2.74**$\diamond$	**-2.73**$\diamond$
21-30	-3.91	-4.84	-3.66	**-3.63**
> 31	-4.32	-5.57	-3.97	**-3.92**

MRR-n is a metric which is defined as the reciprocal rank of the submitted query q after submitting the first n characters of the query. For queries shorter than n characters we define *MRR-n* to be equal to *MRR-*$|q|$. Ranks higher than 10 are considered to be infinitely large (i.e., *MRR-1* and *MRR-3* are equal to 0 if the submitted query is ranked on positions below 10). The MRR metric is used in [18], though in a different evaluation scenario, as discussed in Section 5.

By *wMRR-n* we denote a modification of *MRR-n* weighted by the number of suggestions available for the corresponding query prefix, as used in [2].

MKS (Minimal Keystrokes) is a metric proposed by Duan et al. [12] to evaluate the query misspelling correction algorithms, which is defined as the minimal number of keystrokes a user has to perform in order to submit the query. The minimum is calculated among all possible interactions: the user can type the query's next character or can select the query from the list of suggestions using arrow keys. Despite the fact that it was proposed to evaluate misspelling correction algorithms, MKS can also be used to evaluate query suggestions. By definition, a better system should have lower *MKS*, hence the correlation between the user satisfaction indicator and *MKS* should be negative.

In Table 3, we report the correlation of the effectiveness metrics with the query suggestion success rate across different configurations. As we discussed in Section 7.2, this correlation implicitly includes comparison of different queries. Since for queries of different length the success rates differ (i.e. it is easier for the user to type a short query entirely) we also report the correlation for queries of different length. In order to do this, the queries are split into four bins according to their length: less than 10 characters long; from 10 to 20 characters; from 20 to 30, and a set of queries longer than 30 characters. In addition, we report the correlation on the entire test dataset (length > 0).

On analysing Table 3, we observe that all eight combinations of the proposed metrics (*pSaved* and *eSaved*) and considered examination probability functions (f_{rr}, f_{log}, f_l^i, and f_l^d) perform better than the baseline metrics on each considered subset of queries ($p \leq 10^{-3}$). Comparing *pSaved* and *eSaved* we see that the *pSaved* metric is better correlated with the success rate. Moreover, this observation holds for both machine-learned functions f: $pSaved(f_l^i)$ outperforms $eSaved(f_l^i)$ and $pSaved(f_l^d)$ outperforms $eSaved(f_l^d)$ for each query length bin ($p \leq 10^{-3}$). Considering the *pSaved* metric, we notice that both machine-learned functions, f_l^i and f_l^d lead to a metric that is much better aligned with the user preferences than metrics induced by heuristic functions f_{rr} and f_{log} in each query bin ($p \leq 5 \times 10^{-3}$).

The experimental setting reported in Table 3 highlights that among the studied metrics, *pSaved is the most suitable metric to compare the effectiveness of the query suggestion mechanism across queries and configurations.*

In Table 4, we report the correlation of the difference in effectiveness metrics with the difference in query suggestion success rate. Similarly to Table 3, we split the queries into bins according to their length. Again, the proposed effectiveness metrics outperform metrics used in the literature when the entire dataset considered. However, in contrast to the previous experiment, *pSaved* parameterised by f_l^d is the second best performing metric, less effective than $eSaved(f_l^i)$.

As a result, we can conclude that *changes in ranking as measured by eSaved are better correlated with changes in user preferences* than that of the other considered metrics.

We conjecture that different outcomes of the experiments are caused by the fact that improvements in the ranking of long queries have a higher impact on the overall system performance than improvements for shorter queries and the last experiment reflects this fact. This seems natural from the user's point of view: since long queries are harder to submit, even small improvements in the ranking can be noticed. This observation is also supported by the fact that while $pSaved(f_l^i)$ dominates on short queries, its overall performance is worse than that of $eSaved(f_l^d)$.

On the other hand, as we discussed in Section 6, *eSaved* has higher ability to differentiate changes in the ranking of longer queries than *pSaved*, thus outperforming it in the last experiment (4).

To support this conjecture, we designed an experiment to answer the following question: which bin of queries has the highest impact on the correlation with the user preferences, as reported in Table 4? In order to address this, we artificially improved the alignment of *eSaved* with the user preferences by replacing its value by a linear combination of *eSaved* with the users' satisfaction rate, *SS*:

$$eSaved'(q, \epsilon) \leftarrow (1 - \epsilon)eSaved(q) + \epsilon SS(q)$$

We denote the correlation between differences in the $eSaved'_\epsilon$ "metric" and the success rate SS by $cor(\Delta SS, \Delta eSaved'_\epsilon)$. Further, we numerically calculate the partial derivative of the overall correlation value with respect to ϵ:

$$\left. \frac{\partial \left[cor(\Delta SS, \Delta eSaved'_\epsilon)\right]}{\partial \epsilon} \right|_{\epsilon=0} \quad (7)$$

Table 3: Correlation of the effectiveness metrics with the query suggestion success rate. The correlation was calculated on several subsets of the dataset containing queries with different length. Each experiment corresponds to a column. In each column △ denotes a group of values which statistically significantly outperform other values and do not statistically significant differ from each other.

	> 0	1 - 10	11 - 20	21 - 30	> 31
MRR-1	0.115	0.116	0.139	0.129	0.122
MRR-3	0.243	0.299	0.313	0.279	0.262
wMRR-1	0.094	0.052	0.103	0.104	0.099
wMRR-3	0.154	0.107	0.180	0.176	0.170
MKS	-0.470	-0.180	-0.601	-0.607	-0.875
$eSaved(f_{rr})$	0.816	0.522	0.731	0.871	0.902
$eSaved(f_{log})$	0.827	0.538	0.747	0.882	0.910
$eSaved(f_l^i)$	0.817	0.527	0.731	0.870	0.902
$eSaved(f_l^d)$	0.807	0.502	0.720	0.863	0.896
$pSaved(f_{rr})$	0.849	0.547	0.759	0.918	0.948
$pSaved(f_{log})$	0.838	0.524	0.747	0.916	0.947
$pSaved(f_l^i)$	0.857	**0.561△**	0.768	0.921	0.949
$pSaved(f_l^d)$	**0.860△**	**0.560△**	**0.773△**	**0.922△**	**0.950△**

Replacing *eSaved* by $eSaved'_\epsilon$ sequentially for queries from different bins, we estimate this derivative and report the results in Table 5. Informally, these results show how sensitive is the overall correlation to improvements in the metric on a particular bin of queries. From the table, we observe that the correlation is most sensitive to improvements in the metric on queries which are between 21 and 30 characters long. At the same time, a small improvement of the metric on queries longer than 10 characters leads to almost two times higher improvement in alignment with the user satisfaction than the same change on the queries shorter than 10 characters.

To summarise: on one hand, the *eSaved* metric is more discriminative than *pSaved* for longer queries by its design, and on the other hand the user behaviour (as well as alignment of the metric with it) is very sensitive to changes in longer queries. As a result, changes in *eSaved* demonstrate a better alignment with changes in the user preferences than that of *pSaved*, as can be observed in Table 4.

Overall, our experimental results suggest that the proposed metrics are better aligned with the user behaviour evidenced in the session log than other metrics considered, supporting the user model-based approach to build an effectiveness metric as being promising. Additionally, the experiments demonstrate that the most fruitful direction of improving the proposed metrics is to increase their alignment with user behaviour on long queries. Finally, *pSaved* is shown to be the most suitable metric to compare performances across queries, while changes in rankings measured by the *eSaved* metric correlate better with changes in the user preferences if the set of queries is fixed.

10. CONCLUSIONS AND FUTURE WORK

In this paper, we presented a novel model of the user interactions with the query suggestion mechanisms. We described a machine learning approach to adapt the model parameters to the user behaviour observed in a session log.

Using the described model, we introduced two user model-based evaluation metrics, *pSaved* and *eSaved*. The first metric, *pSaved* is defined as a probability of using a query

Table 4: Correlation of the *difference* in effectiveness metrics with the *difference* in query suggestion success rate. The correlation was calculated on several subsets of the dataset containing queries with different length. Each experiment corresponds to a column. In each column △ denotes a group of values which statistically significantly outperform other values and do not statistically significant differ from each other.

	> 0	1 - 10	11 - 20	21 - 30	> 31
MRR-1	0.557	0.868	0.983	0.924	0.427
MRR-3	0.576	0.931	0.989	0.930	0.486
wMRR-1	0.463	0.588	0.825	0.472	0.198
wMRR-3	0.459	0.549	0.613	0.166	0.229
MKS	-0.484	-0.713	-0.950	-0.805	-0.409
$eSaved(f_{rr})$	0.870	0.981	**0.991**△	**0.956**△	**0.580**△
$eSaved(f_{log})$	0.875	0.981	**0.991**△	**0.957**△	**0.586**△
$eSaved(f_l^i)$	**0.897** △	0.982	**0.990**△	**0.957**△	**0.583**△
$eSaved(f_l^d)$	0.839	0.972	**0.990**△	**0.957**△	**0.580**△
$pSaved(f_{rr})$	0.813	0.965	0.954	0.543	0.303
$pSaved(f_{log})$	0.739	0.933	0.506	0.072	0.202
$pSaved(f_l^i)$	0.839	0.978	0.981	0.819	0.398
$pSaved(f_l^d)$	0.878	**0.991** △	0.987	0.906	0.470

Table 5: Sensitivity of the correlation between the difference of the metric *eSaved* and the difference in the user preferences to small improvements in the metric.

Query length	1 - 10	> 10	11-20	21-30	> 30
$\frac{\partial cor(\Delta SS, \Delta eSaved'_\epsilon)}{\partial \epsilon}$	0.61	1.14	0.04	0.78	0.34

suggestion mechanism while submitting a query. *eSaved* equates to the normalised amount of keypresses a user can avoid due to the deployed query suggestion mechanism.

Our empirical study using a session log encapsulating 6.1M sessions demonstrated that the proposed metrics show the best alignment with the user preferences exhibited in the session log. Among the proposed metrics, our experiments showed that changes in *eSaved* are the most correlated with changes in the user preferences, hence it can be recommended as a target metric in the ranking optimisation. On the other hand, *pSaved* shows the highest correlation with the user preferences across queries. Finally, we experimentally demonstrated that the correlation of the changes in both metrics with the changes in the user behaviour is most sensitive to improvements on long queries, hence making future work in this direction promising.

Since this is the first work to model the user interaction with a query suggestion mechanisms, a variety of extensions can be considered. First of all, the users differ in typing speed, the device they use to select their query from the list of suggestions (e.g., they can use keyboard, mouse or touchpad with their desktop or use a mobile device). All these differences can lead to different patterns in the user behaviour. Consequently, a possible extension of the proposed user model can incorporate these features. This idea is closely related to the work of Carterette et al. [4] which discussed incorporating the user variability into the system-based evaluation paradigm.

Further study of the user behaviour can lead to improvements in the metric alignment with the user satisfaction indicator. However, there are other ways to improve the evaluation of query suggestions, e.g. one can extend a set of queries relevant to the user. As discussed by Zhu et al. [23] in the context of query recommendations, a possible approach is to study the relevance of all queries submitted in the session.

11. REFERENCES

[1] R. Baeza-Yates, C. Hurtado, and M. Mendoza. Query recommendation using query logs in search engines. In *Current Trends in Database Technology*, volume 3268 of *LNCS*, pages 588–596. 2005.

[2] Z. Bar-Yossef and N. Kraus. Context-sensitive query auto-completion. In *WWW '11*.

[3] P. N. Bennett, F. Radlinski, R. W. White, and E. Yilmaz. Inferring and using location metadata to personalize web search. In *SIGIR '11*.

[4] B. Carterette, E. Kanoulas, and E. Yilmaz. Incorporating variability in user behavior into systems based evaluation. In *CIKM '12*.

[5] O. Chapelle, S. Ji, C. Liao, E. Velipasaoglu, L. Lai, and S.-L. Wu. Intent-based diversification of web search results: metrics and algorithms. *Inf. Retr.*, 2011.

[6] O. Chapelle, D. Metlzer, Y. Zhang, and P. Grinspan. Expected reciprocal rank for graded relevance. In *CIKM '09*.

[7] O. Chapelle and Y. Zhang. A dynamic bayesian network click model for web search ranking. In *WWW '09*.

[8] C. L. Clarke, M. Kolla, G. V. Cormack, O. Vechtomova, A. Ashkan, S. Büttcher, and I. MacKinnon. Novelty and diversity in information retrieval evaluation. In *SIGIR '08*.

[9] C. Cleverdon. The Cranfield tests on index language devices. *Aslib Proceedings*, 19(6):173–194, 1967.

[10] K. Collins-Thompson, P. N. Bennett, R. W. White, S. de la Chica, and D. Sontag. Personalizing web search results by reading level. In *CIKM '11*.

[11] N. Craswell, O. Zoeter, M. Taylor, and B. Ramsey. An experimental comparison of click position-bias models. In *WSDM '08*.

[12] H. Duan and B.-J. P. Hsu. Online spelling correction for query completion. In *WWW '11*.

[13] G. E. Dupret and B. Piwowarski. A user browsing model to predict search engine click data from past observations. In *SIGIR '08*.

[14] K. Järvelin and J. Kekäläinen. Cumulated gain-based evaluation of ir techniques. *ACM Trans. Inf. Syst.*, 20(4):422–446, 2002.

[15] F. Radlinski and N. Craswell. Comparing the sensitivity of information retrieval metrics. In *SIGIR '10*.

[16] F. Radlinski, M. Kurup, and T. Joachims. How does clickthrough data reflect retrieval quality? In *CIKM '08*.

[17] M. Sanderson, M. L. Paramita, P. Clough, and E. Kanoulas. Do user preferences and evaluation measures line up? In *SIGIR '10*.

[18] M. Shokouhi and K. Radinsky. Time-sensitive query auto-completion. In *SIGIR '12*.

[19] A. Strizhevskaya, A. Baytin, I. Galinskaya, and P. Serdyukov. Actualization of query suggestions using query logs. In *WWW '12 Companion*.

[20] E. Voorhees. The philosophy of information retrieval evaluation. In *Evaluation of Cross-Language Information Retrieval Systems*, LNCS, pages 355–370. 2002.

[21] E. Yilmaz, M. Shokouhi, N. Craswell, and S. Robertson. Expected browsing utility for web search evaluation. In *CIKM '10*.

[22] Y. Zhang, W. Chen, D. Wang, and Q. Yang. User-click modeling for understanding and predicting search-behavior. In *KDD '11*.

[23] X. Zhu, J. Guo, X. Cheng, and Y. Lan. More than relevance: high utility query recommendation by mining users' search behaviors. In *CIKM '12*.

A General Evaluation Measure for Document Organization Tasks

Enrique Amigó
E.T.S.I. Informática UNED
Juan del Rosal, 16
Madrid, Spain
enrique@lsi.uned.es

Julio Gonzalo
E.T.S.I. Informática UNED
Juan del Rosal, 16
Madrid, Spain
julio@lsi.uned.es

Felisa Verdejo
E.T.S.I. Informática UNED
Juan del Rosal, 16
Madrid, Spain
felisa@lsi.uned.es

ABSTRACT

A number of key Information Access tasks – Document Retrieval, Clustering, Filtering, and their combinations – can be seen as instances of a generic *document organization* problem that establishes priority and relatedness relationships between documents (in other words, a problem of forming and ranking clusters). As far as we know, no analysis has been made yet on the evaluation of these tasks from a global perspective. In this paper we propose two complementary evaluation measures – *Reliability* and *Sensitivity* – for the generic Document Organization task which are derived from a proposed set of formal constraints (properties that any suitable measure must satisfy).

In addition to be the first measures that can be applied to any mixture of ranking, clustering and filtering tasks, Reliability and Sensitivity satisfy more formal constraints than previously existing evaluation metrics for each of the subsumed tasks. Besides their formal properties, its most salient feature from an empirical point of view is their strictness: a high score according to the harmonic mean of Reliability and Sensitivity ensures a high score with any of the most popular evaluation metrics in all the Document Retrieval, Clustering and Filtering datasets used in our experiments.

Categories and Subject Descriptors

B.8 [**Performance and Reliability**]: General

General Terms

Measurement, Performance

Keywords

IR effectiveness measures

1. INTRODUCTION

Some key Information Access tasks can be seen as instances of a generic *document organization* problem that establishes priority (ranking) and relatedness (clustering) relationships between documents. Let us think of a generic *document organization system* as a function from document pairs d, d' into one of these possible relationships: $\succ$, which means that d has more priority than d', and $\sim$, which means that d and d' have some kind of topical equivalence. We will use the notation $\|$ for the cases in which the other two relations do not hold, and the notation $\{d_1, d_2 \dots d_n\}$ to indicate that $d_1 \dots d_n$ are all related via the topical equivalence relation $\sim$.

This general problems subsumes:

Document Ranking. This case is illustrated in Table 1. The gold standard establishes (at least) two priority levels (relevant versus non-relevant), and the system output returns an ordered list with one priority level per document. For clarity, in the table we use a bold font for relevant documents. Note that, in this problem, it is assumed that there is an unlimited amount of irrelevant documents, while the set of relevant documents is limited. Both the gold standard and the system output contain, implicitly, an unlimited set of documents in the last level. The gold standard contains two priority levels (with the documents manually judged) while the system output contains as many levels as returned documents.

Document Filtering. Table 2 illustrates this case; now, both the gold standard and the system output consist of two priority levels (relevant and irrelevant).

Document Clustering is exemplified in Table 3. Now there is only one priority level, and a set of clusters which contain related documents. Both the gold standard and the system output have the same form. Table 4 illustrates the variant of overlapping clustering, where a document may simultaneously appear in more than one cluster.

Evaluation metrics have been extensively discussed for each of these tasks. There are, however, many practical problems where the system must be able both to detect topical relationships (clustering documents) and relative priorities (some clusters are more relevant than others). Let us give a couple of examples:

Alert detection. A number of practical information access problems involve detecting, in an incoming stream of documents, new information that is both novel and of high priority. Online Reputation Management, for instance, involves monitoring online information about an entity (a company, brand, product, person, etc.), clustering texts into the main topics, and establishing which of them have higher priority (for instance, those that may potentially damage the reputation of the entity).

SIGIR'13, July 28–August 1, 2013, Dublin, Ireland.

Gold Standard	System Output
$\mathbf{d_1}, \mathbf{d_2}, \mathbf{d_3}$	$\mathbf{d_1}$
d_4, d_5, d_6, d_7 ..d_n	$\mathbf{d_2}$
	d_6
	$\mathbf{d_3}$
	d_{14}
	d_4, d_5, d_7, ..d_n

Table 1: Example of Document Ranking task. Vertical ordering indicates relative priorities

Goldstandard
$\mathbf{d_1}, \mathbf{d_2}, \mathbf{d_3}$
d_4, d_5, d_6, d_7, d_8
System output
$\mathbf{d_1}, \mathbf{d_2}, d_4$
$\mathbf{d_3}, d_5, d_6, d_7, d_8$

Table 2: Example of filtering task

Search Results Organization. Given the set of top ranked documents retrieved for a query, a mechanism to group related documents and assign priorities between clusters can be used to improve search results in many ways: (i) to enhance search results diversity by maximizing the number of highly relevant topics represented in the top results; (ii) to provide keyword suggestions to refine the query, sampled from the most relevant clusters; (iii) to directly display search results as a ranked list of relevant topics corresponding to alternative query interpretations, subtopics or facets in the retrieved documents.

This type of tasks (and others such as composite retrieval) – which are more complex than the standard ranking and clustering problems – still match the generic Document Organization task as we have defined it. An example is shown in Table 5. In the gold standard there is, for instance, one topic with two documents ($d1 \sim d2$) at the top priority level, and two topics at the second level ($d3 \sim d4$ and $d5 \sim d6$). In the next three priority levels there are two single documents and another topic. The example includes overlapping clusters: for instance, d_5 is relevant for two topics, one in the second priority level and another one in the fourth.

Finally, the (potentially long) list of documents at the bottom of the gold standard ranking ($d_{11}, d_{12}, d_{13}, \ldots d_n$) represents irrelevant documents which are not judged in terms of topical similarity, and are therefore represented via the empty relationship $\|$.

Evaluation measures have been proposed to evaluate clustering outputs in the context of document retrieval [14, 8, 18] and to include the notion of diversity in search results[15, 24, 9]. But, to the best of our knowledge, no measure has been previously designed to evaluate the general document organization problem and all the tasks subsumed by this one.

In order to find appropriate evaluation measures for the generic Document Organization problem, we will focus on the specification of the formal constraints that they should satisfy in each of the subsumed tasks (filtering, clustering and ranking). Our goal is finding an evaluation measure

Gold standard
$\{d_1, d_2, d_3\}, \{d_4, d_5, d_6\}, d_7$
System output
$\{d_1, d_2\}, d_3, \{d_4, d_5, d_6, d_7\}$

Table 3: Example of Clustering task.

Gold standard
$\{d_1, d_2, d_3\}, \{d_4, d_5, d_6\}, \{d_4, d_7\}$
System output
$\{d_1, d_2\}, d_3, \{d_4, d_5, d_6, d_7\}, \{d_6, d_7\}$

Table 4: Example of overlapping clustering

for the general document organization task that (i) satisfies formal constraints for all the tasks; (ii) turns into suitable existing measures when mapped into each of the subsumed tasks.

Our research leads to propose *Reliability* and *Sensitivity* which are, in short, precision and recall over document pair relationships established in the gold standard, with a suitable weighting scheme. Comparing them with state of the art measures for each particular scenario, we find that Reliability and Sensitivity satisfy more formal constraints than previously existing measures in most cases. In addition, its harmonic mean is stricter than previously existing measures – a high score implies high scores with respect to all other standard measures –, which is an interesting property when the application scenario does not clearly prescribe a more specific evaluation measure.

We will start by establishing the set of formal constraints that any suitable metric should satisfy (Section 2); then we present our proposed measures (Section 3) and discuss its application to the different tasks (Section 4). We end by showing how the measures apply to the more complex document organization task, and discussing the main implications of our results.

2. INFORMATION ACCESS MEASURES AND FORMAL CONSTRAINTS

Our approach to measure design is to start defining a set of formal constraints, i.e. a set of formal, verifiable properties that any suitable measure should satisfy. In addition, they explain the nature of different evaluation measure families. We will start by reviewing (or proposing) formal constraints for each of the subsumed tasks, and then merge all collected constraints into a single list of properties for the generalized measures. Table 6 summarize the results of this analysis.

Gold standard	System output
$\{d_1, d_2\}$	d_1
$\{d_3, d_4\}, \{d_5, d_6\}$	d_2
d_7	$\{d_3, d_4\}, \{d_5, d_6\}$
$\{d_5, d_8, d_9\}$	$\{d_5, d_7, d_9\}$
d_{10}	d_8
$d_{11}, d_{12}, d_{13}, \ldots, d_n$	d_{12}
	$d_{10}, d_{11}, d_{13}, \ldots d_n$

Table 5: An example of gold standard and system output for the generic information retrieval task.

Measure	Homo.	Comp.	Rag Bag	Size vs Quantity	Priority	Deepness	Deepness Threshold	Closeness Threshold	Confidence
Set matching	✔	✗	✗	✔					
Entropy based	✔	✔	✗	✔					
Edit distance	✗	✔	✗	✔					
Counting pairs	✔	✔	✗	✗					
Bcubed	✔	✔	✔	✗(overlap)					
MAP, DCG, Q measure					✔	✔	✗	✔	✗
P10					✗	✗	✔	✔	✗
MRR					✔	✔	✔	✗	✗
RBP					✔	✔	✔	✔	✗
UTILITY, F, LAM%					✔				
R*S	✔	✔	✔	✔	✔	✔	✔	✔	✔

Table 6: Formal constraints satisfied by standard measures and R*S

2.1 Document Clustering

[2] provides a detailed analysis of clustering evaluation measures (grouped by families) and the constraints they should satisfy. We briefly describe here these constraints and refer to [2] for its justification and formal description. We will say that the system output produce *clusters* while the gold standard is composed by *classes*. Q represents the quality of a clustering distribution and $a, b, c, d..$ are documents from different classes:

Cluster Homogeneity: This restriction was firstly proposed in [22]. Given a certain system output document distribution, splitting documents that do not belong to the same class, must increase the output quality:

$$Q(\{a, a, a\}, \{b, b\}...) > Q(\{a, a, a, b, b\}...)$$

Although it seems a very basic constraint, in [2] it is shown that measures based in editing distance do not satisfy it.

Cluster Completeness: The counterpart to the first constraint is that documents belonging to the same assessed class should be grouped in the same cluster [2, 22]:

$$Q(\{a, a, a, a, a, \}...) > Q(\{a, a, a\}, \{a, a\}...)$$

Measures based on set matching, such as Purity and Inverse Purity do not satisfy this contraint.

Rag Bag: This constraint states that introducing disorder into a disordered cluster (rag bag) is less harmful than introducing disorder into a clean cluster. That is:

$$Q(\{a, a, a, a\}, \{b, c, d, e\}..) > Q(\{a, a, a, a, b\}, \{c, d, e\}..)$$

In general, all traditional measures fail to comply with this constraint.

Cluster size vs. quantity: A small error in a big cluster is preferable to a large number of small errors in small clusters [2, 19, 22]. This constraint prevents the problem that measures based on counting pairs [19, 13], overweight big clusters. That is:

$$Q(\{a, a, a, a\}, \{a\}, \{b, b\}\{c, c\}\{d, d\}\{e, e\}...) >$$

$$Q(\{a, a, a, a, a\}, \{b\}, \{b\}, \{c\}, \{c\}, \{d\}, \{d\}, \{e\}, \{e\}..)$$

Measures based on counting pairs are sensitive to the combinatory explosion of pairs in big clusters, failing on this constraint.

In [2] it is shown how the above contraints discriminate between four families of evaluation measures for the clustering problem: measures based on set matching (e.g. F measure, Purity and Inverse Purity), entropy-based measures (Entropy, class Entropy, Mutual Information), measures based on counting pairs and edit distance measures. Interestingly, there is only one pair of measures, BCubed Precision and Recall, that satisfies all constraints simultaneously, and forms an independent family. However, we will show in this paper that the extended version of Bcubed for overlapping clustering does not satisfy the last constraint.

2.2 Document Filtering

Filtering is a binary classification problem where there is a relative priority between the two classes: the system must classify each document as positive or negative, being the positive class the one that stores the relevant information. In the filtering scenario all existing measures satisfy a basic constraint:

Priority Constraint Moving a positive (relevant) document from the predicted negative set to the predicted positive set, or moving a negative (irrelevant) document from the predicted positive to the predicted negative set must increase the system output quality. Being d_r and $d_{\neg r}$ a judged relevant/irrelevant document respectively:

$$Q(\{d_r..\}, \{..\}) > Q(\{..\}, \{d_r..\})$$

$$Q(\{..\}, \{d_{\neg r}..\}) > Q(\{d_{\neg r}..\}, \{..\})$$

This constraint is satisfied by every standard measure. Filtering is a basic binary classification task that can be evaluated in multiple ways, but it is difficult to define objectively desirable boundary constraint that discriminate measures. However, there are descriptive properties which are mutually exclusive and explain the nature of different measure families [3]. These properties focus on how the metrics score non-informative outputs $D_{\neg inf}$ depending on the size of the positive set $S(D_{\neg inf})$. A non-informative output is a random distribution of the documents that is independent on the content of the input documents. An "all positive" baseline, for instance, is a non-informative output where the size of the positive set is equivalent to the size of the input set.

For instance, there is a large set of filtering measures that assign a fixed score to every non-informative output: Lam [11], the Macro Average Accuracy [20] and, in general, measures based on correlation such as the Kappa statistic [10]. ($Q(D_{\neg inf}) = constant$). Other family of measures assumes that, if the filtering system does not know anything, returning all is better than removing documents randomly. In this case, the score for a non-informative system is correlated with the size of the positive output set: $(Q(D_{\neg inf}) \propto S(D_{\neg inf}))$ This is the case of the harmonic mean of Precision and Recall over the positive class. Finally, measures such as Accuracy or Utility assign relative weights to documents in each of the cases in the confusion matrix; Depending on how these parameters are set and on the distribution of classes in the input, the optimal positive class size for a non-informative output varies.

2.3 Document Ranking

In order to define a set of constraints for the document ranking (or document retrieval) task, we have to take into account some aspects. First, documents at the top of the ranking must have more weight in the evaluation process: even if the system is able to sort all documents, the user will not be able to explore all of them. The sizes of the relevant and the irrelevant set are expected to be heavily unbalanced: potentially, the amount of irrelevant documents for a given query is (in practice) unlimited. Second, traditional document retrieval is a mixture of filtering and ranking tasks: an optimal system should not only rank the documents, but also decide on the size of the output set, depending on the amount of relevant documents in the collection and the self-assessed quality of the system output. These two features – which are related the fact that the gold standard and the system output take different forms, unlike the filtering and clustering problems – make document retrieval evaluation harder than it seems a priori.

There is a large number of proposed measures in the state of the art. Some of the most popular are: precision at certain recall levels or ranking positions, AUC [12], MAP (Mean Average Precision), Discounted Cumulative Gain [16], Expected Reciprocal Rank (ERR)[25], Q-measure, Binary Preference [4], or Rank Biased Precision [21], among many others. Let us analyze them in terms of formal constraints.

First, the **Priority Constraint** from the filtering problem also applies here (see previous subsection) and it is satisfied by most measures. A notable exception is P@10 (precision at the top ten documents retrieved), given that it is not sensitive to relationships after the tenth position in the system output ranking, and to internal reorderings in the top ten setWe can express this constraint in the context of Document Retrieval evaluation as, being r and $\neg r$ relevant and irrelevant documents respectively, and being $\{d_1, d_2, d_3..d_n\}$ an output ranking:

$$Q(\{..r_{i+1}, \neg r_{i+2}..\}) > Q(\{..\neg r_{i+1}, r_{i+2}..\})$$

Deepness Constraint: The more we go to a deeper point in the output ranking, the less the probability of documents being explored by the user. Therefore, the effect of a document priority relationship in the system quality depends on the depth of the documents in the ranking. Being i<j:

$$Q(\{..r_i, \neg r_{i+1}..\}) - Q(\{..\neg r_i, r_{i+1}..\}) <$$

$$Q(\{..r_j, \neg r_{j+1}..\}) - Q(\{..\neg r_j, r_{j+1}..\})$$

Measures based on traditional correlation, such as AUC or Kendall, do not satisfy this contraint, because they give the same weight to all elements in the ranking. Also, P@10 obviously does not satisfy this contraint.

Deepness Threshold Constraint: Although P@10 does not satisfy the previous two constraints, one motivation for using it is that in some cases it is advisable to assume a practical deepness threshold. In other words, there is a ranking area which will never be explored by the user. We can express this as a constraint by saying that there exists a value n large enough such that retrieving one relevant document at the top of the rank is better than retrieving n relevant documents after n irrelevant documents:

$$Q(\{r_1, \neg r_2, \neg r_3..\neg r_{2n}\}) > Q(\{\neg r_1, \neg r_2..\neg r_{n-1}, r_n..r_{2n}\})$$

We will not include all the formal proofs on how measures satisfy this constraint, due to space availability; we will only discuss the proof that MAP does not satisfy it.

The score for the leftmost distribution in the constraint is $\frac{1}{N_r}$, assuming that there are N_r relevant documents in the collectionWe can prove that the score for the rightmost distribution is always higher:

$$MAP = \frac{1}{N_r}\sum_{i=1}^{i=n}\frac{i}{n+i} > \frac{1}{N_r}\sum_{i=1}^{i=n}\frac{i}{2n} =$$

$$\frac{1}{2nN_r}\sum_{i=1}^{i=n} i = \frac{1}{2nN_r}\frac{(n-1)n}{2} = \frac{(n-1)}{4N_r}$$

which is bigger than $\frac{1}{N_r}$ for any $n > 4$. DCG does not comply with this constraint either: DCG for the first distribution is 1, before normalization. And for the second distribution we have:

$$DCG = \sum_{i=1}^{i=n}\frac{1}{log_2(i+n)} > \sum_{i=1}^{i=n}\frac{1}{log_2(2n)} = \frac{n}{log_2(2n)} > 1$$

For instance, according to MAP or DCG, finding 1,000 relevant documents after 1,000 irrelevant documents is better than having only one relevant document, but at the top of the rank. This is counterintuitive in many practical settings.

The Q-measure is an extension of MAP for multigraded relevance, having a similar behavior. However, the measure ERR does satisfy this constraint (as well as P@10), due to the strong relevance discount for positions deeper in the rank. Measures with similar weighting schemes also satisfy this constraint, but at the cost of failing to satisfy the next one.

Closeness Threshold Constraint: There exists a (short) ranking area which is always explored by the user. For instance, we can assume that the top three documents returned by a search engine for informational queries are always inspected. We formalize this constraint as the counter part of the previous constraint: There exists a value n small enough such that retrieving one relevant document in the first position is worse than n relevant documents after n irrelevant documents:

$$Q(\{r_1, \neg r_2, \neg r_3..\neg r_{2n}\}) < Q(\{\neg r_1, \neg r_2..\neg r_{n-1}, r_n..r_{2n}\})$$

In the case of P@10, n is 9 (i.e. for any n lower than 9, the constraint is satisfied). ERR, on the other hand, does not satisfy the constraint: given its strong discount with ranking depth, one relevant document at the first position has always more weight than n relevant documents after the position n.

The measures RBP and the discounting function proposed by Smucker and Clarke [23] satisfy all the previous constraints. The common characteristic of both measures is that they are based on a probabilistic user behavior model.

However, all proposed measures fail on the following constraint.

Confidence Constraint. The output ranking does not necessarily include all documents in the collection and, therefore, the amount of documents returned is also an aspect of the system quality. The classical TREC ad-hoc evaluation does not consider this aspect, given that the length of the rank is fixed; nevertheless, there is research focused on the prediction of ranking quality, in order to determine when an output rank must be shown to the user. We include this aspect in our constraints by stating that extending the rank with irrelevant documents should decrease the output score:

$$Q(\{d_1, d_2..d_n\}) > Q(\{d_1, d_2..d_n, \neg r_{n+1}\})$$

Given that most measures are based on accumulative relevance weighted by the location in the ranking [5], we can conclude that irrelevant documents at the bottom of the ranking do not affect the score and the constraint is not satisfied. As far as we know, current evaluation measures do not consider this aspect.

In summary, for the tasks subsumed under our document organization problem, the result of our analysis is that (i) in clustering, only the Bcubed measure satisfies all constraints, with the exception of one of them in the case of overlapping clustering; (ii) in the filtering scenario, all measures satisfy the priority constraint, but behave in very different manners with respect to how they score non-informative outputs; and (iii) Finally, in the case of document retrieval, we have detected a few measures that satisfy all constraints except the last one, but none that satisfies all constraints.

Our goal is finding a measure that can be applied to all of the subsumed tasks and to any combination of them (i.e. to the general document organization problem), and that satisfies all constraints coming from each of the subsumed tasks. In the next section we introduce our proposal.

3. PROPOSAL: RELIABILITY AND SENSITIVITY

Our proposal consists of two complementary measures, *Reliability* and *Sensitivity*, with a straightforward initial definition. Let us consider a system output X and a gold standard $\mathcal{G}$, which are both a set of document relationships $r(d,d') \in \{\succ, \prec, \sim\}$. The Reliability (R) of relationships in the system output is the probability of finding them in the gold standard. Reversely, the Sensitivity (S) of predicted relationships is the probability of finding them in the system output when they appear in the gold standard. In other words, R and S are precision and recall of the predicted set of relationships with respect to the true set of relationships:

$$R(\mathcal{X}) \equiv P(r(d,d') \in \mathcal{G} | r(d,d') \in \mathcal{X})$$

$$S(\mathcal{X}) \equiv P(r(d,d') \in \mathcal{X} | r(d,d') \in \mathcal{G})$$

We can express Reliability as a sum of probabilities pondered by the weight of each relationship in $\mathcal{X}$:

$$R(\mathcal{X}) \equiv \sum_{r(d,d')\in\mathcal{X}} P(r(d,d') \in \mathcal{G}) w_{\mathcal{X}}(r(d,d'))$$

We want to observe three restrictions on relationship weights: (i) $w_{\mathcal{X}}(r(d,d')) = f(w_{\mathcal{X}}(d), w_{\mathcal{X}}(d'))$, i.e., the weight of a relationship is a function of the weights of the documents involved. In Document Retrieval, the weight of a document will be related to its probability of being inspected by the user, which is related at least to its position in the ranking; (ii) $w(d) = \sum_{d'} w(r(d,d'))$, i.e., the weight of all relations starting from a document d determines the weight of document d; this restriction prevents the quadratic effect of counting binary relationships and is related to the "size vs quantity" restriction for the clustering problem that we want to satisfy; and finally (iii) the contribution $w(d,d')$ of each d' related to d should be proportional to the weight of d'.

Then, we can express R and S in terms of weights of single documents. Being $w_{\mathcal{X}}(d)$ the weight of d in $\mathcal{X}$ and being $W_{x,d}$ the sum weight of documents related with d:

$$W_{\mathcal{X},d} = \sum_{d'/r(d,d')\in\mathcal{X}} w_x(d')$$

we can compute R and S as:

$$R(\mathcal{X}) = \sum_{r(d,d')\in\mathcal{X}} P(r(d,d') \in \mathcal{G}) \frac{w_x(d')}{W_{x,d}} w_x(d)$$

$$S(v) = \sum_{r(d,d')\in\mathcal{G}} P(r(d,d') \in \mathcal{X}) \frac{w_g(d')}{W_{g,d}} w_g(d)$$

If all documents have the same weight in the distributions, R and S simply turn into the average $R(d)$ and $S(d)$ associated to each document:

$$R(\mathcal{X}) = \text{Avg}_d P(r(d,d') \in \mathcal{G} | r(d,d') \in \mathcal{X})$$
$$S(\mathcal{X}) = \text{Avg}_d P(r(d,d') \in \mathcal{X} | r(d,d') \in \mathcal{G})$$

3.1 Estimating Document Weight Discounting

In the generic document organization task we must assume that there exists a virtually unlimited amount of documents in the collection. Therefore, we must weight documents according to their priority in the system output or in the gold standard. There exist several studies on predicting the weight of a document in the ranking in terms of the probability to be explored by the user. Most of them are based on assumptions over user behavior [6, 7, 23]. However, there is no clear consensus yet on how to model the empirical user behavior. Rather than this, we focus on basic constraints and interpretability as the main criteria to choose a weighting scheme.

We model the weight of the document in the i position as the weight integration between $i-1$ and i. The first constraint is that the sum weight for all documents must be finite. Therefore, we must employ a function with a converging integral. We select $\frac{1}{i^2}$ because it is a simple, soft decay, integrable and convergent function. We leave the refinement of the discounting curve for a latter parameterization step; ideally, our evaluation measure should be as general as possible, and therefore it must have parameters to establish how much of the ranking (v.g. the top 10 vs the top 100) carries on how much of the weight (v.g. 50% or 99% of the overall score) in the evaluation.

According to $\frac{1}{i^2}$, the weight of the document in position i in the priority ordering is:

$$w_{\mathcal{X}}(d) = c_1 \int_{c+i-1}^{c+i} \frac{1}{x^2} dx = c_1 \left(\frac{1}{c+i-1} - \frac{1}{c+i} \right) \quad (1)$$

where c_1 is a normalization factor to ensure that the sum is 1. c is another parameter that moves the function in order to give more or less weight to the high priority documents. Stating that the total sum weight is one:

$$c_1 \int_c^{\infty} \frac{1}{x^2} dx = c_1 \frac{1}{c} = 1$$

Therefore, $c = c_1$. The next constraint is that we should be able to parameterize the weighting curve in an interpretable way. Ideally, we want to be able to set two parameters n and W_n which mean that the first n documents must cover a W_n weight ratio of the overall evaluation score. For instance, we may want to state that the first 30 positions in the ranking ($n = 30$) will have an 80% of the total weight in the evaluation measure ($W_n = 0.8$). Therefore:

$$c \int_c^{c+n} \frac{1}{x^2} dx = W_n \Longrightarrow c = \frac{(1 - W_n)n}{W_n}$$

Now, we can estimate the weight of each document in the system output or in the gold-standard according to Formula 1. Documents at the same priority level share the interval weight. Being $n_{\succ}$ and $n_{=}$ the amount of documents with more and equal relevance than d respectively we can estimate the weight of each document as:

$$w_{\mathcal{X}}(d) = \frac{c_1}{n_{=}} \int_{c+n_{\succ}}^{c+n_{\succ}+n_{=}} \frac{1}{x^2} dx \qquad (2)$$

Smucker and Clarke proposed a discounting model based on exploration time calibration[23] which considers additional aspects such as the relevance and length of documents. Actually, this model is compatible with our proposal: we can incorporate this by replacing the i position of documents with a time function. We leave this analysis for future work.

3.2 Overlapping Clusters

As we mentioned earlier, a document may appear in multiple clusters (corresponding, for instance, to different information nuggets in the document), and therefore it may appear at multiple priority levels. If overlapping between clusters is allowed, a document has potentially a different number of occurrences in the gold and system output distribution. If there exists only one instance of d and d' in both the gold standard and the system output, the probability of coocurrence is 1 when the relationships match. Otherwise, following the extended Bcubed measure proposed in [2], we assume the best possible correspondence between relationships in $\mathcal{X}$ and $\mathcal{G}$. For instance, if two documents are related in the system output less times than in the gold standard, then all the predicted relationships are assumed to be correct. Otherwise, the probability is the ratio of gold relationships per system relationships. Formally, being $|r_{\mathcal{G}}(d, d')|$ and $|r_{\mathcal{X}}(d, d')|$ the number of occurrences of $r(d, d')$ in $\mathcal{G}$ and $\mathcal{X}$ respectively:

$$P(r(d, d') \in \mathcal{G}) = \frac{min(|r_{\mathcal{G}}(d, d')|, |r_{\mathcal{X}}(d, d')|)}{|r_{\mathcal{X}}(d, d')|} \qquad (3)$$

$$P(r(d, d') \in \mathcal{X}) = \frac{min(|r_{\mathcal{G}}(d, d')|, |r_{\mathcal{X}}(d, d')|)}{|r_{\mathcal{G}}(d, d')|} \qquad (4)$$

3.3 Measure Computation

Here we state the method to compute R and S over the general document organization task. We assume that there is a set of prioritized documents $\mathcal{X}_r$ organized by levels and clusters and a special, bottom level containing an unlimited amount of irrelevant/discarded documents $\mathcal{X}_{\neg r}$ (see Table 5). The weight of a single document in the set of prioritized documents $\mathcal{X}_r$ is computed as in Equation 2. The weight of prioritized documents $\mathcal{X}_r$ in the system output is:

$$W(\mathcal{X}_r) = c \int_c^{c+|\mathcal{X}_r|} \frac{1}{x^2} = 1 - \frac{c}{c + |\mathcal{X}_r|}$$

The weight of the long tail of non prioritized documents $\mathcal{X}_{\neg r}$ in the system output is:

$$W_{\mathcal{X}}(\mathcal{X}_{\neg r}) = c \int_{c+|\mathcal{X}_r|}^{\infty} \frac{1}{x^2} = \frac{c}{c + |\mathcal{X}_r|}$$

The sum weight of documents priority related with d is 1 minus the sum weight of documents in the same priority level:

$$W_{\mathcal{X},d,\prec\succ} = 1 - \sum_{d' / \neg(d' \prec\succ_{\mathcal{X}} d)} w_x(d')$$

The probability $P(r(d_{ij}, d_{kl}) \in \mathcal{G})$ for a document relationship between two document occurrences in $\mathcal{X}_r$ is computed as in Equation 3 for both the clustering and priority relationships.

As for the relationships between the unlimited tail $\mathcal{X}_{\neg r}$ and documents in $\mathcal{X}_r$, we must consider that all documents in the infinite set $\mathcal{X}_{\neg r}$ have the same weight. Therefore, the finite amount of relevant documents in the long tail has no effect. Then, any relevant document in $\mathcal{X}_r$ is correctly related with all documents in $\mathcal{X}_{\neg r}$ if it appears between the prioritized documents in $\mathcal{G}_r$. According to Equation 3, being d_{ij} the j occurrence of document d_i in the system output and being $\mathcal{D}_i$ its set of occurrences[1]:

$$P(d_{ij} \succ_{\mathcal{G}} \mathcal{X}_{\neg r}) = \frac{min(|\mathcal{D}_i \cap \mathcal{G}_r|, |\mathcal{D}_i \cap \mathcal{X}_r|)}{|\mathcal{D}_i \cap \mathcal{X}_r|}$$

According to all of this, Reliability over priority relationships can be computed as follows[2]

$$R_{\prec\succ} = \sum_{\substack{d_{ij} d_{kl} \in \mathcal{X}_r \\ r(d_{ij}, d_{kl}) \in \mathcal{X}}} \frac{P(r(d_{ij}, d_{kl}) \in \mathcal{G}) w_x(d_{i,j}) w_x(d_{k,l})}{W_{x,d_{ij},\prec\succ}} +$$

$$\sum_{d_{ij} \in \mathcal{X}_r} P(d_{ij} \succ_g \mathcal{X}_{\neg r}) w_x(d_{ij}) W(\mathcal{X}_{\neg r}) \left(\frac{1}{W_{x,d_{ij},\prec\succ}} + \frac{1}{W_x(\mathcal{X}_r)} \right)$$

Assuming that the documents in the long tail do not have clustering relationships with each other, Reliability over clustering relationships can be computed as follows:

$$R_{\sim} = \sum_{\substack{d_{ij} \in \mathcal{X}_r \\ d_{kl} \in \mathcal{X}_r \\ d_{ij} \sim_x d_{kl}}} \frac{P(d_{ij} \sim_g d_{kl}) w_x(d_{ij}) w_x(d_{kl})}{W_{x,d_{ij},\sim}} + W_x(\mathcal{X}_{\neg r})$$

Sensitivity is computed in the same way, but exchanging $\mathcal{X}$ by $\mathcal{G}$ and x by g. The complexity of this computation is $\mathcal{O}(n^2)$, being n the amount of ranked documents $\mathcal{X}_r$ or prioritized documents $\mathcal{G}_r$.

[1]For the sake of simplicity, we notate $P(d_{ij} \succ \mathcal{X}_{\neg r} \in \mathcal{G})$ as $P(d_{ij} \succ_{\mathcal{G}} \mathcal{X}_{\neg r})$

[2]The first component covers the relationships within documents in $\mathcal{X}_r$. The second and third components cover the relationship $\mathcal{X}_r \rightarrow \mathcal{X}_{\neg r}$ and $\mathcal{X}_{\neg r} \rightarrow \mathcal{X}_r$ respectively.

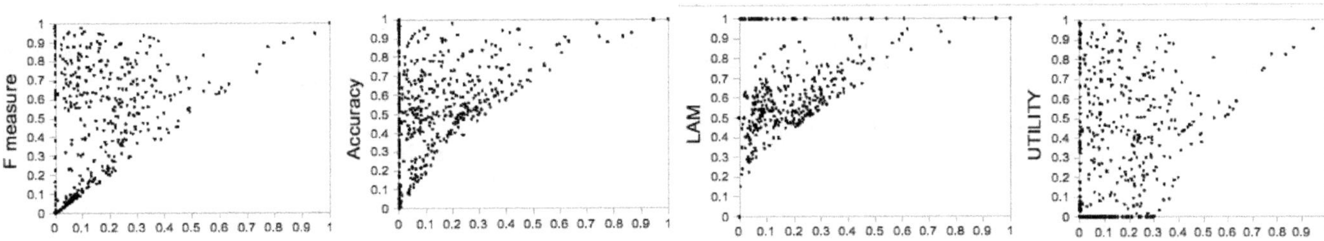

Figure 1: Comparing Evaluation Measures over Document Filtering Task.

4. RELIABILITY AND SENSITIVITY: META-EVALUATION

As far as we know, Reliability and Sensitivity are the first measures which are applicable to the general document organization task. For this reason, our comparison will focus on how R and S behave in each of the subsumed tasks (filtering, clustering, ranking) with respect to previously existing measures.

4.1 Meta-evaluation Criteria

There are many ways of meta-evaluating a new measure. The most direct one consists of comparing measure scores vs. human assessments of quality, or system results in some extrinsic task. Other meta-evaluation criteria focus on the hability to capture information from limited data sets. Some examples are discriminativeness [23], statistical significant differences between systems[21], stability method, swap method, robustness against noisy data, correlation between rankings over different data sets [5], etc. The main drawback of these methods is that a measure can be, for instance, perfectly discriminative under limited data sets without giving information about quality. As an extreme example, the ranking length can be perfectly discriminative but not useful for evaluation purposes.

in this study we want to investigate how useful is to evaluate measures in terms of a basic, intuitive set of formal constraints. According to this, our first meta-evaluation criterion is the ability to satisfy the stated formal constraints. After that formal analysis, and in order to compare measures empirically over data sets, we will assume that current standard measures used by the community are, to a certain extent, reliable: we assume that all of them give some useful information about system quality in certain scenarios. The problem is that, in most cases, we do not know exactly the real scenarios in which the system will be employed. In previous experiments, particularly in the case of clustering and filtering, it has been shown that there can be a very low correlation between measure results [3]. Therefore, we cannot expect to find a measure which is correlated with all of them. However, we can at least ensure that a high score according to the measure implies a high score according to all measures. This is *strictness*. In other words, a good score in a reliable measure should ensure a good system regardless of the environmental conditions. Note that strictness itself is not enough as a meta-evaluation criterion (a measure that always scores zero is the strictest of all). Note also that strictness could easily be achieved by computing a harmonic mean of the most popular measures, but we would have to solve scale-normalization issues and we would end up with a measure that would be hard to interpret, and would not cover all quality aspects in an homogeneous manner. Therefore, and ad-hoc combination of metrics is not the best solution to have a strict measure.

Let us quantify *Strictness* in the following way: we compute, for each measure, all the rank positions obtained by each system output $o \in O$ for each topic and measure. Then we define strictness as the largest difference between a high rank assigned by our measure and a low rank assigned by a traditional measure:

$$\text{Strictness}(m) = -\frac{Max_{o,m'}(Rank_m(o) - Rank_{m'}(o))}{|O|}$$

In order to maintain a correspondence with standard meta-evaluation criteria, we will also compute the *robustness* of measures in terms of the average Spearman correlation of system scores across topics. Being $Rnk(m, t_i)$ the ranking of systems produced by metric m for topic t_i:

$$\text{Robustness}(m) = Avg_{i,j}(\text{Spearman}(Rnk(m, t_i), Rnk(m, t_j)))$$

We now discuss each of the subsumed tasks.

4.2 Clustering Scenario

In the non overlapped clustering scenario where all documents has the same weight, R and S turn into Bcubed Precision and Bcubed Recall:

$$R_{\mathcal{X},\mathcal{G}} \equiv \text{Avg}_d P(r(d,d') \in \mathcal{G} | r(d,d') \in \mathcal{X}) = BR(X)$$

$$S_{\mathcal{X},\mathcal{G}} \equiv \text{Avg}_d P(r(d,d') \in \mathcal{X} | r(d,d') \in \mathcal{G}) = BR(X)$$

Bcubed measures are the only ones that satisfy all the clustering constraints [2]. However, in the extended version for overlapping clustering, the Cluster Size vs Quantity restriction is no longer satisfied. This is due to the fact that, in the extended Bcubed version, all the relationships from one document are computed as a single unit, even when it belongs to several clusters at the same time. The result is that if two documents d and d' are related to each other several times (e.g. they share more than one information nugget), breaking all these relationships is penalized only once. Therefore, splitting n clusters can have less effect than splitting one document from a cluster with size n. The solution provided by R and S consists of considering the document in each different cluster as a separate document. BCubed measures are well-known and have already been studied formally and empirically and compared with other measures in previous work [2]. Therefore, we will focus on the other subsumed tasks for our meta evaluation.

	Accuracy	Utility	Lam%	F Measure	R*S
Rob.	0.3	0.39	0.38	0.49	**0.70**
Strict.	-0.91	-0.91	-0.96	-0.92	**-0.78**

Table 7: Robustness and Strictness achieved by Filtering Evaluation Measures, WEPS2 test set

4.3 Document Filtering Task

4.3.1 *Formal Constraints*

The Filtering scenario consists of distributing a finite set of documents into two priority levels (binary classification). Being $\mathcal{X}_r$ and $\mathcal{G}_r$ the sets of prioritized documents in the system output and gold standard respectively, the correct relationships in the system output are priority relationships between relevant documents in $\mathcal{X}_r$ and irrelevant documents in $\neg\mathcal{X}_r$. Therefore, R corresponds with:

$$R(X) = \text{Avg}_d P(r_g(d, d')|r_x(d, d')) =$$
$$P(\mathcal{G}_r|\mathcal{X}_r)P(\mathcal{X}_r)P(\neg\mathcal{G}_r|\neg\mathcal{X}_r) + P(\neg\mathcal{G}_r|\neg\mathcal{X}_r)P(\neg\mathcal{X}_r)P(\mathcal{G}_r|\mathcal{X}_r) =$$
$$P(\neg\mathcal{G}_r|\neg\mathcal{X}_r)P(\mathcal{G}_r|\mathcal{X}_r)(P(\mathcal{X}_r) + P(\neg\mathcal{X}_r)) = P(\neg\mathcal{G}_r|\neg\mathcal{X}_r)P(\mathcal{G}_r|\mathcal{X}_r)$$

This corresponds with the product of precisions over positive and negative sets in the output. Analogously, Sensitivity corresponds with the product of Recalls over the positive and negative sets.

$$S(X) = P(\neg\mathcal{X}_r|\neg\mathcal{G}_r)P(\mathcal{X}_r|\mathcal{G}_r)$$

Just like any other filtering measure, the combination of R and S (using the F measure) satisfies the priority constraint. Let us denotate the harmonic mean of R and S as R*S. With respect to how R*S scores non-informative outputs, its behavior is a mixture of the other measure families: it assigns a zero-score to the *all-relevant* and *all-irrelevant* baselines, because they are not able to distinguish any useful priority relationship between documents. Other arbitrary partitions receive scores that depend on how the ground truth partitions the test set.

4.3.2 *Empirical meta-evaluation*

For the filtering scenario we employ the evaluation corpus and system results from the second task in the WePS3 competition [1]. The task consisted of classifying Twitter entries [17] that contain a company name as relevant when they do refer to the company and irrelevant otherwise. The test set includes tweets for 47 companies and the training set includes 52 company names. For each company, around 400 tweets were retrieved using the company name as query. The ratio of related tweets per company name is variable, covering both extremely low and high ratios. We will refer to a company tweet set retrieved by a query in a time slot as an input stream or topic. Five research teams participated in the competition, and sixteen runs were evaluated. The organizers included two baseline systems: the placebo system (all true) and its opposite (all false).

Figure 1 shows the correspondence between R*S and standard measures employed in different evaluation campaigns; F represents the harmonic mean of precision and recall over the positive class. The most relevant fact is that a high score in all standard measures is necessary to achieve a high score according to R*S. Table 7 shows the Robustness and strictness of measures (see Section 4.1) in this test set. The strictest measure is R*S (-0.78), followed by Lam% (-0.89). The measures F, Utility and Accuracy achieve -0.92 of Strictness. There exists a clear difference in robustness between R*S and other measures. In this scenario, robustness seems to be correlated with strictness.

4.4 Document Retrieval

4.4.1 *Formal Constraints*

Just like MAP and DCG, Reliability and Sensitivity satisfy the first two constraints, Priority and Deepness. Adding an incorrect relationship produces a score decrease, and the effect of an incorrect relationship depends on the deepness of the related documents in the system output ranking. However, unlike MAP or DCG, Reliability and Sensitivity also satisfy the third constraint, Deepness Threshold. And, unlike MRR, they also satisfy the fourth constraint, Closeness Threshold. Due to space constraints, we do not include here the formal proofs.

Note that the parameters n and W_n offer great flexibility, and permit to accomodate scenarios where only the top documents in the rank matter (as in Web search) as well as recall-oriented scenarios, simply adjusting the parameters accordingly. The formal constraints are satisfied for any paratemer setting. For example, with the setting $W_{30} = 0.8$, ranking 30 relevant documents after 30 irrelevant documents is worse than retrieving one document in the first position, but retrieving five relevant documents in the first 10 positions is better than retrieving only one document at the top 1. The cut point is n=20.

As for the confidence constraint, note that the more we include irrelevant documents in the ranking, the more we include incorrect priority relationships between the priorized documents and the long tail. We could also satisfy this property with measures like RBP by using a discounting score for each irrelevant document, but then the nature of RBP would change and its formal properties would not hold any longer. Table 6 summarizes the results of the formal constraint analysis.

4.4.2 *Empirical Meta-evaluation*

We have used queries 701 to 750 in the GOV-2 collection, which were employed in the TREC 2004 Terabyte Track. The GOV-2 corpus consists of approximately 25 million documents. Therefore, we can assume that the amount of documents in the collection is unlimited for practical purposes. Relevant documents were manually annotated for each query. We consider the results of 60 retrieval systems developed by the participants in the track. Two relevance levels (high and medium) were considered in the human annotation.

Table 8 shows the strictness and robustness[3] of measures. We consider the strictness of all measures against the standard measures MAP, DCP, P@10, MRR, $\text{RBP}_{p=0.8}$ and $\text{RBP}_{p=0.95}$. The strictest measure is R*S with $W_{80} = 30$ (-0.58) followed by MRR (-0.63), MAP (-0.74) and P@10 (-0.75). However, R*S with $W_{80} = 30$ achieves low robustness, while R*S with $n_{80} = 800$ and DCG have higher robustness at the cost of strictness. It seems that there is a trade-off between strictness and robustness. A possible explanation is that the robustness of measures across test cases depends on the amount of data that is considered for the evalua-

[3]Discriminating systems that return short rankings is easy. In order to avoid this noise, we only consider in this test those systems that return at least 1000 documents

Measure	MAP	DCG	P@10	MRR	RBP p=0.8	RBP p=0.95	R*S W_{30}	R*S W_{800}
Robustness	0.55	**0.60**	0.3	0.4	0.28	0.39	**0.35**	0.57
Strictness	-0.89	-0.68	-0.76	-0.63	-0.92	-0.65	**-0.58**	-0.73

Table 8: Robustness and strictness of Document Retrieval Evaluation Measures, GOV2 test set.

Gold Standard	System Output 1
d_1 {d_2 d_3 d_4} {d_4 d_5} {d_6 d_7} {d_6 d_7}	d_1{d_2 d_3 d_4} {d_4 d_5}{d_6 d_7} d_6 d_7
$R_{\prec\succ}$=1 $S_{\prec\succ}$=1 $R_{\sim}$=1 $S_{\sim}$=1	$R_{\prec\succ}$=1 $S_{\prec\succ}$=1 $R_{\sim}$=1 $S_{\sim}$=0.97
System Output 2	**System Output 3**
d_1 {d_2 d_3}{ d_4} {d_4 d_5} {d_6 d_7} {d_6 d_7}	d_1 {d_3 d_4 } {d_4 d_5} {d_6 d_7} {d_6 d_7}
$R_{\prec\succ}$=1 $S_{\prec\succ}$=1 $R_{\sim}$=1 $S_{\sim}$=0.8	$R_{\prec\succ}$=1 $S_{\prec\succ}$=0.86 $R_{\sim}$=1 $S_{\sim}$=0.74
System Output 4	**System Output 5**
d_1 {d_3 d_4 } {d_4 d_5} {d_6 d_7} {d_6 d_7 d_8}	{d_6 d_7} {d_4 d_5} {d_6 d_7} d_1 {d_2 d_3 d_4}
$R_{\prec\succ}$=0.95 $S_{\prec\succ}$=0.85 $R_{\sim}$=0.96 $S_{\sim}$=0.74	$R_{\prec\succ}$=0.64 $S_{\prec\succ}$=0.59 $R_{\sim}$=1 $S_{\sim}$=1

Table 9: Sensitivity and Reliability examples for the generic Document Organization scenario.

tion. Therefore, measures focused on the top of the ranking are less robust. Given that the max function in the strictness definition is very sensitive to outlier systems, we have also computed strictness considering the 10 maximum differences; results were the same.

5. GENERIC DOCUMENT ORGANIZATION SCENARIO

As far as we know, there is no measure that can be directly compared with R*S in the generic document organization scenario as we have defined it. In this section, we illustrate the behavior of R*S across several instances of system outputs. See Table 9. The gold standard consists of seven relevant documents distributed along three priority levels. Each priority level contains two clusters (or information nuggets) and documents 4,6 and 7 appear in two clusters and priority levels simultaneously. The Reliability and Sensitivity over priority and clustering relationships have been computed with $W_10 = 0.8$, i.e., we require that the first 10 occurrences represent 80% of the score.

Of course, Reliability and Sensitivity are maximal for the gold standard. Starting from this, we can identify in the table the following behaviors: (System 1) breaking clusters at low priority levels decreases slightly $S_{\sim}$, (System 2) breaking clusters at high priority levels decreases $S_{\sim}$ to a greater extent; (System 3) Removing one document (d_2) decreases priority and clustering sensitivity; (System 4) removing and adding noisy documents (d_2 and d_8) decreases both sensitivity and reliability scores and in (System 5) we swap all priority levels. Then, clustering is perfect and the priority R and S decrease, but not to zero. Notice that the 10 first documents have only a 80% of weight in the evaluation. There exists a long tail of documents from which this set is priorized.

6. CONCLUSIONS

In this paper we have discussed how some prominent Information Access tasks – Document Retrieval, Clustering and Filtering – can be subsumed under a generic Document Organization task that establishes two kinds of binary relationships between documents: relatedness (which forms clusters) and priority (ranking). We have then introduced two evaluation measures for the document organization problem: Reliability and Sensitivity, which are precision and recall of the predicted set of relationships with respect to the true relationships, with a specific relative weighting scheme between relations. The main contribution of this paper is that R and S can be applied to complex tasks which involve ranking, clustering and filtering at the same time. An example task is online reputation monitoring, where systems have to (i) filter out irrelevant information, (ii) organize relevant information in topics, and (iii) decide which topics have more priority from the point of view of reputation management. R and S are able to provide a unique evaluation measure for this combined problem.

In addition, R and S satisfy all formal constraints in each of the subsumed tasks; in particular, they satisfy more formal constraints than any previous measure in the Document Retrieval task, and they are able to accomodate several retrieval scenarios (from precision-oriented to recall-oriented) via two parameters that establish that the first n levels in the rank carry on a fraction W_n of the overall quality score. Our empirical study indicates that R and S are stricter than standard measures, i.e., a high result with R and S ensures a high result with any other standard measure in all the subsumed tasks. That makes R and S a preferable choice in cases where the application scenario does not clearly point towards any of the previously existing measures, because it guarantees that a good result will still hold according to any other standard measure.

For its application to combined tasks, future work involves extending the set of binary relations – the general principle of R and S can be applied to any kind of relations – together with a a careful analysis on how to assign relative weights to different types of relations; for instance, in certain application scenarios one type of relation (priority or relatedness) may dominate and obscure what is going on with the other, making R and S less transparent and/or useful.

Code to use R and S is available at `http://nlp.uned.es`.

Acknowledgments

This work has been partially funded by EU FP7 project *Limosine* (grant number 288024), a Google Faculty Research Award (*Axiometrics*, project *Holopedia* (grant from the Spanish goverment) and project *MA2VICMR* (grant from the government of Comunidad de Madrid).

7. REFERENCES

[1] E. Amigó, J. Artiles, J. Gonzalo, D. Spina, B. Liu, and A. Corujo. WePS3 Evaluation Campaign: Overview of the On-line Reputation Management Task. In *2nd Web People Search Evaluation Workshop (WePS 2010), CLEF 2010 Conference, Padova Italy*, 2010.

[2] E. Amigó, J. Gonzalo, J. Artiles, and F. Verdejo. A comparison of extrinsic clustering evaluation metrics based on formal constraints. *Inf. Retr.*, 12:461–486, August 2009.

[3] E. Amigó, J. Gonzalo, and F. Verdejo. A comparison of evaluation metrics for document filtering. In *Proceedings of CLEF'11*, CLEF'11, pages 38–49, Berlin, Heidelberg, 2011. Springer-Verlag.

[4] C. Buckley and E. M. Voorhees. Retrieval evaluation with incomplete information. In *Proceedings of the 27th annual international ACM SIGIR conference on Research and development in information retrieval*, SIGIR '04, pages 25–32, New York, NY, USA, 2004. ACM.

[5] B. Carterette. System effectiveness, user models, and user utility: a conceptual framework for investigation. In *Proceedings of the 34th international ACM SIGIR conference on Research and development in Information Retrieval*, SIGIR '11, pages 903–912, New York, NY, USA, 2011. ACM.

[6] B. Carterette, E. Kanoulas, and E. Yilmaz. Simulating simple user behavior for system effectiveness evaluation. In *CIKM*, pages 611–620, 2011.

[7] O. Chapelle and Y. Zhang. A dynamic bayesian network click model for web search ranking. In *WWW*, pages 1–10, 2009.

[8] J. M. Cigarrán, A. Peñas, J. Gonzalo, and F. Verdejo. Automatic selection of noun phrases as document descriptors in an fca-based information retrieval system. In *ICFCA*, pages 49–63, 2005.

[9] C. L. A. Clarke, M. Kolla, G. V. Cormack, O. Vechtomova, A. Ashkan, S. Büttcher, and I. MacKinnon. Novelty and diversity in information retrieval evaluation. In *SIGIR*, pages 659–666, 2008.

[10] J. Cohen. A Coefficient of Agreement for Nominal Scales. *Educational and Psychological Measurement*, 20(1):37, 1960.

[11] G. Cormack and T. Lynam. Trec 2005 spam track overview. In *Proceedings of the fourteenth Text Retrieval Conference 8TREC 2005)*, 2005.

[12] G. V. Cormack and T. R. Lynam. TREC 2005 Spam Track Overview. In *Proceedings of the fourteenth Text REtrieval Conference (TREC-2005)*, 2005.

[13] M. Halkidi, Y. Batistakis, and M. Vazirgiannis. On Clustering Validation Techniques. *Journal of Intelligent Information Systems*, 17(2-3):107–145, 2001.

[14] M. A. Hearst and J. O. Pedersen. Reexamining the cluster hypothesis: Scatter/gather on retrieval results. pages 76–84, 1996.

[15] B. Hu, Y. Zhang, W. Chen, G. Wang, and Q. Yang. Characterizing search intent diversity into click models. In *Proceedings of the 20th international conference on World wide web*, WWW '11, pages 17–26, New York, NY, USA, 2011. ACM.

[16] K. Järvelin and J. Kekäläinen. Cumulated gain-based evaluation of ir techniques. *ACM Trans. Inf. Syst.*, 20:422–446, October 2002.

[17] B. Krishnamurthy, P. Gill, and M. Arlitt. A few chirps about twitter. In *WOSP '08: Proceedings of the first workshop on Online social networks*, pages 19–24, New York, NY, USA, 2008. ACM.

[18] A. Leuski. Evaluating document clustering for interactive information retrieval. In *CIKM*, pages 33–40, 2001.

[19] M. Meila. Comparing clusterings. In *Proceedings of COLT 03*, 2003.

[20] T. M. Mitchell. *Machine learning*. McGraw Hill, New York, 1997.

[21] A. Moffat and J. Zobel. Rank-biased precision for measurement of retrieval effectiveness. *ACM Trans. Inf. Syst.*, 27(1):2:1–2:27, Dec. 2008.

[22] A. Rosenberg and J. Hirschberg. V-measure: A conditional entropy-based external cluster evaluation measure. In *Proceedings of EMNLP-CoNLL 2007*, pages 410–420, 2007.

[23] M. D. Smucker and C. L. Clarke. Time-based calibration of effectiveness measures. In *Proceedings of the 35th international ACM SIGIR conference on Research and development in information retrieval*, SIGIR '12, pages 95–104, New York, NY, USA, 2012. ACM.

[24] S. Vargas and P. Castells. Rank and relevance in novelty and diversity metrics for recommender systems. In *5th ACM Conference on Recommender Systems (RecSys 2011)*, pages 109–116, Chicago, Illinois, October 2011.

[25] E. M. Voorhees. The trec-8 question answering track report. In *In Proceedings of TREC-8*, pages 77–82, 1999.

Modeling Term Dependencies with Quantum Language Models for IR

Alessandro Sordoni
sordonia@iro.umontreal.ca

Jian-Yun Nie
nie@iro.umontreal.ca

Yoshua Bengio
bengioy@iro.umontreal.ca

DIRO, Université de Montréal
Montréal, H3C 3J7, Québec

ABSTRACT

Traditional information retrieval (IR) models use bag-of-words as the basic representation and assume that some form of independence holds between terms. Representing term dependencies and defining a scoring function capable of integrating such additional evidence is theoretically and practically challenging. Recently, Quantum Theory (QT) has been proposed as a possible, more general framework for IR. However, only a limited number of investigations have been made and the potential of QT has not been fully explored and tested. We develop a new, generalized Language Modeling approach for IR by adopting the probabilistic framework of QT. In particular, quantum probability could account for both single and compound terms at once without having to extend the term space artificially as in previous studies. This naturally allows us to avoid the weight-normalization problem, which arises in the current practice by mixing scores from matching compound terms and from matching single terms. Our model is the first practical application of quantum probability to show significant improvements over a robust bag-of-words baseline and achieves better performance on a stronger non bag-of-words baseline.

Categories and Subject Descriptors

H.3.3 [**Information Storage and Retrieval**]: Information Search and Retrieval

Keywords

Density Matrices; Language Modeling; Retrieval Models

1. INTRODUCTION

The quest for the effective modeling of term dependencies has been of central interest in the information retrieval (IR) community since the inception of first retrieval models. However, the gradual shift towards non bag-of-words models is strewn with modeling difficulties. One of the central problems is to find an effective way of representing and scoring documents based on such dependencies. As pointed out by Gao et al. [9], dependencies can be handled in two ways.

The first approach is to extend the dimensionality of the representation space. In early geometrical retrieval models such as the Vector Space Model (VSM), dependencies arising from phrases (compound terms) are represented by defining additional dimensions in the space, i.e. both the phrase and its component single terms are regarded as representation features [8, 21, 28]. For example, *computer architecture* is considered as disjoint from *computer* and *architecture*, which is a strong modeling assumption, and does not take advantage of the semantic relation that generally exists between a compound phrase and its component terms.

The second approach is more principled in such that simple terms are kept as representational units and term dependencies are modeled statistically as joint probabilities, i.e. $p(computer, architecture)$. Proposed dependence models such as n-gram Language Model (LM) for IR [30], biterm LM [31] or the dependence LM [9] adopt such a representation. However, the gain from integrating dependencies was smaller than hoped [35] and it came with higher computational costs due to dependency parsing or n-gram models [13, 30], or unsupervised iterative methods for estimating the joint probability [9].

Recently, non bag-of-words models such Markov random field (MRF) [19], quasi-synchronous dependence model [24] and the query hypergraph model [2] have been proposed. Most of these retrieval models take a log-linear form, which offers a very flexible way of taking into account term dependencies by integrating different sources of evidence, such as proximity heuristics and exact matching. However, the LM is used as a black box to estimate single-term and compound-term influences separately and then the model combines them to compute the final score. We believe that, from a representational point of view, these models have implicitly made a turn back to the first VSM approach in the sense that the dependencies are assumed to represent additional concepts, i.e. atomic units for the purpose of document and query representation, thus disjoint from the component terms [2, 3]. This choice indeed allows for flexible scoring functions. However, the retrieval model boils down to a combination of scores obtained separately from matching single terms and from matching compound dependencies. This is the main cause of the weight-normalization problem [9, 11] which is that a dependency may be counted twice, as a compound and as component terms. In the context of phrases, Sparck Jones et al. note that "the weight of the

SIGIR'13, July 28–August 1, 2013, Dublin, Ireland.

phrase should reflect not the increased odds of relevance implied by its presence as compared to its absence, as a whole unit, but the increased odds compared to the presence of its components words" [11]. When integrating the evidence, the weights for the combination are usually estimated by optimizing a retrieval measure such as mean average precision (MAP). In this sense, a principled probabilistic interpretation of these models is difficult.

The pioneering work by Van Rijsbergen [33] officially formalized the idea that Quantum Theory (QT) could be seen as a "formal language that can be used to describe the objects and processes in information retrieval". The idea of QT as a framework for manipulating vector spaces and probability is appealing. However, the methods that stem from this initial intuition provided only limited evidence about the usefulness and effectiveness of the framework for IR tasks. For example, Piwowarski et al. [25] test if acceptable performance for ad-hoc tasks could be achieved with a quantum approach to IR. The authors represent documents as subspaces and queries as density operators. However, both documents and queries representations are estimated through passage-retrieval like heuristics, i.e. a document is divided into passages and is associated to a subspace spanned by the vectors corresponding to document passages [25]. Different representations for the query density matrix are tested but none of them led to good retrieval performance. Successively, a number of works took inspiration from quantum phenomena in order to relax some common assumption in IR [37, 38]. Zuccon and Azzopardi [38] introduce interference effects into the Probability Ranking Principle (PRP) in order to rank interdependent documents. Although this method achieves good results, it does not make principled use of the quantum probability space and cannot be considered as evidence towards the usefulness of the enlarged probabilistic space. In general, these methods made heuristic use of the concepts of the theory and no clear probabilistic interpretation can be given.

The intrinsic heuristic flavor in preceding approaches motivated some authors to provide evidence to the hypothesis that there exists an IR situation in which classical probabilistic IR fails, or it is severely limited, and it is thus necessary to switch to a more general probabilistic theory [16, 17, 34]. Although these works are theoretically grounded and heavily influenced our general vision of the theory, no clue is given on how to operationalize such results in real-world applications.

In this paper, we propose a novel retrieval framework for modeling term dependencies based on the probabilistic calculus offered by QT. In our model, both single terms and compound dependencies are mathematically modeled as projectors in a vector space, i.e. elementary events in an enlarged probabilistic space. In particular, a compound dependency is represented as a *superposition* event which is a special kind of projector that is neither disjoint from its component terms, nor a joint event. Documents and queries are represented as a sequence of projectors associated to a *quantum language model* (QLM), encapsulated in a particular matrix. The scoring function is a divergence between query and document QLMs. We will show that our model is a generalization of classical unigram LMs. To our knowledge, this work can be seen as the first work to use the quantum probabilistic calculus in order to achieve improvements over state-of-the-art models.

Our contributions are as follows:

1. We propose a novel application of quantum probability to IR.
2. Using this approach, we show significant improvements over a strong baseline bag-of-words model and a strong non bag-of-words model.
3. We propose a new way of representing dependencies without artificially extending the term space and without estimating expensive n-gram probabilities.
4. We show how the new representation of the dependency permits to specify how the dependency behaves with respect to its component terms.
5. In our model, the dependency information is not integrated in the scoring phase, but in the estimation phase. Hence, our model does not suffer the weight-normalization problem.

2. A BROADER VIEW ON PROBABILITY

2.1 The Quantum Sample Space

In quantum probability, the probabilistic space is naturally encapsulated in a vector space, specifically a Hilbert space, noted $\mathbb{H}^n$, but for the sake of simplicity, in this paper we limit ourselves to finite real spaces, noted $\mathbb{R}^n$. We will be using Dirac's notation restricted to the real field, for which a unit vector $\vec{u} \in \mathbb{R}^n$, $\|\vec{u}\|_2 = 1$ and its transpose $\vec{u}^\top$ are respectively written as a *ket* $|u\rangle$ and a *bra* $\langle u|$. Using this notation, the projector onto the direction u writes as $|u\rangle\langle u|$. The inner product between two vectors writes as $\langle u|v\rangle$. Moreover, we note by $|e_i\rangle$ the elements of the standard basis in $\mathbb{R}^n$, i.e. $|e_i\rangle = (\delta_{1i}, \ldots, \delta_{ni})^\top$, where $\delta_{ij} = 1$ iff $i = j$.

Events are no more defined as subsets but as subspaces, more specifically as projectors onto subspaces [23, 34]. Given a 1-dimensional subspace spanned by a ket $|u\rangle$, the projector onto the unit norm vector $|u\rangle$, $|u\rangle\langle u|$, is an elementary event of the quantum probability space, also called a *dyad*. A dyad is always a projector onto a 1-dimensional space. Given the bijection between subspaces and projectors, it is correct to state that $|u\rangle$ is itself an elementary event. For example, if $n = 2$, the quantum elementary events $|e_1\rangle = (1,0)^\top$, $|f_1\rangle = (\frac{1}{\sqrt{2}}, \frac{1}{\sqrt{2}})^\top$, can be represented by the following dyads:

$$|e_1\rangle\langle e_1| = \begin{pmatrix} 1 & 0 \\ 0 & 0 \end{pmatrix}, |f_1\rangle\langle f_1| = \begin{pmatrix} 0.5 & 0.5 \\ 0.5 & 0.5 \end{pmatrix}. \quad (1)$$

Generally, any ket $|v\rangle = \sum_i v_i |u_i\rangle$ is called a *superposition* of the $\{|u_i\rangle\}$ where $\{|u_1\rangle, \ldots, |u_n\rangle\}$ form an orthonormal basis. In order to see the generalization that is taking place, one has to consider that in $\mathbb{R}^n$ there is an infinite number of vectors even if the dimension n is finite. Hence, contrary to the classical case, an infinite number of elementary events can be defined.

2.2 Density Matrices

A quantum probability measure μ is the generalization of a classical probability measure such that (i) for every dyad $|u\rangle\langle u|$, $\mu(|u\rangle\langle u|) \in [0, 1]$ and (ii) it reduces to a classical probability measure for any orthonormal basis $\{|u_1\rangle, \ldots, |u_n\rangle\}$, i.e. $\sum_i \mu(|u_i\rangle\langle u_i|) = 1$. Gleason's Theorem [10] states that,

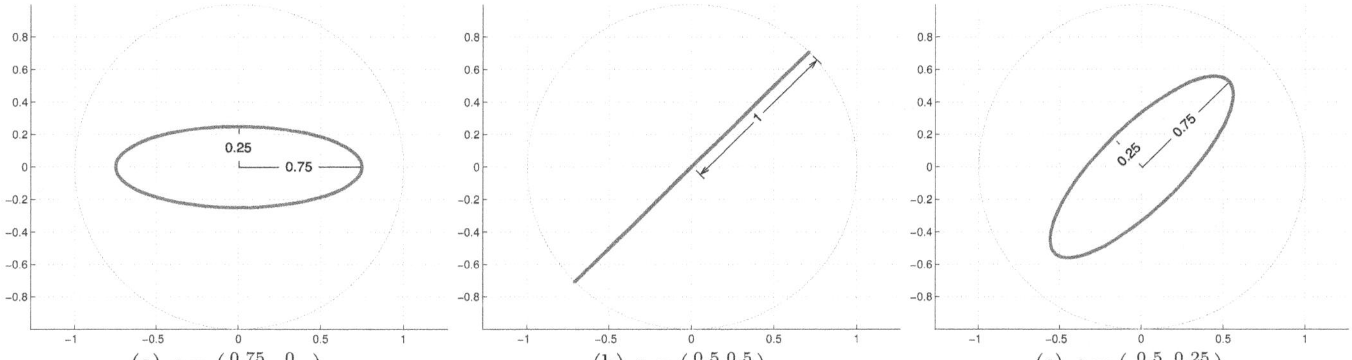

(a) $\rho = \begin{pmatrix} 0.75 & 0 \\ 0 & 0.25 \end{pmatrix}$ (b) $\rho = \begin{pmatrix} 0.5 & 0.5 \\ 0.5 & 0.5 \end{pmatrix}$ (c) $\rho = \begin{pmatrix} 0.5 & 0.25 \\ 0.25 & 0.5 \end{pmatrix}$

Figure 1: The ellipses depict the set of points $\{\rho|u\rangle : |u\rangle \in \mathbb{R}^2\}$. The eigenvalues of ρ define how much each ellipse is stretched along the corresponding eigenvectors. To the left, ρ corresponds to a classical probability distribution. To the center, ρ is a pure state, thus the ellipse degenerates along the eigenvector corresponding to its unit eigenvalue. To the right, a general density matrix for which we vary both the eigenvalues and the eigensystem.

for any real vector space with dimension greater than 2, there is a one-to-one correspondence between quantum probability measures μ and *density matrices* ρ. The form of this correspondence is given by:

$$\mu_\rho(|v\rangle\langle v|) = \text{tr}(\rho|v\rangle\langle v|). \tag{2}$$

A real density matrix is symmetric, $\rho = \rho^\top$, positive semidefinite, $\rho \geq 0$, and of trace 1, $\text{tr}\,\rho = 1$[1]. From now on, the set of $n \times n$ real density matrices would be noted $\mathcal{S}^n$.

By Gleason's theorem, a density matrix can be seen as the proper quantum generalization of a classical probability distribution. It assigns a quantum probability to each one of the infinite dyads. For example, the density matrix:

$$\rho = \begin{pmatrix} 0.5 & 0.5 \\ 0.5 & 0.5 \end{pmatrix}, \tag{3}$$

assigns probabilities $\text{tr}(\rho|e_1\rangle\langle e_1|) = 0.5$ and $\text{tr}(\rho|f_1\rangle\langle f_1|) = 1$. Hence, the event $|f_1\rangle\langle f_1|$ is certain and still there is non-classical uncertainty on $|e_1\rangle\langle e_1|$. Only if $\{|u_1\rangle, \dots, |u_n\rangle\}$ form an orthonormal system of $\mathbb{R}^n$ can the dyads $|u_i\rangle\langle u_i|$ be understood as disjoints events of a classical sample space, i.e. their probabilities sum to one. The relation that ties $|e_1\rangle\langle e_1|$ and $|f_1\rangle\langle f_1|$ is purely geometrical and cannot be expressed using set theoretic operations.

Any classical discrete probability distribution can be seen as a mixture over n elementary points, i.e. a parameter $\vec{\theta} = (\theta_1, \dots, \theta_n)$, where $\theta_i \geq 0$ and $\sum_i \theta_i = 1$. The density matrix is the straightforward generalization of this idea by considering a mixture over orthogonal dyads $\rho = \sum_i v_i |u_i\rangle\langle u_i|$ where $v_i \geq 0$ and $\sum_i v_i = 1$. Given a density matrix ρ, one can find the components dyads by taking its eigendecomposition and building a dyad for each eigenvector. We note such decomposition by $\rho = R\Lambda R^\top = \sum_{i=1}^n \lambda_i |r_i\rangle\langle r_i|$, where $|r_i\rangle$ are the eigenvectors and λ_i their corresponding eigenvalues. This decomposition always exists for density matrices [23].

Conventional probability distributions can be represented by diagonal density matrices. The sample space corresponds to the standard basis $\mathcal{E} = \{|e_i\rangle\langle e_i|\}_{i=1}^n$. Hence, the density matrix corresponding to the parameter $\vec{\theta}$ above can be represented as a mixture over $\mathcal{E}$, i.e. $\rho_\theta = \text{diag}(\vec{\theta}) = \sum_i \theta_i |e_i\rangle\langle e_i|$.

[1]The trace is equal to the sum of the diagonal terms in a matrix.

Consider a vocabulary of two terms $\mathcal{V} = \{a, b\}$. A unigram language model $\vec{\theta} = (0.75, 0.25)$ defined on $\mathcal{V}$ is represented by:

$$\rho_\theta = \frac{3}{4}|e_a\rangle\langle e_a| + \frac{1}{4}|e_b\rangle\langle e_b| = \begin{pmatrix} 0.75 & 0 \\ 0 & 0.25 \end{pmatrix}.$$

Hence, term projectors are orthogonal, i.e. terms correspond to disjoint events. For example, the probability of the term a is computed by $\text{tr}(\rho_\theta|e_a\rangle\langle e_a|) = 0.75$. As conventional probability distributions are restricted to the identity eigensystem, they differ in their eigenvalues, which correspond to diagonal entries. On the contrary, general density matrices can differ also in the eigensystem. For example, the density matrix ρ of Eq. 3 has eigenvector $|f_1\rangle = (\frac{1}{\sqrt{2}}, \frac{1}{\sqrt{2}})^\top$ with eigenvalue 1 and the eigenvector $|f_2\rangle = (\frac{1}{\sqrt{2}}, -\frac{1}{\sqrt{2}})^\top$ with eigenvalue 0. Hence, it can be represented as a one-element mixture containing the projector $\rho = |f_1\rangle\langle f_1|$. When the mixture weights are concentrated into a single projector, the corresponding density matrix is called *pure state*. Otherwise, it is called *mixed state*.

When defined over $\mathbb{R}^n$, density matrices can be seen as ellipsoids, i.e. deformations of the unit sphere (Figure 1) [34]. Classical probability distributions, i.e. diagonal density matrices, are ellipsoids stretched along the identity eigensystem. As quantum probability has access to an infinite number of eigensystems, the ellipsoid can be "rotated", i.e. defined on a different eigensystem. In this work, we will use this additional feature in order to build a more reliable representation of documents and queries taking into account more complex information than single terms.

3. QUANTUM LANGUAGE MODELS

The approach Quantum Language Modeling (QLM) retains the classical Language Modeling for IR as a special case. Hereafter, we will present in details the quantum counterpart of unigram language models. Although it is not explicitly developed in this paper, we argue that arbitrary n-gram models could be modeled as well.

3.1 Representation

In classical bag-of-words language models, a document d is represented by a sequence of i.i.d. term events, i.e.

$\mathcal{W}_d = \{w_i : i = 1, \ldots, N\}$, where N is the document length. Each w_i belongs to a sample space $\mathcal{V}$, corresponding to the vocabulary, of size n. It is assumed that such sequences correspond to a sample from an unknown distribution $\vec{\theta}$ over the vocabulary $\mathcal{V}$, for which we want to gain insight.

A quantum language model assigns quantum probabilities to arbitrary subsets of the vocabulary. It is parametrized by an $n \times n$ density matrix ρ, $\rho \in \mathcal{S}^n$, where n is the size of the vocabulary $\mathcal{V}$. In QLM, a document d is considered as a sequence of M quantum events associated with a density matrix ρ:

$$\mathcal{P}_d = \{\Pi_i : i = 1, \ldots, M\}, \quad (4)$$

where each Π_i is a general dyad $|u\rangle\langle u|$ and represents a subset of the vocabulary. Note that the number of dyads M can be different from N, the total number of terms in the document. The sequence $\mathcal{P}_d$ is constructed from the observed terms $\mathcal{W}_d$: we have to define how to map subsets of terms to projectors. Separating the observed text from the observed projectors constitutes the main flexibility of our model. In what follows, we define a way of mapping single terms and arbitrary dependencies to quantum elementary events. Formally, we seek to define a mapping $m : \mathcal{P}(\mathcal{V}) \rightarrow \mathcal{L}(\mathbb{R}^n)$, where $\mathcal{P}(\mathcal{V})$ is the powerset of the vocabulary and $\mathcal{L}(\mathbb{R}^n)$ is the set of dyads on $\mathbb{R}^n$. As an initial assumption, we set $m(\emptyset) = \mathbb{O}$, where $\mathbb{O}$ is the projector onto the zero vector.

3.1.1 Representing Single Terms

In Section 2.2, we showed that unigram sample spaces can be represented as the set of projectors on the standard basis $\mathcal{E} = \{|e_i\rangle\langle e_i|\}_{i=1}^n$ and unigram language models can be represented as mixtures over $\mathcal{E}$, i.e. diagonal matrices. Therefore, a straightforward mapping from single terms to quantum events is:

$$m(\{w\}) = |e_w\rangle\langle e_w|, \quad (5)$$

where $w \in \mathcal{V}$. This choice associates the occurrence of each term to a dyad $|e_w\rangle\langle e_w|$, and these dyads form an orthonormal basis. Hence, occurrences of single terms are still represented as disjoint events. Consider $n = 3$ and $\mathcal{V} = \{$*computer, architecture, games*$\}$. If $\mathcal{W}_d = \{$*computer, architecture*$\}$ and one applies m to each of the terms, the sequence of corresponding projectors is $\mathcal{P}_d = \{\mathcal{E}_{computer}, \mathcal{E}_{architecture}\}$ where $\mathcal{E}_w = |e_w\rangle\langle e_w|$:

$$\mathcal{E}_{computer} = \begin{pmatrix} 1 & 0 & 0 \\ 0 & 0 & 0 \\ 0 & 0 & 0 \end{pmatrix}, \mathcal{E}_{architecture} = \begin{pmatrix} 0 & 0 & 0 \\ 0 & 1 & 0 \\ 0 & 0 & 0 \end{pmatrix}. \quad (6)$$

Note that if we decide to observe only single terms, $\mathcal{P}_d$ turns out to be the quantum counterpart of classical observed terms $\mathcal{W}_d$, i.e. $M = N$.

3.1.2 Representing Dependencies

In this paper, by dependency, we mean a relationship linking two or more terms and we represent such an entity abstractly by a subset of the vocabulary, i.e. $\kappa = \{w_1, \ldots, w_K\}$. We define the following mapping for an arbitrary dependency κ:

$$m(\kappa) = m(\{w_1, \ldots, w_K\}) = |\kappa\rangle\langle\kappa|, \ |\kappa\rangle = \sum_{i=1}^{K} \sigma_i |e_{w_i}\rangle, \quad (7)$$

where the coefficients $\sigma_i \in \mathbb{R}$ must be chosen such that $\sum_i \sigma_i^2 = 1$, in order to ensure the proper normalization of

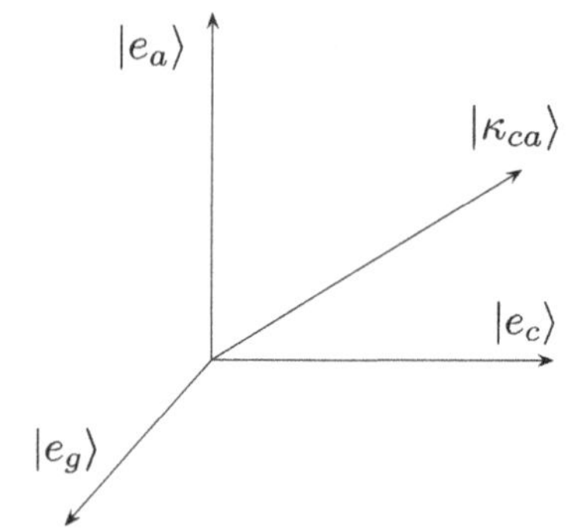

Figure 2: The dependency κ_{ca} is modeled as a projector onto $|\kappa_{ca}\rangle$, i.e. as a superposition event.

$|\kappa\rangle$. The well-defined dyad $|\kappa\rangle\langle\kappa|$ is a *superposition* event. As we showed in Section 2.2, superposition events are justifiable only in the quantum probabilistic space. They are neither disjoint from their constituents $|e_{w_i}\rangle\langle e_{w_i}|$ nor do they solely constitute joint events in the sense of n-grams: here, the compound dependency is not considered as an additional entity, as done in previous models [2, 3, 19, 21]. The proposed mapping allows for the representation of relationships within a group of terms by creating a new quantum event in the same n-dimensional space.

In addition, superposition events come with a flexible way in quantifying how much evidence the observation of dependency κ brings to its component terms. This is achieved by changing the distribution of the σ_i: if one wants to attempt a classical interpretation, the σ_i can be viewed as relative pseudo-counts, i.e. observing $|\kappa\rangle\langle\kappa|$ adds fractional occurrence to the events of its component terms $|e_{w_i}\rangle\langle e_{w_i}|$. To our knowledge, until now this feature has been only modeled heuristically, or not modeled at all. In our framework, it fits nicely in the quantum probabilistic space by specifying how a compound dependency event and its constituent single terms events are related.

As an example, one could model the compound dependency between *computer* and *architecture*, $\kappa_{ca} = \{$*computer, architecture*$\}$, by the dyad $\mathcal{K}_{ca} = |\kappa_{ca}\rangle\langle\kappa_{ca}|$, where $|\kappa_{ca}\rangle = \sqrt{2/3}|e_c\rangle + \sqrt{1/3}|e_a\rangle$ (Figure 2). With respect to the example taken above, the event is represented by the matrix:

$$\mathcal{K}_{ca} = \begin{pmatrix} \frac{2}{3} & \frac{\sqrt{2}}{3} & 0 \\ \frac{\sqrt{2}}{3} & \frac{1}{3} & 0 \\ 0 & 0 & 0 \end{pmatrix}. \quad (8)$$

The superposition coefficients entail that observing $\mathcal{K}_{ca}$ adds more evidence to $|e_c\rangle\langle e_c|$ than to $|e_a\rangle\langle e_a|$.

3.1.3 Choosing When and What to Observe

Once we have defined the mapping m, one must ask three questions:

1. Which compound dependencies to consider?
2. When does such a compound dependency hold in a document?
3. When the compound dependency is detected, should we also consider the projectors for its subsets as observed events?

Regarding the first question, one may (a) use a dictionary of phrases or frequent n-grams, or (b) assume that any

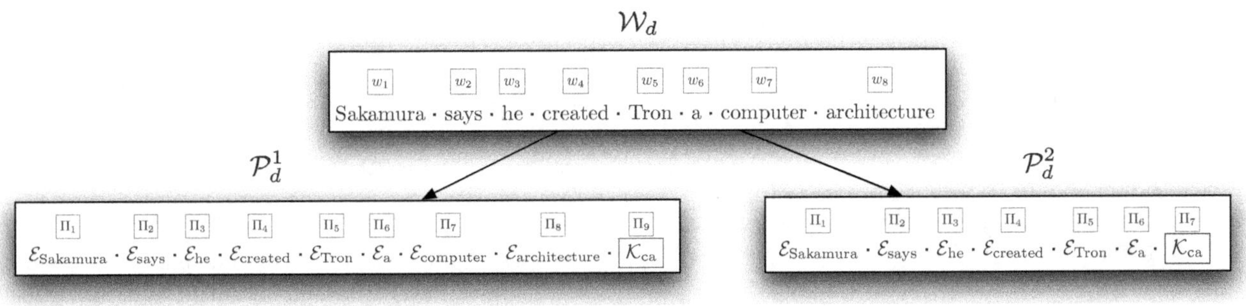

Figure 3: Two possible quantum sequences $\mathcal{P}_d^i$ of an excerpt $\mathcal{W}_d$ from a TREC collection. The observation of *computer architecture* is associated to a superposition projector $\mathcal{K}_{ca} = |\kappa_{ca}\rangle\langle\kappa_{ca}|$ while $\mathcal{E}_w = |e_w\rangle\langle e_w|$ are classical projectors. For $\mathcal{P}_d^2$ we observed only the compound while in $\mathcal{P}_d^1$ we also added its subsets.

subset of terms that appear in short queries are candidate compound dependencies to capture. In this paper, we want to make the approach as independent as possible of any linguistic resource. So the second approach (b) is used. This will also allow us to make a fair comparison with the previous approaches using the same strategy (such as the MRF model [19]).

The second question regards whether such selected compound dependencies hold in a given document. In other words, one has to decide when to add the selected dependency projector into a document sequence $\mathcal{P}_d$. This can be done for example by assuming that the components terms in the dependency appear as a bigram in a document, as biterm or in a unordered window of L terms. Convergent evidence from different works [1, 12, 14, 18, 31, 36] confirms that proximity is a strong indicator of dependence. Therefore, in this work we choose to detect a dependency if its component terms appear in a fixed-window of length L.

The third question regards how to apply the mapping m and can be more easily understood by a practical example. Consider a document $\mathcal{W}_d = \{computer,\ architecture\}$ and a query $\mathcal{W}_q = \{computer, architecture\}$. Once the dependency $\kappa_{ca} = \{computer,\ architecture\}$ has been detected in the document, i.e. the component terms appear next to each other, one can further decide:

1. to map only the dependency, i.e. $\mathcal{P}_d = \{\mathcal{K}_{ca}\}$,
2. to map both the dependency and the component terms, i.e. $\mathcal{P}_d = \{\mathcal{E}_{computer}, \mathcal{E}_{architecture}, \mathcal{K}_{ca}\}$.

These two choices are illustrated in Figure 3. The first choice is a highly non-classical one because it completely steals the occurrence of its component terms. Nevertheless, it becomes a valid choice in our framework. Differently from classical approaches, the fact that we only consider a count for the compound *computer architecture* does not mean that we assume that the terms *computer* and *architecture* do not occur. The dependency event is not disjoint from the single term events, and its occurrence partially entails the occurrence of its component terms. However, this choice is more dangerous because it over-penalizes the component terms: we should know very precisely *when* such a strong dependency is observed and *which coefficients* to assign to it.

The second choice is implicitly done in current dependency models and is at the basis of the weight-normalization problem. From this point of view, the sequence $\mathcal{P}_d$ could be seen as composed by concepts as recently formalized by Bendersky et al. [2, 3]. However, there are crucial differences from that work: (1) we give a clear probabilistic status to such concepts and (2) we do not assume that concepts are atomic units of information, completely unrelated from each other. In classical dependence models, single terms and compound dependencies are scored separately and then the scores are combined together [2, 19, 35]. A critical aspect of such models is that the occurrence of the phrase *computer architecture* will be counted twice - as single terms and as a compound. That is why the score on compound dependencies must be reweighed before integrating it with the independence score [9, 11, 19]. Contrary to classical models, our model does not suffer from such a problem because the evidences brought by the compound dependency as a whole and by its component terms are integrated in the estimation phase. Even if not reported explicitly in the experiments section, conducted experiments show that including projectors for both the dependency and its subsets is much more effective for the ad-hoc task evaluated here and thus this strategy will be preferred throughout this paper. In addition, an algorithm building the sequence of projectors from the document sequence will be presented in Section 4.3.1.

3.2 Estimation

3.2.1 Maximum Likelihood Estimation

Given that a document is represented by a set of observed projectors, one has to find ways to learn a quantum language model ρ to associate with a document. In QT, a number of objective functions have been proposed to estimate an unknown density matrix from a set of projectors: Linear Inversion [23] and Hedged ML [4] are notorious examples. In this work, we use the Maximum Likelihood (ML) formulation proposed in [15], because (1) it can easily be seen as a quantum generalization of a classical likelihood function (2) contrary to linear inversion, ML generates a well-defined density matrix, i.e. $\rho \in \mathcal{S}^n$, and (3) proposed estimation methods remain computationally affordable in high-dimensional spaces.

Given the observed projectors $\mathcal{P}_d = \{\Pi_1, \ldots, \Pi_M\}$ for document d, we define as training criterion for the quantum language model ρ the maximization of the following product proposed in [15] and corresponding in the unigram case to a proper likelihood:

$$\mathcal{L}_{\mathcal{P}_d}(\rho) = \prod_{i=1}^{M} \text{tr}(\rho \Pi_i). \tag{9}$$

The estimate $\widehat{\rho}$ can be obtained by approximately solving the following maximization problem:

$$\begin{aligned} \underset{\rho}{\text{maximize}} \quad & \log \mathcal{L}_{\mathcal{P}_d}(\rho) \\ \text{subject to} \quad & \rho \in \mathcal{S}^n. \end{aligned} \tag{10}$$

This maximization is difficult and must be approximated by using iterative methods. In [15], the following iterative scheme is proposed, also called the "$R\rho R$ algorithm". One introduces the operator:

$$R(\rho) = \sum_{i=1}^{M} \frac{1}{\text{tr}(\rho \Pi_i)} \Pi_i, \tag{11}$$

and updates an initial density matrix $\widehat{\rho}_{(0)}$ by applying repetitive iterations:

$$\widehat{\rho}_{(k+1)} = \frac{1}{Z} R(\widehat{\rho}_{(k)}) \widehat{\rho}_{(k)} R(\widehat{\rho}_{(k)}), \tag{12}$$

where, $Z = \text{tr}(R(\widehat{\rho}_{(k)})\widehat{\rho}_{(k)} R(\widehat{\rho}_{(k)}))$ is a normalization factor in order to ensure that $\widehat{\rho}_{(k+1)}$ respects the constraint of unitary trace [15]. Despite the $R\rho R$ algorithm being a quantum generalization of the well-behaving Expectation Maximization (EM) algorithm, the likelihood is not guaranteed to increase at each step because the nonlinear iteration may overshoot, similarly to a gradient descent algorithm with a too big step size. Characterizing such situations still remains an open problem [27]. In this work, in order to ensure convergence, if the likelihood is decreased at $k+1$, we use the following damped update:

$$\widetilde{\rho}_{(k+1)} = (1-\gamma)\widehat{\rho}_{(k)} + \gamma \widehat{\rho}_{(k+1)}, \tag{13}$$

where $\gamma \in [0, 1)$ controls the amount of damping and is optimized by linear search in order to ensure the maximum increase of the training objective[2]. As $\mathcal{S}^n$ is convex [23], $\widetilde{\rho}_{(k+1)}$ is a proper candidate density matrix. The process stops if the change in the likelihood is below a certain threshold or if a maximum number of iterations is attained.

From an IR point of view, the *metric divergence* problem [22] tells us that the maximization of the likelihood does not mean that the evaluation metric under consideration, such as mean average precision, is also maximized. In the experiments section, we address the two following questions from a perspective closer to IR concerns:

1. Which initial matrix $\widehat{\rho}_{(0)}$ to choose?
2. When to stop the update process?

As the estimation of a quantum document model requires an iterative process, one may believe that the complexity will make the process intractable. In Section 4.5, we provide an analysis of the complexity of the proposed computation, which will show that the process is quite tractable.

3.2.2 Smoothing Density Matrices

The ML estimation presented above suffers from a generalization of the usual zero-probability problem of classical ML, i.e. the estimator assigns zero probability to unseen data [35]. This is also called the zero eigenvalue problem [4]. Bayesian smoothing for density matrices has not yet been proposed. This may be because Bayesian inference in the quantum setting has just started to be the subject of intensive research [5, 34]. In this work, we propose to smooth density matrices by linear interpolation [35]. If $\widehat{\rho}_d$ is a document quantum language model obtained by ML, its smoothed version is obtained by interpolation with the ML collection quantum language model $\widehat{\rho}_c$:

$$\rho_d = (1-\alpha_d)\,\widehat{\rho}_d + \alpha_d\,\widehat{\rho}_c, \tag{14}$$

where $\alpha_d \in [0, 1]$ controls the amount of smoothing. As the set of density matrices $\mathcal{S}^n$ is convex, the resulting ρ_d is a proper density matrix. In this work, we assume that $\alpha_d = \frac{\mu}{(\mu+M)}$, which is the well-known form of the parameter for Dirichlet smoothing [35].

3.3 Scoring

The flexibility of the Kullback Liebler (KL) divergence approach in keeping distinct query and document representations makes it attractive for a candidate scoring function in our new framework. The direct generalization of classical KL divergence was introduced by Umegaki in [32] and is called *quantum relative entropy* or *Von-Neumann* (VN) *divergence*. Given two quantum language models ρ_q and ρ_d for the query and a document respectively, our scoring function is the negative query-to-document VN divergence:

$$\begin{aligned} -\Delta_{VN}(\rho_q \| \rho_d) &= -\text{tr}(\rho_q(\log \rho_q - \log \rho_d)) \\ &\overset{rank}{=} \text{tr}(\rho_q \log \rho_d), \end{aligned} \tag{15}$$

where log applied to a matrix denotes the matrix logarithm, i.e. the classical logarithm applied to the matrix eigenvalues. Rank equivalence is obtained by noting that $\text{tr}(\rho_q \log \rho_q)$ does not depend on the particular document. Denote by $\rho_q = \sum_i \lambda_{qi} |q_i\rangle\langle q_i|$, $\rho_d = \sum_i \lambda_{di} |d_i\rangle\langle d_i|$ the eigendecompositions of the density matrices ρ_q and ρ_d respectively. By substituting into the above equation, the scoring function rewrites as:

$$-\Delta_{VN}(\rho_q \| \rho_d) \overset{rank}{=} \sum_i \lambda_{qi} \sum_j \log \lambda_{dj} \langle q_i | d_j \rangle^2. \tag{16}$$

Compared to a classical KL divergence, the additional term $\langle q_i | d_j \rangle^2$ quantifies the difference in the eigenvectors between the two models. Following the representation introduced in Section 2.2, the VN divergence compares two ellipsoids not only by differences in the "shape" but also by differences in the "rotation".

If a VSM-like interpretation is attempted, one can think about $\{|q_i\rangle\}$, $\{|d_j\rangle\}$ as semantic concepts for the query and the document respectively, whereas the vectors of eigenvalues $\vec{\lambda}_q$, $\vec{\lambda}_d$ denote the importance of the corresponding semantic concepts in the two models. The VN divergence offers a way of matching query concepts by analyzing how much such concepts are related to documents concepts, i.e. $\forall i, j$, $\langle q_i | d_j \rangle^2$. Particularly, $\sum_j \langle q_i | d_j \rangle^2 = 1$. Thus, $\langle q_i | d_j \rangle^2$ can be interpreted as the quantum probability associated with the pure state $|q_i\rangle\langle q_i|$ for the elementary event $|d_j\rangle\langle d_j|$, i.e. $\mu_{q_i}(|d_j\rangle\langle d_j|) = \text{tr}(|q_i\rangle\langle q_i | d_j\rangle\langle d_j|) = \langle q_i | d_j \rangle^2$. Hence, one could rewrite Eq. 16 as:

$$-\Delta_{VN}(\rho_q \| \rho_d) \overset{rank}{=} \sum_i \lambda_{qi}\, \mathbb{E}_{\mu_{q_i}} \left[\log \vec{\lambda}_d\right]. \tag{17}$$

Therefore, the VN divergence scores a document based on the expectation of how important concept $|q_i\rangle$ is in document d even if it does not appear in it explicitly.

[2]Similar damped updates were successfully used in [26] to improve convergence and stability of the loopy belief propagation algorithm.

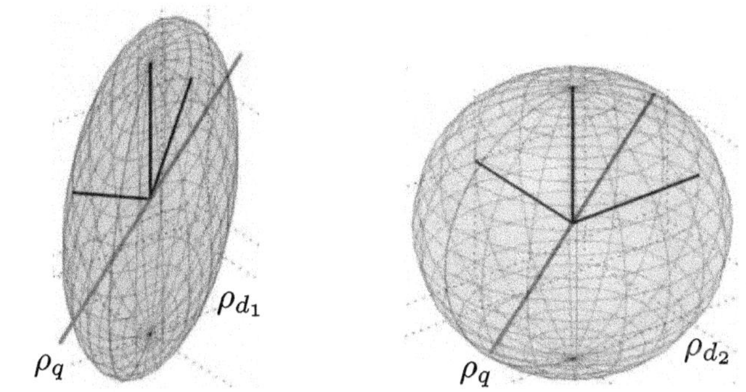

(a) $-\Delta_{VN}(\rho_q \| \rho_{d_1}) \propto -.76$ (b) $-\Delta_{VN}(\rho_q \| \rho_{d_2}) \propto -1.06$

o	$\mathcal{W}_o$	$\mathcal{P}_o$
q	{*computer, architecture*}	$\{\mathcal{E}_c, \mathcal{E}_a, \mathcal{K}_{ca}\}$
d_1	{*computer, architecture, and, games*}	$\{\mathcal{E}_c, \mathcal{E}_a, \mathcal{K}_{ca}, \mathcal{E}_g\}$
d_2	{*computer, games, and, architecture*}	$\{\mathcal{E}_c, \mathcal{E}_g, \mathcal{E}_a\}$

Figure 4: A synthetic example of QLM with a vocabulary of $n = 3$ terms. The orthogonal rays are the eigenvectors of the ellipsoids. ρ_q is not smoothed thus degenerates onto a ray. ρ_{d_1} rotates towards the direction of observed query dependencies and is thus ranked higher.

3.4 Final Considerations

The estimation and scoring process of quantum language models retains classical unigram LMs and KL divergence as special cases. The classical unigram LM is recovered by restricting the maximization in Eq. 10 to diagonal density matrices and including into the sequence of projectors $\mathcal{P}_d$ only an orthonormal basis, such as the elements of $\mathcal{E}$. Classical KL divergence is recovered by noting that if ρ_q and ρ_d are diagonal density matrices, they share the same eigensystem. Hence, $|q_i\rangle = |d_i\rangle$ and $\lambda_{qi} = \theta_{qi}$, $\lambda_{di} = \theta_{di}$, where $\vec{\theta}_q$, $\vec{\theta}_d$ are the parameters of classical unigram LMs for the query and the document respectively. In this setting, $\langle q_i|d_j\rangle^2 = 0$ for $i \neq j$ and the VN divergence reduces to classical KL, i.e. $-\Delta_{VN}(\rho_q\|\rho_d) = -\Delta_{KL}(\vec{\theta}_q\|\vec{\theta}_d) \stackrel{rank}{=} \sum_i \theta_{qi} \log \theta_{di}$.

In Figure 4, we report a synthetic example of the application of the model. We plot the density matrices obtained by the MLE (Section 3.2.1) on the sequence of projectors reported in the table. As usual in ad-hoc tasks, we smooth only the QLMs of the documents. The model corresponding to the query is a projector, i.e. it has two zero eigenvalues, because we did not apply smoothing. If the dependencies are included in the sequence $\mathcal{P}_o$, the MLE rotates the corresponding QLM towards the direction spanned by the observed projector (i.e. $\mathcal{K}_{ca}$). This entails that the model ρ_{d_1} is considered more similar to the query than the model ρ_{d_2} which corresponds to a classical language model.

4. EVALUATION

4.1 Experimental Setup

All the experiments reported in this work were conducted using the open source Indri search engine (version 5.3)[3]. The test collections used are reported in Table 1. We choose the collections in order to vary (1) the collection size and (2) collection type. This will produce a comprehensive test set in order to verify the properties of our approach. All the collections have been stemmed with the Krovetz stemmer. Both documents and queries have been stopped using the standard INQUERY stopword list. For all the methods, the Dirichlet smoothing parameter μ is set to the default Indri value ($\mu = 2500$). The optimization of all the other free parameters for the proposed model and the baselines is done using five-fold cross validation using coordinate ascent [18] with mean average precision (MAP) as the target metric. The performance is measured on the top 1000 ranked documents. In addition to MAP, for newswire collections we report the early precision metric @10 (precision at 10) and for web collections with graded relevance judgements we report the recent ERR@10, which correlates better with click metrics than other editorial metrics [6]. The statistical significance of differences in the performance of tested methods is determined using a two-sided Fisher's randomization test [29] with 25,000 permutations evaluated at $\alpha < 0.05$.

Name	Content	# Docs	Topic Numbers
SJMN	Newswire	90,257	51-150
TREC7-8	Newswire	528,155	351-450
WT10g	Web	1,692,096	451-550
ClueWeb-B	Web	50,220,423	51-200

Table 1: Summary of the TREC collections used to support the experimental evaluation.

4.2 Methodology

Our experimental methodology goes as follows. In a first step, we compare our QLM approach to a unigram Language Modeling baseline (denoted `LM`) based on Dirichlet smoothing [35], which is a strong bag-of-words baseline. This comparison is done by assigning uniform superposition weights to each dependency κ, i.e. $\sigma_i = 1/\sqrt{|\kappa|}$, where $|\kappa|$ is the cardinality of κ (denoted `QLM-UNI`). This step has two main objectives: (1) to test if quantum probability can bring better performance than a standard bag-of-words model and (2) to test if uniform superposition weights are a reasonable baseline setting.

As a second step, we test the proposed model against the strong non bag-of-words MRF model, which has shown to be highly effective especially for large scale web collections [19, 20]. We test the full dependence version of the model (denoted `MRF-FD`) which captures dependencies between all the query terms and thus is the most natural choice for a comparison with our model. However, `MRF-FD` exploits both proximity (#uw) and exact matching (#1). As our model only exploits proximity as an indicator of dependence, we also propose to test the variant `MRF-FD-U`, which is a MRF using only the proximity feature. This could provide interesting insights on how the models score based upon the same evidence.

Finally, we propose a slightly more elaborate version of our model (denoted `QLM-IDF`) in which the superposition weights are no more assumed to be uniform. Instead, we assign to each σ_i the normalized *idf* weight of the corresponding term w_i. The objective is to test if a more reasonable parametrization of superposition weights can improve the retrieval effectiveness.

[3]http://www.lemurproject.org

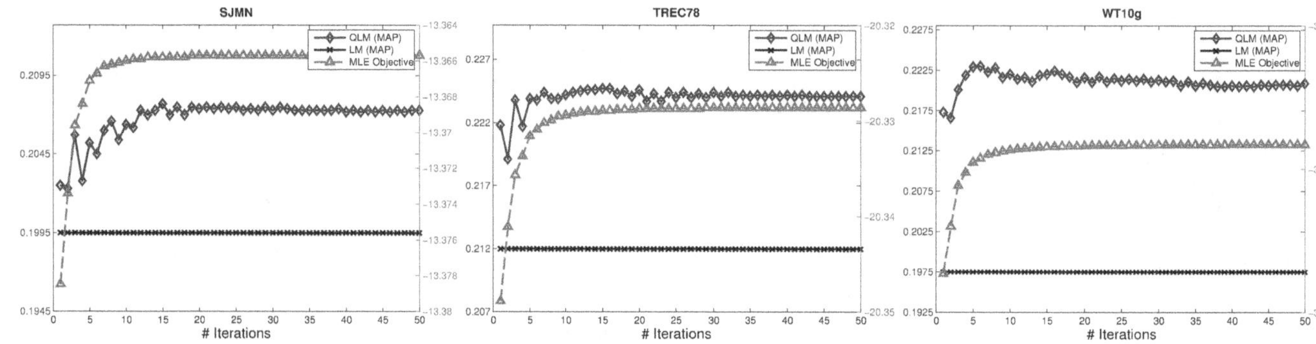

Figure 5: Plots of MAP (QLM-UNI and LM) and MLE objective against the number of updates of the density matrix for SJMN, TREC7-8 and WT10g (left, center and right).

All the results exposed in this paper have been obtained by reranking. We rerank a pool of 20000 documents retrieved using `LM` in order to make a fair comparison between our method and the baselines.

4.3 Setting up QLM

4.3.1 *Building the Sequence of Projectors*

Very similarly to `MRF-FD`, given a query $\mathcal{Q} = \{q_1, \ldots, q_n\}$, we assume that the interesting dependencies to consider correspond to the power set $\mathcal{P}(\mathcal{Q})$[4]. In order to build the set of projectors for the given document we apply Algorithm 1.

Algorithm 1 Builds the sequence $\mathcal{P}_d$ given $\mathcal{W}_d$, $\mathcal{Q}$

Require: $\mathcal{W}_d, \mathcal{Q}$

$\mathcal{P}_d \leftarrow \emptyset$
for $\kappa \in \mathcal{P}(\mathcal{Q})$ **do**
  for $\#(\kappa, \mathcal{W}_d)$ **do**
    $\mathcal{P}_d \leftarrow \mathcal{P}_d \oplus m(\kappa)$ *%Adds the projector to the sequence*
  end for
end for
return $\mathcal{P}_d$

For each dependency κ in $\mathcal{P}(\mathcal{Q})$, the algorithm scans the document sequence $\mathcal{W}_d$. For each occurrence of κ, it adds a projector $m(\kappa)$ to the sequence $\mathcal{P}_d$. The function $\#(\kappa, \mathcal{W}_d)$ returns how many times the dependency κ is observed in $\mathcal{W}_d$. Therefore, the algorithm adds as many projectors as the number of detected compound dependencies. Note that by looping on $\mathcal{P}(\mathcal{Q})$, we are actually implementing the strategy exposed in Section 3.1.3, i.e. adding both the dependence and all of its subsets. Following Section 3.1.3, we choose to parametrize $\#$ as the unordered window operator in Indri ($\#$uw$L$). Therefore, a given dependency κ will be detected if the component terms appear in any order in a fixed-window of length $L = l|\kappa|$. This kind of adaptive parametrization of the window length is state-of-the-art for dependence models such as `MRF-FD` [2, 19]. For all the dependence models, the coordinate ascent for l spans $\{1, 2, 4, 8, 16, 32\}$, which is a robust pool covering different window lengths, including the standard value ($l = 4$) for `MRF-FD`.

[4]In order to keep the retrieval complexity reasonable both for MRF and QLM, we limit ourselves to query term subsets with at most three terms.

4.3.2 *MLE Convergence Analysis*

Before doing any comparisons, we answer the questions related to the construction of a quantum language model, i.e. (1) how to initialize $\widehat{\rho}_{(0)}$? (2) when to stop the update process? In order to help the maximum likelihood process to converge faster, we initialize the matrix $\widehat{\rho}_{(0)}$ to the density matrix corresponding to the classical maximum likelihood language model $\vec{\theta}^{ML}$ of the document or query under consideration. This is a diagonal matrix $\widehat{\rho}_{(0)} = \text{diag}(\vec{\theta}^{ML})$. We also tested with the uniform density matrix, as suggested in [15], but we found that the MAP was severely harmed.

In order to address the second question, we analyze the variation of MAP with respect to the maximum number of iterations $n_{it} \in [1, 50]$. The damping factor γ is optimized over the set of values $\Gamma = \{0, 0.1, ..., 0.9\}$. The iterative process stops before n_{it} if the change in the likelihood is below 10^{-4}. In order to check for possible variations due to the collection type, we plot the iteration-MAP curve for two similar collections, i.e. SJMN and TREC7-8, and a web collection, WT10g. We also plot the training objective in Eq. 10 over the set of topics: $\frac{1}{|\mathcal{R}|}\sum_{d \in \mathcal{R}} \log \mathcal{L}_{\mathcal{P}_d}(\widehat{\rho}_d)$, where $\mathcal{R}$ is the multiset of retrieved documents. The trend is shown in Figure 5. Generally, at any number of iterations, the MAP stays significantly above the baseline. It seems that there is a good correlation between likelihood maximization and MAP, although one can note some overfitting at high number of iterations. Capping by $10 \leq n_{it} \leq 20$ seems a good trade-off between likelihood maximization and MAP. However, to provide a fair comparison with the baselines, we choose to include n_{it} as a free parameter to train by coordinate ascent.

4.4 Results

The results discussed in this section are compactly reported in Table 2.

4.4.1 *Language Modeling Baseline*

From the comparisons with the `LM` baseline, one can see that `QLM-UNI` outperforms `LM` significantly, with relative improvements in MAP going up to 12.1% in the case of WT10g collection and 19.2% for the ClueWeb-B collection. This seems to be in line with the hypothesis formulated in [19], for which dependence models may yield larger improvements for large collections.

The weight-normalization problem seems to be addressed automatically: our model does not need for any combina-

	SJMN		TREC7-8		WT10g		ClueWeb-B	
	P@10	MAP	P@10	MAP	ERR@10	MAP	ERR@10	MAP
`LM`	.3064	.1995	.4230	.2120	.1068	.1975	.0718	.1003
`MRF-FD-U`	.3138	.2071	.4350	.2228	.1136	.2097	.0828	.1103
`MRF-FD`	.3074	.2061	.4460	.2243	.1147	.2146	.0881	.1137
`QLM-UNI`	**.3181**	.2077	**.4480**	.2240	.1162	$.2215^{\alpha\beta}$	$\mathbf{.1015}^{\alpha\beta}$	$\mathbf{.1196}^{\alpha\beta}$
	(+1.4/+3.5)	*(+0.3/+0.8)*	*(+3.0/+0.4)*	*(+0.5/-0.1)*	*(+2.2/+1.3)*	*(+5.6/+3.2)*	*(+22.6/+15.2)*	*(+8.4/+5.2)*
`QLM-IDF`	.3170	**.2093**	.4450	**.2254**	**.1176**	$\mathbf{.2264}^{\alpha\beta}$	$.0997^{\alpha\beta}$	$.1189^{\alpha\beta}$
	(+1.0/+3.1)	*(+1.1/+1.6)*	*(+2.3/-0.2)*	*(+1.2/+0.5)*	*(+3.5/+2.6)*	*(+7.9/+5.5)*	*(+20.4/+13.1)*	*(+7.8/+4.5)*

Table 2: Evaluation of the performance for the five methods tested. Best results are highlighted in boldface. Numbers in parentheses indicate relative improvement (%) in MAP over `MRF-FD-U`/`MRF-FD`. All the results for dependence models are significant with respect to the baseline `LM`. The symbols $^{\alpha}$,$^{\beta}$ means statistical significance over `MRF-FD-U`, `MRF-FD` respectively.

tion weights. Moreover, it is robust across the folds. From an analysis of the optimal values of the parameters obtained across the different folds, we found that optimal window sizes were $l \in \{1, 2\}$. This can be explained by considering that in the current version of QLM, it is possible to decide if the dependency is detected or not, but the model cannot discriminate its "importance". If one decides to increase l, more inaccurate dependencies will be detected and the performance will be deteriorated. However, even with a larger window size, statistical significance over `LM` is maintained. From these considerations, we suggest $l = 2$ as a default setting for our model. Finally, the results endorse that our QLM does not need an engineered estimation of superposition weights to perform well.

4.4.2 Markov Random Fields Baseline

As a second test, we report the results obtained for the `MRF-FD` and `MRF-FD-U` baselines. These have proved to be very robust non bag-of-words baselines [2, 19, 20]. Contrary to our model, MRF does not handle dependency information in the estimation phase. One has to specify the coefficients $(\lambda_T, \lambda_O, \lambda_U)$ for the combination of dependence and independence scores. To limit per-fold overfitting, for the dependence models, we first train combination parameters $(\lambda_f \in \{0, 0.01, ..., 1\})$ then l for each fold. For `MRF-FD-U`, we set $\lambda_O = 0$.

Results show that for SJMN and TREC7-8, `QLM-UNI`, `MRF-FD` and `MRF-FD-U` are essentially equivalent. However, for the two Web collections, our model significantly outperforms both MRF variants. On ClueWeb-B, statistical significance is attained for the two reported measures. As conjectured in [19], noisy web collections could be a more discriminative testbed for dependence models. Optimal l values for `MRF-FD` were very small for SJMN ($l \in \{1, 2\}$) in contrast to the optimal setting for ClueWeb-B ($l \in \{16, 32\}$). In [19], the authors suggest that for homogenous newswire collections a small window is enough to capture useful dependencies, while for large, noisy web collections, a larger span must be set. However, the performances obtained by our model seem to suggest that it can greatly benefit from term dependencies, on a variety of collections, even when a small window size is used. This elucidates the fact that even short range information can be extremely useful if integrated in the estimation phase. In order to get a more comprehensive view on such issues, we trained on the entire set of ClueWeb-B topics three versions of `MRF-FD-U`, each obtained by clamping a different value of $l \in \{1, 2, 4\}$. The best performing model obtained a MAP of 10.91. It seems that our model can exploit this short range information in a better way than MRF models.

4.4.3 Setting Superposition Weights

Our last test aimed at verifying if a more reasonable setting of the superposition weights could further improve retrieval performance. For a dependency $\{w_1, \ldots, w_K\}$, we set $\sigma_i = \sqrt{idf_{w_i} / \sum_i idf_{w_i}}$. This has the effect of attributing a larger count to the more "important" term in the dependency. `QLM-IDF` generally increases MAP. However, this is not the case for ClueWeb-B. From a query-by-query analysis, we noticed that `QLM-IDF` increases the performance for noisy queries by promoting the most "important" terms in unnecessary subsets. For multiword expressions such as ClueWeb-B topics *continental plates* and *rock art*, weighting by *idf* may be misleading by assigning more weight to one of the terms. In this cases, a uniform parametrization is far more effective. This demonstrates that there is still room for improvement by a clever tuning of superposition parameters, for example by leveraging feature functions [2, 3].

4.5 Complexity Analysis

Complexity issues can be tackled by noting that it is not necessary to manipulate $n \times n$ matrices. We associate a dimension for each query term and an additional dimension for a "don't care" term that will store the probability mass for the other terms in the vocabulary. Therefore, a multinomial over n points is reduced to a multinomial over $|\mathcal{Q}| + 1$ points, where $|\mathcal{Q}|$ is the number of unique terms in the query and the additional dimension is simply a relabeling of the other term events. In this way, the QLM to manipulate is $k \times k$, where $k = |\mathcal{Q}| + 1$. The eigendecomposition generally requires $O(k^3)$. The iterative process requires at most $|\mathcal{P}(\mathcal{Q})| = 2^{|\mathcal{Q}|}$ matrix multiplications for the expectation step, where $2^{|\mathcal{Q}|}$ is the maximum number of *unique* projectors in $\mathcal{P}_d$ and 2 matrix multiplications for the maximization step. In the case the likelihood is decreased, $|\Gamma|$ more iterations are done giving a worst-case complexity of $O(n_{it}|\Gamma|2^k + k^3)$, i.e. if each iteration needs damping. We showed that $10 \leq n_{it} \leq 20$ is enough; we use $|\Gamma| = 10$ and k is very small for title queries, which make the process computationally tractable. In practice, we observed that the damping process is very effective and dramatically improves convergence speed. As an example, the mean number of iterations for ClueWeb-B when $n_{it} = 15$ is 7.02 which is orders of magnitude less than $n_{it}|\Gamma| = 150$. Finally, we conjecture that such process could be executed at indexing time, thus eliminating any additional on-line costs.

5. CONCLUSION

In this paper, we presented a principled application of quantum probability for IR. We showed how the flexibility of vector spaces joined with the powerful tools of probabilistic calculus can be mixed together for a flexible, yet principled account of term dependencies for IR. In our model, dependencies are neither represented as additional dimensions, nor stochastically as joint probabilities. They assume a new status as *superposition* events. The relationship of such an event to the traditional term events are encoded by the off-diagonal values in the corresponding projection matrix. Both documents and queries are associated to density matrices estimated through the maximization of a product, which in the classical case reduces to a likelihood. As our model integrates the dependencies in the estimation phase, it has no need for combination parameters. Experiments showed that it performs equivalently to the existing dependence models on newswire test collections and outperforms the latter on web data.

To our knowledge, this work provides the first experimental result showing the usefulness of this kind of probabilistic calculus for IR. The marriage between vector spaces and probability can be endlessly improved in the future. One straightforward direction is to relax the assumption that single terms represent orthogonal projectors. This could lead to a new way of integrating latent directions as estimated by purely geometric methods such as Latent Semantic Indexing (LSI) [7] into a probabilistic model. In this work, we did not exploit the full machinery of complex vector spaces. We do not have a practical justification for the use of the complex field for IR tasks. However, we speculate that this could bring improved representational power and thus remains an interesting direction to explore. At last, we believe that our model could be potentially applied to other fields of natural language processing only by means of a principled Bayesian calculus capable of manipulating density matrices. We hope that this work will foster future research in this direction.

6. ACKNOWLEDGMENTS

We would like to thank the anonymous reviewers for their valuable comments and suggestions.

7. REFERENCES

[1] J. Bai, Y. Chang, H. Cui, Z. Zheng, G. Sun, and X. Li. Investigation of partial query proximity in web search. In *Proc. of WWW*, pages 1183–1184, 2008.

[2] M. Bendersky and W. B. Croft. Modeling higher-order term dependencies in information retrieval using query hypergraphs. In *Proc. of SIGIR*, pages 941–950, 2012.

[3] M. Bendersky, D. Metzler, and W. B. Croft. Parametrized concept weighting in verbose queries. In *Proc. of SIGIR*, pages 605–614, 2011.

[4] R. Blume-Kohout. Hedged maximum likelihood estimation. *Phys. Rev. Lett.*, 105:200504, 2010.

[5] R. Blume-Kohout. Optimal, reliable estimation of quantum states. *New J. Phys.*, 12:043034, 2010.

[6] O. Chapelle, D. Metzler, Y. Zhang, P. Grinspan. Expected reciprocal rank for graded relevance In *Proc. of CIKM*, 2009.

[7] S. Deerwester, S. T. Dumais, G. W. Furnas, T. K. Landauer, and R. Harshman. Indexing by latent semantic analysis. *JASIST*, 41:391–407, 1990.

[8] J. L. Fagan. Automatic phrase indexing for document retrieval. In *Proc. of SIGIR*, pages 91–101, 1987.

[9] J. Gao, J. Y. Nie, G. Wu, and G. Cao. Dependence language model for information retrieval. In *Proc. of SIGIR*, pages 170–177, 2004.

[10] A. Gleason. Measures on the closed subspaces of a hilbert space. *Journ. Math. Mech.*, 6:885–893, 1957.

[11] K. S. Jones, S. Walker, and S. E. Robertson. A probabilistic model of information retrieval: development and comparative experiments. *Inf. Proc. Manag.*, pages 779–840, 2000.

[12] M. Lease. An improved markov random field model for supporting verbose queries. In *Proc. of SIGIR*, pages 476–483, 2009.

[13] C. Lee, G. G. Lee, and M. G. Jang. Dependency structure applied to language modeling for information retrieval. *ETRI*, 28(3):337–346, 2006.

[14] Y. Lv and C. Zhai. Positional language models for information retrieval. In *Proc. of SIGIR*, pages 299–306, 2009.

[15] A. I. Lvovsky. Iterative maximum-likelihood reconstruction in quantum homodyne tomography. *Journ. Opt. B6*, pages S556–S559, 2004.

[16] M. Melucci. Deriving a quantum information retrieval basis. *The Computer Journal*, 2012.

[17] M. Melucci and K. Rijsbergen. Quantum mechanics and information retrieval. *Advanced Topics in Information Retrieval*, 33:125–155, 2011.

[18] D. Metzler and W. Bruce Croft. Linear feature-based models for information retrieval. *Inf. Retr.*, 10(3):257–274, 2007.

[19] D. Metzler and W. B. Croft. A markov random field model for term dependencies. In *Proc. of SIGIR*, pages 472–479, 2005.

[20] D. Metzler, T. Strohman, Y. Zhou, and W. B. Croft. Indri at TREC 2005: Terabyte Track. In *Proc. of TREC*, 2005.

[21] M. Mitra, C. Buckley, A. Singhal, and C. Cardie. An analysis of statistical and syntactic phrases. In *Proc of RIAO*, pages 200–217, 1997.

[22] W. Morgan, W. Greiff, and J. Henderson. Direct maximization of average precision by hill-climbing, with a comparison to a maximum entropy approach. In *Proc. of HLT-NAACL*, pages 93–96, 2004.

[23] M. A. Nielsen and I. L. Chuang. *Quantum Computation and Quantum Information.* Cambridge University Press, 2004.

[24] J. H. Park, W. B. Croft, and D. A. Smith. A quasi-synchronous dependence model for information retrieval. In *Proc. of CIKM*, pages 17–26, 2011.

[25] B. Piwowarski, I. Frommholz, M. Lalmas, and K. van Rijsbergen. What can quantum theory bring to information retrieval. In *Proc. of CIKM*, pages 59–68, 2010.

[26] M. Pretti. A message-passing algorithm with damping. *J. Stat. Mech.*, page P11008, 2005.

[27] J. Řeháček, Z. Hradil, E. Knill, A. I. Lvovsky. Diluted maximum-likelihood algorithm for quantum tomography. *Phys. Rev. A*, 75:042108, 2007.

[28] G. Salton, C. S. Yang, and C. T. Yu. A Theory of Term Importance in Automatic Text Analysis. *JASIST*, 26(1):33–44, 1975.

[29] M. D. Smucker, J. Allan, and B. Carterette. A comparison of statistical significance tests for information retrieval evaluation. In *Proc. of CIKM*, pages 623–632, 2007.

[30] F. Song and W. B. Croft. A general language model for information retrieval. In *Proc. of SIGIR*, pages 279–280, 1999.

[31] M. Srikanth and R. Srihari. Biterm language models for document retrieval. In *Proc. of SIGIR*, pages 425–426, 2002.

[32] H. Umegaki. Conditional expectation in an operator algebra. *Kodai Mathematical Seminar Reports*, 14(2):59–85, 1962.

[33] K. van Rijsbergen. *The Geometry of Information Retrieval.* Cambridge University Press, 2004.

[34] M. K. Warmuth and D. Kuzmin. Bayesian generalized probability calculus for density matrices. *Machine Learning*, 78(1-2):63–101, 2009.

[35] C. Zhai. Statistical language models for information retrieval a critical review. *Found. Trends Inf. Retr.*, 2(3):137–213, 2008.

[36] J. Zhao and Y. Yun. A proximity language model for information retrieval. In *Proc. of SIGIR*, pages 291–298, 2009.

[37] X. Zhao, P. Zhang, D. Song, and Y. Hou. A novel re-ranking approach inspired by quantum measurement. In *Proc. of ECIR*, pages 721–724, 2011.

[38] G. Zuccon and L. Azzopardi. Using the quantum probability ranking principle to rank interdependent documents. In *Proc. of ECIR*, page 357–369, 2010.

Copulas for Information Retrieval

Carsten Eickhoff
Delft University of Technology
Delft, The Netherlands
c.eickhoff@acm.org

Arjen P. de Vries
CWI Amsterdam
Amsterdam, The Netherlands
arjen@acm.org

Kevyn Collins-Thompson
Microsoft Research
Redmond, WA, USA
kevynct@microsoft.com

ABSTRACT

In many domains of information retrieval, system estimates of document relevance are based on multidimensional quality criteria that have to be accommodated in a unidimensional result ranking. Current solutions to this challenge are often inconsistent with the formal probabilistic framework in which constituent scores were estimated, or use sophisticated learning methods that make it difficult for humans to understand the origin of the final ranking. To address these issues, we introduce the use of *copulas*, a powerful statistical framework for modeling complex multi-dimensional dependencies, to information retrieval tasks. We provide a formal background to copulas and demonstrate their effectiveness on standard IR tasks such as combining multidimensional relevance estimates and fusion of results from multiple search engines. We introduce copula-based versions of standard relevance estimators and fusion methods and show that these lead to significant performance improvements on several tasks, as evaluated on large-scale standard corpora, compared to their non-copula counterparts. We also investigate criteria for understanding the likely effect of using copula models in a given retrieval scenario.

Categories and Subject Descriptors

Information Systems [**Information Retrieval**]: Retrieval models

Keywords

Relevance models; Multivariate relevance; Ranking; Probabilistic framework; Data fusion.

1. INTRODUCTION

In response to user queries, today's search systems typically return lists of documents ranked by system estimates of relevance. In traditional IR retrieval models, each document's relevance towards the query is expressed as term overlap between query and document [42]. Early on, researchers began exploring alternative, non-topical document quality criteria such as document recency, credibility or monetary cost. More recently, through a combination of improved algorithms and greatly increased data scale, significant gains in ranking quality and user satisfaction based on employing non-topical factors such as textual complexity [12] or suitability for children [17] have begun influencing the ranking process. Given a scenario such as child-friendly information search, non-topical quality criteria can clearly have a strong influence on usefulness of a document for a specific user. A perfectly relevant document that is not understandable due its complex sentence structure or excessive use of jargon will have significantly diminished user relevance.

Beyond the value of individual relevance factors, there can be complex, non-linear *dependencies* between relevance factors. For example, relevance criteria such as topicality and credibility might appear independent for some document subsets, but extreme values in one dimension may influence the other in a way that is not easily captured by state-of-the-art approaches. As a concrete example, take TREC 2010's faceted blog distillation task [32], that aims at retrieving topically relevant non-factual blog feeds. Here, the relevance space has two dimensions: topicality and subjectivity. Figure 1 shows the distribution of relevance scores for Topic 1171, *"mysql"*, across these two relevance dimensions. We can note an apparent correlation in the lower left part of the graph that weakens as scores increase. To underline this, we computed Pearson's ρ between the two dimensions for the lower score third ($\rho = 0.37$), the upper region ($\rho = -0.4$), as well as the overall distribution ($\rho = 0.18$). Apparently, the dependency structure of the joint distribution of relevance, in this case, is not easily described by a linear model. Consequently, we can expect dissatisfying performance of linear combination models. And, indeed, when inspecting the performance of a linear combination model with empirically learned mixture parameters λ, Topic 1171 receives an average precision of only 0.14, well below the method's average across all topics of 0.25. In the course of this work, we will discuss practical means of addressing cases like the present one and will finally revisit this example to demonstrate the effect of our proposed method.

While the machine learning, information retrieval, data mining and natural language processing communities have significant expertise in estimating topical document relevance and additional criteria in isolation, the commonly applied combination schemes have tended to be *ad hoc* and ignore the problem of modeling complex, multi-dimension dependencies. In practice, they follow statically weighted lin-

SIGIR'13, July 28–August 1, 2013, Dublin, Ireland.

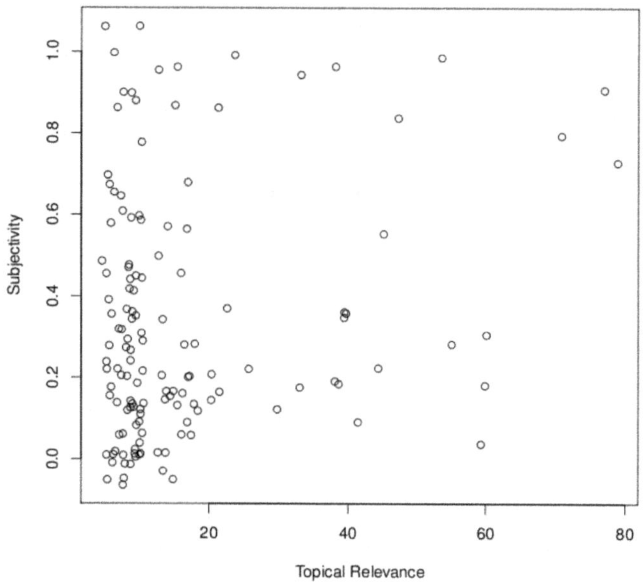

Figure 1: Distribution of bivariate relevance scores for TREC 2010 Blog Track Topic 1171, "mysql".

ear combinations with empirically determined mixture parameters [42] or deploy sophisticated learning to rank techniques that tend to offer only limited insight to humans about why they were weighted highly for relevance. Ideally, we would demand realistic, yet formally-grounded combination schemes that can lead to results that are both effective and with human-interpretable justification.

In a different context, the field of quantitative risk management has devised *copulas*, a flexible, varied class of probability density functions that are designed to capture rich, non-linear dependencies efficiently in multi-dimensional distributions. Copulas work by decoupling the marginal distributions of the data from the underlying dependency structure of the joint distribution. In particular, copulas can account for so-called tail dependencies, i.e., dependencies that play up at the extreme values of the interacting distributions. As an example, let us consider two commodities traded on the stock market, such as rare earth metals and pork bellies. The two commodities are sufficiently different to make the related market segments quasi-independent. However, extreme market situations have been shown to cause investor panics that reach across otherwise independent segments and cause previously unseen interrelationships [9].

This work makes three contributions to the state of the art in relevance modelling. **(1)** We give a detailed introduction to the formal framework of copulas and describe how to estimate them from empirical data. **(2)** Based on a number of sizeable standard data sets such as the Blogs08 collection [32], we demonstrate the merit of using copulas for multivariate relevance estimation. **(3)** In a related effort, we address the task of score fusion based on historic submissions to the TREC *ad hoc* task.
The remainder of this paper is structured as follows: Section 2 gives a historic overview of IR relevance frameworks, prior work on multidimensional relevance models, score fusion approaches, as well as, examples of copula applications from different fields. Section 3 formally introduces the theoretical foundation of copulas and details key techniques in their application. In Sections 4 and 5 we demonstrate their merit at the tasks of estimating multidimensional relevance scores as well as fusing prior TREC runs. Section 6 further discusses the experimental results and aims at identifying those domains of IR for which copulas are most promising. Section 7 concludes the paper with a concise summary of our findings.

2. RELATED WORK

Over the past decades, a wide range of partially overlapping relevance frameworks have been proposed, a few prominent examples include [44, 22, 34, 8]. They unanimously consider relevance as a complex, potentially multidimensional concept that may be composed from a number of constituents. In the further course of this section, we will focus on the practical implementation of formal relevance estimation schemes employed in information retrieval and related disciplines. Schamber *et al.* [45] radically revised the definition of relevance, causing a growing interest in probabilistic relevance modelling in the research community. First openly applied at the third TREC competition, the BM25 retrieval model [43] represents a performance landmark that is still valid today (with slight variations such as the 2004 integration of multiple weighted fields [42]). In 1996, Persin *et al.* [38] introduced the idea of retrieval result lists ranked by their probability of relevance, as an alternative to the previously dominant binary retrieval scenario. Two years later, Ponte and Croft proposed the use of language modelling techniques to determine topical relevance [39]. One of the first notions of non-topical relevance was expressed in Kleinberg's work on hubs and authorities [26] in which the author introduces two document-specific relevance notions independent of the query. Lavrenko and Croft [28, 29] pursued a line of work on dedicated relevance models.
While the formal combination of several individual relevance facets in one model has not been extensively studied, there has been an interesting thread of research on score fusion. The task is to combine the result rankings of multiple independent retrieval systems in order to compensate for local inaccuracies of single engines. Early approaches to the task were based on evidence aggregation in the form of products and sums of scores across individual systems [19]. The fused ranking is based on the absolute value of the cross-system aggregates. Vogt *et al.* [51] first introduced linear interpolation of multiple model rankings for system fusion. Aslam and Montague [5] proposed a probabilistic rank-based method for direct combination of multiple engines. Later on, they devised a similar method based on a majority voting scheme between various retrieval systems [35]. [36] proposed a score normalization scheme that is more robust to outliers in the distribution of relevance than the previously used min/max technique. There has been an extensive body of work on estimating the distribution of relevance scores for document ranking. Recent examples include the work by Arampatzis and Stephenson [4], Kanoulas *et al.* [25], and, Cummins [14]. Manmatha et al. [33] estimated a search engine's score distribution as a mixture of normal and exponential distributions, for relevant and non-relevant documents respectively. They

used the resulting distributions for score fusion across multiple engines, but did not attempt to model dependencies in the joint score distribution, instead treating the scores as independent and averaging probabilities, or discarding 'bad' engines altogether.

In 2002, Wu and Crestani [52] introduced the first of what would become a group of fusion approaches that define an explicit weighting scheme under which the original result lists are combined. [7] and [15] employ various quality notions such as the degree to which a document satisfies a given relevance criterion to dynamically adapt the weighting scheme to the underlying distribution of relevance. In 2005, Craswell *et al.* investigated relevance model combination by linearly combining constituent scores in the log domain [13]. Tsikrika and Lalmas applied Dempster-Shafer theory for the aggregation of independent relevance criteria in web retrieval in the form of belief functions [49]. Gerani *et al.* [21] propose non-linear score transformations prior to the standard weighted linear combination step. Their solid results demonstrate the need for models whose capabilities go beyond linear dependency structures between relevance dimensions.

In recent years, the variety of IR applications has become significantly more diverse. As a consequence, universal relevance models have become less viable in many areas. Tasks such as legal IR, expert finding, opinion detection or the retrieval of very short documents (e.g., tweets) have brought forward strongly customised relevance models tailored towards satisfying a given task (e.g., [24, 6]). Especially for the retrieval of structured (XML) documents, score combination schemes are of central importance to combine evidence across multiple structural fields within a document. Despite the numerous potential issues pointed out by Robertson *et al.* [42], most state-of-the-art approaches to XML retrieval rely on linear models [31]. An advance towards the formal combination of several independent relevance criteria in the form of prior probabilities for language models has been made by Kraaij *et al.* [27] for the task of entry page search. To date, however, most universally applicable relevance models still rely on pure linear combinations of relevance criteria that disregard the underlying data distribution or potential dependencies between the considered dimensions.

Learning to rank (L2R) has been established as an alternative approach for signal combination. The aim is to apply machine learning methods to either directly infer a document ranking or a ranking function from a wide range of features, potentially including the previously-discussed relevance criteria [10, 40, 30]. The downside of this approach is that the resulting models tend to yield only limited insight for humans. The classic approach of developing a unifying formal retrieval model would in our view provide better means to increase not just overall performance, but also our qualitative understanding of the problem domain.

By introducing copulas for information retrieval, this work proposes a way for closing the gap between linear combinations (that break with the probabilistic framework in which the constituent scores were estimated) and non-linear machine-learned models (that offer only limited insight to scientists and users).

Copulas have been traditionally applied for risk analyses in portfolio management [18] as well as derivatives pricing [9] in quantitative finance. Recently, however, there are several successful examples from unrelated disciplines. Renard *et al.* estimate water flow behaviour based on Gaussian copulas [41]. Onken *et al.* apply copulas for spike count analysis in neuroscience [37]. In meteorology, copulas have been used to combine very high-dimensional observations for the task of climate process modelling [47]. To the best of our knowledge, there has been no prior application of the copula framework to information retrieval problems.

3. COPULAS

At this point, we will give a brief introduction of the general theoretical framework of copulas, before applying them to various IR tasks in subsequent sections. For a more comprehensive overview, please refer to [46] for more detail and pointers to further reading.

The term copula was first introduced by Sklar [48] to describe multivariate *cumulative distribution functions* (*cdfs*) that allow for a formal decoupling of observations from dependency structures. Formally, given

$$X = (x_1, x_2, \dots, x_k)$$

a k-dimensional random vector with continuous margins

$$F_k(x) = \mathbb{P}[X_k \leq x]$$

we can map our observations to the unit cube $[0,1]^k$ as

$$U = (u_1, u_2, \dots u_k) = (F_1(x_1), F_2(x_2), \dots F_k(x_k)).$$

This is where our copulas come into play. A k-dimensional copula C describes the joint cumulative distribution function of random vector U with uniform margins.

$$C : [0,1]^k \to [0,1]$$

This approach has two obvious practical benefits: (1) Separating marginals and dependency structure allows for more straightforward estimation or approximation of each component in isolation. (2) An explicit model of dependency is scale-invariant. The copula describes a reference case of dependency on the unit cube $[0,1]^k$ that can be applied to arbitrary random vectors without further adjustment.

A number of key properties make copulas an appealing theoretical framework for a wide number of applications, so we summarize those now.

- Like all cdfs, a copula $C(u_1, u_2, \dots, u_k)$ is increasing in each component u_i

- A marginal component u_i can be isolated by setting all remaining components to 1:

$$C(1, \dots, 1, u_i, 1, \dots, 1) = u_i$$

- If a single component u_i in U is zero, the entire copula is zero:

$$C(u_1, \dots, u_{i-1}, 0, u_{i+1}, \dots, u_k) = 0$$

- Most importantly, we can assume general applicability of the copula framework, since, as a consequence of Sklar's Theorem [48], for each k-dimensional cdf F and all x_i in $[-\infty, \infty]$ and $1 \leq i \leq k$, there exists a copula C with

$$F(x_1, \dots, x_k) = C(F_1(x_1), \dots, F_k(x_k))$$

3.1 Extreme conditions

Before applying the copula framework to problems in information retrieval, let us visit a number of extreme conditions of dependency that frequently occur in IR scenarios. **(1) Independence** of observations is a frequently assumed simplification in IR theory that leads to convenient (if naïve) probabilistic models. In the copula framework, independence of events can be captured by the so-called *independence copula* C_{indep}:

$$C_{indep}(U) = \exp(-\sum_{i=1}^{k} -\log u_i)$$

which is equivalent to the product across all constituent probabilities in U. **(2) Co-monotonicity** describes the case of perfect positive correlation between observations u:

$$C_{coMono}(U) = \min\{u_1, \ldots, u_k\}$$

(3) counter-monotonicity of observations is given in the opposite case of perfect negative correlation:

$$C_{counterMono}(U) = \max\{\sum_{i=1}^{k} u_i + 1 - k, 0\}$$

Consequently, each copula lies within the so-called Fréchet-Höffding bounds [23]:

$$C_{counterMono}(U) \leq C(U) \leq C_{coMono}(U)$$

3.2 Copula families

After having covered the foundations of copula theory let us inspect some concrete examples of copulas that will be used in the course of this work. Three general families of standard copulas have been proposed in the literature, whose corresponding equations are given right after their introduction in this paragraph: **(1) Elliptical copulas** are directly derived from known distributions and are based on standard distribution functions such as the Gaussian distribution or Student's t distribution. Equation 1 shows the Gaussian copula that requires the observed covariance matrix $\Sigma \in \mathbb{R}^{k \times k}$ as a parameter. Φ denotes the cdf of a standard normal distribution and Φ^{-1} its inverse. **(2) Archimedean copulas** are popular as they can be explicitly stated (note that due to their distribution dependency that is not the case for elliptical copulas) and typically depend on only a single degree of freedom. The parameter θ expresses the strength of dependency in the model. Equation 2 shows the Clayton copula whose θ-range is $[-1, \infty)\backslash\{0\}$. $\theta = -1$ represents counter-monotonicity, $\theta \to 0$ gives the independence copula and $\theta \to \infty$ approaches co-monotonicity. Finally, **(3) Extreme value copulas** are robust in cases of extreme observations. The Gumbel copula (Equation 3) has a parameter space of θ in $[1, \infty)$. For $\theta = 1$ we obtain the independence copula, and, for $\theta \to \infty$ we approach co-monotonicity.

$$C_{Gaussian}(U) = \Phi_\Sigma(\Phi^{-1}(u_1), \ldots, \Phi^{-1}(u_k)) \quad (1)$$

$$C_{Clayton}(U) = (1 + \theta(\sum_{i=1}^{k} \frac{1}{\theta}(u_i^{-\theta} - 1)))^{\frac{-1}{\theta}} \quad (2)$$

$$C_{Gumbel}(U) = \exp(-(\sum_{i=1}^{k} (-\log(u_i))^{\theta})^{\frac{1}{\theta}}) \quad (3)$$

Figure 3.2 shows contour plots of a number of bivariate standard copulas. The concrete choice of copula family and instantiation has been frequently reported to depend on the application domain [46]. If no prior knowledge about the dependency structure, e.g., prevalence of asymptotic or tail dependencies, is available, practitioners often resort to goodness-of-fit tests or measures of tail dependency in order to choose an appropriate model. We will describe the use of these techniques in the subsequent sections when applying copulas for information retrieval problems.

3.3 Fitting copulas to observations

In the case of elliptical copulas, the fitting process is limited to calculating means and covariance matrices from the available observations. Here, the only degree of freedom is the concrete choice of distribution function (e.g., Gaussian vs. Student) that best approximates the original distribution that generated the observations. In the non-elliptical case, the task is to determine optimal settings of θ. Commonly, this is achieved by means of maximum likelihood estimates based on the available observations. This is also the approach chosen in this work. It should be noted that there are methods for direct empirical estimations of entire copula functions. The interested reader can find a good overview by Charpentier *et al.* [11] as a starting point for this line of research, the inclusion of which would however go beyond the scope of this initial exploration of copulas for information retrieval.

4. RELEVANCE ESTIMATION

In the previous section, we described the theoretical foundations of copulas including concrete ways of computing $C(U)$ from multivariate observations U. We now detail their application for relevance estimation in information retrieval. First, we separately estimate the probability of relevance $P_{rel}^{(k)}(d)$ and non-relevance $P_{non}^{(k)}(d)$ for a document d, under each of the k criteria (dimensions) – for example, topicality, recency, readability, etc. Next, we assume random observations U_{rel} and U_{non} to derive from these distributions and base two distinct copulas, C_{rel} and C_{non} on them.
Recall that these copulas should capture the dependencies between relevance criteria, in either the relevant (C_{rel}) or the non-relevant (C_{non}) documents retrieved. Since it is difficult to predict where these dependencies have the most effect, it is natural to consider three different general approaches of combining multivariate observation scores U into a single probability of relevance that can be used for resource ranking. **(1)** $CPOS(U_{rel})$ multiplies the independent likelihood of observing U_{rel} with the relevance copula C_{rel}, capturing only dependencies between the likelihoods of relevance. **(2)** $CNEG(U_{rel}, U_{non})$ normalizes the probability of relevance by the non-relevance copula $C_{non}(U_{non})$, capturing only the dependencies between the likelihoods of non-relevance. **(3)** $CODDS(U_{rel}, U_{non})$, finally, multiplies the probability of relevance by the ratio of the two copulas, modelling simultaneously the dependencies between both previous notions.

$$CPOS(U_{rel}) = C_{rel}(U_{rel}) \prod_{i=1}^{k} u_{rel,i}$$

$$CNEG(U_{rel}, U_{non}) = \frac{\prod_{i=1}^{k} u_{rel,i}}{C_{non}(U_{non})}$$

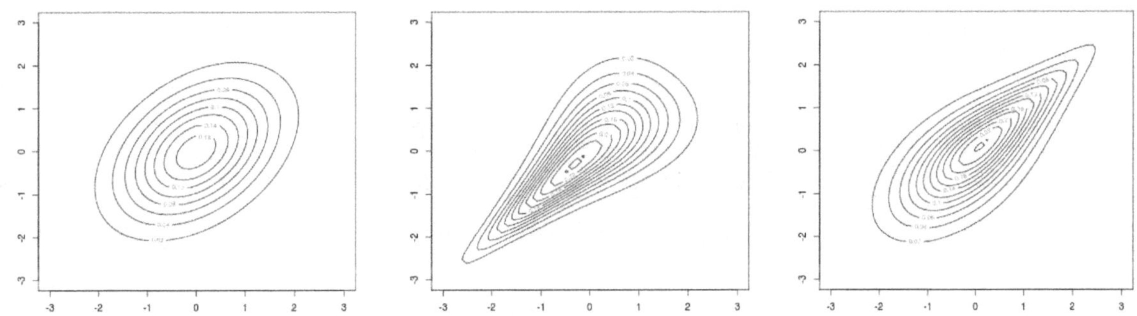

Figure 2: Examples of bivariate copula contour plots. (a) Gaussian copula, (b) Clayton copula with $\theta = 2.0$, (c) Gumbel copula with $\theta = 2.0$.

$$CODDS(U_{rel}, U_{non}) = \frac{C_{rel}(U_{rel})}{C_{non}(U_{non})} \prod_{i=1}^{k} u_{rel,i}$$

As performance baselines, we will compare to three popular combination methods from the literature: **(1)** $SUM(U_{rel})$ sums up the relevance scores across all criteria k and uses the sum as the final ranking criterion [19]. **(2)** $PROD(U_{rel})$ builds the product across all constituents [19]. Probabilistically, this combination scheme assumes independence across all criteria and can be expected to be too naïve in some settings where dependence is given. **(3)** Weighted linear combinations $LIN_{\Lambda}(U_{rel})$ build a weighted sum of constituents $u_{rel,i}$ with mixture parameters λ_i optimized by means of a parameter sweep with step size 0.1 [51]. It should be noted that all optimizations and parameter estimations, both for the baselines as well as for the copula models are conducted on designated training sets that do not overlap with the final test sets. We relied on the original training portion of the respective corpora. In the case that the original corpus did not specify a dedicated training set, we used a stratified 90%/10% split.

$$SUM(U_{rel}) = \sum_{i=1}^{k} u_{rel,i}$$

$$PROD(U_{rel}) = \prod_{i=1}^{k} u_{rel,i}$$

$$LIN_{\Lambda}(U_{rel}) = \sum_{i=1}^{k} \lambda_i u_{rel,i}$$

Based on three different standard datasets and tasks, we will highlight the merit of using copulas over the traditional approaches. Each of the settings specifies 2 individual relevance criteria ($k = 2$) which are crucial for user satisfaction given the retrieval task. Table 1 gives a high-level overview of the relevant corpora that we used. Each of them will be described in more detail in the three following sections. Depending on the strength of tail dependency in the data, we will see varying improvements for the three inspected settings. Comparable as the scenarios appear, there seem to be significant underlying differences in the distribution of relevant documents that influence the benefit from the use of copulas. In Section 6, we will dedicate some room to a detailed investigation of when the use of copula-based retrieval models is most promising.

Table 1: Overview of experimental corpora.

ID	# docs	# topics	# labels	year
Blogs08	1.3M	100	38.2k	2008
Delicious	339k	180	3.8k	2012
ODP	22k	30	1k	2009

4.1 Opinionated blogs

When conducting marketing analyses for businesses, researching customer reviews of products or gauging political trends based on voter opinions, it can be desirable to focus the search process on subjective, non-factual documents. The Text REtrieval Conference (TREC) accounted for this task within the confines of their Blog Track between the years 2006 and 2010 [32]. The aim of the task is to retrieve blog feeds that are both topically relevant and opinionated. Our experimental corpus for this task is the Blogs08 collection specifically created for the venue. The dataset consists of 1.3 million blog feeds and is annotated by more than 38k manually created labels contributed by NIST assessors.

Each document is represented as a two-component vector $U_{rel}^{(2)}$. The first component refers to the document's topical relevance given the query and the second represents its degree of opinionatedness. In order for a document to be considered relevant according to the judges' assessments, it has to satisfy both conditions. Topical relevance was estimated by a standard BM25 model and opinionatedness was determined using the output of a state-of-the-art open source classifier [1]. After an initial evaluation of the domain, we chose Clayton copulas (Equation 2) to represent the joint distribution of topicality and opinionatedness. Table 2 shows a juxtaposition of performance scores for the baselines as well as the various copula methods. The highest observed performance per metric is highlighted by the use of bold typeface, statistically significant improvements (measured by means of a Wilcoxon signed-rank test at $\alpha = 0.05$-level) over all competing approaches are denoted by an asterisk. Of the baseline methods, the score product PROD performs best. However, introducing the use of copulas, we observe that the highest performance was achieved using the *CPOS* copula,

Table 2: Copula-based relevance estimation performance for opinionated blogs ($k = 2$).

Method	P@5	P@10	p@100	BPREF	MRR	MAP
PROD	**0.413**	0.360	0.181	0.289	**0.692**	0.275
SUM	0.400	0.333	0.154	0.255	0.689	0.238
LIN	0.387	0.333	0.162	0.262	0.689	0.245
CPOS	**0.413**	**0.400***	**0.182**	**0.306***	**0.692**	**0.287***
CNEG	0.373	0.373	0.181	0.290	0.545	0.245
CODDS	0.373	0.360	**0.182**	0.283	0.544	0.242

Table 3: Copula-based relevance estimation performance for personalized bookmarks ($k = 2$).

Method	P@5	P@10	p@100	BPREF	MRR	MAP
PROD	0.084	0.079	**0.011**	0.051	0.192	0.043
SUM	0.095	0.095	**0.011**	0.071	0.192	0.055
LIN	0.126	**0.100***	**0.011**	0.077	**0.219***	0.063
CPOS	0.105	0.068	0.01	0.056	0.190	0.047
CNEG	**0.137***	0.090	0.010	**0.079***	0.184	**0.065**
CODDS	0.116	0.074	0.01	0.066	0.202	0.058

which gave statistically significant gains in MAP, Bpref and precision at rank 10 over all the baseline methods.

At this point, we revisit the example query (Topic 1171) that was discussed in the introduction and depicted in Figure 1. For this topic, we observed a clear non-linear dependency structure alongside a lower-than-average linear combination performance of $AP = 0.14$. When applying CPOS to the topic, however, we obtain $AP = 0.22$, an improvement of over 50%.

4.2 Personalized bookmarks

Finding and re-finding resources on the Internet are frequently accompanied and aided by bookmarking. What started as a local in-browser navigation aid, has in recent years become an active pillar of the social web society. Collaborative bookmarking platforms such as *Delicious*, *Furl*, or *Simpy* allow users to maintain an online profile along with bookmarks that can be shared among friends and collaboratively annotated by the user community. Research into tagging behaviour [2] found that a significant amount of the tags assigned to shared media items and bookmarks are of subjective nature and do not necessarily serve as objective topical descriptors of the content. This finding suggests that bookmarking has a strong personal aspect which we will cater for in our experiment. Vallet *et al.* [50] compiled a collection of more than 300k Delicious bookmarks and several million tags to describe them. For a share of 3.8k bookmarks and 180 topics, the authors collected manual relevance assessments along two dimensions, topical relevance of the bookmark given the topic and personal relevance of the bookmark for the user. This dataset is one of the very few corpora whose personalized relevance judgements were made by the actual users being profiled. We conduct a retrieval experiment in which we estimate topical and personal relevance for each document and use Gumbel copula models to model the joint distribution of facets. The set of relevant documents comprises only those bookmarks that satisfy both criteria and were judged relevant in terms of topicality and personal relevance. Table 3 shows an overview of the resulting retrieval performances. *CNEG* stands out as the strongest copula-based model but the overall ranking of systems depends on the concrete metrics evaluated. For some metrics such as precision at rank 10 and MRR, the linear combination baseline prevails, BPREF and precision at 5 documents favour CNEG.

4.3 Child-friendly websites

The third application domain that we will inspect is concerned with the retrieval of child-friendly websites. Children, especially at a young age, are an audience with specific needs that deviate significantly from those of standard web users. Even for adult users it has been shown that focussing the retrieval process on material of appropriate reading level can benefit user satisfaction [12]. In the case of children, this tendency can be expected to be even more pronounced since young users show very different modes of interaction with search engines that reflect their specific cognitive and motor capabilities [16]. Consequently, dedicated web search engines for children should focus their result sets on topically relevant, yet age-appropriate documents. [17] constructed a corpus of 22k web pages, 1,000 of which were manually annotated in terms of topical relevance towards a query as well as the document's likelihood of suitability for children. According to the authors, the class of suitable documents encompasses those pages that were topically relevant for children, presented in a fun and engaging way and textually not too complex to be understood. In our retrieval experiment, we account for both criteria and require documents to be both on topic as well as suitable for children in order to be considered relevant. Table 4 gives an overview of the resulting retrieval performance. In this setting, the various copula models show comparable result quality as the non parametric baselines. Linear combinations with empirically learned weights, however, were consistently the strongest method. We intend to explore the reasons for this in future work. However we note that the distribution of child-suitable ratings has a very large mode at zero, with only a small number of non-zero scores taking a limited number of possible discrete values - limiting the amount of useful dependency information available that copulas could exploit.

Table 4: Copula-based relevance estimation performance for child-friendly websites ($k = 2$).

Method	P@5	P@10	p@100	BPREF	MRR	MAP
PROD	0.240	0.143	0.051	0.221	0.349	0.196
SUM	0.246	0.157	0.052	0.213	0.340	0.200
LIN	**0.320***	**0.187***	**0.071***	**0.275***	**0.357**	**0.235***
CPOS	0.238	0.140	0.053	0.215	0.351	0.200
CNEG	0.242	0.140	0.048	0.223	0.349	0.194
CODDS	0.241	0.143	0.052	0.220	0.349	0.196

5. SCORE FUSION

Previously, we investigated the usefulness of copulas for modelling multivariate document relevance scores based on a number of (largely) orthogonal document quality criteria. Now, we will address a different, closely related problem: *score fusion* (also known as an instance of data fusion). In this setting, rather than estimating document quality from the documents, we attempt to combine the output of several independent retrieval systems into one holistic ranking. This challenge is often encountered in the domains of metasearch or search engine fusion. To evaluate the score fusion performance of copula-based methods, we use historic submissions to the TREC Adhoc and Web tracks. We investigate 6 years of TREC (1995 - 2000) and fuse the document relevance scores produced by several of the original participating systems. Intuitively, this task closely resembles the previously addressed relevance estimation based on individual document properties. In practice, as we will show, the scenario differs from direct relevance estimation in that retrieval systems rely on overlapping notions of document quality (e.g., a variant of *tf/idf* scoring) and are therefore assumed to show stronger inter-criteria dependencies than individual facets of document quality might. Systematically, however, we address a set of document-level scores $U_{rel}^{(k)}$, originating from k retrieval systems, exactly in the same way as we did document quality criteria in the previous section.

As performance baselines, we will rely on two popular score fusion schemes, *CombSUM* and *CombMNZ*[19]. CombSUM adds up the scores of all k constituent retrieval models and uses the resulting sum as a new document score. CombMNZ tries to account for score outliers by multiplying the cross-system sum by $NZ(U)$, the number of non-zero constituent scores.

$$CombSUM(U_{rel}) = \sum_{i=1}^{k} u_{rel,i}$$

$$CombMNZ(U_{rel}) = NZ(U_{rel}) \sum_{i=1}^{k} u_{rel,i}$$

We introduce statistically principled, copula-based extensions of these established baseline methods: corresponding to CombSUM and CombMNZ, we define *CopSUM* and *CopMNZ* that normalize the respective baseline methods by the non-relevance copula.

$$CopSUM(U_{rel}, U_{non}) = \frac{\sum_{i=1}^{k} u_{rel,i}}{C_{non}(U_{non})}$$

$$CopMNZ(U_{rel}, U_{non}) = \frac{NZ(U_{rel}) \sum_{i=1}^{k} u_{rel,i}}{C_{non}(U_{non})}$$

Due to the close relationship to the baseline methods, the effect of introducing copulas is easily measurable. Based on empirical evidence, we employ Clayton copulas to estimate $C_{non}(U_{non})$.

Table 5 compares the baselines and copula methods in terms of MAP gain over the best, worst and median historic system run that were fused. Each performance score is averaged over 200 repetitions of randomly selecting k individual runs with k ranging from 2 to 10 for each year of TREC. Statistically significant improvements over the respective baseline method, *i.e.* of CopSUM over CombSUM and CopMNZ over CombMNZ, are determined by a Wilcoxon signed-rank test at $\alpha = 0.05$ level and are denoted by an asterisk.

Regarding the baseline methods, CombSUM and CombMNZ perform equally well on average, but with a clear dataset bias. On TREC 4, 8 and 9, CombSUM performs consistently better than CombMNZ. For TREC 5, 6 and 7, the inverse is true. With the exception of TREC 4, the fused rankings do not match the performance of the single strongest run that contributed to the fusion.

Introducing the copula methods led to consistent improvements over their non-copula baseline counterparts. In 104 out of 168 cases, the copula-based fusion methods gave statistically significant gains, with only 14 out 168 performing worse than the corresponding baseline method. The copula-based methods achieved, on average, 7% gains over the corresponding baseline when comparing to the strongest fused system, 4% gain on median systems and 2% gain on the weakest systems.

Fusion robustness

There are significant differences in fusion effectiveness between individual editions of TREC. Comparing TREC 4 and TREC 6, for example, we observe that TREC 6 fusion results typically showcase performance losses in comparison to the best original run and very high gains for the weakest systems. We seek an explanation in the imbalance in performance of the original systems. Very weak systems have the potential of decreasing the overall quality of the fused result list by boosting the scores of non-relevant documents. As the number of very weak systems increases, so does the chance for performance losses introduced by fusion. When inspecting the number weak submissions (defined as having an MAP score that is at least 2 standard deviations lower than the average score across all participants) included in our fusion experiments, we find that, indeed, our TREC 6 sample includes ~27% more weak systems than that of TREC 4.

In order to further investigate the influence of weak runs on overall fusion performance and to measure the proposed methods' robustness against this effect, we turn to the 10-system fusion scenario and inject more and more weak systems among the regular ones. Figure 3 shows how the fusion improvement over the single strongest system of TREC 4 is affected as the number of weak submissions ranges from 0 to 9 out of 10. As before, each data point is an average across 200 fusions of randomly drawn runs. In the ideal setting, in which there are no weak systems, we note higher performance gains than in the uncontrolled scenario that was shown in Table 5. As the number of weak systems injected into the fusion increases, performance scores quickly drop. As noted earlier, CombSUM performs slightly better on TREC 4 than CombMNZ. This difference, however, is not further influenced by the number of weak systems. The copula-based fusion methods are more resistant to the influence of weak systems. We note the divide between copula-methods and baseline approaches growing as the number of weak systems increases. Each baseline system score is well-separated from the respective copula-based variant. Error bars in Figure 3 were omitted to prevent clutter.

6. DISCUSSION

In Section 4, we investigated three different domains in which we apply copulas to model the joint distribution of multivariate relevance scores. For each of these settings, we could observe varying degrees of usefulness of the proposed copula scheme. While for child-friendly web search, the linear baseline performed best, we achieved significant improvements in the opinionated blog retrieval setting. At this point, we investigate the reason for this seeming imbalance in performance gains in order to find a way of deciding for which problem domains the application of copulas is most promising.

One of the key properties of copulas is their ability to account for tail dependencies. Formally, tail dependence describes the likelihood that component $u_{rel,i}$ within the observation vector $U_{rel}^{(k)}$ will take on extremely high or low values,

Table 5: Score fusion performance based on historic TREC submissions. Evaluated in percentages of MAP improvements over the best, median, and worst original systems that were fused.

TREC 4	2 runs			4 runs			6 runs			8 runs			10 runs		
	Best	Med.	Worst	Best	Med.	Worst	Best	Med.	Worst	Best	Med.	Worst	Best	Med.	Worst
CombSUM	-9.8	-	118	-4.2	20	1128	0.0	33.5	1709	3.0	39.6	2344	3.9	48.5	3116
CopSUM	-9.6*	-	116	-4.2	20.5*	1136	0.0	33.8*	1721	3.2*	40.0*	2350	4.0	49.2*	3125*
CombMNZ	-9.5	-	116	-5.4	18.3	1071	-1.1	31.6	1675	2.1	38.3	2310	3.6	48.0	3106
CopMNZ	-9.5	-	115	-5.5	18.2	1080	-1.0	31.9*	1689*	1.8	38.6*	2318*	3.8*	48.0	3117*

TREC 5	2 runs			4 runs			6 runs			8 runs			10 runs		
	Best	Med.	Worst	Best	Med.	Worst	Best	Med.	Worst	Best	Med.	Worst	Best	Med.	Worst
CombSUM	-5.6	-	268	-10.6	12.5	614	-6.9	26.5	955	-5.3	34.3	1031	-5.6	40.1	1479
CopSUM	-5.2*	-	274*	-9.9*	13.0*	613	-6.7*	28.0*	972*	-4.9*	35.0*	1050*	-5.2*	43.3*	1503*
CombMNZ	-4.6	-	269	-6.7	17.4	652	-3.5	30.9	986	-2.5	38.2	1074	-3.3	43.5	1526
CopMNZ	-4.5	-	274*	-6.5	17.8*	667*	-3.1*	32.2*	991	-2.4	38.7*	1092	-3.0*	46.0*	1554*

TREC 6	2 runs			4 runs			6 runs			8 runs			10 runs		
	Best	Med.	Worst	Best	Med.	Worst	Best	Med.	Worst	Best	Med.	Worst	Best	Med.	Worst
CombSUM	-18.5	-	486	-24.6	7.8	2235	-24.0	29.6	3950	-22.8	44.9	5585	-22.1	56.9	7685
CopSUM	-17.7*	-	471	-23.1*	9.1*	2279*	-22.9*	32.1*	4075*	-21.2*	48.3*	5699*	-20.8*	58.2*	7702
CombMNZ	-17.0	-	491	-18.6	15.5	2537	-18.1	38.8	4386	-16.7	55.0	6111	-17.3	65.0	8117
CopMNZ	-16.3*	-	490	-17.2*	17.4*	2601*	-17.9	40.5*	4458*	-16.7	59.6*	6202*	-16.4*	66.8*	8170

TREC 7	2 runs			4 runs			6 runs			8 runs			10 runs		
	Best	Med.	Worst	Best	Med.	Worst	Best	Med.	Worst	Best	Med.	Worst	Best	Med.	Worst
CombSUM	-9.3	-	132	-16.2	6.2	303	-11.7	25.9	504	-12.8	30.0	708	-14.5	36.3	863
CopSUM	-9.4	-	145*	-15.8*	6.5*	321*	-11.1*	27.2*	538*	-12.3*	34.1*	734*	-13.8*	39.1*	877
CombMNZ	-8.8	-	130	-13.7	9.4	347	-10.1	28.1	538	-10.9	32.8	745	-13.1	38.5	891
CopMNZ	-8.8	-	139*	-13.3*	10.1*	363*	-10.2	30.5*	565*	-10.7	34.7*	786*	-12.4*	40.4*	922

TREC 8	2 runs			4 runs			6 runs			8 runs			10 runs		
	Best	Med.	Worst	Best	Med.	Worst	Best	Med.	Worst	Best	Med.	Worst	Best	Med.	Worst
CombSUM	-15.9	-	475	-11.6	8.1	1188	-11.5	16.9	3194	-7.7	21.8	2739	-5.4	21.8	3372
CopSUM	-16.1	-	488	-10.1*	8.3	1201	-10.9*	16.7	3195	-7.3*	22.3*	2755	-4.3*	22.4	3397
CombMNZ	-17.2	-	421	-11.8	7.6	1273	-12.9	15.1	3209	-9.8	18.6	2660	-7.2	19.2	3266
CopMNZ	-17.3	-	447*	-11.2	7.9*	1292	-12.8	14.9	3216	-9.2*	19.7*	2685	-6.7*	20.5*	3301*

TREC 9	2 runs			4 runs			6 runs			8 runs			10 runs		
	Best	Med.	Worst	Best	Med.	Worst	Best	Med.	Worst	Best	Med.	Worst	Best	Med.	Worst
CombSUM	-9.0	-	173	-14.9	20.4	473	-15.6	17.4	178	-21.3	18.9	202	-27.9	12.6	204
CopSUM	-8.5*	-	188*	-13.7*	21.2*	499*	-15.3	17.9	182	-20.9	19.2*	207	-26.6*	13.1*	206
CombMNZ	-11.0	-	155	-19.0	14.5	435	-17.4	14.4	172	-25.3	12.6	186	-32.7	4.7	184
CopMNZ	-10.7	-	167	-17.9*	16.0*	432	-17.1	14.7	176	-24.8*	13.0*	190	-30.4*	5.1*	187

as another component $u_{rel,j}$ with $i \neq j$ also takes an extreme value. The strength of this correlation in extreme regions is expressed by the *tail dependency indices* I_U and I_L for upper and lower tail dependency, respectively. Higher values of I signal stronger dependencies in the respective tail regions of the distribution.

$$I_U = P\{X_1 > F_i^{-1}(u_i) | X_2 > F_j^{-1}(u_j)\}$$

$$I_L = P\{X_1 \leq F_i^{-1}(u_i) | X_2 \leq F_j^{-1}(u_j)\}$$

The literature has brought forward a number of estimators of the tail indices. We use the R implementation of Frees *et al.*'s method [20].

Tail index estimates serve as good tools for separating domains where we are likely to observe performance gains (blog and bookmark retrieval) and those that do not match linear combination performance (child-friendly search). Based on the respective copula models that we fit to our observations, the blog retrieval ($I_L = 0.07$) and personalized bookmarking ($I_U = 0.49$) show moderate tail dependencies while the child-friendly web search task has no recognizable dependency among extrema ($I_L = I_U = 0$). Since the comparison of absolute tail index scores across observations is not meaningful, we are interested in a method to further narrow down the expected performance. To this end, we took a closer look at the actual data distribution, and investigated goodness-of-fit tests that are used to determine how well an assumed theoretical distribution fits the empirical observations. The higher the likelihood of our observations to have been generated by the copula models that we estimated, the higher resulting performance we can expect. We apply a standard Anderson-Darling test [3] to determine how well the observations are represented by the copula models. In the personalized bookmarking setting, we obtain $p = 0.47$ and for the blog data $p = 0.67$ for the null hypothesis of the observations originating from the present copula model. As we suspected based on the tail dependency strength, the child-friendly web search data only achieved a probability of fit of $p = 0.046$.

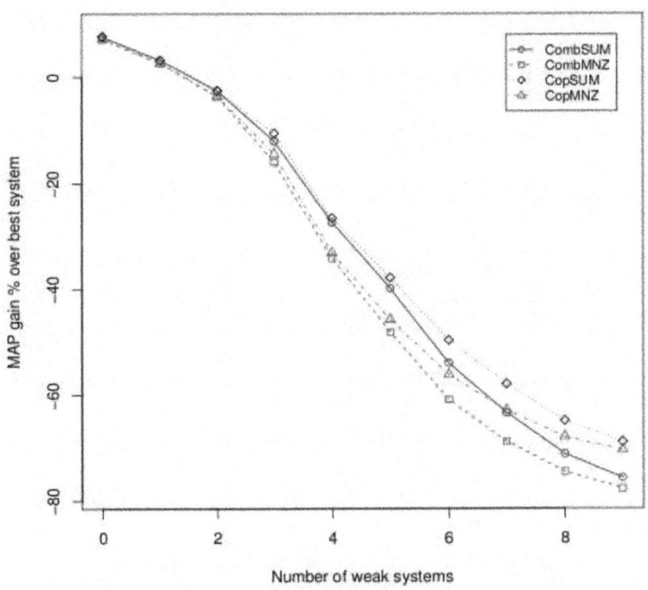

Figure 3: Performance in terms of MAP when $0 \ldots 9$ **out of** 10 **fused original systems are weak.**

To summarize, in this section, we have shown how a combination of tail dependence indices and goodness-of-fit tests can be used to help differentiate between domains that may benefit from copula-based retrieval models and those that may not.

7. CONCLUSION

In this work we introduced the use of *copulas*, a powerful statistical framework for modeling complex dependencies, for information retrieval tasks. We demonstrated the effectiveness of copula-based approaches in improving performance on several standard IR challenges. First, we applied copulas to the task of multivariate document relevance estimation, where each document is described by several potentially correlated relevance criteria. We learned and evaluated copula models for three different IR tasks, using large-scale standard corpora: (1) opinionated blog retrieval; (2) personalized social bookmarking; and (3) child-friendly web search, obtaining significant improvements on the first two of these tasks. Second, we introduced copula-based versions of two existing score fusion methods, COMB-Sum and COMB-MNZ, and showed that these improve the performance of score fusion on historic TREC submissions, in terms of both effectiveness and robustness, compared to their non-copula counterparts. Finally, we investigated the performance differences of copula models between different domains, and proposed the use of tail dependency indices and goodness-of-fit tests to understand the likely effect of using copulas for a given scenario.

In future work, there are a number of interesting challenges remaining in applying copula-based models to information retrieval. **(1)** The independence assumption between individual terms in queries and documents is a long-standing simplification in document and language modelling. Most attempts at incorporating more powerful dependency models into the retrieval process resulted in limited performance improvements at best. We would like to investigate the use of copulas in order to more realistically approximate the complex underlying term dependency structure. **(2)** During our investigation of the blog retrieval scenario, we encountered examples of non-linear multivariate distributions of relevance and briefly pointed out the different correlation regimes that exist within the joint distribution. While the current single-copula models have been shown to outperform linear combination models at capturing such structures, we would like to proceed to inspecting mixture models in which individual copulas account for certain data ranges to represent the underlying regimes better than a single holistic model could. **(3)** This work represents an exploratory study that aims to introduce the copula framework to the information retrieval community. For reasons of simplicity and brevity, it is based on data-driven estimation of copula parameters θ. It would, however, be interesting to build on the large body of previous work on formal modelling of the probability of relevance, to derive custom information retrieval copulas from the assumed distribution of relevance among documents.

8. REFERENCES

[1] Alias-i. LingPipe 3.9.2. http://alias-i.com/lingpipe, 2013.

[2] M. Ames and M. Naaman. Why we tag: motivations for annotation in mobile and online media. In *SIGCHI 2007*. ACM.

[3] TW Anderson and D.A. Darling. A test of goodness of fit. *Journal of the American Statistical Association*, 49, 1954.

[4] Avi Arampatzis and Stephen Robertson. Modeling score distributions in information retrieval. *Information Retrieval*, 2011.

[5] J.A. Aslam and M. Montague. Bayes optimal metasearch: a probabilistic model for combining the results of multiple retrieval systems (poster session). In *Proceedings of SIGIR 2000*, pages 379–381. ACM.

[6] K. Balog, L. Azzopardi, and M. de Rijke. Formal models for expert finding in enterprise corpora. In *Proceedings of SIGIR 2006*, pages 43–50. ACM.

[7] G. Bordogna and G. Pasi. A model for a SOft Fusion of Information Accesses on the web. *Fuzzy Sets and Systems*, 148(1):105–118, 2004.

[8] P. Borlund. The concept of relevance in IR. *JASIST*, 2003.

[9] J.P. Bouchaud and M. Potters. *Theory of financial risk and derivative pricing: from statistical physics to risk management.* Cambridge University Press, 2003.

[10] C. Burges, T. Shaked, E. Renshaw, A. Lazier, M. Deeds, N. Hamilton, and G. Hullender. Learning to rank using gradient descent. In *ICML*, pages 89–96. ACM, 2005.

[11] A. Charpentier, J.D. Fermanian, and O. Scaillet. The estimation of copulas: Theory and practice. *Copulas: From theory to Application in Finance. Risk Publications*, 2007.

[12] K. Collins-Thompson, P.N. Bennett, R.W. White, S. de la Chica, and D. Sontag. Personalizing web search results by reading level. In *CIKM 2011*. ACM.

[13] N. Craswell, S. Robertson, H. Zaragoza, and M. Taylor. Relevance weighting for query independent evidence. In *Proceedings of SIGIR 2005*, pages 416–423. ACM.

[14] Ronan Cummins. Measuring the ability of score distributions to model relevance. In *Information Retrieval Technology*. Springer, 2011.

[15] C. da Costa Pereira, M. Dragoni, and G. Pasi. Multidimensional relevance: A new aggregation criterion. *ECIR 2009*.

[16] A. Druin, E. Foss, L. Hatley, E. Golub, M.L. Guha, J. Fails, and H. Hutchinson. How children search the internet with keyword interfaces. In *Proceedings of the 8th International Conference on Interaction Design and Children*, pages 89–96. ACM, 2009.

[17] C. Eickhoff, P. Serdyukov, and A.P. de Vries. A combined topical/non-topical approach to identifying web sites for children. In *WSDM 2011*. ACM.

[18] P. Embrechts, F. Lindskog, and A. McNeil. Modelling dependence with copulas and applications to risk management. *Handbook of heavy tailed distributions in finance*, 8(329-384):1, 2003.

[19] E. Fox and J. Shaw. Combination of multiple searches. *NIST Special Pub.*, 1994.

[20] E.W. Frees and E.A. Valdez. Understanding relationships using copulas. *North American actuarial journal*, 2(1), 1998.

[21] S. Gerani, C.X. Zhai, and F. Crestani. Score transformation in linear combination for multi-criteria relevance ranking. *ECIR 2012*.

[22] S.P. Harter. Psychological relevance and information science. *JASIS*, 43(9):602–615, 1992.

[23] W. Höffding. Scale-invariant correlation theory. *Schriften des Mathematischen Instituts und des Instituts fur Angewandte Mathematik der Universität Berlin*, 5(3):181–233, 1940.

[24] X. Huang and W.B. Croft. A unified relevance model for opinion retrieval. In *Proceeding of CIKM 2009*, pages 947–956. ACM.

[25] Evangelos Kanoulas, Keshi Dai, Virgil Pavlu, and Javed A Aslam. Score distribution models: assumptions, intuition, and robustness to score manipulation. In *SIGIR 2010*. ACM.

[26] J.M. Kleinberg. Authoritative sources in a hyperlinked environment. *Journal of the ACM (JACM)*, 46(5):604–632, 1999.

[27] W. Kraaij, T. Westerveld, and D. Hiemstra. The importance of prior probabilities for entry page search. In *SIGIR*. ACM, 2002.

[28] V. Lavrenko and W.B. Croft. Relevance based language models. In *Proceedings of SIGIR 2001*, pages 120–127. ACM.

[29] V. Lavrenko and W.B. Croft. Relevance models in information retrieval. *Language modeling for information retrieval*, pages 11–56, 2003.

[30] T.Y. Liu. Learning to rank for information retrieval. *Foundations and Trends in Information Retrieval*, 2009.

[31] W. Lu, S. Robertson, and A. MacFarlane. Field-weighted xml retrieval based on bm25. *Advances in XML Information Retrieval and Evaluation*, pages 161–171, 2006.

[32] C. Macdonald, R.L.T. Santos, I. Ounis, and I. Soboroff. Blog track research at trec. In *SIGIR Forum 2010*. ACM.

[33] R. Manmatha, Toni M. Rath, and Fangfang Feng. Modeling score distributions for combining the outputs of search engines. In *SIGIR 2001*.

[34] S. Mizzaro. Relevance: The whole history. *JASIS*, 1997.

[35] M. Montague and J.A. Aslam. Condorcet fusion for improved retrieval. In *Proceedings of CIKM 2002*, pages 538–548. ACM.

[36] M. Montague and J.A. Aslam. Relevance score normalization for metasearch. In *CIKM 2001*. ACM.

[37] A. Onken, S. Grünewälder, M.H.J. Munk, and K. Obermayer. Analyzing short-term noise dependencies of spike-counts in macaque prefrontal cortex using copulas and the flashlight transformation. *PLoS computational biology*, 5(11):e1000577, 2009.

[38] M. Persin, J. Zobel, and R. Sacks-Davis. Filtered document retrieval with frequency-sorted indexes. *JASIS*, 47(10):749–764, 1996.

[39] J.M. Ponte and W.B. Croft. A language modeling approach to information retrieval. In *Proceedings of SIGIR 1998*, pages 275–281. ACM.

[40] F. Radlinski and T. Joachims. Query chains: learning to rank from implicit feedback. In *SIGKDD*, pages 239–248. ACM, 2005.

[41] B. Renard and M. Lang. Use of a gaussian copula for multivariate extreme value analysis: Some case studies in hydrology. *Advances in Water Resources*, 30(4):897–912, 2007.

[42] S. Robertson, H. Zaragoza, and M. Taylor. Simple BM25 extension to multiple weighted fields. In *CIKM 2004*.

[43] S.E. Robertson, S. Walker, M.M. Hancock-Beaulieu, and M. Gatford. Okapi at TREC-3. Gaithersburgh, MD, 1994.

[44] T. Saracevic. Relevance reconsidered. In *Conference on Conceptions of Library and Information Science*, 1996.

[45] L. Schamber, M.B. Eisenberg, and M.S. Nilan. A re-examination of relevance: toward a dynamic, situational definition. *IPM*, 26(6):755–776, 1990.

[46] T. Schmidt. Coping with copulas. *Risk Books: Copulas from Theory to Applications in Finance*, 2007.

[47] C. Schoelzel, P. Friederichs, et al. Multivariate non-normally distributed random variables in climate research–introduction to the copula approach. *Nonlin. Processes Geophys.*, 15(5):761–772, 2008.

[48] A. Sklar. Fonctions de répartition à n dimensions et leurs marges. *Publ. Inst. Statist. Univ. Paris*, 8(1):11, 1959.

[49] T. Tsikrika and M. Lalmas. Combining evidence for relevance criteria: a framework and experiments in web retrieval. *ECIR 2007*.

[50] D. Vallet and P. Castells. Personalized diversification of search results. In *SIGIR 2012*. ACM.

[51] C.C. Vogt and G.W. Cottrell. Fusion via a linear combination of scores. *Information Retrieval*, 1(3):151–173, 1999.

[52] S. Wu and F. Crestani. Data fusion with estimated weights. In *CIKM 2002*. ACM.

Taily: Shard Selection Using the Tail of Score Distributions

Robin Aly, Djoerd Hiemstra
University Twente
The Netherlands
{r.aly,hiemstra}@ewi.utwente.nl

Thomas Demeester
Ghent University - iMinds
Belgium
thomas.demeester@intec.ugent.be

ABSTRACT

Search engines can improve their efficiency by selecting only few promising shards for each query. State-of-the-art shard selection algorithms first query a central index of sampled documents, and their effectiveness is similar to searching all shards. However, the search in the central index also hurts efficiency. Additionally, we show that the effectiveness of these approaches varies substantially with the sampled documents. This paper proposes Taily, a novel shard selection algorithm that models a query's score distribution in each shard as a Gamma distribution and selects shards with highly scored documents in the tail of the distribution. Taily estimates the parameters of score distributions based on the mean and variance of the score function's features in the collections and shards. Because Taily operates on term statistics instead of document samples, it is efficient and has deterministic effectiveness. Experiments on large web collections (Gov2, CluewebA and CluewebB) show that Taily achieves similar effectiveness to sample-based approaches, and improves upon their efficiency by roughly 20% in terms of used resources and response time.

Categories and Subject Descriptors

H.3.3 [**Information Storage and Retrieval**]: Search process

Keywords

Distributed Retrieval, Database Selection

1. INTRODUCTION

For large collections, search engines have to shard their index to distribute it over multiple machines. Search efficiency can be further increased by shard selection, that is, by querying a small number of promising shards for each query [5]. An important research challenge in this domain is the definition of shard selection algorithms that have to address the following two issues. First, selective shard search should be more efficient than searching all shards, and second, selective shard search should be as effective as searching all shards. In this paper, we investigate the tradeoff between efficiency and effectiveness of sharded search. We propose Taily, a new shard selection algorithm that represents shards by using parametric distributions of the document scores for a query. Taily is much more efficient while showing similar effectiveness, as compared to an exhaustive search.

State-of-the-art shard selection algorithms use a central sample index (CSI) that contains randomly selected documents from each shard [21, 22, 14]. The algorithms use the results of an initial search against the CSI to select the shards to be used in a second, sharded search. In the literature, the efficiency of shard selection algorithms is usually measured by resources used in the sharded search. In this paper, we argue that efficiency measures should also consider the resources spent during the initial search on the CSI, which can be substantial. For example, a common sample size in the literature is four percent [14], which results in a CSI that is bigger than an average shard once there are more than 25 shards. Searching a CSI that is as large as the average shard uses a considerable percentage of the resources required. For the common case that the algorithm selects two shards, the initial search uses roughly one third of the resources required for answering a query. In our experiments we show that our algorithm is more efficient than current sample-based methods, especially when also considering the resources of the initial search, while maintaining similar effectiveness.

Although the query response time is seldom investigated in the shard selection literature, it is often considered more important than the used resources, which are relatively cheap nowadays [9]. Whereas the search in a CSI can use a substantial amount of the total resources, the influence of its execution time on the total query response time can be more severe. In the above example, the initial search would roughly double the response time, assuming the parallel execution of the sharded search. We show that Taily's improvement over the query response time of current shard selection algorithms is particularly strong.

One aspect of sample-based methods that has not been studied so far is the effect of the particular random sample in the CSI on the search effectiveness. One might expect that, if samples are truly random and sufficiently large, different random samples would produce stable effectiveness of the search system in terms of precision or nDCG. We show in this paper that this expectation does not hold in practice. As we show in Section 5, different sample sizes of up to 4%

SIGIR'13, July 28–August 1, 2013, Dublin, Ireland.

of each shard, lead to substantially different effectiveness of the sharded search system. We believe that this variation in effectiveness is a drawback of the sample-based methods tested in this paper.

Like Kulkarni et al. [14] and Arguello et al. [3], Taily is used on clusters of machines in a cooperative search environment. Taily selects one or more shards by estimating the number of documents of a shard that are highly scored in the collection, which we model by the right tail of the score distributions in the collection and the shards. The basic idea of this approach has been proposed by Markov [15]. To estimate these score distributions, we follow the approach by Kanoulas et al. [12], who derive score distributions from statistics of features related to a query's terms (e.g. a term's language model score). Being based on statistics for each term in a vocabulary, Taily belongs to the class of vocabulary-based selection algorithms, which are often biased to larger shards and often show weaker performance than sample-based methods. Our contribution to the shard selection literature are threefold: first, experiments show that its effectiveness is similar or stronger than the effectiveness of sample-based methods, second, compared to a search in a CSI, its processing of feature statistics is more efficient, and results in a lower number of resources used in total and a faster query response time, and finally, compared to sample-based methods, the efficiency and effectiveness do not depend on the size or the sampled documents in a CSI.

The remainder of this paper is structured as follows. Section 2 describes related work on shard selection. Section 3 elaborates on Taily's shard selection algorithm. Section 4 defines the measures that we used to compare our method to state-of-the-art algorithms. Section 5 describes the experiments that we conducted to explore the performance of our search method. Section 6 concludes this paper.

2. RELATED WORK

In this section, we present shard selection algorithms from two classes that are most related to this work. Note that there is also a significant number of works on other approaches to shard selection. Because of space limitations, we refer the interested reader to Kulkarni et al. [14] where a more exhaustive list of related work is presented.

Most of the early shard selection algorithms are vocabulary-based: they represent shards by collection statistics about the terms in the search engine's vocabulary. The popular CORI algorithm by Callan et al. [6] represents a shard by the number of its documents that contain the terms of a vocabulary. The shards are ranked using the INDRI version of the $tf \cdot idf$ score function using the mentioned number as the frequency of each query term. CORI selects a fixed number of shards from the top of this ranking. Xu and Croft [23] build upon this approach by representing them by topical language models. The shards are ranked by the Kullback-Leibner divergence between the language models of the query and the topics. CORI and the algorithm by Xu and Croft characterize a shard by statistics over *all* its documents. We propose that shard selection algorithms should focus on documents with high scores because they contribute most to the system's effectiveness. The gGloss algorithm by Gravano and Garcia-Molina [10] selects shards based on the distribution of the vector space weights, which we refer to as features values. They assume that the distribution of the features is uniform. The algorithm ranks a shard by its expected score value calculated from the expectation of all feature values for a query. In this paper, we also consider the expected score, which we also infer through the expected feature values of the query terms. However, unlike the gGloss algorithm, we assume a gamma distribution of the score instead of a uniform distribution, and focus on the tail of the distribution, which contains the highly scored documents.

Algorithms from the second main class of are called sample-based algorithms because they use a central sample index (CSI) of documents from each shard for shard selection. The REDDE algorithm [21] ranks shards according to the number of the highest ranked documents that belong to this shard, weighted by the ratio between the shard's size and the size of the shard's documents in the CSI. The SUSHI algorithm [22] determine the best fitting function from a set of possible functions that between the estimated ranks of a shard's documents in the central index and their observed scores from the initial search. Using this function, the algorithm estimates the scores of the top-ranked documents of each shard. SUSHI selects shards based on their estimated number of documents among a number of top-ranked documents in the global ranking. REDDE and SUSHI assume that a shard's documents in the CSI are at equidistant ranks in the ranking of the shard. We believe that this assumption may be too strong because the actual ranks vary widely depending on the randomly sampled documents in the CSI, as we found in preliminary experiments. Kulkarni et al. [14] present a family of three algorithms that model shard selection as a process of the CSI documents voting for the shards that they represent. The vote of a shard is the sum of the votes of its documents. The algorithms select shards that have an accumulated vote higher than 0.0001. The three algorithms differ in how they model the strength of a document's vote. In the most effective method Rank-S, the strength of the votes is based on the score from the initial search and decays exponentially according to the rank of the document in this ranking. The base of the exponential decay function is a tuning parameter of the model.

The shard selection algorithm proposed in this paper is vocabulary-based. However, instead of considering all documents in a shard for ranking, it selects shards based on the highly scored documents of a shard similar to the described sample-based methods.

3. SHARD SELECTION USING THE TAIL OF SCORE DISTRIBUTIONS

Before formally introducing our shard selection algorithm in this section, we will explain our reasoning and the intuition behind it.

3.1 Intuition and Reasoning

Abstracting from sharded search, a search engine uses a score function that assigns each document in the collection a score. The documents are then ranked based on that score, and for most effectiveness measures, the top-ranked documents are the most influential. Now, a shard selection algorithm has to identify those shards whose documents can be left out from the complete ranking without hurting the effectiveness. We therefore design our shard selection algorithm to leave out shards with no or only few documents in the top of the complete document ranking. The number of

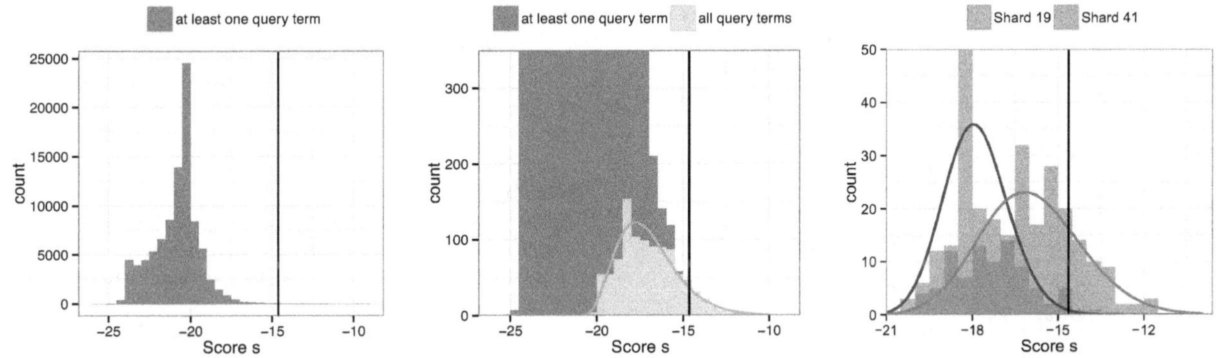

(a) Score distributions of documents with at least one query term.

(b) Score distributions focusing on the right tail.

(c) Score distribution in two shards of documents with all query terms.

Figure 1: Intuition of the shard selection process for the web-track query 843 *pol pot*. The vertical bar indicates the cut-off score of the $n_c = 100$ highest scored documents. The shown distributions are Gamma distributions fitted using the maximum likelihood and multiplied by the number of documents in the distribution.

considered top-ranked documents can vary depending on the search scenario. Our algorithm therefore considers a number of n_c highly scored documents. Expressed differently, these documents are the right tail of the collection's score distribution in response to the given query, and hence we name our shard selection algorithm Taily. Figure 1a shows the score frequency distribution of the query 843 *pol pot* in the Gov2 collection using language model scores. A search engine may want to preserve, e.g., $n_c = 100$ top-ranked documents. For our example, this corresponds to the documents that are assigned a language model score of -14.6 or higher for this query.

The more accurate our model is in the right tail of the score distribution, the more accurate we can expect our shard selection to be. Score distributions are typically dominated by low scores of documents that contain no or only few of the query terms. We do not expect that the tail of these score distributions can be accurately modeled. Instead, we model the score distribution of documents that contain *all* query terms, which include the top-ranked documents for most queries and empirically leads to a better fit of the right tail, see Figure 1b.

Taily selects shards based on the number of documents with a score above the cut-off score of the top-$n_c$documents. To estimate this number, Taily fits the score distribution in each of the shards, from which the probability of a document in this shard with a score above that cut-off point can be readily calculated. Because shards differ in size and absolute numbers of high-scoring documents, a shard with a low right-tail probability might still have a reasonable number of documents with scores above cut-off. We therefore also estimate the total number of documents that participate in the considered score distribution and select shards based on the expected number of documents that are above the cut-off score. For example, Figure 1c shows the empirical and fitted score distribution[1] of the shards 19 and 41 of topical shards generated by Kulkarni and Callan [13]. Most documents in the selected tail of the collection's score distribution belong to shard 41. Therefore, Taily prefers shard 41 over shard 19 for this query.

A popular way to estimate score distributions is to use scores of document samples from the top of the ranking [1]. However, because we avoid the use of a central sample index, this type of methods is not applicable here. Instead, following Kanoulas et al. [12], we infer the query dependent score distribution from query independent feature distributions that are summed in the score function. The parameters of the feature distributions form Taily's shard representation, which can be calculated offline.

In the following, we develop the Taily algorithm more formally. Section 3.2 introduces the used score function and Section 3.3 describes the statistics that form Taily's shard representation. Section 3.4 shows how these statistics are used to estimate the parameters of the score distributions for the shards, and for the whole collection. Section 3.5 describes how the number of documents with all query terms in the whole collection and per shard can be estimated. Using the estimates for the score distribution and the number of documents, we define Taily's shard selection criterion in Section 3.6.

3.2 Notation and Score Functions

We use the following notation throughout this paper. Queries and documents are denoted by lower case q and d respectively. Sets of documents are denoted by $\mathcal{D}$, and particular set is indicated by a subscript. In particular, let $\mathcal{D}_c$ be the set of documents in the total considered collection, and let $\mathcal{D}_1, ..., \mathcal{D}_N$ be the sets of documents of the N shards of this collection. We often refer to either the set of documents in the collection or the shards, for which we use the subscript i. Terms are denoted by lower case t, the query terms of a query q are denoted by $\vec{q}$. The length of document d is denoted by $dl(d)$, the frequency of term t in document d is written $c(t, d)$, and the number of documents from set $\mathcal{D}_i$ that contain term t at least once is given by $c(t, \mathcal{D}_i)$.

Taily infers a query's score distribution from the distributions of the features that constitute the query's score func-

[1]Note that Fig. 1 displays histograms with absolute frequencies. The fitted lines are the estimated density functions (based on the Gamma distribution), rescaled by the total number of documents included and its bin width, in order to allow visual comparison with the histograms.

tion. In general, our algorithm can be used with any score function that is a weighted sum of term-related feature values. Note that we consider score functions independently from their theoretical motivation. To facilitate experiments, which require a particular score function, we focus in this paper on the query likelihood model, as implemented in the Indri search engine[2]. The query likelihood model uses for a term t in a document d a term feature $f_t(d)$, which is defined as follows:

$$f_t(d) = \log\left(\frac{c(t,d) + \mu P(t|\mathcal{D})}{dl(d) + \mu}\right) \quad (1)$$

where $P(t|\mathcal{D}) = \frac{\sum_d c(t,d)}{\sum_d dl(d)}$ is the collection prior of term t, and μ is the Dirichlet smoothing parameter. Note that the term features in (1) are query independent. The score function $s(d)$ of a document d for a query q is a sum of the features for the query terms:

$$s(d) = \sum_{t \in \vec{q}} f_t(d). \quad (2)$$

In this paper we focus on score functions based on features that are related to a single query term. In future work, we plan to extend Taily to capture multi-term features such as ones used in the full dependency model [16], priors such as PageRank or spam scores, see [19] for a possible integration of these features into score functions.

3.3 Statistical Shard Representation

In order to infer the score distributions in shards and the collection, we represent each of them by the distribution parameters of term features. The main statistics of a feature f_t for term t in document set $\mathcal{D}_i$ are the expected value $E_i[f_t]$ and the variance $\text{var}_i[f_t]$ of the feature, which can be calculated as follows:

$$\begin{aligned} E_i[f_t] &= \frac{\sum_{d \in \mathcal{D}_i} f_t(d)}{c(t, \mathcal{D}_i)} && (3) \\ E_i[f_t^2] &= \frac{\sum_{d \in \mathcal{D}_i} f_t(d)^2}{c(t, \mathcal{D}_i)} \\ \text{var}_i[f_t] &= E_i[f_t^2] - E_i[f_t]^2 && (4) \end{aligned}$$

where $E_i[f_t^2]$ is the expected squared feature value. These quantities can be calculated by a single scan through the collection.

The language model score function used in this paper produces negative values. However, the Gamma distribution that we use for the score function is defined for positive values. To be able to shift the score distribution in the next section, we also store for each feature f its minimum value in the collection c:

$$min_c[f] = min\{f(d) | d \in \mathcal{D}_c, c(t,d) > 0\}$$

The expected feature values from (3), the feature variances in (4), and the above minimum values, form the representation used to calculate the score distribution in the shards and the total collection.

3.4 Inferring Score Distributions

Given the shard representation described in the previous section, we derive the distribution parameters of the query specific score distribution. Because the score function used in this paper produces negative scores, we instead consider a score distribution that is shifted by its minimum value, similar to Arampatzis et al. [2]:

$$s^*(d) = s(d) + \sum_{j=1}^{|\vec{f_q}|} min_c[f_j].$$

To keep our notation lean, we continue using s instead of s^* for the score function, keeping in mind that it is now positive defined. For a document set i, the expected score $E_i[s]$ and the score variance $\text{var}_i[s]$ can be derived from the definition of the score function in (2)

$$\begin{aligned} E_i[s] &= \sum_{j=1}^{|\vec{f_q}|} E_i[f_j] + \sum_{j=1}^{|\vec{f_q}|} min_c[f_j] && (5) \\ \text{var}_i[s] &= \sum_{j=1}^{|\vec{f_q}|} \text{var}_i[f_j] && (6) \end{aligned}$$

where $\vec{f_q}$ is the feature vector of the query terms in (2), and f_j is the jth feature in this vector. Equation 6 uses the simplifying assumption that the sum of covariances is zero. Note that we verified the validity of this assumption by repeating our experiment taking covariances into account, which did not result in a significant increase in effectiveness.

According to Kanoulas et al. [12], the distribution of language model scores is gamma distributed. The parameters of the distribution in document set i can be derived from the expected score and the variance by using the method of moments:

$$\begin{aligned} k_i &= \frac{E_i[s]^2}{\text{var}_i[s]} && (7) \\ \theta_i &= \frac{\text{var}_i[s]}{E_i[s]} && (8) \end{aligned}$$

where we used the definition of these parameters. Having the parameters k_i and θ_i for a document set i, we can define its cumulative score distribution function, which yields the probability of documents having a score greater than a score s' in a document set i:[3]

$$cdf_i(s') = P_i(s > s') = 1 - \frac{1}{\Gamma(k_i)} \gamma\left(k_i, \frac{s'}{\theta_i}\right) \quad (9)$$

where Γ is the Gamma function, γ is the incomplete Gamma function, and k_i and θ_i are the distribution parameters defined above. For the case of the whole collection and the example introduced previously, the values of the cumulative distribution function can be visualized as the percentage of documents with a higher score than −14.6 in Figure 1c.

3.5 Documents With All Query Terms

To make the probabilities from the cumulative density functions comparable, Taily uses the number of documents with all query terms in this set. To reduce the strength of assuming independence between the occurrence of query terms [7], we first estimate the number of documents that contain at least one *any* query term Any_i in a document

[2]`http://www.lemurproject.org/indri/`

[3]Note that cumulative distributions are usually defined in terms of the probability in the left tail. We differ from this practice because it simplifies the mathematical formalism used to describe Taily.

set i:

$$Any_i = |\mathcal{D}_i| \left(1 - \prod_{j=1}^{|\vec{q}|} \left(1 - \frac{c(t_j, \mathcal{D}_i)}{|\mathcal{D}_i|}\right)\right)$$

where the term $\prod_{j=1}^{|\vec{q}|} (1 - \frac{c(t, \mathcal{D}_i)}{|\mathcal{D}_i|})$ estimates the number of documents in document set i that have *none* of the query terms. Among the Any_i documents that contain at least one query term, we estimate the number of documents that contain *all* query terms All_i by assuming independence of the term occurrences:

$$All_i = Any_i \prod_{j=1}^{|\vec{q}|} \frac{c(t_j, \mathcal{D}_i)}{Any_i}. \tag{10}$$

where $c(t_j, \mathcal{D}_i)/Any_i$ is the probability that a document with term t_j appears in the documents in $\mathcal{D}_i$ that have at least one of the query term.

Our experiments show that this estimate produces strong and stable results. Important to note here, is that we want an efficient and lightweight algorithm, also during the preprocessing stage. Therefore, even for two-term queries, instead of counting the mutual term occurrences, quadratic in the vocabulary size, we estimate these based on the single-term occurrences.

3.6 Shard Ranking and Selection Criterion

Given the cumulative score distribution cdf_i and estimated number of documents that contain all query terms All_i for both the whole collection and each shard separately, we define Taily's shard selection criteria. Based on our intuition in Figure 1, we first estimate the cut-off score of a fixed number of top-ranked documents in the collection that at least should be in the sharded ranking. Let this number be n_c, which is a parameter of Taily. The probability of a document in the collection to be among the top-ranked documents can be calculated as:

$$p_c = \frac{n_c}{All_c} \tag{11}$$

where All_c is the estimated number of documents in the collection with all query terms. The cut-off score s_c of the top-n_c documents can be estimated using the inverse of the cumulative density function: $s_c = cdf_c^{-1}(p_c)$ where p_c is the probability defined above.

Using the score distribution in a shard i, we can calculate the probability that a document in this shard has a score higher than the cut-off score s_c: $p_i = cdf_i(s_c)$. The number of documents in shard i that have a score above s_c, written n_i, can then be readily estimated[4] by $n_i = All_i\, p_i$. The number of documents in shard i with all query terms is a mere estimation (see (10)), and the sum of estimates All_i for all shards not necessarily equals the overall estimate All_c. Experimentally, this appeared to introduce inaccuracies in the results. As the improvement of score distribution estimates is an ongoing research topic [1], we limit ourselves here to a simple solution. We assume that the estimation of the expected number of documents in the collection n_c is accurate such that (11) holds. A suitably normalized estimate of n_i is hence

$$n_i = All_i\, p_i \, \frac{n_c}{sum_{j=1}^{N} p_j\, All_j} \tag{12}$$

where the term $All_i\, p_i$ is the unnormalized number of documents in $\mathcal{D}_i$ above score s_c and the right term is a normalization constant ensuring that the estimated number of documents above s_c from each shard j add up to the corresponding number of documents in the whole collection, which is n_c.

We are now able to define Taily's shard selection criterion $sel(q)$ for a query q that selects shards with an estimated number of documents in the top-m above a threshold:

$$sel(q) = \left\{ i \middle| i \in 1...N, n_i > v \right\} \tag{13}$$

where i is a shard index, and v is the selection threshold. Note that it can be beneficial for v to be higher than 0 because of the computational costs for including a shard with only very few estimated documents in the top ranks.

4. EFFICIENCY MEASURES

Before we can evaluate Taily, we have to define measures that quantify the efficiency of shard selection algorithms in terms of used resources and response time. To be comparable to related work, we base our measure on the measure by Kulkarni et al. [14], which calculates the resources used by a shard selection algorithm for a query q by the number of documents that the sharded search has to access:

$$\mathrm{C}_R(q) = \sum_{i=1}^{|sel(q)|} \mathcal{D}_i(\vec{q}) \tag{14}$$

where $sel(q)$ are the shards selected by the algorithm and $\mathcal{D}_i(\vec{q})$ is the number of documents in shard i that match at least one of the query terms $\vec{q}$. As discussed in Section 1, the selection algorithm itself can require substantial resources, which should be reflected in the efficiency measure. We therefore extend the above efficiency measure by a component that reflects the costs of executing the selection algorithm. We arrive at our resource efficiency measure $C_{\mathrm{RES}}(q)$ of a query q:

$$C_{\mathrm{RES}}(q) = \mathrm{C}_{SEL}(q) + \mathrm{C}_R(q) \tag{15}$$

where $\mathrm{C}_R(q)$ is measure by Kulkarni et al. from (14), and $\mathrm{C}_{SEL}(q)$ are the costs for executing the selection algorithm for query q. The selection costs C_{SEL} depend on the type of selection algorithm. For sample-based methods, we set the selection costs $\mathrm{C}_{SEL}(q) = CSI(\vec{q})$, where $CSI(\vec{q})$ is the number of documents in the CSI that have at least one query term. For vocabulary based algorithms, we set $\mathrm{C}_{SEL}(q) = N$, where N is the number of shards in the collection, which is the upper bound of the number of entries in the shard representation for any query term.

Additional to the resource usage, the query response time is another important efficiency aspect to consider [18]. In contrast to the used resources, measures for the response time have to take into account that the selected shards are usually processed in parallel, once the selection algorithm has finished. For the search in the selected shards, the costs therefore mainly depend on the shard with the most matching documents. Similar to the methodology in the evaluation of database systems, we measure the response time by the

[4]In fact, we estimate the number of documents that have a score above s_c *and contain all query terms*. This means that we assume that for the shards to be selected, most documents above cut-off contain all query terms. Experimentally, this appears to hold if s_c is reasonably high, see e.g. Figure 1b.

Table 1: Statistics about the collections used in the experiments of this paper (In entries of the form $X \pm Y$, X is the average and Y is the standard deviation. TB=terrabyte track, WT=web track.).

Collection	Documents	Shards	Query set	Query length	Rel. Docs
Gov2	25M	50	TB '04-'06 (701-750)	3.1(±0.97)	180(±148)
ClueWebB	50M	100	WT '09+'10 (1-100)	2.1(±1.36)	49(±42)
ClueWebA	250M	1000	WT '09+'10 (1-100)	2.1(±1.36)	124(±75)

number of accessed data items on the longest execution path (ignoring implementation dependent aspects):

$$C_{\text{TIME}}(q) = C_{SEL}(q) + max_{i=1}^{|sel(q)|}\{\mathcal{D}_i(\vec{q})\}. \qquad (16)$$

where $1, ..., |sel(q)|$ are the selected shards and the other symbols carry the same definition as in (15). We report average values C_{RES} and C_{TIME} over a considered query set, similar to reporting the mean average precision instead of individual average precision values. Note that the measures in this section consider the number of accessed items, which are documents in shards or CSIs, and shards in vocabulary-based methods. Another choice would have been to consider the number of accessed postings for these items in the inverted files of the query terms.

5. EXPERIMENTS

In this section, we describe the experiments that we conducted to evaluate our shard selection algorithm Taily. We aligned our experiments to the ones from the recent publication by Kulkarni et al. [14], to ensure comparability of our work to the state-of-the-art in shard selection. We proceed as follows: first, we describe the experimental setup, second, we describe each experiment and its results, and finally, we discuss the findings.

5.1 Setup

Table 1 describes the collections and query sets that we used. The collections represent modern retrieval collections of a medium to large size. We used the shards defined by the topical clustering algorithm by Kulkarni and Callan [13]. Due to spam, the effectiveness of the search on the full ClueWebA collection of $500M$ documents was weak. We therefore removed the documents whose spam scores were among the 50% highest scores according to the fusion method by Cormack et al. [8].

We implemented the experiments using the hadoop map-reduce framework, directly answering queries and generating statistics from the full text of the collection; similarly to the approach described in [11]. We used the Krovetz stemmer for both the document text and the queries. We did not use stopwording. For the exhaustive search and the searches in the central sample index (CSI), we used the full dependency model [16] with the parameter setting $(0.8, 0.1, 0.1)$ for single term features, unordered term features and ordered term features respectively as recommended by Metzler et al. [17] and used in Kulkarni et al. [14]. The Dirichlet smoothing parameter was set to $\mu = 2500$.

We chose one baseline from each of the two classes of selection algorithms presented in Section 2. As a vocabulary-based algorithm, we used the popular CORI algorithm [6]. As a sample-based algorithm we chose Rank-S by Kulkarni et al. [14], which showed significantly stronger performance than REDDE [21] and SUSHI [22], two other state-of-the-art shard selection algorithms. Note that we added for Rank-S

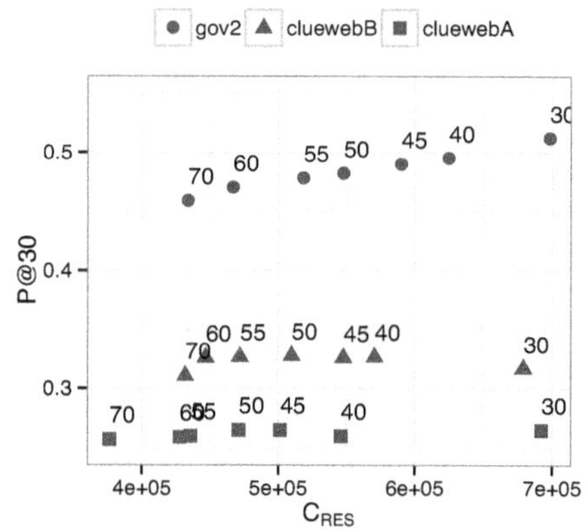

Figure 2: Sensitivity of Taily with n_c=400 according to the threshold parameter v (as indicated in the plot).

the minimum score of the score of the full dependency to make the scores positive. This was not reported by Kulkarni et al. [14] but it was important to achieve results comparable to the ones in the original publication. The documents for the central sample index used by Rank-S were uniformly sampled without replacement from each shard until a percentage P of the shard's size was reached. We ensured that each shard was represented by at least 100 documents. To rule out random effects, we repeated the runs with Rank-S 50 times, producing 50 CSIs with potentially different shards selections. Unless stated otherwise, the reported performance measures are the averages of the 50 repetitions. The average approximates the expected performance for a random CSI of this size. Note that performing statistical significance tests using these expected performance values is mathematically speaking problematic. We still report the results of these tests as an indication of the strength of the performance change. Note that Kulkarni et al. [14] use only a single CSI in their results. Therefore, their numerical results do not necessarily correspond to ours.

The size of the CSI can influence the performance of Rank-S. Unless stated otherwise, we used $P = 0.02, 0.01$ and 0.01 for Gov2, ClueWebB and for ClueWebA respectively. For Gov2 and ClueWebB these settings resulted in a CSI that was roughly as big as an average shard in the respective collection. For ClueWebA we chose $P = 0.01$ because using $P = 0.001$, which corresponds to the size of an average shard, caused poor effectiveness.

We used the effectiveness measures precision at ten, thirty and hundred (P@10, P@30, P@100), mean average precision (*map*), and ndcg at ten (*ndcg*@10). When we focused on a single effectiveness measure, we chose P@30 because it was more stable than P@10 for all selection algorithms but still reflected a precision oriented search task. To mea-

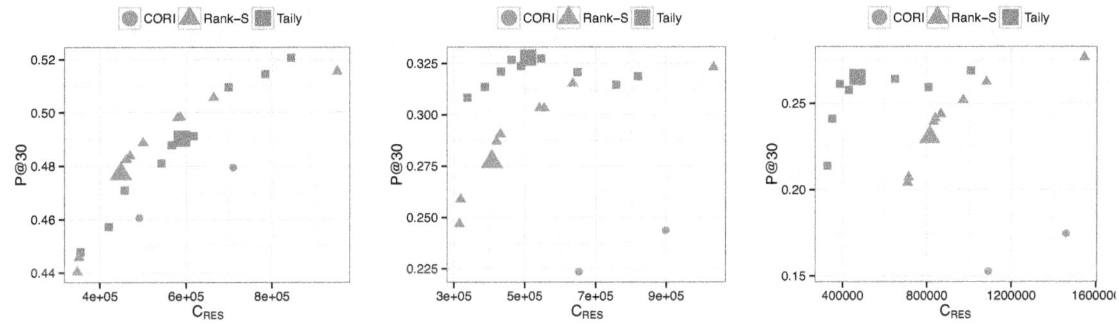

(a) Gov2 (b) Clueweb B (c) Clueweb A

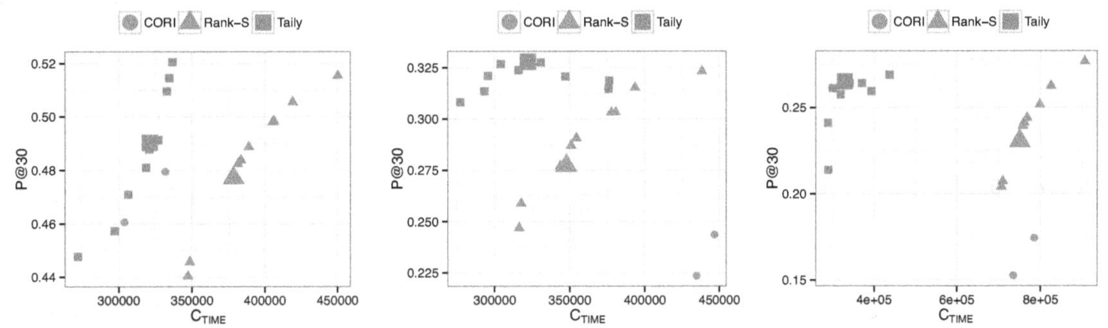

(d) Gov2 (e) ClueweB (f) ClueweA

Figure 3: Efficiency-effectiveness tradeoff for CORI, Rank-S, and Taily. The following tradeoff parameter settings of each method were used. CORI: $n \in \{2,3\}$ (higher values were always outside the limits of the x-axis), Rank-S: $B \in \{2,5,10,30,50,70,100,200,500\}$ (lower values caused lower efficiency), Taily: $n_c \in \{200,250,300,350,400,600,800,1000,1500,2000\}$.

sure efficiency, we used the resource efficiency C_{RES} and the response time C_{TIME} described in Section 4.

5.2 Threshold Parameter

The threshold parameter v, defined in Section 3.6, specifies the minimum number of documents in the right tail of the collection's score distribution that a shard should have to be selected. Figure 2 shows a sensitivity analysis of Taily towards changes of v by displaying the resulting $P@30$ and C_{RES} measures (here, we used a fixed tradeoff parameter of $n_c = 400$ but the results were similar for other values of n_c). The effectiveness of Taily was robust against changes of v, and increased slightly for Gov2. The parameter setting $v = 50$ caused efficiency and effectiveness around the median of the tested values. We chose this parameter setting for the rest of our experiments.

5.3 Efficiency-Effectiveness Comparison

An important characteristic of a shard selection algorithm is the tradeoff it provides between efficiency and effectiveness. A search engine operator may want to invest more resources to ensure high effectiveness, or to make more efficient use of resources and accept worse effectiveness. CORI, Rank-S and Taily each have a parameter that determines the tradeoff between efficiency and effectiveness. For CORI the parameter n states a fixed number of the highest ranked shards that are selected, second, Rank-S uses the parameter B that determines the influence of a CSI document on the selection of the shard it belongs to (see Section 2), finally, Taily uses the parameter n_c that determines the number of top-ranked documents that should be included in the results of the sharded search.

Figure 3 compares the tradeoff that CORI, Rank-S, and Taily provided in the indicated parameter range. The x-axes show the resource usage C_{RES} or the response time C_{TIME}. The y-axes show the effectiveness in terms of precision $P@30$.

Figure 3a-Figure 3c show the tradeoff between C_{RES} and $P@30$. For Gov2 the tradeoff is similar for CORI, Rank-S and Taily at low efficiency values. Rank-S and Taily provide a similar tradeoff between effectiveness and efficiency over all parameter settings. For ClueWebB the efficiency of CORI was always lower than the one of Rank-S and Taily. The effectiveness of Rank-S was lower than the one of Taily for a resource usage of $C_{\text{RES}} < 60,000$. With higher resource usage, both methods had similar effectiveness. For ClueWebA Taily showed a higher effectiveness than Rank-S until $C_{\text{RES}} = 90,000$.

Figure 3d-Figure 3f show the tradeoff between C_{TIME} and $P@30$. For Gov2 CORI performed similar to Taily. All parameter settings of Rank-S had a larger response time than the ones of Taily. To achieve comparable effectiveness, the response time of Rank-S was roughly 15% larger than the one from Taily. For ClueWebB CORI's performance was low. Taily showed higher effectiveness than Rank-S until

Table 2: Effectiveness and efficiency comparison between Taily and Rank-S for the indicated parameter settings. (▲ and ▼ indicate statistically significant improvement or regression respectively compared to the Exhaustive search, using a two-sided t-test with $p\text{−}value<0.05$. Percentages state the efficiency change compared to the Rank-S method.)

Method	P@10	P@30	P@100	map	$ndcg$@10	Shards	C_{RES}		C_{TIME}	
Exhaustive	0.58	0.52	0.42	0.34	0.49	50.0	4.92M		0.51M	
CORI (n=3)	0.57	▼0.48	▼0.36	▼0.25	0.48	3.0	0.71M		0.33M	
Rank-S (B=50 P=0.02)	▼0.55	▼0.48	▼0.37	▼0.24	▼0.45	1.5	0.45M		0.38M	
Taily ($n_c = 400, v = 50$)	0.56	▼0.48	▼0.38	▼0.27	▼0.46	2.6	0.55M	22.1%	0.32M	−15.7%

(a) Gov2

Method	P@10	P@30	P@100	map	$ndcg$@10	Shards	C_{RES}		C_{TIME}	
Exhaustive	0.29	0.32	0.22	0.20	0.24	100.0	10.15M		0.47M	
CORI (n=3)	0.25	▼0.24	▼0.16	▼0.13	0.21	3.0	0.90M		0.45M	
Rank-S (B=50 P=0.01)	0.31	▼0.28	▼0.18	▼0.15	▲0.27	1.5	0.40M		0.34M	
Taily ($n_c = 400, v = 50$)	0.31	0.33	0.22	▼0.18	▲0.27	2.7	0.51M	26.1%	0.32M	−6.5%

(b) CluewebB

Method	P@10	P@30	P@100	map	$ndcg$@10	Shards	C_{RES}		C_{TIME}	
Exhaustive	0.29	0.27	0.18	0.11	0.19	1000.0	48.78M		1.02M	
CORI (n=3)	▼0.20	▼0.17	▼0.11	▼0.06	▼0.14	3.0	1.46M		0.78M	
Rank-S (B=50 P=0.01)	0.29	▼0.24	▼0.15	▼0.08	0.19	2.2	0.90M		0.77M	
Taily ($n_c = 400, v = 50$)	0.30	0.27	0.17	▼0.09	0.20	2.5	0.47M	−47.6%	0.33M	−57.3%

(c) CluewebA

roughly $C_{\text{TIME}} = 40,0000$. For CluewebA CORI's performance is again low. Compared with CluewebB the difference of Rank-S and Taily in terms of C_{TIME} is larger.

The results in Figure 3 show that the effectiveness of Rank-S varies with different settings of B, unlike the results by Kulkarni et al. [14] (their Figures 2 and 3) that suggest that the effectiveness of Rank-S is almost unaffected by the parameter. Because the particular sampled documents in the central indices used by Kulkarni et al. were not available, we did not further investigate these differences. They might be explained by two important differences in the experimental setup: first, we use a smaller CSI size ($P = 0.02$ and $P = 0.01$ vs. $P = 0.04$ by Kulkarni et al.), and second, we report the average performance over random samples, instead of results on a single sample.

5.4 Detailed Effectiveness Analysis

We also investigated the effectiveness in terms of multiple measures at a fixed parameter settings. For CORI we chose a shard cut-off value of $n = 3$. Although larger values sometimes produced better effectiveness, the efficiency was too low to be comparable to Rank-S and Taily. We set the Rank-S parameter $B = 50$ for all three collections because Kulkarni et al. also used this value for CluewebB. For Taily we set $n_c = 400$ and $v = 50$. The efficiency and effectiveness for these parameters is shown as larger points in Figure 3. We also display the performance for the exhaustive search, as a reference. For the displayed efficiency of the exhaustive search, we assumed a parallel search of all shards with zero costs for the selection ($C_{SEL} = 0$ in (15) and (16)).

Table 2a shows the results for the Gov2 collection. CORI shows similar performance than Rank-S and Taily in terms of P@10. The resource efficiency was the lowest among the three methods. The response time C_{TIME} was comparable to the one of Taily. Rank-S showed comparable effectiveness to Taily with only *map* being lower. The resource usage of Rank-S was the lowest among the three runs. The response time was the largest. On average, Taily and Rank-S selected 2.6 and 1.5 shards on average respectively.

Table 2b shows the results for the CluewebB collection. CORI showed weaker efficiency and effectiveness than Rank-S and Taily. Taily's effectiveness was stronger for all efficiency measures. In terms of C_{RES}, Taily used 26.1% more resources than Rank-S, while the response time improved by 6.5%. Note that Rank-S and Taily improved significantly upon exhaustive search for $ndcg$@10. This is possible if top-ranked non-relevant documents in the exhaustive ranking are from shards, which are ignored by the shard selection algorithm. We consider this phenomenon as a property of the data and therefore did not make any further investigations.

Table 2c shows the results for the CluewebA collection. CORI showed weak effectiveness and efficiency. Rank-S performed significantly worse than exhaustive search for P@30, P@100 and *map*. Taily showed similar or better effectiveness compared to Rank-S. Compared to Rank-S, the efficiency improved 47.6% and 57.3% upon Rank-S in terms of C_{RES} and C_{TIME} respectively.

Note that although Taily used more resources in Gov2 and CluewebB than Rank-S for the indicated parameter settings, there exist other parameter settings where this was not the case, see Figure 3. Furthermore, the used effectiveness measures depend on a high coverage of judgments in the top-ranked documents. For CluewebA only roughly 50% of the top-30 documents were judged. This coverage was similar for all investigated shard selection algorithms. As a result, the absolute effectiveness values are not exact. However, we believe that the relative effectiveness comparison among the shard selection algorithms would be similar under complete coverage because the selective rankings are derived from the exhaustive ranking and only differ by few added or removed shards per query, which is likely to average out.

5.5 Influence of Document Sample on Rank-S

The performance of Rank-S depends on the CSI it uses

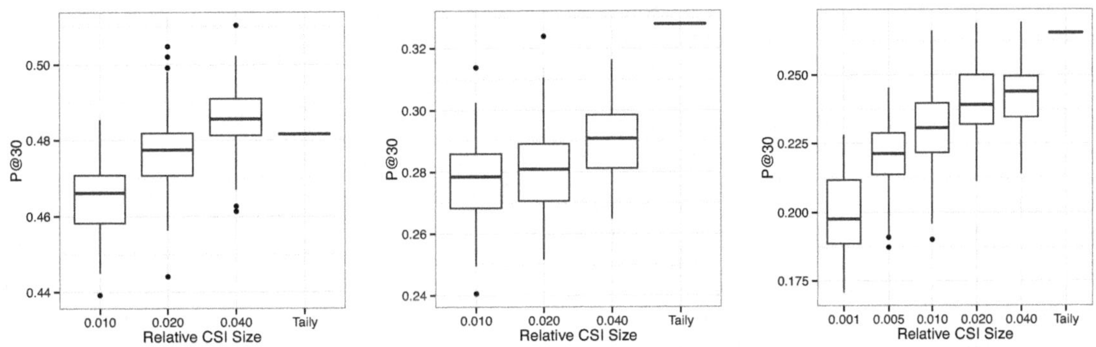

(a) Gov2 (b) Clueweb B (c) Clueweb A

Figure 4: Influence of the document sample on the effectiveness of Rank-S. (Rank-S used $B = 50$. Taily does not use of a CSI and his parameters were $n_c = 400$ and $v = 50$).

for the initial search in two ways: first, the number of documents, assuming that a larger CSI also causes a more accurate selection, and second, exactly which documents are sampled. Variation in performance can influence the comparison of Rank-S and Taily. Therefore, we investigated the performance variability of Rank-S along these axes.

Figure 4 summarizes the results of this experiment, using the $P@30$ measure. As a reference, we also plot the effectiveness of Taily. Figure 4a shows the results for Gov2. The median effectiveness increased by roughly 5% between $P = 0.01$ and $P = 0.04$. The lowest achieved performance was roughly 8% weaker than the median performance. Taily showed similar effectiveness as the median performance of Rank-S with $P = 0.04$.

Figure 4b shows the results for ClueWebB. The median effectiveness was more stable when changing the CSI size than with Gov2. The lowest achieved search performance was roughly 10% lower than the median performance. Taily showed better effectiveness than all measurements for Rank-S.

Figure 4c shows the results for ClueWebA. The median search performance increases by roughly 18% between $P = 0.001$ and $P = 0.04$. The lowest achieved performance was roughly 15% lower than the median performance. Taily's effectiveness was en par with the best-measured effectiveness of Rank-S with $P = 0.02$ and $P = 0.04$.

5.6 Discussion

We discuss the results presented in this section. Taily depends on the following two parameters: the tradeoff parameter n_c that determines the number of high scored documents of the collection, and the threshold parameter v that determines minimum of this estimate for are a shard to be selected, which was introduced to suppress estimation errors. Section 5.2 and Section 5.3 showed that both parameters can be set reliably within a range of values, resulting in strong performance. Nevertheless, the parameter values are unintuitive. For example, the setting of $n_c = 400$ and $v = 50$, used in Section 5.4, means according to the definition of the parameters that shards with 50 documents in the top 400 documents should not be selected. A likely reason for these unintuitive estimates is the crude normalization of the expected values in (12). Therefore, for future work we propose the research of more accurate normalization methods, which possibly improves the performance of Taily further.

The results of the comparison of CORI, Rank-S and Taily yielded a number of findings. First, the performance of the vocabulary-based algorithms shows opposite trends depending on the collection size. While CORI's effectiveness decreases, Taily effectiveness increases. A likely explanation for CORI's performance decrease is its known bias towards bigger shards, which do not necessarily contain many relevant documents, which causes efficiency and effectiveness to drop. Therefore, Taily's approach to model the tail of the score distribution in each shard selects substantially smaller shards with more relevant documents than CORI's approach to model *all* documents. Second, for each parameter setting of Rank-S there was a parameter setting of Taily with higher efficiency and similar or higher effectiveness compared to the former's expected performance. This was in particular true for the response time. This shows that the selection costs C_{SEL} for executing Taily were substantially lower than the ones for Rank-S and Taily's vocabulary-based approach can select shards with a comparable number of relevant documents as Rank-S. Finally, because of the shape of the achieved efficiency - effectiveness tradeoff combinations, we propose that finding tradeoff settings for a given efficiency is easier to achieve for Taily than for Rank-S. An exception is the response time of Taily in Gov2, which increases at a high rate, causing small differences in efficiency to cause large changes in effectiveness.

The effectiveness of Rank-S is strongly correlated with the CSI size. For example, for ClueWebA an increase of the CSI size from $P = 0.001$ to $P = 0.01$ improved the median effectiveness by 16%. At the same time, larger CSI sizes consume more storage space, which also makes them less efficient. Therefore, it is likely that Rank-S does not scale to collections lager than ClueWebA.

6. CONCLUSIONS AND FUTURE WORK

We introduced Taily, a novel shard selection algorithm that is based on highly scored documents in the tail of the collection's score distribution. The scores are assumed to be Gamma distributed and estimated from statistics about features related to the query terms of the language model score function. Taily is therefore a member of vocabulary-based shard selection algorithms that represent shards by statistics of terms in the vocabulary.

We evaluated Taily on three large web collections (Gov2,

ClluewebB and ClluewebA) using topically clustered shards defined by Kulkarni and Callan [13]. Compared to the popular vocabulary-based method CORI [6], Taily showed better efficiency and effectiveness. Compared to Rank-S [14], a state-of-the-art, sample-based shard selection algorithm, Taily achieved similar or better effectiveness using less resources. Especially for larger collections and CSIs, the vocabulary-based Taily used less resources than the sample-based Rank-S although it selected on average more shards. The improvement of the response time compared to Rank-S was larger than the improvement of the resource usage. Taily showed his highest effectiveness with a shorter response time than the shortest response time measured for Rank-S over a wide range of parameters. For ClluewebA, Taily achieved its best performance in roughly 50% of the response time of Rank-S.

Taily does not use document samples and therefore does not need to answer some of the questions that sample-based methods need to answer, such as what samples to take, and what would be a reasonable size of the central sample index (CSI). We investigated possible answers to these questions for Rank-S, and found that the effectiveness of Rank-S decreases with the CSI size. For example, the effectiveness decreased by 20% between using a commonly used CSI size of 4% and 0.1% for the ClluewebA collection, where 0.1% corresponded to the size of an average shard. We also found that, for a given CSI size, the lowest effectiveness of Rank-S in 50 CSIs consisting of different document samples was roughly 10% lower than the median performance. The dependence of effectiveness on CSI size and CSI sample is a weakness of sample-based methods. This weakness can also be seen as an advantage of vocabulary-based methods, like Taily, which do not depend on a CSI.

This work focused on shard selection in a cooperative environment using topically clustered shards. We believe that the basic ideas behind Taily can also be applied to database selection in a uncooperative, federated search scenario [4, 20]. In future work we plan to investigate methods to gather the statistics required by Taily in a federal search scenario, to evaluate whether its performance also applies to this setting.

Acknowledgments

The work reported in this paper was funded by the EU Project AXES (FP7-269980), the Netherlands Organisation for Scientifc Research (NWO) under project 639.022.809, the University of Twente in The Netherlands, Ghent University in Belgium, and iMinds (Interdisciplinary institute for Technology), a research institute founded by the Flemish Government. This work is part of the programme of BiG Grid, the Dutch e-Science Grid, which is financially supported by the Nederlandse Organisatie voor Wetenschappelijk Onderzoek (Netherlands Organisation for Scientific Research, NWO). The authors want to thank the Big Grid team for their outstanding technical support, as well as Jamie Callan and the anonymous reviewers for their fruitful input.

Bibliography

[1] A. Arampatzis and S. E. Robertson. Modeling score distributions in information retrieval. *Information Retrieval*, 14:1–21, 2010. doi: 10.1007/s10791-010-9145-5.

[2] A. Arampatzis, N. Nussbaum, and J. Kamps. Where to stop reading a ranked list? In *TREC'08*, 2008.

[3] J. Arguello, J. Callan, and F. Diaz. Classification-based resource selection. In *CIKM'09*, pages 1277–1286. ACM, 2009. doi: 10.1145/1645953.1646115.

[4] R. Baeza-Yates, C. Castillo, F. Junqueira, V. Plachouras, and F. Silvestri. Challenges on distributed web retrieval. In *ICDE'07*, pages 6–20, 2007. doi: 10.1109/ICDE.2007.367846.

[5] R. Baeza-Yates, V. Murdock, and C. Hauff. Efficiency trade-offs in two-tier web search systems. In *SIGIR'09*, pages 163–170. ACM, 2009. doi: 10.1145/1571941.1571971.

[6] J. P. Callan, Z. Lu, and W. B. Croft. Searching distributed collections with inference networks. In *SIGIR '95*, pages 21–28. ACM, 1995. doi: 10.1145/215206.215328.

[7] W. S. Cooper. Some inconsistencies and misidentified modeling assumptions in probabilistic information retrieval. *ACM Trans. Inf. Syst.*, 13(1):100–111, 1995. doi: 10.1145/195705.195735.

[8] G. V. Cormack, M. D. Smucker, and C. L. A. Clarke. Efficient and effective spam filtering and re-ranking for large web datasets. *CoRR*, abs/1004.5168, 2010.

[9] S. Ganguly, W. Hasan, and R. Krishnamurthy. Query optimization for parallel execution. In *SIGMOD'92*, pages 9–18, NY, USA, 1992. ACM. doi: 10.1145/130283.130291.

[10] L. Gravano and H. Garcia-Molina. Generalizing gloss to vector-space databases and broker hierarchies. In *VLDB'95*, pages 78–89. Morgan Kaufmann Publishers Inc., 1995. ISBN 1-55860-379-4.

[11] D. Hiemstra and C. Hauff. Mapreduce for information retrieval evaluation: "let's quickly test this on 12 tb of data". In *Multilingual and Multimodal Information Access Evaluation*. Springer Verlag, 2010.

[12] E. Kanoulas, K. Dai, V. Pavlu, and J. A. Aslam. Score distribution models: assumptions, intuition, and robustness to score manipulation. In *SIGIR'10*, pages 242–249. ACM, 2010. doi: 10.1145/1835449.1835491.

[13] A. Kulkarni and J. Callan. Document allocation policies for selective searching of distributed indexes. In *CIKM '10*, pages 449–458. ACM, 2010. doi: 10.1145/1871437.1871497.

[14] A. Kulkarni, A. S. Tigelaar, D. Hiemstra, and J. Callan. Shard ranking and cutoff estimation for topically partitioned collections. In *CIKM'12*. ACM, 2012. doi: 10.1007/s10791-006-9014-4.

[15] I. Markov. Modeling document scores for distributed information retrieval. In *SIGIR'11*, pages 1321–1322. ACM, 2011. doi: 10.1145/2009916.2010180.

[16] D. Metzler and W. B. Croft. A markov random field model for term dependencies. In *SIGIR'05*, pages 472–479. ACM, 2005. doi: 10.1145/1076034.1076115.

[17] D. Metzler, T. Strohman, H. Turtle, and W. Croft. Indri at trec 2004: Terabyte track. In *TREC 2004*, 2004.

[18] A. Moffat, W. Webber, J. Zobel, and R. Baeza-Yates. A pipelined architecture for distributed text query evaluation. In *Information Retrieval*, volume 10, pages 205–231. Kluwer Academic Publishers, 2007. doi: 10.1007/s10791-006-9014-4.

[19] D. Nguyen and J. Callan. Combination of evidence for effective web search. In *TREC 2010*, 2010.

[20] M. Shokouhi and L. Si. *Federated search*, volume 5. Now Publishers Inc, 2011. doi: 10.1561/1500000010.

[21] L. Si and J. Callan. Relevant document distribution estimation method for resource selection. In *SIGIR'03*, pages 298–305. ACM, 2003. doi: 10.1145/860435.860490.

[22] P. Thomas and M. Shokouhi. Sushi: scoring scaled samples for server selection. In *SIGIR'09*, pages 419–426. ACM, 2009. doi: 10.1145/1571941.1572014.

[23] J. Xu and W. Croft. Cluster-based language models for distributed retrieval. In *SIGIR'99*, pages 254–261. ACM, 1999.

A Mutual Information-based Framework for the Analysis of Information Retrieval Systems

Peter B. Golbus Javed A. Aslam
College of Computer and Information Science
Northeastern University
Boston, MA, USA
{pgolbus,jaa}@ccs.neu.edu

ABSTRACT

We consider the problem of information retrieval evaluation and the methods and metrics used for such evaluations. We propose a *probabilistic framework* for evaluation which we use to develop new *information-theoretic* evaluation metrics. We demonstrate that these new metrics are powerful and generalizable, enabling evaluations heretofore not possible.

We introduce four preliminary uses of our framework: (1) a measure of conditional rank correlation, *information* τ, a powerful meta-evaluation tool whose use we demonstrate on understanding novelty and diversity evaluation; (2) a new evaluation measure, *relevance information correlation*, which is correlated with traditional evaluation measures and can be used to (3) evaluate a collection of systems simultaneously, which provides a natural upper bound on metasearch performance; and (4) a measure of the similarity between rankers on judged documents, *information difference*, which allows us to determine whether systems with similar performance are in fact different.

Categories and Subject Descriptors

H.3.4 [**Information Storage and Retrieval**]: Systems and Software—*Performance evaluation (efficiency and effectiveness)*

General Terms

Experimentation; Theory; Measurement

Keywords

Information Retrieval, Search Evaluation

1. INTRODUCTION

In order to improve search engines, it is necessary to accurately measure their current performance. If we cannot measure performance, how can we know whether a change was beneficial? In recent years, much of the work on information retrieval evaluation has focused on user models [7, 18] and diversity measures [1, 10, 24] which attempt to accurately reflect the experience of the user of a modern internet search engine. However, these measure are not easily generalized. In this work, we introduce a probabilistic framework for evaluation that encompasses and generalizes current evaluation methods. Our probabilistic framework allows us to view evaluation using the tools of information theory [11]. While our framework is not designed to coincide with user experience, it provides immediate access to a large number of powerful tools allowing for a deeper understanding of the performance of search engines.

Our framework for evaluation is based on the observation that relevance judgments can also be interpreted as a preference between those documents with different relevance grades. This implies that relevance judgments can be treated as a retrieval system, and that evaluation can be considered as the "rank" correlation between systems and relevance judgments. To this end, we develop a probabilistic framework for rank correlation based on the expectation of random variables, which we demonstrate can also be used to compute existing evaluation metrics. However, the true value of our framework lies in its extension to new information-theoretic evaluation tools.

After a discussion of related work (Section 2), we introduce our framework in Section 3. In Section 4, we demonstrate that our framework allows for an information theoretic understanding of Kendall's τ [17], *information* τ, which we use to define a conditional version of the rank correlation between two lists conditioned on a third. In Section 5, we define a new evaluation measure based on our framework: *relevance information correlation.* We validate our measure by showing that it is highly correlated with existing measures such as average precision (AP) and normalized discounted cumulative gain (nDCG). As a demonstration of the versatility of our framework when compared to, for example, user models, we show that our measure can be used to evaluate a collection of systems simultaneously (Section 6), creating an upper bound on the performance of metasearch algorithms. Finally, in Section 7, we introduce *information difference*, a powerful new tool for evaluating the similarity of retrieval systems beyond simply comparing their performance.

SIGIR'13, July 28–August 1, 2013, Dublin, Ireland.

ACM 978-1-4503-2034-4/13/07 ...$15.00.

This material is based upon work supported by the National Science Foundation under Grant No. IIS-1256172. Any opinions, findings and conclusions or recommendations expressed in this material are those of the author(s) and do not necessarily reflect the views of the National Science Foundation (NSF).

2. RELATED WORK

Search systems are typically evaluated against *test collections* which consist of a corpus of documents, a set of topics, and relevance assessments—whether a subset of those documents are *relevant* with respect to each topic.[1] For example, the annual, NIST-sponsored Text REtrieval Conference (TREC) creates test collections commonly used in academic research. The performance of systems is assessed with regards to a specific task. A traditional search task is to attempt to rank all relevant documents above any non-relevant documents. For this task, systems are evaluated in terms of the average trade-off between their *precision* and *recall* with respect to multiple topics. For a given topic, Let $g_i \in \{0, 1\}$ be the relevance grade of the document at rank i, and let R be the number of relevant documents in the collection. At rank k,

$$\text{precision@}k = \frac{\sum_{i=1}^{k} g_i}{k} \tag{1}$$

$$\text{recall@}k = \frac{\sum_{i=1}^{k} g_i}{R} \tag{2}$$

The trade-off between the two is measured by *average precision*, which can be interpreted as the area under the precision-recall curve.

$$AP = \frac{\sum_{i=1}^{\infty} g_i \times \text{precision@}i}{R} \tag{3}$$

Average precision does not include information about document quality and degrees of relevance, and is an inherently recall-oriented measure. It is therefore not suitable for evaluating commercial web search engines.

With the growth of the World Wide Web, test collections began to include graded, non-binary relevance judgments, e.g. $G = \{\text{non-relevant, relevant, highly relevant}\}$ or $G = \{0, \ldots, 4\}$. To make use of these graded assessments, Järvelin and Kekäläinen developed *normalized discounted cumulative gain* (nDCG) [15]. nDCG also has the advantage that it can be evaluated at arbitrary ranks, and can therefore be used for precision-oriented tasks like web search.

Unlike average precision, which has a technical interpretation, nDCG can be best understood in terms of a model of a hypothetical user. In this model, a user will read the first k documents in a ranked list, deriving utility from each document. The amount of utility is proportional to the document's relevance grade and inversely proportional to the rank at which the document is encountered. We first define discounted cumulative gain (DCG).

$$DCG@k = \sum_{i=1}^{k} \frac{2^{g_i} - 1}{\log_2(i+1)} \tag{4}$$

Since the range of DCG will vary from topic to topic, it is necessary to normalize these scores so that an average can be computed. Normalization is performed with regard to an ideal ranked list. If $DCG'@k$ is the maximum possible DCG of any ranked list of documents in the collection then

$$nDCG@k = \frac{DCG@k}{DCG'@k} \tag{5}$$

However, one does not always know how many documents are relevant at each level, and therefore the ideal list used for normalization is only an approximation. Moffat and Zobel [18] introduced a measure, *rank-biased precision* (RBP), that addresses this issue. In RBP, the probability that a user will read the document at rank k is drawn from a geometric distribution, whose parameter, $\beta \in [0, 1)$, models the user's persistence. Given a utility function $u\colon G \to [0, 1]$, commonly defined as

$$u(g) = \frac{2^g - 1}{2^d} \tag{6}$$

where d is the maximum possible relevance grade, RBP is defined as the expected utility of a user who browses according to this model.

$$RBP = (1 - \beta) \sum_{i=1}^{\infty} u(g_i) \times \beta^{i-1} \tag{7}$$

Since RBP is guaranteed to be in the range [0,1) for any topic and β, it does not require normalization.

Craswell et al. [12] introduced the Cascade model of user behavior. In this model, a user is still assumed to browse documents in order, but the probability that a user will view a particular document is no longer assumed to be independent of the documents that were viewed previously, i.e. a user is not assumed to stop at a particular rank, or at each rank with some probability. Instead, the user is assumed to stop after finding a relevant document. This implies that if a user reaches rank k, then all of the $k - 1$ documents ranked before it were non-relevant. Craswell et al. demonstrated empirically that this model corresponds well to observed user behavior in terms of predicting the clickthrough data of a commercial search engine.

Chapelle et al. [7] developed an evaluation measure, *expected reciprocal rank* (ERR), based on the Cascade model. Let R_i denote the probability that a user will find the document at rank i to be relevant. Then in the Cascade model, the likelihood that a user will terminate his or her search at rank r is

$$R_r \prod_{i=1}^{r-1} (1 - R_i). \tag{8}$$

If we interpret the previously defined utility function (Equation 6) as the probability that a user will find a document relevant, i.e. $R_i = u(g_i)$, then we can computed the expected reciprocal rank at which a user will terminate his or her search as

$$ERR = \sum_{r=1}^{\infty} \frac{1}{r} R_r \prod_{i=1}^{r-1} (1 - R_i). \tag{9}$$

In this work, we propose an alternative, information-theoretic framework for evaluation. The first step is to reformulate these measures as the expected outcomes of random experiments. Computing evaluation measures in expectation is

[1]For historical reasons, the set of relevance assessments is often referred to as a *QREL*.

not uncommon in the literature, and we are not the first to suggest that reformulating an evaluation measure as an expectation allows for novel applications. For example, Yilmaz and Aslam [30] formulated average precision as the expectation of the following random experiment:

1. Pick a random relevant document,
2. Pick a random document ranked at or above the rank of the document selected in step 1.
3. Output 1 if the document from step 2 is relevant, otherwise output 0.

Their intention was to accurately estimate average precision while collecting fewer relevance judgments (a process also applied to nDCG [32]). However, this formulation led to new uses, such as defining an information retrieval-specific rank correlation measure, τ_{AP} [31], and a variation of average precision for graded relevance judgments, Graded Average Precision (GAP) [21].

Our work uses pairwise document preferences rather than absolute relevance judgments. The use of preferences is somewhat common in IR. For example, many learning-to-rank algorithms, such as LambdaMart [3] and RankBoost [13], use pairwise document preferences in their objective functions. Carterette et al. [4, 5] explored the collection of preference judgments for evaluation, showing that they are faster to collect and have lower levels of inter-assessor disagreement. More recently, Chandar and Carterette [6] crowdsourced the collection of *conditional* document preferences to evaluate the standard assumptions underlying diversity evaluation, for example that users always prefer novel documents. Relative document preferences can also be inferred from the clickthrough data collected in the logs of commercial search engines [16]. These preferences can be used for evaluation without undertaking the expense of collecting relevance judgments from assessors.

3. A PROBABILISTIC FRAMEWORK FOR EVALUATION

Mathematically, one can view the search system as providing a *total ordering* of the documents ranked and a *partial ordering* of the entire collection, where all ranked documents are preferred to unranked documents but the relative preference among the unranked documents is unknown. Similarly, one can view the relevance assessments as providing a partial ordering of the entire collection: in the case of binary relevance assessments, for example, all judged relevant documents are preferred to all judged non-relevant and unjudged documents, but the relative preferences among the relevant documents and among the non-relevant and unjudged documents is unknown. Thus, mathematically, one can view retrieval evaluation as comparing the partial ordering of the collection *induced by the search system* with the partial ordering of the collection *induced by the relevance assessments.*

To formalize and instantiate a framework for comparing such partial orderings, consider the simplest case where we have two total orderings of objects, i.e., where the entire "collection" of objects is fully ranked in both "orderings." While such a situation does not typically arise in search system evaluation (since not all *documents* are ranked by the retrieval system nor are they fully ranked by relevance assessments), it does often arise when comparing the *rankings of systems* induced by two (or more) evaluation metrics; here Kendall's τ is often the metric used to compare these (total order) rankings.

In what follows, we define a *probabilistic framework* within which to compare two total orderings, and we show how traditional metrics (such as Kendall's τ) are easily cast within this framework. The real power of such a framework is shown in subsequent sections: (1) the framework can be easily generalized to handle the comparison of two partial orderings, such as arise in search system evaluation, and (2) well-studied, powerful, and general information-theoretic metrics can be developed within this generalized framework.

Consider two total orderings of n objects. There are $\binom{n}{2}$ (unordered) pairs of such objects, and a pair is said to be *concordant* if the two orderings agree on the relative rankings of the objects and *discordant* if the two orderings disagree. Let c and d be the number of concordant and discordant pairs, respectively. Then Kendall's τ is defined as follows:

$$\tau = \frac{c-d}{c+d}. \tag{10}$$

If we let C and D denote the *fraction* of concordant and discordant pairs then Kendall's τ is defined as

$$\tau = C - D. \tag{11}$$

Note that $c + d \neq \binom{n}{2}$ if there are ties.[2]

To define a probabilistic framework, we must specify three things: (1) a sample space of objects, (2) a distribution over this sample space, and (3) random variables over this sample space. Let our sample space Ω be all possible $2 \cdot \binom{n}{2}$ *ordered* pairs of distinct objects, and consider a *uniform distribution* over this sample space. For a given ranking R, define a random variable $X_R : \Omega \to \{-1, +1\}$ that outputs $+1$ for any ordered pair concordant with R and -1 for any ordered pair discordant with R.

$$X_R\left[(d_i, d_j)\right] = \begin{cases} 1 & \text{if } d_i \text{ appears before } d_j \text{ in } R. \\ -1 & \text{otherwise.} \end{cases} \tag{12}$$

We thus have a well-defined *random experiment*: draw an ordered pair of objects at random and output $+1$ if that ordered pair agrees with R's ranking and -1 otherwise. Since all ordered pairs of objects are considered uniformly, the *expected value* $E[X_R]$ of this random variable is zero.

Given a second ranked list S, one can similarly define an associated random variable X_S. Now consider the random experiment of *multiplying* the two random variables: the product $X_R \cdot X_S$ will be $+1$ precisely when the pair is *concordant*—i.e. both lists agree that the ordering of the objects is correct ($+1$) or incorrect (-1), and the product will be -1 when the pair is *discordant*—i.e. the lists disagree. In this probabilistic framework, Kendall's τ is the expected value

[2]Kendall defined two means by which τ can account for ties, depending on the desired behavior. Imagine comparing two ranked lists, one of which is almost completely composed of ties. τ_A, defined above, approaches 1. τ_B includes the number of ties in the denominator, and therefore approaches 0. We believe that the former approach is appropriate in this context. Since QRELs are almost exclusively composed of ties (recall that all pairs of unjudged documents in the corpus are considered to be tied), using the latter would mean that effect of the relatively rare meaningful comparisons would be negligible.

of the product of these random variables:

$$\tau = E[X_R \cdot X_S]. \quad (13)$$

The real power of this framework is in the definition of these random variables: (1) the ability to generalize them to compare partial orderings as arise in system evaluation, and (2) the ability to measure the correlation of these random variables using information-theoretic techniques.

4. INFORMATION-THEORETIC RANK CORRELATION

In Section 3, we defined Kendall's τ as the expected product of random variables. The following theorem allows us to restate Kendall's τ equivalently as the mutual information between the random variables.

THEOREM 1. $I(X_R; X_S) = \frac{1+\tau}{2}\log(1+\tau) + \frac{1-\tau}{2}\log(1-\tau)$.

(For a proof of Theorem 1, see Appendix). Unlike Kendall's τ, the mutual information between ranked lists ranges from 0 on lists that are completely uncorrelated to 1 on lists that are either perfectly correlated or perfectly anti-correlated.

If we restrict our attention to pairs of lists that are not anti-correlated, then the relationship is bijective. Given this fact, we define a variant of Kendall's τ, *information* τ:

$$\tau_I(R, S) = I(X_R; X_S) \quad (14)$$

where X_R is the ranked list random variable defined in Equation 12 observed with respect to the uniform probability distribution over all pairs of distinct objects. By reframing Kendall's τ equivalently in terms of mutual information, we immediately gain access to a large number of powerful theoretical tools. For example, we can define a conditional information τ between two lists given a third. For lists R and S given T,

$$\tau_I(R, S \mid T) = I(X_R; X_S \mid X_T). \quad (15)$$

Kendall's τ can tell you whether two sets of rankings are similar, but it cannot tell you why. Information τ can be used as a meta-evaluation tool to find the underlying cause of correlation between measures. We demonstrate the use of information τ as a meta-evaluation tool by using it to analyze measures of the *diversity* of information retrieval systems. In recent years, several diversity measures (e.g. [1, 10, 24]) have been introduced to evaluate how well systems perform in response to ambiguous or underspecified queries that have multiple interpretations. These measures conflate several factors [14], including: a diversity model that rewards novelty and penalizes redundancy, and a measure of ad hoc performance that rewards systems for retrieving highly relevant documents. We wish to know not only whether two diversity measures are correlated, but also the similarity between their component diversity models. Using Kendall's τ, we can observe whether the rankings of systems by each measure are correlated. But even if they are correlated, this could still be for one of two reasons: either both the diversity and the performance components evaluate systems similarly; or else one of the components is similar, and its effect on evaluation is dominant. However, if the measures are correlated when conditioned on their underlying performance components, then this must be due to similarities in their models of diversity.

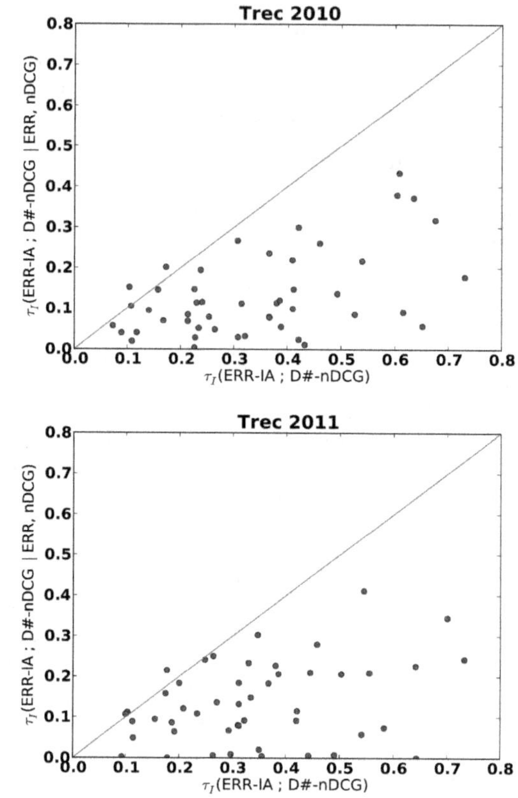

Figure 1: Per-query information τ (conditional rank correlation) between the TREC and NTCIR gold standard diversity measures conditioned on their underlying performance measures.

We measured this effect on the the TREC 2011 and 2012 Web collections [8, 9]. Note that the performance measures are evaluated using graded relevance, while the diversity measures use binary judgments for each subtopic. All evaluations are performed at rank 20. Figure 1 shows the rank correlation between ERR-IA and D#-nDCG, the primary measures reported by TREC and NTCIR [26], when conditioned on their underlying performance models. Each query is computed separately, with each datapoint in the figure corresponding to a different query. Table 1 shows the results of conditioning additional pairs of diversity measures (now averaged over queries in the usual way) on their performance models. The results in Figure 1 are typical of all pairs of measures on a per-query basis.

Our results confirm that while diversity measures are very highly correlated, most of this correlation disappears when one conditions on the underlying performance model. This indicates that most of the correlation is due to the similarity between the performance components and not the diversity components. For example, in TREC 2010, ERR-IA and α-nDCG have an information τ of almost 0.9. However, when conditioned on ERR, the similarity falls to only 0.25. This means that while these two measures are mostly ranking systems for the same reason, that reason is simply ERR. However, of the 0.9 bits that are the same, 0.25 are due to some factor other than ERR. This other factor must presumably be the similarity in their diversity models.

	TREC 2010	TREC 2011
τ_I(ERR-IA ; α-nDCG)	0.8290	0.8375
τ_I(ERR-IA ; α-nDCG | nDCG)	0.4860	0.4434
τ_I(ERR-IA ; α-nDCG | ERR)	0.2499	0.3263
τ_I(ERR-IA ; α-nDCG | nDCG, ERR)	0.2451	0.2805
τ_I(ERR-IA ; D#-nDCG)	0.6390	0.5545
τ_I(ERR-IA ; D#-nDCG | nDCG)	0.3026	0.1728
τ_I(ERR-IA ; D#-nDCG | ERR)	0.1222	0.1442
τ_I(ERR-IA ; D#-nDCG | nDCG, ERR)	0.1239	0.1003

Table 1: TREC 2010 and 2011 information τ (conditional rank correlation) between diversity measures conditioned on ad hoc performance measures.

5. EVALUATION MEASURE

In this section, we demonstrate an extension of our probabilistic framework for evaluation to measuring the correlation between a system and the incomplete ranking generated by a set of relevance judgments. This allows us to define an information-theoretic evaluation measure, *relevance information correlation.* While our measure has novel applications, we will demonstrate that the evaluations produced are consistent with those of existing measures.

To compute mutual information, we must define a sample space, a probability distribution, and random variables. Let the sample space, $\Omega = \{(d_i, d_j)\}$, be the set of all ordered pairs of judged documents. This means that we are ignoring unjudged documents, rather than considering them non-relevant. This is equivalent to computing an evaluation measure on the *condensed list* [23] created by removing all non-judged documents from the list. We define the probability distribution in terms of the QREL to ensure that all ranked lists will be evaluated using the same random experiment. Let $P = U|_{I(g_i \neq g_j)}$, where g_i represents the relevance grade of document d_i, be the uniform probability distribution over all pairs of documents whose relevance grades are not equal. We define a QREL variable Q over ordered pairs of documents as

$$Q\left[(d_i, d_j)\right] = \begin{cases} 1 & \text{if } g_i > g_j \\ 0 & \text{otherwise.} \end{cases} \tag{16}$$

Note that this definition can be applied to both graded and binary relevance judgments.

We now turn our attention to defining a ranked list random variable over ordered pairs of documents (d_i, d_j). If both document d_i and d_j appear in the ranked list, than our output can simply indicate whether d_i was ranked above d_j. If document d_i appears in the ranked list and d_j does not, then we will consider d_i as having been ranked above d_j, and vice versa. If neither d_i nor d_j is ranked, we will output a null value. If we were to instead restrict our attention only to judged document pairs where at least one document is ranked, then a ranked list consisting of a single relevant document followed by some number of non-relevant documents would have perfect mutual information with the QREL—all of the ranked relevant documents appear before all of the ranked non-relevant documents. However, this system must be penalized for preferring all of the ranked non-relevant documents to all of the unranked relevant documents. If we instead use a null value, our example ranked list would almost always output null. This behavior would be independent of the QREL, meaning the two variables will have almost no mutual information. In effect, the null value creates a recall component for our evaluation measure; no system can have a large mutual information with the QREL unless it retrieves most of the relevant documents.

Another problem we must consider is that mutual information is maximized when two variables are completely correlated or completely *anti*-correlated. Consider an example ranked list consisting of a few non-relevant documents followed by several relevant documents and then many more non-relevant documents. Since this example ranked list will disagree with the QREL on almost all document pairs, its random variable will have a very high mutual information with the QREL variable. The system is effectively being rewarded for finding the subset of non-relevant documents that happen to be present in the QREL. To address this, we truncate the list at the last retrieved relevant document prior to evaluation.

Let r_i represent the rank of document d_i in the list S. Then the ranked list variable R_S is defined as

$$R_S\left[(d_i, d_j)\right] = \begin{cases} 1 & \text{if } r_i < r_j \\ 0 & \text{if neither } d_i \text{ nor } d_j \text{were retrieved} \\ -1 & \text{otherwise.} \end{cases} \tag{17}$$

We define our new measure, *Relevance Information Correlation*, as the mutual information between the QREL variable Q and the truncated ranked list variable R

$$RIC(System) = I(R_{System}; Q). \tag{18}$$

RIC is computed separately for each query, and then averaged, as with mean average precision.

In order to compute RIC we must estimate the joint probability distribution of document preferences over Q and R. This could be done in various ways. In this work, we use the maximum likelihood estimate computed separately for each query. Since the MLE requires a large number of observations, RIC is only accurate for recall-oriented evaluation. In future work, we intend to explore other means of estimating $P(Q, R)$ that will allow RIC to be used for precision-oriented evaluation as well.

We also note that RIC has no explicit rank component, and would therefore seem to treat all relevant documents equally independent of the rank at which they were observed. However, there is an *implicit* rank component in that a relevant document that is not retrieved early in the list must be incorrectly ranked below many non-relevant documents. This argument is similar in spirit to Bpref [2].

Our measure is quite novel in its formulation, and makes many non-standard assumptions about information retrieval evaluation. Therefore it is necessary to validate experimentally that our measure prefers the same retrieval systems as existing measures. Note that for two evaluation measures to be considered compatible, it is sufficient that they rank systems in the same relative order; it is not necessary that they always assign systems similar absolute scores. For example, a system's nDCG is often higher than its average precision.

To show that RIC is consistent with AP and nDCG, we computed the RIC, AP, and nDCG of all systems submitted to TRECs 8 and 9. Figure 2 shows the output of RIC plotted against AP (top) and nDCG (bottom) on TRECs 8 (left) and 9 (right) [28, 29]. TREC 8 uses binary relevance

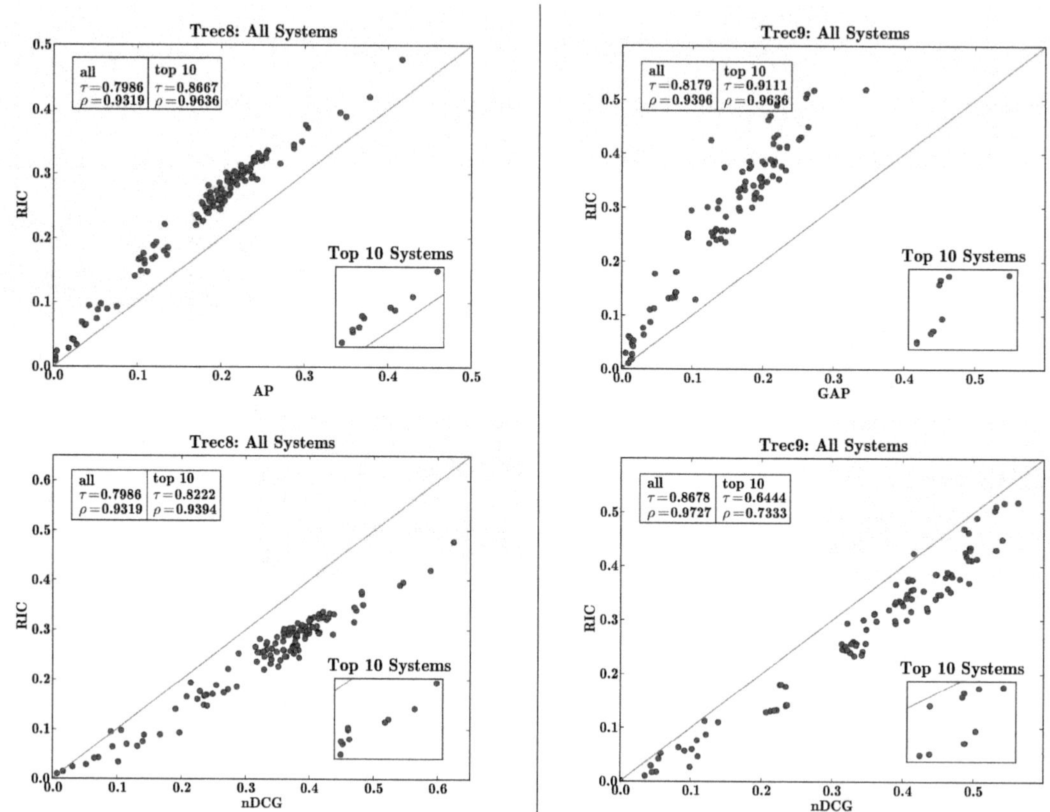

Figure 2: Correlation between RIC and AP (top) and nDCG (bottom). TREC 8 (left) uses binary relevance judgments. TREC 9 (right) uses graded relevance judgments.

	TREC 8	TREC9
(G)AP	0.716	0.648
nDCG	0.713	0.757
MI	0.719	0.744

Table 2: Discriminative power of (graded) AP and nDCG vs. RIC

judgments. TREC 9 uses graded relevance judgments, requiring the use of graded average precision. Inset into each plot is the output of the measures on the top ten systems. For each experiment, we report the Kendall's τ and Spearman's ρ [27] rank correlations for all systems, and for the top ten systems. With Kendall's τ values of at least 0.799 on all systems and 0.644 on top ten systems, the ranking of systems by RIC is still highly correlated with those of both AP and nDCG. However, RIC is not as highly correlated with either AP or nDCG as AP and nDCG are with each other. Note that the correlation between RIC and GAP on TREC 9 is highly monotonic, even if is not particularly linear. This implies that the two measures do rank systems in a consistent relative order, even if RIC is a biased estimator of GAP.

To further validate our measure, we also compute the *discriminative power* [22] of the various measures. Discriminative power is a widely used tool for evaluating a measure's *sensitivity* i.e. how often differences between systems can be detected with high confidence. A high sensitivity can be seen as a necessary, though not sufficient, condition for a good evaluation measure. Discriminative power is defined as the percentage of pairs of runs that are found to be statistically significantly different by some significance test. As per Sakai, we use a two-tailed paired bootstrap test with 1000 bootstrap samples per pair of systems. Our results are displayed in Table 2. As measured by discriminatory power, we see that RIC is at least as sensitive, if not more so, than AP and nDCG.

6. UPPER BOUND ON METASEARCH

In Section 5, we defined an evaluation measure in terms of mutual information. One advantage of this approach is that collections of systems can be evaluated directly by considering the output of their random variables jointly, without their needing to be combined. For a collection of systems, denoted S_1 through S_n, the relevance information correlation can be defined as

$$RIC(S_1, \ldots, S_n) = I(R_{S_1}, \ldots, R_{S_n}; Q) \qquad (19)$$

In this section, we will show that this produces a natural upper bound on metasearch performance that is consistent with other upper bounds appearing in the literature.

We compare our upper bound against those of Montague [19]. Montague describes metasearch algorithms as sorting functions whose comparators, as well as the documents to be sorted, are defined in terms of collections of input systems.

By also using the QREL as input, these algorithms can estimate upper bounds on metasearch performance. These bounds range from the ideal performance that cannot possibly be exceeded by any metasearch algorithm, to descriptions of reasonable metasearch behavior that should be similar to the performance of any quality metasearch algorithm.

Montague defines the following upper bounds on metasearch:

1. Naive: Documents are sorted by comparison of relevance judgments, i.e. the naive upper bound is created by returning all relevant documents returned by any system in the collection above any non-relevant document. Relevant documents not retrieved by any system are not ranked.
2. Pareto: If document A is ranked above document B by all systems, then document A is considered "greater" than document B. Otherwise, the documents are sorted by comparison of relevance judgments.
3. Majoritarian: If document A is ranked above document B by at least half of the systems, then document A is considered "greater" than document B. Otherwise, the documents are sorted by comparison of relevance judgments.

We will compare our direct joint evaluation with these upper bounds, and several metasearch algorithms commonly used as baselines in the IR literature: the CondorcetFuse metasearch algorithm [20], and the comb family of metasearch algorithms [25].

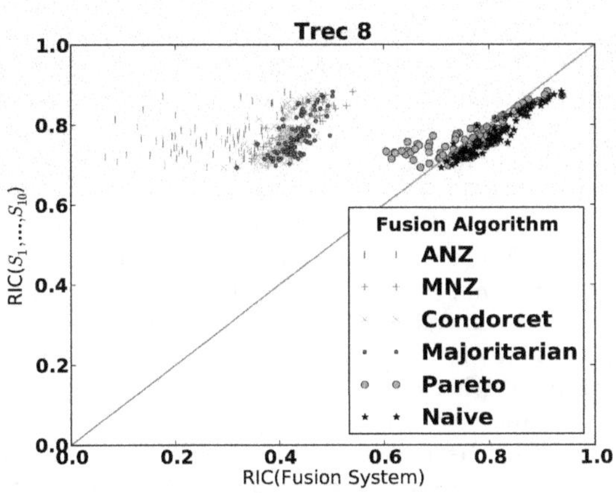

Figure 3: RIC of systems output by metasearch algorithms (Fusion System) versus RIC of systems computed directly ($S_1, \ldots, S_{10}$) without combining.

We examined the direct evaluation and metasearch performance of collections of ten randomly selected systems. Experiments were performed on TREC 8 and 9, with both binary and graded relevance judgments. To conserve space, we only show the results from TREC 8. The results from TREC 9 were highly similar, both when using binary and graded relevance judgments.

Figure 3 shows the RIC of the system output by a metasearch algorithm plotted against the joint RIC of the input systems, and Table 3 shows various measures of their correlation. Montague found that combANZ is inferior to CondorcetFuse and combMNZ, CondorcetFuse and combMNZ

TREC 8	τ	ρ	RMSE
ANZ	0.221	0.330	0.481
MNZ	0.587	0.764	0.351
Condorcet	0.519	0.689	0.362
Majoritarian	0.552	0.735	0.340
Pareto	0.657	0.836	0.044
Naive	0.788	0.931	0.039

Table 3: Correlation between joint distribution and metasearch algorithms (Kendall's τ, Spearman's ρ, root mean square error).

perform comparably to the Majoritarian bound, and the Naive bound is not appreciably better than the Pareto bound. If direct evaluation and the Naive bound are both reasonable estimates of the actual upper bound, then these results should be confirmed by Figure 3 and Table 3, as indeed they are. Note that there is almost no correlation between the joint evalution and the weakest metasearch algorithm, combANZ: combANZ does not approximate the upper bound on metasearch. The correlation improves as the quality of the metasearch algorithm improves, and it does so in a manner consistent with Montague. The correlations between the joint evaluation and the output of combMNZ, CondorcetFuse, and the Majoritarian bound are similar; while they are still biased as estimators, the correlation is beginning to approach monotonicity. Finally, with a root mean square error of 0.039, the joint evaluation estimation of the upper bound is essentially identical to that of the Naive upper bound. If the Naive upper bound is a reasonable estimate of the upper bound on metasearch performance, then so is the joint evaluation of the input systems.

7. INFORMATION DIFFERENCE

In this section, we introduce a novel application of our probabilistic framework. Imagine that you are attempting to improve an existing ranker. On what basis do you decide whether or not your changes are beneficial? One typically evaluates both systems on a number of queries, and measures the difference in average performance. If one system outperforms the other, whether you have made an improvement is clear. But what happens when the systems perform similarly? It could be that your new system is essentially unchanged from your old system, but it is also possible that the two systems chose highly different document and just happened to have very similar evaluation scores. In the latter case, it may be possible to create a new, better system based on a combination of the two existing systems.

We propose to measure the magnitude of the difference between systems in their ranking of documents for which we have relevance information, rather than the magnitude of the difference between their performance. We denote this new quantity as the *information difference* between systems. Our definition of information difference is inspired by the Boolean Algebra symmetric difference operator as applied to information space (see Figure 4).

$$id(S_1, S_2) = I(S_1; Q \mid S_2) + I(S_2; Q \mid S_1) \quad (20)$$

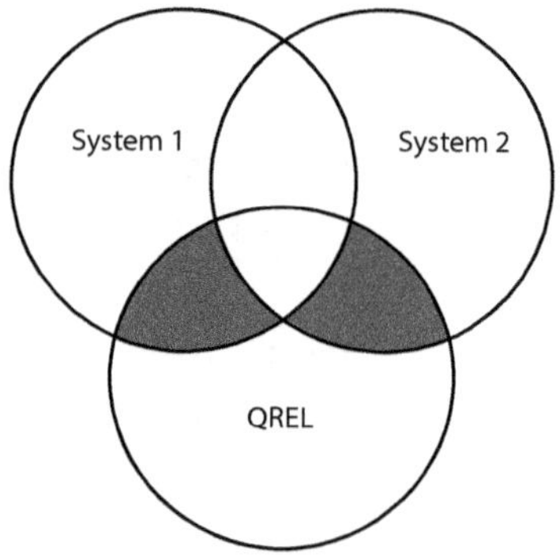

Figure 4: Information difference corresponds to the symmetric difference between the intersections of the systems with the QREL in information space (red portion of the Venn diagram).

As a preliminary validation of information difference, we analyzed the change in AP and information difference between pairs of systems submitted to TREC 8, selected at random. We expect the two to be somewhat directly correlated, since, in general, if two systems rank documents similarly, we would expect them to have similar AP. However, we expect that they will not be highly correlated, since we believe that information difference is much more informative. Our intuition is supported by Figure 5, which shows the magnitude of the change in AP on the horizontal axis, and the information difference on the vertical axis.

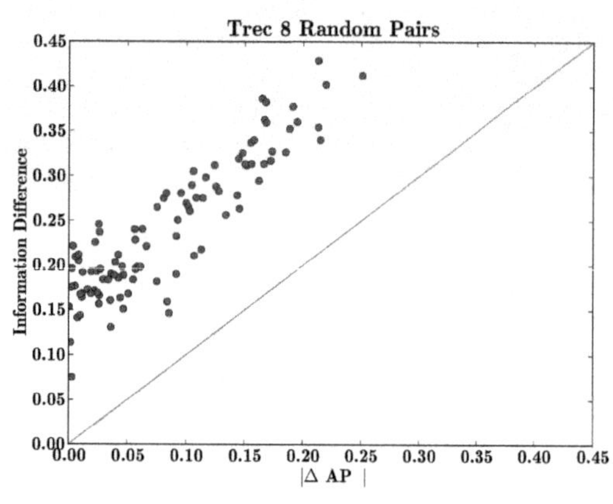

Figure 5: Scatter plot of information difference and the magnitude of change in AP of random pairs of TREC 8 systems.

To demonstrate the utility of information difference, we sorted all the systems submitted to TREC 8 by AP and separated them into twenty equal-sized bins. By construction, each bin contained systems with small differences in performance. Our goal is to distinguish between similar and dissimilar systems within each bin. To this end, all systems within each bin were compared with one other (see Table 4). When the system pairs were sorted by their information difference, both systems in the first 27 pairs were submitted by the same group, whereas sorting by |Δ AP| produced no discernible pattern. It is reasonable to assume that these systems were different instantiations of the same underlying technology. We can therefore conclude that information difference is able to determine whether systems with the same underlying performance are in fact similar, as desired.

Rank	System 1	System 2	*id*	|Δ AP|
1	UB99T	UB99SW	0.010	0.005
2	unc8al32	unc8al42	0.012	0.002
3	fub99tt	fub99tf	0.017	0.000
4	nttd8al	nttd8alx	0.023	0.002
5	ibmg99a	ibmg99b	0.027	0.012
		⋮		
28	isa25t	cirtrc82	0.084	0.004
29	CL99SD	CL99SDopt2	0.086	0.000
30	ok8amxc	ok8alx	0.086	0.006
31	tno8d4	MITSLStd	0.088	0.016
32	uwmt8a2	uwmt8a1	0.089	0.002

Table 4: The systems from TREC 8 were binned by average precision. Information difference and Δ AP were computed for all system pairs within each bin. Sorting by information difference, both systems in the first 27 pairs were submitted by the same group.

8. CONCLUSION

In this work, we developed a probabilistic framework for the analysis of information retrieval systems based on the correlation between a ranked list and the preferences induced by relevance judgments. Using this framework, we developed powerful information theoretic tools for better understanding information retrieval systems. We introduced four preliminary uses of our framework: (1) a measure of conditional rank correlation, *information* τ, which is a powerful meta-evaluation tool whose use we demonstrated on understanding novelty and diversity evalution; (2) a new evaluation measure, *relevance information correlation*, which is correlated with traditional evaluation measures and can be used to (3) evaluate a collection of systems simultaneously, which provides a natural upper bound on metasearch performance; and (4) a measure of the similarity between rankers on judged documents, *information difference*, which allows us to determine whether systems with similar performance are actually different.

Our framework is based on the choice of sample space, probability distribution, and random variables. Throughout this work, we only used a uniform distribution on appropriate pairs of documents. However, not all document pairs are equal. The use of additional distributions is an immediate avenue for improvement that we intend to explore in future work. For example, a geometric distribution may be employed to force our evaluation tools to concentrate their attention at the top of a ranked list.

The primary limitation of our evaluation measure as implemented in this work is that it is only applicable to recall-oriented retrieval tasks. In future work, we intend to develop a precision-oriented version that is applicable to web search. Given such a measure, judgments can be combined in the way systems were in our upper bound on metasearch. In that way, a small number of expensive to produce nominal relevance judgments, a somewhat larger number of somewhat less expensive preference judgments, and a gold-stander ranker could all be used simultaneously to evaluate systems.

Finally, we intend to explore the application of information difference to the understanding of information retrieval models. For example, BM25 and Language Models have long been used as baselines in information retrieval experiments. On the surface, these two models appear to be completely different. And yet, the two share deep theoretical connections [33]. Using information difference, we can determine whether their theoretical similarities outweigh their superficial differences in terms of how they rank documents.

9. REFERENCES

[1] Rakesh Agrawal, Sreenivas Gollapudi, Alan Halverson, and Samuel Ieong. Diversifying search results. In *Proceedings of the Second ACM International Conference on Web Search and Data Mining*, WSDM '09, pages 5–14, New York, NY, USA, 2009. ACM.

[2] Chris Buckley and Ellen M. Voorhees. Retrieval evaluation with incomplete information. In *Proceedings of the 27th annual international ACM SIGIR conference on Research and development in information retrieval*, SIGIR '04, 2004.

[3] Christopher J.C. Burges. From ranknet to lambdarank to lambdamart: An overview. Technical Report MSR-TR-2010-82, Microsoft Research, 2010.

[4] Ben Carterette and Paul N. Bennett. Evaluation measures for preference judgments. In *SIGIR*, 2008.

[5] Ben Carterette, Paul N. Bennett, David Maxwell Chickering, and Susan T. Dumais. Here or there: preference judgments for relevance. In *Proceedings of the IR research, 30th European conference on Advances in information retrieval*, ECIR'08, 2008.

[6] Praveen Chandar and Ben Carterette. Using preference judgments for novel document retrieval. In *Proceedings of the 35th international ACM SIGIR conference on Research and development in information retrieval*, SIGIR '12, 2012.

[7] Olivier Chapelle, Donald Metlzer, Ya Zhang, and Pierre Grinspan. Expected reciprocal rank for graded relevance. In *Proceedings of the 18th ACM conference on Information and knowledge management*, CIKM '09, pages 621–630, New York, NY, USA, 2009. ACM.

[8] Charles L. A. Clarke, Nick Craswell, Ian Soboroff, and Gordon V. Cormack. Overview of the TREC 2010 Web Track. In *19th Text REtrieval Conference*, Gaithersburg, Maryland, 2010.

[9] Charles L. A. Clarke, Nick Craswell, Ian Soboroff, and Ellen M. Voorhees. Overview of the TREC 2011 Web Track. In *20th Text REtrieval Conference*, Gaithersburg, Maryland, 2011.

[10] Charles L.A. Clarke, Maheedhar Kolla, Gordon V. Cormack, Olga Vechtomova, Azin Ashkan, Stefan Büttcher, and Ian MacKinnon. Novelty and diversity in information retrieval evaluation. In *Proceedings of the 31st Annual International ACM SIGIR Conference on Research and Development in Information Retrieval*, SIGIR '08, pages 659–666, New York, NY, USA, 2008. ACM.

[11] Thomas M. Cover and Joy A. Thomas. *Elements of Information Theory*. Wiley-Interscience, 1991.

[12] Nick Craswell, Onno Zoeter, Michael Taylor, and Bill Ramsey. An experimental comparison of click position-bias models. In *Proceedings of the 2008 International Conference on Web Search and Data Mining*, WSDM '08, pages 87–94, New York, NY, USA, 2008. ACM.

[13] Yoav Freund, Raj Iyer, Robert E. Schapire, and Yoram Singer. An efficient boosting algorithm for combining preferences. *J. Mach. Learn. Res.*, 4, December 2003.

[14] Peter B. Golbus, Javed A. Aslam, and Charles L.A. Clarke. Increasing evaluation sensitivity to diversity. In *Journal of Information Retrieval*, To Appear.

[15] Kalervo Järvelin and Jaana Kekäläinen. Cumulated gain-based evaluation of IR techniques. *ACM Transactions on Information Systems*, 20(4):422–446, October 2002.

[16] Thorsten Joachims. Optimizing search engines using clickthrough data. In *Proceedings of the eighth ACM SIGKDD international conference on Knowledge discovery and data mining*, KDD '02, 2002.

[17] M. G. Kendall. A New Measure of Rank Correlation. *Biometrika*, 30(1/2):81–93, June 1938.

[18] Alistair Moffat and Justin Zobel. Rank-biased precision for measurement of retrieval effectiveness. *ACM Trans. Inf. Syst.*, 27(1):2:1–2:27, December 2008.

[19] Mark Montague. *Metasearch: Data Fusion for Document Retrieval*. PhD thesis, Dartmouth College. Dept. of Computer Science, 2002.

[20] Mark Montague and Javed A. Aslam. Condorcet fusion for improved retrieval. In *Proceedings of the eleventh international conference on Information and knowledge management*, CIKM '02, 2002.

[21] Stephen E. Robertson, Evangelos Kanoulas, and Emine Yilmaz. Extending average precision to graded relevance judgments. In *Proceedings of the 33rd international ACM SIGIR conference on Research and development in information retrieval*, SIGIR '10, 2010.

[22] Tetsuya Sakai. Evaluating evaluation metrics based on the bootstrap. In *Proceedings of the 29th annual international ACM SIGIR conference on Research and development in information retrieval*, SIGIR '06, 2006.

[23] Tetsuya Sakai. Alternatives to Bpref. In *Proceedings of the 30th annual international ACM SIGIR conference on Research and development in information retrieval*, SIGIR '07, 2007.

[24] Tetsuya Sakai and Ruihua Song. Evaluating diversified search results using per-intent graded relevance. In *SIGIR*, pages 1043–1052, 2011.

[25] Joseph A. Shaw and Edward A. Fox. Combination of multiple searches. In *The Second Text REtrieval Conference (TREC-2)*, pages 243–252, 1994.

[26] Ruihua Song, Min Zhang, Tetsuya Sakai, Makoto P. Kato, Yiqun Liu, Miho Sugimoto, Qinglei Wang, and Naoki Orii. Overview of the ntcir-9 intent task. In *Proceedings of the 9th NTCIR Workshop*, Tokyo, Japan, 2011.

[27] C. Spearman. The proof and measurement of association between two things. *The American Journal of Psychology*, 1904.

[28] E. M. Voorhees and D. Harman. Overview of the eighth text retrieval conference (TREC-8). In *Proceedings of the Eighth Text REtrieval Conference (TREC-8)*, 2000.

[29] E. M. Voorhees and D. Harman. Overview of the ninth text retrieval conference (TREC-9). In *Proceedings of the Ninth Text REtrieval Conference (TREC-9)*, 2001.

[30] Emine Yilmaz and Javed A. Aslam. Estimating average precision with incomplete and imperfect judgments. In *Proceedings of the 15th ACM international conference on Information and knowledge management*, CIKM '06, 2006.

[31] Emine Yilmaz, Javed A. Aslam, and Stephen Robertson. A new rank correlation coefficient for information retrieval. In *Proceedings of the 31st annual international ACM SIGIR conference on Research and development in information retrieval*, SIGIR '08, 2008.

[32] Emine Yilmaz, Evangelos Kanoulas, and Javed A. Aslam. A simple and efficient sampling method for estimating AP and nDCG. In *Proceedings of the 31st annual international ACM SIGIR conference on Research and development in information retrieval*, SIGIR '08, 2008.

[33] Chengxiang Zhai and John Lafferty. A study of smoothing methods for language models applied to information retrieval. *ACM Trans. Inf. Syst.*, 22(2):179–214, April 2004.

10. APPENDIX

THEOREM 1. $I(X_R; X_S) = \frac{1+\tau}{2}\log(1+\tau) + \frac{1-\tau}{2}\log(1-\tau)$.

PROOF. Denote X_R and X_S as X and Y. Consider the following joint probability distribution table.

		Y	
		-1	1
X	-1	a	b
	1	c	d

Observe that: $a+b+c+d=1$; $C=a+d$, $D=b+c$, and therefore $\tau = a+d-b-c$; and since document pairs appear in both orders, $a=d$ and $b=c$.

The joint probability distribution can be rewritten as follows.

		Y	
		-1	1
X	-1	$\frac{C}{2}$	$\frac{D}{2}$
	1	$\frac{D}{2}$	$\frac{C}{2}$

Observe that the marginal probability $P(X) = P(Y) = (\frac{C}{2}+\frac{D}{2}, \frac{C}{2}+\frac{D}{2}) = (\frac{1}{2}, \frac{1}{2})$.

$$\begin{aligned} I(X;Y) &= KL(P(X,Y)\|P(X)P(Y)) \\ &= \sum_{x,y} p(x,y)\lg\frac{p(x,y)}{p(x)p(y)} \\ &= \sum_{x,y} p(x,y)\lg p(x,y) + \sum_{x,y} p(x,y)\lg\frac{1}{p(x)p(y)}. \end{aligned}$$

Since $P(X,Y) = (\frac{C}{2}, \frac{D}{2}, \frac{C}{2}, \frac{D}{2})$ and $P(X)P(Y) = (\frac{1}{4}, \frac{1}{4}, \frac{1}{4}, \frac{1}{4})$,

$$\begin{aligned} I(X,Y) &= 2\cdot\frac{C}{2}\lg\frac{C}{2} + 2\cdot\frac{D}{2}\lg\frac{D}{2} + 2\cdot\frac{C}{2}\lg 4 + 2\cdot\frac{D}{2}\lg 4 \\ &= C\lg\frac{C}{2} + D\lg\frac{D}{2} + 2C + 2D \\ &= C\lg C - C + D\lg D - D + 2C + 2D \\ &= C\lg C + D\lg D + 1 \\ &= C\lg C + (1-C)\lg(1-C) + 1 \end{aligned}$$

Since $C+D=1$ and $\tau = C-D$, we have that $\tau = 2C-1$, $C = \frac{1+\tau}{2}$ and $D = 1-C = \frac{1-\tau}{2}$.

In terms of C, if H_2 represents the entropy of a Bernoulli random variable ,[3]

$$\begin{aligned} I(X;Y) &= -H_2(C) + 1 \\ &= -H_2\left(\frac{1+\tau}{2}\right) + 1 \\ &= \frac{1+\tau}{2}\lg\frac{1+\tau}{2} + \frac{1-\tau}{2}\lg\frac{1-\tau}{2} + 1 \\ &= \frac{1+\tau}{2}\lg(1+\tau) - \frac{1+\tau}{2} + \frac{1-\tau}{2}\lg(1-\tau) \\ &\quad -\frac{1-\tau}{2} + 1 \\ &= \frac{1+\tau}{2}\lg(1+\tau) + \frac{1-\tau}{2}\lg(1-\tau) \end{aligned}$$

□

COROLLARY 1. *For two ranked lists R and S, $I(X_R; X_S) = 1 - H_2(K)$ where $K = \frac{1-\tau}{2}$ is the normalized Kendall's τ distance between R and S.*

[3] $H_2(p) = -p\lg p - (1-p)\lg(1-p)$. Note that $H_2(p) = H_2(1-p)$.

The Impact of Solid State Drive on Search Engine Cache Management

Jianguo Wang Eric Lo Man Lung Yiu
Department of Computing
The Hong Kong Polytechnic University
{csjgwang, ericlo, csmlyiu}@comp.polyu.edu.hk

Jiancong Tong Gang Wang Xiaoguang Liu
Nankai-Baidu Joint Lab
Nankai University
{lingfenghx, wgzwpzy, liuxguang}@gmail.com

ABSTRACT

Caching is an important optimization in search engine architectures. Existing caching techniques for search engine optimization are mostly biased towards the reduction of random accesses to disks, because random accesses are known to be much more expensive than sequential accesses in traditional magnetic hard disk drive (HDD). Recently, solid state drive (SSD) has emerged as a new kind of secondary storage medium, and some search engines like Baidu have already used SSD to completely replace HDD in their infrastructure. One notable property of SSD is that its random access latency is comparable to its sequential access latency. Therefore, the use of SSDs to replace HDDs in a search engine infrastructure may void the cache management of existing search engines. In this paper, we carry out a series of empirical experiments to study the impact of SSD on search engine cache management. The results give insights to practitioners and researchers on how to adapt the infrastructure and how to redesign the caching policies for SSD-based search engines.

Categories and Subject Descriptors

H.3.3 [**Information Search and Retrieval**]: Search Process

Keywords

Search Engine, Solid State Drive, Cache, Query Processing

1. INTRODUCTION

Caching is an important optimization in search engine architectures. Over the years, many caching techniques have been developed and used in search engines [1, 2, 3, 4, 5, 6, 7, 8, 9, 10, 11, 12]. The primary goal of caching is to improve *query latency* (reduce the query response time). To that end, search engines commonly dedicate portions of servers' memory to cache certain *query results* [1, 5, 7], *posting lists* [2, 3, 6], *documents* [4] and *snippets* [12] in order to avoid excessive disk access and computation.

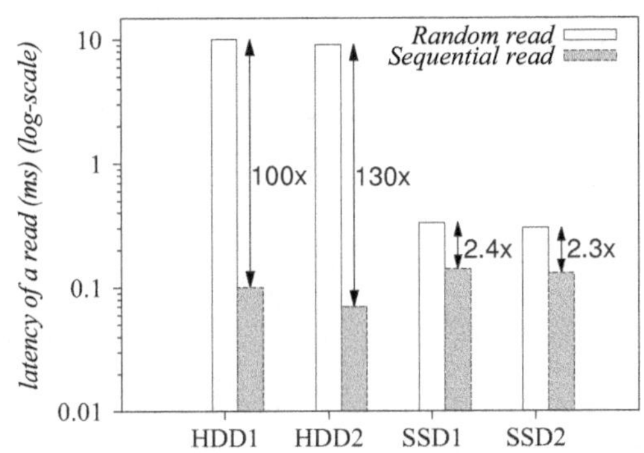

Figure 1: Read latency on two HDDs and two SSDs (for commercial reasons, we do not disclose their brands). Each read fetches 4KB. The OS buffer is by-passed.

Recently, solid state drive (SSD) has emerged as a new kind of secondary storage medium. SSD offers a number of benefits over magnetic hard disk drive (HDD). For example, random reads in SSD are one to two orders of magnitude faster than in HDD [13, 14, 15, 16]. In addition, SSD is much more energy efficient than HDD (around 2.5% of HDD energy consumption [17, 18]). Now, SSD is getting cheaper and cheaper (e.g., it dropped from $40/GB in 2007 to $1/GB in 2012 [19]). Therefore, SSD has been employed in many industrial settings including MySpace [20], Facebook [21], and Microsoft Azure [22]. Baidu, the largest search engine in China, has used SSD to completely replace HDD as its main storage since 2011 [23].

The growing trend of using SSD to replace HDD has raised an interesting research question specific to our community: "*what is the impact of SSD on the cache management of a search engine*?" Figure 1 shows the average cost (latency) of a random read and a sequential read on two brands of SSD and two brands of HDD. It shows that the cost of a random read is 100 to 130 times of a sequential read in HDD. Due to the wide speed gap between random read and sequential read in HDD, the benefit of a cache hit, in traditional, has been largely attributed to the saving of the expensive random read operations. In other words, although a cache hit of a data item could save the random read of seeking the item *and* the subsequent sequential reads of the data when the item spans more

SIGIR'13, July 28–August 1, 2013, Dublin, Ireland.

than one block, the saving of those sequential reads has been traditionally regarded as less noticeable — because the random seek operation usually dominates the data retrieval time.

Since a random read is much more expensive than a sequential read in HDD, most traditional caching techniques have been designed to minimize random reads. The technology landscape, however, has changed if SSD is used to replace HDD. Specifically, Figure 1 shows that the cost of a random read is only about two times of a sequential read in SSD. As such, in an SSD-based search engine infrastructure, the benefit of a cache hit should now attribute to both the saving of the random read and the saving of the subsequent sequential reads for data items that are larger than one block. Furthermore, since both random reads and sequential reads are fast on SSD while query processing in modern search engines involves several CPU-intensive steps (e.g., query result ranking [24, 25] and snippet generations [26, 27]), we expect that SSD would yield the following impacts on the cache management of search engines:

1. Caching techniques should now target to minimize both random reads **and** sequential reads.

2. The size of the data item and the CPU cost of the other computational components (e.g., snippet generation) play a more important role in the effectiveness of various types of caching policies.

In this paper, we carry out a large-scale experimental study to evaluate the impact of SSD on the effectiveness of various caching policies, on all types of cache found in a typical search engine architecture. We note that the traditional metric *cache hit ratio* for evaluating caching effectiveness is inadequate in this study — in the past the effectiveness of a caching policy can be measured by the cache hit ratio because it is a reliable reflection of the actual query latency: a cache hit can save the retrieval of a data item from disk, and the latency improvement is roughly the same for a large data item and a small data item because both require **one** random read, which dominates the time of retrieving the whole data item from disk. With SSD replacing HDD, the cache hit ratio is no longer a reliable reflection of the actual query latency because a larger data item being found in the cache yields a higher query latency improvement over a smaller data item (a cache hit for a larger item can save a number of time-significant sequential reads). In our study, therefore, one caching policy may be more effective than another even though they achieve the same cache hit ratio if one generally caches some larger data items. To complement the inadequacy of cache hit ratio as the metric, our study is based on real replays of a million of queries on an SSD-enabled search engine architecture and **our findings are reported based on actual query latency**.

To the best of our knowledge, this is the first study to evaluate the impact of SSD on search engine cache management. The experimental results here can bring the message "*it is time to rethink about your caching management*" to practitioners who have used or are planning to use SSD to replace HDD in their infrastructures. Furthermore, the results can give the research community insights into the redesign of caching policies for SSD-based search engine infrastructures.

The rest of this paper is organized as follows. Section 2 provides an overview of contemporary search engine architecture and the various types of cache involved. Section 3 presents the set of evaluation experiments carried out and the evaluation results. Section 4 discusses some related studies of this paper. Section 5 summarizes the main findings of this study.

2. BACKGROUND

In this section, we first give an overview of the architecture of the state-of-the-art Web search engines and the cache types involved (Section 2.1). Then we give a review of the various types of caching policies used in Web search engine cache management (Section 2.2).

2.1 Search Engine Architecture

The architecture of a typical large-scale search engine [28, 29, 30] is shown in Figure 2. A search engine is typically composed by three sets of servers: *Web Servers* (WS), *Index Servers* (IS), and *Document Servers* (DS).

Web Servers The web servers are the front-end for interacting with end users and coordinating the whole process of query evaluation. Upon receiving a user's query q with n terms $t_1, t_2, ..., t_n$ [STEP ①], the web server that is in charge of q checks whether q is in its in-memory *Query Result Cache* (QRC) [1, 11, 31, 3, 5, 7, 9, 10]. The QRC maintains query results of some past queries. If the results of q are found in the QRC (i.e., a cache hit), the server returns the cached results of q to the user directly. Generally, query results are roughly the same size and a query result consists of (i) the title, (ii) the URL, and (iii) the snippet [26, 27] (i.e., an extract of the document with terms in q being highlighted) of the top-k ranked results related to q (where k is a system parameter, e.g., 10 [31, 32, 12, 10]). If the result of q is not found in the QRC (i.e., a cache miss), the query is forwarded to an index server [STEP ②].

Index Servers The index servers are responsible for the computation of the top-k ranked result related to a query q. An index server works by: [STEP IS1] retrieving the corresponding *posting list* $PL_i = [d_1, d_2, ...]$ of each term t_i in q, [STEP IS2] intersecting all the retrieved posting lists $PL_1, PL_2, ..., PL_n$ to obtain the list of document identifiers (ids) that contain all terms in q, and [STEP IS3] ranking the documents for q according to a ranking model. After that, the index server sends the ordered list of document ids $d_1, d_2, ..., d_k$ of the top-k most relevant documents of query q back to the web server [STEP ③]. In an index server, an in-memory *Posting List Cache* (PLC) [11, 3, 33] is employed to cache the posting lists of some terms. Upon receiving a query $q(t_1, t_2, ..., t_n)$ from a web server, an index server skips STEP IS1 if a posting list is found in the PLC.

Document Servers Upon receiving the ordered list of document ids $d_1, d_2, ..., d_k$ from the index server, the web server forwards the list and the query q to a document server for further processing [STEP ④]. The document server is responsible for the generating the final result. The final result is a Web page that includes the title, URL, and a snippet for each of the top-k documents. The snippet s_i of a document d_i is query-specific — it is the portion of a document which can best match the terms in q. The generation process is as follows: [STEP DS1] First, the original documents that the list of document ids referred to are retrieved. [STEP DS2] Then, the snippet of each document for query q is generated. There are two levels of caches in the document servers: *Snippet Cache* (SC) [12] and *Document Cache* (DC) [4]. The in-memory Snippet Cache (SC) stores some snippets that have been previously generated for some query-document pairs. If a particular query-document pair is found in the SC, STEP DS1 and STEP DS2 for that pair can be skipped. The in-memory Document Cache (DC) stores some documents that have been previously retrieved. If a particular requested document is in the DC, STEP DS1 can be skipped. As the output, the document server returns the final result (in the form of a Web page with a ranked list of snippets of the k most relevant documents of query q) to the web server [STEP ⑤] and the web server

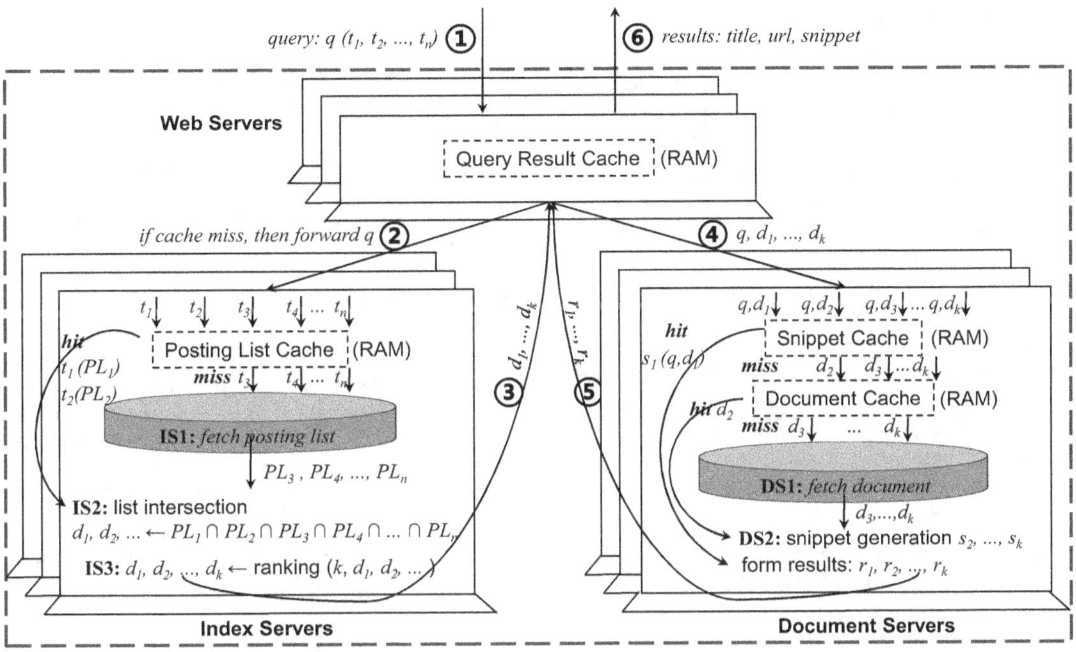

Figure 2: Web search engine architecture

may cache the result in the QRC and then pass the result back to the end user [STEP ⑥].

2.2 Caching Policy

Caching is a widely-used optimization technique to improve system performance [1, 34, 35, 36]. Web search engines use caches in different types of servers to reduce the query response time [11]. There are two types of caching policies being used in search engines: (1) *Dynamic Caching* and (2) *Static Caching*. Dynamic caching is the classic. If the cache memory is full, dynamic caching follows a *replacement policy* (a.k.a. *eviction policy*) to *evict* some items in order to admit the new items [37, 38, 39]. Static caching is less common but does exist in search engines [1, 5, 3, 6, 8, 9, 10]. Initially when the cache is empty, a static cache follows an *admission policy* to select data items to fill the cache. Once the cache has been filled, it does not admit any new items at run-time. The same cache content continuously serves the requests and its entire content is refreshed in a periodic manner [1]. Static caching can avoid the situations of having long-lasting popular items being evicted by the admission of many momentarily popular items as in dynamic caching.

2.2.1 Cache in Web Servers

Query Result Cache (QRC) is the cache used in the web servers. It caches the query results such that the whole stack of query processing can be entirely skipped if the result of query q is found in the QRC. Both dynamic and static query result caches exist in the literature.

Dynamic Query Result Cache Markatos [1] was the first to discuss about the use of dynamic query result cache (D-QRC) in search engines. By analyzing the query logs of Excite search engine, the authors observed a significant temporal locality in the queries. Therefore, they proposed the use of query result cache. Two classic replacement policies were used there: least-recently-used (LRU) and the least-frequently-used (LFU). In this paper, we refer them as D-QRC-LRU and D-QRC-LFU, respectively.

Recently, Gan and Suel [7] have developed a feature-based replacement policy for D-QRC. In this paper, we refer this policy as D-QRC-FB. That policy applies machine learning techniques offline to learn the values of a set of query features from the query log. The cache replacement is then tuned using those values.

Static Query Result Cache Markatos [1] also discussed about the potential use of static caching in search engines. In that work, a static query result cache with an admission policy that analyzes the query logs and fills the cache with the most frequently posed queries was proposed. In this paper, we refer this policy as S-QRC-Freq.

Ozcan et al. [5] reported that some query results cached by S-QRC-Freq policy are not useful because there is a significant number of frequent queries quickly lose their popularities but still reside in the static cache before the next periodic cache refresh. Consequently, they proposed another admission policy that selects queries with high *frequency stability*. Queries with high frequency stability are those frequent queries and the logs show that they remain frequent over a time period. In this paper, we refer to this as S-QRC-FreqStab. Later on, Ismail et al. [8, 9, 10] developed a cost-aware replacement policy for S-QRC. In addition to traditional factors such as the popularity of terms, it also takes into account the latency of a query, as different queries may have different processing time. Nonetheless, its policy has not considered the cost of other expensive steps (e.g., snippet generation) in the whole query processing stack. In this paper, we refer that as S-QRC-CA.

Remark: According to [7], D-QRC-FB has the highest effectiveness among all D-QRC policies. Nonetheless, it requires a lot of empirical tuning on the various parameters used by the machine learning techniques. According to [8, 9, 10], S-QRC-CA is the most stable and effective policy in static query result cache. D-QRC and S-QRC can co-exist and share the main memory of a web server. In [31], the empirically suggested ratios for D-QRC to S-QRC are 6:4, 2:8, and 7:3 for Tiscali, AltaVista, and Excite data, respectively.

2.2.2 *Cache in Index Servers*

Posting List Cache (PLC) is the cache used in the index servers. It caches some posting lists in the memory so that the disk read of a posting list PL of a term t in query q can possibly be skipped. Both dynamic and static posting list caches exist in the literature.

Dynamic Posting List Cache Saraiva et al. [11] were the first to discuss the effectiveness of dynamic posting list caching in index servers. In that work, the simple LRU policy was used. In this paper, we refer this as D-PLC-LRU. In [3, 6], the authors also evaluated another common used policy, LFU, in dynamic PLC, in which we refer this as D-PLC-LFU in this paper. In addition, the authors observed that a popular term tends to have a longer posting list. Therefore, to balance the tradeoff between term popularity and the effective use of the cache (to cache more items), the authors developed a replacement policy that favors terms with a high frequency to posting list length ratio. In this paper, we refer this policy as D-PLC-FreqSize.

Static Posting List Cache Static posting list caching was first studied in [2] and the admission policy was based on selecting posting lists with high access frequency. In this paper, we refer to this as S-PLC-Freq. In [3, 6], the static cache version of D-PLC-FreqSize was also discussed. We refer that as S-PLC-FreqSize here.

Remark: According to [3, 6], S-PLC-FreqSize is the winner over all static and dynamic posting list caching policies.

2.2.3 *Cache in Document Servers*

Two types of caches could be used in the document servers: Document Cache (DC) and Snippet Cache (SC). These caches store some documents and snippets in the memory of the document servers. So far, only dynamic document cache and dynamic snippet cache have been discussed and there is no corresponding static caching technique yet.

Document Cache In [4], the authors observed that the time of reading a document from disk dominates the snippet generation process. So, they proposed to cache some documents in the document servers's memory so as to reduce the snippet generation time. In that work, the simple LRU replacement policy was used and here we refer it as DC-LRU. According to [4], document caching is able to significantly reduce the time for generating snippets.

Snippet Cache In [12], the authors pointed out that the snippet generation process is very expensive in terms of both CPU computation and disk access in the document servers. Therefore, the authors proposed to cache some generated snippets in the document server's main memory. In this paper, we refer this as SC-LRU because it uses the LRU policy as replacement policy.

3. THE IMPACT OF SSD

In this study, we use the typical search engine architecture (Figure 2) to evaluate the impact of SSD on the cache management of the index servers (Section 3.1), document servers (Section 3.2), and the web servers (Section 3.3). We focus on a pure SSD-based architecture like Baidu [23]. Many studies predict that SSD will soon completely replace HDD in all layers [40, 41, 42]. The study of using SSD as a layer between main memory and HDD in a search engine architecture before SSD completely replaces HDD has been studied elsewhere in [43].

Experimental Setting We deploy a Lucene[1] based search engine implementation on a sandbox infrastructure consisting of one index server, one document server, and one web server. All servers are Intel commodity machines (2.5GHz CPU, 8GB RAM), with Windows 7 installed. We have carried out our experiments on two SSDs and two HDDs (evaluated in Figure 1). The experimental results are largely similar and thus we only present the results of using SSD1 and HDD1. In the experiments, the OS buffer is disabled.

We use a real collection of 5.3 million Web pages[2] crawled in the middle of 2008, by Sogou (`sogou.com`), a famous commercial search engine in China. The entire data set takes over 5TB. To accommodate our experimental setup, we draw a random sample of 100GB data. It is a reasonable setting because large-scale Web search engines shard their indexes and data across clusters of machines [23]. As a reference, the sampled data sets in some recent works are 15GB [6], 37GB in [10], and 2.78 million Web pages in [3]. Table 1 shows the characteristics of our sampled data.

Number of documents	11,970,265
Average document size	8KB
Total data size	100GB
Inverted index size	10GB

Table 1: Statistics of Web data

As mentioned in the introduction, the cache hit ratio alone is inadequate to evaluate the effectiveness of caching techniques. So, the experiments are done by a replay of real queries found in Sogou search engine in June 2008[3], and the average end-to-end query latency is reported in tandem with cache hit ratio. The log contains 51.5 million queries. To ensure the replay can be done in a manageable time, we draw a random sample of 1 million queries for our experiments (as a reference, 0.7 million queries were used in [10]). The query frequency and term frequency of our sampled query set follow power-law distribution with skew-factor $\alpha = 0.85$ and 1.48, respectively (see Figure 3). As a reference, the query frequencies in some related work like [11], [7], and [6] follow power-law distribution with α equals 0.59, 0.82, and 0.83, respectively; and the term frequencies in some recent work like [6] follow power-law distribution with $\alpha = 1.06$.

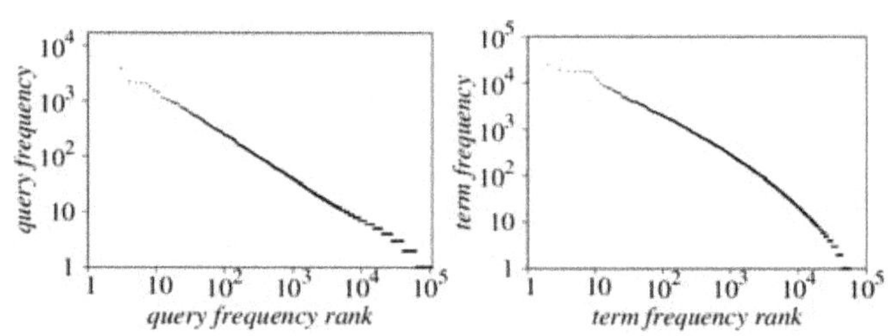

(a) Query frequency distribution (b) Term frequency distribution

Figure 3: Frequency distribution of our query set

In addition, our sampled query set also exhibits the property that the temporal locality of terms is higher than that of queries [11, 3, 6] by observing that the skew-factor α of the query frequency is lower than that of the term frequency. Table 2 shows the characteristics of our query set.

We divide the real query log into two parts: 50% of queries are used for warming the cache and the other 50% are for the replay, following the usual settings [1, 8, 10, 32, 9].

[1] `http://lucene.apache.org`

[2] `http://www.sogou.com/labs/dl/t-e.html`

[3] `http://www.sogou.com/labs/dl/q-e.html`

Number of queries	1,000,000
Number of distinct queries	200,444
Number of terms	1,940,671
Number of distinct terms	82,503
Total size of the posting lists of the distinct terms	3.89GB
Power-law skew-factor α for query frequency	0.85
Power-law skew-factor α for term frequency	1.48

Table 2: Statistics of query log data

In the experiments, we follow some standard settings found in recent work. Specifically, we follow [31, 32, 12, 10] to retrieve the top-10 most relevant documents. We follow [11] to configure the snippet generator to generate snippets with at most 250 characters. Posting list compression is enabled. To improve the experimental repeatability, we use the standard variable-byte compression method [44] in the experiments. The page (block) size in the system is 4KB [45, 46, 47]. When evaluating the caching policy on one type of cache, we disable all other caches in the sandbox. For example, when evaluating the query result cache on the web server, the posting list cache, snippet cache, and document cache are all disabled.

3.1 The Impact of SSD on Index Servers

We first evaluate the impact of SSD on the posting list cache management in an index server. As mentioned, on SSD, a long posting list being found in the cache should have a larger query latency improvement than a short posting list being found because (i) a cache hit can save more sequential read accesses if the list is a long one and (ii) the cost of a sequential read is now comparable to the cost of a random read (see Figure 1).

To verify our claim, Figure 4 shows the access latency of fetching from disk the posting lists of terms found in our query log. We see that the latency of reading a list from HDD increases mildly with the list length because the random seek operation dominates the access time. In contrast, we see the latency of reading a list from SSD increases with the list length at a faster rate.

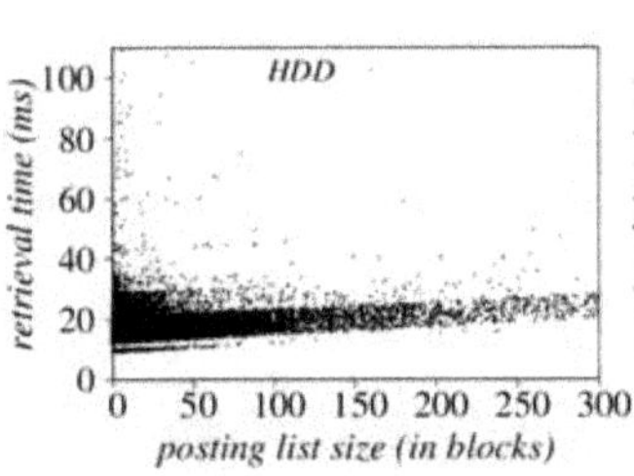

(a) on HDD

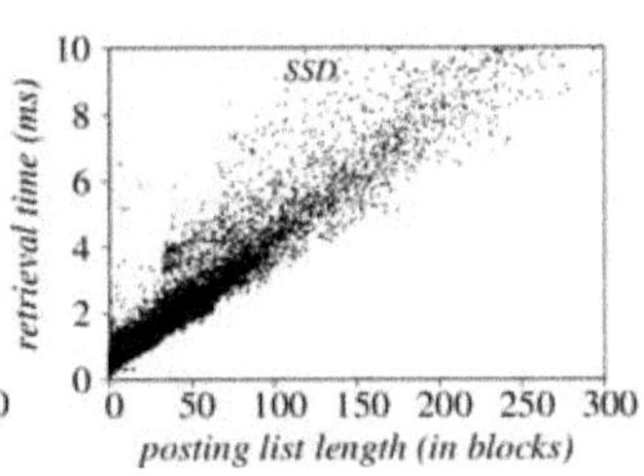

(b) on SSD

Figure 4: Read access latency of posting lists of varying lengths

Based on that observation, we believe that the effectiveness of some existing posting list caching policies would change when they are applied to an SSD-based search engine infrastructure. For example, according to [3, 6], S-PLC-FreqSize has the best caching effectiveness on HDD-based search engines because it favors **popular terms with short posting lists** (i.e., a high frequency to length ratio) for the purpose of caching more popular terms. However, on SSD, a short list being in the cache has **a smaller query latency improvement** than a long list. As such, we believe that design principle is void in an SSD-based search engine infrastructure.

To verify our claim, we carried out experiments to re-evaluate the static and dynamic posting list caching policies on our SSD sandbox. In the evaluation, we focus on the effectiveness of individual caching policy type. The empirical evaluation of the optimal ratio between static cache and dynamic cache on SSD-based search engine architecture is beyond the scope of this paper.

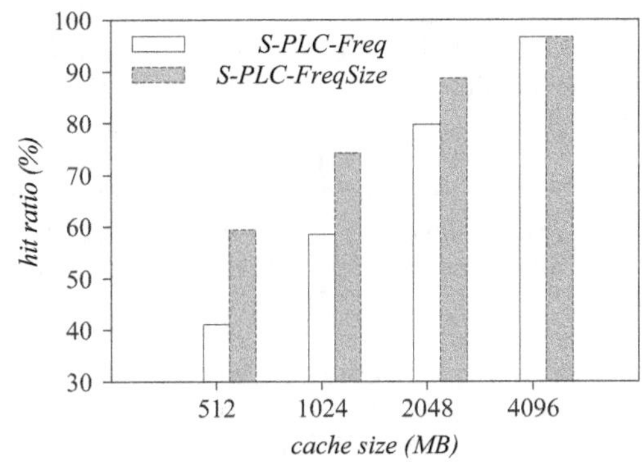

(a) Hit ratio

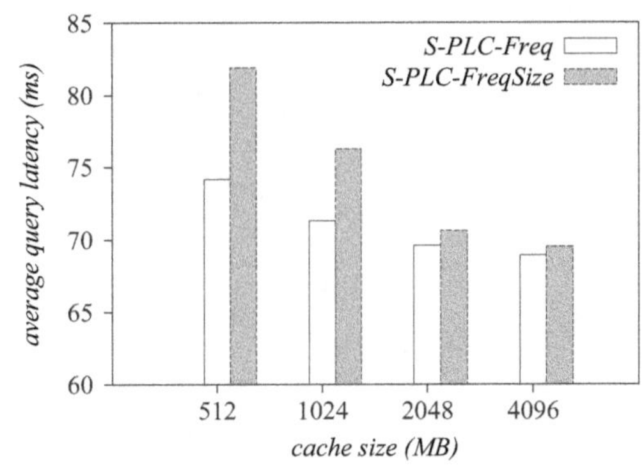

(b) Query latency on SSD

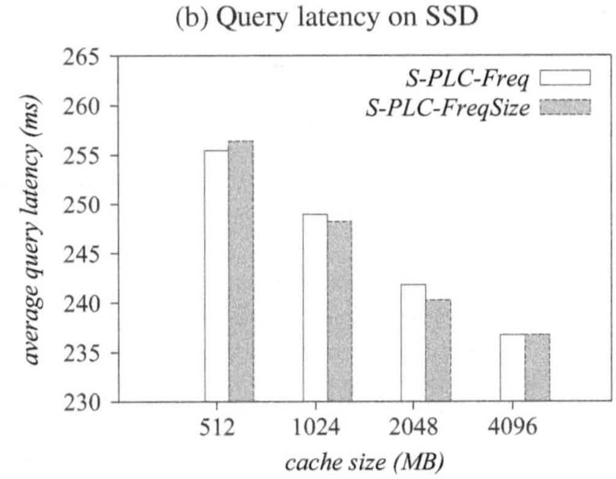

(c) Query latency on HDD

Figure 5: [Index Server] Effectiveness of static posting list caching policies

Reevaluation of static posting list caching policy on SSD We begin with presenting the evaluation results of the two existing static query result caching policies, (1) S-PLC-Freq and (2) S-PLC-FreqSize, mentioned in Section 2.2.2. Figure 5 shows the cache hit ratio and the average query latency of S-PLC-Freq and S-PLC-FreqSize under different cache memory sizes.

Echoing the result in [3, 6], Figure 5(a) shows that S-PLC-FreqSize, which tends to cache popular terms with short posting lists, has a higher cache hit ratio than S-PLC-Freq. The two policies have the same 98% cache hit ratio when the cache size is 4GB because the cache is large enough to accommodate all the posting lists of the query terms (3.89GB; Table 2) in the cache warming phase. The 2% cache miss is attributed to the difference between the terms found in the training queries and the terms found in the replay queries.

Although having a higher cache hit ratio, Figure 5(b) shows that the average query latency of S-PLC-FreqSize is actually longer than S-PLC-Freq in an SSD-based search engine architecture. As the caching policy S-PLC-FreqSize tends to cache terms with short posting lists, the benefit brought by the higher cache hit ratio is watered down by the fewer sequential read savings caused by short posting lists. This explains why S-PLC-FreqSize becomes poor in terms of query latency. Apart from the above, the experimental results above are real examples that illustrate cache hit ratio is not a reliable metric for caching management in SSD-based search engine architectures.

Figure 5(c) shows the average query latency on HDD. We see a surprising result: even on HDD cache hit ratio is not always reliable! Specifically, we see that S-PLC-FreqSize's average query latency is slightly worse than S-PLC-Freq at 512MB cache memory even though the former has a much higher cache hit ratio than the latter. To explain, Figure 6 shows the average size of the posting lists participated in all cache hits (i.e., whenever there is a hit in the PLC, we record its size and report the average).

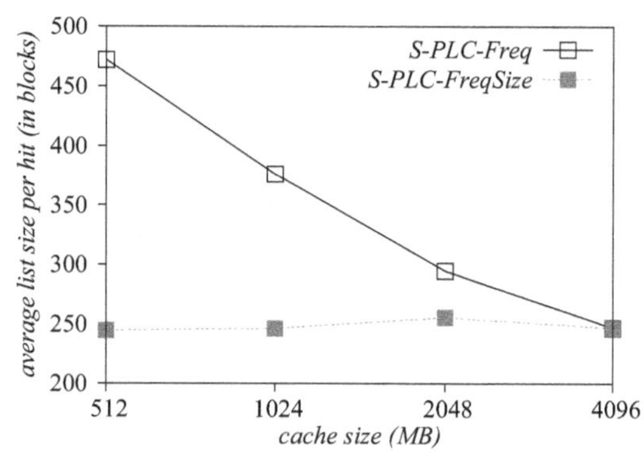

Figure 6: Average list size (in blocks) of all hits in static posting list cache

We see that when the cache memory is small (512MB), S-PLC-Freq keeps the longest (most frequent) posting lists in the cache. In contrast, S-PLC-FreqSize consistently keeps short lists in the cache. At 512MB cache memory, a cache hit under S-PLC-Freq policy can save $470 - 250 = 220$ more sequential reads than S-PLC-FreqSize. Even though sequential reads are cheap on HDD, a total of 220 sequential reads are actually as expensive as two random seeks (Figure 1). In other words, although Figure 5(a) shows that the cache hit ratio of S-PLC-Freq is 20% lower than S-PLC-FreqSize at 512MB cache, that is outweighed by the two extra random seeks saving between the two policies. That explains why S-PLC-Freq slightly outperforms S-PLC-FreqSize at 512MB cache. Of course, when the cache memory increases, S-PLC-Freq starts to admit more short lists into the cache memory, which reduces its benefit per cache hit, and that causes S-PLC-FreqSize to outperform S-PLC-Freq again through the better cache hit ratio.

Reevaluation of dynamic posting list caching policy on SSD We next present the evaluation results of the three existing dynamic query result caching policies, (1) D-PLC-LRU, (2) D-PLC-LFU, and (3) D-PLC-FreqSize, mentioned in Section 2.2.2. Figure 7 shows the cache hit ratio and the average query latency of the three policies under different cache memory sizes.

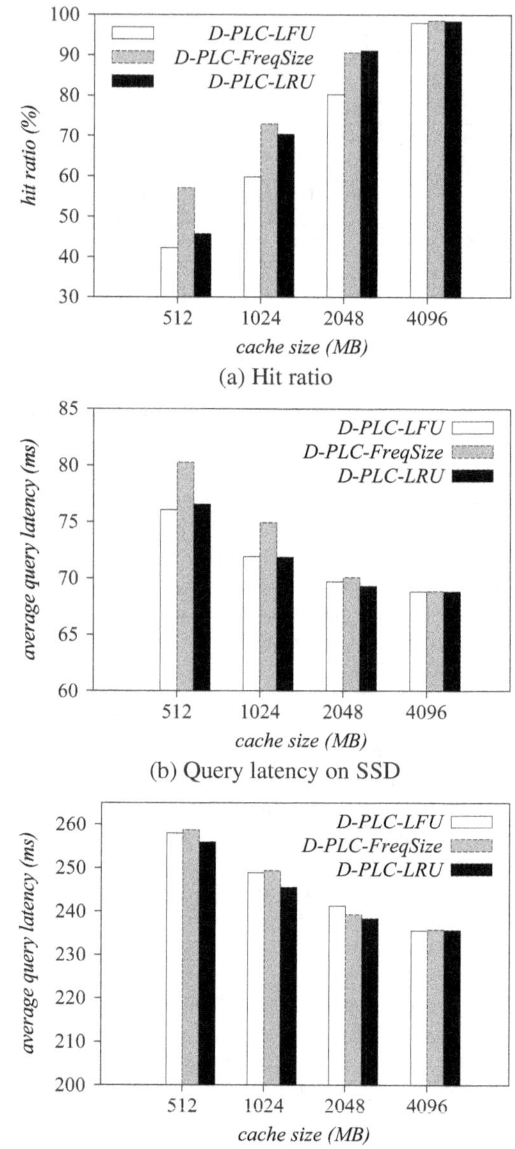

(a) Hit ratio

(b) Query latency on SSD

(c) Query latency on HDD

Figure 7: [Index Server] Effectiveness of dynamic posting list cache policies

First, we also see that while D-PLC-FreqSize has a better cache hit ratio than D-PLC-LFU (Figure 7(a)), its query latency is actually longer than D-PLC-LFU (Figure 7(b)) in SSD-based architecture. This further supports that the claim of favoring terms with high frequency over length ratio no longer sustains in SSD-based search engine architecture. Also, this gives yet another example of the fact that cache hit ratio is not a reliable measure in SSD caching management.

Second, comparing D-PLC-LRU and D-PLC-LFU, we see that while D-PLC-LFU has a poorer cache hit ratio than D-PLC-LRU, their query latencies are quite close in SSD-based architecture. As is shown in [3, 6], the posting list length generally increases with the term frequency, therefore D-PLC-LFU, which favors terms with high frequency, also favors terms with long posting lists. As mentioned, on SSD, the benefit of finding a term with a longer list in cache is higher than that of finding a term with shorter list. This explains why D-PLC-LFU has a query latency close to D-PLC-LRU, which has a higher cache hit ratio.

Figure 7(c) shows the average query latency on HDD. First, we once again see that cache hit ratio is not reliable even on HDD-based architecture. For example, while D-PLC-FreqSize has a higher cache hit ratio than D-PLC-LFU (except when the cache is large enough to hold all posting lists), their query latencies are quite close to each other in an HDD-based architecture. That is due to the same reason that we explained in static caching — Figure 8 shows that D-PLC-LFU can save hundreds of sequential reads more than D-PLC-FreqSize per cache hit when the cache memory is less than 1GB. That outweighs the cache hit ratio difference between the two. In contrast, while D-PLC-LRU has a better cache hit ratio than D-PLC-LFU, they follow the tradition that the former outperforms the latter in latency because Figure 8 shows the size difference of the posting lists that participated in the cache hits (i.e., the benefit gap in terms of query latency) between D-PLC-LRU and D-PLC-LFU is not as significant as the time of one random seek operation. Therefore, D-PLC-LRU yields a shorter query latency than D-PLC-LFU based on its higher cache hit ratio.

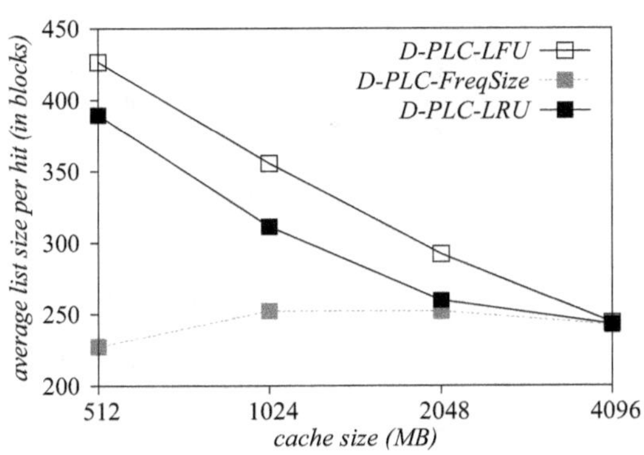

Figure 8: Average list size (in blocks) of all hits in dynamic posting list cache

3.2 The Impact of SSD on Document Servers

We next evaluate the impact of SSD on the cache management of document servers. A document server is responsible for storing part of the whole document collection and generating the final query result. It receives a query q and an ordered list of document ids $\{d_1, d_2, \ldots, d_k\}$ of the k most relevant documents of q from a web server, retrieves the corresponding documents from the disk, and generates the query-specific snippet for each document and consolidates them as a result page. In the process, k query-specific snippets have to be generated. If a query-specific snippet $\langle q, d_i \rangle$ is found in the snippet cache, the retrieval of d_i from the disk and the generation of that snippet are skipped. If a query-specific snippet is not found in the snippet cache, but the document d_i is in found the document cache, the retrieval of d_i from the disk is skipped. In our Web data (Table 1), a document is about 8KB on average. With a 4KB page size, retrieving a document from the disk thus requires one random seek (read) and a few more sequential reads. In traditional search engine architecture using HDD in the document servers, the latency from receiving the query and document list from the web server to the return of the query result is dominated by the k random read operations that seek the k documents from the HDD (see Figure 9(a)). These motivated the use of document cache to improve the latency. As the random reads are much faster on SSD, we now believe that the time bottleneck in the document servers will shift from document retrieval (disk access) to snippet generation (CPU computation). More specifically, the snippet generation process that finds every occurrence of q in d_i and identifies the best text synopsis [26, 27] according to a specific ranking function [27] is indeed CPU-intensive. Figure 9(b) shows that the CPU time spent on snippet generation becomes two times the document retrieval time if SSD is used in a document server. Therefore, contrary to the significant time reduction brought by document cache in traditional HDD-based search engine architectures [26], we believe the importance of document cache in SSD-based search engine architectures is largely diminished. In contrast, we believe the snippet cache is far more powerful in an SSD-based search engine architecture for two reasons: (1) a cache hit in a snippet cache can reduce both the time of snippet generation and document retrieval; and (2) the memory footprint of a snippet (e.g., 250 characters) is much smaller than the memory footprint of a document (e.g., an average 8KB in our Web data). That implies a double-benefit of the use of snippet cache over document cache: the same amount of cache memory in a web server can cache many more snippets than documents, and the benefit of a snippet cache hit is much more significant than the benefit of a document cache hit.

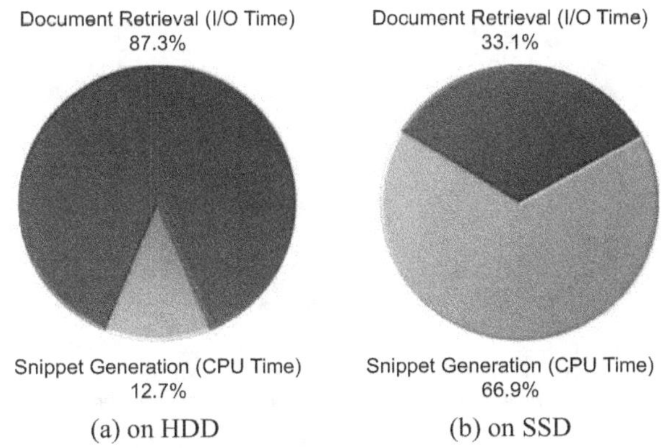

Figure 9: Document retrieval time vs. snippet generation in a document server

To verify our claims, we carried out experiments to vary the memory ratio between the snippet cache and the document cache in our SSD-based sandbox infrastructure. The caching policies in document cache and snippet cache are DC-LRU [4] and SC-LRU [12], respectively. Figure 10 shows the query latency and the hit ratios of the snippet cache and document cache when varying the memory allocation ratio between snippet cache and document cache of 2GB cache memory. Figure 10(a) shows the cache hit ratio of snippet cache increases when we allocate more memory to the snippet cache, but when we continue to allocate more than 2GB $\times$ 40% = 800MB of memory to the snippet cache, the snippet cache hit ratio stays flat because the memory footprint of a snippet is so small that all snippets generated in the warming phase can be resided in the cache. When we go on allocating more memory to the snippet cache even after all snippets could be cached in the memory, it only gives less memory to the document cache. Therefore, the document cache hit ratio in Figure 10(a) continues to drop even when the snippet cache hit ratio has plateaued out. Figure 10(b) shows that when we allocate more memory to the snippet cache (i.e., the document cache has less memory allocated), the query latency drops monotonically before all snippets are in the cache. Furthermore, after all snippets are in the cache and we allocate less memory to the document cache, the query latency almost stays flat. The results indicate that snippet caching is far more ef-

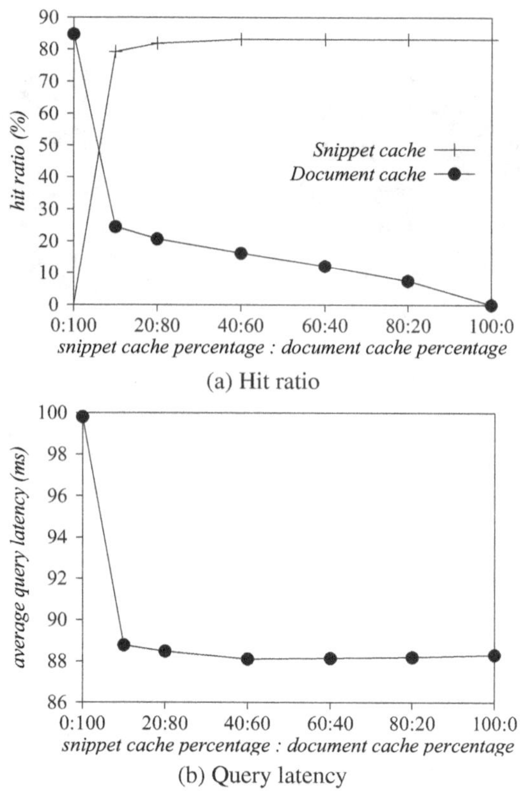

Figure 10: [Document Server] Effectiveness of snippet cache and document cache on SSD

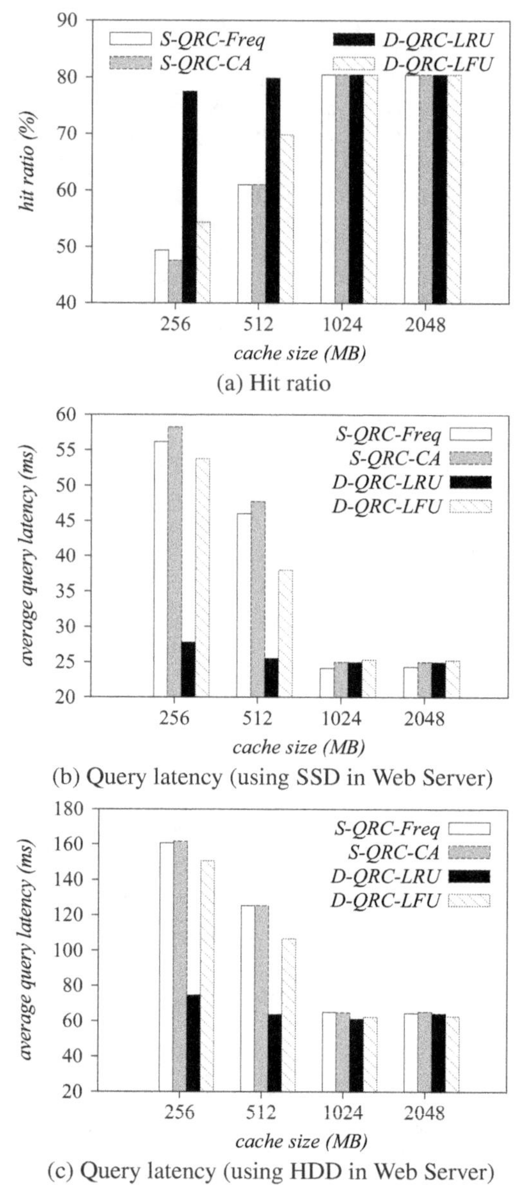

Figure 11: [Web Server] Effectiveness of query result caching policies on SSD and HDD

fective than document caching. The observations above persist for cache memory of size 512MB, 1GB, and 4GB (figures are omitted for space reasons).

3.3 The Impact of SSD on Web Servers

We believe the use of SSD has no impact on the cache management in the web servers because the storage media does not play a major role in web servers (see Figure 2). Therefore, we believe that the use of SSD has no impact on the effectiveness of the caching policies either. Figure 11 shows the cache hit ratio and query latency of four selected query result caching policies: (1) D-QRC-LRU, (2) D-QRC-LFU, and (3) S-QRC-Freq, (4) S-QRC-CA. We see that the tradition holds here: when one policy has a higher cache hit ratio than the others, its query latency is also shorter than the others.[4]

4. RELATED STUDIES

SSD is expected to gradually replace HDD as the primary permanent storage media in both consumer computing and enterprise computing [41, 42, 14, 47, 40] because of its outstanding performance, small energy footprint, and increasing capacity. This has led to a number of studies that aim to better understand the impacts of SSD on different computer systems.

The discussion of the impacts of SSD on computer systems had started as early as in 1995 [48], in which an SSD-aware file system was proposed. Later on, more SSD-aware file systems have been designed, e.g., JFFS [49], YAFFS [50]. After that, the discussion has extended to other components in computer systems, e.g., virtual machine [51, 52], buffer manager [53, 54], I/O scheduler [55], and RAID [56, 57].

The discussion of the impacts of SSD on database systems, our sister field, had started as early as in 2007 [58]. Since then, SSD has become an active topic in database research. The discussions cover the impacts of SSD on database architecture [58, 14, 59], query processing [47, 60], index structures [61, 62, 63] and algorithms [45], data placement and migration [64, 65], transaction management [14, 66, 67] and buffer management [68, 69]. Most concern about the asymmetric performance between slow random write and fast sequential write on SSD [70, 61, 62, 63, 58, 14, 59, 45, 64, 67], some concern about the asymmetric fast read and slow write [68,

[4] In Figure 11(a), the cache hit ratio does not further increase with more than 1024MB of cache memory simply because all query results generated in the warming phase can reside in the cache. Although we claim that SSD has no impact on the cache management in the web servers, Figure 11(b) and Figure 11(c) still show differences in query latency — that is merely due to the other steps (e.g., the posting list retrieval step) in the index server and document server are also sped up by the use of SSD in this experiment.

14, 69, 45, 66], and some concern about the comparable performance between fast random reads and fast sequential reads [47, 60, 45] like what we do in this paper. The recent trend is to exploit the energy efficiency of SSD [71, 72] and its parallelism [73, 74] to fully leverage the power of SSD in large-scale data processing systems.

Baidu first announced their SSD-based search engine infrastructure in 2010 [23], but they did not investigate the impact of SSD on their cache management. The issue of allocating indexes on SSD was recently studied in 2011 [75]. Last year, the issue of maintaining inverted index resided on SSD was also discussed [76]. In [43], the use of SSD as a layer between the RAM and HDD was discussed. Our work focuses on the possibly the next generation of search engine architecture in which SSD completely replaces HDD.

5. CONCLUSIONS AND FUTURE WORK

In this paper, we present the results of a large-scale experimental study that evaluates the impact of SSD on the effectiveness of various caching policies, on all types of cache found in a typical search engine architecture. This study contributes the following messages to our community:

1. Traditional cache hit ratio is no longer a reliable measure of the effectiveness of caching policies and we shall use query latency as the major evaluation metric in SSD-based search engine cache management.

2. The previous known best caching policy in index servers, S-PLC-FreqSize [3, 6], has the worst effectiveness in terms of query latency in our SSD-based search engine evaluation platform. Instead, all the other policies are better than S-PLC-FreqSize in terms of query latency but no clear winner is found.

3. While previous work claims that document caching is very effective and the technique is able to significantly reduce the time of the snippet generation process in the document servers [4], we show that snippet caching is even more effective than document caching in SSD-based search engines. Therefore, snippet caching should have a higher priority of using the cache memory of the document servers in an SSD-based search engine deployment.

4. While SSD can improve the disk access latency of all servers in Web search engines, it has no significant impact on the *cache management* in web servers. Thus, during the transition from an HDD-based architecture to an SSD-based architecture, there is no need to revise the corresponding query result caching policies in the web servers.

As future work, we will next focus on the new bottleneck of query processing in SSD-based web search engine architecture and consider the potential of other cache types (e.g., intersection cache [77]) in the study.

6. ACKNOWLEDGMENTS

This work is partially supported by the Research Grants Council of Hong Kong (GRF PolyU 525009, 521012, 5302/12E), NSFC of China (60903028, 61070014), Key Projects in the Tianjin Science & Technology Pillar Program (11ZCKFGX01100).

7. REFERENCES

[1] Evangelos P. Markatos. On caching search engine query results. *Computer Communications*, 24(2):137–143, 2001.

[2] Ricardo Baeza-Yates and Felipe Saint-Jean. A three level search engine index based in query log distribution. In *SPIRE*, pages 56–65, 2003.

[3] Ricardo Baeza-Yates, Aristides Gionis, Flavio Junqueira, Vanessa Murdock, Vassilis Plachouras, and Fabrizio Silvestri. The impact of caching on search engines. In *SIGIR*, pages 183–190, 2007.

[4] Andrew Turpin, Yohannes Tsegay, David Hawking, and Hugh E. Williams. Fast generation of result snippets in web search. In *SIGIR*, pages 127–134, 2007.

[5] Rifat Ozcan, Ismail Sengor Altingovde, and Özgür Ulusoy. Static query result caching revisited. In *WWW*, pages 1169–1170, 2008.

[6] Ricardo Baeza-Yates, Aristides Gionis, Flavio P. Junqueira, Vanessa Murdock, Vassilis Plachouras, and Fabrizio Silvestri. Design trade-offs for search engine caching. *ACM Trans. Web*, 2:1–28, 2008.

[7] Qingqing Gan and Torsten Suel. Improved techniques for result caching in web search engines. In *WWW*, pages 431–440, 2009.

[8] Ismail Sengor Altingovde, Rifat Ozcan, and Özgür Ulusoy. A cost-aware strategy for query result caching in web search engines. In *ECIR*, pages 628–636, 2009.

[9] Rifat Ozcan, I. Sengor Altingovde, B. Barla Cambazoglu, Flavio P. Junqueira, and Özgür Ulusoy. A five-level static cache architecture for web search engines. *IPM*, 48(5):828–840, 2011.

[10] Rifat Ozcan, Ismail Sengor Altingovde, and Özgür Ulusoy. Cost-aware strategies for query result caching in web search engines. *ACM Trans. Web*, 5:1–25, 2011.

[11] Paricia Correia Saraiva, Edleno Silva de Moura, Novio Ziviani, Wagner Meira, Rodrigo Fonseca, and Berthier Riberio-Neto. Rank-preserving two-level caching for scalable search engines. In *SIGIR*, pages 51–58, 2001.

[12] Diego Ceccarelli, Claudio Lucchese, Salvatore Orlando, Raffaele Perego, and Fabrizio Silvestri. Caching query-biased snippets for efficient retrieval. In *EDBT*, pages 93–104, 2011.

[13] Goetz Graefe. The five-minute rule 20 years later (and how flash memory changes the rules). *CACM*, 52:48–59, 2009.

[14] Sang-Won Lee, Bongki Moon, Chanik Park, Jae-Myung Kim, and Sang-Woo Kim. A case for flash memory SSD in enterprise database applications. In *SIGMOD*, pages 1075–1086, 2008.

[15] Feng Chen, David A. Koufaty, and Xiaodong Zhang. Understanding intrinsic characteristics and system implications of flash memory based solid state drives. In *SIGMETRICS*, pages 181–192, 2009.

[16] Dushyanth Narayanan, Eno Thereska, Austin Donnelly, Sameh Elnikety, and Antony Rowstron. Migrating server storage to SSDs: analysis of tradeoffs. In *EuroSys*, pages 145–158, 2009.

[17] Euiseong Seo, Seon Yeong Park, and Bhuvan Urgaonkar. Empirical analysis on energy efficiency of flash-based SSDs. In *HotPower*, 2008.

[18] Shimin Chen, Phillip B. Gibbons, and Suman Nath. Rethinking database algorithms for phase change memory. In *CIDR*, pages 21–31, 2011.

[19] Flexstar SSD test market analysis. `http://info.flexstar.com/Portals/161365/docs/SSD_Testing_Market_Analysis.pdf`.

[20] MySpace uses fusion powered I/O to drive greener and better data centers. `http://www.fusionio.com/case-studies/myspace-case-study.pdf`.

[21] Releasing flashcache. `http://www.facebook.com/note.php?note_id=388112370932`, 2010.

[22] Microsoft azure to use OCZ SSDs. `http://www.storagelook.com/microsoft-azure-ocz-ssds/`, 2012.

[23] Ruyue Ma. Baidu distributed database. In *SACC*, 2010.

[24] Howard Turtle and James Flood. Query evaluation: strategies and optimizations. *IPM*, 31(6):831–850, 1995.

[25] Andrei Z. Broder, David Carmel, Michael Herscovici, Aya Soffer, and Jason Zien. Efficient query evaluation using a two-level retrieval process. In *CIKM*, pages 426–434, 2003.

[26] Andrew Turpin, Yohannes Tsegay, David Hawking, and Hugh E. Williams. Fast generation of result snippets in web search. In *SIGIR*, pages 127–134, 2007.

[27] Anastasios Tombros and Mark Sanderson. Advantages of query biased summaries in information retrieval. In *SIGIR*, pages 2–10, 1998.

[28] Luiz André Barroso, Jeffrey Dean, and Urs Hölzle. Web search for a planet: The google cluster architecture. *IEEE Micro*, 23(2):22–28, 2003.

[29] Jeffrey Dean. Challenges in building large-scale information retrieval systems: invited talk. In *WSDM*, 2009.

[30] Ricardo Baeza-yates, Carlos Castillo, Flavio Junqueira, Vassilis Plachouras, and Fabrizio Silvestri. Challenges on distributed web retrieval. In *ICDE*, pages 6–20, 2007.

[31] Tiziano Fagni, Raffaele Perego, Fabrizio Silvestri, and Salvatore Orlando. Boosting the performance of web search engines: Caching and prefetching query results by exploiting historical usage data. *TOIS*, 24:51–78, 2006.

[32] I. Sengor Altingovde, Rifat Ozcan, B. Barla Cambazoglu, and Özgür Ulusoy. Second chance: a hybrid approach for dynamic result caching in search engines. In *ECIR*, pages 510–516, 2011.

[33] Jiangong Zhang, Xiaohui Long, and Torsten Suel. Performance of compressed inverted list caching in search engines. In *WWW*, pages 387–396, 2008.

[34] Enric Herrero, José González, and Ramon Canal. Distributed cooperative caching. In *PACT*, pages 134–143, 2008.

[35] Memcached – a distributed memory object caching system. `http://memcached.org/`.

[36] Klaus Elhardt and Rudolf Bayer. A database cache for high performance and fast restart in database systems. *TODS*, 9(4):503–525, 1984.

[37] Laszlo A. Belady. A study of replacement algorithms for a virtual-storage computer. *IBM Systems Journal*, 5(2):78–101, 1966.

[38] Song Jiang and Xiaodong Zhang. LIRS: an efficient low inter-reference recency set replacement policy to improve buffer cache performance. In *SIGMETRICS*, pages 31–42, 2002.

[39] Stefan Podlipnig and Laszlo Böszörmenyi. A survey of web cache replacement strategies. *CUSR*, 35(4):374–398, 2003.

[40] Storage market outlook to 2015. `http://www.storagesearch.com/5year-2009.html`.

[41] Jim Gray. Tape is dead, disk is tape, flash is disk, ram locality is king. `http://research.microsoft.com/en-us/um/people/gray/talks/Flash_is_Good.ppt`, 2006.

[42] Ari Geir Hauksson and Sverrir Ícsmundsson. Data storage technologies. `http://olafurandri.com/nyti/papers2007/DST.pdf`, 2007.

[43] Ruixuan Li, Chengzhou Li, Weijun Xiao, Hai Jin, Heng He, Xiwu Gu, Kunmei Wen, and Zhiyong Xu. An efficient SSD-based hybrid storage architecture for large-scale search engines. In *ICPP*, pages 450–459, 2012.

[44] Falk Scholer, Hugh E. Williams, John Yiannis, and Justin Zobel. Compression of inverted indexes for fast query evaluation. In *SIGIR*, pages 222–229, 2002.

[45] Eran Gal and Sivan Toledo. Algorithms and data structures for flash memories. *CSUR*, 37:138–163, 2005.

[46] Biplob Debnath, Sudipta Sengupta, and Jin Li. FlashStore: High throughput persistent key-value store. In *VLDB*, pages 1414–1425, 2010.

[47] Dimitris Tsirogiannis, Stavros Harizopoulos, Mehul A. Shah, Janet L. Wiener, and Goetz Graefe. Query processing techniques for solid state drives. In *SIGMOD*, pages 59–72, 2009.

[48] Atsuo Kawaguchi, Shingo Nishioka, and Hiroshi Motoda. A flash-memory based file system. In *ATC*, pages 155–164, 1995.

[49] Red Hat Corporation. JFFS2: The journalling flash file system. `http://sources.redhat.com/jffs2/jffs2.pdf`.

[50] Charles Manning. YAFFS: Yet another flash file system. `http://www.aleph1.co.uk/yaffs`.

[51] Han-Lin Li, Chia-Lin Yang, and Hung-Wei Tseng. Energy-aware flash memory management in virtual memory system. *TVLSI*, 16(8):952–964, 2008.

[52] Mohit Saxena and Michael M. Swift. FlashVM: revisiting the virtual memory hierarchy. In *HotOS*, 2009.

[53] Seon-yeong Park, Dawoon Jung, Jeong-uk Kang, Jin-soo Kim, and Joonwon Lee. CFLRU: a replacement algorithm for flash memory. In *CASES*, pages 234–241, 2006.

[54] Hyojun Kim and Seongjun Ahn. BPLRU: a buffer management scheme for improving random writes in flash storage. In *FAST*, pages 1–14, 2008.

[55] Stan Park and Kai Shen. FIOS: a fair, efficient flash I/O scheduler. In *FAST*, 2012.

[56] Cagdas Dirik and Bruce Jacob. The performance of pc solid-state disks (SSDs) as a function of bandwidth, concurrency, device architecture, and system organization. In *ISCA*, pages 279–289, 2009.

[57] Mahesh Balakrishnan, Asim Kadav, Vijayan Prabhakaran, and Dahlia Malkhi. Differential RAID: Rethinking RAID for SSD reliability. *TOS*, 6(2):1–22, 2010.

[58] Sang-Won Lee and Bongki Moon. Design of flash-based DBMS: an in-page logging approach. In *SIGMOD*, pages 55–66, 2007.

[59] Sang-Won Lee, Bongki Moon, and Chanik Park. Advances in flash memory SSD technology for enterprise database applications. In *SIGMOD*, pages 863–870, 2009.

[60] Mehul A. Shah, Stavros Harizopoulos, Janet L. Wiener, and Goetz Graefe. Fast scans and joins using flash drives. In *DaMoN*, pages 17–24, 2008.

[61] Devesh Agrawal, Deepak Ganesan, Ramesh Sitaraman, Yanlei Diao, and Shashi Singh. Lazy-adaptive tree: an optimized index structure for flash devices. *PVLDB*, 2(1):361–372, 2009.

[62] Yinan Li, Bingsheng He, Robin Jun Yang, Qiong Luo, and Ke Yi. Tree indexing on solid state drives. *PVLDB*, 3(1-2):1195–1206, September 2010.

[63] Chin-Hsien Wu, Li-Pin Chang, and Tei-Wei Kuo. An efficient R-tree implementation over flash-memory storage systems. In *GIS*, pages 17–24, 2003.

[64] Ioannis Koltsidas and Stratis D. Viglas. Flashing up the storage layer. *PVLDB*, 1:514–525, 2008.

[65] Mustafa Canim, George A. Mihaila, Bishwaranjan Bhattacharjee, Kenneth A. Ross, and Christian A. Lang. An object placement advisor for DB2 using solid state storage. *PVLDB*, 2(2):1318–1329, August 2009.

[66] Sai Tung On, Jianliang Xu, Byron Choi, Haibo Hu, and Bingsheng He. Flag commit: Supporting efficient transaction recovery in flash-based dbmss. *TKDE*, 24(9):1624–1639, 2012.

[67] Philip A. Bernstein, Colin W. Reid, and Sudipto Das. Hyder – a transactional record manager for shared flash. In *CIDR*, pages 9–20, 2011.

[68] Sai Tung On, Yinan Li, Bingsheng He, Ming Wu, Qiong Luo, and Jianliang Xu. FD-buffer: a buffer manager for databases on flash disks. In *CIKM*, pages 1297–1300, 2010.

[69] Yanfei Lv, Bin Cui, Bingsheng He, and Xuexuan Chen. Operation-aware buffer management in flash-based systems. In *SIGMOD*, pages 13–24, 2011.

[70] Chin hsien Wu, Li pin Chang, and Tei wei Kuo. An efficient B-tree layer for flash-memory storage systems. In *RTCSA*, pages 17–24, 2003.

[71] Dimitris Tsirogiannis, Stavros Harizopoulos, and Mehul A. Shah. Analyzing the energy efficiency of a database server. In *SIGMOD*, pages 231–242, 2010.

[72] Theo Härder, Volker Hudlet, Yi Ou, and Daniel Schall. Energy efficiency is not enough, energy proportionality is needed! In *DASFAA*, pages 226–239, 2011.

[73] Hongchan Roh, Sanghyun Park, Sungho Kim, Mincheol Shin, and Sang-Won Lee. B+-tree index optimization by exploiting internal parallelism of flash-based solid state drives. *PVLDB*, 5(4):286–297, 2011.

[74] Risi Thonangi, Shivnath Babu, and Jun Yang. A practical concurrent index for solid-state drives. In *CIKM*, pages 1332–1341, 2012.

[75] Bojun Huang and Zenglin Xia. Allocating inverted index into flash memory for search engines. In *WWW*, pages 61–62, 2011.

[76] Ruixuan Li, Xuefan Chen, Chengzhou Li, Xiwu Gu, and Kunmei Wen. Efficient online index maintenance for SSD-based information retrieval systems. In *HPCC*, pages 262–269, 2012.

[77] Xiaohui Long and Torsten Suel. Three-level caching for efficient query processing in large web search engines. In *WWW*, pages 257–266, 2005.

Faster Upper Bounding of Intersection Sizes

Daisuke Takuma
IBM Research – Tokyo
6-52, Toyosu, 5-chome, Koto-ku
Tokyo 135-8511 Japan
ta9ma@jp.ibm.com

Hiroki Yanagisawa
IBM Research – Tokyo
6-52, Toyosu, 5-chome, Koto-ku
Tokyo 135-8511 Japan
yanagis@jp.ibm.com

ABSTRACT

There is a long history of developing efficient algorithms for set intersection, which is a fundamental operation in information retrieval and databases. In this paper, we describe a new data structure, a *Cardinality Filter*, to quickly compute an *upper bound* on the size of a set intersection. Knowing an upper bound of the size can be used to accelerate many applications such as top-k query processing in text mining. Given finite sets A and B, the expected computation time for the upper bound of the size of the intersection $|A \cap B|$ is $O((|A| + |B|)/w)$, where w is the machine word length. This is much faster than the current best algorithm for the *exact* intersection, which runs in $O((|A|+|B|)/\sqrt{w}+|A \cap B|)$ expected time. Our performance studies show that our implementations of Cardinality Filters are from 2 to 10 times faster than existing set intersection algorithms, and the time for a top-k query in a text mining application can be reduced by half.

Categories and Subject Descriptors

E.1 [**Data Structures**]: Arrays; H.3.3 [**Information Storage and Retrieval**]: Information Search and Retrieval

Keywords

Indexing; data structure; set intersection; text mining; data mining; top-k

1. INTRODUCTION

Set intersection, which computes the set of the common elements in given sets, is a fundamental operation in many query processing tasks including relational query processing, data mining, and other search tasks. While the output of the set intersection is an enumeration of the elements in the intersection, some applications require only the *size* of the intersection. One example of such applications is *top-k query* in the context of text mining, which extracts top-k most frequent terms in documents for a given search query

SIGIR'13, July 28–August 1, 2013, Dublin, Ireland.

ACM 978-1-4503-2034-4/13/07 ...$15.00.

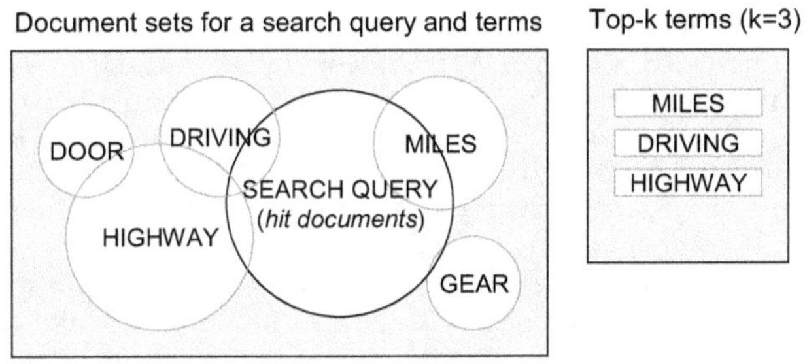

Figure 1: Top-k query retrieves the terms with the top-k largest intersections with the set of documents retrieved by a search query.

(*hit documents*). To process this query, we compute, for each term, the set intersection between (1) the set of hit documents and (2) the set of documents containing the term as illustrated in Figure 1, and then sort the terms with respect to their intersection sizes. An important observation in this kind of top-k query is that an enumeration of the elements of intersections is not necessary, but their sizes alone are sufficient to solve the problem.

The first contribution of our work is to show that the performance of top-k query can be improved by a fast algorithm for computing good *upper bounds* on the sizes of intersections instead of the *exact* ones. The top-k terms retrieved by a top-k query are special in having high frequencies or strong correlations with the search query. Most of the other terms, however, are infrequent and not correlated with the search query. That means they have very small intersections with a set of hit documents compared to those of the top-k terms. Our observations show that intersections for approximately 80% of the terms evaluated in the currently used top-k algorithm are less than 5% of the smallest intersection size (threshold) of the ranked terms. Focusing on this difference between the actual intersection sizes and the threshold, we found that more than 80% of the evaluations of the intersection sizes can be skipped by replacing them with the evaluations of their upper bounds. Our approach of using upper bounds is not limited to the top-k query, but it can be applied to other data analysis algorithms such as frequent item set mining using an inverted index.

The second contribution of our work is to show how to quickly compute an upper bound of the size of the intersection. We propose two data structures for this problem: Single Cardinality Filter (SCF) and Recursive Cardinality

Filter (RCF), both of which share some features with the current best algorithm for *exact* set intersection [13] (the DK algorithm). To make clear our new ideas in SCF and RCF, we should start with the DK algorithm. The DK algorithm constructs, for a given set A, a bit sequence to store a *sketch* of the set A and an auxiliary integer set to keep the original information. The term sketch used here means a data structure that compactly stores a summary of a set to quickly test the membership of an element for the set at the price of some false positive errors. The DK algorithm first computes a sketch of $A \cap B$ using the corresponding sketches (bit sequences) for A and B to filter out unnecessary elements and to select candidate elements of $A \cap B$ in the auxiliary integer sets. Then it compares the candidate elements in the auxiliary integer sets to obtain the exact result. The efficiency of the DK algorithm comes from the filtering by the sketch of $A \cap B$, but we found that the actual computation time of the DK algorithm is dominated by the comparison step. In SCF, we also use the bit sequence to store a sketch for a given set, but unlike the DK algorithm, we use the sketches not for filtering elements but for counting the common elements, and use the auxiliary integer sets not for comparing the elements but for correcting the count. That makes the auxiliary integer sets for SCF far smaller than those for the DK algorithm. Our improvement is that we significantly reduced the time for comparing the elements of the auxiliary integer sets based on the fact that our purpose is to obtain an *upper bound* rather than the *exact* value of $|A \cap B|$. In our methods, the computation time for the bitwise AND operations dominates the whole computation time. The RCF is a variant of SCF that uses another SCF recursively to store the auxiliary integer set. We show that the expected time of the upper bound computation with RCF is $O((|A|+|B|)/w)$, where w is the machine word length, which is faster than the DK algorithm whose expected computation time is $O((|A|+|B|)/\sqrt{w}+|A \cap B|)$. In our performance studies, SCF and RCF are shown to perform from 2 to 10 times faster than the DK algorithm.

In this paper, we use the w-bit word RAM model for the theoretical analysis of the algorithms. In this model, we have access to a random access memory consisting of w-bit words, and the basic operations (such as arithmetic operations, comparison operations, and bitwise Boolean operations) take constant time. In particular, we assume that the popcount operation, which counts the number of true bits in a w-bit machine word, takes constant time. This is a natural assumption because the state-of-the-art CPUs support this operation with this performance. In this model, we can count the number of true bits in a bit sequence of length ℓ in $O(\ell/w)$ time. Note that, in computation models that do not support the popcount operation in constant time, the popcount operation typically takes $O(\log w)$ time [23]. Thus the time complexity of our analysis may become worse by a factor of $O(\log w)$ in another computation model. For example, it may take $O(\ell \log w/w)$ time to count the number of true bits in a bit sequence of length ℓ.

This paper is structured as follows: In the next section, we refer to the related work. Then we describe two new data structures in Section 3 and introduce their applications in Section 4. Section 5 describes our implementations of the applications in detail. We present our experimental results in Section 6. Finally, we conclude in Section 7.

2. RELATED WORK

2.1 Exact Set Intersection

The study of exact set intersection has a long history, and it plays an important role in databases and information retrieval [5, 8]. The *linear merge* algorithm is one of the simplest approaches to intersecting two sets A and B. This algorithm iterates over each element of the sorted arrays of the elements for A and B and compares them in $O(|A| + |B|)$ time. However, when A and B have greatly different sizes, $|A| < |B|$ for example, it is faster to search for each element of A in B. The *binary search* algorithm performs a binary search to quickly check if B contains the elements in A. The theoretical studies of acceleration by exploiting the asymmetry of set sizes go back to [16], which reduced the number of comparisons to $|A| + \log\binom{|A|+|B|}{|A|}$ when $|A| < |B|$. Further improvements include adaptive approaches [4, 5, 12], the use of balanced trees [9, 11], and the use of multicores [21, 22].

The fastest practical algorithm was proposed in [13], effectively using bitwise AND operations to accelerate the algorithm and universal hash functions to skip comparisons between unmatched pairs. It can be seen as a practical improvement of the theoretically fastest algorithm [8], whose expected time complexity is $O((|A| + |B|) \log^2 w/w + |A \cap B|)$. Our algorithm with RCF, whose time complexity is $O((|A| + |B|)/w)$, runs faster than these algorithms both in theory and in practice.

2.2 Approximate Set Intersection

There are many efficient algorithms for computing approximate set intersection sizes [7, 17, 19, 20]. However, since all of these algorithms are sampling-based, the obtained results can be less than the exact value. Our Cardinality Filter is designed to avoid underestimation.

A Bloom filter [10] and its variant, a counting filter [15], are data structures for a set to test whether a given value is a member of the set without false negatives. These data structures can be used to compute an upper bound of the size of the set intersection of two given sets A and B by performing a membership test for each element in the smaller set with the Bloom filter (or the counting filter) of the larger set and count the *true* cases. Since the membership test of the Bloom filter has only false positives and no false negatives, this approach outputs an upper bound of $|A \cap B|$ in $O(\min\{|A|, |B|\})$ time. However, in Section 6, we will show that this is faster than our method only when A and B are strongly asymmetric and that it performs quite poorly in the other cases.

A conjunctive filter [18] is a space-efficient data structure for approximate set intersection, and it can compute a superset of the intersection set. Since the size of the superset of the intersection set is at least the intersection size, we can use the conjunctive filter to calculate the upper bound. However, its computation is not fast because the design of the conjunctive filter puts more emphasis on space-efficiency rather than time-efficiency.

2.3 Top-k problems

The target application of our new data structures presented in this paper is the *top-k query* for text mining, which retrieves the top-k most frequent terms in the documents for a given search query. This is a kind of top-k problem

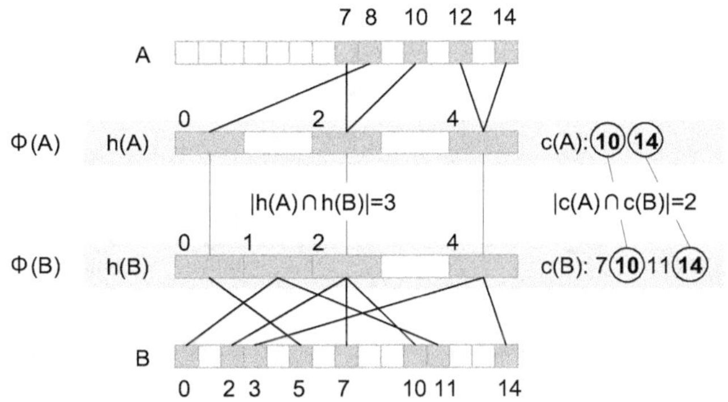

Figure 2: An example of SCFs with $N = 3$ for two sets $A = \{7, 8, 10, 12, 14\}$ and $B = \{0, 2, 3, 5, 7, 10, 11, 14\}$.

[3, 6, 14], which is generally the retrieval of the k highest scoring entries such as the documents having top-k highest relevance scores for a given query. The top-k query corresponds to the case where the entries are the terms and the score of each entry is the intersection size (see Figure 1). The general top-k studies that do not specify the scoring function are orthogonal to our approach since our technique improves the comparison of the scores for the specific case of intersection.

Simitsis et al. [20] studied the top-k query and presented techniques based on pruning and approximate intersection. In this paper, the pruning algorithm is the baseline for evaluating the improvement by using our data structures. We did not consider using their approximate intersection technique since it may return incorrect top-k terms. The scope of our research covers only the exact top-k.

3. CARDINALITY FILTERS

In this section, we propose a new data structure, *Cardinality Filter* (CF), for computing an upper bound on the intersection size of two given sets. First, we give a simple implementation of CF, the Single Cardinality Filter (SCF), in Section 3.1 and then a more efficient variant of SCF, the Recursive Cardinality Filter (RCF), in Section 3.2. Finally we formulate CF as a general data structure in Section 3.3.

Throughout this paper, X denotes a finite set, and the two sets A and B are subsets of X. Our CF works for any set X, but we assume here X is an integer set $X = \{0, 1, \ldots, |X| - 1\}$ for simplicity.

3.1 Single Cardinality Filter

In this section, we describe a new data structure, a *Single Cardinality Filter*, for computing an upper bound of $|A \cap B|$ for two given sets A and B. This data structure is similar to that used by the current fastest algorithm [13] for exact set intersection, in that it uses a bit array. The SCF is designed so that the computation time is significantly reduced because our aim is not to compute the *exact* intersection $A \cap B$ but to compute an upper bound of $|A \cap B|$.

Let us show how to construct the SCF for a given set A. Let h be a universal hash function that maps an element from X to $\{0, 1, \ldots, \lceil |X|/N \rceil - 1\}$, where N is an integer parameter for SCF. The SCF consists of a pair of sets $(h(A), c(A))$, where $h(A)$ is the set of hash values of the elements in A and $c(A)$ is the set of integers that stores all of the elements in A except those that are the smallest in each collision for h. Figure 2 shows an example of the SCFs for sets A and B, where we use the same parameter $N = 3$ for both of the sets. In this example, the elements 7, 8, 10, 12, and 14 in A are mapped to 2, 0, 2, 4, and 4, respectively, by the hash function h. Hence the $h(A)$ is equal to $\{0, 2, 4\}$, and there are three *collisions* for h: $\{8\}$, $\{7, 10\}$, and $\{12, 14\}$. Here, we define the collision as the set of elements that are mapped to the same value by h. That means we refer to a set of a single element as a collision. Hence the set $c(A)$ is equal to $\{10, 14\}$ because the other elements in A are the smallest in their collisions. In the SCF, we store $h(A)$ as a bit sequence of length $\lceil |X|/N \rceil$ and $c(A)$ as an integer array. Intuitively, we can see that the set $h(A)$ stores a sketch of set A and $c(A)$ stores auxiliary information for set A.

Using the SCFs for the two sets A and B with the same hash function h and the integer parameter N, we can efficiently compute an upper bound of $|A \cap B|$. As we will show in a rigorous proof later, $|h(A) \cap h(B)| + |c(A) \cap c(B)|$ is an upper bound of the intersection size. (Recall the example in Figure 2, where $|h(A) \cap h(B)| = 3$, $|c(A) \cap c(B)| = 2$, and $|A \cap B| = 3$.) Intuitively, this is because an element in $A \cap B$ is counted in one of two ways:

- If an element in $A \cap B$ is the smallest in a collision in either A or B (for example, 7 in Figure 2), then it is counted by $|h(A) \cap h(B)|$.
- Otherwise (for example, 10 in Figure 2), it is counted by $|c(A) \cap c(B)|$.

When different elements in A and B have the same hash value, the intersection size may be overcounted ($8 \in A$ and $5 \in B$ in Figure 2). Another case of overcounting is the case of 14 where one element is counted twice by both $|h(A) \cap h(B)|$ and $|c(A) \cap c(B)|$. We can obtain the upper bound quickly by using the fast bitwise AND operations to compute $h(A) \cap h(B)$ and the linear merge algorithm to compute $c(A) \cap c(B)$ (notice that the size of $c(A) \cap c(B)$ is typically far smaller than $|A \cap B|$).

Now we give a rigorous definition of the SCF. Given a positive integer N (*the compression ratio parameter*) and a universal hash function h that maps from X to $H = \{0, 1, \ldots, \lceil |X|/N \rceil - 1\}$, the SCF Φ is defined as a map that maps $A \subseteq X$ to $\Phi(A) = (h(A), c(A)) \in 2^H \times 2^X$ where

$$h(A) = \{h(x) \mid x \in A\} \text{ and}$$
$$c(A) = \{y \in A \mid (\exists x \in A)(x < y, h(x) = h(y))\} .$$

We also respectively define the binary operation $\cap$ between $\Phi(A)$ and $\Phi(B)$ and the size function $|\cdot|$ by

$$\Phi(A) \cap \Phi(B) = (h(A) \cap h(B), c(A) \cap c(B)) \text{ and}$$
$$|\Phi(A)| = |h(A)| + |c(A)| .$$

Using these definitions, we have Theorem 3.1.

THEOREM 3.1. *For any $A, B \subseteq X$, $|A \cap B| \leq |\Phi(A) \cap \Phi(B)|$.*

PROOF. Dividing $A \cap B$ into two disjoint sets, we have $|A \cap B| = |A \cap B \cap c(A) \cap c(B)| + |(A \cap B) \setminus (c(A) \cap c(B))|$, and we have $|\Phi(A) \cap \Phi(B)| = |c(A) \cap c(B)| + |h(A) \cap h(B)|$ by definition. Since $|A \cap B \cap c(A) \cap c(B)| \leq |c(A) \cap c(B)|$, it is sufficient to prove that $|(A \cap B) \setminus (c(A) \cap c(B))| \leq |h(A) \cap h(B)|$.

We can prove this by showing that, for all x and y in $(A \cap B) \setminus (c(A) \cap c(B))$ such that $x \neq y$, we have

$$h(x) \neq h(y).$$

In other words, we must show the restriction of h that maps $(A \cap B) \setminus (c(A) \cap c(B))$ to $h(A) \cap h(B)$ is injective.

First, we verify the image of the restriction of h is contained in $h(A) \cap h(B)$. In other words,

$$\begin{aligned} & x \in (A \cap B) \setminus (c(A) \cap c(B)) \\ & \Rightarrow \quad x \in A \wedge x \in B \\ & \Rightarrow \quad h(x) \in h(A) \wedge h(x) \in h(B) \\ & \Rightarrow \quad h(x) \in h(A) \cap h(B). \end{aligned}$$

Without loss of generality, we can assume $x < y$. Since $y \notin c(A) \cap c(B)$, we know that $y \notin c(A)$ or $y \notin c(B)$. If $y \notin c(A)$, then, by the definition of c, there is no $z \in A$ such that

$$z < y \text{ and } h(z) = h(y).$$

Hence, by the fact that $x \in A$ and the assumption that $x < y$, we know that $h(x) \neq h(y)$ holds. Using a similar argument, we can derive $h(x) \neq h(y)$ if $y \notin c(B)$. Thus, the injectivity holds. □

Now we will analyze the space and time complexities of SCF. We first present Lemma 3.1.

LEMMA 3.1. *The expected size of $c(A)$ is at most*

$$\frac{N|A|^2}{2|X|}.$$

PROOF. Let β_A be the bit array that corresponds to $h(A)$. The length of β_A is $|H| = \lceil |X|/N \rceil$. Since the probability that the hash function h maps an element in A to an arbitrary bit in β_A is $1/|H|$, the probability that this bit in β_A is false is $(1 - 1/|H|)^{|A|}$. Therefore the expected number of true bits in β_A is $|H|(1 - (1 - 1/|H|)^{|A|})$.

The expected size of $c(A)$ is

$$\begin{aligned} |A| - |h(A)| &= |A| - |H|\left(1 - \left(1 - \frac{1}{|H|}\right)^{|A|}\right) \\ &\leq |A| - |H|\left(1 - \left(1 - \frac{|A|}{|H|} + \frac{|A|^2}{2|H|^2}\right)\right) \\ &= \frac{|A|^2}{2|H|} \leq \frac{N|A|^2}{2|X|}, \end{aligned}$$

where the first inequality follows from the inequality $(1 - \epsilon)^n \leq 1 - n\epsilon + n^2\epsilon^2/2$ for $n \geq 1$ and $0 \leq \epsilon \leq 1$. □

From Lemma 3.1 and the fact that the length of bit vector β_A is $|H| = \lceil |X|/N \rceil$, Theorem 3.2 follows directly.

THEOREM 3.2. *The expected space usage of SCF for a set A is at most $\lceil |X|/N \rceil + wN|A|^2/2|X|$ bits.*

There is a second theorem that follows from Lemma 3.1:

THEOREM 3.3. *The expected time complexity of SCF for computing an upper bound of $|A \cap B|$ is $O(|X|/Nw + N(|A|^2 + |B|^2)/|X|)$.*

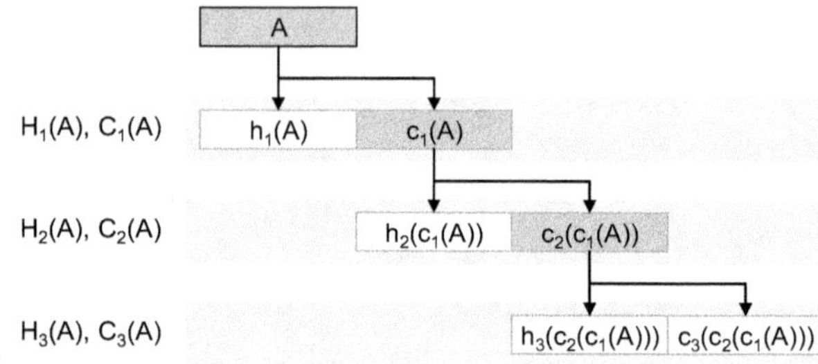

Figure 3: An illustration of a 3-layer RCF for set A.

PROOF. The computation time required for bitwise AND operations between the bit sequences β_A and β_B is $O((|X|/N) \cdot (1/w))$. The computation time for the linear merge algorithm to compute $|c(A) \cap c(B)|$ is $O(|c(A)| + |c(B)|) = O(N(|A|^2 + |B|^2)/|X|)$ by Lemma 3.1. □

Finally we evaluate the accuracy of the SCF. Let us define the *approximation ratio* of SCF Φ for two sets A and B such that $A \cap B \neq \emptyset$ as $|\Phi(A) \cap \Phi(B)|/|A \cap B|$. This number is at least 1 by definition and indicates how close the upper bound is to the exact size. Although we omit the proof due to the space limitation, we present Theorem 3.4.

THEOREM 3.4. *The expected approximation ratio of SCF is at most*

$$1 + \frac{N|A||B|}{|X||A \cap B|}.$$

3.2 Recursive Cardinality Filter

Here we give a variant of the SCF, the *Recursive Cardinality Filter* Φ (RCF), which minimizes the use of the slow linear merge algorithm for computing $|c(A) \cap c(B)|$. We use the same notation Φ for an RCF as used for an SCF, but in this section, Φ always denotes an RCF.

Here is how to construct an RCF for a set A. We first construct an SCF $(h_1(A), c_1(A))$ for the set A as the first layer of the RCF. Here h_i is a hash function $h_i : X \to \{0, \ldots, \lceil |X|/N_i \rceil - 1\}$, c_i is the collision set of h_i, and N_i is a compression ratio parameter for the i-th layer. Then we construct another SCF $(h_2(c_1(A)), c_2(c_1(A)))$ for set $c_1(A)$ as the second layer of the RCF, and replace the set $c_1(A)$ in the first layer data structure with this new SCF. We repeat this process until we obtain the l-th layer, where l is a parameter. Figure 3 illustrates an RCF with three layers.

The resulting *l-layer RCF* can be represented as

$$\begin{aligned} & \Phi(A) = (H_1(A), H_2(A), \ldots, H_l(A), C_l(A)), \text{where} \\ & H_i(A) = h_i(c_{i-1}(c_{i-2}(\ldots c_1(A)\ldots))), \text{ and} \\ & C_i(A) = c_i(c_{i-1}(\ldots c_1(A)\ldots)), \text{ for } i = 1, 2, \ldots, l. \end{aligned}$$

As with an SCF, we define the binary operation and the size function for an RCF as

$$\begin{aligned} \Phi(A) \cap \Phi(B) &= (H_1(A) \cap H_1(B), H_2(A) \cap H_2(B) \\ & \quad \ldots, H_l(A) \cap H_l(B), C_l(A) \cap C_l(B)) \text{ and} \\ |\Phi(A)| &= \sum_{i=1}^{l} |H_i(A)| + |C_l(A)|. \end{aligned}$$

The upper bound $|\Phi(A) \cap \Phi(B)|$ is represented as

$$\sum_{i=1}^{l} |H_i(A) \cap H_i(B)| + |C_l(A) \cap C_l(B)|,$$

and Theorem 3.5 can be easily proved by induction on l.

THEOREM 3.5. $|A \cap B| \leq |\Phi(A) \cap \Phi(B)|$

The best choice of N_i depends on the application, and in Section 5.2, we show how to set N (or N_i) for a specific application. Using an appropriate parameter setting, the time complexity for computing an upper bound of $|A \cap B|$ with an RCF can be improved over that with an SCF.

THEOREM 3.6. *Let l be $\lceil \log \max\{|A|, |B|\} \rceil$, r be a constant larger than 1, and Φ be an l-layer RCF constructed with parameters $N_i = \lfloor 2^{i-1}|X|/r \max\{|A|, |B|\} \rfloor$, where $i = 1, 2, \ldots, l$. The time complexity of computing an upper bound of $|A \cap B|$ for sets A and B with this l-layer RCFs is $O((|A| + |B|)/w)$.*

PROOF. By Lemma 3.1, the expected size of $C_1(A)$ is at most $N_1|A|^2/2|X|$. Since $N_1 = \lfloor |X|/r \max\{|A|, |B|\} \rfloor$, the expected size of $C_1(A)$ is at most $|A|/2r$. Similarly, using Lemma 3.1 for $C_1(A)$ and the definition $N_2 = \lfloor 2|X|/r \max\{|A|, |B|\} \rfloor$, we get the expected size of $C_2(A)$ is at most $|A|/2^2 r$. Repeating this for l layers, we get the expected size of $C_l(A)$ is at most $|A|/2^l r = O(1)$. The length of the bit sequence for $H_i(A)$ is $\lceil |X|/N_i \rceil \leq \lceil r \max\{|A|, |B|\}/2^{i-1} \rceil$. Hence, the time complexity for computing an upper bound of $|A \cap B|$ with RCF is at most

$$O\left(\sum_{i=1}^{l} r \max\{|A|, |B|\}/2^{i-1} \cdot \frac{1}{w}\right) + O(1)$$
$$= O(\max\{|A|, |B|\}/w) = O((|A| + |B|)/w).$$

□

The time complexity for RCF is better than that for the current fastest exact set intersection algorithm [13], whose time complexity is $O((|A| + |B|)/\sqrt{w} + |A \cap B|)$.

3.3 Definition of The Cardinality Filter

We have shown two data structures, SCF and RCF, and they are similar in the sense that they are designed to quickly compute an upper bound of $|A \cap B|$ for two given sets A and B. We define a *Cardinality Filter* (CF) as in Definition 3.1, so both the SCF and RCF can be seen as implementations of a CF. Figure 4 shows the correspondence between the sets and the CFs.

DEFINITION 3.1. *Let X be a set and Λ be a set with operations $\cap : \Lambda \times \Lambda \to \Lambda$ and $|\cdot| : \Lambda \to \mathbb{R}^+ \cup \{0\} = \{x \in \mathbb{R} \mid x \geq 0\}$. A map $\Phi : 2^X \to \Lambda$ is said to be a Cardinality Filter if it satisfies for $\forall A, B \subseteq X$,*

$$|A \cap B| \leq |\Phi(A) \cap \Phi(B)|.$$

4. APPLICATIONS

In this section, we present some applications of CFs. First we describe the general usage of a CF in Section 4.1. Then we give some examples of the top-k query for text mining in Section 4.2 and the frequent item set mining with an inverted index in Section 4.3.

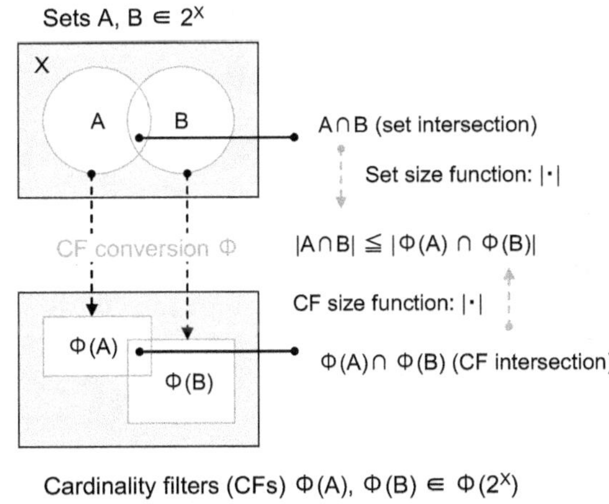

Figure 4: The operation $\Phi(A) \cap \Phi(B)$ for Cardinality Filters $\Phi(A)$ and $\Phi(B)$ is analogous to the set intersection $A \cap B$ for two sets A and B.

4.1 General Usage of Cardinality Filter

We can use CFs to accelerate the evaluation of the inequality of intersection sizes $|A \cap B| > c$. Note that the condition for the CFs is *a necessary condition* of the condition for the original sets: $|A \cap B| > c \Rightarrow |\Phi(A) \cap \Phi(B)| > c$. That means these two conditions are logically equivalent:

1. $|A \cap B| > c$
2. $|\Phi(A) \cap \Phi(B)| > c \quad \wedge \quad |A \cap B| > c$.

Our approach to the acceleration is to substitute the inequality for the intersection size $|A \cap B| > c$ in the target algorithm with $|\Phi(A) \cap \Phi(B)| > c \quad \wedge \quad |A \cap B| > c$. Due to the logical equivalence of the two conditions, this does not change the operation of the target algorithms. In the situation where $|\Phi(A) \cap \Phi(B)| \leq c$ holds for the majority of the inputs, we can skip the computation of $|A \cap B|$. Therefore, if the upper bound can be calculated much faster than the exact value, we can save time.

4.2 Top-k Term Query

First, we show how to apply CF to the top-k query described in Section 1, which is the retrieval of the top-k most frequent terms in documents that are dynamically returned by a search query. Algorithm 1 is known as an efficient algorithm for top-k query [20] and is widely used. In this algorithm, we assume that each term is associated with a posting list, which is a list of IDs of the documents containing a specific term. Algorithm 1 loads the posting list$P[i]$ $(i = 0, 1, \ldots, |P| - 1)$ for each term (Line 2) in descending order of frequency $(|P[0]| \geq |P[1]| \geq \cdots)$, and calculates the intersection size between the set of document IDs for the search query S and the posting list $P[i]$. Pairs of a term and its intersection size $(i, |S \cap P[i]|)$ are put into the temporary queue Q that stores the pairs with the top-k intersection sizes (Lines 7 and 9). The queue is updated only when it is not full (Line 6) or the intersection size $|S \cap P[i]|$ is larger than the minimum intersection size in the queue $|S \cap P[\min(Q)]|$, where $\min(Q)$ denotes the term with the smallest intersection size in the queue (Line 8). This algorithm can terminate its iterations, when both of these con-

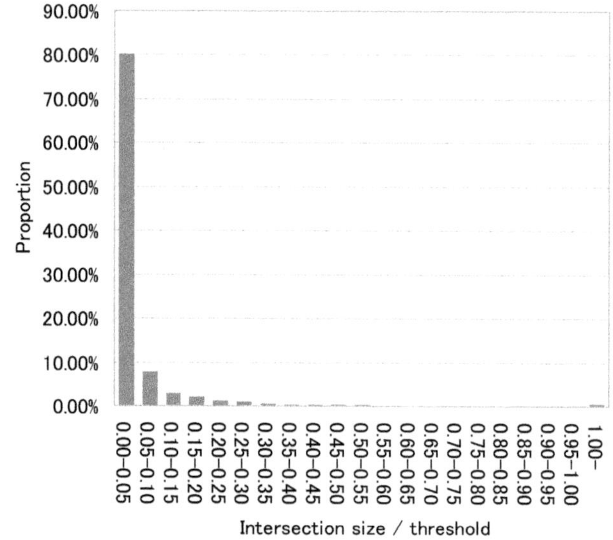

Figure 5: The ratio of the intersection size to the threshold.

ditions are met: (1) the queue is full, and (2) the document frequency of the current term is not more than the minimum intersection size in the queue (Line 3).

Algorithm 1 The top-k query

Input:

P: posting lists sorted in descending order of list size
$|P|$: the number of posting lists
$P[i]$: the posting list for term i ($i = 0, 1, \ldots, |P| - 1$)
S: the documents retrieved by a search query
k: the maximum number of terms to retrieve

1: $Q \leftarrow \emptyset$ // a set of the temporary top-k terms
2: **for** $i = 0, 1, \ldots, |P| - 1$ **do**
3: **if** $|Q| = k$ and $|P[i]| \leq |S \cap P[\min(Q)]|$ **then**
4: break // early out
5: **end if**
6: **if** $|Q| < k$ **then**
7: insert $(i, |S \cap P[i]|)$ into Q
8: **else if** $|S \cap P[i]| > |S \cap P[\min(Q)]|$ **then**
9: insert $(i, |S \cap P[i]|)$ into Q
10: remove the pair $(\min(Q), |S \cap P[\min(Q)]|)$ from Q
11: **end if**
12: **end for**
13: **return** Q

The most time consuming part of this algorithm is the evaluation of the intersection size $|S \cap P[i]| > |S \cap P[\min(Q)]|$ in Line 8. Note that the elements of the intersection $S \cap P[i]$ are not referred to here, and that only the size of the intersection is needed. One important observation is that the intersection size $|S \cap P[i]|$ is typically much smaller than the threshold $|S \cap P[\min(Q)]|$ for most of the posting lists. An example appears in Figure 5, which shows the distribution of the ratios of the intersection size to the threshold $|S \cap P[i]|/|S \cap P[\min(Q)]|$ for real data. The statistics were obtained by testing 309 396 inequalities with 50 top-k term queries ($k = 100$) with $|S|$ ranging from 100 to 100 000 on the 528 545 documents of the NHTSA data [1]. The vertical axis shows the proportion (as a percentage) of the values of $|S \cap P[i]|/|S \cap P[\min(Q)]|$ that fall into each range on the horizontal axis. The range '1.00-' corresponds to the cases for which the inequalities were evaluated as true. The intersection size is at most 20 times as small as the threshold in approximately 80% of the inequalities.

Considering the gaps in the inequalities of the threshold evaluations, we can speed up Algorithm 1 by replacing the threshold condition $|S \cap P[i]| > |S \cap P[\min(Q)]|$ in Line 8 with

$$|\Phi(S) \cap \Phi(P[i])| > |S \cap P[\min(Q)]| \\ \wedge\ |S \cap P[i]| > |S \cap P[\min(Q)]|.$$

As described in Section 4.1, this replacement does not change the results of the algorithm. The CFs for the posting lists $\Phi(P[i])$ ($i = 0, 1, \ldots, |P| - 1$) are created in the indexing phase, and the CF for the hit documents $\Phi(S)$ is created at the beginning of the query processing. The implementation details and the performance improvements will be discussed in Sections 5 and 6, respectively.

4.3 Frequent Item Set mining

Another target application of CF is frequent item set mining. Frequent item set mining is a task to retrieve frequent subsets of items from a transaction database where each transaction is represented as a set of items. An example application is to find frequent combinations of items in purchase records. Given T, a transaction database, $T[t]$, the t-th transaction ($t = 0, 1, \ldots, |T| - 1$), I, a set of all of the items, and s_m, an integer parameter for the minimum size (the minimum support) of the item subsets, our task is to generate

$$\{C \mid C \subseteq I, s(C) \geq s_m\},$$

where $s(C)$ is the *support* of C defined by

$$s(C) = |\{t \mid C \subseteq T[t], t = 0, 1, \ldots, |T| - 1\}|.$$

We say C *has the minimum support* if and only if $s(C) \geq s_m$.

The Apriori algorithm [2] is widely used as a solution for frequent item set mining. Algorithm 2 shows the pseudocode of the Apriori algorithm using an inverted index. It extracts the frequent item sets by iteration for the size of item set n (Line 2). In each iteration, it creates a list of sets L_n, which stores the sets of n items having the minimum support, from the lists L_1 and L_{n-1}. It scans each of the candidate sets of items $C \cup \{i\}$, which consists of a set in L_{n-1} and a set in L_1 (Line 7). Then it checks if the candidate sets have the minimum support:

$$s(C \cup \{i\}) = |P[C] \cap P[\{i\}]| \geq s_m,$$

where it computes the intersection $P[C] \cap P[\{i\}]$ (Line 8). The candidate sets having the minimum support are added to L_n (Line 9). Finally it generates all of the item sets in $L_1, L_2, \ldots$ (Line 13). This algorithm is slightly different from the original Apriori algorithm, which calculate $s(C \cup \{i\})$ by scanning all of the transactions. The difference is that Algorithm 2 uses the inverted index for the items. The inverted index has an advantage when L_1 is small, since the time for the transaction scan is independent of $|L_1|$.

We can apply CF to Algorithm 2 by replacing the inequality in Line 8 with

$$|\Phi(P[C]) \cap \Phi(P[\{i\}])| \geq s_m \quad \wedge \quad |P[C] \cap P[\{i\}]| \geq s_m.$$

We can skip most of the intersections if their sizes are much smaller than the minimum support s_m.

Algorithm 2 The Apriori algorithm on an inverted index

Input:
I: the set of all of the items
$P[\{i\}](i \in I)$: a posting list for i
$(P[C] = \{t \mid C \subseteq T[t], t = 0, 1, \ldots, |T| - 1\})$
s_m: the minimum size of the item subsets

$L_1 \leftarrow \{\{i\} \mid i \in I, s(\{i\}) \geq s_m\}$
for $n = 2, 3, \ldots$ **do**
  if $L_{n-1} = \emptyset$ **then**
    break
  end if
  $L_n \leftarrow \emptyset$
  for each $C \in L_{n-1}$ and each $\{i\} \in L_1$ such that $i \notin C$ **do**
    if $|P[C] \cap P[\{i\}]| \geq s_m$ **then**
      add $C \cup \{i\}$ to L_n
      $P[C \cup \{i\}] \leftarrow P[C] \cap P[\{i\}]$
    end if
  end for
end for
return $\bigcup_{j=1}^{n} L_j$

5. IMPLEMENTATION DETAILS

In this section, we explain the details of our implementation of top-k query processing using a CF.

5.1 Search Query and Posting Lists

First we explain the structure of the data created in the index and in memory. We use the SCF or RCF described in Section 3 for the implementation of the CF. As illustrated in Figure 6, we store in the index the posting list for each term and *a term CF* for each posting list. The posting lists, which are shown as lists of boxes, are stored in the form of a compressed integer array and physically sorted in descending order of size, which is the number of document IDs for each term. The term CFs, which are shown as the boxes below "Term CFs", are also sorted in the same order, but the posting lists and the term CFs are stored in physically separate locations so that the index reader can skip reading the unnecessary parts of the posting lists. In the online phase, given the document ID list retrieved by a search query, *a query CF* is created for the document ID list. The document ID list and the query CF are shown on the left side of Figure 6 in the same form as for the posting lists and the term CFs. The query CF is created in memory, and the upper bound operation is performed on the query CF and each term CF.

One important configuration setting is the compression ratio parameter N. A CF works efficiently when N is set to an appropriate value for its set size, but at the same time, the upper bound can be calculated only for a pair of CFs having same N. In our implementation, we define several candidate values of N (e.g. $N = 1, 2, 5$), and each term CF is created with the most appropriate value in the candidates. In Figure 6, the configurations of N are indicated in the boxes for the term CFs. For the query CF, given the document ID list for a search query, candidate CFs are created for each candidate value of N. In Figure 6, three

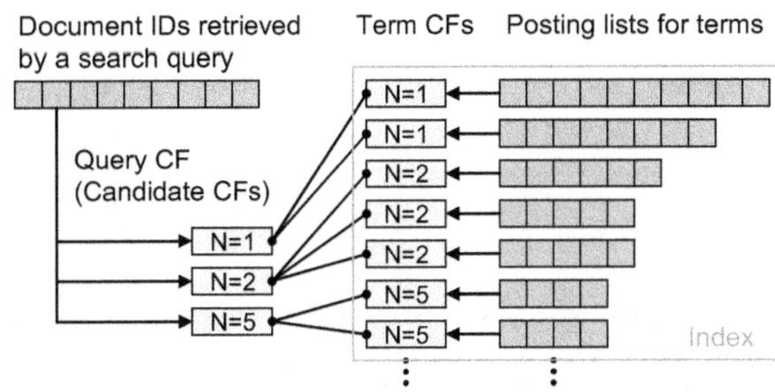

Figure 6: CFs for a query and posting lists.

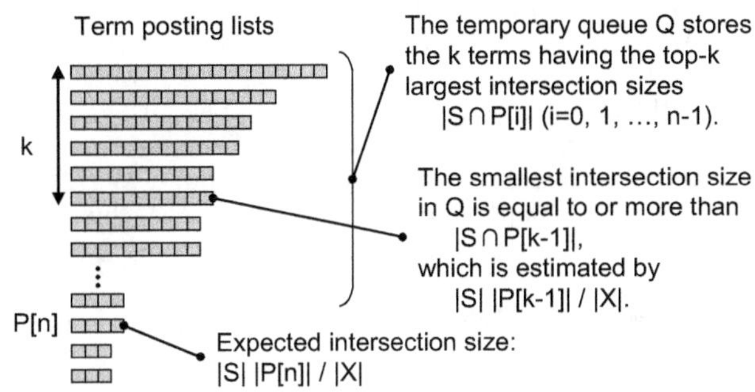

Figure 7: The ratio of the intersection size to the threshold is approximated by $|P[n]|/|P[k-1]|$.

candidate CFs are created with $N = 1, 2, 5$ to be used as a query CF. Then the upper bound is computed between each term CF and one in the candidate CFs with the same value of N as the term CF.

Another feature of the configuration is that we do not create term CFs for very short posting lists because such CFs are not space-efficient. For such posting lists, we use the linear merge algorithm to compute the size of the set intersection.

5.2 Compression Ratio Parameter

The best configuration of the compression ratio parameter N depends on its application, but the example of the configuration for the top-k query gives us clues for general applications. Here, we show how to configure N for the $n+1$-th posting list $P[n]$ using the notation of Section 4.2. Figure 7 illustrates the term posting lists in the form of a list of boxes and the correspondence between the estimated values and the related posting lists. First $|S \cap P[\min(Q)]|$, which is the threshold of the intersection size for a term to be put in the temporary queue Q, is at least $|S \cap P[k-1]|$ since the first k terms are put into Q in every case, and Q is updated only when some $P[i] (i \geq k)$ satisfies $|S \cap P[i]| > |S \cap P[k-1]|$. This means $|S||P[k-1]|/|X|$, which is the expected value of $|S \cap P[k-1]|$ under the assumption of no correlation between S and $P[k-1]$, is a good approximation for $|S \cap P[\min(Q)]|$. Although $|S \cap P[k-1]|$ may become larger or smaller when S and $P[k-1]$ have a positive or negative correlation, $|S \cap P[k-2]|$ or $|S \cap P[k]|$ will be the threshold in either case, and these values should be close to $|S||P[k-1]|/|X|$. Similarly, we can estimate $|S \cap P[n]|$ as $|S||P[n]|/|X|$ for $n \geq k$. Thus, we set N to an integer close to but not larger than $\alpha|P[k-1]|/|P[n]|$, where α is a safety

Name	$\|A\|$	$\|B\|$	Cr
(A) Large / no correlation	1M	1M	1.0
(B) Middle / no correlation	100K	100K	1.0
(C) Small / no correlation	10K	10K	1.0
(D) Asymmetric / no correlation	1M	10K	1.0
(E) Middle / positive correlation	100K	100K	10.0
(F) Middle / negative correlation	100K	100K	0.1

Table 1: Input data with varying the data size (A), (B), and (C), the asymmetry (A) and (D), and the correlation (E), (B), and (F).

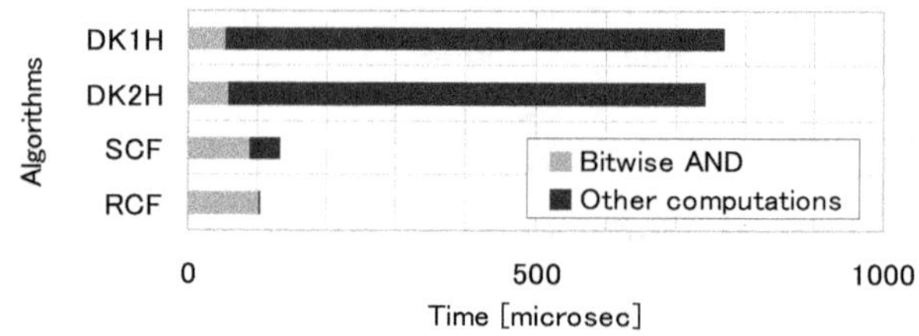

Figure 9: The time breakdown shows that CFs efficiently use bitwise AND operation.

factor. In other words, for this application, we can set N for a set $|A|$ to $\lfloor |X|/r|A| \rfloor$ where r is a constant larger than 1 since $|P[k-1]|$ is linear with the number of documents.

Using this setting of N, the expected space usage of the SCF for a set A is $O(|A|(1+w))$ bits (by Theorem 3.2). The expected time complexity for the upper bound of $|A \cap B|$ is $O(|A| + |B|)$ when $N = |X|/r \max\{|A|, |B|\}$ (by Theorem 3.3).

6. EXPERIMENT

6.1 Improvement of Set Intersection

In this section, we present our speed and size evaluations of CFs compared with known exact set intersection algorithms and the Bloom filter. We compared the computation times for the sizes of two-set intersections or their upper bounds for seven algorithms:

LM the linear merge algorithm described in Section 2.1,

BS the binary search algorithm described in Section 2.1,

DK1H the most practical of the algorithms proposed in [13] with one hash function,

DK2H the two-hash version of DK1H,

BF (upper bound) the algorithm using the Bloom filter described in Section 2.2,

SCF (upper bound) the CF using a single bit array as described in Section 3.1, and

RCF (upper bound) the recursive CF using the bit arrays described in Section 3.2.

All of the algorithms were implemented using C++ and evaluated on a quad core, 64-bit, 2.5-GHz CPU with 4.0 GB of memory. The intersections were calculated in memory for the test data of set pairs which were preloaded into memory before the tests were started. We generated 100 set pairs for each test case and measured the average time for 100 iterations, totalling 10 000 operations. The approximation ratio was also measured to see the relation between the speed and the accuracy.

We used the synthetic test data for set pairs described in Table 1, varying the set sizes, the asymmetry, and the correlation. All of the input sets A and B are subsets in the universe set of 10M elements: $|X| = 10^7$. The column "Cr" is for the correlation between A and B, which we define by $|A \cap B||X|/|A||B|$ (Cr > 1: positive correlation, Cr < 1: negative correlation). The data sets (A), (B), and (C) differ in the size of the sets, but the two input sets of each data set are the same size (the symmetric case). The data sets (A) and (D) are intended to compare the degree of asymmetry for the size differences between the two input sets. The size of the first input set, $|A|$, is set to 1M in both cases, but the size of the other set, $|B|$, differs significantly. The data sets (E), (B), and (F) are used to measure the influence of the correlations between sets. All of these tests have the input sets of the same size, but the intersection size varies from the minimum size (100 elements) to the maximum size (10K elements). We do not consider any cases of biased data such as an integer set that includes dense small numbers and sparse large numbers. Since the tested algorithms except LM and BS are mainly based on hashed values, they do not much depend on the distribution of the elements in each set. Therefore, we used synthetic data in which the elements of each set were uniformly distributed in the universe set. For the compression ratio N, we adopted the policy of "slow but accurate" in this experiment: $N = \lceil \sqrt{|X|/\max\{|A|, |B|\}} \rceil$. Although we can set N to $\lfloor |X|/r|A| \rfloor$ (r is constant) for the top-k query based on the estimate in Section 5.2, we assume a broader application here. The RCF is a 2-layer RCF, and N_2 for the second layer is set to $2N_1$.

Figure 8 shows the computation time and the approximation ratio for each algorithm and each set of data. Each of the six graphs represents the performance on the data set indicated above the graph. The axis for times runs upwards on the left side of each graph, and all of the times are shown in microseconds in all of the graphs. The axis for approximation ratio runs upwards on the right side of each graph. The approximation ratio for the exact algorithms are 1 for all of the data sets. The labels for the series and for the vertical axes are omitted in the graphs for the data sets (B), (C), (D), (E), and (F). As a result, our methods outperformed the other methods by a factor of from 2 to 10 in all of the cases except the asymmetric case, (D), where the Bloom filter has the advantage. Clear differences between SCF and RCF were also observed with the large input sets, (A) and (D). For DK1H and DK2H, we were unable to tune them to run as fast as those in the original paper, which is approximately twice as fast as the linear merge. Even considering this, our proposed methods SCF and RCF still perform the best in all of the cases.

The advantage of SCF and RCF comes from the exploitation of the bitwise AND operations. Figure 9 shows the time breakdown for the data set (B). While the bitwise AND operation takes more time in SCF and RCF than in the DK algorithms, the time for the other operations in SCF and RCF is extremely small compared to the DK algorithms. Although both DK algorithms and CFs use bitwise AND

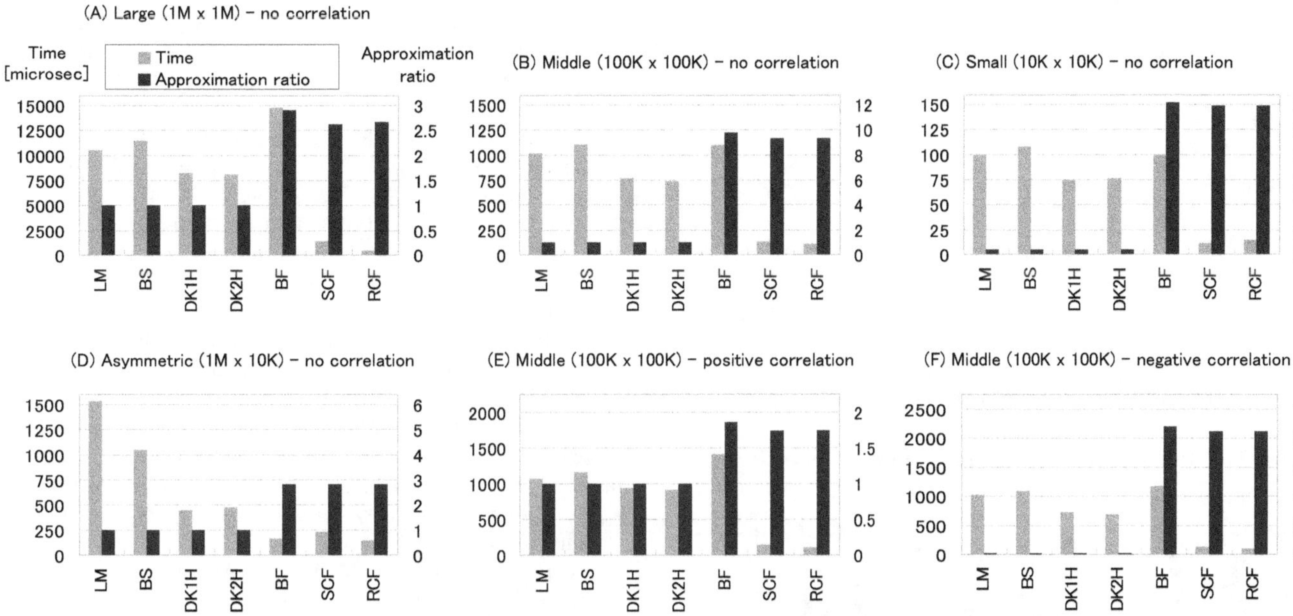

Figure 8: The computation times and intersection approximation ratios measured for known exact algorithms (LM, BS, DK1H, and DK2H), a simple upper bound calculation (BF), and our methods (SCF and RCF).

operations to compute the necessary condition for some of the elements to be contained in the intersection, DK algorithms need to check for each element if it really is a member of the intersection, due to the requirement of exactness. This checking step consumes at least $O(|A \cap B|)$ time. In contrast, the CFs check the membership of the intersection only for the elements that are potentially uncounted. This difference is the essential benefit of computing the upper bound.

6.2 Improvement of Top-k Queries

In this section, we show the performance improvements for the top-k queries. The data used in the experiments was the text data of NHTSA [1], which includes defect and maintenance information for motor vehicles. The total data size was 150 MB and the number of documents was 528 545. We tokenized the text of each document using whitespace as a delimiter and used each token as a term. We varied the number of documents retrieved by each search query ($|S|$ in Section 4.2) from 100 to 100 000. We used five search terms for each size and measured the average time for 50 queries (10 queries for each term). All the algorithms were implemented using Java and evaluated on a quad core, 64-bit, 2.5-GHz CPU with 4.0 GB of memory.

We compared the performance of the top-k query using Algorithm 1 with LM, LM + BS (switching LM and BS at $|A|/|B| = 1/3, 3$), and DK1H as described in Section 6.1 and the improved version of Algorithm 1 with SCF and RCF as described in Sections 4.2 and 5. We set N for SCF and (N_1, N_2) for RCF as in Table 2 using the estimate we introduced in Section 5.2. Figure 10 shows the query processing time for each method. The value of k was set to 100, since this is a frequently used value in text mining. The numbers of documents retrieved by the search queries are displayed on the horizontal axis. If this value is large, each intersection consumes a large amount of time, but only a small

Range of $\lvert P[i]\rvert/\lvert X\rvert$	N, N_1	N_2
$5\% \leq \lvert P[i]\rvert/\lvert X\rvert < 10\%$	1	2
$2\% \leq \lvert P[i]\rvert/\lvert X\rvert < 5\%$	2	4
$1\% \leq \lvert P[i]\rvert/\lvert X\rvert < 2\%$	5	10
$0.5\% \leq \lvert P[i]\rvert/\lvert X\rvert < 1\%$	10	20
$0.2\% \leq \lvert P[i]\rvert/\lvert X\rvert < 0.5\%$	24	48
$0.1\% \leq \lvert P[i]\rvert/\lvert X\rvert < 0.2\%$	47	94
$0.05\% \leq \lvert P[i]\rvert/\lvert X\rvert < 0.1\%$	88	176
$\lvert P[i]\rvert/\lvert X\rvert < 0.05\%$	Not used	Not used

Table 2: Parameter N for top-k query.

number of posting lists are loaded. If this value is small, the computation time for the intersections is small, but many posting lists are read. We can see SCF and RCF performed approximately twice as fast as the other methods.

Figure 11 shows, for each size of the hit document set for the search query, the ratio of the exact intersections skipped by SCF or RCF to the number of evaluated posting lists, except those for the terms that actually rank in the top-k result (skip ratio). We can see that more than 80% of the threshold conditions of intersection were eliminated by the CFs before loading the posting lists of the terms.

7. CONCLUSION

In this paper, we studied the speed of algorithms to compute the upper bounds of the intersection sizes, which has not previously been a focus in the research for the intersection computation. We introduced new data structures, the Single Cardinality Filter and the Recursive Cardinality Filter, to quickly upper bound the size, and we showed they perform much faster than the exact set intersection algorithms and can accelerate the text mining query processing.

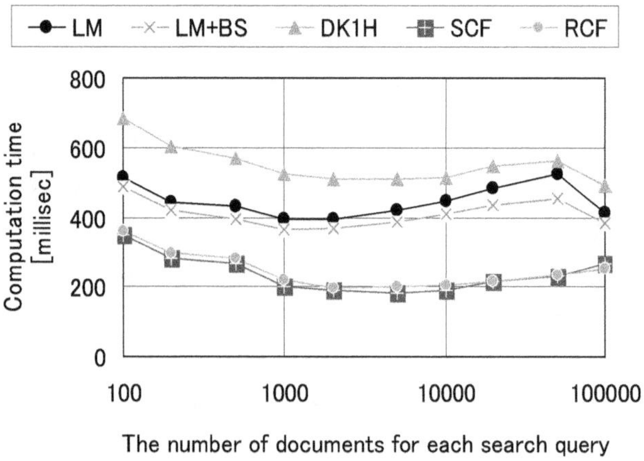

Figure 10: Performance of top-k queries (k=100).

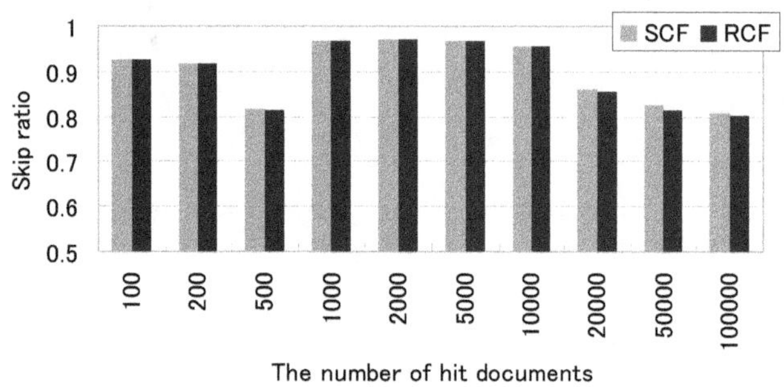

Figure 11: The ratio of skipped exact intersections.

Since a comparison between intersection sizes is a common operation in mining and discovery tasks, CFs are expected to be applied to many analytical queries.

CF presents at least three exciting challenges. First, it would be interesting to study the optional algebraic properties of SCF and RCF that we did not use in this paper. In addition to the property $|A \cap B| \leq |\Phi(A) \cap \Phi(B)|$, SCF and RCF have other algebraic properties such as monotonicity $A \subseteq B \Rightarrow |\Phi(A)| \leq |\Phi(B)|$ and follow the commutative and associative laws for $\cap$, which are important when intersecting three or more sets. Second, although we defined intersection-like operations for CF, union-like operations and exclusions were not studied. A suite of set operations might expand the applications of CF to databases and search engines. Third, a non-parametric implementation of CF is also challenging, since both SCF and RCF have the compression ratio parameter N, which restricts the combinations of sets. To conclude, CF was shown to be capable of speeding up some known algorithms, but still has areas for further algebraic and algorithmic research.

8. REFERENCES

[1] National Highway Traffic Safety Administration. http://www.nhtsa.gov/.

[2] R. Agrawal and R. Srikant. Fast algorithms for mining association rules. In *VLDB*, pages 487–499, 1994.

[3] R. Akbarinia, E. Pacitti, and P. Valduriez. Best position algorithms for efficient top-k query processing. *Information Systems*, 36(6):973–989, 2011.

[4] R. A. Baeza-Yates. A fast set intersection algorithm for sorted sequences. In *CPM*, pages 400–408, 2004.

[5] J. Barbay, A. López-ortiz, and T. Lu. Faster adaptive set intersections for text searching. In *WEA*, pages 146–157, 2006.

[6] H. Bast, D. Majumdar, R. Schenkel, M. Theobald, and G. Weikum. Io-top-k: Index-access optimized top-k query processing. In *VLDB*, pages 475–486, 2006.

[7] K. Beyer, R. Gemulla, P. J. Haas, B. Reinwald, and Y. Sismanis. Distinct-value synopses for multiset operations. *Communications of the ACM*, 52(10):87–95, 2009.

[8] P. Bille, A. Pagh, and R. Pagh. Fast evaluation of union-intersection expressions. In *ISAAC*, pages 739–750, 2007.

[9] G. E. Blelloch and M. Reid-miller. Fast set operations using treaps. In *SPAA*, pages 16–26, 1998.

[10] B. H. Bloom. Space/time trade-offs in hash coding with allowable errors. *Communications of the ACM*, 13(7):422–426, 1970.

[11] M. R. Brown and R. E. Tarjan. A fast merging algorithm. *Journal of the ACM*, 26(2):211–226, 1979.

[12] E. D. Demaine, A. López-Ortiz, and J. I. Munro. Adaptive set intersections, unions, and differences. In *SODA*, pages 743–752, 2000.

[13] B. Ding and A. C. König. Fast set intersection in memory. In *VLDB*, pages 255–266, 2011.

[14] R. Fagin, A. Lotem, and M. Naor. Optimal aggregation algorithms for middleware. *Journal of Computer and System Sciences*, 66(4):614–656, 2003.

[15] L. Fan, P. Cao, J. Almeida, and A. Z. Broder. Summary cache: a scalable wide-area Web cache sharing protocol. *IEEE/ACM Transactions on Networking*, 8(3):281–293, 2000.

[16] F. K. Hwang and S. Lin. A simple algorithm for merging two disjoint linearly ordered sets. *SIAM Journal on Computing*, 1(1):31–39, 1972.

[17] R. Krauthgamer, A. Mehta, V. Raman, and A. Rudra. Greedy list intersection. In *ICDE*, pages 1033–1042, 2008.

[18] D. Okanohara and Y. Yoshida. Conjunctive filter: Breaking the entropy barrier. In *ALENEX*, pages 77–83, 2010.

[19] O. Papapetrou, W. Siberski, and W. Nejdl. Cardinality estimation and dynamic length adaptation for Bloom filters. *Distributed and Parallel Databases*, 28(2-3):119–156, 2010.

[20] A. Simitsis, A. Baid, Y. Sismanis, and B. Reinwald. Multidimensional content exploration. In *VLDB*, pages 660–671, 2008.

[21] S. Tatikonda, F. Junqueira, B. B. Cambazoglu, and V. Plachouras. On efficient posting list intersection with multicore processors. In *SIGIR*, pages 738–739, 2009.

[22] D. Tsirogiannis, S. Guha, and N. Koudas. Improving the performance of list intersection. In *VLDB*, pages 838–849, 2009.

[23] H. S. Warren. *Hacker's Delight*. Addison-Wesley Professional, 2002.

Cache-Conscious Performance Optimization for Similarity Search

Maha Alabduljalil, Xun Tang, Tao Yang
Department of Computer Science
University of California, Santa Barbara
{maha,xtang,tyang}@cs.ucsb.edu

ABSTRACT

All-pairs similarity search can be implemented in two stages. The first stage is to partition the data and group potentially similar vectors. The second stage is to run a set of tasks where each task compares a partition of vectors with other candidate partitions. Because of data sparsity, accessing feature vectors in memory for runtime comparison in the second stage, incurs significant overhead due to the presence of memory hierarchy. This paper proposes a cache-conscious data layout and traversal optimization to reduce the execution time through size-controlled data splitting and vector coalescing. It also provides an analysis to guide the optimal choice for the parameter setting. Our evaluation with several application datasets verifies the performance gains obtained by the optimization and shows that the proposed scheme is upto 2.74x as fast as the cache-oblivious baseline.

Categories and Subject Descriptors

H.3.3 [**Information Search and Retrieval**]: Search Process, Clustering; H.3.4 [**Systems and Software**]: Performance evaluation

Keywords

Similarity search, data traversal, memory hierarchy

1. INTRODUCTION

All Pairs Similarity Search (APSS) [6], which identifies similar objects among a given dataset, has many important applications. For example, collaborative filtering provides recommendations by determining which users have similar tastes [29, 7], search query suggestions identifies queries with similar search results [22], web mirrors and plagiarism recognition [25], coalition detection for advertisement frauds [20], query suggestions [22], spam detection [8, 16, 14], clustering [5], and finally near duplicate detection [12, 30].

The complexity of a naïve APSS can be quadratic to the dataset size. Previous research on expediting similarity computing, developed filtering methods to eliminate unnecessary computations [6, 28, 2], applied inverted indexing to compare vectors only when they share features [18, 21], and used partitioning and parallelization techniques [1]. The LSH based mapping can approximately map vectors to the same bucket when they are potentially similar. However, none of the previously developed methods have considered the impact of memory hierarchy on execution time. The main memory access latency can be 10 to 100 times slower than the L1 cache latency. Thus, the unorchestrated slow memory access can significantly impact performance.

In this paper, we exploit memory hierarchy and develop orthogonal techniques to improve the efficiency of APSS by optimizing data layout and traversal methods. Specifically, we investigate how data traversal affects the use of memory layers. This method is also motivated by the work in query processing [23] and sparse matrix computation that considers cache optimization in computation arrangement.

Similarity comparisons can be performed through a number of tasks where each of them compares a partition of vectors with other candidate vectors [1].

We propose two algorithms PSS1 and PSS2 to exploit the memory hierarchy explicitly. PSS1 splits the data hosted in the memory of each task to fit into the processor's cache and PSS2 coalesces data traversal based on a length-restricted inverted index. We provide an analytic cost model and identify the parameter values that optimize the performance. Hence, the contribution of this paper is a memory-hierarchy aware framework for fast similarity comparison with optimized data layout and traversal.

The rest of this paper is organized as follows. Section 2 reviews background and related work. Section 3 discusses the design framework and PSS1 algorithm for cache-aware data splitting. Section 4 analyzes cost model of PSS1 and demonstrates the impact of the parameters on memory access performance. Section 5 presents the optimization using vector coalescing named PSS2. Section 6 is our experimental evaluation that assess PSS1 and PSS2. Section 7 concludes this paper.

2. BACKGROUND AND RELATED WORK

Following the definition in [6], the APSS problem is defined as follows. Given a set of vectors $d_i = \{w_{i,1}, w_{i,2}, \cdots, w_{i,m}\}$, where each vector contains at most m non-negative features and is normalized to a unit length, then the cosine-based similarity between two vectors is computed as:

$$Sim(d_i, d_j) = \sum_{t \in (d_i \cap d_j)} w_{i,t} \times w_{j,t}.$$

SIGIR'13, July 28–August 1, 2013, Dublin, Ireland.

Two vectors x, y are considered similar if their similarity score exceeds a threshold τ, namely $Sim(x, y) \geq \tau$. The time complexity of APSS is high, especially for a big dataset. There are application-specific methods applied to reduce the complexity. For example, text mining removes stop-words or extremely high frequent features [18]. We use such preprocessing throughout the experiments in Section 6. Generally, there are two groups of optimization techniques developed in the previous work to accelerate APSS.

- **Dynamic computation filtering.** Partially accumulated similarity scores can be monitored at runtime and dissimilar pair of documents can be detected dynamically based on the given similarity threshold without the complete derivation of the total similarity value [6, 28, 21] .
- **Similarity-based grouping in data preprocessing.** The search scope for similarity can be reduced when potentially similar vectors are placed in one group. One approach is to use inverted indexing [28, 18, 21] developed for information retrieval [5]. This approach identifies vectors that share at least one feature, as potentially similar. Hence, it skips unnecessary data traversal while conducting APSS. Another approach is LSH that can approximately map similar vectors into one group [11, 26]. This approach has a tradeoff between precision, recall ratio, and redundant computations when using multiple hash functions. The study in [2] shows that exact comparison algorithms can deliver performance competitive to LSH when computation filtering are used.

  Another approach is partition-based search [1] which statically identifies dissimilar vectors to guide data grouping. Runtime computation avoids the comparison among dissimilar vectors.

Cache optimization for computationally intensive applications is studied in the context of general database query processing [23, 19] and matrix-based scientific computing [10, 9, 27, 4]. Motivated by these studies, we investigate the opportunities of cache-conscious optimization targeting APSS.

3. FRAMEWORK AND CACHE-AWARE DATA SPLITTING

In this section, we give an overview of the partition-based comparison framework [1] and then present the caching optimization strategies as our contributions.

3.1 Framework and basic algorithm

The framework for partition-based similarity search (PSS) consists of two steps. The first step is to divide a dataset into a set of partitions. During this process, the dissimilarity relationship among partitions is identified so that unnecessary comparisons among them are avoided. The second step is to assign a partition to a task and each task compares this partition with other potentially similar partitions.

Dissimilarity-based partitioning identifies dissimilar vectors as much as possible without explicitly computing the product of their features. One approach is to use the following inequality that uses the 1-norm and ∞-norm of each vector.

$$Sim(d_i, d_j) \leq min(||d_i||_\infty ||d_j||_1, ||d_j||_\infty ||d_i||_1) < \tau.$$

The partitioning algorithm sorts the vectors based on their 1-norm values and uses the sorted list to identify dissimilar pairs (d_i, d_j) in complexity $O(n \log n)$ satisfying the inequality $\|d_i\|_1 < \frac{\tau}{\|d_j\|_\infty}$. A different τ value would affect the outcome of the dissimilarity detection in the above partitioning. The details for the above static partitioning is discussed in [1]. This paper focuses on optimizing the task execution after the static partitioning is applied. Note that this scheme can also be applied with LSH when approximations are allowed. When vectors are mapped into a set of dissimilar buckets using LSH, some buckets can still be big and the static partitioning can be further applied to divide such buckets.

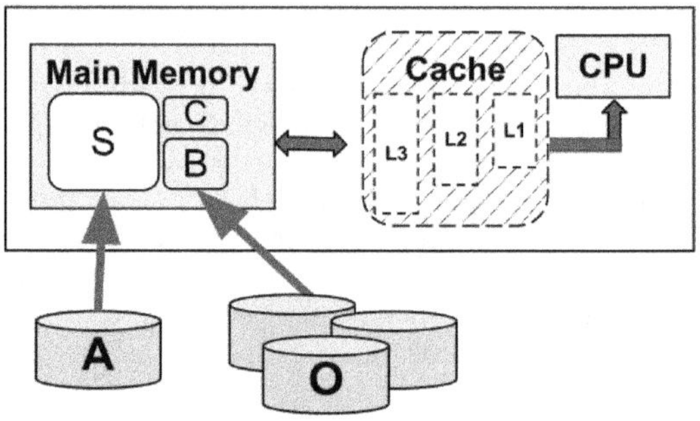

Figure 1: A PSS task compares the assigned partition A with other partitions O.

Figure 1 depicts a task for partition-based similarity search interacting with a CPU core with multiple levels of cache. Two or three cache levels are typical in today's Intel or AMD architecture [17, 15]. We assume that the assigned partition A fits the memory of one machine as the data partitioning can be adjusted to satisfy such an assumption. But vectors of O can exceed memory and need to be fetched gradually from a local or remote storage. In a computer cluster with the distributed file system such as Hadoop, a task can seamlessly fetch data from the file system without worrying about the machine location of data.

The memory used by each task has three areas, as illustrated in Figure 1. 1) Area S: hosts the assigned partition A. 2) Area B: stores a block of vectors fetched from other candidate partitions O at each comparison step. 3) Area C: stores intermediate results temporarily.

Figure 2 describes the function of a PSS task. Each task loads the assigned vectors, whose data structure is in forward index format, into area S. Namely, each vector consists of an ID along with a list of feature IDs and their corresponding weights, stored in a compact manner. After loading the assigned vectors, the task inverts them locally within area S. It then fetches a number of vectors from O, in forward index format, and place them into area B.

Let d_j be the vector fetched from O to be processed (Line 5). For each feature t in d_j, PSS uses the inverted index in area S to find the localized t's posting (Line 10). Then weights of vector d_i from t's posting and d_j contribute a partial score towards the final similarity score between d_j and d_i. After all the features of d_j are processed, the similarity scores between d_j and the vectors in S are validated (Line 17) and only those that exceed the threshold are written to disk. In COMPARE(S, d_j), the dissimilarity of vector d_i in S with d_j can be marked (Line 14) by using a negative value

```
TASK (A, O)
1: Read all vectors from assigned partition A into S
2: Build inverted index of these vectors and store in S
3: repeat
4:    Fetch a set of vectors from O into B
5:    for d_j ∈ B do
6:       COMPARE (S, d_j)
7: until all vectors in O are fetched

COMPARE (S, d_j)
8: Initialize array score of size |S| with zeros
9: r_j ← ||d_j||_1
10: for t ∈ d_j And Posting(t) ∈ S do
11:    for d_i ∈ Posting(t) and d_i is a candidate do
12:       score[i]=score[i]+w_{i,t}×w_{j,t}
13:       if (score[i]+maxw[d_i]×r_j<τ) then
14:          Mark d_i as non-candidate
15:    r_j = r_j − w_{j,t}
16: for i = 1 to |S| do
17:    if score[i]>τ then
18:       Write (d_i, d_j, score[i])
```

Figure 2: PSS task.

for *score*[*i*]. Array *maxw*[ ] contains the ∞-norm value of vector d_i.

3.2 Cache-conscious data splitting

When dealing with a large dataset, the number of vectors in each partition is high. Having a large number of vectors increase the benefits of using inverted indexing as shown in Figure 2. But it has a problem that the accessed areas S or C may not fit in the fast cache. In that case, temporal locality is not exploited, meaning the second access of the same element during any computation will be a cache miss. As we show in the next section, this leads to frequent slow memory access and a significant increase in execution time. Since fast access of each area S, B or C is equally important in the core computation (Lines 12 and 13), one idea is to let area C fit in L1 cache by explicitly dividing vectors of the assigned partition in S into a set of splits and have the task focus on one split at a time.

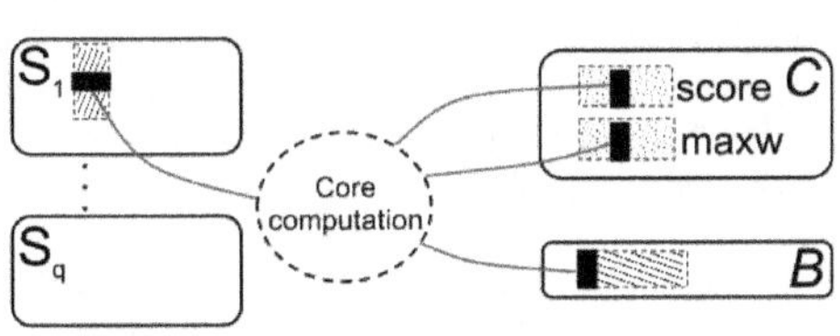

Figure 3: A partition in area S is further divided into multiple splits for each PSS1 task. Four data items are involved in the core computation. The striped area indicates cache coverage.

Figure 3 illustrates this cache-conscious data splitting idea. The corresponding algorithm called PSS1 is shown in Figure 4. First, it divides the hosted vectors in S into q splits. Each split S_i is of size s. PSS1 then executes q comparison sub-tasks. Each sub-task compares vectors from S_i with a vector b_j in B. The access in area C is localized such that array *score*[ ] and *maxw*[ ] can fully fit in L1 cache. This improves temporal locality of data elements for area C and

```
TASK (A, O)
Read and divide A into q splits
Build an inverted index for each split S_i and store in S
repeat
   Fetch a set of vectors from O into B
   for d_j ∈ B do
      for S_i ∈ S do
         COMPARE (S_i, d_j)
until all vectors in O are fetched
```

Figure 4: PSS1 task.

reduces the access time by an order of magnitude. The core computation speeds up as a result.

The data splitting also introduces potential benefits from exploiting the multi-core CPU architecture via threads. Every time a data block from O is fetched into B, there can be multiple threads running in parallel to execute COMPARE(S_i, d_j) where d_j is a vector in B.

The question is, how to determine the s value of each split so that the caches are best utilized? This is discussed next.

4. COST ANALYSIS AND CACHE PERFORMANCE OF PSS1

We model the total execution time of each PSS1 task and analyze how memory hierarchy affects the running time. This analysis facilitates the identification of optimized parameter setting. Table 1 describes the parameters used in our analysis. They represent the characteristics of the given dataset, algorithm variables, and the system setting.

Dataset	
$w_{d,t}$	Weight of feature t in vector d
τ	Similarity threshold
k	Average number of non-zero features in d
Algorithm	
S, B, C	Memory usage for each task
n	Number of vectors to compare per task ($\|O\|$)
s	Avg. number of vectors for each split in S
b	Number of vectors fetched and stored in B
S_i	A split in area S divided by PSS1
q	Number of splits in S
h	Cost for t-posting lookup in table
δ_{total}	Cost of accessing the hierarchical memory
$m_j(X)$	Miss ratio in level j cache for area X
$D_j(X)$	Number of misses in level j cache for area X
D_j	Total number of access misses in level j cache
p_s	Average posting length in the inverted index of each split S_i
p_b	Average posting length in the inverted index of b vectors in B
Infrastructure	
l	Cache line size
e_s, e_b, e_c	Element size in S, B, C respectively
f_s, f_b, f_c	Effective prefetch factor for elements in S, B and C respectively
$\delta_1, \delta_2, \delta_3$	Latency when accessing L1, L2, and L3 cache
δ_{mem}	Latency when accessing main memory
ψ	Cost of addition and multiplication

Table 1: Modeling Symbols

4.1 Task execution time

The total execution time for each task contains two parts: I/O and computation. I/O cost occurs for loading the assigned vectors A, fetching other potentially similar vectors, and writing similarity pairs to disk storage. Notice that in fetching other vectors for comparison, the algorithm always fetches a block of vectors to amortize the startup cost of I/O. For the datasets we have used, read I/O takes about 2% of total cost while write I/O takes about 10-15%. Since I/O cost is the same for the baseline PSS and our proposed schemes, we do not model it in this paper.

For each split, the computation time contains a small overhead for the index inversion of its s vectors. Because the inverted index is built once and reused every time a partition is loaded, this part of computation becomes negligible and the comparison time with other vectors dominates. The core part (Lines 12, 13 in Figure 2) is computationally intensive. Following Table 1, h is the cost of looking up the posting of a feature appeared in a vector in B. Symbol p_s is the average length of postings visited in S_i (only when a common feature exists), so it estimates the number of iterations for Line 10. Furthermore, there are 4 memory accesses in Line 12 and 13, regarding data items $score[i]$, $w_{i,t}$, $w_{j,t}$, and $maxw[d_i]$. Other items, such as r_j, and τ, are constants within this loop and can be pre-loaded into registers. There are 2 pairs of multiplication and addition involved (one in Line 12 and one in Line 13) bringing in a cost of 2ψ. For simplicity of the formula, we model the worst case where none of the computations are dynamically filtered.

For a large dataset, the cost of self-comparison within the same partition for each task is negligible compared to the cost of comparisons with other vectors in O. The execution time of PSS1 task (Figure 4) can be approximately modeled as follows.

$$\text{Time} = q\left[nk(\overbrace{h}^{lookup} + \overbrace{p_s \times 2\psi}^{multiply+add}) + \overbrace{\delta_{total}}^{traverse\ S,B,C} \right]. \quad (1)$$

As s increases, q decreases and the cost of inverted index lookup may be amortized. In the core computation, p_s increases as s increases. More importantly, the running time can be dominated by δ_{total} which is the data access cost due to cache or memory latency. The data access cost is affected by s because of the presence of memory hierarchy. We investigate how to determine the optimal s value to minimize the overall cost in the following subsection.

4.2 Memory and Cache Access of PSS1

Here, we estimate the cost of accessing data in S, B, and C. Define D_0 as the total number of data accesses in performing COMPARE(S_i, d_j) in Figure 4. Define D_j as the total number of data access misses in cache level j. δ_i is the access time at cache level i. δ_{mem} is the memory access time.

$$\delta_{total} = (D_0 - D_1)\delta_1 + (D_1 - D_2)\delta_2 + (D_2 - D3)\delta_3 + D_3\delta_{mem}. \quad (2)$$

To conduct the computation in Lines 12 and 13 of Figure 2, the program needs to access weights of S_i, B, $score[\,]$ and $maxw[\,]$ in C. We model these accesses separately then add them together as follows:

$$D_0 = D_0(S_i) + D_0(B) + D_0(C) = \overbrace{nkp_s}^{S_i} + \overbrace{nk}^{B} + \overbrace{2nkp_s}^{C}. \quad (3)$$

Case		S_i	C	Description
(1)	m_1	$\frac{e_s}{f_s l}$	0	C fits in L1; S_i does not fit L1, but fits in L2.
	m_2	0	0	
	m_3	0	0	
(2)	m_1	$\frac{e_s}{f_s l}$	$\frac{e_c}{f_c l}$	S_i and C do not fit in L1, but fit in L2.
	m_2	0	0	
	m_3	0	0	
(3)	m_1	$\frac{e_s}{f_s l}$	$\frac{e_c}{f_c l}$	C does not fit in L1, but fits in L2; S_i does not fit in L2 but fits in L3.
	m_2	1	0	
	m_3	0	0	
(4)	m_1	$\frac{e_s}{f_s l}$	$\frac{e_c}{f_c l}$	S_i and C do not fit in L2, but fit in L3.
	m_2	1	1	
	m_3	0	0	
(5)	m_1	$\frac{e_s}{f_s l}$	$\frac{e_c}{f_c l}$	C does not fit in L2 but fits in L3; S_i does not fit in L3.
	m_2	1	1	
	m_3	1	0	
(6)	m_1	$\frac{e_s}{f_s l}$	$\frac{e_c}{f_c l}$	S_i and C do not fit in L3.
	m_2	1	1	
	m_3	1	1	

Table 2: Cases of cache miss ratios for split S_i and area C in PSS1 at different cache levels. Column 3 is the cache miss ratio $m_j(S_i)$ for accessing data in S_i. Column 4 is the cache miss ratio $m_j(\mathcal{C})$ for accessing data in $\mathcal{C}$. Column 5 describes the condition of each case.

Define $D_j(X)$ as the total number of data accesses missed in cache level j for accessing area X. $m_j(X)$ is the cache miss ratio to access data for area X in cache level j.

$$\begin{aligned} D_j =& D_j(S_i) + D_j(B) + D_j(C) \\ =& D_{j-1}(S_i) * m_j(S_i) + D_{j-1}(B) * m_j(B) \\ &+ D_{j-1}(C) * m_j(C). \end{aligned} \quad (4)$$

Table 2 lists six cases of miss ratio values $m_j(S_i)$ and $m_j(C)$ at different cache levels j. The miss ratio for B is not listed and is considered close to 0 assuming it is small enough to fit in L1 cache after warm-up. That is true for our tested datasets. For a dataset with long vectors and B cannot fit in L1, there is a small overhead to fetch it partially from L2 to L1. Such overhead is negligible due to the relative small size of B, compared to S_i and C. We explain this table in more details from the following aspects.

- A cache miss triggers the loading of a cache line from next level. We assume the cost of a cold cache miss during initial cache warm-up is negligible and the cache replacement policy is LRU-based. Thus the cache miss ratio for consecutive access of a vector of elements is $\frac{1}{l/e}$ where l is the cache line size and e is the size of each element in bytes. We assume that cache lines are the same in all cache levels for simplicity, which matches the current Intel and AMD architecture.

- The computer system prefetches a few cache lines in advance, in anticipation of using consecutive memory regions [17, 15]. Let f_s be the effective prefetch factor for S_i, and e_s be the element size for S_i. The cache miss ratio for accessing S_i is adjusted as $\frac{e_s}{f_s l}$. Similarly, the cache miss ratio for accessing C is adjusted as $\frac{e_c}{f_c l}$

and the cache miss ratio for accessing B is adjusted as $\frac{e_b}{f_b l}$.

- In Case (1), s is small. C can fit in L1 cache. Thus after initial data loading, its corresponding cache miss ratios $m_1(C_1)$, $m_2(C_1)$, and $m_3(C_1)$ are close to 0. Then $m_1(S_i) = \frac{e_s}{f_s l}$, and $m_2(S_i)$ and $m_3(S_i)$ are approximately 0 since each split can fit in L2 (but not L1). In this case, s is too small, the benefit of using the inverted index does not outweigh the overhead of the inverted-index constructions and dynamic look-up.

- In Case (2), S_i and C can fit in L2 cache (but not L1). $m_1(S_i) = \frac{e_s}{f_s l}$, and $m_1(C) = \frac{e_c}{f_c l}$. $m_2(S_i)$ and $m_3(S_i)$ are approximately 0. Thus δ_{total} is:

$$\delta_{total} = \left[nkp_s(1 - \frac{e_s}{f_s l}) + nkp_s + 2nkp_s(1 - \frac{e_c}{f_c l}) \right] \delta_1 + \left[nkp_s \frac{e_s}{f_s l} + 2nkp_s \frac{e_c}{f_c l} \right] \delta_2. \quad (5)$$

Hence task time is

$$Time = q \left[nk(h + p_s 2\psi) + nkp_s \left(4\delta_1 + (\frac{e_s}{f_s} + \frac{2e_c}{f_c}) \frac{\delta_2 - \delta_1}{l} \right) \right].$$

- As s becomes large in Case (3) to Case (6), S_i and C cannot fit in L2 nor L3, and they need to be fetched periodically from memory if not L3.

We illustrate s value for the optimal case. For the AMD Bulldozer 8-core CPU architecture (FX-8120) tested in our experiments, L1 cache is of size 16KB for each core. L2 cache is of size 2MB shared by 2 cores and L3 cache is of size 8MB shared by 8 cores. Thus 1MB on average for each core. Other parameters are: $\delta_m = 64.52ns$, $\delta_3 = 24.19ns$, $\delta_2 = 3.23ns$, $\delta_1 = 0.65ns$, $l = 64$ bytes. We estimate $\psi = 0.16ns$, $h = 10ns$, $p_s = 10\%s$, $f_c = f_s = 4$ based on the results from our micro benchmark. The minimum task time occurs in Case (2) when S_i and C can fit in L2 cache, but not L1. Thus the constraint based on the L2 cache size can be expressed as

$$s \times k \times e_s + 2s \times e_c \leq 1MB.$$

While satisfying the above condition, split size s is chosen as large as possible to reduce q value. For Twitter data, k is 18, e_s is 28 bytes, and e_c is 4 bytes. Thus the optimal s is around 2K.

To show how the choice of s affects the task execution time in Formula (1), we measure the ratio of the data access time (including the inverted index lookup) over the computation time:

$$\frac{\text{Data-access}}{\text{Computation}} = \frac{4\delta_1 + (\frac{e_s}{f_s} + \frac{2e_c}{f_c}) \frac{\delta_2 - \delta_1}{l} + \frac{h}{p_s}}{2\psi}.$$

This ratio captures the data access overhead paid to perform comparison computation and the smaller the value is, the better. For Twitter benchmark, the above ratio is 8 for optimum case, while it increases to over 25 for Case (3) and Case (4) where more frequent access to L3 cache is required. The data-access-to-computation ratio deduction is supported by experiment results shown in Figure 5. It shows that by selecting s based on our cost function, we are able to reduce the data-access-to-computation ratio from 25 to 8. When an optimum s is chosen, we manage to dramatically reduce the slow cache/memory access out of the whole task execution time.

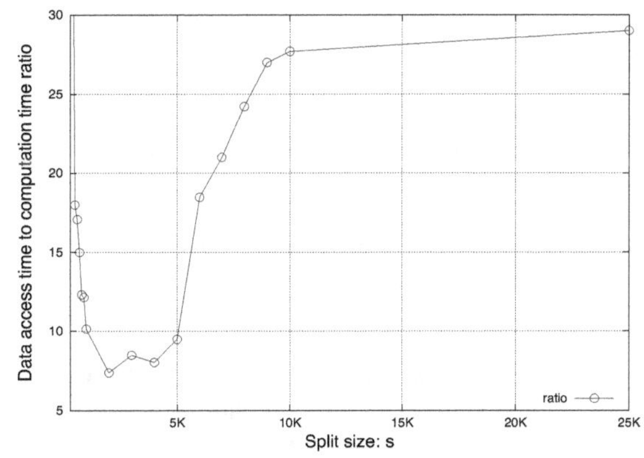

Figure 5: Y axis is the ratio of actual data access time to computation time for Twitter data observed in our experiments.

5. PSS2 WITH FEATURE-BASED VECTOR COALESCING

In PSS1, every time a feature weight from area S_i is loaded to L1 cache, its value is multiplied by a weight from a vector in B. As S_i does not fit in L1 cache, the utilization of L1 for S_i is low. L1 cache usage for S_i is mainly for spatial locality. Namely fetching one or few cache lines for S_i to avoid future L1 cache miss when consecutive data is accessed. The benifit of temporal locality is low, because the same element is unlikely to be accessed again before being evicted, especially for L1 cache due to its small size.

Another way to understand this weakness is that the number of times that an element in L1 loaded for S_i can be used to multiply a weight in B is low before this element of S_i is evicted out from L1 cache. PSS2 is proposed to adjust the data layout and access structure in B in order to increase L1 cache reuse ratio for S_i. The key idea of PSS2 is listed as follows.

- Once an element in S_i is loaded to L1 cache, we compare more vectors in B at each stage. Namely group S_i from S is compared with b vectors in B.

- We coalesce b vectors in B and build an inverted index from these b vectors. The comparison between S_i and b vectors in B is done by intersecting postings of common features in B and S_i.

- The above approach also benefits the amortization of inverted index lookup cost. In PSS1, every term posting lookup for S_i can only benefit multiplication with one element in B. In PSS2, every look up can potentially benefit multiple elements because of vector coalescing.

Figure 7 illustrates the data traversal pattern of PSS2 with $b = 3$. There is one common feature t_3 that appears in both S_i and B. The posting of t_3 in S_i is $\{ w_{1,3}, w_{2,3} \}$

```
PSS2 TASK (A, O)
  Read A and divide it into q splits of s vectors each
  Build an inverted index for each split S_i.
  repeat
     Fetch b vectors from O and build inverted index in B
     for S_i ∈ S do
        COMPARE(S_i, B)
  until all vectors in O are compared

COMPARE (S, B)
  Initialize array score of size s × b with zeros
  for j = 1 to b do
     r_j ← ||d_j||_1
  for Feature t appears in B and S do
     for d_i ∈ Posting(t) in S do
        for d_j ∈ Posting(t) in B and d_i is a candidate do
           score[i][j]=score[i][j]+w_{i,t}×w_{j,t}
           if (score[i][j]+maxw[d_i]×r_j<τ) then
              Mark pair d_i and d_j as non-candidate
     for d_j ∈ Posting(t) in B do
        r_j = r_j − w_{j,t}
  for i = 1 to s do
     for j = 1 to b do
        if score[i][j]>τ then
           Write (d_i, d_j, score[i][j])
```

Figure 6: PSS2 task.

and each iteration of PPS2 uses one element from this list, and multiplies it with elements in the corresponding posting of B which is $\{ w_{4,3}, w_{6,3} \}$. Thus every L1 cache loading for S_i can benefit 2 multiplications with weights in B. In comparison, every L1 loading of weights for S_i in PSS1 can only benefit one multiplication.

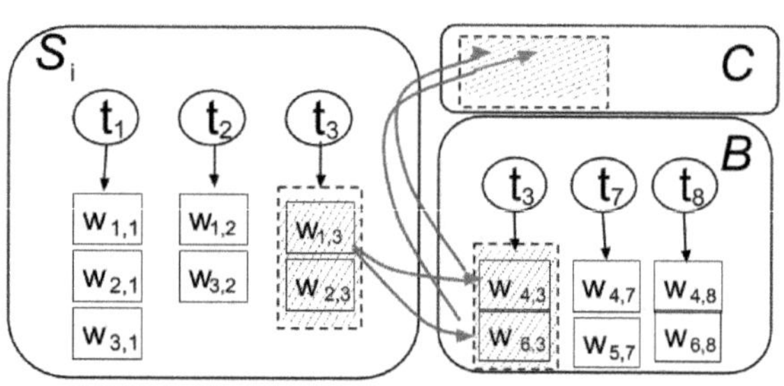

Figure 7: Example of data traversal in PSS2.

Increasing b values expands the size of areas $\mathcal{B}$ and $\mathcal{C}$ to store b vectors and a 2D array $score[][]$. $\mathcal{B}$ and $\mathcal{C}$ may not fit in L1, or even L2 cache anymore. Since L2/L3 cache has higher latency, cache capacity restricts the value of b from being too large. On the other hand, vectors in $\mathcal{B}$ are sparse and b cannot be too small so that there is a sufficient number of vectors sharing a feature after coalescing. Our experiment in Figure 11 discusses this issue in more details.

Similar to PSS1, we can conduct a case-by-case analysis for cache miss ratios of PSS2 based on how S_i, B and $\mathcal{C}$ fit in the different levels of cache. Then we can derive the s and b ranges in each case.

6. EXPERIMENTS

We have implemented PSS, PSS1 and PSS2 in Java. During the evaluation, PSS, PSS1 and PSS2 are applied after data preprocessing. In the default setting, static partitioning [1] is adopted to partition the dataset then, a set of parallel tasks is executed following either PSS2 or PSS1. In another setting (Table 3), LSH [11, 26] is applied first before static partitioning.

We also evaluated another design option we refer to as PSS3. PSS3 follows the previous scientific computing research that views a sparse matrix as a collection of dense small submatrices and employs BLAS3 to perform submatrix multiplication [10, 24, 27]. In this case, we represent the feature vectors in S and B as a set of small submatrices and use a highly optimized BLAS3 library called MTJ [13] for the submatrix multiplication.

The evaluation has the following objectives:

1. Compare PSS1 and PSS2 with the baseline PSS using multiple application datasets. Study how the algorithms behave with different dataset sizes.

2. Evaluate the choice and impact of s value for PSS1 and s and b for PSS2.

3. Illustrate the predicted and observed cache hit ratio. Validate the accuracy of the cost model with respect to the actual execution time.

4. Report the overall parallel performance.

5. Evaluate PSS3 to understand the issues of submatrix multiplication for APSS.

Metrics. We report the running time for different algorithms when the static partitioning is given. Since the number of tasks is fixed, the overall parallel time is proportional to the average task running time. Hence we mainly report the average task running time to evaluate the performance impact of adjusting split size and fetched block size. The cost of self-comparison among vectors within a partition is included when reporting the actual cost. To assess the scalability, we report the overall speedup for the parallel performance, and measure the megaflops number as an additional metric.

6.1 Datasets and experimental setup

The experiments are mainly conducted on a cluster of AMD nodes where each node has 8 cores with 3.1GHz AMD Bulldozer FX8120 and 16GB memory. They run the Hadoop MapReduce environment. In reporting parallel speedup, we have used a bigger cluster of Intel 12-core nodes and each node has dual Intel X5650 six-core processors and 24GB memory. The following five datasets are used.

- Twitter dataset containing 20 million tweets collected from approximately 2 million unique users. The average number of features per vector is 18.32.

- A web dataset containing about 50 million web pages, randomly selected from the Clueweb collection distributed by [3]. The average number of features is 320 per web page.

- Enron email dataset containing 619,446 messages from the Enron corpus, belonging to 158 users with an average of 757 messages per user. The average number of features is 107 per message. The corpus contains large numbers of duplicated emails.

- Yahoo music dataset containing 1,000,990 users rating 624,961 songs to investigate the similarity among songs for music recommendation.
- Google news webpages with over 100K news articles crawled from Google.com. The average number of features per article is 830.

The datasets are preprocessed to follow the TF-IDF weighting after cleaning and stopword filtering [18].

6.2 Comparative studies for execution time and impact of parameters

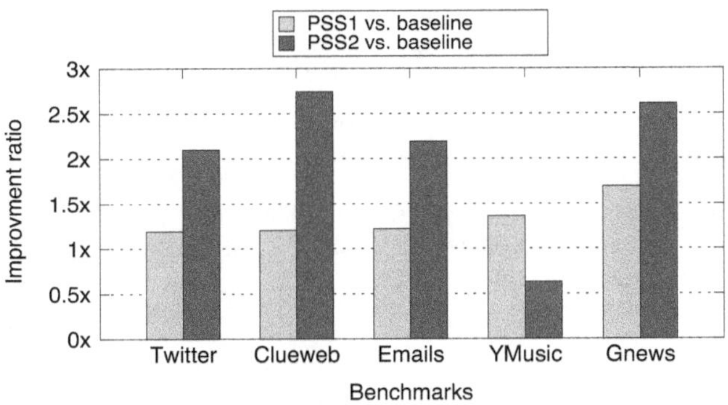

Figure 8: Y axis is ratio $\frac{Time_{PSS}}{Time_{PSS1}}$ and $\frac{Time_{PSS}}{Time_{PSS2}}$. The average task running time includes I/O.

Figure 8 shows the improvement ratio on the average task time after applying PSS1 and PSS2 over the baseline. Namely $\frac{Time_{PSS}}{Time_{PSS1}}$ and $\frac{Time_{PSS}}{Time_{PSS2}}$. PSS is cache-oblivious and each task handles a very large partition that fits into the main memory (but not fast cache). For example, each partition for Clueweb can have around 500,000 web pages. Result shows PSS2 contributes significant improvement compared to PSS1. For example, under Clueweb dataset, PSS1 is 1.2x faster than the baseline PSS while PSS2 is 2.74x faster than PSS. The split size s for PSS1 and s and b for PSS2 are optimally chosen.

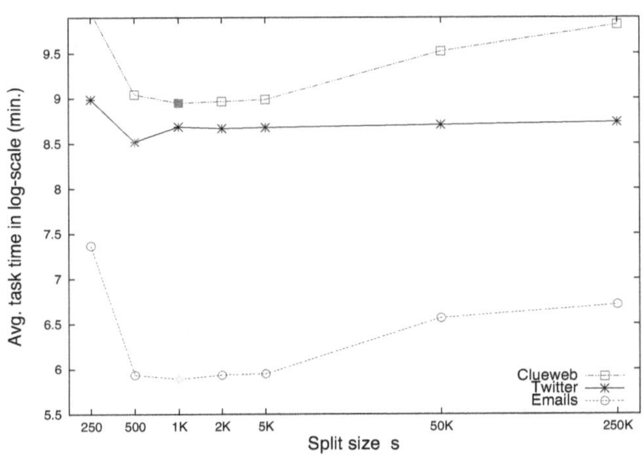

Figure 9: The average running time in *log scale* per PSS1 task under different values for split size s. The partition size S for each task is fixed, $S = s \times q$.

The gain from PSS to PSS1 is achieved by the splitting of the hosted partition data. Figure 9 shows the average running time of a PSS1 task including I/O in log-scale with different values of s. Notice that the partition size ($S = s \times q$) handled by each task is fixed. The choice of split size s makes an impact on data access cost. Increasing s does not change the total number of basic multiplications and additions needed for comparison, but it does change the traversal pattern of memory hierarchy and thus affects data access cost. For all the datasets shown, the lowest value of the running time is achieved when s value is ranged between 0.5K and 2K, consistent with our analytic results.

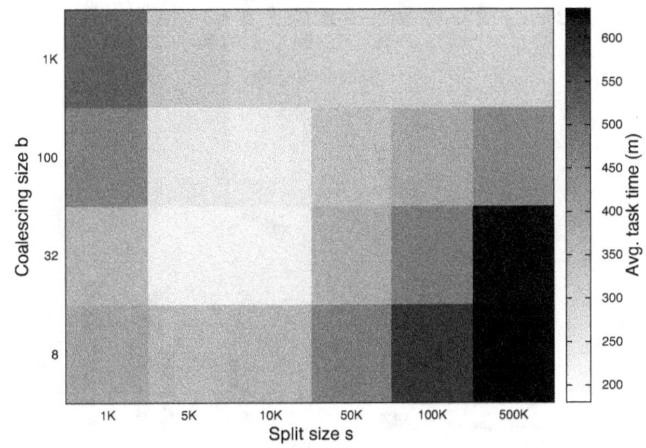

Figure 10: Each square is an $s \times b$ PSS2 implementation (where $\sum s = S$) shaded by its average task time for Twitter dataset. The lowest time is the lightest shade.

The gain of PSS2 over PSS1 is made by coalescing visits of vectors in B with a control. Figure 10 depicts the average time of the Twitter tasks with different s and b, including I/O. The darker each square is, the longer the execution time is. The shortest running time is achieved when $b = 32$ and s is between 5K to 10K. When b is too small, the number of features shared among b vectors is too small to amortize the cost of coalescing. When b is too big, the footprint of area C and B becomes too big to fit into L2 cache.

While PSS1 outperforms PSS in all 5 datasets, there is an exception for Yahoo music dataset. The benefits of PSS2 over PSS1 depend on how many features are shared in area B. The top and bottom parts of Figure 11 show the average and maximum number of features shared among b vectors in area B, respectively. Sharing pattern is highly skewed and the maximum sharing is fairly high. On the other hand, the average sharing value captures better on the benefits of coalescing. The average number shared exceeds 2 or more for all data when b is above 32 (the optimal b value for PSS2) except Yahoo music. In the Yahoo music data, each vector represents a song and features are the users rating this song. PSS2 slows down the execution due to the low intersection of the interest among users.

6.3 Cache Behavior and Cost Modeling

We demonstrate the cache behavior of PSS1 modeled in Section 4.2 with the Twitter dataset. The Linux perf tool is used to collect the cache miss ratio of L1 and L3.

Figure 12 depicts the real cache miss ratios for L1 and L3 reported by perf tool, the estimated L1 miss ratio which is D_1/D_0, and the estimated L3 miss ratio which is D_3/D_2. L1 cache miss ratio grows from 3.5%, peaks when $s = 8K$, and gradually drops to around 9% afterwards when s value in-

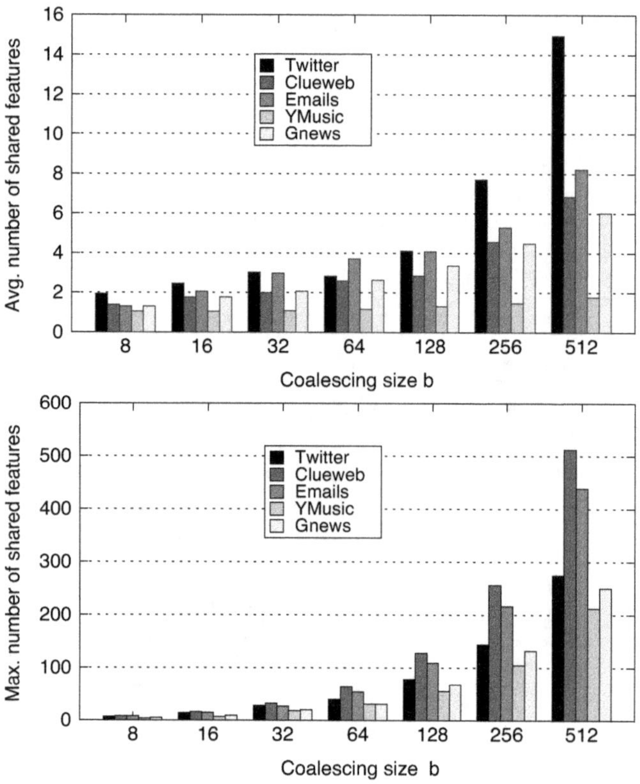

Figure 11: The top is the average number of shared features among b vectors. The bottom is the maximum number of features shared among b vectors.

creases. L3 cache miss ratio starts from 3.65% when s=100, reaches the bottom at 1.04% when s= 5K, and rises to almost 25% when s= 500K. The figure shows that the estimated cache miss ratio approximates the trend of the actual cache miss ratio well.

To validate our cost model, we compare the estimated cost with experimental results in Figure 13. Our estimation of cache miss ratios fits the real ratios quite well, reasonably predicts the trend of ratio change as split size changes. When s is very small, the overhead of building and searching the inverted indexes are too high and thus the actual performance is poor. When s ranges from 50K to 80K, the actual running time drops. This is because as s increases, there is some benefit for amortizing the cost of inverted index lookup. Both the estimated and real time results suggest that the optimum s value is around 2K. Given the optimum s, PSS1 is twice faster than when s is 10K.

6.4 Performance of PSS1 and PSS2 with varying dataset sizes

We also compare the performance of PSS1 and PSS2 with the baseline PSS when the dataset size changes.

Figure 14 shows the average running time of tasks under the three algorithms for four benchmarks with varying input size. We still observe the same trend that PSS1 outperforms the baseline. PSS2 also outperforms PSS1 in all cases except for Yahoo music benchmark. In that case, PSS1 is better than baseline, which is better than PSS2 due to low sharing pattern among the b vectors discussed in Section 6.2.

To reduce the required comparisons with an approximation, we tested the algorithms over an LSH implementation

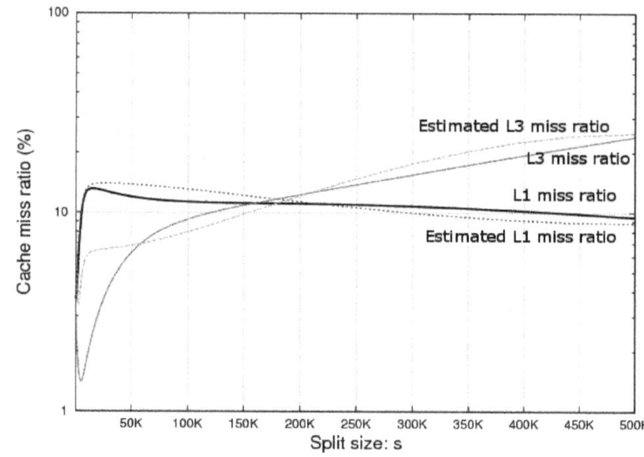

Figure 12: Estimated and real cache miss ratios for PSS1 tasks.

from [26]. LSH is applied first then the static partitioning. Table 3 compares the baseline with PSS2 after applying LSH partitioning over Clueweb dataset with varying sizes. PSS2 is upto 2.55x as fast as PSS for the 50M dataset.

Dataset size	#Buckets	PSS (m)	PSS2 (m)
10 M	176	233.34	98.07
50 M	513	1005.42	394.46

Table 3: PSS and PSS2 task time after LSH mapping for Clueweb. The average number of partitions per bucket is about 6.

6.5 Overall performance and a comparison with PSS3

We assess the overall performance in terms of speedup in processing the entire dataset when varying the number of cores. Figure 15 reports the speedup (parallel time divided by sequential time) for processing Twitter dataset with different numbers of cores in the Intel cluster aforementioned. PSS2 scales well with more computing resources.

We also assess the individual task performance in utilizing the CPU resource by collecting its megaflops rate and compare it with the peak megaflops rate when vectors are dense. Similarity computation can be viewed approximately as a

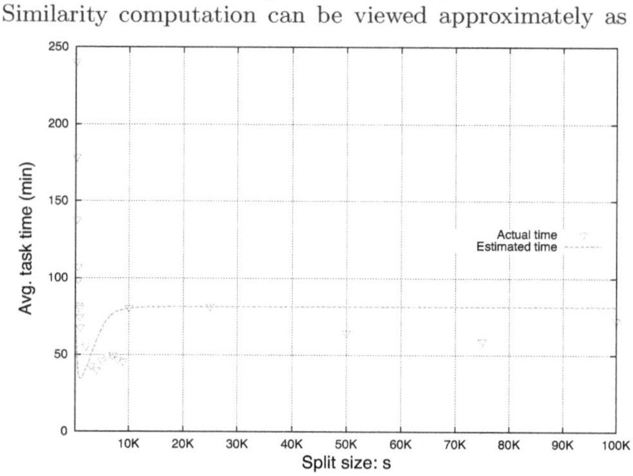

Figure 13: Actual vs estimated average task time for PSS1 in 3M Twitter dataset while split size varies.

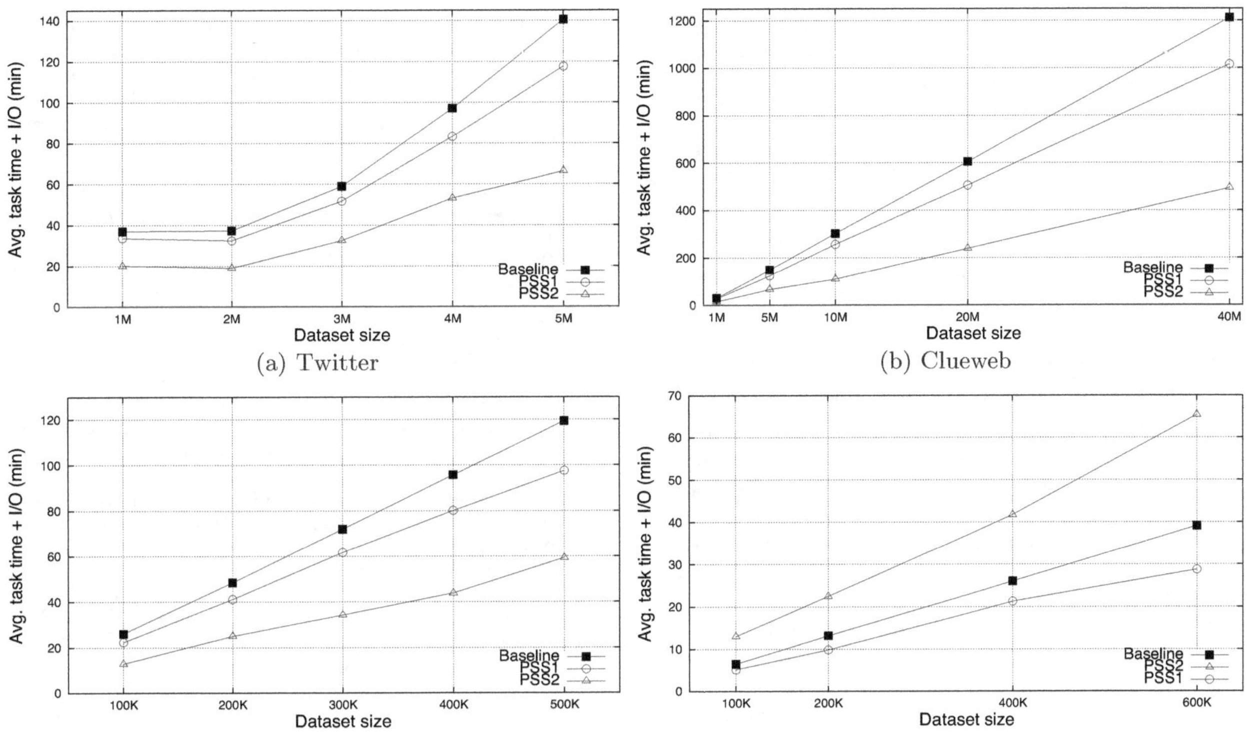

(a) Twitter (b) Clueweb

(c) Emails (d) YahooMusic

Figure 14: Average task running time under Baseline, PSS1 and PSS2 over different datasets.

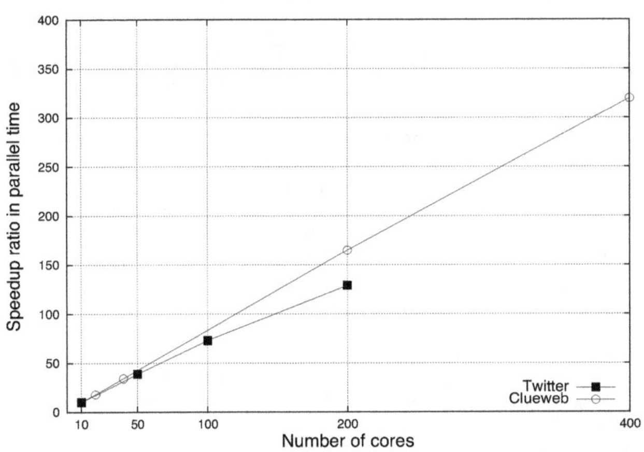

Figure 15: Speedup of PSS2 for processing 20M Twitter and 40M Clueweb with varying numbers of cores.

sparse matrix multiplication together with dynamic computation filtering. We assess the gap between how fast each CPU core can do in terms of peak application performance with a dense matrix and what our scheme has accomplished. First we compare the megaflops performance of our Java code with MTJ [13] from Netlib, which is highly optimized for dense matrix multiplication. The megaflops numbers achieved by a dense matrix multiplication routine (called dgemm) in MTJ achieves 1500 megaflops for matrix dimension 1000 on a single core and achieves 500 megaflops for a small dense matrix. Our scheme achieves 280 megaflops for Twitter benchmark. That is fairly high considering we are dealing with extremely sparse matrices.

In PSS3 design, we represent feature vectors in S and B as a set of small dense submatrices and employ a built-in MTJ BLAS3 dense matrix routine to multiply these submatirces. The advantage of PSS3 is that we leverage MTJ, a highly optimized library for cache performance. The disadvantage is that these small dense matrices still contain many zeros and a BLAS3 routine does not remove the unnecessary computation operations as well as an inverted index does. Figure 16 lists the comparison between PSS3 and PSS2 performance, with the ratio $\frac{Time_{PSS3}}{Time_{PSS2}}$ for different block settings. PSS3 is unfortunately much slower than PSS2. The reason is that vector-feature matrices in the tested similarity applications are extremely sparse and the PSS3 strategy with BLAS3 does not contribute enough benefits to counteract the introduced overhead.

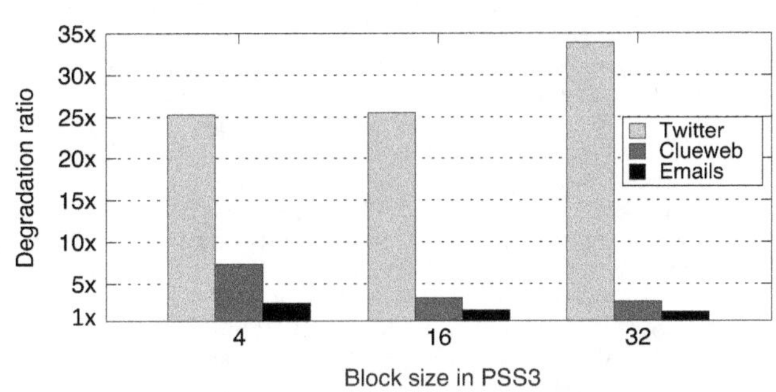

Figure 16: Y axis is ratio $\frac{Time_{PSS3}}{Time_{PSS2}}$. PSS3 is slower than PSS2 in general under different blocking sizes.

Table 4 provides another angle to explain why PSS3 slows down the task. We list the average fill-in ratio of those nonzero submatrices handled by PSS3. Fill-in ratio is the number of stored values which are in fact zero divided by the number of true nonzeros. The fill-in ratio is high and the number of true nonzeros for each block is too low to gain enough benefits with this blocked approach.

Block size	4×4	4×8	4×16	16×16	32×8	32×16
Twitter	2.5	3.7	3.9	6.2	5.3	7.7
Clueweb	2.6	8.2	4.8	5.6	4.4	6.2

Table 4: Average fill-in ratio with different block sizes.

7. CONCLUSIONS

The main contribution of this paper is the development and analysis of cache-conscious data layout and traversal schemes for partition-based similarity search. The key techniques are to 1) split data traversal in the hosted partition so that the size of temporary vectors accessed can be controlled and fit in the fast cache; 2) coalesce vectors with size-controlled inverted indexing so that the temporal locality of data elements visited can be exploited. Our analysis provides a guidance for optimal parameter setting. The evaluation result shows that the optimized code can be upto 2.74x as fast as the original cache-obvious design. Vector coalescing is effective if there is a decent number of features shared among the coalesced vectors.

Acknowledgment

We thank Xifeng Yan, Alexandra Potapova, and Paul Weakliem for their support and feedback, and the anonymous referees for their thorough comments. This work is supported in part by NSF IIS-1118106/0905084 and Kuwait University Scholarship. Equipment access is supported by the Center for Scientific Computing at CNSI/MRL under NSF DMR-1121053 and CNS-0960316. Any opinions, findings, conclusions or recommendations expressed in this material are those of the authors and do not necessarily reflect the views of the National Science Foundation.

8. REFERENCES

[1] Maha Alabduljalil, Xun Tang, and Tao Yang. Optimizing parallel algorithms for all pairs similarity search. In *Proc. of 6th ACM Inter. Conf. on Web Search and Data Mining (WSDM)*, 2013.

[2] Arvind Arasu, Venkatesh Ganti, and Raghav Kaushik. Efficient exact set-similarity joins. In *VLDB'06*.

[3] Language Technologies Institute at Carnegie Mellon University. The clueweb09 dataset, http://boston.lti.cs.cmu.edu/data/clueweb09.

[4] John R. Gilbert Aydin Bulu. Challenges and advances in parallel sparse matrix-matrix multiplication. In *ICPP*, 2008.

[5] Ricardo Baeza-Yates and Berthier Ribeiro-Neto. *Modern Information Retrieval.* Addison Wesley, 1999.

[6] Roberto J. Bayardo, Yiming Ma, and Ramakrishnan Srikant. Scaling up all pairs similarity search. In *Proceedings of WWW*, 2007.

[7] Fidel Cacheda, Víctor Carneiro, Diego Fernández, and Vreixo Formoso. Comparison of collaborative filtering algorithms: Limitations of current techniques and proposals for scalable, high-performance recommender systems. *ACM Trans. Web*, 2011.

[8] Abdur Chowdhury, Ophir Frieder, David A. Grossman, and M. Catherine McCabe. Collection statistics for fast duplicate document detection. *ACM Trans. Inf. Syst.*, 2002.

[9] J. J. Dongarra, Jeremy Du Croz, Sven Hammarling, and I. S. Duff. A set of level 3 basic linear algebra subprograms. *ACM Trans. Math. Softw.*, 16(1):1–17, March 1990.

[10] Iain S. Duff, Michael A. Heroux, and Roldan Pozo. An overview of the sparse basic linear algebra subprograms: The new standard from the blas technical forum. *ACM Trans. Math. Softw.*, 28(2):239–267, June 2002.

[11] Aristides Gionis, Piotr Indyk, and Rajeev Motwani. Similarity search in high dimensions via hashing. In *VLDB*, 1999.

[12] Hannaneh Hajishirzi, Wen tau Yih, and Aleksander Kolcz. Adaptive near-duplicate detection via similarity learning. In *SIGIR*, 2010.

[13] Heimsund Halliday. http://code.google.com/p/matrix-toolkits-java.

[14] Nitin Jindal and Bing Liu. Opinion spam and analysis. In *Proceedings of the international conference on Web search and web data mining*, WSDM '08, pages 219–230, 2008.

[15] David Kanter. Md's bulldozer microarchitecture. *realworldtech.com*, 2010.

[16] Aleksander Kolcz, Abdur Chowdhury, and Joshua Alspector. Improved robustness of signature-based near-replica detection via lexicon randomization. In *Proceedings of KDD*, 2004.

[17] David Levinthal. Performance analysis guide for intel core i7 processor and intel xeon 5500 processors. *Intel*, 2009.

[18] Jimmy Lin. Brute force and indexed approaches to pairwise document similarity comparisons with mapreduce. In *SIGIR*, 2009.

[19] Stefan Manegold, Peter Boncz, and Martin L. Kersten. Generic database cost models for hierarchical memory systems. In *VLDB '02*, 2002.

[20] Ahmed Metwally, Divyakant Agrawal, and Amr El Abbadi. Detectives: detecting coalition hit inflation attacks in advertising networks streams. In *Proceedings of the 16th international conference on World Wide Web*, WWW '07.

[21] Gianmarco De Francisci Morales, Claudio Lucchese, and Ranieri Baraglia. Scaling out all pairs similarity search with mapreduce. In *8th Workshop on LargeScale Distributed Systems for Information Retrieval (2010)*, 2010.

[22] Mehran Sahami and Timothy D. Heilman. A web-based kernel function for measuring the similarity of short text snippets. In *WWW '06*, pages 377–386, 2006.

[23] Ambuj Shatdal, Chander Kant, and Jeffrey F. Naughton. Cache conscious algorithms for relational query processing. In *In Proceedings of the 20th VLDB Conference*, pages 510–521. Morgan Kaufmann Publishers Inc, 1994.

[24] Kai Shen, Tao Yang, and Xiangmin Jiao. S+: Efficient 2d sparse lu factorization on parallel machines. *SIAM J. Matrix Anal. Appl.*, 22(1):282–305, April 2000.

[25] Narayanan Shivakumar and Hector Garcia-Molina. Building a scalable and accurate copy detection mechanism. In *DL'96 (ACM Inter. Conf. on Digital libraries)*, pages 160–168.

[26] Ferhan Ture, Tamer Elsayed, and Jimmy Lin. No free lunch: brute force vs. locality-sensitive hashing for cross-lingual pairwise similarity. In *SIGIR '2011.*

[27] Richard Vuduc, James W. Demmel, Katherine A. Yelick, Shoaib Kamil, Rajesh Nishtala, and Benjamin Lee. Performance optimizations and bounds for sparse matrix-vector multiply. In *ACM/IEEE Conf. on Supercomputing*, 2002.

[28] Chuan Xiao, Wei Wang, Xuemin Lin, and Jeffrey Xu Yu. Efficient similarity joins for near duplicate detection. In *Proceeding of the 17th international conference on World Wide Web*, WWW '08, pages 131–140. ACM, 2008.

[29] Yuan Cao Zhang, Diarmuid Ó Séaghdha, Daniele Quercia, and Tamas Jambor. Auralist: introducing serendipity into music recommendation. In *Proceedings of the fifth ACM international conference on Web search and data mining*, WSDM '12. ACM, 2012.

[30] Shanzhong Zhu, Alexandra Potapova, Maha Alabduljalil, Xin Liu, and Tao Yang. Clustering and load balancing optimization for redundant content removal. In *WWW '12: Inter. Conf. on World Wide Web. Industry Track*, 2012.

A Candidate Filtering Mechanism for Fast Top-K Query Processing on Modern CPUs

Constantinos Dimopoulos, Sergey Nepomnyachiy, Torsten Suel
Computer Science & Eng.
Polytechnic Institute of NYU
constantinos@cis.poly.edu, snepom01@students.poly.edu, suel@poly.edu

ABSTRACT

A large amount of research has focused on faster methods for finding top-k results in large document collections, one of the main scalability challenges for web search engines. In this paper, we propose a method for accelerating such top-k queries that builds on and generalizes methods recently proposed by several groups of researchers based on Block-Max Indexes [15, 10, 13]. In particular, we describe a system that uses a new filtering mechanism, based on a combination of block maxima and bitmaps, that radically reduces the number of documents that have to be further evaluated. Our filtering mechanism exploits the SIMD processing capabilities of current microprocessors, and it is optimized through caching policies that select and store suitable filter structures based on properties of the query load. Our experimental evaluation shows that the mechanism results in very significant speed-ups for disjunctive top-k queries under several state-of-the-art algorithms, including a speed-up of more than a factor of 2 over the fastest previously known methods.

Categories and Subject Descriptors

H.3.3 [**INFORMATION STORAGE AND RETRIEVAL**]: Information Search and Retrieval

General Terms

Algorithms, Performance, Experimentation

Keywords

top-k query processing, early termination, block-max inverted index, docID-oriented block-max index, candidate filtering mechanism, posting bitset, live area computation

1. INTRODUCTION

One of the major problems for large search engines is to keep up with the tremendous growth in the size of the web and the number of queries submitted by users. As discussed in [12], each of these measures increased by several orders of magnitude over the course of a decade. This creates performance challenges in many parts of the search engine architecture, including data acquisition, data analysis, and index maintenance. However, these challenges are particularly acute in the query processing component, whose workload grows with both data size and query load. In fact, one might naively expect query processing costs to increase with the product of these measures, though in practice various techniques are used to limit this increase. In this paper, we focus on such techniques for improving query processing efficiency.

Query processing in search engines is a fairly complex process, typically involving hundreds of features used for ranking, multiple phases that identify promising documents based on subsets of the features, and a distributed architecture that routes queries and results within and between clusters of thousands of machines. However, most systems appear to process a query by first evaluating on each machine a fairly simple ranking function over an inverted index. This results in an initial set of say a few thousand results that is then further processed to identify the best ten or more results to return to the user [26]. We focus on improving this initial step, which is responsible for a significant fraction of the overall work. We assume that this initial step is a ranking function of the form $r(q, D) = \sum_{t \in q} s(t, D)$, i.e., it is the sum of the scores of all the terms occurring in the query. This is a fairly common assumption, and accommodates popular functions such as BM25 as well as approaches based on automatically learning term scores that approximate more complex ranking functions [1].

A straightforward way to execute such a simple disjunctive ranking function is to completely traverse the index structures of all the query terms and compute or retrieve the scores of all the postings. Under this *exhaustive* method, the cost of each query increases linearly with the number of documents, making it very expensive for large collections. To overcome this problem, many researchers have proposed so-called *early-termination* techniques, i.e., techniques for finding the top results without computing or retrieving all posting scores [25, 9, 6, 23, 15, 10]. We focus on *safe* early-termination techniques, which must return the same top results as the exhaustive method [22].

Content of this Paper: Recent work by several groups of researchers [10, 15, 19, 13] has shown significant improvements in performance based on a *Block-Max Index*, first proposed in [10, 15]. This is an index structure that stores maximum scores for groups of postings, thus allowing quick

SIGIR'13, July 28–August 1, 2013, Dublin, Ireland.

skipping, without full evaluation, of sets of postings with low scores. In this paper, we build on this approach to derive new algorithms with additional very significant performance gains. In particular, our contributions are as follows:

(1) We design a general mechanism that can improve the performance of a whole class of query processing algorithms. Given a space budget, we maintain a set of block-max and posting-bitmap structures that can be used to transparently accelerate any DAAT index traversal algorithm. We show how to exploit the aggregated information from the auxiliary structures for aggressive candidate filtering.

(2) We present a space efficient caching policy for storing an optimal set of structures given a query distribution.

(3) We propose an optimized implementation of the mechanism that exploits SIMD instructions of modern CPUs and restricts the critical data structures to L1 cache.

(4) We provide an extensive experimental evaluation that shows significant improvements in query throughput for multiple algorithms. Our fastest results are more than a factor of two faster than the best previous results.

The remainder of this paper is organized as follows. In Section 2 we outline the background and related work. Section 3 describes the proposed filtering mechanism that uses Block-Max Indexes. Next, in Section 4 we present how to augment the mechanism with posting information. Section 5 explains our proposed solutions for the space overhead of the auxiliary structures and Section 6 presents preliminary results on our proposed methods. In Section 7 we show the performance of the filtering mechanisms on several scenarios, whereas in Section 8 we discuss caching policies for our mechanism. Finally, Section 9 presents additional results and Section 10 concludes and discusses future work.

2. BACKGROUND AND PREVIOUS WORK

In this section, we provide some background on inverted indexes, query processing and early termination techniques, Block-Max Indexes, and describe previous work.

2.1 Inverted Indexes

Inverted Indexes: An inverted index [27, 30] is a simple and efficient data structure widely used by large search engines for query processing. This structure allows finding the documents where specific terms occur and can be formally defined as follows. Given a collection of N documents, we assume each document is identified by a unique document ID (docID) between 0 and N-1. An inverted index contains an inverted list L_w for each distinct term w in the collection. Each L_w is a list of postings describing all documents where term w appears in the collection. More specifically, each posting contains the ID of the document (docID) that contains the term w, the number of occurrences of w in the document (the frequency), and potentially additional information such as the exact positions of these occurrences of term w in the document (positions) or other data. Unless stated otherwise, we store docIDs and frequencies such that each posting is of the form (d_i, f_i). There are several ways to layout the inverted lists, but in this work we focus on document-sorted indexes, where postings in each list are sorted by their docIDs d_i; see [18, 16, 6, 8, 23] for work using other layouts.

Index Compression: The inverted lists of frequent terms may contain millions or even billions of postings. To decrease space requirements, inverted lists are usually kept in compressed form. A common approach for docID-sorted indexes is to store the differences between consecutive docIDs in a list in suitably compressed form [30]. Index compression is crucial for search engine performance, and many compression methods have been proposed; see [29, 28, 21] for some recent work. For fast access, inverted lists are usually compressed in blocks of, say, 64 or 128 postings, such that each block can be accessed and decompressed individually. This is done by storing the uncompressed last docIDs and sizes of all blocks in a separate array that can then be used to locate and decompress individual blocks. Here, we compress the inverted lists into blocks of 64 docIDs followed by the corresponding 64 frequencies.

Index Quantization: We usually store each posting as a pair (d_i, f_i). However, it may sometimes be preferable to store postings as (d_i, s_i) where s_i is a score of d_i with respect to w. There are two main motivations for this: (1) to save the cost of computing scores from frequency values and other statistics such as document size and global term frequency, and (2) for scores that cannot be easily computed on the fly as they are derived from complex ranking functions with hundreds of features, using techniques similar to those in [1]. However, storing each s_i as a 32- or 64-bit number would result in very large index sizes. To reduce the size, so-called *index quantization* techniques are used that basically round the floating point score values to one out of a fixed set of, say, 256 distinct values. This may lead to a slight loss in precision during ranking, but guarantees that each score can be stored in only 8 bits. There are several quantization techniques in the literature; see [2, 3, 5, 4]. In this paper, we use the *Global-by-Value* technique proposed in [5], and also used in [11], using 8 bits for each score. All necessary score accumulations can be done directly in integer space, as in [2]. We refer to such an index structure as a *quantized index*, in contrast to a *standard index* storing frequencies values.

Index access: Document-sorted indexes allow fast index traversal during query execution based on a *Document-At-A-Time* (DAAT) approach. In DAAT index traversal, every list has a pointer to a current posting, and all pointers move forward in a synchronized manner as a query is processed. Thus, all postings (and thus documents) to the left of the pointers have already been processed, while postings to the right are yet to be considered. In DAAT, we typical have functions for opening and closing inverted lists for reading, and a function *nextGEQ* that, given a docID d and an open inverted list L, moves the pointer in L forward to the first posting with docID greater or equal to d. In addition, there is a function for retrieving other data (such as frequency or score) associated with the current posting. All decompression operations in the inverted lists are hidden within these functions. In this work, we focus on algorithms that perform DAAT traversal on document-sorted indexes.

2.2 Query Processing and Early Termination

The simplest way to query an inverted index is to ask for all documents containing some (disjunctive) or all (conjunctive) of a set of query terms. Of course, this would return too many results on large document collections, and thus IR systems supporting ranked queries return the highest scoring documents among those that satisfy the condition. Many simple ranking functions have been proposed for this task, including BM25 and the Cosine measure [7]. These functions are typically of the form $r(q, D) = \sum_{t \in q} s(t, D)$, meaning that the score of a document with respect to a query is the sum (or some other simple combination) of the query term scores of the document. In this paper, as in almost all previous work, we assume disjunctive queries with a ranking function of this form, that is, our goal is to return the highest scoring among all documents containing at least one of the query terms.

We note that such disjunctive queries tend to be more expensive than conjunctive queries that only need to score documents containing all query terms. For this reason, many search systems try to use conjunctive queries whenever possible. However disjunctive queries are known to return better results in many situations, and thus it is important for search engines to also support these more expensive types of queries.

Cascade Ranking: The above simple ranking on top of a disjunctive or conjunctive filter is only the first phase of query processing in current search engines. These engines will typically take a limited number k of top-scoring results from the simple ranking, say a few thousand overall, or as little as tens per node on a large cluster of machines, and evaluate a second, more complicated but more precise, ranking function on these results. This process may be repeated with an even more evolved ranking function applied to the top results from this ranking. Thus, we expect our top-k algorithms to be the first phase of such an architecture, and will look at the effect of varying k from 10 to a few thousand.

Early Termination: The main performance bottleneck that we have to deal with is the length of the inverted lists, which can grow to many MBs or even GBs on large collections. As mentioned, a simple algorithm for this problem would compute the score of any document containing at least one of the query terms; we call such an algorithm exhaustive. To avoid scoring many of these documents, early-termination (ET) algorithms have been proposed. We say that an ET algorithm is safe if it outputs exactly the same top k results as an exhaustive algorithm [22]. (In the case of a quantized index, safeness is of course defined with respect to an exhaustive algorithm on the full quantized index.)

There are many safe and unsafe ET algorithms in the literature; see, e.g., [25, 9, 6, 23, 15, 10] for a small sample. Some algorithms keep inverted lists sorted by docID, while others reorganize the lists by score $s(q, D)$, so that all high-scoring postings are encountered early during query processing. In this paper, we focus on safe early termination. All our algorithms keep the inverted lists sorted by docID and use DAAT for index traversal – but our running times also outperform all safe methods with other index layouts.

2.3 ET Algorithms

In this part, we first describe a simple exhaustive algorithm and then outline two basic safe ET algorithms that use DAAT traversal on document-sorted indexes, the WAND algorithm in [9] and the Maxscore algorithm in [25]. Both algorithms store for each inverted list the highest impact score of any posting, called the *maxscore* of the list. Recall that in DAAT traversal, we maintain a pointer to the current posting of each list. Also, we use θ to refer to the current threshold, which is the smallest score that can still make it into the top k results during the execution of the algorithm.

Exhaustive: The simplest query processing algorithm first picks the smallest current docID across all query terms, called *cID*. This can be done using either a loop or a heap, and cID is then fully evaluated. Afterwards, all pointers are moved to at least the next posting after docID cID. We also maintain a heap of the current top-k results, and add cID to this heap if it has a score larger than the current k^{th} highest score.

WAND: This algorithm, proposed in [9], consists of three phases: pivot selection, alignment check, and evaluation. In every iteration, a pivot term is selected by summing up the maxscores of the participating lists in order of increasing current docID, until the sum becomes larger or equal to θ. Next, WAND tries to align the current docIDs of the preceding lists in the ordering with the pivot docID, by moving the pointers in these lists forward to the pivot docID. If this succeeds, and all pointers up to the pivot point to the same docID, then this docID is evaluated, if necessary inserted into the top-k heap, and the current pointer in the pivot list is moved forward. Then we go to the next iteration.

Maxscore: This algorithm was first described in [25]. We focus here on the DAAT versions of the algorithm in [24, 17, 13]. Maxscore splits the query terms into essential and non-essential terms as follows. We sum up the maxscores of the lists from lowest to highest while the sum remains less than θ. The terms that contribute to this sum form the non-essential terms, and the others are the essential terms. The basic idea is that any document that can make it into the top k results must contain at least one essential term. Now we select as candidate, the smallest current docID of any essential list, and evaluate it. Thus, we basically run the exhaustive algorithm on the essential lists only. Of course, as the threshold θ for making it into the top k increases during execution of the algorithm, we may move additional terms from the essential to the non-essential set.

2.4 Block-Max Indexes

The idea of storing and exploiting the maximum impact score of each inverted list was recently and independently extended by two research groups [10, 15], who proposed an augmented index structure called *Block-Max Index* (BM). This structure stores the highest impact score for each block in the inverted lists, where the blocks are defined by the index compression method. Recently in [13], the blocks of the Block-Max structures were decoupled from the index compression and defined on docID space rather than posting distribution. We will refer to Block-Max structures whose blocks are defined by postings as *posting-oriented*, while the ones defined on docID space as *docID-oriented*.

2.5 Previous Work Using Block-Max Indexes

In this paper, we build on the work of [15, 10, 13], where we generalize and extend these ideas by proposing a filtering mechanism that uses Block-Max Indexes to further improve the query processing for disjunctive queries.

More specifically, [10, 15] proposed the posting-oriented BM structure to approximate the score of a block in posting space. The Block-Max Indexes provide score approximations in posting block resolution that enables skipping of compressed blocks. The approach in [15] proposed an enhancement of the WAND [9] algorithm that uses the Block-

Max index, called *BMW*, and operates as follows. After the sorting and pivot selection step as in [9], there is an additional block-max check that tests whether the pivot docID can make it into the top-k results. In case the block-max test fails, BMW can safely skip until the end of the blocks. The work in [10] suggested an algorithm that is built on top of the Maxscore and also uses posting-oriented BM structures. In particular, given a query, the algorithm reads the stored BM information, generates aligned intervals in the docID domain, and computes upper bound scores for each interval. During query processing, each interval's upper bound score is checked whether is larger or equal to the kth highest scoring document seen so far and if the test fails, the algorithm can skip blocks and safely save computations.

Both previous studies show experimentally that these auxiliary indexes provide fast query response times with small space requirements. However, the skipping power offered by posting-oriented BM indexes is limited because the blocks are defined by the index compression method. More recently, a new layout of the BM was proposed [13], where the blocks are defined on the docID domain. The blocks of the BM structure are decoupled from the index compression and their block size can be assigned per-term using the fixed, the expected or the variable block size selection method. The docID-oriented BM indexes provide very fast lookups, because the block-max access can be performed with bit shift operations. The authors in [13] use the variable size selection scheme to deal with the space overhead of the structure and show that several algorithms perform faster using the proposed BM index. We refer to [15, 10, 13] for more details on Block-Max indexes and query processing algorithms using such structures.

In this work, we extend the idea of constructing aligned intervals in docID space and computing interval upper bounds as in [10] by generalizing it on the docID-oriented BM structure [13] with fixed block size. The result is aligned BM blocks for all lists, allowing fast block-maxscore accesses and aggregation of "aligned block" upper bounds. We build on this scheme and propose a filtering mechanism that utilizes docID-oriented BM indexes to discover the "live" blocks in consecutive windows of docID space, which leads to significant performance gains over a series of DAAT algorithms for disjunctive queries. For the remainder of the paper we assume docID-oriented BM using the fixed block size selection method.

3. LIVE BLOCK MECHANISM

In this section we describe our proposed candidate filtering method that exploits the Block-Max index.

Live Area Computation: We can model DAAT query processing algorithms as a sequence of rounds, where in each one we examine whether a specific candidate docID can make it into the top-k results (by evaluating it or safely early terminating). Since our goal is to retrieve the top-k results fast, we can reduce the cost of query processing by minimizing the number of candidate docIDs. In previous works [10, 15, 13], the BM structure is utilized for candidate filtering in an online fashion, meaning that in each round there is a block-maxscore test checking whether the candidate has a chance to be added in the result heap. However, in our approach the aggregation of the upper bound block-maxscores across query terms for consecutive aligned blocks is performed in batch mode and then exploited to aggressively skip blocks. Due to the docID-oriented BM layout, there is no need for the alignment step as needed in [10].

In typical DAAT query processing algorithms, at the end of each round, the candidate docID for the next round is selected. The selection of this document is always preceded by invocation of the nextGEQ() on some lists. Since nextGEQ() usually demands expensive block decompression, we would prefer to make this decision based on the available block-max information. Therefore, given a query with m terms and a threshold θ, we define a block as *live* if the sum of block-max scores across m terms is greater or equal to θ. Thus, we can safely skip the block and avoid redundant decompressions and score calculations when a block is "dead". Remark that in [13] a similar optimization was suggested by the BMM-NLB algorithm, but in their setting there is no enforced block-max alignment.

We extend this idea by computing the live blocks of a *window* of docID space, where window refers to a contiguous docID region. Thus, we calculate block-maxscore sums for all blocks of a window. By definition, only blocks that summed up to more or equal than θ (of the specific window) are live blocks. We will refer to this procedure as *Live Area computation (LA)* of a window. This per-window liveness information is stored in a structure called *Liveness Bitset (LB)*, where each bit corresponds to a block of the window. LB is used for candidate filtering by skipping "dead" blocks. In particular, our mechanism first obtains the next live block from the LB and then provides the first docID of this block to the nextGEQ(). The live area computation is performed prior to query processing to provide efficient filtering oracle for candidate selection. Note that at the end of query processing of each window, we re-use the memory occupied by the LB structure to avoid the costly memory initializations.

Windows: The window size under this setting is crucial since the number of live blocks depends on the most updated θ. When the size of the window is too small, we pay for the construction overhead (LA). On the other hand, if the window size is too large, the effectiveness of the LB would drop due to outdated thresholds. In practice we observed that the appropriate window size should be a function of L1 or L2 cache size. As you advance in docID space (and θ grows), LB becomes more sparse, and hence, more effective. In preliminary experiments we observed that the convergence rate of θ is quite fast.

SIMD: The computation of live areas is performed during query processing (online) per window, thus it must be fast. This process includes the summation of the aligned block-maxscores across terms, the comparison of this sum with θ, and the encoding of the liveness information in LB. Since all inverted lists block-maxes are aligned in docID space, the LA calculation is vectorizable and SIMD capabilities of modern CPUs can be exploited to accelerate this computation. Our calculation of LA is coded for the SSE instruction set and performs the following operations: (i) load 4 consecutive block-maxscores from each query term, (ii) sum the block-maxscores vectors, (iii) compare the results with θ, and (iv) set the corresponding bits in LB. In a nutshell, LA's calculation overhead is negligible because of the natural speed-up of vectorized operations (SSE) and the limitation of LB to L1 cache. Note that SSE also applies to the integer operations used in the quantized index scenario.

In Figure 1, we see an example of LA computation for the 2-term query "cat squirrel" of 4 consecutive block-maxscores.

In this example, the BM scores for both terms are shown in grey, whereas their sum is colored green if the block is live, otherwise it is red. Under this scenario, only the third bit in LB is set. Since we are using SSE for the computation, every step is performed in one instruction. Thus, for any 2-term query we only need 5 instructions instead of 20 to compute the liveness of 4 consecutive blocks. The obtained information can filter all blocks in the window that could not make it into the top-k results and therefore, save decompressions and evaluations.

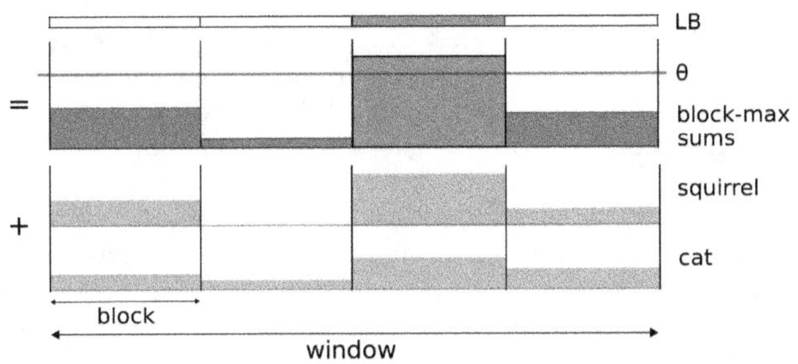

Figure 1: LA computation using terms' BM structures.

Varying Block Size and Threshold: The window-based LA calculation is computed using the most updated θ. The early knowledge of a good threshold makes the filtering mechanism very effective since less blocks will be live. In Figure 2, we show the percentage of live blocks for various block sizes and for different fixed thresholds (θ is not updated). We observe that the number of live blocks decreases when (i) decreasing the size of the block and (ii) providing higher θ. Since larger blocks provide worse block-score approximations, with higher threshold they have better chances of being live. These observations provide a strong evidence about the effectiveness of the proposed filtering mechanism. In practice, when θ is updated per window, the decrease in liveness is more significant (not linear).

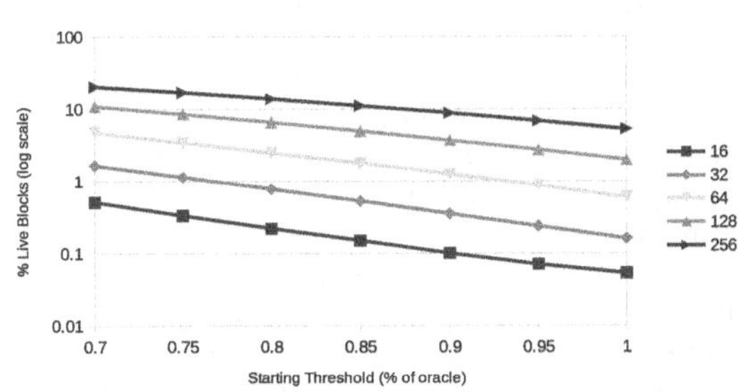

Figure 2: Live block percentage varying block size and fixing the starting threshold, for the TREC06 query trace.

Filtering Mechanism Interface: Our proposed window-based candidate filtering mechanism provides a simple interface that can be easily used by any DAAT query processing algorithm. We now describe the various low-level components of our framework so its adaptation to existing or new algorithms becomes trivial.

In this part, we outline the computation of LB structure and how to utilize it during query processing. First, the LA computation is performed whenever the termination condition of DAAT algorithms occurs. More specifically, these algorithms terminate when the docID of the candidate document is greater than the largest possible docID in the collection. At this point, the algorithms using our mechanism should be adapted to operate in the boundaries of the current window. Thus, whenever the docID of the candidate document exceeds the current window boundaries, the LA computation should be performed with the current θ. This consists of block-maxscores summation, comparison to θ for all blocks of the window, and setting the appropriate bits in the LB. Note that if the BM scores are not available, our mechanism needs direct access to the index to compute them. The liveness information of the LB can be accessed by a core function called *nextPotentialLiveDid*, which given a docID returns the first docID of the current or the next live block. The returned docID and a specific list are then provided to the nextGEQ(). We hide the complexity of this procedure by introducing a new function called *newNextGEQ*, which encapsulates both nextLivePotentialDid() and nextGEQ(). Note that the original nextGEQ() performed on the "live" candidate can still return a docID in a "dead" block. Thus, instead of calling the nextGEQ() the algorithms using our filtering mechanism could just use the new function newNextGEQ.

To sum up, algorithms could use our filtering mechanism by first changing the halting condition to be windows aware, then performing the described LA computation whenever the candidate docID is out of the current window boundary, and finally, by calling the newNextGEQ() instead of nextGEQ(). Hence, our mechanism offers a simple interface to query processing algorithms, by hiding all the complexity behind few functions.

Architecture of the Filtering Mechanism: We now describe how our technique communicates with the available data during query processing. Figure 3 shows our query processing pipeline, which consists of the Index, the Query Processor, the Filter Mechanism and the Filter Cache. The Filter Mechanism has direct bulk access to the Index so that it can generate the augmented structures on-the-fly for lists out of the Filter Cache, as we will describe in Section 5. Hence, the Filter Cache contains augmented structures (such as the BM Index and the LB) that are accessed and exploited by the Filter Mechanism for effective skipping during query processing. The Query Processor uses the core function nextGEQ() to access the Index and move the pointers of the inverted lists. It may also use the Filter Mechanism to request the liveness bit of a docID or the maxscore of a block. In that case, the information is served by the Filter Cache and returned to the Query Processor. Remark that the communication between the Query Processor and the Filter Mechanism can in fact be encapsulated within the newNextGEQ() operator.

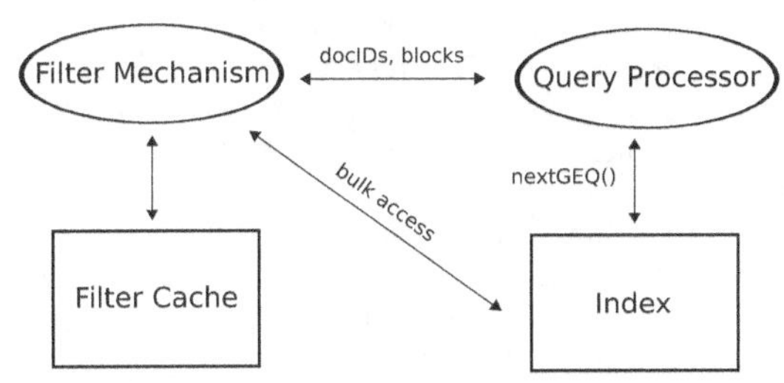

Figure 3: Filtering mechanism architecture.

4. POSTING BITSET (PB)

The LB provides a smart exploitation of the BM structure with performance gains as we will experimentally show in the next section. Its effectiveness to filter candidate docIDs relies solely on the approximation quality of the block-maxscores. The early termination methods of algorithms using BM structures are mainly based on the score approximation. However, we could also filter candidate docIDs using additional information about the postings existence in a block. For example, a block without postings does not contribute to the block-maxscore aggregation in LA. In fact, a block-maxscore is non-zero if and only if the block contains postings. In order to exploit the additional posting existence information of a term we encode it as follows: for a contiguous docID region called *sub-block*, we store a bit describing whether the term contains any posting in it. Thus, for each term we store a *Posting Bitset* (PB), where each bit represents the posting liveness of a specific sub-block. This encoding offers extremely fast accesses to the PB structure (because sub-blocks are docID-oriented).

The PB can be seen as a per-term filtering method that query processing algorithms can benefit from. In particular, this filtering mechanism consists of a basic function called *nextLivePotentialPosting* that given a docID and a list, returns a docID belonging to the current or next populated sub-block of the given list. Moreover, this function can be used to answer whether a term has any postings in a specific region, thus saving redundant computations such as decompressions of blocks and score calculations. Similar to the LB mechanism, the PB filtering technique also requires direct access to the index for construction. The PB structure can be easily combined with the BM index during LA computation to provide finer granularity candidate filtering as we will shortly see.

4.1 LB-PB Mechanism

In the previous section, we proposed the PB structure that provides information about the posting liveness. This structure can be utilized during the LA computation to provide finer granularity filtering. In order to obtain a useful combination of the BM index and the PB, we need to meaningfully select the block size of the sub-blocks. Note that having a sub-block larger than the BM block does not introduce new information. We experimentally observed that a good size for the sub-blocks is 2^{m-3}, where 2^m is the size of the BM block. For the rest of the paper, we assume that the sub-block size is 2^{m-3}.

Our assumption about the sub-block size implies that every BM block is split into 8 sub-blocks. Therefore, for each BM block we have additional information about the posting liveness of its sub-blocks. Utilizing the PB structure in LA computation requires the following steps: first every block-maxscore is duplicated 8 times and masked with 8 sub-block bits, then the sub-block level scores are summed across terms, and finally, we compare the sums with the current most updated θ and set the appropriate bit in the liveness bitset. Note that in our case, the temporary PB structure is 8 times larger than the corresponding structure we used for LB. We will refer to this structure that provides an effective candidate filtering mechanism for the query processing algorithms, as *LB-PB*. Similarly to LB, during query processing the algorithm can provide a docID to the LB-PB to obtain the next live sub-block in the window, avoiding redundant computations such as decompressions and score calculations. Given a docID, the mechanism returns a docID in the current or the next live sub-block. Remark that this filtering technique can exploit both nextLivePotentialDid and nextLivePotentialPosting functions, that now operate on sub-block level, and its complexity can be hidden as well behind the newNextGEQ().

In Figure 4, we describe the live area computation of the query "cat squirrel" for 4 BM blocks using the LB-PB mechanism. The BM scores of both terms are colored in grey, and only the PB of the third block is shown. The non-empty sub-blocks are shaded. The available PB information enables finer block-maxscore granularity on sub-block level. Focusing on the third block, the LA-PB computation includes the multiplication of the posting bitset of the third block of each term with the corresponding BM score. The result is depicted as grey sub-blocks, whereas the summation of the aligned sub-blocks across terms is shown as red or green sub-blocks sums. We can alternatively think this procedure as an alignment step in sub-block resolution. After the LB-PB filtering, only the sixth sub-block of third block was found to be live, while the original LB mechanism would label the entire third block (8 sub-blocks) as live. This example shows the effectiveness of the LB-PB mechanism and its superiority over the simple LB filtering technique.

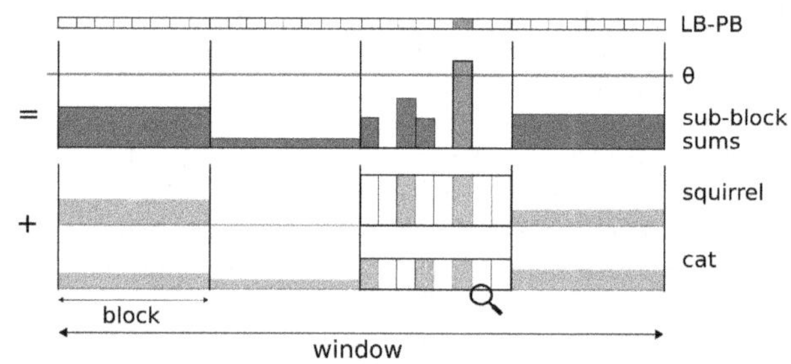

Figure 4: Example of the LB-PB filtering mechanism.

SIMD: Similarly with the LA computation, the calculations of LA when combined with the PB structure can exploit the SIMD opportunities of modern CPUs. All steps of the LA computation of the LB-PB mechanism are vectorizable and therefore, the SSE instruction set is used in the implementation to speed up the calculations.

Varying Block Size and Threshold: Figure 5 presents the percentages of the live sub-blocks for various block sizes and different fixed thresholds. As in Figure's 2 observations, smaller block sizes and higher starting threshold result in less live sub-blocks, as expected. Comparing the percentages of Figure 2 and 5, we observe that the combination of LB and PB leads to less live blocks. These statistics provide evidence that the proposed candidate filtering mechanisms could give significant performance gains.

5. SPACE OVERHEAD

In this section we discuss how to deal with the space overhead of the auxiliary structures.

5.1 Block-Max Index

So far we have not mentioned the space overhead of the BM index needed during the LA computation and we assumed BM resides in memory. In practice, the BM structure

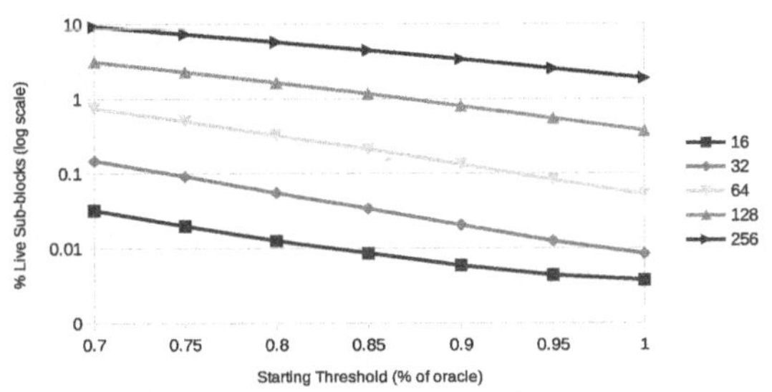

Figure 5: Live sub-block percentage varying block size and fixing the starting threshold, for the TREC06 query trace.

with fixed block size is too large to be memory-resident, so we address the space overhead using the approach in [13], and we will refer to this as *Length-based.* Under this method, the BM for terms with few postings are not stored at all, but generated on-the-fly (OTF), while the BM scores for the rest are undergoing linear quantization (BMQ), such that every block-maxscore is 1-byte (instead of 4). The difference in our setting is that the OTF is now performed per window. The window-based OTF computation involves (i) the decompression of the blocks (docIDs and frequencies), (ii) the score calculation of these docIDs, and (iii) the Block-Max Generation (BMG). We further extend the length-based approach by compressing the quantized Block-Max values (BMQC) of the medium-sized lists. More specifically, we first create a skiplist for non-zero values and then we compress them using a version of PForDelta [29]. This requires decompression of the compressed quantized values during query processing, but its overhead is minimal compared to its space gains.

5.2 Posting Bitset

The size of the sub-block plays a crucial role on the effectiveness of the posting bitset structure. Very large sub-blocks provide poor posting existence information, whereas too small sub-blocks add significant space overhead. Overall, we address the space overhead of the posting bitset structure by following a length-based approach as in the case of the BM structure. A first observation is that for long lists we expect most sub-blocks to be non-empty, hence a PB with all bits set is a decent approximation for it. Instead of storing the actual PBs for such lists, we "fake" them by pointing to a static array of 1's, thus saving this space. We experimentally observed that this approximation of PB does not impair filtering abilities and does not cause a slow down. Moreover, since we already decompress the short lists in OTF BMG, we can use the docIDs to construct the PBs on-the-fly as well. The PB structures are stored in main-memory only for the medium-sized terms. Note that the construction of PB should be also considered under the window-based scenario as described in the previous section.

We will revisit the length-based approach for both structures in Section 8 to achieve a better space/time tradeoff.

6. PRELIMINARY EXPERIMENTS

In this section, we evaluate and compare the performance of the simplest query processing algorithm, the exhaustive, when our filtering mechanisms are applied, with the best previously reported numbers to our knowledge [13] under the scenario of a standard index.

6.1 Experimental Setup

For our experiments, we use the TREC GOV2 dataset that contains 25.2 million web pages. We build inverted index structures with 64 docIDs and frequencies per block, using a version of the PForDelta compression method [31] described in [29], but our ideas also apply to other compression methods. The size of the uncompressed size of the data set is 426GB, whereas its compressed standard index size is 8.75GB and its compressed quantized index 11.97GB. We evaluate our methods using 1000 queries randomly selected from the TREC 2006 and 2005 Efficiency track query set.

We implemented all the algorithms in C++ using BM25 as our ranking function, and return top-10 results unless stated otherwise. For the rest of the paper, we assume docID-oriented BM using the fixed block size selection method with 64 docIDs per block. The experiments were conducted on a single core of an Intel Xeon server with 2.27Ghz and all data structures reside in memory.

6.2 Baseline algorithms

Setup: We begin with a performance comparison of the exhaustive algorithm and its versions that use the LB and the LB-PB mechanisms, called *EX*, *EX-LB* and *EX-LB-PB* respectively, on the standard index. For this experiment we use the following length-based policies for the BM: (i) OTF for lists with length less than 95042, (ii) BMQC for lists between 95042 and 2^{18}, and (iii) BMQ for the remaining ones. Similarly, for the PB structure we use the subsequent length-based rules: (i) OTF for lists with length less than 179758, (ii) maintaining in main memory the posting liveness information for lists with length between 179758 and 2^{22}, and (iii) faking of bitsets for lists larger than 2^{22}. The space requirement for the described policy for the GOV2 data set is $2GBs$, less than 25% of the compressed index, while the use of PB increases the space to $4GBs$. We also compare the performance of the exhaustive algorithm when the filtering methods are applied with the fastest previous results to our knowledge [13]. More specifically, the approach in [13] uses docID-oriented BM structures, variable block size selection methods and both OTF BMG (up to lists of size 2^{15}) and BMQ techniques (on the remaining lists), with $2.76GBs$ space overhead. The authors of [13] were willing to share the code for their fastest algorithm, called BM-OPT, which selects based on the number of query terms the fastest algorithm between BMM, BMM-NLB and BMW.

Exhaustive speed-up: In Table 1, we present the query response times for the BM-OPT algorithm and all versions of the exhaustive algorithm for the TREC06 query trace, when the number of query terms varies. We can see that the LB filtering mechanism makes the exhaustive algorithm faster by a factor of 10, whereas the availability of PB boosts the exhaustive 16 times! The exhaustive algorithm is significantly accelerated by the availability of the LB mechanism achieving average query response time of $13.47ms$. When the LB-PB is used it further reduces the average time to $8.59ms$, 16 times faster over EX. The performance boost of the mechanisms is consistent across varying number of query terms. Table 2 shows the radical decrease in term score evaluations and calls to nextGEQ() when the proposed mechanisms are applied. The reason for the significant reduction in query response times, evaluations and nextGEQ() is the following: at the end of each iteration of any query processing algorithm, the pointers of some or all lists must be moved using the expensive nextGEQ() (which usually includes decompression). Our mechanism checks the LB (or the LB-PB) structure in order to obtain the next live block (or sub-block) and then provides to the nextGEQ() the first docID of this block (or sub-block). Therefore, this test before the call of nextGEQ() moves the pointers much further in docID space and results in much less redundant expensive decompressions, which is the main reason for the significant performance speed-up of our mechanisms.

Comparison with BM-OPT: Furthermore, we see that the performance of both EX-LB and EX-LB-PB outperforms that of BM-OPT. Concerning the space requirements of the algorithms, as mentioned, the EX-LB occupies $2GBs$, less than the $2.76GBs$ needed by the best previous approach. Thus, our filtering method uses less space to achieve faster times compared to the state-of-the-art algorithm, BM-OPT. When the PB structure is also available the space increases to $4GBs$ and EX-LB-PB achieves much faster query response times compared to BM-OPT. Remark that our filtering mechanisms accelerate significantly the simplest query processing algorithm, the exhaustive, which outperforms the state-of-the-art BM-OPT algorithm.

Algorithm	avg	2	3	4	≥ 5
EX	138.98	37.68	97.06	166.39	301.24
EX-LB	13.47	2.71	5.89	16.63	35.08
EX-LB-PB	8.59	2.65	5.07	10.72	18.69
BM-OPT	14.96	3.81	9.91	18.8	34.29

Table 1: Performance of the exhaustive algorithm on the availability of our mechanisms for the standard index and the TREC06 query trace.

Algorithm	Time (ms)	# nextGEQ/query	# evals/query
EX	138.98	4,489,430	4,489,430
EX-LB	13.47	195,080	194,741
EX-LB-PB	8.59	86,792	86,454

Table 2: Number of term score evaluations and calls to nextGEQ for the standard index and the TREC06 query trace.

7. EXPERIMENTS

In this section, we present a performance comparison of widely used DAAT query processing algorithms when our filtering techniques are applied. These algorithms either use (BMM-NLB, BMW) or not (WAND, Maxscore) the BM structure for early termination during query processing.

7.1 LB-PB on DAAT algorithms

In particular, the WAND algorithm was implemented based on [9], Maxscore and BMM-NLB were coded according to [13], while the BMW algorithm based on [15]. All algorithms were modified in order to use the filtering mechanisms interface as previously described.

The performance comparison of these algorithms for the TREC06 and TREC05 query trace when we vary the number of query terms is presented in Table 3 and 4. The significant speed-up of our candidate filtering mechanism over several query processing algorithms shows the effectiveness of the filtering. Table 3 shows that Maxscore outperforms WAND when any filtering method is applied. On algorithms that use the BM index to early terminate documents, BMW is consistently faster from BMM-NLB. We observe that the performance of Maxscore is similar to BMM-NLB and the reason is that BMM-NLB spends too much time during its several cascading filtering steps, which are not very useful when our mechanisms are used. BMW outperforms all algorithms with $6.45ms$ using the LB and $5.74ms$ when PB is also available. A similar performance behavior is observed for the TREC05 query trace in Table 4. Enforcing candidate selection with LB (and LB-PB) in all algorithms consistently accelerates them. However, this was apparent from preliminary experiments, where the simplest algorithm outperformed the state-of-the-art BM-OPT. Due to space limitation, for the remainder of the paper we omit any results for the TREC05.

LB ($2GBs$)					
Algorithm	avg	2	3	4	≥ 5
WAND	11.53	2.51	4.97	13.86	31.15
Maxscore	8.1	2.3	4.17	10.08	19.4
BMM-NLB	8.29	2.13	3.97	10.2	20.38
BMW	6.45	2.03	3.45	7.63	15.44
LB-PB ($4GBs$)					
WAND	8.19	2.59	4.7	10.05	18.23
Maxscore	6.22	2.34	3.93	7.89	12.68
BMM-NLB	6.21	2.21	3.73	7.88	13.06
BMW	5.74	2.18	3.59	7.04	12.03

Table 3: Performance comparison of several DAAT query processing algorithms when LB and LB-PB mechanisms are applied on standard index, for the TREC06 query trace.

LB ($2GBs$)					
Algorithm	avg	2	3	4	≥ 5
WAND	10.22	2.51	5.02	7.56	47.19
Maxscore	5.62	2.18	4.13	5.75	20.37
BMM-NLB	6.19	2.03	3.98	5.66	24.88
BMW	5.35	1.96	3.58	4.89	20.79
LB-PB ($4GBs$)					
WAND	7.66	2.62	5.02	6.9	29.98
Maxscore	5	2.32	4.21	5.41	15.03
BMM-NLB	5.21	2.18	4.06	5.24	17.22
BMW	5.12	2.15	3.93	5.03	17.11

Table 4: Performance comparison of several DAAT query processing algorithms when LB and LB-PB are applied on standard index, for the TREC05 query trace.

8. SPACE/TIME TRADEOFF

In this section, we discuss how we can further optimize both space and time constraints by moving from simple length-based caching policies to cost-based.

8.1 Length-based Caching

In the previous experiments, the performance of our methods and their space requirements were based on decisions governed by the length of the lists, called *Length-based* policies. These policies include (i) OTF computation of BM and PB for short lists, (ii) storing compressed quantized BM for medium lists (BMQC), (iii) faking of PB for long lists, and (iv) storing quantized BM and PB for all remaining lists.

For the previous experiments, the length-based parameters were fixed to specific values using acceptable space requirements to show the effectiveness of our mechanism. Although the length-based caching provides a good space/time tradeoff, it is solely depends on the length of the list. More specifically, it forces short lists' augmented structures (BM and PB) to be computed OTF, whereas it always stores in the Filter Cache these structures for large-sized lists. This is not always optimal, since it is likely that some short terms will occur frequently in the query trace and thus, it may be more beneficial to store their augmented structures rather than computing them OTF. Therefore, we would like to move to policies that take into account the frequency of terms in the query workload and offer better space/time tradeoffs.

8.2 Cost-based Caching

It is common that large web search engines use caching mechanisms so their performance adapts and optimizes to the query workload. Such mechanisms maintain statistics about the terms appearances in the query logs and based on them, decide whether to cache the additional information. The main idea behind such approach is to achieve performance speed-up by using less space smartly. Therefore, we try to maximize the obtained performance gains by following optimal policies for each term according to query statistics and under specific space requirements. We will refer to the proposed policies that are based on a benefit function that takes into account the frequency of the terms in the training query trace, as *Cost-based* policies. In particular, if a short term occurs very frequently in the query log, it would be reasonable to maintain its augmented structures in memory. On the other hand, if a long term does not appear too often in the queries, we refrain from storing it in memory.

The proposed cost-based caching policy follows the next steps: first, for each term we compute a rank under various policies P_i as follows $\frac{time(OTF)-time(P_i)}{space(P_i)} * freq(term)$. The policies for the BM index include the length-based policies (i) OTF, (ii) BMQC and (iii) BMQ. Similarly, the policies for the PB structure consist of (i) OTF, (ii) PB, and (iii) faking of PB. Then, given a space budget, we select the terms (from highest benefit rank to lowest) and store their structures in the Filter Cache. This selection procedure ends when the space requirements are met and thus, for all terms that were not selected by the caching policy, we use OTF (regardless of their length). We obtained the frequency of terms in the query log using as our training set the $99k$ queries from the TREC 2006 Efficiency track query trace and then, applied our method to the remaining $1k$ queries.

In Figure 6, we compare the space/time tradeoff of both caching methods on WAND, BMM-NLB and BMW, when only the LB filtering mechanism is available for the standard index. As expected, given a specific space budget, the cost-based policy always achieves faster times for all the algorithms compared to the length-based approach. Our proposed method is very effective even in scenarios with very limited space constraints. In particular, for space budget of $0.5GBs$, BMW achieves $15.75ms$ using the length-based policy, whereas $10.22ms$ using the cost-based. For the remainder of the paper we will use the cost-based caching approach. Figure 7 shows that when more space is available, using the PB structure accelerates the query processing time. Moreover, we observe that the quantized index can further reduce the query response times, for example Q-BMW-LB-PB for $2GBs$ achieves $4.36ms$.

9. EXTENSIONS

In this section, we provide some additional results. More specifically, we look the performance of our methods for reodered indexes and the impact of increasing top-k on the performance of our techniques.

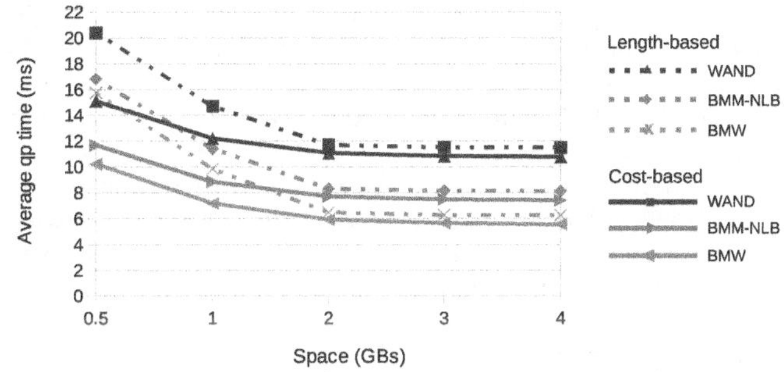

Figure 6: Space/Time tradeoff of Length-based and Cost-based caching on the standard index.

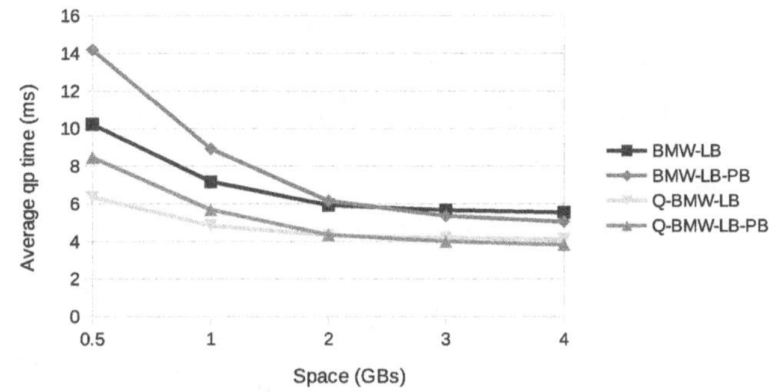

Figure 7: Space/Time tradeoff of Cost-based caching on the availability of LB and LB-PB on the standard and the quantized index.

DocID Reordering: There has been a huge amount of work to reduce the size of the compressed inverted indexes by reordering the docIDs. Under docID reordering, the documents are assigned docIDs using different techniques in order to minimize the index size. The main idea is to assign closeby docIDs to documents sharing lots of terms. A simple and effective method proposed by [20], which first sorts the URLs alphabetically and then assigns docIDs based on this ordering. More sophisticated reordering techniques were proposed in [14], whereas [28] showed that reordering speeds up the conjunctive query processing. Recent work in [15, 13] showed that docID reordering also accelerates the query response times of disjunctive queries. In Table 5 we show the performance of BMW using the cost-based caching policy under the simple reordering method of [20] when varying the number of query terms. For the remainder of the paper, the space requirement of the algorithms using the LB structure is $2GBs$, and $4GBs$ when the PB is also used. As expected reordering gives a speed-up for both filtering mechanisms. In particular, BMW-LB achieves $3.02ms$ average times, whereas BMW-LB-PB performs similarly with $3.04ms$. The reason the performance of BMW-LB-PB is not better is that the reordering changes the distribution of postings in docID space.

Algorithm	avg	2	3	4	≥ 5
BMW-LB	3.02	1.31	2.16	3.25	6.06
BMW-LB-PB	3.04	1.33	2.23	3.3	5.89

Table 5: Impact of docID reordering on BMW on the standard index.

Varying k in Top-k: In this experiment, we show the performance of our methods when k is increased. In Table 6 we see the performance of the filtering mechanisms on BMW as we increase k and vary the number of query terms for the standard and the quantized index. We observe that both mechanisms scale very well, but LB-PB performs better as k increases in both indexes. BMW-LB returns the top-100 results in $13.5ms$. In the quantized index scenario, the query times are further reduced since calculations operate in the integer domain. In particular, Q-BMW-LB-PB returns the top-10 results in $3.83ms$, while the top-1000 in $24.8ms$.

Algorithm	10	50	100	500	1000
BMW-LB	5.93	10.31	13.5	26.88	36.27
BMW-LB-PB	5.06	8.53	11.23	23.33	32.34
Q-BMW-LB	4.32	7.59	10.01	19.72	26.32
Q-BMW-LB-PB	3.83	6.65	8.89	18.09	24.8

Table 6: Impact of top-k on BMW performance on the standard and the quantized index.

10. CONCLUSIONS AND FUTURE WORK

In this paper, we proposed a general filtering mechanism based on docID-oriented Block-Max indexes that significantly improves the performance of several widely used algorithms for safe early termination in disjunctive queries. We present a simple interface that can be easily used by several query processing algorithms. Moreover, we augment the mechanism with an auxiliary structure that maintains posting liveness information for each term and show how it can be exploited to achieve faster query times. We also propose caching techniques that address the space/time tradeoff of our mechanisms and overall, we achieve more than a factor of 2 speed-up over the fastest previous methods.

The future work will introduce additional query processing algorithms that exploit the advanced parallel instruction sets available in modern CPUs (AVX) and faster compression methods that use SIMD operations of current CPUs.

Acknowledgement

This research was supported by NSF Grant IIS-1117829 "Efficient Query Processing in Large Search Engines", and by a grant from Google. Sergey Nepomnyachiy was supported by NSF Grant ITR-0904246 "The Role of Order in Search".

11. REFERENCES

[1] D. Agarwal and M. Gurevich. Fast top-k retrieval for model based recommendation. In *Proc. of the Fifth Int. Conf. on Web Search and Data Mining*, pages 483–492, 2012.

[2] V. N. Anh, O. de Kretser, and A. Moffat. Vector-space ranking with effective early termination. In *Proceedings of the 24th Annual Int. ACM SIGIR Conference on Research and Development in Inf. Retrieval*, 2001.

[3] V. N. Anh and A. Moffat. Impact transformation: effective and efficient web retrieval. In *Proc. of the 25th Annual Int. ACM SIGIR Conf. on Research and Development in Information Retrieval*, pages 3–10, 2002.

[4] V. N. Anh and A. Moffat. Improved retrieval effectiveness through impact transformation. In *Proc. of the 13th Australasian Database Conference*, 2002.

[5] V. N. Anh and A. Moffat. Simplified similarity scoring using term ranks. In *Proc. of the 28th Annual Int. ACM SIGIR Conf. on Research and Development in Information Retrieval*, pages 226–233, 2005.

[6] V. N. Anh and A. Moffat. Pruned query evaluation using pre-computed impacts. In *Proc. of the 29th Annual Int. ACM SIGIR Conf. on Research and Development in Information Retrieval*, 2006.

[7] R. A. Baeza-Yates and B. A. Ribeiro-Neto. *Modern Information Retrieval.* ACM Press / Addison-Wesley, 1999.

[8] H. Bast, D. Majumdar, R. Schenkel, M. Theobald, and G. Weikum. IO-Top-K: Index-access optimized top-k query processing. In *Proceedings of the 32th International Conference on Very Large Data Bases*, 2006.

[9] A. Z. Broder, D. Carmel, M. Herscovici, A. Soffer, and J. Y. Zien. Efficient query evaluation using a two-level retrieval process. In *Proc. of the 12th ACM Conf. on Information and Knowledge Management*, 2003.

[10] K. Chakrabarti, S. Chaudhuri, and V. Ganti. Interval-based pruning for top-k processing over compressed lists. In *Proc. of the 27th Int. Conf. on Data Engineering*, 2011.

[11] R. Cornacchia, S. Héman, M. Zukowski, A. P. de Vries, and P. A. Boncz. Flexible and efficient ir using array databases. *VLDB J.*, 17(1):151–168, 2008.

[12] J. Dean. Challenges in building large-scale information retrieval systems. In *Proceedings of the Second ACM International Conference on Web Search and Data Mining*, 2009.

[13] C. Dimopoulos, S. Nepomnyachiy, and T. Suel. Optimizing top-k document retrieval strategies for block-max indexes. In *Proc. of the Sixth ACM International Conference on Web Search and Data Mining*, 2013.

[14] S. Ding, J. Attenberg, and T. Suel. Scalable techniques for document identifier assignment in inverted indexes. In *Proc. of the 19th Int. Conf. on World Wide Web*, 2010.

[15] S. Ding and T. Suel. Faster top-k document retrieval using block-max indexes. In *Proc. of the 34th Int. ACM SIGIR Conf. on Research and Development in Information Retrieval*, 2011.

[16] R. Fagin. Combining fuzzy information: an overview. *SIGMOD Record*, 31:2002, 2002.

[17] S. Jonassen and S. E. Bratsberg. Efficient compressed inverted index skipping for disjunctive text-queries. In *Proc. of the 33th European Conf. on Information Retrieval*, 2011.

[18] M. Persin, J. Zobel, and R. Sacks-davis. Filtered document retrieval with frequency-sorted indexes. *Journal of the American Society for Information Science*, 47:749–764, 1996.

[19] D. Shan, S. Ding, J. He, H. Yan, and X. Li. Optimized top-k processing with global page scores on block-max indexes. In *Proc. of the Fifth Int. Conf. on Web Search and Data Mining*, 2012.

[20] F. Silvestri. Sorting out the document identifier assignment problem. In *Proc. of the 29th European Conf. on Information Retrieval*, 2007.

[21] F. Silvestri and R. Venturini. Vsencoding: efficient coding and fast decoding of integer lists via dynamic programming. In *Proc. of the 19th ACM Conf. on Information and Knowledge Management*, 2010.

[22] T. Strohman. *Efficient Processing of Complex Features for Information Retrieval.* PhD thesis, University of Massachusetts Amherst, 2007.

[23] T. Strohman and W. B. Croft. Efficient document retrieval in main memory. In *Proc. of the 30th Annual Int. ACM SIGIR Conf. on Research and Development in Information Retrieval*, 2007.

[24] T. Strohman, H. R. Turtle, and W. B. Croft. Optimization strategies for complex queries. In *Proc. of the 28th Annual Int. ACM SIGIR Conf. on Research and Development in Information Retrieval*, 2005.

[25] H. R. Turtle and J. Flood. Query evaluation: Strategies and optimizations. *Inf. Processing and Management*, 31(6):831–850, 1995.

[26] L. Wang, J. J. Lin, and D. Metzler. A cascade ranking model for efficient ranked retrieval. In *Proc. of the 34th Annual Int. ACM SIGIR Conf. on Research and Development in Information Retrieval*, 2011.

[27] I. H. Witten, A. Moffat, and T. C. Bell. *Managing Gigabytes: Compressing and Indexing Documents and Images, Second Edition.* Morgan Kaufmann, 1999.

[28] H. Yan, S. Ding, and T. Suel. Inverted index compression and query processing with optimized document ordering. In *Proc. of the 18th Int. Conf. on World Wide Web*, 2009.

[29] J. Zhang, X. Long, and T. Suel. Performance of compressed inverted list caching in search engines. In *Proc. of the 17th Int. Conf. on World Wide Web*, 2008.

[30] J. Zobel and A. Moffat. Inverted files for text search engines. *ACM Comput. Surv.*, 38(2), 2006.

[31] M. Zukowski, S. Heman, N. Nes, and P. Boncz. Super-scalar RAM-CPU cache compression. In *Proceedings of the 22th Int. Conf. on Data Engineering*, 2006.

Author Index

www.ingramcontent.com/pod-product-compliance
Lightning Source LLC
LaVergne TN
LVHW080106011026
849160LV00013B/1043
* 9 7 8 1 4 5 0 3 2 7 0 2 2 *